Oct. 98

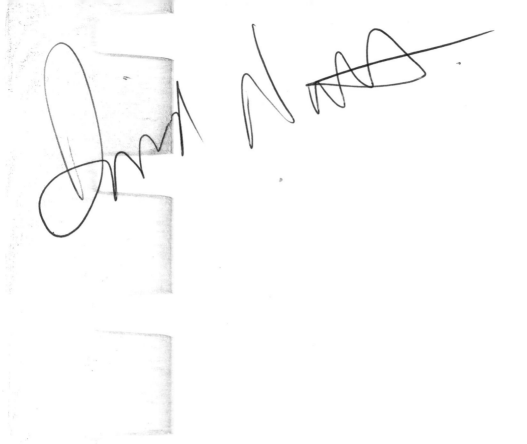

Principles of Addiction Medicine
Second Edition

Allan W. Graham, M.D., FACP, FASAM
Terry K. Schultz, M.D., FASAM

Editors

Bonnie B. Wilford
Associate Editor

American Society of Addiction Medicine, Inc.
Chevy Chase, Maryland
1998

Published by the American Society of Addiction Medicine, Inc.
4601 North Park Avenue, Suite 101
Chevy Chase, Maryland 20815
U.S.A.
Telephone: 301/656-3920
Telefax: 301/656-3815
E-mail: email@asam.org

Principles of Addiction Medicine is a publication of the American Society of Addiction Medicine (ASAM). ASAM is a national medical specialty society of physicians who are concerned about alcoholism and other drug dependencies, and who care for persons affected by those illnesses. For information about ASAM membership, or about the Society's certification program, conferences, policies and publications, contact the American Society of Addiction Medicine, 4601 North Park Ave., Suite 101, Chevy Chase, MD 20815.

ASAM gratefully acknowledges The Rosenstiel Foundation for its generous grant in support of the second edition of *Principles of Addiction Medicine*.

First Edition 1994
Second Edition 1998

Library of Congress Cataloging in Publication Data:

Principles of addiction medicine / edited by
Allan W. Graham and Terry K. Schultz;
associate editor, Bonnie B. Wilford—2nd ed.
p.cm.
Includes bibliographical references and index.
ISBN 1-880425-04-1
1. Substance abuse. 2. Substance abuse—treatment.
3. Substance abuse—diagnosis. 4. Addiction medicine
I. Graham, Allan W. II. Schultz, Terry K.
[DNLM: 1. Substance abuse. WM 270 S941]
RC564.______ 1998
ISBN 1-880425-02-5

Medicine is an ever-changing science. As new research and clinical experience broaden our knowledge, changes in treatment are required. The Editors and publisher of this work have made every effort to ensure that the treatment recommendations and drug dosage schedules herein are accurate and in accord with the standards accepted at the time of publication. Readers are advised, however, that changes may occur in recommended practices as new research emerges.

Printed in the United States of America.

ISBN: 1-880425-04-1

Editors

Allan W. Graham, M.D., FACP, FASAM

Associate Medical Director
Chemical Dependency Treatment Services
Kaiser Permanente
Denver, Colorado

Terry K. Schultz, M.D., FASAM

Alcohol and Drug Abuse Consultant
to The Surgeon General of the U.S. Army
Arlington, Virginia

Associate Editor

Bonnie B. Wilford

Director, Center for Health Services
and Outcomes Research
Arlington, Virginia

Preface to the Second Edition

The second edition of *Principles of Addiction Medicine*, while a publication of the American Society of Addiction Medicine (ASAM), is the product of intensive collaboration among clinicians, researchers, and scholars from ASAM, the National Institute on Alcohol Abuse and Alcoholism (NIAAA) and the National Institute on Drug Abuse (NIDA). As editors, we wish to thank our colleagues for their work, their wisdom, and their devotion in developing this textbook.

The central goal of the book is to improve the medical care given to patients with addictive disorders. With the publication of the second edition, we believe that we have refined and enriched the definition of addiction medicine, described its neuroscientific foundations, and reviewed the most effective techniques and concepts essential to its practice.

The second edition is based on the solid framework established with the first edition of *Principles*, edited by Dr. Norman Miller and Dr. Martin Doot. The new edition has benefited from the generous gifts of time and expertise by ASAM members and by our colleagues in the related disciplines of psychology, sociology, epidemiology, and the basic sciences. Without their support, the textbook would not have been possible.

The scientific advances in addiction medicine have been dramatic in the four years since *Principles* first was published. As a result, the second edition has been extensively revised and updated. All 17 sections reflect the rapidly expanding and emerging knowledge base. To highlight the scientific discoveries that now guide our field, we have invited introductory overview chapters by NIAAA Director Enoch Gordis, M.D., and NIDA Director Alan I. Leshner, Ph.D.

Enoch Gordis has written an overview of the science of alcoholism that is a model of clarity and compression. He discusses the major conceptual advances in alcohol research that have occurred over the past several decades, highlights research progress toward answering the basic questions about alcoholism, and provides some thoughts on scientific advances that are just over the horizon. He explains the tremendous strides in our understanding of the biology and behavior of alcoholism and the implications of this expanded understanding of the disease concept for the future of alcohol treatment.

Alan Leshner has provided an update on the "Decade of the Brain" in terms of how far we have advanced beyond mind-brain dualism. He explains how deep our understanding has become of drug abuse as a special type of chronic relapsing brain disease that is expressed in behavioral ways and within social contexts. His comparison of atherosclerotic heart disease and addictive disorders emphasizes that each is defined by an interaction between the afflicted individual's unique genetic factors and environment.

The editors know that *Principles* will be useful to physicians who specialize in the practice of addiction medicine. Beyond that, we hope that it will prove useful to physicians in primary care, as well as to the wide range of professionals who care for these patients.

Some persons opening this book may ask, "What is addiction medicine and what makes it different from other fields of practice?" Addiction medicine is an interdisciplinary practice specializing in the identification and treatment of persons whose disorders are caused or worsened by their use of addictive substances. These substances have the unique property of promoting continued use in a compulsive manner despite adverse consequences to the user. In our society, the most notable offending substances are nicotine, alcohol, opiates, stimulant drugs, and marijuana. The most common services offered by specialists in addiction medicine are:

- Prevention;
- Diagnosis;
- Detoxification from these substances;
- Consultation with other physicians concerning identification, intervention, and management of patients in hospital or office whose disorders are directly linked to use of these substances;
- Facilitation of patient engagement in treatment programs designed to reduce the progression of the patient's substance- related problems;
- Development of outcomes-based treatment programs for such patients;

- Treatment of medical or psychiatric complications, and relapse;
- Environmental modifications that attempt to alter the social, behavioral, and pharmacologic inputs that support the continuation of substance abuse and dependence; and
- Research into the genetic and neurobiologic aspects of addiction, with the ultimate goal of developing improved treatments (behavioral and pharmacologic) for addictive disorders.

We are grateful to ASAM for giving us the privilege of guiding this work to completion. We also express special thanks to Dr. Dorynne Czechowicz of NIDA and Dr. Raye Litten of NIAAA for helping us in many ways. Lastly, we are indebted to our Associate Editor, Bonnie Wilford, whose expertise both as editor and specialist in the field of addiction medicine has served us well throughout this endeavor.

We welcome your comments, recommendations, criticisms, and engagement, for the field of addiction medicine is rapidly evolving and we are all participants in its growth.

The Editors:
Allan W. Graham, M.D., FACP, FASAM
Terry K. Schultz, M.D., FASAM

Foreword from the American Society of Addiction Medicine

In 1994, the American Society of Addiction Medicine achieved a landmark with publication of its comprehensive textbook, *Principles of Addiction Medicine.* ASAM's purpose in publishing *Principles* was to establish it as the standard textbook of addiction medicine, whose contents reflect state-of-the-art scientific and clinical knowledge of the field.

Given the success of *Principles* in the marketplace and the rapid advances in addiction medicine, ASAM's Board of Directors determined that a second edition of *Principles* ought to be published in 1998.

Principles of Addiction Medicine contains the most current and useful scientific and clinical information for physicians who have a special interest or practice concentration in addiction medicine, for all practicing physicians who wish a comprehensive reference on the subject, and for addiction counselors and other health care professionals. It is, as its size and scope suggest, designed to serve multiple purposes.

At one level, *Principles* is intended to provide background information to augment the faculty presentations at ASAM's Review Courses in Addiction Medicine, which prepare candidates for the certification examinations in addiction medicine. The review courses are open to all physicians—ASAM members and non-members alike—who wish to have an overview and update of clinically relevant information on key topics in addiction medicine.

At a second level, *Principles* is designed as a comprehensive, self-contained text for physicians and other clinicians who wish a comprehensive review of the field of addiction medicine. *Principles* thus joins ASAM's other publications, certification examination, conferences and courses as an expression of the Society's ongoing commitment to help physicians and other health care professionals acquire the knowledge and skills they need to render the highest quality care to addicted patients and their families.

Finally, *Principles of Addiction Medicine* represents the unwavering commitment of ASAM's members to advancing the understanding of addictive disorders on the part of specialist and primary care physicians alike, as well as policymakers and the public, through the presentation of reliable, current information on developments in basic science and clinical practice, as well as the organization and delivery of services.

Clearly, an undertaking of this scope and intensity would not be possible without the contributions of many individuals, whose unstinting enthusiasm for this project is evident in the pages that follow. Foremost among these contributors are the Editors, Allan W. Graham, M.D., and Terry K. Schultz, M.D. *Principles* is the culmination of four years' collaboration in which, as volunteer members of ASAM, Drs. Graham and Schultz co-chaired ASAM's 1995 and 1997 courses on the State of the Art in Addiction Medicine, the 1996 Review Course in Addiction Medicine, and this Second Edition of *Principles of Addiction Medicine*. Throughout, their vision has been to improve patient care by providing addiction medicine specialists and other clinicians with the most current, reliable scientific information that can be drawn from the research and applied in practice. Their colleagues, as well as the many patients who will find effective relief from the pain of addictive disorders as a result of their efforts, have reason to be enormously grateful to Drs. Graham and Schultz.

We also are grateful to the Associate Editor, Bonnie B. Wilford. Mrs. Wilford has successfully edited several ASAM publications and, in doing so, has raised the level of their quality and clinical relevance. As Editor of *ASAM News* and two editions of the *Review Course Syllabus*, as managing editor of the First Edition and as Associate Editor of the Second Edition of *Principles*, Mrs. Wilford has contributed not only her considerable writing, editing and managerial skills, but has brought to the work a dedication to the members of ASAM and to the field of addiction medicine.

Finally, we express gratitude to the authors whose work appears in this volume for their intellectual contributions to this endeavor. The field of addiction medicine is, in all its aspects—prevention, treatment, research, education and public policy—distinguished by a commitment to excellence and a striving to discover the causes of addiction and the most effective means of preventing and treating addictive disorders. The work that appears in this edition of *Principles* exemplifies that excellence.

Thus, to Dr. Graham and Dr. Schultz, to Mrs. Wilford, and to the authors, we proffer our deep esteem and gratitude.

Our success in this unprecedented venture depends on an active, engaged readership as well. With your input, and the continuing leadership of ASAM's Editorial Board and committees, we will fulfill our pledge to make *Principles of Addiction Medicine* the indispensable resource for all who practice in or share our dedication to this most demanding yet rewarding field of medicine.

James F. Callahan, D.P.A.
Executive Vice President and CEO

Contents

Introduction	What We Know: Conceptual Advances in Alcoholism Research *Enoch Gordis, M.D.*	**xvii**
	What We Know: Drug Addiction is a Brain Disease *Alan I. Leshner, Ph.D.*	**xxix**
Section 1.	**Basic Science and Core Concepts**	**1**
CHAPTER 1.	The Epidemiology of Addictive Disorders *Rosa M. Crum, M.D., M.H.S.*	3
CHAPTER 2.	Genetic Influences in Addiction *Robert M. Anthenelli, M.D. and Marc A. Schuckit, M.D.*	17
CHAPTER 3.	Behavioral Models of Addiction *Roy A. Wise, Ph.D. and John E. Kelsey, Ph.D.*	37
CHAPTER 4.	The Neurochemistry of Addiction *David J. Nutt, Ph.D.*	51
CHAPTER 5.	Neuroadaptation in Addiction *Eric J. Nestler, M.D., Ph.D.*	57
CHAPTER 6.	Neurocircuitry Targets in Reward and Dependence *George F. Koob, Ph.D., Amanda J. Roberts, Ph.D., et al.*	73
CHAPTER 7.	Stress as a Factor in Addiction *Pier Vicenzo Piazza and Michel Le Moal*	83
Section 2.	**The Pharmacology of Addictive Drugs**	**95**
CHAPTER 1.	Clinical Pharmacokinetics and Pharmacodynamics: Key Concepts *Donald R. Wesson, M.D.*	99
CHAPTER 2.	The Pharmacology of Alcohol *John J. Woodward, Ph.D.*	103
CHAPTER 3.	The Pharmacology of Sedative-Hypnotics *Steven M. Juergens, M.D., FASAM, and Debra R. Cowley, M.D.*	117
CHAPTER 4.	The Pharmacology of Opioids *Mark S. Gold, M.D., FCP, FAPA*	131
CHAPTER 5.	The Pharmacology of Cocaine, Crack and Other Stimulants *Mark S. Gold, M.D., FCP, FAPA, and Michael J. Herkov, Ph.D.*	137

CHAPTER 6. The Pharmacology of Nicotine 147
John Slade, M.D., FASAM

CHAPTER 7. The Pharmacology of Phencyclidine and the Hallucinogens 153
Marilyn Carroll, Ph.D. and Sandra Comer, Ph.D.

CHAPTER 8. The Pharmacology of Marijuana 163
Mark S. Gold, M.D., FCP, FAPA

CHAPTER 9. The Pharmacology of Steroids 173
Scott Lukas, Ph.D.

CHAPTER 10. The Pharmacology of Inhalants 187
Stephen H. Dinwiddie, M.D.

CHAPTER 11. Future Directions in Research 195
Walter A. Hunt, Ph.D., Roger Brown, Ph.D. and Jerry Frankenheim, Ph.D.

Section 3. Prevention 205

CHAPTER 1. Assessing Individual Risks and Resiliencies 207
Karol L. Kumpfer, Ph.D., Eric Goplerud, Ph.D. and Rose Alvarado, Ph.D.

CHAPTER 2. Prevention Science: Developing Empirical Models for Prevention Intervention 215
Mary A. Jansen, Ph.D. and Michael J. Stoil, Ph.D.

CHAPTER 3. Developing Comprehensive Community Coalitions to Prevent Alcohol, Tobacco and Other Drug Abuse 227
Abraham Wandersman, Ph.D., Robert M. Goodman, Ph.D., M.P.H. and Frances D. Butterfoss, Ph.D., M.S.Ed.

CHAPTER 4. Fitting Prevention into the Continuum of Care 233
Kenneth Hoffman, M.D., M.P.H.

Section 4. Diagnosis and Assessment 247

CHAPTER 1. Principles of Identification and Intervention 249
Jerome E. Schulz, M.D. and Theodore Parran, M.D.

CHAPTER 2. Screening Instruments and Biochemical Screening Tests 263
John Allen, Ph.D. and Raye Z. Litten, Ph.D.

CHAPTER 3. Assessment Instruments 273
David R. Gastfriend, M.D., Sharon L. Baker, Ph.D., Lisa M. Najavits, Ph.D. and Sharon Reif, B.A.

CHAPTER 4. Diagnostic Classification Systems 279
Samuel A. Ball, Ph.D. and Therese A. Kosten, Ph.D.

Section 5. Overview of Addiction Treatment **291**

CHAPTER 1. Natural History of Addiction and Pathways to Recovery 295
George E. Vaillant, M.D.

CHAPTER 2. Myths About the Treatment of Addiction 309
Charles P. O'Brien, M.D. and A. Thomas McLellan, Ph.D.

CHAPTER 3. Traditional Approaches to the Treatment of Addiction 315
Michael M. Miller, M.D., FASAM

CHAPTER 4. Components of Successful Treatment Programs: Lessons from the Research Literature 327
A. Thomas McLellan, Ph.D. and James R. McKay, Ph.D.

CHAPTER 5. What Works in Treatment: Effect of Setting, Duration and Amount 345
John W. Finney, Ph.D. and Rudolf H. Moos, Ph.D.

CHAPTER 6. Linkages of Substance Abuse with Primary Care and Mental Health Treatment 353
Patrick G. O'Connor, M.D., M.P.H. and Douglas M. Ziedonis, M.D., M.P.H.

CHAPTER 7. Use of Patient Placement Criteria in the Selection of Treatment 363
David Mee-Lee, M.D.

CHAPTER 8. Alternative Therapies 371
Tacey Ann Boucher, Thomas J. Kiresuk, Ph.D. and Alan I. Trachtenberg, M.D., Ph.D.

CHAPTER 9. Harm Reduction as an Approach to Treatment 395
Alex Wodak, M.D., FRACP

CHAPTER 10. Addiction and Treatment in the Criminal Justice System 405
Blair Carlson, M.D., M.S.P.H., FACP, FASAM

Section 6. Intoxication, Overdose and Acute Withdrawal **421**

CHAPTER 1. Principles of Detoxification 423
Christine L. Kasser, M.D., Anne Geller, M.D., FASAM, Elizabeth F. Howell, M.D., and Alan A. Wartenberg, M.D., FASAM

CHAPTER 2. Management of Alcohol Intoxication and Withdrawal 431
Michael Mayo-Smith, M.D., M.P.H.

CHAPTER 3. Management of Sedative-Hypnotic Intoxication and Withdrawal 441
Steven J. Eickelberg, M.D., FASAM. and Michael Mayo-Smith, M.D., M.P.H.

CHAPTER 4. Management of Opioid Intoxication and Withdrawal 457
Patrick G. O'Connor, M.D., M.P.H. and Thomas R. Kosten, M.D.

CHAPTER 5. Management of Stimulant, Hallucinogen, Marijuana and Phencyclidine Intoxication and Withdrawal 465
Jeffery N. Wilkins, M.D., Bradley T. Conner and David A. Gorelick, M.D., Ph.D.

CHAPTER 6. Management of Nicotine Withdrawal 487
Terry A. Rustin, M.D., FASAM

Section 7. Pharmacologic Therapies for Addiction 497

CHAPTER 1. Pharmacologic Therapies for Alcoholism 501
Henry R. Kranzler, M.D. and Jerome H. Jaffe, M.D.

CHAPTER 2. Pharmacologic Therapies for Benzodiazepine and Other Sedative-Hypnotic Addiction 517
Donald R. Wesson, M.D., David E. Smith, M.D., FASAM, and Walter Ling, M.D.

CHAPTER 3. Pharmacologic Therapies for Cocaine and Other Stimulant Addiction 531
David A. Gorelick, M.D., Ph.D.

CHAPTER 4. Pharmacologic Therapies for Opioid Addiction 545
Susan Stine, M.D., Ph.D., Borislav Meandzija, M.D. and Thomas R. Kosten, M.D.

CHAPTER 5. Opioid Maintenance Therapies 557
J. Thomas Payte, M.D. and Joan E. Zweben, Ph.D.

CHAPTER 6. Pharmacologic Therapies for Nicotine Dependence 571
Joy M. Schmitz, Ph.D., Jack E. Henningfield, Ph.D. and Murray E. Jarvik, M.D., Ph.D.

CHAPTER 7. Pharmacologic Therapies for Other Drugs and Multiple Drug Addiction 583
Jeffery N. Wilkins, M.D., David A. Gorelick, M.D., Ph.D. and Bradley T. Conner

Section 8. Behavioral Therapies for Addiction 593

CHAPTER 1. Enhancing Motivation to Change 595
James O. Prochaska, Ph.D.

CHAPTER 2. Characteristics of Effective Counselors 609
Kathleen M. Carroll, Ph.D.

CHAPTER 3. Brief Interventions 615
Allan W. Graham, M.D., FACP, FASAM and Michael Fleming, M.D., M.P.H.

CHAPTER 4. Individual Psychotherapy 631
Bruce J. Rounsaville, M.D. and Kathleen M. Carroll, Ph.D.

CHAPTER 5. Network Therapy: An Integration of Therapeutic Approaches at the Office Level 653
Marc Galanter, M.D., FASAM

CHAPTER 6. Aversion Therapy 667
P. Joseph Frawley, M.D.

CHAPTER 7. Community Reinforcement and Contingency Management Interventions 675
Steve T. Higgins, Ph.D., Jennifer W. Tidey, Ph.D., and Maxine L. Stitzer, Ph.D.

Section 9. Twelve Step Programs and Other Interpersonal Therapies 691

CHAPTER 1. Twelve Step Programs 693
Jerome E. Schulz, M.D. and John N. Chappel, M.D., FASAM

CHAPTER 2. Recent Research in Twelve Step Programs 707
Barbara McCrady, Ph.D.

CHAPTER 3. Rational Recovery, SMART Recovery and Non-Twelve Step Mutual Recovery Programs 719
Joseph Gerstein, M.D.

CHAPTER 4. Spiritual Components of the Recovery Process 725
John N. Chappel, M.D., FASAM

Section 10. Medical Disorders in the Addicted Patient 729

CHAPTER 1. Management of Common Medical Problems 731
Alan A. Wartenberg, M.D., FASAM

CHAPTER 2. Nutrition 741
Lawrence Feinman, M.D. and Charles S. Lieber, M.D.

CHAPTER 3. Hepatic Disorders 755
Charles S. Lieber, M.D.

CHAPTER 4. Neurological Effects 775
Anne Geller, M.D., FASAM

CHAPTER 5. Sleep Disorders 793
Allan W. Graham, M.D., FACP, FASAM

CHAPTER 6. Medical Syndromes Associated with Specific Drugs 809
Alan A. Wartenberg, M.D., FASAM

CHAPTER 7. HIV/AIDS, Tuberculosis, and Other Infectious Diseases 825
Harry Haverkos, M.D.

CHAPTER 8. Special Problems of the Elderly 833
James W. Smith, M.D., FASAM

Section 11. Surgery in the Addicted Patient **857**

CHAPTER 1. Surgical Management of the Addicted Patient 859
George W. Nash, M.D., FASAM, and Gordon L. Hyde, M.D., FACS, FASAM

CHAPTER 2. Trauma 863
Carl A. Soderstrom, M.D.

CHAPTER 3. Anesthesia and Analgesia 877
Charles Beattie, M.D., Ph.D., Annie Umbricht-Schneiter, M.D. and Lynette Mark, M.D.

CHAPTER 4. Liver Transplantation 891
Thomas E. Beresford, M.D.

Section 12. Pain Management and Addiction **899**

CHAPTER 1. The Neurophysiology of Pain in Addiction 901
Peggy Compton, R.N., Ph.D. and G. F. Gebhart, Ph.D.

CHAPTER 2. Principles of Pain Treatment in the Addicted Patient 919
Seddon R. Savage, M.D., FASAM

CHAPTER 3. Psychological Approaches to the Management of Pain 945
Edward C. Covington, M.D. and Margaret M. Kotz, D.O.

CHAPTER 4. Prescribing Issues and the Relief of Pain 961
Barry Stimmel, M.D., FASAM

Section 13. Psychiatric Disorders in the Addicted Patient **967**

CHAPTER 1. Substance-Induced Mental Disorders 969
R. Jeffrey Goldsmith, M.D. and Richard K. Ries, M.D.

CHAPTER 2. Comorbid Addiction and Affective Disorders 983
Kathleen T. Brady, M.D., Ph.D., Hugh Myrick, M.D. and Susan Sonne, Pharm.D.

CHAPTER 3. Anxiety Disorders 993
David R. Gastfriend, M.D. and Patrick Lillard, M.D.

CHAPTER 4. Psychotic Disorders 1007
Douglas Ziedonis, M.D., M.P.H., and Steve Wyatt, D.O.

CHAPTER 5. Attention-Deficit/Hyperactivity Disorder, Intermittent Explosive Disorder and Eating Disorders 1029
Frances Rudnick Levin, M.D. and Stephen J. Donovan, M.D.

CHAPTER 6. Other Impulse Control Disorders 1047
Susan L. McElroy, M.D., Cesar A. Soutullo, M.D. and R. Jeffrey Goldsmith, M.D.

CHAPTER 7. Personality Disorders 1063
Linda A. Dimeff, Ph.D., Katherine Anne Comtois, Ph.D. and Marsha M. Linehan, Ph.D.

CHAPTER 8. Integrating Psychotherapy and Pharmacotherapies in Addiction Treatment 1081
Joan E. Zweben, Ph.D.

Section 14. The Family in Addiction 1091

CHAPTER 1. The Family in Addiction 1093
Michael R. Liepman, M.D., FASAM

CHAPTER 2. A Developmental Model of the Alcoholic Family 1099
Stephanie Brown, Ph.D. and Virginia Lewis, M.S.W.

CHAPTER 3. Children in Alcoholic Families: Family Dynamics and Treatment Issues 1111
Hoover Adger, Jr., M.D., M.P.H.

CHAPTER 4. Current Family Treatment Approaches 1115
David Berenson, M.D. and Ellen Woodside Schrier, M.S.W.

Section 15. Alcohol and Drug Use in Children and Adolescents 1127

CHAPTER 1. Screening for Substance Abuse in Children and Adolescents 1129
Robert Cavanaugh, M.D., FAAP, Michelle Pickett, M.D., FAAP and Peter D. Rogers, M.D., M.P.H., FAAP, FASAM

CHAPTER 2. Office Assessment and Brief Intervention with the Adolescent Suspected of Substance Abuse 1145
George D. Comerci, M.D., FAAP

CHAPTER 3. Assessment of the Identified Substance-Abusing Adolescent 1153
Susan Speraw, Ph.D., R.N. and Peter D. Rogers, M.D., M.P.H., FAAP, FASAM

CHAPTER 4. Adolescent Substance Abuse and Psychiatric Comorbidity 1161
Marie E. Armentano, M.D.

Section 16. Women, Infants and Addiction 1171

CHAPTER 1. Understanding Addictive Disorders in Women 1173
Sheila B. Blume, M.D., FASAM

CHAPTER 2. Social Predictors of Drug and Alcohol Use: Implications for Prevention and Treatment 1191
Edith S. Lisansky Gomberg, Ph.D.

CHAPTER 3. Treatment of the Addicted Woman in Pregnancy 1199
Laura J. Miller, M.D.

CHAPTER 4. Treatment Options for Drug-Exposed Infants 1211
Stephen B. Kandall, M.D., FAAP

CHAPTER 5. Developmental Outcomes of Prenatal Exposure to Alcohol and Other Drugs 1223
Sydney L. Hans, Ph.D.

Section 17. Alcohol and Drug Use in the Workplace 1239

CHAPTER 1. Overview of Drug-Free Workplace Programs 1241
Barbara L. Johnson, Esq. and Jonathan D. Quander, Esq.

CHAPTER 2. The Role of the Medical Review Officer 1255
Donald Ian Macdonald, M.D., FASAM, and Robert L. DuPont, M.D., FASAM

CHAPTER 3. Impairment and Recovery in Physicians and Other Health Professionals 1263
G. Douglas Talbott, M.D., FASAM, Karl V. Gallegos, M.D., and Daniel H. Angres, M.D.

Appendix A. Directory of Policy Statements of the American Society of Addiction Medicine 1281

Appendix B. Rapid Reference 1283

SECTION 1. Screening Instruments 1283

SECTION 2. Summary of the DSM-IV Diagnostic Criteria 1287

SECTION 3. Summary of the ICD-10 Diagnostic Criteria 1291

SECTION 4. Crosswalks of the ASAM Patient Placement Criteria, Second Edition (ASAM PPC-2) 1293

SECTION 5. Federal Schedules of Controlled Drugs 1299

SECTION 6. ASAM Addiction Terminology 1301
Emanuel M. Steindler

Index 1305

Introduction

What We Know: Conceptual Advances in Alcoholism Research **xvii**
Enoch Gordis, M.D.

What We Know: Drug Addiction is a Brain Disease **xxix**
Alan I. Leshner, Ph.D.

CONTRIBUTORS

ENOCH GORDIS, M.D.
Director
National Institute on Alcohol Abuse
and Alcoholism
National Institutes of Health
Rockville, Maryland

ALAN I. LESHNER, PH.D.
Director
National Institute on Drug Abuse
National Institutes of Health
Rockville, Maryland

INTRODUCTION

What We Know: Conceptual Advances in Alcoholism Research

Enoch Gordis, M.D.

Alcoholism, like many other serious diseases, results from the interaction of complex biological and behavioral systems. Understanding the systems involved in the development of alcoholism and its consequences, how individual components of biological and behavioral systems interact to produce disease, and how to interrupt this process to prevent disease and reduce harm are the major goals of alcohol research. This is no simple task. It is, however, a very necessary one: it is as likely that alcoholism will yield to one type of intervention or one type of treatment as it is that all cancers will respond to the same regimen of chemotherapy or radiation. Moreover, in today's health care environment, demands by managed care organizations, other third-party payers, state funding agencies, and by the United States Congress for accountability require the same type of safety and efficacy evidence for treatment of alcoholism that is required for all other illnesses. We may believe we know "what works," but it is the evidence of efficacy that will bring financial and patient support.

Today's alcohol researchers are working at the cutting edge of science in many different areas, seeking answers to the most perplexing questions facing the alcoholism field. This overview of the science of alcoholism discusses some of the major conceptual advances in alcohol research that have occurred over the past several decades, highlights research progress toward answering the basic questions in alcoholism, and provides some thoughts on scientific advances that are just over the horizon.

THE PROBLEM OF ALCOHOLISM

Alcoholism is one of our nation's most serious and persistent health problems. Approximately two-thirds of all American adults (ages 18 and older) drink an alcoholic beverage during the course of a year (Midanik & Room, 1992). At least 13.8 million American adults develop problems from drinking (Grant, Harford et al., 1994). Our young people, for whom alcohol remains the number one drug of abuse, also are at risk for developing alcohol-related problems. Recently published data from the National Longitudinal Alcohol Epidemiologic Survey, sponsored by the National Institute on Alcohol Abuse and Alcoholism (NIAAA), which assesses lifetime risk for alcohol use disorders (alcohol abuse and alcohol dependence), provides convincing evidence that the younger an individual is when he or she begins drinking, the greater is his or her chance of developing a clinically diagnosable alcohol use disorder in the future. For example, individuals who begin drinking before age 15 are four times more likely to develop alcohol dependence during their lifetimes than those who begin drinking at age 21 (Grant & Dawson, 1997).

The health problems caused by alcohol use include damage to the brain, liver, gastrointestinal tract, and heart. The relative risk for many alcohol-related illnesses rises along with the quantity of alcohol consumed daily (Boffeta & Garfinkel, 1990). Other consequences of alcohol use include motor vehicle crashes and other injuries, domestic violence, neglect of work and family, and costs to society associated with police, courts, jails, and unemployment. Altogether, the consequences of alcohol abuse and dependence are estimated to cost the Nation almost $100 billion (NIAAA, 1997a) and 100,000 deaths a year (NIAAA, 1993).

MAJOR CONCEPTUAL ADVANCES IN ALCOHOLISM RESEARCH

Several conceptual advances in alcohol research have been instrumental in advancing the study and understanding of alcoholism. These involve acceptance of alcoholism as a disease; the demonstration that a significant portion of vulnerability to alcoholism is inherited; the application of neuroscience to understanding drinking and the phenomena of addiction; the study of "mental processes" involved in alcohol use, abuse, and dependence; new insights into how alcohol damages organs; the demonstration that prevention can be studied rigorously; and new approaches to treatment.

Alcoholism as a Disease. The acceptance of alcoholism as a medical disorder was the conceptual advance that most influenced the direction and shape of alcoholism research. This concept has evolved progressively and with considerable controversy over the past 200 years (Jaffe, 1993). Competing views have included the idea of alcoholism as a symptom of psychological maladjustment or as the arbitrarily delineated upper end of a continuum of drinking (Keller, 1990). The disease concept defines alcoholism as an independent disorder characterized by a craving for alcohol—a dependence, or addiction. As such, it is distinguished from drinking that is merely heavy, problematic, ill advised, or socially unacceptable. Many alcohol-related problems result from misuse of alcohol by persons who are not alcoholic. Nevertheless, the disease concept has sharpened the focus of alcohol research and is helping to remove the stigma from this major chronic disorder.

Gene Involvement in Vulnerability. In the 1970s, rigorous scientific research began to explore the reasons for the common observation that alcoholism runs in families. The question was, does this familial transmission occur through exposure to the environment, or through the inheritance of genes, or both? Adoption and twin studies provided the first evidence of a genetic component in the risk for alcoholism. This conceptual advance has led to an explosion in human and animal genetic work that promises to lead to the development of new treatments and better-focused prevention efforts for those who are most at risk for developing alcohol problems. What is inherited is not yet known. Among the possibilities are differences in a number of biological and psychological reactions to alcohol use, including temperament, initial sensitivity to the rewarding or aversive qualities of alcohol, ability to develop tolerance after repeated exposure, rates and routes of alcohol metabolism, taste preferences, signaling from peripheral sites to the brain after drinking alcohol, and ability to relate memories of drinking experiences to the outcome of such experiences (expectancies).

Neurosciences Applied to Drinking and Addiction. The application of neuroscience techniques in alcohol research has led to an increased understanding of how alcohol actions in the brain are related to the phenomenon of addiction, including how alcohol affects gene proteins and second messengers and expression of these various substances. New imaging techniques have permitted alcohol neuroscientists to study alcohol's effects on the brain in ways not even possible just a decade ago. The puzzling question of how alcohol—a substance that permeates every part of the body, every cell, and distributes in all body water—can have such specific action is being examined. Research on craving, the prelude to relapse, also is yielding important information on the brain mechanisms involved in this phenomenon. This conceptual advance has led to the development, among other things, of new pharmacotherapies for alcoholism, such as naltrexone and acamprosate, and to the possibility of developing "designer" medications targeted at specific alcohol actions.

"Mental Processes" Involved in Alcohol Use, Abuse, and Dependence. Another conceptual advance in alcohol research is the acceptance of "mental processes" in alcohol addiction. This advance has led to increasing emphasis by investigators on the importance of understanding the cognitive processes involved in alcoholism, as well as the biology of alcoholism. As Y. Dudai, the Israeli neuroscientist, has said, "Psychologists must remember that beyond the behavior is a brain, and the biologist must remember that the animal behaved prior to homogenization!" The acceptance of this concept has stimulated very important research into actions that result from alcohol use because they are expected, rather than from the pharmacology of the drug itself. It also has led to studies investigating whether craving, a major cause of relapse in alcoholism treatment, exists intrinsically or is dependent on cues from the environment.

Alcohol's Effects on the Body. Investigating the toxicology of alcohol, or the damage to the body caused by alcohol use, is one of the oldest areas of alcohol research. In addition to understanding what damage occurs (e.g., alcoholic cirrhosis), scientists now are investigating how, or the mechanisms by which, such damage occurs. The demonstration that alcohol use can potentially benefit health also has helped advance the study of alcohol's effects on the body. Increased understanding of alcohol's action on various body systems has led to, among other things, a new understanding of withdrawal and how to safely detoxify patients, discovery of the mechanisms involved in alcoholic liver damage, and recognition of the effects of low doses of alcohol on the fetus. Research has flourished in the last few years on the toxic effects of alcohol on different receptor systems, such as N-methyl-D-aspartate (NMDA), or nitric oxide, and especially of the elaborate cytokine network that has been shown to be involved in alcohol's toxic effects in the liver. Determining how alcohol affects the body both positively and negatively will help researchers to develop medications and other therapies to prevent or limit the damage that alcohol causes and will help clinicians to provide more accurate advice to their patients on the risks and benefits of alcohol use.

Prevention Can Be Studied Rigorously. The demonstration that it is possible to rigorously study approaches to preventing alcohol abuse and alcoholism, including social and regulatory policies, is a welcome occurrence in the alcohol field. This conceptual advance has stimulated a substantial amount of research seeking to define what programs work best with various populations to prevent alcohol-related problems. The findings from prevention research, applied to various public policies, already have been shown to save lives. New approaches to school-based and community prevention also are demonstrating that well-planned prevention programs based on rigorously studied and validated models can significantly reduce the magnitude and extent of our nation's alcohol-related problems.

New Approaches to Treatment. A major change in the alcohol field is the growing acceptance of the need for alcohol treatment research. Today, many trained alcoholism treatment professionals, including physicians, social workers, nurses, and counselors, expect to have access to scientifically validated screening, assessment, diagnostic and treatment tools. Managed care and other aspects of today's health care policy also demand good data. These and other factors have combined to support the need for alcoholism treatment research. This conceptual advance has led to two important developments. First is the rigorous analysis of things that have been done for a long time, such as subjecting traditional treatment approaches to modern clinical trial research. Second is the development of new verbal treatments (such as brief intervention) and new pharmacotherapies (such as naltrexone in the United States and acamprosate in Europe).

THE PROMISE OF RESEARCH

Alcohol research has one fundamental purpose: to develop the knowledge necessary to effectively prevent and treat alcohol abuse and alcoholism and the consequences of these illnesses. From its modest beginnings a quarter century ago, the alcohol research enterprise has expanded to a broad-based program of biomedical and behavioral research in areas such as the epidemiology of alcohol use, abuse, and dependence; alcohol's effects on the brain; the genetics of alcoholism; alcohol's health effects; the effects of public policies on preventing alcohol use disorders; and clinical trials to develop or evaluate alcoholism treatment therapies. Whether research involves understanding the basic mechanisms of alcohol action or the development of a diagnostic manual for use by clinicians, the science of alcoholism is guided by the "promise of research"—that each new discovery made by alcohol researchers will move us closer to our goal of helping those with alcohol-related problems. The highlights of alcohol research discussed below demonstrate how very far alcohol research has progressed toward fulfilling this promise.

The Genetics of Alcoholism. There is ample evidence that a significant portion of the vulnerability to alcoholism is inherited. Genetics researchers are now actively engaged in identifying the genes that confer this vulnerability and in developing ways to apply this information to clinical populations. The task is difficult because alcoholism is considered to be a polygenic disorder, with many different genes contributing only a portion of the vulnerability. The search for the relevant genes is being pursued in several settings.

Collaborative Project on the Genetics of Alcoholism: One important contributor to the study of the genetics of alcoholism is the Collaborative Study on the Genetics of Alcoholism (COGA), a multisite study at six centers. COGA investigators have interviewed hundreds of probands and families, developed a complex computerized pedigree database, and applied statistical genetics and molecular biology techniques to "informative" families. Phenotypic markers shown previously to be relevant to alcohol are incorporated into the study, including biochemical markers, evoked potential responses, and tests of initial sensitivity to alcohol. (Initial sensitivity to alcohol has been shown to be a strong predictor of later alcoholism [Schuckit & Smith, 1996], suggesting the possibility of a biological marker for identifying individuals, as well as groups, who are at greatest risk of developing alcoholism.)

COGA scientists recently have located chromosomal "hot spots"—areas of potential linkage to alcohol dependence—on chromosomes 1, 2, and 7

(Reich, Edenberg et al., in press). Also, the possibility of protective factors is suggested by possible linkage on chromosome 4 for resilience to alcoholism (Reich, Edenberg et al., in press). In addition, locations for the genes involved in the expression of evoked potential responses, a high-risk marker for alcoholism, have been tentatively identified (Begleiter, Porjesz et al., in press). These findings bring us a step closer to finding the specific genes underlying the genetic vulnerability to this chronic disease.

Animal Genetics: The alcohol research field has been a leader in developing animal models for medical inquiry. Many rat and mouse strains have been selectively bred for sensitivity to various effects of alcohol. The development of such strains demonstrates that the selected trait is, to some extent, genetically determined. Studies in selectively bred strains have demonstrated that tolerance and dependence probably are not controlled by a single mechanism, because it is possible to alter alcohol tolerance without affecting alcohol dependence. Similarities between the mouse and human genome give hope that animal work will provide clues that will accelerate the search for alcohol-related genes in humans.

Scientists also are using animals to identify the location of genes responsible for the genetically influenced traits that are thought to underlie responses to alcohol. These traits are known as "quantitative traits" and more than one gene influences the magnitude of a trait. A section of DNA on a chromosome that is thought to influence a quantitative trait is known as a quantitative trait loci (QTL). Using powerful new genetic analysis techniques, researchers have begun to map QTL. Through QTL mapping and analysis, researchers can locate and measure the effects of a single QTL on a trait, or phenotype, and ultimately gain knowledge of the complex physiologic underpinnings of alcohol-related behavior. For example, scientists have identified two loci—*Alcp*1 and *Alcp*2—that appear to have significant gender-specific effects on alcohol consumption in mice (Melo, Shendure et al., 1995). This finding suggests that preference for alcohol, a quantitative trait, may be controlled by different genetic mechanisms in males and females.

Molecular genetic techniques also permit highly selective breeding of mice that express different receptor subtypes on their neurons. Animal models that are devoted to alcohol drinking preferences and methodologies in genetic "knock out" technology and transgenetics all contribute to an understanding of why some people are more vulnerable to developing alcoholism.

Gene-Environment Interactions: Although a significant portion of the vulnerability to development of alcoholism is inherited, ample research indicates that both biological and nonbiological factors influence drinking behavior. For example, even though we can predict that an Asian individual who inherits an $ALDH_2$ (aldehyde dehydrogenase) mutation will be much less likely to develop alcoholism than an individual who does not inherit this mutation, more precise prediction of outcome requires additional knowledge of that individual's cultural context and alcohol-specific expectancies. In recent years, alcohol researchers have begun to test and apply models that emphasize the process by which environmental factors can transform heritable characteristics to either promote or impede the expression of alcohol problems and the reciprocal influence that biological and nonbiological factors can impose over time.

An example of this type of research are the now-classic adoption studies (Cloninger, Bohman & Sigvardsson, 1981), which have identified two alcoholism subtypes that differ in inheritance patterns as well as other characteristics. Type 1 alcoholism, which affects both men and women, requires the presence of a specific genetic background as well as certain environmental factors (e.g., low-socioeconomic status of father). Mild or severe alcohol abuse, adult onset of the disease, a loss of control over drinking, and guilt and fear about alcohol dependence characterize this alcoholism subtype. Individuals with this type of alcoholism generally exhibit high harm avoidance and low novelty-seeking personality traits, and drink primarily to relieve anxiety.

In contrast, Type 2 alcoholism, which occurs more commonly in men than in women, primarily requires a genetic predisposition; environmental factors play only a minor role in its development. Type 2 alcoholism is associated with early onset (before age 25) of both alcohol abuse and criminal behavior and an inability to abstain from alcohol. Type 2 alcoholics exhibit high novelty-seeking personality characteristics and consume alcohol primarily to induce euphoria (Cloninger, Sigvardsson & Bohman, 1996).

Characterizing the specific environmental factors that play a role in the etiology of alcoholism is emerging as a fundamental research issue. Predisposing genetic factors may remain dormant in the absence of environmental cues, while alcoholism may develop in the absence of genetic predisposition. Consequently, it is important not only to identify the principal environmental factors involved in the development of alcoholism, but also the manner and extent to which they interact with genetic factors. Greater knowledge of these factors and their contribution to alcohol problems will enable the design of prevention and early intervention strategies that focus on addressing the environmental risk factors for alcohol abuse and alcoholism.

Alcohol and the Brain. The actions of alcohol that cause intoxication, reinforce drinking behavior, and lead to addiction are based principally in the brain. Alcohol investigators have been vigorously pursuing research to understand the mechanisms in the brain by which alcohol produces these effects. For example, several lines of investigation using animal models have helped scientists to discover two factors—reinforcement and cellular adaptation—that may explain alcohol-dependent behavior. Alcohol is considered to be reinforcing because the ingestion of alcohol, or withdrawal from chronic long-term alcohol use, or sometimes just the sight or smell of an alcoholic drink, increases the probability that an individual will drink. One explanation for reinforcement is that alcohol appears to interact with the brain's reward system, thus stimulating continued use: this is called "positive reinforcement." Relief of abstinence, or negative reinforcement, is another possible mechanism. For example, alcohol-dependent rats undergoing withdrawal have been shown to perform lever press responses for alcohol in an apparent attempt to alleviate withdrawal symptoms (Schulteis, Hyytia et al., 1996). Thus, negative reinforcement also may contribute to continued drinking; its precise mechanism is a subject of current investigation.

When alcohol is chronically present, some neurons seem to adapt to this physiological change by enhancing or reducing their response to normal stimuli. This adaptation is hypothesized to lead to the development of tolerance and dependence. A primary question under investigation is the mechanism of cellular adaptation to the long-term presence of alcohol. One successful approach to exploring cellular adaptation is through molecular genetic studies. Alcohol scientists have uncovered evidence that alcohol can cause changes in cellular communication and functioning by directly influencing the function of specific genes. Sophisticated genetic mapping techniques and related technology may pinpoint exactly which genes are involved. Researchers can selectively investigate the effects of alcohol on specific receptor constituents by directly manipulating genetic material. Data obtained from studies such as these will provide major advances in understanding the process of cellular adaptation to alcohol and thus provide clues about the mechanisms of alcohol dependence, tolerance, and withdrawal.

Alcohol investigators also have evidence that the cellular adaptive changes that occur with alcohol exposure can alter the degree of reinforcement experienced. Thus, adaptation and reinforcement, acting in concert, determine a person's short-term or acute response to alcohol as well as the long-term or chronic craving for alcohol that characterizes dependence. Some adaptive changes may be permanent and are hypothesized to produce the persistent sense of discomfort during abstinence that again leads to relapse. Since relapse is very common among recovering alcoholics, understanding the mechanisms that cause or enable relapse is critical to treating alcohol dependence. Clarification of these processes will enable scientists to develop specifically designed medications and may lead to the design of effective treatment strategies tailored to individual physiology and psychology.

Because alcohol bathes every cell in the body, the challenge is to sort out the critical effects that cause uncontrolled drinking in the face of negative consequences, as well as how alcohol causes brain damage. Following on the discovery of complex cell membranes, neuroscientists began probing the ways in which the brain controls thinking and behavior and movement and other key bodily functions. Current research strongly suggests that alcohol affects multiple neurotransmitter systems in the brain (whereas illicit drugs bind to only one). The specific neurotransmitters involved in the behavioral aspects of alcoholism, the mode of release, and the corresponding receptors involved in these effects now are under investigation. For example, using animal models, scientists have determined precisely the configuration of one serotonin receptor—5-HT_{1B}—that mediates alcohol consumption in mice (Crabbe, Phillips et al., 1996).

Knowledge of the specific receptor binding sites for alcohol may lead to a diagnostic tool for predicting an individual's vulnerability to the development of alcoholism and is invaluable in the design of medications to help individuals reduce their alcohol consumption.

Health Effects of Alcohol Use. Research over the past 25 years has brought about an increasing awareness of alcohol's medical effects and the mechanisms by which these effects occur. There also is growing research evidence that alcohol may have certain beneficial effects. These damaging and protective effects, the mechanisms by which the damage or protection occurs, and the risks and benefits to individuals of using alcohol are under study.

The Liver: Liver damage may be among the most serious consequences of alcohol abuse. Heavy alcohol use may cause liver inflammation and progressive liver scarring (i.e., fibrosis or cirrhosis). Among the mechanisms thought to contribute to liver damage are the release of cytokines, which are substances with inflammatory, fibrogenic, and cell growth-promoting properties, and the formation of free radicals, which are reactive oxygen molecules that can interact with proteins, lipids and DNA, causing damage or death to liver cells. Acetaldehyde, a principal metabolite of alcohol, can form adducts by reacting with cellular proteins, potentially resulting in direct damage to liver cells or stimulation of inflammatory autoimmune reactions in liver tissues. Acetaldehyde protein adducts also may stimulate liver cell collagen synthesis, a process thought to contribute to fibrosis and cirrhosis. A promising approach to preventing fibrosis involves administration of polyunsaturated soybean lecithin, which may promote the breakdown of hepatic collagen.

Cardiovascular System: Alcohol use can contribute to heart and cardiovascular disease. Heavy alcohol consumption can interfere with the mechanical functions of the heart and may cause progressive functional changes and tissue damage, leading to cardiomyopathy and heart failure. Excessive alcohol consumption also is associated with high blood pressure and an increased risk for coronary artery disease and stroke. However, light to moderate drinking appears to be beneficial in preventing coronary artery disease, perhaps by elevating blood levels of high-density lipoprotein or by inhibiting clotting processes that contribute to atherosclerosis and thrombosis.

Neuropsychological Disorders: Alcohol-associated neuropsychological disorders typically involve damage to the limbic system, the diencephalon, and the frontal cerebral cortex of the brain. Among the problems resulting from this damage are deficits in short-term memory, disruption of cognitive and motor functioning, reduced perceptual abilities, and emotional and personality changes. With advances in brain and functional imaging techniques and the development of neurocognitive tests, researchers hope to identify connections between alcohol-associated structural and metabolic changes in the brain and alcohol-associated impairment in mental processes.

Endocrine System: A variety of studies show that alcohol interferes with normal endocrine system activities. Excessive alcohol use may profoundly impair reproductive development and function in both women and men. In postmenopausal women, low-level alcohol consumption may enhance estrogen production, which in turn may provide protection from osteoporosis as well as from coronary heart disease. In premenopausal women, chronic heavy drinking can contribute to many reproductive disorders, including problems with the menstrual cycle, early menopause, and increased risk of spontaneous abortions. Some of these problems have been observed in women classified as social drinkers (two or more standard drinks a day). Women who drink at these levels also may increase their risk for breast cancer. Chronic alcohol exposure may alter the secretion patterns of growth hormone. Consequences of this disruption include numerous metabolic and endocrine changes, because growth hormone regulates levels of other growth stimulators as well as alcohol- and steroid-metabolizing enzymes. In addition, alcohol withdrawal induces marked elevations in glucocorticoid stress hormones. Glucocorticoids in excess may be neurotoxic; thus, glucocorticoid elevations may contribute to the behavioral and neurological changes observed in withdrawal.

Immune System: In healthy individuals, the complex network of lymphoid cells and regulatory cytokines that compose the immune system efficiently detects and eliminates potential pathogens. Alcohol consumption, particularly of a chronic or abusive nature, depresses the immune system by altering the function, regulation, and distribution of lymphoid cells. The result may be immune system dysfunction and an increased susceptibility to infectious disease and cancer. Immunological abnormalities observed with long-term alcohol abuse in humans also include autoimmune processes that damage liver tissues.

Fetal Alcohol Syndrome: Fetal alcohol syndrome (FAS) is a severe alcohol-induced birth defect, consisting of mild facial anomalies, growth retardation, and severe impairment of the central nervous system. Although FAS is associated with chronic, heavy maternal drinking, large individual differences have been observed in the incidence and severity of the disorder in the offspring of drinking women. Children with FAS and alcohol-related birth defects (ARBD)—in which affected individuals exhibit some, but not all, of the attributes of FAS—frequently are described as being hyperactive and impulsive and having short attention spans. Maladaptive behaviors, such as poor judgment, failure to consider the consequences of one's actions, and difficulty perceiving social cues, are common.

Recent studies indicate that the deficits associated with FAS are pervasive and long-lasting and have a marked effect on an individual's ability to live independently. Although many of the physical characteristics of FAS become less prominent after puberty, the intellectual problems endure and the behavioral, emotional, and social problems become more pronounced. Findings from some (but not all) studies of the relationship of quantity, frequency, timing, and pattern of maternal drinking to infant and child outcomes have revealed an association between prenatal alcohol exposure and growth deficits at birth. However, the timing of alcohol exposure, the dose-response, and the effect of maternal drinking patterns at particular stages of fetal development have not yet been defined.

Alcohol-Related Trauma: Alcohol use and abuse can have adverse effects on a wide variety of behaviors, with serious consequences for persons of all ages and backgrounds and for the health and well-being of society. Motor vehicle crashes, falls, fires, and drownings cause more than 75% of deaths from unintentional injuries (NIAAA, 1997b), and alcohol use has been associated with a large percentage of deaths from these causes. Alcohol use also has been linked with high-risk sexual behavior as well as with family and marital violence, homicide, and suicide.

Researchers have theorized that alcohol and injury may interact in two ways. First, the context and the place in which an individual consumes alcohol may result in an increased risk of injury. For example, drinking in bars where the risk of assault may be high increases an individual's exposure to hazardous circumstances. Second, direct biological effects of alcohol may lead to injury by interfering with perception of and responsiveness to potential hazards. The consequences of alcohol's direct biological effects are apparent in the large proportion of motor vehicle-related injuries and deaths associated with alcohol.

Traffic crashes are the leading cause of death for Americans under the age of 35, and alcohol use plays a significant role in these deaths. Encouragingly, the proportion of deaths from alcohol-related traffic crashes has decreased in recent years—a 28% decrease in the number of intoxicated drivers killed in traffic crashes between 1983 and 1993, with reductions of 44% among persons 16 to 20 years of age (NIAAA, 1997c). Research suggests that raising the minimum legal drinking age to 21 has helped to reduce the proportion of alcohol-related highway crashes reported for teenagers (O'Malley & Wagenaar, 1991). Research also has shown that the so-called "zero tolerance" laws aimed at underage drinkers who drive has helped to save young lives (Hingson, Heeren et al., 1994).

Direct associations between alcohol use and other types of injury, such as those associated with aircraft crashes, fires and burns, boating accidents, and violence, are less clear. For example, although associations have been observed between alcohol use by pilots and reduced aircraft safety, these findings must be interpreted with caution because many of the data are based on individual case studies rather than on epidemiologic studies. However, simulated flight experiments clearly show that pilot planning, performance, and vigilance are impaired by acute and hangover effects of alcohol.

Data from numerous studies support a strong relationship between alcohol and various types of violence, including homicides, suicides, and spousal abuse. For example, a review of investigations examining the link between alcohol and homicide revealed that in most studies, more than 60% of persons who committed homicides were drinking at the time of the offense (NIAAA, 1997d). Alcohol use also may increase the risk of becoming a victim of violence and of sustaining injury due to violence. One study has shown that emergency room patients who were injured in violent events were twice as likely to have consumed alcohol than were patients whose injuries were unrelated to violence (NIAAA, 1997d). However, the presence of alcohol in violent episodes does not mean that alcohol itself causes violent behavior. Rather, alcohol is likely to be only one of multiple factors that interact to precipitate violent behavior in some individuals.

Finally, alcohol use is thought to play a role in many risk-taking or sensation-seeking behaviors. For example, research has correlated drinking with high-risk sexual behaviors (those that contribute to the spread of sexually transmitted diseases such as HIV/AIDS). Understanding the role of alcohol in high-risk sexual behavior is of great concern, particularly in view of survey results showing that individuals who met diagnostic criteria for alcohol dependence or abuse or who are heavy or binge drinkers have an increased risk of exposure to human immunodeficiency virus and of developing AIDS (NIAAA, 1997e).

Preventing Alcohol-Related Problems. Historically, programs to prevent alcohol abuse and alcoholism have relied almost exclusively on educational approaches. During the past 10 to 15 years, there has been increasing interest in research into strategies aimed at preventing alcohol problems by altering the social, legal, and economic context in which drinking occurs (Holder & Wallack, 1986).

Prevention encompasses activities or actions ranging from those affecting the whole population through social and regulatory controls to those affecting specific groups, such as adolescents, or the individual. Many of these activities overlap. For example, health warning labels, a product of legislation (social and regulatory control), also are educational. The good news is that, using contemporary tools of science, prevention can be rigorously studied with meaningful results that are generalizable to other populations. Current research evidence shows that some prevention efforts are effective, while others have little or no effect. Having this knowledge will help local communities, the states, and others who have made significant investments in prevention activities develop or refine existing programs to achieve their desired objectives.

Although prevention research is difficult to do, because investigators have little control over activities in the community that may affect outcomes, important results have been obtained in well-designed studies. Alcohol prevention research has shown, for example, that young lives can be saved by two measures: increasing the legal drinking age to 21 (O'Malley & Wagenaar, 1991; Wagenaar, 1986) and setting the maximum blood alcohol limit in young drivers to .02% ("zero tolerance") (Hingson, Heeren & Winter, 1994). School-based programs closely linked to other community activities also have been shown to reduce drinking in preadolescents.

The past few years have seen tremendous progress in specifying and estimating a number of important economic relationships connected to alcohol use. For example, historical analysis (Cook, 1981) and computer modeling (Chaloupka, 1993) indicate that highway deaths and cirrhosis deaths have varied inversely with the price of beverage alcohol and that even heavy drinkers drink less in response to increases in alcohol price. Moreover, overall consumption of beer, wine, and distilled spirits declines in response to increases in the prices or taxes associated with these beverages. But this research also suggests that the small proportion of drinkers with the highest consumption levels may be much less sensitive to price changes than are drinkers who consume at more moderate levels. Several studies also have found that increases in alcoholic beverage taxes and prices are associated with reductions in motor vehicle fatalities and other adverse outcomes that are frequently associated with alcohol consumption. Obviously, the issues involved in using price or taxing policy to address alcohol problems are complex; they involve not just science but economic, social, and political issues as well. Science can contribute to this policy debate, but it is only one of many viewpoints that must be considered (Kenkel & Manning, 1996).

Treating Alcohol Abuse and Alcoholism. The principal goal of alcoholism treatment is to help alcoholics maintain sobriety. Research progress has been made in developing both behavioral strategies and medications, such as naltrexone, to help achieve this goal. These two classes of treatment strategies are not competitive. Rather, research suggests that pharmacologic agents may be combined with verbal therapy to improve treatment outcomes.

Traditional behavioral therapies include exposure to Alcoholics Anonymous, use of disulfiram, group therapy, didactic sessions about alcoholism, teaching about alcoholism as a disease, vocational counseling, or family therapy. Other therapies include "behavior modification" approaches, which emphasize coping skills and techniques patients are taught to recognize and manage situations that allegedly are stressful and trigger relapse. A third approach, especially suggested for the less dependent, is "minimal intervention": instructing the patient about the consequences of drinking, recommending abstinence or reducing drinking, and then leaving the patient to his or her own devices without extensive repeated treatment sessions.

Many of the behavioral treatments that have been used in treating alcoholism evolved informally and are based on clinical judgment and anecdotal information about what works best. Only during the last decade have modern standards of evaluating treatment outcomes, including the use of controls, blinding, and random assignment of subjects, been used to evaluate existing alcoholism treatments. For example, although disulfiram has been used to treat alcoholism since 1949, it was not until 1986 that the efficacy of this medication was subjected to research methods. An individual taking disulfiram experiences uncomfortable physical reactions (e.g., nausea, vomiting, and facial flushing) if he or she drinks alcohol. It was presumed that an individual taking disulfiram would avoid alcohol rather than experience these decidedly unpleasant reactions. However, in a large, multisite, double-blind controlled clinical trial conducted by the Department of Veterans Affairs, researchers found that disulfiram alone did not improve abstinence; rather, patients who wanted to drink simply stopped taking the medication or drank in spite of the aversive reaction (Fuller, Branchey et al., 1986). However, patients who remained in the study and continued to take their disulfiram exhibited fewer drinking days. This research demonstrated the importance of ensuring medication compliance in disulfiram treatment.

A significant advance in understanding what works in alcoholism treatment resulted from a large multisite clinical trial (Project MATCH) initiated by NIAAA. The hypothesis that patients who are appropriately matched to treatments will show better outcomes than those who are unmatched or mismatched is well founded in medicine, behavioral science, and alcoholism treatment. The findings from Project MATCH, however, challenge this notion. In this trial, three specific treatment approaches were evaluated: Twelve Step Facilitation; Cognitive-Behavioral Coping Skills Therapy; and Motivational Enhancement. Project MATCH did not find any decisive match (although patients with low psychiatric severity did better with Twelve Step facilitation therapy than with cognitive-behavioral therapy), leading investigators to speculate that patient-treatment matching does not substantially alter treatment outcome. Treatment in all three approaches resulted in substantial reductions in drinking, with reductions sustained over a 12-month period. Alcoholism treatment also was found to result in decreased alcohol-related problems, other drug use problems, and depression, and improvements in liver functioning. These findings are good news for treatment providers and for patients, who can have confidence that any one of the treatments tested, if well delivered, represents the state of the art in behavioral treatments.

Controlled clinical trials also led to approval of the use of the medication naltrexone as an adjunct to behavioral treatment. A product of neuroscience research, naltrexone, an opiate antagonist, is the first medication approved to help maintain sobriety after detoxification from alcohol since disulfiram's approval in 1949. Studies have shown that, used in combination with verbal therapy, naltrexone prevented relapse better than standard verbal therapy alone (O'Malley, Jaffe et al., 1992, 1996). This coupling of verbal with pharmacological approaches may produce profound changes in the way we view and treat alcoholism. For example, one therapy might continue to function if the other failed, each therapy might increase the efficacy of the other, or verbal and pharmacological therapy might act on the same neural circuits. This last is an especially intriguing possibility for which there already is some evidence in another field. In a study of obsessive-compulsive disorder, positron emission tomography (PET) scans of patients before and after behavioral treatment were compared with PET scans of patients before and after pharmacological treatment. Changes in the scans of patients who had responded to the behavioral treatment resembled changes in patients who had responded to the pharmacological treatment (Baxter, Schwartz et al., 1992).

A variety of other promising medications also are being tested, including the opiate antagonist nalmefene and the European-developed NMDA system inhibitor, acamprosate. The efficacy of fluoxetine and sertraline in treating alcoholics with collateral major depression also is being evaluated. In the future, advances in understanding brain neurochemistry and physiology—particularly the biological bases for alcohol use and the phenomenon of craving—will provide new pharmacotherapeutic possibilities and will have a major impact on the effectiveness and cost of health care in the treatment of alcoholism. Future research will focus on the complex biochemical mechanisms of alcoholism, including the abnormal appetite for alcohol that leads to impaired control over intake, tolerance, and craving.

To find better treatments, researchers are looking for new pharmacotherapies that target the mechanisms of the addiction itself. Increasing knowledge about the brain processes underlying addiction is aiding scientists in this search. For example, drugs that interfere with the reward properties of alcohol may be found to block the phenomenon of craving and become a valuable adjunct to alcoholism treatment. With a more precise understanding of the physiology of alcohol withdrawal, new drugs may be developed that allow improved medical management of the withdrawal syndrome, or reduce the potential for *delirium tremens*. Science also may provide a better understanding of how the withdrawal experience affects both subsequent drinking and the potential for effective treatment. Using pharmacotherapies that control specific clinical features of alcoholism (e.g., craving) in combination with traditional behavioral and verbal therapies has the potential to greatly enhance treatment outcomes.

Refined therapies will benefit many people. For alcohol-dependent individuals, who face the realistic fear of relapse, improved interventions can abate and, optimally, prevent relapse occurrences and halt continuing disease that ultimately can lead to death. For society, which bears the weight of the enormous economic and social costs of problem drinking, improved treatment strategies that heighten the potential for long-term abstinence can lessen this burden and enhance the quality of civic life. New therapies promise to reduce the billions of dollars lost annually from reduced workplace productivity, alcohol-related injuries and illnesses, and alcohol-related premature deaths. Further, more effective treatments can reduce the frequency of the various social tragedies, such as motor vehicle crashes, falls, drownings, fires and burns, crime and family violence, associated with alcohol misuse.

Technological Progress: Scientific progress in unraveling the puzzle that is alcoholism will be aided by increasingly sophisticated research tools and techniques. Animal models are a prime example of techniques that will help define and refine our knowledge concerning who is at risk for developing alcoholism, and why. Developing models with correlate features of the human disease, such as craving or tolerance, will enable scientists to probe the biochemical and physiological mechanisms underlying these features. In turn, the animal models can serve as fundamental tools for developing and assessing treatment measures for the various elements of alcoholism. As one of the first steps in medications development, animal studies can ensure that further tests can be conducted in humans without danger.

Most exciting in the coming years is the very real possibility of using individual brain imaging techniques and combining information derived from different techniques—such as magnetic resonance imaging (MRI), positron emission tomography (PET), and electrophysiological studies—to create new conceptions of the dynamic workings of the brain. At the very least, integrating data from studies that have applied different technologies will help to resolve uncertainties about particular brain pathways and behaviors that regulate responses to alcohol. Computer-aided modeling of cell assemblies will be an additional innovation. Because of the complex pharmacological effects of alcohol and the sheer number of brain regions affected by alcohol, it generally is recognized that a global understanding of alcohol's actions will require sophisticated technological models of networks of brain activity. Brain and behavioral science research also will be able to use computer-aided modeling and imaging techniques that will allow for a better understanding of addictive behaviors and enable early detection of alcohol-related problems.

CONCLUSIONS

The science of alcoholism has made much progress since its early years, when neither science nor the alcohol field believed that research on the causes and consequences of alcohol abuse and alcoholism was necessary. As we move toward the 21st century, there will be many challenges—and many opportunities—for further scientific progress in the alcohol field. Each step toward solving the currently unanswerable questions is a step toward a future in which alcohol-related problems yield to effective, science-based prevention and treatment, and the burden on individuals, families, communities, and nations of alcohol abuse and alcoholism is diminished.

ACKNOWLEDGMENT: The author wishes to acknowledge the outstanding assistance of Ms. Brenda G. Hewitt in the development and preparation of this manuscript.

REFERENCES

Baxter LR, Schwartz JM, Bergman KS et al. (1992). Caudate glucose metabolic rate changes with both drug and behavior therapy for obsessive-compulsive disorder. *Archives of General Psychiatry* 49:681–689.

Begleiter H, Porjesz B, Reich T et al. (in press). Quantitative trait loci analysis of human event-related brain potentials: P3 voltage. *Electroencephalography and Clinical Neurophysiology*.

Boffeta P & Garfinkel L (1990). Alcohol drinking and mortality among men enrolled in an American Cancer Society Prospective Study. *Epidemiology* 1(5):342–348.

Chaloupka FJ (1993). Effects of price on alcohol-related problems. *Alcohol Health and Research World* 17:46–53.

Cloninger CR, Bohman M, & Sigvardsson S (1981). Inheritance of alcohol abuse. *Archives of General Psychiatry* 38:861–868.

Cloninger CR, Sigvardsson S & Bohman M(1996). Type I and Type II alcoholism: An update. *Alcohol Health and Research World* 20(1):30–35.

Cook PJ (1981). The effect of liquor taxes on drinking, cirrhosis, and auto accidents. In MH Moore & DR Gerstein (eds.) *Alcohol and Public Policy: Beyond the Shadow of Prohibition*. Washington, DC: National Academy of Sciences, 255–297.

Crabbe JC, Phillips TJ, Feller DJ et al. (1996). Elevated alcohol consumption in null mutant mice lacking 5-HT_{1B} serotonin receptors. *Journal of Nature Genetics* 14(l):98–101.

Fuller RK, Branchey L, Brightwell DR et al. (1986). Disulfiram treatment of alcoholism. *Journal of the American Medical Association* 256:1449–1455.

Grant BF, Harford TC, Dawson DA, Chou P, DuFour M & Pickering RS (1994). Prevalence of *DSM-IV* alcohol abuse and dependence—United States, 1992. *Alcohol Health and Research World* 183:243–248.

Grant BF & Dawson DA (1997). Age at onset of alcohol use and its association with *DSM-IV* alcohol abuse and dependence: Results from the National Longitudinal Alcohol Epidemiologic Survey. *Journal of Substance Abuse* 9:103–110.

Hingson R, Heeren T & Winter M (1994). Lower legal blood alcohol limits for young drivers. *Public Health Reports* 109:736–744.

Holder HD & Wallack L (1986). Contemporary perspectives for preventing alcohol problems: An empirically-derived model. *Journal of Public Health Policy* 7(3):324–339.

Jaffe JH (1993). The concept of dependence: Historical reflections. *Alcohol Health and Research World* 17(3):188–189.

Keller M (1990). *Models of Alcoholism: From Days of Old to Nowadays*. Piscataway, NJ: Rutgers Center of Alcohol Studies.

Kenkel D & Manning W (1996). Perspectives on alcohol taxation. *Alcohol Health and Research World* 20(4):230–238.

Melo JA, Shendure J, Pociask K & Silver LM (1995). Identification of sex-specific quantitative trait loci controlling alcohol preference in C57BL/6 mice. *Journal of Nature Genetics* 13:147–153.

Midanik LT & Room R (1992). The epidemiology of alcohol consumption. *Alcohol Health and Research World* 16(3):183–190.

National Institute on Alcohol Abuse and Alcoholism (1993). *Eighth Special Report to the U.S. Congress on Alcohol and Health* (Publication No. 94-3699). Bethesda, MD: National Institutes of Health, 13.

National Institute on Alcohol Abuse and Alcoholism (1997a). *Ninth Special Report to the U.S. Congress on Alcohol and Health* (Publication No. 97-4017). Bethesda, MD: National Institutes of Health, 388.

National Institute on Alcohol Abuse and Alcoholism (1997b). *Ninth Special Report to the U.S. Congress on Alcohol and Health* (Publication No. 97-4017). Bethesda, MD: National Institutes of Health, 247.

National Institute on Alcohol Abuse and Alcoholism (1997c). *Ninth Special Report to the U.S. Congress on Alcohol and Health* (Publication No. 97-4017). Bethesda, MD: National Institutes of Health, 251.

National Institute on Alcohol Abuse and Alcoholism (1997d). *Ninth Special Report to the U.S. Congress on Alcohol and Health* (Publication No. 97-4017). Bethesda, MD: National Institutes of Health, 259.

National Institute on Alcohol Abuse and Alcoholism (1997e). *Ninth Special Report to the U.S. Congress on Alcohol and Health* (Publication No. 97-4017). Bethesda, MD: National Institutes of Health, 267.

O'Malley PM & Wagenaar AC (1991). Effects of minimum drinking age laws on alcohol use, related behaviors, and traffic crash involvement among American youth: 1976–1987. *Journal of Studies on Alcohol.* 52:478–491.

O'Malley SS, Jaffe AJ, Chang G, Schottenfeld RS, Mever RE & Rounsaville B (1992). Naltrexone and coping skills therapy for alcohol dependence: A controlled study. *Archives of General Psychiatry* 49:881–887.

O'Malley SS, Jaffe AJ, Chang G et al. (1996). Six-month follow-up of naltrexone and psychotherapy for alcohol dependence. *Archives of General Psychiatry* 53:217–224.

Project MATCH Research Group (1997). Matching Alcoholism Treatments to Client Heterogeneity: Project MATCH posttreatment drinking outcomes. *Journal of Studies on Alcohol* 58(1):7–29.

Reich T, Edenberg H, Goate A et al. (In press). A genome-wide search for genes affecting the risk for alcohol dependence. *Neuropsychiatric Genetics*.

Schuckit MA & Smith TL (1996). 8-year follow-up of 450 sons of alcoholic and control subjects. *Archives of General Psychiatry* 53(3):202–210.

Schulteis G, Hyytia, Heinrichs SC & Koob GF (1996). Effects of chronic ethanol exposure on oral self-administration of ethanol or saccharin by Wistar rats. *Alcoholism: Clinical & Experimental Research* 20(1):164–171.

Wagenaar AC (1986). Preventing highway crashes by raising the legal minimum age for drinking: The Michigan experience 6 years later. *Journal of Safety Research* 17:101–109.

What We Know: Drug Addiction Is a Brain Disease

Alan I. Leshner, Ph.D.

A few years ago, Tommy Lasorda, then-manager of the Los Angeles Dodgers, speaking about a ball player with a drug problem, said:

"How anybody can be dumb enough and weak enough to take it is something that I cannot comprehend. It's crazy. . . . Here's a guy that's making a lot of money and he's got a lot of fame, he's got a family, and yet he puts something inside of him, knowing that this thing could ruin his career—ruin his entire life, and yet they have the weakness to put it into their body.

"That's not a sickness, it's a weakness. A sickness is when you get something—leukemia, you get cancer, or you have a bad heart—that is a sickness. But when you put something inside your body knowing that this is wrong, that to me is a weakness."

In an earlier generation, such comments might have been made in regard to depression. A generation from now—sooner, one hopes—these comments, which reflect a commonly held view of drug addiction, will seem similarly outdated.

The reality, based on 25 years of research, is that drug addiction is a brain disease—a disease that disrupts the mechanisms responsible for generating, modulating, and controlling our cognitive, emotional, and social behavior. Just as many other diseases and disorders once thought to be caused by psychological problems or stress, such as ulcers (NIH, 1994), and schizophrenia (Barondes, Alberts et al., 1997), have been shown to have a physical origin, drug addiction also has been shown to be a disease with a physical basis. However, because of misconceptions about the brain, behavior, and mind, and the resulting societal and cultural biases, there is a "disconnect" between the scientific data and public perceptions and, in many cases, professional perceptions about the nature of addiction and its appropriate treatment.

Although the victims of almost all diseases are viewed with compassion and sympathy, those suffering from most brain diseases are not so fortunate. Malfunction of the kidneys is equated with kidney disease. But malfunction of the brain is equated with being different, eccentric, crazy. Not very long ago, those with mental illnesses were shunned and mistreated, shipped off to asylums, to Bedlam, where their antics provided entertainment for visitors. The public could not understand why someone with depression was emotionally and physically paralyzed or why a person with schizophrenia heard voices or saw apparitions. In the absence of knowledge, these conditions were attributed to other-worldly causes, ranging from weak will to poor parenting. Modern science has shown, of course, that depression and schizophrenia are physical diseases of the brain that manifest themselves—as do all brain diseases and disorders, including autism, stroke, obsessive-compulsive disorder, mania, anorexia, *and* drug addiction—in behavior. The function of the brain is to generate, mediate, and modify behavior—to produce mind. Drug addiction alters the functioning of the brain and changes mind.

The brain of someone addicted to drugs is a changed brain; it is qualitatively different from that of a normal person in fundamental ways, including gene expression (Liu, Nickolenko & Sharpe, 1994; Daunais & McGinty, 1995; Konradi, Leveque & Hyman, 1996; Curran, Akil & Watson, 1996), glucose utilization (Volkow, Gillespie et al., 1996a; London, Cascella et al., 1990), and responsiveness to environmental cues (O'Brien, Childress et al., 1993; Kilgus & Pumariega, 1994; Luborsky, McKay et al., 1995). Whether or not these changes produce physical or psychological addiction, as viewed in a classical sense, is unimportant. What is critical is that drugs change the brain and thereby produce uncontrollable, compulsive drug-seeking and use—the essence of addiction.

A New Paradigm. To create a new paradigm of how addiction develops, it would be helpful to use an analogy to cardiovascular disease and high cholesterol. Although the victim of a heart attack or stroke could be said to bring the disease on him- or herself, once diagnosed, the disease itself is treated, not its long-distant origins. In this more productive concept, it makes little difference whether a disease is brought on by excessive exposure to fat or to abused drugs; one changes the functioning of the arteries and the heart, the other changes the functioning of the brain. Both require treatment.

It is interesting to note that opiate (Pert & Snyder, 1973) and lipoprotein (Brown & Goldstein, 1976) receptors were identified at approximately the same time. How different the reaction to diseases that act through these two classes of receptors! On the one hand, following a massive research effort, extraordinarily effective cholesterol-lowering drugs were developed (Hebert, Gaziano & Chan, 1997) to treat heart disease. These drugs are used extensively by physicians and accepted by the public. On the other hand, until recently there was little interest in developing medications to treat addiction and poor acceptance of those already approved.

Society views addicts as being responsible for their problems. In some sense that is true. Initial drug use is a voluntary behavior. However, over time, users lose control over their drug use, they become *addicted*. To deal with their addiction effectively requires a shift from blaming them and exhorting them to change their evil ways to treating them. The focus must change from who is at fault to what to do about the problem.

Most drug addicts would prefer to stop using drugs. That this proves to be so difficult is, in itself, a demonstration of the reality of the disease. Consider one of the most common addictions, to tobacco. More than 50% of tobacco smokers who have cardiovascular disease and are told that continued smoking will lead to an early death are unable to quit (Rigotti, McKool & Shiffman, 1994). It is not that most smokers are weak-willed, but that nicotine has changed the brains of smokers so that they cannot stop. Mr. Lasorda asks how a successful athlete can ruin his life by taking harmful drugs. The answer is that, given what the drugs have done to him, the addicted athlete no longer has a choice. He has a disease that does not allow him to stop.

THE MIND AND THE BRAIN

To come to terms with the problems of mental diseases in general and drug addiction in particular, the mind-brain dualism of our scientific and philosophical heritage must be discarded. This separation has little heuristic or practical value in light of modern scientific discoveries. Mind and behavior do not exist without brain activity; although the exact mechanisms have yet to be specified, it is obvious that cognition, emotion, learning, and memory all emanate from cohesive brain activity. Absent such activity, there is disordered behavior and loss of mind.

This reality is confronted daily by countless families across the country who are caring for elderly parents with Alzheimer's disease. The body is there—it consumes oxygen, metabolizes sugar, disposes of waste—but the person is gone because the brain no longer works properly.

Alzheimer's disease is an extreme case of a loss of cognitive function and the global deterioration of mind. It is easily recognized for what it is: a brain disease. Other brain diseases can produce more specific effects: hallucinations, seizures, mania, depression. The public and, to some extent, the health professions need to more fully appreciate the fact that changes in the brain lead to behavioral diseases and that addiction is just another such disease.

The repeated administration of abused drugs causes changes in the functioning of the brain—to addiction. Almost all psychoactive drugs activate the mesolimbic dopamine system (Koob, 1996), an area of the brain thought to mediate reward and appetitive behaviors. Although defining the precise mechanisms is the target of an intense research effort, it is known that repeated self-administration of drugs produces a qualitative change in the way the brain functions. The affected individual has an intense need for, and focus on, repeating the drug experience. But there comes a point, as is the case when a depressed person becomes clinically depressed, at which the drug abuser becomes an addict. At that point, it seems as if a figurative "switch" has been thrown and the drug abuser suffers a significant loss in his or her ability to make free choices about continued use of drugs.

Just as depression is more than a lot of sadness, drug addiction is more than a lot of drug use. The addict cannot voluntarily move back and forth between abuse and addiction because the addicted brain is, in fact, different in its neurobiology from the nonaddicted brain.

Addiction, therefore, is not a matter of moral weakness or lack of will. Rather, it occurs when a drug hijacks one's brain, thereby hijacking one's mind, and then one's life. The functioning of those parts of the brain that normally allow one to exercise choice is disrupted. In a way, abused drugs do to the brain what HIV does to the immune system: they attack the very cells that could stop the disease process; in the case of addiction, the cells that allow individuals to regulate and control behavior.

Unfortunately, it is easier to accept the concept of a brain disease when it involves motor function as opposed to behavior. Muhammad Ali is not thought to be weak-willed because he must rely on a wheelchair. Drug-addicted patients should not be seen as weak-willed if they are unable to stop using drugs. Both the Parkinson's patient and the drug addict are suffering from dysfunctions of the dopamine system—the manifestations of one are primarily motor and those of the other primarily behavioral, but both are brain diseases.

BASIC RESEARCH

Chapters in this text amply demonstrate the great strides that have been made in our basic understanding of drug addiction and its underlying mechanisms. Over the past 25 years, scientists have identified the primary receptors for every major class of abused drug and identified the genetic code of and cloned these receptors (NIDA, 1994, 1996; Kilty, Lorang & Amara, 1991; Matsuda, Lolait et al., 1990; Chen, Mestek et al., 1993). They have mapped their locations in the brain and determined the neurotransmitter systems involved (Koob, 1992; Self, in press; Institute of Medicine, 1996); demonstrated activation of these areas during addiction, withdrawal, and craving for drugs (Grant, London et al., 1996; Volkow, Ding et al., 1996b); identified and separated the mechanisms underlying drug-seeking behavior and physical dependence on drugs (Wise & Bozarth, 1985; Maldonado, Saiardi et al., 1997); developed animal models for drug self-administration (Koob, 1995); and, most important of all, demonstrated the importance of the mesolimbic dopamine system as the primary site of the dysfunction caused by abused drugs (Koob, 1992; Schulties & Koob, 1994; Wise, 1996).

A number of recent discoveries demonstrate the exciting possibilities of current research. With knowledge about the gene that codes for the dopamine transporter, the primary target for cocaine, a strain of mice was developed in which this important protein was disabled, or "knocked out" (Giros, Jaber et al., 1996). The animals' response to cocaine thus was altered both physiologically and behaviorally. Although knocking out the dopamine transporter may well have affected other neurotransmitter systems, such as serotonin, this study nonetheless demonstrates that the dopamine transporter is an important mechanism needed for cocaine to exert its influence on the brain.

Another recent significant study (Self, Barnhart et al., 1996) investigated the potential role of D_1 and D_2 dopamine receptors. Using compounds that stimulate either the D_1 or the D_2 dopamine receptor, this study involved rats that had been allowed to self-administer cocaine for two hours, followed by two hours of saline, during which time self-administration diminished or ceased. The subsequent administration of a D_2 agonist led to a dramatic resumption of cocaine seeking, whereas the D_1 agonist had virtually no effect. In a second study, pretreatment with a D_1 receptor agonist suppressed cocaine seeking, whereas the D_2 agonist increased it. This dissociation between the action of D_1 and D_2 receptors opens up a potential line of research for the target of new treatment drugs.

Addictive behaviors may be mediated by both positive and negative reinforcing events, such as withdrawal. A study bearing on the question of whether there are commonalities underlying the withdrawal effects of drugs of abuse recently was reported (Rodriguez de Fonseca, Carrera et al., 1997). It was found that corticotrophin-releasing factor—a hormone that generally is associated with stress response and that also appears to be involved in the mediation of the negative reinforcing events associated with withdrawal from alcohol, cocaine, and opiates—also was elevated in the limbic system after withdrawal from marijuana. The fact that these disparate drugs all cause a similar reaction in the same neural circuitry raises the possibility that all of these drugs, over time, act cumulatively as contributory factors in the development of brain dysfunction and drug addiction.

Self-administration of abused drugs bypasses the cognitive "filters" that are part of normal brain homeostatic function and artificially and powerfully stimulates the mesolimbic dopamine system, producing maladaptive, pathological brain function. For reasons not yet understood, the cognitive world of the addict changes. Everything becomes focused on drugs: thinking about them, talking about them, getting them, and using them. Most people would attribute this obsession with drugs to "psychological" processes. A more likely explanation is that it reflects an underlying change in the relative functioning of various cognitive and reward centers in the brain. The mechanisms that normally override or suppress the activity of the mesolimbic dopamine system are unable to do so in the face of massive "artificial" drug stimulation. It is as if someone receiving direct electrical stimulation of the right-arm dorsal root fibers is told to stop feeling the sensation of tingling or pain in the affected limb. No matter how strong the individual's "will," the person is unable to do so. The repeated stimulation of the mesocortical limbic dopamine system by abused drugs eventually leads to a change in the brain, to the "addiction switch" being turned on, with a consequent loss of control, irrespective of the will of the individual. Author Samuel Taylor Coleridge expressed this idea most eloquently: "My case is a species of madness, only that it is a derangement of the Volition, and not of the intellectual faculties."

TREATMENT RESEARCH

Current research on the neurobehavioral bases of drug addiction is creating a better understanding and appreciation of the uses of older therapies and a greater recognition of opportunities to develop new ones. Most importantly, this knowledge has shown that drug addiction is a treatable disease.

As noted earlier, the fact that addiction is the result of repeated self-administration of drugs should not make people suffering from this disease the objects of derision and contempt, unworthy of sympathy. As with many preventable and treatable diseases—AIDS, heart disease, and emphysema, to name a few—the focus must be on caring for afflicted individuals without allowing public attitudes toward addiction to affect acceptance of proven treatments.

Replacement Therapies. Research shows that methadone maintenance produces significant medical and public health benefits. Methadone is longer-acting than heroin and can serve to stabilize brain function, perhaps stopping the rapid cycling and stimulation of the mesolimbic dopamine system. Because methadone is not injected, the spread of AIDS is curtailed (Metzger, Woody et al., 1993), and children born to methadone-maintained women are much healthier at birth than children born to heroin addicts (Jarvis & Schnoll, 1994). The concept of methadone maintenance has parallels in the pharmacologic management of a number of other chronic conditions, including diabetes, heart disease, and arthritis.

Yet methadone is regarded by many as the substitution of one addiction for another. But if addiction is recognized as a brain disease, then caring for the individual becomes the paramount concern. If a patient with severe heart disease receives an implant of a less than perfect real or artificial heart, it is not thought to be substituting one bad heart for another. The patient is being helped to live longer and better, while the search for an even more effective treatment continues.

Replacement therapy, based on the methadone model, now is widely accepted for the treatment of nicotine addiction. No one suggests that the use of alternative nicotine delivery systems constitutes the substitution of one addiction for another; such delivery systems are seen as part of a comprehensive plan to get people to stop smoking.

Beyond methadone, other replacement therapies, such as LAAM and (as soon as it is approved) buprenorphine, should provide physicians with a variety of medications that can be tailored to the needs of individual patients.

New Treatment Approaches. A brain disease model of addiction requires a broadened search for new treatment modalities. It is essential to study ways to prevent abused drugs from ever reaching the brain, possibly through immunization (Carrera, Ashley et al., 1995) or by modification of the blood-brain barrier. It is necessary to discover mechanisms to block abused drugs from indirectly affecting brain function. For example, cocaine may partly act through its local anesthetic and vasoconstrictive actions. Perhaps the very earliest phase of the cocaine rush is the result of a relative shutdown in cortical function, which releases subcortical structures from tonic inhibitory influences. And consideration must be given to the possibility that some of the effects of abused drugs result from a generalized diffusion of neurotransmitters.

Medications: Replacement therapies and antagonist therapy (such as naltrexone and mecamylamine), and other techniques to block abused drug-receptor coupling serve a valuable function in stabilizing patients and helping them to reduce or eliminate drug use. In addition to directly targeting the drug molecule and its receptor, new medical interventions designed to restore normal brain function (including gene-based therapies) should be explored. Ideally, such medications would affect higher-level brain systems and not necessarily be drug-specific.

Greater consideration should be given to the mechanisms underlying drug craving, relapse, and environmental triggers, which probably involve much more complex mechanisms than simple models of changed neurotransmitter synthesis, altered receptor sensitivity, and up/down-regulation of receptors. Basic research is needed on the homeostatic mechanisms that regulate the interplay between cortical and subcortical structures in the mediation of emotions, memory, and learning. For example, drug experiences are difficult, if not impossible, to forget. The persistence of drug-related memory and its ability to evoke past drug experiences appears to be on par with the power of olfactory memory—an intriguing finding in that olfaction is a chemical sense that bypasses thalamic systems used by other senses and has inputs directly to the limbic system.

Medications that act on other brain systems (for example, glutamatergic or GABAergic) that also are implicated in the effects of drugs of abuse are another possibility. Methods for delivering such psychotherapeutics so that they are active only in specific brain regions may be even more important. The future of medications development for the treatment of all brain diseases lies in therapeutics that do not necessarily target a specific disease but target a specific neurotransmitter system in a particular nucleus in the brain. Using available research findings and new diagnostic tests, the skilled clinician then will be able to prescribe medications to regulate brain function and return it to a degree of normalcy.

Because abused drugs act on the same parts of the brain that allow feelings of pleasure, the challenge is to develop medications that can negate the acute and chronic effects of drugs without blocking the ability to enjoy a romantic dinner, a walk on the beach, or a drive in a new car. Fortunately, the exquisite technologies made available by the fields of molecular biology and neuroscience and the computer-assisted development and design of medications that have a specific structure provide the tools to meet this challenge.

Basic Studies: In addition to medications development, more basic research is required. One exciting area is the neurocognitive aspects of drug addiction. What are the neural bases of just saying "no"? What are the neural bases of making a resolution? Many people have tried to diet. They get up in the morning determined to eat lightly, cut down on calories, and exercise at the end of the day. And they truly believe they can and will follow such a regimen. During the day, however, stress builds, fatigue develops, mood changes, and the diet is viewed as less important than it was in the morning. The would-be dieter thinks: "I will start tomorrow, I really will." And they truly believe they will. Studies are needed to identify the brain systems that mediate changes in the cognitive importance an individual attaches to various activities, thereby modifying his/her behavior depending on mood and affective states. Studies also are needed to investigate the neural mechanisms that mediate "moral fiber" when there is a conflict between needs or desires and intellect. These are not simple issues. In the past, they have been thought of only in psychological terms and have been addressed only with psychological interventions and theories; now, however, we know that neural systems must be involved, and that knowledge is crucial to the development of new technologies that will enable people to be more resolute in any number of behaviors, including refraining from taking drugs.

Another important and frequently overlooked cognitive aspect of drug addiction involves self-recognition and acceptance of the existence of disease. Drug addicts lose their health, families, and careers and still deny they have a problem. They believe that they can stop at any time, if only they want to. The ability to suppress external reality and to deny disease is not unique to drug addicts and is present in other brain diseases (Cutting, 1978). Addicts, however, represent a unique part of the spectrum and should be the subject of neurocognitive research into denial.

Combined Pharmacological and Behavioral Treatments: The treatment of drug addiction requires both behavioral and pharmacological interventions. There is little value in thinking about behavioral therapies as opposed to or in contrast with pharmacological therapies. Drug addiction, like other brain diseases, occurs in a social, environmental, and historical context. The brain functions in response to internal and external chemical cues and in response to feedback and stimulation from the behavior it produces. The brain produces behavior, and evidence from studies of obsessive-compulsive disorder (Schwartz, 1996; Baxter, 1992) indicates that behavioral therapies can produce changes in the brain. The task for treatment is to reverse, or at least to compensate for, the qualitative brain changes that characterize addiction.

Combinations of pharmacological and behavioral treatments for addictive disorders appear to be more beneficial than either component alone (Stitzer & Walsh, 1997). This is true of other diseases as well. For example, cholesterol levels can be dramatically redued through a regimen that combines diet and exercise with cholesterol-lowering drugs. In treating patients with high cholesterol and other chronic conditions, the health professional must determine the best combination of therapies to meet the health needs of the patient, based on access to services, costs, severity of illness, and other risk factors. A similar model, tailoring pharmacological and behavioral treatment approaches to the needs of the addicted patient, is critical for success.

Drug addiction is a brain disease, so brain normalization through pharmacological and behavioral techniques should be the ultimate treatment goal. There will be no "magic bullet" to treat or cure addiction. Pharmacotherapies, however, should be of value in treating the direct acute and chronic brain effects of abused drugs. The success of selective serotonergic reuptake blockers in treating a variety of mental diseases that once were thought to require years of intense therapy provides the hope that addiction medicines more effective than currently can be imagined may one day be developed.

Nevertheless, medications will be only part of the treatment picture. Because of the complexity of addiction and its sequelae, it is likely that many, if not all, addicts will require and benefit from a combination of pharmacological and behavioral interventions. For many addicts, the behavioral interventions employed will have to address at least two sets of problems, and thus will need to incorporate at least two types of therapy. One involves a cognitive approach that will help patients reframe how they relate to and view the world. This would, of necessity, include deconditioning of the environmental cues that elicit drug craving. The other approach is social rehabilitation.

Efforts to treat any disease, be it cancer, stroke, or addiction, often overlook the impact of disease on the person. The cancer patient must learn to live with fear, uncertainty, and anxiety; the stroke patient must accommodate to a loss of function and mental capacity; and the addict must overcome the dysfunction caused by addiction. Those who have lived an addict's life often need professional assistance in learning how to live effectively in the non-drug using world.

The importance of psychosocial interventions in the treatment of addiction has been demonstration in a dose-response study (McLellan, Arndt et al., 1993). Patients in a methadone maintenance program were assigned to three levels of therapy: minimum services (no regular counseling), standard services (regular counseling), and enhanced services (regular counseling plus on-site medical and psychiatric care, family therapy, and employment counseling). None of the subjects receiving minimum services achieved 16 weeks of opiate-free urine samples, whereas 28% of the subjects receiving standard services did so, as did 55% of the subjects receiving enhanced services. Moreover, longer term follow-up indicated that the more intense the services, the better the outcome on a variety of important measures, including drug use, employment, and criminal activity. In short, the more intense the psychosocial intervention, the more effective the pharmacological intervention.

FUTURE RESEARCH ISSUES

Given our expanding knowledge of brain and behavior, new mind-altering drugs and even abusable technologies may be created in the 21st century. Although speculative, it is not too soon to consider the possibility that a technique will be developed to use short-term genetic manipulation of brain cells as a new form of drug abuse and addiction; theoretically, a man-made psychoactive "virus" could be created that would carry instructions to alter neurotransmitter systems and produce entirely novel phenomenal and euphoric states. The potential for genetic manipulation of behavior will make current biomedical ethical issues pale by comparison.

Questions will arise about the abuse of personality-altering drugs, performance-enhancing drugs, cognition-enhancing drugs, anti-aging drugs, and growth-stimulating drugs. Certain drugs, such as LSD, are uniquely rewarding to humans, perhaps because of their unusual cognitive and perceptual effects. The use of LSD has been reported to produce "psychological dependence," a term that conveys ignorance of the underlying physiology. Studies are needed to determine whether the reinforcing effects of LSD ultimately operate through some pathway to the mesolimbic dopamine system, or whether there are other reward pathways and systems subserving higher mental processes such as curiosity or the appreciation of beauty.

The time to start thinking about such issues and society's response to them is now.

CONCLUSIONS: THE FINAL FRONTIER

The disease of addiction begins in the brain, which is the target organ for abused drugs. Within that structure, abused drugs affect specific sites and initiate the cascade of events that can lead from casual drug use to addiction. Unraveling the disease of addiction will require a comprehensive understanding of how a drug occupies a receptor; how the act of occupying a receptor triggers a response in the cell, leading to an electrical impulse; and how that electrical impulse travels through the brain, integrating with other electrical signals emanating from structures responsible for various functions—including learning, memory and forgetting, cognition, attention, and social behavior—and ultimately leads to the qualitative changes that characterize addiction.

Drugs change the brain, possibly forever. They leave something behind that can be exorcised only by knowledge gained through the power of science. As Cocteau wrote: "There exists, therefore, outside alkaloids and habit, a sense for opium, an intangible habit which lives on, despite the recasting of the organism. The dead drug leaves a ghost behind. At certain hours it haunts the house."

The 20th century opened with a golden age in the physical sciences and is closing with a golden age in the biological sciences. Nowhere is this more true than in neurobiology. Incredible progress has been made in understanding brain and behavior, effecting radical changes in the conception and treatment of a variety of diseases previously thought to be little more than weaknesses or bad habits. Genetic research is determining the nature of man. Brain research will determine the nature of mind. The specification of the precise anatomical, biochemical, and physiological mechanisms that determine how the brain works, with the concomitant ability to change those mechanisms, will challenge society as never before. It will be a revolution more profound than those created by Copernicus, Newton, and Einstein: they gave us only time and space.

REFERENCES

Barnard RJ, DiLauro SC & Inkeles SB (1997). Effects of intensive diet and exercise intervention in patients taking cholesterol-lowering drugs. *American Journal of Cardiology* 79(8):11121114.

Barondes SH, Alberts BM, Andreasen NC, Bargmann C, Benes F, Goldman-Rakic P, Gottesman I, Heinemann SF, Jones EG, Kirschner M, Lewis D, Raff M, Roses A, Rubenstein J, Snyder S, Watson SJ, Weinberger DR & Yolken RH (1997). Workshop on schizophrenia. *Proceedings of the National Academy of Sciences* 94(5):1612–1614.

Baxter LR Jr (1992). Caudate glucose metabolic rate changes with both drug and behavior therapy for obsessive-compulsive disorder. *Archives of General Psychiatry* 49(9):681–689.

Brown MS & Goldstein, JL (1976). Receptor-mediated control of cholesterol metabolism. *Science* 191(4223):150–154.

Carrera MR, Ashley JA, Parsons LH, Wirsching P, Koob GF & Janda KD (1995). Suppression of psychoactive effects of cocaine by active immunization. *Nature* 378(6558):727–730.

Chen Y, Mestek A, Liu J, Hurley JA & Yu L (1993). Molecular cloning and functional expression of a mu-opioid receptor from rat brain. *Molecular Pharmacology* 44(1):8–12.

Curran EJ, Akil H & Watson SJ (1996) Psychomotor stimulant-and opiate-induced c-fos mRNA expression patterns in the rat forebrain: Comparisons between acute drug treatment and a drug challenge in sensitized animals. *Neurochemical Research* 21(11):1425–1435.

Cutting J (1978). Study of anosognosia. *Journal of Neurology, Neurosurgery and Psychiatry* 41(6):548–555.

Daunais JB & McGinty JF (1995). Cocaine binges differentially alter striatal preprodynorphin and zif/268 mRNAs. *Brain Research and Molecular Brain Research* 29(2):201–210.

Giros B, Jaber M, Jones SR, Wightman RM & Caron MG (1996). Hyperlocomotion and indifference to cocaine and amphetamine in mice lacking the dopamine transporter. *Nature* 379:606–612.

Grant S, London ED, Newlin DB, Villemagne VL, Liu X, Contoreggi C, Phillips RL, Kimes AS & Margolin A (1996). Activation of memory circuits during cue-elicited cocaine craving. *Proceedings of the National Academy of Sciences* 93(21):12040–12045.

Grundy SM (1997). Primary prevention of coronary heart disease: Role of cholesterol control in the United States. *Journal of Internal Medicine* 241(4):295–306.

Hebert PR, Gaziano JM, Chan KS & Hennekens CH (1997). Cholesterol lowering with statin drugs, risk of stroke, and total mortality. An overview of randomized trials. *Journal of the American Medical Association* 278(4):313–321.

Institute Of Medicine (1996). *Pathways of Addiction: Opportunities in Drug Abuse Research*. Washington, DC: National Academy Press.

Jarvis MA & Schnoll SH (1994). Methadone treatment during pregnancy. *Journal of Psychoactive Drugs* 26(2):155–161.

Kilgus MD & Pumariega AJ (1994). Experimental manipulation of cocaine craving by videotaped environmental cues. *Southern Medical Journal* 87(11):1138–1140.

Kilty JE, Lorang D & Amara SG (1991). Cloning and expression of a cocaine-sensitive rat dopamine transporter. *Science* 254(5031):578–579.

Konradi C, Leveque JC & Hyman SE (1996). Amphetamine and dopamine-induced immediate early gene expression in striatal neurons depends on postsynaptic NMDA receptors and calcium. *Journal of Neuroscience* 16(13):4231–4239.

Koob GF (1996). Drug addiction: The Yin and Yang of hedonic homeostasis. *Neuron* 16(5):893–896.

Koob GF (1995). Animal models of drug addiction. In FE Bloom & DJ Kupfer (eds.) *Psychopharmacology: The Fourth Generation of Progress*. New York, NY: Raven Press, 759–772.

Koob GF (1992). Drugs of abuse: Anatomy, pharmacology, and function of reward pathways. *Trends in Pharmacological Sciences* 13(5):177–184.

Kreek MJ (1992). Rationale for maintenance pharmacotherapy of opiate dependence. *Research Publication—Association for Research in Nervous and Mental Diseases* 70:205–230.

Liu J, Nickolenko J & Sharp FR (1994). Morphine induces c-fos and junB in striatum and nucleus accumbens via D1 and N-methyl-D-aspartate receptors. *Proceedings of the National Academy of Sciences* 91(18):8537–8541.

London E, Cascella NG, Wong DF, Phillips RL, Dannals RF, Links JM, Herning R, Grayson R, Jaffe J & Wagner HN (1990). Cocaine-induced reduction of glucose utilization in human brain. A study using positron emission tomography and [fluorine 18]-fluorodeoxyglucose. *Archives of General Psychiatry* 47(6):567–574.

Luborsky L, McKay J, Mercer D, Johnson S, Schmidt K, McLellan AT & Barber JP (1995). To use or to refuse cocaine—The deciding factors. *Journal of Substance Abuse* 7(3):293–310.

Maldonado R, Saiardi A, Valverde O, Samad TA, Roques BP & Borrelli E (1997). Absence of opiate rewarding effects in mice lacking dopamine D2 receptors. *Nature* 1388(6642):586–589.

Matsuda LA, Lolait SJ, Brownstein MJ, Young AC & Bonner TI (1990). Structure of cannabinoid receptor and functional expression of the cloned cDNA. *Nature* 346(6284):561–564.

McLellan AT, Arndt IO, Metzger DS, Woody GE & O'Brien CP (1993). The effects of psychosocial services in substance abuse treatment. *Journal of the American Medical Association* 269(15):1953–1959.

Metzger DS, Woody GE, McLellan AT, O'Brien, CP, Druly P, Navaline H, DePhilippis D, Stolley P & Abrutyn E (1993). Human immunodeficiency virus seroconversion among intravenous drug users in and out-of-treatment: An 18-month prospective follow-up. *Journal of Acquired Immunodeficiency Syndromes* 6(9):1049–1056.

National Institutes of Health (1994). Helicobacter pylori in peptic ulcer disease. *NIH Consensus Statement* Jan 7–9;12(1):1–23.

National Institutes of Health (1992). Impotence. *NIH Consensus Statement* Dec 7–9;10(4):1–31.

National Institute on Drug Abuse (1994). *Drug Abuse and Drug Abuse Research: The Third Triennial Report to Congress From the Secretary, Department of Health and Human Services*. Bethesda, MD: National Institutes of Health.

National Institute on Drug Abuse (1996). *Drug Abuse and Drug Abuse Research: The Fourth Triennial Report to Congress From the Secretary, Department of Health and Human Services*. Bethesda, MD: National Institutes of Health.

O'Brien CP, Childress AR, McLellan AT & Ehrman R (1993). Developing treatments that address classical conditioning. [please provide title of monograph] *(NIDA Research Monograph 135)*. Rockville, MD: National Institute on Drug Abuse, 71–91.

Pert CB & Snyder SH (1973). Opiate receptor: Demonstration in nervous tissue. *Science* 179(77):1011–1014.

Rigotti NA, Singer DE, Mulley AG Jr & Thibault GE (1991). Smoking cessation following admission to a coronary care unit. *Journal of General Internal Medicine* 6(4):305–311.

Rodriguez de Fonseca F, Carrera MRA, Navarro M, Koob GF & Weiss F (1997). Activation of corticotropin-releasing factor in the limbic system during cannabinoid withdrawal. *Science* 276(5321):2050–2054.

Schulties G & Koob G (1994). Dark side of drug dependence. *Nature* 371(6493):108–109.

Schwartz JM (1996). Systematic changes in cerebral glucose metabolic rate after successful behavior modification treatment of obsessive-compulsive disorder. *Archives of General Psychiatry* 53(2):109–113.

Self DW (in press). The Neurobiology of Relapse. In *Handbook of Drug Abuse.* [city and state of publication?]: CRC Press.

Self DW, Barnhart WJ, Lehman DA & Nestler EJ (1996). Opposite modulation of cocaine-seeking behavior by D_1- and D_2-like dopamine receptor agonists. *Science* 271(5255):1586–1589.

Stitzer ML & Walsh SL (1997). Psychostimulant abuse: the case for combined behavioral and pharmacological treatments. *Pharmacology, Biochemistry and Behavior* 57(3):457–470.

Volkow ND, Gillespie H, Mullani N, Tancredi L, Grant C, Valentine A & Hollister L (1996a). Brain glucose metabolism in chronic marijuana users at baseline and during marijuana intoxication. *Psychiatry Research: Neuroimaging* 67:29–38.

Volkow ND, Ding Y, Fowler JS & Wang G (1996b). Cocaine addiction: Hypothesis derived from imaging studies with PET. *Journal of Addictive Diseases* 15(4):55–71.

Wise RA (1996). Addictive drugs and brain stimulation reward. *Annual Review of Neuroscience* 19:319–340.

Wise RA & Bozarth MA (1985). Brain mechanisms of drug reward and euphoria. *Psychiatric Medicine* 3(4):445–460.

SECTION 1
Basic Science and Core Concepts

CHAPTER 1

The Epidemiology of Addictive Disorders 3
Rosa M. Crum, M.D., M.H.S.

CHAPTER 2

Genetic Influences in Addiction 17
Robert M. Anthenelli, M.D. and Marc A. Schuckit, M.D.

CHAPTER 3

Behavioral Models of Addiction 37
Roy A. Wise, Ph.D. and John E. Kelsey, Ph.D.

CHAPTER 4

The Neurochemistry of Addiction 51
David J. Nutt, Ph.D.

CHAPTER 5

Neuroadaptation in Addiction 57
Eric J. Nestler, M.D., Ph.D.

CHAPTER 6

Neurocircuitry Targets in Reward and Dependence 73
George F. Koob, Ph.D., Amanda J. Roberts, Ph.D., et al.

CHAPTER 7

Stress as a Factor in Addiction 83
Pier Vicenzo Piazza and Michel Le Moal

SECTION COORDINATOR

TERRY K. SCHULTZ, M.D., FASAM
Alcohol and Drug Abuse Consultant
to The Surgeon General of the U.S. Army
Arlington, Virginia

CONTRIBUTORS

Robert M. Anthenelli, M.D.
Department of Psychiatry
Veterans Affairs Medical Center
University of California, San Diego
San Diego, California

Rosa M. Crum, M.D., M.H.S.
Departments of Epidemiology,
Psychiatry and Mental Hygiene
Welch Center for Prevention,
Epidemiology and Clinical Research
The Johns Hopkins Medical Institutions
Baltimore, Maryland

John E. Kelsey, Ph.D.
Whitehouse Professor of Psychology
Department of Psychology
Bates College
Lewiston, Maine

George F. Koob, Ph.D.
Department of Neuropharmacology
The Scripps Research Institute
LaJolla, California

Michel Le Moal
Professor a l'Institut
Universitaire de France
Laboratoire de Psychobiologie des
Comportments Adaptatifs
Universite de Bordeaux
Bordeaux, France

Eric J. Nestler, M.D., Ph.D.
Elizabeth Mears and House Jameson
Professor of Psychiatry and Neurobiology, and
Director, Division of Molecular Psychiatry
Yale University School of Medicine
New Haven, Connecticut

David J. Nutt, Ph.D.
University of Bristol
Psychopharmacology Unit
School of Medical Sciences
University Walk, Bristol, England

Pier Vincent Piazza
Charge de Recherche
Universitaire de France
Laboratoire de Psychobiologie des
Comportments Adaptatifs
Universite de Bordeaux
Bordeaux, France

Amanda J. Roberts, Ph.D.
Department of Neuropharmacology
The Scripps Research Institute
LaJolla, California

Marc A. Schuckit, M.D.
Department of Psychiatry
Veterans Affairs Medical Center
University of California, San Diego
San Diego, California

Roy A. Wise, Ph.D.
Professor of Psychology
Center for Studies in Behavioral Neurology
Department of Psychology
Concordia University
Montreal, Quebec, Canada

CHAPTER 1

The Epidemiology of Addictive Disorders

Rosa M. Crum, M.D., M.H.S.

Some Epidemiologic Principles
Prevalence of Alcohol Use Disorders
Incidence of Alcohol Use Disorders
Prevalence of Drug Use Disorders
Incidence of Drug Use Disorders
Correlates and Suspected Risk Factors
Comorbidity of Alcohol and Drug Addiction

This chapter is organized to cover several areas. First, epidemiologic terms and types of epidemiologic studies are discussed. Second, literature regarding prevalence and incidence rates of alcohol and drug addiction is reviewed. The remainder of the chapter is devoted to discussing some of the correlates and risk factors associated with alcohol and drug addiction.

SOME EPIDEMIOLOGIC PRINCIPLES

Epidemiology "is concerned with the patterns of disease occurrence in human populations and of the factors that influence those patterns" (Lilienfeld & Lilienfeld, 1980). Some basic terms used in epidemiology deserve attention in this chapter, because they are important to understanding the literature and some of the studies reported here. *Prevalence* generally is taken to represent the ratio of the total number of cases of a particular disease, divided by the total number of individuals in a particular population at a specific time. *Incidence* refers to the rate of occurrence of new cases of a disease, divided by the total number at risk for the disorder during a specified period of time (Mausner & Kramer, 1985). Prevalence takes into account both the incidence and duration of a disease, because it depends not only on the proportion of newly developed cases over time, but also on the length of time the disease exists in the population. In turn, the duration of the disorder is affected by the degree of remission and survival from the disease. Incidence generally is taken to represent the risk of disease, whereas prevalence is an indicator of the public health burden in the community (Mausner & Kramer, 1985).

The strength of association for any particular characteristic with the development of a disease generally is represented by the *relative risk*, or the estimated relative risk (often called the *odds ratio*). The relative risk measures the incidence of disease among those with a particular characteristic (such as family history of alcohol addiction), divided by the incidence of disease among those without exposure to this characteristic. If there is no difference in the incidence rates among those with and without the characteristic, the ratio is equal to one. A relative risk greater than one indicates an increased risk of disease associated with this characteristic. A relative risk less than one signifies a lower risk, which may indicate a protective effect associated with this characteristic.

Excellent detailed discussions of epidemiologic studies can be found elsewhere (e.g., Mausner & Kramer, 1985; Lilienfeld & Lilienfeld, 1980). For the purposes of this chapter, epidemiologic studies can be divided into two types: (1) *observational* or (2) *experimental*. Observational studies may include cross-sectional and analytic studies. In cross-sectional studies or surveys, groups of individuals are assessed (by interview or physical examination, for example) at one specified point in time (Mausner & Kramer, 1985). Analytic studies usually are classified as *case-control* (retrospective) or *cohort* (longitudinal, prospective). Analytic studies generally test a hypothesis of a suspected association between a particular exposure (risk factor) and a disease.

In all observational studies, the investigator observes the study participants and gathers information for analysis (Mausner & Kramer, 1985). In contrast, experimental studies, such as randomized clinical trials, are designed by the investigator, study groups are selected, and often an intervention (such as a new type of treatment) is given to one group of participants. With respect to drug and alcohol addiction, experimental studies of humans generally are possible only with treatment or preventive strategies as interventions.

PREVALENCE OF ALCOHOL USE DISORDERS

Several major surveys in the U.S. and internationally have assessed the prevalence of addiction. Comparison of these studies sometimes is difficult because they employ different definitions of addiction. Recent surveys have used structured interviews according to criteria that have become universally recognized, such as the *Diagnostic and Statistical Manual of Mental Disorders* (American Psychiatric Association, 1994), now in its fourth edition, and the *International Classification of Diseases*, now in its 10th revision (World Health Organization, 1992). (See Appendix B for summaries.)

One of the earliest surveys to assess psychiatric and substance use disorder epidemiology is the National Institute of Mental Health's Epidemiologic Catchment Area Program (ECA) (Eaton & Kessler, 1985; Eaton, Kramer et al., 1989b; Robins & Regier, 1991). The baseline interview for this study was conducted between 1980 and 1984, when collaborators in the ECA assessed a probability sample of over 20,000 adult participants in five metropolitan areas in the United States. Using the Diagnostic Interview Schedule (DIS) (Robins, Helzer et al., 1981), diagnoses of substance abuse and dependence were assessed according to criteria from the *Diagnostic and Statistical Manual of Mental Disorders, 3rd Edition* (*DSM-III*; American Psychiatric Association, 1980). Overall rates for alcohol disorders from the ECA survey data were 13.5% for lifetime prevalence, 4.8% for six-month prevalence, and 2.8% for one-month prevalence (Regier, Farmer et al., 1990). However, stratification by gender revealed large rates for men compared with those for women. Lifetime prevalence for men was found to be 23.8%, with a one-year prevalence rate of 11.9% (Helzer, Burnam & McEvoy, 1991). For women, the lifetime prevalence for an alcohol disorder was 4.7%, with a one-year prevalence rate of 2.2% (Helzer, Burnam & McEvoy, 1991). ECA survey results consistently found higher lifetime, one-year and one-month prevalence rates for men than for women across all age and racial groups (Helzer, Burnam & McEvoy, 1991).

More recent studies have included the identification of alcohol use disorders according to the revised third (*DSM-IIIR*) and fourth (*DSM-IV*) editions of the *Diagnostic and Statistical Manuals of Mental Disorders* of the American Psychiatric Association (1987, 1994). Results of the National Comorbidity Survey (NCS), completed in 1990–1992, which was based on *DSM-IIIR* criteria for alcohol abuse and dependence and which used a modified version of the Composite International Diagnostic Interview (CIDI), yielded higher lifetime and 12-month prevalence estimates than previously have been reported. Lifetime prevalence for alcohol abuse without dependence among males was found to be 12.5% and among females was 6.4%. Lifetime prevalence of alcohol dependence was 20.1% for males and 8.2% for females. Twelve-month prevalence estimates from the National Comorbidity Survey also were higher for alcohol abuse without dependence (3.4% for males and 1.6% for females), and alcohol dependence (10.7% for males, and 3.7% for females) (Kessler, McGonagle et al., 1994; Kessler, Crum et al., 1997).

Data from the 1992 National Longitudinal Alcohol Epidemiologic Survey (NLAES), sponsored by the National Institute on Alcohol Abuse and Alcoholism, has provided 12-month estimates of alcohol use disorders based on *DSM-IV* criteria (Grant, Harford et al., 1994). Twelve-month prevalence of alcohol abuse from the NLAES was found to be 4.67% among men and 1.51% among women. For alcohol dependence, the estimates were 2.14% for men and 1.21% for women. Prevalence estimates for *DSM-IV* alcohol dependence also have been provided by the 1990 U.S. National Alcohol Survey (Caetano & Tam, 1995). Twelve-month prevalence findings from this survey fall between the range for the published estimates of the NLAES and the National Comorbidity Survey (5.7% among men, and 2.2% among women).

Some of the differences in estimates found across surveys may be due to differences in the diagnostic instruments used to assess alcohol use disorder criteria, the version of the Diagnostic and Statistical Manual that prevailed at the time the survey was completed, the size of the survey sample and locale of the survey participants (nationally representative samples versus individual communities), as well as specific characteristics of the populations surveyed, including the age range of study participants. For example, the National Comorbidity Survey included a relatively younger population (persons aged 15 to 54 years) than other surveys.

Early population-based surveys that have given us prevalence rates for alcohol addiction include a community survey done in Iceland by Helgason (1964). Along with a number of other conditions, prevalence of alcoholism was studied in this population of 5,395 Icelanders. The study found that 4.5% of the population had alcohol addiction or excessive drinking. Of these, 95% were men. Helgason reported a lifetime expectancy rate of 6.5% for men and 0.4% for women (Helgason, 1964).

In 1939, Fremming (1947) gathered information on 92.3% of the residents born between 1883 and 1887 in the Danish community of Bornholm. Of the total 4,130 probands, he found that the overall prevalence of alcoholism was 1.7%, with a higher prevalence rate of 3.4% for men (Fremming, 1947).

Essen-Moller and colleagues (1956) examined the prevalence of mental disorders in a rural community of Sweden in 1947 (N = 2,550), and were able to interview or gather information on 99.3% of the population. Of the total 1,019 males aged 15 or older, 13.5% had a history of current or lifetime alcohol disorder. Among the 939 females aged 15 and older, only three were found to have an alcohol disorder (0.3% of the female population) (Essen-Moller, 1956).

Most studies have found that prevalence of alcohol disorders is highest among young adults (Helzer, Burnam & McEvoy, 1991). Prevalence rates for the lifetime, year and month all are highest among the ECA survey participants, who are between the ages of 18 and 45. Rates drop among older individuals.

INCIDENCE OF ALCOHOL USE DISORDERS

Data from the Swedish Lundby study has given us one of the few estimates of incidence of alcoholism over a prolonged follow-up period (Ojesjo, Hagnell & Lanke, 1982). The Lundby community was interviewed for the first time in 1947, re-interviewed in 1957 (with 1% lost to follow-up), and then examined again in 1972 (Ojesjo, Hagnell & Lanke, 1982; Ojesjo, 1980; Hagnell, 1966; Essen-Moller, 1956). Of the 1,877 participants in the original survey, 98% of those still alive in 1972 were re-interviewed. The investigators found that, among males, the overall age-adjusted annual incidence of alcoholism was 0.3%. They further found a general decline in incidence with age, with a sharp drop in incidence of alcohol disorders among men beginning in their thirties (Ojesjo, Hagnell & Lanke, 1982). The highest annual incidence for any type of alcohol disorder among men—0.67% annual incidence—was found among the youngest age group: those 10 to 19 years of age (Ojesjo, Hagnell & Lanke, 1982). Of the 925 women examined in the Lundby community in 1972, only three were identified as having an alcohol disorder (Ojesjo, 1980).

Fillmore examined longitudinal data from population-based U.S. samples and also found that incidence rates of problem drinking generally were lower for women than for men, and that incidence rates for both men and women declined with age (Fillmore, 1987a; Fillmore, 1987b). However, her data also showed different patterns of drinking by gender. For example, women tended to develop problems associated with drinking later in life than men, and women were found to have higher rates of remission across all ages relative to men (Fillmore, 1987b).

Data from the ECA surveys on incidence of DIS-identified alcohol disorders are consistent with other studies (Eaton, Kramer et al., 1989a). The estimated annual incidence of DIS-defined alcohol disorders among men was highest for the youngest age group, those aged 18 to 29 (5.8 per 100 person years) and decreased with age, with an overall annual incidence of 3.7 per 100 person years for men. For women, incidence also decreased with age, with an overall incidence of 0.6 per 100 person years. The peak incidence in women also was among those 18 to 29 years of age (1.1 per 100 person years) (Eaton, Kramer et al., 1989a).

PREVALENCE OF DRUG USE DISORDERS

Although several surveys have assessed drug use in the United States, there are relatively few population-based studies that have examined the prevalence and/or incidence of drug use disorders or drug addiction. One such program is the Epidemiologic Catchment Area (ECA) surveys, which have provided estimates on the prevalence of drug use disorders from five metropolitan area communities (Eaton & Kessler, 1985; Anthony & Helzer, 1991). From these data, based on information from the Diagnostic Interview Schedule (Robins, Helzer et al., 1981), which defines diagnoses of drug abuse and dependence using *DSM-III* criteria (American Psychiatric Association, 1980), it is possible to obtain estimates of the prevalence of drug use disorders in the U.S.

Analysis of the ECA surveys yields an overall lifetime prevalence of drug abuse and dependence of 6.2% (Anthony & Helzer, 1991). As discussed with regard to alcohol disorders, men generally have a higher lifetime prevalence of illicit drug use and illicit drug use disorders (Robins, Helzer et al., 1984). Lifetime prevalence of illicit drug use disorders for men in the overall study population was 7.7%; among drug users, lifetime prevalence for men was 21%. In the female population as a whole, lifetime prevalence for illicit drug use disorders was 4.8%; among drug users, it was 19% (Anthony & Helzer, 1991). With age, the lifetime prevalence dropped sharply after the mid-40s, particularly for women. Lifetime prevalence among drug users was found to be 4% for men over the age of 65, and 1% for elderly women. One-year prevalence of illicit drug disorders also was higher for men than for women. The overall one-year prevalence was 2.7%, with a prevalence of 4.1% for men and 1.4% among women (Anthony & Helzer, 1991). Recent data on prevalence of illicit drug disorders has been provided by findings from The National Comorbidity Survey (Kessler, McGonagle et al., 1994). Lifetime prevalence of drug abuse without dependence was found to be 5.4% among males and 3.5% among females. The estimates for lifetime prevalence of drug dependence were 9.2% for males, and 5.9% for females. The NCS also yielded results for 12-month prevalence: for drug abuse without dependence, the estimates were 1.3% among males and 0.3% among females; for drug dependence, 3.8% of the males and 1.9% of the females met the criteria for this disorder.

INCIDENCE OF DRUG USE DISORDERS

As with prevalence data, there also is a paucity of information regarding incidence of drug disorders as a group, with less information available regarding specific types of drug addictions. From the ECA data, it is clear that the incidence of illicit drug use disorders is greater for men than for women across the entire lifespan (Eaton, Kramer et al., 1989a). Overall, the estimated annual incidence was 1.09 per 100 person-years of risk (Eaton, Kramer et al., 1989a). For men, the estimated annual incidence for drug abuse/dependence was 1.66 per 100 person-years of risk, and for women, the estimated annual incidence was 0.66 per 100 person-years of risk. As was the case for alcohol-related disorders, the highest incidence for both men and women was found in the 18 to 29 year old age group; this drops sharply after young adulthood. The incidence of drug disorders was zero among persons 65 years of age and older (Eaton, Kramer et al., 1989a).

CORRELATES AND SUSPECTED RISK FACTORS

A number of correlates and suspected risk factors for alcoholism and drug addiction have been examined. These are discussed in this section for both alcohol and drug addiction, because the suspected risk factors are similar, and there are many findings in common. This section, with few exceptions, thus is restricted to a discussion of a selection of personal or individual characteristics that have been found to be associated with drug and alcohol addiction. The discussion here is by no means exhaustive and only covers a fraction of investigations in this area.

Gender. As discussed earlier, alcohol disorders and alcohol-related problems are more common among men than among women. This consistent finding has been shown in a number of cross-sectional surveys in the U.S. and in other countries (e.g., Kessler, McGonagle et al., 1994, 1997; Grant, Harford et al., 1994; Caetano & Tam, 1995; Helgason, 1964; Helzer, Burnam & McEvoy, 1991; Robins, Helzer et al., 1984; Ojesjo, 1980), as well as in prospective studies (e.g., Fillmore, 1987b; Eaton, Kramer et al., 1989a). Differences in prevalence and incidence between men and women have been attributed to a number of factors. Cultural norms, societal standards, as well as body size and differences in the metabolism of alcohol all may contribute to the finding that women appear to use less alcohol and have lower rates of alcohol addiction. Evidence exists that there has been some increase in heavy alcohol consumption, particularly among younger women (as well as among younger men) (e.g., Knibbe, Drop et al., 1985; Hilton, 1988). Some hypothesize that changes in patterns of drinking among women may be a result of deviations from traditional female social roles, or changes brought about by the increase of women in the labor force, as well as the combined input of home and work environments (Parker & Harford, 1992; Hall, 1992). Many characteristics (such as marital status, full-time employment, ethnicity, age, occupation, and educational level), as well as the occurrence of other life events and the presence of other psychopathology (such as depression), may play a role in gender variability with respect to alcohol consumption and the development of alcohol disorders (e.g., Gorman,

1988; Wilsnack, Klassen et al., 1991). In a recent review, Wilsnack and Wilsnack (1995) assessed drinking and problem drinking among women in the U.S. (Wilsnack & Wilsnack, 1995). They found that certain subgroups of women were more likely to have adverse drinking consequences and higher rates of heavy drinking patterns. These included younger aged women, those in non-traditional jobs, and unmarried women cohabiting with a partner. A history of childhood sexual abuse among women also has been found to be a potential predictor of increased risk for alcohol and drug use disorders (Wilsnack, Vogeltanz et al., 1997).

There also are gender differences with respect to illicit drug disorders. As discussed for alcohol, males (boys and men) generally use illicit drugs more (Anthony & Helzer, 1991; Johnston, O'Malley & Bachman, 1992) and have a higher prevalence of drug use disorders than females (girls and women) (Anthony & Helzer, 1991). The social or cultural restrictions that were mentioned as possible explanations for the decreased prevalence of alcohol use among women also may apply to some types of illicit drug use.

Several studies that have used large community surveys to evaluate particular types of illicit substances have found differences by gender. For example, Adams and Gfroerer (1991) examined characteristics of cocaine users associated with the development of cocaine dependence, using data from the NIDA Household Surveys. Differences between male and female cocaine users at risk for cocaine dependence were found for some sociodemographic characteristics, as well as factors related to drug use (route of administration, and frequency and length of cocaine use) (Adams & Gfroerer, 1991). Moreover, there is evidence that violence associated with drug use differs by gender. In one sample examining cocaine use and violence, it was found that among those reporting violent events, men who regularly used cocaine were more likely to have perpetrated violent crimes, and women who regularly used cocaine were more likely to have been victims of violence (Goldstein, Bellucci et al., 1991).

Age. Prevalence of alcohol disorders may be lower among older adults for a number of reasons. Because the measure of prevalence includes incidence as well as the duration of the disease (Mausner & Kramer, 1985; Lilienfeld & Lilienfeld, 1980), alcoholism may have a lower prevalence among the elderly because (1) the incidence decreases, or (2) the duration of the disorder is reduced, or (3) some combination of these two factors is in effect. If the duration of the disorder is reduced, it may be a result of an increase in remission with age, or a reduction in survival. In other words, with age, prevalence may be reduced because fewer individuals develop the disease, because addiction problems have resolved, or because addicted individuals die earlier. Explanations for a decreased prevalence with age also may include (1) a reduced tolerance to alcohol with age (Vestal, McGuire et al., 1977); (2) poorer recall among older adults; or (3) as a result of a cohort effect (Helzer, Burnam & McEvoy, 1991). Further, the means by which alcohol disorders are identified in young adults may not be applicable to the elderly (Graham, 1986). Surveys that include only household participants may miss many with alcohol disorders who reside in nursing homes; also, older community residents with alcohol disorders may be less willing to participate in household surveys. Although longitudinal analyses show declines in the proportion of older adults who consume alcohol (Adams, Garry et al., 1990), problems related to alcohol use among the elderly may occur at lower levels of consumption, and older adults with alcohol use disorders may be at greater risk for comorbid problems (Dufour & Fuller, 1995; Liberto, Oslin & Ruskin, 1992).

As with alcohol disorders, age correlates with incidence of drug use disorders. The highest prevalence and incidence rates for illicit drug disorders are found among individuals in late adolescence and young adulthood (Anthony & Helzer, 1991). Beyond the fact that incidence is low among older adults, and that survival may be decreased for drug addicts as they age, other factors also may be involved. Prevalence also may be lower among older adults because of a cohort effect. Exposure and availability of illicit drugs differs by birth cohort. For example, older adults living today had no access in their youth to crack cocaine. When evaluating changes in frequency of a disorder (in this case, drug and alcohol addiction), distinctions need to be made between changes that uniformly occur for all age groups during a particular historical period (period effect), changes that occur with age as the individual matures (age effect), and a cohort effect that reflects differences in disease rate for individuals born in different years (O'Malley, Bachman & Johnston, 1988; Kleinbaum, Kupper & Morgenstern, 1982).

Race-Ethnicity. Information on the relationship between alcohol and illicit drug disorders and racial and ethnic background is complex and often conflicting. Some of the inconsistent findings result in part from the relative paucity of data involving ethnic and racial groups, the classifications used for grouping ethnic minorities, the social acceptability of drinking and drug use practices in different groups, and the relationship of socioeconomic status and the availability of health care to minority populations.

The onset of alcohol disorders appears to begin at later ages among African-Americans, and a greater proportion of African-Americans tend to be abstainers relative to Caucasians (Helzer, Burnam & McEvoy, 1991; Caetano & Herd, 1984). However, compared with Caucasians, African-Americans tend to suffer more severe medical consequences, such as relatively high cirrhosis mortality rates (Ronan, 1986, 1987). These elevated rates may be related to issues of socioeconomic status, cultural environment, and access to health care (Herd, 1990; Otten, 1990). Not infrequently, when measures of socioeconomic status (such as household residence or educational level) are taken into account, differences between ethnic minorities and Caucasians are minimized (e.g., Crum, Bucholz et al., 1992). A recent survey found similar drinking patterns between African-Americans and Caucasians. However, differences were found between racial groups when the sample was evaluated by specific sociodemographic characteristics, such as age and income (Herd, 1990). Hispanic-American men tend to have higher lifetime prevalence rates of alcohol disorders than Caucasian men, although a relatively high percentage of Hispanic-American women are abstainers (Helzer, Burnam & McEvoy, 1991; Holck, Warren et al., 1984). However, differences in rates vary across Hispanic ethnic subgroups, so they may reflect factors such as degree of acculturation, country of national origin, and generational status or time since immigration (Caetano, 1988, 1987). It has been shown that a greater proportion of Mexican-Americans report problems with alcohol, and are more liberal in their acceptance of drinking, than other Hispanic groups (Caetano, 1988). Caetano also found that Hispanic-Americans (particularly Hispanic women) who were acculturated to U.S. society tended to drink more and were classified more frequently as heavy drinkers (Caetano, 1987). Recent data on drinking patterns among racial subgroups found that between 1984 and 1992, heavy drinking patterns decreased among white men but not among African-American or Hispanic men. In addition, abstention rates remained essentially unchanged among Hispanic women, but increased in all other subgroups (Caetano & Kaskutas, 1995).

Asian-Americans generally are believed to have some of the lowest levels of alcohol consumption and lowest rates of alcohol disorders. There is some evidence that reduced drinking may result from the discomfort that occurs with the physiological effects of the flushing response present in many individuals of this ethnic background (e.g., Suddendorf, 1989). There also is evidence that genetic heterogeneity may explain differences in rates of alcoholism among certain subgroups (Hsu, Loh et al., 1996; Higuchi, Matsushita et al., 1995). However, as with Hispanic-Americans, the Asian-American population is composed of many subgroups with different backgrounds and cultural drinking practices. Some recent data provide evidence that prevalence rates differ among different groups of Asian-Americans, and that some rates of heavy drinking may not be substantially different from the U.S. as a whole (Chi, Lubben & Kitano, 1989).

Native Americans historically have had higher death rates from alcohol-related disorders than any other ethnic group in the United States (Rhoades, Hammond et al., 1987; Christian, DuFour & Bertolucci, 1989). However, generalizations to all Native Americans cannot be made. Drinking practices are quite varied across tribal groups, and cultural factors as well as socioeconomic factors play a role (Rhoades, Hammond et al., 1987; Christian, DuFour & Bertolucci, 1989).

Patterns of drug use and drug disorders also vary by racial-ethnic group (Anthony & Helzer, 1991). However, less information is available for drug addiction among different ethnic populations than for alcoholism. Data from the ECA surveys found that overall lifetime prevalence of illicit drug use disorders tended to be lower for Hispanic men and women relative to African-Americans or Caucasians and other racial groups, although this did not achieve statistical significance (Anthony & Helzer, 1991). Hispanic women were found to have the lowest lifetime prevalence (Anthony & Helzer, 1991). As with alcohol disorders, there are differences among subgroups of ethnic minorities, and factors such as degree of acculturation are associated with prevalence of drug disorders (e.g., Burnam, Hough et al., 1987; Gfroerer & De La Rosa, 1993). It also has been shown that the relationship of risk factors to drug use among adolescents (such as low family pride, depressed mood, and low self-esteem) also differ by ethnic group (Vega, Zimmerman et al., 1993).

The evaluation of race and its association with alcohol and drug addiction is complex. For example, when examining illicit drug use patterns among different ethnic groups, it is important to consider socioeconomic characteristics (Herd, 1994). One study found that although national survey data indicated a higher prevalence of crack cocaine smoking among some ethnic minorities, when area of neighborhood residence was taken into account, differences in odds of drug use between racial groups were attenuated (Lillie-Blanton, Anthony & Schuster, 1993).

Family History. Alcohol disorders cluster in families. Twin studies (e.g., Kendler, Heath et al., 1992; Kendler, Neale et al., 1994; Hrubec & Omenn, 1981; Kaprio, Koskenvuo et al., 1987), adoption and cross-fostering studies (e.g., Cloninger, 1981; Goodwin, Schulsinger et al., 1973; Sigvardsson, Bohman & Cloninger, 1996), studies involving genetically selected animal models (e.g., Goldman, 1987), genetic segregation analysis (Aston & Hill, 1990), and allelic association (Blum, Noble et al., 1990) have attempted to answer the question of whether the familial relationship is due to genetic transmission or a shared environment. There also have been a number of investigations of physiological and biochemical markers associated with alcoholism (Begleiter & Projesz, 1988; Rausch, Monteiro & Schuckit, 1991; Bailly, Vignau et al., 1993). Many studies examining the familial pattern of alcoholism have demonstrated a possible genetic relationship. In a review of the literature, Cotton found that alcoholics were six times more likely than nonpsychiatric patients to have a history of parental alcoholism (Cotton, 1979). However, approximately one- to two-thirds of individuals who develop alcohol disorders do not have a family history of alcoholism (Cotton, 1979; Schuckit, 1983). Conversely, many individuals whose parents drink do not become alcoholic themselves (West & Prinz, 1987; Ohannessian & Hesselbrook, 1993). Clearly, environmental influences also play a significant role (e.g., Kendler, Gardner & Prescott, 1997; Chilcoat, Dishion & Anthony, 1995).

The relationship of genetic factors to illicit drug disorders is a relatively new and developing field that hopefully will aid us in understanding possible etiologic mechanisms for drug disorders among families (Pickens & Svikis, 1988; Cadoret, Yates et al., 1995). Some recent studies of first and second degree relatives (McCaul, Turkkan et al., 1990) and adoptees (Cadoret, Troughton et al., 1986) have provided further evidence for the importance of familial and potentially genetic mechanisms in the development of drug disorders.

Employment Status and Occupation. Employment, or working for pay, also is related to the prevalence of alcohol disorders (Helzer, Burnam & McEvoy, 1991). For example, McCord found that alcoholics were more frequently unable to work on a regular basis than those who were not alcoholic (McCord & McCord, 1962). Similarly, study results from the ECA have reported that individuals who were unemployed six months or more in the preceding five years had higher prevalence rates of alcoholism (Helzer, Burnam & McEvoy, 1991), and greater risk for development of alcohol disorders (Crum, Bucholz et al., 1992). An assessment of recent trends in drinking-related problems from survey data taken in 1984 and in 1990 found that there were significant increases in reports of two or more social consequences of drinking among the unemployed (Midanik & Clark, 1995). The data also show that prevalence of alcohol disorders differs by type of occupation. For example, higher rates of alcohol addiction have been found among those in occupations typically associated with laborers, "blue-collar" occupations or those in lower socioeconomic levels (e.g., Olkinoura, 1984). There also is evidence that the relationship of employment status with the frequency of alcohol-related health problems show contrasting patterns among men as compared to women (Lahelma, Kangas & Manderbacka, 1995). Recent analyses of the Epidemiologic Catchment Area Surveys also have provided evidence that the effect of alcoholism on lower income status occurs as a result of the indirect and direct effects the disorder has on educational achievement and marriage (Mullahy & Sindelar, 1994).

Unlike the alcohol disorders, data from the ECA did not show an appreciable association of unemployment with illicit drug disorders (Anthony & Helzer, 1991). However, there was a tendency for the probability of illicit drug disorders among employed men to be associated with lower income (Anthony & Helzer, 1991). Further, as with alcoholism, there appear to be differences in prevalence of illicit drug disorders associated with specific occupations (Anthony, Eaton et al., 1992). However, it is not always possible to know which developed first; that is, whether lack of employment led to heavy drinking or drug use, or whether alcohol or drug problems resulted in job loss, inability to obtain work, or selection into a particular type of occupation.

Marital Status. Marital status also has been found to be related to the occurrence of alcohol disorders. Data from the ECA surveys showed that individuals in stable marriages had the lowest lifetime prevalence of alcoholism (8.9%), as opposed to cohabiting adults who had never been married (29.2%) (Helzer, Burnam & McEvoy, 1991). Longitudinal analyses also show that cohabiting women may be at elevated risk for heavy drinking (Wilsnack & Wilsnack, 1995). Cahalan found that a higher percentage of heavy drinkers were single, separated or divorced (Cahalan, Cisin & Crossley, 1969). Some investigators have found that widowhood is associated with the lowest levels of heavy drinking and prevalence of alcohol disorders (Helzer, Burnam & McEvoy, 1991; Cahalan, 1969), whereas other studies have found that late onset drinking in older individuals may be a consequence of death of a spouse and bereavement (e.g., Finlayson, 1988; Rosin & Glatt, 1971). There also is evidence that risks for problematic drinking is higher for women with spouses or partners that drink heavily (Wilsnack & Wilsnack, 1995), and that the quality of marital relationships may vary as a function of the presence of current heavy drinking (McLeod, 1993). Recent prospective data reported by Chilcoat and Breslau (1996) found that the incidence of alcohol disorder symptoms was increased among single or divorced participants relative to those who were married.

Lifetime prevalence rates of illicit drug disorders have also been found to vary appreciably by marital status. Anthony and Helzer found that, for both men and women, and generally across all ages, individuals who lived with a significant other but had never married had the highest lifetime prevalence of drug disorders. Cohabiting unmarried men had a 30.2% lifetime prevalence of an illicit drug disorder, compared to a 3.6% prevalence for married men. Cohabiting women had a lifetime prevalence of 19.9%, as opposed to a rate of 1.8% among women with a stable marital history (Anthony & Helzer, 1992).

Much of the information known about the relationship between marital status and alcohol and drug addiction comes from cross-sectional studies. There are problems in using such data to evaluate the relationship between marital status and the risk of alcohol and drug disorders. Alcohol and drug addiction may predate the time that individuals make decisions about marriage, and problems associated with drinking and drug use may be the reason some individuals remain single, or become separated or divorced. However, some prospective analyses have confirmed findings from cross-sectional data (e.g., Crum, Bucholz et al., 1992; Chilcoat & Breslau, 1996).

Educational Level. Studies of the relationship between educational level and the development of alcoholism often have yielded conflicting results. Educational level often is included as part of broader sociodemographic or social-class characteristics. Some supportive evidence for an association between failure to meet educational goals and risk for alcohol disorders comes from recent cross-sectional surveys (e.g., Helzer, Burnam & McEvoy, 1991), and from prior literature that links the failure to meet social role expectations with the subsequent development of problem behavior (e.g., Jessor & Jessor, 1977; Kellam, Brown et al., 1983).

Utilizing prospective data, it has been shown that leaving school or dropping out of school is associated with an increased risk of alcohol abuse and dependence in adulthood (Crum, Bucholz et al., 1992; Crum, Helzer & Anthony, 1993). Recent analyses of inner city school children, also have provided evidence suggesting that poor educational achievement and some early school behaviors are associated with risk for alcohol use disorders (Crum, Ensminger et al., 1998). Academic competence has been shown to be an important risk factor for problematic drinking behavior among adolescents (Harrison & Luxenburg, 1995; Thomas, 1993; Thomas & Hsiu, 1993). A recent prospective analysis of seniors in high school has provided supportive evidence of an association between poor educational achievement and substance use following high school (Schulenberg, Bachman et al., 1994).

Lifetime prevalence of drug disorders also varies by educational level. Using data from the ECA surveys, Anthony and Helzer showed that for men and women of all ages, lifetime prevalence of illicit drug disorders was highest for those who dropped out of high school, and for those who entered college but failed to earn a degree (Anthony & Helzer, 1991). The lifetime rates were consistently higher for men than for women across all educational levels, but the relative distribution for both sexes was similar with respect to greater prevalence for those who failed to complete an intended level of education (Anthony & Helzer, 1991). Eggert and Herting (1993) found that high-risk youth, defined by adolescents with a history of school problems and/or school dropout, were found to have greater adverse consequences due to drug use as well as greater access to drugs relative to students considered low-risk (those defined as typical high-school students). It also has been shown that performances on some achievement tests are different and lower for substance abusing adolescents relative to a comparison group of student controls (Braggio, Pishkin et al., 1993).

COMORBIDITY OF ALCOHOL AND DRUG ADDICTION

Cross-sectional survey data and clinical studies make clear that individuals who have one alcohol or drug disorder may have another comorbid alcohol or drug use disorder (e.g., Regier, Farmer et al., 1990). Other psychopathologies (such as affective disorders, schizophrenic disorders, and anxiety disorders) also may co-occur with addictions (Regier, Farmer et al., 1990). However, there are few population-based studies that have allowed us to examine this relationship prospectively. The ECA data set provides some of this information. For example, there is evidence that the risk of alcoholism may be increased among individuals who have other psychopathologies, including illicit drug disorders (Crum, Helzer & Anthony, 1993), and cocaine use may be associated with the development of several psychiatric conditions (Anthony & Petronis, 1991). Using data from the ECA surveys of households and institutionalized populations, Regier and colleagues found that, among individuals with a drug disorder, the lifetime prevalence of all alcohol disorder was 47%, and the lifetime prevalence of a psychiatric disorder was 53%. Among those with an alcohol disorder, 37% had a current or prior history of a psychiatric disorder, and lifetime prevalence for a drug disorder was 21% (Regier, Farmer et al., 1990). Recent analyses of lifetime diagnoses of alcohol abuse and dependence from the National Comorbidity Survey also found that individuals with a lifetime history of an alcohol abuse or dependence diagnosis frequently had a history of another lifetime psychiatric or substance use disorder (Kessler, Burnam & McEvoy, 1997). In addition, the analyses indicated that prior psychiatric and substance use disorders may be stronger predictors of alcohol dependence than alcohol abuse. Furthermore, early disorders appear to be better predictors of alcohol dependence among women than among men.

In studying the stages of drug use among adolescents and young adults, several investigators have described a pattern of drug use progression from licit use of tobacco and/or alcohol, to illicit use of marijuana, to the use of other illicit drugs (e.g., Kandel, 1975; Donovan & Jessor, 1983). For example, among most cocaine and crack users, marijuana use is an antecedent. Recent evidence supports gender differences with regard to the significant role of the early licit use of alcohol for young men, and cigarettes for young women (Kandel & Yamaguchi, 1993). Further, there may be differences by gender with respect to the pathways that lead to substance use disorders as well as to the type and severity of psychopathology that develops among individuals with addictions (Luthar, Cushing & Rounsaville, 1996).

As more information from longitudinal studies becomes available, we will be better able to assess these temporal relationships. In addition, future investigations into age of onset and the progression of symptoms with the co-occurrence of other conditions will provide valuable information for clinical treatment, as well as a better understanding of potential etiologic relationships.

CONCLUSIONS

This chapter has attempted to summarize a sampling of major findings in epidemiologic research of alcohol and drug addiction. In contrast to clinical practice, or basic science and laboratory research, epidemiology is a study of populations. As discussed in detail by Kleinbaum and colleagues, it is through this study of populations that epidemiologic research aims to describe the health status and distribution of disease in populations, as well as to identify risk factors and potential etiologic agents of disease, which may enable us to better predict and prevent disease occurrence (Kleinbaum, Kupper & Morgenstern, 1982). These basic principles have been extended to drug and alcohol addiction epidemiology, with the ultimate goals of improving understanding of etiologic mechanisms, identifying targets for intervention, and reducing the prevalence of addictive disorders.

ACKNOWLEDGMENT: This work was supported by a Scientist Development Award for Clinicians from the National Institute on Alcohol Abuse and Alcoholism (AA00168).

REFERENCES

Adams EH & Gfroerer J (1991). Risk of cocaine abuse and dependence. In S Schober & C Schade (eds.) *The Epidemiology of Cocaine Use and Abuse (NIDA Research Monograph 110).* Rockville, MD: National Institute on Drug Abuse, 253–262.

Adams WL, Garry PJ, Rhyne R, Hunt WC & Goodwin JS (1990). Alcohol intake in the healthy elderly. Changes with age in a cross-sectional and longitudinal study. *Journal of the American Geriatric Society* 38:211–216.

American Psychiatric Association (1980). *Diagnostic and Statistical Manual of Mental Disorders, 3rd Ed.* Washington, DC: American Psychiatric Press.

American Psychiatric Association (1987). *Diagnostic and Statistical Manual of Mental Disorders, 3rd Ed., Revised.* Washington, DC: American Psychiatric Press.

American Psychiatric Association (1994). *Diagnostic and Statistical Manual of Mental Disorders, 4th Ed.* Washington, DC: American Psychiatric Press.

Anthony JC, Eaton WW, Mandell W & Garrison R (1992). Psychoactive drug dependence and abuse: More common in some occupations than others? *Journal of Employee Assistance Research* 1(1):148–186.

Anthony JC & Helzer JE (1991). Syndromes of drug abuse and dependence. In LN Robins & DA Regier (eds.) *Psychiatric Disorders in America.* New York, NY: The Free Press, Macmillan, 116–154.

Anthony JC & Petronis KR (1991). Epidemiologic evidence on suspected associations between cocaine use and psychiatric disturbances. In S Schober & C Schade (eds.) *The Epidemiology of Cocaine Use and Abuse (NIDA Research Monograph 110).* Rockville, MD: National Institute on Drug Abuse, 71–94.

Aston CE & Hill SY (1990). Segregation analysis of alcoholism in families ascertained through a pair of male alcoholics. *American Journal of Human Genetics* 46:879–887.

Bailly D, Vignau J, Racadot N, Beuscart R, Servant D & Parquet PJ (1993). Platelet serotonin levels in alcoholic patients: Changes related to physiological and pathological factors. *Psychiatry Research* 47(1):57–88.

Begleiter H & Porjesz B (1988). Potential biological markers in individuals at high risk for developing alcoholism. *Alcoholism: Clinical & Experimental Research* 12(4):488–493.

Blum K, Noble EP, Sheridan PJ, Montgomery A, Ritchie T, Jagadeeswaran P, Nogami H, Briggs AH & Cohn JB (1990). Allelic association of human dopamine D_2 receptor gene in alcoholism. *Journal of the American Medical Association* 263(15):2055–2060.

Braggio JT, Pishkin V, Gameros TA & Brooks DL (1993). Academic achievement in substance-abusing and conduct-disordered adolescents. *Journal of Clinical Psychology* 49(2):282–2911.

Burnam MA, Hough RL, Karno M, Escobar JI & Telles CA (1987). Acculturation and lifetime prevalence of psychiatric disorders among Mexican Americans in Los Angeles. *Journal of Health and Social Behavior* 28:89–102.

Cadoret RJ, Troughton E, O'Gorman TW & Heywood E (1986). An adoption study of genetic and environmental factors in drug abuse. *Archives of General Psychiatry* 43:1131–1136.

Cadoret RJ, Yates, WR, Troughton E, Woodworth G & Stewart MA (1995). Adoption study demonstrating two genetic pathways to drug abuse. *Archives of General Psychiatry* 52(1):42–52.

Caetano R (1987). Acculturation and drinking patterns among U.S. Hispanics. *British Journal of Addiction* 82:789–799.

Caetano R (1988). Alcohol use among Hispanic groups in the United States. *American Journal of Drug and Alcohol Abuse* 14(3):293–308.

Caetano R & Herd D (1984). Black drinking practices in Northern California. *American Journal of Drug and Alcohol Abuse* 10(4):571–587.

Caetano R & Kaskutas LA (1995). Changes in drinking patterns among Whites, Blacks and Hispanics, 1984–1992. *Journal of Studies on Alcohol* 56:558–565.

Caetano R & Tam TW (1995). Prevalence and correlates of DSM-IV and ICD–10 alcohol dependence: 1990 U.S. National Alcohol Survey. *Alcohol & Alcoholism* 30(2):177–186.

Cahalan D, Cisin IH & Crossley HM (1969). *American Drinking Practices. A National Study of Drinking Behavior and Attitudes.* New Haven, CT: College & University Press, 31–36.

Chi I, Lubben JE & Kitano HHL (1989). Differences in drinking behavior among three Asian-American groups. *Journal of Studies on Alcohol* 50(1):15–23.

Chilcoat HD, Dishion TJ & Anthony JC (1995). Parent monitoring and the incidence of drug sampling in urban elementary school children. *American Journal of Epidemiology* 141(1):25–31.

Chilcoat HD & Breslau N (1996). Alcohol disorders in young adulthood: effects of transitions into adult roles. *Journal of Health and Social Behavior* 37(4):339–349.

Christian CM, Dufour M & Bertolucci D (1989). Differential alcohol-related mortality among American Indian Tribes in Oklahoma, 1968–1978. *Social Science and Medicine* 28(3):275–284.

Cloninger CR, Bohman M & Sigvardsson S (1981). Inheritance of alcohol abuse: Cross-fostering analysis of adopted men. *Archives of General Psychiatry* 38:861–868.

Cotton NS (1979). The familial incidence of alcoholism. A review. *Journal of Studies on Alcohol* 40(1):89–116.

Crum RM, Bucholz KK, Helzer JE & Anthony JC (1992). The risk of alcohol abuse and dependence in adulthood: The association with educational level. *American Journal of Epidemiology* 135(9):989–999.

Crum RM, Ensminger ME, Ro M & McCord J (1998). The association of educational achievement and school dropout with risk of alcoholism: A twenty-five-year prospective study of inner-city children. *Journal of Studies on Alcohol* 59:318–326.

Crum RM, Helzer JE & Anthony JC (1993). Level of education and alcohol abuse and dependence in adulthood: A further inquiry. *American Journal of Public Health* 83(6):830–837.

Donovan JE & Jessor R (1983). Problem drinking and the dimension of involvement with drugs. A Guttman Scalogram Analysis of adolescent drug use. *American Journal of Public Health* 73(5):543–551.

Dufour M & Fuller RK (1995). Alcohol in the elderly. *Annual Review of Medicine* 46:123–1432.

Eaton WW & Kessler LG (1985). *Epidemiologic Field Methods in Psychiatry. The NIMH Epidemiologic Catchment Area Program.* Orlando, FL: Academic Press, Inc.

Eaton WW, Kramer M, Anthony JC, Dryman A, Shapiro S & Locke BZ (1989a). The incidence of specific DIS/DSM-III mental disorders: Data from the NIMH Epidemiologic Catchment Area Program. *Acta Psychiatrica Scandinavica* 79:163–178.

Eaton WW, Kramer M, Anthony JC, Chee EML & Shapiro S (1989b). Conceptual and methodological problems in estimation of the incidence of mental disorders from field survey data. In Cooper B & Helgason T (eds.) *Epidemiology and the Prevention of Mental Disorders* (World Psychiatric Association). New York, NY: Routledge, 108–127.

Eggert LL & Herting JR (1993). Drug involvement among potential dropouts and "typical" youth. *Journal of Drug Education* 23(1):31–55.

Essen-Moller E (1956). Individual traits and morbidity in a Swedish rural population. *Acta Psychiatrica et Neurologica Scandinavica* (Suppl) 100:1–160.

Fillmore KM (1987a). Prevalence, incidence and chronicity of drinking patterns and problems among men as a function of age: A longitudinal and cohort analysis. *British Journal of Addiction* 82:77–83.

Fillmore KM (1987b). Women's drinking across the adult life course as compared to men's. *British Journal of Addiction* 82:801–811.

Finlayson RE (1988). Alcoholism in elderly persons: A study of the psychiatric and psychosocial features of 216 inpatients. *Mayo Clinic Proceedings* 63:761–768.

Fremming KH (1947). *Morbid Risk of Mental Diseases and Other Mental Abnormalities in an Average Danish Population (Danish with English Summary).* Copenhagen, Denmark: Ejnar Munksgaard.

Gfroerer J & De La Rosa M (1993). Protective and risk factors associated with drug use among Hispanic youth. *Journal of Addictive Diseases* 12(2):87–107.

Goldman D, Lister RG & Crabbe JC (1987). Mapping of a putative genetic locus determining ethanol intake in the mouse. *Brain Research* 420:220–226.

Goldstein PJ, Bellucci PA, Spunt BJ & Miller T (1991). Frequency of cocaine use and violence: A comparison between men and women. In S Schober & C Schade (eds.) *The Epidemiology of Cocaine Use and Abuse (NIDA Research Monograph 110).* Rockville, MD: National Institute on Drug Abuse, 113–138.

Goodwin DW, Schulsinger F, Hermansen L, Guze SB & Winokur G (1973). Alcohol problems in adoptees raised apart from alcoholic biological parents. *Archives of General Psychiatry* 28:238–243.

Gorman DM (1988). Employment, stressful life events and the development of alcohol dependence. *Drug and Alcohol Dependence* 22:151–159.

Graham K (1986). Identifying and measuring alcohol abuse among the elderly: Serious problems with existing instrumentation. *Journal of Studies on Alcohol* 47(4):322–326.

Grant BF, Harford TC, Dawson DA, Chou P, Dufour M & Pickering R (1994). Prevalence of DSM-IV alcohol abuse and dependence United States, 1992. *Alcohol Health and Research World* 18(3):243–248.

Hagnell O (1966). *A Prospective Study of the Incidence of Mental Disorder.* Lund, Sweden: Svenska Bokforlaget.

Hall EM (1992). Double exposure: The combined impact of the home and work environments on psychosomatic strain in Swedish women and men. *International Journal of Health Services* 22(2):239–260.

Harrison PA & Luxenberg M (1995). Comparisons of alcohol and other drug problems among Minnesota adolescents in 1989 and 1992. *Archives of Pediatric and Adolescent Medicine* 149:137–144.

Helgason T (1964). Epidemiology of mental disorders in Iceland. *Acta Psychiatrica Scandinavica Supplementum* 173:115–132.

Helzer JE, Burnam A & McEvoy LT (1991). Alcohol abuse and dependence. In LN Robins & DA Regier (eds.) *Psychiatric Disorders in America: The Epidemiologic Catchment Area Study.* New York, NY: The Free Press, MacMillan, Inc., 81–115.

Herd D (1990). Subgroup differences in drinking patterns among black and white men: Results from a national survey. *Journal of Studies on Alcohol* 51(3):221–232.

Herd D (1994). Predicting drinking problems among black and white men: Results from a national survey. *Journal of Studies on Alcohol* 55:61–71.

Higuchi S, Matsushita S, Murayama M, Takagi S & Hayashida M (1995). Alcohol and aldehyde dehydrogenase polymorphisms and the risk for alcoholism. *American Journal of Psychiatry* 152(8): 1219–1221.

Hilton ME (1988). Trends in U.S. drinking patterns: Further evidence from the past 20 years. *British Journal of Addiction* 83:269–278.

Holck SE, Warren CW, Smith JC & Rochat RW (1984). Alcohol consumption among Mexican American and Anglo women: Results of a survey along the U.S.-Mexico border. *Journal of Studies on Alcohol* 45(2):149–154.

Hrubec Z & Omenn GS (1981). Evidence of genetic predisposition to alcoholic cirrhosis and psychosis: Twin concordances for alcoholism and its biological end points by zygosity among male veterans. *Alcoholism: Clinical & Experimental Research* 5(2):207–215.

Hsu YP, Loh EW, Chen WJ, Chen CC, Yu JM & Cheng AT (1996). Association of monoamine oxidase A alleles with alcoholism among male Chinese in Taiwan. *American Journal of Psychiatry* 153(9):1209–1211.

Jessor R & Jessor SL (1977). *Problem Behavior and Psychosocial Development: A Longitudinal Study of Youth.* New York, NY: Academic Press.

Johnston LD, O'Malley PM & Bachman JG (1992). *Smoking, Drinking, and Illicit Drug Use among American Secondary School Students, College Students, and Young Adults, 1975–1991; Vol. I, Secondary School Students.* Rockville, MD: National Institute on Drug Abuse.

Kandel D (1975). Stages in adolescent involvement in drug use. *Science* 190:912–914.

Kandel D & Yamaguchi K (1993). From beer to crack: Developmental patterns of drug involvement. *American Journal of Public Health* 83(6):851–855.

Kaprio J, Koskenvuo M, Langinvainio H, Romanov K, Sarna S & Rose RJ (1987). Genetic influences on use and abuse of alcohol: A study of 5638 adult Finnish twin brothers. *Alcoholism: Clinical & Experimental Research* 11(4):349–356.

Kellam SG, Brown CH, Rubin BR & Ensminger ME (1983). Paths leading to teenage psychiatric symptoms and substance use: Developmental epidemiological studies in Woodlawn. In SB Guze, FJ Earls & JE Barrett (eds.) *Childhood Psychopathology and Development.* New York, NY: Raven Press.

Kendler KS, Gardner CO & Prescott CA (1997). Religion, psychopathology, and substance use and abuse; A multimeasure, genetic-epidemiologic study. *American Journal of Psychiatry* 154(3):322–329.

Kendler KS, Heath AC, Neale MC, Kessler RC & Eaves LJ (1992). A population-based twin study of alcoholism in women. *Journal of the American Medical Association* 268(14):1877–1882.

Kendler KS, Neale MC, Heath AC, Kessler RC & Eaves LJ (1994). A twin-family study of alcoholism in women. *American Journal of Psychiatry* 151(5):707–715.

Kessler RC, Crum RM, Warner LA, Nelson CB, Schulenberg J & Anthony JC (1997). Lifetime co-occurrence of DSM-IIIR alcohol abuse and dependence with other psychiatric disorders in the National Comorbidity Survey. *Archives of General Psychiatry* 54(4):313–321.

Kessler RC, McGonagle KA, Zhao S, Nelson CB, Hughes M, Eshleman S, Wittchen H-U & Kendler KS (1994). Lifetime and 12-month prevalence of DSM-III-R psychiatric disorders in the United States. *Archives of General Psychiatry* 51:8–19.

Kleinbaum DG, Kupper LL & Morgenstern H (1982). *Epidemiologic Research.* New York, NY: Van Nostrand Reinhold.

Knibbe RA, Drop MJ, Van Reek J & Saenger G (1985). The development of alcohol consumption in the Netherlands: 1958–1981. *British Journal of Addiction* 80:411–419.

Lahelma E, Kangas R & Manderbacka K (1995). Drinking and unemployment: Contrasting patterns among men and women. *Drug and Alcohol Dependence* 37:71–82.

Liberto JG, Oslin DW & Ruskin PE (1992). Alcoholism in older persons: A review of the literature. *Hospital and Community Psychiatry* 43(10):975–984.

Lilienfeld AM & Lilienfeld DE (1980). *Foundations of Epidemiology, 2nd Ed.* New York, NY: Oxford University Press.

Lillie-Blanton M, Anthony JC & Schuster CR (1993). Probing the meaning of racial/ethnic group comparisons in crack cocaine smoking. *Journal of the American Medical Association* 269(8):993–997.

Luthar SS, Cushing G & Rounsaville BJ (1996). Gender differences among opioid abusers: Pathways to disorder and profiles of psychopathology. *Drug and Alcohol Dependence* 43(3):179–189.

Mausner JS & Kramer S (1985). *Mausner and Bahn Epidemiology: An Introductory Text.* Philadelphia, PA: W.B. Saunders Company.

McCaul ME, Turkkan JS, Svikis DS, Bigelow GE & Cromwell CC (1990). Alcohol and drug use by college males as a function of family alcoholism history. *Alcoholism: Clinical & Experimental Research* (14)3:467–471.

McCord W & McCord J (1962). A longitudinal study of the personality of alcoholics. In DJ Pittman & CR Snyder (eds.) *Society, Culture, and Drinking Patterns.* New York, NY: John Wiley & Sons, 413–430.

McLeod JD (1993). Spouse concordance for alcohol dependence and heavy drinking: evidence from a community sample. *Alcoholism: Clinical & Experimental Research* 17(6):1146–1155.

Midanik LT & Clark WB (1995). Drinking-related problems in the United States: Description and trends, 1984–1990. *Journal of Studies on Alcohol* 56:395–402.

Mullahy J & Sindelar JL (1994). Alcoholism and income: The role of indirect effects. *The Milbank Quarterly* 72(2):359–375.

Ohannessian CM & Hesslebrock VM (1993). The influence of perceived social support on the relationship between family history of alcoholism and drinking behaviors. *Addiction* 88(12):1651–1658.

Ojesjo L (1980). Prevalence of known and hidden alcoholism in the revisited Lundby population. *Social Psychiatry* 15:81–90.

Ojesjo L, Hagnell O & Lanke J (1982). Incidence of alcoholism among men in the Lundby Community Cohort, Sweden, 1957–1972. *Journal of Studies on Alcohol* 43(11):1190–1198.

Olkinuora M (1984). Alcoholism and occupation. *Scandinavian Journal of Work Environment and Health* 10:511–515.

O'Malley PM, Bachman JG & Johnston LD (1988). Period, age and cohort effects on substance use among young Americans: A decade of change, 1976–1986. *American Journal of Public Health* 78(10):1315–1321.

Otten MC, Teutsch SM, Williamson DF & Marks JS (1990). The effect of known risk factors on the excess mortality of black adults in the United States. *Journal of the American Medical Association* 263(6):845–850.

Parker DA & Harford TC (1992). Gender-role attitudes, job competition and alcohol consumption among women and men. *Alcoholism: Clinical & Experimental Research* 16(2):159–165.

Pickens RW & Svikis DS (1988). *Biological Vulnerability to Drug Abuse (NIDA Research Monograph 89).* Rockville, MD: National Institute on Drug Abuse.

Rausch JL, Monteiro MG & Schuckit MA (1991). Platelet serotonin uptake in men with family histories of alcoholism. *Neuropsychopharmacology* 4(2):83–86.

Regier DA, Farmer ME, Rae DS, Locke BZ, Keith SJ, Judd LL & Goodwin FK (1990). Co-morbidity of mental disorders with alcohol and other drug abuse: Results from the Epidemiologic Catchment Area (ECA) Study. *Journal of the American Medical Association* 264(19):2511–2518.

Rhoades ER, Hammond J, Welty TK, Handler AO & Amler RW (1987). The Indian burden of illness and future health interventions. *Public Health Reports* 102(4):361–368.

Robins LN, Helzer JE, Croughan J & Ratcliff KS (1981). National Institute of Mental Health Diagnostic Interview Schedule. *Archives of General Psychiatry* 38:381–389.

Robins LN, Helzer JE, Weissman MM, Orvaschel H, Gruenberg E, Burke JD & Regier DA (1984). Lifetime prevalence of specific psychiatric disorders in three sites. *Archives of General Psychiatry* 41:949–958.

Robins LN & Regier DA (1991). *Psychiatric Disorders in America: The Epidemiologic Catchment Area Study.* New York, NY: The Free Press, Macmillan, Inc.

Ronan L (1986–87). Alcohol-related health risks among Black Americans. *Alcohol Health and Research World* 11(2):36–39, 65.

Rosin AJ & Glatt MM (1971). Alcohol excess in the elderly. *Quarterly Journal of Studies on Alcohol* 32:53–59.

Schuckit MA (1983). Alcoholic men with no alcoholic first-degree relatives. *American Journal of Psychiatry* 140(4):439–443.

Schulenberg J, Bachman JG, O'Malley PM & Johnston LD (1994). High school educational success and subsequent substance use: a panel analysis following adolescents into young adulthood. *Journal of Health and Social Behavior* 35:45–62.

Sigvardsson S, Bohman M, Cloninger CR (1996). Replication of the Stockholm Adoption Study of alcoholism. *Archives of General Psychiatry* 53(8):681–687.

Suddendorf RF (1989). Research on alcohol metabolism among Asians and its implications for understanding causes of alcoholism. *Public Health Reports* 104(6):615–620.

Thomas BS (1993). Drug use in a small Midwestern community and relationships to selected characteristics. *Journal of Drug Education* 23:247–258.

Thomas BS & Hsiu LT (1993). The role of selected risk factors in predicting adolescent drug use and its adverse consequences. *International Journal of the Addictions* 28:1549–1563.

Vega WA, Zimmerman RS, Warheit GJ, Apospori E & Gil AG (1993). Risk factors for early adolescent drug use in four ethnic and racial groups. *American Journal of Public Health* 83(2):185–189.

Vestal RE, McGuire EA, Tobin JD, Andres R, Norris AH & Mezey E (1977). Aging and ethanol metabolism. *Clinical Pharmacology & Therapeutics* 21(3):343–354.

Warner LA, Kessler Rc, Hughes M, Anthony JC & Nelson CB (1995). Prevalence and correlates of drug use and dependence in the United States. Results from the National Comorbidity Survey. *Archives of General Psychiatry* 52(3):219–229.

West MO & Prinz RJ (1987). Parental alcoholism and childhood psychopathology. *Psychological Bulletin* 102(2):204–218.

Wilsnack SC, Klassen AD, Schur BE & Wilsnack RW (1991). Predicting onset and chronicity of women's problem drinking: A five-year longitudinal analysis. *American Journal of Public Health* 81:305–318.

Wilsnack SC, Vogeltanz ND, Klassen AD & Harris TR (1997). Childhood sexual abuse and women's substance abuse: National survey findings. *Journal of Studies on Alcohol* 58(3):264–271.

Wilsnack SC & Wilsnack RW (1995). Drinking and problem drinking in U.S. women. In M Galanter (ed.) *Recent Developments in Alcoholism Volume 12: Women and Alcoholism.* New York, NY: Plenum Press.

World Health Organization (1992). *The ICD-10 Classification of Mental and Behavioural Disorders.* Geneva, Switzerland: The Organization.

CHAPTER 2

Genetic Influences in Addiction

Robert M. Anthenelli, M.D.
Marc A. Schuckit, M.D.

Alcoholism as a Model for Studying Genetic Vulnerability
The Search for Genetically Mediated Markers of Alcoholism
Genetic Aspects of Drug Abuse and Dependence
Genetics of Cigarette Smoking: A Special Case?

Several years ago, the *New York Times* (April 18, 1990) reported that "scientists [had] link[ed] alcoholism to a specific gene[,] . . . opening the 'window of hope' for prevention of a deadly disease." Although the accuracy of the finding on which this headline was based is controversial (Noble, 1993; Goldman, Brown et al., 1994), the story remains historically significant.

Fifty years ago, there were those who doubted they would ever read such a headline (Goodwin, 1989). As our understanding of alcoholism (i.e., alcohol dependence) and other substance use disorders has advanced, so, too, have our ideas about their patterns of transmission. For instance, the moralistic idea of alcoholism as a characterological weakness has given way to the more contemporary view of the condition as a debilitating, heterogeneous group of disorders with multifactorial origins. The importance of environmental, developmental, and social factors championed by Jellinek and others in the 1940s has had to share the stage with growing body of evidence supporting a genetic vulnerability to the disorder. All are important. No one headline tells the whole story.

This chapter reviews the role of genetic factors in the risk for substance abuse and dependence and outlines a methodological approach for study. Because the preponderance of data are from studies on alcohol, this drug is emphasized. Reflecting the clinical nature of this text and the authors' area of expertise, this chapter focuses primarily on human genetic aspects of substance disorders. Interested readers may wish to pursue a more comprehensive review of the animal and preclinical literature (Crabbe, Belknap & Buck, 1994).

ALCOHOLISM AS A MODEL FOR STUDYING GENETIC VULNERABILITY

Traditionally, the search for genetic influences in any complex disorder be-ins with studies of families, twins, and adoptees affected with the condition (Pardes, Kaufmann et al., 1989). These investigations can provide preliminary evidence on the probable importance of genetic factors and serve as the foundation for subsequent research. The following sections briefly review the results of more than three decades of family, twin, and adoption studies in alcoholism. Although these investigations are not unanimous in their results, when taken together, they provide compelling evidence for the importance of genetic factors in this disorder.

Family, Twin, and Adoption Studies of Alcoholism. *Family Studies:* For centuries, philosophers, writers, and clergy have commented on the familial nature of alcoholism. Plutarch's assertion that "drunks beget drunkards" was based on anecdotal observation alone, and it was not until the past few decades that this contention came under careful scientific scrutiny (Goodwin, 1985). The basic design for family studies of any complex illness is to compare the risk for developing the disorder in relatives of probands (individuals manifesting the phenotype or trait) with the rate for relatives of control groups or for the general population (Pardes, Kaufmann et al., 1989).

Numerous studies have shown that rates of alcoholism are substantially higher in relatives of alcoholics than in relatives of nonalcoholics, with children of alcoholics demonstrating a three- to fourfold increased risk for developing the disorder (Schuckit, 1987; Cotton, 1979). This increased risk appears to be relatively specific for alcoholism, with most family studies showing an increased rate for the disorder among relatives of alcoholic probands, while the same group does not show higher rates of schizophrenia or bipolar disorder (Schuckit, 1987, 1986).

Although family studies provide preliminary evidence that alcoholism might be inherited, they are, in themselves, inconclusive. Familial aggregation might also reflect the shared social and developmental influences of being raised in the same environment by biological parents. To disentangle these factors, other approaches are required.

Twin Studies: Research with twins evaluates the relative contributions of genetic and environmental factors by comparing the similarity or concordance rates for illness in pairs of monozygotic twins with those of dizygotic twins. The twin study design allows researchers to estimate the contribution of genetic and environmental effects to the individual's liability for alcoholism and other substance use disorders. The liability identified in twin research generally has three components: (1) additive genetic effects; (2) common environmental effects shared by twins (e.g.. intrauterine environment, parental upbringing); and (3) specific, nonshared environmental experiences (Prescott & Kendler, 1995). Identical twin pairs who share all of their genes should show higher concordance rates for gene-transmitted disorders than should fraternal twin pairs who, like ordinary siblings, generally share only half of their genes (Prescott & Kendler, 1995). On the other extreme, environmentally influenced disorders would show no difference between monozygotic and dizygotic twin pairs so long as both types of twins were exposed to the same childhood environment.

Several major twin studies have directly addressed the concordance rates for alcoholism in identical versus fraternal twins. In Sweden, Kaij found that the concordance rate for alcoholism in male monozygotic pairs was greater than that for dizygotic twins (approximately 60% versus 39%) (Kaij, 1960). Interestingly, the discrepancy between concordance rates increased in proportion to the severity of alcoholism in these male twin pairs, favoring a genetic diathesis. A Veterans Administration twin register study in the United States revealed a similar higher concordance rate for identical male same-sex twin pairs (Hrubec & Omenn, 1981), as did two other smaller studies (Pickens, Svikis et al., 1991; McGue, Pickens & Svikis, 1992); however, not all studies agree (Gurling, Oppenheim & Murray, 1984).

While results among male same-sex twin pairs had consistently demonstrated that genetic factors were important in the etiology of alcoholism in men, results in women were less consistent. Thus, several smaller twin studies found no (McGue, Pickens & Svikis, 1992; Gurling, Oppenheim & Murray, 1984) or relatively little (Pickens, Svikis et al., 1991) genetic influence in females compared to males. However, recently in a large sample of female same-sex twin pairs in the United States, Kendler et al. reported that the concordance for alcoholism was greater in monozygotic than in dizygotic twin pairs (Kendler, Heath et al., 1992).

Other investigations of twins have focused on how genetic factors might influence patterns of drinking and rates of absorption or elimination of ethanol in twins. Two Scandinavian studies of nonalcoholics have found that identical twins are more concordant for quantity and frequency of drinking but not for adverse consequences of drinking (Partanen, Brunn & Markkanen, 1966; Jonsson & Nilsson, 1968). This latter point might reflect the twin sample under study, which was from the general population and not selected for drinking problems per se. Results from twin studies on concordance rates for alcohol absorption or elimination are conflicting, with some studies showing high levels of heritability for these parameters (Vesell, Page & Passananti, 1970; Radlow & Conway, 1978) and others finding no such concordance (Kopun & Propping, 1977). The disparity in results from these studies probably reflects the multiple factors that affect alcohol absorption and metabolism (e.g., use of other drugs, diet, etc.).

Thus, the majority of twin studies support the notion that alcoholism is genetically influenced and that heritable factors might play a role in the quantity and frequency of drinking in both men and women. The lack of unanimity of these studies points to the complexity of these issues and the interaction between genetic and environmental factors.

Adoption Studies. Perhaps the most convincing way to separate genetic from environmental effects is to study individuals separated soon after birth from their biological relatives and raised by nonrelative adoptive parents (Goodwin, 1983). This can be done through classical adoption studies or through a half-sibling approach (Schuckit, 1985).

There have been several half-sibling and adoption studies evaluating the possibility that alcoholism, at least in part, has genetic determinants. Schuckit and colleagues evaluated a group of individuals who had been raised apart from their biological parents but who had either a biological or surrogate parent with alcoholism (Schuckit, Goodwin & Winokur, 1972). Subjects who had a biological parent with severe alcohol problems were significantly more likely to have alcoholism themselves than if their surrogate parent were alcoholic.

Over the past two decades, several adoption studies in Denmark, Sweden, and the United States have yielded similar results. In Denmark, Goodwin and coworkers found that the sons of alcoholics were about four times more likely to be alcoholic than sons of nonalcoholics and that being raised by either nonalcoholic adoptive parents or by biological parents did not affect this increased risk (Goodwin, 1979). Furthermore, although the sons of alcoholics were found to be at highest risk for developing alcoholism, they were no more likely to have other psychiatric disorders (Goodwin, 1983, 1979). As with some of the twin studies cited above, results for women in the Copenhagen Adoption Study were not significant. Similar results were found in another large study, done in Stockholm, Sweden, where Cloninger and colleagues showed significantly higher rates of alcohol abuse in adopted-out sons of biological fathers registered with alcohol problems (Cloninger, Bohman & Sigvardsson, 1981). The Stockholm Adoption Study also suggested that, although significant, genes were less important as risk factors for alcoholism in women than men. Data from two smaller scale adoption studies in Iowa confirmed the results of the larger European studies (Cadoret, Cain & Grove, 1980; Cadoret, Troughton & O'Gorman, 1987); however, Cadoret et al. did find important genetic influences in female adoptees (Cadoret, O'Gorman et al., 1985). In fact, only one study, by Roe, has found contrary results (Roe, 1994), and most authors agree that the disparity probably reflects methodological problems in its design (e.g., small sample size and lack of rigorous diagnostic criteria for alcohol problems in the parents) or differences in the subpopulations of twins studied (Goodwin, 1985, 1983; Cloninger, Bohman & Sigvardsson, 1981).

Summary. The combination of family, twin, and adoption studies strongly suggests that genetic determinants play an important part in the etiology of alcoholism for both men and women. Unfortunately, with the possible exception of cigarette smoking, the case for other types of drug abuse is more complicated and less convincing. We will return to this issue in a later section, but will continue for now, with alcoholism as our "model" for consideration.

THE SEARCH FOR GENETICALLY MEDIATED MARKERS OF ALCOHOLISM

The results of family, twin, and adoption studies offer enough support for genetic factors to justify a search for what might be inherited to increase the risk for this disorder. As a result, a number of laboratories have begun to look for trait or phenotypic markers of a vulnerability toward alcoholism (Schuckit, 1987, 1985). Such markers should be stable, easily measured properties that are themselves under genetic control and either directly influence the alcoholism risk or are linked to genes that affect the development of alcoholism.

The search for biological markers of alcoholism has been guided largely by three related premises. First, it is likely that there are measurable attributes associated with the risk for developing the disorder that differ in the frequency in which they are found in groups of high- and low-risk individuals; second, such properties are present before the illness develops and can be observed during remission from active drug use (Schuckit, 1987); and third, some trait markers may depend on the presence of active drug use for their expression to become overt.

The following sections outline an approach for looking for phenotypic markers of alcoholism. They begin by describing some of the options available for selecting populations at risk for developing the disorder and then address ways in which the homogeneity of these samples can be maximized.

Selecting High-Risk Populations. There are several possible approaches to the study of populations at high risk for the development of substance abuse and dependence, some of which are already paying dividends in the search for biological markers of alcoholism. Each of these methods has its own assets and liabilities, and no one approach is ideal. Choosing a sample for study depends on a number of practical and theoretic considerations: cost factors, the availability of subjects, and the suitability of the sample to the hypothesis being tested are all just some of the factors contributing to this decision (Schuckit, 1985).

Adoptee Samples: Perhaps most informative, but also difficult to perform, are studies of children of alcoholics who have been adopted out and raised by nonalcoholic adoptive parents (Anthenelli & Schuckit, 1990). These offspring are then followed longitudinally to determine differences from control subjects as possible leads to markers that might associate with the risk for developing alcoholism. Although such adoption studies offer the benefit of potentially separating genetic from environmental risk factors, they require years of study and are very expensive. To date, few appropriate groups have been available for study and relatively limited data have been reported (Cadoret, Cain & Grove, 1980; Jacobsen & Schulsinger, 1981; Utne, Hensen et al., 1977); however, continued follow-up of these adoptees may yield useful results.

Family Pedigrees: Another approach is to study a limited number of pedigrees of alcoholics, looking for markers that are present in affected relatives but are absent in nonalcoholic family members (Anthenelli & Schuckit, 1990). Variations of this method are currently in use at a number of centers, usually relying on "multiplex" or "high-density" families in which several members are affected with the disorder. This method is also time-consuming and expensive and, given the disorder's likely multifactorial polygenic origins, runs the risk of missing potential trait markers that may operate in disparate ways in different families (Anthenelli & Schuckit, 1990). As is discussed later, pedigree studies can also provide the framework for more elaborate genetic analyses.

Other "High Risk" Populations: To avoid some of the problems inherent in the two approaches outlined above, most studies of populations at increased risk for alcoholism have examined nonalcoholic relatives of alcoholics from a wide range of families (Schuckit, 1987, 1985). This method usually offers the advantages of a readily accessible control group and can identify potential markers to be intensively studied in more focused (i.e., selected pedigrees) ways (Schuckit, 1985). Most investigators using this method have focused on sons of alcoholic fathers, reflecting the expectation that sons will show higher rates of expression of alcoholism than daughters and the possibility that results from ethanol challenges could vary with the phase of the menstrual cycle (Jones & Jones, 1976).

There are important variations in the designs of studies using these high-risk populations. For example, some researchers have evaluated prepubertal boys in order to observe them before actual exposure to ethanol (Begleiter, Porjesz et al., 1984; Behar, Berg et al., 1983). However, this approach risks missing potential markers that may appear only after puberty or that are triggered following modest alcohol consumption, and it requires a long follow-up period to see if future alcoholism develops (Anthenelli & Schuckit, 1990). Other groups have selected older subjects, usually in their late teens to mid-20s. This decision avoids the problems mentioned above but adds the risk of leaving out early-onset alcoholics while creating the need to match subjects and controls on drinking histories. Such differences in sample selection probably explain some of the variance in the results obtained from these investigations.

Importance of Sample Homogeneity. Regardless of the specific approach selected, it is important to consider several major factors that can influence the results in studies evaluating potential trait markers.

Etiological Heterogeneity: First, when studying complex disorders like alcoholism or other kinds of drug dependence, it is essential to realize that, at best, one's diagnosis rests at the "clinical syndrome" level and that it is likely that many different pathways or etiologies can lead to this combination of symptoms and signs (Anthenelli & Schuckit, 1990; McHugh & Slavney, 1983).

As a result of this etiological heterogeneity and the relatively early stage of this line of research, most investigators have chosen to focus on relatives of severely affected alcoholic individuals in the hope that genetic factors may be most obvious and identifiable in this group (Schuckit, 1987). Hence, we run the risk of identifying genetic factors that may be relevant to only the most severe forms of alcohol abuse.

Comorbidity with Two Separate Disorders: A second, related consideration is that life problems from excessive use of alcohol or other drugs may coexist with other disorders in the same patient. In fact, at least 30% of alcoholics have evidence of preexisting disorders (Schuckit, 1996). For instance, 70% of men with antisocial personality disorder (ASPD) have secondary alcohol problems during the course of their disorder; about 20% of patients during the manic phase of bipolar illness develop severe ethanol-related difficulties; and heroin addicts in methadone rehabilitation show high rates of secondary alcohol problems compared with their rate before treatment (Schuckit, 1996). The phenotypic variations between these groups of "alcoholics" having two disorders is obvious. If these men and women carry genetic factors related to their ASPD, mania, or heroin problems, it could be difficult to identify any inherited influences related to the alcohol dependence. One approach that begins to address the vexing issue of comorbidity is that of *primary versus secondary alcoholism* (Schuckit, 1996; Goodwin & Guze, 1989). Although various meanings have been linked with these terms in the past, one clinically relevant application uses the chronology of development of symptoms to classify alcoholics into two major groups. In primary alcoholism, the major life problems resulting from repeated excessive drinking are observed in men and women with no major preexisting psychiatric illness (Schuckit, 1996; Goodwin & Guze, 1989). In contrast, individuals who develop ethanol-related life problems only after manifesting evidence of bipolar disorder or ASPD (e.g., secondary alcoholics) generally are not included in studies assessing the genetic susceptibility to alcoholism for fear that inherited factors contributing to the primary illness (e.g., ASPD) may obscure genetic determinants predisposing the subject to alcoholism. This distinction has clinical implications, with data from our laboratory and others showing that primary and secondary alcoholics demonstrate significantly different courses (Schuckit, 1985; Hesselbrock, Hesselbrock & Stabenau, 1985) and outcomes at one year (Schuckit, 1985).

Subtypes of Alcoholism: Once the diagnosis of primary versus secondary alcoholism has been made, further classification into distinctive alcoholic subtypes may also increase the homogeneity of the sample population under study. Currently, several overlapping approaches are in use to categorize alcoholics into various subgroups based on family history, age of onset, clinical symptoms, and personality traits (Goodwin, 1983; Schuckit, 1985; McCue, Pickins & Svikis, 1992; Babor, Hofmann et al., 1992). Although each of these methods has its strengths and limitations, the validity of any one method over the others has not yet been established (Penick, Powell et al., 1990; Anthenelli, Smith et al., 1994). Although a review of all of the potential subtypes would require a separate chapter in its own right and is beyond the scope of this discussion, the underlying philosophy behind their use is an attempt to better define subsets of alcoholics who are at increased risk for developing the disorder.

Among the many different subtype classifications currently under study, one theory proposed by Cloninger, Bohman and Sigvardsson, and their colleagues has gained some popularity (Cloninger, Bohman & Sigvardsson, 1981; Cloninger, Sigvardsson et al., 1986; Cloninger, 1987; Bohman, Sigvardsson & Cloninger, 1991; von Knorring, von Knorring et al., 1987). Using a discriminant function analysis of their large sample of Swedish adoptees, this group initially proposed two forms of alcoholism (types 1 and 2) that could be distinguished on the basis of the biological parents' pattern of alcohol abuse and the degree to which postnatal environmental factors affected the inheritance of susceptibility to alcoholism (Cloninger, Bohman & Sigvardsson, 1981; Bohman, Sigvardsson & Cloninger, 1991). Combining results from a variety of personality, clinical, and neuropsychopharmacological studies with the genetic epidemiological findings, these authors elaborated on this theory, expanding its original focus on the importance of gene-environment interactions in alcoholism.

Type 1 or "milieu-limited" alcoholism, thought to predominate among female alcoholics and their male relatives, is characterized by loss of control of drinking after the age of 25, pronounced environmental reactivity to drinking, minimal associated criminality, and "passive-dependent personality traits" marked by high degrees of harm avoidance, reward dependence and low levels of novelty-seeking as measured by Cloninger's Tridimensional Personality Questionnaire (TPQ) (Cloninger, 1987). In contrast, the type 2 or "male-limited" subgroup appears to have an inheritance pattern less dependent on environmental factors for phenotypic expression and has an earlier age of onset, more associated criminal behavior, and a triad of personality traits that run opposite those of the prototypic "milieu-limited" alcoholic (Cloninger, Sigvardsson et al., 1986; Cloninger, 1987; Bohman, Cloninger et al., 1987). This group later refined their theory to include a *third* class of alcoholism, which they call "antisocial behavior or disorder with alcohol abuse" (Cloninger, Sigvardsson et al., 1986; Bohman, Sigvardsson & Cloninger, 1991; Devor & Cloninger, 1989).

Although parts of this theory have been tested (Cloninger, 1987; von Knorring & von Knorring, 1987; Devor & Cloninger, 1989), the results of these investigations must be considered preliminary (Schuckit, 1987). Results from our laboratory and others have tested features of the type 1/type 2 scheme in different populations of subjects in an effort to assess their generality. One major concern surrounds the possible overlap between the male-limited subtype and frank ASPD, for which alcohol problems are only part of the syndrome. For example, when we examined the clinical course of primary alcoholic men (alcoholics without any major preexisting psychiatric disorder), we found that neither classification of these alcoholics into discrete type 1 and type 2 categories nor placing them along a continuum of type 2 characteristics was associated with the severity of their clinical course once age at onset was considered (Irwin, Schuckit & Smith, 1990). In a different sample of male inpatient alcoholics, we further demonstrated that there was significant overlap between type 2 alcoholism and ASPD (Anthenelli, Smith et al., 1994). Using another sample of young, nonalcoholic men at high risk for alcoholism and comparing them with matched controls, we found no difference in personality traits between groups as measured by the TPQ, nor was there any relationship between the severity of the fathers' alcoholism on a type 1/type 2 continuum and the sons' Q scores or their alcohol and drug pattern at an average of 21 years (Schuckit, Irwin & Mahler, 1990; Schuckit & Irwin, 1989). Different laboratories using other samples of alcoholics have found similar results (Penick, Powell et al., 1990; Nixon & Parsons, 1990). Nonetheless, efforts to develop and empirically validate different methods of subtyping alcoholics should remain a priority, and the hypotheses put forward by Cloninger et al. have stirred active interest in this pursuit.

Babor and colleagues (1992) used an empirical clustering technique and described a subgrouping scheme for alcoholics that included type A and type B alcoholics, named after the Roman gods Apollo and Bacchus. Type A alcoholics are characterized by later age at onset, fewer childhood risk factors, less severe dependence, fewer alcohol-related problems, and less psychopathological dysfunction. Type B alcoholics typically exhibit an early onset of alcohol-related problems, higher levels of childhood risk factors and familial alcoholism, greater severity of dependence, multiple substance use, a long-term treatment history, greater psychopathological dysfunction, and greater life stress (Babor, Hofmann et al., 1992; Anthenelli & Tabakoff, 1995). The type A/B dichotomy was replicated in another large sample of alcohol-dependent subjects, even after the exclusion of individuals with ASPD and those with an onset of alcohol dependence before age 25, further supporting this subtyping method's potential usefulness (Schuckit, Tipp et al., 1995).

Summary: An array of study approaches has been used to identify populations at elevated risk for developing alcoholism, usually evaluating children and young adults whose fathers have exhibited relatively severe manifestations of the disorder. Confounding factors such as etiological heterogeneity and the coexistence of two or more disorders in the same individual must be considered in the selection of populations for study and in the subsequent comparison of results. The next section reviews the results of studies of high-risk populations.

Results of Studies of Populations at High Risk for Alcoholism. The studies of alcoholic vulnerability are trying to learn more about the mechanisms by which the increased risk for the disorder is likely to be expressed (Schuckit, 1985). The following sections review evaluations of populations at elevated risk for developing alcoholism, briefly presenting some preliminary results. The characteristics of the sample populations differ for the studies presented here: most results, however, are based on comparisons of high and low-risk groups.

To organize the vast array of findings, we find it convenient to somewhat arbitrarily divide the results regarding possible phenotypic markers into two broad categories: studies evaluating baseline differences in the usual attributes among high-risk and control groups, and alcohol challenge protocols that test for variations in response to ethanol between the two groups. Regarding the latter, an emphasis is placed on the finding of a decreased intensity of reaction to alcohol in sons and daughters of alcoholics (Schuckit, 1987; Anthenelli & Schuckit, 1990).

Studies of Baseline Functioning. *Biochemical Markers:* In keeping with our earlier comments about "prototypic" trait markers, a variety of biochemical gene-products have been evaluated for an association with the alcoholism risk. An array of proteins, antigens, and hormones have been studied in human beings, all of which share the attraction of being under some level of genetic control, while at the same time being relatively accessible for measurement in a variety of tissues. Most of these potential markers were first identified in evaluations comparing alcoholics with nonalcoholic controls and thus run some risk of being "state" markers of heavy drinking (Schuckit, 1985). However, most studies take into consideration the need to assess the stability of the marker over time during periods of abstinence in order to test, at least indirectly, the marker' s potential as a "trait" indicator associated with the predisposition toward alcoholism. Fewer studies have used nonalcoholic high-risk populations (e.g., sons of alcoholics), and these are usually limited by smaller sample sizes.

Among the proteins evaluated, one enzyme system important in the metabolism of ethanol in the liver has been shown to be under genetic control and may provide one of the best examples, to date, of how gene-environment interactions influence the risk for alcoholism (Schuckit, 1987; Wall & Ehlers, 1995). Specifically, about 50% of Asians lack one of the isoenzyme forms of aldehyde dehydrogenase (ALDH), the major enzyme that degrades the first metabolite of ethanol, acetaldehyde, in the liver

(Harada, Agarwal et al., 1983; Suwaki & Ohara, 1985). After imbibing alcohol, affected individuals develop higher blood acetaldehyde levels with associated facial flushing, tachycardia, and a burning sensation in the stomach. Not surprisingly, Asians missing this isoenzyme are less likely than others to drink heavily and appear to have a lower rate of alcoholism (Wall & Ehlers, 1995). Hence, the interaction between a genetically controlled enzyme system and environmental factors such as attitudes about drinking and drunkenness appears to contribute significantly to the lower alcoholism risk among a subgroup of Asians (Wall & Ehlers, 1995).

Monoamine oxidase (MAO), a major degradative enzyme system for many neurotransmitters, may also have potential importance for the risk of developing some subtypes of alcoholism and other substance use disorders (Anthenelli & Tabakoff, 1995). Monoamine neurotransmitters, including dopamine, norepinephrine, and serotonin, have all been implicated in various phenomena related to the risk of developing alcoholism. These phenomena include a preference for consuming alcohol, the development of tolerance to alcohol's rewarding effects, and personality characteristics (e.g., impulsivity) that predispose a person to repeated alcohol-related problems (Anthenelli & Tabakoff, 1995). Humans have two types of MAOs—MAO-A and MAO-B—that are the products of separate genes (Anthenelli & Tabakoff, 1995). Because certain blood cells (i.e., the platelets) also contain MAO-B and since platelet MAO-B activity is correlated with brain MAO-B activity (Bench, Price et al., 1991), scientists have studied platelet MAO extensively as a surrogate for brain MAO-B. Several studies have indicated that low platelet MAO activity might be a marker for type 2 alcoholism (von Knorring, Bohman et al., 1985; Pandey, Fawcett et al., 1988); however, the differences between type 1 and type 2 alcoholics have not been consistent across all studies (Anthenelli, Smith et al., 1995). A recent analysis of data from an ongoing multisite study on the genetics of alcohol demonstrated, however, that regardless of the subgrouping scheme being employed (i.e., type 1 versus type 2, type A versus type B, or primary versus secondary alcoholism), men with an earlier age at onset and more severe course of alcohol-related problems had significantly lower platelet MAO levels than nonalcoholic men (Anthenelli & Tabakoff, 1995; Anthenelli, Tipp et al., 1996). Alternatively, low platelet MAO activity may not be a specific marker for alcoholism per se but may be a more general indicator of a spectrum of disorders marked by disinhibition, impulsive aggression, and a predisposition for alcohol and other drug abuse (Anthenelli & Tabakoff, 1995).

Another platelet enzyme system is also being evaluated for a possible association with the risk of alcoholism. Tabakoff, Hoffman, and colleagues have demonstrated that following *in vitro* stimulation with several activating agents, platelet adenylate cyclase (AC) activity was significantly lower in abstinent alcoholics (Tabakoff & Hofmann, 1989; Tabakoff, Hofmann et al., 1988). AC is an enzyme used by cells, including neurons, to relay signals from a cell's exterior to its interior (Anthenelli & Tabakoff, 1995; Tabakoff & Hoffman, 1989). AC activity levels are genetically determined and are frequently reduced in alcoholics compared with nonalcoholics, even after alcoholics experience long periods of abstinence (Anthenelli & Tabakoff, 1995; Hoffman, Lee et al., 1989). Thus, AC activity levels also may be a marker for alcoholism, although research findings indicate that low AC activity may be characteristic of a different alcoholism subtype than that associated with low MAO activity (Anthenelli & Tabakoff, 1995).

Genetic Polymorphisms: Whereas the biochemical markers discussed above represent gene products (i.e., proteins) associated with some alcoholic phenotypes, researchers have also reported gene variants (i.e., alleles) of specific genes in populations called polymorphisms that might be associated with alcoholism. Although the details of the molecular genetic techniques used to identify such genetic markers are beyond the scope of this chapter, briefly, they involve the meticulous dissection of deoxyribonucleic acid (DNA) into specific nucleotide (e.g., the building blocks of DNA) patterns called markers or microsatellites (for details see Mullan, 1989; Goldman, 1995; Begleiter, 1995). Such markers are then analyzed to determine whether there is *linkage* between the marker and the phenotype (i.e., the marker is transmitted along with the disease in families) or whether there is an *association* between the polymorphism and the phenotype (Cloninger, 1991; Parsian, Todd et al., 1991) (i.e., a given marker allele is more common among those individuals with the disease in a population).

Indeed, as alluded to in the opening paragraphs of this chapter, the first report of an "alcoholism gene" occurred in 1990 when Blum announced that he and his colleagues had identified a gene—an allele of dopamine receptor D2 (DRD2)—that appeared to be implicated in severe cases of alcoholism (Blum, Noble et al., 1990). The subject of much debate

(Noble, 1993; Goldman, Brown et al., 1994; Cloninger, 1991; Parsian, Todd et al., 1991; Holden, 1991; Noble, Blum et al., 1991; Bolos, Dean et al., 1990), the DRD2 controversy remains relevant because it heralded the advent of modem molecular genetic approaches to the complex genetic disease, alcoholism. Interestingly, there is also some evidence to implicate the DRD2 gene in other substance use disorders, leading some investigators to label it a potential "reward gene" (Noble, 1993).

Other molecular measures such as proteins (e.g., MNS) found on red blood cells and the red cells' esterase D enzyme system have been reported to be associated with alcoholism and were previously considered as potential trait markers of alcoholism (Begleiter, 1995; Hill, Goodwin et al., 1980). However, recent data from the ongoing Collaborative Study on the Genetics of Alcoholism (COGA-see below) indicates that neither the esterase D enzyme polymorphism or genotypes could distinguish between alcoholic and nonalcoholic people in more than 2,000 subjects from alcoholic and control families (Begleiter, 1995). Furthermore, linkage analyses for hundreds of sibling pairs in the COGA families revealed no evidence that alcohol dependence was linked to regions on chromosome 13 containing the esterase D gene and the region on chromosome 4 containing the MNS genes (Begleiter, 1995). Thus, these results highlight that reports of associations between biochemical markers and alcoholism need to be viewed with caution until further confirmatory genetic analyses can be performed in larger samples.

Electrophysiologicol Markers: Electrophysiological measurements of brain activity have also been demonstrated as potentially promising neurobehavioral markers that might be associated with the predisposition toward alcoholism, at least among some subgroups of individuals (Schuckit, 1987; Begleiter, Porjesz et al., 1984; Begleiter, 1995). Like the biochemical markers, these parameters are appealing because they can be measured relatively easily and seem to be less influenced by subjective factors such as fatigue or inattention. These indicators are covered elsewhere in this text and are only briefly mentioned here.

Event-related potentials (ERPs) have been used extensively to study information processing in high- and low-risk populations (Anthenelli & Schuckit, 1990). The amplitude of one important component of the ERP, the positive wave observed at approximately 300 msec after a rare but expected stimulus (P300), has been demonstrated to be significantly decreased in about one-third of the sons of alcoholic fathers compared with controls (Begleiter, Porjesz et al., 1984; Hesselbrock, O'Connor et al., 1988). Although some studies do not agree with these results (Polich & Bloom, 1988; Hill, Steinhauer et al., 1988), differences probably reflect variations in the studies' designs, including the sample population chosen. In addition to this elicited brain wave marker, a second approach has relied on measurements of the power of wave forms on the background cortical electroencephalogram (EEG) (Anthenelli & Schuckit, 1990). Male alcoholics and their sons might demonstrate a decreased amount of slow wave (e.g., alpha wave) activity at baseline when compared with controls (Pollock, Volavka & Goodwin, 1983; Volavkak, Pollack et al., 1985). Similarly, our own laboratory has observed that sons of alcoholics differ from lower risk, matched controls at baseline on the amount of activity in one part of the frequency range of alpha waves (i.e., men with a positive family history of alcoholism had more energy in the fast alpha range compared with controls) (Ehlers & Schuckit, 1991). These preliminary results require replication and, as is discussed later, some of these electrophysiological markers also show group differences in response to an ethanol challenge.

Potential Differences in Cognitive Performance: There is disagreement about the relative importance of baseline neurocognitive test results and their relationship to the alcoholism risk (Anthenelli & Schuckit, 1990). Much of this controversy can be attributed to the different sample populations under study. For example, comparisons of family history-positive (FHP) and family history-negative (FFN) subjects identified through their associations with juvenile authorities or from a Danish birth cohort have demonstrated lower verbal intelligence quotients (IQs) for the sons of alcoholics along with decreased auditory word span performance, impaired reading comprehension, a greater number of errors on the Category Test of the Halstead-Reitan Neuropsychological Test Battery, and problems with constructional praxis and abstract problem solving (Gabrielli & Melnick, 1983; Knop, Goodwin et al., 1984; Schaeffer, Parsons & Yohman, 1984; Tarter, Hegedus et al., 1984). In contrast, investigations from our laboratory, using a sample of college students and university employees (Schuckit, Butters et al., 1987), and from other groups selecting children of alcoholics from general population samples (Drake & Vaillant, 1988), have found few significant differences in cognitive performance between groups at higher and lower alcoholism risk (Anthenelli & Schuckit, 1990). Differences in the results might reflect either higher rates of conduct and attention deficit disorders in the group selected because of their behavioral difficulties or environmental factors such as the disparity in the quality of education received. Hence, the association between cognitive variables and future alcoholism remains to be determined.

Personality Profiles: Baseline assessments of personality traits in high- and low-risk populations also provide conflicting results, with several factors likely to have contributed to the confusion (Schuckit, 1987; Anthenelli & Schuckit, 1990). First, during the course of heavy drinking and the period of early recovery, alcoholics are likely to show abnormalities on personality tests that might reflect the sequelae of ethanol's effects on brain functioning or the life stresses and mood swings inherent in an alcoholic style (Schuckit & Haglund, 1982). As a result, studies assessing personality differences in alcoholics may be determining variables that were not observable before the alcoholism developed (Kammeier, Hoffmann & Loper, 1973; Vaillant, 1983; Schuckit, 1989) or that may become normal with continued abstinence. Second, some personality traits that remain following abstinence may reflect other primary psychiatric diagnoses (e.g., ASPD) and not alcoholism per se (Schuckit, 1973). Finally, the diversity of personality measures used, questions about the cross-validity of the various test devices used, the variety of populations studied, and the multiple approaches to data analyses employed make it unlikely to expect unanimity of results (Schuckit, 1987).

With these caveats in mind, it is not surprising that various investigators have obtained different results on personality measures. For example, using a sample of Swedish adoptees, Cloninger et al. adapted information from a behavioral assessment and teacher interviews carried out when the children were 11 years of age and concluded that variations in childhood personality traits encompassed by the "tridimensional" personality theory described earlier (e.g.. high novelty seeking and low harm avoidance) predicted the risk of later alcohol abuse (Cloninger, Sigvardsson & Bohman, 1988). However, other prospective studies have demonstrated few differences between high- and low-risk populations (Schuckit, 1985; Vaillant, 1983). In our own laboratory, studies of high-functioning nonalcoholic young men who differ in their family history for alcoholism revealed few baseline differences in most personality measures, including items of the Minnesota Multiphasic Personality Inventory (MMPI),

FIGURE 1. Mean Blood Alcohol Concentrations

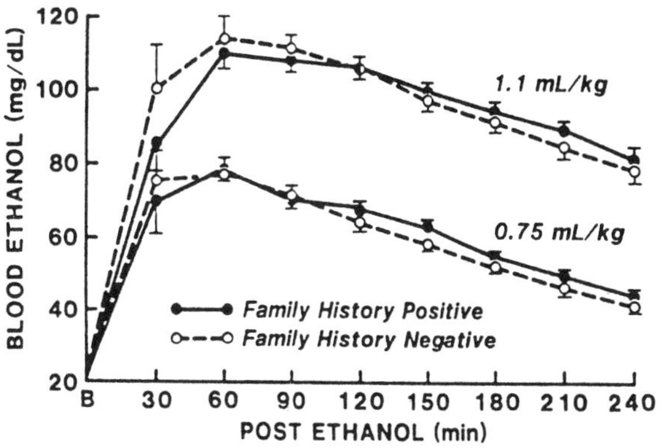

Mean blood alcohol concentrations for 22 matched pairs with positive and negative family histories after drinking 0.75 ml/kg of ethanol and 1.1 ml/kg of ethanol. Bars indicate SEs, and B indicates baseline. (Reproduced with permission from Schuckit MA. Subjective responses to alcohol in sons of alcoholics and control subjects. *Archives of General Psychiatry* 1984; 41:879–884. Copyright 1984, American Medical Association.

Spielberger Trait/State Anxiety Questionnaire, Eysenck Personality Inventory or Rotter's Locus of Control (Anthenelli & Schuckit, 1990; Schuckit, 1983; Morrison & Schuckit, 1983; Saunders & Schuckit, 1981). More recently, preliminary work from our laboratory has demonstrated no significant relationships between any of the 18 TPQ scores and the subject's quantity and frequency of drinking or his family history of alcoholism (Schuckit, Irwin & Mahler, 1990). Although it is too early to draw conclusions from this or any other cross-sectional personality evaluation, it must be remembered that the relationship between personality profiles and the predisposition toward alcoholism remains speculative at this time. Clearly, further research, including long-term follow-up studies using valid, comparable, psychometric instruments that consider the clinical heterogeneity among alcoholics, is needed to test these hypotheses (Schuckit, 1987; Cloninger, Sigvardsson & Bohman, 1988).

Recently, Ebstein et al. (1996) reported an association between a polymorphism of dopamine receptor D4 (DRD4) and the novelty-seeking sub-scale, as measured by Cloninger's TPQ (Cloninger, 1987). That report, along with confirmatory results (Benjamin, Greenberg et al., 1996) published in the same journal issue, provide the first replicated association between a specific genetic polymorphism and a personality trait (Ebstein, Novick et al., 1996). Although the subjects in this study were nonalcoholic normal controls, it is intriguing that a personality trait believed to predict an increased risk for alcoholism might have heritable components.

Alcohol Challenge Studies: Along with the evaluation of baseline functioning, our laboratory and others have documented differences in the response to alcohol between high risk and control populations. Although the details of our approach have outlined extensively elsewhere (Schuckit, 1987; Anthenelli & Schuckit, 1990), we selected otherwise healthy groups of 18- to 25-year-old men who differed mainly in their respective family histories of alcoholism. Sons of primary alcoholic men were selected as higher risk or FHP subjects who were then compared with controls comprised of lower risk FHN individuals. The FHP and FHN subjects were matched on demographic characteristics (e.g., age, sex, race, educational level), along with variables that could influence their response to alcohol, such as quantity and frequency of drinking, substance intake history, height-to-weight ratio, and smoking history (Schuckit, 1987). Each FHP-FHN matched pair was carefully evaluated at baseline and then observed for three to four hours after consuming placebo, 0.75 ml/kg of ethanol, or 11 ml/kg of ethanol (i.e., the equivalent of three to five drinks). The hypothesis behind this alcohol challenge paradigm was that genetic vulnerability toward alcoholism could be mediated through an individual's response to ethanol, the very agent required for the development of the disorder (Anthenelli & Schuckit, 1990).

Before the challenge sessions, the FHP and FHN subjects expressed similar expectations of the effects of ethanol. During the placebo session, there was no evidence of any differences between the two groups for the degree of body sway, the subjective feelings of intoxication, hormone levels, and most electrophysiological evaluations (Anthenelli & Schuckit, 1990; Schuckit, 1988). As shown in Figure 1, after drinking the alcohol, the two family history groups developed similar patterns of blood alcohol concentrations over time, making it unlikely that group differences depended on the rate of absorption or metabolism of ethanol (Anthenelli & Schuckit, 1990; Schuckit, 1984).

Differences in Subjective and Motor Responses: A major consistent difference between FHP and FHN subjects has been in the intensity of their subjective feelings of intoxication after imbibing alcohol (Schuckit, 1987, 1988, 1984; Anthenelli & Schuckit, 1990; Schuckit & Gold, 1988). Using an analog scale and asking subjects to rate the intensity of different aspects of intoxication, including overall

FIGURE 2. Mean Self-Ratings on 0-36 Scale for Intoxication

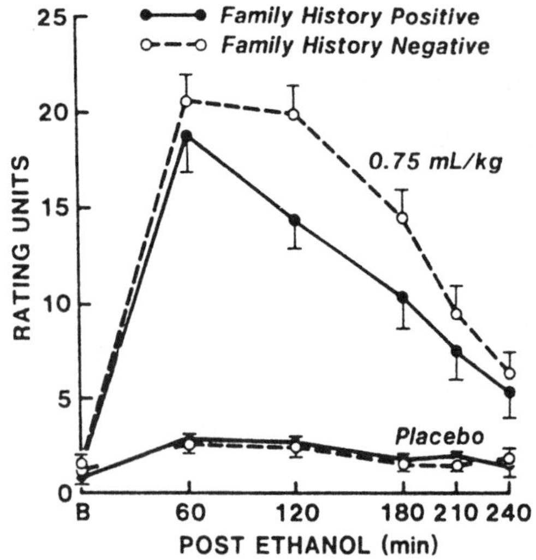

Mean self-ratings on 0–36 scale for intoxication after placebo and after 0.75 ml/kg of ethanol for 23 matched pairs with positive and negative family histories. Bars indicate SEs and B indicates baseline. Reproduced with permission from Schuckit MA. Subjective responses to alcohol in sons of alcoholics and control subjects. *Archives of General Psychiatry* 1984; 41:879–884. Copyright 1984, American Medical Association.

drug effect, level of "high," dizziness, etc., FHP men rated themselves as significantly less intoxicated than did their FHN matched controls after drinking ethanol (Figure 2), with the maximum group difference observed 60 to 120 minutes after the drink had been consumed (Schuckit, 1987, 1988, 1984; Anthenelli & Schuckit, 1990; Schuckit & Gold, 1988).

This decreased intensity of reaction to alcohol was also observed for at least one measure of motor performance. Here, to quantify the level of sway in the upper body, we asked subjects to stand still, with hands at the sides and feet together. Subjects showed a significantly greater increase in body sway after the alcohol challenge, as shown in Figure 3 (Schuckit, 1985), a result corroborated elsewhere in daughters of alcoholics (Lex, Lukas et al., 1988).

Less Intense Neurohormonal Changes: Because changes in subjective feelings and motor performance might be influenced by the differential expectations of the subjects, we next focused on alcohol-related changes in biological systems less likely to be sensitive to volitional control. After an ethanol challenge, FHPs also exhibited less intense change in the levels of cortisol and prolactin, two hormones shown to be altered after ethanol (Schuckit, Gold & Risch, 1987; Schuckit, 1984). Similar results have been observed for the pattern of postdrinking changes in adrenocorticotropic hormone (ACTH), another important hormone in the hypothalamic-pituitary-adrenal axis (Anthenelli & Schuckit, 1990; Schuckit, Risch & Gold, 1988).

Diminished EEG Response: Along with baseline differences in potential electrophysiological markers observed in the two family history groups, sons of alcoholics demonstrated a less intense EEG response to the alcohol challenge (e.g., FHPs had less instability of alpha-range activity of the background cortical EEG) (Ehlers & Schuckit, 1991, 1988). Although there are technical differences between this finding and the reports of Pollock et al., which are beyond the scope of this discussion (Pollock, Volavka & Goodwin, 1983), it is noteworthy that both groups have shown electrophysiological differences between FHPs and FHNs following an ethanol challenge: however, not all studies agree (Polich & Bloom, 1988).

Summary: The results of challenge studies of high-risk populations have provided several potential markers that might be associated with a genetic predisposition toward alcoholism (Anthenelli & Schuckit, 1990). The decreased intensity of reaction to ethanol observed in a number of subjective, motor, hormonal, and electrophysiological measures has been reproduced in various forms by other laboratories in the United States and in Denmark (O'Malley & Maisto, 1985; Pollock, Teasdale et al., 1986). Although the results of alcohol challenge studies are not unanimous (i.e., studies evaluating smaller sample sizes or not controlling for subjects' quantity and frequency of drinking, provide unpredictable results) (Schuckit, 1992), it is hypothesized that a decreased intensity of reaction to lower doses of alcohol might make it more difficult for susceptible individuals to discern when they are becoming drunk at low enough blood levels to be able to stop drinking during an evening. Without this feedback, especially in the setting of a heavy drinking society, predisposed individuals may be inclined to drink more and, thus, run an increased risk for subsequent alcohol-related life problems (Scuckit, 1987). As with the other potential trait markers and hypotheses presented in this chapter, the relationship of these findings to actual alcoholism can be established only with appropriate follow-up evaluations of the high- and low-risk groups. These studies are described next.

Follow-up Studies in Sons of Alcoholics. The study of sons of alcoholics and controls was structured to facilitate a follow-up phase. Thus, interviewers blind to the initial family history and the determination of the level of response to alcohol located all 453 subjects an average of 8.2 years after the time of their initial evaluation (Schuckit, 1995; Schuckit & Smith, 1996). Diagnoses were established using American Psychiatric Association criteria in the *Diagnostic and Statistical Manual of Mental Disorders, 3rd Edition, Revised* (*DSM-IIIR*), as described in detail elsewhere (Schuckit & Smith, 1996). The data revealed that the family history groups had been correctly identified and that the sons of alcoholics had a three-fold increased risk for alcohol dependence. The results also demonstrated a strong and significant relationship between a low level of response to alcohol and the future development of alcoholism. Thus, for example, sons of alcoholics who clearly demonstrated a low level of response to alcohol evidenced almost a 60% risk for alcohol abuse or dependence at follow-up, while the rate of alcoholism was less than 15% in the sons of alcoholics who clearly showed a higher level of sensitivity to alcohol. The relatively small number of FHN controls who showed low levels of response to alcohol at approximately age 20 were also at high risk for future alcoholism. The analyses demonstrated that for this white-collar and relatively highly functional group of men, the low level of response to alcohol was a mediator (or potential direct cause) of the high risk for alcoholism, explaining a great

FIGURE 3. Mean Total-Body Sway Counts

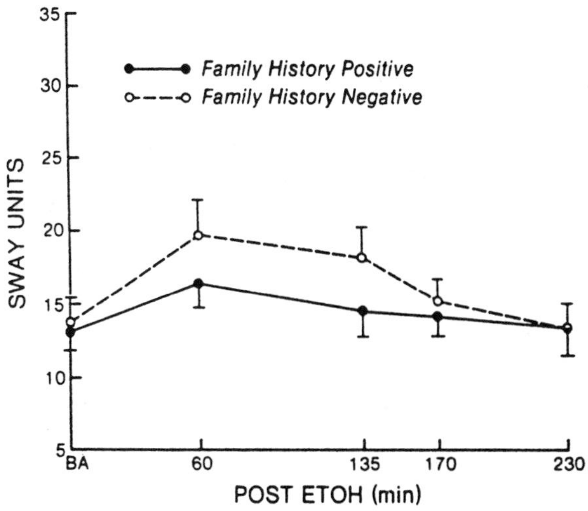

Mean total-body sway counts over time following ingestion of 0.75 ml/kg of ethanol for 34 matched pairs of young men with family histories negative (FHN) and positive (FHP) for alcoholism. Reproduced with permission from Schuckit MA. Ethanol-induced changes in body sway in men at high alcoholism risk. *Archives of General Psychiatry* 1985; 42:375–379. Copyright 1985, American Medical Association.

deal of the ability of family history to predict alcohol abuse or dependence (Schuckit, 1995, 1994).

These studies demonstrate some important attributes regarding genetic influences in the alcoholism risk. First, a family history of alcoholism is associated with increased risk for this disorder among people of diverse socioeconomic classes. Second, it is likely that there are multiple roads into the heightened alcohol risk, with, for example, some individuals developing their alcoholism in part through very high levels of impulsivity associated with the ASPD, but with others increasing their risk for alcoholism through a low level of response to alcohol in the context of a heavy drinking society, and so on. Third, it is not likely that a single gene explains the alcoholism risk, but rather it is multiple genes interacting with environment.

GENETIC ASPECTS OF DRUG ABUSE AND DEPENDENCE

There are a number of reasons why most of the information in this chapter on the genetics of substance abuse relates to alcohol and not to other drugs. Compared with other drug abuse disorders, alcoholism has consistently occurred at high rates in most societies for many decades. Despite some secular variations, overall, the disorder has remained highly prevalent in the population, allowing for its careful study over time. Similarly, enough time has elapsed for multiple generations of families affected with the disorder to be evaluated. These factors have contributed to the relative ease with which family, twin, and adoption study data have been gathered on alcohol dependence and help explain the comparable absence of similar studies of other drugs.

Studies of genetic influences in other types of drug abuse pose additional problems. First, there are many different substances of abuse, and dependency to any one drug might be uniquely related to a heterogeneous group of factors. As we expand the number of drugs and phenotypes under study, the level of complexity increases dramatically, and the relative contributions of genetic, sociocultural, and psychological determinants become even more difficult to discern. Second, the use of most drugs generally comes in waves or "fads," with secular effects taking on added significance compared with the relative stability seen for alcohol over time. For example, after reaching a peak prevalence in the mid-1970s, methaqualone (Quaalude) abuse in teenagers steadily declined in a linear trend as the availability of this drug was limited (O'Malley, Bachman & Johnston, 1988; Anthenelli & Schuckit, 1991). Partly as a result of these period effects, different generations of families have been exposed to different types of drugs, making it more difficult to perform the multigenerational studies described for alcoholism. Finally, ASPD, another syndrome that might have its own separate genetic underpinnings, is frequently associated with secondary drug problems. As was the case for alcoholism, studies of genetic factors in drug abuse will need to control carefully for this confounding diagnosis.

For all of these reasons, with the possible exception of cigarette smoking, it is difficult to marshal consistent evidence regarding genetic determinants as they relate to drugs other than alcohol. Nevertheless, in a manner similar to the approach outlined for alcoholism, the systematic study of genetic influences in drug abuse is beginning to produce some testable hypotheses. This section briefly reviews the information available from family, twin, and adoption studies of drug abuse. In addition, we highlight some preclinical work that offers examples of the ways that genetic influences affecting one category of drug might overlap with those impacting on other substances of abuse.

Some Preclinical Examples. Animal studies have demonstrated some preliminary evidence for the possible role of genetic factors in drug abuse (Crabbe, Belknap & Buck, 1994; Collins, 1986). Differences in the response to an assortment of drugs, including opiates (Collins, Horowitz & Passe, 1977), amphetamines (Anisman, 1975), and barbiturates (Belknap, Ondrusek & Waddington, 1973) in various inbred strains of rodents have been reported (Collins, 1986). However, some investigators believe that the use of more sophisticated selective breeding techniques to develop animal lines with a specific trait for drug-taking (e.g., ones approximating "drug abuse," per se) has lagged behind the models developed for alcoholism (e.g., P line of alcohol-preferring rats) (Collins, 1986; Li, McBride et al., 1986). Also, at the preclinical level, there is evidence that there may be an overlap in the initial reinforcing effects of ethanol, opioids, and psychostimulants that might be mediated via neurons that are part of the ventral tegmental area (VTA)-nucleus accumbens-pallidal-forebrain reward circuit (Koob & Bloom, 1988). Hence, it might be difficult to target genetic factors associated with any one drug and, as described in other chapters of this text, it is possible that genetic factors may play a role in these complex brain systems related to drug sensitivity, neuroadaptation, and reward (Crabbe, Belknap & Buck, 1994).

Human Studies. After the approach outlined above for alcoholism, the majority of studies have focused on the clustering of drug abuse in families. Several studies have documented correlations between drug use by teenagers and substance abuse by older family members (Gfroerer, 1987; Annis, 1974; Pickens & Svikis, 1988; Ripple & Luthar, 1996). For example, a study of opioid dependent probands revealed a prevalence of opiate abuse in family members that far exceeded the lifetime prevalence rate expected in the general population (Maddux & Desmond, 1989). However, these data are more complicated than they first appear. When these authors considered secular trends and the increase in availability of heroin and in the number of heroin-using peers, they found an intergenerational reversal: the siblings of probands had higher rates of opiate abuse than of alcoholism, but the parents of the subjects had higher rates of alcoholism than of opioid dependence. As is the case for alcoholism, family studies do little to sort out potential hereditary effects from environmental effects (Pardes, Kaufmann et al., 1989; Goodwin, 1985).

Twin studies of genetic determinants of abuse of drugs other than alcohol are increasing in number but are still relatively rare (Schuckit, 1986). In general, the studies are limited by small sample sizes, and these investigations frequently focus on several drugs at once (Gershon, 1980; Pedersen, 1981; Gynther, Carey et al., 1995). With these caveats in mind, only tentative conclusions regarding genetic influences on specific drugs of abuse can be reached. However, there is some evidence that identical twins show higher concordance rates for use patterns of nicotine and caffeine (Pedersen, 1981) and for nonalcohol substance abuse (Gynther, Carey et al., 1995; Pickens, Svikis et al., 1991) and that genetic determinants might influence twins' responses to pain and its alleviation by morphine (Liston, Simpson et al., 1981).

Similarly, adoption studies have provided limited data. In the Danish investigation of Goodwin et al., children of alcoholics raised by nonalcoholic adoptive parents were susceptible to alcohol abuse but not to other types of drug dependence (Goodwin, 1985). Perhaps the most informative statement on the genetic vulnerability of drug abuse has come from the Iowa sample of adoptees, which points to the importance of gene-environment interactions in drug abuse (Cadoret, Troughton et al., 1986). Because the adoption agency records from which the investigators obtained their information did not include data on the biological parents' drug abuse history, their conclusions are quite speculative. These authors described two possible genetic routes to drug abuse in this sample. First, drug abuse was correlated with the ASPD, which was itself predicted by the biological parents' own antisocial behaviors. Second, in adoptees with no biological background for ASPD, parental alcohol abuse predicted drug abuse in the subjects. But along with these potential genetic relationships, the authors also showed the importance of environmental factors, in that divorce and psychiatric problems in the adoptive family were associated with the risk for drug abuse. More recently, Cadoret et al. (1995) expanded on their earlier work in a study of male adoptees and again confirmed their earlier model.

GENETICS OF CIGARETTE SMOKING: A SPECIAL CASE?

In contrast to the relatively scant data available regarding heritable factors involved in illicit substance abuse and dependence, results from family, twin, and adoption studies indicate that genetic factors appear to influence cigarette smoking (Hughes, 1986). For instance, in a genetic analysis of aspects of cigarette smoking behavior among male subjects in a large twin registry in the United States, Carmelli et al. reported moderate genetic influences on lifetime smoking practices (Carmelli, Swan et al., 1992). Because cigarette smoking is highly correlated with alcohol consumption and other consummatory behaviors, Swan et al. (1990) adjusted for covariates in a sample of 360 adult male twin pairs and still demonstrated a genetic role for cigarette smoking. Thus, as was the case for alcoholism, smoking researchers are interested in identifying genetic factors that might help tailor prevention and treatment programs for nicotine dependence (Hughes, 1986).

Summary: The systematic study of genetic factors in a predisposition to drug abuse is in its infancy compared with the past three decades of research addressing the biological susceptibility to alcoholism. This gap reflects the relatively stable prevalence of alcoholism in most populations, secular changes in substance abuse, including the faddish nature of drug use, and the increased complexity of studying several different categories of drugs that appear to interact at multiple levels. Although, with the possible exception of cigarette smoking, too few studies are available to draw definite conclusions, our experience with alcoholism can provide some tools applicable to the task.

CONCLUSIONS AND IMPLICATIONS

In the opening paragraphs of this chapter, we alluded to the work being done in molecular genetics and the search for "the gene for alcoholism" (Goodwin, 1989; Blum, Noble et al., 1990). One of the purposes of this chapter has been to provide the reader with much of the "small print" apt to be left out in headlines. As described, much work has preceded the preliminary molecular genetic studies now capturing the news. Our goal has been to organize more than two decades of diverse findings into a format that is understandable and illustrative of the promise of this line of research, while not minimizing the complexity of the issues at hand.

In many ways, the "window of hope" offered by better understanding of the probable genetic influences of alcoholism has already been opened and does not depend solely on identifying gene(s) at a molecular level. The clinical, societal, and research implications of this body of work are already emerging, with results from family, twin, and adoption studies helping to shape programs aimed at preventing the illness by educating children at high risk for alcoholism early on, allowing them to modify their drinking patterns. Individuals already suffering from the disorder are being matched to more appropriate therapies with information obtained in studies of alcoholic subtypes. The stigma once associated with the view of alcoholism as a "moral weakness" is fading with the accumulation of evidence supporting the importance of biological factors. The studies pointing to the importance of gene-environment interactions have demonstrated the need for cooperation among researchers in different disciplines, and they highlight the fact that unitary hypotheses arguing exclusively for any one approach are inadequate in explaining these heterogeneous disorders.

Advances in molecular genetics are adding important information to our understanding of the biological factors associated with the susceptibility to alcoholism. Many potential "candidate" genes have been identified that might be associated with the risk for the disorder (Devor & Cloninger, 1989; Goldman, 1995). Briefly, the rationale behind this approach is similar to that already described as part of our discussion of phenotypic markers. However, here the marker or phenotype (potentially, any of the phenotypic markers mentioned) is explicitly postulated to arise from either an "abnormal" gene product or from the product of a gene "linked" with or close by a gene associated with the disorder (Pardes, Kaufmann & Pincus, 1989). Although the details of the molecular genetic techniques used in this approach are beyond the scope of this discussion and can be found elsewhere (Pardes, Kaufmann & Pincus, 1989; Devor & Cloninger, 1989; Gershon, Merril et al., 1987), recent advances in these areas have sparked a large multicenter effort (the Collaborative Study on the Genetics of Alcoholism or COGA) aimed at "identifying the gene(s) that influence susceptibility to alcoholism" (Goodwin, 1989; Cloninger, 1991). It is hoped that such a coordinated effort might provide insights into how the disorder is transmitted and might expand our knowledge about the biological basis of the inherited factors.

ACKNOWLEDGMENT: Originally published as Anthenelli RM & Schuckit MA (1997). Genetics. In JH Lowinson, P Ruiz, RB Millman & J Langrod (eds.) Substance Abuse: A Comprehensive Textbook. *Baltimore, MD: Williams & Wilkins, 41–51. Reprinted by permission of the publisher.*

REFERENCES

Anisman H (1975). Differential effects of scopolamine and d-amphetamine on avoidance: Strain interactions. *Pharmacology, Biochemistry and Behavior* 3:809–817.

Annis HM (1974). Patterns of intrafamilial drug use. *British Journal of Addiction* 69:361–369.

Anthenelli RM & Schuckit MA. Alcohol and cerebral depressants. In IB Glass (ed.) *The International Handbook of Addiction Behavior*. London, England: Routledge, 57–63.

Anthenelli RM & Schuckit MA (1990). Genetic studies on alcoholism. *International Journal of Addictions* 25:81–94.

Anthenelli RM, Smith TL, Craig CE, Tabakoff B & Schuckit MA (1995). Platelet monoamine oxidase activity levels in subgroups of alcoholics: Diagnostic, temporal, and clinical correlates. *Biological Psychiatry* 1995:38:361–368.

Anthenelli RM, Smith TL, Irwin NM & Schuckit MA (1994). A comparative study of criteria for subgrouping alcoholics: The primary/secondary diagnostic scheme versus variations of the type 1/type 2 criteria. *American Journal of Psychiatry* 151(10):1468–1474.

Anthenelli RM & Tabakoff B (1995). The search for biochemical markers. *Alcohol Health and Research World* 19:176–181.

Anthenelli RM, Tipp J, Li TK, Magnes L, Schuckit MA, Rice J, Warwick D & Nurnberger JI (1996). Platelet monoamine oxidase (MAO) activity, in subgroups of alcoholics and controls: Results from the COGA study. *Alcoholism: Clinical & Experimental Research.*

Babor TF, Hofmann M, Del Boca FK, Hesselbrock VM, Meyer RE, Dolinsky ZS & Rounsaville B (1992). Types of alcoholics 1: Evidence for an empirically derived typology based on indicators of vulnerability and severity. *Archives of General Psychiatry* 49:599–608.

Begleiter H (1995). The collaborative study on the genetics of alcoholism. *Alcohol Health and Research World* 19:228–236.

Begleiter H, Porjesz B, Bihari B & Kissin B (1984). Event-related brain potentials in boys at risk for alcoholism. *Science* 1–27:1493–1496.

Behar D, Berg CJ, Rapoport JL et al. (1983). Behavior and physiological effects of ethanol in hi-risk and control children: A pilot study. *Alcoholism: Clinical & Experimental Research* 7:404–410.

Belknap JK, Ondrusek G & Waddingham S (1973). Barbiturate dependence in mice induced by a single short-term oral procedure. *Physiology and Psychology* 1:394–396.

Bench CJ, Price GW, Lammertsma AA, Cremer JC, Luthra SK, Turton D, Dolan D, Kerder R, Dingemanse J, Da Prada M, Biziere K, McClelland GR, Jamieson VL, Wood ND & Frackowiak SJ (1991). Measurement of human cerebral monoamine oxidase type B (MAO-B) activity with positron emission tomography (PET): A dose ranging study with the reversible inhibitor Ro 19-6. *European Journal of Clinical Pharmacology* 40:169–173.

Benjamin J, Greenberg B, Murphy DL, Lin L, Patterson C & Hamer DH (1996). Population and familial association between the D4 dopamine receptor gene and measures of novelty seeking. *Nature and Genetics* 12:81–84.

Blum K, Noble EP, Sheridan PJ, Montgomery A, Ritchie T, Jagadeeswaran P, Nogami H, Briggs AH & Cohn JB (1990). Allelic association of human dopamine D2 receptor gene in alcoholism. *Journal of the American Medical Association* 263:2055–2060.

Bohman M, Cloninger R, Sigvardsson S & von Knorring AL (1987). The genetics of alcoholisms and related disorders. *Journal of Psychiatric Research* 21(4):447–452.

Bohman M, Sigvardsson S & Cloninger CR (1991). Maternal inheritance of alcohol abuse: Cross-fostering analysis of adopted women. *Archives of General Psychiatry* 38:965–969.

Bolos AM, Dean M, Lucas-Derse S, Ramsberg M, Brown GL & Goldman D (1990). Population and pedigree studies reveal a lack of association between the dopamine D2 receptor gene and alcoholism. *Journal of the American Medical Association* 264:3156–3160.

Cadoret RJ, Cain CA & Grove WM (1980). Development of alcoholism in adoptees raised apart from alcoholic biologic relatives. *Archives of General Psychiatry* 37:561–563.

Cadoret RJ, O'Gorman TW, Troughton E & Heywood E (1985). Alcoholism and antisocial personality: Interrelationships, genetic and environmental factors. *Archives of General Psychiatry* 42:161–167.

Cadoret RJ, Troughton E & O'Gorman TW (1987). Genetic and environmental factors in alcohol abuse and antisocial personality,. *Journal of Studies on Alcohol* 48:1–8.

Cadoret RJ, Troughton E, O'Gorman TW & Heywood E (1986). An adoption study of genetic and environmental factors in drug abuse. *Archives of General Psychiatry* 43:1131–1136.

Cadoret RJ, Yates WR, Troughton E, Woodworth G & Stewart MA (1995). Adoption study demonstrating two genetic pathways to drug abuse. *Archives of General Psychiatry* 52:42–52.

Carmelli D, Swan GE, Robinette D & Fabsitz R (1992). Genetic influence on smoking—A study of male twins. *The New England Journal of Medicine* 327:829–833.

Cloninger CR (1987). Neurogenetic adaptive mechanisms in alcoholism. *Science* 236:410–416.

Cloninger CR (1991). D2 dopamine receptor gene is associated but not linked with alcoholism. *Journal of the American Medical Association* 266:1833–1834.

Cloninger CR, Bohman M & Sigvardsson S (1981). Inheritance of alcohol abuse: Cross-fostering analysis of adopted men. *Archives of General Psychiatry* 38:861–868.

Cloninger CR, Sigvardsson S & Bohman M (1988). Childhood personality predicts alcohol abuse in young adults. *Alcoholism: Clinical & Experimental Research* 12:494–505.

Cloninger CR, Sigvardsson S, Reich T, Bohman M (1986). Inheritance of risk to develop alcoholism. In MC Braude & HM Chao (eds.) *Genetic and Biological Markers in Drug Abuse and Alcoholism (NIDA Research Monograph 66)*. Rockville, MD: National Institute on Drug Abuse, 86–96.

Collins AC (1986). Genetics as a tool for identifying biological markers of drug abuse. In MC Braude & HM Chao (eds.) *Genetic and Biological Markers in Drug Abuse and Alcoholism (NIDA Research Monograph 66)*. Rockville, MD: National Institute on Drug Abuse.

Collins RL, Horowitz GP & Passe DH (1977). Genotype and test experience as determinants of sensitivity and tolerance to morphine. *Behav. Genetics* 7:50.

Cotton NS (1979). The familial incidence of alcoholism. *Journal of Studies on Alcohol* 40:1:89–116.

Crabbe JC, Belknap JK & Buck KJ (1994). Genetic animal models of alcohol and drug abuse. *Science* 264:1715–1723.

Devor EJ & Cloninger CR (1989). Genetics of alcoholism. *Annual Review of Genetics* 23:19–36.

Drake RE & Vaillant GE (1988). Predicting alcoholism and personality disorder in 33-year longitudinal study of children of alcoholics. *British Journal of Addiction* 83:799–807.

Ebstein RP, Novick 0, Umansky R, Priel B, Osher Y. Blaine D,Bennett ER, Nemanov L, Katz M & Belmaker RH (1996). Dopamine D4 receptor (D4DR) rcon III polymorphism associated with the human personality trait of novelty seeking. *Nature and Genetics* 12:78–80.

Ehlers CL & Schuckit MA (1988). EEG responses to ethanol in sons of alcoholics. *Psychopharmacology Bulletin* 24:434–437.

Ehlers CL & Schuckit MA (1991). Evaluation of EEG alpha activity in sons of alcoholics. *Neuropsychopharmacology* 4:199–205.

Gabrielli WF & Mednick SA (1983). Intellectual performance in children of alcoholics. *Journal of Nervous and Mental Disease* 171:444–447.

Gershon ES (1980). Behavorial and biological phatmacogenetics of d-amphetamine. Paper presented at the 3rd International Society for Twin Studies, Jerusalem, Israel, June [Abstract].

Gershon ES, Merril CR, Goldin LR, DeLisi LE, Berrettini VM & Nurnberger JI Jr. (1987). The role of molecular genetics in psychiatry. *Biological Psychiatry* 22:1388–1405.

Gfroerer J (1987). Correlation between drug use by teenagers and drug use by older family members. *American Journal of Drug and Alcohol Abuse* 13:95–108.

Goldman D (1995). Identifying alcoholism vulnerability alleles. *Alcoholism: Clinical & Experimental Research* 19:824–831.

Goldman D, Brown GL, Albaugh B, Robin R, Goodson S, Trunzo M, Akhtar L, Wynne DK, Lucas-Derse S, Bolos A-M, Tokola R, Virkkunen M, Linnoila M & Dean M (1994). D2 receptor genotype and linkage desequilibrium and function in Finnish. American Indian and U.S. Caucasian patients. In ES Gershon & CR Cloninger (eds.) *Genetic Approaches to Mental Disorders.* Washington, DC: American Psychiatric Press, 327–344.

Goodwin DW (1985). Alcoholism and genetics: the sins of the fathers. *Archives of General Psychiatry* 42:171–174.

Goodwin DW (1979). Alcoholism and heredity. *Archives of General Psychiatry* 36:57–61.

Goodwin DW (1983). Familial alcoholism: A separate entity? *Substance and Alcohol Actions-Misuse* 4:129–136.

Goodwin DW (1989). The gene for alcoholism. *Journal of Studies on Alcohol* 50:397–398.

Goodwin DW & Guze SB (1989). *Psychiatric Diagnosis, 4th Ed.* New York, NY: Oxford University Press.

Gurling HM, Oppenheim BE & Murray RM (1984). Depression, criminality and psychopathology associated with alcoholism: Evidence from a twin study. *Acta Genet Med Gemellol (Roma)* 33:333–339.

Gynther LM, Carey G, Gottesman II & Vogler G (1995). A twin study of non-alcohol substance abuse. *Psychiatry Research* 213–220.

Harada S, Agarwal DP, Goedde HW & Ishikawa B (1983). Aldehyde dehydrogenase isozvme variation and alcoholism in Japan. *Pharmacology, Biochemistry and Behavior* 18:151–153.

Hesselbrock VM, Hesselbrock MN & Stabenau JR (1985). Alcoholism in men patients subtyped by family history and antisocial personality. *Journal of Studies on Alcohol* 46:59–64.

Hesselbrock V, O'Connor S, Tasman A & Weidenman M (1988). Cognitive and evoked potential indications of risk for alcoholism in men. In K Kuriyamam, A Takada & H Ishii (eds.) *Biomedical and Social Aspects of Alcohol and Alcoholism.* Amsterdam, The Netherlands: Elsevier Science Publishers.

Hill SY, Steinhauer SR, Zubin J & Baughman T (1988). Event-related potentials as markers for alcoholism risk in high density families. *Alcoholism: Clinical & Experimental Research* 12:368–373.

Hill SY, Goodwin DW, Cadoret R, Osterland CK & Doner SM (1980). Association and linkage between alcoholism and eleven serological markers. *Journal of Studies on Alcohol* 36:981–989.

Hoffman PL, Lee JM & Saito T (1989). Platelet enzyme activities in alcoholics. In K Kiianmaa, B Tabakoff & T Saito (eds.) *Genetic Aspects of Alcoholism.* Helsinki, Finland: Finnish Foundation for Alcohol Studies.

Holden C (1991). Probing the complex genetics of alcoholism. *Science* 251:163–164.

Hrubec Z & Omenn GS (1981). Evidence of genetic predisposition to alcohol cirrhosis and psychosis: Twin concordances for alcoholism and its biological end points by zygosity among male veterans. *Alcoholism: Clinical & Experimental Research* 5:207–212.

Hughes JR (1986). Genetics of smoking: A brief review. *Behavioral Therapy* 17:335–345.

Irwin M, Schuckit MA & Smith TL (1990). Clinical importance of age at onset in type 1 and type 2 primary alcoholics. *Archives of General Psychiatry* 47:320–324.

Jacobsen B & Schulsinger F (1981). Prospective longitudinal research: An empirical basis for the primary prevention of psychosocial disorders. In SA Mednick SA & AE Baert AE (eds.) *The Danish Adoption Register.* Oxford, England: Oxford University Press.

Jones BM & Jones MK (1976). Women and alcohol: Intoxication, metabolism, and the menstrual cycle. In N Greenblatt & MA Schuckit (eds.) *Alcoholism Problems in Women and Children.* New York, NY: Grune & Stratton.

Jonsson E & Nilsson T (1969). Alcoholism in monozygotic and dizygotic twins. *Nor Psykiatr Tidsskr* 49:21.

Kaij L (1960). *Studies on the Etiology and Sequelae of Abuse of Alcohol.* Lund, Sweden: University of Lund Press.

Kendler KS, Heath AC, Neale MC, Kessler RC & Eaves LJ (1992). A population-based twin study of alcoholism in women. *Journal of the American Medical Association* 268:1877–1882.

Kammeier ML Sr, Hoffmann H & Loper RG (1973). Personality characteristics of alcoholics as college freshman and at the time of treatment. *Quarterly Journal of Studies on Alcohol* 34:390–397.

Knop J, Goodwin DW, Teasdale TW, Mikkelsen U & Schulsinger F (1984). A Danish prospective study of young males at high risk for alcoholism. In DW Goodwin, K Van Dusen & SA Mednick (eds.) *Longitudinal Research in Alcoholism*. Boston, MA: Kluwer-Nijhoff.

Koob GF & Bloom FE (1988). Cellular and molecular mechanisms of drug dependence. *Science* 242:715–723.

Kopun M & Propping P (1977). The kinetics of ethanol absorption and elimination in twins and supplementary repetitive experiments in singleton subjects [Abstract]. *European Journal of Clinical Pharmacology* 11:337–344.

Lex BW, Lukas SE, Greenwald NE & Mendelson JH (1988). Alcohol- induced changes in body sway in women at risk for alcoholism: A pilot study. *Journal of Studies on Alcohol* 49:346–350.

Li TK, McBride WJ, Waller MB & Murphy JM (1986). Studies on an animal model of alcoholism. In MC Braude & HM Chao (eds.) *Genetic and Biological Markers in Drug Abuse and Alcoholism (NIDA Research Monograph 66)*. Rockville. MD: National Institute on Drug Abuse.

Liston EH, Simpson JH, Jarvik LF & Guthrie D (1981). Morphine and experimental pain in identical twins. In L Gedda, P Parisi & W Nance (eds.) *Twin research 3: Epidemiological and clinical studies*. New York, NY: Alan R Liss.

Maddox JF & Desmond DP (1989). Family and environment in the choice of opioid dependence or alcoholism. *American Journal of Drug and Alcohol Abuse* 15:117–134.

McGue M, Pickens RW & Svikis DS (1992). Sex and age effects on the inheritance of alcohol problems: A twin study. *Journal of Abnormal Psychology* 101:3, 17.

McHugh PR & Slavney PR (1983). *The Perspectives of Psychiatry*. Baltimore, MD: The Johns Hopkins University Press.

Morrison C & Schuckit MA (1983). Locus of control in young men with alcoholic relatives and controls. *Journal of Clinical Psychiatry* 144:306–307.

Mullan M (1989). Alcoholism and the "new genetics." *British Journal of Addiction* 84:1433–1440.

Nixon SJ & Parsons OA (1990). Application of the tridimensional personality questionnaire to a population of alcoholics and other substance abusers. *Alcoholism: Clinical & Experimental Research* 14:513–517.

Noble EP (1993). The D2 dopamine receptor gene: A review of association studies in alcoholism. *Behavioral Genetics* 23(2):119–229.

Noble EP, Blum K, Ritchie T, Montgomery A & Sheridan PJ (1991). Allelic association of the D2 dopamine receptor gene with receptor-binding characteristics in alcoholism. *Archives of General Psychiatry* 48:648–654.

O'Malley PM, Bachman JG & Johnston LD (1988). Period, age, and cohort effects on substance use among young Americans: A decade of change, 1976–86. *American Journal of Public Health* 78:1315–1321.

O'Malley SS & Maisto SA (1985). Effects of family drinking and expectancies on response to alcohol in men. *Journal of Studies on Alcohol* 46:289–297.

Pandev GN, Fawcett J, Gibbons R, Clark DC & Davis AI (1988). Platelet monoamine oxidase in alcoholism. *Biological Psychiatry* 24:15–24.

Pardes H, Kaufmann CA, Pincus HA & West A (1989). Genetics and psychiatry: Past discoveries. current dilemmas, and future directions. *American Journal of Psychiatry* 164(4):435–443.

Parsian A, Todd RD, Devor EJ, O'Malley KL, Suarez BK, Reich T & Cloninger CR (1991). Alcoholism and alleles of the human D2 dopamine receptor locus. *Archives of General Psychiatry* 48:655–666.

Partanen J, Bruun K & Markkanen T (1966). *Inheritance of Drinking Behavior: A Study on Intelligence, Personality, and Use of Alcohol of Adult Twins*. Helsinki, Finland: Finnish Foundation for Alcohol Studies.

Pedersen N (1991). Twin similarity for usage of common drugs. In L Gedda, P Parisi & W Nance (eds.) *Twin Research 3: Epidemiological and Clinical Studies*. New York, NY: Alan R. Liss.

Pickens RW, Svikis DS & McGue M (1991). Genetic factors in human drug abuse. Paper presented at the Annual Scientific Meeting of the Committee on Problems of Drug Dependence, June [Abstract].

Penick EC, Powell BJ, Nickel EJ, Read MR, Gabrielli WF & Liskow BI (1990). Examination of Cloninger's type I and type II alcoholism with a sample of men alcoholics in treatment. *Alcoholism: Clinical & Experimental Research* 14:623–629.

Pickens RW & Svikis DS (1991). Genetic vulnerability to drug abuse: Biological vulnerability to drug abuse. In *NIDA Research Monograph 89*. Rockville, MD: National Institute on Drug Abuse, 1–7.

Pickens RW, Svikis DS, McGue M, Lykken DT, Heston LL & Clayton PJ (1991). Heterogeneity in the inheritance of alcoholism. *Archives of General Psychiatry* 48:19–28.

Polich J & Bloom FE (1988). Event-related brain potentials in individuals at high and low risk for developing alcoholism: failure to replicate. *Alcoholism: Clinical & Experimental Research* 12:368–373.

Pollock VE, Volavka J & Goodwin DW (1983). The EEG after alcohol administration in men at risk for alcoholism. *Archives of General Psychiatry* 40:857–861.

Pollock VE, Teasdale TW, Gabrielli WF, Knop J (1986). Subjective and objective measures of response to alcohol among young men at risk for alcoholism. *Journal of Studies on Alcohol* 47:297–304.

Prescott CA & Kendler KS (1995). Twin study design. *Alcohol Health and Research World* 19:200–205.

Radlow R & Conway TL (1978). Consistency of alcohol absorption in human subjects. Paper presented at the American Psychological Association, Toronto, Canada, August [Abstract].

Ripple CH & Luthar SS (1996). Familial factors in illicit drug abuse: an interdisciplinary perspective. *American Journal of Drug Alcohol Abuse* 22:147–172.

Roe A (1994). The adult adjustment of children of alcoholic parents raised in foster homes. *Journal of Studies on Alcohol* 5:378–393.

Saunders GR & Schuckit MA (1981). Brief communication: MMPI scores in young men with alcoholic relatives and controls. *Journal of Nervous and Mental Disease* 168:456–481.

Schaeffer KW, Parsons OA & Yohman JR (1984). Neuropsychological differences between familial and nonfamilial alcoholics and nonalcoholics. *Alcoholism: Clinical & Experimental Research* 8:347–358.

Schuckit MA (1992). Advances in understanding the vulnerability to alcoholism. In *Advances in Understanding the Addictive States*. New York, NY: Raven Press, 93–108.

Schuckit MA (1973). Alcoholism and sociopathy—Diagnostic confusion. *Quarterly Journal of Studies on Alcohol* 34:157–164.

Schuckit MA (1995). A long-term study of sons of alcoholics. *Alcohol Health and Research World* 19:172–175.

Schuckit MA (1987). Biological vulnerability to alcoholism. *Journal of Consulting and Clinical Psychology* 55:1–9.

Schuckit MA (1989). Biomedical and genetic markers of alcoholism. In HW Goedde & PD Agarwal (eds.) *Alcoholism: Biomedical and Genetic Aspects*. New York, NY: Pergamon, 290–302.

Schuckit MA (1984). Differences in plasma cortisol after ethanol in relatives of alcoholics and controls. *Journal of Clinical Psychiatry* 45:374–379.

Schuckit MA (1996). *Drug and Alcohol Abuse: A Clinical Guide to Diagnosis and Treatment, 4th Ed*. New York, NY: Plenum Medical Book Company.

Schuckit MA (1985). Ethanol-induced changes in body sway in men at high alcoholism risk. *Archives of General Psychiatry* 42:375–379.

Schuckit MA (1983). Extroversion and neuroticism in young men at higher or lower risk for alcoholism. *American Journal of Psychiatry* 140:1223–1224.

Schuckit MA (1986). Genetic and biological markers in alcoholism and drug abuse. In MC Braude & HM Chao (eds.) *Genetic and Biological Markers in Drug Abuse and Alcoholism (NIDA Research Monograph 66)*. Rockville, MD: National Institute on Drug Abuse.

Schuckit MA (1986). Genetic and clinical implications of alcoholism and affective disorder. *American Journal of Psychiatry* 143:140–147.

Schuckit MA (1994). Low level of response to alcohol as a predictor of future alcoholism. *American Journal of Psychiatry* 151:184–189.

Schuckit MA (1988). Reactions to alcohol in sons of alcoholics and controls. *Alcoholism: Clinical & Experimental Research* 12:465–470.

Schuckit MA (1985). Studies of populations at high risk for alcoholism. *Psychiatric Developments* 3:31–63.

Schuckit MA (1984). Subjective responses to alcohol in sons of alcoholics and control subjects. *Archives of General Psychiatry* 41:879–884.

Schuckit MA (1985). The clinical implications of primary diagnostic groups among alcoholics. *Archives of General Psychiatry* 42:1043–1049.

Schuckit MA (1985). Trait (and state) markers of a predisposition to psychopathology. In LL Judd & P Groves (eds.) *Physiological Foundations of Clinical Psychiatry*. Philadelphia, PA: J.B. Lippincott.

Schuckit MA, Butters N, Lyn L & Irwin M (1987). Neuropsychologic deficits and the risk for alcoholism. *Neuropsychopharmacology* 1:45–53.

Schuckit MA & Gold BO (1988). A simultaneous evaluation of multiple markers of ethanol/placebo challenges in sons of alcoholics. *Archives of General Psychiatry* 45:211–216.

Schuckit MA, Gold E & Risch C (1987). Serum prolactin levels in sons of alcoholics and control subjects. *American Journal of Psychiatry* 144:854–859.

Schuckit MA, Goodwin DW & Winokur GA (1972). A study of alcoholism in half-siblings. *American Journal of Psychiatry* 128:1132–1136.

Schuckit MA & Haglund RM (1982). An overview of the etiologic theories on alcoholism. In N Estes & E Heinemann (eds.) *Alcoholism: Development, Consequences and Interventions*. St. Louis, MO: C.V. Mosby.

Schuckit MA & Irwin M (1989). An analysis of the clinical relevance of type I and type 2 alcoholics. *British Journal of Addictions* 84:869–876.

Schuckit MA, Irwin M & Mahler HIM (1990). The tridimensional personality questionnaire scores for sons of alcoholics and controls. *American Journal of Psychiatry* 147:481–487.

Schuckit MA, Risch SC & Gold ER (1988). Alcohol consumption, ACTH level, and family history of alcoholism. *American Journal of Psychiatry* 145:1391–1395.

Schuckit MA & Smith TL (1996). An 8-year follow-up of 450 sons of alcoholics and control subjects. *Archives of General Psychiatry* 53:202–210.

Schuckit MA, Tipp J, Smith TL, Shapiro E, Hesselbrock V, Bucholz K, Reich T, Nurnberger JI (1995). An evaluation of type A and B alcoholics. *Addiction* 90:1189–1203.

Suwaki J & Ohara H (1985). Alcohol induced facial flushing and drinking behavior in Japanese men. *Journal of Studies on Alcohol* 46:196–198.

Swan GE, Carmelli D, Rosenman RH, Fabsiz RR & Christian JC (1990). Smoking and alcohol consumption in adult male twins: Genetic heritability and shared environmental influences. *Journal of Substance Abuse* 1:39–50.

Tabakoff B & Hoffman PL (1989). Genetics and biological markers of risk for alcoholism. In K Kiianmaa, B Tabakoff & T Saito (eds.) *Genetic Aspects of Alcoholism*. Helsinki, Finland: Finnish Foundation for Alcohol Studies, 127–142.

Tabakoff B, Hoffman PL, Lee AI, Saito T, Willard B & Leon-Jones FD (1988). Differences in platelet enzyme activity between alcoholics and nonalcoholics. *The New England Journal of Medicine* 318:134–139.

Tarter RE, Hegedus AM, Goldstein G, Shell C & Alterman A (1984). Adolescent sons of alcoholics: neuropsycbological and personality characteristics. *Alcoholism: Clinical & Experimental Research* 8:216–222.

Utne HE, Hensen FV, Winkler K, Schulsinger I (1977). Alcohol elimination rates in adoptees with and without alcoholic parents. *Journal of Studies on Alcohol* 38:1219–1223.

Vaillant GE (1983). Natural history of male psychological health. VIII. Antecedents of alcoholism and orality. *American Journal of Psychiatry* 137:181–186.

Vaillant GE (1983). *The Natural History of Alcoholism*. Cambridge, MA: Harvard University Press.

Vesell ES, Page JG & Passananti GT (1970). Genetic and environmental factors affecting ethanol metabolism in man. *Clinical Pharmacology and Therapeutics* 12:192– 201.

Volavka J, Pollock VE, Gabrielli WF & Mednick SA (1985). The EEG in persons at risk for alcoholism. *Recent Developments in Alcoholism* 3:21–36.

von Knorring AL, Bohman M, von Knorring L & Oreland L (1985). Platelet MAO activity as a biological marker in subgroups of alcoholism. *Acta Psychiatrica Scandinavica* 72:51–58.

von Knorring L, von Knorring AL, Smigan L, Lindberg U & Edholm M (1987). Personality traits in subtypes of alcoholics. *Journal of Studies on Alcohol* 48:523–527.

Wall TL & Ehlers CL (1995). Genetic influences affecting alcohol use among Asians. *Alcohol Health and Research World* 19:184–189.

CHAPTER 3

Behavioral Models of Addiction

Roy A. Wise, Ph.D.
John E. Kelsey, Ph.D.

Models of Addiction
The Drug Self-Administration Paradigm
The Conditioned Place-Preference Model
The Brain Stimulation Reward Model
The Reinstatement Paradigm
Recent Dependence Models

There are two major views of addiction, captured in two broad and conceptually independent classes of animal models: "stick" models and "carrot" models. In the former, we are seen to be motivated to avoid the punishing "stick"; in the latter, we are seen to seek the rewarding "carrot." A stick model is a *drive model*; an example is our common-sense notion of hunger. In such models physiological needs are presumed to produce aversive states that become progressively stronger until food or drug is ingested to alleviate the need and the accompanying drive. It is perhaps worth noting that the strongest version of this model, that of Clark Hull, did not long survive the discovery that rats will learn to lever-press for saccharin despite the fact that saccharin fails to satisfy the need for nutrients; stick models have survived much longer in addiction theory than in learning theory.

In contrast, the carrot model is a *positive reinforcement* and *incentive motivational* model; it is concerned with what the subject appears to be working to obtain rather than what it appears to be working to avoid. The carrot exemplifies the external incentive that lures the subject to approach and make contact, whereas the stick exemplifies the painful internal stimulus that drives the addict until relief is found.

MODELS OF ADDICTION

Early attempts to establish animal models of addiction tended to focus on the aversive state of physiological withdrawal distress, on the assumption that, if drugs were freely available, dependence needs would drive the animal to compulsive drug self-administration. Dependence was seen to result from neural adaptations and new homeostatic balances that become necessary, in the adapted animal, for normal function. However, attempts to validate the stick model in the addiction laboratory, like those in the feeding laboratory, have been generally disappointing. For example, when physiological dependence on alcohol finally was produced in laboratory animals, after years of unsuccessful attempts (Mello, 1973), it failed to produce animals that would voluntarily self-administer the drug. As is the case with some human alcoholics, dependent animals continued to refuse freely available alcohol even during acute withdrawal stress (see, for example, Woods, Ikomi & Winger, 1971; Falk, Sampson & Winger, 1972). Moreover, it was difficult to identify a dramatic syndrome of withdrawal distress with other habit-forming drugs, most notably the psychomotor stimulants, nicotine, and marijuana.

With the demonstration that animals will learn to self-administer several drugs compulsively even in the absence of major signs of withdrawal distress (Deneau, Yanagita & Seevers, 1969), the focus of animal models of addiction began to shift away from the early preoccupation with physiological dependence and toward a direct analysis of the habit-forming or "reinforcing" effects of drugs. In addition to the problems mentioned above, dependence theory always had the serious shortcoming of explaining the *maintenance* of drug-seeking without explaining its *acquisition*, whereas the notion of positive reinforcement appeared to offer an explanation of both. Thus, behavioral pharmacologists began to examine drugs in their capacity as positive reinforcers (Thompson & Pickens, 1971), leaning heavily on the teachings of B. F. Skinner (1938) and often ignoring, either out of personal preference or because of the peculiarities of the drug under study, the question of physiological dependence. This work was, for the most part, discussed without any speculation as to subjective states or models of reinforcement; those who speculated did so in the context of the carrot model, stressing the pleasure (Bijerot, 1980) and euphoria (McAuliffe & Gordon, 1974) drugs can bring, while minimizing the importance of the withdrawal distress they can alleviate.

The study of drug self-administration—particularly intravenous drug self-administration—from Skinner's theoretical perspective has been extremely productive. This approach produced, during decades when these drugs were an increasing social problem in North America, robust animal models with obvious relevance to the human conditions of heroin and amphetamine addiction. Examination of the models led to a needed appreciation of the powerful habit-forming properties that drugs can have even in the absence of cultural influences that are unique to humans and even prior to the development of the strong physiological dependence syndromes that accompany some but not all habit-forming drugs. Drug self-administration studies have offered psychiatry a model in which the biological dimensions of addiction can be isolated from the psychodynamic factors that often dominate in the clinic. Finally, oral, intravenous, and intracranial drug self-administration studies each have provided animal models useful in advancing our understanding of reward-related brain mechanisms (Koob & Bloom, 1988; Nestler, 1992; Wise & Bozarth, 1987).

Addictive drugs not only reinforce or "stamp in" (Thorndike, 1898) response habits; they also establish and maintain preferences for previously neutral environmental stimuli with which they become associated. The "conditioned place-preference" paradigm captures this important aspect of drug reward and provides a second animal model of interest to students of addiction. The conditioning of place-preferences—where the rewarding drug injection is given without regard to the behavior of the animal—fits the model of Pavlovian rather than of instrumental conditioning; this kind of conditioning also plays an important, though less obvious and less easily identified, role in lever-pressing studies.

In addition to these relatively pure conditioning models (one based on the paradigm of Skinner and one a variant of the paradigm of Pavlov), there are important models that mix the two paradigms. Of particular interest are studies of the effects of response-independent drug injections on the performance of habits that were established—and in some cases are maintained—with response-contingent reinforcement. The first of these involves the interaction of addictive drugs with brain stimulation reward. Drugs not only can serve as reinforcers in their own right; they can, under some circumstances at least, serve to enhance the effectiveness of other, concurrent, reinforcers. Marijuana and alcohol, for example, are thought to enhance the rewards of food, music, or social or sexual contact. Most addictive drugs enhance the rewarding impact of direct electrical stimulation of lateral hypothalamic and associated reward circuitry (Wise, 1996). Because this enhancement can be precisely controlled and measured, because drug reward appears to summate with rewarding brain stimulation by activating the same neural substrates as are activated by the electrical stimulation itself, and because brain stimulation reward has proven a useful tool for learning about the anatomy and neurochemistry of those substrates, drug-facilitation of brain stimulation reward has developed as a third reward-related paradigm of interest to students of addiction. Finally, the fourth reward-associated model, the "reinstatement model" has been developed as an approach to the study of factors contributing to relapse. In this model, animals are trained to self-administer drugs by lever-pressing and then are given experience in which response-contingent drug reinforcement is no longer available. The lever-pressing habit thus is gradually (though never completely) "extinguished." Then, various stimuli are tested for their ability to temporarily reinstate the response habit, despite the fact that responding continues to go unrewarded. In this paradigm, it is a response-independent "priming" injection of the training drug that appears to most effectively prompt the re-initiation of non-rewarded responding.

Each of these models offers one or more facets of the habit-forming properties of drugs for experimental examination. Although the four paradigms seem largely independent of one another, they each reflect a characteristic of reward-related events. Moreover, it generally is the case that the drugs and doses that are effective in one of these paradigms are similarly effective in the others. For this reason, it has been argued that the four paradigms are four reflections of a common underlying biological phenomenon: the activation of a brain mechanism involving the mesolimbic dopamine system and the output pathways of its targets in nucleus accumbens (Wise, 1989). In addition to these models of reward-related events, there recently has been renewed interest in an aspect of drug dependence that appears to involve a rebound depression, following a variety of chronic drug treatments, of the dopaminergic link in brain reward mechanisms. This chapter deals with each of the four reward models and, briefly, with the new variant of dependence models.

THE DRUG SELF-ADMINISTRATION PARADIGM

The animal model of addiction with the greatest face validity involves the *self-administration* of the drug by the animal. The earliest studies of drug self-administration involved oral intake of ethanol or other drugs. Not all oral intake studies are voluntary intake studies, however; indeed, most animals usually avoid concentrated alcohol solutions when given free access to the other necessities of life. Thus oral alcohol intake often has been forced by giving alcohol in the animals' only source of food, water, or even oxygen; a variety of other forms of coercion also have been used (Falk, Sampson & Winger, 1972). In most cases, intake ceases when the external contingencies are removed. With sufficiently gradual exposure, however, it is possible to establish significant oral ethanol self-administration in rats and monkeys. A particularly effective procedure involves masking the initially aversive taste of ethanol with a sweet incentive, which is gradually reduced as the animal acclimates to the drug (Samson, 1986). Simple ingestion does not, however, offer a persuasive model of human drug self-administration. Addicted humans not only ingest their accustomed drug; they go to great lengths to obtain it. The most convincing animal models of human drug self-administration thus involve the earning of drug by some arbitrary response, rather than the simple consumption of the drug when it is freely available. Simple consumption is designated a "consummatory" response, because it consummates a series of goal-directed acts. The acts that lead up to the final, consummatory, act are variously labeled "preparatory," "appetitive," "instrumental," or "operant" responses.

Skinner's (1938) concept of operant reinforcement has come to dominate the analysis of instrumental behavior. For Skinner, an operant reinforcer is anything that increases the probability of the behaviors that reliably precede it. By this definition, a reinforcer is any habit-forming agent. It is in this context that drug self-administration and drug reinforcement are usually conceived. Thus, to be considered a reinforcer, a drug should not only support consummatory (ingestive) behavior; it should also support operant (preparatory, appetitive, instrumental) behavior. The operant reinforcement model demands that the animal not only take the drug, but also that the animal *earn* the drug. The strongest demonstrations of operant reinforcement involve the demonstration that an animal will learn a normally *unusual* response to earn the drug. The not-infrequent practice of pre-training animals to lever-press for food makes lever-pressing a less unusual response (that is, a response with an elevated baseline rate) and thus compromises attempted demonstrations of operant reinforcement.

Although rats and rhesus monkeys can be trained to work for oral drug reinforcement (Grant & Johanson, 1988; Sinclair, 1974), the more robust demonstrations of drug reinforcement involve the self-administration (usually by lever-pressing) of opiates (Deneau, Yanagita & Seevers, 1969; Weeks, 1962) or psychomotor stimulants (Pickens & Thompson, 1971) through intravenous catheters. In the case of psychomotor stimulants, sub-human animals will self-administer the drug compulsively, resulting in death if drug availability is unlimited (Johanson et al., 1976). Compulsive self-administration can be seen even when low doses are given and no obvious signs of physiological dependence are evident (Deneau, Yanagita & Seevers, 1969). Moreover, animals will simply respond more frequently when increased response demands are made or when dose per injection is reduced, maintaining a relatively constant hourly intake of rewarding amphetamine (Pickens & Thompson, 1971), cocaine (Gerber & Wise, 1989; Pickens & Thompson, 1971), or heroin (Gerber & Wise, 1989). These and other observations (e.g., Yokel & Pickens, 1974) suggest a regulation of hourly drug intake that is seen by many as a mark of goal-directed behavior.

A variant of the self-administration paradigm is the progressive ratio paradigm. In this paradigm, the response demands are gradually escalated, from one response to several hundred per injection in the case of some drugs (Roberts & Richardson, 1992), until the animal no longer is willing to respond. The response requirement at which the animal ceases to respond is termed the "break-point" and is suggested to offer a reflection of the strength of the animal's motivation for the drug in question. A comparison of break-points, it is hoped, can offer some indication of the relative addictive liability of different drug classes.

Most drug self-administration studies are designed to reflect the level of performance of established habits, but in fact the concept of reinforcement initially was intended to reflect *habit formation* rather than level of trained *performance*. The notion of operant reinforcement offers little explanation of the levels of maintenance of an established habit (except, of course, that the habit will extinguish if reinforcement is not maintained). Acquisition studies, on the other hand, offer an animal model of *development of addiction*; they are useful in examining individual differences in addiction susceptibility (Deminiere, Piazza et al., 1989), as well as the effectiveness of manipulations of the animal's physiological state and environmental options (Carroll, Lac & Nygaard, 1989). In general, such factors play a much greater role in the development of addiction when marginal (ED_{50}) doses are given than they play in its control once addiction is established or in its establishment when high doses are given.

One of the reasons that the intravenous drug self-administration paradigm is so well regarded is that intravenous stimulants and opiates control behavior in much the same way as do more natural reinforcers (e.g., Johanson, 1978). However, although there is reason to believe that drug reinforcers and rewarding electrical stimulation of the brain activate the same motivational circuitry that controls such things as food and sexual motivation (Wise & Bozarth, 1987), intravenous drug reinforcement and intracranial stimulation differ from more traditional reinforcers in some important ways (Wise, 1987a). One reason they differ is that they act directly in the depths of the brain, within the neural circuitry of reward; their detection is not delayed, as is the detection of the slower and often less powerful natural reinforcers, by digestion and absorption into the bloodstream or by transduction by peripheral sense organs and transmission across polysynaptic sensory pathways. Thus, whereas drug reinforcement generally follows the laws of operant reinforcement, it can in some ways exert more powerful control over behavior than do more natural rewards (Wise, 1987a). Moreover, the notion of operant reinforcement was never intended as a *complete* explanation of operant habits; there is a powerful role for Pavlovian associations both within the realm of operant behavior and in broader aspects of addiction as well.

THE CONDITIONED PLACE-PREFERENCE MODEL

Addictive drugs not only establish instrumental response habits; they also establish, through Pavlov's (1927) original principle of reinforcement of stimulus-stimulus associations, conditioned attachments to drug-associated environmental stimuli. Such attachments can lead to *de novo* approach responses, never before practiced and never before given response-contingent reinforcement; such approach responses have been suggested (Bindra, 1978) to be the basic elements of all so-called "goal-directed" behavior. Perhaps the most dramatic description of such attachments was provided by Spragg (1940), who documented the course of development of dependence in chimpanzees given daily morphine injections for several months. Spragg describes the following when one of the chimps was weighed and taken back to his cage without the customary injection: "He then grasped the leash in his hand and pulled it back toward the Maternity Building (in which the injection room is located). I let him lead me and he went back, between the Maternity and Nursery Buildings, looking in at each open doorway. He looked in through the open doorway of the injection room, then pulled me into the room after him. . . ." (Spragg, 1940).

The ability of addictive drugs to produce conditioned approach to places that have been associated with the drugs in the past is modeled in the *conditioned place-preference paradigm* (Beach, 1957; Kumar, 1972; Rossi & Reid, 1976). The first systematic study of conditioned place-preferences was done by Beach (1957), who, like Spragg, allowed his animals to walk into the environment that was subsequently associated with morphine injections. Some of Beach's rats, like Spragg's monkeys, had been given repeated doses of morphine and were assumed to be physiologically dependent when the drug was paired with the environment. Thus the animals of Spragg or Beach may have learned to enter the morphine-associated environment because of response-contingent (operant) conditioning; that is, their behavior may have resulted from development of a response habit much like the habit of an animal running in an alleyway for a reward at the end. Subsequent investigators eliminated the possibility of response reinforcement by placing their passive animals directly into the environment that was to be associated with the drug. Subsequent investigators also explored Beach's additional finding that even non-dependent animals developed a preference for the place associated with morphine's effects.

Kumar (1972) should be credited with the design of the modern, prototypical conditioned place-preference paradigm. His animals were tested in a two-compartment apparatus; one compartment had gray floor and walls while the other compartment had black-and-white checkered floor and walls, such that the animals did not have pronounced unconditioned preferences for one compartment over the other. In Kumar's initial experiment, the animals were first made dependent on morphine with doses escalating to 120 mg/kg/day. The animals of one group were subsequently placed for a half-hour in one side of the apparatus *following* their daily maintenance injections, while those of another group were placed in one side of the apparatus for a half-hour *prior to* their maintenance injections. Thus, one group had the drug state associated with one of the two compartments, whereas the other group had the withdrawal state associated with one of the two compartments. The animals were given 14 such pairings and then were withdrawn from morphine for two days. Finally, the partitions between the two compartments were opened and the animals were given a choice between the state-associated compartment and the neutral compartment. Animals given morphine injections in the apparatus preferred the side on which the morphine was given; animals that had been placed in the apparatus during withdrawal periods had no preference for one compartment over the other (but see Bechara & van der Kooy, 1992). Because the conditioned response (approach to the drug-associated compartment) was never permitted prior to the preference test, the conditioned preference for the drug-associated place reflected an acquired approach response that depended on stimulus-stimulus and not stimulus-response conditioning.

While Kumar (1972) thus established the conditioned place-preference paradigm as a paradigm in which approach responses can be established in the absence of response-contingent reinforcement, Kumar's experiment was based on the implicit assumption that morphine was a reward only to a morphine-dependent (and morphine-deprived) animal. Combining the purely Pavlovian pairing of Kumar with the study of non-dependent animals begun by Beach, Rossi & Reid (1976) showed that morphine-conditioned place-preferences can be produced in rats that were not initially dependent. However, because Rossi and Reid's animals received morphine on four consecutive days, it is possible that, even in this study, relief of minor but potentially significant withdrawal symptoms (on the second, third, and fourth days) played a role in the conditioning of place-preference. Evidence that opiate-conditioned place-preferences can be established without any opportunity for relief of opiate withdrawal distress comes from studies in which preferences are established by the first and only opiate injection that the animal ever receives (Mucha, van der Kooy et al., 1982). Even in multiple-injection studies, the possibility of a contribution of dependence can be minimized by extending the period between drug injections from a day to a week or longer.

The conditioned place-preference paradigm has several important advantages. First, the animals are usually tested in the drug-free state one or two days after conditioning; this eliminates any confounding effects of drug intoxication on behavioral performance. Second, unlike the case of the self-administration paradigm, the experimenter controls the dosage of the drug. This is important for statistical comparisons between groups and it is important where the drug is given directly into the brain with the hope of restricting the spread of the drug to adjacent brain regions. Disadvantages are that whereas dose-orderly changes in conditioned place-preference are sometimes demonstrated (Mucha, van der Kooy et al., 1982; Bozarth, 1987), the more usual effects are all-or-none. Another problem is that changes in preference often fail to reflect the development of *absolute* preferences. Although a number of so-called "unbiased" designs have been put forward to address these issues (Carr, Fibiger & Phillips, 1989; van der Kooy, 1987), it is worth noting that strongly rewarding drugs such as morphine and amphetamine establish conditioned place-preferences across a variety of procedural variations (e.g., Mucha & Iversen, 1984); to the authors' knowledge, no major conclusion from a so-called "biased" or "unbalanced" paradigm has been refuted when the same drug and dose were tested in a balanced paradigm.

Rossi and Reid argued that the conditioned place-preference paradigm gives a reflection of the affective response of the animals to the drug and to drug-related stimuli. This assertion has not been challenged in the subsequent literature, but it should not be accepted without careful consideration. The problem lies with the definition of "affective"; even textbooks of motivation avoid formal definitions of such terms (Wise, 1987b). However, Schneirla (1959) has argued forcefully that "*approach* and *withdrawal* are the *only* empirical, objective terms applicable to *all* motivated behavior in *all* animals" (emphasis his). For Schneirla, the approach-withdrawal dichotomy is more fundamental than any other of the ubiquitous dichotomies of motivational writings: pleasure-pain, love-hate, stick-carrot, or reward-punishment. Glickman and Schiff (1967) and others (Wise & Bozarth, 1987) have argued that the ability of a stimulus to elicit approach is the mark of all rewards; indeed, this may be our best independent criterion for identifying a reward. Nonetheless, it should not be casually assumed that the conditioned place preference gives more than unconfirmed hints at the subjective experience of the animals.

Whether the conditioned place-preference paradigm implies anything about the affective responses of animals, it clearly identifies an ability of addictive drugs to establish a new response habit (the habit of "hanging around" the drug environment) in the absence of response-contingent reinforcement. Despite the fact that the drug is never given as an explicit reward for stepping toward the drug-associated compartment, the result of drug-compartment Pavlovian pairings is to induce, *de novo*, an approach response above and beyond that associated with the initial exploration of a novel compartment. The emergence of this approach response is questionably purposive; rather, it appears to reflect an almost reflexive approach toward the drug-associated stimuli. From the Pavlovian perspective, this approach response can be seen as an investigatory reflex that, because of a response-independent association of the compartment with the rewarding drug, comes to be sustained; without the association with reward, exploratory approach tendencies would quickly habituate. Bindra (1978) has argued that the development of such approach habits is fundamental to all appetitive learning.

THE BRAIN STIMULATION REWARD MODEL

Whereas the drug self-administration paradigm and the conditioned place-preference paradigm are seen as relatively pure cases of operant and Pavlovian reinforcement, respectively, the ability of habit-forming drugs to potentiate brain stimulation reward is a mixed paradigm (Wise, 1989). Here, the animal works for operant reinforcement in the form of direct electrical stimulation of the brain, and responding in drug-free conditions is compared to responding after response-independent treatment with addictive drugs (Wise, 1996).

Most addictive drugs are known to increase the rate of responding for brain stimulation reward, and it now seems clear from the curve-shift self-stimulation paradigm (Gallistel, 1987), as predicted by Stein & CD Wise (1973), that such increases usually reflect summation of the rewarding actions of the drugs with the rewarding action of the stimulation (Wise, 1996). This paradigm thus may offer an animal model of the augmentation of the enjoyment of food, music, or sex that are anecdotally suggested to result from "recreational" use of ethanol, cannabis, or cocaine. Because the parameters of stimulation and the dose of drug can each be precisely controlled, this paradigm has been widely used by physiological psychologists (Wise & Rompré, 1989; Wise, 1996). Unlike the self-administration and the place-preference paradigm, this paradigm offers a powerful metric for comparing the reward-relevant effects of different drugs and drug classes (Gallistel, 1987).

At the same time that electrical stimulation of the lateral hypothalamus is serving as an operant reinforcer, it also has proactive "priming" effects on the animal's behavior (Gallistel, Stellar & Bubis, 1974). These response-independent priming effects energize and channel behavior much as does a salted peanut or, unfortunately, as does the first drink or first cigarette after a period of attempted abstinence. The most obvious priming effects are seen when trained animals are, for one reason or another, not responding. Trained rats do not always begin lever-pressing for brain stimulation reward at the start of a session, but if given a "free" sample of rewarding stimulation, the probability that they will begin lever-pressing is greatly increased. This "priming" effect also usually terminates the intermittent periods of non-responding in animals that have temporarily stopped responding during a period of prolonged continuous access to stimulation. However, the proactive effects of brain stimulation reward decay quickly; they are completely lost within one or two minutes (Gallistel, Stellar & Bubis, 1974). Because animals often lever-press more than once per second for rewarding brain stimulation, the priming effect of the previous stimulation usually contributes considerably to the rate of responding of the animal. However, the priming and reinforcing effects of stimulation can be dissociated in a runway task; thus they are independent contributions to response strength and patterns (Gallistel, Stellar & Busis, 1974). One lever-pressing paradigm designated as a brain stimulation reward paradigm (that of Kornetsky, Esposito et al., 1979 and of Markou & Koob, 1991) is a direct measure of the priming effects of stimulation, and reflects the reinforcing effects of the stimulation only secondarily.

Priming and reinforcement effects are usually confounded in operant tasks, each making significant contributions to the rate of responding that was identified by Skinner as the primary measure of operant reinforcement. Indeed, as Skinner's students (Herrnstein, 1971) and physiological psychologists

(Valenstein, 1964) came to realize, simple rate of responding in a lever-press task—particularly if determined at a single level of reinforcement or a single dose response requirement—can easily be misinterpreted. Consequently, the effectiveness of brain stimulation reward are best quantified in the "curve-shift" paradigm in which strength of responding (rate in a lever-press task; running speed in an alleyway) is determined across the full range of effective stimulation levels (Gallistel, 1987; Gallistel, Stellar & Bubis, 1974; Gallistel & Freyd, 1987; Miliaressis, Romprè et al., 1986; Wise, 1996). This paradigm offers essentially a "dose-response" analysis of brain stimulation reward and is valuable in physiological psychology for the same reasons it is valuable in pharmacology (Liebman, 1983). Drugs that shift the curve to the left (such that *less* stimulation is required to produce a given rate of responding) are inferred to augment the rewarding potency of stimulation. Conversely, drugs that shift the curve to the right (such that *more* stimulation is required to sustain responding) are assumed to decrease the rewarding potency of the stimulation.

Two lines of evidence justify the assumption that the ability of a drug to potentiate brain stimulation reward reflects the ability of the drug to serve as a reward in its own right. On a theoretical level, there is the logic of the dose-response paradigm. If a drug is synergizing with the rewarding property of stimulation—reducing the amount of stimulation necessary to produce a given amount of responding (and thus, presumably, a given amount of reward)—then it must be serving the same function (reward) as is served by the stimulation itself. Because drug administration in this paradigm is independent of the animal's behavior, it cannot, by definition, be providing operant reinforcement. However it could be augmenting responding by providing priming and it could also be amplifying the reinforcing impact of the earned brain stimulation. On a more empirical level, the drugs and drug subtypes that have been well-characterized as rewarding in their own right (in self-administration and place-preference tests) appear to potentiate the reward produced by lateral hypothalamic stimulation when they are injected into the same brain sites where their direct rewarding effects have been localized. Amphetamine, cocaine, nicotine, phencyclidine, and morphine, all intravenously self-administered by animals, each cause parallel leftward shifts in the curve-shift paradigm (Wise, 1996). Morphine and mu and delta opioids do so when injected into the ventral tegmental area (Jenck, Gratton & Wise, 1987), where morphine and mu and delta opioids are self-administered (Bozarth & Wise, 1981; Devine & Wise, 1984) and cause conditioned place preferences (Bals-Kubik et al., 1993) in their own right. Similarly, amphetamine both potentiates brain stimulation reward (Colle & Wise, 1988) and also serves as a reward in its own right (Hoebel, Monaco et al., 1983; Carr & White, 1983) when injected into the nucleus accumbens. Phencyclidine, too, has reward-potentiating effects (Carlezon & Wise, 1996a) as well as direct rewarding effects (Carlezon & Wise, 1996b) when injected directly into nucleus accumbens. There have been no reported dissociations of the brain sites where drugs have direct rewarding effects and the brain sites where the same drugs augment the rewarding potency of lateral hypothalamic brain stimulation.

The ability of addictive drugs to potentiate the rewarding effects of more natural reinforcers such as food or sexual contact also can be demonstrated in animal models, though this issue is rarely approached directly. Whereas amphetamine and cocaine are widely viewed as appetite suppressants, low doses of amphetamine can facilitate feeding under some circumstances (Blundell & Latham, 1980). Cannabis facilitates feeding (Hollister, 1971), as do opioid treatments that facilitate brain stimulation reward (Jenck, Quirion & Wise, 1987; Noel & Wise, 1995).

Finally, addictive drugs can potentiate the effects of "conditioned reinforcers." Conditioned reinforcers are initially neutral stimuli that, because they have been associated through Pavlovian conditioning with a primary reinforcer like food, are able to sustain, for a time, an operant response habit (Hyde, 1976). In what appears to be the first demonstration of drug-potentiation of the effectiveness of a conditioned reinforcer, Hill (1970) reported that the psychomotor stimulants, amphetamine, methamphetamine, methylphenidate, and pipradrol increased responding during extinction when responses were followed by the sounds of a dipper that had previously delivered milk reinforcement. This enhancement of rate did not occur in the absence of the sound of the dipper; indeed, when the dipper was not activated, pipradrol decreased responding. Neither did the stimulant increase responding if the sound of the dipper had not been previously associated with the delivery of milk.

A more powerful demonstration of conditioned reinforcement involves the use of a conditioned stimulus to establish a new response habit. Using such a strategy, Beninger, Hanson and Phillips (1981) and Robbins, Watson et al. (1983) reported that pipradrol increased the rate of responding during acquisition of a lever pressing response that was reinforced only with response-contingent presentation of a food-associated conditioned stimulus. Interestingly, variable results have been reported following systemic injections of several doses of amphetamine and cocaine; Beninger, Hanson and Phillips (1981) reported that cocaine differentially increased responding for the conditioned reinforcer but amphetamine did not, and Robbins, Watson et al. (1983) reported the reverse outcome. Taylor and Robbins (1984) subsequently found that injections of amphetamine directly into the nucleus accumbens, where this drug is rewarding in its own right (Carr & White, 1983; Hoebel, Monaco et al., 1983), increased responding for a light that had been paired with water, whereas such injections did not increase responding for a light that had been negatively or randomly paired with water. Inasmuch as these drugs do not increase responding indiscriminately, but only increase responding that is reinforced with a conditioned reinforcer (Beninger, Hanson & Phillips, 1981; Hill, 1970; Robbins, Watson et al., 1983, Taylor & Robbins, 1984), it would seem that these drugs are capable of enhancing the effectiveness of conditioned reinforcers just as they are able to enhance the effectiveness of direct, unconditioned activation of brain reward mechanisms. This, in turn, would suggest that the conditioned reinforcers may activate the same reward mechanism as is activated by the primary reinforcer. The effects of other addictive drugs have not, to our knowledge, been tested for their effects on conditioned reinforcement.

THE REINSTATEMENT PARADIGM

Another mixed paradigm that is important to the understanding of addiction is the reinstatement paradigm (Stewart & de Wit, 1987; Wise, 1989). The reinstatement paradigm is designed as an animal model of "relapse," in which the animal is first trained to lever-press with response-contingent intravenous drug reinforcement. The lever-pressing habit then is extinguished under conditions of nonreinforcement, and, subsequently, the animal is studied to determine what treatments can reinstate, temporarily, the lever-pressing response habit (Davis & Smith, 1976; Gerber & Stretch, 1975). This is a mixed paradigm because the dependent variable (usually lever-pressing) is a response trained and maintained under operant reinforcement but tested with the drug (or associated conditioned stimuli) given in the absence of the operant response and in advance of the period of response assessment. The focus of the reinstatement paradigm is the ability of a response-independent drug injection or drug-associated cue to proactively "prime" or "reinstate" renewed responding in the absence of any further response-contingent reinforcement. Just as the addict becomes more likely to initiate drug-seeking when confronted with the drug or drug-associated cues in the environment (Wikler, 1973), so does the trained animal become more likely to initiate the previously rewarded operant in the presence of the drug cue or drug-associated cues (Stewart & de Wit, 1987). The priming effects discussed in relation to this paradigm would seem to reflect the same phenomenon as the priming effects discussed earlier with relation to brain stimulation reward.

In the reinstatement paradigm, a "taste" of the training drug usually is the most powerful priming stimulus for reinstating previously trained and extinguished habits (de Wit & Stewart, 1981). Other drugs in the same class also are effective; in general, the effective priming stimuli—like the effective rewarding stimuli—are drugs that activate the mesolimbic dopamine system in some way (Stewart, 1984). Indeed, a response-independent injection of the direct dopamine agonist bromocriptine (a reinforcing drug in its own right) appears to be an unusually powerful (supra-normal) stimulus for reinstating lever-press habits trained under either cocaine or heroin reinforcement (Wise, Murray & Bozarth, 1990). Responding thus appears to be triggered by the presence rather than by the absence (withdrawal) of drug in the blood. Of course, high dose priming injections "satiate" the animal for a significant period (de Wit & Stewart, 1981); however, in the case of cocaine, at least, once the period of satiation is over (once the last rewarding injection is "cleared"), the effectiveness of a priming injection becomes independent of time since the last reinforcement (Stewart & de Wit, 1987).

In the case of non-dependent animals trained to self-administer heroin, the opiate antagonist naltrexone actually decreases the probability of renewed responding, whereas the opposite treatment (a response-independent injection of heroin) reinstates responding (Stewart & Wise, 1992; Shaham & Stewart, 1995). These data, taken together, suggest something long taught by Alcoholics Anonymous and other Twelve-Step programs: a taste of the drug is among the most powerful stimuli for craving and for relapse.

Another effective stimulus for reinstating responding in this paradigm is stress. Stress can reinstate responding in both heroin-trained (Shaham & Stewart, 1995) and cocaine-trained animals (Erb, Shaham & Stewart, 1996).

If drugs are effective in reinstating seemingly extinguished drug-seeking, then drug-associated environmental stimuli should have a similar, though perhaps weaker, capacity. Indeed, such stimuli also can reinstate responding during conditions of extinction (Davis & Smith, 1976; de Wit & Stewart, 1981) and can sustain responding during conditions of infrequent reinforcement (Goldberg, Spealman & Kellerher, 1979). Whereas the conditioned stimuli may prove to be most effective if given in a response-contingent manner (Davis & Smith, 1976; Goldberg, Spealman & Kellerher, 1979) they, like the drugs themselves, also are effective when given following a period of no responding (de Wit & Stewart, 1981). Such stimuli, however, are less potent than the optimal dose of the drug itself, and lose their effectiveness as they are repeatedly presented in the absence of the drug (de Wit & Stewart, 1981).

The effectiveness of conditioned stimuli in the reinstatement paradigm thus follows the general principles of Pavlovian conditioning; the conditioned stimulus (CS) has much the same effect as the unconditioned stimulus (UCS) with which it is paired, but depends for its continued effectiveness on repeated pairing with the UCS (Pavlov, 1927). Indeed, it was the loss of effectiveness of a CS given in the continued absence of its associated UCS and the restoration of CS effectiveness occasioned by renewed association of CS with UCS that led Pavlov to introduce the terms "extinction" and "reinforcement" into the psychological literature. The phenomena of Pavlovian conditioning that are revealed in the reinstatement paradigm, in the absence of the confound of operant reinforcement, also contribute significantly to the effectiveness of operant reinforcement within the self-administration paradigm.

RECENT DEPENDENCE MODEL

While reward paradigms have dominated the recent animal models of addiction, dependence models continue to be put forward. One, in particular, has captured recent attention: the dopamine depletion hypothesis (Dackis & Gold, 1985). The dopamine depletion hypothesis was unique among dependence models, in that it first suggested that withdrawal-associated depression of the brain mechanisms of positive reinforcement can be a source of drug craving. The hypothesis was based on evidence that cocaine is rewarding because of its ability to activate the mesolimbic dopamine system (Wise, 1978; Wise & Rompré, 1989), and it postulated that overstimulation of the dopamine system by chronic experience with rewarding cocaine might deplete the system of its transmitter, thus producing a dysphoric state (a state opposite to the drug state) that would, in turn, motivate renewed cocaine-seeking behavior. Such behavior would, in turn, cause a further depletion, a stronger subsequent depression, and ever more vigorous drug-seeking.

Whereas the hypothesis was advanced as an explanation of cocaine craving, it has subsequently been confirmed that extracellular dopamine levels are depressed, particularly in the nucleus accumbens, following cessation of chronic treatment with not only cocaine (Parsons, Smith & Justice, 1991), but by morphine (Acquas, Carboni & DiChiara, 1991; Pothos, Rada et al., 1991), amphetamine, and ethanol (Rosetti, Melis et al., 1991) as well.

These findings are consistent with evidence that the threshold for brain stimulation reward is elevated following chronic cocaine self-administration (Markou & Koob, 1991) and chronic amphetamine treatment (Munn & Wise, 1992). Thus Koob and his coworkers (Koob & Bloom, 1988; Markou & Koob, 1991) have rekindled interest in what are termed the "opponent-process" theories of motivation (Solomon & Corbit, 1974). The essential feature of such theories is that any hedonic state induces in the nervous system a set of compensatory, state-opposite reactions that tend to normalize the mood during the hedonic event and produce a rebound after-effect. When it is a drug that causes the initial hedonic alteration, the opponent process has drug-opposite consequences. To the degree that the opponent process must now be overcome before the previous reward can again cause euphoria, escalating contact with the reward becomes necessary to restore even normal mood.

This model is a variant of classical dependence theory, but it offers the unique postulate that it is the compensatory reactions *of reinforcement mechanism itself* that set up the state that motivates further drug-seeking. This renders moot the fact that opiate reward can be dissociated from the more dramatic classic signs of opiate withdrawal (Deneau, Yanagita & Seevers, 1969; Woods & Schuster, 1971), because the classic signs of withdrawal may not be well correlated with the more critical consequence of withdrawal: depression of the brain's reward circuitry. The postulation of opponent-processes in the reward mechanism is consistent with and builds on the view (Wise, 1978) that brain dopamine plays an important role in the euphorigenic and rewarding effects of addictive drugs and with the fact that several compensatory mechanisms are called into play by perturbations of the dopamine system (Zigmond, Abercrombie et al., 1990).

Although it seems clear that the dopamine system is depressed during at least some drug withdrawal conditions, it remains an open question whether depressed activity in the brain mechanisms of reward is a condition that significantly motivates reward-seeking behavior in lower animals. Depressed dopamine function may be a correlate but not a cause of motivated behavior. This possibility is consistent with the fact that peak withdrawal distress is not a necessary predictor of peak motivation for drug self-administration; it is reinforced by a recent finding with the reinstatement paradigm: opiate antagonists, known to depress the reward mechanism in animals never treated with exogenous opiates (opiate antagonists elevate self-stimulation thresholds of opiate-naive animals: Belluzzi & Stein, 1977; West & Wise, 1988), fail to reinstate heroin-trained lever-pressing (Stewart & Wise, 1992). Whereas response initiation thus may be independent of opponent process states, it is difficult to imagine that drug intake, once initiated, would not be affected to some degree by dependence conditions.

CONCLUSIONS

Animal models of various aspects of addiction are described. The first, *drug self-administration*, has the most obvious relevance to compulsive drug-seeking in humans and seems to reflect, at least in part, the ability of addictive drugs to reinforce response habits as understood within Skinner's (1938) framework of operant reinforcement. The second, *conditioned place-preference*, reflects the ability of animals to form conditioned attachments to the stimuli associated with either passive receipt or active self-administration of those drugs; this paradigm is understood within the framework of Pavlovian (1927) reinforcement. These attachments are a critical part of goal-directed behavior, as even the distal sensory properties of food must gain control over behavior through some form of Pavlovian association with sweetness (an unconditioned incentive) or with the postingestional consequences of food. The Pavlovian association of rewards with previously neutral stimuli plays an important role in the self-administration paradigm as well as the conditioned place-preference paradigm, as is best illustrated by the reinstatement or maintenance of responding by a response-independent presentation of a drug-associated conditioned stimulus after or during a period of response extinction.

The third paradigm, the *brain stimulation reward paradigm*, reflects the ability of low doses of addictive drugs to summate with the effects of response contingent rewarding brain stimulation, apparently because of drug actions within the same reward pathway as is activated by the stimulation itself (Wise & Rompré, 1989). This paradigm offers the experimenter the most direct experimental control over the animal and the rewarding and priming stimuli and offers the most powerful quantitative analysis of the relative impact of different drugs on the brain reward mechanisms. The fourth paradigm, the *reinstatement paradigm*, also reflects the proactive "priming" effects of addictive drugs; this paradigm suggests an explanation for—and a means of studying—the fact that, however difficult it is to resist the first drug administration after a period of abstinence, it is even more difficult to resist the second and subsequent administrations. The reinstatement paradigm offers not only an animal model of relapse to drug-taking but, because drug craving is a presumed correlate of relapse, also offers what may be a reasonable animal model of drug "craving" (Childress, Ehrman et al., 1988). It generally is the case that the same drugs and doses that have reward-relevant actions in one of these paradigms also have reward-relevant actions in the others (Wise, 1989). Thus it is the working hypothesis of an increasing number of investigators that the response-instigating (proactive, incentive-motivational, habit-eliciting) effects and the response-reinforcing (retroactive, habit-establishing) effects are reflections of a common underlying process in the brain.

REFERENCES

Acquas E, Carboni E & DiChiara G (1991). Profound depression of mesolimbic dopamine release after morphine withdrawal in dependent rats. *European Journal of Pharmacology* 193:133–138.

Bals-Kubik R, Ableitner A, Herz A & Shippenberg TS (1993). Neuroanatomical sites mediating the motivational effects of opioids as mapped by the conditioned place preference paradigm in rats. *Journal of Pharmacology and Experimental Therapeutics* 264:489–495.

Beach HD (1957). Morphine addiction in rats. *Canadian Journal of Psychology* 11:104–112.

Bechara A & van der Kooy D (1992). A single brain stem substrate mediates the motivational effects of both opiates and food in nondeprived rats but not in deprived rats. *Behavioral Neuroscience* 106:351–363.

Belluzzi JD & Stein L (1977). Enkephalin may mediate euphoria and drive-reduction reward. *Nature* 266:556–558.

Beninger RJ, Hanson DR & Phillips AG (1981). The acquisition of responding with conditioned reinforcement: Effects of cocaine, (+)-amphetamine and pipradrol. *British Journal of Pharmacology* 74:149–154.

Bijerot N (1980). Addiction to pleasure: A biological and social-psychological theory of addiction. In DJ Lettieri, M Sayers & HW Pearson (eds.) *Theories on Drug Abuse: Selected Contemporary Perspectives.* Rockville, MD: National Institute on Drug Abuse, 246–255.

Bindra D (1978). How adaptive behavior is produced: A perceptual-motivational alternative to response-reinforcement. *Behavioral and Brain Sciences* 1:41–91.

Blundell JE & Latham CJ (1980). Characterization of adjustments to the structure of feeding behavior following pharmacological treatment: Effects of amphetamine and fenfluramine and the antagonism produced by pimozide and methergoline. *Pharmacology, Biochemistry and Behavior* 12:717–722.

Bozarth MA (1987). Conditioned place preference. A parametric analysis using systemic heroin injections. In MA Bozarth (ed.) *Methods of Assessing the Reinforcing Properties of Abused Drugs.* New York, NY: Springer Verlag, 241–274.

Bozarth MA & Wise RA (1981). Intracranial self-administration of morphine into the ventral tegmental area in rats. *Life Sciences* 28:551–555.

Carlezon WA & Wise RA (1996a). Microinjections of phencyclidine (PCP) and related drugs into nucleus accumbens shell potentiate lateral hypothalamic brain stimulation reward. *Psychopharmacology* 128:413–420.

Carlezon WA & Wise RA (1996b). Rewarding actions of phencyclidine and related drugs in nucleus accumbens shell and frontal cortex. *Journal of Neuroscience* 16:3112–3122.

Carr GD, Fibiger HC & Phillips AG (1989). Conditioned place preference as a measure of drug reward. In JM Liebman & SJ Cooper (eds.) *The Neuropharmacological Basis of Reward.* Oxford, England: Clarendon Press, 364–319.

Carr GD & White NM (1983). Conditioned place preference from intra-accumbens but not intra-caudate amphetamine injections. *Life* Sciences. 33:2551–1557.

Carroll ME, Lac ST & Nygaard SL (1989). A concurrently available nondrug reinforcer prevents the acquisition or decreases the maintenance of cocaine-reinforced behavior. *Psychopharmacology* 97:23–29.

Childress AR, Ehrman R, McLellan AT & O'Brien CP (1988). Conditioned craving and arousal in cocaine addiction: A preliminary report. In LS Harris (ed.) *Problems of Drug Dependence 1987.* Rockville, MD: National Institute on Drug Abuse, 74–80.

Colle L & Wise RA (1988). Effects of nucleus accumbens amphetamine on lateral hypothalamic brain stimulation reward. *Brain Research* 459:356–360.

Dackis CA & Gold MS (1985). New concepts in cocaine addiction: The dopamine depletion hypothesis. *Neuroscience and Biobehavioral Reviews* 9:469–477.

Davis WM & Smith SG (1976). Role of conditioned reinforcers in the initiation, maintenance and extinction of drug-seeking behavior. *Pavlovian Journal of Biological Science* 11:222–236.

de Wit H & Stewart J (1981). Reinstatement of cocaine-reinforced responding in the rat. *Psychopharmacology* 75:134–143.

Deminiere JM, Piazza PV, Le Moal M & Simon H (1989). Experimental approach to individual vulnerability to psychostimulant action. *Neuroscience and Biobehavioral Reviews* 13:141–147.

Deneau G, Yanagita T & Seevers MH (1969). Self-administration of psychoactive substances by the monkey: A measure of psychological dependence. *Psychopharmacology* 16:30–48.

Devine DP & Wise RA (1994). Self-administration of morphine, DAMGO, and DPDPE into the ventral tegmental area of rats. *Journal of Neuroscience* 14:1978–1994.

Erb S, Shaham Y & Stewart J (1996). Stress reinstates cocaine-seeking behavior after prolonged extinction and a drug-free period. *Psychopharmacology* 128:408–412.

Falk JL, Sampson HM & Winger G (1972). Behavioral maintenance of high concentrations of blood ethanol and physical dependence in the rat. *Science* 177:811–813.

Gallistel CR (1987). Determining the quantitative characteristics of a reward pathway. In RM Church, ML Commons, JR Stellar & AR Wagner (eds.) *Biological Determinants of Reinforcement.* Hillsdale, NJ: Lawrence Erlbaum Associates, 1–30.

Gallistel CR & Freyd G (1987). Quantitative determination of the effects of catecholaminergic agonists and antagonists on the rewarding efficacy of brain stimulation. *Pharmacology, Biochemistry and Behavior* 26:731–741.

Gallistel CR, Stellar JR & Bubis E (1974). Parametric analysis of brain stimulation reward in the rat: I. The transient process and the memory containing process. *Journal of Comparative and Physiological Psychology* 87:848–859.

Gerber GJ & Stretch R (1975). Drug-induced reinstatement of extinguished self-administration behavior in monkeys. *Pharmacology, Biochemistry and Behavior* 3:1055–1061.

Gerber GJ & Wise RA (1989). Pharmacological regulation of intravenous cocaine and heroin self-administration in rats: A variable dose paradigm. *Pharmacology, Biochemistry and Behavior* 32:527–531.

Glickman SE & Schiff BB (1967). A biological theory of reinforcement. *Psychological Review* 74:81–109.

Goldberg SR, Spealman RD & Kelleher RT (1979). Enhancement of drug-seeking behavior by environmental stimuli associated with cocaine or morphine injections. *Neuropharmacology* 18:1015–1017.

Grant KA & Johanson CE (1988). Oral ethanol self-administration in free feeding rhesus monkeys. *Alcoholism: Clinical & Experimental Research* 12:780–784.

Herrnstein RJ (1971). Quantitative hedonism. *Journal of Psychiatric Research* 8:399–412.

Hill RT (1970). Facilitation of conditioned reinforcement as a mechanism of psychomotor stimulation. In E Costa & S Garattini (eds.) *Amphetamine and Related Compounds.* New York, NY: Raven Press, 781–795.

Hoebel BG, Monaco AP, Hernandez L, Aulisi EF, Stanley BG & Lenard L (1983). Self-injection of amphetamine directly into the brain. *Psychopharmacology* 81:158–163.

Hollister LE (1971). Hunger and appetite after single doses of marijuana, alcohol and dextroamphetamine. *Pharmacology and Therapeutics* 12:44–49.

Hyde TS (1976). The effect of Pavlovian stimuli on the acquisition of a new response. *Learning and Motivation* 7:223–239.

Jenck F, Gratton A & Wise RA (1987). Opioid receptor subtypes associated with ventral tegmental facilitation of lateral hypothalamic brain stimulation reward. *Brain Research* 423:34–38.

Jenck F, Quirion R & Wise RA (1987). Opioid receptor subtypes associated with ventral tegmental facilitation and periaqueductal gray inhibition of feeding. *Brain Research* 423:39–44.

Johanson CE (1978). Drugs as reinforcers. In DE Blackman & DJ Sanger (eds.) *Contemporary Research in Behavioral Pharmacology.* New York, NY: Plenum Press, 325–390.

Johanson CE, Balster RL & Bonese K (1976). Self-administration of psychomotor stimulant drugs: The effects of unlimited access. *Pharmacology Biochemistry and Behavior* 4:45–51.

Koob GF & Bloom FE (1988). Cellular and molecular mechanisms of drug dependence. *Science* 242:715–723.

Kornetsky C, Esposito RU, McLean S & Jacobson JO (1979). Intracranial self-stimulation thresholds: A model for the hedonic effects of drugs of abuse. *Archives of General Psychiatry* 36:289–292.

Kumar R (1972). Morphine dependence in rats: Secondary reinforcement from environmental stimuli. *Psychopharmacologia* 25:332–338.

Liebman JM (1983). Discriminating between reward and performance: A critical review of intracranial self-stimulation methodology. *Neuroscience and Biobehavioral Reviews* 7:45–72.

Markou A & Koob GF (1991). Postcocaine anhedonia: An animal model of cocaine withdrawal. *Neuropsychopharmacology* 4:17–26.

McAuliffe WE & Gordon RA (1974). A test of Lindesmith's theory of addiction: The frequency of euphoria among long-term addicts. *American Journal of Sociology* 79:795–840.

Mello NK (1973). A review of methods to induce alcohol addiction in animals. *Pharmacology, Biochemistry and Behavior* 1:89–101.

Miliaressis E, Rompré PP, Laviolette LP, Philippe L & Coulombe D (1986). The curve-shift paradigm in self stimulation. *Physiology and Behavior* 37:85–91.

Mucha RF & Iversen SD (1984). Reinforcing properties of morphine and naloxone revealed by conditioned place preferences: A procedural examination. *Psychopharmacology* 82:241–247.

Mucha RF, van der Kooy D, O'Shaughnessy M & Bucenieks P (1982). Drug reinforcement studied by the use of place conditioning in rat. *Brain Research* 243:91–105.

Munn E & Wise RA (1992). The effects of escalating doses of d-amphetamine on lateral hypothalamic intracranial self-stimulation. *Society for Neuroscience Abstracts* 18:364.

Noel MB & Wise RA (1995). Ventral tegmental injections of a selective or ? opioid enhance feeding in food-deprived rats. *Brain Research* 673:304–312.

Nestler EJ (1992). Molecular mechanisms of drug addiction. *Journal of Neuroscience* 12:2439–2450.

Parsons LH, Smith AD & Justice JB (1991). Basal extracellular dopamine is decreased in the rat nucleus accumbens during abstinence from chronic cocaine. *Synapse* 9:60–65.

Pavlov IP (1927). *Conditioned Reflexes.* Oxford, England: Oxford University Press.

Pickens R & Thompson T (1971). Characteristics of stimulant reinforcement. In T Thompson & R Pickens (eds.) *Stimulus Properties of Drugs.* New York, NY: Appleton-Century-Crofts, 177–192.

Pothos E, Rada P, Mark GP & Hoebel BG (1991). Chronic morphine increases synaptic dopamine in the nucleus accumbens and naloxone decreases it unless withdrawal is blocked with clonidine. *Brain Research* 566:348–350.

Robbins TW, Watson BA, Gaskin M & Ennis C (1983). Contrasting interactions of pipradrol, d-amphetamine, cocaine, cocaine analogues, apomorphine and other drugs with conditioned reinforcement. *Psychopharmacology* 80:113–119.

Roberts DCS & Richardson NR (1992). Self-administration of psychomotor stimulants using progressive ratio schedules of reinforcement. In A Boulton, G Baker & PH Wu (eds.) *Neuromethods: Animal Models of Drug Addiction.* New York, NY: Humana Press, 233–269.

Rosetti ZL, Melis F, Carboni S & Gessa GL (1991). Marked decrease of extraneuronal dopamine after alcohol withdrawal in rats: Reversal by MK–801. *European Journal of Pharmacology* 200:371–372.

Rossi NA & Reid LD (1976). Affective states associated with morphine injections. *Physiological Psychology* 4:269–274.

Samson HH (1986). Initiation of ethanol reinforcement using a sucrosesubstitution procedure in food- and water-sated rats. *Alcoholism: Clinical & Experimental Research* 10:436–442.

Schneirla TC (1959). An evolutionary and developmental theory of biphasic processes underlying approach and withdrawal. In MR Jones (ed.) *Nebraska Symposium on Motivation.* Lincoln, NE: University of Nebraska Press, 1–42.

Sinclair JD (1974). Rats learning to work for alcohol. *Nature* 249:590–592.

Shaham Y & Stewart, J (1995). Stress reinstates heroin-seeking in drug-free animals: an effect mimicking heroin, not withdrawal. *Psychopharmacology* 119:334–341.

Skinner BF (1938). *The Behavior of Organisms.* New York, NY: Appleton-Century-Crofts.

Solomon RL & Corbit JD (1974). An opponent-process theory of motivation: I. Temporal dynamics of affect. *Psychological Review* 81:119–145.

Spragg SDS (1940). Morphine addiction in chimpanzees. *Comparative Psychology Monographs* 15:1–132.

Stein L & Wise CD (1973). Amphetamine and noradrenergic reward pathways. In E Usdin & SH Snyder (eds.) *Frontiers in Catecholamine Research.* New York, NY: Pergamon Press, 963–968.

Stewart J (1984). Reinstatement of heroin and cocaine self-administration behavior in the rat by intracerebral application of morphine in the ventral tegmental area. *Pharmacology, Biochemistry and Behavior* 20:917–923.

Stewart J & de Wit H (1987). Reinstatement of drug-taking behavior as a method of assessing incentive motivational properties of drugs. In MA Bozarth (ed.) *Methods of Assessing the Reinforcing Properties of Abused Drugs.* New York, NY: Springer Verlag, 211–227.

Stewart J & Wise RA (1992). Reinstatement of heroin self-administration habits: Morphine prompts and naltrexone discourages renewed responding after extinction. *Psychopharmacology* 108:779–84.

Taylor JR & Robbins TW (1984). Enhanced behavioural control by conditioned reinforcers produced by intracerebral injections of d-amphetamine in the rat. *Psychopharmacology* 84:405–412.

Thompson T & Pickens R (1971). *Stimulus Properties of Drugs.* New York, NY: Appleton-Century-Crofts.

Thorndike EL (1898). Animal intelligence: An experimental study of the associative processes in animals. *Psychological Monographs* 8:1–109.

Valenstein ES (1964). Problems of measurement with reinforcing brain stimulation. *Psychological Review* 71:415–437.

van der Kooy D (1987). Place conditioning: A simple and effective method for assessing the motivational properties of drugs. In MA Bozarth (ed.) *Methods for Assessing the Reinforcing Properties of Abused Drugs.* New York, NY: Springer Verlag, 229–240.

Weeks JR (1962). Experimental morphine addiction: Method for automatic intravenous injections in unrestrained rats. *Science* 138:143144.

West TEG & Wise RA (1988). Effects of naltrexone on nucleus accumbens, lateral hypothalamic and ventral tegmental self-stimulation rate/frequency functions. *Brain Research* 462:126–133.

Wikler A (1973). Dynamics of drug dependence: Implications of a conditioning theory for research and treatment. *Archives of General Psychiatry* 28:611–616.

Wise RA (1978). Catecholamine theories of reward: A critical review. *Brain Research* 152:215–247.

Wise RA (1987a). Intravenous drug self-administration: A special case of positive reinforcement. In MA Bozarth (ed.) *Methods of Assessing the Reinforcing Properties of Abused Drugs.* New York, NY: Springer Verlag, 117–141.

Wise RA (1987b). Sensorimotor modulation and the variable action pattern (VAP); Toward a noncircular definition of drive and motivation. *Psychobiology* 15:7–20.

Wise RA (1989). The brain and reward. In JM Liebman & SJ Cooper (eds.) *The Neuropharmacological Basis of Reward.* Oxford, England: Oxford University Press, 377–424.

Wise RA (1996). Addictive drugs and brain stimulation reward. *Annual Review of Neuroscience* 654:192–198.

Wise RA & Bozarth MA (1987). A psychomotor stimulant theory of addiction. *Psychological Review* 94:469–492.

Wise RA, Murray A & Bozarth MA (1990). Bromocriptine self-administration and bromocriptine-reinstatement of cocaine-trained and herointrained lever-pressing in rats. *Psychopharmacology* 100:355–360.

Wise RA & Rompre PP (1989). Brain dopamine and reward. *Annual Review of Psychology* 40:191–225.

Woods JH & Schuster CR (1971). Opiates as reinforcing stimuli. In T Thompson & R Pickens (eds.) *Stimulus Properties of Drugs.* New York, NY: Appleton-Century-Crofts, 163–175.

Woods JH, Ikomi F & Winger G (1971). The reinforcing properties of ethanol. In MK Roach, WM McIsaac & PJ Creaven (eds.) *Biological Aspects of Alcoholism.* Austin, TX: University of Texas Press, 371–388.

Yokel RA & Pickens R (1974). Drug level of *d-* and *l-*amphetamine during intravenous self-administration. *Psychopharmacologia* 34:255–264.

Zigmond MJ, Abercrombie ED, Berger TW, Grace AA & Stricker EM (1990). Compensations after lesions of central dopaminergic neurons: Some clinical and basic implications. *Trends in Neuroscience* 13:290–296.

CHAPTER 4

The Neurochemistry of Addiction

David J. Nutt, Ph.D.

Common Pathways of Drug Action
Individual Factors in Drug Abuse

Addiction is one of the more appealing psychiatric disorders for the psychopharmacologist as it clearly is a disease directly related to pharmacology: drugs are abused specifically because of their actions on brain receptors and neurotransmitters. The sites of actions of most drugs of abuse have become much better understood in the past decade and, with the exception of the solvents, we can construct specific testable hypotheses about the brain neurochemical substrates of most drugs of abuse (see Table 1). This exercise is not merely of scientific interest: it may also have importance for the development of new treatment approaches (see Table 2).

As shown in Table 1, drugs of abuse work through many different mechanisms. Although it is very likely that there is some convergence of action at the level of specific transmitters, this should not be overemphasized to the point that individual targets for the treatment of specific drugs are overlooked.

COMMON PATHWAYS OF DRUG ACTION

Dopamine. Two main mechanisms for convergence of drug action have been identified: dopamine and the endogenous opioid systems. The mesolimbic fronto cortical dopamine system is known to mediate reinforcing actions of various behaviors, such as eating and sex, and much recent work has suggested a clear role in drug abuse. Stimulants such as cocaine release dopamine in both the intermediate way-station of this projection—the nucleus accumbens—and the prefrontal cortex. Similarly reinforcing opioids, such as heroin, increase dopamine release by taking off as GABA-mediated inhibition on the cell bodies in the ventral tegmental area of the brain stem. Alcohol paradoxically also activates the dopamine neurons, perhaps by disinhibiting this inhibition. However, the benzodiazepines do not. The special ability of alcohol to increase dopamine release may explain why it is more euphoric than the benzodiazepines. It is thought that the activating effects of alcohol, as seen on the rising phase of the blood-alcohol curve, could reflect dopamine release. The chronic paranoid state seen in heavy drinkers may reflect dysregulation of the same dopamine system, as can the psychotic sequelae of stimulant use.

A knowledge of the role of dopamine in drug abuse has led to it being targeted for new treatments. One promising approach is to develop drugs which prevent the access of stimulants to their active site. In the case of cocaine this is, at least in part, the dopamine uptake site (transporter). If it were possible to make a drug that bound to a site near to the transporter, it might prevent the binding of cocaine and yet not be addictive itself. Some progress has already been made, in that other dopamine uptake blockers such as GBR can somewhat reduce the reinforcing actions of cocaine, yet have less propensity to be self-administered (an index of abuse liability).

Endogenous Opioids. The brain's endogenous opioid system contains peptides, such as endorphins and enkephalins, that may be reinforcing in themselves. The power of heroin and related opioids to produce addiction is thought to be because they overstimulate this natural pleasure system, and adaptive processes lead to withdrawal and craving that perpetuate drug use.

It is harder to obtain evidence for the release of endogenous opioids than for cocaine, as the opioids are larger molecules that cannot be directly detected by techniques such as HPLC, so brain dialysis studies are very difficult. Most of the evidence for a role of these transmitters comes from indirect measures, especially the ability of antagonists such as naloxone to reduce drug use. As well as blocking the reinforcing actions of the opioids, these drugs will also reduce the self-administration of stimulants and alcohol in animal experiments. Such studies have given the impetus for clinical trials at least in alcoholism, where several well controlled trials have reported it to lead to a better outcome when combined

TABLE 1. Sites of Action of Drugs of Abuse

Drug class	Neurochemical action
Opioids	Agonists at μ opioid receptors
Stimulants	Increase dopamine release
Cocaine	Block dopamine reuptake
Amphetamine	Block dopamine reuptake plus increase dopamine release
Nicotine	Increase dopamine release
Sedatives	
Benzodiazepines	Increase actions of $GABA_A$ receptors
Barbituates	Increase actions of $GABA_A$ receptors plus block EAA receptors
Alcohol(s)	Increase actions of $GABA_A$ receptors plus block EAA receptors
Psychedelics	
LSD-like	? $5\text{-}HT_2$ agonists
Ketamine (angel dust)	EAA block (dissociation)
Cannibis	Cannabinoid receptors
Caffeine	Adenosine receptor blockade

with skilled psychological approaches. The limited data so far suggest that naltrexone acts to reduce the pleasure that a dose of alcohol produces, so a transient lapse to drinking is less likely to progress to a complete relapse. These promising clinical data support some other lines of evidence that alcohol acts to release endogenous opioids.

INDIVIDUAL FACTORS IN DRUG ABUSE

The Role of Efficacy. The concept of pharmacological efficacy is an important one in the addictions. In simple terms, the more a drug does on interacting with its receptor, the greater the efficacy it has. A full agonist has maximal efficacy; antagonists have zero efficacy; and drugs whose efficacy lies in between these extremes are called partial agonists. Generally, the more efficacious the drug, the better it is liked; i.e., the more addictive it is. This is very clear with the opioids, where full agonists such as morphine are preferred to partial agonists such as buprenorphine. Drugs with even greater efficacy than morphine exist: these include fentanyl and derivatives that are called super agonists and are highly sought after by opioid addicts.

Efficacy has a large bearing on the design of new treatments. Maintenance therapy with a full agonist such as methadone is a proven method of treating addiction, the methadone completely substituting for the illicit drug. However, because it is a full agonist, methadone is toxic in overdose, especially if taken by children. Partial agonists are much safer than full agonists, as they will not produce terminal respiratory depression even in overdose. They have other advantages: once in the brain and occupying opioid receptors, they prevent the access of full agonists to these receptors: i.e. act as relative antagonists (hence they are sometimes called agonist/antagonists). If the effect of a dose of agonist such as heroin is blocked, then there is little point in addicts using it, so this behavior begins to extinguish. Antagonists have the same action, but because they can precipitate withdrawal in dependent users and have no pleasurable actions, there is little incentive for addicts to take them. Partial agonists, because they produce some opioid-like actions, are somewhat reinforcing and encourage addicts to stay in a treatment program. If their use can be made compulsory, e.g., on a probation order or under the supervision of a professional body such as the GMC for addicted doctors, then antagonists can be equally effective.

A number of new ideas in opioid antagonist therapy are under investigation. One is the production of a depot injectable naltrexone that might be given under supervision and provide a blockade for perhaps a month. An alternative is a new opioid drug called clocinnamox. This acts as a moderate strength partial agonist (equivalent to codeine), but has a metabolite that appears to be an irreversible antagonist. After an initial experience of pleasure, the drug progressively blocks brain opioid receptors and this action lasts several weeks in primates. It will be interesting to see if this sort of approach is acceptable in the human situation.

Efficacy has a large role to play with other drugs of abuse that are also agonists. Both the benzodiazepines, alcohols such chlormethiazole, and the barbiturates act as agonists at the $GABA_A$ receptor. The alcohols and barbiturates have greater efficacy in increasing the actions of GABA than the benzodiazepines, and this helps explain why they are more abused.

Pharmacokinetic Factors. In addition to drug efficacy, the other main determinant of drug abuse is the rate of brain entry. The faster a reinforcing drug reaches the brain, the more dependence it will produce. Much of the history of drug abuse has been about ways of accelerating the rate of getting drugs into the brain. With cocaine, this has taken the form of refining it from a chewed leaf, which appears to have little euphoriant actions but will provide relief

TABLE 2. Neurochemical Pointers to New Treatments

Opioids	Partial agonists (e.g. buprenophine) Irreversible antagoinists (clocinnamox) G-protein modifiers (P-kinase activators)
Stimulants	
Cocaine	Dopamine reuptake blockers
Amphetamine	Synaptic vesicle stabilizers
Nicotine	Antagonists (mecamylamine) ? full agonists (depolarizing block) ? 5-HT uptake blockers
Sedatives	
Benzodiazepines	Partial agonists, antagonists
Barbituates	Partial agonists, ? EAA modulators
Alcohol(s)	GABA/EAA drugs, e.g. acamprosate Opioid antagonists, e.g. naltrexone 5-HT agonists, e.g. buspirone
Psychedelics	
LSD-like	? 5-HT_2 antagonists
Ketamine (angel dust)	EAA modulators
Cannabis	Cannaboid receptor antagonists
Caffeine	? not required

from mental and physical exhaustion, through a hydrochloride salt that can be inhaled nasally, to a "free base" version (crack) that is more lipophilic and so can be smoked. Of course, both the refined forms can be taken intravenously, although this route is barely faster than smoking as the lungs have such a huge surface area for absorption.

Similar developments have occurred with the opioids: heroin has similar efficacy to morphine, yet is preferred by addicts. The explanation lies in the chemical structure of heroin, which is a diacetylated derivative of morphine. These two substitutions make heroin more lipophilic and so it enters the brain more readily, faster entry giving a better high.

The benzodiazepines in clinical practice all have similar efficacy at the GABA receptor, yet some like diazepam are much more abused than others such as oxazepam. Again, pharmacokinetic factors give the reason. The most liked drugs (diazepam, alprazolam, lorazepam) all have much faster brain entry than the least-liked drugs (oxazepam, chlordiazepoxide). In recent years, both antagonists (e.g., flumazenil) and partial agonists (e.g., bretazenil) at the benzodiazepine receptor have become available. It is conceivable that either class of ligand might be useful in the treatment of benzodiazepine abuse, especially the intravenous injection of temazepam, which is prevalent in certain parts of the U.K. Currently, the only practicable therapeutic drug approach is to prescribe a low abuse benzodiazepine such as chlordiazepoxide.

Prodrugs. These are drugs that require metabolic conversion to the active compound, usually by the liver. This slows their brain entry and so reduces abuse potential. In the case of the benzodiazepines, there are a number of pro-drugs of desmethyldiazepam, such as chlorazepate, that have little street value. LAAM is a prodrug of a methadone derivative that is also available for the treatment of opioid addiction. Of particular interest is the fact that as it requires several hours for effective levels of the active constituent to be formed. LAAM has very little intravenous abuse potential, which should help to reduce the spread of AIDS.

Multiple Sites of Action of Alcohol. Although some drugs, such as the opioids and benzodiazepines, have selective actions on a single receptor, others are less specific. For instance, the barbiturates block excitatory amino acid receptors in addition to potentiating GABA. Cocaine has local anaesthetic as well as dopamine uptake blocking properties. Alcohol (ethanol) is probably the most non-selective of all. Despite this, there is growing evidence that different actions of alcohol are mediated relatively selectively (Table 3). Some actions, such as the release of endogenous opioids, have been discussed already; the other theories are described below.

The ability of alcohol to activate and energize, which is seen predominantly on the rising phase of the blood concentration curve, is thought to be caused by a release of dopamine and/or noradrenaline. Microdialysis studies in animals have shown alcohol increases the levels of both monoamines in the brain. Moreover, in humans this action of alcohol is blocked by depleting these transmitters with the synthesis inhibitor *x*-methyl para tyrosine.

GABA is the main inhibitory transmitter in the brain and is intimately involved in the control of anxiety, as drugs which increase its action (e.g., benzodiazepine and barbiturates) are rapidly acting anxiolytics. Ethanol acts to increase the actions of GABA at low concentrations and then appears directly to mimic the actions of GABA as concentrations rise. The molecular basis of the potentiation of the actions of alcohol has now been worked out and shown to reside in a serine residue in the third intracellular loop of the gamma-2 subunit. When this

TABLE 3. Multiple Mechanisms of Action of Ethanol

Experience	Transmitter
Activation	↑ Noradrenaline: ↑ dopamine
Euphoria	↑ Dopamine: ↑ opioids
Anxiolysis/ataxia	↑ GABA
Sedation/amnesia	↑ GABA + ↓ NMDA
Nausea	Stimulation 5-HT_3 receptors
Withdrawal	↑ Calcium flux:
	↑ L-type channels; ↑ NMDA receptors
	↓ Magnesium
	↓ x-2-adrenoceptor inhibition

is phosphorylated, alcohol can increase the actions of GABA. When this is dephosphorylated or absent (as is found with the short form of the subunit that is missing eight amino acids, including the serine), then alcohol does not enhance GABA and only displays its high concentration action.

In addition to potentiating the actions of the main inhibitory transmitter GABA, alcohol also inhibits the action of the main excitatory transmitter, glutamate. This is the primary sensory transmitter that is responsible for fast interneuronal signalling through activation of AMPA receptors and the laying down of memories through NMDA receptor stimulation. Both these receptors are linked to cation channels and the NMDA one has a very high conductance of calcium ions once open. Appropriate entry of calcium through this channel leads to secondary changes that produce the permanent alterations in neuronal connectivity that we call memory. Excessive influx of calcium ions through this channel leads to cell damage and excitotoxic cell death. Because it is so important, this ion channel is normally kept blocked by a magnesium ion that only leaves the channel when the neuron is highly depolarized. Alcoholics are in a state of severe magnesium depletion and so are relatively deficient in this natural inhibitory factor. This deficit is not apparent when the brain is intoxicated, as alcohol acts to non-competitively block the channel itself. However, during withdrawal, the inhibitory deficiency leads to a hyperexcitable state associated with anxiety and seizures.

The situation in withdrawal is made worse by the adaptive changes that occur in the brain as a consequence of intoxication. As alcohol blocks NMDA-mediated calcium flux, neurons attempt to compensate by increasing both the number of NMDA receptors and the number of another type of calcium channel, the L-type. This means that in withdrawal from alcohol, there is an excess of calcium influx into cells. As alcoholics are commonly in withdrawal on a daily basis, there is a cumulative insult and it is thought that this leads to the neuronal death that characterizes alcoholic dementia. Although NMDA antagonists are at present too new to be considered as potential prophylactic treatments of this state, L-type channel blockers such as nifedipine have been around for years in cardiovascular medicine. As preclinical studies have shown them to be effective against alcohol withdrawal in rodents, perhaps they could be tried in humans.

The NMDA receptor complex may also have a role in the learning of conditioned responses to drugs of abuse, including alcohol. Acamprosate is a new agent for the treatment of alcoholism that has just been licensed in the U.K., although it has been used in France for a number of years. Although its mechanism of action is not yet fully clarified, acamprosate appears to, in part, act at a modulatory site on the NMDA receptor. This may explain its perceived clinical action to reduce craving for alcohol and so improve the long-term outcome of abstinence.

The nausea-inducing actions of alcohol are well known. Recent electrophysiological studies have shown that alcohol acts as an agonist at the 5-HT_3 subtype of 5-HT receptors. This is an ion-channel-linked receptor that is found in very high densities on the vagus nerve. When stimulated by 5-HT, nausea is produced that can be blocked by antagonists of the receptor, such as ondansetron. There is some preliminary evidence that this drug, which is used to treat cytotoxic-induced nausea, may reduce that produced by alcohol, although its great expense means it is unlikely to become commonly used.

ACKNOWLEDGMENT: Originally published as Nutt DJ (1997). The neurochemistry of addiction. Human Psychopharmacology *12:S53–S58. Reprinted by permission of the publisher.*

REFERENCES

Aceto M-D, Bowman E-R, May EL, Harris LS, Woods JH, Smith CB, Medzihradsky R & Jacobson AE (1989). Very long-acting narcotic antagonists: The 14B-p-substituted cinnamolylamino-morphinones and their partial mu agonist codeinone relatives. *Arzneimittel-Forschung: Drug Research* 39:570–575.

Blaine JD, Renault PR, Thomas DB & Whysner JA (1981). Clinical status of methadyl acetate (LAAM). *Annals of the New York Academy of Sciences* 362:101–115.

Collingridge GL (1987). NMDA receptors—Their role in long-term potentiation. *Trends in Neurological Science* 10:288–293.

DiChiara G (1995). The role of dopamine in drug abuse viewed from the perspective of its role in motivation. *Drug and Alcohol Dependence* 38:95–137.

Farrell M, Ward J, Mattick R, Hall W, Stimson GV, Jarlais D, Gossop M & Strang J (1994). Methadone maintenance treatment in opiate dependence: A review. *British Medical Journal* 309:997–1001.

Follesa P & Ticku MK (1996). Chronic ethanol-mediated up-regulation of the N-methyl-D-aspartate receptor polypeptide subunits in mouse cortical neurons in culture. *Journal of Biological Chemistry* 271:13297–13299.

Griffiths RR, McLeod DR, Bigelow GE, Liebson I & Roache JD (1994). Relative abuse liability of idazepam and oxazepam: Behavioural and subjective dose effects. *Psychopharmacology* 84:147–154.

Jasinski DR, Pevnick JS & Griffith JD (1978). Human pharmacology and abuse potential of the analgesic buprenorphine. *Archives of General Psychiatry* 35:501–516.

Johnson RE, Cone EJ, Henningfield JE & Fudala PJ (1989). Use of buprenorphine in the treatment of opiate addiction. 1. Physiologic and behavioral effects during a rapid dose induction. *Clinical Pharmacology and Therapeutics* 46:335–343.

Littleton J (1995). Acamprosate in alcohol dependence: How does it work? *Addiction* 90:1179–1188.

Littleton JM & Little HJ (1988). Dihydropyridine-sensitive Ca channels in the brain are involved in the central nervous system hyper-excitability associated with alcohol withdrawal states. *Annals of the New York Academy of Sciences* 522:199–202.

Malizia AL & Nutt DJ (1995). The effects of flumazenil in neuropsychiatric disorders. *Clinical Neuropharmacology* 18:215–232.

Nutt DJ (1996). Addiction: Brain mechanisms and their treatment implications. *Lancet* 347:31–36.

O'Malley SS, Jaffe AJ, Chang G, Schottenfeld RS, Meyer RE & Rounsaville B (1993). Naltrexone and coping skills therapy for alcohol dependence: A controlled study. *Archives of General Psychiatry* 49(11):881–887.

Potokar J & Nutt DJ (1994). Anxiolytic potential of benzodiazepine receptor partial agonists. *CNS Drugs* 1:305–315.

Rothman RB & Mele J (1991). GBR12909 antagonizes the ability of cocaine to elevate extracellular levels of dopamine. *Pharmacology, Biochemistry and Behavior* 40:187–397.

Shimada S & Kitayama S (1992). Cloning and expression of a cocaine-sensitive dopamine transporter complementary DNA. *Science* 254:576–578.

Ticku MK, Lowrimore P & Lehoullier P (1986). Ethanol enhances GABA-induced 36-Cl-influx in primary spinal cord cultured neurons. *Brain Research Bulletin* 17:123–126.

Ulm RR, Volpicelli JR & Volpicelli LA (1995). Opiates and alcohol self-administration in animals. *Journal of Clinical Psychiatry* 56:5–14.

Volpicelli JR, Alterman AI, Hayashida M & O'Brien CP (1993). Naltrexone in the treatment of alcohol dependence. *Archives of General Psychiatry* 49(11):876–880.

Wafford KA, Burnett DM, Leidenheimer NJ, Burt DR, Wang JB, Kofuji P, Dunwiddie TV, Harris RA & Sikela JM (1991). Ethanol sensitivity of the $GABA_A$ receptor expressed in *Xenopus* oocytes requires 8 amino acids contained in the y2l subunit. *Neuron* 7:27–33.

Weight FF, Peoples RW, Wright JM, Lovinger DM & White G (1993). Ethanol action on excitatory amino acid activated ion channels. In PV Taberner & AAB Badawy (eds.) *Advances in Biochemical Alcoholism Research.* Oxford, England: Pergamon Press.

Whittington MA & Little HJ (1989). Nifedipine prevents the ethanol withdrawal syndrome when administered chronically with ethanol prior to withdrawal. *British Journal of Clinical Pharmacology* 93:385P.

Wolfe SM & Victor M (1969). The relationship of hypomagnesaemia and alkalosis to alcohol withdrawal symptoms. *Annals of the New York Academy of Science* 162:973–984.

CHAPTER 5

Neuroadaptation in Addiction

Eric J. Nestler, M.D., Ph.D.

Neurobiological Context for Drug-Induced Adaptations
Upregulation of the cAMP Pathway: A Model of Neuroadaptation
Adaptations in Neurotransmitters and Receptors
Adaptations in Other Intracellular Messenger Pathways
Adaptations in Gene Expression
Adaptations in Neuronal Morphology and Survival
Future Directions

Drug addiction is a complex phenomenon with important psychosocial causes and consequences. However, at its core, addiction is a biological phenomenon: it is caused by changes that chronic exposure to a biological agent (a drug) produces in a vulnerable physical substrate (the brain). While a complete understanding of addiction will eventually require an appreciation of the ways in which environmental factors (for example, stress) and an individual's genetic composition modify the ability of a drug to influence the brain, a critical step remains the identification of the precise molecular and cellular adaptations that drugs produce in specific neurons to cause the complex behaviors that define an addicted state (Nestler & Aghajanian, 1997).

When a drug of abuse enters the brain, it acts initially on a specific target protein, which, in turn, influences the functioning of neurons that express that protein. The acute protein targets of most of drugs of abuse have by now been very well characterized (Koob & Nestler, 1997) and are covered elsewhere in this text. This chapter focuses on the effects that a drug of abuse exerts on the brain after repeated exposure, which is required to elicit most aspects of addiction.

The working hypothesis advanced in this chapter is that the chronic actions of a drug of abuse on the brain represent adaptations lo the repeated or persistent challenge of the drug's acute effects. As will be seen, many types of adaptation have been identified. Some can be viewed as classical negative feedback (i.e., tolerance), in that the adaptations oppose the acute effects of the drug. Others can be viewed as positive feedback (i.e., sensitization), in that the adaptations lead to sensitized responses to the drug. Still others mediate dependence and withdrawal, in that they underlie an altered physiological state, which leads to a withdrawal syndrome upon cessation of drug exposure.

While examples of each of these adaptations have been identified, critical challenges remain. First, from a clinical perspective, it is not clear which type(s) of adaptation (tolerance, sensitization, or dependence) is the most important contributor to the core clinical features of an addictive disorder (Koob & Nestler, 1997). This question is addressed in other chapters of this text. Second, from a basic neuroscience perspective, it remains difficult to relate adaptations at the molecular and cellular level to behavioral features of addiction. Nevertheless, as will be seen, recent advances in molecular biology (e.g., transgenic, viral vector, antisense oligonucleotide methods) have greatly facilitated this effort. Third, while considerable progress has been made in identifying adaptations that mediate relatively transient aspects of addiction, much less is known about the particularly long-lived adaptations that mediate long-term aspects of addiction, such as drug craving and increased risk for relapse, which can last a lifetime.

NEUROBIOLOGICAL CONTEXT FOR DRUG-INDUCED ADAPTATIONS

Before discussing chronic adaptations to drugs of abuse, a brief overview of the brain's signal transduction pathways will be presented. The classical view of synaptic transmission is that neurotransmitter is released from nerve terminals, in response to a nerve impulse, and then diffuses across the synapse to activate receptor proteins present on the postsynaptic neuron. Such neurotransmitter-receptor activation leads to increases or decreases in the activity of specific ion channels, which either promotes or attenuates the production of nerve impulses in that postsynaptic neuron.

A more complete view of synaptic transmission has been obtained over the past two decades (see Figure 1) (Hyman & Nestler, 1993; Nestler & Greengard, 1994). It is now known that neurotransmitter-receptor activation leads to many more complex effects on the postsynaptic neuron than simply altering ion channel conductance. Thus, virtually every process in a neuron is influenced by a neurotransmitter-receptor signal: this includes changes in the activity of the same or different receptors, in the ability of the neuron to synthesize its own neurotransmitter, and in the neuron's general metabolic activity. Repeated or persistent neurotransmitter-receptor activation also begins to alter more long-term processes, such as gene transcription and protein synthesis. For example, under such conditions, there can be changes in the actual amounts of receptors, channels, neurotransmitter synthetic enzymes, etc. in the postsynaptic neuron.

It is now known that these myriad effects of neurotransmitters (which are viewed as "first messengers") on target neurons are mediated via complex cascades of intracellular messengers, as depicted in Figure 1. These include G proteins, guanine nucleotide binding proteins, that couple receptors (which are associated with the cell membrane) to intracellular processes. Regulation of G proteins then directly affects ion channels as well as the levels of so-called "second messengers" in the target neuron. Prominent second messengers in brain include cAMP, Ca^{2+}, nitric oxide, and the metabolites of phosphatidylinositol (e.g., inositol triphosphate) and arachidonic acid (e.g., prostaglandins). In most cases, altered levels of a second messenger lead to biological responses via changes in protein phosphorylation, a process wherein an enzyme called a protein kinase adds a phosphate group to a specific amino acid residue of a substrate protein and a protein phosphatase removes such phosphate groups. Both protein kinases and protein phosphatases are regulated by second messengers. Because phosphate groups are bulky and highly charged, their addition or removal alters a protein's functional activity. Neurotransmitter-receptor interactions, through the regulation of the phosphorylation state of virtually all types of neuronal protein, account for the diverse physiological responses in target neurons. For example, phosphorylation of receptors alters their ability to be activated by neurotransmitters; phosphorylation of ion channels alters their conductance; phosphorylation of neurotransmitter synthetic enzymes alters their catalytic activity; phosphorylation of ribosomal proteins alters protein synthesis; phosphorylation of transcription factors alters gene expression. Protein phosphorylation can thus be viewed as the major molecular currency underlying signal transduction in the brain.

The other major advance in brain signal transduction in recent years is the appreciation of the role of neurotrophic (or growth) factors. These factors were first characterized for the important role they play in the growth and differentiation of neurons during development (Ip & Yancopoulos, 1996). However, we now know that the factors also play a critical role in the adult brain by regulating the survival of neurons, the maintenance of their differentiated properties, the number and types of synaptic connections they form, and their processes of signal transduction. Thus, the distinction between neurotransmitters and neurotrophic factors has become increasingly arbitrary with respect to their effects on target neurons. Neurotrophic factors also produce most of their effects on the brain via the regulation of protein phosphorylation pathways (Figure 1).

It is in this context, then, that one can begin to formulate the neurobiological basis of adaptations to chronic drug exposure. All drugs of abuse interact initially with a protein located at the extracellular aspect of a synapse (for example, opiates are opioid receptor agonists; cocaine inhibits monoamine reuptake proteins, etc.). However, despite these initial extracellular actions, the many effects that a drug of abuse exerts on the brain, even after an acute exposure, are achieved ultimately via perturbation of intracellular messenger pathways that mediate these extracellular mechanisms. This means that repeated exposure to a drug of abuse leads to repeated or persistent perturbation of these pathways. It is hypothesized that such repeated perturbation triggers neuroadaptive responses in the same and other signaling pathways that gradually accumulate to cause the behavioral abnormalities that characterize addiction.

UPREGULATION OF THE cAMP PATHWAY: A MODEL OF NEUROADAPTATION

The best established adaptation to chronic drug exposure is upregulation of the cAMP pathway, a phenomenon first discovered in cultured neuroblastoma x glioma cells (Sharma, Klee & Nirenberg, 1975) and later demonstrated in neurons (Nestler, Hope &

FIGURE 1. A Working Model of Synaptic Transmission

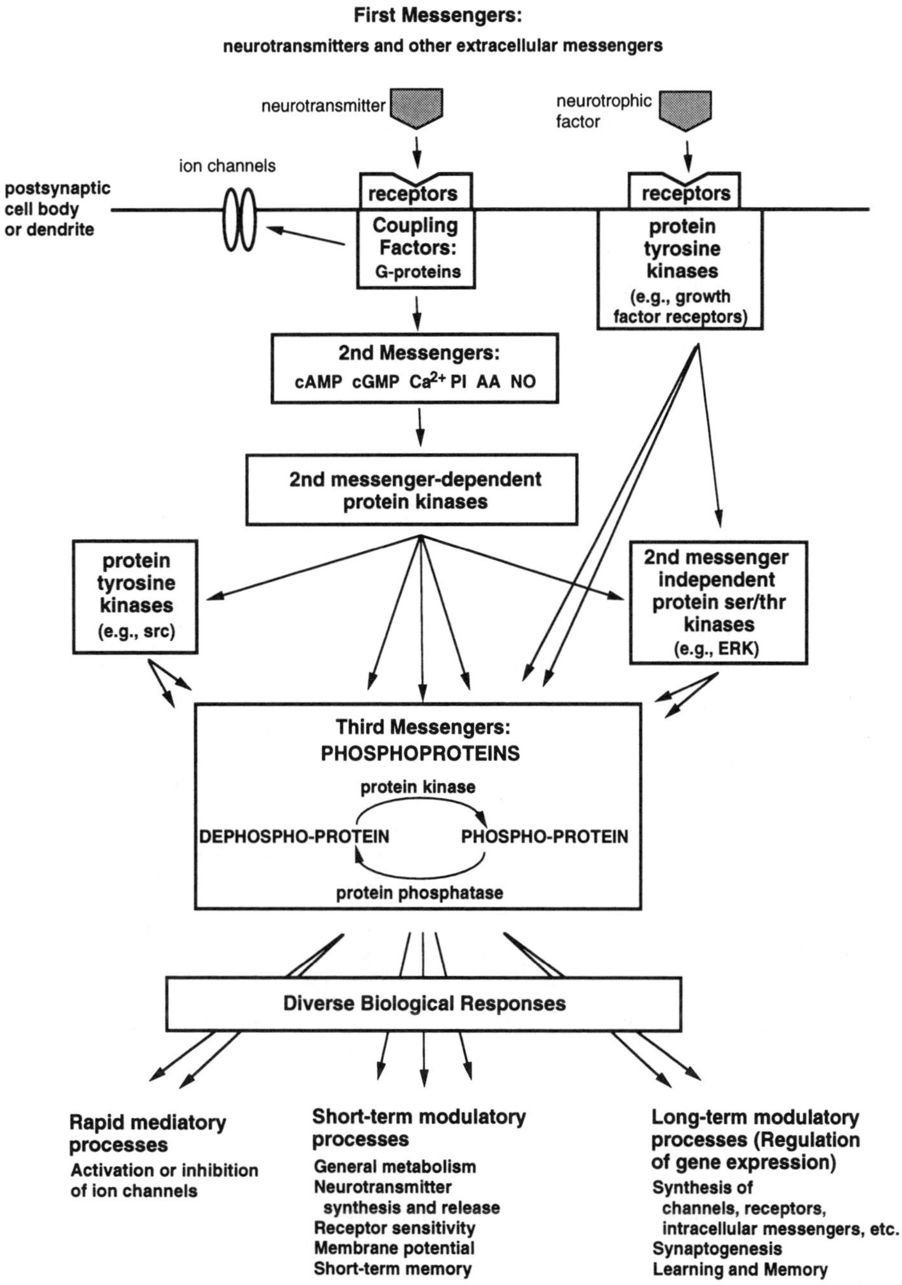

Signal transduction in the brain is mediated via complex cascades of intracellular messengers, involving coupling factors (termed G proteins), second messengers (e.g., cAMP, calcium, nitric oxide, and the metabolites of phosphatidylinositol), and protein phosphorylation (involving the phosphorylation of phosphoproteins by protein kinases and their dephosphorylation by protein phosphatases), in mediating multiple actions of neurotransmitters on their target neurons. Second messenger-dependent protein kinases (e.g., those activated by cAMP or calcium) are classified as protein serine/threonine kinases, since they phosphorylate substrate proteins on serine or threonine residues. Each protein kinase phosphorylates a specific array of substrate proteins and thereby leads to multiple biological responses of the neurotransmitter.

Brain also contains many important intracellular regulatory pathways in addition to those regulated directly by G proteins and second messengers. This includes numerous protein serine/threonine kinases (e.g., the ERKs or MAP kinases), as well as numerous protein tyrosine kinases (which phosphorylate substrate proteins on tyrosine residues), some of which reside in the receptors for neurotrophins and most other growth factors (e.g., the trk proteins), and others that are not associated with growth factor receptors (e.g., src kinase). Each of these various protein kinases are highly regulated by extracellular stimuli. The brain also contains numerous types of protein serine/threonine and protein tyrosine phosphatases, not shown in the Figure, which are also subject to regulation by extracellular and intracellular stimuli.

Widnell, 1993) after chronic administration of opiates. Whereas acute opiate exposure inhibits the cAMP pathway in many types of neurons in the brain (Childers, 1991), chronic opiate exposure leads to a compensatory upregulation of the cAMP pathway in at least a subset of these neurons. This upregulation involves increased levels of adenylyl cyclase, cAMP-dependent protein kinase (protein kinase A), and perhaps other components of this signaling pathway. Upregulation of the cAMP pathway would oppose acute opiate inhibition of the pathway, which would represent a form of tolerance; upon removal of the opiate, the upregulated cAMP pathway would become fully functional and contribute to features of withdrawal (Nestler, Hope & Widnell, 1993).

There is now direct evidence to support this model in neurons of the locus coeruleus (Figure 2), the major noradrenergic nucleus in brain, which have been implicated in opiate physical dependence and somatic symptoms of opiate withdrawal (Koob, Maldonado & Stinus, 1992; Maldonado, 1997). Upregulation of the cAMP pathway in the locus coeruleus appears to increase the intrinsic firing rate of the neurons via activation of a non-selective cation channel (Nestler & Aghajanian, 1997). This increased firing has been related to specific opiate withdrawal behaviors. Increased locus coeruleus activity during withdrawal also is due to increased glutamatergic activation of the neurons (Rasmussen & Aghajanian, 1989; Akaoka & Aston-Jones, 1991). This may be mediated in part via an upregulated cAMP pathway in primary sensory neurons (Crain & Shen, 1996), which would contribute to activation of ascending excitatory inputs to the locus coeruleus. While there has been some debate about the degree to which the locus coeruleus contributes to the overall opiate withdrawal syndrome (Christie, Williams & Osborne, 1997), its cellular and neurochemical homogeneity makes it a useful model system to delineate the precise molecular and cellular mechanisms underlying neuronal adaptations to chronic drug exposure.

Indeed, upregulation of the cAMP pathway also occurs in brain regions implicated in the motivational aspects of drug addiction. For example, chronic administration of opiates, cocaine, or alcohol increases levels of adenylyl cyclase and of protein kinase A in neurons of the nucleus accumbens (Ortiz, Fitzgerald et al., 1995; Unterwald, Fillmore & Kreek, 1995; Schoffelmeer, Voom et al., 1996). However, it remains unclear which of several cell types within this region express this adaptation. The nucleus accumbens, part of the mesolimbic dopamine system, has been implicated in the reinforcing actions of most drugs of abuse (Koob, 1996; Wise, 1996). Upregulation of the cAMP pathway could account for adaptations in the electrophysiological properties observed in these neurons after chronic cocaine (or other stimulant) exposure. Thus, there is an increase in the functional responsiveness of nucleus accumbens neurons to D_1 dopamine receptor activation (Henry & White, 1995). D_1 receptors are thought to produce their physiological effects via coupling with Gs (stimulatory G protein) and activation of the cAMP pathway, and the stimulant-induced supersensitivity to receptor activation occurs

FIGURE 2. Scheme Illustrating Opiate Actions in the LC

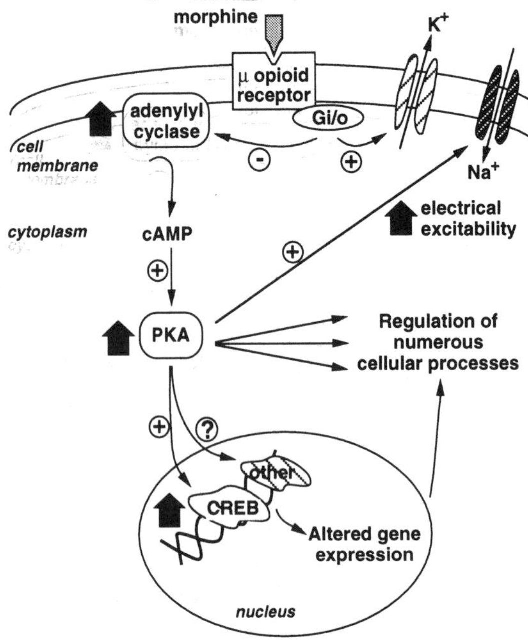

Opiates acutely inhibit LC neurons by increasing the conductance of a K+ channel (light cross-hatch) via coupling with subtypes of Gi and/or Go, and by decreasing a Na+-dependent inward current (dark cross-hatch) via coupling with Gi/o and the consequent inhibition of adenylyl cyclase. Reduced levels of cAMP decrease PKA activity and the phosphorylation of the responsible channel or pump. Inhibition of the cAMP pathway also decreases phosphorylation of numerous other proteins and thereby affects many additional processes in the neuron. For example, it reduces the phosphorylation state of CREB, which may initiate some of the longer-term changes in LC function. *Upward bold ar-rows summarize effects of chronic morphine in the LC.* Chronic morphine increases levels of adenylyl cyclase, PKA, and several phosphoproteins, including CREB. These changes contribute to the altered phenotype of the drug-addicted state. For example, the intrinsic excitability of LC neurons is increased via enhanced activity of the cAMP pathway and Na:+-dependent inward current, which contributes to the tolerance, dependence, and withdrawal exhibited by these neurons. This altered phenotypic state may be maintained in part by upregulation of CREB expression. From Nestler EJ (1996). Under siege: the brain on opiates. *Neuron* 16:897–900.

in the absence of detectable changes in the dopamine receptors themselves. The upregulated cAMP pathway appears to alter the excitability of nucleus accumbens neurons via protein kinase A-mediated phosphorylation of voltage-gated Na^+ and perhaps other ion channels (Zhang, Hu & White, 1998).

Recent work has directly related upregulation of the cAMP pathway in the nucleus accumbens to behavioral aspects of drug action. One current hypothesis, based in part on self-administration studies, is that the upregulated cAMP pathway impairs drug reinforcement mechanisms (tolerance) and contributes to an aversive state during withdrawal (dependence) (Self & Nestler, 1995; Valverde, Tzavara et al., 1996; Self, Genova et al., 1998). However, there is evidence supporting the opposite view using the behavioral paradigm of conditioned reinforcement (Kelley & Holahan, 1997). There also is evidence that an upregulated cAMP pathway may underlie sensitization to the locomotor-activating effects of stimulants (Cunningham & Kelley, 1993; Miserendino & Nestler, 1995). These findings highlight the difficulty in relating a molecular adaptation to behavior, and also the need to utilize multiple behavioral paradigms when addressing this question. The findings also indicate that a single molecular adaptation within one discrete brain region could conceivably contribute simultaneously to aspects of tolerance, sensitization, and dependence.

A role for the cAMP pathway in the chronic actions of opiates or cocaine has been proposed for other discrete regions of the central nervous system, specifically, the ventral tegmental area, periaqueductal gray, and amygdala (Maldonado, Valverde et al., 1995; Tolliver, Ho et al., 1996; Bonci & Williams, 1997; Jolas & Aghajanian, 1997a, 1997b; Punch, Self et al., 1997). Efforts are now underway to better characterize these adaptations and to relate them to specific behavioral aspects of drug action.

ADAPTATIONS IN NEUROTRANSMITTERS AND RECEPTORS

There is a large literature of changes in the levels or activity of several neurotransmitters and their receptors after chronic administration of drugs of abuse. This literature is summarized elsewhere (Kuhar & Pilotte, 1996; Koob, 1996; Wise, 1996) and will not be reviewed here in detail. One limiting feature of this literature is that, in most cases, adaptations in a specific neurotransmitter or receptor have not been related to specific behavioral aspects of drug addiction. Another limiting feature with respect to altered levels of neurotransmitters is the relative lack of insight concerning the molecular and cellular basis of such adaptations. Thus, demonstration of a change in the level of a specific neurotransmitter after a course of drug treatment, for example, by in vivo microdialysis, leaves unanswered the more fundamental question: By what mechanism does this change occur? Such a change could be mediated via altered synthesis, release, reuptake, or breakdown of that neurotransmitter, and would be influenced by the neuronal activity of a host of neuronal cell bodies and terminals within the affected brain region. A major goal of current research is to obtain such mechanistic information, which is now becoming available for certain neurotransmitter-receptor systems.

Adaptations in Dopaminergic Neurotransmission. Given the prominent role of the mesolimbic dopamine system in drug reinforcement, one likely target of adaptations to chronic drug exposure is dopaminergic transmission. Indeed, the most widely cited mechanism of sensitization is enhanced activity of the mesolimbic dopamine system as a consequence of prior drug exposure (Kalivas & Stewart, 1991; Robinson & Berridge, 1993). This could be mediated presynaptically by increased firing of mesolimbic ventral tegmental area dopamine neurons or increased dopamine release from the terminals of these neurons located in the nucleus accumbens and related limbic brain structures. The former has been observed directly by electrophysiological means and could be related to subsensitivity of the neurons' inhibitory D_2-like dopamine autoreceptors (White, Hu et al., 1995). It also could be due to enhanced responsiveness of the neurons to glutamate, as will be discussed below.

Despite this evidence for enhanced dopaminergic transmission after chronic drug exposure, there is growing evidence that during early phases of withdrawal there is a transient reduction in extracellular levels of dopamine in the nucleus accumbens (Kuhar & Pilotte, 1996, Koob, 1996; Wise, 1996). This has been related to the dysphoria or aversion seen during early withdrawal states. These observed changes in dopaminergic transmission highlight the importance of taking into consideration the complex temporal characteristics of any adaptation to drug exposure.

Insight into the molecular basis of alterations in dopamine nerve terminal function as a consequence of drug exposure has remained elusive. This is due in part to the technical difficulty in studying molecular adaptations that might occur selectively within dopaminergic nerve terminals. One possibility is that alterations in dopamine release reflect changes in dopamine cell bodies in the ventral tegmental area. For example, these cell bodies show higher levels of tyrosine hydroxylase, the rate-limiting enzyme in the synthesis of dopamine, after chronic administration of opiates, cocaine, or alcohol (Beitner-Johnson & Nestler, 1991; Sorg, Chen & Kalivas, 1993; Vrana, Vrana et al., 1993). Another possibility is that chronic drug exposure alters levels of expression of the dopamine transporter, the direct target for cocaine and related stimulants, on the nerve terminals. Indeed, alterations in transporter levels have been observed in laboratory animals and people (Cerruti, Pilotte et al., 1993; Malison, Best et al., 1995; Kuhar & Pilotte, 1996; Maggos, Spangler et al., 1997; Volkow, Wang et al., 1996). In addition, mice lacking the dopamine transporter show elevated locomotor activity at baseline and reduced responses to cocaine administration (Giros, Jaber et al., 1996). Still another possibility is that alterations in dopamine release occur at a neural systems level due to altered activation of dopamine terminals by other neural (e.g., glutamatergic) inputs, although this model does not specify the cell types in which molecular adaptations occur to drive such alterations in neurotransmission.

Increased dopaminergic transmission to the nucleus accumbens could also be mediated via increased responsiveness of the neurons to the inhibitory effects of dopamine. This has been observed directly for stimulants, which produce a functional supersensitivity to D1 dopamine receptor activation (Henry & White, 1995). As mentioned above, this supersensitivity appears to be mediated at least in part via upregulation of the cAMP pathway in these neurons, and the subsequent phosphorylation of voltage-gated ion channels. Enhanced inhibitory responses would be further exaggerated by reductions in responsiveness of the neurons to glutamate (see below).

Adaptations in Glutamatergic Neurotransmission. Given the prominent role of glutamatergic neurotransmission in processes of neural plasticity in general (Lisman, Malenka et al., 1997), this, too, is a likely target for adaptations to drugs of abuse. Indeed, alterations in the glutamate system have been observed for both the ventral tegmental area and nucleus accumbens. In the former, there is enhanced responsiveness of dopamine neurons to the activation of AMPA glutamate receptors (White, Hu et al., 1995). This could be mediated by increased expression of specific AMPA receptor subunits in ventral tegmental area neurons observed in response to chronic opiate, cocaine, or alcohol exposure (Fitzgerald, Ortiz et al., 1996). This adaptation could contribute to heightened activity of the mesolimbic dopamine system and, perhaps, drug sensitization. Direct support for this possibility comes from a recent study in which overexpression of specific AMPA receptor subunits selectively within ventral tegmental area neurons, achieved by viral-mediated gene transfer, sensitizes animals to the locomotor-activating and reinforcing effects of morphine (Carlezon, Boundy et al., 1997).

Adaptations in glutamatergic transmission also have been demonstrated in the nucleus accumbens. Here, decreased levels of AMPA and other glutamate receptor subunits have been observed after chronic stimulant exposure (Lu, Chen et al., 1997). This adaptation could contribute to the reduced responsiveness of nucleus accumbens neurons to glutamate, as mentioned earlier (White, Hu et al., 1995; Zhang, Hu et al., 1997).

In addition to changes in neuronal responsiveness to glutamate with chronic drug administration, there are also likely to be changes in the activity of glutamatergic neurons themselves. Glutamatergic neurons in the prefrontal cortex and related limbic cortical regions, as well as in the amygdala, are thought to provide the major excitatory inputs to ventral tegmental area dopaminergic neurons and to their targets in the nucleus accumbens (see Kalivas, 1995). Adaptations in these glutamatergic neurons have, in general, been difficult to demonstrate. This may be due in part to the cellular heterogeneity of these regions, such that adaptations that occur in subpopulations of neurons are not detectable by biochemical means. It also is striking that the effect of chronic drug administration on the electrophysiological properties of neurons in these brain regions are virtually completely unexplored. This represents one of the greatest challenges for future research, since it is likely that cerebral cortex, amygdala, and other limbic structures (e.g., septum, hippocampus) play an important role in the cognitive and affective components of an addicted state.

A role for glutamatergic transmission in drug addiction is supported also by numerous reports that chronic coadministration of glutamate receptor antagonists—particularly NMDA receptor antagonists—can attenuate the development of tolerance to the analgesic effects of opiates as well as of locomotor sensitization to several drugs of abuse (e.g., see Jeziorski, White & Wolf, 1994; Trujillo & Akil, 1994; Kalivas, 1995). Pharmacological inhibitors or antisense oligonucleotide-induced reductions of nitric oxide synthase have been shown to produce similar effects (Kolesnikov, Pan et al., 1997). This enzyme is known to generate a nitric oxide signal in response to NMDA receptor activation, which has been proposed to mediate some of the physiological effects of the receptor. However, interactions between NMDA receptor antagonists and drugs of abuse would appear to be more complex than the former simply blocking the latter. Like opiates, cocaine, and other drugs of abuse, NMDA antagonists (including phencyclidine [PCP] and MK-801) have powerful stimulant and reinforcing actions of their own (indeed, these drugs are abused by humans), and can potentiate the activating and reinforcing effects of drugs of abuse (see Carlezon & Wise, 1996; Vanderschuren, Schoffelmeer et al., 1998). These findings raise the caution that chronic coadministration of NMDA receptor antagonists could conceivably make certain drugs more addictive, regardless of their effects on analgesic tolerance and locomotor sensitization. Clearly, more work is needed to characterize the molecular and cellular basis of the complex interactions between these agents.

Adaptations in Endogenous Opioid Pathways. Endogenous opioid pathways have been implicated in the acute reinforcing effects, not only of opiates (which are opioid receptor agonists), but also for other drugs of abuse, particularly alcohol and nicotine (Koob, 1996; Kreek, 1996). It is conceivable that adaptations in opioid peptides or opioid receptors as a consequence of chronic drug exposure could mediate aspects of addiction. Although it has been difficult, despite a large literature, to demonstrate a role for such adaptations in opiate addiction, there is some evidence that adaptations in endogenous opioid pathways contribute to aspects of stimulant addiction. Thus, chronic administration of cocaine or related stimulants increases levels of expression of specific opioid peptides (particularly dynorphin) and opioid receptors (particularly κ receptors) in specific brain regions, including the nucleus accumbens (Hyman, 1996; Kreek, 1996; Spangler, Zhou et al., 1996). Since dynorphin and κ receptors are believed to mediate aversive effects, it is possible that the concerted upregulation of this peptide and receptor contributes to the dysphoria and negative motivational state seen during drug withdrawal (Figure 3). Given the reported ability of naltrexone (an opioid receptor antagonist) to reduce relapse in alcoholics (O'Malley, Jaffe et al., 1992; Volpicelli, Watson et al., 1992), further study of the role of endogenous opioid pathways in drug addiction is warranted.

ADAPTATIONS IN OTHER INTRACELLULAR PATHWAYS

In addition to upregulation of the cAMP pathway, it is likely that adaptations in many other intracellular signaling pathways occur in response to repeated drug exposure and contribute to the drug-addicted state. As just one example, there is evidence that phospholipase A2 (the first enzyme in the synthesis of prostaglandins and other arachidonic acid metabolites) in the ventral tegmental area influences locomotor responses to stimulants (Reid, Hsu et al., 1996).

Another molecular cite for adaptations to drug exposure is the coupling between receptors and their G proteins. Thus, all known dopamine, opioid, and cannabinoid receptors belong to the family of G protein-coupled receptors. Drug-induced adaptations in the efficacy of this coupling could exert profound effects on receptor function (Nestler & Aghajanian, 1997). Indeed, G protein-coupled receptors display many mechanisms of desensitization after acute exposure to an agonist (Freedman & Lefkowitz, 1996). However, most of these studies have been done in cultured cells in vitro. In addition, it remains unknown whether changes occur in these various mechanisms after chronic drug administration, which could contribute to aspects of tolerance or sensitization.

For example, altered levels of G protein subunits themselves, which have been observed in the ventral tegmental area, nucleus accumbens, and other brain regions, could mediate alterations in drug sensitivity (for references, see Nestler & Aghajanian, 1997). In addition, there might be drug-induced changes in other proteins (e.g., phosducin and RGS [regulators of G proteing signaling] proteins) that modulate G protein function. G protein-coupled receptors are also known to undergo phosphorylation by several types of protein kinases, which in some cases has been shown to lead to desensitization in receptor function, in part by internalization of the receptors from the cell membrane (Freedman & Lefkowitz, 1995). Opioid and dopamine receptors are reported to be phosphorylated (for references, see Nestler & Aghajanian, 1997), although whether such phosphorylation mechanisms are altered after chronic drug exposure remains unknown. One suggestive finding is that a particular type of protein kinase, known to phosphorylate and desensitize several

FIGURE 3. Hypothesized Role of Dynorphin in Drug Addiction

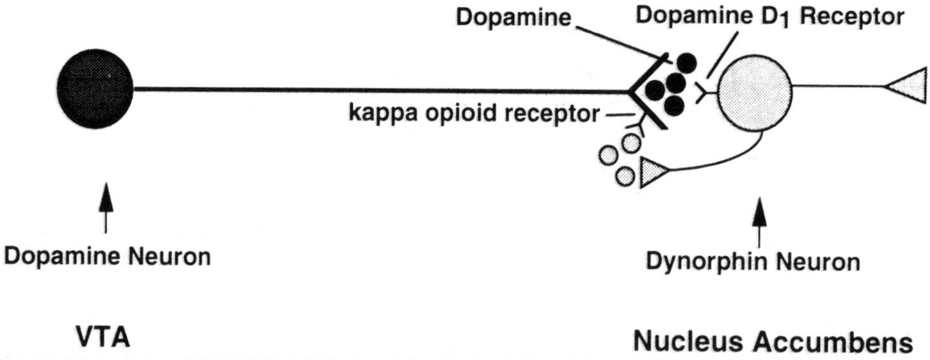

A subset of output neurons in the nucleus accumbens use both dynorphin and the inhibitory amino acid, GABA, as their neurotransmitters. In addition to projecting out of the nucleus accumbens, these neurons have recurrent collateral axons, which feed back within the accumbens itself. The release of dynorphin from these collaterals onto presynaptic terminals of dopamine neurons could act, via inhibitory κ opioid receptors, to decrease dopamine release. As described in the text, dopaminergic transmission to the accumbens leads to increased dynorphin gene expression with the possible consequence that there is increased releasable dynorphin to act as a compensatory "brake" on further dopamine release. Modified from Hyman and Nestler EJ (1996). Initiation and adaptation: A paradigm to understand psychotropic drug action. *American Journal of Psychiatry* 153:151–162.

types of G protein-coupled receptors, is upregulated in the locus coeruleus after chronic morphine administration (Terwilliger, Ortiz et al., 1994). Finally, chronic drug administration could conceivably alter levels of ion channels (for example, inwardly rectifying K^+ channels and voltage-gated Ca^{2+} channels) that mediate some of the acute effects of opioid and D_2-like dopamine receptors (Kovoor, Henry & Chavkin, 1995).

ADAPTATIONS IN OTHER GENE EXPRESSION

As mentioned earlier, perturbation of the brain's signal transduction pathways can lead to changes in gene expression. One prominent mechanism for altered gene expression is regulation of transcription factors, proteins that bind to specific sequences (response elements) in the regulatory (promoter) regions of specific genes and thereby increase or decrease the rate at which those genes are transcribed. Given the relative stability of changes in gene expression, it would make sense that drug-induced adaptations in the transcription of specific genes is an important mediator of drug addiction, particularly, the relatively longer-lasting consequences of drug exposure (Nestler, Hope & Widnell, 1993).

CREB (cAMP response element binding protein), one of the major cAMP-regulated transcription factors in brain, has been implicated in long-term responses to drugs of abuse. This is consistent with the role hypothesized for CREB in mediating several other forms of long-term neural and behavioral plasticity (see Carew, 1996; Martin & Kandel, 1996; Komhauser & Greenberg, 1997). Mutant mice lacking CREB show attenuated development of physical opiate dependence, based on reduced severity of behavioral withdrawal seen upon administration of an opioid receptor antagonist (Maldonado, Blendy et al., 1996). The locus coeruleus is one brain region where this effect of CREB may be mediated (see Figure 2). Thus, chronic opiate administration has been shown to increase levels of CREB phosphorylation and expression in this brain region (see Nestler & Aghajanian, 1997). Moreover, selective reductions in CREB levels in locus coeruleus neurons block the ability of chronic opiate exposure to upregulate some, but not all, components of the cAMP pathway (Lane-Ladd, Pineda et al., 1997). This is associated with attenuated activation of the locus coeruleus during withdrawal and attenuated withdrawal behaviors.

CREB also has been implicated in drug-induced adaptations in the nucleus accumbens and related striatal regions. Chronic administration of opiates or stimulants is reported to alter CREB phosphorylation or expression in these brain regions (Cole, Konradi et al., 1995; Widnell, Self et al., 1996). Genes for opioid peptides (such as dynorphin), which contain CRE sites (the specific sequences of DNA on which CREB acts) and are known to be regulated by chronic drug administration (see above), represent potential targets for CREB in these regions (Hyman, 1996). However, drug-induced alterations in CREB in the nucleus accumbens and related regions have not yet been related directly to drug-regulated behaviors.

The Fos and Jun family of transcription factors have also been studied extensively within the context of addiction. Several are induced rapidly but transiently in the nucleus accumbens and related striatal regions by acute administration of stimulants, opiates, or nicotine. In contrast, chronic drug exposure desensitizes the ability of these proteins to be induced and results instead in the gradual accumulation of novel Fos-like proteins, termed chronic FRAs (Fos-related antigens) (Hope, Nye et al., 1994; Nestler & Aghajanian, 1997). Recent work has identified the chronic FRAs as isoforms of δFosB, a truncated splice variant of the *fosB* gene (Chen, Kelz et al., 1997; Hiroi, Brown et al., 1997). The δFosB isoforms accumulate in brain after repeated drug treatment due to their extraordinary stability and thereby are candidates to serve as molecular switches for long-lived adaptations to drug exposure (Figure 4). Although specific target genes for the δFosB isoforms remain unknown, evidence for their importance in behavioral plasticity to drugs of abuse has been obtained recently: mice lacking the *fosB* gene show enhanced locomotor and reinforcing responses to cocaine (Hiroi, Brown et al., 1997). These findings support a scheme wherein induction of these proteins would represent a relatively stable compensatory adaptation that opposes acute drug action.

FIGURE 4. Hypothetical Scheme of the Gradual Accumulation of the Chronic FRAs versus the Rapid and Transient Induction of C-Fos and the Acute FRAs in the Brain

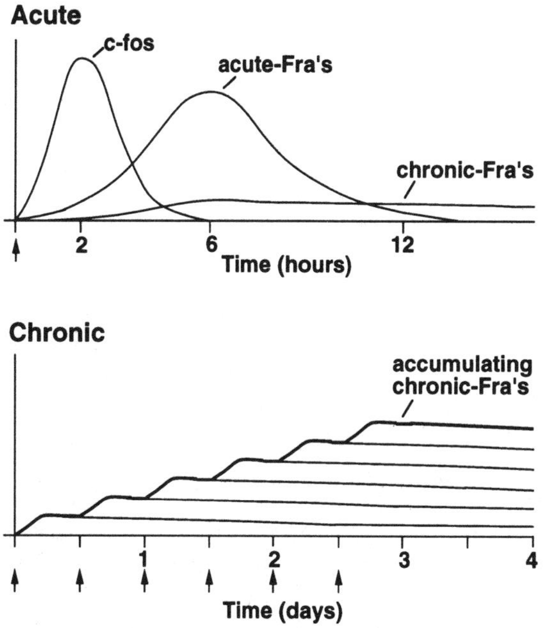

(Top) There are several waves of FRAs (Fos-related antigens) induced by acute exposure to cocaine or some other stimulus. c-Fos is induced rapidly and degraded within several hours of the acute stimulus, whereas the acute FRAs are induced somewhat later and persist somewhat longer than c-Fos. The chronic FRAs are also induced at a low level following a single acute stimulus but persist for many days at low levels (with a half-life of about 7 days). These waves of FRAs form active transcriptional complexes with shifting composition, and functional properties, over time. (Bottom) With repeated stimulation, each acute stimulus induces a low level of chronic FRAs. This is indicated by the lower set of overlapping lines, which indicate chronic FRAs induced by each acute stimulus. The result is a gradual increase in the total level of chronic FRAs with repeated stimuli during a course of chronic treatment. This is indicated by the increasing stepped line in the. graph. The increasing levels of chronic FRAs with repeated stimulation, along with desensitization in the induction of the acute FRAs (not shown in the figure), would result in the gradual induction of significant levels of a long-lasting transcriptional complex with unique functional properties. From Hope BT, Nye HE, Kelz MB, Self DW, Iadarola MJ & Nakabeppu Y (1994). Induction of a long-lasting AP-1 complex composed of altered Fos-like proteins in brain by chronic cocaine and other chronic treatments. *Neuron* 13:1235–1244.

ADAPTATIONS IN NEURONAL MORPHOLOGY AND SURVIVAL

A major goal of current research is to gain insight into the molecular and cellular basis of the more long-lived adaptations in brain function associated with addiction. One possibility, as mentioned above, is that such long-lived adaptations involve relatively stable changes in gene expression. There is now increasing evidence from other systems (Stein-Behrens, Mattson et al., 1994; Hosokawa, Rusakov et al., 1995; Woolley, Weiland et al., 1997; Duman, Henninger et al., 1997) that such changes in gene expression could lead to changes in neuronal function via structural changes in specific neurons, that is, changes in the shape and size of neurons as well as in the number of synaptic connections they form. This might, in addition, even involve changes in neuronal survival.

The best established adaptation of this type in the context of drug addiction is neuronal injury and death elicited by even single doses of any of several amphetamine derivatives (Cadet, Ali et al., 1995; Seiden & Sabol, 1996). For example, methamphetamine has been shown to be directly toxic to dopaminergic neurons, whereas ecstasy (MDMA) is toxic to serotonergic neurons. The mechanism underlying this toxicity is unknown, but appears to involve the selective uptake of the drugs into the respective target neuron (mediated via the dopamine or serotonin transporter, respectively), where the drug's metabolites produce oxidative injury.

In contrast to amphetamine derivatives, however, there is little if any evidence that chronic administration of most other drugs of abuse, including opiates, cocaine, alcohol, cannabinoids, and nicotine, produce overt damage to specific neurons in the brain. Nevertheless, there is evidence for more subtle changes in neuronal structure and morphology. Thus, chronic opiate or cocaine exposure has been shown to decrease levels of neurofilament proteins (the major intermediate filament protein of neurons) and increase levels of glial fibrillary acidic protein (the major intermediate filament protein of glial cells) specifically within the ventral tegmental area (Nestler, Hope & Widnell, 1993; Nestler, 1996). These adaptations are associated, as would be expected, with reduced axoplasmic transport from the ventral tegmental area to the nucleus accumbens and with a reduction in the size of ventral tegmental area dopamine neurons (Figure 5) (Sklair-Tavron, Shi et al., 1996). A major need is to understand the functional consequences of these adaptations. They could, for example, reflect an impairment of mesolimbic dopamine function, which could contribute to aversive withdrawal states. Such an impairment could be viewed as a compensatory adaptation to the repeated activation of the system by the drug. Although these adaptations are clearly suggestive of neural injury, it is critical to emphasize that there is no direct evidence for this interpretation. Indeed, there is considerable evidence for the safety in humans of the long-term administration of the opioid receptor agonist, methadone (Novick, Richman et al., 1993).

Drug-induced adaptations in neuronal morphology raise the interesting possibility that neurotrophic factors could in some way be involved in drug addiction. Indeed, infusion of certain neurotrophic factors (e.g., brain-derived neurotrophic factor [BDNF] or glial-derived neurotrophic factor [GDNF]) into the ventral tegmental area have been shown to prevent and reverse specific molecular adaptations to chronic opiate or cocaine administration (Berhow, Russell et al., 1995). Such infusions also prevent the drug-induced morphological changes seen in ventral tegmental area dopaminergic neurons (see Figure 5) (Sklair-Tavron, Shi et al., 1996). These findings raise the novel possibility that medications that target neurotrophic factors or their signaling pathways could be useful in the treatment of addictive disorders. Clearly, this remains hypothetical, but deserves further investigation.

A related possibility is that some of the effects that chronic exposure to a drug of abuse exerts on target neurons may be mediated via drug-induced adaptations in neurotrophic factor signaling cascades. This possibility is supported by the recent findings that chronic administration of opiates or cocaine alters levels of specific proteins in these cascades specifically within the ventral tegmental area (Berhow, Hiroi et al., 1996a, 1996b).

FUTURE DIRECTIONS

This chapter focused on drug-induced adaptations in representative neurotransmitter, receptor, and post-receptor pathways as mediators of the long-term effects of drugs of abuse on the brain. It is important to highlight that a phenomenon as complex as addiction is likely to be mediated by numerous types of adaptations, many of which have not yet even been identified. One major goal of future research, therefore, is to piece together how multiple molecular and cellular adaptations summate to the complex behavioral changes that characterize addiction. Ultimately, this knowledge will be exploited to develop fundamentally novel treatments for addictive disorders.

Another important goal of future research is to better understand the basis of the drug craving and increased risk for relapse that persists in some addicts for many years. A promising area along these lines are animal models of relapse, in which "drug-seeking behavior" can be stimulated, even after relatively long periods of abstinence, by exposure to the drug itself, by conditioned environmental cues associated with drug exposure, and perhaps most potently by certain forms of stress (Shaham, Rajabi et al., 1996; Shaham, Funk et al., 1997; Self, Barnhart et al., 1996; Piazza & Le Moal, 1996). Stress-induced relapse, which may be particularly relevant to human addiction, could potentially be mediated by any of the many neural and hormonal systems known to be stress-responsive. Most attention has focused on the hypothalamic-pituitary-adrenal axis (for example, corticotropin releasing factor and glucocorticoids), although a role for monoamines, opioid peptides, and cytokines, to name a few, also is worthy of future investigation. As more is learned at the systems level, it will be possible to identify the precise molecular and cellular adaptations in specific neurons that are responsible for stress-induced and other forms of relapse.

The ability of drugs of abuse to alter the brain depends in part on genetic factors: acute drug re-

FIGURE 5. Fluorescence Photomicrographs of Lucifer Yellow-filled Neurons in the Rat Ventral Tegmental Area

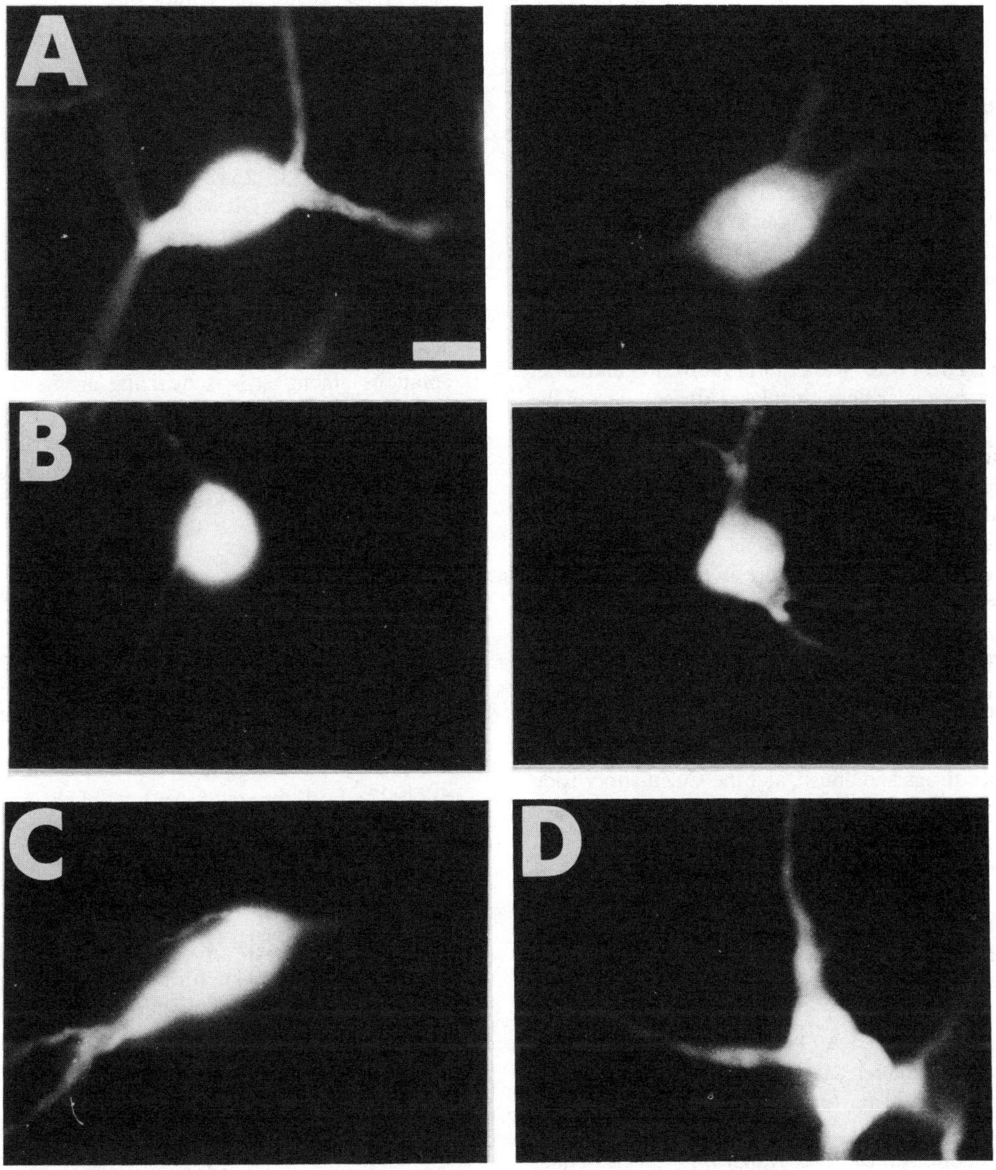

Individual neurons in brain slices at the level of the ventral tegmental area were injected with Lucifer yellow. The slices were then analyzed by immunohistochemistry for tyrosine hydroxylase to determine whether the injected neurons were dopaminergic (TH+) or non-dopaminergic (TH-). All neurons shown in the figure are dopaminergic. *A*, neurons from control rats; *B*, neurons from morphine-treated rats; *C*, neuron from BDNF (brain-derived neurotrophic factor)-treated rat; *D*, neuron from BDNF- and morphine-treated rat. The figure illustrates that chronic morphine administration decreases (by 25%) the size of ventral tegmental area dopaminergic neurons, and that infusion of BDNF into the ventral tegmental area prevents this effect. The effect of morphine is blocked by concomitant treatment with the opioid receptor antagonist, naltrexone, and is not seen for non-dopaminergic neurons within the same brain slice. Bar = 8 m. Sklair-Tavron L, Shi W-X, Lane SB, Harris HW, Bunney BS & Nestler EJ (1996). Chronic morphine induces visible changes in the morphology of mesolimbic dopamine neurons. *Proceedings of the National Academy of Science* 93:11202–11207.

sponses as well as adaptations to repeated drug exposure can vary dramatically depending on the genetic composition of the individual. Genetic factors can also influence the brain's responses to stress and are thus also likely to contribute to stress-induced relapse. Although it has been difficult to identify specific genes that contribute to individual differences in drug and stress vulnerability in laboratory animals and in humans, this works remains of the highest priority since it will greatly inform our understanding of addictive disorders and, ultimately, their treatment and prevention.

REFERENCES

Akaoka A & Aston-Jones G (1991). Opiate withdrawal-induced hyperactivity of locus coeruleus neurons is substantially mediated by augmented excitatory amino acid input. *Journal of Neuroscience* 11:3830–3839.

Beitner-Johnson D & Nestler EJ (1991). Morphine and cocaine exert common chronic actions on tyrosine hydroxylase in dopaminergic brain reward regions. *Journal of Neurochemistry* 57:344–347.

Berhow MT, Hiroi N, Kobierski L, Hyman S & Nestler EJ (1996a). Influence of cocaine on the JAK-STAT pathway in the mesolimbic dopamine system. *Journal of Neuroscience* 15:8019–8026.

Berhow MT, Hiroi N & Nestler EJ (1996b). Regulation of ERK (extracellular signal regulated kinase), part of the neurotrophin signal transduction cascade, in the rat mesolimbic dopamine system by chronic exposure to morphine or cocaine. *Journal of Neuroscience*, 16:4707–4715.

Berhow MT, Russell DS, Terwilliger RZ et al. (1995). Influence of neurotrophic factors on morphine- and cocaine-induced biochemical changes in the mesolimbic dopamine system. *Neuroscience* 68:969–979.

Bonci A & Williams J (1997). Increased probability of GABA release during withdrawal from morphine. *Journal of Neuroscience* 17:796–803.

Cadet JL, Ali SF, Rothman RB & Epstein CJ (1995). Neurotoxicity, drugs and abuse, and the CuZn-superoxide dismutase transgenic mice. *Molecular Neurobiology* 11:155–63.

Carew TJ (1996). Molecular enhancement of memory formation. *Neuron* 16:5–8.

Carlezon WA Jr, Boundy VA, Haile CN, Kalb RG, Neve R & Nestler EJ (1997). Sensitization to morphine induced by viral-mediated gene transfer. *Science* 277:812–814.

Carlezon WA Jr & Wise RA (1996). Rewarding actions of phencyclidine and related drugs in nucleus accumbens shell and frontal cortex. *Journal of Neuroscience* 16:3112–22.

Cerruti C, Pilotte NS, Uhl G & Kuhar MJ (1994). Reduction in dopamine transporter mRNA after cessation of repeated cocaine administration. *Molecular Brain Research* 22:132–138.

Chen J, Kelz MB, Hope BT, Nakabeppu Y & Nestler EJ (1997). Chronic FRAS: Stable variants of ΔFosB induced in brain by chronic treatments. *Journal of Neuroscience* 17:4933–4941.

Childers SR (1991). Opioid receptor-coupled second messenger systems. *Life Sciences* 48:1991–2003.

Christie MJ, Williams JT & Osborne PB (1997). Where is the locus in opioid withdrawal? *Trends in Neuroscience* 18:134–140.

Cole RL, Konradi C, Douglass J & Hyman SE (1995). Neuronal adaptation to amphetamine and dopamine: Molecular mechanisms of prodynoxphin gene regulation in rat striatum. *Neuron* 14:813–823.

Crain S & Shen K (1996). Modulatory effects of Gs-coupled excitatory opioid receptor functions on opioid analgesia, tolerance, and dependence. *Neurochemical Research* 21:1347–1351.

Cunningham ST & Kelley AE (1993). Hyperactivity and sensitization to psychostimulants following cholera toxin infusion into the nucleus accumbens. *The Journal of Neuroscience* 13:2342–350.

Duman RS, Heninger GR & Nestler EJ (1997). A molecular and cellular hypothesis of depression. *Archives of General Psychiatry* 54:597–606, 1997.

Fitzgerald LW, Ortiz J, Hamedani AG & Nestler EJ (1996). Regulation of glutamate receptor subunit expression by drugs of abuse and stress: Common adaptations among cross-sensitizing agents. *Journal of Neuroscience* 16:274–282.

Freedman NJ & Lefkowitz RJ (1996). Desensitization of G protein- coupled receptors. *Recent Progress in Hormone Research* 51:319–351.

Giros B, Jaber M, Jones SR, Wightman RM & Caron MG (1996). Hyperlocomotion and indifference to cocaine and amphetamine in mice lacking the dopamine transporter. *Nature* 379:606–612.

Henry DJ & White FJ (1995). The persistence of behavioral sensitization to cocaine parallels enhanced inhibition of nucleus accumbens neurons. *Journal of Neuroscience* 15:6287–6299.

Hiroi N, Brown J, Haile C, Ye H, Greenberg ME & Nestler EJ (1997). FosB mutant mice: Loss of chronic cocaine induction of Fos-related proteins and heightened sensitivity to cocaine's psychomotor and rewarding effects. *Proceedings of the National Academy of Science* 94:10397–10402.

Hope BT, Nye HE, Kelz MB, Self DW, Iadarola MJ & Nakabeppu Y (1994). Induction of a long-lasting AP-1 complex composed of altered Fos-like proteins in brain by chronic cocaine and other chronic treatments. *Neuron* 13:1235–1244.

Hosokawa T, Rusakov DA, Bliss TV & Fine A (1995). Repeated confocal imaging of individual dendritic spines in the living hippocampal slice: Evidence for changes in length and orientation associated with chemically induced LTP. *Journal of Neuroscience* 15:5560–73.

Hyman S (1996). Addiction to cocaine and amphetamine. *Neuron* 16:901–904.

Hyman SE & Nestler EJ. (1993). *The Molecular Foundations of Psychiatry.* Washington, DC: American Psychiatric Press.

Hyman SE & Nestler EJ. (1996). Initiation and adaptation: A paradigm to understand psychotropic drug action. *American Journal of Psychiatry* 153:151–162.

Ip NY & Yancopoulos GD (1996). The neurotrophins and CNTF: Two families of collaborative neurotrophic factors. *Annual Review of Neuroscience* 19:491–515.

Jeziorski M, White FJ & Wolf ME (1994). MK-801 prevents the development of behavioral sensitization during repeated morphine administration. *Synapse* 16:137–47.

Jolas T & Aghajanian GK (1997). Opioids suppress spontaneous and NMDA-induced inhibitory postsynaptic currents in the dorsal raphe nucleus of the rat in vitro. *Brain Research* 755:229–245.

Kalivas PW (1995). Interactions between dopamine and excitatory amino acids in behavioral sensitization to psychostimulants. *Drug & Alcohol Dependence* 37:95–100.

Kalivas PW & Stewart J (1991). Dopamine transmission in the initiation and expression of drug- and stress-induced sensitization of motor activity. *Brain Research Reviews* 16:223–244.

Kelley A & Holahan M (1997). Enhanced reward related responding following cholera toxin infusion into the nucleus accumbens. *Synapse* 26:46–54.

Kolesnikov Y, Pan Y-X, Babey A, Jain S, Wilson R & Pasternak G (1997). Functionally differentiating two neuronal nitric oxide synthase isoforms through antisense mapping: Evidence for opposing NO actions on morphine analgesia and tolerance. *Proceedings of the National Academy of Sciences USA* 94:8220–8225.

Koob GF (1996). Drug addiction: the yin and yang of hedonic homeostasis. *Neuron* 16:893–896.

Koob GF & Le Moal M (1997). Drug abuse: hedonic homeostatic dysregulation. *Science* 278:52–58.

Koob GF, Maldonado R & Stinus L (1992). Neural substrates of opiate withdrawal. *Trends in Neuroscience* 15:186–191.

Koob GF & Nestler EJ (1997). Neurobiology of drug addiction. *Journal of Neuropsychiatry and Clinical Neuroscience* 9:482–497.

Komhauser J & Greenberg M (1997). A kinase to remember: dual roles for MAP kinase in long-term memory. *Neuron* 18:839–842.

Kovoor A, Henry DJ & Chavkin C (1995). Agonist-induced desensitization of the mu opioid receptor-coupled potassium channel (GIRK1). *Journal of Biological Chemistry* 270:589–595.

Kreek MJ (1996). Opiates, opioids and addiction. *Molecular Psychiatry* 1:232–54.

Kuhar MJ & Pilotte NS (1996). Neurochemical changes in cocaine withdrawal. *Trends in Pharmacological Sciences* 17:260–4.

Lane-Ladd SB, Pineda J, Boundy V et al. (1997). CREB in the locus coeruleus: Biochemical, physiological, and behavioral evidence for a role in opiate dependence. *Journal of Neuroscience* 17:7890–7901.

Lisman J, Malenka R, Nicoll R & Malinow R (1997). Leaning mechanisms: the case for CaM-KII. *Science* 276:2002–2002.

Lu W, Chen H, Xue C & Wolf M (1997). Repeated amphetamine administration alters the expression of mRNA for AMPA receptor subunits in rat nucleus accumbens and prefrontal cortex. *Synapse* 26:269–280.

Maggos C, Spangler R, Zhou Y, Schlussman S, Ho A & Kreek M (1997). Quantitation of dopamine transporter mRNA in the rat brain: mapping effects of "binge" cocaine administration and withdrawal. *Synapse* 26:55–61.

Maldonado R (1997). Participation of noradrenergic pathways in the expression of opiate withdrawal: Biochemical and pharmacological evidence. *Neuroscience & Biobehavioral Reviews* 21:91–104.

Maldonado R, Blendy JA, Tzavara E, Gass P, Roques BP & Hanoune J (1996). Reduction of morphine abstinence in mice with a mutation in the gene encoding CREB. *Science* 273:657–659.

Maldonado R, Valverde O, Garbay C & Roques BP (1995). Protein kinases in the locus coeruleus and periaqueductal gray matter are involved in the expression of opiate withdrawal. *Naunyn-Schmiedebergs Archives of Pharmacology* 352:565–575.

Malison RT, Best SE, Wallace EA et al. (1995). Euphorigenic doses of cocaine reduce [123I]beta-CIT SPECT measures of dopamine transporter availability in human cocaine addicts. *Psychopharmacology* 122:358–362.

Martin KC & Kandel ER (1997). Cell adhesion molecules, CREB, and the formation of new synaptic connections. *Neuron* 17:567–70.

Miserendino MJD & Nestler EJ (1995). Behavioral sensitization to cocaine: Modulation by the cyclic AMP system in the nucleus accumbens. *Brain Research* 674:299–306.

Nestler EJ (1996). Under siege: the brain on opiates. *Neuron* 16:897–900.

Nestler EJ & Aghajanian GK (1997). Molecular and cellular basis of addiction. *Science* 278:58–63.

Nestler EJ & Greengard P (1994). Protein posphorylation and the regulation of neuronal function. In GJ Siegel, RW Albers, B Agranoff & P Molinoff (eds.) *Basic Neurochemistry: Molecular, Cellular, and Medical Aspects* (5th edition). Boston, MA: Little, Brown and Co, 449–474.

Nestler EJ, Hope BT & Widnell K (1993). Drug addiction: A model for the molecular basis of neural plasticity. *Neuron* 11:995–1006.

Novick DM, Richman BL, Friedman JM, Friedman JE, Fried C & Wilson JP (1993). The medical status of methadone maintenance patients in treatment for 11–18 years. *Drug & Alcohol Dependence* 33:235–45.

O'Malley SS, Jaffe AJ, Chang G, Schottenfeld RS, Meyer RE & Rounsaville B (1992). Naltrexone and coping skills therapy for alcohol dependence. A controlled study. *Archives of General Psychiatry* 49:881–887.

Ortiz J, Fitzgerald LW, Charlton M et al. (1995). Biochemical actions of chronic ethanol exposure in the mesolimbic dopamine system. *Synapse* 21:289–298.

Piazza PV & Le Moal ML (1996). Pathophysiological basis of vulnerability to drug abuse: Role of an interaction between stress, glucocorticoids, and dopaminergic neurons. *Annual Review of Pharmacology & Toxicology* 36:359–78.

Punch L, Self DW, Nestler EJ & Taylor JR (1997). Opposite modulation of opiate withdrawal behaviors upon microinfusion of a protein kinase A inhibitor versus activator into the locus coeruleus or periaqueductal gray. *Journal of Neuroscience* 17:8520–8527.

Rasmussen K & Aghajanian GK (1989). Withdrawal-induced activation of locus coeruleus neurons in opiate-dependent rats: Attenuation by lesions of the nucleus paragigantocellularis. *Brain Research* 505:346–350

Reid M, Hsu K, Tolliver B, Crawford C & Berger PS (1996). Evidence for the involvement of phospholipase A2 mechanisms in the development of stimulant sensitization. *Journal of Pharmacology and Experimental Therapeutics* 276:1244–1256.

Robinson TE & Berridge KC (1993). The neural basis of drug craving: an incentive-sensitization theory of addiction. *Brain Research Reviews* 18:247–291.

Schoffelmeer AN, Voom P, Jonker AJ et al. (1996). Morphine-induced increase in D-1 receptor regulated signal transduction in rat striatal neurons and its facilitation by glucocorticoid receptor activation: Possible role in behavioral sensitization. *Neurochemical Research* 21:1417–23.

Seiden LS & Sabol KE (1996). Methamphetamine and methylenedioxymethamphetamine neurotoxicity: possible mechanisms of cell destruction. *NIDA Research Monograph 163*. Rockville, MD: National Institute on Drug Abuse, 251–76.

Self DW, Barnhart WJ, Lehman DA et al. (1996). Opposite modulation of cocaine-seeking behavior by D1-like and D2-like dopamine receptor agonists. *Science* 271:1586–158.

Self DW, Genova LM, Hope BT, Barnhart WJ, Spencer JJ & Nestler EJ (1998). Involvement of cAMP-dependent protein kinase in the nucleus accumbens in cocaine self-administration and relapse of cocaine-seeking behavior. *Journal of Neuroscience* 18:1848–1859.

Self DW & Nestler EJ (1995). Molecular mechanisms of drug reinforcement and addiction. *Annual Reviews of Neurology* 18:463–495.

Shaham Y, Funk D, Erb S, Brown T, Walker C & Stewart J (1997). Corticotropin-releasing factor, but not corticosterone, is involved in stress-induced relapse to heroin-seeking in rats. *Journal of Neuroscience* 17:2605–2614.

Shaham Y, Rajabi H & Stewart J (1996). Relapse to heroin-seeking in rats under opioid maintenance: The effects of stress, heroin priming, and withdrawal. *Journal of Neuroscience* 16:1957–1963.

Sharma SK, Klee WA & Nirenberg M (1975). Dual regulation of adenylate cyclase accounts for narcotic dependence and tolerance. *Proceedings of the National Academy of Science* 72:3092–3096.

Sklair-Tavron L, Shi W-X, Lane SB, Harris HW, Bunney BS & Nestler EJ (1996). Chronic morphine induces visible changes in the morphology of mesolimbic dopamine neurons. *Proceedings of the National Academy of Science* 93:11202–11207.

Sorg BA, Chen SY & Kalivas PW (1993). Time course of tyrosine hydroxylase expression after behavioral sensitization to cocaine. *Journal of Pharmacology and Experimental Therapeutics* 266:424–430

Spangler R, Zhou A, Maggos C et al. (1993). Regulation of kappa opioid receptor mRNA in the rat brain by "binge" pattern cocaine administration and correlation with preprodynorphin mRNA. *Molecular Brain Research* 38:71–76.

Stein-Behrens B, Mattson MP, Chang I, Yeh M & Sapolsky R (1994). Stress exacerbates neuron loss and cytoskeletal pathology in the hippocampus. *Journal of Neuroscience* 14:5373–5380.

Terwilliger RA, Ortiz J, Guitart X & Nestler EJ (1994). Chronic morphine administration increases β-adrenergic receptor kinase (βARK) levels in the rat locus coeruleus. *Journal of Neurochemistry* 63:1983–1986.

Terwilliger RZ, Beitner-Johnson D & Sevarino KA (1991). A general role for adaptations in G-proteins and the cyclic AMP system in mediating the chronic actions of morphine and cocaine on neuronal function. *Brain Research* 548:100–110.

Tolliver B, Ho L, Reid M et al. (1996). Evidence for involvement of ventral tegmental area cyclic AMP systems in behavioral sensitization to psychostimulants. *Journal of Pharmacology and Experimental Therapeutics* 278:1–10.

Tolliver BK, Ho LB, Reid MS & Berger SP (1996). Evidence for involvement of ventral tegmental area cyclic AMP systems in behavioral sensitization to psychostimulants. *Journal of Pharmacology and Experimental Therapeutics* 278:411–420.

Trujillo KA & Akil H (1994). Inhibition of opiate tolerance by non-competitive methyl-D-aspartate receptor antagonists. *Brain Research* 633:178–88, 1994.

Unterwald E, Fillmore J & Kreek M (1991). Chronic repeated cocaine administration increases dopamine D1 receptor-mediated signal transduction. *The European Journal Pharmacology* 318:31–35.

Valverde O, Tzavara E, Hanoune J, Roques BP & Maldonado R (1996). Protein kinases in the rat nucleus accumbens are involved in the aversive component of opiate withdrawal. *European Journal of Neuroscience* 8:2671–8.

Vanderschuren LJMJ, Schoffelmeer ANM, Mulder AH & De Vries TJ (1998). Dizocilpine (MK801): Use or abuse? *Trends in Pharmacological Sciences* 19:79–81.

Volkow ND, Wang GJ, Fowler JS et al. (1996). Cocaine uptake is decreased in the brain of detoxified cocaine abusers. *Neuropsychopharmacology* 14:159–168.

Volpicelli JR, Watson NT, King AC, Sherman CE & O'Brien CP (1995). Effect of naltrexone on alcohol "high" in alcoholics. *American Journal of Psychiatry* 152:613–615

Vrana SL, Vrana KE, Koves TR, Smith JE & Dworkin SI (1993). Chronic cocaine administration increases CNS tyrosine hydroxylase enzyme activity and mRNA levels and tryptophan hydroxylase enzyme activity levels. *Journal of Neurochemistry* 61:2262–2268

White FJ, Hu X-T, Zhang X-F & Wolf ME (1995). Repeated administration of cocaine or amphetamine alters neuronal responses to glutamate in the mesoaccumbens dopamine system. *Journal of Pharmacology and Experimental Therapeutics* 273:445–454.

Widnell KL, Self DW, Lane SB, Russell DS, Vaidya V & Miserendino MJD (1996). Regulation of CREB expression: In vivo evidence for a functional role in morphine action in the nucleus accumbens. *Journal of Pharmacology and Experimental Therapeutics* 276:306–315.

Wise RA (1996). Neurobiology of addiction. *Current Opinions of Neurobiology* 6:243–251.

Woolley CS, Weiland NG, McEwen BS & Schwartzkroin PA (1997). Estradiol increases the sensitivity of hippocampal CA1 pyramidal cells to NMDA receptor-mediated synaptic input: correlation with dendritic spine density. *Journal of Neuroscience* 17:848–59.

Zamanillo D, Casanova E, Alonso-Llamazares A, Ovalle S, Chinchetru MA & Calvo P (1995). Identification of a cyclic adenosine 3',5'-monophosphate-dependent protein kinase phosphorylation site in the carboxy terminal tail of human D1 dopamine receptor. *Neuroscience Letters* 188:183–186.

Zhang X, Hu X & White F (1998). Whole-cell plasticity in cocaine withdrawal: Reduced sodium currents in nucleus accumbens neurons. *Journal of Neuroscience* 18:488–498.

Zhang XF, Hu XT, White FJ & Wolf ME (1997). Increased responsiveness of ventral tegmental area dopamine neurons to glutamate after repeated administration of cocaine or amphetamine is transient and selectively involves AMPA receptors. *Journal of Pharmacology & Experimental Therapeutics* 281:699–706.

CHAPTER 6

Neurocircuitry Targets in Reward and Dependence

George F. Koob, Ph.D.
Amanda J. Roberts, Ph.D., et al.

Neurocircuitry Targets for Acute Ethanol Reinforcement
Neurocircuitry Targets for Ethanol Reinforcement During Dependence
Neurocircuitry Targets for Ethanol Relapse

The purpose of this review is to address the issue of the neurocircuits that are important for the problems associated with reinforcement mechanisms that drive substance dependence on alcohol, or alcoholism. Alcoholism can be defined as a complex behavioral disorder characterized by preoccupation with obtaining alcohol and a narrowing of the behavioral repertoire towards excessive consumption (loss of control over its consumption). It is usually also accompanied by the development of tolerance and dependence and impairment in social and occupational functioning. The *Diagnostic and Statistical Manual of Mental Disorders, 4th Edition* (*DSM-IV*; American Psychiatric Association, 1994) defines dependence on alcohol as a cluster of cognitive, behavioral, and physiological symptoms that indicate that an individual continues to use alcohol despite significant alcohol-related problems, and it lists seven criteria that incorporate these symptoms, three of which must be met over a 12-month period to receive the diagnosis of substance dependence on alcohol (Table 1). For the purposes of this discussion, substance dependence on alcohol, as defined by *DSM-IV*, will be considered to be operationally equivalent to the syndrome of alcoholism. It is recognized that animal models of a complete syndrome are difficult, if not impossible, to achieve. However, it is clear that validated animal models exist for many of the different components of the syndrome, providing a heuristic means by which to pursue the underlying neurobiological basis for the disorder (Table 1).

Several major factors can be distilled from such a definition. One major element is the loss of control over consumption of ethanol or alcohol, or excessive ingestion of ethanol. The other major factor that probably contributes to this overindulgence and overingestion of ethanol has to do with neuroadaptations associated with tolerance and dependence. In this context of substance dependence, there are two major aspects of what one would call the reinforcing actions of ethanol (Table 2). The first would be that ethanol obviously has positive reinforcing effects, and people drink it because it has certain properties that make them want to drink more. However, there is another motivational aspect involving the negative reinforcing properties, and this is an aspect that, perhaps in recent years, has been neglected.

The construct of negative reinforcement refers to the increase in the probability of a response by removal of a stimulus (usually aversive). Negative reinforcement in drug addiction can come from multiple sources. An individual might have a genetic vulnerability for pathology, such as anxiety, that is relieved by self-administering ethanol, e.g., to reduce the anxiety associated with a comorbid anxiety disorder. Alternatively, drinking excessively can produce the pathology that supports a negative reinforcement construct. For example, chronic ethanol may engage the brain stress systems, and drinking may in the short term reduce the stress response. The combination of genetic vulnerability, psychosocial stressors, and drug-reduced stress may constitute a powerful substrate for negative reinforcement. Other areas that are not well-characterized in ethanol research are issues of the conditioned positive reinforcement and conditioned negative reinforcement, at least at the animal model level. These constructs of conditioned positive and conditioned negative reinforcement may be critical for elements associated with protracted abstinence and what has been called relapse vulnerability.

TABLE 1. Animal Models for the Criteria of DSM-IV

DSM-IV	Animal Models
A maladaptive pattern of substance use, leading to clinically significant impairment or distress, occurring at any time in the same 12-month period:	
■ Need for markedly increased amounts of the substance to achieve intoxication or desired effect, or markedly diminished effect with continued use of the same amount of substance.	■ Tolerance to reinforcing effects: ethanol?
■ Presence of a characteristic withdrawal syndrome for the substance, or the substance (or a closely related substance) is taken to relieve or avoid withdrawal symptoms.	■ Increased reward thresholds: ethanol
■ Persistent desire or one or more unsuccessful efforts to cut down or control substance use.	■ Conditioned positive reinforcing effects: ethanol ■ Conditioned withdrawal: ethanol?
■ Substance used in larger amounts or over a longer period than the person intended.	■ Ethanol intake (dependent animals) ■ Ethanol deprivation effect
■ Important social, occupational, or recreational activities are given up or reduced because of substance abuse.	■ Choice paradigms ■ Behavioral economics—loss of elasticity
■ A great deal of time is spent in activities necessary to obtain the substance, to use the substance, or to recover from its effects.	■ Ethanol self-administration during withdrawal
■ Substance use continues despite knowledge of a persistent problem that is likely to be caused or exacerbated by substance use.	■ Progressive ratio responding for ethanol

TABLE 2. Neurotransmitter Implicated in the Motivational Effects of Withdrawal from Drugs of Abuse

↓ Dopamine: "dysphoria"
↓ Opioid peptides: pain, "dysphoria"
↓ Serotonin: pain, "Dysphoria," depression
↓ GABA: anxiety, panic attacks
↑ Corticotropin-releasing: stress factor

NEUROCIRCUITRY TARGETS FOR ACUTE ETHANOL REINFORCEMENT

Significant advances in understanding the neurocircuitry for the positive reinforcing effects of ethanol were greatly facilitated by advances in animal models for drinking. Early paradigms that assessed the reinforcing effects of ethanol typically used an oral preference paradigm whereby animals were allowed to drink ethanol or water. This procedure suffered from numerous methodological problems, however, including failure to provide information regarding the frequency and magnitude of individual drinking episodes (typically, 24-hour preference was recorded), failure to measure meaningful blood ethanol levels, and problems in determining whether sufficient ethanol was ingested to produce pharmacological effects (Samson, 1987). More recently, Samson and colleagues have developed and validated an operant procedure for both limited access to ethanol and more prolonged access (Samson, 1986; Samson, Pfeffer & Tolliver, 1988). A major breakthrough in this area was the development of a training procedure involving access to a sweetened solution and a subsequent "fading in" of ethanol to avoid the aversiveness of the ethanol taste. This produced relatively rapid acquisition of response to ethanol by nondeprived rats and allowed them a choice to respond to either ethanol or water. This ease of training combined with validation by measures of blood alcohol levels has established this procedure as a reliable means of measuring the reinforcing effects of ethanol, and has been a boon to the neuropharmacological analysis of ethanol reinforcement (Samson, Hodge et al., 1993).

An understanding of the neurobiology of the reinforcing effects of ethanol can be approached both from a "bottom-up" and a "top-down" approach. In the top-down approach, one is actually intervening with neuropharmacological manipulations in freely moving, behaving animals. The alternative bottom-up approach is that one can actually set up models at any level of analysis, including the molecular and cellular. Ultimately, the convergence of information from many different sites, systems, and cellular and molecular levels will provide the key to understanding the neurobiology of alcoholism. Ethanol to date does not have a specific neurotransmitter binding site in the brain. However, ethanol-receptive elements within membranes—and a protein component of neuronal membranes in particular—may provide a sensitive site for ethanol actions. The question is, how do these ethanol-receptive elements convey specificity of action, and how does this translate into behavioral action?

Ethanol has been hypothesized to interact with a number of ligand-gated ion channels, and the action on the GABA receptor system has been linked to ethanol reinforcement (Tabakoff & Hoffman, 1992; Deitrich, Dunwiddie et al., 1989). Ethanol allosterically appears to modulate the GABA receptor complex and to basically open the chloride channel and hyperpolarize cells or at least potentiate the hyperpolarization produced by GABA. There has been significant work showing that, at the pharmacological level, one can antagonize the effects of ethanol with GABA antagonists. In addition, the very potent GABA antagonist, SR95531, when microinjected into the basal forebrain, significantly decreased ethanol consumption. The GABA antagonist was injected bilaterally into the nucleus accumbens, bed nucleus of the stria terminalis, and central nucleus of the amygdala. The most sensitive site was the central nucleus of the amygdala (Figure 1).

Significant evidence also supports a role for dopaminergic mechanisms in the mesolimbic dopamine system in alcohol reinforcement. Very low doses of fluphenazine, a dopamine antagonist, injected into the nucleus accumbens, also will block ethanol self-administration at low doses, doses that do not affect water intake (Rassnick, Pulvirenti & Koob, 1992). Injections of an opiate antagonist into the central nucleus of the amygdala also significantly reduce ethanol consumption at lower doses than for other sites such as the nucleus accumbens or lateral ventricle (Heyser, Roberts et al., 1995). Modulation of various aspects of serotonergic transmission, including increases in the synaptic availability of serotonin with precursor loading and blockade of serotonin reuptake, can decrease ethanol intake (Lerner & Steitz, 1979). Antagonists of several serotonin receptor subtypes can also decrease ethanol self-administration. Serotonin-3 receptor antagonists decrease ethanol self-administration (Fadda, Garau et al., 1991; Hodge, Samson et al., 1993),

FIGURE 1. Central Nucleus of Amygdala

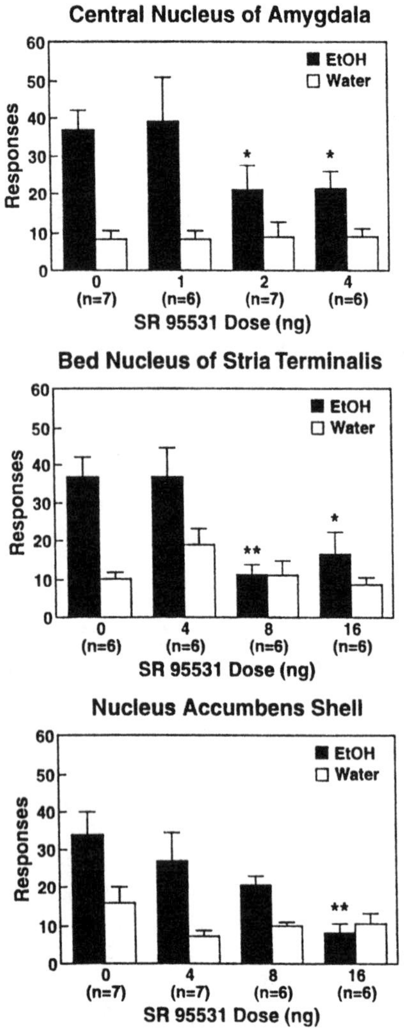

The effects of SR 95531 injections into the central nucleus of the amygdala, the bed nucleus of the stria terminalis, and the shell of the nucleus accumbens on responding for ethanol (EtOH) and water. Data are expressed as the mean (±SEM) number of responses for EtOH and water during 30-min sessions for each injection site. Note the change in the abscissa scale for injections into the bed nucleus of the stria terminalis and the nucleus accumbens shell. Significance of differences from the corresponding saline control values: * $p < 0.05$, ** $p < 0.01$ for EtOH responses, # $p < 0.05$ for water responses (adjusted means test). (Reprinted from *European Journal of Pharmacology*, vol. 283, Hyytiä P, and Koob GF, $GABA_A$ receptor antagonism in the extended amygdala decreases ethanol self-administration in rats, pp 151–159, 1995 with kind permission of Elsevier Science-NL, Sera Burgerhartstraat 25, 1055 KV Amsterdam, The Netherlands.)

and serotonin-2 receptor antagonists, including some with both serotonin-2 antagonist action and serotonin-la agonist activity, can selectively decrease acute ethanol reinforcement (Roberts, Hull et al., in press). Double-blind, placebo-controlled clinical studies have reported that serotonin reuptake inhibitors produced modest decreases in alcohol con-

FIGURE 2. Neuropharmacology of Ethanol Reinforcement

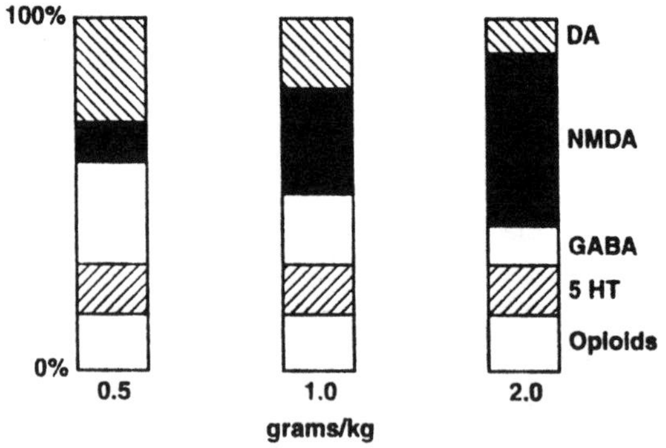

Diagram depicting the hypothesized relative contribution of different neurotransmitter systems of the basal forebrain in the reinforcing actions of alcohol. Note that the relative contribution is hypothesized to change with dose (based on a similar diagram developed for the alcohol drug discrimination stimulus by Dr. Kathleen Grant, Bowman Gray School of Medicine, Wake Forest University, North Carolina). (Reprinted with permission from Koob GF, Rassnick S, Heinrichs S, Weiss F (1994). Alcohol, the reward system and dependence. In B Jansson, H Jörnvall, V Rydberg, L Terenius & BL Vallee (eds.) *Toward a Molecular Basis of Alcohol Use and Abuse*. Basel, Switzerland: Birkhauser Verlag, 103–114.

sumption in humans (Naranjo, Kadlec et al., 1990) and to date these compounds appear to have some utility in decreasing drinking in the treatment of depressed alcoholics (Cornelius, Salloum et al., 1997), but their efficacy may be limited to preventing relapse in alcoholics with no comorbid depression (Kranzler, Burleson et al., 1995). Thus, multiple neurotransmitters have been implicated in the reinforcing effects of ethanol (Figure 2). GABAergic and dopaminergic mechanisms clearly seem to be involved in low-dose effects (Koob, Rassnick et al., 1994). There is also some hint that glutamate is involved in higher dose actions of ethanol. Modulation of the NMDA receptor may also contribute to the intoxicating effects of ethanol (Hoffman, Rabe et al., 1989; Lovinger, White & Weight, 1995), and perhaps to the dissociative effects seen in people with high ethanol blood levels (Tasi, Gastfriend & Coyle, 1995). Ethanol inhibits the functioning of the glutamate receptor complex, again, not by blocking the glutamate binding site, but via a more complex allosteric effect on the receptor complex that results in decreased glutamate-induced Na^+ and Ca^{2+} flux through the receptor ionophore. The hypothesis that ethanol antagonism of the NMDA receptor directly contributes to the reinforcing effects of ethanol remains to be established. In addition, it has long been known that opioid peptide and serotonergic systems could modulate the reinforcing effects of ethanol (Koob, Rassnick et al., 1994).

The circuitry involved in this reinforcing action has as its focal point the reward system that involves both the midbrain, where the dopaminergic system starts, and the basal forebrain, nucleus accumbens, and amygdala (Koob, 1992) (Figure 3). The principle components include the mesocorticolimbic system, the dopaminergic system, the GABA-A receptor, and the opioid peptides. Psychostimulants produce many of their effects through activation of the mesocorticolimbic dopamine system. Ethanol also activates the mesocorticolimbic dopamine system at doses in the intoxicating range (Tsai, Gastfriend & Coyle, 1995; Weiss, Lorang et al., 1993). As noted above, ethanol activates GABAergic function, possibly at specific brain sites (Givens & Breese, 1990). The evidence for an opioid peptide interaction rests largely with pharmacological studies in which opioid peptide antagonists block ethanol self-administration. Regarding specific brain sites for these neurotransmitter interactions, not only is the nucleus accumbens—which receives the dopaminergic projection-important, but perhaps also the central nucleus of the amygdala, a structure long assumed to be involved in hedonic processing in animals and humans (Figure 3). The serotonin and glutamate contributions to this circuitry are not illustrated in Figure 3 but would be hypothesized to interact with the same key structures.

FIGURE 3. Saggital Rat Brain Section

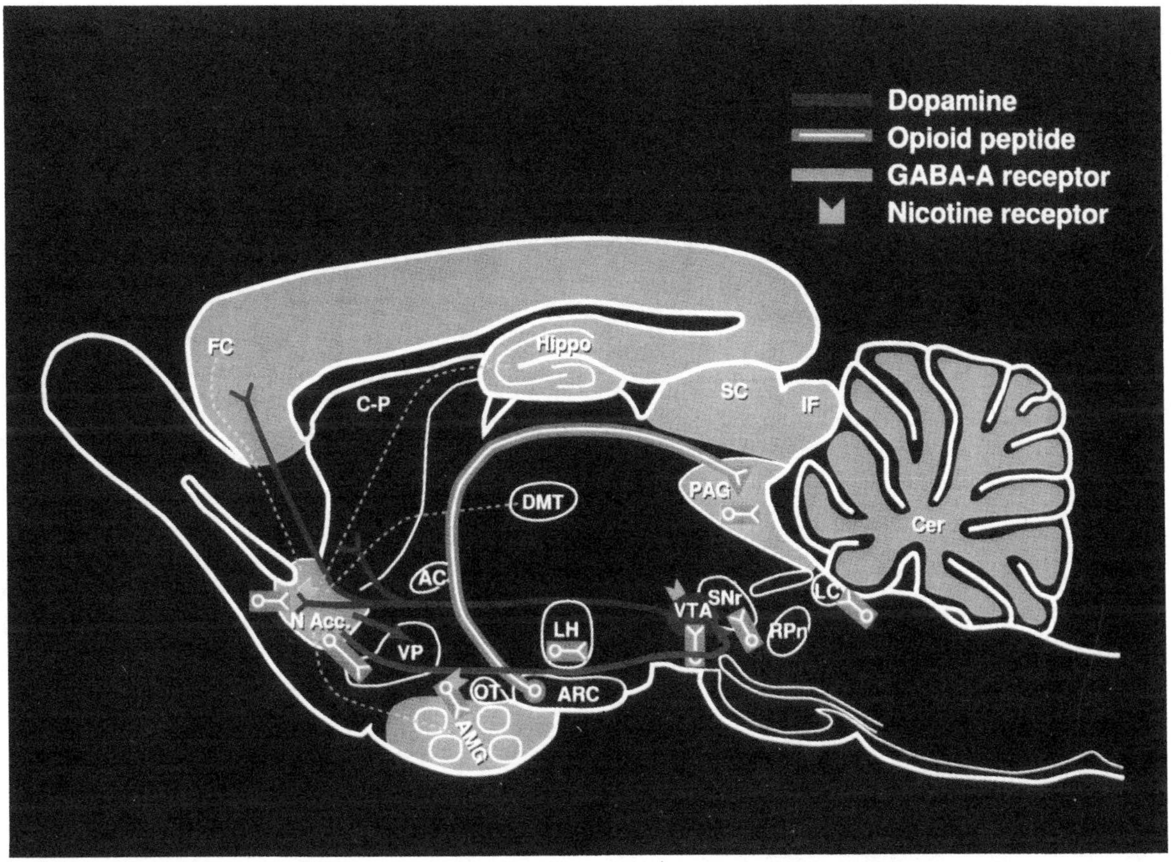

Sagittal rat brain section illustrating a drug (cocaine, amphetamine, opiate, nicotine, and alcohol) neural reward circuit that includes a limbic-extrapyramidal motor interface. VP, ventral pallidum; LH, lateral hypothalamus; SNr, substantia nigra pars reticulate; DMT, dorsomedial thalamus; PAG, periaqueductal gray; OT, olfactory tract; AC, anterior commissure; LC, locus coeruleus; AMG, amygdala; Hippo, hippocampus; Cer, cerebellum, FC, frontal cortex. (Reprinted with permission from Koob GF (1992). Drugs of Abuse: anatomy, pharmacology and function of reward pathways. *Trends in Pharmacological Sciences* 13:177–184.)

NEUROCIRCUITRY TARGETS FOR ETHANOL REINFORCEMENT DURING DEPENDENCE

Much less is known about the neurobiological substrates for other sources of reinforcement associated with dependence. One controversial area is the issue of the contribution of negative reinforcement. Drug taking in the dependent state in some cases involves removal of the aversive consequences of withdrawal. However, one conceptualization is that negative reinforcement derives not from the removal of the physical signs of withdrawal but, rather, removal of a negative affective state. Under this formulation, dependence then becomes defined by the presence of a negative affective state. "The notion of dependence on a drug, object, role, activity, or any stimulus source requires the crucial feature of negative affect experienced in its absence. The degree of dependence can be equated with the amount of negative affect, which may range from mild discomfort to extreme distress" (Russell, 1976). The question of what circuits in the brain are involved in negative reinforcement is the challenge of current research. It is hypothesized that knowledge in this domain will address the nature of the adaptation that takes place when a human moves from limited access to ethanol, to chronic binging, or to chronic drinking on a daily basis.

To address the question of changes in the reward system associated with drug dependence and alcohol dependence, measures of reward function after chronic drug exposure were performed, using the technique of intracranial self-stimulation. Acute administration of many drugs of abuse lower thresholds for brain stimulation reward (Kornetsky & Esposito, 1979). However, after chronic drug administration, thresholds are augmented or increased, which means that there is a decrease in reward during acute withdrawal (i.e., more electrical current is required to activate the neurons of the medial forebrain bundle). For example, during acute ethanol withdrawal, there is a prolonged increase in reward thresholds that lasts up to 72 hours (Schulteis, Markou et al., 1995) (Figure 4). Thus, one can hypothesize that the function of the medial forebrain bundle has been compromised by chronic administration.

A subsequent question is: what is the neurochemical mechanism for such a neuroadaptation? Two different possibilities have been proposed. One is that a within-systems adaptation, whereby some neurotransmitter system that is activated during the acute reinforcing effects of the drug is compromised during withdrawal. Alternatively, in a between-systems adaptation, some other system, not involved in the acute reinforcing effects of the drug, is recruited during chronic administration (Koob & Bloom, 1988).

FIGURE 4. Ethanol Withdrawal

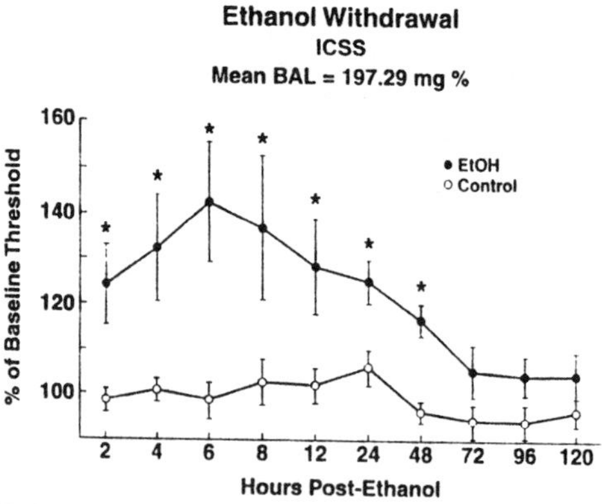

Time-dependent elevation of ICSS current thresholds during ethanol withdrawal. Data are expressed as mean (± SEM) percent of baseline threshold. Thresholds were significantly elevated above control levels at 2–48 hours post-ethanol (* $p < 0.05$). ○, Control condition; ●, ethanol withdrawal condition. (From Schulteis G, Markov A, Cole M & Koob GF (1995). Decreased brain reward produced by ethanol withdrawal. *Proceedings of the National Academy of Science* 92:5880–5884. Reprinted with permission.)

An example of a within-system adaptation is the change in extracellular dopamine observed during withdrawal from ethanol. Animals sustained on a liquid diet show a decrease in extracellular levels of dopamine in the nucleus accumbens (Weiss, Parsons et al., 1996) (Figure 5). Similar effects have been observed for virtually all major drugs of abuse. A unique aspect of this study is that the animals were allowed to self-administer ethanol during this withdrawal, and they self-administered just enough ethanol to return dopamine levels back to normal.

Evidence for between-system adaptation can be found in recent studies of chronic drug effects on corticotropin-releasing factor (CRF). CRF not only mediates hormonal responses to stress by activating the hypothalamic pituitary adrenal axis, but it also appears to mediate behavioral responses to stress independent of this pituitary action (Koob, Heinrichs et al., 1994). During ethanol withdrawal, there is actually a time-related increase in CRF in the amygdala (Figure 6). These results suggest that a brain stress system is recruited during ethanol dependence, forming a between-system neuroadaptation.

To summarize, there are multiple sources of change in neurotransmitters that one can argue may be associated with the transition from drug abuse

FIGURE 5. Neurochemical Response in the Nucleus Accumbens

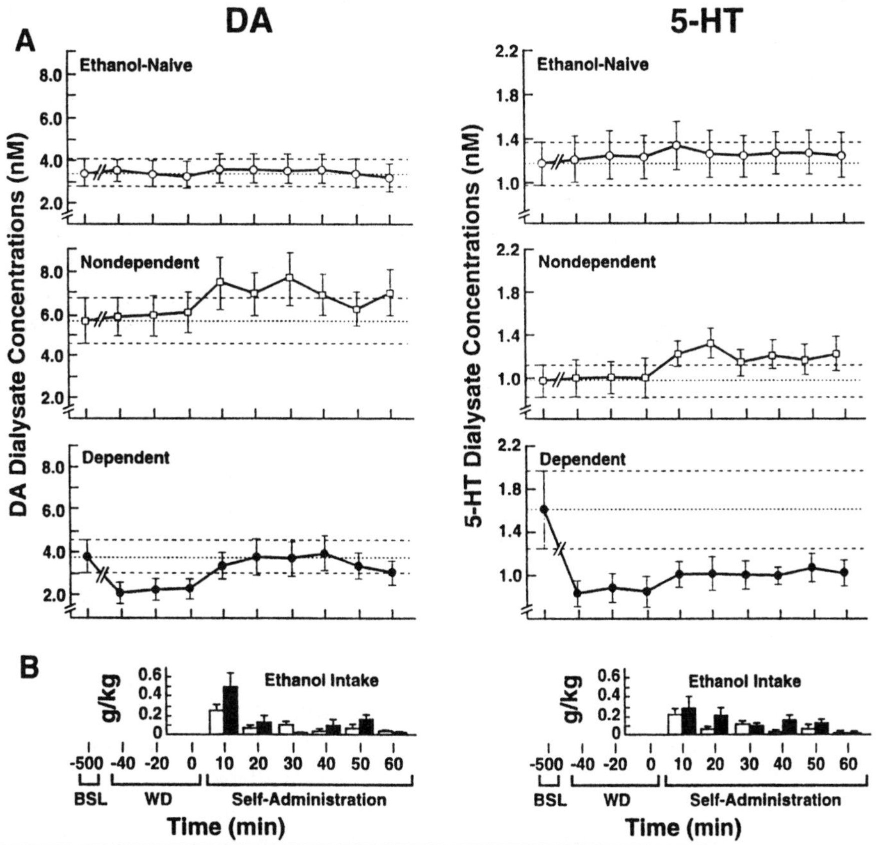

Neurochemical response in the nucleus accumbens subsequent to ethanol withdrawal in dependent animals and during access to ethanol via oral self-administration 8 hours into withdrawal. Dialysate neurotransmitter levels of DA and 5-HT are compared with those in ethanol-naive rats trained to self-administer water. (A) The corresponding dialysate neurotransmitter concentrations are shown in ethanol-naive, nondependent, and dependent animals. Dashed lines represent mean ± SEM prewithdrawal dialysate. (B) Prewithdrawal baseline (BSL) and withdrawal (WD) dialysate concentrations of DA and 5-HT during 8 hours of withdrawal are shown to illustrate the changes in neurotransmitter efflux over the various experimental phases. (From Weiss R, Parsons LH, Schulteis G, Hyytiä P, Lorang MT, Bloom FE & Koob GF (1996). Ethanol self-administration restores withdrawal-associated deficiencies in accumbal dopamine and 5-hydroxytryptamine release in dependent rats. *Journal of Neuroscience* 16(10):3474–3485. Reprinted with permission.)

to drug dependence. With ethanol, there is evidence for changes in dopamine, changes in GABA function, and changes in CRF (Table 2).

Finally, there may be neuroanatomical specificity that impacts on the neuropharmacological specificity outlined above. There is evidence that drugs of abuse preferentially activate different components of the limbic system/extrapyramidal motor system termed the "extended amygdala" (Caine, Heinrichs et al., 1995; Pontieri, Tanda & DiChiara, 1995). The medial aspect (shell) of the nucleus accumbens, the bed nucleus of the stria terminalis, and the central nucleus of the amygdala share a cytoarchitectural similarity that joins these structures into a potential functional entity. Perhaps most intriguing is that the extended amygdala projects very heavily to the lateral hypothalamus and basically forms a long sought after circuit that is responsible for brain stimulation reward and, perhaps, reward in general. Delineation of the elements of this system to promote an understanding of the acute reinforcing effects of ethanol, and further investigation of the elements and the ways in which they change during dependence, ultimately will be critical for our understanding of the neurobiology of drug dependence, in general, and ethanol dependence, in particular.

NEUROCIRCUITRY TARGETS FOR ETHANOL RELAPSE

Perhaps even more challenging for future research is the question of how these neurocircuits change with repeated episodes of ethanol intoxication, chronic (binge) use, and withdrawal. One hypothesis is that the key to understanding relapse lies in the same neurochemical elements that are perturbed

FIGURE 6. Effects of Ethanol Withdrawal on DRF-IR Levels

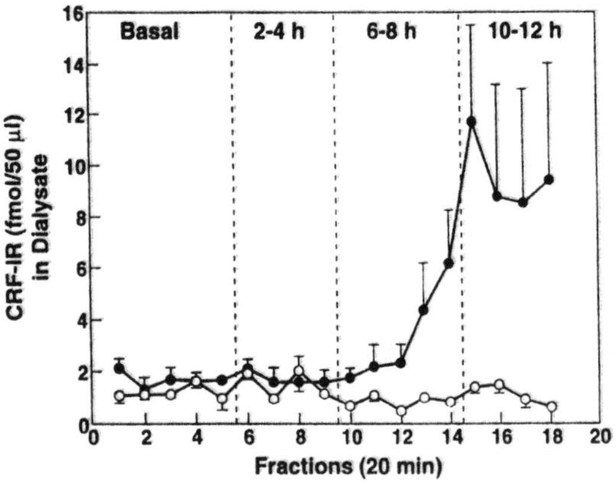

Effects of ethanol withdrawal on CRF-IR levels in the rat amygdala as determined by microdialysis. Dialysate was collected over four 2-hour periods regularly alternated with nonsampling 2-hour periods. The four sampling periods correspond to the basal collection (before removal of ethanol), and 2–4 hours, 6–8 hours, and 10–12 hours after withdrawal. Fractions were collected every 20 min. Data are represented as mean ± SEM (N = 5/group). ANOVA confirmed significant differences between the two groups over time ($p < 0.05$). (From Merlo-Pich E, Lorang M, Yeganeh M, Rodriguez de Fonseca F, Rager J, Koob GF & Weiss F (1995). Increase of extracellular corticotropin-releasing factor-like immunoreactivity levels in the amygdala of awake rats during restraint stress and ethanol withdrawal as measured by microdialysis. *Journal of Neuroscience* 15(8):5439–5447. Reprinted with permission.)

and compromised by repeated ethanol use. Various animal models are under investigation for use as models of excessive drinking and may prove useful for exploring neurochemical bases for this phenomenon. Rats have been shown to increase their ethanol intake during withdrawal, with repeated bouts of chronic exposure and withdrawal episodes, and this withdrawal-associated drinking is sensitive to manipulations of the GABAergic system (Roberts, Cole & Koob, 1996). Repeated episodes of ethanol intoxication in alcoholics can worsen symptoms of dependence (Becker, Diaz-Granados & Weathersby, 1997), and other preclinical studies have shown a "kindling" of some withdrawal symptoms (Moak & Anton, 1996).

Another model of excessive drinking in nondependent rats is the increase in ethanol consumption observed after a period of alcohol deprivation (Heyser, Schulteis & Koob, 1997; Sinclair & Senter, 1967). Termed the "alcohol deprivation effect," this phenomenon has been observed in rodents, monkeys, and humans. Typically, rats trained to lever press for ethanol in daily 30-minute sessions increase their consumption by up to 200% of baseline after five to 14 days of deprivation (Heyser, Schulteis & Koob, 1997). Even more intriguing, this alcohol deprivation effect can be blocked by chronic administration of the anti-relapse drug acamprosate (Heyser, Schulteis et al., 1996). The mechanism of action of acamprosate is still under investigation but may involve modulation of glutamatergic function (Zieglgansberger & Zeise, 1992). Rats also have proven to have increases in release of dopamine in the nucleus accumbens in anticipation of ethanol consumption, and this effect was more pronounced in alcohol-preferring rats than in unselected Wistar rats (Weiss, Lorang et al., 1993). Elucidation of the neurochemical/neurocircuitry basis for the alcohol deprivation effect and other aspects of relapse-related behavior may provide the key to an understanding of the biological basis of vulnerability to relapse.

ACKNOWLEDGMENTS: This is manuscript number 10841-NP from The Scripps Research Institute. This review represents a summary of a presentation entitled "Neurocircuitory Targets in Ethanol Reward and Dependence" at a satellite symposium for the Society for Neuroscience, entitled Approaches for Studying Neural Circuits: Application to Alcohol Research, 1996, in Washington, DC. The authors thank Mike Arends for valuable assistance with manuscript preparation. Originally published as Koob GF, Roberts AJ, Schulteis G, Parsons LH, Heyser CJ, Hyytia P, Merlo-Pich M & Friedbert W (1998). Neurocircuitry targets in ethanol reward and dependence. Alcoholism: Clinical & Experimental Research. *22(1):3–9. Reprinted by permission of the publisher.*

REFERENCES

American Psychiatric Association (1994). *Diagnostic and Statistical Manual of Mental Disorders, 4th Edition.* Washington, DC: American Psychiatric Press.

Becker HC, Diaz-Granados JL & Weathersby RT (1997). Repeated ethanol withdrawal experience increases the severity and duration of subsequent withdrawal seizures in mice. *Alcohol* 14(4):319–326.

Caine SB, Heinrichs SC, Coffin VL & Koob GF (1995) Effects of the dopamine D–1 antagonist SCH 23390 microinjected into the accumbens, amygdala or striatum on cocaine self-administration in the rat. *Brain Research* 692:47–56.

Cornelius JR, Salloum IM, Ehler JG et al. (1997). Fluoxetine in depressed alcoholics: A double-blind, placebo-controlled trial. *Archives of General Psychiatry* 54:700–705.

Deitrich RA, Dunwiddie TV, Harris RA & Erwin VG (1989). Mechanism of action of ethanol: Initial central nervous system actions. *Pharmacology Review* 41:489–537.

Fadda F, Garau B, Marchei F, Colombo G & Gessa GL (1991). MDL 72222, a selective 5-HT3 receptor antagonist, suppresses voluntary ethanol consumption in alcohol-preferring rats. *Alcohol and Alcoholism* 26(2):107–110.

Fitzgerald LW & Nestler EJ (1995). Molecular and cellular adaptations in signal transduction pathways following ethanol exposure. *Clinical Neuroscience* 3:165–173.

Givens BS & Breese GR (1990). Site-specific enhancement of gamma-aminobutyric acid-mediated inhibition of neural activity by ethanol in the rat medial septal area. *Journal of Pharmacology and Experimental Therapeutics* 254:528–538.

Heyser CJ, Roberts AJ, Schulteis G, Hyytia P & Koob GF (1995). Central administration of an opiate antagonist decreases oral ethanol self-administration in rats. *Neuroscience Abstracts* 21:1698.

Heyser CJ, Schulteis G, Durbin P & Koob GF (1996). Chronic acamprosate decreases deprivation-induced ethanol self-administration in rats. RSA/ISBRA Scientific Meeting (Abstract).

Heyser CJ, Schulteis G & Koob GF (1997). Increased ethanol self-administration after a period of imposed ethanol deprivation in rats trained in a limited access paradigm. *Alcoholism: Clinical & Experimental Research* 21:784–791.

Hodge CW, Samson HH, Lewis RS & Erickson HL (1993). Specific decreases in ethanol- but not water-reinforced responding produced by the 5-HT_3 antagonist ICS 205–930. *Alcohol* 10(3):191–196.

Hoffman PL, Rabe C, Moses F & Tabakoff B (1989). N-methyl-D-aspartate receptors and ethanol: Inhibition of calcium flux and cyclic GMP production. *Journal of Neurochemistry* 52:1937–1940.

Hyytia P & Koob GF (1995). $GABA_A$ receptor antagonism in the extended amygdala decreases ethanol self-administration in rats. *European Journal of Pharmacology* 283:151–159.

Koob GF (1992). Drugs of abuse: Anatomy, pharmacology, and function of reward pathways. *Trends in Pharmacological Sciences* 13:177–184.

Koob GF & Bloom FE (1988). Cellular and molecular mechanisms of drug dependence. *Science* 242:715–723.

Koob GF, Heinrichs SC, Menzaghi F, Merio-Pich E & Britton KT (1994). Corticotropin releasing factor, stress and behavior. *Seminars in Neuroscience* 6:221–229.

Koob GF, Rassnick S, Heinrichs S & Weiss F (1994). Alcohol, the reward system and dependence. In B Jansson, H Jörnvall, U Rydberg, L Terenius & BL Vallee (eds.) *Toward a Molecular Basis of Alcohol Use and Abuse* (Experientia supplementum, Vol. 71). Basel, Switzerland: Birkhauser-Verlag, 103–114.

Kornetsky C & Esposito RU (1979). Euphorigenic drugs: Effects on the reward pathways of the brain. *Federal Proceedings* 38:2473–2476.

Kranzler HR, Burleson JA, Korner P et al. (1995). Placebo-controlled trial of fluoxetine as an adjunct to relapse prevention in alcoholics. *American Journal of Psychiatry* 152(3):391–397.

Lerner MR & Steitz JA (1979). Antibodies to small nuclear RNAs complexed with proteins are produced by patients with systemic lupus erythematosus. *Proceedings of the National Academy of Science* 76:5495–5499.

Lovinger DM, White G & Weight FF (1995). Ethanol inhibits NMDA-activated ion current in hippocampal neurons. *Science* 243:1721–1724.

Mereu G, Fadda F & Gessa GL (1984). Ethanol stimulates the firing rate of vigral dopaminergic neurons in unanesthetized rats. *Brain Research* 292:63–69.

Merlo-Pich E, Lorang M, Yaganeh M et al. (1995). Increase of extracellular corticotropin-releasing factor-like immunoreactivity levels in the amygdala of awake rats during restraint stress and ethanol withdrawal as measured by microdialysis. *Journal of Neuroscience* 15:5439–5447.

Moak DH & Anton RF (1996). Alcohol-related seizures and the kindling effect of repeated detoxifications: The influence of cocaine. *Alcohol and Alcoholism* 31(2):135–143.

Naranjo C, Kadlec K, Sanhueza P, Woodley-Remus D & Sellers EM (1990). Fluoxetine differentially alters alcohol intake and other consummatory behaviors in problems drinkers. *Clinical Pharmacology and Therapeutics* 47:490–498.

Pontieri FE, Tanda G & DiChiara G (1995). Intravenous cocaine, morphine, and amphetamine preferentially increase extracellular dopamine in the "shell" as compared with the "core" of the rat nucleus accumbens. *Proceedings of the National Academy of Science* 92:12304–12308.

Rassnick S, Pulvirenti L & Koob GF (1992). Oral ethanol self-administration in rats is reduced by the administration of dopamine and glutamate receptor antagonists into the nucleus accumbens. *Psychopharmacology* 109:92–98.

Roberts AJ, Cole M & Koob GF (1996). Intra-amygdala muscimol decreases operant ethanol self-administration in dependent rats. *Alcoholism: Clinical & Experimental Research* 20:1289–1298.

Roberts AJ, Hull EE, McArthur RA, Post C & Koob GF (in press). Effects of amperozide, 8-OH-DPAT, and FG 5974 on operant responding for ethanol. *Psychopharmacology.*

Russell MAH (1976). What is dependence? In G Edwards, MAH Russell, D Hawks & M MacCafferty (eds.) *Drugs and Drug Dependence.* Westmead, England: Saxon House, 182–187.

Samson HH (1987). Initiation of ethanol-maintained behavior: A comparison of animal models and their implication to human drinking. In T Thompson, PB Dews & JE Barrett JE (eds.) *Advances in Behavioral Phar-*

macology, Neurobehavioral Pharmacology. Hillsdale, NJ: Lawrence Erlbaum Association, 221–248.

Samson HH (1986). Initiation of ethanol reinforcement using a sucrose-substitution procedure in food- and water-sated rats. *Alcoholism: Clinical & Experimental Research* 10:436–442.

Samson HH, Pfeffer AO & Tolliver GA (1988). Oral ethanol self-administration in rats: Models of alcohol-seeking behavior. *Alcoholism: Clinical & Experimental Research* 12:591–598.

Samson HH, Hodge CW, Tolliver GA & Haraguchi M (1993). Effect of dopamine agonists and antagonists on ethanol-reinforced behavior: The involvement of the nucleus accumbens. *Brain Research Bulletin* 30:133–141.

Schulteis G, Markou A, Cole M & Koob GF (1995). Decreased brain reward produced by ethanol withdrawal. *Proceedings of the National Academy of Science* 92:5880–5884.

Sinclair JD & Senter RJ (1967). Increased preference for ethanol in rats following alcohol deprivation. *Psychological Science* 8:11–12.

Tabakoff B & Hoffman PL (1992). Alcohol: Neurobiology. In JH Lowinson, P Ruiz & RB Millman (eds.) *Substance Abuse: A Comprehensive Textbook (2nd edition).* Baltimore, MD: Williams & Wilkins, 152–185.

Tsai G, Gastfriend DR & Coyle JT (1995). The glutametergic basis of human alcoholism. *American Journal of Psychiatry* 152:332–340.

Weiss F, Lorang MT, Bloom FE & Koob GF (1993). Oral alcohol self-administration stimulates dopamine release in the rat nucleus accumbens: Genetic and motivational determinants. *Journal of Pharmacology and Experimental Therapeutics* 267:250–258.

Weiss F, Parsons LH, Schulteis G et al. (1996). Ethanol self-administration restores withdrawal-associated deficiencies in accumbal dopamine and 5-hydroxytryptamine release in dependent rats. *Journal of Neuroscience* 16:3474–3485.

Zieglgansberger W & Zeise ML (1992). Calcium-diacetyl-homotaurinate which prevents relapse in weaned alcoholics decreases the action of excitatory amino acids in neocortical neurons of the rat in vitro. In CA Naranjo & EM Sellers (eds.) *Novel Pharmacological Interventions for Alcoholism.* New York, NY: Springer Verlag, 337–341.

CHAPTER 7

Stress as a Factor in Addiction

Pier Vicenzo Piazza
Michel Le Moal

Experimental Approaches to Studying Stress and Drug Abuse
Influence of Stressors on Drug Self-Administration
Factors Influencing the Behavioral Effects of Stressors
Mechanisms of Stress Action
Does Stress Induce a Drug-Prone Phenotype?

It is well known that, although a large number of people experiment with drugs for variable periods of time, only few of them develop a real addiction, i.e., a compulsive drug use that becomes the main goal-directed activity of the subject (O'Brien, Ehrman & Terns, 1986). Two principal theoretical frames have been used to explain the transition from drug use to addiction. They can be defined as a drug- and an individual-centered vision of addiction, respectively.

The drug-centered vision of addiction views drug abuse as an iatrogenic disease resulting from the changes induced in brain function by chronic drug intake. Drug-induced phenomena, such as tolerance, sensitization and conditioning, would determine a dependent state, which is responsible for the shift from use to abuse (for a review, see Nestler, 1992; Robinson & Berridge, 1993; and White, 1996). According to this hypothesis, the individuals who will develop addiction are the ones who, because of their social environment, have more opportunity to use drugs repeatedly.

The individual-centered vision of addiction considers that drug abuse is a preexisting pathological condition exposed by the drug. Addiction would appear only in certain individuals because their biological features will generate a pathological response to drugs (Piazza & Le Moal, 1996). This pathological response would make the appetitive properties of drugs much greater in some subjects, thus increasing their likeliness to develop a drug addiction.

Research on the influence of stress on drug intake is part of the theoretical frame of the individual-centered vision of addiction. Stress research has contributed to showing that the biological status of an individual plays an important role in determining the propensity to develop drug self-administration, and highlighted the importance of environmental experiences in inducing a drug-prone phenotype.

EXPERIMENTAL APPROACHES TO STUDYING STRESS AND DRUG ABUSE

Humans abuse a large variety of drugs, principally opioids, psychostimulants, alcohol, nicotine, cannabinoids, barbiturates and benzodiazepines. Stress research has mainly focused on opioid and psychostimulant drugs. Consequently, in this review the generic term "drugs of abuse," except when specified otherwise, will refer to these two classes of drugs.

The main core of research on the interaction between stress and drugs of abuse arises from experimental sources and, in particular, from research on the rat. Indeed, although several authors have proposed that stress is positively related to the abuse of both opioid (Kosten, Rounsaville & Kleber, 1986; O'Doherty, 1991) and psychostimulant drugs (Johanson & Fischman, 1989; Gawin, 1991) and to the relapse to such drug abuse, a firm causal link between stress and drug abuse cannot be established on the basis of studies in humans (O'Doherty & Davies, 1987). There are two main reasons for this. First, in humans, the variables under investigation, i.e., the history and the experiences of the subject, cannot be directly manipulated in controlled experimental conditions, but only indirectly assessed on the basis of retrospective self-reports of stress. Second, a reliable measure of the outcome of stress on drug abuse implies that all the individuals have an equal access to drugs under identical environmental conditions. Again, this experimental setting is impossible to be realized in humans.

The experimental study of the interactions between stress and drug abuse in animals allows the experimental conditions described above to be achieved and also permits the study of the biological mechanisms mediating the effect of stress. As reviewed here, these types of investigations have now unveiled some of the biological factors that mediate stress-induced self-administration of drugs of abuse.

Behavioral Studies. The experimental study of drug abuse has been made possible by the discovery that animals self-administer drugs intravenously (Weeks, 1962); this behavior shares many similarities with drug use in humans. First, animals self-administer almost all of the drugs that have been shown to be addictive in humans (Yokel, 1987). The few exceptions are the hallucinogen lysergic acid diethylamide (LSD) and delta-9-tetrahydrocannabinol (THC) (Altman, 1996). Second, the patterns of self-administration of the different drugs in humans and animals are similar (Altman, 1996). Finally, the large individual differences that characterize the human response to drugs of abuse also are found in animals (Piazza & Le Moal, 1996).

Self-administration measures positive reinforcing effects of drugs (Altman, 1996) and best describes what is observed in animals, i.e., the learning of an operant response, such as pressing a lever, that results in the infusion of a drug. In general, changes in the rate of response reinforced by the drug are considered to reflect changes in the sensitivity to its appetitive properties (Altman, 1996; Schuster & Thompson, 1969).

Self-administration usually is studied using three different and complementary approaches, whose features will be briefly outlined here.

1. Acquisition studies evaluate the propensity of an individual to develop drug self-administration. For this purpose, the first contact the individual has with low doses of the drug are studied, and parameters such as threshold or rate of acquisition are taken into account (Piazza & Le Moal, 1996).
2. Retention studies are performed after a prolonged training with high doses of drug and are used to estimate changes in the sensitivity to the reinforcing effects of drugs and the motivation to self-administer drugs (Altman, 1996; Schuster & Thompson, 1969). The individual's sensitivity to drugs is assessed by performing dose-response curves: the dose of the drug per infusion is varied, usually between sessions, and the rate of responding recorded. In the context of retention studies, motivation for self-administering drugs is evaluated principally by means of progressive ratio schedules. In this case, the dose is kept constant and the ratio requirement (number of responses necessary to obtain one infusion) is progressively increased. The highest ratio reached by the subjects (breaking-point) is considered to be an index of their motivation to self-administer drugs.
3. Reinstatement studies are considered as a measure of relapse to drug intake (Shaham & Stewart, 1995). In this case, the behavior is studied after the extinction of previously acquired self-administration. Extinction usually is obtained by substituting the drug with a vehicle solution. Following extinction, administration of stimuli known to induce craving for the drug in abstinent human addicts, such as low doses of the drug, will reinstate responding on the device that elicited the infusion of the drug during acquisition. Rate of responding on this device is the principal measure of reinstatement (Shaham & Stewart, 1995).

Biological Studies. Studies on the biological basis of the effects of stress on drug self-administration have been led by two main complementary research strategies. The first one has investigated stress-induced changes in the activity of the neurobiological substrates of drug-reinforcing effects, the underlying hypothesis being that stressors facilitate drug self-administration by increasing the activity of these neurobiological systems. This research has focused principally on the mesencephalic dopaminergic neurones and, in particular, on their projection to the nucleus accumbens, which is considered to be one of the principal substrates of drug reinforcing effects (Nestler, 1992; Robinson & Berridge, 1993; Koob & Bloom, 1988; Wise, 1996).

The second research strategy has focused on the biological responses to stress and investigated their influence on the reinforcing effects of drugs. The goal of these studies was to identify which specific stress-induced changes mediate the effects of stressors on drug self-administration. These researchers have principally focused on the activity of the hypothalamic-pituitary-adrenal (HPA) axis and, in particular, on glucocorticoid hormones, the final step of this endocrine system. Secretion of glucocorticoids by the adrenal gland is considered to be one of the principal biological adaptations to external aggression (McEwen, De Kloet & Rostene, 1996).

Stress in the Context of Experimental Research. The concept of stress is a very vague one and the term often is used with different meanings. It seems important, therefore, to define stress in the context of experimental research. Models of stress are principally based on the forced exposure to stimuli or situations that normally are avoided by the individual. This is why stress, as studied in animals, probably corresponds to the internal status induced by the exposure to threatening and aversive stimuli. This probably is not a very comprehensive definition of stress, but it seems to be the best reflection of what is generally studied in experimental stress research.

INFLUENCE OF STRESSORS ON DRUG SELF-ADMINISTRATION

Stressful experiences have a large influence on the self-administration of drugs of abuse. They facilitate the acquisition of this behavior, increase the rate of responding during retention, and can precipitate reinstatement (see Table 1 for a summary, as well as Carroll & Meich, 1984; Kanarek & Marks-Kaufman, 1988; Piazza, Deminiere et al., 1990; Goeders & Guerin, 1994; Shaham & Stewart, 1994; Erb, Shaham & Stewart, 1996; Shaham, 1993; Haney, Maccari et al., 1995; Miczek & Mutscheler, 1996; Piazza et al., 1991; Maccari et al., 1991; Hadawy, Alexander et al., 1979; Marks-Kaufman & Lewis, 1994; Schenck, Gorman & Amit, 1990; Wolffgramm & Heyne, 1991; Bozarth, Murray & Wise, 1989; Alexander, Beyerstein et al., 1981; Schenck, Lacelle et al., 1987; Ramsey & Van Ree, 1993; Deminiere et al., 1992). The influence of different forms of stress on the three aspects of self-administration will be analyzed separately.

Acquisition Studies. In adult animals, artificial and physical stressors such as repeated tail pinch (Piazza, Deminiere et al., 1990) (Figure 1a) and electric foot-shocks (Goeders & Guerin, 1994) facilitate the acquisition of the self-administration of psychostimulants such as cocaine and amphetamine. Food restriction is another physical stressor that facilitates the acquisition of psychostimulant, opiate and alcohol self-administration (for review, see Carroll & Meich, 1984; Kanarek & Marks-Kaufman, 1988).

TABLE 1. Stressors that Increase Drug Self-Administration

	Approaches to the study of drug self-administration			
Types of stress	Acquisition	Dose-response	Progressive ratio	Reinstatement
Food restriction	Psychostimulants	Psychostimulants		
		Opiates	Opiates	
		Alcohol	Alcohol	
Tail pinch	Amphetamine			
Foot shocks	Cocaine		Heroin	Heroin
				Cocaine
Restraint	Morphine			
Social aggression	Cocaine	Cocaine		
Social competition	Amphetamine			
Social isolation	Opiates	*Cocaine		
	Alcohol	Heroin		
Witnessing stress	Cocaine			
Prenatal stress	Amphetamine			

Depending on the type of self-adminitration used: facilitation of acquisition; upward shift of the dose-response curve; higher breaking-point; induction of responding on the device previously associated with the infusion of the drug. Note that for social isolation also slightly higher, equal and lower sensitivities to the reinforcing effects of cocaine have been reported.

FIGURE 1. Examples of the Effects of Stress on Drug Self-Administration

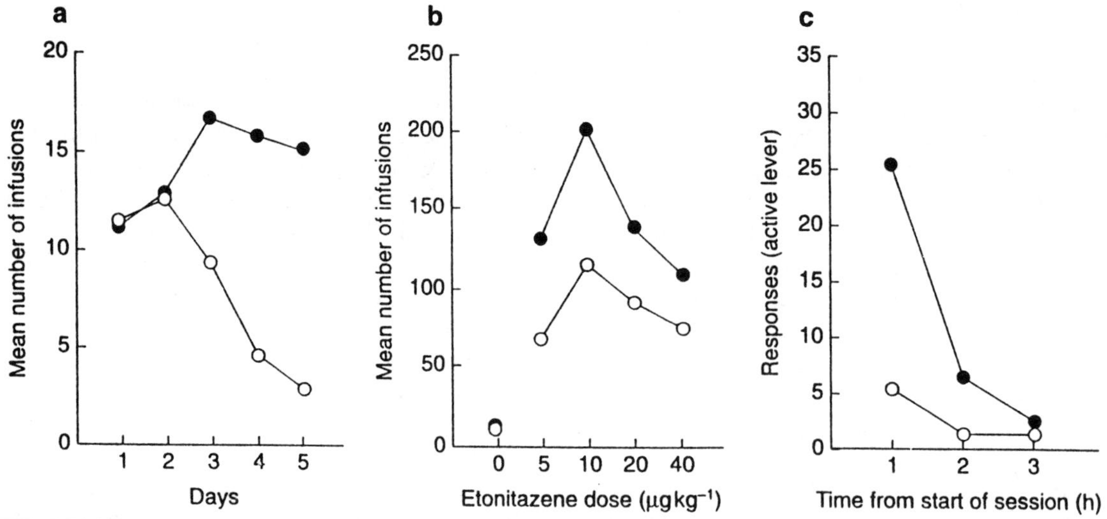

Examples of the effects of stress on intravenous self-administration studied using different approaches. **a:** Acquisition of the self-administration of amphetamine (10 µg/infusion). **b:** Dose-response curves during the retention phase of etonitazene self-administration. **c:** Reinstatement of responding in the device previously associated with drug delivery (active lever) after extinction of heroin self-administration. The stressors are tail-pinch (a), food-restriction (b) and electric foot-shocks (c). Stress facilitates the acquisition of self-administration, induces an upward shift of the dose-response function and triggers reinstatement of drug-seeking behavior. Open circles, controls; closed circles, stress. The effects of the other types of stress cited in Table 1 were very similar to the examples represented here.

Acquisition of psychostimulant self-administration also is enhanced in male and female rats exposed to an aggressive congener (Haney, Maccari et al., 1995) and in male rats raised in colonies at high social competitions, such as mixed colonies. In these colonies, male rats fight to establish and maintain the social hierarchy that will determine access to females (Taylor, Weiss & Rupich, 1987). The maintenance, more than the establishment, of the social hierarchy seems to be the relevant variable here. Thus, if the social hierarchy is constantly renewed by daily changes in the association of the colony's males, acquisition of self-administration decreases (Maccari et al., 1991). Facilitation of the acquisition of morphine (Hadawy, Alexander et al., 1979; Marks-Kaufman & Lewis, 1994) and alcohol (Schenck, Gorman & Amit, 1990; Wolffgramm & Heyne, 1991) oral self-administration, as well as of heroin intravenous self-administration (Deminiere et al., 1992), also is induced by social isolation.

Very early life events, such as prenatal stress, also increase the likelihood of an individual developing amphetamine self-administration (Deminiere et al., 1992). Such an effect has been observed in adult rats whose mothers had been submitted to a restraint procedure during the third and fourth weeks of gestations.

Retention Studies. Changes in dose-response functions for psychostimulant and/or opiate self-administration have been observed after social stress (Miczek & Mutscheler, 1996), social isolation (Alexander, Beyerstein et al., 1981; Schenck, Lacelle et al., 1987; Schenck, Robinson & Amit, 1988) and food restriction (Carroll & Meich, 1984; Kanarek & Marks-Kaufman, 1988) (Figure 1b). In all these cases, the stressors induce an increase in the rate of responding over a large range of doses, resulting in a vertical upward shift of the dose-response function. This type of shift suggests an increase in the reinforcing efficacy of drugs in stressed animals. This idea is confirmed by progressive ratio studies. Thus, over a large range of doses, the breaking point for heroin self-administration has been found to be consistently higher for animals receiving electric foot-shocks than for control rats (Shaham & Stewart, 1994).

Retention studies deserve some methodological considerations. One report (Shaham & Stewart, 1994) showed that although stressed rats had a higher breaking point, they did not differ from controls for the rate of self-administration at fixed low ratios. This result suggests that measuring the rate of responding, under low ratio requirements and high training doses, may not accurately reveal differences in drug-seeking behavior. The use of this type of schedule could explain the large variability observed in the effect of social isolation. Indeed, higher (Schenck, Lacelle et al., 1987), slightly higher (Boyle, Smith & Amit, 1991), equal (Bozarth, Murray & Wise, 1989) or lower (Phillips et al., 1994) sensitivities to cocaine all have been described in socially isolated rats compared with grouped rats. The conditions chosen as controls also could contribute to such variability. In fact, the rate of self-administration of control animals, not isolated ones, is the differentiating factor in some of these reports (Bozarth, Murray & Wise, 1989; Schenck, Lacelle et al., 1987; Boyle, Smith & Amit, 1991). Not surprisingly, the effects of social isolation appeared to be weaker (Bozarth, Murray & Wise, 1989; Boyle, Smith & Amit, 1991) when other conditions that facilitate self-administration, such as printing injections of the drug and pre-test periods of food restriction, were concomitantly used.

Reinstatement Studies. Stressors also increase reinstatement of drug self-administration. In rats in which responding for heroin (Shaham & Stewart, 1995) (Figure 1c) or cocaine (Erb, Shaham & Stewart, 1996) has been extinguished by substituting the drug with a saline solution, a single stressful experience such as exposure to electric foot-shocks induces the reinstatement of responding for the drug. Stress-induced reinstatement seems to be a very robust and well-documented phenomenon. For example, reinstatement was found to be of higher intensity when induced by stress (Shaham, 1996) than when induced by the principal experimental manipulation used to induce reinstatement (Altman et al., 1996), i.e., a non-contingent priming infusion of the self-administered drugs. However, this field of research would benefit by extending these observations to other types of stress in order to provide a degree of generalization to this phenomenon, which, for the moment, is limited to electric foot-shocks.

FACTORS INFLUENCING THE BEHAVIORAL EFFECTS OF STRESSORS

The data reviewed above show that a large variety of stressors can increase the propensity to self-administer drugs of abuse. The following section, by comparing the results obtained using different stress models, will highlight some of the features that increase or decrease the likelihood that a stressful event actually can modify the propensity to self-administer psychostimulant or opioid drugs.

Predictability and Intensity. The predictability of a stimulus to evoke a stress-related response and the intensity of the stressor appear to be important variables in mediating the effects of stress on drug self-administration. Unpredictable stressors have higher effects than predictable ones. For example, it has been shown that unpredictable electric foot-shocks increase the acquisition of cocaine self-administration, whereas identical predictable shocks have no effect (Goeders & Guerin, 1994). Furthermore, stressors, especially when acute, need to be of a certain intensity in order to increase self-administration. For example, unpredictable shocks of around half the intensity of the ones used above (Goeders & Guerin, 1994) do not modify the acquisition of cocaine self-administration (Ramsey & Van Ree, 1993). Similarly, other physical stressors of very short duration, such as exposure to a hot plate for 30 seconds before the self-administration session, fail to modify cocaine intake (Ramsey & Van Ree, 1993). The relationship between the intensity of the stressor and its outcome on drug seeking also is shown by reinstatement studies (Shaham, 1996). Thus, the rate of reinstatement has been found to be a function of the duration of the shocks (Shaham, 1996). However, in the case of prolonged exposure to stress, the duration of the stress seems less important. Similar facilitatory effects on self-administration have been found for stressors that are continuous (Carroll & Meich, 1984; Kanarek & Marks-Kaufman, 1988; Piazza et al., 1991; Maccari et al., 1991; Schenck, Gorman & Amit, 1990; Alexander, Beyerstein et al., 1981; Schenck, Lacelle et al., 1987), as well as for those that are of short duration and administered repeatedly (Piazza, Deminiere et al., 1990; Goeders & Guerin, 1994; Shaham & Stewart, 1994; Haney, Maccari et al., 1995; Miczek & Mutscheler, 1996).

Physical versus Psychological Threats. Although stressors that comprise a physical component, such as electric foot-shock (Goeders & Guerin, 1994) and tail-pinch (Piazza, Deminiere et al., 1990), induce an increase in self-administration, physical aggressions do not seem to be a necessary condition in mediating stress effects. In fact, psychological stress alone also is able to increase drug self-administration. For example, it has been shown that, if a rat witnesses another rat receiving foot-shock, it facilitates the acquisition of cocaine self-administration (Ramsey & Van Ree, 1993). Furthermore, in social aggression experiments, facilitation of self-administration also occurs when the intruder is protected at all times by a screen grid and consequently never submitted to physical attacks (Miczek & Mutscheler, 1996). Some interesting insights regarding the relative "weight" of physical and psychological threats have arisen from the social competition experiment. Here, two potentially stressful conditions were compared in colonies at high competition (mixed colonies of three males and three females) (Maccari et al., 1991). The first was the maintenance of a fixed social hierarchy, which was obtained by maintaining the same component of the colony over one month. The second was the daily reestablishment of the social hierarchy, which was obtained by renewing the male components of the colony every day. Though the inter-male aggression was much higher in the latter, the propensity to develop amphetamine self-administration was higher in males that had to maintain a fixed social hierarchy (Maccari et al., 1991).

Time Contingencies. Both acute and repeated exposure to stress can increase the propensity to develop drug self-administration. However, acute and chronic stress are differently influenced by temporal contingencies. For acute stressors, a short interval between the stressful event and the exposure to the drug appears to be crucial. For example, in the case of restraint stress (Shaham, 1993), facilitation of self-administration has been found if the restraint closely precedes the exposure to the drug, but not if it occurs earlier. However, after prolonged exposure to stress, the interval between the termination of the stress and the exposure to the drug does not seem to be a relevant variable. A facilitation of drug self-administration has been found both when the stressor is continued during the period of test for self-administration (Carroll & Meich, 1984; Kanarek & Marks-Kaufman, 1988; Hadawy, Alexander et al., 1979; Marks-Kaufman & Lewis, 1994; Schenck, Gorman & Amit, 1990; Wolffgramm & Heyne, 1991; Bozarth, Murray & Wise, 1989) and when the stress is terminated weeks before the start of the self-administration session (Piazza, Deminiere et al., 1990; Haney, Maccari et al., 1995; Maccari et al., 1991; Specker, Lac & Carroll, 1994). These observations are important from a pathophysiological point of view. Thus, they indicate that repeated stress can induce long-lasting modifications, determining a drug-prone state that becomes independent from the actual presence of the stressor.

MECHANISMS OF STRESS ACTION

Neurobiological Interaction between Stress and Reward. The results reviewed above clearly show that stress can increase the propensity of an individual to self-administer drugs of abuse. The question that remains to be answered is why stress has such an effect.

One of the most likely explanations is that stress modifies, at the neurobiological level, the motivational and/or reinforcing properties of drugs of abuse. Indeed, one of the effects of stress is to increase the activity of those neurobiological systems involved in motivation and reward (Kalivas & Stewart, 1991; Piazza & Le Moal, in press). As these neurobiological systems also serve as a substrate for drug-induced reinforcement (Nestler, 1992; Robinson & Berridge, 1993; Koob & Bloom, 1988; Wise, 1996), by changing their activity, stressors could enhance the responsiveness to drugs of abuse. Why stressors increase the activity of the biological substrate of reward still remains an open question. However, it recently has been proposed that this could constitute a compensatory attempt to counteract the aversive effects of stress (Piazza & Le Moal, in press).

Mesencephalic dopaminergic neurones seem to be the neurobiological substrate through which stress increases the propensity to self-administer drugs of abuse. The role of these neurones in reward and motivation has been emphasized in several good reviews (Nestler, 1992; Robinson & Berridge, 1993; Koob & Bloom, 1988; Wise, 1996). In particular, the release of dopamine in the nucleus accumbens is considered to be one of the major substrates of the addictive properties of drugs (Nestler, 1992; Robinson & Berridge, 1993; Koob & Bloom, 1988; Wise, 1996).

Several types of acute stress increase dopamine release in the nucleus accumbens (Kalivas & Stewart, 1991). Furthermore, repeated stress induces a long-lasting increase in the release of this neurotransmitter (Kalivas & Stewart, 1991). In particular, in stressed subjects, drug-induced dopamine release is increased (Kalivas & Stewart, 1991). That stress-induced increase in dopamine release could mediate the effects of stress on drug self-administration is supported by a supplementary set of observations. Indeed, when an increase in the activity of the dopaminergic projection to the nucleus accumbens is induced by other means, such as repeated amphetamine injections (Robinson & Berridge, 1993; Piazza, Deminiere et al., 1990; Kalivas & Stewart, 1991) or lesions of specific brain areas (Piazza & Le Moal, 1996), an increase in psychostimulant self-administration similar to the one induced by stress also is observed.

An increase in the levels of glucocorticoid hormones, one of the principal biological responses to stress (McEwen, De Kloet & Rostene, 1996; De Kloet, 1992), could be the link between environmental experiences and mesencephalic dopaminergic neurones. In basal conditions, administration of glucocorticoids at levels that are in the stress range can increase dopamine release in the nucleus accumbens (Piazza et al., 1996), whereas suppression of glucocorticoid secretion has opposite effects (Piazza et al., 1996). During stress, a selective block of stress-induced secretion of glucocorticoids reduces dopamine release by around 50% (Piazza & Le Moal, 1996). Finally, the development of the long-lasting sensitization of the dopaminergic response to psychostimulants and opioids (Deroche et al., 1995; Rouge-Pont, Marinelli et al., 1995) induced by stress is suppressed by the block of corticosterone secretion.

The fact that glucocorticoid hormones, through their action on dopamine release, could increase the behavioral responses to drugs is supported by a supplementary set of data. First, administration of glucocorticoids at levels that are in the stress range increases the propensity to self-administer amphetamines (Piazza et al., 1991). Second, block of stress-induced corticosterone secretion induces a downward shift in the dose-response curve for cocaine self-administration (Deroche, Marinelli et al., 1997), i.e., changes opposite to the ones observed after stress.

A disruption of glucocorticoid secretion also could participate in maintaining the long-term effect of stress. Thus, a long-lasting increase in corticosterone secretion has been observed in several experiments in which a higher propensity to self-administer drugs was induced by stress (Haney, Maccari et al., 1995; Maccari et al., 1991, 1995; Piazza et al., 1991). Furthermore, block of corticosterone secretion can reverse stress-induced sensitization of the dopaminergic and behavioral response to cocaine (Rouge-Pont, Marinelli et al., 1995).

A decrease in hippocampal corticosteroid receptors could be the mechanism mediating the long-lasting increase in corticosterone secretion observed in stressed subjects. These receptors are one of the principal substrates of the inhibitory feedback loop that controls glucocorticoid secretion (McEwen, De Kloet & Rostene, 1996; De Kloet, 1992), and an increase or a decrease in their number has been associated with an increase or a decrease in the secretion of glucocorticoids, respectively (McEwen, De Kloet & Rostene, 1996; De Kloet, 1992). The number of corticosteroid receptors is profoundly reduced (by more than 50%) in subjects made drug-prone by stress (Maccari et al., 1991, 1995). Such a decrease is probably a consequence of the repeated increases in stress-induced glucocorticoid levels (McEwen, De Kloet & Rostene, 1996; De Kloet, 1992). This mechanism, largely observed in the adult (McEwen, De Kloet & Rostene, 1996; De Kloet, 1992), also seems to be involved during early life stages. Thus, if glucocorticoid secretion of the mother is blocked, the decrease in corticosteroid receptors and the increase in glucocorticoid secretion induced by prenatal stress in the offspring also are suppressed (Barbazanges, Piazza et al., 1996).

Figure 2 contains a schematic description of the interaction between stress, glucocorticoids and dopaminergic neurones.

Alternative Mechanisms. The mechanism proposed above should not be considered to be the only one involved in mediating the effects of stress on self-administration. The following section describes some alternatives and presents open questions that may constitute the background for future investigations.

Stress-induced Impulsivity: A deficit in the inhibitory processes that normally operate to control the rewarding effect of a stimulus is considered to be an important dimension of impulsivity (Poulos, Le & Parker, 1995). This type of impairment could contribute to the increase in drug self-administration induced by stress. This idea is prompted by the effects of social aggressions on the rate of responding during time-out periods, i.e., fixed time periods that follow each drug infusion and during which time responding has no scheduled consequences. Whilst, during time out, control animals quickly learn to reduce responding and to wait for the next period of drug availability, stressed rats maintain high rates of responding during these times (Miczek & Mutscheler, 1996). The possibility that an inhibitory deficit is involved in excessive drug consumption also is backed by another recent report showing that the inability to delay gratification predicts alcohol self-administration (Poulos, Le & Parker, 1995).

Although stress-induced impulsivity appears to be an interesting mechanism, its role in the effect of stress is not yet proven. Further experiments should specifically test the actual occurrence of such a change in behavior. Moreover, at the neurochemical level, it would be important to correlate such potential changes in behavior with neurobiological modifications involved in impulsivity, such as a decrease in 5-HT-mediated activity (Soubrie, 1986).

Stress-induced Reinstatement: Different biological mechanisms could mediate stress-induced reinstatement. Although the hypothalamic-pituitary-adrenal axis and dopaminergic neurones still seem

FIGURE 2. Possible Pathophysiological Mechanisms of the Increase in Drug Self-Administration Induced by Stress

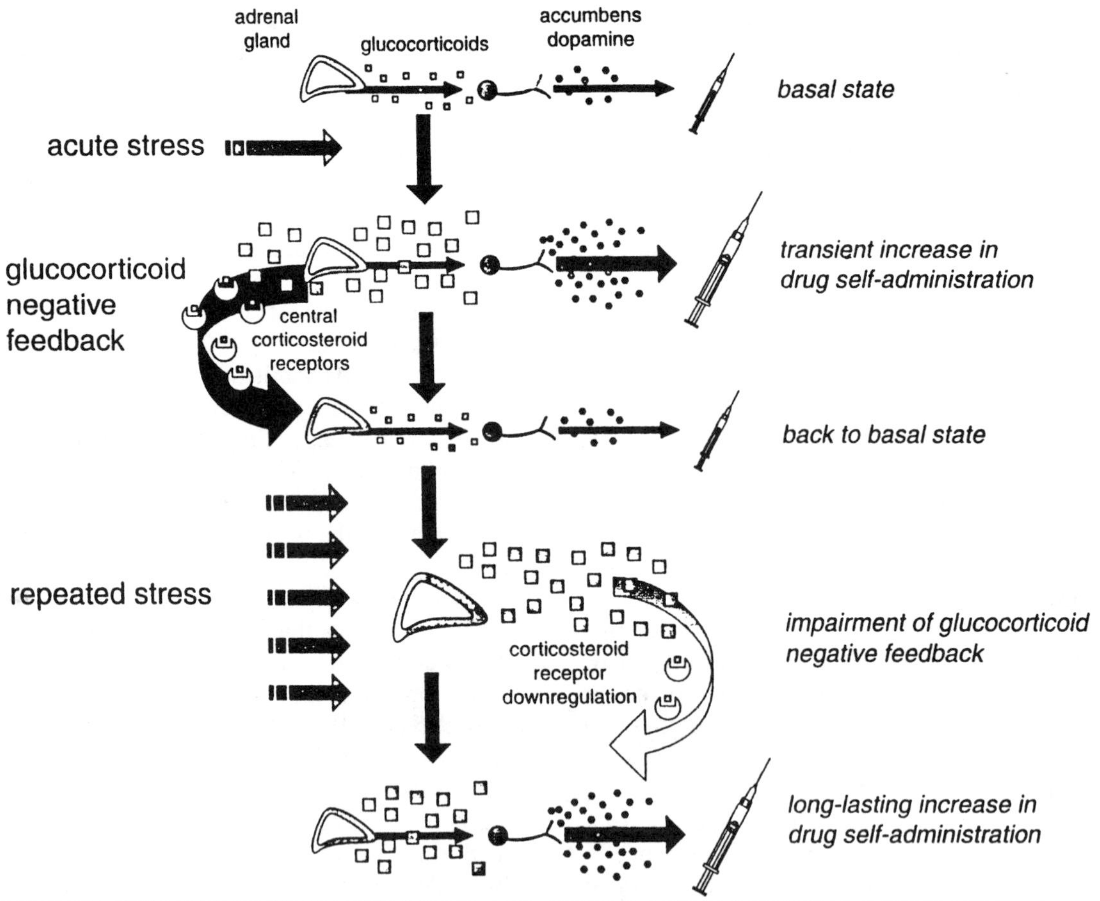

Possible pathophysiological mechanisms of the increase in drug self-administration induced by acute and repeated stress. The interactions of two biological systems are schematically represented as follows: (1) in yellow: the secretion of glucocorticoids from the adrenal gland, one of the principal hormonal responses to stress; (2) in red: the release of dopamine from the meso-accumbens dopaminergic projection, one of the principal neurobiological substrates of the rewarding properties of drugs of abuse. These two systems interact in basal conditions and during stress; the concentrations of glucocorticoids determine the level of dopamine release in the nucleus accumbens. In basal conditions (basal state), glucocorticoid secretion and dopamine release are low, as is sensitivity to drugs of abuse. An acute stress determines an increase in glucocorticoid secretion, which, by enhancing the release of dopamine, result in an increase in the sensitivity to the reinforcing effects of drugs of abuse, which can result in an increase in self-administration. However, activation by glucocorticoids of the negative feedback that controls the secretion of these hormones returns the system to basal levels within 2 hours. Binding of glucocorticoids to hippocampal corticosteroid receptors is a key step in the activation of this negative feedback. The repeated increase in the concentrations of glucocorticoids induced by repeated exposure to stress will progressively impair glucocorticoid negative feedback, and this probably by decreasing the number of central corticosteroid receptors in the hippocampus. The impairment of glucocorticoid negative feedback will result in a long-lasting increase in the secretion of these hormones and in the release of dopamine in the nucleus accumbens. These changes will, in turn, determine a long-lasting increase in the sensitivity to the reinforcing effects of drugs of abuse. The transient increase in glucocorticoids and dopamine observed after acute stress may explain why, in this case, an increase in drug self-administration is found only if the exposure to drug closely follows the stressor. The long-lasting increase in the activity of these two biological factors could explain why, after repeated stress an increase in the sensitivity to drugs, is found also long (weeks) after the end of the stressor.

to play a role, they seem to be involved in reinstatement in a way that differs from that described for drug self-administration.

For example, a concomitant block of dopamine D1 and D2 receptors is needed to block stress-induced reinstatement (Shaham & Stewart, 1996), whereas selective antagonists of either receptors suffice to decrease positive reinforcing effects of drugs (Koob & Bloom, 1988; Wise, 1996). In parallel, although the single injection of glucocorticoids can induce reinstatement (Deroche, Marinelli et al., 1997), blocking the secretion of these hormones does not prevent stress-induced reinstatement of heroin self-administration, which is, in contrast, attenuated by corticotropin-releasing factor (CRF) receptor antagonists (Shaham et al., 1997).

However, it also should be noted that the differences between self-administration and reinstatement could simply reflect the fact that different mechanisms mediate the behavioral response to different drugs of abuse. Thus, the majority of the studies investigating the role of glucocorticoids and dopamine in the mediation of the effects of stress on self-administration concern psychostimulant drugs. In contrast, studies on reinstatement have been performed principally in animals trained to self-administer heroin.

Associative Learning: Learning, in the form of a classical conditioning type of phenomena, also has been evoked to explain certain effects of stress on self-administration (Kanarek & Marks-Kaufman, 1988). In particular, the involvement of associative factors has been suggested by the observation that an acute restraint facilitates morphine self-administration only if it has been paired with (i.e., closely precedes) the onset of the self-administration session (Shaham, 1993).

The data reviewed above propose an alternative explanation to this observation. In the case of acute stress, there must be a close time contingency with the self-administration session, simply because the increase in the secretion of glucocorticoids and in the release of dopamine is transient (Figure 2). Furthermore, associative factors cannot explain the effects of stress as a whole. Thus, stress can facilitate self-administration independently from any time contingency with the exposure to drugs. The best example is the one of prenatal stress (Deminiere et al., 1992). In this case, the stressor occurs months before the exposure to the drug, while the subject is still in a fetal state.

DOES STRESS INDUCE A DRUG-PRONE PHENOTYPE?

In outbred populations of rats, there seems to exist a drug-prone phenotype. As mentioned earlier, large individual differences in the propensity to develop drug self-administration have been described (for a review, see Piazza & Le Moal, 1996), and the propensity of an individual to develop self-administration correlate with the individual's behavior in other experimental situations. For example, the individuals who show the highest locomotor activity when confined in a novel environment, a procedure that can be seen as a model of mild stress, also show the highest propensity to self-administer amphetamine (Piazza, Deminiere et al., 1989).

The data presented in this review suggest that stressful experiences are one of the determinants of a drug-prone phenotype. Indeed, stressors can induce a long-lasting increase in drug self-administration and such an effect can take place at a very early stage of life, as exemplified by prenatal stress (Deminiere et al., 1992). Further support to this idea arises from the comparison of the characteristics of individuals who are spontaneously drug-prone with those of subjects in whom such a predisposition has been induced by stress. Indeed, both from a behavioral and a biological point of view, these two types of individuals are very similar.

Spontaneously predisposed subjects, similar to stressed ones, show a faster acquisition of drug self-administration (Piazza, Deminiere et al., 1989), an upward shift of the dose-response function, and reach higher ratio requirements. They also show a higher level of dopamine release into the nucleus accumbens in response to a drug challenge, and a longer glucocorticoid secretion in response to stress (Piazza et al., 1991). Again, these characteristics are shared by rats made drug-prone by stress. Finally, as described for stressed subjects, the higher dopaminergic activity of individuals who are spontaneously drug-prone seems to be glucocorticoid dependent. These rats are more sensitive to the dopaminergic effect of glucocorticoids (Piazza et al., 1996) and blocking of the secretion of these hormones reduces their dopaminergic hyperactivity.

CONCLUSIONS

To conclude, stress experiences increase the propensity of an individual to develop drug self-administration, inducing a drug-prone phenotype. Stress-induced increases in glucocorticoid secretion, which in turn enhances drug-induced release of dopamine in the nucleus accumbens, seems to be an important substrate of such an effect of stress.

These observations bring three main conclusive considerations. First, they confirm the hypothesis advanced on the basis of correlative human studies (Kosten, Rounsaville & Kleber, 1986; O'Doherty, 1991; Johanson & Fischman, 1989; Gawin, 1991; O'Doherty & Davies, 1987) that stress could be one of the factors facilitating the development of drug abuse in humans. Second, they support the idea that drug abuse is not simply an iatrogenic disease, i.e., a disease induced by chronic drug intake, but that the phenotype of the individual plays an important role in determining the development of such pathological behavior. Third, they highlight the importance of environmental experiences in determining a drug-prone phenotype and consequently the role of environmental factors in the etiology of drug abuse.

The increasing understanding of the biological mechanisms of stress action also could help to develop new therapeutic strategies of drug abuse. On the basis of the evidence described above, the HPA axis could constitute the substrate for the development of new therapies of addiction.

ACKNOWLEDGMENT: Originally published as Piazza PV & Le Moal M (1998). The role of stress in drug self-administration. Trends in Pharmacological Sciences *19:67–74. Reprinted by permission of the publisher.*

REFERENCES

Alexander BK, Beyerstein BL, Hadaway PF & Coambs RB (1981). *Pharmacology, Biochemistry and Behavior* 15:571–576.

Altman J et al. (1996). *Psychopharmacology* 125:285–345.

Barbazanges A, Piazza PV, Le Moal M & Maccari S (1996). *Journal of Neuroscience* 6:3943–3949.

Boyle AE, Smith BR & Amit Z (1991). *Pharmacology, Biochemistry and Behavior* 39:269–274.

Bozarth MA, Murray A & Wise RA (1989). *Pharmacology, Biochemistry and Behavior* 33:903–907.

Carroll ME & Meich RA (1984). *Advanced Behavioral Pharmacology* 4:47–M.

De Kloet ER (1992). Front. *Neuroendocrinology* 12:95–164.

Deminiere JM et al. (1992). *Brain Research* 586:135–139.

Deroche V et al. (1995). *Journal of Neuroscience* 15:7181–7188.

Deroche V, Marinelli M, Le Moal M & Piazza PV (1997). *Journal of Pharmacology and Experimental Therapeutics* 281: 1401–1407.

Maccari S et al. (1995). *Journal of Neuroscience* 15:110–116.

Erb S, Shaham Y & Stewart J (1996). *Psychopharmacology* 128:408–412.

Gawin FH (1991). *Science* 251:1580–1586.

Goeders NE & Guerin GF (1994). *Psychopharmacology* 114:63–70.

Hadaway PF, Alexander BK, Coambs RB & Beyerstein B (1979). *Psychopharmacology* 66:87–91.

Haney M, Maccari R, Le Moal M, Simon H & Piazza PV (1995). *Brain Research* 698:46–52.

Hooks MS, Colvin AC, Juncos JL & Justice JB Jr (1992). *Brain Research* 587:306–312.

Johanson C-E & Fischman MW (1989). *Pharmacology Review* 41:3–52.

Kalivas PW & Stewart J (1991). *Brain Research Review* 16:223–244.

Kanarek RB & Marks-Kaufman R (1988). In RB Kanarek, R Marks-Kaufman & R Van Nostrand (eds.) *Nutrition and Behavior. New Perspectives.* Avi Books, 1–25.

Koob CF & Bloom FE (1988). *Science* 242:715–723.

Kosten TR, Rounsaville BJ & Kleber HD (1986). *Archives of General Psychiatry* 43:733–739.

Nestler EJ (1992). *Journal of Neuroscience* 12:2439–2450.

Maccari S et al. (1991). *Brain Research* 547:7–12.

Marks-Kaufman R & Lewis MJ (1994). *Addictive Behavior* 9:235–243.

McEwen BS, De Kloet ER & Rostene W (1996). *Physiological Review* 66:1221–1188.

Miczek KA & Mutscheler NH (1996). *Psychopharmacology* 128:256–264.

O'Brien CP, Ehrman RN & Terns JN (1986). In SR Goldeberg & IP Stolerman (eds.) *Behavioral Analysis of Drug Dependence.* Academic Press, 329.

O'Doherty F (1991). *Drug and Alcohol Dependence* 29:97–106.

O'Doherty F & Davies BJ (1987). *British Journal of Addictions* 82:127–137.

Phillips GD et al. (1994). *Psychopharmacology* 115:407–418.

Piazza PV et al. (1991). In P Wilner & J Scheel-Kruger (eds.) *The Mesolimbic Dopamine System: From Motivation to Action.* New York, NY: John Wiley & Sons, 473–495.

Piazza PV et al. (1996). *Proceedings of the National Academy of Science* 93:8716–8720.

Piazza PV et al. (1996). *Proceedings of the National Academy of Science* 93:15445–15450.

Piazza PV et al. (1991). *Proceedings of the National Academy of Science* 88:2088–2092.

Piazza PV, Deminiere JM, Le Moal M & Simon H (1990). *Brain Research* 514:22–26.

Piazza PV, Deminiere JM, Le Moal M & Simon H (1989). *Science* 245:1511–1513.

Piazza PV & Le Moal M (in press). *Brain Research Review.*

Piazza PV & Le Moal M (1996). *Annual Review of Pharmacology and Toxicology* 36:359–378.

Poulos CX, Le AD & Parker JL (1995). *Behavior Pharmacology* 6:810–814.

Ramsey NF & Van Ree JM (1993). *Brain Research* 608:216–222.

Robinson TE & Berridge KC (1993). *Brain Research Review* 18:247–291.

Rouge-Pont F, Marinelli M, Le Moal M, Simon H & Piazza PV (1995). *Journal of Neuroscience* 15: 7189–7195.

Schuster CR & Thompson T (1969). *Annual Review of Pharmacology* 9:483–502.

Shaham Y (1993). *Psychopharmacology* 111:477–485.

Shaham Y (1996). *Annals of Behavior Medicine* 18:255–263.

Shaham Y et al. (1997). *Journal of Neuroscience* 17:2605–2614.

Shaham Y & Stewart J (1994). *Psychopharmacology* 114:523–527.
Shaham Y & Stewart J (1995). *Psychopharmacology* 111:334–341.
Shaham Y & Stewart J (1996). *Psychopharmacology* 125:385–391.
Schenck S, Gorman K & Amit Z (1990). *Alcohol* 7:321–326.
Schenck S, Lacelle G, Gorman K & Amit Z (1987). *Neuroscience Letters* 81:227–231.
Schenck S, Robinson B & Amit Z (1988). *Pharmacology, Biochemistry and Behavior* 31:59–62.
Soubrie P (1986). *Behavior Brain Science* 9:319–335.
Specker SM, Lac ST & Carroll ME (1994). *Pharmacology, Biochemistry and Behavior* 48:1025–1029.
Taylor GT, Weiss J & Rupich R (1987). *Physiology and Behaviòr* 39:429–433.
Weeks JR (1962). *Science* 138:143–144.
White F (1996). *Addiction* 91:921–949.
Wise RA (1996). *Current Opinions in Neurobiology* 6:243–251.
Wolffgramm J & Heyne A (1991). *Pharmacology, Biochemistry and Behavior* 38:389–399.
Yokel RA (1987). In MA Bozarth (ed.) *Methods of Assessing the Reinforcing Properties of abused Drugs.* New York, NY: Spring-Verlag, 1–34.

SECTION 2
The Pharmacology of Addictive Drugs

CHAPTER 1

Clinical Pharmacokinetics and Pharmacodynamics: Key Concepts **99**
Donald R. Wesson, M.D.

CHAPTER 2

The Pharmacology of Alcohol **103**
John J. Woodward, Ph.D.

CHAPTER 3

The Pharmacology of Sedative-Hypnotics **117**
Steven M. Juergens, M.D., FASAM, and Debra Cowley, M.D.

CHAPTER 4

The Pharmacology of Opioids **131**
Mark S. Gold, M.D., FCP, FAPA

CHAPTER 5

The Pharmacology of Cocaine, Crack and Other Stimulants **137**
Mark S. Gold, M.D., FCP, FAPA, and Michael J. Herkov, Ph.D.

CHAPTER 6

The Pharmacology of Nicotine **147**
John Slade, M.D., FASAM

CHAPTER 7

The Pharmacology of Phencyclidine and the Hallucinogens **153**
Marilyn Carroll, Ph.D. and Sandra Comer, Ph.D.

CHAPTER 8

The Pharmacology of Marijuana **163**
Mark S. Gold, M.D., FCP, FAPA

CHAPTER 9

The Pharmacology of Steroids 173

Scott E. Lukas, Ph.D.

CHAPTER 10

The Pharmacology of Inhalants 187

Stephen H. Dinwiddie, M.D.

CHAPTER 11

Future Directions in Research 195

Walter A. Hunt, Ph.D., Roger M. Brown, Ph.D. and Jerry Frankenheim, Ph.D.

SECTION COORDINATOR

Mark S. Gold, M.D., FCP, FAPA
Professor, Departments of Psychiatry and Neuroscience
University of Florida Brain Institute
College of Medicine
Gainesville, Florida

CONTRIBUTORS

Roger M. Brown, Ph.D.
Chief, Neuroscience Research Branch
National Institute on Drug Abuse
Rockville, Maryland

Marilyn E. Carroll, Ph.D.
Professor of Psychiatry
University of Minnesota
Medical School
Twin Cities Campus
Minneapolis, Minnesota

Sandra D. Comer, Ph.D.
Assistant Professor
Department of Psychiatry
College of Physicians and Surgeons
Columbia University
New York, New York

Deborah Cowley, M.D.
Professor of Psychiatry and Behavioral Sciences
University of Washington
Seattle, Washington

Stephen H. Dinwiddie, M.D.
Medical Director
Elgin Mental Health Center;
Professor of Psychiatry
Finch University of Health Sciences
The Chicago Medical School
North Chicago, Illinois

Jerry Frankenheim, Ph.D.
Neuroscience and Behavioral Research Branch
National Institute on Drug Abuse
Rockville, Maryland

Michael J. Herkov, Ph.D.
University of Florida Brain Institute
College of Medicine
Gainesville, Florida

Walter A. Hunt, Ph.D.
Chief, Neuroscience and
Behavioral Research Branch
National Institute on Alcohol Abuse and
Alcoholism
Rockville, Maryland

Steven M. Juergens, M.D., FASAM
Assistant Clinical Professor of Psychiatry
University of Washington, and
Medical Director, Virginia Mason
Outpatient Chemical Dependency Program
Seattle, Washington

Scott E. Lukas, Ph.D.
Associate Professor of Psychiatry
(Pharmacology) and
Director, Behavioral Psychopharmacology
Research Laboratory
Harvard Medical School
McLean Hospital
Belmont, Massachusetts

John Slade, M.D., FASAM
Professor of Medicine
The Robert Wood Johnson Medical School
University of Medicine and Dentistry of New Jersey
New Brunswick, New Jersey

John J. Woodward, Ph.D.
Associate Professor
Department of Pharmacology and Toxicology
Medical College of Virginia
Virginia Commonwealth University
Richmond, Virginia

CHAPTER 1

Clinical Pharmacokinetics and Pharmacodynamics: Key Concepts

Donald R. Wesson, M.D.

Pharmacokinetics
Pharmacodynamics
Sources of Information

"Pharmacokinetics" has to do with the absorption, distribution, binding (or distribution) in tissue, biotransformation, and excretion of drugs. "Pharmacodynamics" has to do with the effects of drugs on the body and the mechanism by which drugs produce their effects. Operationally, pharmacokinetics can be viewed as what the body does to a drug, and pharmacodynamics as what the drug does to the body (Benet, 1996). "Pharmacology" is a broader term encompassing not only pharmacokinetics and pharmacodynamics, but also information about a drug's history, source, physical and chemical properties, and uses. "Toxicology" is the study of poisons and medicinal compounds, with a focus on the effects of a compound on tissue.

In clinical practice, the addiction medicine specialist needs a large amount of pharmacological information. Relevant information includes the pharmacology of drugs of abuse, medications used in the treatment of addictive disorders, and the medications used to treat common medical and psychiatric conditions that may coexist with those disorders.

The scientific basis of medical therapeutics for addictive disorders often is incomplete. For example, drug addicts commonly use drugs or medications in amounts, combinations, or ways that have not been studied in humans under laboratory conditions. Indeed, institutional review boards would not approve clinical investigations to administer most of the street drugs in the manner in which they are self-administered by addicts. Therefore, knowledge of "street drug pharmacology" often derives from clinical case reports of medical or psychiatric complications.

Moreover, the increasing ease of international travel makes it possible for drugs of abuse and new patterns of drug use to diffuse across borders quite rapidly, so that physicians must be familiar not only with medications and drugs of abuse from their own countries or regions, but also from other parts of the world. Further complicating the issue, licit drugs that are subject to abuse are marketed in different countries under varying trade names.

The pharmacological information needed by the addiction specialist is widely dispersed in the medical, psychiatric, behavioral and pharmacological literature. This introductory chapter brings together some of the general pharmacological principles that are most relevant to the practice of addiction medicine, applies the general principles to common drugs or medications or situations likely to be encountered, and refers the reader to additional sources of information.

PHARMACOKINETICS

A basic understanding of the pharmacokinetics of drugs of abuse and medications used to treat addictive disorders is important for predicting drug effects, drug interactions, and developing strategies for the treatment of addiction. Further, almost all addiction specialists have occasion to interpret laboratory reports on urine or other body fluids screened for drugs of abuse. Accurate interpretation of urine test results requires detailed information about how drugs are metabolized and how they are excreted. Knowledge of pharmacokinetics has particular application in the work of a medical review officer (MRO; see Section 17).

Metabolic Enzymes. The cytochrome P450 enzymes are the body's primary catalyst of drug and chemical biotransformations. P450 enzymes are involved in the metabolism of hormones and other endogenous chemicals, drugs and medications, and environmental chemicals. Twelve cytochrome P450 gene "families" have been identified in humans and a single cell may contain several different P450 enzymes. These families (e.g., CYP1, CYP2, CYP3) are classified according to the sequence similarities of the individual protein. Members of a family have greater than 40% amino acid sequence identity. The families are subdivided into "subfamilies," which are designated by letter-number combinations: A2, D6, A4. Subfamilies have greater than 55% identical amino acid sequences. The substrate specificity of P450 enzymes is low, and often a drug or chemical is metabolized by more than one enzyme.

Although generally thought of as "liver enzymes," cytochrome P450 enzymes are present in tissues other than in the liver. For example, CYP3A4 in the gastrointestional tract is a significant factor in the poor oral bioavailability of many drugs (Benet, Kroetz & Sheiner, 1996). Age-related decreases in drug metabolism are associated primarily with decreased activity of the P450 enzymes.

Protein Binding. Most drugs or medications are bound in varying degrees to albumin and other proteins in plasma. The unbound faction of psychoactive drugs or medications produces central nervous system effects. A drug's binding capacity in a given patient can be significantly reduced by disease states, such as hypoalbuminemia resulting from liver disease. The effective binding capacity also can be reduced by the presence of other drugs that compete for the binding sites. This effect can lead to unexpected drug-drug interactions. For example, an antibiotic occupying protein-binding sites of a patient's plasma can increase the free faction of a coadministered psychoactive drug and thus produce a greater than anticipated psychoactive effect.

PHARMACODYNAMICS

Drugs and medications can affect cellular function in many different ways, as by impeding or enhancing the action of enzymes, by altering cellular membrane characteristics, or by binding to specialized areas on nerve cells called "receptors."

Receptors. The normal function of many drug receptors is to receive endogenously produced ligands, such as hormones and neurotransmitters. A "ligand" is a substance that produces a pharmacological effect when it attaches to specialized cellular macromolecules (receptors).

Drugs or medications that mimic the effects of these endogenous ligands are called "agonists." Those that are devoid of intrinsic activity but, when bound to receptors, interfere with the binding of agonists at receptors are called "antagonists." Drugs or medications that attach to the receptor, but are not as active as agonists, are called "partial agonists."

Receptors have two specialized physiological functions: the first is binding, and the other is modification of the cell's physiological state. The degree to which a substance binds to a receptor is referred to as its "affinity" for that receptor. The same ligand may attach to different receptors with different degrees of affinity.

Although hundreds of different kinds of receptors and endogenous and exogenous ligands have been identified, the drugs or medications of primary interest to addiction medicine specialists exert their effects on cells by opening or closing ion (e.g., calcium, potassium or chloride) channels, or through G-protein-coupled receptor systems. Examples of ion-gated channels include nicotinic acetylcholine receptors, glutamate receptors, $GABA_A$ receptors, and $5HT_3$ receptors. Receptors for biogenic amines and many peptide hormones use G-protein-coupled receptors. Receptors in this group are hydrophobic proteins that span the plasma membrane in seven alpha-helical segments. The receptors exert their effect on the cell by facilitating the binding of GTP to specific G proteins. GTP binding activates the G protein so that it, in turn, can regulate the activity of enzymes such as adenyl cyclase and phospholipase.

Opiate Receptors. As an example of the role of receptors, let us consider the fact that opiates produce their analgesic and mood-altering effects by binding to various opiate receptors. Pharmacotherapy for opiate dependence includes medications that are agonists, partial agonists, or antagonists at the opiate receptors. An understanding of how these medication affect the mu (opiate) receptor is fundamental to an understanding of opiates' clinical effects and to the skilled prescription of pharmacotherapies for opiate dependence.

Research has identified two types of opiate receptors: μ_1, whose higher affinity is postulated to mediate supraspinal analgesia; and μ_2, which is postulated to mediate respiratory depression and gastrointestinal actions (Satoh & Minami, 1995; Suzuki, Mori et al., 1995; Yasunaga, Motoyana et al., 1996; Zadina, Paul et al., 1996; Zaki, Bilsky et al., 1996).

Continued occupation of the mu receptors alters the electrochemical configuration of those receptors.

TABLE 1. Agonist, Partial Agonist and Antagonist Drugs for the Treatment of Opiate Addiction

Medication	Pharmacological Classification	Current Status
Methadone	Full mu agonist	Available for treatment of opiate dependence only in specially licensed clinics.
LAAM	Pro-drug, full mu agonist	Same as methadone
Buprenophine	Partial mu agonist, kappa antagonist	Investigational for treatment of opiate dependence, Federal Schedule IV, "narcotic."
Nalmephine	Mu antagonist	Not a Federally scheduled controlled drug; any physician can prescribe.
Naltrexone (Trexan®)	Mu antagonist	Not a Federally scheduled controlled drug; any physician can prescribe.

When it is occupied by a mu receptor antagonist, the net effect over time is that the sensitivity of the receptor to the opiate agonists is reduced. In clinical practice, this decreased sensitivity is called "tolerance." The mechanisms of tolerance are not yet fully understood.

Acute Effects of Agonists, Partial Agonists and Antagonists. The effects of agonists, partial agonists, and antagonists differ, depending on what is already occupying the receptor and the degree of tolerance to the drug. For example, in an individual who has no tolerance to opiates, giving increasing amounts of a full *opiate agonist*—such as heroin, morphine or fentanyl—produces progressive opiate effects, including respiratory depression, until death occurs (from respiratory depression).

Administering increasing doses of a *partial agonist,* such as buprenorphine, initially increases the opiate effects, in the same manner as an opiate agonist; however, at some dose, the opioid effects level off and larger doses of the partial agonist produce no additional effects (for the partial agonist buprenorphine, this occurs at 8 mg). This is because partial mu agonists, such as buprenorphine, bind tightly to opiate receptors and produce increasing opiate effects until all the receptor sites are occupied. Because partial agonists have a high affinity for the mu receptor, they may displace full opiate agonists from the receptor and precipitate opiate withdrawal. Additional doses produce no additional effects at the receptor.

In the same individual, giving increasing doses of an *opiate antagonist*—such as naltrexone—produces no opiate effect at any dose. Opiate antagonists attach to the mu receptor tightly, but do not produce an opiate effect. If, however, the receptor is already occupied by an opiate agonist or partial agonist, opiate withdrawal may be precipitated (for examples of opiate agonists, partial agonists and antagonists, see Table 1).

Opiate antagonists apparently do not alter the electrochemical configuration of receptors away from their natural state. If the mu receptor has been altered by exposure to a full opiate agonist, the receptor can be partially reconfigured to its "natural state" with either an opiate antagonist or a partial agonist.

The ability of opiate antagonists or partial agonists to reconfigure mu receptors has led to development of methods of rapid opiate detoxification. For example, infusions of naloxone are used to displace the opiate agonists from their receptors and to reconfigure the receptor into its "natural" state, while the patient's opiate withdrawal symptoms are ameliorated with clonidine or removed from the patient's awareness with general anesthesia.

The dose-effect relationship of agonists, partial agonists and antagonists is schematically depicted in Figure 1.

SOURCES OF INFORMATION

Converging with rapid advances in scientific understanding of areas such as pharmacodynamics and pharmacokinetics, recent increases in monitoring of physician's clinical decisionmaking by third-party payers, managed care organizations and quality assurance entities has resulted in increased interest in the use of clinical practice guidelines to standardize and rationalize treatment practices. Such guidelines are systematically developed statements to assist the practitioner and patient with clinical decisions. Many organizations, including the federal and state governments, professional societies, managed care organizations, third-party payers, and quality assurance and utilization review groups, have been involved in developing guidelines, the best of which are based on solid scientific evidence.

The terminology used in practice guideline development is not standardized and even the terms used

FIGURE 1. Dose-Response Curve of Agonist, Partial Agonist and Antagonist Drugs

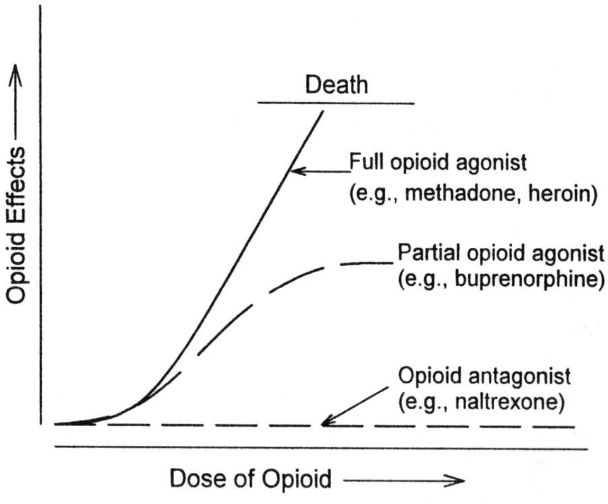

Comparison of the effects of a full opiate agonist, a partial opiate agonist, and an opiate antagonist in an individual whose receptors are not already occupied by an opiate.

to refer to them varies (Kasser, Gillie et al., 1995). The American Medical Association uses the term "practice parameters." In the larger medical literature, practice guidelines are variously referred to as "practice standards," "algorithms," or "protocols." Guidelines are developed through various processes, including clinical consensus of a group of experts, analysis of treatment outcome data, or a systematic review or analysis of published studies. The latter approaches yield "evidence-based" clinical practice guidelines.

Within the American Society of Addiction Medicine, a standing Committee on Practice Guidelines has published guidelines on the pharmacological management of alcohol withdrawal (Mayo-Smith, 1997) and the use of phenytoin in the management of alcohol withdrawal (Kasser, Gillie et al., 1995); others are currently in development. These guidelines reflect the latest developments in pharmacology as well as treatment practice, and represent an excellent tool for physicians and other professionals who wish to incorporate recent developments in pharmacology into their practice decisions.

CONCLUSIONS

The practitioner's need for pharmacological information has never been greater, while the methods of accessing such information are rapidly changing. Incredible amounts of information are accessible on the Internet, and there are many sites that provide information primarily for medical practitioners or scientist who working in the field of psychopharmacology. Access to the National Library of Medicine is available directly or through a number of Internet sites. The ready availability of such information, to both professionals and patients, will be a major force in shaping the future of health care.

REFERENCES

Benet L (1996). General principles: Introduction. In J Hardman, L Limbird, P Molinoff & R Ruddon (eds.) *Goodman and Gillman's The Pharmacological Basis of Therapeutics (9th Edition)*. New York, NY: McGraw-Hill.

Benet L, Kroetz D & Sheiner L (1996). Pharmacokinetics: The dynamics of drug absorption, distribution, and elimination. In J Hardman, L Limbird, P Molinoff & R Ruddon (eds.) *Goodman and Gillman's The Pharmacological Basis of Therapeutics (9th edition)*. New York, NY: McGraw-Hill.

Cone EJ, Yousefnejad D, Hillsgrove MJ, Holicky B & Darwin WD (1995). Passive inhalation of cocaine. *Journal of Analytic Toxicology* 19(6):399–411.

Kasser C, Gillie E, Lame G, Mayo-Smith M, Smith J & Thiessen N (1995). The role of phenytoin in the management of alcohol withdrawal syndrome. *Topics in Addiction Medicine*. Chevy Chase, MD: American Society of Addiction Medicine, 1–9.

Mayo-Smith M (1997). Pharmacological management of alcohol withdrawal: A meta-analysis and evidence-based practice guidelines. *Journal of the American Medical Association* 278(2):144–151.

Satoh M & Minami M (1995). Molecular pharmacology of the opioid receptors. *Pharmacologic Therapy* 68(3):343–64.

Suzuki T, Mori T, Tsuji M, Misawa M & Nagase H (1995). Discriminative stimulus properties of morphine mediated by mu 1-opioid receptors. *European Journal of Pharmacology* 284(1–2):195–198.

Vogl WF & Bush DM (1997). *Medical Review Officer Manual for Federal Workplace Drug Testing Programs: CSAP Technical Report No. 15*. Rockville, MD: Substance Abuse and Mental Health Services Administration.

Yasunaga T, Motoyama S, Nose T, Kodama H, Kondo M & Shimohigashi Y (1996). Reversible affinity labeling of opioid receptors via disulfide bonding: Discriminative labeling of mu and delta subtypes by chemically activated thiol-containing enkephalin analogs. *Journal of Biochemistry (Tokyo)* 120(2):459–65.

Zadina JE, Paul D, Gergen KA, Ge LJ, Hackler L & Kastin AJ (1996). Binding of Tyr-W-MIF-1 (Tyr-Pro-Trp-Gly-NH2) and related peptides to mu 1 and mu 2 opiate receptors. *Neuroscience Letter* 215(1):65–9.

Zaki PA, Bilsky EJ, Vanderah TW, Lai J, Evans CJ & Porreca F (1996). Opioid receptor types and subtypes: The delta receptor as a model. *Annual Review of Pharmacology and Toxicology* 36:379–401.

CHAPTER 2

The Pharmacology of Alcohol

John J. Woodward, Ph.D.

Drugs in the Class
Therapeutic Use and Misuse
Adverse Effects
Addiction Liability
Absorption and Metabolism
Mechanisms of Action
Reinforcing Properties

This chapter reviews alcohol's actions on the body, with special emphasis on sites of action in the brain that may determine some of its addictive properties. It is important to note at the outset that there are relatively few "easy" answers that adequately explain, on a cellular or molecular level, how a simple molecule such as alcohol can have such powerful effects on human behavior.

DRUGS IN THE CLASS

Alcohol is one of the oldest known substances of use and abuse. It is second only to caffeine in incidence of use, and its manufacture, distribution, and sale is of major economic importance.

Despite its pervasive and seemingly sanctioned use by nearly all segments of American society, annual alcohol-related costs in terms of lost productivity and health care are estimated at $136 billion and are expected to increase in the coming years (Public Health Service, 1990). While problem drinking and alcoholism are viewed by a growing number of Americans as legitimate health problems that deserve all of the resources that the medical community can command, there are relatively few pharmacotherapies for alcoholism and alcohol abuse. However, advances in understanding alcohol's effects on cellular processes have yielded several promising areas for drug development.

THERAPEUTIC USE AND MISUSE

Therapeutic Uses. Alcohol currently has a limited spectrum of therapeutic uses, although it was regarded as the elixir of life by medieval alchemists. Ethanol is an excellent solvent and is used in large number of formulations as a vehicle. It is used topically as a disinfectant and is used to reduce fever because of its ability to cool the skin during evaporation. Alcohol has been used to relieve certain types of nerve-related pain, such as that of trigeminal neuralgia.

Systemically administered alcohol has few legitimate medicinal purposes other than the treatment of methanol and ethylene glycol poisoning. Ethanol continues to be used to prevent premature labor. Its use has subsided somewhat due to the development of more selective agents, such as the *B*2 agonist ritodrine which, unlike alcohol, also can reduce the incidence of fetal respiratory distress. However, ethanol remains useful is this regard when circumstances do not favor the use of sympathomimetic agents.

Misuses. Acute alcohol ingestion produces a feeling or warmth as cutaneous blood flow is increased. Gastric secretions usually are increased, although the characteristics of these secretions depends on the concentration of alcohol ingested, with high concentrations (>20%) inhibiting secretions. Continual ingestion of high concentrations of alcohol can lead to erosive gastritis, which can limit absorption of nutrients and vitamins. These nutritional deficiencies are associated with several serious neurological and mental disorders, including brain damage, memory loss, sleep disturbances and psychoses such as Wernicke's and Korsakoff's. Finally, acute and chronic ingestion of alcohol decreases sexual responsiveness in both men and women.

Type 1 alcoholism accounts for about 75% of male alcoholics and is characterized by the following factors: (1) the onset of alcohol-related problems usually occurs after the age of 25; (2) a low degree of spontaneous alcohol-seeking behavior and alcohol-related fighting; (3) psychological dependence, coupled with guilt and fear about alcohol dependence; and (4) a low degree of novelty-seeking and a high degree of harm avoidance and reward dependence.

Type 2 alcoholism involves a much smaller subset of alcoholics, whose characteristics are essentially the opposite of those listed for Type 1 alcoholism. They include infrequent feelings of guilt and fear about alcohol dependence and a low degree of harm avoidance. Although the characteristics of the two types of alcoholism are largely opposite, the acute effects of alcohol on neuronal function that are assumed to underlie alcohol's addictive properties may be consistent, with both mechanisms participating in alcohol's reinforcing properties.

ADVERSE EFFECTS

Acutely, ethanol acts as a sedative-hypnotic, although the quality of sleep often is reduced by ethanol ingestion. In patients with sleep apnea, ethanol increases the frequency and severity of apneic episodes and the resulting hypoxia. Ethanol potentiates the sedative-hypnotic properties of both benzodiazepines and barbiturates, probably reflecting common mechanisms of action on both voltage and ligand-gated ion channels that control neuronal activity. Acute ethanol intoxication is not always associated with sedation or coma; indeed, some intoxicated individuals display violent behavior that requires administration of other sedative or antipsychotic agents. The use of these agents with a severely intoxicated individual must be approached cautiously to prevent respiratory failure.

Chronic use of alcohol is associated with increased risk for the development of several well-characterized disease processes. Probably the best known of these involves deleterious effects on hepatic function. Chronic alcohol exposure in humans results in fat and protein accumulation in hepatocytes that can lead to necrosis and fibrosis. Chronic alcohol use also is associated with an enhanced risk of various cancers, perhaps through changes in liver function that result in increases in activated carcinogens.

Heavy alcohol use during pregnancy can lead to a variety of birth defects and alterations in normal growth and development of the newborn. Fetal alcohol syndrome (FAS) consists of a variety of characteristic symptoms in newborns exposed to alcohol *in utero*. One of three infants born to alcoholic mothers display symptoms of FAS. These include CNS dysfunction such as low IQ and microcephaly, delayed growth, and facial abnormalities among others. FAS generally is associated with heavy drinking, especially early in pregnancy, although it is not known if there is any safe lower limit for alcohol consumption.

ADDICTION LIABILITY

Acute ingestion of alcohol-containing solutions produces pleasurable feelings in most people and can lead to a state of "intoxication" that ranges from a mild inhibition of normal responsible behavior to a state of unconsciousness, depending on the dose and the individual's history of alcohol use. Alcohol's controlled but legal availability characterizes an environment in which its use is tolerated and even encouraged in some settings. Most people who drink moderately conform to social norms and confine their drinking to what are considered appropriate times and places. Alcoholics or problem drinkers, on the other hand, have a diminished ability to adjust their alcohol intake to conform to these social guidelines.

The uncontrolled use of alcohol despite adverse consequences, coupled with the existence of craving and alcohol-seeking behavior, characterize the disease of alcoholism (Morse & Flavin, 1992). Chronic ingestion of alcohol can lead to the development of a degree of tolerance to the intoxicating effects of alcohol such that more alcohol is required to produce noticeable signs of intoxication. Much less tolerance develops to the lethal concentration of alcohol (ethanol), so that an alcoholic may live in a very narrow window of safety with respect to the acute toxicity of ethanol.

During the first 48 hours of alcohol withdrawal, the patient experiences mild agitation, insomnia, restlessness followed by anorexia, tremor, and anxiety. Seizures may appear during this time. In severely dependent patients, these symptoms worsen, and disorientation, confusion, and disordered sensory perception may occur. It is during this latter phase of withdrawal that death may occur in untreated patients.

The severity of these withdrawal symptoms and the individual's wish to avoid them may be a contributing factor that promotes continued drinking in some persons.

ABSORPTION AND METABOLISM

Alcohol is rapidly and efficiently absorbed into the bloodstream from the stomach, small intestine and colon. The rate of absorption is dependent on the gastric emptying time, which can be delayed by the presence of food in the small intestine. Once in the bloodstream, alcohol is rapidly distributed throughout the body and gains access to all tissues, including the fetus in pregnant women.

Alcohol is metabolized primarily in the liver by the actions of alcohol dehydrogenase (ADH) and mixed function oxidases such as P450IIE1 (CYP2E1). Levels of CYP2E1 may be increased in chronic drinkers. ADH converts alcohol to acetaldehyde, which then can be converted to acetate by the actions of acetaldehyde dehydrogenase (ALDH). Small amounts of alcohol can be excreted via the lungs. The odor of the breath is not a reliable indicator of alcohol consumption, since it is due not to alcohol vapor but to impurities in the alcoholic beverage.

The rate of alcohol metabolism by ADH is relatively constant, as the enzyme is saturated at relatively low blood alcohol levels and thus exhibits zero order kinetics (constant amount oxidized per unit of time). Alcohol metabolism is proportional to body weight (and probably liver weight) and averages approximately one ounce of pure alcohol per three hours in adults. Thus, the time for an individual to become sober after even moderate intake of ethanol can be substantial. At present, there do not appear to be any effective "alcohol antagonists" (amethystic agents) that can quickly reverse the intoxicating effects of alcohol, although such an agent is the object of research (see Litten & Allen, 1991, for a review of this topic). The lack of such a substance is undoubtedly due to the myriad interactions between alcohol and the cellular processes that control neuronal activity (as reviewed below). Some candidates for the role of amethystic agent include the opiate antagonist naloxone, which may reverse ethanol-induced respiratory depression, and the experimental benzodiazepine RO 15-4513, which has been reported to reverse some of the signs of alcohol intoxication in certain strains of rats. The clinical utility of such an agent in the treatment of life-threatening alcohol intoxication notwithstanding, there are moral, ethical and medical concerns to be considered in the development of such a drug, since it probably would not reduce the toxicity associated with the chronic ingestion of alcohol.

There are important differences among gender and ethnic groups in the amounts and types of the metabolizing enzymes ADH and ALDH, and these may be important in determining an individual's alcohol use patterns. For example, about half of all persons of Japanese ancestry have a variant of the mitochondrial form of ALDH, which is less able to metabolize acetaldehyde (Goedde, Harada & Agarwal, 1979; Harada, Agarwal & Goedde, 1980; Teng, 1981). Levels of acetaldehyde in these persons after ingestion of alcohol may be 10 times higher than in an individual with the normal mitochondrial variant of ALDH. Thus, in such persons, even small amounts of alcohol can produce the so-called "alcohol flush reaction," which consists of facial flushing, vasodilation, tachycardia and headaches. Nausea, vomiting, edema, and hypotension also can occur at higher levels of alcohol consumption. These symptoms resemble those seen following ingestion of alcohol in patients taking Antabuse® (disulfiram), which inhibits the actions of acetaldehyde dehydrogenase.

Interestingly, the presence of this less-efficient ALDH isozyme appears to have a significant effect on drinking behavior. The presence of the ALDH variant is associated with lower drinking frequencies and amounts of alcohol consumed, suggesting that the ALDH variant is protective against heavy drinking and alcoholism. Conversely, the ALDH variant is rare in Japanese alcoholics with alcoholic liver disease (Harada, Agarwal et al., 1983). Other studies have extended these findings to populations of Taiwanese and Chinese ancestry (Thomasson, Mai et al., 1989). However, the ALDH variant that reduces the individual's ability to metabolize acetaldehyde has not yet been detected in populations of European descent.

Such studies suggest that genetically determined differences in metabolic or other key biochemical processes may play a role in the development of alcohol addiction in certain individuals. This hypothesis is further supported by recent studies by Schuckit (1991), in which sons of alcoholic fathers and sons of non-alcoholic fathers were given an alcohol-containing beverage or a placebo. Using a self-rating scale, sons of alcoholic fathers consistently scored themselves lower than sons of non-alcoholic fathers on feelings of drunkenness, dizziness, drug effect, sleepiness and other subjective characteristics following the alcohol beverage challenge. In separate studies involving sons and daughters of alcoholic and non-alcoholic fathers, similar findings were found when measurements of body sway or ataxia were measured following the alcohol challenge. These findings suggest that sons of alcoholic fathers experience a less intense reaction to alcohol than sons of non-alcoholic fathers, which could be related to the future risk of developing alcoholism in these men. Finally, women generally have been found to possess less gastric mucosal alcohol dehydrogenase activity than men (Frezza, Di Padova et al., 1990). This results in significantly higher blood alcohol levels following alcohol ingestion in women; even more, in fact, than would be expected based solely on differences in liver weight. This may contribute to an enhanced vulnerability of women to the acute and chronic effects of alcohol.

MECHANISMS OF ACTION

Molecular Sites of Action for Alcohol in the Brain. The cellular and molecular actions of alcohol have been pursued with intense interest since the studies of the German scientists Meyer and Overton, who suggested in the early 1900s that alcohol, like other sedative-hypnotic compounds, produces its effects by altering the lipid environment of cell membranes (Figure 1, arrow 1). The relevance of the membrane-disordering action of ethanol as it relates to the profound behavioral effects of ingested alcohol is controversial.

Numerous studies have shown that, while alcohol does indeed induce measurable changes in brain membrane fluidity, these changes are relatively modest, require rather high concentrations of alcohol, and are less than the changes produced by small (1- to 2-degree Centigrade) changes in temperature, which (in intact animals) are not associated with behavioral signs of intoxication (for a review, see Forman & Miller, 1989). This does not exclude the possibility that specific areas of certain neuronal membranes, such as those directly in contact with membrane-spanning receptors or ion channels (Figure 2, arrow 3), may be especially sensitive to pertubation by the physico-chemical nature of the alcohol molecule, but there is as yet no compelling evidence to suggest that this may be true.

This leaves membrane-bound and intracellular proteins as the next likely target for alcohol. Although there is no evidence of a specific receptor for alcohol, it is important to remember that alcohol does interact rather selectively with the enzyme alcohol dehydrogenase in a classic enzyme-substrate complex, suggesting that such an interaction might occur with important brain proteins that could alter their function. The ligand-gated ion channels form a large super-family of functional proteins and may compose a subset of molecular targets that are uniquely sensitive to pertubation by concentrations of alcohol that are behaviorally relevant (Figure 2, arrows 3 and 4).

These proteins all function as gates or pores that allow the passage of certain ions into and out of neurons upon binding of the appropriate neurotransmitter. The presence of a specific neurotransmitter binding site whose occupation is required for activation and opening of the ion channel distin-

FIGURE 1. Representation of a Typical Neuronal Membrane

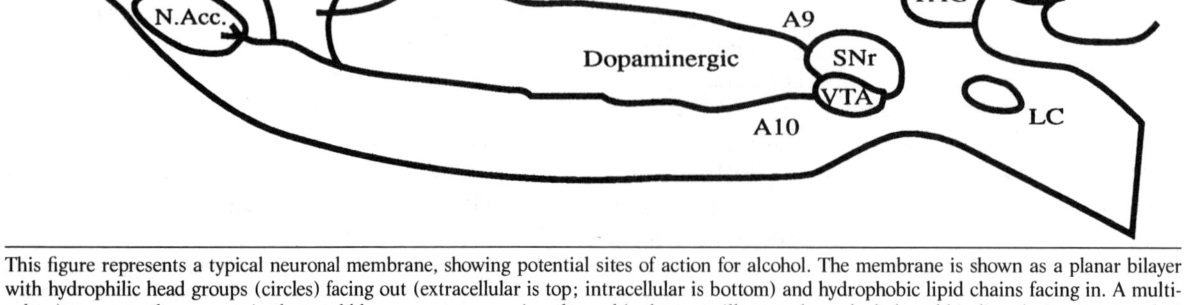

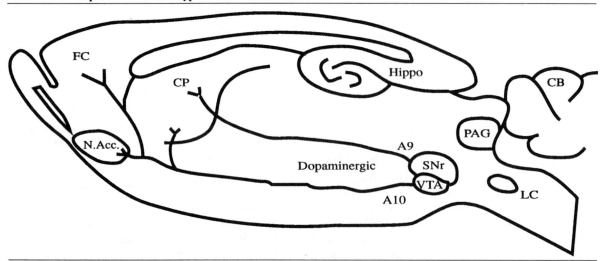

This figure represents a typical neuronal membrane, showing potential sites of action for alcohol. The membrane is shown as a planar bilayer with hydrophilic head groups (circles) facing out (extracellular is top; intracellular is bottom) and hydrophobic lipid chains facing in. A multi-subunit transmembrane protein that could be a receptor or an ion channel is shown to illustrate how alcohol could indirectly (arrows 1 and 2) or directly (arrows 3 and 4) alter its function.

FIGURE 2. Proposed Organization of Ligand-gated Ion Channels

Figure.__________________

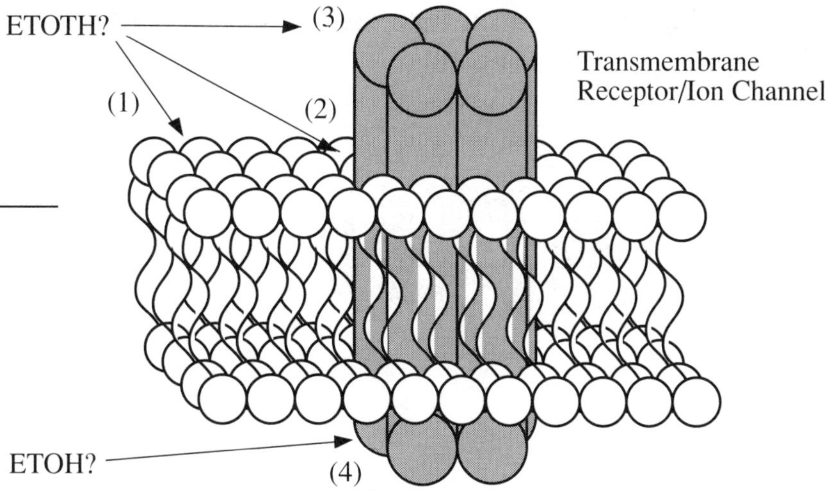

This figure shows the arrangement of four membrane spanning regions (TMI-TMIV) for both glutamatergic and GABAergic, glycinergic, and serotonergic receptors. Note the hairpin structure of the TM II domain of the glutamate receptor that alters the location of the extracellular and intracellular loops as compared to the GABAergic receptor. Sites for phosphorylation by intracellular kinases are also shown. The insert shows a cross-section of a functional ligand-gated channel composed of five sub-units. Notice how the transmembrane regions (M2) face one another and form the central ion pore.

guishes these proteins from the other major class of ion channels, which are activated solely by changes in membrane potential.

Two distinct classes of ligand-gated ion channels appear to be particularly important as potential targets for the actions of alcohol in the brain. These ion channels can be classified as *inhibitory* channels, which include the $GABA_A$ receptor and strychnine-sensitive glycine receptor, and *excitatory* channels, which are composed of glutamate-activated channels (NMDA and non-NMDA) and the $5HT_3$ subtype of serotonin receptors. Activation of the $GABA_A$ and glycine receptors by their respective neurotransmitters usually results in hyperpolarization of neurons due to the inward flux of negatively charged chloride ions. This makes the cell less likely to reach the threshold membrane potential required for firing and is thus thought of as an inhibitory receptor. The NMDA receptor (named after the synthetic selective agonist N-methyl-D-aspartate) and non-NMDA glutamate receptors gate the inward flux of sodium and calcium upon binding of the endogenous neurotransmitters glutamate or aspartate and thus are considered an excitatory receptor that leads to depolarization of neuronal membranes. In brain neurons, the NMDA receptor is especially important since it has a high permeability to calcium which is a trigger for many intracellular processes. The non-NMDA class of glutamate receptors (called the AMPA/Kainate receptors in recognition of their selective agonists) and the $5HT_3$ subtype of serotonin receptors are much less permeable to calcium and most of their current is carried by sodium ions.

Unlike other neurotransmitter receptors, which are composed of a single protein subunit, most of the ligand-gated ion channels are made up of several subunits that assemble to form the functional ion channel. This is perhaps not surprising since the ligand-gated ion channel is composed of two basic components: an extracellular domain that recognizes the neurotransmitter and a membrane-associated domain that forms the ion channel through which the ions flow in or out of the neuron. In a current model of ion channel structure based largely on the proposed organization of the nicotinic aceytlcholine receptor found at the neuromuscular junction, most ligand-gated ion channels are thought to be generally pentameric in structure, with the five sub-units arranged in a circle surrounding a central ion pore (Figure 3). For the $GABA_A$, glycine, and $5HT_3$ receptors, each subunit has four sections that span the membrane (TMI-TMIV) and that are connected by short and long loops of amino acids (Figure 2). Intracellular loop number two, which connects transmembrane sections numbers 3 and 4, is particularly important because it contains specific sequences that are recognized as targets for kinases, which are enzymes that phosphorylate proteins. Phosphorylation is a powerful means of controlling the activity of various receptor proteins and may play

FIGURE 3. Sagital Section of a Rat Brain

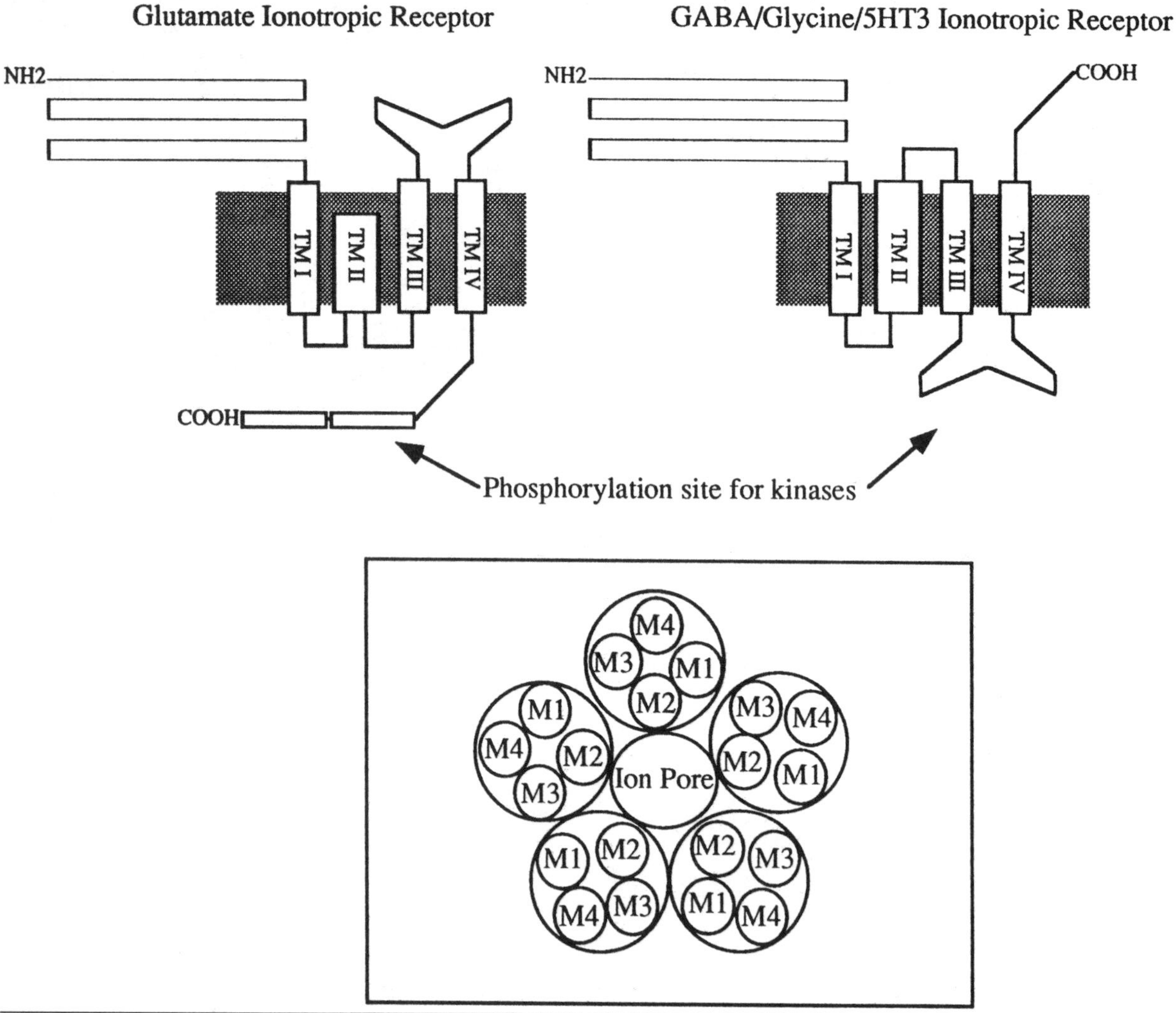

This figure shows the simplified arrangement of dopaminergic fibers thought to be involved in mediating addictive properties of alcohol. Abbreviations: CB (cerebellum), CP (caudate putamen), FC (frontal cortex), Hippo (hippocampus), LC (locus coereleus), N.Acc. (nucleus accumbens), PAG (periaqueductal gray), SNr (substantia nigra-A9 projection), VTA (ventral tegmental area, A10 projection). Alcohol has been shown to increase the firing of the A10 dopaminergic neurons and enhance extracellular levels of dopamine in the nucleus accumbens.

an important role in determining the sensitivity of certain ion channels to the actions of alcohol.

The proposed structure of the glutamate family of ligand-gated channels is somewhat different in that the TMII domain does not completely traverse the membrane but forms a hairpin loop (Figure 2). This places the C-terminus of the subunit inside the neuron where it is subject to regulation by phosphorylation and other cellular processes. In functional ion channels of all types, all of the TMII domains appear to face each other and make up the central ion pore. The ion selectivity of the particular channel is determined largely by the sequence of amino acids in TMII.

The successful cloning and expression of ion channel subunits in experimental systems has greatly enhanced our understanding of the function of these receptors and has allowed for a detailed examination of their sensitivity to ethanol. A brief review of the effects of alcohol on each of these important ion channels follows.

$GABA_A$ Receptors: Screening of DNA libraries has shown that there are at least four different classes of subunits that are used to construct the pentameric $GABA_A$ receptor. Each class of subunits may have multiple members, which differ slightly in their sequence. The theoretical combinatorial associations that may take place between these subunits

can give rise to a bewildering array of $GABA_A$ receptors, which may exhibit differences in their sensitivity to pharmacological agents, including alcohol. Modern molecular biological techniques provide strong evidence that this is indeed the case. Prior to the identification and isolation of cDNAs that code for the various $GABA_A$ receptor subunits, there was controversy as to whether alcohol had significant effects on $GABA_A$ receptor function. In some studies, alcohol was shown to potentiate $GABA_A$ induced currents, while others found no such effects. Recently, alcohol was shown to enhance the GABA-stimulated flux of chloride ions in experimental cells that were genetically engineered to express the γ2 long variant of the GABA receptor, along with α and β subunits (Wafford, Burnett et al., 1991; Wafford & Whiting, 1992). This variant contains an additional 8 amino acids that introduces a site for phosphorylation of the receptor by protein kinsae C. Omission of the γ2L subunit of even substitution of other γ subunits (including the γ2 short variant) resulted in cells that did not show significant potentiation of the GABA-induced chloride flux by alcohol. It should be noted that not all cells that express the g2L variant are sensitive to alcohol suggesting that this subunit may be necessary but not sufficient to confer ethanol sensitivity.

Although it still is not known how the simple addition of a phosphate group to this particular subunit may render the $GABA_A$ receptor sensitive to alcohol, these findings dramatically illustrate that alcohol can no longer be considered non-specific in its actions. These findings have important implications for the etiology of alcoholism, since a variable distribution or expression of $GABA_A$ subunits in important brain regions could dictate to some extent the degree of sensitivity of various individuals to alcohol. For example, several lines of alcohol-preferring rats have been shown to have a greater density of GABAergic terminals in the nucleus accumbens than non-alcohol preferring strains (Hwang, Lumeng et al., 1990). This suggests that enhanced GABAergic function is linked with preference for alcohol in a brain region that has been shown to be an important site for the reinforcing actions of alcohol. Thus, enhanced $GABA_A$ function by alcohol may in some way lead to the increases in dopamine in the nucleus accumbens that are associated with self-administration of alcohol in rats. The actual mechanisms that may underlie this interaction are largely unknown at the present time, but provide a testable hypothesis for linking the acute actions of alcohol on $GABA_A$ receptor function with the reinforcing properties of alcohol.

Glycine Receptors: These receptors have long been known to be important in the spinal cord and recent evidence has shown that they are distributed in higher brain regions as well. Like the $GABA_A$ receptor, activation of glycine receptors leads to neuronal hyperpolarization and inhibition of neuronal firing. Glycine receptors exist as α and β subunits and are found in various combinations throughout the brain and spinal cord. Alcohol as well as anesthetic agents such as halothane and propofol have recently been shown to potentiate glycine-stimulated currents (Mascia, Machu & Harris, 1996). Enhanced inhibition of neuronal firing via potentiation of glycinergic receptors may thus be an important component of the sedative/anesthetic properties of alcohol.

NMDA Receptors: Unlike most receptors, the NMDA receptor requires the presence of two agonists: glutamate and another amino acid (glycine) for activation. These amino acids have distinct binding sites that can be distinguished by different antagonists, which interact selectively with the two binding sites. Antagonism of either of the two sites is sufficient to completely block the ion flux associated with activation of the receptor. In addition to these agonist sites, several drugs such as ketamine, phencyclidine, and an experimental therapeutic agent (MK-801) antagonize the NMDA receptor by binding in the channel pore and blocking ion flux.

The receptor also is unusual in that magnesium (which is relatively plentiful in intracellular and extracellular fluids) blocks activation of the receptor in a voltage-dependent manner. When neurons are relatively quiet and their membrane potential is negative, the agonist actions of glutamate and glycine are counteracted by magnesium blocking the channel. However, when neuronal activity is increased and membrane potential is made more positive via depolarization, the magnesium block is removed and sodium and calcium ions can flow through the ion pore and contribute to the depolarization of the neuron. This conditional activation of the NMDA receptor and its resulting increase in the flux of calcium into neurons has been proposed to be important in mediating cellular events that may underlie complex phenomena such as learning and memory and synaptic plasticity.

Cloning experiments have revealed that the NMDA subtype of glutamate receptor is composed of multiple subunits (NR1, NR2A-D) that co-assemble to form functional channels. The presence of one or more of the NR2 subunits confers unique biophysical and pharmacological properties to the NMDA receptor (see Watkins & Collingridge, 1994). Non-NMDA receptors are made up of multiple subunits as well (GluR1-7) and specific combinations of subunits also yield receptors with distinct properties.

As mentioned earlier, NMDA receptors gate the flux of cations especially sodium and calcium which flow into the neuron when the NMDA receptor binds its natural ligands glutamate and glycine. This leads to a depolarizing or excitatory effect on neurons and this effect is readily antagonized by alcohol (Lovinger, White & Weight, 1989; Hoffman, Moses & Tabakoff, 1989; Dildy & Leslie, 1989). Surprisingly, there is little disagreement with this finding in the literature although differences in the sensitivity to alcohol's inhibitory effects seem to occur in different brain regions. Concentrations of alcohol that are associated with moderate intoxication (25 mM, or approximately 0.1% blood alcohol) inhibit NMDA-stimulated processes such as neurotransmitter release by 20% to 30% (Gothert & Fink, 1989; Woodward & Gonzales, 1990; Gonzales & Woodward, 1990). Higher concentrations produce even greater inhibition.

Alcohol has also been shown to block recombinant NMDA receptors expressed in both oocytes and mammalian cell lines (Kuner, Schoepfer & Korpi, 1993; Masood, Wu et al., 1994; Mirshahi & Woodward, 1995; Lovinger, 1995). There is some evidence that the alcohol sensitivity of NMDA receptor is influenced by the subunits present. However, at this time, no truly alcohol-insensitive combination of NMDA subunits has been described.

The situation with the non-NMDA glutamate receptor is similar although there is some controversy over whether non-NMDA receptors expressed in brain neurons are as sensitive to alcohol as the NMDA subtype. Overall, alcohol's blockade of the activation of excitatory NMDA and non-NMDA receptors are likely to be important in the intoxicating and sedative effects of alcohol.

It is also thought that the antagonism of NMDA receptors may be involved in the rewarding properties of alcohol. NMDA receptors are thought to be important in regulating the release of dopamine in mesolimbic areas such as the nucleus accumbens. For example, using microdialysis techniques, NMDA antagonists have been shown to increase levels of dopamine in the nucleus accumbens (Youngren, Daly & Moghaddam, 1993). These results suggest that glutamate may exert an inhibitory control over dopamine release via NMDA receptors. Thus, ethanol may produce increases in accumbens dopamine by its inhibitory actions on NMDA receptors. In animal studies designed to evaluate the subjective effects of ethanol on behavior, NMDA antagonists can produce ethanol-appropriate lever responding in rats trained to discriminate ethanol from saline (Colombo & Grant, 1992). These results suggest that ethanol does behave as an NMDA antagonist in the intact animal.

NMDA receptors also are altered during chronic exposure to alcohol and appear to be important in mediating some of the signs of alcohol withdrawal. It has been demonstrated (using neuronal cell culture) that chronic exposure to alcohol increases the density of MK801 binding sites (Iorio, Reinlib et al., 1992). Since MK801 is a fairly selective marker for the NMDA receptor, these data suggest that neurons may compensate for the acute inhibitory actions of alcohol on NMDA receptor function by increasing the density of these receptors. This up-regulation of receptor density is a common response of many cell and tissue types to the prolonged presence of receptor antagonists. Since NMDA itself can induce seizure activity in animals, increased numbers of NMDA receptors following chronic alcohol exposure may underlie the increased susceptibility of animals and humans to seizures during abrupt withdrawal from alcohol. Experiments with mice show that NMDA induced seizure activity was elevated in mice made dependent upon alcohol and that the NMDA antagonist MK801 could reduce the severity of these seizures during withdrawal (Grant, Valverius et al., 1990). More recent studies have suggested that the enhancement in NMDA receptor function following chronic alcohol may involve changes in the expression pattern of specific NMDA receptor subunits (Blevins, Mirshahi & Woodward, 1995; Follesa & Ticku, 1995; Snell, Nunley et al., 1996).

Chronic exposure to alcohol also has been shown to increase the density of binding sites for dihydropyridinesensitive, voltage-sensitive calcium channels (Dolin, Little et al., 1987; Messing, Carpenter et al., 1986). These and other voltage-sensitive calcium channels also are inhibited by acute alcohol, although less potently than NMDA-stimulated calcium flux (Leslie, Barr et al., 1983). Increased activation of these channels during withdrawal from chronic alcohol also might contribute to seizure activity and the general enhancement of neuronal activity that accompanies withdrawal.

$5HT_3$ Receptors: As mentioned earlier, the $5HT_3$ receptor also is a ligand-gated ion channel whose

activity is altered by alcohol. Acutely, alcohol has been shown to augment the ion flux through the $5HT_3$ receptor (Lovinger & White, 1991). This ion channel is permeable primarily to monovalent cations, such as sodium and potassium, and thus is thought to be involved in excitatory neurotransmission. In cultured neurons, low doses of ethanol potentiated the currents elicited by activation of the $5HT_3$ receptor. In behavioral studies involving both rats and pigeons, $5HT_3$ receptor antagonists blocked the animal's ability to discriminate ethanol from saline, suggesting that ethanol's acute actions on $5HT_3$ receptors may underlie some of the subjective effects of alcohol (Grant & Barrett, 1991).

Pharmacological Studies Implicating Other Systems. Much of our working knowledge of alcohol's effects on neuronal function comes from studies that have examined the effects of alcohol on various neurotransmitter systems, as well as the ability of known pharmacological agents to mediate alcohol drinking behavior. These studies are important because they may provide new leads to follow in our attempt to understand how alcohol's addictive properties are produced at the molecular and cellular level. A brief review of this literature is presented here.

Adenosine: Adenosine is a major inhibitory neurotransmitter in the brain and may serve as an endogenous anti-epileptic due to its ability to generally inhibit neuronal function. Alcohol has been shown to inhibit the function of one type of adenosine transporter leading to increased extracellular adenosine levels (Diamond, Nagy et al., 1991). Increased synaptic concentrations of adenosine may contribute to some of the effects of acute and chronic alcohol. Adenosine interacts with two receptors: *A1*, which is coupled to inhibition of adenylate cyclase, and *A2*, which is coupled to the stimulation of adenylate cyclase. In cultured cells that express only the A2 receptor, alcohol increases extracellular adenosine, which leads to receptor-stimulated increases in the second messenger cyclic AMP within the cells.

Chronic exposure of these cells to alcohol results in desensitization, such that adenosine stimulation leads to smaller increases in cAMP within the cell. This desensitization is associated with a reduction in the amount of the stimulatory GTP-binding protein G*a*S, which couples various receptors to the stimulation of cAMP production. This reduction in G*a*S results in a heterologous form of desensitization, thereby reducing the effectiveness not only of adenosine but other neurotransmitters, which act via G*a*S to increase cAMP levels. The importance of this finding as it relates to alcohol addiction is unknown but may be important, since regulation of intracellular cAMP levels by a whole variety of neurotransmitters and neuromodulators is important for regulating neuronal activity. Although these studies were performed using a transformed neural cell line, it also has been found that adenosine-stimulated increases in cAMP in blood lymphocytes taken from actively drinking alcoholics was reduced by approximately 76%. These data from alcoholics support the laboratory findings and suggest that chronic alcohol may desensitize receptor-coupled cAMP-mediated signal transduction in a variety of cell types. More work is needed to understand how these changes may influence drinking behavior.

Dopamine: As mentioned above, increases in mesolimbic dopamine are thought to be associated with the reinforcing effects of many drugs of abuse, including alcohol. Electrophysiological studies have demonstrated that alcohol increases the firing of dopamine containing neurons, which arise in the ventral tegmental area (VTA) and project to the nucleus accumbens and other mesolimbic areas (Brodie, Shefner & Dunwiddie, 1990). This could result from alcohol's inhibition of NMDA receptors which may negatively regulate cell firing of these neurons. It should be noted that the concentrations of alcohol required to significantly elevate dopamine neuronal firing in the VTA as measured *in vitro* are relatively high (40 to 200 mM). This may reflect alterations in neuronal excitability that occur during experimental preparation of the tissue slices. Alcohol also has been shown to directly enhance the basal efflux of dopamine from striatal slices, although again, the concentrations required for this effect are very high (Snape & Engel, 1988).

Another approach that has been used to increase our understanding of the role of dopamine in alcohol addiction is the use of pharmacological agonists and antagonists that directly interact with dopamine receptors. Unfortunately, studies using dopamine receptor antagonists to probe the reinforcing properties of alcohol have been limited by the non-specific motor effects of these drugs. The use of dopamine agonists to mimic the effects of alcohol have provided some indirect evidence that dopamine may be involved in alcohol drinking behavior in animals.

The long-acting dopamine agonist bromocriptine, administered systemically, shifted the animals' preference from ethanol to water, especially in those strains of rats that show alcohol preference (Weiss, Mitchiner et al., 1990). Similar findings were demonstrated with another dopamine agonist, apomorphine. These results suggested that administration of direct dopamine agonists reduced the need for alcohol's dopamine-enhancing activity in these animals, such that the "reward state" was achieved at lower alcohol levels. These studies provide compelling but indirect evidence that alcohol's addictive properties involve alterations in mesolimbic dopamine and offer possible sites of action for pharmacotherapies.

Opioids: The involvement of endogenous opioids (endorphins and enkephalins) in alcohol addiction is suggested by several lines of research. One of the first links between alcohol and opioids was suggested by the finding that acetaldehyde could undergo a metabolic reaction with monoamines to form compounds (tetrahydrisoquinolines or TIQs) that were structurally related to morphine (Davis & Walsh, 1970). TIQs also were shown to elicit alcohol drinking behavior and alcohol preference even after cessation of TIQ administration (Meyers, 1989). This hypothesis, while attractive, remains controversial because of the inability to replicate some of these findings and the demonstration that TIQ formation *in vivo* could be accounted by dietary factors rather than direct effects of alcohol (Collins, 1988). Alcohol has been shown to increase the release of certain opioids (such as B-endorphin) from rat pituitary glands, as well as to increase blood levels of B-endorphins in humans (Gianoulakis & Barcomb, 1987; Gianoulakis 1989). If alcohol drinking is mediated in part via opioids, then selective opioid antagonists should inhibit alcohol drinking behavior. Naloxone and naltrexone, two opioid antagonists, have been shown to reduce alcohol intake, although large doses were required to produce these effects (Altshuler, Phillips & Feinhandler, 1980; Sandi, Borell & Gusaz, 1988). Moreover, opiate antagonists reduce consumption of a wide variety of foods and of water (Hynes, Gallagher & Yacos, 1981) and were found not to alter the alcohol preference of rats bred for this trait (Weiss, Mitchiner et al., 1990). Other studies have found that these opiate antagonists reduced alcohol preference, although differences in the methods used to determine these effects may underlie the apparent discrepancies.

Serotonin: As reviewed above, recent advances in receptor cloning and expression have greatly expanded our knowledge of the potential molecular targets for alcohol in the brain. Electrophysiological studies have demonstrated that alcohol enhances cation conductance through $5HT_3$ receptors (Lovinger & White, 1991). These alterations could have important consequences, depending on the location of these receptors and the extent to which they are potentiated. Serotonin also interacts with a number of 5HT-specific receptors that are coupled to various signal transduction pathways. The direct effects of alcohol on these receptor systems are not as well characterized. However, there is a fairly large literature describing the effects on alcohol drinking behavior of various drugs that modulate serotonergic tone. 5HT and 5HT-metabolite levels are reduced in the cerebrospinal fluid of many alcohol abusers, suggesting that reduced 5HT levels or a reduction in 5HT-mediated neurotransmission may predispose certain people to uncontrollable drinking behavior (for a review, see Sellers, Higgins & Sobell, 1992).

It has been suggested that similar deficiencies in 5HT neurotransmission underlie the development of a variety of other disorders, including bulimia and obsessive-compulsive behavior, which also are characterized by a loss of behavioral control. These hypothesis are supported by studies in which certain pharmacological agents that enhance 5HT neurotransmission (such as selective uptake inhibitors) appear to be therapeutically effective in the treatment of these disorders. Similarly, these agents (such as zimeldine, fluoxetine, and sertaline) also have been shown to decrease alcohol intake in both animals and humans. It should be noted that the magnitude of these effects is small ($<20\%$) and is confounded by the finding that increasing synaptic concentrations of 5HT also is associated with reductions in food intake, suggesting that the effect of these drugs on alcohol intake may be non-selective. However, the involvement of the serotonergic system in modulating drinking behavior is supported by a recent report that showed that alcohol consumption was increased in genetic knockout mice lacking the 5-HT1b receptor (Crabbe, Phillips et al., 1996). Food and water consumption was normal in these animals and they were less sensitive to the ataxic effects of alcohol. These types of studies in which specific receptor subunits can be deleted from the animal genome may help unravel the importance of various neurotransmitter systems in alcohol's actions on brain and behavior.

REINFORCING PROPERTIES

A widely accepted tenet of addiction research is that addictive substances, by definition, engender actions that promote further drug-seeking behavior. This concept of positive reinforcement suggests that a positive reward is obtained following ingestion of an addictive substance such as alcohol, and that the desire to re-experience the reward leads to more drinking. However, there also is evidence that alcohol's reinforcing properties may be more of a reflection of its anti-anxiety properties. Certainly, these two mechanisms of reinforcement are not mutually exclusive and probably co-exist to a greater or lesser degree in individuals addicted to alcohol. This is suggested by clinical studies that have led to the classification of two types of alcoholism, based on the appearance of certain alcohol-related problems and the degree of expression of certain personality traits, including novelty seeking, harm avoidance, and reward dependence (Cloninger, 1987). A brief review of the proposed neural basis of reinforcement is presented here.

Animal and human studies have suggested that the biochemical substrates for the reinforcing properties of alcohol and other drugs of abuse involve discrete neuronal pathways in the brain, including the dopaminergic projections to the mesolimbic areas of the forebrain (for a recent review, see Koob, 1992). These neurons (unlike those that reside in the substantia nigra and project to the corpus striatum and are lost in the Parkinsonian patient) originate in the ventral tegmental area and project to discrete areas of the forebrain, including the nucleus accumbens, olfactory tubercle, frontal cortex, amygdala, and the septal area (Figure 3). These areas of the cortex are thought to be involved in translating emotion into action through the activation of motor pathways; thus, they may be important in initiating and sustaining drug-seeking behavior. Lesions of these discrete brain areas in experimental animals reduce motor activity in response to novel environmental stimuli, food presentation, and other factors that normally increase locomotor activity in nonlesioned animals. Conversely, direct injection of dopamine and compounds with dopamine-agonist like properties—such as amphetamine and cocaine—into these areas stimulates locomotor activity. These effects are blocked by prior administration of selective dopamine antagonists. Thus, a "dopamine hypothesis" has emerged, which asserts that all addictive drugs either directly or indirectly increase dopaminergic activity in the mesolimbic areas of the forebrain (DiChiara & Imperato, 1988). This is undoubtedly a simplification of a very complex behavior, but it has a surprisingly impressive amount of experimental data to support it.

The reinforcing properties of alcohol may involve modulation of mesolimbic dopaminergic neurotransmission by several mechanisms which, in the final result, enhance the synaptic concentrations of dopamine in key mesolimbic cortical regions. This is suggested by the locomotor-enhancing effects in animals given low doses of alcohol, which is accompanied by increases in extracellular levels of dopamine as determined by *in vivo* microdialysis in the nucleus accumbens (Imperato & Di Chiara, 1986). In addition, dopamine levels (estimated from dopamine metabolite measurements) following alcohol ingestion are higher in animals genetically selected for alcohol preference over non-preferring strains; again, suggesting a dopamine involvement in the reinforcing properties of alcohol (Fadda, Mosca et al., 1989; Khatib, Murphy & McBride, 1988).

Weiss and colleagues (1992) have carried out a series of elegant studies using *in vivo* microdialysis to monitor extracellular dopamine levels in rats operantly trained to self-administer alcohol. The results of these experiments show that the self-administration of alcohol in rats was accompanied by significant dose-dependent increases in extracellular dopamine levels in the nucleus accumbens. In addition, dopamine levels were elevated to a greater extent in alcohol preferring strains of rats (as compared to non-preferring strains), even though total alcohol consumption over the test period was nearly identical in both strains. These results suggest that the alcohol-preferring strains are sensitized to the dopamine-enhancing effects of alcohol as compared to non-preferring strains, and that this sensitization may be important in determining the degree of alcohol preference in these animals.

Finally, a fascinating finding of these studies was the significant increase in dopamine found only in the alcohol-preferring strains during the 15-minute waiting period prior to the period of alcohol self-administration. This suggests that the expected reward that the ingestion of alcohol may provide these animals is sufficient to enhance activity in this pathway; thus, the genetic differences in this pathway may contribute to the motivational factors that drive alcohol-seeking behavior in certain individuals.

As intriguing as these findings with experimental animal models are, they are not without their problems. For example, animals that have been made physically dependent on alcohol through a schedule-controlled regimen go through withdrawal when that schedule is removed even when alcohol is freely available (Falk & Tang, 1988). Animals undergoing alcohol withdrawal do not perform operant behavior to obtain alcohol, suggesting that the loss of control or craving for alcohol that is associated with the disease of alcoholism is not easily demonstrated in animal models (Samson, 1987).

ACKNOWLEDGMENT: Support for the author's research comes from Grants RO1-AA09986 and KO2-AA00238 from the National Institute on Alcohol Abuse and Alcoholism.

REFERENCES

Altshuler HL, Phillips PE & Feinhandler DA (1980). Alterations of ethanol self-administration by naltrexone. *Life Sciences* 26:679–688.

Blevins T, Mirshahi T & Woodward JJ (1995). Increased agonist and antagonist sensitivity of N-methyl-D-aspartate stimulated calcium flux in cultured neurons following chronic ethanol exposure. *Neuroscience Letters* 200:214–218.

Brodie MS, Shefner SA & Dunwiddie TV (1990). Ethanol increases the firing rate of dopamine neurons of the rat ventral tegmental area in vitro. *Brain Research* 508:65–69.

Cloninger CR (1987). Neurogenetic adaptive mechanisms in alcoholism. *Science* 236:410–416.

Collins MA (1988). Acetaldehyde and its condensation products as markers in alcoholism. In M Galanter (ed.) *Recent Developments in Alcoholism, Vol. 6.* New York, NY: Plenum Press.

Colombo G & Grant KA (1992). NMDA receptor complex antagonists have ethanol-like discriminative stimulus effects. *Annals of the New York Academy of Sciences* 654:421–423.

Crabbe JC, Phillips TJ, Feller DJ, Hen R, Wenger CD, Lessov CN & Schafer GL (1996). Elevated alcohol consumption in null mutant mice lacking 5-HT1b serotonin receptors. *Nature Genetics* 14:98–101.

Davis VE & Walsh MJ (1970). Alcohol, amines, and alkaloids: A possible biochemical basis for alcohol addiction. *Science* 167:1005–1007.

Diamond I, Nagy L, Mochly-Rosen D & Gordon A (1991). The role of adenosine and adenosine transport in ethanol-induced cellular tolerance and dependence: Possible biologic and genetic markers of alcoholism. *Annals of the New York Academy of Sciences* 625:473–487.

DiChiara G & Imperato A (1988). Preferential stimulation of dopamine release in mesolimbic systems: A common feature of drugs of abuse. In M Sandler, C Feuerstein & B Scatton (eds.) *Neurotransmitter Interactions in the Basal Ganglia.* New York, NY: Raven Press.

Dildy JE & Leslie SW (1989). Ethanol inhibits NMDA-induced increases in free intracellular Ca2+ in dissociated brain cells. *Brain Research* 499:383–387.

Dildy-Mayfield JE & Leslie SW (1991). Mechanism of inhibition of N-methyl-D-Aspartate-stimulated increases in free intracellular Ca^{2+} concentration by ethanol. *Journal of Neurochemistry* 56:1536–1543.

Dolin S, Little H, Hudspith M, Pagonis C & Littleton J (1987). Increased dihydropyridine-sensitive calcium channels in rat brain may underlie ethanol physical dependence. *Neuropharmacology* 26:275–279.

Fadda F, Mosca E, Colombo G & Gessa GL (1989). Effects of spontaneous ingestion of ethanol on brain dopamine metabolism. *Life Sciences* 44:281–287.

Falk JL & Tang M (1988). What schedule-induced polydipsia can tell us about alcoholism. *Alcoholism: Clinical & Experimental Research* 12(5):577–585.

Follesa P & Ticku MK (1995). Chronic ethanol treatment differentially regulates NMDA receptor subunit mRNA expression in rat brain. *Molecular Brain Research* 29:99–105.

Forman SA, Miller KW (1989). Molecular sites of anesthetic action in postsynaptic nicotinic membranes. *Trends in Pharmacological Sciences* 10:447–452.

Frezza M, Di Padova C, Pozzato G, Terpin M, Baraona E & Lieber C (1990). High blood alcohol levels in women: The role of decreased gastric alcohol dehydrogenase activity and first-pass metabolism. *The New England Journal of Medicine* 322:95–99.

Gianoulakis C (1989). The effect of ethanol on the biosynthesis and regulation of opioid peptides. *Experientia* 45:428–435.

Gianoulakis C & Barcomb A (1987). Effect of acute ethanol in vivo and in vitro on the B-endorphin system in the rat. *Life Science* 40:19–28.

Goedde HW, Harada S & Agarwal DP (1979). Racial differences in alcohol sensitivity: A new hypothesis. *Human Genetics* 51:331–334.

Gonzales RA & Woodward JJ (1990). Ethanol inhibits N-methyl-D-aspartate-stimulated [^{3}H]norepinephrine release from rat cortical slices. *Journal of Pharmacology and Experimental Therapeutics* 252:1138–1144.

Gothert M & Fink K (1989). Inhibition of N-methyl-D-aspartate (NMDA)- and L-glutamate-induced noradrenaline and acetylcholine release in the rat brain by ethanol. *Naunyn-Schmiedeberg's Archives of Pharmachology* 340:516–521.

Grant KA & Barrett JE (1991). Blockade of the discriminative stimulus effects of ethanol with 5-HT3 receptor antagonists. *Pyschopharmacology* (Berl.) 104:451–456.

Grant KA, Valverius P, Hudspith M & Tabakoff B (1990). Ethanol withdrawal seizures and the NMDA receptor complex. *European Journal of Pharmacology* 176:289–296.

Harada S, Agarwal DP & Goedde HW (1980). Electrophoretic and biochemical studies of human acetaldehyde dehydrogenase isozymes in various tissues. *Life Sciences* 26:1773–1780.

Harada S, Agarwal DP, Goedde HW & Ishikawa B (1983). Aldehyde dehydrogenase isoenzyme variation and alcoholism in Japan. *Pharmacology, Biochemistry and Behavior* 18(Suppl 1):151–153.

Hoffman PL, Moses F & Tabakoff B (1989). Selective inhibition by ethanol of glutamate-stimulated cyclic

GMP production in primary cultures of cerebellar granule cells. *Neuropharmacology* 28:1239–1243.

Hwang BH, Lumeng L, Wu JY & Li TK (1990). Increased number of GABAergic terminals in the nucleus accumbens is associated with alcohol preference in rats. *Alcoholism: Clinical & Experimental Research* 14:503–507.

Hynes MA, Gallagher M & Yacos KV (1981). Systemic and intraventricular naloxone administration: Effects on food and water intake. *Behavioral and Neural Biology* 32:334–342.

Imperato A & Di Chiara G. (1986) Preferential stimulation of dopamine release in the nucleus accumbens of freely moving rats by ethanol. *Journal of Pharmacology and Experimental Therapeutics* 239:219–239.

Iorio KR, Reinlib L, Tabakoff B & Hoffman PL (1992). Chronic exposure of cerebellar granule cells to ethanol results in increased N-methyl-D-aspartate receptor function. *Molecular Pharmacology* 41:1142–1148.

Kalivas PW & Samson HH (1992). The neurobiology of drug and alcohol addiction. *Annals of the New York Academy of Sciences* 654:421–423.

Khatib SA, Murphy JM & McBride WJ (1988). Biochemical evidence for activation of specific monoamine pathways by ethanol. *Alcohol* 5:295–299.

Koob GF (1992). Drugs of abuse: Anatomy, pharmacology and function of reward pathways. *Trends in Pharmacological Sciences* 13:177–184.

Kuner T, Schoepfer R & Korpi, ER (1993). Ethanol inhibits glutamate-induced currents in heteromeric NMDA receptor subtypes. *NeuroReport* 5:297–300.

Leslie SW, Barr E, Chandler J & Farrar RP (1983). Inhibition of fast- and slow-phase depolarization-dependent synaptosomal calcium uptake by ethanol. *Journal of Pharmacology and Experimental Therapy* 225:571–575.

Litten RZ & Allen JP (1991). Pharmacotherapies for alcoholism: Promising agents and clinical issues. *Alcoholism: Clinical & Experimental Research* 15:620–633.

Lovinger DM (1995). Developmental decrease in ethanol inhibition of N-methyl-D-aspartate receptors in rat neocortical neurons: Relation to the actions of ifenprodil. *Journal of Pharmacology and Experimental Therapy* 274:164–172.

Lovinger DM & White G (1991). Ethanol potentiation of 5-hydroxytryptamine$_3$ receptor-mediated ion current in neuroblastoma cells and isolated adult mammalian neurons. *Molecular Pharmacology* 40:263–270.

Lovinger DM, White G & Weight FF (1989). Ethanol inhibits NMDA activated ion current in hippocampal neurons. *Science* 243:1721–1724.

Mascia MP, Machu TK & Harris RA (1996) Enhancement of homomeric glycine receptor function by long-chain alcohols and anesthetics. *British Journal of Pharmacology* 119:1331–1336.

Masood K, Wu C, Brauneis U & Weight FF (1994) Differential ethanol sensitivity of recombinant N-methyl-D-aspartate receptor subunits. *Molecular Pharmacology* 45:324–329.

Messing RO, Carpenter CL, Diamond I & Greenberg DA (1986). Ethanol regulates calcium channels in clonal neural cells. *Proceedings of the National Academy of Science* 83:6213–6215.

Meyers RD (1989). Isoquinolines, beta-carbolines and alcohol drinking: Involvement of opioid and dopaminergic mechanisms. *Experientia* 45:436–443.

Mirshahi T & Woodward JJ (1995) Ethanol sensitivity of heteromeric NMDA receptors: Effects of subunit assembly, glycine and NMDAR1 Mg2+-insensitive mutants. *Neuropharmacology* 34:347–355.

Morse RM & Flavin DK (1992). The definition of alcoholism. *Journal of the American Medical Association* 268:1012–1014.

Samson HH (1987). Initiation of ethanol-maintained behavior: A comparison of animal models and their implication to human drinking. In T Thompson, P Dews & J Barret J (eds.) *Neurobehavioral Pharmacology, Vol. 6; Advances in Behavioral Pharmacology.* New Jersey: Erlbaum Associates.

Sandi C, Borell J & Gusaz C (1988). Naloxone decreases ethanol consumption within a free choice paradigm in rats. *Pharmacology, Biochemistry and Behavior* 29:39–43.

Schuckit MA (1991). A longitudinal study of children of alcoholics. *Recent Developments in Alcoholism* 9:5–19.

Sellers EM, Higgins GA & Sobell MB (1992). 5-HT and alcohol abuse. *Trends in Pharmacological Sciences* 13:69–75.

Snape BM & Engel JA (1988). Ethanol enhances the calcium-dependent stimulus-induced release of endogenous dopamine from slices of rat striatum and nucleus accumbens in vitro. *Neuropharmacology* 27:1097–1101.

Snell LD, Nunley KR, Lickteig RL, Browning MD, Tabakoff B & Hoffman PL (1996). Regional and subunit specific changes in NMDA receptor mRNA and immunoreactivity in mouse brain following chronic ethanol ingestion. *Molecular Brain Research* 40:71–78.

Teng YS (1981). Human liver aldehyde dehydrogenase in Chinese and Asiatic Indians: Gene deletion and its possible implications in alcohol metabolism. *Biochemical Genetics* 19:107–114.

Thomasson HR, Mai XL, Crabb DW, Li TK, Hwu HG, Chen CC, Yeh EK, Wang SP, Lu RB & Yin SJ (1989). Aldehyde dehydrogenase deficiency: Relationship of aldehyde dehydrogenase–2 genotype with risk for alcoholism in Taiwanese. *Clinical Research* 37:898A.

U.S. Public Health Service (1990). *Seventh Special Report to the U.S. Congress on Alcohol and Health.* Washington, DC: National Institutes of Health.

Wafford KA, Burnett DM, Leidenheimer NJ, Burt DR, Wang JB, Kofuji P, Dunwiddie TV, Harris RA & Sikela JM (1991). Ethanol sensitivity of the $GABA_A$ receptor expressed in Xenopus oocytes requires 8 amino acids contained in the gamma 2L subunit of the receptor complex. *Neuron* 7:27–33.

Wafford KA & Whiting PJ (1992). Ethanol potentiation of GABAa receptors requires phosphorylation of the alternatively spliced variant of the $\gamma 2$ subunit. *FEBS Letters* 313:113–117.

Watkins JC & Collingridge GL, eds. (1994). *The NMDA Receptor.* Oxford, England: IRL Press, 503.

Weiss F, Mitchiner M, Bloom FE & Koob GF (1990). Free-choice responding for ethanol versus water in alcohol-preferring (P) and unselected Wistar rats is differentially altered by naloxone, bromocriptine and methysergide. *Pyschopharmacology* 101:178–186.

Weiss F, Hurd YL, Ungerstedet U, Markou A, Plotsky PM & Koob GF (1992). Neurochemical correlates of cocaine and ethanol self-administration. *Annals of the New York Academy of Science* 654:220–241.

Woodward JJ & Gonzales RA (1990). Ethanol inhibition of N-methyl-Daspartate-stimulated endogenous dopamine release from rat striatal slices: Reversal by glycine. *Journal of Neurochemistry* 54:712–715.

Youngren, KD, Daly DA & Moghaddam B (1993). Distinct actions of endogenous excitatory amino acids on the outflow of dopamine in the nucleus accumbens. *Journal of Pharmacology and Experimental Therapeutics* 264:289–293.

CHAPTER 3

The Pharmacology of Sedative-Hypnotics

Steven M. Juergens, M.D., FASAM
Debra Cowley, M.D.

Drugs in the Class
Therapeutic Use and Misuse
Adverse Effects
Addiction Liability
Absorption and Metabolism
Mechanisms of Action
Reinforcing Properties

The benzodiazepines are the primary focus of this chapter, as they have largely supplanted the barbiturate and barbiturate-like sedatives-hypnotics. Benzodiazepines are used for a wide variety of indications. Their use in alcohol withdrawal is covered elsewhere in this text. They also are used as anticonvulsants and muscle relaxants (uses that will not be reviewed here).

DRUGS IN THE CLASS

Sedatives, hypnotics, and anxiolytic drugs are central nervous system (CNS) depressants, traditionally used to reduce anxiety and/or induce sleep. Drugs in the class are listed in Table 1.

Bromide was introduced as a sedative in the 1850s, barbiturates were introduced in the early 1900s, and benzodiazepines were introduced in the early 1960s (Kisnad, 1990). Critical examination of their use continues, with particular attention to concerns about dependence and addiction.

THERAPEUTIC USE AND MISUSE

Therapeutic Uses. Except for the anticonvulsant actions of phenobarbital and its congeners, the barbiturate and other barbiturate-like sedative-hypnotics have a low therapeutic index and low degree of selectivity, so that the therapeutic effect of sedation or anxiolysis is accompanied by CNS depression. Other disadvantages compared to the benzodiazepines are that they induce hepatic enzymes, causing more drug interactions; produce more tolerance, physiological impairment and toxic reactions; have a greater liability for development of dependence; and are more dangerous in overdose (Kisnad, 1990). Unfortunately, there is evidence of some increase in their use in locales where the benzodiazepines have come under more stringent regulation (Weintraub, Singh et al., 1991).

Zolpidem (Ambien®), an imadozopyridine, is a non-benzodiazepine hypnotic with rapid onset, short duration of action, and short half-life (2.5 hours). Its actions are mediated at the type I benzodiazepine receptor subtype (see Mechanisms of Action). Mild rebound insomnia has occurred on the first night after discontinuation. Dose-related dizziness, headaches, nausea, diarrhea and next-day drowsiness occur in a few patients. No fatalities have occurred in overdoses up to 400 mg but deaths have occurred when patients took zolpidem with other drugs that depress the central nervous system. The benzodiazepine receptor antagonist flumazenil appears to be an effective antidote to zolpidem (The Medical Letter, 1993).

Compared with *temazepam* and *triazolam* in normal subjects, zolpidem produces similar impairment of learning, recall, and performance as well as estimates of drug effects. None of the hypnotics was noted as reinforcing (Rush & Griffiths, 1996). However, in those with a history of sedative abuse, zolpidem and triazolam are both reinforcing, although at higher doses triazolam is identified as barbiturate-, benzodiazepine- or alcohol-like nearly twice as often as zolpidem. More nausea and dysphoria were noted with zolpidem (Evans, Funderburk & Griffiths, 1990). While zolpidem appears to have a lower risk of dependence than the benzodiazepines, isolated cases of abuse and withdrawal symptoms have been reported (Braun, 1993; Cavallaro, Regazzetti et al., 1993). Zolpidem is a schedule IV controlled substance, like the benzodiazepines.

Buspirone (Buspar®), an azapirone, is a non-benzodiazepine anxiolytic and partial 5-HT_{1A} receptor agonist. It has a relatively slow onset of action (two to three weeks), does not cause memory impairment or psychomotor deficits, does not potentiate the central nervous effects of alcohol, causes no withdrawal symptoms and, despite the slower onset of action, is comparable to the benzodiazepines in the treatment of anxiety. It has a low abuse potential (Gelenberg, 1994). A study of anxious alcoholics who received weekly relapse prevention therapy in addition to buspirone found buspirone superior to placebo in the reduction of anxiety, the retention in treatment, the reduction of drinking days in follow-up and the delayed return to heavy drinking (Kranzler, Burleson et al., 1994).

Panic disorder responds to benzodiazepines, with *alprazolam* (Xanax®) the drug most extensively studied, although it appears that many benzodiazepines may be effective in short-term treatment, if given in equivalent doses (Cowley & Dunner, 1991). The usual dosage range is the equivalent of 2 to 6 mg of alprazolam daily (Cowley & Dunner, 1991). However, concerns have been raised about the efficacy of long-term use of benzodiazepines for panic disorder. Although alprazolam remains effective during long-term use and dose escalation is rare in patients with panic disorder, dependency and withdrawal symptoms are common. One study demonstrated that panic disorder patients who responded to imipramine or placebo did as well at one year follow-up as patients who responded to alprazolam, without the difficulty with discontinuation (Rickels, Schweizer et al., 1993).

Benzodiazepines have been used for the treatment of generalized anxiety disorder. This often is an indistinct syndrome that coexists with other anxiety and affective disorders. It may be a subsyndromal form of other psychiatric disorders, or may represent an underlying personality disorder (Cowley & Dunner, 1991). Benzodiazepines are indicated for severe generalized anxiety when immediate symptom relief is necessary. Because short acting, high potency benzodiazepines (such as alprazolam) prompt more interdose rebound and dependency, long-acting, low potency benzodiazepines (e.g., chlordiazepoxide 25 to 75 mg/day) are preferred. They are best used for exacerbations of anxiety rather than continuous use, usually one to four weeks (Maxmen & Ward, 1995). Some of these patients may do better with antidepressant medications, other anti-anxiety medications such as buspirone, or other forms of psychosocial intervention. The chronically dysphoric or personality disordered patient may have more difficulty with benzodiazepine addiction and discontinuation of benzodiazepines, so caution is necessary in prescribing (American Psychiatric Association, 1990; Roy-Byrne, 1991; Schweizer, Rickels et al., 1990; Rickels, Schweizer et al., 1990).

Benzodiazepines often are combined with antidepressants to achieve initial symptom relief in patients with depression and anxiety. Alprazolam has been shown to be effective in outpatient treatment of mild depressions, but is not considered a primary pharmacological treatment. In general, benzodiaze-

TABLE 1. Sedative-Hypnotic Drugs

Benzodiazepines
alprazolam (*Xanax®*)
chlordiazepoxide (*Librium®*)
clonazepam (*Klonopin®*)
clorazepate (*Tranxene®*)
diazepam (*Valium®*)
estazolam (*ProSom®*)
flurazepam (*Dalmane®*)
halazepam (*Paxipam®*)
lorazepam (*Ativan®*)
oxazepam (*Serax®*)
prazepam (*Centrax®*)
quazepam (*Doral®*)
temazepam (*Restoril®*)
triazolam (*Halcion®*)
Barbiturates
amobarbital (*Amytal®*)
butabarbital (*Barbased®*, *Butisol®*)
butalbital (in *Fiorinal®*)
pentobarbital (*Nembutal®*)
phenobarbital (*Luminal®*)
secobarbital (*Seconal®*)
Barbiturate-like Drugs
chloral hydrate (*Noctec®*, *Somnos®*)
ethchlorvynol (*Placidyl®*)
ethinamate (*Valmid®*)
glutethimide (*Doriden®*)
meprobamate (*Equanil®*, *Miltown®*)
methaqualone (*Quaalude®*)
methyprylon (*Noludar®*)

pines have not been proved effective as antidepressants (Cowley & Dunner, 1991).

Benzodiazepines are used as an adjunct to the neuroleptics in treating patients with schizophrenia and active psychotic symptomatology who do not respond satisfactorily to neuroleptics alone and as an adjunct in manic bipolar patients (Cohen, 1991).

Benzodiazepine hypnotics are used for transient insomnia, prescribed at the lowest effective dose (e.g., flurazepam 15 mg or triazolam 0.125 mg) in a time-limited fashion, usually for two to three weeks (Pascually, 1991). Tolerance to sedative effects develops within that time, especially with the short half-life agents (American Psychiatric Association, 1990). Rebound insomnia (intense worsening of sleep above baseline levels, following withdrawal of the benzodiazepine) may develop after short-term use. This may lead to patients asking to continue the benzodiazepine for sleep, which should be avoided. Tapering the hypnotic may attenuate the symptoms of rebound insomnia (Pascually, 1991).

Parasomnias, including REM behavior disorder, periodic limb movements during sleep, sleepwalking, and night terrors, may be treated with benzodiazepines, but a careful diagnostic work-up is needed because treatment often is long-term and the risk of relapse to the parasomnias on discontinuation may be high (Pascually, 1991).

Other uses for benzodiazepines include catatonia (lorazepam 1 to 2 mg intramuscularly), acute aggression (i.e., lorazepam 1 to 2 mg orally or infusion every hour until calm), and social phobia (i.e., clonazepam 0.5 to 3 mg daily) (Maxmen & Ward, 1995).

Misuse. The misuse of benzodiazepines can develop when patients are maintained on higher doses and/or for a longer term than is necessary. Lack of clear diagnosis without defined measures of benefit and projected time course of treatment may lead to indiscriminate use. Once begun, a cycle of dependence, withdrawal, continued treatment, and further dependence may develop, with many patients unable to withdraw completely from the benzodiazepine (Rickels, Schweizer et al., 1993; Roache, 1990).

Another concern is the population of patients with polydrug and alcohol addictions who also have anxiety symptoms and phobias. Because of poor history-taking or lack of recognition of what addiction means, such patients may be given benzodiazepines, posing the significant risk of developing an addiction to benzodiazepines, relapsing to their drug of choice, and/or having more difficulty with withdrawal (Roy-Byrne, 1991).

In prescribing benzodiazepines, the physician needs to weigh carefully the potential therapeutic benefit against the risk of dependence, acute and chronic toxicity, and addiction. In the majority of cases, use should be short-term (that is, less than two to four months), on as small a dose as is effective. Longer term use should be reevaluated at regular intervals to ensure that continued use of the benzodiazepine is appropriate and without problems. DuPont (1990) has elucidated a checklist for use in making this determination, the points of which include verifying that:

- The diagnosis, distress and disability warrant use;
- The benzodiazepine is effecting a positive therapeutic response, with appropriate doses and no other drug or alcohol addiction;
- There is no evidence of any benzodiazepine-induced problem; and
- A family member or significant other can confirm the effectiveness of the drug use and the lack of impairment or addiction.

Identification of problems is easier in patients who use benzodiazepines in the context of addiction to multiple drugs and/or alcohol, or if there is clear escalation of the dose. It is more difficult to make a diagnosis of benzodiazepine problems in patients who use the drug at therapeutic doses. Toxic behaviors (such as memory difficulties, psychomotor effects, benzodiazepine-induced depression or anxiety, behavioral disinhibition, or sleep disturbances) may be subtle, unobtrusive or attributed to other causes, so that the physician, family, friends or patient are not aware that their problems are caused by the drug.

When prescribing benzodiazepines, a process of informed consent should take place, including a discussion with the patient on initiation of treatment about the effects of the drugs on memory, psychomotor function (including concerns about driving) and the potential for development of dependence and addiction. If use of a benzodiazepine is contemplated in a patient who is recovering from alcohol or other drug addiction, a consultation with an expert in addiction medicine clearly is indicated.

ADVERSE EFFECTS

Impairment of Memory. Benzodiazepines can induce memory problems. Most studies show the ability to learn new information is impaired (anterograde amnesia) following benzodiazepine administration. This impairment apparently occurs by disrupting the process of transferring information from temporary, short-term memory to longer term memory storage (the consolidation phase) (American Psychiatric Association, 1990). Anterograde amnesia is increased with increased dose, faster absorption, intravenous administration, and higher potency of the benzodiazepines. Tolerance to the anterograde amnesia occurs but is not complete. In chronic users, transient amnesic effects can occur related to post-dose, peak benzodiazepine levels (King 1992). The elderly are more sensitive to the effects of benzodiazepines on memory (American Psychiatric Association, 1990). Of note, cases of amnesia also have been reported with zolpidem (Canaday, 1996).

The increased sensitivity of the elderly may be due, in part, to a lower baseline performance in the elderly so that an equal decrement in a younger and older patient would be more noticeable and have more serious consequences in the elderly (American Psychiatric Association, 1990). In the elderly, benzodiazepines are the drugs that most commonly exacerbate underlying dementia and may cause excess morbidity. The cognitive impairment often appears to develop insidiously as a "late complication" of a drug initially prescribed at a younger age. Some patients may be given other drugs to treat side effects of the benzodiazepines, i.e., neuroleptics given to patients who develop confusion while on benzodiazepines (Larson, Kukull et al., 1987).

Patients have a significant improvement in measures of memory and cognitive functioning following discontinuation of benzodiazepines. Family and staff note that elderly patients who discontinue benzodiazepines are brighter, more energetic, less dysphoric, and substantially more intellectually alert than while on the drug (Salzman, Fisher et al., 1992). However, there is concern that patients withdrawn from long-term therapeutic benzodiazepine use may not have full recovery of cognitive function (Tata, Rollings et al., 1994).

The benzodiazepine-induced memory problems may be unrecognized by patients, family, or clinicians and the true incidence is unknown. Individuals suffering from such memory problems may conclude that nothing worth remembering had happened if they are unable to recall events. In the elderly, memory problems may be blamed on aging rather than the benzodiazepine.

Cognitive and Psychomotor Effects. Benzodiazepines also impair cognitive and motor functioning with acute and chronic dosing, although the effects of chronic administration are not consistent from person to person and may depend on dose and time of drug administration (American Psychiatric Association, 1990). Sedation, drowsiness, ataxia, incoordination, vertigo, and dizziness are common side effects related to dose and individual susceptibility. Tolerance to these effects develops although it may not be complete (American Psychiatric Association, 1990). Impaired visual spatial ability and sustained attention have been found in long-term benzodiazepine users, and patients are often unaware of their reduced ability (Golombeck, Moodley & Lader, 1988). Being elderly, using alcohol, using high doses of benzodiazepine and taking other drugs, i.e., anticholinergics, are associated with increased sensitivity to cognitive and psychomotor effects (American Psychiatric Association, 1990).

Risk of Deleterious Events. Benzodiazepines impair skills of importance to driving. There is epidemiologic evidence of an increased risk of crash involvement in younger and older benzodiazepine users. In older users, their annual rate of involvement in injurious crashes was 50% higher than nonusers. The rate increased as a function of the prescribed dose (Ray, Purushottam & Shorr, 1993). Double blind, placebo controlled studies of healthy volunteers and anxious patients revealed no difference in baseline and/or placebo performances between volunteers and patients. Both groups using benzodiazepine and imadazopyridine anxiolytics demonstrated marked and pervasive driving impairment throughout the 8-day treatment phase, however (O'Hanlon, Vermeeren et al., 1995).

In the elderly, there is a significantly increased risk of falling and hip fracture in current users of long half-life benzodiazepines and this risk does not dissipate after the first 30 days of therapy, indicating no development of tolerance to the impairment (Ray, Griffin & Downey, 1989). Short half-life benzodiazepines also pose considerable hazards to older patients as there are significantly incapacitating psychomotor effects in the first few hours after drug administration which puts patients at risk for falling should they need to void or get out of bed for any reason (Fisch, Bakir et al., 1990).

The use of benzodiazepines in the first weeks after stroke has detrimental effects on recovery of motor function and their routine use in these patients should be avoided (Goldstein et al., 1995).

Other Psychiatric Issues. Behavioral disinhibition reactions with various benzodiazepine may occur, usually associated with higher doses and pretreatment level of hostility (Rothschild, 1992). The use of benzodiazepines is associated with the development of delirium in postoperative patients (Marcantonio, Juarez et al., 1994).

Studies show that significant anxiety and depressive psychopathology remain in many long-term benzodiazepine users while they are using benzodiazepines. However, patients who are able to withdraw successfully from long term benzodiazepine treatment have significantly improved anxiety and depression scores compared to pre-taper baseline (Schweizer, Rickels et al., 1990), implying that benzodiazepines may worsen depression and anxiety long-term. Depression and interdose anxiety have been noted to emerge with benzodiazepine therapy (American Psychiatric Association, 1990). Gains with agoraphobia using alprazolam and exposure therapy are lost after treatment but maintained in patients treated with exposure therapy alone so that the use of benzodiazepines may impair therapeutic progress long-term (Marks, Swinson et al., 1993). Deterioration in mood and social behavior in subjects taking benzodiazepines has been noted by raters but not the subjects themselves so negative effects may be difficult to elicit by self-report (Griffiths, Bigelow & Liebson, 1983).

Benzodiazepines can be a complicating factor in those patients with prior or current chemical dependency. Though existing studies have methodologic difficulties, benzodiazepine abuse and dependence appears greater among alcoholics and addicts (American Psychiatric Association, 1990). The development of alcohol or other drug addiction after primary benzodiazepine dependence, though reported less often than the reverse, has been observed (Wolf, Grohmann et al., 1989). Benzodiazepines are commonly used in suicide attempts. Though safer than barbiturates, there can be fatal overdoses with benzodiazepines, often, though not always, combined with alcohol or other drugs. Some benzodiazepines (diazepam, flurazepam, and temazepam) may be more toxic than others. Completed suicides have been linked with benzodiazepines (Serfaty & Masterton, 1993). The risk of suicide in patients who have been hospitalized for dependence on prescribed narcotics and sedatives is very high in long-term follow-up (Aggulander, Brandt & Allebeck, 1994). Substantial social and occupational impairment have been associated the benzodiazepine addiction as well (Juergens & Morse, 1988).

The high rate of withdrawal symptoms and difficulties with benzodiazepine discontinuation also must be seen as an adverse consequence of their use.

The high potency, short half-life benzodiazepines may have more adverse effects (American Psychiatric Association, 1990). Wysowski and Barash (1991) report that adverse behavioral reactions concerning triazolam, reported to the Spontaneous Reporting System of the Food and Drug Administration, considering the extent of use, were 22 to 99 times those of temazepam for confusion, amnesia, bizarre behavior, agitation, and hallucinations. Higher doses and use in the elderly were associated with more reactions, but the higher incidence occurred even when high dose cases were removed from analysis.

Benzodiazepines are unique in that, with the opioid analgesics, they are the only potentially addicting drug used routinely in medical practice. They are very effective in producing rapid anxiolysis and sedation. However, close monitoring of their use by a physician is necessary as the potential for occurrence of physical dependence, adverse effects, and addiction must be weighed and respected.

ADDICTION LIABILITY

Clinical and descriptive data regarding benzodiazepine addiction are surprisingly inadequate. The data that are available most often have little clinical context and are quite nonspecific (Cole & Chiarello, 1990). There are case reports of benzodiazepine addiction (Juergens & Morse, 1988), and reports documenting populations of benzodiazepine-addicted patients, largely from addiction treatment centers (Busto, Sellars et al., 1986; Finlayson & Davis, 1994). Survey data give evidence of a large number of persons engaged in long-term use of benzodiazepines, and a significant amount of abuse/non-medical use, but it is difficult to translate that into estimates of addiction (Cole & Chiarello, 1990).

Two patterns of benzodiazepine dependence have been described: patients who use only benzodiazepines for long periods of time and those who use them in the context of multiple drug and/or alcohol addiction (and in whom benzodiazepines may not be the primary addicting drug). Patients dependent only on benzodiazepines tend to be older, take lower daily doses for a longer period and have more problems with withdrawal. Benzodiazepine-addicted patients who are multiple-drug users tend to be younger, to take higher daily doses, and to have a higher lifetime benzodiazepine exposure than do patients who use only benzodiazepines. The multiple-drug users also appear more likely to escalate their dose (Busto, Sellars et al., 1986). Isolated, high-dose benzodiazepine addiction is said to be rare. Both groups have significant psychiatric morbidity (Busto, Romach & Sellars, 1996; Finlayson & Davis, 1994).

Physical dependence contributes to the addiction potential of a drug because of the negative reinforcement of withdrawal. That dependence on the benzodiazepines occurs at therapeutic doses is clear and is often a major factor in patients' unsuccessful efforts to discontinue benzodiazepine use.

The benzodiazepine withdrawal syndrome is similar to that produced by barbiturates and barbiturate-like sedative-hypnotics; it can be described as of the sedative-hypnotic type (Roache, 1990). However, distinguishing between withdrawal and rebound anxiety may be difficult. Withdrawal is defined by "new" time-limited symptoms that are not part of the original anxiety state and that begin and end depending on the pharmacokinetics of the particular benzodiazepine; relapse as re-emergence of the original anxiety state; and rebound as an increase in anxiety that is above original baseline levels and may be a combination of relapse and withdrawal (Roy-Byrne, 1991). With abrupt discontinuation, symptoms begin the day after with short and intermediate half-life drugs, within three to eight days of cessation of long-acting benzodiazepines, and are most severe between the second and 18th day after cessation of drug use, again depending on half-life (Busto, Sellars et al., 1986).

With gradual taper, the withdrawal syndrome is the most severe in the last quarter of the taper with short half-life benzodiazepines, but it is the most severe in the first week of abstinence in those using long half-life benzodiazepines. For the most part, the withdrawal syndrome remits by three to five weeks after the taper. However, isolated symptoms such as tinnitus may persist for months (Schweizer, Rickels et al., 1990; Rickels, Schweizer et al., 1993).

Common symptoms of withdrawal include anxiety, irritability, insomnia, fatigue, headache, muscle twitching or aching, tremor, shakiness, sweating, dizziness, and concentration difficulties—all symptoms common in anxiety. Symptoms that are more likely to represent withdrawal rather than a return or exacerbation of the original anxiety are nausea, loss of appetite, depression, derealization, increased sensory perception (smell, light, taste, touch) and an abnormal perception of movement (Roy-Byrne, 1991). Seizures, persistent tinnitus, delirium, confusion, and psychotic symptoms have been reported but are uncommon (American Psychiatric Association, 1990). Depression, mania, and obsessive-compulsive disorder are reported to have been triggered with withdrawal as well (Roy-Byrne, 1991).

The majority (more than 90%) of long-term users of benzodiazepines (i.e., those who have used longer than eight months to a year) experience withdrawal symptoms, whether withdrawn slowly or rapidly (Rickels, Schweizer et al., 1993, 1990; Schweizer, Rickels et al., 1990). Gradual taper of alprazolam after long-term treatment of panic disorder results in significant rebound of panic and anxiety symptoms, exceeding pretreatment levels in 50% to 90% of patients, depending on how it is measured (Rickels, Schweizer et al., 1993). Withdrawal does not appear to worsen if the benzodiazepine is used longer than one year, suggesting that there is a threshold duration of treatment beyond which further drug exposure has little pharmacological influence on the withdrawal experience (Schweizer, Rickels et al., 1990; Rickels, Schweizer et al., 1990). The incidence of withdrawal appears to be less in short-term users (less than six to eight months), although it can develop within weeks, particularly if higher doses of high-potency agents are used (American Psychiatric Association, 1990).

Benzodiazepine withdrawal reactions are reported to be more likely and/or more severe if the drug is: (1) rapidly eliminated; (2) highly potent; (3) discontinued abruptly rather than gradually tapered; (4) used in relatively high doses; and (5) used chronically on a PRN rather than a fixed-dose schedule (Roy-Byrne, 1991) or if the patient (6) has traits of dependency and neuroticism; (7) has mild-to-moderate alcohol use; (8) is female (Schweizer, Rickels et al., 1990); (9) is less well-educated; (10) has more panic, anxiety and depression at baseline (Rickels, Schweizer et al., 1990, 1993) (although panic disorder patients may be more vulnerable to withdrawal than patients with generalized anxiety disorder [Klein, Colin et al., 1994]); (11) has a prior history of alcohol and/or drug abuse; and (12) feels he or she is addicted, weak and "hooked" on these drugs (Roy-Byrne, 1991). The effect of half-life and dose is mitigated when the benzodiazepine is gradually tapered (American Psychiatric Association, 1990). Withdrawal reactions appear to be most severe with the quickly eliminated, high potency benzodiazepines (e.g., alprazolam, lorazepam, triazolam); intermediate with quickly eliminated low-potency (oxazepam) and slowly eliminated, high potency benzodiazepines (clonazepam); and mildest with slowly eliminated, low potency benzodiazepines (diazepam, clorazepate, chlordiazepoxide) (Wolf & Griffiths, 1991).

Relapse with return to benzodiazepine use after withdrawal is another concern. Cognitive behavior therapy is very effective in aiding benzodiazepine discontinuation and preventing relapse in panic disorder. The reduction in the fear of anxiety symptoms is the best predictor of patients' ability to achieve and maintain drug abstinence (Bruce, Spiegel et al., 1995).

The management of sedative-hypnotic withdrawal is discussed in detail in Section 6.

ABSORPTION AND METABOLISM

The pharmacokinetic properties of the sedatives-hypnotics are important considerations in evaluating their addiction potential. The kinetic properties of benzodiazepines (which applies to the barbiturate and barbiturate-like drugs as well) that may contribute to their abuse liability and persistent self-administration of these drugs are summarized in Table 2. Drugs that are potent positive reinforcers or that cause the development of physical dependence and withdrawal symptoms have the most potential for abuse and addiction.

There are four chemical types of benzodiazepines:

2-keto compounds (clorazepate, chlordiazepoxide, diazepam, halazepam, prazepam, flurazepam): All are metabolized to desmethyldiazepam. Clorazepate is rapidly hydrolyzed in the stomach and absorbed with a fast onset of action. They are slowly oxidized in the liver and tend to have long half-lives as desmethyldiazepam has a 30- to 200-hour half-life, with the length increasing with age.

3-hydroxy compounds (lorazepam, oxazepam, temazepam): These active compounds with shorter half-lives are rapidly metabolized by direct conjugation with a glucuronide radical and do not generate active metabolites. Age does not affect half-life.

Triazolo-compounds (alprazolam, triazolam, estazolam): All of these are active, have short half-lives, have active metabolites, and are oxidized.

7-nitro compounds (clonazepam): These are active, have long half-lives, no active metabolites, and are metabolized by nitroreduction (Maxmen & Ward, 1995).

Since all benzodiazepines rapidly enter the brain tissue once in circulation, their onset of action relates to the rapidity of their absorption from the gastrointestinal tract. The most rapidly absorbed benzodiazepines (such as diazepam) may produce more euphoria and be more reinforcing than others (Roache, 1990).

The more highly lipophilic benzodiazepines (Table 3) also are rapidly distributed to peripheral tissue and have high volumes of distribution (such as diazepam). After single doses, the duration of action is shorter, which may be reinforcing as well (Cowley, Roy-Byrne & Greenblatt, 1991).

The rate of elimination after multiple doses is related to the elimination half-life of the parent drug and its metabolites (Table 3). In benzodiazepines with a shorter elimination half-life and little accumulation (i.e., lorazepam and alprazolam), there is more chance of developing withdrawal or rebound symptoms if doses are missed, spaced too far apart, or abruptly discontinued, so that continued use may be related to this negatively reinforcing quality (Cowley, Roy-Byrne & Greenblatt, 1991).

Any agent or disease that interferes with liver enzymes, e.g., cimetidine, disulfiram, can block the oxidative metabolism of 2-keto and triazolo compounds, increasing levels (Maxmen & Ward, 1995). Diazepam, triazolam, alprazolam, and other benzodiazepines are metabolized by cytochrome P450 3A4 which is inhibited by the antidepressants fluoxamine, nefazodone, fluoxetine, sertraline; grapefruit juice, the antimycotics ketoconazole and itraconazole; and other drugs, increasing benzodiazepine levels (Nemeroff, DeVane & Pollock, 1996; Schimder, Greenblatt et al., 1996; Hukkinen, Varhe et al., 1995) and, in the case of high-dose therapy and overdose, lead to toxicity or delayed recovery. Pharmacodynamic factors also are important. There are differences in potency that correlate with receptor binding affinity (e.g., alprazolam binds with greater affinity and is more potent than diazepam). Higher potency agents are associated with more seizures on withdrawal and may induce more severe physical dependence (American Psychiatric Association, 1990; Wolf & Griffiths, 1991). There are clear changes in the pharmacodynamics after multiple doses, affecting the development of tolerance. Patients with panic disorder may have a subsensitivity to benzodiazepines (Roy-Byrne, Cowley et al., 1990).

MECHANISMS OF ACTION

Benzodiazepines act by stereospecifically binding to unique receptors located on a large protein complex located on neurons in the CNS. The effects of barbiturates and alcohol have been linked to this complex, which also contains the receptor for gamma-aminobutyric acid (GABA), the major inhibitory neurotransmitter in the brain and an ion channel

TABLE 2. Pharmacokinetic Properties of Benzodiazepines

Generic name	Dosage equivalent (mg)	Onset of action	Relative Lipophilicity	Active substances	Elimination half-life (hours)[a]	Metabolism
Clonazepam (Klonopin)	0.25	Intermediate	+ 1/2	Clonazepam	18–50	Oxidation Nitro-reduction
Alprazolam (Xanax)	0.5	Intermediate	+ + +	Alprazolam Alphahydroxyalprozelam	6–20 6–10	Oxidation
Triazolam (Halcion)	0.5	Fast	+ + +	Triazolam	1.7–3.0	Oxidation
Lorazepam (Ativan)	1.0	Intermediate	+ + 1/2	Lorazepam	10–20	Conjugation
Estazolam (ProSom)	2	Intermediate	+ +	Estazolam	8–24	Oxidation
Diazepam (Valium and others)	5.0	Fast	+ + + + +	Diazepam Desmethyldiazepam	30–100 30–200	Oxidation
Clorazepate (Tranxene)	7.5	Fast	+ + + +	Desmethyldiazepam[c] Oxazepam	30–200 3–11	Oxidation
Chlordiazepoxide (Librium and others)	10.0	Intermediate	+ + 1/2	Chlordiazepoxide Desmethylchlor-diazepoxide Demoxepam Desmethyldiazepam	5–100 18 14–95 30–200	Oxidation
Oxazepam (Serax)	15.0	Slow	+ +	Oxazepam	3–21	Conjugation
Flurazepam (Dalmane)	30.0	Fast		Flurazepam Hydroxyethylflurazepam Desalkylflurazepam	05–3.5 1–4 48–120	Oxidation
Temazepam (Restoril)	30.0	Slow	+ + +	None	10–12	Conjugation
Quazepam (Doral)	30	Fast	+ + + + +	Quazepam Oxyoquazepam DesalkylFlurazepam[c]	20–120	Oxidation
Buspirone (Buspar)	15–30 (usual dose)	Rapid peak, very slow onset (>7 days)		1-Pyrimidinyl piperazine	2–11	
Zolpidem (AmBien)	10	Rapid		Zolpidem	2.5	

[a] Elimination represents the total for all active metabolites.
[b] Clorazepate is a prodrug that is converted in the stomach to desmethyldiazepam, the active substance in the blood.
[c] DesalkylFlurazepam is identical to N-desalkyl-2-oxoquozepam. Adapted from: Cowley Ds, Roy-Byrne PP & Greenblatt DJ (1991). Benzodiazepines: Pharmacokinetics and Pharmacodynamics. In PP Roy-Byrne & DS Cowley (eds.) Benzodiazepines in Clinical Practice: Risks and Benefits. Washington, DC: American Psychiatric Press, 26–27 (with permission). Additional information from Greenblatt DJ (1991). Benzodiazepines hypnotics: Sorting out the pharmacokinetic facts. Journal of Clinical Psychiatry 52(Suppl):4–10, and Maxmen JS & Ward NG (1995). Antianxiety Agents and Hypnotics. In Psychotropic Drugs: Fast Facts, Second Edition, 260–261 and 315–316, respectively.

TABLE 3. Kinetics and Abuse Potential of Sedative-Hypnotics

Properties that increase potency as a reinforcer:
- High intrinsic pharmacological activity of drug
- Rapid absorption
- Rapid entry into specific brain regions
- High oral bioavailability
- Low protein binding
- Short half-life
- Small volume of distribution
- High clearance.

Factors that promote physical dependence:
- High intrinsic pharmacological activity of drug
- Cumulative drug load (dose, frequency, duration of treatment)
- Small volume of distribution
- Long half-life
- Low clearance.

Factors that promote appearance of the withdrawal syndrome:
- High intrinsic pharmacological activity of drug
- Short half-life
- High clearance
- Rapid exit from specific brain regions
- Small volume of distribution.

Source: Coppell HD, Sellers EM & Busto U (1986). Benzodiazepines as drugs of abuse and dependence. In HD Cappell, FG Blaser, Y Israel, H Halant & W Schmidt (eds.) *Recent Advances in Alcohol and Drug Problems, Vol. 9*. New York, NY: Plenum Press, 63.

through which chloride ions pass (the chloride ion channel) (Figure 1) (Roy-Byrne & Nutt, 1991).

$GABA_A$ receptors are the main site of action of benzodiazepines. The $GABA_A$ receptors appear to assemble as pentameric complexes consisting of several glycoprotein subunits of several major classes (α, β, γ, δ, ϵ, ρ) with various isoforms within each subunit class (e.g., $\alpha_1 - \alpha_6$). The subunit composition in a particular brain region or cell type determines the pharmacological and functional properties of $GABA_A$ receptors. There are at least two $GABA_A$ receptor subtypes: type I and type II. Type I are located in most brain structures and are found in the sensory and motor cortical and subcortical relays. Type II are located in the limbic system, in the striatum, and the spinal cord. Quazepam and zolpidem have affinities for type I and a low affinity for type II, whereas the other benzodiazepines are nonselective. There is no firmly established functional distinction between subtype activation but there is the suggestion that type II may be of particular importance in muscle relaxation and compounds with type I selectivity are hypothesized to produce sedation but little psychomotor effects and little tolerance or dependence (Sanger, Benavides et al., 1994).

GABA promotes the direct opening of chloride-selective ion channels by activating $GABA_A$ receptors. Electrochemical gradients cause the influx of chloride into neurons, which hyperpolarizes the cell and inhibits neuronal activity (Roy-Byrne & Nutt, 1991; Zorumski & Isenberg, 1991). Benzodiazepines act only by potentiating the effects of GABA at these $GABA_A$ receptors and have no action independent of GABA (Roy-Byrne & Nutt, 1991).

A group of endogenous ligands for the benzodiazepine-binding site of the $GABA_A$ receptor have been identified and named "endozepines." Their intrinsic activity is like that of the benzodiazepines in potentiating $GABA_A$ receptor function by acting as positive, allosteric modulators of the receptor (Rothstein, Garland et al., 1992).

Benzodiazepine receptors are uniquely linked with the $GABA_A$ receptors. GABA can enhance the binding of benzodiazepines to the benzodiazepine receptor by increasing benzodiazepine affinity (the "GABA shift"), and benzodiazepines can increase the binding of GABA and the frequency of GABA-induced chloride channel opening (Roy-Byrne & Nutt, 1991).

Barbiturates also are positive modulators of $GABA_A$ receptors by binding to a distinct site on the GABA complex to interact with GABA, which increases the duration of chloride channel opening, in contrast to increasing the frequency, as seen with the benzodiazepines. Barbiturates also can directly increase chloride ion flux, which may explain the greater lethality of barbiturates in overdose (Roy-Byrne & Nutt, 1991). Alcohol also increases the flow of chloride ions, causing sedation and psychomotor impairment, but the mechanism of action is not known (Zorumski & Isenberg, 1991).

The concept of benzodiazepine agonists, antagonists, and inverse agonists has evolved from the complex interaction of benzodiazepines with the $GABA_A$ receptors. Agonists include the commonly used benzodiazepines (alprazolam, diazepam) that increase the affinity of GABA for its receptor, and thus augment GABA-mediated inhibition (Zorumski & Isenberg, 1991). Benzodiazepine antagonists (such as RO15-1788 or flumazenil) have no intrinsic activity, but block the effects of both agonists and inverse agonists by competitive receptor binding (Roy-Byrne & Nutt, 1991). The inverse agonists (such as beta-carboline-3-carboxylic acid ethyl ester [B-CCE]) have the opposite action of the benzodiazepines, decreasing GABA-mediated chloride re-

FIGURE 1. GABA Benzodiazepine Chloride Ionophore Complex

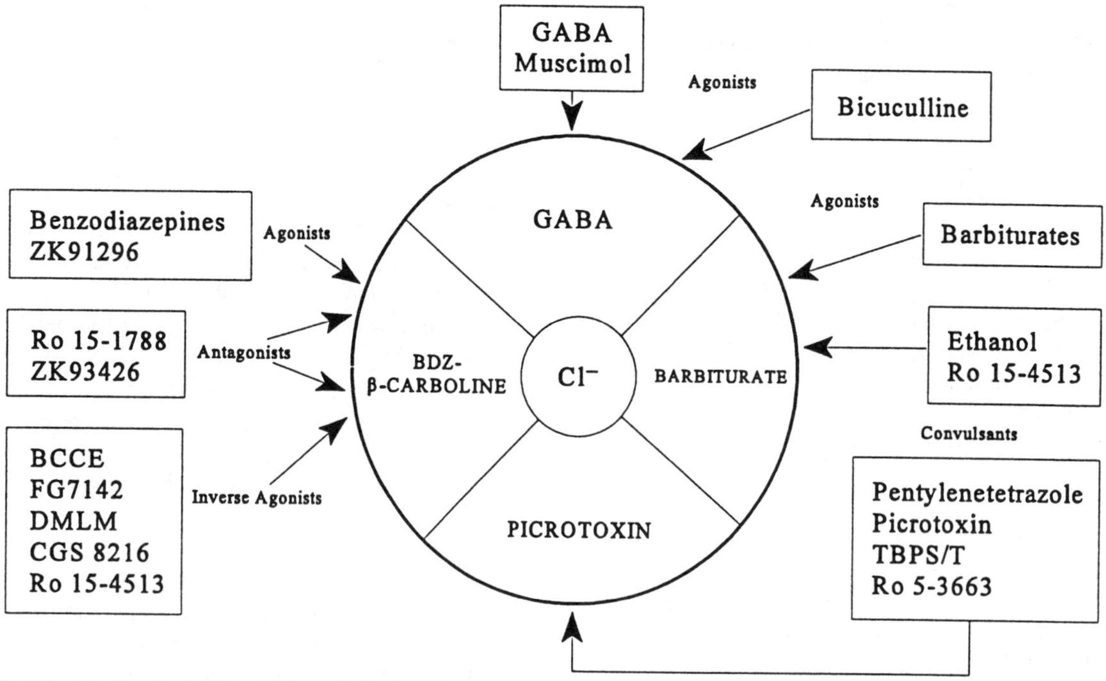

Source: Roy-Byrne PP & Nutt DJ (1991). *Benzodiazepines in Clinical Practice: Risks and Benefits.* Washington, DC: American Psychiatric Press, 7. Reprinted by permission.

sponses, thereby increasing arousal and activation and promoting seizures by increased neuronal excitability (Roy-Byrne & Nutt, 1991; Zorumski & Isenberg, 1991).

There also are sites the GABA complex for convulsants such as picrotoxin which acts to increase chloride ion flux (Zorumski & Isenberg, 1991). With chronic administration of benzodiazepines, there is evidence that changes in gene expression and consequent $GABA_A$ receptor function may be responsible for tolerance and low level, long-term withdrawal symptoms (Sanger, Benavides et al., 1994; Roy-Byrne & Nutt, 1991; Morrow, 1995).

REINFORCING PROPERTIES

The addiction liability of sedatives, hypnotics, and anxiolytics can be assessed by examining the reinforcing effects of these drugs, on the assumption that reinforcing effects are correlated with drug self-ingestion (Roache, 1990). Although in studies using "normal" and mildly anxious subjects, benzodiazepines are not preferred over placebos (Ciraulo & Sarid-Segal, 1991), there are large populations for whom they are reinforcing. In anxious subjects who seek treatment, a significant proportion find diazepam to be a positive reinforcer (deWit, McCracken et al., 1987). Normal volunteers who drink lightly (less than five drinks per week) and moderately (an average of 11 drinks per week) (deWit, Pierri & Johansen, 1989); abstinent alcoholics, children of alcoholics (Ciraulo & Sarid-Segal, 1991; Ciraulo, Sarid-Segal et al., 1996); and occasional recreational users of illicit sedatives without physical dependence as well as abusers (Cole & Chiarello, 1990) have reinforcing responses to benzodiazepines.

Barbiturates, meprobamate, and methaqualone appear to have more euphoric or reinforcing properties than benzodiazepines (Ciraulo & Sarid-Segal, 1991).

There appears to be different relative abuse liability of different benzodiazepines in different individuals. Diazepam, lorazepam, triazolam, and alprazolam have relatively high abuse liability, while oxazepam, halazepam, clorazepate, and possibly chlordiazepoxide do not. The speed of onset of pleasurable effects is an important factor in addiction potential (Ciraulo & Sarid-Segal, 1991).

REFERENCES

Aggulander C, Brandt L & Allebeck P (1994). Suicide and psychopathology in 1,537 patients dependent on prescribed psychoactive medications: Stockholm, Sweden. *American Journal on Addictions* 3:236–240.

American Psychiatric Association (1990). *Task Force Report on Benzodiazepines*. Washington, DC: The Association.

Braun TG (1993). Abuse potential during use and withdrawal psychosis after treatment with the hypnotic zolpidem (Stilnect). *Ugskrift for Laeger* 155:2711–2713.

Bruce TJ, Spiegel DA, Gregg SF & Nuzzarello A (1995). Predictors of alprazolam discontinuation with and without cognitive behavior therapy in panic disorder. *American Journal of Psychiatry* 152:1156–1160.

Busto UE, Romach MK & Sellers EM (1996). Multiple drug use and psychiatric comorbidity in patients admitted to the hospital with severe benzodiazepine dependence. *Journal of Clinical Psychopharmacology* 16:51–57.

Busto U, Sellars EM, Naranjo CA, Cappell HD, Sanchez-Craig M & Simpkins J (1986). Patterns of benzodiazepine abuse and dependence. *British Journal of Addictions* 81:87–94.

Busto U, Sellars EM, Naranjo CA, Cappell HD, Sanchez-Craig M & Sykora K (1986). Withdrawal reactions after long-term therapeutic use of benzodiazepines. *The New England Journal of Medicine* 315:854–589.

Canaday BR (1996). Amnesia possibly associated with zolpidem administration. *Pharmacotherapy* 16:687–689.

Cavallaro R, Regazzetti MG, Cavelli G & Smeraldi E (1993). Tolerance and Withdrawal with Zolpidem (letter). *Lancet* 342:868–869.

Ciraulo DA, Sarid-Segal O, Knapp C, Ciraulo AM, Greenblatt DJ & Shader RI (1996). Liability to alprazolam abuse in daughters of alcoholics. *American Journal of Psychiatry* 153:956–958.

Ciraulo DA & Sarid-Segal O (1991). Benzodiazepines: Abuse liability. In PP Roy-Byrne & DS Cowley (eds.) *Benzodiazepines in Clinical Practice: Risks and Benefits*. Washington, DC: American Psychiatric Press, 157–174.

Cohen S (1991). Benzodiazepines in psychotic and related conditions. In PP Roy-Byrne & DS Cowley (eds.) *Benzodiazepines in Clinical Practice: Risks and Benefits*. Washington, DC: American Psychiatric Press, 59–71.

Cole JO & Chiarello RJ (1990). The benzodiazepines as drugs of abuse. *Journal of Psychiatric Research* 24(Suppl. 2):135–144.

Cowley DS & Dunner DL (1991). Benzodiazepines in anxiety and depression. In PP Roy-Byrne & DS Cowley (eds.) *Benzodiazepines in Clinical Practice: Risks and Benefits*. Washington, DC: American Psychiatric Press, 37–56.

Cowley DS, Roy-Byrne PP & Greenblatt DJ (1991). Benzodiazepines: Pharmacokinetics and pharmacodynamics. In PP Roy-Byrne & DS Cowley (eds.) *Benzodiazepines in Clinical Practice: Risks and Benefits*. Washington, DC: American Psychiatric Press, 21–32.

deWit H, McCracken SM, Uhlenhuth EH & Johansen CE (1987). Diazepam preference in subjects seeking treatment for anxiety. *NIDA Research Monograph 76*. Rockville, MD: National Institute on Drug Abuse, 248–254.

deWit H, Pierri J & Johansen CE (1991). Reinforcing and subjective effects of diazepam in nondrug-abusing volunteers. *Pharmacology, Biochemistry and Behavior* 33:205–213.

DuPont RL (1990). A practical approach to benzodiazepine discontinuation. *Journal of Psychiatric Research* 24:81–90.

Ekedahl AM, Lowenhielm P, Nimeus A, Regnell G & Träskman-Bendz L (1994). Medicine self-poisoning and the sources of the drugs in Lund, Sweden. *Acta Psychiatrica Scandinavica* 89:255–261.

Evans SM, Funderburk FR & Griffiths RR (1990). Zolpidem and triazolam in humans: Behavioral and subjective effects and abuse liability. *Journal of Pharmacology and Experimental Therapeutics* 255:1246–1255.

Finlayson RE & Davis LJ (1994). Prescription drug dependence in the elderly population: Demographic and clinical features of 100 patients. *Mayo Clinic Proceedings* 69:1137–1145.

Fisch HU, Bakir G, Karlaganis G, Minder C & Bircher J (1990). Excessive motor impairment two hours after triazolam in the elderly. *European Journal of Clinical Pharmacology* 38:229–232.

Gelenberg AJ (1994). Buspirone: Seven-year update. *Journal of Clinical Psychiatry* 55:222–229.

Goldstein LB and the Sygen in Acute Stroke Study Investigators (1995). Common drugs may influence motor recovery after stroke. *Neurology* 45:865–871.

Golombeck S, Moodley P & Lader M (1988). Cognitive impairment in long-term benzodiazepine users. *Psychology in Medicine* 18:365–374.

Griffiths RR, Bigelow GE & Liebson I (1983). Differential effects of diazepam and pentobarbital on mood and behavior. *Archives of General Psychiatry* 40:865–873.

Hukkinen SK, Varhe A, Olkkola KT & Neuvonen PJ (1995). Plasma concentrations of triazolam are increased by concomitant ingestion of grapefruit juice. *Clinical Pharmacology and Therapeutics* 58:127–131.

Juergens SM & Morse RM (1988). Alprazolam dependence in seven patients. *American Journal of Psychiatry* 1455:625–627.

King DJ (1992). Benzodiazepines, amnesia and sedation: Theoretical and clinical issues and controversies. *Human Psychopharmacology* 7:79–87.

Kisnad H (1990). Sedative-Hypnotics (not including benzodiazepines). In NS Miller (ed.) *Comprehensive Handbook of Drug and Alcohol Addiction*. New York, NY: Marcel Dekker, 477–502.

Klein E, Colin V, Stolk J & Lenox RH (1994). Alprazolam withdrawal in patients with panic disorder and generalized anxiety disorder: Vulnerability and effect of carbamezepine. *American Journal of Psychiatry* 151:1760–1766.

Kranzler HR, Burleson JA, Del Bocca FK et al. (1994). Buspirone treatment of anxious alcoholics: A placebo-controlled trial. *Archives of General Psychiatry* 51:720–731.

Larson EB, Kukull WA, Buchner D & Reifler BV (1987). Adverse drug reactions associated with global cognitive impairment in elderly persons. *Annals of Internal Medicine* 107:169–173.

Laurigssens BE & Greenblatt DJ (1996). Pharmacokinetic-pharmacodynamic relationships for benzodiazepines. *Clinical Pharmacokinetics* 30:52–76.

Marcantonio ER, Juarez G, Goldman L et al. (1996). The relationship of postoperative delirium with psychoactive medications. *Journal of the American Medical Association* 272:1518–1522.

Marks I, Swinson R, Basoglu M et al. (1993). Alprazolam and exposure alone and combined in panic disorder with agoraphobia. A controlled study in London and Toronto. *British Journal of Psychiatry* 162:776–787.

Maxmen JS & Ward NG (1995). Antianxiety agents. In US Maxmen & NG (eds). *Psychotropic Drugs Fast Facts, Second Ed.* New York, NY: WW Norton and Company, 255–312.

Morrow AL (1995). Regulation of $GABA_A$ receptor function and gene expression in the central nervous system. *International Review of Neurobiology* 38:1–41.

Nemeroff CB, DeVane L & Pollock BG (1996). Newer antidepressants and the cytochrome P450 system. *American Journal of Psychiatry* 153:311–320.

O'Hanlon JF, Vermeeren A, Uiterwizk MMC & Swijgman HF (1995). Anxiolytics' effects on the actual driving performance of patients and healthy volunteers in a standardized test: An integration of three studies. *Neuropsychobiology* 31:81–88.

Pascually R (1991). Benzodiazepines and sleep. In PP Roy-Byrne & DS Cowley (eds.) *Benzodiazepines in Clinical Practice: Risks and Benefits.* Washington, DC: American Psychiatric Press, 37–56.

Ray WA, Griffin MR & Downey W (1989). Benzodiazepines of long and short elimination half-life and the risk of hip fracture. *Journal of the American Medical Association* 262:3303–3307.

Ray WA, Purushottam BT & Shorr RI (1993). Medications and the older driver. *Clinics in Geriatric Medicine* 9:413–438.

Rickels K, Schweizer E, Case G & Greenblatt DJ (1990). Long-term therapeutic use of benzodiazepines: I. Effects of abrupt discontinuation. *Archives of General Psychiatry* 47:899–907.

Rickels K, Schweizer E, Weiss S & Zavodnick S (1993). Maintenance drug treatment for panic disorder. II. Short- and long-term outcome after drug taper. *Archives of General Psychiatry* 50:61–68.

Roache JD (1990). Addiction potential of benzodiazepines and non-benzodiazepine anxiolytics. In B Stimmel (ed.) (CK Erickson, MA Javors & WW Morgan, Guest Eds.) *Addiction Potential of Abused Drugs and Drug Classes.* Binghamton, NY: The Haworth Press, 103–128.

Rothschild AJ (1992). Disinhibition, amnestic reactions, and other adverse reactions secondary to triazolam: A review of the literature. *Journal of Clinical Psychiatry* 53(12 Suppl):69–79.

Rothstein JD, Garland W, Puia G, Guidetti A, Weber R & Costa E (1992). Purification and characterization of naturally occurring benzodiazepine receptor ligands. *Journal of Neurochemistry* 58:2102–2115.

Roy-Byrne PP, Cowley DS, Greenblatt DJ, Shader RI & Hommer D (1990). Reduced benzodiazepine sensitivity in panic disorder. *Archives of General Psychiatry* 47:534–538.

Roy-Byrne PP (1991). Benzodiazepines: Dependence and withdrawal. In PP Roy-Byrne & DS Cowley (eds.) *Benzodiazepines in Clinical Practice: Risks and Benefits.* Washington, DC: American Psychiatric Press, 133–153.

Roy-Byrne PP & Nutt DJ (1991). Benzodiazepines biological mechanisms. In PP Roy-Byrne & DS Cowley (eds.) *Benzodiazepines in Clinical Practice: Risks and Benefits.* Washington, DC: American Psychiatric Press, 5–18.

Rush CR & Griffiths RR (1996). Zolpidem, triazolam, and temazepam: Behavioral and subject-rated effects in normal volunteers. *Journal of Clinical Psychopharmacology* 16:146–157.

Salzman C, Fisher J, Nobel K, Glassman R, Wolfson A & Kelley M (1992). Cognitive improvement following benzodiazepine discontinuation in elderly nursing home residents. *International Journal of Geriatric Psychiatry* 7:89–93.

Sanger DJ, Benavides J, Perrault G et al. (1994). Recent developments in the behavioral pharmacology of benzodiazepine (omega) receptors: Evidence for the functional significance of receptor subtypes. *Neuroscience and Biobehavioral Reviews* 18:355–372.

Schimder J, Greenblatt DJ, Von Moltke LL & Schader RI (1996). Relationship of in vitro data on drug metabolism to in vitro pharmacokinetics and drug interactions: Implications for diazepam disposition in humans (Editorial). *Journal of Clinical Psychopharmacology* 16:267–272.

Schweizer E, Rickels K, Case G & Greenblatt DJ (1990). Long-term therapeutic use of benzodiazepines: II. Effects of gradual taper. *Archives of General Psychiatry* 47:908–915.

Serfaty M & Masterton G (1993). Fatal poisonings attributed to benzodiazepines in Britain during the 1980s. *British Journal of Psychiatry* 163:386–393.

Tata PR, Rollings J, Collins M, Pickering A & Jacobson RR (1994). Lack of cognitive recovery following withdrawal from long-term benzodiazepine use. *Psychological Medicine* 24:203–213.

The Medical Letter on Drugs and Therapeutics (1993). Zolpidem for insomnia. 35:35–36.

Weintraub M, Singh S, Byrne L, Maharay K & Guttmacher L (1991). Consequences of the New York State triplicate benzodiazepine prescription regulation. *Journal of the American Medical Association* 266:2392–2397.

Wolf B & Griffiths RR (1991). Physical dependence on benzodiazepines: Differences within the class. *Drug and Alcohol Dependence* 29:153–156.

Wolf B, Grohmann R, Biber PM, Brenner PM & Ruther E (1989). Benzodiazepine abuse and dependence in psychiatric inpatients. *Pharmacopsychiatry* 22:54–60.

Wysowski DK & Barash D (1991). Adverse behavioral reactions attributed to triazolam in the Food and Drug Administration's spontaneous reporting system. *Archives of Internal Medicine* 151:2003–2008.

Zorumski CF & Isenberg KE (1991). Insights into the structure and function of GABA-benzodiazepine receptor: Ion channels and psychiatry. *American Journal of Psychiatry* 148:162–173.

CHAPTER 4

The Pharmacology of Opioids

Mark S. Gold, M.D., FCP, FAPA

Drugs in the Class
Therapeutic Use and Misuse
Adverse Effects
Addiction Liability
Absorption and Metabolism
Mechanisms of Action
Reinforcing Properties

Until very recently, most of what we know about opiates came from historical accounts, such as the descriptions of Assyrian "poppy" art dating from 4000 B.C. and from studies of Egyptian, Greek and Persian culture. In addition to pain relief, opiates historically have been used for their ability to induce a state of euphoria. In the 19th century, millions of Chinese became addicted to opium after smoking, eating, drinking or sniffing it. In Europe at the time, opiates were used as "tonics," usually in pills of two to three grains, or dissolved in alcohol and drunk as "laudanum." Through use of these products, such notable poets as Samuel Taylor Coleridge and Elizabeth Barret Browning became dependent on opiates (Belkin & Gold, 1991).

DRUGS IN THE CLASS

The principal active ingredient in the ancient medication opium is the alkaloid morphine, and indeed, most modern opiates approximate morphine, either as natural derivatives or as synthetic or semisynthetic compounds. Drugs in this class (see Table 1) act at the opiate receptors in the central nervous system. While all drugs in the class are associated with clinical withdrawal syndromes, those associated with the most severe withdrawal include heroin, methadone, morphine, oxycodone, oxymorphone, and meperidine.

This chapter provides an overview of the major pharmacologic properties of opioid drugs, while the following chapter focuses on the opiate partial agonists and antagonists—the drugs most widely used in the treatment of opiate abuse and dependence.

THERAPEUTIC USE AND MISUSE

Therapeutic Use. Opiates like morphine induce a state of well-being and, at high doses, somnolence. Users report feeling immune to the effects of environmental or psychic distress. Morphine is the prototypical opiate drug, still a mainstay of analgesic therapy, and remarkably effective in both the alleviation of pain and the elimination of anticipatory anxiety.

Misuse. Morphine and heroin have been of considerable scientific interest because of the psychic state they induce, their efficacy as analgesics, antiemetics and other medicinal uses, and because of their propensity to produce tolerance and physical dependence.

With the availability of parenterally administered opiates and the invention of the hypodermic syringe, opiate addiction and withdrawal distress became major worldwide public health problems. By the twentieth century, opioid addiction was a widespread problem in the U.S. In San Francisco, for example, one survey at the turn of the century found that one in every 400 people were abusing opiates. (By comparison, the 1991 National Household Survey found that 2% of the population had used heroin in their lifetime, and the 1992 National High School Senior Survey found a lifetime rate of 1.2%—up from 0.9% in 1991. Opiate emergency room visits also appear to be increasing.)

While the prevalence of heroin addiction in the U.S. today is less than 1%, its contribution to overall drug-related morbidity and mortality is significant. Indeed, opioids play a disproportionate part in the 6,000 deaths attributed to drug abuse each year. At

TABLE 1. Opioid Agonists, Partial Agonists, and Antagonists

Agonists	
	Codeine (various compounds)
	Fentanyl (Sublimaze®)
	Heroin
	Hydrocodone (Tussionex®)
	Hydromorphone (Dilaudid®)
	Morphine
	Methadone
	Meperidine (Demerol®)
	Oxycodone (Percodan®)
	Oxymorphone (Numorphan®)
	Propoxyphene (Darvon®)
Partial Agonists	
	Buprenorphine (Buprenex®)
	Butorphanol (Stadol®)
	Nalbuphine (Nubain®)
	Pentazocine (Talwin®)
Antagonists	
	Naloxone (Narcan®)
	Naltrexone (Trexan®)

least 25% of heroin addicts die within 10 to 20 years of initiating active use, usually as a result of suicide, homicide, accidents and infectious diseases such as tuberculosis, hepatitis and AIDS (Kamerow, Pincus & McDonald, 1988).

ADVERSE EFECTS

In addition to addiction, intravenous use of opiates is associated with diseases introduced by dirty needles contaminated with the blood of previous users, as well as with contaminants and fillers in the drug itself. Less common conditions arising from injection drug use include cellulitis, cerebritis, wound abscess, sepsis, arterial thrombosis, renal infarction and thrombophlebitis. The most common, severe complications of intravenous drug use are bacterial or viral endocarditis, hepatitis and HIV/AIDS. In addition, medical problems associated with the misuse or abuse of opiates (some attributable to the risks that accompany injection drug use) include:

- Accidents, head injuries
- Asthma and breathing problems
- Exposure to HIV infection
- Hepatitis, tuberculosis
- Subacute bacterial endocarditis
- Sexually transmitted diseases
- Ulcers, abscesses and cellulitis
- Memory problems
- Paresthesias.

ADDICTION LIABILITY

The intense experience recalled by addicts as "the high" or "the rush" appears to stimulate opiate use in humans, just as it does in animals. Even though weeks of opiate administration leave the user with more anxiety, dysphoria (as well as the emergence of physical abstinence symptoms on discontinuation or preceding self-administration), the lure of opiate euphoria is not easily resisted. The positive effects of the drug experience apparently outweigh the negative effects and the numerous risks to which the addict is exposed (Gold, 1993).

The diagnosis of opioid addiction is made by using criteria similar to those employed for the diagnosis of other drug addictions. The criteria include a preoccupation with acquisition of the drug, compulsive use in spite of adverse consequences, an inability to reduce the amount of use, and a pattern of relapse to opioids after a period of abstinence.

ABSORPTION AND METABOLISM

Scientists in the early 1970s had preliminary evidence that opiate drugs bind to specific sites in the brain and body, and so cause the numerous and seemingly diverse effects of opiate drugs (Hughes, 1975; Pert & Snyder, 1973; Simon, Hiller & Edelman, 1973). Effects on diarrhea, cough, mood, pain, and so on were quickly and effectively explained by the theory, which correlated the binding of opiates to endogenous opioid receptors in key areas of the brain and body with already recognized functions of these areas (Watson, Akil et al., 1984). While numerous questions remain—such as why every vertebrate and some invertebrates possess opioid receptors, whether endorphins are neurotransmitters of hormones (Mains, Eipper & Ling, 1977), or why authentic morphine and codeine have been found in the mammalian nervous systems (Donnerer, Oka et al., 1986)—the identification of these receptors quickly led to the discovery of naturally-occurring endogenous substances that possess opiate activity (Cox, Goldstein & Li, 1976; Childers, 1991; Mains, Eipper & Ling, 1977).

MECHANISMS OF ACTION

Opioid drugs exert their actions by binding to receptors on cell membranes of neurons and other cells

(Koob & Bloom, 1988). These opiate receptors are multiple in type and function. They have been divided into mu, kappa, delta and lambda subtypes, and a number of important differences among the subtypes have been identified. Kappa receptor activation produces analgesia but, unlike mu and delta, agonists are not self-administered by laboratory animals. Consistent with the self-administration data, it now appears that the kappa agonists are dysphoric rather than euphoric. The 20 or more drugs available that have opioid activity now are defined and categorized in terms of their binding profile or activity at one or another receptor subtype. They are further subdivided into *agonists, antagonists, partial agonists* and *antagonists.* Mu agonists like morphine or heroin generally are administered by injection or smoking. The opiate intoxication state is described as an intense, almost "orgasmic" sense of well-being, referred to as a "high" or "rush." This euphoric state appears to be responsible for the continuation of self-administration and the inability of logical thinking or appreciation of imminent risk or disability to deter drug-taking. Whether the dose of mu agonist also causes nausea and vomiting is not related to the user's feeling of well-being and interest in repeating the experience. Mu agonists inhibit the activity of the LC, which appears essential in the development of the most pronounced features of the abstinence syndrome. Mu opioids also suppress cough, slow the passage of food through the GI system, inhibit diarrhea, decrease urinary voiding, slow respiration, lower pulse rate and blood pressure, reduce anxiety, and provide an overwhelming sense of indifference to physical or psychic "pain"; they are used by addicts for the sense of euphoria or "high" they provide. These effects can be blocked by pretreatment with opiate antagonists (withdrawal can be provoked in tolerant individuals by antagonists as well).

The opiate antagonist naloxone has been shown to reverse electrical brain stimulation analgesia, acupuncture (Pomerantz & Chiu, 1976) and electroacupuncture analgesia (Akil, Mayer & Liebeskind, 1976), and even placebo-induced analgesia (Levine, Gordon & Fields, 1978). These and other studies have led to the widespread belief that all of the three major receptor types for the naturally-occurring opioid peptides are involved in analgesia, but that the mu receptor is most closely related to the actions of morphine; the dissociation of physical dependence and abstinence from analgesic effect is a major pharmaceutical goal of this work.

Since tolerance and physical dependence could be demonstrated to pharmacological administration of opioid peptides (Wei & Loh, 1976), with cross-tolerance between synthetic and natural opiates, it was a natural extension to believe that many of the symptoms of opiate withdrawal could be understood by analysis of the interactions between the mu opioid system and other important neurotransmitter systems, such as the noradrenergic system of the brain (Gold, Dackis et al., 1982; Gold, Redmond & Kleber, 1978). In fact, the characteristic opiate withdrawal syndrome became the model for addicting drugs and focused attention on the physical or autonomic aspects of withdrawal as somehow necessary for addiction. Recently, these relationships have been questioned (Gold & Miller, 1992), primarily as a result of the cocaine and crack epidemics, the obvious addiction liability of cocaine without physical abstinence, and understanding of the dissociation of physical withdrawal and drug-taking (Gold & Miller, 1993).

The Locus Coeruleus in Opiate Withdrawal. Located in the dorsolateral pontine tegmentum of all mammals is the nucleus locus coeruleus, a densely packed cell grouping that was first described by the German neuroanatomist Reil in 1809. The locus coeruleus was named for its bluish color, which derives from the presence of neuromelanin, making it a rather easily identified nucleus on cross section. With the invention of fluorescent staining techniques, this bilateral brain stem nucleus lying along the fourth ventricle beneath the cerebellar peduncles was found to contain the neurotransmitter norepinephrine. The human LC is the largest grouping of NE-containing neurons in the brain consisting of roughly 18,000 cells and the most extensive network of pathways emanating from any nucleus in the brain. The LC is the largest nucleus of central noradrenergic neurons in the mammalian central nervous system, and is the origin of virtually all noradrenergic afferents in the brain (Nakamura & Sakaguchi, 1990). LC neurons extensively innervate many brain sites with highly branched axons. Even single LC neurons project simultaneously to different brain sites from many axonal branches. Ungerstedt has suggested that a single LC cell probably projects to the cerebrum, hippocampus and cerebellum simultaneously, forming a tree of collateral axons (Gold, Dackis et al., 1982). Such a network gives the LC the anatomical capability to integrate the functional activity of many brain regions and influence brain function and reactivity in a very important way.

LC neurons receive sensory input from many or possibly all sensory modalities from the periphery. The LC neurons have a great capacity to undergo axonal sprouting in response to environmental stimuli. When animals are exposed to repeated environmental stimuli such as stress, the LC may attain a greater capacity to affect their target neurons by increasing the density of their terminal axons.

The LC is activated by pain, blood loss, and cardiovascular collapse, but it is generally not aroused by non-threatening stimuli (Amaral & Sinnamon, 1977; Korf, Bunney & Aghajanian, 1974). The importance of LC functioning to the organisms survival is suggested by LC energy metabolism which is unique and characterized by a relative absence of aerobic glucose metabolism and prominent anaerobic and pentose shunt catabolism and by the use of LC neuromelanin as an alternative form of electron transport (Amaral & Sinnamon, 1977).

If the LC hyperactivity seen during opioid withdrawal is responsible for all or a major portion of the opioid withdrawal syndrome, then behavioral patterns associated with electrical activation of the LC also should occur during opiate withdrawal in non-human primates, as was demonstrated by Grant and colleagues in 1988. Other studies have confirmed that the LC cells are hyperactive during withdrawal (Valentino & Wehby, 1989) and that the actual behavioral timeline of opiate withdrawal effects correlates with the *in vivo* activity of LC and increases in G-proteins, adenylate cyclase and cAMP-dependent protein kinase in the rat LC (Rasmussen, Beitner-Johnson et al., 1990).

The recent finding that withdrawal activation of the LC is not observed in isolated slice preparations (Christie, Williams & North, 1987), and by lesions of the paragigantocellularis—the major excitatory input to LC—suggests the importance of this input to the LC hyperactivity in withdrawal and the resultant signs and symptoms (Ennis & Aston-Jones, 1988; Rasmussen & Aghajanian, 1989).

Just as opiates do not remove pain, but rather the alarm or frenzy which accompany pain, lesions of the glutaminergic nucleus paragigantocellularis eliminate LC alarm signals. These lesions, as well as excitatory amino acids antagonist, can suppress opiate withdrawal (Akaoka & Aston-Jones, 1991; Korf, Bunney & Aghajanian, 1974; Tung, Grenhoff & Svensson, 1990). A recent study using antagonists of the N-methyl-d-aspartate (NMDA) subtype of excitatory amino acid receptors lessened morphine withdrawal behaviors while not apparently reversing LC hyperactivity (Rasmussen, Fuller et al., 1991).

REINFORCING PROPERTIES

Endogenous drug reward is great with the opiates and appears to be the primary factor in sustaining drug-taking. However, autonomic withdrawal cannot be ignored as contributing to the generalized discomfort reported objectively and subjectively by opiate addicts (Gold & Miller, 1993). The addict's desire to find more opiates so as to remain "normal," despite numerous health risks, psychiatric and other problems and other addictions, is common. (With much of the emphasis on neurobiology, epidemiology, and co-morbidity, psychological factors involving the overall lack of family support and the level of addiction and other problems in the addict's environment cannot be ignored: the majority of heroin addicts come from single parent families and families where alcoholism and drug use are common. Thus it often is necessary and generally desirable to involve and even treat the entire family at once if the possibility of long-term compliance, and ultimately remission, is to be maximized.)

Opiate Withdrawal Syndrome. Withdrawal from the classic morphine-like opiate is a syndrome now understood to be the mu agonist withdrawal syndrome (Koob & Bloom, 1988; Werling, McMahon & Cox, 1989; Gold, 1993). It is quite variable from person to person, depending on individual factors as well as the specific opiate used and its dose and duration of use. Naturally, withdrawal intensity depends on whether the tolerant and dependent person is given an antagonist like naloxone to provoke withdrawal or whether opiates are slowly discontinued.

The mu withdrawal syndrome from heroin begins within 12 hours of abrupt discontinuation of chronic administration and commonly includes dysphoria, anxiety, yawning, perspiration, lacrimation, rhinorrhea, sleep difficulties, nausea, vomiting, diarrhea, cramps and fever. In summary, the syndrome looks and feels like "the flu." This acute abstinence syndrome is not life-threatening, although it sometimes is difficult to convince the addict and/or the family that the problem will largely pass in less than a week. Clinicians and experienced addicts recognize that the acute withdrawal phase, with its dramatic symptoms, generally is followed by a longer-lasting protracted syndrome that may last for months.

When opioids are rapidly cleared from the mu receptor and are functionally unavailable (as they are by administration of naloxone or naltrexone), neurons in the LC are put into a state of hyperexcitability, also referred to as rebound from chronic inhibition or LC hyperactivity (Gold, Dackis et al., 1982; Gold, Redmond & Kleber, 1978). The resultant noradrenergic hyperactivity and release would be the most critical element in the generation of withdrawal symptoms and signs.

Opiate Consumption as an Acquired Drive. Hyperactivity of the LC may be the cause of the withdrawal syndrome, but clearly opioids are not administered solely to avoid the experience of withdrawal. Opioids, like cocaine, are used for their positive effects. Use of exogenous opioids gives the addict access to the reinforcement reward system, which is believed to be anatomically distinct from the negative/withdrawal system in the LC and elsewhere (Bozarth & Wise, 1984). This positive reward system, normally reserved to reward the performance of species specific survival behaviors, once accessed by exogenous self-administration of drugs of abuse, provides the user with an experience that the brain equates with profoundly important events like eating, drinking and sex. Opioid use thus becomes an acquired drive state that permeates all aspects of human life. Withdrawal from opiate use is mediated by separate neural pathways, which cause withdrawal events to be perceived as life-threatening, and the subsequent physiological and psychological reactions often lead to renewed opiate consumption.

REFERENCES

Akaoka H & Aston-Jones G (1991). Opiate withdrawal-induced hyperactivity of locus coeruleus neurons is substantially mediated by augmented excitatory amino acid input. *Journal of Neuroscience* 11(12):3830–3839.

Akil H, Mayer DJ & Liebeskind JC (1976). Antagonism of stimulation-produced analgesia by naloxone, a narcotic antagonist. *Science* 191:961–962.

Amaral DG & Sinnamon HM (1977). The locus coeruleus: Neurobiology of a central noradrenergic nucleus. *Progress in Neurobiology* 9:147–196.

Arditti J, Bourdon JH, Jean PH, Landi H, Nasset D, Jouglard J & Thirion X (1992). Buprenorphine abuse in a group of 50 drug- use abusers admitted to Marseille Hospital. *Therapie* 47:561–2.

Ball JC, Lange WR, Myers CP & Friedman SR (1988). Reducing the risk of AIDS through methadone maintenance treatment. *Journal of Health and Social Behavior* 29:214–226.

Belkin BM & Gold MS (1991). In NS Miller (ed.) *Comprehensive Handbook of Drug and Alcohol Addiction.* New York, NY: Marcel Dekker, 537–550.

Bozarth MA & Wise RA (1984). Anatomically distinct opiate receptor fields mediate reward and physical dependence. *Science* 224:516–517.

Centers for Disease Control (1989). *HIV/AIDS Surveillance: AIDS Cases Reported through September, 1989.* Washington, DC: U.S. Department of Health and Human Services, Public Health Service (October).

Childers SR (1991). Minireview: Opioid receptor-coupled second messenger systems. *Life Science* 48:1991–2003.

Christie MJ, Williams JT & North AR (1987). Cellular mechanism of opioid tolerance: Studies in single brain neurons. *Molecular Pharmacology* 32:633–638.

Cone E, Holicky B, Pickworth W & Johnson RE (1991). Pharmacologic and behavioral effects of high doses of intravenous buprenorphine. Committee on Problems of Drug Dependence, 53rd Annual Scientific Meeting. Palm Beach, FL, June 16–20.

Cox BM, Goldstein A & Li CH (1976). Opioid activity of a peptide, B-lipotropin (61–91) derived from B-lipotropin. *Proceedings of the National Academy of Science* 73:1821–1823.

Dackis CA, Gold MS & Estroff TW (1989). Inpatient treatment of addiction, Vol. 1. *Treatment of Psychiatric Disorders: A Task Force of the American Psychiatric Association.* Washington, DC: American Psychiatric Press, 1359–1378.

Donnerer J, Oka K, Brossi A, Rice KC & Spector S (1986). Presence and formation of codeine and morphine in the rat. *Proceedings of the National Academy of Science* 83:4566–4567.

Ennis M & Aston-Jones G (1988). Activation of locus coeruleus from nucleus paragigantocellularis: A new excitatory amino acid pathway in brain. *Journal of Neuroscience* 8:3644–3657.

Gastfriend DR, Mendelson JH, Mello NK & Tech SK (1991). Preliminary results of an open trial of buprenorphine in the outpatient treatment of combined heroin and cocaine dependence. Committee on Problems of Drug Dependence, 53rd Annual Scientific Meeting. Palm Beach, FL, June 16–20.

Gold MS (1993). Opiate addiction and the locus coeruleus. *Psychiatric Clinics of North America* 16:61–73.

Gold MS, Dackis CA, Pottash ALC, Sternbach HH, Annitto WJ, Martin D & Dackis CP (1982). Naltrexone, opiate addiction and endorphins. *Medical Research Review* 2(3):211–246.

Gold MS, Redmond DE Jr & Kleber HD (1978). Clonidine in opiate withdrawal. *Lancet* 1(8070):929–930.

Gold MS, Redmond DE Jr & Kleber HD (1978b). Clonidine blocks acute opiate withdrawal symptoms. *Lancet* 2(8090):929–930.

Gold MS & Roehrich H (1987). Treatment of opiate withdrawal with clonidine. *Pharmacology* 1741:29–32.

Gold MS & Miller NS (1992). Seeking drugs/alcohol and avoiding withdrawal: The neuroanatomy of drive states and withdrawal. *Psychiatric Annals* 22:430–435.

Gold MS & Miller NS (1993). Dissociation of craving and relapse in alcohol and cocaine dependence. *Biological Psychiatry.*

Grayson NA, Witkin JM, Katz JL, Cowan A & Rice KC (1991). Actions of buprenorphine on cocaine and opiate mediated effects. Committee on Problems of Drug Dependence, 53rd Annual Scientific Meeting. Palm Beach, FL, June 16–20.

Hughes J (1975). Isolation of an endogenous compound from the brain with properties similar to morphine. *Brain Research* 88:295–308.

Jasinski DR, Pevnick JS & Griffith JD (1978). Human pharmacology and abuse potential of the analgesic buprenorphine. *Archives of General Psychiatry* 35:501–516.

Kamerow DB, Pincus HA & McDonald DI (1988). Alcohol abuse, other drug abuse, and mental disorders in medical practice: Prevalence, costs, recognition, and treatment. *Journal of the American Medical Association* 225:2054–2057.

Koob GF & Bloom FE (1988). Cellular and molecular mechanisms of drug dependence. *Science* 242:715–723.

Korf J, Bunney BS & Aghajanian GK (1974). Noradrenergic neurons: Morphine inhibition of spontaneous activity. *European Journal of Pharmacology* 25:165–169.

Kosten TR, Kleber HD & Morgan C (1989). Role of opioid antagonists in treating intravenous cocaine abuse. *Life Science* 44:887–892.

Kosten TR, Schottenfeld RS, Morgan C, Falcioni J & Ziedon D (1991). Buprenorphine vs. methadone for opioid and cocaine dependence. Committee on problems of Drug Dependence, 53rd Annual Scientific Meeting. Palm Beach, FL, June 16–20.

Levine JD, Gordon NC & Fields HL (1978). The mechanism of placebo analgesia. *Lancet* 2:654–657.

Mains RE, Eipper BA & Ling N (1977). Common precursor to corticotropins and endorphins. *Proceedings of the National Academy of Science* 74:3014–3018.

Nakamura S & Sakaguchi T (1990). Development and plasticity of the locus coeruleus: A review of recent physiological and pharmacological experimentation. *Progress in Neurobiology* 34:505–526.

National Institute of Drug Abuse (1993). *National Household Survey on Drug Abuse: Main Findings, 1991*. Rockville, MD: The Institute (December).

Pert CB & Snyder SH (1973). Opiate receptor: Demonstration in nervous tissue. *Science* 179:1011–1014.

Pomeranz B & Chiu D (1976). Naloxone blockade of acupuncture analgesia: Endorphin implicated. *Life Science* 19:1757–1762.

Rasmussen K, Fuller RW, Stockton ME, Perry KW, Swinford RM & Ornstein PL (1991). NMDA receptor antagonists suppress behaviors but no norepinephrine turnover or locus coeruleus unit activity induced by opiate withdrawal. *European Journal of Pharmacology* 197:9–16.

Rasmussen K, Beitner-Johnson DB, Krystal JH, Aghajanian GK & Nestler EJ (1990). Opiate withdrawal and the rat locus coeruleus: Behavioral, electrophysiological and biochemical cal correlates. *Journal of Neuroscience* 10:2308–2317.

Rasmussen KL & Aghajanian GK (1989). Withdrawal-induced activation of locus coeruleus neurons in opiate-dependent rats: Attenuation by lesions of the nucleus paragigantocellularis. *Brain Research* 505:346–350.

Simon EJ, Hiller JM & Edelman I (1973). Stereospecific binding of the potent narcotic analgesic 3H-etorphine to rat brain homogenate. *Proceedings of the National Academy of Science* 70:1947–1949.

Tung CS, Grenhoff J & Svensson TH (1990). Morphine withdrawal responses of rat locus coeruleus neurons are blocked by an excitatory amino acid antagonist. *Acta Physiologica Scandinavica* 138:581–582.

Valentino RJ & Wehby RG (1989). Locus coeruleus discharge characteristics of morphine-dependent rats: Effects of naltrexone. *Brain Research* 488:126–134.

Vereby K (1991). Laboratory methods for drug and alcohol addiction. In NS Miller (ed.) *Comprehensive Handbook of Drug and Alcohol Addiction*. New York, NY: Marcel Dekker, 809–842.

Vereby K, Gold MS & Mule SJ (1986). Laboratory testing in the diagnosis of marijuana intoxication and withdrawal. In MS Gold (ed.) *Psychiatric Annals* 16(4):235–241.

Watson SJ, Akil H, Khachaturian H, Young E & Lewis ME (1984). Opioid systems: Anatomical, physiological and clinical perspectives. In J Hughes, HOJ Collier, MJ Rance & MB Tyers (eds.) *Opioids Past, Present and Future*. London, England: Taylor & Francis, 145–178.

Wei E & Loh HH (1976). Physical dependence on opiate-like peptides. *Science* 193:1262–1263.

Werling LL, McMahon PN & Cox BM (1989). Selective changes in mu opioid receptor properties induced by chronic morphine exposure. *Proceedings of the National Academy of Science* 86:6393–6397.

CHAPTER 5

The Pharmacology of Cocaine, Crack and Other Stimulants

Mark S. Gold, M.D., FCP, FAPA
Michael J. Herkov, Ph.D.

Drugs in the Class
Therapeutic Use and Misuse
Adverse Effects
Addiction Liability
Absorption and Metabolism
Mechanisms of Action
Reinforcing Properties

This chapter summarizes current patterns of use of cocaine and other stimulants, as well as the cognitive, behavioral, health, and societal consequences of its use and the neurobiologic and psychopharmacological mechanisms underlying its addictive effects.

DRUGS IN THE CLASS

Drugs in this class stimulate the central nervous system by increasing the release of excitatory neurotransmitters (serotonin and dopaminergic). Drugs associated with clinically important problems include cocaine (particularly crack), amphetamines and methamphetamine (see Table 1).

THERAPEUTIC USE AND MISUSE

Therapeutic Use. *Cocaine:* Because of its vasoconstrictive properties, cocaine hydrochloride has therapeutic utility as a topic anesthetic in carefully defined situations such as ENT surgery.

Amphetamines: According to Craig and Weddington (1994), amphetamine preparations became widely available for clinical use in the 1930s. Although used initially for a variety of medical conditions, addiction issues became apparent with the amphetamines during the 1940s in Japan and later during the 1960s in the U.S. Subsequent government regulation of the amphetamines has restricted their use to such a degree that medical use now is limited to conditions such as narcolepsy, childhood hyperkinesis, refractory obesity, and depression (Chiarello & Cole, 1987).

Misuse. *Cocaine:* To the Incas of Peru, cocaine was a gift from the Gods. In our own age, cocaine may better be described as a curse from the Devil. Cocaine abuse causes numerous physical and psychiatric problems for the user, and is associated with violence, crime and other societal ills. While the epidemic of cocaine use appeared to decline throughout the late 1980s to the early 1990s, recent data suggest that this pernicious scourge is again on the rise.

As a rule, pure cocaine is unavailable on the street. Instead it is usually adulterated with other substances (e.g., lactose or glucose) to add weight or provide additional central nervous system (CNS) stimulant effects (e.g., lidocaine, amphetamines or heroin) (Bastos & Hoffman, 1976). The typical concentration of cocaine HCl in street preparations ranges from 10 to 50%; rarely, samples can contain as much as 70% cocaine.

Amphetamines: Amphetamine preparations are illicitly produced in tablet, capsules, powder or crystal form. They are taken orally, intravenously, or by smoking (Craig & Weddington, 1994; King & Ellinwood, 1992).

Methylphenidate: Methylphenidate is structurally related to amphetamines and has essentially the same pharmacological actions, although clinically it serves as a milder stimulant (Chiarello & Cole, 1987).

TABLE 1. Stimulant Drugs

Cocaine hydrochloride

Crack cocaine

Amphetamines
- dextroamphetamine (*Dexedrine®*)
- amphetamine sulfate
- methamphetamine (*Desoxyn®*)

Amphetamine congeners
- benzphetamine (*Didrex®*)
- diethylpropion (*Tenuate®*, *Tepanil®*)
- fenfluramine (*Pondimin®*)
- mazindol (*Mazanor®*, *Sanorex®*)
- phendimetrazine (*Adipost®*, *Bontril®*, *Prelu–2®*)
- phenmetrazine (*Preludin®*)
- phentermine (*Fastin®*, *Obermine®*, *Phentrol®*)

Methylphenidate (*Ritalin®*)

Pemoline (*Cylert®*)

Phenylpropanolamine (over-the-counter cough and cold preparations)

ADVERSE EFFECTS

The adverse effects associated with amphetamine and cocaine abuse are so numerous (Derlet & Albertson, 1989) and severe that it would take an entire book to describe them completely.

Medical Complications. Amphetamines and cocaine produce a number of cardiovascular effects, including arrhythmia, tachycardia sinus bradycardia, ventricular premature depolarization, ventricular tachycardia degenerating to defibrillation, and asystole (Perez-Meyes, DiGiuseppe et al., 1982). Cocaine is known to elevate blood pressure and may underlie many incidents of cerebrovascular accidents (Lichtenfeld, Rubin & Feldman, 1984). Evidence suggests that cocaine can induce spasms in a number of vascular systems, including the coronary arteries (Smith, Lieberman et al., 1987). These spasms can produce myocardial infarction even in a person whose endothelium is otherwise intact (Vitullo, Karam et al., 1989). Cocaine users also frequently develop silent myocardial ischemia (Nadamanee, Gorelick et al., 1989). This problem also may arise during the first weeks of withdrawal. So common is the incidence of myocardial infarction due to cocaine that its occurrence in young patients who lack the usual coronary risk factors suggests a diagnosis of cocaine abuse (Schachne, Roberts & Thompson, 1984). Cocaine addiction can accelerate coronary atherosclerosis. Finally, long-term abuse of cocaine may lead to interstitial fibrosis and eventually to congestive heart failure (Peng, French & Pelikan, 1989). The cardiac effects of cocaine have previously been treated with propranolol and may respond to the calcium channel blocker nitrendipine.

Respiratory Complications: Smoking crack can induce severe chest pain or dyspnea (Weiner & Putnam, 1987). One explanation for this effect may be that cocaine significantly reduces the ability of the lungs to diffuse carbon monoxide (Itkonen, Schnoll & Glassroth, 1984). Often it is this symptom of chest pain that drives patients to seek medical attention.

Other respiratory effects of cocaine smoking include lung damage, pneumonia, pulmonary edema, cough, sputum production, fever, hemoptysis, pulmonary barotrauma, pneumomediastinum, pneumothorax, pneumopericardium, and diffuse alveolar hemorrhage (Murray, Albin et al., 1988) can cause or contribute to asthma (Rebhum, 1988). Respiratory failure, resulting from cocaine-induced inhibition of medullary centers in the brain, may lead to sudden death (Jonsson, O'Meara & Young, 1983).

Recently a new syndrome entered the medical terminology: "crack lung." Individuals with this condition present with the symptoms of pneumonia—severe chest pains, breathing problems, high temperatures, yet x-rays reveal no evidence of pneumonia and the condition does not respond to standard treatments. Anti-inflammatory drugs may relieve symptoms of crack lung. People with this syndrome may suffer oxygen starvation or loss of blood with potentially fatal results.

Sexual Complications: In women, cocaine abuse has adverse effects on reproductive function, including derangement in the menstrual cycle function, galactorrhea, amenorrhea, and infertility. Some women who use cocaine report having greater difficulty achieving orgasm (Smith, Wesson & Apter-Marsh, 1984). While initially producing increased libido and enhanced sexual performance in men, chronic cocaine use leads to reduction in sexual interest, spontaneous orgasm, and impotency.

Cocaine and Pregnancy: Use of amphetamines or, especially, cocaine by pregnant mothers leads to a number of dangerous physical problems for both the mother and the fetus. Pregnancy increases a woman's susceptibility to the toxic cardiovascular effects of cocaine (Woods & Plessinger, 1990). Placental abruption (Pritchard, MacDonald & Gant, 1985) spontaneous abortion, decreased blood flow to the uterus, and reduced fetal oxygen levels all occur with maternal cocaine use. While precise data are unavailable in many parts of the country, between 15 and 25% of babies are born with cocaine already in their system (Bateman & Heagarty, 1989). Infant gestational age, birth weight, head circumference, and length are decreased in infants born to cocaine using women (Bingol, Fuchs et al., 1987; Cherukuri, Minkoff et al., 1989). In fact, a specific syndrome associated with cocaine-addicted infants has been given a name: "jittery baby." Children outside the womb are also vulnerable to their mother's addiction in that cocaine can be passed to infants through breast milk and can be found in milk up to 60 hours after the mother used the drug.

Increases in dopamine in nucleus accumbens and other systems and serotonin systems in brain have been demonstrated for prenatally exposed animals. Prenatal cocaine exposure appears to lead to a marked enhancement of the rates of self-administration for offspring. Prenatal exposure to cocaine alters cocaine reinforcement properties for children and adults (Keller, LeFevre et al., 1996).

Other Adverse Effects: Chronic use of cocaine and other stimulants downregulates DA function in the basal ganglia. As a result of the amphetamines' and cocaine's effects on the primary eating drive, many individuals who use stimulant drugs compulsively lose their appetites and can experience significant weight loss (Jonas & Gold, 1986). The stimulants also have been shown to produce hyperpyrexia, or extremely elevated body temperatures, which can contribute to the development of seizures and death (Loghmanee & Tobak, 1986). Several investigators (Merigian & Roberts 1987; Krohn, Slowman-Kovacs & Leapman, 1988) implicate cocaine in the development of the muscle wasting condition known as rhabdomyolysis.

Different routes of administration can produce different adverse effects. Intranasal use of cocaine, for example, can lead to sinusitis, loss of the sense of smell, atrophy of the nasal mucosa, nosebleeds, perforation of the nasal septum, difficulty in swallowing, and hoarseness (Vilensky, 1982). Ingested cocaine can cause severe bowel ischemia or gangrene due to vasoconstriction and reduced blood flow. Persons who inject cocaine have puncture marks and "tracks," most commonly on their forearms, as seen in those with opioid dependence. HIV infection is associated with cocaine dependence due to the frequent intravenous injections and the increase in promiscuous sexual behavior. As mentioned above, crack smoking can lead to the pneumonia-like symptoms of crack lung. Deaths have occurred from all forms of cocaine administration (Cregler & Mark, 1986; Kosten & Kleber, 1987).

Other medical complications include headache, thallium poisoning, retinal artery occlusion, dermatologic problems, and muscle and skin infarction. Persons who lack the enzyme pseudocholinesterase are at risk for sudden death from cocaine use because the enzyme is essential for metabolizing the drug.

Cocaine abstinence has been reported to be associated with mild cogwheeling and rigidity, and even choreoathetosis, akathesia, and overt parkinsonism with tremor. History of cocaine dependence is commonly associated with more resting hand tremor than alcohol dependence. Tremor correlated with frequency of use of cocaine and was not related to length of abstinence (Bauer, 1989).

Psychiatric Disorders. During chronic, high-dose consumption of stimulants, a "psychosis" may develop, probably more so with amphetamines than with cocaine because of the difficulty of sustaining high chronic blood levels of cocaine. The psychosis is distinguished by paranoid ideation and a well-formed delusional structure. Hyperreactivity, increased sensitivity to environmental stimuli, and hallucinations may follow (Craig & Weddington, 1994; King & Ellingwood, 1992). Stereotyped behaviors, such as repetitive disassembling and reassembling objects, may ensue. Following cessation of prolonged, high-dose use, addicts often report symptoms of despair and fatigue (Lukas, 1991).

Lifetime prevalence rates of psychiatric disorders among cocaine abusers ranges from 75% to 85%. Our experience and those of other investigators have reported important associations between cocaine use and dependence and bipolar disorders, depression, and marijuana and alcohol abuse and dependence. Some investigators have reported comorbidity of up to 25% for bipolar-spectrum illnesses (mania, hypomania, cyclothymia) and up to 50% comorbidity of depression among cocaine abusers. There also is a relationship between cocaine and anxiety disorders with many patients reporting the onset of panic attacks with cocaine use (Gold, 1989). Cocaine use is also associated with borderline and antisocial personality disorders, eating disorders and a history of attention deficit hyperactivity disorder (ADHD).

Features of cocaine-induced psychotic disorder can include delusions and hallucinations that resemble mania or schizophrenia, paranoid type. More commonly, however, the mental disturbances that occur in association with cocaine use resolve within hours to days after cessation of use.

Societal Problems. Abuse of cocaine and other stimulants has been associated with a number of societal problems including accidents, crime and violence. It is now clear that driving under the influence of intoxicating drugs other than alcohol may be an important cause of traffic injuries. Autopsies revealed the presence of cocaine in more than 18% of motor vehicle fatalities in New York City between 1984 and 1987 (Marzuk, Tardiff et al., 1990).

Cocaine use, especially crack and intravenous use, is linked to violence and crime. By 1989, cocaine was the number one cause of emergency room visits in such major U.S. cities as Washington, New York, Atlanta, Chicago, and Los Angeles (NIDA, 1988). Recent cocaine use is associated with a range of violent premature deaths, including accidents, homicides and suicides (Tardiff, Gross et al., 1989). The sale of cocaine is also associated with violence as rivals fight over street profits (Weisman, 1993).

Cocaine has changed society in other ways as well. It has changed professional and nonprofessional sports, altered the process by which businesses screen job candidates and has led to the development of employee assistance programs in the workplace. It has thwarted decades of progress in international diplomacy and threatened the relationships between our nation and other parts of the world.

ADDICTION LIABILITY

Cocaine. The delivery system used to bring cocaine into the body is related to the drug's clinical effects and addiction potential. For example, following intranasal administration of 96 mg of cocaine, peak venous plasma levels of between 150 and 200 ng/ml are reached in 30 minutes. Intravenous administration of 32 mg produce peak venous plasma levels of 250–300 ng/ml after only four minutes. A similar rise in plasma levels occur following the smoking of 50 mg of cocaine base (Foltin & Fischman, 1991). The almost instantaneous high associated with smoking cocaine, along with the affordabiliity of crack (as little as $2 a dose) particularly associated with a rapid progression from use to abuse or dependence, often occurring over weeks to months.

Cocaine HCl is readily converted to base prior to use. The physiological and psychoactive effects of cocaine are similar regardless of the form of cocaine. However, evidence exists showing a greater abuse liability, greater propensity for dependence and more severe consequences when cocaine is smoked or injected compared with intranasal use (Hatsukami & Fischman, 1996). The crucial variables appear to be the immediacy, duration and magnitude of cocaine's effect (Verebey & Gold, 1988).

Amphetamines. Individuals proceed toward amphetamine dependence through phases of use (Craig & Weddington, 1994). Increased use follows the positive reinforcement of euphoria, increased energy, and enhanced social and vocational interactions (King & Ellinwood, 1992). Conditioning to positive effects occurs during the early use of amphetamines.

Amphetamine users discover that higher doses produce greater effects, and that routes of rapid administration, such as intravenous injection or smoking, produce even greater euphoric effects. Tolerance to euphoria develops, followed by even more frequent use of larger quantities (Craig & Weddington, 1994; King & Ellinwood, 1992).

ABSORPTION AND METABOLISM

Cocaine. Cocaine has a plasma half-life of 40 to 60 minutes and can be detected in the urine for up to 36 hours. It remains in the brain for two to three days, although cocaine metabolites can be detected for up to two to three weeks in heavy users and may be found in hair samples for months following use. It is metabolized by the liver into the main metabolites of benzyleconine and ecgonine.

Physiological Effects: The acute physiologic effects result from sympathetic nervous discharge after cocaine releases norepinephrine, epinephrine, and dopamine. Activation of the cardiovascular system results in tachycardia, hyper- or hypotension, chest pain or cardiac arrhythmia and diaphoresis (Hollander, 1995). Central nervous system stimulation lowers seizure threshold and causes other changes such as tremor, arousal electrographic changes, emesis, pupillary dilation, confusion, hyperpyrexia dyskinesias, dystonias, and coma. Peripheral nervous system stimulation results in urinary and bowel delay and retention, muscular contractions, psychomotor agitation or retardation, muscular weakness, respiratory depression and cutaneous flushing (Gold, 1992).

The cocaine-induced feeling of increased alertness is reported subjectively and can be confirmed by electroencephalogram (EEG) and electrocardiogram (ECG) recordings, which show a general desynchronization of brain waves after cocaine administration (Wallach & Gerson, 1971). But there are limits to the degree to which central nervous system activity can be artificially stimulated. After chronic use, or following a prolonged binge, neurotransmitter reserves become depleted leading to exhaustion, depression, insomnia and outright acute toxic psychosis (Gold, Miller & Jonas, 1992).

When cocaine is included in the differential diagnosis, urine testing is necessary. Tolerance and dependence do develop immediately to cocaine and have been demonstrated at wide ranges of doses. Withdrawal from chronic cocaine use also has a predictable and stereotypic, protracted psychological and physiologic course in some addicts.

Psychological Effects: Cocaine's effects as a CNS stimulant leads many users to experience feelings of enhanced physical prowess or mental acuity. However, these feelings are illusory and likely represent enhanced self-confidence and lowered inhibitions.

Once cocaine reaches the brain the user experiences an immediate and intense euphoria, analogous to a sexual orgasm. This sensation may last from seconds to several minutes, depending on the dose, route of administration, and tolerance of the user. Other alterations arising from elevation in mood include giddiness, reduced appetite (at least initially), increased libido (at low doses), forceful boisterousness, poor judgment, decreased problem solving ability, psychomotor acceleration and grandiosity. Cocaine produces a sense of doom and the sensation of being out of control indistinguishable from panic disorder. The subjective feelings of helplessness and hopelessness lead to eventual suicidal thinking and behavior in many cocaine addicts.

At higher doses, cocaine intoxication is virtually indistinguishable from hypomania or frank mania with symptoms of racing thoughts, pressured speech at times being tangential and incoherent. The person may develop frankly psychotic symptoms including hallucinations, delusions and ideas of reference. States of severe transient panic accompanied by a terror of impending death can occur in persons with no preexisting psychopathologic conditions, as can paranoid psychoses (Weinstein, Gottheil et al., 1986; Jeri, Sanchez et al., 1980).

Interactions with Other Drugs: A complication of cocaine abuse is that many users ameliorate some of the unpleasant stimulating effects of the drug by sedating agents such as alcohol or marihuana. The combined use of cocaine and alcohol is common with reports of 62–90% of cocaine abusers also concurrent ethanol abusers (Jatlow, 1993). Cocaine users report that concurrent ethanol use prolongs the "high" and attenuates a number of the unpleasant physical and psychological effects of cocaine. Using cocaine and alcohol together creates a "new drug": cocaethylene, a substance that binds to the dopamine transporter and thus blocks dopamine uptake and increases extracelluar concentrations of dopamine in the nucleus accumbens.

While not entirely clear from anecdotal reports, marijuana may potentiate cocaine's effects. In one study smoking marijuana significantly reduced the latency to peak cocaine euphoria from 1.87 to 0.53 minutes, decreased the duration of dysphoric or bad effects and increased peak cocaine when compared to placebo.

Amphetamines. Amphetamine is a simple organic molecule (Craig & Weddington, 1994). In animals, amphetamine's primary behavioral effects are increased motor behavior, increased arousal, induction of stereotypy, and suppressed food intake; whereas in man, long-term high-dose administration of amphetamines can precipitate an acute paranoid psychosis (Chiarello & Cole, 1987). In animals and man, toxic side effects (which increase with higher doses) reflect autonomic overstimulation (Chiarello & Cole, 1987).

Peak plasma levels of amphetamines after oral use are achieved in one to three hours (Chiarello & Cole, 1987). Amphetamine's plasma half-life ranges from six to 12 hours (Gawin & Ellinwood, 1988, 1989). Euphoria with amphetamine administration persists for up to six hours (Gawin & Ellinwood, 1988, 1989). Binges of amphetamine use may ensue, and can last more than 24 hours, usually with several hours between administrations (Lukas, 1991; Gawin & Ellinwood, 1988, 1989).

Methylphenidate. An oral dose of methylphenidate is quickly absorbed, has a peak plasma level in two hours, rapidly enters the central nervous system, and has a plasma half-life of two hours (Craig & Weddington, 1994).

MECHANISMS OF ACTION

Cocaine. One of cocaine's primary effects in the brain is to block the presynaptic reuptake of neurotransmitters including dopamine, serotonin and norepinephrine within the medial forebrain bundle (MFB). The structures of the MFB (i.e., frontal cortex, nucleus accumbens, and ventral tegmental area) have been identified as being involved in the reinforcing and euphoric effects of cocaine (Ritchie & Greene, 1985). Repeated administration of cocaine enhances the responsivity of dopamine neurons to subsequent challenges so that enhanced basal dopamine tone in the nucleus accumbens may underlie behavioral sensitization. Opioid peptides may play an important role since they appear to modulate mesolimbic dopamine systems. Mu, delta, and kappa opioid receptors have been identified on the mesolimbic dopamine neurons. Enkephalin immunoreactive fibers are also found in the ventral tegmental area and originate in the nucleus accumbens. Both mu and delta opioid receptors agonists increase extracellular dopamine levels in the nucleus accumbens. Tonic control of mesolimbic dopamine neurotransmission by endogenous opioids is suggested by results obtained with enkephalineases inhibitors. Dopamine depletion enhances enkephalin mRNA and cocaine treatment elevates dynorphine content.

Repeated injections of cocaine produces an upregulation of mu-opioid receptors in various mesolimbic areas including nucleus accumbens. The delta opioid receptor antagonist naltrindole attenuates behavioral effects of cocaine and amphetamine (Heidbreder, Shoaib & Shippenberg, 1996).

Tolerance and Dependence: Tolerance to cocaine euphoria develops quickly and has been measured within an hour after a single intravenous dose so that the dose must be escalated or the route and dose changed in order to experience desired effects of equal intensity. In fact, most cocaine addicts recall that their early trials of cocaine yielded the greatest and most satisfying euphoria, even more than that experienced during a cocaine binge. It is not unusual to find in clinical practice cocaine addicts who have reached intranasal doses of 1 to 3 grams per day.

It has become well accepted that the mesolimbic and mesocortical dopaminergic systems are critical in the reinforcing effects of cocaine and also cocaine-induced euphoria. In a recent study of the binge administrations paradigm, cocaine significantly lowers basal dopamine levels but not the magnitude of the response to cocaine itself (Maisonneuve, Ho & Kreek, 1995).

Withdrawal: Until the mid-1980s organized psychiatry discounted the possibility that cocaine use was associated with an abstinence syndrome of any consequence (Grinspoon & Bakalar, 1980; Washton & Gold, 1984, 1983). Recently, however, support for the concept of a (sometimes subtle) cocaine abstinence state has been found (Markou & Koob, 1991; Kokkindis & McCarter, 1990; Gold, 1993; Gold & Miller, 1992). The current edition of the *Diagnostic and Statistical Manual* (*DSM-IV*) of the American Psychiatric Association (1994) recognizes the existence and importance of cocaine withdrawal as: "The essential feature of cocaine withdrawal is the presence of a characteristic withdrawal syndrome that develops within a few hours to several days after the cessation of (or reduction in) cocaine use that has been heavy and prolonged. The withdrawal syndrome is characterized by the development of dysphoric mood accompanied by two or more of the following physiological changes: fatigue, vivid and unpleasant dreams, insomnia or hypersomnia, increased appetite, and psychomotor retardation or agitation. Anhedonia and drug craving can often be present but are not part of the diagnostic criteria. These symptoms cause clinically significant distress or impairment in social, occupational, or other important areas of functioning."

In fact, chronic cocaine use is associated with a withdrawal syndrome that includes prominent psychiatric features which appear related to dopamine deficiency and possibly also a serotonin depletion (Gold, 1993; Gold, 1993). Depression, anxiety, and panic may be consequences of serotonergic depletion. Cocaine has many of the same pharmacological actions on serotonin neurons as it does the dopamine systems. Extracellular 5-HT is significantly decreased in the nucleus accumbens during withdrawal from cocaine self administration (Parsons, Koob & Weiss, 1993). The severity of the serotonin decrease is related to the duration of cocaine binge. Such decreases may be related to depression, panic, insomnia, impulsiveness and even increased aggression. In addition to effects on dopamine, norepinephrine and serotonin, recent research has also identified a possible role of delta, kappa and mu opioid receptors in cocaine addiction (Heidbreder, Shoaib & Shippenberg, 1996; Shippenberg, LeFevour & Heidbreder, 1996; Mello & Negus, 1993). Acutely, cocaine increases extracellular dopamine levels within the nucleus accumbens.

Amphetamines. Acting as indirect sympathomimetic agents, amphetamines exert a variety of pharmacological toxic effects such as central stimulation, anorexia, vasoconstriction, and hyperthermia (Craig & Weddington, 1994; Biel & Bopp, 1978). The (+)enantiomer is two to five times as potent as the (−)enantiomer (Cho, 1990). The non-ionized amphetamine molecule is highly lipophilic, is briskly absorbed through the intestines, and rapidly penetrates the central nervous system (Chiarello & Cole, 1987). Elimination is both by renal excretion and complex biotransformation (Chiarello & Cole, 1987). Amphetamine preparations can be detected in urine for up to two days following last use (Lukas, 1991).

Methylphenidate. Methylphenidate's mode of action is essentially the same as that of the amphetamines (Craig & Weddington, 1994).

REINFORCING PROPERTIES

Cocaine. The major focus of research on cocaine reinforcement has focused on the dopaminergic pathways which originate in the ventral tegmental area and project to the nucleus accumbens. Cocaine reinforcement and withdrawal have been related to dopaminergic function and a dopamine hypothesis proposed to explain addiction and abstinence (Gold & Dackis, 1984; Dackis & Gold, 1985). Recent data suggest that the intense euphoria induced by dopamine transporter inhibitors such as cocaine is associated with initial fast uptake of cocaine into the brain rather than persistence. The peculiarly destructive binge pattern of cocaine abuse may be facilitated by the drugs rapid dissociation from the dopamine transporter *in vivo*, which permits repeat administrations. Although cocaine analogs with higher affinity than cocaine are reinforcing in animals their slower net dissociation from the dopamine transporter may allow adaptive neurochemical changes which cause behavioral tolerance to dopamine transporter occupancy. Withdrawal from repeated intermittent infusions of cocaine produce dopaminergic deficiency in the limbic portions of the nucleus accumbens, the shell of the nucleus accumbens (Pilotte, Sharpe et al., 1996).

While dopamine plays a central role in the rewarding aspects of cocaine, there are at least five dopamine-receptor subtypes and their respective roles in cocaine reinforcement remains to be demonstrated. Studies suggest significant derangement of dopamine function in cocaine addicts with decreases in dopamine D2 and D3 receptors that persist even after protracted cocaine withdrawal. The reduction in D2 receptors is associated with functional changes in the brain that involve among others the orbitofrontal cortex and the cingulate gyrus (Caine & Koob, 1993).

The experience of clinicians with cocaine addicts has helped psychiatry re-focus on the drive for brain reinforcement and place acute abstinence in its proper position (Gold & Miller, 1992). This important new line of research thinking suggests that further progress in treating addicts will not depend upon progress in treating withdrawal but rather in developing new treatments which reduce recidivism and eliminate drive for the drug.

Amphetamines. Craig & Weddington (1994) describe the euphorigenic effects of amphetamines as mediated, in part, by direct neuronal release of dopamine. In addition, amphetamines cause direct neuronal release of norepinephrine and blockade of catecholamine reuptake. Subsequent doses of amphetamines release smaller and smaller quantities of neurotransmitters. Time is required for the nerve terminal to replenish itself. These depletion and replenishment factors could account for increasing doses required for euphoric effects, dysphoria, and recovery after several days due to resynthesis (Cho, 1990). Amphetamines also have weak monoamine oxidase inhibitor effects (Biel & Bopp, 1978).

REFERENCES

American Psychiatric Association (1994). *Diagnostic and Statistical Manual of Mental Disorders, 4th Edition.* Washington, DC: American Psychiatric Press.

Bastos ML & Hoffman DB (1976). Detection and identification of cocaine, its metabolites and its derivatives. In SJ Mulé (ed.) *Cocaine: Chemical, Biological, Clinical, Social and Treatment Aspects.* Ohio: CRC Press, 45.

Bateman DA & Heagarty MC (1989). Passive freebase cocaine ('crack') inhalation by infants and toddlers. *American Journal of Disabled Children* 134:25–27.

Bauer LO (1989). Resting hand tremor in abstinent cocaine dependent alcohol dependent and polydrug dependent patients. *Alcoholism: Clinical & Experimental Research* 20:1196–1201.

Berger P, Gawin F & Kosten TR (1989). Treatment of cocaine abuse with mazindol. *Lancet* 1:283.

Biel JH & Bopp BA (1978). Amphetamines: Structure-activity relationships. In L Iverson, S Iverson & S Snyder (eds.) *Handbook of Psychopharmacology.* New York, NY: Plenum Press, 1–39.

Bingol N, Fuchs M, Diaz V, Stone RK & Gromisch DS (1987). Teratogenicity of cocaine in humans. *Journal of Pediatrics* 110:93–96.

Byck R (1974). *Cocaine Papers: Sigmund Freud.* New York, NY: Stonehill Publishing.

Caine S & Koob GF (1993). Modulation of cocaine self-administration in the rat through D-3 dopamine receptors. *Science* 260:1814–1816.

Casey BL, Ray CA & Piercey MF (1996). Antagonism of cocaine's stimulant effects on local cerebral glucose utilization by the preferential autoreceptor antagonist (+)-AJ 76. *Journal of Neural Transmission* 103:277–285.

Cherukuri R, Minkoff H, Feldman J, Parekh A & Glass L (1989). A cohort study of alkaloidal cocaine (crack) in pregnancy. *Obstetrics and Gynecology* 72:145–151.

Chiarello RJ & Cole JO (1987). The use of psychostimulants in general psychiatry. *Archives of General Psychiatry* 44:286–295.

Cho AK (1990). Ice: A new dosage form of an old drug. *Science* 249:631–634.

Craig RJ & Weddington WJ (1994). Stimulants and cocaine. In NS Miller (ed.) *Principles of Addiction Medicine.* Chevy Chase, MD: American Society of Addiction Medicine.

Cregler LL & Mark H (1986a). Cardiovascular dangers of cocaine abuse. *American Journal of Cardiology* 57:1185–1186.

Cregler LL & Mark H (1986b). Medical complications of cocaine abuse. *The New England Journal of Medicine* 315:1495–1500.

Dackis CA & Gold MS (1985). New concepts in cocaine addiction: The dopamine depletion hypothesis. *Neuroscience and Biobehavioral Reviews* 9(3):469–477.

Dackis CA, Gold MS & Estroff TW (1989). Inpatient treatment of addiction. *Treatments of Psychiatric Disorders: A Task Force Report of the American Psychiatric Association.* Washington, DC: American Psychiatric Association, 1359–1379.

Derlet RW & Albertson TE (1989). Emergency department presentation of cocaine intoxication. *Annals of Emergency Medicine* 18:115–119.

DuPont RL & Gold MS (1995). Withdrawal and reward: Implications for detoxification and relapse prevention. *Psychiatric Annals* 25(11):663–668.

DuPont RL & Voth EA (1995). Drug legalization, harm reduction and drug policy. *Annals of Internal Medicine* 123:461–465.

Foltin RW & Fischman MW (1991). Smoked and intravenous cocaine in humans: Acute tolerance, cardiovascular and subjective effects. *Journal of Pharmacology and Experimental Research* 257:247–261.

Gawin FH (1991). Cocaine addiction: Psychology and neurophysiology. *Science* 251:1580–1586.

Gawin FH & Ellinwood EH (1988). Cocaine and other stimulants. *The New England Journal of Medicine* 318:1173–1182.

Gawin FH & Ellinwood E (1989). Stimulants. In HD Kleber (ed.) *Treatment of Psychiatric Disorders: A Task Force Report of the American Psychiatric Association.* Washington, DC: American Psychiatric Association, 1218–1241.

Giros B, Jaber M, Jones SR, Wightman RM & Caron MG (1996). Hyperlocomotion and indifference to cocaine and amphetamine in mice lacking the dopamine transporter. *Nature* 379:606–612.

Gold MS (1989). *The Good News about Panic, Anxiety, and Phobias.* New York, NY: Villard Books.

Gold MS (1992). Cocaine (and crack). In JH Lowinson, P Ruiz & RB Millman (eds.) *Substance Abuse: A Comprehensive Textbook (2nd Edition).* Baltimore, MD: Williams & Wilkins, 205–221.

Gold MS (1993a). Cocaine. *Drugs of Abuse: A Comprehensive Series for Clinicians (Vol. III).* New York, NY: Plenum Medical Book Co.

Gold MS (1993b). Dopamine depletion hypothesis for acute cocaine abstinence clinical observations, prolactin elevations, and persistent anhendonia/dysphoria. *Neuroendocrinolocy Letters* 15(4):271.

Gold MS (1994). Neurobiology of addiction and recovery: The brain, the drive for the drug and the 12-Step Fellowship. *Journal of Substance Abuse Treatment* 11(2):93–97.

Gold MS & Dackis CA (1984). New insights and treatments: Narcotics and cocaine addiction. *Clinical Therapeutics* 7(1):6–21.

Gold MS & Miller NS (1992). Seeking drugs/alcohol and avoiding withdrawal: The neuroanatomy of drive states and withdrawal. *Psychiatric Annals* 22:430–435.

Gold MS & Miller NS (1994). The biology of addictive and psychiatric disorders. In NS Miller (ed.) *Treating Coexisting Psychiatric and Addictive Disorders.* Center City, MN: Hazelden Foundation, 35–52.

Gold MS, Miller NS & Jonas JM (1992). Cocaine (and crack). In JH Lowinson, P Ruiz & RB Millman (eds.) *Neurobiology in Substance Abuse: A Comprehensive Textbook (2nd Edition).* Baltimore, MD: Williams & Wilkins, 222–236.

Grinspoon L & Bakalar JB (1980). Drug dependence: Non-narcotic agents. In HI Kaplan, AM Freedman & BJ Sadock (eds.) *Comprehensive Textbook of Psychiatry (3rd Edition, Vol. 2).* Baltimore, MD: Williams & Wilkins.

Hatsukami DK & Fischman MW (1996). Crack cocaine and cocaine hydrochloride: Are the differences myth or reality? *Journal of the American Medical Association* 276:1580–1588.

Heidbreder C, Shoaib M & Shippenberg TS (1996). Differential role of delta-opioid receptors in the development and expression of behavioral sensitization to cocaine. *European Journal of Pharmacology* 298:207–216.

Higgins ST, Budney AJ, Bickel WK, Foerg FE, Donham R & Badger GJ (1994). Behavioral treatment of cocaine dependence: Incentives improve outcome in outpatient. *Archives of General Psychiatry* 51:568–576.

Higgins ST, Budney AJ, Bickel WK, Hughes JR, Foerg F & Badger G (1993). Achieving cocaine abstinence with a behavioral approach. *American Journal of Psychiatry* 150:763–769.

Hoffman CK & Goodman PC (1989). Pulmonary edema in cocaine smokers. *Radiology* 172:462–465.

Hoffman RS, Morasco R & Goldfrank LR (1996). Administration of purified human plasma cholinesterase protects against cocaine toxicity in mice. *Clinical Toxicology* 34:259–266.

Hollander JE (1995). The management of cocaine-associated myocardial ischemia. *The New England Journal of Medicine* 333:1267–1272.

Itkonen J, Schnoll A & Glassroth J (1984). Pulmonary dysfunction in "freebase" cocaine users. *Archives of Internal Medicine* 144:2195–2197.

Jaffe JH, Witkin JM, Goldberg SR & Katz JL (1989). Potential toxic interactions of cocaine and mazindol. *Lancet* 8654:111.

Jatlow P (1993). Cocaethylene: Pharmacologic activity and clinical significance. *Therapeutic Drug Monitoring* 15:533–536.

Jeri FR, Sanchez CC, Del Pozo T, Fernandez M & Carbajal C (1980). Further experience with the syndromes produced by coca paste smoking. In FR Jeri (ed.) *Cocaine.* Lima, Peru: Pacific Press.

Jonas JM & Gold MS (1986). Cocaine abuse and eating disorders. *Lancet* 1:390–391.

Jonsson S, O'Meara M & Young JB (1983). Acute cocaine poisoning: Importance of treating seizures and acidosis. *American Journal of Medicine* 75:1061–1064.

Keller RW, LeFevre R, Raucci J, Carlson JN & Glick SD (1996). Enhanced cocaine self-administration in adult rats prenatally exposed to cocaine. *Neuroscience Letters* 205:153–156.

King GR & Ellinwood EH (1992). Amphetamines and other stimulants. In JH Lowinson, P Ruiz & RB Millman (eds.) *Substance Abuse: A Comprehensive Textbook, Second Edition.* Baltimore, MD: Williams & Wilkins, 247–270.

Kokkindis L & McCarter BD (1990). Post cocaine depression and sensitization of brain-stimulation reward: Analysis of reinforcement and performance effects. *Pharmacology, Biochemistry and Behavior* 36:463–471.

Kosten TR & Kleber HD (1987). Sudden death in cocaine abusers: Relation to neuroleptic malignant syndrome. *Lancet* 1(8543):1198–1199.

Kosten TR, Steinberg M & Diakogiannis IA (1993). Crossover trial of mazindol for cocaine dependence. *American Journal of Addictions* 2:161–164.

Krohn KD, Slowman-Kovacs S & Leapman SB (1988). Cocaine and rhabdomyolysis. *Annals of Internal Medicine* 208:639–640.

Kuhar MJ & Pilotte NS (1996). Neurochemical changes in cocaine withdrawal. *TiPS* 17:260–264.

Leshner AI (1996). Molecular mechanisms of cocaine addiction. *The New England Journal of Medicine* 335:128–129.

Lichtenfeld PJ, Rubin DB & Feldman RS (1984). Subarachnoid hemorrhage precipitated by cocaine snorting. *Archives of Neurology* 41:223–224.

Loghmanee F & Tobak M (1986). Fatal malignant hyperthermia associated with recreational cocaine and ethanol abuse. *American Journal of Forensic Medicine and Pathology* 7:246–248.

Lukas S (1991). Cocaine and other stimulants. In *Drug Abuse and Drug Abuse Research (NIDA Research Monograph).* Rockville, MD: National Institute on Drug Abuse, 535–584.

Lukas SE, Sholar M, Kouri E, Fukuzako H & Mendelson JH (1994). Marijuana smoking increases plasma cocaine levels and subjective reports of euphoria in male volunteers. *Pharmacology, Biochemistry and Behavior* 48:715–721.

Maisonneuve IM, Ho A & Kreek MJ (1995). Chronic administration of a cocaine "binge" alters basal extracellular levels in male rats: An in vivo microdialysis study. *Journal of Pharmacology and Experimental Therapeutics* 272:652–657.

Markou A & Koob GF (1991). Post cocaine anhedonia: An animal model of cocaine withdrawal. *Neuropsychopharmacology* 4:17–26.

Marzuk PM, Tardiff K, Leon AC, Stajic M, Morgan EB & Mann JJ (1990). Prevalence of recent cocaine use among motor vehicle fatalities in New York City. *Journal of the American Medical Association* 263:250–256.

Mello NK, Lukas SE, Mendelson JH & Drieze J (1993). Naltrexone-buprenorphine interactions: Effects on cocaine self-administration. *Neuropsychopharmacology* 9:211–224.

Mello NK & Negus SS (1996). Preclinical evaluation of pharmacotherapies for treatment of cocaine and opioid abuse using drug self-administration procedures. *Neuropsychopharmacology* 14:375–424.

Mendelson JH & Mello NK (1996). Management of cocaine abuse and dependence. *The New England Journal of Medicine* 334:965–972.

Merigian KS & Roberts JR (1987). Cocaine intoxication: Hyperpyrexia, rhabdomyolysis, and acute renal failure. *Journal of Toxicology and Clinical Toxicology* 25:135–148.

Miller NS & Gold MS (1992). The psychiatrist's role in integrating pharmacological and nonpharmacological treatments for addictive disorders. *Psychiatric Annals* 22(8):436–440.

Millman RB (1988). Evaluation and clinical management of cocaine abuser. *Journal of Clinical Psychiatry* 49(Suppl 2):27–33.

Murray RJ, Albin RJ, Mergner W et al. (1988). Diffuse alveolar hemorrhage temporally related to cocaine smoking. *Chest* 427–429.

Nadamanee K, Gorelick DA, Josephson MA et al. (1989). Myocardial ischemia during cocaine withdrawal. *Annals of Internal Medicine* 111:876–880.

National Institute on Drug Abuse (1988). Statistical series: Semiannual report: Trend data, July–December. *Drug Abuse Warning Network (Series G, No. 23).* Rockville, MD: Author, 8 ff.

Parsons LH, Koob GF & Weiss F (1996). Extracellular serotonin is decreased in the nucleus accumbens during withdrawal from cocaine self-administration. *Behavioural Brain Research* 73:225–228.

Peng SK, French WJ & Pelikan PCD (1989). Direct cocaine cardiotoxicity demonstrated by endomyocardial biopsy. *Archives of Pathology and Laboratory Medicine* 113:842–845.

Perez-Meyes M, DiGiuseppi S, Ondrusek G, Jeffcoat AR & Cook CE (1982). Free-base cocaine smoking. *Clinical Pharmacology and Therapy* 32:459–465.

Pilotte NS, Sharpe LG, Rountree SD & Kuhar MJ (1996). Cocaine withdrawal reduces dopamine transporter binding in the shell of the nucleus accumbens. *Synapse* 22:87–92.

Pritchard JA, MacDonald PC & Gant NF (1985). *Williams' Obstetrics.* Norwalk, CT: Appleton-Century-Crofts, 395–407.

Rebhum J (1988). Association of asthma and freebase smoking. *Annals of Allergy* 60:339–342.

Ritchie JM & Greene NM (1985). Local anesthetics. In AG Gilman, LS Goodman, TW Rall et al. (eds.) *Goodman and Gilman's The Pharmacological Basis of Therapeutics (7th edition).* New York, NY: Macmillan, 309–310.

Roehrich H & Gold MS (1988). Emergency presentations of crack abuse. *Emergency Medical Service* 17(8):41–44.

Sakurai M, Wirsching P & Janda KD (1996). Design and synthesis of a cocaine-diamide hapten for vaccine development. *Tetrahedron Letters* 37:5479–5482.

Schachne JS, Roberts BH & Thompson PD (1984). Coronary-artery spasm and myocardial infarction associated with cocaine use. *The New England Journal of Medicine* 310:1665–1666.

Shippenberg TS, LeFevour & Heidbreder C (1996). Kappa-opioid receptor agonists prevent sensitization to the conditioned rewarding effects of cocaine. *Journal of Pharmacology and Experimental Therapy* 276:545–554.

Shottenfeld RS, Pakes J, Ziedonis D & Kosten TR (1993). Burprenorphine: Dose-related effects on cocaine and opioid use in cocaine-abusing opioid-dependent humans. *Biological Psychiatry* 34:66–74.

Smith DE, Wesson DR & Apter-Marsh M (1984). Cocaine-and alcohol-induced sexual dysfunction in patients with addictive diseases. *Journal of Psychoactive Drugs* 16:359–361.

Smith HWB, Lieberman HA, Brody SL, Battey LL, Donohue BC & Morris DC (1987). Acute myocardial infarction temporally related to cocaine use. *Annals of Internal Medicine* 107:13–18.

Tardiff DP, Gross EM, Wu J, Stajic M & Millman R (1989). Analysis of cocaine positive fatalities. *Journal of Forensic Science* 34:53–63.

Van Dyke C, Jatlow P, Ungerer J et al. (1978). Oral cocaine: Plasma concentrations and central effects. *Science* 200:211–213.

Verebey K & Gold MS (1988). From coca leaves to crack: The effects of dose and routes of administration in abuse liability. *Psychiatric Annals* 18(9):513–520.

Vilensky W (1982). Illicit and licit drugs causing perforation of the nasal septum. *Journal of Forensic Science* 27:958–962.

Vitullo JC, Karam R, Mekhail N, Wicker P, Engelmann A & Khairallah PA (1989). Cocaine-induced small vessel spasm in isolated rat hearts. *American Journal of Pathology* 135:85–91.

Wallach MB & Gerson S (1971). A neuropsychopharmacological comparison of d-amphetamine, l-DOPA and cocaine. *Neuropharmacology* 10:743.

Washton AM & Gold MS (1983). Intranasal cocaine addiction. *Lancet* 2(8363):1374.

Washton AM & Gold MS (1984). Successful use of naltrexone in addicted physicians and business executives. *Advances in Alcohol and Substance Abuse* 4(2):89–96.

Weinstein SP, Gottheil E, Smith RH & Migrala KA (1986). Cocaine users seen in medical practice. *American Journal of Drug and Alcohol Abuse* 12:341–354.

Weisman GK (1993). Adolescent PTSD and developmental consequences of crack dealing. *American Journal of Orthopedics* 63:553–561.

Weiss SRB, Post RM & Aigner TG (1992). Carbamazepine in the treatment of cocaine-induced disorders. In RR Watson (ed.) *Drug and Alcohol Abuse Reviews: Treatment of Drug and Alcohol Abuse.* Totowa, NJ: Humana Press, 149.

Wiener MD & Putnam CE (1987). Pain in the chest in a user of cocaine. *Journal of the American Medical Association* 258:2087–2088.

Woods JR Jr & Plessinger MA (1990). Pregnancy increases cardiovascular toxicity to cocaine. *American Journal of Obstetrics and Gynecology* 162:529–533.

CHAPTER 6

The Pharmacology of Nicotine

John Slade, M.D., FASAM

Therapeutic Use and Misuse
Adverse Effects
Addiction Liability
Absorption and Metabolism
Mechanisms of Action
Reinforcing Properties

Most tobacco use can be understood as the controlled, orderly ingestion of nicotine to achieve particular pharmacologic effects (USDHHS, 1988). Such use was recognized as addiction by early European observers. Indeed, in 1622, Sir Francis Bacon observed that "The use of tobacco . . . conquers men with a certain secret pleasure so that those who have once become accustomed thereto can hardly be restrained therefrom."

THERAPEUTIC USE AND MISUSE

The only approved therapeutic use for nicotine is as an adjunct to a treatment program for nicotine addiction (Benowitz, 1991; Fiore, 1992; Jarvik & Henningfield, 1993). A number of potential therapeutic uses have been suggested, but none has been established. Conditions that may warrant further study include ulcerative colitis, Parkinson's disease, Alzheimer's disease, obesity, anxiety, depression, schizophrenia, and attention deficit disorder (Levin, Karan & Rosencrans, 1993).

Robinson and Pritchard (1992) have called attention to the way people use cigarettes for a "calming effect on mood" and to achieve "increased mental alertness." Working in the laboratories of the R. J. Reynolds Tobacco Company, they have correlated the EEG changes caused by nicotine from smoking a cigarette with these specific effects (Robinson, Pritchard & Davis, 1992).

Warburton and colleagues (1988) have written about nicotine as a "resource" for smokers. In this view, nicotine produces a variety of benefits in terms of mood control and attention focus. In support of this hypothesis, these researchers cite a series of studies suggesting that nicotine enhances performance. However, these data are far from compelling. They employ simple tasks and often merely compare nicotine-tolerant subjects in a deprived state with non-deprived subjects.

A series of studies early in this century suggested that smoking impairs performance (O'Shea, 1923; Schrumpf-Pierron, 1927). Spilich and colleagues (1992) have provided striking new support for this view. This group conducted a series of tests of cognitive performance on nonsmokers, deprived smokers, and smokers who had just smoked. They found that, on simple tasks, smoking enhanced performance (this result is similar to those cited by Robinson, Pritchard & Davis). However, when the task at hand was more difficult, or when it required the use of long-term memory, smokers who had just smoked did significantly worse than nonsmokers. Deprived smokers scored in an intermediate range. These studies indicate that nicotine, while it may focus attention, interferes with complex functions such as ready access to long-term memory and performance on divided attention tasks. Thus, nicotine has mixed effects on cognitive performance: improved execution of easy tasks and faster reaction times under the influence of nicotine are accompanied by worse performance on more demanding, complex tasks.

ADVERSE EFFECTS

Nicotine itself produces toxicity in novices (MacInnes, 1926) and in persons who are occupationally exposed (Boylan, Brandt et al., 1993). Cognitive impairment is reviewed above. Tobacco use causes a huge variety of morbid complications. Nicotine plays a direct role in some of these (such as Burger's disease), but little or none in others (for example, chronic obstructive pulmonary disease, or COPD).

TABLE 1. Sources of Deaths Caused by Active Smoking

Proximate Cause of Death	Death Toll (Annual)
Cardiovascular	
Heart Disease	150,000
Stroke	26,000
Other	24,000
Cancer	
Lung	112,000
Other	31,000
Nonmalignant Pulmonary Disease	
COPD	62,000
Other (includes pneumonia & influenza)	21,000
TOTAL	426,000

Source: Centers for Disease Control (1991). Smoking-attributable mortality and years of potential life lost—United States. *Morbidity and Mortality Weekly Report* 40:62–71.

The complications of nicotine addiction are legion. Problems arise for the person who directly ingests tobacco products (USDHHS, 1989), as well as for the person who is merely exposed to tobacco smoke, either in the air as tobacco smoke pollution (ETS) (Glantz & Parmley, 1991; EPA, 1992) or transplacentally (Centers for Disease Control, 1991). Table 1 lists the major causes of death related to direct smoking of cigarettes, while Table 2 summarizes the causes of death related to passive smoking.

The data in Table 1 qualify tobacco products by a large margin as the leading cause of preventable death, while those in Table 2 qualify them as the third leading cause of preventable deaths, exceeded only by alcoholic beverages.

Table 3 lists a variety of other problems caused by or highly associated with tobacco products for consumers and for those around consumers. Stopping tobacco use slows down or reverses many of these problems (USDHHS, 1989).

Tobacco use predisposes adolescents to become involved with other psychoactive drugs (Slade, 1993a); thus, tobacco is regarded as a "gateway substance." The phenomenon reflects the fact that tobacco use is a key part of the developmental sequence of psychoactive drug use by adolescents in our culture. This association has important implications for the control and prevention of other drug problems.

Unfortunately, tobacco also synergizes with alcohol in causing a number of medical complications. Persons with alcohol problems are far more likely to smoke, and to smoke heavily, than people without this disease (Hurt, Eberman et al., 1993). Smoking and heavy drinking, in turn, are associated with substantially increased rates of oral and esophageal cancers (USDHHS, 1982; Blot, McLaughlin et al., 1988), pancreatitis (Pitchumoni, Jain et al., 1988), and cirrhosis (Klatsky & Armstrong, 1992). Finally, as long as cigarettes are designed so that they promote household fires when they fall lit into folds of upholstered furniture, alcohol use will continue to combine synergistically with smoking in causing over 1,000 deaths per year among children and adults (McGuire, 1989).

ADDICTION LIABILITY

Henningfield and colleagues (1991) reviewed the psychopharmacology of alcohol, cocaine, heroin and nicotine to sort out whether any one was intrinsically more addicting than the other. Environmental factors were recognized to be of major importance in explaining the ubiquity of nicotine use compared to the other drugs. Each drug was recognized to be a potent agent of addiction, but how they ranked depended on the particular measure under consideration. It is fortunate that the pharmacologic properties of these drugs are not the only determinants of whether addiction will occur. Many of the wide range of environmental factors that interact with agent and host to produce nicotine addiction are potential opportunities for policy change to control the epidemic (USDHHS, 1989; Fisher, Lichtenstein & Haire-Joshu, 1993).

The addiction liability of tobacco results from a complex interplay of environment, host and agent factors (Fisher, Lichtenstein & Haire-Joshu, 1993).

Environmental Factors. Despite the fact that only a fourth of adults smoke, the cigarette is second only to soft drinks and newspapers as the nation's most widely available consumer product. The industry spends over $5 billion each year marketing these products, and they remain astonishingly inexpensive. Family and peer influences also affect the risk of an individual taking up regular tobacco use.

Host Factors. Consistent data show that genetics plays a small role in determining who smokes (Collins, 1990). Behavior problems, attention deficit disorder, and low academic achievement also predict the later use of tobacco products.

Loss of Control Over Use. The regular use of tobacco commonly leads to its compulsive use. The Gallup poll consistently finds that up to three quarters of adults who smoke want to stop (USDHHS,

TABLE 2. Sources of Deaths Caused by Passive Smoking

Proximate Cause of Death	Death Toll (Annual)
Heart Disease	35,000
Cancer other than lung cancer	11,000
Lung Cancer	4,000
Deaths <1 year of age (mostly perinatal)	3,000
TOTAL	53,000

Sources: Glantz SA & Parmley WW (1991). Passive smoking and heart disease. *Circulation* 83:1–12; Centers for Disease Control (1991). Smoking-attributable mortality and years of potential life lost—United States. *Morbidity and Mortality Weekly Report* 40:62–71.

1988). About a third try to stop each year, but only a small number succeed.

Self-administration studies in animals have established that nicotine is a reinforcer (USDHHS, 1988; Collins, 1990). However, although animals will self-administer nicotine, the environment, dose and timing of the reinforcement schedule are more critical than with cocaine.

Human volunteers will lever-press for intravenous nicotine (USDHHS, 1988; Collins, 1990). They experience IV nicotine as pleasurable, and subjects who have experience with a variety of other drugs indicate that the feelings are similar to those induced by cocaine. In studies where *ad lib* smoking is permitted, oral, intravenous, or transdermal administration of nicotine consistently reduces spontaneous smoking rates.

Tolerance. Tolerance (tachyphylaxis) is seen in both animals and humans after single doses of nicotine (USDHHS, 1988; Collins, 1990). Chronic use is associated with the regular ingestion of far larger quantities than initially, even though consumption levels typically remain steady for many years once addiction has become established. However, tolerance is far from complete: the ingestion of as little as 50% more than the usual dose can result in the development of nausea, dizziness, vomiting, headache and dysphoria (Collins, 1990). Tolerance currently is regarded as a clinical manifestation of neural adaptation to nicotine. Smokers actually have an *increased* number of nicotine receptors in the brain compared to nonsmokers, but Collins has suggested that many of these must be inactivated or desensitized.

Withdrawal. A withdrawal syndrome regularly occurs on stopping regular tobacco use. Gruneberg and colleagues (1985) have demonstrated an increase in ingestion of sweet foods with weight gain in rats withdrawn from nicotine. In humans, the syndrome, when it occurs, may begin within a few hours of the last dose and may continue for weeks. Symptoms vary, but prominent ones include: craving for nicotine, irritability, frustration, or anger, anxiety, depression, difficulty concentrating, restlessness, increased appetite or weight gain (APA, 1987; Glassman, Jackson et al., 1988). The prominent signs of nicotine withdrawal involve decreased heart rate and EEG changes (USDHHS, 1988).

The tobacco withdrawal syndrome often is distressing but is not in itself life-threatening. It is promptly relieved by the ingestion of nicotine. Nicotine withdrawal is best understood as a process of reversing neuronal adaptation to nicotine when nicotine levels decline below those to which the brain has become accustomed.

ABSORPTION AND METABOLISM

According to William L. Dunn, Jr., of the Philip Morris Company, ". . . [T]he cigarette is . . . among the most awe-inspiring examples of the ingenuity of man. . . . The cigarette should be conceived not as a product but as a package. The product is nicotine. The cigarette is but one of many package layers. There is the carton, which contains the pack, which contains the cigarette, which contains the smoke. The smoke is the final package. The smoker must strip off all these package layers to get to that which he seeks. . . . Smoke is beyond question the most optimized vehicle of nicotine and the cigarette the most optimized dispenser of smoke" (1972).

The absorption of nicotine depends on pH. At an alkaline pH, unionized nicotine is readily absorbed across either the buccal or the nasal mucosa (Benowitz, 1988; USDHHS, 1988; Henningfield, Radzius et al., 1990). Tobacco products such as cigars, many pipe tobaccos, snuffs and chewing tobaccos present nicotine either as a unionized, vaporized component of smoke or as an alkaline solution of nicotine. In either case, nicotine readily crosses into the capillary bed of the mucous membrane. Alkaline smoke is difficult to inhale because of the irritating qualities of nicotine on the pharynx. (Individuals who switch from cigarettes to cigars or pipes still tend to inhale [Ockene, Pechacek et al., 1987]. This only makes these products more toxic: merely switching from one tobacco product to another is not a safe strategy.)

Smoke from cigarettes and from some pipe tobaccos has an acidic pH. The nicotine in these smokes is ionized and hence is largely dissolved in the aerosol droplets rather than contained in the

TABLE 3. Other Health Problems Related to Tobacco Use

Toxic to User
- Fatal fires
- Peptic ulcer disease
- Burger's disease
- Asthma
- Impotence (men)
- Reduced fertility (women)
- Impaired ability to sustain lactation (women)
- Early menopause (women)
- Oropharyngeal cancers
- Gum recession
- Cataracts
- Impaired wound healing
- Immune suppression
- Impaired mucociliary clearance
- Earlier development of pneumonia in HIV-infected individuals
- Synergy with radon and asbestos in causing lung cancer
- Reduced athletic performance
- Impaired cognitive performance
- Wrinkles

Toxic to Persons Near User
- Fatal fires
- Bronchitis and pneumonia (small children)
- Middle ear effusions (small children)
- Asthma
- Reduced athletic performance
- Reduced performance on standardized achievement tests
- Low birth weight babies
- SIDS

vapor phase. Nicotine in this form is not absorbed across the buccal or nasal mucosa but, because the throat does not perceive these smokes as harsh (compared to cigar smoke), they can be inhaled. The ionized nicotine then is readily absorbed across the respiratory epithelium of the pulmonary alveoli.

Nicotine absorbed in the lungs crosses into the pulmonary venous system. This gives it more rapid access to the brain than nicotine which is absorbed in the mouth. Moreover, inhaling cigarette smoke results in relatively large, brief surges of nicotine in the carotid arteries. Thus, Henningfield, London and Benowitz (1990) found that arterial nicotine levels after smoking a single cigarette were about 60 ng/ml, while simultaneous venous levels were but a third of that amount. The rapid, finely tuned access that nicotine from cigarette smoke has to central nicotinic receptors leads to the observation that cigarettes are more addicting than other tobacco products.

Cigarettes on the U.S. market have a wide range of nicotine delivery (Slade, 1993b). However, except for the "ultra-low" brands, the machine-rated yields bear little relationship to the nicotine levels observed in consumers (Benowitz, Hall et al., 1983). People smoke in ways that largely compensate for the engineering tricks that reduce the amount of nicotine deposited on a filter pad in a smoking machine.

Nicotine is readily absorbed in the stomach, but first-pass metabolism in the liver severely limits the amount of the drug reaching the brain. However, gastrointestinal symptoms that occur in some patients who use nicotine gum probably are related to nicotine dissolved in saliva. (This problem can be minimized by chewing nicotine gum sparingly and keeping it parked between the cheek and gum most of the time. This facilitates buccal absorption.)

Nicotine is readily absorbed across the skin. This is the basis for an occupational illness in tobacco croppers and harvesters, called green tobacco sickness (Boylan, Brandt et al., 1993), as well as the basis for the design of nicotine patches (Jarvik & Henningfield, 1993).

In the body, nicotine has a half life of two hours (USDHHS, 1988). Much of it is transformed into a variety of pharmacologically inactive metabolites, but some is excreted unchanged. The most abundant metabolite is cotinine, which has a half life of 18 hours. Assays for cotinine levels in plasma and urine are available from clinical laboratories. The test can be used as a semi-quantitative index of recent nicotine ingestion. A result below detection limits indicates no tobacco consumption in recent days, but commercially available tests usually are not sensitive enough to detect cotinine derived from nicotine absorbed from environmental tobacco smoke (ETS) (EPA, 1992).

MECHANISMS OF ACTION

Nicotine acts at central and peripheral nicotinic cholinergic receptors, of which there are several subtypes. It is able to act as both an agonist and an antagonist (Rosencrans & Karan, 1993). Its reinforcing actions are thought to be related to central stimulation of these receptors, but Ginzel (1987) has suggested that the peripheral stimulation of vagal nicotinic receptors in the lung by inhaled nicotine also is important in understanding the effects of nicotine on the brain. Cholinergic presynaptic and postsynaptic receptors on neurons in dopaminergic and serotonergic pathways suggest other ways nicotine may act on the brain (Rosencrans & Karan, 1993). It is able to modulate both inhibitory and excitatory elements of a variety of neural pathways. The fact that clonidine ameliorates symptoms of the nicotine withdrawal syndrome (Glassman, Jackson et al., 1984) indicates that nicotine affects some of the same neural pathways as opiates and sedative-hypnotic drugs.

REINFORCING PROPERTIES

In *The Picture of Dorian Gray,* Oscar Wilde observed that "A cigarette is the perfect type of a perfect pleasure. It is exquisite, and it leaves one unsatisfied" (Wilde, n.d.).

Smoking a pack of cigarettes a day for a year results in delivery of 73,000 doses of nicotine to the brain. These doses are not administered at random. Rather, they are paired with an astonishing array of external and internal cues (Fisher, Lichtenstein & Haire-Joshu, 1993). The fantastic amount of conditioning that occurs as tobacco use insinuates itself into every part of an individual's life is at least partially responsible for the fact that those who have been addicted to a variety of drugs often rate nicotine as the most difficult to stop (Henningfield, Radzius et al., 1991).

Nicotine fosters its own self-administration by both positive and negative reinforcement (USDHHS, 1988; Collins, 1990). Relief of withdrawal is the most widely recognized negative reinforcer. On the positive side, the potential for nicotine to induce pleasurable subjective states ("euphoria") often is described by users and has been demonstrated experimentally (Pomerleau & Pomerleau, 1992).

REFERENCES

American Psychiatric Association (1987). *Diagnostic and Statistical Manual, 3rd Edition, Revised.* Washington, DC: American Psychiatric Press.

Benowitz NL (1991). Nicotine replacement therapy during pregnancy. *Journal of the American Medical Association* 266:3174–3177.

Benowitz NL (1988). Pharmacologic aspects of cigarette smoking and nicotine addiction. *The New England Journal of Medicine* 319:1318–1330.

Benowitz NL, Hall SM, Herning RI, Jacob PIII, Jones RT & Osman A-L (1983). Smokers of low-yield cigarettes do not consume less nicotine. *The New England Journal of Medicine* 309:139–142.

Boylan B, Brandt V, Muehlbauer J, Auslander M, Spurlock C & Finger R (1993). Green tobacco sickness in tobacco harvesters—Kentucky, 1992. *Morbidity and Mortality Weekly Reports* 42:237–240.

Blot WJ, McLaughlin JK, Winn DM et al. (1988). Smoking and drinking in relation to oral and pharyngeal cancer. *Cancer Research* 48:3282–3287.

Centers for Disease Control (1991). Smoking-attributable mortality and years of potential life lost—United States. *Morbidity and Mortality Weekly Report* 40:62–71.

Collins AC (1990). An analysis of the addiction liability of nicotine. In CK Erikson, MA Javors & WW Morgan (eds.) *Addiction Potential of Abused Drugs and Drug Classes.* New York, NY: The Haworth Press, 83–103.

Environmental Protection Agency (EPA) (1992). *Respiratory Health Effects of Passive Smoking: Lung Cancer and Other Disorders.* Washington, DC: U.S. Environmental Protection Agency, Office of Research and Development and Office of Air and Radiation (EPA/600/6-90/006F).

Fisher EB, Lichtenstein E & Haire-Joshu D (1993). Multiple determinants of tobacco use and cessation. In CT Orleans & J Slade (eds.) *Nicotine Addiction: Principles and Management.* New York, NY: Oxford University Press.

Ginzel KH (1987). The lungs as sites of origin of nicotine-induced skeletomotor relaxation and behavioral and electrocortical arousal in the cat. In MJ Rand & K Thurau (eds.) *The Pharmacology of Nicotine.* Oxford, England: IRL Press, 269–292.

Glantz SA & Parmley WW (1991). Passive smoking and heart disease. *Circulation* 83:1–12.

Glassman AH, Jackson WK, Walsh T, Roose SP & Rosenfeld B (1984). Cigarette craving, smoking withdrawal, and clonidine. *Science* 266:864–866.

Glassman AH, Stetner F, Walsh T, Raizman PS, Fleiss JL, Cooper TB & Covey LS (1984). Heavy smokers, smoking cessation, and clonidine. *Journal of the American Medical Association* 259:2863–66.

Gruneberg NE, Bowen DJ, Maycock DA & Nespor SM (1985). The importance of sweet taste and caloric contents in the effects of nicotine on specific food consumption. *Psychopharmacology* 87:198–203.

Henningfield JE, Cohen C & Slade JD (1991). Is nicotine more addictive than cocaine? *British Journal of Addiction* 86:565–569.

Henningfield JE, London ED & Benowitz NL (1990). Arterial-venous differences in plasma concentrations of nicotine after cigarette smoking. *Journal of the American Medical Association* 263:2049–2050.

Henningfield JE, Radzius A, Cooper TM & Clayton RR (1990). Drinking coffee and carbonated beverages blocks absorption of nicotine from nicotine polacrilex gum. *Journal of the American Medical Association* 264:1560–1564.

Hurt RD, Eberman KM, Slade J & Karan L (1993). Treating nicotine dependence in patients with other addictive disorders. In CT Orleans & J Slade (eds.) *Nicotine Addiction: Principles and Management*. New York, NY: Oxford University Press.

Jarvik ME & Henningfield JE (1993). Pharmacological adjuncts for the treatment of tobacco dependence. In CT Orleans & J Slade (eds.) *Nicotine Addiction: Principles and Management*. New York, NY: Oxford University Press.

Klatsky AL & Armstrong MA (1992). Alcohol, smoking, coffee, and cirrhosis. *American Journal of Epidemiology* 136:1248–1257.

Levin ED, Karan L & Rosecrans J (1993). Nicotine: An addictive drug with therapeutic potential. *Medicinal Chemistry Research*.

MacInnes CM (1926). *The Early English Tobacco Trade*. London, England: Kegan Paul, Trench, Trubner & Co., Ltd., 19–20.

McGuire A (1989). Fires, cigarettes and advocacy. *Law, Medicine and Health Care* 17:73–77.

Ockene JK, Pechacek TF, Vogt T & Svendsen K (1987). Does switching from cigarettes to pipes or cigars reduce tobacco smoke exposure? *American Journal of Public Health* 77:1412–1416.

O'Shea MV (1923). *Tobacco and Mental Efficiency*. New York, NY: Macmillan.

Pitchumoni CS, Jain NK, Lowenfels AB & DiMagno EP (1988). Chronic cyanide poisoning: Unifying concept for alcoholic and tropical pancreatitis. *Pancreas* 3:220–222.

Pomerleau CS & Pomerleau OF (1992). Euphoriant effects of nicotine in smokers. *Psychopharmacology* 108:460–165.

Robinson JH & Pritchard WS (1992). The role of nicotine in tobacco use. *Psychopharmacology* 108:397–407.

Robinson JH, Pritchard WS & Davis RA (1992). Psychopharmacological effects of smoking a cigarette with typical "tar" and carbon monoxide yields but minimal nicotine. *Psychopharmacology* 108:466–472.

Rosencrans JA & Karan L (1993). Neurobehavioral mechanisms of nicotine action: Role in the initiation and maintenance of tobacco dependence. *Journal of Substance Abuse Treatment* 10:161–170.

Schrumpf-Pierron P (1927). *Tobacco & Physical Efficiency*. New York, NY: Paul B. Hoeber, Inc.

Slade J (1993a). Adolescent nicotine use and dependence. *Adolescent Medicine: State of the Art Reviews* 4(2).

Slade J (1993b). Nicotine delivery devices. In CT Orleans & J Slade (eds.) *Nicotine Addiction: Principles and Management*. New York, NY: Oxford University Press.

Spilich GJ, June L & Renner J (1992). Cigarette smoking and cognitive performance. *British Journal of Addiction* 87:1313–1326.

U.S. Department of Health and Human Services (1989). *Reducing the Health Consequences of Smoking: 25 Years of Progress. A Report of the Surgeon General.* Rockville, MD: Office on Smoking and Health.

U.S. Department of Health and Human Services (1988). *The Health Consequences of Smoking: Nicotine Addiction: A Report of the Surgeon General*. Rockville, MD: Office on Smoking and Health.

U.S. Department of Health and Human Services (1982). *The Health Consequences of Smoking: Cancer. A Report of the Surgeon General*. Rockville, MD: Office on Smoking and Health.

Warburton DM, Revell A, Walters AC (1988). Nicotine as a resource. In MJ Rand & K Thurau (eds.) *The Pharmacology of Nicotine*. Oxford, England: IRL Press, 359–374.

CHAPTER 7

The Pharmacology of Phencyclidine and the Hallucinogens

Marilyn Carroll, Ph.D.
Sandra Comer, Ph.D.

Drugs in the Class
Therapeutic Use and Misuse
Adverse Effects
Addiction Liability
Absorption and Metabolism
Mechanisms of Action
Reinforcing Properties

This chapter reviews the pharmacology of phencyclidine (PCP), lysergic acid diethylamide (LSD) and other drugs that are commonly known as hallucinogens (although PCP and its congeners are from a different class of drugs, the dissociative anesthetics).

DRUGS IN THE CLASS

Hallucinogens consist of a variety of compounds that alter perceptions and feelings (see Table 1). In fact, they only rarely produce hallucinations. The hallucinogenic drugs are similar in that they produce similar subjective effects, there is some cross-tolerance among them, and they respond in similar ways to antagonists. Gilman and colleagues (1990) have classified hallucinogens into five categories: (1) LSD-like drugs, including mescaline, psilocybin and psilocin; (2) drugs that probably are LSD-like, such as DMA, DOM and DMT; (3) drugs that probably are LSD-like and have other properties, such as MDMA (5-methoxy-3, 4-methylenedioxyamphetamine), MDA (3,4-methylenedioxyamphetamine, and other amphetamine derivatives); (4) drugs that probably are not LSD-like, such as 5-hydroxytryptophan; and (5) drugs that are not LSD-like, such as scopolamine and delta 9-THC (Gilman, Goodman et al., 1990). Drugs to be discussed in this chapter include those that are similar to LSD and MDMA, as they are the most commonly abused hallucinogens.

THERAPEUTIC USE AND MISUSE

PCP-like Drugs. PCP-like drugs initially were thought to have scientific value, as they might be used in animal studies to simulate a condition similar to schizophrenia and thereby serve as a model for testing various treatment agents. It was noted very early after PCP was developed that it produced schizophrenic symptoms in normal human subjects and enhanced the disorder in schizophrenic patients. However, research in this area has not advanced, and recent interest in PCP-like drugs has shifted to its pharmacology as it relates to the NMDA receptor complex. PCP-like drugs currently are under investigation for their therapeutic potential in preventing neurological damage due to ischemia. By blocking the release of excitatory amino acids such as glutamate and aspartate, NMDA antagonists (including PCP and dizocilpine) could protect against brain damage resulting from stroke (Olney, Labruyere & Price, 1989).

However, these drugs may have neurotoxic effects of their own. A recent study indicated that their damaging side effects might be minimized by anticholinergics, such as scopolamine, or by drugs such as diazepam or barbiturates that act at the GABA receptor-channel complex (Olney, Labruyere & Price, 1989).

Abuse of phencyclidine, mainly in pill form, peaked in the late 1970s and markedly declined throughout the 1980s and 1990s. The most common route of administration at present is smoking. Phen-

TABLE 1. Hallucinogenic Drugs

Phencyclidine (PCP)

LSD-like drugs
Indolealkylamines
lysergic acid diethylamide (LSD)
psilocybin
psilocyn

Phenylethylamines
mescaline
peyote

Drugs that probably are LSD-like
diethyltryptamine (DET)
dimethyltryptamine (DMT)

Drugs that probably are LSD-like and have other properties
Phenylisopropylamines
3,4-methylenedioxyamphetamine (MDA)
3,4-methylenedioxyethamphetamine (MDEA)
5-methoxy-3,4-methylenedioxymethamphetamine (MDMA)
3-methoxy-4,5-methylenedioxyamphetamine (MMDA)

Drugs that probably are not LSD-like
5-hydroxytryptophan

Drugs that are not LSD-like
Mappine
Nutmeg, mace
Morning glory seeds
Scopolamine

Source: Gilman AG, Goodman LS, Rall TW & Murad F (1990). *Goodman & Gilman's The Pharmacological Basis of Therapeutics, 8th Edition*. New York, NY: Macmillan, 553–557.

cyclidine often is added to marijuana cigarettes, and it is commonly consumed with alcoholic beverages. Street names for PCP are "angel dust" or "crystal," as well as "space base" when it is combined with cocaine.

PCP remains a Schedule II drug, although it is not currently manufactured in the United States except by government contract for animal research.

LSD-like Drugs. LSD also was of interest initially because it was thought that it might be used as an animal model of psychosis, but this line of research was not pursued. Another area of therapeutic interest in LSD involved its use as a psychotherapeutic adjunct to access the subconscious thought processes. LSD also was investigated as a potentially useful treatment for alcoholism (Hollister, Shelton & Krieger, 1969), but its effects were transitory. Finally, at one time LSD was considered as a therapeutic agent for terminal cancer patients, to aid in contemplation and acceptance of their mortality.

LSD-like drugs currently have no therapeutic use and have been placed in federal Schedule I.

MDMA-like Drugs. Psychiatrists were interested in MDA in the 1970s and MDMA in the 1980s as adjuncts to psychotherapy. They felt that the drugs promoted empathy, thus facilitating psychoanalytic work. While the drugs were quietly used in such settings for several years, and several psychiatrists brought litigation in an effort to have the drugs rescheduled to make them more widely available, there currently is no acceptable therapeutic use of MDMA-like drugs and they have been federally classified in Schedule I.

ADVERSE EFFECTS

PCP-like Drugs. There is little evidence that chronic PCP use in adult humans (Luisada, 1981) and monkeys (U.S. Public Health Service, 1993) results in any detectable organ or cellular damage. In monkeys that self-administered PCP for eight years, tests of all organ systems, clinical chemistries, physical examinations and x-rays found no differences between PCP-experienced monkeys and aged-matched control animals. In humans, the form of toxicity most commonly associated with PCP use is behavioral: the rare accounts of PCP toxicity describe it as involving bizarre and/or violent behavior. Such reports have diminished since the preferred route of self-administration has shifted from oral to inhalation, with the attending ability to more carefully titrate dose.

The immediate effects of PCP in humans are not seen in the clinical setting. Instead, the PCP user arrives in the emergency room several hours after drug ingestion, possibly while suffering acute withdrawal effects. Approximately 12 to 15 hours after PCP ingestion, monkeys become agitated, violent and aggressive. It is possible that many of the early reports of human violence and PCP-related homicides were related to the withdrawal effects rather than drug intoxication. It is important to determine the time course of aberrant behavior, although this is difficult to accomplish because use of the drug often provokes retrograde amnesia for the drug-taking event.

Another unusual aspect of PCP toxicity is that users often complain of dysphoric effects long after chronic use has stopped. These reports may be attributed to the fact that PCP is highly fat soluble and is stored for long periods of time in the body fat. During periods of weight loss, there is subsequent mobilization of lipid-stored PCP into blood and brain tissues. Recent laboratory research with rats supports this hypothesis by demonstrating the ability of food deprivation to increase PCP levels in plasma and the brain (Coveney & Sparber, 1990).

A growing body of data on the effects of drugs on the offspring of drug-dependent mothers suggests that the offspring of PCP users may be more vulnerable to adverse effects of PCP than their adult counterparts. Golden and colleagues (1987) studied 94 PCP-exposed neonates and 94 controls and found neurological abnormalities, such as hypertonia and depressed neonatal reflexes, in the exposed group. Another study, which followed 12 exposed infants for 18 months, found a high percentage of medical problems (Howard, Kropenske & Tyler, 1986). At six months, the infants were irritable and hyperresponsive, and later they showed varying degrees of abnormalities in fine-motor, adaptive, language and social skills. A recent study of the offspring of 47 PCP abusers and 38 nonusers found that neurological dysfunction was common in the infants of PCP-abusing mothers (Howard, Kropenske & Tyler, 1986), involving greater apathy, irritability, jitters and abnormal muscle tone and reflexes. Follow-up interviews at six and 15 months, using the Gesell Developmental Exam, revealed impoverished language and lower developmental quotients; however, the long-term outcome for PCP-exposed neonates is not known.

LSD-like Drugs. The effects of LSD-like drugs can occur shortly after oral ingestion, usually within an hour. The duration of action may vary with the type of drug ingested. For example, the effects of LSD may last up to three days, while the effects of psylocybin, psilocin or mescaline may be of a shorter duration, approximately eight to 12 hours. LSD also is 100 times more potent than the other drugs mentioned above. LSD-like drugs are known to cause perceptual changes or "flashbacks" at extended intervals after their use has been terminated. Flashbacks occur in approximately 23% to 63% percent of regular users (Hollister, 1984; Jaffe, 1989).

In addition to the subjective effects of LSD-like drugs, there are physiological side effects such as increased blood pressure, tachycardia, palpitations, tremor, nausea, piloerection, muscle weakness, increased body temperature, blurred vision and ataxia. Contrary to initial reports that gained media attention, there is little scientific evidence that LSD produces congenital abnormalities or that it causes spontaneous abortions.

Regular use of LSD-like drugs has been related to three psychiatric disorders (American Psychiatric Association, 1987):

- A delusional disorder may develop soon after use. It can have a short duration or lead to a protracted schizophrenic-like disorder with persecutory delusions.
- A hallucinogenic mood disorder may result soon after drug use and last for at least 24 hours. (In severe cases, suicide may be attempted.)
- A posthallucination perceptual disorder, characterized by severe flashbacks that lead to major depression, panic disorder and/or suicide, also is seen.

MDMA-like Drugs. MDMA-like drugs produce euphoria, consisting of psychedelic effects like those of mescaline and stimulant effects like those of amphetamine (Seiden & Ricaurte, 1987). These effects last four to six hours, but other subjective effects (such as confusion, depression and anxiety) may last for weeks, even after a single dose. Psychiatric disorders such as chronic paranoid psychosis have been found to result from the use of MDMA-like drugs. Recently, a laboratory study indicated that L-tryptophan produced a rise in serum prolactin levels in controls but not in MDMA users, which suggests a blunting of the serotonergic system (Price, Ricaurte et al., 1989). These findings are consistent with data from animal studies, showing that MDMA-like drugs deplete serotonin and cause degeneration of serotonin nerve terminals (Slikker, Ali et al., 1988).

A number of physiological side effects have been reported after use of MDMA-like drugs, including hyperthermia, cardiac arrest and a blood disorder that affects coagulation (coagulopathy). Studies of physiological changes in animals have focused on alterations in serotonin systems, as noted. There also has been considerable interest in the effects of MDMA-like drugs in the offspring of female rats treated during pregnancy. In a study of the offspring of MDMA-treated pregnant rats, St. Omer and colleagues (1991) found significant retardation of growth and maturational markers, although 5HT levels were not altered in the pups. Others have reported depressed firing of serotonin neurons and reduced food and fluid intake in rat pups. Still others (Grob, Bravo & Walsh, 1990) have minimized the significance of these findings in rats, on the grounds that (1) much higher doses are used in rat studies than the doses typically used by human users; (2) the long-term animal studies indicate that regeneration of damaged serotonin neurons occurs; and (3) MDMA-induced serotonergic neurotoxicity has not been demonstrated clinically. There are no reports of sleep, mood, appetite, sexual or aggressive disorders in chronic MDMA users or in those who have undergone long-term therapy for weight control with fenfluramine (a drug with serotonin neurotoxicity potential at least three times greater than MDMA).

ADDICTION LIABILITY

Tolerance. *PCP-like Drugs:* Tolerance to a drug effect is said to occur when there is a decreased effect after repeated administration of a particular dose of a drug, or when an increasing drug dose is required to produce the same level of drug effect that was previously achieved with a smaller dose. Although systematic studies have not been conducted, chronic PCP users report that they increase their use of PCP over time, and burn patients require increasing doses of ketamine after repeated administration (see Carroll, 1990). More systematic studies using laboratory animals showed that tolerance developed to the effects of PCP on schedule-controlled responding (Smith, 1991), to the effects of both PCP and dizocilpine on adrenocorticotropin and corticosterone release (Pechnick, George & Poland, 1989), and to the cataleptic effects of both PCP and ketamine (Lu, France & Woods, 1992). Tolerance to the effects of PCP and PCP-like drugs presumably is mediated through NMDA receptors, as reported by Manallack, Lodge and Beart (1989), who showed that repeated administration of dizocilpine produced a reduction in the number of cortical NMDA receptors that was correlated with tolerance to some of the behavioral effects produced by dizocilpine. However, other investigators have suggested that different receptor systems are involved in PCP-induced tolerance (Nabeshima, Fukaya et al., 1987). Further studies are needed to evaluate the extent to which the various receptor systems are involved in tolerance produced by PCP and related compounds.

In addition to tolerance that occurs to the effects of PCP-like compounds themselves, recent studies have demonstrated that these compounds also alter morphine-induced tolerance. Although dizocilpine did not alter the analgesic effects produced by acute morphine administration, it did attenuate the development of tolerance to the analgesic effects of morphine (Trujillo & Akil, 1991). Other noncompetitive NMDA antagonists also alter the development of tolerance to morphine-induced analgesia (Hance, Winters et al., 1989), which further suggests that an interaction between noncompetitive NMDA antagonists and the development of tolerance to various opioids exists. Recent studies also have suggested that dizocilpine inhibits the development of tolerance to ethanol (Khanna, Wu et al., 1991) and that it inhibits the development of sensitization to the effects of amphetamine and cocaine (Karler, Clader et al., 1989).

LSD and MDMA-like Drugs: Experimental evidence from laboratory animals has demonstrated that tolerance occurs after repeated administration of LSD, MDMA and related hallucinogens. In laboratory studies, both LSD and mescaline produced increases in the rate and duration of myoclonic jumping behavior (MJB) in rodents (Carvey, Nausieda et al., 1989). Tolerance to MJB rapidly developed after repeated administration of either LSD or mescaline, and cross-tolerance between the two compounds occurred. Tolerance also developed rapidly (within five days) to similar behavioral disruptions that were produced in nonhuman primates after administration of LSD, MDA, mescaline or psilocin (Schlemmer & Davis, 1986). The ability of these hallucinogens to produce behavioral disruptions was highly correlated with their hallucinogenic potencies. In addition, the time course of the development of tolerance to the behavioral effects in nonhuman primates paralleled the development of tolerance to the hallucinogenic effects of these compounds in humans.

Physical Dependence. *PCP-like Drugs:* Physical dependence is characterized by a set of withdrawal signs that follow a specific time course when drug administration is discontinued. The withdrawal signs may be rapidly reversed after acute administration of the drug. Most of what we know about PCP dependence is from experimental studies with animals, since there are only limited reports of drug withdrawal effects in humans. A 1981 study by Tennant and colleagues of 68 chronic PCP users found that one-third of the subjects had sought treatment or medication during a PCP abstinence phase. Withdrawal symptoms that were widely reported involved depression, drug craving, increased appetite and increased need for sleep.

Another way PCP dependence has been documented in humans is in studies of neonates born to PCP-using mothers. Withdrawal signs noted in the infants include diarrhea, poor feeding, irritability, hypertonic reflexes, high-pitched cry and inability to visually track. Similar signs of PCP withdrawal have been noted in laboratory studies with monkeys. Balster and Woolverton (1980) gave rhesus monkeys continuous access to PCP through an intravenous cannula system for 50 days. The monkeys' responses on a lever resulted in PCP infusions. When PCP was replaced with physiological saline, withdrawal signs were apparent, including poor feeding, weight loss, irritability, bruxism, vocalizations, piloerection, tremors, preconvulsive activity, reduced exploratory behavior and impaired motor coordination. The withdrawal syndrome began within four to eight hours after the last infusion of PCP, peaked between 12 and 16 hours, and had dissipated by 24 to 48 hours. These results have been repeated in studies with rats (Wessinger, 1987). Some studies have reported PCP withdrawal effects after as little as two weeks of exposure.

Recent studies with animals have shown that not only a short period of exposure to PCP but low doses result in withdrawal effects when drug administration is terminated. Operant conditioning experiments, in which food deliveries are contingent upon responses on a lever or other manipulandum, are used as sensitive indicators of drug withdrawal effects. A withdrawal-induced suppression in operant responding for food often is seen after termination of doses that produce no observable signs of withdrawal. (These measures also have been used to demonstrate withdrawal effects from drugs that produce no observable signs of withdrawal during abstinence, such as cocaine, caffeine and nicotine.) The most severe reductions in the operant behavioral baselines occurred during the first 48 hours of drug withdrawal, a time when physical signs occur when higher maintenance doses are used. However, the behavioral disruptions often last for protracted periods of time. Although animals reduce their amount of responding on a lever for food, they readily consume food when they are hand-fed. Thus, the decrease in feeding may not be due to illness, but instead may be a motivational deficit that interferes with the ability to work for food.

In the first study that demonstrated disruption in operant behavior during PCP withdrawal, Slifer and colleagues (1984) treated monkeys with continuous intravenous infusions for 10 days; they were required to make 100 responses on a lever for each food pellet. When access to PCP was terminated, the monkeys' responding for food decreased substantially for up to seven days and did not return to normal levels until PCP administration was reestablished. Similar results were found by other investigators, who used monkeys trained to self-administer orally-delivered PCP (there was little difference in the results between self-administered or experimenter-administered PCP). In the monkey studies, there was only a weak relationship between dose and magnitude of the withdrawal effect; the PCP dose, blood levels and magnitude of withdrawal effect were most closely related in rats.

Recent studies have shown that there is cross-dependence between PCP and ketamine, dizocilpine and the (+) isomer of SKF-10,047; however, cross-dependence was not demonstrated with either the (−) isomer or the racemate of SKF-10,047 or with ethanol.

Altering schedule parameters also has been tested with regard to the magnitude of PCP withdrawal-induced behavioral disruptions. In one study in rats, a fixed-ratio (FR) and fixed-interval (FI) schedule were compared. Although the two schedules generated response rates of 0.85 or 0.37 responses per second, and response rates markedly decreased during PCP withdrawal, the two schedules produced similar effects. In contrast, in another study with monkeys, FRs for food were increased from 64 to 128 to 256 to 512 to 1024, with PCP withdrawal effects examined at each value (Carroll & Carmona, 1991). As the FR value increased, PCP withdrawal effects became more pronounced. However, at the two higher FRs, body weights declined and the magnitude of the withdrawal effect showed no further increases.

To examine the effects of food availability, another experiment was conducted in which the FR was held constant at 1024 and the monkeys were either supplemented with 100 g of hand-fed food or not. The amount of responding for earned food remained the same during supplemented and unsupplemented conditions, but when the effects of withdrawal were examined, a disruption in responding occurred only under the supplemented condition. When the monkeys had to earn their entire daily food ration, the withdrawal effect disappeared. These studies suggest that the severity of the PCP withdrawal effect is determined by the behavioral economics of food availability. The magnitude of PCP withdrawal increased as the price (FR of food) increased, but as the price became so high that body weight was lost, the PCP withdrawal effect entirely disappeared. These data support the hypothesis that PCP withdrawal is not an illness state *per se*, but that it affects motivated behaviors.

The results of drug treatment studies during the PCP withdrawal syndrome have been mixed. When monkeys had access to orally-delivered (+)SKF-10,047, the PCP withdrawal-induced disruptions in food-maintained responding were reversed. This was not the case with (−) SKF-10,047 or the racemate of SKF-10,047. Injections of dizocilpine before PCP withdrawal or two days into PCP withdrawal greatly reduced or reversed, respectively, the disruptions in food-reinforced responding. Dizocilpine also dose-dependently reduced PCP self-administration. In contrast, while buprenorphine (a partial mu opiate agonist) also dose-dependently reduced PCP self-administration, it had no effect on PCP withdrawal-induced disruptions in food-maintained responding. When PCP was self-administered concurrently with ethanol and then PCP access was removed, PCP withdrawal effects were as severe as when ethanol had not been available. Thus, ethanol did not alleviate the PCP withdrawal effect, although PCP and ethanol share discriminative stimulus effects (Grant, Knisley et al., 1991).

In other studies, PCP was self-administered concurrently with ethanol or caffeine. When the two drugs were removed simultaneously, the withdrawal disruption was more severe than when PCP was concurrently available with water and PCP alone was withdrawn. Further details of these withdrawal studies may be found in reviews by Willetts, Balster & Leander (1990), Carroll (1990) and the U.S. Public Health Service (1993).

LSD and MDMA-like Drugs: There is no clinical or laboratory evidence of withdrawal effects when access to LSD-or MDMA-like drugs is terminated. This lack of evidence may be due to the fact that these drugs are not used at frequent intervals or in large amounts. Infrequent use may be due to the dysphoric effects sometimes experienced with these drugs.

ABSORPTION AND METABOLISM

PCP-like Drugs. PCP use in humans occurs through either intranasal, intravenous, oral or inhalational routes of administration. The time to peak plasma concentration after oral administration of PCP is 1.5 hours. The bioavailability of PCP by this route of administration is between 50% and 90% (see Busto, Bendayan & Sellers, 1989, for a review). Both PCP and a pyrolytic product, 1-phenylcyclohexene (PC), are absorbed from smoke condensate from parsley cigarettes containing PCP. Peak plasma concentrations occur within 5 to 10 minutes after PCP is smoked, sometimes followed by a second peak one to three hours after inhalation occurs.

The majority of PCP is excreted in urine after intravenous, intranasal and oral administration (Busto, Bendayan & Sellers, 1989). Approximately 20% of the drug is eliminated in urine as PCP, while 80% of the excreted fraction is composed of metabolites (principally 4-phenyl-4-(1-piperidinyl) cyclohexanol), which also are pharmacologically active. Renal clearance of PCP, which is a weak base, depends on both urine pH and on urine flow rate. Under normal urinary pH levels, PCP is eliminated mainly by metabolic processes. However, renal elimination of PCP is slowed when urine is alkalinized and accelerated when urine is acidified. Moreover, when urine output is increased by increasing fluids or by the use of diuretics (e.g., furosemide), renal elimination of PCP also increases. Thus, in the event of PCP overdose, urine acidification and high fluid elimination would increase the elimination of PCP.

Hallucinogens. Several investigators have proposed that MDA-(a major metabolite of MDMA in humans, rodents, and nonhuman primates) is metabolized from MDMA by N-demethylation (Fitzgerald, Blanke et al., 1989; Gollamudi, Ali et al., 1989), although the exact mechanism of this reaction is unclear. While both enantiomers of MDA are formed from MDMA, higher levels of the S(+) isomer of MDA are produced—a significant finding, since the S(+) isomer of MDA (and, to some extent, the R(−) isomer), has been shown to produce a pronounced neurotoxic effect in a number of species. The parent compound, MDMA, also produces a profound neurotoxic effect in laboratory animals. For example, a single subcutaneous injection of MDMA (10 mg/kg) produced a rapid decrease in the enzymatic activity of tryptophan hydroxylase (the rate-limiting enzyme for serotonin biosynthesis) in several brain regions in rats, including the frontal cortex, neostriatum, hippocampus and hypothalamus (Stone, Merchant et al., 1987). Concentrations of 5HT and its metabolite, 5-HIAA, subsequently were reduced in these brain areas. Complete recovery of tryptophan hydroxylase activity did not occur for up to two weeks following the single injection of 10.0 mg/kg MDMA, although 5-HT and 5-HIAA levels returned to control levels by 24 hours after administration of MDMA.

Repeated administration of MDMA (five injections of either 5.0 or 10.0 mg/kg over a 24-hour period) produced a decrease in 5-HT, 5HIAA and tryptophan hydroxylase activity that lasted for up to 110 days. Only transient effects on dopamine systems were noted in this study. Thus, doses of MDMA that were only approximately three to four times greater than that of an acute dose in humans produced a robust, long-acting influence on the serotonergic system.

Several other phenolic and methoxy metabolites are formed from MDMA, including *a*-methyldopamine (which may, in turn, be metabolized to the neurotoxin, 6-hydroxydopamine; Yousif, Fitzgerald et al., 1990). Although it appears fairly clear that administration of either MDMA or MDA results in neurotoxicity in laboratory animals, it is not clear whether it is the substances themselves or their metabolic products that are directly responsible for this neurotoxicity. Further experiments will be helpful in our understanding of the mechanism(s) responsible for MDMA-induced neurotoxicity. Very little is known about the metabolism of LSD.

MECHANISMS OF ACTION

PCP-like Drugs. Many of the behavioral effects produced by PCP are mediated through the N-methyl-D-aspartate (NMDA) excitatory amino acid receptor-channel complex. When either glutamate or NMDA binds to the receptor, the associated channel opens, allowing sodium, calcium and potassium ions to flow into and out of the cell. Under certain conditions, this movement of ions across the cell membrane causes the neuron to "fire," which is a means of communication between adjacent neurons. PCP (as well as TCP, ketamine, dizocilpine and SKF10,047) acts as a noncompetitive antagonist at the NMDA receptor complex. PCP, which binds to a site within the channel, physically prevents the movement of ions across the cell membrane and, in turn, results in a decrease in neuronal firing. However, the binding of PCP within the channel cannot occur unless the channel is initially opened by glutamate, NMDA or other NMDA-like agonists. This requirement was verified experimentally in receptor binding studies, which found that PCP binding was enhanced by NMDA receptor agonists and inhibited by competitive antagonists (see Zukin & Javitt, 1985).

While the noncompetitive antagonists bind to a site within the channel, competitive antagonists such as CGS 19755, NPC 12626, CPP and AP5 bind to the NMDA receptor itself, which resides on the extracellular side of the membrane. Competitive antagonists directly inhibit the excitatory effect of NMDA by binding to the NMDA receptor without opening the channel, which reduces the probability that NMDA or glutamate will bind to and activate the receptor. Both competitive and noncompetitive antagonists are similar in that both reduce neuronal firing.

LSD-like Drugs. LSD, which is structurally related to the neurotransmitter serotonin, produces many of its behavioral effects (possibly including hallucinations) through a serotonergic mechanism. Within the serotonin system, several subtypes of receptors have been characterized. Serotonin, LSD and LSD-like drugs bind postsynaptically to several of these subtypes, including the 5-HT1A, 5HT1B, 5HT1C and 5HT2 sites (Titeler, Lyon & Glennon, 1988). Although LSD binds to several subtypes, the 5HT2 site probably is the most important in its mechanism of action. One line of evidence supporting this hypothesis is that the potency of LSD in binding to 5-HT2 receptors is highly correlated with its hallucinogenic potency in humans (Titeler, Lyon & Glennon, 1988). In addition, many of the effects of LSD also are potently antagonized by compounds selective for 5HT2 receptors (Cunningham & Appel, 1987). Moreover, chronic treatment with a dosing regimen of LSD that produces tolerance to the drug's behavioral and physiological effects also produces a decrease in the number of 5HT2 receptors (Buckholtz, Zhou et al., 1990). Taken together, the evidence strongly supports the notion that the behavioral effects of LSD are mediated through the 5HT2 receptor subtype.

MDMA-like Drugs. Compared to LSD, the pharmacology of MDMA-like compounds is less clear. A significant amount of behavioral evidence initially suggested that dopaminergic receptors mediated the effects of MDMA and other ring-substituted amphetamine derivatives such as MDE and MDA (Glennon, 1989). However, results from receptor binding studies have not supported the notion that dopaminergic receptors mediate the effects of MDMA, since MDMA had the highest affinities for the 5HT and 5HT2 sites, comparable affinities for a-2 adrenergic, M-1 muscarinic cholinergic and H-1 histaminergic sites, and low affinities for the dopamine uptake, D-1 and D-2 dopamine sites (Battaglia, Brooks et al., 1988). Studies of steroisomers of MDMA and MDA showed that the (−) isomers of both compounds produced hallucinogenic effects in humans, presumably through a serotonergic mechanism, while the (+) isomers of these compounds produced stimulatory effects (Lyon, Glennon & Titeler, 1986). Thus, like LSD, the hallucinogenic effects of MDMA probably are mediated through a serotonergic mechanism, although further studies designed to evaluate this hypothesis would help to clarify the issue.

REINFORCING PROPERTIES

PCP-like Drugs. Since there are few studies of PCP-like drugs in humans, and most of those that exist are retrospective accounts by drug users, assessments of addiction liability rely heavily on animal self-administration studies. The reinforcing effects of a drug are determined by demonstrating that self-administration of the drug plus its vehicle (usually water or physiological saline) occurs in excess of self-administration of the vehicle alone. When drug-reinforced behavior is readily achieved in the animal laboratory, it is usually a good predictor that the drug has considerable abuse liability among the human population.

The reinforcing effects of PCP have been studied through use of oral and intravenous routes of self-administration in animals. In monkeys, PCP produces a calming, tranquilizing effect. The intravenous route of self-administration requires that the animal make a specified number of responses on a lever or other manipulandum within a defined timed period, and then a fixed dose of the drug is delivered by an infusion pump via an indwelling venous catheter. A number of studies from different laboratories have demonstrated that intravenously-delivered PCP functions as a reinforcer for rats, dogs, monkeys and baboons.

Drugs that are related to PCP also are self-administered intravenously. These include drugs that have similar mechanisms of action such as ketamine, (+)SKF-10,047, dexoxadrol, cyclazocine and dizocilpine. Phencyclidine and dizocilpine self-administration is more reliably obtained when the animal has a history of self-administration of a drug with similar pharmacological or discriminative stimulus effects. Several studies also have found that drugs that share discriminative stimulus effects with PCP (such as (+)SKF-10,047, ketamine, PCE, TCP and ethanol) are readily substituted for PCP as reinforcers.

Oral PCP self-administration is established by presenting gradually increasing concentrations of PCP after the daily food allotment. After sufficient quantities of PCP are consumed, food is given after a timeout following the drug self-administration session. This procedure provides a long-term stable baseline for examination of variables that modify PCP-reinforced behavior. For instance, alternative non-drug reinforcers such as saccharin reduce PCP-reinforced responding by up to 90% of baseline if the number of responses required to obtain PCP or the fixed-ratio (FR) schedule for PCP is high or the PCP concentration is very low. Free access to food decreases PCP self-administration, while small reductions in the daily food allotment markedly increase PCP self-administration. Concurrent availability of ethanol also reduces PCP-reinforced responding (U.S. Public Health Service, 1993).

A limited amount of information is available concerning drug pretreatment and PCP self-administration. Buprenorphine and dizocilpine pretreatment both resulted in dose-dependent decreases in PCP self-administration; however, potential treatment drugs such as fluoxetine and carbamazepine had no effect. Treatment with other drugs, such as amphetamine or pentobarbital, had a biphasic effect on PCP self-administration: it was increased by low doses and decreased by high doses.

LSD-like Drugs. Hallucinogen abuse ranks fifth in the category of current use among 1991 high school seniors, after alcohol, cigarettes, marijuana, and inhalants. Another recent survey conducted by the Parents Resource Institute for Drug Education (PRIDE) found that LSD use increased among students in grades 9 through 12, from 4.9 to 5.3 percent between 1990 to 1991.

Animal models of LSD self-administration have not been reported in reviews of the drug self-administration literature (Jaffe, 1989; Johanson & Balster, 1978). This is an exception to the general finding that there is a high rate of correspondence between drugs that are self-administered by animals and those that are abused by humans. The discrepancy is believed to be the result of methodological difficulties (e.g., solubility) in the animal laboratory.

MDMA-like Drugs. MDMA-like drugs have been established as reinforcers via the intravenous route for rhesus monkeys (Beardsley, Balster & Harris, 1986), baboons (Lamb & Griffiths, 1987), and rats (Markert & Roberts, 1991). In these studies, MDMA or MDA were substituted for cocaine. It is not known how readily these drugs would be established as reinforcers in animals that are naive to drugs. Overall, MDMA and MDA did not cause the animals to maintain rates of self-administration that were as high as those maintained with cocaine. In one study, a progressive ratio was used in which the animal was required to make a greater number of responses for each succeeding delivery of drug until responding ceased (break point). The results indicated that, over a range of doses, lower break points were maintained with MDA than with cocaine (Markert & Roberts, 1991). Thus, MDMA-like drugs may be less effective reinforcers than cocaine.

Other methods of evaluating the rewarding effects of MDMA-like drugs have concurred with the results of self-administration studies. For instance, another method of assessing the reinforcing effects of MDMA-like drugs has been to determine whether administration of these drugs reduces the threshold of brain stimulation reward (Hubner, Bird et al., 1988). Doses of MDMA ranging from 0.5 to 2 mg/kg significantly lowered the threshold current required to maintain self-stimulation behavior. These results also agreed with the conditioned place preference model for assessing the rewarding effects of drugs. Bilsky, Hui and colleagues (1990) found that MDMA doses ranging from 0.2 to 6.3 reliably produced a conditioned place preference.

REFERENCES

Balster RL & Woolverton WL (1980). Continuous-access PCP self-administration by rhesus monkeys leading to physical dependence. *Psychopharmacology* (Berlin) 70:5–10.

Battaglia G, Brooks BP, Kulsakdinun C & DeSouza EB (1988). Pharmacological profile of MDMA (3,4-methylenedioxymethamphetamine) at various brain recognition sites. *European Journal of Pharmacology* 149:159–163.

Beardsley PM, Balster RL & Harris LS (1986). Self-administration of methylenedioxymethamphetamine (MDMA) by rhesus monkeys. *Drug and Alcohol Dependence* 18:149–157.

Bilsky EJ, Hui YZ, Hubbell CL & Reid LD (1990). Methylenedioxymethamphetamine's capacity to establish place preferences and modify intake of an alcoholic beverage. *Pharmacology, Biochemistry and Behavior* 37(4):633–638.

Buckholtz NS, Zhou D, Freedman DX & Potter WZ (1990). Lysergic acid diethylamide (LSD) administration selectively downregulates serotonin receptors in rat brain. *Neuropsychopharmacology* 3:137–148.

Busto U, Bendayan R & Sellers EM (1989). Clinical pharmacokinetics of non-opiate abused drugs. *Clinical Pharmacokinetics* 16:1–26.

Carroll ME (1990). PCP and hallucinogens. *Advances in Alcohol and Substance Abuse* 9:167–190.

Carroll ME & Carmona G (1991). Effects of food FR and food deprivation on disruptions in food-maintained performance of monkeys during PCP withdrawal. *Psychopharmacology* 104:143–149.

Carvey P, Nausieda P, Weertz R & Klawans H (1989). LSD and other related hallucinogens elicit myoclonic jumping behavior in the guinea pig. *Progress in Neuropsychopharmacology and Biological Psychiatry* 13:199–210.

Coveney JR & Sparber SB (1990). Delayed effects of amphetamine or PCP: Interaction of food deprivation, stress and dose. *Pharmacology, Biochemistry and Behavior* 36:443–449.

Cunningham KA & Appel JB (1987). Neuropharmacological reassessment of the discriminative stimulus properties of d-lysergic acid diethylamide (LSD). *Psychopharmacology* 91:67–73.

Fitzgerald RL, Blanke RV, Rosecrans JA & Glennon RA (1989). Stereochemistry of the metabolism of MDMA to MDA. *Life Science* 45:295–301.

Gilman AG, Goodman LS, Rall TW & Murad F (1990). *Goodman & Gilman's The Pharmacological Basis of Therapeutics, 8th Edition*. New York, NY: Macmillan, 553–557.

Glennon RA (1989). Stimulus properties of hallucinogenic phenalkylamines and related designer drugs: Formulation of structure-activity relationships. In K Asghar & DeSouza (eds.) *Pharmacology and Toxicology of Amphetamine and Related Designer Drugs (NIDA Research Monograph 94)*. Rockville, MD: National Institute on Drug Abuse.

Golden NL, Kuhnert BR, Sokol RJ et al. (1987). Neonatal manifestations of maternal PCP exposure. *Perinatal Medicine* 15:185–191.

Gollamudi R, Ali SF, Newport G, Webb P, Lopez M, Leakey JEA, Kolta M & Slikker W (1989). Influence of inducers and inhibitors on the metabolism in vitro and neurochemical effects in vivo of MDMA. *NeuroToxicology* 10:455–466.

Grant KA, Knisley JS, Tabakoff B, Barrett JE & Balster RL (1991). Ethanol-like discriminative stimulus effects of noncompetitive n-methyl-d-aspartate antagonists. *Behavioral Pharmacology* 2:87–95.

Grob C, Bravo G & Walsh R (1990). Second thoughts on 3,4-methylenedioxymethamphetamine (MDMA) neurotoxicity. *Archives of General Psychiatry* 47:288.

Hance AJ, Winters WD, Quam DD, Benthuysen JL & Cadd GG (1989). Catalepsy induced by combinations of ketamine and morphine: Potentiation, antagonism, tolerance and cross-tolerance in the rat. *Neuropharmacology* 28:109–116.

Hollister LE (1984). Effects of hallucinogens in humans. In BL Jacobs (ed.) *Hallucinogens: Neurochemical, Behavioral, and Clinical Perspectives*. New York, NY: The Raven Press, 19–34.

Hollister LE, Shelton J & Krieger G (1969). A controlled comparison of lysergic acid diethylamide (LSD) and dextroamphetamine in alcoholics. *American Journal of Psychiatry* 125:1352.

Howard J, Beckwith L & Rodning C (1990). *Adaptive Behavior in Recovering Female PCP/Polysubstance Abusers (NIDA Research Monograph 101)*. Rockville, MD: National Institute on Drug Abuse, 86–95.

Howard J, Kropenske V & Tyler R (1986). The long-term effects on neurodevelopment in infants exposed prenatally to PCP. In DH Clouet (ed.) *Phencyclidine: An Update (NIDA Research Monograph 64)*. Rockville, MD: National Institute on Drug Abuse, 237–251.

Hubner CB, Bird M, Rassnick S & Kornetsky C (1988). The threshold lowering effects of MDMA (ecstasy) on brain-stimulation reward. *Psychopharmacology* 95:49–51.

Jaffe JH (1989a). Drug dependence: Opioid nonnarcotics, nicotine and caffeine. In HI Kaplan & BJ Sadock (eds.) *Comprehensive Textbook of Psychiatry, 5th Ed.* Baltimore, MD: Williams & Wilkins, 642–686.

Jaffe JH (1989b). Psychoactive substance abuse disorder. In HI Kaplan & BJ Sadock (eds.) *Comprehensive Textbook of Psychiatry, 5th Ed.* Baltimore, MD: Williams & Wilkins, 642–686.

Johanson CE & Balster (1978). A summary of the results of a drug self-administration study using substitution procedures in rhesus monkeys. *Bulletin of Narcotics* 30:43–54.

Karler R, Clader LD, Chaudhry IA & Turkanis SA (1989). Blockade of "reverse tolerance" to cocaine and amphetamine by MK-801. *Life Science* 45:599–606.

Khanna JM, Wu PH, Weiner J & Kalant H (1991). NMDA antagonist inhibits rapid tolerance to ethanol. *Brain Research Bulletin* 26:643–645.

Lamb RJ & Griffiths RR (1987). Self-injection of d,1-3,4-methylenedioxymethamphetamine (MDMA) in baboon. *Psychopharmacology* 91:268–272.

Lu Y, France CP & Woods JH (1992). Tolerance to the cataleptic effect of excitatory amino acid antagonists in pigeons. In JM Kamonke & EF Domino (eds.) *Multiple Sigma and PCP Receptor Ligands: Mechanisms for Neuromodulation and Neuroprotection*. Ann Arbor, MI: NPP Books, 687–693.

Luisada P (1981). PCP. In JH Lowinson & P Ruiz (eds.) *Substance Abuse: Clinical Problems and Perspectives*. Baltimore, MD: Williams & Wilkins, 209–232.

Lyon RA, Glennon RA & Titeler M (1986). 3,4-methylenedioxymethamphetamine (MDMA): Stereoselective interactions at brain 5-HT1 and 5-HT2 receptors. *Psychopharmacology* 88:525–526.

Manallack DT, Lodge D & Beart PM (1989). Subchronic administration of MK–801 in the rat decreases cortical binding of [3H]D-AP5, suggesting down-regulation of the cortical N-methyl-D-Aspartate receptors. *Neuroscience* 30:87–94.

Markert LE & Roberts DC (1991). 3,4-Methylenedioxyamphetamine (MDA) self-administration and neurotoxicity. *Pharmacology, Biochemistry and Behavior* 39:569–574.

Nabeshima T, Fukaya H, Yamaguchi K, Ishikawa K, Furukawa H & Kameyama T (1987). Development of tolerance and supersensitivity to PCP in rats after repeated administration of PCP. *European Journal of Pharmacology* 135:23–33.

Olney JW, Labruyere J & Price MT (1989). Pathological changes induced in neurons by phencyclidine and related drugs. *Science* 244:1360–1362.

Pechnick RN, George R & Poland RE (1989). Characterization of the effects of the acute and repeated administration of MK-801 on the release of adrenocorticotropin, corticosterone and prolactin in the rat. *European Journal of Pharmacology* 164:257–263.

Price LH, Ricaurte GA, Krystal JH & Heninger GR (1989). Neuroendocrine and mood responses to intravenous L-tryptophan in 3,4-methylenedioxymethamphetamine (MDMA) users. Preliminary observations. *Archives of General Psychiatry* 46(1):20–22.

St. Omer VE, Ali SF, Holson RR, Duhart HM, Scalzo FM & Slikker W (1991). Behavioral and neurochemical effects of prenatal methylenedioxymethamphetamine (MDMA) exposure in rats. *Neurotoxicology and Teratology* 13(1):13–20.

Schlemmer RF & Davis JM (1986). A primate model for the study of hallucinogens. *Pharmacology, Biochemistry and Behavior* 24:381–392.

Seiden LS & Ricaurte GA (1987). Neurotoxicity of methamphetamine and related drugs. In HY Meltzer (ed.) *Psychopharmacology: The Third Generation of Progress*. New York, NY: Raven Press, 359–366.

Slifer BL, Balster Rl & Woolverton WL (1984). Behavioral dependence produced by continuous PCP infusion in rhesus monkeys. *Journal of Pharmacology and Experimental Therapy* 230:339–406.

Slikker W Jr, Ali SF, Scallet AC, Frith CH, Newport GD & Bailey JR (1988). Neurochemical and neurohistological alterations in the rat and monkey produced by orally-administered methylenedioxymethamphetamine (MDMA). *Toxicology and Applied Pharmacology* 94:448–457.

Smith JB (1991). Situational specificity of tolerance to the effects of PCP on responding of rats under fixed-ratio and spaced- respond schedules. *Psychopharmacology* 103:121–128.

Stone DM, Merchant KM, Hanson GR & Gibb JW (1987). Immediate and long-term effects of 3,4-methylenedioxymethamphetamine on serotonin pathways in brain of rat. *Neuropharmacology* 26:1677–1683.

Tennant FS, Rawson RA & McCann M (1981). Withdrawal from chronic phencyclidine dependence with desipramine. *American Journal of Psychiatry* 138:845–847.

Titeler M, Lyon RA & Glennon RA (1988). Radioligand binding evidence implicates the brain 5-HT2 receptor as a site of action for LSD and phenylisopropylamine hallucinogens. *Psychopharmacology* 94:213–216.

Trujillo KA & Akil H (1991). Inhibition of morphine tolerance and dependency by the NMDA receptor antagonist MK–801. *Science* 251:85–87.

U.S. Public Health Service (1993). *Drug Abuse and Drug Abuse Research: The Fourth Triennial Report to Congress from the Secretary, Department of Health and Human Services*. Washington, DC: U.S. Government Printing Office.

Wessinger WD (1987). Behavioral dependence on PCP in rats. *Life Science* 41:355–360.

Willetts J, Balster RL & Leander JD (1990). The behavioral pharmacology of NMDA receptor antagonists. *Trends in Pharmacology* 11:423–428.

Yousif MY, Fitzgerald RL, Narasimhachari N, Rosecrans JA, Blanke RV & Glennon RA (1990). Identification of metabolites of 3,4-methylenedioxymethamphetamine in rats. *Drug and Alcohol Dependence* 26:127–135.

Zukin SR & Javitt DC (1985). Mechanisms of PCP (PCP)-N-methyl-D-aspartate (NMDA) interaction: Implications for drug abuse research. *NIDA Research Monograph* 95. Rockville, MD: National Institute on Drug Abuse, 247–254.

CHAPTER 8

The Pharmacology of Marijuana

Mark S. Gold, M.D., FCP, FAPA

Therapeutic Use and Misuse
Adverse Effects
Addiction Liability
Absorption and Metabolism
Mechanisms of Action
Reinforcing Properties

Marijuana remains the single most commonly used illicit drug in America today. User data reported in 1998 suggest a rising trend in marijuana use. According to the National Monitoring the Future Survey, marijuana use among adolescents is increasing and age of first use is decreasing; in fact, daily marijuana use exceeds daily alcohol use in some surveys of high school seniors.

The physical and psychological problems caused by marijuana use, combined with the millions of people who continue to use the drug alone or with nicotine, alcohol and other drugs, make marijuana consumption a major health issue in the United States.

THERAPEUTIC USE AND MISUSE

Therapeutic Use. Identification of cannabinoid receptors in the brain and its periphery and a candidate ligand suggests that we may soon understand the basis for the seemingly diverse effects of cannabinoids. These findings are the first step in the development of novel cannabinoids for medical use. Cannabinoids may be proven to be safe and effective treatments for a variety of medical problems and in pain management. Of many potential applications, the following lines of evidence suggest that one major function of this novel system is to modulate pain sensitivity. Cannabinoids produce analgesia with nearly the same potency and efficacy as morphine in rodents. The strong correlation between cannabinoid receptor binding affinity and behavioral potency indicate that this effect is mediated by cannabinoid receptors; the analgesic effects of cannabinoids are centrally mediated and have both spinal and supraspinal substrates. Cannabinoids inhibit nociceptive responses in wide dynamic range neurons in the spinal cord and the thalamus, thus illustrating that cannabinoid effects on behavioral measures of pain are due at least in part to the inhibition of neurotransmission within spinothalamic nociceptive pathways.

These findings suggest that endogenous cannabinoids may serve naturally to inhibit the processing of painful inputs. The findings suggest that the dorsolateral periaqueductal gray and dorsal raphe are two sites of action of cannabinoids for the production of antinociceptive effects (Martin, Patrick et al., 1995). Purified and specific pharmacological preparations tested for safety and efficacy and delivered to the site of pathology may find a role in clinical therapeutics. Cannabinoid research also suggests that marijuana is smoked to stimulate the endogenous cannabinoid system. It is believed that smoking marijuana, which delivers high levels of delta-9-tetrahydrocannabinol (THC) and other psychoactive ingredients to the brain over along enough period of time, could induce neuroadaptative changes in this system in a way similar to opiates effects on endorphin systems.

The likely outcome of controlled research studies will be a series of important new compounds that utilize cannabinoid systems to exert their effects but are administered orally, intranasally or as a vapor, and do not produce euphoria. A synthetic cannabinoid, dronabinol (Marinol®) has been developed and used with success, as have potent antiemetic agents such as ondansetron (Zofran®).

Misuse and Abuse. Cannabis abuse and dependence, clinically similar in many ways to alcohol dependence, appears to be increasing. Those who become dependent typically establish a pattern of chronic use that gradually increases in both frequency and amount. With chronic heavy use, there sometimes is a diminution or loss of the pleasurable effects of the substance. Acute withdrawal complaints rarely are reported, although cloudiness and other behavioral signs are common during the months after discontinuation of chronic marijuana smoking.

Recent studies suggest that alcohol no longer is a prerequisite for use of marijuana, but that marijuana use nearly always precedes use of cocaine, crack and heroin (Golub & Johnson, 1994). Thus, marijuana may be the new gateway that allows young people to learn the delivery of drugs to the brain by inhalation (Simmons & Tashkin, 1995). Marijuana smoking may, and now often does, precede tobacco smoking.

ADVERSE EFFECTS

Marijuana smoking has a number of negative health effects. In a recent study, marijuana smokers who did not smoke cigarettes had poor general health and more respiratory infections than did non-marijuana smokers (Polen, Sidney et al., 1993).

Physical Effects. Marijuana produces a number of medical problems, including respiratory disorders and impairments to the immune and reproductive systems that may not be readily apparent to the physician. While many of these disorders may be relieved with symptomatic treatment, abstinence remains the only effective long-term treatment for all conditions associated with marijuana use.

Respiratory Effects: Marijuana and tobacco smoke are very similar, and the effects of marijuana smoking are similar to the effects of tobacco smoking (Gold, 1989). Marijuana smoke contains many of the same carcinogenic components identified in tobacco smoke (Sherman, Aberland et al., 1997), and many other chemicals (e.g. cannabinoids) not found in tobacco (Wallace, Oishi et al., 1994). Chronic marijuana smoking (at least four days a week for six to eight weeks) results in mild air obstruction, which may not be readily reversible with abstinence (Tashkin, Shapiro et al., 1976). Marijuana smoking also causes decreased exercise tolerance, chronic cough, bronchitis and decreased pulmonary function (Tashkin, Shapiro et al., 1976; Tilles, Goldenheim et al., 1986; Henderson, Tennant & Guerry, 1972; Mendelson, Meyer et al., 1972). Decreases in lung function are increased by concurrent use of tobacco cigarettes.

The association between marijuana smoking and lung cancer presents methodological problems stemming from lung cancer's long latency period, the concurrent use of tobacco by many marijuana smokers, and the tendency of patients to not report marijuana use (Gold, 1989). However, studies have shown that marijuana smoke contains elements that are mutagenic, and therefore, likely to be carcinogenic (Seid & Wei, 1979; Wehner, Van Rensburg & Theil, 1980). While both marijuana and tobacco increase the number of inflammatory cells in the lung, they differentially affect the activation of these inflammatory cells, possibly leading to differential effects on lung injury and physiologic consequences, including altered alveolar epithelial permeability (Gil, Kelp et al., 1995).

Cardiovascular Effects: Marijuana smoking almost immediately produces a marked and significant increase in heart rate (Galanter, Weingartner & Vaughn, 1973; Jones, 1977) with inversion or flattening of the T wave on EKG and elevation of ST segment and increased amplitude of the P wave with occasional PVCs (Kochar & Hosko, 1973). These cardiovascular effects can aggravate existing cardiac conditions or hypertension. The tachycardia associated with marijuana use appears to result from parasympathetic and sympathetic stimulation of the cardiac pacemaker; however, it is not clear if beta-adrenergic stimulation is involved (Beaconsfield, Ginsburg & Rainsbury, 1972; Tashkin, Soares et al., 1978). Fortunately, these changes in cardiac function usually can be reversed by abstinence.

Reproductive Effects: THC has mainly inhibitory effects in pituitary leutenizing hormone (LH), prolactin (PRL) and growth hormone (GH) and has no or little effect on the secretion of follicle-stimulating hormone (FSH). The purification and availability of the putative endogenous ligand for the cannabinoid receptor, anandamide (arachidonyl ethanol-amide, anandamide) (ANA) has provided the opportunity to compare the effects of THC and ANA on the female neuroendocrine system in ovariectomized (OVX) rats. Both ANA and THC decrease serum LH level, although THC to a higher degree. No significant differences were observed in serum FSH level. Both drugs decreased serum PRL. Serum GH was increased after THC administration and significantly decreased after ANA. The results indicate that ANA and THC alter pituitary hormone secretion mainly by inhibitory action (Wenger, Toth & Martin, 1995).

Marijuana is reported to decrease plasma testosterone, sperm count and motility (Hembree, Nahas et al., 1976). Marijuana is antiandrogenic and many of its components, including THC, bind to androgen receptors. Whether these antiandrogenic effects result in decreased libido or impaired fertility is not clear (DuPont & Voth, 1995).

Marijuana use can disrupt the female reproductive system: women who use marijuana four or more time a week have shorter menstrual cycles, elevated prolactin levels, and depressed testosterone levels, with galactorrhea occurring in as many as 20% of (Cohen, 1985). Animal studies also show a suppression of ovarian function, interference with gonadotropin and estrogenic activity, and amenorrhea associated with marijuana consumption (Asch, Smith et al., 1981).

Women who smoke marijuana during pregnancy often have children with low birth weights (Tennes, 1984), with the lowest birth weight babies born to those with the highest consumption of marijuana. One study found numerous abnormal responses, including increased startle reflex, tremors, poor self-quieting, and failure to habituate to light, in newborn infants whose mothers used marijuana during pregnancy (Jones & Chernoff, 1984). In addition, THC has been shown to cross the placental barrier, and to accumulate in mother's milk (Fehr & Kalant, 1983).

Immune Impairment: While human studies are contradictory, several do show that marijuana use impairs the immune system, while animal studies provide evidence that marijuana impairs the immune system (Gold, 1989). Marijuana and THC have profound effects on immune responses: both affect acute phase response. In general, THC decreases signals to helper T cells and interferes with macrophage antigen processing. Long-term impairment of the immune system may increase the risk of cancer.

Psychological Effects. In addition to euphoria, users report an increase in hunger and state of relaxation. Panic, anxiety, nausea, dizziness, and a general difficulty in expressing even simple thoughts in words may be associated with marijuana use. While marijuana does not cause a specific psychiatric illness, it can precipitate a psychiatric illness in those with pre-existing illnesses, ranging from panic (Novak, 1980) to paranoia (Naditch, 1974). Visual distortions—including object size and distance (Isbell, Gorodetzsky et al., 1967), decrease in color discrimination, and decrease in ocular motor tracking (Adams, Brown et al., 1975)—have been reported. Decreased detection, recognition and analysis of peripheral visual field light stimuli have been reported (Moskowitz, Sharma et al., 1972). These visual distortions and perceptual problems are special problems for the marijuana-intoxicated driver or worker.

Motor performance is further compromised by the drug intoxication state, with its pleasurable sense of floating and the loss or distortion of the sense of time and failure to calculate proper stopping or braking time. Marijuana use thus is clearly related to driving impairment (Klonoff, 1974; Sharma & Moskowitz, 1972). PET scan studies by Volkow and others (1996) lead to the conclusion that THC is quite persistent in brain, even after acute use and tends to form a depot in cerebellum and elsewhere. This accumulation may explain the serious and consistent performance decrements in flight simulator and driving studies. Tetrahydrocannabinol is second to ethanol as the drug most frequently detected in the blood of drivers cited for impaired driving in the State of Wisconsin (Gil, Kelp et al., 1995).

Marijuana has an adverse effect on cognitive functions and tests, but the *sine qua non* of use appears to be impairment of the ability to learn; this effect is most troublesome, given the frequency of marijuana use by adolescents. Not unlike the hippocampal lesioned animal or insulted man, the presence of marijuana intoxication interferes with the formation of new memories. Students who must learn through listening and repetition may be the most clearly compromised. Voth (1980) and others (Smith & Seymour, 1982) have shown that marijuana interferes with the formation of memories dependent on study; others have reported a more global loss of short-term memory (Lantner, 1982; Roth, Tinklenberg et al., 1977; Clark, Goetz et al., 1979). A recent study of chronic marijuana effects on cognition found that heavy marijuana use (i.e., use seven or more times weekly) was associated with deficits in mathematical skill and verbal expression (Block & Ghoneim, 1993). Foltin and colleagues (1993) recently reported that combinations of a high marijuana dose and a high cocaine dose increased errors on a repeated acquisition task.

Depersonalization and other behavioral effects also have been associated with marijuana use. Marijuana smoking, but not placebo, has been associated with significant depersonalization; other behavioral changes induced by marijuana include disintegration of time sense, sensation of a "high," increased state anxiety, tension, anger and confusion. This study also found that respiration, pulse rate, and systolic blood pressure increased after smoking marijuana and that temporal disintegration was the most significant predictor of depersonalization (Mathew, Wilson et al., 1993).

In a seminal study, Pope and Todd-Yurgelun (1996) followed 65 college students who smoked marijuana regularly and compared them with 64 who smoked occasionally. Urinary cannabinoids were present in all of the heavy users and none of the occasional users. Heavy marijuana use was clearly associated with residual neuropsychological effects. These deficits were found to carryover past acute intoxication and supervised abstinence. Tests for attention, executive functioning and new word learning were significantly impaired by marijuana. In addition, verbal fluency was impaired in many users. These data suggest that multiple brain systems are adversely affected by marijuana. Most profound and consistent effects were seen in brain stem structures and prefrontal regions which sustain attention, shift focus, and promote adaptation to the environment and new learning (Pope & Todd-Yurgelun, 1996).

In the course of clinical treatment of cannabis users, researchers have reported that the use of cannabis more often than every six weeks for approximately two years, leads to changes in cognitive functioning. These changes create a new state of consciousness that can be described as a cannabis-state-dependent effect (Lundqvist, 1995a, 1995b).

Results of a brain event-related potential (ERP) study of selective attention in long-term cannabis users in the unintoxicated state were reported recently by Solowij and co-workers (1995). ERP measures known to reflect distinct components of attention were found to be affected differentially by duration and frequency of cannabis use. The ability to focus attention and filter out irrelevant information, measured by frontal processing negativity to irrelevant stimuli, was impaired progressively with the number of years of marijuana use but was unrelated to frequency of use. The speed of information processing, measured by the latency of parietal P300, was delayed significantly with increasing frequency of use but was unaffected by duration of use. The results suggest that a chronic buildup of cannabinoids produces both short- and long-term cognitive impairments.

ADDICTION LIABILITY

In addition to its apparent detrimental effects on social adjustment and the overall health of the user, long-term use of marijuana has been directly related to subsequent use of other illicit drugs (Clayton & Voss, 1981); marijuana has been called a "gateway drug" (DuPont, 1992). Adolescent marijuana use appears to have been the best of all available predictors of cocaine use (Kandel, Murphy & Karus, 1985).

Use of marijuana is further complicated by its aura as a "safe" drug and by its increase in potency since the 1960s and 1970s. In the past, the most common marijuana cigarette smoked in the U.S. contained approximately 10 mg of THC. More recently, with the advent of selective breeding, there has been an increase in THC content and, consequently, the potency of marijuana cigarettes. In addition, the use of hash oil with the marijuana leaf significantly increases the amount of THC in the combination cigarette (Gold, 1989). This change in potency has been a primary factor in transforming the low-dose, self-experimentation type of marijuana use typical of the 1960s to high-potency, high-reward/reinforcement marijuana use and dependence prevalent in the 1990s.

While there is much debate in the popular press, reproducible tolerance and signs and symptoms of acute physical dependence have been widely reported in man for quite some time. Jones and colleagues (1977, 1988) have clearly demonstrated physical dependence develops to marijuana. The marijuana abstinence syndrome has been reported by Mendelson and co-workers (1972, 1976) and includes many complaints normally associated with opiate withdrawal including insomnia, abstinence, nausea, anorexia, agitation, restlessness, irritability, depression, and tremor. After 21 days of heavy smoking, abrupt cessation of marijuana use was associated with a major abstinence syndrome which begins within 10 hours of cessation of marijuana smoking, peaked within 48 hours and ended by the fifth day of abstinence. Mendelson, Mello and colleagues (1984) have calculated that a THC dose of 3.2 mg/kg of body weight per day for three consecutive weeks induces physical dependence. Marijuana withdrawal may be associated with increased irritability, temper and overt aggression. In animals, marijuana has anti-aggressive effects which could reverse themselves in withdrawal. Laboratory studies of non-human aggression have consistently reported decreased aggressive behavior following the administration of THC. Results indicated that: (1) the effects of marijuana on aggression may be dependent upon the level of provocation and/or aggressive responding; (2) these effects appear to be controlled by the provocation frequencies present immediately after smoking marijuana; (3) marijuana suppresses aggressive responding at high levels of provocation but not at low levels; and (4) the relationship between marijuana smoking and aggression in humans is probable more complex than once assumed (Cherek & Dougherty, 1995).

ABSORPTION AND METABOLISM

While marijuana can be ingested orally, the most common mode of marijuana self-administration is by smoking and inhalation. Marijuana smoke contains more than 150 compounds in addition to the major psychoactive component, THC. Many of the cannabinoids and other complex organic compounds appear to have psychoactive properties; others have not been tested for long- or short-term safety in animals or man.

The pharmacology of marijuana is complex, starting with the volatilized THC produced by the burning of the cigarette and followed by the deep inhalation. Marijuana is rapidly absorbed from the lungs; THC and major metabolites can be traced throughout the body and brain. In the past, there was some debate over whether marijuana's main constituent—THC—acts directly on the central nervous system (CNS) or whether it first must be metabolized to 11-OH delta-9-THC; today, however, it appears that delta-9-THC is directly psychoactive (Lemberger, McMahon & Archer, 1976).

MECHANISMS OF ACTION

When marijuana is smoked, it appears to produce its anticipated and unanticipated effects through specific binding with endogenous THC receptors. Radioligand binding studies with a water-soluble form of cannabinoid have revealed saturable high-affinity sites in the brain that are specific for cannabinoids and that can be inhibited by myelin basic protein in the rat (Nye, Voglmaier et al., 1988). Anandamide (the name given to the structure of arachidonylethanolamide, an arachidonic acid derivative in porcine brain) recently has been shown to inhibit the specific binding of a radiolabeled cannabinoid probe to synaptosomal membranes in a manner typical of competitve ligands. This effect produces a concentration-dependent inhibition of the electrically evoked twitch response of the mouse vas deferens, a characteristic effect of psychotropic cannabinoids. These properties suggest that anandamide may function as a natural ligand for the cannabinoid receptor (Devane, Hanu et al., 1992).

Two subtypes of cannabinoid receptors, CB1 and CB2, have been described (Howlett, Rinaldi-Carmona et al., 1995). Three classes of agonist ligands regulate these receptors: cannabinoid, aminoalkyulindole and eicosanoid derivatives. Brain cannabinoid binding has been correlated with pharmacological properties as well as memory disruption (hippocampus), driving and coordination problems (cerebellum).

In addition, THC binds with the mu receptor, an opioid receptor subtype stimulated by morphine. Chronic marijuana-induced decreased LC activity through the mu-LC connection, could cause LC hyperactivity during withdrawal. Recent data show that AnNH, as previously reported for r9-THC, reduces opiate withdrawal symptoms in mice (Vela, Ruiz-Gaya & Fuentes, 1995). These data support the role of AnNH as an endogenous cannabinoid agonist and provide additional support for a link between the endogenous opioid and cannabinoid systems. This connection may be of critical importance in understanding marijuana dependence and its treatment. Furthermore, the opiate antagonist naloxone has been shown to attenuate the enhanced dopamine (DA) levels associated with THC administration. Naloxone's alteration of THC effects suggest that marijuana engages endogenous brain opioid circuitry, causing an association between these endogenous opioids and DA neurons that appears fundamental to marijuana's euphoric effects. Anandamide (arachidonylethannnolamide; AnNH) is a recently identified natural constituent of mammalian brain tissue that binds with high affinity (Ki = 90 nM vs [3 H]HU-243) to the cannabinoid receptor, and fulfills most of the criteria for consideration as a neurotransmitter. It has been proposed that AnNH may be an endogenous ligand of the cannabinoid receptor. Anandamide has been shown to bind to the cannabinoid receptor. A recent study confirmed that anandamide produced effects similar to THC such as antinociception, hypothermia, hypomotility and catalepsy (Smith, Compton et al., 1994).

It has been shown that extreme tolerance to THC develops quickly and continues for a long time after stopping treatment (Fride, 1995). Tolerance develops to anandamide. Cross-tolerance develops between THC and anandamide. In a recent study, two weeks of daily anandamide (ANA) administration, produce tolerance reversed within one week after cessation of treatment. When mice treated chronically with ANA were challenged with THC, the animals were tolerant to all effects (Fride, 1995). Anandamide produces effects similar to THC, but of shorter duration and with different antinociceptive properties (Adams, Ryan et al., 1995). It is likely that metabolism plays a role in the actions of anandamide. Like THC, anandamide binds to the cannabinoid receptor and produces cannabinoid effects. Low doses of anandamide inhibit the expression of THC's effects in vivo and in vitro (Fride, 1995)

REINFORCING PROPERTIES

Properties that increase reinforcement potential, such as rapid absorption, high intrinsic pharmacological activity of a drug, and rapid entry into specific regions in the brain, are present in the high potency THC of the 1990s. Similarly, the factors that favor physical dependence, such as long half-life, low clearance, cumulative drug load, and high intrinsic pharmacological activity, also are present.

While marijuana is used for the euphoria, or "high," and not to reverse an acute abstinence syndrome, subtle neurochemical changes induced by smoking may make repeat use more likely to occur. Marijuana is self-administered by laboratory animals and appears to have effects on the putative reward neuroanatomy similar to those of other drugs of abuse (Gardner & Lowinson, 1991). Like other drugs, it works as a direct or indirect agonist in the dopaminergic pathways of the medial forebrain (MFB). THC works directly through this mechanism by increasing both basal and stimulated dopamine levels in the MFB (Gardner & Lowinson, 1991). THC appears to act on the putative reward neuroanatomy, as do other drugs of abuse.

In addition, THC binds with the γ receptor, an opioid receptor subtype stimulated by morphine. Chronic γ-decreased LC activity could cause LC hyperactivity during withdrawal (Gold & Miller, 1992). Moreover, the opiate antagonist naloxone has been shown to attenuate the enhanced dopamine levels associated with THC administration. Naloxone's alteration of THC's effects suggest that marijuana causes brain reinforcement through a mechanism similar to that of other drugs, including alcohol and opiates (Gardner & Lowinson, 1991).

REFERENCES

Aceto MD, Scates SM, Lowe JA & Martin BR (1995). Cannabinoid precipitated withdrawal by the selective cannabinoid receptor antagonist, SR 141716A. *European Journal of Pharmacology* 282:R1–R2.

Adams AJ, Brown B, Flom MC et al. (1975). Alcohol and marijuana effects on static visual acuity. *American Journal of Opthalmic Physiology Opt* 52:729–735.

Adams IB, Ryan W, Singer M et al. (1995). Evaluation of the cannabinoid receptor binding and the in vivo activities for the anandamide analog. *Journal of Pharmacology and Experimental Therapeutics* 273:1172–1182.

Asch RH, Smith CG, Siler-Khodor TM & Pauerstein CJ (1981). Effects of delta–9-tetrahydrocannabinol during the follicular phase of the Rhesus monkey (Macaca mulatta). *Journal of Clinical Endocrinology and Metabolism* 52:50–55.

Barrett RL, WIley JL, Balster RL & Martin BR (1995). Pharmacological specificity of Delta-9-THC discrimination in rats. *Psychopharmacology* 118:419–424.

Beaconsfield P, Ginsburg J & Rainsbury R (1972). Marijuana smoking: Cardiovascular effects in man and possible mechanisms. *The New England Journal of Medicine* 287:209–212.

Black GS (1990). *The Partnership Attitude Tracking Study: A Summary Of The Fourth Year Results (Report for the Partnership for a Drug-Free America)*. Rochester, NY: The Gordon S. Black Corporation.

Black GS (1988). Changing attitudes toward drug use. *Reports from The Media-Advertising Partnership for a Drug-Free America, Inc.* Rochester, NY: The Gordon S. Black Corporation.

Block RI & Ghoneim MM (1993). Effects of chronic marijuana use on human cognition. *Psychopharmacology* 110:219–228, 1993.

Bush PJ & Iannotti RJ (1993). Alcohol, cigarette, and marijuana use among fourth-grade urban schoolchildren in 1988/89 and 1990/91. *American Journal of Public Health* 83(1):111–114.

Chait LD & Burke KA (1994). Preference for high-versus low-potency marijuana. *Pharmacology, Biochemistry and Behavior* 49(3):643–647.

Cherek DR & Dougherty DM (1995). Provocation frequency and its role in determining the effects of smoked marijuana on human aggressive responding. *Behavioural Pharmacology* 6:405–412.

Clark WC, Goetz RR, McCarthy RH et al. (1979). Effects of marihuana on pain and verbal memory: A sensory decision theory analysis. In GG Nahas & WDM Paton (eds.) *Marihuana: Biological Effects: Analysis, Metabolism, Cellular Responses, Reproduction and Brain.* New York, NY: Pergamon, 665–680.

Clayton RR & Voss HL (1981). Young men and drugs in Manhattan: A causal analysis. *NIDA Research Monograph 39*. Rockville, MD: National Institute on Drug Abuse, 1–187.

Cohen S (1985). Marijuana and reproductive functions. *Drug Abuse and Alcoholism News* 13:1.

Dalack GW, Glassman AH, Rivelli S, Covey L & Stethner F (1995). Mood, major depression and fluoxetine response in cigarette smokers. *American Journal of Psychiatry* 152:398–403.

Devane WA (1994). New dawn of cannabinoid pharmacology. *Trends in Pharmacological Sciences* 15:40–41.

Devane WA, Hanu L, Breuer A et al. (1992). Isolation and structure of a brain constituent that binds to the cannabinoid receptor. *Science* 258:1946–1949.

DuPont RL (1992). Legalization or prohibition: An interview with Robert L. DuPont, M.D. *University of Florida Facts About Drugs and Alcohol Newsletter* 1(3):1.

DuPont RL & Gold MS (1995). Withdrawal and reward: Implications for detoxification and relapse prevention. *Psychiatric Annals* 25(11):6636–68.

DuPont RL & Voth EA (1995). Legalization, harm reduction and drug policy. *Annals of Internal Medicine* 123:461–465.

Fehr KO & Kalant H (1983). *Addiction Research Foundation/World Health Organization Meeting on Adverse Health and Behavioral Consequences of Cannabis Use.* Toronto, Ontario: Addiction Research Foundation.

Foltin RW, Fischman MW, Pippen PA & Kelly TH (1993). Behavioral effects of cocaine alone and in combination with ethanol or marijuana in humans. *Drug and Alcohol Dependence* 32:93–106.

Fride E (1995). Anandamides: Tolerance and cross-tolerance to delta-9-THC. *Brain Research* 697:83–90.

Fride E & Mechoulam R (1993). Pharmacological activity of the cannabinoid receptor agonist, anandamide, a brain constituent. *European Journal of Pharmacology* 231(2):313–314.

Galanter M, Weingartner H, Vaughn TB et al. (1973). Delta^9-tetrahydrocannabinol and natural marihuana: A controlled comparison. *Archives of General Psychiatry* 28:278–281.

Gardner EL & Lowinson JH (1991). Marijuana's interaction with brain reward systems: Update 1991. *Pharmacology, Biochemistry and Behavior* 40:571–580.

Gil E, Kelp E, Webber M & Taskin DP (1995). Acute and chronic effects of marijuana smoking on pulmonary alveolar permeability. *Life Sciences* 56:2193–2199.

Gold MS (1989). Marijuana. *Drugs of Abuse: A Comprehensive Series for Clinicians, Vol 1.* New York, NY: Plenum Publishing.

Gold MS & Gleaton TJ (1996). Tobacco and marijuana use increases in junior and senior high school students. *Biological Psychiatry* 39:629.

Gold MS & Miller NS (1992). Seeking drugs/alcohol and avoiding withdrawal: The Neuroanatomy of drive states and withdrawal. *Psychiatric Annals* 22(8):430–435.

Gold MS & Miller NS (1994). The biology of addictive and psychological disorders. In NS Miller (ed.) *Treating Coexisting Psychiatric and Addictive Disorders.* Center City, MN: Hazelden, 35–52.

Golub A & Johnson BD (1994). The shifting importance of alcohol and marijuana as gateway substances among serious drug users. *Journal of Studies on Alcohol* 55:607–614.

Hembree WC, Nahas GG, Zeidenberg P et al. (1976). Marijuana effects on human testes. *Clinical Research* 24:272a.

Henderson RL, Tennant FS, Guerry R (1972). Respiratory manifestations of hashish smoking. *Archives of Otolaryngology* 92:248–251.

Howlett AC (1995). Pharmacology of cannabinoid receptors. *Annals Rev Pharmacology and Toxicology* 35:607–634.

Howlett AC, Rinaldi-Carmona M, Calandra B et al. (1996). Characterization of two cloned human CB1 cannabinoid receptor isoforms. *Journal of Pharmacology and Experimental Therapeutics* 278:871–878.

Isbell H, Gorodetzsky CW, Jasinski DR et al. (1967). Effects of (−) trans-tetrahydrocannabinol in man. *Psychopharmacologia* 11:184–188.

Janowsky DS, Meacham MP, Blaine JD et al. (1976). Marijuana effects on simulated flying ability. *American Journal of Psychiatry* 133:383–388.

Jenkins AJ, Darwin WD, Huestis MA, Cone EJ & Mitchell JM (1995). Validity testing of the Accupinch THC Test. *Journal of Analytical Toxicology* 19:5–12.

Jones RT (1977). Human effects in marihuana research findings: 1976. *NIDA Research Monograph 14.* Rockville, MD: National Institute on Drug Abuse, 128–178.

Jones KL & Chernoff GF (1984). Effects of chemical and environmental agents. In RK Creasy & R Resnik (eds.) *Maternal Fetal Medicine.* Philadelphia, PA: W.B. Saunders.

Kandel DB, Murphy D & Karus D (1985). Cocaine use in young adulthood: Patterns of use and psychosocial correlates. *NIDA Research Monograph 61.* Rockville, MD: National Institute on Drug Abuse, 76–110.

Kelly TH, Foltin RW, Emurian CS & Fischman MW (1994). Effects of delta–9-THC on the marijuana smoking, drug choice and verbal reports of the drug liking. *Journal of the Experimental Analysis of Behavior* 61:203–211.

Klonoff H (1974). Marijuana and driving in real-life situations. *Science* 1986:317–324.

Kochar MS & Hosko NJ (1973). Electrocardiographic effects of marijuana. *Journal of the American Medical Association* 225:25–27.

Lanter IL (1982). Marijuana abuse by children and teenagers: A pediatrician's view. In *Marijuana and Youth: Clinical Observations on Motivation and Learning.* Rockville, MD: National Institute on Drug Abuse, 84–92.

Lemberger L, McMahon R & Archer R (1996). The role of metabolic conversion on the mechanisms of actions of cannabinoids. In MS Braude & S Szara (eds.) *Pharmacology of Marihuana, Vol 1.* New York, NY: Raven Press, 125–133.

Lundqvist T (1995a). Chronic cannabis use and the sense of coherence. *Life Sciences* 56:2145–2150.

Lundqvist T (1995b). Specific thought patterns in chronic cannabis smokers observed during treatment. *Life Sciences* 56:2141–2144.

Martin WJ, Patrick SL, Coffin PO, Tsou D & Walker MJ (1995). An examination of the central sites of action of cannabinoid-induced antinocoception in the rat. *Life Sciences* 56:2103–2109.

Mathew RJ, Wilson WH, Humphreys D, Lowe JV & Weithe KE (1993). Depersonalization after marijuana smoking. *Biological Psychiatry* 33:431–441.

Mendelson JH, Babor TF, Kuehnle JC et al. (1976). Behavioral and biological aspects of marihuana use. *Annals of the New York Academy of Sciences* 282:186–210.

Mendelson JH, Mello NK, Lex BW et al. (1984). Marijuana withdrawal syndrome in a woman. *American Journal of Psychiatry* 141:1289–1290.

Mendelson JH, Meyer RE, Rossi AM et al. (1972). Behavioral and biological concomitants of chronic marihuana smoking by heavy and casual users. In *Marijuana: A Signal of Misunderstanding; Technical Papers, Vol. 1.* Rockville, MD: National Institute on Drug Abuse, 68–246.

Mendelson JH, Rossi AM & Meyer RE (eds.) (1974). *The Use of Marihuana: A Psychological and Physiological Inquiry.* New York, NY: Plenum Publishing.

Moskowitz H, Sharma S & McGlothlin W (1972). Effects of marihuana upon peripheral vision and function of the information processing demands in central vision. *Perceptual and Motor Skills* 35:875–882.

Naditch MP (1974). Acute adverse reactions to psychoactive drugs, drug usage and pyschopathology. *Journal of Abnormal Psychology* 83:394–403.

National Institute on Drug Abuse (1993a). *The 1992 National High School Senior Survey*. Rockville, MD: The Institute.

National Institute on Drug Abuse (1993b). *The 1992 National Household Survey.* Rockville, MD: The Institute.

Novak W (1980). *High Culture: Marijuana in the Lives of Americans*. New York, NY: Alfred A. Knopf.

Nye JS, Voglmaier S, Martenson RE & Snyder SH (1988). Myelin basic protein is an endogenous inhibitor of the high-affinity cannabinoid binding site in brain. *Journal of Neurochemistry* 50(4):1170–1178.

Paredes W, Li J, Smith D & Gardner EL (1989). In vivo brain microdialysis studies of delta-9-tetrahydrocannabinol on presynaptic dopamine efflux in nucleus accumbens of the Lewis rat. *Social Neuroscience Abstracts* 15:1096.

Polen MR, Sidney S, Tekawa IS, Sadler M & Friedman GD (1993). Health care use by frequent marijuana smokers who do not smoke tobacco. *Western Journal of Medicine* 158:596–601.

Pope HG & Todd-Yurgelun D (1996). The residual cognitive effects of heavy marijuana use in college students. *Journal of the American Medical Association* 275:521–527.

Rodriguez De Fonseca F, Fernandez-Ruiz JJ, Murphy LL, Cebeira M, Steger RW, Bartke A & Ramos JA (1992). Acute effects of delta-9-tetrahydrocannabinol on dopaminergic activity in several rat brain areas. *Pharmacology, Biochemistry and Behavior* 42(2):269–75.

Roth WT, Tinklenberg JR, Kopell BS et al. (1977). Ethanol and marihuana effects on event-related potentials in a memory retrieval paradigm. *Electroencephalogic and Clinical Neurophysiology* 42:381–388.

Seid DA & Wei ET (1979). Mutagenic activity of marijuana smoke condensates. *Pharmacologist* 21:204.

Shapiro BJ, Tashkin DP & Frank IM (1976). Effects of beta-adrenergic blockade and muscarinic stimulation upon cannabis bronchodilation. In MC Braude & S Szara (eds.) *Pharmacology of Marijuana.* New York, NY: Raven Press.

Sharma S & Moskowitz H (1972). Effect of marihuana on the visual autokinetic phenomenon. *Perceptual and Motor Skills* 35:891–894.

Sherman MP, Aberland EE, Wong VZ, Simmons MS, Roth MD & Taskin DP (1997). Effects of smoking marijuana, tobacco or cocaine alone or in combination on DNA damage in human alveolar macrophages. *Life Sciences* 56:2301–2307.

Simmons MS & Tashkin DP (1995). The relationship of tobacco and marijuana smoking characteristics. *Life Sciences* 56:2185–2191.

Smith DE & Seymour RB (1982). Clinical perspectives on the toxicity of marijuana, 1967, 1981. In *Marijuana and Youth: Clinical Observations on Motivation and Learning.* Rockville, MD: National Institute on Drug Abuse, 61–72.

Smith PB, Compton DR, Welch SP, Razdan RK, Mechoulam R & Martin BR (1994). The pharmacological activity of anandamide, a putative endogenous cannabinoid, in mice. *Journal of Pharmacology and Experimental Therapeutics* 270:219–227.

Solowij N, Miche PT & Fox AM (1995). Differential impairments of selective attention due to frequency and duration of cannabis use. *Biological Psychiatry* 37:731–739.

Stimmel B (1995). Medical marijuana: To prescribe or not to prescribe: That is the question. *Journal of Addictive Diseases* 14:1–4.

Swerdlow NR, Geyer MA, Perry W, Cadenhead K & Braff DL (1995). Drug screening in "normal" controls. *Biological Psychiatry* 38:123–124.

Tashkin DP, Soares JR, Hepler RS, Shapiro BJ & Rachelefsky GS. Cannabis (1978). *Annals of Internal Medicine* 89:539–549.

Tashkin DP, Shapiro BJ, Lee EY & Harper CE (1976). Subacute effects of heavy marijuana smoking pulmonary function in healthy young males. *The New England Journal of Medicine* 294:125–129.

Tennes K (1984). Effect of marijuana on pregnancy and fetal development in the human. *NIDA Research Monograph 44*. Rockville, MD: National Institute on Drug Abuse, 115–123.

Thomas BF, Wei X & Martin BR (1992). Characterization and autoradiographic localization of the cannabinoid binding site in rat brain using [3H]11-OH-delta 9-THC-DMH. *Journal of Pharmacology and Experimental Research* 263(3):1383–90.

Tilles DS, Goldenheim PD, Johnson DC et al. (1986). Marijuana smoking as cause of reduction in single-breath carbon monoxide diffusing capacity. *American Journal of Medicine* 80:601–606.

Tsou K, Patrick SL & Walker JM (1995). Physical withdrawal in rats tolerant to delta-9-THC precipitated by a cannabinoid receptor antagonist. *European Journal of Pharmacology* 280:R13–R15.

Vela G, Ruiz-Gayo M & Fuentes JA (1995). Anandamide decreases naloxone precipitated withdrawal signs in mice chronically treated with morphine. *Neuropharmacology* 34(6):665–668.

Voth HM (1990). *How To Get Your Child Off Marijuana.* Stamford, CT: Patient Care Publications, Inc.

Wall ME, Sadler BM, Brine D et al. (1983). Metabolism, disposition and kinetics of delta-9-tetrahydrocannabinol in men and women. *Clinical and Pharmacologic Therapy* 34:352–363.

Wallace JM, Oishi JS, Barbers RG, Simmons MS & Taskin DP (1994). Lymphocytic subpopulation profiles in bronchoalveolar lavage fluid and peripheral blood and tobacco and marijuana smokers. *Chest* 105:847–852.

Wehner FC, Van Rensburg SJ & Theil PG (1980). Mutagenicity of marijuana smoke and transkei tobacco smoke condensates in the salmonella/microsome assay. *Mutation Research* 77:135–142.

Wenger T, Toth BE & Martin BR (1995). Effects of anandamide (endogenous cannabinoid) on the anterior pituitary hormone secretion in adult ovariectomized rats. *Life Sciences* 56(23/24):2057–2063.

CHAPTER 9

The Pharmacology of Steroids

Scott E. Lukas, Ph.D.

Drugs in the Class
Therapeutic Use and Misuse
Adverse Effects
Addiction Liability
Absorption and Metabolism
Mechanisms of Action
Reinforcing Properties

Within the addiction field, the term *steroids* has come to define those compounds that possess anabolic or tissue-building effects, but because most also have some androgenic properties, they are more appropriately called anabolic-androgenic steroids. This profile of effects distinguishes them from the corticosteroids and the female gonadotrophic hormones, neither of which are subject to abuse. There is a rather long list of anabolic-androgenic steroids that have been produced for both human or veterinary use; the major source of abused steroids is diversion from licit manufacture and distribution, as clandestine laboratory synthesis of these products is very rare. The major distinction between use and abuse is that abusers employ supraphysiologic doses compounds in order to increase muscle growth and performance. It is the consequence of these extremely high doses that results in rather dangerous, but often reversible, organ toxicity.

DRUGS IN THE CLASS

The prototypic hormone, testosterone, is the standard to which all of the synthetic products are compared and it is one of four structurally distinct groups of anabolic-androgenic steroids. The other three groups are: 17α-alkylated derivatives of testosterone, 17β-esterified derivatives of testosterone and modified ring structure analogues (Wilson, 1988). The history of how testosterone and its effects on male sexual development and tissue building were discovered is well detailed by Kochakian (1990). Although hormonal involvement in male sexual development was known in 1849, it was not until 1930 when androsterone (a metabolite of testosterone) was isolated from human urine. In the 1940s, after chemists had succeeded in synthesizing testosterone, their efforts were directed toward separating its anabolic from its androgenic effects and to make a formulation that could be taken orally. The androgenic component of these synthetics have never been completely separated from the anabolic effects; only the relative percentage of the two have been manipulated. Commercially prepared products were used briefly during the second world war to promote wound healing. In 1939, Boje postulated that anabolic-androgenic steroids might not only increase muscle mass, but improve physical performance as well.

The introduction of anabolic-androgenic steroids to the United States has been traced to the 1954 World Weightlifting Championships in Vienna, when the Soviet Union's coach informed the U.S. coach that his team members were taking testosterone (Todd, 1987). In the ensuing years, use of anabolic-androgenic steroids by elite weight lifters, power lifters and bodybuilders increased. Over the years, their use spread to many professional sports, especially those in which strength and body weight were important for success (e.g., football). Testosterone was the drug of choice in the 1950s, which was replaced by more elegant synthetic compounds over the next three decades, primarily because of their slightly higher percent of anabolic versus androgenic effects and their relative resistance to detection by current laboratory tests. Use spread to collegiate and amateur athletes as evidenced by the 50% positive tests obtained by the International Olympic committee during unannounced urine screens in 1984 and 1985 (Yesalis, Anderson et al., 1990a). The 1990s saw a return to the use of testosterone, which is thought to be due to improved gas chromatographic methods of detecting the synthetic compounds and the continued difficulty of accurately detecting exogenously administered testosterone (Lukas, 1993). However, another trend toward using other types of performance-enhancing aids has evolved in the wake of pure anabolic-androgenic steroid abuse.

It often is difficult to determine whether the attraction of the drugs is related to any beneficial effect on the individual's performance, as the drugs rarely are taken in the absence of a training program that includes exercise and sound nutrition (Bahrke & Yesalis, 1994). This concept punctuates the second aspect of anabolic-androgenic steroid abuse among athletes—it usually occurs during training periods, which typically can begin weeks and even months before a competitive event or season. The need for these drugs by most athletes decreases during actual competition, and so the active use can decline. However, with the advent of mandatory urine testing at major athletic events, the risk of being caught also curtails use. Positive urine screens that are collected during the actual competitive event are usually due to the high sensitivity of the analytical methods to detect minute amounts of metabolites that have persisted long since use of the anabolic-androgenic steroid has ceased.

New-Generation "Performance Enhancers." With the advent of more sophisticated urine testing procedures, the likelihood that an athlete can get away with using anabolic-androgenic steroids is decreasing a little. This situation has yielded to the increased popularity of an entirely new generation of performance enhancing drugs that can be taken without detection. These drugs include other hormones such as human growth hormone itself (somatotropin), dihydroepiandrosterone (DHEA), erythropoietin and thyroxine. Other drugs that may enhance performance include the mixed agonist/antagonist opioids such as butorphanol and nalbuphine; the beta adrenergic agonist clenbuterol; "hormone helpers" such as gamma hydroxybutyrate (GHB), clonidine and human chorionic gonadotropin (hCG); and testosterone stimulants such as clomiphene and human chorionic gonadotropin. In addition, a variety of diuretics (acetazolamide, furosemide, spironolactone and triamterene) are used to help clear the anabolic-androgenic steroids and their metabolites from the urine before drug testing. Knowledge of these drugs, where to get them, doses to use and even recipes for adding them to training programs can be found in a number of "underground" guides as well as from a variety of web sites on the world wide net.

At-Risk Populations. Surveys over the past decade have found that athletes are not the only individuals to use and abuse anabolic-androgenic steroids. Abuse has now appeared in adult non-athletes and even in young boys who may to be using them to simply improve their appearance (Yesalis, Kennedy et al., 1993). Women are also using these drugs, but all estimates indicate that the percentage is much lower than in males. These factors pushed the U.S. Congress to enact the Anabolic Steroids Control Act which effectively placed all of these compounds, including testosterone and its many analogues, in Schedule III of the federal Controlled Substances Act (states, of course, have the option of scheduling these drugs even more restrictively under state law). This schedule includes opioids such as nalorphine, stimulants such as benzphetamine and depressants such as butabarbital and thiopental.

The results of the 1994 National Household Survey on Drug Abuse (SAMHSA, 1996a) indicate that overall lifetime use of anabolic-androgenic steroids among all individuals 12 years of age or older is about 0.52%. Except for heroin (0.9%), lifetime use of other drugs such as inhalants (5.8%), cocaine (10.4%), smokeless tobacco (17.2%) marihuana/hashish (31.2%), tobacco cigarettes (73.3%) and alcohol (84.2%) is substantially higher than anabolic-androgenic steroids. The distribution of the anabolic-androgenic steroid problem is age-related as lifetime use was highest in 18- to 25-year-olds (1.1%), followed by 26- to 34-year-olds (1.0%), 12- to 17-year-olds (0.7%) and 35+ year olds (0.2%). Use by males exceeded that by females (0.9 versus 0.2%), and use was equally distributed among Caucasian, African American and Hispanic ethnic groups (about 0.5%). The Monitoring the Future Study for College Students and Young Adults, 1975-1994 (NIDA, 1996b) indicates that use within the past year and within the past 30 days decreased slightly in all age groups, except for those 19 to 28 years old, who demonstrated an increase of 0.1% in both categories from 1993 to 1994. The Monitoring the Future Study for Secondary School Students, 1975–1995 (NIDA, 1996a) indicates that the annual rate of use among 12th graders increased by 0.2% from 1994 to 1995.

Interestingly, when 12th graders were asked "How difficult do you think it would be for you to get each of the following drugs, if you wanted some?", the percent responding either "fairly easy" or "very easy" to get anabolic-androgenic steroids increased by 2.6% from the class of 1994 to the class of 1995. While this may seem to be small, the perceived increase in availability of anabolic-androgenic steroids ranked behind only marihuana, LSD and MDMA, all of which had increased by 3% during the same interval. Thus, it is apparent that anabolic-androgenic steroids are fairly easy to obtain in high schools and their availability is increasing.

THERAPEUTIC USE AND MISUSE

Therapeutic Use. Although one might think that the therapeutic uses of anabolic-androgenic steroids is of less concern to the addiction medicine specialist, in reality, most physicians are asked to give prescriptions for these drugs far more often than they are asked to help treat someone who is dependent on the drugs. Thus, knowledge of these medical situations might help in discussions with a potential abuser because these individuals are likely to be aware of the medical reasons for their prescription and may use such information in their initial attempts to obtain legal medications to support their training or alter their appearance.

Males may receive anabolic-androgenic steroids for replacement therapy when the testicles fail to function, either due to congenital or traumatic factors, or when puberty is delayed and short stature would result. The doses that are prescribed, however, are much lower than those used by bodybuilders. The equivalent of 75 to 100 mg per week of testosterone suffices as replacement, but weight lifters and bodybuilders have reportedly used weekly doses of 1,000 to 2,100 mg of metandienone (Yesalis, Herrick et al., 1988; Freed, Banks et al., 1975). Women are occasionally treated with androgens when metastatic breast cancer has spread to bone. Methyltestosterone is combined with estrogen (Premarin®) to help alleviate some of the signs and symptoms of menopause.

Both males and females might receive the more anabolic agents during treatment of a rare form of hereditary angioedema. Acquired aplastic anemia and myelofibrosis both result in deficiencies of red blood cell production, which is combated with drugs that have equal amounts of anabolic and androgenic effects. Sometimes these drugs can be useful in treating the trauma associated with burns and AIDS. Finally, just as was done in post World War II, steroids with more anabolic activity are useful in treating muscle wasting that is secondary to starvation.

Steroids currently available in the U.S. are shown in Table 1. The list of products available for veterinary use is germane to this discussion because abusers will frequently use preparations that are not labeled for human use when they cannot obtain the desired products. It is an interesting paradox when young bodybuilders profess to be on strict diets and use only the purest of vitamin and dietary supplements, yet they will self-administer drugs for which use in humans has not been approved. Products that are not approved for use in the U.S. typically are obtained by mail order from abroad. Because the testing of these products in some other countries is not as stringent as that in the U.S., patients should be cautioned about using such products. Finally, there is an extensive black market of anabolic-androgenic steroids that supports a rather large percentage of inactive products that are falsely advertised as containing anabolic steroids.

Misuse. Anabolic-androgenic steroids are abused by three distinct populations: (1) athletes who use them to improve performance; (2) aesthetes who use them solely to improve appearance and perhaps gain some weight; and (3) the fighting elite who use them to enhance aggression and fighting skills (Brower, 1989). Identifying to which of the above three populations a patient belongs is the first step to understanding the pattern of use and determining the best treatment plan to follow.

Athletes: Athletes use anabolic-androgenic steroids for only one reason: to improve their performance. Perhaps one of the greatest mistakes a clinician makes in dealing with an athlete is attempting to dissuade their use on the grounds that the drugs cannot improve performance. In fact, this is not true. The older research studies that purported to show that the effects of anabolic-androgenic steroids were no different than placebo suffered from a number of methodological problems, did not control for motivation, and failed to document the amount of physical training. In addition, ethical considerations prevented the investigators from administering extremely high doses, which are considered necessary to achieve the muscle-building effect. Negative findings also have been attributed to the use of only one drug at a time in the research studies, whereas athletes in training typically use multiple drugs in combination. The continued use of these drugs is based on the belief that they increase muscle capacity, reduce body fat, increase strength and endurance, and hasten recovery from injury (Haupt & Rovere, 1984). Many athletes also believe that anabolic-androgenic steroid-assisted training allows the

TABLE 1. Anabolic-Androgenic Steroids

Trade Name	Generic Name	Route	DEA[a]
Human-U.S. available			
Android®	methyltestosterone	p.o.	III
Danocrine®	adanazol	p.o.	N/S
Deca-Durabolin®	nandrolone decanoate	i.m.	III
Delatestryl	testosterone enanthate	i.m.	III
Depo-Testosterone®	testosterone cypionate	i.m.	III
Durabolin®	nandrolone phenpropionate	i.m.	III
Halotestin®	fluoxymesterone	p.o.	III
Metandren®	methyltestosterone	p.o.	III
Oxandrin®	oxandrolone	p.o.	III
Testred®	methyltestosterone	p.o.	III
Virilon®	methyltestosterone	p.o.	III
Winstrol®	stanozolol	p.o.	III
Human-non U.S. available (foreign)			
Anadrol-50®	oxymetholone	p.o.	
Anavar	oxandrolone	p.o.	
Dianabol	methandrostenolone	p.o.	
Finiject 30	bolasterone	i.m.	
Maxibolan	ethylestrenol	p.o.	
	mesterolone	p.o.	
Oranabol	oxymesterone	p.o.	
Primobolan Depot	methenolone enanthate	i.m.	
Primobolan	methenolone	p.o.	
	norethandrolone	p.o.	
Testex Oreton propionate	testosterone propionate	i.m.	
Veterinary-anabolic agents			
Cheque® Drops	mibolerone	p.o.	III
Equipose®	boldenone	i.m.	III
Ralgro®	zeranol	s.c. pellet	Exempt[b]
Winstrol®-V	stanozolol	i.m./p.o.	III
Veterinary-growth promotants			
Finaplix®-H	trenbolone	s.c. pellet	Exempt[b]
Synovex®-H	testosterone/estradiol	s.c. pellet	Exempt[b]
Synovex®-H	trenbolone/estradiol	s.c. pellet	Exempt[b]

[a]DEA Schedule III of the Controlled Substnaces Act or not scheduled (NS)
[b]Exempt as per *Federal Register* 56(169):42935–37, August 30, 1991.

user to increase both the frequency and the intensity of workouts—factors that contribute to any direct benefits of the drugs (Anderson & McKeag, 1985).

In the world of professional weightlifting and body building, anabolic-androgenic steroids are used in three basic patterns: "stacking," "pyramiding," and "cycling." *Stacking* is the practice of using multiple products at the same time. Users believe that the beneficial effects of one drug will compliment those of another, and that they will only achieve real benefits through a specific combination. A *pyramid* plan involves starting with a low dose and then gradually increasing the dose until peak levels are achieved a number of weeks before competition. The individual then slowly decreases or tapers the drug dose down and, because the beneficial effects of anabolic-androgenic steroids persist long after their use has been discontinued, the athlete will be primed for the competitive event. *Cycling* refers to the practice of using different combinations over a period of time in order to avoid the development of tolerance or loss of effectiveness. Thus, different combinations of drugs are used over a six- to 12-week period, after which another drug or combination is substituted.

Aesthetes: Another group of users is composed of young boys who use these drugs primarily to increase their weight or to improve their physical appearance (Buckley, Yesalis et al., 1988; Yesalis, Streit et al., 1989; Wang, Fitzhugh et al., 1994; Tanner, Miller & Alongi, 1995). This desire for weight gain among a group of adolescent boys who are not yet taking anabolic-androgenic steroids may place them at risk for initiating use (Wang, Fitzhugh et al., 1994). This trend is disturbing because these authors noted that a significant number of the boys were unaware of the most dangerous risks associated with anabolic-androgenic steroid use. A recent study of the prevalence of anabolic-androgenic steroid use among sixth to twelfth grade Canadians revealed that 2.8% of the respondents had used these drugs over the past year (Melia, Pipe & Greenberg, 1996). A disturbing trend was that 29.4% of these students reported that they injected the drugs and 29.2% of these reported that they shared needles with friends. Young anabolic-androgenic steroid users are also likely to use other drugs such as marihuana, smokeless tobacco and cocaine (Durant, Rickert et al., 1993). These authors also reported a high percentage of needle sharing behavior among adolescents.

In general, the doses used by adolescents and others who want to improve their appearance are substantially lower than those used by adult athletes (Rogol & Yesalis, 1992). Further, the pattern of lower doses and intermittent cycles of use is likely to obviate the development of major side effects. However, because young boys are often still in transition due to hormonal changes associated with puberty, these drugs can have other significant effects. For example, the epiphyseal plate of the femur can close prematurely and actually stunt a boy's growth (Moore, 1988), which is contrary to what a significant number of adolescents believe. More importantly, these young users may be particularly sensitive to the increased aggressive effects resulting from their use (Rogol & Yesalis, 1992).

Apparently, a substantial proportion of these adolescents are also unaware of the side effects of anabolic-androgenic steroids. Although educational programs have been slow to incorporate these drugs in the lesson plans, the real reason that the public is so unaware of the risks is that these drugs are probably not a severe health hazard when taken intermittently and in low to moderate doses (Rogol & Yesalis, 1992). Because programs that simply emphasize the negative aspects of drugs of abuse are ineffectual at curtailing use (Goldberg, Bents et al., 1991), the health professional should balance the discussion about anabolic-androgenic steroid abuse with the straight facts and not try to overstate the degree of harm. Such actions will only alienate the patient. Unfortunately, these young people know that only a small percentage of users actually experience very serious and deadly outcomes and that it will not happen to them. For the others, the side effects (except for some effects in women) are largely reversible.

Fighting Elite: Very little is known about this population of anabolic-androgenic steroid users. This profile was originally described by Brower (1989) and includes individuals who seek to increase their strength in order to perform their job. Another desired effect is the increase in aggressiveness that may also help them with their jobs. Thus, bouncers at bars, security personnel and even law enforcement officers (Dart, 1991; Swanson, Gaines & Gore, 1991) have been reported to take these drugs.

Personality Profiles. Recent studies of the personalities of anabolic-androgenic steroid abusers by Cooper and colleagues (1996) identified a high rate of abnormal personality traits in a sample of 12 bodybuilders who used anabolic-androgenic steroids compared to a matched group who did not. Along with being heavier than the controls, the users were more likely to score higher on measures of paranoia, schizoid, antisocial, borderline, histrionic, narcissistic and passive-aggressive personality profiles. Further, the incidence of abnormal personality traits before anabolic-androgenic steroid use began was not different from the control group, suggesting that such disturbances are secondary to their use. Users also reported that they believe that anabolic-androgenic steroids not only enhance physical strength and athletic ability, but increase confidence, assertiveness, feelings of sexuality and optimism (Schwerin & Corcoran, 1996).

ADVERSE EFFECTS

A great deal is known about the side effect and toxic profile of these drugs. Side effects generally are reversible with cessation of use (Figure 1). More serious medical consequences and even toxic reactions appear to involve primarily blood chemistry, endocrine function, liver, the cardiovascular system, and the nervous system. Reports that excessive amounts of these drugs lead to certain types of malignant cancers have not been substantiated. Overall, even the more serious side effects have disappeared within three months of discontinuing their use, yet benefits such as increases in lean body mass and

FIGURE 1. Physiologic Signs of Steroid Abuse

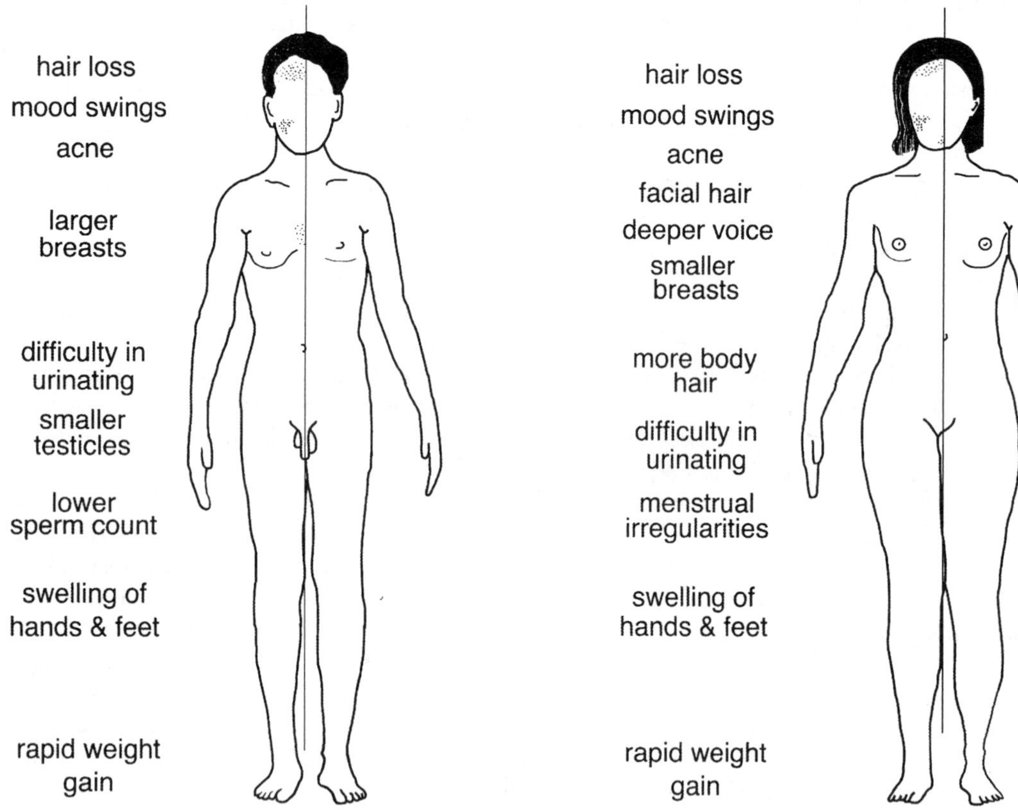

increased diameter of muscle fibers remain (Hartgens, Kuipers et al., 1996).

Administration of the 17-alkylated androgens can cause a dramatic reduction in high-density lipoprotein (HDL) cholesterol, but because there is a nearly equal increase in low-density lipoprotein (LDL) cholesterol, there is no net change in total cholesterol levels (Friedl, 1990). Other agents such as nandrolone and testosterone esters fail to produce this profile (Friedl, 1990; Thompson, Curinane et al., 1989). Although the long-term detrimental effects of altered HDL/LDL ratios are known to predispose humans to atherosclerosis, documented morbidity and mortality as a result of anabolic-androgenic steroid use has been rare (McNutt, Ferenchick et al., 1988; Bowman, 1990). The lack of direct correlations may also be due to the fact that different steroids have varied effects on lipid dynamics (Thompson, Curinane et al., 1989). Thus, while users stack different drugs in order to improve the beneficial effects, this practice may actually afford some protection against these side effects. Further, the relative paucity of coronary vascular disease in athletes who use these drugs may also be due to the fact that other risk factors (e.g., diet, exercise, low body fat) compensate for any negative contribution afforded by the HDL/LDL profile. Such protection, however, may not be present in individuals who use anabolic-androgenic steroids just to improve their appearance and do not engage in athletic activity. Platelet aggregation (Ferenchick, 1990) along with increased red blood cell production and slight increases in systolic blood pressure have been suggested to be important factors that increase an individual's risk for thromboembolic disorders (Wilson, 1988; Lenders, Demacker et al., 1988).

Because testosterone exerts an inhibitory action on the hypothalamic-pituitary axis, administration of natural or synthetic analogs of testosterone decrease testicular size and sperm count (Palacios, McClure et al., 1981; Allen & Suominen, 1984). Residual amounts of active metabolites may keep the levels of FSH and LH low and coupled with the relatively long cycle to produce sperm, the recovery is likely to be slow, but often is complete. Aromatization is the process by which steroid hormones are interconverted. For example, testosterone is converted to estradiol and estrone and high-dose male anabolic-androgenic steroid users can have circulating estrogen levels of normally cycling women (Wilson, 1988). These circulating estrogens exert the usual feminizing effects, such as gynecomastia. Compounds that resist aromatization (e.g., fluoxymesterolone, mesterolone and stanozolol) may not result in the feminizing effects (Kashkin, 1992).

Although a wide variety of medical disorders (and even exercise) can increase the amount of liver enzymes in the blood, this response is primarily limited to the use of oral, 17-alkylated anabolic-androgenic steroids. The relationship between these drugs and elevated enzyme levels exists because: (1) these orally effective drugs are metabolized by the liver, (2) the first pass effect delivers an exceptionally large percentage of the dose to the liver, and (3) abusers typically take excessive doses that further stress liver function. This profile often results in cholestatic jaundice (Pecking, Lejolly & Najean, 1980), but because inflammation and necrosis are not present, the symptoms are limited to an accumulation of bile which spills over into the blood. Interestingly, many bodybuilders use this side effect as a metric of their dosing regimen and titrate themselves to levels that just precipitate jaundice (Lukas, 1994).

Peliosis hepatitis is a disorder characterized by blood-filled cysts scattered throughout the liver; a detailed description of the history of this disorder and its relationship to anabolic-androgenic steroid abuse is presented elsewhere (Karch, 1993). It has been associated with the 17-alkylated androgens, rarely results in symptoms and likely resolves with discontinuation (Westaby, Ogle et al., 1977).

The evidence linking 17-alkylated androgens with hepatic tumors is well established. Except for the fact that the androgen-related adenomas are typically larger, the profile resembles that of women who take birth control pills. The risk for developing hepatocellular adenomas ranges from 1% to 3% of users (Friedl, 1990), and like peliosis hepatitis, these adenomas rarely result in symptoms and are often not documented until a routine autopsy is performed.

Anabolic-androgenic steroids affect the cardiovascular system via their effects on HDL/LDL ratios and other blood products. However, there are reports that these drugs can directly affect myocardial tissue. The bulk of the evidence comes from animal studies in which high doses of methandrostenolone result in myocyte necrosis, cellular edema and mitochondrial swelling (Appell, Heller-Umpfenbach et al., 1983; Behrendt & Boffin, 1977). As these changes cannot be duplicated by exercise alone, it is likely that these effects were responsible for the clinical case report of an anabolic-androgenic steroid user who suddenly died of cardiac arrest (Luke, Farb et al., 1991).

An adverse effect of anabolic-androgenic steroid use during high intensity training periods that is not well documented is the incidence of injury that may occur as a direct result of their use. A recent case of bilateral quadriceps rupture profiles the risks involved (David, Green et al., 1995). While it might seem that the fact that users can train with the drugs beyond what they would be able to tolerate without the drugs is responsible for injuries of this type, it is possible that the growth of muscle mass is not paralleled by an increase in ligament support.

Controversy remains over the degree and extent of the severity of anabolic-androgenic steroid-induced extreme psychiatric effects often referred to as "roid rage." These eruptions of frenzied violent behavior during a cycle of high dose anabolic-androgenic steroids have been described in a few case reports, but no laboratory studies verifying such reactions have been published. More frequently, cases in which psychiatric effects appear associated with drug use have been reported (Annitto & Layman, 1980; Freinhar & Alvarez, 1985; Conacher & Workman, 1989; Pope & Katz, 1987; Wilson, Prange & Lara, 1974).

The constellation of symptoms appears to most closely resemble those of hypomania or mania. The energized user of anabolic-androgenic steroids talks faster, has more energy, sleeps less and is more impulsive, even to the extent of purchasing expensive cars (Pope & Katz, 1987). At the far end of the spectrum, mania may lead to delusions and even hallucinations. Interestingly, many individuals with body dysmorphic disorder present with delusions as well (Phillips, McElroy et al., 1994). Two studies (Perry, Yates & Anderson, 1990; Pope & Katz, 1988) have attempted to standardize the collection of these data and found that using structured interviews, the incidence of a full affective syndrome was present in 22% of a population of 41 bodybuilders (Pope & Katz, 1988). Another 12% displayed psychotic symptoms that clearly emerged during anabolic-androgenic steroid use. The cohort of 20 weight lifters who used anabolic-androgenic steroids experienced more somatic, depressive, anxious, hostile and paranoid complaints than those who did not use these drugs (Perry, Yates & Anderson, 1990).

Empirical evidence of drug effects on aggressive behavior has been obtained using the Karolinska Scale of Personality (Galligani, Renck & Hansen, 1996) and a human laboratory model of aggression, the Point Subtraction Aggression Paradigm or PSAP (Cherek, 1981). Results from the personality scale indicate that a cohort of anabolic-androgenic steroid users exhibit significantly more verbal aggression, impulsiveness, and indirect aggression. Yates, Perry and Murray (1992) reported that three measures of the Buss-Durkee Hostility Inventory (Buss & Durkee, 1957), assault, indirect aggression and verbal aggression were elevated in a group of current or recent anabolic-androgenic steroid users. The PSAP paradigm directly measures the amount of provoked aggressive behavior in the laboratory by ostensibly taking away points (that are worth money) from an individual who believes he is playing against another person. In reality, the subject plays against a computer program and the rate of provocation is controlled by the experimenter. Both aggressive and non-aggressive behavior is recorded, so the effects of various drugs on responding *per se* can be viewed independent from aggressive responding. Using this model, moderately high doses of testosterone cypionate (600 mg, intramuscularly, once a week) can increase aggressive responding in individuals who had not used steroids before (Kouri, Lukas et al., 1995a). Interestingly, animal models have confirmed that anabolic-androgenic steroid administration increases aggressive behavior (Svare, 1990). As weight lifters and bodybuilders have reportedly used weekly doses that exceed three times that used in research studies, it is reasonable to suspect that aggressive behavior can result from these training programs.

Collectively, it appears that anabolic-androgenic steroid use can result in hypomania and even psychotic symptoms, while depression may ensue during withdrawal. The lack of well-controlled prospective studies has prevented a more definitive association between anabolic-androgenic steroid use and psychiatric disorders. It is unlikely that such data will become available in the near future as ethical constraints will preclude the conduct of any double-blind assessments of supraphysiological doses of these drugs.

ADDICTION LIABILITY

Anabolic-androgenic steroid abuse includes a variety of social and psychological components that are not easy to imitate in either animal models or in currently validated methods of assessing abuse liability in human volunteers. The concepts of perception, motivation and expectation play a more pivotal role in the initial use and subsequent abuse of these compounds.

Tolerance. The evidence supporting tolerance development is not strong, although there is a belief among users that cycling is a necessary practice to avoid its development. Twenty percent of a sample of weight lifters believe that tolerance develops, but over 80% believe that dependence develops. Nevertheless, such concerns over lost efficacy with time appear to be without hard empirical evidence. As such, it must be assumed that the escalating doses that elite athletes use are not taken because tolerance develops to their effects, but to increase the magnitude of the desired effects. The doses are increased slowly in order to minimize the side effects or to allow time to acclimate to them. When presented with this fact, some users are likely to confuse their behavior with tolerance.

Dependence. Although evidence of physical dependence on anabolic-androgenic steroids have not been widespread, there are a few detailed reports of clear signs of withdrawal when their use was abruptly stopped (Brower, Eliopulos et al., 1990; Brower, 1992; Brower, Blow et al., 1991). In a study of 49 male weight lifters (Brower, Blow et al., 1991), 84% reported experiencing withdrawal effects and the most frequently reported symptoms were: craving for more steroids (52%), fatigue (43%), depressed mood state (41%), restlessness (29%), anorexia (24%), insomnia (20%), decreased libido (20%), and headaches (20%). Interestingly, 42% of these subjects were dissatisfied with their body image during withdrawal as well. Those who reported being dependent on anabolic-androgenic steroids generally took higher doses, completed more cycles of use and reported more aggressive symptoms than those who did not report being dependent. However, the extent of dependence on anabolic-androgenic steroids in the larger population of users may be considerably smaller as there have been no reported cases of withdrawal effects in female athletes or among patients who have been prescribed high doses for legitimate medical purposes.

Anabolic-androgenic steroids in fact can increase muscle mass and body weight, especially when used along with a regular training program. However, many of the "black market" anabolic-androgenic steroid preparations sold during the late 1980s actually were devoid of any active ingredients, including anabolic-androgenic steroids. In spite of the spread of these counterfeit drugs, users claimed to have experienced improvements in their performance. Herein lies the real difficulty in assessing the abuse liability of these compounds. They are not expected to have immediate beneficial effects and so the delay in any improvement does not raise suspicion that the preparation may be inert. Nevertheless, whether these drugs actually increase muscle mass, improve performance or increase endurance or not is really not the question that confronts the addiction medicine specialist. The fact that anabolic-androgenic steroid-seeking behavior exists and that extremely high doses are used over relatively long periods of time suggests that there is a problem and should trigger further inquiry and subsequent treatment.

Thus, while physical dependence on anabolic-androgenic steroids may be more rare than dependence on other drugs of abuse, the prudent clinician will be ever vigilant to identify the constellation of signs and symptoms that may signify dependence. Attempts to label the withdrawal signs and symptoms as opiate-like or ethanol-like may complicate the issue only because such an effort may conceal a real dependence on these other drugs. Thus, when obvious signs of distress are observed during periods of forced abstinence, it is worthwhile to consider the possibility that the individual may, in fact, be dependent on other drugs. Recently, there have been a few reports of opioid dependence in bodybuilders (Evans, Bowen et al., 1985; McBride, Williamson & Peterson, 1996), and these individuals clearly met criteria for dependence on both drug classes. Thus, the possibility of polydrug abuse should always be considered when dealing with anabolic-androgenic steroid abusers. Interestingly, according to the American Psychiatric Association's *Diagnostic and Statistical Manual of Mental Disorders, 4th Edition* (*DSM-IV*; 1994), the diagnosis of polysubstance dependence cannot be made if the individual meets criteria for dependence on one of the substances; the criteria for polydrug abuse appear to be geared toward identifying individuals who experiment with a number of different drugs.

Diagnostic Classifications. It is apparent from the historical literature that anabolic-androgenic steroid users have met formal criteria for dependence in the American Psychiatric Association's *Diagnostic and Statistical Manual of Mental Disorders, 3rd Edition, Revised* (*DSM-IIIR*; 1987) by having three or more of the following: (1) use continues over longer periods than desired; (2) attempts to stop are unsuccessful; (3) substantial time is spent obtaining, using or recovering from their use; (4) use continues despite knowledge of their harmful effects; (5) physical signs of withdrawal appear upon cessation of use; and (6) they are taken to relieve the withdrawal symptoms (Kashkin & Kleber, 1989). The criteria for the *DSM-IV* are similar, except that a seventh factor of tolerance development, as defined by a need to increase the dose to achieve the desired effect or that a markedly diminished effect occurred with continued use of the same dose, was added.

There is another factor that must be considered when attempting to diagnose anabolic-androgenic steroid abuse. In a study of 108 bodybuilders, Pope and colleagues (1993) noted a rather high percentage of anorexia nervosa and uncovered a body image disorder which they labeled *reverse anorexia*. This condition shares many signs and symptoms of body dysmorphic syndrome (Phillips, 1996). The profile of the former is that they view themselves as being too small and weak, when they are quite large and strong. The incidence of this disorder was 8% among anabolic-androgenic steroid users and was not observed in any of the non users. The authors postulate that these body image disorders may have some influence on an individual's decision to use anabolic-androgen steroids. Because the perceived size, shape and attractiveness of one's body is likely tied to self-esteem (Lombardo, 1992), and in general, men want to be three pounds heavier, taller and have wider shoulders (Wroblewski, 1997), anabolic-androgenic steroid use may be viewed as a way of speeding up the process in order to attain physical attractiveness. This similarity in profiles between body image disorders and drug use might suggest that anabolic-androgenic steroid abusers who present with a profile of body image disturbance may respond to the same treatments that have been used for body dysmorphic syndrome. Serotonin reuptake blockers have been marginally successful in treating body dysmorphic disorder (Hollander, Liebowitz et al., 1989), and while there have been no published studies to this effect with anabolic-androgenic steroid users, fluoxetine has been marginally successful in a small sample of bodybuilders who presented with depression during withdrawal from anabolic-androgenic steroid use (Malone & Dimeff, 1992).

ABSORPTION AND METABOLISM

Anabolic-androgenic steroids are taken either orally or injected deep into the muscle; there is no intravenous formulation, nor is there a smokable product.

By far the greatest influence on subsequent development of toxic side effects is the route of administration. About half of an oral dose of testosterone is metabolized via the first pass effect, so very large doses are needed. Some 17-α-alkylated analogues of testosterone like methyltestosterone resist such metabolism and so can be given orally in smaller doses. The oral route gives rise to a number of 17-alkylated metabolites, which are formed in the liver. This overload, not only of the metabolizing enzymes, but because the doses taken are so high, causes significant stress on this organ.

Testosterone is metabolized to 5-α-dihydrotestosterone (DHT) in certain tissues such as prostate gland, seminal vesicles and pubic skin. As DHT has two to three times the affinity for the androgen receptor as the parent hormone, the effects of testosterone are enhanced in these tissues. One of the more interesting aspects of testosterone's metabolic pathway is that it is converted to estradiol in tissues that contain an aromatase enzyme (Martini, 1982). The biological significance of circulating estrogens in males is unknown, but they may be involved with sex-hormone-binding globulin (SHBG) and lipoproteins. Further, the estrogen that results from this metabolic process may interact with estrogen receptors to produce an anabolic effect (Bardin, Catterall et al., 1990; Svare, 1990). The 17-α-alkylated analogues discussed above are not metabolized to either DHT or estrogen. Instead, they interact with the androgen receptor (Wilson, 1988; Winters, 1990). Thus, the overall profile of relative anabolic to androgenic effects is not only due to the parent compound, but to the profile of metabolites that result. With the advent of widespread use of these drugs during athletic competition, a number of analytical laboratories have been set up to detect either the parent drug or its metabolites (Schanzer, 1996; Catlin, 1987). In addition to providing quantitative analyses of the various synthetic analogues, most labs attempt to measure the testosterone/epitestosterone ratio as a metric of exogenous testosterone administration.

MECHANISMS OF ACTION

About 95% of the testosterone in males is synthesized in the testes, while the remaining 5% comes from the adrenals. The cholesterol used in the synthetic pathway comes from acetate that is stored in the testes, and not from circulating blood levels. Anabolic-androgenic steroids have long been thought to exert their effects in the periphery, primarily by increasing the rate of RNA transcription (see Lukas, 1993, 1996). About half of the circulating testosterone is tightly bound to SHBG, and the other half is lightly bound to albumin, from which it freely dissociates and from whence it can diffuse passively into target cells. After attaching to a steroid receptor in the cytoplasm, the hormone-receptor complex moves into the nucleus where it binds to sites on the chromatin, resulting in new mRNA. If the target tissue is skeletal muscle, then new myofilaments are formed which causes myofibrils to divide (Wilson, 1988; Rogivkin, 1976). As it is not completely understood whether this activity occurs at the supraphysiologic doses typically taken by anabolic-androgenic steroid abusers, another mechanism was sought. It has been suggested that high doses of anabolic-androgenic steroids cross-react with glucocorticoid receptors which control the catabolic rates of protein (Wilson, 1988; Mayer & Rosen, 1977; Raaka, Finnerty & Samuels, 1989). The significance of the anticatabolic effect of these drugs is often ignored in lieu of the more direct effect of these steroids on protein synthesis. It is also possible that the stress of strenuous workouts is not felt by athletes taking these compounds because the stress-induced increase in cortisol is somehow blocked. This action would also permit the workouts to be longer and more vigorous, further improving performance.

It is possible that the physical changes attributed to a direct effect of anabolic-androgenic steroids on protein synthesis may actually be mediated via a direct effect on the central nervous system. Such effects might result in increased motivation and intensity of training to a degree that performance is improved. Increased aggressive behavior may also play a role in the training process. It is likely that the use of supraphysiologic doses of these drugs can have both a direct effect on muscle tissue and an indirect effect by altering emotions like motivation and drive such that the training periods are longer and more productive, resulting in improved performance.

There is provocative new evidence that anabolic-androgenic steroids interact directly with peripheral benzodiazepine receptors in rat brain (Masonis & McCarthy, 1996). These receptors are mitochondrial proteins that are involved with regulating steroid synthesis and transport, so it seems plausible that their activation via exogenous anabolic-androgenic steroids could have an impact on behavior that is mediated by these receptors.

The increase in body weight, especially during the first weeks of use is almost certainly attributed to the stimulation of mineralcorticoid receptors, resulting in sodium and ultimately, water retention as well as increasing amounts of circulating estrogen that has been aromatized from testosterone. This effect gives the muscles, particularly the deltoid, a "puffy" appearance.

The increase in red blood cell production is probably the major reason that long distance runners may use these drugs because endurance, rather than bulk muscle mass, is an asset in this sport. Blood volume probably increases as a result of erythropoietin synthesis. This effect is due to direct action on bone marrow and easily leads to a rise in hematocrit (Narducci, Wagner et al., 1990).

REINFORCING PROPERTIES

Perhaps the most important concept to understand about anabolic-androgenic steroid abuse is that it does not follow typical patterns observed with traditional drugs of abuse such as cocaine, heroin, alcohol, nicotine and marihuana. In this regard, along with most hallucinogens such as LSD, anabolic-androgenic steroids are not self-administered by laboratory animals, although a recent study in male rats demonstrated that these drugs may alter the sensitivity of brain reward systems (Clark, Lindenfeld & Gibbons, 1996). In that study, a two-week treatment with methandrostenolone alone had no effect on brain reward systems, but a 15-week treatment with a cocktail of three different anabolic-androgenic steroids resulted in a shift in the response patterns to brain electrical reward and amphetamine.

The absence of a well-defined pattern of self-administration in animals is confirmed by the finding that humans cannot tell whether they have been given an active anabolic-androgenic steroid or placebo (Ariel & Saville, 1972). Marginal discriminations were made in two studies, but only after a period of extended testing had been employed (Freed, Banks et al., 1975; Crist, Stackpole & Peake, 1983). However, it is likely that it was the side effects of these drugs that were detected, rather than any positive reinforcing effects. As the latter are thought to regulate drug-taking behavior in both humans and animals, the question that remains is "why do humans use and abuse anabolic-androgenic steroids?"

It is well known that if the subjective effects of a psychoactive drug are sufficiently delayed after self-administration, then the drug's reinforcing efficacy decreases and drug-seeking behavior is reduced (Balster & Schuster, 1973). Although there are a few scattered anecdotal reports that high-doses of anabolic-androgenic steroids can elevate mood, no controlled studies have demonstrated that these drugs produce immediate positive mood effects or euphoria. Anabolic-androgenic steroids can act within minutes to hours on cell membrane receptor sites, but the real beneficial effects of such action (e.g., protein synthesis) takes more time.

ACKNOWLEDGMENT: This manuscript was supported by Research Scientist Award KO5 DA00343 from the National Institute on Drug Abuse. The author gratefully acknowledges the technical assistance of Carol Buchanan with its preparation.

REFERENCES

Alen M & Suominen J (1984). Effect of androgenic and anabolic steroids on spermatogenesis in power athletes. *International Journal of Sports Medicine* 5(Suppl):189.

American Psychiatric Association (1994). *Diagnostic and Statistical Manual of Mental Disorders, 4th Edition.* Washington, DC: American Psychiatric Press.

American Psychiatric Association (1987). *Diagnostic and Statistical Manual of Mental Disorders, 3rd Edition, Revised.* Washington, DC: American Psychiatric Press.

Anderson W & McKeag B (1985). *The Substance Use and Abuse Habits of College Student Athletes. Research Paper No. 2.* Mission, KS: National Collegiate Athletic Association.

Annitto WR & Layman WA (1980). Anabolic steroids and acute schizophrenic episode. *Journal of Clinical Psychiatry* 41:143–144.

Appell H, Heller-Umpfenbach B, Feraudi M & Weicker H (1983). Ultra-structural and morphometric investigations on the effects of training and administration of anabolic steroids on the myocardium of guinea pigs. *International Journal of Sports Medicine* 4:268–274.

Ariel G & Saville W (1972). The physiological effects of placebos. *Medicine and Science in Sports* 4:124.

Bahrke MS & Yesalis III CE (1994). Weight training: A potential confounding factor in examining the psychological and behavioural effects of anabolic-androgenic steroids. *Sports Medicine* 18(5):309–318.

Balster RL & Schuster CR (1973). Fixed-interval schedule of cocaine reinforcement: Effect of dose and infusion duration. *Journal of the Experimental Analysis of Behavior* 20(1):119–129.

Bardin CW, Catterall JF, Janne OA et al. (1990). The androgen-induced phenotype. In GC Lin & L Erinoff (eds.) *Anabolic Steroid Abuse (NIDA Research Monograph 102).* Rockville, MD: National Institute on Drug Abuse, 131–141.

Behrendt H & Boffin H (1977). Myocardial cell lesions caused by an anabolic hormone. *Cell and Tissue Research* 181:423–426.

Boje O (1939). Doping. *Bulletin of Health Organization League of Nations* 8:439–469.

Bowman S (1990). Anabolic steroids and infarction. *British Medical Journal* 300:750.

Brower KJ (1989). Rehabilitation for anabolic-androgenic steroid dependence. *Clinics in Sports Medicine* 1:171–181.

Brower KJ (1992). Anabolic steroids: Addictive, psychiatric, and medical consequences. *The American Journal on Addictions* 1(2):100–114.

Brower KJ, Eliopulos GA, Blow FC, Catlin DH & Beresford TP (1990). Evidence for physical and psychological dependence on anabolic-androgenic steroids in weightlifters. *American Journal of Psychiatry* 147:510–512.

Brower KJ, Blow FC, Young JP & Hill EM (1991). Symptoms and correlates of anabolic-androgenic steroid dependence. *British Journal of Addiction* 86:759–768.

Buckley WE, Yesalis CE, Friedl KE, Anderson WA, Streit AL & Wright JE (1988). Estimated prevalence of anabolic steroid use among male high school seniors. *Journal of the American Medical Association* 260:3441–3445.

Buss AH & Durkee A (1957). An inventory for assessing different kinds of hostility. *Journal of Consulting Psychology* 21:343–349.

Catlin DH (1987). Detection of drug use by athletes. In RH Strauss (ed.) *Drugs and Performance in Sports.* Philadelphia, PA: W.B. Saunders, 103–120.

Cherek DR (1981). Effects of smoking different doses of nicotine on human aggressive behavior. *Psychopharmacology* 75:339–345.

Clark AS, Lindenfeld RC & Gibbons CH (1996). Anabolic-androgenic steroids and brain reward. *Pharmacology, Biochemistry and Behavior* 53(3):741–745.

Conacher GN & Workman DG (1989). Violent crime possibly associated with anabolic steroid use. *American Journal of Psychiatry* 146:679.

Cooper CJ, Noakes TD, Dunne T, Lambert MI & Rochford K (1996). A high prevalence of abnormal personality traits in chronic users of anabolic-androgenic steroids. *British Journal of Sports Medicine* 30(3):246–250.

Cowart VS (1987). Some predict increased steroid use in sports despite drug testing, crackdown on supplies. *Journal of the American Medical Association* 257:3025–3029.

Crist DM, Stackpole PJ & Peake GT (1983). Effects of androgenic-anabolic steroids on neuromuscular power and body composition. *Journal of Applied Physiology* 54:366–370.

Dart R (1991). Drugs in the workplace: Anabolic steroid abuse among law enforcement officers. *Police Chief* 58(7):18.

David HG, Green JT, Grant AJ & Wilson CA (1995). Simultaneous bilateral quadriceps rupture: A complication of anabolic steroid abuse. *Journal of Bone and Joint Surgery (British edition)* 77(1):159–160.

Durant RH, Rickert VI, Ashworth CS, Newman C & Slavens G (1993). Use of multiple drugs among adolescents who use anabolic steroids. *The New England Journal of Medicine* 328:922–926.

Elliott D & Goldberg L (1996). Intervention and prevention of steroid use in adolescents. *American Journal of Sports Medicine* 24(6):5–46, 1996.

Evans WS, Bowen JN, Giordano FL & Clark B (1985). A case of stadol dependence (letter). *Journal of the American Medical Association* 253(15):2191–2192.

Ferenchick BS (1990). Are androgenic steroids thrombogenic? *The New England Journal of Medicine* 322:476.

Freed DLJ, Banks AJ, Longson D & Burley PM (1975). Anabolic steroids in athletics: Crossover double-blind trial on weightlifters. *British Medical Journal* 2:471–473.

Freinhar JP & Alvarez W (1985). Androgen-induced hypomania. *Journal of Clinical Psychiatry* 46:354–355.

Friedl KE (1990). Reappraisal of the health risks associated with high doses of oral and injectable androgenic steroids. In GC Lin & L Erinoff (eds.) *Anabolic Steroid Abuse (NIDA Research Monograph 102).* Rockville, MD: National Institute on Drug Abuse, 142–177.

Galligani N, Renck A & Hansen S (1996). Personality profile of men using anabolic androgenic steroids. *Hormones and Behavior* 30(2):170–175.

Goldberg L, Bents R, Bosworth E, Trevisan L & Elliott D (1991). Anabolic steroid education and adolescents: Do scare tactics work? *Pediatrics* 87:283–286.

Hartgens F, Kuipers H, Wijnen JAG & Keizer HA (1996). Body composition, cardiovascular risk factors and liver function in long term androgenic-anabolic steroids using body builders three months after drug withdrawal. *International Journal of Sports Medicine* 17:429–433.

Haupt HA & Rovere GB (1984). Anabolic steroids: A review of the literature. *American Journal of Sports Medicine* 12:469–484.

Hollander E, Liebowitz MR, Winchel R, Klumker A & Klein DF (1989). Treatment of body-dysmorphic disorder with serotonin reuptake blockers. *American Journal of Psychiatry* 146(6):768–770.

Johnson MD, Jay MS, Shoup B & Rickert VI (1989). Anabolic steroid use by male adolescents. *Pediatrics* 83(6):921–924.

Karch SB (1993). Anabolic steroids. *The Pathology of Drug Abuse.* Boca Raton, FL: CRC Press, 355–373.

Karila T, Laaksonen R, Jokelainen K, Himberg JJ & Seppala T (1996). The effects of anabolic androgenic steroids on serum ubiquinone and dolichol levels among steroid abusers. *Metabolism* 45(7): 844–847.

Kashkin KB & Kleber HD (1989). Hooked on Hormones? An anabolic steroid addiction hypothesis. *Journal of the American Medical Association* 262(22):3166–3170.

Kashkin KB (1992). Anabolic Steroids. In JH Lowinson, P Ruiz, RB Millman & JG Langrod (eds.) *Substance Abuse: A Comprehensive Textbook, 2nd Ed.* Baltimore, MD: Williams & Wilkins, 380–395.

Kochakian CD (1990). History of anabolic-androgenic steroids. In GC Lin & L Erinoff (eds.) *Anabolic Steroid Abuse (NIDA Research Monograph 102).* Rockville, MD: National Institute on Drug Abuse, 29–59.

Kouri EM, Lukas SE, Pope HG Jr. & Oliva PS (1995a). Increased aggressive responding in male volunteers following the administration of gradually increasing doses of testosterone cypionate. *Drug and Alcohol Dependence* 40:73–79.

Kouri EM, Pope HG Jr, Katz DL & Oliva P (1995b). Fat-free mass index in users and nonusers of anabolic-androgenic steroids. *Clinical Journal of Sports Medicine* 5(4):223–228.

Lenders JWM, Demacker PN, Vos JA et al. (1988). Deleterious effects of anabolic steroids on serum lipoproteins, blood pressure and liver function in amateur bodybuilders. *International Journal of Sports Medicine* 9:19–23.

Lombardo JA (1992). Anabolic-androgenic steroids. In GC Lin & L Erinoff (eds.) *Anabolic Steroid Abuse (NIDA Research Monograph 102).* Rockville, MD: National Institute on Drug Abuse, 60–73.

Lukas SE (1993). Current perspectives on anabolic-androgenic steroid abuse. *Trends in Pharmacological Sciences* 14:61–68

Lukas SE (1994). *Steroids.* Hillside, NJ.: Enslow Publishers.

Lukas SE (1996). CNS effects and abuse liability of anabolic- androgenic steroids. *Annual Review of Pharmacology and Toxicology* 36:333–357.

Luke J, Farb A, Virmani R & Sample R (1991). Sudden cardiac death during exercise in a weight lifter using anabolic androgenic steroids: Pathological and toxicological findings. *Journal of Forensic Sciences* 35(6):1441–1447.

Malone DA Jr & Dimeff RJ (1992). The use of fluoxetine in depression associated with anabolic steroid withdrawal: A case series. *Journal of Clinical Psychiatry* 53(4):130–132.

Martini L (1982). The 5-alpha-reduction of testosterone in the neuroendocrine structures: Biochemical and physiological implications. *Endocrine Reviews* 3:1–25.

Masonis AE & McCarthy MP (1996). Direct interactions of androgenic/anabolic steroids with the peripheral benzodiazepine receptor in rat brain: Implications for the psychological and physiological manifestations of androgenic/anabolic steroid abuse. *Journal of Steroid Biochemistry and Molecular Biology* 58(56):551–555.

Mayer M & Rosen F (1977). Interaction of glucocorticoids and androgens with skeletal muscle. *Metabolism* 27:937–962.

McBride AJ, Williamson K & Petersen T (1996). Three cases of nalbuphine hydrochloride dependence associated with anabolic steroid use. *British Journal of Sports Medicine* 30(1):69–70.

McNutt RA, Ferenchick GF, Kirlin PC & Hamlin NJ (1988). Acute myocardial infarction in a 22 year old, world-class weightlifter using anabolic steroids. *American Journal of Cardiology* 62:164.

Melia P, Pipe A & Greenberg L (1996). The use of anabolic- androgenic steroids by Canadian students. *Clinical Journal of Sports Medicine* 6(1):9–14.

Moore WB (1988). Anabolic steroid use in adolescents. *Journal of the American Medical Association* 260:3484–3486.

Narducci WA, Wagner JC, Hendrickson TP & Jeffrey TP (1990). Anabolic steroids—A review of the clinical toxicology and diagnostic screening. *Clinical Toxicology* 28(3):287–310.

National Institute on Drug Abuse (1996a). *National Survey Results on Drug Use from The Monitoring The Future Study, 1975–1995, Vol. I.* Bethesda, MD: National Institutes of Health (NIH Publication No. 96-4027).

National Institute on Drug Abuse (1996b). *National Survey Results on Drug Use from The Monitoring The Future Study, 1975–1994, Vol. II.* Bethesda, MD: National Institutes of Health (NIH Publication No. 96-4139).

O'Connor JS, Baldini FD, Skinner JS & Einstein M (1990). Blood chemistry of current and previous anabolic steroid users. *Military Medicine* 155(2):72–75.

Palacios A, McClure RB, Campfield A & Swerdloff RS (1981). Effect of testosterone enanthate on testis size. *Journal of Urology* 26:46–48.

Pecking A, Lejolly JM & Najean Y (1980). Hepatic toxicity of androgen therapy in aplastic anemia. *Nouvelle Revue Francaise D Hematologie* 22:257–265.

Perry PJ, Yates WR & Anderson KH (1990). Psychiatric effects of anabolic steroids: A controlled retrospective study. *Annals of Clinical Psychiatry* 2:11–17.

Phillips KA (1996). Body dysmorphic disorder: Diagnosis and treatment of imagined ugliness. *Journal of Clinical Psychiatry* 57(Suppl 8):61–4; discussion 65.

Phillips KA, McElroy SL, Keck PE Jr, Hudson JI & Pope HG Jr (1994). A comparison of delusional and nondelusional body dysmorphic disorder in 100 cases. *Psychopharmacology Bulletin* 30(2):179–186.

Pope HG Jr & Katz DL (1987). Body-builder's psychosis. *Lancet* 1:863.

Pope HG Jr & Katz DL (1988). Affective and psychotic symptoms associated with anabolic steroid use. *American Journal of Psychiatry* 145(4):487–490.

Pope HG Jr, Katz DL & Hudson JI (1993). Anorexia nervosa and "reverse anorexia" among 108 male bodybuilders. *Comprehensive Psychiatry* 34(6):406–409.

Raaka BM, Finnerty M & Samuels HH (1989). The glucocorticoid antagonist 17 alpha-methyltestosterone binds to the 10S glucocorticoid receptor and blocks agonist-mediated disassociation of the 10S oligomer to the 4S deoxyribonucleic acid-binding subunit. *Molecular Endocrinology* 3:322–341.

Rogivkin BA (1976). The role of low molecular weight compounds in the regulation of skeletal muscle genome activity during exercise. *Medicine and Science in Sports* 8:104.

Rogol AD & Yesalis CE 3d (1992). Anabolic-androgenic steroids and the adolescent. *Pediatric Annals* 21(3): 175, 179, 180–181, 183, 186–188.

Schanzer W (1996). Metabolism of anabolic androgenic steroids. *Clinical Chemistry* 42(7):1001–1020.

Schwerin MJ & Corcoran KJ (1996). Beliefs about steroids: User vs. non-user comparisons. *Drug and Alcohol Dependence* 40(3):221–225.

Substance Abuse and Mental Health Services Administration (1996a). *National Household Survey on Drug Abuse: Main Findings 1994.* Washington, DC: U.S. Government Printing Office (DHHS Publication No. (SMA) 96-3085).

Substance Abuse and Mental Health Services Administration (1996b). *Proceedings of the National Consensus Meeting on the Use, Abuse and Sequelae of Abuse of Methamphetamine with Implications for Prevention, Treatment and Research.* Washington, DC: U.S. Government Printing Office (DHHS Publication Number (SMA) 96-8013).

Svare BB (1990). Anabolic steroids and behavior: A preclinical research prospectus. In GC Lin & L Erinoff (eds.) *Anabolic Steroid Abuse (NIDA Research Monograph 102).* Rockville, MD: National Institute on Drug Abuse, 224–241.

Swanson C, Gaines L & Gore B (1991). Abuse of anabolic Steroids. *FBI Law Enforcement Bulletin* 60(8):19–23.

Tanner SM, Miller DW & Alongi C (1995). Anabolic steroid use by adolescents: Prevalence, motives, and knowledge of risks. *Clinical Journal of Sport Medicine* 5:108–115.

Thompson PB, Curinane AN, Sady SP et al. (1989). Contrasting effects of testosterone and stanozolol on serum lipoprotein levels. *Journal of the American Medical Association* 261:1165–1168.

Todd T (1987). Anabolic steroids: The gremlins of sport. *Journal of Sports History* 14:87–107.

VanItallie TB, Yang MU, Heymsfield SB, Funk RC & Boileau RA (1990). Height-normalized indices of the body's fat-free mass and fat mass: Potentially useful indicators of nutritional status. *American Journal of Clinical Nutrition* 52:953–959.

Wang MQ, Fitzhugh EC, Yesalis CE, Buckley WE & Smiciklas-Wright H (1994). Desire for weight gain and potential risk of adolescent males using anabolic steroids. *Perceptual and Motor Skills* 78:267–274.

Westaby B, Ogle SJ, Paridians FJ, Randall JB & Murray-Lyon IN (1977). Liver damage from long-term methyltestosterone. *Lancet* 1(8032):261–263.

Wilson JD (1988). Androgen abuse by athletes. *Endocrine Review* 9:181–199.

Wilson IC, Prange AJ Jr & Lara PP (1974). Methyltestosterone with imipramine in men: Conversion of depression to paranoid reaction. *American Journal of Psychiatry* 131:21–24.

Winters SJ (1990). Androgens: Endocrine physiology and pharmacology. In GC Lin & L Erinoff (eds.) *Anabolic Steroid Abuse (NIDA Research Monograph 102).* Rockville, MD: National Institute on Drug Abuse, 113–130.

Wroblewski AM (1997). Androgenic-anabolic steroids and body dysmorphia in young men. *Journal of Psychosomatic Research* 42(3):225–234.

Yates WR, Perry P & Murray S (1992). Aggression and hostility in anabolic steroid users. *Biological Psychiatry* 31:1232–1234.

Yesalis CE, Herrick RT, Buckley WE, Friedl KE, Brannon D & Wright JE (1988). Self-reported use of anabolic androgenic steroids by elite powerlifters. *Physiology of Sportsmedicine* 16:91–100.

Yesalis CE, Streit AL, Vicary JR, Friedl KE, Brannon D & Buckley WE (1989). Anabolic steroid use: Indications of habituation among adolescents. *Journal of Drug Education* 19:103–116.

Yesalis C, Anderson W, Buckley W & Wright J (1990a). Incidence of the nonmedical use of anabolic-androgenic steroids. In *Anabolic Steroid Abuse.* Rockville, MD: National Institute on Drug Abuse.

Yesalis CE, Vicary JR, Buckley WE, Streit AL, Katz DL & Wright JE (1990b). Indications of psychological dependence among anabolic-androgenic steroid abusers. In GC Lin & L Erinoff (eds.) *Anabolic Steroid Abuse (NIDA Research Monograph 102).* Rockville, MD: National Institute on Drug Abuse, 196–214.

Yesalis CE, Kennedy NJ, Kopstein AN & Bahrke MS (1993). Anabolic-androgenic steroid use in the United States. *Journal of the American Medical Association* 270(10):1217–1221.

CHAPTER 10

The Pharmacology of Inhalants

Stephen H. Dinwiddie, M.D.

Drugs in the Class
Inhalant Use and Misuse
Adverse Effects
Addiction Liability
Absorption and Metabolism
Mechanisms of Action
Reinforcing Properties

Inhalation long has been recognized as a highly effective means of ingesting many drugs, ranging from nicotine to opiates. It is easy to understand why this might be so: the extensive capillary surface area of the lungs allows rapid absorption, with a consequent "rush" that is described as second in intensity only to direct intravenous injection (Blum, 1984). However, the characteristic shared by the class of agents known variously as solvents, volatile substances, or inhalants is that, unlike most other psychoactive substances, this is the preferred and virtually only route by which these compounds are self-administered.

DRUGS IN THE CLASS

The inhalants comprise a heterogeneous class of addictive substances. Included in this class are paints, spray paints, numerous organic solvents, gasoline and other petrochemicals, and glues; frequently the preparations used by addicts have a variety of compounds with psychoactive properties, as well as other chemicals without such abuse potential, but with toxicities of their own. Some authorities also include in this classification vasodilators such as amyl or butyl nitrite and anesthetics such as nitrous oxide, halothane, or enflurane (Table 1). However, inclusion of the latter agents has been criticized because of substantial differences in factors predisposing to use, consequences of use, and degree of impairment of the user, and it has been suggested that "inhalant abuse" and related terms should be restricted to use of volatile hydrocarbons, excluding users of nitrites and anesthetic gases (Beauvais & Oetting, 1987). This also is the approach taken in the third edition, revised (*DSM-IIIR*) and fourth edition (*DSM-IV*) of the *Diagnostic and Statistical Manuals of Mental Disorders* of the American Psychtriatric Association (1987, 1994); these manuals classify problematic use of the latter agents as "psychoactive substance dependence not otherwise specified."

INHALANT USE AND MISUSE

Even with the class of inhalants restricted in this manner, precise description of the range of substances and their pharmacology and toxicology is a challenging task, both because of the great variety of chemicals that may be used and because many (if not most) agents commonly used by inhalant addicts are a mixture of substances. Thus, relating specific toxic effects to individual agents may not always be possible.

Whatever their precise chemical make-up, most commonly these substances are "sniffed" directly from the container, "huffed" from a rag soaked in the substance and held to the face, or placed in a bag and the vapors repeatedly inhaled. In some cases, the substance may be sprayed directly into the mouth (Sharp & Rosenberg, 1992). Progression from "sniffing" to "huffing" to "bagging" is associated with higher vapor concentrations and may be a sign of increasing familiarity with the misuse of these substances (Linden, 1990). More exotic methods also have been used: there are reports of users increasing vapor concentrations by heating before inhaling, as well as drinking or even attempting to inject these substances (Barnes, 1979).

Misuse of inhalants generally is thought to be most common among younger people; their popularity among adolescents and even preadolescents presumably stems at least in part from their low cost, easy availability, and the fact that these substances can be obtained in small containers that are easily concealed. In addition, unlike most other psychoactive substances, purchase and possession by minors of most inhalants is not illegal (McHugh, 1987). Thus, for many, inhalants may be one of the first psychoactive substances to be used.

In 1979, it was reported that lifetime prevalence of solvent use was 9.8% among adolescents aged 12 to 17 and 16.5% among young adults age 18 to 25 (Fishburn, Abelson & Cisin, 1979). A decade later, it was estimated that nearly 7% of high school seniors had tried inhalants in the preceding year (Crider & Rouse, 1988). More recent data from the Monitoring the Future study indicate that, by 1996, little had changed: 7.6% of twelfth-graders reported inhalant use in the preceding year and 16.6% reported lifetime use. It should be noted, furthermore, that because younger users may be more prone to drop out of school and thus not to be included in such surveys, calculations of use among older stu-

TABLE 1. Chemicals Commonly Found in Inhalants

Product	Chemicals
Adhesives	
Airplane glue	Toluene, ethyl acetate
Rubber cement	Hexane, toluene, methyl chloride, acetone, methyl ethyl ketone, methyl butyl ketone
PVC cement	Trichloroethylene
Aerosols	
Paint sprays	Butane, propane (U.S.), fluorocarbons, toluene, hydrocarbons, "Texas Shoe Shine" (a shoe spray containing toluene)
Hair sprays	Butane, propane (U.S.), fluorocarbons
Deodorants, air fresheners	Butane, propane (U.S.), fluorocarbons
Analgesic spray	Fluorocarbons
Asthma spray	Fluorocarbons
Anesthetics	
Gases	Nitrous oxide
Liquids	Halothane, enflurance
Locals	Ethyl chloride
Cleaning Agents	
Dry cleaning fluid	Tetrachloroethylene, trichloroethane
Spot removers	Tetrachloroethylene, trichloroethane, trichloroethylene
Degreasers	Tetrachloroethylene, trichloroethane, trichloroethylene
Solvents	
Polish remover	Acetone
Paint remover	Toluene, methylene chloride, methanol
Paint thinners	Toluene, methylene chloride, methanol
Correction fluid thinners	Trichloroethylene, trichloroethane
Fuel gas	Butane
Lighter fluid	Butane, isopropane
Fire extinguisher propellant	Bromochlorodifluoromethane
Food Products	
Whipped cream	Nitrous oxide
Whippets	Nitrous oxide
"Room Odorizers"	
"Locker Room" "Rush" "Poppers"	(Iso)amyl nitrite, (iso)butyl nitrite, isopropyl nitrite, butyl nitrite

Source: Sharp CW & Rosenberg NL (1992). Volatile substances. In JH Lowinson, P Ruiz, RB Millman & JG Lagrod (eds.) *Substance Abuse: A Comprehensive Textbook*. Baltimore, MD: Williams & Wilkins. Reprinted by permission.

dents may, if anything, underestimate the true prevalence among adolescents or even preadolescents (Oetting & Beauvais, 1990), while among some economically disadvantaged groups, prevalence of use may be even higher (Beauvais & Oetting, 1988; Mata & Andrew, 1988; Stybel, 1977).

ADVERSE EFFECTS

Complications of use are varied, as might be expected given the heterogeneity of agents and patterns of use. However, one complication deserves special note. Inhalants are cardiac depressants, and hundreds of cases of "sudden sniffing death" have been reported, most likely due to cardiac arrhythmia occurring shortly after using inhalants. The mechanism may involve sensitization of cardiac muscle to the effects of circulating catecholamines, and risk may be even further increased by "bagging," which increases arterial partial pressure of carbon dioxide (Pollard, 1990). Death also may result from vehicular trauma, aspiration, or respiratory depression (al-Alousi, 1989; Anderson, McNair & Ramsey, 1985; Bass, 1970; King, Smialec & Troutman, 1985; Linden, 1990).

The wide variety of inhalants that are abused greatly complicates the task of tracing the connection between a given substance and resultant toxicity. It is nonetheless clear that these agents can cause a wide variety of physical complications, most prominently involving central and peripheral nervous system, lungs, and kidneys (Meadows & Verghese, 1996).

Cortical, cerebellar, and brainstem atrophy have been reported among chronic users; such patients may present with a variety of clinical findings, including cognitive impairment, cranial nerve signs, or evidence of damage to cerebellum or pyramidal tract, while laboratory evaluation may reveal abnormal electroencephalographic (EEG) or brainstem auditory evoked response (BAER) patterns (Hormes, Filley & Rosenberg, 1986; Lazar, Ho et al., 1983; Rosenberg, Spitz et al., 1988; Streicher, Cabow et al., 1981). Patients also may present with complaints of generalized weakness, with examination revealing peripheral neuropathies in addition to CNS findings (Prockop, Alt & Tison, 1974; Streicher, Cabow et al., 1981). Renal complications include metabolic acidosis consistent with distal renal tubular acidosis, acute renal tubular necrosis, and chronic renal failure. Bone marrow suppression and hepatitis also have been reported. A variety of other presentations are possible, including gastrointestinal complaints (nausea, diarrhea, abdominal pain, or vomiting, occasionally with hematemesis) or respiratory complaints. Most inhalants are irritants and thus may cause coughing, wheezing, or upper respiratory tract difficulties; in addition, patients may present with cyanosis or other pulmonary complications secondary to a variety of conditions caused by inhalant use, such as asphyxia, chemical pneumonitis, or methemoglobinemia (Fischman & Oster, 1979; Linden, 1990; Streicher, Cabow et al., 1981).

While several methods are available for detecting organic solvents in body fluids, laboratory assay for the presence of inhalants is not routinely done in clinical practice. Instead, the diagnosis of inhalant intoxication, abuse, or dependence is made on the basis of history and physical examination (Linden, 1990). Users may present with direct evidence of inhalant use, such as residue of solvents on clothing or skin, or an odor of solvents or paint on the user's breath (Linden, 1990; Morton, 1987; Ron, 1986). "Glue-sniffer's rash," conjunctival irritation, or cyanosis also may indicate inhalant use; due to the flammable nature of these compounds, thermal burns also are not uncommon.

ADDICTION LIABILITY

Compared to the large number of persons who have, on a lifetime basis, experimented with inhalants, addiction specifically to these agents appears to be relatively uncommon, with estimates in the range of 0.3% of the population or 3.7% of those who have tried inhalants (Anthony, Arria & Johnson, 1995). There are indications that inhalant use is underrecognized and underreported in adults (Hershey & Miller, 1982), and secondary initiation of inhalant use, after addiction to other drugs, may be more frequent than generally is recognized (Altenkirch & Kindermann, 1986; D'Amanda, Plumb & Taintor, 1977). Moreover, on a lifetime basis, any history of inhalant use appears to be associated with very substantial polysubstance use; thus, it may be that, rather than simply "maturing out," those predisposed to development of addiction merely substitute other drugs for inhalants. Indeed, it has been reported that persons with a history of inhalant use are five to 10 times more likely than non-users to report use of hallucinogens, opioids, stimulants or sedative-hypnotics. In the same population, a history of inhalant use appears to be modestly predictive of later intravenous drug use (Dinwiddie, Reich &

Cloninger, 1991a, 1991b; Schutz, Chilcoat & Anthony, 1994; Johnson, Schutz et al., 1995).

Co-morbid conditions, particularly antisocial personality disorder (ASPD), also appear to be common among those who report a history of inhalant use, at least in some samples (Crites & Schuckit, 1979). In one series, 63% received a diagnosis of ASPD. That disorder, in turn, was found to be associated with elevated rates of alcoholism and secondary depression, which were diagnosed in 68% and 33% of inhalant users, respectively (Dinwiddie, Reich & Cloninger, 1990; 1991a). These associated problems may, in turn, contribute to the apparent high relapse rate and overall difficulty in treating patients who are primarily addicted to inhalants (Dinwiddie, Zorumski & Rubin, 1987; McSherry, 1988; Stybel, 1977); clearly, for some users at least, these substances have powerful rewarding properties and are seen as preferable to other addictive substances.

However, any conclusions regarding the addictive properties of the inhalants must be tempered by possible biases in selection of subjects. It is commonly known that ASPD is associated with the highest odds of having a co-morbid substance use on a lifetime basis (Regier, Farmer et al., 1990). To the extent that substantial inhalant use is associated with high rates of ASPD, it may be that, rather than having particularly pronounced addictive qualities, inhalants simply are used differentially by those with antisocial traits and thus, presumably, higher liabilities toward addiction to any substance—including inhalants. Those without pronounced antisocial traits, on the other hand, may be differentially dissuaded by social forces (such as disapproval of inhalant use within the peer group) or by properties of the inhaled agents themselves.

ABSORPTION AND METABOLISM

Elimination of inhalants can occur through a variety of routes. Nitrites and aromatic hydrocarbons are metabolized via the hepatic microsomal system. For example, toluene is oxidized to benzoic acid, which then is conjugated with glycine to form hippuric acid and eliminated via the kidneys (Morton, 1987). Similar mechanisms come into play for related compounds; metabolism of inhalants creates a wide variety of intermediates, some of which are highly reactive. Halide compounds (such as Freon, methylene chloride and carbon tetrachloride) may be metabolized in a variety of ways; end products of some of these compounds include carbon monoxide (Linden, 1990).

Inhalants also may be excreted via the lungs or kidneys. Aliphatic hydrocarbons may be more likely than aromatic compounds to be eliminated unchanged via the respiratory system. This appears particularly true for ethers, which are reportedly not extensively altered. Ketones appear to be metabolized to their corresponding alcohols (Linden, 1990).

MECHANISMS OF ACTION

The neuropharmacological mechanism by which inhalant intoxication occurs is poorly understood. Once inhaled, these substances are rapidly absorbed via the alveolar capillary beds; peak blood levels may occur within 15 to 30 minutes (Linden, 1990). Highly fat soluble, they are soon stored in high concentrations in lipids within the central nervous system. However, while it is presumed that the inhalants disrupt normal neural function, which systems are most affected and the mechanism by which such disruption occurs is not clear. Even whether specific receptors are affected by these agents remains an unsettled question.

It should be kept in mind that most studies of the pharmacokinetics of inhalants have been carried out on industrial workers exposed to low levels of inhalants for long periods of time. The pharmacology of acute, high-dose exposure to inhalants is poorly understood, and such studies may not be entirely applicable (Morton, 1987).

As mentioned earlier, the intoxication due to inhalants clinically resembles that due to CNS depressants. While there is little evidence from animal studies to suggest the development of tolerance, similarities in action to other CNS depressants suggest that it might nonetheless be possible (Balster, 1987). Human studies are likewise equivocal. Studying a population of young inhalant addicts, Evans and Raistrick (1987b) reported that "clear evidence" of tolerance was seen among habitual users of toluene and butane. These authors also described a withdrawal syndrome beginning 24 to 48 hours after use and lasting two to five days, consisting of sleep disturbance, nausea, shakes, diaphoresis, irritability, and abdominal and chest discomfort. However, because polydrug use is an extremely frequent finding among inhalant users, it has proved difficult to unequivocally identify an inhalant withdrawal state; moreover, the lack of clinical notice of this constellation of symptoms suggests that a withdrawal syndrome purely due to solvent use is not of major clinical significance.

REINFORCING PROPERTIES

Animal research confirms the reinforcing nature of the inhalants. One powerful method of investigating the abuse potential of drugs is to determine whether or not laboratory animals will self-administer the agent in question. The usual paradigm is to infuse the agent via an indwelling catheter in response to bar-pressing. In the case of inhalants, a similar (albeit technically more difficult) approach, using nasal catheters or helmets instead of intravenous lines, has shown that monkeys will self-administer chloroform, lacquer thinner, ether, or nitrous oxide, sometimes at rates of 80 to 100 inhalations per day (Balster, 1987).

This form of behavior is quite similar to what is reported by many chronic inhalant addicts. The duration of action of most inhalants is on the order of a few minutes to half an hour; thus, addicts may repetitively inhale the substance throughout the day, so as to maintain the desired state of intoxication indefinitely (Evans & Raistrick, 1987a; Morton, 1987).

It should be noted that this pattern of use appears to be more typical of the long-term inhalant addict, who may use these compounds preferentially and on a solitary basis. Such behavior probably does not represent the modal inhalant user, and these individuals may represent a subgroup at particular risk for addiction specifically to inhalants. It is probably more common to elicit a history of inhalant use in a group setting in which several adolescents gather to "sniff" these substances. Duration and amount of use, therefore, may be less than in the solitary user.

Obviously, the "rush" obtained by inhaling is reinforcing. In addition, some users report that the odor of the specific substance is rewarding, as well. On the other hand, there also is evidence that use of specific substances is determined largely by availability (Sharp & Rosenberg, 1992). Thus, the role of ancillary rewards such as odor in the process of addiction is unclear.

Clinically, inhalant intoxication resembles intoxication from alcohol or other central nervous system (CNS) depressants, and involves behavioral disinhibition, euphoria, ataxia, and slurred speech. Users also report tinnitus, a sensation of floating, perceptual disturbances, and even visual hallucinations. Following the period of intoxication, users may report fatigue and headache, although "hangovers" apparently are relatively mild and short-lived (Evans & Raistrick, 1987b; Morton, 1987).

CONCLUSIONS

Despite serious health risks, use of inhalants continues to be a widespread and often underrecognized practice, particularly among adolescents and even preadolescents. In this population, inhalant use is associated with numerous conduct difficulties, and many users meet (or will go on to meet) diagnostic criteria for ASPD. Any history of inhalant use also is associated with substantially elevated risk of using other psychoactive substances as well. Thus, while relatively few users become addicted primarily to inhalants, inhalant use appears to be a marker for (and perhaps a risk factor for) significantly elevated risk of exposure and addiction to other substances on a lifetime basis.

Much remains to be learned regarding the toxic effects of specific inhaled agents, their potential for producing tolerance or withdrawal phenomena, and the neurobiological mechanism by which addiction to these agents takes place. The role of social factors, co-morbid psychiatric disorders, and personality traits in predisposing individuals to initiate or maintain use, become addicted, or shift to use of other psychoactive substances also remains to be clarified. More information regarding these areas may benefit not only the physician faced with the need to treat patients addicted to inhalants but, by identifying similarities and differences in action between inhalants and other psychoactive substances, such research may lead to a deeper understanding of the interplay between vulnerability factors—both biological and social—and the process of addiction in general.

REFERENCES

al-Alousi LM (1989). Pathology of volatile substance abuse: A case report and literature review. *Medicine, Science and Law* 29(3):189–202.

Altenkirch H & Kindermann W (1986). Inhalant abuse and heroin addiction: A comparative study on 574 opiate addicts with and without a history of sniffing. *Addictive Behavior* 11:93–104.

American Psychiatric Association (1994). *Diagnostic and Statistical Manual of Mental Disorders, 4th Edition.* Washington, DC: American Psychiatric Press.

American Psychiatric Association (1987). *Diagnostic and Statistical Manual of Mental Disorders, 3rd Edition, Revised.* Washington, DC: American Psychiatric Press.

Anderson HR, MacNair RS & Ramsey JD (1985). Deaths from abuse of volatile substances: A national epidemiological study. *British Medical Journal* 290:304–307.

Anthony JC, Arria AM & Johnson EO (1995). Epidemiological and public health issues for tobacco, alcohol, and other drugs. In JM Oldham & MB Riba (eds.) *American Psychiatric Press Review of Psychiatry, Vol. 14.* Washington, DC: American Psychiatric Press, 15–49.

Balster RL (1987). Abuse potential evaluation of inhalants. *Drug and Alcohol Dependence* 19(1):7–15.

Barnes GE (1979). Solvent abuse: A review. *International Journal of Addiction* 14(1):1–26.

Bass M (1970). Sudden sniffing death. *Journal of the American Medical Association* 212(12):2075–2079.

Beauvais F & Oetting ER (1988). Indian youth and inhalants: An update. In RA Crider & BA Rouse (eds.) *Epidemiology of Inhalant Abuse: An Update (NIDA Research Monograph 85).* Rockville, MD: National Institute on Drug Abuse, 34–48.

Beauvais F & Oetting ER (1987). Toward a clear definition of inhalant abuse. *Interational Journal of Addiction* 22(8):779–784.

Blum K (1984). Solvent and aerosol inhalants. In *Handbook of Abusable Drugs.* New York, NY: Gardner Press, 211.

Crider RA & Rouse BA (1988). Inhalant overview. In RA Crider & BA Rouse (eds.) *Epidemiology of Inhalant Abuse: An Update (NIDA Research Monograph 85).* Rockville, MD: National Institute on Drug Abuse, 1–6.

Crites J & Schuckit MA (1979). Solvent abuse in adolescents at a community alcohol center. *Journal of Clinical Psychiatry* 40:39–43.

D'Amanda C, Plumb MM & Taintor Z (1977). Heroin addicts with a history of glue sniffing: A deviant group within a deviant groupage. *International Journal of Addiction* 12:255–270.

Dinwiddie SH, Reich T & Cloninger CR (1991a). The relationship of solvent use to other substance use. *American Journal of Drug and Alcohol Abuse* 17(2):173–86.

Dinwiddie SH, Reich T & Cloninger CR (1991b). Solvent abuse as a precursor to intravenous drug abuse. *Comprehensive Psychiatry* 32(2):133–40.

Dinwiddie SH, Reich T & Cloninger CR (1990). Solvent use and psychiatric comorbidity. *British Journal of Addiction* 85:1647–56.

Dinwiddie SH, Zorumski C & Rubin EH (1987). Psychiatric correlates of chronic solvent abuse. *Journal of Clinical Psychiatry* 48:334–337.

Evans AC & Raistrick D (1987a). Patterns of use and related harm with toluene-based adhesives and butane gas. *British Journal of Psychiatry* 150:773–776.

Evans AC & Raistrick D (1987b). Phenomenology of intoxication with toluene-based adhesives and butane gas. *British Journal of Psychiatry* 150:769–773.

Fishburne PM, Abelson HI & Cisin I (1979). Inhalants, hallucinogens, and PCP. In *National Survey on Drug Abuse: Main Findings, 1978.* Rockville, MD: National Institute on Drug Abuse, 59–66.

Fischman CM & Oster JR (1979). Toxic effects of toluene. *Journal of the American Medical Association* 241(16):1713–1715.

Hershey CO & Miller S (1982). Solvent abuse: A shift to adults. *International Journal of Addiction* 17(6):1085–1089.

Hormes JT, Filley CM & Rosenberg NL (1986). Neurologic sequelae of chronic solvent vapor abuse. *Neurology* 36:698–702.

Johnson EO, Schutz CG, Anthony JC & Ensminger ME (1995). Inhalants to heroin: A prospective analysis from adolescence to adulthood. *Drug and Alcohol Dependence* 40(2):159–164.

King GS, Smialek JE & Troutman WG (1985). Sudden death in adolescents resulting from the inhalation of typewriter correction fluid. *Journal of the American Medical Association* 253(11):1604–1606.

Lazar RB, Ho SU, Melen O & Daghestani AN (1983). Multifocal central nervous system damage caused by toluene abuse. *Neurology* 33:1337–1340.

Linden CH (1990). Volatile substances of abuse. *Emergency Medical Clinics of North America* 8(3):559–578.

Mata AG & Andrew SR(1988). Inhalant abuse in a small rural south Texas community: A social epidemiological overview. In BA Crider & BA Rouse (eds.) *Epidemiology of Inhalant Abuse: An Update (NIDA Research Monograph 85).* Rockville, MD: National Institute on Drug Abuse, pages 49–76.

McHugh MJ (1987). The abuse of volatile substances. *Pediatric Clinics of North America* 34(2):333–340.

McSherry TM (1986). Program experiences with the solvent abuser in Philadelphia. In RA Crider & BA Rouse (eds.) *Epidemiology of Inhalant Abuse: An Update (NIDA Research Monograph 85).* Rockville, MD: National Institute on Drug Abuse, 106–120.

Meadows R & Verghese A (1996). Medical complications of glue sniffing. *Southern Medical Journal* 89(5):455–462.

Morton HG (1987). Occurrence and treatment of solvent abuse in children and adolescents. *Pharmacologic Therapy* 33:449–469.

Oetting ER & Beauvais F (1990). Adolescent drug use: Findings of national and local surveys. *Journal of Consulting and Clinical Psychology* 58(4):385–94.

Pollard TG (1990). Relative addiction potential of major centrally-active drugs and drug classes—Inhalants and anesthetics. In CK Erickson, MA Javors, WW Morgan & B Stimmel (eds.) *Addiction Potential of Abused Drugs and Drug Classes.* New York, NY: The Haworth Press, 149–165.

Prockop LD, Alt M & Tison J (1974). "Huffer's" neuropathy. *Journal of the American Medical Association* 229(8):1083–1084.

Regier DA, Farmer ME, Rae DS et al. (1990). Comorbidity of mental disorders with alcohol and other drug abuse. *Journal of the American Medical Association* 264(19):2511–2518.

Ron MA (1986). Volatile substance abuse: A review of possible long-term neurological, intellectual and psychiatric sequelae. *British Journal of Psychiatry* 148:235–246.

Rosenberg NL, Spitz MC, Filley CM, Davis KA & Schaumburg HH (1980). Central nervous system effects of chronic toluene abuse—Clinical, brainstem evoked response and magnetic resonance imaging studies. *Neurotoxicology and Teratology* 10:489–495.

Schutz CG, Chilcoat HD & Anthony JC (1994). The association between sniffing inhalants and injecting drugs. *Comprehensive Psychiatry* 35(2):99–105.

Sharp CW & Rosenberg NL (1992). Volatile substances. In JH Lowinson, P Ruiz, RB Millman & JG Langrod (eds.) *Substance Abuse: A Comprehensive Textbook.* Baltimore, MD: Williams & Wilkins, 303–327.

Streicher HZ, Cabow P, Moss A, Kono D & Kaehny WD (1981). Syndromes of toluene sniffing in adults. *Annals of Internal Medicine* 94:758–762.

Stybel LJ (1977). Psychotherapeutic options in the treatment of child and adolescent hydrocarbon inhalers. *American Journal of Psychotherapy* 31:525–532.

CHAPTER 11

Future Directions in Research

Walter A. Hunt, Ph.D.
Roger M. Brown, Ph.D.
Jerry Frankenheim, Ph.D.

Drug Reinforcing Properties
Physical Dependence
Actions on NMDA Receptors
Actions on GABA Receptors
Actions on Second Messengers
Neurotoxicity

Considerable progress is being made in our understanding of how alcohol and other abused drugs affect the brain. The last few years of research have given us real hope that an understanding of the mechanisms underlying alcohol and other drug addictions is not far off. In this chapter, we present the latest findings pertaining to basic biological actions of alcohol and drugs of abuse, the relevance of these actions to clinical conditions, and future prospects.

DRUG REINFORCING PROPERTIES

One exciting area of research involves the manner in which abused drugs are rewarding. Fortunately, there are animal models for testing the reinforcing properties of drugs. With few exceptions, drugs that are reinforcing in animals also are reinforcing in humans (see Kornetsky & Bain, 1992; Collins, Weeks et al., 1984).

Studies with these animal models have led to the development of the "brain reward" hypothesis of drug addiction and have provided a way to begin studying the neuropathological processes underlying addiction. Research on the nature of the "pleasure center" led to the concept of a brain reward circuit that mediates normal rewards (such as those underlying sexual and appetitive behaviors), and that is directly and strongly activated by cocaine, heroin, alcohol and other reinforcing, addictive drugs. According to the model, the feeling of euphoria (i.e., the drug "high") results from activation of this circuit. This concept recently has been refined by Robinson and Berridge (1993), who hypothesize that this neural system attributes "incentive salience" to drug taking and the events and environments surrounding drug taking. *Salience* can be an attribute of drug taking independent of *reward*, especially with chronic drug abuse.

The mesocortical/mesolimbic dopaminergic neural system is a critical component of the "brain reward" circuit and dependence on abused drugs. The dopamine system has been implicated in the reinforcing properties of several of these drugs, including alcohol, cocaine, amphetamine (Koob & Bloom, 1988), heroin (DiChiaro & Imperato, 1988), and nicotine (Pontieri, Tanda et al., 1996; Pich, Pagliusi et al., 1997). However, the different classes of drugs activate the dopamine system by different means. For example, alcohol and amphetamine stimulate the release of dopamine in the nucleus accumbens (Imperato & DiChiara, 1986; Carlsson, 1970), whereas cocaine inhibits its uptake (Moore, Chiueh & Zeldes, 1977; Ritz, Lamb et al., 1987). Evidence also suggests that activation of dopamine receptors in the medial prefrontal cortex contributes to the reinforcing effects of alcohol and cocaine (Hodge, Chiappelle & Samson, 1996; Goeders, Dworkin & Smith, 1986). These results indicate that alcohol and cocaine increase the interaction of dopamine with its receptors in the reward circuit.

A deficiency in the availability of serotonin also may play a role in alcohol-seeking behavior. Alcohol-preferring rats bred at Indiana University have lower concentrations of serotonin and its major metabolite 5-hydroxyindoleacetic acid (5-HIAA) in the nucleus accumbens compared to alcohol non-preferring rats (McBride, Murphy et al., 1990). Reducing the interaction of serotonin with its receptors increases alcohol consumption, whereas enhancing the interaction suppresses consumption (Haraguchi, Samson & Tolliver, 1990; McBride, Murphy et al., 1990). In human alcoholics who develop the disease before age 25, when the disease has a large genetic component, 5-HIAA concentrations in the cerebrospinal fluid are lower than in those developing alcoholism after age 25 (Fils-Aime, Eckardt et al., 1996).

Research using the new genetic knockout technique has provided additional evidence for the role of dopamine and serotonin in the addiction process. Mice lacking the dopamine uptake transporter gene (dopamine transporter knockouts) act as if they have been injected with cocaine or amphetamine, running in their cages at least five times as much as normal mice, and losing weight (Giros, Jaber et al., 1996). Cocaine or amphetamine administration has no effect on locomotor activity in the knockouts. In addition, mice deficient in the serotonin 1B receptor drink greater amounts of alcohol than do normal mice (Crabbe, Phillips et al., 1996)—results consistent with the finding that rats bred for alcohol preference also are deficient in serotonin 1B receptors compared with rats bred for alcohol non-preference (McBride, Chernet et al., 1997). These knockout mice provide an additional tool to help understand addiction to psychomotor stimulants and alcohol.

While the acute neuropharmacological actions of abuse substances appear to be remarkably well understood, the changes in brain function that occur with chronic substance abuse—especially the neuronal changes that underlie addiction, drug craving and relapse—are much less well understood. Animals given repeated injections of cocaine or amphetamine develop a progressive and persistent *sensitization* to their stimulant effects (Robinson & Becker, 1986). It is thought that the same neural processes that underlie sensitization may contribute to the development of compulsive patterns of drug-seeking and drug-taking in addicts (Robinson & Berridge, 1993). One of the neural processes underlying the induction of sensitization may be changes in the *N*-methyl-D-aspartate (NMDA) subtype of excitatory amino acid receptor. These receptors, discussed below, already had been implicated in learning, long-term potentiation, kindling, epilepsy, normal ontogenesis, and other examples of neural and behavioral plasticity.

After chronic exposure to alcohol, dopamine and serotonin release in the nucleus accumbens decreases below pre-exposure levels after withdrawal (Rossetti, Melis et al., 1992; Weiss et al., 1996). In addition, the dependent rats will drink more alcohol than the nondependent ones (Schulteis, Hyytia et al., 1995), and in sufficient amounts to restore dopamine release to pre-exposure levels (Weiss et al., 1996). These responses after withdrawal correspond to an increased threshhold for intracranial self-stimulation, having a similar time-course to overt signs of a withdrawal syndrome (Schulteis, Hyytia et al., 1995). Since these latter two responses are associated with negative affective states, increased alcohol consumption observed during this period may be an attempt to relieve dysphoria that occurs after withdrawal, and thus partially explain the basis for psychological dependence on alcohol.

The persistent changes induced by alcohol and other drugs are the basis of considerable research to find addiction medications. If a drug could reduce craving, the vicious cycle of addiction could be interrupted and relapse prevented. The best clinical example is methadone, which reduces craving for heroin; this is an example of substitution therapy. Treatment of addiction by blocking dopamine or opioid receptors, by neurologic drugs or naltrexone, respectively, generally does not work nearly as well for heroin addiction. All but the most resolute patients simply stop taking the blocker. However, naltrexone is effective in treating alcoholism in some patients when combined with cognitive-behavioral therapy (O'Malley, Jaffe et al., 1992 [also see Section 8 of this text]; Volpicelli, Watson et al., 1995).

PHYSICAL DEPENDENCE

Once drug-taking behavior is established, physical dependence (the need to take a drug to maintain normal physical well-being) may develop, but this depends on what drug is being abused. The classic physical dependence-producing drugs are alcohol, barbiturates, and opiates, although other drugs (such as benzodiazepines and nicotine) also produce characteristic physical signs of withdrawal (or abstinence). For other addicting drugs, such as amphetamine, cocaine or PCP, the abstinence syndrome is mild or nonexistent. Withdrawal of amphetamine, for example, produces drug craving, depressed mood, sleepiness, and hunger for food. Since none of these symptoms are "physical" (in the sense that the convulsions induced by alcohol or barbiturate withdrawal are physical), there is said to be no amphetamine withdrawal syndrome. However, as discussed earlier, the "physical" changes (receptor regulation, gene expression, etc.) underlying the "psychological" symptoms of drug withdrawal may soon be defined. In fact, the dichotomy between "physical signs" and "mental symptoms" of withdrawal is useful only in describing what happens to people when they stop taking a particular class of drug, but it is not important when considering addiction *per se.* A chronic pain patient may be physically dependent on opioids, but is not addicted to them, whereas a "crack" cocaine abuser may be addicted to that drug but not physically dependent on it. Nonetheless, avoidance of abstinence signs is believed to be an important factor in relapse to alcohol, barbiturates, and opiates.

Abstinence from marijuana does not produce signs of physical dependence. The failure to observe an abstinence syndrome following discontinuation of chronic use of delta-9-tetrahydrocannabinol (the major active constituent of marijuana) may result from its long half-life in plasma. This is comparable to the mild syndrome following the withdrawal of methadone or most benzodiazepines, which have long half-lives. However, an opiate antagonist, such as naloxone, can precipitate severe withdrawal signs in chronic methadone-treated animals. A selective cannabinoid antagonist, SR141716A, has been developed by Rinaldi-Carmona and colleagues (1994) and used to demonstrate precipitated cannabinoid withdrawal signs in rodents (Tsou, Patrick & Walker, 1995; Aceto, Scales et al., 1995). These findings may lead to a better understanding of marijuana abuse. SR141716A is proving useful in determining which actions of THC are receptor-mediated and which are not, and may prove to have useful therapeutic actions.

Physical dependence is an important research area for molecular biologists who are interested in cell regulatory mechanisms (see Nestler, 1992; DiChiara & North, 1992; Koob & Bloom, 1988; North, 1989). Understanding the molecular basis of drug action and the process responsible for physical dependence is important, because these mechanisms underlie the switch from seeking drugs for euphoria to seeking drugs to prevent the occurrence of the painful abstinence syndrome. The ability to prevent physical dependence or to reinstate the normal homeostasis of the brain would be a major breakthrough in the search for safe and effective medications.

Drugs of abuse exert their acute effects on the brain by interfering with neurotransmission at specific synapses. Beyond the acute effects, abused drugs produce long-lasting changes in the central nervous system. Like the short-term effects, the long-term consequences involve the activation of specific receptors. But how drug-induced short-term changes in neurons are translated into long-term alterations in neuron function is a major problem in current drug abuse research.

A breakthrough in the study of long-term effects of abused drugs came with the discovery that many of these drugs rapidly activate the transcription of a class of genes called "immediate-early genes." Immediate-early genes previously had been recognized as regulators of specific target genes. A rapidly growing body of evidence suggests that these immediate-early genes play a key role in mediating the drug-induced long-term changes (Nestler, 1992). For example, cocaine and amphetamine profoundly activate the immediate-early gene c-fos in discrete populations of neurons in the brain (Graybiel, Moratalla & Robertson, 1990). In contrast, acute alcohol exposure suppresses pentylenetetrazole-induced c-fos expression (Le, Wilce et al., 1990), whereas alcohol withdrawal seizures increase c-fos mRNA (Dave, Tabakoff & Hoffman, 1990). This effect can be blocked by the anticraving drug acamprosate (Putzke, Spanagel et al., 1996). Thus, drug-induced alterations in the expression of immediate-early genes can influence the transcription of proteins from genetic instructions. This line of research offers a new avenue for exploring the biochemical mechanisms that may be directly involved in the development of tolerance and addiction.

ACTIONS ON *N*-METHYL-D-ASPARTATE (NMDA) RECEPTORS

Most abused drugs have been shown to act directly (PCP, alcohol) or at least indirectly (cocaine, amphetamines, opioids) on the NMDA subtype of the glutamate receptor, which is the predominant excitatory receptor in the brain. The NMDA receptor is inhibited by alcohol and PCP (Hoffman, Rabe et al., 1989; Lovinger, White & Weight, 1989; Lodge & Anis, 1982) at a site within this complex receptor's ion channel. In addition, calcium movements and the release of dopamine and norepinephrine initiated by NMDA also are blocked by alcohol (Dildy-Mayfield, Machu & Leslie, 1991; Gonzales & Woodward, 1990; Hoffman, Rabe et al., 1989; Woodward & Gonzales, 1990). However, not all neurons with NMDA receptors respond to alcohol (Simson, Criswell & Breese, 1993). The subunit composition of the receptor may contribute to alcohol sensitivity (Yang, Criswell et al., 1996).

Long-term treatment with alcohol increases the number of NMDA (Grant, Valverius et al., 1990) and calcium channels (Dolin, Little et al., 1987), which may be related to withdrawal seizures, learning and memory deficits, and brain damage (Hunt & Nixon, 1993). Alterations in specific subunits of the NMDA receptor may be responsible for these effects and are currently under investigation. NMDA receptors and calcium channel antagonists show promise in treating some of these disorders, especially withdrawal seizures (Grant, Valverius et al., 1990; Little, Dolin & Halsey, 1986).

NMDA receptors have been implicated in the induction of tolerance to opioid analgesia, physical dependence (Trujillo & Akil, 1991), and sensitization (which is reverse tolerance) to motor stimulant actions of amphetamines (Karler, Calder & Turkanis, 1991; Wolf & Khansa, 1991) and cocaine (Karler, Calder et al., 1989). Chronic cocaine administration also increases the number of NMDA receptors (Itzhak & Stein, 1992). Tolerance, dependence and sensitization, forms of neural and behavioral plasticity, are antagonized by chronic administration of NMDA antagonists. In addition, inhibitors of nitric oxide synthase, an enzyme that is activated by calcium taken up by neurons after NMDA receptor stimulation, show promise, especially in treating seizures induced by repeated administration of cocaine (Itzhak, 1993).

ACTIONS ON γ-AMINOBUTYRIC ACID (GABA) RECEPTORS

GABA is the major inhibitory neurotransmitter in the brain. Alcohol augments the actions of GABA by facilitating the movement of chloride ions through channels into the neuron (Suzdak, Schwartz et al., 1986). In fact, this action may depend on only an eight amino acid sequence in one of the sub-units of the GABA receptor (Wafford, Burnett et al., 1991). An increased movement of chloride ions into neurons would reduce their excitability and could account for the sedative and anxiolytic properties of alcohol. However, as with the NMDA receptor, not all GABA receptors are affected by alcohol (Criswell, Simson et al., 1993), and the subunit composition may contribute to their sensitivity to alcohol (Duncan, Breese et al., 1995).

Chronic administration of alcohol induces tolerance to the GABA enhancement of chloride movements (Morrow, Suzdak et al., 1988) and increases the activity of the part of GABA receptors on which inverse agonists of benzodiazepines act (Mhatre & Ticku, 1989). This action may underlie in part the seizures and anxiety that occur during a withdrawal syndrome and suggest a usefulness of benzodiazepine antagonists for treating alcohol withdrawal. However, limited studies in rats and humans with flumazenil are inconclusive, and the drug appeared to induce anxiety (Uzbay, Akarsu & Kapaalp, 1995; Nutt, Glue et al., 1993).

ACTIONS ON SECOND MESSENGERS

A number of neurotransmitters act through a cascade of reactions to initiate ion movements across a neuronal membrane. Second messengers, especially adenosine-3',5'-cyclic monophosphate (cAMP), are important in many of these reactions. Neurotransmitter activation of adenylate cyclase, the enzyme responsible for the synthesis of cAMP, is stimulated by alcohol exposure by activating the stimulatory G-protein, an effect that is reversed after chronic exposure (see reviews by Diamond & Gordon, 1994, and Hoffman & Tabakoff, 1990). In cultured neural cells, adenosine activation of cAMP synthesis results from inhibition of adenosine uptake (Nagy, Diamond & Gordon, 1990) and stimulation of adenosine A_2 receptors (Krauss, Ghirnikar et al., 1993).

A recent advance showing considerable promise has been the discovery of a novel form of adenyl cyclase in humans, known as Type VII, located primarily in the granule cell layer of the cerebellum (Hellevuo, Yoshimura et al., 1995). This form of adenyl cyclase is two- to three-fold more sensitive to alcohol than the other forms (Yoshimura & Tabakoff, 1995). Moreover, morphine enhances the stimulation by dopamine of Type VII adenyl cyclase, while inhibiting Type V (Yoshimura, Ikeda & Tabakoff, 1996). These studies provide additional support for the involvement of the cAMP second messenger system in the actions of drugs of abuse.

Such findings may have clinical applications. Adenosine stimulates adenylate cyclase in human lymphocytes and alcohol enhances this process. Chronic alcohol exposure desensitizes adenylate cyclase to this effect of alcohol. Lymphocytes from alcoholics display this desensitization (Diamond, Wrubel et al., 1987). In addition, basal and fluoride-stimulated adenyl cyclase activity in platelets is lower in alcoholics, compared with non-alcoholics (Parsian, Todd et al., 1996). Thus, the differences in adenyl cyclase found in alcoholics might provide a basis for markers to identify those who consume large quantities of alcohol or who are genetically predisposed to alcoholism.

NEUROTOXICITY

Exposure to alcohol and other abused drugs can lead to brain damage. In animal studies, chronic administration of certain drugs and high acute doses of certain stimulants result in irreversible neuropathological alterations in brain structure, electrical activity, and neurochemistry. For example, long-term alcohol and drug abuse can lead to numerous lesions in the brain. Alcohol abuse can induce the reduction in the number of dendritic branches and spines in several areas of the brain, and cognitive deficits, predominantly involving memory (Hunt & Nixon, 1993). Chronic administration of delta-9-tetrahydrocannabinol, the major psychoactive component of marijuana, causes cell loss in the hippocampus of rats (Landfield, Cadwallader & Vinsant, 1988; Scallet, Uemura et al., 1987). Methamphetamine and its related "designer drugs," such as 3,4-methylenedioxyamphetamine (MDA) and 3,4-methylenedioxymethylamphetamine (MDMA, "ecstasy") produce severe, persistent damage to monoamine neuron terminals (Cho, 1990; Kleven & Seiden, 1992). Depending on the drug, the mechanisms of damage may involve several factors, including the hyperactivity of excitotoxins (such as glutamate [NMDA] and nitric oxide), accumulation of free radicals, and loss of neurotrophic factors and cholinergic fibers in the septal-hippocampal area.

An area of research receiving a great deal of attention is excitotoxicity, with its possible role in the development of neurodegenerative diseases. The hallmark of excitotoxicity is the over-stimulation of NMDA receptors. As mentioned earlier, chronic exposure to alcohol leads to an increase in NMDA receptors in the brain. In cultured neural cells, a similar finding is associated with an enhanced ability of NMDA through a cascade of neurodegenerative processes to cause cell death (Chandler, Newson et al., 1993; Iorio, Tabakoff & Hoffman, 1993). Concomitantly, calcium rapidly enters the cell and directly correlates with neuronal toxicity (Ahern, Lustig & Greenberg, 1994). In animals, such a phenomenon may be enhanced, with multiple occurrences of withdrawal seizures (Hunt, 1993). Enhanced NMDA-induced neurotoxicity after alcohol withdrawal can be blocked by NMDA antagonists (Hoffman, Rabe et al., 1995).

These findings suggest that NMDA receptor antagonists may be useful in treating alcohol-induced withdrawal seizures, as well as cocaine-induced seizures. However, acute suppression of NMDA receptor function results in analgesia, amnesia, and a schizophrenia-like syndrome (Javitt & Zukin, 1991), as well as an anticonvulsant action and protection of neurons against the sequelae of ischemia and hypoxia (see Barnes, 1988). In addition, suppression of NMDA function can produce its own type of neuropathology, different from glutamate/NMDA excitotoxicity (Olney, Labruyere & Price, 1989). Work is progressing to find an NMDA antagonist without the undesirable, PCP-like side effects to treat ischemic conditions (e.g., stroke, CNS trauma), convulsions, opiate and alcohol dependence, and other neurological disorders (Choi, 1992; Olney, 1995).

Methamphetamine, MDA, and MDMA toxicity may occur through the formation of the neurotoxin 6-hydroxydopamine (Seiden & Vosmer, 1984) and very toxic superoxide free radicals. Nonenzymic autoxidation of dopamine to toxic quinones also occurs. A recent postmortem study of human chronic methamphetamine abusers (Wilson, Kalasinsky et al., 1996) concluded that methamphetamine had not destroyed the monoamine neuron terminals. However, there were signs of oxidative stress to the dopaminergic neuron terminals. One possible explanation of this finding is that the humans had acquired some tolerance to methamphetamine neurotoxicity; such a tolerance has been demonstrated in rats (Schmidt, Sonsalla et al., 1985).

FUTURE DEVELOPMENTS AND CONCLUSIONS

Addiction to drugs and alcohol is a disease of the brain. To deal with the problems of drug and alcohol abuse and dependence, an understanding of the neural bases of behavioral states associated with addiction is essential. The Decade of the Brain has become an exciting time for research into alcohol and other drug dependence. Rapid breakthroughs are being made in our understanding of the biological basis of addiction, with real promise of more effective treatments on the horizon.

Over the next five to 10 years, significant progress is expected in our knowledge about neurotransmission in the brain. All the known receptors will be cloned, along with a basic understanding about how they operate. This knowledge will help identify the neuronal circuits and the processes regulating reinforcement, dependence, and craving. With the eventual completion of the Human Genome Project, significant progress will be made in identifying genes that underlie the predisposition to alcohol and drug abuse, studies of which currently are under way in animal and human experiments. Knowledge of these genes and the gene products they produce will help locate potential sites for developing new therapeutic agents to treat addiction, and diagnostic tests to identify those individuals most at risk of developing alcoholism or drug abuse. As a result, new drugs for the treatment of addiction will be in clinical trials, with the promise of reducing the consequences of the disease.

The increased understanding of the relationship of brain anatomy, physiology, and pharmacology with drug-seeking behaviors will allow us to develop (1) therapies for correcting neurochemical imbalances created by the abuse of drugs and alcohol and, perhaps, the prevention and treatment of certain neurotoxicities, (2) medications (such as analgesics) that are devoid of abuse liability, and (3) strategies for preventing dependence and craving. The next decade promises to be an exciting time for addiction medicine.

REFERENCES

Aceto MD, Scales SM, Lowe JA & Martin BR (1995). Cannabinoid precipitated withdrawal by the selective cannabinoid receptor agonist, SR141716A. *European Journal of Pharmacology* 282:R1–R2.

Ahern KvB, Lustig HS & Greenberg DA (1994). Enhancement of NMDA toxicity and calcium responses by chronic exposure of cultured neurons to ethanol. *Neuroscience Letters* 16:211–214.

Barnes D (1988). NMDA receptors trigger excitement. *Science* 239:254–256.

Carlsson A (1970). Amphetamine and brain catecholamines. In E Costa & S Garattini (eds.) *Amphetamines and Related Compounds*. New York, NY: Raven Press, 289–300.

Chandler LJ, Newson H, Sumners C & Crews FT (1993). Chronic ethanol exposure potentiates NMDA excitotoxicity in cerebral cortical neurons. *Journal of Neurochemistry* 60:1578–1581.

Cho AK (1990). Ice: A new dosage form of an old drug. *Science* 249:631–634.

Choi DW (1992). Excitotoxic cell death. *Journal of Neurobiology* 23:1261–1276.

Collins RJ, Weeks JR, Cooper MM, Good PI & Russell RR (1984). Prediction of abuse liability of drugs using IV self-administration by rats. *Psychopharmacology* 82:6–13.

Crabbe JC, Phillips TJ, Feller DJ, Hen R, Wenger CD, Lessov CN & Schafer G (1996). Elevated alcohol consumption in null mutant mice lacking 5-HT_{1B} serotonin receptors. *Nature Genetics* 14:96–101.

Criswell HE, Simson PE, Duncan GE, McCown TJ, Herbert JS, Morrow AL & Breese GR (1993). Molecular basis for regionally specific action of ethanol on γ-aminobutyric acid receptors: Generalization to other ligand-gated ion channels. *Journal of Pharmacology and Experimental Therapeutics* 267:522–537.

Dave JR, Tabakoff B & Hoffman PL (1990). Ethanol withdrawal seizures produce increased c-fos mRNA in mouse brain. *Molecular Pharmacology* 37:367–371.

Diamond I & Gordon AS (1994). Rose of adenosine in mediating cellular and molecular responses to ethanol. In B Jansson, H Jornvall, U Rydberg, L Terenius & BL Vallee (eds.) *Toward a Molecular Basis of Alcohol Use and Abuse.* Boston, MA: Birkhauser Verlag.

Diamond I, Wrubel B, Estrin W & Gordon A, (1987). Basal and adenosine receptor-stimulated levels of cAMP are reduced in lymphocytes from alcoholic patients. *Proceedings of the National Academy of Sciences* 84:1413–1416.

DiChiara G & Imperato A (1988). Drugs abused by humans preferentially increase synaptic dopamine concentrations in the mesolimbic system of freely moving rats. *Proceedings of the National Academy of Sciences* 84:1413–1416.

DiChiara G & North RA (1992). Neurobiology of opiate abuse. *Trends in Pharmaceutical Sciences* 13:185–193.

Dildy-Mayfield JE, Machu T & Leslie SW (1991). Ethanol and voltage- or receptor-mediated increases in cytosolic Ca^{2+} in brain cells. *Alcohol* 9:63–69.

Dolin S, Little H, Hudspith M & Littleton JJ (1987). Increased dihydropyridine-sensitive calcium channels in rat brain may underlie ethanol physical dependence. *Neuropharmacology* 26:275–279.

Duncan E, Breese GR, Criswell HE, McCown TJ, Herbert JS, Devaud LL & Morrow AL (1995). Distribution of [^{3}H]zolpidem binding sites in relation to messenger RNA encoding the α1, β2, and γ2 subunits of $GABA_A$ receptors in rat brain. *Neuroscience* 64:1113–1128.

Fils-Aime M-L, Eckardt MJ, George DT, Brown GL, Mefford I & Linnoila M (1996). Early-onset alcoholics have lower cerebrospinal fluid 5-hydroxyindoleacetic acid levels than late-onset alcoholics. *Archives of General Psychiatry* 53:211–216.

Giros B, Jaber M, Jones SR, Wightman RM & Caron MG (1996). Hyperlocomotion and indifference to cocaine and amphetamine in mice lacking the dopamine transporter. *Nature* 379:606–612.

Goeders NE, Dworkin SI & Smith JE (1986). Neuropharmacological assessment of cocaine self-administration into the medial prefrontal cortex. *Pharmacology, Biochemistry and Behavior* 24:1429–1440.

Gonzales RA & Woodward JJ (1990). Ethanol inhibits N-methyl-D-aspartate stimulated [^{3}H]norepinephrine release from rat cortical slices. *Journal of Pharmacology and Experimental Therapeutics* 253:1138–1144.

Grant KA, Valverius P, Hudspith M & Tabakoff B (1990). Ethanol withdrawal seizures and the NMDA receptor complex. *European Journal of Pharmacology* 176:289–296.

Graybiel AM, Moratalla R & Robertson HA (1990). Amphetamine and cocaine induce drug-specific activation of the c-fos gene in striosome-matrix compartments and limbic subdivisions of the striatum. *Proceedings of the National Academy of Sciences* 87:6912–1916.

Haraguchi M, Samson HH & Tolliver GA (1990). Reduction in oral ethanol self-administration in the rat by the

5-HT uptake blocker fluoxetine. *Pharmacology, Biochemistry and Behavior* 35:259–262.

Hellevuo K, Yoshimura M, Mons N, Hoffman PL, Cooper DM & Tabakoff B (1995). The characterization of a novel human adenylyl cyclase which is present in brain and other tissues. *Journal of Biological Chemistry* 270:1631–1638.

Hodge CW, Chappelle AM & Samson HH (1996). Dopamine receptors in the medial prefrontal cortex influences ethanol and sucrose-reinforced responding. *Alcoholism: Clinical & Experimental Research* 19:721–726.

Hoffman PL, Rabe CS, Moses F & Tabakoff B (1989). N-methyl-D-aspartate receptors and ethanol: Inhibition of calcium flux and cyclic GMP production. *Journal of Neurochemistry* 52:1937–1940.

Hoffman PL & Tabakoff B (1990). Ethanol and guanine nucleotide binding proteins: A selective interaction. *FASEB Journal* 4:2612–2622.

Hunt WA (1993). Are binge drinkers more at risk of developing brain damage? *Alcohol* 10:559–561.

Hunt WA & Nixon SJ, eds. (1993). *Alcohol-Induced Brain Damage (NIAAA Monograph 22)*. Rockville, MD: National Institute on Alcohol Abuse and Alcoholism.

Imperato A & DiChiara G (1986). Preferential stimulation of dopamine release in the nucleus accumbens of freely moving rats by ethanol. *Journal of Pharmacology and Experimental Therapeutics* 239:219–228.

Iorio KR, Tabakoff B & Hoffman PL (1993). Glutamate-induced neurotoxicity is increased in cerebellar granule cells exposed chronically to ethanol. *European Journal of Pharmacology* 248:209–212.

Itzhak Y (1993). Nitric oxide (NO) synthase inhibitors abolish cocaine-induced toxicity in mice. *Neuropharmacology* 32:1069–1070.

Itzhak Y & Stein I (1992). Sensitization to the toxic effects of cocaine in mice is associated with the regulation of *N*-methyl-D-aspartate receptors in the cortex. *Journal of Pharmacology and Experimental Therapeutics* 262:464–470.

Javitt C & Zukin SR (1991). Recent advances in the phencyclidine model of schizophrenia. *American Journal of Psychiatry* 148:1301–1308.

Karler R, Calder LD, Chaudry IA & Turkanis SA (1989). Blockade of "reverse tolerance" to cocaine and amphetamine by MK–801. *Life Sciences* 45:599–606.

Karler R, Calder LD & Turkanis SA (1991). DNQX blockade of amphetamine behavioral sensitization. *Brain Research* 552:295–300.

Kleven MS & Seiden LS (1992). Methamphetamine-induced neurotoxicity: Structure activity relationships. In PW Kalivas & HH Sampson (eds.) *The Neurobiology of Drug and Alcohol Addiction.* New York, NY: New York Academy of Science, 292–301.

Koob GF & Bloom FE (1988). Cellular and molecular mechanisms of drug dependence. *Science* 242:715–723.

Kornetsky C & Bain G (1992). Brain-stimulation reward: A model for the study of the rewarding effects of abused drugs. In J Frascella & RM Brown (eds.) *Neurobiological Approaches to Brain Behavior Interaction (NIDA Research Monograph 124).* Rockville, MD: National Institute on Drug Abuse, 73–93.

Krauss SW, Ghirnikar RB, Diamond I & Gordon AS (1993). Inhibition of adenosine uptake by ethanol is specific for one class of nucleotide transporters. *Molecular Pharmacology* 44:1021–1026.

Landfield PW, Cadwallader LB & Vinsant S (1988). Quantitative changes in hippocampal structure following long-term exposure to delta^9-tetrahydrocannabinol: Possible mediation by glucocorticoid systems. *Brain Research* 443:47–62.

Le F, Wilce P, Cassady I, Hume D & Shanley B (1990). Acute administration of ethanol suppresses pentylenetrazole-induced c-fos expression in rat brain. *Neuroscience Letter* 120:271–274.

Little HJ, Dolin SJ & Halsey MJ (1986). Calcium channel antagonists decrease the ethanol withdrawal syndrome. *Life Sciences* 39:2059–2065.

Lodge D & Anis NA (1982). Effects of phencyclidine on excitatory amino acid activation of spinal interneurons in the cat. *European Journal of Pharmacology* 77:203–204.

Lovinger DM, White G & Weight FF (1989). Ethanol inhibits NMDA-activated ion current in hippocampal neurons. *Science* 243:1721–1724.

McBride WJ, Chernet E, Russell RN, Wong DT, Guan X-M, Lumeng L & Li T-K (1997). Regional CNS densities of monoamine receptors in alcohol-naive alcohol preferring P and non-preferring NP rats. *Alcohol* 14:141–148.

McBride WJ, Murphy JM, Lumeng L & Li TK (1990). Serotonin, dopamine and GABA involvement in alcohol drinking of selectively bred rats. *Alcohol* 7:199–205.

Mhatre M & Ticku MJ (1989). Chronic ethanol treatment selectively increases the binding of inverse agonists for benzodiazepine binding sites in cultured spinal cord neurons. *Journal of Pharmacology and Experimental Therapeutics* 251:164–168.

Moore KE, Chiueh CC & Zeldes G (1977). Release of neurotransmitters from the brain in vivo by amphetamine, methylphenidate and cocaine. In EH Ellinwood & MM Kilbey (eds.) *Cocaine and Other Stimulants.* Boston, MA: Plenum Press, 143–160.

Morrow KE, Suzdak PD, Karanian JW & Paul SM (1988). Chronic ethanol administration alters gamma aminobutyric acid, pentobarbital and ethanol-mediated ^{36}C1 uptake in cerebral cortical synaptoneurosomes. *Journal of Pharmacology and Experimental Therapeutics* 246:158–164.

Nagy LE, Diamond I & Gordon AS (1991). cAMP-dependent protein kinase regulates inhibition of adenosine transport by ethanol. *Molecular Pharmacology* 40:812–817.

Nestler E (1992). Molecular mechanisms of drug addiction. *Journal of Neuroscience* 12:2439–2450.

North RA (1989). Drug receptors and the inhibition of nerve cells. *British Journal of Pharmacology* 98:13–28.

Nutt D, Glue P, Wilson S, Groves S, Coupland N & Bailey J (1993). Flumazenil in alcohol withdrawal. *Alcohol and Alcoholism Supplement* 2:337–341.

Olney JW (1995). NMDA receptor hypofunction, excitotoxicity, and Alzheimer's disease. *Neurobiology of Aging* 16:459–461.

Olney JW, Labruyere J & Price MT (1989). Pathological changes induced in cerebrospinal neurons by phencyclidine and related drugs. *Science* 244:1360–1362.

O'Malley SS, Jaffe AJ, Chang G, Rode S, Schottenfeld RS, Meyer E & Rounsaville B (1996). Six-month follow-up of naltrexone and psychotherapy for alcohol dependence. *Archives of General Psychiatry* 53:217–224.

O'Malley SS, Jaffe AJ, Chang G, Schottenfeld RS, Meyer E & Rounsaville B (1992). Naltrexone and coping skills, therapy for alcohol dependence. A controlled study. *Archives of General Psychiatry* 49:881–887.

Parsian A, Todd RD, Cloninger CR, Hoffman PL, Ovchinnikova L, Ikeda H & Tabakoff B (1996). Platelet adenylyl cyclase activity in alcoholics and subtypes of alcoholics. *Alcoholism: Clinical & Experimental Research* 20:745–751.

Pich EM, Pagliusi SR, Tessari M, Talabot-Ayer D, Hooft van Juijsduijnen R & Chiamulera C (1997). Common neural substrates for the addictive properties of nicotine and cocaine. *Science* 275:83–86.

Pontieri FE, Tanda G, Orzi F & DiChiara G (1996). Effects of nicotine on the nucleus accumbens and similarity to those of addictive drugs. *Nature* 382:255–257.

Putzke J, Spanagel R, Tolle TR & Zieglgansberger W (1996). The anti-craving drug acamprosate reduces c-fos expression in rats undergoing ethanol withdrawal. *European Journal of Pharmacology* 317:39–48.

Rinaldi-Carmona M, Barth F, Heaulme M, Shire C, Calandra B, Congy C, Martinez S, Maruani J, Neliat G, Caput D, Ferrara P, Soubrie P, Breliere JC & Fur C (1994). SR141716A, a potent and selective antagonist of the brain cannabinoid receptor. *FEBS Letter* 350:240–244.

Ritz MC, Lamb RJ, Goldberg SR & Kuhar MJ (1987). Cocaine receptors on dopamine transporters are related to self-administration of cocaine. *Science* 237:1219–1223.

Robinson TE & Becker JB (1986). Enduring changes in brain and behavior produced by chronic amphetamine administration: A review and evaluation of animal models of amphetamine psychosis. *Brain Research Reviews* 11:157–198.

Robinson TE & Berridge KC (1993). The neural basis of drug craving: An incentive-sensitization theory of addiction. *Brain Research Reviews* 18:247–291.

Rossetti ZL, Melis F, Carboni S, Diana M & Gessa GL (1992). Alcohol withdrawal in rats is associated with a market fall in extraneuronal dopamine. *Alcoholism: Clinical & Experimental Research* 16:529–532.

Scallet AC, Uemura E, Andrews AM, Craven JM, Rountree RL, Wilson SW, Ali SF, Bailey JR, Paule MG & Slikker W Jr (1990). Morphometric neurohistological studies of rhesus monkeys after chronic marijuana smoke exposure. *Society for Neuroscience Abstracts* 16:1116.

Schmidt CJ, Sonsalla PK, Hanson GR, Peat MA & Gibb JW (1985). Methamphetamine-induced depression of monoamine synthesis in the rat: Development of tolerance. *Journal of Neurochemistry* 44:852–855.

Schulteis G, Hyytia P, Heinrichs SC & Koob GF (1995). Decreased brain reward produced by ethanol withdrawal. *Proceedings of the National Academy of Sciences* 92:5880–5884.

Seiden LS & Vosmer G (1984). Formation of 6-hydroxydopamine in caudate nucleus of the rat brain after a single large dose of methylamphetamine. *Pharmacology, Biochemistry and Behavior* 21:29–31.

Simson PE, Criswell HE & Breese GR (1993). Inhibition of NMDA-evoked electrophysiological activity by ethanol in selected brain regions: Evidence for ethanol-sensitive and ethanol-insensitive NMDA-evoked responses. *Brain Research* 607:9–16.

Suzdak PD, Schwartz RD, Skolnick P & Paul SM (1986). Ethanol stimulates gamma-aminobutyric acid receptor mediated chloride transport in rat brain synaptoneurosomes. *Proceedings of the National Academy of Sciences* 47:1942–1947.

Swift RM, Whelihan W, Kuznetsov O, Buongiorno G & Hsuing H (1994). Naltrexone-induced alterations in human ethanol intoxication. *American Journal of Psychiatry* 151:163–147.

Trujillo KA & Akil H (1991). Inhibition of morphine tolerance and dependence by the NMDA receptor antagonist MK–801. *Science* 251:85–87.

Tsou K, Patrick SL & Walker JM (1995). Physical withdrawal in rats tolerant to delta-9-tetrahydrocannabinol precipitated by a cannabinoid receptor agonist. *European Journal of Pharmacology* 280:R13–R15.

Uzbay TT, Akarsu ES & Kapaalp SO (1995). Effects of flumazenil on ethanol withdrawal syndrome in rats. *Arzneimittelforschung* 45:120–124.

Volpicelli JR, Alterman AI, Hayashida M & O'Brien CP (1992). Naltrexone in the treatment of alcohol dependence. *Archives of General Psychiatry* 49:876–880.

Volpicelli JR, Watson NT, Sherman CE & O'Brien CP (1995). Effect of naltrexone on alcohol high in alcoholics. *American Journal of Psychiatry* 15:613–615.

Wafford KA, Burnett DM, Leidenheimer NJ, Burt DR, Wang JB, Kofuji P, Dunwiddie TV, Harris RA & Sikela JM (1991). Ethanol sensitivity of the $GABA_A$ receptor expressed in Xenopus oocytes requires eight amino acids contained in the gamma2L subunit. *Neuron* 7:27–33.

Wilson JM, Kalasinsky KS, Levey AI, Bergeron C, Reiber G, Anthony RM, Schumk GA, Shannak K, Haycock

JW & Kish SJ (1996). Striatal dopamine nerve terminal markers in human, chronic methamphetamine users. *Nature Medicine* 2:699–703.

Wolf ME & Khansa MR (1991). Repeated administration of MK-801 produces sensitization to its own locomotor stimulant effects but blocks sensitization to amphetamine. *Brain Research* 562:164–168.

Woodward JJ & Gonzales RA (1990). Ethanol inhibition of N-methyl-D-aspartate-stimulated endogenous dopamine release from rat striatal slices: Reversal by glycine. *Journal of Neurochemistry* 54:712–715.

Yang X, Criswell HE, Simson P, Moy S & Breese GR (1996). Evidence for a selective effect of ethanol on NMDA responses: Ethanol affects a subtype of the ifenprodil-sensitive NMDA receptor. *Journal of Pharmacology and Experimental Therapeutics* 278:114–124.

Yoshimura M & Tabakoff B (1995). Selective effects of ethanol on the generation of cAMP by particular members of the adenylyl cyclase family. *Alcoholism: Clinical & Experimental Research* 19:1435–1440.

Yoshimura M, Ikeda H & Tabakoff B (1996). *Mu*-opioid receptors inhibit dopamine-stimulated activity of Type V adenylyl cyclase but enhance dopamine-stimulated activity of Type VII adenylyl cyclase. *Molecular Pharmacology* 50:43–51.

SECTION 3
Prevention

CHAPTER 1

Assessing Individual Risks and Resiliencies **207**
Karol L. Kumpfer, Ph.D., Eric Goplerud, Ph.D. and Rose Alvarado, Ph.D.

CHAPTER 2

Prevention Science: Developing Empirical Models for Prevention Intervention **215**
Mary A. Jansen, Ph.D. and Michael J. Stoil, Ph.D.

CHAPTER 3

Developing Comprehensive Community Coalitions to Prevent Alcohol, Tobacco and Other Drug Abuse **227**
Abraham Wandersman, Ph.D., Robert M. Goodman, Ph.D., M.P.H. and Frances D. Butterfoss, Ph.D., M.S.Ed.

CHAPTER 4

Fitting Prevention into the Continuum of Care **233**
Kenneth Hoffman, M.D., M.P.H.

SECTION COORDINATOR

KENNETH HOFFMAN, M.D., M.P.H.
COL, MC, FS, USA
Director, Center for Addiction Medicine
Department of Preventive Medicine and Biometrics
Uniformed Services University of the Health Sciences
Bethesda, Maryland

CONTRIBUTORS

Rose Alvarado, Ph.D.
Research Associate
Department of Health Education
University of Utah
Salt Lake City, Utah

Frances D. Butterfoss, Ph.D., M.S.Ed.
Associate Professor
Eastern Virginia Medical School
Norfolk, Virginia

Robert M. Goodman, Ph.D., M.P.H.
Associate Professor
Department of Community Health Sciences
School of Public Health and Tropical Medicine
Tulane University
New Orleans, Louisiana

Eric Goplerud, Ph.D.
Associate Administrator
Office of Managed Care
Substance Abuse and Mental Health Services
Administration
Rockville, Maryland

Mary A. Jansen, Ph.D.
Deputy Chief Consultant for Mental Health
U.S. Department of Veterans Affairs
Washington, D.C., and
Professor, Graduate School of Education
George Mason University
Fairfax, Virginia

Karol L. Kumpfer, Ph.D.
Director
Center for Substance Abuse Prevention
Substance Abuse and Mental Health Services
Administration
Rockville, Maryland

Michael J. Stoil, Ph.D.
Conwal, Inc.
McLean, Virginia

Abraham Wandersman, Ph.D.
Professor
Department of Psychology
University of South Carolina
Columbia, South Carolina

CHAPTER 1

Assessing Individual Risks and Resiliencies

Karol L. Kumpfer, Ph.D.
Eric Goplerud, Ph.D.
Rose Alvarado, Ph.D.

A Biopsychosocial Model
Issues in Designing Prevention Programs
Major Types of Prevention Initiatives
Promising Future Directions

Effective approaches to the prevention of substance abuse must address the precursors of alcohol, tobacco and other drug abuse, which are multicausal and differ for each individual and subgroup. This variability significantly complicates the design of effective prevention programs.

Prevention programs typically are organized into a continuum of primary, secondary, and tertiary prevention. The goal of *primary* prevention is to deter or preclude initiation into use of alcohol, tobacco and other drugs. Examples include early educational programs, social skills training, parenting and family programs, and positive youth clubs and activities (Kumpfer, 1991a, 1991b).

The goal of *secondary* prevention is to identify early-stage abusing individuals through assessments and to refer them for treatment.

Tertiary prevention seeks to end compulsive use of alcohol, tobacco and other drugs and to ameliorate the negative consequences of such abuse through treatment and rehabilitation.

A BIOPSYCHOSOCIAL MODEL

Addiction researchers have debated for some time whether biological or environmental factors are the primary cause of addictions, when, in fact, both are important. A biopsychosocial model of addiction (Kumpfer, Trunnell & Whiteside, 1990) should guide efforts at prevention, clinical assessment of at-risk individuals, early intervention, and treatment.

Biological Factors. Because of the promise offered by recent breakthroughs in genetically-linked diseases, many Americans hope geneticists will discover a gene that "causes" alcoholism or drug addiction. Such problems, however, involve a complex interaction of genetic, neurophysiological, and environmental precursors. Therefore, even if a gene for vulnerability to alcohol, tobacco or other abuse were to be found, it is unlikely to provide the total answer to the addiction problem. It seems likely that different genes are associated with the multitude of biological differences found in vulnerable individuals, such as children of alcoholics.

Environmental Factors. Environmental risk and protective factors depend on different experiences in an individual's life and often change predictably over the life span. The resulting resiliency and vulnerability characteristics of individuals also can vary, depending on the transaction between genetic and biological temperament traits, learned psychological characteristics, and environmental factors. For example, Kellam, Werthamer-Larsson, et al. (1991) have found that biologically linked problems of attention-deficit disorder (ADD) and concentration in first graders lead to psychological problems of shy and aggressive behavior and poor achievement in boys and girls, but also to depressive symptoms in girls. Depression then leads to continued poor achievement in boys, but both poor achievement and increased depressive symptoms in girls. These results are particularly important to addiction specialists, because Kellam, Brown and Hendricks (1983) found in an earlier longitudinal study that shy and aggressive behavior in first grade boys was predictive of alcohol, tobacco and other drug abuse by the ages of 16 or 17.

Research by Kumpfer and Turner (1990, 1991) suggests that environmental factors such as substance abuse by peers or family are the final common pathway in adolescent vulnerability to use of alcohol, tobacco and other drugs. Environmental risk factors, organized by realm, involve:

Family environment, including family conflict, poor discipline style, parental rejection of the child, lack of adult supervision or family rituals, poor family management or communication, sexual and physical abuse, parental or sibling modeling of alcohol, tobacco and other drug abuse, and parental approval of the child's use of alcohol, tobacco and other drugs;

School environment, involving lack of school bonding and opportunities for involvement and reward, unfair rules, norms conducive to use of drugs, and school failure because of poor school climate;

Community environment, such as poor community bonding, community norms that condone alcohol, tobacco and other drug abuse, disorganized neighborhoods, lack of opportunities for positive youth involvement, high levels of crime and drug use, endemic poverty and lack of employment opportunities;

Peer factors, such as bonding to an anti-social peer group whose members use alcohol, tobacco and other drugs or engage in other delinquent behaviors.

Family and school climate interact with the child's temperament to influence school and peer adjustment. Although peer influence is the final determinant of alcohol, tobacco and other drug abuse in many youth (Huba & Bentler, 1980; Kumpfer & Turner, 1990, 1991), parental influence is the most important factor in non-use (Coombs, Paulson & Richardson, 1991). High school students who do not engage in such abuse say their parents are their primary source of information about—and their reason for abstaining from—abuse of alcohol, tobacco and other drugs.

Physicians are a primary source of such information to both parents and youth. Brief interventions by physicians can have an impact in reducing addictions by providing realistic and credible scientific information on the health risks of alcohol, tobacco and other drug abuse.

ISSUES IN DESIGNING PREVENTION PROGRAMS

The history of alcohol, tobacco and other drug abuse prevention is one of good intentions, but regrettably little sustained progress. Prevention designers still deal with the addictions as if they were unique disorders and rarely consider their overlap with a broad range of mental and emotional problems. Substance-using youth need: (1) developmentally appropriate programs, (2) culturally-relevant programs, (3) intensive and enduring programs, and (4) targeted and tailored programs.

Historical Models. For many years, a "bandwagon effect" has been apparent, as one approach after another wins sudden popularity and then becomes passé. For example, educational "scare tactics" were popular in the 1940s and 1950s. These were replaced in the 1960s by "affective education programs," which later were found to be ineffectual because they could not singlehandedly modify self-esteem. Alternative activity programs then became briefly popular, but only those activities that involve non-users as role models were found to be effective (Swisher & Hu, 1983).

When the prevention field began to attract behavioral researchers in the 1980s, school curricula that emphasized peer resistance training became popular because they had previously demonstrated effectiveness against tobacco use. These programs were modified for use with alcohol and other drugs, but were found to be less effective for these purposes—particularly in reducing alcohol initiation and use (Pentz, Johnson, et al., 1989). In the 1990s, the community coalition approach has become popular. This approach involves massive community organizing to create infrastructures to support prevention work. While this approach is more likely to be effective than earlier "single-shot" approaches, coalitions can be no more effective than the many prevention interventions they employ.

Supply Reduction versus Demand Reduction Strategies. Supply reduction strategies include destruction of drug crops, confiscation of drug shipments, border patrols, criminal penalties for drug use and dealing, and police actions. Demand reduction strategies include prevention approaches designed to reduce the demand for alcohol and drugs by decreasing precursors of abuse through family, school, community, and peer-focused prevention programs. Over the past several decades, federal programs have allocated ten times more money to supply reduction than demand reduction approaches (Johnston, O'Malley & Bachman, 1991), even though the federal government's own investigative arm concluded in 1992 that supply reduction approaches are not as cost-effective as demand reductions strategies (General Accounting Office, 1992). This review of prevention will consequently focus almost exclusively on demand reduction prevention methods.

The success of prevention programs in changing risk factors such as poor family environment, school and peer groups and other negative community norms and eventually preventing alcohol, tobacco and other drug abuse has been amply debated (Oetting & Beauvais, 1991; Moskowitz, 1989). Research demonstrates that prevention programs can fail at many points, such as failure to address the most critical risk factors, failure to implement the program successfully, and failure to continue the program (Oetting & Beauvais, 1991). Prevention, however, is a relatively new approach and has received very little funding in comparison to costly campaigns used by the tobacco and alcohol industry to promote the use of those substances. In fact, the federal Center for Substance Abuse Prevention (CSAP) is making significant strides in evaluating new models of prevention (Goplerud, 1990).

MAJOR TYPES OF PREVENTION INITIATIVES

There are four primary types of prevention programs, each of which directly relates to one of the four major environmental risk factors for alcohol, tobacco and other drug abuse: community, family, school and peers.

Community Approaches. The broadest types of prevention activities seek to improve communities by reducing crime and changing community norms that foster alcohol, tobacco and other drug abuse, as well as by increasing opportunities for positive community involvement for youth. Although long neglected, probably because of its complexity, community-based prevention currently is very popular because of the success of programs built on this model in reducing tobacco use.

Community coalitions for the prevention of alcohol and drug abuse are springing up around the country with funding from foundations like the Robert Wood Johnson Foundation and federal agencies such as the Center for Substance Abuse Prevention and the Centers for Disease Control and Prevention. These community coalitions provide an opportunity for physicians and other medical professionals to join with diverse community volunteers to plan locally effective prevention approaches.

Typical coalition activities include: (1) community needs assessments to monitor use patterns and trends; (2) coordination of existing prevention services across many different agencies to reduce service gaps and redundancies; (3) legislation and public policy changes to reduce alcohol availability (e.g., licensure of sales outlets, minimum purchase age laws, increased excise taxes, server training and responsibility programs, differential taxation of low-alcohol beverages, advertising restrictions, and elimination of tax deductions for business use of alcoholic beverages); (4) stimulation of funding for family, school, and community agency-based prevention services; and (5) community-wide planning, training, and mobilization of resources.

Family Approaches. Family-focused approaches hold the most promise of long-term, positive impact on a broad range of youth problems (such as alcohol, tobacco and drug abuse, adolescent pregnancy and delinquency, school failure, and unsuccessful life adjustment). Strengthening families through parenting programs, family support, family skills training, and family therapy consistently has been found to reduce risk factors for alcohol, tobacco and other drug abuse, as well as delinquency, conduct disorders, and depression (DeMarsh & Kumpfer, 1985; Kumpfer, 1989; Kumpfer, 1992; Stern, 1992).

Unfortunately, the prevention field has, by and large, bypassed the use of "family" as a major target audience or targeted delivery system for alcohol and other drug messages (Stern, 1992). Prevention specialists generally are trained in school-based approaches and thus have shied away from family-focused approaches because of their lack of training. In addition, recruiting and maintaining families in prevention programs can present difficulties unless attendance barriers (involving child care and transportation) are systematically addressed (Kumpfer, 1991b).

Neglect of family-strengthening approaches as part of comprehensive alcohol, tobacco and other drug abuse prevention initiatives is even more unfortunate today, because the clinical technology to significantly affect families now exists (Kumpfer, 1992). For example, television and videos have the potential to reach the most high-risk families. Even the most isolated and fearful single parent could be effectively reached with powerful media messages, education, and parent skills-training through video and television. Parent education and training videos played in physicians' waiting rooms or distributed through video shops are promising developments in need of evaluation.

Even though family intervention programs are not consistently viewed as prevention strategies, the research shows that any family intervention that reduces family risk factors for alcohol, tobacco and other drug abuse—such as family conflict, child abuse and sexual abuse, child neglect, modeling of use by parents and siblings—and promotes protective factors such as family support, organization and bonding, will reduce rates of alcohol, tobacco and other drug abuse. To be effective, family interventions must be tailored to the ages of the children and the level of dysfunction of the family. For example, family therapy approaches that rely on high-level communications are more appropriate for adolescents, whereas behavioral parent training approaches are more useful for younger children.

School-Based Approaches. For many years, school-based prevention approaches were based on a simple premise: that knowledge changes behavior. While knowledge *does* change behavior under some favorable circumstances (particularly if the message is credible and the audience is open to it), educational approaches to prevention often are not enough.

Peer resistance training programs that teach youth to "Just Say No" are included in almost all school prevention curricula, but their effectiveness for alcohol use is very tenuous. A few studies have found small delays in initiation into alcohol, tobacco and other drug use in youth participating in these programs, but their overall impact does not appear to justify their cost. Dielman, Shope et al. (1989) recently found a delayed "sleeper" effect for alcohol resistance in 9th grade students who were first trained in peer resistance in the 5th grade, but these students participated in annual "booster sessions." Some school-based programs have reduced alcohol, tobacco and other drug abuse in high-risk youth, but other youth have been found to increase their use after exposure to such programs (Moskowitz, 1989). It is possible that a more important use of this 5th- and 6th-grade classroom time would be programs focused on how to choose "good" friends, the importance of avoiding a bad reputation, the importance of good grades to success, understanding subtle peer and media influence, accurate assessment of peer use, and attempts to change the class norms to emphasize success, positive life values, and purpose in life.

To have any lasting impact, school-based prevention approaches must be more intensive than just a six- to 10-session curriculum delivered in the fifth and sixth grades. School-based prevention programs must focus on changing the total school climate to increase school bonding, improve academic achievement and success, and reduce school norms that are conducive to substance abuse. Comprehensive school climate improvement programs such as Project PATHE and HIPATHE have been successful in reducing alcohol, tobacco and drug use (or the precursors of such use) in junior and senior high school students (Gottfredson, 1986; Kumpfer, Turner & Alvarado, 1991).

The American School Health Association and the federal Centers for Disease Control and Prevention are recommending that school health programs no longer have separate curricula for AIDS, alcohol and drug use, teen pregnancy, violence prevention, gang prevention, and other health risks of youth, but rather adopt an integrated, comprehensive school health program. Such an integrated approach has the best chance of success if it remains intensive and is imbedded within a total commitment to school climate improvements to reduce risk factors.

Peer Prevention Approaches. Because association with drug-using peers is consistently found to be the final precursor of alcohol, tobacco and other drug use (Huba & Bentler, 1980; Kumpfer & Turner, 1990, 1991), almost all prevention programs include some type of peer-focused approach. For example, resistance to peer pressure can be increased through involvement in peer resistance training programs. These popular skill-building programs have been shown to delay initiation of drug use (Dielman, Shope et al., 1989; Pentz, Johnson et al., 1989). Unfortunately, peer programs probably target the wrong variable by focusing strictly on peer resistance, rather than on selection of prosocial peers and social/life skills, as does the Life Skills Program of Botvin, Baker et al. (1990) and Platt and Hermalin (1989).

Adolescents are very peer-oriented and should be provided with guidance from parents, teachers, and youth workers on how to choose good friends, what constitutes social acceptance, and how to plan for future happiness. A promising approach that has not yet been evaluated works to increase networking by parents to monitor student activities and support youth in positive problem-solving and social relationships.

PROMISING FUTURE DIRECTIONS

Addiction medicine specialists can be integral participants in prevention activities by:

- Increasing their involvement in patient education, counseling, and advice about alcohol, tobacco and other drug use (using widely available videos, brochures, and other patient education materials);

- Using office visits to conduct risk assessments and brief patient interventions, as well as making referrals for treatment when needed;
- Supporting community coalition planning and activities;
- Promoting public policies, including legislation, that support prevention, early intervention and treatment;
- Endorsing prevention efforts that address protective factors and resiliencies;
- Supporting cultural sensitivity and relevance in prevention efforts; and
- Promoting the involvement of addiction medicine specialists and other health professionals in prevention and public education campaigns.

Increasing Patient Education. Children spend more time watching television than going to school, playing with friends, or doing homework or housework (Flay & Sobel, 1983). Unfortunately, the educational power of television has never been usefully tapped in comparison to the use of television for selling products. Government-subsidized educational television in this country is significantly underfunded compared to that in European and Asian nations. However, there appears to be a dawning awareness that there may be some connection between the rapidly escalating depiction of crime and violence on television and the increased violence our children and adults experience in real life.

According to Postman (1985), "electronic media have decisively and irreversibly changed the character of our symbolic environment. We are now in a culture whose information, ideas and epistemology are given form by television, not by the printed word."

Videos, films, brochures, magazines, and books are useful tools in educating patients about their risk for alcohol, tobacco and other drug problems, and the attendant social and health consequences. In hospital settings, patient and family education classes and discussion groups are a helpful forum for increasing patient knowledge and awareness of the health consequences of substance abuse and the resources available to prevent or address such abuse.

Conducting Risk Assessments and Brief Interventions. If physicians and other health care professionals could identify high-risk patients *before* they develop disabling addictive disorders, those individuals could be treated or referred to remedial services before long-term damage occurs. Predictors of risk include personal and family history, as well as physical examination findings (DuPont, 1989) and the results obtained through use of appropriately selected screening and assessment instruments (see Section 4).

Supporting Community Coalitions. Many community coalitions include physician task forces or involve health professionals in activities such as conducting needs assessments, training, planning and networking.

Promoting Prevention Policies. Through their professional organizations, physicians can provide important support for legislative and other policy initiatives directed toward prevention of alcohol, tobacco and other drug abuse. Such initiatives may address a variety of risk behaviors, such as juvenile delinquency and crime, adolescent sexuality and pregnancy, and family abuse, as well as promoting increased family and community bonding and spirit.

Supporting Resiliency-Focused Prevention Programs. New emphasis is being given to enhancing protective factors and resiliency to drug use in youth, particularly for young people who live in high-risk environments where it would be difficult to reduce their environmental risk exposure.

Researchers have discovered that the more risk factors youth have, the more likely they are to use drugs (Bry, McKeon & Pandina, 1982). Conversely, it could be hypothesized that the more protective factors or resiliency traits youth have, the more likely they are *not* to use drugs. In fact, a shift in emphasis from risk to protective factors could revolutionize the prevention field. The scientific literature on resilient children (Rutter, 1990) who have successfully negotiated high-risk families, schools and neighborhoods is providing increased evidence of the pivotal factors to be emphasized in prevention programs for high-risk youth.

Kumpfer (1994) concludes that there are seven major personal characteristics that increase resiliency. These are *optimism*, *empathy*, *insight*, *intellectual competence*, *self-esteem*, *direction or purpose in life*, and *determination*. These major cognitive resiliency characteristics are associated with specific coping or life skills acquired by resilient children through interaction with their environment, namely: emotional management skills, interpersonal social skills, intrapersonal reflective skills, academic and job skills, ability to restore self-esteem, planning skills, and life skills. Neiger (1991) has argued that *purpose in life* is the most salient variable in resilience, followed by problem-solving ability, self-esteem, and locus of control. Having a positive purpose in life helps high-risk youth create direction and meaning for their lives, which in turn helps them to resist temptations to use drugs or engage in life-threatening activities.

The major questions now facing prevention specialists are (1) how to create resiliency in youth and (2) how to translate these desirable personal characteristics into programs or protective mechanisms to increase resilience to drug use (Rutter, 1990). Methods of fostering such protective mechanisms then could become the primary foci of prevention programs targeting high-risk youth.

Such resiliency factors are developed through a complex transaction between youths and their environment, often involving at least one caring adult who supports a child or adolescent's positive development. In a longitudinal study on the island of Kauai, Werner (1986) found that resilient children of alcoholics were more caring and empathetic toward others, possibly because positive role modeling and family situations required them to be helpful to others.

Promoting Gender, Age, and Cultural Sensitivity and Relevance. To be effective, prevention programs must be gender, age and culturally relevant. Awareness of cultural diversity dictates that prevention programs must be individually tailored to the needs of different populations. Needs assessments directed toward precursors, rather than just incidence and prevalence, are needed and should be analyzed for differences in causes of alcohol, tobacco and other drug abuse by gender, age, and ethnic group. Once such precursors have been identified, interventions that directly target them can be developed and tested.

Supporting the Involvement of Addiction Medicine Specialists and Other Health Professionals in Prevention and Other Public Education Campaigns. Future prevention programs should be comprehensive, relevant to the needs of participants, resiliency-focused, and include interventions of sufficient measure and strength. There is much that addiction medicine specialists can do to foster the development of such programs. Additional research on etiology and prevention approaches could be supported even within clinical practices. Increasing patient education, brief interventions, and modeling appropriate use of legal drugs would be a good start in contributing to the prevention of alcohol, tobacco and other drug abuse.

REFERENCES

Botvin GJ, Baker E, Dusenbury L, Tortu S & Botvin EM (1990). Preventing adolescent drug abuse through a multimodal cognitive-behavioral approach: Results of a 3-year study. *Journal of Consulting and Clinical Psychology* 58(4):1–10.

Bry BH, McKeon P & Pandina RJ (1982). Extent of drug use as a function of number of risk factors. *Journal of Abnormal Psychology* 91(4):273–279.

Chasnoff IJ, Landress HJ & Barrett ME (1990). The prevalence of illicit drug or alcohol use during pregnancy and discrepancies in mandatory reporting in Pinellas County, Florida. *The New England Journal of Medicine* 322:1202–1206.

Coombs RH, Paulson MJ & Richardson MA (1991). Peer vs. parental influence in substance use in Hispanic and Anglo children and adolescents. *Journal of Youth and Adolescents* 20(1):73–88.

DeMarsh J & Kumpfer K (1985). Family environmental and genetic influences on children's future chemical dependency. *Journal of Children in Contemporary Society: Advances in Theory and Applied Research* 18(1–2):49–92.

Dielman TE, Shope JT, Leech SL & Butchart AM (1989). Differential effectiveness of an elementary school-based alcohol misuse prevention program. *Journal of School Health* 59(6):255–263.

DuPont RL (1989). *Stopping Alcohol and Other Drug Abuse Before It Starts: The Future of Prevention (Prevention Monograph Series)*. Rockville, MD: Office for Substance Abuse Prevention.

Felner RD & Silverman M (1991). Prevention of substance abuse and related disorders in childhood and adolescence: A developmentally based, comprehensive ecological approach. *Family and Community Health* 14(3):12–22.

Flay BR & Sobel JL (1983). The role of mass media for preventing adolescent substance abuse. *Preventing Adolescent Drug Abuse: Intervention Strategies (Research Monograph No. 47)*. Rockville, MD: National Institute on Drug Abuse.

General Accounting Office (1992). *Adolescent Drug Use Prevention: Common Features of Promising Community Programs* (GAO/PEMD–92–2). Washington, DC: U.S. Government Printing Office.

Goplerud E (1990). *Breaking New Ground for Youth at Risk: Program Summaries*. Washington DC: U.S. Government Printing Office.

Gottfredson D (1986). An empirical test of school based interventions to reduce the risk of delinquent behavior. *Criminology* 24(4):705–730.

Hawkins DJ, Catalano RR & Miller JY (1992). Risk and protective factors for alcohol and other drug problems in adolescence and early adulthood: Implications for substance abuse prevention. *Psychological Bulletin* 112(1): 64–105.

Huba GL & Bentler PM (1980). The role of peer and adult models for drug taking at various stages of adolescence. *Journal of Youth and Adolescence* 9(5):449–465.

Johnston LD, O'Malley PM & Bachman GM (1991). *Drug Use Among American High School Students, College*

Students, and Young Adults: 1975–1990. Rockville, MD: National Institute on Drug Abuse.

Kellam SG, Brown C & Hendricks F (1983). Relationship of first-grade social adaptation to teenage drinking, drug-use and smoking. *Digest of Alcoholism Theory and Application* 2:20–24.

Kellam SG, Werthamer-Larsson L, Dolan LJ & Brown C (1991). Developmental epidemiologically based preventive trials: baseline modeling of early target behaviors and depressive symptoms. *American Journal of Community Psychology* 19(4):563–584.

Kumpfer KL (1987). Special populations: Etiology and prevention of vulnerability to chemical dependency in children of substance abusers. In BS Brown & AR Mills (eds.) *Youth at High Risk for Substance Abuse.* Rockville, MD: National Institute on Drug Abuse.

Kumpfer KL (1989). The Cinderellas of prevention want to go to the ball, too. In KH Rey, CL Faegre & P Lowery (eds.) *Prevention Research Findings: 1988 (Prevention Monograph 3).* Rockville, MD: Office for Substance Abuse Prevention.

Kumpfer KL (1991a). Children and adolescents and drug and alcohol abuse and addiction: Review of prevention strategies. In NS Miller (ed.) *Comprehensive Handbook of Drug and Alcohol Addiction.* New York, NY: Marcel Dekker.

Kumpfer KL (1991b). How to get hard-to-reach parents involved in parenting programs. In *Parent Training Is Prevention: Preventing Alcohol and Other Drug Problems Among Youth In The Family.* Rockville, MD: Office for Substance Abuse Prevention.

Kumpfer KL (1992). *Strengthening America's families: Promising parenting and family strategies for delinquency prevention. User's Guide.* Washington, DC: Office of Juvenile Justice and Delinquency Prevention, Office of Juvenile Programs, U.S. Department of Justice.

Kumpfer KL (1994). *Promoting Resiliency to AOD Use in High Risk Youth.* Rockville, MD: Center for Substance Abuse Prevention.

Kumpfer KL & Bayes J (1994). Child abuse and alcohol and other drug abuse. In JH Jaffe (ed.) *The Encyclopedia of Drugs and Alcohol.* New York, NY: Macmillan.

Kumpfer KL, Trunnell EP & Whiteside HO (1990). The biopsychosocial model: Application to the addictions field. In R Engs (ed.) *Controversy in the Addictions Field.* Dubuque, IA: Kendall/Hunt Pub. Co.

Kumpfer KL & Turner C (1990). The social ecology model of adolescent substance abuse: Implications for prevention. *The International Journal of the Addictions* 25(4A):435–462.

Kumpfer KL, Turner C & Alvarado R (1991). A community change model for school health promotion. *Journal of Health Education* 22(2):94–110.

Moskowitz J (1989). The primary prevention of alcohol problems: A critical review of the research literature. *Journal of Studies on Alcohol* 50(1):54–88.

Neiger B (1991). Resilient reintegration: Use of structural equations modeling. Dissertation submitted to the faculty of the University of Utah, Department of Health Education.

Oetting ER & Beauvais F (1991). Critical incidents: failure in prevention. *International Journal of the Addictions* 26(7):797–820.

Pentz MA, Johnson C, Dwyer JH, MacKinnon DM, Hansen WB & Flay BR (1989). A comprehensive community approach to adolescent drug abuse prevention: Effects on cardiovascular disease risk behaviors. *Annals of Medicine* 21(3):219–222.

Pihl RO, Peterson J & Finn P (1990). Inherited predisposition to alcoholism: Characteristics of sons of male alcoholics. *Journal of Abnormal Psychology* 99:291–301.

Platt JJ & Hermalin J (1989). Social skill deficit interventions for substance abusers. *Psychology of Addictive Behaviors* 3:114–133.

Postman N (1985). *Amusing Ourselves to Death.* New York, NY: Penguin Books.

Rice DP, Kelman S & Miller LS (1991). Estimates of economic costs of alcohol and drug abuse and mental illness, 1985 and 1988. *Public Health Reports* 106(3):280–291.

Richardson G, Neiger B, Jenson S & Kumpfer KL (1990). The resiliency process. *Journal of Health Education* 21(6):33–39.

Rutter M (1990). Psychosocial resilience and protective mechanisms. In JE Rolf, AS Masten, D Cicchetti et al. (eds.) *Risk and Protective Factors in the Development of Psychopathology.* New York, NY: Cambridge University Press.

Stern A (1992). Family influences on alcohol and other drug-taking behavior: Implications for prevention programming. Paper prepared for the Southwest Regional Center for Drug-free Schools and Communities, Los Angeles, CA.

Swisher JD & Hu TW (1983). Alternatives to drug abuse: Some are and some are not. In TJ Glynn, CG Leukefeld & JP Ludford (eds.) *Preventing Adolescent Drug Abuse: Intervention Strategies (Research Monograph 47).* Rockville, MD: Office for Substance Abuse Prevention.

Tarter RE, Laird SB & Moss HB (1990). Neuropsychological and neurophysiological characteristics of children of alcoholics. In M Windle & J Searles (eds.) *Children of Alcoholics: Critical Perspectives.*

Toffler A (1990). *Power Shift: Knowledge, Wealth and Violence at the Edge of the 21st Century.* New York, NY: Bantam Books.

Werner EE (1986). Resilient offspring of alcoholics: A longitudinal study from birth to age 18. *Journal of Studies on Alcohol* 44(1):34–40.

CHAPTER 2

Prevention Science: Developing Empirical Models for Prevention Intervention

Mary A. Jansen, Ph.D.
Michael J. Stoil, Ph.D.

Challenges in Conducting Prevention Research
Deciding Which Models Are Scientifically Valid
Categorizing Risks for Substance Abuse
Guidelines and Principles for Prevention
Documented Findings from Prevention Science
Future Directions for Prevention Science

The systematic development of an empirical science base in the field of substance abuse prevention is a relatively new endeavor. The effort began in 1975 with the creation of the Division of Epidemiology and Prevention Research at the National Institute on Drug Abuse (NIDA) and continued with the establishment by Congress of the Center for Substance Abuse Prevention in 1986. Together with the National Institute on Alcohol Abuse and Alcoholism (NIAAA), these federal agencies have provided the major impetus for the development of science-based models for the substance abuse prevention field.

To achieve an empirical basis for substance abuse prevention, the efficacy and effectiveness of theoretically-based models must be determined. After efficacy has been established, models must be systematically tested to determine their effectiveness among diverse populations and under varying conditions. The replication process is difficult, however, and generalizability for most prevention models thus has not been established.

The difficulty of replication is inherent in the nature of conducing prevention studies in the community. The good news, however, is that the methods employed in both research and service demonstration programs have improved significantly during the past several years. Additionally, there have been advances in the statistical analysis techniques used in prevention research. As a result, our understanding of the factors which predispose young people toward using illegal substances has improved and we now can link some prevention models to identified risk factors. The next steps are to tease out the effective components from those models, link each of the components to specific risk factors, determine the lowest dosage needed, and determine the generalizability of these models for diverse populations.

CHALLENGES IN CONDUCTING PREVENTION RESEARCH

The conduct of rigorous prevention research in the community is one of the most difficult social science endeavors due to barriers that deter the use of classical experimental designs. These barriers can be grouped into two categories: (1) problems specific to the nature of the desired outcome, i.e., *prevention* of a socially-unacceptable behavior that might not occur; and (2) problems inherent in most community-based social science research.

Problems Specific to Prevention Science. One problem which arises specifically for prevention research results from the fact that most people do not believe that the behavior identified for prevention—substance abuse—will affect them. Potential participants thus are likely to be relatively unconcerned about the outcome and are less likely to maintain participation in a prevention program. Even when initially willing to participate in a prevention program or research study, their commitment is likely to be less strong than it would be if the problem under study already had directly affected their life.

Thus, in contrast to clinical trials of treatment alternatives in which participants believe that their health or lives depend on the outcome, substance abuse prevention research encounters critical issues in recruiting and retaining voluntary participants.

An additional problem is that the measure of outcome for drug abuse prevention research involves participant report of behavior that is disapproved by society and is often illegal. Although the cumulative effects of substance abuse over time are easily detectable, individuals can engage in instances of the behavior without lasting overt symptoms. An accurate measure of whether the behavior occurs therefore relies on self-report. Admitted use of illegal drugs or abuse of alcohol or tobacco could result in a wide variety of penalties, ranging from parental scolding through school expulsion or job loss to incarceration. Study participants—especially in a comparison group which does not receive an intervention—have good reason to avoid self-report of the behavior and little incentive to accurately report such behavior. At the least, research on prevention of substance abuse in the community must maintain elaborate protection of the confidentiality of responses through follow-up; the more fundamental issue, however, is the dubious accuracy of the self-reports on which measures of prevention success are based.

Problems Encountered in Most Social Science Research. The specific difficulties of establishing a science base for substance abuse prevention are compounded by the absence of the ability to control variables in most community-based social science research. There is no way to limit the exposure of comparison or control groups to prevention messages from other sources. There is no way to control—or even effectively monitor—the behavior of subjects under study.

The problems of attrition and accretion of participants is a significant example of the lack of control over participant behavior in a community-based research project. After baseline measurements are assessed, participants frequently drop out and new individuals wish to enter the program under study. Data frequently are available on some individuals at various points in time but unavailable on all participants at each data collection point. For example, if four occasions are identified for data collection, an individual may provide data at baseline and at the third data point, but not be available for the first and final post-intervention data collection. Another individual may provide data at baseline and at the final follow-up but not at either of the two initial post-intervention data collection points. Missing data points due to attrition, and the related failure to take part in every session, become particularly important when subjects who drop out of a study or miss a session are significantly different from subjects who participate fully in every session. Differential attrition between intervention and comparison groups may result in an inability to generalize study results. Even without differential attrition, the volume of missing data points threatens the validity and credibility of the evaluation.

A related issue is the need for survival of a sufficiently large sample size to achieve the statistical power needed to detect the effect of an intervention. Unless enough subjects are present for both baseline and follow-up in treatment and comparison groups, there may be insufficient statistical power to detect small changes. This is especially true when a preventive intervention consists of multiple components which are presumed to have a cumulative impact on behavior. Given the difficulties of retention described earlier, achieving a large enough sample frequently is very difficult. Statistical modeling techniques such as Hierarchical Linear Modeling (HLM) recently have been developed to resolve some of these problems during data analysis (Byrh & Roudenbush, 1993).

The dose-response issue is another problem that is often overlooked in studies of community-based interventions. Community-based prevention studies generally avoid the issue of the impact of dosage by reducing the possibilities to a binary variable (e.g., "participant exposed/not exposed" to the intervention). As a result, prevention science has not identified a precise dose of a given intervention that is required to achieve the desired effect. Significantly, community interventions that attempt even the most crude measurement of dosage have found variations in outcome that can be ascribed to the differences in level of participant exposure (for example, Rhodes, 1990).

Conducting studies of community-level interventions is associated with other methodological problems, including the difficulty of defining and studying entire communities, observation of behavioral change over time, and the credibility of using different samples of community participants for the measurement of each component of the intervention. Many of these issues are discussed in detail in a special issue of the *Journal of Community Psychology* devoted to methodological problems in prevention research (Jansen, 1994).

In addition to the methodological issues described above, the conduct of prevention demonstrations and research studies in the community often is accompanied by an ethical issue that potentially affects the reliability of the research outcome. During the course of a demonstration program or study, it becomes apparent that an individual or family could benefit from referral to, or inclusion in, the program under study. Prevention practitioners often feel professionally bound to include as many participants as possible in a program that they support. Researchers, on the other hand, recognize the need to maintain well-matched intervention and comparison/control groups. From the research perspective, expansion of an intervention to include "needy" members of the comparison group severely compromises the scientific validity of the program outcome. The issue is not easy to resolve, despite the variety of solutions offered: at the end of the day, the program director needs a program-specific plan to resolve the problem on a case-by-case basis.

DECIDING WHICH MODELS ARE SCIENTIFICALLY VALID

The field of community-based prevention of substance abuse has made significant progress in the short time, notwithstanding the methodological problems confronting scientific inquiry. Knowledge has been derived from traditional research techniques, including rigorous experimental studies with randomly-selected intervention and control groups, and quasi-experimental studies utilizing less control over both intervention and comparison populations. In addition, we have recognized that the knowledge base can be legitimately enhanced by utilizing the findings derived from demonstration programs that adopt features of quasi-experimental research.

Traditional research seeks to gain knowledge by holding all variables constant except one or two experimental variations, either through manipulation of the environment or through mathematical surrogates of such manipulation. As described by Springer and Phillips (1994), "The experimental orientation emphasizes using the logic and techniques of the scientific experiment (e.g., control groups) to discern program impact, though often in "quasi" form. The objective is to rule out nonprogram explanations of observed change. The approach also assumes stable and clearly identifiable populations of participants and the ability to select or statistically construct comparable groups not receiving the program intervention" (p. 123).

The benefits of experimental and quasi-experimental research designs are well known. Long-term prospective studies document that preventive interventions can reduce the prevalence of adolescent and young adult substance abuse and anti-social behavior (see, for example, Pentz, Dwyer et al., 1989; Hawkins, Von Cleve & Catalano, 1991; Botvin, Baker et al., 1995; Botvin, Schinke et al., 1995; Perry, Williams et al., 1996).

In contrast, both the drawbacks of quasi-experimental designs and the benefits of applied research embodied in community-based demonstration projects often are misunderstood. The control required by traditional research designs raises questions about whether the resulting findings apply to dynamic programs which may alter the specific details of the program intervention or the population served over time. Recently, some researchers have argued for a broadened conceptualization of what constitutes an acceptable approach to the development of new knowledge, in which evaluation of demonstrations at the community level are a necessary part of the process (Springer & Phillips, 1994; Fetterman 1996).

Field demonstrations apply theoretical findings from experimental and quasi-experimental studies to the complexities of implementation in real-life communities with little experimental control. By repeating similar efforts under a variety of conditions, field demonstrations generate knowledge that links theory to practice. The findings from these types of studies can be judged credible when the evaluations and documentation of field demonstrations meet criteria for methodological rigor appropriate to the format. This is not to say that sloppy research or evaluation methods are acceptable. Rather, it explains why the language discussing methodology and the findings emanating from a well-executed demonstration project differ from the language or rigor in an experimental or quasi-experimental research study.

One of these language differences is the shorthand used to describe the likelihood that a finding is broadly generalizable to a wider universe. Experimental studies employ statistical reliability for this purpose, inferring the probability that observed results are due to random chance. Comparison of a collection of similar demonstration projects does not generate this quantitative measure of inferential probability. Instead, a finding derived from the universe of similar demonstration projects may be described as "repeatedly documented" when supported by multiple examples from demonstrations operating under diverse environmental conditions and when plausible explanations are suggested for the few outcomes, if any, that appear to contradict the finding. A repeatedly documented finding represents the highest level of certainty that can be accorded when the finding is derived from evaluation of multiple demonstration projects: the equivalent of a finding that achieves the consensus statistical significance level in a quasi-experimental study.

Alternatively, findings from demonstration projects should be characterized as "provisional" when documented by a less varied selection of examples. When similar interventions are repeatedly administered to a narrow demographic segment of the target population, it is possible that implementation characteristics, repeated sampling bias or other factors may be responsible for the observed outcomes. "Provisional" applied to findings from evaluation of community-based demonstrations thus implies that parallel observations have been obtained but that alternative hypotheses to explain the results have not yet been eliminated. The elimination of alternative explanations for observations through repeated implementation across disparate community settings is a time-consuming process, but it is well worth the effort. Experimental and quasi-experimental research alone can generate only the beginning of the answers needed to significantly affect the use of drugs in the uncontrolled community environment.

CATEGORIZING RISKS FOR SUBSTANCE ABUSE

Knowledge gained from prior research has led to the conclusion that there are markers for deviant behavior, including substance abuse, and that these markers can be targeted for interventions designed to change the developmental trajectory of youth who may later develop substance abuse disorders. In addition to these behavioral markers, we also know that, in many cases, forces outside the child can exert dramatic influence on behavioral development. Examples include such obvious sources of influence as parental monitoring (Chilcoat, Anthony & Dishion, 1995). Relative poverty has been shown to be a factor in placing urban African-American children at risk for *long-term* substance abuse involvement (Dembo, Williams & Schmeidler, 1994), although *initiation* of drug use among all adolescents is positively correlated with higher socioeconomic status (e.g., Baumrind, 1985; Simcha-Fagan, Gersten & Langer, 1986). In addition, lack of strong bonds to family, school, and pro-social peers has repeatedly been identified as a risk factor for deviant behavior such as juvenile delinquency and early drug abuse (Hawkins, Catalano & Miller, 1992; Elliott, Huizinga & Ageton, 1985).

Prevention science as a field is built on the premise that those individuals with the greatest propensity for developing substance abuse behaviors are those who are exposed to multiple risk factors, sometimes called predictor variables. The field further assumes the existence of mediating variables which influence the way these risk/predictor variables affect an individual's behavior. The prevailing notion is that those most strongly influenced by these negative risk factors also have a deficit of protective factors which can counterbalance the effect of these risk factors.

The citations identified above demonstrate that understanding of the effects of childhood and adolescent risk factors on later behavior largely has been imported into the substance abuse field from other disciplines. Child development studies, educational psychology, and epidemiologic research on physical and mental health have been important sources for the development of models of influences on substance abuse. The impact of this research on the field often is delayed by communication barriers between the disciplines: substance abuse prevention specialists trained in sociology or in the practical issues of social work, for example, are hard-pressed to track advances in experimental and developmental psychology that have important consequences for their work. Thus, the finding that a high percentage of young adult men with substance abuse problems previously were diagnosed with aggressive conduct disorder years earlier (Coie, Terry et al., 1995) was slow to be incorporated among substance abuse risk factors, largely due to its origin in developmental psychology. Similarly, although other mental health problems have long been identified as potential mediating or causal influences on adolescent substance abuse and violence, the epidemiological evidence supporting the importance of such factors (e.g., Regier, Farmer et al., 1990; Milberger, Biederman et al., 1997; Taylor, Chadwick et al., 1996; Weber, Graham et al., 1989) only recently has been reflected in such prevention planning as the Personal Growth Class intervention (Thompson, Horn et al., 1997).

Recently, the Institute of Medicine established a schema for categorizing preventive interventions based on the risk level of the individual or group who appropriately receive the service. When an individual has been diagnosed with early or immediate precursor symptoms for substance abuse, the individual is an appropriate subject for *indicated interventions*. An individual who is a member of a subpopulation identified as being at elevated risk for using drugs, such as children of substance-abusing parents, is described as a candidate for *selected* interventions. Individuals who are part of the population not identified with known risk factors are characterized as appropriate subjects for *universal* preventive interventions (Institute of Medicine, 1994).

The Institute of Medicine typology also can be applied to distinguishing among the vectors from which a risk factor is thought to emanate. Thus, risk factors which affect all individuals present at the community, school or work site level can be described as universal, while risk factors that emanate from the peer or family level can be considered selective and risk factors that are derived from individual characteristics can be described as indicated (Stoil & Jansen, 1997).

We have achieved sufficient confirmation of a relationship between some risk factors and the development of drug use to believe that preventive interventions targeted at these risk factors at certain age or developmental stages will lessen their negative impact and may deliver a protective effect. Although prevention research has identified additional factors correlated with initiation of use, the fact remains that correlation is not synonymous with cause: for most risk factors, the extent of influence on behavior has not been established. Moreover, the cascading effect of intervening with mediating factors is just beginning to be explored.

A further complication is the fact that some individuals never develop drug abuse disorders or other deviant behaviors, despite exposure to a plethora of risk factors. Conversely, some individuals with little or no exposure to any identified risk factors develop deviant lifestyles, including the use of illegal substances. These confounding factors make it difficult to establish a causal link between risk factors, their assumed mediating variables and drug use. This, in turn, complicates the development of effective prevention interventions. Although consensus on a comprehensive listing of risk factors has not been fully achieved, Table 1 depicts a distillation of the elements most often cited and supported by the research literature as of this writing.

TABLE 1 Risk Factors for Substance Abuse, Grouped by IOM Criteria

Universal Risk Factors, Affecting All Populations

Community-Based Influences:

- Accessibility (including economic affordability) of alcohol, tobacco, and drugs;
- Exposure to mass media messages supporting alcohol or drug use;
- High incidence of neighborhood crime and violence;
- Norms condoning substance use; and
- Unsupervised leisure for youth.

School-Based Influences:

- Lack of drug education curriculum;
- Lack of responsiveness to student needs/inability of school to bond with child;
- Norms/policies condoning substance use;
- Physical plant conducive to illicit activities; and
- Poor classroom management.

Risk Factors for Selected Populations

Family Influences:

- Inconsistent interaction with family members;
- Family history of substance abuse;
- Family transmission of socially-deviant values;
- Lack of family monitoring of behavior;
- Latchkey status/no adult supervision;
- Lack of parental—especially maternal—investment in the child;
- Lack of positive adult role models; and
- Very low/very high income.

Peer Influences:

- Inappropriate sexual activity; and
- Ties to deviant peers/gangs (e.g., peers who smoke, drink alcohol, or use drugs).

Risk Factors for Indicated Individuals

Individual Factors:

- Academic failure/school avoidance;
- Aggression/conduct disorder;
- Chronic mental health problems;
- Criminal activity;
- High propensity for risk-taking;
- Impulsivity;
- Inability to regulate/control behavior;
- Lack of future orientation;
- Lack of self-efficacy;
- Lack of social skills/social competence;
- Runaway status/homelessness;
- Sexual/physical victimization (particularly among women); and
- Substance use before age 13.

GUIDELINES AND PRINCIPLES FOR PREVENTION

The National Institute on Drug Abuse (NIDA) has recently identified several prevention principles which can be inferred from observation of prevention efforts against substance abuse and other behaviorally-related conditions (National Institute on Drug Abuse, 1997). While not specifically derived from particular research studies or findings, these principles can provide a common-sense grounding for the conduct of substance abuse prevention. These general principles are paraphrased as follows:

1. Prevention should be designed to enhance protective factors;
2. Prevention efforts should target all forms of drug abuse;
3. Prevention efforts should include skills in conjunction with reinforcement of attitudes against drug use;
4. Substance abuse prevention for adolescents should include interactive methods;
5. Substance abuse prevention should include a parents' or caregivers' component;
6. Prevention efforts should be planned on a multiyear basis;
7. Prevention programming should be adapted to address the specific nature of the problem in the local community;
8. The higher the level of risk of the target population, the more intensive the effort must be and the earlier it must begin.
9. Preventive interventions for substance abuse, as in other health care, should be age-specific, developmentally appropriate, and culturally-sensitive (National Institute on Drug Abuse, 1997).

NIDA concurrently suggested a few observations pertaining to specific settings for substance abuse prevention efforts. These include the following:

- A critical function of community-wide prevention programs is to strengthen norms against drug use;
- To this end, community programs should include media campaigns, policy changes, school and family components;
- School settings offer opportunities to reach all populations;
- Family-focused prevention efforts have a greater impact than prevention efforts conducted in the absence of family settings.

In addition, the Center for Substance Abuse Prevention (CSAP) recently identified guidelines for prevention programming. These guidelines also are based on recent research and can be used to ensure that programs are based on the latest empirical science. Again, these are paraphrased here to underscore their importance and usefulness:

1. Prevention efforts should be based on a clear understanding and definition of the populations and groups to be influenced;
2. Prevention efforts should be focused on specific, realistic goals;
3. The goals of a specific prevention effort should be considered in the context of the larger prevention goals of the community;
4. When available, empirical evidence of effectiveness from comparable programs should be used to select and guide the current effort;
5. A logical conceptual framework should be used to connect the prevention effort with its intended results;
6. The conceptual framework should be based on existing knowledge;
7. The prevention effort should include activities that secure and maintain buy-in of key leaders;
8. The prevention effort should build on related prevention efforts;
9. The prevention effort must be designed and implemented with consideration for different parts of the system;
10. The prevention effort should be carried out through activities consistent with the availability of personnel, resources and realistic opportunities for implementation;
11. Opportunities for leadership across a broad range of participants should be created;
12. Implementation of the prevention effort should be timed to coincide with a period of peak community concern or population's readiness for change;
13. The prevention effort should be designed with sufficient intensity so that results can be sustained;
14. The prevention effort should be designed and implemented for the highest possible quality;
15. The prevention effort should include process and outcome evaluation (Center for Substance Abuse Prevention, 1997).

DOCUMENTED FINDINGS FROM PREVENTION SCIENCE

In addition to the general principles and guidelines, some findings have consistently emerged from demonstration efforts and clinical trials. Using the definitions described earlier, these observations are categorized as repeatedly documented findings. These include:

Life Skills. The transmission of generic life skills at entry into secondary school is associated with reduced initiation of substance abuse among adolescents, with measurable effects retained at least through graduation from high school. Generic "life skills" include problem-solving skills, decision-making skills, resistance skills against adverse peer influences, and social and communication skills. These skills cut across a wide variety of situations encountered by children, adolescents, and adults. The lack of these skills has been correlated with adolescent initiation of substance abuse. Longitudinal follow-up of large scale experimental trials have documented that universal substance abuse prevention efforts incorporating generic life skills training can generate as much as 30 percent reduction in the initiation of substance abuse among adolescents (see, for example, Botvin, Baker et al., 1995; Botvin, Schinke et al., 1995; Caplan, Weissberg et al., 1992; Gilchrist, Schinke et al., 1987; Pentz, 1995).

Controlled experiments of similar interventions applied to preadolescents as universal classroom curricula have shown markedly less impressive results. In several cases, gains in social-cognitive skills were not reflected in significant differences in substance use other than initial tobacco use (Gersick, Grady & Snow, 1988; O'Donnell, Hawkins et al., 1995; Kim, McLeod & Shantis, 1990). There are several possible explanations for this apparent lack of efficacy. A review article by Hall and Zigler (1997) argues that most such research is characterized by major methodological problems. Gersick, Grady and Snow (1988) suggest that even successful skills development conducted prior to adolescence is unlikely to generate immediate results on drug use. "The intervention utilized in this study is based on the assumption that a successful preventive intervention would increase students' decision-making skill levels and problem-solving abilities, and thereby decrease students' tendencies to turn to drug abuse as a way of coping with the stress of adolescence. While it was predicted that some early effect of the skill building on experimentation with gateway drugs would occur, the main impact on serious drug abuse is expected to be cumulative, increasing in measurable strength as use levels rise and as follow-up interventions reinforce the skill development. . . ." (p. 66).

An alternative perspective is offered by Hawthorne (1997), based on a study of the match between skills offered in classroom-based interventions in Australia and predictors for early drug experimentation and use. Hawthorne concluded that the impact of universal classroom-based education on preteen recruitment to drug use or experimentation is likely to be slight because the most potent variables concern the substance use culture of the social network and home environment rather than individual skill or knowledge levels. Hawthorne's conclusion in supported by at least one controlled study in the U.S. (Stevens, Mott & Youells, 1996), which documented the ineffectiveness of both a school-based program and a community intervention in countering the influence of parents and other role models in support of early alcohol use.

Self-Esteem. Activities that improve self-esteem do not consistently affect adolescent substance abuse. Earlier addiction research focused on the self-esteem portion of the self-concept model of personality, using various instruments to explore a proposed relationship between self-esteem and addiction. More recent research has questioned whether low self-esteem is a significant factor in defining a personality that is potentially susceptible to addiction, drug use, or delinquency (see, for example, Schroeder, Laflin & Weis, 1993; Peiser & Heaven, 1996). When substance abuse prevention efforts measure change in self-esteem and self-reported substance abuse as outcomes, no consistent pattern emerges. A consensus panel convened by the Center for Substance Abuse Prevention concluded that improving adolescent self-esteem is not necessarily protective against substance use and that poor self-esteem alone is not predictive of future substance use. Some programs have reported improved self-esteem accompanied either by reduced incidence of drug use or no lasting change in drug use (Kim, McLeod & Shantis, 1990; Ringwalt, Curtis & Rosenbaum, 1990). A few have reported the opposite association, i.e., lower self-esteem scores coupled with reduction in drug use (for example, LoSciuto & Ausetts, 1988).

Pregnant Women. Preventive interventions conducted among pregnant women motivated to participate produce net financial savings in hospital costs. Decisions about providing substance abuse prevention services often are based on the conviction that the consequences of failing to act are too great to ignore, rather than on empirical measures with specific costs and benefits. One promising area of research on the cost-effectiveness of indicated preventive interventions has been with prevention intervention programs for pregnant women who abused alcohol or used drugs during pregnancy (Institute of Medicine, 1994). Such interventions are distinct from traditional addiction treatment, in part because the women are not necessary drug-dependent. The data suggest that although these programs are relatively expensive on a per capita basis, there can be net savings in inpatient neonatal costs (Delaware Department of Health and Human Services, 1990; Emanuel Hospital, 1991).

Clinical trials of such interventions indicate that the level of maternal investment in the program also is a decisive factor in the long-term effectiveness of such interventions (Black, Nair et al., 1994; Hofkosh, Pringle et al., 1995; Nye, Zucker & Fitzgerald, 1996). Specific outcomes observed in clinical trials involving preterm or low birthweight infants—both characteristic of chronic substance abuse during pregnancy—include significant improvement on the Bayley scales of behavioral development at eight months (Parker, Zahr et al., 1992; Hofkosh, Pringle et al., 1996), a more developmentally appropriate home environment at four months (Parker, Zahr et al., 1992; Hofkosh, Pringle et al., 1996) and significantly higher 36-month IQ (Casey, Kelleher et al., 1994).

Parenting Skills. Interventions supporting positive parent interaction with young children have been shown through clinical trials to be associated with promoting positive behaviors during adolescence (Aronen & Kurkela, 1996). Overall cost savings can also be anticipated from prevention interventions serving youth of parents recovering from addiction. In some studies, families with histories of significant drug abuse problems reduced their documented need for other social and health care services following several months of direct contact with prevention intervention programs (Aktan, Kumpfer & Turner, 1996; Alabama Department of Mental Health and Mental Retardation, 1991; Catalano, Haggerty et al., 1997; Mello, 1992).

School-Based Programs. Comprehensive school-focused programs that include community organizations as part of the prevention effort to affect public policy, parent programs, and efforts to change community norms through the media have shown success in changing substance utilization rates among adolescents (Pentz, 1995; Perry, Williams et al., 1996), although the impact of such programs on young children is debatable (Stevens, Mott et al., 1996). A highly significant factor in these findings appears to be reduced perceptions among students of their parents' and friends' acceptance of drug use as normative behavior (Hansen & Graham, 1991).

Repeated Exposure. The extension of preventive interventions through "booster" sessions or through sustained multiyear programs appears critical to promotion of behavioral goals among adolescents. Repeated exposure to a credible, consistent message reinforces acceptance of the message and the desired behaviors conveyed by the message. Individual projects report that booster sessions have greatly increased the likelihood of sustaining reduced rates of substance abuse among adolescents three-to-five years after initial exposure (St. Pierre, Kaltreider et al., 1992; Botvin, Baker et al., 1995). The results of controlled experiments of early interventions addressing school failure and truancy support the need to sustain efforts for several years (Hovacek, Remay et al., 1987; Bry & George, 1992). These findings were confirmed by a national study which conducted secondary analysis on several prevention programs for adolescents (Center for Substance Abuse Prevention, 1994).

It may be that disappointment with the long-term effects of many popular prevention efforts is due largely to the fact that booster sessions to reinforce norms and beliefs are not the norm in prevention programming. Clayton, Cattarello and Johnstone (1996), for example, note that the six-week, single-year intervention known as D.A.R.E. generated some significant intervention effects in attitudes toward drugs in the seventh grade but no discernible effects on drug use throughout a five-year follow-up period. They suggest that the relatively consistent results of such evaluations point to a need for booster sessions to sustain positive effects and greater attention to interrelationships between developmental processes in developing multiyear exposure to prevention programming.

FUTURE DIRECTIONS FOR PREVENTION SCIENCE

A hallmark of the progress made in the field of substance abuse prevention is the increasing number of guideposts available to direct future research. The exploratory research of the 1970s and 1980s can be replaced by studies to confirm or disconfirm the provisional findings which have emerged from observation of demonstration projects. Examples of these include the following:

Interpersonal counseling, mentoring, and other forms of intensive interaction appear to be associated with lessened risk factors (e.g., better school grades, associations with socially deviant peers) among youth at high risk for drug use. In two recent experiments, cohorts of African-American adolescents in Philadelphia received adult mentoring for one year; they averaged better school attendance, fewer arrests per capita, and lower rates of drug use than matched youth who did not receive mentoring (LoSciuto, Rajla et al., 1996). A secondary analysis study of several hundred prevention efforts identified favorable outcomes for 17 programs which offered one-on-one or small group interpersonal counseling to adolescents with histories of drug use (Center for Substance Abuse Prevention, 1994). Analyses of programs with similar activities for young children indicate a less consistent pattern of results (Center for Substance Abuse Prevention, 1994).

Case management and the maintenance of peer support groups appear to be associated with reduced drug or alcohol use among pregnant substance abusers. Available data on substance use at the time of, or following delivery, suggest that maternal use was reduced by a majority of the women (Center for Substance Abuse Prevention, 1993).

The need for *program focus* is suggested by secondary analysis of reported outcomes of more than 300 substance abuse prevention initiatives completed between 1987 and 1993, which led to the conclusion that programs offering more than four types of activities to a single population generally fail to document positive changes in attitudes or behavior (Center for Substance Abuse Prevention, 1994).

Additional future directions for prevention research are derived from the developing model of prevention as a set of interventions designed to counter risk factors for social deviance and substance use. A critical issue for this research is to parcel-out the effect of individual components of intervention and determine an appropriate sequencing of activities. To date, research has concentrated on substantiating effects for multicomponent interventions and relatively few studies have examined the question of whether each component is, in fact, necessary for preventive effects. The rare exceptions, such as the Adolescent Alcohol Prevention Trial (Hansen & Graham, 1991) and the Alcohol Misuse Prevention Study (Shope, Copeland et al., 1993), have provided important insights, respectively, on the synergistic benefits of prevention education curricula that include both normative education and peer refusal skills, and the apparent benefit of delaying exposure to didactic alcohol abuse curriculum until the sixth grade. Additional research is needed to determine the effect of other components of a prevention intervention and their relative ability to achieve the desired effect on their own.

A final direction for new research is raised by observations of the effect of mediating variables on social, health, and environmental influences. Research has begun to explore the mediating effects on prevention efforts of prior substance use and such demographic variables as culture, gender, and ethnicity. Among the results to date are confirmation that health education approaches which have documented significant substance abuse effects with suburban populations (Errecart, Walberg et al., 1991) fail to duplicate these effects with urban, minority populations (D'Elio, Mundt et al., 1993). The field needs a systematic approach to isolating and investigating mediating variables that either enhance or detract from the outcomes of attempts to counter the risk factors for substance abuse.

CONCLUSIONS

The combination of constructing and validating models for the initiation of drug use, with the use of field studies that overcome the challenges confronting community-based research, has added significantly to our understanding of the complex dynamics of substance abuse prevention. Less than a generation ago, the hard evidence available on the effectiveness of preventive interventions was sparse. Our society had tried the legal remedies of Prohibition and the informational approach of offering education about the effects of alcohol, tobacco, and drugs, and found that neither type of intervention was adequate to stem a growing epidemic of drug abuse. We now are aware of approaches that show varying degrees of efficacy, and we have explanatory models that appear to be grounded in rigorously-tested correlations between risk factors and behavior.

Despite these gains, the substance abuse prevention field has not produced hard evidence on the dosage necessary to obtain the desired effects under given circumstances. The field also has not generated empirical evidence of the most effective sequencing of interventions. At best, we can say that repeated "booster" sessions of drug abuse prevention curricula over several years are of greater value to universal preventive interventions than a longer curriculum administered without such sessions. Until the issues of minimum dosage and sequencing of interventions are addressed, the practice of prevention will remain based in part on educated guesses rather than science.

REFERENCES

Aktan GB, Kumpfer KL & Turner CW (1996). Effectiveness of a family skills training program for substance use prevention with inner city African-American families. *Substance Use and Misuse* 31(2):157–175.

Aronen ET & Kurkela SA (1996). Long-term effects of an early home-based intervention. *Journal of the American Academy of Child and Adolescent Psychiatry* 35:1665–1672.

Alabama Department of Mental Health and Mental Retardation (1991). Final report on The Strengthening Black Families Project of the High-Risk Youth Program, submitted to the Office for Substance Abuse Prevention of the Alcohol, Drug Abuse, and Mental Health Administration, U.S. Department of Health and Human Services.

Baumrind D (1985). Familial antecedents of adolescent drug use: A developmental perspective. In CL Jones & RJ Battjes (eds.) *Etiology of Drug Abuse: Implications for Prevention*. Rockville, MD: National Institute on Drug Abuse.

Black MM, Nair P, Knight C, Wachtel R, Roby P & Schuler M (1994). Parenting and early development among children of drug-abusing women: Effects of home intervention. *Pediatrics* 94:440–448.

Botvin GS, Baker E, Dusenbury L, Botvin EM & Diaz T (1995). Long-term follow-up results of a randomized drug abuse prevention trial in a white middle class population. *Journal of the American Medical Association* 273:1106–1112.

Botvin GS, Schinke SP, Epstein JA, Diaz T et al. (1995). Effectiveness of culturally-focused and generic skills training approaches to alcohol and drug abuse prevention among minority adolescents: Two-year follow-up results. *Psychology of Addictive Behaviors* 9(3):183–184.

Bry BH & George FE (1992). Preventive effects of early interventions on the attendance and grades of urban adolescents. *Professional Psychology.*

Byrh & Roudenbush (1993).

Caplan M, Weissberg RP, Grober JS, Sivo PJ, Grady K & Jacoby C (1992). Social Competence promotion with inner city and suburban adolescents: Effects on social adjustment and alcohol use. *Journal of Consulting and Clinical Psychology* 60:56–63.

Casey PH, Kelleher KJ, Bradley RH, Kellogg KW, Kirby RS & Whiteside L (1994). *Archives of Pediatric and Adolescent Medicine* 148:1071–1077.

Catalano RF, Haggerty KP, Gainey RR & Hoppe MJ (1997). *Substance Use and Misuse* 32(6):699–721.

Center for Substance Abuse Prevention (1993). *Signs of Effectiveness in Preventing Alcohol and Other Drug Problems*. Rockville, MD: U.S. Department of Health and Human Services.

Center for Substance Abuse Prevention (1994). *Final Report of the National Structured Evaluation of Alcohol and Other Drug Abuse Prevention*. Unpublished report.

Center for Substance Abuse Prevention (1997). *Guidelines and Principles for Prevention Programming*. Rockville, MD: U.S. Department of Health and Human Services.

Chilcoat H, Anthony J & Dishion TJ (1995). Parent monitoring and the incidence of drug sampling in multiethnic urban children. *American Journal of Epidemiology* 141:25–31.

Clayton RR, Cattarello AM & Johnstone BM (1996). The effectiveness of Drug Abuse Resistance Education (Project DARE): 5-year follow-up results. *Preventive Medicine* 25(3):307–318.

Coie JD, Terry R, Lenox K & Lochman J (1995). Childhood peer rejection and aggression as predictors of stable patterns of adolescent disorder. *Development and Psychopathology* 74:697–713.

Delaware Department of Health and Human Services (1990). Annual Evaluation Report on Delaware Diamond Deliveries Project of the Pregnant and Post-Partum Women and Infants Program, submitted to the Office for Substance Abuse Prevention of the Alcohol, Drug Abuse, and Mental Health Administration, U.S. Department of Health and Human Services.

D'Elio MA, Mundt DJ, Bush PJ & Iannotti RJ (1993). Healthful behaviors: Do they protect African-American urban preadolescents from abusable substance use? *American Journal of Health Promotion* 7:354–363.

Dembo R, Williams A, & Schmeidler J (1994). Psychosocial, alcohol/other drug use, and delinquency differences between urban black and white male high risk youth. *The International Journal of the Addictions* 29:461–483.

Elliott DS, Huizinga D & Ageton SS (1985). *Explaining Delinquency and Drug Use*. Beverly Hills, CA: Sage Publications.

Emanuel Hospital (1991). Final Report on Project Network of the Pregnant and Post-Partum Women and Infants Program, submitted to the Office for Substance Abuse Prevention of the Alcohol, Drug Abuse, and Mental Health Administration, U.S. Department of Health and Human Services.

Errecart MT, Walberg HJ, Ross JG, Gold RS, Fiedler JL & Kolbe LJ (1991). Effectiveness of teenage health teaching modules. *Journal of School Health* 61:26–30.

Fetterman DM (1996). Empowerment evaluation: An introduction to theory and practice. In DM Fetterman, SJ Kaftarian & A Wandersman (eds.) *Empowerment Evaluation: Knowledge and Tools for Self-Assessment and Accountability*. Thousand Oaks, CA: Sage Publications.

Gersick KE, Grady K & Snow DL (1988). Social-cognitive skill development with sixth graders and its initial impact on substance abuse. *International Journal of Psychiatry in Medicine* 16:55–69.

Gilchrist LD, Schinke SP, Trimble JE & Cvetkovich GT (1987). Skills enhancement to prevent substance abuse among American Indian adolescents. *International Journal of the Addictions* 22:869–879.

Hall NW & Zigler E (1997). Drug abuse prevention efforts for young children: A review and critique of existing programs. *American Journal of Orthopsychiatry* 67:134–143.

Hansen WB & Graham JW (1991). Preventing alcohol, marijuana, and cigarette use among adolescents: Peer pressure resistance training versus establishing conservative norms. *Preventive Medicine* 20(13):414–430.

Hawkins JD, Catalano RF & Miller JY (1992). Risk and protective factors for alcohol and other drug problems in adolescence and early adulthood: Implications for substance abuse prevention. *Psychological Bulletin* 112(1):64–105.

Hawkins JD, Von Cleve E & Catalano RF (1991). Reducing early childhood aggression: Results of a primary prevention program. *Journal of the American Academy of Child and Adolescent Psychiatry* 30(2):208–217.

Hawthorne G (1997). Preteenage drug use in Australia: The key predictors and school-based drug education. *Journal of Adolescent Health* 20:384–395.

Hofkosh D, Pringle JL, Wald HP, Switala J, Hinderliter SA & Hamel SC (1995). Early interactions between drug-involved mothers and infants: Within-group differences. *Archives of Pediatric and Adolescent Medicine* 149:665–672.

Hovacek HJ, Remay CT, Campbell FA, Hoffman KP & Fletcher RH (1987). Predicting school failure and assessing early intervention with high-risk children. *Journal of the American Academy of Child and Adolescent Psychiatry* 26:758–763.

Institute of Medicine; Mrazek PJ & Haggerty RJ, eds. (1994). *Reducing Risks for Mental Disorders: Frontiers for Preventive Intervention Research.* Washington, DC: National Academy Press.

Jansen MA, ed. (1994). *American Journal of Community Psychology.*

Kim S, McLeod JH & Shantis C (1990). A short-term outcome evaluation of the "I'm Special" drug abuse prevention program. *Journal of Drug Education* 20:127–138.

LoSciuto L & Ausetts MA (1988). Evaluation of a drug abuse prevention program: A field experiment. *Addictive Behaviors* 13.

LoSciuto L, Rajla AK, Townsend TN & Taylor AS (1996). An outcome evaluation of Across Ages: An intergenerational mentoring approach to drug prevention. *Journal of Adolescent Research* 11(1):116–129.

Mello M (1992). Final report on the YCOSA Targeted Prevention Project of the High-Risk Youth Program, submitted to the Office for Substance Abuse Prevention of the Alcohol, Drug Abuse, and Mental Health Administration, U.S. Department of Health and Human Services.

Milberger S, Biederman J, Faraone SV, Chen L & Jones J (1997). ADHD is associated with early initiation of cigarette smoking in children and adolescents. *Journal of the American Academy of Child and Adolescent Psychiatry* 36:37–44.

National Institute on Drug Abuse (1997). *Preventing Drug Use Among Children and Adolescents: A Research-Based Guide* (NIH Publication 97–4212). Bethesda, MD: National Institute on Drug Abuse.

Nye CL, Zucker RA & Fitzgerald HE (1996). Early intervention in the path to alcohol problems through conduct problems: Treatment involvement and child behavior change. *Journal of Consulting and Social Psychology* 63:831–840.

O'Donnell J, Hawkins JD, Catalano RF, Abbott RD & Day LE (1995). Preventing school failure, drug use, and delinquency among low-income children: Long-term intervention in elementary schools. *American Journal of Orthopsychiatry* 65:87–100.

Parker SJ, Zahr LK, Cole JG, Brecht M-L (1992). Outcome after developmental intervention in the neonatal intensive care unit for mothers of preterm infants with low socioeconomic status. *Journal of Pediatrics* 120:780–785.

Peiser NC & Heaven PCL (1996). Family influences on self-reported delinquency among high school students. *Journal of Adolescence* 19:557–568.

Pentz MA (1995). The school-community interface in comprehensive school health education. In S Stansfield (ed.) *1996 Institute of Medicine Annual Report, Committee on Comprehensive School Health Programs.* Washington, DC: National Academy Press.

Pentz MA, Dwyer JH, MacKinnon DP, Flay BR, Hansen WB, Wang EY & Johnson CA (1989). A multi-community trial for primary prevention of adolescent drug abuse: Effects on drug use prevalence. *Journal of the American Medical Association* 261:3259–3266.

Perry CL, Williams CL, Veblen-Mortenson S, Toomey TL, Komro KA, Anstine PS, McGovern PG, Finnegan JR, Forster JL, Wagenaar AC & Wolfson M (1996). Project Northland: Outcomes of a communitywide alcohol use prevention program during early adolescence. *American Journal of Public Health* 86(6):956–965

Regier DA, Farmer ME, Rae DS, Locke BZ, Keith SJ, Judd LL & Goodwin FK (1990). Comorbidity of mental disorders with alcohol and other drug abuse: Results from the Epidemiologic Catchment Area (ECA) study. *Journal of the American Medical Association* 264:2511–2518.

Rhodes JE (1990). Evaluation report on the Greater Alliance for Prevention System (G.A.P.S.) Project of the High-Risk Youth program, submitted to the Office for Substance Abuse Prevention of the Alcohol, Drug Abuse, and Mental Health Administration, U.S. Department of Health and Human Services.

Ringwalt C, Curtis TR & Rosenbaum D (1990). A first-year evaluation of D.A.R.E. in Illinois. Unpublished study prepared for the Illinois State Police.

Schroeder DS, Laflin MT & Weis DL (1993). Is there a relationship between self-esteem and drug use? Methodological and statistical limitations of the research. *Journal of Drug Issues* 23:645–655.

Shedler J & Block J (1990). Adolescent drug use and psychological health: A longitudinal inquiry. *American Psychologist* 45:612–630.

Shope JT, Copeland LA, Maharg R, Dielman TE & Butchart AT (1993). Assessment of adolescent refusal skills in an alcohol misuse prevention study. *Health Education Quarterly* 20:373–390.

Simcha-Fagan O, Gersten JC & Langer TS (1986). Early precursors and concurrent correlates of patterns of illicit drug use in adolescents. *The Journal of Drug Issues* 16:7–28.

Springer JF & Phillips JL (1994). Policy learning and evaluation design: Lessons from the community partnership demonstration program. *Journal of Community Psychology* (CSAP Special Issue). 22:117–139.

St. Pierre TL, Kaltreider DL, Mark MM & Aiken KJ (1992). Drug prevention in a community setting: A longitudinal study of the relative effectiveness of a three-year primary prevention program in Boys & Girls Clubs across the nation. *American Journal of Community Psychology* 20:673–706.

Stevens MM, Mott LA & Youells F (1996). Rural adolescent drinking behavior: Three-year follow-up in the New Hampshire substance abuse prevention study. *Adolescence* 31:159–166.

Stoil MJ & Jansen MA (1997). Effectiveness of behavioral health promotion: What do we measure, is it credible, and does anyone care? Presentation to the 125th annual meeting of the American Public Health Association, November 11, Indianapolis, IN.

Taylor E, Chadwick O, Heptinstall E & Danckaerts M (1996). Hyperactivity and conduct problems as risk factors for adolescent development. *Journal of the American Academy of Child and Adolescent Psychiatry* 35:1213–1226.

Thompson EA, Horn M, Herting JR & Eggert LL (1997). Enhancing outcomes in an indicated drug prevention program for high-risk youth. *Journal of Drug Education* 27(1):19–41.

Weber MD, Graham JW, Hansen WB, Flay BR & Johnson CA (1989). Evidence for two paths of alcohol use onset in adolescents. *Addictive Behaviors* 14:399–408.

CHAPTER 3

Developing Comprehensive Community Coalitions

Abraham Wandersman, Ph.D.
Robert M. Goodman, Ph.D., M.P.H.
Frances D. Butterfoss, Ph.D., M.S.Ed.

The Role of Community Coalitions
Physicians and Community Partnerships
Resources for Community Coalitions
Attributes of Successful Coalitions

Interest in community approaches to prevention reflects a growing awareness that alcohol, tobacco and other drug use—like other social problems such as teen pregnancy, child abuse, delinquency and school failure—are ". . . not only interrelated and share common roots, but these roots lie in the community" (Benard, 1989). The responsibility for solving these problems rests with the entire community, rather than with solitary institutions such as the family or the school. Indeed, research suggests that coordinated efforts involving schools, law enforcement agencies, civic groups, helping professionals, and other public and private organizations hold the most hope for reducing and preventing abuse of alcohol, tobacco and other drugs (Office for Substance Abuse Prevention, 1990). In short, community-wide problems require community-wide solutions.

The strategies guiding these solutions must involve collaboration among community organizations and institutions, as well as a renewed faith in citizen participation. Coalitions of community agencies, institutions and concerned citizens represent one promising strategy for designing interventions that operate at multiple levels of the social ecology. The rationale for a coalition approach is three-pronged: (1) it creates a positive, supportive and nurturing environment that will, in turn, discourage alcohol, tobacco and other drug use and related social problems; (2) it exemplifies the principles of prevention philosophy: empowerment, mutual problem-solving, decision-making and respect; and (3) it offers the possibility of "whole-system change," rather than addressing symptoms in isolation (Benard, 1989).

THE ROLE OF COMMUNITY COALITIONS

Coalitions have become a "treatment of choice" for assessing the needs of high-risk populations and promoting broad, community-based solutions to health problems. A number of private foundations and granting agencies have begun to require coalition formation as an essential ingredient of the community health promotion programs they support.

Two definitions that capture our understanding of coalitions are: "an organization of individuals representing diverse organizations, factions or constituencies who agree to work together in order to achieve a common goal" (Feighery & Rogers, 1989) and "an organization of diverse interest groups that combine their human and material resources to effect a specific change the members are unable to bring about independently" (Brown, 1984). By these definitions, coalitions are interorganizational, cooperative, and synergistic working alliances.

To date, the literature defines coalitions as important in several ways. First, coalitions allow organizations to become involved in new and broader issues without assuming sole responsibility for managing or developing those issues (Black, 1983). Second, coalitions can solicit widespread public support for issues, actions or unmet needs. Third, coalitions can maximize the power of individuals and groups through joint action; they can increase the "critical mass" behind a community effort by helping individuals achieve objectives beyond the scope of any one individual or organization (Brown, 1984). Fourth, coalitions can minimize duplication of effort and services. This economy of scale can be a positive side effect of improved trust and communication among groups that would otherwise compete for resources (Brown, 1984; Feighery & Rogers, 1989). Fifth, coalitions can help mobilize more talent, resources and approaches to influence an issue than any single organization could achieve alone (Roberts-DeGennaro, 1986a). Sixth, coalitions can provide an avenue for recruiting participants from diverse constituencies, such as political, business, human service, social and religious groups, as well as less organized grassroots groups and individuals (Black, 1983; Feighery & Rogers, 1989). Seventh, the flexible nature of coalitions allows them to exploit new resources in changing situations (Boissevain, 1974).

PHYSICIANS AND COMMUNITY PARTNERSHIPS

Physicians and other health professionals are a key resource to community partnerships fighting alcohol, tobacco and other drug abuse. According to the Physicians' Committee of the Richland (South Carolina) Fighting Back coalition, early recognition, identification and treatment can bring about a significant improvement in the prognosis for an addictive disorder. This community coalition's plan involves health care professionals in providing low-cost or no-cost training to colleagues on screening, identification and referral of addictive disorders; providing print materials to health care professionals for distribution to patients; collaborating on the development of a public awareness campaign and a comprehensive health curriculum; assisting in development of support groups such as Alcoholics Anonymous; and participating in a speaker's bureau.

RESOURCES FOR COMMUNITY COALITIONS

In order to maintain itself, a coalition must acquire the resources to keep going. For coalitions, resources consist primarily of those brought to the organization by its members and those recruited from *external* sources.

A coalition's membership is its primary asset. Several variables related to the members have been associated with organizational maintenance (Prestby & Wandersman, 1985), including the size of the membership, the depth of members' attachment to the mission, and members' personal and political efficacy. Each member brings a different set of resources and skills to the coalition. For instance, one member may provide transportation to or space for meetings, another may contribute staff support, a third may assist in fund-raising, and a fourth may provide access to and influence with relevant policymakers (Knoke & Wright-Isak, 1982). The pooling of member assets is especially significant when participation is voluntary and the coalition has few material resources of its own (Knoke & Wood, 1981; Prestby & Wandersman, 1985). Diversity among members also enables the coalition to reach and represent a larger constituency.

Beyond motivation, the effective maintenance of a coalition requires that members have the skills, or "capacity to participate," needed to operate an effective partnership and to be perceived as legitimate (Gray, 1985). For example, a coalition that worked with problem youth demonstrated that the competence and the performance of members were positively related to coordination among participating organizations and negatively related to conflict (Hall, Clark et al., 1977). A skills training program conducted with members and chairpersons of an advocacy coalition achieved increased reporting of issues by members, improvements in the chairpersons' ability to conduct action-oriented meetings, and overall improved effectiveness of the consumer organization (Balcazar, Seekins et al., 1990).

While coalitions often rely primarily on member resources, they also benefit by linking with resources that are external to the coalition, especially those concerned with policy, planning and services (Butterfoss, Goodman & Wandersman, 1993). Examples of external resources include elected officials and governmental agencies, religious and civic groups, and neighborhood and community development associations. These resources offer special expertise, facilities for meetings, mailing lists, referrals, additional personnel for special projects, grant funding, loans or donations, equipment and supplies, and co-sponsorship of events (Chavis, Florin et al., 1987; Prestby & Wandersman, 1985). On the other hand, external supports may be reduced by funding cutbacks; have small, overworked, inefficient or incompetent staffs; manifest inadequate communication channels; or lack flexible organizational policies (Whetten, 1981).

A coalition's relationships with external resources may be classified along four dimensions: formalization (the degree of official recognition of the relationship), standardization (the degree to which procedures for linking are specified), intensity (the frequency of interactions and flow of resources), and reciprocity (the degree of mutual exchange of resources). High levels of these dimensions are related to greater satisfaction with the collaborative relationship, but also may produce more conflict (Marrett, 1971).

Collaboration with external resources also may be conceptualized along a continuum from mild to intense linkage, in which the stronger the linkage, the greater the trust and investment of time and resources by member agencies (Andrews, 1990).

Access to local communities is an important link for many coalitions (Roberts-DeGennaro, 1986b), particularly those concerned with health promotion. Such coalitions often benefit by linking with individuals and organizations that are active in community affairs.

ATTRIBUTES OF SUCCESSFUL COALITIONS

Organization Structure. Such structure is the aspect of the coalition that obtains the resources and organizes the members. If coalitions are to be viable, they must be able to set goals, offer rewards, and reconcile members' individual needs with the task requirements of the organization. The formalized rules, roles, and procedures of the leadership, as well as the coalition's organizational climate, are important mechanisms for accomplishing these tasks.

Leadership Characteristics. Strong central leadership is an important ingredient in the implementation and the maintenance of coalition activities (Butterfoss, Goodman & Wandersman, 1993). Regardless of size, coalitions tend to have a few core leaders who dominate their activities (Roberts-DeGennaro, 1986b). When these leaders are attentive to and supportive of individual member concerns and are competent in negotiation, garnering resources, problem-solving and conflict resolution, the coalition tends to be more cohesive in reaching peripheral members and in maintaining coalition operations (Brown, 1984). Other important qualities of leadership include: personal resources such as self-efficacy, membership in other community organizations; level of education; degree of political knowledge, commitment, and competence; presence of administrative skills in order to set agendas, run efficient meetings, garner resources, and delegate responsibilities; skill in communication and interpersonal relations; ability to promote equal status and encourage overall collaboration in the member organizations; flexibility; and easy access to the media and decision-making centers of the community (Butterfoss, Goodman & Wandersman, 1993).

Formalized Rules, Roles, and Procedures. Many authors assert that formalization is necessary for the successful implementation and maintenance of collaborative activities. Formalization is the degree to which rules, roles, and procedures are defined precisely. The higher the degree of formalization, the greater the investment of resources and exchanges among agencies; the greater satisfaction with the effort itself; and the more responsible and committed member agencies become. Examples of formalization include: written memoranda of understanding, bylaws, policy and procedures manuals; clearly defined roles; mission statements, goals and objectives; and regular reorientation to the purposes, goals, roles, and procedures of collaboration (Butterfoss, Goodman & Wandersman, 1993).

Formalization promotes "routinization" (or persistent implementation) of the coalition's operations. The more routinized operations become, the more likely they will be sustained (Goodman & Steckler, 1989a, 1989b).

Organizational Climate. Organizational climate reflects the group members' perceptions of several important organizational characteristics. Determining the organizational climate of a coalition helps in assessing its "personality." A coalition's organizational climate may be characterized by relationships among members, volunteer-staff relationships, communication patterns among members and with staff, and the decision-making, problem-solving, and conflict resolution processes.

Volunteer-Staff Relationships. Although not all coalitions have the resources to employ staff, such staff can reduce the burdens placed on a coalition's membership. Member-staff relationships are apt to be more harmonious if all parties are clear about their respective roles and if staff are given latitude to carry out daily tasks (Brown, 1984). Feighery and Rogers (1989) suggest that staff roles should be clarified as soon as a coalition is formed. They believe that in the early stages of the coalition, staff must help educate members to the issues that influence the coalition's mission and strategies, and that staff need to guide members in assuming new roles and responsibilities. Indeed, staff effectiveness may be judged by how well they balance their provision of technical assistance to members with the members' ability to make informed decisions.

Staff seem more likely to improve the atmosphere of a coalition when they possess an appreciation for the voluntary nature of coalitions, and have the organizational and interpersonal skills to facilitate complex collaborative processes (Croan & Lees, 1979).

In a study that asked staff about volunteers, Wandersman and Alderman (1993) found that the relationship between the volunteers and the paid staff is one of negotiation and diplomacy. There are several issues that make this relationship a delicate one. The lack of structure in many volunteer positions often leaves the volunteer unsure of his or her role within the organization; this may contribute to a perceived lack of commitment to the organization.

Communication Patterns. Unimpeded internal communication among the membership and staff may be the most essential ingredient for enhancing the climate of a coalition. The quality of communication has been positively related to coordination and negatively related to conflict (Hall, Clark et al., 1977). Open communication helps the group focus on a common purpose, increases trust and sharing of resources, provides information about one another's programs, and allows members to express and resolve misgivings about planned activities (Andrews, 1990; Feighery & Rogers, 1989). Viable coalitions often have frequent meetings, which members are actively encouraged to attend (Benard, 1989), and a well-developed system of internal communication to keep staff and members informed (Andrews, 1990; Croan & Lees, 1979).

Activities. A coalition must engage in two types of activities: (1) *action strategy activities*—the types of activities the coalition was created to perform (e.g., programs to prevent alcohol, tobacco and other drug abuse), and (2) *maintenance activities*—the activities necessary to maintain the infrastructure of the coalition (e.g., fundraising and recruiting new members).

The coalition must produce more than good feelings among members; it needs to produce the activities it was created to perform. Examples of *action strategy activities* in the early stages of a coalition include creating a mission statement, setting up committees, performing needs assessments and developing a comprehensive plan. In the implementation phase of the coalition, the plan is implemented and prevention activities are carried out. For example, a community partnership might help foster after school activities, parent training, media campaigns, red ribbon campaigns, coping skills programs, and advocacy of policy change.

Internal maintenance activities support the infrastructure of a coalition. All organizations must perform internal maintenance activities such as recruiting members, training leaders, preparing leaders-in-waiting to take over when there is turnover, and fundraising. Prestby and Wandersman (1985) found that such activities are necessary for the survival of an organization. Many voluntary organizations, including community coalitions, appear to slight this area because it does not have the "glitz," visibility or priority of action strategy activities.

Accomplishments. Several experts emphasize the need for coalitions to accomplish "quick wins" and short-term successes so as to increase member motivation and pride and enhance the credibility of the coalition (Brown, 1984; Croan & Lees, 1979). Once a coalition attains a "quick win," it can direct its efforts toward more complex tasks. Short-term successes should not, however, be mistaken for ultimate solutions to chronic health problems and social concerns (Sink & Stowers, 1989).

Program evaluators often discuss two types of program effects, which may be thought of as *short-term* and *long-term* effects. For example, Linney and Wandersman (1991) describe outcomes as the short-term or immediate effects of a program on the recipients of a service or activity.

Outcome evaluation attempts to determine the direct effects of the program: for instance, outcome evaluation may examine the degree to which a drug information program actually increased knowledge of drugs and the perceived risk of drugs.

Impact evaluation is concerned with the long-term and ultimate effects desired by a program. In alcohol, tobacco and other drug prevention programs, the ultimate effects or impacts could include global goals such as reductions in overall drug use or specified goals such as a decrease in arrests for drinking and driving. There is an assumption that a change in *outcome* is necessary to bring about a change in *impacts*.

In addition to evaluating the outcomes produced by the programs of the coalition (outcomes and impacts discusses above), some coalitions are concerned with *systems change,* such as changes in service delivery and system reform (Kagan, 1991). Measurement of system change, such as development of new community linkages and cross-referrals among agencies, is difficult. There are few widely accepted measures and few studies which have attempted to measure such change.

Ultimately, coalitions must evaluate the impact they have on improving the social and health systems and outcomes of the community. Thorough evaluation is one mechanism that is frequently cited for improving outcome effectiveness (Feighery & Rogers, 1989; Andrews, 1990; Wandersman & Goodman, 1990). The authors believe that there is a great need for additional conceptualization and new methodological tools in the assessment of coalition functioning and outcomes.

ACKNOWLEDGMENT: The authors thank the Center for Substance Abuse Prevention for its funding of their program evaluation of local community partnerships in South Carolina. They also thank Michael Klitzner, Ph.D., for his helpful comments on the text.

REFERENCES

Allensworth D & Patton W (1990). Promoting school health through coalition building. *The Eta Sigma Gamma Monograph Series*, 7.

Andrews A (1990). Interdisciplinary and interorganizational collaboration. In A Minahan et al. (eds.) *Encyclopedia of Social Work, 18th Ed.* Silver Spring, MD: National Association of Social Workers.

Balcazar R, Seekins T, Fawcett S & Hopkins B (1990). Empowering people with physical disabilities through advocacy skills training. *American Journal of Community Psychology* 18:281–296.

Benard B (1989). Working together: Principles of effective collaboration. *Prevention Forum* (October):4–9.

Black T (1983). Coalition building—Some suggestions. *Child Welfare* 62:263–268.

Boissevain J (1974). *Friends of Friends.* Oxford, England: Basil Blackwell.

Brown C (1984). *The Art of Coalition Building: A Guide for Community Leaders.* New York, NY: The American Jewish Committee.

Butterfoss F, Goodman R & Wandersman A (1993). Community coalitions for prevention and health promotion. *Health Education Research* 8:315–330.

Carlaw R, Mittlemark M, Bracht N, Luepker R (1984). Organization for a community cardiovascular health program. *Health Education Quarterly* 11:243–252.

Chavis D, Florin P, Rich R & Wandersman A (1987). *The Role of Block Associations in Crime Control and Community Development: The Block Booster Project.* New York, NY: Report to the Ford Foundation.

Croan G & Lees J (1979). *Building Effective Coalitions: Some Planning Considerations.* Arlington, VA: Westinghouse National Issues Center.

Epps J (1986). *Achieving Health for All: A Framework for Health Promotion in Canada.* Toronto, Ontario: Health and Welfare Canada.

Feighery E & Rogers T (1989). Building and maintaining effective coalitions. *How-To Guides on Community Health Promotion, No. 12.* Palo Alto, CA: Stanford Health Promotion Resource Center.

Goodman RM & Steckler A (1989a). A model for the institutionalization of health promotion programs. *Family and Community Health* 11:63–78.

Goodman RM & Steckler A (1989b). A framework for assessing program institutionalization. *Knowledge in Society: The International Journal of Knowledge Transfer* 2(1):57–71.

Gray B (1985). Conditions facilitating interorganizational collaboration. *Human Relations* 38:911–936.

Griffin T (1986). Community-based chemical use problem prevention. *Journal of School Health* 56(9):414–417.

Hall R, Clark J, Giordano P, Johnson P & Van Roekel M (1977). Patterns of interorganizational relationships. *Administrative Science Quarterly* 22:457–473.

Hawkins D & Catalano R (1992). *Communities that Care: Action for Drug Abuse Prevention.* San Francisco, CA: Jossey-Bass.

Johnson CA (1986). Objectives of community programs to prevent drug abuse. *Journal of School Health* 56(9):364–368.

Kagan SL (1991). *United We Stand: Collaboration for Child Care and Early Education Services.* New York, NY: Teachers College Press.

Katz D & Kahn RL (1978). *The Social Psychology of Organizations, 2nd Ed.* New York, NY: John Wiley & Sons.

Klitzner M (1991). *National Evaluation Plan for Fighting Back.* Princeton, NJ: The Robert Wood Johnson Foundation.

Knoke D & Wood JR (1981). *Organized for Action: Commitment in Voluntary Associations.* New Brunswick, NJ: Rutgers University Press.

Knoke D & Wright-Isak C (1982). Individual motives and organizational incentive systems. *Research in the Sociology of Organizations* 1:209–254.

LaLonde M (1974). *A New Perspective on the Health of Canadians: A Working Document.* Toronto, Ontario: Health and Welfare Canada.

Linney JA & Wandersman A (1991). *Prevention Plus III—Assessing Alcohol and Other Drug Prevention Programs at the School and Community Level: A Four Step Guide to Useful Program Assessment.* Rockville, MD: Office for Substance Abuse Prevention.

Marrett C (1971). On the specification of interorganizational dimensions. *Sociology and Social Research* 56:83–99.

McLeroy K, Bibeau D, Steckler A & Glanz K (1988). An ecological perspective on health promotion programs. *Health Education Quarterly* 15:351–377.

Minkler M (1989). Health education, health promotion and the open society: An historical perspective. *Health Education Quarterly* 16:17–30.

Moskowitz J (1989). The primary prevention of alcohol problems: A critical review of the research literature. *Journal of Studies on Alcohol* 50(1):54–88.

National Institute on Drug Abuse (1991). *National Household Survey on Drug Abuse: Highlights 1990.* Rockville, MD: The Institute.

Office for Substance Abuse Prevention (1990). *Citizen's Alcohol and Other Drug Prevention Directory: Resources for Getting Involved.* Rockville, MD: The Office.

Pentz MA, Dwyer JH, MacKinnon DP, Flay BR, Hansen WB, Wang EYI & Johnson CA (1989). A multi-community trial for primary prevention of adolescent drug abuse: Effects on drug use prevalence. *Journal of the American Medical Association* 261:3259–3266.

Prestby JE & Wandersman A (1985). An empirical exploration of a framework of organizational viability: Maintaining block organizations. *The Journal of Applied Behavioral Science* 21(3):287–305.

Roberts-DeGennaro M (1986a). Building coalitions for political advocacy. *Social Work* (July/August):308–311.

Roberts-DeGennaro M (1986b). Factors contributing to coalition maintenance. *Journal of Sociology and Social Welfare* 248–264.

Sink D & Stowers G (1989). Coalitions and their effect on the urban policy agenda. *Administration in Social Work* 13:83–98.

U.S. Department of Health and Human Services (1980). *Evaluation of Health Systems Agency Plans and State Health Plans and Their Development and Use in Review Activities.* Washington, DC: U.S. Government Printing Office.

Wandersman A (1981). A framework of participation in community organizations. *Journal of Applied Behavioral Science* 17:27–58.

Wandersman A & Alderman J (1993). Incentives, barriers and training of volunteers for the American Cancer Society: A staff perspective. *Review of Public Personnel Administration* 13(1):67–76.

Wandersman A & Goodman R (1990). Increasing the effectiveness and efficiency of community coalitions through basic and action research: A concept paper and proposal. Unpublished manuscript.

Whetten D (1981). Interorganizational relations: A review of the field. *Journal of Higher Education* 52:1–27.

Winett R, King A & Altman D (1989). *Health Psychology and Public Health.* New York, NY: Pergamon Press.

CHAPTER 4

Fitting Prevention into the Continuum of Care

Kenneth Hoffman, M.D., M.P.H.

A Multidisciplinary Approach to Prevention
A Community-Based Framework for Prevention
A Methodology for Integrating Prevention with AOD Treatment
The Role of the Health Care Provider

For individuals at any point on the continuum of potential drug use and addiction, there are specific interventions that can be classified as primary, secondary and tertiary prevention. *Primary prevention* attempts to prevent new cases and to reduce disease incidence. It differs from secondary prevention in the population addressed: rather than identifying individuals at risk, as in secondary prevention, primary prevention focuses on healthy populations. In both primary and secondary prevention, disease prevalence is reduced by decreasing the incidence of new disease.

When primary prevention strategies fail, resulting in substance use initiation, experimentation, or heavy and problematic use, it is necessary to move toward *secondary prevention.* In secondary prevention, individuals at risk for disease are identified while their problem is at a sub-clinical level. A successful intervention in secondary prevention is targeted toward preventing a new case from developing. In recognition of the importance of secondary prevention, the American Society of Addiction Medicine has introduced Level 0.5 in the second edition of its *Patient Placement Criteria* (the *PPC-2*, 1996) to address the needs of high-risk individuals who do not meet current criteria for either abuse or dependence.

Tertiary prevention addresses the need of the individual who meets the criteria for a clinical diagnosis and for whom specific individualized treatment is needed to prevent additional complications and comorbid problems. The goal of tertiary prevention is to prevent the disease from running its natural course, to prevent or ameliorate adverse effects of the disease, and to return the individual to the best possible state of health. Tertiary prevention decreases prevalence by decreasing the duration of the disease. Most of the chapters in this text are devoted to tertiary prevention.

By contrast, this chapter focuses on primary and secondary prevention, using lessons learned from the field of preventive medicine and interpolating it with concepts from addiction medicine. The goal is to fit primary and secondary prevention into a continuum of health care that emphasizes the role of the community and social networks as vehicles for preventing the onset of addictive disease. The chapter will describe methods and techniques that provide a framework within which prevention becomes part of the overall continuum of care. Brief assessment and intervention strategies also will be discussed, to provide clinicians with practical tools they can use to help patients at risk for addiction.

Finally, the chapter will present a re-engineering methodology as it has been applied to the addiction field, highlight the need to understand the community in the context of prevention, and discuss the role of the primary care provider in early intervention.

A MULTIDISCIPLINARY APPROACH TO PREVENTION

The Public Health Approach. Traditional public health approaches to prevention have focused on an infectious disease model that identifies the *host*, the *agent* and the *environment.* This model can be applied to the problem of addiction as follows:

- The host is the individual with a genetic predisposition to addiction.
- The agent is the drug of potential abuse.
- The environment is both the geographic location and the social network within which the host operates.

The public health paradigm explains why simple availability of a drug does not inevitably lead to addiction. For example, the individual may not ingest the drug. Or the individual may be relatively immune to developing addiction, so that even heavy and prolonged ingestion does not result in addiction. Or the individual's social network of peers, family and friends may discourage or inhibit use. On the other hand, if use of a given drug is accepted or encouraged, the risk of problem use and addiction climbs.

Epidemiologic, Anthropologic and Demographic Approaches to Prevention. The disciplines that have focused on social networks and community are social epidemiology, anthropology and demography, rather than public health. Each brings unique and valuable perspectives to our understanding of community, using both qualitative and quantitative data analysis.

Social epidemiology relates the standard biomedical model and biological inferences studied in medicine and contrasts those findings with nature and the workings of society. Several social-structural (consensual and conflict) or social-action or interpretive (symbolic interactionism and ethnomethodology) theories form the underpinnings of research in this field.

Social epidemiology is essentially quantitative research, using direct observation and deductive reasoning. Like the traditional discipline of epidemiology, analysis can rely on either secondary data use or primary data collection. Both structured and semi-structured questionnaires can be used. Data may be gathered through focused interviews with video- or audiorecording and transcripts, which are analyzed for content, or through diaries (Morgan, 1997).

Rapid ethnographic assessments draw on the fields of epidemiology and anthropology. A well-designed study defines concepts, collects data, and tests hypotheses. Qualitative research is a "ground-up" approach, emphasizing inductive reasoning. Interviews are conducted to see reality through the eyes of the subject and use a "free format" to avoid social and cultural constraints; such interviews often are conducted in focus groups or through in-depth open discussion (Morgan, 1997; Trotter, 1991).

Although social epidemiology uses small representative samples, studies in this field yield great depth of data, permitting detailed and iterative analysis of different groups, which allows conclusions to be drawn about social networks, cognitive belief systems and decision-making. Questionnaires that reflect the quality of "truth" can be designed and assessed for both their specificity and optimal cut-off values through use of Receiver Operator Characteristic (ROC) curves for structured survey questions, identified to measure identified group typology and domains (Fletcher, 1996).

Anthropology is the study of human beings in culture, within a set of beliefs and behaviors. This is of special importance when trying to understand mental health and behavior as they relate to a broader "web of causality" and "web of healing." The focus of anthropology is on interrelationships rather than sole causative factors. Anthropology works to gain an "insider's" perspective, to search for the telling detail, and to avoid thinking in absolutes. In this discipline, ambiguity and relativism are acceptable. The emphasis is on quality and validity, as they relate cultural "reality" to the data collected. New questions are valued as much as answers. Unexpected findings and leads permit a dynamic shift in focus of the initial study. There is no initial censoring of "necessary" and "superfluous" information. Anthropologists avoid the use of Knowledge, Attitude, Performance (KAP) surveys: they are schooled instead to expect the unexpected (Heggenhougen & Pedersen, 1997).

Anthropology addresses community and social network as complex interactive issues that can be studied through application of rapid ethnographic assessment methods. These attempt to explore and quantify group cognitive systems, linguistics, social networks, and decision modeling (Trotter, 1991; Gladwin, 1989; Bernard, 1988; Milray, 1987). Anthropologic results can be quantified through consensus analysis, using software designed for that purpose (Anthropac®).

Demography, in its narrowest definition, is the study of size and distribution of human populations. There are three important parameters: population fertility, mortality, and migration. In an expanded form, this discipline has been applied to HIV studies, drug use, and a myriad of other social problems. Demographic studies generally use a highly structured data collection process and yield products such as a national population census, vital registration systems, continuous registration systems, and observational surveys (retrospective, cross-sectional, and longitudinal). There is a very high degree of statistical sophistication, including rates and ratios to measures of mortality, fertility and the impact of migration (internal and international). The field of statistics has benefitted from the demographers' development of life tables (ordinary, multi-state, and absorbing, multiple decrement), mixed linear and logistical models (generalized estimating equations), multi-level models (including individual and community variables), grade of membership (GOM) models (which differ from "cluster" models), and geographic information systems (GIS) spatial analyses of population dynamics methods (Suchindran & Koo, 1997).

In summary, there is an interaction between epidemiology, social epidemiology, anthropology and demography as they relate to studies of prevention in addiction. Epidemiology prefers quantitative methods in the context of a biomedical disease model that considers economic, social, political, and cultural factors in disease prevalence, as well as incidence and prevention. Social epidemiology concentrates on health care structure, behavior and policy. It focuses on socio-economic status and issues as they relate to disease and wellness. Research finding can be found in physician-patient relationships and expected behaviors, psychosocial consequences of disease and disability, illness, injury and disease within a social context, health risk behaviors and beliefs (e.g. sexual behaviors and HIV). Anthropology views medicine as a social science. Many studies focus on nutrition and dietary habits and their health consequences; mental illness in different cultures; why people are sick and how they get well. The quest is to define the "good society." Within health care, anthropologists attempt to find associations between establishment of a therapeutic alliance and socioeconomic and cultural differences that separate patient and provider. This requires transcultural iterations to help providers better understand their patients.

Demography's focus on mortality (including infant deaths, abortions, perinatal mortality ratio, and causes of death), fertility (including total fertility rates, proximate determinants of fertility such as intercourse, conception, gestation, and special concerns such as contraception and adolescent pregnancy), and migration (including studies of public health policy, program and social impact on population distribution) have provided powerful statistical tools for examining the effectiveness of primary and secondary prevention.

Drawing on all of these disciplines, there is the potential to design, implement and evaluate primary and secondary prevention programs that effectively address alcohol and other drug problems.

Use of Multidisciplinary Approaches: Lessons from Tobacco Marketing Strategies. The importance of multidisciplinary approaches is best illustrated through examination of tobacco marketing strategies.

The principal goal of the tobacco industry is survival. In order to survive, tobacco companies must induce young people to begin smoking at an early age. This the industry does quite successfully, despite overwhelming evidence of premature deaths associated with tobacco use, the addictive nature of nicotine, and the morbidity cost of smoking. The industry achieves this, in part, by applying its knowledge of group values as they relate to a continuum of normative and conforming behaviors.

Recent legal discovery and court proceedings against the tobacco industry have brought to light the ways in which tobacco marketers use social science research to target and engage potential users. For example, social science research shows that initiation of tobacco use occurs within the context of peers and groups (Hahn, 1990) and is connected to a transition period between adolescence and adulthood (Astone, 1997). The stages through which adolescents typically progress—from pre-initiation to regular use—are highly correlated with sociodemographic, behavioral and psychological risk factors (USDHHS, 1994b). Onset of tobacco use occurs principally in early adolescents, with many reporting withdrawal symptoms while in their teen years (USDHHS, 1994a).

Despite multiple tobacco use prevention policies and programs, the prevalence of smoking among U.S. adolescents has been increasing since 1992 (MMWR, 23 May 1997), with at least 600,000 adolescents beginning to smoke each year (MMWR, 21 July 1995). Tobacco companies have spent billions of dollars on effective initiation strategies, as exemplified by the successful "Joe Camel" campaign beginning in 1988 (MMWR, 21 July 1995; Pierce, 1998; King, 1998). The companies' success appears related to still-secret research in which the tobacco industry defined specific peer groups along a scale of social conformity and specifically targeted brands to the more non-conforming groups (The Washington Post, 1998).

For example, when executives at RJR (Reynolds Tobacco) identified a decline in business in 1974, they determined to reorient the company's marketing focus to young people and set a goal of "capturing" the 14- to 24-year-old group. This would result in 25 years of financial security for the company. The markets' aim was to build loyalty to a specific (RJR) brand of cigarette from the time a new initiate first smoked. The industry knew the importance of brand loyalty: its own market research consistently showed that it is difficult to induce smokers to change brands. Given the large number of potential young smokers, RJR's goal was to increase its share of the youth market.

As a first step, RJR deployed a system called AGEMIX to track smoking rates in youth as young as 12. It developed a test ad campaign for its Camel brand in France, which used focus groups and incentives to establish a potentially successful marketing strategy for the U.S. The market analysis that supported this campaign was not based on individual characteristics that might relate to smoking behavior, but instead focused on defining groups in which smoking was most likely to occur. The analysis was built on prior experience. In a 1969 "Study of Ethnic Markets" commissioned by RJR, the company discovered that its desired market, affluent Blacks, had a new sense of pride and self-confidence. Advertisements based on rural environments, such as the "Marlboro Man" would have minimal impact on this group, whose members were concentrated in urban settings. RJR thus decided to market a specific cigarette brand (Newport) to this group in ways that suggested an affluent lifestyle.

Using a similar approach, RJR in 1984 commissioned a study of "younger adult smokers" (YAS) to better classify the first usual brands young adults smoke (FUBYAS). This was consistent with the company's goal of attracting initial smokers, who were most likely to become loyal smokers. Simply categorizing a YAS as White, Black or other had insufficient marketing precision for this purpose. The YAS analysis instead rated adolescent groups on scales of conformity, assigning each group a thumbnail description of its character. In the study report, the most conforming young adults (by definition, those least likely to initiate tobacco use) were labeled "Goody Goodies." There would be no effort to target this group. On a continuum of degrees of conformity, other groups were classified as "Preps," "GQs" and "Discos"; there might be some potential to induce members of these groups to initiate tobacco use. The groups of greatest interest, however, were at the other end of the conformity continuum, and were labeled "Rockers," "Party-Party" and "Punkers, or Burnouts." These groups were clear marketing targets.

Using these data, RJR re-introduced its Camel brand with a marketing campaign that used the "Joe Camel" character to directly target the "TGIF" and "Heavy Metal" groups. The clear goal was to equate peer acceptance within this type of group with smoking Camel cigarettes.

In conducting its research, RJR successfully employed the basic principles of anthropology and social epidemiology. Successful companies know that they need to understand the culture and the groups that make up the culture. Their goal in research is to "get inside the head" of youth. Successful prevention programs can do no less.

A COMMUNITY-BASED FRAMEWORK FOR PREVENTION

Available Survey Instruments. Several standardized survey instruments and assessment surveys are used in community adolescent studies and individual addiction assessments. A large number of questions are based on the *Youth Risk Factor Surveillance System* (YRBSS), established in 1990 by the Centers for Disease Control and Prevention (CDC) to measure the prevalence of health risk behaviors that begin in youth and contribute to early morbidity and mortality. The YRBSS measures tobacco, alcohol and other drug use; other behaviors that contribute to injuries; unprotected intercourse; dietary behavior; and physical activity. The YRBSS is now used by health agencies and school systems to create awareness of problems, develop programs and set program goals, support health-related legislation, and obtain funding (Everett 1997). The questions are very structured, as illustrated by the following questions addressing tobacco use (others follow a similar pattern) (MMWR, 1994):

- Have you ever tried cigarette smoking? (*lifetime use*)
- At what age were you when you first smoked a whole cigarette? (*age of onset*)
- Have you ever smoked cigarettes regularly? (*at least one a day for at least 30 days = regular use*)
- At what age were you when you first smoked regularly? (*age when use became regular*)
- How many days in the past month did you smoke cigarettes? (*frequency*)
- What number of cigarettes have you smoked per day during the past month? (*quantity*)
- How many days in the past month were cigarettes smoked on school property? (*where*)
- Have you ever tried to quit smoking cigarettes during the past six months? (*quit attempt*)
- Have you ever used chewing tobacco or snuff during past month? (*recent use, other product*)

- Have you ever used chewing tobacco or snuff during past month on school property? (*where*)

Community surveys structured in a manner similar to the YRBSS include the *Maryland Adolescent Survey* and the *Florida Youth Tobacco Survey.* Such surveys are focused on specific problem behaviors and provide only a sociodemographic set of exposure possibilities. Correlations with school items and environmental factors are captured in the *School Health Questionnaire* used in the Child and Adolescent Trial for Cardiovascular Health (CATCH), but individually effective interventions cannot be evaluated (Elder, 1994). Individual problem assessments include the *Problem Oriented Structured Interview for Teenagers (POSIT)*, the Processes and Stages of Change questionnaire, the Fagerstrom questions for nicotine dependence, and the *Self-Administered Nicotine Dependence Scale (SANDS)* (Davis, 1994). These address a broader set of biopsychosocial domains, which can be targeted for specific interventions, but the instruments themselves contain questions that focus more on pathology than on health. An optimal instrument would combine the domain depth of the assessment instruments with the brevity and sharp focus of the community surveys. There is an urgent need to adapt our traditional epidemiological focus on the individual to consider the impact of the peer group as a factor in behavior (Diez, 1998).

Survey Results. Despite their limitations, these survey instruments have been used by the public health community to develop a tremendous amount of knowledge about tobacco use in youth. Among 12- to 17-year-old smokers, for example, approximately 21% are addicted to nicotine (Kandel, 1997). Of adolescents who became regular smokers, 32% will die of a smoking-related disease, at a potential cost of $200 billion and 64 million years of life lost (MMWR, 8 November 1996).

Current state of the art knowledge in prevention has been applied to the seven recommendations from the Centers for Disease Control and Prevention (CDC) for schools to follow to prevent tobacco use and the clinical preventive task force advice to clinicians to provide brief counseling advice (MMWR, 1994), which are summarized in Table 1.

Follow-up surveys show that implementation of these guidelines and community initiatives has had demonstrated success. The Michigan Model for Comprehensive School Health Education model for youth in the 5th through 8th grades, for example, has led to decreased rates of substance use and increased knowledge and skills in resisting use (Shope, 1996). Latent transition analysis (LTA) has been used to compare two models of early adolescent substance use onset as they relate to a school-based substance use prevention program. Such analysis found that students who initiated use with tobacco but not alcohol were more likely to progress to greater degrees of substance use. A normative education prevention program was found to reduce substance use in the 8th grade, except among students who had used tobacco only in the seventh grade (Graham 1991). Effective normative programs emphasize establishing conservative social norms as they relate to substance use (Hansen 1991). When properly implemented (which includes two years of follow-up sessions), programs that teach a combination of social resistance skills and general life skills have achieved a 44% reduction in young drug users and a 66% reduction in polydrug users (Botvin, 1995).

TABLE 1. CDC Recommendations to Prevent Tobacco Use and Addiction

1. Develop and enforce a school policy on tobacco use.
2. Provide instruction about the short- and long-term negative physiologic and social consequences of tobacco use, social influences on tobacco use, peer norms regarding tobacco use, and refusal skills.
3. Provide tobacco use prevention education in kindergarten through 12th grade, intensified in junior high or middle school, and reinforced in high school.
4. Provide program-specific training for teachers.
5. Involve parents and families in support of school-based programs to prevent tobacco use.
6. Support cessation efforts among students and all school staff who use tobacco.
7. Assess tobacco use prevention programs at regular intervals.

Source: Centers for Disease Control and Prevention.

The surveys also have found a number of gender-related differences in relation to prevention. For example, women are more likely to perceive a causal relation between addiction and biological and environmental factors, leading them to believe that the drugs themselves are highly potent and their use is very prevalent. Thus, prevention programs that hope to appeal to women should respond to these perceptions in their design (Kauffman, 1997).

A 1993 meta-analysis of 120 school-based adolescent drug prevention programs identified four major types, which were ranked on a continuum according to the degree of interaction on the part of participants. The meta-analysis found that the most interactive programs were the most effective (Tobler,

1997). In contrast, a 1995 legislative funded comprehensive prevention that provided a K–12th grade continuum of interventions, with special attention to interventions for students 12 to 14 years old, inservice training for staff, prohibition of tobacco use on school property and program evaluation, yet the program was found to be ineffective in changing adolescent tobacco use (Murray, 1992). School-based tobacco prevention programs that do not take into account the social context of adolescent tobacco use have, at best, a weak effect over the long term (Lichtenstein, 1990).

Interactions with the Social Environment. The lesson of these programs is that there may be an interaction between school programs and the external social environment that is too important to ignore (MacKinnon, 1991). Along with individual personality and demographic factors, having family members or friends who use tobacco are commonly accepted predictors of adolescent tobacco use and point to the need for community-based intervention programs with parental involvement (Greenlund, 1997; Jackson, 1997; Hops, 1996; Murray, 1996; Buckhalt, 1992; Sieber, 1990; Ary, 1989; Skinner, 1985). Group value systems have not been explored, except in the context of religious beliefs and conforming to moral norms, both of which appear to have a preventive effect on tobacco use within well-defined groups of adolescents (Swaim, 1996; Pawlek, 1993).

The other key location for preventing initiation of substance use is at the worksite. Section 17 of this textbook covers the classic elements of deterrence (drug testing, employee assistance programs and the role of the health care provider as medical review officer). Beyond their direct effect on workers, however, worksite programs help to establish community norms that are visible to young adults (Zwerling, 1990).

A NEW METHODOLOGY FOR INTEGRATING PREVENTION WITH AOD TREATMENT

Complex relationships between processes and data can be effectively examined through application of an Integrated Definition (IDEF) methodology, with the advantage that IDEF results can be used to design, implement and evaluate the kinds of interventions proposed in this chapter (IDEF-0, 1993; IDEF-1x, 1993). Applied to the addiction field, this methodology allows prevention to be integrated into traditional health care within a precise cost structure. Application of BPR allows best interventions to be based on accumulated data from a community-based and beneficiary-focused health care system.

Integrated Definition (IDEF) modeling is a methodology created by the Air Force in the early 1980s to help contracting officers and vendors describe how money was being spent to build aircraft. However, IDEF is an industrial engineering concept that does more than simply assess workflow. At its most basic level (IDEF-0), the model defines activities as mutually exclusive actions that take time to accomplish. Using IDEF-0, each action can be broken down or deconstructed into a level of detail sufficient to understand how the activity is done. Each activity can be related through inputs and outputs, mechanisms and controls. Something (*input*) has to be transformed or used up (*output*) for the activity to have potential value. For any activity to occur, something has to make it happen (*mechanism*). Such mechanisms might be personnel, equipment or other resources, which have a known cost. *Controls* regulate the activity to ensure consistency or quality. Once defined, current activities can be assessed for their value to the overall production process. Non-value activities (i.e., things no one would want to pay for) can be eliminated, redundant activities combined, and opportunities for improvement identified. An optimized activity model can be built, and serve as the foundation for an optimal data model. Accounting cost methods could be based on the amount of time spent on the activity and the resources required for its accomplishment; this would constitute Activity Based Costing.

The next step (IDEF-1x) is to define data that support the activities. An analysis of current data usually reveals an inefficient data collection process that is highly redundant. Examples include filling out forms and signing in a patient each time a patient visits a treatment center. An improved logical model can be defined in which data are recorded one time only, and changed only as needed. Data collected are justified in terms of the activities they support. Useless or unused data are eliminated from the model. The relational database that evolves thus directly reflects the relationships among the activities. Properly designed, the data model reflects all the business rules that would be built into an automated product, such as an electronic patient record.

By the late 1980s, the Department of Defense (DoD) required that the IDEF methodology be used to develop any automated system. It became the underlying methodology within the DoD Corporate Integrated Management (CIM) initiative, whose purpose was to redesign DoD organizational structures.

Although conceptually a sound methodology, IDEF has not been used effectively in the design of medical information systems or in the redesign of medical care. One of the few applications of this methodology to health care has been in the Army Drug and Alcohol Prevention and Control Program (ADAPCP). Between 1993 and 1995, the Drug and Alcohol Policy Branch at MEDCOM and the Center for Addiction in the Department of Preventive Medicine, Uniformed Services University of the Health Sciences, established current and ideal activity and data models for Army Drug and Alcohol Treatment Clinics through use of the IDEF methodology (Hoffman, 1997, 1995; Hoffman & Keithley, 1994). The IDEF ideal data model was converted into a physical data model in Oracle. It was tested successfully for proof of concept as an electronic patient record at Fort Stewart in 1995 (Hoffman, 1995).

Three steps (initial modeling, validation and workgroup consensus) were involved to create the ideal activity model. Two activity modelers spent eight weeks at the Fort Benning ADAPCP interviewing all personnel. This program was regarded as one of the best in the Army, with a one-year success rate (no relapse) of approximately 90%. The high success rate was attributed to an intensive initial treatment and aftercare program, as well as a very strong community presence and active work with commanders and supervisors. Using IDEF, analysts captured current activities and related them in terms of their Inputs, Outputs, Controls (regulations) and Mechanisms (resources) (ICOMs). This created a current IDEF model, which was described by a detailed definition of current activities and ICOMs. The model was validated through visits to Forts Stewart, Knox, Eustis, Bliss, West Point, and Schofield Barracks. Staff at each location provided suggestions for improvement, which were used to create an ideal model. A rough draft of the model was presented and discussed at the 1993 Clinical Directors' Conference. Through consensus review by 62 ADAPCP Clinical Directors and other experts, the ideal activity model was validated and became the foundation for a logical data model.

Critical and mutually exclusive activities were defined and are presented in outline form in Table 2. (It is useful to note that each of these activities can occur at any level of care in the ASAM *Patient Placement Criteria*, from Level 0.5 to Level IV).

Since activities represent time and resources represent cost, the author and colleagues attempted to do Activity Based Costing (ABC) for both clinical and administrative staff. They found that, although each post had a consistent method of capturing costs for the clinic, the costs did not account for the activities performed. They also found that cost allocations for the same resources differed from one post to the next. This led to the conclusion that costs could not be accurately related to real work done with patients.

While developing the logical data model, the analysts had hoped to engage in the same "bottoms-up" requirement for critical data, because the data model currently in use was form-based. Staff of the Drug and Alcohol Clinics were being asked to manage 14 different forms, including a comprehensive biopsychosocial assessment form that was 14 pages long. The triage form had an incomplete concept of triage and several forms were awkward to use. The most critical requirements for structured data elements were left unstructured within the forms. Specifically, the forms did not contain an integrated summary or a standardized problem list, as well as well-focused treatment descriptions that highlighted education and motivation. In place of these summaries, clinics staff were collecting 92 utilization measures through a separate data collection process. As it related to the activity model, between 15% (counselor) to 80% (clinical director) of the available time was spent in "paperwork," which staff considered "non-value added," except for the perception that accreditation bodies and utilization review personnel wanted it.

Conceptually, the IDEF analysis needed to integrate the business rules described by the activity model into a relational database, and collect supporting information on a justifiable "need to know" basis. Development was complicated by "top-down" data requirements that were not subject to discussion. However, a logical data model was developed through screen flow designs that were integrated into the work flow of patient assessment, treatment planning and treatment implementation.

The resulting prototype was seen as a unique drug and alcohol data system because of the unique drug and alcohol forms. However, the conceptual design was identified as a generic ambulatory care, chronic disease management, and patient-focused model, which had the capacity for outcomes management, provider privileging, and accurate billing for reimbursement. This led to recognition of the importance of the "bottoms-up" approach, which becomes the first recommendation for developing a comprehensive computer patient record. As a side

TABLE 2. Activity Model for All Substance Abuse Treatment Centers

1. Provide Clinical Services		
a. Acquire the patient:	(1) Perform triage:	(a) Conduct triage interview; (b) Determine severity and risk; (c) Recommend disposition.
	(2) Assess patient:	(a) Conduct comprehensive biopsychosocial assessment; (b) Develop summary statement; (c) Recommend course of action.
	(3) Develop initial treatment plan:	(a) Define problems; (b) Identify desired outcomes; (c) Establish goals; (d) Prepare detailed objectives.
	(4) Enroll patient:	(a) Obtain concurrence to initial plan; (b) Provide patient orientation; (c) Set up appointments.
b. Treat the patient:	(1) Provide case management.	
	(2) Provide pharmacotherapy.	
	(3) Provide psychosocial counseling:	(a) Educate patient: i. present factual material; ii. reinforce integration of facts and implications; iii. evaluate patient's understanding. (b) Motivate patient: i. attack problem of denial; ii. explore spiritual aspects of recovery; iii. stimulate personal growth. (c) Empower patient: i. track and evaluate progress; ii. identify obstacles to progress; iii. discuss potential solutions; iv. reinforce motivation.
	(4) Provide health promotion and fitness counseling.	
c. Deliver aftercare services.		
2. Provide External Consultation and Liaison Service		
a. Consult and coordinate with commanders and employers.		
b. Consult and liaise with military health care activities.		
c. Consult and liaise with civilian health care activities.		
d. Consult and liaise with other appropriate activities and individuals.		
e. Consult and liaise with alcohol and drug control officers.		
3. Provide Support Services		
a. Improve the quality and appropriateness of patient care:	(1) Evaluate current performance. (2) Plan and implement improvements. (3) Monitor implementation results.	
b. Train staff:	(1) Provide in-service training. (2) Provide supplemental training. (3) Provide required CEU/CHE/CME training.	
c. Perform management functions:	(1) Plan for and expend resources. (2) Supervise staff. (3) Interact and communicate.	
d. Perform administrative functions:	(1) Capture, maintain and report patient data. (2) Handle communications schedules and requests. (3) Administer office operations.	

benefit, the activity model provided a basis for regulations, business plans and contracts. It also clearly delineated those activities that should be automated and those that should be eliminated.

By using IDEF to streamline "value-added" activities, both access and quality of care should improve. Cost would be reduced through elimination of redundant and unnecessary paperwork and activities.

Most Clinical Directors thought they would be more effective in their jobs if they could spend more time in the community and with patients who had been "discharged" from the clinic. These findings and the Directors' identification of "health promotion" as a treatment activity indicate the importance the APAPCP placed on primary and secondary prevention. Using IDEF, activities such as community interventions and aftercare, which are not at present reimbursed, could be justified.

THE ROLE OF THE HEALTH CARE PROVIDER

Through IDEF and similar methods, integrating prevention into the continuum of care is becoming a standard of care. Under initiatives to "Put Prevention into Practice," a variety of models are being used to teach and motivate individuals to change their behavior. These have been imbedded in practice guidelines advocated by the American Psychiatric Association and the U.S. Clinical Preventive Services Task Force (APA, 1996; USPSTF, 1996).

The specific USPSTF recommendations for early detection of problems with nicotine, alcohol and other drugs are shown in Table 3.

To support such efforts, the federal Center for Substance Abuse Treatment has produced a Treatment Improvement Protocol (TIP) that presents a brief screening instrument based on questions from the CAGE, MAST, AUDIT, POSIT, ASI, DAST, Revised Health Screening Survey (RHSS), and the *Diagnostic and Statistical Manual, 3rd Ed., Revised*, of the American Psychiatric Association (*DSM-IIIR*, 1987) (Winters & Zenilman, 1994). See Appendix B of this text for the 16-question interview form, in which four questions are highlighted for the "short" interview, and a self-administered form reflecting the same questions. Positive responses to four or more of the 16 questions indicate moderate to high risk for alcohol or other drug abuse, which should be assessed further. (Nicotine dependence is not addressed in this survey, unless the patient identifies it as "another drug.")

TABLE 3. General Prevention Practice Guidelines

Tobacco Use

- Tobacco cessation counseling is recommended on a regular basis for all users.
- Pregnant women and parents with children should be counseled on the harmful effects of tobacco on fetal and child health.
- Consider use of nicotine replacement therapy for many users.
- Provide anti-tobacco messages in health promotion programs for children, adolescents and young adults.

Problem Drinking

- Screening to detect problem drinking is recommended for all adult and adolescent patients, using standard history questions or standardized screening questionnaires.
- Routine use of biochemical markers is not recommended for asymptomatic patients.
- Pregnant women should be counseled to stop or limit drinking during pregnancy.
- Although there is insufficient scientific evidence on the impact of light drinking, prudent advice supports abstention.
- All users should be counseled regarding the dangers of driving or performing other potentially dangerous activities after drinking.

Drug Abuse

- Routine screening for drug abuse, either by self-report or drug laboratory screens, is not supported by scientific evidence, but clinicians should ask about them when appropriate (consider the prevalence of drug use and serious consequences in community in which patients live).
- Pregnant women should be counseled regarding the potential adverse effects of drug use on fetal health. Opiate addicts should be placed on methadone maintenance throughout pregnancy.
- Clinicians should be alert to signs and symptoms of drug use, and ask when appropriate.
- Drug-abusing patients should be referred to specialized treatment facilities where available.

Source: American Psychiatric Association and the U.S. Clinical Preventive Services Task Force (APA, 1996; USPSTF, 1996).

Central to all these recommendations is the notion that primary care providers should become comfortable in performing brief assessments of all patients and brief treatment of patients with nicotine, alcohol and other drug problems. The addiction medicine or mental health specialist thus is used as a consultant or referral resource to assist with those patients who exhibit significant psychopathology or who require more intensive treatment than is available in primary care settings.

All patient care requires interaction with the community and personal social network. A supportive network may decrease the intensity of treatment that otherwise would be required.

CONCLUSIONS

The American Society of Addiction Medicine introduced Level 0.5 within the continuum of care to address prevention and early intervention for the alcohol or drug user at high risk for addictive disorders. This has moved addiction intervention into the realm of secondary prevention. However, medical care remains fragmented across the continuum. This chapter has presented a business process reengineering methodology that can be used in the drug and alcohol field to focus on the patient, identifying both the activities and data required to identify problems, develop treatment plans, implement treatment and monitor outcomes. In the context of primary prevention, the "patient" becomes the community, which develops the social norms that encourage or inhibit drug use.

The current practice of prevention remains provider-focused, with heavy reliance on working with individual patients. Research results are weighted toward controlled clinical trials, but show little understanding of the drug abuser's or addict's culture. Research methods generally are employed to develop effective tertiary prevention strategies, including case studies, disease registries and controlled trials. Research methods to develop effective secondary prevention strategies include use of focus groups and the more traditional epidemiologic studies, and risk factor intervention clinical trials. Marketing and anthropological methods and techniques are not valued and social epidemiology has not been well utilized. As the tobacco industry demonstrates through its marketing research, highly effective interventions are possible if group cultures are understood and targeted. Anthropological and social epidemiological research methods are essential in the realm of primary prevention and should be integrated into the continuum of medical research. Appropriate research methods to develop effective primary prevention strategies include focus groups, qualitative studies, marketing and ecological studies.

Primary prevention strategies should be more focused on understanding and effecting changes in groups rather than on individual values and decisions. Ironically, the effectiveness of this approach has been well illustrated by the use of such research by the tobacco industry to induce young adults to overcome their natural aversion to tobacco and initiate tobacco use.

To increase the efficacy of alcohol and drug prevention programs, there is a critical need to understand the evolution of group behaviors as a function of an evolving value system, in the same way we try to better understand individual behaviors. Approaches that integrate community programs with peer-led, interactive school programs in which adolescents take an active role in developing interventions show the greatest potential for preventing tobacco use initiation (Slater, 1998; Tobler, 1997; IOM, 1994; USDHHS-c, 1994).

The views expressed in this article represent those of the author only and should not be construed to represent the official viewpoint of any government agency or organization.

REFERENCES

American Psychiatric Association (APA) (1996). Practice Guideline for the treatment of patients with nicotine dependence. *American Journal of Psychiatry* 153(Suppl. 10):1–31.

Ary DV, Lichtenstein E, Severson H, Weissman W & Seeley JR (1989). An in-depth analysis of male adolescent smokeless tobacco users: Interviews with users and their fathers. *Journal of Behavioral Medicine* 12(5):449–467.

Astone NM, Alexander C, Joffe A & Kanarek N (1997). The social and demographic correlates of smoking among young adults in Maryland. *American Journal of Preventive Medicine* 13(Suppl.)6:25–29.

Bandura A (1977). Self-efficacy: Toward a unifying theory of behavioural change. *Psychological Review* 64(2):191–315.

Bernard R (1988). *Research Methods in Cultural Anthropology*. Newbury Park, CA: Sage.

Botvin GJ, Baker E, Dusenbury L, Botvin EM & Diaz T (1995). Long-term results of a randomized drug abuse prevention trial in a white middle-class population. *Journal of the American Medical Association* 273(14):1106–1112.

Buckhalt JA, Halpin G, Noel R & Meadows ME (1992). Relationship of drug use to involvement in school, home, and community activities: Results of a large survey of adolescents. *Psychological Reports* 70:139–146.

Centers for Disease Control and Prevention (CDC) (1994). Guidelines for school health programs to prevent tobacco use and addiction. *Morbidity and Mortality Weekly Reports* 43(RR-2).

Centers for Disease Control and Prevention (CDC) (1995). Trends in smoking initiation among adolescents and young adults—United States, 1980–1989. *Morbidity and Mortality Weekly Reports*, July 21, 1995.

Centers for Disease Control and Prevention (CDC) (1996). Projected smoking related deaths among youth—United States. *Morbidity and Mortality Weekly Reports*, November 8.

Centers for Disease Control and Prevention (CDC) (1997). Smoking-attributable mortality and years of potential life lost—United States, 1984. *Morbidity and Mortality Weekly Reports*, May 23.

Cinciripini PM, Hecht SS, Henningfield JE, Manley MW, Kramer BS (1997). Tobacco addiction: Implications for treatment and cancer prevention. *Journal of the National Cancer Institute* 89:1852–1867.

Cohen S, Lichtenstein E, Mermelstein R, Kingsolver K, Baer J & Kamarck T (1988). Social support interventions for smoking cessation. In BH Gottlieb (ed.) *Marshalling Social Support: Formats, Processes and Effects*. New York, NY: Sage, 211–240.

Coppotelli HC & Orleans CT (1985). Partner support and other determinants of smoking cessation maintenance among women. *Journal of Consulting and Clinical Psychology* 53:455–460.

Cromwell J, Bartosch WJ, Fiore MC, Hasselblad V & Baker T (1997). Cost-effectiveness of the Clinical Practice Guideline for smoking cessation. *Journal of the American Medical Association* 278(21):1759–1766.

Crouch DJ, Birky MM, Gust SW, Rollins DE, Walsh JM, Moulden JV, Quinlan KE & Beckel RW (1993). The prevalence of drugs and alcohol in fatally injured truck drivers. *Journal of Forensic Sciences* 38(6):1342–1353.

Davis LJ, Hurt RD, Offord KP, Lauger GG, Morse RM & Bruce BK (1994). Self-administered nicotine dependence scale (SANDS): Item selection, reliability estimation and initial validation. *Journal of Clinical Psychology* 30(6):918–930.

DiCLemente CC (1993). Changing addictive behaviors: A process perspective. *Current Directions in Psychological Science* 2:101–106.

Diez-Roux AV (1998). Bringing context back into epidemiology: variables and fallacies in multilevel analysis. *American Journal of Public Health* 88(2):216–222.

Elder JP, McGraw SA, Stone EJ, Reed DB, Harsha DW, Grenne T & Wambsgans KC (1994). CATCH: Process evaluation of environmental factors and programs. *Health Education Quarterly* (Suppl. 2):S107–S127.

Everett SA, Kann L & McReynolds L (1997). The Youth Risk Factor Behavior Surveillance System: Policy and program applications. *Journal of School Health* 67(8):333–335.

Fletcher RH, Fletcher SW & Wagner EH (1996). *Clinical Epidemiology, the Essentials, 3rd Ed.* Baltimore, MD: Williams & Wilkins, 43–74.

Floren AE (1994). Urine drug screening and the family physician. *American Family Physician* 49(6):1441–1447.

Gladwin C (1989). *Ethnographic Decision Tree Modeling.* Newbury Park, CA: Sage.

Graham JW, Collins LM, Wugalter SE, Chung NK & Hansen WB (1991). Modeling transitions in latent stage-sequential processes: A substance use prevention example. *Journal of Consulting and Clinical Psychology* 59(1):48–57.

Greenlund KJ, Johnson CC, Webber LS & Berenson GS (1997). Cigarette smoking attitudes and first use among third through sixth grade students: The Bogalusa Heart Study. *American Journal of Public Health* 87(8):1345–1348.

Gries JA, Black DR & Coster DC (1995). Recruitment to a university alcohol program: Evaluation of social marketing theory and stepped approach model. *Preventive Medicine* 24:348–356.

Hahn G, Charlin VL, Sussman S, Dent CW, Manzi J & Stacy AW (1990). Adolescents' first and most recent use situations of smokeless tobacco and cigarettes: Similarities and differences. *Addictive Behaviors* 15:439–448.

Hansen WB & Graham JW (1991). Preventing alcohol, marijuana, and cigarette use among adolescents: Peer pressure resistance training versus establishing conservative norms. *Preventive Medicine* 20(3):414–430.

Hanson BS, Isacsson SO, Janzon L & Lindell S (1990). Social support and quitting smoking for good. Is there an association? Results from the population study, "Men Born in 1914," Malmo, Sweden. *Addictive Behaviors* 15:221–233.

Heggenhougen HK & Pederson D (1997). Beyond quantitative measures: The relevance of anthropology for public health. In R Detels, WW Holland, J McEwen & GS Omenn (eds.) *Oxford Textbook of Public Health, Third Edition, Vol. 2: The Methods of Public Health.* New York, NY: Oxford University Press, 815–828.

Hoffman KJ (1995). Use of IDEF modeling to develop an Electronic Patient Record for drug and alcohol treatment clinics. *Journal of the Medical Informatics Association*, Symposium Supplement:993.

Hoffman KJ (1997). Demystifying mental health information needs through Integrated Definition (IDEF) activity and data modeling. *Journal of the Medical Informatics Association*, Symposium Supplement :111–116.

Hoffman KJ (1995a). Representing the patient in data. In L Kun (ed.) *Health Care System Infrastructure.* Proc. SPIE 2618.

Hoffman KJ (1995b). Use of IDEF modeling to develop an information management system for drug and alcohol outpatient clinics. In W Grundfest (ed.) *Health Care Policy II: The Role of Technology in the Cost of Health Care: Providing the Solutions.* Proc. SPIE 2499.

Hoffman KJ & Keithley H (1994). Comprehensive modeling of critical health care activities, costs and data needs within the context of addiction rehabilitation. In W Grundfest (ed.) *Health Care Technology Policy I: The Role of Technology in the Cost of Health Care.* Proc. SPIE 2307:412–422.

Hoffman KJ (1994). Adolescent differences in levels of abuse: Implications for alternatives future interventions. Society of Prospective Medicine. Proceedings of the 30th Annual Meeting, March.

Hops H, Duncan TE, Duncan SC & Stoolmiller M (1996). Parent substance use as a predictor of adolescent use: A six-year lagged analysis. *Annals of Behavioral Medicine* 18(3):157–164.

Integration Definition For Function Modeling (IDEF-0), FIPS Pub. 183, Computer Systems Laboratory, National Institute of Standards and Technology, Gaithersburg, MD (issued December 21, 1993).

Institute of Medicine (IOM) (1994). *Growing Up Tobacco Free: Preventing Nicotine Addiction in Children and Youth.* Washington DC: National Academy Press.

Integration Definition for Information Modeling (IDEF-1x), FIPS Pub. 184, Computer Systems Laboratory, National Institute of Standards and Technology, Gaithersburg, MD (issued December 21, 1993).

Jackson C, Henricksen L, Dickinson D & Levine DW (1997). The early use of alcohol and tobacco: Its relation to children's competence and parents' behavior. *American Journal of Public Health* 87(3):359–364.

Kandel D, Chen K, Warner L, Kessler RC & Grant B (1997). Prevalence and demographic correlates of symptoms of last year dependence on alcohol, nicotine, marijuana and cocaine in the U.S. population. *Drug and Alcohol Dependence* 44:11–29.

Kauffman SE, Silver P & Poulin J (1997). Gender differences in attitudes toward alcohol, tobacco, and other drugs. *Social Work* 42(3):231–241.

King C, Siegel M, Celebucki C & Connolly GN (1998). Adolescent exposure to cigarette advertising in magazines. *Journal of the American Medical Association* 279(7):516–520.

Kviz FJ, Clark MA, Crittenden KS, Warnecke RB & Freels S (1995). Age and smoking cessation behaviors. *Preventive Medicine* 24:297–307.

Laufenburg HF & Barton BA (1997). Attitudes of family practice program directors toward mandatory preemployment drug testing. *Family Medicine* 29(9):625–628.

Lemon SJ, Sienko DG & Alguire PC (n.d.). Physician attitudes toward mandatory workplace urine drug testing. *Archives of Internal Medicine* 152(11):2238–2242.

Lichtenstein E, Biglin A, Glasgow RE, Severson H & Ary D (1990). The tobacco use research program at Oregon Research Institute. *British Journal of Addiction* 85:715–724.

Lillsunde P, Korte T, Michelson L, Portman M, Pikkarainen J & Seppala T (1996). Drugs usage of drivers suspected of driving under the influence of alcohol and/or other drugs. A study of one week's samples in 1979 and 1993 in Finland. *Forensic Science International* 77(1–2):119–129.

MacKinnon DP, Johnson CA, Pentz MA, Dwyer JH, Hansen WD, Flay BR & Wang EY (1991). Mediating mechanisms in a school-based drug prevention program: First year effects of the Midwestern Prevention Project. *Health Psychology* 10(3):164–172.

Maryland State Department of Education, Department of Health and Mental Hygiene, and Department of Transportation (1996). *1996 Maryland Adolescent Survey.* Annapolis, MD: The Departments.

Mermelstein R, Cohen S, Lichenstein E, Baer JS & Kamarck T (1986). Social support and smoking cessation and maintenance. *Journal of Consulting and Clinical Psychology* 54:447–453.

Milray L (1987). *Language and Social Networks, 2nd Ed.* Cambridge, MA: Blackwell.

Morgan M (1997). Sociological investigations. In R Detels, WW Holland, J McEwen & GS Omenn (eds.) *Oxford Textbook of Public Health, Third Edition, Vol. 2: The Methods of Public Health.* New York, NY: Oxford University Press, 765–781.

Murray DM, Perry CL, Griffin G, Harty KC, Jacobs DR, Schmid L, Daly K & Pallonen U (1992). Results from a statewide approach to adolescent tobacco use prevention. *Preventive Medicine* 21:449–472.

Murray DM & Short BJ (1997). Intraclass correlation among measures related to tobacco use by adolescents: Estimates, correlates, and applications in intervention studies. *Addictive Behaviors* 22(1):1–12.

Osterloh JD & Becker CE (1990). Chemical dependency and drug testing in the workplace. *Journal of Psychoactive Drugs* 22(4):407–417.

Perz CA, DiClemente CC & Carbonari JP (1996). Doing the right thing at the right time? The interaction of stages and processes of change in successful smoking cessation. *Health Psychology* 15(6):462–468.

Prochaska JO & DiClemente CC (1992). Stages of change in the modification of problem behaviors. In M Hersen, RM Eisler & PM Miller (eds.) *Progress in Behavior Modification.* Sycamore, IL: Sycamore Press, 184–214.

Prochaska JO & DiClemente CC (1986). The transtheoretical approach. In JC Norcross (ed.) *Handbook of Eclectic Psychotherapy.* New York, NY: Brunner/Mazel, 163–200.

Prochaska JO & DiClemente CC (1983). Stages and processes of self-change of smoking: Toward an integrative model of change. *Journal of Consulting and Clinical Psychology* 51:390–395.

Schiwy-Bochat KH, Bogusz M, Vega JA & Althoff H (1995). Trends in occurrence of drugs of abuse in blood and urine of arrested drivers and drug traffickers in the border region of Aachen. *Forensic Sciences International* 71(1):33–42.

Shope JT, Copeland LA, Marcoux BC & Kamp ME (1996). Effectiveness of a school-based substance abuse prevention program. *Journal of Drug Education* 26(4):323–337.

Suchindran CM & Koo HP (1997). Demography and public health. In R Detels, WW Holland, J McEwen & GS Omenn (eds.) *Oxford Textbook of Public Health, Third Edition, Vol. 2: The Methods of Public Health.* New York, NY: Oxford University Press, 829–848.

Winters KC & Zenilman JM, co-chairs (1994). *Simple Screening Instruments for Outreach for Alcohol and Other Drug Abuse and Infectious Diseases: Treatment Improvement Protocol (TIP) No. 11.* Rockville, MD: Center for Substance Abuse Treatment (DHHS Publication No. (SMA) 94-2094).

Zwerling C (1993). Current practice and experience in drug and alcohol testing in the workplace. *Bulletin of Narcotics* 45(2):155–196.

SECTION 4
Diagnosis and Assessment

CHAPTER 1

Principles of Identification and Intervention **249**
Jerome E. Schulz, M.D. and Theodore Parran, M.D., FACP

CHAPTER 2

Screening Instruments and Biochemical Screening Tests **263**
John P. Allen, Ph.D. and Raye Z. Litten, Ph.D.

CHAPTER 3

Assessment Instruments **273**
David R. Gastfriend, M.D., Sharon L. Baker, Ph.D., Lisa M. Najavits, Ph.D. and Sharon Reif, B.A.

CHAPTER 4

Diagnostic Classification Systems **279**
Samuel A. Ball, Ph.D. and Therese A. Kosten, Ph.D.

SECTION COORDINATOR

CHRISTINE L. KASSER, M.D.
Private Practice of Medicine
Germantown, Tennessee

CONTRIBUTORS

John P. Allen, Ph.D.
Treatment Research Branch
Division of Clinical and Prevention Research
National Institute on Alcohol Abuse
and Alcoholism
Rockville, Maryland

Sharon L. Baker, Ph.D.
Clinical Research Associate
Massachusetts General Hospital
and Instructor in Psychology
Harvard Medical School
Boston, Massachusetts

Samuel A. Ball, Ph.D.
Division of Substance Abuse
Department of Psychiatry
Yale University School of Medicine
New Haven, Connecticut

David R. Gastfriend, M.D.
Director of Addiction Services
Massachusetts General Hospital
and Associate Professor of Psychiatry
Harvard Medical School
Boston, Massachusetts

Therese A. Kosten, Ph.D.
Division of Substance Abuse
Department of Psychiatry
Yale University School of Medicine
New Haven, Connecticut

Raye Z. Litten, Ph.D.
Treatment Research Branch
Division of Clinical and Prevention Research
National Institute on Alcohol Abuse
and Alcoholism
Rockville, Maryland

Lisa M. Najavits, Ph.D
Clinical Research Associate
Massachusetts General Hospital
and Instructor in Psychology
Harvard Medical School
Boston, Massachusetts

Theodore Parran, Jr., M.D., FACP
Case-Western Reserve University
School of Medicine
Cleveland, Ohio

Sharon Reif, B.A.
Research Assistant
Massachusetts General Hospital
Boston, Massachusetts

Jerome E. Schulz, M.D.
Clinical Associate Professor
Department of Family Medicine
Eastern Carolina University
School of Medicine
Greenville, North Carolina

CHAPTER 1

Principles of Identification and Intervention

Jerome E. Schulz, M.D.
Theodore Parran, Jr., M.D., FACP

Screening
Assessment
Intervention
Monitoring and Follow-Up Care

All clinicians—and particularly primary care physicians—are in a unique position to identify and help patients with alcohol and other drug problems. Up to 20% of visits to primary care physicians are related to such problems (Bradley, 1994). Patients with alcohol and other drug problems are twice as likely to consult a primary care physician as are patients without such problems (Rush, 1989). Moreover, a recent review of brief interventions for alcohol and drug problems concluded that primary care physicians can help change the course of harmful drinking. Brief interventions are feasible during patient office visits (Bien, Miller & Tongan, 1993; Fleming, Barry et al., 1997).

SCREENING

Many standardized screening techniques are available to determine if a patient has an alcohol and other drug (AOD) problem (see Chapter 2 for a fuller discussion). However, before any attempt is made to assess a patient's alcohol and other drug use, the clinician must establish a relationship of rapport and trust with the patient.

Questions about alcohol and other drug use are most appropriately asked as part of the history of personal habits, such as smoking and coffee drinking. Questions should be asked openly and in a nonjudgmental way to avoid engendering defensiveness on the part of the patient. Assessing adolescents for alcohol and other drug problems is particularly challenging. Physicians must ensure confidentiality and establish trust to be successful in detecting drug/alcohol problems in adolescents.

The most frequently used screening method is the CAGE questionnaire (Mayfield, McLeod & Hall, 1971), which asks: "Have you ever felt the need to **C**ut down on your drinking (or drug use)?," "Have people **A**nnoyed you by criticizing your drinking (drug use)?," "Have you ever felt bad or **G**uilty about your drinking (drug use)?," and "Have you ever needed an **E**ye opener the first thing in the morning to steady your nerves or get rid of a hangover?" The CAGE is 60% to 95% sensitive (that is, likely to identify a problem with alcohol) when two answers are positive, and 40% to 95% specific (Beresford, Blow et al., 1990). CAGE questions concentrate on a patient's lifetime history of alcohol use, but the method does not assess current drinking patterns. Therefore, it may fail to detect early problem drinking if no significant consequences have occurred. Screening for drug use can be accomplished through use of the CAGE, by substituting drug use for drinking in the questions.

It should be recognized that the CAGE is a *screening* tool and cannot be used to diagnose alcohol or drug problems.

Two simple questions can increase the likelihood that screening will detect patients with alcohol problems. The first asks patients if they have ever had drinking problems. The second asks if they have had any alcohol to drink in the last 24 hours. If the answers to both questions are positive, the sensitivity for alcohol problems is 92% (Cyr & Wartman, 1988).

In the past, questions about quantity and frequency of drug or alcohol use were thought to be useless. This belief came from evaluating patients who were already alcoholic or drug dependent and who were in considerable denial about their drug or alcohol use. Those patients tended to minimize and rationalize their drug and alcohol use. On the other hand, patients who are misusing alcohol and other drugs, but who are not yet alcohol- or drug-dependent, have not developed denial and thus usually are willing to tell physicians how often they use alcohol and other drugs and how much they use (Williams, Aitken & Malin, 1985).

If patients do not drink, it is important to ask why they do not; there may be a personal or family history of alcohol problems that should be documented as part of the patient's history. Such an exchange also presents an opportunity for the clinician to do primary prevention by supporting the patient in his or her choice not to use drugs or alcohol. Where there is a history of alcohol or drug problems, the patient chart should be labeled clearly to prevent prescribing any mood-altering drugs that may jeopardize his or her continued recovery. When the family history is positive, the patient should be educated about his or her increased risk of developing drug/alcohol problems.

If a patient does drink alcohol, the CAGE questions should be asked before quantity/frequency questions. One study (not in a primary care setting) showed that the CAGE was significantly less sensitive when administered after quantity/frequency questions had been asked (Steinweg & Worth, 1993). After the CAGE questions, the patient should be asked how many days a week he or she drinks alcohol, how many drinks he or she consumes in an "average" day, and the maximum number of drinks consumed on a single occasion during the preceding month.

From a public health perspective, the research literature demonstrates increased health problems and injuries when alcohol is used in excess of certain levels. For men, the limits for low-risk drinking are no more than two drinks a day and no more than four drinks on a single occasion (at a rate less than one drink per hour). For women and patients over 65, the recommendations are no more than one drink a day and no more than three drinks on a single occasion. (A standard drink is one 12-ounce bottle of beer or wine cooler, one 5-ounce glass of wine, or 1.5 ounces of distilled spirits.) Women reach higher blood levels of alcohol than men after consuming equivalent amounts of alcohol because they are smaller and have less gastric alcohol dehydrogenase to metabolize alcohol. Pregnant patients and those with medical problems complicated by alcohol should abstain completely (NIAAA, 1995).

If a patient is drinking more than the recommended amount of alcohol, is using any illicit drugs, or has one positive answer to the CAGE questions, he or she should be further assessed for alcohol and drug problems.

TABLE 1. Presenting Complaints that are "Red Flags" for Alcohol and Other Drug Problems

- Frequent absences from work or school
- History of frequent trauma/accidental injuries
- Depression
- Anxiety
- Labile hypertension
- Gastrointestinal symptoms
- Sexual dysfunction
- Sleep disorders.

"Red Flags" for AOD Problems. A number of presenting complaints are so frequently seen in patients with alcohol and other drug problems that they are virtual "red flags" to the clinician to consider this as the underlying problem (Table 1). For example, some patients develop recurring "Monday flu" as the result of weekend binge drinking or drug use that requires them to obtain return-to-work slips because of frequent absenteeism. Others have labile blood pressure readings caused by alcohol withdrawal; in fact, withdrawal symptoms and poor medication compliance make treating hypertension a challenge in patients with alcohol and other drug problems.

Family members may present with the same symptoms as the drinking or drug-using patient. Trauma is common secondary to spousal abuse. Children may be seen for abdominal pain, headaches, or school problems.

Patients who abuse drugs other than alcohol may present with a variety of medical problems, each with specific signs and symptoms. Patients who abuse cocaine develop chest pain caused by vasoconstriction of the coronary arteries. Any young patient (< 35 years old) with chest pain should have a urine toxicology screen for cocaine. Intranasal (snorting) use of cocaine causes rhinorrhea, sinus problems, and dental problems. In severe cases, patients may have a perforated nasal septum. Cocaine use also can cause seizures and (rarely) intraventricular hemorrhages. A chronic cough (especially if it produces black sputum) may result from crack cocaine abuse. Marijuana abuse should be considered in adolescents who are experiencing school difficulties, a chronic cough, or worsening of asthmatic conditions.

TABLE 2. Physical Findings Suggestive of Alcohol and Other Drug Problems

- Mild tremor
- Odor of alcohol on breath
- Enlarged, tender liver
- Nasal irritation (suggestive of cocaine insufflation)
- Conjunctival irritation (suggestive of exposure to marijuana smoke)
- Labile blood pressure (suggestive of alcohol withdrawal)
- Tachycardia and/or cardiac arrhythmia
- "After Shave/Mouthwash" syndrome (to mask the odor of alcohol)
- Odor of marijuana on clothing.

ASSESSMENT

Several strategies can be employed to assess patients who screen positive for drug or alcohol problems.

History. The first step is to take an expanded drug and alcohol history. Questions should focus on the consequences of the patient's alcohol and other drug use—blackouts (loss of memory of events while intoxicated), tolerance changes, and withdrawal symptoms. Medical problems that may be clues the patient is abusing drugs or alcohol (Table 2) should be identified. For example, a history of pancreatitis, liver disease, or chronic gastrointestinal problems may signify chronic alcohol abuse. The patient should be asked about social or family problems commonly associated with alcohol and other drug misuse, such as a previous history of arrests for driving under the influence, job loss, financial problems, or family conflicts. Repeated unsuccessful attempts to quit drinking alcohol or using drugs signifies alcohol or drug dependence rather than "problem use." Dependent patients usually need a formal rehabilitation program to help them abstain from drugs and alcohol.

Physical Examination. Many "classic" physical findings of alcohol and other drug problems only become evident later in the disease. More subtle early physical findings are listed in Table 2. For example, mild withdrawal can cause elevated blood pressure, tachycardia, and mild tremor. When patients binge drink, fatty deposits cause the liver to swell and be painful on palpation. Men may try to mask their alcohol use by using too much after shave lotion or mouth wash. Women may use too much perfume or makeup to cover obvious signs of alcohol misuse. The smell of alcohol on a patient's breath is very suggestions of alcohol problems. Hypertensive patients who drink alcohol frequently have wide fluctuations in their blood pressure readings. Alcohol withdrawal elevates the blood pressure, while intoxication may cause falsely low readings.

Laboratory Evaluation. There are no specific laboratory tests that confirm the diagnosis of alcohol or other drug problems. However, there are a number of laboratory tests that can help the clinician evaluate patients for potential alcohol or other drug problems; these are described in Chapter 2.

Blood alcohol levels and urine drug screens can be used to assess patients for possible alcohol and other drug problems; for example, a drug screen may be useful in evaluating an adolescent with school problems. However, these tests are controversial, so it is advisable to obtain the patient's (and/or parent's) permission before initiating such screens; in fact, failure to do so can cause irreparable damage to the physician-patient relationship. Blood and saliva alcohol tests and urine drug screens are critical components of many employee recovery programs (see Section 17).

Assessing the Severity of the Disease. Prior to formulating any treatment plan, physicians routinely assess the severity of the individual patient's disease state. "Staging the disease" is used in hypertension, diabetes, and colon cancer, and certainly is necessary in drug/alcohol dependence. When effective screening tools are used (as outlined above), patients can be identified while their alcohol or other drug problem is marked by moderate to severe psychosocial morbidity and mild to nonexistent physiologic dependence and organ damage.

Clinically, it is helpful to assess the extent of the patient's alcohol or drug dependence within the general domains of physiologic dependence, organ system damage, and psychosocial morbidity (Table 3). This approach provides for a mild, moderate, or severe categorization of disease in each of the aforementioned domains. Stratifying alcohol or other drug problems in this way becomes useful when negotiating a treatment plan with patients across the continuum of readiness for behavior change and severity of disease.

Many other instruments are available for such assessments; see Chapter 3, "Assessment Instruments," for a complete discussion.

INTERVENTION

Once the assessment is complete, the patient should be given specific advice. Many physicians feel that presenting the diagnosis of alcohol or other drug problems or dependence is one of their most uncomfortable and difficult clinical tasks. Their discomfort

TABLE 3. Assessing Levels of Disease Severity

Domains ➧ ➧ Levels	Physiologic Dependence	Organ System Damage	Psychosocial Morbidity
Mild	One or more of the following: ■ Inability to stop ■ Insomnia ■ Irritability ■ Anxiety AUDIT (Quetions 1–3) combined score >5: ■ Frequency (1) ■ Average # of drinks (2) ■ Six or more drinks (3)	One of the following: ■ High normal GGT ■ Memory loss ■ Physical injury ■ Bloodshot eyes ■ Depression ■ Sexual dysfunction ■ High blood pressure ■ Gastritis/ulcers ■ Headaches ■ Osteoporosis	One of the following: CAGE: ■ Cut down (C) ■ Annoyed (A) ■ Guilty (G) AUDIT: ■ Failed expectations (5) ■ Remorse (7) ■ Memory loss (8) ■ Injured self or others (9) ■ Concern expressed by others (10)
Moderate	Any of the above mild symptoms with one or more of the following: ■ Hand tremor ■ "Eye opener" ■ Diaphoresis ■ BAL ≥100 ■ Positive urine toxicology	Two or three of the following: ■ Elevated GGT ■ Memory loss ■ Injury/broken bones ■ Elevated MCV ■ Elevated liver function profile ■ Depression ■ Sexual dysfunction ■ High blood pressure ■ Gastritis/ulcers ■ Headaches ■ Osteoporosis	Two of the following: CAGE: ■ Cut down (C) ■ Annoyed (A) ■ Guilty (G) AUDIT: ■ Failed expectations (5) ■ Remorse (7) ■ Memory loss (8) ■ Injured self or others (9) ■ Concern expressed by others (10)
Severe	Any of the above mild or moderate symptoms with one or more of the following: ■ Hallucinations ■ Seizures ■ DTs ■ BAL >200 ■ Prolonged positive toxicology	Four or more of the following: ■ Elevated GGT ■ Memory loss ■ Injury/broken bones ■ Elevated MCV ■ Elevated liver function profile ■ Depression ■ Sexual dysfunction ■ High blood pressure ■ Gastritis/ulcers ■ Headaches ■ Osteoporosis ■ Hepatomegaly ■ Elevated prothromain time	Positive on three or more of the following: CAGE: ■ Cut down (C) ■ Annoyed (A) ■ Guilty (G) AUDIT: ■ Failed expectations (5) ■ Remorse (7) ■ Memory loss (8) ■ Injured self or others (9) ■ Concern expressed by others (10)

Source: National Institute on Alcohol Abuse and Alcoholism (NIAAA) (1995). *The Physician's Guide to Helping Patients with Alcohol Problems* (NIH Publication No. 95-3769). Rockville, MD: The Institute.

often is caused by lack of knowledge, previous negative experiences, and a lack of appropriate skills. The following guidelines are offered to help physicians overcome these obstacles.

Nonproblem Use: If the patient does not drink or is within the low-risk consumption limits, the physician should provide prevention messages that support the patient's continued positive lifestyle choices. Patients with a positive family history of alcohol or other drug problems should be counseled about their increased risk of developing problems and their need for continued diligence. Patients who are not at risk can be given information about safe limits for alcohol use. In subsequent office visits, they should be screened periodically to verify that they have not developed problems with alcohol or drugs, especially if they have a positive family history.

Problem Drinking/Drug Use: The patient who is not alcohol- or drug-dependent but who is a problem drinker should be encouraged to abstain or cut down on his/her alcohol use. All patients should be strongly encouraged to abstain from all illicit drugs. The physician should articulate the medical concerns, being specific about the patient's alcohol use and the related medical issues. Such patients should be encouraged to verbalize their concerns about their alcohol or other drug use. The goal is for the patient to assume responsibility for deciding on a personal plan, while pursuing abstinence as a goal. If a patient does not wish to abstain, he/she should be asked to agree to a specific limit for alcohol use that is within the "safe" drinking guidelines. The physician should provide such a patient with educational information about low-risk drinking (the National Institute on Alcohol Abuse and Alcoholism publishes an excellent patient handout which helps patients cut down on their drinking and suggests keeping a diary of their progress; NIAAA, 1996). When a physician recommends limits on alcohol consumption, it is essential that the patient be monitored regularly to assess his or her ability to follow the recommended limits.

For the patient who drinks in the "at risk" range but does not meet the criteria for "alcohol abuse" or "alcohol dependence," the clinician should consider making a "problem statement" of "at risk drinking" in the patient's chart, thereby identifying the issue for future reference.

Alcohol/Drug Dependence: When the physician suspects that a patient is alcohol- or drug-dependent, the diagnosis must be presented to the patient (brief intervention). In doing so, the physician is well-advised to follow specific guidelines in order to avoid common pitfalls, to be supportive and caring with the patient, to assess the patient's willingness to change, to determine the severity of the disease, and to negotiate a treatment plan.

Brief Intervention. A brief intervention is a physician/patient interaction, where the diagnosis of alcohol or drug dependence is clearly and concisely presented. This should be accompanied by a recommendation for abstinence and an offer to provide ongoing support. It is very clear from several studies representing community, hospital, and ambulatory settings that brief intervention alone decreases morbidity and mortality at one- and five-year follow-up intervals (Bien, Miller & Tongan, 1993; Buchsbaum, 1994; Fleming, Barry et al., 1997). These data should motivate physicians to adopt a more positive approach to patients with alcohol or drug problems.

TABLE 4. Pitfalls to Avoid When Presenting the Diagnosis: The DEATH Glossary

D: Drinking or drug use details are not relevant; talking with a drunk is not useful. When the diagnosis is presented, patients often launch into long explanations of why their dysfunctional drinking or drug use is really not dysfunctional. It is important to interrupt these discussions and move on. When patients have been actively drinking, they are not able to process much and are emotionally labile. Therefore, the physician's message should be very brief and simple, such as "I am concerned about your drinking and/or drug use; let's schedule a time to talk about it. Please do not drink before that visit, because our time together is too important to have to talk through any alcohol."

E: Etiology. Often patients will insist on an explanation for their addiction (i.e., stress, upbringing, depression, socioeconomic or cultural causes, etc.). However, just as in presenting a diagnosis of hypertension, make the diagnosis and treat the condition, rather than speculating about the cause of the disease.

A: Arguments. Neither the physician nor the patient can hear anything when arguing, and it weakens the therapeutic relationship. It is much better to diffuse arguments with sympathy, respect and support.

T: Threats, guilt and shame do not promote recovery from chemical dependence. If they did, this disease would provide its own cure! It is clear that threats, guilt and shame are rather toxic to the physician/patient relationship.

H: Hedging hurts your credibility. Be clear, concise and to the point. "Agreeing to disagree" with a patient who is precontemplative is much more therapeutic than appearing to be uncertain about and uncomfortable with making and presenting the diagnosis.

Presenting the Diagnosis: In the past, much of the emphasis in presenting the diagnosis centered on the theory that the clinician must confront the patient, overcome the patient's denial, and motivate the patient toward treatment. Too often, this approach has led to arguments, harsh words and, on occasion, the abrupt end of an otherwise therapeutic relationship. Although crisis interventions certainly can be useful in inducing otherwise unwilling patients into treatment, such interventions are neither necessary for most patients nor easy to accomplish in many clinical settings. Use of shame, guilt, threats, confrontation, arguments, and arbitrary treatment plans usually fails to motivate patients and thus should be avoided (Table 4).

In presenting a diagnosis, the SOAPE mnemonic (Support, Optimism, Absolution, Plan, and Explanation) described in Table 5 (Clark, 1981) provides useful guidance. The physician who demonstrates support and optimism about the patient's chances of resolving his or her dependence and its attendant problems increases the likelihood that the patient will cooperate in developing an appropriate treatment plan. It may be helpful for the clinician to copy the SOAPE and DEATH mnemonics (Tables 4 and 5) on a small card and refer to them when preparing to present a diagnosis of alcohol or drug dependence.

Another approach is to use the "Eight Basic Actions" outlined by Whitfield and Barker (1988), who recommend that in one or two sentences, the physician: (1) state the specific diagnosis, (2) say that it is a disease, (3) affirm that it is not the patient's fault, (4) state that it is the patient's responsibility, (5) encourage abstinence, (6) suggest a treatment plan, (7) offer to meet with a family member or supportive friend, and (8) suggest a return visit. Although perhaps not an optimal intervention, merely making these statements in a matter-of-fact, non-judgmental way is of significant therapeutic value.

Assessing the Patient's Readiness to Change. One of the most important new concepts in caring for alcohol- or drug-dependent patients is the issue of assessing the patient's readiness to change his or her behavior. The most widely used model of readiness for behavior change was first articulated by Prochaska and DiClemente (1983) while they were studying smoking cessation. This approach places the initial and often primary emphasis on the patient's willingness to begin to change his or her life, rather than emphasizing the physician's ability to design a treatment plan. In addition to the diagnostic criteria and the severity of the disease, the readiness to change concept introduces the patient's perceptions into the process of forming a treatment plan. Prochaska and DiClemente's model hypothesizes that every patient is at one of six stages of readiness for change with regard to any problem behavior: (1) precontemplation, (2) contemplation, (3) determination/preparation, (4) action, (5) maintenance, or (6) relapse.

A patient who is in the *precontemplation phase* generally does not realize that a problem even exists and thus is not ready to take urgent steps toward its

TABLE 5. Guidelines for Presenting the Diagnosis: The SOAPE Glossary

S: Support. Use phrases such as "we need to work together on this," "I am concerned about you and will follow up closely with you," and "as with all medical illnesses, the more people you work with, the better you will feel." These words reinforce your physician/patient relationship, strengthen the collaborative model of chronic illness management, and help convince the patient that the physician will not just present the diagnosis and leave.

O: Optimism. Most patients have "cut back" on their drinking or drug use several times, quit at times, and perhaps participated in some treatment. They begin to expect failure and relapse, and fear that they never will improve. By voicing a strong, ultimately optimistic message, the physician can help to re-motivate the patient. Use phrases such as, "you will get better," "no one deserves the pain and humiliation of this disease," "treatment works," "you can expect noticeable improvements in most areas of your life," and "with help, you will do well."

A: Absolution. Patients with addictive disorders usually blame themselves and their moral flaws for their addiction. This pervasive sense of guilt, shame, and personal weakness tends to paralyze patients, lessening their ability to consider making life changes and thus perpetuating the addiction cycle. One of the most important things a physician can do it to convince the patient that this is a disease, it is no one's fault, it is the physician's and patient's responsibility to work together toward recovery, and recovery is likely.

P: Plan. Forming a treatment plan is primarily dependent on the patient's readiness for behavior change and the availability of resources. Use phrases such as, "there are many things we can pursue to help you recover," "I want you to seriously consider abstinence as an important aspect in your improvement," "building on what you have tried before is a good place to start," and "what do you think you can do at this point?"

E: Explanatory Model. As in all areas of medical practice, it is important to know what your patient believes regarding his or her illness. Meeting the patient at his or her belief and helping the patient to consider a more therapeutic model is quite important when presenting any diagnosis. Use phrases such as "what is your idea of a person with alcohol or drug problems?," "your illness is not nearly that advanced," "this is an illness that responds to medical intervention and treatment, not a moral weakness," "you have been trying to use willpower by itself to treat a disease; how about adding some treatment to your considerable willpower?"

resolution. Expecting such a patient to accept a referral to AA after one office visit is unrealistic and can set up both the patient and the physician for disappointment. In dealing with such a patient, "agreeing to disagree" about the presence of a drinking problem and following up at a future date is a reasonable course of action.

The patient who is in the *contemplation phase* generally is aware of a problem in his or her life and may be willing to entertain the possibility that such a problem is related to alcohol or drugs. He or she often is willing to discuss the dysfunction caused by substance use. Such a patient usually is willing to discuss treatment options, and is more likely to keep follow-up appointments or to accept referrals for outside opinions than the patient in the precontemplation phase. He or she should be encouraged to develop an action plan.

A patient in the *action phase* is very open to abstinence messages and is more likely to follow through with treatment recommendations than a patient at the earlier phases, especially if those recommendations are the result of a negotiation between the physician and the patient.

Maintenance is the so-called "relapse prevention" phase in which the focus is on maintenance of a behavior change. A patient in this phase still requires intermittent office monitoring, toxicology testing, pharmacotherapy, and ongoing assessment of his or her recovery program.

A patient in *relapse* usually fails to keep appointments and refuses toxicology testing. The patient's feelings of disappointment and shame can present as anger, sarcasm, or even suicidal ideation. Early identification of the risk of relapse and active outreach to the patient at risk is extremely important to restoring the patient's commitment to behavior change. (This is in direct contrast to the traditional clinical practice, in which patients who miss appointments are routinely dropped from the treatment program.)

Assessing the patient's readiness to change allows the physician to negotiate an appropriate patient-centered treatment plans. It also enhances patient compliance, maintains the physician-patient relationship, and reduces staff frustration. It helps physicians with their time management skills, since the patient's stage of readiness is used to set realistic goals for each visit.

Presenting the Diagnosis. Studies suggest that up to 70% of patients with drug and alcohol problems are in either the precontemplation or contemplation stage when initially approached with a diagnosis. Historically, clinicians either have retreated from the diagnosis or adopted a confrontational or authoritarian style if the patient initially resists or disagrees with such a diagnosis. Arguing with the patient and demanding a commitment to behavior change at a time when the patient has not yet recognized the problem or made a self-diagnosis can only weaken the therapeutic relationship and undermine the chance for long-term success. On the other hand, minimizing the importance of the diagnosis by backing off provides the wrong message and reinforces the patient's denial that the disease is a significant factor in his or her life.

The optimal approach to a patient with any type of chronic disease, and particularly alcohol or drug dependence, is to initiate a dialogue and continue it over time to assess the patient's stage of readiness for behavior change. Most patients move from precontemplation to action. At times, some regress through relapse back to precontemplation. Only by maintaining a continuing dialogue about the patient's alcohol and drug dependence can the clinician accurately assess the patient's progress and provide support for positive change.

A large body of clinical research indicates that matching different interventions and frequency of follow-up visits to the patient's actual stage of readiness (the Longitudinal Brief Intervention) leads to decreased morbidity and mortality and improved physician/patient relationships.

Presenting the diagnosis is a discrete independent therapeutic intervention, separate from screening, diagnosis, and forming a treatment plan. Thus, it deserves a discrete office visit and negotiated follow-up to develop an individualized treatment plan.

Negotiating a Treatment Plan. In earlier approaches to patient care, the role of the physician was overemphasized (i.e., the physician formulated the treatment plan, prescribed medications and recommended behavior change, while the patient merely complied with the physician's directives and directions). This physician-centered model of practice was characterized by general noncompliance on the part of patients, with the treatment of alcohol and drug problems no exception.

By contrast, the "negotiated model" for developing a treatment plan shifts the emphasis to include patient participation in the process, leading to much higher levels of patient compliance and satisfaction. The negotiated treatment plan model is applicable to many chronic illnesses in primary care, and is essential when formulating treatment plans with alcohol- and drug-dependent patients. When used appropriately, this patient-centered approach results in treatment plans that are less time-consuming, simpler, more manageable, and more apt to achieve patient compliance.

Prognostic Factors That Influence Patient Outcomes: Several general prognostic indicators are worth evaluating to guide treatment planning and help establish realistic expectations. Positive prognostic factors often indicate either a less severe form or a less advanced stage of alcohol and drug dependence (see Table 3). Such positive factors include the absence of physiologic dependence, an intact family/work life, the presence of a small number of prior treatment episodes (prognosis for sobriety improves if patients have had one to three prior treatment experiences), the absence of other psychiatric diagnoses, and the presence of a long-term monitoring arrangement (e.g., such as that provided by an Employee Assistance Program or a state medical society Physician Effectiveness Program).

Negative prognostic factors point to more severe, advanced, or complicated disease states. They include the presence of intoxication at office visits; loss of job, home or family; a history of multiple unsuccessful treatment attempts; severe physiologic dependence (as marked by a history of convulsions or *delirium tremens*); concomitant psychiatric diagnoses (e.g., schizophrenia, severe post-traumatic stress disorder, or severe depression); and the absence of long-term monitoring.

Engaging Readiness to Change: In negotiating a treatment plan, the severity of the disease and the patient's current state of readiness for change are of primary importance. The relationship between disease stage and the patient's state of readiness, as illustrated in Table 6, provides the framework for developing an individualized treatment plan.

If the patient is *precontemplative* and the severity of the problem is fairly mild, the urgency to intervene beyond an intermittent brief intervention is quite low. Urging such a patient to accept treatment when he or she is not ready to do so threatens the physician-patient relationship and probably is not indicated. If possible, the patient's family members should be encouraged to learn more about alcohol and other drug dependence (either through various readings, family counseling, or participation in Al-Anon). If the problem is moderate in severity, there is more urgency to assess the disease and the patient's readiness to change. Such a patient might be referred to an addiction specialist, presented with medical reasons for not drinking and, if possible, referred for family counseling. If the patient is precontemplative and the problem is severe, a brief intervention should be performed at each visit. Such a patient should be referred to an addiction specialist and given strong medical reasons not to continue his or her drinking or drug use. A crisis intervention should be considered (see below).

If the patient is *contemplative* and the problem is mild, the severity should be assessed frequently (every three to six months), and evidence of dysfunction and disability presented at least yearly. The patient should be encouraged to limit his or her drinking (i.e., move to the action stage) or to abstain. Consideration should be given to referring the family for more education about alcohol and drug dependence. If the disease severity is moderate, evidence of dysfunction and medical reasons not to drink should be reemphasized at least twice a year. The physician should attempt to negotiate an agreement for the patient to be referred to an addiction specialist and the family referred for more education. If the patient is contemplative and the disease is severe, evidence of dysfunction and medical complications should be presented at every visit. A primary care physician should insist on a referral to an addiction specialist, and the family should be referred for more education and crisis intervention, if possible.

Even when patients affirm their willingness to undertake abstinence, it is critical to determine whether they are capable of achieving abstinence. To do so, the physician might negotiate a small change in activities and behaviors, then see the patient for follow-up visits to assess his or her readiness and ability to make changes. Pharmacotherapy is an excellent means to accurately assess "true" readiness.

Helping a Patient Who Is Ready to Change: The following questions provide a useful outline in negotiating a treatment plan with a patient who is ready for change. If possible, answers should be confirmed through interviews with family members and other key informants.

- Is the patient a danger to himself or others? (Suicide and vehicular homicide are serious consequences of alcohol and other drug dependence. Questions about suicidal ideation, impaired judgment while intoxicated, and delirium thus are mandatory when assessing a patient.)
- Has the patient ever been able to stay sober for three or more days? (This question assesses the patient's ability to "self-detoxify.")
- What happened in the past when the patient stopped drinking or using? How serious was the patient's withdrawal syndrome?
- Has the patient ever been able to maintain total abstinence for a long period of time? (Learning

TABLE 6. The Longitudinal Brief Intervention

	Patient Stage	Physician Intervention	Frequency of Follow-up
Precontemplation	No conception of a problem and no plans to change.	Agree to disagree about presence of chemical dependence. Briefly bring up your concern periodically in future. Reassess for a change in readiness.	Follow-up visits as needed for other primary care problems or health maintenance.
Contemplation	Perception that there probably is a problem but ambivalent about change.	Present evidence of dysfunction and disability from the screening and assessment questionnaires, as well as the laboratory and toxicology testing. Be sure to use SOAPE in order to avoid a confrontation.	Schedule follow-up visits to specifically discuss chemical dependence every 3–4 months. Offer a family interview.
Determination	Awareness that a problem definitely exists and something must be done about it.	Problem solve with patient about what forms of action she/he might take. Module 4 can be helpful to negotiate a treatment plan.	Frequent visits, perhaps every 2–4 weeks for a month or more.
Action	Ready for the initiation of behavior change.	Provide strong encouragement and support; assist with referral as needed; encourage family participation; consider pharmacotherapy; collaborate and consult with treatment program staff.	Weekly to every other week.
Maintenance	Incorporation of behavior change into daily routine.	Encourage success; discuss difficulties and problems; encourage compliance with out-patient counseling (aftercare and self-help meetings); reassess pharmacotherapy; monitor for relapse signs; routine toxicology testing; and GGT testing if indicated.	Initially monthly, then decreasing in frequency as appropriate.
Relapse	Reversion back to contemplation or precontemplation with continued substance abuse.	Voice continued optimism; encourage return to determination, action, and maintenance; aid continued treatment and recovery attempts by patient or family members.	Frequently at first, then plan according to the new stage of patient readiness.

what has proved useful in the past and what the patient thinks can be added now is one of the most efficient and effective initial approaches to treatment planning.)

- Why did previous attempts fail to produce sobriety? (Factors that contributed to treatment failures should be identified and addressed.)

Evaluating Treatment Options. Selecting an appropriate treatment program can be difficult. The keys to identifying high-quality treatment programs are similar to the ways in which generalists find specialists for any type of referral. Treatment programs need to be available and affordable to the patient and family. Good treatment programs communicate with the referring physician, coordinate on issues of toxicology testing and laboratory work, are open-minded regarding adjunctive pharmacotherapies, include family members in treatment, and insist on abstinence (Rogers & McMillan, 1992).

If inpatient or outpatient treatment are not options for the patient, Twelve Step support groups can

TABLE 7. Negotiating a Treatment Plan

State ➧ / ➥ Levels*	Precontemplative (30% of patients)	Contemplative (40% of patients)	Ready for Action (30% of patients)	Relapse
Mild	■ Assess disease severity every 6–12 months ■ Periodically perform a brief intervention using SOAPE ■ Consider family referral	■ Assess disease severity every 3–6 months ■ Present evidence of dysfunction and disability using SOAPE* at least once a year ■ Consider family referral	■ Reinstitute what has proved to be successful in the past ■ Form a menu of other treatment options, including counseling, self-help, family/community support, pharmacotherapy ■ Suggest family involvement ■ Very close monitoring and follow-up (weekly phone contact and at least twice a month office visit)	■ Assess magnitude (slip vs binge vs full relapse) ■ Rule out suicidal ideation ■ Encourage return to readiness for action ■ Evaluate for presence of typical relapse patterns ■ Modify prior treatment plan using menu of treatment options ■ Encourage consideration of pharmacotherapy
Moderate	■ Assess disease severity at least every 6 months ■ Periodically perform a brief intervention using SOAPE* ■ Consider referral to an addiction specialist ■ Appeal to medical reasons for not drinking ■ Attempt family referral for more education	■ Assess disease severity and strongly present and reemphasize evidence of dysfunction and disability using SOAPE at least twice a year ■ Negotiate agreement for referral to an addiction specialist ■ Attempt family referral for more education	■ Reinstitute what has proved to be successful in the past ■ Form a menu of other treatment options as above ■ Negotiate additional options that the patient will utilize ■ Strongly suggest family involvement ■ Very close monitoring and follow-up as above ■ Encourage consideration of pharmacotherapy	■ Assess magnitude (slip vs binge vs full relapse) ■ Rule out suicidal ideation ■ Encourage return to readiness for action ■ Evaluate for presence of typical relapse patterns ■ Suggest specific additional treatment options including observed administration pharmacotherapy ■ Attempt closer monitoring system ■ Organize family involvement
Severe	■ Assess disease severity and perform a brief intervention using SOAPE* at each visit ■ Refer to addiction specialist ■ Strongly emphasize medical reasons for not drinking ■ Family referral for more education required ■ Crisis intervention is often essential, best if physician participates	■ Assess disease severity and strongly present and reemphasize evidence of dysfunction and disability using SOAPE* at each visit ■ Refer to addiction specialist ■ Family referral for more education required ■ Crisis intervention is often essential, best if physician participates	■ Detoxification if indicated ■ Reinstitute what has proved to be successful in the past ■ Form treatment option menu ■ Strongly encourage more intense levels of treatment ■ Strongly suggest family involvement ■ Very close monitoring and follow-up as above ■ Strongly encourage observed administration pharmacotherapy	■ Assess magnitude (slip vs binge vs full relapse) ■ Rule out suicidal ideation ■ Evaluate for presence of typical relapse patterns ■ Arrange for more intense levels of treatment ■ Initiate observed administration pharmocotherapy ■ Implement closer monitoring ■ If patient does not return to readiness for action, strongly solicit family support for crisis intervention

*If a change in stage of readiness or level of severity is indicated—go to the appropriate stage/level section of the table.

be recommended as sources of support in helping the patient maintain abstinence from alcohol or drugs (see Section 9). It also may be necessary to detoxify the patient on an outpatient basis (see Section 6).

Guidance in evaluating treatment options is found in the ASAM *Patient Placement Criteria for the Treatment of Substance-Related Disorders, Second Edition* (Mee-Lee, Shulman & Gartner, 1996; see Appendix B for a summary).

Family Referral Resources. Family members frequently have misconceptions about alcohol and drug dependence. It is critically important to assess the family's belief systems and to educate family members toward a more therapeutic approach to this disease.

Resources available include an excellent book entitled "Freeing Someone You Love from Alcohol" (Rogers & McMillan, 1992). After family members have read this or similar books, they are more likely to agree to referral for individual counseling or family therapy. Finally, self-help organizations available to family members include Al-Anon, Alateen, Tough Love, and Families Anonymous. Family members will be much more likely to accept referral to self-help meetings if they have read about the programs and have had a chronic illness concept presented to them by the primary care physician.

In summary, negotiating a treatment program can be rather simple and straightforward if several principles are kept in mind, and there is an accurate assessment of the severity of the disease and the patient's readiness for behavior change. For patients who are willing to consider making changes, the important issues to assess are what treatment options exist, which treatment options are most appropriate for the particular patient, and what treatment options are acceptable to the patient. Answering these questions can result in the development of a surprisingly comprehensive treatment plan. Of equal importance, this plan can be efficiently implemented and managed over time in the primary care setting.

Negotiating a treatment plan is a discrete, independent clinical skill that deserves a separate visit or visits, and should not be appended onto a visit in which the diagnosis is presented. If the patient is not ready to acknowledge a problem, then "agreeing to disagree" is an acceptable option. Frequent follow-up visits, during which the physician expresses ongoing concern about the patient's alcohol or other drug problem, is an acceptable "treatment plan" when working with a precontemplative patient.

Crisis Intervention. Crisis intervention is worth mentioning for several reasons, even though it is beyond the expertise of the generalist. First, over the past three decades, it has become regarded as a potentially successful approach to involving resistant patients in treatment for alcohol or drug dependence. Second, primary care physicians are periodically asked to participate in interventions. Finally, and most importantly, it is a major "invasive procedure" often used to initiate treatment, especially when the patient has severe disease and is in the precontemplation stage. A crisis intervention is a group confrontation with the alcohol- or drug-dependent person. It must be carefully organized, rehearsed, and choreographed by a trained "intervention counselor." Each member of the group should be a significant person in the patient's life, and be prepared to relate several experiences in which the patient's drinking or drug use adversely affected him or her. The weight of all this objective evidence, presented in an orderly way by friends and family members, often overcomes the "wall of denial" erected by many patients, to a degree that the patient can be induced to enter a treatment program. Phrases and techniques that are coached by the intervention counselor include the following: "It's not you, it is the drinking." "It hurts me too much to see you continue in this painful disease." "You did not develop this on purpose, but you've got it." "We care about you, but hate your drinking." "I will not argue; this is what you did, this is when you did it, and this is how it made me feel." This approach is characterized by statements that affirm: (1) positive regard for the individual but rejection of the drinking or drug use, (2) use of specific data about actual events to demonstrate real consequences of the patient's alcohol or drug use, and (3) reinforcing the disease concept through statements about the obvious pain of this progressive illness. This approach allows the patient to relieve his or her guilt, become less defensive and thus more open to getting help with the "disease."

MONITORING AND FOLLOW-UP CARE

Patients should be monitored carefully following brief interventions to assure that they are able to follow the physician's recommendations. Initially, this may require weekly follow-up visits. Seeing the patient regularly gives several "unspoken messages," emphasizing the physician's ongoing concern and availability.

At each visit, the physician should review the patient's progress and give positive reinforcement if the patient has been able to maintain the suggested limits. If there is concern that the patient is not following recommendations, a family member might be asked to verify the patient's history. Biochemical markers such as GGT, CDT, blood or saliva alcohol levels or urine drug screens also might be used to assess patient compliance.

If a patient is not able to follow the recommended limits, the physician should consider referring him or her to an addiction medicine specialist or a formal rehabilitation program. Patients are more willing to follow recommendations if they have proved to themselves that they cannot control their alcohol or other drug use.

It is equally important for the physician to support and monitor the patient who is abstaining from alcohol or drug use. Alcohol- or drug-dependent patients who have entered a formal treatment program should be asked to sign a medical release so that the physician can participate in their aftercare plan. In addition to seeing the patient regularly, the physician should list alcohol or other drug dependence on the problem list in the patient's chart; the patient's "clean and sober" date also might be noted in the chart to remind the physician to provide positive reinforcement and support on recovery anniversaries (usually at one, three, six and nine months and then each year thereafter). This is another way to let the patient know that the physician cares about his or her recovery and supports the patient's continued commitment to recovery. (See Section 17, Chapter 1 for further suggestions on supporting patients in recovery.)

Problems in Recovery: A number of problems are widely encountered by patients early in the recovery process. Depression is common and usually clears without treatment in the first few months. Severe depression, on the other hand, or a history of prior episodes of depression may indicate the need for an antidepressant to reduce the risk of a relapse. Many patients experience sexual dysfunction early in recovery. By raising the issue, the physician can reassure the patient that this a common problem that will resolve with time.

Certain prescription drugs can jeopardize a recovering patient's ability to abstain from alcohol and other illicit drugs. Specifically, benzodiazepines and narcotics should be avoided, since both groups of drugs have abuse potential. Nonpharmacological treatments should be used whenever possible.

In some patients, drug and alcohol body fluid monitoring may be helpful in enhancing motivation. Medications such as naltrexone and disulfiram may be helpful in early recovery (see Section 7). If a patient is attending AA meetings, the physician may need to advise him or her not to let AA members discourage the use of necessary medications; this is particularly true of patients with a co-occurring psychiatric disorder. Although AA's official position is that groups should not interfere with members' medications, some AA members, acting on their own, may urge that all medications be discontinued.

Patients should be monitored for signs of potential relapse (see Section 8). It is possible to anticipate a relapse based on the patient's behavior and then to counsel him or her so as to minimize the risk of relapse and/or to facilitate reentry into treatment.

Physicians often become frustrated with patients who do not want to address their alcohol and other drug problems. It is important to remember that these are chronic disorders, which present an opportunity to work with the patient over time. The physician can continue to reaffirm his or her concern and willingness to help.

Two common dangers are ignoring the problem and "preaching." Both techniques limit the physician's ability to help the patient. An attitude of caring concern is more likely to prevail over the long term. Even if a patient is unwilling to accept help with his or her alcohol or other drug problem, the physician still can help family members by referring them to programs such as Alanon and Alateen.

REFERENCES

Beresford TP, Blow FC, Hill E, Singer K & Lucey MR (1990). Comparison of CAGE questionnaire and computer-assisted laboratory profiles in screening for covert alcoholism. *Lancet* 336:482–485.

Bien TH, Miller WR & Tongan JS (1993). Brief intervention for alcohol problems: A review. *Addiction* 88:315–336.

Bradley KA (1994). The primary care practitioner's role in the prevention and management of alcohol problems. *Alcohol Health & Research World* 18:97–104.

Buchsbaum D (1994). Effectiveness of treatment in general medicine patients with drinking problems. *Alcohol Health & Research World* 18(2):140–145.

Clark WD (1981). Alcoholism: Blocks to diagnosis and treatment. *American Journal of Medicine* 71:285–86.

Cyr MG & Wartman SA (1988). The effectiveness of routine screening questions in the detection of alcoholism. *Journal of the American Medical Society* 259:51–54.

Fleming MF, Barry KL, Manwell LB, Johnson K & London R (1997). Brief physician advice for problem alcohol drinkers. *Journal of the American Medical Association* 277(13):1039–1045.

Mayfield D, McLeod G & Hall P (1971). The CAGE questionnaire: Validation of a new alcoholism screening instrument. *American Journal of Psychiatry* 127:1121–1123.

National Institute on Alcohol Abuse and Alcoholism (NIAAA) (1996). *How to Cut Down on Your Drinking.* Rockville, MD: The Institute.

National Institute on Alcohol Abuse and Alcoholism (NIAAA) (1995). *The Physicians' Guide to Helping Patients with Alcohol Problems* (NIH Publication No. 95-3769). Rockville, MD: The Institute.

Prochaska JO & DiClemente CC (1983). Stages and processes of self-change in smoking: Toward an integrative model of change. *Journal of Consulting and Clinical Psychology* 5:390–95.

Rogers RL & McMillin CS (1992). Choosing a treatment program. In *Freeing Someone You Love From Alcohol.* New York, NY: The Body Press.

Rush BR (1989). The use of family medical practices by patients with drinking problems. *Canadian Medical Association Journal* 140(1):35–38.

Steinweg DL & Worth H (1993). Alcoholism: The key to the CAGE. *American Journal of Medicine* 94:520–23.

Whitfield CL & Barker LR (1995). Alcoholism. In LR Barker, JR Burton & PD Zieve (eds.) *Principles of Ambulatory Medicine.* Baltimore, MD: Williams & Wilkins, 204–231.

Williams GD, Aitken SS & Malin H (1985). Reliability of self-reported alcohol consumption in a general population survey. *Journal of Studies on Alcohol* 46(3):223–227.

CHAPTER 2

Screening Instruments and Biochemical Screening Tests

John P. Allen, Ph.D.
Raye Z. Litten, Ph.D.

Self-Report Screening Instruments
Selecting a Screening Instrument
Screens for Collateral Psychopathology
Biochemical Screening Tests
Tests to Determine the Need for Withdrawal Medication

Initiation of effective alcoholism treatment requires that six sequential questions be accurately answered: (1) Does the patient suffer a problem with alcohol? (2) If so, is the problem one of abuse or of dependence? (3) If dependence, what is the severity? (4) Are other psychiatric problems present? (5) Would medication facilitate alcohol withdrawal? (6) Are there associated medical problems?

A variety of psychometric and laboratory tests have been devised to help clinicians resolve these issues. This chapter discusses popular examples of such measures and suggests how clinicians can employ their results in planning the early stages of treatment, particularly in addressing the first four questions. For medical evaluation see Chapter 1; for treatment of withdrawal, see Section 6.

SELF-REPORT SCREENING INSTRUMENTS

Six widely used self-report screening tests are the CAGE, the Alcohol Use Disorders Identification Test (AUDIT), the Self-Administered Alcoholism Screening Test (SAAST), the MacAndrew Alcoholism Scale, the Adolescent Drinking Inventory (ADI), and the Alcohol Dependence Scale (see Appendix B). Although their purposes and applicability differ somewhat, the value of each is supported by considerable research.

CAGE. Consisting of only four items, the CAGE (Mayfield, McLeod & Hall, 1974; Ewing, 1984) clearly is one of the briefest conceivable self-report screening measures. Three of the questions deal with emotional reactions to one's drinking. The other inquires about morning drinking to relieve withdrawal. Using a cut-off score of two affirmative answers, the CAGE demonstrates impressive sensitivity (the percent of true positive test results) and specificity (the percent of true false negatives) for diagnosis of alcoholism in individuals seeking medical or psychiatric services. The CAGE correlates more highly with a formal diagnosis of alcoholism than do the quantity and frequency of drinking, biochemical measures of excessive drinking, or the age of onset of alcohol use (Fertig, Allen & Cross, 1993). Interestingly, CAGE scores also are moderately associated with emotional distress (Moore & Malitz, 1986; Schofield, 1989) and feelings of powerlessness in one's job situation (Markowitz, 1984).

As with any screening test, the positive predictive value of the CAGE is related to the underlying base rate for the population in which the test is used and saliency of the criterion for which screening is performed. Hence, the CAGE may be expected to perform less efficiently as a screening measure in heterogeneous groups (such as general community samples) than in health-care seeking populations within which underlying alcohol dependence is likely substantially more prevalent and clinically distinctive.

SAAST. The SAAST (Swenson & Morse, 1975) is longer than the CAGE yet can still be administered within ten minutes or less. The SAAST is a variant of the Michigan Alcoholism Screening Test (MAST) (Selzer, 1972) but differs from it in three important respects. The SAAST is more comprehensive and assesses symptoms beyond those covered by the MAST. It may be self-administered via personal computer or written format, rather than given orally to the patient (Davis & Morse, 1987a). Finally, each item contributes equally to derivation of the total score, whereas differential weightings for MAST items may well reflect features idiosyncratic to the original normative sample.

The SAAST reflects six dimensions of alcohol-related problems: loss of control, occupational/social disruption, adverse physical consequences, emotional disturbance/requests for help, concerns by others, and family members' problems with drinking (Davis & Morse, 1987a).

At a positivity criterion of 7, the sensitivity of the SAAST has been reported as high as .91 with a specificity of .93. The test appears at least equally valid when administered via computer (Davis & Morse, 1987a).

In a thought-provoking investigation, Morse and Swenson (1975) found that spouses of alcoholics could complete the measure for their partners and do so at approximately the same level of validity, although the alcoholics themselves tended to acknowledge more alcohol-related problems, such as guilt over drinking and blackouts, phenomena less observable to an outside observer (Davis & Morse, 1987b; Loethen & Khavari, 1990).

AUDIT. The AUDIT (Saunders, Aasland et al., 1993) is one of the most recent additions to the armamentarium of alcoholism screening tests. The AUDIT was developed by the World Health Organization as part of a six-nation study on screening and early intervention for alcohol problems. It consists of two sections, a structured questionnaire and brief clinical exam including questions on previous trauma. The verbal portion is generally employed independently, although addition of the clinical exam section may be useful for alcoholics unaware of or unwilling to disclose alcohol-related symptoms. The interview consists of ten questions on alcohol use (frequency of drinking, average consumption, and peak levels of intake), symptoms of alcohol dependence and alcohol-related problems. For most items, patients are asked to respond based on experiences of the past year rather than "ever," thereby diminishing risk that recovering alcoholics or problem drinkers will be misclassified as currently suffering a drinking problem. At a cutoff score of 8, sensitivities in the normative study generally were in the mid-.90s, with specificities mostly in the mid-.70s to mid-.80s for hazardous drinking, intoxication and alcohol dependence. In a recent study with young adults in the U.S., the AUDIT revealed an internal consistency of .80. In this study, the AUDIT demonstrated a sensitivity of .94 and a specificity of .66 in predicting a *DSM-III* diagnosis of alcohol abuse or dependence (Fleming, Barry & MacDonald, 1991).

Unlike the vast majority of alcohol screening instruments, the AUDIT was designed to detect problems even in their early stages and to be used with community samples as well as with patients in primary health care settings. The AUDIT might well be given in the context of a health risk appraisal (Babor, de la Fuente et al., 1989). It also differs from many alternative scales by virtue of its brevity and ease of comprehension. It also may serve as the basis of brief interventions with patients who have early-stage alcohol problems. The AUDIT appears equally appropriate for men and women, various age groups, and differing ethnic populations (Allen et al., manuscript submitted for publication).

MacAndrew Scale. The MacAndrew Scale (Mac) (MacAndrew, 1965) is the oldest and one of the most extensively researched alcoholism screening instruments in common use. The Mac consists of 49 MMPI items that were found to distinguish male alcoholics from male psychiatric patients. The scale was developed solely on the basis of criteria validity for the diagnosis of alcoholism, but MMPI items referring specifically to drinking were not eligible for inclusion.

As a covert content measure, the Mac is less vulnerable to dissimulation (Otto, Lange et al., 1988) than are some other instruments. At a cut-off score of 24, sensitivity and specificity for the Mac are generally reported in the low .80s.

At least 10 studies have attempted to distinguish psychological characteristics of alcoholics accurately identified by the Mac, as compared with the characteristics of alcoholics who were not detected by the test (Allen, 1991). These studies generally suggest that the accuracy of the Mac is a function of its ability to identify a personality stereotype of alcoholics as more behaviorally expressive, impulsive, sociable, and emotionally distressed than non-alcoholics. Obviously, this personality stereotype is not characteristic of all alcoholics; moreover, it appears that individuals who score low on the Mac may represent a distinct and important subtype of alcoholics (Allen, Faden et al., 1990), perhaps resembling the "Type I" alcoholics posited by von Knorring (von Knorring, Bohman et al., 1985; von Knorring, Oreland & von Knorring, 1987) and Cloninger (1987).

A less widely used adolescent version of the Mac, the Substance Abuse Proclivity Scale (Colligan & Offord, 1990), also has been developed.

Adolescent Drinking Inventory. The Adolescent Drinking Inventory (ADI) (Harrell & Wirtz, 1989) is a 24-item screening scale designed specifically for adolescents. The ADI is intended for alcohol problem screening among adolescents referred for behavioral or emotional problems. Items are written at a fifth grade reading level and the scale has been normed on teenagers 12 through 17 years of age. Questions cover four domains of adolescent problem drinking: loss of control, social effects, psychological problems, and physical symptoms. The first ten items ask respondents to rate symptomatic behaviors on the basis of how well each statement describes their own actions. The remaining questions inquire about frequency of alcohol-related problems over the preceding 12 months.

Internal consistency for the ADI has been reported at .96 and test-retest reliability over a two-week period at .78. The sensitivity of the ADI was .88 and the specificity .82 with independent professional assessment as the criterion.

In addition to providing a total score, the ADI can be used to assess two patterns of drinking: aggressive, rebellious drinking behaviors and "self-medicational" use of alcohol as a means of improving mood. Curiously, male adolescents with an alcoholic father or brother have been found to score significantly higher on the former scale than those referred for psychological evaluation. The two groups did not differ on the self-medicational drinking scale (Harrell & Wirtz, 1989).

Alcohol Dependence Scale. In recent years, interest has grown in conceptualizing alcohol dependence as the "core" feature of alcoholism, as distinct from alcohol consequences and drinking behavior itself. The impetus for this conceptualization of an "alcohol dependence syndrome" was a description by Edwards and Gross (1976), which posited that seven elements constitute the core syndrome: (1) increased tolerance, (2) salience of drink-seeking behavior, (3) narrowing of drinking repertoire, (4) selective awareness of compulsion to drink, (5) withdrawal symptoms when not drinking, (6) relief-avoidance of withdrawal symptoms, and (7) reinstatement of drinking after a period of abstinence.

The Alcohol Dependence Scale (ADS) probably is the most popular instrument in the U.S. and Canada designed to measure alcohol dependence. It consists of 25 self-report questions dealing with drinking patterns, physical and emotional reactions to alcohol, and alcohol withdrawal effects occurring over the previous year.

The ADS was standardized on individuals who voluntarily sought treatment for drinking problems (Skinner & Allen, 1982). Beyond determining psychometric properties of the scale, the normative study explored its relationship to patterns of alcohol use, consequences of drinking, and personal characteristics of subjects. Scores on the ADS correlated with daily alcohol intake, adverse effects of drinking, digestive disorders (Svanum, 1986; Hodgins & Lightfoot, 1989; Dyer, Huebert & Jeune, 1992), number of past episodes of treatment, and patient preferences for treatment outcome. Patients who scored higher on the ADS expressed greater interest in abstinence rather than reduced consumption as the appropriate goal of treatment (Hodgins & Lightfoot, 1989). Unfortunately, alcoholics with higher ADS scores were found to be less likely actually to enter treatment.

Subsequent research has shown that individuals with high ADS scores are more apt to be currently receiving inpatient (rather than outpatient) treatment or to have had inpatient treatment in the past (Dyer, Huebert & Jeune, 1992). Although the ADS does not purport to be a screening measure, it seems able to perform this role as well. A recent study showed it equal in accuracy to the MAST in identifying alcoholics (Ross, Gavin & Skinner, 1990).

SELECTING A SCREENING INSTRUMENT

Alcoholism screening tests differ not only in their validity and reliability, but also in their relative ability to detect alcohol problems in varying stages, in their vulnerability to subjects' duplicity, and in their potential to detect alcohol problems in various populations. Accordingly, all of these factors should be considered in selecting a screening test.

The advantages of the CAGE are primarily its brevity and ability to identify clinically diagnosable alcoholics in health-care seeking populations. Its four questions can be readily integrated into the patient history or description of current complaint interview. The CAGE, however, seems to have difficulties in identifying non-dependence alcohol use problems and its validity is related to the patient's awareness of and willingness to disclose alcohol-related problems and the emotional reactions they elicit.

The AUDIT is slightly longer than the CAGE and is more useful for detecting alcohol-related problems in earlier stages. It also may serve as the basis of brief motivational interventions and, hence, may play a significant role in general medical practice.

The SAAST requires about 10 minutes and is thus slightly more time-consuming than the previous two measures. It can be computer-administered or given in a pencil-and-paper format. That spouses can "vicariously" complete the SAAST for their partners is a second strength. Also, the SAAST can produce separate factor scores for use in assessing various dimensions of alcohol problems.

Admittedly, the Mac scale captures a stereotype of alcoholism. To the extent that the stereotype is accurate, the Mac can serve as an effective screen. The covert content of the scale suggests unique applicability with alcoholics who may deny alcohol-related problems. Since the Mac is embedded in the MMPI, which is commonly included in a psychiatric intake process, it may require no additional patient time for individuals seen in such contexts. Particular caution, however, should be observed in using the Mac with adolescents, non-whites, or patients suffering other addictive behaviors (Gottesman & Prescott, 1989).

The ADI was designed specifically to detect possible alcohol problems in distressed teenagers. As such, it has few competitors. Its factor structure also allows it to identify what appear to be clinically-meaningful subtypes of patients.

Although generally lower in sensitivity and specificity than self-report measures, biochemical measures can corroborate the results of verbal measures. Laboratory tests often are included in standard blood series and thus may require no additional patient or clinician time. Results of laboratory tests may be more compelling to the patient and health care provider in underscoring the need for alcoholism treatment than are self-report measures. Surprisingly, this possible treatment motivational advantage appears to have received little research attention.

SCREENS FOR COLLATERAL PSYCHOPATHOLOGY

Clinicians who treat alcohol problems increasingly are concerned that their patients may suffer psychiatric problems beyond those directly related to excessive alcohol use and that such conditions may have implications for choice of intervention for alcoholism. Since alcoholism and acute alcohol withdrawal may mimic a variety of other emotional problems, it is often wisest to refrain from formally diagnosing other psychiatric problems until the patient has been abstinent for a few weeks. At that time, collateral psychopathology may be more accurately evaluated. Granted the significant amount of time required to conduct a thorough diagnostic evaluation for various psychiatric conditions, it is generally most feasible to screen for major emotional problems and then concentrate full diagnostic efforts only on those which seem likely.

The Brief Symptom Inventory (BSI) (Derogatis, 1975) is highly useful in this regard. The BSI is a shortened version of the popular Symptom Check List 90. It consists of 53 items scored on five-point scales. The inventory assesses global psychiatric distress as well as nine primary symptom dimensions: somatization, obsessive compulsiveness, interpersonal sensitivity, depression, anxiety, hostility, phobic anxiety, paranoid ideation, and psychoticism. Internal consistency reliability for symptom subscales ranged from the mid-.70s to the mid-.80s. Test-retest reliabilities for subscales average about .80 and the global severity score revealed a test-retest reliability of about .90. Moderate convergent and divergent validities have been established with MMPI clinical and content scales (Wiggins, 1966).

Over one hundred published studies have been conducted on the BSI, most of which have yielded favorable results. (Several of the BSI validation studies are reviewed by Derogatis [Derogatis, 1992].) Completion of the inventory requires approximately eight to ten minutes.

BIOCHEMICAL SCREENING TESTS

Another strategy for detecting drinking problems involves the use of biochemical tests, including measures of liver function as well as indicators of alcohol's toxic effects on blood and metabolism. These tests usually are relatively inexpensive and almost all clinical laboratories are able to perform them. Unfortunately, the tests that currently are available are not highly sensitive or specific for alcoholism.

Gamma-glutamyl Transpeptidase (GGT). The serum level of the hepatic enzyme gamma-glutamyl transpeptidase (GGT) is the most widely used and one of the most accurate biochemical markers of alcohol consumption. Several mechanisms have been proposed to explain increase in blood levels of GGT associated with heavy alcohol use (Rosman & Lieber, 1990). Chronic alcohol consumption may stimulate liver cells to synthesize GGT. Second, chronic alcohol exposure may damage liver cell membranes, causing GGT to leak into the circulation. Finally, chronic drinking may precipitate actual cell death, thereby resulting in leakage of GGT into circulating blood. With cessation of drinking, serum levels of GGT typically return to normal values in four to six weeks (Rosman & Lieber, 1990; Salaspuro, 1986).

The sensitivity of GGT for hospitalized alcoholics with liver disease generally is higher than that for hospitalized alcoholics without liver disease or alcoholics in ambulatory settings (Cushman, 1992). Serum GGT levels rarely are significantly elevated in young heavy drinkers, thus lowering its sensitivity for adolescents and young adults (Whitfield, Hensley et al., 1978). Questions also have been raised about the sensitivity of GGT in women (Cushman, 1992; Anton & Moak, 1994).

The specificity of GGT is problematic for alcoholics with liver disease (Cushman, 1992). For example, non-alcoholic liver diseases may raise serum GGT levels. So too, several non-alcohol related conditions can elevate serum GGT levels; these include biliary tract disease, diabetes, pancreatitis, hyperthyroidism, heart failure, high carbohydrate diet, obesity, and use of anticonvulsants and anticoagulants (Rosman & Lieber, 1990; Salaspuro, 1986).

Aspartate Aminotransferase (AST) (also termed oxaloacetic transaminase) and Alanine Aminotransferase (ALT) (or glutamic pyruvic transaminase). These substances are hepatic enzymes involved in metabolism of amino acids. Chronic alcohol use can increase blood levels of both enzymes, presumably due to either damaging the membrane of liver cells or causing cellular death, thereby resulting in leakage into the circulation (Rosman & Lieber, 1990). AST and ALT serum levels usually return to normal ranges several weeks after drinking is stopped (Rosman & Lieber, 1990).

Since significant liver damage must occur before AST and ALT serum levels rise substantially, sensitivity of these markers in detecting alcoholism tends to be low (Rosman & Lieber, 1990; Cushman, 1992). Non-alcoholic liver disease also can increase serum levels of both AST and ALT, though differences in the ratio of AST to ALT may help distinguish these two conditions (Salaspuro, 1986). The ratio of AST to ALT appears to be higher in alcoholic liver disease than in non-alcoholic liver disease (Matloff, Selinger & Kaplan, 1980; Diehl, Potter et al., 1984). Muscular disorders and myocardial infarction also elevate serum AST levels (Rosman & Lieber, 1990).

Mean Corpuscular Volume (MCV). Mean corpuscular red cell volume has been used as a marker of heavy alcohol consumption. Increased MCV may reflect direct toxic effects of alcohol on red blood cells, folic acid deficiency, or advanced liver disease (Rosman & Lieber, 1990).

MCV tends to be less sensitive than GGT (Rosman & Lieber, 1990). As with GGT, however, it appears more sensitive with hospitalized alcoholics than with those in ambulatory clinics (Cushman, 1992). Although elevated MCV might be useful in distinguishing heavy from light drinkers, it appears ineffective in identifying moderate drinkers. In addition, MCV values return to normal only very slowly— sometimes months after drinking ceases (Rosman & Lieber, 1990). This lack of responsiveness appears to limit MCV's value as a marker of alcoholism treatment outcome.

Finally, a variety of pathological conditions other than excessive alcohol use can raise MCV values. These include nutritional deficiencies (vitamin B_{12} and folic acid), hypothyroidism, non-alcoholic liver disease, reticulocytosis, and hematological malignancies (Rosman & Lieber, 1990, 1992).

Carbohydrate-deficient Transferrin (CDT). CDT recently has emerged as a new biochemical marker to measure excessive alcohol consumption. Transferrin is a glycoprotein involved in transporting iron to body tissues. Although the mechanism is unclear, carbohydrate content of transferrin, including sialic acid, galactose, and N-acetylglucosamine, tends to be lower in actively drinking alcoholics, thus the term "carbohydrate-deficient transferrin" (Borg, Beck et al., 1992). It has been estimated that 50 to 80 g of alcohol consumption per day (four to seven drinks per day) for at least one week can significantly elevate CDT levels in alcoholics (Stibler, 1991). CDT currently is more expensive to assay than are the more traditional biochemical tests discussed above. The most common measurement requires an anion-exchange chromatography-radioimmunoassay.

The sensitivity and specificity of CDT appear quite high when the index is used to contrast chronic heavy drinking alcoholics from teetotalers or very light social drinkers (Allen, Litten & Anton, 1992). However, the sensitivity of CDT drops considerably in more heterogeneous, non-alcoholic treatment populations, particularly in distinguishing heavy drinkers from those who consume alcohol at moderate or low levels. In addition, CDT appears to be less sensitive in female drinkers than in male subjects (Anton & Moak, 1994). The validity of CDT in adolescents, older adults, and various ethnic groups remains largely unknown.

CDT appears to have slightly greater validity than standard biochemical markers. In contrasting CDT with GGT, the sensitivities of both generally are similar, while the specificity of CDT is substantially higher than GGT, particularly in patients with nonalcoholic liver diseases (Allen, Litten & Anton, 1992). Unlike GGT and other liver enzyme markers, only some liver diseases can increase serum CDT levels. These include primary biliary cirrhosis, chronic active hepatitis, and hepatic malignoma (Stibler, 1991).

New Tests. Research is underway to develop new markers of high sensitivity and specificity for alcoholism. The most promising include protein-acetaldehyde adducts, 5-hydroxytryptophol, and transdermal devices (Allen, Litten & Anton, 1992).

Absence of a single marker to accurately screen for alcoholism has led to strategies to combine screening tests (Salaspuro, 1986; Allen, Litten & Anton, 1992). Two approaches to combining tests have been employed (Rosman & Lieber, 1990). The first approach, which simply requires that any of the tests be positive, improves sensitivity, but reduces specificity. The second approach, which requires that all tests be positive, sacrifices sensitivity to enhance specificity.

Employing the first strategy, several investigators have shown that combining CDT and GGT markedly increases sensitivity without substantially diminishing specificity. This phenomenon has been observed in various populations, including male and female alcoholics, heavy drinkers, alcoholics with liver disease, alcoholics from different ethnic groups, university students, and unselected populations (Allen, Litten & Anton, 1992).

Discriminant analysis—a multivariate statistical technique designed to identify the optimal additive combination of predictive measures—also has been used (Ryback, Eckardt et al., 1982; Hiller, Alldredge & Massey, 1986). Results of this strategy have been mixed.

A more promising approach involves combining laboratory tests with psychometric instruments. Kristenson and Trell (1982), for example, found that combining GGT with a score from a modified MAST more clearly detected alcoholics than did either measure alone. Olsen and colleagues (1989) reported that the combination of AST and MCV with SAAST scores increased specificity without compromising sensitivity.

Perhaps a more practical strategy is to employ an algorithm based on sequential testing of multiple screening psychometric instruments and biochemical laboratory tests. This approach requires construction of a decision tree (NIAAA, 1987) in which "cruder," less intensive markers or screening items precede the more expensive, more precise measures. The sequencing of items is individualized according to data obtained previously from the patient.

TESTS TO DETERMINE THE NEED FOR WITHDRAWAL MEDICATION

Early in treatment, the physician must determine if medication for alcohol withdrawal is required (see Section 6). If so, dosage and duration must be established.

Clinical Withdrawal Assessment. The Clinical Institute Withdrawal Assessment is a very efficient means of helping to determine the need for medication (Shaw, Kolesar et al., 1981). The scale has been revised and now exists in a ten-item format, the CIWA-Ar (Sullivan, Sykora et al., 1989). Items deal with severity and frequency of a variety of withdrawal symptoms including nausea, tremors, sweating, agitation, and hyperactivity.

Administration of the CIWA-Ar usually requires only about two minutes and the scale can be performed by a nurse each hour or so. The test developers argue that pharmacological support is rarely required if the patient scores below 10. If the total is above 20, they believe medication is recommended. In the mid-ranges of the CIWA-Ar, clinical judgment plays a more prominent role in the decision.

The practical value of the CIWA-Ar has been demonstrated by two investigations (Wartenberg, Nirenberg et al., 1990; Sullivan, Swift & Lewis, 1991). Each contrasted the amount of medication prescribed to withdrawing alcoholics without employment of the CIWA-Ar with dosages given after the CIWA-Ar was implemented in a treatment facility. In both studies, a smaller percentage of patients were medicated when CIWA-Ar results were available, but if medication was required, the doses prescribed were larger. Neither project found differences between the groups in withdrawal complications, lengths of stay or discharge status. The CIWA-Ar thus seems to facilitate more appropriate and more individualized pharmacotherapeutics.

Loading Dose. The CIWA-Ar can be especially helpful if a "loading dose" (Sellers, Naranjo et al., 1983) medication regime is adopted. Under this strategy, patients in alcohol withdrawal receive benzodiazepines approximately every hour until they produce CIWA-Ar scores at safe levels. The benzodiazepine then generally can be discontinued.

Saitz and colleagues (1994) recently confirmed the value of the loading dose strategy by comparing a symptom-triggered with a fixed-schedule intervention in patients admitted for treatment of acute alcohol withdrawal. The fixed-schedule therapy consisted of chlordiazepoxide administered every six hours for 12 doses, while the symptom-triggered therapy allowed medication to be administered hourly as long as the CIWA-Ar score was 8 or greater. Overall, patients in the symptom-triggered group received lower amounts of chlordiazepoxide and completed withdrawal more rapidly than did patients in the fixed-schedule group. At the same time, the severity of withdrawal during treatment and the incidence of seizures or *delirium tremens* were the same for the two groups.

Salloum and colleagues (1995) found that benzodiazepine loading and symptom monitoring by the CIWA-Ar was safe, practical and effective for treating alcohol withdrawal in patients with a collateral psychiatric disorder.

The CIWA-Ar also may identify patient characteristics related to withdrawal severity. For example, alcoholics with co-occurring anxiety diagnoses seem to exhibit more severe withdrawal as measured by the CIWA-Ar than do those who are free of such collateral problems (Johnson, Thevos et al., 1991).

CONCLUSIONS

Ultimately, recognition and management of alcoholism is a clinical responsibility involving multiple medical, psychological, and practical considerations. In this chapter, the authors have attempted to apprise physicians and other clinicians of some of the biochemical and psychometric measures that can inform the decision-making process. With the exception of the Structured Clinical Interview for *DSM-IIIR* (SCID; Hasin, Grant et al., 1992), all are brief, requiring no more than a few minutes of the clinician's and patient's time, and most have been demonstrated by research to be helpful and relevant to alcoholism treatment. Again with the exception of the SCID, administration and scoring of the measures described require minimal training, thus enhancing their clinical utility. Finally, costs of the described tests tend to be quite low. The majority are in the public domain and those that involve a royalty or laboratory charge generally are inexpensive.

As more is learned about the nature and treatment of alcoholism, more refined instruments will be created. Beyond elucidating screening, diagnostic, and medication issues, such instruments can help clinicians determine the intensity and nature of the treatment intervention that is most appropriate for a given patient. Even at present, a useful series of tests exists to help clinicians manage the early stages of alcohol treatment.

REFERENCES

Allen JP (1991). Personality correlates of the MacAndrew Alcoholism Scale: A review. *Psychology of Addictive Behaviors* 5(2):59–65.

Allen JP, Faden V, Miller A & Rawlings R (1990). Subtypes of substance abusers: Personality differences associated with MacAndrew scores. *Psychological Reports* 66(2):691–698.

Allen JP, Litten RZ & Anton R (1992). Measures of alcohol consumption in perspective. In RZ Litten & JP Allen (eds.) *Measuring Alcohol Consumption*. Totowa, NJ: The Humana Press, Inc., 205–226.

Anton RF & Moak DH (1994). Carbohydrate-deficient transferrin and γ-glutamyltransferase as markers of heavy alcohol consumption: Gender differences. *Alcoholism: Clinical & Experimental Research* 18:747–754.

Babor TF, de la Fuente JR, Saunders J & Grant M (1989). *AUDIT: The Alcohol Use Disorders Identification Test: Guidelines for Use in Primary Health Care*. Geneva, Switzerland: World Health Organization.

Bliding G, Bliding A, Fex G & Tornqvist C (1982). Appropriateness of laboratory tests in tracing young heavy drinkers. *Drug and Alcohol Dependence* 10:153–158.

Borg S, Beck O, Helander A, Voltaire A & Stibler H (1992). Carbohydrate-deficient transferrin and 5-hydroxytryptophol: Two new markers of high alcohol consumption. In RZ Litten & JP Allen (eds.) *Measuring Alcohol Consumption: Psychosocial and Biochemical Methods*. Totowa, NJ: The Humana Press, Inc., 148–160.

Brown ME, Anton RF, Malcolm R & Ballanger JC (1988). Alcohol detoxification and withdrawal seizures: Clinical support for a kindling hypothesis. *Biological Psychiatry* 23:507- 514.

Cloninger CR (1987). Neurogenetic adaptive mechanisms in alcoholism. *Science* 236:410–416.

Cloninger CR, Bohman M, Sigvardsson S & von Knorring A (1985). Psychopathology in adopted-out children of alcoholics: The Stockholm adoption study. *Recent Developments in Alcoholism* 3:37–51.

Colligan RC & Offord KP (1990). MacAndrew versus MacAndrew: The relative efficacy of the MAC and the SAP scales for the MMPI in screening male adolescents for substance misuse. *Journal of Personality Assessment* 55(3/4):708–716.

Cushman P (1992). Blood and liver markers in the estimation of alcohol consumption. In RZ Litten & Allen

JP (eds.) *Measuring Alcohol Consumption*. Totowa, NJ: The Humana Press, Inc., 135–147.

Davis LJ & Morse RM (1987a). Age and sex differences in the responses of alcoholics to the Self-Administered Alcoholism Screening Test. *Journal of Clinical Psychology* 43:423–480.

Davis LJ & Morse RM (1987b). Patient-spouse agreement on the drinking behavior of alcoholics. *Mayo Clinic Proceedings* 62:689–694.

Derogatis LR (1975). *Brief Symptom Inventory*. Baltimore, MD: Clinical Psychometric Research.

Derogatis LR (1992). *BSI Administration, Scoring & Procedures Manual-II*. Baltimore, MD: Clinical Psychometric Research.

Devenyi P, Robinson GM, Kapur BM & Roncari DAK (1981). High-density lipoprotein cholesterol in male alcoholics with and without severe liver disease. *American Journal of Medicine* 71:589–594.

Diehl AM, Potter J, Boitnott J, Van Duyn MA, Herlong HF & Mezey E (1984). Relationship between pyridoxal 5′-phosphate deficiency and aminotransferase levels in alcoholic hepatitis. *Gastroenterology* 86:632–636.

Dyer A, Huebert K & Jeune R (1992). Alcohol Dependence Scale: Norms for repeat impaired drivers. Unpublished manuscript.

Edwards G & Gross M (1976). Alcohol dependence: Provisional description of a clinical syndrome. *British Medical Journal* 1:1058–1061.

Ewing JA (1984). Detecting alcoholism: The CAGE questionnaire. *Journal of American Medical Association* 252(14):1905–1907.

Fertig JB, Allen JP & Cross GM (1993). The CAGE as a predictor of heavy alcohol consumption in U.S. Army personnel. *Alcoholism: Clinical and Experimental Research* 17(6):1184–1187.

Fleming MF, Barry KL & MacDonald R (1991). Alcohol Use Disorders Identification Test (AUDIT) in a college sample. *International Journal of the Addictions* 26(11):1173–1185.

Gottesman II & Prescott CA (1989). Abuses of the MacAndrew MMPI Alcoholism Scale: A critical review. *Clinical Psychology Review* 9:223–242.

Grant BF & Towle LH (1990). Standardized diagnostic interviews for alcohol research. *Alcohol Health and Research World* 14(4):340–348.

Harrell AV & Wirtz PW (1989). Screening for adolescent problem drinking: Validation of a multidimensional instrument for case identification. *Psychological Assessment* 1(1):61–63.

Hasin DS (1991). Diagnostic interviews for assessment: Background, reliability, validity. *Alcohol Health and Research World* 15(4):293–302.

Hasin DS, Grant BF, Glick HR & Endicott J (1992). *The Structured Clinical Interview for DSM-III-R, Alcohol/Drug Version (SCID-A/D)*. New York, NY: Department of Research Assessment and Training, New York State Psychiatric Institute.

Haskell WL, Camargo C, Williams PT, Vranizan KM, Krauss RM, Lindgren FT & Wood PD (1984). Effect of cessation and resumption of moderate alcohol intake on serum high-density-lipoprotein subfractions. *The New England Journal of Medicine* 310:805–810.

Hillers VN, Alldredge JR & Massey LK (1986). Determination of habitual alcohol intake from a panel of blood chemistries. *Alcohol and Alcoholism* 21:199–205.

Hodgins DC & Lightfoot LO (1989). Use of the alcohol dependence scale with incarcerated male offenders. *International Journal of Offender Therapy and Comparative Criminology* 33:59–67.

Johnson AL, Thevos AK, Randall CL & Anton RF (1991). Increased severity of alcohol withdrawal in in-patient alcoholics with a co-existing anxiety diagnosis. *British Journal of Addiction* 86(6):719–725.

Kristenson H & Trell E. (1982). Indicators of alcohol consumption: Comparisons between a questionnaire (Mm-MAST), interviews and serum gamma-glutamyl transferase (GGT) in a health survey of middle-aged males. *British Journal of Addiction* 77:297–304.

Laksman MR, Bingham SF, Cushman W, Cutler JA, Dufour M, Harford T & Hanna E (1992). Correlations of chronic alcohol consumption with some of its biochemical markers. *Alcoholism: Clinical & Experimental Research* 16:367.

Litten RZ & Allen JP (1991). Pharmacotherapies for alcoholism: Promising agents and clinical issues. *Alcoholism: Clinical & Experimental Research* 15(4):620–633.

Loethen GJ & Khavari KA (1990). Comparison of the Self-Administered Alcoholism Screening Test (SAAST) and the Khavari Alcohol Test (KAT): Results from an alcoholic population and their collaterals. *Alcoholism: Clinical & Experimental Research* 14(5):756–760.

MacAndrew C (1965). The differentiation of male alcoholic out-patients from non-alcoholic psychiatric out-patients by means of the MMPI. *Quarterly Journal of Studies on Alcohol* 26:238–246.

Markowitz M (1984). Alcohol misuse as a response to perceived powerlessness in the organization. *Journal of Studies on Alcohol* 48(3):225–227.

Matloff DS, Selinger MJ & Kaplan MM (1980). Hepatic transaminase activity in alcoholic liver disease. *Gastroenterology* 86:1389–1392.

Mayfield D, McLeod G & Hall P (1974). CAGE questionnaire: Validation of a new alcoholism screening instrument. *American Journal of Psychiatry* 131(10):1121–1123.

Moore RD & Malitz FE (1986). Underdiagnosis of alcoholism by residents in an ambulatory medical practice. *Journal of Medical Education* 61:46–52.

Morse RM & Swenson WM (1975). Spouse response to a Self-Administered Alcoholism Screening Test. *Journal of Studies on Alcohol* 36:400–405.

National Institute on Alcohol Abuse and Alcoholism (NIAAA) (1987). *Screening for Alcoholism in Primary Care Settings*. Rockville, MD: The Institute, 38–39.

Olsen MW, Morse RM, Davis LJ & O'Brien PC (1989). Discriminant analysis of SAAST and laboratory tests in screening for alcoholism. *Alcoholism: Clinical & Experimental Research* 13:151.

Otto RK, Lange AR, Megargee EI & Rosenblatt AI (1988). Ability of alcoholics to escape detection by the MMPI. *Journal of Consulting and Clinical Psychology* 56:452–457.

Puddey IB, Masarei JRL, Vandongen R & Beilin LF (1988). Serum apolipoprotein A-II as a marker of change in alcohol intake in male drinkers. *Alcohol and Alcoholism* 21:375–383.

Rosman AS & Lieber CS (1990). Biochemical markers of alcohol consumption. *Alcohol Health and Research World* 43:210–218.

Rosman AS & Lieber CS (1992). Overview of current and emerging markers of alcoholism. In RZ Litten & JP Allen (eds.) *Measuring Alcohol Consumption: Psychosocial and Biochemical Methods*. Totowa, NJ: The Humana Press, Inc., 99–134.

Ross HE, Gavin DE & Skinner HA (1990). Diagnostic validity of the MAST and the Alcohol Dependence Scale in the assessment of DSM-III alcohol disorders. *Journal of Studies on Alcohol* 51:506–513.

Ryback RS, Eckardt MJ, Tawlings RR & Rosenthal LS (1982). Quadratic discriminant analysis as an aid to interpretive reporting of clinical laboratory tests. *Journal of the American Medical Association* 248:2342–2345.

Salaspuro M (1986). Conventional and coming laboratory markers of alcoholic and heavy drinking. *Alcoholism: Clinical & Experimental Research* 10:5S–12S.

Saunders JB, Aasland OG, Babor TF, de la Fuente JR & Grant M (1993). Development of the Alcohol Use Disorders Identification Test (AUDIT): WHO collaborative project on early detection of persons with harmful alcohol consumption. II. *Addiction* 88:791–804.

Schofield MA (1989). Contribution of problem drinking to the level of psychiatric morbidity in the general hospital. *British Journal of Psychiatry* 155:229–232.

Sellers EM, Naranjo CA, Harrison M, Devenyi P, Roach C & Sykora K (1983). Diazepam loading: Simplified treatment of alcohol withdrawal. *Clinical & Pharmacological Therapy* 34:214–219.

Selzer ML (1972). The Michigan Alcoholism Screening Test: The quest for a new diagnostic instrument. *American Journal of Psychology* 127(2):1653–1658.

Shaw JM, Kolesar G, Sellers EM, Kaplan HL & Sandor P (1981). Development of optimal treatment tactics for alcohol withdrawal. I. Assessment and effectiveness of supportive care. *Journal of Clinical Psychopharmacology* 1:382–389.

Skinner HA & Allen BA (1982). Alcohol dependence syndrome: Measurement and validation. *Journal of Abnormal Psychology* 91(3):199–209.

Spitzer RL, Williams JBW, Gibbon M & First MB (1992). The Structured Clinical Interview for DSM-III-R (SCID):I. History, rationale, and description. *Archives of General Psychiatry* 49(8):624–629.

Stibler H (1991). Carbohydrate-deficient transferrin in serum: A new marker of potentially harmful alcohol consumption reviewed. *Clinical Chemistry* 37:2029–2037.

Sullivan JT, Swift RM & Lewis DC (1991). Benzodiazepine requirements during alcohol withdrawal syndrome: Clinical implications of using a standardized withdrawal scale. *Journal of Clinical Psychopharmacology* 11(5):291–295.

Sullivan JT, Sykora K, Schneiderman J, Naranjo CA & Sellers EM (1989). Assessment of alcohol withdrawal: The revised Clinical Institute Withdrawal Assessment for Alcohol scale (CIWA-Ar). *British Journal of Addiction* 84:1353–1357.

Svanum S (1986). Alcohol-related problems and dependence: An elaboration and integration. *International Journal of the Addictions* 21(4&5):539–558.

Swenson WM & Morse RM (1975). The use of a self-administered alcoholism screening test (SAAST) in a medical center. *Mayo Clinic Proceedings* 50:204–208.

von Knorring AL, Bohman M, von Knorring L & Oreland L (1985). Platelet MAO activity as a biological marker in subgroups of alcoholism. *Acta Psychiatrica Scandinavica* 72:51–58.

von Knorring L, Oreland L & von Knorring AL (1987). Personality traits and platelet MAO activity in alcohol and drug abusing teenage boys. *Acta Psychiatrica Scandinavica* 75:307–314.

Wartenberg AA, Nirenberg TD, Liepman MR, Silvia LY, Begin AM & Monti PM (1990). Detoxification of alcoholics: Improving care by symptom-triggered sedation. *Alcoholism: Clinical & Experimental Research* 14(1):71–75.

Whitfield JB, Hensley WJ, Bryden D & Gallagher H (1978). Effects of age and sex on biochemical responses to drinking habits. *Medical Journal of Australia* 2:629–632.

Wiggins JS (1966). Substantive dimensions of self-report in the MMPI item pool. *Psychological Monographs: General and Applied* 80(22):42.

Williams JBW, Gibbon M, First M, Spitzer RL, Davies M, Brous J, Howes M, Kone J, Pope H, Rounsaville B & Wittchen HV (1992). The Structured Clinical Interview for DSM-III-R (SCID):II. Multisite test-retest reliability. *Archives of General Psychiatry* 49(8):630–636.

CHAPTER 3

Assessment Instruments

David R. Gastfriend, M.D.
Sharon L. Baker, Ph.D.
Lisa M. Najavits, Ph.D.
Sharon Reif, B.A.

Using Assessment Instruments in Treatment Planning
Characteristics of Valid Assessment Instruments
Instruments for Standardized Assessments
Introducing Assessment Instruments into Practice

At its best, the clinical practice of addiction medicine offers the patient treatments which, because they are tailored to his or her needs, are effective and efficient. The rapid rise in health care costs has alarmed many employers and payers for care, including the Federal Government. Concern over costs, coupled with the perception that much care is unnecessary or provided inefficiently, has given rise to increasingly widespread techniques to manage health benefits and hold clinicians more accountable for services provided (Institute of Medicine, 1990). Clinicians must now continually advocate for their patients' access to quality care while balancing the demands of cost containment.

The field of addiction medicine has been challenged to examine the status of patient evaluation after coming under particular scrutiny by the U.S. Congress, which requested the Institute of Medicine (IOM) to study treatment services for people with alcohol problems. The IOM study noted that society is struggling with two cost versus quality questions that challenge clinicians to rethink our system of care: "First, how do we ensure that people get needed medical care without spending so much that other social objectives are compromised? Second, how do we discourage unnecessary and inappropriate medical services without jeopardizing necessary, high-quality care?" The committee's report "Broadening the Base of Treatment for Alcohol Problems," defined a need for improvements in pretreatment assessment of alcohol problems to facilitate appropriate treatment decisions (Institute of Medicine, 1990).

This thinking represents a departure from the 1980s, when the standard for treatment was to refer patients to the most intensive services they would accept. Current standards look to optimize the match between patient and treatment without relying on the assumption that the most promising treatment for a given patient is the most intensive treatment available. There is growing empirical support for matching strategies, although there is not yet uniformity in the variables used or the methods of implementation (Gastfriend & McLellan, 1997).

Any successful matching strategy must rely initially upon the identification of key matching variables. Mattson and colleagues (1994) reviewed 31 empirical studies of treatment matching and identified at least four categories of clinical variables important to the matching process, including demographics, addiction-specific characteristics such as severity, intrapersonal characteristics such as psychopathology and motivation, and interpersonal function including environmental factors and social support.

Formal assessment instruments may provide the standardization and credibility necessary for effective treatment matching which ideally becomes a critical step in overall treatment planning. Reviewers frequently require providers to assess patients in at least the following areas in order to justify their participation in a particular treatment: (1) diagnosis, (2) severity of addiction, and (3) motivation and rehabilitation potential. These areas roughly correspond to the matching variables identified by Mattson, Allen et al. (1994) and can be assessed using available instruments with known reliability and validity.

The patient placement criteria of the American Society of Addiction Medicine (ASAM, 1996) represent the most significant development to date in the process of establishing a single, standardized set of criteria for matching patients to treatments. The ASAM criteria match patients to levels of care, defined as settings offering discrete treatment intensities. The four major levels of care are hospital, nonhospital inpatient, day treatment and outpatient. First published in 1991, the criteria have since been revised and expanded so that the 1996 second edition (Mee-Lee, Shulman & Gartner, 1996) includes a range of intensities of service within each of the four principal levels of care.

The ASAM patient placement criteria rely on a dimensional approach to assessment that takes into account the full range of clinical variables relevant to the matching process. The six dimensions or problem areas evaluated in matching patients to ASAM levels of care are: (1) acute intoxication and/or withdrawal potential, (2) biomedical conditions and complications, (3) emotional/behavioral conditions and complications, (4) treatment acceptance/resistance, (5) relapse/continued use potential and (6) recovery/living environment.

USING ASSESSMENT INSTRUMENTS IN TREATMENT PLANNING

These considerations demand new approaches to clinical assessment and documentation. Whereas traditionally the patient record served only to communicate clinical data among providers, it has now become crucial in determining what type of care the patient will receive and, indeed, whether the patient will receive care at all. Interest in assessment instruments is no longer limited to research domains now that managed care entities require clinicians to justify and document decisions about treatment. As third-party payers demand increased communication between providers and managed care monitors, uniform assessment becomes a necessity. Patient evaluations that document the assessment process in an objective way offer the distinct advantage of providing justification for any treatment recommendations derived from them.

Formal assessment instruments for treatment planning generally offer several advantages over the conventional clinical interview for both treatment matching and treatment planning. A valid instrument offers a uniform inquiry, comprehensive coverage of essential areas, quantification of data, and standardization of the interpretations of the data. Assessments without instruments cannot provide these features, because interviewers may vary widely in style (e.g., use of open versus closed-ended questions), areas of inquiry (e.g., severity of substance dependence versus psychopathology), depth of inquiry (screening superficially in some areas versus detailed probing in others), units of measure (e.g., severity of drug use may be measured in terms of quantity, frequency, recency, and/or expenditures), and—most importantly—interviewers may vary widely in the assumptions they use in interpretation.

While a plethora of measures exists (Letteri, Nelson & Sayers, 1985), the instruments presented in this chapter have been selected for their utility in treatment matching and treatment planning, their strong psychometric properties (e.g., reliability, validity), and the availability of data on their use. The instruments described provide information in the areas of clinical diagnosis, substance abuse and dependence severity, and/or motivation and treatment readiness. Instruments may be combined to create a comprehensive battery that yields data for matching patients to ASAM levels of care, which presents exciting new possibilities for patient evaluation.

Clinical Diagnosis. Clinical diagnosis is perhaps the most fully developed assessment area because of the general acceptance of the criteria of the *Diagnostic and Statistical Manual of Mental Disorders* of the American Psychiatric Association. The fourth edition, or *DSM-IV* (American Psychiatric Association, 1994) is now widely used. Several clinical interview instruments exist for establishing *DSM-IV* diagnoses of psychoactive substance use disorders.

Of these, the Structured Clinical Interview for *DSM-IV* (SCID; First, Gibbon et al., 1996) is the most readily incorporated into a battery aimed at use in both research and clinical evaluation. Other measures are available, but the requirements for their administration may be less than ideal in most circumstances. The Schedule for Affective Disorders and Schizophrenia (SADS; Endicott & Spitzer, 1978), for example, requires interviewers with graduate degrees and fairly extensive clinical experience and can take up to four hours to administer. The Diagnostic Interview Schedule (DIS; Robins, Helzer et al., 1981) was designed for administration by nonclinicians and proceeds on a symptom-by-symptom basis, with the requirement that each question be read verbatim from a booklet (Hasin, 1991). The DIS also is available in a self-administered, computerized format.

The SCID thus provides a middle ground in terms of structure, level of expertise required for administration and duration of the interview.

Substance Abuse and Dependence Severity. The term severity is used in relation to addiction to refer both to the severity of the addictive behavior itself (that is, the level of dependence and associated risks of withdrawal), and to functional impairment related to the addictive behavior (i.e., the severity of the consequences of that behavior for other areas of life functioning). Assessment of severity for purposes of treatment matching and treatment planning must take into account both uses of the term.

In the second sense of the term, severity is a multidimensional construct. To illustrate this problem, consider two examples: one patient has severe dependence and uses infrequently but in binges of large amounts. These activities are self-destructive in terms of legal violations and physical injury to self and others. Another patient with severe dependence uses regularly without intoxication but with multiple medical, career and family disruptions and losses.

An effective instrument must characterize these differing patterns and yield some absolute level of severity that renders a similarly severe score for both patients. To accomplish this, the instrument must measure severity across multiple dimensions. Of the instruments available for assessing severity, one of the oldest and most widely used is the Addiction Severity Index (ASI; McLellan, Kushner et al., 1992), which was the first to provide a multidimensional assessment of substance abuse severity.

A more recently developed instrument is the Drinker Inventory of Consequences (DrInC; Miller, Tonigan & Longabaugh et al., 1995), which provides a comprehensive assessment of the extent of alcohol problems apart from consumption and dependence.

Motivation and Treatment Readiness. Patient treatment readiness is a fundamental consideration in addictions treatment planning, yet it is often evaluated on an intuitive basis. Clinicians routinely report motivation as a global quality which they believe may predict the patient's likelihood for treatment success. For example, a 1990 pilot study of newly admitted chemically dependent patients found that demographic factors and comorbidity collectively accounted for only one-third of the variance in outcomes, and nurses' global ratings of patients' motivation significantly added to the prediction of outcome (Marc A. Schuckit, personal communication).

Because treatment readiness is a more recent area of investigation, the repertoire of available instruments is less well studied than in the case of diagnosis or severity assessment. However, several promising new instruments are available that assess various aspects of motivation and readiness for treatment. The RAATE-CE (Mee-Lee, 1985, 1988), assesses treatment readiness as a multidimensional construct that combines patient awareness of problems, behavioral intent to change, capacity to anticipate future treatment needs, and medical, psychiatric or environmental impediments. The University of Rhode Island Change Assessment Scale (URICA) assesses Prochaska and DiClementi's (1992) stages of change model. The Stages of Change Readiness and Treatment Eagerness Scale (SOCRATES; Miller & Tonigan, 1996) assesses the three factors of Recognition, Ambivalence and Taking Steps. The Circumstances, Motivation, Readiness, and Suitability Scale (CMRS; DeLeon, Melnick et al., 1994) measures patients' perceptions across the four related domains.

CHARACTERISTICS OF VALID ASSESSMENT INSTRUMENTS

An assessment instrument should demonstrate certain psychometric properties if it is to be accepted for clinical research or routine clinical use. The items that make up the instrument should have clear meanings, should be distinct and parsimonious (i.e., non-redundant), and should relate to one another in a coherent way (i.e., items that are logically connected should be grouped with one another in subscales). Different raters should be able to use the instrument and obtain similar ratings (*inter-rater reliability*) and the same patient should obtain similar results on two different, closely spaced administrations (*test-retest reliability*).

In addition to reliability, an instrument must have demonstrated validity. The instrument and its items should be based on an underlying logical framework, or construct. The instrument should make sense as an effort to assess the intended area: that is, it should demonstrate *face validity.* If an accepted "gold standard" measure exists, a comparative trial between the two instruments should yield similar results, demonstrating *convergent validity.* Different scores should distinguish different outcomes, demonstrating *predictive validity.* Finally, the instrument should obtain different results from those of another instrument designed for a different purpose (*discriminant validity*).

Issues in Self-Report. One of the greatest challenges of clinical assessment in addictions treatment is the reliability of patient self-report. Effective interviewing depends on helping patients to understand the meaning of each question, to organize their recollections, and to avoid defensiveness about their behaviors. In general, the reliability of patient self-report can be improved by using a consistent sequence of questions that progresses from general to specific information and using an interview style that moves from an open-ended to a closed-ended question format.

What follows is the description of a set of instruments that incorporates these principles and that provides a comprehensive assessment capable of yielding sufficient information for treatment matching and/or treatment planning. The battery includes the SCID for *DSM-IV* (First, Gibbon et al., 1994), the Clinical Institute Withdrawal Assessment (CIWA-AR; Sullivan, Sykora et al., 1989), the ASI (McLellan, Kushner et al., 1992) and the RAATE-CE (Mee-Lee, 1985, 1988). This battery is in use in a large-scale study of the validity of the ASAM Patient Placement Criteria for treatment matching, now being conducted by the first author.

INSTRUMENTS FOR STANDARDIZED ASSESSMENTS

The Structured Clinical Interview for DSM-IV (SCID). The Structured Clinical Interview for *DSM-IV* (SCID) is a widely used, semi-structured interview that obtains Axis I and II diagnoses using *DSM-IV* criteria. The SCID is designed for use with psychiatric, medical or community-based normal adults (Spitzer, Williams et al., 1989, 1992). It is composed of one module for each major syndrome group in the *DSM-IV: anxiety disorders, affective disorders, psychotic disorders, and substance use disorders. Each module may stand on its own for assessment of that particular diagnostic syndrome. Each question on the SCID corresponds to a specific DSM-IV* criterion. The questions are sequenced to carefully obey the decision rule process and to yield a diagnosis only if the patient meets all requisite *DSM-IV* criteria.

The SCID is designed for use by a trained clinical evaluator at the master's or doctoral level, although in research settings it has been used by bachelor's level technicians with extensive training. Administration of Axis I and Axis II batteries may require more than two hours each for patients with multiple diagnoses. The Psychoactive Substance Use Disorders module may be administered by itself in 30 to 60 minutes, depending on the extent of the patient's substance use history and current involvement.

For the Psychoactive Substance Use Disorders module, the SCID poses a query for each *DSM-IV* criterion for abuse/dependence, first for alcohol and then for each non-alcohol psychoactive substance. The information is collected in such a way that it is possible to establish lifetime diagnoses, age of onset of first abuse or dependence and current severity.

In a recent study, Kranzler and colleagues (1996) reported on the validity of SCID substance abuse diagnoses using the SCID for *DSM-IIIR*. The researchers were able to demonstrate both concurrent and discriminant validity for both alcohol and drug abuse/dependence diagnoses with a number of related measures, including the ASI, with significance for the most part in the range of $p<.001$. For the comorbid disorders of major depression and antisocial personality, validity was established with a smaller number of concurrent measures in the significance range of $p<.OS$ to $p<.Ol$. Concurrent validity was not demonstrated for comorbid anxiety. Predictive validity using measures of substance use at six-month follow-up generally was good and significant, with some variability across measures for abuse/dependence, but not for comorbid disorders.

One reason for the poorer showing of the SCID in diagnosing comorbid disorders may be that the *DSM-IIIR* version did not assess specifically for substance-induced disorders. Anxiety symptoms, in particular, tend to be high in early abstinence and can be difficult to differentially diagnose. The *DSM-IV* incorporates substance-induced mood disorders and substance-induced anxiety disorders as distinct categories with specific diagnostic criteria. The SCID for *DSM-IV* includes separate modules for obtaining substance-induced diagnoses which are linked to the mood and anxiety modules by specific skip-out instructions. Improved validity for comorbid diagnoses might be expected with the presence of the substance-induced disorder modules.

No published data are available as yet on the interrater reliability of the SCID substance use modules for *DSM-IV*, as it has not been in use for a sufficient period of time. For the SCID for *DSM-IIIR*, interrater reliability for drug abuse/dependence diagnoses in multiple patient populations has been reported as (Kappa) 0.63 and 0.83 for current and lifetime diagnoses, respectively (Williams, Gibbon et al., 1992), and reliability was good for comorbid diagnoses as well (Skre, Onstad et al., 1991).

Because the SCID is constructed around the *DSM-IV*, it uses symptom criteria based upon the loss of behavioral control model for the spectrum of dependence-producing substances. Although it does measure criterion-based symptomatology, the SCID is too limited for a comprehensive treatment evaluation and should be supplemented with an instrument that has been designed for severity assessment, such as the ASI or the DrInC.

Clinical Institute Withdrawal Assessment (CIWA-Ar). Often the first step in conducting an addictions assessment is the establishment of risk associated with the current level of acute intoxication. The CIWA-Ar is a brief scale of 10 items (requiring less than two minutes to administer), which provides a clinical quantification of the severity of the alcohol withdrawal syndrome. The instrument was developed and reliability and validity data obtained on patients in alcohol withdrawal, although it has been shown to be useful in assessing withdrawal from other sedative-hypnotic drugs.

An observer rates the intensity of 10 common withdrawal symptoms and a total score is obtained by summing the ratings from the 10 items. With training, it can be administered by non-medical personnel such as detoxification unit workers or research assistants.

REFERENCES

Abellanas L & McLellan AT (1993). "Stage of change" by drug problem in concurrent opioid, cocaine, and cigarette users. *Journal of Psychoactive Drugs* 25:307–313.

American Psychiatric Association (1994). *Diagnostic and Statistical Manual of Mental Disorders, 4th Edition.* Washington, DC: American Psychiatric Association.

American Society of Addiction Medicine (1991). *Patient Patient Criteria for the Treatment of Substance Abuse Disorders.* Washington, DC: The Society.

Argeriou M, McCarty D, Mulvey K & Daley M (1994). Use of the Addiction Severity Index with homeless substance abusers. *Journal of Substance Abuse Treatment* 11:359–365.

Brown E, Frank D & Friedman A (1995). *Supplementary Administration Manual for the Expanded Female Version of the Addiction Severity Index (ASI) Instrument, The ASI-F.* Herndon, VA: Head & Co., Inc.

DeLeon, G, Melnick G, Kressler D & Jainchill, N (1994). Circumstances, motivation, readiness, and suitability (the CMRS scales): Predicting retention in therapeutic community treatment. *American Journal of Drug & Alcohol Abuse* 20(4):495–515.

DiClementi CC & Hughes SO (1990). Stages of change profiles in outpatient alcoholism treatment. *Journal of Substance Abuse* 2:2172–2175.

Endicott J & Spitzer RL (1978). A diagnostic interview: The Schedule for Affective Disorders and Schizophrenia. *Archives of General Psychiatry* 35(7):837–844.

First M, Gibbon M, Spitzer R & Williams J (1996). *User's Guide for the Structured Clinical Interview for DSM-IV Axis I Disorders, Research Version (SCID I, Version 2.0, February 1996).* New York, NY: Biometrics Research Dept., New York State Psychiatric Institute.

Gastfriend DR, Filstead WJ, Reif S, Najavits LM & Parrella DP (1995). Validity of assessing treatment readiness in patients with substance use disorders. *The American Journal on Addictions* 4(5):254–260.

Gastfriend DR & McLellan AT (1997). Treatment matching: Theoretic and practical implications. *Medical Clinics of North America* 81(4):1–22.

Hasin D (1991). Diagnostic interviews for assessment: Background, reliability, validity. *Alcohol Health and Research World* 15:293–302.

Hodgins D & El-Guebaly N (1992). More data on the Addiction Severity Index: Reliability and validity with the mentally ill substance abuser. *Journal of Nervous and Mental Disease* 180:197–201.

Institute of Medicine (1990). *Broadening the Base of Treatment for Alcohol Problems: A Report of a Study by a Committee of the Institute of Medicine, Division of Mental Health and Behavioral Medicine.* Washington, DC: National Academy Press.

Isenhart C (1994). Motivational subtypes in an inpatient sample of substance abusers. *Addictive Behaviors* 19:463–475.

Kranzler H, Kadden R, Babor T, Tennen H & Rounsaville B (1996). Validity of the SCID in substance abuse patients. *Addiction* 91:859–868.

LaJeunesse C & Thorenson R (1988). Generalizing a predictor of male alcoholic treatment outcomes. *International Journal of Addiction* 23:183–205.

Letteri D, Nelson J & Sayers M (1985). *Alcoholism Treatment Assessment Research Instruments.* Washington, DC: National Institute on Alcohol Abuse and Alcoholism.

Mattson ME, Allen JP, Longabaugh R et al. (1994). A chronological review of empirical studies matching alcoholic clients to treatment. *Journal of Studies on Alcohol* 12(Suppl):1629.

McGahan P, Griffith J, Parente R & McLellan A (1986). Composite scores from the Addiction Severity Index. Pittsburgh, PA: Penn-VA Center for Studies of Addiction (unpublished manuscript).

McLellan AT, Luborsky L & Woody GE (1980). An improved diagnostic evaluation instrument for substance abuse patients: the Addiction Severity Index. *Journal of Nervous and Mental Diseases* 168:26–33.

McLellan AT, Luborsky L, Cacciola J, Griffith J, Evans F, Barr HL & O'Brien CP (1985). New data from the addiction severity index—reliability and validity in three centers. *Journal of Nervous and Mental Disease* 173:412–423.

McLellan AT, Kushner H, Metzger D, Peters R, Smith I, Grissom G, Pettinati H & Argeriou M (1992). The fifth edition of the Addiction Severity Index. *Journal of Substance Abuse Treatment* 9:199–213.

Mee-Lee D (1985). The Recovery Attitude and Treatment Evaluator (RAATE) an instrument for patient progress and treatment assignment. *Proceedings of the 34th International Congress on Alcoholism and Drug Dependence* 424–426.

Mee-Lee D (1988). An instrument for treatment progress and matching: The Recovery Attitude and Treatment Evaluator (RAATE). *Journal of Substance Abuse Treatment* 5:183–186.

Mee-Lee D, Shulman G & Gartner L (1996). *Patient Placement Criteria for the Treatment of Substance-Related Disorders, Second Edition (PPC-2)*. Chevy Chase, MD: American Society of Addiction Medicine.

Miller W & Rollnick S (1991). *Motivational Interviewing; Preparing People to Change Addictive Behavior.* New York, The Guilford Press.

Miller W & Tonigan JS (1996). Assessing drinker's motivations for change: The Stages of Change Readiness and Treatment Eagerness Scale (SOCRATES). *Psychology of Addictive Behaviors* 10(2):81–89.

Miller W, Tonigan JS & Longabaugh R (1995). *The Drinker Inventory of Consequences (DrInC): An Instrument for Assessing Adverse Consequences of Alcohol Abuse. Test Manual* (NIAAA Project MATCH Monograph Series, Volume 4). Rockville, MD: National Institute on Alcohol Abuse and Alcoholism.

Najavits LM, Gastfriend DR, Nakayama EY, Barber J, Blaine J, Frank A, Muenz L & Thase M (1997). A measure of readiness for substance abuse treatment: Psychometric properties of the RAATE research interview. *The American Journal on Addictions* 6:74–82.

Prochaska JO & DiClemente CC (1992). Stages of change in the modification of problem behaviors. *Progress in Behavior Modification* 28:183–218.

Robins LN, Helzer JE, Croughan J & Ratcliff KS (1981). National Institute of Mental Health Diagnostic Interview Schedule. *Archives of General Psychiatry* 38(4):381–389.

Skre I, Onstad S, Torgersen S & Kringlen E (1991). High interrater reliability for the Structured Clinical Interview for DSM-III-R Axis I. *Acta Psychiatrica Scandinavica* 84:167–173.

Smith B, Hoffman N & Nederhoed R (1992). The development and reliability of the RAATE-CE. *Journal of Substance Abuse* 4:355–363.

Spitzer RL, Williams JB, Mirian G & First M (1989). *Instruction Manual for the Structured Interview for DSM-III-R*. New York, NY: Biometrics Research Dept., New York State Psychiatric Institute, May 1.

Spitzer RL, Williams JB, Gibbon M & First MB (1992). The Structured Clinical Interview for DSM-III-R (SCID) I: History, rationale and description. *Archives of General Psychiatry* 49:624–9.

Sullivan JT, Sykora K, Schneiderman J, Naranjo CA & Sellers EM (1989). Assessment of alcohol withdrawal: The revised Clinical Institute Withdrawal Assessment for Alcohol scale (CIWA-AR). *British Journal of the Addictions* 84:1353–1357.

Williams JB, Gibbon M, First MB, Spitzer RL, Davies M, Borus JF; Howes MJ, Kane J, Pope HG Jr & Rounsaville B (1992). The Structured Clinical Interview for DSM-III-R (SCID). II. Multisite test-retest reliability. *Archives of General Psychiatry* 49:630–6.

CHAPTER 4

Diagnostic Classification Systems

Samuel A. Ball, Ph.D.
Therese A. Kosten, Ph.D.

Diagnostic Classification Systems
Reliability and Validity
Distinguishing Substance Effects from Psychiatric Symptoms
Use of Collateral Information
Diagnostic Subtyping

Effective treatment of substance use disorders depends first on establishing a reliable and valid diagnosis, which facilitates communication among providers, as well as treatment planning and reimbursement, and research into causes, courses, and treatment outcomes. This chapter provides an overview of past and current diagnostic systems, with particular emphasis on the *Diagnostic and Statistical Manual of Mental Diseases, Fourth Edition*, of the American Psychiatric Association (*DSM-IV*; 1994) and the "dependence syndrome" construct. Other areas reviewed include: (1) different forms of diagnostic reliability and validity and evidence for this in substance use disorders; (2) methods designed to improve the reliability and validity of alcohol and drug use diagnoses, particularly structured interviews; (3) the shifting emphasis on physiological dependence (i.e., tolerance and withdrawal); and (4) the importance of diagnostic subtypes.

Although there are some important diagnostic distinctions between different substances of abuse (*vis a vis* tolerance, withdrawal, progression to loss of control and impairment), this chapter considers alcohol and the major drug classes as a group. The *DSM-IV* emphasizes these broad behavioral consistencies through the use of general criteria for Substance Intoxication, Withdrawal, Abuse, and Dependence. This common conceptualization is supported by similarities across substances (Carroll, 1995) with regard to their assessment (Rounsaville, Bryant et al., 1993), etiology (Glantz & Pickens, 1992), coexisting psychopathology (Rounsaville, 1982; Rounsaville, Dolinsky et al., 1987), multidimensional typologies (Ball, Carroll et al., 1995), outcome (McLellan, Luborsky et al., 1983; McLellan, Alterman et al., 1994), relapse (Marlatt & Gordon, 1985), and the processes of change (Prochaska, DiClemente & Norcross, 1992).

DIAGNOSTIC CLASSIFICATION SYSTEMS

Diagnostic and Statistical Manuals I-IIIR. The *Diagnostic and Statistical Manuals* (*DSM*) of the American Psychiatric Association (APA) first were published in 1952. Alcoholism and drug addiction were classified as types of "Sociopathic Personality Disturbances" in the original *DSM* and later under the broader category of Personality Disorders in *DSM-II* (1967). Although there was no differentiation by type of drug in the *DSM*, the *DSM-II* did distinguish alcoholism from other types of drug dependence and made some attempt to classify the severity of addiction. However, the *DSM-II* used diagnostic terms such as Dependence, Abuse, Addiction, and Habitual Use, which were ambiguous, subjective and unreliable. The *DSM-II* also reflected definitional confusion and disagreement over whether a diagnosis of alcoholism or drug dependence requires evidence of physical dependence in addition to habitual, compulsive, or hazardous use. This problem has persisted through subsequent revisions.

The *DSM-III* (1980) introduced the term "substance" to refer to all alcohol and drugs and codified the distinction between "abuse" and "dependence" through criteria that were less ambiguous and more operationally defined by a specific number of criteria necessary to diagnose these disorders. Dependence was distinguished from Abuse by the requirement of tolerance or withdrawal. The emphasis on operationally defined criteria for substance use and other psychiatric disorders in the *DSM-III* was directly influenced by the Feighner criteria (1972), which subsequently were refined into the Research Diagnostic Criteria (RDC; Spitzer, Endicott & Robins, 1973). The *DSM-III* conceptualization also was influenced strongly by the "dependence syndrome" construct (Edwards & Gross, 1976), which characterized the clinical features of alcoholism as: (1) narrowing or ritualization of drinking behavior; (2) salience of drink-seeking behavior (despite adverse consequences); (3) tolerance; (4) withdrawal; (5) withdrawal avoidance; (6) compulsion (loss of control, craving, persistent thoughts); and (7) reinstatement liability (returning to prior use levels).

Whereas the *DSM-III* distinguished Abuse from Dependence by the presence of withdrawal or tolerance, the *DSM-IIIR* (1987) de-emphasized the primary importance of the physical aspects of addiction (Rounsaville, Kosten et al., 1986). Moreover, it recognized tolerance and withdrawal as variable across different individuals and drugs (Jaffe, 1985) and regarded them as no better than any other Dependence criteria in terms of reliability or validity. Requiring tolerance or withdrawal in order to make the Dependence diagnosis appeared to have limited value (Rounsaville & Bryant, 1992; Rounsaville, Bryant et al., 1993) because substance users with these symptoms did not differ clinically from those without them. The issue thus was not whether to include tolerance or withdrawal, but rather whether they should be required core symptoms.

The changes in classification for the *DSM-IIIR* also were based on the Edwards and Gross (1976) dependence syndrome, and emphasized physiological, psychological, and behavioral symptoms in a more balanced way, as related to diminished control over use, persistent use despite consequences, and tolerance/withdrawal. This change also allowed for similar criteria across the different substance categories. In addition, the importance of social consequences of use was de-emphasized, because these consequences could be inconsistent across drugs, individuals, and subgroups (Rounsaville, Kosten et al., 1987).

According to the *DSM-IIIR*, Psychoactive Substance Dependence was diagnosed by meeting any three of nine criteria: (1) tolerance; (2) withdrawal; (3) withdrawal avoidance; (4) socially dysfunctional use; (5) use despite problems; (6) cannot stop; (7) salience; (8) pre-occupation, and (9) cannot limit use. In the *DSM-IIIR*, Psychoactive Substance Abuse was a more residual category, defined by hazardous use and related impairment (Rounsaville & Kranzler, 1989). Many individuals who would have met *DSM-III* criteria for Abuse subsequently met the *DSM-IIIR* criteria for Dependence (Rounsaville & Bryant, 1992).

The DSM-IV (1994) (see Appendix B). In the *DSM-IV*, the category of Substance-Related Disorders includes both the Substance Use Disorders (Abuse and Dependence) and the Substance-Induced Disorders. Substance-Induced Disorders include Substance Intoxication and Withdrawal as well as other disorders that may be caused by substance use (e.g., Substance-Induced Persisting Amnestic, Dementia, Delirium, Psychotic, Mood, Anxiety, Sexual Dysfunction, and Sleep Disorders). Table 1 lists the *DSM-IV* criteria for Substance Dependence. These were shortened from nine (in the *DSM-IIIR*) to seven by combining the two withdrawal criteria and "time spent" with "giving up activities." As can be seen, "Tolerance" and "Withdrawal" are listed as the first two criteria in the *DSM-IV*, but (as in the *DSM-IIIR*) physiological dependence is not required for a diagnosis of Substance Dependence.

Substance Abuse is defined as a maladaptive pattern of substance use characterized by hazardous or compulsive use or the presence of role impairment or recurrent legal problems, but without evidence of tolerance or withdrawal. Most individuals who meet the criteria for Substance Abuse and who continue to use eventually will meet the criteria for Dependence. Once the criteria for Dependence have been met in a category, a diagnosis of Abuse no longer can be made.

There are three criteria for Substance Intoxication and Withdrawal: (1) clinically significant substance-specific syndrome due to the recent ingestion (Intoxication) or cessation/reduction (Withdrawal) of a substance; (2) a syndrome associated with significant distress, impairment, or maladaptive psychological/behavioral changes; (3) symptoms that are not accounted for by a medical or psychiatric condition. Substance Intoxication and Withdrawal are distinguished from the other Substance-Induced Disorders (e.g., delirium, mood, sleep, etc.) by the latter requiring additional clinical attention for symptoms which exceed those typically associated with Intoxication and Withdrawal.

In the *DSM-IIIR*, the Substance-Induced Disorders were listed in a separate diagnostic section as Organic Mental Disorders (along with Mental Disorders Due to a General Medical Condition). The *DSM-IV* treats the distinction between "functional" and "organic" as somewhat arbitrary and so eliminates the latter term from its diagnostic system.

TABLE 1. DSM-IV Criteria for Substance Dependence

A maladaptive pattern of substance use, leading to clinically significant impairment or distress, as manifested by three (or more) of the following, occurring at any time in the same 12-month period.

1. Tolerance, as defined by either of the following:
   a. a need for markedly increased amounts of the substance to achieve intoxication or desired effect; or
   b. markedly diminished effect with continued use of the same amount of the substance.
2. Withdrawal, as manifested by either of the following:
   a. the characteristic Withdrawal syndrome for the substance (refer to criteria A and B of the criteria sets for Withdrawal from the specific substances); or
   b. the same (or closely related) substance is taken to relieve or avoid withdrawal symptoms.
3. The substance is taken in larger amounts or over a longer period than was intended.
4. There is a persistent desire or unsuccessful efforts to cut down or control substance use.
5. A great deal of time is spent in activities necessary to obtain the substance (e.g., visiting multiple doctors or driving long distances), use the substance (e.g., chain smoking), or recover from its effects.
6. Important social, occupational, or recreational activities given up or reduced because of substance use.
7. The substance use is continued despite knowledge of having a persistent or recurrent physical or psychological problem that is likely to have been caused or exacerbated by the substance (e.g., current cocaine use despite recognition of cocaine-induced depression, or continued drinking despite recognition that an ulcer was made worse by alcohol consumption).

Specify if:

With Physiological Dependence: Evidence of tolerance or withdrawal (i.e., either item 1 or 2 is present); or

Without Physiological Dependence: No evidence of tolerance or withdrawal (i.e., neither item 1 nor 2 is present.

Source: American Psychiatric Association (1994). *Diagnostic and Statistical Manual of Mental Disorders, 4th Edition*. Washington, DC: American Psychiatric Press, 181. Reprinted by permission.

Although the same criteria sets for Intoxication, Withdrawal, Abuse, and Dependence are applied across most substance classes, it is recognized that the expression of symptoms is different for different substances; thus, they are listed in criteria sets specific to each class. In addition, the *DSM-IV* emphasizes that substances differ in their course (e.g., time from first Intoxication to Dependence) depending on the characteristics of the drug, the route of administration, and the duration of effects. Alcohol, drugs, many medications, and toxins can lead to a diagnosis of Substance Intoxication, Withdrawal, Abuse, or Dependence, with the following exceptions for major categories. Substance Withdrawal cannot be diagnosed for Caffeine, Hallucinogens, Inhalants, or Phencyclidine because they have not been reliably described or do not appear to require clinical attention. For similar reasons, one can be diagnosed with Caffeine Intoxication, but not Abuse or Dependence, and with Nicotine Dependence, but not Abuse or Intoxication.

Miller (1995) has summarized some of the continuing controversy over the *DSM-IV* about the abuse/dependence distinction and the importance of tolerance and withdrawal. The Abuse diagnosis remains problematic because it simultaneously implies a more willful, pathological use and yet the construct of loss of control is central to all four of its symptoms. There also is disagreement as to whether it should be a freestanding or residual category in relation to substance dependence (Hasin, McCloud et al., 1996; Hasin, Trautman et al., 1996). Research seems to suggest that this diagnosis is neither reliable nor valid and seems to be more quantitatively rather than qualitatively different from substance dependence.

Differentiating Abuse and Dependence solely on the basis of tolerance and withdrawal does not appear to be especially relevant clinically or to have strong prognostic implications. Tolerance and Withdrawal also may be misleading phenomena for understanding the process of addiction because both can occur in the absence of loss of control (e.g., taking narcotic analgesics as prescribed). Tolerance in itself is a very complex phenomenon (e.g., behavioral, pharmacologic, genetic), which may develop at different rates for different substances and in different individuals and which may develop even for many medications without clear abuse potential. Some level of tolerance and withdrawal may be observable after a single dose of a drug and thus may be completely unrelated to loss of control or addiction (Miller, 1995).

International Classification of Diseases (ICD-10) (see Appendix B). In 1948, the World Health Organization's (WHO) *International Classification of Diseases* first included classifications for abnormal behavior, but they were not widely accepted, particularly in the U.S. (where four years later the first *DSM* was published). A more widely accepted *ICD* revision in 1969 (around the time the *DSM-II* was published) listed diagnostic categories, but not actual criteria, symptoms, or behaviors. More recent revisions have been more closely related to the *DSM-III, IIIR*, and *IV*. The alcohol dependence syndrome became the basis for the revision of the *ICD* by the WHO expert committee in 1981 (Edwards, Arif & Hodgson, 1981). The alcohol dependence syndrome construct also has been extended to include all other psychoactive substances because they share many of the same symptoms, including tolerance, withdrawal, and drug-seeking behavior. It also was recommended that the term Abuse be replaced by more specific terms such as "unsanctioned" or "hazardous" use.

The 10th edition of the *International Statistical Classification of Diseases and Related Health Problems* (*ICD-10*; WHO, 1992) criteria for Dependence significantly overlaps the *DSM-IIIR* and *DSM-IV*. Although it does not include "cannot limit use," it does include a sense of compulsion and a narrowing of patterns of use. The criteria for Harmful Use, however, are significantly different from the *DSM-IIIR* and *DSM-IV*. Whereas the *DSM* focuses on use despite situations where harm may occur, the *ICD-10* proposes that actual physical or psychological harm has occurred and can be specified, making this diagnosis more restrictive (Rounsaville, Bryant et al., 1993).

Over the past 10 years, the World Health Organization and the federal Substance Abuse and Mental Health Services Administration (SAMHSA) have worked together on the Joint Project on Assessment and Classification of Mental and Alcohol and Drug Related Disorders. The aims of this project have been to improve the accuracy and reliability of psychiatric diagnoses across languages and cultures. Through this multinational project, the *ICD* and *DSM* diagnostic systems for alcohol and drug dependence have been applied to a number of different populations with very different rates and patterns of addiction. The cross-system agreement, reliability, and validity of the *DSM-IIIR* and *DSM-IV* and the *ICD-10* criteria have been evaluated for Substance Dependence and generally are very high (Rounsaville, Bryant et al., 1993; Frances, 1991; Hasin, McCloud et al., 1996). The rates of agreement for Abuse typically have been poor across the systems, which is not surprising given how differently the systems define Abuse. The *DSM-IIIR* and the *DSM-IV* differ substantially from the *ICD-10* for diagnoses of Dependence on marijuana, cocaine and alcohol because of the *ICD-10* requirement for medical (rather than social) impairment from drug use (Rounsaville, Bryant et al., 1993).

RELIABILITY AND VALIDITY

Reliability. In order for a diagnosis to be useful (e.g., communication, treatment planning, research), it must be reliable and valid. The reliability of a diagnosis refers to the accuracy, consistency, and agreement about the classification of an individual and can take several forms: (1) *test-retest reliability* refers to the consistency of the diagnosis at different time points; (2) *inter-rater reliability* refers to the diagnostic agreement between different raters of the same individual; (3) *alternate forms* is the relative equivalence of two similar diagnostic measures; and (4) *internal consistency* is the consistency with which different items of a test are related to the diagnosis.

Research has documented the internal consistency of the dependence syndrome for alcohol (Skinner & Allen, 1982) and other drugs of abuse (Kosten, Rounsaville et al., 1987). Opioid and cocaine dependence syndromes seem to have the strongest internal consistency followed by alcohol, stimulants, and hallucinogens. The sedative and cannabis dependence syndrome constructs seem to have the lowest internal consistency.

Several studies have demonstrated that the inter-rater and test-retest reliability of substance use disorder diagnoses is very good to excellent, based on the substance abuse sections or modules of structured and semi-structured interviews such as the Schedule for Affective Disorders and Schizophrenia (Rounsaville, Rosenberger et al., 1980), the Diagnostic Interview Schedule (Burke, 1986), the Composite International Diagnostic Interview Substance Abuse Module (Cottler, Schuckit et al., 1995), the Structured Clinical Interview for DSM-IIIR (Bryant, Rounsaville et al., 1992; Williams, Gibbon et al., 1992), and the LEAD standard (Kranzler, Rounsaville et al., 1994). The test-retest reliability for the Schedules for Clinical Assessment in Neuropsychiatry (SCAN; Wing et al., 1990) appears to be good to excellent for *ICD-10, DSM-IIIR*, and *DSM-IV* diagnoses of substance dependence across substances and cultural groups (Easton, Meza et al., 1997). However, the test-retest reliability of the diagnosis of substance abuse (*DSM*) or harmful use (*ICD*) has been much less reliable. Moreover, the reliability of many of these instruments is only fair for diagnosing comorbid psychiatric disorders in substance abusers.

Validity. *Validity* refers to the extent to which a diagnosis is a meaningful dimension which can be described and associated with other related dimensions, particularly other current criteria (e.g., impairment in expected life areas) and future outcomes (e.g., symptom changes). Although several studies have found structured and semi-structured interviews to be highly reliable for DSM Axis I and II disorders (see Segal, Hersen & Van Hasselt, 1994), there have been relatively fewer studies which have examined validity of these instruments (Griffin, Weiss et al., 1987; Kranzler, Kadden et al., 1996; Malgady, Rogler & Tyron, 1992) for substance use or psychiatric disorders.

Construct validity refers to the degree to which the substance dependence syndrome or diagnosis is a meaningful hypothetical dimension and usually is established through the correlation of different measures designed to assess the same diagnosis and through factor analysis. An important postulate for the construct validity of the dependence syndrome is that it is unidimensional with a coherent clustering of symptoms along a continuum of severity (Kosten, Rounsaville et al., 1987). A factor analysis of the alcohol dependence syndrome items demonstrated that a single factor accounted for most of the variance (Skinner & Allen, 1982). This is consistent with factor analytic results which suggest that the DSM dependence criteria items load on one general factor (Woody & Cacciola, 1995) and have similar rank orderings (most common to least common) of symptoms across the different major categories. "Use despite adverse consequences" was the most widely endorsed item across drugs whereas the withdrawal items were least endorsed and more strongly associated with high dependence severity.

Research also has supported the construct validity of the dependence syndrome for cocaine (Bryant, Rounsaville & Babor, 1991) and opiates (Kosten, Rounsaville et al. 1987). Woody and Cacciola (1995) have suggested that it may be useful to develop substance-specific dependence severity measures because symptom counts have different meanings (i.e., what constitutes mild, moderate, severe) depending on the type of drug. Skinner (1995) also has questioned the generalizability of the dependence syndrome construct as a severity measure across different drugs of abuse, and ongoing research (Skinner, Woody et al., 1995) will explore the reliability and validity of this single method of scaling severity to determine whether different classes (e.g., high versus low addictive potential) require different methods.

Criterion validity exists when a diagnosis predicts performance on other current measures (concurrent validity) as well as future (e.g., treatment) outcomes (predictive validity). The criteria developed for a diagnostic category should be associated with the course of the disorder, its complications, recovery, and response to treatments.

A number of studies have supported the concurrent validity of the dependence syndrome and diagnosis by relating it to other, more traditional measures of drug and alcohol use (e.g., length of use, amount of use). For alcoholics, the dependence syndrome correlated with daily quantity of alcohol and with lifetime alcohol consumption measures (Skinner & Allen, 1982). Among opiate addicts, the dependence syndrome correlated with recent use measures and severity of withdrawal, but not years of use (Kosten, Jacobsen & Kosten, 1989; Skinner & Goldberg, 1986; Sutherland, Edwards et al., 1986).

Results of a multisite study suggest that dependence symptom counts are moderately correlated with other concurrent measures of substance use amount and frequency and social and occupational impairment (Woody & Cacciola, 1995). Although the concurrent validity of substance abuse diagnoses is very good, the predictive validity is good only for some substances of abuse (Kranzler, Kadden et al., 1996; Kranzler, Tennen et al., 1997). Woody and Cacciola (1995) found that the dependence severity symptom count did not predict outcome. Alcoholism severity was correlated with some measures of treatment outcome at one year, although more strongly for male than female alcoholics (Babor, Cooney & Lauerman, 1987; Orford & Keddie, 1986; Rounsaville, Dolinksy et al., 1987). More severe opiate addiction did predict shorter treatment length at one year follow-up (Kosten, Bianchi & Kosten, 1992). The reliability, concurrent and predictive validity of anxiety and depression diagnoses in substance abusers generally are poor.

Improving Diagnostic Reliability and Validity. Carroll (1995) has summarized many of the methodological problems and issues associated with obtaining a reliable and valid diagnostic assessment of substance use disorders. In addition to intentional lying and unintentional denial, there are many factors common to substance abuse which may decrease the reliability of assessment. Poor educational history, learning, memory, and attention-concentration problems, and histories of head injury can affect the patient's ability to accurately self-report (Maddux & Desmond, 1975). Depression may affect the memory and cognitive attributions for substance abuse. HIV-related complications, including cognitive impairment and changes in mood and personality functioning also can interfere with establishing a reliable diagnosis (Carroll, 1995).

Several limitations are associated with the clinical assessment procedure itself, which limits reliability and validity of diagnoses such as the substance use disorders. For example, self-report measures may be less sensitive to detecting substance abuse problems, but overestimate psychiatric problems. In clinical settings, diagnoses typically are established through a single 30- to 60-minute unstructured interview with a psychiatrist or psychologist, which quickly narrows its focus around a small number of diagnostic possibilities rather than systematically reviewing all DSM disorders. In research settings, diagnoses may be established by research assistants with very minimal clinical training, particularly in distinguishing between substance-related symptoms from the psychiatric symptoms that they can mimic. There have been several attempts to control threats to diagnostic reliability and validity, including the use of structured interviews, collateral informants, and biological validators.

Interview Strategies. Alcohol and drug dependence diagnoses are determined by eliciting information from the patient through careful questioning procedures. Interviewing individuals in a drug- and alcohol-free state, when there is little motivation for or gain from deception, may improve the accuracy of this information. Overall, a standard has emerged in assessing substance abuse that multiple measures should be used (Babor, Cooney & Lauerman, 1987; Connors, Allen et al., 1994; O'Farrell & Maisto, 1987; Rounsaville, Bryant et al., 1993). The factors to be balanced in choosing a format include efficiency, reliability, richness of data, level of training of the personnel, and whether there are cognitive limitations in the patients. Each format (e.g., self-report questionnaire versus interview) has different advantages and disadvantages depending on how the information is obtained (see Carroll, 1995; Maisto, McKay & Connors, 1990).

A number of structured or semi-structured psychiatric interview instruments have been tested for their reliability and validity in diagnosing addiction, including the Structured Clinical Interview for DSM III-R/IV (SCID; Spitzer, Williams et al., 1990), Schedule for Affective Disorders and Schizophrenia (SADS; Endicott & Spitzer, 1978), Diagnostic Interview Schedule (DIS; Robins, Helzer et al., 1981), the Composite International Diagnostic Interview (CIDI; Robins, Wing et al., 1988), the Schedules for Clinical Assessment in Neuropsychiatry (SCAN; Wing, Babor et al., 1990), and the Psychiatric Research Interview for Substance Abuse and Mental Disorders (PRISM; Hasin, McCloud et al., 1996; Hasin, Trautman et al., 1996). (See Chapter 3, "Assessment Instruments," for a complete review.)

Structured interviews lead the diagnostician through a series of questions and probes to obtain additional information. Standardized administration and increased reliability are two advantages of the structured interview over the unstructured interview. Many structured interviews (DIS, CIDI) can be administered by lay or research personnel with less extensive training than a psychiatrist or other physician. Semi-structured interviews (SCAN, SCID, PRISM) permit greater latitude for clinical judgment, typically by a more experienced clinician who explores specific aspects of the patient's problems.

Because they can be administered by lay interviewers, structured interviews may be more efficient for large-scale community survey and psychiatric epidemiological research. In contrast, semi-structured interviews are administered more reliably by a well-trained clinician and are better for smaller scale studies focused on treatment outcome or comorbidity. Finally, the CIDI and SCAN have been translated into several languages for cross-cultural use.

Although the traditional unstructured psychiatric interviews can provide a certain richness of data, they are more likely to miss some diagnoses because they do not systematically assess each drug category (Rounsaville, Rosenberger et al., 1980). In an early study comparing structured clinical interviews (Schedule for Affective Disorders and Schizophrenia; SADS) with a more open-ended psychiatric interview in opiate addicts, Rounsaville and colleagues (1980) found that both diagnostic methods were able to diagnose opiate addiction, but the SADS was better for diagnosing other addictions than the unstructured, psychiatric interview.

DISTINGUISHING SUBSTANCE EFFECTS FROM PSYCHIATRIC SYMPTOMS

Diagnosing psychopathology in addicted individuals can present several challenges, one of which is the difficulty in separating more temporary, substance-induced symptoms (e.g., psychosis, depression) and behaviors required to maintain an addiction (e.g., criminality, manipulation) from more enduring, primary psychiatric disorders (Rounsaville & Kranzler,

1989). Making such a distinction can be very difficult even for an experienced clinician; it may be completely unreliable when made by someone without extensive experience and exposure to substance abuse and psychiatric patients.

To improve reliability and validity and address the potentially confounding effects of substance use, Rounsaville and colleagues (1991) adapted diagnostic systems by developing special interview instructions and excluding obviously substance-related criteria. Psychiatric symptoms not associated with substance use were differentiated by counting them only if they occurred during an extended period of abstinence (for stimulants and hallucinogens) or during a period of steady, unchanging substance use (depressants). More conservative systems have included waiting for a minimum period of abstinence before assessing an individual for a psychiatric disorder or counting only those psychiatric symptoms which chronologically predate the onset of a substance use disorder (see Kadden, Kranzler & Rounsaville, 1995; Schuckit & Monteiro, 1988).

At a minimum, the psychiatric assessment should be delayed until the patient is not intoxicated or experiencing withdrawal and his/her mood and cognitive status have stabilized somewhat. Because a two- to four-week period of abstinence may be impractical for severely addicted individuals, Rounsaville and Kranzler (1989) suggest that a psychiatric diagnosis be delayed until (1) the patient has achieved three to 10 days of abstinence, and (2) a brief mental status examination has been administered to determine that memory and concentration will permit an accurate assessment of the onset, course, and symptoms of the psychiatric disorder.

As reviewed above, the overall reliability and concurrent, predictive, and construct validity of substance use diagnoses are very good, whereas the validity for other psychiatric disorders (e.g., depression, anxiety, antisocial personality) in substance abusers often is fair to poor (Bryant, Rounsaville et al., 1992; Kadden, Kranzler & Rounsaville, 1995; Kranzler, Kadden et al., 1996; Rounsaville, Anton et al., 1991; Williams, Gibbon et al., 1992). Although a trained research technician appears to be capable of obtaining a reliable and valid diagnosis of substance abuse, such an individual may be less experienced at obtaining a reliable and valid comorbid psychiatric diagnosis in substance abusers (see Kranzler, Kadden et al., 1996). This has led some to rely on trained clinicians in studies of psychiatric comorbidity, as well as to develop instruments that specifically focus on standardizing the complicated process of distinguishing substance abuse symptoms from other primary psychiatric symptoms.

Nunes and colleagues (1996) have modified the SCID to focus in detail on the chronological patterning of substance abuse, depressive, and anxiety symptoms, whereas Hasin and colleagues (1995, 1996) have developed a new semi-structured interview (also based on the SCID) specifically to separate substance use effects and symptoms from other psychiatric disorders.

The Psychiatric Research Interview for Substance and Mental Disorders (PRISM; Hasin, Trautman et al., 1996) attempts to control the item-level criterion variance associated with clinical judgment (as in SCID and SCAN) or subject attribution (as in DIS or CIDI) through a very systematic, detailed inquiry into the nature of co-occurring symptoms (chronology, patterning, recency, exacerbation) and the use of explicit rating guidelines for the interviewer. The interview begins with the substance abuse section, which provides a context for the remainder of the psychiatric diagnosis sections. Clear interview instructions for distinguishing organic (substance specific intoxication and withdrawal symptoms) from "non-organic" and primary from secondary disorders are coupled with more standardized probing of areas of diagnostic uncertainty. Preliminary studies suggest that the PRISM has achieved its goal of achieving improved test-retest reliability of comorbid psychiatric disorders in substance abusers (Hasin, Trautman et al., 1996). The reliability of substance *dependence* diagnoses was excellent, although those for substance *abuse* and antisocial personality disorder were poor.

Studies examining the validity of the PRISM currently are underway. On the negative side, the PRISM requires a fair amount of training and can be very time-consuming to administer in substance abuse and dual diagnosis patients, even in its recently modified short form.

USE OF COLLATERAL INFORMATION

A major problem in the area of psychiatric diagnosis is the limited accuracy of a single interview in which patients are asked to provide a history of psychiatric symptoms covering an entire lifetime (Spitzer & Williams, 1980). Structured interviews that incorporate specific diagnostic criteria may provide a good basis for reliable and valid diagnoses, but the data obtained still may be inaccurate if the subject withholds or provides false information. This is particularly likely to be the case for Substance Use and Antisocial Personality Disorder diagnoses, in which the subject may deny or minimize behavior.

There have been two related efforts to improve diagnostic reliability and validity based on inclusion of additional clinical and collateral information: (1) the Best Estimate procedure (Leckman, Sholomskas et al., 1982), and (2) the LEAD standard procedure (Spitzer, 1983). Both of these diagnostic processes involve obtaining collateral sources of information and an overall case review by an expert diagnostician. In studies of the Best Estimate procedure, an expert reviews the blinded records of structured interviews and collateral information from medical records and one or more interviews with the patient's family members. In comparison to a structured interview alone, the Best Estimate procedure yields higher lifetime rates of major and minor depression, alcohol and drug dependence, and especially antisocial personality disorder among opiate-addicted individuals (Kosten & Rounsaville, 1992; Kosten, Anton & Rounsaville, 1992).

An even more comprehensive procedure to evaluate the single diagnostic interview method is the LEAD standard proposed by Spitzer (1983). LEAD is an acronym for **L**ongitudinal, **E**xpert diagnoses based on **A**ll available **D**ata and involves administering: (1) a comprehensive battery of assessments of psychiatric and addiction symptoms by a research associate within the first week of hospitalization, repeated approximately two weeks later by a psychiatrist; (2) interviews with significant others about the patient's alcohol and drug use and psychiatric history; (3) gathering of diagnostic information from other clinical staff by the psychiatrist at the patient's discharge conference; and (4) review of recent and old chart information. After reviewing data in all four of these areas, the expert diagnostician arrives at a LEAD diagnosis. The reliability of the LEAD procedure seems to be excellent for substance abuse disorders, but not for comorbid psychiatric disorders.

Although designed to obtain a diagnosis in clinical practice, the LEAD standard appears to be neither necessary nor cost-effective (Kranzler, Rounsaville et al., 1994; Kranzler, Tennen et al., 1997). It may be useful both as a criterion against which the procedural validity of existing or new diagnostic instruments can be evaluated, or in research on substance use disorders where the need for diagnostic precision is very high (e.g., genetic linkage studies) (Kranzler, Rounsaville et al., 1994; Kranzler, Tennen et al., 1997).

In addition to questionnaires and interviews, several biological measures can help to clarify or contradict self-reports of alcohol and drug use. Alcohol and drugs can be present in biological fluids and tested in blood, urine, breath, and hair; chronic use can cause physiological damage (such as cirrhosis and endocarditis); alcohol and some drugs are associated with stereotypical withdrawal syndromes. However, these are not in themselves valid indicators of addiction. Positive urines may reflect medically indicated or non-dependent use. Physical problems can be consequences of other disease processes and withdrawal symptoms can mimic and be complicated by other medical or psychiatric disorders. Also, stereotypic withdrawal symptoms have been described in only a few drugs, such as opiates or alcohol, and may not appear consistently for all drugs. In addition, all biological markers can be negative, yet addiction can be severe. Clearly, biological tests need to be used in combination with psychological or behavioral assessments.

DIAGNOSTIC SUBTYPING

Follow-up studies consistently find that some addicted patients recover while others show no change or deterioration. This suggests that despite significant developments in the area of assessment, diagnosis, and treatment of addiction, individuals with the same diagnosis can have significantly different responses to the same treatment. The modest or inconsistent predictive validity of the dependence syndrome or diagnosis suggests that there may be a need to evaluate other methods for subtyping individuals who share a common diagnosis.

The DSM System. The *DSM-IV* permits clinicians to subtype Substance Use disorders on the basis of physiological dependence, symptom severity, and recency of use and symptoms. Despite some controversy, DSM-IV subtypes Substance Dependence as either: (1) with physiological dependence, and (2) without physiological dependence based on the presence or absence of tolerance and withdrawal. The diagnosis also can be subtyped based on the recency of use and the presence of one or more abuse or dependence criteria: (1) Sustained Full Remission (no symptoms for at least 12 months); (2) Early Full Remission (no symptoms for one to 12 months); (3) Sustained Partial Remission (one to two criteria met for at least 12 months); (4) Early Partial Remission (one to two criteria for one to 12 months);

(5) On Agonist Medication (e.g., methadone with no symptoms of heroin dependence for at least past month); and (6) In a Controlled Environment. Finally, substance use disorders can be subtyped as mild, moderate, or severe which is consistent with the dimensional scaling of the dependence syndrome described above (Edwards, 1986). The reliability and validity of these three diagnostic subtyping distinctions have not been evaluated empirically. In addition, these diagnostic subtypes of substance dependence communicate little information about the addicted person and his or her frequency, severity, reasons, history of substance use, ability to abstain, and relapse vulnerabilities for the purpose of treatment placement, matching, planning, and evaluating outcome. They also communicate little about the etiology or expected course of the disorder and do not adequately describe the significant heterogeneity found among individuals with this common disorder (see Carroll, 1995).

Single versus Multidimensional Typologies. There have been several attempts to subtype substance abusers based on single dimensions such as comorbid psychopathology, age of onset, family history, gender, and personality. Addicted individuals are likely to have coexisting psychopathology (Rounsaville, Kosten et al., 1986, 1987; Rounsaville, Anton et al., 1991). There is evidence that concurrent psychopathology confers poorer prognosis (McLellan et al., 1983; Rounsaville, Kosten et al., 1986, 1987), is associated with treatment seeking (Carroll & Rounsaville, 1992; Rounsaville & Kleber, 1985), responds to concurrent psychiatric treatment (Woody, McLellan et al., 1984, 1985), and also may have treatment matching implications (Rounsaville & Kranzler, 1989).

Age of onset is another important alcoholism subtyping variable, with earlier onset predicting more severe alcohol-related social problems, drug abuse, coexistent psychopathology, criminality, psychopathy, and familial or genetic risk (Irwin, Schuckit & Smith, 1990; McGue, Pickins & Svikis, 1992; Roy, DeJong et al., 1991; Turnbull, George et al., 1990). These findings tend to be true for drug abusers as well (Robins & Przybeck, 1985). There is an extensive literature (particularly using the MMPI) of subtyping substance abusers on the basis of abnormal personality dimensions, such as neurotic, psychopathic, and psychotic (see Anglin, Weisman & Fisher, 1989; Graham & Strenger, 1988).

Although single dimension subtyping systems have greater clinical appeal from the standpoint of parsimony, they tend to predict a narrower range of outcome than a more comprehensive, multidimensional typology (Babor, Dolinsky et al., 1992). Such a broader theoretical framework helps organize diverse variables into meaningful constructs which may play a role in the etiology, patterning, and course of the disorder. For example, Cloninger's (1987) Type I and II and Babor and colleagues' (1992) Type A and B systems categorize alcoholics into two types. Type I or A alcoholism is characterized by lower heritability, fewer childhood risk factors, later age of onset, less severe dependence, and lower novelty seeking. Type II or B alcoholism is characterized by higher heritability, more childhood risk factors, earlier onset, more severe dependence and psychiatric comorbidity, impulsivity, high novelty seeking, and antisocial behavior.

Ball and colleagues (1995) and Feingold and colleagues (1996) have found that the Type A/B distinction also is reliable and valid for cocaine, opiate, and marijuana users. Type A/B also is a reliable and valid distinction across gender, ethnicity, and treatment settings. In addition, this typology has predicted outcome and response to specific treatment. Type B alcoholics (Babor, Hofmann et al., 1992) and cocaine dependent (Ball, Carroll et al., 1995) individuals exhibit greater substance use severity, associated psychosocial problems, and psychiatric symptoms and may relapse faster than Type As (Babor, Hofmann et al., 1992; Ball, Carroll et al., 1995). One treatment matching study found that Type B alcoholics who received coping skills treatment had better outcomes than those receiving an interactional therapy (Litt, Babor et al., 1992). This finding, however, was not confirmed by Project MATCH (1997), sponsored by the National Institute on Alcohol Abuse and Alcoholism.

CONCLUSIONS

This chapter reviewed past and current diagnostic systems for substance use disorders, with particular emphasis on the *DSM-IV* system. The major diagnostic issues over the past half century have been the increased reliance on the dependence syndrome construct, the operationalization of inclusion/exclusion criteria, the shifting emphasis on the physiological symptoms of addiction (tolerance and withdrawal), and the recognition of addiction as a coherent syndrome which is not subsumed by other addictive disorders.

These developments have stimulated research on the reliability and validity of addiction diagnoses and the important complexity of coexistent psychopathology in the assessment and treatment process. Addicted individuals are not a homogeneous group, but rather differ greatly in the severity of their disorder, the presence and extent of coexistent psychopathology, and on the range of dimensions that may define several subtypes of substance users. Continued research on the complexity of this disorder holds the promise of improved treatment as understanding develops about what types of interventions work best for what types of alcohol and drug users and addicts.

ACKNOWLEDGMENT: Support for the development of this chapter was provided by the National Institute on Drug Abuse Grant R01-DA10012 and Center Grant P50-DA09241.

REFERENCES

American Psychiatric Association (1952). *Diagnostic and Statistical Manual of Mental Disorders* (I:1952, II:1967, III:1980, III-R:1987, IV:1994). Washington, DC: American Psychiatric Press.

Anglin MD, Weisman CP & Fisher DG (1989). The MMPI profiles of narcotics addicts, I: A review of the literature. *International Journal of Addictions* 24:867–880.

Babor TF, Cooney NL & Lauerman RJ (1987). The dependence syndrome concept as a psychological theory of relapse behaviour: An empirical evaluation of alcoholic and opiate addicts. *British Journal of Addiction* 82:393–405.

Babor TF, Dolinsky ZS, Meyer RE, Hesselbrock et al. (1992). Types of alcoholics: Concurrent and predictive validity of some common classification schemes. *British Journal of Addiction* 87:1415–1431.

Babor TF, Hofmann M, Del Boca FK et al. (1992). Types of alcoholics I: evidence for an empirically derived typology based on indicators of vulnerability and severity. *Archives of General Psychiatry* 49:599–608.

Babor TF, Stephens RS & Marlatt GA (1987). Verbal report methods in clinical research on alcoholism: Response bias and its minimization. *Journal of Studies on Alcohol* 12:101–111.

Ball SA, Carroll KM, Babor TF & Rounsaville BJ (1995). Subtypes of cocaine abusers: Support for a Type A-Type B distinction. *Journal of Consulting and Clinical Psychology* 63:115–124.

Bryant K, Rounsaville BJ & Babor TF (1991). Coherence of the dependence syndrome in cocaine users. *British Journal of Addiction* 86:1299–1310.

Bryant K, Rounsaville BJ, Spitzer R & Williams J (1992). Reliability of dual diagnosis: Substance dependence and psychiatric disorders. *Journal of Nervous and Mental Disease* 180:251–257.

Burke JD Jr (1986). Diagnostic categorization by the Diagnostic Interview Schedule (DIS): A comparison with other methods of assessment. In JE Barrett & RM Rose (eds.) *Mental Disorders in the Community: Progress and Challenges*. New York, NY: Guilford Press, 255–279.

Carroll KM (1995). Methodological issues and problems in the assessment of substance use. *Psychological Assessment* 7:349–358.

Carroll KM & Rounsaville BJ (1992). Contrast of treatment-seeking and untreated cocaine abusers. *Archives of General Psychiatry* 49:464–471.

Cloninger CR (1987). Neurogenetic adaptive mechanisms in alcoholism. *Science* 236:410–416.

Connors GJ, Allen JP, Cooney NL & DiClemente CC (1994). Assessment issues and strategies in alcoholism treatment matching research. *Journal of Studies on Alcohol* 12:92–100.

Cottler LB, Schuckit MA, Helzer JE, Crowley T et al. (1995). The DSM-IV field trials for substance use disorders: Major results. *Drug and Alcohol Dependence* 38:59–69.

Easton C, Meza E, Ulug B, Kilic C et al. (1997). Test-retest reliability of the alcohol and drug use disorder sections of the Schedules for Clinical Assessment in Neuropsychiatry (SCAN). *Drug and Alcohol Dependence* 47:187–194.

Edwards G (1986). The alcohol dependence syndrome: A concept as stimulus to enquiry. *British Journal of Addiction* 81:171–183.

Edwards G, Arif A & Hodgson R (1981). Nomenclature and classification of drug- and alcohol-related problems: A WHO memorandum. *Bulletin of the World Health Organization* 59:225–242.

Edwards G & Gross MM (1976). Alcohol dependence: Provisional description of a clinical syndrome. *British Medical Journal* 1:1058–1061.

Endicott J & Spitzer RL (1978). A diagnostic interview: The Schedule for Affective Disorders and Schizophrenia. *Archives of General Psychiatry* 35:837–844.

Feighner JP, Robins E, Guze SB, et al. (1972). Diagnostic criteria for use in psychiatric research. *Archives of General Psychiatry* 26:57–63.

Feingold A, Ball SA, Kranzler HR & Rounsaville BJ (1996). Generalizability of the Type A/Type B distinction across different psychoactive substances. *American Journal of Drug and Alcohol Abuse* 22:449–462.

Frances A, Pincus H, First B, Widiger T et al. (1991). *DSM-IV Options Book: Work in Progress*. Washington, DC: American Psychiatric Press.

Glantz M & Pickens RW, eds. (1992). *Vulnerability to Drug Abuse*. Washington, DC: American Psychological Association.

Graham JR & Strenger VE (1988). MMPI characteristics of alcoholics: A review. *Journal of Consulting and Clinical Psychology* 56:197–205.

Griffin ML, Weiss RD, Mirin SM, Wilson H & Bouchard-Voelk B (1987). The use of the Diagnostic Interview Schedule in drug-dependent patients. *American Journal of Drug and Alcohol Abuse* 13:281–291.

Hasin DS, Babor TF, Grant BF, Room R & Cottler LB (1995). Diagnostic work group report. In JD Blaine,

AM Horton Jr & LH Towle (eds.) *Diagnosis and Severity of Drug Abuse and Drug Dependence* (NIH Publication No. 95-3884). Rockville, MD: National Institute on Drug Abuse, 4–10.

Hasin DS, McCloud S, Li Q & Endicott J (1996). Cross-system agreement among demographic groups: DSM-III, DSM-III-R, DSM-IV, and ICD-10 diagnoses of alcohol use disorders. *Drug and Alcohol Dependence* 41:127–135.

Hasin DS, Trautman KD, Miele GM, Samet S, Smith M & Endicott J (1996). Psychiatric Research Interview for Substance Abuse and Mental Disorders (PRISM): Reliability for substance abusers. *American Journal of Psychiatry* 153:1195–1201.

Irwin M, Schukit M & Smith TL (1990). Clinical importance of age of onset in type 1 and type 2 primary alcoholics. *Archives of General Psychiatry* 47:320–324.

Jaffe JH (1985). Drug addiction and drug abuse. In LS Goodman & A Gilman (eds.) *Goodman & Gilman's The Pharmacological Basis of Therapeutics*. New York, NY: MacMillan.

Kadden RM, Kranzler HR & Rounsaville BJ (1995). Validity of the distinction between "substance-induced" and "independent" depression and anxiety disorders. *American Journal of the Addictions* 4:107–117.

Kosten TA, Anton SF & Rounsaville BJ (1992). Ascertaining psychiatric diagnosis with the family history method in a substance abuse population. *Journal of Psychiatric Research* 26:135–147.

Kosten TA, Bianchi MS & Kosten TR (1992). The predictive validity of the dependence syndrome in opiate addicts. *American Journal of Drug and Alcohol Abuse* 18:145–156.

Kosten TA, Jacobsen LK & Kosten TR (1989). Severity of precipitated opiate withdrawal predicts drug dependence by DSM-III-R criteria. *American Journal of Drug and Alcohol Abuse* 15:237–250.

Kosten TA & Rounsaville BJ (1992). Sensitivity of psychiatric diagnoses based on best estimate procedure. *American Journal of Psychiatry* 149:1225–1227.

Kosten TR, Rounsaville BJ, Babor TF, Spitzer RL & Williams JBW (1987). Substance-use disorders in DSM-III-R: Evidence for the dependence syndrome across different psychoactive substances. *British Journal of Psychiatry* 151:834–843.

Kranzler HR, Kadden RM, Babor TF, Tennen H & Rounsaville BJ (1996). Validity of the SCID in substance abuse patients. *Addiction* 91:859–868.

Kranzler HR, Rounsaville BJ, Kadden RM & Babor TF (1994). Use of the Longitudinal, Expert, All Data procedure for psychiatric diagnosis in patients with psychoactive substance use disorders. *Journal of Nervous and Mental Disease* 182:277–283.

Kranzler HR, Tennen H, Babor TF, Kadden RM & Rounsaville BJ (1997). Validity of the Longitudinal, Expert, All Data procedure for Psychiatric diagnosis in patients with psychoactive substance use disorders. *Drug and Alcohol Dependence* 45:93–104.

Leckman JF, Sholomskas D, Thompson WD, Belanger A & Weissman MM (1982). Best estimates of lifetime psychiatric diagnosis: A methodological study. *Archives of General Psychiatry* 39:879–883.

Litt MD, Babor TF, DelBoca FK et al. (1992). Types of alcoholics II: Application of an empirically derived typology to treatment matching. *Archives of General Psychiatry* 49:609–614.

Maddux JF & Desmond DP (1975). Reliability and validity of information from chronic heroin users. *Journal of Psychiatric Research* 12:87–95.

Maisto SA, McKay JR & Connors GJ (1990). Self-report issues in substance abuse: State of the art and future directions. *Behavioral Assessment* 12:117–134.

Malgady RG, Rogler LH & Tyron WW (1992). Issues of validity in the Diagnostic Interview Schedule. *Journal of Psychiatric Research* 26:59–67.

Marlatt GA & Gordon JR, eds. (1985). *Relapse Prevention: Maintenance Strategies in the Treatment of Addictive Behaviors*. New York, NY: Guilford Press.

McGue M, Pickens RW & Svikis DS (1992). Sex and age effects on the inheritance of alcohol problems: A twin study. *Journal of Abnormal Psychology* 101:3–17.

McLellan AT, Alterman AI, Metzger DS, Grissom GR et al. (1994). Similarity of outcome predictors across opiates, cocaine, and alcohol treatments: Role of treatment services. *Journal of Consulting and Clinical Psychology* 62:1141–1158.

McLellan AT, Luborsky L, Woody GE et al. (1983). Predicting response to alcohol and drug abuse treatments: Role of psychiatric severity. *Archives of General Psychiatry* 40:620–625.

Miller NS (1995). *Addiction Psychiatry: Current Diagnosis and Treatment*. New York, NY: Wiley-Liss, Inc.

Nunes EV, Goehl L, Seracini A et al. (1996). A modification of the Structured Clinical Interview for DSM-III-R to evaluate methadone maintained patients: Test-retest reliabiity. *American Journal on Addictions* 5:241–248.

O'Farrell TJ & Maisto SA (1987). The utility of self-report and biological measures of alcohol consumption in alcoholism treatment outcome studies. *Advances in Behavioral Research Therapy* 9:91–125.

Orford J & Keddie A (1986). Abstinence or controlled drinking in clinical practice: A test of the dependence and persuasion hypotheses. *British Journal of Addiction* 81:495–504.

Prochaska JO, DiClemente CC & Norcross JC (1992). In search of how people change: Application to addictive behaviors. *American Psychologist* 47:1102–1114.

Project MATCH Research Group (1997). Matching alcoholism treatments to client heterogeneity: Project MATCH posttreatment drinking outcome. *Journal of Studies on Alcohol* 5:7–29.

Robins LN, Helzer JE, Croughan J & Ratcliff KS (1981). National Institute of Mental Health Diagnostic Interview Schedule. *Archives of General Psychiatry* 38:381–389.

Robins LN & Przybeck TR (1985). Age of onset of drug use as a factor in drug and other disorders. *Etiology of Drug Abuse: Implications for Prevention (NIDA Research Monograph 56)*. Rockville, MD: National Institute on Drug Abuse, 178–192.

Robins LN, Wing J, Wittchen HU et al. (1988). The Composite International Diagnostic Interview. *Archives of General Psychiatry* 45:1069–1077.

Rounsaville BJ, Anton SF, Carroll K et al. (1991). Psychiatric diagnoses of treatment-seeking cocaine abusers. *Archives of General Psychiatry* 48:43–51.

Rounsaville BJ & Bryant K (1992). Tolerance and withdrawal in the DSM-III-R diagnosis of substance dependence: Utility in cocaine using population. *American Journal of Addictions* 1:50–60.

Rounsaville BJ, Bryant K, Babor TF et al. (1993). Cross system agreement for substance use disorders. *Addiction* 88:337–348.

Rounsaville BJ, Dolinsky ZS, Babor TF & Meyer RE (1987). Psychopathology as a predictor of treatment outcome in alcoholics. *Archives of General Psychiatry* 44:505–513.

Rounsaville BJ & Kleber HD (1985). Untreated opiate addicts. *Archives of General Psychiatry* 42:1072–1077.

Rounsaville BJ, Kosten TR, Weissman et al. (1986). Prognostic significance of psychopathology in treated opiate addicts. *Archives of General Psychiatry* 43:739–745.

Rounsaville BJ, Kosten TR, Williams JBW & Spitzer RL (1987). A field trial of DSM-III-R psychoactive substance dependence disorders. *American Journal of Psychiatry* 144:351–355.

Rounsaville BJ & Kranzler HR (1989). DSM-III-R diagnosis of alcoholism. In A Tasman, RE Hale & AJ Frances (eds.): *Psychiatric Updates*. Washington, DC: American Psychiatric Press, 323–340.

Rounsaville BJ, Rosenberger P, Wilber C et al. (1980). A comparison of the SADS/RDC and the DSM-III: Diagnosing drug abusers. *Journal of Nervous and Mental Disease* 168:90–97.

Rounsaville BJ, Spitzer RL & Williams JBW (1986). Proposed changes in DSM-III substance use disorders: Description and rationale. *American Journal of Psychiatry* 143:463–468.

Roy A, DeJong J, Lamparski D et al. (1991). Mental disorders among alcoholics: Relationship to age of onset and cerebrospinal fluid neuropeptides. *Archives of General Psychiatry* 48:423–427.

Schuckit MA & Monteiro MG (1988). Alcoholism, anxiety and depression. *British Journal of Addiction* 83:1373–1380.

Segal DL, Hersen M & van Hasselt VB (1994). Reliability of the Structured Clinical Interview for DSM-III-R: An evaluative review. *Comprehensive Psychiatry* 35:316–327.

Skinner HA (1995). Critical issues in the diagnosis of substance use disorders. In JD Blaine, AM Horton Jr & LH Towle (eds.) *Diagnosis and Severity of Drug Abuse and Drug Dependence* (NIH Publication No. 95-3884). Rockville, MD: National Institute on Drug Abuse, 71–76.

Skinner HA, Woody GE, Caetano R et al. (1995). Severity work group report: Future directions of research: Next 5 years. In JD Blaine, AM Horton Jr & LH Towle (eds.) *Diagnosis and Severity of Drug Abuse and Drug Dependence* (NIH Publication No. 95-3884). Rockville, MD: National Institute on Drug Abuse, 11–17.

Skinner HA & Allen BA (1982). Alcohol dependence syndrome: Measurement and validation. *Journal of Abnormal Psychology* 91:199–209.

Skinner HA & Goldberg AE (1986). Evidence for a drug dependence syndrome among narcotic users. *British Journal of Addiction* 81:479–484.

Spitzer RL (1983). Psychiatric diagnoses: Are clinicians still necessary? *Comprehensive Psychiatry* 24:399–411.

Spitzer RL, Endicott J & Robins E (1973). Research diagnostic criteria: Rationale and reliability. *Archives of General Psychiatry* 35:773–782.

Spitzer RL & Williams JBW (1980). Classification of mental disorders and DSM-III. In H Kaplan, A Freedman & B Sadock (eds.) *Comprehensive Textbook of Psychiatry*. Baltimore, MD: Williams & Wilkins, 1035–1072.

Spitzer RL, Williams JSW, Gibbon M & First MB (1990). *Structured Clinical Interview for DSM-III-R: Patient Edition*. Washington, DC: American Psychiatric Press.

Sutherland G, Edwards G, Taylor C et al. (1986). The measurement of opiate dependence. *British Journal of Addiction* 82:485–494.

Turnbull JE, George LK, Landerman R et al. (1990). Social outcomes related to age of onset among psychiatric disorders. *Journal of Consulting and Clinical Psychology* 58:832–839.

Williams JBW, Gibbon M, First MB, Spitzer RL et al. (1992). The Structured Clinical Interview for DSM-III-R (SCID), II: Multisite test-retest reliability. *Archives of General Psychiatry* 49:630–636.

Wing JK, Babor T, Brugha T, Burke J et al. (1990). SCAN: Schedules for Clinical Assessment in Neuropsychiatry. *Archives of General Psychiatry* 47:589–593.

World Health Organization (1992). *International Statistical Classification of Diseases and Related Health Problems, 10th Revision*. Geneva, Switzerland: World Health Organization.

Woody GE & Cacciola J (1995). Overview of severity issues as they pertain to DSM-IV. In JD Blaine, AM Horton Jr & LH Towle (eds.) *Diagnosis and Severity of Drug Abuse and Drug Dependence* (NIH Publication No. 95-3884). Rockville, MD: National Institute on Drug Abuse, 37–43.

Woody GE, McLellan, AT, Luborsky L et al. (1984). Psychiatric severity as a predictor of benefits from psychotherapy: The Penn-VA study. *American Journal of Psychiatry* 141:1172–1177.

Woody GE, McLellan AT, Luborsky L et al. (1985). Sociopathy and psychotherapy outcome. *Archives of General Psychiatry* 42:1081–1086.

SECTION 5
Overview of Addiction Treatment

CHAPTER 1

Natural History of Addiction and Pathways to Recovery **295**
George E. Vaillant, M.D.

CHAPTER 2

Myths About the Treatment of Addiction **309**
Charles P. O'Brien, M.D., Ph.D. and A. Thomas McLellan, Ph.D.

CHAPTER 3

Traditional Approaches to the Treatment of Addiction **315**
Michael M. Miller, M.D., FASAM

CHAPTER 4

Components of Successful Treatment Programs: Lessons from the Research Literature **327**
A. Thomas McLellan, Ph.D. and James R. McKay, Ph.D.

CHAPTER 5

What Works in Treatment: Effect of Setting, Duration and Amount **345**
John W. Finney, Ph.D. and Rudolf H. Moos, Ph.D.

CHAPTER 6

Linkages of Substance Abuse with Primary Care and Mental Health Treatment **353**
Patrick G. O'Connor, M.D., M.P.H. and Douglas M. Ziedonis, M.D., M.P.H.

CHAPTER 7

Use of Patient Placement Criteria in the Selection of Treatment **363**
David Mee-Lee, M.D.

CHAPTER 8

Alternative Therapies **371**
Tacey Ann Boucher, B.A., Thomas J. Kiresuk, Ph.D., and Alan I. Trachtenberg, M.D., Ph.D.

CHAPTER 9

Harm Reduction as an Approach to Treatment **395**
Alex Wodak, M.D., FRACP

CHAPTER 10

Addiction and Treatment in the Criminal Justice System **405**
Blair Carlson, M.D., M.S.P.H., FASAM

SECTION COORDINATORS

ANNE GELLER, M.D., FASAM
Associate Professor of Clinical Medicine
Columbia College of Physicians and Surgeons
and Medical Director
Smithers Alcohol Treatment Center
St. Luke's-Roosevelt Hospital
New York, New York

DAVID MEE-LEE, M.D.
Clinical Instructor in Psychiatry
Harvard Medical School
Boston, Massachusetts, and
Consultant in Psychiatry
Massachusetts General Hospital
Boston, Massachusetts

CONTRIBUTORS

Tacey Ann Boucher, B.A.
Research Assistant
Center for Addiction
and Alternative Medicine Research
Minneapolis Medical Research Foundation
Minneapolis, Minnesota

Blair Carlson, M.D., MSPH, FASAM
Medical Director
Chemical Dependency Treatment Services
Kaiser Permanente, Colorado Region, and
Clinical Professor of Medicine
University of Colorado Medical School
Denver, Colorado

John W. Finney, Ph.D.
Health Science Specialist
Program Evaluation and Resource Center
Center for Health Care Evaluation
VA Palo Alto Health Care System and
Stanford University Medical Center
Palo Alto, California

Thomas J. Kiresuk, Ph.D.
Chief Clinical Psychologist
Hennepin County Medical Center, and
Director, Program Evaluation Research Center, and
Director, Center for Addiction and Alternative
Medicine Research
Minneapolis Medical Research Foundation
Minneapolis, Minnesota

James R. McKay, Ph.D.
Penn-VA Center for Studies of Addiction
University of Pennsylvania
Philadelphia, Pennsylvania

A. Thomas McLellan, Ph.D.
Penn-VA Center for Studies of Addiction
University of Pennsylvania
Philadelphia, Pennsylvania

Michael M. Miller, M.D., FASAM
Medical Director
NewStart Alcohol/Drug Treatment Programs
Meriter Hospital, and
Departments of Family Medicine and Practice, Psychiatry, and Internal Medicine
University of Wisconsin Medical School
Madison, Wisconsin

Rudolf H. Moos, Ph.D.
Director, Center for Health Care Evaluation
VA Palo Alto Health Care System and
Stanford University Medical Center
Palo Alto, California

Charles O'Brien, M.D.
Professor of Psychiatry
University of Pennsylvania Medical School
and VA Medical Center
Philadelphia, Pennsylvania

Patrick G. O'Connor, M.D., M.P.H.
Professor of Medicine
Yale University School of Medicine, and
Director, Primary Care Center
Yale New Haven Hospital
New Haven, Connecticut

Alan I. Trachtenberg, M.D., Ph.D.
U.S. Public Health Service Medical Officer
Office of Pharmacological and Alternative Therapies
Center for Substance Abuse Treatment
Rockville, Maryland

George E. Vaillant, M.D.
Professor of Psychiatry
Harvard Medical School, and
Division of Psychiatry
Brigham & Women's Hospital
Boston, Massachusetts

Alex Wodak, FRACP
Director, Alcohol and Drug Service
St. Vincent's Hospital
Darlinghurst, New South Wales
Australia

Douglas Ziedonis, M.D., M.P.H.
Director, Addiction Division
Robert Wood Johnson Medical School
and Senior Researcher
Rutgers Center for Alcohol Studies
Piscataway, New Jersey

CHAPTER 1

Natural History of Addiction and Pathways to Recovery

George E. Vaillant, M.D.

Why Does Addiction Begin?
Why Does Addiction Persist?
Why Does Addiction Cease?

Addiction is a medical disorder with a complex etiology, multiple manifestations of illness, and a varied clinical course. Nevertheless, it may be viewed as a discrete disorder with a discernible natural history. Unlike most medical disorders, however, the risk factors for the onset of addiction are surprisingly independent of the risk factors militating against eventual recovery. The major reason for this paradox is that severity of addiction is associated with both the best and the worst long-term outcomes.

Longitudinal, prospective studies are better suited for analyzing the natural history of addiction (Vaillant, 1988), than are cross-sectional or retrospective studies. In part, this is because schedules of reinforcement are important in determining the effects of drugs on behavior (Morse & Kelleher, 1970). Long-term follow-up helps to clarify the regular sequence of events or schedules under which drugs of abuse are sought and to promote our understanding of the facets of an addict's life that facilitate recovery.

For the purposes of this chapter, the term "addiction" will encompass "substance dependence," as specified in the criteria of the *Diagnostic and Statistical Manual of Mental Disorders, 4th Edition* (*DSM-IV*) of the American Psychiatric Association (1994). For heuristic purposes, the chapter will divide addiction (substance dependence) into two broad facets: (1) addiction without premorbid psychiatric comorbidity—of which alcohol abuse often is an example—and (2) addiction that results in part from efforts at self-medication due to premorbid psychiatric comorbidity—of which heroin and polydrug abuse are outstanding examples. In order to address these two facets of addiction, the chapter will contrast alcohol and heroin addiction.

Alcoholism differs from heroin dependence in many ways. First, alcoholism generally develops slowly over a person's lifetime; it can begin at any age; and it often occurs in individuals who have little premorbid psychosocial pathology. Heroin dependence, by contrast, usually begins in young adults with comorbid personality disorders and/or depression. Such differences arise, in part, because alcohol—like gambling and cigarettes—is highly addicting but a very poor anodyne. In contrast, heroin—like cocaine—relieves, over the short-term, multiple sources of pain. Chronic alcoholism, however, exerts greater long-term effects on the central nervous system than does heroin use. Thus, chronic alcoholism often creates the illusion that it is the result rather than the cause of psychopathology.

In order to describe the natural history of any medical disorder, three questions must be addressed: Why does it begin? Why does it persist? Why does it cease?

WHY DOES ADDICTION BEGIN?

To understand the natural history of any disorder, the major etiologic factors must be kept in mind. To do this, the critical and interactive roles played by host *and* agent *and* environment require attention. When the *agent* causing addiction is readily accessible (inexpensive and/or available at sales outlets that are numerous and often open), or when an agent is available in rapid-acting forms, then abuse will increase. Whenever the *host* is demoralized, ignorant of healthy social drug use, or susceptible to heavy drug using peers, or whenever the host has a high genetic predisposition to abuse the agent or to antisocial personality, or whenever the host is poorly socialized into the culture or is in pain, then drug abuse may increase. Finally, whenever the *environment* makes the agent the recreational drug of choice, or fails to structure healthy drug use practices, or places no taboos upon abuse, or is dysfunctional, then addiction will increase. Thus, in order to understand the cause and course of addiction, we must understand genetics, behavioral psychology, sociology, and economics as well as pharmacology and psychopathology.

Characteristics of the Agent. An important factor in addiction, of course, is the fact that some drugs can produce physiological and psychological habituation. But addiction is far more complicated than mere pharmacology. Thus, the first risk factor to be considered is the *availability of the agent.* Availability has more to do with climate, economics and politics than with pharmacology. In eighteenth century London, the advent of cheap gin as a means of economically disposing of excess grain led to an epidemic of devastating proportions. In contrast, alcohol abuse is rare in countries with grain shortages. This effect is most clearly seen in Moslem countries, where availability is restricted not only by religious laws against alcohol use and the availability of alternative mood-altering recreational drugs, like cannabis, but also by agricultural and climatic patterns that inhibit production of crops from which alcohol may be cheaply produced. In another example, the availability of cheap heroin grown in nearby Burma and Thailand produced an epidemic of heroin abuse among American troops in Viet Nam, even though they lacked other risk factors. In contrast, the shipping restrictions of World War II virtually abolished heroin use in New York City during that war, even among previously intractable addicts who had many risk factors.

A second etiological factor in addiction is *cost.* The ratio of heroin to cocaine abuse is in part a function of relative cost. The prevalence of alcoholism bears a direct relationship to per capita consumption of alcohol, and per capita consumption of alcohol bears a direct relation to cost. Thus, to the extent that social policy affects price structure, these factors also influence alcohol abuse. However, as Moore and Gerstein (1981) have convincingly demonstrated, controlling alcohol abuse by manipulating social policy is a very difficult process.

A third factor affecting the likelihood of addiction is the *rapidity with which the agent reaches the brain.* Cultural patterns that encourage consumption of low-proof alcoholic beverages and that direct that alcohol be drunk only with food—which delays intestinal absorption of alcohol—reduce the likelihood of alcohol dependence. In contrast, drinking practices that encourage high-proof alcohol to be ingested in the absence of food (for example, in bars and in the gin mills at the perimeter of Native American reservations) increase the likelihood of alcohol dependence. All other factors being equal, intravenous short-acting heroin leads to dependence far more rapidly than oral consumption of long-acting methadone.

A fourth risk factor is the agent's *efficacy as a tranquilizer.* Heroin produces effective relief against pain, anger, insomnia, hunger and depression. Thus, heroin is an excellent agent for self-medication. In contrast, alcohol, even in low doses, interferes with sleep architecture, makes depression worse, and is little better than placebo (c.f. barbiturates) in the management of anxiety. (Alcohol is a tranquilizer only to the degree that it reduces guilt, produces muscle relaxation and alters psychological state.) Thus, despite common belief to the contrary, self-medication rarely is a major etiological factor in alcohol dependence.

Characteristics of the Environment. Environment is very important, both as a source of risk for and of protection from addiction. Thus, *occupation* is a fifth contributing factor. Especially dangerous are occupations that break down the time-dependent rituals that help to protect "social" drugs from being consumed around the clock. Occupations like bartending and the diplomatic service put individuals in close contact with alcohol during most of the day. Unemployment and occupations like writing and journalism, which deprive an individual of the structure of the working day, also are associated with increased rates of alcoholism. Prostitution, with its high association with danger, pain and shame, is associated with opiate use in order to make the profession bearable.

A sixth source of risk is the *individual's peer group.* The choice of recreational drug—and thus the rate of addiction—among adolescents and young adults is almost as susceptible to peer fashion as is clothing or music. On the one hand, a common reason for men to shift from a pattern of heavy, prealcoholic drinking to "social" drinking is marriage and its effect on social network. On the other hand, marriage to an alcoholic mate puts the nonalcoholic spouse at risk. However, studies of the children of alcoholic step-parents and adoptive parents suggest that alcohol abuse usually is not environmentally transmitted from parent to child and, despite a vast theoretical literature implicating non-alcoholic spouses as the *cause* of their partners' alcohol abuse, prospective studies indicate that alcoholic spouses create unhappy marriages far more often than unhappy marriages create alcoholic spouses.

Culture is a seventh factor in the risk for addiction. Illegal drugs of abuse often are preferred in deviant subcultures and remain taboo among the law-abiding. For example, passage of the Harrison Narcotic Act in 1914 motivated recovery among the majority of medically-addicted morphine addicts in the U.S., but had little effect on hitherto legal heroin abuse by the New York underworld. In one study that held constant other risk factors like availability and cost, alcohol dependence was five times less common in men of Italian and other Southern European descent compared with Anglo-American ethnic groups (Vaillant, 1995). Such differences, at least in part, can be attributed to variations in cultural attitudes toward alcohol consumption (e.g., Heath, 1975; Greely & McReady, 1980). For example, in the Italian culture, alcohol usually is consumed with meals and, although social alcohol consumption is taught to children, intoxication is proscribed for adults. Conversely, American mores forbid children to learn social consumption of alcohol, drinking often occurs in bars apart from food and, in adults, intoxication historically has been considered humorous or "manly."

An eighth risk factor for addiction is *social instability*, which not only breaks down environmental controls for safe use of the agent, but has a powerful effect on host resistance. One need only examine the interface between Western industrialized cultures and those of developing countries to appreciate that societal change and alcohol abuse often go hand-in-hand. Epidemics of alcoholism may be seen in the aboriginal communities at the fringes of modern Australian cities, at the interface of Native American communities and white settlements, and in the new African cities, with their sudden mix of tribal and European ways. All offer grim testimony that, for individuals to learn the social use of addicting substances, the host must painstakingly learn societal rituals to constrain abuse. By contrast, stable, homogeneous, integrated communities (e.g., Moslem, Hasid, Mormon) increase host resistance to drug use as well as abuse. Stable communities value state change less than do communities in transition.

Characteristics of the Host. The use—without dependence—of highly addicting alcohol is endemic throughout much of the world. In contrast, heroin use, although producing physiological dependence no more severe than alcohol, progresses to dependence more often than not. The differences in differential rates of addiction appear to lie in the host as well as in the drug.

A ninth factor, *genetic predisposition*, may exert its effect because genetically determined sensitivity to the effects of alcohol serves for many as a protective factor (Schuckit, 1995). Early studies noted that unstable childhoods with broken homes and inconsistent upbringing were associated with future alcoholism (McCord & McCord, 1960; Robins, 1966). But more recent studies (Vaillant, 1995) have noted that such association only occurs in the presence of a biologic alcoholic parent. Children raised in alcoholic families are at increased risk for alcoholism only when they are biologically related to the alcoholic family member.

Twin and cross-fostering studies have not clearly implicated genetic factors in heroin addiction. Instead, being reared in a multiproblem family (often, of course, as a result of parental alcohol abuse) predisposes individuals to illegal substance abuse and to abuse of agents like heroin that pharmacologically reduce suffering.

This brings us to the tenth risk factor: *dysfunctional multiproblem families.* Multiproblem families are an etiologic factor in delinquency of all kinds, including illegal and polydrug abuse. If genetic factors are controlled for, however, multiproblem families are less important in the etiology of alcohol dependence. Several studies have shown that the young urban heroin addict cannot easily be distinguished from the young urban delinquent. Heroin addicts have come from broken homes in which maternal supervision and affection in the pre-school years was inadequate, where the father was absent, where there was little family cohesion, and where there often was parent-child cultural disparity. Few heroin addicts have regular work histories before addiction. In short, the heroin addict *begins* drug-seeking behavior more because he or she has had very little opportunity to engage in other competing forms of independent activity than because morphine or heroin *per se* is a powerful reinforcer or temptation. These rather sweeping generalizations have been documented by comparing delinquents and addicts with non-delinquent and non-addict controls who were matched for variables like social class, place of residence, intelligence and ethnic background (Glueck & Glueck, 1950; Chein, Gerard et al., 1964; Vaillant, 1966).

An eleventh major risk factor in host vulnerability to addiction is *comorbid psychiatric disorders.* The most important of these are depression and Axis II cluster B personality disorders (especially antisocial and borderline). Most studies investigating vulnerability to alcoholism have focused on depression as a predisposing factor because both alcoholism and depression tend to occur in the same families, and frequently occur together in the same person (Merikangas & Gelernter, 1990). The common comorbidity of alcoholism and depression has led to the hypothesis that individuals abuse alcohol in order to self-medicate, or to alleviate, their depression. However, prospective study of the natural history of alcoholism indicates that comorbid depression usually is a consequence of, and not an etiological factor for, alcoholism. First, the children of alcoholics often are at environmental risk for depressive disorder because they are reared in dysfunctional alcoholic families and are at risk for alcohol abuse for genetic reasons. Second, the rate of alcoholism among manic-depressive patients, who—according to the self-medication hypothesis—should use alcohol frequently, is not higher than the rate among other psychiatric patients (Woodruff, Guze et al., 1973; Morrison, 1974). Third, biochemical tests that can distinguish between genetically determined (i.e., primary) and environmentally determined (i.e., secondary) depression have found that depressed alcoholics resembled patients with evidence of environmentally-induced depression rather than depressed patients with a family history of depression (Schlesser, Winokur et al., 1980). Fourth, although depression and alcoholism may run in the same families, multigenerational studies have documented that the family linkages for each disorder are genetically separate (Weissman, Gershon et al., 1984; Merikangas & Gelernter, 1990). Fifth, in clinical studies, the use of antidepressants to treat patients with both alcoholism and depression did not alter the course of alcoholism, but abstinence from alcohol in such patients did alleviate the depression (Brown, Irwin & Schuckit, 1988; Dorus, Ostrow et al., 1989).

Three psychiatric disorders do seem to contribute to the risk for alcoholism: antisocial personality (without question), and panic disorder and attention deficit disorder (probably).

Host resistance to heroin dependence and/or polydrug abuse is diminished by many Axis I disorders, including depression and anxiety, and most especially cluster B, Axis II disorders. Antisocial (in women more often labeled borderline) personality is closely associated with dysfunctional families and with polydrug abuse. In the etiology of heroin abuse (and of alcoholism associated with polydrug abuse), antisocial personality is an important factor. Thus, although many delinquent youth abuse alcohol as part of their antisocial behavior, and some become alcoholic, the majority of alcoholics are not sociopathic except as a *result* of their addiction.

At the risk of oversimplification: culture, genes, social networks and sociopathy all play major roles in the facets of addiction that are epitomized by alcohol abuse; sociopathy, dysfunctional childhoods, social alienation, rapidity of action, and psychiatric comorbidity all play major roles in substance abuse that is epitomized by heroin dependence. However, in any single individual, these two etiological clusters will overlap.

Women who develop alcoholism, develop it for the same reasons as men: premorbid antisocial personality, hyperactivity (Glenn & Parsons, 1989), heavy drinking peers (especially spouses), alcoholic biologic relatives, work environments conducive to heavy drinking, and being raised in cultures that forbid drinking and yet encourage drunkenness. Statistically, a woman who develops alcoholism usually manifests more risk factors than an alcoholic male (Svanum & McAdoo, 1991; Blume, 1986).

WHY DOES ADDICTION PERSIST?

Patterns of Relapse. Addiction is a disorder of remissions, relapses, and often premature death. During young adulthood, substance abuse—like multiple sclerosis and obesity—often is *progressive*. After age 40, however, substance abuse may stabilize rather than inexorably progress. Chronic obesity and cigarette consumption are familiar examples of such stabilization. Unlike obesity, however, addiction—whether to legal two-pack-a-day smoking or to illegal crack cocaine binges—often can evolve into stable, lifelong abstinence.

Women with alcoholism are prone to the more fulminant clinical course seen in antisocial men (Fillmore, 1987). This may be because the net effect of having more risk factors, greater shame and thus more denial, and greater difficulty obtaining treatment, puts women at risk for rapid progression of alcohol-related complications. Alcoholic women are more likely than alcoholic men to die from cirrhosis and violence and, in general, they experience more medical complications from alcohol abuse (Ashley, Olin et al., 1977; Blume, 1986). Indeed, women who die from alcoholism and its direct sequelae do so an estimated 11 years earlier than their male counterparts (Krasner, Davis et al., 1977).

To oversimplify, addicted individuals can be divided into those whose addiction has a progressive course (the majority) and those with a nonprogressive, atypical course (a minority). Addicts with a progressive course either continue to abuse substances, despite a worsening of their problems, or they became stably abstinent, usually in response to the consequences of their addiction. As will be discussed below, such abstinence does not occur by chance or due to "burning out" or "maturing out," any more than heavy smokers just grow "tired" or "mature out" of cigarette use.

Surprisingly, among addicts with the progressive form of the disease, no significant differences have been found in the length of dependence that would distinguish those who continue to abuse drugs from those who achieve stable abstinence. Indeed, in alcohol abuse, greater severity of dependence is associated with a greater likelihood of stable abstinence (Vaillant, 1995). Another paradox is that without other risk factors being present, addiction *per se* does not always lead to chronicity. For example, soldiers in Viet Nam who did not have premorbid psychopathology recovered readily from their heroin dependence once availability of the drug and peer support for its use were removed by their return home (Robins, 1974).

In contrast, addicts with atypical course either maintain a relatively stable pattern of intermittent substance abuse without dependence from a young age or return to controlled use of the substance that they once had abused. In general, such atypical addicts have fewer drug-related problems and do not develop physiological dependence. They also experienced a later onset and manifest fewer risk factors.

Because addiction to alcohol and drugs, like food consumption in the obese, can vary rapidly from month to month, studies that examine the same subjects over decades are needed to clarify natural history. Such longitudinal studies support the fact that, unlike most medical disorders, severity ("hitting bottom") paradoxically can facilitate a favorable prognosis. As a result, the severity of the 11 risk factors enumerated above (e.g., genetic loading for alcoholism, criminal history in drug addiction, dysfunctional families, or cultural origins) are not statistically correlated with long-term prognosis (Vaillant, 1988, 1995). Over a lifetime, except for an earlier mean age of onset, the natural history of the heroin subtype of substance abuse does not reveal a worse prognosis than the alcohol subtype. In short-term studies this paradox is less apparent. In clinical studies of addicted individuals, good motivation, high socioeconomic status, marital and employment stability, and lack of criminality all predict good short-term prognoses.

In most long-term studies, the prevalence of addiction declines steadily after age 40 (Vaillant, 1988). For example, examination of the long-term studies illustrated in Table 1 reveals that among alcoholics followed for a couple of decades, or until they were approximately 60 years old, only a third of the patients were still alcohol-dependent at the end of the period of observation (Vaillant, 1995). Few returned to stable asymptomatic drinking, but death and stable abstinence both contributed equally to the observed decline. Several studies indicate that about 2% of all alcoholics achieve stable abstinence each year, with or without treatment. Similar patterns, although not as well documented, are seen for heroin abuse (Vaillant, 1988) and cigarette dependence.

Roughly one-third of alcoholics die before their 60th birthday. Tables 1 and 2 illustrate that the mortality rate for alcoholics at any age is increased two- to three-fold over that of the nonacoholic population. As Table 2 illustrates, most of the premature deaths are from suicide, accident, and heart disease rather than from cirrhosis.

In most alcoholic individuals, the progression from social drinking to alcohol abuse to alcohol dependence occurs gradually, generally over a period of three to 15 years. Dependence occurs somewhat more rapidly in women than in men. In the educated and in men from stable families, progression to alcohol dependence occurs more slowly. Some individuals drink asymptomatically for as long as 20 or 30 years before developing alcohol abuse, and such abuse may never progress to severe dependence. Conversely, antisocial adolescent males exhibit a much more rapid onset of alcoholism, with clear physiological dependence occurring within two to five years. (It must be appreciated, however, that pharmacological tolerance, like high blood pressure or obesity, is a matter of arbitrary definition, rather than an unambiguous state, like pregnancy.) Within a few months of initiating regular use, dependence—in the sense of demonstrable alteration in tolerance to alcohol—occurs in many social drinkers.

To summarize, besides continued abuse and/or death, possible long-term outcomes of substance abuse include stable abstinence or a return to controlled asymptomatic use. In part, outcome depends on habit strength which, in turn, is determined by the duration and severity of dependence. Thus, in adolescents, excessive drinking that meets *DSM-IV* criteria for substance dependence but is of short duration can evolve into a life-long pattern of moderate consumption. If they persist, however, patterns

TABLE 1. Twelve Long-term Follow-up Studies of Alcohol Abuse

Study and nature of sample	Nature of treatment	Type and length of follow-up	Size of original sample	Attrition (%)		Number of survivors followed	Outcome for survivors (%)		
				Lost or refused	Dead		Abstinent	Asymptomatic drinkers[a]	Still alcoholic
Sundby 1967 Clinic; poor prognosis; all classes; ages 30–55	Nonspecific	Record search 20–35 years	1722	2	62	632	64		36
Goodwin, Crane & Guze 1971 Prison; alcoholic only by history; ages 20–35	Nonspecific	Interviews 8 years	c. 111	13	5	93	8	33	59
Lundquist 1973 Inpatient; good prognosis; middle class; ages 30–55	1–4 weeks in hospital	Interviews 9 years	200	0	23	155	37		63
Vaillant 1983 Inpatient; poor prognosis; men and women; ages 30–50	Detoxification; AA oriented; follow-up	Interviews 15 years	96	6	27	71	39	6	55
Ojesjo 1981 Community; good prognosis; age Σ 46	Nonspecific	Interviews 15 years	96	0	26	71	32		68
Vaillant 1996 Community; good prognosis; men; ages 10–20	Nonspecific	Questionnaire/ Interviews 40–50 years	207	11	23	137	29	23	48
Marshall, Edwards & Taylor 1994; alcohol dependent men	Same as above	Interviews 20 years	99	2	43	54	44	30	26
Nordstrom and Berglund 1987 alcohol-dependent men age ca. 32; 70% excellent post-hospital adjustment	Inpatient treatment	Interviews 21 ± 4 years	105	21	NA	84	18	26	56
O'Connor and Daly 1985 men; voluntary first admission; age ca. 48	Inpatient treatment	Questionnaire 20 years	133	30	40	40	67	15	18
Smith et al. 1983 alcohol-dependent women; age ca. 44	Inpatient treatment	Interviews 11 years	103	11[a]	31	61	41[b]		59[b]
Langle et al. 1993 alcohol-dependent men and women; age ca. 38	Inpatient treatment	Interviews 10 years	96	5	22	70	70		30
Cross et al. 1990 men and women; age ca. 48	Inpatient treatment plus AA	Questionnaire 10 years	200	21	22	114	76		24

a. Percent of asymptomatic drinkers is high because it reflects point prevalence. Such outcomes were very unstable over time.
b. Estimated: text not clear.

TABLE 2. Mortality in Prospective Studies of Alcoholism

			Number of deaths from selected causes					
Sample	**Deaths in total sample**	**fo/fe[a]**	**Cardio-vascular**	**fo/fe**	**Cirrhosis**	**fo/fe**	**Accident/murder/suicide**	**fo/fe**
Sundby 1967	1061	2	117	1.6	20	10	149	5
Schmidt and deLint 1972	738	2	258	2	66	12	140	4
Pell and D'Alonzo 1973	102	3	41	3	11	—	4	—
Nicholls, Edwards, and Kyle 1974	309	2.7	71	2	9	23	83	17
Polich, Armor, and Braiker 1981	111	3	23	1.2	8	8	37	10
Marshall, Edwards, Taylor 1994	46	3.6	13	—	4	—	6	—
Vaillant[b]	92	2	23	1.4	7	6	21	10
Brenner 1967	217	3	52	1.8	37	10	44	6
Berglund 1985	497	2.5	144	1.5	21	4	171	8.5

a. Rate of observed deaths among alcoholics divided by rate of expected deaths in the population or of observed deaths in controls, controlling for age.
b. Unpublished current data from the 206 alcohol abusing men in the 2 cohorts described in Vaillant (1995).

of alcohol abuse tend to become more stable (Jessor, 1987; Fillmore, 1987). For example, in an eight-year follow-up study, one-third of felons under 30 who met the criteria for alcoholism successfully returned to asymptomatic drinking (Goodwin, Crane & Guze, 1971). In contrast, a long-term follow-up of Harvard graduates found that, at age 60, the vast majority continued to abuse alcohol; over the long term, return to asymptomatic drinking was rarely successful (Vaillant, 1995). The difference was that a young felon can meet diagnostic criteria for alcoholism with far less chronicity and dependence than can a middle-aged lawyer.

In describing the alcoholic population, early-onset antisocial alcoholics often are called Type 2 and late-onset middle-class alcoholics are called Type 1 (Cloninger, Sigvardsson & Bohman, 1988). This distinction, however, probably is an illusion created by the fact that Type 2 alcoholics are more likely to be premorbidly antisocial and to come from dysfunctional family environments. In addition, alcoholics with a more gradual onset have their illness tempered by maturity.

While often life-saving and providing an opportunity for education, detoxification *per se* rarely alters the natural history of addiction. Three useful analogous situations are going on a successful six-week diet, going to the hospital for diabetic acidosis, and stopping smoking for Lent. All are examples of detoxifications that do not affect the natural history of a disorder. Table 3 summarizes two longitudinal studies of substance abuse. These studies illustrate that, in both the alcohol and heroin types of abuse, detoxification is associated with relapse rates so high that they have little bearing on the natural history of the disorder. The findings in Table 3 are consistent with many other studies that have found that single episodes of detoxification have little effect on addiction (Lindström, 1992).

TABLE 3. Relative Efficacy of Different Modes of Treatment

	Known "treatment" exposures	**% Followed by 1 year of abstinence**
100 Heroin Addicts (followed 20 years)		
Hospital Detoxification	361	3
Short Imprisonment	363	3
Prison and > 1 year of Parole	34	71
Methadone Maintenance	15	67
100 Alcoholics (followed 8 years)		
Hospital Detoxification	c. 1500	3
300+ Visits to AA	19	74

Source: Vaillant GE (1988). What can long-term follow-up teach us about relapse and prevention of relapse in addiction? *British Journal of Addiction* 83:1147–1157.

There are many reasons why detoxification does not alter the long-term course. First, detoxification only addresses the problem of physiological dependence. Detoxification ignores the underlying, inadvertently reinforced, behaviors implicit in the multifactorial etiology of addiction, as outlined above. Second, with chronic use, narcotics may provide little or no conscious gratification, and relatively early in an alcoholic's drinking career, alcohol consumption produces more dysphoria than it relieves (McNamee, Mendelson & Mello, 1968). Thus, once dependence is established, the reinforcing properties of drug self-administration serve in large part to avoid the discomfort of real or imagined withdrawal. Over time, craving and withdrawal symptoms become maintained by many non-pharmacological reinforcers. Friends and holidays, pubs and *bierstuben,* rituals of injection and syringes acquire reinforcing properties and become unconscious stimuli for relapse.

Third, even withdrawal symptoms themselves are not simple physiological responses to the withdrawal of biologically active substances. Withdrawal symptoms, too, are under considerable control of schedules of behavior and past experience. The withdrawal symptoms of monkeys can be effectively relieved by injections of saline, if the saline is administered in settings in which morphine was given in the past (Thompson & Schuster, 1964). On research wards, men who have been abstinent for months can experience acute craving and signs of withdrawal (e.g., lacrimation, runny nose, and gooseflesh) while watching another addict receive an injection of narcotics.

The converse also is true. If morphine-addicted monkeys are given nalorphine, withdrawal symptoms are abruptly precipitated. When morphine-satiated monkeys were given saline instead of nalorphine, withdrawal symptoms still occurred (Goldberg & Schuster, 1966). Studies in humans suggest that the memory of mental discomfort that in the past was relieved by opiates can evoke conditioned withdrawal signs (Dole & Nyswander, 1965). Conversely, in a highly structured laboratory setting (e.g., Sobell & Sobell, 1978; Merry, 1966), active alcoholics who had binged uncontrollably in community settings, could drink alcohol in moderation. In short, the sources of relapse or non-relapse depend on environmental structure as much as they do on pharmacological determinants and conscious motivation.

Fourth, as is implicit in the *DSM-IV* definition of substance dependence, over time drug addiction assumes the characteristics of a career. In someone whose daily life is unpatterned by a job, addiction imposes a very definite and gratifying, if rather stereotyped, pattern of behavior. Having been adolescent "misfits"—both in school and in street gangs—some heroin addicts finally achieve a means of social reinforcement. Thus, drug addiction provides an ersatz occupation, but a very absorbing one. In similar fashion, Hodgson and co-workers (1978) noted that alcohol dependence can be defined by the degree to which alcohol-seeking and consumption become the individual's most salient and preoccupying source of gratification.

To summarize, many of the reinforcing consequences and antecedents of drug addiction have no direct pharmacological basis. For a given individual, the temporal pattern of drug use may be maintained almost entirely by secondary reinforcers. It is not surprising, then, that addicts, upon release from weeks of hospital treatment, can relapse into substance abuse within a few months, despite firm conscious resolutions to the contrary. Not only does a history of poorly patterned social behavior contribute to the initiation of addiction, but the substitute behavioral patterns that evolve due to addiction become strongly associated with relapse. What is needed is for addicts to alter their whole pattern of living.

WHY DOES ADDICTION CEASE?

No known "cure" exists for either alcohol or heroin addiction. Many addicts recover completely without clinical treatment; many addicts experience an inexorably fatal course even with extensive clinical treatment. The natural history of addiction is more often affected by informal, even inadvertent, relapse prevention than it is by many clinical treatment regimens like prolonged hospitalization, psychotherapy and disulfiram.

First, as already noted, the control that a drug exerts over an individual's behavior depends only modestly on its pharmacological properties (Marlatt & Rohsenow, 1980). Thus, to focus too closely on detoxification is to miss the forest for the trees. Second, to a remarkable degree, relapse to drugs is independent of conscious free will and motivation. Finally, most clinical studies of substance abuse have been too brief to clarify the recovery process. On the one hand, it has been repeatedly demonstrated that a majority of treated addicts will be functioning better and using less drugs during a given month *after* treatment than they were during the month immediately prior to admission. This is because in any chronic illness with a fluctuating course, hospitalization usually is sought during clinical nadirs; thus, seeming improvements post-hospitalization may be misinterpreted. On the other hand, due to probability, most clinical studies are overweighed with chronically relapsing patients. Thus, post-hospital treatment failures also are misinterpreted.

Recovery from addiction can occur in two ways: stable abstinence (the only "cure" for two-pack-a-day cigarette smokers) or a less stable return to controlled asymptomatic use (the only "cure" for obesity). Stable abstinence, like "recovery" after surgery from breast cancer, is an actuarial term. As with breast cancer, remissions from addiction of less than two years often are transient. In contrast, if abstinence lasts for more than five years, the odds are likely for both breast surgery patients and addicts that remission will be permanent. As already noted, stable abstinence (defined here as not using the addictive substance for at least the past three years while living in the community) appears relatively independent of the severity of risk factors (Robins, 1974; Vaillant, 1995) or of formal treatment.

Stable abstinence depends on relapse prevention, not detoxification. Relapse prevention is most often achieved by a strict but gratifying regimen to which the addict voluntarily consents and that consistently alters the addict's behavior in the community over time. Perhaps the clearest example of such a regimen is the return of gratifying hospital privileges to addicted physicians on condition that they undergo involuntary random supervised urine testing and attend support groups. Stable abstinence thus requires both carrot and stick.

Often, successful regimens leading to abstinence are not a result of intentional clinical treatment programs. Such regimens can be identified by community studies of the natural history of addicts who recover and contrasting them to addicts who do not recover. The critical ingredients appear to include abstinence that: (1) occurs in the community and lasts for years, not months; (2) results from compulsory supervision or experiencing a consistent aversive experience related to drug use; (3) results from finding a substitute dependency to compete with substance use; (4) results from obtaining a new drug-free, guilt-free social network; and (5) includes inspirational group membership (e.g., discovering a sustained source of hope, inspiration, and self-esteem in religion or Alcoholics Anonymous). In their extensive literature review of remission from abuse of tobacco, food, opiates and alcohol, Stall and Biernacki (1986) identified these same six factors, all of which serve to alter addict's behavior over time and all of which are independent of conscious motivation.

Prolonged Exposure in the Community. In order to be stable, abstinence must be maintained for years in settings that closely resemble those where drugs were consumed in the past. One reason why supervised abstinence (whether under parole, disulfiram or AA) (see Table 3) may be more enduring than voluntary abstinence achieved during hospitalization or during geographic "cures" is that supervised community abstinence occurs in the presence of many secondary reinforcers (other addicts, drug sellers, community stressors, etc.). When secondary reinforcers continue to occur, but in the absence of any reinforcement, they rapidly lose their effectiveness in controlling the addict's behavior.

Compulsory Supervision. As Table 3 suggests, external interventions that restructure the patient's life in the community—such as parole, methadone maintenance, and Alcoholics Anonymous—often are associated with sustained abstinence. The analogy between the treatment of addiction and that of diabetes is helpful. Diabetic patients' control over their illness must take place in the community through sustained self-medication with insulin, altered life habits and through rituals that continue to remind the patient that relapse always is possible. Willpower, alone, is all too fallible. In diabetes, such conscious awareness of relapse is maintained by daily rituals like urine testing and dietary restrictions and substitutions. Studies of delinquent opiate addicts and of drug-dependent physicians note that the rituals of enforced parole and/or compulsory urine testing are vastly more effective than punishment or hospitalization.

Compulsory supervision is not successful if it just punishes; rather it also needs to alter an addict's schedule of reinforcement and provide alternative sources of gratification. For example, in Table 3, parole required weekly proof of employment in heroin addicts who previously were convinced that they could not hold a job. Parole-enforced work provided structure to the addict's life, and structure interferes with addiction. In addition, parole—like disulfiram and painful alcohol-induced medical complaints—provided an external source of vigilance against relapse. Finally, parole also alters old social networks—a common source of relapse.

Compulsory abstinence from alcohol is similarly reinforced by events contingent on alcohol use that systematically and negatively alter the consequences of alcohol consumption. These events, rather than will power or warnings about liver disease (which is painless), remind the alcoholic that alcohol is an "enemy." Such contingent events can be medical consequences (e.g., painful stomach problems exacerbated by alcohol consumption), or legal consequences (e.g., probation), or disulfiram.

Substitute Dependencies. Principles of behavior modification also help to explain why substitute dependencies (i.e., competing behaviors) are useful in altering an addict's behavior. The importance of providing a competing dependency to prevent relapse is illustrated by the failure of disulfiram administration alone to prove more effective than placebo in facilitating long-term abstinence from alcohol use (Mottin, 1973). Disulfiram punishes alcohol use, but it does not provide a competing behavior. Substitute dependencies can take many different forms, ranging from the somewhat maladaptive (e.g., chain smoking, compulsive working or gambling) to the clinically designed models (e.g., being sure continuously to sip a glass of soda at cocktail parties or becoming "addicted" to methadone).

New Social Networks. Formation of new stable social relationships often is associated with remission in substance abuse patients (Vaillant, 1988). The most familiar example is epitomized by the refrain "wedding bells are breaking up that old gang of mine." New social networks help extinguish many of the secondary reinforcers associated with relapse. Drug-free communities like Phoenix Houses offer perhaps the best example of such networks. Such communities do not ask the addict to bond to family members to whom they feel guilty, or to non-addicts with whom they cannot identify. Phoenix House asks the addict to bond with a familiar group of companions whose only novel characteristic is that they do not use drugs. During recovery, it is especially valuable for alcoholics to associate with people they have not hurt in the past. This is true in part because shame and guilt are among the few dysphoric emotions that are relieved by alcohol. Thus, studies suggest that while marital therapy is good for family stability and communication, it has little effect on the long-term course of alcohol abuse (Orford & Edwards, 1977).

Inspirational Group Membership. In *The Varieties of Religious Experience,* William James (1902) articulated the close relationship between religious conversion and recovery from intractable addiction. Sudden "conversion" to abstinence also is triggered through what Knupfer (1972) called "strangely trivial" but significant accidents. Instead of being miraculous, however, such "conversion" experiences often have been incubating for some time. Always the psychic task of successful treatment is to convert alcohol from friend to foe. Both evangelical religious involvement and participation in Alcoholics Anonymous (AA) can effect such conversion. Like AA, intense religious involvement also provides group forgiveness and relieves feelings of shame over past relapses that may fuel future relapses. Group membership also provides a "new nonstigmatized identity," cited as important by Stall and Biernacki (1986). Enhanced hope and/or self-esteem assists addicts in maintaining abstinence.

Alcoholics Anonymous and inspirational residential communities both provide the other three ingredients found in naturalistic studies of relapse prevention: compulsory supervision, substitute dependencies and a nonaddicted, nondelinquent, non-guilt inducing social network. As Table 3 suggests, stably abstinent individuals are more likely to attend AA meetings frequently than are those who relapse (Vaillant, 1995). Although the jury is still out as to whether the associated AA attendance is a cause or consequence of abstinence, the strong association of AA utilization with abstinence cannot be attributed to premorbid social stability (Vaillant, Clark et al., 1983) or even to prior motivation for abstinence (Miller et al., 1992). Mann and colleagues (1991) offered evidence that increasing AA membership may be partly responsible for the recently observed declines in cirrhosis morbidity and mortality in Canada and in the U.S. By observing differential rates of rising AA membership, of rising utilization of alcohol clinics, and of declining rates of cirrhosis in contrasting American states, the investigators noted that no significant relationship could be observed between increase in professional treatment services and declining cirrhosis rates. However, decreases in per capita alcohol consumption and increases in AA membership both were significantly and independently associated with declining rates of cirrhosis (Mann, Smart et al., 1991).

Increasingly, the five factors described above are becoming the basis of clinical relapse prevention programs. Methadone maintenance programs can provide not only compulsory supervision by requiring random urine screens but also provide a direct substitute for heroin. Court-mandated commitment to therapeutic communities also effects sustained alterations in community behavior through compulsory supervision, substitute dependency, self-esteem building, and drug-free social networks. These same principles also apply to abstinence-focused cognitive-behavioral techniques. Cognitive-behavioral programs, in addition to providing positive feedback for successful abstinence and facilitating the recall of alcohol-related negative experiences, often include developing a plan to stop drinking that enlists the help of others, ways of recognizing an imminent unconscious relapse, providing substitutes for drinking, and developing social supports that help reinforce sobriety (Marlatt & Gordon 1985).

Abstinence. Although many highly regarded treatment programs consider sustained abstinence the only desirable treatment outcome, the effects of abstinence on the alcoholic's physical and psychological well-being rarely have been examined over prolonged periods of time. Certainly, abstinence does not automatically restore an alcoholic's physical and psychological health. Prospective studies of community samples (Vaillant, 1995) have noted that abstinence, if maintained for more than three years, improved the psychological health and quality of life of securely abstinent alcoholics, but such beneficial effects of abstinence may take several years to develop. For example, divorce and depression are common among newly abstinent alcoholics who must readjust to their familial responsibilities and occupational roles. In some studies, the short-term death rate among abstinent alcoholics was similar to that among progressive alcoholics. Kurtines and colleagues (1978) found that newly abstinent alcoholics were "less normal" on several measures of psychological functioning than were alcoholics who had been abstinent for more than four years. Thus, abstinence should not be considered in isolation but in a context of overall social rehabilitation that may require years.

A related but rarely studied question in the natural history of addiction is how long abstinence must last before it can be considered secure. Many treatment outcome studies follow their subjects for only six to 12 months. Long-term follow-up studies of abstinent alcoholics, however, have demonstrated that relapse rates still were as high as 40% after two years of abstinence. After additional years of abstinence, however, relapse rates fell dramatically. For example, in one study, only 7% of 37 men who had achieved six years of abstinence from alcohol eventually relapsed over the next 15 years of follow-up (Vaillant, 1996a, 1996b).

Return to Asymptomatic Drinking. Several studies of less than two years' duration have suggested that the natural history of alcohol dependence includes not only abstinence but also a return to asymptomatic drinking (Edwards & Grant, 1980; Sobell & Sobell, 1978). Compared with individuals who remained alcoholic or who became abstinent, the alcoholic careers of such controlled drinkers were significantly less symptomatic and the presence of physiological dependence was extremely rare. In this sense, such outcomes are comparable to individuals with high blood pressure or diabetes who can control their illness by life changes and diet alone.

More prolonged follow-up, however, has demonstrated that, even in these selected individuals, return to controlled drinking is a very *unstable* outcome (Edwards, 1985; Pendery, Maltzman & West, 1982; Miller et al., 1992). In one study, by age 60, only six of 42 men once classified as stable asymptomatic drinkers still qualified as such (Vaillant, 1995); the others either had relapsed, become stably abstinent, left the study or had been reclassified as not meeting the criteria for alcohol abuse. Similarly, Helzer and colleagues (1985) found that among 1,289 clinically treated alcoholics, fewer than 2% returned to asymptomatic drinking for more than two years.

In summary, when clinicians plan interventions, they must determine where patients are in the natural history of their disorder. In the *initial* phases of the treatment career of any alcoholic, a trial of return to controlled drinking is almost always worth the effort (Sanchez-Craig & Lei, 1988). Once such efforts have been documented to fail, clinician and patient should focus on abstinence as the actuarial goal of choice.

CONCLUSIONS

On the one hand, we must cease to conceptualize addiction as simply a more or less voluntary use of a psychoactive drug in order to provide self-medication, self-indulgence, or the relief of physiologic withdrawal symptoms. Instead, we must conceive of addiction as a career—as a whole constellation of conditioned, unconscious behaviors more akin to destructive fingernail biting than to self-medication. If we view addiction as a loss of behavioral plasticity, the importance of behavior modification techniques begins to make sense. Then, clinicians can understand why abstinence, parole, methadone maintenance and Alcoholics Anonymous may be superior to insight, conventional detoxification, disulfiram and scripted admonitions to "cut down." Sustained community interventions serve to impose a structure on the addict's life. Such structure interferes with unconscious drug-seeking behavior based on conditioned withdrawal symptoms and secondary reinforcers.

On the other hand, the natural history of chronic substance dependence also must evoke our compassion. Active substance dependence produces enormous suffering. To deny palliation through short-term hospitalization to addicts because we are not always certain that such an intervention will alter the natural history of their illness is as inhumane as denying short-term hospital palliation to patients with multiple sclerosis and diabetes because it does not alter the natural history of their diseases. First, if detoxification does not always cure, it reduces mortality and suffering. Second, no matter how refractory addiction seems, addicts should not be excluded from medical insurance coverage, from treatment by emergency departments and by detoxification centers, or from shelters for the homeless. One of the great lessons to be learned by prolonged follow-up of addicts is that stable remission may occur among the most unlikely prospects. Finally, at least 12 controlled cost-benefit studies (Jones & Vischi, 1979; Reiff, Griffith et al., 1981) conclude that the expense of providing treatment is more than repaid by declines in medical care utilization, in lost time from work and in benefit costs related to sickness and accidents. To understand the natural history of addiction, we must track more than drug use.

REFERENCES

Ashley MJ, Olin JS, le Riche WH, Kornaczewski A, Schmidt W & Rankin JG (1977). Morbidity in alcoholics: Evidence for accelerated development of physical disease in women. *Archives of Internal Medicine* 137:883–887.

Berglund M (1985). Cerebral dysfunction in alcoholism related to mortality and long-term social adjustment. *Alcoholism: Clinical & Experimental Research* 9:153–157.

Blume SB (1986). Women and alcohol: A review. *Journal of the American Medical Association* 256:1467–1470.

Brenner B (1967). Alcoholism and fatal accidents. *Quarterly Journal of Studies on Alcohol* 28:517–528.

Brown SA, Irwin M & Schuckit MA (1988). Changes in depression among abstinent alcoholics. *Journal of Studies on Alcohol* 49:412–417.

Chein I, Gerard D, Lee R et al. (1964). *The Road to H.* New York, NY: Basic Books.

Cloninger CR, Sigvardsson S & Bohman M (1988). Childhood personality predicts alcohol abuse in young adults. *Alcohol: Clinical & Experimental Research* 12(4):494–505.

Cros GM et al. (1990). Alcoholism treatment: A ten-year follow-up study. *Alcoholism: Clinical & Experimental Research* 14:169–173.

Dole VP & Nyswander M (1965). A medical treatment for diacetylmorphine (heroin) addiction. *Journal of the American Medical Association* 193:646–650.

Dorus W, Ostrow DG, Anton R et al. (1989). Lithium treatment of depressed and nondepressed alcoholics. *Journal of the American Medical Association* 162:1646–1652.

Edwards G & Grant M, eds. (1980). *Alcoholism Treatment in Transition*. London, England: Croom Helm.

Edwards G (1985). A later follow-up of a classic case series: D.L. Davies' (1962) report and its significance for the present. *Journal of Studies on Alcohol* 46:181–190.

Fillmore KM (1987). Women's drinking across adult life course as compared to men's: A longitudinal and cohort analysis. *British Journal of Addiction* 82:801–812.

Glenn SW & Parsons OA (1989). Alcohol abuse and familial alcoholism: Psychosocial correlates in men and women. *Journal of Studies on Alcohol* 50:116–127.

Glueck S & Glueck E (1950). *Unraveling Juvenile Delinquency*. New York, NY: Commonwealth Fund.

Goldberg S & Schuster CR (1966). Classic conditioning of the Morphine withdrawal syndrome. *Federation Proceedings* 25:261.

Goodwin DW, Crane JB & Guze SB (1971). Felons who drink: An 8-year follow-up. *Quarterly Journal of Studies on Alcohol* 32:136–147.

Greely A & McReady WC (1980). *Ethnic Drinking Subcultures*. New York, NY: Praeger.

Heath DB (1975). A critical review of ethnographic studies of alcohol use. In RJ Gibbins et al. (eds) *Research Advances in Alcohol and Drug Problems (2nd edition)*. New York, NY: John Wiley & Sons.

Helzer JE, Robins LN, Taylor JR et al. (1985). The extent of long-term moderate drinking among alcoholics discharged from medical and psychiatric treatment facilities. *The New England Journal of Medicine* 312(26):1678–1685.

Hodgson RT, Stockwell T, Rankin H et al. (1978). Alcohol dependence: The concept, its utility and measurement. *British Journal of Addictions* 73:339–342.

James W (1902). *The Varieties of Religious Experience*. London, England: Longmans Green.

Jessor R (1987). Problem-behavior theory psychosocial development and adolescent problem drinking. *British Journal of Addiction* 82:331–342.

Jones KR & Vischi TR (1979). Impact of drug abuse and mental health on treatment of medical care utilization. *Medical Care* 17(Suppl):1–81.

Krasner N, Davis M, Portmann B & Williams R (1977). Changing pattern of alcohol liver disease in Great Britain: Relation to sex and signs of autoimmunity. *British Medical Journal* 1:1497–1500.

Knupfer G (1972). Ex-problem drinkers. In M Roff, L Tobins & M Pollack (eds.) *Life History Research and Psychopathology*. Minneapolis, MN: University of Minnesota Press, 256–280.

Kurtines WM, Ball LR & Wood GH (1978). Personality characteristics of long-term recovered alcoholics: A comparative analysis. *Journal of Consulting and Clinical Psychology* 46:971–977.

Langle G et al. (1993). Ten years after—The post-treatment course of alcoholism. *European Psychiatry* 8:95–100.

Lindström L (1992). *Managing Alcoholism*. Oxford, England: Oxford University Press.

Lundquist GAR (1973). Alcohol dependence. *Acta Psychiatrica Scandinavica* 49:332–340.

Mann RE, Smart R, Anglin L & Edward A (1991). Reductions in cirrhosis deaths in the United States: Associations with per capita consumption and AA membership. *Journal of Studies on Alcohol* 52:361–365.

Marlatt GA & Gordon JR, eds. (1985). *Relapse Prevention: Maintenance Strategies in the Treatment of Addictive Behaviors.* New York, NY: Guilford Press.

Marlatt G & Rohsenow DJ (1980). Cognitive processes in alcohol use: Expectancy and the balanced placebo design. In NK Mello (ed.) *Advances in Substance Abuse: Behavioral and Biological Research.* Greenwich, CT: JAI Press.

Marshall EJ, Edwards G & Taylor C (1994). Mortality in men with drinking problems: A 20 year follow-up. *Addiction* 89.

McCord W & McCord J (1960). *Origins of Alcoholism.* Stanford, CA: Stanford University Press.

McNamee HB, Mendelson JH & Mello NK (1968). Experimental analysis of drinking patterns of alcoholics, concurrent psychiatric observations. *American Journal of Psychiatry* 124:1063–1069.

Merikangas KR & Gelernter CS (1990). Comorbidity for alcoholism and depression. *Psychiatric Clinics of North America* 13:613–632.

Merry J (1966). The loss of control myth. *Lancet* 1:1257–1258.

Miller WR et al. (1992). Long-term follow-up of behavioral self-control training. *Journal of Studies on Alcohol* 53:249–261.

Moore NIH & Gerstein DR, eds. (1981). *Alcohol and Public Policy: Beyond the Shadow of Prohibition.* Washington, DC: National Academy Press.

Morrison JR (1974). Bipolar affective disorder and alcoholism. *American Journal of Psychiatry* 131:1130–1133.

Morse WH & Kelleher RT (1970). Schedules as fundamental determinants of behavior. In WN Schoenfeld (ed.) *The Theory of Reinforcement Schedules.* New York, NY: Appleton Century Crofts.

Mottin JL (1973). Drug induced attenuation of alcohol consumption. *Quarterly Journal of Studies on Alcohol* 34:444–472.

Nicholls P, Edwards G & Kyle E (1974). A study of alcoholics admitted to four hospitals II: General and cause-specific mortality during follow-up. *Quarterly Journal of Studies on Alcohol* 35:841–855.

Nordstrom G & Berglund M (1987). Type 1 and Type 2 alcoholics (Cloninger and Bohman) have different patterns of successful long-term adjustment. *British Journal of Addiction* 82:761–769.

O'Connor A & Daly J (1985). Alcoholics: A twenty year follow-up study. *British Journal of Psychiatry* 146:645–647.

Ojesjo L (1981). Long-term outcome in alcohol abuse and alcoholism among males in the Lundby general population, Sweden. *British Journal of Addiction* 76(4):391–400.

Orford J & Edwards G (1977). *Alcoholism.* Oxford, England: Oxford University Press.

Pell S & D'Alonzo CA (1973). A five year mortality study of alcoholics. *Journal of Occupational Medicine* 15:120–125.

Pendery ML, Maltzman IM & West LJ (1982). Controlled drinking by alcoholics? New findings and a reevaluation of a major affirmative study. *Science* 217:169–175.

Polich JM, Armor J & Braiker HB (1981). *The Course of Alcoholism.* New York, NY: John Wiley & Sons.

Reiff S, Griffith B, Forsythe AB et al. (1981). Utilization of medical services by alcoholics participating in a health maintenance organization outpatient treatment program: Three year follow-up. *Alcoholism: Clinical & Experimental Research* 5:559–562.

Robins LN (1966). *Deviant Children Grown Up: A Sociological and Psychiatric Study Sociopathic Personality.* Baltimore. MD: Williams & Wilkins.

Robins LN (1974). The Vietnam drug user returns. In *Special Action Office Monograph Series A (No. 2).* Washington, DC: U.S. Government Printing Office.

Sanchez-Craig M & Lei H (1986). Disadvantages to imposing the goal of abstinence on problem drinkers: An empirical study. *British Journal of Addiction* 81:505–512.

Schlesser MA, Winokur G & Sherman BM (1980). Hypothalamic-pituitary-adrenal axis activity in depressive illness. *Archives of General Psychiatry* 37:737–743.

Schmidt W & deLint J (1972). Causes of death of alcoholics. *Quarterly Journal of Studies on Alcohol* 33:171–185.

Schuckit MA (1995). A long-term study of sons of alcoholics. *Alcohol Health and Research World* 19(3):172–175.

Sobell MB & Sobell L (1978). *The Behavioral Treatment of Alcohol Problems.* New York, NY: Plenum Press.

Smith EM, Cloninger CR & Bradford S (1983). Predictors of mortality in alcoholic women: A prospective follow-up study. *Alcoholism: Clinical & Experimental Research* 7:237–243.

Stall R & Biernacki P (1986). Spontaneous remission from the problematic use of substances: An inductive model derived from a comparative analysis of the alcohol, opiate, tobacco and food/obesity literatures. *International Journal of the Addictions* 21:1–23.

Sundby P (1967). *Alcoholism and Mortality.* Oslo, Norway: Universitets Forlaget.

Svanum S & McAdoo WG (1991). Parental alcoholism: An examination of male and female alcoholics in treatment. *Journal of Studies on Alcohol* 52:127–132.

Thompson T & Schuster CR (1964). Morphine self-administration, food reinforce, and avoidance behaviors in rhesus monkeys. *Psychopharmacologia* 5:87–94.

Vaillant GE (1966a). A long-term follow-up of male alcohol abuse. *Archives of General Psychiatry* 53:243–249.

Vaillant GE (1966b). A 12 year follow-up of New York narcotic addicts: III. Some social and psychiatric characteristics. *Archives of General Psychiatry* 15:599–609.

Vaillant GE (1988). What can long-term follow-up teach us about relapse and prevention of relapse in addiction? *British Journal of Addiction* 83:1147–1157.
Vaillant GE (1995). *Natural History of Alcoholism, Revisited.* Cambridge, MA: Harvard University Press.
Vaillant GE, Clark W, Cyrus C et al. (1983). The natural history of alcoholism: An eight year follow-up. *American Journal of Medicine* 75:455–466.
Weissman MM, Gershon ES, Kidd KK et al. (1984). Psychiatric disorders in the relatives of probands with affective disorders. *Archives of General Psychiatry* 41:13–21.
Woodruff RA, Guze SB, Clayton PJ & Carr D (1973). Alcoholism and depression. *Archives of General Psychiatry* 28:97–100.

CHAPTER 2

Myths About the Treatment of Addiction

Charles P. O'Brien, M.D., Ph.D.
A. Thomas McLellan, Ph.D.

Is Addiction a Voluntary Disorder?
Comparison to Other Medical Disorders
Addiction Treatment is a Worthwhile Medical Endeavor

Although addictions are chronic disorders, there is a tendency for most physicians and for the general public to perceive them as being acute conditions such as a broken leg or pneumococcal pneumonia. In this context, the acute-care procedure of detoxification has been thought of as appropriate "treatment." When the patient relapses, as most do sooner or later, the treatment is regarded as a failure. However, contrary to commonly held beliefs, addiction does not end when the drug is removed from the body (detoxification) or when the acute post-drug-taking illness dissipates (withdrawal). Rather, the underlying addictive disorder persists, and this persistence produces a tendency to relapse to active drug-taking. Thus, although detoxification, as explained by Mattick and Hall (1996, p. 97), can be successful in cleansing the person of drugs and withdrawal symptoms, detoxification does not address the underlying disorder, and thus is not adequate treatment.

As we shall discuss, addictions are similar to other chronic disorders such as arthritis, hypertension, asthma, and diabetes. Addicting drugs produce changes in brain pathways that endure long after the person stops taking them. Further, the associated medical, social, and occupational difficulties that usually develop during the course of addiction do not disappear when the patient is detoxified. These protracted brain changes and the associated personal and social difficulties put the former addict at great risk of relapse. Treatments for addiction, therefore, should be regarded as being long-term, and a "cure" is unlikely from a single course of treatment.

IS ADDICTION A VOLUNTARY DISORDER?

One reason why many physicians and the general public are unsympathetic towards the addict is that addiction is perceived as being self-afflicted: "they brought it on themselves." However, there are numerous involuntary components in the addictive process, even in the early stages. Although the choice to try a drug for the first time is voluntary, whether the drug is taken can be influenced by external factors such as peer pressure, price, and, in particular, availability. In the U.S., there is a great deal of cocaine in all areas of the country, and in some regions the availability of heroin is widespread. Nonetheless, it is true that, despite ready availability, most people exposed to drugs do not go on to become addicts. Heredity is likely to influence the effects of the initial sampling of the drug, and these effects are in turn likely to be influential in modifying the course of continued use. Individuals for whom the initial psychological responses to the drug are extremely pleasurable may be more likely to repeat the drug-taking and some of them will develop an addiction. Some people seem to have an inherited tolerance to alcohol, even without previous exposure (Schuckit, 1994). At some point after continued repetition of voluntary drug-taking, the drug "user" loses the voluntary ability to control its use. At that point, the "drug misuser" becomes "drug addicted" and there is a compulsive, often overwhelming involuntary aspect to continuing drug use and to relapse after a period of abstinence. We do not yet know the mechanisms involved in this change from drug-taking to addiction, and we are searching for pharmacological mechanisms to reverse this process.

COMPARISON TO OTHER MEDICAL DISORDERS

The view of addiction as a chronic medical disorder puts it in a category with other conditions that show a similar confluence of genetic, biological, behavioral, and environmental factors. There are many examples of chronic illnesses that are generally accepted as requiring life-long treatment. Here, we will focus on only three: adult-onset diabetes, hypertension, and asthma. Like substance use disorders, the onset of these three diseases is determined by multiple factors, and the contributions of each factor are not yet fully specified. In adult-onset diabetes and some forms of hypertension, genetic factors have a major, though not exclusive, role in the etiology. Parenting practices, stress in the home environment, and other environmental factors are also important in determining whether these diseases actually get expressed, even among individuals who are genetically predisposed. Behavioral factors are also important at the outset in the development of these disorders. The control of diet and weight and the establishment of regular exercise patterns are two important determinants of the onset and severity. Thus, although a diabetic, hypertensive, or asthmatic patient may have been genetically predisposed and may have been raised in a high-risk environment, it is also true that behavioral choices such as the ingestion of high sugar and/or high-cholesterol foods, smoking, and lack of exercise also play a part in the onset and severity of their disorder.

Treatment Results. Almost everyone has a friend or relative who has been through a treatment program for addiction to nicotine, alcohol, or other drugs. Since most of these people have a relapse to drug-taking at some time after the end of treatment, there is a tendency for the general public to believe that addiction treatment is unsuccessful. However, this expectation of a cure after treatment is unrealistic, just as it is for other chronic disorders. The persistent changes produced by addiction are still present and require continued maintenance treatment, either psychosocial or pharmacological or a combination. As with other chronic disorders, the only realistic expectation for the treatment of addiction is patient improvement rather than cure. Consistent with these expectations, studies of abstinence rates at one year after completion of treatment indicate that only 30% to 50% of patients have been able to remain completely abstinent throughout that period, although an additional 15% to 30% have not resumed compulsive use (Gerstein & Harwood, 1990; Gerstein, Judd & Rovner, 1979).

Successful treatment leads to substantial improvement in three areas: reduction of alcohol and other drug use; increases in personal health and social functions; and reductions in threats to public health and safety. All these domains can be measured in a graded fashion with a method such as the Addiction Severity Index (ASI) (McLellan, Luborsky et al., 1980). In the ASI, a structured interview determines the need for treatment in seven independent domains. These measurements allow us to see addiction, not as an all-or-none disease, but in degrees of severity across all the areas relevant to successful treatment.

FIGURE 1. Admission Severity Profiles of Two Patients Admitted for Drug Misuse

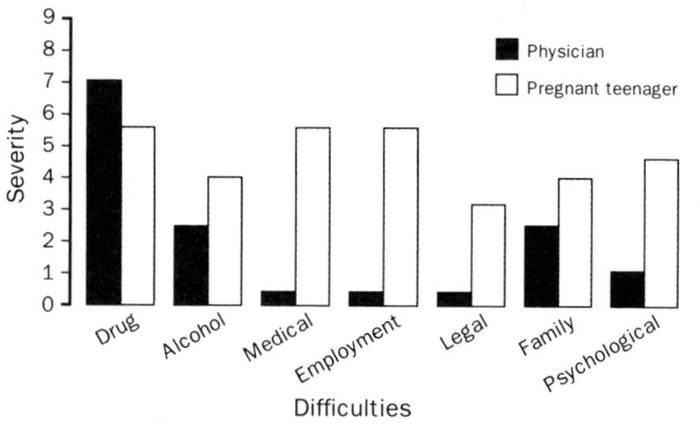

As assessed by Addiction Severity Index.

Success rates for treatment of addictive disorders vary according to the type of drug and the variables inherent in the population being treated. For example, prognosis is much better in opioid addicts who are professionals, such as physicians or nurses, than in individuals with poor education and no legitimate job prospects, who are addicted to the same or even lesser amounts of opioids obtained on the street and financed by crime. Figure 1 compares the AST profiles of two patients admitted to our treatment program. One was a resident physician who had few personal or professional difficulties except for heavy compulsive cocaine use. The other patient was a pregnant teenager, who was admitted while in premature labor induced by cocaine. The profile shows less drug use in the young woman, but in other areas shown to be important determinants of the outcome of treatment, she has severe problems. The types of treatment needed by these two patients are clearly different. Although the treatment of the physician will be challenging, his prognosis is far better than that of the young woman.

Success rates for the treatment of various addictive disorders are shown in Table 1. Improvement is defined as a greater than 50% reduction on the drug-taking scale of the ASI. Another measure of the success of addiction treatment is the monetary savings that it produces. That addiction treatment is

TABLE 1. Success Rates for Addictive Disorders

Disorder	Success rate (%)*
Alcoholism[8]	50 (40–70)
Opioid dependence[9]	60 (50–80)
Cocaine dependence[10]	55 (50–60)
Nicotine dependence[11]	30 (20–40)

* Follow-up 6 mo. Data are median (range).

cost-effective has been shown in many studies in North America. For example, in one study in California, the benefits of alcohol and other drug treatment outweighed the cost of treatment by four- to 12-fold, depending on the type of drug and the type of treatment.

There has been progress in the development of medications for the treatment of nicotine, opioid, and alcohol addictions. For heroin addicts, maintenance treatment with a long-acting opioid such as methadone, l-α-acetylmethadol (LAAM), or buprenorphine can also be regarded as a success. The patient may be abstinent from illegal drugs and capable of functioning normally in society while requiring daily doses of an orally administered opioid medication—in very much the same way that diabetic patients are maintained by injections of insulin and hypertensive patients are maintained on beta blockers to sustain symptom improvements. Contrary to popular belief, patients properly maintained on methadone do not seem "drugged." They can function well, even in occupations requiring quick reflexes and motor skills, such as driving a subway train or motor vehicle. Of course, not all patients on methadone can achieve high levels of function. Many street heroin addicts, such as the young cocaine-dependent woman in Figure 1, have multiple additional psychosocial difficulties, are poorly educated, and misuse many drugs. In such cases, intensive psychosocial supports are necessary in addition to methadone; even then, the prognosis is limited by the patient's ability to learn skills for legitimate employment.

Nicotine is the addicting drug that has the poorest success rate (Table 1). That these success rates are for individuals who came to a specialized clinic for the treatment of their addiction implies that the patients tried to stop or control drug use on their own but have been unable to do so. Of those who present for treatment for nicotine dependence, only about 20% to 30% have not resumed smoking by the end of 12 months.

Treatment Compliance. Studies of treatment response have uniformly shown that patients who comply with the recommended regimen of education, counseling, and medication that characterizes most contemporary forms of treatment have typically favorable outcomes during treatment and longer-lasting post-treatment benefits (Miller & Hester, 1986; Moos, Finney & Cronkite, 1990; Simpson & Savage, 1980; Hubbard, Marsden et al., 1989; De Leon, 1994). Thus, it is discouraging for many practitioners that so many drug-dependent patients do not comply with the recommended course of treatment and subsequently resume substance use. Factors such as low socioeconomic status, comorbid psychiatric conditions, and lack of family or social supports for continuing abstinence are among the most important variables associated with lack of treatment compliance, and ultimately to relapse after treatment (Havassy, Wasserman & Hall, 1995; McLellan, Druley et al., 1980; Alterman & Cacciola, 1991).

Patient compliance is also especially important in determining the effectiveness of medications in the treatment of substance dependence. Although the general area of pharmacotherapy for drug addiction is still developing, in opioid and alcohol dependence there are several well-tested medications that are potent and effective in completely eliminating the target problems of substance use. Disulfiram has proven efficacy in preventing the resumption of alcohol use among detoxified patients. Alcoholics resist taking disulfiram because they become ill if they take a drink while receiving this medication; thus compliance is very poor (O'Brien, Woody & McLellan, 1986).

Naltrexone is an opioid antagonist that prevents relapse to opioid use by blocking opioid receptors. It is a nonaddicting medication that makes it impossible to return to opioid use, but it has little acceptance among heroin addicts, who simply do not comply with this treatment. Naltrexone is also helpful in the treatment of alcoholism. Animal and human studies have shown that the reward produced by alcohol involves the endogenous opioid system. After patients are detoxified from alcohol, naltrexone reduces craving and blocks some of the rewarding effects of alcohol if the patient begins to drink again (Volpicelli, Alterman et al., 1992; O'Malley, Jaffe et al., 1992). Naltrexone also decreases relapse rates (Figure 2) (Volpicelli, Alterman et al., 1992). Although compliance is substantially better for naltrexone in the treatment of alcoholism than in opioid addiction, efforts to improve compliance are pivotal in the treatment of alcoholism. Continuing clinical research in this area is focused on the development

FIGURE 2. Effect of Naltrexone Hydrochloride on Relapse Rates in Alcoholics

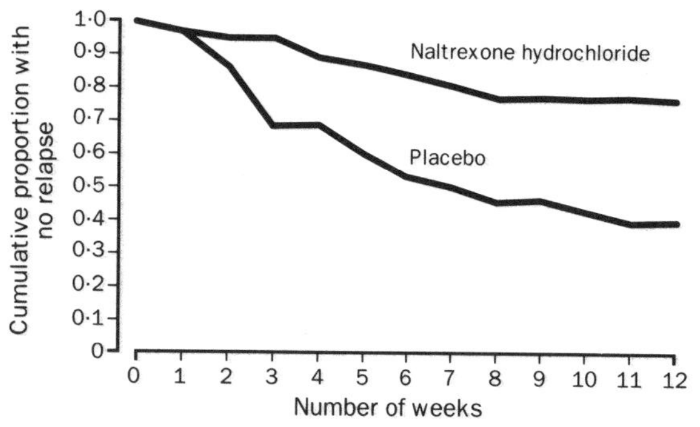

of longer-acting forms of these medications and behavioral strategies to increase patient compliance.

The diseases of hypertension, diabetes, and asthma are also chronic disorders that require continuing care for most, if not all, of a patient's life. At the same time, these disorders are not necessarily unremitting or unalterably lethal, provided that the treatment regimen of medication, diet, and behavioral change is followed. This last point requires emphasis. As with the treatment of addiction, treatments for these chronic medical disorders heavily depend on behavioral change and medication compliance to achieve their potential effectiveness. In a review of over 70 outcome studies of treatments for these disorders (summarized in Table 2), patient compliance with the recommended medical regimen was regarded as the most significant determinant of treatment outcome. Less than 50% of patients with insulin-dependent diabetes fully comply with their medication schedule (Graber, Davidson et al., 1992), and less than 30% of patients with hypertension or asthma comply with their medication regimens (Horowitz, 1990; Dekker, Dieleman et al., 1993). The difficulty is even worse for the behavioral and diet changes that are so important for the maintenance of short-term gains in these conditions. Less than 30% of patients in treatment for diabetes and hypertension comply with the recommended diet and/or behavioral changes that are designed to reduce risk factors for reoccurrence of these disorders (Clark, 1991; Kurtz, 1990). It is interesting in this context that clinical researchers have identified low socioeconomic status, comorbid psychiatric conditions, and lack of family support as the major contributors to poor patient compliance in these disorders (see Clark, 1991, for discussion of this work). As in addiction treatment, lack of patient compliance with the treatment regimen is a major contributor to reoccurrence and to the development of more serious and more expensive "disease-related" conditions. For example, outcome studies show that 30% of insulin-dependent diabetic patients, and about 50% to 80% of hypertensive and asthmatic patients, have a reoccurrence of their symptoms each year and require at least restabilization of their medication and/or additional medical interventions to re-establish symptom remission (Graber, Davidson et al., 1992; Horowitz, 1990; Dekker, Dieleman et al., 1993; Clark, 1991; Kurtz, 1990). Many of these reoccurrences also result in more serious additional health complications. For example, limb amputations and blindness are all-too-common consequences of treatment non-response among diabetic patients (Sinnock, 1985; Herman & Teutsch, 1985). Stroke and cardiac disease are often associated with exacerbation of hypertension (Schaub, Steiner & Vetter, 1993; Gorlin, 1991).

TABLE 2. Compliance and Relapse in Selected Medical Disorders

	Compliance and relapse
IDDM	
Medication regimen	<50%
Diet and foot care	<30%
Relapse*	30–50%
Hypertension†	
Medication regimen	<30%
Diet	<30%
Relapse*	50–60%
Asthma	
Medication regimen	<30%
Relapse*	60–80%

* Retreatment within 12 mo. by physician at emergency room or hospital. †Requiring medication. Sources are refs 33 and 34; for a complete list of references please write to CPO'B. IDDM = insulin-dependent diabetes mellitus.

There are, of course, differences in susceptibility, onset, course, and treatment response among all the disorders discussed here, but at the same time, then are clear parallels among them. All are multiply determined, and no single gene, personality variable, or environmental factor can fully account for the onset of any of these disorders. Behavioral choices seem to be implicated in the initiation of each of them, and behavioral control continues to be a factor in determining their course and severity. There are no "cures" for any of them, yet there have been major advances in the development of effective medications and behavioral change regimens to reduce or eliminate primary symptoms. Because these conditions are chronic, it is acknowledged (at least in the treatment of diabetes, hypertension, and asthma) that maintenance treatments will be needed to ensure that symptom remission continues. Unfortunately, other common features are their resistance to maintenance forms of treatment (both medication and behavior aspects) and their chronic, relapsing course. In this regard, it is striking that many of the patient characteristics associated with non-compliance are identical for these acknowledged "medical" disorders and addictive disorders; and the rates of reoccurrence are also similar.

ADDICTION TREATMENT IS A WORTHWHILE MEDICAL ENDEAVOR

A change in the attitudes of physicians is necessary. Addictive disorders should be considered in the category with other disorders that require long-term or life-long treatment. Treatment of addiction is about as successful as treatment of disorders such as hypertension, diabetes, and asthma, and it is clearly cost-effective. We believe that the prominence and severity of concerns about the public health and public safety associated with addiction have made the public, the press, and public policy officials understandably desperate for a lasting solution, and disappointed that none has yet been developed. As with treatments for these other chronic medical conditions, there is no cure for addiction. At the same time, there are a range of pharmacological and behavioral treatments that are effective in reducing drug use, improving patient function, reducing crime and legal system costs, and preventing the development of other expensive medical disorders. Perhaps the major difference among these conditions lies in the public's and the physician's perception of diabetes, hypertension, and asthma as clearly medical conditions, whereas addiction is more likely to be perceived as a social problem or a character deficit. It is interesting that despite similar results, at least in terms of compliance or reoccurrence rates, there is no serious argument against support by contemporary health care systems for diabetes, hypertension, or asthma, whereas this is very much in question with regard to the treatments for addiction. Is it not time that we judged the "worth" of treatments for chronic addiction with the same standards that we use for treatments of other chronic diseases?

ACKNOWLEDGMENTS: Supported by VA Medical Research Service and NIDA Grant P50-DA-05186. We thank Dr. Debrin Goubert for her assistance with the review of medical literature. Originally published as O'Brien CP & McLellan AT (1996). Myths about the treatment of addiction. Lancet *347:237–240. Reprinted by permission of the publisher.*

REFERENCES

Alterman AI & Cacciola JS (1991). The antisocial personality disorder in substance abusers: Problems and issues. *Journal of Nervous and Mental Disease* 179:401–409.

Armor DJ, Polich JM & Stambul HB (1976). *Alcoholism and Treatment*. Santa Monica, CA: RAND Corporation Press.

Ball JC & Ross A (1991). *The Effectiveness of Methadone Maintenance Treatment*. New York, NY: Springer-Verlag.

Clark LT (1991). Improving compliance and increasing control of hypertension: Needs of special hypertensive populations. *American Heart Journal* 121:664–669.

Dekker FW, Dieleman FE, Kaptein AA & Mulder JD (1993). Compliance with pulmonary medication in general practice. *European Respiratory Journal* 6:886–890.

De Leon G (1994). The therapeutic community: Study of effectiveness. *NIDA Treatment Research Monograph 84*. Rockville, MD: National Institute on Drug Abuse.

Fiore MC, Smith SS, Jorenby DE & Baker TB (1994). The effectiveness of the nicotine patch for smoking cessation. *Journal of the American Medical Association* 271:1940–1946.

Fuller RK, Branchey L, Brightwell DR et al. (1986). Disulfiram treatment of alcoholism. *Journal of the American Medical Association* 256:1449–1555.

Gerstein DR, Harwood H & Suter N (1994). *Evaluating Recovery Services: The California Drug and Alcohol Treatment Assessment (CALDATA)*. Sacramento, CA: California Department of Alcohol and Drug Programs (Executive Summary: Publication No. ADP94–628).

Gerstein D & Harwood H (1990). *Treating Drug Problems, Vol I*. Washington, DC: National Academy Press.

Gerstein D, Judd LL & Rovner SA (1979). Career dynamics of female heroin addicts. *American Journal of Drug and Alcohol Abuse* 6:1–23.

Gorlin R (1991). Hypertension and ischemic heart disease: The challenge of the 1990s. *American Heart Journal* 121:658–663.

Graber AL, Davidson P, Brown A, McRae J & Woolridge K (1992). Dropout and relapse during diabetes care. *Diabetic Care* 15:1477–1483.

Harrison WH (1993). *Harrison's Internal Medicine*. New York, NY: Raven Press.

Havassy BE, Wasserman D & Hall SM (1995). Social relationships and cocaine use in an American treatment sample. *Addiction* 90:699–710.

Herman WH & Teusch SM (1985). Diabetic renal disorders. Diabetes data, National Diabetes Data Group. Bethesda, MD: National Institutes of Health.

Higgins ST, Budney AJ, Bickel WK, Foerg F, Donham R & Badger GJ (1994). Incentives improve outcome in outpatient behavioral treatment of cocaine dependence. *Archives of General Psychiatry* 51:568–576.

Horowitz RI (1990). Treatment adherence and risk of death after a myocardial infarction. *Lancet* 336:542–545.

Hubbard RL, Marsden ME, Rachel JV, Harwood HJ, Cavanaugh ER & Ginzburg HM (1989). *Drug Abuse Treatment: A National Study of Effectiveness*. Chapel Hill, NC: University of North Carolina Press.

Institute of Medicine (1989). *Prevention and Treatment of Alcohol Problems: Research Opportunities*. Washington, DC: National Academy Press.

Kurtz SM (1990). Adherence to diabetic regimes: Empirical status and clinical applications. *Diabetic Education* 16:50–59.

Mattock RP & Hall W (1996). Are detoxification programmes effective? *Lancet* 347:97–100.

McLellan AT, Druley KA, O'Brien CP & Kron R (1980). Matching substance abuse patients to appropriate treatments. A conceptual and methodological approach. *Drug and Alcohol Dependence* 5:189–193.

McLellan AT, Luborsky L, O'Brien CP & Woody GE (1980). An improved evaluation instrument for substance abuse patients: The Addiction Severity Index. *Journal of Nervous and Mental Disease* 168:26–33.

Miller WR & Hester RK (1986). The effectiveness of alcoholism treatment methods: What research reveals. In WR Miller & N Heather (eds.) *Treating Addictive Behaviors: Process of Change*. New York, NY: Plenum Press.

Moos RH, Finney JW & Cronkite RC (1990). *Alcoholism Treatment: Context, Process and Outcome*. New York, NY: Oxford University Press.

National Center for Health Statistics (1989). Public use datatape documentation. Hyattsville, MD: The Center.

O'Brien CP, Woody GE & McLellan AT (1986). A new tool in the treatment of impaired physicians. *Philadelphia Medicine* 82:442–446.

O'Malley SS, Jaffe AJ, Chang G, Schottenfeld RS, Meyer RE & Rounsaville B (1992). Naltrexone and coping skills therapy for alcohol dependence. *Archives of General Psychiatry* 49:881–887.

Schaub AF, Steiner A & Vetter W (1993). Compliance to treatment. *Journal of Clinical Experience in Hypertension* 15:1121–1130.

Schuckit MA (1994). Low level of response to alcohol. *American Journal of Psychiatry* 151:184–189.

Simpson D & Savage L (1980). Drug abuse treatment readmissions and outcomes. *Archives of General Psychiatry* 37:896–901.

Sinnock P (1985). Hospitalization for diabetes. Diabetes data, National Diabetes Data Group. Bethesda, MD: National Institutes of Health.

Volpicelli JR, Alterman AI, Hayashida M & O'Brien CP (1992). Naltrexone in the treatment of alcohol dependence. *Archives of General Psychiatry* 49:876–880.

CHAPTER 3

Traditional Approaches to the Treatment of Addiction

Michael M. Miller, M.D., FASAM

The Minnesota Model
Variations on Traditional Approaches
Criticisms of Traditional Approaches
Other Approaches to Treatment

Diagnosing and treating patients is the foundation of what clinicians do in addiction medicine. The *American College Dictionary* defines "to treat" as "to deal with (a disease, patient, etc.) in order to relieve or cure." This definition goes to the heart of many controversies in addiction treatment: How does professional treatment "deal with" the addiction and the addict? Is treatment focused on patients or conditions? Is anyone "cured," or is the problem only arrested or managed?

Treatment of addiction is a complex process (Gitlow, 1988) that requires engagement of the patient and establishment of a therapeutic contract. It involves biomedical, behavioral, emotional, cognitive, spiritual, family systems and socioenvironmental interventions (congruent with the biopsychosocial, familial and spiritual aspects of the addictive disorders being treated). Various approaches and modalities have been used over the years to meet the clinical needs of the patient with active addictive disease. As a frame of reference for descriptive purposes, this chapter provides an overview of traditional approaches to addiction treatment. It first examines an addiction treatment approach widely employed in the U.S., before contrasting this treatment model with other approaches.

THE MINNESOTA MODEL

Historical Development. Models of treatment derive from models of disease, and early interventions for alcohol problems derived from models of alcohol use as illegal behaviors or forms of insanity or depravity; hence, the public inebriate was jailed or placed in an asylum. While there was some appreciation that episodic intemperance, loss of control, and inability to abstain might be features of a disease process that made alcoholics different from non-alcoholic drinkers or total abstainers, the 20th century dawned with few special facilities, special clinicians or special paradigms for medical management of alcohol addiction.

Indeed, medical science was primitive, in the area of alcohol addiction, in the first half of the 20th century: even though the syndrome of *delirium tremens* was well described by early Greek physicians, the pathophysiology of this syndrome was not confirmed as due to acute alcohol abstinence until 1953 (Thompson, 1978). Alcoholics Anonymous (AA) had developed a model of alcoholism as disease and a model of alcohol treatment in the 1930s, but the AA approach was not initially embraced by medical professionals and so became a "self-help" approach rather than a modality of professional treatment.

Although there were significant developments in alcoholism treatment theory and practice on the East Coast as early as the 1800s, professional treatment of alcoholism in America largely adopted an approach referred to as the "Minnesota Model" of treatment. Developed at the Willmar State Hospital in Minnesota in the late 1940s (Anderson, 1981), the model attempted to provide some restorative intervention for chronic alcoholics who were institutionalized in state hospitals alongside the chronically mentally ill. The model suggested that if one approached alcohol problems through the "disease concept" elucidated by the founders of Alcoholics Anonymous (1976), one would find various components of the addictive process—such as dysfunctional behaviors, attitudes, thought patterns, emotional response patterns, interpersonal interactional styles and orientations to the transcendent. Originators of the model then assembled professionals from a variety of disciplines to create a rehabilitation team that could address the many needs of the alcoholic. Thus, a physician would assess general health status and the impact of chronic ethanol exposure on body organs and physiology; a psychologist would assess mental health status, including affective states, defense mechanisms, reality testing and cognitive capacity; nurses would assess general functional level in the hospital milieu; and chaplains would assess the patient's capacity and style of relating to transcendence. With input from all these professionals, a rehabilitation plan would be devised. Treatment would involve physicians, nurses, psychologists, social workers, family counselors, vocational rehabilitation counselors, clergy, AA members and others, and was focused on restoration of function in terms of physiology, affective stability, coping, interpersonal relations, spirituality, intimacy, vocational capacity, avocational repertoire, etc.

The Minnesota Model of clinical intervention at first was applied in the state hospital setting, over a duration of six months. A cornerstone of this process was introduction of the patient to the principles of Alcoholics Anonymous, education about AA and alcoholism, and participation in AA groups within the hospital setting. The results of these interventions were encouraging.

As it became possible to deinstitutionalize schizophrenic patients through the application of phenothiazine medications, social skills training and vocational rehabilitation, it also became possible to deinstitutionalize alcoholic patients through the application of a multidisciplinary treatment process. Life skills training, vocational rehabilitation and community AA participation all were part of the discharge plan that allowed institutionalized alcoholics to reenter the community with function largely restored to premorbid levels. This treatment process, applied over six months, came to be referred to as "alcohol rehabilitation."

The treatment process followed patients outside institutional walls when the founders of the Minnesota Model left Willmar State Hospital and attempted to apply their treatment approach to patients who had not yet reached the point of admission to a state institution. Some of the founders of the Minnesota Model became affiliated with Hazelden Rehabilitation Center in Center City, Minnesota, while others became affiliated with the Lutheran General Hospital Treatment Center in Park Ridge, Illinois (Doot, 1994). Having condensed the period of inpatient rehabilitation to four and then to two months from the original six (and having found success at these shorter lengths of stay), the founders decided to receive patients from general hospitals, from AA clubhouses or from the community and to treat them in a private setting over a four- to six-week period, using the techniques developed at Willmar. The success of this new form of treatment led to its replication, especially in Minnesota, where a number of private facilities began to offer rehabilitation services to alcoholics.

The model featured intensive rehabilitation services, offered in an institutional setting, to patients who had been successfully stabilized after acute alcohol withdrawal. It involved a team of professionals from various disciplines, treating ambulatory patients who resided together in a setting that created a therapeutic milieu. The model was an intensive, acute intervention. It was so restorative for some patients that it was referred to by many recipients as "getting the cure." In much of North America, it became the standard of practice (Goodwin, 1991). When commercial health insurance plans began to define alcohol rehabilitation services as a covered benefit, insurance provided the financial underpinnings that allowed treatment centers offering this standard treatment modality to proliferate.

As the Minnesota Model became the prevailing approach to professional medical care for the alcoholic, it became possible for students or outside observers to lose sight of the fact that this model was almost uniquely American in application, relatively recent in origin and based more on empirical links to AA than on theoretically-derived therapeutic designs that had been subjected to the rigors of double-blind comparisons to other forms of treatment. In some regions of America, especially the Northeast, the Minnesota Model never became the predominant paradigm. Further, therapeutic communities, methadone maintenance clinics, and public mental health centers used approaches that were not designed around the Minnesota Model. Nonetheless, the Minnesota Model became the normative model for hospital-based professional treatment of alcoholism in the private sector.

Goals of Treatment. The Minnesota Model makes assumptions about the features of the addiction process and the components of the disease of alcoholism, and then targets as treatment outcomes the resolution of deficits seen in the alcoholic patient. Thus, untreated alcoholic patients are viewed as having knowledge deficits about the fact that alcoholism is a disease; knowledge deficits about the features of alcoholism and its progression over time; knowledge deficits about AA and how to make use of AA groups and sponsors; shame and guilt about being alcoholic; and knowledge deficits about what is to be confronted during recovery. Further, alcoholics are viewed as having developed an atrophy of emotional skills; an atrophy of their social support network; an atrophy of their repertoire of social and avocational activities; an atrophy of their personal responsibilities and other values; an atrophy in their prayer life; and often a variety of physical sequelae to chronic ethanol exposure. All of these are viewed as constituting part of the progressive functional deterioration of the alcoholic over time.

Components of Treatment. The components of traditional addiction treatment include didactic seminars, to resolve knowledge deficits; group psychotherapy, to identify defenses, overcome denial and build skills in alternative methods of handling affective material; orientation to AA; and, sometimes, family services to aid the family in traversing a parallel process of recovery, including involvement in Al-Anon. The formal structure of a traditional inpatient alcohol rehabilitation program has been well described in the literature (Kaufman & Hann, 1991).

Stages of Change. In the therapeutic milieu of a traditional Minnesota Model 28-day inpatient program, patients often progress predictably through various stages of personal metamorphosis. In the first week, the patient may be completing "detoxification" and consequently experiencing cognitive or psychomotor slowness, impairing much of the psychological changes targeted for "rehabilitation." Following this phase (or immediately upon admission for patients who are not experiencing acute alcohol abstinence symptoms), patients may exhibit extreme denial about their need to be in treatment at all. The patient may not view his or her drinking as problematic (denial), may not view the problem as significant (minimization), and may attribute difficulties to other etiologies or other persons (projection). The patient may view himself or herself as not fitting into the milieu, as different from other patients, as having unique individual needs, and as being misunderstood by the staff. The therapeutic task of the clinician at this stage is to consistently, firmly and dispassionately provide information about the nature of addiction, so that the patient gradually is exposed to clinical vignettes with which he or she can identify; to use confrontational methods in group therapy settings to try to overpower the patient's denial system; and to facilitate a cohesive therapeutic milieu within the patient's living environment.

Traditional inpatient treatment involves placing individuals into a closed living environment with ample free time for development of leisure skills, but also for social mingling, so that newly entering patients gradually feel more socially at ease with their peers in treatment and can begin to identify with them and their stories as well as bond with them emotionally (Yalom, 1975). These processes within the milieu facilitate the patient becoming more comfortable in the group therapy setting, so that denial decreases and the patient's pathological sense of specialness diminishes. In the first week, patients may be assigned behavioral tasks in group therapy, including introducing themselves to other patients in the group, writing an autobiography, writing a journal cataloging the history of their drug use and its consequences over time, or making a collage of pictures cut from magazines that represent feeling states the patient could identify for others in the group. These behavioral exercises serve purposes beyond completion of the tasks assigned: they serve as "ice-breakers" by which the patient can be introduced to peers in the group therapy setting and be received by the group members. They also help peers to become familiar with the new patient's life history and disease progression, and also with the patient's emotional and interpersonal style.

The physician may be able to identify deficits in the patient's verbal or written history and to point to these deficits as examples of the patient's denial system and minimization processes. Senior members of the group may identify with the new group member, pointing out that they also exhibited denial and projection during their first days in treatment. Identification and bonding with the group are essential to the process of developing trust among group members, in the therapist, and in the group process itself (Yalom, 1975).

In summary, the first week of traditional inpatient rehabilitation generally finds the patient in denial, angry, feeling apart and unaware of what will lie ahead.

The second week of 28-day Minnesota Model treatment generally finds the patient becoming more acclimated to group therapy, less angry and defensive, and more bonded to the milieu. The therapeutic task of the clinician remains focused on decreasing the extent to which the patient's defense mechanisms (especially denial) prevent self-awareness and behavioral and affective change. The patient usually is assigned to "complete" the first of the Twelve Steps of Alcoholics Anonymous, through encouragement to identify himself or herself as being "powerless over alcohol," which involves an awareness of alcoholism as a disease process rather than a personality flaw, moral weakness or social depravity; an awareness of the power of addiction to control one's life (through processes such as loss of predictable control of alcohol consumption and inability to consistently abstain without periodic relapse); and an acknowledgement that the patient does, indeed, fit into the cohort of individuals afflicted with the disease of alcohol addiction. Attendance at AA meetings, both within the institutional setting and in community-based AA meetings, facilitates acceptance of these new attitudes and beliefs. Further, patients are encouraged to identify ways in which their lives "have become unmanageable," and to attribute this situation to the effects of alcohol consumption (rather than projecting it onto some other factor). Patients often are provided with written outlines of questions to be addressed in writing, to be shared with the clinician in private session and/or with other patients in a group therapy ("First Step") session. The patient's presentation of a "First Step" in group therapy—more specifically, the patient's sharing of his or her response to the provocative items in the typed outline of the "First Step Guide" provided by the clinician—is an intensely emotional experience and a powerful catharsis, in which the patient often undergoes an emotional and cognitive metamorphosis within the 60 to 90 minutes of the group therapy session.

During this time, the patient ideally experiences a marked decrease in denial and defensiveness, a sense of acceptance by the group and by the therapist, and begins to incorporate a sense of personal acceptance despite the alcohol or other drug problem and their adverse consequences.

In summary, the end of the second week finds the patient less defensive, more clearly identified with peers and with the disease of alcoholism or drug addiction, more self-aware and more self-accepting.

In many traditional 28-day Minnesota Model programs, the third week incorporates family involvement in the treatment process. Not only is the family encouraged to attend educational seminars about the nature of addiction, but also is encouraged to meet with the patient and to discuss experiences associated with the patient's drinking. This can occur in an individual family therapy session, in a multiple-family group therapy session, or in a session in which the patient's family is brought into the group therapy milieu. This powerful therapeutic event occurs after two weeks of intensive therapy, which has decreased the patient's denial and defensiveness sufficiently that the patient can be open to the input of the family. Yet, input from the family often serves to even more thoroughly assault the remnants of the patient's denial system. Again, after the family material has been introduced, the more senior members of the therapeutic cohort can identify with the patient, normalize the experience, validate the individual and counterbalance the narcissistic blows that accompany the introduction of highly charged emotional material from the family. Further, the therapist has the challenge of balancing confrontation with support, balancing a therapeutic attack on destructive narcissism with ego supports, and balancing acceptance of personal flaws with an attenuation of the shame experienced by the patient.

Concurrent with the family exercises, which deepen the patient's endorsement of the First Step of AA, the patient is given written exercises to complete in group therapy or individual therapy, to promote acceptance of the Second and Third Steps of AA. Written assignments often facilitate these processes. At this point, the patient is expected to begin to exhibit some of the personality features seen in the recovering alcoholic that are described in Step Two and Step Three, including acknowledgment that individual willpower is insufficient to overcome the power of addiction, and "surrender" of the pathologically narcissistic aspects of will that attempt to control other persons and events.

In summary, the third week finds the patient experiencing humility, bonding with others and finding increased comfort with AA participation. Further, an increased awareness of the spiritual aspects of the human condition accompanies the patient's introduction to Steps Two and Three.

The fourth week is a time of intense activity. The patient is able to look back on several metamorphoses he or she has experienced regarding his or her basic orientation to Step One of AA. Denial and projection are markedly reduced. Bonding to others is high. The patient now is a senior member of the treatment cohort, and not only welcomes newcomers to the group, but identifies with their early struggles and serves as a role model for incoming patients. Discharge planning consumes much staff and patient energy, and brings focus to the patient's ambivalence about leaving the emotional security of the inpatient environment. Discharge meetings with the patient's employer, vocational counselor, corrections officer, social worker or subsequent caregiver may be scheduled. Simultaneously, the patient is challenged to delve deeper into the recovery process, by "doing a Fourth Step" and "doing a Fifth Step" before leaving inpatient treatment. This involves adhering to those aspects of the Twelve Steps of AA that address introspection into one's history, behaviors, and values. Values clarification, cathartic sharing with another person, and an increased orientation to the spiritual components of the individual's personal life accompany the Fourth Step and Fifth Step exercises. At this point, many treatment programs involve members of the chaplaincy staff to meet with patients and hear their "Fifth Step" presentations in private.

Thus, the patient engaged in traditional Minnesota Model rehabilitation services in a 28-day inpatient program is expected to complete many therapeutic assignments, and to experience many therapeutic events, in a sequence that is largely preprogrammed by the design of the individual's week-by-week experiences in the treatment setting. Experienced clinicians can observe patients in group therapy sessions and identify styles of alertness, personal awareness, defensiveness, group participation, sense of connection with others and to the transcendent, that typify their particular stages of treatment.

VARIATIONS ON TRADITIONAL APPROACHES

Treatment Settings. Traditional inpatient addiction treatment is offered in a variety of hospital and nonhospital settings. In fact, Hazelden's inpatient facilities in Center City, Minnesota, are located outside a general hospital. The facilities largely resemble a private psychiatric hospital in a pastoral location. Hazelden essentially has evolved into an intake and detoxification facility where a staff of nurses and counselors is available around the clock to provide withdrawal management in a hospital-type unit, connected to treatment units designed for patients who do not require acute withdrawal management. The clinical safety and success of this format led to the observation that facilities in which patients reside and receive inpatient rehabilitation can be freestanding residential facilities that do not require 24-hour-a-day medical staff, or even licensure as a hospital facility. Hence, there are two settings for traditional addiction services: hospitals and freestanding residential settings. Many states have developed licensure and facility standards for nonhospital inpatient addiction services. Of course, many medical and psychiatric hospitals use regular inpatient beds to offer post-detoxification addiction rehabilitation services as well.

The next evolution of the Minnesota Model involved offering services to outpatients (Schneider & Herbert, 1992). Treaters hypothesized that there were curative elements in the psychoeducational process of seminars, films and bibliotherapy, in the group therapy process, and in the process of orientation to AA, that could prove beneficial even to patients not living in the inpatient milieu. Persons with stable lives outside the treatment setting (a home to live in, an intact family, and a daily activity structure such as a job or full-time school in order to maintain productivity and self-esteem) were deemed good candidates for outpatient services that resembled inpatient Minnesota Model treatment. These were not designed to emulate ambulatory psychiatric care, with one or several individual sessions a week for an open-ended period; rather, they were akin to psychiatric partial hospitalization or day treatment services and were referred to as intensive outpatient (IOP) services for addiction.

The changes the patient was expected to undergo in intensive outpatient programs were identical to those expected of patients in inpatient treatment. One of the clinical challenges for the therapist was to try to create for patients not only group cohesiveness, but also a therapeutic milieu among the outpatient cohort, to allow them to experience the curative aspects of close peer connections.

Intensive outpatient programs proved extremely popular and quite effective when patients were properly pre-screened for appropriateness of placement. For example, by 1983, there were about 10 providers of inpatient addiction treatment in the Minneapolis-St. Paul area, but about 40 providers of intensive outpatient treatment. A feature of outpatient treatment preferred by patients, families, and especially employers, was that it allowed patients to remain in school or on the job while experiencing the benefits of addiction treatment. Clinically, the patient avoided the sometimes disruptive transition from the sheltered inpatient setting to the challenges of work and home life. Discharge anxiety was less often a problem with outpatient than with inpatient care, and some clinicians believed that the risk of relapse also was reduced.

Minnesota Model treatment also was offered in residential care facilities (which are analogous to extended care facilities for general medical conditions) and halfway houses (which espouse AA and Minnesota Model approaches but provide far less professional therapeutic contact while providing a structured healthy and sober environment in which recovery can take deeper root over time).

Duration of Treatment. Changes in the duration of treatment occurred even before the Minnesota Model left the Willmar State Hospital. The duration of intensive treatment evolved from six months to two months, to four weeks. Access to treatment was enhanced when patients experienced fewer financial barriers as a result of shorter inpatient stays, and the availability of private insurance coverage for addiction treatment led to an expansion of the supply of treatment providers. When the Minnesota legislature established mandated insurance benefits for addiction treatment and specified that private insurers must reimburse for up to 28 days of inpatient care, the 28-day length of stay became entrenched as the standard duration of inpatient treatment. Intensive outpatient services were established for four- to six-week periods.

Longer durations of treatment were offered to patients whose addiction was deemed to be intense, whose relapse potential was thought to be high, or when the risks attendant on relapse were deemed more critical. Thus, patients with cocaine addiction who entered traditional inpatient programs often were placed in a separate therapy group, with a different psychoeducational curriculum, more emphasis on Narcotics Anonymous than on Alcoholics Anonymous, and an average length of stay of six weeks rather than four. The proliferation of intensive outpatient services, coupled with clinicians' increased comfort with their use, led to the observation that patients could be "stepped down" from inpatient settings to outpatient settings at a point determined by their clinical progress. The duration of inpatient care thus could be shortened, with patients continuing to receive intensive therapy as outpatients. The emergence of "managed care" has fostered further scrutiny of the duration of inpatient treatment, which recently has decreased to an average of eight days.

Conditions Treated. The Minnesota Model originally was designed for the rehabilitation of alcoholics. At first, patients with other drug addictions were discouraged from participating in the same treatment groups as alcoholics. If the Minnesota Model was used for patients with opiate, cocaine, or even prescription sedative addictions, they were placed in separate facilities or in separate therapy groups. Only as psychoeducational curricula came to address the common features of all chemical addictions were all patients with addictive disorders provided service in the same therapy groups as alcoholics.

Eventually, other conditions were approached with the Minnesota Model methods and orientations to Twelve Step recovery processes. Patients with compulsive disorders involving gambling, overeating, food restriction, purging, exercise or sexual behaviors were referred to self-help programs designed to meet their needs (Gamblers Anonymous, Overeaters Anonymous, etc.), and professional services were developed to transcend the gains patients could make with self-help alone.

Providers of Treatment. The first caregivers in Minnesota Model treatment programs were recovering alcoholics who either were themselves graduates of treatment programs or who had extensive experience with AA and solid recoveries from their own addictions. Counselors eventually were required to have a credential certifying competence to provide professional services. The credential generally involved, at a minimum, demonstrated completion of a program of counselor training; such training programs generally involved apprenticeships of six to 18 months' duration. Certified counselors gradually took into their ranks individuals who did not have a personal history of addiction and recovery; recovering and non-recovering certified counselors were more likely to be reimbursed for professional services than were recovering counselors without an educational credential.

Today, the addiction counselor credential is granted to mental health therapists, nurses, and even some physicians. In some jurisdictions (such as Wisconsin), state certification of treatment programs requires that diagnoses and treatment plans be determined by certified counselors, with their credentials carrying more authority in the addiction treatment arena than even medical licensure. More recently, given the complexities of addictive disorders and the psychiatric comorbidities so common in addicted patients, the addiction counselor certification has sometimes been required to be supplemented by further credentials, such as a master's degree in a clinical mental health discipline.

The entry of physicians into the arena of Minnesota Model addiction treatment is a more recent development. While physicians often have been expected to administer physical examinations to patients admitted to hospital or even residential addiction treatment programs, and medical oversight of counselor activities has been required by the Joint Commission on Accreditation of Healthcare Organizations, direct physician involvement in clinical care of addicted patients generally has been relegated to acute withdrawal management (rather than addiction rehabilitation). The exception has been the care of physicians and other health care professionals being treated for alcohol or drug addiction (Talbott, 1993). In such cases, recovering or non-recovering physicians have been direct therapists (or co-therapists with addiction counselors) in group therapy sessions in inpatient or intensive outpatient Minnesota Model treatment facilities. The *Patient Placement Criteria* of the American Society of Addiction Medicine (*PPC*; Hoffmann, Halikas et al., 1991; *PPC-2*; Mee-Lee, Shulman et al., 1994) have suggested the proper role for the physician in the management (as opposed to the monitoring) of addiction care.

Customers for Treatment. Traditionally, the party primarily concerned with care of addictive disorders has been the patient with the addiction problem. More recently, however, a number of other parties have become involved. As self-pay has played a decreasing role in the financing of addiction treatment over the past 30 years, the parties paying for services have become very interested in the care given, in what setting and at what financial cost. Employers are indirect utilizers of services, for they need to have employees restored to a premorbid functional level; as purchasers of service, they are very interested parties. Other purchasers include patients and their families; employers who offer health care services as a fringe benefit and who, because of decisions to self insure, may directly purchase addiction treatment services; or unions that offer health care services to members and may directly purchase addiction treatment services. More recently, managed care entities such as health maintenance organizations and behavioral health management firms have been given the authority to direct purchasers of addiction treatment services toward or away from certain providers.

Providers must be aware of the multitude of customers for treatment services and be sensitive to the different needs of different customers. Therapeutic alliances with patients always have been important, but now collaborative alliances with employers, employee assistance professionals and managed care entities require attention.

Recipients of Treatment. Traditional addiction treatment focuses on the individual drug addict or alcoholic. The patient is encouraged to work a program of personal recovery, using the Steps of AA, and to accept personal responsibility for change. Simultaneously, family members are encouraged to work their own personal programs of recovery through Al-Anon, to accept personal responsibility for their own change, and not to focus solely on the issues of the addict.

However, with alternative models of care, the focus of treatment can extend beyond the individual in isolation, and address the addict's family, marriage or social network. Thus, family members can be brought into the treatment arena, not simply to provide data about the patient, but as subjects of the treatment process itself. There is now a rich literature on family treatment in alcoholism (Steinglass, 1976; Young & Liepman, 1991). The marital unit also can be a focus of treatment; in fact, some treatment models require spousal participation before the individual addict is accepted into services (Gallant, Rich et al., 1970; Talbott, 1993). Finally, a variety of other significant persons in the addict's social network can be brought into the treatment process as well.

CRITICISMS OF TRADITIONAL APPROACHES

Program Model. The most frequent criticism of traditional Minnesota Model treatment is that it is not individualized and non-specific, with a predetermined psychoeducational curriculum offered to every patient, regardless of the diagnosis, severity or chronicity of illness, with a fixed length of stay offered to all patients. Compared to other areas of medical practice, such as cancer chemotherapy or management of glucose intolerance, the lack of treatment variation in the face of patient diversity is viewed as a major deficit of Minnesota Model treatment. External utilization reviewers and case managers often raise specific objections to the notion that inpatient treatment is required for psychoeducational material to be conveyed to the patient. Lack of variation in length of stay, regardless of patients' varied responses to the treatment experience, also is criticized. The harshest criticisms label fixed-program and fixed-length addiction treatment experiences as unscientific, not thoughtfully developed, prepackaged and promoted, designed to meet institutional needs over patient needs, or even unethical.

Diagnosis Determines Treatment. One of the features of programmatically-designed treatment experiences is that the duration and content of treatment are determined at the time of admission. Clinical criteria may need to be applied to determine if a diagnosis of alcoholism or other drug dependence is present; however, once the diagnosis is made and objectively verified by quality assurance measures, then a full course of prescribed treatment can be expected to follow when traditional Minnesota Model approaches are employed. Pretreatment clinical activity focuses almost exclusively on the confirmation of a diagnosis, rather than on more refined assessment measures such as severity of condition, presence of co-morbid conditions, or other discriminating variables that might differentiate the treatment provided to a given patient. In traditional addiction treatment, if a diagnosis has been confirmed, then the services to be rendered 14 days after admission, or 25 days after admission, can be fairly accurately estimated regardless of individual patient characteristics.

Rewarding Process versus Change. In traditional Minnesota Model treatment, successful completion of the treatment program's fixed process is the goal of treatment and thus the measure of success or failure of the treatment episode. Accordingly, successful attendance at psychoeducational sessions and successful completion of assignments from the counselor are considered measures of a good treatment outcome. Discharge summaries and quality assurance monitors often describe success in terms of completion of the process of program-designed treatment, whereas more detailed analyses of treatment outcome tend to examine specific changes in functional level, elimination of life problems attendant to alcohol or drug use and biopsychosocial changes (see Table 1).

Acute Intervention for Chronic Problems. Finally, intensive alcoholism rehabilitation methods that focus on acute interventions and short-term outcomes do not seem complementary to the newest definitions of alcoholism (Morse & Flavin, 1992) and models of chronic disease management. Long-term management strategies are not incompatible with Minnesota Model theories or AA concepts; in fact, the original program design for services at the Lutheran General Hospital Alcoholism Treatment Program, over three decades ago, incorporated three months of aftercare (Doot, 1994). But longer-term models have not been emphasized by inpatient facilities to the same extent as short-term management strategies.

TABLE 1. Therapeutic Changes Addressed in Addiction Treatment

Behavioral Changes
- Eliminate alcohol and other drug use behaviors
- Eliminate other problematic behaviors
- Expand repertoire of healthy behaviors
- Develop alternative behaviors

Biological Changes
- Resolve acute alcohol and other drug withdrawal symptoms
- Physically stabilize the organism
- Develop sense of personal responsibility for wellness
- Initiate health promotion activities (e.g., diet, exercise, safe sex, sober sex)

Cognitive Changes
- Increase awareness of illness
- Increase awareness of negative consequences of use
- Increase awareness of addictive disease *in self*
- Decrease denial

Affective Changes
- Increase emotional awareness of negative consequences of use
- Increase ability to tolerate feelings without defenses
- Manage anxiety and depression
- Manage shame and guilt

Social Changes
- Increase personal responsibility in all areas of life
- Increase reliability and trustworthiness
- Become resocialized: reestablish sober social network
- Increase social coping skills: with spouse or partner, with colleagues, with neighbors, with strangers

Spiritual Changes
- Increase self-love and esteem; decrease self-loathing
- Reestablish personal values
- Enhance connectedness
- Increase appreciation of transcendence.

OTHER APPROACHES TO TREATMENT

Treatment Modalities. There are many modalities of addiction treatment other than those applied in the traditional 28-day Minnesota Model. One that antedated the Minnesota Model is the psychoanalytic model, which emphasized individual psychotherapy, professional services and non-behavioral theories of drive reduction and conflict resolution, more so than involvement in self-help groups, abstinence and other behavior changes. There are self-help models that differ from Alcoholics Anonymous and its analogues (such as Al-Anon, NA, CA, and OA). Among the best-known is Rational Recovery (RR), which also emphasizes group process and self-help (see Section 9). There are individual psychotherapy models other than the psychoanalytic model. Rational-emotive therapy and cognitive-behavioral therapy have been successfully applied to improve the functioning of alcoholics and drug addicts. Some treatment models use behavioral analysis to identify cues to and triggers of relapse and attempt to decrease relapse potential specifically (as opposed to the Minnesota Model, which focuses more intently on resolution of denial and improvements in treatment acceptance). Beyond various psychotherapeutic, behavioral and self-help modalities, there are pharmacotherapies, described elsewhere in this text.

Treatment of drug addictions through approaches developed outside the traditional model of alcoholism treatment has led to development of modalities that have benefits for patients with all kinds of addictions, including alcoholism. The standard modalities of treatment for heroin addiction and other drug addictions include the Minnesota Model—referred to by the drug treatment community as "chemical dependency treatment," offered in settings referred to as "CD treatment centers." But the cornerstones of treatment services—as conceptualized by the National Institute on Drug Abuse and as funded by NIDA before its treatment services sections were reorganized into the Center for Substance Abuse Treatment—are methadone maintenance (a specialized subset of pharmacotherapeutic approaches to addiction treatment) and therapeutic communities (specialized residential settings, different from chemical dependency halfway houses, which may or may not incorporate the philosophies of Narcotics Anonymous). Methadone maintenance and therapeutic communities certainly differ from the Minnesota Model modality; in fact, one of the clinical challenges of contemporary addiction treatment is to make simultaneously available for patients those aspects of methadone maintenance and NA-oriented treatment that patients may need.

The other leg of the "four-legged stool" of drug treatment services (the first three "legs" of which are chemical dependency treatment centers, therapeutic communities, and methadone maintenance) has been the so-called "drug-free outpatient" modality, employed in many public-sector clinics that see patients in individual or group sessions without methadone and without use of the Minnesota Model type day treatment or intensive outpatient services. Note that while this description of four modalities of drug treatment does, in fact, differentiate on the basis of modalities and philosophies of care, it also differentiates strongly among settings for care.

Services for the patient with cocaine dependence may closely mirror services offered to alcoholics in traditional intensive outpatient or inpatient chemical dependency treatment settings. However, different approaches have been developed for cocaine dependency management. Certainly, the use of periodic urine drug screening is a modality used more often in the treatment of drug addicts than alcoholics. Also, contingency contracting (Calsyn & Saxon, 1987) may be more applicable in some cases of drug treatment than in alcohol treatment. The behavioral methods of identification of conditioned cues, role-playing strategies for dealing with situations that pose a high risk of relapse, and other relapse prevention techniques all are especially important in the management of cocaine dependence. Traditional Minnesota Model programs have expanded their approaches to include these modalities in addition to traditional denial-reduction group therapy modalities, for patients with all sorts of addiction problems, but the roots of some of these different methodologies in other-than-alcoholism treatment settings is to be acknowledged. Obviously, the specific pharmacotherapeutic strategies for management of cocaine withdrawal and cocaine dependence differ from those in alcoholism or opiate withdrawal management or rehabilitation.

It is the area of nicotine addiction that has seen the development of even more different therapeutic modalities, many of which are being incorporated into traditional alcoholism treatment approaches and settings. It was the nicotine treatment area that brought into greater focus behavioral analysis and behavior therapy for habituated or compulsive tobacco use. It was the nicotine treatment area that developed brief office interventions that could be employed in sequential, seven-minute office visits with a primary care physician. It was in the treatment of nicotine addiction that the theories of motivational analysis first were applied (Prochaska & DiClemente, 1992; Prochaska, DiClemente & Norcross, 1992).

The addiction field overall now is embracing the concepts of motivational analysis (Miller, 1983; Miller & Rollnick, 1991). This clearly is a different psychotherapeutic modality than abstinence-based treatment in groups through fixed chemical dependency programs. Further, the brief office management techniques developed by Babor and others (Babor & Grant, 1992; Babor, Korner et al., 1987; Babor, Ritson & Hodgson, 1986; Bien, Miller & Tonigan, 1993), have brought a new dimension to what addiction medicine physicians can do in the office for an individual or couple, and have provided guidance for general physicians as they attempt to address alcohol and other drug use problems in their practices.

Treatment Intensities. With the publication of the ASAM *Patient Placement Criteria* (Hoffmann, Halikas et al., 1991; Mee-Lee, Shulman et al., 1994), there has been an increased focus on individualization of treatment and on defining treatment necessity according to features of the illness and of the patient, rather than relying simply on the presence of a diagnosis of addiction. The basic model of service utilization parallels the utilization management methods applied in other areas of medical practice, suggesting that the intensity of clinical service should be a function of a quantified severity of clinical illness. The task of defining treatment intensity, as defined by the levels of care of the *PPC* and *PPC-2*, involves defining intensity of service as something other than duration or setting of service. This is a major departure from the Minnesota Model, for which the inpatient setting and a four-week duration of treatment often were considered the standard of excellence. The ASAM *PPC* and *PPC-2* thus have placed new emphasis on what is designated as Level I services, including general outpatient care, ongoing care after completion of intensive program-type services, individual care in lieu of group therapy and program-type intensive outpatient services, and brief office interventions.

Treatment Continuum. One of the challenges of contemporary addiction treatment is to provide appropriate initial placement of patients into services of appropriate intensity and to move them from one level of care to another over time, all the while respecting the chronic relapsing and remitting nature of addiction. Such shifting of treatment intensities over time requires that a full range of services be available, with a mechanism by which patients can access them. (Access usually includes ability to pay for services, so insurance reimbursement for a variety of intensities of care is critical.)

It should be pointed out that the full continuum of care for alcohol and other drug use problems includes preventive, diagnostic and therapeutic services for alcohol or drug use, abuse and dependence, as well as case finding, emergency services, consultation, withdrawal management, rehabilitation and monitoring services. The 1990 Institute of Medicine Report describes the role of general physicians in the detection and management of alcohol problems, and describes ideal interfaces between specialist care, generalist care and community-based services that lie outside the formal health care delivery system (IOM, 1990). Understanding the continuum of care also must include understanding the role of non-addictionists in delivering treatment services.

An issue often overlooked in considering the continuum of care is that of periodic monitoring to assess how well a patient is maintaining gains achieved through treatment. One of the basic definitions of "therapy" is that it is a process that promotes change; however, the models of Prochaska and DiClemente demonstrate that *maintenance* of change is a crucial component of lasting behavioral change. In addiction treatment, there is a place for periodic "check-in" sessions after a patient no longer needs weekly "recovery group" sessions. Such check-in sessions can be individual meetings or involve spouses, employers or other members of the patient's social network. The frequency of such sessions can be tapered before all professional contacts cease. Periodic—often random—drug urine screens frequently are a component of monitoring services.

Public Sector versus Private Sector Approaches. For a variety of reasons, addiction services available in the private sector and those available through public sector reimbursement often are not the same. The addiction treatment field, with traditional program-model treatment, may have its origins in the public sector, but its proliferation in the 1970s and 1980s was a phenomenon largely of the private sector. For-profit hospital programs promoted services that had predictable lengths of stay and were significant sources of institutional revenues (Reader & Sullivan, 1993). Public sector programs, often required to offer services to relatively large numbers of patients with limited resources, could not afford to design delivery systems that relied on expensive hospital-based treatment models. Outpatient services therefore were emphasized, as exemplified by the services of the Haight Ashbury Free Clinic in San Francisco.

Moreover, federal block grants and state levies for addiction services often funded services beyond the types of benefits covered by commercial insurers. Thus, halfway houses, therapeutic communities, and methadone maintenance programs have proliferated in the public but not the private sector. As a result, patients *without* insurance often have been unable to access chemical dependency treatment programs, while patients *with* insurance have been unable to access halfway houses.

One of the more recent developments in addiction treatment has been the application of managed care processes to the addiction field. Widely applied in private-sector settings and now often seen in the public sector, managed care involves many utilization and reimbursement management components. Managed care also may involve case management. Whereas case management approaches may seem new to private sector providers, they have been the hallmark of mental health and addiction services in outpatient public facilities at least since the Community Mental Health Center movement of the 1960s.

Patient-Treatment Matching. One of the fundamental challenges in delivering addiction treatment services in the 1990s—whether in the public or private sector—is to maximize treatment efficacy and efficiency. Patients ideally should receive the type of service that will most predictably generate the maximal treatment outcome, provided in the setting that is least restrictive and least expensive (without compromising outcome), delivered by the optimal provider and collateral parties. The process of matching patients to treatment intensity, setting, modality and provider (Annis, 1988) is well-described in the 1990 Institute of Medicine Report (IOM, 1990). It seems certain that treatment matching philosophies will guide delivery system design in the 1990s, with or without the advent of government-initiated health care reform. The basic premise of patient-treatment matching is that, as demonstrated by data on treatment outcome, there are subsets of patients who do better or worse than others in a given modality of service (McLellan, Woody et al., 1983). Finding which patients do better, what patient characteristics contribute to differential outcomes, and what aspects of treatment contribute to differential outcomes thus is the first step in a matching process (McLellan, Woody et al., 1983). Such matching ideally will result in referral of a given patient to a particular treatment modality/setting/provider that is expected to have the greatest probability of success in addressing the patient's problem. Most matching studies to date have examined gross differences in treatment (such as intensity or setting) rather than differences in specific elements of treatment (such as whether group therapy, family therapy or vocational rehabilitation is offered) (McLellan & Alterman, 1991).

Care Management. The final aspect of addiction treatment, which differs from traditional addiction care, involves management of the treatment process itself by entities external to the provider and the patient. While the term "managed care" often is used pejoratively by addiction specialists, the management of care involves complex interactions of reimbursement management, utilization management, case management and outcomes management, which can prove beneficial not only to individual patients but especially to populations of patients.

CONCLUSIONS

Some therapists lament that the rehabilitation model of addiction treatment has been supplanted in recent years by an acute-care model. Their concern is that addictive disorders are being approached as acute problems in general medical-surgical care, and that the major functional improvements to be derived from intensive inpatient addiction rehabilitation (Table 1) may no longer be attainable in an era of managed care. A similar concern is that newer treatment philosophies driven by managed care attempt only to resolve symptoms of addictive disease, without addressing the underlying pathophysiology of addiction.

On the other hand, the rehabilitation model can be applied to an intensive phase of addiction service (following withdrawal management, as needed, to stabilize the patient physiologically) that can involve a variety of modalities and settings. The key in approaching an analysis of addiction treatment is to examine the desired outcomes of treatment and to explore the curative aspects of any given treatment modality. Certainly, there have been demands to link the intensity of addiction services to the severity of disease symptoms. While severity of illness generally is measured at a given point in time, it does not necessarily follow that the overall disease process is to be ignored. Instead, newer treatment approaches suggest that a given intervention should focus on a specific aspect of the disease process at a point in time, with the intensity of service dictated by what is required for the given therapeutic activity to have a reasonable chance of success.

Even given the current shift of much private sector treatment from inpatient to outpatient settings, there is no reason to abandon the rehabilitation model or to suppose that utilization managers will not approve clinical efforts aimed at rehabilitation of the patient. One need only look at the changes that have occurred in the rehabilitation of patients with brain or spinal cord injuries to see how overall rehabilitation goals can be maintained, even in outpatient settings. Therapeutic change thus remains an appropriate object of therapeutic energy.

REFERENCES

Alcoholics Anonymous (1976). *Alcoholics Anonymous, 3rd Ed.* New York, NY: Alcoholics Anonymous World Service, Inc., 4, 12.

Anderson DJ (1981). *Perspectives on Treatment: The Minnesota Experience.* Center City, MN: Hazelden Foundation.

Annis H (1988). *Patient Treatment Matching in the Management of Alcoholism (NIDA Research Monograph 90).* Rockville, MD: National Institute on Drug Abuse.

Babor TF, Korner P, Wilbur P & Good F (1987). Screening and early intervention strategies for harmful drinkers.

Initial lessons learned from the Amethyst project. *Australian Drug and Alcohol Review* 6:325–339.

Babor TF, Ritson BE & Hodgson RJ (1986). Alcohol-related problems in the primary health care setting: A review of early intervention strategies. *British Journal of Addictions* 81:23–46.

Babor TF & Grant M (1992). *Project on identification and management of alcohol-related problems. Report on Phase II: A randomised clinical trial of brief interventions in primary health care.* Geneva, Switzerland: World Health Organization, 1–266.

Barnhart CL (1962). *American College Dictionary*. New York, NY: Random House.

Bien TH, Miller WR & Tonigan JS (1993). Brief interventions for alcohol problems: A review. *Addiction* 88:315–336.

Calsyn DA & Saxon AJ (1987). A system for uniform application of contingencies for illicit drug use. *Journal of Substance Abuse Treatment* 4:41–47.

Doot M (1994). Personal communication.

Gallant DM, Rich A, Bey E & Terranova L (1970). Group psychotherapy with married couples: A successful technique in New Orleans Alcoholism Clinic Patients. *Journal of the Louisiana State Medical Society* 122:41–44.

Gitlow SE (1988). An overview. In SE Gitlow & HS Peyser (eds.) *Alcoholism: A Practical Treatment Guide*. Philadelphia, PA: Grune & Stratton.

Goodwin DW (1991). Inpatient treatment of alcoholism—New life for the Minneapolis Plan. *The New England Journal of Medicine* 325(11):804–806.

Hoffmann NG, Halikas JA, Mee-Lee D & Weedman RD (1991). *Patient Placement Criteria for the Treatment of Psychoactive Substance Use Disorders*. Washington, DC: American Society of Addiction Medicine.

Institute of Medicine (1990). *Broadening the Base of Treatment for Alcohol Problems*. Washington, DC: National Academy Press.

Kaufman RB & Hann SB (1991). Description of Hospital-based programs. In J Westermeyer & RS Krug (eds.) *Substance Abuse Services: A Guide to Planning and Management*. Chicago, IL: American Hospital Association.

Lewis D (1992). Inpatient consultation service models. Faculty Development Training Program of the National Institute on Drug Abuse and the National Institute on Alcohol Abuse and Alcoholism, Madison, WI.

McLellan AT & Alterman AI (1991). Patient treatment matching: A conceptual and methodological review with suggestions for future research. *NIDA Research Monograph 106*. Rockville, MD: National Institute on Drug Abuse, 114–135.

McLellan AT, Woody GE, Luborsky L, O'Brien CP & Druley KA (1983). Increased effectiveness of substance abuse treatment. A prospective study of patient-treatment "matching." *Journal of Nervous and Mental Disease* 171(10):597–605.

Mee-Lee D, Shulman G & Gartner L (1994). *Patient Placement Criteria for the Treatment of Substance Use Disorders, Second Edition (PPC–2)*. Chevy Chase, MD: American Society of Addiction Medicine.

Miller WR (1983). Motivational interviewing with problem drinkers. *Behavioral Psychotherapy* 11:147–172.

Miller WR & Rollnick S (1991). *Motivational Interviewing: Preparing People to Change Addictive Behavior.* New York, NY: Guilford Press.

Morse RM & Flavin DK (1992). The definition of alcoholism (The Joint Committee of the National Council on Alcoholism and Drug Dependence and the American Society of Addiction Medicine to Study the Definition and Criteria for the Diagnosis of Alcoholism. *Journal of the American Medical Association* 268(8):1012–1014.

Prochaska JO & DiClemente CC (1992). Stages of change in the modification of problem behaviors. In M Hersen, RM Eisler & PM Miller (eds.) *Progress in Behavior Modification*. Sycamore, IL: Sycamore Press.

Prochaska JO, DiClemente CC & Norcross JC (1992). In search of how people change: Application to addictive behaviors. *American Psychologist* 47:1102–1114.

Reader JW & Sullivan KA (1993). Private and public insurance. In JH Lowinson, RB Millman & P Ruiz (eds.) *Substance Abuse: A Comprehensive Textbook*. Baltimore, MD: Williams & Wilkins.

Schneider RJ & Herbert M (1992). Substance abuse day treatment and managed health care. *Journal of Mental Health Administration* 19(1):119–124.

Steinglass P (1976). Experimenting with family treatment approaches to alcoholism, 1950–1975: A review. *Family Process* 15:97–123.

Talbott GD (1993). Extended treatment components in the Georgia Impaired Health Professionals Program. Presentation to the 24th Annual Medical-Scientific Conference, American Society of Addiction Medicine, Los Angeles, CA.

Thompson WL (1978). Management of alcohol withdrawal syndromes. *Archives of Internal Medicine* 138:278–283.

Yalom ID (1975). *The Theory and Practice of Group Psychotherapy, 2nd Ed.* New York, NY: Basic Books, 11.

Young SL & Liepman MR (1991). Family behavior loop mapping enhances treatment of alcoholism. *Family and Community Health* 13(4):72–83.

CHAPTER 4

Components of Successful Treatment Programs: Lessons from the Research Literature

A. Thomas McLellan, Ph.D.
James R. McKay, Ph.D.

Parameters of the Literature Review
Treatment Programs: What are They For, What Should They Do?
Research on Treatment Process Factors Related to Outcomes

Problems of substance abuse and dependence produce dramatic costs to society in terms of lost productivity, social disorder and, of course, health care utilization (National Institute on Drug Abuse, 1991; Merrill, 1993). Over the past 20 years, many of the traditional forms of addiction treatment (such as methadone maintenance, Therapeutic Communities, outpatient drug-free programs and others) have been evaluated multiple times and shown to be effective (McLellan, Luborsky et al., 1980; Sells & Simpson, 1980; Hubbard & Marsden, 1986; Ball & Ross, 1991; Institute of Medicine, 1990; Gerstein & Harwood, 1990). Importantly, this research has shown that the benefits obtained from addiction treatments typically extend beyond the reduction of substance use, to areas that are important to society as a whole, such as reduced crime, reduced risk of infectious diseases and improved social function (McLellan, Luborsky et al., 1980; Ball & Ross, 1991; Institute of Medicine, 1990; Gerstein & Harwood, 1990). Finally, research findings indicate that the costs associated with the provision of substance abuse treatment provide three- to seven-fold returns to the employer, the health insurer and to society within three years following treatment (Holder, Longabaugh et al., 1991; Gerstein & Harwood, 1990).

How Do These Results Translate into Recommendations for Providing High-Quality Treatment? While the conclusions from this line of research are important and gratifying, they are not adequate to inform important clinical questions regarding the delivery of addiction treatment services. Simply knowing that those who stay in treatment longer have better outcomes does not help when the funding and duration of treatment in "real world" settings is regularly reduced (McLellan & Weisner, 1996). Further, research demonstrating that highly specialized and resource-intensive treatments work with highly selected samples of patients may not be helpful to "real world" treatment providers who have no prospects of accessing those treatments and very few of the patients on whom the treatment was tested. This is particularly true at the level of the community-based public sector treatment programs, which have been forced to operate under limited budgets, with little access to sophisticated services. How can research in the treatment setting inform these providers? How can these providers use information from research studies to upgrade or expand their treatment efforts within the practical constraints of budget and personnel available?

PARAMETERS OF THE LITERATURE REVIEW

In response to these questions, the authors have reviewed the existing treatment outcome literature to summarize the available knowledge regarding the important patient and treatment factors that have been shown to influence the outcomes of addiction rehabilitation treatments. This is an important *first step* in recognizing and recommending proven, practical and cost-effective treatment strategies that can be implemented by community treatment programs. The review did not include the literature on detoxification methods, on adolescent treatment, or on smoking cessation treatment so that it could better focus on standard rehabilitation treatments for drug and alcohol dependence, typically following detoxification. The adolescent drug abuse treatment literature was not reviewed because it is still a developing field and there is a paucity of pertinent outcome studies in this area.

From a methodological perspective, this review included only those clinical trials, treatment matching or health services studies in which the patients were alcohol- or drug-dependent by contemporary criteria; where the treatment provided was a conventional form of rehabilitation (any setting or modality); and where there were measures of either treatment processes or patient change during the course of treatment, as well as post-treatment measures of outcome (as defined later in the chapter). Finally, the review included methadone maintenance (as well as its long-acting form, levo-alpha-acetyl methadol [LAAM]) as part of the general category of outpatient rehabilitation treatments, rather than create a special category.

The review that follows first discusses some of the basic assumptions underlying rehabilitation forms of addiction treatment (e.g., patients eligible for rehabilitation, realistic goals of rehabilitation, etc.), since they set the stage for the clinical methods currently in use and for the types of studies that appear in the research literature. The discussion then turns to considerations regarding definitions of "outcome," the types of treatments that were included in the review and the methodological standards set for articles to be included. With these assumptions and considerations in mind, the chapter then reviews the most significant treatment process contributors to the outcomes of addiction treatment.

TREATMENT PROGRAMS: WHAT ARE THEY FOR, WHAT SHOULD THEY DO?

Patients for Whom Rehabilitation Is Designed. *Detoxification* is a relatively brief, usually medical procedure designed to stabilize the physical and emotional effects of recent termination of heavy alcohol and/or drug use. In contrast, *rehabilitation* is a much longer process, usually involving multidisciplinary staff, that is designed for substance dependent patients who have gotten past the initial detoxification/stabilization part of addiction treatment but who still have problems controlling their use of alcohol and/or drugs and who are in need of behavioral change to regain control of their urges to use substances.

Purposes of Addiction Rehabilitation. The major purposes of rehabilitation treatments for alcohol and drug addiction are:

1. To prevent return to active substance use that would require detoxification/stabilization;
2. To assist the patient in developing control over urges to use alcohol and/or drugs (usually through attaining and sustaining total abstinence from all drugs and alcohol); and
3. To help the patient to regain (or attain for the first time) improved personal health and social function, as both a secondary part of the rehabilitation function and because these improvements in lifestyle are important for maintaining sustained control over substance use.

Rehabilitation Methods. There is a very wide range of professional opinions regarding the *underlying reasons* for the loss of control over alcohol and drug abuse (genetic predispositions, acquired metabolic abnormalities, learned negative behavioral patterns, self-medication of underlying psychiatric or physical medical problems, character flaws, lack of family and community support for positive function, etc.). For this reason, there is an equally wide range of treatment methods that have been applied to "correct" or ameliorate these underlying problems and to provide continuing support for the targeted patient changes. These have included such diverse elements as psychotropic medications to relieve underlying psychiatric problems, "anti-craving" medications to relieve alcohol and drug craving, acupuncture to correct acquired metabolic imbalances, educational seminars, films and group sessions to correct false impressions about alcohol and drug use, group and individual counseling and therapy sessions to provide insight, guidance and support for behavioral changes, and peer help groups (e.g., Alcoholics Anonymous, Narcotics Anonymous, Cocaine Anonymous) to provide continued support for the behavioral changes thought to be important for sustained improvement.

At this writing, inpatient rehabilitation programs can be divided into three general categories (Hubbard, Marsden et al., 1989):

1. Inpatient hospital-based treatment (no longer common): typically 7 to 11 days in duration.
2. Non-hospital "residential rehabilitation": 30 to 90 days.
3. Therapeutic Communities: six months to two years.

Outpatient forms of treatment (at least abstinence-oriented treatments) typically range from 30 to 120 days (Hubbard, Marsden et al., 1989). Many of the more intensive forms of outpatient treatment (e.g., intensive outpatient, day hospital) begin with full or half-day sessions, five or more times per week for approximately one month. As the rehabilitation progresses, the intensity of the treatment is reduced to shorter duration sessions (one to two hours) delivered twice weekly to semi-monthly.

The final part of outpatient rehabilitation generally is called "continuing care" or "aftercare" and features bi-weekly to monthly group support meetings (in association with parallel activity in self-help groups), continuing for as long as two years (McKay, Cacciola et al., 1996). Maintenance forms of treatment (e.g., methadone or LAAM) are designed to be of indeterminate length—indeed, some are intended to continue throughout the life of the patient.

Outcomes to Be Expected from Addiction Treatments. The authors have argued in earlier work (McLellan, Woody et al., 1996, 1995) that outcome expectations for addiction treatment should not be confined simply to reduction of alcohol and drug use, since the public, the payers of treatment and even the patients themselves are interested in a broader definition of "rehabilitation." Further, the authors have argued that for addiction treatments to be worthwhile to the multiple stakeholders who are involved in treatment, the positive effects of addiction treatment should be sustained beyond the end of the treatment period and continue for at least six to 12 months. Most of the experienced researchers in the drug abuse field have taken a similar, broad view of outcome expectations for addiction treatments (see Simpson & Savage, 1980; Anglin, Speckart et al., 1989; Anglin & Hser, 1990; De Leon, 1984; Hubbard & Marsden, 1986). Thus, in the review that follows, the authors have attempted to characterize outcomes broadly in terms of improved health, social function and reductions in public health and safety concerns, rather than focusing only on reduced substance use, and to present findings from post-treatment evaluations. Thus, this review gives greater attention to studies in which multiple outcomes were measured six to 12 months after inpatient discharge or at the same points during the course of outpatient care.

RESEARCH ON TREATMENT PROCESS FACTORS RELATED TO OUTCOMES

Patient factors have been much more widely studied than treatment setting, modality, process and service factors as predictors of outcome from addiction treatments. Perhaps the major reason for this is that, while there have been many reliable and valid measures of various patient characteristics, there are still very few measures of treatment setting (Moos, 1974) or treatment services (McLellan, Grissom et al., 1993; Barber, Mercer et al., 1996). Recent developments in the psychotherapy field have led to the creation of manual-based treatments and, with them, appropriate measures of treatment fidelity and integrity. More recently, the multi-site study of patient treatment matching (Project MATCH, 1997) sponsored by the National Institute on Alcohol Abuse and Alcoholism (NIAAA) has brought several new manuals for the three treatments that were studied as part of that project, as well as additional manuals for measuring patient and treatment characteristics. The following sections review several dimensions or characteristics of treatment that have been studied and that have shown some relationship to post-treatment outcomes.

Treatment Setting. A large number of studies have investigated potential differences in outcome between various forms of inpatient and outpatient treatments. In the field of rehabilitation from alcohol dependence, there have been several important studies of the role of treatment setting. For example, studies by McCrady, Noel et al. (1986) and Alterman, McLellan et al. (1994) randomly assigned alcohol-dependent patients to an equal length (28–30 days) of either inpatient or day hospital treatment. Comparisons of many outcome measures in both studies showed essentially no significant differences among the groups, suggesting that the setting of care might not be an important contributor to outcome. A review of the literature on inpatient and outpatient alcohol rehabilitation by Miller and Hester (1986) also concluded that, across a range of study designs and patient populations, inpatient care provided no significant advantage over outpatient care in the rehabilitation of alcohol dependence, despite the substantial difference in costs. It is important to note that a widely cited study by Chapman-Walsh et al. (1995) did find a significant difference in outcome favoring an inpatient program. This difference was shown among employed alcohol-dependent patients who were assigned to either an inpatient program or to a very non-intensive form of outpatient treatment (largely Alcoholics Anonymous meetings).

In the field of cocaine dependence treatment, there also have been several studies examining the role of treatment setting. Again, while there are problems with high attrition rates, there is evidence indicating that outpatient treatments for cocaine dependence can be effective, even for patients with relatively limited social resources. In a recent study, Alterman, McLellan et al. (1994) compared the effectiveness of four weeks of intensive, highly structured day hospital (DH) treatment (27 hours weekly) with that of inpatient (INP) treatment (48 hours weekly) for cocaine dependence. The subjects were primarily inner city, male African-Americans treated at a Veterans Administration Medical Center. The INP treatment completion rate of 89% was significantly higher than the DH completion rate of 54%. However, at seven months post-treatment, self-reported outcomes indicated considerable improvements for both groups in terms of reductions in drug and alcohol use, family/social, legal, employment, and psychiatric problems. The finding of reduced self-reported cocaine use was supported by urine screening results. Both self-report and urine data indicated 50% to 60% abstinence rates for both groups at the follow-up assessment.

Similar findings have been shown in field studies of private substance abuse treatment programs that treat primarily cocaine and cocaine-plus-alcohol-dependent patients (Pettinati, Meyers et al., 1993; McLellan, Alterman et al., 1994; Havassy, Wasserman et al., 1995). In all of these studies, patients who were assigned to one of several outpatient treatment programs were less likely to complete treatment than those assigned to the inpatient programs, but those who did complete treatment showed equal levels of improvement and outcome in the two settings. It is important to note that *virtually all studies of this type have shown greater engagement and retention of patients in inpatient settings*. This is particularly significant in that the majority of this research was conducted among patients who were willing to accept random assignment to either treatment.

There have been at least two attempts to formalize clinical decision processes regarding who should and should not be assigned to inpatient and outpatient settings of care (the Cleveland Criteria and the Patient Placement Criteria of the American Association of Addiction Medicine [1990, 1994]). McKay, Alterman et al. (1994) failed to show evidence for the predictive validity of the Cleveland placement criteria, at least when applied to the assignment of alcohol- and drug-dependent patients to inpatient and day hospital treatment. That is, there were no significant differences in the six-month outcomes of those who met Cleveland criteria for inpatient treatment, who had been randomly assigned to either inpatient care or day hospital treatment. In a similar study evaluating the psychosocial predictors from the ASAM Patient Placement Criteria, McKay, Cacciola et al. (1996) did find at least partial support for the predictive validity of these placement variables, although a full evaluation was not possible.

The most recent version of the ASAM criteria (1994) has attempted to make very fine-grained decisions regarding placements to levels of care according to the amount and quality of medical supervision and monitoring. Research is needed to determine the predictive validity of these finer distinctions and whether patients in settings and modalities with more medical supervision actually receive more medical contact or services than patients in settings where they are not expected to receive such services. Studies in progress by Mee-Lee and Gastfriend may inform our understanding about these clinical decision criteria.

Length of Treatment and Compliance with Treatment. Perhaps the most robust and pervasive indicator of favorable post-treatment outcome in all forms of substance abuse rehabilitation has been length of stay in treatment. Virtually all studies of rehabilitation have shown that patients who stay in treatment longer and/or attend the most treatment sessions have the best post-treatment outcomes (Simpson & Savage, 1980; Hubbard, Marsden et al., 1989; De Leon, 1984; Ball & Ross, 1991). Specifically, several studies have suggested that outpatient treatments of less than 90 days are more likely to result in early return to drug use and generally poorer response than shorter terms (Ball & Ross, 1991; Simpson & Savage, 1980; Des Jarlais, Hagan et al., 1995).

Although length of stay is a very robust, positive predictor of treatment outcome, the nature of this relationship remains ambiguous. Clearly, one possibility is that patients who enter treatment gradually acquire new motivation, skills, attitudes, knowledge, and supports over the course of their stay in treatment; that those who stay longer acquire more of these favorable attributes and qualities; and that the gradual acquisition of these qualities or services is the reason for the favorable outcomes. A less attractive but equally plausible possibility is that better motivated and better adjusted patients come into treatment ready and able to change; that the decisions they made to change their lives were made in advance of their admission and because of this greater motivation and treatment readiness they are likely to stay longer in treatment and to do more of what is recommended. These two interpretations of the same facts have very different implications for treatment practice. If treatment gradually produces positive changes over time, it is obviously clinically sound practice to retain patients longer so as to provide them with more benefits. On the other hand, if well-motivated, high-functioning, compliant patients enter treatment with the requisite skills and supports necessary to do well, then length in treatment could be irrelevant to their outcome. More research is needed on this important point.

Participation in AA/NA/CA. Alcoholics Anonymous (AA) is, of course, recognized as a social organization and not a formal treatment. For this reason, and because of the anonymous quality of the group, not much research has been done to evaluate this important part of substance abuse rehabilitation until recently (Project MATCH, 1997). While there always has been consensual validation for the value of AA and other peer support forms of treatment, the past few years have witnessed a new evidence that patients who have participated in AA, NA or other form of peer support group, who have a sponsor, or who have participated in similar fellowship activities have much better abstinence records than patients who have received rehabilitation treatments but have not continued in AA (Miller, Brown et al., 1995). McKay, Alterman, McLellan et al. (1994) found that participation in post-treatment self-help groups predicted better outcome among a group of cocaine or alcohol dependent veterans in a day hospital rehabilitation program. Timko, Moos et al., (1994) found that more AA attendance was associated with better one-year outcomes among previously untreated problem drinkers, regardless of whether they received inpatient, outpatient, or no other treatment.

There has been less research on the use of self-help organizations among cocaine and/or opiate dependent patients. However, a recent study of cocaine patients participating in outpatient counseling and psychotherapy showed that, while only 34% attended a cocaine anonymous (CA) meeting, 55% of them became abstinent, as compared with only 38% of those who did not attend CA. Interestingly, there were very few background characteristics that differentiated those who attended CA from those who did not (Weiss et al., 1996).

It is important to note that in contemporary substance abuse treatment, AA has become synonymous with the last part of rehabilitation: aftercare. Virtually all alcohol dependence rehabilitation programs and most cocaine dependence rehabilitation programs refer patients to AA programs, with instructions to find a sponsor, to "share and chair" at meetings, and to attend 90 meetings in 90 days as a continued commitment to sobriety. Thus, while the research studies done to date generally have suggested that the peer support component of rehabilitation is valuable, it also is difficult to sort out the extent to which AA attendance constitutes an active ingredient of successful treatment and/or the extent to which it simply is a marker of treatment compliance. In this regard, McLatchie and Lomp (1988) found that infrequent or irregular attendance at AA following discharge from residential treatment was associated with a poorer prognosis than either regular attendance or no attendance. Finally, citing a relative paucity of well-controlled studies of the effect of AA participation on drinking among alcoholics, Vaillant (1996) concluded that "The jury is still out" (p. 269).

The Therapist or Counselor Who Provides the Treatment. There is a growing body of research suggesting that the drug or alcohol abuse counselor or therapist can make an important contribution to the engagement and participation of the patient in treatment and to the post-treatment outcome. Perhaps the clearest example of the role of the counselor in at least individual counseling is a study of methadone-maintained patients, all within the same treatment program and all receiving the same methadone dose, who were randomly assigned to receive counseling or no counseling in addition to the methadone (McLellan, Woody et al., 1988). Results were unequivocal, showing that 68% of patients assigned to the no counseling condition failed to reduce drug use (confirmed by urinalysis) and 34% of these patients required at least one episode of emergency medical care. In contrast, no patient in the counseling groups required emergency medical care, 63% showed sustained elimination of opiate use and 41% showed sustained elimination of cocaine use over the six months of the trial.

A study by Fiorentine (1996) as part of a larger "Target Cities" evaluation also showed the contribution of counseling in drug rehabilitation. Group was the most common counseling modality (averaging 9.5 sessions per month), followed by Twelve Step meetings (average 7.5 times per month) and individual counseling (average 4.7 times per month). Greater frequency of both group and individual counseling sessions were shown to decrease the likelihood of relapse over the subsequent month and the subsequent six months. One important contribution of this study, given the above cautions regarding the role of simple length of stay in determining treatment outcome (see above), is that the relationships shown between more counseling and lower likelihood of relapse to cocaine use were seen even among patients who completed treatment, that is, having approximately the same tenure in the programs. Thus, it may be that beyond the simple effects of attending a program, more involvement with counseling activities is important to improved outcome.

Many important questions remain in this area. While there is clear indication that patients who meet with a counselor during treatment have better outcomes than those who have no counselor, and that there are significant differences in outcome for patients treated by different counselors, there is little indication regarding which qualities of the counselor (personal, educational, philosophical, etc.) are important in determining who should and should not be a counselor and whether a particular counselor is likely to have good or bad outcomes with assigned patients. It is important to note that the relationships of counseling to outcomes have been examined primarily for individual therapy and counseling and it is not known whether the relationships also will be found in studies of group therapy settings.

At least four studies of addiction treatment have documented between-therapist differences in patient outcomes. These differences have emerged both among professional psychotherapists with doctoral level training and among paraprofessional counselors. Luborsky, McLellan et al. (1985) found outcome differences in a variety of areas between nine professional therapists who provided ancillary psychotherapy to methadone maintenance patients. McLellan, Woody et al. (1988) found that assignment to one of five methadone maintenance counselors resulted in significant differences in treatment progress over the following six months. Specifically, patients transferred to one counselor achieved significant reductions in illicit drug use, unemployment, and number of arrests while concurrently reducing their average methadone dose. In contrast, patients transferred to another counselor evidenced increased unemployment and illicit drug use, while their average methadone dose went up. In a study of two different interventions for problem drinkers, Miller, Taylor and West (1980) found significant differences between paraprofessional therapists in the percentage of their patients who improved at six-month follow-up. These percentages varied from 25% for the least effective therapist to 100% for the most effective therapist. Finally, McCaul et al. (1990) reported significant differences in post-treatment drinking rates and several other outcomes among alcohol-dependent patients assigned to different individual counselors within an alcohol treatment program.

As noted above, although it is relatively clear that therapists and counselors differ considerably in the extent to which they are able to help their patients achieve positive outcomes, it is less clear what distinguishes more effective from less effective therapists. In an experimental study of two different therapist styles, Miller, Benefield and Tonigan (1993) found that a client-centered approach that emphasized reflective listening was more effective for problem drinkers than a directive, confrontational approach. In a review of the literature on therapist differences in substance abuse treatment, Najavits and Weiss (1994) concluded that "The only consistent finding has been that therapists' in-session interpersonal functioning is positively associated with greater effectiveness" (p. 683). Among indicators of interpersonal functioning are the ability to form a helping alliance (Luborsky, Crits-Christoph et al., 1986), measures of the level of accurate empathy (Miller, Tonigan & West, 1980; Valle, 1981), and a measure of "genuineness," "concreteness" and "respect" (Valle, 1981).

It should be noted that there are a variety of certification programs for counselors (Committee on Addiction Rehabilitation [CARF] and Certified Addictions Counselor [CAC]) as well as other professions treating addicted patients (American Society of Addiction Medicine; American Academy of Psychiatrists in Addiction; recent added certification for psychologists through the American Psychological Association). These added qualification certificates are offered throughout the country, usually by professional organizations. While the efforts of these professional organizations to bring needed training and proficiency to the treatment of addicted persons is commendable, there are not yet any published studies validating whether patients treated by "certified" addictions counselors, physicians or psychologists have better outcomes than patients treated by non-certified individuals. This is an important gap in the existing literature and the results of such studies would be quite important for the licensing efforts and health policy decisions of many states and health care organizations.

Medications. At this writing, a great deal of research is being sponsored by both the National Institute on Alcoholism and Alcohol Abuse and the National Institute on Drug Abuse toward developing useful medications for the treatment of addicted persons. Great progress has been made over the past

10 years in the development of new medications and in the application of existing medications for the treatment of particular conditions associated with substance dependence and for particular types of addicted patients. This section summarizes only some of the clearest results from the use of medications in the treatment of addiction and provides citations for more comprehensive medication reviews for the interested reader. Two types of medications are discussed: agonist and antagonist or blocking medications.

Agonist Medications: Methadone has been an approved agonist medication for the maintenance treatment of opiate dependence for more than 25 years. The long-acting form of methadone (48 to 72 hours' duration), levo-alpha-acetyl methadol (LAAM) has received approval of the Food and Drug Administration (FDA) and has been accepted by 16 states for use in the same way as methadone (that is, LAAM is available only at methadone maintenance programs). Buprenorphine is a partial opiate agonist that has been widely used in Europe and in the U.S. It is thought to have some advantages over methadone in that it produces much fewer (often no) withdrawal symptoms.

Among the most robust findings in the treatment literature is the relationship between dose of methadone and general outcome in methadone treatment (Ball & Ross, 1991; D'Aunno & Vaughn, 1992; Institute of Medicine, 1990). Higher doses are more effective than lower doses. In a well-controlled double-blind multi-site VA study, Ling, Charuvastra et al. (1976) found that 100 mg of methadone per day was superior to 50 mg, as indicated by staff ratings of global improvement and by a drug use index comprised of weighted results of opiate urine tests. In a more recent randomized, double-blind study, Strain, Stitzer et al. (1993) compared 50 mg and 20 mg of methadone with a 0 mg placebo-only group. They found orderly dose-response effects on treatment retention, and they found that 50 mg was more effective than 20 mg or 0 mg at decreasing opiate and cocaine use, as measured by urinalysis results. In a randomized double blind comparison of moderate (40 to 50 mg) and high (80 to 100 mg) dose methadone, Strain, Stitzer et al. (1993) found a significantly lower rate of opiate-positive urine specimens among patients who received a high dose of methadone (53% versus 62%). They concluded that although the higher dose was more effective, substantial opiate use can persist even among patients treated with 80 to 100 mg per day of methadone. There are many other studies of opiate agonist medications, but space limitations do not permit more detail here.

Antagonist and Abuse Blocking Agents: Naltrexone has been used for more than 20 years in the treatment of opiate dependence. Naltrexone is an orally administered opiate antagonist that blocks actions of externally administered opiates, such as heroin, by competitively binding to opiate receptors. More recently, naltrexone (marketed under the trade name Revia®) has been found to be effective in the treatment of alcohol dependence (Volpicelli, Alterman et al., 1992; O'Malley, Jaffe et al., 1992). Naltrexone at 50 mg/day has been approved by the FDA for use with alcohol-dependent patients since independent studies have shown it to be a safe, effective pharmacological adjunct for reducing heavy alcohol use among alcohol-dependent patients. Its mechanism of action appears to be the blocking of at least some of the euphoria produced by alcohol consumption, again through competitive binding of the opiate receptors (Volpicelli, Alterman et al., 1992; O'Malley, Jaffe et al., 1992).

With regard to other medications designed to block the effects of an abused drug, disulfiram (Antabuse®) has been used the longest and most pervasively in the treatment of alcohol dependence. While both of these medications can be used for extended periods, in practice they generally are prescribed for about one to three months as part of a more general rehabilitation program that includes behavioral change strategies (see review by Anton, 1996).

Many agents have been tried as blocking agents in the treatment of cocaine dependence and, while this literature is quite large, it is to date disappointing. At this writing, there is no convincing evidence that any of the various types of cocaine-blocking agents are truly effective for even brief periods of time or for even a significant minority of affected patients. Research continues in this important area, but no treatment-relevant recommendations are possible at this time.

While the use of opiate and alcohol antagonists or blocking agents is increasing, as addiction medicine physicians become more comfortable with the prescription of adjunctive medications (Jaffe, Rounsaville et al., 1996) and as more substance dependence is treated by primary care physicians in office settings (Fleming, Barry et al., 1997), there still are relatively few patients who receive—or practitioners who prescribe—these medications, and the available literature in this area still does not provide an unambiguous conclusions regarding the parameters that are most effective when using these medications. For example, a recent cautionary article warned about an unusually high rate of deaths (particularly suicides) among opiate-dependent individuals who were transferred to naltrexone (Rawson et al., 1996).

The responsible and appropriate use of antagonist or blocking medications in treatment of addictive disorders may be among the most important topics for future research in the treatment field. The past 10 years has witnessed innovation and discovery in this area, but there still is reluctance on the part of some physicians to prescribe these medications (Institute of Medicine, 1990). At this time, there is a need for long-term studies of patients who have been prescribed these medications, as well as of the most appropriate and efficient mix of psychosocial and pharmacological services that will maximize the effectiveness of rehabilitation for various types of addicted patients.

Provision of Specialized Services. The majority of patients admitted to addiction treatment have significant addiction-related problems in one or more areas of their lives, such as medical status, employment and self-support, family relations and/or psychiatric function (see, for example, McLellan & Weisner, 1996). As discussed earlier, the severity of these problems generally is predictive of response during treatment as well as post-treatment outcome. Studies have documented that strategies designed to direct and focus specialized services to these addiction-related problems can be applied in standard clinical settings and can be effective in improving the results of addiction treatment. Again, this conclusion follows more than a decade of research showing that the addition of professional marital counseling (McCrady, Noel et al., 1986; Stanton & Todd, 1982), psychotherapy (Carroll, Rounsaville et al., 1994; Woody, McLellan et al., 1995) and medical care (Fleming, Barry et al., 1997) produces clinically and significantly better outcomes from addiction treatment. It should be noted that the majority of these adjunctive forms of therapy and services have been most clearly associated with improved personal health and social function following treatment and less related to reduced alcohol and drug use. In addition, and not surprisingly, these treatments have been shown to be effective only with those patients who have more severe problems in the target area (matching effect); that is, if there has been no indication of a relatively severe problem in the target area, typically there has been no evidence that the provision of the target therapy is effective or worthwhile (see Woody, McLellan et al., 1984).

A recent study by Milby and colleagues (1996) illustrates the importance of providing supplemental social support services to homeless, substance-dependent (typically cocaine- and alcohol-dependent) individuals, based on a study of patients who sought health care services from the Birmingham (AL) Health Care for the Homeless Coalition. In a study funded by the National Institute on Drug Abuse and the National Institute on Alcohol Abuse and Alcoholism (which was not focused specifically on patients who sought addiction treatment), 176 subjects were recruited and randomized into one of two programs, which were conducted in separate facilities:

Usual Care (UC): Patients in this program received twice-weekly Twelve Step-oriented individual and group counseling, medical evaluation and referral for diagnosed conditions. Referrals for housing and vocational services were made to other agencies by counselors.

Enhanced Care (EC): These patients received day treatment five days a week for 5.5 hours per day. Transportation and lunch were provided. Day treatment was group-oriented around a community model. Multiple education and psychologically oriented groups were provided on various topics and themes. Each client had an individual counselor and an individual treatment plan, with regularly supervised reviews of progress. After two months, EC subjects graduated to a four-month work-therapy phase, during which day treatment was reduced to two afternoons per week and the remaining time was involved in the supervised rehabilitation of dilapidated housing that ultimately would be used by the program for drug-free housing (including housing for the subjects themselves). Minimum wages were paid and subsidized housing was available to participants during the work therapy phase. Importantly, participation in this second phase was *contingent on drug-free urines* (monitored weekly on randomly selected days) and continued participation in the day treatment program.

Outcomes were measured at several points following admission and included multiple domains that were considered important to the "value" of the treatment program to the supporting agencies. With regard to treatment retention, 131 of the 176 individuals entered one of the two programs. Usual care (UC) patients attended an average of 0.6 days per week, or 29% of expected attendance. In contrast, Enhanced Care (EC) patients attended an average of 2.5 days per week, or 48% of expected attendance. At six month follow-up, the EC patients showed significantly lower levels of cocaine, alcohol and opiate use than the UC patients. In addition, the EC patients were two times more likely to be employed and four times less likely to be homeless than the UC patients. Some of these significant group differences disappeared at 12 months. Although there were problems with the very low number of subjects recruited (approximately 10% of the total homeless population). The results are important in that the differences between the groups were substantial and important from a health policy perspective, and because these individuals were *not* applying for substance abuse treatment. The treatment was available from the project and was offered to individuals who wanted only health screening services. Despite the lack of initial motivation for these services, the supplemental services included as part of addiction treatment were associated with significant and broad improvements. These data are reminiscent of the findings in the criminal justice system, where addiction treatments added to standard probation or parole typically were found to improve the effects of those interventions (Cornish, Metzger et al., 1996; Wexler, Falkin et al., 1990; Inciardi, 1997).

Milby and colleagues (1996) have suggested that the reasons their study was able to show significant differences is that the interventions were aimed at severely affected individuals, the components of the care provided were both necessary and desirable to the subjects, and the enhanced intervention was potent and well implemented. Milby believes that both addiction-focused interventions (e.g., drug counseling, aftercare, AS/NA) and survival services (drug-free housing, employment or self-support skills) are necessary for effective treatment, but that neither is sufficient alone. Similar findings have emerged from studies of "Target Cities" projects in Los Angeles and Philadelphia (Anglin & Hser, 1990; McLellan et al., 1998), which showed that the provision of supplemental social services such as drug-free housing, medical screening and referral, parenting classes and employment counseling were able to be integrated effectively into standard outpatient drug abuse treatment through use of clinical case managers, and that those patients who were assigned to "enhanced" service programs showed 20% to 40% improvements over patients assigned to standard outpatient programs.

Matching Patients with Treatments. The past two decades have witnessed substantial research on attempts to "match" patients with particular problems to the specific treatment types, modalities or settings that are thought to be best suited to their needs. The approach to patient-treatment matching that has received the greatest attention from treatment researchers involves attempting to identify the characteristics of individual patients that predict the best response to different forms of substance abuse treatment (e.g., cognitive-behavioral versus Twelve Step, or inpatient versus outpatient) (Mattson, Allen et al., 1994; Project MATCH Research Group, 1997). Another approach to matching is to assess patients' problem severity in a range of areas at intake and then to add those specific treatment services indicated by the assessment to the standard substance abuse treatment protocol (McLellan & Gastfriend, 1996). This approach has the potential to be particularly helpful for the polyproblem substance abuser, as most substance abuse-focused interventions are not designed to also address serious co-occurring medical, psychiatric, family, or legal problems.

Substance abusers with comorbid psychiatric problems may be particularly good candidates for the addition of focused, specialized services, in the form of professionally-delivered psychotherapy, psychotropic medications, greater treatment intensity or structure, or a combination of all three. For example, recent studies suggest that tricyclic antidepressants may reduce both drinking and depression levels in alcoholics with major depression (Mason, Kocsis et al., 1996; McGrath, Nunes et al., 1996). Similarly, the anxiolytic buspirone may reduce drinking in alcoholics with a comorbid anxiety disorder (Kranzler & McLellan, 1995). Highly structured relapse prevention interventions may also be more effective in decreasing cocaine use, as compared to less structured interventions, in cocaine abusers with comorbid depression (Carroll, Rich & Rounsaville, 1995).

Woody and colleagues have evaluated the value of individual psychotherapy when added to paraprofessional counseling services in the course of methadone maintenance treatment (Woody, Luborsky et al., 1983). In that study, patients were randomly assigned to receive standard drug counseling alone (DC group) or drug counseling plus one of two forms of professional therapy: supportive-expressive psychotherapy (SE) or cognitive-behavioral psychotherapy (CB) over a six-month period. Results showed that patients who received psychotherapy showed greater reductions in drug use, more improvements in health and personal function and greater reductions in crime than those receiving counseling alone. Stratification of patients according to their levels of psychiatric symptoms at intake showed that the main psychotherapy effect was in those patients with greater than average levels of psychiatric symptoms. That is, patients with low symptom levels made considerable gains with counseling alone and there were no differences between groups. However, patients with more severe psychiatric problems showed few gains with counseling alone but substantial improvements with the addition of the professional psychotherapy.

The effect of adding additional, professionally-delivered treatment services to a basic methadone program also was investigated by McLellan, Arndt et al. (1993). In this study, patients were randomly assigned to receive (1) methadone only, (2) methadone plus standard counseling, or (3) methadone and counseling plus on-site medical, psychiatric, employment, and family therapy services (the "enhanced" condition). Although these additional services were not "matched" to patients on an individual basis, most of the patients in the study were polydrug abusers with relatively high problem levels in other areas. On most outcome measures, the best results were obtained in the enhanced condition, followed by methadone plus counseling and methadone alone. Improvements in the enhanced condition were significantly better than those in the methadone plus counseling condition in the areas of employment, alcohol use, criminal activity, and psychiatric status. These results demonstrate the value of providing additional professional treatment services to polyproblem substance abusers, even when these services are not "matched" to specific problems at the level of the individual patient.

Another type of substance abuser who can pose particular problems for outpatient treatment is the cocaine-dependent patient who is unable to achieve remission from cocaine dependence early in outpatient treatment. Several randomized studies suggest that highly structured cognitive-behavioral treatment is particularly efficacious with such individuals. In two outpatient studies with cocaine abusers, those with more severe cocaine problems at intake had significantly better cocaine use outcomes if they received structured relapse prevention rather than interpersonal or clinical management treatments (Carroll, Rounsaville et al., 1994, 1991). In a third study, cocaine dependent patients who continued to use cocaine during a four-week intensive outpatient treatment program (IOP) had much better cocaine use outcomes if they subsequently received aftercare that included a combination of group therapy and a structured relapse prevention protocol delivered through individual sessions, rather than aftercare that consisted of group therapy alone (McKay, Cacciola et al., 1996).

McLellan and colleagues recently attempted a different type of matching research in two inpatient and two outpatient private treatment programs (McLellan, Grissom & Brill, 1996). Patients in the study (N = 130) were assessed with the ASI at intake and placed in a program that was acceptable to both the EAP referral source and the patient. At intake, patients also were randomized to either the standard or "matched" services conditions. In the standard condition, the treatment program received information from the intake ASI, and personnel were instructed to treat the patient in the "standard" manner, as though there was no evaluation study ongoing. The programs were instructed to not withhold any services from patients in the standard condition. Patients who were randomly assigned to the matched services condition also were placed in one of the four treatment programs and ASI information was forwarded to that program. For these patients, the programs agreed to provide at least three individual sessions in the areas of employment, family/social relations, or psychiatric health, delivered by a professionally trained staff person to improve functioning in those areas when a patient evidenced a significant degree of impairment in one or more of these areas at intake. For example, a patient whose intake ASI revealed significant impairments in the areas of social and psychiatric functioning would receive at least six individual sessions, three by a psychiatrist and three by a social worker.

The standard and matched patients were compared on a number of measures, including number of services received while in treatment, treatment completion rates, intake to six-month improvements in the seven problem areas assessed by the ASI, and other key outcomes at six months. The following results were obtained. First, matched patients received significantly more psychiatric and employment services than standard patients, but not more family/social services or alcohol and drug services. Second, matched patients were more likely to complete treatment (93% versus 81%), and showed more improvement in the areas of employment and psychiatric functioning than the standard patient. Third, while matched and standard patients had sizable and equivalent improvements on most measures of alcohol and drug use, matched patients were less likely to be re-treated for addiction-related problems during the six-month follow-up period. These findings suggest that matching treatment services to adjunctive problems can improve outcomes in key areas and also may be cost-effective by reducing the need for subsequent treatment due to relapse.

Limitations of the Matching Approach: It is difficult to argue against the face validity of a treatment approach that stresses the importance of providing additional services to address co-occurring medical, economic, psychiatric, family, and legal problems. After all, standard addiction-focused interventions are not designed to address serious problems in other areas. If left untreated, co-occurring problems can increase the risk for poor treatment response and poor post-treatment outcome. And in some cases, it may be impossible to even initiate treatment for a substance abuse problem until treatment for severe co-occurring problems has been provided. In addition to benefits for the patients, the matching of services to problems approach also can reduce stress levels in clinicians who treat polyproblem individuals, provided that a team approach to treatment is taken and regular lines of communication are established among clinicians involved with a case.

The primary limitation of this approach concerns the potential lack of resources available to support it at a time of health care cost containment. Funding may not be available for adjunctive services in areas such as medical and psychiatric care unless the level of problem severity is sufficiently high that these co-occurring disorders can be considered "primary," or at least critical to the substance use problem. Recent research has shown that addiction treatment programs vary widely in the number and frequency of adjunctive services they provide (McLellan, Grissom et al., 1993b), which may reflect differences between programs in the funding available for such services. Obviously, it is impossible to match services to problems if the appropriate services are not available. The scarcity of resources underlies the need for accurate assessment and diagnosis of co-occurring problems, so as to assure that patients who are more in need of such services will stand a better chance of receiving them. Also, not all services may be potent enough to make a significant impact on the target problem area. For example, despite the importance of employment-related problems in predicting treatment outcome, and despite the range of interventions that have been developed to improve employment and self-support among substance-dependent patients (see Bradley, French & Rachal, 1994), there is little evidence (Hall, Loeb et al., 1981, is an exception) that this type of specialized service is effective in improving the post-treatment employment rates of patients or in improving their abstinence from drugs.

A *caveat* also is in order concerning the addition of family or couples therapy (i.e., conjoint therapy) to addictions treatment. In studies in which couples behavioral marital therapy has been compared to other forms of outpatient treatment for alcoholics, it has frequently produced superior outcomes (Holder, Longabaugh et al., 1991). However, there is less evidence that conjoint therapy is effective with polyproblem individuals or drug abusers, and there is some indication that it can produce worse outcomes with some patients under certain conditions. Longabaugh and colleagues (1995) randomized patients to three 20-session outpatient social learning-based conditions that varied in the amount of conjoint therapy included (0, 4, or 8 sessions). Analyses indicated that the 8 conjoint session condition was least effective for patients with either the worst or best relationship situations, as indicated by degree of investment in relationships on the part of the patient and degree of support for abstinence from significant others. Additional analyses with the same sample indicated that according to the perceptions of both the patient and significant other, family functioning showed equal improvement from pre- to post-treatment in individually focused (0 conjoint sessions) and the relationally focused (4 or 8 conjoint sessions) conditions. However, the individually focused condition actually produced greater improvements in family functioning for patients characterized by a high degree of dependence on others (McKay, Longabaugh et al., 1993).

The results of this study raise the possibility that for patients with serious family or social problems, a limited number of conjoint treatment sessions may do more harm than good, especially if these sessions are substituted for standard alcohol or drug sessions. In these cases, providing a limited number of conjoint sessions may in a sense "open a can of worms" by encouraging both the patient and significant other to air feelings of anger, hurt, or disappointment, but not providing enough time to work through the problems that have been identified.

CONCLUSIONS

In this review, the authors have attempted to identify patient variables and treatment process variables that have been shown to be important in determining the outcome of addiction rehabilitation efforts. Review of the research in this area suggests the following three points:

First, *research to date has conclusively established that treatment can be effective, but there are only preliminary indications at this time as to why treatment is effective or what it is within treatment that makes it effective.* Treatment researchers are only now beginning to develop the measures and models that will be necessary for the exploration of questions regarding why treatment works. If the outcomes research field is really to inform contemporary community treatments, then it will be necessary to move beyond the question of *whether* treatment works, to the question of *how* treatment works. In turn, this will require a methodology shift from the simple evaluation or comparison of treatment outcomes to the parametric study of the various types of treatment and their relationship to the target outcomes.

The suggested methodology will require measurement of more than just the target outcomes at a post-treatment follow-up point. Careful recording of the treatment services and processes provided during treatment will be necessary, as will concurrent monitoring of during-treatment changes in patient attitude, cognition, motivation, affect and behavior that are the interim goals of these processes. These types of "dose response" or "dose ranging" designs ultimately will permit the discovery of the important therapeutic milestones that patients must achieve along their route to recovery and the "active ingredients" within a treatment that are responsible for those milestones and, ultimately, for lasting outcomes following treatment. This is a line of research that has been called for by several within the field (DeLeon, Simpson, Finney) but the present review has uncovered very few studies that have pursued this direction. Thus, an important message from this chapter is a call to the treatment research field for more systematic work on this line of investigation.

Second, *some patients have better prognoses at the start of treatment than others.* The variables that suggest better prognosis include: (1) low severity of dependence and psychiatric symptoms at admission; (2) motivation beyond the pre-contemplation stage of change; (3) being employed or self supporting; and (4) having family and social supports for sobriety.

Third, *some treatment variables have been reliably shown to produce better and more enduring outcomes.* The treatment variables associated with better outcome in rehabilitation include: (1) staying in treatment (at least outpatient treatment) longer and being more compliant with treatment; (2) having an individual counselor or therapist and more counseling sessions during treatment; (3) receiving proper medications—both anti-craving medications and medications for adjunctive psychiatric conditions; (4) participating in voucher-based behavioral reinforcement interventions; (5) participating in AA, CA or NA following treatment; and (6) having supplemental social services provided for adjunctive medical, psychiatric, and/or family problems.

In summary, it is important to note that none of these patient or treatment variables showed a completely unambiguous record of prediction, although all have shown replicated evidence across more than one type of primary drug problem (alcohol, cocaine or opiates) and in more than one research evaluation. An important point, suggested by Miller and Holder in their recent review of the alcohol rehabilitation field (1994), is that many of the currently applied treatment practices and processes have not been shown to be importantly associated with treatment outcome, and many have not been studied at all. And there are a number of therapeutic practices and procedures that remain prevalent in the field that have not shown indication of success. Clearly, more research is needed to identify the "active ingredients" of treatment and the minimal effective dose of these ingredients.

ACKNOWLEDGMENTS: Supported by grants from the Center for Substance Abuse Treatment, the National Institute on Drug Abuse and the Robert Wood Johnson Foundation. A version of this paper was submitted as part of the work of the Institute of Medicine Committee on Community Based Addiction Treatments.

REFERENCES

Abellanas L, Meyers K, Metzger DS & McLellan AT (1993). Latino/a IDUS: Do their risk behaviors differ from those IDUs of other racial groups? In L Harris (ed.) *Problems of Drug Dependence 1993 (NIDA Research Monograph)*. Rockville, MD: National Institute on Drug Abuse.

Allison M & Hubbard RL (1982). *Drug Abuse Treatment Process: A Review of the literature (TOPS Research Monograph)*. Raleigh, NC: Research Triangle Press.

Alterman AI, Droba M & McLellan AT (1992). Response to day hospital treatment by patients with cocaine and alcohol dependence. *Hospital and Community Psychiatry* 43(9):930–932.

Alterman A, McKay J, Mulvaney F & McLellan AT (1996). Prediction of attrition from day hospital treatment in lower socioeconomic co-dependent men. *Drug and Alcohol Dependence* 40:227–233.

Alterman AI, McLellan AT, O'Brien CP et al. (1994). Effectiveness and costs of inpatient versus day hospital cocaine rehabilitation. *Journal of Nervous and Mental Disease* 182:157–163.

Alterman AI, McLellan AT & Schiffman RB (1993). Psychopathology, quantity of treatment and improvement? *Journal of Nervous and Mental Disease* 181(9):576–582.

Anglin MD & Hser Y (1990). Legal coercion and drug abuse treatment. In J Inciardi (ed.) *Handbook on Drug Control in the United States.* Westport, CT: Greenwood Press.

Anglin MD, Speckart GR, Booth MW & Ryan TM (1989). Consequences and costs of shutting off methadone. *Addictive Behaviors* 14:307–326.

Armor DJ, Polich JM & Stambul HB (1976). *Alcoholism and Treatment.* Santa Monica, CA: RAND Corporation.

Azrin NH, Sisson RW, Meyers RW & Godley M (1982). Alcoholism treatment by disulfiram and community reinforcement therapy. *Journal of Behavior Therapy and Experimental Psychiatry* 13:105–112.

Babor TF, Dolinsky Z, Rounsaville BJ & Jaffe JH (1988). Unitary versus multidimensional models of alcoholism treatment outcome: An empirical study. *Journal of Studies on Alcohol* 49(2):167–177.

Ball JC & Ross A (1991). *The Effectiveness of Methadone Maintenance Treatment.* New York, NY: Springer-Verlag.

Barber JP, Mercer D, Krakauer I & Calvo N (1996). Development of an adherence/competence rating scale for individual drug counseling. *Drug and Alcohol Dependence* 43:125–132.

Bradley CJ, French MT & Rachal JV (1994). Financing and cost of standard and enhanced methadone treatment. *Journal of Substance Abuse Treatment* 11:433–442.

Carroll KM, Rich C & Rounsaville BJ (1995). Differential symptom reduction in depressed cocaine abusers treated with psychotherapy and pharmacotherapy. *Journal of Nervous and Mental Disease* 183(4):251–259.

Carroll KM, Power MD, Bryant K & Rounsaville BJ (1993). One-year follow-up status of treatment-seeking cocaine abusers: Psychopathology and dependence severity as predictors of outcome. *Journal of Nervous and Mental Disease* 181:71–79.

Carroll KM, Rounsaville BJ & Gawin FH (1991). A comparative trial of psychotherapies for ambulatory cocaine abusers: Relapse prevention and interpersonal psychotherapy. *American Journal of Drug and Alcohol Abuse* 17:229–247.

Carroll KM, Rounsaville BJ, Gordon LT et al. (1994). Psychotherapy and pharmacotherapy for ambulatory cocaine abusers. *Archives of General Psychiatry* 51:177–187.

Carroll KM, Rounsaville BJ, Rich C, Gordon LT et al. (1994). One-year follow-up of psychotherapy and pharmacotherapy for cocaine dependence: Delayed emergence of psychotherapy effects. *Archives of General Psychiatry* 51(12):989–997.

Chapman-Walsh et al. (1995).

Cloninger CR (1987). Neurogenetic adaptive mechanisms in alcoholism. *Science* 236:410–416.

Cornish J, Metzger D, Woody G et al. (1996). Naltrexone pharmacotherapy for opioid dependent federal probationers. *Journal of Substance Abuse Treatment.*

Crits-Christoph P, Baranackie K, Beck AT, Carroll K, Luborsky L & McLellan AT (1992). Meta-analysis of therapist effects in psychotherapy outcome studies. *Psychotherapy Research.*

D'Aunno T & Vaughn TE (1992). Variations in methadone treatment practices: Results from a national study. *Journal of the American Medical Association* 267:253–258.

De Leon G (1984). *The Therapeutic Community: Study of Effectiveness (Treatment Research Monograph No. 84.* Rockville, MD: National Institute on Drug Abuse, 128.

Des Jarlais DC, Hagan H, Friedman SR et al. (1995). Maintaining low HIV seroprevalence in populations of injecting drug users. *Journal of the American Medical Association* 274:1226–1231.

Edwards G, Orford J, Egert S et al. (1977). Alcoholism: A controlled trial of treatment and advice. *Journal of Studies on Alcohol* 38:1004–1031.

Finney JW, Moos RH & Chan DA (1981). Length of stay and program component effects in the treatment of alcoholism: A comparison of two techniques for process analyses. *Journal of Consulting and Clinical Psychology* 49:120–131.

Fiorentine (1996).

Fleming MF, Barry KL, Manwell LB, Johnson K & London, R (1997). Brief physician advice for problem alcohol drinkers: A randomized controlled trial in community-based primary care practices. *Journal of the American Medical Association* In press.

French MT & Martin RF (submitted). The costs of drug abuse consequences: A summary of research findings.

Gerstein D & Harwood H, eds. (1990). *Treating Drug Problems, Vol. 1.* Washington DC: National Academy Press.

Gossop M, Johns A & Green L (1986). Opiate withdrawal: Inpatient versus outpatient programmes and preferred versus random assignment. *British Medical Journal* 293:103–104.

Gottheil E, McLellan AT & Druley KA (1990). Length of stay, patient severity and treatment outcome: An example from the field of alcoholism. *Journal of Studies on Alcohol.*

Greenstein R, O'Brien CP, Woody G & McLellan AT (1981). Naltrexone: A short-term treatment alternative for opiate dependence. *American Journal of Alcohol and Drug Abuse* 8(1):291–296.

Hall SM, Loeb P, LeVois P & Cooper J (1981). Increasing employment in ex-heroin addicts II: Methadone maintenance sample. *Behavioral Medicine* 12:453–460.

Havassy BE, Hall SM & Wasserman DA (1991). Social support and relapse: Commonalities among alcoholics, opiate users, and cigarette smokers. *Addictive Behaviors* 16(5):235–246.

Havassy BE, Wasserman D & Hall SM (1995). Social relationships and cocaine use in an American treatment sample. *Addiction* 90:699–710.

Hayashida M, Alterman AI, McLellan AT et al. (1989). Comparative effectiveness of inpatient and outpatient detoxification patient with mild-to-moderate alcohol withdrawal syndrome. *The New England Journal of Medicine* 320:358–365.

Hesselbrock V, Meyer R & Keener J (1985). Psychopathology in hospitalized alcoholics. *Archives of General Psychiatry* 42:1050–1055.

Higgins ST, Delaney DD, Budney AJ et al. (1991). A behavioral approach to achieving initial cocaine abstinence. *American Journal of Psychiatry* 148:1218–1224.

Holder HD, Longabaugh R, Miller WR & Rubonis A (1991). The cost effectiveness of treatment for alcohol problems: A first approximation. *Journal of Studies on Alcohol* 52:517–540.

Hubbard RL & Marsden ME (1986). Relapse to use of heroin, cocaine and other drugs in the first year after treatment. In *Relapse and Recovery in Drug Abuse (NIDA Research Monograph 72)*. Rockville, MD: National Institute on Drug Abuse.

Hubbard RL, Marsden ME, Rachal JV, Harwood HJ, Cavanaugh ER & Ginzburg HM (1989). *Drug Abuse Treatment: A National Study of Effectiveness*. Chapel Hill, NC: University of North Carolina Press.

Inciardi JA (1997). Introduction: A response to the war on drugs. In JA Inciardi (ed.) *Drug Treatment and Criminal Justice*. Newbury Park, CA: Sage Publication.

Institute of Medicine (1990). *Broadening the Base of Treatment for Alcohol Problems*. Washington DC: National Academy Press.

Jaffe AJ, Rounsaville B, Chang G, Schottenfeld RS, Meyer RE & O'Malley SS (1996). Naltrexone, relapse prevention, and supportive therapy with alcoholics: an analysis of patient treatment matching. *Journal of Consulting and Clinical Psychology* 64(5):1044–1053.

Joe GW, Simpson DD & Sells SB (1992). Treatment process and relapse to opioid use during methadone maintenance. *American Journal of Drug and Alcohol Abuse* 19:124–130.

Kadden RM, Cooney NL, Getter H & Litt MD (1990). Matching alcoholics to coping skills or interactional therapies: Post treatment results. *Journal of Consulting and Clinical Psychology* 57:698–704.

Kranzler HR & McLellan AT (1995). Pharmacotherapies for alcoholism: Evolving theoretical and methodological perspectives. In H Kranzler (ed.) *Substance Abuse Treatment*. Baltimore, MD: Williams & Wilkins.

Lawental E, McLellan AT, Grissom G, Brill P & O'Brien CP (1996). Coerced treatment for substance abuse problems detected through workplace urine surveillance: Is it effective? *Journal of Substance Abuse* 8(l):115–128.

Ling W, Charuvastra VC, Kaim SC & Klett CJ (1976). Methadyl acetate and methadone as maintenance treatments for heroin addicts. *Archives of General Psychiatry* 33:709–720.

Lipton DS & Maranda MJ (1983). Detoxification from heroin dependency: An overview of method and effectiveness. *Advances in Alcohol and Substance Abuse* 2:31–55.

Longabaugh R, Wirtz PW, Beattie MC, Noel N & Stout R (1995). Matching treatment focus to patient social investment and support: 18 month follow-up results. *Journal of Consulting and Clinical Psychology* 63:296–307.

Luborsky L, Crits-Cristoph P, McLellan AT & Woody GE (1986). Do psychotherapists vary much in their effectiveness? The answer within four outcome studies. *American Journal of Orthopsychiatry* 56(4).

Luborsky L, McLellan AT, Woody GE & O'Brien CP (1985). Therapist success and its determinants. *Archives of General Psychiatry* 42:602–611.

Mason BJ, Kocsis JH, Ritvo EC & Cutler RB (1996). A double-blind, placebo-controlled trial of desipramine for primary alcohol dependence stratified on the presence or absence of major depression. *Journal of the American Medical Association* 275:761–767.

Mattick RP & Hall W (1996). Are detoxification programmes effective? *Lancet* 347:97–100.

Mattson ME, Allen JP, Longabaugh R, Nickless CJ, Connors GJ & Kadden RM (1994). A chronological review of empirical studies matching alcoholics to treatment. *Journal of Studies on Alcohol* 12(Suppl):16–29.

McCaul et al. (1990). [Effect of counselor selection]

McCrady BS, Noel NE, Abrams DB, Stout RL, Nelson HF & Hay WM (1986). Comparative effectiveness of three types of spouse involvement in outpatient behavioral alcoholism treatment. *Journal of Studies on Alcohol* 47:459–467.

McCrady BS, Stout R, Noel N, Abrams D et al. (1991). Effectiveness of three types of spouse-involved behavioral alcoholism treatment. *British Journal of Addiction* 86(11):1415–1424.

McGrath PJ, Nunes EV, Stewart JW, Goldman D, Agosti V, Ocepek-Welikson K & Quitkin FM (1996). Imipramine treatment of alcoholics with primary depression: A placebo-controlled clinical trial. *Archives of General Psychiatry* 53(3):232–240.

McKay J, Alterman A, McLellan AT & Snider E (1995). Inpatient versus day hospital rehabilitation for alcoholics: A comparison of experimental and naturalistic designs. *Journal of Consulting and Clinical Psychology*.

McKay J, Cacciola J, Alterman A, McLellan AT & Wirtz P (1996). An initial evaluation of the psychosocial dimensions of the American Society on Addiction Medicine criteria for inpatient versus intensive outpatient substance abuse rehabilitation. *Journal of Studies on Alcohol*.

McKay J, Cacciola J, McLellan AT, Alterman A & Durell J (1996). Characteristics of recipients of supplemental security income (SSI) benefits for drug addicts and alcoholics. *Archives of General Psychiatry*.

McKay J, McLellan AT, Alterman A, Cacciola J, Rutherford M & O'Brien CP (1996). Predictors of participation in aftercare sessions and self-help groups following completion of intensive outpatient treatment for substance abuse. *Journal of Studies on Alcohol*.

McKay JR, Alterman AI & McLellan AT (1991). Does achieving goals of addiction treatment predict better outcomes? *Alcoholism: Clinical & Experimental Research* 15:383.

McKay JR, Alterman AI, McLellan AT, Snider C et al. (1994). Treatment goals, continuity of care, and outcome in a day hospital substance abuse rehabilitation program. *American Journal of Psychiatry* 151:254–259.

McKay JR, Cacciola J, McLellan AT, Alterman AI & Wirtz PW (1997). An initial evaluation of the psychosocial dimensions of the ASAM criteria for inpatient and day hospital substance abuse rehabilitation. *Journal of Studies on Alcohol* 58:239–252.

McKay JR, Longabaugh R, Beattie MC, Maisto SA & Noel N (1993). Does adding conjoint therapy to individually-focused alcoholism treatment lead to better family functioning? *Journal of Substance Abuse* 5:45–60.

McKay JR, McLellan AT & Alterman AI 91992). An evaluation of the Cleveland Criteria for Inpatient Treatment of Substance Abuse. *American Journal of Psychiatry* 149:1212–1218.

McLatchie BH & Lomp KG (I 988). Alcoholics Anonymous affiliation and treatment outcome among a clinical sample of problem drinkers. *American Journal of Drug & Alcohol Abuse* 14:309–324.

McLellan et al. (1998).

McLellan A T, Alterman AI, Metzger DS et al. (1994). Similarity of outcome predictors across opiate, cocaine, and alcohol treatments: Role of treatment services. *Journal of Consulting and Clinical Psychology* 62(6):1141–1158.

McLellan AT, Alterman AI, Woody GE, Metzger D, McKay J & O'Brien CP (1995). Great expectations: A review of the concepts and empirical findings regarding substance abuse treatment. In *Alcohol and Substance Dependence*. London, England: Royal Task Force on Substance Dependence.

McLellan AT, Arndt IO, Woody GE & Metzger D (1993). Psychosocial services in substance abuse treatment?: A dose-ranging study of psychosocial services. *Journal of the American Medical Association* 269(15):1953–1959.

McLellan AT & Ball JC (1995). Is methadone treatment effective? In R Rettig (ed.) *A Re-Evaluation of Federal Regulations on Methadone Treatment*. Washington, DC: Institute of Medicine Press.

McLellan AT, Ball JC & Rosen L (1981). Pretreatment source of income and response to methadone maintenance: A follow-up study. *American Journal of Psychiatry* 138(6):785–789.

McLellan AT, Ball JC, Rosen L & O'Brien CP (1981). Pretreatment source of income and response to methadone maintenance: A follow-up study. *American Journal of Psychiatry* 6:785–789.

McLellan AT, Cacciola J, Kushner H, Peters R, Smith I & Pettinati H (1992). The fifth edition of the Addiction Severity Index: Cautions, additions and normative data. *Journal of Substance Abuse Treatment* 9(5)461–480.

McLellan AT & Durell J (1995). Evaluating substance abuse and psychiatric treatments: Conceptual and methodological considerations. In L Sederer (ed.) *Outcomes Assessment in Clinical Practice*. Baltimore, MD: Williams & Wilkins.

McLellan AT, Griffith J, Childress AR & Woody GE (1984). The psychiatrically severe drug abuse patient: Methadone maintenance or therapeutic community. *American Journal of Drug and Alcohol Abuse* 10(1):77–95.

McLellan AT & Gastfriend D (1996).

McLellan AT, Grissom G & Brill P (1996). Improved outcomes from treatment service "matching" in substance abuse patients: A controlled study. *Archives of General Psychiatry*.

McLellan AT, Grissom G, Durell J, Alterman AI, Brill P & O'Brien CP (1993). Substance abuse treatment in the private setting: Are some programs more effective than others? *Journal of Substance Abuse Treatment* 10:243–254.

McLellan AT, Grosman DS, Blaine JD & Haverkos HW (1993). Acupuncture treatment for drug abuse: A Technical review. *Journal of Substance Abuse Treatment*.

McLellan AT & Hunkeler E (1996, in press). Relationships between patient satisfaction and patient performance in addiction treatment. *American Journal of Psychiatry*.

McLellan AT, Luborsky L, Cacciola J & Griffith J (1985). New data from the Addiction Severity Index: Reliability and validity in three centers. *Journal of Nervous and Mental Disease*.

McLellan AT, Luborsky L, O'Brien CP & Woody GE (1980). An improved diagnostic instrument for substance abuse patients: The Addiction Severity Index. *Journal of Nervous and Mental Disease*.

McLellan AT, Luborsky L, O'Brien CP & Druley KA (1982). Is treatment for substance abuse effective? *Journal of the American Medical Association* 247:1423–1428.

McLellan AT, Luborsky L, Woody GE, Druley KA & O'Brien CP (1983). Predicting response to alcohol and drug abuse treatments: Role of psychiatric severity. *Archives of General Psychiatry* 40:620–625.

McLellan AT, Luborsky L, Woody GE, O'Brien CP & Druley KA (1983). Increased effectiveness of substance abuse treatment: A prospective study of patient-treatment "matching." *Journal of Nervous and Mental Disease* 171(10):597–605.

McLellan AT, O'Brien CP, Luborsky L, Woody GE & Kron R (1981). Are the addiction-related problems of substance abusers really related? *Journal of Nervous and Mental Disease* 169(4):232–239.

McLellan AT & Weisner C (1996). Achieving the public health potential of substance abuse treatment: Implications for patient referral, treatment "matching" and outcome evaluation. In W Bickel & R DeGrandpre (eds.) *Drug Policy and Human Nature*. Baltimore, MD: Wilkins & Wilkins.

McLellan AT, Woody GE, Luborsky L & Goehl L (1988). Is the counselor an "active ingredient" in substance abuse rehabilitation? *Journal of Nervous and Mental Disease* 176:423–430.

McLellan AT, Woody GE, Luborsky L, O'Brien CP & Druley KA (1982). Is treatment for substance abuse effective? *Journal of the American Medical Association* 247:1423–1427.

McLellan AT, Woody GE, Metzger D, McKay J, Alterman AI & O'Brien CP (1995). Evaluating the effectiveness of treatments for substance use disorders: Reasonable expectations, appropriate comparisons. In D Fox (ed.) *The Milbank Foundation Volume on Health Policy Issues*. New York, NY: Milbank Foundation Press.

McLellan AT, Woody GE, Metzger D, McKay J, Alterman AI & O'Brien CP (1996). Evaluating the effectiveness of treatments for substance use disorders: Reasonable expectations, appropriate comparisons. *The Milbank Quarterly* 74(1):51–85.

Mee-Lee D (1988). An instrument for treatment progress and matching: The Recovery Attitude and Treatment Evaluator (RAATE). *Journal of Substance Abuse Treatment* 5:183–186.

Mee-Lee D, Shulman J & Gartner L (1996). *Patient Placement Criteria for the Treatment of Substance-Related Disorders, Second Edition* (ASAM *PPC-2*). Chevy Chase, MD: American Society of Addiction Medicine.

Merrill J (1993). *The Cost of Substance Abuse to America's Health Care System, Report 1: Medicaid Hospital Costs*. New York, NY: Columbia University Center on Addiction and Substance Abuse.

Milby et al. (1996).

Miller WR, Benefield RG & Tonigan JS (1993). Enhancing motivation for change in problem drinking: A controlled comparison of two therapist styles. *Journal of Consulting and Clinical Psychology* 61:455–461.

Miller WR & Hester RK (1986). Inpatient alcoholism treatment: Who benefits? *American Psychologist* 41:794–805.

Miller WR, Brown JM, Simpson TL et al. (1995). What works? A methodological analysis of the alcohol treatment outcome literature. In RK Hester & WR Miller (eds.) *Handbook of Alcoholism Treatment Approaches: Effective Alternatives*. Boston, MA: Allyn and Bacon, 12–44.

Miller WR & Holder (1994).

Miller WR & McCready (1989).

Miller WR, Taylor CA & West JC (1980). Focused versus broad-spectrum behavior therapy for problem drinkers. *Journal of Consulting and Clinical Psychology* 8:590–601.

Moos RH (1974). *Evaluating Treatment Environments*. New York, NY: John Wiley & Sons.

Moos RH, Finney JW & Cronkite RC (1990). *Alcoholism Treatment: Context, Process and Outcome*. New York, NY: Oxford University Press.

Najavits LM & Weiss RD (1994). Variations in therapist effectiveness in the treatment of patients with substance use disorders: An empirical review. *Addiction* 89(6):679–688.

National Institute on Drug Abuse (1991). *See How Drug Abuse Takes the Profit Out of Business*. Rockville, MD: The Institute.

National Institute on Drug Abuse (n.d.).

Nunes E, Quitkin, F Brady R & Post KT (1994). Antidepressant treatment in methadone maintenance patients. *Journal of Addictive Diseases* 13(3):13–24.

O'Farrell TJ, Cutter HS & Floyd FJ (1985). Evaluating behavioral marital therapy for male alcoholics: Effects on marital adjustment and communication from before to after treatment. *Behavior Therapy* 16(2):147–167.

Office of Technology Assessment (1983). *The Effectiveness and Costs of Alcoholism Treatment (Health Technology Case Study 22)*. Washington DC: The Office.

O'Malley SS, Jaffe AJ, Chang G, Schottenfeld RS, Meyer RE & Rounsaville B (1992). Naltrexone and coping skills therapy for alcohol dependence. *Archives of General Psychiatry* 49:881–887.

Pettinati HM, Meyers K, Jensen JM, Kaplan F & Evans BD (1993). Inpatient vs outpatient treatment for substance abuse revisited. *Psychiatric Quarterly* 64:173–182.

Powell BJ, Campbell JL, Landon JF, Liskow BI et al. (1995). A double-blind, placebo-controlled study of nortriptyline and bromocriptine in male alcoholics subtyped by comorbid psychiatric disorders. *Alcoholism: Clinical & Experimental Research* 19(2):462–468.

Prochaska JO & DiClemente CC (1983). Stages and processes of self-change of smoking: Toward an integrative model of change. *Journal of Consulting and Clinical Psychology* 51:390–395.

Prochaska JO, DiClemente CC & Norcross JC (1992). In search of how people change: Applications to addictive behaviors. *American Psychologist* 47(9):1102–1114.

Project MATCH Research Group (1997). Matching alcoholism treatments to client heterogeneity: Project MATCH posttreatment drinking outcomes. *Journal of Studies on Alcohol* 58:7–29.

Rawson et al. (1996).

Rounsaville BJ, Dolinsky ZS, Babor TF & Meyer RE (1987). Psychopathology as a predictor of treatment outcome in alcoholics. *Archives of General Psychiatry* 44:505–513.

Rounsaville BJ, Glazer W, Wilber CH, Weissman MM & Kleber HD (1983). Short-term interpersonal psychotherapy in methadone-maintained opiate addicts. *Archives of General Psychiatry* 40:630–636.

Rounsaville BJ, Weissman MM, Crits-Christoph K, Wilber C & Kleber H (1982). Diagnosis and symptoms of depression in opiate addicts: Course and relationship to treatment outcome. *Archives of General Psychiatry* 39:151–156.

Saxe L, Dougherty D, Esty K & Fine M (1983). *The Effectiveness and Costs of Alcoholism Treatment (Health Technology Case Study 22).* Washington, DC: Office of Technology Assessment.

Schuckit MA (1985). The clinical implications of primary diagnostic groups among alcoholics. *Archives of General Psychiatry* 42:1043–1049.

Sells SB & Simpson DD (1980). The case for drug abuse treatment effectiveness, based on the DARP research program. *British Journal of Addiction* 75:117–131.

Shaw JA, Donley P, Morgan, DW & Robinson JA (1975). Treatment of depression in alcoholics. *American Journal of Psychiatry* 132(6):641–644.

Simpson D & Savage L (1980). Drug abuse treatment readmissions and outcomes. *Archives of General Psychiatry* 37:896–901.

Stanton MD & Todd T (1982). *The Family Therapy of Drug Abuse and Addiction.* New York, NY: Guilford Press.

Stockwell T, Bolt E & Hooper J (1986). Detoxification from alcohol at home managed by general practitioners. *British Medical Journal* 292:733–735.

Stockwell T, Bolt L, Milner I, Puch P & Young I (1990). Home detoxification for problem drinkers: Acceptability to clients, relatives, general practitioners and outcome after 60 days. *British Journal of Addiction* 85:61–70.

Stockwell T, Bolt L, Milner I, Russell G, Bolderston H & Hugh P (1991). Home detoxification from alcohol: Its safety and efficacy in comparison with inpatient care. *Alcohol and Alcoholism* 26:645–650.

Strain EC, Stitzer ML, Liebson IA & Bigelow GE (1993). Methadone dose and treatment outcome. *Drug and Alcohol Dependence* 33:105–117.

Strain, Stitzer ML, Liebson IA & Bigelow GE (1994). Buprenorphine versus methadone in the treatment of opioid-dependent cocaine users. *Psychopharmacology* 116:401–406.

Timko C, Moos RH, Finney JW & Moos BS (1994). Outcome of treatment for alcohol abuse and involvement in Alcoholics Anonymous among previously untreated problem drinkers. *Journal of Mental Health Administration* 21:145–160.

Vaillant GE (1996). *The Natural History of Alcoholism.* Cambridge, MA: Harvard University Press.

Valle S (1981). Interpersonal functioning of alcoholism counselors and treatment outcome. *Journal of Studies on Alcohol* 42:783–790.

Volpicelli JR, Alterman AI, Hayashida M & O'Brien CP (1992). Naltrexone in the treatment of alcohol dependence. *Archives of General Psychiatry* 49:876–880

Walsh DC, Hingson R, Merrigan D et al. (1991). A randomized trial of treatment options for alcohol-abusing workers. *The New England Journal of Medicine* 325:775–782.

Weiss et al. (1996).

Wexler HK, Falkin GP & Lipton DS (1990). Outcome evaluation of a prison therapeutic community for substance abuse treatment. *Criminal Justice and Behavior* 17(1):71–92.

Woody GE, Luborsky L, McLellan AT et al. (1983). Psychotherapy for opiate addicts: Does it help? *Archives of General Psychiatry* 40:639–645.

Woody GE, McLellan AT, Luborsky L et al. (1984). Psychiatric severity as a predictor of benefits from psychotherapy. *American Journal of Psychiatry* 141(10):1171–1177.

Woody GE, McLellan AT, Luborsky L & O'Brien CP (1995). Psychotherapy in community methadone programs: A validation study. *American Journal of Psychiatry* 152(9):1302–1308.

Zanis D, Metzger DS & McLellan AT (1994). Employment patterns among methadone maintenance clients. *Journal of Substance Abuse Treatment.*

CHAPTER 5

What Works in Treatment: Effect of Setting, Duration and Amount

John W. Finney, Ph.D.
Rudolf H. Moos, Ph.D.

Treatment Settings
Duration and Amount of Treatment
Implications for Policymakers and Service Providers

Substance abuse treatment researchers sometimes feel that their work is overlooked by policymakers and treatment providers. This has not been the case for researchers studying the effects of different treatment settings and different treatment durations/amounts, where variations on those treatment dimensions have readily apparent, short-term cost implications. Several research reviews have examined the relative effectiveness of alcohol treatment in inpatient and outpatient settings (Annis, 1986; Mattick & Jarvis, 1994; Miller & Hester, 1986; Saxe, Dougherty et al., 1983) and of variations in treatment duration and amount (e.g., Babor, 1994; Bien, Miller & Tonigan, 1993; Mattick & Jarvis, 1994; Miller & Hester, 1986). Focusing on controlled studies employing random assignment or matching on patient pretreatment variables, each of these reviews concluded there was no evidence for the superiority of inpatient over outpatient treatment (a similar conclusion has been reached in reviews of drug abuse treatment research by Anglin & Hser, 1990 and Crits-Christoph & Siqueland, 1996, but see Budde, Rounsaville & Bryant, 1992), or of longer or more intensive treatment over briefer or less intensive treatment. The same reviews also point out, however, that certain types of patients might benefit more from inpatient/residential or longer/more intensive treatment.

In this chapter, the authors re-examine the research evidence on the effects of treatment settings, duration, and amount, drawing heavily on recent reviews of these topics (Finney, Hahn & Moos, 1996; Finney & Moos, 1996, 1998; Monahan & Finney, 1996; Moos & Finney, 1996a, 1996b). The primary focus is research on treatment for alcohol use disorders, although research on treatment of drug abuse also is considered. The authors argue that research findings have been extrapolated to populations beyond those involved in the studies and that key issues remain to be addressed. Those issues include determining whether certain types of patients benefit more from treatment in inpatient/residential settings, whether certain types of patients benefit from longer or more intensive treatment, and whether, perhaps for many patients, treatment should be less intensive, but spread out over longer periods.

TREATMENT SETTINGS

Rationales for Inpatient and Outpatient Treatment. Four main rationales have been put forward for the superiority of inpatient/residential substance abuse treatment settings. One is that such settings provide a respite for patients, (1) removing them from environments that are perpetuating their addiction, and (2) allowing their efforts toward abstinence to be consolidated. Second, it has been argued that inpatient/residential settings allow patients to receive more treatment because (1) they are less likely to drop out of treatment, (2) treatment is more intensive, and (3) patients are more effectively linked with aftercare. A third rationale is that inpatient/residential settings provide medical/psychiatric care (inpatient settings) and/or tangible and emotional support (inpatient and residential settings) to patients who otherwise would not have access to such care or support. Finally, some proponents argue that inpatient treatment suggests to patients that their problems are more severe than would be the case if treatment were offered in an outpatient setting.

Arguments in favor of outpatient treatment also have focused on the patient's usual life situation, but the advantages of leaving the patient in, rather than removing him or her from, that context are stressed. Proponents have suggested that outpatient treatment provides an opportunity for more accurate assessments of the antecedents of substance use and for testing coping skills in real-life situations while the patient remains in a supportive therapeutic relationship. Thus, the theory goes, greater generalization of learning should take place than would be the case in the atypical environment of an inpatient treatment program (see Annis, 1986). In addition, it has been suggested that outpatient treatment mobilizes help in the patient's natural environment—as from a family physician or self-help groups—to a greater extent than does inpatient or residential treatment. Finally, proponents have argued that outpatient treatment results in a morg successful transition to aftercare when, for example, a patient begins to attend self-help group meetings near his or her home while still in treatment.

Review of Relevant Research. In a recent review of research on inpatient versus outpatient treatment for alcohol abuse, Finney, Hahn and Moos (1996) considered 14 relevant studies, including several studies not included in prior reviews. In these studies, inpatient treatment took various forms, but usually was provided in an acute inpatient setting. In one study, the planned alterative to inpatient treatment was inpatient detoxification; in another, it was a wait-list control. In the remaining studies, the planned outpatient treatment ranged from day hospital programs, to individual and group outpatient treatment, including brief advice, to self-help group participation in Alcoholics Anonymous. Overall, the studies varied substantially in the content and amount of index treatment and aftercare.

The investigators initially summarized the studies' findings through use of a "box-score" approach—that is, tallying whether inpatient/residential treatment was found to be significantly superior or inferior to or not different from the comparison condition in each study. Of the 14 studies, seven yielded significant setting effects on one or more drinking-related outcome variables at one or more follow-up points. In five studies, the outcome difference favored inpatient over outpatient treatment; in the other two, the outcome difference favored day hospital over inpatient treatment. Patients in the "superior" setting usually received more treatment. When patients treated in outpatient settings did not first receive inpatient detoxification, they tended to show poorer outcomes than did patients treated in inpatient settings.

The box-score approach to synthesizing the research literature has serious limitations. Nonsignificant differences between groups may simply reflect lack of statistical power; significant findings may emerge by chance when multiple tests for treatment effects are conducted and not adjusted for "experimentwise" error. Indeed, Finney, Hahn and Moos (1996) found that the seven studies yielding significant setting effects had greater statistical power and conducted more treatment contrasts, on average, than the studies with no difference in outcome.

The shortcomings of box-score reviews prompted the development of meta-analytic techniques that used between-group effect sizes (Cooper & Hedges, 1994). A between-group effect size is the difference in the average post-treatment functioning of two groups, divided by the pooled standard deviation of outcome scores within the two groups. An effect size (ES) allows one to determine by how many standard deviation units, or by what proportion of standard deviation unit, the functioning of one group is superior to that of another.

Initially, the authors had not conducted an ES analysis because the number of studies was small and it was felt that following the conventions of assigning a zero ES to findings simply reported as "nonsignificant," and of assigning the smallest possible ES consistent with $p < .05$ for findings simply reported as "statistically significant," could yield distorted results. However, after submitting the manuscript reporting the box-score review, the authors were able to obtain additional data from several investigators. When the average, cross-study ESs were calculated, only the three-month follow-up ES was significantly different from zero (for more details, see Finney & Moos, 1996).

The significant ES of .22 at three months favored inpatient treatment but was small in magnitude. Nevertheless, in terms of Rosenthal and Rubin's (1982) "binomial effect size display," an ES of that magnitude is associated with a "success rate" of .55 in the inpatient group compared to .45 in the outpatient or comparison group. However, this more positive perspective on the setting effect at three-month follow-up is offset, at least to some extent, by the nonsignificant average cross-study ESs at six- and 12-month follow-ups, and by the cost differences in the treatments offered. In addition, it should be noted that a randomized trial of inpatient versus day hospital treatment for cocaine abuse found no setting differences in outcome (Alterman, O'Brien et al., 1994; cf. Budde, Rounsaville & Bryant, 1992) and that reviews of the relevant research (by Anglin & Hser, 1990; Crits-Christoph & Siqueland, 1996) on outpatient methadone maintenance and outpatient drug-free treatment reported few differences in outcomes in comparison with residential therapeutic community programs.

These findings lead the authors to question the representativeness of the patients included in the existing studies of inpatient and outpatient alcohol treatment (Finney, Hahn & Moos, 1996). The reports for eight of the 14 studies did not indicate the percentage of patients in treatment who participated in the research. In the other six studies, the percentage of patients who participated were 14% (McLachlan & Stein, 1982), 22% (McKay, Cacciola et al., 1997—two studies), 25% (Pittman & Tate, 1972), 54% (Chapman & Huygens, 1988), and 61% (Walsh, Hingson et al., 1991). In general, existing studies have examined a restricted set of patients and often have excluded patients with major medical or psychiatric disorders, and/or an inability to commute to treatment. Three studies focused specifically on patients who presented for treatment at private hospitals, two focused on first admission patients, and one focused on workers in an Employee Assistance Program. Thus, the findings may not generalize well to populations of more impaired individuals and/or those with fewer social resources.

Is there evidence that such impaired patients would benefit more from inpatient or residential treatment? A diagnosis of a serious psychiatric disorder often has been an exclusion criterion in studies of inpatient versus outpatient alcohol treatment (see Finney, Hahn & Moos, 1996), precluding its examination as a matching variable. However, Ritson (1968) found that patients in outpatient treatment who had personality disorders tended to have poor outcomes; no relationship was found between personality disorders and outcome among inpatients.

With respect to social resources, Kissin, Platz and Su (1970) reported that more socially competent alcoholic patients experienced better outcomes in outpatient treatment, whereas socially unstable patients had better outcomes following inpatient treatment. Among both alcoholic and drug abuse patients with middle-level psychiatric severity in a study by McLellan, Luborsky et al. (1983), those who had more serious family, legal, and/or employment problems experienced poorer outcomes when exposed to outpatient treatment.

Scattered research findings, such as these, formed part of the basis for the *Patient Placement Criteria* of the American Society of Addiction Medicine (ASAM) (Mee-Lee, Shulman & Gartner, 1996). The criteria attempt to match patients to five levels of care: (1) early intervention; (2) outpatient treatment; (3) intensive outpatient/partial hospitalization treatment; (4) residential/inpatient treatment; and (5) medically managed intensive inpatient treatment. Placement decisions are based on a patient's standing on six dimensions: (1) acute intoxication and/or withdrawal potential; (2) biomedical conditions and complications; (3) emotional/behavioral conditions or complications; (4) treatment acceptance/resistance; (5) relapse/continue use potential; and (6) recovery/living environment. More research is needed to determine the validity of these criteria and other patient-setting matching systems (for an initial effort with respect to an earlier version of the ASAM criteria, see McKay, Cacciola et al., 1997).

As a concluding comment, the authors point out that research on treatment settings has focused on the relative *effectiveness* of inpatient and outpatient treatment. Not typically addressed in such studies is the relative capability of different settings to *retain* patients in treatment. The few studies that have examined this issue (e.g., Alterman, O'Brien et al., 1994; Bell, Williams et al., 1994; McKay, Alterman et al., 1995; Pettinati, Meyers et al., 1993; Stecher, Andrews et al., 1994) often have found a higher proportion of inpatients complete treatment, although with no difference in outcome when follow-ups were conducted. Whether the enhanced treatment retention afforded by inpatient/residential settings would lead to better outcomes for certain types of patients (e.g., those with few social resources) remains to be determined.

A more fundamental issue not addressed in existing studies is the relative *attractiveness* of treatment in each of the two types of settings; that is, their ability to induce (certain types of) persons to seek treatment. In randomized trials, patients have already opted for treatment. Under normal conditions of treatment delivery, inpatient/residential programs may be more effective than outpatient programs in attracting to treatment homeless individuals and persons without access to transportation. If inpatient/residential programs are not available, administrators of such facilities may be able to point to "reduced demand" as evidence to support cutbacks in substance abuse treatment services.

DURATION AND AMOUNT OF TREATMENT

This section reviews the evidence on the effectiveness of brief interventions, longer versus shorter stays in inpatient/residential treatment, and the effects of participation in outpatient aftercare.

Brief Interventions. Three reviews have reported considerable support for the effectiveness of brief interventions for alcohol use disorders. Babor (1994) and Bien, Miller & Tonigan (1993) concluded that brief interventions were more effective than no intervention, and, in many cases, as effective as more extensive interventions. Among 43 treatment approaches considered by Miller, Brown et al. (1995), brief interventions had the highest score on the authors' effectiveness criterion. Moreover, Project MATCH (Project MATCH Research Group, 1997), a major multi-site treatment trial, found a planned four sessions of motivational enhancement treatment to be as effective as cognitive-behavioral and Twelve Step facilitation treatments that were offered in 12 planned sessions. Several points should be kept in mind when considering this evidence, however. First, Bien, Miller, and Tonigan (1993) reported that the average study effect size favoring brief interventions over a control condition was .38. This effect size falls in between what Cohen (1988) termed a "small" and a "medium" effect. However, each study's effect size was calculated for a single drinking-related outcome. The usual practice in a meta-analysis is to calculate an average effect size for all drinking-related outcomes or for different classes of drinking-related outcomes at each follow-up point (see Mattick & Jarvis, 1994). Such an approach might have yielded a smaller effect of brief intervention versus no intervention.

Second, Jonson, Hermansson et al. (1995) note that the brief interventions in some of the studies reviewed by Bien, Miller, and Tonigan (1993) were considered to be more extended interventions in other studies. As one example, Monahan and Finney (1996) calculated that the average patient in the single-session "advice" condition in the well-known study by Edwards, Orford et al. (1977) actually received more than 30 hours of assessment and treatment during the year that other participants were receiving extended "treatment." Thirty hours typically would be classified as extended treatment.

In a 1995 review, Miller, Brown et al. classified a brief intervention that was not significantly inferior to a more extensive intervention as considered "effective"—it received an effectiveness score of +1 (the more extensive comparison intervention received a score of −2). Thus, studies finding no difference in treatment outcome constituted "positive evidence" for the effectiveness of brief interventions. This aspect of Miller, Brown et al.'s (1995) box-scoring system combines cost and effectiveness, two dimensions that should be considered separately so that their relationship can be determined from independent data.

Finally, in Project MATCH (Project MATCH Research Group, 1997), patients attended proportionately more of the four planned sessions of motivational enhancement therapy, on average, than they did of the 12 planned sessions of Twelve Step Facilitation and cognitive-behavioral treatment. In addition, all patients received eight hours of assessment prior to treatment and five follow-up contacts at three-month intervals, all of which may have had therapeutic impact. Overall, the difference in treatment intensity between the motivational enhancement and the other two conditions was not as large as it might at first appear.

Studies of brief interventions most often have been conducted with clients of low to moderate severity in terms of their alcohol use disorders (Babor, 1994). Research is needed to examine the effectiveness of brief interventions among patient populations that vary more substantially in severity. At present, however, low to moderate alcohol severity patients with positive life contexts and without severe skills deficits appear to be the best candidates for brief interventions. In this vein, Edwards, Orford et al. (1977) noted the social stability of the patients in their classic study of brief advice versus treatment and suggested that "patients with a lesser degree of social support might . . . be less able to respond to the advice regimen—extrapolation to a population of homeless men would be risky" (p. 1021).

Even with these caveats, the evidence supporting the effectiveness of low-cost brief interventions is impressive. Miller and Sanchez (1993) offered the acronym "FRAMES" to identify the six "active ingredients" of brief interventions they believe contribute to change in drinking behavior: **F**eedback of personal risk or impairment, emphasis on personal **R**esponsibility for change, clear **A**dvice to change, a **M**enu of alternative change options, therapeutic **E**mpathy, and enhancement of patients' **S**elf-efficacy or optimism. Bien, Miller and Tonigan (1993) also note that many brief interventions have included ongoing follow-through contacts with patients. Overall, the

FRAMES elements may help patients enhance their motivation to change their drinking behavior; ongoing contacts may supply the support needed by some individuals to maintain such change.

Length of Stay in Inpatient/Residential Treatment. Miller and Hester (1986) and Mattick and Jarvis (1994) reviewed several randomized trials comparing different lengths of inpatient or residential treatment for alcohol abuse. The consistent finding was no difference in outcome. In contrast, many naturalistic studies of substance abuse treatment have found longer stays in treatment to be associated with better outcomes, even a reduction in premature mortality (Bunn, Booth et al., 1994). For example, longer episodes of inpatient care (Peterson, Swindle et al., 1994; Timko, Finney & Moos, 1995), extended care (Moos, King & Patterson, 1996), community residential care (Moos, Pettit & Gruber, 1995; Rosenheck, Frisman & Gallup, 1995; Simpson, 1981), and therapeutic communities (Condelli & Hubbard, 1994) have been associated with better substance use outcomes and psychosocial functioning, as well as lower readmission rates for subsequent inpatient care.

In addition, Monahan and Finney (1996) found that amount of treatment for alcohol abuse, indexed by treatment in inpatient, residential, and day hospital settings, was related to treatment group abstinence rates across 150 treatment groups included in 100 studies. On average, patients in the high intensity treatment groups received 148 hours of treatment in comparison with 14 hours for patients in the low intensity groups. After patient social stability, program ownership (private for-profit versus other), and several study design features were taken into account, the more intensively treated patients had a 15% higher abstinence rate than did the less intensively treated patients.

It may be that beneficial effects of longer stays in inpatient/residential treatment apply only to more impaired patients with fewer social resources. For example, Welte, Hynes et al. (1981) found no relationship between LOS and outcome of alcoholism treatment for higher social stability patients; in contrast, for patients with lower social stability, those with longer stays had better outcomes (but see Gottheil, McLellan & Druley, 1992).

Outpatient Care Following Inpatient Treatment. Most clinicians recommend additional outpatient treatment to maintain or enhance the therapeutic gains achieved during inpatient/residential or intensive outpatient (e.g., day hospital) treatment. Outpatient treatment attempts to provide the ongoing support needed to continue a course of sobriety or to limit the course of a relapse. Ito and Donovan's (1986) review suggests a link between such "aftercare" participation and positive outcomes for alcohol abuse. Hawkins and Catalano (1985) arrived at a similar conclusion with respect to substance abuse treatment.

Recent individual studies have yielded similar findings. Timely outpatient mental health care, as reflected by two or more visits in the month after discharge from inpatient substance abuse care, was related to lower subsequent readmission rates (Peterson, Swindle et al., 1994; Moos, Mertens & Brennan, 1995). A randomized trial (O'Farrell, Choquette et al., 1993) also linked aftercare, which was offered over the course of a full year, to better outcomes in a sample of married alcoholic patients.

Taken together, these reviews of treatment intensity, length of stay, and aftercare suggest that an effective strategy may be to provide lower intensity addiction treatment for a longer duration—that is, treatment spread out at a lower rate over a longer period. As O'Brien and McLellan (1996) note: "The persistent changes produced by addiction . . . require continued maintenance treatment . . ." (p. 237). They point out that there are many chronic diseases, such as diabetes, hypertension, and asthma, that "are generally accepted as requiring life-long treatment" (p. 237).

The effectiveness of spreading substance abuse treatment over a longer period is suggested by the positive findings for outpatient care following inpatient treatment and for brief interventions that incorporate extended contacts with patients. This strategy also is consistent with the findings from Project MATCH, where the four planned sessions of motivational enhancement therapy spread over a three-month period were as effective as the 12 planned sessions of Twelve Step facilitation or cognitive-behavioral therapy also provided over three months. More extended treatment may improve patient outcomes because it provides patients with ongoing support and the potential to discuss and resolve problems prior to the occurrence of a full-blown relapse. In this vein, brief interventions may be most effective for relatively healthy patients who have intact community support systems. Patients who have severe substance dependence, concomitant psychiatric disorders, and/or deficient social resources appear to be appropriate candidates for longer and more intensive (see Higgins, Budney et al., 1993; Crits-Christoph & Siqueland, 1996) treatment to address their multiple disorders.

IMPLICATIONS FOR POLICYMAKERS AND SERVICE PROVIDERS

Past research on substance abuse treatment settings, amount, and duration, along with reviews of this research, have had a positive impact on health care policy: They have called into question the blanket application of expensive forms of treatment. For example, in the U.S. in the early 1980s, insurance coverage for alcohol treatment often was available only for inpatient care. If a socially stable individual wanted covered treatment, inpatient treatment was the only option.

At this point, however, the pendulum may have swung too far in the other direction. Findings for the selected populations in prior studies have been used to justify denying inpatient/residential treatment, and more intensive or extensive treatment to persons who may need such treatment. An important agenda over the next decade will be to determine whether certain types of patients derive greater benefit from inpatient/residential treatment or longer-term/more intensive treatment.

With respect to treatment setting, the authors believe that the best approaches for treatment providers today are those recommended in previous reviews: (1) provide outpatient treatment for those individuals who have sufficient social resources and no serious medical/psychiatric impairment; (2) use less costly intensive outpatient treatment options for patients who have failed with brief interventions or for whom a more intensive intervention seems warranted, but who do not need the structured environment of a residential setting; (3) retain residential options for those with few social resources and/or a living environment that is a serious impediment to recovery, and (4) reserve inpatient treatment options for individuals with serious medical/psychiatric conditions.

With respect to treatment duration and amount, existing research indicates that uncomplicated patients should be provided less intensive treatment; patients with more complex disorders should receive more intensive treatment. For many patients, outpatient treatment, in some cases following an initial episode of residential care, should be provided over an extended period.

Overall, it should be kept in mind that, although very important from a cost perspective, the setting of treatment for substance abuse, and to a lesser extent the duration and amount of treatment, are distal variables in relation to patients' post-treatment functioning. Other treatment variables, such as the treatment modality (Finney & Monahan, 1996; Miller, Brown et al., 1995), treatment services (McLellan, Arndt et al., 1993; McLellan, Grissom et al., 1993), and therapists characteristics (Hser, 1995: Najavits & Weiss, 1994) should have a more direct effect on patient's post-treatment functioning.

REFERENCES

Alterman AI, O'Brien CP, McLellan AT et al. (1994). Effectiveness and costs of inpatient versus day hospital cocaine rehabilitation. *Journal of Nervous and Mental Disease* 182:157–163.

Anglin MD & Hser Y-I (1990). Treatment of drug abuse. In M Tonry and JQ Wilson (eds.) *Drugs and Crime (Vol. 13)*. Chicago, IL: University of Chicago Press.

Annis HM (1986). Is inpatient rehabilitation cost effective? Con position. *Advances in Alcohol and Substance Abuse* 5:175–190.

Babor TF (1994). Avoiding the horrid and beastly sin of drunkenness: Does dissuasion make a difference? *Journal of Consulting and Clinical Psychology* 62:1127–1140.

Bell DC, Williams ML, Nelson R & Spence RT (1994). An experimental test of retention in residential and outpatient programs. *American Journal of Drug and Alcohol Abuse* 20:331–340.

Bien TH, Miller WR & Tonigan JS (1993). Brief interventions for alcohol problems: A review. *Addiction* 88:315–336.

Budde D, Rounsaville F & Bryant K (1992). Inpatient and outpatient cocaine abusers: Clinical comparisons at intake and one-year follow-up. *Journal of Substance Abuse Treatment* 9:337–343.

Bunn JY, Booth BM, Loveland Cook CA, Blow FC & Fortney JC (1994). The relationship between mortality and intensity of inpatient alcoholism treatment. *American Journal of Public Health* 84: 211–214.

Chapman PLH & Huygens I (1988). An evaluation of three treatment programmes for alcoholism: An experimental study with 6- and 18-month follow-ups. *British Journal of Addiction* 83:67–81.

Cohen J (1988). *Statistical Power Analysis for the Behavioral Sciences (2nd Ed.)*. Hillsdale, NJ: Lawrence Erlbaum.

Condelli WS & Hubbard RL (1994). Relationship between time spent in treatment and client outcomes from therapeutic communities. *Journal of Substance Abuse Treatment* 11:25–33.

Cooper H & Hedges LV (eds.) (1994). *The Handbook of Research Synthesis*. New York, NY: Russell Sage Foundation.

Crits-Christoph P & Siqueland L (1996). Psychosocial treatment for drug abuse: Selected review and recommendations for national health care. *Archives of General Psychiatry* 53:749–756.

Edwards G, Orford J, Egert S et al. (1977). Alcoholism: A controlled trial of "treatment" and "advice." *Journal of Studies on Alcohol* 38:1004–1031.

Finney JW, Hahn AC & Moos RH (1996). The effectiveness of inpatient and outpatient treatment for alcohol abuse: The need to focus on mediators and moderators of setting effects. *Addiction* 91:1773–1796.

Finney JW & Monahan SC (1996). The cost effectiveness of treatment for alcoholism: A second approximation. *Journal of Studies on Alcohol* 57:229–243.

Finney JW & Moos RH (1996). Effectiveness of inpatient and outpatient treatment for alcohol abuse: Effect sizes, research design issues, and explanatory mechanisms (Response to Commentaries). *Addiction* 91:1813–1820.

Finney JW & Moos RH (1998). Psychosocial treatments for alcohol use disorders. In PE Nathan & JM Gorman (eds.) *Treatments that Work*. New York, NY: Oxford University Press, 156–166.

Gottheil E, McLellan AT & Druley KA (1992). Length of stay, patient severity and treatment outcome: Sample data from the field of alcoholism. *Journal of Studies on Alcoholism* 53:69–75.

Hawkins JD & Catalano RF (1985). Aftercare in drug abuse treatment. *International Journal of the Addictions* 20:917–945.

Higgins ST, Budney AJ, Bickel WK, Hughes JR, Foerg F & Badger, G (1993). Achieving cocaine abstinence with a behavioral approach. *American Journal of Psychiatry* 150:763–769.

Hser Y-I (1995). Drug treatment counselor practices and effectiveness. *Evaluation Review* 19:389–408.

Ito J & Donovan DM (1986). Aftercare in alcoholism treatment: A review. In WR Miller & N Heather (eds.) *Treating Addictive Behaviors: Processes of Change*. New York, NY: Plenum, 435–452.

Jonson H, Hermansson U, Ronnberg S, Gyllen-Hammar C & Forsberg L (1995). Comments on brief intervention of alcohol problems: A review of a review. *Addiction* 90:1118–1120.

Kissin B, Platz A & Su WH (1970). Social and psychological factors in the treatment of chronic alcoholism. *Journal of Psychiatric Research* 8:13–27.

Mattick RP & Jarvis T (1994). In-patient setting and long duration for the treatment of alcohol dependence? Out-patient care is as good. *Drug and Alcohol Review* 13:127–135.

McKay JR, Alterman AI, McLellan AT, Snider EC & O'Brien CP (1995). The effect of random versus nonrandom assignment in a comparison of inpatient and day hospital rehabilitation for male alcoholics. *Journal of Consulting and Clinical Psychology* 63:70–78.

McKay JR, Cacciola JS, McLellan AT, Alterman AI & Wirtz PW (1997). An initial evaluation of the psychosocial dimensions of the American Society of Addiction Medicine criteria for inpatient versus intensive outpatient substance abuse rehabilitation. *Journal of Studies on Alcohol* 58:239–252.

McLachlan JFC & Stein RL (1982). Evaluation of a day clinic for alcoholics. *Journal of Studies on Alcohol* 43:261–272.

McLellan AT, Arndt IO, Metzger DS, Woody GE & O'Brien CP (1993). The effects of psychosocial services in substance abuse treatment. *Journal of the American Medical Association* 269: 1953–1959.

McLellan AT, Grissom GR, Brill P, Durell J, Metzger DS & O'Brien CP (1993). Private substance abuse treatments: Are some programs more effective than others? *Journal of Substance Abuse Treatment* 10:243–254.

McLellan AT, Luborsky L, Woody GE, O'Brien CP & Druley KA (1983). Predicting response to alcohol and drug abuse treatments: Role of psychiatric severity. *Archives of General Psychiatry* 40:620–625.

Mee-Lee D (1998). Use of patient placement criteria in the selection of treatment. In AW Graham & TK Schultz (eds.) *Principles of Addiction Medicine, Second Edition*. Chevy Chase, MD: American Society of Addiction Medicine.

Mee-Lee D, Shulman G & Gartner L (1996). *Patient Placement Criteria for the Treatment of Substance-Related Disorders, Second Edition.* Chevy Chase, MD: American Society of Addiction Medicine.

Miller WR, Brown JM, Simpson TL et al. (1995). What works? A methodological analysis of the alcohol treatment outcome literature. In RK Hester & WR Miller (eds.) *Handbook of Alcoholism Treatment Approaches: Effective Alternatives.* Boston, MA: Allyn and Bacon, 12–44.

Miller MR & Hester RK (1986). Inpatient alcoholism treatment: Who benefits? *American Psychologist* 41:794–805.

Miller WR & Sanchez VC (1993). Motivating young adults for treatment and lifestyle change. In G Howard (ed.) *Issues in Alcohol Use and Misuse by Young Adults.* Notre Dame, IN: University of Notre Dame Press.

Monahan SC & Finney JW (1996). Explaining abstinence rates following treatment for alcohol abuse: A quantitative synthesis of patient, research design, and treatment effects. *Addiction* 91:787–805.

Moos RH & Finney JW (1996a). Inpatient and outpatient treatment for substance abuse: Implications for VA services. *VA Health Services Research & Development Forum* June, 4–5.

Moos R & Finney J (1996b). *Inpatient and Outpatient Treatment for Substance Abuse: Current Findings and Implications for VA Services.* Palo Alto, CA: Department of Veterans Affairs Health Care System, Psychiatry Services and Center for Health Care Evaluation: HSR&D Field Program.

Moos RH, King M & Patterson M (1996). Outcomes of residential treatment of substance abuse in hospital- versus community-based programs. *Psychiatric Services* 47:68–74.

Moos RH, Mertens J & Brennan P (1995). Program characteristics and readmission among older substance abuse patients: Comparisons with middle-aged and younger patients. *Journal of Mental Health Administration* 22:332–345.

Moos RH, Pettit E & Gruber V (1995). Longer episodes of community residential care reduce substance abuse patients' readmission rates. *Journal of Studies on Alcohol* 56:433–443.

Najavits LM & Weiss RD (1994). Variation in therapist effectiveness in the treatment of patients with substance use disorders: An empirical review. *Addiction* 89:679–688.

O'Brien CP & McLellan AT (1996). Myths about the treatment of addiction. *Lancet* 347:237–240.

O'Farrell TJ, Choquette KA, Cutter HSG, Brown ED & McCourt WF (1993). Behavioral Marital Therapy with and without additional couples relapse prevention sessions for alcoholics and their wives. *Journal of Studies on Alcohol* 54:652–666.

Peterson K, Swindle R, Phibbs C, Recine B & Moos R (1994). Determinants of readmission following inpatient substance abuse treatment: A national study of VA programs. *Medical Care* 32:535–550.

Pettinati HM, Meyers K, Jensen JM, Kaplan F & Evans BD (1993). Inpatient vs outpatient treatment for substance abuse revisited. *Psychiatric Quarterly* 64:173–182.

Pittman DJ & Tate RL (1972). A comparison of two treatment programs for alcoholics. *Journal of Social Psychiatry* 18:183–193.

Project MATCH Research Group (1997). Matching alcoholism treatment to client heterogeneity: Project MATCH posttreatment drinking outcomes. *Journal of Studies on Alcohol* 58:7–29.

Ritson B (1968). The prognosis of alcohol addicts treated by a specialised unit. *British Journal of Psychiatry* 114:1019–1029.

Rosenheck R, Frisman L & Gallup P (1995). Effectiveness and cost of specific treatment elements in a program for homeless mentally ill veterans. *Psychiatric Services* 46:1131–1139.

Rosenthal R & Rubin DB (1982). A simple, general purpose display of magnitude of experimental effect. *Journal of Educational Psychology* 74:166–169.

Saxe L, Dougherty D, Esty K & Fine M (1983). *The Effectiveness and Costs of Alcoholism Treatment (Health Technology Case Study 22)*. Washington, DC: Office of Technology Assessment.

Simpson DD (1981). Treatment for drug abuse: Follow-up outcomes and length of time spent. *Archives of General Psychiatry* 38:875–880.

Stecher BM, Andrews CA, McDonald L et al. (1994). Implementation of residential and nonresidential treatment for the dually diagnoses homeless. *Evaluation Review* 18:689–717.

Timko C, Finney JW & Moos RH (1995). Short-term treatment careers and outcomes of previously untreated alcoholics. *Journal of Substance Abuse* 7:43–59.

Walsh DC, Hingson RW, Merrigan DM et al. (1991). A randomized trial of treatment options for alcohol-abusing workers. *New England Journal of Medicine* 325(11):775–782.

Welte J, Hynes G, Sokolow L & Lyons JP (1981). Effect of length of stay in inpatient alcoholism treatment on outcome. *Journal of Studies on Alcohol* 42:483–491.

CHAPTER 6

Linkages of Substance Abuse with Primary Care and Mental Health Treatment

Patrick G. O'Connor, M.D., M.P.H.
Douglas M. Ziedonis, M.D., M.P.H.

Linkages between Substance Abuse and Primary Care Services
Linkages between Substance Abuse and Mental Health Services
Mechanisms to Improve Coordination of Services

As a clinical problem, substance abuse rarely stands alone as an isolated issue in a given patient. Such patients typically also are at risk for significant medical problems (Cherubin & Sapira, 1993; Eckardt, Horford et al., 1981; O'Connor, Selwyn & Schottenfeld, 1994) and mental health disorders (Ziedonis & Brady, 1997). Thus, providing comprehensive care for this population involves much more than simply providing addiction treatment services. Careful attention must be given to screening for and diagnosing co-occurring medical and psychiatric disorders. In addition, basic health care services need to be provided for any problems that are found.

Because patients with substance abuse problems present in primary care, psychiatric, and addiction treatment settings, clinicians in all three settings must be aware to screen for co-existing medical, psychiatric and substance abuse problems. Most patients who present for treatment have multiple problems and comorbidities, which may worsen the prognosis for any individual problem. To help such patients, linkages across services and cross-training of staff are essential.

Most patients with co-occurring disorders could be treated in an integrated manner in any of the three settings. Instead, however, treatment often occurs in a linear and parallel fashion. In such cases, linkages between services may be crucial not only to improving outcomes but also to providing continuity of care. Cross-consultation in all three settings could help in earlier detection and treatment planning.

The development of integrated and linked services can be facilitated through shared values and mutual respect for the specialized services provided in each setting. Although improving linkages of services may add initial costs to develop the system, improved continuity of services can save costs and improve quality of care. The effectiveness of such linkages between services is increasingly being evaluated in managed care organizations. Because of the complexity of these issues, it is unusual that they can each be addressed by one provider or at one setting. However, newer approaches have been under development to form linkages between substance abuse, medical and mental health services in order to enhance health care services to this population and to make them more integrated and comprehensive (Samet, Stein & O'Connor, 1995b) (Table 1). This chapter reviews the importance of linkages between substance abuse, primary care and mental health services, with an emphasis on describing newer approaches to linking and integrating such services.

LINKAGES BETWEEN SUBSTANCE ABUSE AND PRIMARY CARE SERVICES

"Primary care" by definition implies the provision of first-contact and continuing health care services. Primary care providers are the clinicians who would most typically provide "medical" services to substance users who are engaged in ongoing health care. In addition, because substance users tend not to form linkages with primary care providers they often may resort to non-primary care providers such as emergency rooms for episodic, urgent and emergent care.

TABLE 1. Models for Linking Care

Models for Linking Primary Care and Substance Abuse Treatment
- Distributive Model
- Primary Assessment and Triage
- Drug Treatment Program Linked to Primary Care

Models for Linking Mental Health and Substance Abuse Treatment
- Assertive Community Treatment Team
- Integrated Treatment
- Motivation-Based Dual Diagnosis Treatment
- Consultation Services

Barriers to Linkages with Primary Care Services. There are a variety of reasons to explain the barriers to effective linkages between substance abuse and primary care services. Most substance abuse treatment programs do not have direct access to "on site" medical services and are left to rely on the existing health care system to access these services. In addition, substance abuse treatment program personnel may not be familiar with the variety of medical issues for which this population may be at risk. From the perspective of primary care providers, substance users may be perceived as "difficult" and undesirable as patients (Gerbert, Maguire et al., 1991). In addition, primary care providers are likely to be poorly educated about substance abuse issues and ill equipped to manage this population (Lewis, Niven et al., 1987). All of these factors may lead to mistrust or misunderstanding between substance abuse treatment providers, primary care providers and substance users themselves (O'Connor, Selwyn & Schottenfeld, 1994). However, the complex nature of medical problems in this patient population speak clearly to the need for generalist physicians to play a major role in the care of substance abusing patients (Lewis, 1997).

Models of Medical Care for Substance Abusers. A variety of efforts have focused on the development of formal models for linking medical and substance abuse treatment services. These efforts have primarily occurred since the onset of the HIV epidemic among drug users (Samet, Stein & O'Connor, 1995b). Depending on which model is considered, the "site" where these linkages occur may vary. Examples of three specific models were the subjects of a recent review by Samet, Stein and O'Connor (1995b) (Table 1).

The *Distributive Model* describes that system of care with drug users which occurs most commonly. In this approach patients are "distributed to a variety of sites" for primary care which may include private physician offices or hospital-based clinics and community health centers (Samet, Stein & O'Connor, 1995b). As it is, this approach is left to rely upon an unselected group of primary care providers whose interest and skill in caring for this population may vary widely. In addition, given that many substance users may be uninsured, their access to both the primary health care system in the distributive model and to substance abuse treatment programs in general may be greatly inferior. In part, to address some of these issues, new models of providing medical care to drug users have been developed.

The *Primary Assessment and Triage Model* was first described by Samet, Libman et al. (1995a). In this model, developed specifically for HIV infected drug users without primary care, a multidisciplinary assessment with a facilitated access to medical services is provided. The assessment occurred in a specific clinic, the "Diagnostic Evaluation Unit" which was established at Boston City Hospital for the purpose of linking drug users to services. In their study, 95% of patients successfully completed referral to primary care and basic assessments of immune status, syphilis serology, hepatitis B serology, and tuberculosis exposure were obtained in 92% of the patients. Not only did this setting demonstrate an effective model for linking drug users to medical services, it also demonstrated that this model could be effective in improving the attitudes and confidence of medical students in the care of individuals with HIV infection. Although this model was not designed specifically to link drug users to substance abuse treatment, it clearly would have applicability to this need. A similar model was developed at Rhode Island Hospital in which multidisciplinary intake procedures take place directly within the general primary care clinic (Samet, Stein & O'Connor, 1995b).

In the *Drug Treatment Program Linked to Primary Care Model*, the linkage between substance abuse treatment programs with the provision of primary care is designed to be stronger. In this model medical services and substance abuse treatment are delivered together "on site" typically within a substance abuse treatment program (Samet, Stein & O'Connor, 1995b). This model was first described by Selwyn et al. in a description of a program at Montefiore Hospital in New York City (Selwyn, Feingold et al., 1989). Medical services were provided on site in a methadone maintenance program for individuals with HIV infection. The goal of the program was to enhance compliance with antiretroviral therapy, prophylaxis for Pneumocystis pneumonia, and chemoprophylaxis and chemotherapy for tuberculosis. In this study, 100% of patients accepted therapy for active tuberculosis and 82% for tuberculosis chemoprophylaxis, while 69% of subjects accepted antiretroviral therapy (Selwyn, Feingold et al., 1989).

In a follow-up report, the authors reported that 81% of patients enrolled in methadone maintenance utilized primary care providers in a study which included HIV positive and HIV negative drug users (Selwyn, Budner et al., 1993). Similarly, O'Connor et al. reported the results of an "on site" primary care program for drug users (O'Connor, Molde et al., 1992). Unlike Selwyn's program, which was physically within the confines of a methadone maintenance program, the program reported by O'Connor, Molde et al. (1992) was adjacent (next door to) a methadone maintenance clinic in their system. Referred to as "The Central Medical Unit," this program provides services to HIV positive and HIV negative drug users enrolled in methadone maintenance and other substance abuse treatment programs. In addition, this program provides medical services for individuals enrolled in alcohol treatment. As with other such models, the program developed at Yale placed emphasis on the provision of services to drug users with HIV infection. Among 120 HIV-infected drug users studied by this group, 81% accepted pneumococcal vaccination, 49% received influenza vaccination, and 36% received hepatitis B vaccination. In addition, the vast majority of these patients accepted assessment of their immune function and a prescription of antiretroviral therapy when indicated (O'Connor, Molde et al., 1992).

The model described by Selwyn and O'Connor offers a "one stop shopping" approach, which brings substance abuse treatment and primary care services into close proximity. Among other benefits, this approach can increase the convenience associated with obtaining medical services and enhanced communication between drug treatment and primary care providers. Among the disadvantages of this approach is that it relies on patients to be enrolled in drug treatment and thus does not specifically provide services for those not enrolled in drug treatment. In addition, these approaches do not provide continuity of primary care services beyond patient enrollment in drug treatment and patients lose access to primary care once they drop out of treatment.

LINKAGES BETWEEN SUBSTANCE ABUSE AND MENTAL HEALTH SERVICES

Psychiatric symptoms are commonly associated with substance use disorders, and many patients in either the mental health, addiction, or primary care treatment settings have both a substance use disorder and a psychiatric disorder. These patients have been labeled as having a "dual diagnosis," however the dually diagnosed represent a very heterogeneous population and there tends to be different subtypes of dual diagnosis combinations. The psychiatric symptoms may be a primary psychiatric disorder or secondary to the effects of a general medical condition, medications, or substance use.

The National Comorbidity Study (Kessler, McGonagle et al., 1994) and the Epidemiological Catchment Area study (Regier, Farmer et al., 1990), both with population-based samples, reported high rates of co-existing psychiatric and substance use disorders. In general population studies, about 35% of the population will have a psychiatric disorder during their lifetime and about 20% meet current criteria (Kessler, McGonagle et al., 1994; Robbins & Regier, 1991).

Substance use disorders are very common among psychiatric patients, and psychiatric disorders are common among patients in substance abuse treatment. In mental health treatment settings, the current substance abuse rates range from 40 to 80%, and polysubstance abuse is common (Ziedonis & Fisher, 1996). A recent outpatient study at the Connecticut Mental Health Center found 45% of psychiatric patients had a current substance use disorder, the majority of these dually diagnosed had low motivation to stop using substances, and the level of motivation varied according to the specific substance of abuse (Ziedonis & Trudeau, 1997).

Dually diagnosed patients often are difficult to treat and can be a challenge to both clinical treatment and the delivery system. These patients require innovative, integrated, and coordinated services to address multiple problems. Treatment of the dually diagnosed requires collaboration across many treatment philosophies and systems, including agencies providing alcohol and drug prevention and treatment, mental health treatment, criminal justice/legal services, social and welfare services, general health care treatment, vocational rehabilitation services, housing agencies, and educational systems (Ries, 1994).

Two important assessment and treatment matching factors in any clinical setting are the patient's acknowledgment of a problem and their motivational level to address this problem. Psychiatric and primary care settings are similar in that patients usually do not present requesting treatment for substance abuse. They often minimize their problems and are poorly motivated to seek help to address the problem. Patients in the addiction setting may not believe they have a co-existing psychiatric disorder and attribute the symptoms only to early recovery. The difference in motivational levels according to treatment setting is a factor in understanding the differences in regards to treating dual diagnosis in different settings. Patients may accept the need for help for only the psychiatric problem, only the substance abuse problem, both problems, or neither problem.

Barriers to Linkages with Mental Health Services. Unfortunately, multiple barriers limit the coordination of substance abuse and mental health services, including the lack of a unified clinical model/philosophy between the two systems. Barriers exist at all levels of organization, including federal, state, local, and individual treatment agency. A lack of coordination has resulted in services being fragmented, duplicated, disorder focused, and unaccountable to the dually diagnosed (Baker, 1991).

System barriers to coordination include policy and planning barriers. There is a lack of mandate to develop coordinated or integrated services for the dually diagnosed. Often there is little or no communication or collaboration among the various departments and levels of government that have separate administrative structures, constituencies, mandates, and target groups. This lack of communication or collaboration is seen at all organizational levels. There are different federal, state, and local planning cycles within the addiction and mental health treatment systems. The perceived social contract with the mental health and addiction treatment system differs. The mental health system's contract includes pursuing/removing unmotivated troubled patients (suicidal, homicidal, or unable to care for themselves) and the legal system provides mechanisms to remove these individuals. By contrast, the addiction system's contract is to provide services to those who seek treatment (more motivated or treatment stipulated in lieu of jail). As a result, the mental health system has assertive community outreach teams, but the addiction treatment system does not. Other organizational barriers to treatment include the fact that substance abuse and psychiatric treatment programs often are administered and funded by separate agencies, may be physically located in separate places, and their staff are not cross-trained. The different systems have separate and confusing streams of funding for different categories of disabilities. Current reimbursement inhibits integration of services because there are separate funding streams for addiction and mental health treatment, the span of coverage limits the types of services that can be provided in different settings, and third party reimbursement mechanisms focus on the primary diagnosis. Staff have become inhibited in providing full or accurate diagnosis based on the rules of some reimbursement plans. Data collection and needs assessment are separate in the two systems, limiting the sharing of information and documenting the clear need for coordinated and integrated treatment services for the dually diagnosed. These separate political jurisdictions has created a barrier that is particularly difficult with patients with multiple and difficult problems (Baker, 1991; Ries, 1994).

Agencies delivering substance abuse and psychiatric services operate according to different goals and objectives. They are separated by different sponsorship, geography, and operating principles. They employ different eligibility criteria and deal only with parts of the needs of individuals and families. Categorical approaches perpetuate the existing patterns of specialist and single function agencies dealing with even smaller aspects of larger problems. Screening, assessment, and referral are based on the primary diagnosis and not the complexity of the co-existing disorders. Often no single person or agency takes the primary responsibility for case management and coordinating services. Deciding on the appropriate level of care for the dually diagnosed can be difficult given the different criteria for mental illness (suicidal, homicidal, grossly psychotic, or unable to care for themselves) versus addiction (American Society of Addiction Medicine, 1997). Fortunately, the ASAM criteria are being expanded to include the unique issues of the dually diagnosed; however, mental health system staff generally are unaware of these criteria and are guided by another set of criteria.

Agencies do not provide a wide range of services to respond to the complex needs of some individuals. As a result, agencies often select the less impaired patients on the basis of the type of disability, the difficulty of presenting symptoms, the perceived manageability of the patient, their ability to pay, or some other characteristic (Grusky, Tierney et al., 1985). Unfortunately, being dually diagnosed makes you a more complicated patient with a worse prognosis, and therefore more likely to be excluded from treatment. As local program leaders feel the pressure to do more for less, the difficult patient is "turfed" to other systems. Leaders try to strengthen their organization by limiting the commitment of resources, the range of services, and the types of patients they will serve (Aiken, Dewar et al., 1975).

Developing new dual diagnosis services in either system is limited by staff's resistance to change, ongoing turf battles, regulations and reimbursement rules, lack of program evaluation/treatment outcome data, lack of standards for dual diagnosis treatment services, lack of incentives to develop programs, and lack of training. Clinicians are poorly cross-trained in assessing and treating coexisting disorders. The staff may stigmatize the other disorder due to lack of training and mentoring. The different treatment philosophies tend to cause misunderstanding between groups and limit coordination and collaboration. There is tension between a harm reduction versus abstinence goal; however, a more over-arching model might include both goals. The mental health setting and staff often are unprepared to do assessments such as urine toxicology and Breathalyzer, and the barriers to this include lack of equipment, training, and integration into the standard of care. Professional ideologies define what is proper professional behavior and the right approach to providing service. Differences in professional perspectives interfere with staff working together, particularly because different staff members are likely to view the main problems of a multiple-problem patient in different ways (Baker, 1982).

In the new era of capitation, behavioral health "carve-outs," and managed care, there is a strong desire to provide both comprehensive services (having the necessary resources and types of help are present and available to patients to meet all their needs) and a full continuity of care (services to an individual are comprehensive and coordinated for a particular episode and over time and is responsive to changes in the person's needs).

Models of Mental Health Care for Dually Diagnosed Substance Abusers. Treatment of the dually diagnosed client requires addressing both the psychiatric and substance use disorders in a comprehensive, coordinated, and integrated manner. This is more likely to occur when changes occur at multiple levels of organization, including federal, state, local, and agency. New clinical models and mechanisms of coordination have been and must continue to develop to facilitate coordination and integration of services on all levels. Three types of treatment models have been used to address the needs of the dually diagnosed: sequential, parallel, and integrated (Ries, 1994). In the sequential treatment model, the patient receives treatment in one system (the addiction or mental health) and then in the other system. The order of the sequencing is based on clinical and philosophical criteria. The parallel treatment model requires that the patient be simultaneously in treatment in both the mental health and addiction treatment system. Both the sequential and parallel models require coordination of services across agencies. In recent years, the integrated model has been favored and research supports this approach (Ries, 1994). In this model, the patient receives treatment from one program that integrates treatment approaches and provides comprehensive treatment. The integrated models articulate needed changes in values/philosophy and approach to clinical practice (Table 2). The dually diagnosed population is very heterogeneous and treatment models must consider these differences. In addition, dual diagnosis occurs in both the mental health and the substance abuse treatment system, and therefore coordination and integration of services must occur in

TABLE 2. Components of Integrated Models for Treating the Substance-Abusing Mentally Ill

- Early diagnosis and case identification
- Outreach services
- A focus on treatment engagement
- Continuity of care between treatment components
- Assistance applying for entitlements (income, medical, etc.)
- 24-hour crisis stabilization services
- Psychosocial rehabilitation
- Pharmacotherapy
- Optimizing the use of natural support systems
- Case management services
- Patient-specific treatment appropriate to:
  - Mental health and substance abuse diagnoses
  - Severity of both diagnoses
  - Disability
  - Motivation
  - Compliance
  - Phase of treatment
  - Cultural orientation.

Sources: Davidson, L, Simsarian J & Marcus K (1993). *Providing Services to Persons Dually Diagnosed with Prolonged Mental Illness and Substance Abuse: A Report.* White Paper prepared for the Connecticut Department of Mental Health; Ziedonis D, Simsarian J, Carroll D et al. (1997). *Department of Mental Health and Addiction Service's Dual Diagnosis Task Force Report.* Hartford, CT: The Department; Ries R (1994). *Assessment and Treatment of Patients with Coexisting Mental Illness and Alcohol and Other Drug Abuse (CSAT Treatment Improvement Protocol No. 9).* Rockville, MD: Center for Substance Abuse Treatment.

both settings. Beyond improving service coordination, some states, local networks, and agencies have created a third treatment track for the dually diagnosed to better integrate services.

Several integrated models have developed within the mental health system to integrate substance abuse treatment for the dually diagnosed, including the Assertive Community Treatment Team Model (Drake, Bartels et al., 1993), the Integrated Model (Minkoff, 1994), the Stages of Treatment Model (Osher & Kofoed, 1989), and the Motivation Based Dual Diagnosis Treatment Model (Ziedonis & Fisher, 1996). These models share similar clinical values, including an empathic approach, coordination of services, comprehensive services, case management, and outreach efforts. Psychosocial and medication treatments for both disorders must be integrated into the treatment plan when appropriate. These models recognize that dual diagnosis clinical treatment also must be linked in a system of care with housing, entitlements, rehabilitation, legal, and community services.

The *Assertive Community Treatment Team Model* (Drake, Bartels et al., 1993) is a stage-wise, cognitive-behavioral substance abuse treatment integrated into comprehensive community mental health services that include outreach, case-management, and medications. Multidisciplinary teams serve as the primary clinician for a relatively small number of patients, and are involved in the patient's treatment in all settings. The teams are outpatient-oriented and execute intensive case management within the patient's natural environment. The model incorporates Osher and Kofoed's (Osher & Kofoed, 1989) five stages of dual diagnosis treatment: engagement, persuasion, coercion, relapse prevention, and action.

The *Integrated Treatment Model* (Minkoff, 1994) emphasizes case management care in an integrated manner that recognizes the parallels between psychiatric and substance use disorders. Both disorders are chronic relapsing conditions with biological underpinnings. Both illnesses are stigmatized. Individuals often deny or minimize the presence or impact of both disorders. In this model, after a substance abuse or psychiatric relapse, there is a stabilization period prior to rehabilitation. The integrated model attempts to address both problems simultaneously and recognizes the parallels between the two disorders.

The *Motivation-Based Dual Diagnosis Treatment Model* builds on the values and philosophy of the previous two models; however, it emphasizes a treatment matching strategy based on the type of psychiatric and substance use disorders, the severity of the disorders, and the motivational level to address the addiction problem (Ziedonis & Fisher, 1996). This model focuses on integrating substance abuse treatment techniques into mental health treatment. In the MBDDT model, the patients' motivational level is determined using the five motivational stages of Prochaska and DiClemente. Each stage is matched with specific addiction treatment psychosocial approaches: motivational enhancement therapy (MET), Twelve Step recovery, and relapse prevention. Traditional psychiatric psychosocial treatments are blended (social skills training, cognitive-behavioral therapies, etc). Additional treatment strategies include vocational exploration, self-care skills, sleep hygiene, case management, money management, and practical problem-solving. Specific social skills training includes medication management, relationship skills, communication skills, stress management skills, and leisure skills. Other ingredients of treatment include medications (for both the psychiatric and substance abuse problems), psychoeducation, vocational rehabilitation, behavioral contracting, peer-support counseling, and family involvement.

The three dual diagnosis treatment models share common principles of providing dual diagnosis services that are patient centered, comprehensive, empower patients, are racially and culturally appropriate, are flexible and responsive, focus on patient strengths, are normalized and integrated within natural supports, and meet social needs for service (Table 2). In addition, service systems for the dually diagnosed should be accountable, committed to continual improvement, and coordinated (Davidson, Simsarian & Marcus, 1993).

Substance Abuse Prevention Among Individuals with Psychiatric Disorders. The coordination of services should include the link between treatment and prevention services, and the dually diagnosed population provides an opportunity to develop prevention strategies that target a high risk group to develop a second disorder. Substance abuse prevention efforts might be aimed at primary prevention (to prevent the secondary disorder of substance abuse) and at secondary prevention (to do early detection and implementation of an intervention to stop the progression from use to abuse). Prevention efforts can be extended into the community support services of residential services, vocational programs, and social clubs. The use of prevention audio-visual materials, peer support programs, healthy coping skills development, and drug resistance skill training could all promote healthy relationships and non-chemical ways to improve one's well-being. Such programs could reinforce the cultural shift of addressing substance abuse problems and integrating treatment within a mental health setting (Ziedonis, 1995).

MECHANISMS TO IMPROVE COORDINATION OF SERVICES

Coordination of services improve when the extent of collaboration and exchange among separate agencies in a community increases while recognizing the integrity and autonomy of these agencies. Baker has described four key elements that require coordination in a service delivery system: programs, resources, patients, and information. "Programs" includes all the services necessary to provide a continuum of care. "Resources" includes all the needed funds and necessary autonomy. "Patients" includes the treatment of all the needs of eligible patients. "Information" includes centralized patient recordkeeping, knowledge about availability of resources, and continuous feedback about patients, resources, and programs (Baker, 1991).

On an inter-organizational level, agencies are motivated to improve coordination because of a need to obtain resources (money, personnel, support, recognition, patients, and information) and control over uncertain environmental conditions (Blostein, 1983). In the basic exchange model, agreeing about what each organization should be doing facilitates coordination (Levine & White, 1961). Also, mandating by law or administrative regulations can force coordination. Another approach is voluntary inter-organizational interaction that is standardized through formal agreements. The formal agreements may stipulate sharing facilities, information about particular patients, or personnel.

Several mechanisms to improve coordination have been described (Table 3) (Baker, 1991). These include co-location of services from different agencies in the same physical setting, sharing information and developing a referral system for directing patients who need assistance to agencies that meet their needs, and having a centralized intake and referral (a single point of access to full range of services). In addition, interagency networks provide three mechanisms of linkages (multidisciplinary team, bilateral coordination, and multilateral coordination). Case management can be a method or process for ensuring that patients are provided needed services in a coordinated, effective, and efficient manner through the use of a case manager and core service agency. Some agencies share staff to improve coordination. Financing models include the use of funding arrangements to encourage coordination such as incentive programs, strengthening local entities to manage funding of services, and capitation of funds. Providing education and training across agencies offers a means of teaching the value of coordination (Baker, 1991).

TABLE 3. Principles for Service Coordination Across Agencies

- Organizational changes do no necessarily lead to coordination.
- Success depends on the leadership of responsible individuals.
- Funding incentives are crucial.
- Service providers must perceive benefits.
- Shared information systems are required.
- State and local governments need a common service strategy.
- Formal inter-organizational agreements facilitate coordination.
- Responsibility to a common superordinate authority.
- Coordination is difficult to achieve outside of major urban areas.
- Travel times exceeding 45 minutes interferes with coordination.
- Relevant staff training and education necessary.
- Shared ideology that supports coordination helpful.
- Coordination is a slow, evolutionary process.
- Coordination is primarily a consensus-building process.

Source: Table based on discussion in Baker F (1991). *Coordination of Alcohol, Drug Abuse and Mental Health Services (Technical Assistance Publication Series No. 4)*. Rockville, MD: Center for Substance Abuse Treatment.

On a state level, task forces and councils can provide a mechanism for separate state agencies to attempt to better coordinate their efforts to solve certain problems. In Connecticut, the Governor's Blue Ribbon Task Force on Substance Abuse recommended to Governor John Rowland the creation of an Addictions Council to develop a single, integrated system of services based on a comprehensive statewide plan. This coordinated system would attempt to maximize coordination, purchasing power, and outcome measurement for state agencies funding prevention, intervention, treatment, and enforcement efforts. Membership includes the heads of agencies that are impacted by substance abuse (e.g. Departments of Mental Health and Addiction Services, Public Health, Corrections, Children and Families, Social Services, Education) the Judicial Branch, legislative leadership, major business representatives including the insurance industry. The Council promotes a coordinated statewide effort and presents to the Governor a summation and integration of individual agency substance abuse budgets with overarching goals and outcome measures. The Council provides a mechanism in which to better coordinate resources for addiction services (prevention, treatment, and criminal justice system). The Task Force recognized the special needs of the dually diagnosed and the problems with interagency coordination of services. The Task Force encouraged the newly created Department of Mental Health and Addiction Services (which blended the two separate departments) to focus on improving service coordination (Kraus, Segal et al., 1996).

One of the first initiatives of the Connecticut Department of Mental Health and Addiction Services was to develop a Task Force on Dual Diagnosis Services. This Task Force consisted of leaders in the addiction treatment community and mental health treatment community who represented different public and private organizations within the state. The group developed a Behavioral Health treatment model for the state, a dual diagnosis subtyping system, a training curriculum and plan, modifications in the state screening and intake process to assess for both problems and to assess motivational level for substance abuse problems, and a dual diagnosis service system with multiple levels to provide continuity of care. The Task Force recommendations encouraged increased integration of mental health and addiction services within agencies and increased coordination between agencies within the five networks in the state (Ziedonis, Simsarian et al., 1997).

On an intra-organizational level, service integration attempts to bring an agency's programs into a single system, requiring the individual organization to change and adapt in order to integrate services. For example, a community mental health center may provide substance abuse services in one unit and mental health outpatient services in another. The dually diagnosed patient may get bounced between these units receiving no specialized or integrated services unless the organization mandates integration. Community mental health centers, health maintenance organizations, neighborhood health centers, and youth opportunity centers are all examples of organizations that can be designed to integrate service by providing decentralization of care to areas of high need, shifting resources between programs, co-locating mental health and substance abuse services, and operationally sequencing services to eliminate duplication and wasted time (Baker, 1991; March, 1968).

On an individual consultant level, mental health and addiction services can be coordinated through a *Consultation Service Model* in either the mental health or addiction setting (Greenfield, Weiss & Tohen, 1995; Ziedonis, 1995). Substance abuse consultation liaison service to inpatient psychiatric programs can include assessment, treatment planning, and specific service delivery (such as dual diagnosis group therapy, detoxification, and continuing care planning) (Greenfield, Weiss & Tohen, 1995). Substance abuse consultation to mental health outreach teams can include urine toxicology and Breathalyzer systems, diagnosis training, and infectious disease training (especially for HIV, tuberculosis, and hepatitis). Consultation by both substance abuse and mental health specialists to care delivery administrators can include strategic plan development, promotion of a unified philosophy and model for behavioral health problems, creation of triage algorithms, and designing staff training programs. These same tasks also are particularly relevant for developing improved emergency department management. Lastly, the specialist in addiction psychiatry may be able to provide consultation to substance abuse programs concerning patient assessment and treatment, pharmacologic management of psychiatric disorders, focused brief psychotherapy, and family assessment and therapy (Kraus, Ziedonis & Segal, 1998).

CONCLUSIONS

Integrated, comprehensive care of patients with mental health, substance abuse, and general medical problems produces improved patient outcomes. Barriers to delivery can be systematically removed to benefit these patients. Coordination of services is a slow, evolutionary, consensus-building process requiring skilled leadership, financial incentives, and commitments to mutually agreed upon goals.

REFERENCES

Aiken M, Dewar R, DiTomaso N, Hage J & Zeitz G (1975). *Coordinating Human Services: New Strategies for Building Service Delivery Systems*. San Francisco, CA: Jossey-Bass.

Baker F (1982). Effects of value systems on service delivery. In HC Shulberg & M Killilea (eds.) *The Modern Practice of Community Mental Health*. San Francisco, CA: Jossey-Bass, 246264.

Baker F (1991). *Coordination of Alcohol, Drug Abuse, and Mental Health Services (Technical Assistance Publication Series No. 4)*. Rockville, MD: Center for Substance Abuse Treatment.

Blostein S (1983). The Coordination Dimensions Scale: A tool to assess interorganizational relationships. *Journal of Sociology and Social Welfare* 10:424–439.

Cherubin CE & Sapira JD (1993). The medical complications of drug addiction and the medical assessment of the intravenous drug user: 25 years later. *Annals of Internal Medicine* 119:1017–1028.

Davidson L, Simsarian J & Marcus K (1993). *Providing Services to Persons Dually Diagnosed with Prolonged Mental Illness and Substance Abuse: A Report.* White Paper prepared for the Connecticut Department of Mental Health.

Drake RE, Bartels SJ, Teague GB, Noordsy DL & Clark RE (1993). Treatment of substance abuse in severely mentally ill patients. *Journal of Nervous and Mental Disease* 181:606–611.

Eckardt MJ, Horford TC, Kaelber CT et al. (1981). Health hazards associated with alcohol consumption. *Journal of the American Medical Association* 246:648–666.

Gerbert B, Maguire BT, Bleecker T, Coates TJ & McPhee SJ (1991). Primary care physicians and AIDS. Attitudinal and structural barriers to care. *Journal of the American Medical Association* 266:2837–2842.

Greenfield SF, Weiss RD & Tohen M (1995). Substance abuse and the chronically mentally ill: A description of dual diagnosis treatment services in a psychiatric hospital. *Community Mental Health Journal* 31:265–277.

Grusky O, Tierney KJ, Holstein J et al. (1985). Models of local mental health delivery systems. *American Behavioral Scientist* 28:685–703.

Kessler RC, McGonagle KA, Zhao S et al. (1994). Lifetime and 12-month prevalence of DSM-III-R psychiatric disorders in the United States. Results from the National Comorbidity Survey. *Archives of General Psychiatry* 51:8–19.

Kraus ML, Segal SR, Frantz AH & Ziedonis DM (1996). *Governor's Blue Ribbon Task Force on Substance Abuse*. Hartford, CT: State of Connecticut.

Kraus ML, Ziedonis DM & Segal SR (1998). A community hospital's ambulatory addiction program. *Connecticut Medicine* 62:89–93.

Levine S & White PE (1961). Exchange as a conceptual framework for the study of interorganizational relationships. *Administrative Science Quarterly* 5:583–601.

Lewis DC (1997). The role of the generalist in the care of the substance-abusing patient. *Medical Clinics of North America* 81:831–843.

Lewis DC, Niven RG, Czechowicz D & Trumble JG (1987). A review of medical education in alcohol and other drug abuse. *Journal of the American Medical Association* 257:2945–2948.

March MS (1968). The neighborhood center concept. *Public Welfare* 26:97–111.

Mee-Lee D, Shulman G & Gartner L (1996). *Patient Placement Criteria for the Treatment of Substance-Related Disorders, Second Edition*. Chevy Chase, MD: American Society of Addiction Medicine.

Minkoff K (1994). Models for addiction treatment in psychiatric populations. *Psychiatric Annals* 24:412–417.

O'Connor PG, Molde S, Henry S, Shockor WT & Schottenfeld RS (1992). Human Immunodeficiency Virus infection in intravenous drug users: A model for primary care. *American Journal of Medicine* 93:382–386.

O'Connor PG, Selwyn PA & Schottenfeld RS (1994). Medical progress: Medical care for injection drug users with human immunodeficiency virus infection. *The New England Journal of Medicine* 331:450–459.

Osher FC & Kofoed L (1989). Treatment of patients with psychiatric and psychoactive substance abuse disorders. *Hospital and Community Psychiatry* 40:1025–1030.

Regier DA, Farmer ME, Rae DS et al. (1990). Comorbidity of mental disorders with alcohol and other drug abuse. Results from the Epidemiologic Catchment Area (ECA) Study. *Journal of the American Medical Association* 264:2511–2518.

Ries R (1994). *Assessment and Treatment of Patients with Coexisting Mental Illness and Alcohol and Other Drug Abuse (CSAT Treatment Improvement Protocol No. 9)*. Rockville, MD: Center for Substance Abuse Treatment.

Robbins LN & Regier DA (1991). *Psychiatric Disorders in America.* New York, NY: Free Press.

Samet JH, Libman H, LaBelle C et al. (1995a). A model clinic for the initial evaluation and establishment of primary care for persons infected with human immunodeficiency virus. *Archives of Internal Medicine* 155:1629–1633.

Samet JH, Stein MD & O'Connor PG (1995b). Models of medical care for HIV-infected drug users. *Substance Abuse* 16:131–139.

Selwyn PA, Budner NS, Wasserman WC & Arno PS (1993). Utilization of on-site primary care services by HIV-seropositive and seronegative drug users in a methadone maintenance program. *Public Health Reports* 108:492–500.

Selwyn PA, Feingold AR, Iezza A et al. (1989). Primary care for patients with human immunodeficiency virus (HIV) infection in a methadone maintenance treatment program. *Annals of Internal Medicine* 111:761–763.

Ziedonis D & Brady K (1997). Dual diagnosis in primary care. Detecting and treating both the addiction and mental illness. *Medical Clinics of North America* 81:1017–1036.

Ziedonis D, Simsarian J, Carroll D et al. (1997). *Department of Mental Health and Addiction Service's Dual Diagnosis Task Force Report*. Hartford, CT: The Department.

Ziedonis DM (1995). Substance abuse prevention strategies for psychiatric patients. In RH Coombs & DM Ziedonis (eds.) *Handbook on Drug Abuse Prevention:*

A Comprehensive Strategy to Prevent the Abuse of Alcohol and Other Drugs. Boston, MA: Allyn & Bacon, 445–469.
Ziedonis DM & Fisher W (1996). Motivation-based assessment and treatment of substance abuse in patients with schizophrenia. *Directions in Psychiatry* 16:1–8.
Ziedonis DM & Trudeau K (1997). Motivation to quit using substances among individuals with schizophrenia: Implications for a motivation-based treatment model. *Schizophrenia Bulletin* 23:229–238.

CHAPTER 7

Use of Patient Placement Criteria in the Selection of Treatment

David Mee-Lee, M.D.

Limited Models and Levels of Care
The ASAM Patient Placement Criteria
The Multiple Uses of Patient Placement Criteria
Implications for Clinicians, Programs, Payers and Policy

In a health care environment in which the focus too often is on cost-containment rather than clinical integrity, it is increasingly important to attain conceptual clarity as to the definition and delivery of high-quality treatment services. Care givers and care managers now face more than ever before, demands for cost-effectiveness and a clear demonstration of value in health care delivered or managed. The tendency to perpetuate a narrow range of models and services for all patients renders the treatment field continually vulnerable to arbitrary funding, reimbursement, or benefit limits, under the control of individuals and organizations unfamiliar with treatment. To conceptualize and define services and levels of care only according to the availability of funding or health care coverage pushes providers to "treat the reimbursement, rather than the patient."

LIMITED MODELS AND LEVELS OF CARE

It has long been known that treatment is effective, but that no one treatment model or level of care is effective for all patients (Institute of Medicine, 1990, p. 149). There has been over a decade of more widespread knowledge of patient placement criteria for assigning patients to a variety of levels of care within a continuum of care based on multidimensional severity or level of functioning (Cleveland Criteria of the Northern Ohio Chemical Dependency Treatment Directors Association, Hoffmann, Halikas & Mee-Lee, 1987; the National Association of Addiction Treatment Providers (NAATP) Criteria, Weedman, 1987). Yet many patients still receive one treatment model, based on diagnosis alone. If a patient meets the diagnostic criteria for alcoholism or other drug addiction, a single treatment model and level of care is offered for primary treatment, as if addiction is an acute illness responsive to an episode of primary treatment followed by aftercare.

Of such addiction treatment, which is *program-based* rather than *clinically-driven*, it can be said that "one size fits all." However, to protect access to high quality treatment and conserve health care resources, there is a need for providers and payers to continue to strive for conceptual clarity on how to provide for a range of options tailored to patient needs and implement complex patient placement criteria.

Such matching of patient needs to treatment services has been increasingly studied, with one major study showing that we still face significant challenges in demonstrating effective outcomes for theoretical and clinical concepts of matching (Project Match Research Group, 1997). The Institute of Medicine's report on *Broadening the Base of Treatment for Alcohol Problems* defined treatment as the broad range of services, including identification, brief intervention, assessment, diagnosis, counseling, medical services, psychiatric services, psychological services, social services, and follow-up, for persons with alcohol and other drug problems. The overall goal of treatment is, to reduce or eliminate the use of alcohol or other drugs as a contributing factor to physical, psychological, and social dysfunction and to arrest, retard, or reverse the progress of any associated problems (IOM, 1990, p. 46).

This definition informs payers and providers of the need for assessment and treatment that goes far beyond the necessary, but not sufficient, determination of diagnosis and entry into a program or level of care that provides little variety of treatment options for the broad range of patient needs. But the report also posed a comprehensive and complex question whose answer remains yet unresolved: "Which individuals, with what kinds of alcohol or other drug problems, are likely to respond to what kinds of treatments by achieving what kinds of goals when delivered by which kinds of practitioners?" (IOM, 1990, p. 143).

Past and current research address aspects of this challenging question. But there has not been a coherent integration of findings that can guide the front-line clinician in day to day decisions about tailoring care to patient's specific needs. The field lacks a common approach and classification system meaningful to a diverse set of clinicians and patient populations, as regards: (1) kinds of individuals treated, (2) kinds of alcohol or other drug problems, (3) kinds of treatment, (4) kinds of goals, and (5) kinds of practitioners.

Consensus on these issues would help clinicians and payers use and pay for components of treatment in a rational and individualized treatment manner that would move the addiction treatment field away from ideology and fixed programs to an assessment-based, clinically-driven, outcomes-oriented, continuum of care. Such would allow treatment planning and placement to be truly individualized in a patient-friendly, respectful, efficient and effective, clinically-sophisticated manner.

However, it is not just the lack of conceptual clarity and research consensus that has provoked administrators, payers and employers to arbitrarily cut funding, limit reimbursement and increase the pressures on addiction treatment personnel to do more and more with less and less. Providers, practitioners and payers have themselves failed to adopt and fund treatments that do have consensus and demonstrated efficacy. (Hester & Miller, 1995; Bickel & McLellan, 1996). The result of such ideological and clinical constriction often is the inefficient and ineffective use of resources on treatment that is neither individualized nor assessment-based; and inadvertent collusion to allow the funding of a continuum of care that is too narrow and limited to effectively utilize a broader range of services that have demonstrated value.

THE ASAM PATIENT PLACEMENT CRITERIA

The role and current status of patient placement criteria has gained more attention as the proportion of the population enrolled in some type of managed care plan has increased (Center for Substance Abuse Treatment, 1995; Morey, 1996; Gastfriend & McLellan, 1997; McGee & Mee-Lee, 1997). Within this context, the *Patient Placement Criteria for the Treatment of Substance-Related Disorders* of the American Society of Addiction Medicine (Mee-Lee, Shulman & Gartner, 1996) has gained new prominence.

Reviews of the ASAM Criteria have pointed to the advantages and disadvantages of the criteria, the need for more validity studies and better inter-rater reliability in the assessment dimensions, and the limitations of the four levels of care (Center for Substance Abuse Treatment, 1995; Book, Harbin et al., 1995; Morey, 1996; McKay, Cacciola et al., 1997; Gastfriend & McLellan, 1997; McGee & Mee-Lee, 1997). These observations are relevant to the first edition of the ASAM criteria, published in 1992 (Hoffmann, Halikas et al., 1991), and to its predecessor, the Cleveland Criteria (IOM, 1990; McKay, McLellan & Alterman, 1992). Issues related to the need for a broader continuum of care, better definition of the assessment dimensions, and elimination of any perceived bias toward more intensive levels of care have been addressed in the second edition. While more needs to be done, the evolutionary improvement process continues.

Consensus-driven criteria such as those developed for ASAM remain to be validated empirically. Gastfriend and colleagues have initiated a four year, controlled, randomized, prospective trial of the ASAM *Patient Placement Criteria*, involving nine collaborative treatment sites and funded by the National Institute on Drug Abuse. With the urgency to preserve and improve the current addiction treatment service continuum, and the need for conceptual clarity to give direction and vision to the design and testing of treatment services, the ASAM Criteria serves a valid role in the here and now, to help shape the dialogue as the treatment field struggles to improve care for a variety of patient needs.

In such a system, diagnosis is necessary to ensure the need for addiction treatment rather than, or in addition to, mental health treatment. But beyond that, the addiction field requires use of *criteria* to guide proper patient placement; *practice guidelines* to promote effective individualized treatment modalities; and *outcomes data* to continuously improve both the criteria and guidelines. Patient placement criteria cannot address all of the necessary elements inherent in the complex question posed by the Institute of Medicine. However, they do provide direction to the elements of what kinds of individuals (assessment guided by six dimensions); with what kinds of alcohol and other drug problems (specific dimensional priorities from the multidimensional severity or level of functioning profile); and what kinds of treatments, goals and practitioners (levels of care and levels of service in a continuum of care delivered by a variety of disciplines appropriate to those levels and intensity of services).

Improving the ASAM Patient Placement Criteria. When the first edition of the ASAM Criteria was released in 1991, the private sector of the addiction treatment field was just beginning to realize the full impact of increasing managed care, which was eventually to see the closure of many inpatient hospital and residential programs. Since then, as managed care enrollment has grown dramatically in both the private and public sectors, more that 20 states require their publicly funded treatment programs to use the ASAM Criteria in the original form or a modified version. While not universally accepted by providers, payers and managed care organizations, the ASAM Criteria have defined the dialogue about placement criteria and the continuum of addiction care.

The original ASAM Criteria consisted of admission, continued stay and discharge criteria and defined four levels of care (separate for adults and adolescents) that reflected two years' work by two task forces of addiction treatment specialists, involving counselors, psychologists, social workers and physicians. The National Association of Addiction Treatment Providers (NAATP) joined with ASAM to create the criteria, based on a review of the literature and careful clinical consensus representing many years of addiction treatment experience. The task forces integrated and revised the Cleveland Criteria of the Northern Ohio Chemical Dependency Treatment Directors Association (NOCDTDA) with the NAATP criteria. Both NOCDTDA and NAATP agreed to allow a third set of national criteria to supersede their organizations' documents, despite considerable investments of time, effort and financial resources in developing the separate criteria.

Ten draft sets of criteria were produced after seven two-day, face-to-face meetings and innumerable phone calls and individual working sessions. Over 1,300 sets of field review draft criteria were distributed; feedback from these reviews and 15 field test sites were entered into the computerized database. The draft criteria were modified to accommodate the field test results.

Key features of the development process of the second edition (ASAM *PPC-2*) included the following:

- Response to questionnaires, roundtable discussions, Coalition for National Clinical Criteria meetings and general feedback from the field since 1991 resulted in the identification of a variety of gaps and areas for improvement;
- Subcommittees representing 126 different organizations within the Coalition, including ASAM committee members, prepared drafts of revised sections or new additions, which were distributed for field review;
- Reviewers were invited to participate in the field review and seventy, from a wide variety of organizations and field interests, including providers, payers, professional organizations, managed care organizations, industry and state and federal agencies gave detailed feedback; and
- Revisions to the drafts were made by a small working group based on widespread field and ASAM member leadership review; the final draft was approved by the Executive Committee of the Board of Directors of ASAM. The PPC-2 was reformatted to allow easier comparison of levels of service. However, not all sections were revised. What was revised and what was added was shaped by feedback from the field on perceived inadequacies and gaps.

The ASAM PPC-2: What Changed and What Didn't? The same six assessment dimensions were retained in *PPC-2*, with the exception that dimension 5, Relapse Potential, was expanded to Relapse/Continued Use Potential to recognize that some individuals have not achieved a period of recovery, from which to relapse. For them, assessment of the potential for continued use is determined to guide the decision on whether twenty four hour containment is necessary for any imminent, dangerous consequences of continued use of alcohol or other drugs.

In the adult criteria, Levels I and IV were not revised except for minor modifications made to update diagnostic terminology consistent with the *Diagnostic and Statistical Manual of Mental Disorders, 4th Edition* (American Psychiatric Association, 1994). For Level II, new criteria were developed to separate Intensive Outpatient, designated Level II.1, from Partial Hospitalization, Level II.5. In Level III, three levels of care were added to the original Medically-Monitored Intensive Inpatient now designated Level III.7. But, like Levels I and IV, only minor modifications updating the terminology to accord with the fourth edition of the American Psychiatric Association's *Diagnostic and Statistical Manual of Mental Disorders* (*DSM-IV*; 1994) were made to Level III.7.

The new Level III additions were in response to public sector concerns for criteria for halfway houses, extended residential and therapeutic communities. Hence the development of Clinically-Managed, Low Intensity Residential Treatment designated Level III.1; Clinically-Managed Medium Intensity Residential (III.3); and Clinically-Managed Medium/High Intensity Residential (III.5). Other new additions were: Early Intervention Services (Level 0.5) for individuals who do not meet criteria for a substance use disorder, but who are at high risk for alcohol or other drug problems e.g., DUI clients, school based early intervention; and Opioid Maintenance Therapy (OMT) to address methadone and levo-alpha-acetylmethadol (LAAM); and five levels of detoxification services criteria to match varying severities of withdrawal management needs in assessing Dimension 1, Acute Intoxication and/or Withdrawal Potential.

In the adolescent criteria, while criteria for Early Intervention Services, which have application to both adults and adolescents, were included, no specific revision of the adolescent criteria was done. This was not because such a revision would not be useful, but that was not an expressed priority from the field. With limited human and financial resources, this edition of necessity could not address the adolescent criteria.

THE MULTIPLE USES OF PATIENT PLACEMENT CRITERIA

The Role of Patient Placement Criteria in Individualized Treatment. If the addiction field is ever to realize the specificity of individualized treatment as articulated in the Institute of Medicine's question, the continuing tendency for reimbursement-driven treatment will necessarily be replaced with clinically-driven and eventually, outcomes-driven, individualized treatment. Although most clinicians agree that treatment should be individualized and based on assessment, their treatment plans often are similar, if not identical, across the population of patients they treat (Miller & Hester, 1986). This has changed little in the past ten years, with many programs still using the same pre-printed treatment plans, and listing generic problems, goals, objectives and strategies for every patient admitted.

Noting the strong influence reimbursement and the current payment system has on the failure of treatment programs to adopt effective research innovations, Bickel and McLellan pose the question: "Can management by outcome invigorate substance abuse treatment?" (Bickel & McLellan, 1996). Changing the system so that incentives are given for treatment outcome, they suggest, would move providers from the focus on process and enhance both treatment and cost-effectiveness.

FIGURE 1. Components of Individualized Treatment

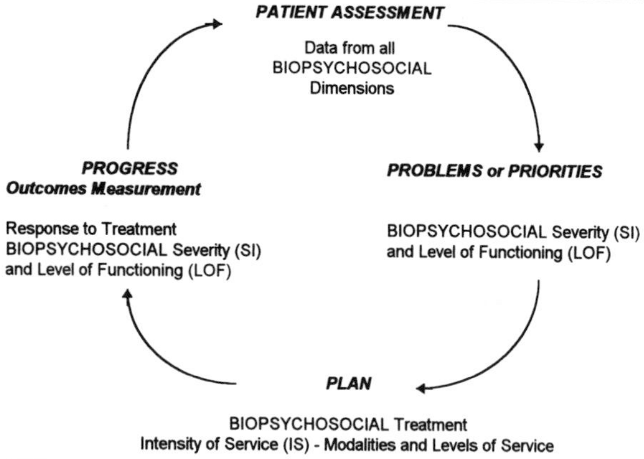

Conceptualizing individualized treatment as a continuous quality improvement cycle of ongoing assessment, treatment planning, progress or outcomes measurement, cycling back to assessment of what is working well or not (see Figure 1), has patient placement criteria, like diagnosis, being necessary, but not sufficient for good treatment outcome. As with the treatment of other disorders, the severity and level of functioning of the alcoholism or other drug addiction should determine the match to type and intensity of treatment, not diagnosis alone. Placement criteria are necessary as guidelines to the utilization of a broad continuum of care, but insufficient to provide the specificity of treatment planning for the particular severity and multidimensional functioning of any one individual.

Improved outcomes necessarily need a range of levels of care, but require integration of a broad range of services and treatment strategies to match services to needs (Gastfriend & McLellan, 1997). Thus, multidimensional patient placement criteria, as the ASAM Criteria are, play an important role in: (1) defining assessment dimensions to profile severity and level of functioning; (2) providing a common language, definition and description of a continuum of levels of service; (3) profiling a variety of patient severities and functioning that guide placement for the site of individualized services, matched to assessed needs; and (4) promoting the infrastructure needed to generate outcomes data that can be compared across systems and patient populations.

Patient placement criteria are an important resource and impetus to promote flexible, cost-effective treatment that conserves scarce health care resources. They give the addiction field guidelines that can encourage clinicians, payers and policymakers to broaden and fund the scope of available treatment options by placing greater emphasis on the continuum of care and encouraging flexible movement throughout the continuum.

The Role of Patient Placement Criteria in Providing and Managing Care. Improved communication between and among all involved in care, requires a common, unifying perspective on addiction. Understanding addiction as a biopsychosocial illness in its etiology, expression and treatment offers several advantages: it promotes productive integration of diverse perspectives; it explains clinical heterogeneity while preserving common clinical dimensions; it necessitates multidimensional assessment; and it promotes matching through comprehensive, individually-prescribed treatment. An additional advantage is that it reflects and promotes a holistic systems approach to assessing the clinical, social and economic impact of addiction on society.

In an increasingly cost-conscious, managed care environment, all systems and agencies involved in this biopsychosocial illness are realizing the cross-systems impact that addiction invokes. French and Martin (1996) provide a comprehensive overview of the cost estimates for drug abuse consequences that touch biomedical and perinatal services costs; the costs of psychiatric and mental health comorbidity; and the societal costs of crime, state and federal payments, and the cost special education programs.

Providers and managers of care must now think not only of clinical needs, but also of social needs if outcomes success is to be achieved (McGee & Mee-Lee, 1997). An expensive acute care hospitalization for detoxification, or a substance-induced, psychiatric emergency will likely only be soon repeated if attention is not paid to the patient's homelessness or transportation or childcare needs.

Thus the ASAM Patient Placement Criteria's focus on six dimensions to define biopsychosocial severity and level of functioning: (1) potential for acute intoxication and/or withdrawal; (2) biomedical conditions and complications; (3) emotional/behavioral conditions or complications; (4) treatment acceptance/resistance; (5) relapse/continued use potential; and (6) recovery environment (PPC-2, 1996), provides a useful structure to focus problem and priority identification.

Placing patients into appropriate treatment involves matching severity of illness and level of functioning with intensity of service. It is the process of moving from biopsychosocial assessment to determination of diagnoses and then a multidimensional profile. Dimensions that show high severity or low functioning allow for ready identification of specific problems that require priority attention. Specific services are designed into the treatment plan to address those priorities, and the "dose" of these services, define the resulting treatment plan. The least intensive, but safe level of service that allows the delivery of this treatment plan, determines the placement decision. Thus the patient placement decision is the final decision step in the process of providing and managing care (Gastfriend & McLellan, 1997) (See Figure 2).

Such a common language and decision tree process would allow payers and managed care organizations to know exactly how treatment programs and clinicians make decisions about patient placement and ongoing care, while at the same time facilitating communication between and among all parties involved in treatment and payment decisions.

The Role of Patient Placement Criteria in Monitoring Treatment Outcomes. Treatment outcomes often are thought of as *post-treatment* outcomes, typically involving a range of follow-up periods, from six months to two years, and tracking a wide variety of indicators involving alcohol and other drug use, healthcare utilization, family and vocational functioning, and legal involvement. Early outcomes work examined whether addiction treatment as a whole "worked" and produced behavior change. Then, comparisons of levels of care were examined, using gross divisions of inpatient versus outpatient treatment.

Without agreement on definitions of assessment dimensions and levels of care however, this outcomes research mirrors the difficulties of research before there was consensus on specific diagnostic criteria. Before the conceptual clarity and specificity of the later editions of the *Diagnostic and Statistical Manual of Mental Disorders* of the American Psychiatric Association, comparison of outcomes research on depression, for example, suffered from a variety of diagnostic criteria that made comparison of findings cumbersome, if not impossible. Outcomes research focused only on level of care and placement criteria has been an important refinement of the broad question of whether treatment works. However, more focused outcomes research has blossomed as the

FIGURE 2. Decision Tree to Match Assessment and Treatment Placement

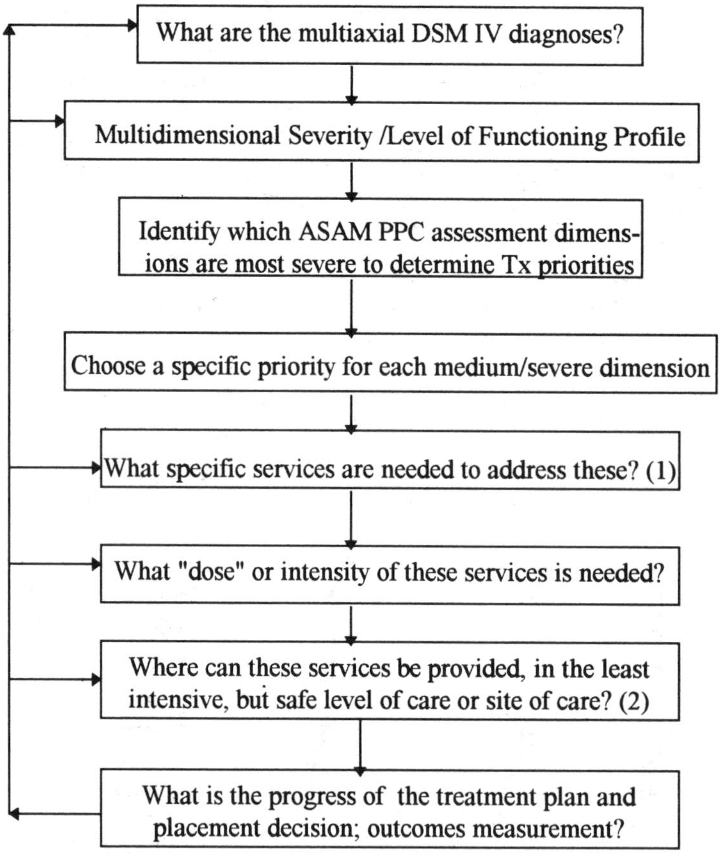
What are the multiaxial DSM IV diagnoses?
Multidimensional Severity /Level of Functioning Profile
Identify which ASAM PPC assessment dimens-ions are most severe to determine Tx priorities
Choose a specific priority for each medium/severe dimension
What specific services are needed to address these? (1)
What "dose" or intensity of these services is needed?
Where can these services be provided, in the least intensive, but safe level of care or site of care? (2)
What is the progress of the treatment plan and placement decision; outcomes measurement?

NOTES: (1) Consider services for each ASAM dimension (e.g., detoxification services for Dimension 1, medical services for Dimension 2, mental health services for Dimension 3, motivational interviewing/counseling/intervention for Dimension 4). (2) If medically managed treatment is necessary, a Level IV setting is used; if medically monitored treatment is appropriate, a Level III setting, "23-hour bed" or hospital-based partial hospitalization program may be appropriate.

"matching hypothesis" gained support (Project Match, 1997).

Conceptual clarity in outcome evaluation requires that other dimensions be considered besides just post-treatment outcome. Tonigan considers three dimensions critical: the purpose of the evaluation (addressing the programmatic value or worth versus collection of information to improve existing treatment services); the unit of analysis for the evaluation (individual versus group-based evaluation); and whether the post-treatment experience will be examined longitudinally or cross-sectionally (Tonigan, 1995).

Outcomes also might be conceptualized as *proximal* outcomes (short-term measures of patient satisfaction, engagement, attendance, and empathic connection that can provide feedback to a clinician to allow more immediate treatment planning improvement in almost real time); *process* outcomes (evaluation of assessment, treatment planning, service options and quality improvement mechanisms to identify skills, services or systems issues likely to affect outcome (e.g., failure to identify a specific priority and strategy in an assessment dimension rated as severe; or failure of the patient to receive a recommended level of care due to non-existence, waiting list, transportation or funding problems); and *post-treatment* outcomes as traditionally described above. (Filstead, personal communication, 1997).

As the treatment and research field can reach some consensus on conceptual clarity, clinicians and others involved in care will increasingly be able to apply the overwhelming diversity of instruments, tools, findings and guidelines to each aspect necessary to improve outcomes: (1) more accurate diagnosis; (2) better inter-rater reliability and validity in the development of a multidimensional severity or level of functioning profile; (3) more focused, pertinent problem/priority identification; (4) better targeted strategies having proven effectiveness; (5) more broadly trained practitioners, skilled in a variety of methodologies to promote greater flexibility to respond to individualized, assessed needs.

The outcome of a patient's treatment plan is monitored by assessing the changing biopsychosocial severity of illness and functioning for improvement or deterioration in any or all of the dimensions (but particularly the high-severity dimensions). Patient placement is informed by the ongoing repetition of this cycle and process, as the regularly assessed multidimensional profile is matched with the appropriate intensity of service (see Figures 1 and 2).

Outcome evaluation then, is interwoven in the progress evaluation of an individual's specific treatment plan, or in the *proximal* and *post-treatment* results of a group of subjects. It is interwoven in the *process* of the quality of biopsychosocial assessment, multidimensional profiling and priority identification and the specificity of matched services for the individual; but also in the variety and eclecticism of services available for the range of needs in the target service population. Outcome evaluation also is woven into the ongoing behavior change of the individual and group in producing less harm and progressing toward full recovery.

Patient placement criteria (PPC) provide a foundation and common language of multidimensional assessment areas, and a continuum of care that can help create and develop the infrastructure needed to move from fixed, program-driven to assessment-based, clinically-driven to outcomes-oriented, individualized treatment. The structure that PPC provides to the assessment and treatment process allows for a variety of feedback loops. These can inform and improve the interaction between placement criteria and each stage of assessment, priority identification and treatment matching.

Outcomes measurement loops and feeds back to: (1) sharpen refinement on which assessment dimensions should be discarded, added or improved in PPC; (2) differentiate between two or more compared levels of care, as to whether there are intrinsic differences, or whether essential differences lie in the mix and intensity of specific strategies and services; and (3) identify levels of care and services that should be added to or deleted from the continuum of care.

TABLE 1. Transition to Outcomes-Oriented Services

Implications for Personnel:
- Better training in biopsychosocial theories, modalities of treatment, assessment, outcomes research and documentation skills.
- Increased interdisciplinary functioning and teamwork.
- Increased individualized treatment and thorough case management.
- Increased reliance on research.

Implications for Public/Private Sector Programs:
- One quality and a single system of care that integrates public and private programs.
- One common set of criteria that are clinically-based rather than program-based.
- Consensus on outcomes evaluation models and measures
- Increase interdependence through improved incentives and equalization of over/under capacities.

Implications for Programs:
- Flexible lengths of stay in all levels of service.
- Overlapping levels of care for better continuity and efficiency.
- Expanded intensities of service, involving a wide continuum of service.
- More modalities of treatment from all biopsychosocial schools of thought.
- Innovative program structures that preserve the milieu yet allow individualized treatment.
- Development of proximal, process and post-treatment outcomes evaluation.

Implications for Payers:
- Reimburse or fund all levels of care.
- Increase incentives for less costly care and outcomes management.
- Fund thorough case management.
- Expand understanding of "medical necessity" to incorporate biopsychosocial severity.

IMPLICATIONS FOR CLINICIANS, PROGRAMS, PAYERS AND POLICY

The "re-tooling" of the addictions treatment system necessary to promote individualized treatment and the move to outcomes-driven treatment, requires a paradigm shift that has broad implications for personnel, programs, payment systems and the public and private sectors.

If clinicians are to be able to deliver high quality treatment while demonstrating fiscal responsibility, increased attention must be given to more flexible models of care, informed by research findings of demonstrated effective strategies and services. Greater accountability and shrinking resources preclude the selection of inefficient care offered by programs with a single level of care and a unitary treatment protocol for all patients, unrelated to patients' clinical heterogeneity assessed or (too often) not assessed.

As the population of patients in need of treatment becomes increasingly diverse—representing polydrug users; comorbid psychopathology, younger, psychologically and socially impoverished patients who are more diverse in gender and ethnicity—so too must the staff mix become more diverse. As assessment, level of functioning and severity of illness become multidimensional, old definitions of medical necessity that focused only on physical and psychiatric problems must give way to multidimensional profiles that allow better matching and diminish inefficient assignments to inappropriate levels of service.

Placing patients in appropriate treatment represents high-quality clinical care, respectful human concern, good financial and public health policy and sensible application of treatment outcome research. With payment, funding and policy changes, clinicians and programs can be incentivized to develop systems of care more innovative and effective than what currently exists.

Unless and until there is conceptual clarity and a broad interdisciplinary and cross-systems approach to PPC, we will likely continue with fragmented care and compromised outcomes. With a common focus and language, there lies the hope of approaching the level of clinical sophistication needed to answer the Institute of Medicine's comprehensive question and improve outcomes for the individuals we serve.

Note: Summaries of the ASAM Patient Placement Criteria for Adolescents and Adults are presented in Appendix B.

REFERENCES

American Psychiatric Association (1994). *Diagnostic and Statistical Manual of Mental Disorders, 4th Edition.* Washington, DC: American Psychiatric Association.

Bickel WK & McLellan AT (1996). Can management by outcome invigorate substance abuse treatment? *The American Journal on Addictions* 5:281–291.

Book J, Harbin H, Marques C, Silverman C, Lizanich-Aro S & Lazarus A (1995). The ASAM and Green Spring alcohol and drug detoxification and rehabilitation criteria for utilization review. *The American Journal on Addictions* 4:187–197.

Center for Substance Abuse Treatment (1995). *Treatment Improvement Protocol on Patient Placement Critera* (TIP No. 13; DHHS Publication No. (SMA) 95-3021). Rockville, MD: Center for Substance Abuse Treatment.

French MT & Martin RF (1996). The costs of drug abuse consequences: A summary of research findings. *Journal of Substance Abuse Treatment* 13:453–466.

Gastfriend DR & McLellan AT (1997). Treatment matching—Theoretic basis and practical implications. *Medical Clinics of North America* 81(4):945–966.

Hester RK & Miller WR (eds.) (1995). *Handbook of Alcoholism Treatment Approaches—Effective Alternatives.* Needham Heights, MA: Allyn and Bacon.

Hoffmann NG, Halikas JA & Mee-Lee D (1987). *The Cleveland Admission, Discharge, and Transfer Criteria: Model for Chemical Dependency Treatment Programs.* Cleveland, OH: Northern Ohio Chemical Dependency Treatment Directors Association.

Hoffmann NG, Halikas JA, Mee-Lee D & Weedman RD (1991). *Patient Placement Criteria for the Treatment of Psychoactive Substance Use Disorders.* Washington, DC: American Society of Addiction Medicine.

Institute of Medicine (1990). *Broadening the Base of Treatment for Alcohol Problems.* Washington, DC: National Academy Press.

McGee MD & Mee-Lee, D. (1997) Rethinking patient placement: The human services matrix model for matching services to needs. *Journal of Substance Abuse Treatment* 14(2):141–148.

McKay JR, Cacciola J, McLellan AT, Alterman AI & Wirtz PW (1997). An initial evaluation of the psychosocial dimensions of the ASAM criteria for inpatient and day hospital substance abuse rehabilitation. *Journal of Studies on Alcohol* 58:239–252.

McKay JR, McLellan AT & Alterman AI (1992). An evaluation of the Cleveland Criteria for inpatient treatment of substance abuse. *American Journal of Psychiatry* 149:1212–1218.

Mee-Lee D, Shulman G & Gartner L (1996). *Patient Placement Criteria for the Treatment of Substance-Related Disorders, Second Edition* (ASAM PPC-2). Chevy Chase, MD: American Society of Addiction Medicine.

Miller WR & Hester RK (1986). Matching problem drinkers with optimal treatments. In WR Miller & N Heather (eds.) *Treating Addictive Behaviors: Processes of Change.* New York, NY: Plenum Publishing Co.

Morey LC (1996). Patient placement criteria: Linking typologies to managed care. *Alcohol Health & Research World* 20:36–44.

Project MATCH Research Group (1997). Matching alcoholism treatments to client heterogeneity: Project MATCH posttreatment drinking outcomes. *Journal of Studies on Alcohol* 58:7–29.

Tonigan JS (1995). Issues in alcohol treatment outcome assessment. In JP Allen & M Columbus (eds.) *Assessing Alcohol Problems—A Guide for Clinicians and Researchers* (NIAAA Treatment Handbook Series 4; NIH Publication No. 95-3745). Rockville, MD: National Institute on Alcohol Abuse and Alcoholism, 143–154.

Weedman RD (1987). *Admission, Continued Stay and Discharge Criteria for Adult Alcoholism and Drug Dependence Treatment Services.* Irvine, CA: National Association of Addiction Treatment Providers.

CHAPTER 8

Alternative Therapies

Tacey Ann Boucher, B.A.
Thomas J. Kiresuk, Ph.D.
Alan I. Trachtenberg, M.D., Ph.D.

Overview of Complementary and Alternative Medicine (CAM)
Acupuncture/Electro-Acupuncture
Biofeedback
Nutrition/Vitamins
Hypnosis
Hallucinogens
Transcendental Meditation
Herbal Remedies
Restricted Environmental Stimulation (REST)
Transcranial Neuroelectric Stimulation (TENS)
Other Therapies
Culturally Specific Therapies
Spirituality/Prayer
Efficacy and Effectiveness of CAM

Addiction medicine has several treatment components that at present are labeled "Complementary" or "Alternative" Medicine (CAM). These components have not received special attention until recently, when scientific publications and the popular press have raised awareness of the treatment methods and their widespread use by the general public. In addition, recent surveys suggest that a large percentage of physicians are willing to consider the possibility that alternative medicine holds promise for the treatment of symptoms and disease. Scientific inquiry by academics and practitioners has begun and, while outcome data may not be available for many of these treatments, preliminary findings suggest that some may have efficacy. Further, it seems reasonable to suggest that some alternative treatments may offer symptomatic relief and/or benefits when the treatments are compatible with the patient's belief system.

The goal of this chapter is to provide basic information for (1) researchers and practitioners unfamiliar with CAM for the treatment of substance abuse, (2) clinicians who need to answer questions by patients who are using or interested in using CAM therapies, and (3) clinicians considering treatment alternatives for patients who have special needs and for whom traditional therapies have been ineffective or unacceptable.

To this end, the chapter will review several of the most frequently utilized or promising therapies, such as acupuncture, biofeedback, and nutrition. For each modality, a brief description is followed by a summary of the current state of the science. There also is a discussion of some of the primary debates and questions that confront both researchers and practitioners with regard to CAM.

OVERVIEW OF COMPLEMENTARY AND ALTERNATIVE MEDICINE (CAM)

The use of complementary and alternative medicine (CAM) extends around the world and, in many countries, constitutes the major form of treatment. The American Medical Association estimates that Americans spend over $10 billion annually on CAM treatments (Cronan, Kaplan et al., 1989). Other research suggests that U.S. consumers use CAM therapies for a wide variety of conditions, visiting CAM providers more frequently than they do primary care physicians (Eisenberg, Kessler et al., 1993). Use of CAM does not appear restricted by social class, educational levels, or gender (Anderson & Anderson, 1987; Hadley, 1988; Visser & Peters, 1990; Eisenberg, Kessler et al., 1993).

Patient and physician surveys are not the only indication of CAM's increasing prevalence. For instance, CAM is finding its way into medical school curricula, while leaders in health care and legislators debate coverage for alternative medicine. Changes in terminology from "unconventional" or "alternative" to "complementary" and "integrative" speak to the increasing alliance of disciplines.

The lack of a "magic bullet" to treat substance use disorders and the high rates of relapse from available treatments may help to explain the influx of CAM into addiction medicine relative to other specialties. Physicians may be more willing to refer or recommend patients to CAM practitioners for complaints that conventional medicine has been unable to eliminate. For example, the appearance of crack cocaine in the 1980s probably contributed to the popularity of acupuncture in treatment centers and drug courts throughout the U.S.

CAM and Substance Misuse. Some of the landmarks in the history of addiction medicine demonstrate the recurrent interaction of standard practice with modalities and practices considered by many to be "alternative." In the late 1800s, for example, sanitaria for persons with alcohol and opiate disorders offered, among other things, saline and electric baths. At the turn of the century, street vendors sold remedies for every complaint imaginable, including substance abuse. The remedies themselves could be addicting, were not regulated, and often contained a variety of ingredients—including morphine, cocaine, or even gold (Morgan, 1981). In the mid-1900s, treatment took a spiritual path as individuals participating in Alcoholics Anonymous and other self-help groups were instructed to turn their lives over to a Higher Power (Miller, 1990; Chappel, 1993). Today, Twelve Step programs and other programs based on the Alcoholics Anonymous (AA) model are the most popular forms of treatment in the U.S. (Vaillant, Clark et al., 1993; Peteet, 1993). More recently, the use of acupuncture, nutrition, and even homeopathy has been increasing for the treatment for substance abuse disorders, despite the lack of conclusive research regarding the efficacy of these modalities.

Although there have been many significant findings during the past two decades regarding the physiological, neurochemical, and pharmacological basis of addiction, many scientists and physicians are no longer searching for a "magic bullet," but a combination of therapies to prevent or treat addictive disease. Efforts to broaden the practitioner's treatment arsenal have run parallel with the growing popular acceptance of CAM. Addiction treatment programs increasingly use a combination of conventional and CAM methods, as in the use of acupuncture in conjunction with counseling and AA. Within the past three decades, researchers have begun to take an active role in exploring the potential CAM therapies for the treatment of addictive disorders. The fluid nature of CAM and the changing nature of addiction medicine provide a rich and variable field for research.

Defining CAM. CAM generally is conceptualized as those medical systems, interventions, applications, theories or claims that are not part of the dominant or conventional medical system. Attempts to create an operational definition have been limited in part by changing attitudes, as well as a growing body of clinical experience and scientific data.

The label "CAM" may be applied to entire systems of medicine such as Ayurvedic Medicine, a specific modality or therapy such as massage or ear acupuncture, a profession or practice such as naturopathy, or an explanation of efficacy such as spiritual rather than behavioral or neurochemical. The particular use of a modality also may be considered CAM, such as the use of dietary restrictions and recommendations for the prevention of relapse to drugs and alcohol, in contrast to heart disease or diabetes, for which dietary treatments are conventional. Similarly, spirituality has become a standard of care in addiction medicine through Twelve Step programs, but not for the treatment of cancer. Definitions of CAM also have been unable to distinguish between certain lifestyle choices and therapeutic regimes, such as a vegetarian diet, prayer, art therapy, or meditation. This chapter will not resolve these problems of definition but will attend to those practices commonly understood to be representative of CAM.

Researching CAM. Although the application of "Western" research methodology to the realm of CAM research is relatively recent, it would be short-sighted to assume that the difference between CAM and conventional therapies is that the former are unproved and the latter are proven. While there is scant knowledge about the efficacy of CAM modalities, it is generally accepted that many treatments currently recommended by U.S. physicians also lack adequate evidence of efficacy (Goldstein, 1989). Nevertheless, the relative absence of scientific validation is particularly detrimental to physician acceptance of CAM (Schachter, Weingarten & Kahan, 1993; Himmel, Schulte & Kochen, 1993; Visser & Peters, 1990; Wharton & Lewith, 1986; Hadley, 1988; Marshall, 1992; Berman, Singh et al., 1995). At present, case studies, clinic data, and pilot studies with inadequate power, randomization, and/or controls comprise the majority of CAM research.

Controlled research has become an integral part of the process of confirmation or refutation of medical interventions. Skepticism of new treatments is justified because numerous treatments throughout history have been initially applied with enthusiasm, only later to be found ineffective or even detrimental (Shapiro & Morris, 1978). Neither conventional nor CAM modalities should be excluded from this process simply on the basis of their origin. However, it is important for researchers studying CAM to have an understanding of the special methodological problems inherent in researching some of these treatments.

In particular, difficulties arise around the issue of standardization. Other obstacles, such as blindedness, also need to be considered. Acupuncture has become the most thoroughly researched and utilized CAM modality for the treatment of substance abuse in the U.S. The methodological challenges inherent to CAM and substance abuse research may be illustrated by the acupuncture experience (McLellan, Grossman et al., 1993).

Standardization: A large percentage of CAM therapies are rooted in philosophies and theories that focus on the individual rather than on a disease entity. For example, in traditional acupuncture, a person addicted to alcohol may be diagnosed in a number of ways, such as "damp heat condition of the liver" or "kidney yin heart deficiency." Treatment delivery would vary according to the diagnosis.

In the interests of clinical expediency and research, acupuncture treatment protocols for addictive disorders have been standardized in the U.S. The protocol was derived from the clinical practice at Lincoln Hospital in New York and was adopted by the National Association of Detoxification Acupuncturists (NADA). The method consists of three to five needles placed in each ear, and is referred to as bilateral auricular acupuncture (Smith & Khan, 1988; Culliton & Kiresuk, 1996; Brumbaugh, 1993).

However, the issue of standardization is controversial. The number of needles and the placement may vary from one practitioner to another, as may the use of unilateral or bilateral auricular placement or the use of other body points. The needles may or may not be moved or twirled. The skin may or may not be penetrated. Electrical current and moxibustion may or may not be used. The number of sessions attended over a given period of time also varies widely. As a result of this variation, it cannot be said that the acupuncture treatment experience as it exists in practice has been adequately researched.

Other Methodological Issues: These issues remain complex. If standardized points are to be used, how should these points reliably be identified? Some practitioners locate points by experience or by the responses of individual patients, while others use a galvanometer that measures skin impedance or conductivity. This relates to the level of practitioner experience. While it would be ideal to conduct double-blind studies of acupuncture, only an untrained practitioner could be blinded to whether they were delivering a true or sham treatment. However, an untrained acupuncturist lacks the skills to know by site or patient reaction whether they are needling the appropriate location, thereby calling into question treatment reliability. To date, reliability has taken priority over blindedness, and a double-blind trial of acupuncture has not been conducted.

Regarding appropriate control groups, the identification of appropriate placebo or sham needling points has been somewhat controversial. This is, in part, due to the inability of the majority of studies to find significant variation between true and sham treatment groups (Avants, Margolin et al., 1995; Lipton, Brewington & Smith, 1994; McLellan, Grossman et al., 1993; Washburn, Fullilove et al., 1993).

There are other important debates. For example, electro-acupuncture has been shown to release endorphins and this has been hypothesized to be the primary mechanism of action in the relief of opiate withdrawal symptoms. However, unstimulated needles have not been shown to release endorphins (McLellan, Grossman et al., 1993). If one accepts that the endorphin system is an important mechanism for the efficacy of acupuncture in treating drug abuse (McLellan, Grossman et al., 1993; Brewington, Smith & Lipton, 1994; Kosten, Kreck et al., 1986; Pomeranz, 1987), further investigation of electro-acupuncture is warranted.

Finally, researchers have failed to design a fair or standard set of expectations for acupuncture. Trials of acupuncture may deal with several stages of addiction, from detoxification (the majority of animal studies) to relapse prevention (U.S. human trials). Whether acupuncture is most effective for any particular stage of treatment is a question yet to be addressed.

Many practitioners and researchers question whether CAM can be accurately evaluated using conventional standards for research. Due to variations in philosophy, the individualization of treatments, and the difficulties in assigning appropriate placebos, some researchers and practitioners claim that Western science is not capable of assessing the efficacy of alternative medicine. However, before CAM therapies are further integrated into the health care system by physicians, clinics, and managed care organizations, they must be subjected to evaluation using methodologically sound research strategies (Lewith, Kenyon & Lewis, 1996). In the interim, it seems wise to maintain a reasonable skepticism while not arbitrarily discounting any approach that may improve treatment outcomes or reduce somatic complaints associated with addictive disorders.

Placebo and Non-Specific Effects. Particular attention has been paid to the relationship of CAM to placebo effects. At this time, the extent to which the effects of modalities like acupuncture are the result of placebo effects, rather than neurophysiologically induced treatment effects, remains unclear. Classically defined, a placebo effect is an effect that occurs after the administration of a therapeutically inactive substance. An example of a placebo treatment would be the substitution of a sugar pill in place of active medication. If the patient's physiological response to the sugar pill is similar to the effects that normally would result from active treatment, a placebo effect has occurred. Non-specific effects are effects that occur after treatments that do not use medication or procedures that have known or presumed mechanisms of action. In conventionally treated alcoholics, nonspecific treatments (as defined by Frank) such as information, evaluation only, advice, encouragement, and exhortation have been shown to have salutary effects (Miller & Hester, 1980; Miller & Baca, 1983; Powell, Penick et al., 1985; McLellan, Luborsky et al., 1985).

This is of more than academic interest, since variously defined placebo and nonspecific treatments are reputed to be as effective as certain forms of surgery, influence the effectiveness and action of medications and hypnosis analgesia in dentistry, enhance tolerance of pain, increase survival rates in the elderly, reduce post-surgical length of stay and requests for pain medication and, in certain individuals and cultures, cause death (Adler & Cohen, 1975; Justice, 1987; Lefcourt, 1973; Mumford, Schlesinger & Glass, 1982; Richter, 1957). Jerome Frank's work (1973) on the role of persuasion in healing has been followed by many reviews of the topic, indicating its importance in any form of treatment delivery (Kiresuk, 1988; Bowers & Clum, 1988; Shapiro, Struening & Shapiro, 1980).

Early accusations that the therapeutic effect of alternative therapies such as acupuncture were attributable to suggestibility stimulated experimentation on animals and an investigation of the inhibitory effects of naloxone on humans under hypnosis. Both lines of inquiry indicated that the effects of acupuncture were not explained by suggestion. The role of nonspecific effects in acupuncture or other alternative approaches to addiction has not been studied.

However, it should be noted that the placebo and its effects are not simple concepts. For example, Shapiro recounts conflicting finds in placebo research (Kiresuk, 1988). Efforts to replicate research findings have failed, even when identical procedures were used on highly similar populations and when the same subjects were given identical placebo stimuli in different environments. The placebo effect has not been consistently identified with particular patient characteristics that would label certain individuals as "placebo reactors," nor has it been found to be consistently related to the attributes of suggestibility, acquiescence, social desirability, dependency, external locus of control, and particular psychopathology.

In a major review and critique of the placebo literature, Kienle and Kiene (1996) challenge the commonly accepted 35% placebo effect concept popularized by Beecher. They found that Beecher had been misquoted in 10 of the 15 studies referring to him.

In their review of often-cited placebo studies, Kienle and Kiene have pointed out that the possibility of a specific effect being produced by a procedure never can be entirely ruled out. The authors state:

> "Precisely this possibility must be taken into account in the context of ligation of the internal mammary arteries. The first step in this operation, after all, is parasternal local anesthesia. However, such parasternal injections of local anesthetic agents are regarded in 'neural therapy' as the 'fundamental treatment for all cardiac diseases' (p. 45). . . . in the case of a therapy, in order to exclude the specific components it is necessary to know all the specific modes of action. At best, however, scientists can only know those modes of action that already have been discovered and already known

> to them as such. Consequently, there can never be any certainty that all specific modes of action have been excluded" (p. 40).

Kienle and Kiene make observations relevant to the many forms of CAM that are conceived of as dealing with the total system of the body's mental and physical energy, equilibrium, and self-sustaining tendencies:

> "It must be borne in mind that the term "placebo" will only be applied to the imitation of a treatment, not to all those therapeutic endeavors aimed at mobilizing the body's self-healing powers" (p. 40).
>
> "If our analyses erase doubts about the existence of the placebo effect in its narrow sense (i.e., true therapeutic effects achieved by mere imitation of a therapy), it does not rule out the possibility that the patient's self-healing powers may be influenced by a wide variety of non-pharmacological approaches" (p. 51).

Finally, these authors provide a statement that can serve as our recommendation regarding placebo concepts and CAM:

> "In our opinion, one should be particularly cautious about dismissing therapeutic procedures used in other cultures . . . [placebo] may all too easily mask our own ignorance and lack of understanding when research attempts at understanding would be more appropriate" (p. 51).

ACUPUNCTURE/ELECTRO-ACUPUNCTURE

In 1973, Wen noted that opium addicts being treated with post-surgical analgesic electro-acupuncture reported relief from withdrawal symptoms (Wen & Cheung, 1973). Wen conducted a series of studies using electro-acupuncture on addicted rodents and humans; his preliminary results suggested that opiate withdrawal symptoms could be mitigated through use of electro-acupuncture (Brewington, Smith & Lipton, 1994). Research on humans combined naloxone with EA, yielding a drug-free rate of 51% at one-year follow-up. Wen's distinction between craving and abstinence and between detoxification and subsequent psychosocial rehabilitation underlie the importance of his research (Wen & Cheung, 1973; Wen & Teo, 1975; Wen, 1979).

Five animal studies of electro-acupuncture have been conducted using opiate-addicted rats and mice, each demonstrating a significant decrease in morphine withdrawal symptoms in the EA group compared to controls (Brewington, Smith & Lipton, 1994). Findings suggest that EA may alleviate symptoms associated with addiction to various substances and may be responsible for various neurophysiologic changes observed. However, there have been no systematic controlled studies of electro-acupuncture for the treatment of substance abuse in humans. Further, the majority of studies have been criticized for faulty methodology, such as inadequate controls or, in the animal studies, excessive electrical current. To date no significant negative side effects have been reported.

Research in the United States has focused on daily auricular acupuncture therapy without electrical stimulation, based on a three- to five-point auricular acupuncture protocol established by Smith and colleagues at Lincoln Hospital in New York (Smith & Khan, 1988). Smith began treating detoxifying drug addicts with acupuncture in the mid-1970s, and his early clinical research showed promising results. Smith's protocol was used in the first two placebo-controlled studies conducted by Bullock and colleagues (Bullock, Umen et al., 1987; Bullock, Culliton & Olander, 1989), and the method subsequently was adopted as the standard treatment by the 4,000-member National Acupuncture Detoxification Association (NADA).

Both EA and acupuncture are based on the belief that health is determined by a balanced flow of *qi*, the vital life energy present in all living organisms. Practitioners identify 12 major energy pathways, called meridians, each linked to a specific internal organ or system. Thousands of acupoints exist along the meridians; in a traditional treatment setting, the practitioner places approximately 10 to 12 small stainless steel needles into the skin at points consistent with the diagnosis. This is said to help correct and re-balance the flow of energy and consequently to restore health. During EA, the needle is linked to a small device that delivers mild electricity to the acupuncture site.

A proposed hypothesis of addiction states that when naturally occurring endogenous opioids (e.g., enkephalins and endorphins) occupy specific receptor sites in the brain, individuals experience well-being and the absence of craving. Drugs such as ethanol may displace endogenous opioids by acting as agonist binding sites, over time inhibiting the production of the natural endorphins. Craving may be linked to the deficiency of enkephalins and endorphins, as well as other genetic or ethanol-related neurochemical deficits (McLellan, Grossman et al.,

1993; Brewington, Smith & Lipton, 1994; Kosten, Kreck et al., 1986; Culliton & Kiresuk, 1996).

The work of Pomeranz and Steiner provides support for the use of acupuncture to treat addictions. The work of Pomeranz suggests that acupuncture stimulates peripheral nerves, which send messages to the brain to release endorphins (Pomeranz, 1987). Steiner reported that acupuncture has been shown to alter levels of other central neurotransmitters, including serotonin and norepinephrine, and also to affect regulation of hormones such as prolactin, oxytocin, thyroid hormone, corticosteroid, and insulin (Steiner, May & Davis, 1982). These findings suggest a preliminary model for the efficacy of acupuncture for the treatment of pain, opiate and alcohol addiction.

Acupuncture has been studied in the treatment of heroin, alcohol, cocaine and nicotine addiction. Trials have shown detoxification success rates comparable to methadone for the treatment of opiate withdrawal. Several reviews of the literature have outlined study findings to date (see Table 1).

In brief, two controlled studies of alcoholic populations conducted by Bullock and colleagues (Bullock, Umen et al., 1987; Bullock, Culliton & Olander, 1989) resulted in significantly improved program attendance and less self-reported need for alcohol among the acupuncture group. The second study also found that placebo subjects self-reported over two times the number of drinking episodes and had twice the number of admissions to a hospital detoxification unit than did the subjects treated with acupuncture. A third study, by Worner, Zeller et al. (1992), found no significant differences between acupuncture, sham acupuncture, and standard treatment. However, the Bullock and Worner studies are difficult to compare because of differences in protocols and methods of analysis (Culliton & Kiresuk, 1996).

The first large-scale RCT to study the efficacy of acupuncture for the treatment of alcoholism, funded by the National Institute on Alcohol Abuse and Alcoholism, is expected to be completed in 1998.

Smith has reported positive outcomes in open clinical trials of acupuncture for the abuse of cocaine, "crack" cocaine, and other substances in 1,500 volunteers in New York City (Smith, 1988). However, the results of the first randomized placebo-controlled research study, conducted by Bullock et al. (N=438), showed that cocaine use did not differ significantly in the acupuncture and control groups posttreatment (Bullock, Pheley et al., 1997).

BIOFEEDBACK

Biofeedback did not develop out of any single healing tradition or discipline, but evolved in the 1950s and 1960s from several disciplines, including electronics and psychophysiology. Researchers envisioned a wide range of possible applications for the new modality (Winer, 1977). The 1960s were especially active periods of research into biofeedback. While the concept of controlling physiological functions was not new in the West, the outstanding finding of early work was that highly specific responses could be learned (Winer, 1977).

Research on the effects of biofeedback for substance abuse has been varied and the outcomes have been questionable. Some confusion has arisen as a result of the variety of biofeedback methods used. In the early 1970s, EEG alpha biofeedback was discounted as largely ineffective, particularly for the treatment of substance abuse. The addition of theta brainwave training to the alpha protocol has resulted in generally positive clinical reports (Fahrion, 1995; Peniston & Kulkosky, 1990), although there have been no controlled studies to evaluate these claims. Other researchers have turned to EMG or thermal biofeedback techniques (Denney, Baugh et al., 1991; Taub, Steiner et al., 1994). Recent advances in measurement devices have expanded biofeedback possibilities (Alternative Medicine, 1994).

TABLE 1. Review Articles: Acupuncture in the Treatment of Substance Misuse

Author(s)	Year	Focus	Drug(s)
Culliton, Kiresuk	1996	General review	multiple
Brewington, Smith, Lipton	1994	Review of efficacy	multiple
Brumbaugh	1994	Summary of practice	multiple
Brumbaugh	1993	History and protocol	multiple
McLellan, Grossman, Blaine, Haverkos	1993	Research methodology	multiple
Ter Riet	1990	Meta-analysis	multiple
Smith, Kahn	1989	General review	multiple
Whitehead	1978	Review of efficacy	multiple
Blum, Newmeyer, Whitehead	1978	Review of neurochemical mechanisms	opiates

Alpha-theta biofeedback attempts to rectify psychophysiological deficits by enhancing certain EEG frequencies. Although the method is controversial, there is some evidence to suggest that chemically dependent individuals may exhibit lower levels of alpha activity (8–11 Hz), suggesting elevation of beta-endorphin levels, which correlate with anxiety (Peniston & Kulkosky, 1989; Fahrion, 1995). Such individuals also may fail to produce appropriate theta activity (4–7 Hz), which has been linked to insight and resolution of unconscious issues (Cowan, 1993; Fahrion, 1995). Researchers have proposed that teaching patients to improve their alpha-theta levels provides an effective tool for the treatment of addictive disorders. It also has been hypothesized that perceived self-mastery and control over physiological states and stress may be linked to recovery (Cowan, 1993). However, due to a paucity of rigorous research, the true mechanism linking biofeedback to the treatment of substance abuse is unknown, as is the extent of treatment efficacy.

In the 1970s and 1980s, the Menninger Center for Applied Psychophysiology began using alpha-theta brainwave training to treat patients suffering from addictive disorders, with results that were generally positive. This work was modified by Peniston in the late 1980s, sparking a wave of research. Studies to date have shown similar responses regardless of the patient's drug of choice, although biofeedback has not yet been applied to methamphetamine addiction (Fahrion, 1995). The first large randomized study of alpha-theta training for addiction is being conducted by Fahrion in the Kansas Prison System, using group training equipment. Preliminary results from this study indicate that alpha-theta feedback plus conventional treatment is significantly more effective than conventional treatment alone (Fahrion, 1995). Previous studies of alpha-theta feedback have suggested effects on various measures of mood and personality associated with clinical outcomes (Fahrion, Walters et al., 1992; Peniston & Kulkosky, 1990). The studies have not yet controlled for the placebo and nonspecific effects inherent in increments of any therapy.

EMG biofeedback teaches the subject to reduce muscle tension rather than effect brainwaves. Research linking EMG biofeedback to the treatment of addictions has been scarce. The findings of case studies have been mixed, and only one randomized controlled trial has been conducted (by Taub, Steiner et al., in 1994), with EMG biofeedback as one of the four treatment arms (N = 125). The study found support for the use of EMG biofeedback for use in the prevention of relapse in alcoholics, and the EMG group did significantly better than the control group at the end of treatment and at follow-up.

Research has demonstrated that the use of alcohol or nicotine results in poor performance during biofeedback sessions. The ability of smokers to modulate blood pressure is restricted when compared to non-smokers and the ability to manipulate skin temperature appears to be greatest in non-smokers and impossible for those who smoke just prior to the biofeedback session (DeGood & Valle, 1978; Birnbaumer, Elbert et al., 1992; Grimsley, 1990; Schneider, Elbert et al., 1993).

NUTRITION/VITAMINS

Food and nutrition long have played an important role in various healing traditions. For example, in Traditional Chinese Medicine, food is categorized by its energetic qualities. Prevention-oriented prescriptions are emphasized, but in the case of illness, dietary interventions are tailored according to the physical characteristics of the patient and the illness disturbance (Alternative Medicine, 1994). Western medical traditions also have recognized the importance of nutrition, using foods and vitamins for the treatment of disease. Moreover, Western science has demonstrated links between basic vitamin-mineral deficiencies and some severe, chronic and even terminal diseases, such as iron and anemia, vitamin C and scurvy, or vitamin D and rickets. Conventional medicine also has begun to incorporate nutritional substances in the prevention, reduction, and elimination of various disease states, such as the use of lithium for the treatment of bipolar disorders (Schou, 1997).

An increasing number of clinical settings have begun to incorporate nutritional therapies. The American Dietetic Association has taken the position that improved nutritional status can improve the efficacy of addiction treatment through the effects of supplements, modified diets, and nutrition education (Beckley-Barrett & Mutch, 1990). Some advocates of nutritional therapy attribute depression and other ailments commonly found in drug users to nutritional deficits, undiagnosed hypoglycemia, and unidentified food allergies, and claim that these ailments can be treated through special diets, exercise, and vitamin and mineral supplements.

While scientists seem to agree that excessive intake of alcohol and other drugs may cause a number of nutritional deficiencies, including malnutrition

(Werbach, 1991; Mohs, Watson & Leonard-Green, 1990; Watson & Mohs, 1990), the link between nutritional disorders and addiction has not been fully accepted. Further, the belief that special diets or nutritional supplements may be viable adjunctive or stand-alone treatments for addictive disorders has not been adequately researched.

Preliminary human studies have shown positive results for nutritional programs or supplements used in the treatment of alcoholism, including increased abstinence, reduced craving, and decreased depression (Biery, Williford & McMullen, 1991; Mathews-Larson & Parker, 1987; Brown, Blum & Trachtenberg, 1990; Blum, Trachtenberg et al., 1988). In the early 1980s, one study of alcoholics conducted in a VA medical center compared a standard treatment group (which employed counseling and Twelve Step meetings) to a standard treatment group with the addition of a whole foods diet, nutritional supplements, and nutritional education. After six months, 81% of the nutrition group compared to 38% of the control group had maintained abstinence (Guenther, 1983). A clinical study followed patients through a 28-day treatment program that involved both counseling and nutrition. One year posttreatment, 74% of those treated for alcoholism remained abstinent (Beasley, Grimson et al., 1991). A third study conducted a six-month follow-up of 100 patients who had received six weeks of outpatient counseling and nutritional therapy; the researchers reported that 81% were abstinent from alcohol (Mathews-Larson & Parker, 1987).

Preliminary studies of amino acid supplementation also have shown promising results for the treatment of alcohol and cocaine abusers; however, no large-scale controlled trials have been conducted. Amino acid supplements were tested in an open trial on 30 alcoholic patients and 30 patients addicted to cocaine. Rates of relapse were 13% for the alcohol group and 20% for the cocaine group, and 53% and 87% respectively for the placebo controls (Blum, Trachtenberg et al., 1988). However, detailed experimental or clinical studies are limited, and published studies frequently are outdated, lack methodological rigor, or lack adequate sample size (Mohs, Watson & Leonard-Green, 1990).

Preliminary animal studies of the effects of various nutrients on withdrawal and free choice ethanol consumption also have shown promise (Werbach, 1991; Collipp, Kris et al., 1984; Eriksson, Pekkanen et al., 1980; Pekkanen, 1980; Forander, Kohonen & Suomalainen, 1958; Pekkanen, 1980; Register, Marsh et al., 1972; Rogers, Pelton & Williams, 1956). The majority of human and animal studies have been restricted to alcohol abuse, neglecting the impact of nutritional therapies on other types of addiction. Research on nutrition has been slow because of the lack of resources to follow up on promising preliminary results (Alternative Medicine, 1994).

HYPNOSIS

Hypnotic suggestion in one form or another has been used in healing throughout the world since ancient times, and was a focal point of treatment in early Greek healing temples (Alternative Medicine, 1994). However, the roots of modern hypnosis can be traced to the 18th century work of Franz Anton Mesmer. Mesmer used what he called "magnetic healing" to treat a variety of psychological and psychophysiological disorders (Alternative Medicine, 1994). Hypnotic methods have varied widely across time and still vary among practitioners (Katz, 1980). Despite controversy over the validity of hypnosis, historically it has been one of the most important techniques of psychotherapy (Katz, 1980).

In 1958, the American Medical Association (AMA) formally sanctioned the use of hypnosis as a valid medical treatment, and in the past 50 years the clinical application of hypnosis by physicians, dentists, psychologists, and other health professional for numerous ailments, including addictive disorders, has increased (Alternative Medicine, 1994). Hypnosis attempts to place patients in a state of attentive and focused concentration. Practitioners typically either lead patients through relaxation and mental imagery exercises, often using suggestion, or teach clients a form of self-hypnosis that can be practiced at home. Contrary to popular folklore, patients must be willing to undergo hypnosis, and despite being relatively unaware of their external environment, are capable of responding to stimuli (Alternative Medicine, 1994).

Research and clinical reports have repeatedly demonstrated that hypnotic methods are capable of generating notable changes in memory, cognition, perception, and physiology in susceptible subjects (Katz, 1980). Studies have shown that hypnosis may result in decreased sympathetic nervous system activity, oxygen consumption and carbon dioxide elimination, lowered blood pressure and heart rate, and increased activity in certain kinds of brain waves (Spiegel, Bloom et al., 1989). However, the difficulties in defining hypnosis, the inability to externally measure the presence of hypnotic states, and the lack of standardized methods in research have hampered efforts at systematic evaluation (Stoil, 1989). Moreover, the mechanism of action of hypnosis is unknown.

To say that "hypnosis" has been used as a treatment for an addictive disorder means that the patient could have been exposed to any of 20 or more strategies, including suggestions to reduce urges, symptom substitution, ego strengthening, or cue sensitization (Katz, 1980). Therefore, it is difficult to compare the few controlled studies that have been conducted. However, practitioner claims of cure rates as high as 95% have never been verified through controlled research (Haxby, 1995). Several case studies using either hypnotherapy or self-hypnosis for the treatment of substance abuse have reported successful outcomes (Page & Handley, 1993; Orman, 1991), and some clinical data has demonstrated high rates of abstinence (Johnson & Karkut, 1994; Schwartz, 1992).

Generally the results of controlled trials have not supported these preliminary findings. A review of four studies conducted prior to 1975 evaluated hypnosis negatively (Miller, Brown et al., 1995), and more recent studies have demonstrated some short-term benefits that were not maintained through follow-up (Rabkin, Boyko et al., 1984; Hyman, Stanley et al., 1986; Lambe, Osier & Franks, 1986). Moreover, hypnosis research has been criticized for lack of proper controls, insufficient follow-up, and poor reporting of data (Johnston & Donoghue, 1971; Katz, 1980; Holroyd, 1980). Most researchers and modern practitioners believe that hypnosis alone is not an effective therapy, although it may enhance the effects of other therapies (Haxby, 1995; Stoil, 1989).

HALLUCINOGENS

The hallucinogenic properties of lysergic acid diethylamide (LSD) were discovered by Hofmann in 1943 (Abraham, Aldridge & Gogia, 1996). Upon introduction to the United States and Europe in the late 1940s and 1950s, this and other potent agents became available to large populations for religious, recreational, and scientific purposes. By the mid-1960s, it appeared that medicine had found a new tool for generating insights into the mechanisms of nerve cell transmission or the phenomenology of schizophrenia, as well as a potential treatment for a number of psychiatric disorders (Riedlinger, Riedlinger, 1994).

However, beginning in 1968 a series of papers were published on the potential dangers of hallucinogens and, by the mid-1970s, the majority of investigations of therapeutic uses of hallucinogens had ceased (Halpern, 1996; Abraham, Aldridge & Gogia, 1996). It is difficult to know which came first, political and societal pressure to abandon research, or the belief that models of therapy were lacking validity (McKenna, 1996; Abraham, Aldridge & Gogia, 1996; Halpern, 1996). Only recently, with the introduction of new agents such as ibogaine, has there been a resurgence of interest in the potential utility of hallucinogens.

It is hypothesized that craving may be attenuated through the use of agonist/antagonists of the neurotransmitter serotonin (5-HT) (Halpern, 1996). LSD, like DMT, mescaline, and psilocybin, is characterized by a serotonergic pharmacology (McKenna, 1996) and is an agonist/antagonist at the discrete serotonin receptors 5-HT^1 and 5-HT^2. If serotonin mediates reward-related behavior, then LSD and other hallucinogens may exhibit anti-craving features (Halpern, 1996). Ibogaine also has an impact on serotonergic pharmacology and is an NMDA antagonist. Preclinical data suggest that these compounds are effective in attenuating the development of tolerance and in decreasing the symptoms of dependence on all abused substances examined to date (Popik, Layer & Skolnick, 1995).

During the 1960s and 1970s, the use of LSD to treat alcoholism was examined more thoroughly than any other therapeutic application of hallucinogenic agents. Reviews of these studies are mixed (Halpern, 1996; Abraham, Aldridge & Gogia, 1996; Ludwig, Levine & Stark, 1970). Studies of hallucinogens conducted in the 1960s and 1970s have been criticized on the basis of their varied methodology, dosing, and criteria for improvement, as well as their failure to adhere to the now-accepted double-blind, placebo-controlled standards. It now appears that, while case studies and data from open trials resulted in encouraging findings, controlled studies failed to replicate these results (Halpern, 1996). A review of the controlled studies conducted during that era suggests that, in the majority of studies, there were no differences between treatment and control groups and that LSD may even possess some anti-therapeutic effects (Ludwig, Levine & Stark, 1970).

Based on a review of single dose studies, it has been suggested that the anti-addictive properties offered by hallucinogens may be of limited duration. Peak-theories recommend dosing at intervals that would provide the addict a continuous or steady-state benefit, perhaps every one or two months (Halpern,

1996). However, prior to consideration of further testing involving dosing, the clinical difficulties of administering hallucinogenic agents to patients must be addressed. Besides their current status as Schedule I controlled substances, these include: (1) the need to monitor patients for hours or even days after the agent is administered to minimize adverse effects, (2) the need for therapists to be extensively trained as guides for the sessions, and (3) the degree of adjustment and accommodation that would be required by psychotherapists wishing to incorporate these drugs into practice (Riedlinger & Riedlinger, 1994).

The root bark of a West African shrub, Tabernanthe iboga yields the psychoactive indole alkaloid known as ibogaine (Rezvani, Overstreet & Lee, 1995). Ibogaine is a stimulant, but at high doses has hallucinogenic properties. Historically, ibogaine has been used in ritual by various indigenous populations, and has been used by hunters and warriors to help them stay awake for long periods. Like the classic hallucinogens, ibogaine is classified as a Schedule I controlled drug by the U.S. Drug Enforcement Administration (Popik, Layer & Skolnick, 1995). However, ibogaine is available throughout much of the European community, and in some locations is available as a treatment for substance abuse (Sheppard, 1994). Extremely high doses of ibogaine may be fatal (Popik, Layer & Skolnick, 1995).

Studies have been conducted to document the effects of ibogaine on a variety of animal populations. It has been shown to attenuate alcohol intake and reduce cocaine preference (Rezvani, Overstreet & Lee, 1995; Sershen, Hashim & Lajtha, 1994). Other research has focused on the impact of ibogaine on dopaminergic systems, opioid systems, serotonergic systems, intracellular calcium regulation, cholinergic systems, *g*-aminobutyric acidergic systems, voltage-dependent sodium channels, glutamatergic systems, *s* receptors, and adrenergic systems (see Popik, Layer & Skolnick [1995] for a review). Because ibogaine appears to be dose, setting, sex, and species specific, further testing is necessary.

Anecdotal reports regarding the efficacy of ibogaine as a treatment for substance abuse have been impressive, and preliminary human case studies using single doses of 700 to 1,800 mg of ibogaine for the treatment of heroin addiction have been encouraging but inconclusive (Sheppard, 1994). Despite its use on clinical populations in Europe, no controlled clinical data are available on the use of ibogaine for the treatment of addiction.

TRANSCENDENTAL MEDITATION

Transcendental Meditation (TM) was introduced to the U.S. in the 1960s by the Maharishi Mahesh Yogi as a simplified form of yoga (Alternative Medicine, 1994). Derived from the ancient Vedic tradition of India, TM is a significant component of the modern version of Ayurvedic medicine (O'Connell & Alexander, 1995). Proponents claim that TM is a truly holistic modality that addresses physiological, psychological, spiritual, and environmental/social factors. However, the Maharishi Mahesh Yogi and TM have been accused of deceptive practices and fraud. Some critics even cite evidence of considerable harm they claim can result from the practice of TM (Singer, 1992; Alexander, 1992; Chopra, 1992; Tompkins, 1992; Skolnick, 1992). Since its introduction, TM has been used for stress management and health maintenance, as well as a cure for conditions such as high blood pressure, chronic pain, and addiction.

TM philosophy holds that repetitive or perpetual stressors (chronic stress) may result in an ineffective or destructive stress response, producing homeostatic imbalance or disease in the body. TM proponents contend that substance abuse arises in an attempt to achieve homeostasis: "substance abuse is an attempt to optimize one's psychophysiological state [using] exogenous chemicals" (Walton & Levitsky, 1995). They add that substance abuse results in increased imbalance, distress, and eventually more drug use. Therefore, the objective of TM is to optimize psychophysiological function and balance, simply and naturally, thus interrupting the cycle of drug use and need for addiction. Proponents clearly state that this view does not exclude the possibility that genetic factors predisposing some individuals to addiction. Mechanisms involved in the maintenance of homeostasis may be affected by genetic differences, inclining these individuals toward substance abuse (Walton & Levitsky, 1995).

Studies indicate that during TM, physiological arousal is significantly decreased compared to simply resting with the eyes closed, as indicated by lowered respiration rate, skin conductance level, and plasma lactate level. Studies also have shown that in as little as four months, TM significantly increases serotonin and reduces cortisol, and that TM results in a more rapid mobilization, habituation, and stability of autonomic response to stressful stimuli than various control conditions (O'Connell & Alexander, 1995). The implications of these findings for addiction medicine have been reviewed in several publications (O'Connell & Alexander, 1995).

Over 30 studies have been conducted on the efficacy of TM for the treatment of substance abuse and addiction. While rates of success have ranged from 65% in a controlled study of recidivist alcoholics (with two-year follow-up) to 98% in a retrospective analysis of drug use among TM program participants, most of the studies have lacked rigorous methods and appropriate controls. Methodological difficulties have included a failure to control for the type of drug(s) used, the subject's history of use, or the severity of misuse. Moreover, studies often are retrospective, lack appropriate randomization and controls, are rarely blinded, and are usually conducted by researchers affiliated with the Maharishi University.

Gelderloos, Walton, Orme-Johnson and Alexander (1991) reviewed 24 studies and positively evaluated all of them despite often serious methodological flaws. Success in these studies was measured by "discontinued or reduced use"; however, reduced use was never quantified and abstinence not reported separately. Moreover, for 10 of the 24 studies, the authors simply cited a percentage of subjects who "succeeded," without adequately defining the criteria by which that was assessed.

Most recently, TM, biofeedback, and electro-neurotherapy were compared in a randomized controlled trial conducted by Taub, Steiner, Weingarten and Walton (1994). At two-year follow-up, the TM and biofeedback groups significantly increased their number of non-drinking days compared to the electric neurotherapy and AA/counseling controls. However, because non-drinking days were used as the primary indicator, rather than rates of abstinence, these findings are difficult to interpret and compare.

HERBAL REMEDIES

The use of herbal remedies to treat illness dates back to prehistoric times. The earliest written records detailing the use of medicinal herbs are found in Mesopotamian clay tablets, dated earlier than 2,000 BC. Numerous cultures have produced descriptions and systems of herbal medicine. Between 2,000 BC and 1 AD, the Chinese, Greek, and East Indian peoples all created materia medica that involved reviews of up to 1,000 substances. The current version of the Chinese materia medica (1977) contains over 5,500 entries (Alternative Medicine, 1994). While less than 10% of plants today have been extensively studied for medicinal applications, about 25% of Western medicines contain plant material (Alternative Medicine, 1994; McKenna, 1996). Further, the modern use of nearly 75% of plant-derived pharmaceutical products directly correlates with their traditional uses (Mack, 1997).

Critics argue that synthetic compound screening and combinatorial chemistry are more efficient and legitimate methods for determining pharmaceutical leads than pursuing ancient nostrums based on anecdotal evidence (Mack, 1997). Proponents point to the prevalence of plant materials in modern medicines and speak of the advantages of acknowledging thousands of years of experimentation and folk knowledge. For example, the Chinese ethnopharmacopoeia is written, taught in medical schools, and has been used and revised over thousands of years.

Difficulties in herbal research include: (1) the lack of a methodology capable of studying the herb as a whole, rather than its component parts or derivatives, (2) difficulties in securing a standardized preparation of herbs and herbal compounds, so that the results of trials will be reliable and valid, and (3) the cost of meeting FDA guidelines for the introduction of new pharmaceuticals. Because botanicals are not patentable (although they can be patented for use) producers of herbal remedies may not recover their expenses, and pharmaceutical companies will not risk the loss (Mack, 1997; Alternative Medicine, 1994). While many herbal remedies have few or no side effects, others can be toxic if improperly administered.

Despite these barriers, some research on herbal medicines for the treatment of addictive disorders has been conducted. The majority of this research has been conducted on traditional Chinese herbs. For example, Leguminosae Pueraria lobata (kudzu) is a perennial vine native to eastern Asia which also is widely available in the southern U.S. (Keung & Vallee, 1993; Althoff, 1994). An extract from the root, radix pueraria, has been used in traditional Chinese medicine for thousands of years as an antipyretic, antidiarrhetic, diaphoretic, antiemetic, amethystic, as well as an anti-inebriation agent (Keung & Vallee, 1993; Xie, Lin et al., 1994). An "anti-drunkenness" effect was first noted in 600 AD, and radix pueraria was described as a treatment for alcoholism circa 1580 (Keung & Vallee, 1993).

The mechanism of radix pueraria for the treatment of alcohol abuse is as yet elusive, although it seems unlikely that the herb works through either the ADH or the ALDH enzyme systems (Keung, 1993; Keung, Lazo et al., 1995). It has been hypothesized that kudzu may work through the serotonergic systems of the brain or through the calcium channels regulator (Lee, 1996).

One of the primary animal models used in the research of kudzu and its isoflavones, diadzin and diadzein, for the treatment of alcoholism (Keung & Vallee, 1993; Keung, Lazo et al., 1995) has been soundly criticized (McMillen & Williams, 1995; Piercy & Myers, 1995; Lankford, Roscoe et al., 1991; Lankford & Myers, 1994). However, four studies using Wistar (P) rats reported similar findings, including decreased peak blood alcohol levels, shortened sleep time induced by ethanol intoxication, and reduced free choice ethanol intake (Xie, Lin et al., 1994; Lee, 1996). Research currently is underway at Harvard on the use of kudzu for the treatment of alcoholism in humans, and an herbal compound containing kudzu is under investigation by the Center for Addiction and Alternative Medicine Research in Minneapolis.

Other herbs and herbal compounds have been identified by practitioners as effective in the reduction of craving and as adjuncts to the process of detoxification (Petri & Takach, 1990; Shanmugasundaram, Subramaniam et al., 1986), but virtually no work has been done to assess their efficacy.

RESTRICTED ENVIRONMENTAL STIMULATION (REST)

The late 1950s and 1960s marked the beginning of academic interest in research on sensory deprivation and restricted environments' effects on the mind and body (Lilly, 1956; Suedfeld, 1964; Lawes, 1963). By the 1970s, interest had expanded to include research on the effects of restricted environmental stimulation therapies (REST) on smoking and drinking behaviors (Suedfeld, Landon et al., 1972; Suedfeld & Ikard, 1974; Jacobson, 1971; Suedfeld & Best, 1977; Rank & Suedfeld, 1978).

Chamber REST and flotation REST are two methods used to produce a sensory-deprivation environment. In chamber REST, the individual is placed in a light- and sound-proof room for 12 to 24 hours, or longer, with only a comfortable bed, a toilet, and access to food. Flotation REST also takes place in an enclosed room or capsule, where the individual lies in a pool of water heated to skin temperature and supersaturated with Epsom salts to a specific gravity of 1.26 to 1.28. There the individual floats effortlessly for 30 to 150 minutes (Borrie, 1990–1991).

Researchers and practitioners have suggested a number of potential psychological and psychotherapeutic uses for REST in both adolescent and adult populations. By isolating the individual from the majority of sensory stimuli (visual, auditory, tactile, gustatory, and olfactory), REST attempts to reduce stress and increase introspection, allowing the body to re-balance and heal (Borrie, 1990–1991).

Various studies have shown that REST may result in a number of significant biochemical changes, including reduced plasma and urinary cortisol levels, plasma renin, ACTH, and aldosterone levels, lowered blood pressure, and enhanced EEG alpha activity following treatment (Turner & Fine, 1983; Barabasz, Barabasz & Mullin, 1983; McGrady, Turner et al., 1987; Borrie, 1990-1991). It also has been hypothesized that REST may stimulate the release of beta-endorphins and thus stimulate the brain's reward mechanism. REST has been offered by advocates as an alternative method, in place of alcohol or drugs, to stimulate pleasure centers.

The majority of clinical research involving REST and addictive disorders has focused on smoking behavior. In preliminary quasi-experimental and clinical designs, chamber REST has shown better results in smoking cessation than floatation REST. There is some evidence to indicate that chamber REST may result in significant reductions in smoking behavior, which may be sustained through a two-year follow-up (Suedfeld, 1990; Suedfeld & Ikard, 1974; Suedfeld, Landon et al., 1972). There also is some evidence to suggest that REST is more effective when combined with other treatment modalities. A six-month follow-up of a multimodal program using REST, self-management, and social support found an 88% rate of abstention. Another study combined REST with hypnosis and reported abstinence rates of 47% at four months posttreatment (Barabasz, Baer et al., 1986). While floatation REST has been considered unsuccessful for promoting smoking cessation (Borrie, 1990-1991), there is some evidence that the psychotic-like symptoms of persons intoxicated with PCP and LSD may be diminished using this therapy, and that floatation REST may be useful for the treatment of drug withdrawal symptoms (Borrie, 1990–1991).

Less research has been conducted on REST for the treatment of alcohol consumption, although preliminary studies of both floatation and chamber REST have shown positive results (Rank & Suedfeld, 1978; Borrie, 1990–1991).

TRANSCRANIAL NEUROELECTRIC STIMULATION (TENS)

Transcranial or cranial neuroelectric stimulation (TENS)—originally called "electrosleep"—was used in the 1950s for the treatment of insomnia (Brewington, Smith & Lipton, 1994). In a typical TENS session, surface electrodes are placed in the mastoid region (behind the ear) and, similar to electro-acupuncture, stimulated through use of a low amperage and frequency alternating current.

Several studies have examined the role of TENS in the treatment of addictions, particularly with opiates, but evidence in support of the therapy is weak. In a review of the literature by Brewington, Smith and Lipton (1994), three studies were identified as having somewhat positive results for the treatment of opiates. However, serious methodological flaws and a fourth study reporting that TENS is less effective than methadone reduce confidence in these findings (Gossop, Bradley et al., 1984). A fifth study, by Gariti, Auriacombe et al. (1992), was a randomized, double-blind study of hospitalized opiate and cocaine users who were detoxified by use of TENS. The rate of completion for the 12-day study was 88%. However, other than a comfortable detoxification, there were no significant differences between the active and placebo groups.

There have been fewer studies conducted on TENS use in alcohol-addicted populations, and available studies have focused primarily on reduction of anxiety and depression levels rather than consumption. These studies have either had serious methodological difficulties or yielded findings that failed to provide adequate support (Patterson, Patterson et al., 1993; Patterson, Krupitsky et al., 1994; Brewington, Smith & Lipton, 1994). More recently, Taub, Steiner, Weingarten and Walton (1994) conducted a study of TENS for the treatment of alcoholism. Even when administered in conjunction with AA and counseling, these investigators failed to find support for TENS as an effective treatment.

OTHER THERAPIES

Several other CAM therapies have been used to treat addictive disorders. At this time, clinical and controlled data on efficacy is lacking. A brief description of each follows.

Light Therapy. Light Therapy probably is best known for its use as a treatment for Seasonal Affective Disorder (SAD), a depressive disorder characterized by seasonal onset. While a specific mechanism of action for the efficacy of light therapy has not been identified, SAD may be linked to serotonin deficits. A connection between SAD and some cases of substance abuse has been proposed on the basis of preliminary case studies (Satel & Gawin, 1989; McGrath & Yahia, 1993) and basic science research (Dilsaver & Majchrzak, 1988). However, studies looking for seasonal patterns of alcoholism have produced contradictory findings (Eastwood & Stiasny, 1978; Poikolainen, 1982). Currently, proponents suggest the use of light therapy as an adjunct to standard treatment modalities for those patients with seasonal patterns of dependence.

Yoga and Tai-chi. Yoga is a discipline that has been practiced in India for thousands of years. In the West, the art known as yoga has adopted segments from this traditional lifestyle and involves postures, breathing, and meditation. Over 70 years of scientific research have shown that, through the practice of yoga, a person can learn to control certain physiological parameters, including blood pressure, cardiac and respiratory function, and brain waves (Alternative Medicine, 1994). It has been suggested that there may be some potential in the use of yoga for the treatment of addictive disorders and their related consequences. The rationale for using yoga sounds similar to that of biofeedback, although no scientific evidence exists regarding the mechanism of action. One pilot study (N = 59) has been conducted on the use of yoga for the treatment of opiate misuse (Shaffer & LaSalvia, 1997). All subjects received daily doses of methadone and the treatment group was taught hatha yoga, while the controls participated in traditional psychodynamic group therapy. The investigators found no significant differences in outcomes between the treatment group and the controls.

Tai-chi is a form of mid-range boxing that has been practiced in China for centuries. The philosophy and practice of Tai-chi applies the principles of Yin and Yang and the five-element theory. These principles also serve as the foundation of Traditional Chinese Medicine, practiced for thousands of years (Jou, 1991). As the popularity of Tai-chi increases in North America, it has been suggested that Tai-chi may assist individuals in the process of withdrawal and relapse prevention. No studies have been published on the efficacy of Tai-chi for the treatment of addictive disorders.

Eye Movement Desensitization and Reprocessing. Eye movement desensitization and reprocessing (EMDR) is a relatively new psychological method based on the belief that eye movement, such as the rapid eye movement (REM) experienced during sleep, can stimulate the brain's self-healing capacities (Coates, 1996). Research to date has focused on patients dealing with the psychological consequences of traumatic events such as sexual assault, combat, or grief (Shapiro, Vogelmann-Sine & Sine, 1994; Montgomery & Ayllon, 1994; Silver, Brooks & Obenchain, 1995). EMDR has been recommended for the treatment of addicts who have a history of mental trauma and who have progressed through the initial stage of withdrawal. Proponents believe that EMDR may aid recovery by helping addicts to confront their denial and distortions (Shapiro, Vogelmann-Sine & Sine, 1994). Research on the efficacy of EMDR for the treatment of substance abuse is ongoing.

Homeopathy. The theory of homeopathy was first described 200 years ago by Samuel Hahnemann (Abbott & Stiegler, 1996). In the early part of the 19th century, homeopathy was introduced to the U.S., where its apparent success in treating cholera won it many allies. By 1900, there were 22 medical schools, more than 100 hospitals, and around 15,000 practitioners in the U.S. dedicated to the practice of homeopathy. However, with the introduction of effective pharmacotherapies in the 1920s and the standardization of conventional physician training programs, homeopathic hospitals and schools all but disappeared from the U.S. (Alternative Medicine, 1994). Only recently has interest in homeopathy been increasing.

Homeopathy is based on the "Law of Similars," derived in part from observations made by Hippocrates. The law states that certain pharmacologically active substances are able to cure symptoms similar to those which they cause: "like cures like" (Anonymous, 1995). Hahnemann began testing this hypothesis by administering small doses of various substances to healthy volunteers to determine the agents' symptom profiles. He then administered the substances to patients by giving them substances that evoked symptoms similar to the patient's symptom profile (Mirman, 1994). Classical homeopathy asserts that each patient should receive one remedy tailored to his or her particular needs, while pluralist practitioners often prescribe several tinctures to a single patient.

The aspect of homeopathic theory that most disturbs critics is that many of the remedies are "potentized" by dilution with a water-alcohol solution. The final concentration may be diluted to a concentration as low as 10:30 or 10:20,000—far beyond the point at which any molecules of the medicine can be detected in the solution (Alternative Medicine, 1994). To date, no one has been able to provide an adequate explanation for the possible mechanism of homeopathy. Moreover, meta-analyses and reviews of homeopathic research have come to different conclusions regarding the efficacy of the modality (Reilly, Taylor et al., 1994; Kleijnen, Knipschild & Ter Reit, 1991; Hill & Doyon, 1990; Bellavite, 1990; Walach & Righetti, 1996; Kurz, 1992).

Homeopathy is being used to treat substance abuse in parts of Europe, including the U.K. and—to a lesser extent—in the United States. To date, no research on the treatment of substance abuse has been published. Several directions for future research have been suggested in previous texts (Alternative Medicine, 1994).

Relaxation Training. Relaxation training can take a number of forms, and sometimes is considered to be either a form of or a component of meditation. On the other hand, "relaxation" groups sometimes are used as controls in meditation research. Due to the variety of definitions and methods, studies of relaxation training may be difficult to compare. For the purposes of this chapter, relaxation does not include the practice of TM (see above).

In general, the intent of relaxation training in treating substance abuse has been to provide a substitute for the sedative effects of drugs such as alcohol and tobacco. However, the validity of this philosophy has been questioned, as many drugs may be consumed for their euphoric, rather than tranquilizing, effects (Klajner, Hartman & Sobell, 1984; Surawy & Cox, 1986). Further, relaxation training for the treatment of substance abuse has not fared well in evaluations of past research (Holder, Longabaugh et al., 1991; Miller, Brown et al., 1995). While one study did show a reduction in measures of anxiety with the use of relaxation training, the reduction was not linked to consumption (Ormrod & Budd, 1991). Finally, biofeedback (Taub, Steiner et al., 1994) has been shown to be more effective as the relaxation for treating substance use disorders, as measured by abstinence rates.

Flower Essence/Aromatherapy. Flower Essence elixirs are created when the "energy resonance" of flowers floating in a bowl of water is absorbed by water molecules. The resulting elixir is consumed and, advocates claim, promotes gentle healing in the body by "adjusting the vibrational frequency" of an individual's cells. The elixirs are thought to be free of negative effects (Morrison, 1995).

Aromatherapy is a branch of herbal medicine in which the aroma of fragrant essential oils extracted from various forms of vegetation is inhaled, applied to the skin, or ingested orally. Advocates believe that the oils promote the prevention and treatment of disease, that each oil has special pharmacologic properties, and that they function by easily penetrating bodily tissues because of their small molecular size.

There have been clinical reports to suggest that these two modalities are being used for the treatment of substance abuse. However, no data are available on their efficacy.

CULTURALLY SPECIFIC THERAPIES

Cultural differences exist regarding the use and meaning of psychoactive drugs. For example, psychoactive substances have been used in religious ceremonies or rituals across cultures and time, from the use of alcohol in Jewish and Christian ceremonies to the use of peyote by Native Americans, or opium in certain Hindu marriages (Westermeyer, Lyfoung et al., 1991). Cultural differences in treatment philosophies and modalities also exist. Below we discuss the case of Native American treatment of alcohol abuse. Many of the issues raised in this example are applicable to the debates regarding other culturally specific treatments.

Despite the absence of national data on prevalence, it has long been recognized that alcohol is a major drug of abuse among Native Americans, who have a mortality rate from alcoholism three to four times greater than the U.S. average (Seale & Muramoto, 1993). Further, Native Americans tend to do poorly in standard addiction treatment programs, as measured by reported rates of relapse (Kivlahan, Walker et al., 1985; Query, 1985; Hanson, 1985). American Indian tribes are recognized as having unique cultures, heritage and needs. Thus it has been suggested that treatment services for this and other minority populations need to be more sensitive to the cultural perspectives and issues of importance to the populations served (Hanson, 1985).

The range of Native American practices used for the treatment of drug and alcohol abuse is quite diverse, including sweat lodges, herbs, cultural reeducation, peyote rituals, and sun dances (Hall, 1986; Beauvais & La Boueff, 1985). Although cultural supports are given attention by some treatment centers, the availability of culturally specific programs is limited, and funding is scarce (Seale & Muramoto, 1993).

The lack of agreement among treatment professionals and the literature regarding the meaning of "culturally-specific" or "culturally-appropriate" treatments have made replication and research difficult. The terms imply that the programs are in some way designed for, adapted to, or responsive to the needs of the individual, based on his or her cultural heritage. However, the essential differences between culturally-specific and non-specific programs have not been defined. Moreover, there are no standards for defining the cultural competence of counselors, or formal policies in place for regulating referrals of clients to culturally specific treatment programs.

Despite the argument that cultural identification may influence the patient's response to treatment (Babor & Mendelson, 1986; Iber, 1986; Flores, 1985–1986; Hall, 1986), research results have been contradictory (Beauvais, 1992; Brady, 1995; Flores, 1985–1986; Hanson, 1985; Parker, Jamous et al., 1991; Rhodes, Mason et al., 1988; Beauvais & La Boueff, 1985; Westermeyer & Peake, 1983; Westermeyer & Neider, 1986; Gutierres, Russo & Urbanski, 1994). There has been some evidence to suggest that Native Americans who withdraw temporarily from their cultural communities may have better rates of recovery (Westermeyer & Peake, 1983). Conclusions and recommendations have been drawn from epidemiologic data, as controlled research has not been conducted.

However, at this point, research on treatment outcomes has failed to separate the cultural influences from the demographic differences among ethnic groups, using the appropriate statistical controls (Babor & Mendelson, 1986). Not all tribes or individuals are going to respond identically to any given situation (Beauvais & La Boueff, 1985), and ethnicity is not the only factor to be considered, as substance abuse problems also vary with age, gender, education, and socioeconomic status (Seale & Muramoto, 1993; Westermeyer & Peake, 1983). Further, researchers have failed to consider the possibility that culturally specific programs also may be used to treat non-native peoples (Babor & Mendelson, 1986), a point which, if verified, could contribute to future support and funding.

SPIRITUALITY/PRAYER

Although spirituality and religion frequently are used in the prevention and treatment of substance abuse, drugs and alcohol also have been used during religious rituals and in the quest for transcendence.

However, there is some evidence to suggest that for some individuals, participation in new religions may actually relieve psychiatric symptoms and psychological distress, including substance abuse and dependence. Through the provision of a community, the New Religious Movements (NRMs) may serve a "halfway house" function, helping participants recover and reintegrate into the mainstream (Muffler, Langrod et al., 1997).

Indigenous therapies for the treatment of addictions often have incorporated aspects of the spiritual. Spirit dancing, peyote ceremonies, and Shakerism have been used by Native Americans; spiritual churches, "Voodoo" and Black Hebrew divine healing by African-Americans. Hispanic traditions have used Curanderismo, Pentecostalism and Espiritismo for the treatment of addictions (Singer & Borrero, 1984). For example, in Espiritismo it is believed that people may be made ill or cured by spirits. The treatment of spiritists, then, involves mediums who perform spiritual consultations and conduct cleansing rituals (Singer & Borrero, 1984; Muffler, Langrod et al., 1997). Healing that addresses a patient's faith and culture may be an effective method of treatment (Muffler, Langrod et al., 1997; Miller, 1997).

Evangelical and Pentecostal churches teach individuals seeking treatment to pray and to depend on God. This belief teaches that by accepting Jesus Christ as savior, an individual may be "born again," free himself or herself from the mistakes of the "former" life, and thus recover. Programs like Teen Challenge developed with the belief that religious conversion is the only reality capable of combating addictions (Muffler, Langrod et al., 1997).

Mainline Christianity—Protestant and Catholic—is more frequently associated with addiction treatment than other religious or spiritual forms. Historical programs emphasized religious values, but have been transformed into more secular approaches. The majority of efforts sponsored by Protestant and Catholic churches have been institutionalized and are housed in hospitals or community centers rather than church facilities. The influence of earlier Protestant treatment efforts, and the emphasis on religious values, still is seen in popular Twelve Step programs such as Alcoholics Anonymous and Narcotics Anonymous. Successful completion of the steps in these programs requires that members turn their lives over to God or some Higher Power.

Religious involvement is the third major source of help for individuals trying to change involuntary habits. In a large number of studies, epidemiological research has demonstrated a negative correlation between personal "religiousness" and substance use (Benson, 1992). However, there has been no direct research into spirituality/prayer as a treatment for substance abuse. A body of research does provide evidence that spiritual healing can occur even when psychological factors have been controlled, as in plant or animal research (Hodges & Scofield, 1995). However, whether prayer is a nonspecific treatment or whether it is efficacious has yet to be determined. Studies on the efficacy of prayer and spirituality are necessary to further its potential use in the treatment of substance abuse, primarily in relapse prevention.

EFFICACY AND EFFECTIVENESS OF CAM

There may be confusion regarding the benefits to be obtained from CAM and indeed, for any current treatment of addictive disorders. In the treatment of medical conditions, benefits may consist of alleviation or cure of the underlying illness or disease. In this sense, antibiotic treatment of certain forms of respiratory illness may be considered efficacious. On the other hand, many treatments can be shown to be effective in dealing with symptoms related to cancer, even though the underlying condition does not improve. In addiction treatment, even if proper controls cannot be put together to adequately show efficacy, treatments that lack efficacy may still have "effectiveness" for some populations. If the treatment procedure helps make the patient accessible to treatment, if drop-out rates are reduced, if employment rates improve or other side effects are alleviated, then that treatment has effectiveness and may be worthwhile. At this time, probably all addiction treatment—conventional and CAM— can be considered potentially effective but not efficacious.

Spontaneous Remission. The addiction literature is full of evidence that some individuals "mature out" of their substance abuse (Klingemann, 1991; Stall & Biernacki, 1986; Klingemann, 1992; Tuchfield, 1981; Prugh, 1986). The most familiar example of addicts maturing out or spontaneously remitting can be seen in the many recovered nicotine addicts. Another well-known example of addicts who spontaneously stopped using is the American servicemen who stopped using heroin on their return from Vietnam. In addition, we know that the majority of humans who use psychoactive drugs (including nicotine, caffeine and alcohol), never misuse substances (Kalant, 1989).

If there are interventions that can interrupt addiction or increase the probability of spontaneous remission or maturing out, then these would be valuable tools in the clinical armamentarium. Many of the CAM treatments described in this chapter may serve this purpose.

Drop-outs and Relapse. Conventional treatment approaches to substance abuse have been criticized on a number of levels. Drop-out rates from most treatment programs are extremely high; rates of 50% or more are common for alcohol misuse and 75% to 85% for cocaine or crack cocaine addiction (Hoffman, Caudill et al., 1994; Vaillant, Clark et al., 1993; Chappel, 1993; Mammo & Weinbaum, 1991). Some facilities do not include drop-out rates in their outcome data and significantly inflate their rates of success and misrepresent their capabilities to the general public. A 25% overall success rate (success measured as abstinence) is typical within conventional treatment facilities. Further, despite the substantial amount of time, energy, and money expended by conventional treatment facilities, there has been scant assessment of the effect of their programs on costs to society or reduction in arrest rates.

Critics also have pointed out that treatment facilities often are not available or accessible to special populations and the high rate of drop-out and relapse of these special populations suggests that their needs are not being met. Further, critics question whether current programs are unable to handle the full scope of physiological, sociological, and psychological problems of clients, all of which must be addressed during recovery. The increasing treatment reliance in the U.S. on the Minnesota Model and the prominence of the Twelve Step self-help groups (AA, NA, CA, etc.) despite the lack of controlled research demonstrating the efficacy of these programs has been questioned (Chiauzzi & Liljegren, 1993; Hester, 1994; Holder, Longabaugh et al., 1991).

One way to combat these deficiencies would be to increase the frequency, intensity, and/or types of treatment services offered. Many studies have indicated that increasing the number of modalities provided increases rates of treatment success (Hoffman, Caudill et al., 1994). In this context, Alternative Medicine (AM) approaches promise to expand and enrich the treatment continuum and improve overall treatment outcome.

CONCLUSIONS

There are several reasons to consider the use of CAM. Some treatments show promise in preliminary clinical reports and early research efforts, which suggest that at least effectiveness (as described above) may be expected. In addition, however, many of the treatments described in this chapter have the capacity to elicit salubrious changes in personal and interpersonal status. One of the lessons of biofeedback, yoga, Tai-chi, relaxation, transcendental meditation, is that the individual can learn to control mental and physical processes. In that way, the gateway to the concept of self-efficacy is opened. A common concept underlying many of CAMs is the elicitation and strengthening of natural healing processes. This concept of self-healing may be one of the learning experiences of the patients.

These aspects may help account for the current excitement and curiosity about use of CAM. It has been demonstrated that patients are finding their way through conventional and CAM systems, even in the absence of secure information regarding efficacy. It is the responsibility of therapists to help these individuals by providing information regarding the potential benefits and dangers of CAM, and to be open to the possibility that they may be avenues for personal and interpersonal growth in addition to narrowly defined symptom reduction and management.

REFERENCES

Abbott A & Stiegler G (1996). Support for scientific evaluation of homeopathy stirs controversy. *Nature* 383.

Abraham HD, Aldridge AM & Gogia P (1996). The psychopharmacology of hallucinogens. *Neuropsychopharmacology* 14:285–298.

Adler R & Cohen N (1975). Behaviorally conditioned immunosuppression. *Psychosomatic Medicine* 33:333–340.

Alexander CN (1992). Closing the chapter on Maharishi Ayur-Veda (Letter). *Journal of the American Medical Association* 267(10):1337.

Alternative Medicine (1994a). *Alternative Medicine: Expanding Medical Horizons: A Report to the National Institutes of Health on Alternative Medical Systems and Practices in the United States* (NIH Publication Number 94-066). Rockville, MD: National Institute on Drug Abuse.

Althoff S (1994). Weed for alcoholics. *Natural Health* 24(2):18.

Anderson E & Anderson P (1987). General practitioners and alternative medicine. *Journal of the Royal College of General Practitioners* 37:52–55.

Anonymous (1995). What is Homeopathy: BOIRON Reference Guide, France: BOIRON.

Anonymous (1994). Much ado about nothing? *Consumer Reports* 59(3):201–206.

Avants SK, Margolin A, Chang P, Kosten TR & Birch S (1995). Acupuncture for the treatment of cocaine addiction. *Journal of Substance Abuse Treatment* 12(3):195–205.

Babor RF & Mendelson JH (1986). Ethnic/religious differences in the manifestation and treatment of alcoholism. *Annals of the New York Academy of Sciences* 472:46–59.

Barabasz AF, Baer L, Sheehan DV & Barabasz M (1986). A three-year follow-up of hypnosis and restricted environmental stimulation therapy for smoking. *International Journal of Clinical & Experimental Hypnosis* 34(3):169–181.

Barabasz M, Barabasz AF & Mullin CS (1983). Effects of brief Antarctic isolation on absorption and hypnotic susceptibility—preliminary results and recommendations: A brief communication. *International Journal of Clinical and Experimental Hypnosis* 31(4):235–238.

Beasley JD, Grimson RC, Bicker AA, Closson WJ, Heusel CA & Faust FI (1991). Follow-up of a cohort of alcoholic patients through 12 months of comprehensive biobehavioral treatment. *Journal of Substance Abuse Treatment* 8(3):133–142.

Beauvais F (1992). An integrated model for prevention and treatment of drug abuse among American Indian youth. *Journal of Addictive Diseases* 11(3):63–81.

Beauvais F & LaBoueff S (1985). Drug and Alcohol abuse intervention in American Indian communities. *The International Journal of the Addictions* 20(1):139–171.

Beckley-Barrett LM & Mutch PB (1990). Position of The American Dietetic Association: Nutrition Intervention in treatment and recovery from chemical dependency. *Journal of the American Dietetic Association* 90(9):1274–1277.

Bellavite P (1990). Research in homeopathy: Data, problems and prospects (Review) (Italian). *Annali dell Istituto Superiore di Sanita* 26(2):179–187.

Benson PL (1992). Religion and substance use. In JF Schumaker (ed.) *Religion and Mental Health*. New York, NY: Oxford University Press, 211–220.

Berman BM, Singh BK, Lao L, Singh BB, Ferentz KS & Hartnoll SM (1995). Physicians' attitudes toward complementary or alternative medicine: A regional survey. *Journal of the American Board of Family Practice* 8(5):361–366.

Biery JR, Williford JH & McMullen EA (1991). Alcohol craving in rehabilitation: Assessment of nutrition therapy. *Journal of the American Dietetic Association* 91(4):463–466.

Birnbaumer N, Elbert T, Rockstroh B, Kramer J, Lutzenberger W & Grossmann P (1992). Effects of inhaled nicotine on instrumental learning of blood pressure responses. *Biofeedback and Self Regulation* 17(2):107–123.

Blum K, Newmeyer JA & Whitehead C (1978). Acupuncture as a common mode of treatment for drug dependence: Possible neurochemical mechanisms. *Journal of Psychedelic Drugs* 10(2):105–115.

Blum K, Trachtenberg MC, Elliott CE et al. (1988). Enkephalinase inhibition and precursor amino acid loading improves inpatient treatment of alcohol and polydrug abusers: Double-blind placebo-controlled study of the nutritional adjunct SAAVE. *Alcohol* 5(6):481–493.

Borrie RA (1990–1991). The use of restricted environmental stimulation therapy in treating addictive behaviors (Review). *International Journal of the Addictions* 25(7A–8A):995–1015.

Bowers TG & Clum GA (1988). Relative contribution of specific and nonspecific treatment effects: Meta-Analysis of placebo-controlled behavior therapy research. *Psychological Bulletin* 103(3):315–323.

Brady K (1995). Prevalence, consequences and costs of tobacco, drug, and alcohol use in the United States. In CM Circa (ed.) *Training About Alcohol and Substance Abuse for All Primary Care Physicians*. Proceedings of a conference sponsored by the Josiah Macy, Jr. Foundation, October 2–5, 1994, Phoenix, AZ.

Brewington V, Smith M & Lipton D (1994). Acupuncture as a detoxification treatment: An analysis of controlled research. *Journal of Substance Abuse Treatment* 11(4):289–307.

Brown RJ, Blum K & Trachtenberg MC (1990). Neurodynamics of relapse prevention: A neuronutrient approach to outpatient DUI offenders. *Journal of Psychoactive Drugs* 22(2):173–187.

Brumbaugh AG (1994). Acupuncture. In NS Miller (ed.) *Principles of Addiction Medicine*. Chevy Chase, MD: American Society of Addiction Medicine.

Brumbaugh AG (1993). Acupuncture: New perspectives in chemical dependency treatment. *Journal of Substance Abuse Treatment* 10(1):35–43.

Bullock ML, Culliton PD & Olander RT (1989). Controlled trial of acupuncture for severe recidivist alcoholism. *Lancet* 1(8652):1435–1439.

Bullock ML, Kiresuk TJ, Pheley AM, Culliton PD & Lenz SK (1998). Auricular acupuncture in the treatment of cocaine abuse. *The Journal of Substance Abuse Treatment* 15(2):1–8.

Bullock ML, Umen AJ, Culliton PD & Olander RT (1987). Acupuncture treatment of alcoholic recidivism: A pilot study. *Alcoholism, Clinical & Experimental Research* 11(3):292–295.

Chappel J (1993). Long-term recovery from alcoholism. *Recent Advances in Addictive Disorders* 16(1):177–187.

Chiauzzi E & Liljegren S (1993). Taboo topics in addiction treatment. An empirical review of clinical folklore. *Journal of Substance Abuse Treatment* 10(3):303–316.

Chopra D (1992). Closing the chapter on Maharishi Ayur-Veda (Letter). *Journal of the American Medical Association* 267(10):1338.

Coates C (1996). Sympathetic threads. *Common Boundary* 40–45.

Collipp PJ, Kris VK, Castro-Magana M et al. (1984). The effects of dietary zinc deficiency on voluntary alcohol drinking in rats. *Alcoholism* 8(6):556–59.

Cowan JD (1993). Alpha-theta brainwave biofeedback: The many possible theoretical reasons for its success. *Biofeedback* 21(2):11–16.

Cronan TA, Kaplan RM, Posner L, Blumberg E & Kozin F (1989). Prevalence of the use of unconventional remedies for arthritis in a metropolitan community. *Arthritis & Rheumatism* 32(12):1604–1607.

Culliton P & Kiresuk T (1996). Overview of substance abuse acupuncture treatment research. *Journal of Alternative and Complementary Medicine* 2(1):149–159.

DeGood DE & Valle RS (1978). Self-reported alcohol and nicotine use and the ability to control occipital EEG in a biofeedback situation. *Addictive Behaviors* 3:13–18.

Denney MR, Baugh JL & Hardt HD (1991). Sobriety outcome after alcoholism treatment with biofeedback participation: A pilot inpatient study. *International Journal of the Addictions* 26(3):335–341.

Dilsaver SC & Majchrzak MJ (1988). Bright artificial light produces subsensitivity to nicotine. *Life Sciences* 42:225–230.

Eastwood MR & Stiasny LS (1978). Psychiatric disorder, hospital admission, and season. *Archives of General Psychiatry* 35:769–771.

Eisenberg DM, Kessler RC, Foster C, Norlock FE, Calkins DR & Delbanco TL (1993). Unconventional medicine in the United States. Prevalence, costs, and patterns of use. *The New England Journal of Medicine* 328(4):246–52.

Eriksson K, Pekkanen L & Russi M (1980). The effects of dietary thiamin on voluntary ethanol drinking and ethanol metabolism in the rat. *British Journal of Nutrition* 43(1):1–13.

Fahrion SL (1995). Human potential and personal transformation. *Subtle Energies* 6(1):55–88.

Fahrion SL, Walters ED, Coyne L & Allen T (1992). Alterations in EEG amplitude, personality factors, and brain electrical mapping after alpha-theta brainwave training: A controlled case study of an alcoholic in recovery. *Alcoholism: Clinical & Experimental Research* 16(3):547–552.

Flores PJ (1985–1986). Alcoholism treatment and the relationship of Native American cultural values to recovery. *The International Journal of the Addictions* 20(11–12):1707–1726.

Forander O, Kohonen J & Suomalainen H (1958). *Quarterly Journal of Studies on Alcohol* 19:379–387.

Frank J (1973). *Persuasion and Healing*. Baltimore, MD: The Johns Hopkins University Press.

Gariti P, Auriacombe M, Incmikoski R et al. (1992). A randomized double-blind study of neuroelectric therapy in opiate and cocaine detoxification. *Journal of Substance Abuse* 4(3):299–308.

Gelderloos P, Walton KG, Orme-Johnson D & Alexander CN (1991). Effectiveness of the Transcendental Meditation program in preventing and treating substance misuse: A review. (Review). *International Journal of the Addictions* 26(3):293–325.

Goldstein A (1989). Introduction. In A Goldstein (ed.) *Molecular and Cellular Aspects of the Drug Addictions*. New York, NY: Springer-Verlag, xiii–xviii.

Gossop M, Bradley B, Strang J & Connell P (1984). The clinical effectiveness of electrostimulation vs oral methadone in managing opiate withdrawal. *British Journal of Psychiatry* 144:203–208.

Grimsley D (1990). Nicotine effects on biofeedback training. *Journal of Behavioral Medicine* 13(3):321–326.

Guenther RM (1983). Nutrition and alcoholism. *Journal of Applied Nutrition* 35(1):44–46.

Gutierres SE, Russo NF & Urbanski L (1994). Sociocultural and psychological factors in American Indian drug use: Implications for treatment. *International Journal of the Addictions* 29(14):1761–1786.

Hadley C (1988). Complementary medicine and the general practitioner: A survey of general practitioners in the Wellington area. *New Zealand Medical Journal* 101:766–768.

Hall RL (1986). Alcohol treatment in American Indian populations: An indigenous treatment modality compared with traditional approaches. *Annals of the New York Academy of Sciences* 472:168–178.

Halpern JH (1996). The use of hallucinogens in the treatment of addiction. *Addiction Research* 4(2):177–189.

Hanson B (1985). Drug treatment effectiveness: The case of racial and ethnic minorities in America—Some research questions and proposals. *The International Journal of the Addictions* 20(1):99–137.

Haxby D (1995). Treatment of nicotine dependence (Review). *American Journal of Health-System Pharmacy* 52(3):265–281.

Hester R (1994). Outcome research: Alcoholism. In M Galanter & H Kleber (eds.) *The American Psychiatric Press Textbook of Substance Abuse Treatment*. Washington, DC: American Psychiatric Press, 35–43.

Hill C & Doyon F (1990). Review of randomized trials of homeopathy. *Revue and Epidemiologie et de Sante Publique* 38(2):139–147.

Himmel W, Schulte M & Kochen MM (1993). Complementary medicine: Are patients' expectations being met by their general practitioners? *British Journal of General Practice* 43(371):232–235.

Hodges RD & Scofield AM (1995). Is spiritual healing a valid and effective therapy. *Journal of the Royal Society of Medicine* 88:203–207.

Hoffman JA, Caudill BD, Koman JJ & Luckey JW (1994). Comparative cocaine abuse treatment strategies: Enhancing client retention and treatment exposure. *Journal of Addictive Diseases* 13(4):115–128.

Holder H, Longabaugh R, Miller W & Rubonis A (1991). The cost effectiveness of treatment for alcoholism: A first approximation. *Journal of Studies on Alcohol* 52(6):517–540.

Holroyd J (1980). Hypnosis treatment for smoking: An evaluative review. *The International Journal of Clinical and Experimental Hypnosis* 28(4):341–357.

Hyman G, Stanley R, Burrows G & Horne D (1986). Treatment effectiveness of hypnosis and behavior therapy in smoking cessation: A methodological refinement. *Addictive Behaviors* 11(4):355–365.

Iber FL (1986). Treatment and recovery in alcoholism: Contrast between results in white men and those in special populations. *Annals of the New York Academy of Sciences* 472:189–194.

Jacobson GR (1971). Sensory Deprivation and Field Dependence in Alcoholics. Unpublished doctoral dissertation, Illinois Institute of Technology.

Johnson D & Karkut R (1994). Performance by gender in a stop-smoking program combining hypnosis and aversion. *Psychological Reports* 75(2):851–857.

Johnston EJ & Donoghue JR (1971). Hypnosis and smoking: A review of the literature. *The American Journal of Clinical Hypnosis* 13(4):265–272.

Jou TH (1991). *The Tao of Tai-Chi Chuan: Way to Rejuvenation*. Warwick, NY: Tai-Chi Foundation.

Justice B (1987). *Who Gets Sick: Thinking and Health*. Houston, TX: Peak Press.

Kalant H (1989). The nature of addiction: An analysis of the problem. *Molecular and Cellular Aspects of the Drug Addictions*. New York, NY: Springer-Verlag, 1–28.

Katz N (1980). Hypnosis and the addictions: A critical review. *Addictive Behaviors* 5:41–47.

Keung WM (1993). Biochemical studies of a new class of alcohol dehydrogenase inhibitors from Radix puerariae. *Alcoholism: Clinical & Experimental Research* 17(6):1254–1260.

Keung WM, Lazo O, Kunze L & Vallee BL (1995). Daidzin suppresses ethanol consumption by Syrian golden hamsters without blocking acetaldehyde metabolism. *Proceedings of the National Academy of Sciences* 92(19):8990–8993.

Keung WM & Vallee BL (1993). Daidzin and daidzein suppress free-choice ethanol intake by Syrian golden hamsters. *Proceedings of the National Academy of Sciences* 90(21):10008–10012.

Kienle GS & Kiene H (1996). Placebo effect and placebo concept: A critical methodological and conceptual analysis of reports on the magnitude of the placebo effect. *Alternative Therapies* 2(6):39–54.

Kiresuk TJ (1988). The placebo effect: Public policy and knowledge transfer. *Knowledge: Creation, Diffusion, Utilization* 9(4):435–475.

Kivlahan DR, Walker D, Donovan DM & Mischke HD (1985). Detoxification recidivism among urban American Indian alcoholics. *American Journal of Psychiatry* 142(12):1467–1470.

Klajner F, Hartman L & Sobell M (1984). Treatment of substance abuse by relaxation training: A review of its rationale, efficacy and mechanisms. *Addictive Behaviors* 9(1):41–55.

Kleijnen J, Knipschild P & Ter Riet G (1991). Clinical trials of homeopathy. *British Medical Journal* 302(6772):316–323.

Klingemann HK (1992). Coping and maintenance strategies of spontaneous remitters from problem use of alcohol and heroin Switzerland. *International Journal of the Addictions* 27(12):1359–1388.

Klingemann HK (1991). The motivation for change from problem alcohol and heroin use. *British Journal of Addiction* 86(6):727–744.

Kosten TR, Kreck MJ, Ragunath J & Kleber HB (1986). A preliminary study of beta endorphin during chronic naltrexone maintenance treatment in ex-opiate addicts. *Life Sciences* 31(1):5559.

Kurz R (1992). Clinical medicine vs. Homeopathy. *Paditrie und Padologie* 27(2):37–41.

Lambe R, Osier C & Franks P (1986). A randomized controlled trial of hypnotherapy for smoking cessation. *Journal of Family Practice* 22(1):61–65.

Lankford MF & Myers RD (1994). Genetics of Alcoholism: Simultaneous presentation of a chocolate drink diminishes alcohol preference in high drinking HAD rats. *Pharmacology, Biochemistry and Behavior* 49(2):417–225.

Lankford MF, Roscoe AK, Pennington SN & Myers RD (1991). Drinking of high concentrations of ethanol versus palatable fluids in alcohol-preferring (P) rats: Valid animal model of alcoholism. *Alcohol* 8:293–299.

Lawes TGG (1963). Schizophrenia, "Sernyl", and sensory deprivation. *British Journal of Psychiatry* 109:243–250.

Lee DY (1996). Animal Studies of NPI-028 for Addiction (herbal compound). Unpublished data.

Lefcourt H (1973). The functions of illusions of control and freedom. *American Psychologist* 28(3):417–425.

Lewith GT, Kenyon JN & Lewis PJ (1996). *Complementary Medicine: An Integrated Approach*. Oxford, England: Oxford University Press.

Lilly JC (1956). *Mental Effects of Reduction of Ordinary Levels of Physical Stimuli on Intact, Healthy Persons* (Psychiatric Research Reports, No. 5). Washington, DC: American Psychiatric Association.

Lipton DS, Brewington V & Smith M (1994). Acupuncture for crack-cocaine detoxification: Experimental evaluation of efficacy. *Journal of Substance Abuse Treatment* 11(3):205–215.

Ludwig A, Levine J & Stark L (1970). *LSD and Alcoholism: A Clinical Study of Treatment Efficacy*. Springfield, IL: Charles C Thomas.

Mack A (1997). Biotechnology turns to ancient remedies in quest for sources of new therapies. *The Scientist* 11(1):8–9.

Mammo A & Weinbaum D (1991). Some factors that influence dropping out from outpatient alcoholism treatment facilities. *Journal of Studies on Alcohol* 54(1):92–101.

Marshall R (1992). Integration of alternative and orthodox practices among general practitioners in Auckland, New Zealand. In W Andritzky (ed.) *Yearbook of Cross-Cultural Medicine and Psychotherapy*. Berlin, Germany: VWB—Verlag fur Wissonschaft und Bildung, 133–143.

Mathews-Larson J & Parker RA (1987). Alcoholism treatment with biochemical restoration as a major component. *International Journal of Biosocial Research* 9(1):92–104.

McGrady A, Turner JW, Fine TH & Higgins JT (1987). Effects of biobehaviorally-assisted relaxation training on blood pressure, plasma renin, cortisol, and aldosterone levels in borderline essential hypertension. *Clinical Biofeedback and Health: An International Journal* 10(1):16–25.

McGrath RE & Yahia M (1993). Preliminary data on seasonally related alcohol dependence. *Journal of Clinical Psychiatry* 54(7):260–262.

McKenna DJ (1996). Plant hallucinogens: Springboards for psychotherapeutic drug discovery. *Behavioural Brain Research* 73:109–115.

McLellan AT, Grossman DS, Blaine JD & Haverkos HW (1993). Acupuncture treatment for drug abuse: A technical review. *Journal of Substance Abuse Treatment* 10(6):569–576.

McLellan A, Lubrosky L, Cacciola J et al. (1985). New data from the Addiction Severity Index. Reliability and validity in three centers. *Journal of Nervous and Mental Diseases* 172:412–423.

McMillen BA & Williams HL (1995). Volitional consumption of ethanol by fawn-hooded rats: Effects of alternative solutions and drug treatments. *Alcohol* 12(4):345–350.

Miller WR (1990). Spirituality: The silent dimension in addiction research. The 1990 Leonard Ball Oration. *Drug and Alcohol Review* 9:259–266.

Miller WR (1997). Spiritual aspects of addictions treatment and research. *Mind/Body Medicine* 2(1):37–43.

Miller W & Baca L (1983). Two-year follow-up of Bibliotherapy and therapist-directed controlled drinking training for problem drinkers. *Behavioral Therapy* 14:441–450.

Miller WR, Brown JM, Simpson TL et al. (1995). What works? A methodological analysis of the alcohol treatment outcome literature. In RK Hester & WR Miller (eds.) *Handbook of Alcoholism Treatment Approaches: Effective Alternatives (2nd edition)*. Boston. MA: Allyn and Bacon, 12–44.

Miller W & Hester R (1980). The addictive behaviors: Treatment of alcoholism, drug abuse, smoking and obesity. *Treating the Problem Drinker: Modern Approaches*. Oxford, England: Pergamon Press.

Mirman JI (1994). *What the Hell Is Homeopathy?* New Hope, MN: New Hope Publishers.

Mohs ME, Watson RR & Leonard-Green T (1990). Nutritional effects of marijuana, heroin, cocaine, and nicotine. *Journal of the American Dietetic Association* 90(9):1261–1267.

Montgomery R & Ayllon T (1994). Eye movement desensitization across subjects: Subjective and physiological measures of treatment efficacy. *Journal of Behavior Therapy and Experimental Psychiatry* 25(3):217–230.

Morgan HW, ed. (1981). *Drugs in America: A Social History, 1800–1980*. Syracuse, NY: Syracuse University Press.

Morrison H (1995). Nature's Prozac. *Natural Health* 25(3):80–88.

Muffler J, Langrod JG, Richardson JT & Ruiz P (1997). Religion. In JH Lowinson, P Ruiz, RB Millman & JG Langrod (eds.) *Substance Abuse: A Comprehensive Textbook, 3rd edition*. Baltimore, MD: Williams and Wilkins, 492–499.

Mumford E, Schlesinger H & Glass G (1982). The effects of psychological intervention on recovery from surgery and heart attacks: An analysis of the literature. *American Journal of Public Health* 7 2(2):141–151.

O'Connell DF (1995). Possessing the self: Maharishi Ayur-Veda and the process of recovery from addictive diseases. In DF O'Connell & CN Alexander (eds.) *Self Recovery: Treating Addictions Using Transcendental Meditation and Maharishi Ayur-Veda*. New York, NY: Harrington Park Press, 459–496.

O'Connell DF & Alexander CN (1995). Introduction: Recovery from addictions using Transcendental Meditation and Maharishi Ayur-Veda. In DF O'Connell & CN Alexander (eds.) *Self Recovery: Treating Addictions Using Transcendental Meditation and Maharishi Ayur-Veda*. New York, NY: Harrington Park Press, 1–12.

Orman D (1991). Reframing of an addiction via hypnotherapy: A case presentation. *American Journal of Clinical Hypnosis* 33(4):263–271.

Ormrod J & Budd R (1991). A comparison of two treatment interventions aimed at lowering anxiety levels and alcohol consumption amongst alcohol abusers. *Drug and Alcohol Dependence* 27(3):233–243.

Page R & Handley G (1993). The use of hypnosis in cocaine addiction. *American Journal of Clinical Hypnosis* 36(2):120–123.

Parker L, Jamous M, Marek R & Camacho C (1991). Traditions and innovations: A community-based approach to substance abuse prevention. *Rhode Island Medical Journal* 74:281–286.

Patterson M, Krupitsky E, Flood N, Baker D & Patterson L (1994). Amelioration of stress in chemical dependency detoxification by transcranial electrostimulation. *Stress Medicine* 10:115–126.

Patterson MA, Patterson L, Winston JR & Patterson SI (1993). Electrostimulation in drug and alcohol detoxification: Significance of stimulation criteria in clinical success. *Addiction Research* 1:130–144.

Pekkanen L (1980). Effects of thiamin deprivation and antagonism on voluntary ethanol intake in rats. *Journal of Nutrition* 110:937–944.

Peniston EG & Kulkosky PJ (1990). Alcoholic personality and alpha-theta brainwave training. *Medical Psychotherapy* 3:37–55.

Peniston EG & Kulkosky PJ (1989). Alpha-theta brainwave training and beta-endorphin levels in alcoholics.

Alcoholism: Clinical & Experimental Research 13(2):271–279.

Peteet JR (1993). A closer look at the role of a spiritual approach in addictions treatment. *Journal of Substance Abuse Treatment* 10(3):263–267.

Petri G & Takach G (1990). Application of herbal mixtures in rehabilitation after alcoholism. *Planta Medica* 56(6):692–693.

Piercy KT & Myers RD (1995). Tomato juice, chocolate drink, and other fluids suppress volitional drinking of alcohol in the female Syrian golden hamster. *Physiology and Behavior* 57(6):1155–1161.

Poikolainen K (1982). Seasonality of alcohol-related hospital admissions has implications for prevention. *Drug and Alcohol Dependence* 10:65–69.

Pomeranz B (1987). Scientific basis of acupuncture. *Acupuncture: Textbook and Atlas*. Berlin, Germany: Springer-Verlag.

Popik P, Layer RT & Skolnick P (1995). 100 years of ibogaine: Neurochemical and pharmacological actions of a putative anti-addictive drug. *Pharmacological Reviews* 47(2):235–253.

Powell B, Penick E, Read M & Ludwig A (1985). Comparison of three outpatient treatment interventions: A twelve-month follow-up of men alcoholics. *Journal of Studies on Alcohol* 46(4):309–312.

Prugh T (1986). Recovery without treatment. *Alcohol Health and Research World* 11(1)(24):71–72.

Query JMN (1985). Comparative admission and follow-up study of American Indians and whites in a youth chemical dependency unit on the North Central Plains. *The International Journal of the Addictions* 20(3):489–502.

Rabkin SW, Boyko E, Shane F & Kaufer J (1984). A randomized trial comparing smoking cessation programs utilizing behaviour modification, health education, or hypnosis. *Addictive Behaviors* 9:157–173.

Rank D & Suedfeld P (1978). Positive reactions of alcoholic men to sensory deprivation. *The International Journal of the Addictions* 13(5):807–815.

Register UD, Marsh SR, Thurston DT et al. (1972). Influence of nutrients on intake of alcohol. *Journal of the American Dietetic Association* 61:159–162

Reilly D, Taylor M, Beattie N et al. (1994). Is evidence for homeopathy reproducible? *Lancet* 344(8937):1601–1606.

Rezvani AH, Overstreet DH & Lee Y (1995). Attenuation of alcohol intake by ibogaine in three strains of alcohol-preferring rats. *Pharmacology, Biochemistry and Behavior* 52(3):615–620.

Rhodes ER, Mason RD, Eddy P, Smith EM & Burns TR (1988). The Indian Health Service approach to alcoholism among American Indian and Alaska Natives. *Public Health Reports* 103(6):621–627.

Richter C (1957). On the phenomenon of sudden death in animals and man. *Psychosomatic Medicine* 72(3):191–198.

Riedlinger TJ & Riedlinger JE (1994). Psychedelic and entactogenic drugs in the treatment of depression. *Journal of Psychoactive Drugs* 26(1):41–55.

Rogers LL, Pelton RB & Williams RJ (1956). Amino acid supplementation and voluntary alcohol consumption by rats. *Journal of Biological Chemistry* 220(1):321–323.

Satel SL & Gawin FH (1989). Seasonal cocaine abuse. *American Journal of Psychiatry* 146:534–535.

Schachter L, Weingarten MA & Kahan EE (1993). Attitudes of family physicians to nonconventional therapies. *Archives of Family Medicine* 2:1268–1270.

Schneider F, Elbert T, Heimann H et al. (1993). Self-regulation of slow cortical potentials in psychiatric patients: Alcohol dependency. *Biofeedback and Self Regulation* 18(1):23–32.

Schou M (1997). Forty years of lithium treatment (Review). *Archives of General Psychiatry* 54(1):21–23.

Schwartz J (1992). Methods of smoking cessation (Review). *Medical Clinics of North America* 76(2):451–476.

Seale JP & Muramoto ML (1993). Substance abuse among minority populations. *Primary Care Clinics in Office Practice* 20(1):167–180.

Sershen H, Hashim A & Lajtha A (1994). Ibogaine reduces preference for cocaine consumption in C57BL/6 by mice. *Pharmacology, Biochemistry and Behavior* 47:13–19.

Shaffer HJ & LaSalvia TA (1997). Comparing Hatha Yoga with dynamic group psychotherapy for enhancing methadone maintenance treatment: A randomized clinical trial. *Alternative Therapies in Health and Medicine* 3(4):57–66.

Shanmugasundaram E, Subramaniam U, Santhini R & Shanmugasundaram K (1986). Studies on brain structure and neurological function in alcoholic rats controlled by an Indian medicinal formula (SKV). *Journal of Ethnopharmacology* 17:225–245.

Shapiro A & Morris L (1978). *Placebo Effects in Medical and Psychological Therapies: Handbook of Psychotherapy and Behavior Change*. New York, NY: John Wiley & Sons.

Shapiro A, Struening E & Shapiro E (1980). The reliability and validity of a placebo test. *Journal of Psychiatric Research* 55:253–290.

Shapiro F, Vogelmann-Sine S & Sine LF (1994). Eye movement desensitization and reprocessing: Treating trauma and substance abuse. *Journal of Psychoactive Drugs* 26(4):379–391.

Sheppard SG (1994). A preliminary investigation of ibogaine: Case reports and recommendations for further study. *Journal of Substance Abuse Treatment* 11(4):379–385.

Silver S, Brooks A & Obenchain J (1995). Treatment of Vietnam War veterans with PTSD: A comparison of eye movement desensitization and reprocessing, biofeedback, and relaxation training. *Journal of Traumatic Stress* 8(2):337–342.

Singer MT (1992). Closing the chapter on Maharishi Ayur-Veda (Letter). *Journal of the American Medical Association* 267(10):1337.

Singer M & Borrero MG (1984). Indigenous treatment of alcoholism: The case of Puerto Rican spiritism. *Medical Anthropology* 8(4):246–73.

Skolnick AA (1992). Closing the chapter on Maharishi Ayur-Veda (Letter). *Journal of the American Medical Association* 267(10):1339–1340.

Smith MO (1988). Acupuncture treatment for crack: Clinical survey of 1500 patients treated. *American Journal of Acupuncture* 16(3):241–247.

Smith MO & Khan I (1988). An acupuncture programme for the treatment of drug-addicted persons. *Bulletin on Narcotics* 40(1):35–41.

Spiegel D, Bloom JR, Kraemer HC & Gottheil E (1989). Effect of psychosocial treatment on survival of patients with metastatic breast cancer. *Lancet* 2(8668):888–891.

Stall R & Biernacki P (1986). Spontaneous remission from the problematic use of substances: An inductive model derived from a comparative analysis of the alcohol, opiate, tobacco, and food/obesity literatures. *International Journal of the Addictions* 21(1):1–23.

Steiner RP, May DL & Davis AW (1982). Acupuncture therapy for the treatment of tobacco smoking addiction. *American Journal of Chinese Medicine* 10(1–4):107–121.

Stoil M (1989). Problems in the evaluation of hypnosis in the treatment of alcoholism. *Journal of Substance Abuse Treatment* 6:31–35.

Suedfeld P (1964). Attitude manipulation in restricted environments: I. Conceptual structure and response to propaganda. *Journal of Abnormal and Social Psychology* 68:242–247.

Suedfeld P (1990). Restricted environmental stimulation and smoking cessation: A fifteen-year progress report. *International Journal of the Addictions* 25:861–888.

Suedfeld P & Best JA (1977). Satiation and sensory deprivation combined in smoking therapy: Some case studies and unexpected side-effects. *The International Journal of the Addictions* 12(2–3):337–359.

Suedfeld P & Ikard F (1974). The use of sensory deprivation in facilitating the reduction of cigarette smoking. *Journal of Consulting and Clinical Psychology* 42:888–895.

Suedfeld P, Landon PB, Pargament R & Epstein YM (1972). An experimental attack on smoking: Attitude manipulation in restricted environments, III. *International Journal of the Addictions* 7:721–733.

Surawy C & Cox T (1986). Smoking behaviour under conditions of relaxation: A comparison between types of smokers. *Addictive Behaviors* 11(2):187–191.

Taub E, Steiner SS, Weingarten E & Walton KG (1994). Effectiveness of broad spectrum approaches to relapse prevention in severe alcoholism: A long-term, randomized, controlled trial of transcendental mediation, EMG biofeedback and electronic neurotherapy. *Alcoholism Treatment Quarterly* 11(1/2):187–220.

Ter Riet G, Kleijnen J & Knipschild P (1990). A meta-analysis of studies into the effect of acupuncture on addiction. *British Journal of General Practice* 40(338):379–382.

Tompkins VD (1992). Closing the chapter on Maharishi Ayur-Veda (Letter). *Journal of the American Medical Association* 267(10):133139.

Tuchfield BS (1981). Spontaneous remission in alcoholics: Empirical observations and theoretical implications. *Journal of Studies on Alcohol* 42(7):626–641.

Turner JW & Fine TH (1983). Effects of relaxation associated with brief restricted environmental stimulation therapy (REST) on plasma cortisol, ACTH and LH. *Biofeedback and Self-Regulation* 8(1):115–126.

Vaillant G, Clark W, Cyrus C et al. (1993). Prospective study of alcoholism treatment: Eight year follow-up. *The American Journal of Medicine* 75:455–463.

Visser GJ & Peters L (1990). Alternative medicine and general practitioners in The Netherlands: Towards acceptance and integration. *Family Practice* 7(3):227–232.

Walach H & Righetti M (1996). Homeopathy: Principles, status of research, research design. *Wiener Klinische Wochenschrift* 108(20):654–63.

Walton KG & Levitsky D (1995). A neuroendocrine mechanism for the reduction fo drug use and addiction by transcendental meditation. In DF O'Connell & CN Alexander (eds.) *Self Recovery: Treating Addictions Using Transcendental Meditation and Maharishi Ayur-Veda*. New York, NY: Harrington Park Press, 89–118.

Washburn AM, Fullilove RE, Fullilove MT et al. (1993). Acupuncture heroin detoxification: A single-blind clinical trial. *Journal of Substance Abuse Treatment* 10(4):345–351.

Watson RR & Mohs ME (1990). Effects of morphine, cocaine, and heroin on nutrition. *Alcohol, Immunomodulation, and AIDS* 325:413–418.

Wen HL (1979). Acupuncture and electrical stimulations (AES) Outpatient detoxification. *Modern Medicine in Asia* 15:39–43.

Wen HL & Cheung SYC (1973). Treatment of drug addiction by acupuncture and electrical stimulation. *Asian Journal of Medicine* 9:138–141.

Wen HL & Teo SW (1975). Experience in the treatment of drug addiction by electro-acupuncture. *Modern Medicine in Asia* 11:23–24.

Werbach MR (1991). Alcoholism. *Nutritional Influences on Mental Illness: A Sourcebook of Clinical Research.* Tarzana, CA: Third Line Press, 18–47.

Westermeyer J, Lyfoung T, Westermeyer M & Neider J (1991). Opium addiction among Indochinese refugees in the U.S.: Characteristics of addictions and their opium use. *American Journal of Drug and Alcohol Abuse* 17(3):267–277.

Westermeyer J & Neider J (1986). Cultural affiliation among American Indian alcoholics: Correlations and change over a ten-year period. *Annals of the New York Academy of Sciences* 472:179–188.

Westermeyer J & Peake E (1983). A ten-year follow-up of alcoholic Native Americans in Minnesota. *American Journal of Psychiatry* 140(2):189–194.

Wharton R & Lewith G (1986). Complementary medicine and the general practitioner. *British Medical Journal* 292(6534):1498–500.

Whitehead PC (1978). Acupuncture in the treatment of addiction: A review and analysis. *International Journal of the Addictions* 13(1):1–16.

Winer LR (1977). Biofeedback: A Guide to the clinical literature. *American Journal of Orthopsychiatry* 47(4):626–638.

Worner TM, Zeller B, Schwarz H, Zwas F & Lyon D (1992). Acupuncture fails to improve treatment outcome in alcoholics. *Drug & Alcohol Dependence* 30(2):169–173.

Xie CI, Lin RC, Antony V et al. (1994). Daidzin, an antioxidant isoflavonoid, decreases blood alcohol levels and shortens sleep time induced by ethanol intoxication. *Alcoholism: Clinical & Experimental Research* 18(6):1443–1447.

CHAPTER 9

Harm Reduction as an Approach to Treatment

Alex Wodak, M.D., FRACP

What is Harm Reduction?
Harm Reduction and Drug Treatment
Alternatives to Harm Reduction

Harm reduction policies and programs span prevention and treatment. They aim to decrease the adverse health, social and economic consequences of drug use without *necessarily* diminishing drug consumption (Wodak & Saunders, 1995). This approach has gained increasing support over the last decade, while more conventional approaches increasingly have appeared ineffective, expensive and counterproductive (Nadelmann, 1989; Riley, 1996).

WHAT IS HARM REDUCTION?

Defining Harm Reduction. The term "harm reduction," sometimes also known as "harm minimization," has not been defined by an official body and consequently has been used with a bewildering variety of interpretations (Strang, 1993). The ambiguity of the term adds to the confusion of an area already complicated by lack of terminological clarity and excessive emotional fervor. The alcohol and drug field also is characterized by attempts to force dichotomous categorizations even though most phenomena in the discipline are distributed on a continuum. Harm reduction is better considered as a difference in emphasis rather than a radically departure from conventional responses.

A more expanded view of harm reduction emphasizes maximizing the potential benefits of mood-altering substances as an aim additional to minimizing potential harms. Accordingly, emphasis is given to more judicious use of dependence-producing medications. For example, sub-optimal utilization of opioids in the management of cancer pain is common and often results in considerable distress from inadequate pain relief. Sub-therapeutic doses of analgesics are prescribed largely because of excessive fears of inducing drug dependence in patients with very limited life expectancy. Similarly, the possibility that medicinal use of cannabis might ameliorate distressing symptoms of AIDS (Kassirer, 1997) concerns many harm reduction supporters who favor the same kind of rigorous evaluation of costs and benefits as in other medical attempts to prolong life or alleviate suffering.

Although harm reduction approaches are not intended primarily to reduce consumption of drugs, this often is an unintended long-term result. For example, random breath testing was introduced to reduce the incidence of alcohol-related road crash deaths and serious injuries by deterring intoxicated citizens from driving. This has had the unanticipated benefit of encouraging many car drivers, who form the majority of the adult population, to consume less alcohol. Similarly, many drug users who have attended needle exchange programs for some time canvass the idea of achieving abstinence and request referral to drug treatment (Lurie, Reingold et al., 1993; Heimer, in press).

History of Harm Reduction. Although harm reduction often is misrepresented as a recent development in the alcohol and drug field, it has a long history. Like the character in Molière's "Le Bourgeois Gentilhomme" who said, "Good heavens! I have been speaking in prose for 40 years without knowing it!," some clinicians and policymakers have discovered that they have long been practicing harm reduction. In ancient China, authorities attempted unsuccessfully to limit alcohol consumption as a means of preventing inebriated citizens falling into wintry canals and freezing to death. Although it was not possible to eliminate public intoxication, the simple installation of barriers around the canals was found to effectively prevent such deaths. Compulsory safety belt legislation was introduced in the 1960s in a number of countries when authorities became alarmed by increasing numbers of alcohol-related road crash deaths. Efforts at that time to reduce per capita alcohol consumption were singularly unsuccessful. Ensuring that almost all car drivers wore safety belts while driving had no effect on alcohol consumption or drunk driving but did dramatically reduce alcohol-related road crash deaths and serious injuries. Support for harm reduction policies and programs increased in the mid-1980s following the recognition of the HIV pandemic and the realization that uncontrolled epidemics involving injecting drug users had immense health, social and economic costs.

Misconceptions about Harm Reduction. Harm reduction often is misconstrued as dismissing any role for law enforcement. On the contrary, harm reduction usually involves a far closer partnership between law enforcement and health. Police have become persuaded of the importance of not interfering with the functioning of needle exchange and methadone programs in order to ensure that significant community benefits are not jeopardized. Health workers have come to better understand the considerable difficulties of illicit drug law enforcement and the importance of collaborative work in certain areas, such as reducing alcohol-related violence. In many countries where harm reduction has been well accepted for some years, police have begun to reverse earlier opposition to methadone programs and supported expansion of drug treatment. They also have been influenced by impressive evidence of crime reduction following enrollment in methadone (Maddux & Desmond, 1979) and increasing concern that excessive reliance on use reduction inevitably leads to serious corruption among police officers.

Although sometimes misrepresented as a radical threat to conventional policies, harm reduction has received support from prestigious international health authorities. "A concern often expressed about harm reduction strategies is their potential for communicating a message condoning drug use. Such concerns have been expressed, for instance, concerning mass media programs that encourage drinking groups to nominate a nondrinking 'designated driver,' since this message might seem to condone drunkenness in the other group members, and concerning those that provide information about methods for solvent inhalation that reduce the risk of fatalities and other harm. Often these concerns could be alleviated by targeting the message to those already involved in hazardous drug use. In considering such strategies, it should be kept in mind that the public health sector has always been in favor of reducing the immediate drug-related harm, even if this involves some risk of a more distant hazard or can be seen as condoning drug use" (World Health Organization, 1993).

For some, harm reduction is simply the thin edge of an ugly wedge of drug legalization. For others in more hostile environments, achieving even minimal harm reduction is a major accomplishment while talk of substantial drug policy reform is a luxurious distraction. A third group are convinced that the major benefits achieved in many communities from harm reduction justifies taking reform further, including rigorously evaluating some forms of controlled availability of currently illicit drugs.

It is difficult to deny that harm reduction has in some countries appeared to open up drug policy as an issue. But this is not in itself reason enough to permanently suppress all consideration of harm reduction policies and programs.

Examples of Harm Reduction Approaches. Needle exchanges and methadone maintenance programs are the most commonly quoted exemplars of harm reduction. The rationale for needle exchange is to increase the supply of sterile injecting equipment while decreasing the availability of contaminated injecting equipment in order to reduce the spread of HIV among injecting drug users. At the time of their introduction in many countries in the late 1980s, there was a fear that the benefit of reducing HIV spread might be at the cost of inadvertently increasing drug consumption. No evidence has emerged over the last decade to support this fear (Lurie, Reingold et al., 1993). In many parts of the world, increased demand for treatment followed the introduction of needle exchange programs (Lurie, Reingold et al., 1993; Heimer, in press).

Methadone maintenance programs provide an oral, legal and long half-life drug as a replacement for an intravenous, illegal and short half-life drug. Enrollment in methadone programs is associated with multiple benefits (Ward, Mattick & Hall, 1998) including decreased mortality, morbidity, HIV infection (Caplehorn & Ross, 1995) and crime. Social functioning also improves (Ward, Mattick & Hall, 1998). Supporters of harm reduction welcome these benefits while accepting that all patients continue to consume a mood altering substance (methadone) and a small proportion continue to inject (considerably reduced quantities of) heroin. Better, they argue, to have a patient taking methadone who is well, employed, not committing crime, HIV negative and occasionally injects heroin than someone who intermittently engages in drug-free treatment but has become HIV positive, commits crime, is unemployed, injects heroin frequently but does not take methadone.

Official Responses to Harm Reduction. "Harm reduction" has been explicitly accepted as national drug policy in a number of developed countries, including Australia, Canada and France. A national meeting of senior Australian politicians declared in 1985 that "the aim [of drug policy] is to minimize the harmful effects of drugs on Australian society" (Department of Health, 1985).

Although the United Nations International Drug Control Programs (UNDCP) is responsible for coordinating international illicit drug law enforcement and global supply control initiatives, even this organization has recently provided muted endorsement of harm reduction (Executive Director, 1994):

> "In recent years the increased attention on drug abuse has led to an intense debate on how best to reduce the damage inflicted on the individual and society. Insofar as UNDCP is involved in this debate its position can be only the following: there is no fixed formula, no panacea to remedy the global ill of drug abuse. Entrenched confrontation at the national and international levels must be tempered with pragmatism. While ridding the world of drug abuse remains a central objective, it is a long-term goal. Therefore, the most useful short-term outlook should aim to contain the immediate threat to society."

A recent document drawn up by an Expert Committee of the World Health Organization used the term "harm reduction" in the sense of preventing adverse consequences of drug use without setting out primarily to reduce drug consumption (World Health Organization, 1993). This interpretation of harm reduction has existed comfortably and apparently without controversy in an organization that carefully positions itself in the middle ground of the family of nations. Examples of harm reduction referred to included needle exchange to control the spread of HIV among injecting drug users, nicotine patches for tobacco users and attempts to reduce physical injuries associated with alcohol intoxication by making environments in which people drink less dangerous. The committee commented that "in the harm minimization approach attention is directed to the careful scrutiny of all prevention and treatment strategies in terms of their intended and unintended effects on levels of drug-related harm" (World Health Organization, 1993).

A series of international conferences on the Reduction of Drug Related Harm have been held annually following an initial conference in Liverpool, United Kingdom in 1990. In 1996, an International Harm Reduction Association and an Asian Harm Reduction Network was established. Other regional harm reduction networks are planned. The first National Harm Reduction Conference in the United States was held in Oakland, California, September 17–20, 1996, organized by the National Harm Reduction Coalition.

Almost all developed countries with a significant presence of injecting drug use have established needle exchange programs. As federal funding is still prohibited for these programs in the United States, the scale of implementation of needle exchange is limited to areas that choose to mount local initiatives, through which 55 needle exchange programs provided almost eight million syringes annually (Wodak & Lurie, 1997). Programs in some other developed countries, such as Sweden, also are quite restricted. In 1994, needle programs exchanged over ten million syringes from over 4,000 outlets in Australia. A few developing countries have established needle exchange programs, and such programs also have been established in Russia.

Methadone programs now operate in all countries belonging to the European Union and are growing very rapidly in Austria, Belgium, France, Germany and Spain. Methadone programs exist in a number of Asian countries including Nepal, Thailand and Hong Kong. A number of developing countries are likely to establish methadone programs in the next few years.

The growing international acceptance of methadone was confirmed in a recent survey carried out by the Health Department of Canada (Ruel, 1996). Long-term methadone maintenance was accepted in sixteen countries by 1995 including Australia, Canada, Denmark, Finland, France, Germany, Hong Kong, Hungary, Israel, Italy, Mexico, The Netherlands, New Zealand, Spain, Switzerland and the United States. Three countries (Belgium, England and Sweden) regarded methadone with eventual withdrawal as the only acceptable form of treatment. Controls and regulations differed considerably. Switzerland had the highest number of patients/million (2,000) followed by Hong Kong (1,818), Belgium (1,000), Australia (964), Netherlands (732), Denmark (542), New Zealand (495), Spain (459) and the United States (441).

Methadone programs for inmates now operate in correctional systems in five countries, pilot needle exchange for inmates is being evaluated in prisons in Switzerland and Germany, while bleach for decontamination of needles and syringes is provided to prisoners in 13 countries (Dolan, Wodak & Penny, 1995).

Reduction of drug-related harm is the most logical target of national and international drug policy. Decreasing drug consumption is but one possible means of achieving this end.

Public Support for Harm Reduction. Strong community support for needle exchange has been demonstrated in two community opinion surveys in Australia, where 90% of respondents supported needle exchange in a survey in New South Wales (Schwartzkopf, Spooner et al., 1990), while the proportion of Western Australian respondents supporting needle exchange increased from 76% to 87% after participants heard a brief tape explaining the rationale for the program (Lenton, 1994). Although anticipated public opposition to needle exchange programs often is used by opponents to justify maintenance of the United States ban, a national public opinion poll found 66% of respondents supported such programs (Henry J. Kaiser Family Foundation, 1996).

While these opinion surveys are encouraging, authorities in several countries have encountered local opposition to the establishment of needle exchange and methadone treatment programs. Opposition is not unique to these services as local communities often oppose other drug treatment services and even fire stations or other public utilities which are well accepted if located elsewhere.

HARM REDUCTION AND DRUG TREATMENT

Harm reduction has had a significant effect on drug treatment, changing the focus from the rapid achievement of a drug-free state to acceptance of incremental improvements that are the best that particular individuals in particular circumstances can manage at particular times. Clinicians working in a harm reduction framework are generally very conscious of the considerable difficulties often experienced by many drug dependent persons disadvantaged by poverty, poor housing, racial discrimination, unemployment, limited educational opportunities and squalid neighborhoods with high crime rates. Objectives in harm reduction treatment settings generally are negotiated between clinician and patient with the latter largely determining specific goals and targets.

Harm reduction also encourages clinicians to take a more generic and broader view of alcohol and drug problems and their amelioration. Treatment and prevention are regarded as indivisible parts of the same whole.

Harm reduction has broadened treatment from an exclusive preoccupation with intensive and expensive treatment for alcoholics to the additional provision of brief and inexpensive interventions for the far larger number of problem drinkers. This shift in emphasis is justified by the epidemiological observation that it is the very large number of persons with moderately heavy aggregate consumption who account for the majority of alcohol related problems in society rather than the small number of very conspicuous, severely dependent drinkers with a far higher relative risk of developing alcohol related problems (Kreitman, 1986).

Harm reduction principles also have been applied to detoxification services. Non-medical (or social) detoxification provides a supportive (but inexpensive) environment where the carefully selected and trained staff and calm surroundings become "the tranquilizer" and the expensive costs of doctors, nurses, medical investigations and medications are avoided. Multiple vitamins are provided to reduce the incidence of alcohol-related brain damage. These facilities are generally well accepted by street populations who otherwise often gravitate to expensive hospital beds. Non-medical detoxification centers accept that many of their residents will return on multiple occasions, each time possibly making an incremental improvement. The modest achievement of a safe and comfortable detoxification for all residents is regarded as the core objective. Even in this population, some achieve enduring abstinence (which is regarded as a bonus).

Harm reduction also has influenced smoking cessation programs. As smokers who cut down their consumption frequently soon resume previous level of consumption or compensate by subconsciously adjusting their inhalation to maintain previous blood nicotine and tar levels, the application of harm reduction to cigarette smokers not infrequently has been questioned. The use of nicotine substitution (as chewing gum, skin patches and nasal sprays) has many parallels with methadone maintenance programs for heroin users (Russell, 1993). In both cases, a less damaging variant of the addictive substance is provided for a period during which the powerful reinforcing cues supporting continuation of drug seeking behavior are allowed to dissipate gradually. It is accepted in both cases that some may continue the less damaging addictive substance for a lengthy period, a tiny minority even continuing indefinitely.

When methadone maintenance is provided in countries that are sympathetic to harm reduction, adequate doses (> 60 mg/day) are generally provided for a duration that is largely determined by the patient and may extend for more than two years. These characteristics of treatment have been demonstrated repeatedly to maximize benefits (Ward, Mattick & Hall, 1998). Methadone may be provided under supervision of a general practitioner who has completed a brief training course. Vigorous efforts are made to provide sufficient treatment to match demand.

In harm reduction settings, patients undergoing drug treatment often are encouraged to negotiate treatment goals and parameters with clinicians. Cycles of remission and relapse tend to be regarded as part of the natural history of drug dependence, rather than a reflection of poor motivation. Harm reduction treatments generally emphasize evidence-based clinical practice, rather than moral, religious or spiritual aspects of care. Retention in treatment is stressed and correlated with favorable outcomes. Harm reduction treatments often favor minimal improvements for many rather than heroic gains for the few. Drug treatment in a harm reduction framework is regarded as similar to the management of many relapsing medical conditions, rather than as an offshoot of law enforcement.

Outcomes of Harm Reduction Approaches. *Methadone Treatment:* There is compelling evidence for the effectiveness of methadone treatment against a range of important outcomes drawn from a large literature including some randomized controlled studies and a vast number of observational studies (Ward, Mattick & Hall, 1998). Methadone treatment has been demonstrated to reduce deaths from drug overdose, total mortality, morbidity, HIV risk behavior, HIV seroprevalence, HIV seroincidence, unemployment rates and crime. The plausibility and consistency of these findings is extremely impressive. Improved outcomes are seen with higher doses of methadone, strengthening the confidence in these findings. Cost effectiveness rarely has been investigated, but the estimated cost of methadone treatment is very small in comparison with other treatment modalities, incarceration or no treatment. Methadone programs also are far more successful than other treatment modalities in attracting and retaining large numbers of drug users. In general, retention in drug treatment is closely linked to satisfactory outcomes. Methadone availability was limited during the 1980s in all European countries, with a high (> 50 cases/million) total number of AIDS cases among injecting drug users, such as Spain, France, Italy, Ireland and Portugal (M. Resienger, personal communication). Methadone was more available in most countries with a low prevalence of AIDS among injecting drug users (< 30 cases), such as Germany, Netherlands, Denmark, Belgium and the United Kingdom. Availability of methadone and needle exchange programs was linked. The three European countries with the highest percentage of injecting drug users in methadone treatment (Denmark, Netherlands and the United Kingdom) have long had extensive needle exchange programs. Early implementation of harm reduction policies and programs has been associated with persistently low HIV seroprevalence rates in a number of cities around the world (Des Jarlais, Hagan et al., 1995) and impressive claims have been made for an averted HIV epidemic in Britain based on harm reduction programs (Stimson, 1996a).

Comparison of the HIV epidemics in Australia and the United States are illuminating (Wodak & Lurie, 1997). It was estimated that 14% of the 1.5 million injecting drug users in the 96 metropolitan areas of the United States with a population over 500,000 are infected with HIV (Holmberg, 1996). The proportion of annual AIDS cases in the United States attributed to injecting drug use increased from 12% in 1981 to 28% in 1993 with a corresponding decline from 74% to 47% in the proportion of cases attributed to homosexually active men (National Research Council, 1995). The United States epidemic is even more injecting drug user-dominated than AIDS data suggest. Fifty percent of incident HIV infections are estimated to occur among injecting drug users, excluding infections from injecting drug users to sex partners and children (Holmberg, 1996).

Yet prevalence of HIV infection is consistently low (less than 5%), among injecting drug users in Australia who do not report male-to-male sexual contact (Kaldor, Elford et al., 1993). A 1995 survey involving 1005 attendees at 21 needle exchanges in all states found that 1.0% of attendees with no history of male-to-male sexual contact were HIV-positive (MacDonald, Wodak et al., 1997). Injecting drug users accounted for 2.5% of AIDS cases in Australia in 1994 (Wodak & Lurie, in press). The HIV epidemic in Australia started later in Australia than in the United States. Consequently, AIDS cases per head of population in the two countries converged after the early 1980s. However, they began to diverge again after 1988, probably reflecting the growing HIV epidemic among injecting drug users in the United States and the relative lack of such an epidemic in Australia.

Needle Exchange: Six studies of needle exchange funded by the U.S. government concluded that these programs reduce HIV transmission and do not lead to increased drug use (National Commission on Acquired Immune Deficiency Syndrome, 1991; United States General Accounting Office, 1993a; Lurie, Reingold et al., 1993; Satcher, 1995; National Research Council and Institute of Medicine, 1995; Office of Technology Assessment, 1995).

As more data has become available over time, confidence in the findings of these major studies has increased immeasurably (Wodak & Lurie, 1997). The plausibility that needle exchange schemes would reduce HIV spread among injecting drug users is high. Comparisons of needle exchange attendees with non-attenders have generally shown a reduction in risk behavior among the former. A reduction of at least one third in the incidence of HIV among injecting drug users who attended needle exchange programs was estimated using a mathematical model. A single study (Hagan, Des Jarlais et al., 1995), as yet unreplicated, demonstrated that non-exchange attendees had a seven to eight fold greater risk of infection with hepatitis B or hepatitis C than injecting drug users who attended a needle exchange.

A recent ecological study of needle exchange programs and HIV seroprevalence among injecting drug users involved 29 cities in many countries where serial data on HIV seroprevalence was available (Hurley, Jolley & Kaldor, 1996) . Mean initial seroprevalence was approximately 3% in both cities that subsequently introduced needle exchange and those that did not. Mean terminal seroprevalence was considerably lower in locations with a needle exchange program (6%) than those without (21%).

The mean annual increase in seroprevalence, weighted according to the number of subjects sampled, was 3.6% in cities without and 0.2% in cities with needle exchange programs. Although a standard methodology for measurement of HIV seroprevalence between and within cities was not used, it is difficult to envisage any systematic design flaw capable of producing these results. Virtually all court challenges mounted in the United States against needle exchange have been dismissed. Public support for needle exchange in opinion surveys was demonstrated in Australia and the United States. It was estimated in Australia (Feacham 1995), that exchanging 10 million needles and syringes in 1991 cost $8 million, prevented 2,900 HIV infections and saved $220 million at a cost per life year saved of $280 million. Cost-effectiveness analyses estimated that needle exchange programs in the United States can generally prevent an HIV infection for between $4,000 and $12,000 (Kahn, 1993). Using conservative assumptions drawn from published studies, it was estimated that between 4,000 and 10,000 HIV infections could have been prevented in the United States had needle exchange programs been implemented at the same rate as in Australia. These infections will ultimately cost up to half a billion U.S. dollars in HIV/AIDS treatment costs (Lurie & Drucker, 1997).

ALTERNATIVES TO HARM REDUCTION

Societal responses to illicit drug use once were divided into law enforcement, education and treatment. A more contemporary division has been supply reduction, demand reduction and harm reduction.

Demand Reduction. "Demand reduction" typically involves a range of educational measures, including mass campaigns, school campaigns and programs directed at established drug users and high risk groups. Treatment of drug users is classified as a form of demand reduction. Supply reduction involves attempts to reduce crop production, drug production, drug transport from countries of origin to countries of destination (interdiction), drug entry to the country of destination (customs), drug distribution (police) and financial surveillance.

Some measures clearly intended to reduce demand also reduce supply and *vice versa*. For example, methadone treatment might be regarded as simply reducing demand for drugs in a small number of heroin dependent individuals. But those seeking entry to methadone maintenance programs are usually severely dependent and probably include many of the heaviest consumers in the community. Removing these individuals from the heroin market will have a significant effect on demand. As many of these users also are likely to traffick in drugs, their entry into treatment may temporarily disrupt the heroin supply system somewhat.

Supply Reduction. "Supply reduction," also sometimes referred to as "use reduction," forms the core of traditional international drug policy. The paramount aim of use reduction is to decrease consumption of (usually illicit) mood altering substances. Any reduction in harm is regarded as a bonus.

Use reduction is based on the implicit premise that adverse consequences of drug use are closely correlated with consumption. This relationship is valid in the case of legal drugs like alcohol and tobacco. Both drugs have significant intrinsic toxicity and adverse health consequences correlate closely with individual or societal consumption. Consumption of alcohol and tobacco correlates closely with changes in price or availability. Decreases in price or increases in availability of alcohol and tobacco almost invariably result in increased consumption and worse health outcomes. The converse also is true. Above a threshold, alcohol toxicity increases, linearly for some conditions, exponentially for others and in a J curve relationship for other conditions (Edwards, Anderson et al., 1994). Tobacco toxicity is generally linear but there seems to be no threshold below which smokers can consume with impunity.

Among developed countries, one of the strongest supporters of use reduction is the United States. The Anti-Drug Abuse Act passed by Congress in 1988 stated in 5252-B that "it is the declared policy of the United States to create a Drug-Free America by 1995." Members of Congress who supported the Anti-Drug Abuse Act did so notwithstanding the fact that this lofty policy goal clearly was not achievable within the specified seven year time frame. Whether drug consumption or drug-related harm is considered the more appropriate target of U.S. government policy clearly was answered in a recent official policy statement declaring that "we must come to terms with the drug problem in its essence: use itself. Worthy efforts to alleviate the symptoms of epidemic drug abuse—crime and disease for example—must continue unabated. But a largely ad-hoc attack on the holes in the dike can have only an indirect and minimal effect on the flood itself" (The White House, 1989).

Contrasts between Harm Reduction and Alternative Approaches. One of the most fundamental differences between the harm reduction and use reduction approaches is the judgement implicit in harm reduction that it is more effective to establish and reach achievable but suboptimal goals than to nominate but fail to reach unachievable and utopian goals. The public health tradition accepts that incremental improvements often are all that can be achieved in areas of great complexity and difficulty. Aggregate results from the combination of multiple interventions often are very rewarding although each intervention produces relatively minor benefit.

An elderly and somewhat decrepit Groucho Marx responded to the question, "What do you think of old age?" by noting that it was better than the alternative. This remark encapsulates the spirit of harm reduction. Harm reduction programs do not pretend to be a panacea, always producing complete success for all, but they do have a strong case to be regarded as more effective than alternative approaches relying almost exclusively on supply reduction.

Outcomes of Alternative Approaches. A recent review of the global illicit drug situation by a body charged with responsibility for international supply reduction concluded that "countries that are not suffering from the harmful consequences of drug abuse are the exception rather than the rule" (International Narcotics Control Board, 1993). This deterioration in the global illicit drug situation has occurred despite progressive strengthening of illicit drug law enforcement over several decades.

Illicit drug use was a problem in only a few developed countries a generation ago. During the 1960s, illicit drug use spread to a number of developed countries. During the 1980s, illicit drug use began to spread to most developing countries. By the early 1990s, it was estimated that there were over 5 million drug injectors (Mann, Tarantola & Netter, 1992) spread over more than 120 countries (Stimson & Choopanya, in press). These changes reflected a steady growth in global cultivation and production of illicit drugs. Technological changes in transport, communications and computers made movement of contraband substances and profits around the globe much easier for drug traffickers while control of illicit drug trafficking became much more difficult for law enforcement authorities.

This inexorable deterioration of the global illicit drug situation was accompanied by increasingly serious consequences of illicit drug use. Soon after the AIDS epidemic was first recognized in the early 1980s, it was recognized that HIV had spread alarmingly among and from populations of injecting drug users in several developed countries including the United States. HIV has irrevocably changed the nature of injecting drug use and has had an equally dramatic influence on the way injecting drug use is now perceived. Hepatitis C is now recognized to be globally more prevalent among injecting drug users than HIV including those countries where HIV prevalence has reached alarming levels (Garfein, Vlahov et al., 1996). Although there is still some uncertainty about the natural history of hepatitis C, it is apparent that this infection results in considerable mortality and morbidity, albeit in a smaller proportion and after a longer interval than HIV infection. Multidrug resistant tuberculosis has appeared as a significant health problem in some countries and is now recognized to be closely associated with uncontrolled HIV epidemics in injecting drug users.

Demand Reduction Approaches: There is a large literature evaluating the effectiveness of efforts to reduce demand for illicit substances using educational programs. There is little evidence of significant and sustained reduction in demand from mass-audience, school-based, or specially targeted educational campaigns (Cohen, 1993). Some educational programs have demonstrated improvements in knowledge, others in attitudes, some in both. But evidence of reduced consumption, or more significantly, a reduction in drug-related problems, is scant.

Demand for illicit substances appears to be greater in populations with high levels of youth unemployment, poor housing, limited educational opportunities, poor health services and neglected, crime-ridden neighborhoods. It is difficult to assess the role of these factors in stimulating demand for drugs. Lack of data for the influence of these factors on demand should not be taken as evidence that they are unimportant.

Supply Reduction Approaches: A substantial literature, including empirical (Riley, 1996; Commission on Narcotic Drugs, 1995) and theoretical (Riley, 1996; Wisotsky, 1986; Thornton, 1991; Center for Strategic and International Studies, 1993) studies document the relative ineffectiveness of supply reduction and predict continuing failure. An impressive study commissioned by the United States Army and carried out by the RAND Corporation evaluated the return on a one dollar investment in a variety of measures designed to reduce the societal cost of cocaine. The return was 17 cents for crop reduction and eradication in South America, 32 cents for interdicting transport of cocaine between South America and the United States, 52 cents for U.S. customs and police and $7.48 for drug treatment of cocaine users (Rydell & Everingham, 1994). The ineffectiveness of supply reduction and likelihood of continuing failure prompted a review body to despair that "over the past two decades in Australia we have devoted increased resources to drug law enforcement, we have increased the penalties of drug trafficking and we have accepted increasing inroads on our civil liberties as part of the battle to curb the drug trade. All the evidence shows, however, not only that our law enforcement agencies have not succeeded in preventing the supply of illicit drugs to Australian markets but that it is unrealistic to expect them to do so. If the present policy of prohibition is not working then it is time to give serious consideration to the alternatives, however radical they may seem" (Parliamentary Joint Committee on the National Crime Authority, 1989). Consideration of alternatives (Nadelmann, 1992) is now beginning in a number of countries and has even been undertaken by the research arm of the Congress (United State General Accounting Office, 1993b).

The experience of most countries and the international experience has been that global drug production has for decades increased almost every year apart from occasional reductions in production caused by bad weather in growing areas. Illicit drug use is spreading to more and more countries around the world. The range of drugs used has increased. Many countries have experienced an exponential growth in drug-related crime and other adverse outcomes including drwg-related deaths. The response to this national and global deterioration of the illicit drug situation has been an ever-increasing emphasis on attempts to restrict the supply of illicit drugs. International collaboration has increased. More funds have been allocated to attempts to reduce drug cultivation and production. Penalties for drug trafficking or drug use have been increased. Drug squads have been expanded. The number of prison inmates serving sentences for drug related offenses has increased. Financial surveillance has been intensified.

Strengthening supply reduction has required ever-increasing funding at a time of growing scarcity of public resources. Greater inroads have been made into civil liberties and corruption of the criminal justice system also has increased. A comparison of the effectiveness of harm reduction and supply reduction suggests that attempted harm elimination has rarely been successful while attempted harm reduction has rarely failed. To many, harm reduction has been a way of curbing the excesses of a drug policy which has unrealistically emphasized supply reduction.

The alarming possibility exists that supply reduction may have inadvertently exacerbated health problems. Emphasis on supply reduction and public health goals may be inimical. Anti-opium policies adopted in Hong Kong (1945), Thailand (1959) and Laos (1972) were followed by the disappearance of opium smoking which was replaced by heroin injecting (Westermeyer, 1976), setting the scene for a later epidemic of HIV infection beginning among injecting drug users in Thailand in 1988, which then seeded uncontrolled epidemics involving the general populations of Thailand, Burma, Malaysia, Vietnam, China and India.

CONCLUSIONS

It is likely that harm reduction will be accepted increasingly as a legitimate component of a modern response to mood altering drugs along with efforts to decrease demand and restrict supplies. A more effective response to the problems of illicit drugs requires a better balance of these elements rather than an almost exclusive reliance on supply reduction. If, as expected, harm reduction is accepted increasingly around the world, including the United States (in spirit if not name), treatment for drug users will change considerably with outcomes increasingly satisfactory for drug users, clinicians and communities.

REFERENCES

Caplehorn JRM & Ross MW (1995). Methadone maintenance and the likelihood of risky needle sharing. *International Journal of Addiction* 30(6):685–698.

Center for Strategic and International Studies (1993). *The Transnational Drug Challenge and the New World Order: New Threats and Opportunities.* Washington, DC: The Center.

Cohen J (1993). Achieving a reduction in drug-related harm through education. In N Heather, A Wodak, E Nadelmann & P O'Hare (eds.) *Psychoactive Drugs and Harm-reduction: From Faith to Science.* London, England: Whurr Publishers, 65–76.

Commission on Narcotic Drugs (1995). *Economic and Social Consequences of Drug Abuse and Illicit Trafficking: An Interim Report.* Vienna, Austria: United Nations Economic and Social Council.

Department of Health (1985). *National Campaign Against Drug Abuse.* Canberra, Australia: Australian Government Publishing Service, 2.

Des Jarlais DC, Hagan H, Friedman SR et al. (1995). Maintaining low HIV seroprevalence in populations of injecting drug users. *Journal of the American Medical Association* 274:1226–1231.

Dolan K, Wodak A & Penny R (1995). AIDS behind bars: Preventing HIV spread among incarcerated drug injectors (Editorial). *AIDS* 9:825–832.

Edwards G, Anderson P, Babor TF et al. (1994). *Alcohol Policy and the Public Good.* Oxford, England: Oxford University Press, 41–74.

Executive Director, United Nations International Drug Control Program (1994). 37th Session of the Commission on Narcotic Drugs. Vienna, 13th April.

Feacham RGA (1995). *Valuing the Past . . . Investing in the Future. Evaluation of the National HIV/AIDS Strategy 1993–94 to 1995–96.* Canberra, Australia: Commonwealth Department of Human Services and Health; Australian Government Publishing Services.

Garfein RS, Vlahov D, Galai N, Doherty MC & Nelson KE (1996). Viral infections in short-term injection drug users: The prevalence of the hepatitis C, B, human immunodeficiency and human T-lymphotropic viruses. *American Journal of Public Health* 86:655–661.

Hagan H, Des Jarlais DC, Friedman SR, Purchase D & Alter MJ (1995). Reduced risk of hepatitis B and hepatitis C among injection drug users in the Tacoma syringe exchange program. *American Journal of Public Health* 85:1531–1537.

Heimer R (1997). Needle exchange as a conduit to drug treatment. *Journal of Substance Abuse Treatment* (in press).

Henry J. Kaiser Family Foundation (1996). *The Kaiser Survey on Americans and AIDS/HIV.* Menlo Park, CA: Author.

Holmberg SD (1996). The estimated prevalence and incidence of HIV in 96 large US metropolitan areas. *American Journal of Public Health* 86:642–654.

Hurley S, Jolley D & Kaldor J (1996). In S Hurley & JRG Butler (eds.) *An Economic Evaluation of Aspects of the Australian HIV/AIDS Strategies.* Canberra, Australia: Australian Government Publishing Service, 56–60.

International Narcotics Control Board (INCB) (1993). *Report of the International Narcotics Control Board for 1993.* Vienna, Austria: INCB.

Kahn JG (1993). Are NEPs cost-effective in preventing HIV infection? In P Lurie, AL Reingold, B Bowser, D Chen et al. (eds.) *The Public Health Impact of Needle Exchange Programs in the United States and Abroad* (Volume I). San Francisco, CA: University of California.

Kaldor J, Elford J, Wodak A, Crofts JN & Kidd S (1993). HIV prevalence among IDUs in Australia: A methodological review. *Drug and Alcohol Review* 12:175–184.

Kassirer JP (1997). Federal foolishness and marijuana (Editorial). *The New England Journal of Medicine* 336:366–367.

Kreitman N (1986). Alcohol consumption and the prevention paradox. *British Journal of Addiction* 81:353–363.

Lenton S. (1994). *Illicit Drug Use, Harm Reduction and the Community: Attitudes to Cannabis Law and Needle and Syringe Provision in Western Australia* (Technical Report). Perth, Australia: National Centre for Research into the Prevention of Drug Abuse.

Lurie P & Drucker E (1996). *An Opportunity Lost: Estimating the Number of HIV Associated with the U.S. Government Opposition to Needle Exchange Programs.* Presented at XI International Conference on AIDS, Vancouver, British Columbia, July 7–12.

Lurie P, Reingold AL, Bowser B et al. (1993). *The Public Health Impact of Needle Exchange Programs in the United States and Abroad* (Vol. I). San Francisco, CA: University of California.

MacDonald M, Wodak A, Ali R et al. (1997). HIV prevalence and risk behaviour in needle exchange attenders: A national study. The Collaboration of Australian Needle Exchanges. *Medical Journal of Australia* 166(5):237–240.

Maddux JF & Desmond DP (1979). Crime and drug abuse: An area analysis. *Criminology* 19:281–302.

Mann JM, Tarantola DJM & Netter TW (1992). *AIDS in the World. The Global AIDS Policy Coalition.* Cambridge, MA: Harvard University Press, 406–411.

Nadelmann E (1989). Drug prohibition in the United States: Costs, consequences and alternatives. *Science* 245(4921):939–947.

Nadelmann E (1992). Thinking seriously about alternatives to drug prohibition. *Daedalus* 121:85–132.

National Commission on Acquired Immune Deficiency Syndrome (1991). *The Twin Epidemics of Substance Use and HIV.* Washington, DC: Author.

National Research Council and Institute of Medicine (1995). *Preventing HIV Transmission. The Role of Sterile Needles and Bleach.* Washington, DC: National Academy Press.

Office of Technology Assessment (1995). *The Effectiveness of AIDS Prevention Efforts.* Washington, DC: Author.

Parliamentary Joint Committee on the National Crime Service (1989).

Riley KJ (1996). *Snow Job?: The War Against International Cocaine Trafficking.* New Brunswick, NJ: Transaction Publishers.

Ruel J-M (1996). *International Survey of the Use of Methadone in the treatment of Narcotic Addiction.* Ottawa, Canada: Health Canada.

Russell MAH (1993) Reduction of smoking-related harm: The scope for nicotine replacement. In N Heather, A Wodak, E Nadelmann & P O'Hare (eds.) *Psychoactive Drugs and Harm-reduction: From Faith to Science.* London, England: Whurr Publishers, 153–167.

Rydell CP & Everingham SS (1994). *Controlling Cocaine. Supply Versus Demand Programs.* Santa Monica, CA: RAND Drug Policy Research Center.

Satcher D (1995). *Note to Jo Ivey Boufford.* Available from the Drug Policy Foundation, 4455 Connecticut Avenue, NW, Suite B500, Washington, DC, 20008.

Schwartzkopf J, Spooner S, Flaherty B et al. (1990). *Community Attitudes to Needle & Syringe Exchange and to Methadone Programs* (A 90/6). Sydney, Australia: New South Wales Department of Health.

Stimson GV (1996). Has the United Kingdom averted an epidemic of HIV–1 infection amongst drug injectors? (Editorial). *Addiction* 91(8):1085–1088.

Stimson GV & Choopanya K (in press). Global perspectives on drug injecting. In GV Stimson, DC des Jarlais & A Ball (eds.) *Drug Injecting and HIV Infection: Global Dimensions and Local Responses.*

Strang J (1993). Drug use and harm reduction: Responding to the challenge. In N Heather, A Wodak, E Nadelmann & P O'Hare (eds.) *Psychoactive Drugs and Harm-reduction: From Faith to Science.* London, England: Whurr Publishers, 3–20.

Thornton M (1991). *The Economics of Prohibition.* Salt Lake City, UT: University of Utah Press.

United States General Accounting Office (1993b). *Confronting the Drug Problem: Debate Persists on Enforcement And Alternative Approaches* (Report No. GAO/GGD–93–82). Washington, DC: U.S. Government Printing Office.

United States General Accounting Office (1993a). *Needle Exchange Programs: Research Suggests Promise as an AIDS Prevention Strategy* (Report No. GAO/HRD–93–60). Washington, DC: U.S. Government Printing Office.

Ward J, Mattick R & Hall W (1998). *Methadone Maintenance Treatment and Other Opioid Replacement Therapies.* Amsterdam, The Netherlands: Harwood Academic Publishers.

Westermeyer J (1976). The pro-heroin effects of anti-opium laws in Asia. *Archives of General Psychiatry* 33:1135–1139.

White House (The) (1989). *Drug Control Strategy.* Washington, DC: Government Printing Office, 11.

Wisotsky S (1986). *Breaking the Impasse in the War on Drugs.* Westport, CT: Greenwood Press.

Wodak A & Lurie P (1997). A tale of two countries: Attempts to control HIV among injecting drug users in Australia and the United States. *Journal of Drug Issues* 27(1):117–134.

Wodak A & Saunders W (1995). Harm reduction means what I choose it to mean (Editorial). *Drug and Alcohol Review* 14:269–271.

World Health Organization Expert Committee on Drug Dependence (1993). *WHO Technical Report Series* (Twenty-eighth Report). Geneva, Switzerland: World Health Organization.

CHAPTER 10

Addiction and Treatment in the Criminal Justice System

Blair Carlson, M.D., M.S.P.H., FASAM

Drugs and Crime
The Criminal Justice System and Sentencing Discretion
Drug Abuse Treatment in Legal Systems
Does Coerced Treatment Work?
Therapeutic Communities
Methadone Maintenance
Outpatient Drug-Free Treatment
DARP, TOPS, DATOS, CALDATA and CDATE
Race, Drugs, and Criminal Justice

Interest in the rehabilitation of criminals and their reintegration into communities paled in the mid–1970s and was replaced by a culture of retribution that continues today (Travis, Schwartz & Clear, 1992). Fueled by the public's fears of rising crime rates and the unfortunate and undeserved notion that when it comes to criminal rehabilitation, "nothing works," an epidemic of incarceration began (Lipton, 1995), precipitated by the "War on Drugs" and the drug laws of the 1980s. It now follows that jails and prisons house more persons who are addicted to drugs than at any other time in the history of the United States, and that the drug-addicted population includes a disproportionately large number of minority group members (Mauer, 1997).

Is it appropriate to incarcerate persons found guilty of nonviolent property or drug crimes who are not a real risk to society? Will they be evaluated for drug problems and get treatment? Would not it better serve society's interests if such offenders received sentences (sanctions) in which treatment was central to the stipulations set by a court? Should not physicians use their influence to intercede on behalf of the drug addict and demand a policy that puts a priority on treatment rather than incarceration? Knowing, as we do, that treatment works, can addiction medicine specialists use our influence to convince uninformed voters and legislators that many of the people being locked up are sick with the disease of addiction?

What follows is an overview of the relationship between the criminal justice system and drug abuse treatment as it stands today, an investigation of how we got where we are, examples of successful rehabilitation initiatives, and observations concerning our nation's current needs. It is written in the hope that more physicians will become interested in the plight of the much-maligned criminal addict and "accept the responsibility" (Dole, 1974) to become involved in the shaping of public policy.

DRUGS AND CRIME

Laws to control the use of drugs—that is, laws to restrict the use of opioids and other drugs to the realm of controlled medical or research use—did not exist in America prior to the 19th century (Musto, 1987). Early in that century, morphine and codeine were isolated from crude opium; by mid-century, cocaine had been separated and crystallized. Subsequently, the hypodermic needle and syringe came into use, and, late in the century, morphine was diacetylated and heroin became available. Opioids and cocaine were staples in patent medicines and soft drinks, as well.

In time, the rising importation of crude opium stoked the fires of the reformers who began to agitate for controls. In 1860, Pennsylvania passed an antimorphine law and, in 1897, Illinois enacted a law against cocaine. The federal government initiated a mini-war on drugs with the District of Columbia Pharmacy Act of 1906 restricting the prescribing of "habit-forming drugs." A month later, Congress enacted the Pure Food and Drug Act, requiring patent medicines containing narcotics, including cannabis, to be labeled before they could be shipped across state lines. By 1919, the Harrison Narcotic Act of 1914 had been examined by the Supreme Court and the pieces were in place to make it a crime to participate in the transfer and/or use of narcotics except for medical purposes (Musto, 1987).

The Comprehensive Drug Abuse and Control Act of 1970 combined several earlier laws into one and also ranked drugs according to perceptions of dangerousness. In this act, as in the Drug Abuse Control Amendments of 1965, the constitutional foundation for federal anti-drug legislation shifted from tax power at the time of the Harrison Act to the broader commerce power where it remains today. It did not provide for, and in fact repealed, mandatory minimum sentences for drug offenses that had been in force since the 1951 Hale Boggs Act (Musto, 1987; United States Sentencing Commission, 1995).

The Sentencing Reform Act of 1984 established the United States Sentencing Commission and directed it to promulgate a system of mandatory sentencing guidelines for federal judges. The Anti-drug Abuse Acts of 1986 and 1988 established mandatory minimum sentences for some drug-defined crimes including a five-year mandatory minimum sentence for the first offense possession of 5 grams of base cocaine (United States Sentencing Commission, 1995; National Council on Crime and Delinquency, 1996). Mandatory minimum sentencing has had a profound effect on treatment plans in that when mandatory minimum sentences are applied, they preclude alternative sanctions packaged to include substance abuse treatment in a community corrections environment.

Crimes associated with illicit drug use by persons who need drug abuse treatment include the drug-defined crimes of attempted possession, simple possession, possession with intent to distribute, distribution, and the manufacture of illegal substances. Other crimes associated with illicit drug use and the transfer of illicit drugs from one person to another include the predatory crimes of assault, theft, burglary, and robbery. Prostitution and crimes of deceit, such as fraud and confidence games, occur regularly among those who are heavily involved with illicit drugs (Chaiken & Chaiken, 1990; Hunt, 1990). Finally, violent crimes are not uncommon in the public trading of drugs and to a lesser extent, when under the influence of drugs. In the latter circumstance, while the evidence is "pervasive" that there is an association between substance abuse and violence, "the temporal order of substance abuse and aggression does not indicate a causal role for intoxicants" (Fagan, 1990).

Predatory crimes and illicit drug abuse coexist in certain social groups; however in other groups that abuse illicit drugs, there is little or no predatory criminal activity (Chaiken & Chaiken, 1990). A temporal sequence where drug addiction leads to predatory activity in order to support a habit is not a regular finding. In fact, in groups where predatory activities and drug abuse coexist, the criminality often preceded the addiction (Chaiken & Chaiken, 1990; 1982).

In the RAND Inmate Survey, only 26% of those who used illicit drugs cited their drug use as a factor in the commission of predatory crimes, and, in fact, criminal behavior often preceded drug use in that study (Chaiken & Chaiken, 1982). It is more likely that a deviant environment is responsible for both drug abuse and criminal behavior where these behaviors coexist (Fagan & Weiss, 1990; Kandel, Simcha-Fagan & Davies, 1986).

In the case of illicit drug use, especially heroin and cocaine, those who use "enough to have associated legal problems tend to be so enmeshed in other deviance and adjustment problems as to make attempts to untangle the exact sequence of the onset of drug use and criminal behavior a futile and perhaps trivial pursuit" (Wish & Johnson, 1986). Based on inmate interviews, Chaiken has calculated the criminal activity for "heavily involved" heroin addicts working at their criminal trade at 239 crime days per year in a California sample and 228 crime days per year in a Texas inmate cohort (Chaiken & Chaiken, 1990; Chaiken & Chaiken, 1982). This survey also indicated that a small number of offenders engage in assault, robbery, and drug dealing at very high rates (Chaiken & Chaiken, 1990; Chaiken & Chaiken, 1982; Visher, 1986). A controversial proposal would selectively and systematically identify these predators for incapacitation in hopes of dramatically reducing crime; however, it is likely that much more study is needed before a "trustworthy prediction instrument" is available (Visher, 1986). The ability to identify—and subsequently incapacitate—high-risk offenders is important if only because the public is more likely to support alternatives to incarceration for those addicts who are not a risk to public safety.

Regardless of which comes first in the drug-crime nexus, persons who commit predatory crimes and are heavily involved with drugs, particularly heroin, cocaine, and/or multiple drugs, commit crimes with far greater frequency than the same individuals when they are not as involved with drugs (Chaiken & Chaiken, 1990). Not only do predatory offenders who use large amounts of many different drugs or are heavily involved with drugs commit more crimes over a longer time than less drug involved offenders, but reduction in drug use and crime rate is seen when these persons enter treatment (Chaiken & Chaiken, 1990). For example, in a study of methadone maintenance patients, property crime days in the year that followed their first daily use of heroin were compared as a ratio to crime days per year in the year following their last daily use. The reduction in crime varied from 8.3:1 in Anglos to 6.3:1 in a Chicano cohort (Chaiken & Chaiken, 1990; Anglin & Speckart, 1986; Anglin, 1987); thus, where the association of drug use and crime is a strong one, treatment interventions directed at the drug use can be expected to reduce crime (Anglin & Hser, 1990; Lipton, 1995).

THE CRIMINAL JUSTICE SYSTEM AND SENTENCING DISCRETION

It is logical to see the criminal justice system as having three component systems: police systems, court systems, and corrections systems (Travis, Schwartz & Clear, 1992). Because each of these components have different legal roots, infrastructures, and accountability, criminal justice has been referred to as a non-system. Nevertheless, there is a enough interdependence among the three to justify the term.

Individuals who enter the system, enter it as an arrestee. If charged with a crime, the arrestee becomes a defendant. If found guilty, the defendant becomes an offender (although the term offender often is used loosely to describe a suspect). What exists is a funnel-shaped flow through the system, at each step of which there are broad discretionary opportunities that methodically remove individuals from the flow. Where discretion exists, there are rules: statutes, case law, regulations, and guidelines.

Sheldon Glueck is said to have described the American criminal justice system as a "clumsy admixture of the oil of discretion and the water of rule" (Travis, Schwartz & Clear, 1992). A standard textbook on criminal justice provides the following hypothetical example of how the funnel works in practice: out of 5,000 possible felonies based on citizen complaint or observation by an authority, no more than 1,100 adult arrests result and 600 of these arrestees are charged with a crime. Of the remainder, 100 are dismissed and 400 are resolved by guilty pleas (half to misdemeanors). One hundred cases go to trial, resulting in 70 convictions (West Publishing Company, 1989).

When there are discretionary opportunities in the system, it is possible for arrestees, defendants, and offenders to be engaged in treatment as part of, or in lieu of, sanctions. Treatment interventions are most likely to be effective when there is an established relationship (statutory or otherwise) between treatment systems and the criminal justice system. For example, diversion programs provide a formal structure for a prosecutor to not charge if an arrestee agrees to comply with treatment. This is a charge-bargain—a form of plea bargain. Other prosecutors prefer to charge and then make the treatment provision a condition of probation following a guilty plea or conviction. This is a sentence-bargain form of a plea bargain (West Publishing Company, 1989). These pre-charge and postcharge decisions may result in a disposition for nearly half of all arrestees. As mentioned earlier, judicial discretion in sentencing has been limited recently by sentencing guidelines and legislatively mandated minimum sentences for certain crimes or for certain offenders. Sentencing guidelines are commonly structured so that the severity of offense (principally drug amount in the case of drug-defined crimes) appears along one axis of a grid while the other axis carries offender characteristics. The judge has only to find the cell where the two intersect in order to find the sentence range that must be used (Hutchison, Yellen et al., 1994).

An intermediate sanction for commission of a crime lies between imprisonment and simple probation and is a concept that is very important to drug treatment under criminal justice surveillance. The term implies a more intensive supervision than simple probation, may include urine monitoring and treatment in a community, and is best used in lieu of incarceration (Petersilia & Turner, 1993).

If these programs are to relieve prison overcrowding, they must be used for offenders who would otherwise be sent to prison. Problems occur when judges and other officials use intermediate sanctions, under a strict sentencing philosophy, for offenders who might better be placed in low intensity supervision. When this happens, technical violations of intensive supervised probation (ISP) occur that often draw unmeasured and extreme consequences, such as revocation of probation; hence, offenders who would be on simple probation where technical violations are less likely to occur, are instead imprisoned and, of course, prison beds are not saved. Consequently, there exists a net-widening effect as a result of such policy, and it becomes difficult to demonstrate the effectiveness insofar as reducing prison costs where intermediate sanctions are concerned (Tonry & Lynch, 1996).

As of late 1996, the American Correctional Association reported the existence of approximately 1,000 state and federal prisons and 3,000 jails in the United States. By the end of 1995, there were over 1.6 million persons in prisons and jails, or 600 persons per 100,000 U.S. residents, up from 461 per 100,000 in 1990 (Bureau of Justice Statistics, 1996). In addition, 3.8 million persons were on probation or parole (Bureau of Justice Statistics Press Release, 1996).

The number of individuals within these systems who might benefit from substance abuse treatment is not known precisely; however, estimates range from two-thirds to three-fourths of prison inmates (General Accounting Office, 1991). Drug Use Forecasting (DUF) data indicated that the median percentage of males who tested positive for at least one illicit drug at the time of arrest at a DUF site was 66% in 1994 (National Institute of Justice, 1995).

DRUG ABUSE TREATMENT IN LEGAL SYSTEMS

After 1919, the large numbers of addicts in the federal prison system led to the establishment of two Public Health Service "farms" in Lexington, Kentucky, in 1935 and Fort Worth, Texas, in 1938. The patients of these institutions were to be detoxified from drugs, usually heroin, and then to be rehabilitated as inpatients. These institutions became known first as hospitals and later as clinical research centers where they provided the first systematic data on treatment outcome of drug abusers (Pickens & Fletcher, 1991). While the centers were intended to house federal prisoners, volunteers also could be treated there and, in fact, made up most of the admissions. These volunteers often left soon after detoxification but then relapsed within six to 12 months (Rasor & Maddux, 1978). It was thought that the lack of community follow-up played a role in the 87% to 96% relapse rate, yet these failures in treatment simply confirmed, for some, an already existing belief that narcotic addiction was incurable (Pickens & Fletcher, 1991; Lipton, 1995).

In the late 1950s, the therapeutic community of Synanon was founded and soon claimed to have remarkable success with narcotic addicts (Yablonsky, 1965). Despite the lack of objective outcome data to support the community's claims, it became clear that some narcotic addicts had, at the least, become drug-free, prompting the opening of other therapeutic communities. Daytop Village opened in New York in 1964, Phoenix House in 1968, and others soon followed (De Leon, 1986). There are now many therapeutic communities throughout the world.

It soon followed that Dole and Nyswander were able to show that providing a legal opiate drug under medically controlled conditions to a group of 22 narcotic addicts resulted in reducing criminal behaviors and inducing prosocial behaviors, as well (Dole & Nyswander, 1965). Their success was soon replicated, and methadone maintenance remains a staple in the treatment of heroin and other opiate addiction (Kreek, 1991).

The guarded acceptance of the concept of civil commitment and the high relapse rates following discharge from the Lexington and Fort Worth facilities led the federal government to design its own civil commitment program. The Narcotic Addict Rehabilitation Act of 1966 (NARA) provided for civil commitment of narcotic addicts in order to keep them in treatment after detoxification. Title IV of the act provided for the development of community aftercare programs and for the training of drug abuse professionals (Leukefeld, 1991). These programs were the beginnings of the network of publicly funded community drug treatment programs such as we know today.

The three modalities of treatment most closely associated with the successful treatment of addicts in the criminal justice system are methadone maintenance, drug-free outpatient, and drug-free residential treatment. Methadone maintenance is the only modality limited to one type of drug addict. Therapeutic communities and drug-free outpatient programs treat abusers of all varieties of drugs including cocaine and other stimulants, hallucinogens, depressant drugs, multiple drugs, and alcohol.

The 1980s and 1990s have seen cocaine users, especially base cocaine users, appear in ever-increasing numbers before the criminal justice system (Inciardi, 1997). Criminal justice surveillance in the form of professional monitoring or criminal justice referral to these treatment programs has the effect of improving retention in treatment where criminal justice involved patients do at least as well as those patients who are not involved with the criminal justice system in any way (Collins & Allison, 1983).

Outcome studies that evaluate each of these modalities are made difficult by a number of problems: the heterogeneous nature of the population under study, the recidivistic course of both drug use and criminal behaviors, attrition that shrinks sample size, ethical problems associated with the design of randomized controlled studies, and the inability of this population to avoid compromising whatever randomization is attempted (DeLeon, 1984; Bale, Van Stone et al., 1980; Anglin & Hser, 1990).

Pretreatment versus posttreatment comparisons of the same individuals or groups avoid some of the design problems, but as the immediate pretreatment period is characterized by intense involvement in drugs and crime, the posttreatment improvement may be due, in part, to regression toward the mean. Using a pretreatment period of at least three to five years and dividing the postadmission period into time in treatment and out of treatment minimizes this latter problem. Similarly, the problems with the lack of control groups has been minimized by taking advantage of natural experiments such as the California Civil Commitment Study described below and the closing or privatization of methadone maintenance clinics (McGlothlin & Anglin, 1981). More sophisticated analytic and statistical techniques also have helped to minimize the bias resulting from the lack of experimental design (Anglin & Hser, 1990; Lipton, 1995).

Outcome variables used to measure criminal justice drug abuse treatment success are generally harm-reduction measures such as reduction in days using drugs per year, reduction in crime days per year, rearrest rates, time elapsed until rearrest, and rates of reincarceration as opposed to measuring only the number of subjects attaining abstinence or no longer committing crime. A crime day is any day that a subject commits one or more crimes, thus capping criminal activity at one crime per day. Other means of summarizing statistics on crimes include crime days per unincarcerated year or crime days as a percent of total days during any time period (Chaiken & Chaiken, 1990).

It is worth noting that one finds the term "readdiction" used in the narcotic addict treatment outcome literature. The investigators are well aware that addiction has a lifelong connotation, but the term readdiction is simply used to denote return to daily drug use.

DOES COERCED TREATMENT WORK?

Workers in the field of drug abuse treatment are witness to a common event when they see family or employer, euphemistically referred to as a "rational authority" (Inciardi, 1988), force the issue of "getting help" in the case of persons with a substance abuse problem. The notion that an individual must want to get help in order to change a substance abuse behavior continues to engender pessimism in the case of court-ordered coercion of an addict into treatment (Anglin & Hser, 1990; Lipton, 1995). Clearly, the legal system can serve as a catalyst to encourage persons with substance abuse problems to engage in and maintain treatment (Collins & Allison, 1983; Anglin & Hser, 1990; Nurco, Hanlon et al., 1995). In fact, many narcotic addicts may have little interest in treatment until they come under criminal justice surveillance (Maddux, 1988; Lipton, 1995).

Evidence that legal coercion can be a successful motivating force has been available for some time (Anglin, 1988). In a study of nearly 1,000 subjects admitted into court-enforced treatment from 1962 to 1964 under the California Civil Addict Program (CAP), there was a significant reduction in drug use in a treatment group when compared to a serendipitously provided control group inadvertently released from supervision by procedural errors. Realistic harm-reduction outcome measures were compared between the treated group and the released group who was not treated but was similar in other respects to the group coerced into treatment. On follow-up, the decrease in the drug related arrest rate was 19% greater in the treatment group, which also exhibited a 40% greater reduction in non-drug arrests. The treatment group spent less time involved in property crimes (12% greater reduction), committed fewer crimes (32% greater reduction), and spent less time with daily narcotic use (15% greater reduction). The treated group spent 29% more time under legal supervision, largely due to supervised community aftercare. Because the follow-up was conducted over an 11- to 13-year period, the control group also experienced some reduction in drug use and crime due in part to "maturing out" of their addiction (Anglin, Brecht et al., 1986; Biernacki, 1986).

In the CAP, drug addiction and criminality were seen to be chronic conditions such that "the same perspective should be applied to narcotic addiction control as many mental health professionals take toward intervention with the chronically mentally ill: such interventions require a lengthy, if not lifetime, management program." Further, it was thought that "should relapse to narcotic use, property crime, or dealing become apparent, only a short return to the inpatient facility, at most 30 to 90 days, is required to detoxify addicts and ready them for release again" (Anglin, 1988).

The fact that coerced treatment can be effective is additionally supported by an evaluation of methadone maintenance treatment provided to a group of male subjects who were divided into three groups based on whether they had entered treatment under no, moderate, or high legal coercion. Follow-up indicated a reduction of heroin use during treatment to one fifth of the pretreatment level in each group, the coerced as well as the volunteer cohort (Anglin, Brecht & Maddahian, 1990). A later study of similar design involved a more diverse group of subjects, including women and Latino subjects, and noted there was substantial improvement in level of narcotic use, criminality, and social functioning regardless of whether or not the treatment involvement was coerced or voluntary (Brecht, Anglin & Jung-Chi Wang, 1993).

A means of professional monitoring of offenders with substance abuse problems was established in 1972 after discussion among a number of federal agencies (Weinman, 1992). The model became known as Treatment Alternatives to Street Crime (TASC), and it was charged to identify, assess, refer to treatment, and monitor opiate abusing defendants charged with nonviolent crimes. The TASC professional reported to both the treatment professionals and the criminal justice system alike, both of which became supportive of the project.

The principles of TASC continue to foster a partnership between the criminal justice system and the drug treatment community, (although funding and the name may be different in various communities). In addition, TASC-like programs now work with probation and parole populations, as well.

The Treatment Outcomes Prospective Study (TOPS) showed that TASC clients remained in treatment six to seven weeks longer than voluntary or other criminal justice treatment referrals (Hubbard, Marsden et al., 1989). Another major contribution of TASC was to identify and refer to treatment a large number of persons who had never been in treatment before. In 1986, two thirds of their clients were new to any form of treatment (Weinman, 1992). A RAND study compared 1,000 subjects who were referred to a TASC program with another 1,000 subjects who were referred to routine criminal justice processing. The study indicated that TASC had favorable effects highly influenced by site and offender characteristics. For example, TASC often had a stronger effect among those offenders who were more problematic (Longshore & Turner, 1996).

Treatment-oriented special courts (drug courts) evolved in order to process the large numbers of nonviolent drug-related cases overwhelming dockets and probation departments. Between 1980 and 1989, drug arrests had increased 134% while the number of total arrests had increased only 37% (Belenko & Dumanovsky, 1993). The Dade county, Florida, drug court was the first drug court of its kind, and it is perhaps the best known. The court was established in 1989 by administrative order of the chief judge of Florida's 11th judicial circuit for the purpose of diverting arrestees who had no history of violent crimes, had not been arrested for drug trafficking, and who had no more than two felony convictions. Other drug courts prefer to have a guilty plea or conviction before providing a deferred sentencing arrangement that includes treatment (Belenko, 1996). In both cases, the offender is referred to treatment and then monitored by the court. This process allows the court to provide a measured and immediate judicial consequence for a return to drug use, lack of participation in treatment, or commission of a new crime. The impact of the drug courts on recidivism when compared to other alternatives remains to be determined.

The RAND corporation evaluated the First Time Drug Offender (FTDO) program in Maricopa County, Arizona, using an experimental design whereby participants were randomized into one of four probation tracks, one of which was the FTDO drug court track. There was no significant difference between the FTDO group and the "regular probation with drug testing" group in recidivism rates, rates of rearrest on drug charges, or technical violations of probation. The FTDO group did, however, have a lower prevalence of violations for drug use, 10% versus 26% for other probationers (Deschenes & Greenwood, 1995).

THERAPEUTIC COMMUNITIES

In contrast to the absence of objective data to measure the claimed successes of the Synanon Community, a number of other drug-free therapeutic communities (TCs) that followed have been extensively evaluated (DeLeon, 1984; De Leon, Wexler & Jainchill, 1982; De Leon & Schwartz, 1984; De

Leon, Melnick et al., 1993; Wexler, Falkin & Lipton, 1990; Pan, Scarpitti et al., 1993; Wexler & Williams, 1986; Wexler, 1996; Condelli & Hubbard, 1994; Inciardi, 1997).

Defining or describing a drug-free therapeutic community is no easy task, at least in a short form. De Leon put it this way:

> "The therapeutic community is a total treatment environment that provides a residential 24-hour-per-day learning experience in which a drug user's transformations in conduct, attitudes, values, and emotions are introduced, monitored, and mutually reinforced as part of the daily regime. . . . The essential dynamic in the TC is mutual self-help. Thus, the day-to-day activities are conducted by the residents themselves. In their jobs, groups, meetings, recreation, and personal and social time, it is the residents who constantly transmit to each other the main messages and expectations of the community" (De Leon, 1986).

The conversion of the antisocial lifestyles of criminal addicts to the prosocial behaviors of parolees who have a chance of remaining drug-free and law-abiding is no simple matter. Nevertheless, the total environments described briefly above by De Leon are able to affect change in a sufficient number of criminal addicts to offer some hope for a successful and humane societal response to the problem of drugs and crime.

For example, 75% of the 75 graduates of the 1970–1971 Phoenix House were crime- and drug-free five years after completion of the program. There were, however, 162 dropouts who did not fare as well. Still, 31% of dropouts were crime- and drug-free while 56% could be judged improved. Time in program (TIP) correlated with better outcomes (De Leon, Wexler & Jainchill, 1982). Retention in therapeutic communities remains a problem. In a study of the rates in a seven TC consortium over February 1 to August 15, 1979, 87.8% of the clients dropped out at least once, and across all seven programs, the 12-month retention rates ranged from only 4% to 21% (De Leon & Schwartz, 1984).

The Oregon Cornerstone program is a 32-bed coeducational facility located on the grounds of the Oregon State Hospital in Salem, Oregon, where prison inmates may spend the last ten to twelve months of their sentence. In a study of one cohort (N = 43) three years after graduation, 37% had no arrests, 51% had no convictions, and 74% had served no prison time. As noted in the Phoenix House study, the non-graduates who served as a comparison sample did not fare as well, although time in program correlated with higher rates of success (Field, 1989).

A multi-stage program in Delaware combines an in-prison TC with a work release TC followed by an aftercare program during parole (Inciardi, 1997). An 18-month follow-up perceived those offenders who completed all three programs as having fared best in terms of arrest rate and several measure of drug and alcohol use. For example, 77% were arrest-free at 18 months. A comparison group (N = 180) of individuals who were randomly assigned to a traditional work-release program fared less well with only 46% being arrest-free at 18 months ($p < .05$). Of those who did not complete all three programs but did participate in some portion, e.g., the in-prison TC or the work-release TC, improvement correlated positively with time in program. Several measures of alcohol and other drug use paralleled the arrest rate findings in that those subjects who completed both the in-prison and work release programs were more successful in reducing drug use.

The Amity In-prison Therapeutic Community is a 200-bed residential unit at the R.J. Donovan Medium Security Prison at San Diego. It has been in operation for over five years and is in the process of its five-year evaluation (Wexler, 1996). It is similar to the Delaware program in that the in-prison component is accompanied by a next-stage community TC in the area. The treatment sample was randomly selected from eligible volunteers. Results of evaluation at 24 months after completion of both the in-prison and aftercare TCs indicated that, of the 43 subjects completing both programs, only seven (16.3%) were reincarcerated, whereas 52 out of 80 subjects (65%) within the control group were returned to custody ($p < .001$). Also, six of 16 (56.3%) prison TC completers who were aftercare dropouts were also returned to custody ($p < .001$). Of those who had been reincarcerated, the mean time until reincarceration was greater for those subjects who had completed both programs (429 days) than for those who had dropped out of aftercare (295 days) or who had received no treatment at all (215 days).

Clearly, therapeutic communities located in prisons and in communities have a role in harm reduction where the criminal addict is concerned. Retention remains a problem, but for those willing to undergo the changes in behaviors that are possible in the TC environment, success is a common event. Certainly, incarceration time is best spent participating in an in-prison therapeutic community or, as an alternative to incarceration, a more productive form of incapacitation can often be found through community TCs.

METHADONE MAINTENANCE

Methadone maintenance treatment has been documented by prospective studies initiated in 1964, and by numerous other prospective and retrospective studies, to be medically safe and very effective in achieving its primary treatment goal: that is, "significant reduction or cessation of illicit narcotic (opiate, usually heroin) use" (Kreek, 1991). However, "despite their high crime rates, criminal incomes, and economic consequences, many heroin addicts are quite successful at avoiding or limiting their contacts with the two major institutions of social control that address their behavior: methadone treatment and the criminal justice system" (Johnson, Goldstein et al., 1985).

Methadone maintenance, or any other treatment for that matter, will not be effective unless the opiate addict can be engaged in treatment in the first place. A means of engaging more opiate addicts in treatment is desirable, though not yet available. In the meantime, methadone maintenance continues to offer success in the management of a difficult subset of addicted individuals.

Some examples of significant harm reduction associated with methadone maintenance have appeared earlier in chapter, but there are others. In one of the few randomized studies used in evaluating substance abuse treatment, Dole began 12 inmate-volunteers, who had been randomized into treatment, on methadone in the final ten days of jail time and referred them to a methadone maintenance clinic at the time of release. Of this group, none returned to daily heroin use and 9 of the 12 had no further convictions in the 50-week follow-up period. Of 16 volunteers who were randomized into a control group, all relapsed to daily heroin use and 15 of the 16 were convicted of new crimes during the follow-up period (Dole, Robinson et al., 1969).

In a Swedish study, 34 heroin-dependent patients who had applied for methadone maintenance were randomized to methadone maintenance or non-methadone outpatient. In the methadone treatment group, 12 of the original 17 still were in treatment after two years, had not returned to "regular" heroin use, had not been imprisoned, and had not been expelled from treatment. On the other hand, only one of the non-methadone treatment group met these criteria. After two years, members of the control group were allowed to reapply for methadone maintenance. Of the 9 who did so, 8 subjects had not returned to regular heroin use at five years. Also, at five years, 13 of the original 17 who were randomized into treatment were still in treatment and had not returned to regular heroin use. The 13th member had remained in treatment, despite a return to regular use, but eventually stopped the regular use of heroin (Gunne & Gronbladh, 1984).

Events have created natural experiments where comparisons can be made. For example, the closing of the Bakersfield, California Methadone Maintenance Clinic in 1976 allowed for a comparison between 88 clients of that clinic who could not avail themselves of a distant alternate clinic and 88 clients of an enrolled-elsewhere comparison group. Fifty-four percent of the terminated clients returned to daily heroin use, while 31% of the comparison group were daily users of illicit narcotics. Arrest and incarceration rates were twice those of the comparison sample (McGlothlin & Anglin, 1981).

In a unique program in New York City's central jail facilities on Rikers Island, inmates with "more chronic and severe social and personal deficits than other addicts applying for treatment" were started on methadone while incarcerated and referred to dedicated slots in community methadone maintenance programs at release. These subjects were more likely to apply for treatment after release and to be in treatment at 26 weeks after release than those who underwent a seven-day detoxification while incarcerated. In addition, inmates at Rikers Island who are in a methadone maintenance program at the time of their arrest can be maintained while incarcerated and referred back to their clinic at release (Magura, Rosenblum et al., 1993).

Finally, not all methadone maintenance programs are alike, and "programs oriented more toward rehabilitation and long-term maintenance that delivered more counseling services had better patient outcomes than programs providing fewer patient services" (Ball & Ross, 1991). Unfortunately, the Drug Abuse Treatment Outcome Study (DATOS), which collected data on subjects in treatment in the years 1991 through 1993, indicates that the level of counseling and other services has fallen off, with the lowest level found in methadone maintenance clinics (Etheridge, Craddock et al., 1995).

Physicians who are knowledgeable about drug addiction must dispel the many negative myths about methadone and help the public and other physicians to understand the value of methadone maintenance treatment in the reduction of illicit drug use and crime.

OUTPATIENT DRUG-FREE TREATMENT

The roots of the drug-free outpatient programs are said to lie in the Community Mental Health Centers Act of 1963. Individual counseling, along with vocational, educational, and other community assistance, became a model of service delivery in substance abuse treatment (Brown, 1990). In the 1970s, these programs treated mostly young non-opiate abusers, but later many opiate addicts entered these programs (Anglin & Hser, 1990). TOPS found that when drug-free outpatient clients remained more than 26 weeks in treatment, the odds ratio (compared to 1.00 for the comparison group who were in treatment <1 week) was 0.47 ($p < .01$) for involvement in predatory illegal acts and 1.95 ($p < .05$) for full-time employment (Hubbard, Marsden et al., 1989). The favorable outcomes were mainly in those subjects who were not daily users of opiates and used in conjunction with other drugs or used only non-opiates (Anglin & Hser, 1990). Drug-free outpatient programs often serve a monitoring function for clients under criminal justice surveillance. As with methadone maintenance clinics, those that provide a full range of services, such as vocational, educational, and family counseling, are more likely to be helpful to their clients. They provide valuable support to addicts in the community, can be scaled to meet budgetary requirements, and are available to nudge contemplators toward changes in behavior.

DARP, TOPS, DATOS, CALDATA AND CDATE

After Title IV of the Narcotic Addict Rehabilitation Act (NARA) aided in the establishment of a community drug abuse treatment system, the first of several programs to monitor these publicly funded programs was the Drug Abuse Reporting Program (DARP). It described the subjects entering treatment, the treatment system itself, and gathered treatment outcome data. Outcomes were reported for methadone maintenance, residential drug-free, outpatient drug-free, and detoxification only. The distribution of clients to the different modalities was not a random one. Over the period of 1969 to 1974, data was collected on nearly 44,000 subjects in 52 programs. The DARP reported that of this sample, "virtually all had some criminal history" (Lehman & Simpson, 1990). In all modalities, and over all client characteristics, the more favorable outcomes correlated with longer time in treatment. About 40% of the study subjects had entered treatment on probation, parole, or were awaiting trial. By the time of the 12-year follow-up interview, 71% of the sample had relapsed one or more times to daily opioid use. Still, only 25% were using opioids daily by the twelfth year, and it had been three years or longer since 63% had last used daily (Joe, Chastain et al., 1990). Those treated in a TC one or more times had the most favorable year–12 outcomes on drug abuse, alcohol use, employment, and time in jail (Marsh, Joe et al., 1990). In the 12-year follow-up of persons who had quit daily opiate use, 61% said that they were in treatment "when it happened," but not necessarily the original DARP treatment (Lehman & Simpson, 1990). Each addict had been in an average of six separate treatment programs at the time of the 12-year follow-up, thus pointing out the problems inherent in evaluating long-term outcomes from a single treatment facility (Marsh, Joe et al., 1990). The DARP data "consistently showed that the overall posttreatment outcomes of methadone maintenance, therapeutic community, and drug-free outpatient groups were significantly more favorable than for the detoxification only and the intake only (no treatment) groups" (Simpson, Joe & Barrett, 1990).

As the community based drug abuse treatment system evolved, the second evaluation project, the Treatment Outcome Prospective Study (TOPS) looked at samples of 11,750 clients admitted to 41 programs over the period 1979 to 1981. Again, longer time in treatment was associated with better outcomes, both in terms of drug use and criminal activity. Those who entered treatment who were married, older, better educated, held better employment records, were more psychologically sound, and had fewer arrests, did better in treatment. Many who entered treatment at the time of the TOPS project reported multiple substance abuse in contrast to the earlier cohort of the DARP who were mostly heroin addicts. TOPS also included clients who entered treatment under criminal justice referral through Treatment Alternatives to Street Crime (TASC) and found that these clients did as well or better than those who were in treatment voluntarily. Three annual admission cohorts were followed one month after entry into treatment and at three intervals during treatment. Samples of each cohort were interviewed after treatment at three months, one year, two years, and three to five years. On follow-up of a sample that spent >3 months in a residential community, 61% had committed "serious predatory illegal acts" in the year before admission, but less than 20% of the sample were found to have committed these crimes over the past year at three to five years after treatment. A cohort sample who had spent >3 months in a methadone program saw a reduction in the prevalence of regular heroin use from 63.5% before entering treatment to 17.5% at the three-to-five-year follow-up. Only 27.1% of a drug-free outpatient sample that spent >3 months in treatment worked full-time, but by the three-to-five-year follow-up, 49.7% were working full time. Such are examples of the favorable outcomes as indicated by TOPS.

Not as successful was the reduction of "heavy alcohol use," which was modest at best in those who had spent >3 months in each of the three modalities and no better than the sample populations that had spent <3 months in treatment. While 33.4% of a drug-free outpatient sample reported heavy alcohol use in the year before treatment, 26.9% reported heavy alcohol use at three to five years after treatment. Those in residential or methadone maintenance fared no better. It may be that some subjects had substituted alcohol for other drugs during and after treatment.

The Drug Abuse Treatment Outcome Study (DATOS) is evaluating clients who entered treatment between 1991 and 1993. It is a multi-year study with very few results yet available. It will, as did DARP and TOPS, look at methadone maintenance, therapeutic communities, and drug-free outpatient clinics.

The California Drug and Alcohol Treatment Assessment (CALDATA) reported the cost of treatment to be 209 million dollars in a large California sample of publicly funded programs while saving 1.5 billion dollars, due mostly to a reduction in crime (Gerstein, Johnson et al., 1994).

The Correctional Drug Abuse Treatment Effectiveness project (CDATE) is gathering the results of 25 years of correctional evaluation research with special attention being given to drug treatment offered to all levels of offenders. The project has been undertaken by the National Development and Research Institutes, Inc. (NDRI) in New York (Lipton, 1995).

RACE, DRUGS, AND CRIMINAL JUSTICE

The history of the interface between drug use and the criminal justice system in the United States is leavened with racial issues, likely based on both fear of minorities and fear of drugs. This has been especially true where drug use and associated criminal behavior has been linked to Chinese, Hispanic, Puerto Rican, and African-American minority groups (Musto, 1987). To be sure, many Americans and many American politicians know very little about illicit drug use or criminal justice (and understand little about minorities, as well). This lack of understanding results in a reliance on tragic anecdotes of the Willie Horton variety and hand-me-down stereotyping of the "crazed dope fiend." The topic of drugs and crime, therefore, is open to populist tirades and political demagoguery. The Sentencing Commission has elegantly documented that the laws targeting persons associated with crack cocaine use were generated by the unfounded but oft-repeated belief that the University of Maryland basketball star, Len Bias, died in 1986 of a "crack overdose." A year after his death, testimony at the trial of his accused supplier established that Bias and his friends were snorting powdered cocaine hydrochloride, not crack cocaine (United States Sentencing Commission, 1995).

There is evidence that public opinion is not driving political rhetoric about the need to "get tough" on criminal addicts, but that the reverse may be true. That is, public concern is more often driven by political and media initiatives, not crime rates or drug use (Beckett, 1997; Cullen, Clark & Wozniak, 1985).

The association of crime, cocaine trafficking, and minorities (usually African-Americans) was made early in the twentieth century (Musto, 1987) and revived with the advent of crack cocaine in the mid–1980s. Congress enacted the Anti-Drug Abuse Act of 1986 that established the 100 to 1 ratio between powdered cocaine hydrochloride and crack cocaine. This act was followed by the Anti-Drug Abuse Act of 1988, which set forth mandatory minimum penalties for the simple possession of crack cocaine (United States Sentencing Commission, 1995). These legislative initiatives superseded sentencing guidelines that were implemented in 1987 and tied the hands of federal judges and the Sentencing Commission, as well. The adverse effects on minorities were foreseeable (Tonry, 1995). Congress was persuaded that crack cocaine was far more addicting than other forms of cocaine and also was responsible for more violent crime. The fact that powdered cocaine hydrochloride is easily converted (with some sodium bicarbonate and a household oven) to crack cocaine, notwithstanding. Congress also arbitrarily decided that "possession of as little as 5 grams means individuals (carrying such amounts) in most instances are dealers, not users" (United States Sentencing Commission, 1995). The result here is that an individual found in possession of as little as 5 grams of crack cocaine (equal to 1 tablespoon of sugar in the author's kitchen) and who is convicted in a federal court, even of a first offense, will receive five years in a federal prison without parole. If, on the other hand, the individual is convicted in a state court, there may be a great deal of judicial discretion in the sentencing process even though all states have instituted some forms of mandatory minimum sentencing for certain crimes.

The Sentencing Commission found the 100 to 1 ratio to be unduly high despite some concerns about the dangers of crack cocaine and also noted that the "vast majority" of those affected by "such an exaggerated ratio" are racial minorities (United States Sentencing Commission, 1995). In April 1997, the Sentencing Commission recommended that congress change the current "trigger" amount of cocaine and mandate a five-year minimum sentence to somewhere between 25 and 75 grams of crack cocaine and 125 and 375 grams of powdered cocaine hydrochloride, about a 1:5 ratio (Conaboy, 1997).

In a July 1997 letter to the President of the United States, the Attorney General recommended that the amounts be set at 25 grams for crack cocaine and 250 grams for the powder, a 1:10 ratio. As of early 1998, Congress had taken no action on the matter.

The Sentencing Project, a scholarly watchdog of sentencing policy, notes that 73.7% of all persons sentenced to state prison for possession of any drug are African-American and 16% of those sentenced are Hispanic, (totaling 90% of all state prison sentences for drug possession).

African-Americans represent about 12% of the U.S. population, 13% of those Americans who used drugs in the past month, according to the National Household Survey, 35% of those who are arrested for drug possession, 55% of those who are convicted, and 74% of those citizens sentenced to state prisons because of possession of an illicit drug (Mauer, 1995).

Drug arrests increased from 471,000 in 1980 to 1,247,000 in 1989. During that period, the proportion of arrestees who are African-American rose from 24% to 39%. Residential racial segregation and the targeting of Black neighborhoods sweep African-Americans into the criminal justice system and carry along working class Blacks who are vital to neighborhoods (Mauer, 1995). Prosecutorial policies (including, but not limited to, the decision to prosecute in the federal system) also result in a larger number of African-Americans being incarcerated for drug offenses.

Marc Mauer and Tracy Huling of the Sentencing Project cite a survey published by the *Los Angeles Times* on May 21, 1995, stating that "not a single white offender had been convicted of a crack cocaine offense in a federal court serving the Los Angeles metropolitan area since 1986, despite the fact that whites comprise a majority of crack users." During the same period, hundreds of white cocaine traffickers were prosecuted in state courts. While federal prosecutors contend that they target high-level traffickers, the *Times* analysis found that "many African-Americans charged in the federal court were low-level dealers or accomplices in the drug trade" (Mauer, 1995).

Finally, tougher sentencing policies, including mandatory minimum sentences, have disproportionately affected AfricanAmerican drug offenders. For example, in 1994, 82% of all women sentenced for a drug offense were African-American (Mauer, 1995). Many of them, no doubt, were mothers. Skilled legal advice during this process could have dramatically affected these outcomes, but such legal advice would be a luxury for disadvantaged minority youth and there are no drug courts in the federal system.

Michael Tonry, Sonorsky Professor of Law and Public Policy at the University of Minnesota, notes that "there is a consensus among scholars and policy analysts that most of the Black punishment disproportions result not from racial bias or discrimination within the system but from patterns of Black offending and of Black criminal records. Drug law enforcement is the conspicuous exception. Blacks are arrested and confined in numbers grossly out of line with their use or sale of drugs." Professor Tonry goes on to say, "the war on drugs and the set of harsh crime control policies in which it was enmeshed were undertaken to achieve political, not policy objectives. It is the adoption for political purposes with foreseeable disparate impacts, the use of disadvantaged Black Americans as a means to achieving politicians' electoral ends, that must in the end be justified. It cannot" (Tonry, 1995).

CONCLUSIONS

Clearly, the responsibility for solving the problems associated with the criminality tied to drug use itself, the associated criminality not tied directly to use, the consequences of crime to victims, and the terrible personal consequences experienced by addicts and their families seem to lie at the feet of the criminal justice system (The American College of Physicians, The National Commission on Correctional Health Care, & The American Correctional Health Services Association, 1992). What role is there for physicians here?

Vincent Dole, as he delivered the Distinguished Scientist Lecture to an annual meeting of the American Society of Addiction Medicine stated that "the existence of this society (ASAM) bears witness to the official recognition of addicts as sick persons, deserving serious study and medical treatment when appropriate." Dr. Dole described addiction as a public health problem. Later, others defined correctional health care as a public health opportunity and urged that a public policy agenda for criminal justice should "take advantage of the period of confinement" in order to detect, educate, counsel, and treat infectious diseases (Glaser & Greifinger, 1993).

One place where addiction, crime, and infectious diseases come together before health care workers is under criminal justice surveillance. These are opportunities to detect, educate, counsel, and treat addiction as well as the HIV infections, tuberculosis, and other disorders in a population that rarely seeks medical care when not in custody. Dole saw a need for physicians to be involved in the criminal justice system in 1974, when he said, "it is the duty of physicians to be aware of medical conditions in jails and of the effects of incarceration on prisoners. They owe this service to the community both as health professionals and as influential citizens" (Dole, 1974).

Finally, a compassionate nudge from another physician on the subject of correctional populations and our professionalism comes from Alvin J. Thompson, the American Medical Association's representative to the National Commission on Correctional Health Care, who said: "Professionalism in medicine depends on our ability to provide quality care to the least of us" (Anno, 1982).

Hopefully, physicians will find a way to influence policy makers on behalf of our chemically dependent patients, wherever they may be, but especially where they are relatively helpless before the law.

REFERENCES

Anglin MD, Brecht ML, Woodward A & Bonett DG (1986). An empirical study of maturing out: Conditional factors. *International Journal of the Addictions* 21(2):1011–1027.

Anglin MD (1987). *Narcotics Use and Crime: A Multisample, Multimethod Analysis*. Los Angeles, CA: Department of Psychology, University of California at Los Angeles.

Anglin MD (1988). The efficacy of civil commitment in treating narcotic addiction. In CG Leukefeld & FM Tims (eds.) *Compulsory Treatment of Drug Abuse: Research and Clinical Practice (NIDA Research Monograph 86)*. Rockville, MD: National Institute on Drug Abuse, 8–34.

Anglin MD & Hser Y (1990). Treatment of drug abuse. In M Tonry and JQ Wilson (eds.) *Drugs and Crime*. Chicago, IL: The University of Chicago Press, 393–460.

Anglin MD & Speckart G (1986). Narcotics use, property crime, and dealing: Structural dynamics across the addiction career. *Journal of Quantitative Criminology* 2:355–375.

Anno BJ (1982). The role of organized medicine in correctional health care. *Journal of the American Medical Association* 247(21):2923–2925.

Bale RN, Van Stone WW, Kuldau JM, Engelsing TM, Elashoff RM & Zarcone VPJ (1980). Therapeutic communities vs. methadone maintenance. *Archives of General Psychiatry* 37:179–193.

Ball JC & Ross A (1991). *The Effectiveness of Methadone Maintenance Treatment: Patients, Programs, Services, and Outcomes*. New York, NY: Springer Verlag.

Belenko S (1996). *Comparative Models of Treatment Delivery in Drug Courts*. Washington, DC: The Sentencing Project.

Beckett K (1997). Political preoccupation with crime leads, not follows, public opinion. *Overcrowded Times* 8(5):1–11.

Belenko S & Dumanovsky T (1993). *Special Drug Courts: Program Brief*. Washington, DC: Bureau of Justice Assistance.

Biernacki P (1986). *Pathways from Heroin Addiction: Recovery Without Treatment*. Philadelphia, PA: Temple University Press.

Brecht M, Anglin MD & Jung-Chi Wang (1993). Treatment effectiveness for legally coerced versus voluntary methadone maintenance clients. *American Journal of Drug and Alcohol Abuse* 19(1):89–106.

Brown BS (1990). The growth of drug abuse treatment systems. In JA Inciardi (ed.) *Handbook of Drug Control in the United States*. New York, NY: Greenwood Press, 51–70.

Bureau of Justice Statistics (1996a). *Prison and Jail Inmates, 1995*. Washington, DC: The Bureau.

Bureau of Justice Statistics (1996b). Probation and Parole Population Reaches Almost 3.8 Million (press release). Washington, DC: The Bureau.

Chaiken JM & Chaiken MR (1982). *Varieties of Criminal Behavior*. Santa Monica, CA: The RAND Corporation.

Chaiken JM & Chaiken MR (1990). Drugs and predatory crime. In M Tonry & JQ Wilson (eds.) *Drugs and*

Crime. Chicago, IL: The University of Chicago Press, 203–240.

Collins JJ & Allison M (1983). Legal coercion and retention in drug treatment. *Hospital and Community Psychiatry* 34(12):1145–1149.

Conaboy RP (1997). *Commission Recommends New Cocaine Sentencing Policy*. Washington, DC: United States Sentencing Commission.

Condelli WS & Hubbard RL (1994). Client outcomes from therapeutic communities. In FM Tims, G De Leon & N Jainchill (eds.) *Therapeutic Community: Advances in Research and Application (NIDA Research Monograph 144)*. Rockville, MD: National Institute on Drug Abuse, 80–98.

Cullen FT, Clark GA & Wozniak JF (1985). Explaining the get-tough movement, can the public be blamed? *Federal Probation* 45(2):16–24.

De Leon G (1986). The therapeutic community for substance abuse: Perspective and approach. In G De Leon & JTJ Ziegenfuss (eds.) *Therapeutic Communities for Addictions: Readings in Theory, Research, and Practice*. Springfield, IL: Charles C. Thomas, 5–18.

De Leon G, Melnick G, Schocket D & Jainchill N (1993). Is the therapeutic community culturally relevant? Findings on race/ethnic differences in retention in treatment. *Journal of Psychoactive Drugs* 25(1):77–86.

De Leon G & Schwartz S (1984). Therapeutic communities: What are the retention rates? *American Journal of Drug and Alcohol Abuse* 10(2):267–284.

De Leon G, Wexler HK & Jainchill N (1982). The therapeutic community: Success and improvement rates 5 years after treatment. *The International Journal of the Addictions* 17(4):703–747.

De Leon G (1984). Program-based evaluation research in therapeutic communities. In FM Tims & JP Ludford (eds.) *Drug Abuse Treatment Evaluation: Strategies, Progress, and Prospects (NIDA Research Monograph 51)*. Rockville, MD: National Institute on Drug Abuse, 69–87.

Deschenes E & Greenwood P (1995). Drug court or probation? An experimental evaluation of Maricopa County's drug court. *The Justice System Journal* 18(1):55–73.

Dole V (1991). Addiction as a public health problem. *Alcoholism: Clinical & Experimental Research* 15(5):749–752.

Dole V & Nyswander M (1965). A medical treatment for diacetylmorphine (heroin) addiction: A clinical trial with methadone hydrochloride. *Journal of the American Medical Association* 193(8):646650.

Dole VP (1974). Medicine and the criminal justice system. *Annals of Internal Medicine* 81:687–689.

Dole VP, Robinson R, Orraca J, Towns E, Searcy P & Caine E (1969). Methadone treatment of randomly selected criminal addicts. *The New England Journal of Medicine* 280(25):1372–1375.

Etheridge RM, Craddock SG, Dunteman GH & Hubbard RL (1995). Treatment services in two national studies of community-based drug abuse services. *Journal of Substance Abuse* 7(1):9–26.

Fagan J (1990). Intoxication and aggression. In M Tonry & JQ Wilson (eds.) *Drugs and Crime*. Chicago, IL: University of Chicago Press, 241–320.

Fagan J & Weis JG (1990). *Drug Use and Delinquency Among Inner City Youth*. New York, NY: Springer-Verlag.

Field G (1989). The effects of intensive treatment on reducing the criminal recidivism of addicted offenders. *Federal Probation* 53:5156.

General Accounting Office (1991). *Drug Treatment: Despite New Strategy, Few Federal Inmates Receive Treatment*. Washington, DC: U.S. General Accounting Office.

General Accounting Office (1991). *Drug Treatment: State Prisons Face Challenges in Providing Services*. Washington, DC: U.S. General Accounting Office.

Gerstein DR, Johnson RA, Harwood HJ, Fountain D, Suter N & Malloy K (1994). *Evaluating Recovery Services: The California Drug and Alcohol Treatment Assessment*. Sacramento, CA: Department of Alcohol and Drug Programs.

Glaser JB & Greifinger RB (1993). Correctional health care: A public health opportunity. *Annals of Internal Medicine* 118:139–145.

Gunne L & Gronbladh L (1984). The Swedish methadone maintenance program. In G Serban (ed.) *The Social and Medical Aspects of Drug Abuse*. Jamaica, NY: Spectrum Publications, 205–213.

Hubbard RL, Marsden ME, Rachal JV, Harwood HJ, Cavanaugh ER & Ginzburg HM (1989). *Drug Abuse Treatment: A National Study of Effectiveness*. Chapel Hill, NC: The University of North Carolina Press.

Hunt DE (1990). Drugs and consensual crimes: Drug dealing and prostitution. In M Tonry & JQ Wilson (eds.) *Drugs and Crime*. Chicago. IL: University of Chicago Press, 159–202.

Hutchison TW, Yellen D, Young D & Kipp MR (1994). *Federal Sentencing Law and Practice*. Saint Paul, MN: West Publishing.

Inciardi JA (1988). Some considerations on the clinical efficacy of compulsory treatment: Reviewing the New York experience. In CG Leukefeld & FM Tims (eds.) *Compulsory Treatment of Drug Abuse: Research and Clinical Practice (NIDA Research Monograph 86)*. Rockville, MD: National Institute on Drug Abuse, 126–138.

Inciardi JA (1997). Introduction: A response to the war on drugs. In JA Inciardi (ed.) *Drug Treatment and Criminal Justice*. Newbury Park, CA: Sage Publication.

Joe GW, Chastain RL, Marsh KL & Simpson DD (1990). Relapse. In DD Simpson & SB Sells (eds.) *Opioid Addiction and Treatment*. Malabar, FL: Robert E. Krieger Publishing, 121–136.

Johnson BD, Goldstein PJ, Preble E, et al. (1985). *Taking Care of Business: The Economics of Crime by Heroin Users*. Lexington, MA: Lexington Books.

Kandel DB, Simcha-Fagan O & Davies M (1986). Risk factors for delinquency and illicit drug use from adolescence to young adulthood. *Journal of Drug Issues* 1667–1690.

Kreek MJ (1991). Using methadone effectively: Achieving goals by application of laboratory, clinical, and evaluation research and by development of innovative programs. In RW Pickens, CG Leukefeld, & CR Schuster (eds.) *Improving Drug Abuse Treatment (NIDA Research Monograph 106)*. Rockville, MD: National Institute on Drug Abuse, 245–266.

Lehman WEK & Simpson DD (1990). Predictions of 12 year outcomes. In DD Simpson & SB Sells (eds.) *Opioid Addiction and Treatment*. Malabar, FL: Robert E. Krieger Publishing, 203–220.

Lehman WEK & Simpson DD (1990). Criminal involvement. In DD Simpson & SB Sells (eds.) *Opioid Addiction and Treatment*. Malabar, FL: Robert E. Krieger Publishing, 157–176.

Leukefeld CG (1991). Opportunities for enhancing drug abuse treatment with criminal justice authority. In RW Pickens, CG Leukefeld & CR Schuster (eds.) *Improving Drug Abuse Treatment (NID Research Monograph 106)*. Rockville, MD: National Institute on Drug Abuse, 328–337.

Lipton DS (1995). The effectiveness of treatment for drug abusers under criminal justice surveillance. *National Institute of Justice Research Report*. Washington, DC: National Institute of Justice.

Longshore D & Turner S (1996). Drug treatment for criminal offenders. *RAND Drug Policy Research Center Newsletter* 5(1):4–5.

Maddux JF (1988). Clinical experience with civil commitment. In C Leukefeld, G Tims & FM Tims (eds.) *Compulsory Treatment of Drug Abuse: Research and Clinical Practice (NIDA Research Monograph 86)*. Rockville, MD: National Institute on Drug Abuse, 35–56.

Magura S, Rosenblum A, Lewis C & Joseph H (1993). The effectiveness of in-jail methadone maintenance. *The Journal of Drug Issues* 23(1):75–99.

Marsh KL, Joe GW, Simpson DD & Lehman WEK (1990). Treatment history. In DD Simpson & SB Sells (eds.) *Opioid Addiction and Treatment*. Malabar, FL: Robert E. Krieger Publishing, 137–156.

Mauer M & Huling T (1995). *Young Black Americans and the Criminal Justice System: Five Years Later*. Washington, DC: The Sentencing Project.

Mauer M (1997). *Intended and Unintended Consequences: State Racial Disparities in Imprisonment*. Washington, DC: The Sentencing Project.

McGlothlin WH & Anglin MD (1981). Shutting off methadone: Costs and benefits. *Archives of General Psychiatry* 38:885–892.

Musto DF (1987). *The American Disease: Origins of Narcotic Control* (Expanded Edition). New York, NY: Oxford University Press.

National Council on Crime and Delinquency (1996). *National Assessment of Structured Sentencing*. Washington, DC: Bureau of Justice Assistance.

National Institute of Justice (1995). *Drug Use Forecasting: 1994 Annual Report on Adult and Juvenile Arrestees*. Washington, DC: U.S. Department of Justice.

Nurco DN, Hanlon TE, Bateman RW & Kinlock TW (1995). Drug abuse treatment in the context of correctional surveillance. *Journal of Substance Abuse Treatment* 12(1):19–27.

Pan H, Scarpitti FR, Inciardi JA & Lockwood D (1993). Some considerations on therapeutic communities in corrections. In JA Inciardi (ed.) *Drug Treatment and Criminal Justice*. Newbury Park, CA: Sage Publications, 30–43.

Petersilia J & Turner S (1993). Intensive probation and parole. In M Tonry (ed.) *Crime and Justice: A Review of Research (Volume 17)*. Chicago, IL: University of Chicago Press, 281–335.

Pickens RW & Fletcher BW (1991). Overview of treatment issues. In RW Pickens, CG Leukefeld, & CR Schuster (eds.) *Improving Drug Abuse Treatment (NIDA Research Monograph 106)*. Rockville, MD: National Institute on Drug Abuse, 1–19.

Simpson DD, Joe GW & Barrett ME (1990). Introduction. In DD Simpson & SB Sells (eds.) *Opioid Addiction and Treatment*. Malabar, FL: Robert E. Krieger Publishing, 1–24.

The American College of Physicians, The National Commission on Correctional Health Care & The American Correctional Health Services Association (1992). The crisis in correctional health care: The impact of the national drug control strategy on correctional health services. *Annals of Internal Medicine* 117(1):71–77.

Tonry M & Lynch M (1996). Intermediate sanctions. In M Tonry (ed.) *Crime and Justice: A Review of Research (Volume 20)*. Chicago, IL: University of Chicago Press, 99–144.

Tonry M (1995). *Malign Neglect: Race, Crime, and Punishment in America*. New York, NY: Oxford University Press.

Travis LF III, Schwartz MD & Clear TR (1992). The setting. In LFI Travis, MD Schwartz & TR Clear (eds.) *Corrections: An Issues Approach*. Cincinnati, OH: Anderson Publishing, 5–53.

United States Sentencing Commission (1995). *Special Report to the Congress: Cocaine and Federal Sentencing Policy*. Washington, DC: The Commission.

Visher CA (1986). The Rand inmate survey: A reanalysis. In A Blumstein, J Cohen, JA Roth & CA Visher (eds.) *Criminal Careers and "Career Criminals" (Volume II)*. Washington, DC: National Academy Press, 161–211.

Weinman B (1992). A coordinated approach for drug-abusing offenders: TASC and parole. In CG Leukefeld & FM Tims (eds.) *Drug Abuse Treatment in Prisons and Jails (NIDA Research Monograph 118)*. Rockville, MD: National Institute on Drug Abuse, 232–245.

West Publishing (1989). *The American Criminal Justice Process: Selected Rules, Statutes, and Guidelines*. Saint Paul, MN: Author.

Wexler HK (1996). The Amity Prison TC Evaluation: Inmate Profiles and Reincarceration Outcomes. Presented at the California Department of Corrections, Youth and Adult Correctional Agency, Sacramento, CA, November.

Wexler HK, Falkin GP & Lipton DS (1990). Outcome evaluation of a prison therapeutic community for substance abuse treatment. *Criminal Justice and Behavior* 17(1):71–92.

Wexler HK & Williams R (1986). The Stay'n Out therapeutic community: Prison treatment for substance abusers. *Journal of Psychoactive Drugs* 18(3):221–230.

Wish ED & Johnson BD (1986). The impact of substance abuse on criminal careers. In A Blumstein, J Cohen, JA Roth & CA Visher (eds.) *Criminal Careers and "Career Criminals" (Volume II)*. Washington, DC: National Academy Press, 52–88.

Yablonsky L (1965). *The Tunnel Back: Synanon*. New York, NY: Macmillan.

SECTION 6
Intoxication, Overdose and Acute Withdrawal

CHAPTER 1

Principles of Detoxification **423**
Christine Kasser, M.D., Anne Geller, M.D., FASAM, Elizabeth Howell, M.D., and Alan Wartenberg, M.D., FASAM

CHAPTER 2

Management of Alcohol Intoxication and Withdrawal **431**
Michael F. Mayo-Smith, M.D., M.P.H.

CHAPTER 3

Management of Sedative-Hypnotic Intoxication and Withdrawal **441**
Steven J. Eickelberg, M.D., FASAM, and Michael F. Mayo-Smith, M.D., M.P.H.

CHAPTER 4

Management of Opioid Intoxication and Withdrawal **457**
Patrick G. O'Connor, M.D., M.P.H., and Thomas R. Kosten, M.D.

CHAPTER 5

Management of Stimulant, Hallucinogen, Marijuana and Phencyclidine Intoxication and Withdrawal **465**
Jeffery N. Wilkins, M.D. and David A. Gorelick, M.D., Ph.D.

CHAPTER 6

Management of Nicotine Withdrawal **487**
Terry A. Rustin, M.D., FASAM

SECTION COORDINATOR

MICHAEL F. MAYO-SMITH, M.D., M.P.H.
Associate Chief of Staff/Ambulatory Care
Department of Veterans Affairs Medical Center
Manchester, New Hampshire, and
Assistant Professor of Medicine
Harvard Medical School
Boston, Massachusetts

CONTRIBUTORS

Bradley T. Conner
University of California at Los Angeles
Los Angeles, California

Steven J. Eickelberg, M.D., FASAM
President, PerforMax
Private Practice of Sport Psychiatry,
Addiction Medicine and Psychiatry,
Occupational and Organizational Psychiatry
Scottsdale, Arizona

David A. Gorelick, M.D., Ph.D.
Chief, Treatment Branch
Intramural Research Program
National Institute on Drug Abuse, and
Adjunct Professor of Psychiatry
University of Maryland School of Medicine
Baltimore, Maryland

Christine L. Kasser, M.D.
Private Practice of Medicine
Germantown, Tennessee

Thomas R. Kosten, M.D.
Chief of Psychiatry
Veterans Affairs Connecticut Hospital
West Haven, Connecticut, and
Professor of Psychiatry
Yale University School of Medicine and
Yale New Haven Hospital
New Haven, Connecticut

Patrick G. O'Connor, M.D., M.P.H.
Director, Primary Care Center
Yale New Haven Hospital, and
Associate Professor of Medicine
Yale University School of Medicine
New Haven, Connecticut

Terry A. Rustin, M.D., FASAM
Assistant Professor
Department of Psychiatry and Behavioral Sciences
University of Texas Medical School
Houston, Texas

Jeffery N. Wilkins, M.D.
Chief, Clinical Psychopharmacology Unit
Department of Veterans Affairs Medical Center
West Los Angeles, and
Adjunct Professor of Psychiatry
UCLA School of Medicine
Los Angeles, California

CHAPTER 1

Principles of Detoxification

Christine L. Kasser, M.D.
Anne Geller, M.D., FASAM
Elizabeth Howell, M.D.
Alan Wartenberg, M.D., FASAM

Definitions
Goals of Detoxification
General Principles of Management
Modifications for Special Populations
Detoxification Settings
Considerations in Selecting a Setting

The treatment of patients who are under the influence of, or experiencing withdrawal from, substance-related disorders requires an understanding of the natural history and variants of such syndromes; a complete assessment of the patient's individual medical, psychiatric, and social issues; and a knowledge of the uses and limitations of a variety of interventions, including—but not limited to—pharmacotherapies. Memorization of protocols will not serve as well as a full appreciation of the basic and clinical science of Addiction Medicine. All therapies must be individualized to specific patients' needs and adjusted appropriately to their response to treatment.

DEFINITIONS

Substance refers to a drug (including alcohol and nicotine) that is mood-altering. A variety of *substance-related disorders* may result from exposure to mood-altering drugs.

The diagnosis of *substance dependence* may be made when cognitive, behavioral, and physiologic signs and symptoms indicate that an individual continues to use a substance despite significant substance-related problems (APA, 1994). Substance dependence may occur with or without neuroadaptation. Physiologic dependence and/or tolerance may develop with continued exposure to certain substances as neuroadaptation occurs.

Tolerance is the ability to use greatly increased amounts of a substance with diminished intoxicating effect. *Neuroadaptation* is present if a withdrawal syndrome occurs with cessation of or reduction in use of a substance.

Withdrawal syndrome is the predictable constellation of signs and symptoms following abrupt discontinuation of, or rapid decrease in, intake of a substance that has been used consistently for a period of time. The signs and symptoms of withdrawal usually are the opposite of the direct pharmacologic effects of a drug. Substances in a given pharmacologic class produce similar withdrawal syndromes; however, the onset, duration, and intensity are variable, depending on the particular agent used, the duration of use, and the degree of neuroadaptation. Evidence for the cessation of or reduction in use of a substance may be obtained by history or toxicology. Additionally, the clinical picture should not correspond to any of the organic mental syndromes, such as organic hallucinosis (APA, 1994). Withdrawal may, however, be superimposed on any organic mental syndrome.

The term *detoxification* implies a clearing of toxins. However, for individuals with physiologic substance dependence, detoxification is defined as the management of the withdrawal syndrome.

GOALS OF DETOXIFICATION

Detoxification can be said to have three immediate goals: (1) to provide a safe withdrawal from alcohol or other drug(s) of dependence and enable the patient to become free of non-prescribed medications; (2) to provide a withdrawal that is humane and that protects the patient's dignity; and (3) to prepare the patient for ongoing treatment of his or her dependence (CSAT, 1995a):

To provide a safe withdrawal from the drug(s) of dependence and enable the patient to become drug-free. Many risks are associated with withdrawal, some influenced by the setting. For persons who are severely dependent on alcohol, abrupt, untreated cessation of drinking may result in withdrawal delirium, seizures (which may be recurrent), marked hyperautonomic signs, or death. Other sedative-hypnotics also may produce life-threatening withdrawal syndromes. Withdrawal from opiates and stimulants produces severe discomfort but generally is not life-threatening. It may, however, present a danger to those who are debilitated by advanced HIV disease, medical sequelae of addiction, advanced age, coronary artery disease, and other medical problems. Moreover, risks to the patient and society are not limited to the severity of the patient's physical disturbance, particularly when the detoxification is conducted in an outpatient setting. Outpatients experiencing withdrawal symptoms may self-medicate with alcohol or other drugs, and the interaction between prescribed medication and self-administered drugs may result in an overdose.

To provide a withdrawal that is humane and thus protects the patient's dignity. A caring staff, a supportive environment, sensitivity to cultural issues, confidentiality, and the selection of appropriate detoxification medication (if needed) all are important to providing humane withdrawal. However, staff must be firm as well as sympathetic and have experience in dealing with difficult behaviors that often accompany detoxification.

To prepare the patient for ongoing treatment of his or her dependence on alcohol or other drugs. During detoxification, patients may form therapeutic relationships with treatment staff or other patients, and may become aware of alternatives to an alcohol- or drug-using lifestyle. Detoxification is an opportunity to offer patients information and to motivate them for longer term treatment.

Managed care organizations and other third-party payers often regard detoxification as separate from other phases of alcohol and other drug treatment, as though detoxification occurred in isolation from such treatment. In clinical practice, this separation cannot exist: detoxification is but one component of a comprehensive treatment strategy.

GENERAL PRINCIPLES OF MANAGEMENT

Some detoxification procedures are specific to particular drugs of dependence, while others are based on general principles of treatment and are not drug-specific. Here, the general principles are presented first, followed by specific treatment protocols for each drug class.

Initial medical assessment should include evaluation of predicted withdrawal severity and medical or psychiatric comorbidity. Because there is a risk of serious adverse consequences for some patients who undergo withdrawal, an initial medical assessment is important in order to determine the need for medication and medical management.

The severity of a given patient's withdrawal cannot always be predicted with accuracy. However, helpful information to obtain in the initial assessment includes the amount and duration of a patient's use of alcohol and/or other drugs, the severity of the patient's prior withdrawal experiences (if any), as well as the medical and psychiatric history.

The Clinical Institute Withdrawal Assessment of Alcohol-Revised (CIWA-Ar) is used widely in clinical and research settings for initial assessment and ongoing monitoring of alcohol withdrawal signs and symptoms (see the Appendix for the CIWA-Ar instrument).

The initial medical assessment should facilitate selection of an appropriate level of care for detoxification. Detoxification may take place in a variety of inpatient and outpatient settings. Multiple instruments have been designed to facilitate selection of an appropriate level of care. ASAM's *Patient Placement Criteria for the Treatment of Substance-Related Disorders, Second Edition (ASAM PPC-2)* (Mee-Lee, Shulman & Gartner, 1996) contains detailed guidelines for matching patients to an appropriate intensity of services for detoxification.

Every means possible should be used to ameliorate the patient's withdrawal signs and symptoms. Medication should not be the only component of treatment. Psychological support is extremely important in reducing the patient's distress during detoxification.

The duration of detoxification is not a clearly defined, discrete period of time. Because detoxification often requires a greater intensity of services than other types of treatment, there is a practical value in defining a period during which a person is "in detoxification." The detoxification period usually is defined as the time during which the patient receives detoxification medications, even though some signs and symptoms may persist for a much longer period. Another way of defining the detoxification period is by measuring the duration of withdrawal signs or symptoms. However, the duration of these symptoms may be difficult to determine in a correctly medicated patient, because symptoms of withdrawal are largely suppressed by the medication.

Patients may have prolonged withdrawal signs or symptoms, or protracted abstinence syndrome. The existence of a protracted abstinence syndrome has been the subject of considerable controversy (Geller, 1994). Physicians often find it difficult to distinguish symptoms caused by drug withdrawal from those caused by a patient's underlying mental disorder, if one is present. The signs and symptoms of protracted withdrawal thus are not as predictable as those of acute withdrawal. Some patients may be predisposed to a protracted withdrawal.

Acute withdrawal syndromes produce measurable signs that researchers can study in animals under controlled laboratory conditions; protracted withdrawal in patients, on the other hand, often is confined to distress symptoms that cannot be studied in animals.

The plan of care for detoxification should be individualized. There is considerable variation among patients in terms of signs and symptoms of withdrawal. The best outcomes are obtained by tailoring the detoxification regimen to meet the needs of individual patients. The initial plan of care for detoxification should be adjusted to reflect the patient's response to the treatment provided.

There are two general strategies for pharmacologic management of withdrawal: (1) suppression of withdrawal by a cross-tolerant medication, and (2) decreasing signs and symptoms of withdrawal by alteration of another neuropharmacological process. Either, or both together, may be used to manage withdrawal syndromes effectively. In order to suppress withdrawal with cross-tolerant medication, a longer-acting medication typically is used to provide a milder, controlled withdrawal. Examples include use of methadone for opiate detoxification and chlordiazepoxide for alcohol detoxification. Medications that are not cross-tolerant are used to treat specific signs and symptoms of withdrawal. Examples include use of clonidine for opiate or alcohol withdrawal.

Detoxification alone rarely constitutes adequate treatment. The provision of detoxification services without continuing treatment in an appropriate level of care constitutes less than optimum use of limited resources. The appropriate level of care and content of treatment following detoxification must be clinically determined, based on the individual needs of the patient. Biopsychosocial factors to be considered in determining the continuing treatment plan include medical and psychiatric conditions, motivation, relapse potential, and available support system. These factors correspond to the dimensions of illness described in the *ASAM PPC-2*.

Many individuals undergo detoxification more than once, and some do so many times. Alling (1992) describes a pattern in young persons who return for several detoxification episodes, observing that individuals with a history of alcohol or drug dependence of short duration "often are unrealistically optimistic about being able to remain drug-free following detoxification." When recently dependent persons return for repeat detoxification, it generally is with a more realistic expectation of what is needed to remain free from alcohol and other drugs.

O'Brien, Childress, and McLellan (1991) point out that compliance and relapse in addictive disease are comparable to rates of relapse in other illnesses, such as diabetes and hypertension. Therefore, they recommend comparable long-term treatment.

In fact, during certain predictable phases of recovery, addicted persons are at increased risk of relapse. However, relapse can occur at any point in recovery. The relapsed patient is an appropriate candidate for detoxification and continuing treatment, including relapse prevention education.

After detoxification, the physiological functioning of the brain gradually returns to its predependent state; however, the cells may not be exactly the same as they were before the onset of dependence. If a person who has undergone detoxification resumes use of any drug in the same class as that on which he or she has been physiologically dependent, neuroadaptation would occur more rapidly than it did the first time (Cochin & Kornetsky, 1964).

MODIFICATIONS FOR SPECIAL POPULATIONS

Patients in several groups require special consideration during detoxification.

Pregnant and Nursing Women. Special concerns attend detoxification during pregnancy. For example, withdrawal from opiates can result in fetal distress, which can lead to premature labor or miscarriage (LJ Miller, 1994; Mitchell, 1994). Opioid substitution therapy, coupled with good prenatal care, generally is associated with good maternal and fetal outcomes (LJ Miller, 1994; Mitchell, 1994; Kreek, 1979). Although offspring of women on opioid maintenance therapy tend to have a lower birthweight and smaller head circumference than drug-free newborns, no developmental differences at six months of age have been documented. Use of clonidine in pregnant women should be considered investigational and done only in the setting of a research protocol.

Federal panels recommend that all pregnant and nursing women should be advised of the potential risks of drugs that are excreted in breast milk (CSAT, 1993a; CSAT, 1995a). Nevertheless, they advise that detoxification protocols should not be modified for nursing women unless there is specific evidence that the detoxification medication enters the breast milk in amounts that could be harmful to the nursing infant (CSAT, 1995a; CSAT, 1993a). Women who are using benzodiazepines, antidepressants, or antipsychotic medications should not breastfeed (CSAT, 1995a).

For a more detailed discussion, see Section 16.

Persons Who Are HIV-Positive. A diagnosis of HIV does not change the indications for detoxification medications, which can be used in HIV-positive persons in the same way they are used in uninfected patients. A federal panel advises that the detoxification process need not be altered by the presence of HIV (CSAT, 1993c; 1993e; 1995a).

Patients with Other Medical Conditions. *Brain-injured patients* are at risk for seizures (CSAT, 1995a). If an alcohol- or other drug-abusing patient who has sustained trauma to the head becomes delirious, it is imperative to determine the exact cause of the delirium. Slower medication tapers should be used in patients with seizure disorders (CSAT, 1995a). Dosages of anticonvulsant medications should be stabilized before sedative-hypnotic withdrawal begins.

Patients with *cardiac disease* require continued clinical assessment (Chiang & Goldfrank, 1990). Because a withdrawal seizure—or even the physiologic stress of withdrawal—may complicate the patient's cardiac condition, it may be necessary to withdraw the drug at a slower-than-normal rate. Treatment providers also should be alert to the possibility of interactions between cardiac medications and the agents used to manage detoxification.

Severe *liver or renal disease* can slow the metabolism of both the drug of abuse and the detoxification medication. Use of shorter-acting detoxification drugs and a slower taper are appropriate for such patients but require precautions against drug accumulation and oversedation (Chiang & Goldfrank, 1990).

Pain patients do not require detoxification from prescribed medications unless they meet the *DSM-IV* criteria for opiate abuse or dependence (CSAT, 1995a). However, treatment providers should exercise caution when prescribing medications for chronic pain patients with a history of addictive disorders.

Patients with Psychiatric Comorbidities. It is difficult to assess accurately underlying psychopathology in a patient who is undergoing detoxification (CSAT, 1995a). Drug toxicity or organic psychiatric symptoms (particularly with amphetamines and cocaine, hallucinogens or phencyclidine) can mimic psychiatric disorders. For this reason, physicians should conduct a thorough psychiatric evaluation after two to three weeks of abstinence.

At the time they are evaluated for detoxification, some patients with underlying psychiatric disorders already are using antidepressants, neuroleptics, anxiolytics, or lithium. Although staff may believe that such patients should discontinue all psychoactive drugs immediately, a federal panel advises that this course of action may not be in the best interest of the patient (CSAT, 1995a). Abrupt cessation of psychotherapeutic medications may cause withdrawal symptoms or re-emergence of symptoms of the underlying psychopathology. Thus, decisions about discontinuing the medication should be deferred temporarily. (If, however, the patient has been abusing the prescribed medication or the psychiatric condition clearly was caused by the the patient's alcohol or other drug abuse, the rationale for discontinuing the medication is more compelling.)

During detoxification, some patients decompensate into psychosis, depression, or severe anxiety. In such cases, careful evaluation of the withdrawal medication regimen is of paramount importance. If the decompensation is the result of inadequate dosing with the withdrawal medication, the appropriate response is to increase that medication. If it appears that the dose of the withdrawal medication is adequate, other medications may need to be added. Before selecting that alternative, however, it is important to consider the potential side effects of the additional medication and the possibility of interaction with the withdrawal medication. If withdrawal medications are adequate and appropriate but the patient continues to decompensate, non-addicting psychotropic medications (such as antipsychotics or antidepressants) may be indicated for the treatment of psychoses, depression, or anxiety emerging during withdrawal.

After detoxification is completed, the patient's need for medications should be reassessed. A trial period with no medications may be indicated.

Adolescents. Adolescents in detoxification pose somewhat different clinical issues than do adults. Chief among these is that physical dependence generally is not as severe and the adolescent patient's response to detoxification usually is more rapid than that of the adult (CSAT, 1995a; 1993d). On the other hand, adolescents are not as accustomed to pain as adults and thus may be more resistant to simple procedures, such as having blood drawn. Adolescents also are notorious for leaving treatment against medical advice.

Adolescents undergoing detoxification need a structured environment that is nurturing and supportive. They should be housed separately from adults. Decisions about involving family in treatment should be made on a case-by-case basis and should reflect an assessment of family functioning.

Note: Federal regulations allow methadone detoxification of adolescents, but state regulations vary. Methadone detoxification is rare in this age group.

Elderly Persons. Older patients are less likely than younger patients to exhibit hyperautonomic effects of drug use but are more likely to experience deleterious effects. Because many elderly persons are taking a number of prescription and over-the-counter drugs, the possibility of drug interactions cannot be ignored. Elderly persons with alcohol and other drug disorders also have an increased likelihood of medical comorbidities.

For these reasons, detoxification in a medically monitored or medically managed setting often is required (CSAT, 1995a). Dosages may need to be reduced because of slowed metabolism or coexisting medical disorders. A complete assessment and careful monitoring of the patient for comorbid conditions (such as respiratory or cardiac disease, or diabetes) is essential (Wartenberg & Nirenberg, 1995).

Patients in Criminal Justice Settings. Persons who are incarcerated or in detention in holding cells or elsewhere should be assessed for dependence on alcohol or other drugs, as untreated withdrawal from alcohol and sedative-hypnotics can be life-threatening (CSAT, 1995a; 1994b). Heroin withdrawal is not life-threatening to a healthy individual, but it can be very difficult for the patient.

Patients who have been on maintenance therapy before being incarcerated should continue to receive their usual dosage of medication if the expected period of incarceration is less than two weeks. If it is to be longer, the maintenance therapy should be discontinued gradually. Individuals who are on methadone maintenance may experience severe withdrawal symptoms if the medication is stopped abruptly. Indeed, methadone abstinence symptoms may persist for weeks or months and include severe vomiting and diarrhea, which may result in complications. Pain may be severe and intractable.

Detoxification protocols need not be modified for incarcerated persons, except to the extent that state laws restrict the use of methadone or LAAM in criminal justice settings. In such cases, linkages with local methadone detoxification programs are advised.

In dealing with incarcerated patients, the physician needs to be aware that, in most prisons, there is an underground market for psychoactive medications. Patients may try to deceive caregivers about their dependence so as to obtain drugs for sale to others. For this reason, prison medical staff need special training in patient assessment and detoxification (CSAT, 1994b).

DETOXIFICATION SETTINGS

Detoxification is conducted in both inpatient and outpatient settings. Both types of settings initiate recovery programs that may include referrals for problems such as medical, legal, psychiatric, and family issues.

Inpatient Detoxification. Inpatient detoxification is offered in medical hospitals, psychiatric hospitals, and medically managed residential treatment programs.

Alling (1992) cites as the advantages of *inpatient* detoxification that (1) "the patient is in a protected setting where access to substances of abuse is restricted," (2) "the withdrawal process may be safer, especially if the patient is dependent upon high levels of sedative-hypnotic drugs, since the clinician can observe him or her closely for serious withdrawal symptoms, and medications can be adjusted," and (3) "detoxification can be accomplished more rapidly than it can in an outpatient setting." He describes the advantages of *outpatient* detoxification as: (1) "it is much less expensive than inpatient treatment," (2) "the patient's life is not a disrupted as it is during inpatient treatment," and (3) "the patient does not undergo the abrupt transition from a protected inpatient setting to the everyday home and work settings."

Outpatient Detoxification. Outpatient detoxification usually is offered in community mental health centers, AOD abuse treatment clinics, and private clinics. *Intensive outpatient programs* offer a minimum of nine hours a week of professionally directed evaluation and treatment in a structured environment. Examples include day or evening programs in which patients attend a full spectrum of treatment programming but live at home or in special residences. Some programs provide medical detoxification. Many programs have established linkages through which they may refer patients to behavioral and psychosocial treatment. One strength of these programs is the daily contact between patients and staff (CSAT, 1994a).

In *nonintensive outpatient programs*, patients attend regularly scheduled sessions that usually total no more than 9 hours of professionally directed evaluation and treatment per week. These programs may provide detoxification services. Treatment approaches and philosophies in staffing of outpatient programs vary considerably. Some offer only assessments; in others, counseling may continue for a year or longer. A majority of programs provide one or two weekly patient visits and may deliver psychiatric or psychological counseling and other services, such as resource referral and management. Many combine counseling with Twelve Step recovery.

Emergency Departments. The emergency department often serves as a gateway to detoxification services. Detoxification programs may rely on emergency department staff to assess and initiate treatment for patients with medical conditions or medical complications that occur during detoxification. For social model programs, emergency departments often serve as a safety net for patients who need medical treatment. For the addict who has overdosed or who is experiencing a medical complication of abuse, the emergency department may be the initial point of contact with the health services system and serve as a source of case identification and referral to detoxification.

Certain illnesses treated in emergency departments may mimic, mask, or resemble symptoms of withdrawal from alcohol and other drugs. Urine and blood toxicology testing may assist emergency department staff in making the correct diagnosis.

Methadone Maintenance (Maintenance Pharmacotherapy) Programs. These clinics, which must be licensed by the Food and Drug Administration, the Drug Enforcement Administration, and state regulatory agencies, are the only settings in which methadone maintenance may be conducted for opiate addicts.

CONSIDERATIONS IN SELECTING A SETTING

Treatment providers should consider detoxification settings and patient matching within the context of two fundamental principles of high-quality patient care. The first is that the patient's needs should drive the selection of the most appropriate setting. The severity of the patient's withdrawal symptoms and the intensity of care required to ensure appropriate management of these symptoms are of primary importance.

The best detoxification setting for a given patient may be defined as the least restrictive, least expensive setting in which the goals of detoxification can be met. The ability to meet this standard assumes that treatment choices always are based primarily on a patient's clinical needs.

A comprehensive evaluation of the patient often indicates what therapeutic goals might be achieved realistically during the time allotted for the detoxification process.

Pressures to achieve cost savings are having a significant effect on the selection of treatment settings for detoxification. Many insurance companies, managed care organizations, and other payers have adopted stringent policies concerning reimbursement for alcohol and other drug detoxification services. Such policies govern not only the setting in which the services are provided but also the maximum number and duration of detoxification episodes that are covered benefits.

Many physicians report that current policies concerning reimbursement for services are problematic from the perspective of patient care. Such policies are characterized as giving insufficient weight to the variety of factors that affect the selection of a setting in which the patient has the greatest likelihood of achieving satisfactory detoxification. Some persons in need of detoxification, for example, may not be appropriate candidates for outpatient detoxification because of environmental impediments, such as a spouse who is using alcohol or other drugs. Such a patient may be more appropriately detoxified in a residential setting, such as a recovery house or other residential environment that is free of alcohol and other drug use.

In a recent review (CSAT, 1995a), panelists convened by the federal Center for Substance Abuse Treatment expressed concern that important clinical decisions often are driven by economic rather than clinical considerations. They affirmed that the dominant principle in patient placement is that detoxification is cost-effective only if it is appropriate to the needs of the individual patient.

Use of the ASAM Patient Placement Criteria. The *ASAM PPC-2* is intended for use as a clinical tool for matching patients to appropriate levels of care. The criteria reflect a clinical consensus of adult and adolescent treatment specialists and incorporate the results of a comprehensive peer review by professionals in addiction treatment. The ASAM criteria describe levels of treatment that are differentiated by the following characteristics: (1) degree of direct medical management provided, (2) degree of structure, safety, and security provided, and (3) degree of treatment intensity provided.

The ASAM criteria offer a variety of options, on the premise that each patient should be placed in a level of care that has the appropriate resources (staff, facilities, and services) to assess and treat that patient's substance use disorder.

ACKNOWLEDGMENT: The authors express their gratitude to Sidney Schnoll, M.D., Ph.D., FASAM, and Michael Mayo-Smith, M.D., for their contributions as reviewers of this manuscript.

REFERENCES

Alling FA (1992). Detoxification and treatment of acute sequelae. In JH Lowinson, P Ruiz & RB Millman (eds.) *Substance Abuse: A Comprehensive Textbook*. Baltimore, MD: Williams & Wilkins, 402–415.

American Psychiatric Association (1994). *Diagnostic and Statistical Manual of Mental Disorders, Fourth Edition*. Washington, DC: American Psychiatric Association.

Center for Substance Abuse Treatment (1995a). *Detoxification from Alcohol and Other Drugs* (Treatment Improvement Protocol (TIP) Series, Number 19). Rockville, MD: Department of Health and Human Services, DHHS Publication No. (SMA) 95-3046.

Center for Substance Abuse Treatment (1993d). *Guidelines for Improving the Treatment of Alcohol and Other Drug-Abusing Adolescents* (Treatment Improvement Protocol (TIP) Series, Number 4). Rockville, MD: Department of Health and Human Services, DHHS Publication No. (SMA) 93.

Center for Substance Abuse Treatment (1994a). *Intensive Outpatient Treatment for Alcohol and Other Drug Abuse* (Treatment Improvement Protocol (TIP) Series, Number 8). Rockville, MD: Department of Health and Human Services, DHHS Publication No. (SMA) 94-2077.

Center for Substance Abuse Treatment (1995b). *LAAM in the Treatment of Opioid Addiction* (Treatment Improvement Protocol (TIP) Series, Number 22). Rockville, MD: Department of Health and Human Services, DHHS Publication No. (SMA) 95-3052.

Center for Substance Abuse Treatment (1995c). *Matching Treatment to Patient Needs in Opioid Substitution Therapy* (Treatment Improvement Protocol (TIP) Series, Number 20). Rockville, MD: Department of Health and Human Services, DHHS Publication No. (SMA) 95-3049.

Center for Substance Abuse Treatment (1994b). *Planning for Alcohol and Other Drug Abuse Treatment for Adults in the Criminal Justice System* (Treatment Improvement Protocol (TIP) Series, Number 17). Rockville, MD: Department of Health and Human Services, DHHS Publication No. (SMA) 93.

Center for Substance Abuse Treatment (1993a). *Pregnant, Substance-Using Women* (Treatment Improvement Protocol (TIP) Series, Number 2). Rockville, MD: Department of Health and Human Services, DHHS Publication No. (SMA) 93-1998.

Center for Substance Abuse Treatment (1993e). *Screening for Infectious Diseases Among Substance Abusers* (Treatment Improvement Protocol (TIP) Series, Number 6). Rockville, MD: Department of Health and Human Services, DHHS Publication No. (SMA) 93.

Center for Substance Abuse Treatment (1993b). *State Methadone Treatment Guidelines* (Treatment Improvement Protocol (TIP) Series, Number 1). Rockville, MD: Department of Health and Human Services, DHHS Publication No. (SMA) 93-1991.

Center for Substance Abuse Treatment (1993c). *Treatment for HIV-Infected Alcohol and Other Drug Abusers* (Treatment Improvement Protocol (TIP) Series, Number 15). Rockville, MD: Department of Health and Human Services, DHHS Publication No. (SMA) 93.

Chiang W & Goldfrank L (1990). The medical complications of drug abuse. *Medical Journal of Australia* 152:83–88, January.

Cochin J & Kornetsky C (1964). Development and loss of tolerance to morphine in the rat after single and multiple injections. *Journal of Pharmacological and Experimental Therapeutics* 145:1–10.

Geller A (1994). Management of protracted withdrawal. In NS Miller (ed.) *Principles of Addiction Medicine, First Edition*. Chevy Chase, MD: American Society of Addiction Medicine.

Kreek MJ (1979). Methadone disposition during the perinatal period in humans. *Pharmacology, Biochemistry and Behavior* 11:7–13.

Mee-Lee D, Shulman G & Gartner L (1996). *Patient Placement Criteria for the Treatment of Psychoactive Substance Use Disorders, 2nd Edition* (*ASAM PPC-2*). Chevy Chase, MD: American Society of Addiction Medicine.

Miller LJ (1994). Detoxification of the Addicted Woman in Pregnancy. In NS Miller (ed.) *Principles of Addiction Medicine, First Edition*. Chevy Chase, MD: American Society of Addiction Medicine.

Mitchell JL (1994). Treatment of the Addicted Woman in Pregnancy. In NS Miller (ed.) *Principles of Addiction*

Medicine, First Edition. Chevy Chase, MD: American Society of Addiction Medicine.

O'Brien CP, Childress AR & McLellan AT (1991). *Conditioning Factors May Help to Understand and Prevent Relapse in Patients Who Are Recovering from Drug Dependence* (NIDA Research Monograph Number 106). Rockville, MD: National Institute on Drug Abuse, DHHS Publication No. (ADM) 91-1754.

Wartenberg AA & Nirenberg TD (1995). Alcohol and drug abuse in the older patient. In W Reichel (ed.) *Care of the Elderly: Clinical Aspects of Aging, Ed. 4.* Baltimore, MD: Williams & Wilkins, 133–141.

CHAPTER 2

Management of Alcohol Intoxication and Withdrawal

Michael F. Mayo-Smith, M.D., M.P.H.

Alcohol Intoxication
Alcohol Withdrawal

The management of alcohol intoxication and withdrawal is one of the most frequently encountered issues in Addiction Medicine. Effective approaches, with a strong scientific basis, have been developed to reduce the incidence of serious complications.

ALCOHOL INTOXICATION

Clinical Picture. As blood alcohol concentration rises, so too does the clinical effect on the individual (Herrington, 1987). At a blood alcohol concentration between 20 mg % and 99 mg %, loss of muscular coordination begins. Changes in mood, personality and behavior accompany these blood alcohol levels. As the blood alcohol level rises to 100 mg % to 199 mg %, neurologic impairment occurs, accompanied by prolonged reaction time, ataxia, incoordination and mental impairment.

At a blood alcohol level of 200 mg % to 299 mg %, very obvious intoxication is present, except in those with marked tolerance. Nausea and vomiting may occur, as well as marked ataxia. As the level rises to 300 mg % to 399 mg %, hypothermia may occur, as well as severe dysarthria and amnesia, with Stage I anesthesia.

At blood alcohol levels between 400 mg % and 799 mg %, the onset of alcoholic coma occurs. The precise level at which this occurs depends on tolerance: some persons experience coma at levels of 400 mg %, while others do not experience it until the level approaches 600 mg %.

Serum levels of alcohol between 600 and 800 mg % often are fatal. Progressive obtundation develops, accompanied by decreases in respiration, blood pressure and body temperature. The patient may develop urinary incontinence or retention, while reflexes are markedly decreased or absent. Death may occur from the loss of airway protective reflexes (with subsequent airway obstruction by the flaccid tongue), from pulmonary aspiration of gastric contents or from respiratory arrest arising from profound CNS depression.

Management of Alcohol Intoxication. Management of alcohol intoxication and overdose remains supportive. The most important goal is to prevent severe respiratory depression and to protect the airway to prevent aspiration. Even with very high blood alcohol levels, survival is probable as long as the respiratory and cardiovascular systems can be supported. As with all patients with impaired consciousness, intravenous glucose and thiamine should be given, but these are of particular importance in alcohol intoxication. Ethanol can impair gluconeogenesis, with an increased risk of hypoglycemia, and chronic alcoholism places the individual at increased risk of thiamine deficiency. It also is important to assess whether the patient has ingested other drugs in addition to the alcohol, as these may further suppress the central nervous system and alter the approach to treatment.

Alcohol is rapidly absorbed, so induction of emesis or gastric lavage usually is not indicated unless a substantial ingestion has occurred within the preceding 30 to 60 minutes, or unless other drug ingestion is suspected. Ipecac-induced emesis may be useful at the scene, e.g., with children at home, if it can be given within a few minutes of exposure. Similarly, gastric lavage is indicated only if the patient presents in the emergency department soon after ingestion. Activated charcoal does not efficiently absorb ethanol but may be given if other toxins were ingested.

Enhancement of elimination has only a very limited role to play. Over 90% of alcohol is oxidized in the liver and, at the levels seen clinically, the rate of oxidation follows zero-order kinetics, i.e., it is independent of time and concentration of the drug. Elimination thus occurs at a fixed rate, with the level falling approximately 20mg/dl/hour. In extreme cases, hemodialysis can be used, as it efficiently removes alcohol, but it is rarely needed because supportive care usually is sufficient. Hemoperfusion and forced diuresis are not effective. High doses of oral or intravenous fructose will moderately increase alcohol metabolism. Large fructose doses, however, cause gastrointestinal upset, lactic acidosis, hyperuricemia and osmotic diuresis, which make this approach of little clinical value.

At present there is no known agent that is effective as an alcohol antagonist, reversing the effects of alcohol in the same manner that naloxone reverses opiate intoxication. While human laboratory studies have shown that CNS stimulants such as amphetamine and caffeine can overcome some of the sedation and psychomotor impairment produced by acute alcohol intoxication, they are not useful clinically. Such stimulants have significant toxicities, which limit their use in higher doses. In patients with clinically significant alcohol ingestions, they would pose the risk of producing a mixed CNS depressant/stimulant intoxication (Gorelick, 1993). Benzodiazepine antagonists such as flumazenil do not block or reverse alcohol intoxication (Broaden & Goa, 1991).

The acutely intoxicated patient may exhibit some agitation as part of the intoxication syndrome. This is best managed non-pharmacologically. Support and reassurance can go a long way in dealing with agitation in an acutely intoxicated patient. On rare occasions, if pharmacologic intervention is needed to manage an mildly or moderately intoxicated individual's behavior in a medical setting, intramuscular administration of a rapid onset, short-acting benzodiazepine (such as lorazepam), alone or in combination with a neuroleptic agent such as haloperidol, can be useful. Caution must be exercised in regard to a potential synergistic response between the alcohol already in the patient's system and an exogenously administered sedative-hypnotic, so this approach should be used only as a last resort and not in individuals with high blood alcohol levels.

ALCOHOL WITHDRAWAL

Pathophysiology of Alcohol Withdrawal. Goldstein and Goldstein proposed in 1961 that dependency develops as a cell or organism makes homeostatic adjustments to compensate for the primary effect of a drug (Goldstein & Goldstein, 1961). As detailed in Section 2, the primary effect of alcohol on the brain is depressant. With chronic exposure, there are compensatory adjustments to this chronic depressant effect, with downregulation of inhibitory systems and upregulation of excitatory systems. With abrupt abstinence from alcohol, these relative deficiencies in inhibitory influences and relative excesses in excitatory influences are suddenly unmasked, leading to the appearance of withdrawal phenomena. The withdrawal symptoms last until the body readjusts to the absence of the alcohol and establishes a new equilibrium.

Two neurotransmitter systems appear to play a central role in the development of alcohol withdrawal. Alcohol exerts its effects in part by directly or indirectly enhancing the effect of GABA, a major inhibitory neurotransmitter. GABA mediates typical sedative-hypnotic effects such as sedation, muscle relaxation and a raised seizure threshold. Chronic alcohol intake leads to an adaptive suppression of GABA activity. A sudden relative deficiency in GABA neurotransmitter activity is produced with alcohol abstinence, and is believed to contribute to the anxiety, increased psychomotor activity and predisposition to seizures seen in withdrawal.

While alcohol enhances the effect of GABA, it inhibits the sensitivity of autonomic adrenergic systems, with a resulting upregulation with chronic alcohol intake. The discontinuation of alcohol leads to rebound overactivity of brain and peripheral noradrenergic systems. Increased sympathetic autonomic activity, arising from increased neuronal activity in the locus ceruleus area of the brain stem, contributes to such acute manifestations as tachycardia, hypertension, tremor, diaphoresis, and anxiety. Norepinephrine and its metabolites are elevated in plasma, urine and cerebral spinal fluid during withdrawal; levels of metabolites correlate significantly with the sympathetic nervous system signs of withdrawal (Hawley Major et al., 1985).

Research is beginning to identify a large number of other neural effects of chronic alcohol intake, including effects on neuronal calcium channels, on glutamate receptors, on cyclic AMP systems and on the hypothalamic-pituitary-adrenal neuroendocrine axis. However, the importance of these in producing the clinical manifestations of alcohol withdrawal and their implications for treatment is uncertain at this time.

Clinical Picture. "If the patient be in the prime of life and if from drinking he has trembling hands, it may be well to announce beforehand either delirium or convulsions" (Hippocrates, circa 400 BC). As this quote reveals, the relationship of heavy alcohol intake to certain syndromes has been recognized since ancient times. However, it was not until the eighteenth century that the clinical manifestations of alcohol withdrawal were clearly delineated. As is evident in the following writings of Sutton, the vivid descriptions of severe withdrawal written at that time remain relevant today:

> "It is preceded by tremors of the hands, restlessness, irregularity of thought, deficiency of memory, anxiety to be company, dreadful nocturnal dreams when the quantity of liquor through the day has been insufficient; much diminution of appetite, especially an aversion to animal food; violent vomiting in the morning and excessive perspiration from trivial causes. Confusion of thought arises to such height that objects are seen of the most hideous forms, and in positions that it is physically impossible they can be so situated; the patients generally sees flies or other insects; or pieces of money which he anxiously desires to possess. . . ."

For the most part, clinicians believed that these symptoms were a consequence of alcohol itself, and it was not until the second half of the twentieth century that their relationship to the cessation of chronic alcohol intake—a relationship taken for granted today—was established. In 1953, Victor and Adams reported their careful observations of 286 consecutive alcoholic patients admitted to an innercity hospital, revealing the consistent relationship of the cessation of alcohol to the emergence of clinical symptoms (Victor & Adams, 1953). Their findings were supported in 1955 by a study by Isbell and colleagues, in which 10 former morphine addicts were given large quantities of alcohol for seven to 87 days and then withdrawn abruptly without sedation (Isbell et al., 1955).

Over the next two decades, the concept of an alcohol withdrawal syndrome was firmly established by further animal and human studies, and diagnostic criteria based on empirical observation were developed.

The current understanding of the alcohol withdrawal syndrome is reflected in the diagnostic criteria of the American Psychiatric Association's *Diagnostic and Statistical Manual of Mental Disorders, 4th Edition* (1994), as summarized in Table 1.

Hallucinations: In mild alcohol withdrawal, patients may experience perceptual distortions of a visual, auditory and tactile nature. Lights may seem too bright or sounds too loud and startling. A sensation of "pins and needles" may be experienced. In more severe cases of withdrawal, these misperceptions may develop into frank hallucinations. Visual hallucinations are most common and frequently involve some type of animal life, such as seeing a dog or rodent in the room. Auditory hallucinations may begin as unformed sounds (such as clicks or buzzing) and progress to formed voices. In contrast to the auditory hallucinations of schizophrenia, which may be of religious or political significance, these voices often are of friends or relatives and frequently are accusatory in nature. Tactile hallucinations may involve a sensation of bugs or insects crawling on the skin.

TABLE 1. DSM IV Diagnostic Criteria for Alcohol Withdrawal (291.8)

A. Cessation of (or reduction in) alcohol use that has been heavy and prolonged.

B. Two (or more) or the following, developing within several hours to a few days after Criterion A:
   (1) autonomic hyperactivity (e.g., sweating or pulse rate greater than 100)
   (2) increased hand tremor
   (3) insomnia
   (4) nausea or vomiting
   (5) transient visual, tactile, or auditory hallucinations or illusions
   (6) psychomotor agitation
   (7) anxiety
   (8) grand mal seizures

C. The symptoms in Criterion B cause clinically significant distress or impairment in social, occupational, or other important areas of functioning.

D. The symptoms are not due to a general medical condition and are not better accounted for by another mental disorder.

Specify if: With Perceptual Disturbances

In milder cases of withdrawal, the patient's sensorium is otherwise clear and the patient retains insight that the hallucinations are not real. In more severe withdrawal, this insight may be lost. In the past, it was thought that the hallucinations could become chronic, developing into a state labeled "chronic alcoholic hallucinosis." However, with improved psychiatric nosology and more careful clinical observation, the existence of this entity has not been confirmed and it is not contained in current diagnostic classifications.

Withdrawal Seizures: Grand mal seizures are another manifestation of alcohol withdrawal. Withdrawal seizures occurred in 23% of the patients studied by Victor and Adams, in 33% of the patients in Isbell's study who drank for 48 to 87 days, and in 11% of placebo-treated patients who were enrolled in prospective controlled studies examining the effectiveness of benzodiazepines in symptomatic withdrawal (Mayo-Smith, Cushman et al., 1997). Withdrawal seizures usually begin within eight to 24 hours after the patient's last drink and may occur before the blood alcohol level has returned to zero. Most are generalized major motor seizures, occurring singly or in a burst of several seizures occurring over a period of one to six hours.

Although less than 3% of withdrawal seizures evolve into status epilepticus, alcohol withdrawal has been found to be a contributing cause in up to 15% of status epilepticus patients. Seizures peak 24 hours after the last drink, corresponding to the peak of withdrawal-induced EEG abnormalities, which include increased amplitude, a photomyoclonic response, and spontaneous paroxysmal activity. These EEG abnormalities are transient, in keeping with the brevity of the convulsive attacks. Except for this brief period following withdrawal, the incidence of EEG abnormalities in patients with withdrawal seizures is not greater than in the normal population. The risk of withdrawal seizures appears to be in part genetically determined, and is increased in patients with a history of prior withdrawal seizures or who are undergoing concurrent withdrawal from benzodiazepines or other sedative-hypnotic drugs.

There also is evidence that the risk of seizures increases as an individual undergoes repeated withdrawals (Booth & Blow, 1993). This association has been described as a "kindling effect," which refers to animal studies demonstrating that repeated subcortical electrical stimulation is associated with increases in seizure susceptibility (Ballenger & Post, 1978). Animal studies have supported this kindling hypothesis in alcohol withdrawal, demonstrating that submitting animals to repeated alcohol withdrawal episodes increases their risk of withdrawal seizures.

Alcohol Withdrawal Delirium: Withdrawal is highly individualized in both severity and duration. For up to 90% of patients, withdrawal does not progress beyond the milder symptoms described above, peaking between 24 and 36 hours and gradually subsiding. In others, however, the manifestations steadily worsen and can progress into a severe life-threatening delirium accompanied by an autonomic storm: hence the term *delirium tremens* (DTs). DTs generally appear 72 to 96 hours after the last drink.

In its classic presentation, DTs are marked by all the signs and symptoms of mild withdrawal in a much more pronounced form, with the development of marked tachycardia, tremor, diaphoresis and fever. The patient develops global confusion and disorientation to place and time. The patient may become absorbed in a separate psychic reality, often believing himself or herself to be in a location other than the hospital, and misindentifies staff as personal acquaintances. Hallucinations are frequent and the patient may have no insight into them. Without this insight, they can be extremely frightening to the patient, who may react in a way that poses a threat to his or the staff's safety. Marked psychomotor activity may develop, with severe agitation in some cases or continuous low level motor activity in others, with activities such as efforts to get out of bed lasting for hours. Severe disruption of the normal sleep-wake cycle also is common, and may be marked by the absence of clear sleep for several days.

The duration of the delirium is variable, lasting an average of two to three days in most studies. In some cases the delirium is relatively brief, lasting only a few hours before the patient regains orientation. In others the patient remains delirious for several days, with reports of periods as long as 50 days before the confusion clears (Wolf, Shaughnessy & Middleton, 1993).

As noted, severe withdrawal develops in only a minority of individuals. While accurate knowledge of patient characteristics that put them at risk for severe withdrawal would be of great use clinically, well done research on this question has been very limited. Surprisingly, the amount of daily intake and duration of heavy drinking have not been consistently correlated with severity of withdrawal, although clearly a certain amount is required to induce dependence. There is evidence, however, that individuals with a high alcohol level at the time of presentation (greater than 300 mg/dl) or who present after having a withdrawal seizure appear to be at higher risk for progressing to severe withdrawal or DTs.

Older individuals appear at higher risk for developing confusion and delirium when undergoing withdrawal. This confusion in older patients may not involve the severe autonomic manifestations of classic DTs and may be a manifestation of the increased susceptibility of older persons to development of delirium with any significant medical illness or hospitalization (Kraemer, Mayo-Smith & Calkins, 1997).

Assessment of the Patient. The first step in managing the patient with alcohol withdrawal is to perform an assessment for the presence of medical and psychiatric problems. Chronic alcohol intake is associated with the development of many acute and chronic medical problems. The clinician needs to determine whether these are acute conditions that require hospital treatment or chronic conditions that may alter the approach to management of withdrawal because they might be significantly exacerbated by the development of withdrawal or its treatment.

Pertinent laboratory tests generally include complete blood count, electrolytes, magnesium, calcium, phosphate, liver enzymes, urine drug screen, pregnancy test (when appropriate), and Breathalyzer or blood alcohol level. Others, depending on suspected coexisting conditions, may include skin test for tuberculosis, chest x-ray, electrocardiogram, and tests for viral hepatitis, other infections, or sexually transmitted diseases.

General management also involves maintaining adequate fluid balance, correction of electrolyte deficiencies, and attendance to the patient's nutritional needs. Patients in early withdrawal often are overhydrated, so that aggressive hydration usually is not necessary unless there have been significant fluid losses from vomiting or diarrhea. Supportive care and reassurance from nursing personnel are important elements of comfortable detoxification and serve to facilitate continuing treatment.

Supportive non-pharmacologic care is an important and useful element in the management of all patients undergoing withdrawal. Simple interventions such as reassurance, reality orientation, monitoring of signs and symptoms of withdrawal, and general nursing care are effective. In controlled trials, they were sufficient to manage 85% of emergency room patients and 60% of inpatients (Shaw, 1981; Naranjo, 1983). It is important to note that these measures do not prevent the development of major complications such as seizures and are not adequate by themselves to manage the patient with severe withdrawal or delirium, in which case pharmacological intervention is required.

Alcohol Withdrawal Severity Scales: Because alcohol withdrawal involves a constellation of nonspecific findings, efforts have been made to develop structured withdrawal severity assessment scales to objectively quantify the severity of withdrawal. A number of such scales have been published in the literature. The most extensively studied and best known is the Clinical Institute Withdrawal Assessment-Alcohol, or CIWA, and a shortened version known as the CIWA-A revised, or CIWA-Ar (see Appendix B). The CIWA-Ar has well-documented reliability, reproducibility and validity based on comparisons to ratings of withdrawal severity by experienced clinicians. The CIWA-Ar and similar scales require two to five minutes to complete and have been shown to be useful in a variety of settings, including detoxification units, psychiatric units and general medical/surgical wards. Such scales allow rapid documentation of the patient's signs and symptoms and provide a simple summary score that facilitates accurate and objective communication among staff.

In the case of the CIWA-Ar, a score of 9 or less indicates mild withdrawal, a score of 10 to 18 indicates moderate withdrawal, and a score above 18, severe withdrawal. Moreover, it has been shown that high scores are predictive of the development of seizures and delirium; thus, use of the CIWA-Ar can contribute to appropriate triage of patients to levels of treatment.

Pharmacologic Management of Alcohol Withdrawal. The medical literature on the pharmacological management of alcohol withdrawal recently has been comprehensively reviewed as part of the American Society of Addiction Medicine's efforts to develop evidence-based Clinical Practice Guidelines (Mayo-Smith, Cushman et al., 1997). This review of the evidence indicated that the cornerstone of pharmacologic management of withdrawal is the use of benzodiazepines (see chapter 3 of this section).

Benzodiazepines: Benzodiazepines are pharmacologically cross-tolerant with alcohol and have the similar effect of enhancing the effect of GABA-induced sedation. A specific benzodiazepine receptor site has been identified on the GABA receptor complex. It is believed that the provision of benzodiazepines alleviates the acute deficiency of GABA neurotransmitter activity that occurs with sudden cessation of alcohol intake.

Well-designed studies consistently have shown that benzodiazepines are more effective than placebo in reducing the signs and symptoms of withdrawal. In addition, meta-analysis of prospective placebo controlled trials of patients admitted with symptomatic withdrawal has shown a highly significant reduction in seizures, with a risk reduction of 7.7 seizures/100 patients treated, as well as in delirium, with a risk reduction of 4.9 cases of delirium/100 patients treated.

Trials comparing different benzodiazepines indicate that all are similarly efficacious in reducing signs and symptoms of withdrawal. However, longer-acting agents such as diazepam and chlordiazepoxide may be more effective in preventing seizures. Longer-acting agents also may contribute to an overall smoother withdrawal course, with a reduction in breakthrough or rebound symptoms. On the other hand, pharmacologic data and clinical experience suggest that longer-acting agents can pose a risk of excess sedation in some patients, including the elderly and those with significant liver disease. In such patients, shorter-acting agents such as lorazepam or oxazepam may be preferable.

Another consideration in the choice of benzodiazepine is the rapidity of onset. Certain agents with rapid onset of action (such as diazepam, alprazolam and lorazepam) demonstrate greater abuse potential than those with slower onset of action (such as chlordiazepoxide or oxazepam). This consideration may be of relevance in an outpatient setting or for patients with a history of benzodiazepine or other substance abuse. However, when rapid control of symptoms is needed, medications with faster onset offer an advantage.

A final consideration in the choice of benzodiazepine is cost, as these agents vary considerably in price. Given the evidence of equal efficacy, if a particular agent is available to a practitioner or program at a lower cost, this is a legitimate factor to consider.

Studies have indicated that non-benzodiazepine sedative-hypnotics also are effective in reducing the signs and symptoms of withdrawal, but non-benzodiazepine agents have not been as extensively studied and the size of studies with them is not adequate to draw conclusions as to their degree of effectiveness in reducing seizures and delirium. Benzodiazepines have a greater margin of safety, with a lower risk of respiratory depression, as well as overall lower abuse potential than do the non-benzodiazepine agents. Phenobarbital, a long-acting barbiturate, still is used by some programs, as it is long-acting, has well-documented anticonvulsant activity, is inexpensive and has low abuse liability

Determining the Dose: In the majority of studies examining the effectiveness of various medications for withdrawal, the medications were given in fixed amounts at scheduled times (such as chlordiazepoxide 50 mg every six hours) and were given for periods of five to seven days. However, it has been shown that many patients can go through withdrawal with only minor symptoms even though they receive little or no medication. An alternative to giving medication on a fixed schedule is known as symptom-triggered therapy. In this approach, the patient is monitored using a structured assessment scale and given medication only when symptoms cross a threshold of severity. Well-designed studies have demonstrated that this approach is as effective as fixed-dose therapy, but results in the administration of significantly less medication and a significantly shorter duration of treatment (Saitz, 1994). This approach also facilitates the delivery of large amounts of medication quickly to patients with rapidly escalating withdrawal and reduces the risk of undertreatment that may arise with the use of fixed doses.

For programs specializing in the management of addiction, use of a symptom-triggered approach with the utilization of a severity scale offers significant advantages. However, there may be situations in which the provision of fixed doses remains appropriate. For example, with patients admitted to general medical or surgical wards, the nursing staff may not have the training or experience to implement the regular use of scales to monitor patients. In certain patients, such as those with severe coronary artery disease, the clinician may wish to prevent the development of even minor symptoms of withdrawal. Finally, because a history of past withdrawal seizures is a risk factor for seizures during a withdrawal episode, and because withdrawal seizures usually occur early in the course of withdrawal, some practitioners administer fixed doses to patients with a history of withdrawal seizures.

Whenever fixed schedule doses are given, it is very important that allowance be made for the provision of additional medication should the fixed dose prove inadequate to control symptoms. Treatment should allow for a degree of individualization so that patients can receive large amounts of medication rapidly if needed.

In all cases, medications should be administered by a route that has been shown to have reliable absorption. Therefore, the benzodiazepines should be administered orally or, when necessary, intravenously. An exception is lorazepam, which has good intramuscular and sublingual absorption. In the past, intramuscular (IM) administration was commonly used. However, for most agents IM absorption is extremely variable, leading to problems when rapid control of symptoms is necessary and also with delayed appearance of oversedation when large amounts are administered.

Examples of some treatment regimens consistent with current recommendations are shown in Table 2.

Other Agents: Beta adrenergic blocking agents, such as atenolol and propanolol, as well as centrally acting alpha adrenergic agonists, such as clonidine, also are effective in ameliorating symptoms in pa-

TABLE 2. Examples of Specific Medication Treatment Regimens

Monitoring
Monitor the patient every 4 to 8 hours using the CIWA-Ar until the score has been below 8–10 for 24 hours; use additional assessments as needed.

Symptom-triggered Medication Regimens
Administer one of the following medications every hour when the CIWA-Ar is ≥ 8–10:
- Chlordiazepoxide 50 to 100 mg
- Diazepam 10 to 20 mg
- Oxazepam 30 to 60 mg
- Lorazepam 2 to 4 mg

(Other benzodiazepines may be used at equivalent substitutions.)

Repeat the CIWA-Ar one hour after every dose to assess need for further medication.

Structured Medication Regimens
The physician may feel that the development of even mild to moderate withdrawal should be prevented in certain patients (for example, for patients experiencing a myocardial infarction) and may therefore order medication to be given on a predetermined schedule. One of the following regimens could be used in such circumstances:
- Chlordiazepoxide 50 mg every 6 hours for four doses, then 25 mg every 6 hours for 8 doses.
- Diazepam 10 mg every 6 hours for four doses, then 5 mg every 6 hours for eight doses.
- Lorazepam 2 mg every 6 hours for 4 doses, then 1 mg every 6 hours for eight doses.

(Other benzodiazepines may be substituted at equivalent doses.)

It is very important that patients receiving medication on a predetermined schedule be monitored closely and that additional medication be provided should the doses given prove inadequate.

Agitation
For the patient who displays increasing agitation or hallucinations that have not responded to oral benzodiazepines alone, one of the following medications may be used:
- Haloperidol 2 to 5 mg IM alone or in combination with 2 to 4 mg of lorazepam.
- Intravenous diazepam given slowly every 5 minutes until the patient is lightly sedated. Begin with 5 mg for two doses, then if needed increase to 10 mg for two doses, then 20 mg every 5 minutes.

Given the risk of respiratory depression, the patient needs to be closely monitored, with equipment for respiratory support immediately available.

Other phenothiazines and benzodiazepines may be substituted at equivalent doses.

tients with mild to moderate withdrawal, primarily by reducing the autonomic nervous system manifestations of withdrawal. However, these agents do not have known anticonvulsant activity, and the studies to date have not been large enough to determine their effectiveness in reducing seizures or delirium. Beta blockers offer a particular problem in this regard because delirium is a recognized, albeit rare, side effect of these drugs. In addition, there is concern that selective reduction in certain manifestations of withdrawal may mask the development of other significant withdrawal symptoms and make it difficult to utilize withdrawal scales to guide therapy.

Carbamazepine has been widely used in Europe for alcohol withdrawal, and it has been shown to be equal in efficacy to benzodiazepines for patients with mild to moderate withdrawal. It is without significant toxicity when used in seven-day protocols for alcohol withdrawal and is associated with less psychiatric distress and a faster return to work. Carbamazepine does not potentiate the CNS and respiratory depression caused by alcohol, does not inhibit learning (an important side effect of larger doses of benzodiazepines) and has no abuse potential. It has well-documented anticonvulsant activity and prevents alcohol withdrawal seizures in animal studies. However, studies of adequate size are currently unavailable to assess its efficacy in preventing withdrawal seizures or delirium. It is currently available only in oral form, making it difficult to titrate doses rapidly for the more symptomatic or rapidly worsening patient. The benzodiazepines thus remain the recommended agents.

Carbamazepine sometimes is used as an adjunctive agent, as in patients who have a history of recurrent withdrawal seizures, with prominent mood liability during withdrawal or with concurrent benzodiazepine withdrawal.

Neuroleptic agents, including the phenothiazines and the butryphenone haloperidol, demonstrate some effectiveness in reducing the signs and symptoms of withdrawal, and for a period of time were used extensively for that purpose. However, these agents are less effective than benzodiazepines in preventing delirium and actually lead to an increase in the rate of seizures. Neuroleptic agents are widely used to calm agitated patients and are useful for this purpose in the setting of alcohol withdrawal as well. However, they should not be used alone, but always in conjunction with a benzodiazepine, and agents with less effect on the seizure threshold, such as haloperidol, should be selected.

It long has been recognized that magnesium levels often are low during alcohol withdrawal. Closer study has found that magnesium levels usually are normal on admission, but then drop during the course of withdrawal before spontaneously returning to normal as withdrawal symptoms subside. Only one randomized trial of magnesium during withdrawal has been performed, and that study found no difference in severity of withdrawal or rate of seizures, even after adjustment for magnesium levels. Providing supplemental oral magnesium to patients with a documented low magnesium level is without significant risk, but routine administration of magnesium, either oral or intramuscular, for withdrawal no longer is recommended.

One agent whose use for the management of alcohol withdrawal still is occasionally encountered is alcohol itself. Case series describing oral or intravenous alcohol for the prevention or treatment of withdrawal symptoms have been published, but no controlled trials evaluating the safety or relative efficacy—either compared to placebo or to benzodiazepines—have been performed. Intravenous alcohol infusions require close monitoring because of the potential toxicity of alcohol. As a pharmacologic agent, ethyl alcohol has numerous adverse effects, including its well known hepatic, gastrointestinal and neurologic toxicities, as well as its effects on mental status and judgment. Given the proven efficacy and safety of benzodiazepines, the use of alcohol for detoxification is discouraged by addiction specialists.

Phenytoin: The routine use of phenytoin has been advocated as a method to prevent the occurrence of withdrawal seizures, and there is some evidence from early trials that it may be effective for this purpose. However, more recent and more methodologically sound trials have failed to show evidence that phenytoin is effective in preventing recurrent withdrawal seizures. Moreover, studies have shown that appropriately used benzodiazepines are extremely effective in preventing withdrawal seizures and that the addition of phenytoin does not lead to improved outcomes (Kasser et al., 1994). For these reasons, the routine use of phenytoin has been for the most part abandoned.

Thiamine: A final agent with an important role in the management of patients withdrawing from alcohol is thiamine. Alcoholics are at risk for thiamine deficiency, which may lead to Wernicke's disease and the Wernicke-Korsakoff syndrome. Wernicke's disease is an illness of acute onset characterized by the triad of mental disturbance, paralysis of eye movements and ataxia. The ocular abnormality usually is weakness or paralysis of abduction (sixth nerve palsy), which is invariably bilateral though rarely symmetric. It is accompanied by diplopia, strabismus and nystagmus. The ataxia primarily affects gait and stance. Mental status changes most commonly involve a global confusional-apathetic state, but in some patients a disproportionate disorder of retentive memory is apparent.

Wernicke's disease is a neurologic emergency that should be treated by the immediate parenteral administration of thiamine, with a dose of 50 mg intravenously and 50 mg intramuscularly. Delay in provision of thiamine increases the risk of permanent memory damage. The provision of intravenous glucose solutions may exhaust a patient's reserve of B vitamins, acutely precipitating Wernicke's disease, and thus always should be accompanied by the administration of thiamine in the alcoholic patient. Ocular palsies may respond within hours, while the gait and cognitive functions improve more slowly.

As the apathy, drowsiness and confusion recede, the patient may be left with a sometimes permanent defect in retentive memory and learning known as Korsakoff's psychosis. To reduce the risk of these sequelae, all patients presenting with alcohol withdrawal should receive 50 to 100 mg of thiamine at the time of presentation, followed by several weeks of oral supplementation. As noted, patients with symptoms of Wernicke's disease, those who are to receive glucose-containing IV solutions, and those at high risk of malnutrition should receive their initial dose parenterally.

Location of Treatment Services. After it became clear that pharmacological therapy is able to significantly reduce the incidence of major complications, it became common practice to admit patients to the hospital to provide three to seven days of medication. However, such intensive therapy is unnecessary for many patients, and increasing interest has been shown in managing withdrawal on an outpatient basis. Such therapy clearly is less expensive than the inpatient altenative, but is an area of some current controversy because the factors that may be used to identify patients for whom this therapy is appropriate have not been clearly delineated. Nevertheless, for patients with only mild withdrawal, no history of seizures or DTs and no concurrent significant medical or psychiatric problems, such an approach seems reasonable.

Such patients should have a responsible individual to monitor them, they should be seen on a daily basis until they have stabilized, and transportation to emergency medical services should be available.

In addition, many programs are concentrating on sharply reducing their lengths of stay for patients undergoing withdrawal. Patients may be treated in an observation unit or admitted for a one-day stay. If significant withdrawal symptoms do not develop, and the withdrawal is easily controlled with little or no medication, patients can be safely discharged or transferred to an intensive outpatient rehabilitation program. Patients experiencing severe withdrawal, however, need the close monitoring and nursing support of an inpatient unit.

Management of the Patient After a Withdrawal Seizure. The patient who presents after having a withdrawal seizure raises a number of management issues. It is important to recognize that not all seizures in alcohol-dependent patients are due to withdrawal. In epidemiological studies, it is clear that the rate of epilepsy and seizures rises with the amount of an individual's alcohol intake. Alcoholics are at higher risk for seizures unrelated to withdrawal. A careful history of the temporal relationship of alcohol intake to the seizure should be obtained, and the diagnosis of withdrawal seizure should be made only if there is a clear history of a marked decrease or cessation of drinking in the 24 to 48 hours preceding the seizure.

All patients who present with their first seizure warrant hospital admission for observation and evaluation. At a minimum, this should a thorough neurologic exam and brain imaging, with lumbar puncture and EEG also appropriate in many cases. Patients who have a known history of withdrawal seizures and who present with a seizure that can clearly be attributed to withdrawal may not require a full repeat evaluation. If the seizure was generalized and without focal elements, and if a careful neurologic examination reveals no evidence of focal deficits, there is no suspicion of meningitis and there is no history of recent major head trauma, additional testing has an extremely low yield and may be safely omitted.

As noted, there is a 6- to 12-hour period during which there is an increased risk of seizures. Withdrawal seizures often are multiple, with a second seizure occurring in one case out of four. For the patient who presents with a withdrawal seizure, rapid treatment is indicated to prevent further episodes. The parenteral administration of a rapid-acting benzodiazepine such as diazepam or lorazepam is effective. Several studies have shown that phenytoin is no more effective than placebo in preventing recurrent seizures. Initial treatment should be followed up by oral doses of long-acting benzodiazepines over the ensuing 24 to 48 hours.

Management of the Patient with Delirium. The patient who progresses to delirium raises a number of special management issues. Older studies showed a mortality rate of up to 30% in DTs, but with modern care, mortality has been reduced to less than 1% (Kiam, 1972). The principles of successful treatment are adequate sedation and meticulous supportive medical care. Such patients require close nursing observation and supportive care, which frequently necessitates admission to an intensive care unit. Careful management of fluids and electrolytes is important, given the patient's inability to manage his own intake and the presence of marked autonomic hyperactivity.

Delirium often is encountered in patients admitted for acute medical problems whose alcohol dependence was not recognized and whose withdrawal was not adequately treated. A high index of suspicion for the development of infection—whose presenting signs may be masked by the fever, tachycardia and confusion of the underlying delirium—is essential, as is careful management of other co-existing medical conditions.

The use of cross-tolerant sedative-hypnotics has been shown to reduce mortality in DTs and is recommended (Kasser et al., 1998). However, such medications have not been shown to reverse the delirium or reduce its duration. The goal is to sedate the patient to a point of light sleep. This will control the patient's agitation, preventing behavior posing a risk to him- or herself and to staff, and allowing provision of necessary supportive medical care. The use of intravenous benzodiazepines with rapid onset, such as diazepam, has been shown to provide more rapid control of the patient's symptoms. An example of a widely used regimen is given in Table 2.

The main complication is respiratory depression. Whenever this approach is used, providers should have equipment and personnel immediately available to provide respiratory support if needed. One advantage of diazepam is that its peak onset occurs within five minutes of intravenous administration. This allows the provider to deliver repeat boluses and titrate sedation quickly without fear of a delayed appearance of oversedation. Once established, delirium can be expected to last for a number of hours, so diazepam offers another advantage in that its longer half-life helps maintain sedation with less chance of breakthrough agitation. Massive doses of benzodiazepines may be needed to control the agitation of patients in DTs, with hundreds and even thousands of milligrams of diazepam or its equivalent used over a course of treatment. The practitioner should not hesitate to use whatever amounts are needed to control the agitation.

There have been reports of the use of continuous intravenous drips of short-acting agents such as lorazepam or triazolam. Existing evidence suggests that while this approach is no more effective than the use of boluses of longer acting agents, such an approach has proved extremely expensive.

In the agitated patient, benzodiazepines can be supplemented with the addition of neuroleptic agents such as haloperidol. As has been discussed, such agents should not be used alone, and agents with less effect on seizure threshold, such as haloperidol, should be used. In patients whose withdrawal is not readily controlled with oral benzodiazepines and who are beginning to demonstrate signs of agitation, intramuscular administration of a combination of lorazepam and a neuroleptic such as haloperidol often is effective in calming the patient, thus avoiding the need to use intravenous administration.

CONCLUSIONS

It is important to remember that successful management of withdrawal is only the first, and sometimes the most easily achieved, step toward the primary goal of treating the patient's underlying alcohol dependence. Development of a treatment plan for the dependence and engagement of the patient in treatment are critical components of withdrawal and must not be overlooked.

REFERENCES

Alldredge BK & Lowenstein DH (1993). Status epilepticus related to alcohol abuse. *Epilepsia* 34:1033–1037.

American Psychiatric Association (1994). *Diagnostic and Statistical Manual of Mental Disorders, 4th Edition.* Washington, DC: American Psychiatric Press.

Ballenger JC & Post RM (1978). Kindling as a model for alcohol withdrawal syndromes. *British Journal of Psychiatry* 133:1–14.

Booth BM & Blow FC (1993). The kindling hypothesis: Further evidence from a U.S. national study of alcoholic men. *Alcohol and Alcoholism* 28:593–598.

Broaden RN & Goa KL (1991). Flumazenil: A reappraisal of its pharmacological properties and therapeutic efficacy as a benzodiazepine antagonist. *Drugs* 42(6):1061–1089.

Goldstein DB & Goldstein A (1961). Possible role of enzyme inhibition and repression in drug tolerance and addiction. *Biochemistry and Pharmacology* 8:48.

Gorelick DA (1993). Overview of pharmacologic treatment of alcohol and other drug addictions: Intoxication, withdrawal and relapse prevention. *Psychiatric Clinics of North America* 16(1):141–156.

Hawley RJ, Major LF, Schulman EA & Linnoila M (1985). Cerebrospinal fluid 3-methoxy-4-hydroxyphenylglycol and norepinephrine levels in alcohol withdrawal: Correlations with clinical signs. *Archives of General Psychiatry* 42(11):1056–1062.

Herrington RE (1987). Alcohol abuse and dependence: Treatment and rehabilitation. In R Herrington, G Jacobson & D Benzer (eds.) *An Alcohol and Drug Abuse Handbook*. St. Louis, MO: Warren H. Green, Inc., 180–219.

Isbell H, Fraser HF, Wikler A, Bellevile MA & Eisenman AJ (1955). An experimental study of the etiology of "rum fits" and delirium tremens. *Quarterly Journal of Studies of Alcohol* 16:1–33.

Kasser C et al. (1998). ASAM Clinical Practice Guideline on the role of phenytoin in the management of alcohol withdrawal syndrome. *Topics in Addiction Medicine, Vol. 1, No. 1*. Chevy Chase, MD: American Society of Addiction Medicine.

Kasser C et al. (1998). Management of alcohol withdrawal delirium. ASAM clinical practice guideline. Manuscript in preparation.

Kiam SC & Klett CJ (1972). Treatment of delirium tremens: A comparative evaluation of four drugs. *Quarterly Journal of Studies on Alcohol* 33:1065–1072.

Kraemer K, Mayo-Smith MF & Calkins R (1997). Impact of age on severity, course and complications of alcohol withdrawal. *Archives of Internal Medicine* 157:2234–2241.

Mayo-Smith MF, Cushman P, Hill AJ et al. (1997). Pharmacological management of alcohol withdrawal: A meta-analysis and evidence-based practice guideline. *Journal of the American Medical Association*.

Victor M & Adams RD (1953). Effect of alcohol on the nervous system. *Research Publication of the Association for Research in Nervous and Mental Diseases* 32:526–3

Wolf KM, Shaughnessy AF & Middleton DB (1993). Prolonged delirium tremens requiring massive doses of medication. *Journal of the American Board of Family Practice* 6:502–504.

CHAPTER 3

Management of Sedative-Hypnotic Intoxication and Withdrawal

Steven J. Eickelberg, M.D., FASAM
Michael F. Mayo-Smith, M.D., M.P.H.

Sedative-Hypnotic Intoxication and Overdose
Sedative-Hypnotic Withdrawal

Sedative-hypnotic medications decrease activity, moderate excitement, exert a calming effect, produce drowsiness and facilitate sleep. Sedative-hypnotic agents are among the most widely used prescription medications in the U.S., and misuse of and dependence on these medications have occurred since their introduction.

SEDATIVE-HYPNOTIC INTOXICATION AND OVERDOSE

Clinical Picture. The signs and symptoms of sedative-hypnotic intoxication and overdose are similar for the various drugs in the class. Mild to moderate toxicity presents with slurred speech, ataxia and incoordination similar to that seen with alcohol intoxication. On occasion, particularly in the elderly, a paradoxical agitated confusion and even delirium may be produced. With more severe intoxication, stupor and coma develop. With the older non-benzodiazepine agents, toxicity may progress, ultimately leading to fatal respiratory arrest or cardiovascular collapse. Overdose of these older agents also may be associated with a variety of agent-specific clinical manifestations, such as bullous skin lesions with barbiturates ("barb blisters"), details of which can be found in textbooks on toxicological emergencies (Osborn & Goldfrank, 1994).

An additional problem with several of the older sedative-hypnotics is that, with regular use, tolerance may develop to the drugs' therapeutic effects but not to their lethal effects. The maintenance dose then may approach the lethal dose and the therapeutic index decreases. Toxicity and overdose thus can occur with only small increases over the individual's regular intake.

On the other hand, benzodiazepines virtually never lead to death when ingested by themselves. A lethal dose has not been established for any of the benzodiazepines and there are very few well-documented cases of death due to ingestion of benzodiazepines alone. Those that have occurred involved newer, short-acting high potency benzodiazepines such as alprazolam and triazolam (Litovitz, 1987) or administration of benzodiazepines by an intravenous route. Moreover, the benzodiazepines are free of toxic effects on peripheral (non-CNS) organ systems, either with long-term use or in acute overdose.

Despite their safety, benzodiazepines continue to be a major cause of overdose and continue to pose a significant problem because, while safe by themselves, they act synergistically with other agents when ingested together. Mixed overdoses, such as those involving benzodiazepines in combination with alcohol, major tranquilizers, antidepressants or opiates, can be fatal. This is true of the non-benzodiazepine agents as well.

Management of Sedative-Hypnotic Intoxication and Overdose. Assessment and maintenance of the airway and, when necessary, ventilatory support, form the cornerstone of management of sedative-hypnotic overdose. Many of the benzodiazepines agents slow gut motility and some—such as phenobarbital, meprobamate, glutethimide and ethchlorvynol—can form concretions in the stomach. Therefore, evacuation of the GI tract with a large-bore orogastric tube is the next step, provided an active gag reflex is elicited or the airway is protected by intubation. A slurry of 1.0 g/kg activated charcoal together with a dose of cathartic should be given. Repeated doses of activated charcoal, at 0.5 to 1.0 g/kg every two to four hours (or a similar amount delivered by slow continuous nasogastric infusion) may be helpful, particularly for barbiturate or other non-benzodiazepine ingestions. Some of these agents have an extensive entero-hepatic circulation, and repeated doses of charcoal have been shown to speed their elimination. Alkalinization of the urine may also be helpful in the elimination of phenobarbital, but forced diuresis has not been shown to be helpful for any drugs in the class. In extreme cases, hemoperfusion may have a role.

Measurement of serum levels can be helpful in documenting the identity and amounts of agents ingested, as well as in tracking levels over time. However, immediate clinical management is based on the patient's condition rather than serum levels.

Flumazenil is a competitive antagonist with very weak agonist properties at the benzodiazepine receptor (Howland, 1994). It can reverse the sedative effects of benzodiazepines, but not of the other agents or alcohol. Overall, it has found a role in reversing the effects of short-acting benzodiazepines such as midazolam after medical procedures. It also may be used when benzodiazepines have been ingested alone as an overdose. In such settings, slow IV titration in amounts not exceeding 1 mg is recommended, with monitoring for the recurrence of sedation. The effects of flumazenil are short-lived and symptoms may return in 30 to 60 minutes. Moreover, its use has been associated with seizures and cardiac arrhythmias. These adverse effects are more likely to occur when it is administered rapidly in large amounts and in patients who have co-ingested a substance capable of causing seizures, particularly the tricyclic antidepressants (Spivey, 1992). Persons who are physiologically dependent on benzodiazepines are at high risk of seizures when they are administered flumazenil. Flumazenil thus has not found a role as part of the standard "coma cocktail" and its use in mixed overdoses or in patients who have used benzodiazepines chronically is limited by the risk of adverse effects.

SEDATIVE-HYPNOTIC WITHDRAWAL

Clinical Picture. The use of most sedative, hypnotic, and/or anxiolytic drugs can result in the development of addiction and/or pharmacologic-physiologic dependence. (In this chapter, "dependence" is used to refer to the host's neurophysiological adaptation to regular or chronic sedative-hypnotic use. The definition of dependence includes: adaptation to substance use that leads to an abstinence syndrome upon the abrupt cessation of use.) Withdrawal is tantamount to, and is defined by, the signs and symptoms contained within the abstinence syndrome. The evolutionary development of dependence to sedative-hypnotic compounds is similar across the classes of barbiturates, non-barbiturate-non-benzodiazepine agents and the benzodiazepines.

All of the sedative-hypnotic drugs covered in this chapter are substances that currently, or in the recent past, have enjoyed widespread use and possess well-documented and clinically important dependence and withdrawal characteristics. Marked similarities exist between the withdrawal syndromes seen with barbiturates, non-barbiturate-non-benzodiazepine drugs, and the benzodiazepines; these resemble the acute alcohol withdrawal syndrome in many ways. Differences in withdrawal syndrome characteristics among sedative-hypnotic compounds primarily reflect differences in the rate at which dependence is induced, the temporal onset of symptoms upon discontinuation, and the severity of symptoms.

A clinically significant sedative-hypnotic withdrawal syndrome is most apt to occur following the discontinuation of daily therapeutic dose (low dose) use for at least four to six months or, at doses that exceed two to three times the upper limit of recommended therapeutic dosing (high dose), for more than two to three months. The time course and severity of the sedative-hypnotic withdrawal syndrome reflects the influences of three pharmacological factors (Figure 1): (1) dose, (2) duration of use, and (3) duration of drug action. (For the purposes of this discussion, duration of drug action is directly related to the elimination half-life at steady-state conditions.) Clinical research with benzodiazepines has identified additional drug and host factors that influence the onset and severity of the withdrawal syndrome; these factors are discussed in the following sections.

There are no pathognomonic signs or symptoms of sedative-hypnotic withdrawal. Table 1 outlines the spectrum of signs and symptoms that are most commonly experienced during the course of withdrawal. Considerable variation exists among patients in terms of the signs and symptoms of the abstinence syndrome. Although Figure 1 appears to indicate that withdrawal follows a smooth and predictable course, most patients experience significant moment-to-moment quantitative and qualitative variations in their signs and symptoms. The areas under the curves in Figure 1 outline the potential time course and withdrawal severity characteristics. The multitude of signs and symptoms outlined in Table 1 illustrates that, in the absence of the knowledge that a patient is withdrawing from a sedative-

FIGURE 1. Time-Course of Sedative-Hypnotic Withdrawal

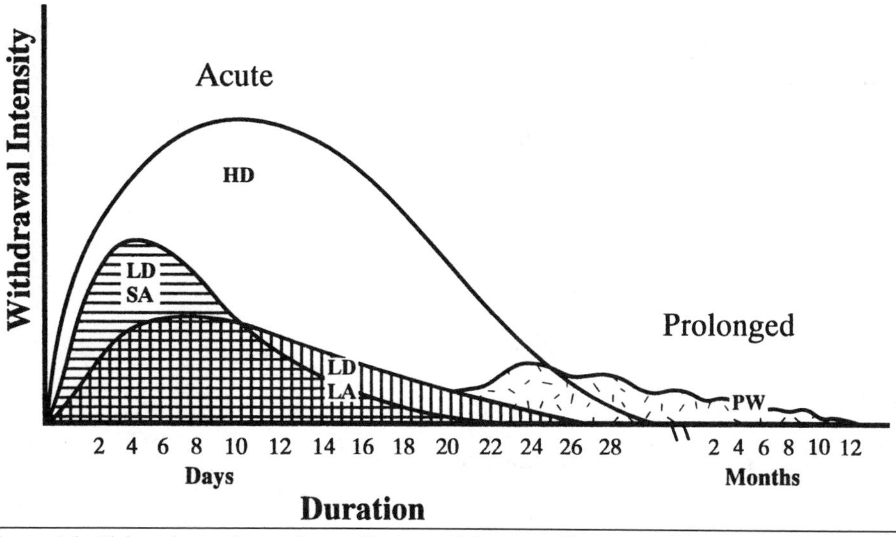

Time course and potential withdrawal intensity as influenced by dose and duration of drug action. HD = High Dose; LD = Low or Therapeutic Dose; SA = Short-Acting; LA = Long-Acting; PW = Prolonged Withdrawal.

hypnotic, an extensive medical and/or psychiatric differential diagnoses would be entertained to explain the patient's condition.

Barbiturates: Medical literature evidenced an emerging awareness of barbiturate dependence and an abstinence syndrome in the 1940s. The first American paper (Isbell, 1950) directly addressing the barbiturate withdrawal syndrome was followed by a clinical study which chronicled the signs and symptoms of the barbiturate abstinence syndrome following chronic use (Isbell & Altschul, 1950). Further studies quantified, with high dose use, the duration of barbiturate ingestion necessary for mild, moderate, and severe withdrawal symptoms to occur (Fraser, Wikler et al., 1958; Isbell & White, 1953). The first evidence that an abstinence syndrome could occur following long-term, therapeutic dose (low-dose) barbiturate use was published nearly two decades later (Covi, Lipman et al., 1973; Epstein, 1980).

Treatment of barbiturate withdrawal with barbiturate substitution was reported as early as 1953 (Isbell & White, 1953). In 1970 and 1971, Smith and Wesson reported on a protocol that uses a phenobarbital substitution, stabilization, and tapering technique to treat barbiturate dependence. Their technique remains the "gold standard" for the management of all sedative-hypnotic classes or mixed sedative-hypnotic withdrawal.

Non-Barbiturate-Non-Benzodiazepine Agents: The medical literature contains case reports documenting the full spectrum of sedative-hypnotic withdrawal signs and symptoms from this group of compounds. Of greatest concern are the multitude of reports documenting severe withdrawal syndromes marked by delirium, psychosis, hallucinations, hyperthermia, cardiac arrests, and death (Essig, 1964; Sadwin & Glen, 1958; Lloyd & Clark, 1959; Phillips, Judy & Judy, 1957; Swanson & Okada, 1963; Flomenbaum & Gumby, 1971; Swartzburg, Lieb & Schwartz, 1973; Vestal & Rumack, 1974).

Benzodiazepines: Benzodiazepine use, dependence, and withdrawal are much more thoroughly researched than with other classes of sedative-hypnotic compounds. Soon after chlordiazepoxide (Librium®, 1960) and diazepam (Valium®, 1963) became available commercially, clinical reports were published documenting a high dose discontinuation withdrawal syndrome with severe characteristics (seizures, depression, delirium, psychosis) (Hollister, Motzenbecker & Degan, 1961; Hollister, Bennett et al., 1963; Essig, 1966). Reports of a withdrawal syndrome following the discontinuation of long-term use of benzodiazepines at therapeutic doses were published within the next decade (Covi, Park & Lipman, 1969; Covi, Lipman et al., 1973). It now is well established that benzodiazepine dependence, withdrawal, and difficulties discontinuing chronic benzodiazepine use are influenced by multiple pharmacological and host factors (as discussed in upcoming sections).

Signs and Symptoms of Discontinuation. The signs and symptoms experienced following the discontinuation of benzodiazepine use have been ca-

TABLE 1. Sedative-Hypnotic Withdrawal

	Withdrawal Severity	
Withdrawal Factors	**Mild–Moderate**	**Severe**
ADRENERGIC-AUTONOMIC	Anxiety Restlessness Agitation Nausea Vomiting Yawning Insomnia Hypertension Tachycardia Mydriasis	Autonomic hyperactivity Vital sign instability Hyperpyrexia
MUSCULOSKELETAL	Tremor Weakness Fasciculations Spasms Cramping Hyperreflexia	
NEUROPSYCHIATRIC	Sensory Hypersensitivity —Light —Sound —Touch —Smell Light headedness Dizziness Depression Depersonalization Derealization Confusion Difficulty expressing thoughts	Psychosis Delusions Hallucinations Mania Catatonia Delirium Seizure
OTHER	Lethargy Fatigue Loss of drive Loss of appetite Tinnitus Nightmares/Vivid dreams Metallic taste	

tegorized and attributed to at least four different etiologies: (1) symptom recurrence or relapse, (2) rebound, (3) pseudowithdrawal, and (4) true withdrawal.

Symptom recurrence or relapse is characterized by the recurrence of symptoms (such as insomnia or anxiety) for which the benzodiazepine originally was taken. The symptoms are similar in character to the condition that existed prior to drug treatment. Relapse may occur following discontinuation, with or without the prior existence of benzodiazepine dependence. Reemergence of symptoms is quite common, exceeding 60% to 80% for anxiety and insomnia disorders (Rickels, Case et al., 1986a; Greenblatt, Miller & Shader, 1990). Symptom recurrence can present rapidly or slowly over days to months following drug discontinuation.

Rebound is marked by the development of symptoms, within hours to days of drug discontinuation, that are qualitatively similar to the disorder for which the benzodiazepine initially was prescribed.

However, the symptoms are transiently more intense than they were prior to drug treatment. Insomnia and anxiety disorders are the best studied examples of this syndrome (Rickels, Fox & Greenblatt, 1988). Rebound symptoms are of short duration and are self-limited (Greenblatt, Miller & Shader, 1990), which distinguishes this syndrome from relapse.

Pseudowithdrawal and over-interpretation of symptoms may occur when expectations of withdrawal lead to the experiencing of abstinence symptoms. This effect has been observed in study patients who discontinued placebo medication or continued benzodiazepine use but believed that the benzodiazepine had been discontinued (Winokur, 1981). In addition, expectations of symptoms often are negatively influenced by concerns registered by the media, press, friends, and/or physician(s).

True withdrawal is marked by the emergence of psychological and somatic signs and symptoms following the discontinuation of benzodiazepines in an individual who is physically dependent on the drug. The withdrawal syndrome can be suppressed by the reinstitution of the discontinued benzodiazepine or another cross-tolerant sedative-hypnotic. Withdrawal from benzodiazepines results from a reversal of the neuroadaptive changes in the central nervous system that were induced by chronic benzodiazepine use. Withdrawal reflects a relative temporal and temporary diminution of central nervous system GABA-ergic neuronal inhibition.

Considerable individual variations and variability over time occur with each patient who discontinues benzodiazepine use. The benzodiazepine withdrawal syndrome has been documented to include any of the spectrum of signs and symptoms listed in Table 1. Any combination of signs and symptoms may be experienced with varying severity throughout the initial one to four weeks of abstinence. None of the signs or symptoms of the abstinence syndrome are pathognomonic of benzodiazepine withdrawal. Many signs and symptoms are identical to the symptoms of anxiety or depressive disorders. The most common *symptoms* include: tremor, muscle twitching, nausea and vomiting, impaired concentration, restlessness, anorexia, blurred vision, irritability, insomnia, sweating, and weakness. Common clinical *signs* include tachycardia, hypertension, hyperreflexia, mydriasis, and diaphoresis. The presence of neuropsychiatric symptoms, including perceptual distortions and hypersensitivity to light, sound, and touch are common. Many believe these "sensory-perceptual symptoms" are most indicative of neurophysiological withdrawal, but they rarely occur in the absence of some of the aforementioned adrenergic or anxiety symptoms. Lack of clinical signs should not be considered tantamount to the absence of a withdrawal syndrome.

The clinical withdrawal picture can consist primarily of *subjective symptoms*, accompanied by few or no concurrently observable hyper-adrenergic signs or vital sign fluctuations (as is seen with acute alcohol withdrawal).

Combinations of the above discontinuation syndromes often coexist. For example, considerable overlap exists between the symptoms of relapse in anxiety and insomnia disorders and the signs and symptoms of rebound and withdrawal. Clinical techniques that treat, minimize and attenuate benzodiazepine abstinence symptoms also effectively alleviate rebound. As a result, attention to sorting out rebound from withdrawal is unnecessary (if not impossible). However, symptom recurrence or relapse are common. Clinicians thus must be attuned to the emergence or persistence of clinically important symptoms of relapse during and after the period of acute withdrawal.

Role of the GABA-Benzodiazepine Receptor Complex. Benzodiazepine action in the central nervous system is mediated by the Gamma-amino-butyric acid benzodiazepine receptor complex (GABA-BZD-R-complex; Haefly, 1975; Costa, 1975). Work by numerous investigators has shown that GABA is the primary central nervous system inhibitory neurotransmitter. Activation of the GABA receptor induces the opening of a neuronal, membrane-bound chloride ion channel, located within the GABA-BDZ-R-complex. Neuronal inhibition results from neuronal membrane hyperpolarization secondary to the flow of chloride ions down the electrochemical gradient into the neuron. Benzodiazepines bind allosterically to a "benzodiazepine receptor" (recently named the Omega receptor), located on the GABA-BDZ-R-Complex. Benzodiazepines positively modulate and influence the GABA-chloride channel relationship.

A series of studies by Miller, Greenblatt and colleagues (1988a, 1988b, 1989, 1990; Miller, 1991) illustrate that in mice, behavioral tolerance and discontinuation syndromes are temporally associated with molecular/receptor level adaptations. The investigators reported that as tolerance to the ataxia-inducing effects of lorazepam developed behaviorally, benzodiazepine and GABA receptors were down-regulated (through decreased receptor number, decreased GABA-receptor function, and diminished protein synthesis for GABA receptors). After lorazepam was administered for four weeks, it was abruptly discontinued. Concurrent with signs of withdrawal, GABA-receptors were up-regulated and GABA-receptor complex function was enhanced (as evidenced by greater affinity for GABA, increased affinity of the benzodiazepine receptor for benzodiazepines, and increased benzodiazepine receptor number).

The rate of onset of behavioral tolerance to alprazolam and clonazepam followed by an abstinence syndrome upon abrupt discontinuation was similarly computed and then compared with lorazepam in a subsequent report (Miller, 1991). Alprazolam tolerance and withdrawal developed more rapidly (four days for tolerance; two days for withdrawal) than was the case with lorazepam and clonazepam, which were similar (seven days for tolerance; four days for withdrawal) (Miller, Greenblatt et al., 1988a, 1988b; Miller, 1991). These studies also demonstrated that tolerance is primarily a pharmacodynamic, neuroadaptive phenomenon (brain and plasma levels remained constant throughout the period of chronic administration).

File (1993) has commented that it is premature to link our current observations of neurochemical changes to behavior etiologically, since multiple potential explanations exist. Events may: (1) be independent yet occur simultaneously, (2) reflect neuroadaptive changes resulting from compensatory mechanisms, or (3) be causally linked. Despite numerous unanswered questions, it is apparent that the primary neuroadaptive response occurs at the GABA-BDZ-R-complex. This system then influences changes in other neurotransmitter systems, depending on the neuroanatomical location of the GABA-BDZ-receptor complex. The benzodiazepine discontinuation syndrome subsequently is influenced, if not mediated, by numerous neurotransmitter systems.

Pharmacological Characteristics Affecting Withdrawal. Pharmacological factors are primarily responsible for the relationship between various benzodiazepines and the clinical manifestations of benzodiazepine withdrawal syndrome.

Pharmacokinetics: Benzodiazepine pharmacokinetics determine the onset of discontinuation symptoms following chronic use. Cessation of use is followed by declining blood levels of drug at receptor sites, brain, blood, and peripheral tissues, with the rate of decline determined primarily by the elimination half-life. The onset, duration, and severity of the withdrawal syndrome correlate with declining serum levels of drug (Hollister, Motzenbecker & Degan, 1961; Tyrer, Rutherford & Huggett, 1981; Schweizer & Rickels, 1990; Miller, Greenblatt et al., 1988a, 1988b, 1989).

Onset of withdrawal from short-acting benzodiazepines (such as lorazepam, oxazepam, triazolam, alprazolam, and temazepam) occurs within 24 hours of cessation of use (Busto, 1986; Rickels, 1986b), with peak severity of withdrawal following within one to five days (Busto, Sellers et al., 1986; Rickels, Case et al., 1986b; Schweizer & Rickels, 1990). With long-acting benzodiazepines (such as diazepam, chlordiazepoxide, and clonazepam), onset of withdrawal occurs within five days of cessation (Busto, Sellers et al., 1986) and withdrawal severity peaks at one to nine days (Hollister, Bennett et al., 1960; Schweizer & Rickels, 1990).

Duration of acute withdrawal, from the temporal onset to the resolution of symptoms, can be as long as seven to 21 days for short-acting and 10 to 28 days for long-acting benzodiazepines. While there is no difference in the type or number of withdrawal symptoms following discontinuation of short- or long-acting benzodiazepines (Rickels, Case et al., 1986b; Schweizer & Rickels, 1990), withdrawal symptoms from short-acting benzodiazepines are experienced as being more intense (compared to the symptoms associated with long-acting drugs) following abrupt discontinuation (Tyrer, Rutherford & Huggett, 1981; Busto, Case et al., 1986; Rickels, Sellers et al., 1986b; Schweizer & Rickels, 1990).

Dosage and Duration of Use: Higher doses and longer use place patients at greater risk for increased withdrawal severity. Daily benzodiazepine use for 10 days or even less can lead to transient insomnia when the medication is stopped. A withdrawal syndrome frequently follows discontinuation of short-term (< 2 to 3 months') therapeutic (low-dose) use, but most symptoms, if present at all, are rated as mild (e.g., insomnia) and are easily managed. On discontinuation of long-term (> 1 year) therapeutic dose (low-dose) use, withdrawal is common and is experienced as moderate to severe symptoms by 20% to 100% of patients (Rickels, Case et al., 1986b; Noyes, Garvey et al., 1988; Schweizer & Rickels, 1990). Discontinuation of high dose (> 4 to 5 times the high end of the therapeutical range for more than six to 12 weeks) benzodiazepine use leads to moderate withdrawal in all patients, and severe withdrawal signs and symptoms in most patients (Hollister, Motzenbecker & Degan, 1961; Hollister, Bennett et al., 1963).

Beyond one year of continuous benzodiazepine therapy, the duration of use becomes a less important factor in the severity of acute withdrawal (Rickels & Schweizer, 1990). Use beyond one year may, however, predispose patients for prolonged withdrawal sequelae.

Potency: Tolerance to the sedative and hypnotic effects develops most rapidly to shorter acting, higher potency benzodiazepines such as triazolam and alprazolam. Withdrawal from these agents may be more intense and requires more aggressive attention and longer periods of medical monitoring than is the case with other benzodiazepines (Dickinson, Rush & Radcliffe, 1990; Malcolm, Brady et al., 1993).

Host Factors Affecting Withdrawal. In addition to the aforementioned pharmacological influences, host factors are implicated in both patients' susceptibility to benzodiazepine dependence and their difficulty in discontinuing benzodiazepines once they become dependent. Clinically important patient factors include:

Psychiatric Comorbidity: The primary clinical indications for benzodiazepine use is in the treatment of insomnia, anxiety, thought and mood disorders. It follows that patients with chronic psychiatric disorders, maintained on benzodiazepines for more than three to six months will, in addition to their psychiatric condition (adequately treated or not), possess benzodiazepine physiologic dependence. Numerous benzodiazepine discontinuation studies highlight the high (40% to 100%) prevalence of active concurrent psychiatric disorders at intake of study participants (Rickels, Case et al., 1986b; Schweizer & Rickels, 1990; Rickels & Schweizer, 1990; Malcolm, Brady et al., 1993; Romach, Busto et al., 1995; Busto, Sellers et al., 1996). Most of these studies demonstrate a positive correlation between the patient's degree of psychopathology, withdrawal symptom severity, and inability to discontinue use.

Rickels, Case and colleagues (1986b) reported on 119 patients who were discontinuing benzodiazepines after long-term use of therapeutic doses. They noted a 90% prevalence of initial, active psychopathology, with current diagnoses that included generalized anxiety disorder, 44%; panic disorder, 27%; depression, 14%; and other, 7%. Patients with greater psychopathology required more support and assurance. The intensity of the withdrawal syndrome was noted to be partially a function of the degree of psychopathology and other premorbid personality variables.

Rickels and Schweizer (1990) studied abrupt and tapered discontinuation of long-term, therapeutic-dose benzodiazepine use. They found that 79% to 84% of patients possessed clinically significant, active symptoms of anxiety and/or depression at intake (primary psychiatric diagnoses included generalized anxiety disorder, panic disorder and major depression). They reported significantly greater withdrawal severity in patients who had more initial psychopathology, dependent personality disorder or neuroticism.

Clinicians conducting benzodiazepine discontinuation thus must obtain psychiatric histories while remaining vigilantly watchful for, and prepared to manage, the emergence or reemergence of psychiatric disorders. Clinicians also must be aware that patients with psychiatric symptoms or disorders often experience more severe withdrawal symptoms and have greater difficulty discontinuing use.

Concurrent Other Substance Use: Concurrent regular use of other dependence-producing substances increases the complexity of the benzodiazepine abstinence syndrome and the patient's clinical situation as a whole. Additional sedative-hypnotic substance use contributes to a withdrawal syndrome of increased severity and less predictable course. For example, opioid substance withdrawal contributes an additional cluster of signs and symptoms. Anxiety, agitation, irritation, hyper-arousal, and the adrenergic components of opioid and benzodiazepine withdrawal are additive, often overlap, and lead to an exacerbation of symptoms. Psychomotor stimulant withdrawal symptoms contribute factors from the opposite end of the withdrawal spectrum (e.g., apathy, hypersomnia and lethargy). When stimulant withdrawal is combined with sedative-hypnotic withdrawal, the clinical picture is remarkable for symptoms of severe agitation, depression, irritability, and somatosensory hypersensitivity.

At least four factors emphasize the need for clinicians to be aware of the high co-occurrence of alcoholism, anxiety disorders, and/or benzodiazepine dependence and their potential influence on the benzodiazepine withdrawal syndrome:

- A high percentage of alcoholics use benzodiazepines regularly. Concurrent use is reported to range from 29% (Busto, Sellers et al., 1982) to 33% (Busto, Simpkins & Sellers, 1983) to 76% (Ciraulo, Barnhill et al., 1988).
- The comorbidity rate of alcohol abuse and anxiety disorders is reported at 18% to 19% (Regier, Farmer et al., 1990).
- Alcoholics have a high propensity for dependence on benzodiazepines (Ciraulo, Barnhill et al., 1988; Sellers, Farmeret et al., 1993).
- Rickels, Schweizer and colleagues (1990) reported that moderate alcohol use (exceeding one

beer or drink per day) is a more significant predictor of benzodiazepine withdrawal severity than dose or half-life of the drug.

Busto, Romach and Sellers (1996) and Malcolm, Brady et al. (1993) have shown that patients with high-dose benzodiazepine use who present for inpatient addiction treatment exhibit a high rate (70%, Busto; 96%, Malcolm) of concurrent dependence on other substances. Almost 100% of these patients reported histories of dependence on other substances. DuPont (1988) reported that > 20% of newly admitted patients to inpatient addiction treatment reported using benzodiazepines at least weekly; 73% of heroin users reported greater than weekly use; and > 15% of heroin users used benzodiazepines daily. In addition, a high rate of benzodiazepine use in methadone maintenance clinics is supported by numerous clinical surveys.

Consequently, clinicians must be aware of, and/or suspect, benzodiazepine use in patients with any substance use disorder. Conversely, in high-dose benzodiazepine users, other substance use must be assumed until it is ruled out.

Family History of Alcohol Dependence: Mood changes associated with liability for benzodiazepine abuse (and increased propensity to develop dependence) have been reported following controlled clinical administration of diazepam and alprazolam in adult sons of severe alcoholics (Ciraulo, Barnhill et al., 1988, 1989; Cowley, Roy-Byrne et al., 1991, 1992). Similar findings with alprazolam were reported recently in adult daughters of alcoholics (Ciraulo, Sarid-Segal et al., 1996). This predisposition to abuse benzodiazepines is important because at least one study implicates a linkage of paternal history of alcoholism with increased withdrawal severity in patients discontinuing alprazolam use (Dickinson, Rush & Radcliffe, 1990).

Concurrent Medical Conditions: Benzodiazepine withdrawal should be avoided during acute medical or surgical conditions because the physiological stress of withdrawal can adversely and unnecessarily affect the course of the acute medical condition. On the other hand, continued benzodiazepine use rarely has a negative effect on acute medical conditions. The goal of therapy for a patient dependent on benzodiazepines, during an acute medical situation, is to provide adequate stabilization of the benzodiazepine dose and prevention of withdrawal.

Clinicians need to be secure in their understanding of the indications for discontinuing long-term benzodiazepine use in patients who have chronic medical conditions. This is particularly true when evaluating the discontinuation of sedative-hypnotics in patients with conditions that are significantly influenced by adrenergic and psychological stress factors (i.e., cardiac arrhythmia, asthma, SLE, inflammatory bowel disease, etc.). The risks of exacerbating the medical condition during acute withdrawal or a protracted withdrawal course may outweigh the longer-term benefits of benzodiazepine discontinuation. In general, patients with chronic medical conditions experience benzodiazepine withdrawal more severely than others. Clinicians and patients must be aware that during withdrawal, difficulties in managing the medical condition (i.e., diabetes, cardiovascular disease, thyroid disease, arthritis, etc.) may emerge.

Age: Hepatic microsomal enzyme oxidase system (MEOS) efficiency decreases with age. Elderly patients may have elimination half-lives that are two to five times slower than the rate in younger adults for benzodiazepines eliminated through the MEOS (all benzodiazepines except for lorazepam, temazepam, and oxazepam). The withdrawal syndrome for elderly persons who are discontinuing oxidatively metabolized benzodiazepines may be quite prolonged and/or approach the severity of high-dose withdrawal secondary to the pharmacokinetic factors of aging. The withdrawal course can become especially pernicious following discontinuation of long-acting benzodiazepines that are metabolized to sedative-hypnotic compounds with longer elimination half-lives (such as diazepam, chlordiazepoxide, and flurazepam).

Gender: World-wide, women are prescribed benzodiazepines twice as often as men; hence, twice as many women are likely to become dependent on these drugs (Gabe, 1993). Possibly compounding this demographic trend are reports that female gender was a significant predictor of increased withdrawal severity in patients undergoing tapered cessation of long-term, therapeutic benzodiazepine use (Rickels, Schweizer et al., 1990). (However, gender was not implicated as an influential factor with *abrupt* cessation of long-term, therapeutic dose use [Schweizer, Rickels et al., 1990].)

Patient Evaluation. Evaluating patients for benzodiazepine cessation and detoxification requires a combination of clinical, diagnostic, consultation and liaison, counseling, and pharmacologic management skills. To be consistently effective and successful, the clinician must be flexible and able to tolerate ambiguities and variations in the course of withdrawal and to support the patient who experiences significant apprehension and anxiety.

Patient Evaluation and Assessment. Components of the clinical evaluation and assessment of the patient typically include the following steps:

Step 1: Determine the reason(s) that the patient or referral source is seeking evaluation of sedative-hypnotic use and/or discontinuation. Determine the indication(s) for the patient's drug use. A discussion with the referring physician should be standard practice. Discussion with any other referring person(s) or close family members often is helpful. Seek evidence to answer the question of whether the patient's use is improving the quality of his or her life or causing significant disability and/or exacerbating the original condition.

Step 2: Take a sedative-hypnotic use history, including, at a minimum, the dose, duration of use, substance(s) used and the patient's clinical response to sedative-hypnotic use currently and over time. The history should include any attempts at abstinence, symptoms experienced with changing the dose, and reasons for increasing or decreasing the dose. The history also should include behavioral responses to sedative-hypnotic use and any adverse or toxic side-effects. For long-term users, a determination of the current pharmacological and clinical efficacy should be sought.

Step 3: Elicit a detailed accounting of other psychoactive drug use (including medical and non-medical, prescribed and over-the-counter drugs), as well as current use of alcohol and prior sequelae of use. The history also should include abstinence attempts and/or prior periods of abstinence, in addition to prior withdrawal experiences.

Step 4: Take a psychiatric history, including current and past psychiatric diagnoses, hospitalizations, suicide attempts, treatments, psychotherapy, and therapists (names and locations).

Step 5: Take a family history of substance use, psychiatric, and medical disorders.

Step 6: Take a current and past medical history of the patient, including illnesses, trauma, surgery, medications, allergies, and history of loss of consciousness, seizure(s), or seizure disorder.

Step 7: Take a psychosocial history, including current social status and support system.

Step 8: Perform a physical and mental status examination.

Step 9: Conduct a laboratory urine drug screen for substances of abuse. An alcohol Breathalyzer (if available) often is helpful in providing evidence of substance use which was not provided in the history. Depending on the patient's profile, EKG, HIV testing, TB testing, a blood chemistry panel, liver enzymes, CBC, and/or pregnancy testing may be indicated.

Step 10: Complete an individualized assessment, taking into account all aspects of the patient's presentation and history and, in particular, focusing on factors that would significantly influence the presence, severity, and time course of withdrawal.

Step 11: Arrive at a differential diagnosis, including a comprehensive listing of considered and/or possible diagnoses. This greatly aids and guides clinical management decisions as the patient's symptoms diminish, emerge or change in character during and after drug cessation.

Step 12: Determine the appropriate setting for detoxification.

Step 13: Determine the most efficacious detoxification method. In addition to proven clinical and pharmacological efficacy, the method selected should be one that the physician and clinical staff in the detoxification setting are comfortable with and experienced in administering.

Step 14: Obtain the patient's informed consent.

Step 15: Initiate detoxification. Ongoing physician involvement is central to appropriate management of detoxification. Subsequent to the patient assessment, development of the treatment plan, and obtaining patient consent, the individualized discontinuation program should be initiated. The physician closely monitors and flexibly manages (adjusting as necessary) the dosing or detoxification strategy to provide the safest, most comfortable and efficacious course of detoxification. To achieve optimal results, the physician and patient will need to establish a close working relationship.

Management of Detoxification. For patients who are dependent on sedative-hypnotics, there are two primary options for the detoxification process: (1) tapering, or (2) substitution and tapering.

Tapering: Although carefully controlled studies comparing tapering methods are lacking, gradual dose reduction is the most widely used and most logical method of benzodiazepine discontinuation. The taper method is primarily indicated for use in: (1) an outpatient ambulatory setting; (2) patients with therapeutic-dose benzodiazepine dependence; (3) patients who are dependent only on benzodiazepines; and (4) patients who can reliably present for regular clinical follow-up during and after detoxification.

With the taper method, the patient is slowly and gradually weaned from the benzodiazepine on

TABLE 2. Sedative-Hypnotic Withdrawal Substitution Dose Conversions

Drug	Dose(mg)
Benzodiazepines	
Alprazolam (Xanax)	0.5
Chlordiazepoxide (Librium)	25
Clonazepam (Klonopin)	1–2
Clorazepate (Tranxene)	15
Diazepam (Valium)	10
Estazolam (ProSom)	2
Flurazepam (Dalmane)	15
Lorazepam (Ativan)	2
Oxazepam (Serax)	10
Quazepam (Doral)	15
Temazepam (Restoril)	15
Triazolam (Halcion)	0.25
Barbiturates	
Pentobarbital (Nembutal)	50–100
Secobarbital (Seconal)	100
Butalbital (Fiorinal)	100
Amobarbital (Amytal)	100
Phenobarbital	30
Nonbarbiturates-Nonbenzodiazepines	
Ethchlorvynol (Placidyl)	300
Glutethimide (Doriden)	250
Methyprylon (Noludar)	200
Methaqualone (Quaalude)	300
Meprobamate (Miltown)	400
Carisoprodol (Soma)	700
Chloral Hydrate (Notec)	500

which he or she has been dependent, using a fixed-dose taper schedule. The dose is decreased on a weekly to every-other-week basis. The rate of discontinuation for long-term users (> one year) should not exceed 5 mg diazepam equivalents (Table 2) per week or 10% of the current (starting) dose, per week, whichever is smaller. For the final 20% of the taper, the rate and/or dose reduction schedule should be slowed to half the previous dose reduction per week and the reductions accomplished at twice the original tapering interval. If symptoms of withdrawal occur, the dose should be increased until the symptoms resolve and the subsequent taper schedule is commenced at a slower rate.

Patients who are unable to complete a simple taper program should be reevaluated and, if indicated, an alternative detoxification method chosen. Some patients may require the use of a substitution and taper program and/or require a short period of hospitalization to receive the monitoring and support necessary to complete the drug discontinuation.

Substitution and Tapering: Substitution and tapering methods employ cross-tolerant long-acting benzodiazepines (chlordiazepoxide or clonazepam) or phenobarbital as substitutes, at equipotent doses, for the sedative-hypnotic(s) on which the patient is dependent. Three substitution and taper paradigms are presented below, each of which is useful in different clinical situations dictated by patient compliance, the severity of dependence, the presence of other substance dependence, the clinical setting, etc.

Chlordiazepoxide, clonazepam and phenobarbital are the most widely used substitution agents for a number of important reasons:

- At steady state, there is negligible inter-dose serum level variation with these drugs;
- With tapering, a more gradual reduction in serum levels diminishes the incidence of withdrawal symptom emergence; and
- Each of the three drugs has low abuse potential (phenobarbital is lowest, followed by clonazepam and then chlordiazepoxide). Phenobarbital has the added advantages of not inducing behavioral disinhibition and possessing broad clinical efficacy in the management of withdrawal from all classes of sedative-hypnotic agents. Clinical experience shows that phenobarbital is most useful and effective in patients with polysubstance dependence, high-dose dependence, and in patients with unknown dose or erratic "polypharmacy" drug use.

Uncomplicated Substitution and Taper: This method is used in outpatient settings for patients who are discontinuing short half-life benzodiazepines or for those who are unable to tolerate gradual tapering. Substitution also can be conducted in an inpatient or intensive outpatient or day-hospital setting for reliable patients who are discontinuing high-dose use. The procedure requires an accurate knowledge of the patient's current daily dose of sedative-hypnotics.

1. Calculate the equivalent dose of chlordiazepoxide, clonazepam, or phenobarbital, using the Substitution Dose Conversion Table (Table 2).

Individual variation in clinical responses to "equivalent" doses can vary by a factor of 2 to 3; therefore, close clinical monitoring of patient response to substitution is necessary. Adjustments to the initially calculated dose schedule are to be expected.

2. Provide the substituted drug in a divided dose: e.g., three to four doses per day.
3. In an *outpatient setting,* while the substituted agent is achieving steady state levels on a fixed dose schedule, provide the patient with PRN doses of the benzodiazepine he or she has been using to suppress symptoms of withdrawal (in doses up to the daily amount he or she had been receiving prior to the institution of substitution) for the first week only, then discontinue the PRN drug dosing.

   In an *inpatient setting,* provide doses of the substitute agent as needed (PRN) for signs of withdrawal. The PRN drug substitution should be prescribed in addition to the fixed-dose scheduled medication, while awaiting steady state levels, which are achieved within four to seven days.
4. Stabilize the patient on an adequate substitution dose (same dose on consecutive days without the need for regular PRN doses). This usually is accomplished in five to seven days.
5. Gradually reduce the dose. This usually is accomplished through reductions of 30 to 60 mg of phenobarbital (or equivalent) per day (as tolerated) for the first 80% of the taper. Hold the taper schedule for any symptoms of withdrawal and stabilize the patient for at least 24 hours prior to reinstituting the process.
6. The final 20% of the taper is accomplished through a reduction of 15 to 30 mg of phenobarbital (or equivalent) per day, or every other day, depending on the patient's response.

Sedative-Hypnotic Tolerance Testing: This method is employed when the degree of dependence is difficult to determine. This situation is common in high dose, erratic dose, illicit source, polysubstance, or alcohol plus sedative-hypnotic use. Pentobarbital is used because of its rapid onset of action, short half-life, easy to monitor signs of toxicity, and the ease with which it can be replaced by phenobarbital once a patient has been stabilized.

1. 200 mg pentobarbital is given orally every two hours for 24 to 48 hours.
2. Doses are held for signs of toxicity (intoxication), which develop in the following progression at increasing serum levels: fine lateral sustained nystagmus; coarse nystagmus; slurred speech; ataxia; and somnolence. Doses are held with the development of coarse nystagmus and slurred speech and subsequently resumed on resolution of the signs of toxicity.
3. After 24 to 48 hours, the total amount of administered pentobarbital is divided by the number of days it was administered. This amount is the 24-hour stabilizing dose.
4. The stabilizing dose is administered in divided doses over the next 24 hours to assure adequate substitution. The patient's response determines the indications for dose upward or downward adjustments in the dose.
5. Once the patient is stable on a consistent dose for 24 hours, phenobarbital is substituted for pentobarbital (Table 2).
6. A gradual reduction of the phenobarbital dose is conducted, as described above.

Withdrawal Emergence PRN Phenobarbital Substitution: This procedure is best used in a 24-hour medically monitored setting. It provides the smoothest and most effective treatment for sedative-hypnotic withdrawal for patients who are unable to complete outpatient tapering regimens, for high-dose users or polysubstance dependent patients, and for patients who have considerable comorbid psychopathology.

1. Signs and symptoms of withdrawal are treated as needed (PRN) hourly with 30 to 60 mg of phenobarbital for two to seven days. The period of PRN dosing is determined by the duration of action of the substance(s) the patient is discontinuing.
2. The patient is monitored hourly to assure adequate dosing. Ideally, a balance is achieved between the signs and symptoms of withdrawal and of phenobarbital intoxication.
3. When the patient has received similar 24-hour phenobarbital dose totals for two consecutive days, the total dose for those two days then is divided by two to arrive at the stabilizing dose.
4. The stabilizing dose is given in divided dose increments over the next 24 hours. This may require medication administration every three to four hours for patients with high tolerance.
5. A gradual taper is initiated, as described above.

Patients often can be transferred from an inpatient setting to an intensive daily (medically monitored) outpatient program once they are stabilized on the tapering portion of the protocol.

Adjunctive Withdrawal Management Measures. *Carbamazepine:* Adjunctive carbamazepine therapy is not yet widely used, although clinical protocols and patient selection for this method are being studied. Six reports on small clinical trials using carbamazepine showed encouraging but mixed effectiveness and utility (Klein, Uhde et al., 1986; Klein, Colvin et al., 1994; Ries, Roy-Byrne et al, 1989, 1991; Garcia-Borresuerro et al., 1990; Schweizer, Rickels et al., 1991). It is clear that carbamazepine lacks clinical indications for use in patients with high-dose dependence, polysubstance dependence, unreliable histories of benzodiazepine dose, dependence on sedative-hypnotics other than benzodiazepines, and older age. Adverse consequences of carbamazepine use can include neutropenia, thrombocytopenia and hyponatremia, necessitating initial and ongoing laboratory evaluation and monitoring.

Propranolol: Tyrer and colleagues (1981) clearly demonstrated that propranolol alone does not affect the rate of successful benzodiazepine discontinuation or the incidence of withdrawal symptoms for discontinuation of chronic benzodiazepine use. However, propranolol treatment does diminish the severity of adrenergic signs and symptoms of withdrawal. Propranolol is not cross-tolerant with sedative-hypnotic drugs and should not be used as the sole therapeutic agent in managing sedative-hypnotic withdrawal. Propranolol can be used, in doses of 60 to 120 mg per day, as an adjunct to one of the aforementioned withdrawal methods. However, clinicians need to be mindful that propranolol treatment will diminish (or "hide") some of the very symptoms and signs that are monitored to determine substitution doses.

Clonidine: Clonidine has been shown to be ineffective in treating benzodiazepine withdrawal. In this study, doses sufficient to decrease serum levels of norepinephrine metabolites had minimal attenuating effect on the benzodiazepine withdrawal syndrome. One significant result of the study was the demonstration that increased norepinephrine activity plays a small role in the overall benzodiazepine withdrawal syndrome.

Buspirone: Buspirone is a non-benzodiazepine anxiolytic drug that is not cross-tolerant with benzodiazepines or other sedative-hypnotic drugs. Schweizer, Rickels et al. (1986) demonstrated that buspirone substitution in patients undergoing abrupt or gradual benzodiazepine discontinuation failed to protect against the symptoms of withdrawal.

Sodium Valproate: Anecdotal reports indicate that sodium valproate is effective in attenuating the benzodiazepine withdrawal syndrome. Valproate possesses GABA-ergic actions and anticonvulsant effects and is an attractive candidate for larger clinical studies of its utility in managing benzodiazepine withdrawal.

Cognitive-Behavioral Therapy: Two studies (Spiegel, 1994; Otto, Pollack et al., 1993) demonstrate that adding cognitive-behavioral therapy to alprazolam discontinuation, in patients with panic disorder, improved the rates of successful discontinuation. Spiegel, Bruce et al. (1994) reported that patients in the combined taper and cognitive-behavioral therapy group had greater rates of abstinence from alprazolam at six months than those who underwent taper alone.

Addiction treatment is indicated for nearly all patients with substance abuse, addiction, or chemical dependence, as defined by the *Diagnostic and Statistical Manual of Mental Disorders, 4th Edition* (American Psychiatric Association, 1994). Among sedative-hypnotic users, treatment most often is indicated for the polysubstance users, high-dose users, and/or patients in whom compulsive use (addiction) is identified. The support, education, and recovery training available in most treatment programs are valuable to many patients who are dependent on sedative-hypnotics. On the other hand, patients with long-term, therapeutic use problems should not be coerced to participate in programs designed to treat addictive or compulsive drug use problems, as they often feel out of place and unable to relate to patients with addictive disorders.

Alternatively, in the spirit of individualizing treatment, some components of treatment may be of use to therapeutic-dose users. Participation in specific components of treatment, tailored to their needs, can be helpful and non-threatening. Those patients who choose to participate in treatment often discover an immense source of support and encouragement in addition to learning and developing coping skills that facilitate drug discontinuation and abstinence.

Prolonged Benzodiazepine Withdrawal. *Clinical Picture:* Some physicians (Smith & Wesson, 1983; Smith & Seymour, 1991; Landry, Smith et al., 1992) report, and clinical experience confirms, that a small proportion of patients, following long-term benzodiazepine use, experience a prolonged syndrome in which withdrawal signs and symptoms persist for weeks to months following discontinuation. This prolonged withdrawal syndrome is noted for its irregular and unpredictable day-to-day course and qualitative and quantitative differences in symptoms from both the pre-benzodiazepine use state and the acute withdrawal period. Patients with prolonged withdrawal often experience slowly abating, albeit characteristic, waxing and waning symptoms of insomnia, perceptual disturbances, tremor, sensory hypersensitivity(ies), and anxiety.

Smith and Wesson (1982) propose that protracted (prolonged) symptoms reflect long-term receptor site adaptations. Higgitt and Fonagy (1993) propose that a comprehensive etiologic model of the prolonged withdrawal syndrome must include a psychological component that can be explained through cognitive and behavioral models. They observe that many patients with persistent withdrawal symptoms resemble patients with somatization disorders. These patients often experience acute withdrawal more severely and may be "sensitized to anxiety." In addition to a potential lack of effective coping mechanisms away from benzodiazepines, such patients often possess a perceptual and/or cognitive style that leads to apprehensiveness, body sensation amplification and mislabeling, and misinterpretation.

Management of Prolonged Withdrawal: Before entertaining the existence of a prolonged withdrawal syndrome, the physician must rule out psychiatric conditions. A distinguishing characteristic of protracted withdrawal from anxiety disorders is the gradual diminution and eventual resolution of symptoms with benzodiazepine withdrawal.

Propranolol in doses of 5 to 20 mg four times a day often is helpful in attenuating anxiety or tremors. Lower doses of sedating antidepressant medications such as trazodone, amitriptyline, imipramine, or doxepin are helpful in treating insomnia. Frequent clinical follow-up for education, supportive psychotherapy, and/or regular reassurance are strongly advised. Frequent reassessment of the working diagnosis is recommended.

REFERENCES

Allgulander C (1986). History and current state of sedative-hypnotic drug abuse. *Acta Psychiatrica Scandinavica* 73(5):465–478.

American Psychiatric Association (1994). *Diagnostic and Statistical Manual of Mental Disorders, 4th Edition.* Washington, DC: American Psychiatric Association, 886.

Busto U, Romach MK & Sellers EM (1996). Multiple drug use and psychiatric comorbidity in patients admitted to the hospital with severe benzodiazepine dependence. *Journal of Clinical Psychopharmacology* 16:51–57.

Busto U, Sellers EM & Naranjo CA et al. (1986). Withdrawal reaction after long-term therapeutic use of benzodiazepines. *The New England Journal of Medicine* 315:854–859.

Busto U, Sellers EM, Sisson B et al. (1982). Benzodiazepine use and abuse in alcoholics. *Clinical Pharmacology and Therapeutics* 31:207–208.

.Busto U, Simpkins J & Sellers EM (1983). Objective determination of benzodiazepine use and abuse in alcoholics. *British Journal of Addiction* 78:429–435.

Ciraulo DA, Barnhill JG, Ciraulo MM, Greenblatt DJ et al. (1989). Parental alcoholism as a risk factor in benzodiazepine abuse: A pilot study. *American Journal of Psychiatry* 146(10):1333–1335.

Ciraulo DA, Barnhill JG, Greenblatt DJ et al. (1988). Abuse liability and clinical pharmacokinetics of alprazolam in alcoholic men. *Journal of Clinical Psychiatry* 49:333–337.

Ciraulo DA, Sarid-Segal O, Knapp C, Ciraulo AM, Greenblatt DJ & Shader RI (1996). Liability to alprazolam abuse in daughters of alcoholics. *American Journal of Psychiatry* 153:956–958.

Covi L, Park LC & Lipman RS (1969). Factors affecting withdrawal response to certain minor tranquilizers. In JO Cole & JR Wittenborn (eds.) *Drug Abuse: Social and Pharmacological Aspects.* Springfield, IL: Charles C Thomas, 93–108.

Covi L, Lipman RS, Pattison JH, Derogatis LR & Uhlenhuth EH (1973). Length of treatment with anxiolytic sedatives and response to their sudden withdrawal. *Acta Psychiatrica Scandinavica* 49:51–64.

Costa E, Guidotti A et al. (1975). Evidence for the involvement of GABA in the actions of benzodiazepines. In E Costa & P Greengard (eds.) *Mechanisms and Actions of Benzodiazepines.* New York, NY: Raven Press, 141–161.

Cowley DS, Roy-Byrne PP, Hommer DW et al. (1991). Sensitivity to benzodiazepines in sons of alcoholics. *Biological Psychiatry* 29:104–112.

Cowley DS, Roy-Byrne PP, Gordon C et al. (1992) Response to diazepam in sons of alcoholics. *Alcoholism: Clinical & Experimental Research* 16:1057–1063.

Dickinson W, Rush PA & Radcliffe AB (1990). Alprazolam use and dependence: A retrospective analysis of 30 cases of withdrawal. *Western Journal of Medicine* 152(5):604–608.

DuPont RL (1988). Abuse of benzodiazepines: The problems and solutions. *American Journal of Drug and Alcohol Abuse* 14S:1–69.

Epstein RS (1980). Withdrawal symptoms from chronic use of low-dose barbiturates. *American Journal of Psychiatry* 137(1):107–108.

Essig CF (1964). Addiction to nonbarbiturate sedative and tranquilizing drugs. *Clinical Pharmacology and Therapeutics* 5(3):334–343.

Essig CF (1966). Newer sedative drugs that can cause states of intoxication and dependence of barbiturate type. *Journal of the American Medical Association* 196(8):126–129.

File SE (1993). The biology of benzodiazepine dependence. In C Hallstrom (ed.) *Benzodiazepine Dependence*. New York, NY: Oxford University Press, 95–118.

Flemenbaum A & Gumby B (1971). Ethchlorvynol (Placidyl) abuse and withdrawal. *Diseases of the Nervous System* 32:188–191.

Fraser HF, Wikler A, Essig CF et al. (1958). Degree of physical dependence induced by secobarbital or phenobarbital. *Journal of the American Medical Association* 166:126–129.

Gabe J (1993). Women and tranquilizer use; A case study in the social politics of health and health care. In C Hallstrom (ed.) *Benzodiazepine Dependence*. New York, NY: Oxford University Press, 350–363.

Garcia-Borresuerro D et al (1990). Treatment of benzodiazepine withdrawal symptoms with carbamazepine. *Psychiatry and Clinical Neuroscience* 241:145–150.

Greenblatt DJ, Miller LG & Shader RI (1990). Benzodiazepine discontinuation syndromes. *Journal of Psychiatric Research* 24(Suppl):73–79.

Haefly W (1975). Possible involvement of GABA in the central actions of benzodiazepines. In E Costa & P Greengard (eds.) *Mechanism of Action of Benzodiazepines*. New York, NY: Raven Press, 162–202.

Higgitt A & Fonagy P (1993). Benzodiazepine dependence syndromes and syndromes of withdrawal. In C Hallstrom (ed.) *Benzodiazepine Dependence*. New York, NY: Oxford University Press, 58–70.

Hollister LE, Motzenbecker FP & Degan RO (1961). Withdrawal reactions for chlordiazepoxide (Librium). *Psychopharmacologia* 2:63–68.

Hollister LE, Bennett LL, Kimbell I, Savage C & Overall JE (1963). Diazepam in newly admitted schizophrenics. *Diseases of the Nervous System* 24:746–750.

JHowland MA (1994). Flumazenil. In LR Goldfrank, NE Flemenbaum, NA Lewin, RS Weisman, MA Howland & RS Hoffman (eds.) *Toxicologic Emergencies*. Norfolk, CT: Appleton & Lange, 805–810.

Ilsbell H (1950). Addiction to barbiturates and the barbiturate abstinence syndrome. *Annals of Internal Medicine* 33:108–121.

Ilsbell H, Altschul S et al. (1950). Chronic barbiturate intoxication: An experimental study. *Archives of Neurology and Psychiatry* 64:1–28.

Ilsbell H & White WM (1953). Clinical characteristics of addictions. *American Journal of Medicine* 14:558–565.

Klein RL, Uhde TW et al. (1986). Preliminary evidence for the utility of carbamazepine in alprazolam withdrawal. *American Journal of Psychiatry* 143:336–336.

Klein RL, Colvin V et al. (1994). Alprazolam withdrawal in patients with panic disorder and generalized anxiety disorder: Vulnerability and effect of carbamazepine. *American Journal of Psychiatry* 151:1760–1766.

Landry MJ, Smith DE, McDuff DR & Baughman OL (1992). Benzodiazepine dependence and withdrawal: Identification and medical management. *Journal of the American Board of Family Practice* 5:167–176.

Litovitz T (1987). Fatal benzodiazepine toxicity. *American Journal of Emergency Medicine* 5:472–473.

Littrell RA, Hayes LR & Stillner V (1993a). Carisoprodol (Soma): A new and cautious perspective on an old agent. *Southern Medical Journal* 86(7):753–756.

Littrell RA, Sage T & Miller W (1993b). Meprobamate dependence secondary to carisoprodol (Soma) use. *American Journal of Alcohol and Drug Abuse* 19(1):133–134.

Lloyd EA & Clark LD (1959). Convulsions and delirium incident to glutethimide (Doriden). *Diseases of the Nervous System* 20:1–3.

Malcolm R, Brady TK et al. (1993). Types of benzodiazepines abused by chemically dependent inpatients. *Journal of Psychoactive Drugs* 25(4):315–319.

Miller L (1991). Chronic benzodiazepine administration: From patient to gene. *Journal of Clinical Pharmacology.* 31:492–495.

Miller L, Greenblatt DJ et al. (1988a). Chronic benzodiazepine administration I: Tolerance is associated with benzodiazepine receptor down regulation and decreased $GABA_A$ receptor function. *Journal of Pharmacology and Experimental Therapeutics* 246(1):170–176.

Miller L, Greenblatt DJ et al. (1988b). Chronic benzodiazepine administration II: Discontinuation syndrome is associated with up regulation of $GABA_A$ receptor complex binding and function. *Journal of Pharmacology and Experimental Therapeutics* 246(1):177–181.

Miller L, Greenblatt DJ et al. (1989). Chronic benzodiazepine administration III: Up regulation of $GABA_A$ receptor binding and function associated with chronic benzodiazepine antagonist administration. *Journal of Pharmacology and Experimental Therapeutics* 248:1096–1101.

Miller L, Greenblatt DJ et al. (1990). Chronic benzodiazepine administration IV: A partial agonist produces behavioral effects without tolerance or receptor alterations. *Journal of Pharmacology and Experimental Therapeutics* 254(1):33–38.

Noyes R, Garvey MJ, Cook BL & Perry PJ (1988). Benzodiazepine withdrawal: A review of the evidence. *Journal of Clinical Psychiatry* 49:382–389.

Osborn H & Goldfrank LR (1994). Sedative-hypnotic agents. In LR Goldfrank, NE Flomenbaum, NA Lewin, RS Weisman, MA Howland & RS Hoffman (eds.) *Toxicologic Emergencies*. Norfolk, CT: Appleton & Lange, 787–804.

Otto MN, Pollack MH, Sachs GS et al. (1993). Discontinuation of benzodiazepine treatment: Efficacy of cognitive behavioral therapy for patients with panic disorder. *American Journal of Psychiatry* 150:1485–1490.

Phillips RM, Judy FR & Judy HE (1957). Meprobamate addiction. *Northwest Medicine* 56:453–454.

Regier DA, Farmer ME et al. (1990). Comorbidity of mental disorders with alcohol and other drug abuse. Results from the epidemiologic catchment area (ECA) study. *Journal of the American Medical Association* 264(19):2511–2518.

Rickels K, Case WG, Downing RW et al. (1986a). One-year follow-up of anxious patients treated with diazepam. *Journal of Clinical Psychopharmacology* 6:32–36.

Rickels K, Case WG, Schweizer E et al. (1986b). Low-dose dependence in chronic benzodiazepine users: A preliminary report. *Psychopharmacology Bulletin* 22:407–415.

Rickels K, Fox IL & Greenblatt DJ (1988). Clorazepate and lorazepam: Clinical improvement and rebound anxiety. *American Journal of Psychiatry* 145:312–317.

Rickels K, Schweizer E et al. (1990). Long-term therapeutic use of benzodiazepines. I. Effects of abrupt discontinuation. *Archives of General Psychiatry* 47:899–907.

Ries R et al. (1991). Benzodiazepine withdrawal: Clinician's ratings of carbamazepine treatment versus traditional taper methods. *Journal of Psychoactive Drugs* 23(1):73–76.

Ries R, Roy-Byrne PP et al. (1989). Carbamazepine treatment for benzodiazepine withdrawal. *American Journal of Psychiatry* 146(4):536–537.

Romach M, Busto U, Somer GR et al. (1995). Clinical aspects of chronic use of alprazolam and lorazepam. *American Journal of Psychiatry* 152:1161–1167.

Sadwin A & Glen RS (1958). Addiction to glutethimide (Doriden). *American Journal of Psychiatry* 115:469–470.

Schweizer E & Rickels K (1986). Failure of buspirone to manage benzodiazepine withdrawal. *American Journal of Psychiatry* 143:1590–1592.

Schweizer E, Rickels K, Case WG & Greenblatt DJ (1991). Carbamazepine treatment in patients discontinuing long-term benzodiazepine therapy. Effects on withdrawal severity and outcome. *Archives of General Psychiatry* 48:448–452.

Schweizer E & Rickels K (1990). Long-term use of benzodiazepines. II. Effects of gradual taper. *Archives of General Psychiatry* 47:908–915.

Sellers EM, Ciraulo DA, DuPont RL et al. (1993). Alprazolam and benzodiazepine dependence. *Journal of Clinical Psychiatry* 54(Suppl 10):64–75.

Smith DE & Wesson DR (1970). A new method for treatment of barbiturate dependence. *Journal of the American Medical Association* 213:294–295.

Smith DE & Wesson DR (1971). A phenobarbital technique for withdrawal of barbiturate abuse. *Archives of General Psychiatry* 24:56–60.

Smith DE & Wesson DR (1982). Low-dose benzodiazepine withdrawal syndrome: Receptor site mediated. *California Society for the Treatment of Alcoholism and Other Drug Dependencies News* 9:1–5.

Smith DE & Wesson DR (1983). Benzodiazepine dependency syndromes. *Journal of Psychoactive Drugs* 15:85–95.

Smith DE & Seymour RB (1991). Benzodiazepines. In NS Miller (ed.) *Comprehensive Handbook of Drug and Alcohol Addiction*. New York, NY: Marcel Dekker, 405–426.

Spiegl DA, Bruce TJ, Gregg SF & Nuzzarello A (1994). Does cognitive behavioral therapy assist slow-taper alprazolam discontinuation in panic disorder? *American Journal of Psychiatry* 151:876–881.

Spivey WH (1992). Flumazenil and seizures: Analysis of 43 cases. *Clinical Therapeutics* 14:292–305.

Swanson LA & Okada T (1963). Death after withdrawal of meprobamate. *Journal of the American Medical Association* 184:780–781.

Swartzburg M, Lieb J & Schwartz AH (1973). Methaqualone withdrawal. *Archives of General Psychiatry* 29:46–47.

Tyrer P, Rutherford D & Huggett (1981). Benzodiazepine withdrawal symptoms and propanolol. *Lancet* 1:520–522.

Vestal R & Rumack B (1974). Glutethimide dependence: Phenobarbital treatment. *Annals of Internal Medicine* 80:670–673.

Winokur A & Rickels K (1981). Withdrawal and pseudowithdrawal reactions from diazepam therapy. *Archives of Clinical Psychiatry* 42:442–444.

Woods SW, Nagy LM, Koleszar AS, Krystal JH, Heninger GR & Charney DS (1992). Controlled trial of alprazolam supplementation during imipramine treatment of panic disorder. *Journal of Clinical Psychopharmacology* 12:32–8.

CHAPTER 4

Management of Opioid Intoxication and Withdrawal

Patrick G. O'Connor, M.D., M.P.H.
Thomas R. Kosten, M.D.

Opioid Intoxication
Opioid Withdrawal

This chapter reviews the clinical features of opioid intoxication and withdrawal. The opioid class includes: (1) substances that are directly derived from the opium poppy (such as morphine and codeine), (2) the semisynthetic opioids (such as heroin), and (3) the purely synthetic opioids (such as methadone and fentanyl). These compounds share several pharmacological effects, including sedation, respiratory depression and analgesia, as well as the common clinical features of intoxication and withdrawal.

OPIOID INTOXICATION

Clinical Picture. While mild or moderate intoxication (as evidenced by euphoria or sedation) with opioids usually is not life-threatening, severe intoxication or overdose is a medical emergency that requires immediate attention. In a retrospective analysis of consecutive cases of presumed opioid overdose in patients initially managed by emergency medical service (EMS) personnel in an urban setting, 16% of the patients were either dead or in full cardiopulmonary arrest at the time of the initial EMS evaluation (Sporer, Firestone & Isaacs, 1996). Opioid overdose can be treated successfully, if patients present in a timely manner and general principles of overdose management (as well as specific therapies for opioid overdose) are employed.

The pharmacological actions responsible for opioid intoxication and overdose involve a specific set of opioid receptors, particularly those in the central nervous system (Martin, 1983; Jaffe & Martin, 1990). These opioid receptors include the mu, kappa and delta types, which also interact with endogenous substances, including the endorphins (Bozarth & Wise, 1984). Of primary concern in the management of overdose are interactions with mu receptors in the central nervous system (CNS), which can lead to sedation and respiratory depression. The mechanism of respiratory depression with opioids presumably is direct suppression of respiratory centers in the brain stem and medulla (Martin, 1983).

Myosis ("pinpoint pupils") is an important pharmacological effect that can be used as a sign to identify possible opioid intoxication. Other pharmacological effects of the opioids, including gastrointestinal hyposecretion and dysmotility, are less important when considering opioid intoxication.

Diagnosis of Opioid Intoxication or Overdose. As with most clinical challenges, evaluation of opioid intoxication begins with the careful collection of patient data through a careful history and physical examination (Table 1). An important issue in the patient with moderate to severe respiratory depression is the immediate initiation of pharmacological and supportive therapies to ameliorate morbidity and prevent mortality.

When historical information concerning opioid use can be obtained (including the specific drug, amount, and time of last use), either directly from the patient or from friends and family members, this information can supplement available hospital records. In addition to asking about opioid abuse, it is important to ask about use of other drugs or alcohol because of the likelihood of polydrug abuse (Gould & Kleber, 1974; Kosten, Gawin et al., 1986). Identification of polydrug use has important implications for patient management; for example, identification of the frequent co-occurrence of heroin and benzodiazepine overdose may indicate the need for additional therapy directed at reversing the benzodiazepine component of the overdose with flumazenil (Dunton, Schwam et al., 1988). This also applies to cases of suspected opioid overdose in children who are at high risk of co-occurring opioid and benzodiazepine toxicity and may require management of

TABLE 1. Diagnosis of Opioid Overdose

History
- Opioid use (ask about drug, amount, time of last use)
- Polydrug abuse
- Use multiple sources of information (family, hospital records, etc.)

Findings on Physical Examination
- Central nervous system depression
- Respiratory depression
- Myosis
- Needle tracks

Laboratory Tests
- Rule out hypoglycemia, acidemia, fluid and electrolyte abnormalities
- Perform toxicology screens for opioids and other drugs.

both upon presentation for medical care (Perry & Shannon, 1996).

Physical examination of the intoxicated patient may find CNS and respiratory depression, as well as pinpoint pupils and direct evidence of drug use, such as needle track marks or soft tissue infection.

The laboratory can provide important supportive information in the evaluation of opioid intoxication.

In addition, acute mental status changes from HIV-related opportunistic infections may mimic those of opioid intoxication (O'Connor, Selwyn & Schottenfeld, 1994). Patients who present with symptoms of such intoxication also may have other important causes of depressed mental status, such as hypoglycemia, acidemia, or other fluid and electrolyte disorders. Thus, toxicology screening should be performed immediately in emergency settings (American Medical Association, 1987). Urine toxicology is preferred because urine contains higher concentrations of drugs and their metabolites than serum. Results usually are qualitative, indicating only the presence or absence of specific substances. Even when the results of toxicologic screening are available after acute management has been initiated, drug screening may support the diagnosis of drug intoxication, and also may reveal the presence of other drugs not suspected on initial evaluation. For example, benzodiazepine abuse is common among patients with opioid dependence, and some benzodiazepines (such as alprazolam) may not be readily detectable by standard urine techniques. Newer approaches involving the examination of serum may be useful in documenting previously unsuspected benzodiazepine abuse (Rogers, Hall et al., 1997).

Kellerman and colleagues (1987) examined the impact of drug screening in suspected overdose in a study of 405 adult patients who presented to an emergency department. While initial clinical management did not change significantly on the basis of toxicology results, there were implications for treatment beyond the acute event. Poor follow-up of drug screening also was demonstrated in a study of alcohol intoxication in motor vehicle crash patients. In the second study, none of 47 patients who had alcohol levels between 200 and 500 mg per deciliter were referred for a substance abuse follow-up visit (Chang & Astrachan, 1988). Thus, toxicology screening is useful not only for acute management, but also for planning care after discharge from the acute setting (O'Connor, Samet & Stein, 1994).

Opioid use and overdose may also be complicated by the effects of substances use to "cut" the drugs purchased on the street. Along with "inert" substances present to add bulk, "active" substances including dextromethorphan, lidocaine and scopolamine may be present. One report of overdoses that contained significant amounts of scopolamine documented the potential clinical importance of this problem (MMWR, 1996).

Although the classic "triad" of opioid overdose (respiratory depression, coma, and pinpoint pupils) commonly alerts clinicians to the possibility of opioid overdose, atypical presentations may cause some initial confusion. In a study of 43 hospitalized patients who received naloxone for a clinically suspected narcotic overdose, only two overdose patients had this classic triad, suggesting that a high index of suspicion should be maintained in certain patients who may have atypical presentations (Whipple, Quebbeman et al., 1994).

Management of Opioid Intoxication or Overdose. In a case of suspected opioid intoxication, general supportive management must be instituted simultaneously with the specific antidote, naloxone (Table 2). Adult basic life support and adult advanced cardiac life support need to be available (American Heart Association, 1992a, 1992b). The physician needs to assure that an adequate airway is established and that respiratory and cardiac function are appropriately assessed and managed. Adequate intravenous access is essential so that fluids and pharmacological agents can be administered as needed. Finally, frequent monitoring of vital signs and cardiorespiratory status is required until it is clearly established that the patient has successfully cleared the opioid and any other intoxicating substances from the system.

In the course of managing patients with suspected opioid overdose, clinicians need to simulta-

TABLE 2. Management of Opioid Overdose

General Supportive Management
- Assess and clear airway
- Support ventilation (if needed)
- Assess and support cardiac function
- Give intravenous fluids

Specific Pharmacologic Therapy
- Naloxone hydrochloride: 0.4 to 0.8 mg initially, repeated as necessary.

neously be aware of the co-occurrence of acute medical problems and the exacerbation of chronic medical problems often seen in this population (O'Connor, Selwyn & Schottenfeld, 1994; Cherubin & Sapira, 1993). For example, prolonged hypoxia in overdose survivors can result in rhabdomyolysis and myocardial infarction (Melandri, Re et al., 1996). Other more common issues such as acute infections, trauma and chronic liver disease may have major implications in overdose patients (Cherubin & Sapira, 1993).

Pharmacological Therapies for Opioid Intoxication or Overdose. When a patient presents to an emergency department with pinpoint pupils and respiratory depression, pharmacological therapy for opioid dependence should be instituted immediately. Naloxone hydrochloride, a pure opioid antagonist, can effectively reverse the central nervous system effects of opioid intoxication and overdose. An initial intravenous dose of 0.4 to 0.8 mg will quickly reverse neurologic and cardiorespiratory depression. The onset of action of intravenously administered naloxone, as manifested by antagonism of opioid overdose, is approximately two minutes. Overdose with more potent (fentanyl) or longer-acting opioids (methadone) may require higher doses of naloxone given over longer periods of time, thus necessitating the use of ongoing naloxone infusion.

In patients who do not respond to multiple doses of naloxone, alternative causes of unresponsiveness must be considered. Along with the need to monitor patients for continued naloxone requirements, another important consideration to anticipate in administering naloxone is the possibility of initiating a significant withdrawal syndrome.

Follow-Up Care for Opioid Intoxication or Overdose. Pharmacologic management of opioid overdose is relatively straightforward in comparison to the challenge of engaging opioid dependent patients in medical care and substance abuse treatment following overdose management. In one study of 77 patients admitted to the hospital for management of opioid overdose, 64% left hospital against medical advice after an average stay of less than six hours and only half the subjects seemed interested in counseling (Seidler, Stuhlinger et al., 1996). Despite these and similar findings, clinicians who treat overdose patients should establish the need for ongoing substance abuse treatment as the major goal of patient management, while caring for overdose-related complications.

OPIOID WITHDRAWAL

Clinical Picture. Withdrawal from opioids results in a specific constellation of symptoms. Although some opioid withdrawal symptoms overlap withdrawal from sedative-hypnotics, opioid withdrawal generally is considered less likely to produce severe morbidity or mortality. Clinical phenomena associated with opioid withdrawal include neurophysiologic rebound in the organ systems on which opioids have their primary actions (Jaffe, 1990). Thus, the generalized central nervous suppression that occurs with opioid use is replaced by increased CNS activity.

The severity of opioid withdrawal varies with the dose and duration of drug use. The time to onset of opioid withdrawal symptoms depends on the half-life of the drug being used. For example, withdrawal may begin four to six hours after last use of heroin, but up to 36 hours after last use of methadone (Gunne, 1959).

Neuropharmacologic studies of opioid withdrawal have supported the clinical picture of increased central nervous system noradrenergic hyperactivity (Jaffe, 1990; Gunne, 1959). Therapies to alter the course of opioid withdrawal (such as clonidine) are designed to decrease this hyperactivity, which occurs primarily at the locus ceruleus. Evidence for the role of noradrenergic hyperactivity in opioid withdrawal is provided by studies showing elevated norepinephrine metabolite levels (Crawley, Laberty & Roth, 1979).

Diagnosis of Opioid Withdrawal. Opioid withdrawal involves a constellation of clinical manifestations (Table 3). Early findings may include abnormalities in vital signs, including tachycardia and hypertension. Bothersome CNS system symptoms include restlessness, irritability and insomnia. Opioid craving also occurs in proportion to the severity of physiologic withdrawal symptoms. Pupillary dilation can be marked. A variety of cutaneous and mucocutaneous symptoms (including lacrimation, rhinorrhea, and piloerection—known as "gooseflesh") can

TABLE 3. Clinical Manifestations of Opioid Withdrawal

Vital Signs
- Tachycardia
- Hypertension
- Fever

Central Nervous System
- Restlessness
- Irritability
- Insomnia
- Craving
- Yawning

Eyes
- Pupillary dilation
- Lacrimation

Nose
- Rhinorrhea

Skin
- Piloerection

Gastrointestinal
- Nausea
- Vomiting
- Diarrhea

occur as well. Patients frequently report yawning and sneezing. Gastrointestinal symptoms, which initially may be mild (anorexia), can progress in moderate to severe withdrawal to include nausea, vomiting and diarrhea. Combined with intense craving, this combination of symptoms frequently leads to relapse to drug use.

As with the onset of withdrawal, the duration also varies with the drug used. For example, the meperidine abstinence syndrome may peak within 8 to 12 hours and last only four to five days (Jaffe, 1990), whereas heroin withdrawal symptoms generally peak within 36 to 72 hours and may last for seven to 14 days (Dole, 1972).

A protracted abstinence syndrome has been described, in which a variety of symptoms may last beyond the typical acute withdrawal period (Schuckit, 1989). Findings in prolonged and protracted abstinence can include mild abnormalities in vital signs and continued craving (Wen, Ho & Wen, 1984). Despite the extensive literature on protracted withdrawal, a universal definition and diagnostic criteria are lacking, making diagnosis difficult in individual patients (Satel, Kosten et al., 1993).

Management of Opioid Withdrawal. As in the management of opioid intoxication and overdose, management of withdrawal involves a combination of sound general supportive measures and specific pharmacological therapies. It is very important for the physician to do a thorough evaluation to ascertain that other medical illnesses are not complicating the opioid withdrawal. In patients hospitalized for medical illnesses, the severity of their underlying clinical conditions can alter the selection of withdrawal therapy (O'Connor, Samet & Stein, 1994). Along with the assessment of general health problems, it is important to obtain objective information to help guide the management of patients undergoing opioid withdrawal. Thus, a physical examination to detect specific findings consistent with withdrawal is important both to establish the diagnosis and to follow patients through their treatment.

General supportive measures for managing withdrawal include providing a safe environment and adequate nutrition, as well as reassuring patients that their symptoms will be taken seriously. The decision as to whether to perform opioid detoxification on an outpatient or inpatient basis depends on the presence of comorbid medical and psychiatric problems, the availability of social support (e.g., family members to provide monitoring and transportation) and the presence of polydrug abuse. The preferred method of detoxification also may affect this decision; for example, methadone detoxification is legally restricted by federal legislation to inpatient settings or specialized licensed outpatient drug treatment programs (Federal Register, 1989).

In the course of managing opioid withdrawal, clinicians also need to be able to address medical problems seen in this population (O'Connor, Selwyn & Schottenfeld, 1994; Cherubin & Sapira, 1993). Issues such as acute bacterial infections and HIV-related problems may complicate withdrawal presentation and management.

Pharmacologic Therapies for Opioid Withdrawal. A variety of pharmacological therapies have been developed to assist patients through a safer, more comfortable opioid withdrawal. These therapies involve the use of opioid agonists (e.g., methadone), an alpha-2 adrenergic agonist (clonidine), an opioid antagonist (naltrexone) in combination with clonidine, and a mixed opioid agonist/antagonist (buprenorphine).

Methadone detoxification is based on the principle of cross-tolerance, in which one opioid is replaced with another and then slowly withdrawn. Methadone has distinct advantages over heroin in this regard, because it is orally effective and has a long half-life. Withdrawal from heroin typically is managed with initial doses of methadone in the range of 15 to 20 mg (Fultz & Senay, 1975). This dose often is sufficient to control symptoms in heroin users over a 24-hour period, although additional methadone can be given as required by clinical symptoms. The dose should be maintained through the second or third day and then slowly tapered by approximately 10% to 15% per day, as guided by patients' symptoms and clinical findings (Jaffe, 1990; Fultz & Senay, 1975). Patients withdrawing from high doses of methadone obtained on the street or other potent opioids may require higher doses of methadone to control withdrawal symptoms.

Clonidine is an alpha-2 agonist that is used primarily for the treatment of hypertension, but it also has been efficacious in managing opioid withdrawal (Gold, Redmond & Kleber, 1978; Gold, Pottash et al., 1980). Clonidine has been demonstrated to diminish norepinephrine release (presumably by binding to the alpha-2 receptors), thereby decreasing norepinephrine turnover during opioid withdrawal (Laberty & Roth, 1980). Charney and colleagues (1981) demonstrated that clonidine eased the withdrawal to a drug-free state in patients who were abruptly withdrawn from methadone. In opioid withdrawal, clonidine seems to be most effective in suppressing autonomically mediated signs and symptoms of abstinence, but less effective for subjective symptoms (Jasinski, Johnson & Kocher, 1985).

Clonidine typically is used in higher doses for detoxification than for treating hypertension. Suggested dosing regimens have included initial total daily doses of up to 1.2 mg in divided increments (Schuckit, 1988). A typical initial regimen of 0.2 mg orally every four hours has been recommended. Such a dosing regimen has been used with some success in outpatients treated with clonidine for heroin withdrawal (O'Connor, Waugh et al., 1992). As with methadone, clonidine can be tapered after the third day by approximately 0.2 mg each day (or every other day), as dictated by the symptoms.

Clonidine may be administered for a total of 10 to 14 days. A benzodiazepine (such as oxazepam) may be beneficial as adjuvant therapy for insomnia and muscle cramps. Patients undergoing clonidine detoxification need to be monitored for hypotension and fatigue. While the hypotensive effects of clonidine generally are well-tolerated in the context of pure opioid withdrawal, ongoing illicit drug use and comorbid medical problems (such as sepsis) can make hypotension more likely. In addition to its physiologic effects, clonidine may also have a beneficial effect on craving for opioids (Dawe & Gray, 1995).

Recently, clonidine has been compared to lofexidine as a treatment for opioid detoxification. In one study, 28 patients stabilized on methadone were randomized to clonidine or lofexidine, and similar suppression of opioid withdrawal symptoms was observed (Kahn, Mumford et al., 1997). Lofexidine may have some of the beneficial effects of clonidine in this situation, with fewer clonidine-related side effects including hypotension (Kahn, Mumford et al., 1997).

A newer method of opioid withdrawal uses clonidine in combination with naltrexone, which is a potent long-acting narcotic antagonist that has been used clinically to help maintain patients opioid-free after detoxification from heroin (Kosten & Kleber, 1984). Sometimes referred to as "rapid" detoxification, this approach is designed to shorten the time course of acute withdrawal. A combination of clonidine and naltrexone has been used with inpatients to induce abrupt and safe withdrawal from methadone (Riordan & Kleber, 1980; Charney, Heninger & Kleber, 1986). The clonidine/naltrexone combination also can be used in outpatients to provide abrupt opioid withdrawal over five days (Kleber, Topazian et al., 1987; Vining, Kosten & Kleber, 1988). While the clonidine/naltrexone approach results in a more intensive initial withdrawal during Day 1 of naltrexone induction, this approach may have enhanced efficacy in starting patients on blocking doses of naltrexone.

Clonidine and clonidine/naltrexone detoxification also has been demonstrated to be feasible in primary care settings as a way of initiating substance abuse treatment by primary care providers O'Connor, Waugh et al. (1992). In one recent study, 125 subjects were detoxified using one of these two methods: 70% (88/125) were successful, including 42% (24/57) of clonidine and 94% (64/68) of clonidine/naltrexone ($p < 0.001$) detoxifications (O'Connor, Waugh et al., 1995). Although treatment assignment was not randomized in this study, these results support the potential feasibility of both approaches in primary care settings (O'Connor, Waugh et al., 1995).

More recently, "ultra rapid" detoxification has been proposed as a very short (one-day) method of opioid detoxification (Pesslich, Loimer et al., 1989). In this approach, patients are placed under heavy sedation or general anesthesia and given intravenous naloxone or oral naltrexone so that acute withdrawal takes place while the patient is in the unconscious state (Loimer, Schmid et al., 1990; Loimer, Lenz et al., 1991; Loimer, Hofmann & Chaudhry, 1993). In this technique, patients may require intubation and mechanical ventilation during detoxification. While the rapidity of this approach may seem attractive, it has not been evaluated in a rigorous randomized clinical trial and suffers from the risk inherent to general anesthesia (Stephenson, 1997).

Another recent development in opioid detoxification involves use of buprenorphine, a drug that combines the characteristics of methadone and naltrexone by virtue of its actions as both a partial opioid agonist and a potent opioid antagonist (Jasinski, Pevnick & Griffith, 1978). Like methadone, buprenorphine is a potent analgesic that can be given once a day to block withdrawal symptoms in opioid-dependent patients (Mello & Mendelson, 1980). The initial work on use of buprenorphine for detoxification examined the efficacy of sublingual buprenorphine (in doses of 2, 4, and 8 mg sublingually) as an agent for opioid detoxification from methadone or heroin (Kosten & Kleber, 1986). This early work supported the role of buprenorphine in providing an effective and comfortable withdrawal. Buprenorphine also has been used as a transitional agent between heroin and naltrexone (Kosten, Morgan et al., 1989; Kosten, Morgan & Kleber, 1992).

Although specific protocols have yet to be established, buprenorphine appears to be effective for opioid detoxification. One study compared a low dose of buprenorphine (0.6-1.2 mg/day) to clonidine and found buprenorphine to be superior in alleviating subjective and objective opioid withdrawal symptoms (Nigam, Ray & Tripathi, 1993). In another study, a three-day buprenorphine regimen was found to have similar efficacy to a five-day clonidine regimen although the buprenorphine group had more effective early relief of withdrawal symptoms (Cheskin, Fudala & Johnson, 1994). Buprenorphine has also been demonstrated to be superior to both clonidine and lefetamine for detoxifying methadone maintained patients from long term methadone (Janiri, Mannelli et al., 1994). Finally, rapid detoxification using buprenorphine with naltrexone may provide some of the advantages of the rapid clonidine/naltrexone detoxification with more easily tolerated withdrawal symptoms (O'Connor, Carroll et al., 1995).

Follow-Up Care for Opioid Withdrawal. As with the management of opioid overdose, medical detoxification is an important first step in treating opioid addiction. It must be made clear that detoxification alone, without plans for ongoing drug treatment, is not adequate to manage patients (O'Connor, Samet & Stein, 1994). Thus, at the initiation of detoxification, arrangements for ongoing drug abuse treatment need to be assured.

CONCLUSIONS

The management of opioid intoxication and withdrawal requires that physicians be familiar with the basic pharmacologic properties of opioids and the clinical manifestations of opioid overdose and withdrawal. Patients experiencing intoxication and withdrawal require careful evaluation and supportive management. In addition, specific pharmacological therapies such as naloxone and clonidine may play a major role in the management of these conditions.

REFERENCES

American Heart Association, Emergency Cardiac Care Committee and Subcommittees (1992a). Adult advanced cardiac life support. *Journal of the American Medical Association* 268:2199–2241.

American Heart Association, Emergency Cardiac Care Committee and Subcommittees (1992b). Adult basic life support. *Journal of the American Medical Association* 268:2184–2198.

American Medical Association, Council on Scientific Affairs (1987). Scientific issues in drug testing. *Journal of the American Medical Association* 257:3110–3114.

Bozarth MA & Wise RA (1984). Anatomically distinct opiate receptor fields mediate reward and physical dependence. *Science* 224:514–517.

Chang G & Astrachan BN (1988). The emergency department surveillance of alcohol intoxication after motor vehicle accidents. *Journal of the American Medical Association* 260:2533–2536.

Charney DS, Heninger GR, Kleber HD et al. (1986). The combined use of clonidine and naltrexone as a rapid, safe, effective treatment for abrupt withdrawal from methadone. *American Journal of Psychiatry* 143:831–837.

Charney DS, Sternburg DE, Kleber HD, Heninger GR & Redmond DE (1981). The clinical use of clonidine in abrupt withdrawal from methadone. *Archives of General Psychiatry* 38:1273–1277.

Cherubin CE & Sapira JD (1993). The medical complications of drug addiction and the medical assessment of the intravenous drug user: 25 years later. *Annals of Internal Medicine* 119(10):1017–1028.

Cheskin LJ, Fudala PJ & Johnson RE (1994). A controlled comparison of buprenorphine and clonidine for acute detoxification from opioids. *Drug and Alcohol Dependence* 36(2):115–121.

Crawley JN, Laberty RN & Roth RH (1979). Clonidine reversal of increased norepinephrine metabolite levels during morphine withdrawal. *European Journal of Pharmacology* 57:247–255.

Dawe S & Gray JA (1995). Craving and drug reward: a comparison of methadone and clonidine in detoxifying opiate addicts. *Drug and Alcohol Dependence* 39(3):207–12.

Dole VP (1972). Narcotic addiction, physical dependence and relapse. *The New England Journal of Medicine* 286:988–992.

Dunton AW, Schwam E, Pittman V, McGrath J, Hendler J & Siegel J (1988). Flumazenil. U.S. Clinical Pharmacology Studies. *European Journal of Anesthesiology* 581–595.

Federal Register (1989). Methadone: Rules and Regulations. *The Federal Register* 54:8954.

Fultz JM & Senay EC (1975). Guidelines for the hospitalized narcotic addicts. *Annals of Internal Medicine* 82:815–818.

Gold MS, Pottash AC, Sweeney DR & Kleber HD (1980). Opiate withdrawal using clonidine. *Journal of the American Medical Association* 243:343–346.

Gold M, Redmond DE & Kleber HD (1978). Clonidine blocks acute opiate withdrawal symptoms. *Lancet* 2:599–600.

Gould LC & Kleber HD (1974). Changing patterns of multiple drug use among applicants to a multimodality drug treatment program. *Archives of General Psychiatry* 31:408–415.

Gunne LN (1959). Noradrenaline and adrenaline in the rat brain during acute and chronic morphine administration and during withdrawal. *Nature* 184:150–151.

Jaffe JH (1990). Drug addiction and drug abuse. In AG Gilman, TW Rall, AS Nies & P Taylor (eds.) *Goodman and Gilman's The Pharmacological Basis of Therapeutics, 8th Edition*. New York, NY: Pergamon Press, 522–573.

Jaffe JH & Martin WR (1990). Opioid analgesics and antagonists. In AG Gilman, TW Rall, AS Nies & Taylor P (eds.) *Goodman and Gilman's The Pharmacological Basis of Therapeutics, 8th Edition*. New York, NY: Pergamon Press, 485–521.

Janiri L, Mannelli P, Persico AM, Serretti A & Tempesta E (1994). Opiate detoxification of methadone maintenance patients using lefetamine, clonidine and buprenorphine. *Drug and Alcohol Dependence* 36(2):139–145.

Jasinski DR, Johnson DR & Kocher TR (1985). Clonidine and morphine withdrawal: Differential effects on signs and symptoms. *Archives of General Psychiatry* 42:1063–1066.

Jasinski DR, Pevnick JS & Griffith JD (1978). Human pharmacology and abuse potential of the analgesic buprenorphine. *Archives of General Psychiatry* 35:510–516.

Kahn A, Mumford JP, Rogers GA & Beckford H (1997). Double-blind study of lofexidine and clonidine in the detoxification of opiate addicts in hospital. *Drug and Alcohol Dependence* 44(1):57–61.

Kellerman AL, Fikn SD, Logerford JP & Copass MK (1987). Impact of drug screening and suspected overdose. *Annals of Emergency Medicine* 16:1206–1216.

Kleber HD, Topazian M, Gaspari J, Riordan CE & Kosten TR (1987). Clonidine and naltrexone in the outpatient treatment of heroin withdrawal. *American Journal of Drug and Alcohol Abuse* 13:1.

Kosten TR, Gawin FH, Rounsaville BJ & Kleber HD (1986). Cocaine use among opioid addicts: Demographic and diagnostic factors in treatment. *American Journal of Drug and Alcohol Abuse* 12:1–16.

Kosten TR & Kleber HD (1986). Buprenorphine detoxification from opioid dependence: A pilot study. *Life Sciences* 42:635–641.

Kosten TR & Kleber HD (1984). Strategies to improve compliance with narcotic antagonists. *American Journal of Drug and Alcohol Abuse* 10:249–266.

Kosten TR, Morgan C & Kleber HD (1992). Phase II clinical trials of buprenorphine: Detoxification and induction onto naltrexone. *NIDA Research Monograph 121*. Rockville, MD: National Institute on Drug Abuse, 101–119.

Kosten TR, Morgan CH, Krystal JH, Price LH, Charney DS & Kleber HD (1989). Rapid detoxification procedure using buprenorphine and naloxone. *American Journal of Psychiatry* 147:1349.

Laberty R & Roth RH (1980). Clonidine reverses the increased norepinephrine increase during morphine withdrawal in rats. *Brain Research* 182:482–485.

Loimer N, Hofmann P & Chaudhry H (1993). Ultrashort noninvasive opiate detoxification [Letter]. *American Journal of Psychiatry* 150(5):839.

Loimer N, Lenz K, Schmid R & Presslich O (1991). Technique for greatly shortening the transition from methadone to naltrexone maintenance of patients addicted to opiates. *American Journal of Psychiatry* 148(7):933–5.

Loimer N, Schmid R, Lenz K, Presslich O & Grunberger J (1990). Acute blocking of naloxone-precipitated opiate withdrawal symptoms by methohexitone. *British Journal of Psychiatry* 157:748–52.

Martin WR (1983). Pharmacology of opioids. *Pharmacology Reviews* 35:283–323.

Melandri R, Re G, Lanzarini C et al. (1996). Myocardial damage and rhabdomyolysis associated with prolonged hypoxic coma following opiate overdose. *Journal of Toxicology and Clinical Toxicology* 34(2):199–203.

Mello MK & Mendelson JH (1980). Buprenorphine suppresses heroin use by heroin addicts. *Science* 207:657–659.

Morbidity and Mortality Weekly Reports (1996). Scopolamine poisoning among heroin users—New York City, Newark, Philadelphia, and Baltimore, 1995 and 1996. *Morbidity and Mortality Weekly Reports* 45(22):457–60.

Nigam AK, Ray R & Tripathi BM (1993). Buprenorphine in opiate withdrawal: A comparison with clonidine. *Journal of Substance Abuse Treatment* 10(4):391–394.

O'Connor PG, Carroll KM, Shi JM, Schottenfeld RS, Kosten TR & Rounsaville BJ (1995). A randomized trial of three methods of primary care-based outpatient opioid detoxification. *Journal of General Internal Medicine* 10(s):47.

O'Connor PG, Samet JH & Stein MD (1994). Management of hospitalized intravenous drug users. Role of the internist. *American Journal of Medicine* 96:551–558.

O'Connor PG, Selwyn PA & Schottenfeld RS (1994). Medical management of injection-drug users with HIV infection. *The New England Journal of Medicine* 331:450–459.

O'Connor PG, Waugh ME, Carroll KM, Rounsaville BJ, Diagkogiannis IA & Schottenfeld RS (1995). Primary care-based ambulatory opioid detoxification: The results of a clinical trial. *Journal of General Internal Medicine* 10:255–260.

O'Connor PG, Waugh ME, Schottenfeld RS, Diakogiannis IA & Rounsaville BJ (1992). Ambulatory opiate detoxification and primary care: A role for the primary care physician. *Journal of General Internal Medicine* 7:532–534.

Perry HE & Shannon MW (1996). Diagnosis and management of opioid- and benzodiazepine-induced comatose overdose in children. *Current Opinions in Pediatrics* 8(3):243–7.

Presslich O, Loimer N, Lenz K & Schmid R (1989). Opiate detoxification under general anesthesia by large doses of naloxone. *Journal of Toxicology and Clinical Toxicology* 27(4–5):263–70.

Riordan CE & Kleber HD (1980). Rapid opiate detoxification with clonidine and naloxone. *Lancet* 1:1039–1080.

Rogers WO, Hall MA, Brissie RM & Robinson CA (1997). Detection of alprazolam in three cases of methadone/benzodiazepine overdose. *Journal of Forensic Sciences* 42(1):155–6.

Satel SL, Kosten TR, Schuckit MA & Fischman MW (1993). Should protracted withdrawal from drugs be included in DSM-IV? *American Journal of Psychiatry* 150(5):695–704.

Schuckit MA (1989). Opiates and other analgesics. In *Drug and Alcohol Abuse: A Clinical Guide to Diagnosis and Treatment, 3rd Ed.* New York, NY: Plenum Publishing Co., 118–142.

Schuckit N (1988). Clonidine and the treatment of withdrawal. *Drug Abuse and Alcoholism Newsletter* 17:1–4.

Seidler D, Stuhlinger GH, Fischer G et al. (1996). After antagonization of acute opiate overdose: A survey at hospitals in Vienna. *Addiction* 91(10):1479–87.

Sporer KA, Firestone J & Isaacs SM (1996). Out-of-hospital treatment of opioid overdoses in an urban setting. *Academy of Emergency Medicine* 3(7):660–667.

Stephenson J (1997). Experts debate merits of 1-day opiate detoxification under anesthesia. *Journal of the American Medical Association* 277(5):363–4.

Vining E, Kosten TR & Kleber HD (1988). Clinical utility of rapid clonidine naltrexone detoxification for opioid abusers. *British Journal of the Addictions* 83:567–575.

Wen HL, Ho WK & Wen PY (1984). Comparison of the effectiveness of different opioid peptides in depressing heroin withdrawal. *European Journal of Pharmacology* 100:155–162.

Whipple JK, Quebbeman EJ, Lewis KS, Gottlieb MS & Ausman RK (1994). Difficulties in diagnosing narcotic overdoses in hospitalized patients. *Annals of Pharmacotherapy* 28(4):446–50.

CHAPTER 5

Management of Stimulant, Hallucinogen, Marijuana and Phencyclidine Intoxication and Withdrawal

Jeffery N. Wilkins, M.D.
Bradley T. Conner
David A. Gorelick, M.D., Ph.D.

Stimulants
Hallucinogens
Marijuana
Phencyclidine (PCP)
Multiple Drug Withdrawal
Special Populations

This chapter reviews the treatment of intoxication and acute withdrawal states from the use of stimulants such as cocaine and methamphetamine (including their smokable forms "crack" and "ice"), marijuana, phencyclidine (PCP), and hallucinogens such as lysergic acid diethylamide (LSD), 3, 4-methylene-dioxymethamphetamine (MDMA, "Ecstasy"), and N,N-dimethyltryptamine (DMT). It also reviews the treatment of withdrawal from multiple sedative-hypnotics and sedative-hypnotics plus other drugs. The psychiatric and medical complications are considered separately, since they often are treated with different modalities and in different settings (e.g., psychiatric versus medical emergency rooms). Not all of the substances reviewed here have defined treatments for intoxication, overdose, or withdrawal (see Table 1.)

Successful treatment of acute intoxication, overdose, or withdrawal can facilitate entry into addiction treatment, as by reducing uncomfortable withdrawal symptomatology that negatively reinforces drug taking. Even when successful, these early stages of treatment often are followed by relapse to substance abuse, with patients reentering a "revolving door" of repeated detoxification programs. For drugs without a physiologically prominent withdrawal syndrome, such as marijuana, LSD, PCP, and MDMA, there may be little benefit to short-term treatment focused on alleviating acute withdrawal, as opposed to longer term treatment of addiction. Thus, short-term treatment of acute intoxication or withdrawal does not obviate the need for longer term treatment of addiction.

Pharmacological treatment of drug intoxication/overdose generally follows one of three approaches (Gorelick, 1993): (1) increased clearance of drug from the body, either by increasing catabolism, increasing excretion, or both; (2) blockade of the neuronal site to which the drug binds to exert its effect (e.g., use of naloxone to block the opiate receptor in the treatment of opiate overdose); and (3) counteracting effects of the drug through some other neuropharmacological action. Pharmacological treatment of any drug withdrawal syndrome generally follows one of two approaches (Gorelick, 1993): (1) suppression by a cross-tolerant medication from the same pharmacological class, usually a longer-acting one to provide a milder, controlled withdrawal (as in the use of the opioid methadone for opiate detoxification) and (2) decreasing signs and symptoms of withdrawal by targeting alternative neurochemical or receptor systems that mediate withdrawal (as in the use of the non-opiate clonidine to treat opiate withdrawal).

TABLE 1. Presence of Clinically Significant Intoxication or Withdrawal Syndrome

Substance	Intoxication	Withdrawal
Stimulants	Yes	Yes
Marijuana	Yes	No
Hallucinogens	Yes	No
Phencyclidine	Yes	No

For a variety of reasons, many of these pharmacologic approaches to treatment are not appropriate for the drugs reviewed in this chapter. There may be no practical method for altering drug clearance (as with hallucinogens and marijuana), or no specific drug receptor site has been identified. Even when a receptor site has been identified, there may not yet exist a clinically approved antagonist (i.e., PCP and marijuana). Finally, current understanding of the neuropharmacological processes mediating intoxication or withdrawal may be too limited to suggest appropriate pharmacological interventions.

STIMULANTS

Stimulant Intoxication. The acute psychomotor stimulant effect of cocaine, amphetamine, and methamphetamine, including restlessness, irritability, tremor, talkativeness, anxiety, lability of mood, headache, chills, vomiting, and sweating (Weiss, Greenfield & Mirin, 1994), are principally attributable to increases in central nervous system (CNS) catecholamine neurotransmitter activity. Enhanced catecholamine activity occurs through stimulant-mediated blockade of the neurotransmitter presynaptic reuptake pumps (e.g., by cocaine) and by presynaptic release of catecholamines (e.g., by amphetamines) (Gawin & Ellinwood, 1988; Johanson & Fischman, 1989). These neuropharmacological actions suggest that blocking catecholamine presynaptic binding sites or postsynaptic receptors might be effective treatment for stimulant intoxication. However, no such medication used to date has proven clinically effective in blocking or attenuating the desirable or reinforcing aspects of stimulant intoxication (Gorelick, 1995).

Another method of attenuating the effects of cocaine intoxication would be to decrease the availability of cocaine by increasing its metabolism. This has been performed in animal studies through activation of cocaine's major metabolic enzyme, plasma butyrylcholinesterase (BChE, E.C.3.1.1.8) (Gorelick, 1997).

Table 2 provides an overview of treatment for the psychiatric and medical complications of stimulant intoxication.

Psychological/Behavioral Effects of Stimulant Intoxication: In addition to the desired euphoric or reinforcing effect, stimulants may produce various psychiatric complications ranging from less disabling manifestations such as behavioral disinhibition, bruxism, and hypervigilance, to compulsive or stereotyped behavior, paranoia, and psychosis (Gawin & Ellinwood, 1988). Table 3 lists the mental status findings for acute cocaine and stimulant intoxication. Panic reactions are common, and may evolve into a panic disorder (Schuckit, 1989). This may be exacerbated by anxiety elicited by the physiological symptoms commonly associated with stimulant use. For example, the user's fear of having a heart attack may be exacerbated by heart palpitations and hyperventilation caused by the stimulant.

Repeated or high-dose stimulant use may result in initial suspiciousness and hypervigilance developing into pronounced paranoia or psychosis, with well-formed delusions, ideas of reference, hallucinations, and social withdrawal (King & Ellinwood, 1992). The hallucinations are commonly auditory or tactile (e.g., formication, the tactile hallucination of insects crawling under one's skin). Visual hallucinations are much less common; their presence suggests a possible neurologic etiology. This psychosis can closely resemble acute schizophrenia; many patients are mistakenly diagnosed with schizophrenia (Karch, 1993). Although users typically remain oriented and alert, the delusional state may impair judgment, cognition, and attention. Very severe intoxication may produce a delirium similar to toxic reactions with PCP, including extreme emotional lability, enhanced strength, decreased awareness of pain, and unpredictable, sometimes violent, behavior (Wetli & Fisbain, 1985).

At high doses, cocaine or amphetamines can precipitate an organic brain syndrome (OBS), with disorientation, hallucinations, paranoia, bruxism, and stereotyped behaviors such as repeated touching (Schuckit, 1989). Patients should be evaluated for an acute neurological lesion (e.g., intracranial bleeding) and preexisting neurological disease or psychopathology before any pharmacological treatment is initiated. The OBS generally is self-limited, with treatment following the guidelines as for other OBS.

Treatment of the Psychological/Behavioral Effects of Stimulant Intoxication: Initial clinical evaluation should rule out possible medical problems (such as hyperthyroidism) or pre-existing psychopathology

TABLE 2. Treatment of Cocaine and Other Stimulant Intoxication

Clinical Problem	Moderate Syndrome	Severe Syndrome
Anxiety, agitation:	Reassurance, observation in quiet, nonthreatening atmosphere	Diazepam or other benzodiazepine
Delusions, psychosis:	Neuroleptic only if necessary	Potent neuroleptic (e.g., haloperidol)
Hyperthermia:	Monitor body temperature closely	If b.t. > 102°F (oral), external cooling with cold water, ice packs; and if needed, hypothermic blanket; can use haloperidol
Seizures:	Diazepam (5–10 mg, < 5mg/min., IV), phenytoin, or phenobarbital (25–50 mg, IV)	For repeated seizures, use diazepam via nasogastric tube instead of IV
Hypertension:	Monitor blood pressure closely	If diastolic b.p. > 120 for 15 mins., use phentolamine (2–10 mg, IV over 10 mins.)
To increase drug excretion:	Ammonium chloride, if renal and hepatic function normal, to achieve pH < 6.6	*(same as for moderate intoxication)*
Oral overdose:	Gastric lavage with nasogastric tube (if patient conscious) or after intubation (if patient comatose)	*(same as for moderate intoxication)*
Sympathetic N.S. overactivity (hypertension, tachycardia, and respiratory effects):		Propranalol (with phentolamine or nitropursides or labetalol)
Toxicological analysis:	Draw blood and urine	*(same as for moderate intoxication)*

Note: The division between "moderate" and "severe" is only a guideline (e.g., hypertension may become severe while other clinical problems remain moderate). References: O'Connor et al. (1992); Weiss & Mirin (1988).

(especially panic or affective disorder), as well as confirm the presence of stimulants by toxicologic analysis of body fluids. Once medical or psychiatric causes have been excluded, the patient should be isolated in a quiet area to minimize sensory stimulation and reassured that the effects of the stimulant will dissipate within a few hours as the drug is cleared from the body. If reassurance alone proves inadequate, anti-anxiety drugs such as chlordiazepoxide (10 to 25 mg orally) or diazepam (10 to 30 mg orally) may be administered, repeated as needed every 30 to 60 minutes (Schuckit, 1989). If parenteral benzodiazepines are needed, diazepam (10 to 12 mg IM) may be effective (Chang & Kosten, 1992).

The initial treatment approach for stimulant-induced psychosis is non-pharmacological (Khantzian & McKenna, 1979). Patients should be treated in a calm, non-threatening atmosphere, with sensory stimuli (such as bright lights and noise) kept to a minimum to avoid exacerbating hallucinations and/or delusions. Treatment staff should appear calm and confident, but remain alert for possible aggressive outbursts. No sudden movements should be made in the patient's presence, and any treatment procedure should be carefully explained before it is initiated (Kosten & Kleber, 1988).

If symptoms persist, pharmacological intervention may be necessary, e.g., to prevent or reduce aggressive outbursts. There is little systematic evidence directly comparing neuroleptics with benzodiazepines, but there is some evidence that the latter offer medical advantages. Neuroleptics may worsen the sympathomimetic and cardiovascular effects of cocaine (Goldfrank & Hoffman, 1991) and produce a syndrome of hyperthermia and rapid death (Kosten & Kleber, 1988). If neuroleptics are needed, one of high potency, such as haloperidol (5 to 20 mg/day

TABLE 3. Psychological/Behavioral Effects of Acute Cocaine/Stimulant Intoxication

"Abnormal" overall behavior and appearance	x
Disoriented to person, place, date, or situation	none
Dysfunctional immediate, recent, remote memory	x
Inappropriate direction and degree of affect	xx
Altered mood: depressed	x/xxx
Altered mood: overly elated	xxx
Confused, disorganized	xx
Hallucinations	xxx
Delusions	none/xxx
Bizarre behavior	xx
Suicidal or danger to self	xxx
Homicidal or danger to others	xxx
Poor judgment	xxx

Relative weighting: x = mild, xx = moderate, xxx = marked; / = common/rare. See text for references.

orally or IM, for up to four days), is preferred because of its minimal anticholinergic activity (Ungar, 1989). Haloperidol is especially useful in controlling aggression (Beebe & Walley, 1994). Past concerns that haloperidol might lower the seizure threshold (Gold, 1992) or produce Parkinsonian side effects (acute stiffness, dystonia) (Roberts, 1987; Kumor, Sherer & Jaffe, 1986) have not been supported by more recent data (Callaway & Clark, 1994). While chlorpromazine has shown efficacy in safely treating children with severe amphetamine poisoning (Callaway & Clark, 1994), presumably through its reduction of increased motor activity, overall it is not preferred. Less potent neuroleptics, such as chlorpromazine, have been associated with anticholinergic or hypotensive episodes (Smart & Anglin, 1987), and may possibly inhibit the metabolism of amphetamine (Weiss, Greenfield & Mirin, 1994). Benzodiazepines avoid the disadvantages of neuroleptics and may protect against the sympathomimetic and adverse cardiovascular effects of cocaine (Goldfrank & Hoffman, 1991). However, benzodiazepines should be used with some caution because they may exacerbate the potential for aggressive outbursts (Schuckit, 1989).

A delusional or psychotic patient should be hospitalized until the episode has safely passed. The syndrome usually abates within a few days if no more stimulants are ingested (Schuckit, 1989). Psychiatric symptoms that persist beyond four or five days suggest an etiology other than stimulant use (Hurlbut, 1991).

Physical restraints, to control agitation or violent behavior, should be avoided unless absolutely necessary. The use of restraints can increase risk of hyperthermia and rhabdomyolysis, with a resulting risk of renal failure from myoglobinuria (Hurlbut, 1991).

Medical Effects of Stimulant Intoxication: Medical complications associated with cocaine and stimulant intoxication are summarized in Table 4. Hyperthermia, vasoconstriction, hypertension, tachycardia, and palpitations may accompany acute stimulant intoxication. Hyperthermia may occur independently of other symptoms and suggests a more severe prognosis (Callaway & Clark, 1994; Weiss, Greenfield & Mirin, 1994). Acute hyperthermia may lead to reversible coagulopathy and renal failure. Other symptoms may include myocardial ischemia, arrhythmia, and dyspnea (Goldfrank & Hoffman, 1992). Severe cases may progress to cardiogenic shock, myocardial infarction, and death. Other systemic effects may include cerebral and pulmonary edema, hemorrhage, rhabdomyolysis, myoglobinuria, nephrotoxicity, and hyperkalemia (Callaway & Clark, 1994; Karch, 1993).

The medical aspects of cocaine intoxication can be divided into three phases (Weiss, Greenfield & Mirin, 1994). The first phase presents with the psychological/behavioral effects described above and mild physiological effects (usually not requiring specific treatment). The second phase includes myocardial ischemia or infarction (usually reflected in chest pain), seizures, malignant encephalopathy, incontinence, and ventricular dysrhythmias. The third (premorbid) phase is characterized by coma, paralysis, and fixed and dilated pupils.

Management of Stimulant Intoxication: The first priority in the management of severe acute stimulant intoxication is maintenance of basic life-support functions, including airway patency and ventilation (O'Connor, Chang & Shi, 1992). Vital signs, cardiac, and neurologic status should be monitored closely, with treatment for shock implemented if necessary. Elevated body temperature (over 102 degrees F. orally) should be managed aggressively to avert hyperthermic crisis (e.g., external body cooling measures, including ice packs, cold water, ice water gastric lavage, and hypothermic blankets) (Beebe & Walley, 1994; Callaway & Clark, 1994, Schuckit, 1989). If hyperthermia is not treated aggressively, the patient may develop rhabdomyolysis and renal failure (Callaway & Clark, 1994).

Intravenous diazepam (5 to 10 mg at no more than 5 mg/min.) is recommended for seizures stem-

TABLE 4. Medical Complications of Cocaine/ Stimulant Intoxication

Organ System	Medical Effects
HEENT	Pupillary dilation; sudden headache; bruxism; stereotyped movements (picking, stroking)
Pulmonary	Increased respiration rate and depth; possible dyspnea; pulmonary edema, respiratory failure.
Cardiovascular	Pulse will usually increase 30–50% above normal; blood pressure will usually increase 15–20% above normal. Skin pallor due to vasoconstriction; possible circulatory failure; tachycardia; myocardial ischemia, arrhythmia. If severe, then possibility of myocardial infarction and cardiogenic shock.
Neurologic	Tremor, hyperreflexia; twitching of small muscles (esp. face, fingers, and feet); tics (generalized); cold sweating, flushing; preconvulsive movements (tonic and clonic jerks). Possibility of seizures, coma, and paralysis of medullary brain center, cerebral edema.
Gastrointestinal	Possible nausea and vomiting
Urogenital	Possible renal failure. Possible incontinence
Body temperature	Mildly elevated to possible malignant hyperthermia
Other	Possible rhabdomyolysis; hepatic insufficiency.

Gold (1992); O'Connor, Chang & Shi (1992); Miller (1991); Milhorn (1991); Carroll (1990); Selden et. al. (1990); Leikin et al. (1989); Schuckit (1989); Hyner & McKinney (1986).

ming from cocaine or amphetamine intoxication (Beebe & Walley, 1994; Weiss, Greenfield & Mirin, 1994). Resuscitation equipment should be available in case the diazepam precipitates respiratory depression. For repeated seizures, intubation is recommended after intravenous diazepam administration, which could cause apnea or laryngospasm (Schuckit, 1989). Seizure activity can also be managed with phenytoin or a short-acting barbiturate such as pentobarbital sodium (25 to 50 mg, IV) (O'Connor, Chang & Shi, 1992; Beebe & Walley, 1994; Kunisaki & Augenstein, 1994).

Blood pressure should be monitored closely to avoid CNS hemorrhage from malignant hypertension (Schuckit, 1989). Hypertension lasting more than 15 minutes should be promptly treated. In many cases, hypertension will respond to sedation with a benzodiazepine (Goldfrank & Hoffman, 1991). If this is insufficient, vasodilation with phentolamine (2 to 10 mg IV, over 10 minutes) or, in more serious cases, sodium nitroprusside infusion (0.5–10 mcg/kg/min) can be used. There is some evidence that this approach improves coronary perfusion, and no evidence that rapid lowering of blood pressure compromises peripheral (including cerebral) circulation in otherwise intact patients. Animal studies suggest that calcium channel blockers (e.g., nimodipine, verapamil, diltiazem) are not consistently useful (Ansah, Wade & Shockley, 1993; Abel & Wilson, 1992), and may actually increase CNS toxicity (Derlet & Albertson, 1989; Hollander, 1995). However, no systematic human studies have been performed.

Previous research supported the use of beta- or mixed alpha- and beta-adrenergic blockers, such as propranolol or labetalol, to reduce stimulant-induced overactivity of the sympathetic nervous system. Pre-clinical and some clinical studies suggest that beta-blockers may actually exacerbate cocaine-related cardiovascular toxicity, leading to recommendations against their use and in favor of benzodiazepines (Callaway & Clark, 1994; Goldfrank & Hoffman, 1991; Hollander, 1995; Ramoska & Sacchetti, 1985). Propranolol may create or increase hypertension, possibly by increasing vascular resistance (Callaway & Clark, 1994). An alternative approach is vasodilation by administration of sodium nitroprusside or phentolamine (Weiss, Greenfield & Mirin, 1994). No large case series or controlled clinical trials have directly compared the efficacy or safety of vasodilation versus adrenergic blockade.

The treatment of cocaine-associated myocardial ischemia or infarction resembles that for non-cocaine-associated ischemia, with the exception of avoiding use of beta-adrenergic blockers, including labetolol (Hollander, 1995). Initial treatment includes oxygen, benzodiazepine for sedation, nitroglycerin for vasodilation, and aspirin for antiplatelet action, while evaluation is continuing. Further treatment can include phentolamine and/or verapamil to reverse cocaine-induced coronary artery vasoconstriction. If the diagnosis of myocardial infarction is established, treatment can proceed to angioplasty or thrombolysis.

Gastric lavage may be helpful if the stimulant was taken orally (Schuckit, 1989). If the patient is conscious, a nasogastric tube can be used; intubation is preferred if the patient is unconscious.

Acidification of urine may increase elimination of amphetamine, but probably has little role in the treatment of cocaine or methamphetamine intoxication. There is some controversy regarding its clinical usefulness even for amphetamine (Callaway & Clark, 1994; Weiss, Greenfield & Mirin, 1994). Administration of ammonium chloride (500 mg orally, every three to four hours) to lower urine pH below 6.6 will inhibit almost all renal reabsorption of amphetamine (because of its basic pKa of 9.9) and increase its excretion (Chang & Kosten, 1992; Vree & Henderson, 1980). Acidification is contraindicated if renal or hepatic function is abnormal (Weiss, Greenfield & Mirin, 1994), or in overdose situations when plasma acidification may compromise cardiovascular function (Hurlbut, 1991).

In a medical emergency, the clinical picture may be confusing and the patient history unreliable or impossible to obtain (Schwartz, 1988). Urine and/or blood samples for toxicological analysis should always be obtained to determine what drugs, if any, the patient has taken. Even if an apparently adequate history is obtained from the patient or collateral informants, toxicological analysis is essential because other drugs (e.g., alcohol, opiates, or sedative-hypnotics) may have been ingested either intentionally (e.g., to temper the stimulant's unwanted effects) (Gold, 1992) or unknowingly (e.g., as adulterants or by misrepresentation).

Stimulant Withdrawal. *Clinical Picture:* Abrupt cessation of stimulant use is associated with depression, anergia, anhedonia, increased drug craving, increased appetite, hypersomnolence, and increased REM sleep (Gillin, Pulviranti et al., 1994; Lago & Kosten, 1994; Weiss, Greenfield & Mirin, 1994). These symptoms have been attributed to decreased CNS dopamine activity. The initial period of intense symptoms is commonly termed the "crash," but most symptoms are mild and self-limited.

One early study of cocaine addicts in outpatient treatment described a triphasic withdrawal syndrome lasting several weeks (Gawin & Kleber, 1986; see Table 5), but this pattern has not been found in prospective inpatient studies of cocaine withdrawal (Gill, Gillespie et al., 1991; Gorelick, Stauffer et al., 1997; Satel, Price et al., 1991; Weddington, Brown et al., 1991), possibly because inpatients were not exposed to cocaine-associated environmental stimuli. Because stimulant withdrawal is not medically serious and usually is short-term and self-limiting, pharmacological treatment has focused more on long-term treatment of addiction than on short-term treatment of acute withdrawal. Most clinical trials that began medication during the early withdrawal period have continued medication for at least several weeks, with the goal of also treating the addiction itself (Gorelick, 1995; see also Section 7, Chapter 3).

Medical Effects of Stimulant Withdrawal: Myocardial ischemia has been associated with stimulant withdrawal (Nademanee, Gorelick et al., 1989), with coronary vasospasm considered a possible contributing factor. The ischemia usually presents during the first week of withdrawal. Other medical effects of stimulant withdrawal are relatively minor, including a variety of nonspecific aches and pains, tremors, chills, and involuntary motor movement (Franz, 1985; Khantzian & McKenna, 1979). These rarely require specific medical treatment. However, as with any patient, it is prudent to conduct a thorough medical evaluation, including physical examination and electrocardiogram, in order to rule out a concurrent medical problem. Urine testing for stimulants and other drugs of abuse, in addition to aiding the diagnosis, can be helpful in reinforcing the patient's incentive to remain abstinent.

Management of Stimulant Withdrawal: The stimulant withdrawal syndrome has been hypothesized to be the result of decreased levels of dopamine activity in the brain resulting from chronic stimulant exposure (Dackis & Gold, 1985). This so-called "dopamine deficiency" hypothesis of withdrawal has not been consistently supported by clinical studies (Gill, Gillespie et al., 1991; Satel, Price et al., 1991; Volkow, Fowler et al., 1992), but has generated use of dopamine agonists to treat cocaine withdrawal. Most commonly used are bromocriptine and amantadine, two medications already marketed for the treatment of Parkinsonism, which is also a dopamine deficiency disease. In animal studies, single doses of bromocriptine have shown promise in reversing manifestations of cocaine withdrawal (Markou & Koob, 1992), but clinical trials have yielded inconsistent results (Gorelick, 1995; Teller & Devenyi, 1988). The dopamine amino acid precursor L-dopa, also used to treat Parkinsonism, was effective in reducing cocaine withdrawal symptoms in one small inpatient case series (Wolfson & Angrist, 1990). No controlled clinical trial has directly compared the benefits of medication versus a supportive milieu.

Symptoms of stimulant withdrawal are best treated supportively by allowing the patient to sleep and eat as much as necessary (Siegel, 1984). Short-acting benzodiazepines such as lorazepam may be

TABLE 5. Symptoms and Treatment of Cocaine Withdrawal (Model of Gawin & Kleber)

Phase	Time Course	Symptoms	Treatment
Crash	Starts right after binge	Stimulant craving	Assess neurological and physical status. Take blood and urine samples.
Initial crash		Intense dysphoria—depression, anxiety, agitation	Obtain history of other drug use and prior psychiatric disorders.
Middle crash	Starts 1–4 hours after binge	Craving replaced by desire for sleep, despite insomnia	Observe closely, take precautions against suicide if necessary.
		Dysphoria may self-medicate with other drugs	Delay clinical evaluation until after hypersomnia/crash.
Late crash	Lasts 3–4 days	Hypersomnia, increased appetite	Allow patient 3–4 days in quiet room to recover and sleep and eat as much as needed.
Withdrawal			
Honeymoon phase	Lasts 12 hours to 4 days	Normalization of sleep	Evaluate for other drug use and premorbid psychopathology.
		Fairly normal mood (only mild dysphoria)	Pharmacotherapy for stimulant withdrawal has not yet been established.
		Reduced craving	
Dysphoria, craving	Lasts 6–18 weeks	Withdrawal symptoms emerge—depression, lethargy, anhedonia	Initiate outpatient program (e.g., group support meetings, individual psychotherapy, education, urine monitoring, steps to avoid drug-taking situations, etc.).
		Reemergence of craving	
Extinction	Lasts months to years	Gradual return of mood, interest in environment, and ability to experience pleasure	Relapse prevention techniques and participation in long-term self-help groups (e.g., Twelve Step).
		Gradual extinction of periodic craving episodes	

References: Gawin & Kleber (1986); Gawin & Ellinwood (1988); Schuckit (1989); King & Ellinwood (1992).

helpful in selected patients who develop agitation or sleep disturbance (Pearsall & Rosen, 1992). Lisuride (a dopamine receptor agonist) has been used to reduce increased REM sleep and improve mood (Gillin, Pulviranti et al., 1994), but has not yet been subjected to controlled trials. Severe or persistent depression may require antidepressant treatment (Weiss, Greenfield & Mirin, 1994). Neuroleptics are contraindicated because of their potential for dysphoric side effects; they have been considered to increase drug craving (Extein & Dackis, 1987). The risk of relapse is high during the early withdrawal period, in part because drug craving is easily triggered by encounters with or thinking of drug-associated stimuli. This issue is better addressed by psychosocial treatment, such as behavioral therapy techniques of desensitization and cue extinction, than by medication (Gawin & Ellinwood, 1988).

Administration of a cross-tolerant or similarly acting stimulant has not been systematically evaluated as a short-term treatment for stimulant withdrawal. Tricyclic antidepressants have been used because, like cocaine, they inhibit presynaptic neurotransmitter reuptake, and because depression is a common symptom of stimulant withdrawal. No controlled clinical trials have evaluated the effectiveness of tricyclic antidepressants for this purpose.

HALLUCINOGENS

Hallucinogen Intoxication. *Clinical Picture:* Despite differences in chemical structure, both the serotonin-related hallucinogens (such as psilocybin or DMT) and the phenylethylamine hallucinogens (such as mescaline, MDMA, or dimethoxymethylamphetamine [DOM]) share enough clinical similarities with LSD to be classified as LSD-like hallucinogens (Abraham, Aldridge & Gogia, 1996; Martin & Sloan, 1971). The subjective experience of hallucinogen intoxication is heavily determined by set and setting, i.e., the expectations and personality of the user, coupled with the environmental and social conditions of use. In general, perception is heightened and distorted, with alterations in the sense of time, space, and body boundaries (Weiss & Millman, 1991). Cognition may range from clarity to confusion and disorientation, although reality testing usually remains intact.

Psychological/Behavioral Effects of Hallucinogen Intoxication: The psychological and behavioral effects associated with hallucinogen intoxication are summarized in Table 6 (also see Section 2). Mood and emotional state can vary from euphoria and feelings of spiritual insight to depression, anxiety, and terror.

A "bad trip" usually takes the form of an anxiety attack or panic reaction, with the user feeling out of control (Weiss, Greenfield & Mirin, 1994; Kulig, 1990). Ongoing sensory bombardment, coupled with a distortion in the sense of time, may cause the user to fear permanent brain damage. An experience of depersonalization may precipitate the fear of losing one's mind permanently. Panic reactions are commoner in those who have limited experience with hallucinogens, but previous "positive" experiences with LSD provide no guarantee against adverse reaction (Ungerleider & Pechnick, 1992). Acute psychotic reactions are rare; however, psychologically normal users may go into a transient psychosis or a latent psychopathology may be triggered. An LSD-induced psychotic state can result in unprovoked violence based on paranoid delusions (Bowers, 1972).

Hallucinogen ingestion may result in an acute toxic delirium characterized by delusions, hallucinations, agitation, confusion, paranoia, and inadvertent suicide attempts (Weiss, Greenfield & Mirin, 1994). The inadvertent suicide attempts may manifest in patient's attempts to fly or perform other impossible activities.

LSD psychosis, despite its resemblance to paranoid schizophrenia, may often be differentiated from schizophrenia by several diagnostic signs (Ungerleider & Pechnick, 1992). In particular, schizophrenia is suggested by auditory rather than visual hallucinations, a history of prior mental illness, or a lack of development of drug tolerance. Unlike schizophrenic patients, the LSD patient usually retains at least partial insight that his symptomatology is drug-related.

Medical Effects of Hallucinogen Intoxication: The medical effects of hallucinogen intoxication are summarized in Table 7. Acute medical complications of LSD are rare, but convulsions and hyperthermia have been reported (Rosenberg, Pentel et al., 1986). Body temperature should be monitored and any elevation treated promptly. Dry skin, increased muscle tone, agitation, and seizures are warning signs of a potential hyperthermic crisis. Patients may not respond to anticonvulsant medication until body temperature is lowered.

Because LSD is rapidly absorbed when taken orally, ipecac-induced vomiting and gastric lavage usually are not helpful, and may exacerbate the patient's psychological condition. There is no evidence that LSD binds to charcoal. Gastric lavage should be

TABLE 6. Psychological/Behavioral Effects of Hallucinogen, Marijuana, and PCP Intoxication

	LSD	Marijuana	PCP	MDMA
"Abnormal" overall behavior and appearance	xx	x	xxx	x
Disoriented to person, place, date, or situation	xx	none	xx	none
Dysfunctional immediate, recent, remote memory	x	xx	xx	x
Inappropriate direction and degree of affect	xxx	x	xxx	xx
Altered mood: depressed	xx	x	xx	x
Altered mood: overly elated	xxx	xx	xx	xxx
Confused, disorganized	xx	xx	xxx	x
Hallucinations	xxx	x	xxx	x
Delusions	x/xxx	xxx	xx	?
Bizarre behavior	xxx	x	xxx	?
Suicidal or danger to self	xx	xx	xx	?
Homicidal or danger to others	xx	x	xxx	x
Poor judgment	x/xxx	xxx	xxx	xx

Relative weighting: x = mild, xx = moderate, xxx = marked; / = common/rare; ? = insufficient research. See text for references.
MDMA = 3, 4-methylenedioxymethamphetamine

considered if psilocybin is involved, especially when there is any doubt as to the identity of the ingested mushrooms (Schwartz & Smith, 1988). However, of 886 samples purported to be psilocybin over an 11-year period, only 28% were hallucinogenic mushrooms, while 31% were LSD or PCP, and 37% contained no drug at all (Renfroe & Messinger, 1985).

Medical emergencies associated with MDMA intoxication commonly involve hyperthermia, and may include a syndrome of hyperthermia, seizures, cardiac arrhythmia, disseminated intravascular coagulation, rhabdomyolysis, and acute renal failure (Green, Cross & Goodwin, 1995; Henry, Jeffreys & Dawling, 1992) which can lead to death. This syndrome may be related to both the intrinsic stimulant-like hyperthermic properties of MDMA and its use in "rave" dance clubs, where individuals have become dehydrated from exertion in a warm, crowded environment. Patients presenting with suspected MDMA toxicity should promptly receive intravenous fluids and intravenous dantrolene (Henry, Jeffreys & Dawling, 1992). Hyperthermia can be treated successfully with tepid wet towels, ice packs, cooling sponge baths, and rectal acetaminophen (Hayner & McKinney, 1986).

Management of Hallucinogen Intoxication: The first goal of treatment is the physical safety of the patient and others. The patient should be placed in a quiet environment with minimal sensory input, but should not be left alone because of the risk of unintended self-injury (due to delusions or hallucinations) or of suicide (due to depression). The presence of a familiar person usually is comforting. Unless the patient presents in an acutely agitated or threatening state, physical restraints are contraindicated because they may exacerbate anxiety and increase the risk of rhabdomyolysis associated with LSD-induced muscle rigidity and spasms. The use of "gentle restraints," combined with muscle massage and individualized counseling, may be helpful (Miller, Gay et al., 1992). The "talk-down" or reassurance technique is the commonest form of treatment for adverse reactions to hallucinogens. The clinician, in a concerned and nonjudgmental manner, discusses the patient's anxiety reaction, stressing that LSD's effects are temporary and that the patient will completely recover.

For patients who are unresponsive to reassurance alone, benzodiazepines are the traditional drug of choice because they sedate and relax muscle rigidity and spasms (Strassman, 1984). When the onset of action of oral medication is too slow, or the patient will not take oral medication, intramuscular lorazepam (2 mg, repeated hourly as needed) may be effective. If benzodiazepines are insufficient, a high potency neuroleptic such as haloperidol (5 to 10 mg orally or 2 mg intramuscularly) is recommended. Haloperidol can reduce psychotic reactions, but must be used cautiously, as neuroleptics can lower the seizure threshold. Although some researchers believe this threat is over-emphasized (Callaway & Clark, 1994), this is a relevant factor because hallucinogens may be cut with adulterants (such as strychnine) that have proconvulsant activity (Ungerleider & Pechnick, 1992). Anti-Parkinsonism medication, such as benztropine or trihexphenidyl, should be available to treat acute dystonic reactions or other possible acute neuroleptic side effects (Strassman, 1984). Phenothiazines are contraindicated because they have been associated with poor

TABLE 7. Physical Effects of Hallucinogen and Marijuana Intoxication

Organ System	LSD	MDMA	Marijuana	PCP (stage I)	PCP (stage II)	PCP (stage III)
HEENT	Pupillary dilation	Bruxism; headache; trismus	Slight pupillary constriction; dose-related conjunctival injection; decreased intraocular pressure; altered color vision; possible headache; possible nystagmus.	Horizontal nystagmus, later vertical also; lid reflex lost, "blank stare"; variable pupil size, often miotic; laryngeal/pharyngeal reflexes hyperactive	Corneal reflex lost, "roving eyes," disconjugate gaze; pupils midposition and reactive; laryngeal/pharyngeal reflexes diminished	"Eyes open coma," hippus, increasing pupillary dilation; laryngeal/pharyngeal reflexes absent
Pulmonary	Mucosal irritation; bronchodilation		Mildly increased respiratory rate, tidal volume and minute volume	Moderately increased respiratory rate (25% above normal)	Periodic breathing, apnea, possible pneumonia or pulmonary edema	
Cardiovascular	Elevated blood pressure and heart rate	Elevated heart rate variable to tachycardia; hypertension progressing to hypotension; palpitations; disseminated intravascular coagulation.	Sinus tachycardia; increased cardiac output; reduced peak exercise performance; peripheral vasodilation; orthostatic hypotension in large doses	Mildly elevated pulse rate and blood pressure	Moderately elevated	Greatly elevated (100% above normal), spikes in blood pressure, high-output failure
Neurologic	Increases in reflexes, muscular tremors, convulsions; muscular weakness; seizures; flushing and chills.	Tremor; tight jaw muscles; hypertonicity of the body;	Mild tremor; decreased coordination and strength; decreased ability to perform complex motor tasks	Conscious but with lack of concentration; illogical speech, agitation, muscle rigidity, repetitive movements, grimacing; increased deep tendon reflexes; diaphophoresis, flushing, lacrimation, hypersalivation	Stupor to mild coma, tonic-clonic seizures on stimulation; deep pain response intact; generalized muscle rigidity, muscle twitching; diaphophoresis, lacrimation, flushing, hypersalivation	Deep coma, tonic-clonic seizures to status epilepticus, possible stroke; deep pain response absent; generalized myoclonus, opisthotonic or decerebrate posturing, muscle rigidity; deep tendon reflexes absent; diaphophoresis, flushing, hypersalivation

Gastrointestinal	Occasional nausea and vomiting	Nausea; decreased appetite.	Dry mouth; antiemetic effect; possible nausea.	Nausea, vomiting	Protracted vomiting	Nausea; dry mouth
Urogenital	Contraction of uterus, urinary retention	Renal failure from overdose	Urinary retention	Renal failure from overdose.		
Body Temperature	Elevated; possible hyperthermia	Possible malignant hyperthermia	Mildly elevated, possible hypothermia in children.	Normal to mildly elevated	Moderately elevated	Possible malignant hyperthermia
Other	Piloerection; temporary elevation of free fatty acids	sweating; rhabdomylosis from overdose.	Decreased testosterone level.	Rhabdomylosis from overdose.		

MDMA = 3, 4-methylenedioxymethamphetamine
Sources: Gold (1992); O'Conner, Chang, & Shi (1992); Miller (1991); Milhom (1991); Carroll (1990); Selden et al. (1990); Leikin et al. (1989); Schuckit (1989); Hayner & McKinney (1986).

outcomes (including death in patients on DOM) (Leikin, Krantz et al., 1989) and may exacerbate an unsuspected anticholinergic poisoning.

Patients usually recover sufficiently after several hours to be released into the care of a responsible relative or friend. If psychosis does not resolve within one or two days, ingestion of a longer-acting drug such as PCP or DOM should be suspected (Schuckit, 1989). Any symptoms persisting beyond one to two days raise the strong likelihood of a preexisting or concurrent psychiatric or neurological condition. Psychiatric problems lasting over a month probably are related to preexisting psychopathology.

The predominant treatment for a bad trip or panic attack is general reassurance, rather than medication. A severe panic attack or extreme agitation may require a benzodiazepine or short-acting barbiturate, such as diazepam (10 to 30 mg PO) (Weiss, Greenfield & Mirin, 1994). Chlorpromazine is contraindicated if the substance causing the panic attack is not known. If the substance ingested has anticholinergic action, such as PCP, belladonna, or scopolamine, there is the possibility of coma and cardiorespiratory failure if chlorpromazine or other anticholinergic phenothiazines are administered (Henderson, 1994).

Treatment for hallucinogen-induced delirium generally follows that for simple intoxication, i.e., isolate the patient and minimize sensory input until effects of the drug have worn off. Reassurance that the delirium will abate as the drug is metabolized may also be helpful. Pharmocological treatment is not necessary in most cases. It may be beneficial to avoid medication so as to not confuse the clinical picture. If medication is needed, one with few anticholinergic properties is preferable for the reasons listed above, e.g., diazepam (15 to 30 mg orally, repeating 5 to 20 mg every four hours as needed) (Weiss, Greenfield & Mirin, 1994).

The use of 3,4-methylenedioxymethamphetamine (MDMA, "ecstasy") recently has increased because of its popularity in so-called "rave" dance clubs and its reputation as an enhancer of psychological insight. The psychiatric complications of MDMA intoxication and their treatment are similar to those of other LSD-like hallucinogens. Residual symptoms, including anxiety, insomnia, and psychotic symptoms, can persist for several weeks (Allen, McCann & Ricaurte, 1993; Green, Cross & Goodwin, 1995; Hayner & McKinney, 1986).

Hallucinogen Withdrawal. There is no evidence to suggest the existence of any clinically significant withdrawal syndrome associated with discontinuation of hallucinogen use (Khantzian & McKenna, 1979; Ungerleider & Pechnick, 1992). The rapid development of tolerance (within three to four days) may explain in part why use of LSD-like drugs generally is intermittent.

There currently is no role for medication in the treatment of hallucinogen withdrawal.

MARIJUANA

Marijuana Intoxication. *Clinical Picture:* The effects of marijuana are now known to be mediated by specific cannabinoid receptors on nerve cells (Adams & Martin, 1996; Musty, Reggio & Consroe, 1995) whose regional distribution in the human brain is consistent with the known effects of marijuana (Glass, Dragunow & Faull, 1997).

Psychological/Behavioral Effects of Marijuana Intoxication: Psychological set and social setting contribute substantially to the psychological manifestations of marijuana intoxication. The most common adverse effects are depersonalization (commonly associated with altered time sense) (Mathew, Wilson et al., 1993), acute panic (associated with anxiety), and delirium. Individuals with a history of panic anxiety appear more susceptible to marijuana-induced anxiety (Szuster, Pontius & Campos, 1988).

Psychotic states resulting from marijuana intoxication are rare (Hurlbut, 1991), and may be due in some cases to adulterants such as PCP or LSD. Table 6 summarizes the mental status findings for marijuana intoxication. The realization that there is some cognitive impairment may cause anxiety, further contributing to a heightened sense of loss of control. As the intoxication intensifies, it may progress to a panic state requiring treatment intervention. Delirium, usually as a result of a large dose, may result in depersonalization and derealization. Associated hallucinations (visual and auditory) and paranoia are possible. Oral ingestion yields a higher incidence of adverse reactions than does smoking. Since no immediate psychological effects are experienced, users may ingest larger quantities than expected before they experience the delayed, cumulative effect of a larger dose.

Medical Effects of Marijuana Intoxication: The physiological effects of acute marijuana intoxication are generally mild (Table 7), not usually associated with medical complications, and rarely require medical treatment. There are no established cases of human fatalities from cannabis overdose (Grinspoon & Bakalar, 1992). Single doses of THC (the psychoactive chemical in marijuana) lower testosterone and sperm count in men, but there is no evidence that these changes affect fertility.

Management of Marijuana Intoxication: Both panic and psychosis tend to be self-limited and usually resolve with supportive reassurance. If immediate pharmacological intervention is needed to control agitation, benzodiazepines are preferred to neuroleptics, although there are no controlled studies to confirm this. Psychosis usually responds promptly to low doses of antipsychotic medication (Schnoll & Daghestani, 1986). Physical restraints should be avoided unless essential for safety.

Advances in psychopharmacology may some day provide a specific antidote for marijuana intoxication. A synthetic, highly specific cannabinoid receptor antagonist has recently been developed, which blocks the effects of marijuana in animals (Adams & Martin, 1996; Compton, Aceto et al., 1996; Musty, Reggio & Consroe, 1995). This compound (SR141716A) currently is undergoing initial Phase I trials in humans. Should this or a similar compound prove safe and effective, it could be used to treat marijuana intoxication in the same way that naloxone acts on opiate intoxication.

Marijuana Withdrawal. *Clinical Picture:* Acute marijuana withdrawal is associated with a generally mild syndrome including irritability, restlessness, anorexia, insomnia, diaphoresis, nausea, diarrhea, muscle twitches, and flu-like symptoms (Wesbeck, Schuckit et al., 1996; Duffy & Milin, 1996; Hyman & Tesar, 1994). Other physiological signs may include mild increases in heart rate, blood pressure, and body temperature (Grinspoon & Bakalar, 1992; Schuckit, 1989). Onset of withdrawal symptoms usually is within 24 hours of cessation, with a peak after two to four days and resolution within one to two weeks. Only a minority of even chronic, heavy marijuana users appear to develop a noticeable syndrome (Wesbeck, Schuckit et al., 1996).

Management of Marijuana Withdrawal: Marijuana withdrawal rarely requires medical treatment or hospitalization. Residential treatment may be helpful in some cases of severe psychological dependence to avoid early relapse and promote entry into long-term treatment. In cases of severe withdrawal insomnia, the serotonergic antidepressant trazodone has been reported helpful (Duffy & Milin, 1996).

PHENCYCLIDINE (PCP)

Phencyclidine Intoxication. *Clinical Picture:* Treatment of the acute medical and psychiatric effects of PCP intoxication depends on which of three stages of intoxication the patient is manifesting (Gorelick & Balster, 1995; Rappolt, Gay & Farris, 1980): Stage I—conscious, with psychological effects but (at most) mild physiological effects; Stage II—stuporous or in a light coma, yet responsive to pain; or Stage III—comatose and unresponsive to pain.

Psychological/Behavioral Effects: Table 6 summarizes the psychological and behavioral effects of PCP intoxication and overdose. The time course of psychological effects is highly variable and unpredictable, so that even a recovering patient should be kept under observation until all symptoms have resolved (typically at least 12 hours) (Woolf, Vourakis & Bennett, 1980). Patients may "emerge" from one stage of intoxication to the next; that is, a stuporous or comatose patient in Stage II or III may enter Stage I and become agitated and delirious (Milhorn, 1991; Rappolt, Gay & Farris, 1980). Similarly, a conscious patient in Stage I may suddenly become comatose (Baldridge & Bessen, 1990). The entire clinical episode may require up to six weeks to resolve (Schuckit, 1989).

The psychiatric manifestations of Stage I intoxication can resemble a variety of psychiatric syndromes, making differential diagnosis difficult in the absence of toxicology results or a history of recent PCP intake. Common syndromes seen in treatment settings include delirium, psychosis without delirium, catatonia, hypomania with euphoria, and depression with lethargy. Agitated or bizarre behavior, with increased risk of violence, can occur with any psychiatric presentation (Gorelick & Balster, 1995; Hurlbut, 1991).

Medical Effects: PCP intoxication at the mild Stage I desired by users is associated with few serious medical complications (see Table 7) (Gorelick & Balster, 1995). Common medical complications include nystagmus, hypertension, tachycardia, ataxia, dysarthria, numbness, and hyperreflexia (Weiss, Greenfield & Mirin, 1994). In one study, renal failure and rhabdomyolysis were reported as a possible complication of PCP intoxication (Karch, 1993).

The tachycardia and hypertension seen in Stage I intoxication can be treated with beta-blockers such as propranolol, or calcium channel blockers such as verapamil, although there are no controlled trials to substantiate their efficacy. By contrast, Stage II and III intoxication are medical emergencies that require treatment in a comprehensive medical setting. The focus is on maintaining life-support functions and hastening PCP elimination from the body to shorten the duration of intoxication (Gorelick & Balster, 1995).

Tables 8 and 9 summarize medical treatments for acute PCP intoxication. PCP elimination can be hastened by acidification of urine to below pH 5 and forced diuresis, which increase renal clearance of PCP up to ten-fold. This can be done by administration of ammonium chloride—2.75 mEq/kg in 60 ml of saline every six hours through nasogastric tube and 2 gm of IV ascorbic acid in 500 ml of IV fluid every 6 hours (Weiss, Greenfield & Mirin, 1994). IM ascorbic acid has also been used successfully (Giannini, Loiselle et al., 1987). Caution should be exercised to avoid causing metabolic acidosis, especially in the presence of drugs such as barbiturates and salicylates whose renal clearance is delayed by acidification. Another pharmacokinetic approach currently undergoing animal testing is administration of antiPCP monoclonal antibody binding fragments (Valentine, Mayersohn et al., 1996). These antibody fragments bind to PCP molecules in the blood and other peripheral tissues and prevent them from entering the brain. IV injection of such antiPCP antibody fragments can reverse the behavioral and neurologic effects of a PCP dose (Valentine, Mayersohn et al., 1996) while decreasing brain concentration of PCP up to 80% (Valentine & Owens, 1996). Further research is needed to establish the safety and efficacy of this antibody approach in humans.

Management of Phencyclidine Intoxication: Mild Stage I PCP intoxication is best treated nonpharmacologically. The patient should be isolated in a quiet room, with close, unobtrusive observation, eliminating as much external stimuli as possible. Reassuring, reality-oriented communication ("talking down") should be provided only as long as the patient appears receptive. Frequent or intrusive contact or aggressive medical intervention may exacerbate the situation and should be avoided. Urine acidification may increase renal clearance of PCP, but is of doubtful clinical utility at this level of intoxication (Gorelick, Wilkins & Wong, 1986). Cranberry juice, commonly used as a urine acidifier in the non-medical setting, has not been clearly shown to decrease urine pH (Soloway & Smith, 1988). Pharmacological treatment, when needed, is aimed at sedation or reduction of PCP-induced psychotic

TABLE 8. Procedures for Managing Acute PCP Intoxication

Procedure	Stage I	Stage II	Stage III
Continually assess consciousness	Yes	Yes	Yes
Monitor vital signs (body temp., resp. rate, pulse rate, blood pressure)	Yes	Yes	Yes
Collect specimens (blood, urine)	Yes	Yes	Yes
Cooling procedures	No	Loosen clothing, use sponge, ice, and fans	Sponge and use ice as needed
Urinary bladder catheterization	No	Yes	Yes
Gastric lavage	No	If necessary	Yes
Oral suctioning	Only if necessary	Gently as needed	Yes
Tracheobronchial suctioning	No	Only if necessary	Yes; frequently, as needed
Orotracheal intubation	No	Only if necessary	Yes
Nueromuscular blockade and mechanical ventilation	No	If necessary	If necessary

Source: Milhorn TH (1991). Diagnosis and management of phencyclidine intoxication. *American Family Physician* 43 (4):1293–1302 (with permission from Dr. Milhorn).

TABLE 9. Medications for Treating PCP Intoxication

Medication	STAGE I (conscious)	STAGE II (stuporous to unconscious; deep pain response intact)	STAGE III (unconscious, no deep pain response)
Syrup of ipecac	Not indicated	Not indicated	Not indicated
Activated charcoal	Not indicated	If needed	50–150 mg initially, then 30–40 g every 6–8 hours
Diazepam (*Valium®*)	For agitation: 10–30 mg orally or 2.5 IV, up to 25 mg total	For muscle rigidity: same dosage, IM or IV, as for agitation in Stage I	For muscle rigidity: same as for Stage II. For status epilepticus: 5–10 mg IV, to 30 mg total
Lorazepam (Ativan®)	For agitation: 2–4 mg IM as needed	Not indicated	Not indicated
Haloperidol (Haldol®)	For psychosis: 5–10 mg	Not indicated	Not indicated
5% dextrose in lactated Ringer's sol.	Not indicated	1.5 times maintenance	(as for Stage II)
Ascorbic acid	Not indicated	For urine acidification: 0.5–1.5 g every 4–6 hours as needed to reduce urine pH to <5.5	(as for Stage II)
Hydralazine (*Alazine®*, *Apresoline®*)	Not indicated	For hypertension: 5–10 mg IV	For hypertension: 10–20 mg IV
Propranolol (*Inderal®*)	Not indicated	For hypertension: 1 mg IV every 30 mins as needed up to 8 mg total	(as for Stage II)
Diazoxide (*Hyperstat®*)	Not indicated	Not indicated	For hypertension: 300 mg IV
Feresemide (Lasix®)	Not indicated	For increased urinary output: 20–40 mg IV every 6 hours	(as for Stage II)
Aminophylline	Not indicated	For bronchospasm: 250 mg IV	(as for Stage II)
Naloxone (*Narcan®*)	Not indicated	0.4 IV if respiratory rate < 12/minute	(as for Stage II)
50% dextrose in water	Not indicated	50 mL IV	(as for Stage II)
Diphenhydramine (*Benadryl®*)	50 mg IV	Not indicated	Not indicated

IV = intravenous; IM = intramuscular.
Source: Milhorn TH (1991). Diagnosis and management of phencyclidine intoxication. *American Family Physician* 43 (4):1293–1302 (with permission from Dr. Milhorn).

behavior (Gorelick & Balster, 1995; Zukin & Zukin, 1992). Benzodiazepines are effective, but may delay renal clearance of PCP at high doses (Milhorn, 1991). If intramuscular medication is needed, diazepam may be given (Weiss, Greenfield & Mirin, 1994).

If a neuroleptic is employed for its anti-psychotic properties, high potency medications such as haloperidol or droperidol are preferred because they are less likely to produce anticholinergic or cardiovascular side effects that might exacerbate PCP's own anticholinergic and cardiovascular effects. Because neuroleptics may lower the seizure threshold, they should be avoided if seizures are a concern. No controlled trials have directly compared the efficacy and safety of benzodiazepines versus neuroleptics (Gorelick & Balster, 1995; Zukin & Zukin, 1992).

Although a specific PCP receptor has been identified (part of the NMDA-glutamate excitatory amino acid neurotransmitter receptor complex), no clinically useful receptor antagonist has yet been developed (Gorelick & Balster, 1995).

Ketamine is a PCP analogue, legally marketed as an anesthetic, that has pharmacological effects similar to those of PCP. These include rewarding psychological effects, so that ketamine has enjoyed increasing popularity as a substance of abuse in recent years (Dotson, Ackerman & West, 1995). The spectrum of psychiatric complications from ketamine intoxication appears similar to that from PCP (Siegel, 1978), but there are very little published data on the treatment of ketamine intoxication.

Phencyclidine Withdrawal. *Clinical Picture:* Although PCP withdrawal can occur in animals given large daily doses, physiological withdrawal does not appear to be common in human PCP users, even chronic heavy users (Gorelick & Balster, 1995; Weiss, Greenfield & Mirin, 1994; Carroll, 1990). One study of 68 chronic PCP users reported that one-third sought treatment for symptoms associated with cessation of PCP use, which included depression, anxiety, irritability, hypersomnolence, and craving for PCP (Tennant, Rawson & McCann, 1981), although it was not clear to what extent these represented a true withdrawal syndrome. Tricyclic antidepressants such as desipramine may reduce the psychological symptoms associated with discontinuation of PCP use, but there is no evidence that such treatment actually improves the outcome of PCP addiction (Giannini, Loiselle et al., 1993; Tennant, Rawson & McCann, 1981).

Prolonged Psychiatric Sequelae (Flashbacks) of Phencyclidine Withdrawal: All hallucinogens and PCP have the potential to trigger long-lasting (days to weeks) psychiatric sequelae, ranging from prolonged states of anxiety or depression to both mild and pronounced psychotic states. The risk for prolonged psychiatric reactions appears to depend on several factors: the patient's premorbid psychopathology, the number of prior exposures to the drug, and history of polydrug use (Strassman, 1984). Prolonged reactions occasionally are reported in apparently well-adjusted individuals who have no obvious risk factors. Some users, while maintaining otherwise normal functioning, suffer from perceptual disorders that may last for years, including auditory and visual hallucinations such as afterimages seen from moving objects (Weiss & Millman, 1991). Prolonged psychotic reactions to PCP almost always are associated with premorbid psychopathology (Erard, Luisada & Peele, 1980; Gwirtsman, Winkop et al., 1984).

Treatment of prolonged anxiety or depression is usually psychosocial, but may involve medication if symptoms become severe enough. Treatment of prolonged psychosis essentially follows guidelines for treatment of chronic functional psychosis. Patients may present with wide-ranging symptomatology, including apathy, insomnia, hypomania, dissociative states, formal thought disorder, hallucinations, delusions, and paranoia. An observation period of at least several days with no or minimal medication (e.g., sedatives) is helpful to ensure an accurate diagnosis. The term "flashback" has been given to brief episodes (usually lasting a few seconds) in which aspects of a previous hallucinogenic drug experience are unexpectedly reexperienced. Flashbacks are fairly rare and are associated principally with the LSD-like hallucinogens (Schick & Smith, 1970), although they can occur following use of MDMA, PCP, and, occasionally, marijuana (Weiss, Greenfield & Mirin, 1994). Flashbacks can precipitate considerable anxiety, particularly if the original drug experience had negative overtones. Re-experience of perceptual effects is most common, but somatic and emotional components of the original experience can re-occur too. Flashbacks may occur spontaneously or be triggered by stress, exercise, another drug (such as marijuana), or a situation reminiscent of the original drug experience. Not knowing when another flashback may occur can be quite unsettling to some patients.

Flashbacks almost always are brief and self-limiting. Treatment usually involves no more than alleviating anxiety with supportive reassurance. Over time, flashbacks tend to decrease in frequency, duration, and intensity, as long as no further hallucinogens are taken (Strassman, 1984). Benzodiazepines may be helpful in treating secondary anxiety. Neuroleptics are not indicated, as haloperidol has been reported to transiently worsen flashbacks (Moskowitz, 1971; Strassman, 1984). Recent case reports suggest that selective serotonin reuptake inhibitor antidepressants or naltrexone may help reduce flashbacks (Lerner, Oyffe et al., 1997; Young, 1997). Flashbacks occurring more than a year after the original drug experience suggest the probability of another etiology, such as a functional psychosis (Mirin & Weiss, 1991).

MULTIPLE DRUG WITHDRAWAL

Multiple Sedative-Hypnotics. Withdrawal from dependence on multiple sedative-hypnotic/anxiolytic agents, including alcohol, is best managed like withdrawal from a single such drug, by using tapering dosages of a single, longer-acting sedative-hypnotic (Gorelick, Wilkins & Wong, 1986; Schuckit, 1989). It usually is safest to focus on managing withdrawal of the longer-acting drug, while keeping alert to atypical symptomatology. The time course of withdrawal from multiple sedative-hypnotics/anxiolytics is more unpredictable than from single drugs, e.g., there may be a bimodal time course of symptomatology if one drug is short-acting and the other longer-acting. The dose tapering rate usually should not exceed 10% a day. Safe withdrawal may be facilitated by use of an anti-convulsant such as carbamazepine (Tegretol®), even in the absence of epilepsy or withdrawal seizures. Carbamazepine has proved effective in clinical trials of withdrawal from single sedative-hypnotics (Ries, Cullison et al., 1991), but has not yet been studied in withdrawal from multiple drugs.

Sedative-Hypnotics/Other Drugs. In the pharmacological management of patients withdrawing from both sedative-hypnotics/anxiolytics and CNS stimulants (such as cocaine or amphetamine), it is preferable to treat the sedative-hypnotic/anxiolytic withdrawal first, since this poses the most difficulty and medical risk. For concurrent addiction to sedative-hypnotics/anxiolytics and opiates, concurrent pharmacological treatment is recommended (Gorelick, Wilkins & Wong, 1986; Schuckit, 1989). The patient may be stabilized on an opiate (preferably oral methadone, although codeine can be used if methadone is not available) at the same time that the sedative-hypnotic/anxiolytic dose is tapered by 10% per day. Once sedative-hypnotic/anxiolytic withdrawal has been completed, opiate withdrawal can begin. Clonidine has been suggested as adjunctive treatment for such mixed sedative-hypnotic/opiate withdrawal, since it can alleviate withdrawal symptoms from both drug classes, but this has not been systematically evaluated.

SPECIAL POPULATIONS

Adolescents. There has been little systematic study of drug intoxication or withdrawal in adolescents. Recent research suggests that symptoms of drug dependence and withdrawal similar to those in adults are present in adolescent substance abusers (Stewart & Brown, 1995), suggesting that adolescents may respond to the same treatment methods used in adults. Future clinical research is needed to determine optimal treatment approaches for adolescents.

Women. There has been little systematic study of possible gender differences in the treatment of intoxication/overdose and withdrawal. Limited anecdotal evidence suggests that pharmacological treatment for women can be similar to that for men, taking into account possible gender differences in medication pharmacokinetics. One area requiring special attention is the effects of intoxication/overdose and withdrawal and their treatment on pregnancy and the fetus. For example, the benefit to mother and fetus of successful withdrawal treatment must be weighed against the possible ill effects on the fetus of medications such as benzodiazepines and anticonvulsants (Briggs, Freeman & Jaffe, 1990), and the risks of inadequately treated withdrawal. Another area in need of further research is the influence of the menstrual cycle on intoxication and withdrawal and their treatment.

The Elderly. Little information is available regarding pharmacologic treatment of intoxication/overdose and withdrawal in the elderly and how it might differ from treatment in younger individuals. Benzodiazapines should be used with caution in elderly patients because of an increased risk of development of overdose, dependency, and withdrawal above normal populations (Shorr & Robin 1994). The elderly are more susceptible to medication-induced delirium, so any medication must be used cautiously in this population (Sumner & Simons, 1994). The recommended dosing approach is to "start low and go slow," i.e., start the medication at a lower dose and increase the dose in smaller increments than would be used in younger individuals. Because delirium may present with diverse clinical features, it should be considered in any elderly patient with a change in mental status, personality, or behavior.

REFERENCES

Abel FL & Wilson SP (1992). The effects of nimodipine on cocaine toxicity. *American Journal of the Medical Sciences* 303:372–378.

Abraham HD, Aldridge AM & Gogia P (1996). The psychopharmacology of hallucinogens. *Neuropsychopharmacology* 14:285–298.

Adams IB & Martin BR (1996). Cannabis: pharmacology and toxicology in animals and humans. *Addiction* 91:1585–1614.

Allen RP, McCann UD & Ricaurte GA (1993). Persistent effects of (+)3,4-methylenedioxymethamphetamine (MDMA, "Ecstasy") on human sleep. *Sleep* 16:560–564.

Ansah T-A, Wade LH & Shockley DC (1993). Effects of calcium channel entry blockers on cocaine and amphetamine-induced motor activities and toxicities. *Life Sciences* 53:1947–1956.

Aronow R, Miceli JN & Done AK (1980). A therapeutic approach to the acutely intoxicated PCP patient. *Journal of Psychoactive Drugs* 12:259–267.

Baldridge BE & Bessen HA (1990). Phencyclidine. *Emergency Medicine Clinics of North America* 8(3):541–549.

Beebe DK & Walley EJ (1994). Ice: A new drug of concern. *Journal of the Mississippi State Medical Association* 35:225–227.

Benazzi F & Mazzoli M (1991). Psychiatric illness associated with "ecstasy" (letter). *The Lancet* 338:1520.

Bost RO (1988). 3,4-Methylenedioxymethamphetamine (MDMA) and other amphetamine derivatives. *Journal of Forensic Science* 33:576–587.

Bowers MB Jr (1972). Acute psychosis induced by psychotomimetic drug abuse: 2. *Archives of General Psychiatry* 27:440–442.

Briggs GG, Freeman RK & Yaffe SJ (1990). *Reference Guide to Fetal and Neonatal Risk: Drugs in Pregnancy and Lactation, 3rd Edition*. Baltimore, MD: Williams & Wilkins.

Callaway CW & Clark RF (1994). Hyperthermia in psychostimulant overdose. *Annals of Emergency Medicine* 24:68–75.

Carroll ME (1990). PCP and hallucinogens. *Advances in Alcohol and Substance Abuse* 9(1–2):167–190.

Chang G & Kosten TR (1992). Emergency management of acute drug intoxication. In JH Lowinson, P Ruiz, RB Millman & JG Langrod (eds.) *Substance Abuse: A Comprehensive Textbook (2nd Edition)*. Baltimore, MD: Williams & Wilkins, 437–445.

Compton DR, Aceto MD, Lowe J & Martin BR (1996). *In vivo* characterization of a specific cannabinoid receptor antagonist (SR141716A): Inhibition of D^9-tetrahydrocannabinol-induced responses and apparent agonist activity. *Journal of Pharmacology and Experimental Therapeutics* 277:586–594.

Dackis CA & Gold MS (1985). Pharmacological approaches to cocaine addiction. *Journal of Substance Abuse Treatment* 2:139–145.

Derlet RW & Albertson TE (1989). Potentiation of cocaine toxicity with calcium channel blockers. *American Journal of Emergency Medicine* 7:464–468.

Devenyi P (1989). Cocaine complications and pseudocholinesterase. *Annals of Internal Medicine* 110:167–168.

Dotson JW, Ackerman DL & West LJ (1995). Ketamine abuse. *Journal of Drug Issues* 25:751–757.

Duffy A & Milin R (1996). Case study: Withdrawal syndrome in adolescent chronic cannabis users. *Journal of American Academy of Child Adolescent Psychiatry* 35:1618–1621.

Ellison JM & Jacobs D (1986). Emergency psychopharmacology: A review and update. *Annals of Emergency Medicine* 15:962–968.

Erard R, Luisada PV & Peele R (1980). The PCP psychosis: Prolonged intoxication or drug precipitated functional illness? *Journal of Psychedelic Drugs* 12(3–4):235–250.

Extein I & Dackis CA (1987). Brain mechanisms in cocaine dependency. In AM Washton & MS Gold (eds.) *Cocaine: A Clinician's Handbook*. New York, NY: Guilford Press, 73–84.

Foulks EF & Pena JM (1995). Ethnicity and psychotherapy. A component in the treatment of cocaine addiction in African Americans. *Psychiatric Clinics of North America* 18:607–20.

Franz DN (1985). In AG Gilman, LS Goodman, TW Rall & F Murad (eds.) *The Pharmacological Basis of Therapeutics (7th edition)*. New York, NY: Macmillan, 582–588.

Gawin FH (1986). Neuroleptic reduction of cocaine-induced paranoia but not euphoria? *Psychopharmacology* 90:142–143.

Gawin FH & Ellinwood E (1988). Cocaine and other stimulants. *The New England Journal of Medicine* 318(18):1173–1182.

Gawin FH & Kleber HD (1986). Abstinence symptomatology and psychiatric diagnosis in cocaine abusers. *Archives of General Psychiatry* 43:107–113.

Giannini AJ, Loiselle RH, Graham BH et al. (1993). Behavioral response to buspirone in cocaine and phencyclidine withdrawal. *Journal of Substance Abuse Treatment* 10:523–527.

Giannini AJ, Loiselle RH, DiMarzio LR & Giannini MC (1987). Augmentation of haloperidol by ascorbic acid in phencyclidine intoxication. *American Journal of Psychiatry* 144:1207–1209.

Gill K, Gillespie, HK, Hollister LE et al. (1991). Dopamine depletion hypothesis of cocaine dependence: A test. *Human Psychopharmacology* 6:25–29.

Gillin JC, Pulviranti L, Withers N, Golshan S & Koob G (1994). The effects of lisuride on mood and sleep during acute withdrawal in stimulant abusers: A preliminary report. *Biological Psychiatry* 35:843–849.

Glass M, Dragunow M & Faull RLM (1997). Cannabinoid receptors in the human brain: A detailed anatomical and quantitative autoradiographic study in the fetal, neonatal and adult human brain. *Neuroscience* 77:299–318.

Gold MS (1992). Cocaine (and crack): Clinical aspects. In JH Lowinson, P Ruiz, RB Millman & JG Langrod (eds.) *Substance Abuse: A Comprehensive Textbook, 2nd Edition*. Baltimore, MD: Williams & Wilkins, 205–221.

Gold MS, Miller NS & Jonas JM (1992). Cocaine (and crack): Neurobiology. In JH Lowinson, P Ruiz, RB Millman & JG Langrod (eds.) *Substance Abuse: A Comprehensive Textbook, 2nd Edition*. Baltimore, MD: Williams & Wilkins, 222–235.

Goldfrank LR & Hoffman RS (1991). The cardiovascular effects of cocaine. *Annals of Emergency Medicine* 20:165–175.

Goldfrank LR & Hoffman RS (1992). The cardiovascular effects of cocaine: Update 1992. *Acute Cocaine Intoxication, NIDA Research Monograph 123*. Rockville, MD: National Institute on Drug Abuse, 70–108.

Gorelick D, Wilkins J &Wong C (1986). Diagnosis and treatment of chronic phencyclidine abuse. *NIDA Research Monograph 64* [title of monograph?]. Rockville, MD: National Institute on Drug Abuse, 218–228.

Gorelick DA (1993). Overview of pharmacological treatment approaches for alcohol and other drug addiction: Intoxication, withdrawal, and relapse prevention. *Psychiatric Clinics of North America* 16(1):141–156.

Gorelick DA (1995). Pharmacologic therapies for cocaine addiction. In NS Miller & MS Gold (eds.) *Pharmacologic Therapies for Drug and Alcohol Addiction*. New York, NY: Marcel Dekker, 143–157.

Gorelick DA (1998). Enhancing cocaine metabolism with butyrylcholinesterase as a treatment strategy. *Drug and Alcohol Dependence* 48:159–165.

Gorelick DA & Balster RL (1995). Phencyclidine (PCP). In FE Bloom & DJ Kupfer (eds.) *Psychopharmacology: The Fourth Generation of Progress*. New York, NY: Raven Press, 1767–1776.

Gorelick DA, Stauffer R, Zubieta J-K & Frost JJ (1997). Phenomenology of inpatient cocaine withdrawal. *Problems of Drug Dependence 1996, NIDA Research Monograph 174*. Rockville, MD: National Institute on Drug Abuse, 185.

Green AR, Cross AJ & Goodwin GM (1995). Review of the pharmacology and clinical pharmacology of 3,4-methylenedioxymethamphetamine (MDMA or "Ecstasy"). *Psychopharmacology* 119:247–260.

Grinspoon L & Bakalar JD (1981). Marijuana. In JH Lowinson & P Ruiz (eds.) *Substance Abuse: Clinical Problems and Perspectives*. Baltimore, MD: Williams & Wilkins, 140–147.

Grinspoon L & Bakalar JD (1992). Marihuana. In JH Lowinson, P Ruiz, RB Millman & JG Langrod (eds.) *Substance Abuse: A Comprehensive Textbook, 2nd Edition*. Baltimore, MD: Williams & Wilkins, 236–246.

Grof S (1980). *LSD Psychotherapy*. Pomona, CA: Hunter House, 233–237.

Gwirtsman HE, Winkop W, Gorelick DA et al. (1984). Phencyclidine intoxication: Incidence, clinical patterns and course of treatment. *Research Communications in Psychology, Psychiatry and Behavior* 9:405–410.

Hayner GN & McKinney H (1986). MDMA: The dark side of ecstasy. *Journal of Psychoactive Drugs* 18(4):341–347.

Henderson LA (1994). Adverse reactions to LSD. In LA Henderson & WJ Glas (eds.) *LSD: Still With Us After All These Years*. New York, NY: Lexington Books, 77–98.

Henry JA, Jeffreys CJ & Dawling S (1992). Toxicity and deaths from 3,4-methylenedioxymethamphetamine ("ecstasy"). *Lancet* 340:384–387.

Hoffman RS, Henry GC, Howland MA, Weisman RS, Weil L & Goldfrank LR (1992). Association between life-threatening cocaine toxicity and plasma cholinesterase activity. *Annals of Emergency Medicine* 21:247–253.

Hoffman RS, Morasco MS & Goldfrank LR (1996). Administration of purified human plasma cholinesterase protects against cocaine toxicity in mice. *Clinical Toxicology* 34:259–266.

Hollander JE (1995). The management of cocaine-associated myocardial ischemia. *The New England Journal of Medicine* 333:1267–1272.

Hurlbut KM (1991). Drug-induced psychoses. *Emergency Medicine Clinics of North America* 9(1):31–52.

Johanson CE & Fischman MW (1989). The pharmacology of cocaine related to its abuse. *Pharmacological Review* 41:3–52.

Karch SB (1993). *The Pathology of Drug Abuse*. Boca Raton, FL: CRC Press.

Khantzian EJ & McKenna GJ (1979). Acute toxic and withdrawal reactions associated with drug use and abuse. *Annals of Internal Medicine* 90:361–372.

King GR & Ellinwood EH Jr (1992). Amphetamines and other stimulants. In JH Lowinson, P Ruiz, RB Millman & JG Langrod (eds.) *Substance Abuse: A Comprehensive Textbook, 2nd Edition*. Baltimore, MD: Williams & Wilkins, 247–270.

Kosten T & Kleber H (1988). Rapid death during cocaine abuse. *American Journal of Drug and Alcohol Abuse* 14:335–346.

Kulig K (1990). LSD. *Emergency Medicine Clinics of North America* 8(3):551–558.

Kumor K, Sherer M & Jaffe J (1986). Haloperidol-induced dystonia in cocaine addicts. *Lancet* 2:1341–1342.

Kunisaki TA & Augenstein WL (1994). Drug- and toxin-induced seizures. *Emergency Medicine Clinics of North America* 12:1027–1055.

Lago JA & Kosten TR (1994). Stimulant withdrawal. *Addiction* 89:1477–1481.

Leikin JB, Krantz AJ, Zell-Kanter M, Barkin RL & Hryhorczuk DO (1989). Clinical features and management of intoxication due to hallucinogenic drugs. *Medical Toxicology & Adverse Drug Experiences* 4(5):324–350.

Lerner AG, Oyffe I, Isaacs G & Sigal M (1997). Naltrexone treatment of hallucinogen persisting perception disorder. *American Journal of Psychiatry* 154:437.

Markou A & Koob GF (1992). Bromocriptine reverses the elevation in intracranial self-stimulation thresholds observed in a rat model of cocaine withdrawal. *Neuropsychopharmacology* 7:213–224.

Martin W & Sloan J (1971). Pharmacology and classification of LSD-like hallucinogens. In W Martin (ed.) *Hanbuch der experimentellen Pharmakologie* (Vol. 45, Part 2). Berlin, Germany: Springer verlag, 305–368.

Mathew RJ, Wilson WH, Humphreys D, Lowe JV & Weithe KE (1993). Depersonalization after marijuana smoking. *Biological Psychiatry* 33:431–441.

Milhorn TH (1991). Diagnosis and management of phencyclidine intoxication. *American Family Physician* 43(4):1293–1302.

Miller NS (1991). Special problems of the alcohol and multiple-drug dependent: Clinical interactions and detoxification. In RJ Frances & SI Miller (eds.) *Clinical Textbook of Addictive Disorders*. New York, NY: Guilford Press, 194–218.

Miller PL, Gay GR, Ferris KC & Anderson S (1992). Treatment of acute adverse psychedelic reactions: "I've tripped and I can't get down." *Journal of Psychoactive Drugs* 24(3):277–279.

Mirin SM & Weiss RD (1991). Substance abuse and mental illness. In RJ Frances & SI Miller (eds.) *Clinical Textbook of Addictive Disorders*. New York, NY: Guilford Press, 271–298.

Moskowitz D (1971). Use of haloperidol to reduce LSD flashbacks. *Military Medicine* 136:754–757.

Moskowitz RA & Byrd T (1983). Rescuing the angel within: PCP related self-emulation. *Psychosomatics* 24:402–406.

Musty RE, Reggio P & Consroe P (1995). A review of recent advances in cannabinoid research and the 1994 International Symposium, on Cannabis and Cannabinoids. *Life Sciences* 56:1933–1940.

Nademanee K, Gorelick DA, Josephson MA et al. (1989). Myocardial ischemia during cocaine withdrawal. *Annals of Internal Medicine* 111:876–880.

O'Connor PG, Chang G & Shi J (1992). Medical complications of cocaine use. In TR Kosten & HD Kleber (eds.) *Clinician's Guide to Cocaine Addiction: Theory, Research, and Treatment*. New York, NY: Guilford Press, 241–272.

Om A, Ellahham S, Ornato JP et al. (1993). Medical complications of cocaine: Possible relationship to low plasma cholinesterase enzyme. *American Heart Journal* 125:1114–1117.

Pearsall HR & Rosen MI (1992). Inpatient treatment of cocaine addiction. In TR Kosten & HD Kleber (eds.) *Clinician's Guide to Cocaine Addiction: Theory, Research, and Treatment*. New York, NY: Guilford Press, 314–334.

Ramoska E & Sacchetti A (1985). Propranol-induced hypertension in treatment of cocaine intoxication. *Annals of Emergency Medicine* 14:1112–1113.

Rappolt RT, Gay GR & Farris RD (1980). Phencyclidine (PCP) intoxication: Diagnosis in stages and algorithms of treatment. *Clinical Toxicology* 16:509–529.

Renfroe C & Messinger TA (1985). Street Drug Analysis: An eleven-year perspective on illicit drug alteration. *Seminar on Adolescent Medicine* 1:247–258.

Ricaurte G, Bryan G, Strauss L, Seiden L & Schuster C (1985). Hallucinogenic amphetamine selectively destroys brain serotonin nerve terminals. *Science* 229:986–988.

Ries R, Cullison S, Horn R et al. (1991). Benzodiazepine withdrawal: Clinicians' ratings of carbamazepine treatment versus traditional taper methods. *Journal of Psychoactive Drugs* 23:73–76.

Roberts D (1987). Self-increased self-administration of cocaine following haloperidol. *Pharmacology, Biochemistry and Behavior* 26:37–43.

Rosenberg J, Pentel P, Pond S, Benowitz N & Olson K (1986). Hyperthermia associated with drug intoxication. *Critical Care Medicine* 14(11):964–969.

Roth D, Alacron FJ, Fernandez JA, Preston RA & Bourgoignie JJ (1988). Acute rhabdomyolysis associated with cocaine intoxication. *The New England Journal of Medicine* 319:673–677.

Satel SL, Price LH, Palumbo JM et al. (1991). Clinical phenomenology and neurobiology of cocaine abstinence: A prospective inpatient study. *American Journal of Psychiatry* 148(12):1712–1716.

Schick JFE & Smith DE (1970). An analysis of the LSD flashback. *Journal of Psychedelic Drugs* 3:13–19.

Schindler CW, Carmona GN, Goldberg SR et al. (1996). Influence of butyrylcholinesterase (BChE) on cocaine–induced motor activity in rats. *Society for Neuroscience Abstracts* 22(Part 3):1930.

Schnoll SH & Daghestani AN (1986). Treatment of marijuana abuse. *Psychiatric Annals* 16:249–254.

Schuckit MA (1989). *Drug and Alcohol Abuse: A Clinical Guide to Diagnosis and Treatment (3rd edition)*. New York, NY: Plenum Publishing.

Schwartz RH (1988). Urine testing in the detection of abuse. *Archives of Internal Medicine* 148:2407–2412.

Schwartz RH & Smith DE (1988). Hallucinogenic mushrooms. *Clinical Pediatrics* 27(2):7073.

Selden BS, Clark RF & Curry SC (1990). Marijuana. *Emergency Medicine Clinics of North America* 8(3):527–539.

Sherer MA, Kumor KM, Jaffe JH et al. (1989). Effects of intravenous cocaine are partially attenuated by haloperidol. *Psychiatry Research* 27:117–125.

Shorr RI & Robin DW (1994). Rational use of benzodiazepines in the elderly. *Drugs and Aging* 4:9–20.

Shulgin AT (1986). The background and chemistry of MDMA. *Journal of Psychoactive Drugs* 18(4):291–303.

Siegel RK (1978). Phencyclidine and ketamine intoxication: A study of four populations of recreational users. *Phencycledine (PCP) Abuse: An Appraisal, NIDA Research Monograph 21*. Rockville, MD: National Institute on Drug Abuse, 119–147.

Siegel RK (1984). Cocaine smoking disorders: Diagnosis and treatment. *Psychiatric Annals* 14:728–732.

Smart RG & Anglin L (1987). Do we know the lethal dose of cocaine? *Journal of Forensic Sciences* 32:303–312.

Soloway MS & Smith RA (1988). Cranberry juice as a urine acidifier. *Journal of the American Medical Association* 260:1465.

Stewart DG & Brown SA (1995). Withdrawal and dependency symptoms among adolescent alcohol and drug abusers. *Addiction* 90:627–635.

Strassman RJ (1984). Adverse reactions to psychedelic drugs: A review of the literature. *Journal of Nervous and Mental Disease* 172(10):577–595.

Sumner AD & Simons RJ (1994). Delirium in the hospitalized elderly. *Cleveland Clinic Journal of Medicine* 61:258–262.

Szuster RR, Pontius EB & Campos PE (1988). Marijuana sensitivity and panic anxiety. *Journal of Clinical Psychiatry* 49:427–429.

Teller DW & Devenyi P (1988). Bromocriptine in cocaine withdrawal—Does it work? *International Journal of the Addictions* 23:1197–1205.

Tennant FS (1986). The clinical syndrome of marijuana dependence. *Psychiatric Annals* 16(4):225–242.

Tennant FS, Rawson RA & McCann M (1981). Withdrawal from chronic phencyclidine dependence with desipramine. *American Journal of Psychiatry* 138:845–847.

Ungar JR (1989). Current drugs of abuse. In GR Schwartz, N Bukar, BK Hanke, MA Mangeben, T Mayer & JR Ungar (eds). *Emergency Medicine: The Essential Update*. Philadelphia, PA: WB Saunders, 210–224.

Ungerleider JT & Pechnick R (1992). Hallucinogens. In JH Lowinson, P Ruiz, RB Millman & JG Langrod (eds.) *Substance Abuse: A Comprehensive Textbook, 2nd Edition*. Baltimore, MD: Williams & Wilkins, 280–289.

Valentine JL & Owens SM (1996). Antiphencyclidine monoclonal antibody therapy significantly changes phencyclidine concentrations in brain and other tissues in rats. *Journal of Pharmacology and Experimental Therapeutics* 278:717–724.

Valentine JL, Mayersohn M, Wessinger WD, Arnold LW & Owens SM (1996). Antiphencyclidine monoclonal Fab fragments reverse phencyclidine-induced behavioral effects and ataxia in rats. *Journal of Pharmacology and Experimental Therapeutics* 278:709–716.

Volkow ND, Fowler JS, Wolf AP et al. (1992). Effects of chronic cocaine abuse on postsynaptic dopamine receptors. *American Journal of Psychiatry* 147:719–724.

Vree TB & Henderson PTH (1980). Pharmacokinetics of amphetamine: In vivo and in vitro studies of the factors governing their elimination. In J Cadwell (ed.) *Amphetamines and Related Stimulants: Chemical, Biological, Clinical, and Social Aspects*. Boca Raton, FL: CRC Press.

Weddington WW, Brown BS, Haertzen CA et al. (1991). Comparison of amantidine and desipramine combined with psychotherapy for treatment of alcoholism and drug abuse. *American Journal of Alcohol and Drug Abuse* 17(2):137–152.

Weiss CJ & Millman RB (1991). Hallucinogens, phencyclidine, marijuana, inhalants. In RJ Frances & MI Sheldon (eds.) *Clinical Textbook of Addictive Disorders*. New York, NY: Guilford Press, 146–170.

Weiss RD, Greenfield, SF & Mirin SM (1994). Intoxication and withdrawal syndromes. In SE Hyman (ed.) *Manual of Psychiatric Emergencies*. Boston, MA: Little, Brown & Co., 217–227.

Wetli CV & Fisbain D (1985). Cocaine-induced psychosis and sudden death. *Journal of Forensic Sciences* 30:873–880.

Wesbeck GA, Schuckit MA, Kalmijn JA, Tipp JE, Bucholz KK & Smith TL (1996). An evaluation of the history of a marijuana withdrawal syndrome in a large population. *Addiction* 9:1469–1478.

Wolfsohn R & Angrist B (1990). A pilot trial of levodopa/carbidopa in early cocaine abstinence. *Journal of Clinical Psychopharmacology* 10:440–442.

Woolf DS, Vourakis C & Bennett G (1980). Guidelines for management of acute phencyclidine intoxication. *Critical Care Update* 7(6):16–24.

Yang G, Chun J, Arakawa–Uramoto H et al. (1996). Anticocaine catalytic antibodies: A synthetic approach to improved antibody diversity. *Journal of the American Chemical Society* 118:5881–5890.

Young CR (1997). Sertraline treatment of hallucinogen persisting perceptual disorder. *Journal of Clinical Psychiatry* 58:85.

Young T, Lawson GW & Gacono CB (1987). Clinical aspects of phencyclidine (PCP). *International Journal of the Addictions* 22:1–15.

Zukin SR & Zukin RS (1992). Phencyclidine. In JH Lowinson, P Ruiz, RB Millman & JG Langrod (eds.) *Substance Abuse: A Comprehensive Textbook, 2nd Edition*. Baltimore, MD: Williams & Wilkins, 290–302.

Zweben JE & O'Connell K (1992). Strategies for breaking marijuana dependence. *Journal of Psychoactive Drugs* 24(2):165–171.

CHAPTER 6

Management of Nicotine Withdrawal

Terry A. Rustin, M.D., FASAM

Management of Withdrawal
Treatment of Nicotine Withdrawal in Smokers Who Do Not Intend to Quit Smoking

Nicotine withdrawal is thought to be present after daily use of nicotine for at least several weeks and when abrupt cessation of nicotine use or reduction in the amount of nicotine used is followed within 24 hours by at least four of the following signs or symptoms: (1) craving for nicotine, (2) irritability, frustration or anger, (3) anxiety, (4) difficulty concentrating, (5) restlessness, (6) decreased heart rate, or (7) increased appetite or weight gain.

MANAGEMENT OF WITHDRAWAL

Clinical Picture. The symptoms that accompany abrupt cessation of tobacco use are variable in intensity and duration. At lower levels of dependence, patients experience less severe withdrawal symptoms (Jarvik & Henningfield, 1988).

Withdrawal signs and symptoms typically include anxiety, increased appetite, craving, irritability, decreased heart rate, restlessness, and difficulty concentrating.

The management of nicotine withdrawal typically involves: (1) reversing withdrawal symptoms at the receptor level, (2) reducing somatic and psychological withdrawal symptoms, (3) treating or preventing craving for nicotine (and thus preventing relapse), (4) reducing other symptoms that develop after smoking cessation, and (5) making smoking aversive.

Pharmacotherapies for Nicotine Withdrawal. Pharmacologic agents used in the management of nicotine withdrawal include:

Lobeline: Lobeline antagonizes nicotine peripherally at the acetylcholine-N receptor site and has thus been promoted as an agent to reduce the central agonist effects of nicotine. However, very little lobeline crosses the blood-brain barrier, and it therefore has little activity in the central nervous system. Lobeline has not been demonstrated to be a reliable aid in smoking cessation.

Silver acetate: Silver acetate has been available for decades as a smoking cessation aid. After ingesting silver acetate, many smokers find that cigarette smoke takes on a disagreeable taste. Evidence for its effectiveness, however, has not been demonstrated.

Benzocaine: Benzocaine produces local anesthesia in the mouth, reducing the sensory pleasure of smoking. It does not affect the response to nicotine, and has not been shown to improve smoking cessation rates.

Buspirone: Buspirone (BuSpar®) has been used to treat the anxiety associated with nicotine withdrawal, with conflicting results. Some studies show short-term benefit (Hilleman, Mohiuddin et al., 1992), while others do not (Robinson, Pettice et al., 1992), but none has evaluated buspirone's long-term efficacy.

Benzodiazepines: Benzodiazepines also have been used to treat the anxiety often associated with smoking cessation; most addiction medicine specialists would resist the use of these drugs for a relatively benign withdrawal state. Glassman and colleagues (1984) used alprazolam (Xanax®) as the active placebo drug in a study of clonidine versus active placebo versus inactive placebo in smoking cessation; subjects in the clonidine and alprazolam groups described reduced anxiety and irritability, but only those on clonidine described a reduction in craving for a cigarette.

Scopolamine: Scopolamine transdermal patches (Transderm ScÜp®) have been used at Fair Oaks Hospital in New Jersey. The logic for the use of scopolamine (or other anticholinergic drugs) is based on nicotine's role as an acetylcholine receptor agonist (Benowitz, 1988), but the data on anticholinergic treatment still are preliminary.

Ondansetron: One small study evaluated the effectiveness of ondansetron (Zofran®), a selective serotonin blocking agent used as an antiemetic in chemotherapy, for use in smoking cessation (Cropp & Gora-Harper, 1995). The trial did not clearly demonstrate a beneficial effect of the drug.

Clonidine: While investigating the use of clonidine (Catapres®) for the treatment of hypertension, Glassman noted that some of the subjects reported a decrease in their "urge to smoke"; he followed this observation with a series of trials that evaluated clonidine's potential as an adjunctive medication in the treatment of nicotine dependence (Glassman, Jackson et al., 1984; Glassman, Stetner et al., 1988). Clonidine, in doses of 0.1 to 0.2 mg, two to three times a day, or the use of the clonidine patch, appears to reduce the urge to smoke. The long-term data on clonidine, however, suggest that used alone, it does not alter cessation rates after the initial treatment. Combining clonidine with smoking cessation therapy may help to improve success rates.

Buproprion: In 1997, a sustained-release form of buproprion (Zyban®) was approved for the treatment of nicotine dependence. Buproprion is a selective presynaptic dopamine reuptake inhibitor, approved for the treatment of depression as Wellbutrin®. Buproprion first was proposed as a smoking cessation aid in 1989 by Linda Ferry after she noted that some patients treated with it for depression reported a decreased desire to smoke (Ferry, Robbins et al., 1992; Ferry & Burchette, 1994). Larger controlled studies have confirmed that buproprion reduces the desire to smoke and improves quit rates at levels comparable to those seen with nicotine patches (Hurt, Dale et al., 1992), and concomitant use of bupriοprion and a nicotine patch produced higher quit rates than buproprion alone (Fiore, Leischow et al., 1997). The mechanism of its action in nicotine dependence has not been well clarified; although buproprion is effective as an antidepressant with dopaminergic properties, its effectiveness in smoking cessation appears to be distinct from its antidepressant properties. Buproprion is the first non-nicotine agent approved by the Food and Drug Administration (FDA) for treatment of smoking cessation, and its approval presages the development of other medications targeting the biochemical basis of nicotine dependence.

Nicotine Replacement Therapies. While several of the non-nicotine agents just described reduce nicotine withdrawal symptoms and signs, they do not replace the nicotine from which the individual is withdrawing. Anxiety, restlessness, hunger, confusion and irritability and sleep disturbances may last for several weeks after the last cigarette and may be too much for the smoker to handle. While none of these symptoms represent a serious medical problem, they are sufficiently uncomfortable that patients are unwilling to tolerate them, and they are frequently the cause of relapses back to smoking (Henningfield, 1990). Therefore, physicians can contribute to patients' recovery from nicotine dependence by treating their withdrawal symptoms (Henningfield, 1984a; Henningfield & Woodson, 1989; Jarvik & Henningfield, 1988; Pomerleau & Pomerleau, 1988).

Treatment of nicotine withdrawal symptoms has taken on greater importance as hospitals, treatment centers, public agencies, and outpatient clinics have adopted smokefree policies. Whether or not programs using these facilities choose to address the nicotine dependence of their clients and patients, they cannot avoid addressing their smoking—smoking is not permitted in most of these facilities. Thus, the treatment of nicotine withdrawal symptoms has become an important issue for physicians, nurses, and counselors, and the patients they treat.

Nicotine replacement therapies substitute pharmacologic nicotine for tobacco nicotine in approximately equal dosages for purposes of detoxification. Thus, an individual smoking 40 Marlboro cigarettes daily ingests 30 to 60 mg of nicotine, depending on how the cigarette is smoked (Benowitz, Hall et al., 1983). The nicotine in the cigarette can be replaced by using a pharmacologic product containing nicotine, but without the toxic constituents of tobacco; this alleviates the symptoms of nicotine withdrawal and permits gradual detoxification from nicotine.

Providing nicotine substitution relieves many, though not all, nicotine withdrawal symptoms, because the pharmacokinetic profile of nicotine replacement products do not mimic the pharmacokinetic profile of tobacco products (cigarettes or smokeless tobacco). Specifically, smoking a cigarette produces a rapid rise in the arterial nicotine level, exposing the brain to a bolus of nicotine. None of the nicotine replacement products act that rapidly. There are three options when using nicotine replacement: (1) nicotine maintenance (stay on the product indefinitely instead of using tobacco); (2) gradual nicotine withdrawal (progressive reductions in nicotine dose); and (3) sudden nicotine withdrawal (switching from tobacco to nicotine replacement and then stopping the nicotine replacement without weaning). The products discussed here are approved only for detoxification, not for maintenance; however, since most of these products are available without a prescription, there is nothing to prevent individuals from using them indefinitely.

Currently, three nicotine replacement products are available in the United States: nicotine polacrilex (available without a presciption), the nicotine transdermal systems (some brands available without a prescription and some brands requiring one), and nicotine nasal spray (prescription only). A nicotine inhaler is available in Europe and eventually may be approved by the FDA.

Nicotine Nasal Spray and Nicotine Inhalers: Nicotine is absorbed across the nasal mucosa with the nasal spray (Russell, 1991) and the nasal inhaler (Robinson, Pettice et al., 1992) and from the mouth and pharynx with the nicotine oral inhaler (Tnnesen, Norregaard et al., 1993). In these studies, the patients using a nasal or oral nicotine inhaler had abstinence rates at one year about three times higher than patients using placebo inhalers. Untoward effects were minimal (involving burning, coughing and nausea), and addiction to the inhalers was not reported. Absorption of nicotine from the nasal spray (Nicotrol NS®) is only minimally impaired when the patient has an upper respiratory infection; absorption is delayed, however, by the concomitant use of a nasal decongestant (Lunell, Molander & Andersson, 1995).

Nicotine Polacrilex: Nicotine polacrilex ("nicotine gum," Nicorette®) is a resin to which nicotine has been bound; it is available in small pieces in a unit dose pack, each piece containing either 2 mg or 4 mg of nicotine. Because of incomplete bioavailability, only about half of the nicotine in each piece is actually absorbed. The product has been available in the U.S. since 1984 and has been used successfully in conjunction with behavioral therapy, with frequent medication checks but no professional therapy, and by itself with no therapy (Pomerleau & Pomerleau, 1988; Hughes, Gulliver et al., 1989; McGovern & Lando, 1992). The data suggest that nicotine polacrilex works best when the patient is able to chew enough to raise the venous blood level to more than 12 ng/ml (Henningfield & Woodson, 1989a), which may require 25 or 30 pieces a day (smokers routinely reach venous levels of 25 ng/ml and reach bolus arterial levels of 70 ng/ml; Henningfield, London & Benowitz, 1990). Use of the 4 mg size may improve quit rates in highly dependent smokers (Herrera, Franco et al., 1995).

Nicotine polacrilex has a number of advantages. It is patient controlled; that is, it is available whenever patients feel they need the effects of nicotine (as in moments of stress, at times when they usually use tobacco, or when they anticipate a relapse). Smoking is an oral behavior, and nicotine polacrilex is an oral product; this may help some patients cope with their symptoms. When patients chew their nicotine polacrilex rapidly, they can achieve a rapid rise in their nicotine levels, providing symptomatic relief rather quickly. Since the product is available in small unit doses (2 mg of nicotine in each piece), the patient can smoothly titrate the nicotine dose down to zero. The gum is relatively convenient to carry because it is sold in plastic unit dose packages. Finally, the gum can be helpful for patients who are in danger of relapse; when tempted to smoke, they can chew a piece of the gum instead.

There are a number of disadvantages to nicotine polacrilex as well. Gum chewing is simply not socially acceptable in many situations, and some patients do not consider nicotine polacrilex to be the serious medication it is because it is provided in the form of a gum. Chewing 25 or 30 pieces of nicotine polacrilex a day may cause tempero-mandibular jaw syndrome (TMJ) or sore muscles in the jaw and neck. Patients may object to holding the saliva (in which the nicotine is dissolved) in their mouths while the nicotine is absorbed across the buccal membrane. Some patients respond by swallowing the saliva; stomach acid prevents most of this nicotine from being absorbed, and it makes patients nauseated as well. The product has a sharp, peppery taste that few find appealing and which may limit its acceptance. To overcome this, some patients chew a piece of flavored gum or drink a beverage to mask the unpleasant flavor; this acidifies the oral environment sufficiently to ionize the nicotine (a weak base) and prevent its absorption across the buccal mucosa (Henningfield, Radzius et al., 1990).

Nicotine Transdermal Systems: The nicotine transdermal systems ("NTS," "the patches") obviate some of the problems inherent in the use of nicotine polacrilex. They are inobtrusive and easy to use; patients apply a patch once daily beneath their clothing and do not have to think about it again until the next morning. The patch provides steady-state nicotine levels (avoiding the peaks and valleys of smoking or nicotine polacrilex), which keep patients out of withdrawal without giving them the euphoria found with cigarettes. The patient controls the dose by making a once-daily decision to apply a patch. The patches are available in several strengths, allowing stepwise titration; lower doses have the same mechanisms and nicotine concentrations in the reservoirs, but have smaller surface areas.

There are several significant disadvantages to the patches. Skin reactions are quite common, ranging from minor problems involving itching and redness to bullae and hyperpigmentation. While the patches allow stepwise titration, there are only a few sizes available, and cutting the patches is not recommended—a patch fragment may not adhere well, and nicotine, vaporized by body heat, may escape from the cut surface. The patches are expensive: a one-month supply costs about $100, and now that they are available over-the-counter, many insurance plans will not pay for them. The patches cannot provide a bolus dose of nicotine when the patient desires one; although some patients develop interesting rituals involving rubbing the patches to "squeeze" some extra nicotine into their systems; in reality, it takes several hours to boost the nicotine level, and rubbing the patch does not alter the rate of absorption.

Patches deliver a predictable dosage of nicotine over 24 hours, but each patch contains a great deal more than the delivered dose of nicotine in its reservoir. Concern has been raised that patients may intentionally or unintentionally leave a previous day's patch on after placing a new one, thus administering a larger than intended dose. Concerns have also been raised that children or pets might ingest a discarded patch, leading to toxicity. At least one study (Matsushima, Prevo & Gorsline, 1995) found that the family dog is in little serious danger from ingesting a discarded nicotine patch.

Another problem is that patients tend to put their full faith in the device alone and fail to make the lifestyle changes necessary for long-term abstinence. Outcome studies suggest that nicotine dependence counseling will improve cessation rates (Smith & Winters, 1995), but few patients actually enroll in formal cessation programs after purchasing patches. The pharmaceutical companies that manufacture nicotine transdermal systems have developed self-help materials, call-in 800 numbers, and a variety of other creative counseling solutions, but these strategies are not often used. Thus, most patches are used as pharmacologic supports alone, without significant therapy.

Single-case reports have offered anecdotal data suggesting that the patches can produce other untoward effects associated with nicotine, including coronary artery spasm (Ottervanger, Festen et al., 1995) and brief psychosis (Foulds & Toone, 1995). No consistent pattern of such untoward events has been identified.

Four brands of patches are currently marketed: Habitrol®, Nicoderm®, ProStep®, and Nicotrol®. While all contain nicotine, they are not generically equivalent; each patch incorporates a different

TABLE 1. Nicotine Transdermal Systems Compared (from Manufacturer's Literature)

Incidence of any skin reaction (regardless of severity)	
Habitrol® (CIBA-GEIGY)	35%
Nicoderm® (Marion Merrell Dow)	47%
ProStep® (Lederle)	54%
Nicotrol® (Parke-Davis)	47%
Amount of nicotine in the reservoirs	
Habitrol® 21 mg (CIBA-GEIGY)	52.5 mg
Nicoderm® 21 mg (Marion Merrell Dow)	114.0 mg
ProStep® 22 mg (Lederle)	30.0 mg
Nicotrol® 15 mg (Parke-Davis)	24.9 mg
Average steady-state nicotine levels (range)	
Habitrol® 21 mg (CIBA-GEIGY)	13.0 ng/ml (9–17)
Nicoderm® 21 mg (Marion Merrell Dow)	17.0 ng/ml (10–26)
ProStep® 22 mg (Lederle)	11.0 ng/ml (6–17)
Nicotrol® 15 mg (Parke-Davis)	8.7 ng/ml (5–12)

mechanism of nicotine delivery, with very different pharmacokinetic profiles. Table 1 summarizes several distinguishing aspects of these products, using data provided by the manufacturers: their rates of skin irritation, the amount of nicotine in their reservoirs, and their average steady-state nicotine levels.

The patches are clearly different from each other. For example, ProStep produces the most rapid increase in nicotine levels when first applied, but has the widest range of nicotine levels; Habitrol produces the least variation from peak to trough but has the slowest increase in nicotine levels when first applied. Nicotrol is marketed as a "16-hour patch," which may help to decrease nighttime restlessness, but it leaves the patient with a negligible nicotine blood level on awakening. Nicoderm produces higher peak nicotine levels than the others, but contains more nicotine in its reservoir than the others (114 mg); a discarded Nicoderm patch would therefore be the most likely brand of patch to be hazardous to children or pets if inadvertently ingested or chewed.

Advertising for the patches emphasizes the differences and purported superiority of one brand over another. However, no head-to-head studies comparing the different brands of patches have been done, and methodological differences between studies on specific brands of patches preclude any conclusions about their relative effectiveness. Regardless of claims made on television commercials, there are no data suggesting an advantage to a gradual titration plan or a single-dose-then-quit plan, nor data to suggest an advantage of 16-hour patch use over 24-hour patch use. The finding that many patients have disturbed sleep while using a patch may be due to nicotine withdrawal (i.e., not enough nicotine) in some patients and to nicotine excess in others (Salin-Pascual, de la Fuente et al., 1995; Wetter, Fiore et al., 1995).

Combined Use of Patch and Gum: The FDA has made no comments on the use of patch and gum concomitantly. Since both deliver pure nicotine, concomitant use of the two agents would be expected to raise the nicotine blood level additively, with a pharmacokinetic profile intermediate between the two. Combined patch and gum may be helpful in patients with intense nicotine dependence or rapid nicotine metabolism, in whom one agent alone is insufficient to control withdrawal symptoms. Studies indicate that combinations of patch and gum facilitate dose titration (filling the gap between patches of different sizes) and allow for intermittent temporary dose increases when patients feel an increased desire to smoke (Kornitzer, Boutsen et al., 1995). Physicians must make their own clinical decisions in such cases, documenting their reasoning.

Detoxification Schedules. The pharmaceutical companies have recommended certain titration schedules for their products, but there are scant data to support these recommendations. Some physicians have been led to believe that one patch has the ability to treat a patient more rapidly than another because it has a shorter recommended titration schedule. However, no comparative data on shorter versus longer titration schedules exist.

When smokers are viewed as addicted to nicotine and tobacco, it becomes clear that imposing a rigid detoxification schedule is countertherapeutic. All active addicts protect their chemicals, none more ardently than smokers. Detoxification from nicotine, like detoxification from other drugs, requires personal attention from the physician, observation of objective data, negotiation with the patient, and considerable patience. Most outpatients require two to four months of progressive detoxification; while some will return, smokefree, after a month with 20 unused patches, others will continue to need pharmacologic supports at six months. In an inpatient addiction treatment program, where staff can control the environment and the medication, most patients can be detoxified over two or three weeks without significant complications by progressively reducing the size of the patch.

Advice to Patients. When prescribing the patch, physicians should attempt to engage the patient in a smoking cessation program or to create one; patches and nicotine polacrilex should be viewed as adjunctive therapies. Formal smoking cessation programs may not be more efficacious than brief physician advice, encouragement, and supervision (Stapleton, Russell et al., 1995).

When prescribing a nicotine replacement product, the physician must educate the patient about the product's use and potential untoward effects. The following is a suggested list of useful information for patients:

- Neither the patch nor the gum produces a nicotine bolus like a cigarette; instead, they are designed to provide steady-state nicotine levels to prevent withdrawal.
- There is one brand of nicotine nasal spray, one brand of nicotine gum and four brands of nicotine patches; they are not equivalent. Patients should use the same brand consistently.
- The FDA has approved the gum, the patch and the spray for detoxification from nicotine; they are not approved for long-term maintenance.
- While primarily intended for the treatment of smokers, the gum, the patch and the spray can also be used for detoxification from smokeless tobacco.
- Using two different products at the same time is appropriate under certain circumstances.
- Lifestyle changes are essential; patients should participate in a smoking cessation program of some kind.
- Patients should follow up with the physician at regular intervals.

Patient advice specific to the nicotine transdermal systems includes the following:

- Minor skin irritation from the patches usually responds to over-the-counter hydrocortisone cream; the patient should contact the physician if a rash persists.
- It is good practice to remove the old patch each morning, bathe the site, then apply the new patch to a different site; this precludes leaving the old patch on (still supplying nicotine) and reduces skin irritation.
- Patients should avoid handling the medicated side of the patch: nicotine is on its surface, so if the patient touches the surface and then touches the eye, severe irritation can result. In addition, han-

dling the adhesive surface reduces its adhesive qualities.

- Patients should not attempt to cut the patch.
- If the patient should feel lightheaded or dizzy after placing the first patch (indicating nicotine overdose), he or she should remove the patch, flush the area with cold (not hot) water, and hold an ice cube over the area to reduce absorption.

Patient advice specific to nicotine polacrilex includes this information:

- The patient should not use another kind of gum, candy or a beverage while using the nicotine gum. The resulting acidification of the oral environment prevents nicotine absorption.
- Patients should chew the gum until the peppery taste becomes evident; then "park" the gum in the buccal pouch for several minutes; then chew it again. Most of the nicotine is absorbed in 20 minutes.
- Whitish patches in the mouth or irritation to the buccal mucosa or gums should be evaluated by the physician or dentist.

Titrating the Dose. Accurate prescribing is a hallmark of the knowledgeable physician. Patients can titrate their own doses of nicotine polacrilex, but the physician is responsible for prescribing the appropriate dose of nicotine in the patch. Using serum cotinine levels to determine a patient's degree of nicotine dependence would be a logical method of determining proper dosage, but cotinine levels are not readily available, are expensive to determine, and would create a delay in initiating therapy. As an alternative, the author has used the Fagerström Test for Nicotine Dependence, which correlates well with cotinine levels (Heatherton, Kozlowski et al., 1991); in 1,000 patients, there have been no significant incidents of excessive dosing. (Note that this is Fagerström's second version of the test; the earlier version, known as the Fagerström Tolerance Questionnaire, has been superseded by this version.) A slightly revised version, altered to modify Fagerström's European terminology to reflect the cultural background of U.S. patients is included as Table 2.

The Fagerström test is easily incorporated into patient evaluations, with the questions asked as part of the drug use history and the score recorded as part of the vital signs. Patients who score 7 to 10 on the Fagerström are classified as having a high degree of nicotine dependence and started on the 21 mg patch; those scoring 4 to 6 have a moderate degree of nicotine dependence and are started on the 14 mg patch. Those scoring below 4 have a light degree of nicotine dependence and need no patch at all; if the patient insists, he or she is prescribed the 7 mg size. At appropriate intervals, the physician reduces the patch to the next smaller size. These intervals may be as short as four days in hospitalized patients, or as long as a month in outpatients.

TREATMENT OF NICOTINE WITHDRAWAL IN SMOKERS WHO DO NOT INTEND TO QUIT SMOKING

Physicians frequently confront the clinical problem of having a nicotine-dependent patient in the hospital for a medical or surgical condition (Miller, Smith et al., 1997). With the patient in a smoke-free environment, but not by choice, many physicians choose to treat their patient's symptoms of nicotine withdrawal in preference to having them either suffer these symptoms or give them permission to smoke. Either nicotine polacrilex or the nicotine patch work well in these situations; the choice of route of administration is based on the patients' preferences and medical conditions. The same principles apply to patients in residential or hospital addiction treatment programs (Campbell, Wander et al., 1995).

With more addiction treatment programs beginning to address nicotine dependence in the context of other alcohol and drug treatment, this will be an increasingly important issue in the years ahead.

CONCLUSIONS

Research into smoking cessation techniques has increased significantly over the past 15 years. These studies vary considerably, however, in the rigor of their methodology and the appropriateness of their patient selection criteria. Studies that exclude subjects with alcoholism, depression, emphysema and heart disease do not reflect real-world clinical practice as well as studies that include such subjects. Some researchers also use their own definitions of "success," "improved," "relapse," and "lapse." Practitioners who seek direction from the research literature must, as always, review these reports with care.

Relapse is at least as common in nicotine dependence as in other addictions: indeed, a meta-analysis of 39 controlled smoking cessation trials showed that half of the subjects who quit smoking in a spectrum of treatment programs had relapsed by the end

TABLE 2. Fagerström Test for Nicotine Dependence (Revised)

1. How soon after you wake up do you smoke your first cigarette?

within 5 min	3 points
5–30 min	2 points
31–60 min	1 point
after 60 min	0 points

2. Do you find it hard not to smoke in places that you shouldn't smoke, such as in church, in school, in a movie, on the bus, in court or in a hospital?

Yes	1 point
No	0 points

3. Which cigarette would you hate most to have to give up?

The first one in the morning	1 point
Any other one	0 points

4. How many cigarettes do you smoke each day?

10–fewer	0 points
11–20	1 point
21–30	2 points
31 or more	3 points

5. Do you smoke more in the first few hours after waking up than you do during the rest of the day?

Yes	1 point
No	0 points

6. Do you still smoke, even if you are so sick that you are in bed most of the day, or if you have the flu or a severe cough?

Yes	1 point
No	0 points

Total .... ________ points

Fagerström Score	Start with
7–10	21 mg patch
4–6	14 mg patch
<4	7 mg patch

of the first week and that 88% had relapsed by the end of the first year (Kottke, 1989). Part of the reason for this low success rate is apparent in a study by Frank and colleagues (1991). They found that 87% of those who had successfully quit smoking did so completely on their own, with no outside assistance; less than 4% stopped under the supervision of a physician. In addition, few persons made use of all the other things that addiction specialists know can help people recover: the support of family or friends, mutual-help groups, group therapy, and detoxification medications.

The use of nicotine replacement products and/or buproprion add important elements to reduce the discomfort of nicotine withdrawal and improve the success rate of smokers attempting to quit. Nicotine polacrilex has been modestly successful in helping subjects stop smoking; the best results have been seen when the gum is used as part of a multimodality treatment program (McGovern & Lando, 1992; Murray, Bailey et al., 1996). Most of the studies on the nicotine transdermal systems have included only minimal therapy; still, use of an active patch has doubled the success rates over placebo patches in several studies (Abelin, Mullin et al., 1989; Gourlay, Forbes et al., 1995; Hurt, Dale et al., 1992; Tnnesen, Norregaard et al., 1991; Transdermal Nicotine Study Group, 1991), although the effects sizes in real-world settings have been small (Mankani, Garabrant & Homa, 1996). Buproprion may significantly reduce relapse by normalizing the smoker's neurotransmitter/receptor balance (multiple studies in press). Further research on the mechanisms by which these agents exert their beneficial effects will provide clinicians with improved strategies and new agents.

REFERENCES

Abelin T, Muller P, Buehler A, Vesanen K & Imhof PR (1989). Controlled trial of transdermal nicotine patch in tobacco withdrawal. *The Lancet* 1:7–10.

Benowitz NL (1988). Pharmacologic aspects of cigarette smoking and nicotine addiction. *The New England Journal of Medicine* 319:1318–1330.

Benowitz NL, Hall SM, Herning RI, Jacob P III, Jones RT & Osman A-L (1983). Smokers of low-yield cigarettes do not consume less nicotine. *The New England Journal of Medicine* 309:139–142.

Campbell BK, Wander N, Stark MJ & Holbert T (1995). Treating cigarette smoking in drug-abusing clients. *Journal of Substance Abuse Treatment* 12:89–94.

Casey K (1987). *If Only I Could Quit: Recovery from Nicotine Addiction*. Center City, MN: Hazelden Educational Materials.

Cropp CD & Gora-Harper ML (1995). Ondansetron use for smoking cessation. *Annals of Pharmacotherapy* 29:1041–1042.

Dawley HH (1989). Toward a smoke-free VA. *VA Practitioner* 4:47–65.

Delaney GO (1988). Tobacco dependence in treating alcoholism. *New Jersey Medicine* 85:131–132.

Ferguson T (1987). *The No-Nag, No-Guilt, Do-It-Your-Own-Way Guide to Quitting Smoking*. New York, NY: Ballantine Books.

Ferry LH & Burchette RJ (1994). Efficacy of buproprion for smoking cessation in non-depressed smokers. *Journal of Addictive Diseases* 13:9A.

Ferry, LH, Robbins, AS, Scariati AM, Abbey DE & Burchette RJ (1992). Enhancement of smoking cessation using the antidepressant buproprion (abstract). *Circulation* (abstract supplement) 86:I-167.

Fiore, MN, Leischow S, Nides M, Reynard R & Ferry LH (1997). Comparison of buprioprion with and without nicotine patches for smoking cessation (submitted for publication).

Fiore MN, Novotny TE, Pierce JP, Giovino GA, Hatziandreu EJ, Newcomb PA, Surawicz TS & Davis RM (1990). Methods used to quit smoking in the United States; Do cessation programs help? *Journal of the American Medical Association* 263:2760–2765.

Foulds J & Toone B (1995). A case of nicotine psychosis? *Addiction* 90:435–437.

Frank E, Winkleby MA, Altman DG, Rockhill B & Fortmann SP (1991). Predictors of physicians' smoking cessation advice. *Journal of the American Medical Association* 266:3139–3144.

Glassman AH, Jackson WK, Walsh T, Roose SP & Rosenfeld B (1984). Cigarette craving, smoking withdrawal, and clonidine. *Science* 266:864–866.

Glassman AH, Stetner F, Walsh T, Raizman PS, Fleiss JL, Cooper TB & Covey LS (1988). Heavy smokers, smoking cessation, and clonidine. *Journal of the American Medical Association* 259:2863–66.

Gourlay SG, Forbes A, Marriner T, Pethica D & McNeil JJ (1995). Double blind trial of repeated treatment with transdermal nicotine for relapsed smokers. *British Medical Journal* 311:363–366.

Heatherton TF, Kozlowski LT, Frecker RC & Fagerstrom KO (1991). The Fagerstrom Test for Nicotine Dependence: A revision of the Fagerstrom Tolerance Questionnaire. *British Journal of Addictions* 86:1119–1127.

Henningfield JE (1984a). Pharmacologic basis and treatment of cigarette smoking. *Journal of Clinical Psychiatry* 45:24–34.

Henningfield JE (1984b). Behavioral pharmacology of cigarette smoking. In T Thompson & PB Dews (eds.) *Advances in Behavioral Pharmacology, Vol. 4*. New York, NY: Academic Press, 131–210.

Henningfield JE (1990). Understanding nicotine addiction and physical withdrawal. *Journal of the American Dental Association* Jan(Suppl):2s–6s.

Henningfield JE, London ED & Benowitz NL (date?). Arterial-venous differences in plasma concentrations of nicotine after cigarette smoking. *Journal of the American Medical Association* 263:2049–2050.

Henningfield JE, Radzius A, Cooper TM & Clayton RR (1990). Drinking coffee and carbonated beverages blocks absorption of nicotine from nicotine polacrilex gum. *Journal of the American Medical Association* 264:1560–1564.

Henningfield JE & Woodson PP (1989). Behavioral and physiologic aspects of nicotine dependence: The role of nicotine dose. *Progress in Brain Research* 79:303–312.

Herning RI, Jones RT, Benowitz NL & Mines AH (1983). How a cigarette is smoked determines blood nicotine levels. *Clinical Pharmacology and Therapeutics* 33:84–90.

Herrera N, Franco R, Herrera L, Partidas A, Rolando R & Fagerström KO (1995). Nicotine gum, 2 and 4 mg, for nicotine dependence: A double-blind placebo-controlled trial with a behavior modification support program. *Chest* 108:447–451.

Hilleman DE, Mohiuddin SM, DelCore MG & Sketch MH (1992). Effect of buspirone on withdrawal symptoms associated with smoking cessation. *Archives of Internal Medicine* 152:350–352.

Hoffman EH (1991). *Recovery from Smoking: Quitting with the Twelve Step Process*. Center City, MN: Hazelden Educational Materials.

Holroyd J (1980). Hypnosis treatment for smoking: An evaluative review. *International Journal of Clinical and Experimental Hypnosis* 28:341–357.

Hughes JR, Gulliver SB, Amora G, Mireault GC & Fenwick JF (1989). Effects of instructions and nicotine on smoking cessation, withdrawal symptoms and self-administration of nicotine gum. *Psychopharmacology* 99:486–491.

Hurt RD, Dale LC, Offord KP, Bruck BK, McClain FL & Eberman KM (1992). Inpatient treatment of severe nicotine dependence. *Mayo Clinic Proceedings* 67:823–828.

Hurt RD, Sachs D & Glover E (1997). Buproprion for smoking cessation (accepted for publication).

Jarvik ME & Henningfield JE (1988). Pharmacological treatment of tobacco dependence. *Pharmacology, Biochemistry and Behavior* 30:279–294.

Jeanne E (1989). *Twelve Steps for Tobacco Users: For Recovering People Addicted to Nicotine*. Center City, MN: Hazelden Educational Materials.

Kornitzer M, Boutsen M, Bramaix M, Thijs J & Gustavsson G (1995). Combined use of nicotine patch and gum in smoking cessation: a placebo-controlled clinical trial. *Preventive Medicine* 24:41–47.

Kottke TE (1989). The smoke-free hospital: A smoke-free worksite. *New York State Journal of Medicine* 89:38–42.

Lunell E, Molander L & Andersson M (1995). Relative bioavailability of nicotine from a nasal spray in infectious rhinits and after use of a topical decongestant. *European Journal of Pharmacology* 48:71–75.

Mankani SK, Garabrant DH & Homa DM (1996). Effectiveness of nicotine patches in a workplace smoking cessation program: An eleven-month follow-up study. *Journal of Occupational and Environmental Medicine* 38:184–189.

Matsushima D, Prevo ME & Gorsline J (1995). Absorption and adverse effects following topical and oral administration of three transdermal nicotine products to dogs. *Journal of Pharmacy Science* 84:365–369.

McGovern PG & Lando HA (1992). An assessment of nicotine gum as an adjunct to Freedom from Smoking cessation clinics. *Addictive Behaviors* 17:137–147.

Miller NH, Smith PM, DeBusk RF, Sobel DS & Taylor CB (1997). Smoking cessation in hospitalized patients. Results of a randomized trial. *Archives of Internal Medicine* 24;157(4):409–15.

Mulligan SC, Masterson JG, Devane JG & Kelly JG (1990). Clinical and pharmacokinetic properties of a transdermal nicotine patch. *Clinical Pharmacology and Therapeutics* 47:33–337.

Murray RP, Bailey WC, Daniels K, Bjornson WM, Kurnow K, Connett JE, Nides MA & Kiley JP (1996). Safety of nicotine polacrilex gum used by 3,094 participants in the Lung Health Study. *Chest* 109:438–445.

Ottervanger JP, Festen JM, de Vries AG & Stricker BH (1995). Acute myocardial infarction while using the nicotine patch. *Chest* 107:1765–1766.

Pomerleau OF & Pomerleau CS (1988). *Nicotine Replacement: A Critical Evaluation*. New York, NY: Alan R. Liss.

Richmond RL, Kehoe L & de Almeida Neto AC (1997). Effectiveness of a 24-hour transdermal nicotine patch in conjunction with a cognitive behavioural programme: One year outcome. *Addiction* 92:27–31.

Robinson MD, Pettice YL, Smith WA, Cederstrom EA, Sutherland DE & Davis H (1992). Buspirone effect on tobacco withdrawal symptoms: A randomized placebo-controlled trial. *Journal of the American Board of Family Practice* 5:1–9.

Russell MAH (1991). The future of nicotine replacement. *British Journal of Addiction* 86:653–658.

Rustin TA (1991). Recovery-oriented nicotine addiction therapy. In J Corcores (ed.) *The Clinical Management of Nicotine Dependence*. New York, NY: Springer verlag, 119–135.

Rustin TA (1994). *Quit and Stay Quit: A Personal Program to Stop Smoking*. Center City, MN: Hazelden Educational Materials.

Rustin TA (1997). Incorporating nicotine dependence into addiction treatment. *Journal of Addictive Diseases*, in press.

Quit and Stay Quit: A Personal Program to Stop Smoking. Center City, MN: Hazelden Educational Materials.

Salin-Pascual RJ, de la Fuente JR, Galicia-Polo L & Drucker-Colin R (1995). Effects of transdermal nicotine on mood and sleep in nonsmoking major depressed patients. *Psychopharmacology* (Berlin) 121;476–479.

Schwartz JL (1987). *Review and Evaluation of Smoking Cessation Methods: United States and Canada, 1978–1985*. Bethesda, MD, National Institutes of Health, DHHS Pub. No. 87–2940.

Shipley R (1990). *QuitSmart: A Guide to Freedom from Smoking Cigarettes*. Durham, NC: JB Press.

Smith MD, McGhan WF & Lauger G (1995). Pharmacist counseling and outcomes of smoking cessation. *American Pharmacist* NS35(8):20–29.

Smith TM & Winters FD (1995). Smoking cessation: A clinical study of the transdermal nicotine patch. *Journal of the American Osteopathic Association* 95:655–662.

Solberg LI, Maxwell PL, Kottke TE, Gepner GJ & Brekke ML (1990). A systematic primary care office-based smoking cessation program. *Journal of Family Practice* 30:647–654.

Stapleton JA, Russell MA, Feyerabend C, Wiseman SM, Gustavsson G, Sawe U & Wiseman D (1995). Dose effects and predictors of outcome in randomized trial of transdermal nicotine patches in general practice. *Addiction* 90:31–42.

Tnnesen P, Norregaard J, Mikkelsen K, Jorgensen S & Nilsson F (1993). A double-blind trial of a nicotine inhaler for smoking cessation. *Journal of the American Medical Association* 269:1268–1271.

Tnnesen P, Norregaard J, Simonsen K & Sawe U (1991). A double-blind trial of a 16-hour transdermal nicotine patch in smoking cessation. *The New England Journal of Medicine* 325:311–315.

Transdermal Nicotine Study Group (1991). Transdermal nicotine for smoking cessation: Six-month results from two multicenter controlled clinical trials. *Journal of the American Medical Association* 266:3133–3148.

Wetter DW, Fiore MC, Baker TB & Young TB (1995). Tobacco withdrawal and nicotine replacement influence objective measures of sleep. *Journal of Consulting and Clinical Psychology* 63:658–667.

SECTION 7
Pharmacologic Therapies for Addiction

CHAPTER 1

Pharmacologic Therapies for Alcoholism **501**
Henry R. Kranzler, M.D. and Jerome H. Jaffe, M.D.

CHAPTER 2

Pharmacologic Therapies for Benzodiazepine and Other Sedative-Hypnotic Addiction **517**
Donald R. Wesson, M.D., David E. Smith, M.D., FASAM, and Walter Ling, M.D.

CHAPTER 3

Pharmacologic Therapies for Cocaine and Other Stimulant Addiction **531**
David A. Gorelick, M.D., Ph.D.

CHAPTER 4

Pharmacologic Therapies for Opioid Addiction **545**
Susan Stine, M.D., Ph.D., Borislav Meandzija, M.D., and Thomas R. Kosten, M.D.

CHAPTER 5

Opioid Maintenance Therapies **557**
J. Thomas Payte, M.D. and Joan Ellen Zweben, Ph.D.

CHAPTER 6

Pharmacologic Therapies for Nicotine Dependence **571**
Joy M. Schmitz, Ph.D., Jack E. Henningfield, Ph.D., and Murray E. Jarvik, M.D., Ph.D.

CHAPTER 7

Pharmacologic Therapies for Other Drug and Multiple Drug Addiction **583**
Jeffery N. Wilkins, M.D., David A. Gorelick, M.D., Ph.D., and Bradley T. Conner

SECTION COORDINATORS

RAYE Z. LITTEN, PH.D.
Treatment Research Branch
National Institute on Alcohol Abuse and Alcoholism
Rockville, Maryland

DAVID A. GORELICK, M.D., PH.D.
Chief, Pharmacotherapy Section
Intramural Research Program
National Institute on Drug Abuse, and
Adjunct Professor of Psychiatry
University of Maryland School of Medicine
Baltimore, Maryland

CONTRIBUTORS

Bradley T. Conner
University of California at Los Angeles
Los Angeles, California

Jack E. Henningfield, Ph.D.
Associate Professor
Department of Psychiatry and Behavioral Sciences
The Johns Hopkins University
School of Medicine, and
Vice President, Research and Health Policy
Pinney Associates
Bethesda, Maryland

Jerome H. Jaffe, M.D.
Adjunct Clinical Professor of Psychiatry
University of Maryland
School of Medicine
Baltimore, Maryland

Murray E. Jarvik, M.D., Ph.D.
Chief, Psychopharmacology Unit
Veterans Affairs Medical Center
West Los Angeles
UCLA School of Medicine
Los Angeles, California

Thomas R. Kosten, M.D.
Associate Professor
Department of Psychiatry
Yale University School of Medicine
New Haven, Connecticut

Henry R. Kranzler, M.D.
Professor of Psychiatry and
Associate Scientific Director,
Alcohol Research Center
University of Connecticut School of Medicine
Farmington, Connecticut

Walter Ling, M.D.
Director, Matrix/UCLA Alcoholism and
Addiction Medicine Service, and
Associate Chief of Psychiatry for Substance Abuse
West Los Angeles VA Medical Center, and
Professor and Chief of Substance Abuse Programs
Department of Psychiatry and Behavioral Sciences
University of California, Los Angeles
Los Angeles, California

Borislav Meandzija, M.D.
Assistant Professor
Department of Psychiatry
Yale University School of Medicine
New Haven, Connecticut

J. Thomas Payte, M.D.
Founder and Medical Director
Drug Dependence Associates
San Antonio, Texas

Joy M. Schmitz, Ph.D.
Associate Professor
Department of Psychiatry and Behavioral Sciences
University of Texas Medical School
Houston Health Science Center
Houston, Texas

David E. Smith, M.D., FASAM
Founder, Medical Director and President
Haight Ashbury Free Clinics, and
Associate Clinical Professor of
Occupational Health and Clinical Toxicology
University of California, San Francisco
San Francisco, California

Susan Stine, M.D., Ph.D.
Director, Opiate Treatment Program
VA Connecticut Healthcare System
West Haven, Connecticut, and
Yale University School of Medicine
New Haven, Connecticut

Donald R. Wesson, M.D.
Associate Director of Research
Los Angeles Addiction
Treatment Research Center, and
Associate Clinical Professor of Psychiatry
University of California, San Francisco
San Francisco, California

Jeffery N. Wilkins, M.D.
Chief, Clinical Psychopharmacology Unit
Veterans Administration Medical Center
West Los Angeles, and
Adjunct Professor of Psychiatry
UCLA School of Medicine
Los Angeles, California

Joan E. Zweben, Ph.D.
Clinical Professor of Psychiatry
University of California, San Francisco
and Executive Director
14th Street Clinic and
East Bay Community Recovery Project
Oakland, California

CHAPTER 1

Pharmacologic Therapies for Alcoholism

Henry R. Kranzler, M.D.
Jerome H. Jaffe, M.D.

Alcohol Sensitizing Agents
Drugs that Directly Reduce Alcohol Consumption
Agents Affecting Other Neurotransmitter Systems
Drugs in the Treatment of Postwithdrawal Affective Disturbances

Among the major challenges in the months after an alcoholic stops drinking are the prevention of relapse to drinking and the management of persistent emotional and physiological disturbances.

This chapter reviews the literature on use of medications for the prevention of such relapse to drinking. It will focus specifically on those developments that are of interest to the clinician, although it also will review developments that are likely to yield important clinical advances in the future. The authors' intention is not to review the literature exhaustively; rather, they refer the reader to a number of other recently published reviews that are complementary to the material covered here (Jaffe, Kranzler & Ciraulo, 1992; Gorelick, 1993; Litten, Allen & Fertig, 1996; Meza & Kranzler, 1996).

Pharmacological agents can be used to deter alcohol consumption in several ways. Alcohol sensitizing drugs make the ingestion of alcohol aversive or hazardous. Some drugs appear to reduce alcohol intake by reducing the reinforcing effects of alcohol or by reducing the urge or craving to ingest alcohol. The treatment of persistent psychiatric symptoms is also postulated to reduce the risk of relapse by removing motivation to use alcohol as "self-medication" to control such symptoms. Each of these approaches to pharmacotherapy will be discussed in detail below.

ALCOHOL SENSITIZING AGENTS

Sensitizing agents alter the body's response to alcohol, thereby making its ingestion unpleasant or toxic. Disulfiram and carbimide are the only two drugs of this type that are currently used in the treatment of alcoholism. Both inhibit aldehyde dehydrogenase (ALDH), the enzyme that catalyzes the oxidation of acetaldehyde to acetic acid. If alcohol is ingested after this enzyme is inhibited, blood acetaldehyde levels rise. As a result, the disulfiram-ethanol reaction (DER) develops which, although to some degree idiosyncratic, generally varies in intensity both with the dose of the aversive drug and the amount of alcohol ingested. In its mild form, the syndrome includes warmth and flushing of the skin, especially that of the upper chest and face; heart rate increases; palpitations; and decreased blood pressure. There may also be nausea, vomiting, shortness of breath, sweating, dizziness, blurred vision, and confusion. Most reactions last about 30 minutes and are self-limited, but occasionally they may be life-threatening, even after relatively small amounts of alcohol.

The DER can sometimes be quite severe and may include marked tachycardia. Hypotension is sometimes accompanied by bradycardia, or even cardiac arrest secondary to vagal stimulation associated with retching or vomiting. Cardiovascular collapse, congestive failure, and convulsions have also been reported. While severe reactions are usually associated with high doses of disulfiram (over 500 mg/day), combined with more than two ounces of alcohol, deaths have occurred with lower dosage and after a single drink (Lindros, Stowell et al., 1981; Peachey, Brien et al., 1981; Peachey, Maglana et al., 1981; Sellers, Naranjo & Peachey, 1981).

The reactions seen after carbimide generally are milder than those produced by disulfiram. The two agents also differ significantly in their metabolism and in the onset and duration of effects, carbimide having a more rapid onset of effects, but a shorter duration of action. Hypoglycemics and trichomonacides also may produce unpleasant effects when combined with ethanol, as a consequence of their inhibition of ALDH. However, given their other actions, these drugs generally are unsuitable for use as sensitizing agents in the treatment of alcoholism.

The use of alcohol sensitizing agents has intuitive appeal. Consequently, these drugs long have been used in the rehabilitation of alcoholic patients (Favazza & Martin, 1974), despite the absence of methodologically sound evaluations demonstrating their clinical efficacy. Most studies undertaken prior to this decade failed to include measures of compliance or adequate controls, both of which are now generally considered essential elements in the evaluation of the efficacy of a medication for treatment of alcohol dependence (Kranzler, Mason et al., 1997). Except for the VA Cooperative Study (see below), only a few studies of disulfiram have incorporated these elements, and those studies generally have had small samples or have used ill-defined outcome measures.

The efficacy of alcohol sensitizing agents in the prevention or limitation of relapse in alcoholics remains to be demonstrated. However, in selected samples of alcoholics with whom special efforts are made to insure compliance, these drugs may be of utility. Unfortunately, though, at the present time there are no guidelines that can be offered either to identify patients for whom disulfiram is most likely to have a beneficial effect or for matching specific psychosocial interventions to enhance compliance.

Disulfiram (Antabuse®). Disulfiram is almost completely absorbed after oral administration. It is rapidly metabolized to diethyldithiocarbamate (DDC), which in turn is degraded to diethylamine and several other substances, including carbon disulfide. The detection of carbon disulfide in breath provides a measure of compliance. Since disulfiram inhibits ALDH by binding to it irreversibly, renewed enzyme activity requires the synthesis of new protein. This is the basis for the admonition to avoid alcohol consumption for at least two weeks from the time disulfiram is last ingested, since it may produce the DER.

Adverse effects from disulfiram are common. In addition to its effects on ALDH, disulfiram inhibits a variety of other enzymes including dopamine beta-hydroxylase (DBH). Although disulfiram reduces clearance rates of chlordiazepoxide and diazepam, benzodiazepines that do not require hydroxylation prior to excretion (e.g., lorazepam, oxazepam) are not altered. Disulfiram also may reduce the clearance, increase the elimination half-life, and lead to higher peak plasma levels of desipramine and imipramine (Ciraulo, Barnhill & Boxenbaum, 1985). Clearance of phenytoin and warfarin are also reduced, and dosage adjustments are required to avoid adverse effects (Hoyumpa & Schenker, 1982; Sellers, Naranjo & Peachey, 1981). Thus, in addition to the toxicity of the DER caused by the accumulation of acetaldehyde, adverse effects of disulfiram or its metabolites can occur as a result of multiple drug interactions, alterations in levels of normal body constituents and neurotransmitters, and other toxic effects.

Common side effects of disulfiram include drowsiness, lethargy, peripheral neuropathy, hepatotoxicity, and hypertension. The inhibition of DBH by disulfiram and its metabolite DDC results in increased dopamine levels. The exacerbation of psychotic symptoms in schizophrenics and occasionally their appearance in nonschizophrenics, as well as the development of depression, may be linked to this action. Alcoholics with low cerebrospinal fluid DBH activity are more likely to develop dysphoric or psychotic symptoms in response to disulfiram (Major, Lerner et al., 1979; Sellers, Naranjo & Peachey, 1981).

Although disulfiram has been used in the treatment of alcoholism for many years, problems in designing adequate experiments have made it difficult to assess its efficacy. Its approval by the FDA preceded the implementation of rigorous requirements for efficacy that now must be satisfied for a drug to be marketed in the United States. In the few controlled studies that have been conducted, the difference in outcome between subjects taking disulfiram and those given placebo is minimal. One problem is that patients may easily determine what they are taking, making it impossible to implement a double-blind study. Another problem has been poor ascertainment of compliance.

In a large, multicenter study conducted by the Veterans Administration Cooperative Studies Group, more than 600 male alcoholics were assigned randomly to groups receiving either 1 mg of disulfiram per day or a therapeutic dosage of 250 mg/day, or to a control group that was told they were not receiving disulfiram. Patients assigned to the disulfiram groups were told they were being given the drug, but neither patients nor staff knew the dosage. The capsules provided to patients in the different groups were indistinguishable and all contained riboflavin, which permitted the monitoring of compliance. Among the significant findings were the following:

- There was a direct relationship between compliance with drug therapy (in all three groups) and complete abstinence.
- Among patients who resumed drinking, those taking a therapeutic dosage of disulfiram had significantly fewer drinking days than did patients in the other two groups.
- However, in terms of a variety of outcome measures, including length of time to first drink, unemployment, social stability, or number of men totally abstinent, there was no significant difference among the three groups.

The authors concluded that disulfiram may be helpful in reducing the frequency of drinking in men who cannot remain abstinent (Fuller, Branchey et al., 1986), although they conceded that such a finding may have arisen by chance (given the large number of statistical analyses).

Disulfiram usually is given orally. Because there is an increased risk of side effects and toxic hazards as the dosage is increased, the daily dosage prescribed in the United States has been limited to 250–500 mg/day. However, efforts to titrate the dose of disulfiram in relation to a challenge dose of ethanol indicate that some patients require in excess of 1 g/day of disulfiram to reach blood levels sufficient to produce the DER (Brewer, 1984). Moveover, the clinical use of a challenge dose of ethanol to demonstrate to the patient the potential for adverse effects of disulfiram in combination with alcohol generally is not used in the U.S., even though it is thought to enhance the efficacy of the medication (Brewer, 1984). Disulfiram also has been given by subcutaneous implantation of 100 mg tablets (Esperal®) in the abdominal wall (Wilson, Davidson & Blanchard, 1980). Blood levels of disulfiram and DDC after implantation probably are too low in most cases to exert alcohol sensitizing effects for a period long enough to justify the implant, and benefits seen after implantation have been attributed primarily to psychological factors (Bergstrom, Ohlin et al., 1982; Sellers, Naranjo & Peachey, 1981). Such psychological factors may interact or overlap with factors related to compliance, which was shown by Fuller and colleagues (1986) to be a potent predictor of treatment outcome.

Many practitioners believe that by enhancing compliance with disulfiram it is possible to increase the individual's commitment to abstinence from alcohol. Consequently, a variety of other approaches to the enhancement of compliance with disulfiram therapy have been employed (reviewed by Allen & Litten, 1992). These include the use of incentives provided to the patient (e.g., less restrictive probation, money, continued participation in a treatment program), contracting with the patient and a significant other to commit themselves to the patient's taking disulfiram, providing additional information to the patient (e.g., concerning settings in which disulfiram may be most useful, providing the results of carbon disulfide breath tests), and behavioral training and social support. A trial program of stimulus control training, role playing, communication skills and vocational counseling improved outcome in disulfiram-treated patients (Azrin, Sisson et al., 1982). Enhancement of compliance with disulfiram therapy generally requires substantial effort (Azrin, Sisson et al., 1982); consequently, use of the drug outside of a well-organized treatment program probably is not warranted.

Patients should be warned carefully about the hazards of disulfiram, including the need to avoid over-the-counter preparations containing alcohol and drugs that interact adversely with disulfiram. A warning also should be provided regarding the potential for a DER precipitated by alcohol used in food preparation. There is some controversy about the ethics of prescribing disulfiram to anyone except those who want to use it, who seek abstinence, and who have no psychological or medical contraindications. Nevertheless, disulfiram has been incorporated as a mandatory element in some court-related programs.

Calcium Carbimide (Temposil®). Like disulfiram, calcium carbimide inhibits ALDH. In contrast to the effect of disulfiram, the enzyme inhibition produced by carbimide is reversible, so that its duration of action is less than one day. In order to ensure continued alcohol sensitizing effects, the usual 50 mg dose ordinarily must be given twice a day. It has been suggested that the rapid onset of effects, combined with short duration of action, may make the drug useful for intermittent use (Peachey & Annis, 1985). Intermittent use might also reduce the potential for adverse effects associated with chronic administration. As with disulfiram, the intensity of the carbimide-ethanol reaction is related both to the dose of the drug and to the dose of alcohol. The reaction is variable, however, both among individuals and in the same individual on different occasions.

Calcium carbimide does not inhibit the same wide range of enzyme systems that disulfiram does, nor is it associated with as many adverse drug interactions or the potential to produce psychosis, drowsiness, or lethargy (Sellers, Naranjo & Peachey, 1981). However, hepatitis more severe than that seen with disulfiram has been reported to occur with calcium carbimide (Vasquez, Diaz de Otazu et al., 1983). Although calcium carbimide is in clinical use in Europe and in Canada, it is not available in the U.S.

Peachey and colleagues (1989a) published the first randomized, placebo-controlled study of calcium carbimide. In a crossover study, they showed that alcohol consumption was significantly reduced from pre-treatment levels to the same extent during both the experimental and control treatment periods. Patients reported no more symptoms and had no more medical problems during carbimide treatment than during placebo treatment, and there was no evidence of hepatotoxicity (Peachey, Annis et al., 1989a).

DRUGS THAT DIRECTLY REDUCE ALCOHOL CONSUMPTION

Several neurotransmitter systems appear to influence the reinforcing or discriminative stimulus effects of ethanol: endogenous opioids, catecholamines (especially dopamine), serotonin (5-HT), and excitatory amino acids (such as glutamate) (Kranzler, Burleson et al., 1995). Although these systems probably function interactively in their effects on drinking behavior, they will be discussed separately here.

Opioidergic Agents. It has been suggested that some of the reinforcing effects of alcohol consumption are mediated by effects at opioid receptors. While there is evidence that the condensation products of ethanol metabolites and catecholamines (including tetrahydroisoquinolines, or TIQs) interact with opioid receptors (Cohen & Collins, 1970), such condensation products appear not to play a significant role in the maintenance of alcohol consumption (Amit, Smith et al., 1982). In animal models, ethanol in high concentrations also influences opioid receptors (Hiller, Aangel & Simon, 1981). Evidence that the opioid antagonist naltrexone decreases ethanol consumption in animals (Myers, Borg & Mossberg, 1986) suggests that some of the reinforcing effects of alcohol may be mediated through opioid neurotransmission.

Results from two double-blind, placebo-controlled trials of naltrexone in alcoholics have shown it to be efficacious in the prevention of relapse to heavy drinking (Volpicelli, O'Brien et al., 1992; O'Malley, Jaffe et al., 1992). Based on these studies, naltrexone is the first agent to receive approval by the FDA for the treatment of alcoholism since the introduction of disulfiram 50 years ago. In the 12-week study by Volpicelli and colleagues (1992), the medication was provided to alcohol-dependent veterans initially as an adjunct to an intensive day treatment program. Naltrexone was well tolerated and resulted in significantly less craving for alcohol and fewer drinking days. The active medication also limited the progression of drinking from initial sampling of alcohol to operationally-defined relapse. Study subjects who drank while taking naltrexone reported less euphoria, which may indicate that naltrexone blocked the endogenous opioid system's contribution to alcohol's "priming effect" (Volpicelli, Watson et al., 1995). In a related laboratory study of nonproblem drinkers, naltrexone was found to reduce the reinforcing (i.e., stimulant) effects and increase the unpleasant (i.e., sedative) properties of initial alcohol consumption (Swift, Whelihan et al., 1994).

O'Malley and colleagues (1992) replicated and extended the findings of Volpicelli, O'Brien et al. (1992) by examining the effects of naltrexone in ambulatory alcoholics who also received either supportive or relapse prevention psychotherapy. These investigators found that naltrexone was well tolerated and was superior to placebo in reducing the number of drinking days, the total number of drinks consumed, and in the frequency of alcohol-related problems measured during the 12-week treatment period.

In addition to the main effect of the medication, naltrexone interacted differentially with the psychotherapy provided. Naltrexone was more efficacious in preventing the initiation of drinking in combination with supportive therapy than when paired with coping skills training. On the other hand, once the subject sampled alcohol, naltrexone plus coping skills training was better at preventing a full-blown relapse.

An analysis of the reasons for relapse in the study by O'Malley and colleagues indicated that naltrexone differentially affected craving for alcohol, alcohol's reinforcing properties, the experience of intoxication, and the chances of continued drinking following a slip (O'Malley, Jaffe et al., 1996a). These investigators also found that naltrexone may be most beneficial among alcoholics who have higher levels of craving and poorer cognitive functioning (Jaffe, Rounsaville et al., 1996).

During a posttreatment follow-up period, O'Malley, Jaffe et al. (1996b) found that the beneficial effects of naltrexone diminished gradually over time. Moreover, abstinence during treatment strongly predicted whether subjects met criteria for alcohol abuse or dependence at a six-month, posttreatment follow-up. These findings suggest that patients who are unable to remain abstinent during acute treatment might benefit from naltrexone treatment for longer than the 12-week duration of treatment in these initial studies.

However, in a recent study, Volpicelli, Rhines et al. (1997) found that, overall, naltrexone failed to reduce the risk of relapse to heavy drinking. These investigators found that compliance with naltrexone treatment was variable and that only among highly-compliant subjects (23 of 49 who received placebo and 28 of 48 who received naltrexone), was the active medication significantly better than placebo with respect to the percentage of patients who drank, the percentage of patients who relapsed, and total drinks consumed. These findings underscore the need to understand more clearly the factors that underlie medication compliance among alcoholics, since the enhancement of compliance is necessary if medication therapy is to play a meaningful role in the routine clinical care of alcohol-dependent patients.

In summary, although naltrexone is a promising treatment for alcohol dependence, the number of patients treated in published double-blind studies of the drug has been modest (N < 300; O'Malley, Croop et al., 1995; Volpicelli, Rhines et al., 1997), and longer-term outcome studies are lacking. A number of studies currently are underway to further evaluate the range of patients for whom naltrexone is efficacious, its optimal duration of use and the most appropriate psychosocial treatments to be used in combination with the medication. In addition, based on promising initial results in the treatment of alcoholism obtained with the opioid antagonist nalmefene (Mason, Ritvo et al., 1994), further research with that medication currently is under way.

Catecholaminergic Agents. There is evidence from animal studies that adrenergic systems are involved in the reinforcing effects of ethanol (Lewis, 1990; Wise & Routtenberg, 1983). In outpatient alcoholics, the beta blocker atenolol decreased the desire to drink compared to placebo (Horwitz, Kraus & Gottlieb, 1987). However, a one-year follow-up study of the effects of continued treatment with atenolol on relapse prevention showed no advantage for the active drug (Gottlieb, Kraus et al., 1990).

Based on *in vivo* microdialysis in rats (Di Chiara & Imperato 1988), dopamine also has been implicated in the reinforcing effects of ethanol. In a placebo-controlled clinical trial, Borg (1983) found bromocriptine, a dopamine agonist, useful in relapse prevention. During a six-month trial, bromocriptine produced significantly improved outcomes, both in terms of alcohol craving and in psychosocial functioning. The level of ethanol consumption also was substantially reduced in the bromocriptine-treated patients, but no statistical comparison was made with the placebo-treated group. Dongier and colleagues (1991) reported that bromocriptine was more effective than placebo in the reduction of psychopathologic symptoms in alcohol-dependent subjects. However, the active and placebo groups showed a comparable (though marked) decrease in alcohol consumption. Given renewed interest in the role that dopamine plays in mediating the reinforcing effects of a variety of drugs of abuse (for a review, see Gardner, 1997), further evaluation of the efficacy of dopaminergic medications for the treatment of alcoholism, including that occurring together with dependence on other drugs (such as cocaine), would appear to be justified.

Serotonergic Agents. Naranjo and colleagues (1986), Gorelick (1989), and LeMarquand and colleagues (1994a, 1994b) have reviewed the extensive experimental literature that links 5-HT neurotransmission to alcohol consumption. Animal studies have linked 5-HT to aggression and readiness to ingest alcohol (Roy, Linnoila & Virkkunen, 1987), while human studies have linked low levels of 5-HT with violent and suicidal behavior and with alcoholism (Roy, Linnoila & Virkkunen, 1987). In rodents, 5-HT precursors and selective serotonin reuptake inhibitors (SSRIs) consistently decrease ethanol consumption (LeMarquand, Pihl & Benkelfat, 1994a; Naranjo, Sellers & Lawrin, 1986).

In humans, the data on the effects of SSRIs on alcohol consumption are more limited, and the results are less consistent. Both acute (Amit, Brown et al., 1985) and chronic (Naranjo, Sellers et al., 1984) administration of zimelidine, an SSRI that was removed from clinical trials due to toxicity, have shown that zimelidine reduces ethanol consumption. Other SSRIs that have been tested in humans to determine their effects on alcohol consumption include fluoxetine (Gerra, Caccavari et al., 1992; Gorelick & Paredes, 1992; Kabel & Petty, 1996; Naranjo, Kadlec et al., 1990; Kranzler, Burleson et al., 1995), citalopram (Naranjo, Sellers et al., 1987; Balldin, Berggren et al., 1994; Naranjo et al., 1995), viqualine (Naranjo, Sullivan et al., 1989), and fluvoxamine (Kranzler, Del Boca et al., 1993).

When alcoholics on an inpatient unit were given the opportunity to drink alcohol, fluoxetine pretreatment initially reduced alcohol consumption, but the effect did not persist (Gorelick & Paredes, 1992). Using a crossover design, Gerra, Caccavari et al. (1992) compared the effects of fluoxetine, acamprosate (discussed in detail below), and placebo in family-history-positive (FHP) and family-history-negative (FHN) alcoholics. They found that both active medications were superior to placebo in reducing the number of drinks consumed. However, the effect of fluoxetine was significant only in the FHP patients, while acamprosate produced a significant reduction only in the FHN patients. Kranzler and colleagues (1995) conducted a 12-week, placebo-controlled trial of fluoxetine in combination with coping skills psychotherapy in 101 alcohol-dependent subjects. They found no overall advantage to the active drug on drinking outcomes. In a further analysis of the data, the investigators (Kranzler, Burleson et al., 1996) found that, among the subgroup of patients with high levels of both premorbid vulnerability and alcohol-related problems, fluoxetine appeared to reduce the beneficial effects of coping skills training. Kabel and Petty (1996) found no effect of fluoxetine compared with placebo among severe alcoholics recruited from an alcoholism treatment program at a Veterans Affairs Medical Center.

The results obtained with several other SSRIs suggest that most of the drugs in this group are well tolerated (one exception being fluvoxamine [Kranzler, Del Boca et al., 1993]) and that they reduce drinking in non-depressed, heavy drinkers. The magnitude of the decrease, however, generally has not been large, with reductions typically in the range of 15% to 20% from pretreatment levels and the effects being limited to subgroups of heavy drinkers (Balldin, Berggren et al., 1994) or to the early period in treatment (Naranjo, Bremner & Lanctot, 1995). Despite these modest effects, a role may emerge for SSRIs in combination with other medications to which patients are refractory or to which they respond only partially.

AGENTS AFFECTING OTHER NEUROTRANSMITTER SYSTEMS

Acamprosate® (calcium acetylhomotaurinate), an amino acid derivative, is a particularly promising therapeutic agent. It is approved for use in a number of European countries and recently began clinical trials in the U.S. Acamprosate affects both gamma-aminobutyric acid (GABA) and excitatory amino acid (i.e., glutamate) neurotransmission. Based on its profile of clinical effects, Littleton (1995, 1996) has argued that acamprosate works by decreasing craving. While craving long has been criticized as a nonspecific, overused term (Kozlowski & Wilkinson 1987), Littleton (1995, 1996) has elaborated a compelling theory of the phenomenon, based on empirical findings from both the laboratory and the clinic. It is in this context that he seeks to explain the observed clinical effects of acamprosate.

Initially evaluated in a single-center trial in France, acamprosate was shown over a three-month treatment period to be twice as effective as placebo in reducing the rate at which alcoholics returned to drinking (Lhuintre, Moore et al., 1985). A subsequent three-month, multicenter study in France provided additional evidence for the use of acamprosate in postdetoxified alcoholics (Lhuintre, Moore et al., 1990). A large, multicenter study in France (Paille, Guelfi et al., 1995) showed a dose-response relationship for the medication over 12 months of active treatment, followed by six months of single-blind placebo. In this study, acamprosate generally was associated with significantly better rates of clinic attendance and more abstinent days, with the high-dose acamprosate showing the best outcomes, the placebo group the poorest outcomes, and the low-dose acamprosate group intermediate on these measures. More recently, acamprosate also has been shown to enhance treatment retention and the maintenance of abstinence among alcoholics in a six-month study in Belgium (Pelc, Le Bon et al., 1996).

In a multicenter study in Austria (Whitworth, Fischer et al., 1996), alcoholic patients were treated with acamprosate or placebo for 12 months and then followed up for an additional 12 months. During treatment, acamprosate-treated patients were significantly less likely to return to drinking, an effect that persisted during the post-treatment follow-up. Sass, Soyka et al. (1996) conducted a multicenter study in Germany, which also included 12-month treatment and post-treatment follow-up periods. These investigators found that acamprosate was superior to placebo with respect to treatment retention. Patients receiving the active medication also were more likely to remain abstinent during both the active treatment and follow-up periods.

In a multicenter study in Belgium, Netherlands, and Luxembourg, alcoholics were treated with either acamprosate or placebo for six months and then were followed up for an additional six months (Geerlings, Ansoms & van der Brink, 1997). Acamprosate-treated patients were significantly more likely to complete treatment and to remain abstinent during the treatment period than were placebo-treated patients. However, the beneficial effects, although evident at follow-up, did not reach statistical significance during the post-treatment period.

Together, these studies in more than 3,000 patients (a substantially greater number than have been studied with naltrexone) provide strong evidence of the efficacy of acamprosate in alcoholism rehabilitation. Further, the medication has a benign side-effect profile, with gastrointestinal symptoms most prominent. Based on these findings, the drug appears to have a promising future for the treatment of alcohol dependence. However, published studies of acamprosate have not employed standardized psychotherapeutic approaches. Consequently, an important goal of future studies should be to examine the interactive effects of psychotherapy with the medication. Further, studies are needed to identify subgroups of alcoholics who may be most responsive to acamprosate.

Summary. To date, the most promising agents that directly reduce alcohol consumption are the opiate antagonists (e.g., naltrexone) and acamprosate. Further research is required with these agents to identify the circumstances under which they are most efficacious, specifically including which patient groups, dosage schedules, duration of therapy, and concomitant psychosocial treatments are optimal for the use of these medications. Further, trials that compare and/or combine medications that show initial promise for relapse prevention (including SSRIs) are needed to determine the best strategies for pharmacotherapy in relapse prevention.

DRUGS IN THE TREATMENT OF POSTWITHDRAWAL AFFECTIVE DISTURBANCES

While many alcoholics feel considerably better after their acute withdrawal symptoms abate, for many others the anxiety, insomnia, and general distress of the acute withdrawal syndrome merge imperceptibly into a postwithdrawal state that may last for weeks or months. Some aspects of this post-acute withdrawal (e.g., irritability, insomnia) are referred to as "protracted withdrawal." Other symptoms may represent the emergence of diagnosable psychiatric disorders. Whether the treatment of either the persistent withdrawal symptoms or co-morbid disorders will result in a generally better outcome in alcoholic patients remains uncertain.

Multiple factors may play a causal role in the production of mood disturbances in the postwithdrawal period, including: (1) heavy alcohol intake; (2) acute and protracted withdrawal; (3) alcohol-induced CNS damage; (4) CNS damage from indirect effects of alcohol (e.g., head trauma, thiamine deficiency); (5) social, economic, and interpersonal losses; (6) antecedent psychiatric disorders; and (7) a cluster of signs and symptoms that may be referred to as the "defeat/depression/hypophoria cluster."

Most of the studies of the efficacy of pharmacotherapy for mood disturbances were carried out before the full extent of this diagnostic heterogeneity was recognized (Ciraulo & Jaffe, 1981). Consequently, treatment usually was directed at target symptoms of depression and anxiety in unselected groups of detoxified alcoholics. Under these circumstances, unless the patient samples are unusually homogeneous by chance or the drug in question works powerfully across diagnostic and etiological categories, consistent positive findings are unlikely.

There is now renewed interest in the incidence and prevalence of comorbid psychiatric disturbances among patients seeking treatment for alcohol abuse/dependence. It is evident that the majority of alcoholics who seek treatment meet lifetime criteria for psychiatric disorders in addition to alcoholism. Among the more common of these disorders are major depression, bipolar disorder, antisocial personality disorder, drug dependence, borderline personality disorder, phobias, and attention deficit disorder, residual type (hyperactivity syndrome) (Behar & Winokur, 1979; Mullaney & Trippett, 1979; Nace, Saxon & Shore, 1983; Wood, Wender & Reimherr, 1983; Ross, Glaser & Germenson 1988).

Among the drugs that have been used or proposed as treatment for anxiety and depression in the postwithdrawal state are tricyclic antidepressants, selective serotonin reuptake-inhibiting antidepressants, benzodiazepines and other anxiolytics, phenothiazines and other dopaminergic blockers, and lithium. The use of these drugs in alcoholics requires careful consideration of the potential for adverse effects in this patient population, attributable to co-morbid medical disorders (which are often present among alcoholics) and the pharmacokinetic effects of acute and chronic alcohol consumption. For example, it has been shown that chronic ethanol administration increases clearance of imipramine and desipramine, thereby reducing the therapeutic potential of these medications (Ciraulo, Alderson et al., 1982; Ciraulo, Barnhill & Jaffe, 1988). Moreover, disulfiram may interact with these and other medications used to treat comorbid psychiatric disorders in alcoholics (Ciraulo, Barnhill & Boxenbaum, 1985; Gorelick, 1993). Although indications for the use of these medications in alcoholics are similar to those for non-alcoholic populations and can be arrived at only through careful psychiatric diagnosis, the choice of medications should take into account the increased potential for drug interactions among alcoholics.

Tricyclic Antidepressants (TCAs). TCAs have been widely used in the treatment of alcoholic patients. However, because alcoholics have been routinely excluded from antidepressant trials, only recently has firm evidence of their efficacy in such patients become available. In most studies, a therapeutically inadequate dosage was used and no effort was made to compensate for the fact that both cigarette smoking and heavy drinking can stimulate liver enzymes that metabolize drugs (Ciraulo & Jaffe, 1981). Ciraulo, Alderson et al. (1982) have shown that the intrinsic clearance of imipramine in alcoholics is 2.5 times that of controls. After a standard 150-mg dose of imipramine, alcoholics have steady-state concentrations of imipramine and its metabolites that are subtherapeutic. The effect on imipramine clearance is greater than that on desipramine clearance (Ciraulo, Barnhill & Jaffe, 1988).

Nunes, McGrath et al. (1993) conducted an open-label study in which alcoholics with primary major depression or dysthymic disorder who responded to imipramine treatment were randomly assigned to continue on imipramine or switch to placebo. Despite a small sample size, there was a trend for the active drug to prevent a relapse to depression and heavy drinking. In a study of outpatient alcoholics with primary depression, imipramine treatment was found to result in a modest improvement in depressive symptoms, but no overall effect on drinking measures (McGrath, Nunes et al., 1996). These investigators did find that effective treatment of depression was associated with decreased risk of heavy drinking, with those patients responding to imipramine having the lowest risk of heavy drinking. However, it is unclear whether adequate treatment of depression resulted in a decrease in drinking, or improvement in drinking led to a reduction in depressive symptoms.

The efficacy of pharmacotherapy for secondary depression in alcoholics has also recently been demonstrated (Mason, Kocsis et al., 1996). In this study, in which desipramine or placebo treatment was initiated after a median of eight days of abstinence, the active drug was found to be superior in reducing both depressive symptoms and heavy drinking. The antidepressant response that was observed suggests that the common practice of requiring a period of two to four weeks before initiating antidepressant therapy may be excessive.

Even if one accepts the view that most instances of postwithdrawal depression and "blues" will spontaneously remit within a few days to several weeks (Schuckit, 1983; Brown & Schuckit, 1988), there are some patients whose severe and persistent depression requires treatment. In these cases, TCAs may be employed. However, both because alcoholics may be less compliant with the recommended dosage than are nonalcoholic depressives and because heavy drinking and smoking may increase clearance of TCAs (Ciraulo, Alderson et al., 1982; Ciraulo, Barnhill & Jaffe, 1988; see Sands Knapp et al., 1995, for a review), the monitoring of plasma levels is recommended.

Selective Serotonin Reuptake Inhibitors. There are a limited number of studies with serotonin reuptake-inhibiting antidepressants, such as fluoxetine, in the treatment of major depression in alcoholics. A small, open-label study of inpatient, depressed, suicidal alcoholics showed that fluoxetine reduced depressive symptoms and alcohol consumption (Cornelius, Salloum et al., 1993). More recently, a 12-week, placebo-controlled, double-blind study by these investigators showed fluoxetine to be superior in reducing both depressive symptoms and total alcohol consumption in 51 patients diagnosed with major depression and alcohol dependence (Cornelius, Salloum et al., 1997). Similarly, in a placebo-controlled trial of fluoxetine for relapse prevention in alcoholics (Kranzler, Burleson et al., 1995), the subgroup with current major depression showed a greater reduction in depressive symptoms in response to the active drug. However, the size of the subsample was too small in that study to permit a meaningful evaluation of the effect of reduced depression on alcohol consumption.

Benzodiazepines (BZs) and Other Anxiolytics. BZs are widely used in the treatment of acute alcohol withdrawal. However, anxiety, depression, and sleep disturbances can persist for months following withdrawal. Consequently, it is unclear where withdrawal ends and other causes of anxiety and disturbed sleep begin. Nonetheless, most nonmedical personnel involved in the treatment of alcoholism are opposed to the use of medication that can induce any variety of dependence.

The increased risk of dependence notwithstanding, there may be an important role for the judicious use of BZs in alcoholics. The dropout rate from alcoholism rehabilitation may be very high, often as the result of a relapse to drinking. To the degree that early relapse is a result of continued withdrawal-related symptoms (e.g., anxiety, depression, insomnia) that can be suppressed by low doses of BZs, such use may enhance retention in treatment (Kissin, 1977). Moreover, for some patients, BZ dependence—if it does occur—may be more benign than alcoholism.

These important potential benefits must be weighed against the risk both of BZ overdose and of physical dependence on the drug. While BZs alone are comparatively safe, even in overdose, their combination with other brain depressants (including alcohol) can be lethal. Although there is little doubt that alcoholics are vulnerable to developing dependence on the BZs, the probability of abuse and dependence may be lower than generally is believed (Bliding, 1978; Marks, 1978; Ciraulo, Barnhill et al., 1990). However, dependence on both alcohol and BZs may increase depressive symptoms and BZ dependence may be more difficult to treat than alcoholism alone (Sokolow, Welte et al., 1981).

The BZs currently available for clinical use vary substantially in terms of pharmacokinetics, acute euphoriant effects and frequency of reported dependence. It is likely, therefore, that not all BZs have the same potential for abuse. Kissin (1977) believed that chlordiazepoxide was the BZ of choice for use in alcoholics. Wolf and colleagues (1990) offer evidence that diazepam, lorazepam, and alprazolam may have greater abuse potential than chlordiazepoxide and clorazepate. Bliding (1978) reported low levels of abuse with oxazepam. Jaffe, Ciraulo et al. (1983) found that, in recently detoxified alcoholics, halazepam produces minimal euphoria even at supratherapeutic doses. A number of partial BZ agonist and mixed BZ agonist/antagonist drugs now in development may offer an advantage over approved BZs for use in alcoholics.

Buspirone, a nonbenzodiazepine anxiolytic, appears to exert its effects largely via its agonist activity at serotonergic autoreceptors. It is equal to diazepam in the relief of anxiety and associated depression in outpatients with moderate to severe anxiety. Buspirone may, however, have several advantages: it is less sedating than diazepam or clorazepate, does not interact with alcohol to impair psychomotor skills, and does not appear to have abuse liability.

A double-blind, placebo-controlled trial of buspirone in alcoholics (Bruno, 1989) showed significantly greater retention in treatment and greater decreases in alcohol craving, anxiety, and depression scores in buspirone-treated patients. Although both groups showed significant declines in alcohol consumption during the study, buspirone treatment did not differentially reduce alcohol consumption. Tollefson and colleagues (1992) reported an advantage for buspirone over placebo in abstinent alcoholics with comorbid generalized anxiety disorder. These investigators found that buspirone-treated subjects were less likely to discontinue treatment prematurely and had greater reductions in anxiety than did placebo-treated subjects. While a subjective, global measure of improvement in drinking was observed for the active drug group, measures of alcohol consumption were not reported in this study. Kranzler, Burleson et al. (1994) also found that, in anxious alcoholics, buspirone was superior to placebo in terms of retention in treatment. The active drug also delayed relapse to heavy drinking and, during a six-month posttreatment follow-up period, it reduced the number of drinking days. The beneficial effects of buspirone on both anxiety and drinking were most evident among the patients with the highest baseline anxiety scores.

In contrast to these three reports, a recent placebo-controlled study by Malcolm and colleagues (1992) showed the drug to have no advantage over placebo in treatment retention or on anxiety or drinking measures in an anxious, severely alcohol-dependent patient sample. While there appears to be a role for buspirone in the treatment of anxiety in alcoholics, further research is needed to identify the most appropriate patient group in which to use the drug.

Phenothiazines and Other Dopaminergic Blockers. These drugs are of obvious importance in the treatment of alcoholics with comorbid psychotic disorders (e.g., schizophrenia). Several studies have also compared the effects of dopaminergic blockers with those of placebo on symptoms of anxiety, tension, or depression during the postwithdrawal phase (Behar & Winokur, 1979; Rada & Kellner, 1979; Smith, 1978). As with most studies of TCAs, patients on placebo also showed substantial improvement and the differences in favor of the active drugs were not great. In one study, a low dosage of thioridazine was superior to placebo in the reduction of tension and insomnia, but the placebo group did better in terms of work and activity (Hague, Wilson et al., 1976).

The selective dopaminergic receptor blocker, tiapride, also was studied in depressed and anxious alcoholics (Shaw, Majumdar et al., 1987). Although the study's findings are limited by a high dropout rate, subjects treated with the active drug drank less and had longer periods of abstinence than the placebo-treated patients. Tiapride-treated patients also showed less neuroticism, anxiety, and depression; expressed greater satisfaction with their social situations and physical health; and exhibited fewer physical complications of alcoholism (Shaw, Majumdar et al., 1987). At present, given the equivocal results of trials of antipsychotics in alcoholics and the potential for adverse effects, such as tardive dyskinesia, long-term use of these medications in alcoholics without coexistent psychotic disorder is not warranted.

Lithium. Several placebo-controlled studies of lithium for alcoholism have been reported. The initial study by Kline, Wren et al. (1974) involved 73 male veterans who had high scores on the Zung Self-Rating Scale for depression. Thus, all subjects were depressed by this criterion, but those with diagnoses of unipolar and bipolar depression were excluded. At the end of the 48-week double-blind treatment period, only 16 lithium and 14 placebo patients were still in the study. The Zung scores for those remaining on lithium were comparable to those on placebo, but lithium patients had experienced significantly fewer days of pathological drinking and hospitalization for alcoholism.

A study by Merry, Reynolds et al. (1976) began with 71 patients, 48% of whom were considered depressed, based on their scores on the Beck Depression Inventory (BDI). At the end of an average of 41 weeks of treatment, BDI scores were improved for both groups, with patients in the lithium group doing somewhat better than those in the placebo group. Among those categorized as depressed at the start of treatment, patients on lithium had spent significantly fewer days drinking and incapacitated by drinking compared to those on placebo. This comparison, however, involved only nine "depressed" patients on lithium and seven "depressed" patients on placebo.

Lithium also has been studied in young, institutionalized delinquents with histories of aggressive behavior and in prisoners with histories of recurrent patterns of violent behavior following minimal provocation (Kellner & Rada, 1979). In these studies, violent, angry behavior decreased with lithium treatment, while other forms of sociopathic behavior did not. Since alcoholism is particularly prevalent and has a particularly poor prognosis among these groups, these studies of lithium in prisoners and delinquents may have substantial clinical relevance. Lithium may produce its clinical effects in alcoholics via increased serotonergic tone (Zucker & Branchey, 1985).

Fawcett and colleagues (1987) found that compliance with either lithium or placebo was associated with abstinence in alcoholics who were not selected for coexistent depression. Moreover, compliant patients taking active medication who had therapeutic serum levels (0.4 meq/l or greater) were abstinent more often than were compliant subjects with subtherapeutic lithium levels. After the first six months, however, even those subjects who were compliant early in the study tended to stop taking their medication. Nevertheless, the association between early compliance and sobriety persisted, suggesting that the beneficial effects of lithium are greatest in the early months after detoxification. The beneficial effect of lithium did not appear to be mediated by an antidepressant effect, since it did not affect mood in those patients who were depressed.

Dorus and colleagues (1989) conducted a multicenter, double-blind placebo-controlled trial in depressed and nondepressed alcoholic veterans. A total of 457 male alcoholics, of whom approximately one-third were depressed, were randomly assigned to receive either 600 or 1,200 mg per day of lithium or a comparable number of placebo capsules. No significant differences between lithium-treated and placebo-treated patients were found on any of a variety of outcome measures, including number of drinking days, alcohol-related hospitalizations, and severity of depression. The lack of efficacy was observed for both the depressed and the non-depressed groups. This large, carefully conducted trial suggests that lithium should be reserved for the treatment of those alcoholics with comorbid bipolar disorder.

CONCLUSIONS

In general, with the exception of the central role that BZs play in the treatment of alcohol withdrawal, pharmacotherapy has not yet had a demonstrably large effect on alcoholism treatment. However, recent developments, including approval of naltrexone for relapse prevention in the U.S. and Europe, and of acamprosate in Europe, suggest that the use of medications eventually may contribute substantially to the treatment of alcoholism. Nevertheless, there remain a considerable number of unstudied questions that must be examined before medications can be widely employed in the treatment of alcohol dependence. In addition to the issues discussed earlier in regard to specific agents (e.g., concerning the optimal duration of use of naltrexone), the safety and efficacy of medications for treatment of alcohol dependence must be examined in women, in various ethnic and racial groups, and in adolescent and geriatric populations. Data on pharmacotherapy for relapse prevention in these groups are virtually nonexistent (Gorelick, 1993).

Increasingly, psychiatric comorbidity is being recognized as an important determinant of the effectiveness of alcoholism rehabilitation. Persistent psychiatric disturbances interfere with psychosocial treatments. Thus, pharmacologic agents effective in treating psychiatric symptomatology may provide important benefits for relapse prevention. Anxiolytics that appear to have little abuse potential, such as buspirone, and antidepressants that also may influence ethanol intake, such as desipramine and fluoxetine, warrant careful evaluation in the treatment of anxious and depressed alcoholics.

However, the relationship between substance use and psychiatric symptomatology is complex (Meyer, 1986). Drugs that ameliorate persistent mood and anxiety symptoms will not necessarily produce changes in alcohol consumption once a significant degree of alcohol dependence develops. This may be so even if pathological mood states were important in the initiation of heavy drinking. Once the neuroadaptive changes and the complex learning that constitute the dependence syndrome occur, alcohol dependence becomes autonomous (Edwards & Gross, 1976; Wikler, 1980), and does not resolve simply because one major contributing factor is brought under control. Efforts to change pathological alcohol use patterns must accompany any treatment, including pharmacotherapy, aimed at control of pathological mood states. The challenge for those treating alcoholics is to combine medication effectively with psychotherapy and self-help group participation (Meza & Kranzler, 1996).

Drugs that directly affect alcohol consumption may be most useful as adjuncts to cognitive-behavioral, relapse prevention treatment (O'Malley et al., 1992). In this regard, the drugs that appear most promising are naltrexone and acamprosate. Multiple studies of these medications, administered in conjunction with psychotherapy, currently are underway. As the research literature on the use of these drugs grows, it will be possible to assess their utility in conjunction with a variety of psychotherapies or as one element in a multimodal program for the treatment of alcoholism. Efforts to match medications with specific subgroups of alcoholics also are a promising strategy.

As is true of the use of medications to treat comorbid psychopathology, the use of medications to reduce drinking must be integrated with psychosocial treatment. Although medications have not become a mainstream therapy in alcoholism treatment programs, combining medications with self-help group participation may represent a particular challenge (Meza & Kranzler, 1996). Abstinence-oriented groups such as Alcoholics Anonymous see the alcohol sensitizing agents as supportive of their goal of total abstinence and are willing to work with physicians around the issue of proper dosage, compliance, and early detection of side effects. For alcoholic patients who participate in self-help groups, it may be necessary to communicate the view that effective pharmacotherapy of associated anxiety and mood disturbances is complementary, rather than competitive, with abstinence-oriented change and support systems. Similarly, the use of medications to reduce the risk of relapse through direct effects on craving or drinking behavior should be seen as potentially additive or synergistic to self-help efforts.

It does not seem unduly optimistic to predict that by early in the new millenium, a number of medications will have been convincingly demonstrated to be efficacious for the treatment of comorbid psychopathology and/or the prevention of relapse in alcoholics. In anticipation of these developments, attention also must be directed to enhancing the acceptability of these medications to the alcoholism treatment community as a standard ingredient in alcoholism rehabilitation (Meza & Kranzler, 1996).

REFERENCES

Allen JP & Litten RZ (1992). Techniques to enhance compliance with disulfiram. *Alcoholism: Clinical & Experimental Research* 16:1035–1041.

Amit Z, Brown Z, Sutherland A, Rockman G, Gill K & Selvaggi N (1985). Reduction in alcohol intake in humans as a function of treatment with zimelidine: Implications for treatment. In CA Naranjo & EM Sellers (eds.) *Research Advances in New Psychopharmacological Treatments for Alcoholism*. Amsterdam, Holland: Elsevier.

Amit Z, Smith BR, Brown ZW & Williams RL (1982). An examination of the role of TIQ alkaloids in alcohol intake: Reinforcers, satiety agents or artifacts. In F Bloom, J Barchas & M Sandler et al. (eds.) *Beta-Carbolines and Tetrahydroisoquinolines*. New York, NY: Alan R. Liss, Inc.

Azrin NH, Sisson RW, Meyers R & Godley M (1982). Alcoholism treatment by disulfiram and community reinforcement therapy. *Journal of Behavior Therapy and Experimental Psychiatry* 13:105–112.

Balldin J, Berggren U, Engel J, Eriksson M, Hard E & Soderpalm B (1994). Effect of citalopram on alcohol intake in heavy drinkers. *Alcoholism: Clinical & Experimental Research* 18:1133- 1136.

Behar D & Winokur G (1979). Research in alcoholism and depression: A two-way street under construction. In RW Pickens & LL Heston (eds.) *Psychiatric Factors in Drug Abuse*. New York, NY: Grune & Stratton, 125–152.

Bergstrom B, Ohlin H, Lindblom PE & Wadstein J (1982). Is disulfiram implantation effective? *Lancet* 1:49–50.

Bliding A (1978). The abuse potential of benzodiazepines with special reference to oxazepam. *Acta Psychiatrica Scandinavica* 24(Suppl):111–116.

Borg V (1983). Bromocriptine in the prevention of alcohol abuse. *Acta Psychiatrica Scandinavica* 68:100–110.

Brewer C (1984). How effective is the standard dose of disulfiram? A review of the alcohol-disulfiram reaction in practice. *British Journal of Psychiatry* 144:200–202.

Brown SA & Schuckit MA (1988). Changes in depression among abstinent alcoholics. *Journal of Studies on Alcohol* 49:412–417.

Bruno F (1989). Buspirone in the treatment of alcoholic patients. *Psychopathology* 22(Suppl 1):49–59.

Ciraulo DA & Jaffe JH (1981). Tricyclic antidepressants in the treatment of depression associated with alcoholism. *Journal of Clinical Psychopharmacology* 1:146–150.

Ciraulo DA, Alderson LM, Chapron DJ, Jaffe JH, Subbarao B & Kramer PA (1982). Imipramine disposition in alcoholics. *Journal of Clinical Psychopharmacology* 2:2–7.

Ciraulo DA, Barnhill J & Boxenbaum HG (1985). Pharmacokinetic interaction of disulfiram and antidepressants. *American Journal of Psychiatry* 142:1373–1374.

Ciraulo DA, Barnhill JG & Jaffe JH (1988). Clinical pharmacokinetics of imipramine and desipramine in alcoholics and normal volunteers. *Clinical Pharmacology and Therapeutics* 43:509–518.

Ciraulo DA, Barnhill JG, Jaffe JH, Ciraulo AM & Tarmey MF (1990). Intravenous pharmacokinetics of 2-hydroxyimipramine in alcoholics and normal controls. *Journal of Studies on Alcohol* 51:366–372.

Cohen G & Collins MS (1970). Alkaloids from catecholamines in adrenal tissues: Possible role in alcoholism. *Science* 167:1749–1751.

Cornelius JR, Salloum IM, Cornelius MD et al. (1993). Fluoxetine trial in suicidal depressed alcoholics. *Psychopharmacology Bulletin* 29:195–199.

Cornelius JR, Salloum IM, Ehler JG et al. (1997). Fluoxetine in depressed alcoholics: A double-blind, placebo-controlled trial. *Archives of General Psychiatry* 54:700–705.

DiChiara G & Imperato A (1988). Drugs abused by humans preferentially increase synaptic dopamine concentrations in the mesolimbic system of freely moving rats. *Proceedings of the National Academy of Sciences* 85:5274–5278.

Dongier M, Vachon L & Schwartz G (1991). Bromocriptine in the treatment of alcohol dependence. *Alcoholism: Clinical & Experimental Research* 15:970–977.

Dorus W, Ostrow DG, Anton R, Cushman P, Collins JF, Schaefer M, Charles HL, Desai P, Hayashida M, Malkerneker U, Willenbring M, Fiscella R & Sather MR (1989). Lithium treatment of depressed and nondepressed alcoholics. *Journal of the American Medical Association* 262:1646–1652.

Edwards G & Gross MM (1976). Alcohol dependence: Provisional description of a clinical syndrome. *British Medical Journal* 1:10581061.

Favazza AR & Martin P (1974). Chemotherapy of delirium tremens: A survey of physicians' preferences. *American Journal of Psychiatry* 131:1031–1033.

Fawcett J, Clark DC, Aagesen CA, Pisani VD, Tilkin JM, Sellers D, McGuire M & Gibbons RD (1987). A double-blind, placebo-controlled trial of lithium carbonate therapy for alcoholism. *Archives of General Psychiatry* 44:248–256.

Fuller RK, Branchey L, Brightwell DR, Derman RM, Emrick CD, Iber FL, James KE, Lacoursiere RB, Lee KK, Lowenstam I, Maany I, Neiderhiser D, Nocks JJ & Shas S (1986). Disulfiram treatment of alcoholism: A Veteran's Administration Cooperative Study. *Journal of the American Medical Association* 256:1449–1455.

Gardner E (1997). Brain reward mechanisms. In JN Lowinson, P Ruiz, RB Millman & J Lagrod (eds.). *Substance Abuse: A Comprehensive Textbook, 3rd Edition*. Baltimore, MD: Williams & Wilkins, 51–85.

Geerlings PJ, Ansoms C & van den Brink W (1997). Acamprosate and prevention of relapse in alcoholics. *European Addiction Research* 3:129–137.

Gerra G, Caccavari R, Delsignore R, Bocchi R, Fertonani G & Passeri M (1992). Effects of fluoxetine and Ca-acetyl-homotaurinate on alcohol intake in familial and nonfamilial alcohol patients. *Current Therapeutic Research* 52:291–295.

Gorelick DA (1993). Recent developments in pharmacological treatment of alcoholism. In M. Galanter (ed.) *Recent Developments in Alcoholism, Vol. 11.* New York, NY: Plenum Publishing Co., 413–427.

Gorelick DA (1989). Serotonin uptake blockers and the treatment of alcoholism. In M Galanter (ed.) *Recent Developments in Alcoholism*, Vol. 7. New York, NY: Plenum Publishing Co., 267–281.

Gorelick DA & Paredes A (1992). Effect of fluoxetine on alcohol consumption in male alcoholics. *Alcoholism: Clinical & Experimental Research* 16:261–265.

Gottlieb L, Kraus ML, Segal S & Horwitz RI (1990). Beta-blocker therapy does not prevent long-term alcohol relapse. *Clinical Research* 38:694A.

Hague WH, Wilson LG, Dudley DL & Cannon DS (1976). Post-detoxification drug treatment of anxiety and depression in alcoholic addicts. *Journal of Nervous and Mental Disease* 162:354–359.

Hesselbrock MN, Hesselbrock VM, Tennen H, Meyer RE & Workman KL (1983). Measurement of depression in alcoholics. *Journal of Clinical Consulting Psychology* 51:399–405.

Hiller JM, Aangel LM & Simon EJ (1981). Multiple opiate receptors: Alcohol selectively inhibits binding to delta receptors. *Science* 214:468–469.

Horwitz RI, Kraus ML & Gottlieb LD (1987). The efficacy of atenolol and the mediating effects of craving in the outpatient management of alcohol withdrawal. *Clinical Research* 35:348A.

Hoyumpa AM & Schenker S (1982). Major drug interactions: Effect of liver disease, alcohol and malnutrition. *Annual Review of Medicine* 33:113–149.

Jaffe JH, Ciraulo DA, Nies A, Dixon R & Monroe L (1983). Abuse potential of halazepam and diazepam in patients recently treated for acute alcohol withdrawal. *Clinical Pharmacology and Therapeutics* 34:623–630.

Jaffe JH, Kranzler HR & Ciraulo DA (1992). Drugs Used in the Treatment of Alcoholism. In J Mendelson & N Mello (eds.) *Medical Diagnosis and Treatment of Alcoholism.* New York, NY: McGraw-Hill, Inc., 421–461.

Jaffe AJ, Rounsaville B, Chang G, Schottenfeld RS, Meyer RE & O'Malley SS (1996). Naltrexone, relapse prevention and supportive therapy with alcoholics: An analysis of patient treatment matching. *Journal of Consulting and Clinical Psychology* 64:1044–1053.

Kabel DI & Petty F (1996). A double blind study of fluoxetine in severe alcohol dependence: Adjunctive therapy during and after inpatient treatment. *Alcoholism: Clinical & Experimental Research* 20:780–784.

Kellner R & Rada RT (1979). Pharmacotherapy of personality disorders. In JM Davis & D Greenblatt (eds.) *Psychopharmacology Update: New and Neglected Areas.* New York, NY: Plenum Press, 55–103.

Kissin B (1977). Medical management of the alcoholic patient. In B Kissin & H Begleiter (eds.) *The Biology of Alcoholism—Volume 5. Treatment and Rehabilitation of the Chronic Alcoholic.* New York, NY: Plenum Publishing Co., 55–103.

Kline NS, Wren JC, Cooper TB, Varga E & Canal 0 (1974). Evaluation of lithium therapy in chronic and periodic alcoholism. *American Journal of Medical Sciences* 268:15–22.

Kozlowski LT & Wilkinson DA (1987). Use and misuse of the concept of craving by alcohol, tobacco, and drug researchers. *British Journal of Addiction* 82:31–36.

Kranzler HR, ed. (1995). *The Pharmacology of Alcohol Abuse.* New York, NY: Springer verlag.

Kranzler HR, Burleson JA, Brown J & Babor TF (1996). Fluoxetine treatment seems to reduce the beneficial effects of cognitive-behavioral therapy in Type B alcoholics. *Alcoholism: Clinical & Experimental Research* 20:1534–1541.

Kranzler HR, Burleson JA, Del Boca FK et al. (1994). Buspirone treatment of anxious alcoholics: A placebo-controlled trial. *Archives of General Psychiatry* 51:720–731.

Kranzler HR, Burleson JA, Korner P et al. (1995). Placebo-controlled trial of fluoxetine as an adjunct to relapse prevention in alcoholics. *American Journal of Psychiatry* 152:391–397.

Kranzler HR, Del Boca F, Korner P & Brown J (1993). Adverse effects limit the usefulness of fluvoxamine for the treatment of alcoholism. *Journal of Substance Abuse Treatment* 10:283–287.

Kranzler HR, Mason B & Modesto-Lowe V (1998). Prevalence, diagnosis and treatment of comorbid mood disorders and alcoholism. In HR Kranzler & BJ Rounsaville (eds.) *Dual Diagnosis: Substance Abuse and Comorbid Medical and Psychiatric Disorders.* New York, NY: Marcel Dekker, 107–136.

Kranzler HR, Mason BJ, Pettinati HM & Anton RF (1997). Methodological issues in pharmacotherapy trials with alcoholics. In M Hertzman & D Feltner (eds.) *The Handbook of Psychopharmacology Trials.* New York, NY: New York University Press, 213–245.

LeMarquand D, Pihl RO & Benkelfat C (1994a). Serotonin and alcohol intake, abuse, and dependence: Findings of animal studies. *Biological Psychiatry* 36:395–421.

LeMarquand D, Pihl RO & Benkelfat C (1994b). Serotonin and alcohol intake, abuse, and dependence: Clinical evidence. *Biological Psychiatry* 36:326–337.

Lewis M (1990). Alcohol: Mechanisms of addiction and reinforcement. *Advances in Alcohol and Substance Abuse* 9:47–66.

Lhuintre JP, Moore N, Saligaut C et al. (1985). Ability of calcium bis acetyl homotaurinate, a GABA agonist, to prevent relapse in weaned alcoholics. *Lancet* 1:1014–1016.

Lhuintre JP, Moore N, Tran G et al. (1990). Acamprosate appears to decrease alcohol intake in weaned alcoholics. *Alcohol & Alcoholism* 25:613–622.

Lindros Ko, Stowell A, Pikkarainen P & Salaspuro M (1981). The disulfiram (Antabuse)-alcohol reaction in male alcoholics: Its efficient management by 4-methylpyrazole. *Alcoholism: Clinical & Experimental Research* 5:528–530.

Litten RZ, Allen JP & Yertig J. (1996). Pharmacotherapies for Alcohol problems: A review of research, with focus on developments since 1991. *Alcoholism: Clinical & Experimental Research* 20:859–876.

Littleton J (1995). Acamprosate in alcohol dependence: How does it work? *Addiction* 90:1179–1188.

Littleton J (1996). The neurobiology of craving: Potential mechanisms for acamprosate. In M Soyka (ed.) *Acamprosate in Relapse Prevention of Alcoholism.* Berlin, Germany: Springer verlag, 27–46.

Major LF, Lerner P, Ballenger JK, Brown GL, Goodwin FK & Lovenberg W (1979). Dopamine beta-hydroxylase in the cerebrospinal fluid: Relationship to disulfiram induced psychosis. *Biological Psychiatry* 14:337–344.

Malcolm R, Anton RF, Randall CL, Johnston A, Brady K & Thevos A (1992). A placebo-controlled trial of buspirone in anxious inpatient alcoholics. *Alcoholism: Clinical & Experimental Research* 16:1007–1013.

Marks J (1978). *The Benzodiazepines: Use, Misuse, Abuse*. Lancaster, England: MTP Press, Ltd.

Mason BJ, Kocsis JH, Ritvo EC et al. (1996). A double-blind, placebo-controlled trial of desipramine for primary alcohol dependence stratified on the presence or absence of major depression. *Journal of the American Medical Association* 275:761–767.

Mason BJ, Ritvo EC, Morgan RO et al. (1994). A double-blind, placebo-controlled pilot study to evaluate the efficacy and safety of oral nalmefene HCL for alcohol dependence. *Alcoholism: Clinical & Experimental Research* 18:1162–1167.

McGrath PJ, Nunes EV, Stewart JW et al. (1996). Imipramine treatment of alcoholics with primary depression. *Archives of General Psychiatry* 53:232–240.

Merry J, Reynolds CM, Bailey J & Coppen A (1976). Prophylactic treatment of alcoholism by lithium carbonate. *Lancet* 2:481–482.

Meyer RE (1986). How to understand the relationship between psychopathology and addictive disorders: Another example of the chicken and the egg. In RE Meyer (ed.) *Psychopathology and Addictive Disorders*. New York, NY: Guilford Press.

Meza E & Kranzler HR (1996). Closing the gap between alcoholism research and practice: The case of pharmacotherapy. *Psychiatric Services* 47:917–920.

Mullaney JA & Trippett CJ (1979). Alcohol dependence and phobias: Clinical description and relevance. *Psychiatry* 135:565–573.

Myers RD, Borg S & Mossberg R (1986). Antagonism by naltrexone of voluntary alcohol selection in the chronically drinking macaque monkey. *Alcohol* 3:383–388.

Nace CP, Saxon JJ & Shore N (1983). A comparison of borderline and nonborderline alcoholic patients. *Archives of General Psychiatry* 40:54–56.

Naranjo CA, Bremner KE & Lanctot KL (1995). Effects of citalopram and a brief psycho-social intervention on alcohol intake, dependence, and problems. *Addiction* 90:87–99.

Naranjo CA, Kadlec KE, Sanhueza P, Woodley-Remus D & Sellers EM (1990). Fluoxetine differentially alters alcohol intake and other consummatory behaviors in problem drinkers. *Clinical Pharmacology and Therapeutics* 47:490–498.

Naranjo CA, Sellers EM & Lawrin M (1986). Modulation of ethanol intake by serotonin uptake inhibitors. *Journal of Clinical Psychiatry* 47(Suppl):16–22.

Naranjo CA, Sellers EM, Roach CA, Woodley DV, Sanchez-Craig M & Sykora K (1984). Zimelidine-induced variations in alcohol intake by nondepressed heavy drinkers. *Clinical Pharmacology and Therapeutics* 35:374–381.

Naranjo CA, Sellers EM, Sullivan JT, Woodley DV, Kadlec K & Sykora K (1987). The serotonin uptake inhibitor citalopram attenuates ethanol intake. *Clinical Pharmacology and Therapeutics* 41:266–274.

Naranjo CA, Sullivan JT, Kadlec KE, Woodley-Remus DV, Kennedy G & Sellers EM (1989). Differential effects of viqualine on alcohol intake and other consummatory behaviors. *Clinical Pharmacology and Therapeutics* 46:301–309.

Nunes EV, McGrath PJ, Quitkin FM et al. (1993). Imipramine treatment of alcoholism with comorbid depression. *American Journal of Psychiatry* 150:963–965.

O'Malley SS, Croop RS, Wroblewski JM, Labriola DF & Volpicelli JR (1995). Naltrexone in the treatment of alcohol dependence: A combined analysis of two trials. *Psychiatric Annals* 25:681–688.

O'Malley SS, Jaffe AJ, Chang G, Schottenfeld RS, Meyer RE & Rounsaville B (1996b). Six-month follow-up of naltrexone and psychotherapy for alcohol dependence. *Archives of General Psychiatry* 53:217–224.

O'Malley SS, Jaffe AJ, Chang G, Schottenfeld RS, Meyer RE & Rounsaville B (1992). Naltrexone and coping skills therapy for alcohol dependence: A controlled study. *Archives of General Psychiatry* 49:894–898.

O'Malley SS, Jaffe AJ, Rode S et al. (1996a). Experience of a "slip" among alcoholics treated with naltrexone or placebo. *American Journal of Psychiatry* 153:281–283.

Paille FM, Guelfi JD, Perkins AC, Royer RJ, Steru L & Parot P (1995). Double-blind randomized multicentre trial of acamprosate in maintaining abstinence from alcohol. *Alcohol & Alcoholism* 30:239–247.

Peachey JE & Annis H (1985). New strategies for using the alcohol-sensitizing drugs. In CA Naranjo & EM Sellers (eds.) *Research Advances in New Psychopharmacological Treatments for Alcoholism*. New York, NY: Excerpta Medica, 199–218.

Peachey JE, Annis HM, Bornstein ER, Sykora K, Maglana SM & Shamai S (1989a.). Calcium carbimide in alcoholism treatment. Part 1: A placebo-controlled, double-blind clinical trial of short-term efficacy. *British Journal of Addiction* 84:877–887.

Peachey JE, Annis HM, Bornstein ER, Sykora K, Maglana SM & Shamai S (1989b). Calcium carbimide in alcoholism treatment. Part 2: Medical findings of a short-term, placebo-controlled, double-blind clinical trial. *British Journal of Addiction* 84:1359–1366.

Peachey JE, Brien JF, Roach CA & Loomis CW (1981a). A comparative review of the pharmacological and toxicological properties of disulfiram and calcium carbimide. *Journal of Clinical Psychopharmacology* 1:21–26.

Peachey JE, Maglana S, Robinson GM, Hemy M & Brien JF (1981b). Cardiovascular changes during the calcium carbimide-ethanol interaction. *Clinical Pharmacology and Therapeutics* 29:40–46.

Pelc I, Le Bon O, Lehert P & Verbanck P (1996). Acamprosate in the treatment of alcohol dependence: A 6-month postdetoxification study. In M Soyka (ed.) *Acamprosate in Relapse Prevention of Alcoholism*. Berlin, Germany: Springer verlag, 133–142.

Rada RR & Kellner R (1979). Drug treatment in alcoholism. In JM Davis & D Greenblatt (eds.) *Psychopharmacology Update: New and Neglected Areas*. New York, NY: Grune & Stratton, Inc., 105–144.

Ross HE, Glaser FB & Germanson T (1988). The prevalence of psychiatric disorders in patients with alcohol and other drug problems. *Archives of General Psychiatry* 45:1023–1031.

Roy A, Linnoila M & Virkkunen M (1987). Serotonin and alcoholism. *Substance Abuse* 8:21–27.

Sands BF, Knapp CM & Ciraulo DA (1995). Interaction of alcohol with therapeutic drugs and drugs of abuse. In HR Kranzler (ed.) *The Pharmacology of Alcohol Abuse*. New York, NY: Springer verlag, 475–512.

Sass H, Soyka M, Mann K & Zieglgansberger W (1996). Relapse prevention by acamprosate: Results from a placebo controlled study on alcohol dependence. *Archives of General Psychiatry* 53:673–680.

Schuckit M (1983). Alcoholic patients with secondary depression. *American Journal of Psychiatry* 140:711–714.

Sellers EM, Naranjo CA & Peachey JE (1981). Drugs to decrease alcohol consumption. *The New England Journal of Medicine* 305:12551262.

Shaw GK, Majumdar SK, Waller S et al. (1987). Tiapride in the long- term management of alcoholics of anxious or depressive temperament. *British Journal of Psychiatry* 150:164–168.

Smith CM (1978). *Alcoholism: Treatment*. Montreal, Ontario: Eden Press.

Sokolow L, Welte J, Hynes G & Lyons J (1981). Multiple substance use by alcoholics. *British Journal of Addiction* 76:147–158.

Swift RM, Whelihan W, Kuznetsov O et al. (1994). Naltrexone-induced alternations in human ethanol intoxication. *American Journal of Psychiatry* 151:1463–1467.

Tollefson G D, Montague-Clouse J & Tollefson SL (1992). Treatment of comorbid generalized anxiety in a recently detoxified alcohol population with a selective serotonergic drug (Buspirone). *Journal of Clinical Psychopharmacology* 12:19–26.

Vasquez JJ, Diaz de Otazu R, Guillen FJ, Zozaya J & Pardo FJ (1983). Hepatitis induced by drugs used as alcohol aversion therapy. *Diagnostic Histopathology* 6:29–37.

Volpicelli JR, O'Brien C, Alterman A & Hayashida M (1992). Naltrexone in the treatment of alcohol dependence. *Archives of General Psychiatry* 49:867–880.

Volpicelli JR, Watson NT, King AC et al. (1995). Effect of naltrexone on alcohol "high" in alcoholics. *American Journal of Psychiatry* 152:613–615.

Volpicelli JR, Rhines KC, Rhines JS, Volpicelli LA, Alterman AI & O'Brien CP (1997). Naltrexone and alcohol dependence: Role of subject compliance. *Archives of General Psychiatry* 54:737–742.

Whitworth AB, Fischer F, Lesch OM et al. (1996). Comparison of acamprosate and placebo in long-term treatment of alcohol dependence. *Lancet* 347:1438–1442.

Wikler A (1980). *Opioid Dependence*. New York, NY: Plenum Publishing Co.

Wilson A, Davidson WJ & Blanchard R (1980). Disulfiram implantation: A trial using placebo implants and two types of controls. *Journal of Studies on Alcohol* 41:429–436.

Wise RA & Routtenberg A (1983). Ethanol and brain mechanisms of reward. In B Kissin & H Begleiter (eds.) *The Pathogenesis of Alcoholism. Biological Factors*. New York, NY: Plenum Publishing Co., 77–105.

Wolf B, Iguchi MY & Griffiths RR (1990). Sedative/tranquilizer use and abuse in alcoholics currently in outpatient treatment: Incidence, pattern and preference. In LS Harris (ed.) *Problems of Drug Dependence, 1989* (NIDA Research Monograph No. 95). Rockville, MD: National Institute on Drug Abuse, 376–377.

Wood D, Wender PH & Reimherr FW (1983). The prevalence of attention deficit disorder, residual type, or minimal brain dysfunction, in a population of male alcoholic patients. *American Journal of Psychiatry* 140:95–98.

Zucker DK & Branchey L (1985). Lithium, CNS serotonergic tone, and intoxication. *American Journal of Psychiatry* 142:886–887.

CHAPTER 2

Pharmacologic Therapies for Benzodiazepine and Other Sedative-Hypnotic Addiction

Donald R. Wesson, M.D.
David E. Smith, M.D., FASAM
Walter Ling, M.D.

Neuroadaptation versus Physiologic Dependence
Biological Vulnerabilities
Issues in Diagnosing and Treating Dependence on Sedative-Hypnotics
Indications for Initiating Withdrawal
Benzodiazepine Withdrawal Syndromes
Pharmacologic Management of Withdrawal
Post-Withdrawal Treatment

The pharmacological classification of sedative-hypnotics draws attention to the therapeutic applications of these drugs. Sedative-hypnotics generally are prescribed to treat anxiety and insomnia. They are known as "depressants" because, in high doses, they obtund consciousness and reduce respiration. In overdose, they can produce coma and death.

The term "depressants" should be used with caution in referring to the sedative-hypnotics because of the potential for confusion with depression as a mood disorder. This potential for confusion is compounded by the observation that clinical depression often is present in individuals who are sedative-hypnotic dependent; in such persons, chronic use of sedative-hypnotics appears to cause or exacerbate clinical depression.

While the usual effect of sedative-hypnotics is sedation or sleep induction, under some conditions, sedative-hypnotics may result in disinhibition that can be perceived subjectively by a drug user as stimulation and by others as aggressive or agitated behavior.

Alcohol has a pharmacological profile that qualifies it as a sedative-hypnotic. By convention, however, alcohol generally is considered in a class by itself.

Benzodiazepine agonists usually are included in the category of sedative-hypnotics. In contrast to the generic term "sedative-hypnotic," which by convention may refer to barbiturates and medications of several different chemical classes, "benzodiazepines" refers to a class of medications that are variations on a common chemical structure.

In medical therapeutics, the benzodiazepines have largely replaced the short-acting barbiturates and other non-barbiturate sedative-hypnotics that were available before 1960. More recently, imidazopyridine derivatives (e.g., alpidem, zolpidem [Ambien®] and zopiclone) have been introduced; these drugs share some pharmacodynamic properties of benzodiazepines, but are not related chemically.

Some disorders previously treated with benzodiazepines are now being treated with the newer generations of antidepressants. For example, in the treatment of panic disorder, alprazolam (Lydiard, Lesser et al., 1992), clonazepam (Rosenbaum, Moroz & Bowden, 1997), and diazepam (Noyes, Burrows et al., 1996) have shown efficacy in controlled clinical trials. The tricyclic antidepressant imipramine also is an efficacious treatment of panic disorders. In a large, multicenter study comparing imipramine, alprazolam and placebo, both alprazolam and imipramine produced better results than the placebo. Improvement occurred within the first or second week for subjects treated with alprazolam and by the fourth week in subjects treated with imipramine. By the end of week 8, the effects of alprazolam and imipramine were similar (Drug Treatment of Panic Disorder, 1992). A small placebo-controlled study comparing imipramine with alprazolam found that more patients in the imipramine plus placebo group were able to tolerate the taper schedule (Woods, Nagy et al., 1992).

More recently, the efficacy of the specific serotonin reuptake inhibitor (SSRI) paroxetine in reducing the frequency of panic attacks has been established (Oehrberg, Christiansen et al., 1995). Clinical trials have found that paroxetine is as effective as clomipramine in the treatment of panic disorder (Lecrubier & Judge, 1997; Lecrubier, Bakker et al., 1997). The Food and Drug Administration (FDA) approved paroxetine (Paxil®) for treatment of panic disorder in 1996. Some clinicians opine that the SSRIs now are the treatment of choice for panic attacks (Sheehan & Hartnett-Sheehan, 1996).

Of the benzodiazepines, alprazolam appears to have had the most widespread clinical use in the treatment of panic attacks. Physiological dependence is common because alprazolam is prescribed in relatively high doses (2 to 6 mg/day) and pharmacotherapy often continues for months, if not years. (The trials demonstrating efficacy of benzodiazepines in ameliorating panic attacks are trials of eight to 12 weeks.) The pharmacology of benzodiazepines and imidazopyrines (e.g., alpidem, zolpidem [Ambien] and zopiclone) is described in detail in Section 2.

This chapter focuses on the treatment of physical dependence on benzodiazepines and the imiazopyrines and discusses other prescription sedative-hypnotics in terms of their similarities or differences from benzodiazepines. In the final section, the chapter discusses treatment of patients who ingest sedative-hypnotics in addition to other psychoactive drugs, and the post-detoxification pharmacotherapy of sedative-hypnotic dependence.

NEUROADAPTATION VERSUS PHYSIOLOGIC DEPENDENCE

Chronic exposure to sedative-hypnotics induces alterations in brain function at the neuroreceptor level; these changes are termed "neuroadaptation." An understanding of physical dependence is best achieved through an understanding of how benzodiazepines and other sedative-hypnotics interact with the brain receptors.

Benzodiazepines exert their physiological effects by attaching to a subunit of gamma aminobutyric acid (GABA) receptors. The GABA receptor is made up of an ion channel and several subunits that bind to different drugs: one subunit binds GABA, another benzodiazepines, and another barbiturates. The receptor subunits that are separate from, but functionally coupled to the GABA receptor, are said to be allosterically bound to the GABA receptor. The subunit that binds benzodiazepines has been designated the benzodiazepine receptor (Squires & Braestrup, 1977; Braestrup, Albrechtsen & Squires, 1977; Mohler & Okada, 1977).

Benzodiazepines that enhance the effect of GABA are called agonists. Although receptors typically are named for the endogenous ligand that is an agonist at the receptor, the natural ligand for the benzodiazepine receptor still has not been identified. Several endogenous nonbenzodiazepine compounds have been identified that attach to the receptor; however, it has not been established that these compounds attach to the receptor during normal physiological function.

GABA is the major inhibitory neurotransmitter in the brain, and GABA synapses, distributed throughout the brain and spinal cord, comprise as many as 40% of all synapses. The physiological function of GABA synapses is to modulate the polarization of neurons. The GABA receptor does this by opening or closing chloride ion channels (ionophores). Opening chloride channels allows more chloride ions to enter neurons. The influx of negatively charged chloride ions increases the electrical gradient across the cell membrane and makes the neuron less excitable. Closing the channels decreases electrical polarization and makes the cell more excitable. Attachment of an agonist at the benzodiazepine receptor facilitates the effect of GABA (i.e., opens the chloride channel). The clinical effects are anxiety reduction, sedation, and increased seizure threshold.

Substances that attach to the benzodiazepine receptor and close the channel produce an opposite effect: they are anxiogenic and lower the seizure threshold. Compounds such as betacarboline that produce an effect that is the opposite of the benzodiazepine agonists are termed "inverse agonists." Some compounds attach to the benzodiazepine receptor but neither increase nor decrease the effect of GABA. In the absence of a benzodiazepine agonist or inverse agonist, these compounds are neutral ligands (i.e., they attach to the receptor and block the effects of both agonists and inverse agonists). Consequently, neutral agonists are called "antagonists." If the receptor is occupied by an agonist or inverse agonist, a neutral agonist will displace the agonist or inverse agonist. (Displacement of a benzodiazepine agonist has clinical utility. For example, the benzodiazepine antagonist flumazenil [Romazicon®, previously designated Ro 15-1788] was marketed in the U.S. in 1992 to reverse the sedation produced by a benzodiazepine following a surgical procedure or overdose.)

The interaction of benzodiazepine receptors with their ligand is extremely complex. Attachment of the ligands can alter the pharmacology of the receptor (e.g., alter the number of receptors or change the affinity of the ligand for the receptor). With chronic exposure to benzodiazepines, there is evidence that the functional coupling of the benzodiazepine receptor with the GABA receptor is decreased.

BIOLOGICAL VULNERABILITIES

In the addiction literature, it is common to read that benzodiazepines are likely to be abused by individuals who have a history of sedative-hypnotic abuse or "polydrug" abuse. This statement is true, but the underlying reasoning is circuitous. After sedative-hypnotic dependence has occurred, it is fairly certain that the individual is at risk for sedative abuse, dependence, or both if he or she resumes use of a sedative-hypnotic drug. However, predicting in advance who will abuse or become dependent on a sedative-hypnotic is a much less certain enterprise.

Studies of the reinforcing properties of benzodiazepines show that the benzodiazepines are not effective reinforcers for most individuals (Chutuape & de Wit, 1994; de Wit, Johanson & Uhlenhuth, 1984). A growing body of evidence suggests that benzodiazepines are euphorogenic for some individuals. In one study, for example, the mood-elevating effects of alprazolam were experienced more intensely by daughters of alcoholics than by subjects with no history of parental alcohol dependence (Ciraulo, Sarid-Segal et al., 1996). Similar results were found in sons of alcoholics (Cowley, Roy-Byrne et al., 1992, 1994). Animal studies suggest that coadministration of non-psychoactive medications can affect the development of physical dependence. Coadministration of nifedipine, a calcium channel blocker, was found to facilitate development of physical dependence in the rat on barbital but not diazepam (Suzuki, Mizoguchi et al., 1995).

A hotly debated issue is the vulnerability of alcohol abusers to benzodiazepine abuse and dependence. Both alcohol and benzodiazepines enhance the effects of GABA at the $GABA_A$ receptor complex. One concern is that the combination of alcohol and benzodiazepines may result in increased neurocognitive and behavioral toxicity (Hollister, 1990). Another is that alcohol, through its effect on receptor function, may increase the likelihood of uncoupling of the benzodiazepine receptor. *In vitro* data suggest that alcohol can produce alterations of $GABA_A$ receptor binding and function (Klein, Mascia et al., 1995).

ISSUES IN DIAGNOSING AND TREATING DEPENDENCE ON SEDATIVE-HYPNOTICS

Benzodiazepine dependence differs from most other drug dependencies because, for most persons, benzodiazepines do not produce desirable mood-altering effects. Most patients develop sedative-hypnotic dependence while being treated for an anxiety disorder or insomnia. Thus, the majority of such patients have an underlying disorder that must be addressed either before or after detoxification.

Clinical trials with patients treated for panic disorder with benzodiazepines provide useful insights into therapeutic dose benzodiazepine tolerance and the issues to be considered when initiating benzodiazepine discontinuation.

Some drug abusers become sedative-hypnotic dependent while using sedative-hypnotics purchased on the black market for self-medication of symptoms caused by stimulant or opiate abuse.

With the exception of alcohol, sedative-hypnotics are not often primary drugs of abuse; that is, they are not taken daily to produce intoxication. Even among drug abusers, sedative-hypnotic abuse usually is intermittent and only rarely results in physical dependence.

Treatment strategies for sedative-hypnotic dependence cannot be separated from the realities of evolving health care delivery. Physicians often are in the position of devising not the optimal treatment plan, but one that can be negotiated with the patient and the payer. The realities of today's fractured health care dictate rethinking pharmacological treatment strategies for sedative-hypnotic dependence. Health care payers and the agents of managed care may have simplistic and unrealistic criteria for assigning patients to level of care. (By contrast, ASAM's *Patient Placement Criteria* are clinically derived and should be followed whenever possible.) Some—if not most—of the assessment and treatment of sedative-hypnotic dependence thus must be accomplished on an outpatient basis. The assessment and treatment of physical dependence is more complex for the physician and carries more risk for the patient on an outpatient than on an inpatient basis. For example, in an inpatient setting, the patient's access to medications can be better controlled, the patient's response to medications can be closely observed, and the patient is not tempted to drive an automobile while experiencing toxicity or withdrawal symptoms.

The uncertainties associated with outpatient management of withdrawal can be reduced by establishing clear goals, employing a systematic assessment procedure, and devising a clearly defined treatment protocol. Assessment and treatment protocols help the physician to systematically accumulate the information needed to initiate treatment and monitor treatment progress. Well-structured assessment and treatment protocols also are useful in negotiating with treatment payers and managed care entities around payment for the treatment the patient needs. Detailed medical records can be important in documenting the patient's clinical course and adverse events, and can buttress the physician's argument for a more intensive level of care, when needed.

INDICATIONS FOR INITIATING WITHDRAWAL

Presence of a Substance Use Disorder. From the point of view of an addiction medicine specialist, a primary reason for discontinuing treatment with a sedative-hypnotic drug is a concomitant substance use disorder involving a second (or multiple) drug(s). It is impossible to adequately assess the therapeutic benefits or risks of treatment of an underlying disorder with sedative-hypnotic drugs while a patient is concomitantly abusing alcohol, cocaine or other substances.

Development of Physical Dependence. Physical dependence on sedative-hypnotics (principally benzodiazepines) is a cause for concern, but it may be an acceptable state if: (1) the medication is medically indicated; (2) the medication is still effective in ameliorating symptoms and is not producing significant behavioral or organ toxicity; and (3) the patient has not been diagnosed with a substance use disorder.

Distinguishing Physical Dependence from Substance Use Disorder. Patients may be physically dependent on a benzodiazepine but not have a substance abuse disorder. In the minds of many patients and physicians, physical dependence is synonymous with addiction or a substance abuse disorder. An unfortunate choice of terms in the *Diagnostic and Statistical Manual of Mental Disorders, 4th Edition* (American Psychiatric Association, 1994) (*DSM-IV*) adds to the confusion. The *DSM-IV* diagnostic criteria for substance abuse were developed primarily for drugs not used in a medical context. In the *DSM-IV* nomenclature, "drug dependence" refers to a disorder more severe than "drug abuse." "Physical dependence" and "characteristic withdrawal syndrome" are diagnostic criteria included in "drug dependence," but physical dependence alone is not sufficient to establish a diagnosis of a benzodiazepine-related substance abuse disorder. (This seemingly arcane distinction often is lost.) Some patients conclude that they are addicted if they stop a medication and withdrawal symptoms emerge.

The diagnostic criteria are sufficiently broad that they can reasonably accommodate abuse of and dependence on prescription drugs used in a medical context. *DSM-IV* diagnosis of "substance dependence" requires a maladaptive pattern of substance use leading to clinically significant impairment or distress (American Psychiatric Association, 1994). Seven criteria are listed; three or more criteria are required for a diagnosis of substance dependence. The first two criteria are tolerance and drug withdrawal; a diagnosis of substance abuse disorder requires at least one other of the five remaining criteria.

Sensible use of the diagnostic criteria requires some interpolation and judgment, taking into consideration the medical context and the nature of the patient's underlying problem. For example, Criteria 3 and 4 relate to a patient's loss of control over drug-taking behavior, i.e., "the drug often is used in larger amounts or over a longer period than intended," or "there is persistent use, or unsuccessful efforts to cut down or control substance use." In a medical context, a patient would fulfill these criteria if he or she frequently took more of the medication than was prescribed, stealthily obtained the medication from multiple physicians, or insisted on using it beyond the duration intended by the prescribing physician.

Criteria 5 involves the patient spending a great deal of time in activities necessary to obtain the substance or to recover from its effects (this would include seeing multiple physicians to obtain additional prescriptions). Criteria 6 involves the patient giving up important social, occupation, or recreational activities because of substance use. Criteria 7 involves continued use of the medication even though the patient is experiencing a physical or psychological problem that is caused or exacerbated by continued use of the substance.

Other Indications. Beyond a substance use disorder, there are other reasons for initiating withdrawal of a sedative-hypnotic drug; for example, if the treatment is inducing difficulties with memory, or producing adverse behavioral reactions such as irritability, anger, rage or hostility.

Benzodiazepines and Memory: Knowledge about the amnestic effects of benzodiazepines derives from many sources, including animal studies (Dickinson-Anson, Mesches et al., 1993), clinical case reports of patients' experiences, experiments with nonpatient volunteers (Ott, Rohloff et al., 1988; Fleishaker, Sisson et al., 1993; Ingum, Beylich & Moriand, 1993), studies of recall in patients undergoing medical procedures, studies of neurocognitive function in patients receiving long-term treatment with benzodiazepines and after benzodiazepine discontinuation (Tonne, Hiltunen et al., 1991). Some studies suggest that the amnestic effect produced by benzodiazepines and alcohol are mediated through the benzodiazepine receptor linked to $GABA_A$ (Dickinson-Anson, Mesches et al., 1993). Other studies have found that the benzodiazepine antagonist flumazenil blocks sedation, but not the amnesic effects of the midazolam (Curran & Birch, 1991). The knowledge base of benzodiazepines and their effects on memory is far from complete.

Experimental studies often use memory tasks that are unique to the laboratory situation. This has led some to question the generalizability of the laboratory data (Moussaoui, 1986). There are no experimental data on subjects given high doses of benzodiazepines.

Memory is a complex process requiring integration of many aspects of neurocognitive function. At some dose, all benzodiazepines can produce impairment of memory. Considerable evidence suggests that benzodiazepine-induced memory defects are produced because the drug impairs the transfer of newly acquired information to long-term storage (Barbee, 1993):

> "The memory impairment is for events following the ingestion of the benzodiazepine. This type of memory impairment, often referred to as 'anterograde amnesia,' is similar to an alcohol 'blackout.' Amnesia may be partial or complete for a interval of time. The memory impairment is dose dependent and more profound as the dose of the benzodiazepine is increased. Unlike the memory impairment produced by anticholinergic medications such as scopolamine, recall of information acquired before the ingestion of the benzodiazepine is not impaired" (Barbee, 1993).

The term "retrograde amnesia" can be a source of confusion because it is used to refer to different timeframes in the medical and pharmacology literature, and in the legal and lay literature. In the medical and pharmacologic literature, the term "anterograde amnesia" refers to the inability to remember events *following* the ingestion of a drug, while "retrograde amnesia" refers to the inability to remember events that *preceded* drug ingestion. The literature on benzodiazepines contains mentions of retrograde amnesia (Ott, Rohloff et al., 1988), but the references are to contrast retrograde amnesia with anterograde amnesia. No studies have conclusively established that benzodiazepines produce retrograde amnesia. In fact, some studies suggest that small to moderate doses of a benzodiazepine may produce enhanced recall of events that occurred prior to drug ingestion (Ott, Rohloff et al., 1988).

Benzodiazepine-induced memory impairment is not merely a function of sedation. In an experimental study of healthy volunteers, midazolam-induced sedation was reversed by the benzodiazepine antagonist flumazenil, whereas the memory impairment was not (Curran & Birch, 1991). In contrast, acute effects (neuropsychological impairment in humans) of diazepam were observed in memory measures at all times. Given subjects' very prolonged BZ use, it is possible to predict that tolerance to the memory effects never fully develops (Gorenstein, Bernik & Pompeia, 1994).

The amnestic effects of benzodiazepines are useful properties in anesthetic practice (Deppe, Sipperly et al., 1994; Berggren, Eriksson et al., 1983), but in other therapeutic uses, memory impairment is an undesirable side effect.

Paradoxical Reactions: Although the benzodiazepines generally have the effect of reducing anxiety and anger, some patients respond to these drugs with an increase in anger, rage or hostility. Because the effect is contrary to the expected effect, it often is referred to as a "paradoxical reaction." This effect has been mentioned episodically in the medical literature (Lader & Petursson, 1981; Lader & Morton, 1991; Freedman, 1990; Goldney, 1977; Hall & Zisook, 1981; Feldman, 1986). The reasons that some individuals respond paradoxically are not well understood. Set and setting are factors, as demonstrated by the fact that paradoxical reactions are reported as frequent in prison populations (Brown, 1978) and in patients with borderline personality disorders (Cole & Kando, 1993).

BENZODIAZEPINE WITHDRAWAL SYNDROMES

Withdrawal from high doses of sedative-hypnotics can be severe and even life-threatening. Therapeutic doses of benzodiazepines taken for months to years produce physiologic dependence and a significant discontinuation syndrome in about 50% of patients (Tyrer, 1993). Management of these withdrawal syndromes is described in detail in Section 6.

Symptom Rebound. After cessation of a benzodiazepine, an intensified return of the symptoms (such as insomnia or anxiety) for which the benzodiazepine was prescribed is called "symptom rebound." The term comes from sleep research in which rebound insomnia is commonly observed following sedative-hypnotic use. Symptom rebound lasts a few days to weeks following discontinuation (American Psychiatric Association Task Force on Benzodiazepine Dependency, 1990). Symptom rebound is the most common withdrawal syndrome resulting from prolonged benzodiazepine use.

Symptom Reemergence (or recrudescence). Patients' symptoms of anxiety, insomnia or muscle tension abate during benzodiazepine treatment. When the benzodiazepine is stopped, symptoms return to the same level as before the benzodiazepine therapy was initiated. The reason for distinguishing between symptom rebound and symptom reoccurrence is that symptom reoccurrence suggests that the original symptoms have not been adequately treated, whereas symptom rebound suggests a form of withdrawal syndrome (American Psychiatric Association Task Force on Benzodiazepine Dependency, 1990).

Some patients can ingest therapeutic doses of benzodiazepines for many months or years and then abruptly stop them without developing symptoms other than those that were present before benzodiazepine treatment. Others patients taking the same doses of benzodiazepines over long periods develop new symptoms after the benzodiazepine is stopped. Such symptoms can be disabling and last many months.

Protracted Withdrawal. Some clinicians have described a more prolonged benzodiazepine withdrawal syndrome that is severe and disabling (Ashton, 1991; O'Connor, 1993). Whether a protracted benzodiazepine withdrawal syndrome exists is a matter of clinical controversy. Some authorities attribute the signs and symptoms that occur after discontinuation to symptom reemergence.

Waxing and waning intensity of symptoms is characteristic of the low-dose protracted benzodiazepine withdrawal syndrome. Patients sometimes are asymptomatic for several days, then, without apparent reason, they become acutely anxious. Often, there are concomitant physiological signs (such as dilated pupils, increased resting heart rate and elevated blood pressure). The intense waxing and waning of symptoms is important in distinguishing low-dose withdrawal symptoms from symptom reemergence.

Protracted benzodiazepine withdrawal has no pathognomonic signs or symptoms. The differential diagnosis includes agitated depression, generalized anxiety disorder, panic disorder, partial complex seizures, and schizophrenia. Other symptoms that have been attributed to protracted benzodiazepine withdrawal include anxiety, increased sensitivity to sound, light and touch (Lader, 1990), tinnitus (Busto, Fornazzari & Naranjo, 1988), and psychotic depression. The time course of symptom resolution is the primary differentiating feature between symptoms generated by withdrawal and symptom reemergence. Symptoms from protracted benzodiazepine withdrawal wax and wane but gradually subside with continued abstinence, whereas symptom reemergence and symptom sensitization do not.

Clinicians in the early 1980s hypothesized that low-dose benzodiazepine withdrawal is mediated by neuroadaptation of the GABA receptor (Wesson & Smith, 1982); however, neurochemical evidence was lacking. The pathophysiology of a protracted withdrawal syndrome from benzodiazepines remains incomplete. Some drugs or medications may facilitate neuroadaptation by increasing the affinity of benzodiazepines for their receptors. Phenobarbital, for example, increases the affinity of diazepam to benzodiazepine receptors (Skolnick, Concada et al., 1981; Olsen & Loeb-Lundberg, 1981). Prior treatment with a barbiturate has been found to increase the intensity of withdrawal symptoms (Covi, Lipman et al., 1973). Patients at increased risk for development of the low-dose withdrawal syndrome are those with a family or personal history of alcoholism, those who use alcohol daily, or those who concomitantly use other sedatives. Case control studies suggest that patients with a history of addiction, particularly to other sedative-hypnotics, are at high risk for low-dose benzodiazepine dependence (Ciraulo, Barnhill et al., 1988). The short-acting, high-milligram potency benzodiazepines appear to produce a more intense low-dose withdrawal syndrome.

A protracted withdrawal syndrome has been described for most drugs that induce physical dependence, including alcohol (Geller, 1991). The signs and symptoms generally attributed to protracted withdrawal syndromes consist of irritability, anxiety, insomnia and mood instability.

The Dependence/Withdrawal Cycle. When dependence arises during therapeutic treatment, it often occurs in a predictable sequence of phases. The clinical course described here most often occurs during long-term treatment of a generalized anxiety disorder, panic disorder, or severe insomnia.

Stages in the development of benzodiazepine dependence include:

Pre-Treatment Phase: Even before treatment, the distressing symptoms of anxiety or insomnia vary in intensity from day to day, depending on life stresses and the waxing and waning of the patient's underlying disorder.

Therapeutic Response Phase: When treatment with a benzodiazepine is started, patients often have initial side effects, such as drowsiness. Tolerance to unwanted sedation usually develops within a few days, and the patient's overall level of symptoms decreases. The therapeutic phase, in which the patient's symptoms are ameliorated or reduced by benzodiazepine treatment, may last for months to years.

Symptom Escape and Dosage Escalation Phase: During long-term treatment, benzodiazepines may lose their effectiveness in controlling symptoms. For some patients, this "symptom escape" coincides with a period of increased life stress; for others, no unusual psychological stressor is apparent. Patients often are aware that the medication "no longer works" or that its effect is qualitatively different.

As the usual dose of benzodiazepines loses effectiveness, the patient may increase his or her benzodiazepine consumption in the hope that symptoms again will be controlled. As the daily dose increases, the patient may develop subtle benzodiazepine toxicity that is difficult to diagnose without psychometric assessment. This is a common clinical problem that generally goes unrecognized. It has not received sufficient research attention, and evidence at this time is scanty and indirect. Although many studies have demonstrated that acute doses of benzodiazepines impair cognitive function, there has been little study of the effect of benzodiazepines over prolonged periods of use. One psychometric study, which compared long-term benzodiazepine users with subjects who were benzodiazepine-abstinent, found that the long-term benzodiazepine users performed poorly on tasks involving visual-spatial ability and sustained attention (Golombok, Moodley & Lader, 1988). Clinically, the patient may not be aware that his or her impairment is benzodiazepine-induced. Coping skills that previously were bolstered by the benzodiazepine become compromised. Some patients make suicidal attempts or exhibit self-defeating behavior that otherwise would be out of character.

The symptom escape phase does not appear to be an invariable consequence of long-term benzodiazepine treatment. Some patients are vulnerable to developing withdrawal symptoms; others are not. Patients who have experienced symptom escape and dosage escalation appear most likely to have a protracted withdrawal syndrome.

Withdrawal Phase: When patients stop taking the benzodiazepine or their daily dose falls below 25% of the peak maintenance dose, patients may become increasingly symptomatic. Such symptoms may be the result of symptom rebound, symptom reemergence, or the beginning of a protracted withdrawal syndrome. The symptoms that occur during this phase may be a mixture of symptoms that were present during the "pre-treatment phase" and new symptoms. During the first few weeks, it is not possible to know exactly what is producing such symptoms or to estimate their duration.

Symptoms of the same type that occurred during the pre-treatment phase suggest symptom rebound or symptom reemergence. New symptoms, particularly alterations in sensory perception, suggest the beginning of a protracted withdrawal syndrome. Increasing the benzodiazepine dose reduces the symptoms, not because the benzodiazepines have not completely lost effectiveness but because the withdrawal syndrome is reversed; however, symptom reduction will not be as complete as during the initial therapeutic phase.

Resolution Phase: The duration of the resolution phase is highly variable. Most patients experience symptom rebound lasting only a few weeks, while others have a severe, protracted abstinence syndrome that lasts months to over a year. During early abstinence, the patient's symptoms generally vary in intensity from day to day. If abstinence from benzodiazepines is maintained, symptoms will gradually return to their baseline level. An encouraging finding of one discontinuation study was that "patients who were able to remain free of benzodiazepines for at least five weeks obtained lower levels of anxiety than before benzodiazepine discontinuation" (Rickels, Schweizer et al., 1990).

The physician's response during the withdrawal phase is critical to achieving a resolution. Some physicians interpret patients' escalating symptoms as evidence of patients' "need" for benzodiazepine treatment and reinstitute higher doses of benzodiazepines or switch to another benzodiazepine. Reinstitution of any benzodiazepine usually does not achieve satisfactory symptom control and may prolong the recovery process. Formal benzodiazepine withdrawal, using one of the strategies described below, generally achieves the best long-term outcome.

PHARMACOLOGIC MANAGEMENT OF WITHDRAWAL

Benzodiazepine withdrawal strategies must be tailored to suit three possible dependence situations: (1) high-dose withdrawal (following use of doses greater than the recommended therapeutic doses for more than one month); (2) low-dose withdrawal (following use of doses below those in the upper range of Table 1); and (3) a combined high-dose and low-dose withdrawal (following daily high doses for more than six months), in which both a high-dose sedative hypnotic withdrawal syndrome and a low-dose benzodiazepine withdrawal syndrome occur.

High-Dose Benzodiazepine Withdrawal. Abrupt discontinuation of a sedative-hypnotic in patients who are severely physically dependent can result in serious medical complications and even death. There are three general strategies for safely withdrawing patients from sedative-hypnotics, including benzodiazepines.

The first is to use *decreasing doses of the drug of dependence*. Gradual reduction of the benzodiazepine of dependence is used primarily in medical settings to treat dependence arising from treatment of an underlying condition. The patient must be cooperative, able to adhere to dosing regimens, and not concurrently abusing alcohol or other drugs.

The second method is to *substitute phenobarbital for the addicting agent* and gradually withdraw the substitute medication (Smith & Wesson, 1970, 1971). The pharmacologic rationale for phenobarbital substitution is that phenobarbital is long-acting, so that little change in blood levels of phenobarbital occurs between doses. This allows the safe use of a progressively smaller daily dose. Phenobarbital is safer than the shorter-acting barbiturates, the lethal dose of phenobarbital is many-fold higher than the toxic dose, and the signs of toxicity (such as sustained nystagmus, slurred speech, and ataxia) are easy to observe. Finally, phenobarbital intoxication usually does not produce disinhibition, so most patients view it as a medication rather than as a drug of abuse.

Phenobarbital substitution also can be used to withdraw patients who have lost control of their benzodiazepine use or who are polydrug dependent.

The third method, used for patients with a dependence on both alcohol and a benzodiazepine, is to *substitute a long-acting benzodiazepine*, such as chlordiazepoxide, and taper it over one to two weeks.

The method selected depends on the particular benzodiazepine, the involvement of other drugs of dependence, and the clinical setting in which the detoxification is to take place.

Stabilization Phase: The patient's history of drug use during the month preceding treatment is used to compute the stabilization dose of phenobarbital. Although many addicts exaggerate the number of pills they are taking, the patient history remains the best guide to initiating pharmacotherapy for withdrawal. Patients who have overstated the amount of drug they are taking will become intoxicated during the first day or two of treatment. Such intoxication is easily managed by omitting one or more doses of phenobarbital and recalculating the daily dose.

The patient's average daily sedative-hypnotic dose is converted to phenobarbital equivalents and the daily amount divided into three doses. (The conversion equivalents for various benzodiazepines and for other sedative-hypnotics appears in Table 2.)

The computed phenobarbital equivalent is given in three or four doses daily. If the patient is using significant amounts of other sedative-hypnotics (including alcohol), the amounts of all the drugs are converted to phenobarbital equivalents and added together (for example, 30 cc of 100 proof alcohol is equated to 30 mg of phenobarbital for withdrawal purposes). The maximum starting phenobarbital dose is 500 mg per day.

Before each dose of phenobarbital is given, the patient is checked for signs of phenobarbital toxicity; these include sustained nystagmus, slurred speech or ataxia. Of these, sustained nystagmus is the most reliable. If nystagmus is present, the scheduled dose of phenobarbital is withheld. If all three signs are present, the next two doses of phenobarbital are

TABLE 1. Characteristics of Syndromes Related to Benzodiazepine Withdrawal

Syndrome	Signs/Symptoms	Time Course	Response to Reinstitution of Benzodiazepine
High-dose withdrawal	Anxiety, insomnia, nightmares, major motor seizures, psychosis, hyperpyrexia, death.	Begins 1 or 2 days after a short-acting benzodiazepine is stopped; 3–8 days after a long-acting benzodiazepine is stopped.	Signs and symptoms reverse 2 to 6 hours following a hypnotic dose of a benzodiazepine.
Symptom rebound	Same symptoms that were present before treatment.	Begins 1 to 2 days after a short-acting benzodiazepine is stopped; 3–8 days after a long-acting benzodiazepine is stopped. Lasts 7 to 14 days.	Signs and symptoms reverse 2 to 6 hours following a hypnotic dose of a benzodiazepine.
Protracted, low-dose withdrawal	Anxiety, agitation, tachycardia, palpitations, anorexia, blurred vision, muscle cramps, insomnia, nightmares, confusion, muscle spasms, psychosis, increased sensitivity to sounds and light and paresthesias.	Signs and symtoms emerge 1–7 days following discontinuation of the benzodiazepine or after reduction of the benzodiazepine to below the usual therapeutic dose.	Sings and symptoms reverse 2 to 6 hours following a sedative dose of a high-potency benzodiazepine.
Symptom reemergence	Recurrence of the same symptoms that were present before taking a benzodiazepine (e.g., anxiety, insomnia).	Symptoms emerge when benzodiazepine is stopped and continue unabated with time.	Signs and symptoms reverse 2 to 6 hours following usual therapeutic dose of a benzodiazepine.

withheld and the daily dose of phenobarbital for the following day is halved.

If the patient is in acute withdrawal and has had or is in danger of having withdrawal seizures, the initial dose of phenobarbital is administered by intramuscular injection. If nystagmus and other signs of intoxication develop one to two hours after the intramuscular dose, the patient is in no immediate danger of barbiturate withdrawal. Patients are maintained on the initial dosing schedule of phenobarbital for two days. If the patient has neither signs of withdrawal nor phenobarbital toxicity (slurred speech, nystagmus, unsteady gait), then phenobarbital withdrawal is initiated.

Withdrawal Phase: Unless the patient develops signs and symptoms of phenobarbital toxicity or sedative-hypnotic withdrawal, the phenobarbital dose is decreased by 30 mg per day. Should signs of phenobarbital toxicity develop during withdrawal, the daily phenobarbital dose is decreased by 50% and the 30 mg per day withdrawal continued from the reduced phenobarbital dose. Should the patient have objective signs of sedative-hypnotic withdrawal, the daily dose is increased by 50% and the patient restabilized before the withdrawal is continued.

Low-Dose Benzodiazepine Withdrawal. Most patients experience only mild to moderate symptom rebound, which disappears after a few days to a week. No special treatment is needed. However, the patient may need reassurance that rebound symptoms are common and that they will subside.

Some patients experience severe symptoms that may be quite unlike previous symptoms. The phenobarbital regimen described above will not be adequate to suppress these symptoms to tolerable levels. For such patients, there are several pharmacologic options.

One strategy is to increase the phenobarbital dose to 200 mg per day and then to slowly taper the phenobarbital over several months.

Another approach is to block somatic symptoms, such as tachycardia, with propranolol. A dose of 20 mg every six hours can be used, alone or in combination with phenobarbital, to reduce low-dose benzodiazepine withdrawal symptom intensity (Tyrer, Rutherford & Huggett, 1981). This schedule is contin-

TABLE 2. Benzodiazepines and Sedative-Hypnotics and Their Phenobarbital Withdrawal Equivalents

Generic Name	Trade Name	Common Therapeutic Indication(s)	Therapeutic Dose Range (mg/day)	Dose Equal to 30 mg of phenobarbital withdrawal (mg)[b]
Benzodiazepines				
alprazolam	Xanax	sedative, anti-panic	0.75–6	1
chlordiazepoxide	Librium	sedative	15–100	25
clonazepam	Klonopin	anti-convulsant	0.5–4	2
clorazepate	Tranxene	sedative	15–60	7.5
diazepam	Valium	sedative	4–40	10
estazolam	ProSom	hypnotic	1–2	1
flumazenil	Mazicon	benzodiazepine antagonist	NA	NA
flurazepam	Dalmane	hypnotic	15–30	15
halazepam	Paxipam	sedative	60–160	40
lorazepam	Ativan	sedative	1–16	2
midzaolam	Versed	IV sedative	NA	NA
oxazepam	Serax	sedative	10–120	10
prazepam	Centrax	sedative	20–60	10
quazepam	Doral	hypnotic	15[a]	15
temazepam	Restoril	hypnotic	15–30[a]	15
triazolam	Halcion	hypnotic	0.125–0.50	0.25
Barbiturates				
amobarbital	Amytal	sedative	50–100	100
butabarbital	Butisol	sedative	45–120	100
butalbital	Fiorinal, Sedapap	sedative/analgesic[c]	100–300	100
pentobarbital	Nembutal	hypnotic	50–100[c]	100
secobarbital	Seconal	hypnotic	50–100[c]	100
Others				
buspirone	BuSpar	sedative	15–60	—[d]
choral hydrate	Noctec, Somnos	hypnotic	250–1000	500
ethchlorvynol	Placidyl	hypnotic	500–1000	500
glutethimide	Doriden	hypnotic	250–500	250
meprobamate	Miltown, Equanil, Equagesic	sedative	1200–1600	1200
methylprylon	Noludar	hypnotic	200–400	200

NA Not applicable
[a]Usual hypnotic dose
[b]Phenobarbital withdrawal conversion equivalence is not the same as therapeutic dose equivalency. Withdrawal equivalence is the amount of the drug that 30 mg of phenobarbital will substitute for and prevent serious high-dose withdrawal signs and symptoms.
[c]Butalbital is usually available in combination with opiate or non-opiate analgesics.
[d]Not cross-tolerant with barbiturates.

ued for two weeks and then stopped. Even after phenobarbital withdrawal is complete, propranolol can be used episodically as needed to control tachycardia, increased blood pressure and anxiety. However, continuous propranolol therapy for more than two weeks is not recommended, because propranolol itself may result in symptom rebound when discontinued after prolonged use (Glaubiger & Lefkowitz, 1977).

POST-WITHDRAWAL TREATMENT

Withdrawal usually is successful when the patient cooperates, but many patients do not remain abstinent. For patients with an underlying anxiety disorder, relapse may mean that the patient is unable or unwilling to tolerate the symptoms that emerge following detoxification. For patients with a dual diagnosis, outcomes other than drug abstinence must be considered. Fortunately there are now pharmacologic alternatives to benzodiazepines and the older sedative-hypnotics for treatment of anxiety. In addition, cognitive-behavioral therapies and other psychotherapeutic and behavioral treatments for anxiety have shown efficacy.

Detoxification alone is not adequate treatment of sedative-hypnotic dependence, but rather the first step in the recovery process. Adjunctive use of medications such as carbamazepine, imipramine, and buspirone have been found to result in significantly higher discontinuation rates—carbamazepine (91%), buspirone (85%), and imipramine (79%)—compared to placebo (58%) (Rickels, Case et al., 1990).

Because of its low abuse potential and benign side effects, buspirone would seem a likely candidate for treatment of anxiety following benzodiazepine discontinuation. Buspirone appears to act as a serotonin HT1A partial agonist (Taylor & Moon, 1991). However, in a crossover study, buspirone did not appear to lessen the intensity of benzodiazepine withdrawal (Schweizer & Rickels, 1986). There is some suggestion that patients with a history of benzodiazepine abuse are resistant to the anxiolytic effects of buspirone (Schweizer, Rickels & Lucki, 1986). Buspirone does not appear to be efficacious in management of panic disorders (Sheehan, Raj et al., 1993) or social phobias. On the other hand, some success has been reported with the use of buspirone in post-detoxification treatment of generalized anxiety in alcoholics (Tollefson, Montague-Clouse & Tollefson, 1992).

Because benzodiazepines may cause or exacerbate cognitive impairment in the elderly, buspirone may be a particularly useful alternative to the benzodiazepines for managing anxiety in elderly patients (Steinberg, 1994).

Supportive individual psychotherapy or self-help recovery group support is virtually always needed as part of the recovery plan for patients who have a sedative-hypnotic substance abuse disorder.

CONCLUSIONS

Benzodiazepines have many therapeutic uses. In the treatment of some conditions, such as panic disorders, long-term use of benzodiazepines is an appropriate strategy. Physical dependence is not always an avoidable complication. Before initiating a course of prolonged therapy, the physician should discuss with the patient the possibility that the patient will develop new or intensified symptoms when use of the benzodiazepine is discontinued.

For patients whose benzodiazepine dependence develops during pharmacotherapy, benzodiazepine dependence does not necessarily amount to a substance use disorder. To label it as substance abuse unnecessarily stigmatizes patients and their psychiatrists.

ACKNOWLEDGMENTS: Writing of this chapter was supported in part by NIDA grant Rl8 DA6082 to Friends Medical Sciences Research Center, Inc., and RO1 DA06038 to Merritt Peralta Institute in Oakland, California. The authors wish to acknowledge the assistance of Susan Steffens and Gantt Galloway, Pharm.D., in the preparation of this manuscript.

REFERENCES

American Psychiatric Association (1994). *Diagnostic and Statistical Manual of Mental Disorders*, 4th Edition. Washington, DC: American Psychiatric Association, 886.

American Psychiatric Association Task Force on Benzodiazepine Dependency (1990). *Benzodiazepine Dependency, Toxicity, and Abuse.* Washington, DC: American Psychiatric Press.

Apelt S & Emrich HM (1990). Sodium valproate in benzodiazepine withdrawal (Letter). *American Journal of Psychiatry* 147:950–951.

Ashton H (1991). Protracted withdrawal syndromes from benzodiazepines. *Journal of Substance Abuse Treatment* 8:19–28.

Barbee JG (1993). Memory, benzodiazepines, and anxiety: integration of theoretical and clinical perspectives. *Journal of Clinical Psychiatry* 54(Suppl):86–97; discussion 98–101.

Berggren L, Eriksson I, Mollenholt P & Wickbom G (1983). Sedation for fibreoptic gastroscopy: A comparative study of midazolam and diazepam. *British Journal of Anaesthesia* 55:289–96.

Braestrup C, Albrechtsen R & Squires R (1977). High densities of benzodiazepine receptors in human cortical areas. *Nature* 269:702–704.

Brown CR (1978). The use of benzodiazepines in prison populations. *Journal of Clinical Psychiatry* 39:219–222.

Busto U, Fornazzari L & Naranjo CA (1988). Protracted tinnitus after discontinuation of long-term therapeutic use of benzodiazepines. *Journal of Clinical Psychopharmacology* 8:359–362.

Chutuape MA & de Wit H (1994). Relationship between subjective effects and drug preferences: Ethanol and diazepam. *Drug and Alcohol Dependence* 34:243–251.

Ciraulo DA, Barnhill JG, Greenblatt DJ et al. (1988). Abuse liability and clinical pharmacokinetics of alprazolam in alcoholic men. *Journal of Clinical Psychiatry* 49:333–337.

Ciraulo DA, Sarid-Segal O, Knapp C, Ciraulo AM, Greenblatt DJ & Shader RI (1996). Liability to alprazolam abuse in daughters of alcoholics. *American Journal of Psychiatry* 153:956–958.

Cole JO & Kando JC (1993). Adverse behavioral events reported in patients taking alprazolam and other benzodiazepines. *Journal of Clinical Psychiatry* 54(Suppl):49–61; discussion 62–63.

Covi L, Lipman RS, Pattison JH, Derogatis LR & Uhlenhuth EH (1973). Length of treatment with anxiolytic sedatives and response to their sudden withdrawal. *Acta Psychiatrica Scandinavica* 49:51–64.

Cowley DS, Roy-Byrne PP, Godon C et al. (1992) Response to diazepam in sons of alcoholics. *Alcoholism: Clinical & Experimental Research* 16:1057–1063.

Cowley DS, Roy-Byrne PP, Radant A et al. (1994). Eye movement effects of diazepam in sons of alcoholic fathers and male control subjects. *Alcoholism: Clinical & Experimental Research* 18:324–332.

Curran HV & Birch B (1991). Differentiating the sedative, psychomotor and amnesic effects of benzodiazepines: A study with midazolam and the benzodiazepine antagonist, flumazenil. *Psychopharmacology* 103:519–23.

Deppe SA, Sipperly ME, Sargent AI, Kuwik RJ & Thompson DR (1994). Intravenous lorazepam as an amnestic and anxiolytic agent in the intensive care unit: A prospective study. *Critical Care Medicine* 1994; 22:1248–52.

de Wit H, Johanson CE & Uhlenhuth EH (1984). Reinforcing properties of lorazepam in normal volunteers. *Drug and Alcohol Dependence* 13:31–41.

Dickinson-Anson H, Mesches MH, Coleman K & McGaugh JL (1993). Bicuculline administered into the amygdala blocks benzodiazepine-induced amnesia. *Behavioral & Neural Biology* 60:1–4.

Drug treatment of panic disorder. Comparative efficacy of alprazolam, imipramine, and placebo. Cross-National Collaborative Panic Study, Second Phase Investigators *British Journal of Psychiatry* 1992, 160:191–205.

Farre M, de la Torre R, Gonzalez ML et al. (1997). Cocaine and alcohol interactions in humans: neuroendocrine effects and cocaethylene metabolism. *Journal of Pharmacology and Experimental Therapeutics* 283:164–176.

Feldman MD (1986). Paradoxical effects of benzodiazepines. *North Carolina Medical Journal* 47:311–312.

Fleishaker JC, Sisson TA, Sramek JJ, Conrad J, Veroff AE & Cutler NR (1993). Psychomotor and memory effects of two adinazolam formulations assessed by a computerized neuropsychological test battery. *Journal of Clinical Pharmacology* 33:463–469.

Freedman DX (1990). Benzodiazepines: Therapeutic, biological and psychosocial issues. Symposium summary. *Journal of Psychiatric Research* 24(Suppl 2):169–174.

Geller A (1991). Protracted abstinence. In NS Miller (ed.) *Comprehensive Handbook of Drug and Alcohol Addiction.* New York, NY: Marcel Dekker, 905–913.

Glaubiger G & Lefkowitz R (1977). Elevated beta-adrenergic receptor number after chronic propranolol treatment. *Biochemical and Biophysical Research Community* 78:720–725.

Goldney RD (1977). Paradoxical reaction to a new minor tranquilizer. *Medical Journal of Australia* 1:139–140.

Golombok S, Moodley P & Lader M (1988). Cognitive impairment in long-term benzodiazepine users. *Psychological Medicine* 18:365–374.

Gorenstein C, Bernik MA & Pompeia S (1994). Differential acute psychomotor and cognitive effects of diazepam on long-term benzodiazepine users. *International Clinical Psychopharmacology* 9:145–153.

Griffiths R & Roache J (1985). Abuse liability of benzodiazepines. A review of human studies evaluating subjective and/or reinforcing effects. In D Smith & D Wesson (eds.) *The Benzodiazepines: Current Standards for Medical Practice.* Hingham, MA: MTP Press, 209–225.

Hall RC & Zisook S (1981). Paradoxical reactions to benzodiazepines. *British Journal of Clinical Pharmacology* 11(Suppl 1):99S–104S.

Harrison M, Busto U, Naranjo CA, Kaplan HL & Sellers EM (1984). Diazepam tapering in detoxification for high-dose benzodiazepine abuse. *Clinical Pharmacology and Therapeutics* 36:527–533.

Henning RJ & Wilson LD (1996). Cocaethylene is as cardiotoxic as cocaine but is less toxic than cocaine plus ethanol. *Life Sciences* 59:615–627.

Hollister LE (1990). Interactions between alcohol and benzodiazepines. *Recent Developments in Alcohol* 8:233–239.

Hollister LE, Bennett LL, Kimbell I, Savage C & Overall JE (1963). Diazepam in newly admitted schizophrenics. *Diseases of the Nervous System* 24:746–750.

Ingum J, Beylich KM & Moriand J (1993). Amnesic effects and subjective ratings during repeated dosing of flunitrazepam to healthy volunteers. *European Journal of Clinical Pharmacology* 45:235–240.

Jatlow P, Elsworth JD, Bradberry CW et al. (1991) Cocaethylene: A neuropharmacologically active metabolite associated with concurrent cocaine-ethanol ingestion. *Life Sciences* 48:1787–1794.

Klein RL, Mascia MP, Whiting PJ & Harris RA (1995). $GABA_A$ receptor function and binding in stably transfected cells: Chronic ethanol treatment. *Alcoholism: Clinical & Experimental Research* 19:1338–1344.

Lader M (1990). Drug development optimization—Benzodiazepines. *Agents and Actions Supplements* 29:59–69.

Lader M & Morton S (1991). Benzodiazepine problems. *British Journal of Addictions* 86:823–828.

Lader M & Petursson H (1981). Benzodiazepine derivatives—Side effects and dangers. *Biological Psychiatry* 16:1195–1201.

Lecrubier Y & Judge R (1997). Long-term evaluation of paroxetine, clomipramine and placebo in panic disorder. Collaborative Paroxetine Panic Study Investigators. *Acta Psychiatrica Scandinavica* 95:153–60.

Lecrubier Y, Bakker A, Dunbar G & Judge R (1997). A comparison of paroxetine, clomipramine and placebo in the treatment of panic disorder. Collaborative Paroxetine Panic Study Investigators. *Acta Psychiatrica Scandinavica* 95:145–52.

Lydiard RB, Lesser IM, Ballenger JC, Rubin RT, Laraia M & DuPont R (1992). A fixed-dose study of alprazolam 2 mg, alprazolam 6 mg, and placebo in panic disorder. *Journal of Clinical Psychopharmacology* 12:96–103.

McElroy SL, Keck PE Jr & Lawrence JM (1991). Treatment of panic disorder and benzodiazepine withdrawal with valproate (Letter). *Journal of Neuropsychiatry and Clinical Neuroscience* 3:232–233.

Modell JG (1997). Protracted benzodiazepine withdrawal syndrome mimicking psychotic depression (Letter). *Psychosomatics* 38:160–161.

Möhler H & Okada T (1977). Benzodiazepine receptors: Demonstration in the central nervous system. *Science* 198:849–851.

Moussaoui D (1986). Benzodiazepines and memory. *Encephale* 12:315–319.

Nabeshima T, Tohyama K & Kameyama T (1988). Reversal of alcohol-induced amnesia by the benzodiazepine inverse agonist Ro 15-4513. *European Journal of Pharmacology* 155:211–7.

Noyes R Jr, Burrows GD, Reich JH et al. (1996). Diazepam versus alprazolam for the treatment of panic disorder. *Journal of Clinical Psychiatry* 57:349–55.

O'Connor R (1993). Benzodiazepine dependence—A treatment perspective and an advocacy for control. *NIDA Research Monograph* Rockville, MD: National Institute on Drug Abuse, 266–269.

Oehrberg S, Christiansen PE, Behnke K et al. (1995). Paroxetine in the treatment of panic disorder. A randomised, double-blind, placebo-controlled study. *British Journal of Psychiatry* 167:374–9.

Olsen R & Loeb-Lundberg F (1981). Convulsant and anticonvulsant drug binding sites related to GABA-regulated chloride ion channels. In E Costa, G DiChiari & G Gessa (eds.) *GABA and Benzodiazepine Receptors.* New York, NY: The Raven Press.

Ott H, Rohloff A, Aufdembrinke B & Fichte K (1988). Anterograde and retrograde amnesia after lormetazepam and flunitrazepam. *Psychopharmacology Series* 6:180–93.

Ozdemir V, Bremner KE & Naranjo CA (1994). Treatment of alcohol withdrawal syndrome. *Annals of Medicine* 26:101–105.

Pevnick JS, Jasinski DR & Haertzen CA (1978). Abrupt withdrawal from therapeutically administered diazepam. *Archives of General Psychiatry* 35:995–998.

Randall T (1992). Cocaine, alcohol mix in body to form even longer lasting, more lethal drug. *Journal of the American Medical Association* 267:1043–1044.

Richens A, Davidson DL, Cartlidge NE & Easter DJ (1994). A multicentre comparative trial of sodium valproate and carbamazepine in adult onset epilepsy. *Journal of Neurology, Neurosurgery, and Psychiatry* 57:682–687.

Rickels K, Case WG, Schweizer E, Garcia-Espana F & Friedman R (1990). Benzodiazepine dependence: management of discontinuation. *Psychopharmacology Bulletin* 26:63–68.

Rickels K, Schweizer E, Case WG & Greenblatt DJ (1990). Long-term therapeutic use of benzodiazepines. 1. Effects of abrupt discontinuation [published erratum appears in *Archives of General Psychiatry* 1991 Jan;48(1):51]. *Archives of General Psychiatry* 47:899–907.

Robinson GM, Sellers EM & Janecek B (1981). Barbiturate and hypnosedative withdrawal by a multiple oral phenobarbital loading technique. *Clinical Pharmacology and Therapeutics* 30:71–76.

Rosenbaum JF, Moroz G & Bowden CL (1997). Clonazepam in the treatment of panic disorder with or without agoraphobia: A dose-response study of efficacy, safety, and discontinuance. Clonazepam Panic Disorder Dose-Response Study Group. *Journal of Clinical Psychopharmacology* 17:390–400.

Roy-Byrne PP, Ward NG & Donnelly P (1989). Valproate in anxiety and withdrawal syndromes. *Journal of Clinical Psychiatry* 50:44–48.

Salloum IM, Cornelius JR, Daley DC & Thase ME (1995). The utility of diazepam loading in the treatment of alcohol withdrawal among psychiatric inpatients. *Psychopharmacology Bulletin* 31:305–310.

Schechter MD (1997). Discrimination of cocaethylene in rats trained to discriminate between its components. *European Journal of Pharmacology* 320:1–7.

Schweizer E & Rickels K (1986). Failure of buspirone to manage benzodiazepine withdrawal. *American Journal of Psychiatry* 143:1590–1592.

Schweizer E, Rickels K, Case WG & Greenblatt DJ (1991). Carbamazepine treatment in patients discontinuing long-term benzodiazepine therapy. Effects on withdrawal severity and outcome. *Archives of General Psychiatry* 48:448–452.

Schweizer E, Rickels K & Lucki I (1986). Resistance to the anti-anxiety effect of buspirone in patients with a history of benzodiazepine use (Letter). *The New England Journal of Medicine* 314:719–720.

Sellers EM, Naranjo CA, Harrison M, Devenyi P, Roach C & Sykora K (1983). Oral diazepam loading: Simplified treatment of alcohol withdrawal. *Clinical Pharmacology and Therapeutics* 34:822–826.

Sheehan DV & Harnett-Sheehan K (1996). The role of SSRIs in panic disorder. *Journal of Clinical Psychiatry* 57 (Suppl 10):51–8, discussion 59–60.

Sheehan DV, Raj AB, Harnett-Sheehan K, Soto S & Knapp E (1993). The relative efficacy of high-dose buspirone and alprazolam in the treatment of panic disorder: A double-blind placebo-controlled study. *Acta Psychiatrica Scandinavica* 88: 1–11.

Skolnick P, Concada V, Barker J et al. (1981). Pentobarbital: dual action to increase brain benzodiazepine receptor affinity. *Science* 211:1448–1450.

Smith D & Wesson D (1970). A new method for treatment of barbiturate dependence. *Journal of the American Medical Association* 213:294–295.

Smith D & Wesson D (1971). A phenobarbital technique for withdrawal of barbiturate abuse. *Archives of General Psychiatry* 24:56–60.

Squires RF & Braestrup C (1977). Benzodiazepine receptors in rat brain. *Nature* 266:732–734.

Steinberg JR (1994). Anxiety in elderly patients. A comparison of azapirones and benzodiazepines. *Drugs and Aging* 5:335–345.

Suzuki T, Mizoguchi H, Motegi H, Awano H & Misawa M (1995). Effects of nifedipine on physical dependence on barbital or diazepam in rats. *Journal of Toxicological Sciences* 20:415–425.

Taylor DP & Moon SL (1991). Buspirone and related compounds as alternative anxiolytics. *Neuropeptides* 19(Suppl):15–19.

Tollefson GD, Montague-Clouse J & Tollefson SL (1992). Treatment of comorbid generalized anxiety in a recently detoxified alcoholic population with a selective serotonergic drug (buspirone). *Journal of Clinical Psychopharmacology* 12:19–26.

Tonne U, Hiltunen AJ, Vikander B et al. (1991). Neuropsychological changes during steady-state drug use, withdrawal and abstinence in primary benzodiazepine-dependent patients. *Acta Psychiatrica Scandinavica* 91:299–304.

Tyrer P, Rutherford D & Huggett (1981). Benzodiazepine withdrawal symptoms and propranolol. *Lancet* 1:520–527.

Tyrer P (1993). Benzodiazepine dependence: A shadowy diagnosis. *Biochemical Society Symposium* 59:107–119.

Wesson DR & Smith DE (1982). Low dose benzodiazepine withdrawal syndrome: Receptor site medicated. *California Society for the Treatment of Alcoholism and Other Drug Dependencies News* 9:1–5.

Winokur A, Rickels K, Greenblatt DJ, Snyder PJ & Schatz NJ (1980). Withdrawal reaction from long-term, low-dosage administration of diazepam. A double-blind, placebo-controlled case study. *Archives of General Psychiatry* 37:101–105.

Woods SW, Nagy LM, Koleszar AS, Krystal JH, Heninger GR & Charney DS (1992). Controlled trial of alprazolam supplementation during imipramine treatment of panic disorder. *Journal of Clinical Psychopharmacology* 12:32–8.

CHAPTER 3

Pharmacologic Therapies for Cocaine and Other Stimulant Addiction

David A. Gorelick, M.D., Ph.D.

Goals of Treatment
Pharmacological Mechanisms
Choice of Medication
Special Treatment Situations
Future Prospects

Pharmacological treatment of cocaine addiction is widely practiced in the United States, as evidenced by results of a recent anonymous mail survey of physicians practicing addiction medicine, which found that 59% of respondents used medications to help prevent relapse after initial abstinence. Fifteen different medications were reported used, despite the physicians' own doubts about their effectiveness (Gorelick, Halikas & Crosby, 1994). This reflects the absence of consensus on effective pharmacotherapy for cocaine addiction and the paucity of replicated, scientifically rigorous studies supporting the efficacy of any particular medication (Gorelick, 1993, 1995). Despite this state of knowledge, both clinical and scientific interest in pharmacological treatment continues to be stimulated by the often disappointing success rate of current psychosocial treatment approaches.

This chapter reviews the current state of pharmacological treatment of cocaine addiction, including choice of medication, as well as medication use in special populations such as women and patients with other psychiatric diagnoses (so-called "dual diagnosis" patients). Emphasis is on the use of medication in clinical practice, rather than on research findings or preclinical pharmacology. (For more detailed coverage of the latter topic, see Section 2 on the pharmacology of cocaine and other stimulants.) The overwhelming majority of both the clinical and clinical research literature deals with cocaine, rather than other stimulants such as the amphetamines or methylphenidate; thus, there is little mention of the latter in this chapter. The extent to which findings with cocaine addiction can be extrapolated to other stimulant addictions remains unclear.

GOALS OF TREATMENT

The goals of pharmacologic treatment are the same as for any other treatment modality; that is, to help patients abstain from cocaine use and regain control over their lives. The behavioral mechanisms by which medication achieves these goals are poorly understood, and may vary among individual patients and medications. In theory, medication could shift the balance of reinforcement away from cocaine-taking in favor of other behaviors by several mechanisms: (1) reducing or eliminating the positive reinforcement from taking a cocaine dose (for example, reduce the euphoria or "high"); (2) reducing or eliminating a subjective state (such as "craving") that predisposes to taking cocaine; (3) reducing or eliminating negative reinforcement from taking a cocaine dose (as by reducing withdrawal-associated dysphoria); (4) making cocaine-taking aversive; or (5) increasing the positive reinforcement obtained from non-cocaine taking behaviors. Currently available medications are considered to act by one or more of the first three mechanisms, and these mechanisms are the focus of current research in medications development. No current medication or research addresses the fourth mechanism (which would be analogous to use of disulfiram in treating alcoholism). The fifth mechanism is crucial to successful treatment by ensuring that other behaviors are reinforced to replace cocaine taking as the latter is extinguished, but such medications do not exist. In current practice, this mechanism is engaged by psychosocial interventions that address issues such as vocational rehabilitation, the patient's social network, and use of leisure time.

Because of the importance of this mechanism, and other factors, medication is almost never used by itself without some psychosocial treatment component. There are few controlled clinical trials explicitly comparing the efficacy of medication used with and without psychosocial treatment (Carroll, Rounsaville et al., 1994; Henningfield & Singleton, 1994), so the relative contributions of pharmacological and psychosocial treatments are unknown. The type, intensity, and duration of psychosocial treatment that should accompany pharmacologic treatments are questions with little systematic or scientific data to guide clinical decision-making. At a minimum, one would expect that addressing psychosocial factors that influence medication compliance would enhance treatment outcome.

PHARMACOLOGICAL MECHANISMS

At least four pharmacological approaches are potentially useful in the treatment of cocaine addiction (Gorelick, 1993; 1995): (1) substitution treatment with a cross-tolerant stimulant (analogous to methadone maintenance treatment of opiate addiction); (2) treatment with an antagonist medication that blocks the binding of cocaine at its site of action (true pharmacological antagonism, analogous to naltrexone treatment of opiate addiction); (3) treatment with a medication that functionally antagonizes the effects of cocaine (e.g., reduces the reinforcing effects of or craving for cocaine); (4) alteration of drug metabolism to either enhance its elimination from the body or change its metabolite profile (analogous to disulfiram treatment of alcoholism). No medication currently is approved by the Food and Drug Administration for the treatment of cocaine addiction, chiefly because no medication has met the scientifically rigorous standard of consistent, statistically significant efficacy in replicated, controlled clinical trials. Most current clinical and research attention has focused on the second and third approaches mentioned above—reducing or blocking cocaine's actions either directly at its neuronal binding site (true pharmacological antagonism) or indirectly by otherwise reducing its reinforcing effects. The first approach has seen limited use, with one controlled clinical trial not showing efficacy. The fourth approach has not been used clinically, but has shown promise in some animal studies.

Cocaine has two major neuropharmacological actions: blockade of presynaptic neurotransmitter reuptake pumps, resulting in psychomotor stimulant effects, and blockade of sodium ion channels in nerve membranes, resulting in local anesthetic effects (Johanson & Fischman, 1989). Cocaine's positively reinforcing effects are believed to derive from its blockade of the dopamine reuptake pump, causing presynaptically released dopamine to remain in the synapse and enhancing dopaminergic neurotransmission (Koob & Bloom, 1988). Cocaine's local anesthetic effects are believed to contribute to cocaine-induced kindling, the phenomenon whereby previous exposure to cocaine sensitizes the individual so that later exposure to low doses produces an enhanced response.

CHOICE OF MEDICATION

Antidepressants. *Heterocyclic Antidepressants:* Tricyclic and other heterocyclic antidepressants are the most widely used and best studied class of medications used in the treatment of cocaine addiction. Their use is based both on the clinical observation of frequent depressive symptoms among cocaine addicts seeking treatment and on their pharmacological mechanism of increasing biogenic amine neurotransmitter activity in synapses by inhibiting presynaptic neurotransmitter reuptake pumps, thus ameliorating a hypothesized neurotransmitter deficiency, especially of dopamine, caused by chronic cocaine use.

Desipramine was the first medication found effective in an outpatient, double-blind, controlled clinical trial (Gawin, Kleber et al., 1989), a finding which received wide publicity even before the complete study was published in a peer-reviewed journal. As a result, desipramine is the best studied of the tricyclic antidepressants, with more than a half-dozen double-blind, controlled clinical trials in the published literature. Typical doses are 150 to 300 mg per day (about 2.5 mg/kg), similar to those used in the treatment of depression. While an early meta-analysis found desipramine significantly effective in reducing relapse to cocaine use, but not in initiating abstinence (Levin & Lehman, 1991; Delucchi, 1992), later and larger controlled trials have not confirmed desipramine's efficacy (Arndt, Dorozynsky et al., 1992; Campbell, Thomas et al., 1994; Carroll, Nich & Rounsaville, 1995), or have found it effective only for short durations (four or six weeks, but not eight or 12 weeks) and in less severely addicted patients (Carroll, Rounsaville et al., 1994; Kosten, Morgan et al., 1992b).

Retrospective data analyses suggest that some patient characteristics may account for the differential efficacy of desipramine in different studies; for example, patients with depression (Ziedonis & Kosten, 1991) and without antisocial personality disorder (Arndt, McLellan et al., 1994) may respond best to desipramine.

One factor that may influence efficacy is plasma level of medication. Preliminary evidence from some clinical trials suggests that desipramine may have a therapeutic "ceiling" in terms of plasma level, with steady state plasma levels above 200 ng/ml associated with poorer outcome than lower levels (Khalsa, Gawin et al., 1993). This "ceiling" effect may be related, in part, to anecdotal reports that, at higher desipramine doses (and presumably higher plasma levels), some patients have subjective effects that they experience as somewhat similar to those produced by cocaine itself, with consequent stimulation of cocaine craving (Weiss & Mirin, 1989). These findings would support keeping desipramine at moderate dose levels, rather than pushing for the maximum tolerated dose, and adjusting the dose downward if the patient is taking concomitant medication (such as methadone) that inhibits desipramine metabolism.

There is no obvious pharmacologic rationale for preferring desipramine over other heterocyclic antidepressants. Limited open-label experience with imipramine and maprotiline, at antidepressant doses, found them effective in reducing cocaine use over periods of several weeks (Brotman, Witkie et al., 1988). Imipramine (150 mg/day) was not effective in reducing methamphetamine use in a 180-day controlled clinical trial, although it did improve treatment retention (Galloway, Newmeyer et al., 1996a).

No unexpected or medically serious side effects have been reported to date from clinical trials of tricyclic antidepressants. However, patients who relapse to cocaine use while still on medication could, in theory, be at increased risk of cardiovascular side-effects. Both cocaine and the tricyclics have quinidine-like membrane effects which, when superimposed, could lead to cardiac arrhythmias or sudden death. The concurrent administration of cocaine and desipramine (blood levels above 100 ng/ml) to research volunteers has produced additive increases in heart rate and blood pressure (Fischman, Foltin et al., 1990. This potential cardiotoxicity, although not yet actually observed in any clinical trial, should be considered when prescribing tricyclics for patients with other cardiovascular risk factors, such as a history of coronary artery disease, arrhythmia or recent myocardial infarction.

Selective serotonin reuptake inhibitors (SSRIs): Antidepressants that specifically block the presynaptic serotonin reuptake pump have attracted interest because of the role of serotonin in inhibiting appetitive behaviors and their efficacy in reducing alcohol and food intake (Gorelick, 1993; Sellers, Higgins et al., 1991). The SSRI fluoxetine attenuates cocaine's behavioral effects in animals (Howell & Byrd, 1995) and its positive psychological effects in human research volunteers (Walsh, Preston et al., 1994). While two of four open-label pilot studies with fluoxetine (20 to 60 mg daily in methadone-maintained cocaine abusers) or sertraline (200 mg daily) were promising (Batki, Manfredi et al., 1993; Kosten, Kosten et al., 1992a; Pollack & Rosenbaum, 1991), four recently completed double-blind, controlled clinical trials have not found any advantage for fluoxetine (20, 40, or 60 mg daily) over placebo (Batki, Washburn et al., 1996a; Covi, Hess et al., 1995; Grabowski, Rhoades et al., 1995), although treatment retention was improved in two of the studies. Thus, the early promise of SSRIs in the treatment of cocaine addiction has not been borne out.

Recent open-label case series have reported fluoxetine (20 mg daily) effective in reducing or eliminating drug use for two weeks to several months in amphetamine abusers participating in outpatient treatment (Polson, Fleming & O'Shea, 1993).

Monoamine oxidase inhibitors: The rationale for use of monoamine oxidase (MAO) inhibitors lies in their effect of increasing brain levels of biogenic amine neurotransmitters by inhibiting a major catabolic enzyme. Limited open-label experience with phenelzine, at antidepressant doses of 30 to 90 mg daily, suggests that this medication may reduce both cocaine and other stimulant use (Brewer, 1993; Maletzky, 1977). However, its clinical usefulness may be limited by the need for dietary and concomitant medication restrictions to avoid precipitating a hypertensive crisis, as well as by the theoretical possibility of potentiating cocaine-induced effects should patients relapse to cocaine use while still taking the medication. Some have argued that fear of such an aversive, potentially life-threatening reaction is what motivates abstinence while taking an MAO inhibitor (Brewer, 1993), making the mechanism of action analogous to that of disulfiram for alcoholism.

Current research is focusing on newer selective MAO inhibitors that act only on MAO type B, the predominant type in the brain, while sparing MAO type A, the predominant type in the GI tract. It is inhibition of MAO in the GI tract that produces a hypertensive crisis ("cheese reaction") after ingestion of tyramine-containing foods or certain catecholaminergic medications. Selegiline (Eldepryl®), marketed for the treatment of Parkinsonism, is fairly selective for MAO B at recommended doses (10 mg/day) and is being studied as a treatment for cocaine addiction, although one small, open-label outpatient study found it ineffective (Tennant, Tarver et al., 1993).

Other antidepressants: The "second generation" antidepressant buproprion (Wellbutrin®) has attracted interest because it increases brain dopamine activity by binding to the same presynaptic dopamine reuptake site as does cocaine. Although well-tolerated by cocaine addicts at antidepressant doses (100 mg tid), a double-blind, placebo-controlled trial among inpatients found no significant effect on cocaine craving (Hollister, Krakewski et al., 1992), and a multisite outpatient controlled clinical trial in methadone-maintained cocaine addicts found no signficant effect on cocaine use (Margolin, Avants & Kosten, 1995).

Ritanserin, a 5-HT_2 receptor antagonist used as an antidepressant, was not effective in reducing cue-elicited cocaine craving during a controlled clinical trial (Ehrman, Robbins et al., 1996). Its effect on cocaine use is still under evaluation.

Dopamine Agonists (Anti-Parkinson agents). A variety of dopamine agonist medications have been tried for the treatment of cocaine addiction, based on the dopamine depletion hypothesis (Dackis & Gold, 1985), although the data supporting the hypothesis in human subjects are equivocal (Gill, Gillespie et al., 1991). Dopamine agonists, by stimulating synaptic dopamine activity, would ameliorate the effects of decreased dopamine activity caused by cessation of cocaine use, such as anhedonia, anergia, depression, and cocaine craving. In rats, dopamine receptor agonists such as bromocriptine and lisuride reduce cocaine self-administration and reverse the reduced metabolic rate and elevated intracranial self-stimulation threshold produced in dopaminergic mesocorticolimbic brain areas after cessation of chronic cocaine administration (Clow & Hammer, 1991; Markou & Koob, 1992; Pulvirenti & Koob, 1994).

Bromocriptine and amantadine, both marketed for the treatment of Parkinsonism (another dopamine deficiency condition), are the most commonly used dopamine agonist medications. Open-label and double-blind studies of the effects of single and chronic doses of bromocriptine (0.625 to 10 mg daily) or lisuride (0.4 to 4.0 mg daily) on cocaine craving among hospitalized cocaine addicts have yielded mixed results, with some studies showing significant reductions in craving (Dackis, Gold et al., 1987; Extein, Gross et al., 1989; Wang, Kalbfleisch et al., 1994) and others showing no effect (Teller & Devenyi, 1988; Kranzler & Bauer, 1992; Gillin, Pulvirenti et al., 1994; Eiler, Shaefer et al., 1995).

Results of outpatient double-blind clinical trials also are inconclusive. Several such trials from one research group have consistently found bromocriptine (2.5 to 10 mg daily) better than placebo, but used psychological symptoms, rather than actual cocaine use, as the outcome measure, making the relevance of the results to addiction treatment unclear (Giannini, Folts et al., 1989). Of two small (7 and 29 patients, respectively), short-term (10 and 15 days, respectively) outpatient trials using urine toxicology results as the outcome measure, the first found an increase in cocaine-negative urine tests, but had no placebo comparison group (Tennant & Sagherian, 1987) and the second found no significant decrease in cocaine-positive urine tests (Moscovitz, Brookoff & Nelson, 1993). A third, larger (69 patients) placebo-controlled trial also found no significant effect on cocaine use (Hill, Wilkins & Gorelick, 1996).

One factor limiting the use of bromocriptine is side effects such as headache, nausea, and abdominal cramps. These tend to be related to high individual doses (2.5 mg or more) and rapid dose escalation, and can be avoided by use of low starting doses, divided daily doses (tid or qid) and limiting dose increases to no oftener than every three days. Bromocriptine should be used very cautiously in postpartum women because of an increased risk of vasospastic complications and seizures (Bakht, Kirshon et al., 1990).

Results of clinical trials of amantadine have been disappointing. Only one of six well-designed double-blind, placebo-controlled studies found that amantadine (200–400 mg daily) reduced cocaine use more than placebo (Alterman, Droba et al., 1992; Arndt, McLellan et al., 1992; Kampman, Volpicelli et al., 1996; Kolar, Brown et al., 1992; Kosten, Morgan et al., 1992b; Weddington, Brown et al., 1991). Two other small positive double-blind studies (7 and 10 patients, respectively) either had no placebo group (Tennant & Sagherian, 1987) or did not use cocaine use as an outcome measure (Giannini, Folts et al., 1989).

Stimulants. By analogy with methadone maintenance treatment of opiate addiction (see Chapters 4 and 5 of this section), maintenance treatment of cocaine addicts with stimulant medication might be clinically beneficial in reducing cocaine craving and use. As with methadone, advantages might include use of the less medically risky oral route of administration (versus injected or smoked cocaine), use of pure medication of known potency (thus avoiding contaminant effects or inadvertent overdose), and use of a medication with slower onset and longer duration of action (thus avoiding "rush"/"crash" cycling) (Gorelick, 1998).

Several orally active psychomotor stimulants marketed for the treatment of attention deficit disorder, narcolepsy, and/or as appetite suppressants (anorexiants) have been used to implement the substitution approach, with only limited success. Early case reports using methylphenidate (50 to 70 mg daily) in outpatients with definite or possible attention deficit disorder were positive (Khantzian, Gawin et al., 1984). However, in a later series of five patients without attention deficit disorder who were treated for two to five weeks with increasing doses up to 100 mg daily (recommended doses for attention deficit disorder or narcolepsy are 10 to 60 mg daily), methylphenidate was actually detrimental (Gawin, Riordan & Kleber, 1985). Cocaine craving and use increased in four patients, and there was concern about the abuse potential of methylphenidate (which is classified in Schedule II of the federal Controlled Substances Act). Another Schedule II anorexiant, phenmetrazine (Preludin®), also increased cocaine use in a small, open-label outpatient study when used at or slightly above the recommended dose of 50 to 75 mg daily (Tennant, Tarver et al., 1993).

Several marketed stimulants with less abuse potential (Schedule IV) have given disappointingly mixed results. Pemoline (75 to 225 mg daily for several weeks) reduced cocaine use in one case series of outpatients with attention deficit/hyperactivity disorder (ADHD), but not in another series of outpatients with and without ADHD (Margolin, Avants & Kosten, 1996; Weiss, Pope & Mirin, 1985). Diethylpropion (up to 75 mg daily for two weeks) did not reduce cocaine craving (both spontaneous and cocaine-cue elicited) among inpatients in a double-blind trial (Alim, Rose et al., 1995). Mazindol, which blocks cocaine binding to the presynaptic dopamine reuptake pump, was effective in one of two small open-label outpatient studies (Berger, Gawin & Kosten, 1989; Tennant, Tarver et al., 1993), but ineffective in two double-blind outpatient studies (at 1 or 2 to 4 mg daily) (Kosten, Steinberg & Diakogiannis, 1993; Margolin, Avants & Kosten, 1995).

In principle, cocaine itself, in a slow onset formulation or route of administration, might be used for agonist maintenance treatment, as slow onset transdermal or transbuccal nicotine is used to treat addiction to rapid onset smoked nicotine (cigarettes) (Gorelick, 1998). Oral cocaine (in the form of coca tea) has been used successfully to reduce cocaine smoking in an open-label case series in Lima, Peru (where oral cocaine products are legal) (Llosa, 1994).

Neuroleptics. The neuroleptics marketed in the U.S. for treatment of psychosis, which are potent dopamine receptor antagonists (chiefly D_2 subtype), do not significantly alter cocaine craving or use, as evidenced by clinical experience with cocaine-abusing schizophrenics who received chronic neuroleptic treatment (Brady, Anton et al., 1990; Gawin, 1986). The neuroleptic flupenthixol, not marketed in the U.S. but available in Canada and Europe, was reported to markedly decrease cocaine craving and use in 10 Bahamian "crack" cocaine addicts followed for 9 to 62 weeks (Gawin, Allen & Hamblestone, 1989). Preliminary results of an ongoing double-blind, outpatient trial of flupenthixol in the U.S. suggest that it is significantly superior to placebo in retaining cocaine addicts in treatment and initiating abstinence (Gawin, Khalsa et al., 1993). The advantage of flupenthixol over other neuroleptics may be twofold: (1) decanoate depot formulation allows biweekly IM administration, thereby eliminating compliance problems found with daily oral medication, and (2) at low doses (10 to 20 mg IM every two weeks), it has a possible preferential action on presynaptic dopamine autoreceptors over postsynaptic receptors, which would lead to increased synaptic dopamine levels (making low-dose flupenthixol functionally equivalent to a dopamine agonist).

Caution should be exercised when prescribing any neuroleptic to cocaine users because of their potential vulnerability to the neuroleptic malignant syndrome, based on their presumed cocaine-induced dopamine depletion (Kosten & Kleber, 1988). Cocaine or amphetamine users also may be at greater risk for neuroleptic-induced movement disorders (Decker & Ries, 1993) and for cardiovascular side effects from clozapine (Hameedi, Sernyak et al., 1996).

Anticonvulsants. Anticonvulsants have been used in the treatment of cocaine addiction because they block the development of cocaine-induced kindling in animals. Kindling (increased neuronal sensitivity to a drug because of prior intermittent exposure) has been hypothesized as a neurophysiological mediator of cocaine craving in humans (Halikas & Kuhn, 1990). Carbamazepine (Tegretol®) has been the most studied. Two of three open-label outpatient studies found it effective in reducing cocaine use at doses (200 to 1,000 mg daily) and plasma levels (4-8 fg/ml) less than those usually required for the treatment of epilepsy (Halikas, Kuhn et al., 1992; Montoya, Llosa et al., 1992; Tennant, Tarver et al., 1993), with some suggestion that cocaine addicts might be especially sensitive to carbamazepine side effects. However, four of five recent double-blind outpatient trials found no significant effect on cocaine craving or use at similar doses and plasma levels (Campbell, Thomas et al., 1994; Cornish, Maany et al., 1995; Halikas, Crosby et al., 1997; Kranzler, Bauer et al., 1995; Montoya, Levin et al., 1995).

Another anticonvulsant, valproic acid, was not effective in a small, open-label study at doses (500 to 1,000 mg daily) typically used for the treatment of epilepsy (Tennant, Tarver et al., 1993). Phenytoin (300 mg daily) significantly reduced cocaine use in a double-blind outpatient trial, especially at serum concentrations above 6.0 fg/ml (Crosby, Pearson et al., 1996).

Amino Acids. The amino acid l-DOPA, a precursor for the synthesis of catecholamines, has been used to increase brain dopamine levels in the treatment of cocaine addiction, both alone and in combination with carbidopa, a peripheral amino acid decarboxylase inhibitor that prevents systemic side effects by blocking the conversion of l-DOPA to dopamine outside the brain. This approach is successful in the treatment of Parkinsonism, a known disorder of brain dopamine deficiency, but has had only mixed success in short-term, open-label studies of cocaine addiction at doses in the low range of those used to treat Parkinsonism (Rosen, Flemenbaum, et al., 1986; Tennant, Tarver et al., 1993). L-Tyrosine, the amino acid precursor of L-DOPA, reduced cocaine craving in a small (12 patients) double-blind study of inpatients (Cold, 1996), but was not effective in reducing cocaine use in two outpatient clinical trials at 2 g every 8 hours (open-label) or 800 or 1,600 mg twice daily (double-blind) (Galloway, Frederick et al., 1996b; Thomas et al., 1996).

The use of amino acid mixtures, either alone or with other nutritional supplements (vitamins and minerals), has been widely publicized in the drug abuse treatment field, encouraged by their freedom from the regulations imposed on prescription medications and their perceived safety and absence of side effects. Proprietary mixtures including tyrosine and l-tryptophan, the amino acid precursor of serotonin, have been marketed with claims of efficacy (Blum, Allison et al., 1988), but a double-blind, 28-day cross-over study found no significant effect of tyrosine and tryptophan (1 g of each daily) on cocaine craving or withdrawal symptoms (Chadwick & Gregory, 1990).

Lithium. Both double-blind and open-label studies have found lithium, at doses and plasma levels used in the treatment of bipolar disorder, ineffective for the treatment of cocaine addiction, except in patients with comorbid bipolar or cyclothymic disorder (Nunes, McGrath et al., 1990).

Calcium Channel Blockers. Calcium channel blockers have been suggested as treatment for cocaine addiction because of their effects on neurotransmitter release and inhibition of cocaine's behavioral reinforcing effects in some, but not all, studies of rodents and human research volunteers (Gorelick, 1995; Reid, Pabello et al., 1997; Schindler, Tella et al., 1995). However, diltiazem and nifedipine showed no efficacy in a recent open-label outpatient case series (Tennant, Tarver et al., 1993), nor did nimodipine reduce cocaine craving in a double-blind inpatient study (Rosse, Alim et al., 1994).

Other Medications. Fenfluramine, a serotonin releasing agent marketed as an appetite suppressant, was not effective in reducing cocaine use in a double-blind trial among methadone-maintained cocaine addicts (Batki, Bradley et al., 1996b).

Medication Combinations. Concurrent use of two different medications is being studied in the hope of enhancing efficacy while minimizing side effects, either by acting on a single neurotransmitter system by two different mechanisms or by acting on two different neurotransmitter systems. Concurrent open-label use of the dopaminergic agents bupropion and bromocriptine in outpatient cocaine addicts has been found safe, with some suggestion of efficacy (Montoya, Preston et al., 1996a).

The combined use of the dopamine releaser phentermine and the serotonin releaser fenfluramine, each marketed as an appetite suppressant, has received substantial publicity as the so-called "phen-fen" treatment for obesity and substance abuse. This medication combination has achieved some success in the outpatient treatment of cocaine addiction (Rothman, Gendron & Hitzig, 1994). Widespread use has been inhibited by concerns over serious long-term toxicity, including primary pulmonary hypertension (Abenhaim, Moride et al., 1996) and valvular heart disease (Connolly, Crary et al., 1997). The combination of pemoline (a dopamine releaser marketed for the treatment of attention deficit disorder) and fenfluramine has also been used with some reported success (Rothman, 1995).

SPECIAL TREATMENT SITUATIONS

Mixed Addictions. *Opiate addiction:* Concurrent opiate use, including addiction, is a common clinical problem among cocaine addicts. Some addicts use cocaine and opiates simultaneously (as in the so-called "speedball") to enhance the drugs' subjective effect. Up to 20% or more of opiate addicts already in methadone maintenance treatment abuse cocaine for a variety of reasons, including continuation of prior polydrug abuse, replacement for the "high" no longer obtained from opiates, self-medication for the sedative effects of high methadone doses, or attenuation of opiate withdrawal symptoms (Schottenfeld, Pakes et al., 1993). Three different pharmacologic approaches have been used for the treatment of such dual cocaine and opiate addiction: (1) adjustment of methadone dose, (2) maintenance with another opiate medication, (3) addition of a medication targeting the cocaine addiction.

Higher methadone doses (usually 60 mg or more daily) generally are associated with less opiate use by patients in methadone maintenance. This relationship also holds in general for cocaine use among methadone maintenance patients (Tennant & Shannon, 1995), although exceptions have been reported (Grabowski, Rhoades et al., 1993). Increasing the methadone dose as a contingency in response to cocaine use can be effective in reducing such use (and more so than decreasing the methadone dose in response to a cocaine-positive urine sample) (Stine, Freeman et al., 1992; Tennant & Shannon, 1995). There is some evidence that cocaine use can lower serum methadone concentrations (Tennant & Shannon, 1995).

Buprenorphine is a mixed opiate agonist (partial mu receptor agonist/kappa receptor antagonist) marketed as a parental opiate analgesic. Administered sublingually, it can be as effective as high-dose methadone as a maintenance treatment for opiate dependence, although not yet approved for marketing for this indication. Its advantages over methadone (a pure mu receptor agonist) lie in buprenorphine's milder withdrawal syndrome and higher therapeutic index (i.e., safety in overdose). Early open-label studies in opiate addicts who used cocaine (but who were not necessarily cocaine-dependent) found that cocaine use was reduced along with opiate use (Kosten, Rosen et al., 1992c), but double-blind clinical trials found no significant effect of buprenorphine on cocaine use, even when opiate use was substantially reduced (Johnson, Jaffe & Fudala, 1992; Strain, Stitzer et al., 1994). More recent studies in patients who were dually dependent on both opiates and cocaine suggest that cocaine use may be reduced at higher buprenorphine doses (12 to 16 mg daily) (Montoya, Gorelick et al., 1996b; Schottenfeld, Pakes et al., 1993).

Naltrexone is a mu receptor antagonist marketed for maintenance treatment of opiate dependence. Anecdotal evidence is inconsistent as to whether cocaine use is reduced in opiate addicts on naltrexone maintenance (at a usual dose of 50 mg daily). No controlled clinical trials have directly evaluated naltrexone's efficacy in cocaine dependence, except for one open-label study in outpatients dually dependent on cocaine and alcohol, which found naltrexone (50 mg daily) of no benefit (Carroll, Ziedonis et al., 1993).

Non-opiate medications for the treatment of cocaine addiction frequently are evaluated in methadone-maintained, opiate-dependent outpatients because the methadone maintenance component ensures good treatment retention and compliance, making medication trials easier to conduct and complete. A variety of the medications discussed above, including desipramine, amantadine, bromocriptine, and fluoxetine, have been studied in methadone-maintained cocaine addicts, with inconsistent results, but no studies have explicitly and directly compared medication efficacy in methadone-maintained versus opiate-free cocaine addicts. Pharmacodynamic and pharmacokinetic interactions between methadone and the other treatment medication could account for some of the variability in results, although these interactions have not been well studied. Methadone maintenance has been found to increase desipramine plasma levels by inhibiting desipramine metabolism (Kosten, Gawin et al., 1990; Maany, Dhopesh et al., 1989).

Alcoholism: Alcoholism is a common problem among cocaine addicts, both in the community and in treatment settings, with rates of comorbidity as high as 90% (Gorelick, 1992). Alcohol use by cocaine addicts is associated with poorer outcome

(Gorelick, 1992; Carroll, Ziedonis et al., 1993), which may be related to a variety of factors, including production of the toxic and psychoactive metabolite cocaethylene (Gorelick, 1992), stimulation of cocaine craving by alcohol (Gorelick, 1992), and alteration of medication metabolism by the hepatic effects of alcohol (which has not been directly studied in cocaine addicts).

Two medications used in the treatment of alcoholism have received open-label trials in the treatment of outpatients dually dependent on cocaine and alcohol. Disulfiram (Antabuse®), at the dose commonly used to treat alcoholism (250 mg daily), substantially decreased both cocaine and alcohol use (Carroll, Ziedonis et al., 1993; Higgins, Budney et al., 1993). Naltrexone (Revia®), a mu opiate receptor antagonist now marketed for the treatment of alcoholism (O'Mara & Wesley, 1994), did not significantly reduce cocaine or alcohol use at doses used for the treatment of opiate or alcohol dependence (50 mg daily) (Carroll, Ziedonis et al., 1993).

Psychiatric Comorbidity. Treatment-seeking cocaine addicts have high rates of psychiatric co-morbidity (i.e., psychiatric diagnoses other than another substance use disorder), with rates as high as 65% for lifetime disorders and 50% for current disorders (Rounsaville, Anton et al., 1991; Thevos, Brady et al., 1993). The commonest comorbid disorders tend to be major depression, bipolar spectrum, phobias, and posttraumatic stress disorder. Personality disorders also are common among treatment-seeking cocaine addicts, with rates as high as 69% (Weiss, Mirin et al., 1993). The commonest is antisocial personality disorder, which is associated with poor response to treatment (Arndt, McLellan et al., 1994).

In general, medication addressing the comorbid psychiatric disorder can successfully reduce cocaine use, even when the medication is not very effective in cocaine addicts without psychiatric comorbidity. Examples include lithium (at doses and plasma levels effective for bipolar disorder) in cocaine addicts with bipolar or cyclothymic disorder (Nunes, McGrath et al., 1990), desipramine (at antidepressant doses) in depressed cocaine addicts (Ziedonis & Kosten, 1991), and bromocriptine and methylphenidate in cocaine addicts with adult attention deficit disorder (Cocores, Patel et al., 1987; Khantzian, Gawin et al., 1984). This pattern suggests that psychiatric symptomatology is a significant contributing factor to cocaine use, and is circumstantial evidence supporting the self-medication hypothesis of drug use in this population (Khantzian, 1985).

Although schizophrenia is not a common comorbid psychiatric disorder among cocaine addicts, cocaine use, if not abuse, is common among treatment-seeking schizophrenic patients (Shaner, Khalsa et al., 1993). Scattered case reports suggest that at least some medications used in cocaine addicts, such as mazindol (Seibyl, Brenner et al., 1992) and imipramine/desipramine, can be effective in cocaine-abusing schizophrenics. Because post-psychotic depression is associated with cocaine abuse in schizophrenic patients, imipramine (150 to 200 mg daily) has been reported effective in reducing cocaine abuse when used to treat post-psychotic depression (Siris, Kane et al., 1988), although attention must be paid to potential pharmacokinetic interactions with neuroleptics and anti-cholinergic interactions with anti-Parkinson medications (Siris, Sellew et al., 1988). Use of cocaine or amphetamines also may exacerbate or provoke neuroleptic-induced movement disorders (Decker & Ries, 1993).

Medical Comorbidity. Very little data have been systematically or prospectively collected to guide the pharmacotherapy of cocaine addiction in medically ill patients, making this an important issue for future clinical research. Prudent clinical practice would require a careful medical evaluation of any patient prior to starting medication, with special attention to medical conditions common in cocaine addicts. Such conditions would include viral hepatitis and alcoholic liver disease, which might alter the metabolism of prescribed medications, and HIV infection. The presence of the latter necessitates caution in prescribing medications with a known potential for inhibiting white blood cell production or other aspects of immune function, such as carbamazepine.

Gender-Specific Issues. Women tend to be excluded from or underrepresented in many clinical trials of cocaine abuse pharmacotherapy (Gorelick, Montoya & Johnson, 1998), in part because of concern, embodied in former FDA regulations, over risk to the fetus and neonate should a female subject become pregnant. Thus, there is a substantial lack of information that addresses gender-specific issues of pharmacotherapy in general (Yonkers, Kando et al., 1992) or cocaine abuse pharmacotherapy specifically. This situation should improve in the future now that FDA and NIH regulations require appropriate representation of women in clinical trials. Meanwhile, clinicians must deal on an ad hoc basis with the treatment implications of possible gender differences in medication pharmacokinetics (such as those due to differences in body mass and composition) and in pharmacodynamics (such as those due to the menstrual cycle or exogenous hormones such as oral contraceptives) (Yonkers, Kando et al., 1992).

In the absence of direct, systematic data, caution should be used when prescribing medication for pregnant addicts and those with pregnancy potential, keeping in mind both medication risks and the risks of continued cocaine use. Most medications used for the treatment of cocaine addiction (such as tricyclic antidepressants, fluoxetine, bupropion, and bromocriptine), appear to have little potential for morphologic teratogenicity or disruption of pregnancy, although there are little or no data on behavioral teratogenicity (Miller, 1994). Some exceptions are amantadine (which has been associated with pregnancy complications), lithium (which is associated with cardiac malformations and neonatal toxicity), and neuroleptics (which may be associated with nonspecific congenital anomalies and neonatal withdrawal). Bromocriptine should be used cautiously in the postpartum period because of the risk of vasospastic complications and seizures (Bakht, Kirshon et al., 1990).

Age. Although adolescents make up a substantial minority of heavy cocaine users, they have been excluded from clinical trials of cocaine abuse pharmacotherapy because of legal and informed consent considerations. Based on the scarcity of published case reports, it appears that medication is very little used in the treatment of adolescent cocaine addiction (Center for Substance Abuse Treatment, 1993).

FUTURE PROSPECTS

Future progress in pharmacologic treatment for cocaine addiction is likely to come from development of new medications with novel mechanisms of action, rather than use of existing medications developed for other indications. One exception may be the stimulant maintenance approach, which warrants further evaluation using medications with less abuse potential (pemoline, diethylpropion) than those studied to date (methylphenidate), perhaps even a slow onset (e.g., oral) form of cocaine itself. More sophisticated patient-treatment matching, taking into account both patient characteristics that influence treatment response (severity of addiction, psychiatric comorbidity, concomitant medications) and characteristics of the psychosocial treatment accompanying medication, may improve the efficacy of both existing and newly developed medications (Carroll, Rounsaville et al., 1994).

New medications should evolve from improved understanding of the neuropharmacology of cocaine addiction and animal studies of the interactions of cocaine with novel compounds (Gorelick, 1995; Witkin, 1994). Studies with compounds that bind tightly to the same presynaptic dopamine transporter site as does cocaine, but without producing as robust reinforcing subjective effects (such as the experimental compound GBR-12909), suggest that these may be useful in treatment as functional cocaine "antagonists." Other neuropharmacologic approaches being studied in animals (and, in some cases, in humans) for possible therapeutic use include selective stimulation or blockade of dopamine receptor subtypes (e.g., Glowa & Wojnicki, 1996), stimulation of κ-opioid receptors (Kuzmin, Semenova et al., 1997; Woolfolk & Holtzman, 1996), blockade of excitatory amino acid receptors (Pulvirenti, Balducci & Koob, 1997), and stimulation of $GABA_B$ receptors (Roberts, Andrews & Vickers, 1996). These manipulations have been reported to reduce cocaine self-administration in animals, presumably by their indirect influence on the dopaminergic "reward" systems activated by cocaine (Koob & Bloom, 1988).

The failure of existing medications to show consistent efficacy in the treatment of cocaine addiction has prompted growing interest in pharmacokinetic approaches, i.e., preventing ingested cocaine from entering the brain and/or enhancing its elimination from the body (Gorelick, 1977). The former could be implemented by active or passive immunization to produce binding antibodies which keep cocaine from crossing the blood-brain barrier. The latter could be implemented by administration of the enzyme (butyrylcholinesterase) which catalyzes cocaine hydrolysis or by immunization with a catalytic antibody. These pharmacokinetic approaches have shown promise in attenuating cocaine's effects in animals, but have not yet been studied in humans.

Regardless of which medications show promise in the future, their adoption into and use in clinical practice should be guided by acceptable scientific proof of efficacy and safety, based on data from replicated, well-designed, controlled clinical trials.

REFERENCES

Abenhaim L, Moride Y, Brenot F et al. (1996). Appetite-suppressant drugs and the risk of primary pulmonary hypertension. *The New England Journal of Medicine* 335:609–616.

Alim TN, Rosse RB, Vocci FJ, Jr, Lindquist T & Deutsch SI (1995). Diethylpropion pharmacotherapeutic adjuvant therapy for intpatient treatment of cocaine dependence: A test of the cocaine-agonist hypothesis. *Clinical Neuropharmacology* 18:183–195.

Alterman AI, Droba M, Antelo R, et al. (1992). Amantadine may facilitate detoxification of cocaine addicts. *Drug and Alcohol Dependence* 31:19–29.

Arndt IO, Dorozynsky L, et al. (1992). Desipramine treatment of cocaine dependence in methadone-maintained patients. using amantadine or desipramine. *Archives of General Psychiatry* 49:888–893.

Arndt IO, McLellan AT, Dorozynsky L et al. (1994). Desipramine treatment for cocaine dependence. *Journal of Nervous and Mental Disease* 182:(3)151–156.

Bakht FR, Kirshon B, Baker T et al. (1990). Postpartum cardiovascular complications after bromocriptine and cocaine use. *American Journal of Obstetrics and Gynecology* 162:1065–1066.

Batki SL, Manfredi LB et al. (1993). Fluoxetine for cocaine dependence in methadone maintenance: Quantitative plasma and urine cocaine/benzoylecgonine concentrations. *Journal of Clinical Psychopharmacology* 13(4)243–250.

Batki SL, Washburn AM, Delucchi K & Jones RT (1996a). A controlled trial of fluoxetine in crack cocaine dependence. *Drug and Alcohol Dependence* 41:137–142.

Batki SL, Bradley M, Herbst M, et al. (1996b). A controlled trial of fenfluramine in cocaine dependence. *NIDA Research Monograph 162*. Rockville, MD: National Institute on Drug Abuse, 148.

Berger R, Gawin F & Kosten TR (1989). Treatment of cocaine abuse with mazindol. *Lancet* 283.

Blum K, Allison D, Trachtenberg MC et al. (1988). Reduction of both drug hunger and withdrawal against advice rate of cocaine abusers in a 30-day inpatient treatment program by the neuronutrient tropamine. *Current Therapeutic Research* 43:1204–1214.

Brady K, Anton R, Ballenger JC et al. (1990). Cocaine abuse among schizophrenic patients. *American Journal of Psychiatry* 147:1164–1167.

Brewer C (1993). Treatment of cocaine abuse with monoamine oxidase inhibitors. *British Journal of Psychiatry* 163:815–816.

Brotman AW, Witkie SM et al. (1988). An open trial of maprotiline for the treatment of cocaine abuse. *Journal of Clinical Psychopharmacology* 8:125–127.

Campbell JL, Thomas HM, Gabrielli W, Liskow BI & Powell BJ (1994). Impact of desipramine or carbamazepine on patient retention in outpatient cocaine treatment: Preliminary findings. *Journal of Addictive Diseases* 13:191–199.

Carroll KM, Ziedonis D, O'Malley S et al. (1993). Pharmacologic interventions for alcohol- and cocaine-abusing individuals. *American Journal on Addictions* 2(1):77–79.

Carroll KM, Rounsaville BJ, Gordon LT, Nich C, Jatlow P, Bisighini RM & Gawin FH (1994). Psychotherapy and pharmacotherapy for ambulatory cocaine abusers. *Archives of General Psychiatry* 51:177–187.

Carroll KM, Nich C & Rounsaville BJ (1995). Differential symptom reduction in depressed cocaine abusers treated with psychotherapy and pharmacotherapy. *Journal of Nervous and Mental Disease* 183:251–259.

Center for Substance Abuse Treatment (1993). Guidelines for the treatment of alcohol- and other drug-abusing adolescents. *Treatment Improvement Protocol (TIP) Series 4*. Rockville, MD: CSAT.

Chadwick MJ & Gregory DL (1990). A double-blind amino acids, L- tryptophan and L-tyrosine, and placebo study with cocaine-dependent subjects in an inpatient chemical dependency treatment center. *American Journal of Drug and Alcohol Abuse* 16:275–286.

Clow DW & Hammer RP (1991). Cocaine abstinence following chronic treatment alters cerebral metabolism in dopaminergic reward regions. *Neuropsychopharmacology* 4(1):71–75.

Cold JA (1996). NeuRecover-SA™ in the treatment of cocaine withdrawal and craving, a pilot study. *Clinical Drug Investigation* 12:1–7.

Connolly HM, Crary JL, McGoon MD et al. (1997) Valvular heart disease associated with fenfluramine-phentermine. *The New England Journal of Medicine*, in press.

Corcores JA, Patel MD et al. (1987). Cocaine abuse, attention deficit disorder and bipolar disorder. *Journal of Nervous and Mental Disorders* 175(7):431–432.

Cornish JW, Maany I, Fudala PJ, Neal S et al. (1995). Carbamazepine treatment for cocaine dependence. *Drug and Alcohol Dependence* 38:221–227.

Covi L, Hess JM, Kreiter NA & Haertzen CA (1995). Effects of combined fluoxetine and counseling in the outpatient treatment of cocaine abusers. *American Journal of Drug and Alcohol Abuse* 21:327–344.

Crosby RD, Pearson VL, Eller C et al. (1996). Phenytoin in the treatment of cocaine abuse: A double-blind study. *Clinical Pharmacology and Therapeutics* 59:458–468.

Dackis CA, Gold MS, Sweeney DR et al. (1987). Single-dose bromocriptine reverses cocaine craving. *Psychiatry Research* 20:261–264.

Dackis CA, Gold MS (1985). Pharmaocological approaches to cocaine addiction. *Journal of Substance Abuse Treatment* 2:139–145.

Decker KP & Ries RK (1993). Differential diagnosis and psychopharmacology of dual disorders. *Psychiatric Clinics of North America* 16:(4)703–718.

Delucchi KL (1992). Research on desipramine in the treatment of cocaine abuse: A critique of Levin and Lehman's meta-analysis. *Journal of Clinical Psychopharmacology* 12(5):367–369.

Ehrman RN, Robbins SJ, Cornish JW et al. (1996). Failure of ritanserin to block cocaine cue reactivity in humans. *Drug and Alcohol Dependence* 42:167–174.

Eiler K, Schaefer MR, Salstrom D & Lowery R (1995). Double-blind comparison of bromocriptine and placebo in cocaine withdrawal. *American Journal of Drug and Alcohol Abuse* 21:65–79.

Extein IL, Gross DA, Gold MS et al. (1989). Bromocriptine treatment of cocaine withdrawal symptoms. *American Journal of Psychiatry* 146:403.

Fischman MW, Foltin RW, Nestadt G et al. (1990). Effects of desipramine maintenance on cocaine self-administration by humans. *Journal of Pharmacology and Experimental Therapeutics* 253(2):760–770.

Galloway GP, Newmeyer J, Knapp T, Stalcup SA & Smith D (1996a). A controlled trial of imipramine for the treatment of methamphetamine dependence. *Journal of Substance Abuse Treatment* 13:493–497.

Galloway GP, Frederick SL, Thomas S et al. (1996b). A historically controlled trial of tyrosine for cocaine dependence. *Journal of Psychoactive Drugs* 28:305–309.

Gawin FH (1986). Neuroleptic reduction of cocaine-induced paranoia but not euphoria? *Psychopharmacology* 90:142–143.

Gawin FH, Allen D & Humblestone B (1989). Outpatient treatment of "crack" cocaine smoking with flupenthixol decanoate. *Archives of General Psychiatry* 46:322–325.

Gawin FH, Khalsa ME, Brown J et al. (1993). Flupenthixol treatment of crack users: Initial double-blind results. *NIDA Research Monograph 132*. Rockville, MD: National Institute on Drug Abuse, 319.

Gawin FH, Kleber HD, Byck R, et al. (1989). Desipramine facilitation of initial cocaine abstinence. *Archives of General Psychiatrey* 46:117–121.

Gawin FH, Riordan CA & Kleber HD (1985). Methylphenidate use in non-ADD cocaine abusers—A negative study. *American Journal of Drug and Alcohol Abuse* 11:193–197.

Giannini AJ, Folts DJ, Feather JN et al. (1989). Bromocriptine and amantadine in cocaine detoxification. *Psychiatry Research* 29:11–16.

Gill K, Gillespie HK, Hollister LE et al. (1991). Dopamine depletion hypothesis of cocaine dependence. *Human Psychopharmacology* 6:25–29.

Gillin JC, Pulvirenti L, Withers N, Golshan S & Koob G (1994). The effects of lisuride on mood and sleep during acute withdrawal in stimulant abusers: A preliminary report. *Biological Psychiatry* 35:843–849.

Glowa JR & Wojnicki FHE (1996). Effects of drugs on food- and cocaine-maintained responding. III: Dopaminergic antagonists. *Psychopharmacology* 128:351–358.

Gorelick DA (1995). Pharmacologic therapies for cocaine addiction. In NS Miller & MS Gold (eds.) *Pharmacological Therapies for Drug and Alcohol Addictions*. New York, NY: Marcel Dekker, 143–157.

Gorelick DA (1993). Overview of pharmacologic treatment approaches for alcohol and other drug addiction: Intoxication, withdrawal, relapse prevention. *Psychiatric Clinics of North America* 16(1):141–156.

Gorelick DA (1992). Alcohol and cocaine: Clinical and pharmacological interactions. *Recent Developments in Alcoholism* 11:37–56.

Gorelick DA (1998). The rate hypothesis and agonist substitution approaches to cocaine abuse treatment. *Advances in Pharmacology* 42:995–997.

Gorelick DA (1997). Enhancing cocaine metabolism with butyrylcholinesterase as a treatment strategy. *Drug and Alcohol Dependence*. 48:159–165

Gorelick DA, Halikas JA & Crosby RD (1994). Pharmacotherapy of cocaine dependence in the United States: Comparing scientific evidence and clinical practice. *Substance Abuse* 15:209–213.

Gorelick DA, Montoya ID & Johnson EO (1998). Sociodemographic representation in published studies of cocaine abuse pharmacotherapy. *Drug and Alcohol Dependence*. 49:89–93

Grabowski J, Rhoades H, Elk R et al. (1993). Methadone dosage, cocaine and opiate abuse. *American Journal of Psychiatry* 150(4):675.

Grabowski J, Rhoades H, Elk R, Schmitz J, Davis C, Creson D & Kirby K (1995). Fluoxetine is ineffective for treatment of cocaine dependence or concurrent opiate and cocaine dependence: Two placebo-controlled, double-blind trials. *Journal of Clinical Psychopharmacology* 15:163–174.

Halikas JA & Kuhn KL (1990). A possible neurophysiological basis of cocaine craving. *Annals of Clinical Psychiatry* 2:79–83.

Halikas JA, Kuhn KL, Carlson GA et al. (1992). The effect of carbamazepine on cocaine use. *American Journal on Addictions* 1(1):30–39.

Halikas JA, Crosby RD, Pearson VL & Graves NM (1997). A randomized double-blind study of carbamazepine in the treatment of cocaine abuse. *Clinical Pharmacology and Therapeutics* 62:89–105.

Hameedi FA, Sernyak MJ, Naqvi SA & Kosten TR (1996). Near syncope associated with concomitant clozapine and cocaine use. *Journal of Clinical Psychiatry* 57:371–372.

Henningfield JE & Singleton EG (1994). Managing drug dependence: Psychotherapy or pharmacotherapy? *CNS Drugs* 1(5):317–322.

Higgins ST, Budney AJ, Bickel WK et al. (1993). Disulfiram therapy in patients abusing cocaine and alcohol. *American Journal of Psychiatry* 150(4):675–676.

Hill JL, Wilkins JN & Gorelick DA (1996). Double-blind outpatient trial of bromocriptine for treatment of cocaine abuse. *NIDA Research Monograph 162*. Rockville, MD: National Institute on Drug Abuse, 145.

Hollister LE, Krajewski K, Rustin T & Gillespie H (1992). Drugs for cocaine dependence: Not easy. *Archives of General Psychiatry* 49:905.

Howell LL & Byrd LD (1995) Serotonergic modulation of the behavioral effecs of cocaine in the squirrel monkey. *Journal of Pharmacology and Experimental Therapeutics* 275:1551–1559.

Johanson CE & Fischman MW (1989). The pharmacology of cocaine related to its abuse. *Pharmacological Review* 41:3–52.

Johnson RE, Jaffe JH, Fudala PJ (1992). A controlled trial of buprenorphine treatment for opioid dependence. *Journal of the American Medical Association* 267(20):2750–2755.

Kampman K, Volpicelli JR, Alterman A, Cornish J, Weinrieb R, Epperson L, Sparkman T & O'Brien CP (1996). Amantadine in the early treatment of cocaine dependence: a double-blind, placebo-controlled trial. *Drug and Alcohol Dependence* 41:25–33.

Khalsa ME, Gawin FH, Rawson R et al. (1993). A desipramine ceiling in cocaine abusers. *NIDA Research Monograph 132*. Rockville, MD: National Institute on Drug Abuse, 318.

Khantzian EJ, Gawin FH, Riordan C et al. (1984). Methylphenidate treatment of cocaine dependence: A preliminary report. *Journal of Substance Abuse Treatment* 1:107–112.

Khantzian EJ (1985). The self-medication hypothesis of addictive disorders: Focus on heroin and cocaine dependence. *American Journal of Psychiatry* 142:1259–1264.

Kolar A, Brown B, Weddington W, Haertzen C, Michaelson B & Jaffe J (1992). Treatment of cocaine dependence in methadone maintenance clients: a pilot study comparing the efficacy of desipramine and amantadine. *International Journal of the Addictions* 27:849–868.

Koob GF & Bloom FE (1988). Cellular and molecular mechanisms of drug dependence. *Science* 242:715–723.

Kosten TR, Gawin FH, Morgan C et al. (1990). Evidence for altered desipramine disposition in methadone-maintained patients treated for cocaine abuse. *American Journal of Alcohol and Drug Abuse* 16:329–336.

Kosten TR & Kleber HD (1988). Rapid death during cocaine abuse: A variant of the neuroleptic malignant syndrome? *American Journal of Drug and Alcohol Abuse* 12:(3)335–346.

Kosten TA, Kosten TR, Gawin FH et al. (1992a). An open trial of sertraline for cocaine abuse. *American Journal on Addictions* 1(4):349–353.

Kosten TR, Morgan CM, Falcione J, Schottenfeld RS (1992b). Pharmacotherapy for cocaine-abusing methadone-maintained patients using amantadine or desipramine. *Archives of General Psychiatry* 49:894–898.

Kosten TR, Rosen MI, Schottenfeld R et al. (1992c). Buprenorphine for cocaine and opiate dependence. *Psychopharmacology Bulletin* 28:15–19.

Kosten TR, Steinberg M & Diakogiannis IA (1993). Crossover trial of mazindol for cocaine dependence. *American Journal on Addictions* 2:161.

Kranzler HR & Bauer LO (1992). Bromocriptine and cocaine cue reactivity in cocaine-dependent patients. *British Journal of Addiction* 87:1537–1548.

Kranzler HR, Bauer LO, Hersh D, Klinghoffer V (1995). Carbamazepine treatment of cocaine dependence: a placebo-controlled trial. *Drug and Alcohol Dependence* 38:203–211.

Kuzmin AV, Semenova S, Gerrits MA, et al. (1997) κ-Opioid receptor agonist U50,488H modulates cocaine and morphine self-administration in drug-naive rats and mice. *European Journal of Pharmacology* 321:265–271.

Levin FR & Lehman AF (1991). Meta analysis of desipramine as an adjunct in the treatment of cocaine addiction. *Journal of Clinical Psychopharmacology* 11:374–378.

Llosa T (1994). The standard low dose of oral cocaine used for treatment of cocaine dependence. *Substance Abuse* 15:215–220.

Maany I, Dhopesh V et al. (1989). Increase in desipramine serum levels associated with methadone treatment. *American Journal of Psychiatry* 146:1611–1613.

Maletzky BM (1977). Phenelzine as a stimulant drug antagonist. *International Journal of the Addictions* 12(5):661–665.

Margolin A, Kosten TR, Petrakis I et al. (1991). Bupropion reduces cocaine abuse in methadone-maintained patients. *Archives of General Psychiatry* 48:87.

Margolin A, Avants SK & Kosten TR (1995). Mazindol for relapse prevention to cocaine abuse in methadone-maintained patients. *American Journal of Drug and Alcohol Abuse* 21:469–481.

Margolin A, Avants SK & Kosten TR (1996). Pemoline for the treatment of cocaine dependence in methadone-maintained patients. *Journal of Psychoactive Drugs* 28:301–304.

Markou A & Koob GF (1992). Bromocriptine reverses the elevation in intracranial self-stimulation thresholds observed in a rat model of cocaine withdrawal. *Neuropsychopharmacology* 7(3):213–224.

Miller LJ (1994). Psychiatric medication during pregnancy: Understanding and minimizing risks. *Psychiatric Annals* 24:69–75.

Montoya ID, Preston K, Cone EJ, Rothman R & Gorelick DA (1996a). Safety and efficacy of bupropion in combination with bromocriptine for treatment of cocaine dependence. *American Journal on Addictions* 5:69–75.

Montoya I, Gorelick D, Preston K et al. (1996b). Buprenorphine for treatment of dually-dependent (opiate and cocaine) individuals. *NIDA Research Monograph 162*. Rockville, MD: National Institute on Drug Abuse, 178.

Montoya ID, Levin FR, Fudala P & Gorelick DA (1995). Double-blind comparison of carbamazepine and placebo for treatment of cocaine dependence. *Drug and Alcohol Dependence* 38:213–219.

Montoya ID, Llosa T, Hess JM et al. (1992). Open-label carbamazepine reduces cocaine use in cocaine-dependent patients with and without abnormal EEG. *Biological Psychiatry* 31:142a.

Moscovitz H, Brookoff D & Nelson L (1993). A randomized trial of bromocriptine for cocaine users presenting to the emergency department. *Journal of General Internal Medicine* 8:1–4.

Nunes EV, McGrath PJ, Wager S et al. (1990). Lithium treatment for cocaine abusers with bipolar spectrum disorders. *American Journal of Psychiatry* 147(5):655–657.

O'Mara NB & Wesley LC (1994). Naltrexone in the treatment of alcohol dependence. *Annals of Pharmacotherapy* 28:210–211.

Pollack MH & Rosenbaum JF (1991). Fluoxetine treatment of cocaine abuse in heroin addicts. *Journal of Clinical Psychiatry* 52:1.

Polson RG, Fleming PM & O'Shea JK (1993). Fluoxetine in the treatment of amphetamine dependence. *Human Psychopharmacology* 8:55–58.

Pulvirenti L & Koob GF (1994). Lisuride reduces intravenous cocaine self-administration in rats. *Pharmacology, Biochemistry and Behavior* 47:(4)819–822.

Pulvirenti L, Balducci C & Koob GF (1997). Dextromethorphan reduces intravenous cocaine self-administration in the rat. *European Journal of Pharmacology* 321:279–283.

Reid LD, Pabello NG, Cramer CM & Hubbell CL (1997). Isradipine in combination with naltrexone as a medicine for treating cocaine abuse. *Life Sciences* 60:119–126.

Roberts DCS, Andrews MM & Vickers GJ (1996). Baclofen attenuates the reinforcing effects of cocaine in rats. *Neuropsychopharmacology* 15:417–423.

Rosen H, Flemenbaum A, Slater V et al. (1986). Clinical trial of carbidopa–1- dopa combination for cocaine. *American Journal of Psychiatry* 143:1493.

Rosse RB, Alim TN, Fay-McCarthy M et al. (1994). Nimodipine pharmacotherapeutic adjuvant therapy for inpatient treatment of cocaine dependence. *Clinical Neuropharmacology* 17:348–358.

Rothman RB (1995). Treatment of alcohol and cocaine addiction by the combination of pemoline and fenfluramine: A preliminary case series. *Journal of Substance Abuse Treatment* 12:449–453.

Rothman RB, Gendron T & Hitzig P (1994). Combined use of fenfluramine and phentermine in the treatment of cocaine addiction. *Journal of Substance Abuse Treatment* 11:(3)273–275.

Rounsaville BJ, Anton SF, Carroll K, Bude D et al. (1991). Psychiatric diagnoses of treatment-seeking cocaine abusers. *Archives of General Psychiatry* 48:43–51.

Schindler CW, Tella SR, Prada J & Goldberg SR (1995). Calcium channel blockers antagonize some of cocaine's cardiovascular effects, but fail to alter cocaine's behavioral effects. *Journal of Pharmacology and Experimental Therapeutics* 272:791–798.

Schottenfeld R, Pakes J, Ziedonis D & Kosten T (1993). Buprenorphine: Dose-related effects on cocaine and opioid use in cocaine-abusing opioid-dependent humans. *Biological Psychiatry* 34:66–74.

Seibyl JP, Brenner L, Krystal JH et al. (1992). Mazindol and cocaine addiction in schizophrenia. *Biology and Psychiatry* 31:1172–1183.

Sellers EM, Higgins GA, Tomkins DM et al. (1991). Opportunities for treatment of psychoactive substance use disorders with serotonergic medications. *Journal of Clinical Psychiatry* 52(Suppl 12):49–54.

Shaner A, Khalsa ME, Roberts L, Wilkins J et al. (1993). Unrecognized cocaine use among schizophrenic patients. *American Journal of Psychiatry* 150:758–762.

Siris SG, Kane JM, Frechen K, Sellew AP et al. (1988). Patterns of previous drug abuse in patients presenting with postpsychotic depression. *Psychopharmacology Bulletin* 24:256–259.

Siris SG, Sellew AP, Frenchen K, Cooper TB et al. (1988). Antidepressants in the treatment of post-psychotic depression in schizophrenia: Drug interactions and other considerations. *Clinical Chemistry* 34:837–840.

Stine SM, Freeman M et al. (1992). Effect of methadone dose on cocaine abuse in a methadone program. *American Journal on Addictions* 1(4):294–303.

Strain EC, Stitzer ML, Liebson IA & Bigelow GE (1994). Buprenorphine versus methadone in the treatment of opioid-dependent cocaine users. *Psychopharmacology* 116:401–406.

Teller DW & Devenyi P (1988). Bromocriptine in cocaine withdrawal: Does it work? *International Journal of the Addictions* 23:1197–1205.

Tennant F, Shannon J (1995). Cocaine abuse in methadone maintenance patients is associated with low serum methadone concentrations. *Journal of Addictive Diseases* 14:67–74.

Tennant F, Tarver A, Sagherian A et al. (1993). A placebo-controlled elimination study to identify potential treatment agents for cocaine detoxification. *The American Journal on Addictions* 2:299–308.

Tennant FS & Sagherian AA (1987). Double-blind comparison of amantadine and bromocriptine for ambulatory withdrawal from cocaine dependence. *Archives of Internal Medicine* 147:109–112.

Thevos AK, Brady KT, Grice D, Dustan L & Malcolm R (1993). A comparison of psychopathy in cocaine and alcohol dependence. *The American Journal on Addictions* 2:279–286.

Thomas HM, Campbell J, Laster L, et aL. (1996). Efficacy of two doses of tyrosine in retaining crack cocaine abusers in outpatient treatment. *NIDA Research Monograph 162* Problems of Drug Dependence, 1995: Proceedings of the 57th Annual Scientific Meeting, The College on Problems of Drug Dependence, Inc. Rockville, MD: National Institute on Drug Abuse, 148.

Walsh SL, Preston KL, Sullivan JT, Fromme R & Bigelow GE (1994) Fluoxetine alters the effects of intravenous cocaine in humans. *Journal of Clinical Psychopharmacology* 14:396–407.

Wang RIH, Kalbfleisch J, Cho JK et al. (1994). Bromocriptine, desipramine, and trazodone alone and in combination to cocaine dependent patients. *NIDA Research Monograph 141*. Rockville, MD: National Institute on Drug Abuse, 437.

Weddington WW, Brown BS, Haertzen CA et al. (1991). Comparison of amantidine and desipramine combined with psychotherapy for treatment of alcoholism and drug abuse. *American Journal of Alcohol and Drug Abuse* 17(2):137–152.

Weiss RD & Mirin SM (1989). Tricyclic antidepressants in the treatment of alcoholism and drug abuse. *Journal of Clinical Psychiatry* 50(Suppl 7):4–9.

Weiss RD, Mirin SM, Griffin ML, Gunderson JG & Hufford C (1993). Personality disorders in cocaine dependence. *Comprehensive Psychiatry* 34:145–149.

Weiss RD, Pope HG & Mirin SM (1985). Treatment of chronic cocaine abuse and attention deficit disorder, residual type, with magnesium pemoline. *Drug and Alcohol Dependence* 15:69–72.

Witkin JM (1994). Pharmacotherapy of cocaine abuse: Preclinical development. *Neuroscience and Biobehavioral Reviews* 18:121–142.

Woolfolk DR & Holtzman SG (1996). The effects of opioid receptor antagonism on the discriminative stimulus effects of cocaine and d-amphetamine in the rat. *Behavioural Pharmacology* 7:779–787.

Yonkers KA, Kando JC, Cole JO & Blumenthal S (1992). Gender differences in pharmacokinetics and pharmacodynamics of psychotropic medication. *American Journal of Psychiatry* 149:587–595.

Ziedonis DM & Kosten TR (1991). Pharmacotherapy improves treatment outcome in depressed cocaine addicts. *Journal of Psychoactive Drugs* 23(4):417–425.

CHAPTER 4

Pharmacologic Therapies for Opioid Addiction

Susan M. Stine, M.D., Ph.D.
Borislav Meandzija, M.D.
Thomas R. Kosten, M.D.

Acute Withdrawal
Chronic Dependence and Protracted Abstinence
Pharmacotherapies for Acute Withdrawal
Maintenance Pharmacotherapies

Studies on the nature of opioid addiction have described an abstinence syndrome characterized by two phases (Himmelsbach, 1942; Martin & Jasinski, 1969): during the relatively brief initial phase, opioid-dependent patients experience acute withdrawal, followed by the more chronic signs of a protracted abstinence syndrome. Current pharmacotherapeutic strategies are based on this distinction.

ACUTE WITHDRAWAL

This syndrome is precipitated by withdrawal from opioids and consists of a wide range of symptoms for various lengths of time. The symptoms include gastrointestinal distress (such as diarrhea and vomiting), thermal regulation disturbances, insomnia, muscle pain, joint pain, marked anxiety and dysphoria. Although these symptoms generally include no life-threatening complications, the acute withdrawal syndrome causes marked discomfort, often prompting continuation of opioid use, even in the absence of any opioid-associated euphoria (also see Section 6).

CHRONIC DEPENDENCE AND PROTRACTED ABSTINENCE

In patients with a chronic history of opiate dependence, acute withdrawal and detoxification are only the beginning of treatment. Himmelsbach (1942), reporting on 21 prisoners addicted to morphine, observed that "physical recovery requires not less than six months of total abstinence." Factors he measured included temperature, sleep, respiration, weight, basal metabolic rate, blood pressure and hematocrit. The times required for return to baseline ranged from one week to about six months. Martin and Jasinski (1969) reported in a subsequent study that this phase persisted for six months or more following withdrawal and that it was associated with "altered physiological function." They found decreased blood pressure, decreased heart rate and body temperature, miosis and a decreased sensitivity of the respiratory center to carbon dioxide, beginning about six weeks after withdrawal and persisting for 26 to 30 or more weeks. They also found increased sedimentation rates (which persisted for months) and questionable EEG changes.

Martin and Jasinski also postulated a relationship between the protracted abstinence syndrome and relapse. Based on similar observations, Dole (1972) concluded that "human addicts almost always return to use narcotics" after hospital detoxification. In this paper, he reviewed the relative importance of metabolic and conditioned factors in relapse and concluded that the underlying drive is metabolic, arguing that "psychological factors are only triggers for relapse." The concept of protracted abstinence has been controversial, but remains a useful model for scientific hypothesis testing and development of new therapeutic approaches. Accordingly, Dole recommended methadone maintenance treatment, even though "it does establish physical dependence." Since, as Dole pointed out, methadone continues physical dependence, protracted abstinence may remain a problem later whenever detoxification from methadone is undertaken. Fortunately, the recent development of new pharmacological agents may prove to decrease this problem. In addition to biological considerations, psychosocial concomitants of opioid dependence also necessitate longer, more specialized adjunct treatments for these additional problems.

PHARMACOTHERAPIES FOR ACUTE WITHDRAWAL

Slow Methadone Detoxification. Clinically, one must distinguish between withdrawal from short-acting opioids such as heroin (plasma half-life of morphine, the main metabolite: 3 to 4 hours) and long-acting opioids such as methadone (plasma half-life: 13 to 47 hours). For short-acting opioids, the natural course of withdrawal generally is relatively brief, but more intense and associated with a higher degree of discomfort than with long-acting opioids. However, it should be noted that there is considerable individual variation, so that strong early withdrawal symptoms from methadone are possible, as are delayed severe heroin withdrawal symptoms.

One treatment strategy that employs this general principle is stabilization of heroin addicts on methadone, followed by a slow decrease in methadone dose. Initially, methadone may be given in 5 mg increments as the physical signs of abstinence begin to appear (Jackson & Shader, 1973), up to a total of 10 to 20 mg over the first 24 hours. Recently, larger methadone doses have been required in treating patients who use heroin of greater purity and who have larger opioid habits; for such patients, a routine starting dose might be 20 mg rather than 5 mg.

Once a stabilizing dose has been reached, methadone is tapered by 20% a day for inpatients, leading to a one- to two-week procedure; alternatively, the dose is tapered by 5% per day for outpatients, in a withdrawal lasting as long as six months (Margolin & Kosten, 1991). Senay and colleagues (1977) studied the effects of rapid (reductions of 10% of initial dose per week) and gradual (3% per week) withdrawals under double-blind conditions. They found that the 10% weekly decrements were associated with higher drop-out rates, increased illicit opioid use and elevated levels of subjective distress. The authors recommended a withdrawal rate of about 3% per week from methadone maintenance.

On such a regimen, successful detoxification may be achieved by as many as 80% of inpatients and 40% of outpatients, when success is measured by completion of detoxification and a successful naloxone challenge test. The longer duration of the procedure and discomfort make the outpatient detoxification with methadone especially vulnerable to patient drop-out and continuing illicit opioid use.

Clonidine Detoxification. Gold and colleagues (1978) reported amelioration of opioid withdrawal symptoms by use of clonidine and postulated that both morphine and clonidine blocked activation of the locus ceruleus, a major noradrenergic nucleus that shows increased activity during opioid withdrawal. While opioids exert their effect through opiate receptors, clonidine activates alpha-2 adrenergic receptors. Consequently, clonidine does not possess the opioid-associated physical dependence and abuse potential.

In a subsequent outpatient study (Washton & Resnick, 1980), clonidine was reported to "reduce or eliminate most of the commonly reported withdrawal symptoms," including lacrimation, rhinorrhea, restlessness, muscle pain, joint pain and gastrointestinal symptoms. However, symptoms such as lethargy and insomnia persisted. Sedation and dizziness due to orthostatic hypotension were reported as the most significant side effects of clonidine.

The protocol involved administration of 0.1 mg of clonidine every four to six hours as needed for withdrawal discomfort on the first day, followed by an increase in clonidine of 0.1 or 0.2 mg per day, to a maximum of 1.2 mg, according to each patient's blood pressure and withdrawal symptoms. The average maximum dose used in the study was 0.8 mg. Toward the end of the detoxification period (days 5 to 7 in heroin detoxification), the clonidine dose was tapered by 0.1 to 0.2 mg daily to avoid rebound hypertension, headaches and the reemergence of withdrawal symptoms. Success was defined as becoming opiate-free in 10 days and undergoing a naloxone challenge without opioid withdrawal. In this study (Washton & Resnick, 1980), 80% of methadone-maintained patients (taking 5 to 40 mg per day), but only 36% of heroin-dependent patients, were successfully detoxified. Another study (Charney, Sternberg et al., 1981) confirmed the 80% completion rate for methadone withdrawal using clonidine, but found that withdrawal symptoms of anxiety, restlessness, insomnia and muscle aches were the most resistant to clonidine treatment. In an outpatient study comparing a slow methadone taper (at 1 mg decrements starting from a 20 mg daily methadone dose) with a clonidine detox over 10 to 13 days, Kleber and colleagues (1985) demonstrated equal effectiveness and 40% successful detoxification completion. In a six-month follow-up, about a third of each group had maintained abstinence. However, the authors noted that clonidine offered some advantages for outpatient detoxification, in that it poses minimal risk of diversion to illicit use, it is not a controlled substance and therefore is more widely available to general physicians, and it shortens the detoxification period from 20 days (for the methadone taper) to 10 to 13 days.

Some reports indicate clonidine does not induce euphoria (Gold, Redmond & Kleber, 1978), while other reports exist of reinforcing properties associated with this drug in animals (Asin & Wirtshafter, 1985). The reinforcing properties are relatively weak (Davis & Smith, 1977) and are not morphine-like in nature in animals. Although there have been case reports of street abuse of clonidine (Lauzon, 1992), this has not become a widespread problem.

Combined Clonidine and Naltrexone Treatment. While clonidine alone "ameliorates signs and symptoms, it does not alter the time course of opiate withdrawal" (Kleber, Riordan et al., 1985). The authors found that addition of the opioid antagonist naltrexone to clonidine shortened the duration of withdrawal without increasing patient discomfort. However, the small naltrexone doses used in this study were clinically impractical, because they were not commercially available. Vining, Kosten & Kleber (1988) compared two rapid outpatient opioid withdrawals (over four and five days), using clonidine and naltrexone. In this study, the smallest naltrexone dose was 12.5 mg, or one-quarter of a scored 50 mg naltrexone tablet (Trexan®). In the four-day protocol, subjects underwent a naloxone challenge test, followed by clonidine therapy administered three times a day. The first naltrexone dose of 12.5 mg was given in the afternoon of the first day, after preloading with clonidine at 0.2 to 0.3 mg. Naltrexone was increased to 25 mg on the second day, 50 mg on the third day, and 100 mg on day four. Clonidine was given at 0.1 to 0.3 mg three times per day, as needed, for the first three days, and three times at 0.1 mg on the fourth day.

The authors reported that 75% of patients successfully completed detoxification and were discharged on maintenance doses of naltrexone. There was no difference in withdrawal symptoms or severity between the four- and five-day protocols. Subject ratings indicated a "relatively comfortable" withdrawal for the majority. Persistent symptoms included anxiety, restlessness, insomnia, joint pain and muscle aches. Diazepam 10 mg twice a day on days 1 and 2 was found to be very effective for persistent restlessness and muscle aches. In addition, clonidine lowered blood pressure significantly, but caused no clinical problems as a result. In summary, the authors found that combined clonidine and naltrexone therapy had the advantage of "being more rapid and probably more successful in the outpatient setting." The completion rate of 75% (compared to 40% for methadone or clonidine alone) is another significant advantage. Finally, the initiation of naltrexone during withdrawal eased the patients' transition into naltrexone maintenance treatment.

Buprenorphine Detoxification and Use in Agonist to Antagonist Transition. Buprenorphine, a long-acting partial opioid agonist described in more detail in the maintenance pharmacotherapy section of this chapter, was used in several experimental studies (Kosten & Kleber, 1988; Bickel, Stitzer et al., 1988) as a transitional agent between agonists (such as methadone or heroin) and antagonists (such as naloxone or naltrexone). In one study, Kosten and Kleber (1988) substituted buprenorphine at 2, 4 and 8 mg for 20 to 30 mg of methadone of heroin for one month without precipitating substantial withdrawal symptoms, although buprenorphine may act as an opioid antagonist at doses as low as 8 mg. After chronic administration, buprenorphine produces less physical dependence than do pure agonists, as suggested by the minimal withdrawal symptoms that occur when buprenorphine is stopped. After one month of buprenorphine stabilization, the drug was abruptly discontinued and a small dose of naltrexone was given 24 hours later. The investigators observed that the transition to buprenorphine generally was well tolerated. The subsequent abrupt discontinuation of buprenorphine was associated with "minimal withdrawal" in the 2 and 4 mg buprenorphine groups, and a low dose of naltrexone (1 mg) did not precipitate withdrawal. However, subjects in the 8 mg group reported a more substantial increase in withdrawal symptoms when buprenorphine was stopped.

Because of these properties, Kosten examined whether buprenorphine might facilitate the transition from opioid agonists to antagonists in a three-step process: (1) buprenorphine substitution for agonists such as methadone, (2) buprenorphine induced reduction in physical dependency, and (3) discontinuation of buprenorphine with rapid introduction of naltrexone. In a study testing that hypothesis, Kosten and colleagues (1989) used intravenous naloxone to challenge five opioid-addicted patients who were maintained on 3 mg sublingual buprenorphine. Induction onto naltrexone was attempted in all of those patients who completed 30 days on buprenorphine. The buprenorphine discontinuation and induction onto naltrexone included blinded discontinuation of the buprenorphine followed by double-blind placebo-controlled challenges with high dose naloxone. Five male opioid-addicted patients maintained on buprenorphine 3 mg sublingually for one month as outpatients were abruptly discontinued from buprenorphine by blinded, placebo substitution and enlisted in a placebo-controlled, double-blind challenge with intravenous naloxone at 0.5 mg/kg. The naloxone was given over a 20-minute period using a 10 mg/ml solution. Significant withdrawal symptoms were precipitated. However, the severity of withdrawal was about two-thirds the severity for methadone patients (Abstinence Rating Scale = 22; SD = 9.3) and less than a third of the full Abstinence Rating Scale score of 45. Moreover, five hours after this naloxone challenge, withdrawal symptoms were at baseline levels and oral naltrexone was given at either 12.5 mg or 25 mg without precipitating further withdrawal symptoms. The authors felt that the withdrawal syndrome was milder for buprenorphine than for pure opioid agonists, "suggesting a partial resetting of the opioid receptors by the antagonist activity of buprenorphine."

The use of buprenorphine stabilization of opioid addicts before transitioning to naltrexone also has the advantage of psychosocial stabilization prior to detoxification. This approach may therefore represent a compromise treatment between acute detoxification and long-term treatment of chronic dependence (discussed below).

The foregoing techniques (clonidine/naltrexone and buprenorphine/naltrexone) may be combined in a clinical protocol that places methadone patients or heroin addicts on buprenorphine for several weeks in order to stabilize them and get them engaged in the psychosocial aspects of treatment followed by rapid transition to naltrexone using clonidine to relieve any withdrawal symptoms caused by stopping the buprenorphine. Such combination approaches are reviewed in Stine and Kosten (1992). These studies generally have been small pilot studies and larger clinical trials studying buprenorphine to naltrexone transitions with and without clonidine are needed and have potential to lead to shorter, more cost-effective treatment alternatives (to long-term maintenance) for patients who need more treatment than brief detoxification.

Other Drug Combinations for Detoxification. Very rapid inpatient detoxification from opiates using sedatives and anesthetics in combination with opiate antagonists has also been reported. Loimer and associates (1990) reported a protocol involving barbiturate anesthesia with methohexitone (100 mg intravenous pretreatment, followed by 400 mg intravenously) and naltrexone (10 mg intravenously). This protocol successfully detoxified patients from opiates in 48 hours, but required intensive medical treatment (intubation, artificial ventilation) and entailed the risk of anesthesia, and therefore is controversial.

A subsequent study by this group, using a similar strategy, employed midazolam (a short-acting benzodiazepine used to induce anesthesia), but this protocol nevertheless continues to require supervised intravenous medication administration. Moreover, data relating to longer term effectiveness are not available. These methods also do not address psychosocial rehabilitation issues.

MAINTENANCE PHARMACOTHERAPIES

Antagonist Maintenance with Naltrexone. Naltrexone is a long-acting opioid antagonist that provides complete blockade of opioid receptors when taken at least three times per week for a total weekly dose of about 350 mg (Kosten & Kleber, 1984). Because the opioids' reinforcing properties are completely blocked, naltrexone is theoretically an ideal maintenance agent in the rehabilitation of opioid addicts. However, this optimistic theoretical perspective is contradicted by clinical reality, as reflected in treatment retention rates of only 20% to 30% over six months. Multiple factors appear to account for such poor retention rates (Kleber, 1987).

Opioid antagonists, unlike methadone, do not provide any narcotic effect. If antagonists are stopped, there is no immediate reminder in the form of withdrawal. In addition, craving for narcotics may continue during naltrexone treatment. Nevertheless, for some patients (such as health care professionals, business executives or probation referrals), for whom there is an external incentive to comply with naltrexone therapy and to remain drug-free, naltrexone has been very effective. A pharmacological approach to patient non-compliance may be the development of an injectable, long-acting depot preparation of naltrexone, which would eliminate the need for daily intake. Other supportive measures to increase compliance include family therapy and several behavior modification approaches (Kosten & Kleber, 1984).

Clinically, naltrexone is initiated following acute withdrawal from opioids. There should be at least a five- to seven-day opioid-free period for the short-acting narcotics and a seven- to 10-day period for the long-acting agents. This, of course, does not apply to withdrawal medicated with the naltrexone-clonidine combination (see above). The initial dose of naltrexone used generally is 25 mg on the first day, followed by 50 mg daily or an equivalent of 350 mg weekly, divided into three doses (100, 100 and 150 mg). The main reason for the reduced dose on day 1 is the potential for gastrointestinal side effects, such as nausea and vomiting. This occurs in about 10% of patients taking naltrexone. In most cases, GI upset is relatively mild and transient, but in some cases it may be so severe as to cause discontinuation of the naltrexone. The most serious (but far less frequent) naltrexone side effect is the potential for liver toxicity; however, 50 mg daily has been given safely to opioid addicts (Brahen, Capone & Capone, 1988).

In summary, although naltrexone has not lived up to expectations, for selected cases of opioid dependence it may represent the best form of maintenance pharmacotherapy.

Agonist Maintenance with Methadone. The initial pharmacological rationale for long-term methadone maintenance was its ability to relieve the protracted abstinence syndrome and to block heroin euphoria (Dole, 1972; Kosten, 1990). However, an equally important benefit of longer term maintenance has since proved to be the opportunity it affords for psychosocial stabilization in the context of symptom relief. Good treatment retention, improved psychosocial adjustment and reduced criminal activity are among the benefits reported (Cooper, Altman et al., 1983; Dole, 1972). No serious side effects are associated with continued methadone use (Kleber, 1987). Minor side effects, such as constipation, excess sweating, drowsiness, decreased sexual interest and performance, have been noted. In addition, neuro-endocrine studies have shown normalization of stress hormone responses and reproductive functioning (both of which are significantly disrupted in heroin users) after several months of stabilization on methadone (Kreek, 1981). Women stabilized on methadone generally have an uneventful pregnancy. Newborns of methadone-maintained women may experience opioid withdrawal symptoms, but these are readily treatable. Long-term follow-up of 27 children who had been exposed to methadone *in utero* found no cognitive impairment in the preschool years (Kaltenbach & Finnegan, 1988). (For detailed protocols, see the Chapter 5.)

A series of large-scale studies has emerged showing that patients maintained on doses of 60 mg a day or more had better treatment outcomes than those maintained on lower doses and that dosages below 60 mg appear inadequate for most patients (Hartel, Selwyn et al., 1988; Hartel, Schoenbaum et al., 1989; Hartel, 1989/1990; Ball & Ross, 1991; Capelhorn & Bell, 1991). These studies also confirm that medical decisions should not be based on public biases but on scientific knowledge and clinical evaluation. The study by Ball and Ross (1991) in particular revealed that opiate use was directly related to methadone dose levels and that the effectiveness of methadone was even greater for patients on a 70 mg dose and was still more pronounced for patients on 80 mg a day or more. Another factor recently mandating higher doses is the purity of street heroin: opioid cross-tolerance implies that the amount of heroin needed to produce euphoria would be prohibitively expensive for someone maintained on a sufficiently high dose of methadone. However, today's high purity street heroin has required even higher methadone doses to achieve cross-tolerance.

High doses and pure street drugs also may increase the risk of toxicity if patients try to override the cross-tolerance with street heroin since tolerance to respiratory depression may not be as complete as that to euphoria. The functional biological distinction between these pharmacological effects in animal and binding studies resulted in the proposal of two subclasses of mu receptors (Pasternak & Wood, 1986; Pasternak, 1993; Reisine & Pasternak, 1996), although receptor cloning experiments have not yet confirmed the existence of these mu subclasses (Chen, Mestek et al., 1993; Reisine & Bell, 1993).

Many diverse factors may, in theory, significantly modify the pharmacological effectiveness of methadone. Three types of factors which have been demonstrated to significantly modify the metabolic breakdown of methadone in the body, and thus potentially its pharmacological effectiveness are: (1) chronic diseases, including chronic liver disease, chronic renal disease, and possibly other diseases; (2) drug interactions, including interactions of methadone with rifampin and phenytoin in man, possibly with ethanol and disulfiram, and also, by inference from animal studies, interactions of methadone with phenobarbital, diazepam, desipramine, and other drugs, as well as with estrogen steroids, cimetidine, and antiviral agents used in treatment of HIV (Friedland, Schwartz et al., 1992); and (3) altered physiological states, in particular, pregnancy. The liver in particular may play a central role in several aspects of methadone disposition, including not only methadone metabolism and clearance but also storage and subsequent release of unchanged methadone.

In a study by Kreek and colleagues (1978), unchanged methadone persisted in the liver for up to six weeks and methadone disposition was significantly altered only in a patient subgroup with moderately severe but compensated cirrhosis. These factors have been reviewed in detail by Kreek (1986) and also in Stine (1997).

Multiple medical problems result from direct and/or indirect effects of opioid use. Chronic liver disease is the most common problem. For example, 50% to 60% of all heroin addicts entering methadone maintenance have biochemical evidence of chronic liver disease either secondary to infection (hepatitis B and C) or alcohol-induced liver disease. Chronic liver disease in all its forms has major implications for medication use. For instance, opioid medications for treatment of dependence such as methadone, LAAM, and buprenorphine, medications commonly prescribed to treat other diseases that are prevalent in drug users, such as tuberculosis (e.g., Isoniazid®, Rifampin®), as well as drugs used to treat or prevent opportunistic infections (such as trimethopram-sulfamethoxazole) and some antiretroviral agents (such as Didanosine®) may have hepatotoxic influence (O'Connor, Selwyn & Schottenfeld, 1994; Kreek, Garfield et al., 1976; Sawyer, Brown et al., 1993; Schwartz, Brechbuhl et al., 1990). Other diseases commonly coexisting with chronic opioid dependence that can affect maintenance pharmacotherapy are bacterial infections and tuberculosis, particularly "extrapulmonary" manifestations of tuberculosis in HIV-infected individuals (Braun, Byers et al., 1990; Barnes, Bloch et al., 1991) and drug-resistant tuberculosis (Small, Shafer et al., 1993; MMWR, 1991).

With the increasing number of HIV-infected patients in methadone maintenance programs, potential interactions between methadone and antiviral agents used in the treatment of HIV are particularly important to define. A study of possible interactions between methadone and zidovudine (Azidothymidine®, or AZT) has shown that serum levels of methadone are not affected by this drug, but that some patients who receive methadone maintenance treatment may show a potentially toxic increase in serum levels of AZT (Friedland, Schwartz et al., 1992). However, these authors caution against making changes in the dosage of AZT; instead, they suggest careful clinical monitoring for signs of dose-related AZT toxicity in such patients.

The assessment of new antiretroviral drug efficacy, as well as the determination of patients' prognosis and rate of disease progression, were revolutionized in 1996 with the introduction of commercial assays which quantitate the amount of HIV RNA in plasma. The introduction of new antiretroviral agents has raised justifiable hope of a new therapeutic era for HIV-infected patients but has also introduced new complexities due to potential drug toxicities and drug interactions. This is also an issue of current research.

Recently, the AIDS epidemic has led to methadone maintenance being accorded added importance because intravenous heroin use is a major vector for HIV transmission. Given that there are over a million chronic intravenous heroin users in the U.S., the magnitude of this problem becomes clear. Prevalence studies in New York City from 1984 to 1985 found that less than 10% of methadone-maintained patients who entered treatment before 1978 were HIV-positive, compared to more than half of street heroin addicts (Des Jarlais, Friedman et al., 1992). Similarly, a prospective study in Philadelphia found an HIV seroconversion rate four times higher in active intravenous heroin users than in methadone maintenance patients (Metzger, Woody et al., 1993). Other studies also documented a dramatically reduced HIV seroprevalence rate for successfully methadone-maintained patients, compared to active intravenous drug users (Barthwell, Senay et al., 1989; Novick, Joseph et al., 1990; Tidone, Sileo et al., 1987). Methadone maintenance thus appears to be extremely effective in reducing injection-related risk factors for HIV.

The importance of psychosocial treatment as an adjunct to methadone pharmacotherapy also was emphasized by the Ball and Ross study (1991), and recent refinements of this component as well as treatment matching studies of the appropriate treatment intensity for patients with varying disability are an active focus of clinical research (Avants, Ohlins & Margolin, 1996). In general, for successful rehabilitation, length of treatment with methadone is best seen in terms of years rather than months. For many patients, five to 10 years—or even a lifetime—of methadone maintenance may be needed. However, most programs attempt to withdraw their patients after about a year of treatment (Kleber, 1987). At that time, the pharmacological component of protracted withdrawal may still present a problem, but the slow decrease in methadone dose plus ongoing therapeutic support and the context of greater psychosocial stability render this problem more manageable.

From an organizational and public health perspective, early treatment termination, illicit use of non-narcotic substances (such as cocaine or alcohol), and diversion of the take-home dose of methadone to the illicit market remain significant issues for most methadone maintenance programs. While concurrent substance use remains a problem (initially, 20% to 50% of methadone patients use cocaine, and 25% to 40% abuse alcohol), several effective treatment interventions have been developed, including behavioral approaches and pharmacological interventions. Diversion of take-home-bottles is of concern to every methadone maintenance program, although its impact on illicit opioid use remains small (methadone accounts for about 4% of opioids used on the street). Diversion could be eliminated by using levo-alpha-cetylmethadol (LAAM), a methadone alternative, which has a duration of action of up to three days and thus obviates the need for take-home dosing (Ling, Charuvastra et al., 1976; Kleber, 1987) and also by the use of buprenorphine-naloxone combination medication currently in development (see below).

In summary, methadone maintenance, which traditionally has been one of the safest and most effective treatments for chronic opioid addiction, has received added importance in the current AIDS epidemic and has also received recent clinical research activity to refine psychosocial, medical and pharmacological aspects of the treatment.

LAAM: A New Agonist Maintenance Agent. The 1993 approval by the Food and Drug Administration (FDA) of levo-alpha-acetylmethadol (LAAM) for the treatment of opiate addiction represents the first and only alternative to methadone for opiate substitution in over thirty years of drug treatment. LAAM is a derivative of methadone with a duration of action up to three days, which makes a three times per week dosing schedule possible. The principal disadvantage of such a long duration of action is the time necessary to reach a steady state and to stabilize patients at an appropriate comfort level. However, with increased recognition of the shortcomings of methadone maintenance (e.g., incomplete suppression of withdrawal due to rapid metabolism in some patients, need for daily dosing, and diversion of take-home doses), this new alternative offers a distinct improvement for some patients.

After oral administration, LAAM is well absorbed in the gastrointestinal tract. It is metabolized by sequential n-demethylation to nor-LAAM and dinor-LAAM, with a half-life of approximately two hours for the removal of one N-methyl group. Both nor-LAAM and dinor-LAAM are potent opiate agonists, more potent in fact than the parent drug (RTI, 1984; Nickander, Booher & Miles, 1974; Smits, 1974; Smits & Booher, 1973; Foldes, Shivaku et al., 1979), with the former being three to six times more active than methadone and the latter about equivalent to methadone. The combined pharmacological effects of LAAM and its active metabolites are greater after oral administration than after parenteral administration.

In a large clinical trial (N=430), Ling, Charuvastra et al. (1976) compared a fixed dose of LAAM (80 mg three times weekly) to two different doses of methadone (50 or 100 mg daily) over a 40-week period. LAAM was found to be as safe as methadone, as no serious adverse reactions were observed. The investigators found a somewhat larger drop-out rate for the LAAM group than for the two methadone groups, with most terminations occurring in the early weeks of the study, during dose stabilization. This suggests that individualizing the dose may be more difficult with LAAM than with methadone, because of LAAM's longer half-life. However, after the initial stabilization LAAM appeared to reduce illicit opioid use between weeks 8 and 40 of the study, which compares very favorably with the 100 mg methadone group and is significantly better than the 50 mg methadone group.

The delayed onset of action of LAAM poses a danger that some individuals will use additional doses in an attempt to get high, possibly triggering an overdose. The absence of take-home doses should minimize this risk. LAAM should be used cautiously in patients with known hepatic or respiratory disease, or cardiac conduction defects. Interactions with alcohol, sedatives, tranquilizers, antidepressants, or benzodiazipines carry serious risk of overdose for persons maintained on LAAM, thus it should be administered cautiously in persons who abuse any of these drugs.

Although the essential requirements for LAAM maintenance are the same as for methadone maintenance, there are special categories of patients who may find LAAM particularly attractive, such as persons reliant upon public transportation, persons for whom employment or education schedules conflict with daily clinic attendance, parents of small children—primarily single mothers—and patients who rapidly metabolize on daily doses of methadone and report that it does not "hold" them for the entire 24 hours or that it causes unwanted acute sedation.

In summary, LAAM offers the advantage of less frequent dosing and thus eliminates the need for take-home bottles. On the other hand, it is more difficult to adjust the dose during the initial phase of treatment. This limitation can be overcome by initiating treatment with methadone and then switching the patient to LAAM (Kosten, 1990).

Buprenorphine: A New Type of Maintenance Pharmacotherapy. Buprenorphine, the long-acting partial opioid agonist mentioned earlier in this chapter as an agent useful for detoxification, has been tested as an alternative to methadone maintenance treatment. Approval by the FDA is anticipated shortly. Buprenorphine is classified as a morphine-like (mu) partial agonist and kappa antagonist (Martin, Eades et al., 1976), producing ceiling effects on several measures and under some conditions blocking the effects of pure agonists. The larger the dose of buprenorphine administered, the longer is the duration of the antagonist effect. Ceiling effects are seen on respiration since buprenorphine produced an inverted U-shaped dose-effect curve (Doxey, Everitt et al., 1977). Its potential advantages include a higher degree of safety than methadone, coupled with an ameliorated withdrawal syndrome. Jasinski and colleagues (1978) showed that buprenorphine maintenance (8 mg/day, sc) attenuated the subjective and physiological effects of high doses of morphine (60 to 120 mg, sc) for up to 30 hours. A delayed withdrawal syndrome of mild severity occurred, suggesting that buprenorphine does not produce significant physical dependence in humans. Although buprenorphine's potential for abuse and dependence is much less than that of full opioid agonists, several instances of buprenorphine abuse have been reported across the globe (e.g., Strang, 1985; Pickworth, Johnson et al., 1993).

Buprenorphine maintenance studies using daily doses as diverse as 1.5 to 16 mg daily (Resnick, Resnick & Galanter, 1991; Resnick, Galanter et al., 1992; Kosten & Kleber, 1991) have consistently demonstrated treatment retention rates comparable to those for methadone maintenance therapy. The optimal dosage regimen has yet to be determined. In a study of buprenorphine given sublingually at doses of 2 and 6 mg daily compared to methadone doses of 35 to 65 mg, Kosten, Schottenfeld et al. (1993) reported significantly higher levels of illicit opioid use in the two buprenorphine groups, both by self-report and urine toxicology screens. In addition, continued opioid withdrawal symptoms were associated with the 2 mg buprenorphine group; these may have caused greater illicit use. Treatment retention, another outcome measure, also favored methadone over buprenorphine (retention averaged 20 weeks in the methadone groups versus 16 weeks in the buprenorphine-treated groups). The authors concluded that methadone was "clearly superior" to the two buprenorphine doses used. However, a slightly higher dose of buprenorphine (8 mg daily) was equivalent to methadone 60 mg daily in abstinence rates from heroin.

Another outpatient study, by Johnson and colleagues (1992) also demonstrated equivalent treatment retention and reduction in illicit opioid use with buprenorphine at 8 mg daily and methadone at 65 mg daily. Dose ranging studies (Bickel, Stitzer et al., 1988; Schottenfeld, Pakes et al., 1993) have suggested that further increases in buprenorphine dose to doses as high as 16 mg daily may further improve abstinence from opiates. Schottenfeld and colleagues (1993) compared 4, 8, 12 and 16 mg of buprenorphine daily in an open study with ascending and then tapering dosing schedule, with each dose given for 21 days. They found a clear buprenorphine dose-effect on illicit opioid use. At 16 mg daily of buprenorphine, 64.7% of subjects were abstinent for three weeks, compared to only 27.3% at 4 mg. However, there was no placebo or methadone comparison in this study and only half of the subjects completed.

A unique characteristic of buprenorphine may be its ability to decrease use of cocaine as well as illicit opiates. Studies in non-human primates (Carroll, Carmona et al., 1992; Mello, Mendelson et al., 1989, 1992; Winger, Skjodageer & Woods, 1992) that have been taught to self-administer cocaine have shown robust dose-dependent decreases (up to 60 to 97%) in cocaine self-administration when these monkeys are treated with buprenorphine.

Reports of a buprenorphine effect on cocaine use among human opiate addicts have been more equivocal. In a double-blind, placebo controlled study by Johnson, Fudala and Jaffe (1992) that compared buprenorphine 8 mg daily with methadone 20 mg or 60 mg daily, cocaine use was comparable in all subgroups at baseline, and there was no significant difference in cocaine use in any of the treatment groups. Schottenfeld, Pakes et al. (1993), on the other hand, in the above cited buprenorphine dose-ranging study (from 4 mg to 16 mg daily), found that subjects who were dependent on both opiates and cocaine significantly decreased their cocaine use with increasing doses of buprenorphine. A large multi-site study supported by a collaboration of the Veterans Administration Cooperative Studies Program (VA/CSP) and NIDA Medications Development Division (NIDA/MDD), which was designed as a labeling study for buprenorphine, recently has been completed. This study is expected to contribute to the clarification of dosing issues.

The diversion potential of buprenorphine has been theorized to be less than that of methadone because of the combined agonist-antagonist effects. A study is in progress also supported by VA/CSP and NIDA/MDD of a buprenorphine/naloxone combination sublingual tablet that promises to further reduce the risk of diversion to intravenous abuse.

In summary, buprenorphine shows much promise as an alternative to methadone and naltrexone maintenance. It is well accepted by patients, has a mild withdrawal syndrome facilitating its discontinuation, it reduces opioid and possibly cocaine abuse, and it has greater safety and lower diversion potential than agonists such as methadone.

REFERENCES

Asin K & Wirtshafter D (1985). Clonidine produces a conditioned place preference in rats. *Psychopharmacology* 85:383–385.

Avants SK, Ohlin R & Margolin A (1996) Matching methadone-maintained patients to psychosocial treatments. In SM Stine & TR Kosten (eds.) *New Treatments for Opiate Dependence*. New York, NY: Guilford Press, 3:149–170.

Ball JC & Ross A (1991). *The Effectiveness of Methadone Maintenance Treatment*. New York, NY: Springer-Verlag.

Barnes PF, Bloch AB, Davidson PT & Snider DE Jr (1991). Tuberculosis in patients with human immunodeficiency virus infection. *The New England Journal of Medicine* 1644–1650.

Barthwell A, Senay E, Marks R & White R (1989). Patients successfully maintained with methadone escaped human immunodeficiency virus infection. *Archives of General Psychiatry* 46:957–958.

Bickel WK, Stitzer ML, Bigelow GE, Liebson IA, Jasinski DR & Johnson RE (1988). A clinical trial of buprenorphine: Comparison with methadone in the detoxification of heroin addicts. *Clinical Pharmacology and Therapeutics* 43:72–78.

Brahen LS, Capone TJ & Capone DM (1988). Naltrexone: Lack of effect on hepatic enzymes. *Journal of Clinical Pharmacology* 28:64–70.

Braun MM, Byers RH, Heyward WL et al. (1990). Acquired immunodeficiency syndrome and extrapulmonary tuberculosis in the United States. *Archives of Internal Medicine* 150:1913–1916.

Capelhorn JRM & Bell J (1991). Methadone dosage and retention of patients in maintenance treatment. *Medical Journal of Australia* 154:195–199.

Carroll ME, Carmona GN, May SA, Buzalsky S & Larson C (1992). Buprenorphine effects on self-administration of smoked cocaine base and orally delivered phencyclidine, ethanol and saccharin in rhesus monkeys. *Journal of Pharmacology and Experimental Therapeutics* 261:26–37.

Charney DS, Sternberg DE, Kleber HD, Heninger GR & Redmond DE (1981). The clinical use of clonidine in abrupt withdrawal from methadone. *Archives of General Psychiatry* 38:1273–1277.

Chen Y, Mestek A, Liu J, Hurley JA & Yu L (1993). Molecular cloning and functional expression of a mu-opioid receptor from rat brain. *Molecular Pharmacology* 44:8–12.

Cooper JR, Altman F, Brown B & Czechowicz D (1983). *Research on the Treatment of Narcotic Addiction: State of the Art*. Rockville, MD: National Institute on Drug Abuse.

Davis WM & Smith SG (1977). Catecholaminergic mechanisms of reinforcement. Mechanisms of reinforcement: Direct assessment by drug self-administration. *Life Sciences* 20:483–492.

Des Jarlais DC, Friedman SR, Woods J & Milliken J (1992). HIV infection among intravenous drug users: Epidemiology and emerging public health perspectives. In JH Lowinson, P Ruiz & RB Millman (eds.) *Substance Abuse: A Comprehensive Textbook*. Baltimore, MD: Williams & Wilkins, 734–743.

Dole VP (1972). Narcotic addiction, physical dependence and relapse. *The New England Journal of Medicine* 286:988–992.

Dole VP & Nyswander ME (1965). A medical treatment for diacetylmorphine (heroin) addiction. *Journal of the American Medical Association* 193:646–650.

Doxey JC, Everitt JE, Frank LW & MacKenzie JE (1977). A comparison of the effects of buprenorphine and morphine on the blood gases of conscious rats. *British Journal of Pharmocology* 60:118P.

Foldes BS, Shivaku Y, Matsuo S & Morita K (1979). The influence of methadone derivatives on the isolated myenteric plexus-longitudinal muscle preparation of the guinea pig ileum. *Advances in Pharmacological Research and Practice: Proceedings of the Congress of the Hungarian Pharmacological Society* 5:165–170. 201.

Friedland A, Schwartz E, Brechbuhl AB, Kahl P, Miller M & Selwyn P (1992). Pharmacokentic interactions of zidovudine and methadone in intravenous drug using patients with HIV infection. *Journal of the Acquired Immune Deficiency Syndrome* 5:619–626.

Gold MS, Redmond DE & Kleber HD (1978). Clonidine in opiate withdrawal. *Lancet* 11:929–930.

Gold ME, Redmond DC & Kleber HD (1978). Clonidine blocks acute opiate-withdrawal symptoms. *Lancet* 2:599–602.

Hartel D, Selwyn PA, Schoenbaum EE et al. (1988). Methadone maintenance treatment and reduced risk of AIDS and AIDS-specific mortality in intravenous drug users [Abstract 8526]. *4th International Conference on AIDS*, Stockholm, Sweden, June.

Hartel D, Schoenbaum EE, Selwyn PA et al. (1989). Temporal patterns of cocaine use and AIDS in intravenous drug users in methadone maintenance [Abstract]. *5th International Conference on AIDS*, Stockholm, Sweden, June.

Hartel D (1989–1990). Cocaine use, inadequate methadone dose increase risk of AIDS for IV drug users in treatment. *NIDA Notes* 5(1).

Himmelsbach CK (1942). Clinical studies of drug addiction: Physical dependence, withdrawal and recovery. *Archives of Internal Medicine* 69:766–772.

Jackson AH & Shader RI (1973). Guidelines for the withdrawal of narcotic and general depressant drugs. *Diseases of the Nervous System* 34:162–166.

Jasinski DR, Pevnick JS & Griffith JD (1978). Human pharmacology and abuse potential of the analgesic buprenorphine. *Archives of General Psychiatry* 35:501–516.

Johnson RE, Fudala PJ & Jaffe JH (1992). A controlled trial of buprenorphine for opioid dependence. *Journal of the American Medical Association* 267:2750–2755.

Kaltenbach K & Finnegan L (1988). Children exposed to methadone in-utero: Cognitive ability in preschool years. *NIDA Research Monograph 81*. Rockville, MD: National Institute on Drug Abuse.

Kleber HD (1987). Treatment of narcotic addicts. *Psychiatric Medicine* 3:389–418.

Kleber HD, Riordan CE, Rounsaville B, Kosten T, Charney D, Gaspari J, Hogan I & O'Connor C (1985). Clonidine in outpatient detoxification from methadone maintenance. *Archives of General Psychiatry* 42:391–394.

Kosten TR & Kleber HD (1988). Buprenorphine detoxification from opioid dependence: A pilot study. *Life Sciences* 42:635–611.

Kosten TR (1990). Current pharmacotherapies for opioid dependence. *Psychopharmacology Bulletin* 26:69–74.

Kosten TR & Kleber HD (1984). Strategies to improve compliance with narcotic antagonists. *American Journal of Drug and Alcohol Abuse* 10:249–266.

Kosten TR & Kleber HD (1991). Buprenorphine detoxification from opioid dependence: A pilot study. *Life Sciences* 42:635–641.

Kosten TR, Krystal JH, Charney DS, Price LH, Morgan CH & Kleber HD (1989). Rapid detoxification from opioid dependence. *American Journal of Psychiatry* 146:1349.

Kosten TR, Schottenfeld R, Ziedonis D & Falcioni J (1993). Buprenorphine versus methadone maintenance for opioid dependence. *Journal of Nervous and Mental Disease*.

Kreek MJ, Garfield JW, Gutjahr CL & Giusti LM (1976). Rifampin-induced methadone withdrawal. *The New England Journal of Medicine* 294:1104–1106.

Kreek MJ, Oratz, M & Rothschild MA (1978). Hepatic extraction of long- and short-acting narcotics in the isolated perfused rabbit liver. *Gastroenterology* 75:88–94.

Kreek MJ (1981). Medical management of methadone-maintained patients. In JH Lowinson & P Ruiz (eds.) *Substance Abuse: Clinical Problems and Perspectives*. Baltimore, MD: Williams & Wilkins, 660–673.

Kreek MJ (1986). Factors modifying the pharmacological effectiveness of methadone. *NIDA Monograph*.

Lauzon P (1992). Two cases of clonidine abuse/dependence in methadone-maintained patients. *Journal of Substance Abuse Treatment* 9(2):125–7

Ling W, Charuvastra VC, Kaim SC & Klett CJ (1976). Methadyl Acetate and methadone as maintenance treatments for heroin addicts. *Archives of General Psychiatry* 33:709–720.

Loimer N, Schmid R, Lenz K, Presslich O & Grunberger J (1990). Acute blocking of naloxone-precipitated opiate withdrawal symptoms by methohexitone. *British Journal of Psychiatry* 157:748–52.

Margolin A & Kosten TR (1991). Opioid detoxification and maintenance with blocking agents. In NS Miller (ed.) *Comprehensive Handbook of Drug and Alcohol Addiction*. New York, NY: Marcel Dekker, 1127–1141.

Martin WR & Jasinski DR (1969). Physiological parameters of morphine dependence in man—Tolerance, early abstinence, protracted abstinence. *Journal of Psychiatric Research* 7:9–17.

Martin WR, Eades CG, Thompson JA, Huppler RE & Gilbert PE (1976). The effects of morphine- and nalorphine-like drugs in the nondependent and morphine-dependent chronic spinal dog. *Journal of Pharmocology and Experimental Therapy* 197:517–532.

Mello NK, Mendelson JH, Bree MP & Lukas SE (1989). Buprenorphine suppresses cocaine self-administration by Rhesus monkeys. *Science* 245:859–862.

Metzger DS, Woody GE, McLellan AT, O'Brien CP, Druley P, Navaline H, DePhilippis D, Stolley P & Abrutyn E (1993). Human immunodeficiency virus seroconversion among intravenous drug users in- and out-of-treatment: An 18 month prospective follow-up. *Journal of Acquired Immune Deficiency Syndrome* 6:1049–1056.

MMWR (1991b). Nosocomial transmissions of multidrug-resistant tuberculosis among HIV-infected persons—Florida and New York, 1988–1991. *Morbidity and Mortality Weekly Reports* 40:585–602.

Nickander R, Booher R & Miles H (1974) L-a-acetylmethadol and its N-demethylated metabolites have potent opiate actions in guinea pig isolated ileum. *Life Sciences* 41:2011–2017.

Novick DM, Joseph H, Croxson TS, Salsitz EA, Wang G, Richman BL, Poretsky L, Keefe JB & Whimbey E (1990). Absence of antibody to human immunodeficiency virus in long-term, socially rehabilitated methadone maintenance patients. *Archives of Internal Medicine* 150:97–99.

O'Connor PG, Selwyn PA & Schottenfeld RS (1994). Medical care for injection drug users with human immunodeficiency virus infection. 331(7):450–459.

Pasternak GW & Wood PJ (1986). *Life Sciences* 38:1889–1898.

Pasternak GW (1993). *Neuropharmacology* 16:1–18.

Pickworth WB, Johnson RE, Holicky BA & Cone EJ (1993). Subjective and physiologic effects of intravenous buprenorphine in humans. *Clinical Pharmocology and Therapeutics* 53:570–576.

Research Triangle Institute (1984). Bioavailability and pharmacokinetics/pharmacodynamics of l-a-acetylmethadol and its metabolites: metabolism and pharmacokinetics of drugs. *Final Report for Contract #771-80-3705, Task #2,* September.

Reisine T & Bell GI (1993). Molecular biology of opioid receptors. Trends. *Neuroscience* 16:506–510.

Reisine T & Pasternak G (1996). Opioid analgesics and antagonists. In JG Hardman & LE Limbird (eds.) *Goodman and Gilman's Pharmacological Basis of Therapeutics, 9th Edition*. New York, NY: McGraw-Hill, 521–557.

Resnick RB, Resnick E & Galanter M (1991). Buprenorphine responders: A diagnostic subgroup of heroin addicts? *Progress in Neuro-Psychopharmacology and Biological Psychiatry* 15:531–538.

Resnick RB, Galanter M, Pycha C, Cohen A, Grandison P & Flood N (1992). Buprenorphine: An alternative to methadone for heroin dependence treatment. *Psychopharmacology Bulletin* 28(1):109–113.

Sawyer RC, Brown LS, Narong PG & Li R (1993). Evaluation of a possible pharmacological interaction between rifampin and methadone in HIV seropositive injecting drug users. In *Abstracts of the Ninth International Conference on AIDS/Fourth STD World Congress, Berlin, Germany, June 6–11*. London, England: Wellcome Foundation, 501 Abstract.

Schottenfeld RS, Pakes J, Ziedonis D & Kosten TR (1993). Buprenorphine: Dose-related effects on cocaine-abusing opioid dependent humans. *Biological Psychiatry*.

Schwartz EL, Brechbuhl AB, Kahl P Miller MH, Selwyn PA & Friedland GH (1990). Altered pharmacokinetics of zidovudine in former IV drug-using patients receiving methadone. In *Abstracts of the Sixth International Conference on AIDS, San Francisco, June 20–24, Vol* 3. San Francisco, CA: University of California, 194. Abstract.

Senay EC, Dorus W, Goldberg F & Thornton W (1977). Withdrawal from methadone maintenance. *Archives of General Psychiatry* 34:361–367.

Small PM, Shafer RW, Hopewell PC, Singh SP, Murphy MJ, Desmond E, et al. (1993). Exogenous reinfection with multidrug- resistant Mycobacterium tuberculosis in patients with advanced HIV infection. *The New England Journal of Medicine* 328:1137–1144.

Smits SE (1974) The analgesic activity of l-a-acetylmethadol and two of its metabolites in mice. *Research in Commun. Chemistry, Pathology and Pharmacology* 8:575–578.

Smits SE & Booher R (1973). Analgesic activity of some of the metabolites of methadone and a-acetylmethadol in mice and rats. *Federation Proceedings* 32:764.

Stine SM & Kosten TR (1992). Use of drug combinations in treatment of opioid withdrawal. *Journal of Clinical Psychopharmacology* 12(3):203–209.

Stine SM (1997). New Developments In Methadone Treatment And Matching Treatments To Patient. In SM Stine & TR Kosten (eds.) *New Treatments for Opiate Dependence*. New York, NY: Guilford Press, 3:121–172.

Strang J (1985). Abuse of buprenorphine. *Lancet* 725.

Tidone L, Sileo F, Goglio A & Borra GC (1987). AIDS in Italy. *American Journal of Drug and Alcohol Abuse* 13(4):485–486.

Vining E, Kosten TR & Kleber HD (1988). Clinical utility of rapid clonidine-naltrexone detoxification for opioid abusers. *British Journal of Addiction* 83:567–575.

Washton AM & Resnick RB (1980). Clonidine for opiate detoxification: outpatient clinical trials. *American Journal of Psychiatry* 137:1121–1122.

Winger G, Skjoldager P & Woods JH (1992). Effects of buprenorphine and other opioid agonists and antagonists on alfentanil and cocaine reinforced responding in rhesus monkeys. *Journal of Pharmacology and Experimental Therapeutics* 261:311–317.

CHAPTER 5

Opioid Maintenance Therapies

J. Thomas Payte, M.D.
Joan E. Zweben, Ph.D.

Unique Aspects of Opioid Addiction
Clinical Issues in Maintenance Pharmacotherapy
Maintenance Treatment Using Methadone
Maintenance Treatment Using LAAM
Maintenance Treatment Using Buprenorphine
Psychosocial Interventions
Growth, Controversy and Future Challenges

Of an estimated 600,000 opiate addicts in the United States, approximately 115,000 are involved in opioid agonist treatment (OAT) using methadone and LAAM maintenance, making it the largest single treatment intervention attempting to address the needs of this population (NIH-CDC, 1997). Thirty-five years of extensive research and clinical experience have somewhat quieted the passions about this approach, and public health concerns combined with an extensive educational effort have made this treatment somewhat more available to those who need it. It also is apparent that for each patient in an existing treatment slot, there are approximately five sufferers of opioid addiction for whom OAT is not available (Payte, 1997b). Nonetheless, physicians may be startled by the discrepancy between the benefits documented by scientific research and the public's perceptions of opioid agonist treatment, and for this reason it is necessary to begin with a description of the context in which this treatment takes place.

The use of opioids as a maintenance pharmacotherapy began with the use of methadone by Vincent Dole and Marie Nyswander in the 1960s (Dole & Nyswander, 1965). Negative attitudes have been common since that time among physicians, other treatment staff, patients and the general public. These attitudes often stem from the perception that methadone treatment is "just substituting one addicting drug for another." Rather than a simple substitution or replacement for illicit opioids, OAT involves a stabilization or correction of a possible lesion or defect in the endogenous opioid system (Dole, 1988; Goldstein, 1991). The neurobiological mechanism remains poorly understood even among physicians, and will be elaborated later in this chapter.

This simple intervention, by reducing craving and preventing withdrawal, virtually eliminates the hazards of needles, frees the patient from preoccupation with obtaining illicit opioids, and enhances overall function, thus enabling the patient to utilize available psychosocial interventions. Nevertheless, a set of regulatory requirements unmatched by anything in medicine contributes further to the stigmatization of the modality and creates many barriers to providing treatment for those who need it. Despite recent review of regulatory barriers and capacity, misunderstanding and negative attitudes continue to influence daily practice (Rettig & Yarmolinsky, 1995).

Negative attitudes affect medical practice in a variety of ways (Zweben & Payte, 1990). Physicians in other medical settings sometimes refuse to treat a patient who discloses that he or she is on maintenance pharmacotherapy. Patients are occasionally told that they must withdraw from maintenance pharmacotherapy in order to receive treatment for other medical conditions. A physician may withhold needed symptomatic medication, thus causing unnecessary discomfort and pain. Patients are keenly sensitive to disgust, distrust, and a begrudging manner and often will conclude that needed medical treatment is not worth tolerating an adversarial relationship with the health care provider. Although long-standing educational efforts have modified negative attitudes in many quarters, they are still common enough to constitute a hazard to quality care of these patients.

Contrary to common beliefs, many heroin addicts enter opioid agonist treatment with great ambivalence and want to discontinue maintenance treatment as soon as possible. Indeed, the original hope of many practitioners, policymakers, and regulators was that methadone could be used to transition patients to a drug-free lifestyle and then be withdrawn. This has not proved to be the case. Repeated studies suggest that only 10% to 20% of patients who discontinue methadone are able to remain abstinent (McLellan, 1983), a range consistent with clinical impressions and the findings of subsequent studies (Ball & Ross, 1991). The known risks associated with discontinuing OAT with predictable relapse to IV heroin become increasingly critical when viewed in the context of the HIV epidemic. This, when seen along with the proved safety and efficacy of long-term methadone treatment, suggests that long-term—even indefinite—OAT is appropriate and even essential in a significant proportion of OAT patients.

> "Treatment should be continued as long as the patient continues to benefit from treatment, wishes to remain in treatment, remains at risk of relapse to heroin or other substance use, suffers no significant adverse effects from continued methadone maintenance treatment, and as long as continued treatment is indicated in the professional judgment of the physician" (Payte & Khuri, 1993a).

Patients do seek to discontinue maintenance for non-medical but very real and practical reasons (e.g., transportation or scheduling difficulties) and to escape continued disruption of their lives associated with the burdensome restrictions, regulations, and structure of the treatment delivery system. For patients who attempt withdrawal, it is important for practitioners to provide encouragement along with the best medical and supportive treatment available, without fostering unrealistic expectations or unnecessary guilt, and to provide a means for rapid readmission in the event of relapse or impending relapse to the use of illicit opiates (ASAM, 1991).

UNIQUE ASPECTS OF OPIOID ADDICTION

Although this chapter will focus on medical aspects of opioid agonist therapy, it is commonly agreed that addictive disorders are complex phenomena involving the interaction of biologic, psychosocial, and cultural variables, all of which need to be addressed for treatment to be most effective. As a medical modality based on proper use of opioid agonist medication, it should be clear that the medication itself is central to and the foundation of the treatment modality. However, favorable treatment outcomes require that the medical intervention be integrated into a host of other therapies and supportive and rehabilitative activities. Much of the destructive behavior of professionals results from inappropriate expectations, especially the belief that heroin addicts could stay off opiates if they were sufficiently motivated.

Vincent Dole has always held the view that there is something unique about opioid addiction that made it difficult for patients to remain free of illicit heroin for extended periods of time. In their early work, Dole and Nyswander postulated the existence of a "metabolic disease" (Dole & Nyswander, 1967), a view supported and refined by subsequent biomedical research. Dole won the Albert Lasker Clinical Medicine Research Award in 1988 for his work in this area. He summarized his views in a paper in the *Journal of the American Medical Association* (Dole, 1988), in which he said:

> "It is postulated that the high rate of relapse of addicts after detoxification from heroin use is due to persistent derangement of the endogenous ligand-narcotic receptor system and that methadone in an adequate daily dose compensates for this defect. Some patients with long histories of heroin use and subsequent rehabilitation on a maintenance program do well when the treatment is terminated. The majority, unfortunately, experience a return of symptoms after maintenance is stopped. The treatment, therefore, is corrective but not curative for severely addicted persons. A major challenge for future research is to identify the specific defect in receptor function and to repair it. Meanwhile, methadone maintenance provides a safe and effective way to normalize the function of otherwise intractable narcotic addicts."

In Dole's view, the persistent receptor disorder results from chronic opiate use, leading to down-regulation of the modulating system and possibly also to a suppression of endogenous ligands. Avram Goldstein supported the concept of a metabolic disease as well as a genetic predisposition to that disease (Goldstein, 1991). Goldstein stressed that genetic influence carries an exceptional vulnerability to the disease in the presence of environmental influences. Kreek suggests that multiple genes may account for different degrees of vulnerability to developing addiction (Kreek, 1992). Recent work supports the view that heroin addiction has genetic underpinnings in a proportion of users (Pickens, 1997). Further research is needed to define the metabolic disease process and the respective roles of genetic predisposition and environmental exposure to a substance. A key question for future research is whether it is possible to restore normal functioning without maintenance therapy, and if so, how to accomplish this.

CLINICAL ISSUES IN MAINTENANCE PHARMACOTHERAPY

Maintenance pharmacotherapy is based on the use of a medication to maintain chronic opioid users in a normal state for 24 hours or more, avoiding any impairment in the form of sedating, obtunding, or euphoric effects and preventing the onset of the withdrawal syndrome associated with active opioid addiction. For opioid agonist (maintenance) treatment *per se*, the sole criterion of success is a reduction/cessation of illicit opioid use—which allows for the broader goals of restoration of function and improved quality of life (Goldstein, 1991). Cessation of opioid agonist treatment should never be a criterion of success as practitioners are encouraged to focus on improved social integration and quality of life issues for the sufferers of chronic opioid addiction, rather than the relentless pursuit of eliminating all medication as the primary goal of treatment.

Kreek (1992) outlines the goals of treatment and the properties of desirable opioid agonist medications as follows:

Goals for Pharmacotherapy:

1. Prevention or reduction of withdrawal symptoms.
2. Prevention or reduction of drug craving.
3. Prevention of relapse to use of addictive drug.
4. Restoration to or toward normalcy of any physiological function disrupted by chronic drug abuse.

Profile for Potential Psychotherapeutic Agents:

1. Effective after oral administration.
2. Long biological half-life (> 24 hours).
3. Minimal side effects during chronic administration.
4. Safe, i.e., no true toxic or serious adverse effects.
5. Efficacious for a substantial percentage of persons with the disorder.

Initial Dose and Induction. In most cases, patients being evaluated for admission to maintenance pharmacotherapy are experiencing some degree of objective withdrawal syndrome. The initial dose can be expected to provide relief of discomfort associated with withdrawal. The initial dose of methadone is no more than 30 mg in most cases. The induction phase allows for subsequent careful adjusting of dose to realize the elimination of drug craving and the prevention of withdrawal while avoiding risk of intoxication or overdose associated with accumulation of methadone (Kaufman, Payte & McLellan, 1995; Payte & Khuri, 1993a). During the induction phase it is helpful to observe patients three to four hours after receiving a dose of methadone or LAAM.

Maintenance. Once a stable dose is established based on demonstration of desired clinical effects, elimination of craving and prevention of withdrawal, the maintenance phase has begun. Maintenance continues until such a time that there is a reason to alter the treatment. Most methadone maintained patients do well on a dose range of 60 to 120 mg daily, although some patients require less and some require more.

Medical Maintenance. According to current federal and most state methadone regulations, the maximum number of consecutive doses dispensed for consumption away from the program is six, with at least one observed dose each week. The earliest a patient is eligible for this level of take-home privilege is at three years, if a variety of other criteria are met. This applies regardless of extent of psychosocial rehabilitation or quality of recovery.

Medical maintenance generally refers to reduced attendance to one or two visits per month, with a minimum number of supportive services, in selected stable patients. Two models have emerged. The first involved Des Jarlais, Joseph, Dole, and Nyswander as a feasibility study (1985). This model was subsequently reported by Novick. According to the Novick model, medical maintenance is defined as the treatment of rehabilitated methadone maintenance patients in a general medical setting (rather than in a licensed clinic). Selection criteria called for a minimum of five years in treatment, with essentially perfect compliance for a period of three years. Results are excellent in terms of retention and very low rates of substance abuse or lost medication (Novick & Joseph, 1991; Novick, Joseph et al., 1994; Novick, Pascarelli et al., 1988).

The other model, by Senay, differed in several ways. Admission to the study was based on performance rather than time in treatment, with six months of excellent performance qualifying a patient for participation. The reduced attendance and services were carried out in a methadone program with continued periodic counseling and urine drug screens. The Senay model also demonstrated an excellent treatment outcome (Senay, Barthwell et al., 1994, 1993).

An obvious advantage to both models is a reduced level or intensity of care and cost of treatment, making more resources available to those just entering treatment while stable rehabilitated patients benefit from ongoing OAT with a minimum of cost and disruption of lives.

Pain Management. The under-treatment of pain in methadone- and LAAM-maintained patients remains a serious problem. In cases of acute pain associated with surgery, trauma, or dental work the physicians or dentists involved assume the maintenance dose should relieve any pain and further treatment should not be needed. Some perhaps fear that a methadone-maintained addict might become dangerous if given opioid analgesia or perhaps there are those who simply don't care. The minimum essentials of management of acute pain in OAT patients were summarized as follows in the *Journal of Maintenance in the Addictions* (Payte, 1997a):

"Patients being maintained with methadone or LAAM require special considerations for acute pain management in surgical or trauma situations. OAT patients are often denied any analgesia and serious under-treatment of pain is common. Maintenance patients develop full tolerance to the analgesic effects of the maintenance dose of methadone. During OAT a cross-tolerance develops to all opioid agonist drugs accounting for the 'blockade' effect. Early research demonstrated that stable OAT patients could not distinguish 20 mg IV morphine from IV saline. Hence: *The usual maintenance dose does not provide any analgesia, and adequate analgesia will require higher doses of opioid agonists given more frequently than in the non-tolerant patient.*

"Methadone has a half-life of 24–36 hours, but analgesic effects are from four to six hours, similar to morphine in both potency and duration. Morphine, Dilaudid®, codeine, etc. are appropriate in the OAT patient. Mixed agonist/antagonists (pentazocine, butorphanol, nalbuphine) and partial agonists (buprenorphine) *must not be used* as they will precipitate opioid withdrawal syndrome. Meperidine and propoxyphene should be avoided due to risk of seizures at the higher doses required to produce analgesia in OAT patients.

"In summary: (1) Continue maintenance treatment without interruption; (2) Provide *adequate individualized* doses of opioid agonists, which must be titrated to the desired analgesic effect. The proper dose is *enough!* and (3) Doses should be given more frequently and on a schedule rather than 'as needed for pain' (PRN)."

Pregnancy and Opioid Agonist Treatment. Of the various topics covered in this chapter, issues relating to opioid agonist treatment during pregnancy remain the most controversial and emotionally charged. This is largely due to the neonatal opioid withdrawal syndrome (NOWS) that is clearly the most visible and dramatic sequela of passive addiction in the neonate. Efforts to treat, prevent, and minimize neonatal opioid withdrawal have predominated since the results of the first 13 pregnancies were reported in 1969 (Wallach, Jerez & Blinick, 1969). This issue is addressed in detail in Section 16.

Hepatitis C. The hepatitis C virus (HCV) was isolated in 1988, with the first serologic test for HCV antibody available in 1990. It is estimated that 1.8% of the U.S. population is infected and that the overall mortality rate is 2% (8,000 to 10,000 deaths per year) (Alter, 1997). Since accurate identification became possible, studies suggest that the prevalence in intravenous drug users ranges from 50% to 90% (Barthwell & Gibert, 1993; Novick, Reagan et al., 1997), with some providers reporting even higher rates when they are able to test all their clinic patients.

Novick and his colleagues (1997) concluded that by 1978 to 1983, HCV had become well established in the addict population. High rates are found even in those with short histories. A recent report found 71.4% of those with less than a year of injection drug use were positive, and among those with histories greater than ten years, the rate was 91.7%. Once infected, it is estimated that 20% to 40% will develop liver disease and that, of that subgroup, 20% to 40% will develop liver cancer (Cahoon-Young, 1997).

HCV is a blood-borne pathogen transmitted by direct contact with blood or blood products, usually contaminated needles in the addict population. Injection drug use is considered the risk factor for acquisition in about 35% of reported cases. HCV also may be spread by sexual contact, but the risks are considered lower (Barthwell & Gibert 1993). Inasmuch as the risk factors are similar, it is not surprising that over 90% of injection drug users who are HIV-positive are co-infected with hepatitis C (Cahoon-Young, 1997).

Approximately 50% to 75% of acute HCV infections in adults are asymptomatic. If symptoms are present, they include the following:

- Flu-like illness
- Fatigue, malaise, fever, chills

- Anorexia, loss of appetite
- Nausea and occasional vomiting
- Dark urine (the color of cola drinks)
- Vague abdominal discomfort, especially in right quadrant
- Jaundice, with yellow eyes, skin and mucous membranes

Tong and el-Farra (1996) described the course of HCV infection in 125 patients with a history of injection drug use. The mean age of initiating drug use was 23.1 years, with presentation to a tertiary care center in California occurring approximately 20 years later (Liver Center, Pasadena). The most common presenting symptoms were fatigue, abdominal pain, anorexia, and weight loss. The initial workup indicated 26% had chronic hepatitis, 37% had chronic active hepatitis, 36% had cirrhosis, and 0.8% had hepatocellular carcinoma. In the subgroup of patients with short histories, alcohol use did not appear to influence progression of liver disease, but others (Novick, Reagan et al., 1997) have found otherwise in longer term users, and have hypothesized an additive and possibly synergistic effect of alcohol and HCV on the liver.

Currently, alpha interferon treatments are under study, but are often difficult to access and are poorly tolerated by patients. Changes in eligibility policies regarding liver transplantation make these difficult if not impossible to obtain. Viral titres are obtainable but do not presently appear to have a clear relationship to symptomatology; however they can be used to develop additional antiviral treatments.

Well-established programs are seeing an increasing number of patients who are becoming ill and dying. It is important that programs develop educational interventions to encourage health practices (such as complete elimination of alcohol) likely to prolong the period of good health. Advocacy will be needed to ensure that patients have access to emerging treatments.

Patients with Dual Disorders. The high comorbidity of psychiatric disorders and substance abuse (Regier, Farmer et al., 1990; Kessler, McGonagle et al., 1994) obliges drug abuse treatment providers to equip themselves to address both problems. In addition, psychiatric severity (as measured by the Addiction Severity Index) strongly predicts clinical outcome (O'Brien, Woody & McLellan, 1984). Woody and his colleagues (1986) examined the efficacy of two kinds of professional psychotherapy and drug abuse counseling typically provided in methadone programs as a function of global psychiatric status ratings of the patients. They found that low-severity patients benefited from both drug abuse counseling (focused on current life problems) and psychotherapy (supportive-expressive and cognitive-behavioral approaches). Those with high levels of psychiatric symptoms were lower in all areas of pretreatment functioning, and did not improve as much as patients with less severe problems. However, the addition of psychotherapy did maximize their improvement in many areas. Professionally trained therapists, integrated into the ongoing program, improve outcome for these difficult patients.

Depression and dysthymia are common coexisting disorders in the opiate using population in treatment. Rounsaville and Kleber (1985) compared opiate addicts with similar severity and duration of use, and found those seeking treatment had higher lifetime rates of dysphoric disorders and current major depression. Life crises and depressive symptoms posed a substantial risk of relapse, which lessened for those who remained in treatment (Kosten, Rounsaville & Kleber, 1986). Antidepressant medications can be prescribed in conjunction with opioid agonist treatment without ill effects, although lower doses of tricyclics may be desirable in some patients (Maany, Dhopesh et al., 1989). For patients at high risk, or those known for poor compliance, antidepressants can be dispensed with opioid agonist medication. Anxiety disorders are also common, with symptoms abating with a combination of an adequate methadone dose and the provision of counseling or psychotherapy over a period of time (Musselman & Kell, 1995).

Schizophrenia is relatively uncommon in opioid treatment programs (O'Brien, Woody & McLellan, 1984; Rounsaville, Weissman et al., 1982), although most programs have some of these patients. Some observers, using historical references and clinical observations, have proposed that opioids have antipsychotic properties (Comfort, 1977; Verebey, 1982). Clinicians have described a subgroup of patients, like the one who referred to methadone as his "sanity syrup," who appear calmed and stabilized by it; when their doses drop, they become disorganized. It also is likely that the high structure characteristic of many programs has a beneficial effect on these patients, providing a sense of safety and security to their world.

It is common to find reports of a high incidence of personality disorders, particularly antisocial personality disorder in the heroin using population, but it is important to view these findings with caution. Criteria in the *Diagnostic and Statistical Manual of*

Mental Disorders prior to *DSM-IV* (APA, 1994) failed to distinguish behaviors characteristic of alcohol and drug users from personality qualities that were more enduring. The self-preoccupation of the opioid agonist treatment patient in the stabilization phase (comparable to other patients who are newly abstinent or in early recovery) was too readily interpreted as narcissistic preoccupation characteristic of a personality disorder. In addition, symptoms of post traumatic stress disorder (PTSD) can be mistaken for personality disorders. As our appreciation grows of the high prevalence of emotional trauma sequelae in addicted populations, clinicians have noted that apparent lack of feelings and/or interpersonal connection can represent numbing symptoms (e.g., feelings of detachment or estrangement, restricted range of emotions) of PTSD in some patients. It is important to be attentive to these potential confusions because personality disorders, particularly antisocial personality disorder, carry a poor prognosis and often evoke negative staff attitudes. It also is advisable to be wary of psychiatric disorders diagnosed upon admission or shortly thereafter, as many patients look more pathological than they will after their medication has been stabilized and they have begun to make use of psychosocial services.

MAINTENANCE TREATMENT USING METHADONE

Heroin versus Methadone. The active opioid addict typically suffers rapid and wide swings from a brief "high," fading into a period of normalcy, which can be described as the "comfort zone." This is followed by beginnings of subjective withdrawal, which soon develops into the full objective withdrawal syndrome typical of opioid addiction. This cycle is especially marked with intravenous injection of potent short acting opioids such as heroin. A full cycle from sick to high to normal to sick can occur within 24 hours or less (Figure 1).

Steady-State. Methadone, regularly administered at steady-state, is present at levels sufficient to maintain normalcy (comfort zone) throughout a 24-hour dose period. With the next maintenance dose there is a gradual rise in blood level reaching a peak at about three to four hours after the dose. Typically the peak level is less than two times the trough level. There is a gradual decline over the remainder of the 24-hour period back to the trough level. At no time does the rate or extent of change in blood levels cause a sensation of being "high" or result in withdrawal syndrome. The sensation of the "rush" is associated with a very rapid increase in blood levels to a point somewhat in excess of the established opioid tolerance. The "high" is experienced during the time the levels remain in excess of tolerance (Figure 2).

The safe and effective introduction of methadone requires an understanding of steady-state pharmacological principles (Benet, Kroetz & Sheiner, 1996). In general, steady-state levels are reached after a drug is administered for four to five half-lives. Methadone has a half-life of 24–36 hours. The clinical significance is that with daily dosing, a significant portion of the previous dose remains in the bloodstream, resulting in increased peak and trough methadone levels following the second dose and subsequent doses. Thus the levels of methadone increase daily, even without an increase in dose. The rate of increase levels off as steady-state is achieved at four to five half-lives (five to eight days; see Figure 3).

Duration and Dose. Since the "regulatory counterattack" (Courtwright, Joseph & DesJarlais, 1989) of the early 1970s, regulators have responded to a self-imposed question: How long should treatment last and how much methadone should be given? Ill-fated efforts to limit duration of treatment occurred initially at the federal level and later became an issue for some individual state methadone authorities. Based on extensive review of the research literature on the prognosis of patients who have withdrawn from methadone and the established safety of continued maintenance treatment, the American Society of Addiction Medicine supports the principle that methadone maintenance treatment (MMT) is most effective as a long-term modality (ASAM, 1991).

Dose: Until recently, clinical practice in relation to methadone dosing has been guided by regulation and treatment philosophy, rather than clinical judgment. The development of an affordable technology to measure blood levels as well as clear documentation of the need for adequate dose to achieve positive outcome (Ball & Ross, 1991) has improved treatment practices in many settings. Efforts to establish dose should be focused on achieving and maintaining the desired clinical response rather than adherence to arbitrary dose practices set by policy or regulation. There is no scientific or clinical basis for an arbitrary dose ceiling on methadone or other agonist medication (Kaufman, Payte & McLellan, 1995). Despite the presence of abundant evidence in the research literature, it is still common to find inadequate dosing. When a patient continues to use heroin, the first response should be to ensure adequacy of dose. Once dose has been determined

FIGURE 1. Heroin-Simulated 24-Hour Dose/Response

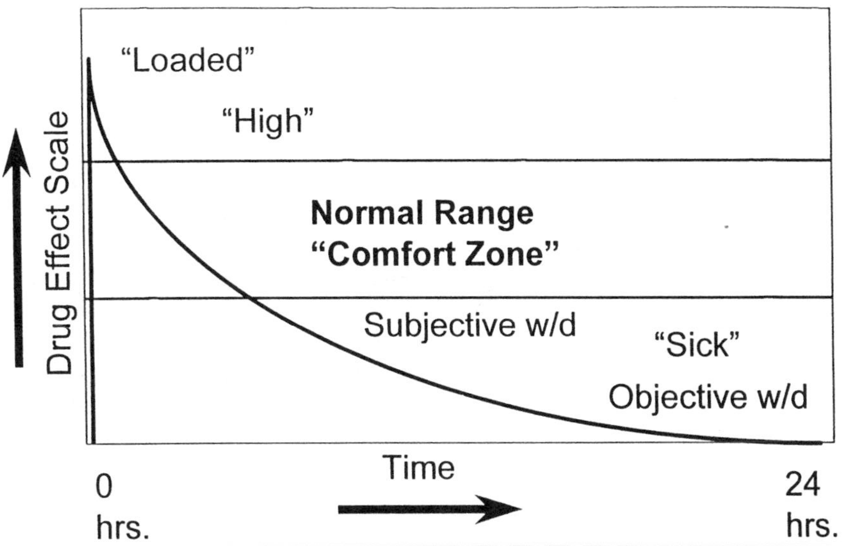

to be adequate, appropriate behavioral and psychosocial interventions can be effective.

Techniques to Assure Adequacy of Dose: The proper dose of methadone is "enough." How much is enough? "The amount required to produce the desired response for the desired duration of time, with an allowance for a margin of effectiveness and safety" (Payte & Khuri, 1993a). In most cases, clinical observation and patient reporting are adequate to make appropriate dose determinations.

Blood Levels in Dose Determination: In the methadone clinic setting, patients occasionally experience problems in maintaining stability on a given dose of methadone. Statements such as, "My dose isn't holding me"; "I wake up sick every morning"; "My dose only lasts a few hours"; "I have drug hunger every night"; "I get sleepy at work but start getting sick by bedtime," are common in OAT programs. These clinical problems may not respond to simple dose adjustments.

As early as 1978, it was suggested that serial methadone levels could result in dramatic clinical improvement, with a "flattening of the curve" associated with a divided dose regimen in methadone maintenance patients who were experiencing problems on a single daily dose (Walton, Thornton & Wahl, 1978). Researchers in the early 1980s compared 24-hour methadone levels in two groups of patients, all receiving 80 mg daily. The two groups were composed of patients doing very well in treatment and a group doing poorly in terms of drug use, compliance, etc. The results showed the stable group to have a mean of 410 ng/ml at 24 hours, while the poor performers had a mean of 101 ng/ml (Tennant, Rawson et al., 1984). It has become clear that the same dose may vary in efficacy among individuals and that patients doing poorly may be a result of inadequate dosing rather than being "bad patients."

Several researchers support blood levels greater than 150 to 200 ng/ml at all times for optimum results (Dole, 1988; Holmstrand, Anggard & Gunne, 1978; Loimer & Schmid, 1992). There is growing consensus that levels above 400 ng/ml may represent an optimum level in providing adequate cross-tolerance to make ordinary doses of IV heroin ineffective (nonreinforcing) during OAT (Loimer, Schmid et al., 1991).

Methadone peak, trough, and mean levels and the rate of elimination (half-life) may be influenced by several factors. Inter-individual differences in the metabolism of methadone, poor absorption, changes in urinary pH, effects of concomitant medications, diet, and even vitamins are among the possible factors that may influence the 24-hour dose-response curve of methadone. Pregnancy, particularly during the third trimester, is associated with significant decrease in trough methadone levels, suggesting increased rates of metabolism of methadone (Pond, Kreek et al., 1985).

Methadone blood levels are useful when the clinical picture does not agree with the typical or expected response to a given dose of methadone, as in the case of a patient taking 100 mg observed daily who is in early withdrawal before the end of the 24-hour period. Levels may be very useful in suspected drug interactions (discussed later in this chapter), to ensure adequacy of current dose, and to document the "need" for a certain dose, particularly doses in excess of 120 mg. Blood levels can identify patients who may benefit from a divided dose regimen or demonstrate the effectiveness of divided dose regimen.

Procedure for Obtaining Blood Levels: Ideally, peak blood levels should be drawn at three (two to four) hours after a dose and the trough at 24 hours after the dose. Patients already on a divided dose,

FIGURE 2. Methadone 24 Hour . . . at Steady-State

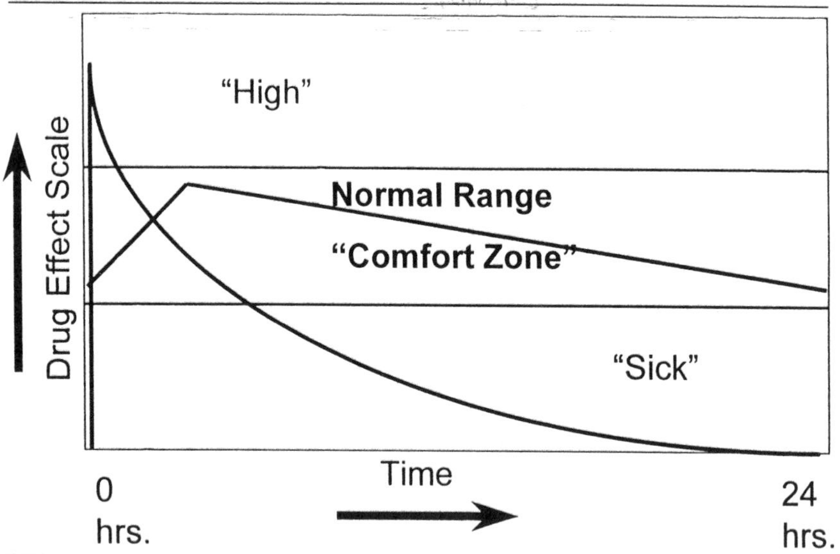

such as every 12 hours, should have two- to three-hour and 12-hour specimens. A trough level alone, while providing useful information, fails to indicate the rate of change over the time-course of a dose.

Interpretation: Blood levels are interpreted in the context of a clinical presentation for which the lab values can supplement clinical judgment in those more difficult cases. The trough level at 24 hours should be at least 150 to 200 ng/ml or more, and ideally 400 ng/ml or more. The higher levels may be necessary in patients who require a cross-tolerant or blockade level. The peak level at two to four hours should be no more than twice the trough level. A peak/trough ratio of 2 or less is ideal (peak/trough = ratio). Ratios greater than 2 suggest rapid metabolism. The *rate of change* is of greater clinical significance than the actual levels. For example, a patient with a 24-hour level of 350 ng/ml after a peak of 1,225 ng/ml (1,225/350 = 3.5 indicating rapid metabolism) may be experiencing early opioid withdrawal, while a patient with a trough of 150 ng/ml and a peak of 250 ng/ml (250/150 = 1.7 indicating a normal metabolism) may be very comfortable.

The clinical examples referred to above can best be illustrated with brief case histories.

Patient A was admitted in December 1991, using $150 heroin daily. He was disabled and under treatment for a severe seizure disorder, using carbamazepine. Based on his clinical presentation, the daily dose was gradually adjusted to 180 mg daily. At that time, he was symptomatic in less than 24 hours. Initial methadone levels were 118 ng/ml at three hours and < 25 ng/ml at 24 hours. The dose was gradually increased while the dosing interval was decreased, until the patient was receiving 100 mg methadone every six hours. The result was a modest improvement in peak/trough ratio from 9.8 to 5.8, but levels remained well below therapeutic levels. Cimetidine was added to inhibit metabolism and the patient clinically stabilized at methadone 100 mg and cimetidine 300 mg every six hours. Mean levels at two and six hours were 219 and 136 ng/ml, with a ratio of 1.6. Despite the low levels, the marked flattening of the curve provided excellent stability over the dosing interval.

Patient B, a 39-year-old female, was admitted November 21, 1994. She was an insulin dependent diabetic with a severe seizure disorder, alcoholism in remission, chronic opioid addiction, bulimia, anxiety, and depression. Phenytoin 400 mg daily provided adequate control of seizure activity. Based on persistent craving and withdrawal, methadone levels were performed December 2, showing a peak of 38 ng/ml and 0 ng/ml at 24 hours while on methadone 100 mg once daily. Methadone was gradually increased to 100 mg every 6 hours, resulting in dramatic clinical improvement, with 3/6 hour levels of 224/101 = 2.2. The final stabilizing dose was 120 mg every six hours (254/155 = 1.6), providing an excellent clinical response (Grudzinskas, Woosley et al., 1996).

The preceding examples are not common in clinical practice but do illustrate the need for flexibility in pursuit of the goals of providing effective treatment, comfort and relief for the patient by making sound decisions based on clinical presentation supported by appropriate laboratory procedures. It also should be apparent that any effort to set a specific ceiling or maximum dose of methadone, LAAM, or other opioid agonist by policy or regulation is not based on any scientific, clinical or laboratory evidence. Such efforts are destined to be counterproductive. Where arbitrary dose ceilings are applied, the patients are denied adequate care and physicians are limited in the exercise of their clinical judgment.

FIGURE 3. Steady-State Simulation—Maintenance Pharmacotherapy Attained after 4–5 Half-Times, 1 Dose/Half-Life

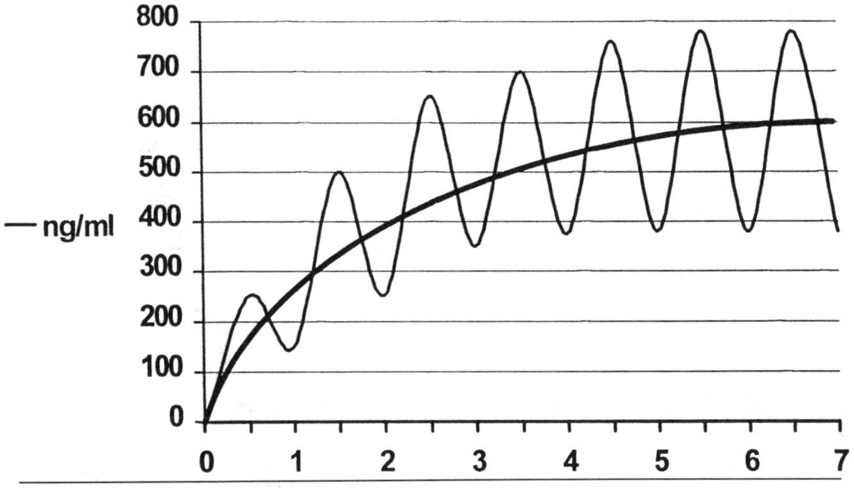

Time (multiples of elimination half-lives)
Daily dose remains constant to steady-state.

Methadone-Drug Interactions. At a 1995 College on Problems of Drug Dependence (CPDD) Symposium, clinical examples were cited in which concomitant medications could either induce or inhibit CYP-450 activity on methadone metabolism (Grudzinskas, Woosley et al., 1996). It was stressed that considerable flexibility in dosing may be required to stabilize some patients whose metabolism has been altered by drug interactions or inter-individual differences. Metabolism of methadone is largely a function of enzyme activity in the liver. The group of enzymes is known as CYP-450 enzymes. Drugs that stimulate or induce CYP-450 activity can precipitate opioid withdrawal by accelerating metabolism, thus shortening duration and diminishing intensity of the effect of methadone. Other drugs tend to inhibit this enzyme activity, slowing the metabolism and extending the duration of the drug effect (see Table 1).

MAINTENANCE TREATMENT USING LAAM

Levo-alpha-acetylmethadol (LAAM) was developed in 1948. By 1952, LAAM had been observed to suppress opioid withdrawal for more than 72 hours (Fraser & Isbell, 1952). LAAM was evaluated in opioid addiction in the late 1960s and 1970s, ignored in the 1980s, and resurrected by the National Institute on Drug Abuse (NIDA) Medications Development Division in 1990. The final study, called the labeling assessment study, was conducted in 26 methadone programs (Fudala, Vocci et al., 1997). LAAM was approved for use in the treatment of opioid addiction by the Food and Drug Administration (FDA) in 1993 (Marion, 1995).

LAAM, a derivative of methadone, is similar to methadone in terms of its safety profile, side effects, drug interactions, and efficacy. LAAM differs from methadone in its suppression of opioid withdrawal for 72 hours and in some cases longer. With a slow onset and long duration of action, it is given every other day or thrice weekly. The extended action is due to sequential metabolism to nor-LAAM and dinor-LAAM, both of which are more potent and longer acting than the parent drug.

Conversion from methadone to LAAM is simple, with the LAAM dose being 1.2 to 1.3 times the methadone dose given every 48 hours, with a 0–40% increase in LAAM dose for a 72-hour interval. At this time there are no provisions for a LAAM take-home dose, so daily methadone must be provided for emergencies, necessary travel, etc., at 80% of the 48-hour LAAM dose.

LAAM has not been studied in pregnancy, so patients who become pregnant are converted to methadone. For women of child-bearing age, monthly pregnancy tests are required.

LAAM is not recommended for nursing mothers and persons under 18 years of age, simply because studies have not been done in these populations (Marion, 1995).

Aside from the greater comfort enjoyed by some patients, the principal advantages of LAAM are evident early in treatment in the form of reduced travel, disruption, and clinic attendance, without the need for take-home doses. Patients in work settings in which drug testing occurs are greatly relieved by the absence of toxicology screens to detect LAAM. Later in treatment, the lack of provision for take-home medication results in disadvantages, because of the need for more travel, disruption, and clinic attendance on the part of patients who would qualify for methadone take-home privileges.

TABLE 1. Methadone–Drug Interactions

Drugs that induce CYP-450 enzyme activity:
- Rifampin
- Phenytoin
- Ethyl Alcohol
- Barbiturates
- Carbamazepine

Drugs that inhibit CYP-450 enzyme activity:
- Cimetidine
- Ketoconazole
- Erythromycin

MAINTENANCE TREATMENT USING BUPRENORPHINE

Buprenorphine is a partial agonist at the mu and kappa opioid receptors. Pharmacological studies show that buprenorphine combines a strong affinity for the opioid receptors with a low intrinsic activity. Another significant advantage is that as a partial agonist with antagonist properties, buprenorphine has a considerable margin of safety with little chance for a lethal overdose. Since the mid-1970s, when the potential benefits of buprenorphine in opioid addiction first were noted, extensive clinical investigations have been carried out.

Buprenorphine has been widely used as an injectable analgesic. Intravenous buprenorphine has been reported as a significant drug of abuse in Europe, New Zealand, and Australia. At the time of this writing, final FDA approval is expected for two sublingual tablet forms. One is a single product and the other a combination of naloxone and buprenorphine. It is expected that the combination product will virtually eliminate the potential for diversion to IV use. Numerous studies have confirmed the safety and efficacy of buprenorphine in maintenance treatment. Studies have found that an 8 mg dose of buprenorphine is equivalent to methadone doses of 35 to 60 mg in terms of retention and opioid-positive urines. High dose methadone is uniformly superior to low dose methadone and lower doses of buprenorphine (Johnson & Fudala, 1992; Kosten, Schottenfeld et al., 1993; Ling, Rawson & Compton, 1994). A later study found that 8 mg buprenorphine did not compare favorably with methadone doses of 80 mg per day (Ling, Wesson et al., 1996). This suggests that doses in the range of 16 mg/d or more might be required in some cases.

PSYCHOSOCIAL INTERVENTIONS

Physicians working in clinics focused on opioid maintenance pharmacotherapy typically find that counseling and case management components range widely in quality and comprehensiveness. In many states, the introduction of methadone was permitted only if accompanied by a serious rehabilitative effort, but recent changes in funding have undermined efforts to maintain comprehensive services. Inasmuch as medication makes other changes possible, but does not magically produce them, it is important to preserve the capacity of programs to provide a broad spectrum of care.

Psychosocial interventions in many programs are implemented by drug counselors, who range widely in their educational level and professional training. The counselor's task is to identify and address specific problems in the areas of drug use, physical health, interpersonal relationships (including family interaction), psychological problems, and educational or vocational goals (Zweben, 1991). Short- and long-term treatment plans provide structure for the counseling sessions and a tool by which to monitor patient progress and quality of care. The counselor also serves as case manager, initiating screening for medication and other program services, attending to issues concerning program rules, privileges, and policies, and providing links to other agencies.

Clinics with access to professionally trained staff may offer psychotherapy for selected patients in the program. Typically, this is more common in programs involved in research or professional training. Motivational enhancement strategies (Miller & Rollnick, 1991; Miller, Zweben et al., 1994) have been introduced to address patient resistance to giving up alcohol, cocaine and continuing (even if reduced) heroin use. This approach offers an alternative to harsh confrontation, encouraging counselors to meet patients wherever they are prepared to begin and move forward from there. Other psychological issues and interventions are reviewed in Zweben (1991).

The philosophy of providing comprehensive services is supported by recent research. McLellan and his colleagues (McLellan, 1983; McLellan, Alterman et al., 1994; McLellan, Arndt et al., 1993; McLellan, Grissom et al., 1997) have demonstrated that the addition of enhanced on-site professional services was more effective than basic counseling alone. Quality, quantity, and the match with the patient's specific problem areas (e.g., vocational, family, psychiatric) all led to demonstrably better outcomes in a variety of populations examined. A quality assurance process which monitors and encourages a close fit between the patient's needs and actual services delivered is likely to produce the best outcome, in contrast to a "cookie cutter" approach in which most patients receive a similar mix of services.

Phase programs permit the individualizing of treatment within a highly structured, systematic process that allows the patient to move forward, obtaining tangible markers of progress. Hoffman and Moolchan (1994) have described one such model, divided into three phases: intensive stabilization, commitment, and rehabilitation. Staff/patient ratios can be adjusted according to the levels of support and assistance required by patients in each stage, and specific activities can be tailored to individual needs. Services can be provided on site, or through a network of referral sources in the community. In the later stages, patients can be tracked into a tapering phase or a medical maintenance phase, with a reinforcement phase as a follow-up.

GROWTH, CONTROVERSY AND FUTURE CHALLENGES

Any physician who becomes involved in the treatment of an opioid maintenance patient has an important task beyond that of medical practitioner: education and advocacy. A few minutes spent educating family members, clinical providers, and others can have a major impact on softening the stigma and improving the way the patient is treated in a variety of systems of care. The patient who feels the physician is knowledgeable and concerned will make far greater efforts to comply with treatment recommendations.

An issue which merits attention, though there is little literature, is that of the middle class population using illicit opiates who would not consider seeking treatment in the current system which delivers OAT. A study of Empire Blue Cross and Blue Shield (EBCBS) subscribers in the New York metropolitan area indicated approximately 141,000 opiate users were insured between 1982 and 1992, and that at the end of the study, 85,000 still were currently insured by EBCBS (Eisenhandler & Drucker, 1993). The authors suggested that there is a large population of mainstream, working, insured opiate users who are not well described because they are not reached by government agencies, which historically have been the source of data on opiate users. Clinicians observe that many of these patients are referred to more "middle class" treatment facilities, in which staff who are not knowledgeable about opiate addiction may harbor negative attitudes towards those who use this class of drugs. Some of these patients substitute alcohol or benzodiazepines as a more socially acceptable remedy. Many of the longer term opiate users clearly would be candidates for OAT, if the treatment system were comparable to that for other medical conditions. In the interim, they will make themselves known by presenting for assessment and treatment for HIV disease and, more recently, HCV.

Oversight and Regulatory Challenges. Since the early 1970s, methadone maintenance and withdrawal treatment have been influenced by regulations promulgated by the Food and Drug Administration (FDA), in consultation with the National Institute on Drug Abuse (NIDA) and the Drug Enforcement Administration (DEA). In addition, some states have adopted their own regulations, most of which are based on—but which may be more restrictive than—the federal regulations. There is little question that these regulations, in their current form, have failed to ensure the quality of patient care and have had some unintended consequences (Dole, 1995; Dole, 1992; Rettig & Yarmolinsky, 1995).

As of early 1998, major changes are under way. The most significant is a transition of primary federal oversight responsibilities from FDA to the federal Center for Substance Abuse Treatment (CSAT). Major revisions of regulations, guidelines, and standards are expected to accompany this transition.

CSAT has sponsored a study on the feasibility and impact of an accreditation system for methadone providers. This ambitious study is being conducted by the Research Triangle Institute (RTI), working in collaboration with the Commission on Accreditation of Rehabilitation Facilities (CARF). CSAT and CARF are developing accreditation standards for OAT. It is likely that the outcome of this process will play a significant role in the manner and extent of involvement of managed care with OAT programs in the future.

Driving the need for such a restructuring is an urgent need to increase access to treatment while improving and ensuring the quality of that treatment. This is a formidable task, given the reluctance of policymakers to commit needed resources, both financial and human, to ensure success. The changes now taking place and under consideration do allow for some optimism.

REFERENCES

Alter MJ (1997). Epidemiology of Hepatitis C. *NIH Consensus Development Conference on Management of Hepatitis C.* Bethesda, MD: National Institutes of Health, 67–70.

American Psychiatric Association (1994). *Diagnostic and Statistical Manual of Mental Disorders; Fourth Edition (DSM-IV)*. Washington, DC: American Psychiatric Press.

American Society of Addition Medicine (1991). *American Society of Addiction Medicine Policy Statement on Methadone Treatment.* Washington, DC: American Society of Addiction Medicine.

Ball JC & Ross A (1991). *The Effectiveness of Methadone Maintenance Treatment.* New York, NY: Springer-Verlag, 283.

Barthwell AG & Gibert CL (1993). *Screening for Infectious Diseases Among Substance Users: Treatment Improvement Protocol (TIP)* (Series 6). Rockville, MD: U.S. Department of Health and Human Services.

Benet LZ, Kroetz DL & Sheiner LB (1996). Pharmacokinetics: The dynamics of drug absorption, distribution, and elimination. In JG Hardman, LE Limbird, PB Molinoff & RW Ruddon (eds.) *Goodman & Gilman's The Pharmacological Basis of Therapeutics.* New York, NY: McGraw-Hill, 23.

Cahoon-Young B (1997). Prevalence of hepatitis C virus in women: Who's getting it, why and co-infection with HIV. *Perspective on the Epidemiology, Treatment and Interventions for the Hepatitis C Virus.* Sponsors: Haight Ashbury Free Clinics, Inc., Diagnostic Support Services, 14th Street Clinic and Medical Group. San Francisco, March 20, 1997.

Comfort A (1977). Morphine as an antipsychotic. Relevance of a 19th-century therapeutic fashion. *Lancet* 2(8035):448–449.

Courtwright D, Joseph H & DesJarlais D (1989). Methadone maintenance—Interview with Vincent Dole. *Addicts Who Survived: An Oral History of Narcotic Use in America, 1923–1965.* Knoxville, TN: The University of Tennessee Press, 331–343.

de Cubas MM & Field T (1993). Children of methadone-dependent women: developmental outcomes. *American Journal of Orthopsychiatry* 63(2):266–276.

Des Jarlais DC, Joseph H, Dole VP & Nyswander ME (1985). Medical maintenance feasibility study. *NIDA Research Monograph* 58(10):101–110.

Dole VP (1988). Implications of methadone maintenance for theories of narcotic addiction. *Journal of the American Medical Association* 260(20):3025–3029.

Dole VP (1992). Hazards of process regulations. The example of methadone maintenance. *Journal of the American Medical Association* 267(16):2234–2235.

Dole VP (1995). On federal regulation of methadone treatment. *Journal of the American Medical Association* 274(16):1307.

Dole VP & Nyswander M (1965). A medical treatment for diacetylmorphine (heroin) addiction—A clinical trial with methadone hydrochloride. *Journal of the American Medical Association* 193(8):646–650.

Dole VP & Nyswander ME (1967). Heroin addiction—A metabolic disease. *Archives of Internal Medicine* 120(1):19–24.

Edelin KC, Gurganious L, Golar K, Oellerich D, Kyei-Aboagye K & Adel Hamid M (1988). Methadone maintenance in pregnancy: consequences to care and outcome. *Obstetrics and Gynecology* 71(3 Pt 1):399–404.

Eisenhandler J & Drucker E (1993). Opiate dependency among the subscribers of a New York area private insurance plan. *Journal of the American Medical Association* 269(22):2890–2891.

Finnegan LP (1986). Neonatal abstinence syndrome: assessment and pharmacotherapy. In FF Rubaltelli & B Granati (eds.) *Neonatal Therapy: An Update.* New York, NY: Elsevier, 122–146.

Finnegan LP (1991). Treatment issues for opioid-dependent women during the perinatal period. *Journal of Psychoactive Drugs* 23(2):191–201.

Finnegan LP, Connaughton JF Jr., Kron RE & Emich JP (1975). Neonatal abstinence syndrome: Assessment and management. *Addictive Diseases: An International Journal* 2(1):141–158.

Fraser HF & Isbell H (1952). Actions and addiction liabilities of alpha-acetylmethadol in man. *Journal of Pharmacology and Experimental Therapy* 105:458–465.

Fudala PJ, Vocci F, Montgomery A & Trachtenberg AI (1997). Levomethadyl acetate (LAAM) for the treatment of opioid dependence: A multisite, open-label study of LAAM safety and an evaluation of the product labeling and treatment regulations. *Journal of Maintenance in the Addictions* 1(2):9–39.

Geraghty B, Graham EA, Logan B & Weiss EL (1997). Methadone levels in breast milk. *Journal of Human Lactation* 13(3):227–230.

Goldstein A (1991). Heroin addiction: Neurobiology, pharmacology, and policy. *Journal of Psychoactive Drugs* 23(2):123–133.

Grudzinskas CV, Woosley RL, Payte JT et al. (1996). The documented role of pharmacogenetics in the identification and administration of new medications for treating drug abuse. NIDA Research Monograph 162:60–63.

Harper RG, Solish GI, Purow HM et al. (1974). The effect of a methadone treatment program upon pregnant heroin addicts and their newborn infants—Short-term, ambulatory detoxification of opiate addicts using methadone. *Pediatrics* 54(3):300–305.

Hoegerman G & Schnoll S (1991). Narcotic use in pregnancy. *Clinical Perinatology* 18(l):51–76.

Hoffman JA & Moolchan ET (1994). The phases-of-treatment model for methadone maintenance: Implementation and evaluation. *Journal of Psychoactive Drugs* 26(2):181–197.

Holmstrand J, Anggard E & Gunne LM (1978). Methadone maintenance: Plasma levels and therapeutic outcome. *Clinical Pharmacology and Therapeutics* 23(2):175–180.

Jarvis M, Knisely J & Schnoll S (1996). Changes in metabolism of methadone during pregnancy. *NIDA Research Monograph* 174:129.

Jarvis MA & Schnoll SH (1994). Methadone treatment during pregnancy. *Journal of Psychoactive Drugs* 26(2):155–161.

Johnson RE & Fudala PJ (1992). Background and design of a controlled clinical trial (ARC 090) for the treatment of opioid dependence. *NIDA Research Monograph* 128(24):14–24.

Kaltenbach K, Comfort M, Rajagopal D & Kumaraswamy G (1996). Methadone maintenance of > 80 mg during pregnancy. *NIDA Research Monograph* 174:128.

Kaltenbach K & Finnegan LP (1984). Developmental outcome of children born to methadone maintained women: a review of longitudinal studies. *Neurotoxicology and Teratology* 6(4):271–275.

Kaltenbach K & Finnegan LP (1987). Perinatal and developmental outcome of infants exposed to methadone in-utero. *Neurotoxicology and Teratology* 9(4):311–313.

Kaltenbach K, Silverman N & Wapner R (1993). Methadone maintenance during pregnancy. In MW Parrino (ed.) *State Methadone Treatment Guidelines. Center for Substance Abuse Treatment: Treatment Improvement Protocol (TIP)* (Series No. 1). Rockville, MD: U.S. Department of Health and Human Services, 85–93.

Kaltenbach KA (1994). Effects of in-utero opiate exposure: new paradigms for old questions. *Drug and Alcohol Dependence* 36(2):83–87.

Kaufman J, Payte JT & McLellan AT (1995). Treatment standards and optimal treatment. In RA Rettig & A Yarmolinski (eds.) *Institute of Medicine—Federal Regulation of Methadone Treatment.* Washington, DC: National Academy Press, 185–216.

Kessler RC, McGonagle KA, Zhao S et al. (1994). Lifetime and 12-month prevalence of *DSM-III-R* psychiatric disorders in the United States. Results from the National Comorbidity Survey. *Archives of General Psychiatry* 51(l):8–19.

Kosten TR, Rounsaville BJ & Kleber HD (1986). A 2.5-year follow-up of depression, life crises, and treatment effects on abstinence among opioid addicts. *Archives of General Psychiatry* 43(8):733–738.

Kosten TR, Schottenfeld R, Ziedonis D & Falcioni J (1993). Buprenorphine versus methadone maintenance for opioid dependence. *Journal of Nervous and Mental Disease* 181(6):358–364.

Kreek MJ (1979). Methadone disposition during the perinatal period in humans. *Pharmacology, Biochemistry and Behavior* 11(Suppl):7–13.

Kreek MJ (1992). Rationale for Maintenance Pharmacotherapy of Opiate Dependence. In CP O'Brien & JH Jaffee (eds.) *Addictive States.* Research Publications: Association for Research in Nervous and Mental Disease. New York, NY: Raven Press, 205–230.

Ling W, Rawson RA & Compton MA (1994). Substitution pharmacotherapies for opioid addiction: From methadone to LAAM and buprenorphine. *Journal of Psychoactive Drugs* 26(2):119–128.

Ling W, Wesson DR, Charuvastra C & Klett CJ (1996). A controlled trial comparing buprenorphine and methadone maintenance in opioid dependence. *Archives of General Psychiatry* 53(5):401–407.

Loimer N & Schmid R (1992). The use of plasma levels to optimize methadone maintenance treatment. *Drug and Alcohol Dependence* 30(3):241–246.

Loimer N, Schmid R, Grunberger J, Jagsch R, Linzmayer L & Presslich O (1991). Psychophysiological reactions in methadone maintenance patients do not correlate with methadone plasma levels. *Psychopharmacology* (Berlin) 103(4):538–540.

Maany I, Dhopesh V, Arndt IO, Burke W, Woody G & O'Brien CP (1989). Increase in desipramine serum levels associated with methadone treatment. *American Journal of Psychiatry* 146(12):1611–1613.

Mackie-Ramos RL & Rice JM (1988). Group psychotherapy with methadone-maintained pregnant women. *Journal of Substance Abuse Treatment* 5(3):151–161.

Marion IJ (ed.) (1995). LAAM in the treatment of opiate addiction. *Center for Substance Abuse Treatment: Treatment Improvement Protocol (TIP)* (Series No. 22). Rockville, MD: U.S. Department of Health and Human Services.

McLellan AT (1983). Patient characteristics associated with outcome. In JR Cooper, F Altman, BS Brown & D Czechowicz (eds.) *Research on the Treatment of Narcotic Addiction: State of the Art* (NIDA Monograph Series). Rockville, MD: National Institute on Drug Abuse Treatment, 500–529.

McLellan AT, Alterman AI, Metzger DS et al. (1994). Similarity of outcome predictors across opiate, cocaine, and alcohol treatments: role of treatment services. *Journal of Consulting and Clinical Psychiatry* 62(6):1141–1158.

McLellan AT, Arndt IO, Metzger DS, Woody GE & O'Brien CP (1993). The effects of psychosocial services in substance abuse treatment. *Journal of the American Medical Association* 269(15):1953–1959.

McLellan AT, Grissom GR, Zanis D, Randall M, Brill P & O'Brien CP (1997). Problem-service 'matching' in addiction treatment. A prospective study in 4 programs. *Archives of General Psychiatry* 54(8):730–735.

Miller WR & Rollnick S (1991). *Motivational Interviewing: Preparing People to Change Addictive Behavior.* New York, NY: Guilford Press.

Miller WR, Zweben A, DiClemente CC & Rychtarik RG (1994). *Motivational Enhancement Therapy Manual* (Project Match Series Monograph No. 2). Rockville, MD: U.S. Department of Health and Human Services.

Musselman DL & Kell MJ (1995). Prevalence and improvement in psychopathology in opioid dependent patients participating in methadone maintenance. *Journal of Addictive Diseases* 14(3):67–82.

NIH-CDC (1997). Effective medical treatment of heroin addiction. *NIH Consensus Statement.* Bethesda, MD: National Institutes of Health.

Novick DM & Joseph H (1991). Medical maintenance: the treatment of chronic opiate dependence in general medical practice. *Journal of Substance Abuse Treatment* 8(4):233–239.

Novick DM, Joseph H, Salsitz EA et al. (1994). Outcomes of treatment of socially rehabilitated methadone maintenance patients in physicians' offices (medical maintenance): Follow-up at three and a half to nine and a fourth years. *Journal of General Internal Medicine* 9(3):127–130.

Novick DM, Pascarelli EF, Joseph H et al. (1988). Methadone maintenance patients in general medical practice. A preliminary report. *Journal of the American Medical Association* 259(22):3299–3302.

Novick DM, Reagan KJ, Croxson TS, Gelb AM, Stenger RJ & Kreek MJ (1997). Hepatitis C virus serology in parenteral drug users with chronic liver disease. *Addiction* 92(2):167–171.

O'Brien CP, Woody GE & McLellan AT (1984). Psychiatric disorders in opioid-dependent patients. *Journal of Clinical Psychiatry* 45(12 Pt 2):9–13.

Payte JT (1997a). Clinical take-homes (Column). *Journal of Maintenance in the Addictions* 1(2):103–104.

Payte JT (1997b). Methadone maintenance treatment: The first thirty years. *Journal of Psychoactive Drugs* 29(2):149–153.

Payte JT & Khuri ET (1993a). Principles of Methadone Dose Determination. In M Parrino (ed.) *CSAT State Methadone Treatment Guidelines. Treatment Improvement Protocol (TIP)* (Series No. 1). Rockville, MD: U.S. Department of Health and Human Services, 47–58.

Payte JT & Khuri ET (1993b). Treatment Duration and Patient Retention. In MW Parrino (ed.) *State Methadone Treatment Guidelines. Center for Substance Abuse Treatment: Treatment Improvement Protocol (TIP)* (Series No. 1). Rockville, MD: U.S. Department of Health and Human Services, 119–124.

Pickens RW (1997). Genetic and other risk factors in opiate addiction. *NIH Consensus Development Conference on Effective Medical Treatment of Heroin Addiction.* Bethesda, MD: National Institutes of Health, 33–36.

Pond SM, Kreek MJ, Tong TG, Raghunath J & Benowitz NL (1985). Altered methadone pharmacokinetics in methadone-maintained pregnant women. *Journal of Pharmacology and Experimental Therapeutics* 233(1):1–6.

Regier DA, Farmer ME, Rae DS et al. (1990). Comorbidity of mental disorders with alcohol and other drug abuse. Results from the Epidemiologic Catchment Area (ECA) Study. *Journal of the American Medical Association* 264(19):2511–2518.

Rettig R & Yarmolinsky A (eds.) (1995). *Institute of Medicine—Federal Regulation of Methadone Treatment.* Washington, DC: National Academy Press.

Rounsaville BJ & Kleber HD (1985). Untreated opiate addicts. How do they differ from those seeking treatment? *Archives of General Psychiatry* 42(11):1072–1077.

Rounsaville BJ, Weissman MM, Wilber CH & Kleber H (1982). The heterogeneity of psychiatric diagnosis in treated opiate addicts. *Archives of General Psychiatry* 39:161–169.

Senay EC, Barthwell A, Marks R & Bokos PJ (1994). Medical maintenance: an interim report. *Journal of Addictive Diseases* 13(3):65–69.

Senay EC, Barthwell AG, Marks R, Bokos P, Gillman D & White R (1993). Medical maintenance: a pilot study. *Journal of Addictive Diseases* 12(4):59–76.

Soepatmi S (1994). Developmental outcomes of children of mothers dependent on heroin or heroin/methadone during pregnancy. *Acta Paediatrica Supplement* 404(9):36–39.

Swift RM, Dudley M, DePetrillo P, Camara P & Griffiths W (1989). Altered methadone pharmacokinetics in pregnancy: implications for dosing. *Journal of Substance Abuse* 1(4):453–460.

Tennant FS Jr, Rawson RA, Cohen A, Tarver A & Clabough D (1984). Methadone plasma levels and persistent drug abuse in high dose maintenance patients. *NIDA Research Monograph* 49(8):262–268.

Tong MJ & el-Farra NS (1996). Clinical sequelae of hepatitis C acquired from injection drug use. *Western Journal of Medicine* 164(5):399–404.

Verebey K (ed.) (1982). Opioids in mental illness: Theories, clinical observations and treatment possibilities. *Annals of the New York Academy of Sciences* 398:ix.

Wallach RC, Jerez E & Blinick G (1969). Pregnancy and menstrual function in narcotics addicts treated with methadone. The Methadone Maintenance Treatment Program. *American Journal of Obstetrics and Gynecology* 105(8):1226–1229.

Walton RG, Thornton TL & Wahl GF (1978). Serum methadone as an aid in managing methadone maintenance patients. *International Journal of Addiction* 13(5):689–694.

Wittmann BK & Segal S (1991). A comparison of the effects of single- and split-dose methadone administration on the fetus: ultrasound evaluation. *International Journal of Addiction* 26(2):213–218.

Woody GE, McLellan AT, Luborsky L, O'Brien CP & Lubursky L (1986). Psychotherapy for substance abuse [published erratum appears in *Psychiatric Clinics of North America* 1990 Mar; 13(1): xiii]. *Psychiatric Clinics of North America* 9(3):547–562.

Zweben JE (1991). Counseling issues in methadone maintenance treatment. *Journal of Psychoactive Drugs* 23(2):177–190.

Zweben JE & Payte JT (1990). Methadone maintenance in the treatment of opioid dependence. A current perspective. *Western Journal of Medicine* 152(5):588–599.

CHAPTER 6

Pharmacologic Therapies for Nicotine Dependence

Joy M. Schmitz, Ph.D.
Jack E. Henningfield, Ph.D.
Murray E. Jarvik, M.D., Ph.D.

Biobehavioral Mechanisms of Tobacco Dependence
Treatment of Tobacco Dependence
Other Areas of Medication Development
Combining Behavioral and Pharmacological Approaches

Nicotine can be delivered in many ways. By far the most prevalent and hazardous vehicle for delivering nicotine is the tobacco cigarette. Of the 46.3 million Americans who currently smoke (CDC, 1994), most are dependent on nicotine and would like to quit, but find it difficult to give up tobacco. Chronic smokers are at significantly higher risk than nonsmokers to develop tobacco-related illnesses, including cardiovascular diseases, lung and other cancers, stroke, and chronic obstructive pulmonary diseases (USDHHS, 1988). Tobacco-attributable deaths account for approximately 20% of all deaths each year in the United States (McGinnis & Foege, 1994). The treatment of tobacco dependence continues to play a prominent role in efforts to reduce the substantial morbidity and mortality caused by cigarette smoking. Indeed, it is arguably far more cost-effective to treat drug dependence than to treat the serious health consequences of smoking (Becker, Windsor et al., 1993).

The past decade represents a period of remarkable innovation in pharmacological approaches to smoking cessation. Medications with proven efficacy for smoking cessation include nicotine replacement therapies and a non-nicotine medication. Additional nicotine and non-nicotine formulations also show promise or have valuable, albeit limited, applications. The rationale for these interventions is based on the pathophysiology of tobacco dependence, characterized by neuroadaptation, tolerance, withdrawal, and nicotine reinforcement (Henningfield, Schuh & Jarvik, 1994). To the extent that nonpharmacological factors contribute to the development and maintenance of cigarette smoking, some form of behavioral intervention remains the cornerstone of all tobacco dependence treatment programs (Henningfield & Singleton, 1994). Appropriate integration of behavior and pharmacologic therapy has proven to be most effective in the treatment of drug dependence (Kirby, Schmitz & Stitzer, 1997).

This chapter begins by summarizing the extensive literature on the biological basis of tobacco dependence, followed by a review of the medications presently approved by the Food and Drug Administration (FDA) for the treatment of tobacco dependence. These include nicotine polacrilex, transdermal nicotine, nicotine nasal spray, nicotine inhaler, and bupropion. Other medications that have been the focus of clinical investigation, but are not currently approved for use in the treatment of tobacco dependence, will be presented. The chapter closes with a discussion of a successful behavioral-pharmacologic interface for smoking cessation.

BIOBEHAVIORAL MECHANISMS OF TOBACCO DEPENDENCE

Scientific investigation has shown that biological and behavioral mechanisms are fundamental determinants of tobacco dependence. Repeated exposure to nicotine, a psychoactive agent, leads to neuroadaptations that support drug-seeking behavior and the development of tolerance. In addition to the direct reinforcing effects of nicotine administration, associated environmental stimuli can serve as powerful (secondary) reinforcers relevant to maintaining drug-seeking behavior. Dependence is further characterized by signs and symptoms of withdrawal upon interruption or termination of this cycle. Most regular smokers are probably dependent, in varying degrees, upon nicotine.

Nicotine Delivery Kinetics. The nicotine delivery system is partially related to its dependence-producing effects (Henningfield & Keenan, 1993). Tobacco smoke inhalation is the fastest and the most efficient method of drug delivery to the brain. In less than 10 seconds of inhalation, approximately 25% of the nicotine reaches the brain, a rate that may be twice as fast as intravenous delivery (Benowitz 1990, 1992). Further, smoke inhalation produces high arterial concentrations of nicotine which may be five to 10 times higher than those observed in venous blood or produced by nicotine patch administration (Henningfield, Stapleton et al., 1993; Henningfield, 1995). Behaviorally, this extremely rapid transit time of nicotine to the brain makes the drug a powerful reinforcer of smoking behavior (Oldendorf, 1992). The pharmacokinetic profile of inhaled nicotine is unmatched by any other currently available form of nicotine delivery. Indeed, this knowledge recently prompted the FDA to conclude that nicotine in tobacco products is a drug and cigarettes are nicotine delivery devices under the federal Food, Drug, and Cosmetic Act, and therefore subject to FDA regulation.

Neurobiological Actions. On the molecular level, nicotine appears to exert most of its effects in the brain by interacting with neuronal nicotinic receptors (nAChRs) on the membranes of target cells (Wonnacott, 1990). Several brain areas containing high densities of nAChRs have been implicated in the behavioral effects of nicotine. In particular, nAChRs are found in both the nucleus accumbens and ventral tegmental area (VTA), areas involved in the mesolimbic dopamine (DA) system. Nicotine's involvement with the DA system may resemble activity found in other dependence-producing drugs (amphetamine, cocaine, morphine, alcohol). Whereas brain nAChRs may mediate some of the beneficial effects of nicotine such as cognitive enhancement, arousal and negative affect (Sherwood, 1993), our understanding of the relationship between nAChR activity and effects on behavior remains incomplete. Chronic nicotine exposure results in an increase in the number of brain nicotinic receptors, known as receptor upregulation (Balfour, 1991). This form of neuroadaptation may occur to varying degrees in different individuals, perhaps in relation to level of dependence on nicotine (Fagerström & Säwe, 1996). It generally is assumed that this process of receptor upregulation is critical to the development of tolerance to and/or dependence on nicotine.

Primary and Secondary Reinforcing Effects. Animals and humans will choose to self-administer nicotine over placebo, confirming that nicotine can function as a positive reinforcer (Henningfield & Goldberg, 1983; Pomerleau, 1992; Stolerman & Shoaib, 1991). On subjective measures of euphoria, nicotine produces elevated drug liking scores relative to placebo (Henningfield, Miyasato & Jasinski, 1985). Anecdotally, smokers often report that nicotine improves cognitive function and helps to regulate mood. Upon cessation of smoking, nicotine dependent cigarette persons experience impaired cognitive function which can be prevented or reversed by nicotine administration (Heishman, Taylor & Henningfield, 1994). Nicotine also may modulate mood and some types of behavioral performance in nondependent cigarette smokers (Heishman, Taylor & Henningfield, 1994; Hughes, 1991a). Nicotine can produce reinforcing effects due to its administration which leads to release of dopamine and other neurohormones which also mediate the reinforcing effects of cocaine and other addictive drugs (Di Chiara & Imperato, 1988; Henningfield, Schuh & Jarvik, 1995; Imperato, Mulas & Di Chiara, 1986). Nicotine also produces reinforcing effects by providing relief of withdrawal symptoms, modulation of mood, and weight control (Henningfield, Miyasato & Jasinski, 1985).

The reinforcing effects of nicotine can be conditioned to stimuli associated with smoking. From an operant learning model, the smoker associates smoking a cigarette in specific situations with the rewarding effects of nicotine. Eventually, specific environmental situations, such as after a meal, with coffee or an alcoholic beverage, or around other smokers, become powerful cues capable of eliciting conditioned responses. Experimental studies have shown that exposure to environmental cues associated with smoking can elicit physiological responses consistent with conditioning effects (Rickard-Figueroa & Zeichner, 1985; Samuet & Dittmar, 1985), and that pattern of responsivity may be related to risk for smoking relapse (Niaura, Rohsenow et al., 1988; Niaura, Abrams et al., 1989). Moreover, sensory aspects of smoking behavior—including the handling, taste, and smell of the smoke—acquire powerful and persistent reinforcing effects which are not surprising in light of the approximately 75,000 pairings of such stimuli with each puff-delivered dose of nicotine self-administered by a pack-per-day smoker each year.

Tolerance. Within the course of a single day, cigarette smokers develop tolerance to many of the effects of nicotine, yet regain sensitivity after overnight abstinence from smoking. Individuals appear to differ in their sensitivity to nicotine, starting with initial exposure. The rate of development of tolerance following continued exposure to nicotine also varies across individuals. The "sensitivity" model of tolerance suggests that individual differences in vulnerability to tolerance and dependence are related to constitutional factors (i.e., initial sensitivity to nicotine) and environmental factors (Pomerleau, Collins et al., 1993). Persons with high innate sensitivity experience more intense aversive and rewarding effects of nicotine. For those individuals, initial exposure to nicotine leads quickly to the enhancement of functional tolerance. Conversely, other persons are relatively insensitive to nicotine and have limited capability to develop tolerance and, depending on prevailing environmental and social conditions, may never become smokers. "Chippers" (light smokers who smoke no more than five cigarettes per day at least four days per week) appear to be relatively insensitive to nicotine (Shiffman, Zettler-Segal et al., 1992) and are able to smoke without developing additional tolerance and dependence. Findings from animal and human studies generally have supported the hypothesis that tolerance to nicotine is linked to initial sensitivity (e.g., Collins & Marks, 1991; Pomerleau, Hariharan et al., 1993). However, the evidence to date, while provocative, is limited and awaits further examination of innate differences in sensitivity in people with different levels of nicotine exposure and smoking patterns.

Withdrawal. Withdrawal symptoms, as described in the *Diagnostic and Statistical Manual of Mental Disorders, Fourth Edition* (American Psychiatric Association, 1994), or *DSM-IV*, are believed to be due primarily to nicotine deprivation. Diagnostically, the presence of at least four of the following signs occurring within 24 hours of abrupt cessation of nicotine use or reduction in the amount of nicotine use constitutes nicotine withdrawal: (1) dysphoric or depressed mood, (2) insomnia, (3) irritability, frustration, or anger, (4) anxiety, (5) difficulty concentrating, (6) restlessness, (7) decreased heart rate, and (8) increased appetite or weight gain. Most symptoms of withdrawal reach maximal intensity 24 to 48 hours after cessation and gradually diminish over a period of two weeks. That the abstinence symptoms are nicotine-specific has been shown repeatedly in controlled laboratory studies (e.g., Henningfield & Nemeth-Coslett, 1988; Pickworth, Herning & Henningfield, 1989; Snyder, Davis & Henningfield, 1989) and in clinical trials of nicotine replacement therapy (e.g., Hughes, Gust et al., 1991; Schneider, Jarvik & Forsythe, 1984). In general, the administration of nicotine produces relief of these symptoms, however, the degree of relief is related to the dose of the nicotine administered.

Summary. Biobehavioral factors explain the development of nicotine dependence, human cigarette smoking behavior, and treatment challenges. For heavily dependent smokers, the first cigarette of the day is smoked within minutes of awakening. The rapid delivery of nicotine to the brain produces nearly immediate pharmacologic effects, and, in some cases, reversal of withdrawal symptoms. Most smokers regulate their nicotine intake by smoking a certain number of cigarettes per day that allow them to achieve the desired effects of smoking while minimizing withdrawal discomfort (Benowitz, 1992). Learning takes place such that stimuli paired with smoking can function to maintain smoking behavior controlled by nicotine. Taken together, these strong behavior controlling effects of cigarette smoking suggest that treatment of nicotine dependence can be accomplished based on the modifications of underlying biobehavioral mechanisms.

TREATMENT OF TOBACCO DEPENDENCE

The management of drug dependence is recognized as involving the integration of psychotherapeutic and medication-based approaches (Henningfield & Singleton, 1994). In the case of tobacco dependence, pharmacological developments over the past decade have outpaced all other forms of treatment (Fiore, Bailey et al., 1996; Shiffman, 1993; The Smoking Cessation Clinical Practice Guideline Panel and Staff, 1996). Medications with proven efficacy can help smokers deal with the nicotine dependence aspect of tobacco smoking. While nicotine delivering medications continue to dominate the armamentarium of approved indications, non-nicotine medications have recently been introduced.

Nicotine Replacement Therapy (NRT). The most widely used and accepted pharmacological treatment of nicotine addiction involves using nicotine itself as an agonist drug replacement. In essence, NRT provides the dependent smoker with a safer form of nicotine delivery, one that mimics some of the pharmacological effects but with lower abuse liability. None of the kinetic profiles of NRT resemble the arterial concentration spike, or rapid entry of nicotine to the brain created from inhaling nicotine into the lungs (Henningfield, 1995). The pharmacokinetics of several forms of NRT vary widely from each other and in comparison to the cigarette. Implications of these differences will be discussed in the following sections.

All forms of NRT have been shown to adequately suppress pharmacologically mediated withdrawal symptoms, and, to some extent, maintain a level of tolerance that attenuates the reinforcing properties of smoking. NRT medications are approved for use as temporary aids while the individual develops alternate behavioral patterns to maintain a smoke-free lifestyle. Long-term use of NRT, while infrequent, appears to be significantly less harmful than the risks of continued smoking and may be an appropriate application for people who have difficulty sustaining abstinence from tobacco. All forms of NRT are superior to their respective placebos, with highest efficacy rates achieved when NRT is used as an adjunct to behaviorally-based counseling (see Table 1).

Nicotine Polacrilex: The use of nicotine polacrilex ("gum") was approved by the FDA in 1984, and thereafter marketed under the trade name Nicorette®. It is currently dispensed with 2 mg or 4 mg of nicotine bound to an ion-exchange resin and incorporated into a gum base. "Chewing" the gum releases nicotine, which then is absorbed into the circulation solely across the buccal mucosa (Sachs, 1989); however, the exact amount of nicotine released and its bioavailability are largely determined by how the gum is chewed. Even when the gum is used according to the recommended "chew and park" technique, only 54% of the nicotine is extracted, whereas 46% remains bound to the ion-exchange resin (Benowitz, Jacob & Savanapridi, 1987). The bioavailability of nicotine from nicotine polacrilex varies across individuals but averages about 50% of the labeled dose. Clinical trials have reported plasma nicotine concentrations of 8–13.3 μg/L and 22.5 μg/L achieved with *ad libitum* use of 2 mg and 4 mg gum, respectively (Schneider, Lunell et al., 1996). Blood levels peak about 20 to 30 minutes after administration of a dose.

Numerous research studies have demonstrated the clinical efficacy of nicotine gum in suppressing withdrawal symptoms and improving abstinence outcomes (Hughes, 1991b, 1993; Lam, Sze et al., 1987; Silagy, Mant et al., 1994; Tang, Law & Wald, 1994). The 4 mg strength is indicated for the treatment of the more highly dependent smoker who smokes 25 or more cigarettes per day or has a score of greater than 6 on the Fagerström Test for Nicotine Dependence (Glover, Sachs et al., 1996; Herrera, Franco et al., 1995; Kornitzer, Kittel et al., 1987; Sachs, 1995). The main benefit of the gum formulation is its ability to provide the patient with "on demand" ability to obtain small amounts of nicotine. Conversely, the main limitation of this NRT formulation is that some patients are unwilling or unable to comply with the chew and park dosing procedure.

Transdermal Nicotine: The first transdermal delivery systems were approved by the FDA in 1991. The patch releases nicotine that permeates the skin, is absorbed through the capillary bed, then passes into the blood stream. Currently available patches are approved and proven effective when worn for 24 hours (Habitrol®, Prostep®), 16 hours (Nicotrol®), or 16 or 24 hours (Nicoderm CQ®); however, pa-

TABLE 1. Comparison of NRT Products

Dimension	Gum (4 mg)	Patch	Nasal Spray	Oral Inhaler
Availability	OTC	OTC	Rx	Rx
Flexible dosing	yes	no	yes	yes
Allows for extinction of sensory/ritual reinforcers	no	yes	no	no
Speed of onset (T_{max})	10 mins	2–12 hrs	5–10 mins	15 mins
Frequency of use (doses per day)	9–20	1	13–20	6–16
Effort required for proper use	high	low	moderate	high
Mimics oral/behavioral aspects of smoking	no	no	no	yes
Primary side effects	mouth/throat soreness	topical skin irritation	nose/throat irritation, runny nose	cough, throat irritation

tients who experience persistent sleep disturbances should remove the patch before going to bed for the night, regardless of the brand (Fiore, Smith et al., 1993). They come in dosing regimens of 21-14-7 mg (Habitrol, Nicoderm CQ), 15-mg (Nicotrol), or 22-11 mg (Prostep).

The relative effectiveness of the different patch brands has not been directly evaluated, but the differences in dosing parameters, such as speed of delivery and peak blood level, suggest that people who are either intolerant or refractory to one patch brand might benefit from another. The patches also differ widely in the characteristics of their behavioral support programs. Persons smoking more than 10 cigarettes per day are generally instructed to start with the strongest dose of a brand. Lower level smokers begin on the intermediate level dose. For the patch brands that provide a step down weaning regimen of patches, dose weaning should be achieved over a period of two to six weeks following four to eight weeks on the initial dose. Patients vary widely in their dosing needs, duration of treatment required, as well as need for a weaning regimen (Sachs, 1994). Transdermally-delivered nicotine has a relatively slower rising time, with peak levels occurring within two to 10 hours after application (depending on the patch), compared to nicotine gum and other NRT systems (Benowitz, 1993; Henningfield, 1995).

Nicotine patches relieve withdrawal symptoms in abstinent subjects (e.g., Levin, Westman et al., 1994) and significantly increase quit rates over those produced by placebo treatment (Hughes, 1995; Silagy, Mant et al., 1994; Tang, Law & Wald, 1994; Fiore, Bailey et al., 1996). The hypothesis that heavily dependent subjects might benefit from higher transdermal nicotine doses that produce more adequate replacement has received mixed support (Jorenby, Smith et al., 1995; Dale, Hurt et al., 1995). However, it recently has been shown that low dependent smokers (defined on the basis of serum cotinine level) are substantially more successful in quitting smoking with transdermal nicotine (15 mg) compared to placebo (Paoletti, Fornai et al., 1996).

The main benefits of the transdermal formulations may be relative ease of use and high degree of compliance with dosing regimens compared to other systems (Jorenby, Keehn & Flore, 1995). The major limitation may be the absence of moment-to-moment dosage control that some patients find important.

Nicotine Nasal Spray: A relatively faster NRT system is the nicotine nasal spray (NNS), approved by the FDA in 1996. The nasal spray is used by pressing a pumping mechanism that delivers aerosolized nicotine across the nasal mucosa. One dose consists of one squirt in each nostril, for a total of 1.0 mg of nicotine. Patients are instructed to administer 13 to 20 doses per day. Primary side effects (such as nose/throat irritation, runny nose, watering eyes, coughing) generally decrease as tolerance develops over the first seven days of use. Compared to the other replacement systems, nasal delivery causes a faster rise in plasma nicotine concentrations. One study reported a mean rise time of 11.5 minutes to reach peak venous blood levels of 8.1 ng/ml of nicotine following a single dose of 1 mg NNS (Johansson, Olsson et al., 1991).

Results from three independent studies have clearly demonstrated that NNS is more effective than placebo spray in producing sustained one-year abstinence rates (Sutherland, Stapleton et al., 1992; Hjalmarson, Franzon et al., 1994; Schneider, Olmstead et al., 1995). The more aggressive nicotine dosing capability of the nasal system may make it especially useful for highly addicted smokers. The main limitation of this formulation is that some patients do not tolerate the nasal and throat irritation.

Nicotine Inhaler: The nicotine inhaler, or "puffer," received FDA approval in 1997. The puffing device is assembled by sliding a nicotine cartridge into a plastic reusable holder. The cartridge consists of a porous plug impregnated with 10 mg of nicotine and 1 mg of menthol. Menthol is added to reduce the irritating effect of nicotine (Leischow, 1994). Each mouthpiece delivers up to 400 puffs of vaporized nicotine. The amount of nicotine obtained depends on number of puffs and temperature of the air passing through the plug. At room temperature, one puff delivers up to 13 micrograms of nicotine or the equivalent of about 10% to 20% of the nicotine obtained by puffing on a cigarette. At lower ambient air temperatures, less nicotine is extractable from the device and nicotine dosing capability is probably negligible in cooler outdoor settings. It takes at least 80 puffs from the inhaler to obtain the nicotine delivery typically provided by one cigarette (Leischow, Nilsson et al., 1996), although some people obtain negligible dose levels with even more intensive puffing procedures (Schuh, Schuh et al., 1997). In clinical trials, subjects generally are instructed to puff frequently, using at least four inhalers per day at a rate of about 100 puffs per use. Importantly, nicotine inhaled via the mouthpiece is absorbed mainly in the mouth and throat, rather than through the lungs, so that the kinetics more closely resemble those of 2 mg nicotine gum than the other formulations.

To date, three randomized, placebo-controlled studies have examined the efficacy of the nicotine inhaler for smoking cessation. These studies found higher rates of abstinence in the first few months for the active inhaler group compared with the placebo inhaler group (Schneider, Olmstead et al., 1996; Leischow, Nilsson et al., 1996; Tonnesen, Norregaard et al., 1993). Like nicotine gum, proper use of the inhaler appears to be related to the probability of success (Tonnesen, Norregaard et al., 1993). Using too few inhalers per day can result in dosing that is inadequate to suppress withdrawal symptoms. The major benefit of the inhaler formulation is that its use comes close to mimicking that of smoking a cigarette, which some patients find useful. The major limitation is the inability to extract adequate doses of nicotine to replace those obtained by smoking cigarettes.

Comparison of NRTs: The previous sections clearly indicate that each of the four different nicotine replacement delivery systems is effective in reducing withdrawal symptoms and improving abstinence outcomes. Consequently, a much broader range of NRT options is now available to the smoker and to the clinician. Understanding the distinguishing features of each delivery system is the first step toward individualizing NRT based on specific patient characteristics. Eight clinically relevant dimensions by which each product can be compared are as follows:

1. Availability. To date, only the polacrilex and transdermal delivering medications are available without a prescription. Both of these preparations are known as being generally safe, with low abuse potential (Henningfield & Keenan, 1993). Although there is less experience with the NNS and nicotine inhaler, a recent study demonstrated low potential for abuse relative to cigarettes (Schuh, Schuh, Henningfield, & Stitzer, 1997).
2. Flexible dosing. This dimension is related to the smokers ability to self-titrate nicotine dosage. All NRT products, with the exception of the patch, offer this type of flexibility. For some, self-titration provides a sense of control when experiencing acute high-risk smoking situations.
3. Allows for extinction of sensory/ritual reinforcers. Inversely related to the second dimension is the system's allowance for extinction of sensory/ritual reinforcers. The passive, inflexible administration of the patch weakens the associations between nicotine delivery in smoking-related situations, whereas self-administration of the acute systems (gum, NNS, inhaler) may continue to strengthen associative cues or triggers to smoke.
4. Speed of onset. The nasal spray and the patch have the fastest and slowest rates of nicotine absorption, respectively. It should be noted, however, that all of the systems are substantially slower than nicotine delivery from cigarettes.
5. Frequency of use. Except for the once-a-day dosing regimen of the patch, all of the NRT products require repeated dosing, spaced evenly throughout the day, in order to maintain adequate venous nicotine levels.
6. Effort required for proper use. This dimension can be rated on a scale from low (i.e., simple instruction, minimal effort) to high (i.e., detailed instruction, concentrated effort). The ease of application associated with the nicotine patch affords it the lowest effort rating. High effort ratings are given for the nicotine gum and the oral inhaler, because effective levels of nicotine absorption from either product depend on careful adherence to application instructions. Moreover, the work requirement per dose is highest for the inhaler, where the subject must puff 80–100 times to obtain the nicotine delivery typically provided by one cigarette.
7. Mimics oral/behavioral aspects of smoking. Both the gum and inhaler formulations provide oral sensory stimulation and behavioral activity, and use of the inhaler partially mimics the smoking of a cigarette.
8. Primary side effects. Commonly reported side effects for each nicotine medication consist mostly of local symptoms that are mild and transient. At present, the adverse effect profile of the nasal spray appears to be the least favorable of all the NRT preparations. In one large clinical trial (Sutherland, Stapleton et al., 1992) more than 80% of patients using the active spray reported nose/throat irritation, watering eyes, and coughing during the first week of use. Despite the frequency of these unpleasant experiences, dropout rates were low, suggestive of high tolerability.

Bupropion HCl: The first non-nicotine agent approved by the FDA for use in smoking cessation is the sustained-release formulation of bupropion hydrochloride, marketed as Zyban®. The antidepressant bupropion is of the aminoketone class, structurally dissimilar to other known antidepressant agents. Its mechanism of action as a smoking cessation aid is unknown, however it is presumed to act through noradrenergic and dopaminergic mechanisms as it can produce amphetamine-like stimulant effects (Ascher, Cole et al., 1995). The recommended dosing regimen is one 150 mg tablet in the morning for the first three days, increasing to 150 mg twice daily by the fourth day.

Careful patient screening is important to ensure that persons at risk for seizures or who are taking antidepressants or several other medications are not given bupropion. Patients in clinical trials also were limited to no more than two alcoholic beverages per week.

Smokers are instructed to use the medication for one week prior to quitting smoking, and for at least seven weeks after quitting. The most commonly reported side effects include dry mouth and difficulty in sleeping.

Information on the efficacy of bupropion is derived from two placebo-controlled, double-blind trials in nondepressed cigarette smokers (data on file, Glaxo Wellcome Inc.). In both studies, bupropion was used as an adjunct to smoking cessation counseling, with patients coming for weekly visits over the first seven weeks of the studies. In the dose-response trial, 615 male and female smokers received one of four treatments: bupropion SR 50 mg BID, bupropion SR 150 mg QD, bupropion SR 150 mg BID, or placebo. Results showed a dose-related increase in quit rates at end-of-treatment and 12-month follow-up, with bupropion SR at both 150 and 300 mg/day significantly more effective than placebo. A second multicenter trial (N = 893) compared bupropion SR 300 mg/day, the Habitrol 21 mg transdermal nicotine patch formulation, and the combination of these medications. Highest rates of continuous abstinence (through week 10) were observed for the bupropion/patch group (51%), compared to either individual treatment alone, although only the comparison with the patch group (32%) achieved statistical significance (p 0.01). General withdrawal symptoms were reduced, but relief of craving was erratic, leading to labeling indicating only that relief of craving varied across sites in clinical trials. The main benefit of bupropion may be the convenience of an oral medication that needs to be taken only two times per day. The main limitation may be the variety of contraindications to ensure that patients are not put at undue risk of seizures or adverse drug interactions.

OTHER AREAS OF MEDICATION DEVELOPMENT

This section summarizes the status of other state-of-the-art pharmacologic treatments and combinations of treatments that are being tested for smoking cessation. In most cases, conclusions about efficacy, safety, and abuse liability are tentative, pending additional research.

Nicotine Tablet. A new NRT product, a sublingual tablet (2 mg), has been developed and is the focus of an ongoing double-blind, placebo-controlled clinical trial (N = 241) in the United States (Glover, 1997). In this study, subjects are instructed to use 20 to 40 tablets per day for three months, then taper use by 25% for another three months. Complete abstinence rates at three months clearly favor the active (33%) over placebo (17%) group. The kinetic profile of the sublingual tablet is intended to be most similar to nicotine polacrilex with respect to dosing parameters. As such, the tablet may provide an alternative for smokers who would like to have the ability to respond to urges to smoke but are unable or unwilling to use nicotine gum.

Other Non-Nicotine Agents. Another intriguing treatment approach involves the use of agents that target symptoms associated with cigarette smoking or smoking cessation. Nicotine withdrawal, for example, results in considerable negative affect (Hall, Munoz et al., 1993), and for some smokers, may represent the emergence of preexisting psychopathology (Goldstein, 1987; Hughes & Hatsukami, 1987). In addition, both past and present history of depression predicts worse outcomes for smoking cessation (Anda, Williamson et al., 1990; Covey, Glassman & Stetner, 1990; Glassman, Helzer et al., 1990; Hughes, Hatsukami et al., 1986). Thus, it is conceivable that antidepressant medications may counteract withdrawal symptoms and, in some smokers, treat an underlying disorder.

Only a handful of studies have evaluated the role of antidepressants in depressed smokers. As described earlier, the antidepressant, bupropion, has now been approved as efficacious in the treatment of nicotine dependence in nondepressed persons. Ferry and colleagues (1992) reported higher cessation rates in bupropion-treated smokers compared to placebo-treated smokers; however, subjects with the highest depression scores were least likely to stop smoking in either group. In another preliminary study, fluoxetine treatment prior to quitting significantly reduced subsyndromal depressive symptoms in smokers with a history of depression (Dalack, Glassman et al., 1995; Niaura, Goldstein et al., 1995). Hall, Reus et al. (1996) found that subjects receiving nortriptyline had better long-term treatment outcome than placebo subjects, but that treatment effectiveness was not related to having a history of depression. At present, with the exception of bupropion, the potential role of antidepressant medications for smokers in general, as well as for smokers with a depression history is unclear.

As with antidepressants, selective anxiolytic medications could be useful in smokers for whom anxiety is a prominent symptom. In a recent randomized, double-blind, placebo-controlled trial, buspirone significantly increased smoking cessation rates in high-anxiety smokers compared to placebo-treated high-anxiety smokers (Cinciripini, Lapitsky et al., 1995). All subjects received medication in conjunction with cognitive-behavioral treatment. No differences were found at three-month follow-up, however, suggesting that the buspirone advantage was short-lived. Moreover, a second trial failed to support the differential usefulness of buspirone in high versus low anxiety smokers (Schneider, Olmstead et al., 1996).

NRT Combinations. Combining nicotine replacement products is a promising new approach to increase cessation rates over that achieved by a single delivery system. For example, findings from recent studies suggest that the transdermal patch with nicotine gum is more effective than either treatment alone (Fagerström, Schneider & Lunell, 1993; Kornitzer, Boutsen et al., 1995). Similarly, preliminary outcome results on the efficacy of combining transdermal patch with nicotine spray (Sutherland, 1997) or with nicotine inhalers (Westman, 1997) are encouraging. Another form of combination use is the sequential use of nicotine patch to achieve tobacco abstinence then follow-up use of nicotine gum or inhaler to sustain abstinence (Henningfield, 1995).

The therapeutic effects of nicotine medications in combination with other non-nicotine agents have been evaluated in a few recent studies. Rose and colleagues (1989, 1994a, 1994b) have conducted a series of treatment studies based on an agonist-antagonist model. Specifically, co-administration of nicotine and mecamylamine is expected to reduce the number of receptors that would otherwise be available to respond to the nicotine from cigarettes. With fewer receptor sites open, the reinforcing effects of smoking are reduced. Support for this novel treatment model comes from a randomized, double-blind, placebo-controlled clinical trial (N = 48), in which the concurrent administration of oral mecamylamine with transdermal nicotine produced higher rates of continuous abstinence compared to patch treatment alone (at 12 months, 37.5% versus 4.2%, respectively). Efforts to develop a single transdermal patch containing nicotine and mecamylamine are underway.

The rationale for adding an antidepressant to NRT is based on evidence that affective symptomatology related to nicotine withdrawal, if left untreated, could contribute to relapse after smoking cessation. Support for this approach was provided by the use of bupropion in combination with the Habitrol nicotine patch which showed a trend, albeit nonsignificant, of improved efficacy of the patch plus bupropion combination when compared to the patch alone (data on file, Glaxo Wellcome Inc.). However, in a randomized double-blind study with another antidepressant, 101 smokers received either the combination of fluoxetine (20 mg/day) and nicotine inhaler (6–12 units/day recommended) or placebo and inhaler (Blondal, 1997). Fluoxetine began 16 days prior to quit day. Contrary to the hypothesis, fluoxetine did not improve abstinence rates when combined with nicotine inhaler in this unselected group of smokers. Further studies are needed to determine whether this treatment combination might significantly benefit a subgroup of high depressive smokers.

COMBINING BEHAVIORAL AND PHARMACOLOGICAL APPROACHES

In the case of tobacco dependence treatment, both pharmacological and behavioral interventions can be efficacious independently, but best results are often achieved when the two types of therapy are combined (Hughes, 1995). In fact, Henningfield and Singleton (1994) argued that medication-based therapy or treatment implies that in addition to dispensing a medication, fundamentals of therapeutics (namely, individualized prescription, advice giving, regular follow-up) were practiced. Beyond these fundamentals of therapeutic intervention, it is clear that as attention to behavioral aspects of the dependency are increasingly addressed, so is treatment efficacy increasingly improved. Presumably, this is because nicotine medications address biological factors of dependence (e.g., by suppressing withdrawal), while behavior therapy addresses environmental and behavioral aspects of dependence by teaching alternate coping skills to manage cravings and other relapse factors.

Recently, Lichtenstein and Glasgow (1997) proposed a framework that recognizes the interrelatedness of interventions as they exert their influence on three key factors that influence quitting: dependence, motivation, and environmental supports and barriers. For example, a new medication might target dependence, while in a secondary fashion serve to raise one's motivation or readiness to quit. Likewise, coping skills might reduce barriers to quitting (e.g., presence of a smoking spouse), while at the same time, help the highly-dependent smoker handle cravings and other withdrawal-related symptoms. The effectiveness of combined treatment programs depends on the treated individual's ability and willingness to comply with the requirements of both treatment interventions. In the case of pharmacotherapy, this means taking required medications in the correct doses over a specified time period. In behavioral interventions, this often involves daily self-monitoring and coping skills training.

Combining pharmacotherapy and behavioral interventions has long been advocated in clinical settings. With the availability of NRT over-the-counter, recent attempts have been made to develop combined packages that can be disseminated into a public-health or population-focused arena. For example, Nicotrol NS (nasal spray) offers the Pathways to Change® Program, a set of individualized guidelines for quitting smoking, along with a toll-free telephone hotline service for additional assistance. Bupropion provides the smoker with a free personalized smoking cessation program (Advantage Plan®), consisting of support materials, telephone counseling, and individualized progress reports. Data are lacking on whether consumers actually use these support programs and to what extent these programs enhance the effectiveness of the pharmacological treatment.

CONCLUSIONS

The U.S. population has been giving up smoking in increasing numbers. In 1993, the quit ratio, or proportion of ever-smokers who are now ex-smokers, was 49.6%, representing almost half of an estimated 46 million former smokers (CDC, 1994). This significant trend (USDHHS, 1989) reflects myriad influences over the past two decades. One important influence has been the increasing availability of effective smoking cessation programs, based on a sophisticated body of empirical research. This has been most demonstrable in the development of new medications. Effective pharmacotherapies, however, do not obviate the need for effective behavioral interventions. Indeed, the application of combined treatments is likely to best "cover" the range of factors maintaining tobacco smoking. The next challenge in the evolution of smoking cessation treatment will be to increase our ability to provide individualized therapy in large populations and thereby contribute to further improvements in the cost-efficacy of combined treatments.

ACKNOWLEDGMENT: This research was supported in part by a grant from the National Institute on Drug Abuse to Dr. Schmitz (R01 DA08888).

REFERENCES

American Psychiatric Association (1994). *Diagnostic and Statistical Manual of Mental Disorders, 4th Edition.* Washington, DC: The Association.

Anda RF, Williamson DF, Escobedo LG, Mast EE, Giovino GA & Remington PL (1990). Depression and the dynamics of smoking. *Journal of the American Medical Association* 264:1541–1545.

Ascher JA, Cole JO, Colin JN et al. (1995). Bupropion: A review of its mechanism of antidepressant activity. *Journal of Clinical Psychiatry* 56:395–401.

Balfour DJK (1991). The neurochemical mechanisms underlying nicotine tolerance and dependence. In JA Pratt (ed.) *The Biological Basis of Drug Tolerance and Dependence.* London, England: Academic Press, 121–151.

Becker DM, Windsor R, Ockene JK et al. (1993). Setting the policy, education, and research agenda to reduce tobacco use. *Circulation* 88:1381–1386.

Benowitz NL (1990). Clinical pharmacology of inhaled drugs of abuse: Implications in understanding nicotine dependence. In CN Chiang & RL Hawks (eds.) *Research Findings on Smoking of Abused Substances (NIDA Research Monograph 99).* Rockville, MD: National Institute on Drug Abuse, 12.

Benowitz NL (1992). Cigarette smoking and nicotine addiction. *Medical Clinics of North America* 76:415–437.

Benowitz NL (1993). Nicotine replacement therapy: What has been accomplished—Can we do better? *Drugs* 45:157–170.

Benowitz NL, Jacob P III & Savanapridi C (1987). Determinants of nicotine intake while chewing nicotine polacrilex gum. *Clinical Pharmacology and Therapeutics* 41:467–473.

Blondal T (1997). New pharmacological treatments for nicotine dependence. Presented at the 3rd Annual Meeting of The Society for Research on Nicotine and Tobacco, Nashville, TN, June.

Centers for Disease Control (1994). Cigarette smoking among adults—United States, 1993. *Morbidity and Mortality Weekly Reports* 43:925–930.

Cinciripini PM, Lapitsky L, Seay S, Wallfisch A, Meyer WJ & Vunakis H (1995). A placebo-controlled evaluation of the effects of buspirone on smoking cessation: Differences between high- and low-anxiety smokers. *Journal of Clinical Psychopharmacology* 15:182–191.

Collins AC & Marks MJ (1991). Progress towards the development of animal models of smoking-related behaviors. *Journal of Addictive Diseases* 10:109–126.

Covey LS, Glassman AH & Stetner F (1990). Depression and depressive symptoms in smoking cessation. *Comprehensive Psychiatry* 31:350–354.

Dalack GW, Glassman AH, Rivelli S & Lirio C (1995). Mood, major depression, and fluoxetine response in cigarette smokers. *American Journal of Psychiatry* 152:398–403.

Dale LC, Hurt RD, Offord KP, Lawson GM, Croghan IT & Schroeder DR (1995). High-dose nicotine patch therapy: Percentage of replacement and smoking cessation. *Journal of the American Medical Association* 274:1353–1358.

DiChiara G & Imperato A (1988). Opposite effects of Mu and Kappa Opiate Agonists on dopamine release in the nucleus accumbens and in the dorsal caudate of freely moving rats. *Journal of Pharmacology and Experimental Therapeutics* 244:1067–1080.

Fagerström KO & Säwe U (1996). The pathophysiology of nicotine dependence: Treatment options and the cardiovascular safety of nicotine. *Cardiovascular Risk Factors* 6:135–143.

Fagerström KO & Schneider NG (1989). Measuring nicotine dependence: A review of the Fagerström Tolerance Questionnaire. *Journal of Behavioral Medicine* 12:159–182.

Fagerström KO, Schneider NG & Lunell E (1993). Effectiveness of nicotine patch and nicotine gum as individual versus combined treatments for tobacco withdrawal symptoms. *Psychopharmacology* 111:271–277.

Ferry LH, Robbins AS, Scariati PD et al. (1992). Enhancement of smoking cessation using the antidepressant bupropion hydrochloride. *Circulation* (Suppl)86:I-671. Abstract.

Fiore MC, Smith SS, Jorenby DE & Baker TB (1993). The effectiveness of the nicotine patch for smoking cessation: A meta-analysis. *Journal of the American Medical Association* 271:1940–1947.

Fiore MC, Bailey WC, Cohen SJ et al. (1996). *Smoking Cessation.* Clinical Practice Guideline No 18. Rockville, MD: Agency for Health Care Policy and Research (AHCPR Publication No. 96-0692).

Fisher EB Jr, Lichtenstein E, Haire-Joshu D, Morgan GD & Rehberg HR (1993). Methods, successes, and failures of smoking cessation programs. *Annual Review of Medicine* 44:481–513.

Glassman AH, Helzer JE, Covey LS, Cottler LB, Stetner F, Tipp JE & Johnson J (1990). Smoking, smoking cessation and major depression. *Journal of the American Medical Association* 264:1546–1549.

Glover ED (1997). Safety and efficacy of a nicotine sublingual tablet for smoking cessation: 3-month preliminary data. Presented at the 3rd Annual Meeting of The Society for Research on Nicotine and Tobacco, Nashville, TN.

Glover ED, Sachs DPL, Stitzer ML, Rennard SI, Wadland WC, Pomerleau OF, Nowak RT, Daughton DM, Glover PN, Hughes JR & Gross J (1996). Smoking cessation in highly dependent smokers with 4 mg nicotine polacrilex. *American Journal of Health Behavior* 20:319–332.

Goldstein A (1987). Criteria of a pharmacologic withdrawal syndrome. *Archives of General Psychiatry* 44:392.

Hall SM, Munoz RF, Reus VI & Sees KL (1993). Nicotine, negative affect, and depression. *Journal of Consulting and Clinical Psychology* 5:761–767.

Hall SM, Reus VI, Munoz RF, Sees KL, Humfleet G & Frederick S (1996). Nortriptyline and cognitive-behavioral treatment of cigarette smoking. Paper presented at the scientific meeting of the College on Problems of Drug Dependence, San Juan, Puerto Rico.

Hajek P (1996). Current issues in behavioral and pharmacological approaches to smoking cessation. *Addictive Behaviors* 21:699–707.

Heishman SJ, Taylor RC & Henningfield JE (1994). Nicotine and smoking: A review of effects on human performance. *Experimental and Clinical Psychopharmacology* 2:345–395.

Henningfield JE (1995). Nicotine medications for smoking cessation. *The New England Journal of Medicine* 333:1196–1203.

Henningfield JE & Goldberg SR (1983). Nicotine as a reinforcer in human subjects and laboratory animals. *Pharmacology, Biochemistry and Behavior* 19:989–992.

Henningfield JE & Keenan RM (1993). Nicotine delivery kinetics and abuse liability. *Journal of Consulting and Clinical Psychology* 61:743–750.

Henningfield JE & Nemeth-Coslett R (1988). Nicotine dependence: Interface between tobacco and tobacco-related disease. *Chest* 93:37S–55S.

Henningfield JE & Singleton EG (1994). Managing drug dependence: Psychotherapy or pharmacotherapy? *CNS Drugs* 1(5):317–322.

Henningfield JE, Miyasato K & Jasinski DR (1985). Abuse liability and pharmacodynamic characteristics of intravenous and inhaled nicotine. *Journal of Pharmacology and Experimental Therapeutics* 234:1–12.

Henningfield JE, Schuh LM & Jarvik ME (1995). Pathophysiology of tobacco dependence. In FE Bloom & DJ Kupfer (eds.) *Psychopharmacology: The Fourth Generation of Progress.* NY: Raven Press.

Henningfield JE, Stapleton JM, Benowitz NL, Grayson RF & London ED (1993). Higher levels of nicotine in arterial than in venous blood after cigarette smoking. *Drug & Alcohol Dependence* 33:23–9.

Herrera N, Franco R, Herrera L, Partidas A, Rolando R & Fagerstrom KO (1995). Nicotine gum, 2 and 4 mg, for nicotine dependence. *Chest* 108:447–451.

Hjalmarson A, Franzon M, Westin A & Wiklund O (1994). Effect of nicotine nasal spray on smoking cessation: A randomized placebo-controlled, double-blind study. *Archives of Internal Medicine* 154:2567–2572.

Hughes JR (1991). Distinguishing withdrawal relief and direct effects of smoking. *Psychopharmacology* 104:409–410.

Hughes JR (1991). Combined psychological and nicotine gum treatment for smoking: A critical review. *Journal of Substance Abuse* 3:337–350.

Hughes JR (1993). Pharmacotherapy for smoking cessation: Unvalidated assumptions, anomalies, and suggestions for future research. *Journal of Consulting and Clinical Psychology* 61:751–760.

Hughes JR (1995). Combining behavioral therapy and pharmacotherapy for smoking cessation: An update. In LS Onken, JD Blaine & JJ Boren (eds.) *Integrating Behavioral Therapies with Medications in the Treatment of Drug Dependence (NIDA Research Monograph 150)*. Rockville, MD: National Institute on Drug Abuse, 92–109.

Hughes JR & Hatsukami D (1987). In reply. *Archives of General Psychiatry* 44:392.

Hughes JR, Hatsukami DK, Mitchell JE & Dahlgren LA (1986). Prevalence of smoking among psychiatric outpatients. *American Journal of Psychiatry* 143:993–997.

Hughes JR, Gust SW, Skoog K, Keenan RM & Fenwick JW (1991). Symptoms of tobacco withdrawal: A replication and extension. *Archives of General Psychiatry* 48:52–59.

Imperato A, Mulas A & Di Chiara G (1986). Nicotine preferentially stimulates dopamine release in the limbic system of freely moving rats. *European Journal of Pharmacology* 132:337–338.

Johansson CJ, Olsson P, Bende M, Carlsson T & Gunnarsson PO (1991). Absolute bioavailability of nicotine applied to different nasal regions. *European Journal of Clinical Pharmacology* 41:585–588.

Jorenby DE, Keehn DS & Flore MC (1995). Comparative efficacy and tolerability of nicotine replacement therapies. *CNS Drugs* 3:227–236.

Jorenby DE, Smith SS, Fiore MC, Hurt RD, Offord KP, Croghan IT, Hays JT, Lewis SF & Baker TB (1995). Varying nicotine patch dose and type of smoking cessation counseling. *Journal of the American Medical Association* 274:1347–1352.

Kirby K, Schmitz J & Stitzer ML (1997). Integrating behavioral and pharmacological treatments. In BA Johnson & J Roache (eds.) *Drug Addiction and Its Treatment: Nexus of Neuroscience and Behavior*. New York, NY: Raven Press, 403–419.

Klesges RC, Ward KD & DeBon M (1996). Smoking cessation: A successful behavioral/pharmacologic interface. *Clinical Psychology Review* 16:479–496.

Kornitzer M, Kittel F, Dramaix M & Bourdoux P (1987). A double-blind study of 2 mg versus 4 mg nicotine-gum in an industrial setting. *Journal of Psychosomatic Research* 31:171–176.

Kornitzer M, Boutsen M, Dramaix M, Thijs J & Gustavsson G (1995). Combined use of nicotine patch and gum in smoking cessation: A placebo-controlled trial. *Preventive Medicine* 21:41–47.

Lam W, Sze PC, Sacks HS & Chalmers TC (1987). Meta-analysis of randomised controlled trials of nicotine chewing-gum. *Lancet* 27–30.

Leischow SJ (1994). The nicotine vaporizer. *Health Values* 18:4–9.

Leischow SJ, Nilsson F, Franzon M, Hill A, Otte P & Merikle EP (1996). Efficacy of the nicotine inhaler as an adjunct to smoking cessation. *American Journal of Health and Behavior* 20:364–371.

Levin ED, Westman EC, Stein RM, Carnahan E, Sanchez M, Herman S, Behm FM & Rose JE (1994). Nicotine skin patch treatment increases abstinence, decreases withdrawal symptoms, and attenuates rewarding effects of smoking. *Journal of Clinical Psychopharmacology* 14:41–49.

Lichtenstein E & Glasgow RE (1997). A pragmatic framework for smoking cessation: Implications for clinical and public health programs. *Psychology of Addictive Behaviors* 11:142–151.

McGinnis JM & Foege WH (1994). Actual causes of death in the United States. *Journal of the American Medical Association* 270:2207–12.

Niaura R, Abrams D, Demuth B, Pinto R & Monti P (1989). Responses to smoking-related stimuli and early relapse to smoking. *Addictive Behaviors* 14:419–428.

Niaura RS, Rohsenow DJ, Binkoff JA, Monti PM, Pedraza M & Abrams DB (1988). Relevance of cue reactivity to understanding alcohol and smoking relapse. *Journal of Abnormal Psychology* 97:133–152.

Niaura R, Goldstein MG, Depue J, Keuthen N, Kristeller J & Abrams D (1995). Fluoxetine, symptoms of depression, and smoking cessation. Paper presented at the Society of Behavioral Medicine's Annual Meeting, March.

Oldendorf WH (1992). Some relationships between addiction and drug delivery to the brain. *NIDA Research Monograph 120: Bioavailability of Drugs to the Brain and the Blood-Brain Barrier*. Rockville, MD: National Institute on Drug Abuse, 13–25.

Paoletti P, Fornai E, Maggiorelli F, Puntoni R, Viegi G, Carrozzi L, Corlando A, Gustavsson G, Säwe U & Giuntini C (1996). Importance of baseline cotinine plasma values in smoking cessation: Results from a double-blind study with nicotine patch. *European Respiratory Journal* 9:643–651.

Pickworth WB, Herning RI & Henningfield JE (1989). Spontaneous EEG changes during tobacco abstinence and nicotine substitution in human volunteers. *Journal of Pharmacology and Experimental Therapeutics* 251:976–982.

Pomerleau OF (1992). Nicotine and the central nervous system: Behavioral effects of cigarette smoking. *American Journal of Medicine* 93:1A2S–1A7S.

Pomerleau OF, Collins AC, Shiffman S & Pomerleau CS (1993). Why some people smoke and others do not:

New perspectives. *Journal of Consulting and Clinical Psychology* 61:723–731.

Pomerleau OF, Hariharan M, Pomerleau CS, Cameron OG & Guthrie SK (1993). Differences between smokers and never-smokers in sensitivity to nicotine: A preliminary report. *Addiction* 88:113–118.

Rickard-Figueroa K & Zeichner A (1985). Assessment of smoking urge and its concomitants under an environmental smoking cue manipulation. *Addictive Behaviors* 10:249–256.

Rose JE, Sampson A, Levin ED & Henningfield JE (1989). Mecamylamine increases nicotine preference and attenuates nicotine discrimination. *Pharmacology, Biochemistry and Behavior* 32:933–938.

Rose JE, Behm FM, Westman EC, Levin ED, Stein RM & Ripka GV (1994a). Mecamylamine combined with nicotine skin patch facilitates smoking cessation beyond nicotine patch treatment alone. *Clinical Pharmacology and Therapeutics* 56:86–99.

Rose JE, Behm FM, Westman EC, Levin ED, Stein RM, Lane JD & Ripka GV (1994b). Combined effects of nicotine and mecamylamine in attenuating smoking satisfaction. *Experimental and Clinical Psychopharmacology* 2:328–344.

Sachs DPL (1989). Nicotine polacrilex: Practical use requirements. *Current Pulmonology* 10:141–159.

Sachs DPL (1994). The use and efficacy of nicotine patches. *Journal of Smoking Related Diseases* 5:183–193.

Sachs DPL (1995). Effectiveness of the 4-mg dose of nicotine polacrilex for the initial treatment of high-dependent smokers. *Archives of Internal Medicine* 155:1973–1980.

Samuet JL & Dittmar A (1985). Heat loss and anticipatory finger vasoconstriction induced by a smoking of a single cigarette. *Physiology and Behavior* 35:229–232.

Schneider NG, Jarvik ME & Forsythe AB (1984). Nicotine versus placebo gum in the alleviation of withdrawal during smoking cessation. *Addictive Behaviors* 9:149–156.

Schneider NG, Lunell E, Olmstead RE & Fagerström KO (1996). Clinical pharmacokinetics of nasal nicotine delivery: A review and comparison to other nicotine systems. *Clinical Pharmacokinetics* 31:65–80.

Schneider NG, Olmstead R, Nilsson F, Mody F, Franzon M & Doan K (1996). Efficacy of a nicotine inhaler in smoking cessation: A double-blind, placebo-controlled trial. *Addiction* 91:1293–1306.

Schneider NG, Olmstead RE, Sloan K, Steinberg C, Daims R & Brown HV (1996). Buspirone in smoking cessation: A placebo-controlled trial. *Clinical Pharmacology and Therapeutics* 60:568–575.

Schneider NG, Olmstead R, Mody FV, Doan K, Franzon M, Jarvik ME & Steinberg C (1995). Efficacy of a nicotine nasal spray in smoking cessation: A placebo-controlled, double-blind trial. *Addiction* 90:1671–1682.

Schuh KJ, Schuh LM, Henningfield JE & Stitzer ML (1997). Nicotine nasal spray and vapor inhaler: Abuse liability assessment. *Psychopharmacology* 130:352–361.

Sherwood N (1993). Effects of nicotine on human psychomotor performance. *Human Psychopharmacology* 8:155–84.

Shiffman S (1993). Smoking cessation treatment: Any progress? *Journal of Consulting and Clinical Psychology* 61:718–722.

Shiffman S, Zettler-Segal M, Kassel J, Patsy J, Benowitz NE & O'Brien G (1992). Nicotine elimination and tolerance in non-dependent cigarette smokers. *Psychopharmacology* 109:449–456.

Silagy C, Mant D, Fowler G & Lodge M (1994). Meta-analysis on efficacy of nicotine replacement therapies in smoking cessation. *Lancet* 343:139–142.

Snyder FR, Davis FC & Henningfield JE (1989). The tobacco withdrawal syndrome: Performance decrements assessed on a computerized test battery. *Drug and Alcohol Dependence* 23:259–266.

Stolerman IP & Shoaib M (1991). The neurobiology of tobacco addiction. *Trends in Pharmacologic Science* 12:467–473.

Sutherland G (1997). New pharmacological treatments for nicotine dependence. Presented at the 3rd Annual Meeting of The Society for Research on Nicotine and Tobacco, Nashville, TN.

Sutherland G, Stapleton JA, Russell MAH et al. (1992). Randomised controlled trial of nasal nicotine spray in smoking cessation. *Lancet* 340:324–329.

Tang JL, Law M & Wald N (1994). How effective is nicotine replacement therapy in helping people to stop smoking? *British Medical Journal* 308:21–6.

The Smoking Cessation Clinical Practice Guideline Panel and Staff, Agency for Health Care Policy and Research (1996). Smoking Cessation Clinical Practice Guideline. *Journal of the American Medical Association* 275:1270–1280.

U.S. Department of Health and Human Services (1988). *The Health Consequences of Smoking: Nicotine Addiction. A report of the Surgeon General* (DHHS Publication No. CDC 88-8406). Washington, DC: U.S. Government Printing Office.

U.S. Department of Health and Human Services (1989). *Reducing the Health Consequences of Smoking: 25 years of progress. A Report of the Surgeon General* (DHHS Publication No. (CDC) 89-8411). Washington, DC: U.S. Government Printing Office.

Westman EC (1997). New pharmacological treatments for nicotine dependence. Presented at the 3rd Annual Meeting of The Society for Research on Nicotine and Tobacco, Nashville, TN.

Wonnacott S (1990). Characterization of brain nicotine receptor sites. In S Wonnacott, MAH Russell & IP Stolerman (eds.), *Nicotine Psychopharmacology: Molecular, Cellular, and Behavioural Aspects.* New York, NY: Oxford University Press, 226–265.

CHAPTER 7

Pharmacologic Therapies for Other Drug and Multiple Drug Addiction

Jeffery N. Wilkins, M.D.
David A. Gorelick, M.D., Ph.D.
Bradley T. Conner

Marijuana
Anabolic Steroids
Caffeine
Phencylidine
Hallucinogens
Inhalants
Nicotine/Other Drugs
Opiates/Other Drugs
Experimental Hallucinogen Treatment for Addiction

Pharmacological treatment of individuals with addiction can follow at least five different strategies (Gorelick, 1993). Patients can be given medications with pharmacological actions similar to those of the target drug (i.e., cross-tolerant agonists), with the goal of substitution (e.g., methadone employed for opioid dependence, nicotine for tobacco dependence). A second approach is to use antagonists or receptor blockers, with the goal of preventing or blunting the action of the target drug (e.g., use of the opiate receptor antagonist naltrexone in the treatment of opiate dependence). A third approach is use of medications that alter neural mechanisms mediating reinforcement or drug craving (other than by acting at the same drug receptor). A fourth approach is to increase drug metabolism or clearance from the body, with the goal of reducing the intensity and/or duration of drug effects. A final approach is to use medication to produce a conditioned aversion to the drug, with the goal of reducing or reversing the reinforcing qualities of the target drug (e.g., disulfiram [Antabuse®] in the treatment of alcoholism).

This chapter focuses on pharmacological therapies for the following single substances: marijuana, anabolic steroids, caffeine, phencyclidine (PCP), hallucinogens (e.g., lysergic acid diethylamide [LSD], 3,4-methylenedioxymethamphetamine [MDMA, "ecstasy"], N,N-dimethyltryptamine [DMT], mescaline), and inhalants (volatile substances, including solvents), and for the following mixed addictions: nicotine with other drugs, multiple sedative-hypnotics and sedative-hypnotics with other drugs, opiates with other drugs (alcohol, cocaine), and cocaine with PCP. Few of the potential treatment strategies listed above have been tried with these drugs. In almost all cases, the pharmacological treatments described must be considered experimental or unproven, in that they lack any rigorous clinical data (e.g., from controlled clinical trials) to support their use. Therefore, in most cases the mainstay of treatment is psychosocial modalities.

This chapter closes with a discussion of the potential use of hallucinogenic drugs as pharmacological agents in the treatment of addiction. This use of hallucinogens received considerable attention in the 1950s and 1960s, then waned for a variety of social, legal, and ethical reasons. It has recently gained renewed attention.

MARIJUANA

There is no recognized or proven role for medication in the short- or long-term treatment of marijuana abuse or dependence. No medication has any substantial body of clinical experience to support its use, much less been subjected to controlled clinical trials. L-tryptophan, the amino acid precursor of serotonin, has been used in some patients, but it is unclear to what extent its effects went beyond its ability to induce sedation and sleep (Zweben & O'Connell, 1992). Trazodone, an antidepressant which tends to induce sleep by increasing serotonin activity, has been used to treat cases of severe insomnia associated with marijuana withdrawal (Duffy & Milin, 1996). Aside from such limited adjunctive use of medication, there does not appear to be any current role for pharmacologic treatment of marijuana abuse or dependence. The mainstay of treatment remains psychosocial (see Section 8).

Future research in psychopharmacology may well change this picture (see Section 2). A specific marijuana (cannabinoid) receptor has been identified on nerve cell membranes (Adams & Martin, 1996; Musty, Reggio & Consroe, 1995), with a regional distribution in human brain consistent with the known effects of marijuana (Glass, Dragunow & Faull, 1997). An endogenous ligand (the unsaturated fatty acid anandamide) for the receptor has been identified (Adams & Martin, 1996; Di Marzo, Fontana et al., 1994; Musty, Reggio & Consroe, 1995). In principle, the development of specific cannabinoid receptor agonists or antagonists could lead to pharmacological treatment for marijuana abuse, using either the strategy of cross-tolerant agonist substitution or of receptor blockade. A synthetic, highly specific cannabinoid receptor antagonist has recently been developed, which blocks the effects of marijuana in animals (Adams & Martin, 1996; Compton, Aceto et al., 1996; Musty, Reggio & Consroe, 1995). This compound (SR141716A) is undergoing initial Phase I trials in humans.

ANABOLIC STEROIDS

There is no clear consensus on the treatment of anabolic steroid abuse, and no pharmacological treatment with proven efficacy (Kashkin, 1992). Adjunctive pharmacological treatment of patients taking anabolic steroids may be useful in three areas: steroid-induced violence and aggressive behavior, steroid-induced depression, and detoxification using tapering doses of steroid medications. Low-dose neuroleptics (e.g., phenothiazine-equivalent doses of about 200 mg daily) have been reported effective for managing steroid-induced psychosis, hostility, and agitation (Weiss, Greenfield & Mirin, 1994), although these symptoms are usually self-limited with cessation of steroid use even in the absence of medication. In contrast, tricyclic antidepressants have been associated with exacerbation of steroid-induced psychological symptoms (Wilson, Prang & Lapp, 1974). In non-psychotic patients, antidepressants may be useful in reducing craving and steroid use (Kashkin & Kleber, 1989), possibly because major depression may be associated with withdrawal from steroids (Pope & Katz, 1988). Because of the possible risk of steroid-related prostatic hypertrophy or cardiotoxicity, antidepressants with less anticholinergic and cardiac activity are recommended (Kashkin, 1992). In theory, this would make the selective serotonin reuptake inhibitors the antidepressants of choice, although there is no published systematic clinical experience to confirm this.

Two case reports have described patients with apparent steroid withdrawal syndromes. One patient showed opiate-like symptoms which responded to clonidine (Tennant, Black & Voy, 1988), but this observation has never been confirmed. A second patient had a long-lasting (more than two months) withdrawal syndrome associated with severe depression, including suicidal ideation, insomnia, loss of appetite, and diminished motivation, as well as paranoia and derealization (Allnut & Chaimowitz, 1994). This patient did not respond to desipramine (250 mg/day), even when augmented with haloperidol or lithium, or to fluoxetine and haloperidol. His symptoms did respond to electroconvulsive therapy (ECT) followed by maintenance desipramine.

Further research is needed to determine the appropriate role, and efficacy, of medications and ECT in the treatment of anabolic steroid abuse and withdrawal.

CAFFEINE

Caffeine is the most commonly used psychoactive drug in the world (Gilbert, 1984). When used chronically through ingestion of beverages (coffee, tea, cocoa, and colas), chocolate, and many over-the-counter and prescription medications, caffeine can produce many of the signs of addiction, including craving (Greden & Walters, 1992), a high degree of tolerance (Robertson, Wade et al., 1981), and withdrawal (Hofer & Battig, 1994; Griffiths, Bigelow & Liebson, 1986). Signs and symptoms of caffeine withdrawal include tachycardia, decreased motor activity, headaches, fatigue, and lethargy (Griffiths, Bigelow & Liebson, 1986; Hofer & Battig, 1994). Despite this convincing empirical evidence, the Diagnostic and Statistical Manual of Mental Disorders of the American Psychiatric Association (*DSM-IV*; 1994) does not list a withdrawal syndrome associated with caffeine. Withdrawal symptoms tend to begin about 19 hours after last caffeine intake, peak during the first 48 hours, and resolve by one week (Griffiths, Bigelow & Liebson, 1986).

The pharmacological treatment of choice for individuals wishing to stop or decrease caffeine use is a rapidly tapering regimen of caffeine. Detoxification to complete abstinence, rather than reduction in use appears to be more effective at preventing relapse (Greden & Walters, 1992). There is no viable substitute medication to offset caffeine withdrawal and diminish caffeine craving (Greden & Walters, 1992). An individual who drinks six cups of coffee per day could be placed on the following six-day tapering regimen: 1st day—five cups caffeinated coffee/one cup decaffeinated; 2nd day—four cups caffeinated coffee/two cups decaffeinated, and so forth to the 6th day—no cups caffeinated coffee/six cups decaffeinated. Alternatively, especially in patients with severe dependence, caffeine pills may be used, starting at one gram per day. Treatment also should include patient education about the adverse consequences of chronic caffeine use and about the variety of products and medications that contain caffeine. Increased water intake and sugarless mints have been suggested to help patients alleviate caffeine craving.

PHENCYCLIDINE (PCP)

PCP is a synthetic dissociative anesthetic which gained popularity as an abused drug in the 1960s and is no longer legally available in the U.S. (Gorelick & Balster, 1995). A synthetic analogue, ketamine, is still clinically used and legally marketed in the U.S., although subject to the same abuse (Dotson, Ackerman & West, 1995). There is little systematic experience with pharmacological treatment of PCP addiction. Almost all published studies involve psychosocial treatment approaches, which usually have poor long-term success rates (Daghestani & Schnoll, 1989; Gorelick & Wilkins, 1989; Gorelick, Wilkins & Wong, 1989). Both the tricyclic antidepressant desipramine and the anxiolytic buspirone have significantly improved psychological symptoms such as depression in small outpatient controlled clinical trials, but neither medication significantly reduced PCP use when compared with a double-blind placebo (Giannini, Loiselle et al., 1993; Giannini, Malone et al., 1986). There is no published experience with pharmacological treatment of ketamine abuse (Dotson, Ackerman & West, 1995).

PCP in Combination with Cocaine or Marijuana. PCP often is smoked with cocaine ("spacebasing") or marijuana ("primos"). There is very little literature on the treatment of these dual addictions, and no clinical trial has demonstrated any medication as effective. The antidepressant desipramine has been used because of its possible effectiveness in the treatment of separate PCP or cocaine addiction. In a double-blind study of 20 chronic PCP/cocaine users, desipramine (200 mg daily) significantly lessened symptoms associated with withdrawal, but had less effect on actual drug use (Giannini, Loiselle & Giannini, 1987).

HALLUCINOGENS

Hallucinogens are a varied group of plant-derived alkaloids and synthetic compounds which have in common the ability to produce sensory, perceptual, and cognitive changes without impairing level of consciousness or orientation (i.e., with a clear sensorium) (Abraham, Aldridge & Gogia, 1996). These include compounds which influence serotonergic neurotransmission, such as lysergic acid diethylamide (LSD), psilocybin, and N,N-dimethyltryptamine (DMT), and those which influence catecholaminegic neurotransmission, such as mescaline and amphetamine analogues such as 3,4-methylenedioxymethamphetamine (MDMA, "ecstasy"). There are no currently available pharmacological treatments for hallucinogen abuse (Abraham, Aldridge & Gogia, 1996; Smith & Seymour, 1994). Several retrospective case reports suggest that chronic treatment with monoamine oxidase (MAO) inhibitors (e.g., phenelzine) or selective serotonin reuptake inhibitors (SSRIs) (e.g., fluoxetine, sertraline) can reduce the acute psychological effects of LSD, while chronic treatment with tricyclic antidepressants (e.g., imipramine, desipramine) or lithium may enhance LSD effects (Bonson & Murphy, 1996). These findings, if confirmed by more systematic studies, raise the possibility of using pharmacological treatment to minimize the immediate positive (reinforcing) psychological effects of hallucinogens, thus contributing to effective treatment.

Meanwhile, the mainstay of treatment remains psychosocial intervention, which may require residential treatment in patients with severe personality disorganization. Prolonged psychotic reactions appear to occur chiefly in individuals with pre-existing psychiatric problems, and can be difficult to distinguish from hallucinogen-induced precipitation or exacerbation of a preexisting psychotic disorder such as schizophrenia (Boutros & Bowers, 1996). Regardless of etiology, these psychotic reactions may require treatment with anti-psychotic medication (Boutros & Bowers, 1996; Smith & Seymour, 1994). Low doses of a high potency neuroleptic have been recommended, e.g., 2 to 5 mg of haloperidol (Giannini, 1994).

LSD use has been associated with perceptual abnormalities such as illusions, distortions and hallucinations persisting or recurring intermittently for long periods (up to years) after the last LSD use (hallucinogen persisting perception disorder in *DSM-IV*) (Abraham, Aldridge & Gogia, 1996; Smith & Seymour, 1994). When these abnormalities occur after a period of normal perceptual functioning, they are termed "flashbacks." Several recent case reports suggest that sertraline or naltrexone may be helpful in the treatment of both persisting perceptual abnormalities or flashbacks (Young, 1997; Lerner, Oyffe et al., 1997). Some anecdotal experience indicates that neuroleptics such as haloperidol may transiently worsen flashbacks (Moskowitz, 1971; Strassman, 1984). These perceptual disorders may be associated with secondary depression or anxiety disorders such as panic and agoraphobia. In such cases, treatment with benzodiazepines or SSRI antidepressants has been reported helpful (Smith & Seymour, 1994).

INHALANTS

Inhalants are a heterogeneous group of abused substances that include adhesives, aerosols, anesthetics, gasoline, cleaning agents, food products, paint, and room odorizers, comprising many different chemical agents with different properties, effects, and toxicities (Miller & Gold, 1990; Smart, 1986) (see also Section 2, Chapter 10). Because these agents are legal, they are generally inexpensive and readily available. Many inhalant abusers entering treatment are concurrently abusing other substances, especially alcohol and marijuana (Dinwiddie, Zorumski & Rubin, 1987; Smart, 1986).

There are no pharmacological treatments for inhalant addiction (Jumper-Thurman & Beauvais, 1992). The mainstay of treatment is psychosocial, although no specific technique has proven efficacy (Richardson, 1989; Smart, 1986). Psychosocial treatment is best conducted in a supportive, non-confrontational atmosphere, and directed toward developing basic social and personal skills (Jumper-Thurman & Beauvais, 1992). When severe psychiatric sequelae are present or inhalant use cannot be otherwise controlled, inpatient treatment has been recommended, although there is still a high relapse rate. A thorough medical evaluation at the start of treatment is important, since chronic inhalant use is commonly associated with neurologic and hepatic toxicity (Jumper-Thurman & Beauvais, 1992; Richardson, 1989; Smart, 1986).

NICOTINE/OTHER DRUGS

Nicotine/Alcohol. An estimated 90% of alcoholic patients are also cigarette smokers (Burling & Ziff, 1988), possibly in order to antagonize some of alcohol's CNS-depressant properties (Mintz, Boyd et. al., 1985). Many clinicians and treatment programs do not attempt to simultaneously curtail concurrent alcohol and nicotine addiction, in the belief that this would place too great a burden on the patient. Consequently, alcoholic patients often are discouraged from quitting smoking so as not to jeopardize their recovery (Bobo, Gilchrist et al., 1987; Miller, Hedrick & Taylor, 1983). This laissez-faire approach to the smoking behavior of alcoholics has been questioned because nicotine does appear to facilitate alcohol use and vice versa (Henningfield, Clayton & Pollin, 1990; Hughes, 1993; Shiffman, 1986). There is no empirical support for the traditional notion that simultaneous quitting of both alcohol and nicotine might increase the risk of relapse to drinking (Bien & Burge, 1991). The few published studies of smoking cessation treatment (including nicotine replacement) among alcoholic patients (most in treatment and already abstinent from alcohol) suggest that smoking cessation treatment is as successful in this group as it is among non-alcoholics and that smoking cessation does not increase the risk of relapse to drinking (Hughes, 1993). Conversely, any smoking cessation strategy for individuals who drink alcohol should probably include some attention to the moderation, if not cessation, of alcohol use.

Given the known reciprocal interactions between alcohol and nicotine use, further systematic research is warranted to determine the possible disadvantages and benefits to treating alcohol and nicotine addiction simultaneously. For example, medications used separately for the treatment of alcoholism (e.g., disulfiram, naltrexone) or nicotine dependence (e.g., nicotine gum) should be evaluated when used concurrently in the treatment of nicotine and alcohol dependence.

Nicotine/Other Drugs. Treatment for nicotine dependence often is neglected in the context of other addictions, largely because of the belief that smoking cessation might have an adverse effect on abstinence from other drugs. This belief is not supported by the limited research done to date. Addicted patients often express a strong interest in quitting smoking, and doing so does not adversely affect their future course (Hurt, Eberman et al., 1994; Burling, Marshall & Seidner, 1991; Sees & Clark, 1993). Preliminary research has shown that some dopaminergic receptor antagonists may indirectly block cravings for nicotine as well as stimulants (Wilkins, 1997). No clinical treatment trials have yet addressed the issue of concurrent pharmacological treatment for nicotine dependence (e.g., with nicotine replacement therapy) and other drug dependence (e.g., methadone maintenance therapy for heroin dependence). One issue that should be addressed by such trials is the potential for pharmacokinetic interactions between the medications involved.

OPIATES/OTHER DRUGS

Opiates/Alcohol. Alcoholism is a common problem among opiate-dependent individuals, including those in methadone maintenance treatment (Chatham, Rowan-Szal et al., 1995; Shaffer & LaSalvia, 1992). Concurrent treatment with disulfiram, at the same doses used to treat alcoholism alone, can be effective in reducing alcohol intake among methadone maintenance patients (Liebson, Bigelow & Flamer, 1973). The careful medication monitoring and incentives for compliance that are possible in a methadone maintenance program may make disulfiram treatment more effective than it is in other treatment settings.

Opiates/Cocaine. Cocaine use is common among opiate addicts, even among those in methadone maintenance treatment (Hartel, Schoenbaum et al., 1995; Kosten, Morgan et al., 1992; Shaffer & LaSalvia, 1992). One pattern of concurrent use is simultaneous ("speed balling"), which is considered to provide a qualitatively better subjective experience ("high") than either drug alone (Walsh, Sullivan et al., 1996). An ideal pharmacological treatment would reduce use of both drugs, since cocaine and heroin use are highly associated in patients on methadone maintenance (Dunteman, Condelli & Fairbank, 1992; Hartel, Schoenbaum et al., 1995). The opiate antagonist naltrexone has been suggested for treating these two addictions, although it does not alter the subjective effects of cocaine when cocaine and an opiate are experimentally administered together (Walsh, Sullivan et al., 1996).

Buprenorphine, a partial opioid agonist (mu-opioid agonist, kappa-opioid antagonist) marketed in the U.S. as a parenteral opiate analgesic, is as effective (given sublingually) as methadone for substitution treatment of opiate dependence (Johnson, Eissenberg et al., 1995; Strain, Stitzer et al., 1996). Some animal drug self-administration studies have suggested that it might also be effective in reducing cocaine use (Rodefer, Mattox et al., 1997). While several clinical trials found no influence of buprenorphine on cocaine use among opiate addicts (at doses which significantly decreased opiate use), a few trials using higher doses (12 to 16 mg sl daily) have found a significant reduction in cocaine use (Montoya, Gorelick et al., 1996; Schottenfeld, Pakes et al., 1993). In human laboratory studies, low doses of buprenorphine (2 to 4 mg sl) do not reduce the acute effects of cocaine, but rather enhance them (Foltin & Fischman, 1994; Rosen, Pearsall et al., 1993), as would be expected from the "speed ball" combination of cocaine with an opiate. Thus, the mechanism for buprenorphine's reduction of cocaine use at higher doses remains unclear.

EXPERIMENTAL HALLUCINOGEN TREATMENT FOR ADDICTION

An early clinical use of LSD was as pharmacological treatment for a variety of psychiatric disorders (Abraham, Aldridge & Gogia, 1996; Strassman, 1995). Within four years of its discovery, LSD (Delysid®) was marketed as an adjunct to psychotherapy (Kurtzweil, 1997; Ulrich & Patten, 1991). It was given in small doses to lower psychological defenses and speed the psychotherapeutic process (Strassman, 1995; Henderson, 1994; Neill, 1987). Since LSD was considered to induce a "model" temporary psychosis, it was hoped that study of LSD's chemistry and effects might unlock some of the neurochemical mysteries of psychiatric disorders. The literature accompanying Delysid recommended that psychiatrists themselves take it to better understand the subjective experience of their schizophrenic patients (Strassman, 1995; Henderson, 1994).

Alcoholic patients were treated with relatively large oral doses of LSD (up to 1,500 micrograms in early studies, up to 600 micrograms in later studies) to simulate or induce the experience of "bottoming out," considered by many the turning point in their recovery (Abraham, Aldridge & Gogia, 1996; Hoffer, 1967). Some researchers claimed better treatment success when subjects reported having life-affirming or spiritual experiences, based on LSD's "psychedelic" (mind-expanding) properties. This psychedelic approach became popular in the U.S. and Canada (Osmond, 1957). LSD administration was viewed as the centerpiece of therapy, in the context of creating a directed psychedelic or "peak" emotional experience. A specialized treatment approach evolved, with trained therapists using specific cues and props, including special music, eye shades, and photographs of relatives. By the late-1960s, LSD and other hallucinogens such as mescaline and psilocybin had been given to thousands of patients, with successful treatment reported in open trials for alcoholism (Kurland, Savage et al., 1971), heroin addiction (Savage & McCabe, 1973), neurotic disorders, and the pain and depression of terminally ill patients (Strassman, 1984). However, almost all studies had significant methodologic limitations, and most better controlled clinical trials failed to demonstrate any advantage for LSD therapy over conventional therapy for alcoholism (Abraham, Aldridge & Gogia, 1996). LSD administration in medical and research settings was considered safe, with low rates of psychosis and suicidality and little or no potential for addiction or overdose (Strassman, 1984, 1995; Cohen, 1960).

As use of hallucinogens spread outside the medical setting in the mid-1960s, reports of adverse reactions and behavioral toxicity increased sharply. The resulting controversy included criticism of hallucinogenic drug research for inadequate controls and follow-up (Smart, Storm et al., 1967). Studies that claimed no therapeutic efficacy for hallucinogenic drugs were in turn criticized for their own methodology, including failure to administer the hallucinogenic drug in the appropriate context and with clinicians adequately trained in LSD-assisted therapy (Grof, 1980). The issue of double-blind controls remained problematic. No adequate placebo could be found, since it soon became clear to both subject and clinician whether a placebo or LSD had been administered. Further criticism of LSD research in humans was fueled by a report of LSD-induced chromosomal damage, which was later disproved (Dishotsky, Loughman et al., 1971). Before these scientific questions could be resolved, LSD and other hallucinogenic drugs were reclassified as Schedule I drugs, defining them as having a high potential for abuse and no known medical uses (Kurtzweil, 1997). This action stopped virtually all clinical research with hallucinogens in the U.S. (Ungerleider & Pechnick, 1992).

The Food and Drug Administration (FDA) has recently approved several preliminary studies of hallucinogenic drugs in humans, so that future research eventually may resolve the question of the therapeutic usefulness of hallucinogens (Kurtzweil, 1997). In addition to LSD, other hallucinogenic drugs to be studied include MDMA ("ecstasy"); ibogaine, derived from the West African plant Tabernanthe iboga; DMT (Strassman & Qualls, 1994); psilocybin, derived from mushrooms; and ketamine. MDMA has attracted interest as an alternative to LSD because of its shorter duration of action and milder hallucinogenic properties (Strassman, 1995). However, concerns about its serotonergic neurotoxicity remain to be resolved (Allen, McCann & Ricaurte, 1993; Green, Cross & Goodwin, 1995). Studies of mescaline, derived from the peyote cactus, and of psilocybin are underway in Germany and Switzerland, respectively (Hermle, 1994; Vollenweider, Schrfetter et al., 1994).

Ibogaine has recently attracted interest because of anecdotal reports from the Netherlands that a single high-dose (> 1 g) treatment alleviated withdrawal symptoms and produced long-term abstinence (> 3 months) in heroin and polydrug addicts (Popik, Layer & Skolnick, 1995; Sheppard, 1994). Phase I studies in the U.S. have been approved by the FDA, but no clinical trials have yet been conducted. Concern about possible ibogaine toxicity has limited its use. Several deaths have been associated with the administration of ibogaine, and neurotoxicity, especially in the cerebellum, has been reported in animal studies (Kurtzweil, 1997; Popik, Layer & Skolnick, 1995). Ibogaine's mechanism of action remains unclear, since it influences several different neurotransmitter systems (Popik, Layer & Skolnick, 1995; Sershen, Hashim & Lajtha, 1997). In many, but not all, rodent studies, ibogaine pretreatment reduced cocaine and heroin self-administration and blunted the locomotor stimulation produced by cocaine (Dworkin, Gleeson et al., 1995; Maisonneuve & Glick, 1992; Sershen, Hashim & Lajtha, 1994, 1997).

The use of hallucinogens in treating depression also is under investigation (Riedlinger & Redlinger, 1994). The presumed benefits to psychotherapy include a lessening of patient's "fear responses" that often inhibit their ability to deal with traumatic situations, facilitation of interpersonal dyadic relationships with therapists, spouses, and others in their social support network, and accelerating formation of the therapist/patient relationship (Riedlinger & Riedlinger, 1994).

CONCLUSIONS

This chapter has reviewed approaches to pharmacological treatment of addiction to several individual drugs of abuse, including marijuana, anabolic steroids, caffeine, PCP, and inhalants, as well as to some common mixed addictions, including nicotine/alcohol, nicotine/other drugs, multiple sedative-hypnotics, sedative-hypnotics/other drugs, opiates/alcohol, and cocaine/PCP. In most cases, there is little or no published literature to guide the choice of pharmacological treatment and no clinical trials supporting the efficacy of any treatment. Thus, the mainstay of treatment for marijuana, anabolic steroid, PCP, hallucinogen, or inhalant abuse is psychosocial interventions. The use of pharmacological treatment remains a question for which the physician must rely almost exclusively on his or her own experience and judgment, with very little help from the medical or scientific literature. Future research may alter this situation and spur the development of effective new pharmacological treatments. Two intriguing areas now gaining attention are compounds that interact with cannabinoid receptors in the brain (such as specific "marijuana antagonists") and the use of hallucinogenic drugs in the treatment of addiction.

REFERENCES

Abraham HD, Aldridge AM & Gogia P (1996). The psychopharmacology of hallucinogens. *Neuropsychopharmacology* 14:285–298.

Adams IB & Martin BR (1996). Cannabis: pharmacology and toxicology in animals and humans. *Addiction* 91:1585–1614.

Allen RP, McCann UD & Ricaurte GA (1993). Persistent effects of (±)3,4-methylenedioxymethamphetamine (MDMA, "Ecstasy") on human sleep. *Sleep* 16:560–564.

Allnut S & Chaimowitz G (1994). Anabolic steroid withdrawal depression: A case report. *Canadian Journal of Psychiatry* 39:317–318.

American Psychiatric Association (1987). *Diagnostic and Statistical Manual of Mental Disorders, 3rd Edition, Revised*. Washington, DC: American Psychiatric Association.

Bien TH & Burge R (1991). Smoking and drinking, a review of the literature. *International Journal of the Addictions* 25(12):1429–1454.

Bobo JK (1992). Nicotine dependence and alcoholism epidemiology and treatment. *Journal of Psychoactive Drugs* 24(2):123–129.

Bobo JK, Gilchrist LD, Schilling II RF, Noach B & Schinke SP (1987). Cigarette smoking cessation attempts by recovering alcoholics. *Addictive Behaviors* 12:209–215.

Bonson KR & Murphy DL (1996). Alterations in responses to LSD in humans associated with chronic administration of tricyclic antidepressants, monoamine oxidase inhibitors or lithium. *Behavioural Brain Research* 73:229–233.

Boutros NN & Bowers Jr MB (1996). Chronic substance-induced psychotic disorders: State of the literature. *Journal of Neuropsychiatry and Clinical Neurosciences* 8:262–269.

Budney AJ, Higgins ST, Hughes JR & Bickel WK (1993). Nicotine and caffeine use in cocaine-dependent individuals. *Journal of Substance Abuse* 5(2):117–130.

Burling TA, Marshall GD & Seidner AL (1991). Smoking cessation for substance abuse inpatients. *Journal of Substance Abuse* 3(3):269–276.

Burling TA & Ziff DC (1988). Tobacco smoking: A comparison between alcohol and drug abuse inpatients. *Addictive Behaviors* 13:185–190.

Carroll ME (1990). PCP and hallucinogens. *Advances in Alcohol and Substance Abuse* 9(1–2):167–190.

Chatham LR, Rowan-Szal GA, Joe GW, Brown BS & Simpson DD (1995). Heavy drinking in a population of methadone-maintained clients. *Journal of Studies on Alcohol* 56:417–422.

Cohen S (1960). Lysergic acid diethylamide: Side effects and complications. *Journal of Nervous and Mental Disease* 139:30–40.

Compton DR, Aceto MD, Lowe J & Martin BR (1996). *In vivo* characterization of a specific cannabinoid receptor antagonist (SR141716A): Inhibition of D^9-tetrahydrocannabinol-induced responses and apparent agonist activity. *Journal of Pharmacology and Experimental Therapeutics* 277:586–594.

Daghestani AN & Schnoll SH (1989). Phencyclidine abuse and dependence. *Treatments of Psychiatric Disorders* (Vol. 2). Washington, DC: American Psychiatric Association, 1209–1218.

Di Marzo V, Fontana A, Cadas H et al. (1994). Formation and inactivation of endogenous cannabinoid anandamide in central neurons. *Nature* 372:686–691.

Dinwiddie, SH, Zorumski CF & Rubin EH (1987). Psychiatric correlates of chronic solvent abuse. *Journal of Clinical Psychiatry* 48:334–337.

Dishotsky NI, Loughman WD, Mogar RE & Lipscomb WR (1971). LSD and genetic damage. *Science* 172(3982):431–440.

Dotson JW, Ackerman DL & West JL (1995). Ketamine abuse. *Journal of Drug Issues* 25:751–757.

Duffy A & Milin R (1996). Case study: Withdrawal syndrome in adolescent chronic cannabis users. *Journal of American Academy of Child and Adolescent Psychiatry* 35:1618–1621.

Dunteman GH, Condelli WS & Fairbank JA (1992). Predicting cocaine use among methadone patients: Analysis of findings from a national study. *Hospital and Community Psychiatry* 43:608–611.

Dworkin SI, Gleeson S, Meloni D, Koves TR & Martin TJ (1995). Effects of ibogaine on responding maintained by food, cocaine and heroin reinforcement in rats. *Psychopharmacology* 117:257–261.

Foltin RW & Fischman MW (1994). Effects of buprenorphine on the self-administration of cocaine by humans. *Behavioural Pharmacology* 5:79–89.

Giannini AJ (1994). Inward the mind's I: Description, diagnosis, and treatment of acute and delayed LSD hallucinations. *Psychiatric Annals* 24(3):134–136.

Giannini AJ, Loiselle RH & Giannini MC (1987). Space-based abstinence: alleviation of withdrawal symptoms in combinative cocaine-phencyclidine abuse. *Clinical Toxicology* 25(6):493–500.

Giannini AJ, Loiselle RH, Graham BH et al. (1993). Behavioral response to buspirone in cocaine and phencyclidine withdrawal. *Journal of Substance Abuse Treatment* 10:523–527.

Giannini AJ, Malone DA, Giannini MC, Price WA & Loiselle RH (1986). Treatment of depression in chronic cocaine and phencyclidine abuse with desipramine. *Journal of Clinical Pharmacology* 26:11–214.

Gilbert RM (1984). Caffeine consumption. In GA Spiller (ed.) *The Methylxanthine Beverages and Foods: Chemistry, Consumption, and Health Effects*. New York, NY: Alan R. Liss, 85–213.

Glass M, Dragunow M & Faull RLM (1997). Cannabinoid receptors in the human brain: A detailed anatomical and quantitative autoradiographic study in the fetal, neonatal and adult human brain. *Neuroscience* 77:299–318.

Gorelick DA (1993). Overview of pharmacological treatment approaches for alcohol and other drug addiction: Intoxication, withdrawal, and relapse prevention. *Psychiatric Clinics of North America* 16(1):141–156.

Gorelick DA & Balster RL (1995). Phencyclidine (PCP). In FE Bloom & DJ Kupfer (eds.) *Psychopharmacology: The Fourth Generation of Progress*. New York, NY: Raven Press, 1767–1776.

Gorelick DA & Wilkins JN (1986). Special aspects of human alcohol withdrawal. *Recent Developments in Alcoholism* 4:283–305.

Gorelick DA & Wilkins JN (1989). Inpatient treatment of PCP abusers and users. *American Journal of Drug and Alcohol Abuse* 15:1–12.

Gorelick DA, Wilkins JN & Wong C (1989). Outpatient treatment of PCP abusers. *American Journal of Drug and Alcohol Abuse* 15:367–374.

Greden JF & Walters A (1992). Caffeine. In JH Lowinson, P Ruiz, RB Millman & JG Langrod (eds.) *Substance Abuse: A Comprehensive Textbook* (2nd edition). Baltimore, MD: Williams & Wilkins, 357–370.

Green AR, Cross AJ & Goodwin GM (1995). Review of the pharmacology and clinical pharmacology of 3,4-methoxydioxymethamphetamine (MDMA or "Ecstasy"). *Psychopharmacology* 119:247–260.

Griffiths RR, Bigelow GE & Liebson IA (1986). Human coffee drinking: Reinforcing and physical dependence producing effects of caffeine. *Journal of Pharmacology and Experimental Therapeutics* 239(2):416–425.

Grof S (1980). *LSD Psychotherapy*. Pomona, CA: Hunter House.

Hartel DM, Schoenbaum EE, Selwyn Paet al. (1995). Heroin use during methadone maintenance treatment: The importance of methadone dose and cocaine use. *American Journal of Public Health* 85:83–88.

Henderson LA (1994). About LSD. In LA Henderson & WJ Glass (eds.) *LSD: Still With Us After All These Years*. New York, NY: Lexington, 37–54.

Henningfield JE, Clayton R & Pollin W (1990). Involvement of tobacco in alcoholism and illicit drug use. *British Journal of Addiction* 85:279–292.

Henningfield JE, Cohen C & Slade JD (1991). Is nicotine more addictive than cocaine? *British Journal of Addiction* 86(5): 565–569.

Hermle L (1994). Arylalkanamin-induced effects in normal volunteers—On the significance of research in hallucinogenic agents for psychiatry. *Neuropsychopharmacology* 10(3S Part 1):764S.

Hoffer A (1967). A program for the treatment of alcoholism: LSD, malvaria and nicotinic acid. In HA Abramson (ed.) *The Use of LSD in Psychotherapy*. New York, NY: Bobbs-Merrill Co., 343–406.

Hofer I & Battig K (1994). Cardiovascular, behavioral, and subjective effects of caffeine under field conditions. *Pharmacology, Biochemistry, and Behavior* 48:899–908.

Hughes JR (1993). Treatment of smoking cessation in smokers with past alcohol/drug problems. *Journal of Substance Abuse Treatment* 10:181–187.

Hurt RD, Eberman KM, Croghan IT et al. (1994). Nicotine dependence treatment during inpatient treatment for other addictions: A prospective intervention trial. *Alcoholism: Clinical & Experimental Research* 18:867–872.

Johnson RE, Eissenberg T, Stitzer ML, Strain EC, Liebson IA & Bigelow GE (1995). A placebo controlled clinical trial of buprenorphine as a treatment for opioid dependence. *Drug and Alcohol Dependence* 40:17–25.

Jumper-Thurman P & Beauvais F (1992). Treatment of volatile solvent abusers. In CW Sharp, F Beauvais & R Spence (eds.) *Inhalant Abuse: A Volatile Research Agenda* (Research Monograph 129). Rockville, MD: National Institute on Drug Abuse, 203–213.

Kashkin KB (1992). Anabolic steroids. In JH Lowinson, P Ruiz, RB Millman & JG Langrod (eds.) *Substance Abuse: A Comprehensive Textbook* (2nd edition). Baltimore, MD: Williams & Wilkins, 380–397.

Kashkin KB & Kleber HD (1989). Hooked on hormones? An anabolic steroid addiction hypothesis. *Journal of the American Medical Association* 262(22):3166–3170.

Kosten TR, Morgan CM, Falcione J & Schottenfeld RS (1992). Pharmacotherapy for cocaine-abusing methadone-maintained patients using amantadine or desipramine. *Archives of General Psychiatry* 49:894–898.

Kurland A, Savage C, Pahnke WN, Grof S & Olson JE (1971). LSD in the treatment of alcoholics. *Pharmakopsychiatrie Neuropsychopharmakologie* 4:83–94.

Kurtzweil P (1997). Medical possibilities for psychedelic drugs. Food and Drug Administration (FDA) Homepage (http://www.fda.gov/fdac/features/795_psyche.html).

Lerner AG, Oyffe I, Isaacs G & Sigal M (1997). Naltrexone treatment of hallucinogen persisting perception disorder. *American Journal of Psychiatry* 154:437.

Liebson I, Bigelow G & Flamer R (1973). Alcoholism among methadone patients: A specific treatment method. *American Journal of Psychiatry* 130:483–485.

Maisonneuve IM & Glick SD (1992). Interactions between ibogaine and cocaine in rats: *In vivo* microdialysis and motor behavior. *European Journal of Pharmacology* 212:263–266.

Miller NS & Gold MS (1990). Organic solvents and aerosols: An overview of abuse and dependence. *Annals of Clinical Psychiatry* 2:85–92.

Miller WR, Hedrick KE & Taylor CA (1983). Addictive behaviors and life problems before and after behavioral treatment of problem drinkers. *Addictive Behaviors* 8:403–412.

Mintz J, Boyd G, Rose JE, Charuvastra VC & Jarvik ME (1985). Alcohol increases cigarette smoking: A laboratory demonstration. *Addictive Behaviors* 10:203–207.

Montoya I, Gorelick D, Preston K et al. (1996). Buprenorphine for treatment of dually-dependent (opiate and cocaine) individuals. *NIDA Research Monograph 162: Problems of Drug Dependence 1995.* Rockville, MD: National Institute on Drug Abuse, 178.

Moskowitz D (1971). Use of haloperidol to reduce LSD flashbacks. *Military Medicine* 136:754–757.

Musty RE, Reggio P & Consroe P (1995). A review of recent advances in cannabinoid research and the 1994 international symposium on cannabis and the cannabinoids. *Life Sciences* 56:1933–1940.

Neill JR (1987). "More than medical significance": LSD and American psychiatry, 1953 to 1966. *Journal of Psychoactive Drugs* 19(1):39–45.

Osmond H (1957). A review of the clinical effects of psychotomimetic agents. *Annals of the New York Academy of Sciences* 66(3):418–434.

Perkins KA, Sexton JE, DiMarco A, Grobe JE, Scierka A & Stiller RL (1995). Subjective and cardiovascular responses to nicotine combined with alcohol in male and female smokers. *Psychopharmocology* 119:205–212.

Pope HG & Katz DL (1988). Affective and psychotic symptoms associated with anabolic steroid use. *American Journal of Psychiatry* 145(4):487–490.

Popik P, Layer RT & Skolnick P (1995). 100 Years of ibogaine: Neurochemical and pharmacological actions of a putative anti-addictive drug. *Pharmacological Reviews* 47:235–253.

Reidlinger TJ & Reidlinger JE (1994). Psychedelic and entactogenic drugs in the treatment of depression. *Journal of Psychoactive Drugs* 26:41–55.

Richardson H (1989). Volatile substance abuse: Evaluation and treatment. *Human Toxicology* 8:319–322.

Ries R, Cullison S, Horn R et al. (1991). Benzodiazepine withdrawal: Clinicians' ratings of carbamazepine treatment versus traditional taper methods. *Journal of Psychoactive Drugs* 23:73–76.

Robertson D, Wade D, Workman R, Woosley RL & Oates JA (1981). Tolerance to the humeral and hemodynamic effects of caffeine in man. *Journal of Clinical Investigation* 67:1111–1117.

Rodefer JS, Mattox AJ, Thompson SS & Carroll ME (1997). Effects of buprenorphine and an alternative nondrug reinforcer, alone and in combination on smoked cocaine self-administration in monkeys. *Drug and Alcohol Dependence* 45:21–29.

Rosen MI, Pearsall HR, McDougle CJ, Price LH, Woods SW & Kosten TR (1993). Effects of acute buprenorphine on responses to intranasal cocaine: A pilot study. *American Journal of Drug and Alcohol Abuse* 19:451–464.

Savage C & McCabe L (1973). Residential psychedelic (LSD) therapy for the narcotic addict: A controlled study. *Archives of General Psychiatry* 28(6):808–814.

Schottenfeld RS, Pakes J, Ziedonis D & Kosten TR (1993). Buprenorphine: Dose-related effects on cocaine and opioid use in cocaine-abusing opioid-dependent humans. *Biological Psychiatry* 34:66–74.

Schuckit MA (1989). *Drug and Alcohol Abuse: A Clinical Guide to Diagnosis and Treatment* (3rd edition). New York, NY: Plenum Publishing Co.

Sees KL & Clark HW (1993). When to begin smoking cessation in substance abusers. *Journal of Substance Abuse Treatment* 10(2):189–195.

Sershen H, Hashim A & Lajtha A (1994). Ibogaine reduces preference for cocaine consumption in C57BL/6By mice. *Pharmacology, Biochemistry and Behavior* 47:13–19.

Sershen H, Hashim A & Lajtha A (1997). Ibogaine and cocaine abuse: Pharmacological interactions at dopamine and serotonin receptors. *Brain Research Bulletin* 42:161–168.

Shaffer HJ & LaSalvia TA (1992). Patterns of substance use among methadone maintenance patients. *Journal of Substance Abuse Treatment* 9:143–147.

Sharp CW & Rosenberg NL (1992). Volatile substances. In JH Lowinson, P Ruiz, RB Millman & JG Langrod (eds.) *Substance Abuse: A Comprehensive Textbook* (2nd edition). Baltimore, MD: Williams & Wilkins, 303–327.

Sheppard SG (1994). A preliminary investigation of ibogaine: Case reports and recommendations for further study. *Journal of Substance Abuse Treatment* 11:379–385.

Shiffman S (1986). A cluster-analytic classification of smoking relapse episodes. *Addictive Behavior* 11: 295–307.

Smart RG, Storm T, Baker EFW & Solursh L (1967). *Lysergic Acid Diethylamide (LSD) in the Treatment of*

Alcoholism. West Toronto, Canada: University of Toronto Press.

Smart RG (1986). Solvent use in North America: Aspects of epidemiology, prevention and treatment. *Journal of Psychoactive Drugs* 18(2):87–96.

Smith DE & Seymour RB (1994). LSD: History and toxicity. *Psychiatric Annals* 24(3):145–147.

Strain EC, Stitzer ML, Liebson IA & Bigelow GE (1996). Buprenorphine versus methadone in the treatment of opioid dependence: Self-reports, urinalysis, and addiction severity index. *Journal of Clinical Pharmacology* 16:58–67.

Strassman RJ (1984). Adverse reactions to psychedelic drugs: A review of the literature. *Journal of Nervous and Mental Disease* 172(10):577–595.

Strassman RJ & Qualls CR (1994). Dose-response study of N,N-dimethyltryptamine in humans. I. Neuroendocrine, autonomic, and cardiovascular effects. *Archives of General Psychiatry* 51:85–97.

Strassman RJ (1995). Hallucinogenic drugs in psychiatric research and treatment: Perspectives and prospects. *Journal of Nervous and Mental Disease* 183:127–138.

Tennant F, Black DL & Voy RS (1988). Anabolic steroid dependence with opioid-type features. *The New England Journal of Medicine* 319:578.

U.S. Department of Health and Human Services (1988). *The Health Consequences of Smoking: Nicotine Addiction. A Report of The Surgeon General, U.S. Department of Health and Human Services, Office on Smoking and Health* (DHHS Publication No. (CDC) 88-8406). Washington, DC: U.S. Government Printing Office.

Ulrich RF & Patten BM (1991). The rise, decline, and fall of LSD. *Perspectives in Biology and Medicine* 34(4):561–578.

Ungerleider JT & Pechnick RN (1992). Hallucinogens. In JH Lowinson, P Ruiz, RB Millman & JG Langrod (eds.) *Substance Abuse: A Comprehensive Textbook* (2nd edition). Baltimore, MD: Williams & Wilkins, 280–289.

Victor BS, Lubetsky M & Greden JF (1981). Somatic manifestations of caffeinism. *Journal of Clinical Psychiatry* 42:185–188.

Vollenweider FX, Schrfetter C, Leenders K & Angst J (1994). Ketamine and psilocybin model psychoses: Psychopathology and FDG-PET. *Neuropsychopharmacology* 10(3S Part 1):771S.

Walsh SL, Sullivan JT, Preston KL, Garner JE & Bigelow GE (1996). Effects of naltrexone on response to intravenous cocaine, hydromorphone and their combination in humans. *The Journal of Pharmacology and Experimental Therapeutics* 279:524–538.

Weiss CJ & Millman RB (1991). Hallucinogens, phencyclidine, marijuana, inhalants. In RJ Frances & MI Sheldon (eds.) *Clinical Textbook of Addictive Disorders*. New York, NY: Guilford Press, 146–170.

Weiss RD, Greenfield, SF & Mirin SM (1994). Intoxication and withdrawal syndromes. In SE Hyman (ed.) *Manual of Psychiatric Emergencies*. Boston, MA: Little, Brown & Co., 279–293, 217–227.

Wilkins JN (1997). Pharmacotherapy of schizophrenic patients with comorbid substance abuse. *Schizophrenia Bulletin* 23:215–228.

Wilson IC, Prang AJ & Lapp PP (1974). Methyltestosterone and imipramine in men: Conversion of depression to paranoid reaction. *American Journal of Psychiatry* 131:21–24.

Young CR (1997). Sertraline treatment of hallucinogen persisting perception disorder. *Journal of Clinical Psychiatry* 58:85.

Zweben JE & O'Connell K (1992). Strategies for breaking marijuana dependence. *Journal of Psychoactive Drugs* 24(2):165–171.

SECTION 8

Behavioral Therapies for Addiction

CHAPTER 1

Enhancing Motivation to Change 595
James O. Prochaska, Ph.D.

CHAPTER 2

Characteristics of Effective Counselors 609
Kathleen M. Carroll, Ph.D.

CHAPTER 3

Brief Interventions 615
Allan W. Graham, M.D., FACP, FASAM and Michael Fleming, M.D., M.P.H.

CHAPTER 4

Individual Psychotherapy 631
Bruce J. Rounsaville, M.D. and Kathleen M. Carroll, Ph.D.

CHAPTER 5

Network Therapy: An Integration of Therapeutic Approaches at the Office Level 653
Marc Galanter, M.D., FASAM

CHAPTER 6

Aversion Therapy 667
P. Joseph Frawley, M.D.

CHAPTER 7

Community Reinforcement and Contingency Management Interventions 675
Steve T. Higgins, Ph.D., Jennifer W. Tidey, Ph.D., and Maxine L. Stitzer, Ph.D.

SECTION COORDINATOR

ALLAN W. GRAHAM, M.D., FACP, FASAM
Associate Medical Director
Chemical Dependency Treatment Services
Kaiser Permanente
Denver, Colorado

CONTRIBUTORS

Kathleen M. Carroll, Ph.D.
Associate Professor of Psychiatry
Yale University School of Medicine
New Haven, Connecticut

Michael Fleming, M.D., M.P.H.
Department of Family Practice
University of Wisconsin Medical School
Madison, Wisconsin

P. Joseph Frawley, M.D.
Private Practice of Medicine
Santa Barbara, California

Marc Galanter, M.D., FASAM
Professor of Psychiatry and
Director, Division of Alcoholism and Drug Abuse
New York University School of Medicine
New York, New York

Stephen T. Higgins, Ph.D.
Professor of Psychiatry and Psychology
Human Behavioral Pharmacology Laboratory
Department of Psychiatry
University of Vermont
Burlington, Vermont

James O. Prochaska, Ph.D.
Director and Professor
Cancer Prevention Research Center
University of Rhode Island
Kingston, Rhode Island

Bruce J. Rounsaville, M.D.
Director of Research
Division of Substance Abuse, and
Professor of Psychiatry
Yale University School of Medicine
and Connecticut Mental Health Center
New Haven, Connecticut

Maxine L. Stitzer, Ph.D.
Department of Psychiatry
The Johns Hopkins University
Baltimore, Maryland

Jennifer W. Tidey, Ph.D.
Human Behavioral Pharmacology Laboratory
Department of Psychiatry
University of Vermont
Burlington, Vermont

CHAPTER 1

Enhancing Motivation to Change

James O. Prochaska, Ph.D.

The Stages of Change
Recruitment into Treatment
Retention in Treatment
Progress in Treatment
Principles and Processes of Change
Treatment Outcomes

What moves people to take action? The answer to this key question depends on what type of action is to be taken. What moves them to start therapy? What motivates people to continue therapy? What moves people to progress, or to continue to progress after therapy? Answers to these questions can provide better alternatives to one of the addiction field's most pressing concerns: What types of treatment programs have the greatest effects on entire populations at risk for addiction?

What motivates people to change? The answer to this question depends in part on where they start. What motivates people to begin thinking about change can be different from what motivates them to prepare to take action. Once prepared, different forces can move them actually to take the action or, once the action is taken, to maintain the state of change. We also need to be concerned about the forces that move people backward, that cause them to regress or relapse back to their addictive behaviors.

Fortunately, the answers to this complex set of questions may be simpler or at least more systematic than the questions themselves. To appreciate these answers, we need to begin by considering the author's model of change (Prochaska & DiClemente, 1983; Prochaska, DiClemente & Norcross, 1992; Prochaska, Norcross & DiClemente, 1994).

THE STAGES OF CHANGE

Change is a process that unfolds over time through a series of stages: precontemplation, contemplation, preparation, action, maintenance and termination.

Precontemplation is the stage in which an individual is not intending to take action in the foreseeable future, usually measured as the next six months. Individuals may be in this stage because they are uninformed or underinformed about the consequences of their behavior. Or they may have tried to change a number of times and become demoralized at their inability to do so. (Individuals in both of these categories tend to avoid reading, talking or thinking about their high-risk behaviors. They are characterized in some other models as "resistant" or "unmotivated," or not ready for therapy or health promotion. In fact, traditional treatment programs often are not ready for such individuals and are not motivated to match their needs.

Persons in the precontemplation stage underestimate the benefits of change and overestimate its costs. Typically, they are not aware that they are making such mistakes, so it is difficult for them to change. Many remain "stuck" in the precontemplation stage for years, doing considerable damage to themselves and others. There appears to be no inherent motivation for individuals to progress from one stage to the next. These are not like stages of human development, in which children have inherent motivation to progress from crawling to walking, even though crawling works very well and learning to walk can be painful and embarrassing.

The author and colleagues have identified two major forces that can move individuals to progress out of the precontemplation stage. The first is *developmental events.* In our research, the mean age of smokers who reach long-term maintenance is 39. Those of us who have lived through age 39 know that it is indeed a "mean" age. It is an age to reevaluate how we have been living and whether we want to die from the way we have been living or enhance the quality and quantity of the second half of our lives.

The second naturally occurring force is *environmental events.* However, such events do not always lead to a predictable response. A good example of this unpredictability involves a couple who both were heavy smokers. Eventually their dog, a pet of many years, died of lung cancer. This moved the wife to quit smoking, whereas her husband bought a new dog. So even the same events can be processed differently by different people.

There has been a widespread belief that individuals with addictive disorders must "hit bottom" before they will become motivated to change, so family, friends, and physicians wait helplessly for a crisis to occur. But how often do people turn 39 or have a dog die? When people show the first signs of a serious physical illness, such as cancer or cardiovascular disease, others around them mobilize to help them seek early intervention. With these disorders, we understand that early interventions often are lifesaving and we would not wait for such patients to "hit bottom," but the same reaction has not occurred to persons with addictive disorders. To respond to this dichotomy, experts in the addiction field have created an environmental event—the planned intervention—to help addicted patients progress past the precontemplation stage.

Contemplation is the stage in which individuals intend to take action within the next six months. At this stage, they are more aware of the benefits of change, but also remain acutely aware of its costs. When people begin to seriously contemplate giving up their favorite substances, their awareness of the costs of changing can increase. There is no free change. This balance between the costs and benefits of change can produce profound ambivalence, in which the individual develops a type of "love-hate" relationship with an addictive substance. Such ambivalence can keep the individual "stuck" in this stage for long periods of time. We often characterize this phenomena as "chronic contemplation" or "behavioral procrastination." Persons caught up in such ambivalence are not ready for traditional action-oriented programs.

Preparation is the stage in which persons intend to take action in the immediate future, usually measured as the next month. Such individuals have a plan of action, such as going to a recovery group, consulting a counselor, talking with their physician, buying a self-help book or relying on a self-change approach. These are the persons who should be recruited for action-oriented treatment programs.

Action is the stage in which individuals have made specific overt modifications in their lifestyles within the past six months. Since action is observable, behavior change often has been equated with action. But in the author's Transtheoretical Model, action is only one of six stages. Not all modifications of behavior count as action in this model. The individual must attain a criterion that professionals agree is sufficient to reduce his or her risk of disease. In smokers, for example, only total abstinence counts. With alcoholism and alcohol abuse, there is disagreement: many experts believe that only total abstinence can be effective, while others accept controlled drinking as effective action.

Maintenance is the stage in which people are working to prevent relapse, but they do not apply change processes as frequently as do people in action. They are less tempted to relapse and increasingly more confident that they can sustain their changes. Based on temptation and self-efficacy data, maintenance is estimated to last from six months to about five years.

One of the common reasons that people relapse early in the action stage is that they are not well-prepared for the prolonged effort needed to progress to maintenance. Many think the worst will be over in a few weeks or a few months. However, if they ease up on their efforts to change too early, they are at great risk of relapse.

To prepare people for what is to come, we encourage them to think of overcoming an addiction as akin to running a marathon rather than a sprint. They may have wanted to enter the Boston Marathon, but if they had little or no preparation, they understand that they could not succeed and thus would not enter the race. With a little preparation, they might run for several miles before falling to the side. Only those who are well-prepared could maintain their efforts mile after mile.

In the Boston Marathon metaphor, people know they have to be well-prepared if they are to survive "Heartbreak Hill," which the runners hit after 20 miles. What is the behavioral equivalent of Heartbreak Hill? The best evidence we have suggests that the majority of relapses occur at times of emotional distress. Periods of depression, anxiety, anger, boredom, loneliness, stress and distress are the times when we are at our emotional and psychological weakest.

How does the average American cope with such troubling times? The average American drinks more, eats more, smokes more and takes more drugs to cope with emotional distress. It is not surprising, therefore, that people struggling to overcome addictions will be at greatest risk of relapse when they face distress without their substance of choice. We cannot prevent emotional distress from occurring. But we can help to prevent relapse if our patients have been prepared to cope with distress without falling back on addictive substances.

If so many Americans rely on oral consumptive behavior as a way to manage their emotions, what is the healthiest oral behavior they could use? Talking with others about one's distress is a means of seeking support that can help to prevent relapse. Another healthy alternative that can be relied on by large numbers of people is exercise. Not only does physical activity help to manage moods, stress and distress, but the recovering addict derives multiple physical and mental health benefits. Exercise thus should be prescribed to all sedentary patients with addictive disorders. A third healthy alternative is some form of deep relaxation, such as meditation, yoga, prayer, massage or deep muscle relaxation. Letting the stress and distress drift away from one's muscles and one's mind helps to keep the person moving forward, even at the most tempting of times.

Termination is the stage in which individuals have zero temptation and 100% self-efficacy. No matter whether they are depressed, anxious, bored, lonely, angry or stressed, they are sure they will not return to their old unhealthy habits as a way of coping. It is as if they had not acquired such habits in the first place. In a study of former smokers and alcoholics, the author and colleagues found that fewer than 20% of each group had reached the criteria of "no temptation" and "total self-efficacy" (Snow, Prochaska & Rossi, 1992). While the ideal is for the patient to be cured or totally recovered, it must be recognized that, for many people, the best we can do is help them achieve a lifetime of maintenance.

Next, we apply the stages of change model to understand how we can motivate many more people at each of the five phases of planned intervention for addiction disorders. These phases are: (1) recruitment, (2) retention, (3) progress, (4) process, and (5) outcomes.

RECRUITMENT INTO TREATMENT

Too few studies have paid attention to one of the "skeletons in the closet" of professional treatment programs for the addictions, which is that such programs recruit or reach too few people with addictive disorders. For example, across all diagnoses in the newest edition of the *Diagnostic and Statistical Manual of Mental Disorders* (*DSM-IV*; American Psychiatric Association, 1994), in their lifetimes fewer than 25% of persons with these disorders ever enter professional treatment programs. Among smokers, fewer than 10% ever participate in professional smoking cessation programs (USDHHS, 1990).

Given that the addictive disorders are among the most costly of contemporary conditions—to the individuals, their families and friends, their employers, their communities and their health care systems—we must motivate many more people to participate in appropriate programs. No longer can we be prepared to treat the addictions on a case-by-case basis. Instead, we must develop programs that can reach addicted individuals on a population basis. However, the early results of such efforts are not encouraging (Luepker, Murray et al., 1994; Glasgow, Terborg et al., 1995; Ennett, Tabler et al., 1994). Whether such trials were conducted at worksites, schools or across entire communities, the results have been remarkably similar: no significant effects compared to the control conditions. If we examine one of these trials more closely, we may find suggestions at to what went wrong.

The Minnesota Heart Health Study targeted smoking as one of a group of heart health risk behaviors. Nearly 90% of the smokers in treated communities reported seeing media stories about smoking, but the same was true with smokers in the control communities. More significantly, only about 12% of smokers in the treatment and control communities reported that their physicians had talked to them about smoking in the past year. If we look at what percentage participated in the most powerful behavior change programs (clinics, classes and counselors), we find that only 4% of the smokers participated. Offered free smoking cessation clinics, only 1% of smokers are recruited (Lichtenstein & Hollis, 1992). We simply cannot have much impact on the health of the population if our best treatment programs reach so few people in need.

Motivating Populations at Risk to Accept Help. How do we motivate many more people with addictive disorders to seek appropriate help? By changing our paradigms and our practices. There are two paradigms that we need to consider changing. The first is an *action-oriented paradigm*, which construes behavior change as an event that can occur quickly, immediately, discretely and dramatically. Treatment programs that are designed to help patients immediately stop abusing substances are implicitly or explicitly designed for the portion of the population that is in the preparation stage.

The problem here is that across 15 unhealthy behaviors in a representative population—20,000 HMO members—fewer than 20% are prepared to take action (Rossi, 1992). The general rule of thumb can be summed up as "40, 40, 20": 40% in precontemplation, 40% in contemplation and 20% in preparation. Thus, when we offer action-oriented interventions, we are implicitly recruiting from fewer than 20% of the at-risk population. If we are to meet the needs of entire populations with addictive disorders, we must design interventions for the 40% in precontemplation and the 40% in contemplation.

Offering stage-matched interventions and applying proactive or outreach recruitment methods in three large clinical trials, the author and colleagues have been able to motivate 80% to 90% of smokers to enter into treatment (Prochaska, Velicer et al., 1997a, 1997b). This is a quantum increase in terms of our ability to move many more people to take the action of starting therapy.

The second paradigm change that is required is movement away from a passive-reactive approach and toward a *proactive approach.* Most professionals have been trained to be passive-reactive: that is, they passively wait for patients to seek their services, and then they react. However, the majority of persons with addictive disorders never seek such services.

The passive-reactive paradigm is designed to serve populations with acute conditions. The pain, distress or discomfort of such conditions can motivate people to seek the services of health professionals. But the major killers of our time are chronic conditions caused in large part by chronic life-style problems, like the addictive disorders. If we are to treat the addictions seriously, we must learn to reach out to entire populations and offer them stage-matched therapies. There are regions of the National Health Service in Great Britain that are training health professionals in these new paradigms. Over 4,000 physicians, nurses, counselors and health educators have been trained to proactively interact at each stage of change with their entire patient populations who smoke or abuse alcohol, drugs and food.

What happens if professionals change only one paradigm and proactively recruit entire populations to action-oriented interventions? This approach was attempted by one of the nation's largest managed care organizations (Lichtenstein & Hollis, 1992). In that experiment, physicians spent time with every smoker to encourage them to sign up for a state-of-the-art, action-oriented clinic. If the patients did not respond, nurses spent up to 10 minutes with each, trying to convince them to sign up. This was followed by 12 minutes of time with a health educator, and a phone call at home from a counselor.

Working from a base rate of 1% participation, this intensive recruitment protocol motivated 35% of smokers who were in the precontemplation stage to enroll in the clinic. But only 3% showed up, 2% completed, and none achieved sustainable change. From a combined contemplation and preparation group, 65% signed up, 15% showed up, 11% completed, and some unmeasured percent sustained change.

Reviewing the evidence from this and other studies, we believe we can answer the question: What would motivate a majority of people to participate in a professional treatment program for an addictive disorder? One answer is professionals who are motivated and prepared to proactively reach out to entire populations and offer them interventions that match whatever stage of change they are in.

RETENTION IN TREATMENT

What motivates people to continue in therapy? Or conversely, what moves clients to terminate counseling quickly and prematurely, as judged by their counselors? A meta-analysis of 125 studies found that nearly 50% of clients drop out of treatment (Wierzbicki & Pekarik, 1993). Across studies, there were few consistent predictors of premature termination, except substance abuse, minority status, and lower educational level. While important, these variables did not account for much of the variance in drop-outs among programs.

There are now at least five studies that have adopted a stage model perspective to examine drop-outs from treatment programs on substance abuse, smoking, obesity, and a broad spectrum of psychiatric disorders. These studies found that stage-related variables were better predictors than demographics, type and severity of problem and other problem-related variables. Figure 1 presents the stage profiles of three groups of patients with a broad spectrum of psychiatric disorders (Medeiros & Prochaska, 1997; Prochaska, Norcross & DiClemente, 1994). In the former study, the authors were able to predict with 93% accuracy which patients would fall into each of three groups: (1) premature terminators, (2) early but appropriate terminators, and (3) continuers in therapy (Medeiros & Prochaska, 1997).

Figure 1 shows that the pre-therapy profile of the entire group who dropped out quickly and prema-

FIGURE 1. Pre-Therapy Stage Profiles for Premature Terminators, Appropriate Terminators and Continuers

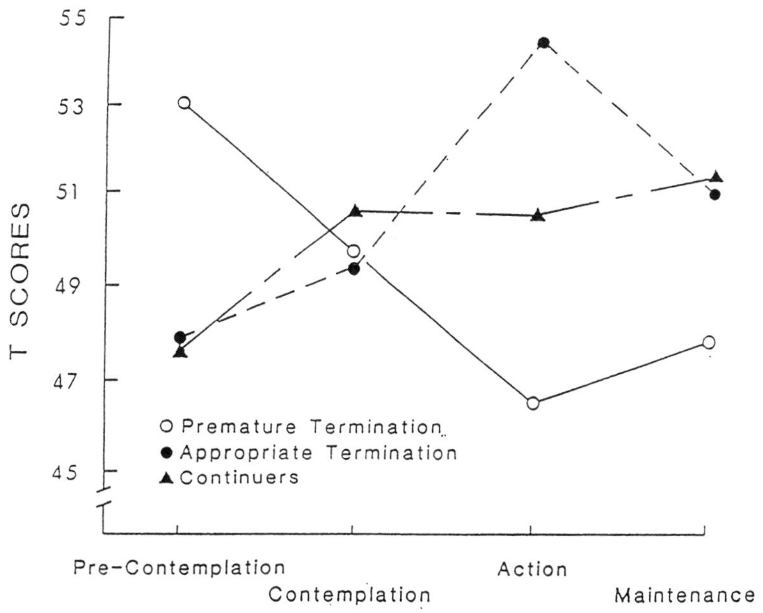

turely (40%) was a profile of people in the precontemplation stage. The 20% who finished quickly but appropriately had a profile of patients who were in the action stage at the time they entered therapy. Those who continued in longer term treatment were a mixed group, the majority of whom were in the contemplation stage.

We cannot treat people in the precontemplation stage as if they are starting in the same place as those in the action stage and expect them to continue in therapy. If we try to pressure them to take action when they are not prepared to do so, should we expect to retain them in therapy? Or do we drive them away and then blame them for not being sufficiently motivated or ready for our action-oriented interventions?

With patients in the action stage who enter treatment for an addictive disorder, what would be an appropriate approach? One alternative would be to provide relapse prevention strategies. But would relapse prevention strategies make any sense with the 40% of patients who enter in the precontemplation stage? What might be a good match here? We would recommend a drop-out prevention approach, since we know these patients are likely to leave early if they do not receive help.

With persons in the precontemplation stage who start treatment, the therapist might share key concerns: "I'm concerned that therapy may not have a chance to make a significant difference in your life, because you may be tempted to leave early." The therapist then might explore whether the patient has been pressured to enter therapy. How do they react when someone tries to pressure or coerce them into quitting an addiction when they are not ready? Can they articulate a response if they feel pressured or coerced by the therapist? It may be most appropriate to encourage them to take steps only where they are most ready to succeed.

Four studies with stage-matched interventions allow us to examine retention rates of persons who entered treatment while in the precontemplation stage. What is clear is that when treatment is matched to stage, people in the precontemplation continue at the same high rates as those who started in the preparation stage. This result held for clinical trials in which patients were recruited proactively, as well as in participants recruited reactively. Unfortunately, these studies have been done only with smokers. But if they hold up across other addictive disorders, we will be able to offer a practical answer to the question: What motivates people to continue in therapy? The answer seems to be: Receiving treatments that match their stage.

PROGRESS IN TREATMENT

What moves people to progress in therapy and to continue to progress after therapy? Figure 2 presents an example of what is called the *stage effect.* The

FIGURE 2. Percentage of Smokers Who Maintained Abstinence Over 18 Months

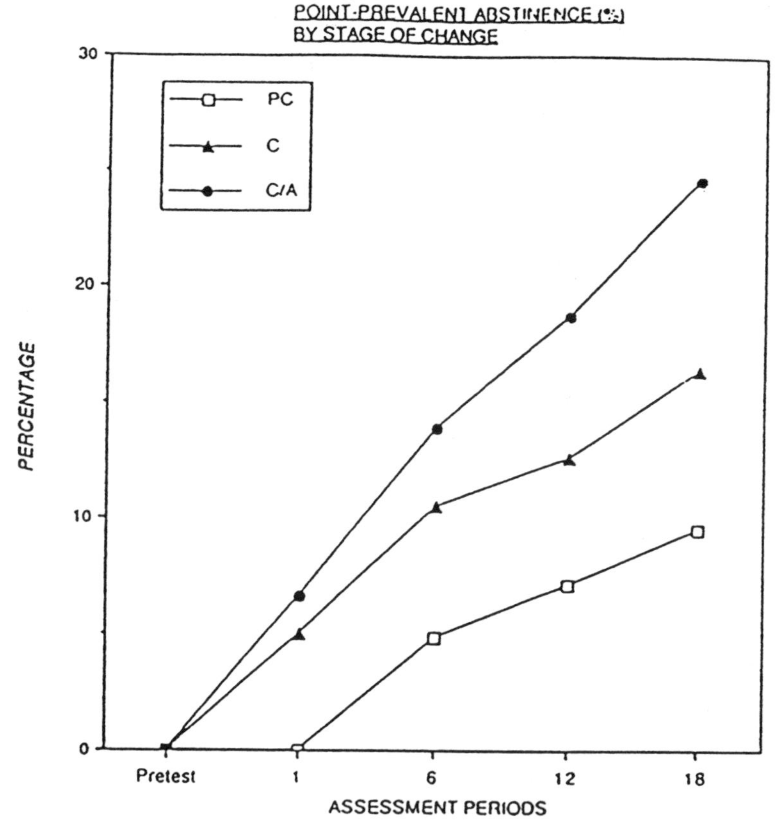

Note: Groups were in the following stages at the time of entry into treatment: Precontemplation (PC), Contemplation (C) and Preparation (C/A) (N = 570).

stage effect predicts that the amount of successful action taken during and after treatment is directly related to the stage people are in at the start of treatment (Prochaska, DiClemente & Norcross, 1992). In this example, interventions with smokers ends at six months. The group of smokers who were in the precontemplation stage at the time they started show the least amount of effective action, as measured by abstinence at each assessment point. Those who started in the contemplation stage made significantly more progress. And those who entered treatment already prepared to take action were most successful at every assessment.

The stage effect has been found to exist across a variety of problems and populations, including rehabilitation programs for brain injury and recovery from anxiety and panic disorders (Beitman, Beck et al., 1994).

A strategy for applying the stage effect clinically involves setting realistic goals for brief encounters with patients at each stage of change. A realistic goal would be to help the individual progress by one stage through brief therapy. If the patient moves relatively quickly, then it may be possible to help them progress by two stages. The results to date indicate that, if clients progress one stage in one month, they double the chance that they will take effective action by six months. If they progress through two stages, they increase their chances of taking effective action three- to four-fold (Prochaska, Velicer et al., 1997a). Setting such realistic goals can enable many more people to enter therapy, continue in therapy, progress in therapy and continue to progress after therapy.

As managed care organizations move to briefer and briefer therapies for the addictions and other disorders, there is a danger that most health professionals will feel pressured to produce immediate action. If this pressure is transferred to patients who are not prepared for such action, we will repeat our past failures; that is, we will not engage most patients in treatment or retain them there. We can help move a majority of patients to progress in relatively brief encounters, but only if we set realistic goals for them and for ourselves.

PRINCIPLES AND PROCESSES OF CHANGE

To help motivate patients to progress from one stage to the next, clinicians need to understand the principles and processes of change.

Principle 1: The benefits of change must increase before individuals will progress from precontemplation to contemplation. In a meta-analysis, the author and colleagues found that in 12 of 12 studies, benefits were perceived as greater in the contemplation than the precontemplation stage (Prochaska, Velicer et al., 1994). This pattern held true across 12 problem behaviors, including cocaine use, smoking, delinquency, obesity, inconsistent condom use, unsafe sexual behaviors, sedentary life styles, high-fat diets, sun exposure, radon testing, and avoidance of mammography screening.

A technique based on this principle would be to ask a patient in the precontemplation stage to recount all the benefits of a proposed change such as quitting smoking or starting to exercise. Most persons can list four or five. The clinician then can let them know that there are 8 to 10 times that amount, and challenge them to double or triple their list by the time of the next meeting. If their list of benefits for exercising starts to indicate many more motives, such as a healthier heart, healthier lungs, more energy, healthier immune system, better moods, less stress, better sex life, and enhanced self-esteem, they will be more motivated to begin to seriously contemplate changing.

Principle 2: The costs of change must decrease before individuals will progress from contemplation to action. In a series of studies, the author and colleagues found that the perceived costs of changing were lower in the action stage than in the contemplation stage (Prochaska, Velicer et al., 1994).

Principle 3: The relative balance between the benefits and costs of change must cross over for people to be prepared to take action. In the author's experience, the costs of change were perceived as greater than the benefits by patients at the precontemplation stage, but the benefits were perceived to exceed the costs by patients at the action stage (Prochaska, Velicer et al., 1994). The single exception involved quitting cocaine use, for which the study population was largely inpatient. We interpret this exception to mean that the actions of these individuals may have been more under social controls of residential care than under self-control.

It should be noted that, if we used raw scores to assess these patterns, we often would find that the benefits of changing ranked higher than the costs, even for individuals in the precontemplation stage. It is only when we use standardized scores that the patterns become clear. Thus, compared to their peers in other stages, persons in the precontemplation stage underestimate the benefits and overestimate the costs of change.

Principle 4: The strong principle of progress holds that, to progress from precontemplation to effective action, the benefits of change must increase by one standard deviation (Prochaska, 1994).

Principle 5: The weak principle of progress holds that, to progress from contemplation to effective action, the costs of change must decrease by one-half standard deviation.

What is striking here is that we believe we have discovered mathematical principles for how much positive motivation must increase and how much negative motivation must decrease. Such principles can produce much more sensitive assessments for guiding interventions, giving professionals and patients feedback to help them understand when therapeutic efforts are producing progress and when they are failing. Together, we can modify our methods if we are not seeing as much movement as is needed for the patient to become adequately prepared for action.

Principle 6: It is essential to match particular processes of change to specific stages of change. Table 1 presents the empirical integration that the author and colleagues have found between processes and stages of change. Guided by this integration, one would apply the following processes with patients in precontemplation:

Consciousness raising involves increasing awareness about the causes, consequences and treatments of a particular problem. Interventions that can increase awareness include observation, confrontation, interpretation, feedback and education (such as bibliotherapy). Some techniques, like confrontation, are high-risk in terms of retention and are not recommended as much as motivational enhancement methods such as personal feedback about the current and long-term consequences of continuing with the addiction. Increasing the costs of not changing is the corollary of raising the benefits of changing.

Dramatic relief involves emotional arousal around one's current behavior and the relief that can result from change. Fear, inspiration, guilt and hope are some of the emotions that can move people to contemplate changing. Psychodrama, role playing, grieving, and personal testimonies are examples of techniques that can move people emotionally.

TABLE 1. Stages of Change in Which Change Processes Are Most Emphasized

	Stages of Change				
	Precontemplation	Contemplation	Preparation	Action	Maintenance
Processes	Consciousness raising				
	Dramatic relief				
	Environmental reevaluation				
		Self-reevaluation			
			Self-liberation		
				Contingency management	
				Helping relationship	
				Counterconditioning	
				Stimulus control	

Earlier behavior change literature concluded that interventions like education and fear arousal did not motivate behavior change. Unfortunately, many interventions were evaluated by their ability to move people to immediate action. Processes like consciousness raising and dramatic relief are intended to move people to contemplation rather than immediate action. Therefore, we should assess their effectiveness according to whether they produce the progress they are expected to produce.

Environmental reevaluation combines both affective and cognitive assessments of how an addiction affects one's social environment and how changing it would affect that environment. Empathy training, values clarification and family or network interventions can facilitate such reevaluation.

Here is brief media intervention aimed at smokers in precontemplation: A man clearly in grief says, "I always feared that my smoking would lead to an early death. I always worried that my smoking would cause lung cancer. But I never imagined it would happen to my wife."

Beneath his grieving face appears this statistic: 50,000 deaths per year are caused by passive smoking, the California Department of Health.

In 30 seconds, this message has achieved consciousness raising, dramatic relief and environmental reevaluation. No wonder such media interventions have been found to be important components of smoking cessation campaigns.

Self-reevaluation combines both cognitive and affective assessments of one's self-image, free from an addiction. Imagery, healthier role models and values clarification are techniques that can move people evaluatively. Clinically, we find people first looking back and reevaluating how they have been as addicted individuals. As they progress into preparation, they begin to develop a future focus as they imagine how their lives will be free from addiction.

Self-liberation is both the belief that one can change and the commitment and re-commitment to act on that belief. Techniques that can enhance such change involve public rather than private commitments. Motivational research also suggests that if people only have one choice, they are not as motivated as if they have two choices. Three is even better, although having four choices does not seem to enhance motivation. Thus, wherever possible, we try to provide people with three of the best choices for applying each process. With smoking cessation, for example, we used to believe only one commitment really counted and that was quitting cold turkey. We now know there are at least three good choices: (1) cold turkey, (2) nicotine replacement, and (3) nicotine fading. Asking patients to choose the alternative they believe would be most effective for them and to which they would be most committed can enhance their motivation and self-liberation.

Counterconditioning requires the learning of healthier behaviors that can substitute for addictive behaviors. We just discussed three healthier alternatives to smoking. Earlier we discussed healthier alternatives for coping with emotional distress rather than relapsing. Counterconditioning techniques tend to be quite specific to a particular behavior and include desensitization, assertion, and cognitive counters to irrational self-statements that can elicit distress.

Contingency management involves the systematic use of reinforcements and punishments for taking steps in a particular direction. Since we find that successful self-changers rely much more on reinforcement than punishment, we emphasize reinforcements for progressing rather than punishments for regressing. Contingency contracts, overt and covert reinforcements and group recognition are procedures for increasing reinforcement and incentives that increase the probability that healthier responses will be repeated.

To prepare people for the longer term, we teach them to rely more on self-reinforcements then social reinforcements. We find clinically that many individuals expect much more reinforcement and recognition from others than what others actively provide. Too many relatives and friends can take action for granted too quickly. Average acquaintances typically generate only a few positive consequences early in action. Self-reinforcement obviously is much more under the control of the patient and can be given more quickly and consistently when temptations to lapse or relapse are resisted.

Stimulus control involves modifying the environment to increase cues that prompt healthier responses and to decrease cues that undermine commitment to change. Avoidance, environmental reengineering (such as removing addictive substances and paraphernalia) and attending self-help groups can provide stimuli that elicit healthier responses and reduce risks for relapse.

Helping relationships combine caring, openness, trust and acceptance as well as support for changing. Rapport building, a therapeutic alliance, counselor calls, buddy systems, sponsors and self-help groups all can be excellent resources for social support. If people become dependent on such support to maintain change, we need to take care in fading out such supports, lest termination of therapy becomes a condition for relapsing.

Competing theories of therapy have implicitly or explicitly advocated alternative processes of enhancing motivation for change. Is it cognitions that move people or emotions? Is it values, decisions or dedication? Are contingencies what incentivize us or are we controlled by environmental conditions or conditioned habits? Or is it the therapeutic relationship that is the common healer across all therapeutic modalities?

Our answer to each of these questions is "yes." Therapeutic processes originating from competing theories can be compatible when they are combined in a stage-matched paradigm. With patients in earlier stages of change, we can enhance motivation through more experiential processes that produce healthier cognitions, emotions, evaluations, decisions and commitments. In later stages, we seek to build on such solid preparation and motivation by emphasizing more behavioral processes that can help condition healthier habits, reinforce those habits, and provide physical and social environments that support healthier lifestyles that are freer from addictions.

TREATMENT OUTCOMES

What happens when we combine all of these principles and processes of change to help patients and entire populations to move toward action on their addictions? We will examine a series of clinical trials applying stage-matched interventions to see what lessons we might learn about the future of behavioral health care generally and treatment of the addictions specifically.

In a large-scale clinical trial, the author and colleagues compared four treatments: (1) one of the best home-based action-oriented cessation programs (Standardized); (2) stage-matched manuals (Individualized); (3) expert system computer reports plus manuals (Interactive); and (4) counselors plus computers and manuals (Personalized). Participants (739 smokers) were randomly assigned to one of the four treatments (Prochaska, DiClemente et al., 1993).

In the computer condition, participants completed by mail or telephone 40 questions that were entered into our central computers and generated feedback reports. These reports informed participants about their stage of change, the benefits and costs of changing and their use of change processes appropriate to their stages. At baseline, participants were given positive feedback on what they were doing correctly and guidance on which principles and processes they needed to apply in order to progress. In two progress reports delivered over the ensuing six months, participants also received positive feedback on any improvement they made on any of the variables. With this assistance, demoralized and defensive smokers could begin to progress without having to quit and without having to work too hard. Smokers in the contemplation stage could begin taking small steps, such as delaying their first cigarette in the morning for an extra 30 minutes. They could choose small steps that would increase their self-efficacy and help them become better prepared for quitting.

In the personalized condition, smokers received four proactive counselor calls over the six-month intervention period. Three of the calls were based on the computer reports. Counselors reported much more difficulty in interacting with participants without any progress data. Without scientific assessments, it was much harder for both clients and counselors to tell whether any significant progress had occurred since their last interaction.

Figure 3 presents point prevalence abstinence rates for each of the four treatment groups over 18 months, with treatment ending at six months. The two self-help manual conditions paralleled each other for 12 months. At 18 months, the stage-matched manuals moved ahead. This is an example of a *delayed action effect*, which we often observe with stage-matched programs specifically and others have observed with self-help programs generally. It takes time for participants in early stages to progress all the way to action. Therefore, some treatment effects that are measured by action will be observed only after considerable delay. However, it is encouraging to find treatments producing therapeutic effects months and even years after treatment ended.

The computer alone and the computer plus counselor conditions paralleled each other for 12 months. At that point, the effects of the counselor condition flattened out, while the computer condition effects continued to increase. We can only speculate as to the delayed differences between these two conditions. Participants in the personalized condition may have become somewhat dependent on the social support and social control of the counselor calling. The last call was after the six-month assessment and benefits would be observed at 12 months. Termination of the counselors could result in no further progress because of the loss of social support and control. The classic pattern in smoking cessation clinics is rapid relapse beginning as soon as the treatment is terminated. Some of this rapid relapse could well be due to the sudden loss of social support or social control provided by the counselors and other participants in the clinic.

The next test was to demonstrate the efficacy of the expert system when applied to an entire population recruited proactively. With over 80% of 5,170

FIGURE 3. Point-Prevalence Abstinence (%) for Four Treatment Groups at Pre-Test and at 6, 12 and 18 Months

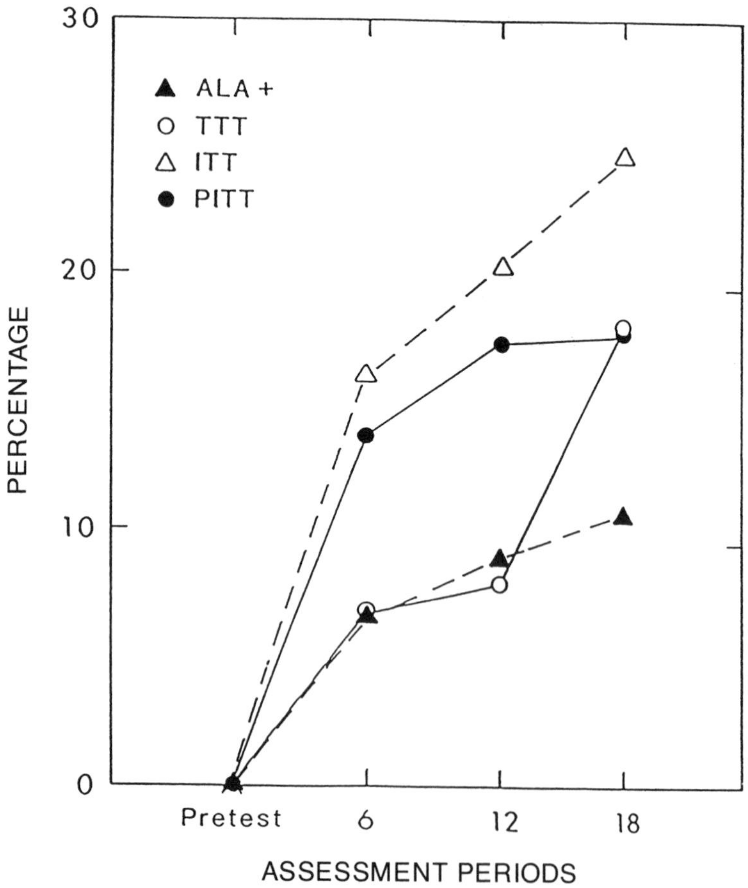

Note: ALA + = standardized manuals; TTT = individualized stage-matched manuals; ITT = interactive computer reports; PITT = personalized counselor calls.

smokers participating and fewer that 20% in the preparation stage, we demonstrated significant benefit of the expert system at each six-month follow-up (Prochaska, Velicer et al., 1997b). Furthermore, the advantages over proactive assessment alone increased at each follow-up for the full two years assessed. The implications here are that expert system interventions in a population can continue to demonstrate benefits long after the intervention has ended.

We then showed replication of the expert system's efficacy in an HMO population of 4,000 smokers with 85% participation (Prochaska, Velicer et al., 1997a). In the first population-based study, the expert system was 34% more effective than assessment alone; in the second, it was 31% more effective. These replicated differences were clinically significant as well. While working on a population basis, we were able to produce the level of success normally found only in intense clinic-based programs with low participation rates of much more selected samples of smokers. The implication is that once expert systems are developed and show effectiveness with one population, they can be transferred at much lower cost and produce replicable changes in new populations.

Enhancing Interactive Interventions. In recent benchmarking research, the author and colleagues have been trying to create enhancements to our expert system to produce even better outcomes. In the first enhancement, in an HMO population, we added a personal hand-held computer, which was designed to bring the behavior under stimulus control (Prochaska, Velicer et al., 1997a). This commercially successful innovation was an action-oriented intervention that did not enhance our expert system program on a population basis. In fact, the expert system alone was twice as effective as the system plus the enhancement. There are two principal implications here: (1) more is not necessarily better, and (2) providing interventions that are mis-matched to stage can make outcomes markedly worse.

Counselor Enhancements. In the HMO population, counselors plus expert system computers outperformed expert systems alone at 12 months. But at 18 months, the counselor enhancement had declined while the computers alone had increased. Both interventions produced identical outcomes (e.g., 23.2% abstinence rates), which are excellent for an entire population. Why did the effect of the counselor condition decline after the intervention? Our leading hypothesis is that people can become dependent on counselors for the social support and social monitoring that they provide. Once these social influences are withdrawn, people may do worse. The expert system computers, on the other hand, may maximize self-reliance. In a current clinical trial, the author and colleagues are fading out counselors over time as a method of dealing with dependency on the counselor. If fading is effective, it will have implications for how counseling should be terminated: gradually over time rather than suddenly.

We believe that the most powerful change programs will combine the personalized benefits of counselors and consultants with the individualized, interactive and data-based benefits of expert system computers. But to date we have not been able to demonstrate that the more costly counselors, who had been our most powerful change agents, actually add value over computers alone. These findings have clear implications for the cost-effectiveness of expert systems for entire populations in need of health promotion programs.

Interactive versus Non-Interactive Interventions. Another important aim of the HMO project was to assess whether interactive interventions (computer-generated expert systems) are more effective than non-interactive communications (self-help manuals) when controlling for number of intervention contacts (Prochaska, Velicer et al., 1997). At 6, 12, and 18 months for groups of smokers receiving a series of 1, 2, 3 or 6 interactive versus non-interactive contacts, the interactive intervention (expert system) outperformed the non-interactive manuals in all four comparisons. In three of the comparisons (1, 2 and 3), the difference at 18 months was at least five percentage points, a difference between treatment conditions assumed to be clinically significant. These results clearly support the hypothesis that interactive interventions will outperform an equal number of non-interactive interventions.

These results support our assumption that the most powerful health promotion programs for entire populations will be interactive. In the clinical literature, it is clear that interactive interventions like behavioral counseling produce greater long-term abstinence rates (20% to 30%) than do non-interactive interventions such as self-help manuals (10% to 20%). It should be kept in mind that these traditional action-oriented programs were implicitly or explicitly recruiting for populations in the preparation stage. Our results indicate that even with proactively recruited smokers, where less than 20% were in the preparation stage, the long-term abstinence rates are in the 20% to 30% range for the interactive interventions and in the 10% to 20% range for the non-interactive interventions. The implications are clear. Providing interactive interventions via computers are likely to produce greater outcomes than relying on non-interactive communications, such as newsletters, media or self-help manuals.

CONCLUSIONS

The author and colleagues believe that the future of health promotion programs lies with stage-matched, proactive and interactive interventions. Much greater effects can be generated by proactive programs because of much higher participation rates, even if efficacy rates are lower. We further believe that proactive programs can produce outcomes comparable to traditional reactive programs. It is counterintuitive to believe that outcomes with persons whom we reach out to help can be as positive as outcomes with people who call us for help, but that is what informal comparisons strongly suggest. Comparing 18-month follow-ups for all subjects who received our three expert system reports in a previous reactive study and in our current proactive study, the abstinence curves are remarkably similar (Prochaska, DiClemente et al., 1993; Prochaska, Velicer et al., 1997a).

The results with counseling plus computer conditions are even more impressive. Proactively recruited smokers who worked with counselors and computers had higher abstinence rates at each followup than did the smokers who had called for help. One of the differences is that the proactive counseling protocol had been revised and improved to reflect previous data and experience. The conclusion is, however, that if we reach out and offer people improved behavior change programs that are appropriate for their stage, we probably can produce efficacy or abstinence rates at least equal to those we produce with those who reach out to us for help. Unfortunately, there is no experimental design that could permit us to randomly assign people to proactive versus reactive recruitment programs. We are left with informal but provocative comparisons.

If these results continue to be replicated, therapeutic programs will be able to produce unprecedented effects on entire populations. We believe that these effects require adjustments in professional practice: (1) from an action paradigm to a stage paradigm; (2) from reactive to proactive recruitment; (3) from expecting participants to match the needs of our programs to having our programs match the needs of participants; and (4) from clinic-based to population-based programs that apply the field's most powerful individualized and interactive intervention strategies.

REFERENCES

American Psychiatric Association (1994). *Diagnostic and Statistical Manual of Mental Disorders, 4th Edition*. Washington, DC: American Psychiatric Press.

Beitman BD, Beck NC, Deuser W, Carter C, Davidson J & Maddock R (1994). Patient stages of change predicts outcome in a panic disorder medication trial. *Anxiety* 1:64–69.

Ennett ST, Tabler NS, Ringwolt CL & Fliwelling RL (1994). How effective is drug abuse resistance education? A meta-analysis of Project DARE outcome evaluations. *American Journal of Public Health* 84:1394–1401.

Glasgow RE, Terborg JR, Hollis JF, Severson HH & Boles SM (1995). Take Heart: Results from the initial phase of a work-site wellness program. *American Journal of Public Health* 85:209–216.

Lichtenstein E & Hollis J (1992). Patient referral to smoking cessation programs: Who follows through? *The Journal of Family Practice* 34:739–744.

Lichtenstein E, Nothwehyr F & Gray C (1995). Changes in adult cigarette smoking in the Minnesota Heart Health Program. *American Journal of Public Health* 85:201–208.

Luepker RV, Murray DM, Jacobs DR et al. (1994). Community education for cardiovascular disease prevention: Risk factor changes in the Minnesota Heart Health Program. *American Journal of Public Health* 84:1383–1393.

Medeiros ME & Prochaska JO (1997). Predicting termination and continuation status in psychotherapy using the Transtheoretical Model. Manuscript under review.

Prochaska JO (1994). Strong and weak principles for progressing from Precontemplation to Action based on twelve problem behaviors. *Health Psychology* 13:47–51.

Prochaska JO & DiClemente CC (1983). Stages and processes of self-change of smoking: Toward an integrative model of change. *Journal of Consulting and Clinical Psychology* 51:390–395.

Prochaska JO, DiClemente CC & Norcross JC (1992). In search of how people change: Applications to the addictive behaviors. *American Psychologist* 47:1102–1114.

Prochaska JO, DiClemente CC, Velicer WF & Rossi JS (1993). Standardized, individualized, interactive and personalized self-help programs for smoking cessation. *Health Psychology* 12:399–405.

Prochaska JO, Norcross JC & DiClemente CC (1994). *Changing for Good*. New York, NY: William Morrow & Co., Inc.

Prochaska JO, Velicer WF, Fava J, Ruggiero L, Laforge R & Rossi J (1997a). Counselor and stimulus control enhancements of a sage matched expert system for smokers in a managed care setting. Manuscript under review.

Prochaska JO, Velicer WF, Fava J, Rossi J & Tsoh (1997b). A stage matched expert system intervention with a total population of smokers. Manuscript under review.

Prochaska JO, Velicer WF, Rossi JS, Goldstein MG, Marcus BH, Rakowski W, Fiore C, Harlow L, Redding CA, Rosenbloom D & Rossi SR (1994). Stages of change and decisional balance for twelve problem behaviors. *Health Psychology* 13:39–46.

Rossi JS (1992). Stages of change for 15 health risk behaviors in an HMO population. Paper presentation at 13th meeting of the Society for Behavioral Medicine, New York, NY.

Snow MG, Prochaska JO & Rossi JS (1992). Stages of change for smoking cessation among former problem drinkers: A cross-sectional analysis. *Journal of Substance Abuse* 4:107–116.

U.S. Department of Health and Human Services. (1990). *The Health Benefits of Smoking Cessation: A Report of the Surgeon General* (DHHS Publication No. CDC 90-8416). Washington, DC: U.S. Government Printing Office.

Wierzbicki M & Pekarik G (1993). A meta-analysis of psychotherapy dropout. *Professional Psychology: Research and Practice* 29:190–195.

CHAPTER 2

Characteristics of Effective Counselors

Kathleen M. Carroll, Ph.D.

Implications of Therapist Variability
Therapist Characteristics Associated with Variability in Treatment Outcome
Therapist Attributes
Therapist Behaviors

Many factors may explain variability in the outcome of behavioral treatments for substance use disorders; some of the most frequently evaluated are the treatments themselves and the characteristics of the patients who participate in treatment. However, the effectiveness of behavioral therapies also is dependent, to varying degrees, on the therapists who deliver them. Yet therapists and the nature of their contributions to treatment outcomes remain a comparatively underresearched area in the treatment of substance use disorders (Crits-Christoph, Beebe & Connolly, 1990; Najavits & Weiss, 1994).

While therapists and therapist effects often receive little attention in reports of clinical trials, they can have tremendous influence on treatment retention and outcome. In many cases, the magnitude of therapist effects may be larger than the effects of the treatment itself. For example, in a meta-analysis of therapist effects on psychotherapy outcomes, Crits-Christoph and colleagues (1991) reported that up to 72.9% of outcome variance, depending on the outcome measure used, was associated with the therapists delivering the treatment.

Single studies involving a range of substance-abusing populations also have noted large differences across therapists in rates of retention and outcome. McLellan and colleagues (1988), after assigning 61 methadone maintenance patients to four new therapists, reported statistically and clinically significant differences across the therapists in patient outcomes, including percent of positive urinalyses, methadone dose, and employment status. In their groundbreaking evaluation of manual-guided psychotherapy and counseling among methadone maintenance patients, Luborsky and colleagues (1985) found that effect sizes across nine therapists ranged from a weak .13 to a very robust .74. As in the McLellan study, these considerable differences in therapist effectiveness did not appear to be associated with patient characteristics, therapist caseloads, or other therapist or program characteristics. Miller and colleagues (1980) found that therapist success rates ranged from 25% to 100% among nine paraprofessional therapists treating alcoholics; moreover, therapist effects accounted for over half the variance in drinking outcomes for up to a year following treatment. McCaul and Svikis (1991) reported that rates of successful client discharge varied from 17% to 54% among seven counselors, with dropout rates varying from 14% to 61%. Analysis of therapist effects in Project MATCH indicated that the magnitude of therapist effects on drinking outcomes ranged from 1% to 12% of the variance in drinking outcomes (depending on the treatment evaluated and whether the treatment was delivered in an outpatient or aftercare setting), even after controlling for patient baseline variables (Project MATCH Research Group, in press). However, almost all significant therapist effects could be traced to a single outlier therapist, usually one whose outcomes were poorer than those of the other therapists delivering the same treatment.

Variability in outcome due to therapists has been reviewed by Najavits and Weiss (1994), who noted that substantial levels of therapist variability have been found across a wide range of studies in the addictions, which have spanned a range of therapist characteristics, patient characteristics, treatment modalities, treatment settings, and other features. Thus, there is consensus that a great deal of variability in substance abuse treatment outcomes may be associated with the therapists implementing the treatment.

IMPLICATIONS OF THERAPIST VARIABILITY

Treatment efficacy research seeks to control extraneous sources of variability so that meaningful conclusions can be drawn regarding a treatment's effectiveness with a given population. In such studies, large therapist effects are a critical problem because even moderate variability can lead to false positive conclusions about treatment effects and thus reduce statistical power (Carroll, 1997; Crits-Christoph, Beebe & Connolly, 1990). Therefore, it is essential to attempt to minimize therapist variability in implementing treatment. The Crits-Christoph meta-analysis (1991) indicated that several methodological features were associated with the magnitude of therapist effects. Studies that employed more highly experienced therapists and that used treatment manuals were found to have a significantly lower magnitude of therapist effects. While those data are correlational, they do suggest that there are several strategies, particularly the use of rigorous methods associated with the technology model of psychotherapy research (e.g., use of manuals and therapist selection criteria), which investigators can use to minimize therapist effects in clinical outcome research.

From a clinical point of view, therapist variability may be extremely useful in pointing to therapist characteristics that can mediate good versus poorer outcomes in substance abuse treatment, and thus to strategies that may improve therapist performance and patient outcome. For example, much might be learned from studying "outlier" therapists—both those who are very effective versus those who have particularly poor outcomes. The following section briefly summarizes the status of knowledge on the influence of various therapist characteristics on outcome; for a more comprehensive review, see Najavits and Weiss (1994).

THERAPIST CHARACTERISTICS ASSOCIATED WITH VARIABILITY IN TREATMENT OUTCOME

It should be noted that a number of methodologic limitations have hampered researchers' ability to draw firm conclusions about specific therapist characteristics and outcome. For example, in most studies, the number of therapists studied has been small, limiting both power to detect significant differences by characteristic and increasing the likelihood of chance findings. Very few prospective studies have been done, so those that do exist tend to be retrospective and exploratory, again capitalizing on chance. Similarly, in most studies therapists have been "nested" within treatments; that is, a single therapist has performed only one type of treatment. As a result, it is difficult to distinguish effects associated with particular therapist characteristics from effects of the treatments themselves. Moreover, in no study of therapist characteristics have patients been randomly assigned to therapists, and thus findings of characteristics associated with effective therapists may be confounded by any number of variables (e.g., more skillful or experienced therapists may be assigned more difficult, poorer-prognosis patients). Finally, the few studies that have reported on therapist effects and characteristics tend to be more tightly controlled clinical trials that use selected therapists and comparatively rigorous therapist training procedures; these procedures are designed to reduce variability in therapist performance and restrict both the range of therapist characteristics of interest and outcome variability.

Najavits and Weiss (1994) noted that therapist characteristics associated with specific outcomes could be broadly classified into two main areas: *therapist attributes* and *therapist behaviors and processes*; this is analogous to Beutler's (1994) distinction between therapist traits and more mutable therapist states.

THERAPIST ATTRIBUTES

As in the larger psychotherapy outcome literature (see Beutler, Machado & Neufeldt, 1994; Blatt, Sanislow et al., 1996), few "gross" therapist attributes have been consistently related to outcomes of substance abuse treatment (Najavits & Weiss, 1994). For example, no therapist demographic characteristic (gender, age, education, ethnicity) has been identified as strongly related to outcomes in more than a study or two. However, Beutler, Machado and Neufeldt (1994) noted that, while the evidence does not suggest that therapist age, sex, or ethnicity plays a major role in therapy outcome, a "tentative rule of thumb" emerging from the general psychotherapy outcome literature is that similarity on these dimensions facilitates retention in therapy. This rule of thumb appears to apply in treatment of substance use disorders as well (Nurco, Shaffer et al., 1988).

Similarly, while therapist recovery status has been held by many practitioners to be an important determinant of treatment response, McLellan and colleagues' review of over 50 studies that compared the recovery status of clinicians predicted little about therapists' effectiveness (McLellan, Woody et al., 1988). In an evaluation of therapist characteristics based on over 80 therapists participating in Project MATCH, very few of the large number of therapist attributes studied, including recovery status, were significant predictors of drinking outcomes in patients and no attribute consistently predicted outcome across treatment types (Project MATCH Research Group, in press).

There is some evidence to suggest that other therapist attributes may be associated with improved outcomes in the treatment of substance use disorders; however, these typically reflect findings from single studies in which there were few controls over the variables of interest or potential confounds. Luborsky and colleagues (1985) found moderate positive correlations between the therapists' adjustment and interest in helping (as rated by colleagues) and outcome among methadone-maintained opiate addicts. Sanchez-Craig and colleagues (1991) reported better outcomes among patients treated for heavy drinking by more-experienced rather than less-inexperienced therapists. Rosenberg and colleagues (1976) reported that alcohol counselors who were female, older, and more introverted had better outcomes. Therapists who were rated by colleagues as more effective were higher in dominance and less deferential, as rated by the Edwards Personal Preference Schedule (Thrower & Tyler, 1986). Rohrer, Thomas and Yasenchak (1992) reported that, when 60 patients in a residential treatment center were asked to describe the ideal addictions counselor, the most highly ranked descriptors included "understanding," "caring," "experienced," and "honest."

It is of note that few studies of therapists treating substance-abusing patients have explored the potential negative effects of poor therapist adjustment, given the limited training, education, and supervision found among some clinicians in substance abuse treatment programs. In their review of the general psychotherapy literature, Beutler, Machado and Neufeldt (1994) remarked that, while good therapist adjustment may be an important but not necessary determinant of positive outcome, the effects of poor therapist adjustment and emotional problems is an area that deserves further research.

THERAPIST BEHAVIORS

Although few gross therapist attributes appear to be strongly associated with outcome, research on therapist variables linked to treatment process has been more promising. Among the most consistent findings in the general psychotherapy literature is that a positive therapeutic relationship is associated with better outcome (Horvath & Luborsky, 1993; Horvath & Symonds, 1991). This appears to be true in the treatment of substance use disorders as well. Luborsky and colleagues (1985) found high and significant correlations between Helping Alliance Questionnaire ratings and drug use, employment, legal, and psychological outcomes among methadone-maintained opiate addicts. In Project MATCH, patient and therapist ratings of the therapeutic alliance were found to be significant predictors of retention and drinking outcomes in the outpatient arm of the study, even after controlling for a range of other sources of variance (including patient and therapist demographic characteristics, drinking history, setting, and treatment type) (Connors, Carroll et al., 1997). Carroll and colleagues (1997) found that the level of the therapeutic alliance between patient and therapist predicted outcomes for a psychotherapy control condition among cocaine-dependent patients. In addition, there were significant correlations between measures of the therapeutic alliance, where the better the therapeutic alliance, the more therapists adhered to the treatment manual. This suggests that a good therapeutic relationship may make it easier for therapists to deliver treatment; conversely, delivery of interventions of demonstrated efficacy may facilitate the therapeutic alliance. Finally, continuity of the patient-clinician relationship over long periods of time, as opposed to reassigning patients to new therapists, has been associated with better outcomes among drug abusers (Cohen, Garey et al., 1980; McCaul & Svikis, 1991).

Several investigators have evaluated the impact of the therapist's style on outcomes. Miller, Benefield and Tonigan (1993) demonstrated that a directive, confrontational counselor style was associated with significantly more resistance on the part of patients and poorer one-year outcomes than was a more empathic, client-centered style. This finding appears to be consistent with several studies from the general psychotherapy literature, which point to a negative relationship between therapist directiveness and outcome (see Beutler, Machado & Neufeldt, 1994;

Patterson & Forgatch, 1985); however, it also has been noted that some patients seem to benefit from a directive therapist style. Better outcomes also have been associated with higher levels of counselor interpersonal skills, particularly empathy (Miller & Baca, 1983; Valle, 1981).

Another process variable that has been linked to improved patient outcomes is the therapist's level of adherence to a particular, well-defined treatment approach. This reflects the increased emphasis on careful specification of treatment delivery through the use of treatment manuals and the related emphasis on empirically validated treatments. Luborsky and colleagues (1985) evaluated therapist effects in manual-guided psychotherapies for methadone-maintained opioid addicts and found that the degree to which therapists delivered interventions associated with the treatment manual and refrained from delivering interventions associated with comparison approaches (e.g., treatment "purity") was significantly associated with improved outcomes. While research on the relationship between adherence to manual guidelines and outcome has yielded mixed results (see Stiles & Shapiro, 1994), Beutler and colleagues, in their review, note that "Therapists who use psychotherapy manuals to guide their interventions . . . appear to enhance therapeutic benefit over those who do not use such structured intervention packages. One may also compare the moderate effect size obtained by therapists who use manuals with the low effect size attributable to therapist theoretical orientation" (Beutler, Machado & Neufeldt, 1994, p. 259). Thus, how effectively a therapist delivers a treatment ultimately may be more important than the specific type of treatment delivered.

IMPLICATIONS AND CONCLUSIONS

To summarize, research on therapist effectiveness and therapist characteristics associated with outcomes in the treatment of substance use disorders largely parallels that of the general psychotherapy literature in several ways. First, the magnitude of therapist effects on patient outcomes can be substantial—in some cases, larger than the effect of the treatment itself. Strategies for reducing the magnitude of therapist variability in clinical trials include use of experienced therapists, treatment manuals, and assigning fewer cases to each therapist. Second, despite the magnitude of outcome variability due to therapist effects, relatively little is known about therapist characteristics associated with effectiveness in the treatment of the addictions. While gross therapist characteristics such as sex, race, age, and recovery status appear to have little impact on outcome, process-related variables such as therapist empathy, ability to establish a positive therapeutic relationship, use of a client-centered, non-confrontational style, and application of a well-specified treatment approach have been more consistently tied to positive outcomes.

Although we have far to go in the evaluation and understanding of therapist effects, therapist characteristics, and their contribution to outcomes, what guidelines for selecting therapists to work with substance-abusing patients can be derived from the existing data? First, *ne front crede*—don't trust appearances. The data suggest that we cannot tell an effective therapist from his or her surface features, or vita. Rather, effectiveness appears to be associated with therapist behaviors and how the therapist interacts with his or her patients. Thus, selection of therapists is likely to be best approached through review of taped examples of a therapist's work, with particular attention to the therapist's ability to establish and maintain therapeutic relationships, to use a non-confrontational style, to maintain an appropriate level of focus on the patient's target symptoms, and to implement techniques associated with empirically validated forms of treatment.

The good news in all of this is that it appears to be the mutable therapist features that matter; a given therapist's effectiveness appears to be associated with characteristics that are, at least theoretically, subject to change through greater training or experience. However, it remains to be seen whether and to what degree characteristics like the capacity to establish effective therapeutic relationships can be improved through training or other interventions. In fact, Henry and colleagues (1993) found that while training in dynamic therapy for depression did alter the technical aspects of therapists' technique, there was some evidence of deterioration in interpersonal aspects of treatment.

Beyond training, alternate methods of enhancing therapist effectiveness rarely have been explored. McCaul and Svikis (1991) suggested that therapist performance might be enhanced through clear definition of desired performance goals and providing the therapist with regular feedback on those goals (rates of patient retention, urine outcomes, etc.). For example, clinicians might receive bonuses or other incentives (e.g., conference attendance) for meeting defined performance objectives (such as fewer positive urines or higher rates of employment among patients) or using a compensation system more akin to those in private practice, where clinicians who do not retain their patients are not rewarded.

Overall, effectiveness among therapists who deliver substance abuse treatment appears more closely related to what they do and how well they do it than to who they are. Areas particularly worthy of further research include patient-therapist matching; the careful study of outlier therapists, both effective and ineffective; determinants of common elements of therapies that affect outcome; determinants of variance in performance for a single therapist; the "trainability" of characteristics such as the ability to foster effective working relationships; the effects of training and supervision on the performance of substance abuse therapists; the extent to which therapists who closely identify themselves with a single therapeutic orientation can effectively implement a dissimilar treatment; evaluation of therapist behaviors that facilitate periods of behavior change within therapy; and further study of therapist characteristics and attributes, including skillfulness, treatment structure, and self-disclosure.

ACKNOWLEDGMENT: Support was provided by the National Institute on Drug Abuse Grants P50 DA09241, RO1 DA10679, and K02 DA00248.

REFERENCES

Beutler LE, Machado P & Neufeldt S (1994). Therapist variables. In AE Bergin & SL Garfield (eds.) *Handbook of Psychotherapy and Behavior Change, 4th edition.* New York, NY: John Wiley & Sons, 229–269.

Blatt SJ, Sanislow CA, Zuroff DC & Pilkonis PA (1996). Characteristics of effective therapists: Further analyses of data from the National Institute of Mental Health Treatment of Depression Collaborative Research Program. *Journal of Consulting and Clinical Psychology* 64:1276–1284.

Carroll KM (1997). Manual guided psychosocial treatment: A new virtual requirement for pharmacotherapy trials? *Archives of General Psychiatry* 54:923–928.

Carroll KM, Nich C & Rounsaville BJ (1997). Contribution of the therapeutic alliance to outcome in active versus control psychotherapies. *Journal of Consulting and Clinical Psychology* 65:510–514.

Cohen GH, Garey RE, Evans A & Wilchinsky M (1980). Treatment of heroin addicts: Is the client-therapist relationship important? *The International Journal of the Addictions* 15:207–214.

Connors GJ, Carroll KM, DiClemente CC, Longabaugh R & Donovan DM (1997). The therapeutic alliance and its relationship to alcoholism treatment participation and outcome. *Journal of Consulting and Clinical Psychology* 65:588–598.

Crits-Christoph P, Baranackie K, Kurcias J et al. (1991). Meta-analysis of therapist effects in psychotherapy outcome studies. *Psychotherapy Research* 1:81–91.

Crits-Christoph P, Beebe KL & Connolly MB (1990). Therapist effects in the treatment of drug dependence: Implications for conducting comparative treatment studies. In LS Onken & JD Blaine (eds.) *Psychotherapy and Counseling in the Treatment of Drug Abuse (NIDA Research Monograph 104).* Rockville, MD: National Institute on Drug Abuse, 39–49.

Henry WP, Strupp HH, Butler S, Schacht TE & Binder JL (1993). Effects of training in time-limited dynamic psychotherapy: Changes in therapist behavior. *Journal of Consulting and Clinical Psychology* 61:434–440.

Horvath AO & Luborsky L (1993). The role of the therapeutic alliance in psychotherapy. *Journal of Consulting and Clinical Psychology* 61:561–573.

Horvath AO & Symonds BD (1991). Relation between working alliance and outcome in psychotherapy: A meta-analysis. *Journal of Counseling Psychology* 38:139–149.

Luborsky L, McLellan AT, Woody GE, O'Brien CP & Auerbach A (1985). Therapist success and its determinants. *Archives of General Psychiatry* 42:602–611.

McCaul ME & Svikis DS (1991). Improving client compliance in outpatient treatment: Counselor-targeted interventions. In RW Pickens, CG Leukefeld & CR Schuster (eds.) *Improving Drug Abuse Treatment (NIDA Research Monograph 106).* Rockville, MD: National Institute on Drug Abuse, 204–217.

McLellan AT, Woody GE, Luborsky L & Goehl L (1988). Is the counselor an 'active ingredient' in substance abuse rehabilitation? An examination of treatment success among four counselors. *Journal of Nervous and Mental Disease* 176:423–430.

Miller WR & Baca LM (1983). Two-year follow-up of bibliotherapy and therapist-directed controlled drinking training for problem drinkers. *Behavior Therapy* 14:441–448.

Miller WR, Benefield RG & Tonigan JS (1993). Enhancing motivation for change in problem drinking: A controlled comparison of two therapist styles. *Journal of Consulting and Clinical Psychology* 61:455–461.

Miller W, Taylor C & West J (1980). Focused versus broad-spectrum behavior therapy for problem drinkers. *Journal of Consulting and Clinical Psychology* 48:590–601.

Najavits LM & Weiss RD (1994). Variations in therapist effectiveness in the treatment of patients with substance use disorders: An empirical review. *Addiction* 89:679–688.

Nurco DN, Shaffer JW, Hanlon TE, Kinlock TW, Duszynski KR & Stephenson P (1988). Relationships between client/counselor congruence and treatment outcome among narcotic addicts. *Comprehensive Psychiatry* 29:48–54.

Patterson GR & Forgatch MS (1985). Therapist behavior as a determinant for client noncompliance: A paradox for the behavior modifier. *Journal of Consulting and Clinical Psychology* 53:846851.

Project MATCH Research Group (in press). Therapist effects in three treatments for alcohol problems. *Psychotherapy Research*.

Rohrer GE, Thomas M & Yasenchak AB (1992). Client perceptions of the ideal addictions counselor. *The International Journal of the Addictions* 27:727–733.

Rosenberg CM, Gerrein JR, Manohar V & Liftik J (1976). Evaluation of training in alcoholism counselors. *Journal of Studies on Alcohol* 37:1236–1246.

Sanchez-Craig M, Spivak K & Davila R (1991). Superior outcome of females over males after brief treatment for the reduction of heavy drinking: Replication and report of therapist effects. *British Journal of Addiction* 86:867–876.

Stiles WB & Shapiro DA (1994). Disabuse of the drug metaphor: Psychotherapy process-outcome correlation. *Journal of Consulting and Clinical Psychology* 62:942–948.

Thrower J & Tyler J (1986). Edwards Personal Preference Schedule correlates of addiction counselor effectiveness. *International Journal of Addiction* 21:191–193.

Valle SK (1981). Interpersonal functioning of alcoholism counselors and treatment outcome. *Journal of Studies on Alcohol* 42:783–790.

CHAPTER 3

Brief Interventions

Allan W. Graham, M.D., FACP, FASAM
Michael S. Fleming, M.D., M.P.H.

Practical Problems in Clinical Practice
Intervening in the Continuum of Use
Integrating Brief Interventions into Primary Care

The disease of alcoholism and the behaviors of harmful drinking contribute to the hospitalization of 11% to 22% of patients in the United States (Moore, Bone et al., 1989) and a similar proportion of medical outpatient visits (Cleary, Miller et al., 1988; Cyr & Wartman, 1988; Goldberg, Ries et al., 1991; Adams, Barry & Fleming, 1996; Fleming, Barry et al., 1997). Physicians routinely under-identify patients with alcohol use problems, a reality attributed to physician practice patterns (Roche, Guray & Saunders, 1991), attitudes (Clark, 1981), education (Delbanco, 1992b), and medical record use. Once alcohol abuse is identified, discussion of the problem with patients is inconsistent and referral to appropriate continuing care infrequent (Goldberg, Ries et al., 1991). Physician behaviors can change, however, coincident with increased confidence in their own management skills and with the implementation of systems for identifying problem drinking and drug use (Wallace, Cutler & Haines, 1988; Graham, 1991).

PRACTICAL PROBLEMS IN CLINICAL PRACTICE

Early identification of hazardous alcohol use is easy and intervention, effective. Screening instruments such as the CAGE, MAST (Michigan Alcoholism Screening Test; see Appendix B of this text) and AUDIT (Alcohol Use Disorders Identification Test) can readily identify persons who are alcohol-dependent (Mayfield, Mcleod & Hall, 1974; Selzer, Vinokur & Van Rooijen, 1975; Ewing, 1984; Skinner, Holt et al., 1986; Bush, Shaw et al., 1987; Cyr & Wartman, 1988; Saunders, Aasland et al., 1993). Consumption questions that inquire about quantity, frequency and binge use have been found to identify at-risk drinkers who were not identified by the CAGE questions (Adams, Barry & Fleming, 1996). Moreover, research shows that many patients self-identify past problems with drinking when asked (Cyr & Wartman, 1988; Goldberg, Ries et al., 1991; Graham, 1991). Hence, screening interviews should gather basic information in an objective, straightforward, and non-judgmental fashion.

After a potential alcohol use problem has been identified, brief interventions that consist of as little as a single visit can be delivered and are associated with 20% to 50% decreases in consumption and adverse effects (Chick, Lloyd & Crombie, 1985; Wallace, Cutler & Haines, 1988; Babor & Grant, 1992; Fleming, Barry et al., 1997). However, changing addictive behaviors requires more than education. Specific strategies for brief intervention need to be implemented.

Individuals are most likely to make behavior changes when they perceive that they have a problem (DiClemente, Fairhurst et al., 1991; Prochaska & DiClemente, 1983), when they feel they can be effective in making a change (Bandura, 1977), and when they are active participants in setting the goals to be achieved (Miller & Rollnick, 1991; Ockene, Quirk et al., 1988).

Motivation can be enhanced by patient-centered interviewing and should incorporate the following elements (Delbanco, 1992a; Miller & Rollnick, 1991; Ockene, Quirk et al., 1988; Rollnick, Heather et al., 1992):

- Offering empathic, objective feedback of data;
- Meeting patient expectations;
- Working with ambivalence;
- Assessing the patient's readiness for change;
- Assessing barriers and strengths;
- Reinterpreting past experience in light of current medical consequences;

TABLE 1. Treatment Efficacy Associated with Coexisting Medical Problems

Motivation for making a behavior change is greatly increased when a patient becomes aware that the behavior is causally related to a current medical illness. Examples of increased intervention efficacy are listed below. It is important that health care providers make the most of these moments when patients are receptive to change.

TOBACCO

Differential smoking cessation rates measured one year after intervention demonstrate the effects of motivation and concurrent medical illness on successfully quitting.

Intervention	Quit Rate	Reference
Baseline yearly quit rate	2.5%	Fiscella, 1996
Hospital based stop-smoking consult service, no physician quit message	2.5%	Orleans, 1990
Physician counsel to quit	4.0%	Fiscella, 1996
With pregnant women	8%	Law, 1995
Community volunteers for quit studies	8–22%	Silagy, 1994
With nicotine replacement	15–25%	Silagy, 1994
Smoking clinic patients	10–22%	Silagy, 1994
With nicotine replacement	21–36%	Silagy, 1994
Victims of myocardial infarction	32%	Taylor, 1990
With nurse-managed intervention	61%	Taylor, 1990
Surgical oncology patients "usual care"	43%	Stanislaw, 1994
With nurse intervention	75%	Stanislaw, 1994

ALCOHOL

Effectiveness of alcohol use interventions is similarly subject to the differential effects of motivational state and of previously experienced alcohol-related life problems.

Intervention	Use after 6–24 months	Reference
At-risk drinkers, attending medical clinic	15% reduction	Wallace, 1988
Physician counsel to quit	30% reduction	Wallace, 1988
Health provider quit counsel	40% reduction	WHO, 1996
GGT feedback several times yearly	26% fewer sick days	Kristenson, 1983
	55% fewer hospital days	Kristenson, 1983
Alcoholics requesting treatment	90% reduction	Graham, 1995
	80% reduction	Project MATCH, 1997
Alcoholics receiving liver transplantation	80% abstinence	Knechle, 1992

- Negotiating a follow-up plan; and
- Providing hope.

Health care providers who address lifestyle issues in medical contexts increase the effectiveness of their messages. *Timing and context* are important: during an alcohol-related illness, a patient's motivation to change may be heightened. Building a *co-operative alliance* is more effective in changing behavior than is an authoritarian stance (Roche, Guray & Saunders, 1991; Delbanco, 1992a, 1992b: Miller & Rollnick, 1991; Ockene, Quirk et al., 1988). The physician's words can have a major influence on future abstinence, frequency of drinking episodes, and behavioral impairment (Walsh, Hingson et al., 1992). Negotiating *appropriate goals* for cessation of drinking and other negative behaviors is a key to success (Sanchez-Craig & Lei, 1986). Providing a *menu of options* helps to tailor treatment to the patient's learning style, motivational level, and the services available. Assuring a *plan for follow-up,* with objective, measurable, non-judgmental goals, appears to enhance outcome (Kristenson, Ohlin et al., 1983). Telephone contacts can be an important adjunct in improving compliance (Scivoletto, DeAndrade & Castel, 1992; Wasson, Gaudette et al., 1992).

INTERVENING IN THE CONTINUUM OF USE

Early identification of alcohol use problems is easier if clinicians begin to view such use along a continuum, rather than as a dichotomy between "alcoholic" and "non-alcoholic" use. Viewing such a continuum requires that the focus be broadened to include (1) persons whose drinking patterns have just started to cause life problems and (2) persons with an increased risk of future problems, injury, or harm. A simple categorization by levels of use (abstinent, light use, hazardous use, harmful use, and dependent) predicts the increasing probability of adverse consequences (Babor & Grant, 1992). "Hazardous use" can be defined as a level of alcohol consumption that is associated with a measurably increased risk of adverse consequences, such as trauma or accidents. "Harmful use" is a consumption pattern that is contributing to a current problem or problems, such as esophagitis, gastritis, hypertension, insomnia, depression, or difficulties with interpersonal relationships. "Dependent use" is commonly marked by physical withdrawal symptoms (e.g., tremor, diaphoresis, nausea, vomiting, and diarrhea) and the continued, compulsive use of alcohol in spite of adverse consequences.

Over the past decade, brief intervention studies in general hospitals, physicians' offices, and public health centers have demonstrated that a surprisingly large percentage of heavy drinkers and alcoholics can reduce their intake by 20% to 50% after very brief counseling, while others seem unresponsive to months of care (Babor & Grant, 1992; Chick, Lloyd & Crombie, 1985; Edwards, Orford et al., 1977; Elvy, Wells & Baird, 1988; Kristenson, Ohlin et al., 1983; Nilssen, 1991; Persson & Magnusson, 1989; Wallace, Cutler & Haines, 1988). In an effort to explain these differences, investigators recently have focused on motivation and readiness to change (Bandura, 1977; DiClemente, Fairhurst et al., 1991; DiClemente & Hughes, 1990; Miller & Rollnick, 1991; Ockene, Quirk et al., 1988; Prochaska & DiClemente, 1983; Rollnick, Heather et al., 1992). A number of these trials are summarized in Table 2.

In England, Edwards and colleagues (1977) studied the effects of treatment intensity on outcome by following 100 male, married, outpatient alcoholics. After evaluation, couples were randomly assigned to receive brief advice or moderately intensive treatment, and then followed prospectively. The advice group received a "sympathetic, constructive" message that attainment of the goals of reducing alcohol-related problems was in their own hands; the drinkers were encouraged to practice total abstinence from alcohol use, to return to work, and to attempt to make their marriages viable.

The treatment group received an average of three weeks' inpatient alcoholism treatment, psychiatric outpatient counseling (mean: 9.7 appointments, 30 minutes each), and monthly social worker visits with spouses. With 94% follow-up at one year, no major differences in outcome were found between the two groups; both showed marked improvement, as evidenced by a 40% decrease in self-assessed alcohol-related problems, a 50% decrease in spouse-rated "hardship," and an average longest abstinence of 15 weeks. Edwards concluded that "a reasonably intensive and conventional treatment regimen confers no additional benefit over an extremely simple approach."

Even at 10 years, there still was no difference between the brief advice and treatment groups (Edwards, Oppenheimer et al., 1983). Of the initial 100 patients, 68 were interviewed; 18 (18%) were deceased (representing 2.5 times the expected age-adjusted mortality rate; five had died by suicide). Of those interviewed, 28% were abstinent; 12% were drinking, with "good outcomes"; 13% were drinking, with "equivocal outcomes"; and 47% were drinking, with poor outcomes.

How does one explain the fact that the minimal intervention group did so well and that the more intensively counseled patients did not fare better? Sample size, statistical power, evaluation instruments, treatment approaches, patient mix, and the natural course of the disease all play a role, but an adequate answer has yet to be found.

In Sweden, Kristenson and colleagues (1983) added important evidence about the efficacy of brief interventions when they published a report of 585 male heavy drinkers who were followed for two to six years. The men were part of a large public health initiative to reduce middle-aged health risks. In the study, 11,643 men (aged 40 to 48) were invited to a medical screening; of the 585 who attended, 6.6% had gamma-glutamyltranspeptidase (GGT) levels in the top decile (greater than or equal to 84 IU/liter) and were invited to participate. Consumption data showed that 54% of these men drank more than 40 grams of ethanol a day, 22% consumed 20 to 40 grams a day, and 24% drank less that 20 grams a day (11.7 grams ethanol equals 1.25 ounces of liquor, 4 ounces of wine, or 12 ounces of beer). A substantial number of study participants had symptoms consistent with alcoholism: 30% experienced physical withdrawal and 20% were early morning "relief" drinkers.

Patients were randomly assigned to control or intervention groups. Intervention patients received GGT tests monthly, physician visits every three months to discuss the GGT values, and a treatment goal of moderation of drinking. "Control group" patients were sent a letter informing them of their impaired liver tests, encouraged to live as usual but

TABLE 2. Critical Review of Brief Advice Intervention Trials

Author	Site/ Location	Selection Process	Sample Size	Population of Interest	Intervention Protocol	Follow-Up/ Drop Out	Results
Sanchez-Craig, 1980	Ontario, Canada (Regular intake clients at the Clinical Institute of the ARF and newspaper ads)	Screening questionnaire—Criteria: no physical pathology, no participation in AA, 10 yrs or less of problem drinking (interfere with work, health, relationships)	N = 70 Exp 1 = 35 Exp 2 = 35	Males who are problem drinkers	Exp 1: Controlled drinking intervention: self-monitoring problem-solving; controlled drinking. Exp 2: Abstinence model: self-monitoring, problem-solving.	1 month	Differences in compilation in the groups. Those in controlled drinking group were more compliant with treatment.
Kristenson et al., 1983	Malmo, Sweden (Community health centers)	Males responding to a screening invitation for cardiovascular disease, diabetes, & heavy drinking	N = 585 Exp = 317 Cont = 268	Males ages 46–53	Exp: Consultation every 3 months with physician, monthly GGT, monthly contact with nurse. Cont: Informed of GGT by letter. Told to cut down. Further liver tests in 2 yrs.	Time: 2,4,5 yrs Drop out: unclear	GGT values reduced in both groups. Significant reduction in sick days, hospital days, & mortality in experimental group compared to control group. Alcohol use not determined.
Chick et al., 1985	Edinburgh, Scotland (Royal Edinburgh Hospital)	Consecutive admissions of at least 48 hours duration	N = 156 Exp = 78 Cont = 78	Males ages 18–65 in one of four medical wards	Exp: Counseling with nurse up to 1 hour plus self-help booklet. Cont: Nurse assessment only.	Time: 12 mos. Drop out: Exp = 12% Cont = 18%	No significant difference in alcohol consumption at 12 mos. Intervention group: 1. Reduced problems 2. Reduced GGT
Heather et al., 1986	GP offices in Scotland	Questionnaire in doctor's office. Males drinking 35+ units/wk. Females 20+ units/wk.	N = 104 A: 34 B: 32 C: 38	Males and females ages 18–65 in general medical settings	A: DRAMS—Leaflet for GP, medical record card, checklist of complications, drinking diary card, self-help book. B: Simple advice, no follow-up. C: No intervention.	Time: 6 mos. Drop out: A = 15% B = 6% C = 16%	No significant differences between groups. All showed decrease in consumption and improved well-being.

Wallace et al., 1988	England (Rural and small urban general practices)	Mailed questionnaire & in-practice questionnaire. Males 35+ units units/wk. Females 20+ units/wk.	N = 909 Exp: M N = 319 F N = 131 Cont: M N = 322 F N = 137	Male and female patients in general medical practices	Exp: Physician assessment, booklet, told to cut down. Cont: No advice unless patient requested or evidence of liver impairment.	Time: 6 and 12 months Drop out: 6 mos, males = 15%, females = 13%. 12 mos, males = 19%, females = 17%.	At 6 and 12 mos, significant reduction in drinking for experimentals compared to controls. Male experimentals: 1. Reduced GGT 2. Reduced BP.
Persson and Magnusson, 1989	Sweden (Out-patient clinics)	Questionnaires and GGT levels	N = 78 Exp = 36 Cont = 42	Patients ages 15–70 attending outpatient clinics. Consumption: males 200+ gms/wk, females 150+ gms/wk, or GGT greater than 0.6.	Exp: Doctor interview, monthly follow-up with nurse, quarterly follow-up with doctor, advice to cut down. Cont: Initial questionnaire, no discussion about consumption, blood sample at 12 mos.	Time: 12 mos. Drop out: 0%	Consumption, GGT, triglycerides, and sick days decreased in experimental group. Sick days increased in control group. No follow-up alcohol data on control group.
Drummond et al., 1990	United Kingdom (Hospital alcohol clinic)	Consecutive pts. in a hospital alcohol clinic	N = 40 Exp 1 = 20 Exp 2 = 20	Males who met criteria for problem drinking	Exp 1: Counseling and advice w/ routine follow-up in alcohol clinic. Exp 2: Initial counseling and advice and returned to physician for follow-up.	6 month follow-up	Both groups reduced drinking; improved problem-solving status
Anderson and Scott, 1992	England (8 group practices in the Oxford Regional Health Authority)	Self-administered questionnaires, disseminated in office and by mail. Consumption: 350+ gms/wk.	N = 154 Exp = 80 Exp = 74	Males ages 17–69 in general medical practice settings	Exp: Physician advice for 10 mins. & self-help book. Cont: No advice.	Time: 12 mos. Drop out: Exp = 31% Cont = 39%	Males in advice group showed significant decrease in consumption compared to control group.

TABLE 2. Critical Review of Brief Advice Intervention Trials (*Continued*)

Author	Site/ Location	Selection Process	Sample Size	Population of Interest	Intervention Protocol	Follow-Up/ Drop Out	Results
Maheswaran et al., 1992	England (Hypertensive clinic at Dudley Road Hospital)	Referral by general practitioners. Consumption of 20+ units/wk.	N = 45 Exp = 22 Cont = 23	Males drinking more than 20 units of alcohol	Exp: 10–15 min session with advice to cut down or abstain; advice reinforced at follow-up visits. Cont: No intervention.	Time: 8 wks. Drop out: Exp = 5% Cont = 13%	Significantly greater reduction in alcohol consumption and in standing diastolic BP in experimental group.
Senft, 1994	Kaiser Permanente primary care clinics in Oregon	AUDIT screening instrument given to patients entering clinic for routine care	N = 220	Adults attending managed care clinics	Exp 1: 15-min physician visit. Exp 2: Multiple contacts with counselor. Cont: No treatment.	12 months. Drop out rate = 31%	No difference between the groups in any of the outcome measures of interest.
Buchsbaum, 1994	University of Virginia primary care clinic, downtown Richmond	Face-to-face diagnostic interview using DIS	N = 100	Adults attending a university teaching hospital	Exp: 15-min. counseling session with physician or nurse. Cont: Health booklet	12 months. Drop out rate = 40%	No difference between the groups in any of the outcome measures of interest.
Burge, et al., 1995	San Antonio, TX University-based family medicine residency (Primarily Hispanic population)	Screening interview for all adult Hispanic patients ages 18–65 with regular appointments	N = 175 Cont = 46 Exp 1 = 40 Exp 2 = 42 Exp 3 = 47	Males and females ages 18–65 attending university-based primary care clinics	Exp 1: Physician intervention with brochure and follow-up chklist. Exp 2: Six one-hour patient education sessions. Exp 3: Physician intervention and patient education session. Cont: Routine medical care.	12 and 18 mos. Drop out: 30% didn't complete base. 12 and 18 mos. 26% of pts didn't attend.	No differences in groups in alcohol consumption, ASI variables, and GGT (all improved).

WHO, 1996	WHO 10-nation study. Combination of settings.	Males 350+ gms/wk. Females 225+ gms/wk.	N = 1,655 M = 1,356 F = 299	Cross-cultural	A: Control group—20-min interview. B. Interview, 5 mins of advice. C. Interview, 5 mins. of advice, 15 mins. of counseling, self-help manual.	Time: Minimum 6 mos. Ave. 9 mos. Drop out: 25% varying by center	Significant reduction in alcohol use found in both experimental groups. No difference between brief and extended experimental groups.
Israel, 1996	Primary care practices in Cambridge, Ontario	Trauma questions as screening tool to patients ages 18–65	N = 105 Exp = 56 Cont = 58	Adults attending 42 private practices	Exp: 30-min visit, 20-min follow-up + GGT every 2 mos with nurse educator Cont: Self-help booklet + 1 GGT.	Drop out rate 12 mos = 30%	Decreased alcohol use both groups. Significantly greater reduction in GGT levels, psychosocial problems, & physician visits in experimentals.
Fleming and Barry, 1997	64 community-based primary care physicians in 10 counties in Wisconsin	In-office questionnaire given to all patients ages 18–65 with regular appointments. Males 15+ drinks/wk; females 12+ drinks/wk, binge, or positive CAGE.	N = 774 Exp = 392 Cont = 382	Males and females ages 18–65 attending primary care clinics	Exp: Two 15-min physician visits, self-help book, drinking diary cards, drinking contract, 2 nurse follow-up calls. Cont 1: General health booklet. Cont 2: No health booklet, no intervention.	Time: 6 and 12 mos. Drop out: 6 mos = 6% 12 mos = 8%	Significant reduction in 7-day alcohol use, binge drinking, hospital days, and emergency department visits in experimental group compared to control group.

TABLE 3. Edwards: England, 1983

	Advice (N = 46)		Treatment (N = 46)	
	Intake	1 year	Intake	1 year
Age (years)	40.9		40.9	
Self-rated trouble score	5.2	3.2	5.1	3.1
Wife-rated hardship score	5.4	2.8	6.0	3.0
Self-rated drinking problems				
moderate to serious		37%		33%
Wife-rated drinking problems				
moderate to serious		52%		60%
Longest abstinence past year		15.3 wks		15.8 wks
A.A. meetings past year		4.8		7.2
Any A.A. attendance		33%		60%
After 10 years, no statistically significant differences between groups.				
Drinking status				
Abstinent		28%		
Social drinking with "good outcome"		12%		
Drinking with equivocal outcome		13%		
Uncontrolled drinking, poor outcome		47%		
Decreased		18%		
Attempted suicides		38%		
Excessive use of psychoactive drugs		44%		
Working >39 weeks of the past 52 weeks		76%		
A.A. attendance: never		38%		
slight contact		22%		

to restrict their alcohol consumption, and invited back two years later for new liver tests. Follow-up results at two and four years showed equal decreases for both groups in GGT values of 28 IU and 40 IU, respectively. The intervention group showed significantly fewer sick days (29 versus 52 days per year) and hospital days (4.1 versus 9.1 days per year), and lower rates of mortality (1.5% versus 3.3%) than did the controls.

In England and Scotland, Wallace and colleagues (1988) studied the impact of physicians' advice to reduce drinking on patients with excessive alcohol consumption. These patients were part of a larger study evaluating the effects of physician intervention on heart disease. Of the study group, 909 subjects had drinking patterns deemed excessive and were enrolled in a randomized, prospective study.

Every participant received advice on smoking, exercise, and diet, as well as an educational booklet. While the controls received no specific advice about drinking, the intervention group was given advice by their physicians about the potentially harmful effects of their current drinking, shown a histogram comparing their weekly intake with national norms, given an informational booklet about sensible drinking, and scheduled for a follow-up appointment one month later. On return visits, physicians reviewed drinking diaries and blood tests.

Twelve months later (with 82% follow-up), both the control and intervention groups showed statistically significant reductions in alcohol consumption. The intervention group showed a twofold greater reduction compared to controls ($p<0.001$ men, $p<0.05$ women). No substantial change in cigarette consumption, exercise frequency, or weight reduction occurred in either group.

In a multinational study for the World Health Organization, Babor and colleagues (Babor & Grant, 1992; WHO, 1996) initiated a program evaluating the effects of brief intervention on heavy drinkers. In the study, 1,490 nonalcoholic heavy drinkers were recruited from primary care clinics, hospitals, and work sites in eight different countries. Subjects were randomly assigned to a "control" group (who received a 20-minute health interview), a simple "advice" group (who received an interview plus five minutes of advice about sensible drinking or abstinence), a "brief counseling" group (who received an interview, advice, 15 minutes of counseling and a self-help manual), or an "extended counseling" group (who received four counseling sessions).

TABLE 4. Kristenson: Sweden, 1983

For 4 yrs per-intake:	Control		Intervention		p value
Sick days/person/year	25		24		NS, p>0.05
N =	144		163		
Subjects at intake: N =	212		317		
Follow-up:	**2 yr**	**4 yr**	**2 yr**	**4 yr**	
Sick days/person/year	38	52	28	29	p<0.05
N =	138	94	160	90	
Hospitalizations:					
days/person/year	9.1		4.1		
from accidents	15%		10%		
from mental disorders	28%		20%		
N =	180		195		
Mortality:	9 (3.3%)		4 (1.5%)		
N =	212		261		
GGT Decrease in IU/liter	27	35	28	44	p<0.05
N =	212	212	261	261	

TABLE 5. Wallace: England and Scotland, 1988

	Men		Women	
	Control	Treated	Control	Treated
Intake				
Age (years)	41	41	44	43
Drinking concerns	52%	54%	51%	53%
Ethanol (grams/day)	73	71	42	40
Drinks per week (est.)	36	35	21	20
(13 grams ethanol = 1 drink = 12 oz beer = 5 oz wine = 1.25 oz liquor)				
12 Month Follow-up (82% of 909 patients)				
Ethanol (grams/day)	64	51	35	27
Drinks per week (est.)	32	25	17	14
Amount of decrease	12%	28% p <0.001	17%	32% p <0.05
GGT (IU/liter)				
Intake	27	28	12	14
12 months	28	25 p <0.01	12	14 NS, p <0.05
"Excessive drinking" (men > 40 gms/day; women > 24 gms/day)				
Intake	100%	100%	100%	100%
12 months	74%	56% p <0.001	71%	52% p <0.05

At six months (with 75% follow-up), the investigators found a clinically meaningful and statistically significant reduction in alcohol use for men in the intervention groups compared to controls. Alcohol consumption (average daily intake) decreased for 40% of the controls, compared to 52% to 58% in the intervention groups. Intensity of drinking (number of drinks on a typical drinking day) decreased by more than one drink a day for 42% of the controls, compared to 62% to 65% of the intervention subjects. For men, simple advice appeared to be as effective as brief or extended counseling. For women, significant and equal reductions in consumption were seen in both control and intervention groups. (Although many drinkers had reduced their consumption at six months, 45% of the men and 53% of the women were still drinking in the "hazardous" range.)

A systematic, office-based, screening-intervention program has been described by Israel and colleagues

(1996): 15,686 patients attending private practices of 42 Canadian physicians were asked five questions related to any past history of trauma (Skinner, Holt et al., 1984). This technique identified 62% to 85% of the expected number of problem drinkers. A sample of problem drinkers was randomized and prospectively assigned to either (1) simple advice or (2) cognitive-behavioral counseling of three hours delivered over a period of one year. After one year with 70% completing follow-up, the advice group reported a 46% reduction in alcohol use but showed no significant decrease in GGT levels, physician visits, or psychosocial problems. In contrast, the counseled patients reported larger reductions in alcohol use (70%) and showed significant decreases in GGT (32%), physician visits (34%), and psychosocial problems (85%). There is a notably larger effect size in this study than those seen in Wallace's study.

Physicians rated the following factors as important to the success of the program: a non-threatening detection instrument, the nurse providing a comprehensive assessment within the context of a lifestyle evaluation, counseling that did not brand the patient as alcoholic, initiating screening in the waiting room, and the use of alcohol-related questions only if there is a good chance that a problem is present.

Physician time was estimated to be 17 minutes per patient identified as having an alcohol problem. The total physician time was 9,500 minutes to identify 596 positive patients: 0 minutes for screening the 13,486 patients who were negative on the trauma questions asked in the waiting room, two minutes per "trauma-positive" patient for asking follow-up questions about weekly alcohol consumption (N = 2,382), and 10 minutes per patient to assess the persons who were drinking in the hazardous range (> 14 drinks per week) (N = 596). Nurse counseling time was three hours per positive patient, or 1,800 hours for the one year follow-up contacts. The cost per patient in this study is readily calculated by the following equation: [nurse salary ÷ 596 patients] + {[(average physician salary) × (9,500 minutes v minutes worked yearly)] ÷ 596} = cost per at-risk drinker identified. An estimated cost of $80 per at-risk drinker results if nurse salary is $35,000 and physician salary is $150,000; an estimated saving of three office visits is expected over the ensuing two years, as well as a decrease in hospitalizations and medications (not evaluated in this study).

Two community-based, primary care, brief intervention trials have recently reported 12-month follow-up results: Project TrEAT (**Tr**ial for **E**arly **A**lcohol **T**reatment) and GOAL (**G**uiding **O**lder **A**dult **L**ifestyles) (Fleming, Barry et al., 1997). They are the first large clinical trials designed for the U.S. health care system to test the efficacy of brief physician advice on reducing alcohol use by at-risk and problem drinkers. Previous studies have been conducted outside the United States.

Project TrEAT, conducted in the practices of 64 physicians, studied adults aged 18 to 64 (Fleming, Barry et al., 1997). Project GOAL, conducted in the practices of 87 physicians, studied adults aged 65 and over. All physicians who participated in these randomized, controlled clinical trials were family physicians or internists practicing in 10 southern Wisconsin counties.

Project TrEAT screened 17,695 patients for problem drinking using a Health Screening Survey and randomized 774 patients into either a control (N = 382) or intervention group (N = 382). Project GOAL screened 6,047 patients and randomized 159 into a control (N = 71) or intervention group (N = 88). Both trials achieved follow-up rates of >90%. Patients in the control groups received no advice from their physicians about their alcohol use, except at their own request or as part of usual care unrelated to the study.

The main outcome measures for Project TrEAT included alcohol use, health status, legal events, drug use, and health care utilization. No significant differences were found between the intervention and control groups at baseline on alcohol use, age, social-economic status, smoking status, rates of depression or anxiety, frequency of conduct disorders, lifetime drug use, or health care utilization. At the time of the 12-month follow-up, there was a significant reduction in alcohol use ($p < .001$), as well as in episodes of binge drinking ($p < .001$) and frequency of excessive drinking ($p < .001$). Chi-square tests of independence revealed a significant relationship between group status and lengths of hospitalization over the 12-month study period for men and women ($p < .01$). Long-term follow-up data collection is ongoing; 24-month follow-up surveys have been completed and 36-month interviews are in progress. A cost-benefit analysis also is in progress, with results to be announced in 1998.

The main outcome measures for Project GOAL included alcohol use, emergency department visits, and hospital days and showed similar reductions in alcohol use, episodes of binge drinking, and frequency of excessive drinking.

TABLE 6. Israel: Canada, 1996

Patients screened = 15,686	Problem drinkers found = 548:	"Just quit"	131
		Offered referral	417
		Accepted referral	231
		Entered study	105
		Follow-up at 1 year	83

	Advice		Brief Counseling	
	Intake	1 Yr	Intake	1 Yr
Drinks/4 weeks	139	75	152	46
Ethanol (grams/day, est.)	70	37	76	23
		$p < 0.003$	$p < 0.0001$	
Amount of decrease		46%		70%
Psychosocial problems	13.4	8.8	18.3	2.7
		NS, $p > 0.05$	$p < 0.001$	
Amount of decrease		34%		85%
GGT (IU/liter)	53	47	62	42
	NS, $p > 0.05$	$p < 0.02$		

Physician Visits per year	Intake	1 Yr	2 Yr	Intake	1 Yr	2 Yr
(N = 29, to 15 HMO doctors)						
(estimated from published graph)	2.9 ± 0.6	4.6	3.6	2.9 ± 0.6	2.6	1.3
Amount of change		Not reported				−34%
Reported significance			NS			$p < 0.05$
	Between group significance by ANOVA: $p < 0.02$					

Lifestyle Risk Assessment. Graham (1991) demonstrated the successful combined use of several screening techniques with the patients and medical staff in a small community hospital. Ninety-eight patients who had been admitted for general medical problems agreed to participate in a voluntary lifestyle interview. The medical staff showed a high reliability (90%) for recording alcohol use problems in the medical records. The physicians also wrote follow-up plans specific to the alcohol problems 71% of the time. In a further study, an intervention team (achieving 93% participation and screening 543 patients) found 64 patients (12%) to be positive on the SMAST and/or CAGE screens (scores greater than or equal to 2), plus an additional 23 patients (4%) who previously were identified as late-stage alcoholics and who were not screened. Of the 64 positive patients, all were offered follow-up interviews with an alcohol specialist: 37% refused, 46% accepted the offer, and 16% left within 48 hours and were not seen. Family practitioners and internists showed a high reliability (92%) for recording alcohol problems in the discharge summaries; surgeons performed less well, listing the alcohol problem only 50% of the time.

The lifestyle risk assessments (Graham, 1991) were performed through use of a simple instrument that asked questions about the use of cigarettes, alcohol, regular exercise, diet, and stress management. The interviews were performed by an addiction specialist nurse and the results placed on the front of the patient's chart for physician review. High rates of patient satisfaction were found (92% of patients solicited agreed to participate; 55% said they "enjoyed" the experience, 44% found it "O.K.," while less than 1% "disliked" the interview).

Readiness to Change Assessment. Research over the past decade has shown that individuals appear to change behaviors in association with a number of stages, involving precontemplation, contemplation, action, and maintenance (DiClemente, Fairhurst et al., 1991; DiClemente & Hughes, 1990; Prochaska & DiClemente, 1983). People typically shift back and forth among these stages, reflecting changing levels of motivation. Using these principles, Rollnick and colleagues (1992) created a 12-question "readiness to change" questionnaire for use in matching intervention techniques with a given patient's stage of change. The patient's stage does appear to be a significant predictor of future changes in alcohol consumption

FIGURE 1. A Lifestyle Risk Assessment Form

Date:

Name:

Age:

Why have you come today? What's wrong?

Injuries
Since your 18th birthday: (Yes, No)
Have you had a fracture or dislocation?
Have you been injured in a traffic accident?
Have you injured your head?
Have you been injured in a fight?
Have you been injured after drinking?

Exercise
Do you exercise regularly? (Yes, No)
Times per week for 20 mins or more? ____

Stress and Social Network
Do you feel under stress?
(Constantly, Often, Occasionally, Infrequently)
With whom do you live?
(Alone, Spouse, Other relative, Group, Other)

Smoking
Have you ever smoked? (Yes, No)
How many cigarettes daily do you smoke? ____

Diet
Do you regulate your diet for:
Cholesterol? (Yes, No)
Salt (sodium) (Yes, No)
Total calories or fat? (Yes, No)

Alcohol Use
Have you ever had a drinking problem? (Yes, No)
Has anyone in your family had a drinking problem? (Yes, No)
Have you ever felt you should cut down on your drinking? (Yes, No)
Have people annoyed you by criticizing your drinking? (Yes, No)
Have you ever felt bad or guilty about your drinking? (Yes, No)
Have you ever had a drink first thing in the morning to steady your nerves or get rid of a hangover? (Yes, No)
How many drinks do you have on a typical drinking day? ____
(1 drink = 12 oz beer = 5 oz wine = 1.25 oz liquor)
How many days a week do you generally drink? ____

(Heather, Rollnick & Bell, 1993). Matching stage of change with treatment choices would appear to be important for treatment planning, allocating resources, and developing referral plans.

INTEGRATING BRIEF INTERVENTIONS INTO PRIMARY CARE

Screening procedures can be applied to whole communities and large populations with minimal resources. The goal of brief intervention programs is to decrease alcohol use and associated problems in at-risk drinkers; the target population is the 20% of U.S. adults who are at risk for, or who are experiencing, serious alcohol-related adverse effects and who, for the most part, are non-dependent drinkers. This goal can be achieved by a variety of health care professionals, including nurses' aides, staff nurses, counselors, psychologists, social workers, physicians, and other clinicians. Brief interventions are inexpensive and can be incorporated into routine clinical practice; they are much less costly than a single emergency department visit for an alcohol-related injury.

Implementation of clinical protocols for screening and brief intervention needs to be approached as a systems issue. Health care settings are complex systems with multiple competing agendas. Implementation strategies include convincing payers (such as employers and governmental agencies) and administrators (including insurance companies and health care maintenance organizations) to provide financial support and leadership. Payers and administrators will need to be convinced that the prevention and treatment of alcohol problems will reduce overall health care costs, improve the health of their enrolled populations, and reduce other hidden social costs. Ongoing U.S. trials are expected to provide solid research data to support widespread application of screening and brief intervention strategies. The study by Israel (1996) already provides benchmarks for estimating the power of the intervention effects.

Primary medical care systems need to incorporate screening and brief intervention protocols routinely in the course of clinical care and prevention activities, including routine examinations (e.g., sports physicals, well woman exams and insurance physicals), treatment of acute medical problems (e.g., trauma, infections, anxiety and headaches), management of chronic conditions (e.g., depression, hypertension and diabetes) and prevention programs (e.g., breast cancer screening, nutrition and diet counseling, and immunizations). Strategies include the use of self-administered screening tests such as the AUDIT or the trauma questions, the use of lifestyle questions including alcohol consumption as part of routine vital signs, or the use of computerized reminder systems to cue clinicians to screen patients for alcohol problems. Reminder systems can be attached to the front of the client's medical record or in another prominent location. Clinical protocols such as the one illustrated in Figure 1 can be placed on a card and taped to a desk or wall in clinical areas. Self-help booklets, alcohol diary cards, lists of meetings of self-help groups such as Alcoholics Anonymous, and referral information with phone numbers and names of addiction medicine specialists can assist clinicians and clients in establishing follow-up plans and strategies.

Measuring provider performance, assessing patient outcomes, and providing feedback to the staff are important steps that enhance provider participation, morale, and enthusiasm about screening and the effectiveness of intervention. Efficient data collection, management, and analysis are needed to facilitate feedback and to promote meaningful outcome evaluation. Providers need to "buy in" to the process and to feel that they are effective clinically if systematic interventions are to work.

Providers generally need skills training workshops and incentives to make brief interventions an essential clinical activity. These workshops should focus on skills training activities that use role play exercises and standardized clients. Contemporary medical training has emphasized technology-based, physician-centered decisionmaking to the relative exclusion of skills training in effective listening, patient negotiation, and dealing with ambivalence. Physicians tend to blame patients for lack of compliance and for denial, failing to have been taught that the physician's own interviewing skills and negotiating style have great influence on patient compliance and outcome. The National Institute on Alcohol Abuse and Alcoholism has supported the development of a number of skills training curricula that have been shown to increase the clinical skills of providers (Murray & Fleming, 1996). Alternatively, medical offices may decide to assign a specific staff member to the intervention-counseling role, which has been shown to be very effective and well received both by patients and providers.

Incentives will be needed and these must include financial reimbursement for this clinical activity, paid time to attend training workshops, and quality improvement peer review programs. Moreover, disincentives and barriers to implementation must be examined and changed. In the current health care system, it often is difficult for primary care providers to receive compensation for alcohol and drug screening and treatment. "Carved out" contracts (those that separate mental health and addiction services

FIGURE 2. Steps for Screening and Brief Intervention

STEP 1: Ask about alcohol use:
- a. Inquire about the patient's alcohol consumption;
- b. Use the CAGE questionnaire.

STEP 2: Assess for alcohol problems:
- a. Alcohol-related medical problems;
- b. Alcohol-related behavioral problems;
- c. Alcohol dependence.

STEP 3: Advise appropriate action:
- a. If alcohol dependence is suspected:
  (1) advise him or her to abstain;
  (2) refer the patient to a specialist.
- b. If the patient is at risk for or evidences alcohol poblems:
  (1) advise him or her to cut down;
  (2) set a drinking goal.

STEP 4: Monitor the patient's progress.

from other medical care) may exacerbate this problem and create significant barriers to providers and therapists.

Quality improvement programs implemented throughout a health care system can provide a unique opportunity to change provider practice behaviors. The establishment of monitoring systems to examine rates of alcohol screening in persons being treated for hypertension, depression, or anxiety disorders may be able to significantly change practice patterns and increase identification rates.

Another important component of the systems approach is the integration of specialized treatment into general medical care. Addiction treatment historically has operated outside the traditional medical care system. Many addiction treatment programs are self-standing, community-based organizations. Lack of communication between these specialized treatment programs and the primary care provider can have a serious adverse effect on a patient's long-term sobriety. In contrast to referrals between other specialties of medicine, addiction treatment programs do not routinely send treatment plans or discharge summaries to the primary care provider. Alcohol and drug specialists do not routinely call the patient's provider to coordinate and develop a long-term treatment plan. Reciprocally, primary care providers can increase communication by sending referral letters to addiction treatment specialists. One way to better integrate treatment and to increase communication is to locate addiction treatment programs that are physically near to medical care facilities. Providers are more likely to refer clients to a trusted colleague whose office is located down the hall than to a stranger located many miles away, operating in a different care delivery system. Similarly, patients are more likely to arrive at that colleague's office if it is close at hand.

Referrals to other care providers should be tracked in order to optimize follow-up attendance, in recognition of the substantial dropout rate that occurs when patients are sent elsewhere for treatment. Feedback loops need to be created to optimize follow-up attendance. Managed care organizations can potentially be very effective agents for developing internal feedback loops which promote patient follow-up and which evaluate medical service utilization. However, such feedback loops will work only if providers are given adequate time, technologies, and personnel resources to implement them.

Confidentiality concerns over sharing information between medical care providers and addiction treatment programs need to be handled smoothly yet with the highest level of concern for the patient's privacy. If "at-risk drinking" is the problem identified, then the stigma incurred by labeling a patient alcoholic or chemically dependent is avoided. At-risk or hazardous drinking designations do not carry the burden of legal scrutiny that the "chemical dependency" label requires.

If providers and addiction treatment specialists perceive themselves as working together as part of the same interdisciplinary team, then patients will be more likely to receive coordinated, comprehensive care—the best kind of care available.

CONCLUSIONS

In the health care field, there has been a movement away from employing extensive and costly alcohol and drug treatment programs and toward developing low-cost, innovative treatment technologies for addressing varying levels of severity of alcohol and drug problems. The impetus for this change stems in part from budgetary contraints and their consequent restrictions on time available for clinical services.

In health care settings, brief interventions have been used in two ways: (1) as a stand-alone, self-help, self-guided strategy for changing drinking or drug use behavior and (2) as a referral strategy to motivate individuals to seek further help for their alcohol or drug problems. The former is deemed suitable for nondependent or risky drinkers, while the latter is considered appropriate for dependent or severe problem drinkers. Findings on brief intervention with individuals who are at risk for alcohol problems thus far support the application of this treatment technology in a variety of health care settings. Further consideration needs to be given to devising new methods of incorporating brief intervention technology into routine care as conducted in these settings.

REFERENCES

Adams WL, Barry KL & Fleming MF (1996). Screening for problem drinking in older primary care patients. *Journal of the American Medical Association* 276(24):1964–1967.

Anderson P & Scott E (1992). The effect of general practitioners' advice to heavy drinking men. *British Journal of Addiction* 87:1498–1508.

Babor T & Grant M (1992). *Project on Identification and Management of Alcohol Related Problems*. Report on Phase II: A Randomized Clinical Trial of Brief Interventions in Primary Health Care. Geneva, Switzerland: World Health Organization.

Bandura A (1977). *Social Learning Theory*. Englewood Cliffs, NJ: Prentice-Hall.

Buchsbaum DG (1994). A brief intervention trial in a primary care sample of dependent drinkers. Presented at the NIAAA Working Group on Screening and Brief Intervention, Miami, FL, January.

Burge S (1995). Brief intervention trial in a Hispanic primary care sample. Presented the annual meeting of the Society of Teachers of Family Medicine, New Orleans, LA, May 2.

Bush B, Shaw S, Cleary P, Delbanco T & Aronson M (1987). Screening for alcohol abuse using the CAGE questionnaire. *American Journal of Medicine* 82:231–235.

Chick J, Lloyd G & Crombie E (1985). Counseling problem drinkers in medical wards: A controlled study. *British Medical Journal* 290:965–967.

Clark W (1981). Alcoholism: Blocks to diagnosis and treatment. *American Journal of Medicine* 71:271–286.

Cleary P, Miller M, Bush B, Warburg M, Delbanco T & Aronson M (1988). Prevalence and recognition of alcohol abuse in a primary care population. *American Journal of Medicine* 85:466–471.

Cyr M & Wartman S (1988). The effectiveness of routine screening questions in the detection of alcoholism. *Journal of the American Medical Association* 259(1):51–54.

Delbanco T (1992a). Enriching the doctor-patient relationship by inviting the patient's perspective. *Annals of Internal Medicine* 116(5):414–418.

Delbanco TL (1992b). Patients who drink too much: Where are their doctors? *Journal of the American Medical Association* 267(5):702–703.

DiClemente C, Fairhurst S, Velasquez M, Prochaska J, Velicer W & Rossi J (1991). The process of smoking cessation: An analysis of pre-contemplation, contemplation, and preparation stages of change. *Journal of Consulting and Clinical Psychology* 59(2):295–304.

DiClemente C & Hughes S (1990). Stages of change profiles in outpatient alcoholism treatment. *Journal of Substance Abuse* 2:217–235.

Drummond D, Thom B, Brown C, Edwards G & Mullan M (1990). Specialist versus general practitioner treatment of problem drinkers. *Lancet* 336:915–918.

Edwards G, Orford J, Eggert S et al. (1977). Alcoholism: A controlled trial of "treatment" and "advice." *Journal of Studies on Alcohol* 38(5):1004–1031.

Edwards G, Oppenheimer E, Duckitt A, Sheehan M & Taylor C (1983). What happens to alcoholics? *Lancet* 2(8344):269–271.

Elvy G, Wells J & Baird K (1988). Attempted referral as intervention for problem drinking in the general hospital. *British Journal of Addiction* 83:83–89.

Ewing J (1984). Detecting alcoholism. *Journal of the American Medical Association* 252:1905–1907.

Fiscella K & Franks P (1996). Cost-effectiveness of the transdermal nicotine patch as an adjunct to physicians' smoking cessation counseling. *Journal of the American Medical Association* 275(16):1247–51.

Fleming MF, Barry KL, Adams W, Manwell LB & Krecker P (1996). A trial of early alcohol treatment in older adults. Presented at the annual Wisconsin Research and Education Network, Wausau, WI.

Fleming MF, Barry KL, Manwell LB, Johnson K & London R (1997). Brief physician advice for problem alcohol drinkers: A randomized controlled trial in community-based primary care practices. *Journal of the American Medical Association* 277(13):1038–1045.

Goldberg HI, Ries RK et al. (1991). Alcohol counseling in a general medicine clinic: A randomized controlled trial of strategies to improve referral and show rates. *Medical Care* 29(7 Suppl):JS49–JS57.

Graham AW (1991). Screening for alcoholism by life-style risk assessment in a community hospital. *Archives of Internal Medicine* 151(5):958–964.

Graham AW (1995). Positive outcomes after brief hospital interventions in patients seeking treatment for alcoholism (abstract). *Journal of Addictive Diseases* 14(1):139.

Heather N, Rollnick S & Bell A (1993). Predictive validity of the readiness to change questionnaire. *Addiction* 88:1667–1677.

Heather N, Whitton B & Robertson I (1986). Evaluation of a self-help manual for media-recruited problem drinkers: Six-month follow-up results. *British Journal of Clinical Psychology* 25:19–34.

Israel Y, Hollander O et al. (1996). Screening for problem drinking & counseling by the primary care physician-nurse team. *Alcoholism: Clinical & Experimental Research* 20(8):1443–1450.

Knechtle SJ, Fleming MF, Barry KL, Steen D, Pirsch JD, Hafez GR, D'Alessandro AM, Reed A, Sollinger HW, Belzer FO & Kalayoglu M (1992). Liver transplantation for alcoholic liver disease. *Surgery* 112(4):694–703.

Kristenson H, Ohlin H, Hulten-Nosslin M, Trell E & Hood B (1983). Identification and intervention of heavy drinking in middle-aged men. Results and follow-up of 24–60 months of long-term study with randomized controls. *Alcoholism: Clinical & Experimental Research* 7(2):203–209.

Law M & Tang JL (1995). An analysis of the effectiveness of interventions intended to help people stop smoking. *Archives of Internal Medicine* 155(18):1933–1941.

Maheswaran R, Beevers M & Beevers D (1992). Effectiveness of advice to reduce alcohol consumption in hypertensive patients. *Hypertension* 19:79–84.

Mayfield D, Mcleod G & Hall P (1974). The CAGE questionnaire: Validation of a new alcoholism screening instrument. *American Journal of Psychiatry* 131:1121–1123.

Miller W & Rollnick S (1991). *Motivational Interviewing: Preparing People to Change Addictive Behavior*. New York, NY: Guilford Press.

Moore R, Bone L, Geller G, Mamon J, Stokes E & Levine D (1989). Prevalence, detection, and treatment of alcoholism in hospitalized patients. *Journal of the American Medical Association* 261(3):403–407.

Murray M & Fleming M (1996). Prevention and treatment of alcohol-related problems: An international medical education model. *Academic Medicine* 71(11):1204–1210.

Nilssen O (1991). The Tromso Study: Identification of and a controlled intervention on a population of early-stage risk drinkers. *Preventive Medicine* 20:518–528.

Ockene J, Quirk M, Goldberg R, Kristeller J et al. (1988). A residents' training program for the development of smoking intervention skills. *Archives of Internal Medicine* 148:1039–1045.

Orleans CT, Rotberg HL, Quade D & Lees P (1990). A hospital quit-smoking consult service: Clinical report and intervention guidelines. *Preventive Medicine* 19(2):198–212.

Persson J & Magnusson P (1989). Early intervention in patients with excessive consumption of alcohol: A controlled study. *Alcohol* 6:403–408.

Prochaska J & DiClemente C (1983). Stages and processes of self-change of smoking: Toward an integrative model of change. *Journal of Consulting and Clinical Psychology* 51(390–395).

Project MATCH Research Group (1997). Matching alcoholism treatments to client heterogeneity: Project MATCH posttreatment drinking outcomes. *Journal of Studies on Alcohol* 58:7–29.

Roche A, Guray C & Saunders J (1991). General practitioners' experiences of patients with drug and alcohol problems. *British Journal of Addiction* 86:263–275.

Rollnick S, Heather N, Gold R & Hall W (1992). Development of a short 'readiness to change' questionnaire for use in brief, opportunistic interventions among excessive drinkers. *British Journal of Addiction* 87:743–754.

Sanchez-Craig M (1980). Random assignment to abstinence or controlled drinking in a cognitive-behavioral program: Short-term effects on drinking behavior. *Addictive Behaviors* 5:35–39.

Sanchez-Craig M & Lei H (1986). Disadvantages to imposing the goal of abstinence on problem drinkers: An empirical study. *British Journal of Addiction* 81:505–512.

Saunders J, Aasland O, Babor T, De La Fuente J & Grant M (1993). Development of the alcohol use disorders identification test (AUDIT): WHO collaborative project on early detection of persons with harmful alcohol consumption, II. *Addiction* 88:791–804.

Scivoletto S, DeAndrade A & Castel S (1992). The effect of a 'recall system' in the treatment of alcoholic patients. *British Journal of Addiction* 87:1185–1188.

Selzer M, Vinokur A & Van Rooijen I (1975). A self-administered Short Michigan Alcoholism Screening Test (SMAST). *Journal of Studies on Alcohol* 36:117–126.

Senft RA (September 1994). Drinking patterns and health: Implementing a randomized trial of screening and brief intervention in an HMO setting. Presented at the NIAAA Primary Care Prevention Working Group meeting, Rockville, MD.

Silagy C, Mant D, Fowler G & Lodge M (1994). Meta-analysis on efficacy of nicotine replacement therapies in smoking cessation. *Lancet* 343(8890):139–142.

Skinner H (in press). Early identification of addictive behaviors using a computerized lifestyle assessment. In J Baer, G Marlatt & R McMahon (eds.) *Addictive Behaviors Across the Lifespan: Prevention, Treatment, and Policy Issues*. Newbury Park, CA: Sage Publications.

Skinner H, Holt S, Sheu W & Israel Y (1986). Clinical versus laboratory detection of alcohol abuse: The Alcohol Clinical Index. *British Medical Journal* 292:1703–1708.

Skinner H, Allen B, McIntosh M & Palmer W (1985). Lifestyle assessment: Applying microcomputers in family practice. *British Medical Journal* 290:212–214.

Skinner H, Holt S, Schuller R, Roy J & Israel Y (1984). Identification of alcohol abuse using laboratory tests and a history of trauma. *Annals of Internal Medicine* 101:847–851.

Stanislaw AE & Wewers ME (1994). A smoking cessation intervention with hospitalized surgical cancer patients: A pilot study. *Cancer Nursing* 17(2):81–6.

Taylor CB, Houston-Miller N, Killen JD & DeBusk RF (1990). Smoking cessation after acute myocardial infarction: Effects of a nurse-managed intervention. *Annals of Internal Medicine* 113:118–123.

Wallace P, Cutler S & Haines A (1988). Randomised controlled trial of general practitioner intervention in patients with excessive alcohol consumption. *British Medical Journal* 297:663–668.

Walsh DC, Hingson RW, Berrigan DM et al. (1992). The impact of a physician's warning on recovery after alcoholism treatment. *Journal of the American Medical Association* 267(5):663–667.

Wasson J, Gaudette C, Whaley F et al. (1992). Telephone care as a substitute for routine clinic follow-up. *Journal of the American Medical Association* 267(13):1788–1793.

WHO Brief Intervention Group (1996). A cross-national trial of brief interventions with heavy drinkers. *American Journal of Public Health* 86(7):948–955.

CHAPTER 4

Individual Psychotherapy

Bruce J. Rounsaville, M.D.
Kathleen M. Carroll, Ph.D.

History
Population Served
Group versus Individual Therapy
Treatment Methods
Review of the Treatment Literature
Uses of Individual Psychotherapy in the Treatment of Substance Abuse

Given the place of this chapter in a volume describing a variety of therapeutic approaches to substance abuse that have been applied in an individual modality (e.g., community reinforcement therapy), this chapter focuses on those aspects of individual therapy that are unique to the one-to-one format of treatment delivery. While this chapter presents guidelines on individual therapy that are applicable to those dependent on alcohol and other drugs, we will concentrate the empirical literature reviews of drugs other than alcohol, as the extensive literature on psychosocial treatments for alcoholics has been reviewed elsewhere (Miller & Heather, 1986; Institute of Medicine, 1990; Babor, 1994).

HISTORY

The history of individual psychotherapy for substance abusers has been one of importation of methods first developed to treat other conditions. Thus, when psychoanalytic and psychodynamic therapies were the predominant modality for treating most mental disorders, published descriptions of the dynamics of substance abuse or of therapeutic strategies arose from using this established general modality to treat the special population of drug abusers (Blatt, McDonald et al., 1984). Likewise, with the development of behavioral techniques, client-centered therapies, and cognitive behavioral treatments, earlier descriptions based on other types of patients were followed by discussions of the special modifications needed to treat substance abusers. Psychosocial approaches that originated for the treatment of substance abusers, such as Alcoholics Anonymous (AA) and therapeutic communities, have emphasized large and small group treatment settings. Although always present as a treatment option, individual psychotherapy has not been the predominant treatment modality for drug abusers since the 1960s, when inpatient Twelve Step-informed milieu therapy, group treatments, methadone maintenance, and therapeutic community approaches came to be the fixtures of substance abuse treatment. In fact, these newer modalities derived their popularity from the failures of dynamically informed ambulatory individual psychotherapy when it was used as the sole treatment for substance abusers. The problems reported for this form of treatment were premature termination, reaction to anxiety-arousing interpretations with resumption of substance use, erratic attendance at sessions, difficulties posed by attending sessions while intoxicated, and failure to pay fees because money was spent on drugs and alcohol (Brill, 1977; Nyswander, Winick et al., 1958).

Given these difficulties, it is a wonder that this approach has not been abandoned entirely. However, some inspection of what went wrong with outpatient dynamic therapy when applied to substance abusers may suggest the modifications that are needed when attempting to deliver individual treatment to this population. Briefly, dynamic psychotherapy is based on an overall conception that explains all symptoms as arising from underlying psychological conflicts that are at least partly beyond the patient's awareness (unconscious). The major goal of this therapy is to help the patient become aware of these conflicts and to seek healthier methods of achieving wishes and aims that previously have been disavowed. According to this view of psychopathology, the actual symptom choice (e.g., depression, phobia, drug abuse) is less the focus of treatment because symptom substitution is likely to take place if the presenting symptom is removed without resolving the underlying conflict. The process of the therapy relies heavily on discovering one's conflicts through an unstructured, exploratory, and anxiety-arousing procedure of attempting to say everything that comes to mind (free association). A major strategy for discovering unconscious conflicts is the analysis of transference, a process by which the patient begins to develop thoughts and feelings about the therapist that are derived from those originally experienced in other, formative relationships outside of therapy. To facilitate this exploratory process and development of transference, the therapist typically assumes a neutral, passive stance and provides a minimum in the way of advice, support, or instruction (Bibring, 1954; Alexander & French, 1946).

There are several reasons why this approach was poorly suited to the needs of substance abusers when it was offered as the sole ambulatory treatment. First, the lack of emphasis on symptom control and the lack of structure in the therapist's typical stance allowed the patient's continued drug or alcohol use to undermine the treatment. Therapists did not develop methods for addressing the patient's needs to acquire coping skills because this removal of symptoms was seen as palliative and likely to result in symptom substitution. As a result, substance use often continued unabated while the treatment focused on underlying dynamics. Limit setting by the therapist was to be avoided so as to maintain neutrality, and no clear guidelines were provided for dealing with intoxication during sessions. Dropout was a likely outcome because patients believed that their primary presenting problem was not being addressed and because little progress could be made in the exploratory dynamic goals of treatment if drug and alcohol use was not first brought under control. The major strategy that is now common to all currently practiced psychotherapies for substance abusers is to place primary emphasis on controlling or reducing drug use, while pursuing other goals only after substance use has been at least partly controlled. This means that either: (1) the individual therapist employs techniques designed to help the patient stop substance use as a central part of the treatment, or (2) the therapy is practiced in the context of a comprehensive treatment program in which other aspects of the treatment curtail the patient's use of drugs (such as methadone maintenance, disulfiram for alcoholics, or residential treatment).

A second major misfit between individual dynamic therapy and substance abusers is its anxiety-arousing nature, coupled with the lack of structure provided by the neutral therapist. Because substance abusers frequently react to increased anxiety or other dysphoric affects by resuming substance use, it is important to introduce anxiety-arousing aspects of treatment only after a strong therapeutic alliance has been developed or within the context of other supportive structures (e.g., inpatient unit, strong social support network, methadone maintenance) that guard against relapse to substance use when the patient experiences heightened anxiety and dysphoria in the context of therapeutic exploration.

Individual psychotherapy has become a resurgent approach since the 1980s, as the limitations of other modalities have become apparent (e.g., methadone maintenance without ancillary services) (Dole, Nyswander & Warner, 1976; Ball & Ross, 1991), and necessary modifications in technique have been made to address the factors underlying earlier failures. As is reviewed below, growing evidence indicates that individual psychotherapy can be an effective modality with substance abusers, and a series of studies has been conducted with the aim of guiding the context and timing for delivery of individual therapy to substance abusers.

POPULATION SERVED

To address the issue of when and with whom individual psychotherapy might best be used, it is useful to consider first when psychotherapy appears to be indicated, and second, the conditions that are best suited for an individual form of treatment.

When Is Psychotherapy Indicated? Is psychotherapy necessary in the treatment of substance abuse? What are the alternatives to psychotherapy? Of course, many, if not most, individuals who use psychoactive substances either do not become abusers of these substances or eventually stop or limit their substance use without formal treatment (Brunswick, 1979; O'Donnell, Voss et al., 1976; Robins & Davis, 1974; Robins, 1979). Most of those who seek treatment do so only after numerous unsuccessful attempts to stop or reduce drug use on their own (Robins, 1979). For those who seek treatment, the alternatives to some form of psychotherapy are either structural (e.g., sequestration from access to drugs and alcohol in a residential setting) or pharmacologic. Removal from the substance-using setting is a useful and sometimes necessary part of substance treatment but is seldom sufficient, as is shown by the high relapse rates typically seen from residential detoxification programs or incarceration during the year following the patient's return to his or her community (Hubbard, Rachal et al., 1984; O'Donnell, 1969; Simpson, Joe & Brady, 1982; Vaillant, 1966).

Psychotherapy and Pharmacotherapy. The most powerful and commonly used pharmacologic approaches to drug abuse are maintenance on an agonist that has an action similar to that of the abused drug (e.g., methadone for opioid addicts, nicotine gum for cigarette smokers), use of an antagonist that blocks the effect of the abused drug (e.g., naltrexone for opioid addicts), the use of an aversive agent that provides a powerful negative reinforcement if the drug is used (e.g., disulfiram for alcoholics) and use of agents that reduce the desire to use the abused substance (e.g., naltrexone and acamprosate for alcoholics). Although all of these agents are widely used, they are seldom used without the provision of adjunctive psychotherapy, because, for example, naltrexone maintenance alone for opioid dependence is plagued by high rates of premature dropout (Kleber & Kosten, 1984; Rounsaville, 1995), and disulfiram use without adjunctive psychotherapy has not been shown to be superior to placebo (Fuller, Branchey et al., 1986; Allen & Litten, 1992). In particular, the large body of literature on the effectiveness of methadone maintenance points to the success of methadone maintenance in retaining opioid addicts in treatment and reducing their illicit opioid use and illegal activity (Ball & Ross, 1991). However, there is a great deal of variability in the success across different methadone maintenance programs, which is in part due to wide variability in the provision and quality of psychosocial services (Ball & Ross, 1991; Corty & Ball, 1987).

The shortcomings of even powerful pharmacotherapies delivered without psychotherapy were convincingly demonstrated by McLellan and colleagues at the Philadelphia VA Medical Center (McLellan, Arndt et al., 1993). Ninety-two opiate addicts were randomly assigned to receive: (1) methadone maintenance alone, without psychosocial services, (2) methadone maintenance with standard psychosocial services, which included regular individual meetings with a counselor, and (3) enhanced methadone maintenance, which included regular counseling plus access to on-site psychiatric, medical, employment and family therapy, in a 24-week trial. In terms of drug use and psychosocial outcomes, the best outcomes were seen in the enhanced methadone maintenance program, with intermediate outcomes for the standard methadone services, and the poorest outcomes were related to the methadone alone condition. Although a few patients did reasonably well in the methadone-alone condition, 69% had to be transferred out of that condition within three months of the study inception because their substance use did not improve or even worsened, or because they experienced significant medical or psychiatric problems which required a more intensive level of care. Results from this study suggest that although methadone maintenance alone may be sufficient for a small subgroup of patients, the majority will not benefit from a purely pharmacological approach and best outcomes are associated with higher levels of psychosocial treatments.

Even when the principal treatment is seen as pharmacologic, psychotherapeutic interventions are needed to complement the pharmacotherapy by: (1) enhancing the motivation to stop substance abuse by taking the prescribed medications, (2) providing guidance for use of prescribed medications and management of side effects, (3) maintaining motivation to continue taking the prescribed medication after the patient achieves an initial period of abstinence, (4) providing relationship elements to prevent premature termination, and (5) helping the patient to develop the skills to adjust to a life without drug and alcohol use. Those elements that psychotherapy can offer to complement pharmacologic approaches are likely to be needed even if "perfect" pharmacotherapies are available. This is because the effectiveness of even the most powerful pharmacotherapies is limited by patients' willingness to comply with them, and the strategies found to enhance compliance with pharmacotherapy (monitoring, support, encouragement, education) are inherently psychosocial. Moreover, the provision of a clearly articulated and consistently delivered psychosocial treatment in the context of a primarily pharmacologic treatment is an important strategy for reducing noncompliance and attrition, thereby enhancing outcome in clinical research and treatment (Carroll, 1996).

Moreover, the importance of psychotherapy and psychosocial treatments is reinforced by recognition that the repertoire of pharmacotherapies available for treatment of drug abusers is limited to a handful, with the most effective agents limited in their utility to treatment of dependence on opioids (Senay, 1989; Jaffe & Kleber, 1989; O'Brien & Woody, 1989) and alcohol (Fuller, Branchey et al., 1986; Volpicelli, Alterman et al., 1992, O'Malley, Jaffe et al., 1992, Whitworth, Fischer et al., 1996; Sass, Soyka et al., 1996). Effective pharmacotherapies for abuse of cocaine, marijuana, hallucinogens, sedative-hypnotics, and stimulants have yet to be developed and talking therapies remain the principal approaches for the treatment of substance abuse involving these classes of drugs (Kosten & McCance, 1995; McCance-Katy & Kosten, n.d.; Meyer, 1992; Kleber, 1989; Kosten, 1989).

GROUP VERSUS INDIVIDUAL THERAPY

If psychotherapy is necessary for at least a substantial number of treatment-seeking drug abusers, when is individual therapy a better choice than other modalities, such as family therapy or group therapy? Because group therapy has become the modal format for psychotherapy of drug abusers, evaluation of the role of individual therapy should take the strengths and weaknesses of group therapy as its starting point.

A central advantage of group over individual psychotherapy is economy, which is a major consideration in an era of generally skyrocketing health care costs and increasingly curtailed third-party payments for substance abuse treatment. Groups typically have a minimum of six members and a maximum of two therapists, yielding at least a threefold increase in the number of patients treated per therapist hour. Although the efficacy of group versus individual therapy has not been systematically studied with drug abusers, there is no evidence from other populations that individual psychotherapy yields superior benefits (Smith, Glass & Miller, 1980). Moreover, nearly all major schools of individual psychotherapy have been adapted to a group format.

In addition to the general concept that group therapy may be just as good as but less expensive than individual therapy, there are aspects of group therapy that can be argued to make this modality more effective than individual treatment of drug abusers. For example, given the social stigma attached to having lost control of substance use, the presence of other group members who acknowledge having similar problems can provide comfort. Related to this, other group members who are farther along in their recovery from addiction can act as models to illustrate that attempting to stop drug and alcohol use is not a futile effort. These more advanced group members can offer a wide variety of coping strategies that may go beyond the repertoire known even by the most skilled individual therapist. Moreover, group members frequently can act as "buddies" who offer continued support outside of the group sessions in a way that most professional therapists do not. Finally, the "public" nature of group therapy, with its attendant aspects of confession and forgiveness coupled with the pressure to publicly confess slips and transgressions, provides a powerful incentive to avoid relapse. Being able to publicly declare the number of days sober and the fear of having to publicly admit to "falling off the wagon" are strong forces pushing a substance abuser toward recovery. This public affirmation or shaming may be all the more crucial in combating a disorder that is characterized by a failure of internalized mechanisms of control. Drug abusers have been characterized as having poorly functioning internal self-control mechanisms (Khantzian, 1978, 1985; Wurmser, 1979) and the group process provides a robust source of external control. Moreover, because the group is composed of recovering substance abusers, members may be better able to detect each other's attempts to conceal relapse or early warning signals for relapse than would an individual therapist who may not have a history of substance abuse.

Given these strengths of group therapy, what are the unique advantages of individual therapy that may justify its greater expense? First, a key advantage for individual therapy is that it provides privacy. Although self-help groups such as Alcoholics Anonymous attempt to protect the confidentiality of group members by asking for first names only and routine group therapy procedures involve instructions to members to keep identities and content of sessions confidential, participation in group therapy always risks a breach in confidentiality, especially in small communities. Although publicly admitting to one's need for help may be a key element of the recovery process, it is a step that is very difficult to take, particularly when the problems associated with substance abuse have not yet become severe. Public knowledge of drug and alcohol abuse can still be the ruin of careers and reputations, despite the more widespread acknowledgment of the prevalence of these disorders that occurred since the 1980s.

Second, the individualized pace of individual therapy allows the therapist more flexibility in addressing the patient's problems as they arise, whereas group therapy may be out of sync with some members while suiting the needs of the majority. This is particularly an issue for open groups that add new members throughout the life of the group, necessitating repetition of many therapeutic elements so as to acquaint new members with the group's history and to address the needs of individuals who have just begun treatment.

Third, from the patient's point of view, individual therapy allows a much higher percentage of therapy time to concentrate on issues that are uniquely relevant to that individual. Members of therapy groups usually have the experience of spending many hours discussing issues that are not problems for them, and the individual tailoring of therapy sessions to fit particular needs ultimately may be more efficient.

Fourth, logistical issues make individual therapy more practical in many settings. Given the decentralization of much mental health service delivery, individual therapy is most feasible for many mental health professionals or medical practitioners, who may not have a caseload of substance abusers that is large enough to conduct group treatment. If group therapy is to be started with a new group, it may be many weeks before enough members are screened to be entered into a new group, resulting in patients' discouragement and high dropout rates while awaiting the onset of treatment. If group therapy involves addition to an ongoing group, this can present formidable obstacles to joining. Also, unless group therapy is offered in the context of a large clinic or practice with many ongoing groups, scheduling may be very difficult for those patients whose employer is not apprised of the need for treatment.

Fifth, the process and structure of individual therapy may confer unique advantages for dealing with some kinds of problems presented by patients. For example, individual therapy may be more conducive to the development of a deepening relationship between the patient and therapist over time, which may allow exploration of relationship elements not possible in group therapy. Alternatively, patients with particular personality disorders, such as schizoid patients, may be unable to become involved with other group members, as may avoidant patients, who are so shy that they cannot bring themselves to attend group sessions.

TREATMENT METHODS

Most schools of therapy, with widely varying rationales and strategies, have been adapted for potential use with substance abusers in an individual format. Rather than focus on specific techniques associated with the different approaches, this chapter focuses on two topics that can guide the individual therapy of substance abusers within a variety of different schools: (1) the specialized knowledge needed to apply individual psychotherapy to drug abusers, and (2) the common goals and strategies that must be addressed by individual psychotherapists.

Areas of Specialized Knowledge Needed to Work with Drug Abusers. This section bases its recommendations on the assumption that most individual psychotherapists who attempt to work with substance abusers obtained their first psychotherapy experience and training with other groups of patients, such as those typically seen at inpatient or outpatient general psychiatric clinics. This assumption is based on the status of substance abuse treatment as a subspecialty placement within training programs for the major professional groups practicing psychotherapy, such as psychologists, psychiatrists, and social workers. Thus, to treat substance abusers, the task for the typical psychotherapist is to acquire necessary new knowledge and modify already learned skills.

The principal areas of knowledge to be mastered by the beginning therapist are the pharmacology, use patterns, consequences, and course of addiction for the major types of abused substances. For therapy to be effective, it is useful not only to obtain textbook knowledge about frequently abused substances, but also to become familiar with street knowledge of such drugs (e.g., slang names, favored routes of administration, prices, and availability) and the clinical presentation of individuals when they are intoxicated or experiencing withdrawal from the various abused substances.

This knowledge has many important uses in the course of individual therapy with substance abusers. First, it fosters a therapeutic alliance by allowing the therapist to convey an understanding of the addict's problems and the world in which the addict lives. This is an especially important issue when the therapist is from a different racial or social background from the drug-abusing patient. In engaging a patient in treatment, it is important to emphasize that the patient's primary presenting complaint is likely to be substance abuse, even if many other issues also are likely to be amenable to psychotherapeutic interventions. Hence, if the therapist is not comfortable and familiar with the nuances of problematic drug and alcohol use, it may be difficult to forge an initial working alliance. Moreover, by knowing the natural history of substance abuse and the course of drug and alcohol effects, the clinician can be guided in helping the patient to anticipate problems that will arise in the course of initiating abstinence. For example, knowing the typical type and duration of withdrawal symptoms can help the addict recognize the transient nature of those symptoms and develop a plan for successfully completing an outpatient detoxification.

Second, knowledge of drug actions and withdrawal states is critical to diagnosing comorbid psychopathology and helping the addict to understand and manage dysphoric affects. It has been observed in clinical situations and demonstrated in laboratory conditions (Mendelson & Mello, 1966; Mirin, Meyer & McNamme, 1980; Nathan & O'Brien, 1971; Gawin & Ellinwood, 1988) that most abused substances such as opioids or cocaine are capable of producing constellations of symptoms that mimic psychiatric syndromes such as depression, mania, anxiety disorders, or paranoia. Many of these symptomatic states are completely substance-induced and resolve spontaneously when substance use is stopped. It often is the therapist's job to determine whether or not presenting symptoms are part of an enduring, underlying psychiatric condition or a transient, drug-induced state. If the former, then simultaneous treatment of the psychiatric disorder is appropriate; if the latter, reassurance and encouragement to maintain abstinence usually are the better course.

The need to distinguish transient substance-induced affects from enduring attitudes and traits also is an important task of psychotherapy. Affective states have been shown to be linked closely with cognitive distortions, as Beck and colleagues have demonstrated in their delineation of the cognitive distortions associated with depression (Beck, 1967). While experiencing depressive symptoms, a patient is likely to have a profoundly different view of himself or herself, of the future, of the satisfactions available in life, and of his or her important interpersonal relationships. These views are likely to change radically with remission of the depressive symptoms, even if the remission of symptoms was induced by pharmacotherapy and not by psychotherapy or actual improvement in life circumstances (Simons, Garfield & Murphy, 1984). Because of this tendency for substance-related affective states to greatly color the patient's view of self and the world, it is important for the therapist to be able to recognize these states so that the associated distorted thoughts can be recognized as such rather than being taken at face value. Moreover, it is important that the patient also be taught to distinguish between sober and substance-affected conditions and to recognize when, in the colloquial phrase, it is "the alcohol talking" and not the person's more enduring sentiments.

Third, learning about drug and alcohol effects is important in the detection of patients who have relapsed or have come to sessions intoxicated. It is seldom useful to conduct psychotherapy sessions when the patient is intoxicated and, when this happens, the session should be rescheduled for a time when the patient can participate while sober. For alcoholics, noticing the smell of alcohol or using a Breathalyzer is a useful technique for detecting intoxication, but such immediate aids are not available for other drugs of abuse. The clinician then must rely on his or her own clinical skills to determine whether or not the patient is drug-free and able to participate fully in the psychotherapy.

Another area of knowledge to be mastered by the psychotherapist is an overview of treatment philosophies and techniques for the other treatments and self-help groups that are available to substance-abusing patients. As noted above, the early experience of attempting individual psychotherapy as the sole treatment of the more severe types of drug abuse has been marked by failure and early dropout. Hence, for many substance abusers, individual psychotherapy is best conceived of as a component in a multifaceted program of treatment to help the addict overcome a chronic, relapsing condition. In fact, one function of individual psychotherapy can be to help the patient choose which additional therapies to take advantage of in his or her attempt to cease substance abuse. Thus, even when the therapist is a solo practitioner, he or she should know when detoxification is necessary, when inpatient treatment is appropriate, and what pharmacotherapies are available.

Another major function of knowing about the major alternative treatment modalities for substance abuse is to be alert to the possibility that different treatments may provide contradictory recommendations that may confuse the patient or foster the patient's attempts to sabotage treatment. Unlike a practitioner whose treatment is likely to be sufficient, the individual psychotherapist does not have the option of simply instructing the patient to curtail other treatments or self-help groups while individual treatment is taking place. Rather, it is vital that the therapist attempt to adjust his or her own work in order to bring the psychotherapy in line with the other treatments.

A common set of conflicts arises between the treatment goals and methods employed by professional therapists and the predominant Twelve Step self-help movements such as Alcoholics Anonymous, Cocaine Anonymous, and Narcotics Anonymous. For example, the recovery goal for many who espouse a Twelve Step approach is a life of complete abstinence from psychotropic medications. This can come into conflict with professional advice when the therapist recommends use of psychopharmacologic treatment for patients with coexisting psychiatric disorders such as depression, mania, or anxiety. Although the Twelve Step literature supports use of appropriately prescribed medications of all kinds, many individual members draw the line at prescribed psychotropics. In the face of disapproval from fellow members of self-help groups, patients may prematurely discontinue psychotropic medications and experience relapse of psychological symptoms, with consequent return to substance abuse. To avoid this occurrence, it is important, when psychotropic medications are recommended or prescribed, to warn the patient about the apparently contradictory messages that he or she may receive between the Twelve Step admonition to lead a drug-free life and the clinician's support of the use of prescribed psychotropic medications.

One way of approaching this issue is to describe the psychiatric condition for which the medications are prescribed as a disease separate from the substance abuse, and to impress upon the patient that the prescribed medications are as necessary for the treatment of this separate condition as insulin would be for diabetes. The fact that the medications are intended to affect brain functioning and attendant mental symptoms, while insulin affects other parts of the body, is less important than the concept that two diseases are present and not one.

A second common area of conflict between some forms of psychotherapy and the Twelve Step philosophy is the role played by family members. The Al-Anon approach tends to suggest that family members get out of the business of attempting to control the substance abuser's use of drugs and alcohol, and separate meetings are held for dealing with family members' and drug abusers' issues. In contrast, many therapists encourage involvement of family members in dealing with family dynamics that may foster substance use and/or in acting as adjunctive therapists (Anton, Hogan et al., 1981; Stanton & Todd, 1982). As with the use of psychotropic medications, the major way of preventing a patient's confusion is to anticipate the areas of contradictory advice and to provide a convincing rationale for the therapist's recommendations. In doing so, it is advisable to acknowledge that different strategies appear to work for different individuals and that alternative approaches might be employed sequentially if the initial plan fails.

Common Issues and Strategies for Psychotherapy with Substance Abusers. This section reviews issues presented by substance abusers that must be addressed, if not emphasized, by any type of individual psychotherapy that is to be effective. As noted in reviewing the difficulties encountered by early psychodynamic practitioners, the central modification that is required of psychotherapists is always to be aware that the patient being treated is a substance abuser. Hence, even when attempting to explore other issues in depth, the therapist should devote at least a small part of every session to monitoring the patient's most recent successes and failures at controlling or curtailing substance use and being willing to interrupt other work to address slips and relapses when they occur.

Implicit in the need to remain focused on the patient's substance use is the requirement that psychotherapy with these patients entails a more active therapist stance than does treatment of patients with other psychiatric disorders, such as depression or anxiety disorders. This is related to the fact that the principal symptom of substance abusers, compulsive use, is at least initially gratifying, and that it is the long-term consequences of substance use that induce pain and the desire to stop. In contrast, the principal symptoms of depression or anxiety disorders are inherently painful and alien. Because of this key difference, psychotherapy with substance abusers typically requires both empathy and structured limit-setting, whereas the need for limit setting is less marked in psychotherapy with depressed or anxious patients. Beyond these key elements, this section also elaborates on the following set of psychotherapy tasks: (1) setting the resolve to stop drug use, (2) teaching coping skills, (3) changing reinforcement contingencies, (4) fostering management of painful affects, and (5) improving interpersonal functioning.

Although various schools of thought about therapeutic action and behavior change may differ in the degree to which emphasis is placed on these different tasks, some attention to these areas is likely to be involved in any successful treatment.

Setting the Resolve to Stop. Cummings (1979) has noted that substance abusers most often enter treatment not with the goal to stop such use, but to return to the days when drug and alcohol use was enjoyable. The natural history of substance abuse (Robins, 1979) typically is characterized by an initial period of episodic use, lasting months to years, during which the consequences of such use are minimal and use is perceived as beneficial. Even at the time of treatment-seeking, which usually occurs only after substance-related problems have become severe, patients usually can identify many ways in which they want or feel the need for drugs or alcohol; hence, they have difficulty developing a clear picture of what life without drugs might be like.

To be able to achieve and maintain abstinence or controlled use, substance abusers need a clear conception of their treatment goals. Several investigators (DiClemente, Prochaska & Gibertini, 1985; Prochaska & DiClemente, 1986; see Chapter 1 of this Section) have postulated stages in the development of substance abusers' thinking about stopping use, beginning with precontemplation, moving through contemplation, and culminating with determination as the ideal cognitive set with which to derive the greatest benefit from treatment.

Regardless of the treatment type, an early task for psychotherapists is to gauge the patient's level of motivation to stop substance use by exploring his or her treatment goals. In doing this, it is important to challenge overly quick or glib assertions that the patient's goal is to stop using substance altogether. One way to approach the patient's likely ambivalence toward treatment goals is to attempt an exploration of the patient's perceived benefits from abused substances or perceived needs for them. To obtain a clear report of the patient's positive attitudes toward substance use, it may be necessary to elicit details of the patient's early involvement with drugs and alcohol. When the therapist has obtained a clear picture of the patient's perceived needs and desires for abused substances, it is important to counter these by exploring the advantages of a drug-free life.

As noted above, while virtually all types of psychotherapy for substance abusers address the issue of motivation and goal-setting to some extent, motivational therapy or interviewing (Miller & Rollnick, 1991; Miller, Zweben et al., 1992) makes this the sole initial focus of treatment. Motivational approaches, which usually are quite brief (e.g., two to four sessions), are based on principles of motivational psychology and are designed to produce rapid, internally motivated change by seeking to maximize patients' motivational resources and commitment to abstinence. Active ingredients of this approach are hypothesized to include objective feedback as to personal risk or impairment, emphasis on personal responsibility for change, clear advice to change, a menu of alternative change options, therapist empathy, and facilitation of patient self-efficacy (Miller, Zweben et al., 1992). A substantial body of empirical evidence (Babor, 1994; Holder, Longabaugh et al., 1991) supports the efficacy of motivational approaches with alcoholics, but these approaches have not yet been widely applied or evaluated with drug-abusing populations. Motivational approaches are intuitively appealing, however, given that patients' commitment to abstinence has been found to be a predictor of treatment success in cocaine abusers (Hall, Havassy & Wasserman, 1991).

One major controversy in this area is whether controlled use can be an acceptable alternative treatment goal to abstinence from all psychoactive drugs (Douglas, 1986; Cook, 1988). Many, if not most, patients enter treatment with a goal of controlled use, especially of alcohol (Sanchez-Craig & Wilkinson, 1986/1987), and failure to address the patient's presenting goal may result in failure to engage the patient. At the heart of the issue is whether or not drug abuse is seen as a categoric disease, for which the only treatment is abstinence, or a set of habitual dysfunctional behaviors that are aligned along a continuum of severity (Edwards & Gross, 1976). For illicit drugs of abuse (such as cocaine and heroin), it is unwise for a professional therapist to take a position that advocates any continued use of illicit drugs, because such a stance allies the therapist with illegal and antisocial behavior. Even advocates of controlled use as an acceptable treatment goal usually acknowledge that substance abusers with more severe dependence should seek an abstinence goal. In practice, the therapist cannot force the patient to seek any goal that the patient does not choose. The process of arriving at an appropriate treatment goal frequently involves allowing the patient to make several failed attempts to achieve a goal of controlled substance use. This initial process may be needed to convince the patient that an abstinence goal is more appropriate.

Teaching Coping Skills. The most enduring challenge of treating substance abusers is to help the patient avoid relapse after achieving an initial period of abstinence (Marlatt & Gordon, 1985). A general tactic for avoiding relapse is to identify sets of circumstances that increase an individual's likelihood of resuming substance use and to help the patient anticipate and practice strategies (e.g., refusal skills, recognizing and avoiding cues for craving) for coping with these high-risk situations. For example, approaches that emphasize the development of coping skills include cognitive-behavioral approaches such as relapse prevention (Marlatt & Gordon, 1985; Kadden, Carroll et al., 1992), in which a systematic effort is made to identify high-risk situations and master alternative behaviors and coping skills intended to help the patient avoid drug use when these situations arise. A postulate of this approach is that proficiency in a variety of coping skills that are generalizable to a variety of problem areas will help foster durable change. Evidence is emerging that points to the durability and, in some cases, the delayed emergence of effects of coping skills treatments for substance abusers (Carroll, Rounsaville et al., 1994; O'Malley, Jaffe et al., in press). For other approaches, enumeration of risky situations and development of coping skills is less structured (Luborsky, 1984; Rounsaville, Gawin & Kleber, 1985) and embedded in a more general exploration of patients' wishes and fears.

Changing Reinforcement Contingencies. Edwards and colleagues (Edwards & Gross, 1976; Edwards, 1986; Edwards, Arif & Hodgson, 1981) have noted that a key element of deepening dependence on substances is the rise of substance-related behavior to the top of an individual's list of priorities. As substance abuse worsens, it can take precedence over concerns about work, family, friends, possessions, and health. As compulsive substance use becomes a part of every day, previously valued relationships or activities may be given up so that the rewards available in daily life are narrowed progressively to those derived from substance use. When substance use is brought to a halt, its absence may leave the patient with the need to fill the time that had been spent using drugs or alcohol and to find rewards that can substitute for those derived from use. The ease with which the patient can rearrange priorities is related to the level of achievement prior to the person's becoming a substance abuser and the degree to which substance use has destroyed or replaced valued relationships, jobs, or hobbies. Since the typical course of illicit substance abuse entails initiation of compulsive use between the ages of 12 and 25, many drug and alcohol abusers come to treatment never having achieved satisfactory adult relationships or vocational skills. In such cases, achieving a drug- and alcohol-free life may require a lengthy process of vocational rehabilitation and development of meaningful relationships. Individual psychotherapy can be important to this process by helping to maintain the patient's motivation throughout the recovery process and by exploring factors that have interfered with achievement of rewarding ties to others.

An example of an approach that actively changes reinforcement contingencies is the approach developed by Higgins and colleagues (Higgins, Delaney et al., 1991; Higgins & Budney, 1993), which incorporates positive incentives for abstinence into a Community Reinforcement Approach (CRA) (Sisson & Azrin, 1989). This strategy has four organizing features which are grounded in principles of behavioral pharmacology: (1) drug use and abstinence must be swiftly and accurately detected, (2) abstinence is positively reinforced, (3) drug use results in loss of reinforcement, and (4) emphasis on the development of competing reinforcers to drug use (Higgins & Budney, 1993).

Fostering Management of Painful Affects. Marlatt and colleagues (Marlatt & Gordon, 1980) have demonstrated that dysphoric affects are the most commonly cited precipitant for relapse, and many psychodynamic clinicians (Khantzian, 1985; Wurmser, 1979) have suggested that failure of affect regulation is a central dynamic underlying the development of compulsive substance use. Moreover, surveys of psychiatric disorders in treatment-seeking substance abusers concur in demonstrating high rates of depressive disorders (Hesselbrock, Meyer & Keener, 1985; Khantzian & Treece, 1985; Rounsaville, Weissman et al., 1982). A key element in developing ways to handle powerful dysphoric affects is learning to recognize and identify the probable cause of these feelings. This difficulty in differentiating among negative emotional states has been identified as a common characteristic among substance abusers (Khantzian, 1985; Wurmser, 1979). To foster the development of mastery over dysphoric affects, most psychotherapies include techniques for eliciting strong affects within a protected therapeutic setting and then enhancing the patient's ability to identify, tolerate, and respond to them appropriately. Given the demonstrated efficacy of pharmacologic treatments for affective and anxiety disorders (Beckman & Leber, 1985) and the high rates of these disorders seen in treatment-seeking substance abusers, the individual psychotherapist should be alert to the possibility that the patient may benefit from combined treatment with psychotherapy and medications. Moreover, as recent evidence points to the difficulty many substance users face in articulating strong affect (Keller, Carroll et al., 1995), which may have an impact on treatment response (Taylor, Parker & Bagby, 1990), clinicians should be alert to the need to assess and address difficulties in expression of affect and cognition when working with substance abusers in psychotherapy.

Improving Interpersonal Functioning and Enhancing Social Supports. A consistent finding in the literature on relapse to substance abuse is the protective influence of an adequate network of social supports (Marlatt & Gordon, 1985; Tims & Leukefeld, 1986). Gratifying friendships and intimate relationships provide a powerful source of rewards to replace those obtained by drug and alcohol use, and the threat of losing those relationships can furnish a strong incentive to maintain abstinence. Issues typically presented by substance abusers are loss of or damage to valued relationships that occurred when using substances was the principal priority, failure to have achieved satisfactory relationships even prior to having initiated substance abuse, and inability to identify friends or intimates who are not, themselves, substance abusers. For some types of psychotherapy, working on relationship issues is the central focus of the work (e.g., interpersonal therapy or supportive-expressive treatment), while for others, this aspect is implied as a part of other therapeutic activities, such as identifying risky and protective situations (Marlatt & Gordon, 1985). A major potential limitation of individual psychotherapy as the sole treatment for substance abusers is its failure to provide adequate social supports for those patients who lack a supportive social network of persons who are not substance abusers. Individual psychotherapy can fill only one to several hours per week of a patient's time.

Again, while most approaches address these issues to some degree in the course of treatment, approaches that strongly emphasize the development of social supports are traditional counseling approaches, Twelve Step Facilitation (Nowinski, Baker & Carroll, 1992), and other approaches that underline the importance of involvement in self-help groups. Self-help groups offer a fully developed social network of welcoming individuals who are understanding and personally committed to leading a substance-free life. Moreover, in most urban and suburban settings, self-help meetings are held daily or several times weekly, and a sponsor system is available to provide the recovering substance abuser with individual guidance and support on a 24-hour basis, if necessary. For psychotherapists working with substance abusers, encouraging the patient to become involved in a self-help group can provide a powerful source of social support that can protect the patient from relapse while the work of therapy progresses.

REVIEW OF THE TREATMENT LITERATURE

As noted above, early efforts to engage and treat drug users with dynamically oriented individual psychotherapy as the sole treatment have been marked by failure. This has led researchers to focus increasingly on the evaluation of psychotherapy for substance users in terms of the context in which individual psychotherapy is delivered most effectively, as well as the types of substance abusers most likely to benefit from individual psychotherapy. Hence, the following section reviews empiric evidence for the effectiveness of individual psychotherapy in various treatment settings, with special emphasis on identifying those types of drug users who may respond to this form of treatment. In this section, we emphasize findings from the comparatively few studies that have used rigorous methodologies associated with the technology model of psychotherapy research (Waskow, 1984; Carroll & Rounsaville, 1991). These methodologic features include random assignment to treatment conditions, specification of treatments in manuals, selection of well-trained therapists committed to the type of approach they conduct in the trial, extensive training of therapists, ongoing monitoring of therapy implementation, multidimensional ratings of outcome by independent evaluators who are blind to the study treatment received by the patient, and adequate sample sizes. We have concentrated on studies of opiate and cocaine abusers, as the more extensive literature on psychosocial treatments of alcohol has received detailed review elsewhere (Miller & Heather, 1986; Institute of Medicine, 1990; Babor, 1994).

Psychosocial Treatments for Opioid Dependence: Outpatient Drug-Free Treatment. As noted in an earlier review (Rounsaville & Kleber, 1985), outpatient drug-free treatment is a catch-all term for heterogeneous programs that are defined by the fact that they offer pharmacologic treatments and rely on psychotherapy or counseling as the core of treatment. To date, large-scale naturalistic evaluations have suggested that outpatient drug-free treatment may be as effective as other forms of treatment, such as methadone maintenance and therapeutic communities (Hubbard, Rachel et al., 1984; Hubbard, Marsden et al., 1989; Sampson, Savage & Lloyd, 1979). However, interpretation of findings from these studies is confounded by their numerous methodologic limitations, most important of which are substantial selection biases, since less severely addicted patients tended to be seen in the outpatient drug-free treatment programs evaluated and the more severely and chronically addicted individuals were treated in methadone maintenance programs or therapeutic communities. Further, because the type of psychotherapy or counseling administered in the various outpatient drug-free treatment settings that were evaluated rarely was specified, these studies offer little guidance regarding the effectiveness of particular psychotherapeutic treatments in outpatient drug-free treatment settings or the types of addicts for whom such treatments may be most appropriate. Finally, because the outpatient drug-free treatment programs evaluated typically were multimodality programs (composed of individual, group, and/or family therapy, often in combination with self-help groups, vocational counseling, and the like), the unique contribution of individual psychotherapy to outcome in these programs was difficult to determine.

Narcotic Antagonist Programs. Individual psychotherapy offered in the context of narcotic antagonist programs has been found to have a positive effect on the most significant drawback associated with this approach: that of very high dropout rates during the induction and stabilization phases (Kosten & Kleber, 1984). In the only published randomized clinical trial evaluating individual psychotherapy in the context of naltrexone treatment, Resnick and colleagues (1981) randomly assigned 66 addicts to intensive weekly individual therapy (described as supportive and insight-oriented) or to low-intervention case management. Sixty-three percent of the subjects who received counseling were successfully inducted into naltrexone treatment, as compared with 48% of the noncounseled addicts, a non-significant difference. Significant differences between the treatment groups emerged during the stabilization phase, however; of 37 subjects successfully inducted, 77% (17/22) of the group receiving counseling remained in treatment through one month, in contrast to 33% (5/15) of the controls.

The study by Resnick and colleagues (1981) also demonstrated differential responsiveness to psychotherapy by different types of addicts. The Resnick study included two types of addicts: those coming to treatment from the street, and those entering treatment after having been maintained on a methadone program. When results were analyzed by subjects' treatment history (street versus post-methadone), it was found that the provision of psychotherapy had little effect for the post methadone maintenance group; whereas the addition of psychotherapy significantly increased rates of successful naltrexone induction and stabilization for the street addicts (45% versus 12%).

Methadone Maintenance. A number of investigations have examined the value of individual counseling in the context of methadone maintenance programs. Notwithstanding the methodologic flaws inherent in many of them (including nonrandom assignment to treatments, poorly defined outcome measures, vaguely defined study treatments, and failure to protect treatment integrity), these studies consistently suggest that the provision of counseling within methadone maintenance programs can be of benefit in reducing attrition and improving compliance with treatment. In a naturalistic study, Janke (1976) found that switching from a primarily "medical model" methadone program to a more "heavily psychotherapeutic" program resulted in higher rates of successful program completion in two very large (N = 887) samples of methadone-maintained addicts, but few changes in other indicators of outcome were seen. Studies by Ramer and colleagues (1971), as well as Senay and colleagues (1973), compared outcome for addicts who received full-service methadone maintenance (which included individual counseling) to outcome for addicts assigned to methadone only, where staff was instructed to withhold psychological support. In both studies, the power to detect group differences was undercut by the staff's tendency to offer counseling on demand to subjects in the methadone-only group. In the Senay (1973) study, the counseled group was found to have better program attendance than the methadone-only group, although differences in illicit drug use, employment, and illegal activity were not seen. In the Ramer (1971) study, less attrition was found among the addicts who made use of counseling and other ancillary services; it also was noted that subjects who made the most use of these services tended to be those with higher levels of psychopathology.

Only a few well-designed randomized clinical trials have evaluated professional psychotherapy as an adjunct to standard full-service methadone maintenance. In one of the first, which has become the classic study of the benefits of individual psychotherapy in the context of methadone maintenance, Woody and colleagues (1983) randomly assigned 110 patients entering a methadone maintenance program to a six-month course of one of three treatments: drug counseling alone, drug counseling plus supportive-expressive psychotherapy (SE), or drug counseling plus cognitive-behavioral psychotherapy (CB). Although the SE and CB groups did not differ significantly from each other on most measures of outcome, subjects who received either form of professional psychotherapy evidenced greater improvement in more outcome domains than did the subjects who received drug counseling alone. Further, gains made by the subjects who received professional psychotherapy were sustained over a 12-month follow-up period, while subjects who received drug counseling alone evidenced some attrition of gains (Woody, McLellan et al., 1985, 1987). Differential responsiveness to treatment by both presence and type of addict's psychopathology was found: addicts with low levels of psychopathology tended to show significant improvement regardless of the treatment received, but those with higher levels of psychopathology were likely to improve only if they received professional psychotherapy (Woody, McLellan et al., 1984). Addicts with antisocial personality disorder tended not to benefit from treatment, while those with concurrent depressive disorders showed improvements in all areas assessed (Woody, McLellan et al., 1985).

In a recent replication of this study with psychiatrically impaired patients in community methadone maintenance programs, Woody and colleagues (1995) evaluated supportive-expressive psychotherapy versus supplemental drug counseling for 84 methadone-maintained subjects who were interviewed at one and six months following a 24-week course of therapy. Patients assigned to the supportive-expressive condition had significantly lower doses of methadone and fewer cocaine-positive urines, but no significant differences in the proportion of opiate-positive urines during treatment. No significant differences between the groups was seen at one-month follow-up, although patients in both conditions maintained the gains they made during treatment. However, at six-month follow-up, diminishment of gains was seen for subjects receiving drug counseling only, and several significant differences favoring the supportive-expressive therapy emerged. These findings point to the durability of the effects of psychotherapy, particularly for psychiatrically impaired methadone-maintained opiate addicts. The findings also suggest that the benefits of psychotherapy are generalizable to community drug treatment programs and are not limited to treatment settings in academic centers.

Rounsaville and colleagues (1983) randomly assigned addicts who had been maintained on methadone for at least six weeks to either weekly interpersonal psychotherapy (IPT) or a low-contact condition, in which the patient met with a therapist for one 20-minute session per month. The study was marked by low rates of patient recruitment (less than 5% of all eligible subjects opted to participate) and poor treatment retention. Although subjects in both conditions showed significant improvements over baseline levels on most measures of outcome, significant differences between treatment groups were not found. Further, differential treatment responsiveness by depressed versus non-depressed subjects was not seen in this investigation. Rounsaville and Kleber (1985) noted that, in contrast to the study by Woody and colleagues (1983), there were important differences in implementation of the study treatments that may have accounted for the failure to demonstrate a psychotherapy effect. These included several factors: (1) the option to participate in psychotherapy was offered at least six weeks after patients enrolled in the methadone program, providing ample time for resolution of depressive symptoms as well as opportunity to become fully engaged with program staff and ongoing group therapy, both of which may have undercut patients' motivation to become involved in individual psychotherapy; and (2) the provision of psychotherapy was not well-integrated into the existing methadone program, and subjects were seen for psychotherapy at a site physically separated from the methadone program. This resulted in a low recruitment rate for the study, which in turn may have resulted in a preponderance of poor prognosis patients entering the study (e.g., as a "last resort" before being administratively discharged).

Behavioral Treatments for Opioid Dependence. Recognizing that methadone maintenance may curtail opioid use but often has little effect on other illicit substance use, particularly cocaine use (Kosten, Rounsaville & Kleber, 1987), a variety of behavioral approaches have been evaluated to reduce illicit substance use among methadone-maintained opiate-addicted persons. Several features of standard methadone-maintenance treatment (daily attendance, frequent urine monitoring, reinforcing properties of methadone) have offered behavioral researchers an opportunity to control reinforcers available to patients and hence to evaluate the effects of both positive and negative contingencies on outcome within methadone-maintenance programs.

Negative Contingencies: Several studies have evaluated negative contingency contracting, which requires specific improvements in behavior (typically, submission of drug-free urines) for continued methadone treatment, with failure to improve or comply resulting in dose reduction, detoxification, or termination of treatment. Liebson and colleagues (1978) found that this procedure increased compliance with disulfiram treatment for alcoholic methadone-maintained opiate-addicted persons. Several studies have demonstrated that approximately 40% to 60% of subjects are able to reduce or stop illicit substance use under threat of dose reduction or treatment termination (e.g., Dolan, Black et al., 1985; McCarthy & Borders, 1985; Nolimal & Crowley, 1990; Saxon, Calsyn et al., 1993). However, fully half of the subjects in these studies do not reduce their substance use under these conditions and are forced to leave treatment. Often, patients who do not comply with behavioral requirements and hence are terminated are those with more frequent or severe polysubstance use (Dolan, Black et al., 1985; Saxon, Calsyn et al., 1993). These studies thus demonstrate that, although negative contingencies may reduce or stop illicit substance use in some methadone-maintenance patients, these somewhat draconian procedures also may have the undesirable effect of terminating treatment for those more severely impaired patients who have difficulty complying and who may need treatment most (Stitzer, Bickel et al., 1986)

Positive Contingencies: Several types of positive contingencies have been evaluated in the context of methadone maintenance. Methadone take-home privileges contingent on reduced drug use is an attractive approach because it capitalizes on an inexpensive reinforcer that is potentially available in all methadone-maintenance programs. Stitzer and colleagues (1986) did extensive work in evaluating methadone take-home privileges as a reward for decreased illicit drug use. In a series of well-controlled trials, this group of researchers demonstrated: (1) the relative benefits of positive over negative contingencies (Stitzer, Bickel et al., 1986); (2) the attractiveness of take-home privileges over other incentives available within methadone-maintenance clinics (Stitzer & Bigelow, 1978); (3) the effectiveness of targeting and rewarding drug-free urines over other, more distal behaviors such as group attendance (Iguchi, Lamb & Platt, 1993); and (4) the benefits of using take-home privileges contingent on drug-free urines over noncontingent take-home privileges (Stitzer, Bickel et al., 1986).

Several studies have evaluated methadone dose increases as contingent reinforcers. Stitzer and colleagues (1986) compared the effect of methadone dose increases that were contingent on drug-free urines with blind dose increases. Over an eight-week period, both groups reduced opiate use from baseline levels; however, the contingent dose increase was significantly superior to the blind dose increase in producing drug-free urines (74% versus 48% opiate-free urines). This finding could not be attributed to the effect of dose increases producing methadone satiation that could reduce use of illicit opiates, because subjects in the blind dose condition actually received higher doses of methadone than those in the contingent dose condition. Higgins and colleagues (1986) also showed the effectiveness of contingent (for opiate-free urines) versus noncontingent methadone dose increases.

Extinction of Conditioned Craving: Childress and colleagues (1984, 1993) conducted a series of studies evaluating the effectiveness of procedures intended to reduce conditioned responses to stimuli associated with drugs through repeated exposure to such stimuli. Their study group demonstrated cue reactivity, including both physiological (changes in galvanic skin response and skin temperature) and subjective (withdrawal-like symptoms, craving) responses in both opiate and cocaine-abusing persons who were exposed to drug-related stimuli, such as handling drug paraphernalia, watching videotapes of individuals preparing and using drugs, and negative mood states (Childress, McLellan & O'Brien, 1988a). Repeated exposure to these stimuli in controlled laboratory settings has been associated with extinction of some conditioned responses, particularly decreases in craving (McLellan, Childress et al., 1986)

To evaluate the utility of extinction procedures as an adjunct to drug treatment, 56 methadone-maintained addicted persons were randomly assigned to one of three groups: (1) a combination group that received cognitive-behavior therapy, extinction, and relaxation training; (2) a group that received cognitive-behavioral therapy and relaxation training without extinction; and (3) a group that received drug counseling alone (McLellan, Childress et al., 1986). The group that received extinction training evidenced reduction in subjective craving for opiates with repeated extinction sections. However, although both groups that received cognitive-behavioral therapy had significantly better six-month outcomes than the group that received drug counseling alone, the two therapy groups were not significantly different from each other, suggesting that the extinction procedure added no greater relative benefit over the cognitive-behavioral therapy plus relaxation training. The authors suggested several factors that may have undercut the power of the outpatient extinction procedure, including the need to use individualized stimuli and the need to consider modifying variables such as affect or cognitive set. Similar findings have been reported for extinction procedures with cocaine patients (Childress, Ehrmann et al., 1988b), where extinction of craving to some cocaine cues has been demonstrated, but it is not yet clear whether extinction generalizes to other cues more difficult to control in laboratory-treatment settings, or whether extinction of craving has an appreciable difference on drug use (Childress, Hole et al., 1993)

Behavioral Treatments for Cocaine Dependence. Some of the most exciting findings pertaining to the power of psychosocial treatments have been the recent reports of Higgins and colleagues (1991, 1994) of the effectiveness of a program incorporating positive incentives for abstinence, reciprocal relationship counseling, and disulfiram into a Community Reinforcement Approach (CRA) approach (Sisson & Azrin, 1989). In this program, urine specimens are required three times weekly. Abstinence, assessed through drug-free urine screens, is reinforced through a voucher system in which patients receive points redeemable for items consistent with a drug-free lifestyle, such as movie tickets, sporting goods, and the like, but patients never receive money directly. To encourage longer periods of consecutive abstinence, the value of the points earned by the patients increases with each successive clean urine specimen, and the value of the points is reset when the patient produces a drug-positive urine screen. In a series of well-controlled clinical trials, Higgins has demonstrated: (1) high acceptance, retention and rates of abstinence for patients randomized to this approach (85% completed a 12-week course of treatment, while 65% achieved six or more weeks of abstinence) relative to standard Twelve Step-oriented substance abuse counseling (Higgins, Delaney et al., 1991; Higgins, Budney et al., 1993a); (2) rates of abstinence did not decline when less valuable incentives, such as lottery tickets, were substituted for the voucher system (Higgins, Budney et al., 1993a); and (3) the value of the voucher system itself (as opposed to other program elements) in producing good outcomes by comparing the behavioral system with and without the vouchers (Higgins, Budney et al., 1994).

Although a variety of individual psychotherapeutic approaches to the treatment of cocaine abuse have been described (Anker & Crowley, 1981; Galanter, 1986; Schiffer, 1988), clinical trials evaluating their effectiveness thus far have been few. In a pilot study evaluating the efficacy of purely psychotherapeutic treatments for ambulatory cocaine abusers, Carroll and colleagues (1991) randomly assigned 42 subjects to either relapse prevention (a cognitive-behavioral approach) or IPT adapted for cocaine abusers. Rates of attrition were significantly higher in IPT than in relapse prevention, with 62% of those in IPT failing to complete a 12-week course of treatment, as compared to 33% of those in relapse prevention. On most measures of outcome, significant differences by treatment type were not seen but did emerge when subjects were stratified according to pretreatment severity of cocaine abuse. Among the subgroup of more severe users, subjects who received relapse prevention were significantly more likely to achieve abstinence (54% versus 9%) than were subjects in IPT, whereas subjects with lower levels of abuse improved regardless of treatment received.

These findings were replicated by the authors group in a more recent study evaluating both psychotherapy (cognitive-behavioral relapse prevention or clinical management, a psychotherapy control condition) and pharmacotherapy (desipramine or placebo) in a 2x2 factorial design for 139 cocaine abusers in a 12-week abstinence initiation trial (Carroll, Rounsaville et al., 1994). After 12 weeks of treatment, all groups showed significant reductions in cocaine use, but significant main effects for medication or psychotherapy condition were not found for treatment retention, reduction in cocaine use, or other outcomes. However, exploratory analyses suggested a disordinal interaction of baseline severity with psychotherapy, which was consistent with that found in the earlier study (Carroll, Rounsaville & Gawin, 1991): higher severity patients had significantly better outcomes, including fewer urine toxicology screens positive for cocaine, when they were treated with relapse prevention compared with supportive clinical management (28% versus 47% of screens). Subsequent exploratory analyses also suggested better retention and cocaine outcomes for depressed subjects who were treated with relapse prevention over clinical management (Carroll, Nich & Rounsaville, 1995).

Finally, one year follow-up of subjects in this study indicated possible 'sleeper effects' for relapse prevention (Carroll, Rounsaville et al., 1994). That is, significant continuing improvement across time for cocaine outcomes (days of use, ASI composite scores) was seen for subjects who had received relapse prevention compared with clinical management. These findings suggest delayed emergence of effects for cognitive-behavioral relapse prevention, which may reflect subjects' implementation of the generalizable coping skills learned during treatment. Moreover, these data underline the importance of conducting follow-up studies of substance abusers and other groups, as delayed effects may occur after cessation of acute treatment.

Trends in Psychosocial Treatments for Drug Dependence. The empirical evidence reviewed here and the literature on psychosocial treatments of alcoholism reviewed elsewhere suggest the following:

First, most studies to date suggest that individual psychotherapy is superior to control conditions as treatment for substance abusers. This is consistent with the bulk of findings from psychotherapy efficacy research in areas other than substance use, which suggests that the effects of many psychotherapies are clinically and statistically significant and are superior to no treatment and placebo conditions (Lambert & Bergin, 1994).

Second, no specific type of individual psychotherapy has been shown consistently to be superior as treatment for substance abusers or for other types of patients (Smith, Glass & Miller, 1980). However, behavioral and cognitive-behavioral therapies may show particular promise (Lambert & Bergin, 1994).

Third, in studies examining the differential effectiveness of psychotherapy on those substance abusers with and without coexisting psychopathology (Woody, McLellan et al., 1985; Carroll, Rounsaville & Gawin, 1991; Carroll, Nich & Rounsaville, 1995), the results indicate with some consistency that those therapies shown to be generally effective were differentially more effective with patients who presented with high levels of general psychopathology or depression (Woody, McLellan et al., 1984, 1985, 1995; Carroll, Rounsaville & Gawin, 1991; Carroll, Nich & Rounsaville, 1995).

Fourth, the effects of even comparatively brief psychotherapies appear to be durable among substance users (Woody, McLellan et al., 1987), as they are among other populations (Lambert & Bergin, 1994). Recent evidence suggests that, while the benefits of individual psychotherapy may not be immediately apparent with respect to control or treatment-as-usual conditions, meaningful gains may emerge after the termination of treatment (Carroll, Rounsaville et al., 1994; O'Malley, Jaffe et al., in press; Woody, McLellan et al., 1995), perhaps as patients have more time to implement or practice the skills acquired during treatment. Further research is needed to determine whether delayed benefits of individual psychotherapy in substance abusers are specific to the forms of treatment where this effect has so far been identified (coping skills treatment with cocaine abusers in the study by Carroll and colleagues, and supportive-expressive therapy with methadone-maintained opiate addicts in the study by Woody and colleagues) or is a more general effect of psychotherapy.

USES OF INDIVIDUAL PSYCHOTHERAPY IN THE TREATMENT OF SUBSTANCE ABUSE

From the preceding summary of empiric findings, it is clear that the empirical literature offers only the most general sort of guidance regarding the choice of which individual psychotherapy is likely to be useful for which type of substance abuser and when in the course of treatment it should be offered. Hence, the following recommendations are made on the basis of clinical experience rather than research evidence. With this caveat, it is suggested that individual psychotherapy may have the following uses: (1) to introduce a substance abuser into treatment, (2) to treat patients with low levels of substance dependence, (3) to treat failures of other modalities, (4) to complement other ongoing treatment modalities for selected patients, and (5) to help the patient solidify gains following achievement of stable abstinence.

Psychotherapy as an Introduction to Treatment. As noted previously, a key advantage of individual therapy is the privacy and confidentiality that it affords. This aspect may make individual therapy or counseling an ideal setting to clarify the treatment needs of patients who are in early stages (i.e., contemplation, precontemplation) of thinking about changing their substance use habits (Prochaska & DiClemente, 1986). For individuals with severe dependence or severe substance-related problems who deny the seriousness of their involvement, a course of individual therapy in which the patient is guided to a clear recognition of the problem may be an essential first step toward more intensive approaches such as residential treatment or methadone maintenance. An important part of this process may involve allowing the patient to fail one or more times at strategies that have a low probability of success, such as attempting to cut down on substance use without stopping or attempting outpatient detoxification. A general principle underlying this process is the successive use of treatments that involve greater expense and/or patient involvement only after less intensive approaches have been shown to fail. Hence, brief individual treatment can serve a cost-effective triage function.

Psychotherapy for Patients with Mild to Moderately Severe Substance Dependence. Although less studied with nonalcoholic drug abusers, the drug dependence syndrome concept (Edwards, Arif & Hodgson, 1981) has received considerable attention in the study of alcoholism. This concept, first described by Edwards and colleagues (1976), suggests that drug dependence is best understood as a constellation of cognitions, behaviors, and physical symptoms that underlie a pattern of progressively diminished control over drug use. This dependence syndrome is conceived of as aligned along a continuum of severity, with higher levels of severity associated with poorer prognosis and the need for more intensive treatment, and lower levels of severity requiring less intensive interventions. The dependence syndrome construct has generated a large empiric literature suggesting its validity with alcoholics (Edwards, 1986). Moreover, several scales have been developed for gauging the severity of alcohol dependence (Skinner, 1981; Stockwell, Hodgson et al., 1979; Chick, 1980). Generally, however, measures of quantity and frequency of alcohol use show a high correlation with dependence severity, and similar quantity/frequency indices for other drugs of abuse may be an adequate gauge of dependence severity. Evidence from studies of individuals who are mildly to moderately dependent on alcohol indicates that a brief course of psychotherapy is sufficient for many to achieve substantial reduction in or abstinence from drinking (Miller & Heather, 1986; Babor, 1994; Sanchez-Craig & Wilkinson, 1986/1987; Edwards, 1986; Wallace, Cutler & Haines, 1988). Although these findings have yet to be replicated with other types of substance abusers, they are likely to be generalizable.

Failures from Other Modalities. Although numerous predictors of treatment outcome for substance abusers have been identified (Luborsky & McLellan, 1978; McLellan, Alterman et al., 1994; Carroll, Powers et al., 1993), few are robust, and still fewer have been evaluated regarding the issue of matching patients to treatments (McLellan, O'Brien et al., 1980). As a result, choice of treatments often involves a degree of trial and error. Each type of treatment has its strengths and weaknesses and may prove a better or worse 'fit' for particular patients. For example, individual therapy is more expensive but more private than group therapy, more enduring and less disruptive to normal routine than residential treatment, and less troubled by side effects and medical contraindications than pharmacotherapies. Each of these advantages may be crucial to a patient who has responded poorly to alternative therapies.

Psychotherapy as Ancillary Treatment. In considering psychotherapy as part of an ongoing comprehensive program of treatment, it is useful to distinguish between treatment of opioid addicts and alcoholics, for which powerful pharmacologic approaches are available, and treatment of other drugs of abuse, for which strong alternatives to psychosocial treatments are still unavailable (Kosten & McCance, 1995). For alcoholics, naltrexone, acamprosate and disulfiram have demonstrated strong potential to reduce relapse rates. However, the effectiveness of disulfiram in the absence of a strong psychosocial treatment was no greater than placebo (Fuller, Branchey et al., 1986) and studies demonstrating efficacy for naltrexone and acamprosate have studied these medications only in the context of a comparatively intense psychosocial intervention (Volpicelli, Alterman et al., 1992; O'Malley, Jaffe et al., 1992; Sass, Soyka et al., 1996; Whitworth, Fischer et al., 1996).

For opioid abusers, the modal approach is methadone maintenance, which is used with the majority of those in treatment, while an alternative pharmacotherapy, naltrexone, can be highly potent for the minority who choose this approach. Because of their powerful and specific pharmacologic effects, either to satisfy the need for opioids or to prevent illicit opioids from yielding their desired effect, these agents, provided that they are delivered with at least minimal counseling, may be sufficient for many opioid addicts (McLellan, Alterman et al., 1994). The choice of those who might benefit from additional individual psychotherapy can be guided by the unique but robust empiric findings of Woody and colleagues (1984, 1985) and McLellan, O'Brien et al. (1980), which suggest that psychotherapy is most likely to be of benefit to those opioid addicts with high levels of psychiatric symptoms as measured by the Addiction Severity Index (ASI) (McLellan, O'Brien et al., 1980) or with a diagnosis of major depression as defined in the revised third edition (*DSM-IIIR*; American Psychiatric Association, 1987) or the fourth edition (*DSM-IV*; American Psychiatric Association, 1994) of the *Diagnostic and Statistical Manual of Mental Disorders.* Because the benefits of psychotherapy may be maximized when instituted relatively soon after admission to treatment, screening instruments such as the ASI (McLellan, O'Brien et al., 1980) or the Beck Depression Inventory (Beck, Ward & Mendelson, 1970) could be used to quickly identify those with psychopathology or depression, alerting staff to the need to refer these clients for psychotherapy.

For non-opioid drugs of abuse, an active search for effective pharmacotherapies is under way. The mainstay of treatment for non-opioid drugs of abuse remains some form of psychosocial treatment offered in a group, family, residential, or individual setting. For cocaine use, forms of treatment that have empirical support at this time include behavioral and cognitive-behavioral treatments (Carroll, Rounsaville et al., 1994; Higgins, Budney et al., 1994). Some evidence suggests that these forms of treatment may be of particular benefit to cocaine abusers who have greater severity of cocaine dependence (Carroll, Rounsaville et al., 1994), have substantial depressive symptoms (Carroll, Nich et al., 1995), or who have substantial family support (Higgins, Budney et al., 1994). However, there is at this point no strong empirical evidence as to the optimal duration of treatment, nor are there clear guidelines for matching patients to treatment. For other types of drug abuse, in the absence of empirically validated guidelines, the choice of an individual form of psychotherapy for this population can be based on such factors as expense, logistical considerations, patient preference, or the clinical "fit" between the patient's presenting picture and the treatment modality (e.g., family therapy is ruled out for those without families).

Psychotherapy Following Achievement of Sustained Abstinence. As noted above, a substance abuser who is experiencing frequent relapses or who is only tenuously holding on to abstinence may be a poor candidate for certain types of psychotherapy, particularly those that involve bringing into focus painful and anxiety-provoking clinical material as an inevitable part of helping the patient master dysphoric affects or avoid recurrent failures in establishing enduring intimate relationships. In fact, some arousal of anxiety or frustration can occur with most types of psychotherapy, even those that are conceived of as being primarily supportive. Because of this, individual psychotherapy may be most effective for many individuals only after they have achieved abstinence using some other method such as residential treatment, methadone maintenance, or group therapy. Given the vulnerability to relapse, which can extend over a lifetime, and the frequency with which dysphoric affects or interpersonal conflict are noted as precipitants of relapse (Marlatt & Gordon, 1980), individual psychotherapy may be especially indicated for those whose psychopathology or disturbed interpersonal functioning is found to endure following the achievement of abstinence. Given findings pointing to the delayed emergence of effects of individual psychotherapy for both cocaine (Carroll, Rounsaville et al., 1994) and opioid (Woody, McLellan et al., 1995) addicts, psychotherapy aimed at these enduring issues can be helpful not only for these problems, independent of their relationship to drug use, but also as a form of insurance against the potential that these continuing problems eventually will lead to relapse.

REFERENCES

Alexander F & French T (1946). *Psychoanalytic Therapy: Principles and Applications*. New York, NY: Ronald Press.

Allen JP & Litten RZ (1992). Techniques to enhance compliance with disulfiram. *Alcoholism: Clinical & Experimental Research* 16:1035–1041.

American Psychiatric Association (1994). *Diagnostic and Statistical Manual of Mental Disorders, 4th Edition*. Washington, DC: American Psychiatric Press.

American Psychiatric Association (1987). *Diagnostic and Statistical Manual of Mental Disorders, 3rd Edition, Revised*. Washington, DC: American Psychiatric Press.

Anker AL & Crowley TJ (1982). Use of contingency contracts in specialty clinics for cocaine abuse. In LS Harris LS (ed.) *Problems of Drug Dependence, 1981 (NIDA Research Monograph 41)*. Rockville, MD: National Institute on Drug Abuse, 452–459.

Anton RF, Hogan I, Jalali B et al. (1981). Multiple family therapy and naltrexone in the treatment of opioid dependence. *Drug and Alcohol Dependence* 8:157–168.

Babor TF (1994). Avoiding the horrid and beastly sin of drunkenness: Does dissuasion make a difference? *Journal of Consulting and Clinical Psychology* 62:1127–1140.

Ball JC & Ross A (1991). *The Effectiveness of Methadone Maintenance Treatment*. New York, NY: Springer-Verlag.

Beck AT, Rush AJ, Shaw BF & Emery G (1979). *Cognitive Therapy of Depression*. New York, NY: Guilford Press.

Beck AT, Ward CH & Mendelson M (1970). An inventory for measuring depression. *Archives of General Psychiatry* 4:461–471.

Beck AT (1967). *Depression: Clinical, Experimental and Theoretical Aspects*. New York, NY: Hoeber.

Beckman EE & Leber WR (1985). *Handbook of Depression: Treatment, Assessment and Research*. Homewood, IL: Dorsey Press.

Bibring E (1954). Psychoanalysis and the dynamic psychotherapies. *Journal of American Psychoanalysis Association* 2:745–770.

Blatt S, McDonald C, Sugarman A & Wilber C (1984). Psychodynamic theories of opiate addiction: New directions for research. *Clinical Psychology Review* 4:159–189.

Brill L (1977). The treatment of drug abuse: evolution of a perspective. *American Journal of Psychiatry* 134:157–160.

Brunswick AF (1979). Black youth and drug use behavior. In GM Beschner & AS Friedman (eds.) *Youth Drug Abuse*. Lexington, MA: Lexington Books, 52–66.

Carroll KM, Rounsaville BJ & Gawin FH (1991). A comparative trial of psychotherapies for ambulatory cocaine abusers: Relapse prevention and interpersonal psychotherapy. *American Journal of Drug and Alcohol Abuse* 17:229–247.

Carroll KM (1996). Manual-guided psychosocial treatment: A new virtual requirement for pharmacotherapy trials? Under review.

Carroll KM & Rounsaville BJ (1991). Can a technology model be applied to psychotherapy research in cocaine abuse treatment? In LS Onken & JD Blaine (eds.) *Psychotherapy and Counseling in the Treatment of Drug Abuse (NIDA Research Monograph 104)*. Rockville, MD: National Institute on Drug Abuse, 91–104.

Carroll KM, Nich C & Rounsaville BJ (1995). Differential symptom reduction in depressed cocaine abusers treated with psychotherapy and pharmacotherapy. *Journal of Nervous and Mental Disease* 183:251–259.

Carroll KM, Powers MD, Bryant KJ & Rounsaville BJ (1993). One-year follow-up status of treatment-seeking cocaine abusers: Psychopathology and dependence severity as predictors of outcome. *Journal of Nervous and Mental Disease* 181:71–79.

Carroll KM, Rounsaville BJ, Gordon LT, Nich C, Jatlow PM, Bisighini RM & Gawin FH (1994). Psychotherapy and pharmacotherapy for ambulatory cocaine abusers. *Archives of General Psychiatry* 51:177–187.

Carroll KM, Rounsaville BJ, Nich C, Gordon LT, Wirtz PW & Gawin FH (1994). One year follow-up of psychotherapy and pharmacotherapy for cocaine dependence: Delayed emergence of psychotherapy effects. *Archives of General Psychiatry* 51: 989–997.

Chick J (1980). Alcohol dependence: methodological issues in its measurement: Reliability of the criteria. *British Journal on Addiction* 75:175–186.

Childress AR, Ehrman RN, McLellan AT et al. (1988b). Conditioned craving and arousal in cocaine addiction: A preliminary report. In LS Harris (ed.) *Problems of Drug Dependence, 1987 (NIDA Research Monograph No 81)*. Rockville, MD: National Institute on Drug Abuse, 74–80.

Childress AR, Hole AV, Ehrman RN et al. (1993). Cue reactivity and cue reactivity interventions in drug dependence. In LS Onken, JD Blaine & JJ Boren (eds.) *Behavioral Treatments for Drug Abuse and Dependence (NIDA Research Monograph 137)*. Rockville, MD: National Institute on Drug Abuse, 73–95.

Childress AR, McLellan AT & O'Brien CP (1984). Assessment and extinction of conditioned withdrawal-like responses in an integrated treatment for opiate dependence. In *Problems of Drug Dependence, 1983 (NIDA Research Monograph)*. Rockville, MD: National Institute on Drug Abuse, 202–210.

Childress AR, McLellan AT & O'Brien CP (1988a). Classically conditioned responses in cocaine and opioid dependence: A role in relapse? In BA Ray (ed.) *Learning Factors in Substance Abuse (NIDA Research Monograph 84)*. Rockville, MD: National Institute on Drug Abuse, 25–43.

Cook CCH (1988). The Minnesota Model in the management of drug and alcohol dependency: Miracle, method or myth? Part I. The philosophy and the program. *British Journal on Addiction* 83:625–634

Corty E & Ball JC (1987). Admissions to methadone maintenance: Comparisons between programs and implications for treatment. *Journal of Substance Abuse Treatment* 4:181–187.

Cummings N (1979). Turning bread into stones: Our modern anti-miracle. *American Psychology* 1979;34:1119–1129.

DiClemente CC, Prochaska JO & Gibertini M (1985). Self-efficacy and the stages of self-change of smoking. *Cognitive Therapy Research* 9(2):181–200.

Dolan MP, Black JL, Penk WE et al. (1985). Contracting for treatment termination to reduce illicit drug use among methadone maintenance treatment failures. *Journal of Consulting and Clinical Psychology* 53:549–551.

Dole VP, Nyswander ME & Warner A (1976). Methadone maintenance treatment: A ten-year perspective. *Journal of American Medical Association* 235:2117–2119.

Douglas DB (1986). Alcoholism as an addiction: The disease concept reconsidered. *Journal on Substance Abuse Treatment* 3:115–120

Edwards G (1986). The alcohol dependence syndrome: A concept as stimulus to enquiry. *British Journal on Addiction* 81:171–183.

Edwards G, Arif A & Hodgson R (1981). Nomenclature and classification of drug and alcohol related problems. *Bulletin of the WHO* 59:225–242

Edwards G & Gross MM (1976). Alcohol dependence: Provisional description of a clinical syndrome. *British Medical Journal* 1:1058–1061.

Fuller R, Branchey L, Brightwell D et al. (1986). Disulfiram treatment of alcoholism: A Veterans Administration cooperative study. *Journal of the American Medical Association* 256:1449–1455.

Galanter M (1986). Social network therapy for cocaine dependence. *Advances in Alcohol and Substance Abuse* 12:159–175.

Gawin FH & Ellinwood EH (1988). Stimulants: Actions, abuse, and treatment. *The New England Journal of Medicine* 318:1173–1183.

Hall SM, Havassy BE & Wasserman DA (1991). Effects of commitment to abstinence, positive moods, stress, and coping on relapse to cocaine use. *Journal of Consulting and Clinical Psychology* 59:526–532.

Hesselbrock MN, Meyer RE & Keener JJ (1985). Psychopathology in hospitalized alcoholics. *Archives of General Psychiatry* 42:1050–1055.

Higgins ST, Stitzer ML, Bigelow GE et al. (1986). Contingent methadone delivery: Effects on illicit opiate use. *Drug and Alcohol Dependence* 17:311.

Higgins ST & Budney AJ (1993). Treatment of cocaine dependence through the principles of behavior analysis and behavioral pharmacology. In LS Onken, JD Blaine & JJ Boren (eds.) *Behavioral Treatments for Drug and Alcohol Dependence (NIDA Research Monograph 137)*. Rockville, MD: National Institute on Drug Abuse, 97–121.

Higgins ST, Budney AJ, Bickel WK & Hughes JR (1993a). Achieving cocaine abstinence with a behavioral approach. *American Journal of Psychiatry* 150:763–769.

Higgins ST, Budney AJ, Bickel WK & Badger GJ (1994). Participation of significant others in outpatient behavioral treatment predicts greater cocaine abstinence. *American Journal of Drug and Alcohol Abuse* 20:47–56.

Higgins ST, Budney AJ, Bickel WK, Foerg FE, Donham R & Badger GJ (1994). Incentives improve outcome in outpatient behavioral treatment of cocaine dependence. *Archives of General Psychiatry* 51:568–576.

Higgins ST, Delaney DD, Budney AJ, Bickel WK, Hughes JR, Foerg F & Fenwick JW (1991). A behavioral approach to achieving initial cocaine abstinence. *American Journal of Psychiatry* 148:1218–1224.

Holder HD, Longabaugh R, Miller WR & Rubonis AV (1991). The cost effectiveness of treatment for alcohol problems: A first approximation. *Journal of Studies on Alcohol* 52:517–540.

Hubbard RL, Marsden ME, Rachal JV, Harwood JH, Cavanaugh ER & Ginzburg HM (1989). Drug abuse treatment: A national study of effectiveness. Chapel Hill, NC: University of North Carolina Press.

Hubbard RL, Rachal JV, Craddock SG & Cavanaugh ER (1984). Treatment Outcome Prospective Study (TOPS): Client characteristics and behaviors before, during, and after treatment. In FM Tims & JP Ludford (eds.) *Drug Abuse Treatment Evaluation: Strategies, Progress, and Prospects (NIDA Research Monograph 51)*. Rockville, MD: National Institute on Drug Abuse, 42–68.

Iguchi MY, Lamb RJ & Platt JJ (1993). Contingent reinforcement of group participation versus drug-free urines in a methadone maintenance program. Paper presented at the College on Problems of Drug Dependence.

Institute of Medicine (1990). *Broadening the Base of Treatment for Alcohol Problems*. Washington, DC: National Academy Press.

Jaffe JH & Kleber HD (1989). Opioids: General issues and detoxification. In TB Karasu (ed.) *Treatments of Psychiatric Disorders*. Washington, DC: American Psychiatric Association Press, 1309–1331.

Janke P (1976). Differential effects on completion of treatment in a medical versus psychotherapeutic model for methadone maintenance. Paper presented to the Third National Drug Abuse Conference, New York, March 25–29.

Kadden R, Carroll KM, Donovan D, Cooney N, Monti P, Abrams D, Litt M & Hester R (1992). Cognitive-behavioral coping skills therapy manual: A clinical research guide for therapists treating individuals with alcohol abuse and dependence. In *Project MATCH Monograph Series, Volume 3* (DHHS Publication No. (ADM) 92–1895). Rockville, MD: National Institute on Alcohol Abuse and Alcoholism.

Keller DS, Carroll KM, Nich C & Rounsaville BJ (1995). Differential treatment response in alexithymic cocaine abusers: Findings from a randomized clinical trial of psychotherapy and pharmacotherapy. *The American Journal on Addictions* 4:234–244.

Khantzian EJ & Schneider RJ (1986). Treatment implications of a psychodynamic understanding of opioid addicts. In RE Meyer (ed.) *Psychopathology and Addictive Disorders*. New York, NY: Guilford Press, 1986.

Khantzian EJ & Treece C (1985). DSM-III psychiatric diagnosis of narcotic addicts. *Archives of General Psychiatry* 42:1067–1071.

Khantzian EJ (1978). The ego, the self and opiate addiction: theoretical and treatment considerations. *International Review of Psychoanalysis* 5:189–198.

Khantzian EJ (1985). The self-medication hypothesis of addictive disorders: Focus on heroin and cocaine dependence. *American Journal of Psychiatry* 142:1259–1264.

Kleber HD, ed. (1989). Psychoactive substance use disorders (not alcohol). In TB Karasu (ed.) *Treatments of Psychiatric Disorders*. Washington, DC: American Psychiatric Press, 1183–1484.

Kleber HD & Kosten TR (1984). Naltrexone induction: psychologic and pharmacologic strategies. *Journal of Clinical Psychiatry* 45:29.

Kosten TR (1989). Pharmacotherapeutic interventions for cocaine abuse: matching patients to treatments. *Journal of Nervous and Mental Disease* 177:379–389.

Kosten TR & Kleber HD (1984). Strategies to improve compliance with narcotic antagonists. *American Journal on Drug and Alcohol Abuse* 10:249–266.

Kosten TR, Rounsaville BJ & Kleber HD (1987). A 2.5 year follow-up of cocaine use among treated opioid addicts: Have our treatments helped? *Archives of General Psychiatry* 44:281–284.

Kosten TR & McCance-Katz E (1995). New pharmacotherapies. In JM Oldham & MB Riba (eds.) *American Psychiatric Press Review of Psychiatry, Vol. 14*. Washington, DC: American Psychiatric Press, 105–126.

Lambert MJ & Bergin AE (1994). The effectiveness of psychotherapy. In AE Bergin & SL Garfield (eds.) *Handbook of Psychotherapy and Behavior Change, Fourth Edition*. New York, NY: John Wiley & Sons, 123–149.

Liebson IA, Tommasello A & Bigelow GE (1978). A behavioral treatment of alcoholic methadone patients. *Annals of Internal Medicine* 89:342–344.

Luborsky L & McLellan AT (1978). Our surprising inability to predict the outcomes of psychological treatments with special reference to treatments for drug abuse. *American Journal on Drug and Alcohol Abuse* 5:387–398.

Luborsky L (1984). *Principles of Psychoanalytic Psychotherapy: A Manual for Supportive-Expressive (SE) Treatment*. New York, NY: Basic Books.

Marlatt GA & Gordon GR (1980). Determinants of relapse: Implications for the maintenance of behavior change. In PO Davidson & SM Davidson (eds.) *Behavioral Medicine: Changing Health Lifestyles.* New York, NY: Brunner/Mazel, 410–452.

Marlatt GA & Gordon J, eds. (1985). *Relapse Prevention.* New York, NY: Guilford Press.

McCance-Katz E & Kosten TR (in press). Overview of potential treatment medications for cocaine dependence. To appear in P Bridge, N Chiang & B Tai (eds.) *Medication Development for the Treatment of Cocaine Dependence: Issues in Clinical Efficacy Trials (NIDA Research Monograph).* Rockville, MD: National Institute on Drug Abuse.

McCarthy JJ & Borders OT (1985). Limit setting on drug abuse in methadone maintenance treatment. *American Journal of Psychiatry* 142:1419–1423.

McLellan AT, Childress AR, Ehrman R et al. (1986). Extinguishing conditioned responses during opiate dependence treatment: Turning laboratory findings into clinical procedures. *Journal on Substance Abuse Treatment* 3:33–40.

McLellan AT, Luborsky L, O'Brien CP et al. (1980). An improved diagnostic evaluation instrument for substance abuse patients: The Addiction Severity Index. *Journal of Nervous and Mental Disease* 168:26–33.

McLellan AT, O'Brien CP, Kron R et al. (1980). Matching substance abuse patients to appropriate treatments. *Drug and Alcohol Dependence* 5:189–195.

McLellan AT (1983). Patient characteristics associated with outcome. In JR Cooper, F Altman & BS Brown (eds.) *Research on the Treatment of Narcotic Addiction: State of the Art.* Rockville, MD: National Institute on Drug Abuse.

McLellan AT, Alterman AI, Metzger DS, Grissom GR, Woody GE, Luborsky L & O'Brien CP (1994). Similarity of outcome predictors across opiate, cocaine, and alcohol treatments: Role of treatment services. *Journal of Consulting and Clinical Psychology* 62:1141–1158.

McLellan AT, Arndt IO, Metzger DS, Woody GE & O'Brien CP (1993). The effects of psychosocial services in substance abuse treatment. *Journal of the American Medical Association* 269: 1953–1959.

Mendelson JH & Mello NK (1966). Experimental analysis of drinking behavior in chronic alcoholics. *Annals of the New York Academy of Science* 133:828–845.

Meyer RE (1992). New pharmacotherapies for cocaine dependence, revisited. *Archives of General Psychiatry* 49:900–904.

Miller WE & Heather N, eds (1986). *Treating Addictive Behaviors.* New York, NY: Plenum Press.

Miller WR & Rollnick S (1991). *Motivational Interviewing: Preparing People to Change Addictive Behavior.* New York, NY: Guilford.

Miller WR, Zweben A, DiClemente CC & Rychtarik RG (1992). Motivational enhancement therapy manual: A clinical research guide for therapists treating individuals with alcohol abuse and dependence. In *NIAAA Project MATCH Monograph Series, Vol. 2.* Rockville, MD: National Institute on Alcohol Abuse and Alcoholism.

Mirin SR, Meyer RE & McNamme B (1980). Psychopathology and mood duration in heroin use: acute and chronic effects. *Archives of General Psychiatry* 33:1503–1508.

Nathan PE & O'Brien JS (1971). An experimental analysis of the behavior of alcoholics and nonalcoholics during prolonged experimental drinking: A necessary process of behavior therapy? *Behavioral Therapy* 2:455–476.

Nolimal D & Crowley TJ (1990). Difficulties in a clinical application of methadone-dose contingency contracting. *Journal on Substance Abuse Treatment* 7:219–224.

Nowinski J, Baker S & Carroll KM (1992). Twelve-step facilitation therapy manual: A clinical research guide for therapists treating individuals with alcohol abuse and dependence. *NIAAA Project MATCH Monograph Series, Vol. 1.* Rockville, MD: National Institute on Alcohol Abuse and Alcoholism.

Nyswander M, Winick C, Bernstein A, Brill I & Kauger G (1958). The treatment of drug addicts as voluntary out-patients: A progress report. *American Journal on Orthopsychiatry* 28:714- 727.

O'Brien CP & Woody GE (1989). Antagonist treatment: Naltrexone. In TB Karasu (ed.) *Treatments of Psychiatric Disorders.* Washington, DC: American Psychiatric Press, 1332–1340.

O'Donnell JA, Voss HL, Clayton RR, Slatin GT & Room RGW (1976). Young men and drugs: A nationwide survey. *NIDA Research Monograph 5.* Rockville, MD: National Institute on Drug Abuse.

O'Donnell JA (1969). Narcotic addicts in Kentucky. *Public Health Service Publication, 1981.* Washington, DC: U.S. Government Printing Office.

O'Malley SS, Jaffe AJ, Chang G, Schottenfeld RS, Meyer RE & Rounsaville B (1992). Naltrexone and coping skills therapy for alcohol dependence. *Archives of General Psychiatry* 49:881–887.

O'Malley SS, Jaffe AJ, Chang G, Rode S, Schottenfeld R, Meyer RE & Rounsavile BJ (in press). Six month follow-up of naltrexone and psychotherapy for alcohol dependence. *Archives of General Psychiatry.*

Prochaska JO & DiClemente C (1986). Toward a comprehensive model of change. In WR Miller & N Heather (eds.) *Treating Addictive Behaviors: Processes of Change.* New York, NY: Plenum Press, 3–27.

Ramer BS, Zaslove MO & Langan J (1971). Is methadone enough? The use of ancillary treatment during methadone maintenance. *American Journal of Psychiatry* 127:1040–1044. Republished as Depression: causes and treatment. Philadelphia: University of Pennsylvania Press, 1972.

Resnick RB, Washton AM & Stone-Washton N (1981). Psychotherapy and naltrexone in opioid dependence. In LS Harris (ed.) *Problems of Drug Dependence, 1980 (NIDA Research Monograph 34).* Rockville, MD: National Institute on Drug Abuse, 109–115.

Robins LN & Davis DH (1974). How permanent was Vietnam drug addiction? *American Journal on Public Health* 64(Suppl):38–43.

Robins LN (1979). Addicts' careers. In RI Dupont, A Goldstein, J O'Donnell & B Brown (eds.) *Handbook on Drug Abuse.* Rockville, MD: National Institute on Drug Abuse.

Rounsaville BJ, Gawin FH & Kleber HD (1985). Interpersonal psychotherapy (IPT) adapted for ambulatory cocaine abusers. *American Journal on Drug and Alcohol Abuse* 11:171–191.

Rounsaville BJ, Glazer W, Wilber CH et al. (1983). Short-term interpersonal psychotherapy in methadone-maintained opiate addicts. *Archives of General Psychiatry* 40:629–636.

Rounsaville BJ & Kleber HD (1985). Psychotherapy/counseling for opiate addicts: strategies for use in different treatment settings. *International Journal of the Addictions* 20:869–896.

Rounsaville BJ, Weissman M, Kleber HD et al. (1982). Heterogeneity of psychiatric diagnosis in treated opiate addicts. *Archives of General Psychiatry* 39:161–166.

Rounsaville BJ (1995). Can psychotherapy rescue naltrexone treatment of opioid addiction? In L Onken & J Blaine (eds.) *Potentiating the Efficacy of Medications: Integrating Psychosocial Therapies with Pharmaco-Therapies in the Treatment of Drug Dependence (NIDA Research Monograph 105).* Rockville, MD: National Institute on Drug Abuse, 37–52.

Sampson DD, Savage LJ & Lloyd MR (1979). Follow-up evaluation of treatment of drug abuse during 1969 to 1972. *Archives of General Psychiatry* 36:772–780.

Sanchez-Craig M & Wilkinson DA (1986/1987). Treating problem drinkers who are not severely dependent on alcohol. *Drugs and Society.* 1(2/3):39–67.

Sass H, Soyka M, Mann K & Zieglgansberger W (1996). Relapse prevention by acamprosate. *Archives of General Psychiatry* 53:673–680.

Saxon AJ, Calsyn DA, Kivlahan DR et al. (1993). Outcome of contingency contracting for illicit drug use in a methadone maintenance program. *Drug and Alcohol Dependence* 31:205–214.

Schiffer F (1988). Psychotherapy of nine successfully treated cocaine abusers: Techniques and dynamics. *Journal on Substance Abuse Treatment* 1:131–137.

Senay E (1989). Methadone maintenance. In TB Karasu (ed.) *Treatments of Psychiatric Disorders.* Washington, DC: American Psychiatric Press, 1341–1358.

Senay EC, Jaffe JH, DiMenza S et al. (1973). A 48-week study of methadone, methadylacetate, and minimal services. *Psychopharmacology Bulletin* 9:37.

Simons AD, Garfield SL & Murphy GE (1984). The process of change in cognitive therapy and pharmacotherapy for depression. *Archives of General Psychiatry* 41:45–51.

Simpson DD, Joe GW & Bracy SA (1982). Six-year follow-up of opioid addicts after admission to treatment. *Archives of General Psychiatry* 39:1318–1326.

Sisson RW & Azrin NH (1989). The community reinforcement approach. In RK Hester & WR Miller (eds). *Handbook of Alcoholism Treatment Approaches.* New York, NY: Pergamon, 242–258.

Skinner HA (1981). Primary syndromes of alcohol abuse: Their management and correlates. *British Journal on Addiction* 76:63–76.

Smith M, Glass C & Miller T (1980). *The Benefits of Psychotherapy.* Baltimore, MD: The Johns Hopkins Press.

Stanton MD & Todd TC, eds. (1982). *The Family Therapy of Drug Abuse and Addiction.* New York, NY: Guilford Press, 393–402.

Stitzer ML, Bickel WK, Bigelow GE et al. (1986). Effect of methadone dose contingencies on urinalysis test results of polydrug-abusing methadone maintenance patients. *Drug and Alcohol Dependence* 18:341–348.

Stitzer ML & Bigelow GE (1978). Contingency management in a methadone maintenance program: Availability of reinforcers. *International Journal on Addiction* 13:737–746.

Stockwell T, Hodgson R, Edwards G et al. (1979). The development of a questionnaire to measure severity of alcohol dependence. *British Journal on Addiction* 74:79–87.

Taylor GJ, Parker JD & Bagby RM (1990). A preliminary investigation of alexithymic in men with psychoactive substance dependence. *American Journal of Psychiatry* 147:1228–1230.

Tims F & Leukefeld C, eds. (1986). RAUS—Relapse and recovery in drug abuse. *NIDA Research Monograph.* Rockville, MD: National Institute on Drug Abuse.

Vaillant GE (1966). Twelve-year follow-up of New York addicts. *American Journal of Psychiatry* 122:727–737.

Volpicelli JR, Alterman AI, Hayashida M & O'Brien CP (1992). Naltrexone in the treatment of alcohol dependence. *Archives of General Psychiatry* 49:876–880.

Wallace P, Cutler S & Haines A (1988). Randomised controlled trial of general practitioner intervention in patients with excessive alcohol consumption. *British Medical Journal* 297:663–668.

Waskow IE (1984). Specification of the technique variable in the NIMH Treatment of Depression Collaborative Research Program. In JBW Williams & RL Spitzer (eds.) *Psychotherapy Research: Where Are We and Where Should We Go?* New York, NY: Guilford, 81.

Whitworth AB, Fischer F, Lesch OM et al. (1996). Comparison of acamprosate and placebo in long-term treatment of alcohol dependence. *Lancet* 347:1438–1442.

WHO Brief Intervention Study Group (1996). A cross-national trial of brief interventions with heavy drinkers. *American Journal of Public Health* 86:948–955.

Wikler A (1980). *Opioid Dependence: Mechanisms and Treatment.* New York, NY: Plenum Press.

Woody GE, Luborsky L, McLellan AT et al. (1983). Psychotherapy for opiate addicts: does it help? *Archives of General Psychiatry* 40:639–645.

Woody GE, McLellan AT, Luborsky L et al. (1984). Severity of psychiatric symptoms as a prediction of benefits from psychotherapy: The Veterans Administration-Penn study. *American Journal of Psychiatry* 141:1172–1177.

Woody GE, McLellan AT, Luborsky L et al. (1985). Sociopathy and psychotherapy outcome. *Archives of General Psychiatry* 42:1081–1086.

Woody GE, McLellan AT, Luborsky L & O'Brien CP (1985). Sociopathy and psychotherapy outcome. *Archives of General Psychiatry* 42:1081–1086.

Woody GE, McLellan AT, Luborsky L & O'Brien CP (1987). Twelve-month follow-up of psychotherapy for opiate dependence. *American Journal of Psychiatry* 144:590–596.

Woody GE, McLellan AT, Luborsky L & O'Brien CP (1995). Psychotherapy in community methadone programs: A validation study. *American Journal of Psychiatry* 152:1302–1308.

Wurmser L (1979). *The Hidden Dimension: Psychopathology of Compulsive Drug Use*. New York, NY: Jason Aronson.

CHAPTER 5

Network Therapy

Marc Galanter, M.D., FASAM

Conditioning and Conditioned Cues
Social Cohesiveness as a Vehicle for Reinforcing Change
Network Therapy in Office Practice
Principles of Network Treatment

In recent years, there has been considerable progress toward developing psychosocial modalities specific to the treatment of addiction. Indeed, the situation is quite different than it was when Alcoholics Anonymous (AA) emerged over half a century ago in a climate of inadequate physician attention to the rehabilitation of alcoholics. Professionals in the addictions field now have access to a variety of therapeutic techniques. These include variants of cognitive therapy, motivational enhancement, and family and group therapy modalities, all tailored to the needs of the patient with alcohol or drug disorder. The clinician in office practice, however, often is uncertain as to how to integrate these approaches to meet the needs of a given patient. On the face of it, there is no obvious relationship, for example, between the use of cognitively oriented approaches such as relapse prevention, and the engagement of family support to secure improved motivation.

To address this dilemma, this chapter will examine a comprehensive modality that has been disseminated to practitioners over the past two decades, and more recently standardized and studied in the clinical research setting. It is designed to provide clinicians with the means of integrating a variety of approaches developed specifically for management of the addicted patient.

Support for addiction treatment itself has itself expanded over time, and recognition of the severity of the problem in the 1970s initially led to an increase in resources for inpatient care. The availability of beds in designated units increased by 62% from 1977 to 1984, with all of the net gain in the private sector (NIAAA, 1987). Also at this time, the "Minnesota model" for inpatient management (Cook, 1988), based on a protracted inpatient stay, became a standard of treatment for many middle-class addicts. A recent wave of cost containment initiatives, however, has led bed occupancy rates in non-public facilities to fall as low as 60% by 1990 (Anonymous, 1990), and even lower more recently. This decline has been fueled by a lack of empirical support for the relative advantage of inpatient over ambulatory care (Institute of Medicine, 1990).

Managing addicted patients in office practice may in fact be less costly, but reports on its relative effectiveness in standard office practice have not been positive. In an early survey of psychiatrists in practice, Hayman (1956) found that very few professed an appreciable degree of success in treating alcoholics in office practice. No difference in outcome was found when outpatients were offered individual therapy as a treatment added to medical monitoring alone (Braunstein, Powell et al., 1983), nor was insight-oriented therapy found to enhance the effectiveness of outpatient milieu treatment for alcoholism (Olson, Ganley et al., 1981). Indeed, Vaillant (1981), commenting on alcoholism treatment, said "The greatest danger of this is wasteful, painful psychotherapy that bears analogy to someone trying to shoot a fish in a pool. No matter how carefully he aims, the refracted image always renders the shot wide of its mark." As conventionally practiced, individual therapy does not appear to be an effective tool for addiction rehabilitation.

A number of issues, however, can be considered in formulating a new approach to augmenting office-based therapy. Recent years have witnessed both research-based and clinically-based support for the importance of securing abstinence as an initial step in addiction treatment, rather than awaiting results of an exploratory therapy (Nathan & McCrady, 1986/1987; Gitlow & Peyser, 1980; Gallant, 1987). This position has been strengthened by the widespread acceptance of Alcoholics Anonymous, which is strongly oriented toward abstinence. To implement a regimen of abstinence, clinical researchers have developed a number of structured techniques, focusing on cognitive-behavioral change (Marlatt & Gordon, 1985; Annis, 1986) and interpersonal support from family and peers (Stanton & Thomas, 1982; Kaufman & Kaufman, 1979; Galanter, 1993a). We thus shall consider how these approaches can be adapted to an office practice oriented toward individual therapy so as to promote abstinence and effective rehabilitation.

This integrated approach is called "network therapy" because it draws on the support of a group of family and peers who are introduced into therapy sessions. The term derives from the work of Speck and Attneave (1974), who used a large support group drawn from the patient's family and social network as a tool for psychiatric management. These networks were used for both psychological and practical aid in addressing acute psychiatric illness, so as to avert a hospitalization until the acute symptoms remitted. Once mobilized, the network became available to aid in ambulatory rehabilitation as well.

To define what this approach must accomplish, it is first necessary to examine some unique characteristics of the substance dependence syndrome.

In this chapter, we shall first consider the clinical implications of the conditioned abstinence syndrome in terms of its relevance to relapse prevention techniques directed at the conditioned cues that precipitate substance use. We then will examine the role of social cohesiveness in stabilizing the substance-abusing patient in treatment, and define how family members and peers can be integrated into the patient's treatment in the office setting so as to make use of this potent vehicle for reinforcing abstinent behavior. Clinical examples and the particulars of the integrated technique then will be given. Altogether, therefore, the integration of relapse prevention technique into a therapeutic approach which brings family and peer members into the individual treatment setting will be presented under the rubric of network therapy.

CONDITIONING AND CONDITIONED CUES

For many clinicians, the problems of relapse and loss of control, embodied in the criteria for substance dependence in the *Diagnostic and Statistical Manual of Mental Disorders, 4th Edition* of the American Psychiatric Association (*DSM-IV*; 1994), epitomize the pitfalls inherent in addiction treatment. Because addicted patients typically experience pressure to relapse and ingest alcohol or drugs, they are seen as poor candidates for stable treatment. The concept of "loss of control" has been used to describe addicts' inability to reliably limit consumption once an initial dose is taken (Gallant, 1987).

Conditioned Abstinence. These clinical phenomena generally are described anecdotally, but can be explained mechanistically as well, by recourse to the model of conditioned withdrawal, one that relates the pharmacology of dependency-producing drugs to the behaviors they produce. Wikler (1973), an early investigator of addiction pharmacology, developed this model to explain the spontaneous appearance of drug craving and relapse. He pointed out that drugs of dependence typically produce compensatory responses in the central nervous system at the same time that their direct pharmacologic effects are felt, and these compensatory effects partly counter the drug's direct action. Thus, when an opiate antagonist is administered to addicts maintained with morphine, latent withdrawal phenomena are unmasked. Similar compensatory effects are observed in alcoholics maintained with alcohol, who evidence evoked response patterns characteristic of withdrawal while still clinically intoxicated (Begleiter & Porjesz, 1979).

Wikler studied addicts maintained with morphine and then thrown into withdrawal with a narcotic antagonist. After several trials of precipitated withdrawal, he found that a full-blown withdrawal response could be elicited in his subjects when a placebo antagonist was administered. He concluded that the withdrawal had been conditioned and was later elicited by a conditioned cue, in this case the syringe used to administer the placebo. This hypothesized mechanism was later confirmed by O'Brien and colleagues (1977), who elicited conditioned withdrawal by using sound tones as conditioned cues. This conception helps to explain addictive behavior outside the laboratory.

A potential addict who has begun to drink or use another drug heavily may be repeatedly exposed to an external stimulus (such as a certain mood state) while drinking. Subsequent exposure to these cues may thereby produce conditioned withdrawal symptoms, subjectively experienced as craving. A dramatic example of this phenomenon is seen among heroin addicts, in whom a severe withdrawal syndrome may emerge when they return to the neighborhoods where they previously have used heroin, even after years away from the drug. In this case, the setting of the neighborhood itself serves as a cue that produces the symptoms and signs of withdrawal (McAuliffe, 1982; Galanter, 1983).

Implications for Treatment. This model helps to explain why relapse is such a frequent and unanticipated aspect of addiction treatment. Exposure to conditioned cues (ones that were repeatedly associated with drug use) can precipitate reflexive drug craving during the course of therapy, and such cue exposure also can initiate a sequence of unconditioned behaviors that lead addicts to relapse unwittingly into drug use.

Loss of control can be the product of conditioned withdrawal, described by Ludwig and colleagues (1978) and long recognized on a practical level by members of Alcoholics Anonymous. The sensations associated with the ingestion of an addictive drug, such as the odor of alcohol or the euphoria produced by opiates, are temporally associated with the pharmacologic elicitation of a compensatory response to that drug and can later produce drug-seeking behavior. For this reason, the first drink can serve as a conditioned cue for further drinking. Patients therefore have a very limited capacity to control consumption once a single dose of drug has been taken.

Case 1: A 30-year-old cocaine addict undergoing treatment was abstinent and well-motivated for two months but occasionally drank socially. One evening he sought out a cocaine dealer on an impulse and purchased and then insufflated 1 g of cocaine. After returning home, he bought more cocaine and continued to take the drug over the course of the entire night. Examination of this sequence of events in his next therapy session revealed that he had been sitting in a restaurant bar that evening with a date whom he knew to use cocaine. After having two drinks, he had gone to the rest room—a place where he had occasionally used cocaine before entering treatment. It was after this that he bought the cocaine. The patient acknowledged that he had been exposed to a number of cues that had been associated with his previous cocaine consumption: a sexually charged situation with a cocaine user, consumption of alcohol, and a physical setting in which he had used cocaine in the past.

Changes in mood state also can become conditioned stimuli for drug seeking behavior, and the addict can become vulnerable to relapse through reflexive response to a specific affective state. Such phenomena have been described clinically by Khantzian (1985) as self-medication. Such mood-related cues, however, are not necessarily mentioned spontaneously by the patient in conventional therapy. This is because the triggering feeling may not be associated with a memorable event, and the drug use may avert emergence of memorable distress.

More dramatic is the phenomenon of affect regression, which Wurmser (1977) observed among addicted patients studied in a psychoanalytic context. He pointed out that when addicts suffer narcissistic injury, they are prone to a precipitous collapse of ego defenses and the consequent experience of intense and unmanageable affective flooding. In the face of such vulnerability, they handle stress poorly and may turn to drugs for relief. This vulnerability can be considered in light of the model of conditioned withdrawal, in which drug seeking can become an immediate reflexive response to stress, thereby undermining the stability and effectiveness of a patient's coping mechanisms.

The model of conditioned drug seeking has been applied to development of treatment techniques, to training patients to recognize drug-related cues, and to avert relapse. Annis (1986), for example, has used a self-report schedule to assist patients in identifying the cues, situations, and moods that are most likely to lead them to alcohol craving. Marlatt (1985) evolved an approach he described as "relapse prevention," whereby patients are taught strategies for avoiding the consequences of the alcohol-related cues they have identified. A similar conception has been used to extinguish cocaine craving through cue exposure in a clinical laboratory (Childress, McLellan et al., 1988).

These approaches can be introduced as part of a single-modality behavioral regimen, but they also can be used in expressive and family-oriented psychotherapy. For example, Ludwig and colleagues (1978) suggested the approach of cognitive labeling; namely, associating drinking cues with readily identified guideposts to aid the patient in consciously averting the consequences of prior conditioning. Similarly, the author has described (1983) a process of guided recall to explore the sequence of antecedents in given episodes of craving or drinking slips that were not previously clear to the patient. These approaches can occur concomitant with an examination of general adaptive problems in an exploratory therapy.

The conditioning approach described here is useful in understanding the relationship between the pharmacology and behaviors associated with drugs of abuse. The test of an explanatory approach, however, is whether it yields options that can be adapted to practice. This means that a stable ongoing treatment (one in which cues related to drug seeking can be addressed) must be secured.

In light of this need for practical application, this chapter next will consider the interpersonal modality necessary to secure an addicted patient's engagement in treatment and compliance. This approach has been termed "network therapy" because specific family members and friends are enlisted to provide ongoing support for recovery. This approach will be considered by examining the role of social cohesiveness in securing treatment.

SOCIAL COHESIVENESS AS A VEHICLE FOR REINFORCING ABSTINENCE

Social cohesiveness is defined as the sum of all forces that act on members of a group to keep them engaged (Cartwright & Zander, 1962). It can be an important factor in binding a patient to the therapeutic context, even when he or she is inclined to drop out. Dependency on a therapist, affinity for members of a therapy group, or bonds to spouse and children in family therapy all are examples of this phenomenon.

Cohesiveness is particularly important in relation to addiction rehabilitation, as it often is the principal vehicle for retaining the addicted patient in therapy when relapse is threatening. Let us first consider its role in peer-led and established professional programs for addiction, after which we will examine how it can be developed in an office-based modality to secure patients' engagement in addiction rehabilitation.

Peer-Led Programs. In studies of the emergence of cohesiveness in AA and other mutual-help groups, the author and colleagues have found that when inductees become engaged, they experience an improvement in emotional well-being. This enhanced well-being stabilizes conformity with the group's norms, as compliance is operantly reinforced by a positive affective response to involvement in the group (Galanter, Talbott et al., 1990; Galanter, 1990). Drug-free therapeutic communities also promote intense relatedness among members as a vehicle for addiction rehabilitation (De Leon, 1989). Alcoholism also has been treated by recourse to group practices in cohesive subcultures. This is seen in peyote rituals in Native American communities in the southwestern United States and in espiritismo practices among Puerto Rican Americans (Albaugh & Anderson, 1974; Singer & Borrero, 1984).

AA in particular provides an example of how group cohesiveness can be highly influential in addiction rehabilitation. At AA meetings, reinforcement for involvement is regularly provided as members are given effusive, ritualized approval by the group, both when they speak informally and when they recount their histories at anniversaries of their sobriety. An individual member develops close ties to a member who serves as a sponsor to supervise recovery, and this relationship is a predictor of good outcome (Emrick, 1989). On an institutional level as well, the AA approach has been integrated into hospital-based programs, encouraging patients to sustain ties to fellow AA members after discharge (Cook, 1988). In a study of physicians who successfully completed an AA-oriented residential program, the author and colleagues found that, even two years after discharge, they attended more than five AA meetings each week and were in contact with their AA sponsors twice a week (Galanter, Talbott et al., 1990).

Importantly, AA also illustrates the feasibility of combining strong, cohesive ties with cognitive-behavioral techniques. For example, members are inculcated to avoid the "persons, places and things" that are cues to drinking. They also learn mottos and phrases that serve as cognitive labels for avoidance of problem attitudes and situations (Ludwig, Bendfeldt et al., 1978). These aspects of the Twelve Step approach illustrate how the labeling of cues for conditioned withdrawal can be wedded to a social therapy, thereby enhancing the addict's motivation to apply such labeling in avoiding relapse. AA members are reinforced when they discuss the avoidance of cues at AA meetings or with their sponsors in the organization.

Unfortunately, however, many addicted patients reject the option of involvement in AA, while others drop out after their initial meetings (Brandsma, Maultsby & Welsh, 1980). Accordingly, there is a strategic advantage in a therapeutic approach that draws on preexisting cohesive ties—those of family and close friends—as a starting point in treatment. The latter approach also can protect against early dropping out, which might take place in a self-help group setting populated by relative strangers. It also can help the therapist to encourage a reluctant patient to continue attendance at AA meetings.

Professionally Led Treatment. Professionals also can draw on a network of cohesive relationships to enhance the outcome of treatment. For example, an evaluation of the outcome of Speck and Attneave's network therapy for psychotic patients

(Schoenfeld, Halevey & Hemley-van-der Velden, 1986) demonstrated that considerable benefit derived from use of existing social ties to family and friends. Enhanced outcome was reported as well when the community reinforcement techniques developed by Hunt and Azrin (1973) were augmented by greater social relatedness in a club-like setting (Mallams, Godley et al., 1982). Similarly, the author and colleagues (Galanter, Castaneda & Salamon, 1987) effected higher rates of retention and social recovery by integrating a peer-led format into a professionally directed alcohol treatment program.

Not surprisingly, the cohesiveness and support offered by group and family therapy has been found effective in rehabilitating addicted patients. Yalom, Bloch et al. (1978) reported on benefits derived when interactional group therapy was used as an adjunct to recovery techniques. Couples group therapy also has been shown to benefit alcoholics and to diminish the likelihood of treatment dropout (Gallant, Rich et al., 1970; McCrady, Stout et al., 1991). Even counseling of spouses of alcoholics in the absence of their alcoholic partners ultimately yielded effective treatment (Dittrich & Trapold, 1984). Observations like these have led experienced clinicians to develop addiction rehabilitation techniques based on expertise in the practice of family therapy and have yielded a number of clinical monographs on the use of established family therapy techniques in addiction (Stanton & Thomas, 1982; Kaufman & Kaufman, 1979; Steinglass, Bennett et al., 1987).

NETWORK THERAPY IN OFFICE PRACTICE

Having examined the need for introducing behavioral techniques and social cohesion into ongoing treatment of the addicted patient, this chapter next considers the model of network therapy for addiction (Galanter, 1993; Galanter, 1987). It offers a pragmatic approach to augmenting conventional individual therapy that draws on these recent advances to enhance the effectiveness of office management.

Couples. A cohabiting couple will provide the first example of how natural affiliative ties can be used to develop a secure basis for rehabilitation. Couples therapy for addiction has been described in both ambulatory and inpatient settings, and good marital adjustment has been found to be associated with a diminished likelihood of dropping out and a positive overall outcome (Stanton & Thomas, 1982; Kaufman & Kaufman, 1979; McCrady, Stout et al., 1991; Dittrich & Trapold, 1984; Galanter, 1987; Noel, McCrady et al., 1987; Moos & Moos, 1984).

It is recognized, however, that a spouse must be involved in an appropriate way. Constructive engagement should be distinguished from a co-dependent relationship (Cermak, 1986) or overly involved interaction, which is thought to be a problem in recovery. Indeed, couples managed with a behavioral orientation showed greater improvement in alcoholism than those treated with interactional therapy, where attempts were made to engage them in relational change (O'Farrell, Cutter & Floyd, 1985). It is therefore important for clinicians to accord each member of the couple an appropriate and differentiated role, so that the spouse is not placed in a position of pressing the patient to comply with treatment. Thus we will consider here a simple, behaviorally oriented device for making use of the marital relationship: namely, working with a couple to enhance the effectiveness of disulfiram therapy.

The use of disulfiram has yielded relatively little benefit overall in controlled trials, when patients are responsible for taking their doses on their own (Fuller & Williford, 1980). This is largely because this agent is effective only when it is ingested as instructed, typically on a daily basis. Alcoholics who forget to take required doses likely will resume drinking in time. Indeed, such forgetting often reflects the initiation of a sequence of conditioned drug-seeking behaviors.

Although patient characteristics have not been shown to predict compliance with a disulfiram regimen (Schuckit, 1985), changes in the format of patient management have been found to have a beneficial effect on outcomes (Brubaker, Prue & Rychtarik, 1987). For example, the involvement of a spouse in observing the patient's consumption of disulfiram yields a considerable improvement in outcome (Keane, Foy et al., 1984; Azrin, Sisson et al., 1982; Galanter, 1989). Patients alerted to taking disulfiram each morning by this external reminder are less likely to experience conditioned drug seeking when exposed to addictive cues and are more likely to comply on subsequent days with the dosing regimen.

The technique (Galanter, 1993) also helps in clearly defining the roles in therapy of both the alcoholic and spouse, typically the wife, by avoiding the spouse's need to monitor drinking behaviors she cannot control. The spouse does not actively remind the alcoholic to take each disulfiram dose. She merely notifies the therapist if she does not observe the pill being ingested on a given day. Decisions about managing compliance are then shifted to the therapist, and the couple does not become entangled in a dispute over the patient's attitude and the possibility of secret drinking. By means of this technique, a majority of alcoholics in one clinical trial (Galanter, 1993) experienced marked improvement and sustained abstinence over the period of treatment.

A variety of other behavioral devices shown to improve outcome can be incorporated into this couples format. For example, it has been found (Stark, Campbell & Brinkerhoff, 1990) that scheduling the first appointment for as soon as possible after the initial telephone contact improves outcome by diminishing the possibility of an early loss of motivation. Spouses also can be engaged in history taking at the outset of treatment to minimize the introduction of denial into the patient's representation of the illness (Liepman, Nierenberg & Begin, 1989). The initiation of treatment with such a technique is illustrated in the following case report.

Case 2: A 39-year-old alcoholic man was referred for treatment. Both the patient and his wife were initially engaged by the psychiatrist in a telephone exchange so that all three could plan for the patient to remain abstinent on the day of the first session. They agreed that the wife would meet the patient at his office at the end of the work day on the way to the appointment. This would ensure that cues presented by his friends going out for a drink after work would not lead him to drink. In the session, an initial history was taken from the spouse as well as the patient, allowing her to expand on the negative consequences of the patient's drinking, thereby avoiding his minimizing of the problem. A review of the patient's medical status revealed no evidence of relevant organ damage, and the option of initiating his treatment with disulfiram was discussed. The patient, with the encouragement of his wife, agreed to take his first dose that day, continue under her observation, and then be evaluated by his internist within a few days. Subsequent sessions with the couple were dedicated to dealing with implementation of this plan, and concurrent individual therapy was initiated as well.

Patients who take disulfiram in this manner have acquired a cognitive label to help them avoid a sudden and unanticipated relapse. The potential efficacy of this approach is illustrated by the reaction of the patient described in Case 2, an attorney who experienced a precipitous collapse of psychological defenses on receiving an incorrect report about his share of the partnership's profits. If he had been taking disulfiram as described here, his knowledge of a potential disulfiram reaction could have alerted him to avoid going out to get a drink. Patients who are maintained with disulfiram, as described, for an initial year of recovery thus have the opportunity to deal in therapy with the issues that precipitate craving, without exposing themselves unduly to the threat of relapse. In the lawyer's case, this would have allowed him to address the psychodynamic underpinnings of his job-related anxieties in the therapy, rather than by reflexive drinking.

It is important to clarify certain aspects of engaging a collateral in the treatment, particularly a spouse. Long-standing conflicts between members of an alcoholic couple should not be allowed to interfere with the disulfiram monitoring. For example, the spouse should not be placed in a role in which he or she must demand compliance. This is why the patient is vested with the responsibility of ingesting the disulfiram so that he is clearly seen by his spouse; her role is only to notify the therapist in a telephone message if she does not see him taking his pill on a given morning. Discussions of compliance *per se* therefore are initiated by the therapist and not by the spouse. In this way, the role of the spouse as enforcer is eliminated. This is compatible with the approach suggested by Al-Anon, which encourages the spouse to avoid responsibility for managing the partner's drinking problem.

Larger Networks. In an evaluation of family treatment for alcohol problems reported by the Institute of Medicine, McCrady concluded that "research data support superior outcomes for family-involved treatment, enough so that the modal approach should involve family members and carefully planned interventions" (Institute of Medicine, 1990). Indeed, the idea of the therapist's intervening with family and friends to start treatment was introduced by Johnson (1986) as one of the early ambulatory techniques in the addiction field (Gitlow & Peyser, 1980; Gallant, 1987). More broadly, the availability of greater social support to patients has been shown to be an important predictor of positive outcome in addiction (McLellan, Woody et al., 1983).

In light of this, it is important to consider what would serve as a useful paradigm for using family and social supports in office treatment. This can be used as well to enhance the stability of the technique for disulfiram observation already described.

The demonstrated utility of directive and behaviorally oriented approaches for preventing relapse might protect against an unstructured exploration of the family as a system. There are, however, two options for stabilizing abstinence: the ecologic and the problem-solving family treatment. The ecologic approach, developed by Minuchin and colleagues (1967) and others, emphasizes the engagement of resources from the patient's family and social environment. It presumes that the pathology is embedded in the broader social context and acknowledges that this context must be used to effect recovery. Problem-solving family therapy, developed by Haley (1977) and others, relies on an initial assessment of the principal presenting symptom, and subsequent treatment is directed at the problem itself, rather than primarily at restructuring the family relations. By means of these approaches, the therapist can develop an option that parallels the community reinforcement behavioral approach used in multimodality clinics (Hunt & Azrin, 1973).

The author reported a positive outcome for this approach with a series of 60 patients treated in network therapy (Galanter, 1993). These patients attended one network session a week for an initial month and subsequent sessions less frequently, typically bimonthly after a year of ambulatory care. Individual therapy was carried out concomitantly once or twice a week. On average, the networks had 2.3 members, and the most frequent participants were mates, peers, parents or siblings.

Case 3: Friends of a 46-year-old alcohol-dependent man sought out consultation to secure his abstinence. At the psychiatrist's suggestion, they brought him along with them to a conjoint session, where he avowed that he could stop drinking on his own. An agreement was made among the network members, the patient and the psychiatrist that they would maintain contact so that they could act together in case the patient's suggested approach did not succeed. Two months later, after the patient had required brief hospitalization for detoxification following a relapse into drinking, members of the network prevailed on him to come for treatment. The patient and network members then agreed that he would participate in individual therapy and would meet with the network and psychiatrist at regular intervals. The patient suffered a relapse six months later; one of the network members consulted the psychiatrist and stayed with the patient in his home for a day to ensure that he would not drink. He and other network members then brought the patient to the psychiatrist's office to reestablish a plan for abstinence.

This case illustrates how members of the network can help to counter the patient's inclination to deny his drinking problem in the initial stages of engagement and during relapse as well. It shows the value of the network in providing the psychiatrist with the means of communicating with a relapsing patient and of assisting in reestablishment of abstinence.

On the other hand, it points to the quandary posed to the clinician who deals with a disorder in which a nonpsychotic patient is subject to uncontrolled, damaging behavior. To what extent should members of the network be encouraged to intervene in the patient's life? Is it proper for the clinician to support their pressing an intoxicated patient to let one of them stay in his home? To exercise proper caution, the therapist must carefully assess the motives and judgment of network members, as well as the patient's capacity to respond positively to their intervention. The therapist must anticipate as much as possible the patient's response to an intervention, both during intoxication and later. Despite a clear need for caution, though, it should be noted that members of AA have for years assumed an active role in helping fellow members terminate relapses into drinking. This aspect of AA underlines the meaningful support that persons close to a recovering person can provide. Incidentally, their support can be instrumental in helping the therapist ensure that the addicted patient is motivated to attend AA meetings and become engaged.

The network is, however, most valuable during conjoint sessions with the patient when it supports the therapist's suggestions for helping the patient avoid relapse. For example, network involvement can be vital in countering the patient's denial of his or her own vulnerability to relapse. As illustrated in the following case vignette, an effective intervention need involve no more than the network members' providing advice in the therapy session. The weight of the patient's relationship with his own chosen network members and his ability to respond to their efforts to help him are potent tools in securing compliance. In the following case, the network members were instrumental in ensuring that the patient would remove himself from conditioned environmental cues for substance use during the period of early abstinence.

Case 4: A 23-year-old man who had insufflated heroin for a year had recently begun using it intravenously. He abused alcohol and marijuana as well. In a psychiatric consultation that he solicited, he agreed to bring in his uncle, his cousin and a friend for support and to take naltrexone each day under the observation of the uncle. In the ensuing session with this network, he expressed reluctance to move to his parents' house temporarily to provide a setting that would help him avoid friends who would expose him to regular drinking and marijuana use. After discussing the importance of this added security with his network members and the psychiatrist, he concurred with the consensus that he did need the move temporarily. On the basis of their input, he conceded that it was more important at the moment to avoid the drug cues of his peer group than to insist on independence from his parents.

Sustaining the Network. Yalom (1974) has described anxiety-reducing tactics that he used in therapy groups with alcoholics to avert disruptions and promote cohesiveness. These included setting an agenda for the session and using didactic instruction. In the network format, a cognitive framework can be provided for each session by starting out with the patient's recounting events related to cue exposure or substance use since the last meeting. Network members then are expected to comment on this report to ensure that all are engaged in a mutual task with correct, shared information. Their reactions to the patient's report are addressed as well.

Case 5: An alcoholic began one of his early network sessions by reporting a minor lapse in abstinence. This was disrupted by an outburst of anger from his older sister. She said that she had "had it up to here" with his frequent unfulfilled promises of sobriety. The psychiatrist addressed this source of conflict by explaining in a didactic manner how behavioral cues affect vulnerability to relapse. This didactic approach was adopted in order to defuse the assumption that relapse is easily controlled and to relieve consequent resentment. He then led members in planning concretely with the patient how he might avoid further drinking cues in the period preceding their next conjoint session.

This case illustrates the importance of maintaining an appropriate therapeutic milieu in the network sessions. In volunteering to participate, members agree to help the patient but not to subject their own motives to scrutiny. In this, the network format therefore differs materially from the systemic family therapy approach, as it avoids subjecting network members to the demands of addressing their own motives. The didactic or intellectualized approach, as used in Case 5, thus can be helpful in neutralizing excessive anger that may be felt toward the patient, without scrutinizing the reasons for a member's anger.

In addition, the patient himself is expected to help maintain amicable relations with network members to protect the supportive milieu. This is made explicit in both network and individual sessions. For example, if a network member is absent for a few sessions, the patient is expected to discuss the matter with that member and to resolve any outstanding issues in order to promote the member's return. Any difficulty the patient may experience in carrying out this role is viewed as an issue to be addressed in individual sessions.

The network therefore is conceived of as an active collaboration in which conflicts are minimized to ensure optimal function, as they would be on the work site or in a sports team. When led effectively, members are inclined to be effective team members. They develop a positive transference toward the therapist and are willing to support the therapist's views.

Conditioned Withdrawal and Anxiety. Patients undergoing detoxification from chronic depressant medication often experience considerable anxiety, even when the dose is reduced gradually (American Psychiatric Association, 1990). The expectation of distress (Monti, Rohsenow et al., 1988), coupled with conditioned withdrawal phenomena, may cause patients to balk at completing a detoxification regimen. In individual therapy, the psychiatrist would have little leverage at this point. When augmented with network therapy, however, the added support can be valuable in securing the patient's compliance.

Case 6: A patient elected to undertake detoxification from chronic use of diazepam (approximately 60 mg per day). In network meetings with the patient, her husband and her friend, the psychiatrist discussed the need for added support toward the end of her detoxification. As her daily dose was brought to 2 mg t.i.d., she became anxious, said that she had never intended to stop completely and insisted on being maintained permanently with that low dose. Network members supportively but explicitly pointed out that this had not been the plan. She then agreed to the original detoxification agreement, and her dose was reduced to zero over six weeks.

The Contingency Contract. Contingency contracting, as used in behavioral treatment (Hall, Cooper et al., 1977), stipulates that an unpalatable contingency will be applied if a patient carries out a prohibited symptomatic behavior. Crowley (1984) successfully applied this technique to rehabilitating cocaine addicts by preparing a written contract with each patient, stating that a highly aversive consequence would be initiated for any use of the drug. For example, for an addicted physician, a signed letter in which the physician admitted addiction was prepared for mailing to the state licensing board. This approach can be adapted to the network setting as well.

Case 7: A patient regularly attended network and individual therapy sessions and also attended Narcotics Anonymous. Nonetheless, he frequently slipped into cocaine use. In a network session, he agreed to random weekly urinalyses and collection of urine samples by his friend, a member of the network. In discussion with network members, he further agreed to prepare a letter to his employer indicating that he was an addict and not suitable to remain on the job. The patient signed an agreement stating that the letter should be mailed by the psychiatrist if any of his weekly urinalyses revealed that he had ingested cocaine. He remained substance free with this regimen over the ensuing year, and his improved status was discussed in network sessions over that time. He continued to be substance free after the contingency was discontinued as well.

Complementing Individual Therapy. Psychotherapeutic approaches have been found to yield improved outcomes when combined with certain addiction treatments, such as AA (Emrick, 1989), methadone maintenance (Woody, Luborsky et al., 1983) and cocaine management techniques (Rounsaville, Gawin & Kleber, 1985). In the context of network therapy, individual expressive sessions can complement the abstinence orientation of network meetings if the therapist closely attends to conditioned cues for substance use. Once abstinence is stabilized, network sessions can augment the psychotherapy with support for the patient's general social recovery.

Even after the patient's abstinence is apparently stable, it is important to examine in therapy the patient's thoughts about drinking, dreams related to substance use and responses to environmental drinking cues. On the one hand, they alert the patient to the need to be aware of the long-term risk of relapse. In addition, they provide revealing clues to ongoing conflicts, which may be apparent only in their expression in the symbolism of addiction.

Although network sessions may be terminated before long-term individual therapy comes to an end, it is essential to make clear that the network members should be available if the patient experiences difficulties in the future, as illustrated in the next case vignette.

Case 8: An alcoholic woman had been seen in network and individual sessions for 16 months and had been abstinent for a year. Because of her stability, a final network session was scheduled with her husband and two friends. Discussion there initially focused on her successful recovery, as evidenced by her beginning employment in the previous month. Those present then agreed that any of the network members could contact the therapist if the patient relapsed in the future. The patient indicated that she would discuss any lapse in abstinence with both the network members and the therapist.

Empirical Research. Two studies recently have been added to the body of empirical research on network therapy. In one, the technique was standardized relative to a structured treatment manual and, in the second, an assessment was made of the feasibility of training clinicians in the technique.

Standardization. Contemporary research on psychosocial treatment modalities requires the development of a structured manual explaining the ways in which the treatment is carried out in the clinical setting. It is only in this manner that reliability can be achieved across clinicians in the application of therapy techniques. Such a manual, 122 pages in length, was developed for Network Therapy (Galanter & Keller, 1994). Using the manual, 17 clinicians were trained in the network technique and then tested for their ability to distinguish network procedures in a reliable manner from conventional family systems therapy. For both modalities, videotaped segments of respective sessions were shown and scored by mental health professionals. The treatments were found to be differentiable with a high degree of reliability.

The Network Therapy Rating Scale employed with the latter group of subjects was applied in a second study, in which the efficacy of clinical training was assessed in terms of the results of treatment of addicts in a clinical context. In the second study (Galanter, Keller et al., in press), 19 third-year psychiatric residents without experience in addictions treatment or in outpatient therapy were given a 13-hour course in network therapy. They then undertook the treatment of cocaine addicts and were supervised by clinicians experienced in the network therapy technique. Altogether, 24 patients were treated over the course of 24 weeks. While the patients were in treatment, 79% of the urine samples obtained each week were negative for cocaine, and 42% of the patients produced clean urines during the three weeks immediately before termination of treatment. Overall, this outcome, along with treatment retention rates, compared favorably with those reported in several studies of cocaine treatment in the medical literature in which experienced therapists were employed. These results suggest that naive mental health trainees can be taught to apply network therapy for effective treatment management.

PRINCIPLES OF NETWORK TREATMENT

The following is an abstract of the manual for applying Network Therapy. It can be adapted to the needs of a given patient and to the relative availability of potential network members.

Begin a Network as Soon as Possible

1. It is important to see the patient promptly, as the window of opportunity for openness to treatment generally is brief. A week's delay can result in loss of motivation or relapse to drinking.
2. If the patient is married, engage the spouse early on, preferably at the time of the first telephone call. Point out that addiction is a family problem. The spouse generally can be enlisted in assuring that the patient arrives at the office with a day's sobriety.
3. In the initial interview, frame the exchange so that a good case is built for the grave consequences of the patient's addiction, and do this before the patient can introduce his or her system of denial. This approach avoids putting the spouse or other network members in the awkward position of having to contradict a close relative.
4. Make clear that the patient needs to be abstinent, beginning immediately. (A tapered detoxification may be necessary with some drugs, such as the sedative-hypnotics.)
5. Start an alcoholic patient on disulfiram treatment as soon as possible, in the office at the time of the first visit, if possible. Instruct the patient to continue taking disulfiram under the observation of a network member.
6. Start to build a network for the patient at the first visit, involving the patient's family members and close friends.
7. From the very first meeting, consider how to ensure the patient's sobriety until the next meeting and plan that with the network. Initially, their immediate companionship, a plan for daily AA attendance, and planned activities all may be necessary.

Manage the Network with Care

1. Include persons who are close to the patient, who have a longstanding relationship with him or her, and who are trusted. Avoid members with substance problems. Avoid superiors and subordinates at work, as they have an overriding relationship with the patient independent of friendship.
2. Get a balanced group. Avoid a network composed solely of the parental generation, or of younger people, or of persons of the opposite sex. Sometimes a nascent network selects itself for a consultation if the patient is reluctant to address his or her own problem. Such a group will go on to supportively engage the patient in the network, with careful guidance from the therapist.
3. Assure that the mood of meetings is trusting and free of recrimination. Do not allow the patient or the network members to be made to feel guilty or angry in meetings. Explain issues of conflict in terms of the problems presented by addiction, rather than engaging in discussions around personality conflicts.
4. Set a directive tone by giving explicit instructions to support and ensure abstinence. A feeling of teamwork should be promoted, with no psychologizing or impugning of members' motives.
5. Meet as frequently as necessary to ensure abstinence—perhaps once a week for a month, every second week for the next few months, and every month or two by the end of a year.

6. Assure that the network has no agenda other than to support the patient's abstinence. As that abstinence is stabilized, the network can help the patient plan for a new drug-free lifestyle. Do not allow the network be distracted by issues of family relations, or allow the focus to shift to other members' problems.

Keep the Network's Agenda Focused

1. *Maintain Abstinence:* The patient and the network members should report at the outset of each session any exposure of the patient to alcohol or drugs. The patient and network members should be instructed as to the nature of relapse and should work with the clinician to develop a plan to sustain abstinence. Cues to conditioned drug-seeking should be examined.
2. *Support the Network's Integrity:* Everyone has a role in this: the patient is expected to assure that network members keep their meeting appointments and stay involved with the treatment. The therapist sets meeting times and summons the network for any emergency, such as relapse. (The therapist does whatever is necessary to secure stability of the membership if the patient is having trouble doing so.) Members of the network are responsible for attending network sessions and engaging in other supportive activities with the patient.
3. *Secure Future Behavior:* The therapist should combine any and all modalities necessary to ensure the patient's stability. This may involve establishing a stable, drug-free residence; avoiding substance abusing friends; attending Twelve Step meetings; using medications such as disulfiram or blocking agents; observing urinalysis; and obtaining ancillary psychiatric care. Written agreements may be useful. This may involve a mutually acceptable contingency contract, with penalties for violation of understandings.

Make Use of AA and Other Self-Help Groups

1. Patients should be expected to attend meetings of AA or related groups at least two to three times, with follow-up discussion in therapy.
2. If a patient has reservations about these meetings, the therapist should try to help them understand how to deal with them. Issues such as social anxiety should be explored if they make a patient reluctant participate. Generally, resistance to AA can be related to other areas of inhibition in a person's life, as well as to the denial of addiction.
3. As with other spiritual involvements, the therapist should not probe the patient's motivation or commitment to AA, once he or she has engaged. The therapist should allow the patient to work out issues on his/her own, but be prepared to listen as needed.

CONCLUSIONS

The model of addictive behavior and office-based treatment presented here deals with the influence of pharmacologically conditioned drinking cues on relapse into substance dependence, and it uses a cognitive-behavioral approach to averting relapse. To engage addicted patients while treatment is applied and to motivate them to overcome the effect of addictive cues, a network of persons close to the patient can be brought into the therapy sessions to augment the individual treatment. Specific network techniques draw on the variety of relationships among the patient, the family and peers.

ACKNOWLEDGMENT: This chapter was adapted in part from articles by the author in the Journal of Psychiatric Treatment and Evaluation *(1983;5:551),* Advances in Alcohol and Substance Abuse *(1987;6:159), and* Psychiatric Annals *(1989;19:226), and the manual* Network Therapy for Alcohol and Drug Abuse *(Basic Books, 1993).*

REFERENCES

Albaugh BJ & Anderson PO (1974). Peyote in the treatment of alcoholism among American Indians. *American Journal of Psychiatry* 131:1247–1250.

American Psychiatric Association (1990). *Benzodiazepine Dependence, Toxicity, and Abuse: A Task Force Report of the American Psychiatric Association*. Washington, DC: American Psychiatric Association.

American Psychiatric Association (1994). *Diagnostic and Statistical Manual of Mental Disorders, 4th Edition.* Washington, DC: American Psychiatric Press.

Annis HM (1986). A relapse prevention model for treatment of alcoholics. In WE Miller & N Heather (eds.) *Treating Addictive Behaviors: Processes of Change*. New York, NY: Plenum Publishing Co.

Anonymous (1990). Nation's treatment providers forced to ration care. *Alcoholism and Drug Abuse Week* Feb. 28 (newsletter).

Azrin NH, Sisson RW, Meyers R & Godley M (1982). Alcoholism treatment by disulfiram and community reinforcement therapy. *Journal of Behavioral Therapy and Experimental Psychiatry* 13:105–112.

Begleiter H & Porjesz B (1979). Persistence of a subacute withdrawal syndrome following chronic ethanol intake. *Drug and Alcohol Dependence* 4:353–357.

Brandsma JM, Maultsby MC & Welsh RJ (1980). *Outpatient Treatment of Alcoholism: A Review and Comprehensive Study*. Baltimore, MD: University Park Press.

Braunstein WB, Powell BJ, McGowan JF & Thoreson RW (1983). Employment factors in outpatient recovery of alcoholics: A multi-variate study. *Addictive Behavior* 8:345–551.

Brubaker RG, Prue DM & Rychtarik RG (1987). Determinants of disulfiram acceptance among alcohol patients: A test of the theory of reasoned action. *Addictive Behavior* 12:43–52.

Cartwright D & Zander A (1962). *Group Dynamics: Research and Theory*. Evanston, IL: Row, Peterson.

Cermak TL (1986). *Diagnosing and Treating Codependence*. Minneapolis, MN: Johnson Institute Books.

Childress AR, McLellan AT, Ehrman R & O'Brien CP (1988). Classically conditioned responses in opioid and cocaine dependence: A role in relapse? In Ray BA (ed.) *Learning Factors in Substance Abuse (NIDA Research Monograph 84)*. Rockville, MD: National Institute on Drug Abuse.

Cook CCH (1988). The Minnesota Model in the management of drug and alcohol dependency: Miracle, method, or myth? *British Journal of Addiction* 83:625–634.

Crowley TJ (1984). Contingency contracting treatment of drug-abusing physicians, nurses, and dentists. In J Grabowski, ML Stitzer & JF Henningfeld (eds.) *Drug Abuse Treatment (NIDA Research Monograph 46)*. Rockville, MD: National Institute on Drug Abuse.

De Leon G (1989). Therapeutic communities for substance abuse: Overview of approach and effectiveness. *Bulletin of the Society of Psychology of Addictive Behavior* 3:140–147.

Dittrich JE & Trapold MA (1984). A treatment program for wives of alcoholics: An evaluation. *Bulletin of the Society of Psychology of Addictive Behavior* 3:91–102.

Emrick CD (1989). Alcoholics Anonymous: Membership characteristics and effectiveness as treatment. In M Galanter (ed.) *Recent Developments in Alcoholism, Vol 7.* New York, NY: Plenum Publishing Co.

Fuller RK & Williford WO (1980). Life-table analysis of abstinence in a study evaluating the efficacy of disulfiram. *Alcoholism: Clinical & Experimental Research* 4:298–301.

Galanter M (1993). Network therapy for substance abuse: A clinical trial. *Psychotherapy* 30:251–258.

Galanter M (1993a). Network therapy for addiction: a model for office practice. *American Journal of Psychiatry* 150:28–36.

Galanter M (1990). Cults and zealous self-help movements: A psychiatric perspective. *American Journal of Psychiatry* 147:543–551.

Galanter M (1989). Management of the alcoholic in psychiatric practice. *Psychiatric Annals* 19:266–270.

Galanter M (1987). Social network therapy for cocaine dependence. *Advances in Alcohol and Substance Abuse* 6:159–175.

Galanter M (1983). Cognitive labelling: Psychotherapy for alcohol and drug abuse: An approach based on learning theory. *Journal of Psychiatric Treatment and Evaluation* 5:551–446.

Galanter M, Castaneda R & Salamon I (1987). Institutional self-help therapy for alcoholism: Clinical outcome. *Alcoholism: Clinical & Experimental Research* 11:424–429.

Galanter M & Keller D (1994). *Network Therapy for Substance Abuse: A Therapist's Manual*. New York, NY: Basic Books.

Galanter M, Keller D & Dermatis H (in press). Network therapy for addiction: Assessment of the clinical outcome of training. *American Journal of Drugs and Alcohol.*

Galanter M, Talbott D, Gallegos K & Rubenstone E (1990). Combined Alcoholics Anonymous and professional care for addicted physicians. *American Journal of Psychiatry* 147:64- 68.

Gallant DM (1987). *A Guide to Diagnosis, Intervention, and Treatment.* New York, NY: W.W. Norton.

Gallant DM, Rich A, Bey E & Terranova L (1970). Group psychotherapy with married couples. *Journal of the Louisiana State Medical Society* 122:41–44.

Gitlow SE & Peyser HS (1980). *A Practical Treatment Guide*. New York, NY: Grune & Stratton.

Haley J (1977). *Problem Solving Therapy*. San Francisco, CA: Jossey-Bass.

Hall SM, Cooper JL, Burmaster S & Polk A (1977). Contingency contracting as a therapeutic tool with methadone maintenance clients. *Behavioral Research Therapy* 15:438–441.

Hayman M (1956). Current attitudes toward alcoholism of psychiatrists in Southern California. *American Journal of Psychiatry* 112:485–493.

Hunt GM & Azrin NH (1973). A community-reinforcement approach to alcoholism. *Behavioral Research Therapy* 11:91–104.

Institute of Medicine (1990). *Broadening the Base of Treatment for Alcohol Problems*. Washington, DC: National Academy Press.

Johnson VE (1986). *How to Help Someone Who Doesn't Want Help*. Minneapolis, MN: Johnson Institute Books.

Kaufman E & Kaufman PN, eds. (1979). *Family Therapy of Drug and Alcohol Abuse*. New York, NY: Gardner Press.

Keane TM, Foy DW, Nunn B & Rychtarik RG (1984). Spouse contracting to increase Antabuse compliance in alcoholic veterans. *Journal of Clinical Psychology* 40:340–344.

Khantzian EJ (1985). The self-medication hypothesis of addictive disorders: Focus on heroin and cocaine dependence. *American Journal of Psychiatry* 142:1259–1264.

Liepman MR, Nierenberg TD & Begin AM (1989). Evaluation of a program designed to help family and significant others to motivate resistant alcoholics to recover. *American Journal of Drug and Alcohol Abuse* 15:209–222.

Ludwig AM, Bendfeldt F, Wikler A & Cain RB (1978). "Loss of control" in alcoholics. *Archives of General Psychiatry* 35:370–373.

Mallams JH, Godley MD, Hall GM & Meyers RJ (1982). A social-systems approach to resocializing alcoholics in the community. *Journal of the Study of Alcoholism* 43:1115–1123.

Marlatt GA & Gordon J (1985). *Relapse Prevention: Maintenance Strategies in the Treatment of Addictive Behaviors*. New York, NY: Guilford Press.

McAuliffe WE (1982). A test of Wikler's theory of relapse: The frequency of relapse due to conditioned withdrawal sickness. *International Journal of Addiction* 17:19–33.

McCrady BS, Stout R, Noel N, Abrams D & Fisher-Nelson H (1991). Effectiveness of three types of spouse-involved behavioral alcoholism treatment. *British Journal of Addiction* 86:1415–1424.

McLellan AT, Woody GE, Luborsky L, O'Brien CP & Druly KA (1983). Increased effectiveness of substance abuse treatment: A prospective study of patient-treatment "matching." *Journal of Nervous and Mental Disorders* 171–597–605.

Minuchin S, Montalvo B, Guerney BG, Rusman BL & Schumer F (1967). *Families of the Slums*. New York, NY: Basic Books.

Monti PM, Rohsenow DJ, Abrams DB & Binkoff JA (1988). Social learning approaches to alcohol relapse: Selected illustrations and implications. In BA Ray (ed.) *Learning Factors in Substance Abuse (NIDA Research Monograph 84)*. Rockville, MD: National Institute on Drug Abuse.

Moos RH & Moos BS (1984). The process of recovery from alcoholism, III: Comparing functioning in families of alcoholics and matched control families. *Journal of the Study of Alcoholism* 45:111–118.

National Institute on Alcohol Abuse and Alcoholism (NIAAA) (1987). *Alcohol and Health*. Washington, DC: U.S. Government Printing Office.

Nathan PE & McCrady BS (1986/1987). Bases for the use of abstinence as a goal in the treatment of alcohol abusers. *Drugs and Society* 1(2/3):109–131.

Noel NE, McCrady BS, Stout RL & Fisher-Nelson H (1987). Predictors of attrition from an outpatient alcoholism treatment program for couples. *Journal of Studies on Alcohol* 48:229–235.

O'Brien CP, Testa T, O'Brien TJ, Brady JP & Wells B (1977). Conditioned narcotic withdrawal in humans. *Science* 195:1000–1002.

O'Farrell TJ, Cutter HSG & Floyd FJ (1985). Evaluating behavioral marital therapy for male alcoholics: Effects on marital adjustment and communication before and after treatment. *Behavioral Therapy* 16:147–167.

Olson RP, Ganley R, Devine VT & Dorsey GC (1981). Long-term effects of behavioral versus insight-oriented therapy with inpatient alcoholics. *Journal of Consulting and Clinical Psychology* 49:866–877.

Rounsaville BJ, Gawin FH & Kleber HD (1985). Interpersonal psychotherapy adapted for ambulatory cocaine users. *American Journal of Drug and Alcohol Abuse* 11:171–191.

Schoenfeld P, Halevey J & Hemley-van-der Velden E (1986). The long-term outcome of network therapy. *Hospital & Community Psychiatry* 37:373–376.

Schuckit MA (1985). A one-year follow-up of men alcoholics given disulfiram. *Journal of Studies on Alcohol* 46:191–195.

Singer M & Borrero MG (1984). Indigenous treatment for alcoholism: The case of Puerto Rican spiritualism. *Medical Anthropology* 8:246–273.

Speck R & Attneave C (1974). *Family Networks*. New York, NY: Vintage Books.

Stanton MD & Thomas TC, eds. (1982). *The Family Therapy of Drug Abuse and Addiction*. New York, NY: Guilford Press.

Stark MJ, Campbell BK & Brinkerhoff CV (1990). "Hello, may we help you? A study of attrition prevention at the time of the first phone contact with substance-abusing clients. *American Journal of Drug and Alcohol Abuse* 15:209–222.

Steinglass P, Bennett LA, Wolin SJ & Reiss D (1987). *The Alcoholic Family*. New York, NY: Basic Books.

Vaillant GE (1981). Dangers of psychotherapy in the treatment of alcoholism. In MH Bean & NE Zinberg (eds.) *Dynamic Approaches to the Understanding and Treatment of Alcoholism*. New York, NY: Free Press.

Wikler A (1973). Dynamics of drug dependence. *Archives of General Psychiatry* 28:611–616.

Woody GE, Luborsky L, McLellan AT, O'Brien CP, Beck AT, Blaine J, Herman I & Hole A (1983). Psychotherapy for opiate addicts: Does it help? *Archives of General Psychiatry* 40:639–645.

Wurmser L (1977). Mrs. Pecksniff's horse? Psychodynamics of compulsive drug use. In JD Blaine & DS Julius (eds.) *Psychodynamics of Drug Dependence (NIDA Research Monograph 12)*. Rockville, MD: National Institute on Drug Abuse.

Yalom ID (1974). Group therapy and alcoholism. *Annals of the New York Academy of Science* 233:85–103.

Yalom ID, Bloch S, Bond G & Zimmerman E (1978). Alcoholics in interactional group therapy. *Archives of General Psychiatry* 35:419–425.

CHAPTER 6

Aversion Therapy

P. Joseph Frawley, M.D.

Principles of Training and Conditioning
Uses of Aversion Therapy in Treatment
Safety of Aversion Therapy
Acceptability of Aversion Therapy
Criticisms of Aversion Therapy
Aversion Therapy as Part of a Multimodality Treatment Program

Aversion therapy, or counterconditioning, is a powerful tool in the treatment of alcohol and other drug addiction. Its goal is to reduce or eliminate the "hedonic memory" or craving for a drug and to simultaneously develop a distaste and avoidance response to the substance. Unlike punishments (jail, firings, fines, divorce, hangovers, cirrhosis, and the like), which often are delayed in time from the use episode, aversion therapy relies on the immediate association of the sight, smell, taste and act of using the substance with an unpleasant or aversive experience. This treatment is not designed to appeal to the logical part of the person's brain, which often is all too aware of the negative consequences of alcohol and other drug use, but to the part of the brain where emotional attachments are made or broken through experienced associations of pleasure or discomfort. Aversion therapy provides a means of achieving control over injurious behavior for a period of time, during which alternative and more rewarding modes of response can be established and strengthened (Bandura, 1969).

People Need Care; Behavior Needs Modification. It is important not to confuse aversion with punishment. In punishment, it is the person who receives the negative consequence, while in aversion therapy the negative consequence is *only* paired with the act of using the drug. This has a very important benefit to self-esteem. While the patient is engaging in positive recovery activities, he or she is receiving immediate positive support for this new way of behaving and thinking. It is only when the patient is using the substance that he or she experiences immediate and consistent discomfort. Hence, self-esteem is rebuilt by separating the drug from the person (Smith, 1982).

In non-addict populations, hangovers have been cited as a significant reason to cut down or stop drinking (Smith, Bookner & Dreher, 1988). However, the hangover is delayed from the actual use of the alcohol; for the alcohol addict, who drinks for the immediate euphorogenic effects of alcohol, the hangovers often are ineffective in producing aversion, since they are delayed in time from the use of the substance whose immediate effect was experienced as pleasant or euphoric. Moreover, the discomfort of the hangover, while logically understood to be due to drinking, is blamed on "drinking too much" (i.e., weakness) rather than drinking at all (disease); moreover, alcohol may be used to cure the withdrawal ("hair of the dog"), which ensures that emotionally the alcohol is perceived as the solution, not the problem.

Disulfiram (Antabuse®) is not an aversion treatment. In aversion therapy for alcohol addiction, alcohol is not absorbed into the system (Smith, 1982). With disulfiram, alcohol must be absorbed and metabolism begun for it to produce its toxic effect (Ritchie, 1980). Aversion relies on safe but uncomfortable experiences that can be repeated, while disulfiram reactions can be life-threatening, even in healthy people. For this reason, patients today are not given alcohol at the same time that they are prescribed disulfiram. As a result, they have not actually experienced getting sick on disulfiram while drinking. Thus, disulfiram does not change the way the addict feels about the alcohol. He or she may fear the consequence of drinking on disulfiram, similar to the fear of being arrested for drinking and driving, but still retains the euphoric recall of past episodes of drinking alcohol and hence the craving for the alcohol itself. Aversion works to eliminate or reduce the euphoric recall through the recording of new negative experiences with the drug (Cannon, Baker et al., 1986).

Spontaneous Aversions Are Common. The capacity to develop aversions is a biological defense mechanism. Silva and Rachman (1987) published a study of 125 students and hospital employees. One hundred five (84%) had a history of natural aversions. There were an average of 3.5 aversions per person (females > males) and 70.1% had been present since childhood.

PRINCIPLES OF TRAINING AND CONDITIONING

Ivan Pavlov noted that the repetitive pairing of a bell with food would soon lead to a "conditioned response" of salivation on the part of dogs to the sound of the bell alone, even with no food present. This type of pairing or training is called *classical conditioning.*

B.F. Skinner expounded on the observation that the nervous system is so constructed that organisms will reduce or avoid behavior that is consistently paired with negative consequences, and increase behavior that is rewarded. This type of learning is called *operant conditioning.* Both types of learning can be shown to occur in addiction (Hoeschen, 1991). Aversion therapy uses these principles in reversing the drug-rewarded learning and conditioned reflex to seek drugs.

The development of an aversion can be very specific. Inadequate treatment can occur when aversion is developed only to one type of alcoholic beverage (Lemere & Voegtlin, 1940; Quinn & Henbest, 1967). In professional alcohol addiction treatment, for example, 50% of trials may be with the addict's favorite brand or type of liquor, but the other trials include a whole range of alcoholic beverages (Lemere, Voegtlin et al., 1942; Smith, 1982).

Repetition is an essential part of training and conditioning (Schwartz, 1978). Adequate trials are needed to develop an aversion (Lemere, Voegtlin et al., 1942) and to maintain and reinforce it to prevent extinction (Voegtlin, Lemere et al., 1941; Smith, Frawley & Polissar, 1991).

Addicts Already Have Been Conditioned by the Drug Prior to Entry into Treatment. Studies of alcoholics have found that they increase the number of swallows and amount of salivation in response to the sight of alcohol, as compared to non-alcoholics (Pomerleau, Fertig et al., 1983). Studies of smokers seeking to quit cigarettes show that those who are least likely to quit will have a much larger conditioned drop in pulse (presumably to compensate for the increase in pulse rate caused by smoking) when presented with a cigarette, than those who will successfully quit (Niaura, Abrams et al., 1989). Cocaine-dependent addicts have progressively increasing drops in skin temperature and increased galvanic skin response (a sign of arousal) when watching progressively more intense and explicit pictures of cocaine use. These responses can be shown to decay in strength the longer the addict is away from the drug.

The presence of these phenomena suggest that one of the consequences of addiction is that the body becomes conditioned to drink or use in the presence of drug stimuli. This may contribute to the sensation of physical craving experienced by addicts. The availability of drugs such as heroin or cocaine in the environment also influences craving (Sherman, Zinser et al., 1989; Weddington, Brown et al., 1990; Gawin & Kleber, 1986).

USES OF AVERSION THERAPY IN TREATMENT

Aversion Therapy in Smoking Cessation. It is estimated that over 80% of smokers wish to quit but feel compelled to continue smoking because of the difficulty of stopping; indeed, the annual spontaneous recovery rate for smokers is less than 5% (Sachs, 1991). Sachs (1986, 1991) reviewed modern smoking cessation treatments and concluded that programs that use rapid smoking aversion had superior outcomes. Hall (1985) and Lando (1977) reported in separate studies that the best results were reported by programs in which aversion was combined with several other modalities, including relapse prevention, relaxation training, written exercises, contract management, booster sessions of aversion, and group support. In patients with cardiopulmonary disease, Hall has provided data both for and against the use of satiation aversion. In one study (1983), patients treated with health motivation, self-management, film models and verbal commitment had better outcomes than those treated with satiation aversion, relaxation training and role play. In 1984, on the other hand, Hall reported that those on a waiting list had no abstinence compared with those treated with satiation aversion, who achieved a 50% two-year abstinence. The safety of satiation smoking has been evaluated by Hall and colleagues (1984), who found no myocardial ischemia or significant arrhythmia in a group of 18 treated patients. Five patients with ischemic changes on the treadmill did not experience these changes during the satiation treatment.

Much of the research on aversion therapy for smoking cessation has focused on improved outcomes with aversive smoking (puffing or inhaling smoke from the cigarette in a rapid manner to induce nicotine toxicity, often including nausea) (Erickson, Tiffany et al., 1983). While nicotine is taken into the system during this treatment, the aversion developed to smoking is adequate to prevent relapse despite the transient presence of nicotine in the bloodstream during treatment. Faradic aversion (mild electric stimulus applied to the forearm) has been used commercially for smoking cessation since 1972 (Smith, 1988). With faradic aversion, the smoke is not inhaled, but merely puffed. Inhaling during faradic aversion may lead to early relapse because of maintenance of the nicotine dependence (Berecz, 1972). One advantage of this form of treatment is that less medically sophisticated staff can supervise the administration of the treatment. In both forms of treatment, the patient personally administers the aversive agent (rapid smoking or electric stimulus) to him- or herself, while the therapist serves as a coach. In the case of the faradic aversion, each time that the patient brings the cigarette toward his or her lips, a mild electric stimulus is administered automatically by a nine-volt battery. The stimulus is activated by a string attached to the smoker's wrist. The therapist also instructs the patient in relapse prevention methods, behavior and dietary changes, which assist in abstinence and comfort during the initial period following smoking cessation. Smith (1988) contacted 59% of 556 patients treated with this method in a commercial program and found that 52% had achieved continuous abstinence at one year.

Aversion Therapy for Alcohol Addiction. The spontaneous recovery rate for alcoholism is influenced by a variety of factors, including severity of problems, age and the presence of a psychiatric disorder. Nevertheless, the annual spontaneous recovery rate estimated by Vaillant in his study of the natural history of alcoholism was 2% to 3% (Vaillant, 1983). In 1949, Voegtlin and Broz published a 10.5-year follow-up of 3,125 patients treated with aversion therapy. One-year abstinence rates of 70% were reported using chemical aversion therapy with minimal counseling.

There are three well-conducted controlled trials of aversion therapy. Boland and colleagues (1978) evaluated the six-month abstinence rates for 50 low-socioeconomic status alcoholics, using lithium as a chemical aversive agent. Twenty-five patients given emetic aversion with lithium had 36% total abstinence, as compared to 12% for the 25 patients given control treatment ($p < 0.05$). Cannon, Baker and Wehl (1981) divided 20 VA patients into three groups and found that there was little difference in outcome between seven patients given chemical aversion and those given control treatment (both groups, however, had extremely high abstinence rates: 170/180 days for the chemical aversion group versus 158/180 days for the control group). Both did better than seven patients receiving faradic aversion. However, the groups were small, there may have been some ceiling effect, and the subjects had to drink some alcohol during the actual testing sessions, which could counteract any aversion being developed.

In the private sector, Smith and Frawley (1990) compared 249 inpatients receiving aversion therapy as part of a multimodality treatment program with 249 inpatients from a large (> 9,000 patient) treatment registry of patients receiving multimodality treatment, but no aversion therapy. All were matched on 17 baseline characteristics. Of the patients receiving aversion therapy, 84.7% had total abstinence from alcohol at six months, compared with 72.2% in the control group ($p<0.01$); at one year, 79% of those treated with aversion had maintained abstinence, versus 67% of those without such treatment ($p < 0.05$). The group showing the greatest benefit from aversion therapy seemed to be the daily drinkers (84% versus 67% at six months, $p < 0.001$).

While the majority of patients in the study were treated with chemical aversion therapy, a subsample of 28 patients received faradic aversion instead. The decision to prescribe faradic aversion instead of chemical aversion within clinical practice usually is based on the patient's medical condition. If the patient has a medical contraindication to chemical aversion therapy, then faradic is prescribed. In this study, the 11.5% of patients treated with faradic did not have significantly better outcomes than controls. Jackson and Smith (1978) reported that patients receiving faradic or chemical aversion based on medical indications had outcomes similar to each other. Jackson and Smith (1978) reported that patients selected in this way had nearly identical abstinence rates.

Nausea Aversion. As reported by Smith (1982), "The usual treatment session involves having the patient take nothing except clear liquids by mouth for six hours prior to treatment. This reduces the likelihood of aspiration of solid stomach contents during treatment. The patient, after receiving a full explanation of the treatment procedure, is taken to the treatment room, which is small in size and has shelves containing all types of alcoholic beverages along the walls. It also has cut-outs of various liquor advertisements on the walls. The intent is to have the majority of the patient's visual stimuli associated with alcohol beverages and visual cues for drinking. The patient is seated in a comfortable chair with an attached large emesis basin. The patient receives an injection of pilocarpine and ephedrine to induce an autonomic arousal and an oral dose of emetine. The emetic effect begins in approximately five to eight minutes. Prior to that time, the patient is given two 10-ounce glasses of warm water with a small amount of added salt. The water provides a volume of easily vomited material, while the salt content tends to counteract the excessive loss of electrolytes during the procedure. Shortly before the expected onset of nausea, the nurse administering the treatment pours a drink of the patient's preferred alcoholic beverage and mixes it with an equal amount of warm water. The patient then is instructed to smell the beverage and to take a small mouthful, swish it around in the mouth to get the full flavor of it, and then to spit it out into the basin. This 'sniff, swish, and spit' phase is designed to insure that the patient has well-defined visual, olfactory and gustatory sensations associated with the preferred beverage prior to the onset of the aversive stimulus of nausea. The nausea and vomiting ensue shortly thereafter and the procedure is altered to that of 'sniff, swish, and swallow.' The alcoholic beverage swallowed is shortly returned as emesis so that no significant amount of alcohol is retained to be absorbed, an event that would negate the treatment. After an intensive conditioning session in the treatment room, lasting 20 to 30 minutes, the patient is returned to the hospital room, where 30 minutes later, another drink of alcoholic beverage is given containing an oral dose of emetine and tartar emetic, which induces a slower-acting residual nausea lasting up to three hours. The average patient receives five treatment sessions, which are given every other day over a 10-day period of time."

Faradic Aversion Therapy for Alcohol. As reported by Smith (1982), "During each session, a pair of electrodes is attached to the forearm of the dominant hand and placed approximately two inches (0.05 dm) apart. The electrodes are attached to an electrostimulus machine capable of delivering 1 to 20 mA (DC, constant current). The faradic therapist runs an ascending series of test stimuli to determine the level of stimulus perceived as aversive by the patient on that particular day (there is a relatively wide variance between patients and within the same individual from day to day).

"The treatment paradigm consists of pairing an aversive level of electrostimulation with the sight, smell, and taste of alcoholic beverages. At the direction of the therapist (forced choice trial) the patient reaches for a bottle of alcoholic beverage, pours some of it in a glass and tastes it without swallowing. Electrostimulus onset occurs randomly throughout the entire behavior continuum, from reaching for the bottle through tasting the alcoholic beverage. The number of electrostimuli with each trial varies from one to eight. An additional 10 free choice trials are designed so that the patient is negatively reinforced, with removal of the aversive stimulus if he or she selects a nonalcoholic choice such as fruit juice. The patient is instructed not to swallow any alcohol at any time throughout the faradic session, and this behavior is closely monitored by the therapist."

Sessions last 20 to 45 minutes, depending on the speed of the individual patient. Following the aversion conditioning session in the treatment room, the patient returns to his or her room, listens to a relaxation tape, makes a list of positive changes with sobriety and contrasts these with negative consequences of continued use.

Aversion Therapy for Marijuana Dependence. The spontaneous recovery rate from marijuana dependence is not known and, like that for alcohol and nicotine, probably is dependent on multiple factors. Chemical aversion with emetine has been used for marijuana by Morakinyo (1983). In clinical practice, aversion therapy for marijuana uses faradic aversion (Smith, Schmeling & Knowles, 1988). The protocol for faradic aversion is similar to that of the treatment for alcohol, but uses a variety of bongs, drug paraphernalia and visual imagery. An artificial marijuana substitute and marijuana aroma are used in treatment. A one-year abstinence rate of 84% was reported following five days of treatment, combined with three weekly group sessions on self-management techniques (Smith, Schmeling & Knowles, 1988).

Aversion Therapy for Cocaine or Amphetamine Dependence. The spontaneous recovery rate from cocaine or amphetamine dependence is not known. Rawson and colleagues (1986) followed 30 patients who had requested information about stopping cocaine, but had not used treatment for an eight-month period; 47% were reported at the follow-up point to be using cocaine at least monthly. No total abstinence figures are available. Frawley and Smith (1990) reported the use of chemical aversion for the treatment of snorting cocaine dependence. In this treatment, an artificial cocaine substitute called Articaine® was developed from tetracaine, mannitol and quinine. Patients snorted this substance and paired this with nausea induced by emetine. Of those so treated, 56% were continuously abstinent and 78% currently abstinent (i.e., for the prior 30 days) at six months following treatment; at 18 months, 38% were continuously abstinent and 75% currently abstinent. For those treated for both alcohol and cocaine, 70% were continuously and currently abstinent from cocaine at six months and 50% were continuously abstinent and 80% currently abstinent at 18 months following treatment.

Frawley and Smith (1992) reported a 53% one-year continuous abstinence rate in 156 cocaine/amphetamine dependent patients treated with aversion. This was based on a 73% follow-up rate. Outcomes for chemical and faradic aversion were not significantly different. This report also compared patients treated for alcohol and cocaine problems before the institution of cocaine aversion, when only aversion therapy for alcohol was available, with those who received aversion therapy for both alcohol and cocaine. The addition of the aversion for cocaine produced statistically significant improved abstinence rates in this population. The increase in cocaine abstinence in the second group compared to the first (55% versus 88%) is greater than the decrease in follow-up rate from the first to the second group (84% versus 64%). Because of the lower follow-up rate in the second study, this research needs replication.

Aversion for Heroin Addiction. Copemann (1976) employed a unique approach to aversion therapy by pairing aversive stimuli to cognitive images of heroin use. Patients were asked to verbalize only after they had conjured up a strong mental image. A second part of the treatment asked addicts to conjure images of socially appropriate behavior, involving employment, education or non-drug entertainment. Latency to verbalization was measured. Copemann found that, at baseline, addicts could rapidly conjure up positive thoughts about heroin use, but had significant delays in conjuring up thoughts about rewarding non-drug activities. Subjects were in a half-way house for heroin addicts and received group therapy in conjunction with relaxation therapy in addition to the aversion treatment. A faradic stimulator was used. Once addicts had conjured up drug images, faradic aversion was applied. At other times, addicts were given 15 seconds to conjure images of non-drug socially appropriate behavior to prevent aversion from being applied. With this training over an average of 15 sessions (with a range of 5 to 25), latency for drug-related images increased while that for socially appropriate images decreased. Thirty of 50 patients completed the treatment and, at 24 months, 80% (24 of 30) were reported to be still drug-free.

SAFETY OF AVERSION THERAPY

Faradic aversion has virtually no unwanted side effects and has been found to be safe for patients with pacemakers and pregnant women (because the current only travels between two electrodes on the arm).

To be eligible for chemical aversion therapy, patients must be free of medical contraindications such as esophageal varices, serious coronary artery disease or active gastrointestinal pathology. Emetine today is given only orally, thus effectively eliminating the risk of cardiotoxic effects of i.m. emetine, since very little of the orally administered emetine is absorbed (Kattwinkel, 1949; Loomis, 1986). Emetine exerts its principal action by irritating the GI tract, hence stimulating the afferent vagus nerve to stimulate the vomiting center in the medulla. Oral emetine is effective in stimulating nausea in over 95% of cases, while intramuscular emetine produces nausea only 30% to 40% of the time, probably through excretion in the bile (Klatskin & Friedman, 1948; Loomis, 1986). Pilocarpine and ephedrine are not used in patients with asthma or serious hypertension, while tartar emetic is held for patients with excessive diarrhea or prolonged nausea. Smith, Frawley and Polissar (1991, unpublished data) found that there was no increased incidence of medical utilization or hospitalization in the six months after treatment in a group treated with aversion therapy, as compared to matched controls treated without aversion.

There are some contraindications to covert sensitization, similar to those for chemical aversion; however, with this therapy emesis can be prevented in most cases. The drawback to covert aversion therapy is that the induction of nausea or other aversive state is not as predictable as with medication and requires more patient preparation (Elkins, 1975).

Satiation therapy with nicotine has been studied by Hall and colleagues (1984) in 18 patients (nine men and nine women; average age 45.8 years) with pulmonary and cardiac disease. Nine had definite or probably cardiac ischemia, but none showed ischemic changes during rapid smoking. Premature ventricular contractions were not increased above baseline by rapid smoking.

ACCEPTABILITY OF AVERSION THERAPY

Selecting the appropriate treatment for a patient involves the patient having full informed consent. The practitioner needs to counsel the patient about the risks of continuing the addiction and the risks, benefits and expected outcomes of alternative methods of treatment. Studies of patients who voluntarily received aversion therapy do not show higher rates of leaving against medical advice than are found in patients in Minnesota Model programs (Smith & Frawley, 1990; Gilmore, 1985; Patton, 1979).

Chemical aversion therapy has been reviewed and approved as treatment for alcoholism by the National Center for Health Services Research and Health Care Technology Assessment (Carter, 1987), the body charged with determining which services should be reimbursable under Medicare. A 1987 CHAMPUS demonstration project recommended coverage for chemical aversion therapy for alcoholism (Mendes, 1992). A California Medical Association Scientific Advisory Panel approved aversion therapy as appropriate treatment when incorporated in a multimodality program (California Medical Association, 1984). The American Society of Addiction Medicine includes aversion therapy as an appropriate part of treatment for alcoholism and other drug dependencies (ASAM, 1986). The American Medical Association's Council on Scientific Affairs (1987) indicated that the available research on the efficacy of faradic aversion for alcohol was weak, but that there was moderate support for the efficacy of chemical aversion. There was some support for both faradic and rapid smoking aversive techniques. However, the report emphasized that there have been few controlled trials. The Office of Technology Assessment of the U.S. Congress found that aversion therapy was effective for some patients under some conditions (Saxe, Dovaterty et al., 1983).

CRITICISMS OF AVERSION THERAPY

Much of the criticism of aversion therapy is similar to the criticism of treatment in the field of addiction in general and stems from the lack of multiple well-designed controlled trials and the need to identify which treatment is appropriate for a given patient (Institute of Medicine, 1990; Saxe, Dovaterty et al., 1983). Wilson (1987) has summarized a variety of criticisms of aversion therapy. These include: (1) greater medical expense than some other forms of treatment, (2) intrusiveness of aversion and (3) the theoretical framework of aversive conditioning. While aversion therapy is more expensive than some other forms of treatment, the CHAMPUS demonstration project did compare costs of CHAMPUS beneficiaries admitted to the hospital with other forms of treatment and found the average cost to be slightly less for aversion therapy (which may be partially attributable to the shorter length of stay for aversion).

The principle that when the outcomes for treatment are the same that the least intrusive treatment should be tried first is brought up by Wilson (1987) and has been echoed by Carter (1987). As further work is done on patient-treatment matching, patients for whom aversion is clearly more effective should be offered this treatment before less effective but less intrusive treatment. Smith, Frawley and Polissar (1991) found significantly better outcomes in males and daily drinkers and Boland, Mellor and Revusky (1978) found significantly better outcomes with indigent male alcoholics with the use of aversion. This work should be replicated.

The theoretical framework of aversion conditioning as a treatment does not exclude the need to develop alternative modes of behavior as part of a multimodality treatment program. Silva and Rachman (1987) have demonstrated that aversions are common and can last a long time. Cannon, Baker et al. (1986) have demonstrated a relationship between the strength of an aversion and the duration of abstinence following treatment.

AVERSION THERAPY AS PART OF A MULTIMODALITY TREATMENT PROGRAM

Relapse to alcohol and drug use is the result of a variety of factors. Patients who report that aversion therapy greatly reduced their urges have the best outcome (Frawley & Smith, 1992). In addition to craving, however, relapse may be related to reflex-conditioned responses to drink or use in response to either external cues such as being around others using or drinking or going to parties, or may be in response to internal cues such as negative or positive emotional states (Frawley & Smith, 1992; Marlatt & Gordon, 1980). The development of new appropriate responses to these emotional states and a change in the recovering person's associations remain important goals for treatment. Aversion therapy does not interfere with their development, but instead enhances the readiness of the patient to avoid the alcohol or drug and thus prepares him or her for new approaches and patterns that do not involve chemicals. Frawley and Smith (1992) found that the use of support groups was associated with improved abstinence in patients treated with aversion for cocaine and methamphetamine dependence.

CONCLUSIONS

Aversion therapy is an important tool to help patients achieve abstinence from alcohol and other drugs of dependence. The knowledgeable clinician should be aware of the risks, benefits and expected outcomes for this approach to treatment.

ACKNOWLEDGMENT: The author wishes to acknowledge the assistance of James W. Smith, M.D., who has reviewed the manuscript and assisted in much of the research on aversion therapy.

REFERENCES

American Medical Association (1987). Aversion therapy (Report of the Council on Scientific Affairs). *Journal of the American Medical Association* 258(18):2562–2566.

American Society of Addiction Medicine (1986). *Statement on Treatment for Alcoholism and Other Drug Dependencies.* Washington, D.C., American Society of Addiction Medicine.

Bandura A (1969). *Principles of Behavior Modification.* New York, NY: Holt, Rinehart and Winston, 509.

Berecz JM (1972). Reduction of cigarette smoking through self-administered aversion conditioning: A new treatment model with implications for public health. *Social Science and Medicine* 6:57–66.

Boland FJ, Mellor CS & Revusky (1978). Chemical aversion treatment of alcoholism: Lithium as the aversive agent. *Behavior Research and Therapy* 16:401–409.

California Medical Association (1984). *Medical Practice Question: Is Aversion Therapy for the Treatment of Alcoholism Considered accepted medical practice or Is It Investigational?* (Report of Scientific Advisory Panels on General and Family Practice and Internal Medicine and the Committee on Alcoholism and Other Drug Dependence). San Francisco, CA: California Medical Association.

Cannon DS, Baker TB, Gino A & Nathan PE (1986). Alcohol-aversion therapy: Relation between strength of aversion and abstinence. *Journal of Consulting and Clinical Psychology* 54(6):825–830.

Cannon DS, Baker TB & Wehl CK (1981). Emetic and electric shock alcohol aversion therapy: Six- and twelve-month follow-up. *Journal of Consulting and Clinical Psychology* 49(3):360–368.

Carter E (1987). Chemical aversion therapy for the treatment of alcoholism. *Health Technology Assessment Reports, 4.* Washington, DC: National Center for Health Care Services Research and Health Care Technology Assessment.

Copemann CD (1976). Drug addiction: II. An aversive counterconditioning technique for treatment. *Psychological Reports* 38:1271–1281.

Elkins RL (1985). Aversion therapy for alcoholism: Chemical, electrical, or verbal imaginary? *The International Journal of the Addictions* 10(2):157–209.

Erickson LM, Tiffany ST, Martin EM & Baker TB (1983). Aversive smoking therapies: A conditioning analysis of therapeutic effectiveness. *Behavior Research and Therapy* 21(60:595–611.

Frawley PJ & Smith JW (1992). One-year follow-up after multimodal inpatient treatment for cocaine and methamphetamine dependence. *Journal of Substance Abuse Treatment* 9(4):271–286.

Frawley PJ & Smith JW (1990). Chemical aversion therapy in the treatment of cocaine dependence as part of a multimodal treatment program: Treatment outcome. *Journal of Substance Abuse Treatment* 7:21–29.

Gawin FH & Kleber HD (1986). Abstinence symptomatology and psychiatric diagnosis in cocaine abusers. *Archives of General Psychiatry* 43:107–113.

Gilmore K (1985). *Hazelden Primary Residential Treatment Program: 1983 Profile and Patient Outcome.* Center City, MN: Hazelden Foundation.

Hoeschen LE (1991). The pharmacokinetics and pharmacodynamics of alcohol and drugs of addiction. In NS Miller (ed.) *Comprehensive Handbook of Drug and Alcohol Addiction.* New York, NY: Marcel Dekker, 745–746.

Institute of Medicine (1990). *Broadening the Base of Treatment for Alcohol Problems.* Washington, DC: National Academy of Sciences.

Jackson TR & Smith JW (1978). A comparison of two aversion treatment methods for alcoholism. *Journal of Studies on Alcohol* 39(1):187–191.

Kattwinkel EE (1949). Death due to cardiac disease following the use of emetine hydrochloride in conditioned-reflex treatment of chronic alcoholism. *The New England Journal of Medicine* 240(25):995–997.

Klatskin G & Friedman H (1948). Emetine toxicity in man: Studies on the nature of early toxic manifestations, their relation to the dose level, and their significance in determining safe dosage. *Annals of Internal Medicine* 28:892–915.

Lemere F & Voegtlin (1940). Conditioned reflex therapy of alcoholic addiction: Specificity of conditioning against chronic alcoholism. *California and Western Medicine* 53(6):1–4.

Lemere F, Voegtlin WL, Broz WR, O'Hollaren P & Tupper WE (1942). Conditioned reflex treatment of chronic alcoholism: VII technic. *Diseases of the Nervous System* 3(8):59–62.

Loomis TA (1986). *Emetine Risk Analysis for the Shadel Hospitals Aversion Therapy Program.* Arlington, VA: Drill, Freiss, Hays, Loomis & Shaffer.

Marlatt GA & Gordon JR (1980). Determinants of relapse: Implications for the maintenance of behavior change. In PO Davidson & SM Davidson (eds.) *Behavioral Medicine: Changing Health Lifestyles.* New York, NY: Bruner/Mazel.

Mendes E (1992). Letter to The Honorable Jamie L. Whitten, Chairman, Committee on Appropriations, House of Representatives, Washington, DC.

Niaura R, Abrams D, Demuth B, Pinto R & Monti P (1989). Responses to smoking-related stimuli and early relapse to smoking. *Addictive Behaviors* 14:419–428.

Patton M (1979). *The Outcomes of Treatment: A Study of Patients Admitted to Hazelden in 1976.* Center City, MN: Hazelden Foundation.

Pomerleau OF, Fertig J, Baker L & Cooney N (1983). Reactivity to alcohol cue in alcoholics and non-alcoholics: Implications for a stimulus control analysis of drinking. *Addictive Behaviors* 8:1–10.

Quinn JT & Henbest R (1967). Partial failure of generalization in alcoholics following aversion therapy. *Quarterly Journal of Studies on Alcohol* 28:70–75.

Rawson RA, Obert JL, McCann MJ & Mann AJ (1986). In LS Harris (ed.) *Cocaine Treatment Outcome: Cocaine Use Following Inpatient, Outpatient and No Treatment (NIDA Research Monograph Series 67).* Rockville, MD: National Institute on Drug Abuse, 271–277.

Ritchie JM (1980). The aliphatic alcohols. In AG Gilman, LS Goodman & A Gilman (eds.) *The Pharmacological Basis of Therapeutics, 6th Ed.* New York, NY: Macmillan.

Sachs DPL (1991). Advances in smoking cessation treatment. *Current Pulmonology* 12:139–198.

Sachs DPL (1986). Cigarette smoking: Health effects and cessation strategies. *Clinics in Geriatric Medicine* 2(2):337–363.

Saxe L, Dovaterty D, Esty K, Fine M (1983). Research on the effectiveness of alcoholism treatment. *Health Technology Case Study 22: The Effectiveness and Costs of Alcoholism Treatment.* Washington, DC: Office of Technology Assessment, U.S. Congress, 43–53.

Schwartz B (1978). *Psychology of Learning and Behavior, Chapter 4, Pavlovian Conditioning.* New York, NY: W.W. Norton & Co., 55.

Sherman JE, Zinser MC, Sideroff SI & Baker TB (1989). Subjective dimensions of heroin urges: Influence of heroin-related and affectively related stimuli. *Addictive Behaviors* 14:611–623.

Silva P & Rachman S (1987). Human food aversions: Nature and acquisition. *Behavior Research and Therapy* 25(6):457–468.

Smith C, Bookner S & Dreher F (1988). Effects of alcohol intoxication and hangovers on subsequent drinking. *NIDA Research Monograph 90.* Rockville, MD: National Institute on Drug Abuse, 366.

Smith JW (1988). Long-term outcome of clients treated in a commercial stop smoking program. *Journal of Substance Abuse* 5:33–36.

Smith JW (1982). Treatment of alcoholism in aversion conditioning hospitals. In EM Pattison & E Kaufman (eds.) *Encyclopedic Handbook of Alcoholism.* New York, NY: Gardner Press, 874–884.

Smith JW & Frawley PJ (1990). Long-term abstinence from alcohol in patients receiving aversion therapy as part of a multimodal inpatient program. *Journal of Substance Abuse Treatment* 7:77–82.

Smith JW, Frawley PJ & Polissar L (1991). Six- and twelve-month abstinence rates in inpatient alcoholics treated with aversion therapy compared with matched inpatients from a treatment registry. *Alcoholism: Clinical & Experimental Research* 15(5):862–870.

Vaillant GE (1983). *The Natural History of Alcoholism: Causes, Patterns and Paths to Recovery.* Cambridge, MA: Harvard University Press, 128.

Voegtlin WL & Broz WR (1949). The conditioned reflex treatment of chronic alcoholism. X. An analysis of 3125 admissions over a period of ten and a half years. *Annals of Internal Medicine* 30:580–597.

Voegtlin WL, Lemere F, Broz WR & O'Hollaren P (1941). Conditioned reflex therapy of chronic alcoholism: IV. A preliminary report on the value of reinforcement. *Quarterly Journal of Studies on Alcohol* 2(3):505–511.

Weddington WW, Brown BS, Haertzen CA, Cone EJ, Dax EM, Herning RI & Michaelson BS (1990). Changes in mood, craving, and sleep during short-term abstinence reported by male cocaine addicts. *Archives of General Psychiatry* 47:861–868.

Wilson GT (1987). Chemical aversion conditioning as a treatment for alcoholism: A re-analysis. *Behavior Research and Therapy* 25(6):503–516.

CHAPTER 7

Community Reinforcement and Contingency Management Interventions

Steven T. Higgins, Ph.D.
Jennifer W. Tidey, Ph.D.
Maxine L. Stitzer, Ph.D.

Conceptual Framework
Community Reinforcement Approach
Contingency Management Interventions
Treatment of Cocaine Dependence
Treatment of Opioid Dependence

This chapter reviews the efficacy of the Community Reinforcement Approach (CRA) and contingency-management procedures for treating alcohol and drug dependence. CRA and contingency management are based in the theoretical framework of operant conditioning, which is the study of how reinforcing and punishing environmental consequences alter the form and frequency of voluntary behavior. The chapter describes how drug use and abuse are conceptualized within an operant framework, and reviews controlled studies on the efficacy of CRA and contingency management in the treatment of drug dependence. These interventions have been researched most extensively with regard to treating alcohol, cocaine, and opioid dependence, which are the main foci of this chapter. The review is restricted to controlled studies published in peer-reviewed journals. The only exceptions are where an uncontrolled study is mentioned as the first in a series of studies that included a controlled trial.

CONCEPTUAL FRAMEWORK

Within an operant framework, drug use is considered a case of operant response that is maintained, in part, by the reinforcing effects of the drugs involved (Goldberg & Stolerman, 1986). The reliable scientific observation that abused drugs function as reinforcers with humans and laboratory animals provides sound scientific support for that position (Griffiths, Bigelow & Henningfield, 1980; Henningfield, Lukas & Bigelow, 1986). Alcohol, cocaine, opioids and most other drugs that are abused by humans are voluntarily self-administered by a variety of species (Young & Herling, 1986). Neither a prior history of drug exposure nor physical dependence are necessary for these drugs to support ongoing and stable patterns of voluntary drug use in otherwise normal laboratory animals. These commonalities across species and drugs provide strong empirical support for the position that reinforcement is a fundamental determinant of drug use and abuse.

Within this framework, all physically intact humans are assumed to possess the necessary neurobiological systems to experience drug-produced reinforcement and hence to develop drug use, abuse, and dependence. Genetic or acquired characteristics (e.g., family history of alcoholism, other psychiatric disorders) are recognized as important factors that affect the probability of developing drug dependence, but they are not deemed to be necessary conditions for the problem to emerge. Instead, drug use is considered a normal, learned behavior that falls along a continuum ranging from patterns of little use and few problems to excessive use and many untoward effects, including death. The same processes and principles of learning are assumed to operate across this continuum.

Treatments developed within this framework are designed to assist in reorganizing the physical and social environments of drug abusers in an effort to systematically weaken the influence of reinforcement obtained through drug use and related activities, by increasing the availability and frequency of reinforcement from alternative activities, especially those that are incompatible with a drug-abusing lifestyle. The following discussion illustrates how this general strategy is implemented in CRA and contingency-management interventions.

COMMUNITY REINFORCEMENT APPROACH

In titling the Community Reinforcement Approach (CRA), the term "community" was used to underscore the important role played by socially-mediated environmental consequences in the remediation of substance abuse problems (cf, Hunt & Azrin, 1973). The term "reinforcement" was included to recognize the central role of this behavioral principle in substance abuse and in all aspects of CRA.

The seminal CRA study was conducted with 16 severe alcoholics admitted to a state hospital for treatment of alcoholism (Hunt & Azrin, 1973). These 16 men were divided into eight pairs that were matched on employment history, family stability, previous drinking history, and education. They were randomly assigned to receive CRA plus standard hospital care or standard care alone. (Standard hospital care consisted of 25 one-hour didactic sessions involving lectures and audio-visuals on Alcoholics Anonymous [AA], alcoholism, and related medical problems.)

CRA was designed to rearrange and improve the quality of reinforcers obtained by patients through their vocational, family, social, and recreational activities. The goal was for these reinforcers to be operational and of high quality when the patient was sober, but unavailable if and when drinking resumed. Importantly, plans for rearranging these reinforcers were individualized to conform to the specifics of each patient's situation.

The first step was to address any immediate barriers to treatment participation, such as pending legal matters or other crises. For pressing legal matters, for example, staff would help put the patient in touch with an appropriate lawyer. The next priority was vocation. Vocational counseling was provided, based on what subsequently became known as Job Club (Azrin & Besalel, 1980). Marital and family therapy was initiated during hospitalization and continued after discharge. Couples and other family members received training in positive communication skills to facilitate negotiation of contracts for reciprocally reinforcing changes in each other's behavior, including alcohol abstinence on the part of the patient (Azrin, Naster & Jones, 1973). For those without family, attempts were made to identify someone in the community who was willing to serve as a surrogate family member. Additionally, social counseling was implemented to develop or reinstate social interactions with other friends, relatives, and members of community groups who had low tolerance for drinking, and to discourage interactions with drinkers (i.e., attempts were made to decrease the availability and acceptability of drinking opportunities). To further this process, staff renovated a former tavern to serve as an alcohol-free social club that patients and their wives could attend for social activities. Lastly, patients were taught to solve problems that had previously resulted in drinking and participated in behavioral rehearsal with the therapist to acquire new and more effective skills for resolving these situations without drinking. Following discharge from the hospital, CRA patients received a tapered schedule of counseling sessions, beginning on a once or twice weekly basis during the first month and then a once monthly basis across the next several months.

During the six-month follow-up period after hospital discharge, time spent drinking was 14% for participants in CRA versus 79% for those in standard treatment. Time unemployed was 5% for CRA participants versus 62% for those in standard treatment, and time away from family was 16% for CRA participants versus 36% for those in standard treatment. Time spent institutionalized was 2% for CRA participants versus 27% for those in standard treatment (Figure 1). Each of these differences was statistically significant.

Improving CRA. CRA subsequently was expanded to include disulfiram therapy, with monitoring by a significant other to ensure medication compliance, additional counseling directed toward anticipating and avoiding potential crises, a "buddy" system in which individuals in the alcoholic's neighborhood volunteered to be available to give assistance with practical issues like repairing cars, etc., and a switch from individual to group counseling to reduce the total number of counselor hours needed to implement the treatment (Azrin, 1976). Twenty matched pairs of hospitalized alcoholic men were randomly assigned to receive this "improved" CRA or a standard hospital program. The standard program was similar to that described above, but also included advice to take disulfiram. Nothing beyond advice was provided to facilitate disulfiram therapy among those who received standard treatment.

FIGURE 1. Comparison of the CRA and Control Groups on Key Dependent Measures

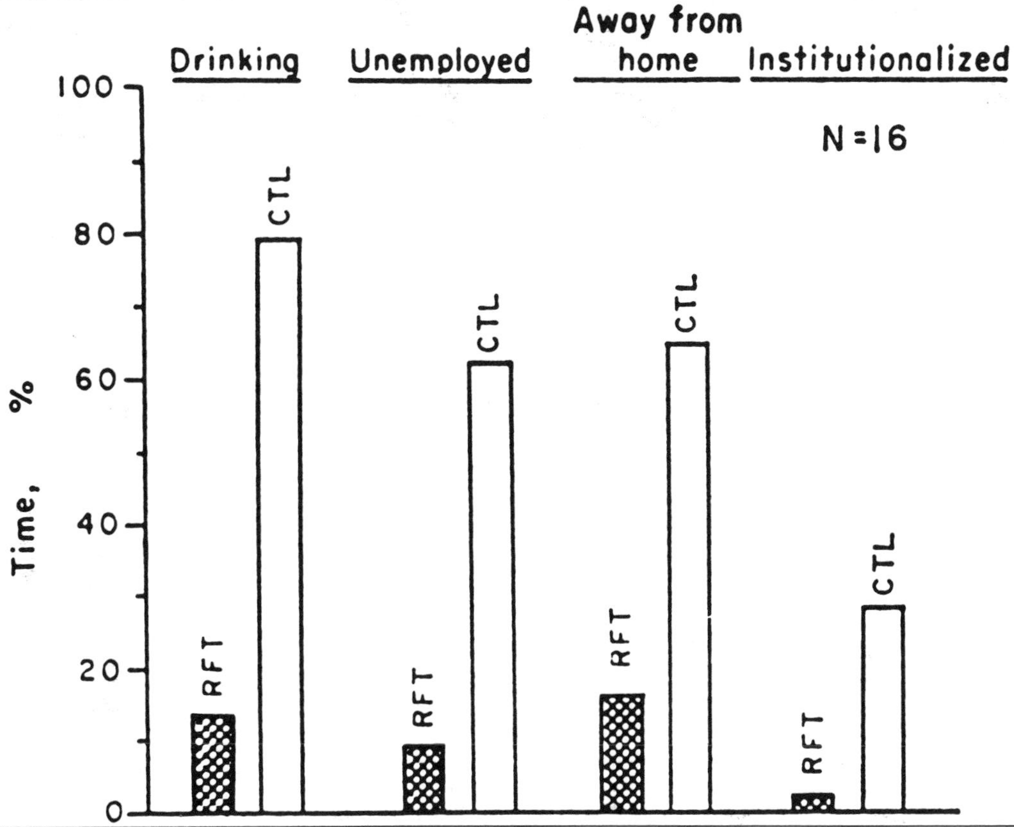

Comparison of the CRA and control groups on key dependent measures during the 6 months of follow-up following hospital discharge: mean percentage of time spent drinking, unemployed, away from home, and institutionalized. From Hunt GM & Azrin NH (1973). A community-reinforcement approach to alcoholism. *Behaviour Research and Therapy* 11:91104. Reprinted by permission.

During the six months after hospital discharge, outcomes achieved by participants in CRA were significantly better than for those who participated in standard treatment in terms of percent of time spent drinking (2% for CRA versus 55% for control), time unemployed (20% for CRA versus 56% for control), time away from family (7% for CRA versus 67% for control), and time spent institutionalized (0% for CRA versus 45% for control). The CRA group spent 90% or more time abstinent during a two-year follow-up period; comparable data were not reported for the standard treatment group.

Social Club. A subsequent study examined the effects of adding the social club described above to a standard regimen of outpatient counseling for alcoholism (Mallams, Godley et al., 1982). The social club was designed to have the social atmosphere and presumably the social reinforcement associated with taverns, but without alcohol. Individuals had to be abstinent to attend. Forty male and female alcoholics were randomly assigned to a group that received systematic encouragement to attend the social club or to a control group that was informed about the existence of the club but received no encouragement to attend. Outcomes were evaluated via a 36-item questionnaire that assessed drinking habits and social adjustment patterns. No significant differences between the treatment groups were discerned in the intake questionnaire scores. At three-month follow-up, drinking in the experimental group decreased significantly from a baseline average of 4.67 ounces of alcohol consumed daily to 0.85 ounces. By contrast, there was no significant change in daily alcohol consumption in the control group, with baseline and posttreatment values at 3.56 and 3.32 ounces, respectively. Significantly greater improvements in the experimental than control group also were observed in ratings of behavioral impairment and time spent in heavy-drinking situations, but not in time spent institutionalized.

This study experimentally isolated the efficacy of the social club, independent of the other elements of

CRA, and extended this component of the CRA intervention to alcoholics enrolled in outpatient treatment.

Disulfiram Therapy. A fourth study dissociated the effects of monitored disulfiram therapy from the other aspects of CRA (Azrin, Sisson et al., 1982). In a parallel-groups design, 43 male and female alcoholic outpatients were randomly assigned to receive traditional treatment and traditional disulfiram therapy (no attempt to influence compliance), traditional therapy plus disulfiram therapy involving significant others to monitor compliance, or CRA in combination with disulfiram therapy and significant-other monitoring. CRA in combination with disulfiram and compliance procedures produced the greatest reductions in drinking, disulfiram in combination with compliance procedures but without CRA produced intermediate results, and the poorest results were observed with the traditional treatment and disulfiram therapy. For example, mean number of days drinking during the sixth month of follow-up was 16.4, 7.9, and 0.9 for the traditional, disulfiram plus compliance, and disulfiram plus full CRA groups, respectively. Interestingly, additional analyses indicated that married patients did equally well with the full CRA treatment package or disulfiram plus compliance procedures alone. Only single subjects appeared to need the package of CRA treatment plus monitored disulfiram to achieve abstinence.

This was the first full report on the efficacy of CRA with less-impaired outpatients. With these less impaired individuals, treatment group differences were noted on measures of drinking only, whereas in the prior studies with more severe hospitalized alcoholics, differences also were discerned on measures of time institutionalized and employed.

Helping Significant Others. The same group of investigators adapted CRA for use with the significant others of treatment-resistant alcoholics (Sisson & Azrin, 1986). Twelve significant others were randomly assigned to receive the CRA intervention (N = 7) or a standard program (N = 5) involving group instruction about alcohol and the disease model of alcoholism. The adapted CRA intervention included education about alcohol problems, information and discussion of the positive consequences of not drinking, assistance in involving the alcoholic in activities that might compete with drinking, increasing the involvement of the significant other in social and recreational activities, and training in how to respond to drinking episodes (including dangerous situations) and how to recommend treatment entry to the alcoholic family member.

There was no evidence of improvement in the control group, in that none of the alcoholics entered treatment during the three-month follow-up and their drinking remained unchanged. In the CRA group, by contrast, six of the seven alcoholics entered treatment and the average frequency of drinking decreased from pretreatment levels of almost 25 days per month to fewer than five days per month posttreatment.

Conclusions. This series of experimental studies is relatively unique in the field of alcoholism treatment research in terms of its programmatic nature and excellent outcomes. Several CRA research projects are underway at the University of New Mexico in an effort to replicate these findings in a different setting and to extend them to the treatment of homeless substance abusers. (The authors are not aware that the results of these projects have appeared in peer-reviewed journals.) CRA in combination with contingency-management procedures has been extended with success to the outpatient treatment of cocaine and opioid dependence and studies on those advances are reviewed below. Additionally, the efficacy of several aspects of the CRA approach—including skills training, relationship counseling, and monitored disulfiram therapy—have been evaluated more extensively since the publication of this original series of studies and their efficacy generally has been supported (see Hester & Miller, 1995).

CONTINGENCY MANAGEMENT INTERVENTIONS

The goal of contingency-management interventions is to arrange environmental contingencies to systematically weaken drug use and strengthen drug abstinence. Contingencies are arranged so that reinforcing or punishing events occur contingent on drug use (more typically a biological marker of recent drug use) or on other behavior deemed important in the treatment process, such as compliance with an adjunct medication regimen or regular attendance at counseling sessions. Often, but not always, contingency management procedures are implemented through written behavioral contracts. That is, a written document is prepared that carefully specifies, in objective detail, the desired behavior change, the consequences to follow success or failure in making that change, and the temporal boundaries for completing the contract. Often, but not always, contingency contracts are used as a component of a more comprehensive treatment intervention.

With regard to the treatment of alcohol abuse and dependence, contingency management procedures have been investigated for their efficacy in directly reducing drinking and for increasing compliance with disulfiram therapy and treatment participation.

Directly Reducing Drinking. In one of the earliest controlled clinical reports, Miller and colleagues (Miller, Hersen & Eisler, 1974) demonstrated the efficacy of a contingency-management intervention in an outpatient male with a 20-year history of alcoholism. The intervention consisted of the subject earning a $3 book of coupons that could be exchanged for meals, clothing, etc., contingent on each zero breath alcohol level (BAL) submitted. BALs decreased from an average of approximately 0.11% at baseline to 0.005% during the contingent-reinforcement period.

Those results set the stage for Miller (1975) to examine whether contingent reinforcement could be used to reduce chronic public drunkenness. Twenty alcoholic men were selected from among a group of recent arrestees for public drunkenness in a city jail (in Jackson, MS) and randomly assigned to an experimental or control group. By reducing their drinking, those in the experimental group earned housing, employment, medical care, and meals through several cooperating social service agencies located in the area. Sobriety was assessed through direct staff observation of gross intoxication and randomly administered BALs. BALs of less than 0.01% maintained services, while BALs of 0.01% or more, or observation of gross intoxication by agency personnel, resulted in an immediate termination of services for five days. Subjects in the control group received the same goods and services independent of BALs or intoxication. Subjects in the contingent-reinforcement and control groups were arrested an average of 1.7 ± 1.2 and 1.4 ± 1.1 times during a two-month baseline period. During the two-month intervention period, arrests decreased to a mean of 0.3 ± 0.5 in the contingent group, while remaining relatively unchanged at 1.3 ± 0.8 in the control group. Additionally, mean hours of employment per week increased in the experimental group but not the control group.

To the authors' knowledge, the only other published report of a controlled study on the use of contingency management procedures to directly reduce drinking involved three controlled case studies (Brigham, Rekers et al., 1981). In this study, three adolescent alcohol abusers, 13 to 15 years of age, received points plus $1 for each day of alcohol abstinence (measured with self-reports, parental reports and/or BALs). Points were exchanged for special privileges. A response-cost contingency also was used, in which subjects were required to pay $1 for each episode of alcohol use. The contingencies led to 82% to 100% reductions in the frequency of drinking across the three subjects.

Increasing Treatment Compliance. Alcohol abuse and attendant behavioral problems are a frequent cause of discharge from methadone treatment (Bickel, Marion & Lowinson, 1987). The authors know of three experimental reports supporting the efficacy of contingencies for increasing disulfiram compliance and decreasing drinking in this population (Bickel, Rizzuto et al., 1989; Liebson, Bigelow & Flamer, 1973; Liebson, Tommasello & Bigelow, 1978). The initial report on this topic described preliminary evidence from six subjects, indicating that requiring alcoholic methadone-maintenance patients to ingest disulfiram as a condition for obtaining their daily methadone dose increased disulfiram compliance and reduced drinking (Liebson, Bigelow & Flamer, 1973). That report was followed up by a well-controlled study (Liebson, Tommasello & Bigelow, 1978) in which 23 alcoholic methadone patients were randomly assigned to one of two groups: 13 patients received methadone treatment contingent on compliance with a recommended course of disulfiram therapy; that is, failure to ingest disulfiram resulted in the start of a 21-day methadone detoxification and clinic dismissal. The option of resuming disulfiram therapy remained available throughout the 21-day detoxification. The 10 control subjects also received a recommendation of disulfiram therapy, but noncompliance with that recommendation had no effect on their methadone treatment. All subjects received hospital detoxification from alcohol before beginning the study. During the 180-day study period, subjects in the methadone-contingent group spent 2% of study-days drinking, as compared to 21% for the control group. Bickel and colleagues (1989) replicated those findings using a within-subject design in three alcoholic methadone maintenance patients.

Robichaud, Strickler and colleagues (1979) used a within-subject reversal design to evaluate the efficacy of mandated disulfiram therapy in a study conducted with 21 industrial employees referred for drinking-related problems on the job. Treatment consisted exclusively of mandatory supervised disulfiram ingestion. The main dependent variable was absenteeism. Treatment duration lasted an average of 10.6 months. Median absenteeism rates, which had been 9.8% during a 24-month baseline period, decreased significantly to 1.7% during treatment. The authors know of no other controlled studies examining the efficacy of disulfiram in employer-referred patients.

Gallant and colleagues conducted a series of experimental studies that examined the efficacy of mandated treatment in criminal justice populations (Gallant, Bishop et al., 1968a, 1973; Gallant, Faulkner et al., 1968b). In the initial study (Gallant, Bishop et al., 1968a), 84 repeat public-drunkenness offenders were randomly assigned to one of four treatment conditions: (1) six months of mandated weekly group therapy, (2) six months of mandated group therapy plus thrice weekly observed disulfiram ingestion, (3) thrice weekly observed disulfiram therapy only, and (4) usual sentence and informal suggestion from the judge to attend the alcoholism clinic. For participants in Groups 1, 2 and 3, noncompliance was to result in individuals automatically being sent to court for a minimum 60-day sentence. However, the authors noted that law enforcement officials failed to adhere to this plan (i.e., contingencies were not systematically enforced). Fewer than 10% of the assigned subjects were available for the six-month follow-up evaluation, which precluded drawing any meaningful conclusions from the study. Results were no better in a follow-up study by the same group that included an inpatient treatment component (Gallant, Bishop et al., 1973). Finally, Ditman and colleagues (1967) reported similarly poor results in the ability of mandated treatment to significantly affect outcome with chronic public drunkenness offenders. If nothing else, this series of studies provides additional reason to appreciate the positive results achieved with this population by Miller (1975) in the study described above.

In contrast to the poor results of compulsory treatment with public drunkenness offenders, Gallant, Faulkner and colleagues (1968b) reported relatively good success with compulsory treatment of alcoholics with more serious criminality. Nineteen criminal alcoholics were randomized to either a group for which attendance in outpatient alcoholism treatment was a parole requirement, or a control group for which attendance after the first appointment was urged but not required. Criminal alcoholics were defined as persons who recently served a sentence of one year or more in a state penitentiary for a major offense that was directly or indirectly associated with alcoholism. Subjects in the compulsory group were instructed that failure to attend a scheduled clinic visit was a violation of parole, for which they would be returned to prison to serve out their time (typically several years). Ninety percent (9/10) of treatment-compulsory subjects attended treatment regularly for at least six months, compared to only 11% (1/9) of treatment-voluntary subjects. At one year, 70% (7/10) of contingent subjects were found to have been abstinent and working during the parole year, while 78% (7/9) of treatment-voluntary subjects were either in prison or had violated parole and were at large.

What variables account for the outcome differences observed between the studies conducted with the public drunkenness offenders and the more serious criminals cannot be determined with confidence. However, three possibilities merit mention: First, law enforcement officials appeared to be more willing to enforce the contingencies with the serious criminals than with the public-drunkenness offenders. Second, the more serious offenders faced lengthier sentences for noncompliance than did the public-drunkenness offenders. Third, there is a possibility that the positive results observed with the serious offenders may have been due to chance. The authors know of no replications of the results from this study.

Ersner-Hershfield, Connors and Maisto (1981) examined the effectiveness of contingencies to promote treatment program attendance for DUI offenders. Sixty-seven male and female participants were randomly assigned to either a program based on principles of self-control and behavioral assessment or to a program consisting of alcohol education, relaxation training and guided reevaluations of situations associated with drinking and driving. Half of the subjects in each treatment group also participated in a deposit system in which they paid $50 at the first session and received a $5 check in each subsequent session for attending and turning in self-reports of drinking. No differences were found for the main effect of self-control versus alcohol-education training, but subjects in the two refundable-deposit groups had fewer unexcused absences than subjects in the no-deposit groups (9 versus 16). Readers interested in the efficacy of compulsory treatment for DUI offenders also may want to examine a report by Ries (1982). The report was not published in a peer-reviewed journal and hence is not described in detail in this review, but it provides evidence suggesting that one year of compulsory treatment can reduce DUI recidivism during the year of treatment.

Conclusions. The use of contingency-management procedures in the treatment of alcohol abuse is less extensive than with other forms of substance abuse, partly because of the difficulty of objectively monitoring alcohol intake. Unlike the case with most illicit drugs, in which urinalysis provides an objective marker of drug use during the several days preceding the test, the only practical objective measure of alcohol use is BAL, which provides evidence only about use during the few hours preceding the test. Considering that alcohol often is abused in an episodic or binge manner, this absence of a good biological marker with an appropriate detection duration makes it difficult to arrange consistent contingencies to directly reinforce or punish alcohol use. The reports by Miller (1975) and Brigham, Rekers et al. (1981) illustrate that this difficulty can be surmounted by relying on a combination of observations by others in the subject's natural environment, in combination with randomly scheduled BALs. The fact that neither of those studies appears to have been followed up might suggest that doing so is relatively cumbersome.

An alternative strategy is to target behaviors that are more readily monitored and incompatible with alcohol use, which is the rationale behind the use of monitored disulfiram therapy and compulsory treatment. The study by Azrin, Sisson et al. (1982) on the use of monitored disulfiram therapy as part of CRA and the studies described above with alcoholic methadone maintenance patients illustrate how reinforcing disulfiram compliance can be effective when the contingencies are managed systematically. The criminal justice system would seem to be an ideal setting for making greater use of compulsory disulfiram therapy as a less expensive alternative to incarceration, but the controlled studies needed to evaluate the efficacy of that strategy are not available. As the studies by Gallant and colleagues on compulsory treatment illustrate, getting consequences implemented in a systematic and timely manner by the criminal justice system is no small challenge and probably is the greatest obstacle to wider use of compulsory disulfiram therapy in that setting. Overall, contingency management appears to have more to offer alcohol treatment in general and treatment of alcoholic offenders in particular than currently is being realized. Perhaps current interest in cost-effective alternatives to the incarceration of substance abusers will cause a revisiting of some of these topics. If so, it is essential that controlled clinical trials be part of that revisiting so that answers to some of the same vexing questions that have been facing us for more than three decades might be obtained.

TREATMENT OF COCAINE DEPENDENCE

Community Reinforcement Approach. Techniques tested and demonstrated to be effective in the treatment of alcoholics recently have been successfully adapted for use with cocaine-dependent individuals. Several controlled trials were completed at the University of Vermont demonstrating the efficacy of an intervention that combining CRA and a contingency management approach to the outpatient treatment of cocaine dependence. Two trials were conducted comparing CRA in combination with contingent voucher-based reinforcement to standard outpatient drug abuse counseling (Higgins, Delaney et al., 1991; Higgins, Budney et al., 1993a). The first of these two trials was 12 weeks in duration and assigned consecutive clinic admissions to the respective treatment groups, while the second trial was 24 weeks and randomly assigned patients to the two treatment groups. In both trials, CRA-plus-vouchers retained patients in treatment significantly longer than did standard counseling and resulted in significantly longer periods of documented cocaine abstinence. For example, in the randomized trial, 58% of patients assigned to the CRA-plus-vouchers treatment completed 24 weeks of treatment, versus 11% of those assigned to standard counseling. Further, 68% and 42% of patients in the CRA-plus-vouchers group were documented to have achieved eight and 16 weeks of continuous cocaine abstinence, versus 11% and 5% of those in the counseling group. Follow-up assessments were conducted at 9 and 12 months after treatment entry into the randomized trial (Higgins, Budney et al., 1995). Significantly greater cocaine abstinence was documented via urinalysis at 9- and 12-month follow-ups in the CRA-plus-vouchers group than in the standard counseling group, while both groups showed comparable and significant improvements on the Addiction Severity Index (ASI).

While these trials were focused on treatment of cocaine dependence, approximately 60% of the cocaine-dependent individuals were also alcohol-dependent and an even larger number abused alcohol. As described above, monitored disulfiram therapy is a core component of CRA and thus was offered to all individuals who reported evidence of concurrent alcohol dependence or abuse. As a first step toward assessing the contribution of that element of treatment to outcome, a chart review was conducted with 16 individuals who met criteria of the revised third edition of the *Diagnostic and Statistical Manual of Mental Disorders* (*DSM-IIIR*; American Psychiatric Association, 1987) for cocaine dependence and alcohol abuse and/or dependence (Higgins, Budney et al., 1993b). Subjects were chosen on the basis of having ≥ 2 weeks on and off disulfiram therapy, which permitted an opportunity to assess for associated benefits. Both drinking and cocaine-positive urinalysis results were more than twofold lower while on, rather than off, disulfiram therapy.

That uncontrolled study was followed up by two randomized trials. Carroll, Ziedonis et al. (1993) reported results from a pilot trial in which 18 outpatients being treated for alcohol and cocaine abuse were randomized to receive disulfiram or naltrexone therapy. Disulfiram therapy resulted in threefold or greater reductions in drinking and cocaine use, as compared to naltrexone therapy. Finally, a larger randomized trial on the efficacy of disulfiram therapy was completed recently by Carroll and colleagues, and again alcohol and cocaine use were significantly reduced by disulfiram therapy (Carroll et al., in press).

Conclusions: These studies illustrate that CRA combined with contingency management is an efficacious treatment for cocaine dependence. Importantly, the studies provided some of the earliest evidence that cocaine dependence could be managed effectively in outpatient settings. In the course of assessing the efficacy of this combined treatment, it was learned that the majority of patients also were alcohol-dependent and that observation provided an opportunity to apply monitored disulfiram therapy to this population. Subsequent controlled trials completed at another site demonstrated that monitored disulfiram therapy is effective in decreasing cocaine and alcohol abuse in abusers of both substances. Those positive results stand in stark contrast to the largely negative results that have been observed with almost all of the other pharmacotherapies for cocaine dependence tested to date (Mendelson & Mello 1996).

Lastly, the voucher system that was the main feature of the contingency management component of this combined intervention has been shown to be efficacious in reducing cocaine use in several controlled trials (described below). Overall, the basic treatment strategy underlying CRA and contingency management has resulted in several important and distinct advances in the quest to develop empirically-based and effective treatments for cocaine dependence.

Contingency Management Interventions. As was noted above, the primary contingency management procedure used in combination with CRA in the studies conducted at the University of Vermont was one in which patients earned vouchers exchangeable for retail items contingent on documentation (by urinalysis) of recent cocaine abstinence. The voucher system was in effect for Weeks 1 to 12 of a 24-week intervention, with a $1.00 state lottery ticket awarded for each cocaine-negative urinalysis test during treatment Weeks 13 to 24. The value of the vouchers increased with each consecutive cocaine-negative specimen delivered, and cocaine-positive specimens reset the value of vouchers back to their initial level. Those who were continuously abstinent (all cocaine negative urine tests) earned the equivalent of $997.50 during Weeks 1 to 12 and $24 during Weeks 13 to 24.

In a randomized trial examining the efficacy of this voucher program, 40 patients were assigned to receive CRA with or without the voucher program (Higgins, Budney et al., 1994). Treatment was 24 weeks in duration and the voucher versus no-voucher difference was in effect during Weeks 1 to 12 only. Both treatment groups were treated the same after Week 12. Seventy-five percent of patients in the group with vouchers completed 24 weeks of treatment, compared to 40% in the group without vouchers. Average duration of continuous cocaine abstinence documented via urinalysis in the two groups were 11.7 ± 2.0 weeks in the vouchers group versus 6.0 ± 1.5 in the no-vouchers group (Figure 2). At the end of the 24-week treatment period, significant decreases from pretreatment scores were observed in both treatment groups on the ASI family/social and alcohol scales, with no differences between the groups. Both groups also decreased on the ASI drug scale, but the magnitude of change was significantly greater in the voucher than the non-voucher groups, and only the voucher group showed a significant improvement on the ASI psychiatric scale. These ASI results remained the same at follow-up assessments completed at 9 and 12 months after entry into treatment (Higgins, Budney et al., 1995).

Because this trial of vouchers was conducted in a small metropolitan area, an important question was whether the findings had generality to inner-city cocaine abusers. Thus, a controlled trial was completed to examine the efficacy of the voucher program described above with cocaine-abusing methadone maintenance patients in a clinic located in Baltimore, Maryland (Silverman, Higgins et al.,

FIGURE 2. Mean Durations of Continuous Cocaine Abstinence

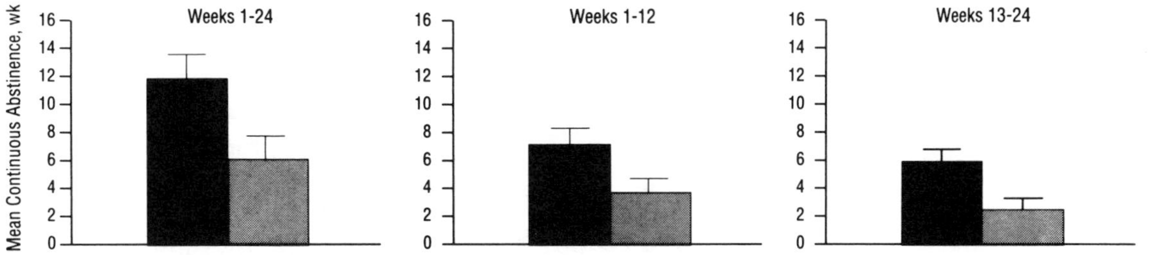

Mean durations of continuous cocaine abstinence documented via urinalysis testing in each treatment group during weeks 1–24, 1–12, and 13–24 of treatment. Solid and shaded bars indicate the voucher and no-voucher groups, respectively. Error bars represent + S.E.M. From Higgins ST, Budney AJ, Bickel WK, Foerg FE, Donham R & Badger GJ (1994). Incentives improve treatment retention and cocaine abstinence in ambulatory cocaine-dependent patients. *Archives of General Psychiatry* 51:568–576. Reprinted by permission.

1996). During a 12-week study, subjects in the experimental group (N = 19) received vouchers exchangeable for retail items, contingent on cocaine-negative urinalysis tests. A matched control group (N = 18) received the vouchers independent of urinalysis results and according to a schedule that was yoked to the experimental group. Both groups received a standard form of outpatient drug abuse counseling. Cocaine use was substantially reduced in the experimental group, but remained relatively unchanged in the control group (Figure 3). Both treatment groups were followed for one month after termination of the voucher intervention. Abstinence decreased in the contingent group compared to levels observed during the intervention period, but remained significantly above levels observed in the control group during Weeks 1 and 4 of that month of follow-up.

The efficacy of this voucher intervention has been or is being investigated in projects underway at several centers around the U.S.; particularly exciting is that some of these projects include studies in pregnant abusers and other cocaine-using populations of special concern.

An approach combining day-treatment (same as day-hospital but in a nonmedical setting) with access to work therapy and housing, contingent on drug abstinence, has been demonstrated to be efficacious with homeless substance abusers (72% primary crack cocaine abusers) (Milby, Schumacher et al., 1996). Subjects were 176 homeless individuals who met diagnostic criteria for one or more substance abuse disorders. They were randomized to receive enhanced or usual care. Enhanced care involved two months of five-day-a-week clinic attendance, transportation to and from the clinic, clinic-provided lunch, psychoeducational groups and individualized counseling. During the last four months of the six-month treatment, intensity of day-treatment was reduced, and subjects were eligible to participate in a work-therapy program refurbishing condemned houses and also to reside in the refurbished housing for a modest rental fee. Participation in the work program and housing were contingent on drug abstinence documented through weekly, random urinalysis testing. Usual care consisted of twice-weekly drug abuse counseling, medical evaluation and treatment for identified problems, and referral to community agencies for housing and vocational services. Usual care was provided without a specified end-point, although the frequency of services decreased as subjects progressed.

At the two-month assessment, the percent of urinalysis results that were positive for cocaine had decreased significantly from a baseline of approximately 60% to 30% in the enhanced group. Comparable values in the usual-care group were 55% to 65%. The percent of cocaine-negative results tended to remain greater in the enhanced than the usual-care group at the 6- and 12-month follow-up assessments, but those differences no longer were statistically significant. Enhanced care also produced greater reductions than usual care in alcohol use at each of the assessments and fewer days of homelessness at the 6- and 12-month assessments. Only enhanced care produced significant baseline to 12-month improvements in employment.

Conclusions: There remains little doubt that cocaine abuse can be reduced through contingency management interventions. The authors know of no other treatment about which an equally unequivocal statement can be made. Nonetheless, it also is the case that many important issues remain to be addressed in developing this approach to treating cocaine abuse. One important issue is that not all patients respond equally well to the intervention (Higgins, Budney et al., 1994; Silverman, Higgins et al., 1996). Those with more severe baseline levels

FIGURE 3. Longest Duration of Sustained Cocaine Abstinence

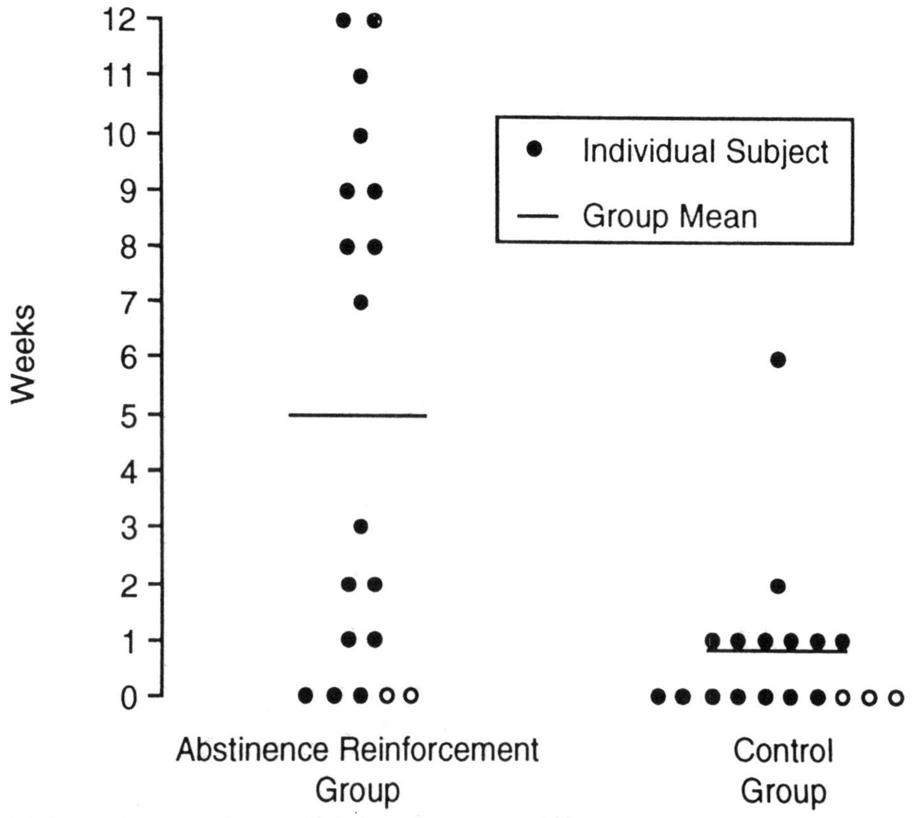

Longest duration of sustained cocaine abstinence achieved during the 12-week voucher condition. Each data point indicates data from an individual subject and the lines represent group means. Subjects in the reinforcement and control conditions are displayed in the left and right columns, respectively. Open circles represent early study drop outs. From Silverman K, Higgins ST, Brooner RK et al. (1996). Sustained cocaine abstinence in methadone maintenance patients through voucher-based reinforcement therapy. *Archives of General Psychiatry* 53:409–415. Reprinted by permission.

of cocaine use, for example, appear to benefit less or sometimes not at all from the intervention (Silverman, Higgins et al., 1996). Whether these individuals simply need a larger magnitude consequence or a qualitatively different intervention is unclear. Another issue is how interventions like this might be deployed in community clinics, where resources to support material incentives are limited or nonexistent and regular urinalysis testing often is not a routine part of patient care.

In sum, an impressive degree of progress has been made in this area of treatment research, but a great deal more remains to be done.

TREATMENT OF OPIOID DEPENDENCE

Methadone and other opioid substitution therapies represent an important modality for the treatment of opioid abuse, with close to 100,000 persons presently receiving such treatment in the U.S (Bigelow & Preston, 1995). These treatments have demonstrated efficacy in suppressing heroin use and associated criminal activity (Ball & Ross, 1991), but do not directly address the full range of problems that opioid abusers bring to treatment. Polysubstance abuse is common among these patients, with cocaine being the most serious and prevalent secondary substance of abuse (Silverman, Bigelow et al., in press). Other interventions are needed to provide adequate treatment for this population.

Community Reinforcement Approach. The authors are aware of only one published controlled study involving CRA in the treatment of opioid dependence. In a randomized trial, CRA in combination with the voucher program described above was compared to standard drug abuse counseling in 39 opioid-dependent individuals who were undergoing a buprenorphine detoxification (Bickel, Amass et al., in press). Buprenorphine is a partial mu-opioid agonist that currently is being evaluated as a substitution pharmacotherapy for opioid dependence (Bickel & Amass, 1995). CRA in this study generally was delivered in the same manner as in the studies with cocaine-dependent individuals described above. The voucher program was modified so that one-half of the available vouchers could be earned via drug-free urinalysis test results and the other half by participating in activities specified as part of CRA therapy.

Subjects assigned to the CRA-plus-vouchers group were significantly more likely to complete the 24-week detoxification protocol (53% versus 20%) and to achieve eight or more weeks of continuous abstinence from illicit opioids (47% versus 15%). There were no other significant differences between the two groups.

Conclusions: The results of the study by Bickel and colleagues demonstrate the utility of combined use of CRA and voucher-based reinforcement procedures for improving outcomes in opioid-replacement therapy. As is described below, the efficacy of various contingency management procedures with this population is well established. An important next step is to assess what effect CRA alone has on treatment outcomes in patients undergoing opioid replacement therapy. The authors are aware of only one trial on that topic, which was conducted at the University of New Mexico, but are not aware that a report of that study has appeared in a peer-reviewed journal.

Contingency Management Interventions. A number of potential reinforcers, such as use of medication take-homes, money, etc., can be identified within the context of a daily methadone dispensing clinic for use in contingency management procedures. The methadone take-home privilege, in which an extra daily dose of methadone is dispensed to the patient for ingestion on the following day, offers a convenient and effective incentive for use in abstinence reinforcement protocols (Stitzer & Bigelow, 1978) and is one of the most potent positive reinforcers available within the context of routine clinic operation. Studies by Stitzer and colleagues (1982) and Iguchi et al. (1988) examined take-home incentives in methadone patients who chronically supplemented with benzodiazepines. When take-home privileges could be earned for providing drug-free urines, temporary abstinence was observed in about 50% of study patients during the contingent take-home intervention, which lasted 12 to 20 weeks. Magura and colleagues (1988) found that one-month contracting for contingent take-home privileges resulted in 34% of their polydrug-abusing subjects achieving abstinence, whereas Milby, Garrett et al. (1978) found a similar percentage of clients responding to a take-home incentive program with increased numbers of consecutive drug-free urines, as required by the contingent intervention. Most of these studies focused on selected groups of identified polydrug abusers and used within-subject designs to evaluate the efficacy of contingent take-home programs for improving treatment outcomes.

A more recent controlled clinical trial was conducted by Stitzer and colleagues (1992) to examine take-home incentive effects in 54 newly admitted methadone maintenance patients, who were randomly assigned to receive take-home privileges under contingent or noncontingent conditions. In the contingent condition, the first take-home privilege was available after a relatively short (e.g., two-week) period of demonstrated abstinence from supplemental drugs, in an attempt to provide relatively immediate reinforcement for positive behavior change. The conditional probability that a patient would improve on drug use was 2.5 times greater for the contingent than for the noncontingent study condition, whereas the probability of worsening on the drug use measure was two times greater for the noncontingent than for the contingent group. Overall, 32% of contingent patients achieved sustained periods of abstinence during the intervention (mean 9.4 weeks; range 5 to 15 weeks) compared to approximately 10 percent in the control group (Figure 4). The beneficial effect of contingent take-home delivery was replicated within the group of noncontingent patients, who switched to the contingent intervention after their six-month evaluation in the main study (partial crossover design). In this case, 28% improved substantially and achieved, on average, 15.5 drug-free weeks. In both the main study and the partial crossover, as well as in a recent analysis of the characteristics of take-home earners in clinical practice (Kidorf & Stitzer, 1994), lower rates of drug-positive urines early in treatment predicted improvement under the contingent take-home program, but patients using cocaine and benzodiazepines were equally likely to respond.

Take-homes can be used in combination with other programmed consequences as a treatment package. A study by McCaul and colleagues (1984) examined the effects of an incentive package on relapse to opiate drug use during a 90-day ambulatory methadone detoxification. Patients selected for the study had submitted 50% opiate-positive urines during a baseline period and were randomly assigned to a control or contingent intervention con-

FIGURE 4. Improvement in Urine Test Results

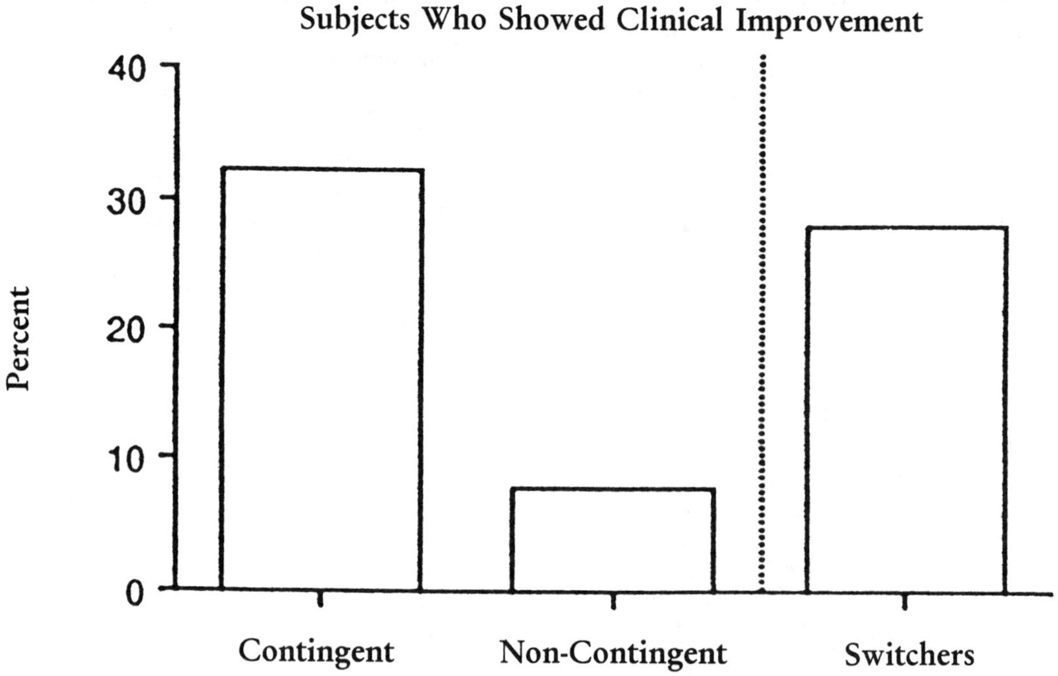

Percentages of subjects whose urine test results improved 10% or more from baseline to intervention periods and submitted at least 12 consecutive drug-free tests during the intervention period are shown for the original contingent and noncontingent take-home groups and also for the group of noncontingent subjects who received delayed exposure to the contingent protocol later in treatment. From Stitzer ML, Iguchi MY & Felch LJ (1992). Contingent take-home incentive: Effects on drug use of methadone maintenance patients. *Journal of Consulting and Clinical Psychology* 60(6):927–934. Reprinted by permission.

dition. In the contingent group, opiate-free urines resulted in a take-home day and $10 cash, whereas opiate-positive urines resulted in increased counseling contact, urine sample collection, and data questionnaire requirements for patients. The contingent procedure was shown to be effective for promoting sustained periods of opiate abstinence and delaying relapse.

Another effective consequence for reducing supplemental drug use is a methadone dose change. Impressive suppression of opiate use during ambulatory methadone detoxification was achieved in a study in which the contingent incentive for opiate-free urines was the opportunity to increase the methadone dose by up to 20 mg, an opportunity that remained active only so long as urines were opiate-free (Higgins, Stitzer et al., 1986). Suppression of opiate use was shown to be specifically related to the contingency between increased methadone dose and drug use, because the benefits were not apparent in a group that could receive noncontingent increases in their methadone dose. Another study extended evaluation of dose change incentives by showing that decreases in polydrug abuse could be demonstrated during methadone maintenance both when methadone dose was increased above original maintenance levels as a result of drug-free urines and when dose was decreased below original maintenance levels as a consequence of drug-positive urines (Stitzer, Bickel et al., 1986).

Regarding still other reinforcers, the study by Silverman and colleagues (1996) described above demonstrated the efficacy of contingent voucher-based reinforcement for reducing cocaine abuse among methadone-maintenance patients. Reductions in drug use during ambulatory detoxification also were reported in a controlled trial by Hall, Bass et al. (1979), using small amounts of money ($4 to $10 per sample) to reinforce submitting drug-free urines. Carroll, Chang et al. (1995) were unsuccessful in a recent attempt to use a small amount of contingent monetary reinforcement (subjects could earn $15 weekly for three consecutive negative urine screens) in conjunction with weekly prenatal care and relapse prevention groups to increase drug abstinence in a group of pregnant methadone-maintained patients (N = 7). Compared to a randomized control group who received standard methadone treatment (N = 7), no increases in drug abstinence were observed in the intervention group. While one can only speculate as to the reason for the negative results in this study, requiring three consecutive negative tests in order to earn a reinforcer may have been too large a response requirement considering the relatively low amounts of monetary reinforcement used.

The possible influence of reinforcer delay and response requirement in the study by Carroll et al. is supported by the results of a study by Rowan-Szal and colleagues (1994), who examined the influence of response requirement and reinforcement delay on the efficacy of low-cost reinforcers in decreasing supplemental drug abuse and increasing counseling participation among methadone maintenance patients. Subjects could earn stars exchangeable for low-cost retail items (vouchers for gasoline, coffee mugs, etc.), contingent on attending individual and group counseling sessions. Stars earned also were displayed on bulletin boards in counselors' offices. Subjects were randomized to three groups, referred to as high reward (four stars required per back-up reinforcer), low reward (eight stars required per reinforcer), and delayed reward (stars could not be redeemed for back-up reinforcers until the end of the three-month intervention). Only the high reward condition resulted in significant reductions in drug use and increases in counseling attendance.

Treatment Termination Contracting. Another commonly used intervention that has received research evaluation is the contingent availability of further methadone treatment. Treatment termination contracting provides a means of formulating specific behavioral improvement objectives for poorly performing methadone patients, with the consequence of noncompliance being dose reduction and termination from treatment. The studies with mandated disulfiram therapy were described above. They demonstrated that treatment outcome could be dramatically improved for severely alcoholic methadone patients by using the threat of treatment termination to motivate participation in a monitored disulfiram program at the clinic. McCarthy and Borders (1985) showed that structured treatment involving the threat of termination for failure to meet specified standards of drug-free urine submissions could improve outcomes on measures of opiate drug use during treatment.

Conclusions: Structured contingency programs have considerable efficacy as a means of reducing chronic supplemental drug use by methadone and other opioid-replacement patients. The studies reviewed above demonstrate that positive incentives (including methadone take-home privileges, vouchers, money, and methadone dose changes), when used in a contingent manner, can delay relapse during detoxification and reduce supplemental drug use during maintenance treatment. Future research needs to focus on ways to optimize the utility and cost-effectiveness of incentives that are readily available in the context of methadone clinic operation, to further characterize patients who do and do not respond to treatment, and to develop and evaluate more potent reinforcers for their ability to influence the drug use of more severely dependent polydrug abusers. Negative incentives also can be used in contingent arrangements to promote periods of abstinence from supplemental drug use among opioid-replacement patients. However, positive incentives have the advantage of keeping patients in treatment, whereas negative incentives, particularly those involving methadone dose decrease or threat of treatment termination, run the risk of resulting in treatment dropout.

An interesting issue that deserves additional research is whether there are any patient characteristics associated with response to positive versus negative incentive procedures. A second issue is whether multiple incentives can be used together to increase the potency of contingency management procedures for improving outcomes during opioid-replacement treatment.

CONCLUSIONS

This chapter has reviewed how, within an operant framework, drug use is considered a normal, learned behavior that can be fruitfully conceptualized to fall along a continuum ranging from light use with no problems to heavy use with many untoward effects. The same basic learning processes are assumed to operate across the drug-use continuum. Treatment strategies based on this conceptual framework look to weaken the reinforcement obtained from drug use and related activities and to enhance the material and social reinforcement obtained from other sources, especially from participation in activities deemed to be incompatible with a drug-abusing lifestyle. Community reinforcement and contingency management procedures are based on this general strategy and have been demonstrated in controlled studies to be effective in treating alcohol, cocaine, and opioid dependence. CRA and contingency management offer no "magic bullets" for the treatment of these disorders and, as discussed above, much more remains to be learned about each of them. Those limitations notwithstanding, the research reviewed in this chapter provides a compelling case that CRA and contingency management procedures offer a wide range of empirically-based and effective strategies for managing some of the most challenging aspects of alcohol, cocaine, and opioid dependence.

ACKNOWLEDGMENT: Preparation of this chapter was supported by Grants RO1 DA09378 and RO1 DA08076 from the National Institute on Drug Abuse.

REFERENCES

American Psychiatric Association (1987). *Diagnostic and Statistical Manual of Mental Disorders, 3rd Edition, Revised*. Washington, DC: American Psychiatric Press.

Azrin NH (1976). Improvements in the community-reinforcement approach to alcoholism. *Behaviour Research and Therapy* 14:339–348.

Azrin NH & Besalel VA (1980). *Job Club Counselor's Manual.* Baltimore, MD: University Park Press.

Azrin NH, Naster BJ & Jones R (1973). Reciprocity counseling: A rapid learning based procedure for marriage counseling. *Behaviour Research and Therapy* 11:364–382.

Azrin NH, Sisson RW, Meyers R & Godley M (1982). Alcoholism treatment by disulfiram and community reinforcement therapy. *Journal of Behavior Therapy & Experimental Psychiatry* 13:105–112.

Ball JC & Ross A (1991). *The Effectiveness of Methadone Maintenance Treatment.* New York, NY: Springer-Verlag.

Bickel WK & Amass L (1995). Buprenorphine treatment of opioid dependence: A review. *Experimental and Clinical Psychopharmacology* 3:477–489.

Bickel WK, Amass L, Higgins ST, Badger GJ & Esch RA (in press). Effects of adding behavioral treatment to opioid detoxification with buprenorphine. *Journal of Consulting and Clinical Psychology.*

Bickel WK, Marion I & Lowinson JH (1987). The treatment of alcoholic methadone patients: A review. *Journal of Substance Abuse Treatment* 4:15–19.

Bickel WK, Rizzuto P, Zielony RD et al. (1989). Combined behavioral and pharmacological treatment of alcoholic methadone patients. *Journal of Substance Abuse* 1:161–171.

Bigelow GE & Preston KL (1995). Opioids. In FE Bloom & DJ Kupfer (eds.) *Psychopharmacology: The Fourth Generation of Progress.* New York, NY: Raven Press, 1731–1744.

Brigham SL, Rekers GA, Rosen AC, Swihart JJ, Pfrimmer G & Ferguson LN (1981). Contingency management in the treatment of adolescent alcohol drinking problems. *Journal of Psychology* 109:73–85.

Carroll KM, Chang G, Behr H, Clinton B & Kosten TR (1995). Improving treatment outcome in pregnant, methadone-maintained women. *The American Journal on Addictions* 4:56–59.

Carroll KM, Ziedonis D, O'Malley S, McCance-Katz E, Gordon L & Rounsaville B (1993). Pharmacologic interventions for alcohol- and cocaine-abusing individuals: A pilot study of disulfiram vs. naltrexone. *The American Journal on Addictions* 2:77–79.

Carroll ME, Lac ST & Nygaard SL (1989). A concurrently available nondrug reinforcer prevents the acquisition or decreases the maintenance of cocaine-reinforced behavior. *Psychopharmacology* 97:23–29.

Ditman KS, Crawford GG, Forgy EW, Moskowitz H & MacAndrew C (1967). A controlled experiment on the use of court probation for drunk arrests. *American Journal of Psychiatry* 124:64–67.

Ersner-Hershfield SM, Connors GJ & Maisto SA (1981). Clinical and experimental utility of refundable deposits. *Behavioral Research and Therapy* 19:455–457.

Gallant DM, Bishop MP, Faulkner MA et al. (1968a). A comparative evaluation of compulsory (group therapy and/or Antabuse) and voluntary treatment of the chronic alcoholic municipal court offender. *Psychosomatics* 9:306–310.

Gallant DM, Bishop MP, Mouledoux A, Faulkner MA, Brisolara A & Swanson WA (1973). The revolving-door alcoholic. *Archives of General Psychiatry* 28:633–635.

Gallant DM, Faulkner M, Stoy B, Bishop MP & Langdon D (1968b). Enforced clinic treatment of paroled criminal alcoholics. *Quarterly Journal of Studies on Alcohol* 29:77–83.

Goldberg SR & Stolerman IP (eds.) (1986). *Behavioral Analysis of Drug Dependence.* Orlando, FL: Academic Press, Inc.

Griffiths RR, Bigelow GE & Henningfield JE (1980). Similarities in animal and human drug taking behavior. In NK Mello (ed.) *Advances in Substance Abuse: Behavioral and Biological Research, Vol. 1.* Greenwich, CT: JAI Press, 1–90.

Hall SM, Bass A, Hargreaves WA & Loeb P (1979). Contingency management and information feedback in outpatient heroin detoxification. *Behavioral Therapy* 10:443–451.

Henningfield JE, Lukas SE & Bigelow GE (1986). Human studies of drugs as reinforcers. In SR Goldberg & IP Stolerman (eds.) *Behavioral Analysis of Drug Dependence.* Orlando FL: Academic Press, Inc, 69–122.

Hester RK & Miller WR (eds.) (1995). *Alcohol Treatment Approaches: Handbook of Effective Alternatives.* Boston, MA: Allyn & Bacon.

Higgins ST, Budney AJ, Bickel WK, Foerg FE, Donham R & Badger GJ (1994). Incentives improve treatment retention and cocaine abstinence in ambulatory cocaine-dependent patients. *Archives of General Psychiatry* 51:568–576.

Higgins ST, Budney AJ, Bickel WK, Foerg FE, Ogden D & Badger GJ (1995). Outpatient behavioral treatment for cocaine dependence: One-year outcome. *Experimental and Clinical Psychopharmacology* 3:205–212.

Higgins ST, Budney AJ, Bickel WK, Hughes JR & Foerg F (1993b). Disulfiram therapy in patients abusing cocaine and alcohol. *American Journal of Psychiatry* 150:675–676.

Higgins ST, Budney AJ, Bickel WK, Hughes JR, Foerg F & Badger G (1993a). Achieving cocaine abstinence with a behavioral approach. *American Journal of Psychiatry* 150:763–769.

Higgins ST, Delaney DD, Budney AJ et al. (1991). A behavioral approach to achieving initial cocaine abstinence. *American Journal of Psychiatry* 148:1218–1224.

Higgins ST, Stitzer ML, Bigelow GE & Liebson IA (1986). Contingent methadone delivery: Effects on illicit-opiate use. *Drug and Alcohol Dependence* 17:311–322.

Hunt GM & Azrin NH (1973). A community-reinforcement approach to alcoholism. *Behaviour Research and Therapy* 11:91104.

Iguchi MY, Stitzer ML, Bigelow GE & Liebson IA (1988). Contingency management in methadone maintenance: Effects of reinforcing and aversive consequences on illicit polydrug use. *Drug and Alcohol Dependence* 22:1–7.

Kidorf M & Stitzer ML (1994). Characteristics of methadone patients responding to take-home incentives. *Behavioral Therapy* 25:109–121.

Liebson IA, Bigelow GE & Flamer R (1973). Alcoholism among methadone patients: A specific treatment model. *American Journal of Psychiatry* 130(4):483–485.

Liebson IA, Tommasello A & Bigelow GE (1978). A behavioral treatment of alcoholic methadone patients. *Annals of Internal Medicine* 89:342–344.

Magura S, Casriel C, Goldsmith DS, Strug DL & Lipton DS (1988). Contingency contracting with polydrug-abusing methadone patients. *Addictive Behaviors* 13(1):113–118.

Mallams JH, Godley MD, Hall GM & Meyers RJ (1982). A social-systems approach to resocializing alcoholics in the community. *Journal of Studies on Alcohol* 43:1115–1123.

McCarthy JJ & Borders OT (1985). Limit setting on drug abuse in methadone maintenance patients. *American Journal of Psychiatry* 142(12):1419–1423.

McCaul ME, Stitzer ML, Bigelow GE & Liebson IA (1984). Contingency management interventions: Effects on treatment outcome during methadone detoxification. *Journal of Applied Behavior Analysis* 17(l):35–43.

Mendelson JH & Mello NK (1996). Management of cocaine abuse and dependence. *The New England Journal of Medicine* 334:965–972.

Milby JB, Garrett C, English C, Fritschi O & Clarke C (1978). Take-home methadone: Contingency effects on drug-seeking and productivity of narcotic addicts. *Addictive Behaviors* 3(3–4):215–220.

Milby JB, Schumacher JE, Raczynski JM et al. (1996). Sufficient conditions for effective treatment of substance abusing homeless persons. *Drug and Alcohol Dependence* 43:23–38.

Miller PM (1975). A behavioral intervention program for chronic public drunkenness offenders. *Archives of General Psychiatry* 32:915–918.

Miller PM, Hersen M & Eisler RM (1974). Relative effectiveness of instructions, agreements, and reinforcement in behavioral contracts with alcoholics. *Journal of Abnormal Psychology* 83(5):548–553.

Ries RE (1982). *The Traffic Safety Effectiveness of Educational Counseling Programs for Multiple Offense Drunk Drivers.* Washington, DC: Department of Transportation, National Highway Traffic Safety Administration.

Robichaud C, Strickler D, Bigelow G & Liebson I (1979). Disulfiram maintenance employee alcoholism treatment: A three-phase evaluation. *Behavior Research & Therapy* 17:618–621.

Rowan-Szal G, Joe GW, Chatham LR & Simpson DD (1994). A simple reinforcement system for methadone clients in a community-based treatment program. *Journal of Substance Abuse Treatment* 11:217–223.

Silverman K, Bigelow GE & Stitzer ML (in press). Treatment of cocaine abuse in methadone maintenance patients. In ST Higgins & JL Katz (eds.) *Cocaine Abuse Research: Pharmacology, Behavior, and Clinical Application.* San Diego, CA: Academic Press.

Silverman K, Higgins ST, Brooner RK et al. (1996). Sustained cocaine abstinence in methadone maintenance patients through voucher-based reinforcement therapy. *Archives of General Psychiatry* 53:409–415.

Sisson RW & Azrin AH (1986). Family-member involvement to initiate and promote treatment of problem drinkers. *Journal of Behaviour Research and Therapy* 17:15–21.

Stitzer ML, Bickel WK, Bigelow GE & Liebson IA (1986). Effect of methadone dose contingencies on urinalysis test results of polydrug-abusing methadone-maintenance patients. *Drug and Alcohol Dependence* 18(4):341–348.

Stitzer ML & Bigelow GE (1978). Contingency management in a methadone maintenance program: Availability of reinforcers. *International Journal of the Addictions* 13:737–746.

Stitzer ML, Bigelow GE, Liebson IA & Hawthorne JW (1982). Contingent reinforcement for benzodiazepine-free urines: Evaluation of a drug abuse treatment intervention. *Journal of Applied Behavior Analysis* 15(4):493–503.

Stitzer ML, Iguchi MY & Felch LJ (1992). Contingent take-home incentive: Effects on drug use of methadone maintenance patients. *Journal of Consulting and Clinical Psychology* 60(6):927–934.

Young AM & Herling S (1986). Drugs as reinforcers: studies in laboratory animals. In SR Goldberg & IP Stolerman (eds.) *Behavioral Analysis of Drug Dependence.* Orlando FL: Academic Press, Inc., 9–67.

SECTION 9
Twelve Step Programs and Other Interpersonal Therapies

CHAPTER 1

Twelve Step Programs 693
Jerome E. Schulz, M.D. and John N. Chappel, M.D., FASAM

CHAPTER 2

Recent Research in Twelve Step Programs 707
Barbara S. McCrady, Ph.D.

CHAPTER 3

Rational Recovery, SMART Recovery and Non-Twelve Step Mutual Recovery Programs 719
Joseph Gerstein, M.D., FACP

CHAPTER 4

Spiritual Components of the Recovery Process 725
John N. Chappel, M.D., FASAM

SECTION COORDINATOR

JEROME E. SCHULZ, M.D.
Associate Clinical Professor of Family Medicine
Eastern Carolina University
School of Medicine
Greenville, North Carolina

CONTRIBUTORS

John N. Chappel, M.D., FASAM
Professor, Department of
Psychiatry and Behavioral Sciences
University of Nevada at Reno School of Medicine
and Medical Director, Alcohol and Drug Programs
West Hills Hospital
Reno, Nevada

Joseph Gerstein, M.D., FACP
Assistant Clinical Professor of Medicine
Harvard Medical School
Boston, Massachusetts

Barbara S. McCrady, Ph.D.
Rutgers Center of Alcohol Studies
Rutgers—The State University of New Jersey
Piscataway, New Jersey

CHAPTER 1

Twelve Step Programs

Jerome E. Schulz, M.D.
John N. Chappel, M.D., FASAM

Alcoholics Anonymous
Narcotics Anonymous
Cocaine Anonymous
Family Support Groups
Al-Anon
Alateen
Adult Children of Alcoholics
The Physician's Role

Today, millions of people worldwide are living fuller and more complete lives because of their involvement in Twelve Step recovery groups. This discussion of recovery groups will emphasize Alcoholics Anonymous (AA) and its basic philosophy. Several other programs, including Al-Anon, Alateen, Narcotics Anonymous and Adult Children of Alcoholics, also will be described.

ALCOHOLICS ANONYMOUS

History. AA was founded in 1935 by a stockbroker (Bill W.) and a physician (Dr. Bob) (Schulz, 1991). Bill W. was an alcoholic who had a spiritual experience during his fourth detoxification in December 1934, following a visit from a recovering alcoholic friend. For several months, he attempted without success to convert other alcoholics—although he remained sober himself—and subsequently became involved in a religious group called the Oxford Movement. When a business venture failed during a trip to Akron, Ohio, Bill W.'s thoughts turned to alcohol as a means to ease the pain. As his preoccupation and compulsion grew stronger, he knew he had to talk to another alcoholic to keep from drinking. He contacted a local member of the Oxford Movement and asked for the name of an alcoholic with whom he might talk. A meeting was arranged with Dr. Bob, who was unenthusiastic and intended to stay no longer than 15 minutes. The meeting lasted several hours and marked the beginning of Alcoholics Anonymous. Over the following months, Bill W. and Dr. Bob began to formulate the basic philosophy of Alcoholics Anonymous: reaching out to other alcoholics to help them stay sober.

The principles that came to guide the organization were published in *Alcoholics Anonymous* (widely known as the "Big Book") (AA, 1976a) in 1939. This publication represented the final break from the Oxford Movement and any apparent connection with a particular religious orientation. It established AA for all alcoholics, including atheists and agnostics.

Overview and Philosophy. The preamble of *Alcoholics Anonymous*, which frequently is read at the beginning of AA meetings, points out many important facts about how AA works: "Alcoholics Anonymous is a fellowship of men and women who share their experience, strength and hope with each other that they may solve their common problem and help others to recover from alcoholism. The only requirement for membership is a desire to stop drinking. There are no dues or fees for AA membership; we are self-supporting through our own contributions. AA is not allied with any sect, denomination, politics, organization or institution; does not wish to engage in any controversy; neither endorses nor opposes any causes. Our primary purpose is to stay sober and help other alcoholics to achieve sobriety" (AA, 1976a).

The Twelve Steps of AA (Table 1) describe both the spiritual basis and the necessary actions which form the backbone of recovery for AA members. It is important to point out that AA is a spiritual, not a religious, program: as the AA preamble states, AA "is not allied with any sect or denomination."

TABLE 1. The Twelve Steps of Alcoholics Anonymous

We:
1. Admitted we were powerless over alcohol; that our lives had become unmanageable;
2. Came to believe that a Power greater than ourselves could restore us to sanity;
3. Made a decision to turn our will and our lives over to the care of God as we understood Him;
4. Made a searching and fearless moral inventory of ourselves;
5. Admitted to God, to ourselves, and to another human being the exact nature of our wrongs;
6. Were entirely ready to have God remove all these defects of character;
7. Humbly asked Him to remove our shortcomings;
8. Made a list of all persons we had harmed, and became willing to make amends to them all;
9. Made direct amends to such people wherever possible, except when to do so would injure them or others;
10. Continued to take personal inventory and, when we were wrong, promptly admitted it;
11. Sought through prayer and meditation to improve our conscious contact with God as we understood Him, praying only for knowledge of His will for us and the power to carry that out; and
12. Having had a spiritual experience (awakening) as the result of these steps, we tried to carry this message to alcoholics, and to practice these principles in all our affairs.

The Twelve Steps have been applied effectively to many other problems in life, such as gambling, sex, emotions and eating disorders. They require a willingness to change and become a healthy human being who can live harmoniously with others.

The Twelve Traditions (Table 2) are the guidelines that help Alcoholics Anonymous groups survive and function smoothly. The traditions grew out of experiences that threatened AA's existence. It took 13 years to develop these protective principles. There are now more than 96,000 AA groups with more than two million members in 146 countries worldwide (Anonymous, 1996); all are guided by the Twelve Traditions, yet no individual or group is "in charge."

The General Service Office in New York City serves as a clearinghouse for AA information and publications, under the direction of the General Service Board, which is composed of both alcoholics and nonalcoholics. Neither the Office nor the Board has any authority over AA members or groups. Both are responsible to the AA groups and report annually at the General Service Conference attended by members selected by groups in the United States and Canada. This large, loosely structured, leaderless, democratic system works because AA closely follows the Twelve Traditions.

Each AA group is autonomous (as defined in the fourth tradition). This tradition allows AA groups to vary widely in how they apply the Twelve Steps and Twelve Traditions.

Membership in AA is simple to obtain: all that is required is to attend a meeting and, according to the third tradition, "have a desire to stop drinking." There is no formal application process or paperwork. Groups may have a phone list so individuals can support and help each other between meetings, but participation is strictly optional. Each member is encouraged to develop his or her own personal phone list for use in times of need.

Meetings. AA holds both open and closed meetings. Anyone may attend an open meeting, whereas closed meetings are restricted to alcoholics. AA meetings usually open with the reading of the Serenity Prayer (Table 3), after which each participant introduces himself or herself by saying, "My name is ____ and I'm an alcoholic." A brief (10-minute) business meeting often follows. At open meetings, a speaker usually gives the classic AA talk about how it was, what happened, and how it is now. Speakers frequently talk for an hour or more and almost never use notes or scripts, because they believe that such spontaneity helps them "talk from the heart and not the head."

In closed meetings, group members may discuss one of the Twelve Steps, a specific topic (such as resentments, fear or anger) or the Alcoholics Anonymous Big Book, which serves as the textbook of AA. An important part of the Big Book, entitled "How it Works" (Chapter 5), often is read at the beginning of AA meetings. The Twelve Steps are part of "How It Works" and also are discussed in the AA publication, *Twelve Steps and Twelve Traditions* (1952)—the "12 by 12"—which describes the important aspects of each of the steps and traditions.

AA meetings usually last one hour, and most meetings close with the Lord's Prayer or the Serenity Prayer. Many newcomers initially are uncomfortable with the apparent Christian orientation expressed by the Lord's Prayer; however, in the context of AA, the prayer is viewed as a commonly remembered ritual that reminds group members of their need for

TABLE 2. The Twelve Traditions of Alcoholics Anonymous

1. Our common welfare should come first; personal recovery depends on AA unity.
2. For our group purpose there is but one ultimate authority—a loving God as He may express Himself in our group conscience. Our leaders are but trusted servants; they do not govern.
3. The only requirement for AA membership is a desire to stop drinking.
4. Each group should be autonomous except in matters affecting other groups or AA as a whole.
5. Each group has but one primary purpose—to carry its message to the alcoholic who still suffers.
6. An AA group ought never endorse, finance, or lend the AA name to any related facility or outside enterprise, lest problems of money, property and prestige divert us from our primary purpose.
7. Every AA group ought to be fully self-supporting declining outside contributions.
8. Alcoholics Anonymous should remain forever nonprofessional, but our service centers may employ special workers.
9. AA, as such, ought never be organized, but we may create service boards or committees directly responsible to those they serve.
10. Alcoholics Anonymous has no opinion on outside issues; hence, the AA name ought never be drawn into public controversy.
11. Our public relations policy is based on attraction rather than promotion; we need always maintain personal anonymity at the level of press, radio, and film.
12. Anonymity is the spiritual foundation of all our traditions, ever reminding us to place principles before personalities.

something other than self in maintaining sobriety. In fact, each group can use any ritual it wishes to open or close its meeting.

Meetings often are followed by socializing over coffee to give members a chance to continue to talk about the meeting topic or just to interact without alcohol—a new experience for most alcoholics. It also gives the newcomer a chance to get to know the other group members.

Types of Groups. As AA has grown, many special groups have developed because of the autonomous nature of each AA group. When patients report they felt uncomfortable at an AA meeting, referral to a special interest group may be helpful. Most large metropolitan areas have special meetings for women, young people, seniors, gays and lesbians, African-Americans and other ethnic groups. Nonsmoking AA meetings are becoming very common. In many areas, there are special meetings for professionals such as nurses, physicians, lawyers and clergy.

One special group for physicians, psychologists, dentists, veterinarians, educators and anyone with a doctoral degree is International Doctors in AA (IDAA). IDAA was founded in upstate New York in 1947 by several physicians (three from Canada) and a psychologist. The program is based on the principles of Alcoholics Anonymous. There are more than 6,000 members internationally, many of whom attend the annual IDAA meeting which is held in different parts of the country (and Canada). Any physician interested in IDAA can get more information or join by contacting the IDAA secretary at P.O. Box 199, Augusta, MO 63332, by E-mail at IDAAdickMc@aol.com, or by telephone at (314) 228-4102.

Sponsorship. Sponsorship is a basic AA concept. A sponsor generally is someone of the same sex who has been in AA for at least one year. The sponsor becomes a mentor and role model for the newcomer and is an example of how the AA program works. Newcomers are asked to call their sponsors whenever they are thinking about drinking or having problems (which almost always is the case with newcomers). It is common for a newcomer to talk with his or her sponsor on the phone between meetings and to meet with the sponsor regularly to discuss progress.

Newcomers are urged to find a sponsor as soon as possible, and groups often appoint temporary sponsors. AA will provide temporary contacts through the local treatment facilities committee. These temporary contacts can introduce the newcomer to local meetings and members of the fellowship. Sponsorship frequently is a lifelong relationship. After some time in recovery, the AA member may be asked to sponsor a new member. In one 10-year follow up, 91% of alcoholics who became sponsors were in stable sobriety (Cross, Morgan et al., 1990).

Anniversaries. Sobriety anniversaries are important milestones in AA. Many groups give a

TABLE 3. The Serenity Prayer of Alcoholics Anonymous

"God grant me the serenity to accept the things I cannot change, the courage to change the things that I can, and the wisdom to know the difference."

"chip" (a poker chip) to the newcomer attending his or her first AA meeting. When the newcomer reaches into his or her pocket for drinking money, the chip is a reminder not to drink. Newcomers are given a new chip (different colors) at one, two, three, six, nine and 12 months, signifying their continuing sobriety and commitment to recovery.

Some groups give out medallions instead of chips. A medallion may have the Serenity Prayer on one side and something about AA on the other side, along with the number of years the member has been sober. Medallions are given out at three, six and nine months and then each year thereafter. Anniversaries are special times in AA and may be celebrated with a cake and party.

The "dry date," which is the first drug- or alcohol-free day, is an important date for physicians to acknowledge. This date can be put on the patient's problem list along with the diagnosis of alcoholism. Physicians can show support and interest in the patient's recovery by acknowledging anniversaries.

AA Slogans. Several studies have shown that alcoholics suffer permanent cognitive deficits due to their chronic alcohol intake. AA has many slogans and sayings that are repeated frequently at meetings. For alcoholics, these simple slogans are a way to overcome cognitive deficits. By learning AA's slogans, physicians can use them to help their alcoholic patients. When recovering alcoholics are having difficulty, these simple slogans can redirect their thinking and make them less likely to use alcohol or other mood-altering chemicals to overcome their frustration. The physician's commitment to the patient's recovery is obvious when the physician knows enough about AA to use the slogans.

"One day at a time" is one of the oldest slogans in AA. This slogan emphasizes a basic AA philosophy—that the alcoholic has to be concerned only with today. They may go on a roaring drunk tomorrow, but they need to stay sober just today. Along with drinking problems, alcoholics have all kinds of fears and irrational concerns about what may happen tomorrow, next week or in the next hundred years. This simple five-word slogan helps them live in the present and take care of just today's problems.

"Easy does it" is another frequently heard slogan. Alcoholics early in recovery tend to want to get everything resolved immediately. They expect years of problems somehow to be resolved the minute they become sober. They frequently want to go on diets, start exercising, quit smoking, and resolve all their personal conflicts. This behavior usually fails and can result in a relapse. "Easy does it" helps them realize they need to go slowly.

"Let go and let God" emphasizes the spiritual aspect of AA. For alcoholics, attempts to control their drinking can spill over into trying to exert excessive control over other areas of their lives. This behavior can cause frustration in sobriety. The slogan helps the alcoholic realize that there is a Higher Power ("God, as we understand Him") to help them if they can just "let go."

"Keep it simple" is directed toward the alcoholic's knack for complicating things. In AA, members are told not to drink, to go to meetings, to read the Big Book, to work the steps and to reach out to other suffering alcoholics (doing Twelfth Step work).

HOW is an acronym frequently heard at AA meetings. It stands for **h**onesty, **o**penness and **w**illingness. The steps of AA require members to be honest with themselves, with their Higher Power and with the people around them. For many alcoholics, this is the first time in their lives (or at least in many years) that they have been truly honest. Openness helps alcoholics overcome their narrow-minded attitudes and their lack of ability to share what they are feeling. They are encouraged to be open to new ideas and to share their true feelings. They need to stop putting up the "front" that they worked so hard to develop while they were drinking.

HALT is an acronym that warns alcoholics not to get too **h**ungry, **a**ngry, **l**onely or **t**ired. An excess of any of these feelings can lead to relapse.

"First things first" emphasizes that alcoholics always must remember: staying sober is the most important priority in their lives.

Serenity Prayer. The Serenity Prayer (Table 3) is basic to AA. It offers a simple solution to many frustrations that alcoholics (and, for that matter, everyone) experience in life. Almost all AA meetings either open or close with this prayer. Alcoholics use the Serenity Prayer during the day to help them deal with frustrating and stressful situations.

AA Promises. An essential aspect of recovery in AA is the "Promises," which AA says will happen if a person works the AA program to the best of his/her ability. The promises are as follows:

"If we are painstaking about this phase of our development, we will be amazed before we are halfway through. We are going to know a new freedom and a new happiness. We will not regret the past nor wish to shut the door on it. We will comprehend the word serenity and we will know peace.

"No matter how far down the scale we have gone, we will see how our experience can benefit others.

That feeling of uselessness and self-pity will disappear.

"We will lose interest in selfish things and gain interest in our fellows. Self-seeking will slip away.

"Our whole attitude and outlook upon life will change. Fear of people and of economic insecurity will leave us. We will intuitively know how to handle situations which used to baffle us. We will suddenly realize that God is doing for us what we could not do for ourselves.

"Are these extravagant promises? We think not! They are being fulfilled among us—sometimes quickly, sometimes slowly. They will always materialize if we work for them" (Anonymous, 1976b).

The promises frequently are read at the beginning or end of AA meetings. They help AA members realize that life without alcohol can be rich and rewarding.

Outcomes. Since 1968, the membership of AA has grown at a remarkable rate, averaging 6% to 7% annually. These membership figures probably err on the low side, as there are many AA groups that do not register with the General Service Office and thus are not included in the membership estimate. This steady rate of growth has occurred despite a historically high dropout rate. In five surveys over the period 1977 to 1989, analysis "strongly suggests that about half those who come to AA are gone within three months" (Anonymous, 1989).

Although the causes of this continuing high dropout rate are not known, some reasons can be inferred. There probably are three main sources of resistance to AA. The first is *resistance to external pressure*, whether it comes from loved ones, friends, work, or the court system. Health care professionals, as objective third parties, can help to reduce this resistance through cognitive restructuring by emphasizing both the care behind the pressure and especially the benefits of working a program of recovery in AA.

The second source of resistance is *denial*. Addiction is said to be the only disease that tells the sufferer he or she does not have it. The connection of the pain in the alcoholic's life to the use of alcohol is one of the most effective counters to denial.

The third source of resistance is *AA itself*. There is much misinformation about AA, usually based on hearsay or erroneous media reports. In a study of 407 professionals in recovery from alcoholism, Bissell and Haberman (1984) found the following mistaken beliefs about AA:

- It is a religious organization that may be fanatic or cult-like.
- It is a kind of folk medicine with no scientific basis.
- As a substitute for alcohol, it is an equally unhealthy addiction.
- The members are of a lower social class.

A health care professional who is knowledgeable about AA can do much to dispel or correct these erroneous beliefs.

Despite the high dropout rate, many people continue to participate in AA. The proportion of the membership with recent, intermediate, and long-term sobriety has remained relatively stable. In 1996 these proportions were 27% sober less than one year, 28% sober between one and five years, and 45% sober over five years. The most recent survey showed that the average length of sobriety of AA members exceeds six years (Anonymous, 1996).

NARCOTICS ANONYMOUS

History. "We cannot change the nature of the addict or addiction. We can help to change the old lie 'Once an addict, always an addict' by striving to make recovery more available. God help us to remember this difference" (Narcotics Anonymous, 1983)—this is the basic premise of Narcotics Anonymous (NA). Narcotics Anonymous was established at the U.S. Public Health Service Hospital in Lexington, Kentucky, in 1947 (Peyrot, 1985). Dan Carlson, who had been treated as a patient at Lexington, helped spread NA to New York City in 1948. In 1953 a group of AA members, who also were addicts, started an NA group in Sun Valley, California. The seed from which NA grew, this group emphasized the need for NA to closely follow the Twelve Steps and Twelve Traditions of AA. NA was formed because of the discomfort many narcotic and other drug addicts felt when attending AA meetings. At NA meetings, members are able to share problems related to drugs other than alcohol. The Twelve Steps are the same, except for Step One, which in NA states, "We admitted we were powerless over our addiction, that our lives had become unmanageable," and the NA Twelfth Step, which states, "Having had a spiritual awakening as the result of these steps, we tried to carry the message to addicts and to practice these principles in all our affairs." By refocusing from a specific substance (alcohol) to addiction, NA was able to include all drugs.

NA's philosophy is that drug addiction is a disease that is progressive, lifelong and involves more than the use of drugs. Recovery is based on abstinence from all mood-altering drugs, including alcohol. Through the Twelve Steps, the addict is encouraged to work toward freedom, goodwill, creative action and personal growth.

Certain characteristics are typical of addicts in early recovery because the drugs they use are illegal. Manipulation and suspicion are very commonly seen. Other group members can help newcomers identify these problems in themselves and give them helpful suggestions about how to overcome them. The goal of recovery is more than abstinence from mood-altering chemicals—it is to live life so that mood-altering chemicals are no longer needed to experience positive feelings. By associating with other people in recovery, the addict is able to see the benefits of being "straight and clean."

Structure and Meetings. The structure of NA is almost identical to that of AA. The basic unit is the "group." Like AA, groups have area service boards and a World Service Office, which reports to a 15-member World Service Board of Trustees. Two-thirds of the members of the board are recovering addicts with at least five years of abstinence. Five nonaddicts also serve on the Board. The World Service Office is the information center for NA.

NA meetings are similar to those of AA and generally can be classified as discussion, step or speaker meetings. Sponsorship is an integral part of the NA program and all newcomers are urged to find a sponsor (Sponsorship, 1983). AA slogans and sayings also are used in NA.

Literature. NA has its own "Big Book," entitled *Narcotics Anonymous* (1983), which outlines the principles of NA and contains the personal stories of early NA members. *Welcome to Narcotics Anonymous* is an excellent NA pamphlet that explains to the newcomer the principles of NA. This is a valuable resource for patients interested in NA. The pamphlet states: "Our message is simple: We have found a way to live without using drugs and we are happy to share it with anyone for whom drugs are a problem."

Staying Clean on the Outside is another resource to give to patients when they leave a treatment program. For people in communities without an NA group, the World Service Office provides an *NA Group Starter Kit* that describes how to start an NA group.

COCAINE ANONYMOUS

With the national epidemic of cocaine addiction surfacing over the past 25 years, Cocaine Anonymous groups have started in many metropolitan areas across the country. These groups are based on the Twelve Steps and are open to anyone suffering from addiction to cocaine. Most cocaine addicts also attend either Narcotics Anonymous or Alcoholics Anonymous meetings. At NA and AA, they can find people with longer periods of being chemically free. Most cocaine addicts also are addicted to other drugs and alcohol.

FAMILY SUPPORT GROUPS

If one estimated that there are 20 million alcoholics in the U.S. and that the life of each alcoholic affects four other individuals, then approximately 80 million persons are affected by alcoholism in some way. This estimate is very close to the findings of a Gallup poll, which found that 24% of persons interviewed said that their life had been affected by an alcoholic in some way (Robertson, 1988).

AL-ANON

As the field of alcohol and drug addiction has become more sophisticated, the concept of addiction being a family disease has emerged. Everyone in the family is affected—not just the identified alcoholic or addict. With this understanding, Twelve Step support groups for the family members of alcoholics have grown rapidly. These support groups all emphasize that even if the person who is addicted to drugs or alcohol continues to use, the family members can get help. The emphasis is on helping the family member, not the drug- or alcohol-addicted person.

The oldest family program is Al-Anon, which was started by Lois Wilson (wife of Bill Wilson). Early in the history of AA, wives frequently would accompany their husbands to AA meetings. While the men were having their meeting, the wives would get together to talk and support each other. Many members of these groups tried to follow the Twelve Steps and to apply them to their own lives. They began to see that they also were affected by alcoholism and that they needed help and support in their recovery. In 1950, Lois Wilson and several other spouses started their own Central Service Center and published the first Al-Anon literature—*Purposes and Suggestions for Al-Anon Family Groups*. Focusing on themselves, not the alcoholic, was the major theme of their work. This simple philosophy was revolutionary in its meaning and application to people who

TABLE 4. The Al-Anon Preamble

The Al-Anon Family Groups are a fellowship of relatives and friends of alcoholics who share their experience, strength, and hope in order to solve their common problems. We believe alcoholism is a family illness and that changed attitudes can aid recovery.

Reprinted from *This is Al-Anon*, by permission of Al-Anon Family Group Headquarters, Inc.

previously had spent most of their energy and time concentrating on the alcoholic.

Philosophy. Like AA, Al-Anon is a spiritual (not religious) program based on Twelve Steps. The steps are similar to AA's, with the exception of Step Twelve, which states: "Having had a spiritual awakening as the result of these steps, we tried to carry this message to others, and to practice these principles in all our affairs." There are two main ideas stressed by Al-Anon (Anthony, 1977). The first is that alcoholism is a disease. This principle is emphasized in the Al-Anon Preamble (Table 4) (read at the opening of most Al-Anon meetings) to help members learn to free themselves of feeling responsible for the alcoholic's disease.

The second major Al-Anon principle emphasizes that the program is for the person, not the alcoholic. This idea is emphasized in the Al-Anon welcome: "We welcome you to the (name of the group) and hope you will find in this fellowship the help and friendship we have been privileged to enjoy. We who live, or who have lived, with the problem of alcoholism understand as perhaps few others can. We, too, were lonely and frustrated, but in Al-Anon we discover that no situation is truly hopeless and that it is possible for us to find contentment, and even happiness, whether or not the alcoholic continues to drink. We urge you to try our program. It has helped many of us find solutions that lead to serenity. So much depends on our own attitudes, and as we learn to place our problem in its true perspective, we find it loses its power to dominate our thoughts and our lives" (Al-Anon, 1981).

The Al-Anon program teaches people to look at what they can do to feel better about themselves and to caringly "let go" of the alcoholic. This concept is called "tough love," which means stopping "enabling" behaviors and making the alcoholic responsible for the consequences of his or her drinking and alcoholism. Al-Anon describes this idea in a pamphlet called *Detachment* (1979). Members are encouraged to "let go of our obsession with another's behavior and begin to lead happier and more manageable lives." Al-Anon helps members learn:

- Not to suffer because of the action or reactions of other people;
- Not to allow ourselves to be used or abused in the interest of another's recovery;
- Not to do for others what they should do for themselves;
- Not to manipulate situations so others will eat, go to bed, get up, pay bills, etc.;
- Not to cover up another's mistakes or misdeeds;
- Not to create a crisis;
- Not to prevent a crisis if it is in the natural course of events.

Newcomers often come into Al-Anon with resentments and anger that they have not previously acknowledged. Al-Anon helps them view the alcoholic as someone with a disease instead of someone who is "trying to get them." Step One points out that they are powerless over alcohol and that they have no control over the alcoholic. Steps Two and Three help the person reach outside herself or himself for help from a "Higher Power." "Letting go" of control and trusting a Higher Power are basic concepts of Al-Anon.

Membership and Meetings. The third tradition of Al-Anon states: "The only requirement for membership is that there be a problem of alcoholism in a relative or friend." There are over 15,000 Al-Anon groups in the U.S. and Canada. Al-Anon meetings usually start with the Serenity Prayer, the preamble and the welcome, and are followed by introductions. There are speaker, discussion and step meetings. The meetings emphasize sharing, support and encouragement to work on oneself.

Meetings usually last an hour and have a standard closing: "The opinions expressed here were strictly those of the persons who gave them. Take what you like and leave the rest. A few special words to those of you who haven't been with us long: Whatever your problems, there are those among us who have had them too. If you try to keep an open mind, you will find help. You will come to realize that there is no situation too difficult to be bettered and no unhappiness too great to be lessened. We aren't perfect. The welcome we give you may not show the warmth we have in our hearts for you. After a while, you'll discover that though you may not like all of us, you'll love us in a very special way—the same way we already love you" (Al-Anon, 1981).

The leader then emphasizes that everything said in the meeting is considered confidential. Frequently there is a social time after the meeting for further support and sharing.

Literature. In 1966 Al-Anon published *Al-Anon Family Groups* (1966), which is equivalent to the Big Book in AA. This book sets down the basic principles of Al-Anon and tells the stories of the founders. *Al-Anon's Twelve Steps & Twelve Traditions* (1981) discusses the steps and traditions from an Al-Anon perspective. *One Day at a Time in Al-Anon* (1973) is a daily meditation guide that many members read for inspiration and guidance. Al-Anon also publishes over 50 pamphlets on special topics such as men in Al-Anon, denial, alcoholism as a family disease and adult children of alcoholics. (Pamphlets are available from Al-Anon Family Group Headquarters, Inc., P.O. Box 862, Midtown Station, New York, NY 10018-0862, or a local Al-Anon office.)

ALATEEN

Alateen is a separate program of Al-Anon Family Groups. Started by a California teenager in 1957, Alateen is specifically for teenagers and follows the Al-Anon steps and traditions. Every Alateen group has an active Al-Anon member who serves as a sponsor for the group. The sponsor provides guidance and stability to the group and helps the group stay focused on the Twelve Steps and Twelve Traditions. A key to being a good sponsor is to guide without dominating. The group can hold a group inventory and decide to get a new sponsor if the relationship is unsatisfactory. Alateen meetings frequently meet at the same place as Al-Anon but in different rooms. Many schools have Alateen meetings. A referral to Alateen can be made through the local Al-Anon office.

Alateen has its own literature especially directed to teenagers. In *Hope for Children of Alcoholics–Alateen* (1973), there is a chapter devoted to explaining alcoholism in terms teenagers can understand. Alcoholics are described as anyone and not necessarily "skid row bums." The sources of the alcoholic's obsession, addiction and compulsion are defined. The family disease concept is discussed, with an emphasis on denial, anger, anxiety and adolescents' feelings about being "caught in the middle." The alcoholic is described as sick and unable to control his or her alcohol intake or reactions. The slogans are explained and one chapter contains personal stories to help teenagers feel that they are not alone. At the end of the book, there is a detailed discussion of how to start an Alateen group. A special page labeled "Remember" encourages group members to focus on the common problem of alcoholism and not to gossip, waste time, be impatient, or talk about what happens in the group outside of the group. As the members become older, they are encouraged to join Al-Anon to continue their recovery.

ADULT CHILDREN OF ALCOHOLICS

Adult Children of Alcoholics (ACOAs) is a new movement which has developed rapidly over the past 25 years. In the early 1960s, researchers began trying to identify common characteristics of adults raised in alcoholic homes. Books published because of this research (Black, 1982; Wegscheider, 1981) were the impetus for starting support groups for these individuals (by some estimates, as many as 30 to 40 million people). Because the movement grew rapidly, it did not have the advantage of time to develop and mature as did AA and Al-Anon, and many different groups developed. Al-Anon started having special meetings for adult children of alcoholics. Groups such as the National Association for Children of Alcoholics started. There was a lack of clarity about what the groups should and should not do. Many groups had no one who had any extended time in recovery to help provide guidance and direction. Some groups emphasized therapy over support with heavy confrontation instead of relying on the Twelve Steps and Twelve Traditions. Although these problems still exist in some groups, most ACOA groups have matured and now offer excellent support for adult children of alcoholics.

Adult children of alcoholics have certain common characteristics. One is a need to control (Cermak & Rosenfeld, 1987). When faced with stressful life situations, adult children of alcoholics frequently try to increase their control of the situation even when doing so is impossible. Denial, dishonesty, secretiveness and suppression of feelings are characteristics commonly seen in alcoholic families. Woititz (1981) has described these and other characteristics of adult children of alcoholics, which include not knowing normal behavior, problems finishing projects, severe self-judging, difficulty having fun, problems with relationships and being impulsive. If physicians are aware of these common characteristics, they can identify patients who are adult children of alcoholics. Until they are identified, these individuals can be overutilizers of the medical system and frustrating for physicians to treat. By referring patients to ACOA, physicians can be instrumental in helping them start a program of recovery.

Meetings. Most ACOA meetings last one and a half hours. They usually start with the Serenity Prayer and a welcome. The Twelve Steps, the problem (which describes what happens when a person is reared in an alcoholic home), and the solution (which describes what ACOA recommends for recovery) often are read. At some meetings, the characteristics are read. A member may talk about a step or characteristic and how it affects his or her life. Then each member of the group has the opportunity to share his or her feelings about the topic or talk about any other concerns he or she may have. The meeting usually closes with a prayer (the Lord's Prayer). Members are invited to socialize after meetings.

Newcomers are encouraged to attend six meetings to help them become comfortable with the group and develop the trust that is essential to recovery. Sponsors are an important part of ACOA, and newcomers are encouraged to get a sponsor. Most groups have phone lists and encourage members to call each other for support. As with AA and Al-Anon, an important part of recovery in ACOA is reaching out to others. ACOA members are willing to take people to meetings and can be a helpful resource for physicians.

THE PHYSICIAN'S ROLE

To be able to help alcoholics and drug addicts, physicians need to be familiar with recovery support groups, especially the Twelve Step programs. Such groups offer patients a number of resources:

- Attending group meetings helps overcome the patient's feelings of "terminal uniqueness" and isolation (Bassin, 1975; Canavan, 1983).
- Groups educate patients about the disease process of addiction and hold out the hope of recovery.
- Group members offer newcomers unconditional support as they struggle with early recovery, which the group characterizes as a positive, joyful experience.
- Groups help members learn basic social skills. Members become less self-obsessed and more aware of the feelings of others.
- Groups provide a "reality base" for addicts in recovery, overcoming the isolation and thinking disorders that prevent addicts from comprehending the potential consequences of their behavior and illuminating errors and dangers in the member's thinking.
- Groups help members with the inevitable setbacks experienced in recovery.
- Groups help members constructively use the time formerly occupied by alcohol and drug use.

Making Referrals to Twelve Step Programs. In the 1996 triennial Alcoholics Anonymous (AA) member survey, only 8% of newcomers reported coming to meetings through a physician's referral. This finding is unfortunate, because AA and other self-help programs can be a valuable resource for physicians in helping their addicted patients.

There are several ways to refer patients. AA has a listed phone number in most cities and will provide volunteers to contact the patient and explain AA. After obtaining the patient's permission, the physician should initiate contact with the self-help group in the patient's presence. Giving the patient the telephone number with a recommendation to call usually is not successful. Sisson and Mallams (1981) randomly assigned newly diagnosed alcoholics to two types of referral. The first group was told to call AA and go to a meeting. The second group was put in direct contact with an AA member while in the physician's office. None of the first group attended a meeting; all of the second group did.

Most addiction treatment programs incorporate a strong self-help component and will encourage patients to attend Twelve Step meetings as a regular part of their aftercare program.

Alcoholics Anonymous: The physician may find it helpful to keep a list of AA members willing to do "Twelfth Step" work. Some physicians accompany patients to AA meetings (nonalcoholic physicians may be allowed to attend closed meetings if they are with patients, or the physician may select an open AA meeting). Although such attendance is time-consuming for the physician, it demonstrates to the patient the physician's sincere belief in the importance of AA to recovery. Physicians can obtain a current list of nearby AA meetings from the local AA office (frequently listed in directories as "Intergroup" or "Central Office"). Such lists usually include a brief description of the type of meeting, whether it is a special interest group, and if it is nonsmoking. A summary, published by AA, of how physicians can help alcoholic patients is included as Table 5.

Narcotics Anonymous (NA): Referrals to NA are similar to those for AA. NA often has a listed phone number; many treatment programs also have lists of NA meetings. If neither of these resources is available, the Narcotics Anonymous World Service Office

TABLE 5. Communicating with Addicted Patients About Recovery

1. If you think your patient is an alcoholic, tell him (her).
2. Tell him he's suffering from an illness, not a moral weakness.
3. Tell him alcoholism is progressive and can only get worse if the alcoholic continues to drink.
4. Tell him his illness is treatable.
5. Try to get him to admit his troubles are caused by drinking, not the other way around.
6. Tell him where help is available—clinics, detox units, therapy groups, etc.
7. Tell him about AA.
8. Go to an AA meeting yourself to see how it works.
9. Get a local AA meeting list.
10. Get to know some AA members for referral purposes.

in Van Nuys, California, can provide help and a wealth of information about NA.

Al-Anon: In most cities, Al-Anon has a listed phone number. If not, the AA office often will provide the location and times of Al-Anon meetings. The more physicians know about Al-Anon, the more effectively they can make referrals. An excellent way to learn is to talk with Al-Anon members about their experiences with the program and to attend a meeting. It is also helpful to have a list of Al-Anon members who are willing to take people to Al-Anon meetings.

Adult Children of Alcoholics (ACOA): Because there is considerable variation in ACOA groups, physicians must be familiar with the groups to which they refer patients. Good groups usually have members who have been involved in other Twelve Step programs, and who provide stability and experience. A group can offer support and caring when the pain of being an adult child of an alcoholic begins to surface. The group should not allow "cross-talk" (confrontation or interruptions), so that the meeting feels "safe" to the new member. The purpose of ACOA groups is "to shelter and support newcomers in confronting denial; to comfort those mourning their early loss of security, trust and love; and to teach the skills for reparenting themselves with gentleness, humor, love and respect" (Jacobson, 1987).

Many therapists with special training conduct therapy groups for adult children of alcoholics. These groups include confrontation and feedback to help patients break through the denial and minimization of the consequences of being raised in an alcoholic home. The therapist must be able to direct the group and to provide support when patients begin to open up and to give up control. Both these processes can be terrifying for an adult child of an alcoholic. Therapy groups can show the patient that conflict can be resolved in a healthy manner, which is quite different from the destructive methods commonly used in alcoholic homes.

In helping an ACOA patient, the physician should work from the principle that, because alcoholism is an inherited disease, the patient is at high risk for alcoholism or drug addiction. Patients need to be carefully screened and referred if there is any suggestion of an addictive disorder. Although ACOA patients may appear to be emotionally stable, they often are fragile under their carefully constructed external shell. They need to be treated with care, understanding and gentleness by the physician.

Potential Problems with Referrals. Patient objections to AA and other self-help groups typically are expressed in the following ways (Anonymous, 1982):

"I don't believe in all that God stuff." AA is a spiritual program that is not allied with any particular religion and does not require the members to believe in anything except a Higher Power ("God, as we understand Him"). There are many atheists and agnostics in AA. *Alcoholics Anonymous* (the Big Book) contains an entire chapter for agnostics (Chapter 4), which the physician may recommend to patients who offer this objection.

"I don't like to talk in a group." There is no requirement to talk at an AA meeting. Members can say they "pass" if they do not wish to talk in front of the group.

"I can't stand all the smoke." Nonsmoking group meetings now are available in most geographic areas. In others, large groups divide into smoking and nonsmoking sections.

"I don't have a way to get there." Transportation usually can be arranged for an interested newcomer by calling AA.

"I don't want anyone to know about my drinking." Anonymity is a basic concept of AA. Things said in a meeting stay there; no AA member has the right to break the anonymity of another member.

"I can't stay sober." The third tradition of AA clearly states: "The only requirement for AA membership is a desire to stop drinking." Many old-timers spent a long time attending meetings before they were able to stay sober, and they understand the plight of the newcomer.

Group Problems: The patient may have difficulty identifying with the members of his or her self-help group. If the patient has attended a meeting several times and still has this feeling, he or she should be referred to a different group. In large metropolitan areas, there are many varieties of self-help groups (involving young people, senior citizens, gays/lesbians, nonsmokers, women, African-Americans, Hispanic-Americans, et al.).

Compliance: Although AA as an organization encourages members to cooperate with their physicians, individual AA members may give patients inappropriate advice about stopping essential drugs, such as antidepressants, disulfiram or other medications. If patients are using these medications, it is important to caution them about this possibility. Frequently, communication between the physician and the patient's sponsor can overcome this problem.

Gender Orientation: Women sometimes have problems with AA because of the masculine perspective of most AA literature. However, AA groups now are very receptive to women, who do well in the program. There also are AA meetings exclusively for women.

Limitations of Twelve Step Groups. Physicians need to understand the limitations of AA and other Twelve Step approaches (Anonymous, 1972):

- AA does not solicit members; it will only reach out to people who ask for help.
- AA does not keep records of membership (although some AA groups will provide phone lists for group members).
- AA does not engage in research.
- There is no formal control or follow-up on members by AA.
- AA does not make any medical or psychiatric diagnoses. Each member needs to decide if he or she is an addict.
- AA as a whole does not provide housing, food, clothing, jobs or money to newcomers (although individual members may do this).
- AA is self-supporting through its own members' contributions; it does not accept money from any outside sources.

Making the Referral Work. It is important for the patient to choose a "home group." Such a group functions as an extended family, in which the patient can learn to know other members on a more personal level (improving social skills is important in early sobriety). The home group offers an opportunity to begin service work long before the recovering person is ready to work the Twelfth Step. Setting up chairs, making coffee, chairing meetings, and performing other activities helps to promote responsible behavior. The home group also can help the newcomer develop a phone list of people in the group to call for support between meetings—a practice that is associated with a decreased risk of relapse (Sheeren, 1988).

The physician also can help the addict choose a sponsor. New members often are reluctant to make such a choice because they distrust their ability to select the "right" person. By suggesting that the patient choose a *temporary* sponsor, the physician can help overcome this obstacle. It also may be helpful to tell the patient that selecting a sponsor is a step toward recovery. Patients should be encouraged to select sponsors who are of the same sex and who have at least one year's continuous sobriety (this is not a hard rule; the quality of sobriety is more important than the quantity). The sponsor should be a member of the patient's home group.

When referring a patient to Al-Anon, the physician should emphasize that it takes time to become comfortable with the group. Indeed, the physician may wish to recommend that the patient attend a minimum of six meetings before deciding about the helpfulness of Al-Anon. As with AA, sponsorship by a member is a strong component of the program.

Supporting Recovery. The patient who participates in a self-help group may show certain warning signs of an impending relapse. Early in sobriety, patients often experience excessive euphoria, which can lead to overconfidence and relapse.

The first sign of a potential relapse may be an unwillingness to discuss the recovery program with the physician. This behavior may mean that the patient has decreased the frequency of or stopped attending meetings. This can lead to the "dry drunk syndrome," which is characterized by irritability and unwillingness to share feelings. The patient loses his or her reality base and reverts to distorted thinking. New resentments and a multitude of other negative feelings can lead to drinking to relieve the pain. At this point, patients may request mood-altering chemicals to relieve anxiety. This is a "red flag" that a relapse may be imminent.

Physician monitoring of recovery has been shown to increase the probability of a successful outcome for addicted physicians (Shore, 1987). The physician can perform such monitoring through the recovery status examination (Chappel, 1992). The following questions will help the physician and patient in monitoring the progress of recovery:

Question: "What are you working on in your program of recovery?" The response of a patient working a solid program will be straightforward and open to follow-up questions. If the response is vague, confused, or irritable, a red flag is raised and more inquiry and support are needed.

Question: "What are you working on with your sponsor?" The presence of a sponsor has been shown to reduce the risk of relapse (Sheeren, 1988). Serving as a sponsor later in recovery has an even more powerful association with long-term sobriety (Cross, Morgan et al., 1990).

Question: "What steps are you working on?" Individuals in good recovery usually are working on Steps 10, 11 and 12. Occasionally, they return to work on earlier steps that have particular significance for them. The hallmark of good recovery is responding to this question with ease and openness. The absence of step work indicates that there is little, if any, work done on recovery.

Question: "What meetings are you attending?" In this area, quantity matters. Vaillant found that attendance at more than 300 AA meetings over an eight-year period was associated with stable sobriety (Vaillant, 1983). Active AA members averaged three meetings a week (infrequent or sporadic meeting attendance is a danger signal in persons with less than five years' sobriety).

Question: "What are you doing with your home group?" As described above, a home group plays an important role in recovery. Patients' responses to this question will provide useful information about their recovery support system and sense of responsibility for service work.

Question: "How are you using your phone list?" Patients' willingness and ability to talk to other recovering persons is critical to sustaining sobriety. This is the foundation on which AA was built. As discussed earlier, use of a phone list is associated with significantly reduced risk of relapse (Sheeren, 1988).

The kind of brief recovery status examination outlined here provides the physician with useful information about the patient's progress—or lack of progress—in recovery. The questions stimulate patients' thinking about what it means to work a program of recovery. Using the information elicited, physicians often can make suggestions about their patients' recovery and decrease the likelihood of a relapse.

The physician can do other simple things to show an interest in his or her patients' recovery. For example, anniversaries are important occasions for celebrations in AA. By noting the "dry date" (the last day the patient used any mood-altering substance) in the patient's chart, the physician can acknowledge achievement of a year of sobriety. Alcoholism and drug addiction should be included on patients' problem lists (with their permission). This helps prevent inadvertent prescribing of medications that may endanger recovery.

Physicians also can counsel patients during high risk times, such as periods of extreme stress. Encouraging the patient to attend more meetings during such periods can prevent relapse. Patients frequently complain to their physicians about AA; by listening patiently to patients' concerns and then encouraging them to keep attending meetings, the physician can allow patients to vent their frustration while maintaining attendance at meetings. Physicians also can learn the AA slogans and use them to reinforce what the patient is hearing at meetings.

CONCLUSION

Twelve Step programs have over 62 years' experience in helping alcoholics, addicts and family members recover from addiction and its consequences. Almost all patients afflicted with addictive disease will have a more rewarding recovery if they actively participate in a Twelve Step program. Physicians can play an important role by helping their patients understand these programs and encouraging them to participate in meetings.

Physicians need to know how to use Twelve Step and other support groups effectively to help alcoholics, addicts, and family members recover from the disease of drug and alcohol addiction. By learning what programs are available in the community and mastering a few basic concepts, physicians can be a valuable resource to patients struggling to recover from the devastating effects of addictive disease.

REFERENCES

Alcoholics Anonymous (1989). *Comments on AA's Triennial Surveys, 1989*. New York, NY: Alcoholics Anonymous World Service, Inc.

Alexander J (1941). Alcoholics Anonymous. *The Saturday Evening Post* 213:9–12.

Anonymous (1976a). *Alcoholics Anonymous*. New York, NY: Alcoholics Anonymous World Service, Inc.

Anonymous (1976b). *Alcoholics Anonymous*. New York, NY: Alcoholics Anonymous World Service, Inc., 83–84.

Anonymous (1982). *AA as a Resource for the Medical Profession*. New York, NY: Alcoholics Anonymous World Service, Inc.

Anonymous (1996). *AA Membership Survey*. New York, NY: Alcoholics Anonymous World Service, Inc.

Anonymous (1989). *AA Membership Survey*. New York, NY: Alcoholics Anonymous World Service, Inc.
Anonymous (1972). *A Brief Guide to Alcoholics Anonymous*. New York, NY: Alcoholics Anonymous World Service, Inc.
Anonymous (1966). *Al-Anon Family Groups*. New York, NY: Al-Anon Family Group Headquarters, Inc.
Anonymous (1981). *Al-Anon's Twelve Steps & Twelve Traditions*. New York, NY: Al-Anon Family Group Headquarters, Inc.
Anonymous (1973). *Alateen—Hope for Children of Alcoholics*. New York, NY: Al-Anon Family Group Headquarters, Inc.
Anonymous (1984). *Another Look*. Van Nuys, CA: Narcotics Anonymous World Service Office, Inc.
Anonymous (1979). *Detachment*. New York, NY: Al-Anon Family Group Headquarters, Inc.
Anonymous. *Grapevine*. New York, NY: Alcoholics World Service, Inc.
Anonymous (1983). *Narcotics Anonymous*. Van Nuys, CA: World Service Office, Inc.
Anonymous (1973). *One Day at a Time in Al-Anon*. New York, NY: Al-Anon Family Groups Headquarters, Inc.
Anonymous (1975). Ten tips from Alcoholics Anonymous for family doctors. *Medical Times* 103(6):74–76.
Anonymous (1983). *Sponsorship*. Van Nuys, CA: Narcotics Anonymous World Service Office, Inc.
Anonymous (1983). *The Triangle of Self-Obsession*. Van Nuys, CA: World Service Office, Inc.
Anonymous (1952). *Twelve Steps and Twelve Traditions*. New York, NY: Alcoholics Anonymous World Service, Inc.
Anthony M (1977). Al-Anon. *Journal of the American Medical Association* 238(10):1062–1063.
Bassin A (1975). Psychology in action. *American Psychologist* 30(6):695–696.
Bissell L & Haberman PW (1984). *Alcoholism in the Professions*. New York, NY: Oxford University Press.
Black C (1982). *It Will Never Happen to Me!* Denver, CO: M.A.C. Printing and Publishing Division.
Canavan D (1983). Impaired physicians program-support groups. *Journal of the Medical Society of New Jersey* 80(11):953–954.
Cermak T & Rosenfeld A (1987). Therapeutic considerations with adult children of alcoholics. *Advances in Alcohol & Substance Abuse* 6(4):17–32.
Chappel JN (1992). Effective use of AA and NA in treating patients. *Psychiatric Annals* 22:409–418.
Cross GM, Morgan CW, Mooney AJ, Martin CA & Rafter JA (1990). Alcoholism treatment: A ten year follow up study. *Alcoholism: Clinical & Experimental Research* 14(2):169–173.
Harrison PA, Hoffman NG & Sneed SC (1988). Drug and alcohol addiction treatment outcome. In NS Miller (ed.) *Comprehensive Handbook of Drug and Alcohol Addiction*. New York, NY: Marcel Dekker, 1163–1197.
Jacobson S (1987). The 12-step program and group therapy for adult children of alcoholics. *Journal of Psychoactive Drugs* 19(3):253–255.
Peyrot M (1985). Narcotics Anonymous: Its history, structure and approach. *International Journal of Addiction* 20(10):1509–1522.
Robertson N (1988). *Getting Better Inside Alcoholics Anonymous*. New York, NY: Ballantine Books.
Schulz J (1991). 12-Step programs in recovery from drug and alcohol addiction. In N Miller (ed.) *Comprehensive Handbook of Drug and Alcohol Addiction*. New York, NY: Marcel Dekker, 1255–1271.
Sheeren M (1988). The relationship between relapse and involvement in Alcoholics Anonymous. *Journal of Studies on Alcohol* 49:104–106.
Shore JE (1987). The Oregon experience with impaired physicians on probation: An eight year follow-up. *Journal of the American Medical Association* 257(21):2931–2934.
Sisson RW & Mallams JH (1981). The use of systematic encouragement and community access procedures to increase attendance at Alcoholics Anonymous and Al-Anon meetings. *American Journal of Drug Abuse* 8(3):371–376.
Vaillant GE (1983). *The Natural History of Alcoholism: Causes, Patterns, and Paths to Recovery.* Cambridge, MA: Harvard University Press.
Wegscheider S (1981). *Another Chance*. Palo Alto, CA: Science and Behavior Books.
Woititz J (1981). *Adult Children of Alcoholics*. Pompano Beach, FL: Health Communications, Inc.

CHAPTER 2

Recent Research in Twelve Step Programs

Barbara S. McCrady, Ph.D.

Structure of AA
Operation of the AA Program
AA and Treatment
Utilization of AA
AA and Population Subgroups
Processes of Change
Effectiveness of AA
Issues in Measurement

The past five years have witnessed an explosion of research on Alcoholics Anonymous (AA). Despite earlier skepticism about the possibility of conducting research on AA, researchers have utilized a range of methodologies, including ethnographic methods, epidemiological studies, longitudinal studies of treatment-seeking and non-treatment seeking populations, controlled clinical trials, and meta-analyses to develop a body of new research about AA that has some coherence, confirms some previous findings and beliefs, and challenges others. McCrady and Miller (1993) have reviewed AA research up to the early 1990s. This chapter provides a review of research on AA reported from 1992 through 1996, inclusive, and addresses several major topics, including the structure and functioning of AA, patterns of utilization, the unique experiences and views of AA among specific population groups, and processes of change and outcomes associated with involvement with AA and other Twelve Step programs. The chapter concludes with methodological comments and directions for future research. Research on other Twelve Step programs for substance use disorders is very limited, but will be included where relevant data exist.

STRUCTURE OF AA

Results of a multinational study of AA in eight different countries provide a rich picture of the structure and functioning of AA in different cultural contexts (Mäkelä, Arminen et al., 1996). Study countries included the United States (California), Finland, Iceland, Sweden, Austria, Switzerland, Poland, and Mexico. Ethnographic and survey methods were used in complementary fashion to provide data.

The study documented the international diffusion of AA. The rate of growth of AA from 1981 through 1990 was almost 60% greater in the rest of the world than in the United States (11.5% versus 7.2%). AA developed first in countries similar to the U.S. in language or culture, then spread to other countries. Americans directly influenced the development of AA in approximately half the study countries; natives visiting the United States were responsible for the development of AA in their own countries in the other half of the study countries. The General Service Office in New York provided direct advice and assistance to the development of AA in all study countries (Mäkelä, 1993).

The formal structure of AA was similar in all study countries, although the number of levels of hierarchy varied, with the most levels in the U.S., Mexico, and Finland. AA in all countries had various structures to support publishing activities, service systems, and conferences, and in all countries except Poland (where AA is a newer organization), the majority of members were active in attending AA assemblies, conferences or roundups. Income sources to support AA varied widely among study countries, with some countries relying primarily on member contributions (100% of income in Sweden; 51% in the U.S.), while contributions represented a small portion of income in Poland and Mexico. Profits from publishing accounted for almost half of the income of AA in countries that had active publishing programs (U.S., Finland, Mexico, French-speaking Switzerland). The structure of AA at the local level also varied across study sites. For example, in Austria, German-speaking Switzerland, Poland, and Mexico more than 70% of the groups were small (fewer than 20 members). The availability of "special interest" groups also varied widely. In the U.S., such groups were quite common; in Finland, Sweden, and Mexico special interest groups were somewhat common. The most common "special" meetings were gay/lesbian meetings, which were available in six of the eight study countries, and women's meetings, available in five study countries. Member contributions were solicited at meetings in all study countries, and the distribution of group expenses was similar across countries.

The demography of AA members also varied across countries. The proportion of women in AA varied from 10% in Mexico to 44% in Switzerland, and was not directly related to the prevalence of female alcoholism in study countries. The age distribution of AA members also varied, with the high prevalence of young people under the age of 30 in Mexico (32%) and Iceland (30%), and the lowest prevalence in Finland (7%) and German speaking Switzerland (8%). Socioeconomic status (SES) also varied, with members in Austria and Sweden having the highest SES among study countries, and Mexico having more urban workers and rural poor (Mäkelä, 1993).

OPERATION OF THE AA PROGRAM

Research by Mäkelä et al. (1996) and others (Montgomery, Miller & Tonigan, 1993; Tonigan, Ashcroft, & Miller, 1995) documents both the consistency and the heterogeneity in the practice of AA across AA members, AA groups, and countries. Mäkelä (1993) noted that in no study country were cross-talk (i.e., confrontation or interruptions) and negative feedback accepted during AA meetings. Meetings in different countries also tended to emphasize different steps to the same degree: Steps 1 to 3 and 4 to 9 received fairly equal attention, while Steps 10 through 12 were attended to in only 10% to 15% of the meetings. Among members with at least a year of sobriety, more than two-thirds of members reported doing Twelfth Step work. In other ways, the practice of AA differed across cultures. For example, interpretations of the concept of a Higher Power varied substantially: 30% to 50% of AA members in Iceland, Mexico, Poland, and German-speaking Switzerland viewed the Higher Power as a Christian god, but only 13% held this perspective in Sweden. The Lord's Prayer was common at meetings in the U.S. and Iceland, but rare in Austria, Finland, France or Poland. Use of sponsors also varied considerably; more than 70% of U.S. and Mexican members had a sponsor, but only 30% of Polish members had a sponsor. Behavior during meetings also showed considerable cultural variation, particularly in the degree of physical and personal intimacy. For example, eye contact, body contact, holding hands, and applause, common in most countries, were rare in Finland and Iceland.

Complementing the cross-national studies of Mäkelä and his colleagues, Tonigan and colleagues reported two studies examining the group environment of several different AA meetings in the United States (Montgomery, Miller & Tonigan, 1993; Tonigan, Ashcroft & Miller, 1995). Groups were similar on many dimensions, but seemed to differ in the degree of cohesiveness that members experienced and the amount of aggressiveness they perceived. Groups were similar in how often different steps were discussed, and all placed more emphasis on both the early steps (surrender), and the later steps (maintenance) than on the middle, action-oriented steps (Tonigan, Toscova & Miller, 1996). All groups were seen as encouraging spirituality and discouraging innovation (Montgomery, Miller & Tonigan, 1993).

AA AND TREATMENT

AA is not alcoholism treatment; it is a self-help or mutual help movement. Mäkelä and colleagues (1996) pointed clearly to the differences between AA meetings and therapy, particularly in the rules of discourse, requirements for involvement, and hierarchical structures. There are, however, intimate links between AA and health care delivery generally, and addictions treatment in particular, that have been examined in several studies.

AA and Twelve Step Treatment Programs. AA and professional treatment are linked to differing degrees in different countries and cultures. Mäkelä et al. (1996) reported that AA organized meetings within treatment institutions in all their study countries. Institutional Twelve Step-oriented treatment programs were common in the U.S., Finland, Mexico, French-speaking Switzerland, Sweden, and Iceland, and were an important pathway into treatment in most of these countries. Only in the U.S. and

Iceland, however, was Twelve Step treatment the predominant model and did recovering staff form a substantial proportion of treatment professionals. The close interrelationship between Twelve Step ideology and professional treatment was clearly documented by Mavis and Stöffelmayr (1994). They studied 36 publicly funded inpatient and outpatient treatment programs in the United States. They found that staff of residential programs were more likely to be in recovery from alcohol or drug dependence, or to have family members in recovery than outpatient staff, and that they held AA-related beliefs more strongly than did outpatient staff. Not surprisingly, the degree to which staff supported AA philosophy for their clients was related to the number of recovering staff. Importantly, clients' satisfaction with their treatment program was positively correlated with the degree to which staff endorsed AA beliefs and the degree to which AA-related materials were part of the treatment program.

AA and Health Care Professionals. Two studies have examined health care providers' views of AA. Roche, Parle, et al. (1995) polled physicians (1,365 responded) in postgraduate training programs about their views of alcoholism and treatment. AA was rated "effective" by 82% of respondents. In contrast, only 52% rated inpatient rehabilitation programs as effective, and approximately 35% rated brief physician advice or cognitive behavioral treatment as effective. Morgenstern and McCrady (1992) surveyed members of the American Society of Addiction Medicine, psychologist members of the Society for a Psychology of Addictive Behaviors, psychologists involved with Psychologists Helping Psychologists, and first authors of published treatment research studies. Respondents rated the perceived importance to recovery of 35 different treatment processes. Overall, facilitating commitment to AA was rated as 15th in importance, with other aspects of treatment, such as helping clients accept responsibility for change, preparing clients for relapse, and decreasing denial, being seen as most important. However, among clinicians who subscribed to a disease model of treatment, facilitating commitment to AA was ranked fifth in importance.

UTILIZATION OF AA

AA members enter the program by a number of routes, including self-referral or referral by family or friends, referral from treatment centers, or through coercion from the legal system, employers, or social welfare system.

Population surveys provide information on utilization of AA in the general and alcohol-problem populations. Hasin and Grant (1995) examined data from the National Health Interview Survey of 43,809 adults in the United States. Among the survey population, 5.78% had attended AA at some point in their lives. Room and Greenfield's (1993) household survey of 2,058 adults revealed similar results: 10% of men and 8% of women had attended AA at some point. Room and Greenfield further distinguished between AA attendance for personal problems with drinking and AA attendance for other reasons, and found that only 3.1% of respondents had attended AA for themselves in their lifetime. Weisner, Greenfield and Room (1995) reported that AA attendance among respondents with a history of alcohol dependence or social consequences from their drinking was even higher (22% and 15%, respectively). Their data also suggest, over the period 1979 to 1990, that the probability of attending AA has increased among young men (from 1.4% in 1979 to 5.8% in 1990) and among those with more evidence of alcohol dependence (from 11% to 22%) and more social consequences of drinking (from 4% to 15%). Such increases may be due to increased treatment resources and more mandatory referrals to treatment.

A different perspective on the utilization of AA is provided by studies of patterns of help-seeking among individuals seeking assistance for an alcohol problem. Narrow, Regier, et al. (1993), using data from the Epidemiological Catchment Area Survey, reported that, among individuals with substance abuse disorders who sought help, 36% used AA and other voluntary support services, compared to 83% who used professional services. Timko, Finney and colleagues examined treatment utilization among individuals who first contacted an information and referral center, or who underwent alcohol detoxification. One year later, 75% had sought treatment: 18% had attended only AA or another self-help group (24% of help-seekers); 25% had sought outpatient treatment (33% of help-seekers), and 32% had sought inpatient/residential treatment (43% of help-seekers). AA involvement was high among treatment seekers, with 66% of outpatients and 68% of inpatients also attending AA (Timko, Finney et al., 1993). At the three-year follow-up point, only 16% had received no assistance for their drinking problems. Among those who delayed help-seeking, AA was utilized more often: 39% attended only AA, 26% sought outpatient treatment, and 34% received inpatient/residential treatment (Timko, Finney et al., 1995).

Although there has been considerable controversy about the current criminal justice practice of mandating individuals to attend AA, little research has examined the actual process of criminal justice referral to AA. Speiglman (1994) selected four counties in California that varied in the degree to which they used presentencing screening strategies to deal with repeat Driving Under the Influence (DUI) offenders. Two of the four counties referred cases to AA, referring 37% to 40% of cases. Interestingly, those offenders who were represented by private attorneys were more likely to be referred to AA than those who had public representation. However, among offenders also mandated to parole or to participate in probation-defined treatment, the vast majority (88% to 97%) were required to attend AA. Frequency of attendance was also specified, and typically was two to three meetings per week.

Patterns of Utilization of AA. Both cross-sectional and longitudinal studies provide information about patterns of utilization of AA. Data from the Epidemiological Catchment Area Study (Narrow, Regier et al., 1993) suggest that individuals who attend AA or other self-help groups make about twice as many visits to meetings as to professional treatment. Alcoholics attending AA averaged 44.8 visits/person/year, or just under one meeting per week. Data from Timko, Finney et al. (1993) also suggest fairly substantial utilization rates among AA attenders, with subjects who attended AA with or without outpatient treatment remaining involved, on average, for about six months, with an average rate of attendance of two meetings per week. Subjects who received inpatient treatment were involved longer, but at the same frequency of attendance.

Several innovative methodologies have been used to study patterns of affiliation over time. McCrady, Epstein and Hirsch (1996) examined weekly records of AA attendance among outpatients and reported three distinct patterns of affiliation: (1) positive affiliation, characterized by either immediate, regular attendance or gradually increasing attendance over the course of treatment, (2) negative affiliation, characterized by initially higher rates of attendance, which decreased over the course of treatment, and (3) non-affiliation, characterized by little or no involvement. Morgenstern, Kahler et al. (1996) identified three distinct patterns of post-treatment involvement with AA that were similar to those of McCrady and colleagues within treatment findings. Optimal responders attended meetings daily and often sought advice from AA members, partial responders attended meetings frequently but rarely sought advice from AA members, and non-responders did not engage with AA. Humphreys, Moos and Finney (1995), in studying patterns of change over time, noted that subjects who were able to attain stable abstinence over a three-year period initially were actively involved with AA, attending approximately two meetings per week for the first year. However, AA involvement decreased over the following two years so that, although remaining abstinent, subjects on average attended AA rarely, averaging about one meeting per month.

Mäkelä (1994) studied anniversary announcements published in a Finnish AA newsletter to track continued membership with AA over time. Over three consecutive years, he found that the probability of remaining sober and involved with AA was about 67% for those with one year of sobriety, 85% for those with two to five years sobriety, and 90% for those with more than five years of sobriety.

Finally, Smith (1993) conducted semi-structured interviews with members of AA with at least two years' sobriety to characterize patterns of social affiliation with AA. She described three patterns of affiliation: those who were affiliative from the beginning of involvement, those who were socially distant at first but later became more involved, and those who remained distant from interactions with other group members despite continued attendance at AA meetings. Those who affiliated gradually seem to have followed a common pattern, first forming a connection with one person in AA, then focusing on specific content of stories told at meetings and through the literature, working the steps with encouragement from the sponsor without much group affiliation, and finally performing some service work within the organization despite personal discomfort.

Factors Associated with Successful Affiliation with AA. AA clearly includes a membership diverse in age, gender, ethnicity, severity of alcohol dependence, and a variety of other personal characteristics. Research to identify characteristics of those more likely to affiliate with AA is directed toward identifying those factors that are most associated with successful affiliation, and does not imply that individuals without those characteristics will not affiliate. A number of individual studies have reported characteristics predictive of affiliation with AA, including male gender (Room & Greenfield, 1993), more serious alcohol problems (Caetano, 1993; Hasin & Grant, 1995; Morgenstern, Labouvie et al., in press; Timko, Finney et al., 1993), greater commitment to abstinence (Morgenstern, Labouvie et al., in press), more social support to stop drinking (Hasin & Grant, 1995), less support from and more stress in marriage/intimate relationship (Humphreys, Finney & Moos, 1994), less psychological problems such as depression or poor self-esteem (Timko, Finney et al., 1993), use of more avoidant style for coping with problems (Humphreys, Finney et al., 1994), and having a greater desire to find meaning in life (Project MATCH Research Group, 1997). Most findings, however, are supported by only one recent study. Findings are contradictory for some variables, such as education, where affiliation is predicted by greater education among whites but less education among Hispanic-Americans; or marital status, where unmarried status predicts affiliation among Hispanics (Caetano, 1993), but being married in general predicts affiliation in population surveys. In a meta-analysis of 107 research articles about AA, Emrick, Tonigan et al. (1993) concluded that five variables were most predictive of AA affiliation: a history of use of external supports to cope with problems, loss of control drinking, a greater daily quantity of alcohol consumed, greater physical dependence, and greater anxiety about drinking.

Factors Associated with Unsuccessful Affiliation with AA. Virtually no research has examined the question converse to predicting affiliation: prediction of those least likely to affiliate with AA. The sole empirical finding suggests that those employed problem drinkers who have many resources at their worksite are unlikely to affiliate with AA (Humphreys, Finney et al., 1994). More anecdotal writings have suggested that certain subgroups might find affiliation with AA more difficult (work in this area is reviewed below).

AA AND POPULATION SUBGROUPS

Two contrasting views of AA lead to different predictions about AA and different population subgroups. One perspective suggests that AA is a program of recovery for alcoholics and that the common experience of alcoholism should supersede superficial individual differences. Because AA groups are autonomous, individual meetings may take on the character of the predominant population in attendance, allowing for meetings that could be comfortable for persons of different backgrounds. In the United States, "special interest" groups for certain subpopulations (e.g., women, gays and lesbians, and young people) are very common (Mäkelä, Arminen et al., 1996).

An alternative perspective states that because AA was developed by educated, middle-aged, white, Christian, heterosexual males, its relevance to the young or elderly, persons of color, non-Christians, gays and lesbians, or women, is suspect. AA's own triennial surveys have revealed an increase in the proportion of women in AA, as well as a decrease in the age of AA members (cited in Mäkelä, Arminen et al., 1996), and observation of AA meetings clearly reveals a full diversity among the membership. Research data about the relevance of AA to various subgroups are limited.

Women. Three recent articles examined women and AA. Smith (1992) recruited a convenience sample of women attending AA and compared them with women in outpatient alcoholism treatment. The women in AA tended to be older, were more likely to be employed, and showed some evidence of having more severe drinking problems than the women in the other comparison groups. Kaskutas (1994) studied women attending Women for Sobriety (WFS) meetings, approximately 25% of whom also attended AA. The women attended AA for reasons somewhat different than for attending WFS: AA was seen as the program most crucial to their staying sober, although the fellowship, support, sharing, and spirituality in AA were all seen as important as well. The women perceived WFS as most valuable for the nurturing atmosphere, involvement with an all-women's program, and being exposed to positive female role models. The women in the sample also reported reasons they did not attend AA, including feeling that they did not fit in, perceiving AA as too punitive and focused on shame and guilt, disagreement with program principles related to powerlessness, surrender, and reliance on a Higher Power, and perceiving AA as male-dominated. Beckman (1993), in a review of the literature on AA, Twelve Step-oriented treatment and women, concluded that women were underrepresented in studies of AA, but that AA involvement seemed to be associated with more positive drinking outcomes.

Cultural, Racial, and Ethnic Subgroups. Literature on cultural, ethnic, and racial subgroups and alcoholism in general is quite limited, and research on AA involvement for these groups is even more limited. Caetano (1993) reported data from national household surveys on the acceptance of the disease concept by different U.S. ethnic groups and also described AA utilization data for different groups. He found that endorsement of several aspects of the disease concept, including viewing alcoholism as an illness, believing that drinking problems get worse without help, and that abstinence is necessary for alcoholics, was comparable for white, African-American, and Hispanic-American men and women. However, Hispanic-American and African-American respondents were more likely than whites to see alcoholics as morally weak, to believe that alcoholics drink "because they want to," and to endorse controlled drinking as a goal for alcoholics. Caetano reported that all groups studied had positive views of AA, as they were likely to recommend AA as a therapy for alcohol problems, and recommended AA more than any other resource. Some variability in support for AA was noted, with 97% of Hispanics, 94% of whites, 87% of African-Americans, and only 76% of Asian-Americans recommending AA as a resource.

In terms of actual utilization of AA, Caetano also reported, among those with drinking problems, that Hispanic-Americans were more likely to have had contact with AA (12%) than either whites or African-Americans (5%). He also reported, among those involved with the criminal justice or welfare system, that whites were more likely than African-Americans or Hispanic-Americans to have been involved with AA. In contrast, in samples drawn from primary health care settings, African-Americans were more likely to have been involved with AA than whites or Hispanic-Americans.

Positive utilization of AA by different cultural groups may be related to the ways that local meetings reflect the nature of the individuals attending the meetings. Hoffman (1994) conducted a participant observer study of Hispanic AA groups in the Los Angeles area. From his observations, he concluded that the groups had a character quite different from Anglo meetings. He noted in particular, the use of "rough therapy," in which criticism, ridicule, boasting, competitiveness, and sexually aggressive behavior toward women were common. He suggested that these behaviors were a way to maintain a "machismo" value within AA. Although he believed that the environment of the Hispanic-American meetings was conducive to involvement for Hispanic males, he suggested that these same qualities made the meetings particularly inapt for females or gay men.

Age-Specific Groups. No studies reported in the past five years have focused specifically on the experience of either youth or elderly persons in AA. Several studies of adolescent treatment, however, suggest a strong association between AA/NA involvement and abstinence. These studies are reviewed below in the section on the effectiveness of AA.

Gays and Lesbians. Research on the experience of gays and lesbians in relation to AA also is very limited. One ethnographic study (Hall, 1994) recruited lesbians in recovery for at least one year. All respondents were familiar with AA; 74% were actively involved. Hall identified three sources of tension for the lesbians in AA. First was the tension between a sense of assimilation and a sense of differentiation. Women felt that AA was a program in which people of very different backgrounds could relate because of their common concerns but also at times viewed AA as a white, male, heterosexist organization. Second, they noted the value of the authority of AA as a prescription for sobriety but at times viewed AA more as a program that provided a set of tools for recovery. The perceived sexist language in the AA literature and the lack of focus on lesbian issues made following the program prescriptively a difficult task. Finally, the women experienced tension between the strongly individual focus of AA and their perception of the importance of examining issues in a cultural context.

PROCESSES OF CHANGE

Two types of studies have examined the actual processes of involvement with AA—studies of AA members themselves, and studies of Twelve Step-oriented treatment programs.

Brown and Peterson (1991) surveyed AA members' views of the relative importance of aspects of the AA program. Working the steps, having a sponsor, telling their story at a meeting, and daily meditations were seen as most important. In a second sample, members of AA, as well as other Twelve Step groups, were surveyed. Respondents believed in a Higher Power, that they would recover with the help of their Higher Power, and that they were powerless over alcohol or another problem for which they sought help. Additionally, respondents reported a number of behavioral changes to facilitate recovery, including attending meetings, avoiding people, places and things associated with their problem, making amends, working the Fourth and Fifth Steps, praying, telling their story at a meeting, and maintaining a regular pattern of sleep.

Snow, Prochaska, and Rossi (1994) used a broader theoretical model to describe the types of cognitive and behavioral processes used by AA members to facilitate change. Half of their sample were current members of AA; another 35% had attended at some point. Current members of AA were more likely to use helping relationships, stimulus control ("people, places and things"), and behavioral management strategies to maintain sobriety. Those who attended more frequently used more behavioral processes of change. Snow, Prochaska and Rossi (1994) also examined the processes of change used by those with the strongest affiliation to AA, and found that those with the greatest affiliation reported greater importance for helping relationships, stimulus control, behavior management, and consciousness raising processes.

Morgenstern, Kahler et al. (1996) reported that the processes used in AA depended on the degree of involvement with AA. Those subjects who attended daily meetings and turned to other AA members for advice also were more likely to have a sponsor, work the steps, be involved with AA service, read AA literature, and pray.

Processes of Change in Twelve Step Treatment. An alternative approach to studying affiliation with AA is to study the process of acceptance of Twelve Step beliefs during treatment. McCrady, Epstein and Hirsch (1996), reporting on an outpatient sample, found that among outpatients in treatment designed to facilitate AA involvement, 50% had a sponsor by the end of treatment, 57% reported working the initial steps in AA, and 36% reported being involved with AA activities and socializing with other AA members. Morgenstern and colleagues (1996) found that, during Twelve Step-oriented residential or outpatient treatment, participants became more accepting of several beliefs, including their own powerlessness over alcohol and the existence of a Higher Power.

EFFECTIVENESS OF AA

AA as a Correlate of Outcome. One of the most consistent and robust findings is that of a correlation between AA attendance and positive drinking outcomes. Hoffmann and Miller (1992), in an evaluation of 8,087 patients treated in 57 different inpatient and outpatient Minnesota-model type programs, reported that those attending AA at one-year follow-up were 50% more likely to be abstinent than those not attending AA. Studies of smaller samples produced similar results: patients who received inpatient chemical dependency treatment were more likely to be abstinent if they were attending AA or Narcotics Anonymous (NA) (Johnson & Herringer, 1993); for adolescents involved with a combined treatment/wilderness program, AA/NA attendance was the strongest predictor of abstinence, and those not attending AA/NA were four times as likely to relapse (Kennedy & Minami, 1993); a review of studies of women receiving alcohol treatment suggested that women involved in AA or Twelve Step-oriented treatment had better outcomes than women not involved with AA (Beckman, 1993). Even in pharmacotherapy studies, AA attendance predicted positive outcomes and was a stronger predictor than medication compliance (Pisani, Fawcett et al., 1993). Similar results have been reported for NA involvement: Christo and Graney (1995) found that NA attendance was correlated with less drug use six months after treatment ($r = -.31$). Meta-analysis of the role of AA in treatment outcomes found a modest correlation between AA involvement and drinking outcomes ($r_w = .21$) and generally found stronger relationships between AA involvement and outcome in outpatient than inpatient samples (Tonigan, Toscova & Miller, 1996). Studies of AA members who were recruited through AA rather than treatment programs also find an association between AA involvement and positive outcome: McBride (1991) found a strong correlation ($r = .71$) between length of AA involvement and length of abstinence.

Studies of nontreatment seeking populations provide a similar view of the association between AA involvement and outcome. Humphreys and colleagues (1994) recruited a sample of 631 individuals who either contacted an alcohol information and referral center or presented for detoxification without further treatment. The sample was followed for three years (70% follow-up rate) to determine pathways into change. A total of 298 subjects were involved with AA at some point during the follow-up. Those involved with AA were more likely to be abstinent, drank less, were intoxicated less frequently, had fewer alcohol-related problems or symptoms of alcohol dependence and reported greater self-efficacy for resisting alcohol (Timko, Finney et al., 1995).

Evaluation of Twelve Step-Oriented Treatments. AA and Twelve Step-oriented treatments have close conceptual links in adherence to the classic disease conception of alcoholism, emphasis on abstinence, the importance of AA involvement, and working the Twelve Steps. Differences between Twelve Step treatment programs and AA, however, are substantial, and the two should not be equated. Unfortunately, the empirical literature often ignores this distinction and reports results of Twelve Step-oriented treatments as though they are studies of AA. Several important studies evaluating Twelve Step-oriented treatments have been reported in the past five years and, while not on AA *per se*, provide important information about the effectiveness of programs philosophically allied with AA principles. As noted above, Hoffmann and Miller (1992) reported the largest single group evaluation of Twelve Step-oriented programs. Subjects were predominantly male (70%), young (70% between 20 and 39), high school or college educated (70%), and employed (60% to 70%, depending on the sample). Most had a diagnosis of alcohol dependence. Six-month follow-ups (almost 75% of the sample) revealed an abstinence rate of 67% to 75% among subjects from whom they collected follow-up data; with 60% to 68% abstinence rates at 12-month follow-up (approximately 60% follow-up rate). Hoffmann and Miller estimated that, if all subjects lost to follow-up had relapsed, then abstinence rates would have been approximately 56% to 65% at six months and 34% to 42% at 12 months. Kennedy and Minami (1993) and Alford, Koehler and Leonard (1991) reported similarly positive outcomes for Twelve Step-oriented treatment with adolescents: 47% of Kennedy and Minami's sample were abstinent at one-year follow-up; 48% of males and 70% of females in the Alford sample were abstinent at one year; 40% of the males and 61% of the females were abstinent at two years. Three randomized clinical trials of outpatient treatments have included a treatment modality designed to facilitate involvement with AA.

In studies of alcoholics (McCrady, Epstein & Hirsch, in preparation) and cocaine abusers (Wells, Peterson et al., 1994), relapse prevention treatment was found to be more effective than Twelve Step-oriented treatment on some outcomes variables, but outcomes were similar across most variables. The Project MATCH Research Group (1997) found that Twelve Step facilitation treatment was more effective than cognitive behavioral therapy for outpatients (but not aftercare patients) who did not show psychiatric symptoms, but outcomes were comparable with more psychiatrically impaired patients.

Psychological Correlates of AA Affiliation. A final important outcome related question is the degree to which AA involvement is associated with positive functioning in other life areas. Popular criticism of AA asserts that, although sober, AA members have become psychologically dependent on AA and therefore are poorly adjusted, though sober. The research literature contradicts this perspective. Three recent studies are of relevance. Christo and Sutton (1994) studied 200 addicts in recovery and involved with Narcotics Anonymous and found that longer abstinence was associated with lower levels of anxiety. Humphreys, Finney and Moos (1994) reported that greater involvement with AA was associated with more active cognitive and behavioral coping and less avoidant coping, as well as more social support from friends. In a meta-analysis of the AA literature, Emrick, Tonigan et al. (1993) also found a positive association between AA involvement and improved psychological adjustment.

Mediators of the Influence of AA on Outcomes. Research has gone beyond merely examining correlations between AA involvement and drinking outcomes to examine what aspects of AA involvement relate to drinking outcomes. Montgomery, Miller and Tonigan (1995) distinguish AA *attendance* from AA *involvement*, which includes, in addition to attendance, the degree of involvement with different aspects of AA such as participation during meetings, having a sponsor, leading meetings, working specific steps or doing Twelfth Step work (Tonigan, Toscova & Miller, 1996). Montgomery, Miller and Tonigan (1995) reported that AA involvement and attendance were moderately correlated (.45); however, involvement, not attendance, correlated with post-treatment alcohol consumption ($r = -.44$) in a sample of patients in an inpatient Twelve Step treatment program.

A meta-analysis of the literature on AA (Emrick, Tonigan et al., 1993) found a significant association between participating in AA activities and drinking outcomes (r_w's $> .20$). Aspects of participation most strongly associated with positive outcomes included being more involved with AA than during previous periods of AA involvement, leading meetings, having a sponsor, and doing Twelfth Step work.

Two studies have examined mediators of the relationship between AA and positive outcome. Christo and Graney (1995) found that, although neither spiritual beliefs nor believing in addiction as a disease predicted drug use outcomes, both predicted NA attendance, which was related to reduced drug use. Morgenstern and colleagues (in press) examined a complex set of mediational pathways to abstinence after Twelve Step-oriented treatment. They found that several variables predicted affiliation with AA after treatment, including perceived past and future harm from alcohol use, anticipated benefits from abstinence, degree of commitment of abstinence, and drinking problem severity. In turn, affiliation with AA one month after treatment predicted that subjects would use behavioral coping strategies to stay abstinent and would have a greater commitment to abstinence six months after treatment. AA affiliation one month after treatment was also a strong predictor of six-month drinking status. Regression analyses of AA affiliation and problem severity in Step 1, and use of active change processes in Step 2 increased the predictability of six-month drinking outcomes. Entering change processes into the model decreased the degree to which AA affiliation predicted drinking, suggesting that AA leads to a positive drinking outcome in part because it enhances individuals' general use of strategies for dealing with alcohol.

ISSUES IN MEASUREMENT

Definitional Issues. Recent research has approached the definition of AA involvement from a richer and more complete conceptual framework. Older studies classified subjects into simple categories—those who attended AA and those who did not. Somewhat more sophisticated studies measured attendance quantitatively, defining greater attendance as indicative of greater affiliation. More recent research has approached affiliation as a multidimensional construct that includes attendance, endorsement of the central beliefs of AA, use of behavioral strategies suggested by AA, use of cognitive strategies suggested by AA, degree of involvement with the organization as an organization, and degree of subjective sense of affiliation with AA. In at least one study, a multidimensional measure of AA involvement yielded two factors, one reflecting attendance, the other reflecting other aspects of involvement (Tonigan, Connors & Miller, 1996). Although correlated, the two scales shared only 40% of the variance.

Advances in Measurement. Three groups have developed measures of AA involvement. The Project MATCH research group developed the Alcoholics Anonymous Involvement Scale (AAIS; Tonigan, Connors & Miller, 1996), a 13-item measure to assess meeting attendance, membership in AA, attending 90 meetings in 90 days, having a sponsor or serving as a sponsor, working the steps, and having a spiritual awakening. Test-retest reliability for items, subscales, and the total scale was good, with most reliability scores above .90. Internal consistency also was good for a treatment-seeking sample. Brown and Peterson (1991) developed a 53-item questionnaire, the Brown-Peterson Recovery Progress Inventory (B-PRPI), to assess both cognitive and behavioral aspects of AA involvement. Split-half reliability of the measure was above .90. Morgenstern, Kahler et al. (1996) developed two measures of AA involvement: the Recovery Interview, which assesses nine aspects of AA involvement, and the Addiction Treatment Attitude Questionnaire, which measures beliefs and intentions related to the Twelve Step model, including degree of commitment to AA, abstinence, commitment to lifetime abstinence, intention to avoid high risk situations, and belief in alcoholism as a disease. Internal consistency of the Recovery Interview was .87.

CONCLUSIONS

This chapter has reviewed a substantial body of research on AA. Research has documented the diffusion of AA throughout the world. AA seems to maintain substantially the same structure across cultures, although there is variability in the complexity of the formal organization. AA also maintains the same essential core program cross-culturally. Variability in the program often is reflective of cultural differences, as in the views of the nature of a Higher Power or the degree of intimacy expressed in groups. Even within a culture, there is considerable variability in the atmosphere of different AA groups, a finding that is consistent with AA's emphasis on the autonomy of the individual group. AA and formal treatment are closely tied in some cultures, and many health care and addictions professionals adhere to the philosophy underlying AA and perceive AA as effective.

AA is fairly widely utilized in the United States: 6% to 10% of the population has attended AA at some point, with that rate doubling or tripling among those with drinking problems. Utilization is growing most quickly among young men, who are also most likely to be mandated to treatment. Increasingly, the legal system is referring individuals to attend AA. When individuals seek help voluntarily, a substantial proportion use AA, either as their sole source of assistance or in conjunction with formal treatment. Most commonly, individuals seem to become actively involved for several months, going to meetings about twice a week. There is, however, considerable variability in patterns of affiliation with some individuals becoming increasingly committed over time, while others gradually slip away from the program. Longer term involvement is less common, but those who stay with AA for more than a year are very likely to continue their involvement for many years.

AA is such a heterogeneous organization that it is difficult to draw generalizations about who is most or least likely to affiliate with AA. There is little evidence of problems with affiliation among specific subpopulations, but concerns about aspects of the AA program have been documented, particularly among women. It may be that the presence of "special interest" groups and modifications of the program at the local level address specific concerns. Overall, data suggest that individuals with more severe problems, more concern about their drinking and a greater commitment to staying abstinent, less support from their spouse, a history of turning to others for support, and a greater desire to find meaning in their lives may be most likely to affiliate with AA.

Substantial research on the process of change and outcomes associated with AA involvement has been reported in the past five years. AA involvement is clearly correlated with positive outcomes, both in drinking and psychological functioning. Research supports that members actively use the core of the AA program: they attend meetings, work the steps, get a sponsor, and tell their story at meetings. The more active they are with AA, the better are their outcomes. Part of the positive impact of AA seems to be through clear cognitive and behavioral changes that members make. Studies of formal treatments that draw from the core beliefs of AA have yielded more mixed findings.

Finally, there is increased methodological sophistication and creativity in research into AA. Concepts of AA involvement capture more fully the core of the AA program, while several new measures that have good psychometric properties have been developed. Diverse and complementary methodologies have contributed to a richer, data-based understanding of AA, which should continue to expand over the next decade.

REFERENCES

Alford GS, Koehler RA & Leonard J (1991). Alcoholics Anonymous–Narcotics Anonymous model inpatient treatment of chemically dependent adolescents: A 2-year outcome study. *Journal of Studies on Alcohol* 52:1181–126.

Beckman LJ (1993). Alcoholics Anonymous and gender issues. In BS McCrady & WR Miller (eds.) *Research on Alcoholics Anonymous: Opportunities and Alternatives.* New Brunswick, NJ: Rutgers Center of Alcohol Studies, 233–248.

Brown HP & Peterson JH (1991). Assessing spirituality in addiction treatment and follow-up: Development of the Brown-Peterson Recovery Progress Inventory (B-PRPI). *Alcoholism Treatment Quarterly* 8:21–50.

Caetano R (1993). Ethnic minority groups and Alcoholics Anonymous: A review. In BS McCrady & WR Miller (eds.) *Research on Alcoholics Anonymous: Opportunities and Alternatives.* New Brunswick, NJ: Rutgers Center of Alcohol Studies, 209–232.

Christo G & Graney C (1995). Drug users' spiritual beliefs, locus of control and the disease concept in relation to Narcotics Anonymous attendance and six-month outcomes. *Drug and Alcohol Dependence* 38:51–56.

Christo G & Sutton S (1994). Anxiety and self-esteem as a function of abstinence time among recovering addicts attending Narcotics Anonymous. *British Journal of Clinical Psychology* 33:198–200.

Emrick CD, Tonigan JS, Montgomery H & Little L (1993). Alcoholics Anonymous: What is currently known? In BS McCrady & WR Miller (eds.) *Research on Alcoholics Anonymous: Opportunities and Alternatives.* New Brunswick, NJ: Rutgers Center of Alcohol Studies, 41–76.

Hall JM (1994). The experiences of lesbians in Alcoholics Anonymous. *Western Journal of Nursing Research* 16:556–576.

Hasin DS & Grant BF (1995). AA and other help seeking for alcohol problems: Former drinkers in the U.S. general population. *Journal of Substance Abuse* 7:281–292.

Hoffman F (1994). Cultural adaptations of Alcoholics Anonymous to serve Hispanic populations. *International Journal of the Addictions* 29:445–460.

Hoffmann NG & Miller NS (1992). Treatment outcomes for abstinence-based programs. *Psychiatric Annals* 22:402–408.

Humphreys K, Finney JW & Moos RH (1994). Applying a stress and coping framework to research on mutual help organizations. *Journal of Community Psychology* 22:312–327.

Humphreys K, Moos RH & Finney JW (1995). Two pathways out of drinking problems with professional treatment. *Addictive Behaviors* 20:427–441.

Johnson E & Herringer LG (1993). A note on the utilization of common support activities and relapse following substance abuse treatment. *Journal of Psychology* 127:73–78.

Kaskutas LA (1994). What do women get out of self-help? Their reasons for attending Women for Sobriety and Alcoholics Anonymous. *Journal of Substance Abuse Treatment* 11:185–195.

Kennedy B & Minami M (1993). The Beech Hill Hospital/Outward Bound Adolescent Chemical Dependency Treatment Program. *Journal of Substance Abuse Treatment* 10:395–406.

Mäkelä K (1993). International comparisons of Alcoholics Anonymous. *Alcohol Health & Research World* 17:228–234.

Mäkelä K (1994). Rates of attrition among the membership of Alcoholics Anonymous in Finland. *Journal of Studies on Alcohol* 55:91–95.

Mäkelä K, Arminen I, Bloomfield K et al. (1996). *Alcoholics Anonymous As a Mutual-help Movement.* Madison, WI: University of Wisconsin Press.

Mavis BE & Stöffelmayr BE (1994). Program factors influencing client satisfaction in alcohol treatment. *Journal of Substance Abuse* 6:345–354.

McBride JL (1991). Abstinence among members of Alcoholics Anonymous. *Alcoholism Treatment Quarterly* 8:113–121.

McCrady BS, Epstein EE & Hirsch LS (1996). Issues in the implementation of a randomized clinical trial that includes Alcoholics Anonymous: Studying AA-related behaviors during treatment. *Journal of Studies on Alcohol* 57:604–612.

McCrady BS, Epstein EE & Hirsch LS (in preparation). Enhancing behavioral couples therapy with Relapse Prevention or AA: Six month outcomes.

McCrady BS & Miller WR (1993). *Research on Alcoholics Anonymous: Opportunities and Alternatives.* New Brunswick, NJ: Rutgers Center of Alcohol Studies.

Montgomery HA, Miller WR & Tonigan JS (1993). Differences among AA groups: Implications for research. *Journal of Studies on Alcohol* 54:502–504.

Montgomery HA, Miller WR & Tonigan JS (1995). Does Alcoholics Anonymous involvement predict treatment outcome? *Journal of Substance Abuse Treatment* 12:241–246.

Morgenstern J, Frey R, McCrady B, Labouvie E & Neighbors C (1996). Examining mediators of change in traditional chemical dependency treatment. *Journal of Studies on Alcohol* 57:53–64.

Morgenstern J, Kahler CW, Frey RM & Labouvie E (1996). Modeling therapeutic response to 12-step treatment: Optimal responders, nonresponders, and partial responders. *Journal of Substance Abuse* 8:45–59.

Morgenstern J, Labouvie E, McCrady BS, Kahler CW & Frey RM (in press). Affiliation with Alcoholics Anonymous following treatment: A study of its therapeutic effects and mechanisms of action. *Journal of Consulting and Clinical Psychology.*

Morgenstern J & McCrady BS (1992). Curative processes in the treatment of alcohol and drug problems: Behavioral and disease model perspectives. *British Journal of Addiction* 87:615–626.

Narrow WE, Regier DA, Rae DS, Manderscheid RW & Locke BZ (1993). Use of services by persons with mental and addictive disorders. *Archives of General Psychiatry* 50:95–107.

Pisani VD, Fawcett J, Clark DC & McGuire M (1993). The relative contributions of medication adherence and AA meeting attendance to abstinent outcome for chronic alcoholics. *Journal of Studies on Alcohol* 54:115–119.

Project MATCH Research Group (1997). Matching alcoholism treatments to client heterogeneity: Project MATCH posttreatment drinking outcomes. *Journal of Studies on Alcohol* 58:7–29.

Roche AM, Parle MD, Stubbs JM, Hall W & Saunders JB (1995). Management and treatment efficacy of drug and alcohol problems: What do doctors believe? *Addiction* 90:1357–1366.

Room R & Greenfield T (1993). Alcoholics Anonymous, other 12-step movements and psychotherapy in the U.S. population, 1990. *Addiction* 88:555–562.

Smith AR (1993). The social construction of group dependency in Alcoholics Anonymous. *Journal of Drug Issues* 23:689–704.

Smith LN (1992). A descriptive study of alcohol-dependent women attending Alcoholics Anonymous, a regional council on alcoholism and an alcohol treatment unit. *Alcohol & Alcoholism* 27:667–676.

Snow MG, Prochaska JO & Rossi JS (1994). Processes of change in Alcoholics Anonymous: Maintenance factors in long-term sobriety. *Journal of Studies on Alcohol* 55:362–371.

Speiglman R (1994). Mandated AA attendance for recidivist drinking drivers: Ideology, organization, and California criminal justice practices. *Addiction* 89:859–868.

Timko C, Finney JW, Moos RH & Moos BS (1995). Short-term treatment careers and outcomes of previously untreated alcoholics. *Journal of Studies on Alcohol* 56:597–610.

Timko C, Finney JW, Moos RH, Moos BS & Steinbaum DP (1993). The process of treatment selection among previously untreated help- seeking problem drinkers. *Journal of Substance Abuse* 5:203–220.

Tonigan JS, Ashcroft F & Miller WR (1995). AA group dynamics and 12-step activity. *Journal of Studies on Alcohol* 56:616–621.

Tonigan JS, Connors GJ & Miller WR (1996). Alcoholics Anonymous Involvement (AAI) Scale: Reliability and norms. *Psychology of Addictive Behaviors* 10:75–80.

Tonigan JS, Toscova R & Miller WR (1996). Meta-analysis of the literature on Alcoholics Anonymous: Sample and study characteristics moderate findings. *Journal of Studies on Alcohol* 57:65–72.

Weisner C, Greenfield T & Room R (1995). Trends in the treatment of alcohol problems in the U.S. general population, 1979–1990. *American Journal of Public Health* 85:55–60.

Wells EA, Peterson PL, Gainey RR, Hawkins JD & Catalano RF (1994). Outpatient treatment for cocaine abuse: A controlled comparison of relapse prevention and twelve step approaches. *American Journal of Drug and Alcohol Abuse* 20:1–17.

CHAPTER 3

Rational Recovery, SMART Recovery and Non-Twelve Step Recovery Programs

Joseph Gerstein, M.D., FACP

Traditional Programs
Non-Traditional Programs
Program Characteristics
The Need for Alternative Approaches

A number of programs offer alternatives to the traditional Twelve Step approach for persons with alcohol and other drug problems. (A listing, including contact information, appears in Table 1.) These programs are best categorized as Traditional (i.e., derived from or related directly to the Twelve Step approach and with a clear spiritual context) and Non-Traditional (Fox, 1995).

TRADITIONAL PROGRAMS

Traditional programs include Alcoholics Victorious (an arm of the Institute for Christian Living); CALIX (which has a Catholic orientation and considers itself a supplement to AA); and JACS, or Jewish Alcoholics, Chemically Dependent Persons and Significant Others Foundation (this group considers itself a supplement to AA). Some prominent proprietary programs have broadened the scope of the Twelve Step approach by grafting a "coping skills" component onto their curricula. In the Hazelden Program, Rational-Emotive Behavior Therapy (REBT), a public-domain concept originated by Dr. Albert Ellis, is used extensively: a large segment of the Hazelden catalogue of proprietary pamphlets, books, audio tapes and videos features items related to REBT. Although patients and programs could follow the aphoristic advice of Bill W. to "take what you want and leave the rest," few are encouraged to do so.

In the "reworking" category are groups such as *We Agnostics*, which has chapters in New York City and San Francisco. This group employs Twelve Step methods, but has reworded the steps to eliminate references to a deity or higher power (Cleveland & Arlys, 1989). As with traditional Twelve Step programs, participants refer to themselves emphatically as "alcoholics" and victims of a disease and plan life-long attendance at meetings.

NON-TRADITIONAL PROGRAMS

Non-traditional programs include Men For Sobriety (MFS) and Women For Sobriety (WFS), Secular Organizations for Sobriety (SOS), Rational Recovery^{sm}, and SMART Recovery^{sm}.

Moderation Management is a non-abstinence based program that favors controlled drinking.

Men For Sobriety. This program proposes to help men recover from problem drinking through discovery of self, gained by sharing experiences, hopes and encouragement with other men. It recognizes men's complex role in today's society and the process of self-discovery leading to a sense of self-value and self-worth in recovery from alcoholism. Program methods involve exchanging information, positive reinforcement of personal progress, cognitive strategies that emphasize positive thinking, imagery and "letting the body help" (relaxation/meditation techniques, diet and exercise).

Women For Sobriety. Founded in 1975 by Jean Kirkpatrick, a sociologist, WFS promotes a "take charge of your life" attitude for women (as expressed through the philosophy, "Our first conscious act is to remove negativity from our lives"). Several of the other tenets of the program are clearly congruent with cognitive-behavioral concepts: "Problems bother me only to the degree I permit them to;

I am what I think; The past is gone forever; I am a competent woman and have much to give to life." In this program, spirituality is a goal in recovery, but is to be achieved through working toward the highest realization of one's self. The program is based on the belief that women have different reasons for drinking and different needs from men in recovery (e.g., women drink because of frustration, loneliness, emotional deprivation and various kinds of harassment) and that issues arising from women's cultural socialization are not sufficiently understood in male-dominated treatment programs (Kasl, 1992).

Secular Organizations for Sobriety. Founded in 1986 by James Christopher, SOS groups are most accurately depicted as support groups. Major tenets of SOS are that sobriety is the number one priority in the alcoholic's or drug addict's life; the support of other alcoholics or addicts is a vital adjunct to recovery; confidentiality and anonymity are critical in this endeavor; one's sobriety should not be made contingent upon belief in or reliance on a mystical or supernatural force. SOS does not subscribe to the notion that there is "one right way" to get and stay sober; instead, it encourages membership in more than one self-help organization when and if the individual finds that beneficial. Participants also are encouraged to take responsibility for their own sobriety and to give themselves credit for having stayed sober on a daily basis.

Rational Recovery.sm Founded in 1986 by social worker Jack Trimpey, Rational Recoverysm (RR) originally embraced two major modalities: Addictive Voice Recognition Techniquesm (AVRT) and Rational-Emotive Behavior Therapy (REBT). It was in this form that it spread across the country and underwent initial assessment (Galanter, 1993). Each RR group had a lay "coordinator" and a professional advisor. Today, the RR program consists of AVRT alone and is categorized as an educational rather than a treatment process.

AVRT sets up a dichotomy between thoughts and feelings that support continued use of intoxicating substances (The Addictive Voice) and those that support abstinence ("you"). Trimpey (1996) localizes the Addictive Voice to the midbrain (or reptilian brain) and the "you" voice to the forebrain. He then suggests that the Addictive Voice be divorced from the "you" by categorizing it as "it," i.e. "other" or alien. Trimpey argues that recovery is not a process but an event: a moment when an irreversible decision is made to separate the "you" from the "it." Commitment thus is crucial. The training involves learning to deal with the seductive, disguised subtleties of the Addictive Voice, which he suggests be named "The Beast." Meetings apparently involve learning the technique and learning, "with the help of group members more experienced and sophisticated, the conniving blandishments of The Beast . . . this is where the rational thinking comes in." Group coordinators are lay persons. Trimpey now speaks explicitly of his program as a "cure" for alcoholism and labels it explicitly as educational as opposed to therapeutic (Trimpey, 1996).

SMART Recovery.sm Sponsored by the not-for-profit Alcohol and Drug Abuse Self-Help Network, Inc., SMART (**S**elf-**M**anagement **A**nd **R**ecovery **T**raining) Recoverysm is an evolving program that is dedicated to constantly integrating the latest scientific information into its format. Group coordinators are volunteers, mainly "graduates" of the program with some volunteer professionals. At present, 200 groups across the U.S. (and several in Canada) use a four-module program.

The *Motivational Module* recognizes that not all individuals attending mutual-help group meetings have arrived at the action phase and that moving them into the action phase is as important as moving those in the action phase into sobriety. The Spiral of Change (Prochaska, Norcross & DiClemente, 1994) is explained to participants, followed by a series of exercises.

The *DISARM Module* (**D**estructive **S**elf-talk **A**wareness and **R**efusal **M**ethod) is designed to prompt recall of the persistently negative experiences consequent to drinking and/or drug use. It requires the individual to be aware of the ambivalent thoughts that are transiting his/her brain. Behavioral "thought-stopping" devices are also encouraged at this stage, e.g., the stout rubber band worn on the wrist and snapped against the inside of the wrist at the first hint of the urge; the list of substance abuse-induced calamities carried in the shirt pocket and viewed at the first hint of the urge. The goal here is to move from the rational into the behavioral mode of functioning. The types of irrational, self-convincing statements that encourage or excuse drinking are discussed and refuted. The differences between the short- and long-term benefits of drinking or not drinking are emphasized.

The third module is the *REBT* (Rational-Emotive Behavior Therapy) construct and includes both a detailed explanation of the basic philosophical approach ("People are disturbed not by things, but by the view they take of them," Epictetus, 1st Century BCE) and the role of REBT in defusing intense emotions before they reach a level at which they inhibit rational thinking (rage, depression), rather than containing them at the cooler level (anger or sadness). The goal at every meeting is to do at least one ABC(DE) exercise, wherein the participants learn to recognize and dispute the irrational beliefs that are creating their "hot" emotions before the distress rises to the level that it provokes an urge to drink or use drugs.

The fourth module deals with *lifestyle changes*: new people, new hobbies, new volunteer activities, new career choices. Filling the void left by the absence of alcohol or drugs is not easy for many people, and the examples of how various attendees have accomplished this feat are helpful to the others in a group. Writing a specific plan is emphasized. Rehearsals for important events such as job interviews, weddings and holidays are done in the group setting. Relaxation/meditation training instruction is used periodically to demonstrate the natural approach to enhancing the brain's chemical milieu.

Moderation Management. Moderation Management (MM) is a group harm-reduction program targeted at alcohol abusers or problem drinkers, with the goal of preventing progression to alcohol dependence. Participants must abstain for 30 days before joining a group. MM provides information about alcohol, moderate drinking guidelines and limits, drink monitoring exercises, goal-setting techniques, and self-management strategies. The program also attempts to help members find moderation and balance in the rest of their lives.

PROGRAM CHARACTERISTICS

Most alternative programs share the following elements:

Permanent Abstinence. Except for one (Moderation Management), all alternative programs advocate permanent abstinence for those who are afflicted with serious drug/alcohol problems or dependency. Some recognize the reality that certain serious and persistent alcohol abusers can return to social, non-abusive drinking, but believe that the frequency of this is so low as to make the data almost irrelevant; therefore, they find it imprudent not to make abstinence the goal of the treatment process.

Recognition of the Importance of Choice in Addiction Care. This is the implicit or explicit essence of all the non-traditional groups. Most attendees of and participants in these programs have attended Twelve Step meetings and found themselves unable or unwilling to participate fully. A few enjoy the fellowship and support and continue to attend, although the alternative program is usually their chosen pathway to sobriety.

Rejection of the "Disease Concept." Some groups, such as Women for Sobriety, appear to accept the disease paradigm, though they may quibble about the details. Others do not consider addiction a disease. Some consider the question irrelevant.

TABLE 1. Alternative Mutual Help and Self-Help Programs

Alcoholics Victorious (The Institute for Christian Living) Westview Business Center 620 Mendelssohn Avenue, #105 Golden Valley, MN 55427-4351 Phone: 612/593-1791
CALIX (The Society) 7601 Wayzata Blvd. Minneapolis, MN 55426 Phone: 612/546-6209
JACS (Jewish Alcoholics, Chemically Dependent Persons and Significant Others Foundation) 197 Broadway, Room M-7 New York, NY 10002 Phone: 212/473-4747
Moderation Management Network, Inc. P.O. Box 6005 Ann Arbor MI 48106 Phone: 810/788-8040
Men For Sobriety P.O. Box 618 Quakertown, PA 18951 Phone: 1-800/333-1606
Rational Recovery[sm] P.O. Box 800 Lotus, CA 95651 Phone: 1-800/303-2873
Secular Organizations For Sobriety P.O. Box 5 Buffalo, NY 14215-0005 Phone: 716/834-2922
SMART Recovery[sm] c/o Alcohol and Drug Abuse Self-Help Network, Inc. 24000 Mercantile Road, Suite 11 Beachwood, OH 44122 Phone: 216/292-0220
Women For Sobriety P.O. Box 618 Quakertown, PA 18951 Phone: 1-800/333-1605

Absence of Labeling. Most alternative groups do not focus on the necessity of the participant's admission that he or she is an "alcoholic" or "addict." Many people begin to attend meetings while in the preparation phase, or occasionally even while in the contemplation phase, and can benefit from the meetings by gradually moving toward the action phase; these individuals may be able to accept the severity of their situation only gradually. Additionally, most alternative groups are not interested in members developing an identity as "an alcoholic" or "an addict"; they prefer that participants feel as much like a normal person as possible, since their recovery may depend on their self-image and self-acceptance.

Rejection of the Concept of a Lifetime in Recovery. Most of the alternative groups take the view that although a participant must know that he/she never can drink or use drugs again, individuals nonetheless can recover from an addiction and get on with their lives without becoming part of the "recovery culture." The object of such groups is to return members to the routine of everyday life, albeit with an altered lifestyle. Such groups tend to want participants not to develop dependence on a group to replace dependence on a drug. Generally, about a year is considered a fair trial of a program, after which it is felt that an individual, unless he/she wishes to continue in a leadership capacity, should be preparing to return to a lifestyle of lifetime sobriety without reference to a "treatment" component.

Acceptance of Pharmacologic Therapy. Although Twelve Step programs do not prohibit the use of medically prescribed drugs, many Twelve Step members are sceptical of the practice. Most alternative programs, on the other hand, encourage the appropriate use of anxiolytics (or, preferably, antidepressants) for anxiety disorders, antidepressants for depression and anti-craving drugs, such as naltrexone.

Unity of the Addictions. Some alternative groups maintain a focus solely on alcohol abuse. SMART Recovery and Secular Organizations for Sobriety explicitly invite participation by those with alcohol and other drug problems, emphasizing the unity of the fundamental issues in all addictions. This approach also recognizes the fact that many participants are experiencing problems with more than one addictive substance.

Frequency of Meetings. Most alternative groups place less emphasis on frequent attendance at meetings than do Twelve Step groups, typically suggesting participation in one to two meetings per week (with "homework").

Cross-talk. Cross-talk (i.e., confrontation and interruption) is encouraged by alternative groups. Groups are kept small to encourage discussion and remain small because of "graduations."

THE NEED FOR ALTERNATIVE APPROACHES

Hester and Miller (1989) reviewed the alcoholism treatment outcomes literature and concluded that:

- No single approach to treatment is superior for all individuals. In fact, different individuals respond to quite different treatment approaches.
- The state of the art is an array of empirically-supported alcoholism treatment options.
- The appropriate question is not "Which treatments are best?" but rather, "Which types of individuals are most appropriate for a given program?"; "For this individual, which approach is most likely to succeed?"; "Is it possible to match individuals to optimal treatments, thereby increasing treatment effectiveness and efficiency?"

CONCLUSIONS

We have probably not seen the last of these non-traditional group creations. Just as in religions, there are different tastes, styles, emphases and depths. It is interesting that in recent Yale studies of the efficacy of naltrexone, the coping skills (cognitive-behavioral therapy) groups that emphasized preventing lapses from escalating to relapses had the lowest rates of relapse, and the supportive therapy groups that emphasized abstinence had the highest rates of absolute abstinence. Based on this experience, it is possible that we will see another bevy of non-traditional programs, each with permutations that appeal to one or another niche segment of substance abusers. Through emphasis on specific programs, emerging areas of scientific knowledge will seek to achieve specific goals for various subgroups of persons with addictive disorders.

REFERENCES

Chiauzzi E (1993). Taboo topics in addiction treatment: An empirical review of clinical folklore. *Journal of Substance Abuse Treatment* 10:303–316.

Cleveland M & Arlys G (1989). *The Alternative 12 Steps: A Secular Guide to Recovery*. New York, NY: Health Communications.

Fox V (1998). *Addiction, Change and Choice: The New View of Alcoholism*. Tucson, AZ: See Sharp Press.

Galanter M, Egelko S & Edwards H (1994). Rational Recovery: Alternative to AA for addiction? *American Journal of Drug Abuse* 19(4):499–510.

Hester RK & Miller WR (1989). *Handbook of Alcoholism Treatment Approaches: Effective Alternatives*. New York, NY: Pergamon Press, 11–12.

Kasl CD (1992). *Many Roads, One Journey: Moving Beyond the 12 Steps*. New York, NY: Harper Collins.

Lindstrom L (1992). *Managing Alcoholism: Matching Clients to Treatments*. New York, NY: Oxford University Press.

Marlatt GA & Tapert SF (1993). Harm reduction: Reducing the risks of addictive behaviors. In JS Baer, GA Marlatt & RJ McMahon (eds.) *Addictive Behaviors Across the Lifespan: Prevention, Treatment, and Policy Issues*. Newbury Park, CA: Sage Publications.

Miller WR & Rollnick S (1991). *Motivational Interviewing: Preparing People to Change Addictive Behavior*. New York, NY: Guilford Press.

Mooney AJ, Eisenberg A & Eisenberg H (1992). *The Recovery Book*. New York, NY: Workman, 324.

O'Malley SS, Jaffe AJ, Chang G, Schottenfeld RS, Meyer RE & Rounsaville B (1992). Naltrexone and coping skills therapy for alcohol dependence: A controlled study. *Archives of General Psychiatry* 49:881–887.

Prochaska J, Norcross JC & DiClemente CC (1994). *Changing for Good*. New York, NY: Avon Books.

Schaler JA (1995). The Addiction Belief Scale. *International Journal of the Addictions* 30(2):117–134.

Schaler JA (1997). Addiction beliefs of treatment providers: Factors explaining variance. *Addiction Research* 4:367–384.

Shaffer HJ & Jones SB (1989). *Quitting Cocaine: The Struggle Against Impulse*. Lexington, MA: Lexington Books.

Trimpey J (1996). *Rational Recovery: The New Cure for Substance Addiction*. New York, NY: Pocket Books.

Tuchfeld BS (1981). Spontaneous remission in alcoholics: Empirical observations and theoretical implications. *Journal of Studies on Alcohol* 42:626–641.

Velten E (1993). Self-help and self-directed change. *Annual Review of Addiction Research and Treatment* 3:199–220.

Waterhouse GJ, Roback HB, Moore RF & Martin PR (1997). Perspectives of treatment efficacy with the substance dependent physician: A national survey. *Journal of Addictive Diseases* 16(1):123–138.

Chapter 4

Spiritual Components of the Recovery Process

John N. Chappel, M.D., FASAM

Spirituality and Health Professionals
Benefits of Spirituality
Attainment of Spiritual Health
Spirituality in Clinical Practice

Spirituality can be defined as the relationship between an individual and a transcendent or higher being or force or mind of the universe (Peterson & Nelson, 1987). This relationship is personal to the individual and does not require affiliation with any religion; in fact, religion is not necessary for a person to have a spiritual experience or to develop his or her own spirituality. While spirituality does not require religion, it does require theology: i.e., a theory of this higher being, mind, or power.

SPIRITUALITY AND HEALTH PROFESSIONALS

According to Lukoff, Lu and Turner (1992), "Health professionals have not accorded religious and spiritual issues in clinical practice the attention warranted by their prominence in human experience." Medical undergraduate and specialty training virtually ignores religious and spiritual issues. Even psychiatry offers little or no instruction in this area which can so often have a profound effect on patients' lives (Sansone, Khatain & Rodenhauser, 1990). The reasons for this omission are rooted in two important influences. The first, and perhaps most important, is that modern medical ethics demand that physicians provide equal care regardless of their patients' (or their own) religious beliefs (American Psychiatric Association, 1990). The second is the explosion in medical technology and the resulting emphasis on biomedical issues in medical education and practice.

The loss of psychosocial knowledge and skill in medical education led to development of the biopsychosocial model, which now is taught in most medical schools and which has had some impact on medical practice, particularly in family medicine. Hiatt (1986) and Kuhn (1988) augmented Engel's work by proposing an expansion to a biopsychosocial/spiritual model, on the grounds that adding spiritual approaches could help unify the technical aspects of medicine with such diverse matters as medical ethics and attitudinal influences in healing. There is little evidence that this suggestion has had any influence on medical education or practice.

Addiction medicine, however, cannot ignore spiritual issues. If former patients are asked about the factors leading to long-term recovery from alcohol or other drug addictions, a large number mention spiritual experiences or motivation. The most important source of such spiritual experiences in recovery is participation in a Twelve Step program, such as Alcoholics Anonymous (AA). The Twelve Step approach to spiritual experience is one that specialists in addiction medicine should understand, clinically support and communicate to their colleagues who care for alcohol- and other drug-addicted patients.

BENEFITS OF SPIRITUALITY

Why should an individual make any effort to develop spirituality or work on their spiritual health? The main reason for making the effort has to do with the benefits that result:

Humility. Khantzian and Mack (1989) state that "the power and awe engendered by an outside universe and our humble place in it instill a sense of a force or power greater than ourselves." They argue that this experience "may be a step in the direction of taming and transforming infantile omnipotence and serving in early childhood to establish a capacity for object love." "In this context God serves as a 'self-object' in transition from self love to object love and provides much needed authority and structure within the self."

Humility can be a powerful stimulus for healing by engendering honesty and a willingness to accept help. In humility, we know ourselves as fallible individuals who make mistakes. It then is unnecessary to make excuses, blame others, or tell lies when a problem arises.

Inner Strength. The experience of a higher power within oneself leads to a sense of being able to deal with adversity. This makes it possible for the individual to face painful situations and to continue the struggles that so often are necessary in life.

A Sense of Meaning and Purpose. Spiritual experience often leads to a greater interest and intention in living. This may be as specific as promoting healing in medical practice or as general as working to improve or sustain the quality of life on earth. This experience is a major reason for associating service with spiritual health.

Robert Coles, a child analyst, spent years studying children from different cultures and various religious backgrounds. He concluded that most, if not all, children struggle with the concept of God and attempt to find meaning and purpose in their lives. His concluding comment is: "So it is that we connect with one another, move in and out of one another's lives, teach and heal and affirm one another, across space and time—yet how young we are when we start wondering about it all, the nature of the journey and of the final destination!" (Coles, 1990).

Acceptance and Tolerance. The internal experience of being accepted and cared for by a power greater than oneself leads to acceptance of oneself. This is the first step toward accepting others as they are. Acceptance and tolerance are facilitated by humility, with the individual recognizing the fact that it is difficult enough to live his or her own life without trying to direct, control, or destroy the lives of others.

Harmony. Closely related to acceptance is the experience of being in harmony with the universe. This experience leads to an interest in preserving and protecting our environment. It also leads to a sense of connectedness to all other human beings and living things.

Other qualities could be described, including the sobriety that is so important in addiction medicine. There is, however, more benefit to be derived from focusing on a few key issues rather than dwelling on complex theoretical issues which atheist and agnostic health care professionals can more justifiably ignore.

Booth (1991) described spirituality as "an inner attitude that emphasizes energy, creative choice, and a powerful force for living. . . . There are four qualities that increasingly reflect healthy spirituality the more we develop them in our lives. They are truth (honesty), energy (vitality), love, and acceptance." AA puts it more simply: "Spirituality is the ability to get our minds off ourselves" (Pittman, 1988).

ATTAINMENT OF SPIRITUAL HEALTH

The attainment of physical and mental health requires more than the belief that they can be experienced. Both require active effort and practice on the part of each individual. The roles of exercise, nutrition, and physiologic monitoring have been well established. Less is known about the relationship between body and mind, but most of us practice thinking, problem-solving, management and expression of feelings, and the maintenance of long-term relationships in a social support system.

What areas of practice and exercise are needed if we are to attain and maintain a relationship with a higher power? Five activities could be postulated as useful in this area:

Prayer. Attempts to communicate with a higher power have been effective for many people. Books have been written on how to pray. One simple fact to remember is that communication with another includes listening as well as talking. Anyone can pray: at issue are the results. As one recovering alcoholic said, "I came into this program a drunken atheist. Today I pray. . . . As an atheist, I faked prayer in the beginning. The results have altered my view of the cosmos. . . . This change in a drunken, hardcore, cynical atheist is a miracle beyond human comprehension" (AA, 1985).

Maintaining an Open Mind. Clearing the mind through meditation may be a way of opening one's self to the experience of a higher power. Many persons experience new ideas and energy—in addition to mental and physical benefits—when they practice meditation. The best results appear to be obtained through disciplined practice.

Discussion. We can learn much from the experience of others. Unfortunately, social prohibitions make discussion about spiritual issues difficult; for example, military personnel are cautioned not to discuss religion because of the arguments and fights that so often ensue. Anxiety at the prospect of ridicule and rejection poses another barrier to discussion of spiritual issues. The Twelve Step programs, by valuing personal experience and refusing to evaluate or judge anyone's experience, have created a forum where people can be comfortable discussing their spiritual beliefs and experiences or lack of them.

Reading. The recorded thoughts and experiences of others can be useful in developing one's own ideas and experiences. The classic literature of each of the world's great religions provides examples that often are stimulating and inspiring. Kurtz and Ketcham (1992) have gathered stories from both religious and secular sources to illustrate the spirituality of imperfection.

Religious Activity. Worship services in all religions are designed to help participants strengthen their contact with a higher power and improve their spiritual health. (That this activity alone is insufficient to attain spiritual health is evidenced by the unspiritual behavior of many when they are not in a place of worship.)

As yet there are no empirical data to support the relationship of these activities to healing. The amount of time and energy that should be devoted to the attainment of spiritual health is unknown. In this regard, it is useful to recall the example of aerobic exercise. Although the aspects of such exercise are easily measurable, it took years for scientists to demonstrate its beneficial effect on physical health and longevity. Those of us who had experienced the benefits of aerobic exercise in our own lives did not wait for the controlled studies. We made the effort, noted how much better we felt, and modified our lifestyles.

The same is true of activities that contribute to mental and spiritual health. As potentially beneficial activities (such as Step 11) are identified and practiced on a regular basis, it will be possible to measure their effects on different areas of health.

SPIRITUALITY IN CLINICAL PRACTICE

The specialist in addiction medicine or addiction psychiatry must have a working knowledge of the potential role of spirituality in enhancing recovery from alcoholism and other drug addictions. Knowledge and skill in supporting a patient's spiritual experience and the work necessary to develop and maintain spiritual health do *not* require spiritual beliefs on the part of the health care professional. The atheist or agnostic physician is at no greater disadvantage than is the physician who smokes or is overweight in helping patients deal with those problems. In any case, it is important that the physician refrain from any attempt to persuade the patient to adopt a particular set of religious beliefs. In this context, the physician is offered the following guidelines, which have been adapted from principles articulated by the American Psychiatric Association (1990):

- Maintain respect for each patient's beliefs.
- Obtain information about the religious or ideologic orientation and beliefs of patients so that they can be attended to in the course of treatment.
- If conflict arises in relation to such beliefs, handle it with a concern for the patient's vulnerability to the physician's attitudes.
- Develop empathy for the patient's sensibilities and particular beliefs.
- Do not impose one's own religious, anti-religious, or ideologic concepts in the course of therapeutic practice.

Some patients may wish to enter a religiously based treatment program. There is no reason to discourage them. After studying several programs in New York and surveying the literature, Muffler, Langrod and Larson (1992) concluded that "religious programs have demonstrated successful outcomes comparable to those of secular treatment regimens. Religious commitment and treatment by religious practitioners are playing a vital role for many in addictive treatment care."

Know Alcoholics Anonymous. This program is recommended because it provides the best practical example of a spiritual program that is not a religion. This fact is not always recognized in the professional literature. For example, Galanter (1990), although he recommends the clinical use of AA, refers to it as a zealous self-help group and compares it to cults. After describing Bill W.'s initial spiritual experience, he states that "Bill went on from this experience to preach to other alcoholics and, as with the cultic groups described above, the forces of shared belief and group cohesiveness have become central in the engagement process of AA." The key fact missed in this description is that, after a few months of preaching that failed to sober up a single alcoholic, Bill W. stopped preaching and began sharing his experience. It took less than three years for AA to discover that a religious approach did not work for many alcoholics. AA then separated from the Oxford Movement and only included a uniquely personal spiritual experience with a higher power as each individual alcoholic understood this concept.

Inquire About the Benefits Associated with Spiritual Health. These include the humility, inner strength, sense of meaning and purpose, evidence of acceptance and tolerance, and sense of harmony with others and the world already described. Kurtz and Ketcham (1992) add gratitude and forgiveness as benefits of spiritual health; indeed, their research in this area found that "the experience of being able to forgive was preceded by some experience of being forgiven."

CONCLUSIONS

Although powerful arguments can be made against including spiritual issues in addiction medicine, an even stronger case can be made for their inclusion. The experiences of so many recovering alcoholics and other drug addicts cannot be ignored. As physicians, it is useful for us to practice acceptance of the varied spiritual experiences of our patients and to support them as helping their recovery.

As practitioners of addiction medicine and addiction psychiatry, we have an obligation to demonstrate knowledge and skill in supporting spiritual issues in treatment of addictive disorders.

REFERENCES

Alcoholics Anonymous (1976). *AA: Alcoholics Anonymous: The Story of How Many Thousands of Men and Women Have Recovered from Alcoholism, 3rd Ed.* New York, NY: Alcoholics Anonymous World Service, Inc.

Alcoholics Anonymous (1985). *AA: Best of the Grapevine.* New York, NY: AA Grapevine, Inc.

American Psychiatric Association (1990). Committee on Religion and Psychiatry: Guidelines regarding possible conflict between psychiatrists' religious commitments and psychiatric practice. *American Journal of Psychiatry* 47:542.

Anonymous (1944). Bill W.: Basic concepts of Alcoholics Anonymous. *New York State Medical Journal* 44:1805–1810.

Anonymous (1978). *Webster's New Twentieth Century Dictionary.* Ann Arbor, MI: Collins World Publishing.

Booth L (1991). *When God Becomes a Drug: Breaking the Chains of Religious Addiction and Abuse.* New York, NY: Tarcher/Perigree Books.

Coles R (1990). *The Spiritual Life of Children.* Boston, MA: Houghton-Mifflin Co.

Craigie FC, Liu IY, Larson DB & Lyons JS (1988). A systematic analysis of religious variables in the Journal of Family Practice, 1976–1986. *Journal of Family Practice* 27:509–513.

Cross GM, Morgan CW, Mooney AJ, Martin CA & Rafter JA (1990). Alcoholism treatment: A ten year followup study. *Alcoholism: Clinical & Experimental Research* 14(2):169–173.

Galanter M (1990). Cults and zealous self-help movements: A psychiatric perspective. *American Journal of Psychiatry* 147(5):543–551.

Hiatt JF (1986). Spirituality, medicine and healing. *Southern Medical Journal* 79:736–743.

Khantzian EJ & Mack JE (1989). Alcoholics Anonymous and contemporary psychodynamic theory. In M Galanter (ed.) *Recent Developments in Alcoholism.* New York, NY: Plenum Press, 67–89.

Kuhn C (1988). A spiritual inventory of the medically ill patient. *Psychiatric Medicine* 6:87–89.

Kurtz E & Ketcham K (1992). *The Spirituality of Imperfection: Modern Wisdom From Classic Stories.* New York, NY: Bantam Books.

Lukoff D, Lu F & Turner R (1992). Toward a more culturally sensitive DSM-IV. *Journal of Nervous and Mental Disorders* 180(11):673–682.

Muffler J, Langrod JG & Larson D (1992). "There is a balm in Gilead": Religion and substance abuse treatment. In J Lowinson (ed.) *Substance Abuse: A Comprehensive Textbook.* Baltimore, MD: Williams & Wilkins, 584–595.

Peterson EA & Nelson K (1987). How to meet your client's spiritual needs. *Journal of Psychological Nursing* 25:34–39.

Pittman B (1988). *Stepping Stones to Recovery.* Seattle, WA: Glen Abbey Books, Inc.

Sansone RA, Khatain K & Rodenhauser P (1990). The role of religion in psychiatric education: A national survey. *Academic Psychiatry* 14:34–38.

Thomsen R (1975). *Bill W.* New York, NY: Perennial Library, Harper and Row.

Veach TL & Chappel JN (1992). Measuring spiritual health: A preliminary study. *Substance Abuse* 13(3):139–147.

SECTION 10
Medical Disorders in the Addicted Patient

CHAPTER 1

Management of Common Medical Problems **731**
Alan A. Wartenberg, M.D., FASAM

CHAPTER 2

Nutrition **741**
Lawrence Feinman, M.D. and Charles S. Lieber, M.D.

CHAPTER 3

Hepatic Disorders **755**
Charles S. Lieber, M.D.

CHAPTER 4

Neurological Effects **775**
Anne Geller, M.D., FASAM

CHAPTER 5

Sleep Disorders **793**
Allan W. Graham, M.D., FACP, FASAM

CHAPTER 6

Medical Syndromes Associated with Specific Drugs **809**
Alan A. Wartenberg, M.D., FASAM

CHAPTER 7

HIV/AIDS, TB and Other Infectious Diseases **825**
Harry W. Haverkos, M.D.

CHAPTER 8

Special Problems of the Elderly **833**
James W. Smith, M.D., FASAM

SECTION COORDINATORS

ALAN A. WARTENBERG, M.D., FASAM
Medical Director
Addiction Recovery Program
Faulkner Hospital, and
Assistant Professor of Medicine
Tufts University
School of Medicine
Boston, Massachusetts

ALLAN W. GRAHAM, M.D., FACP, FASAM
Associate Medical Director
Chemical Dependency Treatment Services
Kaiser Permanente
Denver, Colorado

CONTRIBUTORS

Lawrence Feinman, M.D.
Associate Professor of Medicine
Mt. Sinai School of Medicine, and
Chief, Section on Gastroenterology
Veterans Affairs Medical Center
Bronx, New York

Anne Geller, M.D., FASAM
Associate Professor of Clinical Medicine
Columbia College of Physicians and Surgeons, and
Medical Director
Smithers Alcohol Treatment Center
St. Luke's-Roosevelt Hospital
New York, New York

Harry W. Haverkos, M.D.
Medical Officer
Office of Antiviral Drug Products
U.S. Food and Drug Administration
Rockville, Maryland, and
Staff Physician
Division of Infectious Diseases
Department of Medicine
Walter Reed Army Medical Center
Washington, D.C.

Charles S. Lieber, M.D.
Professor of Medicine & Pathology
Mt. Sinai School of Medicine (CUNY), and
Director, Alcohol Research and Treatment Center
Veterans Affairs Medical Center
Bronx, New York

James W. Smith, M.D., FASAM
Medical Director
Shick Shadel Hospital, and
Clinical Associate Professor
Department of Psychiatry and Behavioral Sciences
University of Washington School of Medicine
Seattle, Washington

CHAPTER 1

Management of Common Medical Problems

Alan A. Wartenberg, M.D., FASAM

Ischemic Heart Disease
Hypertension
Diabetes Mellitus
Cancer
Sexually Transmitted Diseases
Retroviral Infections
Hepatitis
Tuberculosis
Infections Associated with Parenteral Drug Use

A careful medical evaluation ideally should begin with a comprehensive history performed by an empathic physician who is trained in both general medical and addictive disorders. Complex, expensive and even risky diagnostic evaluations are not a substitute for a thorough basic clinical evaluation.

The physician must be aware of the general health problems that can develop independent of a patient's addiction, those problems that may interact in a variety of ways with the addiction, and those that usually are seen only in patients with addiction. Knowledge of the specific effects of the many chemical agents that are used and abused is required. Diagnostic and treatment approaches, which may differ in the patient with addiction, must be understood. The alcohol- or drug-addicted patient may present with all of the medical problems seen in any general population. While the addictive disorder may have greater or lesser influences on the presentation of other illnesses, in most cases the management of medical disorders in the patient with addiction does not differ from that of any other patient. However, compliance issues, drug interactions and safety considerations may play a role in management decisions. Patients also may not have a history of close and trusting relationships with medical professionals. In some cases, both the patient and the physician may believe that there is a "hidden agenda" and may engage in rationalization, minimalization or denial of symptoms. In other cases, there may be a somatic focus and a multiplicity of symptoms that are difficult to interpret.

It should be stressed that the occurrence of a medical problem in a patient with addiction does not mean that addiction is necessarily the cause; a thorough history, examination, appropriate laboratory testing and thoughtful consideration of the differential diagnosis are indicated.

An acute medical illness provides an important opportunity to leverage a patient's positive motivations to change his or her alcohol and other drug use. Physical illness is a powerful biologic means of getting the patient's attention and initiating behavior change. For example, giving advice to quit smoking after a patient has had a myocardial infarction leads to a 32% to 61% quit rate, as measured one year later (Taylor, Houston-Miller et al., 1990). However, delivering similar advice at the time of a routine office visit leads to only a 4% quit rate, which is only marginally better than the baseline yearly quit rate of 2.5% (Fiscella & Franks, 1996). Physicians and other providers need to make the most of the "teachable moments" that medical illnesses and their patients' symptomatic complaints provide. Helping patients understand the links between their diseases and their substance use can leverage behavior change.

Patients with serious medical problems require special attention to their emotional needs, since the anxiety associated with diagnosis and treatment of medical problems can be a strong trigger for relapse. Every effort should be made to present information in a supportive manner; it may be appropriate in some cases to temporize discussion of abnormal findings until the patient is past the withdrawal period and has established a trusting relationship with the physician and counseling staff. In other cases, information must be presented more urgently. Careful assessment of the patient's emotional state, including the presence or risk of depression and suicidal ideation, should be part of the overall evaluation. In some cases, psychiatric consultation and treatment may be warranted.

If the attending physician does not have a background in general medicine, it is important that consulting physicians with appropriate training be available to assist in management, particularly when the other medical problems are, or are likely to become, unstable. Consultants ideally should have or develop skills in addiction medicine, so that they can operate as part of the team, interact with the patient in an empathic and supportive manner, and understand the context of the treatment of medical issues in the treatment of the patient's addiction issues.

ISCHEMIC HEART DISEASE

The review of systems in all patients should include questions regarding risk factors for coronary disease (family history, smoking history, presence of elevated cholesterol, history of diabetes, sedentary lifestyle) and specific questions regarding presence of chest pain or pressure, atypical anginal presentations (neck, jaw or arm pain, etc.), palpitations or cardiac awareness, dizziness or syncope, dyspnea and edema. Physical examination generally is unrevealing in the asymptomatic patient at rest, but blood pressure, pulse and respiratory rate should be recorded, and a careful cardiovascular and pulmonary examination performed, including inspection, palpation, percussion and auscultation of the chest. If the history or examination is suggestive, an electrocardiogram and chest x-ray may be appropriate. It must be stressed that a normal resting electrocardiogram does not rule out the presence of organic heart disease. Similarly, the presence of nonspecific changes in ST segments or T waves, poor R wave progression or non-diagnostic Q waves does not necessarily indicate the presence of heart disease. Cardiologist readings of EKGs should not be uncritically accepted; the attending physician must put them into the context of the patient's overall clinical presentation.

In patients with chest pain or discomfort brought on by specific situations such as heavy exercise, emotion or exposure to cold, avoidance of the precipitating factor should be encouraged. The use of sublingual nitroglycerine for rare events may be appropriate treatment, but in most cases treatment with regular scheduled medication is indicated. Beta blockers are very useful drugs, but may present problems in the patient with addiction when compliance is an issue, particularly in those abusing alcohol and other sedative-hypnotics, since abrupt discontinuation of beta blockers may cause exacerbation of angina and precipitate myocardial infarction, and this may be further exacerbated by the hyperautonomic state induced by sedative withdrawal.

Long-acting nitrates can be very useful drugs. These include transdermal nitroglycerine patches and long-acting oral forms. Tolerance and tachyphylaxis to oral nitrates occurs; the use of newer forms (isosorbide mononitrate) and regimens involving longer intervals between doses may reduce this event (Fung, 1993). Calcium channel blockers may be the most useful drugs in patients with addictive disorders, since they do not cause as much vasodilatation (with consequent headache, dizziness or flushing) as nitrates (which also may be exacerbated by alcohol), and they are not associated with a rebound syndrome if they are abruptly discontinued. The choice of medication should be based on individual patient characteristics. The use of beta blocking drugs in patients using cocaine who present with chest pain is controversial; nitrates and calcium channel blockers may be safer choices, or use of concomitant alpha blocking agents can be considered.

Congestive heart failure is treated with diuretics, angiotensin-converting enzyme inhibitors and digitalis glycosides. Cardiomyopathy, including alcoholic cardiomyopathy, may respond poorly to digitalis, with increased likelihood of digitalis toxicity (Zakhari, 1991). Evaluation should exclude other causes of heart failure, and echocardiography can be helpful in differentiating systolic from diastolic dysfunction, which may require differing therapies. Since alcoholic cardiomyopathy can coexist with ischemic heart disease, absolute abstinence from alcohol must be stressed in all patients with congestive heart failure. The once-common practice of prescribing "medicinal" alcohol, which may reduce afterload by producing vasodilatation, as well as having an anxiolytic effect, must be decried in the patient with an addictive disorder. Alcohol and other sedative-hypnotic withdrawal, opiate withdrawal, and the abuse of stimulants—particularly cocaine—may markedly exacerbate the manifestations of ischemic heart disease, producing unstable angina, infarction, arrhythmias, worsening congestive failure, and sudden death.

HYPERTENSION

In patients who present with untreated hypertension, or in those who have discontinued treatment, it may be appropriate to monitor blood pressures without pharmacologic treatment if the patient is without symptoms, there are no signs of target organ damage (left ventricular hypertrophy, hypertensive retinopathy, proteinuria or renal insufficiency), and the blood pressure is not in a range associated with risk of cerebrovascular events (generally > 200/100). In pregnancy, there may be cause for concern even if the blood pressure is in the "normal" range, since such pressure actually may be indicative of preeclampsia.

Expectant management, with appropriate treatment of any withdrawal syndromes, salt restriction and rest may decrease blood pressure within one or two days. If blood pressure remains elevated, medical evaluation is warranted if not previously carried out. In elderly patients, elevated blood pressure readings may result from "lead-pipe" arteries with significant calcification. If high pressures are found in the absence of evidence of target organ effects, and particularly if there are differences between the left and right arm, consideration should be given to a spurious elevation. Cannulation of the artery with direct measurement of the blood pressure may be necessary in some cases.

Work-up for secondary hypertension may be warranted in younger patients, those without family histories of hypertension, histories suggestive of episodic hypertension, presence of abdominal or flank bruits on examination, or in those where screening laboratory evaluation suggests a secondary cause (hypokalemia, urinary sediment abnormalities). Evaluation should include, in addition to a complete history and physical examination, serum electrolytes, urinalysis, BUN/creatinine, fasting blood sugar and a lipid profile (the latter should be done when the patient is well past any abstinence syndrome). A screening electrocardiogram may be useful, particularly in the patient whose hypertension is likely to be of longer standing. A chest x-ray may be obtained where coarctation of the aorta is suspected on the basis of younger age, carotid-femoral pulse delay, difference in blood pressure between arms or lower blood pressure in the legs.

More elaborate evaluation should be limited to patients in whom the screening evaluation is suggestive, and generally can be carried out on an elective basis.

Patient education is critical in the treatment of hypertension. Since hypertension seldom is associated with symptoms, the patient must understand the need for long-term therapy and follow-up, and the importance of not discontinuing therapy without adequate supervision. In many cases, non-drug trials of weight loss, smoking cessation, stress reduction and anxiety management techniques should be tried before drug treatment. Asymptomatic patients should rarely, if ever, be treated on the basis of a single elevated pressure. In the presence of addiction, a period of observation in the absence of the abused drug may be rewarded with normalization of the blood pressure without other intervention.

DIABETES MELLITUS

The management of diabetes in the patient with addiction may be particularly challenging. The caloric load of alcohol, particularly in the form of beer, may lead to obesity. Alcohol-induced malnutrition may deplete glycogen stores, and alcohol impairment of gluconeogenesis may increase likelihood of hypoglycemia. Abstinence syndromes may be associated with high levels of catecholamines and cortisol, and may increase the chance of infection; the injection drug user may experience a number of severe infections that affect diabetic control.

In patients presenting with diabetic ketoacidosis, insulin therapy is required. Hyperglycemia in excess of 400 mg% also generally requires insulin, although expectant management with aggressive treatment of abstinence syndromes may cause a decrease in blood sugar. A trial of abstinence from alcohol and other drugs, in combination with appropriate diet, is warranted in patients with blood glucose in the 200 to 300 range or less. Oral hypoglycemic drugs may be effective with less chance of producing acute hypoglycemia. As with hypertension, treatment of diabetes in the asymptomatic patient rarely is indicated on the basis of one abnormal reading. Serial determinations of fasting blood sugar and two-hour postprandial blood sugars generally are adequate for diagnosis. Glucose tolerance tests, measurement of serum insulin and other more sophisticated tests are indicated only in selected cases where the diagnosis is in doubt.

Close monitoring of the patient for relapse is particularly important in the diabetic patient, since continued use of the same dose of insulin or an oral agent may become dangerous in the presence of alcohol or other drug intoxication or an abstinence syndrome. It may be appropriate to allow the patient to have mild hyperglycemia early in recovery, since the deleterious effects of hypoglycemia may be more damaging. When a firm sobriety program is established, tighter control may be more desirable and more readily attainable.

CANCER

Patients with addiction may be at greater risk for various cancers, either because of the inherent carcinogenicity of their drug (alcohol, tobacco), associated infections (hepatitis C), or other environmental or dietary factors associated with their addiction. Patients entering treatment should have a screening evaluation adequate to detect both the risk and the presence of cancer. Such evaluation should be followed by an educational and counseling program to reduce subsequent risk of cancer and increase chances of early detection and treatment.

A history of weight loss, malaise, weakness, unexplained fever, chills or night sweats can suggest a number of chronic illnesses, including cancer. More specific symptoms, such as hemoptysis, change in bowel habits, hoarseness, dysphagia, etc., may suggest specific cancers. Physical examination can reveal abnormal skin lesions, enlarged lymph nodes, hepatosplenomegaly, ascites or pleural effusions, prostate nodules, etc. Laboratory screens may show anemia, abnormal liver function tests, positive hepatitis B or C studies, hypercalcemia, occult blood in the stool or a pulmonary lesion.

Many treatment programs include a "medical aspects" series designed to discuss not only the effects of addiction, but to educate patients about common problems such as heart disease and cancer. While the focus must remain on the patients' addiction, it is possible to evaluate individual patients for the risk and presence of cancer, as well as to educate patients in groups about reduction of risk factors (especially smoking cessation). Patients should be referred for routine, periodic screening studies; it may be inappropriate to carry out such studies while the patient is in addiction treatment. In the patient where the presence of cancer is a serious possibility, more urgent evaluation can be recommended.

SEXUALLY TRANSMITTED DISEASES

Patients with addictive disorders may be more likely to develop sexually transmitted diseases (STDs) for a variety of reasons. The disinhibiting and amnestic effects of alcohol and the sedative-hypnotic drugs may promote casual sexual activity without protective precautions. Both women and men may engage in prostitution, either directly for drugs (as is common with crack cocaine) or for money for drugs. Increased numbers of partners increase the likelihood of exposure to STDs. Ulcerating lesions, such as those of genital herpes, may increase the infectious potential of other STDs, including HIV infection (Moss & Kreis, 1990). A complete history of sexual activity should be obtained from all patients, including those being evaluated for addictive disorders. Symptoms of recurrent ulcers, genital or perianal lesions, and oral or dermatologic manifestations should be sought, and physical examination should include careful evaluation where appropriate. In patients with symptoms of penile or vaginal discharge, particularly where known contact has occurred, gram stain and culture should be obtained, for both Neisseria gonorrheae and chlamydia species. Other STDs, including chancroid and granuloma inguinale, may require specialized stains and culture. Herpetic infections may have a typical presentation, but special stains (Tzanck preparation) may be needed to demonstrate typical giant cells when the presentation is unusual.

Treatment depends on the particular microbiology. A single intramuscular dose of ceftriaxone (250 mg), followed by doxycycline 100 mg po twice daily for seven days is adequate for uncomplicated gonorrhea and any associated chlamydial infection. More complicated STDs may require consultation with infectious disease specialists and more extensive treatment (Centers for Disease Control, 1993b).

Syphilis has become a more complicated issue in the HIV era, and there has been a worldwide increase in prevalence. Serologic tests for syphilis (STS) commonly are performed in many programs, with most using the Rapid Plasma Reagin (RPR). It is not uncommon for IDUs to have a false biologic positive (FBP) STS; in some cases it may be indicative of bacterial endocarditis or collagen-vascular disease, but in most it is a non-specific reaction to repeated exposure to injected antigens. A confirmatory test, such as the fluorescent treponemal antibody-absorbed (FTA-ABS) or microhemaglutination assay-Treponema pallidum (MHA-TP), must be done before a diagnosis of syphilis is made. There have, however, been case reports of advanced syphilis with negative confirmatory studies (Hook, 1992).

In cases where the typical primary genital, anal or oral lesion is present, treatment is uncomplicated, and generally consists of a single intramuscular dose of 2.4 million units of benzathine penicillin; the same treatment is adequate for dermatologic manifestations of secondary syphilis, or the early latent phase (Hook, 1992; Centers for Disease Control, 1993b). If the infection cannot be dated, treatment is more problematic. There is controversy over the routine use of lumbar puncture in unselected patients, or even in those with known or suspected HIV infection. In patients with symptoms compatible with neurosyphilis, lumbar puncture should be carried out, as should usual studies, including CSF VDRL (Dowell, Ross et al., 1992; Holton, Larrsen et al., 1992). If neurosyphilis (asymptomatic or symptomatic) is proven or strongly suspected, more aggressive treatment with 10 to 14 days of parenteral penicillin is required.

Because of the increased virulence of syphilis in the HIV-positive individual, as well as the possible increased resistance to usual treatment, all patients with positive syphilis confirmatory tests should be considered for HIV testing, and all HIV-positive individuals should be tested for syphilis. Despite the controversy over treatment, it probably is reasonable to treat the patient with three weekly intramuscular injections of 2.4 million units of benzathine penicillin, while re-checking the RPR titer after several months. Failure to reduce the titer should lead to repeat treatment, and failure of second courses may be followed by evaluation for neurosyphilis and more aggressive treatment (Hook, 1992; Centers for Disease Control, 1993b). Ceftriaxone therapy may be more effective in these cases (Dowell, Ross et al., 1992).

RETROVIRAL INFECTIONS

The advent of the human immunodeficiency syndrome has had catastrophic consequences for homosexual and bisexual men, injecting drug users who share infected paraphernalia, sexual partners of those infected, children born to infected mothers, and those who received contaminated blood products or organ donations in the period before HIV antibody testing was available. Other forms of exposure—such as from infected patients to health professionals exposed to needle sticks or mucocutaneous contact with infected material—rarely occur; very rare reports of individuals infected by health care professionals, or through exposure to infected secretions through skin or mucous membranes in more casual settings, have occurred and have had the unfortunate effect of creating an atmosphere of fear.

The relationship of AIDS and substance abuse has been reviewed (Wartenberg, 1991a, 1991b; Karan, 1990; Selwyn & O'Connor, 1992). Physicians who work with individuals at risk for HIV infection should develop a working knowledge base of usual presentations and treatment. Research evidence suggests that IDUs can make significant changes in their risk behaviors, and that needle exchange programs can reduce HIV seroconversion and serve as an entry to drug treatment (Watters, Estilio et al., 1994). Physicians need to be more involved in the treatment of IDUs in a variety of care settings (O'Connor, Molde et al., 1993; Wartenberg, Nirenberg & Clifford, 1994).

The physician should be able to provide HIV risk assessment, to educate patients about how to reduce their risk behaviors, and to assess patients for the appropriateness of HIV antibody testing. It has been shown that testing is well-accepted by many alcohol and drug treatment populations (Magura, Shapiro et al., 1990; Quinn, Groseclose et al., 1992). However, in some patients, HIV antibody testing itself—as well as a positive test result—may increase anxiety and depression (Ostrow, 1986; Perry, Jacobsberg et al., 1990), and promote premature leaving of treatment, relapse to drug use and/or other self-destructive behaviors (Wartenberg, Nirenberg & Clifford, 1994). In some cases, severe depression and suicidal ideation may result (Marzuk, Tierney & Tardiff, 1988; Perry, Jacobsberg et al., 1990).

HIV antibody testing, subsequent CD4 count stratification, and determination of viral load allow the physician and patient to develop plans tailored to the patient's unique clinical profile and preferences. Early intervention, further observation without therapy, or aggressive multi-drug treatment all have their place, based on objective laboratory data. Treatment is so effective now that an optimistic approach can be taken in pretest counseling with most individuals at risk. The availability of protease inhibitors has dramatically improved the prognosis for HIV-infected patients. In fact, the mortality from continued injection drug dependence (about 10% per year) far exceeds the HIV death rate for newly diagnosed patients.

Treatment strategies and medication protocols are changing so quickly that HIV management often is best handled by an integrated infectious disease team, including physician specialists, nurse coordinators, and social service liaison personnel.

Special problems of women with HIV infection deserve special attention (Anastos & Palleja, 1991), including screening for cervical neoplasia, sexually transmitted diseases and attention to the domestic safety of the woman and her family.

For more detailed information, consult Chapter 7 in this Section.

HEPATITIS

Hepatitis C virus (HCV) infection appears to be the most common form of infectious hepatitis in patients with addictive disorders; serologic evidence of infection may be present in up to 90% of injection drug users (IDUs) and up to 25% of alcoholics and non-injecting patients (Fingerhood, Jasinski & Sullivan, 1993). HCV results in chronic hepatitis in 80% of infected patients and cirrhosis in 20% to 35% (Sharara, Hunt & Hamilton, 1996). This slowly progressive disease is the leading cause of end-stage liver disease requiring transplantation and also is strongly associated with the development of hepatocellular carcinoma. The average time from infection to cirrhosis is 21 years and to hepatocellular carcinoma, 29 years. Morbidity and mortality begin to increase about 10 to 30 years after viral acquisition. Progression is more rapid with concomitant use of alcohol. Disease activity can be assessed by liver biopsy and by measurement of HCV RNA levels.

Interferon-α2b currently is the only FDA-approved drug therapy for HCV infection; the recommended treatment course is 3 million units, subcutaneously, three times weekly for six months. Response rates are 50%, but relapses occur in 70% of patients after the initial course, yielding a sustained response rate of less than 20%. Nonetheless, cost-benefit analyses suggest interferon is as effective an intervention as cholesterol-lowering therapies for vascular disease or as screening mammography for breast cancer (Kim, Poterucha et al., 1997).

Interferon is not recommended in patients with major psychiatric problems because of the risk of relapse and worsening of depression. Additionally, interferon cannot be recommended if patients continue to use alcohol, as this practice renders the interferon even less effective. Current follow-up data suggest that patients with advanced cirrhosis are not likely to benefit from interferon. Finally, controversy surrounds treatment recommendations for patients with normal or minimally elevated serum aminotransferase levels. Watchful waiting appears to be a common approach, given the lack of long-term prognostic data for these patients.

Hepatitis B also is very common but is associated with clinically apparent infection in a minority of patients. Acute infection with hepatitis B may produce the usual rheumatological prodrome, with chronic hepatitis occurring in about 10% and associated development of cirrhosis and hepatocellular carcinoma in a significant minority. Diagnosis is by the usual serological tests; persistent hepatitis B surface antigen and E antigen are common and hyperglobulinemia often is seen. Outbreaks of delta virus co-infection with hepatitis B, associated with high mortality, have occurred among IDUs. Treatment with interferon-a has shown promise in chronic hepatitis B and has shown a high success rate in clearing the virus and decreasing hepatic inflammation (Korenman, Baker et al., 1991), with demonstrated cost-effectiveness (Dusheiko & Roberts, 1995).

TUBERCULOSIS

After many decades of reduced prevalence, recent years have witnessed a dramatic increase in cases of pulmonary tuberculosis. This epidemic is linked to the epidemic of HIV disease, but unlike HIV, can be transmitted via casual and household contact. Indeed, tuberculosis has become increasingly prevalent in poorer inner city areas; it also is endemic in many areas of Asia, Africa and South and Central America (Bates & Stead, 1993), from which immigrants come to the United States. It should be noted that IDUs have always had a higher rate of tuberculosis than the non-injecting population, and this apparently occurs in crack cocaine users as well (Centers for Disease Control, 1991).

The presentation of tuberculosis in the patient with addiction, or even the patient co-infected with HIV, usually is not different from the non-drug using population, and generally is pulmonary, involving the upper lobes. Cough, weight loss, night sweats and hemoptysis are common.

Diagnosis is via tuberculin skin testing, typical radiographic features, special sputum stains and culture. There is a high rate of anergy in patients who are co-infected with HIV. Recommendations include placing purified protein derivative (PPD) 5 units intradermally, along with at least two control skin tests (mumps, candida, tetanus, etc.). A negative PPD with a positive control (3 mm) makes tuberculous infection highly unlikely. While a positive PPD traditionally has been considered to be 10 mm or more, the HIV-positive individual may have a positive response at 5 mm or more (Barnes, Le & Davidson, 1993). There have been suggestions that anergic patients who are HIV-infected be considered for chemotherapy for prophylaxis of tuberculosis (Selwyn, Schell & Alcabes, 1992), but this strategy has not proved worthwhile (Hawken, Meme et al., 1997).

Treatment is with isoniazid 300 mg daily for six to 12 months; preliminary evidence suggests that this is effective even in HIV-infected individuals (Small, Scheckter et al., 1991). Treatment may be complicated by addiction-related issues (see below). When medical treatment is combined with drug treatment, compliance can be excellent (Selwyn, Feingold et al., 1989; Samet, Libman et al., 1992; O'Connor, Molde et al., 1993).

Treatment of active pulmonary tuberculosis has been complicated by the appearance of multidrug resistant organisms (MDR-TB) and the prophylaxis of those exposed to these organisms may be similarly complicated. Some of this resistance may have been fostered by individuals who take their medication on an intermittent or irregular basis; this is very common among IDUs, particularly those who are not receiving treatment. A variety of regimens (usually involving isoniazid, rifampin and pyrazinamide) are commonly effective in M. tuberculosis, but streptomycin, ethambutol, cycloserine and other agents may need to be used in MDR-TB (Kent, 1993). While MDR-TB thus far has been limited to outbreaks in a few geographic locations, there is increasing fear of further spread. Strong efforts to detect, treat and prevent tuberculosis infection in patients with addictive disorders need to be part of the effort to prevent this tragedy.

Atypical mycobacterial disease, particularly M. avium, M. intracellulare and M. scofulaceum—usually referred to as the M. avium-intracellulare complex (MAI or MAC)—is an AIDS-defining opportunistic infection in HIV-infected patients, as pulmonary tuberculosis has been designated (Centers for Disease Control, 1992). It produces nonspecific symptoms of anorexia and weight loss, fever, night sweats, malaise and diarrhea. Definitive diagnosis is by positive culture of blood or bone marrow, liver or lymph node, but diagnosis may be presumptive. MAI occurs in patients with profound immunosuppression, often with CD4 counts of less than 50 (Young, 1988; Beck, 1991).

INFECTIONS ASSOCIATED WITH PARENTERAL DRUG USE

Local Infections. The injecting drug user (IDU) may experience cellulitis, abscess formation and septic thrombophlebitis. Subcutaneous injection may produce induration and loss of elasticity, particularly with sclerosing drugs such as pentazocine. Intramuscular injection is particularly likely to produce abscess, but necrotizing fascitis, gas gangrene and pyomyositis also may occur (Cherubin, 1971; Biederman & Hiatt, 1987). Causative organisms generally are staphylococcus aureus or epidermitis, streptococci and gram-negative bacilli. Unusual complications related to injection into veins in the neck, subclavian area, or femoral triangle may occur, including mycotic aneurysm; compartmental syndromes with potential for limb loss may be seen (Stein, 1990).

Systemic Infections. An astounding array of infections may occur in the IDU. A full discussion is beyond the scope of this chapter; the reader is referred to Levine and Sobel's exhaustive text (1991) and to other pertinent reviews (Stein, 1990; Cherubin & Sapira, 1993). Septic emboli to the lung may produce pneumonia and lung abscess. Acute and sub-acute bacterial endocarditis (usually with staphylococcal species, but also with pseudomonas species, candida, anaerobes and other organisms) are very common in IDUs (Levine, 1991). Intravenous cocaine use may be associated with an elevated rate of endocarditis, perhaps because of increased frequency of injection or reduced need to solubilize cocaine solutions with heat (Chambers, Morris & Tauber, 1987). Group A beta-hemolytic streptococcal septicemia (associated with severe toxicity, fever, renal failure and cardiovascular collapse), with resulting high mortality, has been reported in IDUs (Bartter, Dascal et al., 1988; Lentner, Giger & O'Rourke, 1990). Osteomyelitis (often involving unusual sites such as the sternoclavicular joint, pubic symphysis and intervertebral spaces) is common, as is septic arthritis (Chanrasekar & Narulla, 1986).

Systemic candidal and other fungal infections may be seen in IDUs (Leen & Brettle, 1991). This is complicated in patients with HIV disease, in whom widespread fungal infections (including nocardiosis with brain and pulmonary abscess and disseminated aspergillosis) may be seen. Infections that disseminate to arteries within the brain may form pseudo-aneurysms and rupture (mycotic aneurysm). Contaminated paraphernalia or poor technique also may be responsible for a number of cases of pyomyositis. Tetanus, clostridial myonecrosis and malaria have become less common. With any long-standing or untreated infection, amyloidosis may occur (Menchel, Cohen et al., 1983) and can cause renal insufficiency.

Diagnosis of infectious complications is by history, examination, gram stain of available material, culture and serologic testing. The use of non-prescribed antibiotics by IDUs is widespread and may make culture difficult or impossible. It is not uncommon for IDUs with fever to be discharged from emergency departments with prescriptions for oral antibiotics even if a source of fever is not readily apparent. However, since studies have shown a high rate of serious disease (including pneumonia, endocarditis and other system infections) in this population, it would appear warranted to admit IDUs with fever for further evaluation and treatment (Marantz, Linzer et al., 1987; Samet, Shevitz et al., 1990).

Other Complications of Parenteral Drug Use. Most IDUs do not inject sterile purified material with aseptic technique, although some IDUs (particularly those with a medical or nursing background) may inject sterile drugs meant for parenteral use (such as morphine, meperidine, fentanyl, or pentazocine). Injected drugs also may include heroin or cocaine powders, adulterated with lactose or quinine and dissolved in contaminated water or even saliva; crushed tablets with a variety of fillers and stabilizers (including talc) put into suspension; liquids meant for oral use but given parenterally (methadone or codeine-containing cough syrups); and even boiled preparations of fentanyl patches, marijuana leaves, and other unusual combinations. (While most parenteral drug use is intravenous, drugs also may be given intramuscularly and subcutaneously by injection.) The issue of needle exchange has been highly controversial, with some addiction professionals strongly opposed on the grounds that it encourages continued drug use.

Patients may present with complications related to unusual adulterants, such as strychnine, acute or chronic injection of particulate matter such as talc, or local systemic toxic reactions to the injected drug itself. Of greater significance are the complications related to the injection of infected material, either through lack of aseptic technique and injection of skin organisms, or through the sharing of injection paraphernalia with individuals infected with hepatitis B or C, the human immunodeficiency virus (HIV), and other organisms. Complications have been extensively reviewed (Stein, 1990; Cherubin & Sapira, 1993). Some older reviews from the pre-HIV era also are well worth reading (see, for example, Louria, Hensle & Rose, 1967).

CONCLUSIONS

Patients with addictive disorders may be seen in medical, surgical, obstetrical or psychiatric units or outpatient clinics, and may be under the care of physicians of different specialties. Only a minority receive care in dedicated units for treatment of addiction. The addiction medicine specialist may be called upon to see the patient in consultation, or may be the attending physician. In whatever setting such patients are encountered, it is critical that they be afforded the same respect and dignity accorded any patient. Health professionals often have very negative attitudes toward patients with addictive disorders, and this frequently leads to escalating negative behaviors on the part of both patient and staff. The addiction medicine specialist—whether physician, nurse, social worker, psychologist or other dedicated health professional—thus must assist not only in the medical evaluation and management of the patient, but also in establishing firm behavioral contracts to assure that the mutual obligations of patient and staff are safely and effectively met. Improved attitudes, knowledge and skills on the part of caregivers can promote better care within the medical mainstream.

REFERENCES

AIDS and Chemical Dependency Committee, American Medical Society on Alcoholism and Other Drug Dependencies (1988). *Guidelines for Facilities Treating Chemical Dependency Patients at Risk for AIDS and HIV Infection, 2nd Ed.* New York, NY: American Medical Society on Alcoholism and Other Drug Dependencies.

Anastos K & Palleja S (1991). Caring for women at risk of HIV infection. *Journal of General Internal Medicine* 6(Suppl):S40–46.

Barnes PF, Le HQ & Davidson PT (1993). Tuberculosis in patients with HIV infection. *Medical Clinics of North America* 77:1369–1390.

Bartter T, Dascal A, Carrol K & Curley FJ (1988). "Toxic strep syndrome": A manifestation of group A streptococcal infection. *Archives of Internal Medicine* 140:1421–1424.

Bates JH & Stead WW (1993). The history of tuberculosis as a global epidemic. *Medical Clinics of North America* 77:1205–1217.

Beck K (1991). Mycobacterial disease associated with HIV infection. *Journal of General Internal Medicine* 6(Suppl):S19–23.

Biderman P & Hiatt JR (1983). Management of soft-tissue infections of the upper extremity in parenteral drug abusers. *American Journal of Surgery* 154:526–528.

Centers for Disease Control (1991). Crack cocaine use among persons with tuberculosis: Contra Costa county. *Morbidity and Mortality Weekly Reports* 40:485–489.

Centers for Disease Control (1992). 1993 Revised classification system for infection and expanded surveillance case definition for AIDS among adolescents and adults. *Morbidity and Mortality Weekly Reports* 41(RR-17):1–19.

Centers for Disease Control (1993a). Recommendations for HIV testing services for inpatients and outpatients in acute care hospital settings, and technical guidance on HIV counseling. *Morbidity and Mortality Weekly Reports* 42(RR-2):1–17.

Centers for Disease Control (1993b). Sexually transmitted diseases treatment guidelines. *Morbidity and Mortality Weekly Reports* 42(RR-14):1–102.

Chambers HF, Morris L & Tauber MG (1987). Cocaine use and the risk of endocarditis in intravenous drug abusers. *Annals of Internal Medicine* 106:833–836.

Chandrasakar PH & Narula AP (1986). Bone and joint infections in intravenous drug abusers. *Review of Infectious Diseases* 8:904–911.

Cherubin CE (1971). Infectious disease problems of narcotics addicts. *Archives of Internal Medicine* 128:309–313.

Cherubin CE & Sapira JD (1993). The medical complications of drug addiction and the medical assessment of the intravenous drug user: 25 years later. *Annals of Internal Medicine* 119:1017–1028.

Dowell ME, Ross PG, Musker DM, Cate TR & Baughn RE (1992). Response of latent syphilis or neurosyphilis to ceftriaxone therapy in persons infected with human immunodeficiency virus (HIV). *American Journal of Medicine* 93:481–488.

Dusheiko GM & Roberts JA (1995). Treatment of chronic type B and C hepatitis with interferon alfa: An economic appraisal. *Hepatology* 22(6):1863–1873.

Farber HW, Fairman RP & Glauser FL (1982). Talc granulomatosis: Laboratory finding similar to Sarcoidosis. *American Review of Respiratory Diseases* 125:259–261.

Fingerhood MI, Jasinski DR & Sullivan JT (1993). Prevalence of hepatitis C in a chemically dependent population. *Archives of Internal Medicine* 153:2025–2030.

Fiscella K & Franks P (1996). Cost-effectiveness of the transdermal nicotine patch as an adjunct to physicians' smoking cessation counseling. *Journal of the American Medical Association* 275(16):1247–1251.

Fung HL (1993). Clinical pharmacology of organic nitrates. *American Journal of Cardiology* 72(Suppl):9C–15C.

Gifford RW Jr (1993). The fifth report of the Joint National Commission on detection, evaluation and treatment of high blood pressure. *Archives of Internal Medicine* 153:154–183.

Hawken MP, Meme HK, Elliott LC et al. (1997). Isoniazid preventive therapy for tuberculosis in HIV-1-infected adults: Results of a randomized controlled trial. *AIDS* 11(7): 875–882.

Holton PD, Larrsen RA, Leal ME & Leedon JM (1992). Prevalence of neurosyphilis in HIV-infected patients with latent syphilis. *American Journal of Medicine* 93:9–12.

Hook EW (1992). Management of syphilis in human immunodeficiency. *American Journal of Medicine* 93:477–479.

Kaku DA & Lowenstein DH (1990). Emergence of recreational drug use as a major risk factor for stroke in young adults. *Annals of Internal Medicine* 113:821–827.

Kaplan MH, Hall WW, Susin M, Pahwa S, Salahuddin SZ & Hellman C (1991). Syndrome of severe skin disease, eosinophilia and dermatopathic lymphadenopathy in patients with HTLV-II complicating HIV infection. *American Journal of Medicine* 91:300–309.

Karan LD (1990). Primary care for AIDS and chemical dependency. *Western Journal of Medicine* 152:538–542.

Kent JH (1993). The epidemiology of multidrug-resistant tuberculosis in the United States. *Medical Clinics of North America* 77:1391–1409.

Kim WR, Poterucha RR, Hermans JE et al. (1997). Cost-effectiveness of 6 and 12 months of interferon-α therapy for chronic hepatitis C. *Annals of Internal Medicine* 127:866–874.

Korenman J, Baker B, Waggoner J, Everhart JE, Di Bisceglie AM & Hoofnagle JH (1991). Long-term remission of chronic hepatitis B after alpha interferon therapy. *Annals of Internal Medicine* 114:629–634.

Lee H, Swanson P, Shorty VS, Zack JA, Rosenblatt JD & Chen IS (1989). High rate of HTLV-II infection in seropositive i.v. drug abusers in New Orleans. *Science* 244:471–475.

Lee HH, Weiss SH, Brown LS, Mildvan D, Shorty V & Saravolatz L (1990). Patterns of HIV-1 and HTLV-I/II in intravenous drug abusers from the Middle Atlantic and central regions of the USA. *Journal of Infectious Diseases* 162:347–352.

Leen CL & Brettle RP (1991). Fungal infections in drug users. *Journal of Antimicrobial Chemotherapy* 28:83–96.

Lentner AL, Giger O & O'Rourke E (1990). Group A beta hemolytic streptococcal bacteremia and intravenous substance abuse: a growing clinical problem? *Archives of Internal Medicine* 150:89–93.

Levine DP (1991). Infectious endocarditis in intravenous drug users. In DP Levine & JD Sobel (eds.) *Infections in Intravenous Drug Abusers*. New York, NY: Oxford University Press, 231–185.

Louria D, Hensle T & Rose J (1967). The major medical complications of heroin addiction. *Annals of Internal Medicine* 67:1–22.

Magura S, Shapiro JL, Grossman J, Siddiqui Q, Lipton DS, Amann KR, Koger J & Gehan K (1990). Reactions of methadone patients to HIV antibody testing. *Advances in Alcohol and Substance Abuse* 8:97–111.

Marantz PR, Linzer M, Feiner C, Feinstein SA, Kozin AM & Friedland GH (1987). Inability to predict diagnosis in febrile intravenous drug abusers. *Annals of Internal Medicine* 106:823–828.

Marzuk PM, Tierney H & Tardiff K (1988). Increased risk of suicide in persons with AIDS. *Journal of the American Medical Association* 259:1333–1337.

Menchel S, Cohen D, Gross E, Fragione B & Gallo G (1983). AA protein-related amyloidosis in drug addicts. *American Journal of Pathology* 112:195–199.

Miller A, Taub H, Spinak A, Pilipski M & Brown LK (1991). Lung function in former intravenous drug abusers: the effect of ubiquitous cigarette smoking. *American Journal of Medicine* 90:678–684.

Moss GB & Kreis JK (1990). The interrelationship between HIV infection and other sexually transmitted diseases. *Medical Clinics of North America* 74:1674–1660.

O'Connor PG, Molde S, Henry S, Shockcor WT & Schottenfeld RJ (1993). Human immunodeficiency virus infection in intravenous drug users: A model for primary care. *American Journal of Medicine* 93:382–385.

Ostrow DG (1986). Psychiatric consequences of AIDS: An overview. *International Journal of the Neurosciences* 29:1–3.

Perry SW, Jacobsberg LB, Fishman B, Weiler PH, Gold JW & Francis AJ (1990). Psychological responses to serological testing for human immunodeficiency virus. *Acquired Immune Deficiency Syndrome* 4:145–152.

Quinn TC, Groseclose SL, Spence M, Provost O & Hook EW 3rd (1992). Evaluation of the human immunodeficiency virus epidemic among patients attending sexually transmitted disease clinics: a decade of experience. *Journal of Infectious Diseases* 165:541–544.

Rubin AM (1987). Neurological complications of intravenous drug abuse. *Hospital Practice* (15 April):279–288.

Salanova V & Taubner R (1984). Intracerebral hemorrhage and vasculitis secondary to amphetamine use. *Postgraduate Medical Journal* 60:429–430.

Samet JH, Libman H, Stegler KA, Dhawan RK, Chen J, Shevitz AH, Dewees-Dunk R, Levinson S, Kufe D & Craven D (1992). Compliance with zidovudine therapy in patients infected with HIV type 1: A cross-sectional study in a municipal hospital clinic. *American Journal of Medicine* 92:495–502.

Samet JH, Shevitz A, Fowle J & Singer DE (1990). Hospitalization decision in febrile intravenous drug users. *American Journal of Medicine* 89:53–57.

Selwyn PA, Feingold AR, Iessa A, Satyadeo M, Colley J, Torres R & Shaw JFM (1989). *Annals of Internal Medicine* 111:761–763.

Selwyn PA & O'Connor PG (1992). Diagnosis and treatment of substance abusers with HIV infection. *Primary Care* 19:119–156.

Selwyn PA, Schell BM & Alcabes B (1992). High risk of active tuberculosis in HIV-infected drug users with cutaneous anergy. *Journal of the American Medical Association* 268:504–509.

Sharara AI, Hunt CM & Hamilton JD (1996). Hepatitis C. *Annals of Internal Medicine* 125(8):658–668.

Small PM, Scheckter GF, Goodman PC, Sande MA, Chaisson RE & Hopewell PC (1991). Treatment of tuberculosis in patients with advanced human immunodeficiency virus infection. *The New England Journal of Medicine* 324:289–294.

Stein MD (1990). Clinical review: Medical complications of intravenous drug use. *Journal of General Internal Medicine* 5:249–257.

Taylor CB, Houston-Miller N, Killen JD & DeBusk RF (1990). Smoking cessation after acute myocardial infarction: Effects of a nurse-managed intervention. *Annals of Internal Medicine* 113:118–123.

Wartenberg AA (1991a). Into whatever houses I enter: HIV and injecting drug use (editorial). *Journal of the American Medical Association* 271:151–152.

Wartenberg AA (1991b). HIV disease in the intravenous drug user: Role of the primary care physician. *Journal of General Internal Medicine* 6(Suppl):35–40.

Wartenberg AA, Nirenberg TD & Clifford P (1994). Patient perceptions of adverse consequences to HIV antibody testing in the chemical dependency treatment setting: Risks of elopement, relapse, depression and suicidal ideation. *Journal of Substance Abuse*.

Watters JK, Estilo MJ, Clark GL & Lorvick J (1994). Syringe and needle exchange as HIV/AIDS prevention for injection drug users. *Journal of the American Medical Association* 271.

Young LS (1988). Mycobacterium avium complex infection. *Journal of Infectious Diseases* 157:863–867.

Zakhari S (1991). Vulnerability to cardiac disease. *Recent Developments in Alcoholism* 9:225–260.

CHAPTER 2
Nutrition

Lawrence Feinman, M.D.
Charles S. Lieber, M.D.

Nutritive Value of Alcoholic Beverages
Alcohol and Appetite
Alcohol and Nutritional Status
Water-Soluble Vitamins
Fat-Soluble Vitamins
Pathogenesis of Liver Disease
Nutritional Therapy

Alcohol contributes 4.5% of Americans' total calories (Scheig, 1970)—10% for adult drinkers. Ethanol may provide more than half the daily energy needs in heavy drinkers.

NUTRITIVE VALUE OF ALCOHOLIC BEVERAGES

Alcoholic beverages contain little of nutritive value except water, variable amounts of carbohydrate, and ethanol, which can serve as an energy source, but whose metabolic impact is profound. The carbohydrate content of alcoholic beverages is nil for whiskey, cognac or vodka, from 2 to 10 g/L for red or dry white wine, 30 g/L for beer or dry sherry, and as much as 120 g/L for sweetened white or port wines. The content of protein and vitamins in these beverages is extremely low, except for beer. An individual would have to drink a liter of beer daily to satisfy his need for nicotinic acid, 15 to 20 liters for protein, and 25 liters for thiamin. Iron content may be appreciable, especially in wines. Occasionally the amounts of iron, lead or cobalt actually reach harmful levels. The significance of congener content is still debated (Feinman & Lieber, 1988).

Although the combustion of ethanol in a bomb calorimeter yields 7.1 kcal/g, its biological value is less when compared to carbohydrates. Despite higher total caloric intakes (alcohol included), drinkers are not more obese than nondrinkers (Gruchow, Sobocinski et al., 1985). Subjects given additional calories as alcohol under metabolic ward conditions fail to gain weight (Lieber, Jones & DeCarli, 1965). Isocaloric substitution of ethanol for carbohydrate, as 50% of total calories in a balanced diet, results in a decline in body weight; when given as additional calories, ethanol causes less weight gain than calorically equivalent carbohydrate or fat (Pirola & Lieber, 1972). Others have reported variable responses to additional calories as ethanol (Crouse & Grundy, 1984): lean individuals did not gain weight, but half of the obese individuals did gain some weight. Others could detect no weight changes in healthy men over a two-week period, using moderate amounts of alcohol (Contaldo, D'Arrigo et al., 1989), 75 g/day substituted on a calorie basis for all foods in the diet, while others detected a drop in weight in alcoholic men after only four days of a substantial dose of alcohol, 40% to 60% of calories (168 g/day for a 70 kg man) substituted for glucose (Reinus, Heymsfield et al., 1989). The meaning of these findings would have been clearer had the weight changes been large enough for body composition studies to have been done.

The increase in metabolism caused by ethanol consumption probably contributes to the failure of ethanol to consistently support body weight or to promote weight gain. For example, oxygen consumption after ethanol ingestion increases in normal subjects, and more so in alcoholics. Substitution of ethanol for carbohydrates increases the metabolic rate of humans and rodents. Also, an increase in thermogenesis occurs in humans and rats fed ethanol: a 15% increase in thermogenesis occurred in rats after only 10 days of ethanol intake (Stock & Stuart, 1974). Although some of the energy wastage was attributable to brown fat thermogenesis in rats (Rothwell & Stock, 1984) and is suppressible by sympathectomy, most of it is not. Studies in "normal" males whose usual alcohol intake was less than five alcoholic beverages per day showed a thermic effect of small doses of ethanol (20 grams) (Westrate, Wunnink et al., 1990). Diet-induced thermogenesis (DIT) was increased during the time of maximal ethanol oxidation, compared to the effects of an isocaloric control meal not containing ethanol. Recently, it was found that either addition of ethanol to the diet or substitution of it for other foods increased 24-hour energy expenditure and decreased fat oxidation in man (Suter, Schutz & Jequier, 1992).

Thus, alcoholic beverages provide little nutritive value aside from calories; as an energy source, alcohol is not as adequate as equivalent carbohydrate.

ALCOHOL AND APPETITE

Alcohol intake appears to be "unregulated" for the moderate drinker, so that alcohol intake in the range of 20 g/day supplements rather than displaces macronutrient-derived calories (de Castro & Orozco, 1990), thereby adding 140 kcal/day. Even intakes in the range of 50 g/day generally were taken as additional calories, although at these levels alcohol began to be substituted for sucrose calories (Colditz, Giovannucci et al., 1991). When individuals had been classified as restrained versus unrestrained eaters, it was found that alcohol consumption increased the amount of food taken by restrained eaters (Polivy & Herman, 1976a, 1976b). Patients admitted to hospital with severe liver disease typically are anorectic.

ALCOHOL AND NUTRITIONAL STATUS

Patients admitted to hospitals for medical complications of alcoholism have a history of inadequate dietary protein intake (Patek, Post & Ratnoff, 1948) and have signs of protein malnutrition (Mendenhall, Bongiovanni et al., 1985). For this group of hospitalized patients, anthropomorphic measurements indicate impaired nutrition: height/weight ratio is lower, muscle mass estimated by creatinine/height index is reduced, and triceps skin folds are thinner. Continued drinking is associated with weight loss while abstinence is associated with weight gain, both in patients with and without liver disease.

It is clear from many reports that the average patient who drinks to excess is not malnourished, or is so to a lesser extent than those hospitalized for medical problems. Patients with moderate intakes of alcohol, and even those admitted for alcohol rehabilitation, may hardly differ nutritionally from controls.

The wide variation in nutritional status that exists in alcohol drinkers prompts a closer look at what they eat. Moderate alcohol intake in which alcohol accounts for less than 16% of total calories (alcohol included) is associated with a slightly elevated energy intake (Gruchow, Sobocinski et al., 1985; de Castro & Orozco, 1990). Despite comparable levels of physical activity, there is no weight gain compared to nondrinkers, perhaps because of the energy considerations discussed above. Intake of alcohol above 23% of calories (Hillers & Massey, 1985) is associated with a beginning substitution of alcohol for carbohydrate calories (Colditz, Giovannucci et al., 1991), at which point women begin to exhibit loss of weight. When the percentage of calories as alcohol exceeds 30%, significant decreases in protein and fat intake occur; the intake of vitamins A, C and thiamine may fall below the recommended dietary allowances (Hillers & Massey, 1985). Calcium, iron and fiber intake also are appreciably lowered (Gruchow, Sobocinski et al., 1985). Decreased dietary intake has been considered a major cause of malnutrition in alcoholic cirrhotics.

In summary, alcoholism is characterized by a broad spectrum of malnutrition, with the vast majority of alcoholics having slight if any detectable impairment. However, when alcohol intake approaches about 25% of daily calories, deficient intake of important nutrients becomes likely. Alcoholics with medical complications requiring hospitalization generally have severe nutritional deficits.

Protein. The effect of ethanol *per se* on overall protein metabolism, measured as nitrogen balance, is to spare nitrogen when given as additional calories, but to cause increased urinary urea when used as an isocaloric substitute for carbohydrate. An increase in urea nitrogen could reflect protein that has escaped small bowel absorption and has been converted to ammonia in the colon and subsequently to urea by the liver. Ethanol causes impaired hepatic amino acid uptake, increased serum branched chain amino acids, impaired protein secretion from the liver (probably related to alterations in microtubules), decreased gluconeogenesis and retention of proteins in enlarged hepatocytes (Lieber, 1992). Manipulation of dietary protein is not suggested during active alcoholism. In the abstinent patient with cirrhosis, protein requirements are not abnormal.

Carbohydrates. The clinical problems of carbohydrate metabolism include hyperglycemia, which is common, but is rarely severe or life-threatening; hypoglycemia, which is uncommon, mostly occurs in conjunction with fasting or prolonged very poor intake (except in children), and can be lethal; and disaccharide (mostly lactose) malabsorption.

Hyperglycemia: In large population studies, alcohol intake correlates with hyperglycemia. Aside from patients with chronic pancreatitis and endocrine (insulin) insufficiency, there is no ready explanation for this. Insulin resistance caused by alcohol has been demonstrated in healthy subjects using the insulin clamp technique (Yki-Järvinen & Nikkilä, 1985), whereby glucose utilization can be measured during glucose infusions at steady blood glucose and insulin levels.

Hypoglycemia: In the fed state, when liver glycogen is abundant, glycogenolysis supports blood glucose levels. In the fasting state, the following pathways that can support blood glucose are interfered with by concomitant metabolism of alcohol: gluconeogenesis from amino acids, formation of glucose from glycerol, lactate, and galactose. The increase in NADH/NAD ratio due to hepatic metabolism of alcohol is partly responsible for these metabolic changes. Changes in enzyme activities relevant to various metabolic steps of gluconeogenesis have been noted. From a clinical standpoint, hypoglycemia should be suspected when an alcohol imbiber exhibits altered mental status (even in the fed state, especially in children). Provision of glucose, usually intravenously, is simple and effective.

Lipids. Alcohol ingestion is associated with fatty infiltration of the liver, hyperlipidemia, and ketosis, each of which is largely explained by the effects that alcohol has upon the metabolism of lipids (Lieber & Pignon, 1989).

Fatty liver is composed of triglycerides having fatty acids derived from dietary sources, when available, but of endogenously synthesized ones when dietary fatty acids are not available. High-fat diets increase the amount of fat that accumulates. Low-fat diets, high-protein diets and even hypocaloric diets lessen the amount of fat that accumulates as a result of alcohol ingestion, but do not completely prevent fatty liver. Dietary fat composed of triglycerides of medium chain length causes less hepatic fat accumulation than fat containing triglycerides of long-chain fatty acids.

The administration of ethanol to man consistently results in hyperlipidemia; the extent is modified by associated dietary and pathologic conditions. The major elevation occurs in serum triglycerides, with some cholesterol elevation; the involved lipoproteins are very low density lipoproteins (VLDL) and chylomicrons, dietary particles formed by the intestines. High-density lipoproteins (HDL) also are increased by ethanol. Alcoholic hyperlipemia usually is composed mostly of VLDL, but may sometimes have increased chylomicrons. Hyperlipemia usually is absent with severe liver injury (e.g., cirrhosis), where hypolipemia may occur.

Some patients may have marked hyperlipemia during alcohol ingestion. This probably represents an underlying genetic defect in lipid metabolism in addition to the effects of alcohol, such as hyperchylomicronemia (Type I), due to decreased post-heparin lipoprotein lipase activity, carbohydrate sensitive hyperlipidemia, diabetes, obesity, pancreatitis or other diseases.

The treatment of alcohol-induced hyperlipidemia consists of abstinence from alcohol and provision of a normal diet. The lipemia should rapidly disappear. Persistent hyperlipemia requires investigation for genetic or other causes not related to alcohol.

Moderate alcohol intake, except for a recent study of pre-menopausal women which showed increased HDL_2 and HDL_3, is associated with an increase in the fasting levels of a species of high-density lipoprotein cholesterol (HDL_3), whose significance regarding risk for heart disease (unlike that of HDL_2), has not been formally established. Therefore, it is not clear whether any decreased risk for coronary heart disease associated with moderate alcohol intake can be attributed to increased levels of HDL due to alcohol. HDL_2 increases with more substantial alcohol intake but, at that level of consumption, alcohol is not cardio-protective and may even be deleterious.

Alcohol intake often is accompanied by ketosis, with minimal or absent acidosis. Blood glucose usually is normal. The extent of ketosis will be underestimated unless care is taken to measure beta hydroxybutyrate as well as acetoacetate (more common to diabetic ketosis). Abstinence from alcohol and return to normal diet usually is all that is required. Fluid and electrolytes may be given. Insulin usually is not necessary.

WATER-SOLUBLE VITAMINS

Thiamine. Thiamine deficiency usually is present in alcoholics in our society, and is responsible for Wernicke-Korsakoff syndrome and Beri beri heart disease; it also may contribute to polyneuropathy. When prolonged thiamine deprivation was induced in the Rhesus monkey, neuroanatomical lesions comparable to the human syndrome were produced without the need for concomitant alcohol intake.

Thiamine intake certainly will be insufficient for those alcoholics who rely on alcoholic beverages for most of their energy needs. However, when obvious deficiency symptoms are not present, it is difficult for the physician to assess thiamine status. Blood thiamine concentration is not often used clinically.

Thiamine should be provided to all alcoholics because, as a group, they suffer an appreciable incidence of thiamine deficiency. It is difficult to clinically assess any but the most glaring thiamine deficiency syndromes; it is important to reverse early neurologic disease, and thiamine replacement is easy and safe. Fifty mg/day of thiamine should be given parenterally until oral intake can be established, followed by 50 mg/day orally for weeks, or longer if neurologic problems persist.

Riboflavin. When there is a general lack of B vitamin intake, riboflavin deficiency may be encountered. Alcoholics tend to shun dairy products, an important source of riboflavin. Deficiency was found in 50% of a small group of patients whose medical complications were severe enough to warrant hospital admission (Rosenthal, Adham et al., 1973). While none exhibited the classic signs of riboflavin deficiency (cheilosis, glossitis, angular stomatitis), they had an abnormal activity coefficient (AC), which returned to normal two to seven days after intramuscular replacement with 5 mg riboflavin daily.

Riboflavin is readily absorbed from a saturable site in the proximal small bowel, excreted in the urine when ingested in excess, and has no described toxicity. It usually is given to alcoholic patients as part of a multivitamin preparation.

Pyridoxine. Neurologic, hematologic, and dermatologic disorders can be caused in part by pyridoxine deficiency. Pyridoxine deficiency, as measured by low plasma pyridoxal-5'-phosphate (PLP), was reported in over 50% of alcoholics without hematologic findings or abnormal liver function tests. Inadequate intake may partly explain low plasma PLP, but increased destruction (acetaldehyde playing a role) and reduced formation also seem to be important.

Clinical management generally involves provision of pyridoxine in the usual multivitamin dosage unless neuropathy or pyridoxine responsive anemia has been diagnosed. Since ataxia due to sensory neuropathy has been ascribed to toxicity from as little as 200 mg of pyridoxine per day, the indiscriminate use of large doses of this vitamin must be avoided.

Folic Acid. Alcoholics tend to have a low folic acid status when they are drinking heavily and their folic acid intake is reduced (World, Ryle et al., 1984). Malnourished alcoholics without liver disease also absorb folic acid less well, when compared to their better nourished counterparts (Halsted, Robles & Mezey, 1971). It has not been clearly shown, however, that either protein deficiency or alcohol (Halsted, Robles & Mezey, 1971; Lindenbaum & Lieber, 1971) decreases folate absorption. Thus, it remains unclear what aspects of malnutrition adversely affect folate absorption and under what clinical circumstances alcohol may interfere with folate absorption.

Alcohol accelerates the production of megaloblastic anemia in patients with depleted folate stores and suppresses the hematologic response to folic acid in folic acid-depleted patients (Sullivan & Herbert, 1964). Alcohol given acutely causes a decrease in serum folate, partly explained by increased urinary excretion (Russell, Rosenberg et al., 1983); alcohol given chronically to monkeys decreases hepatic folate levels, partly due to the inability of the liver to retain folate (Tamura, Romero et al., 1981) and perhaps partly due to increased urinary and fecal losses (Tamura & Halsted, 1983).

The clinical approach to folate deficiency without anemia is straightforward. A diet providing adequate folate, perhaps with additional folate, will replete stores in a matter of weeks. If malabsorption persists after this period, evaluation for causes other than folate deficiency should be instituted. When the patient is anemic, the diagnostic evaluation is more complex (Lindenbaum, 1982). In addition to folate deficiency, the direct effect of alcohol on the bone marrow, liver disease, hypersplenism, bleeding, iron deficiency, infection, and the use of anticonvulsants all are commonly encountered, and will exert separate and combined influences on the hematologic picture. It should be kept in mind that in well-nourished alcoholics folic acid deficiency is a rare cause of anemia (Eichner, Buchanan et al., 1972) and, moreover, that a search for folic acid deficiency (serum or red cell folate levels) as an explanation for anemia is unwarranted unless some or all of the morphologic features of the vitamin deficiency are present (involving macroovalocytes, hypersegmentation of polymorphonuclear leukocytes, or megaloblastosis of the bone marrow).

Vitamin B_{12}. Alcoholics do not commonly get vitamin B_{12} deficiency. Serum vitamin B_{12} levels usually are normal in patients with folate deficiency, whether they have cirrhosis or not. The low prevalence of clinically significant deficiency is probably due to the large body stores of vitamin B_{12} and the reserve capacity for absorption, since there are several factors in the context of alcoholism which would favor depletion. Pancreatic insufficiency, for example, results in decreased vitamin B_{12} absorption as measured by Schilling test. In this situation, there is insufficient lumenal protease activity and alkalinity, which normally serve to release vitamin B_{12} from "r" protein, secreted by salivary glands, intestines, and possibly stomach. Alcohol ingestion also has been shown to decrease vitamin B_{12} absorption in volunteers after several weeks of intake (Lindenbaum & Lieber, 1975).

Vitamin C. The vitamin C status of alcoholic patients (mostly admitted to hospital) is poorer than that of nonalcoholics, as measured by serum ascorbic acid, peripheral leukocyte ascorbic acid, or urinary ascorbic acid after an oral challenge (Bonjour, 1979). In addition to a lower mean ascorbic acid level for the alcoholic group compared to controls, some 25% of patients with Laennec's cirrhosis had serum ascorbic acid levels below the range of healthy controls (Bonjour, 1979). Ascorbic acid levels are low in alcoholic patients with and without liver disease.

When alcohol exceeds 30% of total calories, vitamin C intake generally falls below recommended dietary allowances (Gruchow, Sobocinski et al., 1985). However, inadequate ascorbic acid intake provides only a partial explanation for low ascorbic acid levels. For patients who are not clearly scorbutic, it is unknown if their low ascorbic acid levels have clinical significance. Daily supplementation with 175 to 500 mg of ascorbic acid may be necessary for weeks to months to restore plasma ascorbate and urinary ascorbate to normal (Bonjour, 1979).

FAT-SOLUBLE VITAMINS

Vitamin A. The interaction of alcoholism with vitamin A is of particular interest because it involves the intake and possibly the absorption of the vitamin and its metabolism; and because there is evidence that alcohol may modulate the role of vitamin A in hepatotoxicity.

Vitamin A ingestion is not significantly below normal for Americans who drink up to a mean of 400 calories of alcohol per day (or less than 20% of total calories) (Gruchow, Sobocinski et al., 1985), since the vitamin A density of the nonalcoholic portion of the diet approximates that eaten by control populations. Americans who consume 24% of their energy as alcohol ingest 75% of the RDA for vitamin A (Hillers & Massey, 1985). Since the RDA for vitamin A is falling (Olson, 1987), these drinkers still may not have significantly subnormal intakes. Intense alcoholism (in which 50% or more of energy is derived from alcohol) may be associated with even less vitamin A intake. The effect of alcohol on vitamin A absorption in man was shown to be inhibitory (17% reduction by 120 ml of wine) in a single study (Althausen, Uyeyama & Loran, 1960). When fat malabsorption due to chronic alcoholic pancreatitis occurs, vitamin A absorption is further reduced.

Hepatic vitamin A stores are decreased by alcohol consumption, whether vitamin A intake is low, normal or high. In humans, hepatic vitamin A levels progressively decrease with increasing severity of lesions to cirrhosis (Leo & Lieber, 1985) inducible by alcohol (Leo, Kim & Lieber, 1986).

The clinical consequences of altered vitamin A levels include an increased incidence of night blindness. There is a poor correlation of serum retinol, retinyl esters, retinol binding protein, and albumin with tissue stores. The correlation of serum vitamin A with tissue stores is especially complicated by liver disease, protein deficiency and zinc deficiency. Hepatic alterations from low vitamin A intake includes the presence of multivesicular lysosomes and is potentiated by concomitant alcohol intake. Hepatotoxicity—including fibrosis—of increased vitamin A also is potentiated by concomitant alcohol.

Therapy is complicated by several factors: the difficulty in assessing tissue stores of vitamin A, the toxicity of high doses of vitamin A, the potential toxicity of even normal doses of vitamin A concomitant with continued intake of alcohol (or other microsome inducing drugs), and the difficulty of monitoring vitamin A hepatotoxicity in the presence of continued alcohol intake. Therefore, vitamin A replacement should be modest for patients who cannot be assured an alcohol- and drug-free environment. More liberal vitamin A replacement may be considered for those who can be confirmed as deficient and who can be assured abstinence from alcohol. Deficiency would be established as night blindness (or abnormal dark adaptation) with low serum vitamin A (<30 μg/dL or 1.4 μM/L). Determination of hepatic vitamin A, while ideal, is not practical. Vitamin A at doses of 3,000 to 5,000 units/day for several weeks would be an adequate trial. A low serum zinc (< 80 μg/dL) should prompt simultaneous replacement with $ZnSO_4$. Zinc also might be given subsequent to a failed trial of vitamin A. (It must be stressed that these recommendations are not based on rigorous clinical trials.)

Vitamin D. It is clear that alcoholics have illnesses related to abnormalities of calcium, phosphorus, and vitamin D homeostasis. They have decreases in bone density and bone mass, increased susceptibility to fractures, and increased osteonecrosis. Low blood calcium, phosphorus, magnesium, and 25 (OH) vitamin D have been reported, indicating disturbed calcium metabolism.

In patients with alcoholic liver disease, vitamin D deficiency probably derives from too little vitamin D substrate which results from poor dietary intake, malabsorption due to cholestasis and/or pancreatic insufficiency, and insufficient sunlight.

Osteomalacia in patients with liver disease should be treated by increasing intake of vitamin D_3, ultraviolet irradiation therapy, and correction of fat malabsorption, to keep plasma calcium, phosphorus, and 25-OH D normal.

Vitamin K. Vitamin K deficiency in alcoholism arises when there is an interruption of fat absorption due to pancreatic insufficiency, biliary obstruction or intestinal mucosal abnormality secondary to folic acid deficiency. Inadequacy of dietary vitamin K is not a likely cause of clinical deficiency unless there is concomitant sterilization of the large gut, a reliable source of the vitamin. Alcohol-induced hepatocyte injury interferes with utilization of available vitamin K, with a consequent drop in blood levels of clotting factors (II, VII, IX, X) whose syntheses depend on this vitamin. Vitamin K serves as a cofactor for the microsomal carboxylase reaction that results in posttranslational modification of these proteins, the conversion of glutamic acid residues to gamma-carboxyglutamic acid residues, necessary for function. Abnormally high levels of inactive factor II (prothrombin) are found in the plasma (Blanchard, Furie et al., 1981) in the presence of cirrhosis or vitamin K deficiency. If there is doubt as to whether hepatocellular dysfunction or lack of availability of vitamin K to the liver is responsible for low vitamin K dependent clotting factors in the blood, a trial of intramuscular vitamin K is helpful.

Vitamin E and Selenium. Although malnutrition has been dismissed as the sole cause of liver disease in the alcoholic for lack of evidence and the abundant data about the direct hepatotoxicity of ethanol have been reviewed, it remains necessary to consider the possibility that—in the setting of alcoholism, with the known attributes of ethanol metabolism—specific nutrients and metabolic intermediates, had they been more abundant, might have prevented hepatotoxicity.

Acetaldehyde is produced as the first product of ethanol metabolism. The harmful effects of acetaldehyde derive from its abilities to link covalently to proteins and to foster lipid peroxidation. It activates collagen-producing mesenchymal cells, forms protein adducts with microsomal cytochrome P4502El, tubulin, fatty acid binding protein, and others, some of which form neoantigens: the mechanisms by which these events result in cell damage are beyond the scope intended here. Acetaldehyde causes lipid peroxidation in isolated perfused livers, and evidence supports the occurrence of lipid peroxidation after ethanol administration in nonhuman primates (Shaw, Jayatilleke & Lieber, 1981) and in humans (Shaw, Rubin & Lieber, 1983). Lipoperoxidation long ago was proposed as a mechanism of alcohol-induced hepatotoxicity and increasingly is accepted.

Cysteine, which is a constituent of glutathione, along with glutamic acid and glycine, has the capacity via its mercaptan group to react with acetaldehyde, thereby rendering it less toxic. Glutathione is a major cell scavenger of toxic free radicals, and also spares and potentiates the function of other of the cells' guardians against peroxidative, free radical or electrophylic attack, such as vitamin E. Hepatic glutathione is depressed by ethanol, in part due to acetaldehyde, which may selectively deplete the mitochondria of glutathione (Hirano, Kaplowitz et al., 1992). The liver cell thus is left vulnerable to all manner of injuries mediated by peroxidative or other (electrophylic) mechanisms. Chronic ethanol feeding in rats depresses hepatic methionine synthetase with eventual fall in liver S-adenosyl-L-methionine levels. It is of great interest that glutathione levels can be restored by providing S-adenosyl-L-methionine, thereby lessening hepatotoxicity as measured by leakage of mitochondrial glutathione dehydrogenase into the blood stream (Lieber, Casini et al., 1990). This may be a prototypical example of a nutrient in relative deficiency, by the criterion that its provision in supernormal amounts counteracts expected deleterious events.

Vitamin E and selenium can be discussed jointly, since they serve a protective role as antioxidants and interact physiologically. Vitamin E and selenium behave synergistically: vitamin E reduces selenium requirements, prevents its loss from the body and maintains it in an active form; selenium spares vitamin E and reduces the requirement for the vitamin.

Vitamin E deficiency only recently has been recognized as a complication of alcoholism. Alcoholic patients with chronic pancreatitis, especially with fat malabsorption, were reported to have low serum vitamin E levels. One would anticipate that symptomatic deficiency would be delayed by large body stores in adults. Although vitamin E seems well "positioned" metabolically, when relatively deficient, to be important in allowing ethanol to cause hepatotoxicity by the mechanisms discussed, further evidence is needed, especially at early stages of ethanol-induced liver damage, to confirm its role in human disease. No special dietary recommendations for vitamin E can be made for the alcoholic at this time.

Selenium metabolism is of great theoretic interest to hepatologists in view of the proposed lipoperoxidative mechanism of drug- and alcohol-induced liver injury (Lieber, 1987). Serum selenium levels were noted to be low in alcoholics, especially with liver disease, but this could be a consequence of liver injury since other, nonalcoholic patients with liver disease also have low levels. No recommendations for dietary modification of selenium intake in alcoholism are appropriate now.

Polyunsaturated Lecithin. Choline deficiency can cause fatty liver in rats. However, there is no evidence that dietary choline deficiency causes human liver disease or is a part of ethanol-induced human liver disease. Additionally, choline therapy is not effective when alcohol intake is continued, probably reflecting low choline oxidase activity in human liver. Current evidence shows no relevance of choline deficiency hepatotoxicity to that induced by ethanol in humans or in experimental animals, and it is unlikely that choline supplementation could be provided safely as treatment.

Polyunsaturated lecithin (PUL) affords protection from alcohol-induced cirrhosis in the baboon mode (Lieber, Casini et al., 1990). Polyenylphosphatidylcholine decreases alcohol-induced oxidative stress in subhuman primates, which may be relevant to its protective effects (Lieber, Leo et al., 1997). Neither the choline nor the linoleate moiety is protective when present in the diet, except as polyene phosphatidylcholine. PUL counteracts the acetaldehyde-induced increase in collagen accumulation *in vitro* (Casini, Cunningham et al., 1991; Li, Kim et al., 1993). PUL increases collagenase activity. It has been suggested that a failure of collagen breakdown via collagenase leads to cirrhosis (Maruyama, Feinman et al., 1982).

PUL can in no ordinary sense be considered deficient in the diets of alcoholics: however, should provision of dietary PUL in clinical trials prove to be effective in preventing alcoholic fibrosis, then it can be designated as a "super nutrient" able to correct a relative deficiency.

Minerals and Electrolytes. *Salt and Water Retention in Cirrhosis.* Alcoholics with chronic liver disease often have disorders of water and electrolyte balance. Sodium and water retention are clinically apparent as peripheral edema, ascites, and pleural effusions. Patients may have weight gain, increasing abdominal girth, ankle swelling, and respiratory difficulties or umbilical herniation as further complications. Not only is sodium retained avidly, but a water load cannot be excreted normally. Low body potassium may result from vomiting, diarrhea, hyperaldosteronism, muscle wasting, renal tubular acidosis, and diuretic therapy. Potassium depletion may contribute to the appearance of renal vein ammonia and worsen hepatic encephalopathy.

Patients with cirrhosis and fluid overload may require urgent relief, as when ascites and pleural effusion are causing respiratory difficulties or when imminent rupture of an umbilical hernia may result in lethal peritonitis. Thoracentesis and/or paracentesis should be performed promptly. Usually, however, there is no rush to diuresis patients, once a diagnostic tap has shown the fluid to be a non-infected transudate. Treatment is eventually aimed at preventing recurrence of fluid retention. Dietary management combines sodium and water restriction. It is difficult to provide a palatable diet on a long-term basis, with less then 0.5 to 1 gram of sodium and 1,500 ml of total fluid daily. At least these amounts are recommended with addition of spironolactone, followed, if necessary, by small doses of diuretics (hydrochlorthiazide or furosemide) to achieve an initial daily weight loss of no more than 0.5 kg. More rapid weight loss probably is safe when the patient has mobilizable peripheral edema and can be observed carefully. Accelerated diuresis risks renal failure. Use of prostaglandin inhibitors such as nonsteroidal anti-inflammatory drugs (NSAID) carries the potential risk of altering renal hemodynamics and precipitating renal failure. Careful monitoring for the development of hypokalemia (or hyperkalemia), hyponatremia and renal failure must be undertaken. For patients in whom a reasonable program of salt and water restriction and diuretic therapy is not successful, a peritoneal-venous (LeVeen) shunt may be useful. The best results have been obtained for patients without encephalopathy, coagulopathy, or severe jaundice.

Zinc. Zinc is an essential element for humans. Deficiency has resulted in growth retardation, male hypogonadism, rough dry skin, disordered taste, poor appetite and mental lethargy. Zinc is absorbed from the small bowel, and absorption appears to increase when deficiency is present. Among the enzymes that contain zinc are hepatic alcohol dehydrogenase (which converts ethanol to acetaldehyde); a similar enzyme, ocular retinol dehydrogenase (which converts retinol to retinal); and hepatic and erythrocyte superoxide dismutases (which serve to protect against oxidative damage).

Alcoholic cirrhosis is associated with abnormalities of zinc homeostasis, although the clinical implications are uncertain. Patients have low plasma zinc, low liver zinc, and an increase in urinary zinc. Acute ethanol ingestion, however, does not cause zincuria (Sullivan, 1962). The low zinc status of chronic alcoholics with cirrhosis is thought to be due to decreased intake and decreased absorption as well as increased urinary excretion. Many Americans have a diet that is marginal in zinc; poor protein intake is one reason. Alcoholics fall into several of the groups with marginal intake. It is interesting that zinc absorption was shown to be low in alcoholic cirrhotics but not in cirrhosis of other etiologies (Valberg, Flanagan et al., 1985). Some instances of night blindness not fully responsive to vitamin A replacement (see the discussion of vitamin A) have responded to zinc replacement. The possibility that human hypogonadism of alcoholism may involve perturbations of vitamin A and zinc interactions has been raised.

Currently the therapeutic use of zinc in alcoholism is restricted to the treatment of night blindness not responsive to vitamin A.

Magnesium. Chronic alcoholism is associated with magnesium deficiency: alcoholics have low levels of blood magnesium and low levels of body exchangeable magnesium; symptoms in alcoholics resemble those in patients with magnesium deficiency of other etiologies; alcohol ingestion causes magnesium excretion; upon withdrawal from alcohol magnesium balance is positive; hypocalcemia in alcoholics may only be responsive to magnesium repletion. The correlation of magnesium content of blood with that of other tissues, and with the severity of clinical symptoms in individual cases is imperfect, although it is statistically obvious among groups. Magnesium replacement should be seriously considered for symptomatic patients with measurably low serum magnesium, for anorectic patients with low serum magnesium, and for hypocalcemic alcoholics not responsive to calcium replacement. The majority of alcoholics will replete body stores of magnesium readily from normal dietary sources.

Iron. Alcoholics may be iron-deficient as a result of the several gastrointestinal lesions to which they are prone and which may bleed (esophagitis, esophageal varices, gastritis, duodenitis). Iron overload of the liver was described in Bantus who consumed alcoholic beverages prepared in iron containers, which thereby contributed a large amount of elemental iron to their diet. In most alcoholics, the iron content of the liver is normal or only modestly elevated, although there may be stainable iron in reticuloendothelial cells, possibly due to hepatic necrosis or bouts of hemolysis. It is unclear whether increased intestinal absorption of iron due to alcohol or hepatic uptake of iron from serum in established alcoholic liver disease contributes significantly to an increase in hepatic iron. Iron therapy should be restricted to clear states of deficiency.

Alcoholism has been reported to result in qualitative changes in transferrin, the serum transport protein for iron: a higher fraction of molecules bear a reduced sialic acid content. This provides a useful test for chronic alcohol consumption. The synthesis of transferrin is decreased at the stage of alcoholic cirrhosis and so is serum transferrin concentration. At the stage of alcoholic fatty liver, the serum transferrin concentration is normal, although both catabolic rate and presumably synthesis are increased. The significance of these changes in transferrin is not yet apparent.

THE PATHOGENESIS OF LIVER DISEASE

Undernutrition is common in one subset of alcoholics and is an important cause of illness for them. It is not surprising that disturbances in nutrition should have been considered for the etiology of alcoholic liver disease. The following section will review the evidence that alcohol is hepatotoxic of itself and how nutritional factors, in the setting of alcoholism, may influence the pathogenesis of liver disease. Lastly, this chapter will discuss the prospects for providing special nutrients to forestall the development of alcoholic cirrhosis.

Malnutrition. Malnutrition has not been shown to cause cirrhosis in human adults in the absence of other etiologic factors. Starvation *per se* does not cause prominent hepatic lesions in adult humans

(Sherlock & Walshe, 1948), certainly not those of alcoholic liver disease. However, experimental animals such as rodents are susceptible to the development of fatty liver and fibrosis when placed on a choline deficient diet. The inappropriate extrapolation of this observation to human disease was a source of confusion for a long time: it will be discussed in detail below. It has been shown, however, that malnourished cirrhotic patients, especially those on parenteral nutrition, may be deficient in choline and bear some liver function abnormalities (Chawla, Wolf et al., 1989). These patients may respond to choline supplementation with raised plasma choline (Chawla, Wolf et al., 1989).

Direct Hepatotoxic Effect of Alcohol. The role of nutrition in the pathogenesis of alcoholic liver injury (fatty liver, hepatitis, and cirrhosis) has been investigated from the perspectives of epidemiology, clinical therapeutic trials, and animal experimentation: the direct toxic effect of ethanol had in each case to be considered, and was confirmed (Lieber & DeCarli, 1991).

It appears that alcohol *per se*, given in sufficient quantities, can cause fatty liver in man (and lower animals) despite the presence of an otherwise adequate diet. The lipid and protein composition of the diet have modulating effects on the amount and/or types of fat that accumulate in the liver. For example, reduction of dietary fat to 10% of total calories (but not lower) greatly lessens, but does not completely eliminate, hepatic fat accumulation. Fatty acids of chain length found in the diet accumulate in the liver when available from the diet; otherwise endogenously synthesized fatty acids deposit. Long chain fatty acids in the diet have a greater tendency than medium chain fatty acids to promote fatty liver in the presence of ethanol. Reduction of dietary protein intake to deficient levels (4% of total calories) increases the fat accumulation caused by concomitant ethanol. However, provision of 25% of total calories as protein, which exceeds the usually recommended amount of dietary protein, will not eliminate hepatic fat accumulation. The amount of fat accumulating in the ethanol induced fatty liver is but one parameter of damage, and must be considered along with distortion of organelles such as mitochondria, the endoplasmic reticulum and plasma membranes and, also to be considered, are metabolic derangements involving impaired respiration and energy production, fatty acid oxidation and susceptibility to acetaldehyde toxicity, which are caused by ethanol intake.

The role of nutrition in the pathogenesis of alcoholic hepatitis has been studied in much less detail. It is a lesion considered too severe to be induced in volunteers.

The incidence of alcoholic cirrhosis has been linked to per capita ethanol consumption. The studies of Lelbach (1967) also show the direct influence of the accumulated alcohol consumption on the incidence of chronic liver disease. The beverage source of ethanol did not seem to be important, and concomitant malnutrition was not noted to be an influence. The implied direct effect of ethanol in causing hepatic fibrosis and cirrhosis has been confirmed in the baboon model of hepatic injury (Lieber, DeCarli & Rubin, 1975).

The direct hepatotoxic effect of ethanol has been shown histologically and biochemically in both alcoholics and nonalcoholics regardless of dietary variation in fat, protein, vitamins, and ordinary lipotropes. Epidemiologic surveys, beginning with the observations that decreased cirrhosis mortality correlated with the decreased availability of alcohol during the First World War in Europe and Prohibition in the U.S., went on to observe that the incidence of cirrhosis increases with the accumulated alcohol intake (g/kg/day times years) (Lelbach, 1975), women being susceptible at lower alcohol intakes than men.

The role of nutrition in the recovery from alcoholic liver injury was studied before its pathogenesis was understood. A normal protein, fat, and vitamin enriched diet yielded a clinical response in cirrhosis, including greater longevity (Patek & Post, 1941; Patek, Post & Ratnoff, 1948; Morrison, 1946).

The significance of congeners (Feinman & Lieber, 1988), moderate dosages of alcohol, genetic factors, and marginal nutritional deficiencies in alcohol related tissue injury and in the recovery phase is not yet clear.

NUTRITIONAL THERAPY

The nutritional therapy of alcoholism is directed at the prevention of illness, the treatment of documented or presumed deficiencies, and the management of complications.

The management of observed deficiencies of protein and calories is straightforward in the absence of organ damage. Nervous system damage due to thiamine lack is serious and treatable with a great margin of safety, therefore thiamin deficiency should be presumed if not definitely disproved. Parenteral therapy with 50 mg of thiamine per day should be given until similar doses can be taken by mouth. Riboflavin and pyridoxine should be given routinely at the doses usually contained in standard multivitamin preparations. Adequate folic acid replacement can be accomplished with the usual hospital diet. Additional replacement is optional unless deficiency is severe. Vitamin A replacement should be given only for well-documented deficiency, and to patients whose abstinence from alcohol is assured (see the preceding discussion of hepatotoxicity of hypervitaminosis A with alcohol). Vitamin A at dosages of 3,000 micrograms/day may then be given. Zinc replacement should be given for night blindness that is unresponsive to vitamin A replacement. Magnesium replacement is recommended for symptomatic patients with low serum magnesium. Where iron has been clearly diagnosed as deficient, it may be replaced in the usual manner orally.

A diet providing 25 to 35 kcal and 1 to 1.25 grams of protein per kg ideal body weight, not unlike that advocated for healthy adults, should be attempted. Lipids should constitute 30% to 35% of calories and carbohydrate 40%. If patients with alcoholic hepatitis cannot achieve these intakes, it is uncertain whether force-feeding by stomach tube or parenteral routes is desirable. However, it seems likely that the severely anorectic patient will benefit from nasogastric feeding with an energy-dense mixture such as Isocal-HCN®, or from intravenous supplementation with a standard amino acid mixture and glucose. The usefulness of proteins or amino acids of special composition is much less certain. In general, nutritional support of patients with alcoholic liver disease restores nutritional parameters and liver function tests but does not improve short-term (one month) mortality (Schenker & Halff, 1993).

Parenteral therapy with conventional mixtures of amino acids to provide at least 80 g of protein equivalents per day has been fairly safe in terms of avoiding hepatic encephalopathy.

Dietary aspects of management of hepatic encephalopathy consist of diminishing protein intake to about 20 grams of protein per day for a patient who can eat, but to zero in the comatose. Such drastic reductions can be maintained only for a day or two. Every attempt must be made to provide sufficient calories to forestall catabolism of endogenous protein, which would contribute to encephalopathy and is deleterious in its own right. Dietary protein is increased in a stepwise fashion, with continual monitoring for return of encephalopathy, until a satisfactory protein intake is achieved (0.5 to 1.0 g/kg ideal body weight per day). As discussed earlier, if anorexia precludes adequate intake of energy and nitrogen, nasogastric feeding or parenteral infusions may be given.

Provision of dietary protein of unusual quality, such as vegetable protein lower in aromatic amino acids than casein, for example, or the use of keto analogues of essential amino acids to lower the overall nitrogen load while providing the carbon skeletons of these amino acids, or the use of oral (Hepatic Aid®) or intravenous (F080) amino acid mixtures high in branched-chain amino acids and low in aromatic amino acids, have not been consistently more successful than standard mixtures in well-controlled studies. Thus, mixtures such as Hepatic Aid® and F080, although theoretically attractive because they represent a partial reversal of the blood amino acid profile seen in hepatic encephalopathy (increased aromatic amino acid concentrations and lowered branched chain amino acids), nonetheless are more expensive, inadequately tested against appropriate amino acid or protein controls in the presence of comparable energy sources, and deficient in cystine, cysteine, and glutathione (Chawla, Lewis et al., 1984). They have induced decrease in plasma tyrosine and cystine of unknown significance (Millikan, Henderson et al., 1983).

CONCLUSIONS

Alcoholic beverages contain little of nutritive value other than calories. Ethanol-derived calories are not as adequate as carbohydrate-derived calories, for which several metabolic theories have been offered in explanation. As alcohol consumption increases, especially above 25% of daily calories, intake of other nutrients falls significantly and contributes to malnutrition. Ethanol intake alters the metabolism of other foodstuffs.

Alcohol intake *per se* is a cause of cirrhosis in adult humans, whereas nutritional deficiency is not. However, there is evidence that, in the setting of alcoholism, several nutrients might be capable of preventing hepatotoxicity had they been provided in greater abundance. These "supernutrients," such as S-adenosyl-L-methionine and polyunsaturated lecithin, will undergo prospective clinical trials.

REFERENCES

Althausen TL, Uyeyama K & Loran K (1960). Effects of alcohol on absorption of vitamin A in normal and gastrectomized subjects. *Gastroenterology* 38:942.

Blanchard RA, Furie BC, Jorgensen M, Kruger SF & Furie B (1981). Acquired vitamin K-dependent carboxylation deficiency in liver disease. *The New England Journal of Medicine* 305:242–248.

Bonjour JP (1979). Vitamins and Alcoholism, 1. Ascorbic acid. *International Journal of Vitamin and Nutrition Research* 49:434–441.

Breen KJ, Buttigieg R, Iossifidis S, Lourensz C & Wood B (1985). Jejunal uptake of thiamin hydrochloride in man: influence of alcoholism and alcohol. *American Journal of Clinical Nutrition* 42:121126.

Casini A, Cunningham M, Rojkind M & Lieber CS. (1991). Acetaldehyde increased procollagen type I and fibronectin gene transcription in cultured rat fat-storing cells through a protein synthesis-dependent mechanism. *Hepatology* 13:758–765.

Chawla RK, Lewis FW, Kutner MH, Bate DM, Roy RG & Rudman D (1984). Plasma cysteine, cystine, and glutathione in cirrhosis. *Gastroenterology* 87:770–776.

Chawla RK, Wolf DC, Kutner MH & Bonkovsky HL (1989). Choline may be an essential nutrient in malnourished patients with cirrhosis. *Gastroenterology* 97:1514–1520.

Colditz GA, Giovannucci E, Rimm EB, Stampfer MJ, Rosner B, Speizer FE, Gordis E & Willett WC (1991). Alcohol intake in relation to diet and obesity in women and men. *American Journal of Clinical Nutrition* 54:49–55.

Contaldo F, D'Arrigo E, Carandente V, Cortese C, Coltorti A, Mancini M, Taskinen M-R & Nikkila EA (1989). Short-term effects of moderate alcohol consumption on lipid metabolism and energy balance in normal men. *Metabolism* 38:166–171.

Crouse JR & Grundy SM (1984). Effects of alcohol on plasma lipoproteins and cholesterol and triglyceride metabolism in man. *Journal of Lipid Research* 25:486–496.

Dancy M, Evans G, Gaitonde MK & Maxwell JD (1984). Blood thiamin and thiamine phosphate ester concentrations in alcoholic and non-alcoholic liver diseases. *British Medical Journal* 289:79–82.

de Castro JM & Orozco S (1990). Moderate alcohol intake and spontaneous eating patterns of humans: Evidence of unregulated supplementation. *American Journal of Clinical Nutrition* 52:246–253.

Eichner ER, Buchanan B, Smith JW & Hillman RS (1972). Variations in the hematologic and medical status of alcoholics. *American Journal of Medical Sciences* 273:35–42.

Feinman L & Lieber CS (1988). Toxicity of ethanol and other components of alcoholic beverages. *Alcoholism: Clinical & Experimental Research* 12:2–6.

Gruchow HW, Sobocinski KA, Barboriak JJ & Scheller JG (1985). Alcohol consumption, nutrient intake and relative body weight among US adults. *American Journal of Clinical Nutrition* 42:289–295.

Halsted CH, Robles EZ & Mezey E (1971). Decreased jejunal uptake of labeled folic acid (^{3}H-PGA) in alcoholic patients: role of alcohol and nutrition. *The New England Journal of Medicine* 285:701–706.

Herbert V (1986). Folate deficiency. *Book of Abstracts*. XXI Congress of the International Society of Haematology, Sydney, Australia, 11–12:216.

Hillers VN & Massey LK (1985). Interrelationships of moderate and high alcohol consumption with diet and health status. *American Journal of Clinical Nutrition* 41:356–362.

Hirano T, Kaplowitz N, Tsukamoto H, Kamimura S & Fernandez–Checa JC (1992). Hepatic mitochondrial glutathione depletion and progression of experimental alcoholic liver disease in rats. *Hepatology* 16:1423–1427.

Kawase T, Kato S & Lieber CS (1989). Lipid peroxidation and antioxidant defense systems in rat liver after chronic ethanol feeding. *Hepatology* 10:815–821.

Lelbach WK (1967). Leberschaden bei chronischen Alkoholismus. *Acta Hepatosplenology* (Stutg) 14:9–39.

Lelbach WK (1975). Cirrhosis in the alcoholic and its relation to the volume of alcohol abuse. *Annals of the New York Academy of Sciences* 252:85–105.

Leo MA & Lieber CS (1982). Hepatic vitamin A depletion in alcoholic liver injury. *The New England Journal of Medicine* 307:597–601.

Leo MA & Lieber CS (1985). New pathway for retinol metabolism in liver microsomes. *Journal of Biological Chemistry* 260:5228–5231.

Leo MA, Kim C & Lieber CS (1986). Increased vitamin A in esophagus and other extrahepatic tissues after chronic ethanol consumption in the rat. *Alcoholism: Clinical & Experimental Research* 10:487–492.

Li J-J, Kim C-I, Leo MA, Mak KM, Rojkind M & Lieber CS (1993). Polyunsaturated lecithin prevents acetaldehyde-mediated hepatic collagen accumulation by stimulating collagenase activity in cultured lipocytes. *Hepatology* 15:373–381.

Lieber CS (1987). Alcohol and the liver. In IM Arias, MS Frenkel & JHP Wilson (eds.) *Liver Annual-VI*. Amsterdam, The Netherlands: Excerpta Medica, 163–240.

Lieber CS (1991). Perspectives: Do alcohol calories count? *American Journal of Clinical Nutrition* 54:976–982.

Lieber CS (1991). Alcohol, liver, and nutrition. *Journal of the American College of Nutrition* 10:602–632.

Lieber CS (1992). *Medical and Nutritional Complications of Alcoholism: Mechanisms and Management*. New York, NY: Plenum Press, 589.

Lieber CS & DeCarli LM (1991). Hepatotoxicity of ethanol. *Journal of Hepatology* 12:394–401.

Lieber CS & Pignon J-P (1989). Ethanol and Lipids. In JC Fruchart & J Shepherd (eds.) *Human Plasma Lipoproteins: Chemistry, Physiology and Pathology*. Berlin, NY: Walter De Gruyter and Co., 245–289.

Lieber CS, Jones DP & DeCarli LM (1965). Effects of prolonged ethanol intake: Production of fatty liver despite adequate diets. *Journal of Clinical Investigation* 44:1009–1021.

Lieber CS, DeCarli LM & Rubin E (1975). Sequential production of fatty liver, hepatitis and cirrhosis in subhuman primates fed ethanol with adequate diets. *Proceedings of the National Academy of Sciences* 72:437–441.

Lieber CS, Casini A, DeCarli LM, Kim C, Lowe N, Sasaki R & Leo MA (1990). S-adenosyl-L-methionine attenuates alcohol-induced liver injury in the baboon. *Hepatology* 11:165–172.

Lieber CS, DeCarli LM, Mak KM, Kim CI & Leo MA (1990). Attenuation of alcohol-induced hepatic fibrosis by polyunsaturated lecithin. *Hepatology* 12:1390–1398.

Lieber CS, Robins S, Li J-J, DeCarli LM, Mak KM, Fasulo JM & Leo MA (1994). Phosphatidylcholine protects against fibrosis and cirrhosis in the baboon. *Gastroenterology* 106:161–168.

Lieber CS, Leo MA, Aleynik SI, Aleynik MK & DeCarli LM (1997). Polyenylphosphatidylcholine Decreases Alcohol-Induced Oxidative Stress in the Baboon. *Alcoholism: Clinical & Experimental Research* 21:375–379.

Lindenbaum J (1982). Alcohol and the hematologic system. In CS Lieber (ed.) *Medical Disorders of Alcoholism: Pathogenesis and Treatment*. Philadelphia, PA: W.B. Saunders, 313–362.

Lindenbaum J & Lieber CS (1971). Effects of ethanol on the blood, bone marrow, and small intestine of man. In MK Roach, WM McIssac & PJ Creaven (eds.) *Biological Aspects of Alcohol*, Vol. III. Austin, TX: University of Texas Press, 27–45.

Lindenbaum J & Lieber CS (1975). The effects of chronic ethanol administration on intestinal absorption in man in the absence of nutritional deficiency. *Annals of the New York Academy of Science* 252:228–234.

Lumeng L (1978). The role of acetaldehyde in mediating the deleterious effect of ethanol on pyridoxal 5'-phosphate metabolism. *Journal of Clinical Investigation* 62:286293.

Maruyama K, Feinman L, Fainsilber Z, Nakano M, Okazaki I & Lieber CS (1982). Mammalian collagenase increases in early alcoholic liver disease and decreases with cirrhosis. *Life Science* 30:1379–1384.

Mendenhall C, Bongiovanni G, Goldberg S, Miller B, Moore J, Rouster S, Schneider D, Tamburro C, Tosch T, Weesner R, and The VA Cooperative Study Group on Alcoholic Hepatitis (1985). VA cooperative study on alcoholic hepatitis III: Changes in protein-calorie malnutrition associated with 30 days of hospitalization with and without enteral nutritional therapy. *Journal of Parenteral and Enteral Nutrition* 9:590–596.

Millikan WJ Jr, Henderson JM, Warren WD, Riepe SP, Kutner MH, Wright-Bacon L, Epstein C & Parks RB (1983). Total parenteral nutrition with F080 in cirrhotics with subclinical encephalopathy. *Annals of Surgery* 197:294–304.

Morrison LM (1946). The response of cirrhosis of the liver to an intensive combined therapy. *Annals of Internal Medicine* 24:465–478.

Olson JA (1987). Recommended dietary intakes (RDI) of Vitamin A in humans. *American Journal of Clinical Nutrition* 45:704–716.

Patek AJ & Post J (1941). Treatment of cirrhosis of the liver by a nutritious diet and supplements rich in vitamin B complex. *Journal of Clinical Investigation* 20:481–505.

Patek AJ, Post J & Ratnoff OB (1948). Dietary treatment of cirrhosis of the liver. *Journal of the American Medical Association* 138:543–549.

Pirola RC & Lieber CS (1972). The energy cost of the metabolism of drugs including alcohol. *Pharmacology* 7:185–196.

Polivy J & Herman CP (1976a). Effects of alcohol on eating behavior: Disinhibition or sedation? *Addictive Behaviors* 1:121–125.

Polivy J & Herman CP (1976b). Effects of alcohol on eating behavior: Influences of mood and perceived intoxication. *Journal of Abnormal Psychology* 85:601–606.

Reinus JF, Heymsfield SB, Wiskind R, Casper K & Galambos JT (1989). Ethanol: Relative fuel value and metabolic effects *in vivo*. *Metabolism* 38:125–135.

Rosenthal WS, Adham NF, Lopez R & Cooperman JM (1973). Riboflavin deficiency in complicated chronic alcoholism. *American Journal of Clinical Nutrition* 26:858–860.

Rothwell NJ & Stock MJ (1984). Influence of alcohol and sucrose consumption on energy consumption and brown fat activity in the rat. *Metabolism* 33:768–771.

Russell RM, Rosenberg IH, Wilson PD, Iber FL, Oaks EB, Giovetti AC, Otradovec CL, Karwoski BS & Press AW (1983). Increased urinary excretion and prolonged turnover time of folic acid during ethanol ingestion. *American Journal of Clinical Nutrition* 38:64–70.

Scheig R (1970). Effects of ethanol on the liver. *American Journal of Clinical Nutrition* 23:467–473.

Schenker S & Halff GA (1993). Nutritional therapy in alcoholic liver disease. *Seminars in Liver Disease* 13:196–209.

Shaw S, Jayatilleke E & Lieber CS (1981). Hepatic lipid peroxidation: Potentiation by chronic alcohol feeding and attenuation by methionine. *Journal of Laboratory and Clinical Medicine* 98:417–435.

Shaw S, Rubin KP & Lieber CS (1983). Depressed hepatic glutathione and increased diene conjugates in alcoholic liver disease: Evidence of lipid peroxidation. *Digestive Diseases and Sciences* 28:585–589.

Sherlock S & Walshe V (1948). Effect of undernutrition in man on hepatic structure and function. *Nature* 161:604.

Stock MJ & Stuart JA (1974). Thermic effects of ethanol in the rat and man. *Nutrition and Metabolism* 17:297–305.

Sullivan JF (1962). Effect of alcohol on urinary zinc excretion. *Quarterly Journal of Studies on Alcohol* 23:216–220.

Sullivan LW & Herbert V (1964). Suppression of hematopoiesis by ethanol. *Journal of Clinical Investigation* 43:2048–2062.

Suter PM, Schutz Y & Jequier E (1992). The effect of ethanol on fat storage in healthy subjects. *The New England Journal of Medicine* 326:983–987.

Tamura T & Halsted CH (1983). Folate turnover in chronically alcoholic monkeys. *Journal of Laboratory and Clinical Medicine* 101:623–628.

Tamura T, Romero JJ, Watson JE, Gong EJ & Halsted CH (1981). Hepatic folate metabolism in the chronic alcoholic monkey. *Journal of Laboratory and Clinical Medicine* 97:654–661.

Tomasulo PA, Kater RMH & Iber FL (1968). Impairment of thiamin absorption in alcoholism. *American Journal of Clinical Nutrition* 21:1341–1344.

Valberg LS, Flanagan PR, Ghent CN & Chamberlain MJ (1985). Zinc absorption and leukocyte zinc in alcoholic and nonalcoholic cirrhosis. *Digestive Diseases and Sciences* 30:329–333.

Westrate J, Wunnink I, Deurinberg P & Hautvast JGAJ (1990). Alcohol and its acute effects on resting metabolic rate and diet induced thermogenesis. *British Journal of Nutrition* 64:413–425.

World MJ, Ryle PR, Jones D, Shaw GK & Thompson AD (1984). Differential effect of chronic alcohol intake and poor nutrition on body weight and fat stores. *Alcohol and Alcoholism* 19:281290.

Yki-Järvinen H & Nikkilä EA (1985). Ethanol decreases glucose utilization in healthy man. *Journal of Clinical Endocrinology and Metabolism* 61:941–945.

CHAPTER 3

Hepatic Disorders

Charles S. Lieber, M.D.

Magnitude of the Problem
Mechanisms of Toxicity
Organ Damage
To Drink or Not to Drink?
Future Trends

Alcoholism affects virtually all organs of the body. Associated disorders are very common and, in the elderly, the number of alcohol-related hospitalizations are similar to those of myocardial infarction (Adams, Yuan et al., 1993).

MAGNITUDE OF THE PROBLEM

Approximately 20% to 40% of all persons admitted to general hospitals have alcohol-linked problems; often, they are undiagnosed alcoholics who are being treated for the consequences of their drinking.

The most severe functional and structural alterations occur in the liver, and cirrhosis of the liver (usually as a complication of alcoholism) is a common cause of death. In a prospective survey of U.S. Veterans, it was found that, within 48 months, more than half of those with cirrhosis, and two-thirds of those with cirrhosis plus alcoholic hepatitis, had died (Chedid, Mendenhall et al., 1991). This outcome is more severe than that of many cancers, yet it is attracting much less concern, among both the public and the medical profession. This may be due, at least in part, to the prevailing, pervasive and pernicious perception that not much can be done about this major public health issue. However, new insights in the pathophysiology of the alcohol-use disorders now allow for prospects of earlier recognition and more successful efforts at prevention and treatment, prior to the medical and social disintegration of the patient.

MECHANISMS OF TOXICITY

Alcohol is a small molecule, both water and lipid soluble. It therefore readily permeates all organs of the body and affects most of their vital functions (Lieber, 1992).

Alcohol and Nutrition. Ethanol is not only a psychoactive drug. Besides its pharmacologic action, it has a substantial energy value (7.1 kcal/g). It is almost as energy dense as fat and is more so than carbohydrates or proteins. In many societies, alcoholic beverages are considered part of the food supply, whereas in others, alcohol is consumed mainly for its mood-altering effects. In the alcoholic, alcohol represents on the average 50% of the total dietary energy intake. As a consequence, alcohol displaces many normal nutrients of the diet, resulting in primary malnutrition and associated symptomatology, foremost that of folate, thiamine and other vitamin B deficiencies. Alcohol also impairs the activation and utilization of nutrients, and secondary malnutrition may result from either maldigestion or malabsorption caused by gastrointestinal complications associated with alcoholism, mainly pancreatic insufficiency.

Alcohol also promotes nutrient degradation. At the tissue level, alcohol replaces various normal substrates, and the most seriously affected organ is the liver, which contains the bulk of the body's enzymes capable of sustaining ethanol metabolism. Ethanol acts as a preferred substrate and displaces up to 90% of the liver's normal fuel which is fat (Lieber, 1992). Consequently, fat accumulates, resulting in a fatty liver, the first stage of alcoholic liver disease.

Originally, it was believed that liver disease in the alcoholic was due exclusively to malnutrition. Subsequently, as reviewed elsewhere (Lieber, 1992; Lieber & DeCarli, 1991), the hepatotoxicity of ethanol has been established by the demonstration that, in the absence of dietary deficiencies, and even in the presence of protein-, vitamin-, and mineral-enriched diets, ethanol produces fatty liver (Lieber, Jones & DeCarli, 1965) with striking ultrastructural lesions (Lane & Lieber, 1966) both in rats and in humans, and fibrosis with cirrhosis in nonhuman primates (Lieber & DeCarli, 1974).

Although ethanol is rich in energy (7.1 kcal/g), chronic consumption of substantial amounts of alcohol is not associated with the expected effect on body weight (Lieber, 1991). In addition to mitochondrial inefficiency secondary to chronic ethanol consumption and acetaldehyde toxicity, some of the energy deficit could be attributed to induction of the microsomal ethanol oxidizing system (a metabolic pathway that oxidizes ethanol without associated chemical energy production).

Metabolic disorders associated with alcohol oxidation by alcohol dehydrogenase: The oxidation of ethanol via the alcohol dehydrogenase pathway results in the production of acetaldehyde with loss of H which reduces NAD to NADH. The large amounts of reducing equivalents generated overwhelm the hepatocyte's ability to maintain redox homeostasis and a number of metabolic disorders ensue (Figure 1) (Lieber, 1992), including hyperlactacidemia which contributes to the acidosis and also reduces the capacity of the kidney to excrete uric acid, leading to secondary hyperuricemia. The latter is aggravated by the alcohol-induced ketosis and acetate-mediated enhanced ATP breakdown and purine generation (Faller & Fox, 1982). Hyperuricemia explains, at least in part, the common clinical observation that excessive consumption of alcoholic beverages frequently aggravates or precipitates gouty attacks. The increased NADH also opposes gluconeogenesis, thereby promoting a cause of hypoglycemia, and raises the concentration of α-glycerophosphate which favors lipogenesis by trapping fatty acids. In addition, excess NADH may promote fatty acid synthesis directly. The net result is fat accumulation with enlargement of the liver.

Adverse effects resulting from microsomal ethanol oxidation, its induction and interactions with other chemicals: Almost four decades ago, another pathway for alcohol metabolism was discovered, namely the microsomal ethanol oxidizing system (MEOS) (Lieber & DeCarli, 1968, 1970). Unlike ADH, MEOS is strikingly inducible by chronic ethanol consumption. The key enzyme of the MEOS is the ethanol-inducible cytochrome P4502E1 (2E1) which is increased four- to 10-fold in liver biopsies of recently drinking subjects (Tsutsumi, Lasker et al., 1989), with a corresponding rise in mRNA (Takahashi, Lasker et al., 1993). Other cytochromes P450 (1A2, 3A4) may also be involved (Tsyrlov, Salmela et al., 1996). This induction contributes to

FIGURE 1. Abnormalities After Ethanol Abuse

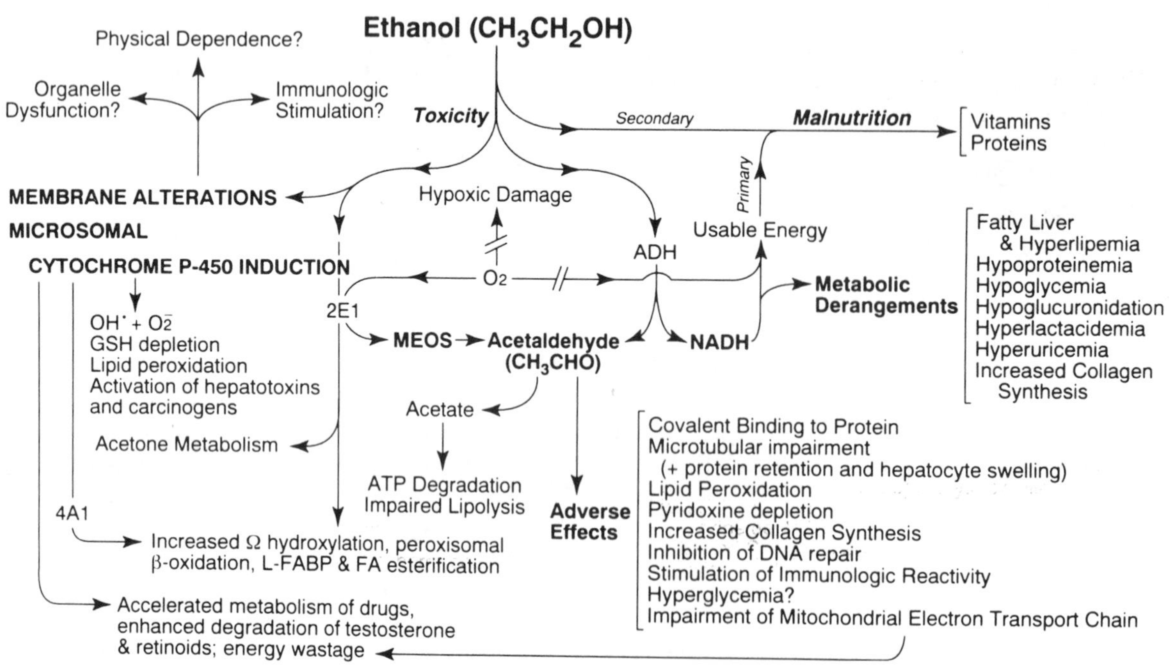

Hepatic, nutritional, and metabolic abnormalities after ethanol abuse. Malnutrition, whether primary or secondary, can be differentiated from metabolic changes or direct toxicity, resulting partly from redox changes, or effects secondary to microsomal induction, including increased oxidative stress and acetaldehyde production.

the ethanol tolerance that develops in the alcoholic and spills over to other drugs that are microsomal substrates (Figure 2).

The tolerance of the alcoholic to various psychoactive drugs has been generally attributed to central nervous system adaptation (Kalant, Khanna & Marshman, 1970) but, in addition, metabolic adaptation must be considered, because the clearance rate of many drugs from the blood is enhanced in alcoholics (Misra, Lefèvre et al., 1971). Indeed, controlled studies have shown that chronic administration of pure ethanol with non-deficient diets either to rats or man (under metabolic ward conditions) results in a striking increase in the rate of blood clearance of ethanol meprobamate (Salaspuro & Lieber, 1978), pentobarbital (Misra, Lefèvre et al., 1971) and propranolol (Pritchard & Schneck, 1977; Sotaniemi, Anttila et al., 1981). Similarly, increases were found in the metabolism of antipyrine (Sotaniemi, Anttila et al., 1981), tolbutamide (Carulli, Manenti et al., 1971; Kater, Roggin et al., 1969; Kater, Tobon, Iber et al., 1969), warfarin (Kater, Roggin et al., 1969), diazepam (Sellman, Kanto et al., 1975) and rifamycin (Grassi & Grassi, 1975). The metabolic drug tolerance persists several days to weeks after the cessation of alcohol consumption, and the duration of recovery varies with each drug (Hetu & Joly, 1985). During that period, the dosage of these drugs has to be increased to offset the accelerated breakdown.

In addition to the oxidation of ethanol, 2E1 also has an extraordinary capacity to activate many xenobiotics to highly toxic metabolites. These include industrial solvents such as bromobenzene (Hetu, Dumont & Jolly, 1983) and vinylidene chloride (Siegers, Heidbuchel & Younes, 1983), as well as anesthetics such as enflurane (Kharasch & Thummel, 1993; Tsutsumi, Leo et al., 1990) and halothane (Takagi, Ishii et al., 1983), commonly used medications, such as isoniazid and phenylbutazone (Beskid, Bialek et al., 1980), illicit drugs (e.g., cocaine) and over-the-counter analgesics such as acetaminophen, paracetamol, or N-acetyl-*p*-aminophenol, shown to be a good substrate for human 2E1 (Raucy,

FIGURE 2. Schematic Representation of Ethanol-Drug Interactions

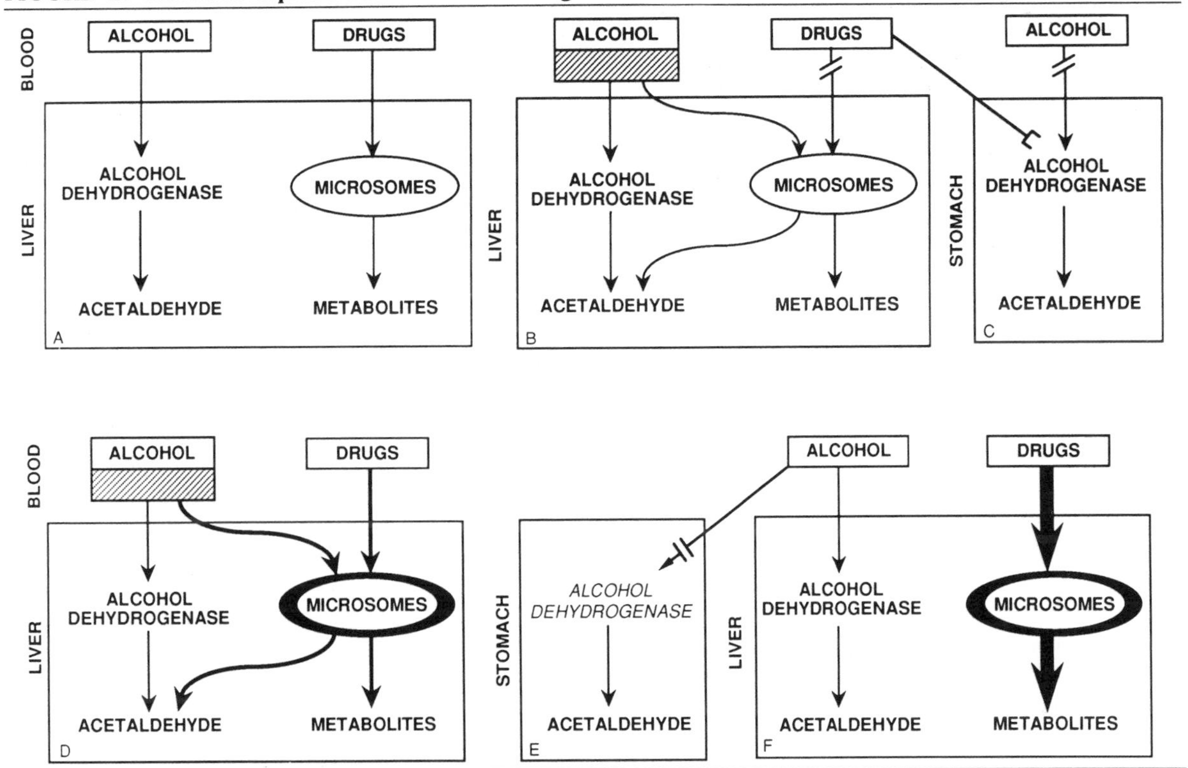

Schematic representation of ethanol-drug interactions involving the ADH pathway and microsomes. (A) Hepatic metabolism by alcohol by ADH and drugs by microsomes; (B) inhibition of hepatic microsomal drug metabolism in the presence of high concentrations of ethanol, in part through competition for a common microsomal detoxification process; (C) inhibition of gastric ethanol metabolism by drugs; (D) microsomal induction after chronic alcohol consumption and its contribution to accelerated hepatic metabolism of ethanol at high blood levels; (E) decreased gastric ADH activity and gastric ethanol metabolism after chronic alcohol abuse; (F) increased hepatic drug metabolism and xenobiotic activation because of the persisting microsomal induction after withdrawal from long-term alcoholism (Lieber, 1994).

Lasker et al., 1989). The induction of 2E1 explains the increased vulnerability of the heavy drinker to the toxicity of these substances.

Among alcoholic patients, hepatic injury associated with acetaminophen has been described following repetitive intake for headaches (including those associated with withdrawal symptoms), dental pain, or the pain of pancreatitis. Amounts well within the accepted tolerable rate (2.5–4 g) have been incriminated as the cause of hepatic injury in alcoholic patients (Black, 1984; Seeff, Cucherini et al., 1986). It is likely that the enhanced hepatotoxicity of acetaminophen after chronic ethanol consumption is caused, at least in part, by an increased microsomal production of reactive metabolite(s) of acetaminophen. Consistent with this view is the observation that, in animals fed ethanol chronically, the potentiation of acetaminophen hepatotoxicity occurs after ethanol withdrawal (Sato, Matsuda & Lieber, 1981), at which time production of the toxic metabolite may be at its peak, since at that time competition by ethanol (Figure 2B) for a common microsomal pathway has been withdrawn (Figure 2F). Thus, maximal vulnerability to the toxicity of acetaminophen occurs immediately after cessation of drinking, when there is also the greatest need for analgesia, because of the headaches and other symptoms associated with withdrawal. This also explains the synergistic effect between acetaminophen, ethanol and fasting (Whitecomb & Block, 1994), since all three deplete reduced glutathione (GSH), thereby contributing to the toxicity of each compound because GSH provides one of the cell's fundamental mechanisms for the scavenging of toxic free radicals. Furthermore, 2E1 promotes the generation of active oxygen species which are toxic in their own right and may overwhelm the antioxidant system of the liver and other tissues with striking consequences. A similar effect may also be produced by the free hydroxy-ethyl radical generated from ethanol by 2E1. A depletion in the steady state levels of hepatocellular GSH, in synergy with other conditions, leads to hepatocellular necrosis and liver injury (Israël, Speisky et al., 1992).

Acute ethanol administration also inhibits GSH synthesis and produces an increased loss from the liver (Speisky, MacDonald et al., 1985). GSH is selectively depleted in the mitochondria (Hirano, Kaplowitz et al., 1992) and may contribute to the striking alcohol-induced alterations of that organelle. Alpha-tocopherol, the major antioxidant in the membranes, is depleted in patients with cirrhosis (Leo, Rosman & Lieber, 1993). This deficiency in the defense systems, coupled with increased acetaldehyde, oxygen and other free radical generation (by the ethanol-induced microsomes), may contribute to liver damage via lipid peroxidation and also via enzyme inactivation (Dicker & Cederbaum, 1988). Replenishment of GSH can be achieved by administration of GSH precursors such as acetylcysteine, or S-adenosyl-L-methionine (SAMe) (Lieber, Casini et al., 1990) (Figure 3).

Contrasting with the inductive effect of long-term ethanol consumption, after short-term administration, inhibition of hepatic drug metabolism is seen, primarily because of its direct competition for a common metabolic process involving cytochrome P-450 (Lieber, 1992) (Figure 2B). Methadone exemplifies this dual interaction. Whereas long-term ethanol consumption leads to increased hepatic microsomal metabolism of methadone and decreased levels in the brain and liver, short-term administration inhibits microsomal demethylation of methadone and enhances brain and liver concentrations of the drug (Borowsky & Lieber, 1978). These effects are of clinical relevance since approximately 50% of the patients taking methadone have an alcohol use disorder. The combination of ethanol with tranquilizers and barbiturates also results in increased drug concentrations in the blood, sometimes to dangerously high levels, commonly observed in suicides.

Ethanol, carcinogens and vitamin A: Heavy alcohol consumption is associated with an increased incidence of alimentary, respiratory tract and breast cancers (Garro, Espina et al., 1992). Even moderate alcohol consumption leads to an increased risk of rectal cancer in men and women, and of breast cancer in women (Garro & Lieber, 1990; Schatzkin, Jones et al., 1987; Willett, Stampfer et al., 1987). A low daily intake (10 to 40 grams), especially as beer, results in a 1.5 to 3.0-fold risk of rectal and, to a lesser extent, of colon cancer in both genders, but predominantly in men. One pathogenic factor is the effect of ethanol on enzyme systems participating in the cytochrome P-450-dependent activation of carcinogens. Alcoholics are commonly heavy smokers, and there is a synergistic effect of alcohol consumption and smoking on cancer development, with long-term ethanol consumption enhancing the mutagenicity of tobacco-derived products (Lieber, Garro et al., 1986).

Alcohol also influences carcinogenesis in many other ways (Garro & Lieber, 1990), one of which involves vitamin A. Ethanol consumption depresses hepatic levels of vitamin A in animals and in man (Leo & Lieber, 1982) (Figure 4), even when given

FIGURE 3. Link Between Accelerated Acetaldehyde Production and Increased Free Radical Generation

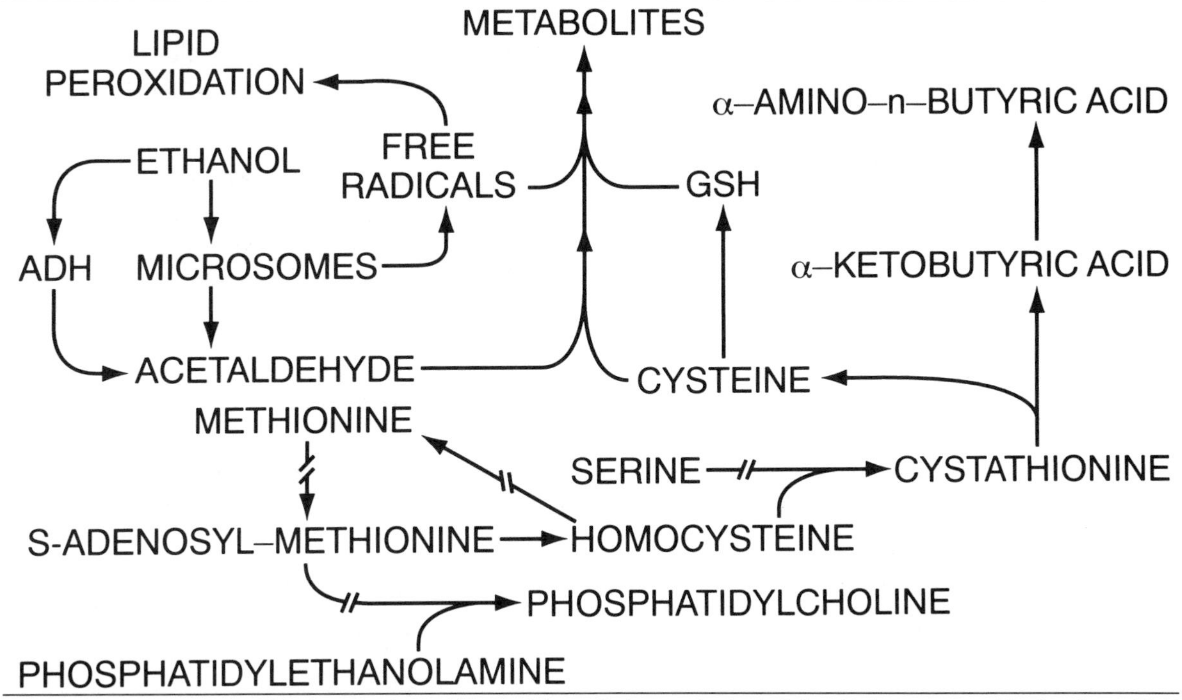

Link between accelerated acetaldehyde production and increased free radical generation by the induced/microsomes, resulting in enhanced lipid peroxidation. with metabolic blocks due to alcohol, folate deficiency and/or alcoholic liver disease, illustrating possible beneficial effects of GSH, and its precursors (including S-adenosylmethionine [SAMe]) as well as phosphatidylcholine (Lieber, 1997a); see explanation in text.

with diets containing large amounts of vitamin A (Sato, Matsuda & Lieber, 1981). This reflects, in part, accelerated microsomal degradation of the vitamin via pathways of microsomal retinol metabolism, inducible by either ethanol or drug administration (Leo, Kim & Lieber, 1987; Leo & Lieber, 1985). Deficiency of vitamin A, which plays a key role in the maintenance of the integrity of normal mucosal linings, has been invoked in the pathogenesis of cancerous lesions. Supplementation of the alcoholic's diet with vitamin A, however, is complicated by the fact that excess vitamin A is hepatotoxic (Leo & Lieber, 1988). Long-term ethanol consumption enhances the latter effect, resulting in striking morphologic and functional alterations of the mitochondria (Leo, Arai et al., 1982), along with hepatic necrosis and fibrosis (Leo & Lieber, 1983). Thus, in heavy drinkers, there is a narrowed therapeutic window for vitamin A.

Contrasting with retinoids, the toxicity of which is well established, the toxicity of beta-carotene is not settled. Heretofore, there was a consensus that no obvious a-carotene toxicity exists. It must be noted, however, that in nonhuman primates, enhanced toxicity of a-carotene in the presence of ethanol has been observed (Leo, Kim et al., 1992). Furthermore, a-carotene increased pulmonary cancer and cardiovascular complications in smokers (Alpha-Tocopherol, Beta Carotene Cancer Prevention Study Group, 1994). This effect was confirmed in a more recent study (Omenn, Goodman et al., 1996) and was also found to be related to the amount of alcohol consumed (Albanes, Heinonen et al., 1996; Leo & Lieber, 1994), suggesting again that the toxicity resulted from an alcohol β-carotene interaction. Thus, caution must be exercised with a-carotene supplementation in the drinker. It is noteworthy that an interaction between ethanol and β-carotene occurs not only at high alcohol levels (Ahmed, Leo et al., 1994), but also with relatively moderate intake, namely 30 grams (or 2 drinks) a day (Forman, Beecher et al., 1995). Thus, moderate consumption is not only associated with "beneficial effects" (discussed below), but also with some definite risks.

Toxicity of Acetaldehyde. Ethanol oxidation produces acetaldehyde (Figure 1), a highly toxic metabolite with extraordinary reactivity, resulting in binding to a variety of proteins. In turn, acetaldehyde-protein adduct formation interferes with the activity of many key enzymes and repair systems, and thus becomes an important cause of direct toxicity at the

FIGURE 4. Hepatic Vitamin A Levels

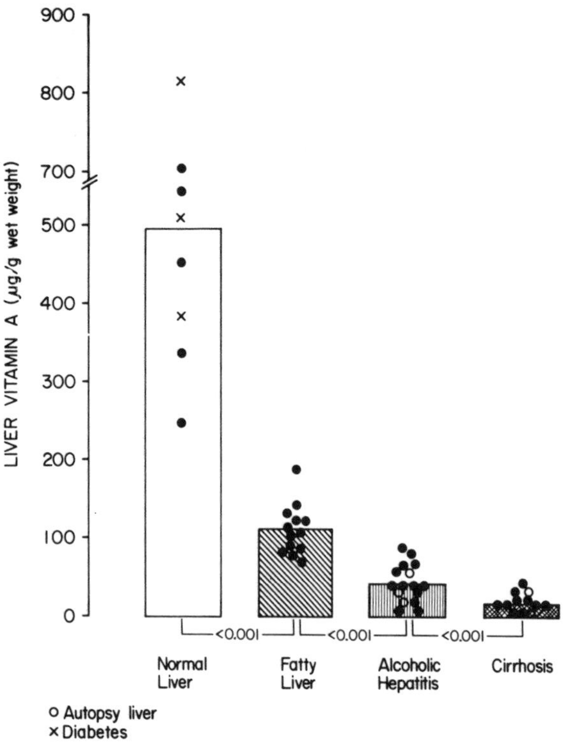

Hepatic vitamin A levels in subjects with normal livers and various stages of alcoholic liver injury. Figures below the graph denote p values (Leo & Lieber, 1982).

tissue level, eventually resulting in cell necrosis. Indeed, minute concentrations of acetaldehyde (as low as 0.05 mol/L) were found to impair the repair of alkylated nucleoproteins (Espina, Lima et al., 1988). The toxicity is associated with a significant reduction in the capacity of the liver to utilize oxygen (Lieber, Baraona et al., 1989) and there is uncoupling of oxidation with phosphorylation in mitochondria damaged by chronic ethanol consumption (Arai, Leo et al., 1984). Moreover, acetaldehyde promotes GSH depletion, free radical-mediated toxicity, and lipid peroxidation. By binding to the tubulin of the microtubules, acetaldehyde seriously impairs the secretion of proteins from the liver into the plasma, with a corresponding hepatic retention (Baraona, Leo et al., 1977). The increases in lipid, protein, water (Wondergem & Davis, 1994), and electrolytes result in enlargement of the hepatocytes, the experimental counterpart of the ballooning of the hepatocyte seen in the alcoholic. Acetaldehyde adducts promote collagen production and may also serve as neoantigens, generating an immune response in mice (Israël, Hurwitz et al., 1986) and in humans (Hoerner, Behrens et al., 1986, 1988; Niemela, Klajner et al., 1987). Acetaldehyde also crosses the placenta (Karl, Gordon et al., 1988), and may contribute to the development of fetal alcohol syndrome, the most prevalent cause of preventable congenital abnormality (Abel & Sokol, 1991).

Effect of gender, interactions with age, hormones and heredity and role of gastric ADH. For a given dose of alcohol, blood concentrations achieved in women are higher than in men. This effect is particularly striking in alcoholic women, but it is also of great significance for social drinking in normal women. Indeed, normal women develop higher blood concentrations than men because women are usually smaller than men, but the amount of alcohol offered to them in social settings does not take this gender difference into account. Furthermore, the alcohol consumed is distributed in a 12% smaller water space (Frezza, Di Padova et al., 1990) because of a difference in body composition (more fat and less water in women). Moreover, less of the alcohol is broken down in the stomach and more reaches the peripheral blood because women also have lower gastric ADH activity than men (Frezza, Di Padova et al., 1990), at least when below the age of 50 years (Seitz, Egerer et al., 1993). This effect is much more striking in alcoholic than in nonalcoholic women. These gender differences, however, are already obvious at levels of social drinking. Thus, a moderate dose for men is not necessarily moderate for women. Moderate drinking is presently defined as not more than two drinks per day in men, and only one drink per day in women (Dietary Guidelines for Americans, 1995), a drink being defined as 12 ounces of regular beer, 5 ounces of wine, or 1.5 ounces of distilled spirits (80 proof).

Peripheral blood concentrations of alcohol represent the difference between the amount of ethanol that reaches the circulation and the amount metabolized. Thus, if the rate of entry is close to the rate of oxidation, even moderate differences in the bioavailability of ethanol may result in striking blood-concentration changes, with substantial effects on the brain and other tissues. The lower rate of first-pass metabolism in normal women as compared to normal men (Frezza, Di Padova et al., 1990) and the even lower rate in alcoholic women as compared to normal women (Frezza, Di Padova et al., 1990) or in alcoholic men as compared to nonalcoholic men (DiPadova, Worner et al., 1987; Frezza, Di Padova et al., 1990) all parallel changes in gastric ADH and are consistent with a role for gastric ethanol oxidation. Taken together, the observations described above suggest that the differences in gastric ADH activity between men and women do, at least in part, explain the differences in blood ethanol concentrations.

Inhibition of gastric ADH and the increased blood ethanol concentrations by aspirin (Roine, Gentry et al., 1990), as well as the differential effects of H_2-blockers on first-pass metabolism (Caballeria, Baraona, et al., 1989; Di Padova, Roine et al., 1992) also follow these patterns. Those H_2-blockers that inhibit gastric ADH activity *in vitro* (Caballeria, Baraona, et al., 1989; Baraona, Yokoyama et al., 1991; Palmer, Frank et al., 1991; Seitz, Simanowski et al., 1992) (Figure 2C) also increase blood alcohol concentrations *in vivo* (Hernández-Muñoz, Caballeria et al., 1990). Although questioned at first, such increases in blood level have now been confirmed (Palmer, Frank et al., 1991; Fraser, Hudson et al., 1992) for a low alcohol dose of 0.15 g/kg, and are particularly striking after repetitive consumption of small doses (Gupta, Baraona & Lieber, 1995), a pattern common in social drinkers. The H_2-blocker effect on blood alcohol concentrations has also been shown with higher doses of ethanol (Di Padova, Roine et al., 1992; Guram, Howden & Hott, 1991; Seitz, Veith et al., 1984; Sharma, Gentry et al., 1995) with an associated increase in intoxication scores (Feely & Wood, 1982), but these effects at higher ethanol dosage are still the subject of controversy.

It must be pointed out, however, that some of the negative investigations used dilute concentrations of alcohol (e.g., Raufman, Notar-Francesco et al., 1993), at which gastric first pass metabolism (FPM) is minimal (Roine, Gentry et al., 1991). In addition, significant ethanol metabolism (and inhibition by H_2-blockers) has been recently confirmed in cultured gastric cells (Haber, Gentry et al., 1996; Mirmiran-Yazdy, Haber et al., 1995). In any event, in contemporary social settings, women are commonly served amounts of alcohol comparable to those given to men. Making women aware of their increased vulnerability might strengthen their resolve to resist the social pressures that may lead to inappropriate levels of consumption.

There also are ethnic differences in gastric ADH. The human gastric mucosa possess an ADH isoenzyme (sigma-ADH) that is not present in the liver and which is absent or markedly decreased in activity in a large percentage of Japanese subjects (Baraona, Yokoyama et al., 1991). Moreno and Parés (1991) isolated a sigma-ADH with similar characteristics (a new class IV ADH; Parés, Cederlund et al., 1992) for which a full-length cDNA has been obtained and the complete amino acid sequence deduced (Satre, Zgombic-Knight & Duester, 1994; Yokoyama, Baraona & Lieber, 1994); its gene also has been fully cloned and localized to chromosome 4 (Yokoyama, Baraona & Lieber, 1996). Increased bioavailability secondary to a low level of σ-ADH may thus influence the severity of medical problems related to drinking.

Women differ from men not only in terms of gastric ethanol metabolism. Hepatic ADH activity is suppressed by testosterone and its derivatives (Teschke & Wiese, 1982) and, indeed, ADH activity in the livers of women is significantly higher than in men although, after the age of 53 in men and 50 in women, the sex difference is no longer apparent (Maly & Sasse, 1991). Of course, ADH activity, measured *in vitro* is only one of the determinants of ethanol metabolism *in vivo* and discrepancies between the two are not uncommon (Zorzano & Herrera, 1990).

The menstrual cycle is important for women's metabolism of alcohol, in part through its effects on gastric emptying (Wald, Van Thiel et al., 1982). Gastric emptying is delayed during the luteal phase of the menstrual cycle, which is characterized by high estradiol and progesterone. Gastric emptying is one of the factors that determines the time of exposure of ethanol to gastric ADH metabolism, as well as speed of intestinal absorption. Thus, blood alcohol concentrations and related effects of alcohol intake vary somewhat over the menstrual cycle. Chronic ethanol consumption also has a profound interaction with testosterone metabolism, resulting in a castration-like effect in men (Lieber, 1992).

There is evidence that the progression to more severe liver injury is accelerated in women (Rankin, 1977), and that the incidence of chronic advanced liver disease is higher among women than among men with a similar history of alcohol misuse (Morgan & Sherlock, 1977). A daily alcohol intake of 40 g in men (3 drinks), but only 20 g in women resulted in a statistically significant increase in the incidence of cirrhosis in a well-nourished population (Parrish, Dufour et al., 1993; Pequignot, Tuyns & Berta, 1978).

The mechanism whereby the female gender potentiates alcohol-induced liver damage is not known but could relate to hormonal status. Indeed, both endogenous and exogenous (i.e., contraceptive) female hormones have been shown to result in some impairment of liver function in a significant number of women (Lieber, 1993). Elevated acetaldehyde concentrations in women compared to men may also explain why ethanol causes tissue damage more rapidly in women than men (Fukunaga, Sillanaukee & Eriksson, 1993). A sex-specific cytochrome P450 has been invoked as a cause of sex- and species-related differences in drug toxicity in rats (Kato & Yamazoe, 1992). Similarly, long-term ethanol consumption was associated with increases in the content of a specific cytochrome (P4504A1), and more so in male than in female rats (Ma, Baraona & Lieber, 1993); the microsomal ω-hydroxylation of lauric acid was significantly greater and the rise in males (89%) was significantly higher than in females (4%). Products of omega-oxidation increase liver cytosolic fatty acid-binding protein (L-FABPc) content and peroxisomal beta-oxidation (Kaikaus, Sui et al., 1993), an alternate pathway for fatty acid disposition. L-FABP is a major contributor to the ethanol-induced increase in liver cytosolic proteins (Pignon, Bailey et al., 1987) and plays a role in protecting the liver against the excess accumulation of free fatty acids by binding them and thereby making them less reactive. Whereas the ethanol-induced increase in fatty acid-binding capacity provided an excess of binding sites for the fatty acids in male rats, the increase in females was barely sufficient (Shevchuk, Baraona et al., 1991). Moreover, the difference in fatty acid accumulation was compounded by a lesser compensatory increase in omega oxidation after chronic alcohol consumption in females compared to males. Under these circumstances the risk for development of a deleterious accumulation of fatty acids in the liver is increased, thereby potentially contributing to the enhanced vulnerability of females to alcohol-induced hepatotoxicity.

Gender also modulates the pathologic response to ethanol in extrahepatic tissues. This may involve cancer of the breast (Longnecker, Berlin et al., 1988; Lowenfels & Zevola, 1989), and gastric ulcer (Rabinovitz, Van Thiel et al., 1989). The degree of brain shrinkage in alcoholics was found by Mann and colleagues (1992) to be similar in men and women, despite significantly shorter ethanol exposure in the women.

In summary, gender differences in response to alcohol, suspected for centuries, are now objectively documented, with one of the most striking differences being the increased bioavailability of alcohol in women. Thus, sex must be recognized as one of the determinants of alcohol metabolism and hence of the severity of alcoholic liver injury, a factor of increasing significance because male/female differences in drinking are smaller than they were a generation ago, especially in terms of drinking by young women (Gomberg, 1993).

The elderly may drink less alcohol, but this is offset by age-related decreases in body fluids which result in a lower volume of distribution for ethanol, and thus higher blood alcohol concentrations for a given level of consumption. Prognosis is also age-related. For example, one-year mortality was 50% among cirrhotics over the age of 60, versus 7% for those under 60 years (Potter & James, 1987). Many other organs are also differentially affected. There is an effect of social drinking on intellectual capacities as a function of age. Linnoila and colleagues (1980) found that, with increased blood alcohol concentrations, tests of perception and attention decrease progressively, and that the older subjects perform less well than the younger ones at all blood alcohol concentrations. The most common clinical interactions of alcohol and drugs concern the psychotropic medications frequently used by the elderly. The alcoholic is also particularly prone to osseous abnormalities such as fractures (Nilsson, 1970), osteoporosis (Saville, 1965), and osteonecrosis (Solomon, 1973). It is evident that the elderly alcoholic is at even greater risk for these complications given the normal bone loss that occurs with advancing age. Although the thesis that moderate alcohol intake increases the risk of non-insulin dependent diabetes has been challenged (Stampfer, Colditz et al., 1988), studies have reported such a risk (Colditz, 1990). Even modest amounts of ethanol in elderly men impair glucose oxidation and cause insulin resistance which, because of lack of compensatory insulin secretion, results in deterioration of glucose tolerance (Boden, Chen et al., 1993). This vulnerability of the geriatric population, as well as their other special needs discussed in greater detail before (Korsten & Lieber, 1983), should be taken into account in the treatment of these patients.

The role of heredity in the development of alcoholism in men is well established (Lumeng & Crabb, 1994), and it has now been shown to play a major role in the etiology of alcoholism in women as well (Kendler, Heath et al., 1992). The dopamine D_2 gene has been incriminated (Blum, Noble et al., 1990; Higuchi, Muramatsu et al., 1994), but this is disputed (Bolos, Dean et al., 1990; Gejman, Ram et al., 1994). Individual differences in rates of ethanol metabolism also appear, in part, to be genetically controlled, and it is suspected that genetic factors influence the severity of alcohol-induced liver disease (Lumeng & Crabb, 1994). Indeed, preliminary results (Day, Bashir et al., 1991) indicated different

ADH3 allele frequencies in patients with alcohol-related end-organ damage compared to controls, suggesting that genetically determined differences in alcohol metabolism may, in part, explain differences in susceptibility to disease (possibly through enhanced generation of toxic metabolites), but this has been questioned (Poupon, Napalas et al., 1992). 2E1 also is polymorphic and some alleles have been reported to predispose to alcoholic liver disease by some, but not by others. Similarly, a significant association of a particular restriction fragment length polymorphism (RFLP) haplotype of the COL1A2 locus with alcoholic cirrhosis has been reported (Weiner, Eskreis et al., 1988) but questioned by others (Bashir, Day et al., 1992). That susceptibility to alcoholic liver disease is in part genetically determined has been shown by twin studies (Hrubec & Omenn, 1981) and, recently, a significant association was found between the occurrence of the "null" genotype and that of alcoholic liver cirrhosis (Savolainen, Pajarinen et al., 1996).

ORGAN DAMAGE

Alcoholic Liver Disease. *Clinical and pathological presentations, pathogenesis:* Because of its intrinsic toxicity, alcohol can injure the liver even in the absence of dietary deficiencies (Lieber, 1992). Fatty liver, the first manifestation of alcoholic liver disease, can begin within days of heavy drinking. This is followed by early fibrosis, which in turn can be associated with alcoholic hepatitis. Eventually, there is irreversible damage leading to severe fibrosis, and subsequently, to cirrhosis. The various clinical manifestations of alcoholic liver disease are well documented (Lieber, 1992) and will not be reviewed here.

Fibrosis as a result of necrosis and inflammation is thought to be the underlying mechanism of alcoholic cirrhosis. However, cirrhosis commonly develops without an apparent intermediate stage of alcoholic hepatitis, both in alcoholics (Hasumura, Minato et al., 1985; Worner & Lieber, 1985) and in baboons given alcohol (Lieber, Robins et al., 1994). Indeed, independently of necrosis and inflammation, alcohol directly affects stellate cells in the liver (also called lipocytes, Ito, or fat-storing cells) causing the deposition of collagen, the characteristic protein of the fibrous tissues, first deposited around the terminal hepatic venules (perivenular fibrosis). Long-term alcohol consumption transforms stellate cells into collagen-producing myofibroblast-like cells (Friedman, 1993; Mak & Lieber, 1988). *In vitro*, these cells respond to acetaldehyde with a further increase in collagen (Moshage, Casini & Lieber, 1990) and its messenger mRNA (Casini, Cunningham et al., 1991). Phospholipids, the backbone of all cellular membranes, are the primary targets of peroxidation and can be strikingly altered by ethanol (Yamada, Mak & Lieber, 1985). In baboons given alcohol, phosphatidylcholine is generally depleted in the liver (Lieber, Robins & Leo, 1994b) and especially in liver mitochondria (Arai, Gordon & Lieber, 1984), causing a marked decrease in cytochrome oxidase activity and oxygen consumption. This deficiency was correctable *in vitro* by replenishing phospholipid (Arai, Gordon & Lieber, 1984). When the alcohol-fed baboons were given polyenylphosphatidylcholine, a polyunsaturated phospholipid mixture extracted from soybeans, hepatic phosphatidylcholine and the activity of phosphatidylethanolamine methyltransferase were restored (Lieber, Robins & Leo, 1994a), the number of transformed stellate cells was reduced, and septal fibrosis ($p < 0.001$) as well as cirrhosis was fully prevented (Lieber, DeCarli et al., 1990; Lieber, Robins & Leo, 1994a).

Cirrhosis, which results from an imbalance between the degradation and production of collagen, may represent the failure of degradation to keep pace with synthesis. Indeed, in transformed stellate cells, polyenylphosphatidylcholine (PPC) (Li, Kim et al., 1992) and its active phospholipid species dilinoleoylphosphatidylcholine (DLPC) (Lieber, Robins & Leo, 1994b) suppress the acetaldehyde-mediated increase in collagen accumulation, most likely by stimulating collagenase activity. The role of collagenase has also been shown indirectly in humans by the correlation between the severity of alcoholic fibrosis and the activity of a circulating collagenase inhibitor, the tissue inhibitor of metalloproteinase (Li, Rosman et al., 1994).

Cytokines such as transforming growth factor β and tumor necrosis factor α also stimulate fibrogenesis. Furthermore, tumor necrosis factor α may contribute to the anorexia and muscle wasting associated with severe liver disease (McClain, Hill et al., 1993).

Derangements of the immune system occur in alcoholic liver disease (Paronetto, 1993), but whether they are a consequence or a cause of the liver injury remains debatable. Viral hepatitis due to hepatitis B or C virus commonly accompanies chronic hepatitis in alcoholics. Even in the absence of risk factors such as intravenous drug use, portal or lobular inflammation is strongly associated with the hepatitis C virus in alcoholics (Rosman, Paronetto et al., 1993). This suggests that alcohol may favor the acquisition, replication, or persistence of the virus, which can potentiate associated liver disorders.

Treatment and prevention of liver disease: The traditional approach toward alcoholism is based on treatment of underlying psychological and behavioral problems, coupled with treatment of late-stage medical complications. The latter efforts focus on the management of the consequences of cirrhosis, such as ascites and bleeding. These traditional approaches, though helpful, have not impacted on the prevalence of the disease, and come too late to revert the liver to normal. Better understanding of how alcohol affects the liver allows for earlier and more direct avenues to prevent or counteract alcohol's effects. These efforts include a focus on early detection of alcoholism, utilizing, in part, biochemical markers of heavy drinking, such as carbohydrate-deficient transferrin (CDT); screening, among heavy consumers, for signs of medical complications (for instance, through the use of traditional "liver" tests); and reducing the task of treatment to manageable size by focusing major therapeutic efforts on susceptible subgroups. Indeed, only a minority of heavy drinkers eventually develop the major complications such as liver cirrhosis. In the absence of practical accepted genetic markers, individuals vulnerable to develop the more severe complications can be recognized empirically through the early detection of lesions (such as perivenular fibrosis) which indicate that the patient has already entered the process of liver fibrosis and may therefore rapidly progress to the ultimate stages of cirrhosis. These individuals should be the subject of especially intense treatment, such as the correction of nutritional deficits, when present, and efforts at curbing alcohol consumption.

Some agents that can be viewed as "supernutrients" have been found to be effective in nonhuman primates. These include S-adenosylmethionine for the treatment of early aspects of alcohol-induced liver injury (Lieber, Casini et al., 1990) and polyunsaturated lecithin for the prevention of fibrosis (Lieber, DeCarli et al., 1990; Lieber, Robins et al., 1994a). Both of these compounds are now being tested in humans. In patients who have either spontaneous hepatic encephalopathy or a high hepatic "discriminant function" (based on elevated prothrombin time and bilirubin), prednisolone (40 mg/day for 28 days) improves survival.

Helicobacter (H.) pylori infection potentially contributes to hepatic encephalopathy because of its high urease activity, which promotes the conversion of urea to ammonia, one of the precipitating factors of hepatic precoma and coma. It was shown that various antibiotics, including tetracyclines (Lieber & Lefèvre, 1957, 1959) and ampicillin (Meyers & Lieber, 1976), effectively suppress gastric conversion of urea to ammonia. A corresponding beneficial effect in patients with cirrhosis was observed, particularly in the presence of associated azotemia (Lieber & Davidson, 1960; Lieber & Lefèvre, 1958). The encephalopathy can also be alleviated by judicious adjustment of dietary protein (avoiding both deficiency and excess), and by decreasing colonic production and absorption of NH_3 with lactulose, a nonabsorbable disaccharide that acidifies the colon content through fermentation.

Oxandrolone therapy is also associated with a beneficial effect in moderately malnourished patients (Mendenhall, Anderson et al., 1984). Propylthiouracil has been suggested for the treatment of alcoholic hepatitis (Orrego, Kalant et al., 1979; Orrego, Blake et al., 1987), and colchicine for the treatment of alcoholic cirrhosis (Kershenobich, Vargas et al., 1988). Additional controlled trials are presently ongoing.

A multitude of other "hepatoprotective" agents have been proposed, but they are not yet fully validated in humans. Finally, liver transplantation, originally not applied to alcoholic liver disease, is now increasingly being considered for individuals who have stopped drinking (Kumar, Stauber et al., 1990).

Gastrointestinal and Pancreatic Complications. Alterations in salivary secretion and enlargement of the parotid glands are common in patients with alcoholic liver injury. Esophageal complications of alcohol use include an increased incidence of esophageal (and oropharyngeal) cancer, especially in those who smoke.

A serious complication in the alcoholic is GI bleeding. In alcoholics presenting with upper GI bleeding, acute hemorrhagic gastritis is found in 25% to 36% (Katz, Pitchumoni et al., 1976). Other sources of blood loss in the alcoholic are esophageal varices (40%), peptic ulceration, Mallory-Weiss lesions, duodenitis, and esophagitis. Chronic gastritis is also common in the alcoholic, in part because of *H. pylori* infection (Lieber, 1997b). Indeed, chronic gastritis generally resolves with the eradication of the microbe (Uppal, Lateef et al., 1991).

Diarrhea may occur for a variety of reasons, including ethanol-exacerbated lactase deficiency, especially in non-Caucasians.

Alcoholic pancreatitis, another major complication, is considered a "chronic" form of pancreatitis because it is associated with irreversible changes in function and structure. Alcoholic pancreatitis generally develops after 10 to 15 years of heavy drinking. Episodic heavy drinking in alcoholics often precipitates relapses. A high serum amylase level is compatible with the diagnosis of pancreatitis, but the test is not entirely specific or always sensitive enough since the amylase may be within the normal range in patients with long-standing fibrotic disease. Conversely, other intra-abdominal processes (including biliary tract disease, intestinal infarction, perforated ulcer, and pelvic emergencies) may increase the serum amylase. Various theories have been proposed to explain alcohol-induced pancreatitis (Lieber, 1992), including oxidative damage mediated by free radicals. A major functional consequence of chronic pancreatitis is its exocrine deficiency with reduced secretion of digestive enzymes (amylase, lipase, etc.).

Endocrine Pathology. Alcohol activates the hypothalamic-pituitary-adrenal axis, resulting in increased ACTH release, but the adrenocortical response diminishes with chronic use of ethanol. Although acute administration increases plasma cortisol concentrations, the stimulatory response to ethanol is blunted after chronic ethanol exposure. Alcohol stimulates adrenal medullary secretion of catecholamines. Alcohol use decreases plasma testosterone, an effect that reflects both a decrease in production and an increase in metabolic clearance of the hormone. Hypogonadism and feminization are consistent hallmarks of cirrhosis. Clinically, loss of pubic hair and libido are present in males, menstrual disorders are common in females, and vascular spiders are seen in both.

Hematologic Disorders. Megaloblastic anemia resulting from folate deficiency is a common cause of anemia in the alcoholic. The mean corpuscular volume (MCV) is typically increased, but may be normal when iron deficiency coexists. Severe folate deficiency may cause thrombocytopenia and granulocytopenia as well, but thrombocytopenia also appears to result from a direct toxic effect of ethanol on hematopoiesis. Folate deficiency interferes with homocysteine disposition (Figure 3). It has been associated with elevated plasma homocysteine concentrations noted in alcoholics (Hultberg, Berglund et al., 1993), and hyperhomocysteinemia has been incriminated in the development of premature vascular disease (Stampfer, Malinow et al., 1992). Sideroblastic changes are usually encountered in malnourished alcoholics. Alcoholic liver injury itself may result in a number of red blood cell abnormalities.

Musculoskeletal, Renal and Dermatologic Complications. Fractures of the femoral neck, the wrist, vertebrae and ribs are especially common even after mild trauma. Because of demineralization, alcoholics have a five- to 10-fold greater risk of incurring a fracture than do nonalcoholics. Myopathy in the alcoholic is either acute or chronic. In acute myopathy, one or more groups of muscles become painful, tender and swollen, and this is often associated with increases in serum concentrations of creatine kinase and LDH. In chronic myopathy, pain is a less prominent feature but there is proximal muscle wasting and weakness. Myoglobinuria may occur and lead to renal failure.

Chronic as well as acute alcohol intoxication results in major electrolyte and acid-base disturbances (Lieber, 1992), as well as a host of other abnormalities (such as proteinuria), as yet largely uncharted.

Among the dermatologic lesions characteristic of heavy alcohol consumption are facial edema, rosacea, rhinophyma, psoriasis and discoid eczema. Dermatoses also arise from nutritional deficiencies: pellagra (erythema followed by hyperkeratosis and desquamation) and zinc deficiency (desquamative or bullous lesions).

Cardiovascular Effects. Moderate drinkers (two drinks/day) have lesser mortality due to coronary complications compared to total abstainers (Boffetta & Garfinkel, 1990). Postulated mechanisms include increased high density lipoproteins (HDL). An increase in HDL concentrations after alcohol ingestion was demonstrated in animals and has since been widely observed in human beings (Devenyi, Robinson et al., 1981). When the role of HDL in cholesterol transport and its protective effect against atherosclerosis became apparent, it made sense to postulate that the decreased incidence of coronary heart disease in moderate drinkers might be due to the ethanol-induced elevation of HDL. HDL is a heterogeneous group of lipoproteins with two major subclasses: the less dense HDL_2, epidemiologically associated with a reduction in coronary heart disease, and the more dense HDL_3, not clearly related to coronary heart disease prevention. Indeed, agents or conditions that are thought to affect coronary heart disease through HDL (such as exercise and being female) have been shown to increase HDL_2, not HDL_3. It had first been reported that the increase in HDL after alcohol consumption involves both HDL_2 and HDL_3, with a major change in

HDL_2 (Taskinen, Valimaki et al., 1982). However, these observations were made in alcoholics with a relatively high intake of alcohol. It is now well recognized that large amounts of alcohol have adverse effects, and it is generally agreed that such high intakes are not associated with protection against coronary heart disease (Devenyi, Robinson et al., 1981). Haskell and colleagues (1984) reported that administration of moderate doses of alcohol (about 0.5 to 2.2 oz or 12 to 51 g or absolute ethanol per day) raised concentrations of HDL_3 but not concentrations of HDL_2, and that upon abstention from moderate consumption, concentrations of HDL_3, not of HDL_2, decreased. Thus, the conclusion of Hartung and colleagues (1983) that "nonexercisers can maintain concentrations of HDL similar to those of individuals who jog regularly by ingesting three beers a day" must be reassessed in the light of the fact that the HDL subfractions involved appear to be different in the two groups.

Thus, we can distinguish three partially overlapping stages in the relationship between alcohol, coronary heart disease, and HDL:

(1) Moderate alcohol intake is associated with a decreased incidence of coronary heart disease and with increased concentrations of HDL_3. It is not known for sure whether HDL_3 has an impact on the incidence of coronary heart disease or whether the "protective" effect of moderate drinking is secondary to some mechanism unrelated to HDL, such as plasminogen activation, decreased platelet aggregation (perhaps because of the acetaldehyde-mediated increase in prostacyclins) (Guivernau, Baraona & Lieber, 1987), or wine congeners. In fact, whether the "protection" is due primarily to alcohol rather than to some other associated factor is not yet settled, since occasional drinkers also show such relative protection with amounts as low as one drink a week (Boffeta & Garfinkel, 1990), or one glass of wine a month (Gronbaek, Henriksen & Becker, 1995); (2) In the absence of severe liver injury, high alcohol intake results in increased concentrations of HDL, primarily HDL_2, but at that level of alcohol intake there is no evidence of "protection" against coronary heart disease; (3) When alcohol consumption is associated with severe liver disease, concentrations of the HDL fractions decrease. Thus, with higher alcohol intakes, adverse effects predominate.

Alcoholic cardiomyopathy with myocardial fiber hypertrophy and fibrosis can be found in patients who have been drinking heavily for at least 10 years. The diagnosis of alcoholic cardiomyopathy is one of exclusion (Lieber, 1992). There are no specific and easily performed tests to identify the disorder. Some of the metabolic effects that have been demonstrated in other tissues may apply to the heart as well, including the toxic effects of fatty-acid ethyl esters. Episodes of heavy alcohol consumption may also result in cardiac arrhythmias. Ethanol has a pressor effect in normotensive individuals and its chronic consumption has been linked to the prevalence of hypertension in alcoholics, which contributes to an increased incidence of strokes.

Neurologic Complications. The various syndromes associated with brain atrophy, neuritis and other sequelae of chronic alcohol consumption and associated thiamine, pyridoxine and other nutritional deficiencies have been reviewed in detail elsewhere (Victor, 1992). Physical signs comprise alcohol tolerance, alcohol withdrawal, and an inability to control alcohol intake. The mesolimbic dopaminergic systems, and the gamma-aminobutyric acid-A and *N*-methyl-D-aspartate (NMDA) receptors have been implicated as mediators of various aspects of the symptomatology, including tolerance and withdrawal signs. Withdrawal from alcohol produces a wide range of symptoms, which may appear following abrupt cessation or marked diminution of alcohol intake. Early manifestations include anxiety, tremulousness, diaphoresis, insomnia, anorexia, and nausea. Withdrawal (generalized major motor) seizures may occur from seven to 48 hours following cessation of alcohol consumption. They are usually self-limited, rarely exceed six episodes over a period of several hours, and seldom proceed to *status epilepticus. Delirium tremens*, characterized by profound confusion, disorientation, hallucination, agitation, tremulousness, and tachycardia, represents the most severe stage of alcohol withdrawal. A benzodiazepine should be administered to produce a calm state. To that end, chlordiazepoxide (Librium®) is most commonly used. The patient should be closely observed and the dosage repeated in four to six hours if symptoms persist. It is essential to treat early and to titrate the dose for each patient individually, rather than to adopt a fixed schedule. Thiamine (100 mg), given intravenously or intramuscularly, is recommended empirically.

To prevent relapse, self-help groups, such as Alcoholic Anonymous, are helpful. Treatment with disulfiram (Antabuse®) can also be a successful deterrent, although this has been the subject of debate. By inhibiting aldehyde dehydrogenase, disulfiram increases blood acetaldehyde, resulting in an aversive reaction of flushing, nausea and hypotension. It should not be given to those subjects (common in

Oriental populations) with a genetic defect in aldehyde dehydrogenase, detectable by a flushing reaction on drinking even small amounts of alcohol. Disulfiram may be safely instituted three days following cessation of alcohol intake. Patients should be evaluated following detoxification for underlying hepatic and cardiovascular disease. Naltrexone has been found to reduce craving in short-term studies (three to six months). Continuation of treatment appears to be necessary, and longer follow-up studies are in progress to determine whether benefits persist.

TO DRINK OR NOT TO DRINK?

Medical disorders related to alcoholism which affect virtually all tissues of the body represent a major but neglected public health issue. Even at moderate intake, adverse consequences may ensue, although "protective" cardiovascular effects also may be produced. The latter prompted recommendations of moderate consumption but, for those, one must take associated circumstances into account. When intact judgment and motor coordination are essential (as in driving), temporary cessation of alcohol intake is, of course, advisable. Abstinence may also be appropriate under other special circumstances, such as pregnancy, since even moderate amounts of alcohol may adversely affect the fetus. The question remains whether, under ordinary circumstances, people should be advised to engage in moderate drinking to "protect" their coronary arteries. It must be emphasized that the introduction of moderate drinking into the life of an abstainer involves the unpredictable risk of loss of control, with the potential for social and medical disintegration. By contrast, in a moderate drinker who has demonstrated the capacity to maintain intake at an acceptable level, there is no compelling reason to change his or her lifestyle and eliminate a pleasurable and possibly beneficial habit. Thus, one's past capacity to keep consumption within socially and medically acceptable bounds is probably the most useful guide in deciding whether to drink (moderately) or not drink. On the other hand, heavy alcohol consumption must always be discouraged, because its obvious adverse effects cannot be prevented through nutritional manipulations (Lieber & DeCarli, 1974; Lieber, Jones & DeCarli, 1965). Moreover, recommendations should not be based on limited observations taken out of context. For instance, the fact that the population of France still has one of the highest rates of alcohol intake in the world, and that coronary heart disease mortality rates there are lower than in many other developed countries, should not necessarily lead to adoption of the French drinking pattern, since in France the possible benefits of alcohol in the prevention of coronary heart disease are canceled out by increased rates of mortality from other causes of death. Indeed, a recent study, using two independent sources of data, demonstrated a very high alcohol-related premature mortality rate in the French population. Furthermore, in comparison with the United States, alcohol-related mortality rates were far higher in France. Moreover, a recommendation for moderate consumption of alcohol could lead to an overall increase in alcohol intake, since the level of average consumption of alcohol in the population appears to correlate with the frequency of heavy drinking. The latter, in turn, may result in an increase in morbidity and mortality.

FUTURE TRENDS

Despite recent decreases in overall alcohol consumption, there is an opposite trend in the young, especially women (Gomberg, 1993). Therefore, one can predict that alcohol-related disorders will remain a major issue in the foreseeable future. To date, intervention has been focused mainly on the prevention and treatment of alcohol abuse and dependence and the therapy of severe sequelae of alcohol-related disorders such as cirrhosis of the liver. However, treatment of alcohol abuse and dependence has not as yet been codified, and a recent massive eight-year research project by the National Institute on Alcohol Abuse and Alcoholism failed to find that matching clients with particular treatment methods improves treatment outcomes (Project MATCH Research Group, 1997). In addition to these traditional efforts, it now appears relevant and appropriate to intervene at early stages of the medical disorders using a truly public health approach that is based on identification of individuals at risk (i.e., heavy drinkers identified not only through questionnaires, but also by biologic markers) and early detection of the various associated medical disorders. Such an approach is in keeping with the disease concept of alcoholism. Treatment of these medical complications should take advantage of the newly acquired knowledge on how alcohol causes injuries to the various tissues. There are therapeutic agents that can boost the body's defenses against the toxic manifestations of alcohol excess by restoring the antioxidant status and repairing the phospholipid alterations in the membrane, as well as by interrupting the body's exaggerated response to injury, such as inordinate scarring, which ultimately may lead to irreversible cirrhosis and its disastrous sequelae. However, there is a relative disinterest of the medical profession in such an approach. By contrast, the public appears to be sensing such a need and sometimes is turning to "alternate" therapies with uncontrolled herbal and "nutritional supplements," which are of dubious efficacy and inherently dangerous because of their lack of safety profiles and standardization.

It behooves the medical profession to fill the gap by using recently acquired knowledge and resulting validated therapies. Thereby, even a small decrease in the frequency or duration of medical and social complications associated with alcohol excess would largely offset the costs of early intervention and of the research efforts still needed in that field, not to mention the benefit of a significant reduction in human suffering.

ACKNOWLEDGMENTS: The original studies reviewed here were supported by National Institutes of Health grants AA05934, AA11115, AA07275, the Department of Veterans Affairs, and the Kingsbridge Research Foundation. The skillful preparation of this manuscript by Joan Jennings and Shawn Dickerson is gratefully acknowledged.

REFERENCES

Abel EL & Sokol RJ (1991). A revised conservative estimate of the incidence of FAS & its economic impact. *Alcoholism: Clinical & Experimental Research* 15:514–524.

Adams WI, Yuan Z, Barboriak JJ et al. (1993). Alcohol-related hospitalizations of elderly people: Prevalence and geographic variation in the United States. *Journal of the American Medical Association* 270:1222–1225, 1993.

Albanes D, Heinonen OP, Taylor PR et al. (1996). α-tocopherol and β-carotene supplements and lung cancer incidence in the Alpha-Tocopherol, Beta-Carotene Cancer Prevention Study: Effects of base-line characteristics and study compliance. *Journal of the National Cancer Institute* 88:1560–1571.

Ahmed S, Leo MA & Lieber CS (1994). Interactions between alcohol and beta-carotene in patients with alcoholic liver disease. *American Journal of Clinical Nutrition* 60:430–436.

The Alpha-Tocopherol, Beta-Carotene Cancer Prevention Study Group (1994). The effect of vitamin E and beta carotene on the incidence of lung cancer and other cancers in male smokers. *The New England Journal of Medicine* 330:1029–1035.

Arai M, Leo MA, Nakano M et al. (1984). Biochemical and morphological alterations of baboon hepatic mitochondria after chronic ethanol consumption. *Hepatology* 4:165–174.

Arai M, Gordon ER & Lieber CS (1984). Decreased cytochrome oxidase activity in hepatic mitochondria after chronic ethanol consumption and the possible role of decreased cytochrome aa3 content and changes in phospholipids. *Biochimica Biophysica Acta* 797:320–327.

Baraona E, Leo MA, Borowsky SA et al. (1977). Pathogenesis of alcohol-induced accumulation of protein in the liver. *Journal of Clinical Investigation* 60:546–554.

Baraona E, Yokoyama A, Ishii H et al. (1991). Lack of alcohol dehydrogenase isoenzyme activities in the stomach of Japanese subjects. *Life Sciences* 49:1929–1934.

Bashir R, Day CP, James OFW et al. (1992). No evidence for involvement of type I collagen structural genes in "genetic predisposition" to alcoholic cirrhosis. *Journal of Hepatology* 16:316–319.

Beskid M, Bialek J, Dzieniszewski J et al. (1980). Effect of combined phenylbutazone and ethanol administration on rat liver. *Experimental Pathology* 18:487–491.

Black M (1984). Acetaminophen hepatotoxicity. *Annual Review of Medicine* 35:577–593.

Blum K, Noble EP, Sheridan PJ et al. (1990). Ailelic association of human dopamine D2 receptor gene in alcoholism. *Journal of the American Medical Association* 263:2055–2060.

Boden G, Chen X, Desantis R et al. (1993). Effects of ethanol on carbohydrate metabolism in the elderly. *Diabetes* 42:28–34.

Boffetta P & Garfinkel L (1990). Alcohol drinking and mortality among men enrolled in an American Cancer Society prospective study. *Epidemiology* 1:342–348.

Bolos AM, Dean M, Lucas-Derse S et al. (1990). Population and pedigree studies reveal a lack of association between the dopamine D2 receptor gene and alcoholism. *Journal of the American Medical Association* 264:356–360.

Borowsky SA & Lieber CS (1978). Interaction of methadone and ethanol metabolism. *Journal of Pharmacology and Experimental Therapeutics* 207:123–129.

Caballeria J, Baraona E, Deulofeu R et al. (1991). Effects of H_2 receptor antagonists on gastric alcohol dehydrogenase activity. *Digestive Diseases & Sciences* 36:1673–1679.

Caballeria J, Baraona E, Rodamilans M et al. (1989). Effects of cimetidine on gastric alcohol dehydrogenase activity and blood ethanol levels. *Gastroenterology* 96:388- 392.

Carulli N, Manenti F, Gallo M et al. (1971). Alcohol-drugs interaction in man: Alcohol and tolbutamide. *European Journal of Clinical Investigation* 1:421–424.

Casini A, Cunningham M, Rojkind M et al. (1991). Acetaldehyde increases procollagen type I and fibronectin gene transcription in cultured rat fat-storing cells through a protein synthesis-dependent mechanism. *Hepatology* 13:758–765.

Chedid A, Mendenhall CL, Gartside P et al. and the VA Cooperative Study Group (1991). Prognostic factors in alcoholic liver disease. *American Journal of Gastroenterology* 86:210–216.

Colditz GA (1990). A prospective assessment of moderate alcohol intake and major chronic diseases. *Annals of Epidemiology* 1:167–177.

Day CP, Bashir R, James O et al. (1991). Investigation of the role of polymorphisms at the alcohol and aldehyde dehydrogenase loci in genetic predisposition to alcohol-related end-organ damage. *Hepatology* 14:798–801.

Devenyi P, Robinson GM, Kepen BM et al. (1981). High density lipoprotein cholesterol in male alcoholics with and without severe liver disease. *American Journal of Medicine* 71:589–594.

Dicker E & Cederbaum AI (1988). Increased oxygen radical-dependent inactivation of metabolic enzymes by liver microsomes after chronic ethanol consumption. *FASEB Journal* 2:2901–2906.

Di Padova C, Roine R, Frezza M et al. (1992). Effects of ranitidine on blood alcohol levels after ethanol ingestion: Comparison with other H_2-receptor antagonists. *Journal of the American Medical Association* 267:83–86.

Di Padova C, Worner TM, Julkunen RJK et al. (1987). Effects of fasting and chronic alcohol consumption on the first pass metabolism of ethanol. *Gastroenterology* 92:1169–1173.

Espina N, Lima V, Lieber CS et al. (1988). *In vitro* and *in vivo* inhibitory effect of ethanol and acetaldehyde on O^6methylguanine transferase. *Carcinogenesis* 9:761–766.

Faller J & Fox IH (1982). Evidence for increased urate production by activation of adenine nucleotide turnover. *The New England Journal of Medicine* 307:1598–1602.

Feely J & Wood AJ (1982). Effect of cimetidine on the elimination and actions of ethanol. *Journal of the American Medical Association* 247:2819–2821.

Forman MR, Beecher GR, Lanza E et al. (1995). Effect of alcohol consumption on plasma carotenoid concentrations in premenopausal women: A controlled dietary study. *American Journal of Clinical Nutrition* 62:131–135.

Fraser AG, Hudson M, Sawyer AM et al. (1996). Short report: The effect of ranitidine on post-prandial absorption of a low dose of alcohol. *Alimentary Pharmacology & Therapeutics* 6:267–271.

Frezza M, Di Padova C & Pozzato G (1990). High blood alcohol levels in women: The role of decreased gastric alcohol dehydrogenase activity and first-pass metabolism. *The New England Journal of Medicine* 322:95–99.

Friedman SL (1993). The cellular basis of hepatic fibrosis: Mechanisms and treatment strategies. *The New England Journal of Medicine* 328:1828–35.

Fukunaga T, Sillanaukee P & Eriksson CJP (1993). Occurrence of blood acetaldehyde in women during ethanol intoxication: Preliminary findings. *Alcoholism: Clinical & Experimental Research* 17:1198–1200.

Garro AJ, Espina N, McBeth D et al. (1992). Effects of alcohol consumption on DNA methylation reactions and gene expression: Implications for increased cancer risk. *European Journal of Cancer Prevention* 3:19–23.

Garro AJ & Lieber CS (1990). Alcohol and cancer. *Annual Review of Pharmacology and Toxicology* 30:219–249.

Gejman PV, Ram A, Gelernter J et al. (1994). No structural mutation in the dopamine D_2 receptor gene in alcoholism or schizophrenia. Analysis using denaturing gradient gel electrophoresis. *Journal of the American Medical Association* 271:204–208.

Gomberg ESL (1993). Women and alcohol: Use and abuse. *Journal of Nervous and Mental Diseases* 181:211–219.

Grassi GG & Grassi C (1975). Ethanol-antibiotic interactions at hepatic level. *International Journal of Clinical Pharmacology* 11:216–225.

Gronbaek M, Henriksen JH & Becker U (1995). Carbohydrate-deficient transferrin-A. Valid marker of alcoholism in population studies? Results from the Copenhagen City Heart Study. *Alcoholism: Clinical & Experimental Research* 19:457–461.

Guivernau M, Baraona E & Lieber CS (1987). Acute and chronic effects of ethanol and its metabolites on vascular production of prostacyclin in rats. *Journal of Pharmacology and Experimental Therapy* 140:59–64.

Gupta AM, Baraona E & Lieber CS (1995). Significant increase of blood alcohol by cimetidine after repetitive drinking of small alcohol doses. *Alcoholism: Clinical & Experimental Research* 19:1083–1087.

Guram M, Howden CW & Holt S (1991). Further evidence for an interaction between alcohol and certain H_2-receptor antagonists. *Alcoholism: Clinical & Experimental Research* 15:1084–1085.

Haber PS, Gentry T, Mak KM et al. (1996). Metabolism of alcohol by human gastric cells: Relation to first-pass metabolism. *Gastroenterology* 111:863–870.

Hartung GH, Foreyt JP, Mitchell RE et al. (1983). Effect of alcohol intake on high-density lipoprotein cholesterol levels in runners and inactive men. *Journal of the American Medical Association* 249:747–750.

Haskell WL, Camargo C Jr, Williams PT et al. (1984). The effect of cessation and resumption of moderate alcohol intake on serum high-density lipoprotein subfractions: A controlled study. *The New England Journal of Medicine* 310:805–810.

Hasumura Y, Minato Y, Nishimura M et al. (1985). Hepatic fibrosis in alcoholics: Morphologic characteristics, clinical diagnosis and natural course. *Pathobiology of Hepatic Fibrosis* 7:13–24.

Hernández-Muñoz R, Caballeria J, Baraona E et al. (1990). Human gastric alcohol dehydrogenase: Its inhibition by H_2-receptor antagonists, and its effect on the bioavailability of ethanol. *Alcoholism: Clinical & Experimental Research* 14:946–950.

Hetu C, Dumont A & Joly J-G (1983). Effect of chronic ethanol administration on bromobenzene liver toxicity in the rat. *Toxicology and Applied Pharmacology* 67:166- 167.

Hetu C & Joly J-G (1985). Differences in the duration of the enhancement of liver mixed-function oxidase activities in ethanol-fed rats after withdrawal. *Biochemical Pharmacology* 34:1211–1216.

Higuchi S, Muramatsu T & Murayama M (1994). Association of structural polymorphism of the dopamine D2 receptor gene and alcoholism. *Biochemical & Biophysical Research Communications* 204:1199–1205.

Hirano T, Kaplowitz N, Tsukamoto H et al. (1992). Hepatic mitochondrial glutathione depletion and progression of experimental alcoholic liver disease in rats. *Hepatology* 16:1423–1427.

Hoerner M, Behrens UJ, Worner TM et al. (1988). The role of alcoholism and liver disease in the appearance of serum antibodies against acetaldehyde adducts. *Hepatology* 8:569–574.

Hoerner M, Behrens UJ, Worner T et al. (1986). Humoral immune response to acetaldehyde adducts in alcoholic patients. *Research Communications in Molecular Chemistry, Pathology & Pharmacology* 54:3–12.

Hoffman PL & Tabakoff B (1996). Alcohol dependence: A commentary on mechanisms. *Alcohol & Alcoholism* 31:333–340.

Hrubec Z & Omenn GS (1981). Evidence of genetic predisposition to alcoholic cirrhosis and psychosis: Twin concordances for alcoholism and its biological end points by zygosity among male veterans. *Alcoholism: Clinical & Experimental Research* 5:207–215.

Hultberg B, Berglund M, Andersson A et al. (1993). Elevated plasma homocysteine in alcoholics. *Alcoholism: Clinical & Experimental Research* 17:687–689.

Israël Y, Hurwitz E, Niëmelä O et al. (1986). Monoclonal and polyclonal antibodies against acetaldehyde-containing epitopes in acetaldehyde-protein adducts. *Proceedings of the National Academy of Sciences* 83:7923–7927.

Israël Y, Speisky H, Lança AJ et al. (1992). Metabolism of hepatic glutathione and its relevance in alcohol induced liver damage. *Cellular and Molecular Aspects of Cirrhosis* 216:25–37.

Kaikaus RM, Sui Z, Lysenko N et al. (1993). Regulation of pathways of extramitochondrial fatty acid oxidation and liver fatty acid-binding protein by long-chain monocarboxylic fatty acids in hepatocytes. *Journal of Biological Chemistry* 268:26866–26871.

Kalant H, Khanna JM & Marshman J (1970). Effect of chronic intake of ethanol on pentobarbital metabolism. *Journal of Pharmacology* 175:318–324.

Karl PI, Gordon BH, Lieber CS et al. (1988). Acetaldehyde production and transfer by the perfused human placental cotyledon. *Science* 242:273–275.

Kater RMH, Roggin G, Tobon F et al. (1969). Increased rate of clearance of drugs from the circulation of alcoholics. *American Journal of Medicine and Science* 258:35–39.

Kater RMH, Tobon F & Iber FL (1969). Increased rate of tolbutamide metabolism in alcoholic patients. *Journal of the American Medical Association* 207:363–365.

Kato R & Yamazoe Y (1992). Sex-specific cytochrome P450 as a cause of sex- and species-related differences in drug toxicity. *Toxicology Letter* 64/65:661–667.

Katz D, Pitchumoni CS, Thomas E et al. (1976). The endoscopic diagnosis of upper gastrointestinal hemorrhage: Changing concepts of etiology and management. *Digestive Diseases* 21:182–189.

Kendler KS, Heath AC, Neale MC et al. (1992). A population-based twin study of alcoholism in women. *Journal of the American Medical Association* 268:1877–1882.

Kershenobich D, Vargas F, Garcia-Tsao G et al. (1988). Colchicine in the treatment of cirrhosis of the liver. *The New England Journal of Medicine* 318:1709–1713.

Kharasch ED & Thummel KE (1993). Identification of cytochrome P4502E1 as the predominant enzyme catalyzing human liver microsomal defluorination of sevoflurane, isoflurane, and methoxyflurane. *Anesthesiology* 79:795–807.

Korsten MA & Lieber CS (1983). The elderly alcoholic. In EB Feldman (ed.) *Nutrition in the Middle and Later Years*. Littleton, MA: John Wright PSG, Inc., 5:93–106.

Kumar S, Stauber RE, Gavaler JS et al. (1990). Orthotopic liver transplantation for alcoholic liver disease. *Hepatology* 11:159–164.

Lane BP & Lieber CS (1966). Ultrastructural alterations in human hepatocytes following ingestion of ethanol with adequate diets. *American Journal of Pathology* 49:593–603.

Leo MA, Arai M, Sato M et al. (1982). Hepatotoxicity of vitamin A and ethanol in the rat. *Gastroenterology* 82:194–205.

Leo MA, Kim CI & Lieber CS (1987). NAD^{++}dependent retinol dehydrogenase in liver microsomes. *Archives of Biochemistry and Biophysics* 259:241–249.

Leo MA, Kim CI, Lowe N et al. (1992). Interaction of ethanol with β-carotene: Delayed blood clearance and enhanced hepatotoxicity. *Hepatology* 15:883–891.

Leo MA & Lieber CS (1982). Hepatic vitamin A depletion in alcoholic liver injury. *The New England Journal of Medicine* 307:597–601.

Leo MA & Lieber CS (1983). Hepatic fibrosis after long term administration of ethanol and moderate vitamin A supplementation in the rat. *Hepatology* 3:1–11.

Leo MA & Lieber CS (1985). New pathway for retinol metabolism in liver microsomes. *Journal of Biochemistry* 260:5228–5231.

Leo MA & Lieber CS (1988). Hypervitaminosis A: A liver lover's lament. *Hepatology* 8:412–417.

Leo MA & Lieber CS (1994). Beta carotene, vitamin E and lung cancer (letter). *The New England Journal of Medicine* 331:612–613.

Leo MA, Rosman AS & Lieber CS (1993). Differential depletion of carotenoids and tocopherol in liver disease. *Hepatology* 17:977–986.

Li J-J, Kim C-I, Leo MA et al. (1992). Polyunsaturated lecithin prevents acetaldehyde-mediated hepatic collagen accumulation by stimulating collagenase activity in cultured lipocytes. *Hepatology* 15:373–381.

Li J-J, Rosman AS, Leo MA et al. (1994). Tissue inhibitor of metalloproteinase is increased in the serum of precirrhotic and cirrhotic alcoholic patients and can serve as a marker of fibrosis. *Hepatology* 19:1418–23.

Lieber CS (1991). Perspectives: Do alcohol calories count? *American Journal of Clinical Nutrition* 54:976–982.

Lieber CS, ed. (1992). *Medical and Nutritional Complications of Alcoholism: Mechanisms and Management.* New York, NY: Plenum Press.

Lieber CS (1993). Women and alcohol: Gender differences in metabolism and susceptibility. In EL Gomberg & TD Nirenberg (eds.) *Women and Substance Abuse*. Norwood, NJ: Ablex Publishing Corp., 1–17.

Lieber CS (1994). Alcohol and the liver: 1994 update. *Gastroenterology* 106:1085–1105.

Lieber CS (1995). Medical disorders of alcoholism. *The New England Journal of Medicine* 333:1058–1065.

Lieber CS (1997a). Pathogenesis and treatment of liver fibrosis: 1997 update. *Digestive Diseases* 15:42–66.

Lieber CS (1997b). Gastric ethanol metabolism and gastritis: Interactions with other drugs, helicobacter pylori, and antibiotic therapy 1957–1997. *Alcoholism: Clinical & Experimental Research* 21:1360–1366.

Lieber CS (1998). Hepatic and other medical disorders of alcoholism: From pathogenesis to treatment. *Journal of Studies on Alcohol* 59:9–25.

Lieber CS, Baraona E, Hernández-Muñoz R et al. (1989). Impaired oxygen utilization: A new mechanism for the hepatotoxicity of ethanol in sub-human primates. *Journal of Clinical Investigation* 83:1682–1690.

Lieber CS & Davidson CS (1960). Complications resulting from renal failure in patients with liver disease. *Archives of Internal Medicine* 106:749–752.

Lieber CS & DeCarli LM (1968). Ethanol oxidation by hepatic microsomes: Adaptive increase after ethanol feeding. *Science* 162:917–918.

Lieber CS & DeCarli LM (1970). Hepatic microsomal ethanol oxidizing system: *In vitro* characteristics and adaptive properties *in vivo*. *Journal of Biological Chemistry* 245:2505–2512.

Lieber CS & DeCarli LM (1974). An experimental model of alcohol feeding and liver injury in the baboon. *Journal of Medical Primatology* 3:153–163.

Lieber CS & DeCarli LM (1991). Hepatotoxicity of ethanol. *Hepatology* 12:394–401.

Lieber CS, Casini A, DeCarli LM et al. (1990a). S-adenosyl-L-methionine attenuates alcohol-induced liver injury in the baboon. *Hepatology* 11:165–172.

Lieber CS, DeCarli LM, Mak KM et al. (1990b). Attenuation of alcohol-induced hepatic fibrosis by polyunsaturated lecithin. *Hepatology* 12:1390–1398.

Lieber CS, Garro A, Leo MA et al. (1986). Alcohol and cancer. *Hepatology* 6:1005–1019.

Lieber CS, Jones DP & DeCarli LM (1965). Effects of prolonged ethanol intake: Production of fatty liver despite adequate diets. *Journal of Clinical Investigation* 44:1009–1021.

Lieber CS & Lefèvre A (1957). Effect of oxytetracycline on acidity, ammonia and urea in gastric juice in normal and uremic subjects. *CR Soc. Biology* (Paris) 151:1038–1042.

Lieber CS & Lefèvre A (1958). Ammonia and intermediary metabolism in hepatic coma: Value of the determination of blood ammonia in the diagnosis and management of cirrhosis. *Acta Clinica Belgica* 13:328–357.

Lieber CS & Lefèvre A (1959). Ammonia as source of gastric hypoacidity in patients with uremia. *Journal of Clinical Investigation* 38:1271–1277.

Lieber CS, Robins SJ, Li J et al. (1994a). Phosphatidylcholine protects against fibrosis and cirrhosis in the baboon. *Gastroenterology* 106:152–159.

Lieber CS, Robins SJ & Leo MA (1994b). Hepatic phosphatidylethanolamine methyltransferase activity is decreased by ethanol and increased by phosphatidylcholine. *Alcoholism: Clinical & Experimental Research* 18:592–595.

Linnoila M, Erwin CW, Ramm D et al. (1980). Effects of age and alcohol on psychomotor performance of men. *Journal of Studies on Alcohol* 41:488–541.

Longnecker MP, Berlin JA, Orza MJ et al. (1988). A meta-analysis of alcohol consumption in relation to risk of breast cancer. *Journal of the American Medical Association* 260:652–656.

Lowenfels AB & Zevola SA (1989). Alcohol and breast cancer: An overview. *Alcoholism: Clinical & Experimental Research* 13:109–111.

Lumeng L & Crabb DW (1994). Genetic aspects and risk factors in alcoholism and alcoholic liver disease. *Gastroenterology* 107:572–578.

McClain C, Hill D, Schmidt J et al. (1993). Cytokines and alcoholic liver disease. In CS Lieber (ed.) *Alcoholic Liver Disease* (Seminars in Liver Disease, Vol. 13, No. 2). New York, NY: Thieme Medical Publishers, 170–182.

McGinnis JM & Foege WH (1993). Actual causes of death in the United States. *Journal of the American Medical Association* 270:2207–2212.

Ma X, Baraona E & Lieber CS (1993). Alcohol consumption enhances fatty acid ω-oxidation, with a greater increase in male than in female rats. *Hepatology* 18:1247–1253.

Mak KM & Lieber CS (1988). Lipocytes and transitional cells in alcoholic liver disease: A morphometric study. *Hepatology* 8:1027–1033.

Maly PI & Sasse D (1991). Intraacinar profiles of alcohol dehydrogenase and aldehyde dehydrogenase activities in human liver. *Gastroenterology* 101:1716–1723.

Mann K, Batra A, Gunther A et al. (1992). Do woman develop alcoholic brain damage more readily than men? *Alcoholism: Clinical & Experimental Research* 16:1052–1056.

Marik P & Mohedin B (1996). Alcohol-related admissions to an inner city hospital intensive care unit. *Alcohol & Alcoholism* 31:393–396.

Mendenhall CL, Anderson S, Garcia-Pont P et al. (1984). Short-term and long-term survival in patients with alcoholic hepatitis treated with oxandrolone and prednisolone. *The New England Journal of Medicine* 311:1464–1470.

Meyers S & Lieber CS (1976). Reduction of gastric ammonia by ampicillin in normal and azotemic subjects. *Gastroenterology* 70:244–247.

Mirmiran-Yazdy SA, Haber PS, Korsten MA et al. (1995). Metabolism of ethanol in rat gastric cells and its inhibition by cimetidine. *Gastroenterology* 108:737–742.

Misra PS, Lefèvre A, Ishii H et al. (1971). Increase of ethanol meprobamate and pentobarbital metabolism after chronic ethanol administration in man and in rats. *American Journal of Medicine* 51:346–351.

Moreno A & Parés X (1991). Purification and characterization of a new alcohol dehydrogenase from human stomach. *Journal of Biological Chemistry* 266:1128–1133.

Morgan MY & Sherlock S (1977). Sex-related differences among 100 patients with alcoholic liver disease. *British Medical Journal* 1:939–941.

Moshage H, Casini A & Lieber CS (1990). Acetaldehyde selectively stimulates collagen production in cultured rat liver fat-storing cells but not in hepatocytes. *Hepatology* 12:511–518.

Niemela O, Klajner F, Orrego H et al. (1987). Antibodies against acetaldehyde-modified protein epitopes in human alcoholics. *Hepatology* 7:1210–1214.

Niki E (1987). Interaction of ascorbate and α-tocopherol. *Annals of the New York Academy of Science* 493:186–199.

Nilsson BE (1970). Conditions contributing to fracture of the femoral neck. *Acta Chirurgica Scandinavica* 136:338–384.

Omenn GS, Goodman GE, Thornquist MD et al. (1996). Effects of a combination of beta-carotene and vitamin A on lung cancer and cardiovascular disease. *The New England Journal of Medicine* 334:1150–1155.

Orrego H, Kalant H, Israel Y et al. (1979). Effect of short-term therapy with propylthiouracil in patients with alcoholic liver disease. *Gastroenterology* 76:105–115.

Orrego H, Blake JE, Blendis LM et al. (1987). Long-term treatment of alcoholic liver disease with propylthiouracil. *The New England Journal of Medicine* 317:1421–1427.

Palmer RH, Frank WO, Nambi P et al. (1991). Effects of various concomitant medications on gastric alcohol dehydrogenase and the first-pass metabolism of ethanol. *American Journal of Gastroenterology* 86:1749–1755.

Parés A, Cederlund E, Moreno A et al. (1992). Class IV alcohol dehydrogenase (the gastric enzyme). Structural analysis of human σσ-ADH reveals class IV to be variable and confirms the presence of a fifth mammalian alcohol dehydrogenase class. *F.E.B.S. Letter* 303:69–72.

Paronetto F (1993). Immunologic reactions in alcoholic liver disease. In CS Lieber (ed.) *Alcoholic Liver Disease* (Seminars in Liver Disease, Vol. 13, No. 2). New York, NY: Thieme Medical Publishers, 183–195.

Parrish KM, Dufour MC, Stinson FS et al. (1993). Average daily alcohol consumption during adult life among decedents with and without cirrhosis: The 1986 National Mortality Followback Survey. *Journal of Studies on Alcohol* 54:450–456.

Pequignot G, Tuyns AJ & Berta JL (1978). Ascitic cirrhosis in relation to alcohol consumption. *International Journal of Epidemiology* 7:113–120.

Pignon J-P, Bailey NC, Baraona E et al. (1987). Fatty acid-binding protein: A major contributor to the ethanol-induced increase in liver cytosolic proteins in the rat. *Hepatology* 7:865–871.

Potter JF & James OFW (1987). Clinical features and prognosis of alcoholic liver disease in respect of advancing age. *Gerontology* 33:380–387.

Poupon RE, Napalas B, Coutelle C et al. and the French Group for Research on Alcohol and Liver (1992). Polymorphism of the alcohol dehydrogenase, alcohol and aldehyde dehydrogenase activities: Implications in alcoholic cirrhosis in white patients. *Hepatology* 15:1017–1022.

Pritchard JF & Schneck DW (1977). Effects of ethanol and phenobarbital on the metabolism of propranolol by 9000 g rat liver supernatant. *Biochemistry and Pharmacology* 26:2453–2454.

Project MATCH Research Group (1997). Matching alcoholism treatments to client heterogeneity: Project MATCH Posttreatment Drinking Outcomes. *Journal of Studies on Alcohol* 58:7–29.

Rabinovitz M, Van Thiel DH & Dindzans V et al. (1989). Endoscopic findings in alcoholic liver disease Does gender make a difference? *Alcohol* 6:465–468.

Rankin JG (1977). The natural history and management of the patient with alcoholic liver disease. In MM Fisher & JG Rankin (eds.) *Alcohol and the Liver.* New York, NY: Plenum Press, 365–381.

Raucy JL, Lasker JM, Lieber CS et al (1989). Acetaminophen activation by human liver cytochromes P450IIE1 and P4501A2. *Archives of Biochemistry & Biophysics* 271:270–283.

Raufman JP, Notar-Francesco V, Raffaniello RD et al. (1993). Histamine–2 receptor antagonists do not alter serum ethanol levels in fed, nonalcoholic men. *Annals of Internal Medicine* 118:488–494.

Roine R, Gentry RT, Hernández-Muñoz R et al. (1990). Aspirin increases blood alcohol concentrations in humans after ingestion of ethanol. *Journal of the American Medical Association* 264:2406–2408.

Roine RP, Gentry RT, Lim RT Jr. et al. (1991). Effect of concentration of ingested ethanol on blood alcohol levels. *Alcoholism: Clinical & Experimental Research* 15:734–738.

Rosman AS, Paronetto F, Galvin K et al. (1993). Hepatitis C virus antibody in alcoholic patients: Association with the presence of portal and/or lobular hepatitis. *Archives of Internal Medicine* 153:965–969.

Salaspuro MP & Lieber CS (1978). Non-uniformity of blood ethanol elimination: Its exaggeration after chronic consumption. *Annals of Clinical Research* 10:294–297.

Sato C, Matsuda Y & Lieber CS (1981). Increased hepatotoxicity of acetaminophen after chronic ethanol consumption in the rat. *Gastroenterology* 80:140–148.

Satre MA, Zgombic-Knight M & Duester G (1994). The complete structure of human class IV alcohol dehydrogenase (retinol dehydrogenase) determined from the ADH 7 gene. *Journal of Biological Chemistry* 269:15606–15612.

Saville PD (1965). Changes in bone mass with age and alcoholism. *Journal of Bone and Joint Surgery* 47:429–499.

Savolainen VT, Pajarinen J, Perola M et al. (1996). Glutathione-*S*-transferase GST M1 "null" genotype and the risk of alcoholic liver disease. *Alcoholism: Clinical & Experimental Research* 20:1340–1345.

Schatzkin A, Jones Y, Hoover RN et al. (1987). Alcohol consumption and breast cancer in the Epidemiologic Follow-up Study of the First National Health and Nutrition Examination Survey. *The New England Journal of Medicine* 316:1169–1173.

Seeff LB, Cucherini BA, Zimmerman HJ et al. (1986). Acetaminophen hepatotoxicity in alcoholics: A therapeutic misadventure (Clinical review). *Annals of Internal Medicine* 104:399–404.

Seitz HK, Veith S, Czygan P et al. (1984). *In vivo* interactions between H_2-receptor antagonists and ethanol metabolism in man and in rats. *Hepatology* 4:1231–1234.

Seitz HK, Simanowski UA, Egerer G et al. (1992). Human gastric alcohol dehydrogenase: *In vitro* characteristics and effect of cimetidine. *Digestion* 51:80–85.

Seitz HK, Egerer G, Simanowski UA et al. (1993). Human gastric alcohol dehydrogenase activity: Effect of age, sex and alcoholism. *Gut* 34:1433–1437.

Sellman R, Kanto J, Raijola E et al. (1975). Human and animal study on elimination from plasma and metabolism of diazepam after chronic alcohol intake. *Acta Pharmacology & Toxicology* 36:33–38.

Sharma R, Gentry RT, Lim RT Jr et al. (1995). First pass metabolism of alcohol: Absence of diurnal variation and its inhibition by cimetidine after an evening meal. *Digestive Diseases & Sciences* 40:2091–2097.

Shevchuk O, Baraona E, Ma X-L et al. (1991). Gender differences in the response of hepatic fatty acids and cytosolic fatty acid- binding capacity to alcohol consumption in rats. *Proceedings of the Society for Experimental Biology and Medicine* 198:584–590.

Siegers C-P, Heidbuchel K & Younes M (1983). Influence of alcohol, dithiocarb and (+)-catechin on the hepatotoxicity and metabolism of vinylidene chloride in rats. *Journal of Applied Toxicology* 3:90–95.

Solomon L (1973). Drug-induced arthropathy and necrosis of the femoral head. *Journal of Bone and Joint Surgery* (Br) 55:246–261.

Sotaniemi EA, Anttila M, Rautio A et al. (1981). Propranolol and sotalol metabolism after a drinking party. *Clinical Pharmacology and Therapeutics* 29:705–710.

Speisky H, MacDonald A, Giles G et al. (1985). Increased loss and decreased synthesis of hepatic glutathione after acute ethanol administration: Turnover studies. *Biochemistry Journal* 225: 565.

Stampfer MJ, Colditz GA, Willett WC et al. (1988). A prospective study of moderate alcohol drinking and risk of diabetes in women. *American Journal of Epidemiology* 128:549–558.

Stampfer MJ, Malinow R, Willett WC et al. (1992). A prospective study of plasma homocyst(e)ine and risk of myocardial infarction in US physicians. *Journal of the American Medical Association* 268:877–881.

Takagi T, Ishii H, Takahashi H et al. (1983). Potentiation of halothane hepatotoxicity by chronic ethanol administration in rat: An animal model of halothane hepatitis. *Pharmacology, Biochemistry and Behavior* 18(Suppl 1):461–465.

Takahashi T, Lasker JM, Rosman AS et al. (1993). Induction of cytochrome P–4502E1 in the human liver by ethanol is caused by a corresponding increase in encoding messenger RNA. *Hepatology* 17:236–245.

Taskinen M-R, Valimaki M, Nikkila EA et al. (1982). High density lipoprotein subfractions and postheparin plasma lipases in alcoholic men before and after ethanol withdrawal. *Metabolism* 31:1168–1174.

Teschke R & Wiese B (1982). Sex-dependency of hepatic alcohol metabolizing enzymes. *Journal of Endocrinologic Investigation* 5:243–250.

Tsutsumi M, Lasker JM, Shimizu M et al. (1989). The intralobular distribution of ethanol-inducible P450IIE1 in rat and human liver. *Hepatology* 10:437–446.

Tsutsumi R, Leo MA, Kim CI et al. (1990). Interaction of ethanol with enflurane metabolism and toxicity: Role of P450IIE1. *Alcoholism: Clinical & Experimental Research* 14: 174–179.

Tsyrlov IB, Salmela KS, Kessova IG et al. (1996). Effect of combined ethanol and 3-methylcholanthrene treatment on hepatic microsomal P4502E1 and P4501A2 in rats. *Alcoholism: Clinical & Experimental Research* 20:37a.

Uppal R, Lateef SK & Korsten MA (1991). Paronetto F, Lieber CS (1991). Chronic alcoholic gastritis: Roles of ethanol and *Helicobacter pylori*. *Archives of Internal Medicine* 151:760–764.

USDA and USDHHS (1995). *Dietary Guidelines for Americans*. Washington, DC: U.S. Department of Agriculture and U.S. Department of Health and Human Services, Home and Garden Bulletin No. 232, Fourth Edition, December.

Victor M (1992). The effects of alcohol on the nervous system: Clinical features, pathogenesis, and treatment. In CS Lieber (ed.) *Medical and Nutritional Complications of Alcoholism: Mechanisms and Management*. New York, NY: Plenum Medical Book Co., 413–457.

Wald A, Van Thiel DH, Hoechstetter L et al. (1982). Effect of pregnancy on gastrointestinal transit. *Digestive Diseases & Sciences* 27:1015–1018.

Weiner FR, Eskreis DS, Compton KV et al. (1988). Haplotype analysis of a type I collagen gene and its association with alcoholic cirrhosis in man. *Molecular Aspects of Medicine* 10:93–194.

Whitecomb DC & Block GD (1994). Association of acetaminophen hepatotoxicity with fasting and ethanol use. *Journal of the American Medical Association* 272:1845–1850.

Willett WC, Stampfer MJ, Colditz GA et al. (1987). Moderate alcohol consumption and the risk of breast cancer. *The New England Journal of Medicine* 316:1174–1180.

Wondergem R & Davis J (1994). Ethanol increases hepatocyte water volume. *Alcoholism: Clinical & Experimental Research* 18:1230–1236.

Worner TM & Lieber CS (1985). Perivenular fibrosis as precursor lesion of cirrhosis. *Journal of the American Medical Association* 254:627–630.

Yamada S, Mak KM & Lieber CS (1985). Chronic ethanol consumption alters rat liver plasma membranes and potentiates release of alkaline phosphatase. *Gastroenterology* 88:1799–806.

Yokoyama H, Baraona E & Lieber CS (1994). Molecular cloning of human class IV alcohol dehydrogenase: cDNA. *Biochemistry Biophysiology Res. Commun.* 203:219–224.

Yokoyama H, Baraona E & Lieber CS (1996). Molecular cloning and chromosomal localization of ADH7 gene encoding human class IV δ ADH. *Genomics* 31:243–245.

Zorzano A & Herrera E (1990). *In vivo* ethanol elimination in man, monkey and rat: A lack of relationship between the ethanol metabolism and the hepatic activities of alcohol and aldehyde dehydrogenases. *Life Sciences* 46:223–230.

CHAPTER 4

Neurological Effects

Anne Geller, M.D., FASAM

Alcohol
Cocaine
Heroin
Marijuana
Sedative-Hypnotics
Volatile Inhalants

All drugs that produce euphoria affect the nervous system acutely during intoxication. Chronic use can result in neuroadaptive changes which are the basis for tolerance and dependence. This chapter is not concerned with those effects which are integral to the action of the drug itself, but is focused on neurological impairments which may occur as a consequence of drug use in some individuals. For the most part, the concern will be with structural neurological damage occurring after chronic drug use; however, both transient symptoms and complications arising from a single episode of use will be mentioned when they are of importance for a specific drug. Alcohol is the drug of abuse with the most extensive medical consequences and its adverse effects on the nervous system are both common and diverse. The neurological complications of alcoholism thus constitute the largest segment of this chapter. Because alcohol has such a significant impact on neurological function, it is a potential confounding variable in clinical studies of neurological effects in abusers of other drugs, who are frequently also drinking heavily, if not alcoholically. Head traumas occur more frequently among drug abusers than the general population and may complicate the clinical presentation, as do compression neuropathies, a consequence of prolonged immobility or loss of pain perception in the drugged state. Finally, neurological consequences of poor nutrition and personal neglect may add to the overall picture.

ALCOHOL

The traditional picture of central nervous system damage due to alcohol focused, not surprisingly, on striking clinical syndromes. These were often irreversible resulting in death or serious disability, and occurred most frequently in debilitated alcoholics after years of addictive drinking with general neglect of health and nutrition. Wernicke described the acute delirium with ophthalmoplegia and ataxia in 1881. Six years later, Korsakoff (1887) noted the remarkable chronic impairment of memory with relative preservation of other cognitive capacities which occurred in some alcoholics. Around the same time, Maudsley (1879) wrote of a more generalized impairment of cognitive abilities which he had observed in alcoholics resembling the last stages of senile dementia. These three syndromes, Wernicke's encephalopathy, Korsakoff's psychosis and alcoholic dementia, were to constitute the basis of entries in textbooks on brain damage due to alcoholism for almost a century. The work of Peters (1936) on the thiamine-deficient pigeon provided insight into the nature of Wernicke's encephalopathy, and the link between Wernicke's encephalopathy and Korsakoff's psychosis became increasingly apparent as more patients survived the acute encephalopathy as a result of thiamine treatment, only to reveal subsequent difficulties with memory.

The nutritional (thiamine deficiency) etiology of Wernicke's encephalopathy having been clearly established, what then of Korsakoff's psychosis and alcoholic dementia? Although deficiency of thiamine and perhaps other vitamins may contribute to the cause of these disorders, a direct toxic action of alcohol itself on the brain has been postulated by a number of workers (Freund, 1973; Walker & Hunter, 1978). Long-term alcohol administration to nutritionally supplemented rats has been shown to result in severe neuronal damage (Riley & Walker, 1978).

Freund and Ballinger have demonstrated that chronic alcohol abuse (defined as consumption of more than 80 gm of absolute alcohol a day for more than 10 years) results in loss of muscarinic cholinergic receptors in the frontal cortex (Freund & Ballinger, 1988). They also showed loss of muscarinic receptors and sparing of benzodiazepine receptors in the putamen. This loss of muscarinic receptors occurs in histologically normal brains in the absence of significant atrophy and gross dementia. These findings suggest that alcohol toxicity does not simply result in a random loss of neurons, but in region- and receptor-specific effects. A direct action of alcohol itself, in addition to the nutritional deficits which may occur after long-term alcohol abuse, is consistent with many of the more recent observations regarding alcohol-related brain damage. These observations come from a number of different sources: pneumoencephalograms (PEGs), computed tomographic (CT) scans, magnetic resonance imaging (MRI), positron emission tomography (PET), autopsy material and event-related potential (ERP) studies in man as well as chronic ethanol treatment (CET) in animals. Alcohol itself appears to produce a continuum of impairments beginning possibly with those which are mild and probably transient in heavy social drinkers (Parker & Noble, 1977; Parker, Beirnbaum et al., 1979), followed by significant and partly reversible deficits in alcoholics, and ending with the chronic, severe picture of alcoholic dementia. Other events such as acute thiamine deficiency, head trauma and hepatic failure may be superimposed on this picture.

There are many different factors which are involved in the ways in which drinking alcoholic beverages can adversely effect the brain, which include:

1. Direct action on nerve cells, particularly nerve cell membranes (Von Wartburg, 1979).
2. Effects on neurotransmitters, receptors, second-messenger systems (Hoffman, Tabakoff et al., 1987; Tabakoff, Hoffman et al., 1988).
3. Chronic changes in membranes, neurotransmitters or receptors resulting in dependence (Tabakoff, Hoffman et al., 1988).
4. Poor food intake and malabsorption, resulting in vitamin deficiency, particularly thiamine, pyridoxine, niacin (Wollman, Smith & Stephen, 1968).
5. Associated metabolic changes.
6. Reduction in cerebral blood flow (Berglund & Ingvar, 1976).
7. Damage to other organs indirectly resulting in CNS effects, for example, hepatic encephalopathy.

Undoubtedly as one progresses along the scale from heavy social drinking to severe chronic alcoholism, more factors come into play and the chances of sustaining some degree of nervous system impairment increase. There is, however, considerable individual variability. Some alcoholics suffer severe brain damage, whereas others, at the same age with similar drinking histories and socioeconomic backgrounds, are only minimally impaired. Some evidence exists for genetic factors increasing vulnerability to end-organ damage due to alcohol (Blass & Gibson, 1977; Hrubeck & Omenn, 1981).

Table 1 lists, for convenient reference, the major alcohol-related syndromes with brief summaries of clinical findings, pathological lesions and etiology when known.

Intermediate Brain Syndrome. The intermediate brain syndrome is not technically a diagnosis. It is a term originally coined by Bennett in 1960 to describe the impairment in cognitive abilities observed in many alcoholics coming to treatment. These deficits range from mild, detectable only by neuropsychological testing, to moderate when clinicians can observe defects in memory, thinking and problem-solving abilities which may interfere with the patient's ability to participate in treatment and to return to work. The impairment is not severe enough, however, to be correctly labeled Korsakoff's psychosis or alcoholic dementia, or to require institutionalization of the patient. Awareness of these impairments is important for the clinician in treatment planning and in return-to-work counseling. Alcoholics toward the more severe end of the cognitive impairment spectrum have been observed to be less able to participate in treatment and to have poorer outcome, but this requires further investigation (Leber & Parsons, 1980; Gregson & Taylor, 1977).

The particular abilities most affected by excessive alcohol intake have been remarkably consistent over a wide range of studies involving males and females of different socioeconomic and ethnic groups (Parsons, 1977; Parsons & Farr, 1981). General intelligence and verbal abilities are intact. The IQ as measured on the Wechsler Adult Intelligence Scale (WAIS) is normal. Difficulties occur with abstract thinking and problem-solving abilities as measured on the Halsted Category Test or the Shipley Hartford. Visual spatial and perceptual motor abilities are also impaired. New learning, both verbal and visual, is significantly impaired in alcoholics compared to age-matched controls.

Evidence from CT studies suggest that one-half to two-thirds of alcoholics develop brain atrophy

TABLE 1. Major Alcohol-Related Syndromes

Syndrome	Clinical Findings	Lesion/Etiology
Intermediate brain syndrome	1. May be difficulty in new learning, some concreteness, lack in mental flexibility. 2. Impairment on neuropsychological testing.	Occurs in alcoholics with normal nutritional status. Could be subclinical nuritional deficiency and direct neurotoxic effect of alcohol.
Wenicke's encephalopathy	1. Disorientation 2. Confusion 3. Nystagmus 4. Ocular palsies 5. Ataxia	Mid-brain punctate hemorrhages. Nutritional (thiamine) deficiency with or without additional genetically determined enzyme deficiency.
Korsakoff's psychosis	1. Profound deficit in new learning (recent memory) 2. Some deficits in remote memory 3. Intelligence and verbal abilities usually preserved 4. May confabulate	Mid-brain gliosis. basal forebrain frequently follows Wernicke's encephalopathy. Can occur alone. Permanent syndrome not seen in uncomplicated thiamine deficiency. Only partially responsive to thiamine. Possible neurotoxic component.
Alcoholic dementia	1. Global decline in intellectual functions; memory affected but not predominantly 2. Apathy, irritability, emotional liability	Etiology unclear. Direct neurotoxic effect of alcohol and possible subclinical nutritional deficiencies, trauma, metabolic components.
Central pontine myelinolysis	1. Rapid-onset paraparesis or quadriparesis 2. Dysarthria 3. Dysphagia	Edema of the pons 2° electrolyte disturbance. Hypoatremia.
Marchiafava-Bignami	1. Gradual-onset dementia with psychosis 2. Convulsions 3. Focal symptom aphasia	Degeneration of corpus callosum related to alcohol. Etiology unknown.
Alcoholic cerebellar degeneration	1. Acute onset with Wernicke's encephalopathy 2. Subacute onset alone 3. Market gait ataxia 4. Little arm ataxia or dysarthria	Degeneration of Purkinje cells in cerebellar vermis. Possibly mainly due due to thiamine lack. Possibly a direct neurotoxic effect of alcohol. Not dose-related. Possible genetic susceptibility.
Alcoholic polyneuropahy	1. Gradual onset of symmetrical loss of sensation in toes, fingers 2. Symmetrical motor loss, beginning distally 3. Loss of reflexes	Degeneration of myelin sheaths of peripheral nerves. Thiamine deficiency.
Optic neuropathy (tobacco-alcohol amblyopia)	1. Acute or subacute onset of impaired vision 2. Central scotomata.	Thiamine deficiency.

and/or ventricular dilation (Lishman, Jacobson & Acker, 1987). This may occur in some quite early in their drinking careers. Others appear to be unaffected despite long drinking histories. The reasons for these differences are not clear, though genetic factors may play a role. The severity of CT changes and abnormalities in evoked potentials seem to be greater in family history-positive than family history-negative alcoholics (Begleiter, Porjesz & Kissin, 1982). Age is also a factor. In a recent study (Pfefferbaum, Rosenbloom et al., 1988), widened sulci were found, even in younger alcoholics, and appeared to be correlated with lifetime alcohol consumption. Ventricular enlargement, on the other hand, was more prominent in older patients. Measurements of brains at autopsy confirm the CT findings that brain tissue is commonly affected in alcoholics; brain weight tends to be lower, ventricular volume increased, and sulci widened (Torvik, Lindboe & Rodge, 1982; Harper & Krie, 1985). Positron emission tomography (PET) and cerebral blood flow (CBF) studies have been conducted to investigate brain pathophysiology in alcoholic patients. Compared with age-matched controls, long-term abstinent alcoholics with memory impairments showed lower glucose use than controls, particularly in the frontal cortex, thalamus and basal ganglia (Eckardt, Rohrbaugh et al., 1988). Cerebral blood flow studies have shown decrements in blood flow correlated with life-time alcohol consumption (Risberg & Berglund, 1987). In young (less than 40-year-old) alcoholics, CBF showed abnormal regional patterns (Dally, Luft et al., 1988). Particularly marked was decreased blood flow to the frontal regions.

Just as marked improvement in neuropsychological functioning has been noted in some alcoholics who maintain abstinence, certain CT scan parameters have also shown improvement with abstinence. This reversibility of brain atrophy was first shown by Carlen et al. (Carlen, Wortzmann et al., 1978), and this has subsequently been confirmed by other groups (Artmann, Gall et al., 1981; Ron, Acker et al., 1982). Patients who remain abstinent show increased brain density and decreased ventricular size. In a five-year follow-up study (Muvroner, Bergman et al., 1989), alcoholics who had been abstinent for the five-year period had less brain atrophy, both cortical and subcortical, than they had on initial examination after detoxification. However, they still showed more atrophy than an age-matched control group.

Cerebral blood flow studies have also shown improvements in blood flow with abstinence and treatment (Ishikawa, Meyer et al., 1986). Magnetic resonance imagining of the intracranial cerebrospinal fluid (CSF) volume has shown a highly significant reduction after five weeks of abstinence (Schroth, Naegele et al., 1988). This reduction could not be accounted for only by de- and re-hydration of the brain. Other effects such as the rise of protein synthesis after alcohol withdrawal and a subsequent increase in dendritic growth may be important.

The number of withdrawals from alcohol appears to be related to poorer memory test performance in both males and females (Glenn, Parsons et al., 1988). Females showed the same amount of performance errors with a shorter duration of alcohol use and withdrawals than males. Interestingly, Freund in 1970 had shown that shuttle box performance in mice was markedly impaired in a group given 24-hour withdrawals four times over a five-week period compared with mice who were kept continuously alcohol dependent during that period.

Of great concern to clinicians is the extent to which functional deficits observed in most alcoholics in early (up to one month) abstinence can be reversed if abstinence is sustained. Parsons and Leber (1981) reviewed 21 neuropsychological studies in which recovery had been assessed after one month to four years of abstinence. Eight percent of the studies indicated that significant improvement is to be expected. Different functions appear to recover at different times. At the end of one month, verbal learning and sensory and motor capabilities improve. However, abstracting ability and visual spatial learning remain impaired. Older alcoholics show the least improvement. Abstracting abilities and perceptual motor abilities show improvement between three and six months of abstinence. Even in the longer studies, the alcoholics as a group, though improved from their initial testing, remained impaired relative to controls. For the individual alcoholic it would seem that some are left with no detectable impairment if abstinence is sustained, whereas others, older, and/or with greater initial impairment, show only partial recovery. Alcoholics who resume drinking (even though not at their earlier levels) tend to have more impaired neuropsychological test findings during treatment than eventual abstainers (Fabian & Parsons, 1983). However, when examined at six months or one year after treatment, resumers are much more impaired than abstainers.

It is important to recognize that the majority (75%) of alcoholics coming to treatment have some degree of cognitive impairment. It may be mild and transient in some. In others, it may be severe enough to seriously limit the patient's ability to participate in traditional cognitively oriented treatment. In these cases, longer-term residential treatment may be indicated to permit maximum recovery to take place in an alcohol-free environment. In yet others, the degree of cognitive impairment observed requires careful counseling to permit a successful return to work. Cognitive rehabilitation may be productively used with selected patients (Goldstein, 1987).

Blackouts. Although not strictly a consequence of chronic alcohol use, blackouts, episodes of transient anterograde amnesia occurring exclusively during intoxication, would seem to be related in some way to deficits in learning and memory observed in long-term heavy drinkers. Blackouts appear to be associated with a rapid rise in the blood alcohol level and can occur in naive drinkers having their first drinking experience. However, repeated blackouts can be said to be pathognomonic of alcoholic drinking, mainly because to experience such a devastating event as to be totally unable to recall a large segment of one's awake activities, and not to change one's drinking practices to prevent this from ever occurring again, indicates a quite abnormal positive value of intoxication for the individual. Interestingly, blackouts have been little studied since Goodwin's (1971) work 20 years ago. Alcoholics were given alcohol and their behavior studied. Five episodes of anterograde amnesia were recorded. There did not appear to be any predictive factors. The alcoholics behaved during the blackout in a "normal" intoxicated manner. Immediate recall was intact, however, no permanent memories were formed. The mechanism for this acute failure of memory consolidation is not known. Clearly in susceptible people the memory system becomes less tolerant than other systems to high blood alcohol concentrations (BACs). (The average BAC in Goodwin's [1971] patients was 300 mg %.)

Alcohol's inhibitory effects on the N-methyl-D-aspartate (NMDA) receptor, thought to be involved in long-term potentiation, may be a factor. Long-term potentiation refers to those changes in neuronal biochemistry and physiology which perpetuate the brain signals long after those evoked through neurotransmission have decayed (Lister, Eckardt & Weingartner, 1987). Inhibition of responses at the NMDA receptor may contribute to the cognitive impairments associated with intoxication by preventing transfer from short- to long-term memory processes. The effects of calcium channel blockers on alcoholic blackouts would be interesting to study. Clinically, the alcoholic blackout shares many features with the syndrome of transient global amnesia (Fisher, 1982) which is essentially a period of anterograde amnesia occurring in older people without warning. The etiology is not known, but it may be a form of transient ischemic attack in the posterior cerebral circulation. Perhaps the most instructive comparison between an alcoholic having experienced a blackout and a person who had just had an episode of transient global amnesia lies in the affective response to the event. Patients after an episode of transient global amnesia are uniformly terrified. Not to have any recollection of a period of time during which one was walking, talking, and generally acting in the world appears to evoke a radical fear in normal adults. "Who was the I who was acting on the stage while the monitoring self, the remembering self, was absent?" "What did I do?" "What might I do?" "Tell me it will never happen again." The alcoholic's calm acceptance of blackouts as an unremarkable part of the drinking experience smells of the *belle indifference* of the hysteric. Indeed, it is a measure of the intensity of denial in this disease.

Wernicke's Encephalopathy. Wernicke described the clinical picture and pathology of the syndrome that bears his name in his textbook of 1881, and it has been little changed since. What is seen is a relatively abrupt onset of a confusional state, accompanied by unsteadiness of gait and visual difficulties. Objectively the patient is confused, disoriented, and often apathetic, and has ataxia of the lower limbs, nystagmus, and partial or complete ophthalmoplegia. A tremor may be observed and a peripheral neuropathy is usually present, but may be difficult to test in the acute situation.

Wernicke's encephalopathy is clearly related to thiamine deficiency. This syndrome has been observed not only in alcoholics, but also in malnourished prisoners of war and in intractable vomiting from many causes. Indeed, one of Wernicke's original patients was a seamstress with persistent vomiting following sulfuric acid poisoning. The mechanism by which thiamine deficiency results in the characteristic lesions in the midline periventricular structures of the brainstem and diencephalon is not yet clear. These regions have been shown to undergo metabolic and histological changes that may not normalize even after prolonged thiamine administration. An episode of severe thiamine deficiency has been shown to result in increased consumption and accelerated metabolism of alcohol in rats even after six months of a normal diet (Martin, Adinoff et al., 1989). Furthermore, the previously thiamine-deficient rats showed greater CNS sensitivity to alcohol at a given blood alcohol concentration.

Brain energy metabolism is decreased in chronic alcoholics, as is the rate of formation of thiamine pyrophosphate. Thiamine pyrophosphate, a cofactor for ketoglutarate dehydrogenase, is reduced in thiamine deficiency, and this is accompanied by decreased aspartate, glutamate and gamma aminobutyric acid (GABA) (Butterworth, 1989). Brain cell death could result from compromised cerebral energy metabolism and local accumulation of lactase. Transketolase may be irreversibly decreased, which may make those with genetically low levels especially vulnerable. An interesting observation with potential therapeutic usefulness is that damage from thiamine deficiency is similar to that seen with excitotoxic amino acids. The administration of an antagonist of NMDA receptors (a subclass of glutamate receptors through which excitotoxic damage is mediated) has been shown to decrease the thalamic damage in thiamine deficient rats (Langlais, Mair & McEntree, 1988).

The treatment for Wernicke's encephalopathy is high-dose thiamine (100 mg) given immediately intravenously and twice a day intramuscularly until the patient can take medication by mouth. Improvement in the ophthalmoplegia usually occurs within a few hours of thiamine treatment. The acute confusional state clears more slowly over several days. The ataxia may clear completely or partially over a period of days or weeks. Some patients may be left with a permanent residual deficit in coordination. Fifty to 84% of patients with Wernicke's encephalopathy will be revealed to have Korsakoff's psychosis as their acute confusional state clears. It should be noted that very few, if any, patients with Wernicke's encephalopathy whose etiology is related to alcohol abuse will again regain completely normal cognitive capacity.

In a series from Boston City Hospital, 2.2% of autopsies had lesions in the mid-brain, and in a similar study in Australia (Victor & Laureno, 1978), Wernicke's encephalopathy was diagnosed at autopsy in 2% of the brains examined (Harper, 1979). The latter study is interesting in that it corroborated earlier observations that patients whose brains showed the characteristic lesions at autopsy had not exhibited the classic Wernicke signs while alive. Indeed, only 14% of the Australian series had been suspected prior to death. Hypotension and lethargy occurred clinically as frequently as did the classic triad of confusion, ataxia and ophthalmoplegia. Twenty percent had died suddenly and unexpectedly. Lishman (1981) has suggested that possibly because of widespread use of vitamins the condition has become less fulminating and subclinical forms of the disease might be occurring. Recurrent attacks of subclinical encephalopathy over the years would explain why, in alcoholics, the memory difficulties following Wernicke's encephalopathy tend to remain, whereas in nutritionally depleted prisoners they respond to thiamine.

If lesions do develop to Wernicke location without being clinically apparent as the autopsy evidence indicates, then high-potency vitamin replacement should be given as often as possible. Indeed, fortification of alcoholic beverages with thiamine, as suggested by Canterwell and Criqui (1978), would be a reasonable idea.

Korsakoff's Psychosis. Korsakoff's psychosis is linked to Wernicke's encephalopathy by common pathological findings and common etiology. Victor, whose 1953 paper is the classic of modern clinical studies of the neurological complications of alcohol abuse, entitled his 1971 book *The Wernicke-Korsakoff Syndrome*, and it is frequently referred to by that compound name. Nevertheless, it should be noted that not all patients with Wernicke's encephalopathy develop the amnestic confabulatory psychosis of Korsakoff. Furthermore, many cases of Korsakoff's psychosis develop their amnestic difficulties insidiously without any preceding history of Wernicke's encephalopathy.

The most striking feature of patients with Korsakoff's psychosis is a severe memory impairment for ongoing events: these patients are unable to find their way around the ward or to remember the names of staff and other patients. Memory for remote events, both public and personal, is spotty and vague. Some make up stories, confabulate, to cover the memory gaps, but many do not do this and it is not a necessary part of the syndrome. This devastating memory deficit occurs in some pure cases in the absence of any other clinical signs of intellectual deterioration. Intelligence on the WAIS is preserved. These patients can think, speak and calculate numbers with customary speed and efficiency. Immediate memory as tested by the digit span is normal, but information can be retained at most for a few minutes after which it rapidly dissipates. Because patients with Korsakoff's psychosis may be articulate, even witty, and may appear superficially intact, the gross memory defect can be overlooked by the casual observer.

Many cases diagnosed as Korsakoff's psychosis are not pure in the sense that though the striking memory impairments are present, so too are other cognitive deficits. Indeed, one of the "pure" Korsakoff patients studied so carefully by Mair, Warrington and Weiskrantz (1979) for nine years began to show a general intellectual deterioration two years before his death. This is not surprising when one considers that patients with Korsakoff's psychosis are subject to the same factors which produce cognitive deficits in other alcoholics. Most cases of Korsakoff's psychosis are found to have, in addition to marked anterograde and retrograde amnesia, less marked visuoperceptive and problem-solving impairments. It has been suggested Korsakoff's psychosis represents one end of a continuum of alcohol damage with the mild often transient memory deficits of most younger alcoholics being near the other end, and perhaps the alcoholic blackout representing the beginning. This does not seem to be the case (Butters & Granholm, 1987). There is an abrupt discontinuity between the severity of memory impairments of patients with Korsakoff's psychosis and those with similar age and drinking history. Furthermore, alcoholics who do not have Korsakoff's psychosis have predominantly poor visual memory, whereas both verbal and visual memory are severely impaired in affected patients. Patients with Korsakoff's psychosis are extremely sensitive to distraction and proactive interference; that is, when trying to remember a current task, items from previous tasks keep intruding. Without acute trauma such as thiamine deficiency alcohol results only in mild to moderate memory deficits.

The retrograde amnesia of Korsakoff's psychosis is temporally graded, affecting recent events much more than distant events. This was thought to be a result of anterograde amnesia, much as one sees in a considerably milder form in other alcoholics. That is, events do not get encoded in the permanent memory and thus cannot be recalled. Anyone trying to get a clear, temporally ordered, history from an alcoholic in a detoxification unit knows how fuzzy recollection for events over the recent past can be. However, the situation in Korsakoff's psychosis is different. An unusual clinical opportunity occurred when an eminent scientist developed Korsakoff's psychosis at the age of 65, two years after the publication of his autobiography in 1981. He was tested by Butters (1984) on events recorded in his own autobiography. He showed a marked retrograde amnesia for his own history with sparing of events only from his remote past. Clearly, this could not be due to a deficit in learning, since these events had obviously at one time been known and recorded by him.

In contrast to amnestic syndromes of other etiologies, patients with Korsakoff's psychosis frequently display apathy, lack of initiative, and profound lack of insight, suggesting a cortical component.

Once established, Korsakoff's psychosis in alcoholics is not notably responsive to thiamine. Nevertheless, thiamine and multivitamin supplements should be given to affected patients in order to assist any improvement and attenuate further damage should drinking recur. In Victor's 1971 series, one-quarter of the patients showed complete clinical recovery, one-half partial recovery, and the remainder were unchanged. The extent of more subtle neuropsychological deficits in those 25% who recovered clinically is unknown. The time over which recovery may take place can extend beyond one year. In an elegant study (Mair, Warrington & Weiskrantz, 1979) correlating neuropsychological findings with pathology in patients studied for several years prior to death, the critical lesions for the memory deficit appeared to be bilaterally in the medial nuclei of the mammillary bodies and bilaterally between the wall of the third ventricle and the medical dorsal nucleus of the thalamus. Arendt, Bigl et al. (1983), however, suggest that the critical area affected in alcoholic patients with Korsakoff's psychosis may be the basal forebrain, the major source of cholinergic input to the cerebral cortex and hippocampus. They found that the number of neurons was reduced by 70% in the basal forebrain of patients with Korsakoff's psychosis.

Cerebrospinal fluid levels of metabolites of norepinephrine, dopamine, and serotonin have been shown to be reduced in patients with Korsakoff's psychosis. Improvement in memory has been found with the alpha 2-adrenergic agonist clonidine (McEntree, Mair & Langlais, 1984), and also with the serotonin reuptake blocker fluvoxamine (Martin, Adinoff et al., 1989). In neither study could the drug effects be said to be dramatic, but either could be promising leads for therapy in the future.

Alcoholic Dementia. Alcoholic dementia has been a rather neglected condition clinically, pathologically, and etiologically. There is no question that a substantial proportion of alcoholics (8% in one series) become demented (Lishman, 1981). This dementia is not clinically distinguishable from dementia due to other causes. There is a progressive deterioration in all cognitive abilities. Acquisition and use of new information is impaired along with general problem-solving abilities. There may be increasing difficulty with remote memory as well. Inappropriate social behavior and personal neglect occur in the later stages. Apathy, irritability, emotional lability, and undue truculence may also be present, as in other dementias. Alcoholic dementia usually develops insidiously against a background of chronic inebriation, and may not be recognized by the patient's family, who attribute the behavior to simple drunkenness. Only when the patient is detoxified may the picture become clear. As mentioned above, cerebral atrophy is a very common finding in CT scans of alcoholics. Computed tomographic scans of patients with alcoholic dementia have not been compared to those of nondementia alcoholics. It would seem likely that cerebral atrophy would be worse among demented alcoholics. Pathological findings have included neuronal degeneration and loss, which are patchy and diffuse throughout the cerebral cortex. The characteristic plaques and tangles seen in the presenile and senile dementias have been rarely observed in the brains of alcoholics with dementia (Lynch, 1960).

Alcoholism accounted for 7% of demented patients in three current surveys (Lishman, 1981), and was at least as common as multi-infarct dementia. In a series from the Maudsley Hospital, 50 alcoholics had been labeled as having Korsakoff's psychosis and 13 as having alcoholic dementia. Half of the patients with Korsakoff's psychosis had an acute onset. The others had a more gradual and insidious onset. Those patients with Korsakoff's psychosis of gradual onset had global deficits as well as the severe memory impairments, and they resembled the alcoholic dementias in having a later age of onset and also a better prognosis for improvement. Two-thirds of the alcoholic dementias and "gradual-onset" Korsakoff patients showed some improvement.

Cerebral Trauma. Alcoholics, because of drunkenness, are particularly prone to accidents of all kinds. The shrunken brain, fragile blood vessels and delayed clotting time make them more vulnerable to serious complications of head trauma such as subdural and epidural hematomas. Alcoholics constitute a large percentage of patients admitted to neurosurgical wards because of significant head trauma. The actual incidence of this among alcoholics is difficult to ascertain. Significant head trauma was reported in 7% of alcoholics having seizure. Severe craniocerebral trauma can produce focal deficits such as hemiparesis in addition to more diffuse cerebral dysfunction. Minor degrees of unreported or unnoticed head trauma may contribute to intellectual deterioration in some alcoholics.

Hepatic and Other Metabolic Encephalopathies. Alcoholism is the leading cause of cirrhosis of the liver. Some patients with cirrhosis will develop liver failure and subsequent hepatic encephalopathy. Other metabolic derangements such as electrolyte imbalance, hypoglycemia, and respiratory alkalosis are also more common in alcoholics than in the general population. Delirium, particularly if prolonged or repeated, may lead to long-term or permanent cognitive impairments. Again, this may contribute to a picture of intellectual deterioration in the alcoholic.

Central Pontine Myelinolysis and Marchiafava-Bignami Disease. In Victor and Laureno's 1978 series (Victor & Laureno, 1978), central pontine myelinolysis was found in only 0.25% of autopsied cases and Marchiafava-Bignami disease in less than 0.05%. Patients with central pontine myelinolysis are rarely diagnosed before death, though advances in CT scanning now make this a possibility. Clinically, the condition appears as a rapidly evolving paraparesis or quadriparesis in a patient who is confused and usually lethargic. Pseudobulbar symptoms, dysarthria, and dysphagia are prominent. Severe electrolyte aberrations are found, particularly hyponatremia, which are thought to be the cause of the syndrome (Messert, Orrison et al., 1979). Central pontine myelinolysis occurs in conditions other than alcoholism. The course is usually progressively downhill to death, but with recognition and prompt correction of the electrolyte imbalance, recovery can occur. At autopsy the pons is edematous with central destruction of myelin.

Marchiafava-Bignami disease is rare. It was thought to be limited to Italian males who drank red wine, but one of Victor's cases was a black woman who drank any type of alcoholic beverage. There is a slow onset of mental symptoms which may be manic, paranoid, or delusional, often accompanied by intellectual deterioration. Convulsions and various focal neurological signs are frequent. The course is downhill, usually over several years. The pathology is distinctive with symmetrical necrosis of the corpus callosum. The etiology is unknown and there is no treatment.

Deficiencies of Vitamins Other than Thiamine. Deficiencies of niacin, pyridoxine, and pantothenic acid occur in alcoholics and are associated with nervous system disorders (Victor, Adams & Collins, 1989). Riboflavin and folic acid deficiency also occur in alcoholics, but the evidence that either deficiency results in nervous system disease is quite flimsy. Niacin deficiency disease (pellagra) is rare in developed countries. However, Serdau recently collected 22 cases of alcoholic pellagra in France (Serdau, Hausser-Hauw & Laplane, 1988). The clinical triad of pellagra, i.e., dermatitis, diarrhea, and dementia, consists of erythematous skin lesions, gastrointestinal symptoms of anorexia and diarrhea, and neurological systems, including confusion, hypertonus and myoclonus. Peripheral neuropathy may also occur. Early symptoms of fatigue, apathy, anorexia, insomnia and irritability are nonspecific and may be misdiagnosed as depression. In Serdau's autopsy cases, all were neglected, undernourished, and cachectic, and most belonged to the classical category of clochards, tramps with no fixed abode. When hospitalized they were given thiamine and pyridoxine but not niacin. These cases emphasize the importance of multivitamin replacement for alcoholics. Pyridoxine and pantothenic acid deficiency give rise to peripheral neuropathies, the latter being associated with the burning feet syndrome (severe dysesthesias manifested by burning pain in the extremities). They occur in conjunction with other B vitamin deficiencies.

Alcoholic Cerebellar Degeneration. The unsteady gait, clumsy movements, and slurred speech, manifestations of the acute effects of alcohol on the cerebellar system, are the familiar hallmarks of drunkenness. Alcoholic cerebellar degeneration results in a less diffuse but unfortunately often permanent clinical picture. The gait is primarily affected, being broad based and unstable. Lower limb ataxia is usually severe, but involvement of the upper limbs is minimal. Dysarthria and nystagmus are rare. The ataxia may appear acutely as a component of Wernicke's encephalopathy or it may evolve more gradually in isolation. When it appears as part of Wernicke's encephalopathy, about 50% of the cases will recover completely from the ataxia (Dreyfus, 1974); however, a much smaller proportion of those in whom the ataxia occurs alone will demonstrate significant recovery.

The pathology is quite specific, and consists of degeneration of the neurocellular elements of the cerebellar cortex, particularly the Purkinje cells, with an interesting restriction to the anterior and superior parts of the vermis. It should be noted that characteristic lesions have been found in autopsy material from patients who have not manifested the ataxia in life.

In a comparison (Estrin, 1987) of ataxic and nonataxic alcoholics, there were no differences on measures of coordination such as hand-eye coordination or reaction time. There was also a lack of any dose-response effect with regard to alcohol and ataxia. Indeed, the annual and lifetime consumption of alcohol was actually lower in the ataxic individuals. This suggests either greater variations in individual susceptibility or a nutritional etiology.

The association of cerebellar degeneration with Wernicke's encephalopathy points to a thiamine deficiency etiology. The condition, as Korsakoff's psychosis, is not dramatically responsive to thiamine, which nevertheless should be given for all the reasons outlined above for Korsakoff's psychosis. A direct toxic effect of alcohol on the cerebellum has been suggested and may contribute to the fixed structural lesions (Barnes & Walker, 1980).

Alcoholic Polyneuropathy. Damage to the peripheral nerves may occur in alcoholics either as a result of associated nutritional deficiencies, specifically thiamine, or as a result of trauma, most frequently compression neuropathies. In alcoholic polyneuropathy, the sensory, motor, and autonomic systems may all be affected. There is degeneration of the myelin sheath with resulting impairment of nerve conduction velocities, and there may be direct axonal damage with reduced nerve action potential.

As with other nutritional polyneuropathies, impairment begins distally, is symmetrical, and usually starts with sensory symptoms in the form of abnormal, unpleasant sensations; i.e., dysesthesias. The usual progression of symptoms is from dysesthesia, often burning or tingling sensations in the toes and soles of the feet, to actual loss of sensation, numbness, loss of vibratory and position sense, to motor involvement with loss of dorsiflexion of the feet; i.e., bilateral footdrop. Progression marches proximally and slowly over a period of months, with sensation being lost in the classic glove and stocking fashion and motor involvement spreading from the more distal muscle groups to the more proximal. If the condition is severe, cranial nerves may become involved. When involvement is predominantly motor and more proximal than distal, an alcoholic myopathy should be suspected, since both complications may co-exist (Johnson, Eisenhofer & Lambie, 1986).

Autonomic System. *Sympathetic:* Alcoholism may be associated with sympathetic dysfunction affecting both blood pressure regulation and thermoregulation. The cause of the association between regular alcohol use and hypertension is unclear, but it may in part be due to sympathetic overactivity. During alcohol withdrawal increased sympathetic nerve activity is likely to be responsible for the hypertension, tremor, sweating, and tachycardia. Orthostatic hypotension occurring in some alcoholics during withdrawal may be a consequence of sympathetic nervous system dysfunction. Peripheral sympathetic nerve damage can also affect sweating, which may be lost in a glove and stocking distribution. In a study of thermoregulatory response to heat stress, alcoholics were found to have higher temperatures after heat exposure, with reduced weight loss and impaired distal sweating. Hypothermia conversely can occur in Wernicke's encephalopathy and, as noted previously, the lesions of the latter may be present without the diagnostic clinical signs. This may further contribute to instability of heat regulation in alcoholics.

Parasympathetic: Vagal nerve degeneration has been seen in alcoholic patients manifesting dysphagia and dysphonia, and vagal neuropathy has been shown to result in depressed heart rate responses in alcoholics. Damage to the vagus can be demonstrated by diminished heart rate responses to standing, to sustained hand grip, to atropine, or to Valsalva's maneuver. In diabetics, vagal neuropathy has been suggested as a cause of acute death. It is not clear whether this is the case in alcoholics; however, autonomic dysfunction may be related to cardiomyopathy.

Central sleep apnea and hypoapnea are common in chronic alcoholics and show associations with central nervous system damage and vagal neuropathy.

Impotence, partial or complete, is quite common in male alcoholics and sacral neuropathy may contribute to impaired sexual function. It is important that this issue be addressed directly. It is usually of much concern to the patient, but is rarely mentioned spontaneously. Reassurance can be offered that with abstinence and daily thiamine, some improvement is to be expected, though this may require several months.

Alcoholic peripheral neuropathy responds very well to thiamine, the time course for recovery being dependent upon the severity of the condition. Complete recovery can be expected in most patients within several months to a year. Some, however, present with such severe initial deficits that only partial recovery occurs.

Abnormalities in electromyographic studies are often found in alcoholics without clinical signs of peripheral neuropathy, indicating an occult form of the disease (Lefebre D'Amour, Shahani et al., 1979).

Optic Neuropathy. Optic neuropathy is frequently referred to as tobacco-alcohol amblyopia, though there is little evidence for other than a straightforward nutritional etiology, as in alcohol neuropathy. The onset of impaired vision can be acute or subacute. Central scotomata, particularly for red test objects, are found on examination. Dizziness may accompany the visual impairment and symptoms and signs of a general polyneuropathy are frequently present. Treatment and prognosis is as for polyneuropathy.

Nerve Trauma. It is good medical practice to inquire closely into the drug and alcohol intake of any patient presenting with nerve compression syndrome, since chemical dependency is one of the common causes. Most physicians are familiar with "Saturday night palsy," which is a brachial plexus compression. Other nerve compression can result from "passing out" in any number of positions, which can compromise blood flow to peripheral nerves, resulting in ulnar, peroneal and other nerve palsies. Perhaps the subclinically damaged state (Lefebre D'Amour, Shahani et al., 1979) of the peripheral nerves contributes to the frequency with which this condition develops in alcoholics. The prolonged ischemia is thought to produce demyelination. Recovery is expected to take place over a few weeks. Thiamine supplements would be prudent in alcoholics with compression neuropathies because of the possibility of underlying nutritional deficiency.

Stroke. There is a higher than normal incidence of hemorrhagic stroke and other intracranial bleeding among heavy users of alcohol, with an association of strokes or strokelike episodes within 24 hours of a drinking binge. Studies in rats have shown graded contractile responses in cerebral arterioles in an alcohol concentration range of 10 to 500 mg/ml. Two calcium antagonists, nifedipine and verapamil, were shown to prevent alcohol-induced vasospasm, suggesting a possible therapeutic approach to hypertension and stroke in heavy alcohol users. Moderate alcohol consumption (three to nine drinks a week) was found to be associated with increased subarachnoid hemorrhage in women (Altura, 1986). The association between alcohol and stroke may be related to hypertension, cerebral artery spasm, and increased bleeding tendency.

Seizures. Alcohol and epilepsy have been linked together since the time of Hippocrates. The relationship is complex. The prevalence of epilepsy in the general population ranges from 0.23 to 2.4% (Chan, 1985) and alcoholism 6.6 to 10.6% (Devatag, Mandich et al., 1983). The increased seizures in alcoholics may be due to withdrawal, to metabolic changes such as hypoglycemia or electrolyte imbalance, or to head trauma and infection for which alcoholics are at greater risk. It is, however, very important to remember that alcoholics may have seizures from non-alcohol-related causes as well. In a series from Denver (Earnest, Feldman et al., 1988) of 195 cases in seizures in alcoholics, 59% were due to alcohol withdrawal, 20% to head trauma, 5% to vascular disorders, and 2% to tumors. In a prospective study of 250 patients with first alcohol-related seizures, CT scan showed that 6.2% had an intracranial lesion. Most common were subdural hematoma and hygroma. Other conditions included neurocysticercosis, aneurysm, glioma and cerebral infarction. In 3.9%, the clinical management was changed by the scan results, emphasizing the importance of a complete neurological workup in alcoholics presenting with first seizures. On the other hand, it is also important to be alert to the possible role of alcohol in new-onset seizures in adults. In one series, 23% of adults with new-onset seizures had no other factor but alcohol abuse (Dam, Fugslang et al., 1985).

In their classic study, Victor and Adams (1978) found that in 241 alcoholic patients with seizures carefully selected to exclude those with known other causes (e.g., head trauma), 90% of the seizures occurred within the first seven to 48 hours of alcohol withdrawal. This tight association between seizures and alcohol withdrawal has recently been questioned by Ng, Hanser et al. (1988), who instead found a relationship between current alcohol intake and seizures. In their study, 16% of the first seizures occurred outside the withdrawal period and the rest exhibited an apparently random timing since the last drink. In spite of this, the preponderance of evidence from both human and animal studies indicates that the period of alcohol withdrawal is one in which there is intense CNS hyperexcitability and an increased propensity for seizures. Devetag (1983), in his series, has assigned seizures in alcoholics according to the following categories: (1) solitary convulsive seizures in alcoholics with no prior history of seizures and no other potentially epileptogenic disease, and no association with withdrawal, 21%; (2) withdrawal seizures, 21%; (3) seizures in alcoholics with other potentially epileptogenic disease, 20%; and (4) recurrent seizures in alcoholics not previously epileptic and not suffering from any other potentially epileptogenic condition, and not associated with withdrawal, 37%.

Repeated episodes of drinking and withdrawal are thought to predispose to seizures due to a kindling phenomenon (Post, Unde & Roy Byrne, 1987), though the evidence is conflicting at present. Given the various causes of seizures in alcoholics, it is obvious that no blanket statement can be made about treatment. A complete neurological workup should be done on all first seizures and treatment accordingly planned. In a large series from San Francisco General Hospital (Simon, Alldredge & Lowenstein, 1988), the effectiveness of intravenous phenytoin was assessed in a double-blind placebo-controlled study. For patients presenting with seizures in the period of alcohol withdrawal, 1,000 mg phenytoin given intravenously was no more effective than placebo in preventing a second seizure.

Seizures are quite rare in detoxification units, and there is no clear evidence that any of the commonly used detoxification agents is better than any other in preventing seizures during the withdrawal period. In one series of 227 patients admitted for withdrawal from alcohol (Lechtenberg & Worner, 1988), 83 were determined to have risk factors other than alcohol predisposing them to seizures. All were placed on a standard chlordiazepoxide withdrawal regimen. None had seizures.

Anticonvulsant medication is not indicated for those patients whose seizures have been only related to alcohol withdrawal or intake and who have no other risk factors. For patients who, independent of their drinking, have clinical reasons for being placed on an anticonvulsant regimen, careful monitoring is essential. Medication compliance in alcoholics is notoriously poor. Alcohol interferes with drug metabolism through its induction of the microsomal ethanol oxidizing system (MEOS). In an actively drinking alcoholic, drug levels will be unexpectedly high, whereas during periods of abstinence levels may be subtherapeutic.

Anosognosia. Denial or unawareness accompanies many neurological disorders. Anosognosia has been described for right hemiplegia, blindness, loss of memory, hemiballismus, sexual impotence, and incontinence due to central nervous system damage (Fisher, 1989). Schizophrenics treated with neuroleptics may not acknowledge the grossly disturbing movements of tardive dyskinesia (Myslobodsky, Tomer et al., 1986), and patients with Parkinsonian gait and tremor may be unperturbed by their defects. Early stages of dementia are often characterized by poor judgment, lack of concern, and uncharacteristic rudeness, of which the patient is unaware. Confabulation accompanies anosognosia, indeed is part of it. The patient acts as if he can move his limbs, see, or remember normally because he is unaware that he cannot. Patients with Korsakoff's psychosis are usually, at least partially, unaware of the amnesia and may confabulate. It seems possible that the dense denial seen, particularly in some older alcoholics, may have a neurological as well as a psychological basis. Alcoholics near the end of the continuum of central nervous system damage may show evidence of some memory loss, perseveration, unconcern, inappropriate responses, concreteness, loss of volition or impulsiveness, which are manifestations of cerebral dysfunction. They remain unimpressed by a huge body of evidence demonstrating the consequences of their drinking. They adhere to alternative explanations of events in spite of direct confrontation with the falsity of their beliefs. They seem incapable of changing cognitive set from seeing themselves as normal social drinkers to problem drinkers. They do not respond to the usual therapeutic interventions, nor do they seem capable of responding to the social pressures of a rehabilitation environment with even token verbal compliance. While it is true that they do not present with the gross damage customarily seen in patients with anosognosia, an organic explanation for their intransigence seems plausible. It certainly reduces staff frustration in these difficult cases.

COCAINE

Cocaine use by any route can result during intoxication in a variety of neurological problems. Cocaine is both a local anesthetic and a powerful sympathomimetic, and its neurological effects are related to these properties (Table 2). Of 47 patients in whom stroke followed cocaine use, the mean age was 32 years and all routes of administration were represented (Klonoff, Andrews & Obana, 1989). Over half of the patients who were studied, either angiographically or at autopsy, had intracranial aneurysms or anterior venous malformations.

Convulsions. The convulsant effects of cocaine are most likely related to its local anesthetic effects and are similar to those of lidocaine (Rowbotham, 1988). Seizure activity begins in the temporal lobe and then becomes generalized (Matsuzaki, 1978). In single seizures the EEG should be normal soon after the seizure. Multiple seizure and status are associated with high blood levels such as are seen following the internal rupture of a cocaine-filled condom swallowed for smuggling purposes by a body packer. A patient who presents with a cocaine-induced seizure should have a thorough assessment. If no cause other than cocaine use is found, there is no indication for treatment with anticonvulsants, since they do not protect against cocaine-induced seizures, and there is no evidence to suggest that the patient is at increased risk for seizures other than those associated with drug use.

Headaches. Headaches in cocaine abusers are common complaints both during intoxication and for several weeks into abstinence. During intoxication the prodromal significance of head pain signalling focal deficits and vascular catastrophes should not be overlooked. There is a report of *de novo* migraine-like headaches arising during cocaine intoxication and withdrawal (Satel & Gawin, 1989). The association of migraine with serotonin dysregulation and the known effects of cocaine as a potent inhibitor of serotonin reuptake present a possible causal link.

Dystonic Reactions. Cocaine may lower the threshold for dystonic reactions induced by neuroleptic drug. Six of seven chronic cocaine users developed dystonic reactions after taking haloperidol (Choy Kwong & Lipton, 1989). In one case, a dystonic reaction developed in association with withdrawal from cocaine alone without the concomitant use of neuroleptics.

It should be noted that the neurological complications of cocaine are acute effects related to intoxication and withdrawal. Anecdotally, headache has been reported for weeks following abstinence from cocaine. However, there are no formal studies of long-term neurological consequences of cocaine use.

HEROIN

Opinion is divided with regard to whether or not there exist specific damages and deficits resulting from the use of opiates and not as consequences of the method of use, lifestyle, or adulterants mixed

TABLE 2. Acute and Chronic Effects of Cocaine

Condition	Timing	Observation
Stroke	Intoxication	Intracerebral hem: 49% frequency associated Cerebral infarction: 22% A-V malformations
Seizures	Intoxication	Single Multiple Status epilepticus associated with high blood levels
Transient neurological symptoms	Intoxication	Dizziness Blurred vision Ataxia Tinnitus Transient hemiparesis
Headache	Intoxication Withdrawal Early abstinence	Can be *de novo* migraine
Dystonia	Withdrawal	

with the drug. The following neurological complications have been described (Richter & Baden, 1969; Richter & Rosenberg, 1968; Hall & Karp, 1973; Rounsaville, Novelly & Kleber, 1991; Stamboulis, Psimaras & Malliara-Loulakaki, 1988).

1. Mononeuropathy
2. Chronic polyneuropathy
3. Brachia and lumbar plexitis
4. Guillain-Barre syndrome
5. Transverse myelitis (from postmortem examinations)
6. Central pontine myelinolysis
7. Delayed postanoxic encephalopathy
8. Diffuse cortical impairment.

The pathogenesis of the peripheral nervous system complications remains obscure. It has been considered that the heroin-quinine adulterant mixture may either cause a toxic change in nerve or muscle tissue, or it may stimulate a hypersensitivity response. The question of long-term central nervous system damage from opiates remains open, since in practice it is difficult to find a group of long-term opiate addicts who have been exposed to steady high doses of the opiate in pure form using sterile techniques, who have not contaminated the picture by abusing other drugs, especially alcohol, and have not had a history of head injury. One such study is available (Strang & Gurling, 1989). Seven subjects had been using British pharmaceutical heroin for 17 to 23 years, were in their 50s at the time of examination, and were using little or no alcohol. Three of the seven had a history of alcohol abuse for periods of six months, one year, and 17 years. In this group of seven, both greater CT scan abnormalities (similar to alcohol) and neuropsychological deficits were observed compared to age-matched controls. There was, however, no consistent relationship between their intake of heroin and CT changes or neuropsychological impairment.

MARIJUANA

The data on long-term central nervous system damage in heavy users of cannabis is at present inconclusive. There have been reports of memory impairment, reduced capacity for sustained attention, slower rates of processing, and perceptual motor impairment as well as a number of negative studies (Souief, 1976; Wig & Varma, 1977).

In five out of eight controlled studies, persistent short-term memory deficits were detected in chronic cannabis smokers. Two studies involved long-term follow up. In one (Page, Fletcher & Tone, 1988), 30 marijuana-dependent Costa Rican men, compared with 31 matched controls on tests of memory, had scores which were lower, but not significantly, in 1973. When reevaluated 11 years later, they showed significant impairment of short-term memory and attention compared with non-users. A reevaluation study (Mendhiratta, Varma et al., 1988) in India of heavy bhang (marijuana) users, charas (hashish) smokers, and controls was conducted after 11 years. All the users had continued use over this period. The tests of intelligence, memory and perceptual motor functions, which were used initially, were repeated. Additional deterioration in the users was seen on digit span, speed and accuracy tests, reaction time and Bender Visumotor Gestalt Test. In a small but well-controlled study of 10 cannabis-dependent adolescents compared with nine non-drug-abusing adolescents and eight who had abused drugs, but not cannabis, significant differences were obtained on the Benton Visual Retention Test and the Wechsler Memory Prose Passages (Schwartz, Grunewald et al., 1989). Retesting after six weeks showed improvement in the cannabis-dependent group, but residual impairment remained.

SEDATIVE-HYPNOTICS

There have been few studies on the long-term effects of prolonged heavy use of sedative-hypnotics alone (Bergman, Borg & Holm, 1980; Hendler, Cimini et al., 1980; Lader, Ron & Peterson, 1984; Petursson, Gudjonsson & Lader, 1983; Poser, Poser et al., 1983; Bergman, Borg et al., n.d.; Golombok, Moodley & Lader, 1988). Bergman and his associates (1980) investigated patients using only sedative-hypnotics (barbiturates, benzodiazepines, or meprobamate) but no other drugs and compared them to a pair-matched control group from the general population. These 55 sedative-hypnotic users showed a pattern of neuropsychological deficits similar to that seen in alcoholics. Thirty-eight of these patients were reevaluated five years later (Bergman, Borg et al., n.d.). There was overall neuropsychological improvement; however, half the group showed signs of intellectual impairment at follow-up. Twenty-nine patients had CT scans, which showed an increased prevalence of dilation of the ventricles, but unlike alcoholics, not of widened cortical sulci. There was correlation between impaired neuropsychological status (visual spatial skills) on the initial evaluation and continuing drug abuse at follow-up. Unfortunately, the authors reported that 11 of the patients

TABLE 3. Chronic Effects of Inhalants

Substance	Source	Symptoms
Gasoline	Fuel	Tremor, ataxia, myoclonus, chorea, encephalopathy (Doulehan, Hirsch & Brillman, 1983)
Halogenated hydrocarbons	Degreasers Spot remover Typewriter correction fluid	CNS edema, hemorrhages
h-Hexane	Glues, cements	Peripheral neuropathy
Methanol	Often in solvents	Blurred vision, photophobia, blindness, basal ganglia hemorrhage
Methyl-n-butyl ketone	Paints, inks, resins	Peripheral neuropahty
Nitrous oxide		Sensory disturbances, ataxia, impotence, multiple sclerosis-like syndrome (Layzer, 1978)
Toluene	Solvents: paint thinners, glues, lacquers	Peripheral neuropathy, optic neuropahty, ataxia, severe muscle weakness, encephalopathy (Streicher, Gabow & Moss, 1981)
Trichloroethane	Typewriter correction fluid	Diffuse CNS damage

were showing signs of alcohol abuse at follow-up, but they did not separate this group in the final results. Three studies (Hendler, Cimini et al., 1980; Petursson, Gudjonsson & Lader, 1983) have reported neuropsychological impairment in chronic benzodiazepine users. Patients taking high doses of benzodiazepines for long periods of time perform poorly on tests involving visual spatial abilities and sustained attention, a pattern of impairment consistent with deficits in posterior cortical function. Unlike alcoholics, these patients function normally on tests of frontal function such as verbal fluency and card sorting. It is not yet known whether these impairments persist after a drug-free period.

VOLATILE INHALANTS

Solvent abuse is rare outside the adolescent population. Unfortunately, abuse of volatile inhalants may be associated with permanent central nervous system damage. Most act like general anesthetics, with a similar picture of acute intoxication. Chronic central nervous system damage may be a consequence of the euphorigenic substance itself, or of other toxic components in the product, e.g., glue, cement, degreaser, paint, antifreeze, which is being inhaled. Some products also cause peripheral nerve damage. These substances are generally highly fat soluble and diffusely toxic to the nervous system, producing a wide array of dysfunctions, including ataxia, myoclonus, chorea, tremor, optic neuropathy and sensory and motor neuropathies as well as seizures and encephalopathy. Table 3 summarizes some of the consequences of specific inhalant abuse.

CONCLUSIONS

Since euphorigenic drugs have, by definition, their site of action in the CNS and produce their effects by distorting its normal function, it is not surprising that acute and chronic neurological symptoms are common among addicts. As a general rule, the more nonspecific and diffuse the actions of the drug, the more widespread its functional perturbations will be. Alcohol and the inhalants, for example, have effects on nerve cell membranes and on ion transport systems as well as on catecholamine levels and produce diverse pictures of neurological impairment. Opioid drugs whose actions are more targeted toward specific receptor systems have few reported neurological consequences. Stimulant drugs, again acting more discretely on the CNS, have acute effects which, except for hyperexcitability phenomena, are secondary to their effects on the cardiovascular system and minor, or questionable, chronic direct neurological consequences. Of particular interest are the more subtle effects on memory, problem-solving, mental flexibility, curiosity, motivation, and affect, which have been studied to some extent in alcoholics but much less with other drug abusers. For the past 100 years, attention has been focused on striking clinical syndromes and the absence of such has been taken to imply a lack of CNS toxicity of the particular drug. In fact, it is chastening to remember that accepted clinical wisdom of 25 years ago was that alcohol did not cause CNS damage provided nutrition was adequate. We need more probing neuropsychological studies than those currently available to be able to say with confidence that a specific abused drug is without long-term effects on the central nervous system.

ACKNOWLEDGMENTS: Originally published as Geller A (1991). Neurological effects of drug and alcohol addiction. In NS Miller (ed.) Comprehensive Handbook of Drug and Alcohol Addiction. *New York, NY: Marcel Dekker, 599–621. Reprinted by permission of the publisher.*

REFERENCES

Altura BM (1986). Introduction to the symposium and overview. *Alcoholism: Clinical & Experimental Research* 10:557–559.

Altura BM, Altura BT & Gebrewold A (1983). Alcohol induced spasms of cerebral blood vessels: Relation to cerebro vascular accidents and sudden death. *Science* 220:331–333.

Arendt T, Bigl V, Arendt A & Tennstedt A (1983). Loss of neurons in the nucleus basalis of Meynert in Alzheimer's disease, paralysis agitans and Korsakoff's disease. *Acta Neuropathologica* 61:101–108.

Artmann H, Gall MV, Hacker H & Herrlick J (1981). Reversible enlargement of cerebro spinal fluid spaces in chronic alcoholics. *American Journal of Neuroradiology* 2:23–27.

Barnes DE & Walker DW (1980). Neuronal loss in hippocampus and cerebellar cortex in rats prenatally exposed to ethanol. *Alcoholism* 4:209.

Begleiter H, Porjesz & Kissin B (1982). Brain dysfunction in alcoholics with and without a family history of alcoholism. *Alcoholism: Clinical & Experimental Research* 6:136.

Bennett AE (1960). Diagnosis of intermediate stage of alcoholic brain disease. *Journal of the American Medical Association* 172:1143–1146.

Berglund M & Ingvar DH (1976). Cerebral blood flow and its regional distribution in alcoholism and Korsakoff's patients. *Journal of Studies on Alcohol* 37(5):586–597.

Bergman H, Borg S & Holm L (1980). Neuropsychological impairment and exclusive abuse of sedatives or hypnotics. *American Journal of Psychiatry* 137:215–217.

Bergman H, Borg S, Engelbrektson K & Vikander B (n.d.). Dependence on sedative hypnotics: Neuropsychological impairment, filed dependence and clinical course in a five year follow up study. *British Journal of Addiction.*

Blass JP & Gibson GE (1977). Abnormality of a thiamine requiring enzyme in patients with Wernicke-Korsakoff syndrome. *The New England Journal of Medicine* 297:1367–1370.

Butters N (1984). Alcoholic Korsakoff's syndrome: An update. *Seminars in Neurology* 4:229–247.

Butters N & Granholm E (1987). The continuity hypothesis: Some conclusions and their implications for the etiology and neuropathology of alcoholic Korsakoff's syndrome. In OA Parsons, N Butters & PE Nathan (eds.) *Neuropsychology of Alcoholism: Implications for Diagnosis and Treatment.* New York, NY: Guilford Press.

Butterworth RF (1989). Effects of thiamine deficiency on brain metabolism: Implications for the pathogenesis of the Wernicke-Korsakoff syndrome. *Alcohol* 24:271–279.

Canterwell BS & Criqui MH (1978). Prevention of the Wernicke-Korsakoff syndrome. A cost benefit analysis. *The New England Journal of Medicine* 299:285–289.

Carlen PL, Wortzmann G, Holgate RC, Wilkinson DA & Rankin JG (1978). Reversible cerebral atrophy in recently abstinent alcoholics measured by computed tomography scans. *Science* 200:1076–1078.

Chan AWK (1985). Alcoholism and epilepsy. *Epilepsia* 26:323–333.

Choy Kwong M & Lipton RB (1989). Dystonia related to cocaine withdrawal: A case report and pathogenic hypothesis. *Neurology* 39:996.

Coulehan JL, Hirsch W & Brillman J (1983). Gasoline sniffing and lead toxicity in Navajo adolescents. *Pediatrics* 71:113–117.

Dally S, Luft A, Ponsin JC, Girre C, Mamo H & Fournier E (1988). Abnormal pattern of cerebral blood flow distribution in young alcohol addicts. *British Journal of Addiction* 83:105–109.

Dam AM, Fugslang , Frederiksen A, Svarre Olsen U & Dam M (1985). Late onset epilepsy: Etiologies, types of seizures and value of clinical investigation, EEG and computerized tomography scan. *Epilepsia* 26:227–231.

Devatag F, Mandich G, Zaiotti G & Toffolo GG (1983). Alcoholic epilepsy: Review of a series and proposed classification and etiopathogenesis. *Harvard Journal of Neurologic Science* 4:275–284.

Dreyfus PM (1974). Diseases of the nervous system in chronic alcoholics. In Kissin & Begleiter (eds.) *Biology of Alcoholism, Vol. 3.* New York, NY: Plenum Press, 265–290.

Earnest MP, Feldman H, Marx JA, Harris JA, Biltech M & Sullivan LP (1988). Intracranial lesions shown by CT scans in 259 cases of first alcohol-related seizures. *Neurology* 38:1561–5.

Eckardt MG, Rohrbaugh JW, Rio D, Rawlings RR & Coppola R (1988). Brain imaging in alcoholic patients. *Advances in Alcohol and Substance Abuse* 7:59–71.

Estrin WJ (1987). Alcoholic cerebellar degeneration is not a dose dependent phenomenon. *Alcoholism: Clinical & Experimental Research* 11:372–275.

Fabian MS & Parsons OA (1983). Differential improvement of cognitive functions in recovering alcoholic women. *Journal of Abnormal Psychology* 92:87–89.

Fisher CM (1989). Neurologic frequents II. Remarks on anosognosia, confabulation, memory and other topics and an appendix on self-observation. *Neurology* 39:127–132.

Fisher CM (1982). Transient global amnesia. *Archives of Neurology* 39:605–608.

Freund G (1970). Alcohol, barbiturate and bromide withdrawal symptoms in mice. In NK Mello & J Mendelson (eds.) *Recent Advances in Studies in Alcoholism.* Rockville, MD: National Institute on Mental Health, 453–471.

Freund G (1973). Chronic central nervous system toxicity of alcohol. *Annual Review of Pharmacology* 13:217–227.

Freund G & Ballinger WE (1988). Loss of cholinergic muscarinic receptors in the frontal cortex of alcohol abusers. *Alcoholism: Clinical & Experimental Research* 12:630–638.

Freund G & Ballinger WE (1989). Neuroreceptor changes in the putamen of alcohol abusers. *Alcoholism: Clinical & Experimental Research* 13:213–217.

Glenn SW, Parsons OA, Sinha R & Stevens L (1988). The effects of repeated withdrawals from alcohol on the memory of male and female alcoholics. *Alcohol* 23:337–342.

Goldstein G (1987). Recovery, treatment and rehabilitation in chronic alcoholics. In OA Parsons, N Butters & PE Nathan (eds.) *Neuropsychology of Alcoholism Implications for Diagnosis and Treatment.* New York, NY: Guilford Press.

Goodwin DW (1971). Blackouts and alcohol induced memory dysfunction. In NK Mello & JH Mendelson (eds.) *Recent Advances in Studies in Alcohol.* Rockville, MD: National Institute on Mental Health.

Golombok S, Moodley P & Lader M (1988). Cognitive impairment in long term benzodiazepine users. *Psychology and Medicine* 18:365–374.

Gregson RAM & Taylor GM (1977). Prediction of relapse in male alcoholics. *Journal of Studies on Alcohol* 38:1749–1760.

Hall JH & Karp HR (1973). Acute progressive pontine disease in heroin abuse. *Neurology* 23:6.

Harper C (1979). Wernicke's encephalopathy: A more common disease than realized. A neuropathological study of 51 cases. *Journal of Neurology, Neurosurgery and Psychiatry* 42:226–231.

Harper C & Krie J (1985). Brain atrophy in chronic alcoholic patients: A quantitative pathological study. *Journal of Neurology, Neurosurgery and Psychiatry* 48:211–217.

Hendler N, Cimini C, Terence MA & Long DA (1980). A comparison of cognitive impairment due to benzodiazepines and narcotics. *American Journal of Psychiatry* 137:828–830.

Hoffman PL, Tabakoff B, Szabo G, Suzdak PD & Paul SM (1987). Effects of an imidazodiazepine, Ro 15 4513 on the incoordination and hypothermia produced by ethanol and pentobarbital. *Life Science* 41:611–619.

Hrubeck Z & Omenn GS (1981). Evidence for genetic predisposition for alcoholic cirrhosis and psychosis. Twin concordances for alcoholism and its biological end points. *Alcoholism* 5:207–214.

Ishikawa Y, Meyer JS, Tanahasi N, Hata T, Velez M, Fann WE, Kandula P, Motel KF & Rogers RE (1986). Abstinence improves cerebral perfusion and brain volume in alcohol neurotoxicity without Wernicke-Korsakoff syndrome. *Journal of Cerebral Blood Flow and Metabolism* 6:86–94.

Johnson RH, Eisenhofer G & Lambie DG (1986). The effects of acute and chronic ingestion of ethanol on the autonomic nervous system. *Drug and Alcohol Dependence* 18:319–328.

Klonoff DC, Andrews BT & Obana WG (1989). Stroke associated with cocaine use. *Archives of Neurology* 46:989–993.

Korsakoff SS (1887). Disturbance of psychic function in alcoholic paralysis and its relation to the disturbance of the psychic sphere in multiple neuritis of non-alcoholic origin. *Vestnik Psichiatrii Vol IV*, fasicle 2.

Lader MM, Ron M & Peterson M (1984). Computed axial brain tomography in long term benzodiazepine users. *Psychology and Medicine* 14:203–206.

Langlais PJ, Mair RG & McEntree WJ (1988). Acute thiamine deficiency in the rat: Brain lesions amino acid MK-801 pre-treatment. *Society for Neuroscience Abstracts* 14:313.

Layzer RR (1978). Myeloneuropathy after prolonged exposure to nitrous oxide. *Lancet* 2:1227–1228.

Leber WR & Parsons OA (1980). Neuropsychological Functioning and Clinical Progress in Alcoholics. Presented at the Southwestern Psychological Association 26th Annual Meeting, Oklahoma City.

Lechtenberg R & Worner TM (1988). Prospective Study of Seizure Risk Management of Alcoholics During Inpatient Detoxification. International Symposium on Alcohol and Seizures, Washington, DC.

Lefebre D'Amour M, Shahani BT, Young RR & Bird KT (1979). The importance of studying neural nerve conduction and late responses in the evaluation of alcoholics. *Neurology* 29:1600–1604.

Lishman WA, Jacobson RR & Acker C (1987). Brain damage in alcoholism: Current concepts. *Acta Medica Scandinavica* 717(Suppl):5–17.

Lishman WA (1981). Cerebral disorder in alcoholism. Syndromes of impairment. *Brain* 104:1–20.

Lister RG, Eckardt M & Weingartner H (1987). Ethanol intoxication and memory: Recent developments and new directions. In M Galanter (ed.) *Recent Developments in Alcoholism* 5:115–125.

Lynch MJG (1960). Brain lesions in chronic alcoholism. *Archives of Pathology* 69:342–353.

Mair WGP, Warrington EK & Weiskrantz L (1979). Memory disorder in Korsakoff's psychosis. A neuropathological and neuropsychological investigation of two cases. *Brain* 102:749–783.

Martin PR, Adinoff B, Echardt MJ, Stapleton JM, Bone GAH, Rubinow DR, Lane EA & Linnoila M (1989). Effective pharmacotherapy of alcohol amnestic disorder with fluvoxamine. *Archives of General Psychiatry* 46:617–621.

Martin PR, Impeduglia G, Giri PR & Karanian J (1989). Acceleration of ethanol metabolism by past thiamine deficiency. *Alcoholism: Clinical and Experimental Research* 13:457–460.

Matsuzaki M (1978). Alterations in pattern of EEG activities and convulsant effect of cocaine following administration in the rhesus monkey. *Electroencephalography Clinical Neurophysiology* 45:1–15.

Maudsley H (1879). *The Pathology of Mind, 3rd Ed.* London, England: Macmillan.

McEntree WJ, Mair RG & Langlais PJ (1984). Neurochemical pathology in Korsakoff's psychosis: Implications for other cognitive disorders. *Neurology* 34:648–652.

Mendhiratta SS, Varma VK, Dang R, Malhotra AK, Das K & Nehra R (1988). Cannabis and cognitive functions: A re-evaluation study. *British Journal of Addiction* 83–749–753.

Messert B, Orrison WW, Hawkins MJ & Quaglier CE (1979). Central pontine myelinolysis. Considerations of etiology, diagnosis and treatment. *Neurology* 29:147–160.

Muvroner A, Bergman H, Hindmarsh T & Telakioi T (1989). Influence of improved drinking habits on brain atrophy and cognitive performance in alcoholic patients: A 5-year follow up study. *Alcoholism: Clinical & Experimental Research* 13:137–141.

Myslobodsky MS, Tomer R, Holden T, Kempler S & Sigal M (1986). Cognitive impairment in patients with tardive dyskinesias. *Journal NMD* 173:156–160.

Ng SK, Hanser WA, Brust JC & Susser M (1988). Alcohol consumption and withdrawal in new onset seizures. *The New England Journal of Medicine* 319:666–73.

Page JB, Fletcher J & Tone WR (1988). Psychosocial cultural perspectives on chronic cannabis use: The Costa Rican follow-up. *Journal of Psychoactive Drugs* 20:57–65.

Parker ES & Noble EP (1977). Alcohol consumption and cognitive functioning in social drinkers. *Journal of Studies on Alcohol* 38(7):1224–1232.

Parker ES, Beirnbaum IM, Boyd RA & Noble EP (1979). Neuropsychological decrements as a function of alcohol intake in male students. *Alcoholism: Clinical & Experimental Research* 4:330–334.

Parsons OA (1977). Neuropsychological deficits in alcoholics: Facts and fancies. *Alcoholism: Clinical & Experimental Research* 1(1):51–56.

Parsons OA & Farr SP (1981). The neuropsychology of alcohol and drug use. In S Filskow & T Boll (eds.) *Handbook of Clinical Neuropsychology*. New York, NY: John Wiley and Sons.

Parsons OA & Leber WR (1981). The relationship between cognitive dysfunction and brain damage in alcoholics. *Alcoholism* 5:326–343.

Peters RA (1936). The biochemical lesion in Vitamin B_1 deficiency. *Lancet* 1:1161–1165.

Petursson H, Gudjonsson GA & Lader MM (1983). Psychometric performance during withdrawal from long term benzodiazepine treatment. *Psychopharmacology* 81:345–349.

Pfefferbaum A, Rosenbloom M, Cousan K & Jernigan TL (1988). Brain CT changes in alcoholics: Effects of age and alcohol consumption. *Alcoholism: Clinical & Experimental Research* 12:81–85.

Poser W, Poser S, Roscher D & Argyrakis A (1983). Do benzodiazepines cause cerebral atrophy? *Lancet* 1:715.

Post RM, Unde TW & Roy Byrne PP (1987). Correlates of anti-manic response to carbamazepine. *Psychiatric Research* 21:71–83.

Richter RW & Baden MM (1969). Neurological complications of heroin addiction. *Trans American Neurological Association* 94:330–332.

Richter RW & Rosenberg RN (1968). Transverse myelitis associated with heroin addiction. *Journal of the American Medical Association* 206:1255–1257.

Riley JN & Walker DW (1978). Morphological alterations in hippocampus after long-term alcohol consumption in mice. *Science* 201(4356):646–648.

Risberg J & Berglund M (1987). Cerebral blood flow and metabolism in alcoholics. In OA Parsons, N Butters & PE Nathan (eds.) *Neuropsychology of Alcoholism*. New York, NY: Guilford Press.

Ron MA, Acker W, Shaw GK & Lishman WA (1982). Computerized tomography of the brain in chronic alcoholism: A survey and follow up study. *Brain* 105:497–514.

Rounsaville BJ, Novello RA & Kleber HAD (1991). Neuropsychological impairment in opiate addicts: Risk factors. In RB Millman, P Cushman & J Lowinson (eds.) *Recent Developments in Drug and Alcohol Use*. New York, NY: Annals of the New York Academy of Sciences.

Rowbotham MC (1988). Neurologic aspects of cocaine abuse. *Western Journal of Medicine* 149:442–448.

Satel D & Gawin FH (1989). Migraine-like headache and cocaine use. *Journal of the American Medical Association* 261:2995–2996.

Schroth G, Naegele T, Klose V, Mann K & Peterson D (1988). Reversible brain shrinkage in abstinent alcoholics measured by MRI. *Neuroradiology* 30:385–389.

Schwartz RH, Grunewald PJ, Klitzner M & Fedio P (1989). Short-term memory impairment in cannabis dependent adolescents. *American Journal of Diseases of Children* 143:1214–1219.

Serdau M, Hausser-Hauw C & Laplane D (1988). The clinical spectrum of alcoholic pellagra encephalopathy. *Brain* 111:829–842.

Simon RP, Alldredge BK & Lowenstein DH (1988). Alcohol symposium proceedings. *Epilepsia* 29:492–497.

Souief MI (1976). Differential association between chronic cannabis use and brain function deficits. *Annals of the New York Academy of Science* 282:323–43.

Stamboulis E, Psimaras A & Malliara-Loulakaki S (1988). Brachial and lumbar plexitis as a reaction to heroin. *Drug and Alcohol Dependence* 22:205–207.

Stamfer MJ, Colditz GA, Willett WC, Speizer FE & Hennekens CH (1988). A prospective study of moderate alcohol consumption and the risk of coronary disease and stroke in women. *The New England Journal of Medicine* 319:267–273.

Strang J & Gurling H (1989). Computerized tomography and neuropsychological assessment in long term high dose heroin addicts. *British Journal of Addiction* 84:1012–1019.

Streicher HZ, Gabow PA & Moss AH (1981). Syndromes of toluene sniffing in adults. *Annals of Internal Medicine.*

Tabakoff B, Hoffman PL, Lee JM, Saito T, Willard B et al. (1988). Differences in platelet enzyme activity between alcoholics and nonalcoholics. *The New England Journal of Medicine* 318:134–139.

Tabakoff B & Hoffman PL (1987). Biochemical pharmacology of alcohol. In HY Meltzer (ed.) *Psychopharmacology: The Third Generation of Progress*. New York, NY: The Raven Press, 1521–1526.

Torvik A, Lindboe CF & Rodge S (1982). Brain lesions in alcoholics. A neuropathological study with clinical correlations. *Journal of Neurology Science* 56:233–248.

Victor M, Adams RA & Collins GH (1989). *The Wernicke-Korsakoff Syndrome and Related Neurologic Disorders Due to Alcoholism and Malnutrition, 2nd Ed.* Philadelphia, PA: Davis.

Victor M, Adams RD & Collins GH (1971). *The Wernicke-Korsakoff Syndrome*. Philadelphia, PA: Davis.

Victor M & Laureno R (1978). Neurologic complications of alcohol abuse: Epidemiological aspects. *Advances in Neurology* 19:603–617.

Von Wartburg JP (1979). Effects of alcohol on membrane structure and function. *Alcoholism* 3:46–47.

Walker DW & Hunter BE (1978). Short-term memory impairment following chronic alcohol consumption in rats. *Neuropsychologia* 16:545–554.

Wernicke C (1881). *Lehrbuch der Gehirnkrankheiten*. Berlin, Germany: Kassel.

Wig NN & Varma VK (1977). Patterns of long-term heavy cannabis use in North India and its effects on cognitive functions: A preliminary report. *Drug and Alcohol Dependence* 2:211–219.

Wollman H, Smith TC & Stephen GW (1968). Effects of respiratory and metabolic alkalosis on cerebral blood flow in man. *Journal of Applied Physiology* 24:60–65.

CHAPTER 5

Sleep Disorders

Allan W. Graham, M.D., FACP, FASAM

Office Considerations
Evaluating Sleep
Sleep Architecture in Alcoholics
Medical Matters Affecting Sleep
Management of Insomnia
Neurobiology and Physiology

Alcoholics commonly complain to their physicians about poor sleep: about their inability to go to sleep in the absence of drinking alcohol and about their trouble staying asleep. Physicians generally are reluctant to prescribe sedative-hypnotics for these patients because of the potential for habituation, particularly in these genetically and behaviorally vulnerable patients. The result often is annoyance or reticence on the part of the physician; for the patients, the results are often frustration and exploration of over-the-counter remedies.

Sleep research is revealing the anatomic and physiologic properties of sleep—normal and abnormal—in alcoholics and in relation to alcohol, drugs, and environmental influences. The astute clinician can now make a number of recommendations to the chemically dependent patient about the predictable course of insomnia in early recovery and about techniques, medications, and other practices which may ameliorate insomnia during the first few months of abstinence. This chapter will provide: (1) suggestions for systematically assessing sleep in the office, (2) treatment recommendations, pharmacologic and behavioral, which may be tailored to various clinical settings, and (3) an overview of sleep mechanisms in normal and chemically dependent persons.

Sleep is a manifestation of a complex interplay of cyclic, neurobiologic processes involving multiple regions of the brain extending from the pons and midbrain (including the ascending reticular activating system, the locus coeruleus, and the raphe nuclei), to the caudal diencephalon (including the thalamus, hypothalamus, and subthalamus), to the suprachiasmatic nucleus and the basal forebrain (including the nucleus basalis of Meynert), and terminating in the hippocampus and the cerebral cortex, with branching influences on the neurohormonal regulatory systems in the pineal gland and the hypothalamic-pituitary-adrenal axis (Jones, 1994). Alcohol, nicotine, caffeine, and other drugs of addiction powerfully affect each of these neuroregulatory systems; and their effects on brain physiology take considerable time to change even after the substances have been removed from the body.

Prolonged disturbances of sleep following alcohol withdrawal are manifestations of the protracted nature of the alcohol withdrawal syndrome. Clearly, withdrawal insomnia reflects the fact that the elimination of a psychoactive substance from the body is only the first of many steps required for new balances in neuroregulation to be achieved. The concept of a "protracted abstinence syndrome" refers to the hours, days, or months that may be required for neuronal systems to readjust after the removal of a psychoactive substance. As they discuss treatment strategies, patients and providers both need to be cognizant of the fact that different time frames are required for resolution of different withdrawal symptoms and findings.

A number of clinical studies of sleep in chemically dependent patients have expanded the neurobiological understanding of sleep dysfunctions. Chronic insomnia in alcoholics, abstinent for one to two months, may represent a protracted abstinence syndrome, which for many continues to improve over time. Studies suggest the possibility that permanent damage to sleep mechanism may result from prolonged, heavy alcohol intake; patients with such injuries may never be able to regain normal sleep functions. Patients in this latter category probably have degenerative changes in sleep-modulating circuits, analogous to the degenerative changes seen elsewhere in alcoholic syndromes, such as Wernicke-Korsakoff's; indeed, many patients with dementias

TABLE 1. Important Features of Sleep

- Time to falling asleep (sleep onset latency)
- Awakenings
- Slow-wave sleep (SWS) time
- Rapid eye movement (REM) sleep time
- Sleep efficiency (% time asleep while in bed)
- Percent REM sleep (REM as a percent of total sleep)
- Restfulness or quality of sleep
- Daytime napping
- Daytime functioning

(Korsakoff's, Alzheimer's, and Parkinson's) suffer from chronic insomnia and share some similar, structural abnormalities, notably degenerative changes in selected regions of the thalamus (Lugaresi, 1992). As our understandings of the neurocircuitry and neurochemistry of sleep improve, alcoholic insomnias will be increasingly defined at the cellular and integrated circuit level. Improved fundamental understandings of the neurobiology of sleep and of addiction lead ultimately to more specific and effective management strategies for both.

OFFICE CONSIDERATIONS

What does it mean when a patient complains about sleeping problems? How does a busy physician or counselor evaluate the complaint appropriately?

First, the steps for evaluation need to be linked to the treatment goals that the patient and provider establish. Perhaps one of the major impediments to dealing with sleep problems is the lack of mutually agreed upon goals and, consequently, agreed upon expectations. The provider may well be aware that many issues contribute to causing the patient's seemingly simple complaint; the patient, however, may wish to believe that the problem can be simply solved with a medication or other remedy. The task before the provider and patient then becomes one of negotiating a plan—a task that can be made manageable and satisfying if reasonable and achievable goals are defined.

Second, a useful practical belief is that if a patient complains of a sleeping problem, then a problem does exist. The problem may not be as the patient envisions it, or the problem may not have the causes or antecedent connections that the patient attributes to it; but a sleep complaint points toward some kind of issue needing further clarification and, generally, some kind of plan.

The Four As of a brief intervention (as recommended by the National Cancer Institute for smoking intervention) can help the provider in addressing sleep complaints: ask, advise, assist, and assure follow-up.

Ask: Define adequately the scope of the patient's sleeping problems, associated medical disorders, and stage of withdrawal.

Advise: Provide feedback to the patient about the objective results in terms understandable to him or her. Couch objective findings in simple words, emphasizing the chemical and physiological basis of the patient's problems. This approach helps him understand that it is a brain disease which is being battled, not "just a bad habit" or "a moral weakness." Patients truly know they are different than the other 90% of people who don't have these addiction problems; they gain strength from hearing their own suspicions validated, particularly in structural/chemical brain terms.

Assist the Patient in Making a Change: Support prior personal behavioral efforts that have been helpful for promoting sleep. Allow the patient to make a list of steps for creating a positive expectancy that sleep will improve. Review steps for getting ready to go to bed, for using the bed only for sleep and not for a place to worry about the next day's problems. Negotiate the pros and cons of pharmacologic interventions, encouraging patient input about the balance of benefits and liabilities of each approach.

Assure a Follow-up Appointment: At the follow-up, review the sleep log, evaluate the outcomes of the plan, and provide empathic support over the time interval that the brain is rebalancing.

Each treatment setting will impose different challenges. The principles, however, remain the same: listen to the patient's expectations; assess realistically the future course based on the medical, psychiatric, and emotional issues identified; negotiate achievable, mutually acceptable goals; and measure what you do applying the results to modifying the plan on the next visit.

EVALUATING SLEEP

Both patient and physician benefit from a systematic evaluation of sleep complaints. Careful scrutiny of a limited number of features, assessable in the office, provides reassurance to the patient and builds rapport around a subject which appears medically benign to the physician but is often inordinately important to the patient. Gillin and Byerley (1990) provide an informative and clinically useful summary of the general principles and practices of diagnosing and managing insomnia which are relevant to the alcoholic's needs. Sophisticated sleep laboratory studies generally are not necessary for an adequate sleep assessment unless the patient's clinical signs and symptoms suggest other diagnoses that complicate the substance abuse problem. Even then, most such medical problems can be identified by careful history and physical and do not require the expense and distraction of one or two nights in a sleep lab. A standardized, self-administered sleep inventory may help to quantify the sleep problems, to track changes in sleep over several weeks, and to identify associations with environmental and pharmacologic triggers not otherwise apparent (Spielman, Nuners & Glovinsky, 1996).

The cyclic structure of sleep can be broken into several simple stages and phenomena which patients can commonly recall in the office during an initial interview or can self-evaluate at home. The first phenomenon, sleep onset latency, is the time it takes to fall asleep after closing one's eyes with the intent to go to sleep. Most persons require three to 15 minutes for this process. Debate can exist concerning the exact time of onset of the first stage of sleep (requiring electroencephalographic measurement to determine), but a serviceable clinical estimation can be obtained by simply asking the patient to recall the previous night and how long it took to fall asleep.

The next important measure is the number of awakenings and the length of time awake before returning to sleep. Most people cycle through stages I and II (early onset, non-rapid eye movement sleep, NREM), followed by stages III and IV (slow-wave sleep, SWS), and then move into rapid eye movement sleep (REM, sometimes called "paradoxical sleep") every one to two hours throughout the night, with the length of the cycle shortening and the amount of time spent in stages III and IV (SWS) becoming briefer as the night progresses. Patients can give reasonably good estimates of the number of awakenings and time awake, although they cannot accurately estimate REM time (when most dreaming occurs) or time in SWS. (However, in patients using benzodiazepines for sleep, a notable discrepancy can exist between what the patient recalls and what EEG findings demonstrate [Schneider-Helmert, 1988]. These patients may grossly overestimate sleep time, perhaps because of an amnesic effect of the medication.) Measurements of SWS, REM, and other NREM sleep are not clinically feasible without sleep EEGs; but for most clinical purposes, these estimates are not essential for a useful and productive patient encounter.

Sleep efficiency is the percentage of time asleep while in bed. The basic data for estimating efficiency requires recording the time of going to bed, estimating of total minutes awake through the night, and listing the time of arising; calculations can be easily done in the office if deemed useful. Efficiency can be increased by the recommendation that patients get out of bed when they are unable to fall back asleep within 30 minutes. Alternative activities (reading, cleaning the house, or taking a warm bath) are commonly recommended as preferable to lying in bed waiting to go to sleep and reinforcing the expectation and frustration of being unable to sleep.

Quality of sleep can be estimated crudely using a discriminant scale of 1 to 4, for excellent, good, fair, or poor. Similarly, a Lichert scale from 1 to 10 could be used with the patient placing a mark on the line to estimate the quality from poor to excellent for each night. These techniques allow for a semi-quantitative estimate of the entire night's sleep by the patient, and they commonly reveal patterns of change over the weeks between office visits. Correlations with other environmental, emotional, and personal health factors may become apparent if the patient also includes a nightly "Comments" column for these factors. Finally, daytime functional status should be appraised; drowsiness, work performance, and irritability are domains worthy of patient comments. Number and duration of daytime naps are a useful parameter, particularly in the elderly who are more likely to supplement their nocturnal sleep with daytime napping.

If the patient keeps a flow sheet with this information, he or she often feels more in control of his or her sleep recovery, especially when it is proceeding slowly. The data help to quantify the protracted nature of the withdrawal course and provide feedback about the healing process. Commonly, improvements over four weeks' time are much easier to point out to patients with a flow sheet than if unaided memory is used alone. Further, using a flow sheet or sleep log permits focused questioning about particularly good or poor nights, which may elicit information not previously considered relevant by the patient. Naturally, any medications, alcohol, or other drugs should be recorded on the flow sheet with times of their use. The sleep log can provide motivational leverage for maximizing the therapeutic utility of an otherwise annoying symptom: "Doctor, I can't sleep."

SLEEP ARCHITECTURE IN ALCOHOLICS

Acute alcohol use in social drinkers or in recently abstinent alcoholics produces an initial sedative effect (brisk sleep onset, decreased REM, and increased slow-wave sleep) which gives way later in the night to increased REM disruptions, decreased slow-wave sleep, and more frequent awakenings (Williams & Rundell, 1981). Further nights of drinking are associated with a loss of the initial sedative effects of alcohol and the emergence of sleep fragmentation.

Active alcoholics with insomnia show long sleep onset latency, frequent awakenings, fragmented shifts in sleep stages ("fractured sleep"), decreased sleep efficiency, decreased total sleep time, decreased SWS (stages III and IV), and increased percent REM without a change in total REM time (Gillin, Smith et al., 1990; Shinba, Murashima & Yamamoto, 1994; Johnson, Burdick et al., 1970). With abstinence, these alcoholics demonstrate slow improvement over the first one to four months in all parameters. In the first few weeks after drinking stops (in patients who average over 300 grams of ethanol per day) awakenings decrease from 124 per night to 36, especially decreasing during REM; stage changes decrease from 84 to 51 per night; and sleep onset latency decreases from 29 minutes to 21 minutes (Williams & Rundell, 1981). After four months, many abstinent alcoholics still have difficulty maintaining normal REM sleep, often experiencing interruptions, and decreased amounts of stage IV sleep. At one to two years of abstinence, some alcoholics continue to demonstrate increased awakenings, REM interruptions, and decreased stage IV sleep. Age and years of heavy drinking accounted for nearly 50% of the variance in decreased amounts of stage IV sleep in these patients. The findings of Shinba's group suggest a potentially irreversible character of the alcohol-related insomnia in some patients (Shinba, Murashima & Yamamoto, 1994). Twenty-four of their 40 insomniac-alcoholic men had reduced or stopped alcohol intake for more than five years; these patients still experienced sleep problems, most commonly restless sleep (38%) and frequent awakenings (28%). (Shinba's study failed to identify the number of subjects who were abstinent.) Insomnia appeared to be dose related; of alcoholics with insomnia, 70% consumed more that 300 grams ethanol per day over the prior three months compared to non-insomniacs having only 17% drinking in that range. Following acute alcohol withdrawal, alcoholics have decreased amounts of SWS, a deficit which slowly improves over the next one to four months (Allen, Wagman & Funderburk, 1977). After a period of abstinence, repeat alcoholization of these subjects showed an association between the rapid development of decreased SWS and poor treatment outcome. The subgroup of alcoholics having especially low amounts of SWS during abstinence appears to have differences in neurocircuity that may be related to: (1) more advanced degenerative disease, (2) more "residual tolerance" (Allen and Wagman's term), or (3) genetically pre-determined differences in SWS generation. Much further study is needed to separate out these competing hypotheses.

Many of the sleep changes noted above in alcoholic insomnia are also typical of changes seen in patients with assorted dementias, with schizophrenia, and with prior brainstem or midbrain injuries (particularly from trauma or infection).

MEDICAL MATTERS AFFECTING SLEEP

A host of medical disorders can adversely affect the chemically dependent person's sleep. The following discussion reviews the most frequent diagnoses to be considered when the patient complains of insomnia.

Psychiatric disorders account for 30% to 60% of patients with long term insomnia (i.e. sleep problems persisting longer than three weeks) (Gillin & Byerley, 1990). The list of these disorders is long and includes alcohol and other drug dependence, major affective disorder, bipolar mood disorder, panic and generalized anxiety disorders, obsessive-compulsive disorder, borderline personality, post-traumatic stress disorder, and anorexia nervosa. Alcohol and substance abuse, of course, aggravates all of these psychiatric illnesses and is a commonly associated comorbid diagnosis. Most alcohol-related insomnia will improve significantly after one to two months of abstinence; if this improvement fails to appear, a careful evaluation should be undertaken to identify any previously unrecognized psychiatric disorders.

Psychoactive drugs with stimulant properties, such as cocaine and amphetamines, impair sleep onset and maintenance. Conversely, the withdrawal of depressant drugs (such as alcohol, benzodiazepines, and opiates) produces rebound stimulation and subsequent sleep impairment. The half-life of a drug is a usefully predictor for estimating the onset of withdrawal symptoms and withdrawal duration. Five half-lives are required to remove 95% of a drug from the system; typically, withdrawal will be manifest by the time 50% to 75% of a drug has left; for alcohol, this may be 12 to 24 hours after the last drink, whereas for some benzodiazepines, it may be five to seven days.

TABLE 2. Factors Contributing to Insomnia

Age

Medications

Psychoactive substance use and abuse

Coexistent medical disorders
- COPD and asthma
- Angina, especially with prior myocardial infarction
- Esophageal reflux
- Arthritis, arthralgias, musculoskeletal pain syndromes
- Periodic limb movement (restless legs, myoclonus, hypnic jerks)
- Obstructive sleep apnea
- Head injury
- Dementia
- Korsakoff's syndrome
- Parkinson's disease
- Menopausal changes
- Hyperthyroidism

Coexisting psychiatric disorders
- Depression (major affective disorder)
- Bipolar mood disorder
- Panic and generalized anxiety disorder
- Obsessive-compulsive disorder
- Borderline personality disorder
- Post-traumatic stress disorder
- Anorexia nervosa

Home environment
- Conditioned anxiety

Working environment
- Job dissatisfaction
- Shift work
- Flying across multiple time zones

Medications are common disrupters of sleep and careful review of the side-effect profile of each prescribed drug is a rewarding habit for both clinician and patient. Many medications can adversely affect sleep architecture (Obermeyer & Benca, 1996), but their symptomatic benefits may outweigh their negative neurologic impact. In hypertension management, β-blockers decrease sleep continuity but generally do not cause much clinical insomnia. In arthritis, aspirin and non-steroidal antiinflamatory drugs (NSAIDs) increase awakenings and decrease sleep efficiency in normal subjects (Murphy, Myers & Badia, 1996), but the benefits in terms of pain reduction in symptomatically afflicted arthritics generally outweighs the potential for mild sleep disturbance. Similarly, for respiratory problems, although theophylline bronchodilators and inhaled selective β-agonists can increase sleep latency and decrease sleep continuity, their benefits on breathing generally outweigh their liabilities. Chronic opiate or codeine use is associated with decreased total sleep, decreased sleep continuity, and decreased percentage of sleep as REM; there is a coincident increase in daytime somnolence. For depression, tricyclics typically induce daytime somnolence, increase total sleep, and decrease sleep latency; selective serotonin reuptake inhibitors (SSRIs), however, increase sleep latency, increase REM latency, and decrease sleep continuity, while monoamine oxidase inhibitors (MAOIs) decrease total sleep and increase sleep latency. Medication effect profiles need to be carefully considered for both their positive and negative impacts on sleep. While most of these effects are of little clinical importance for most patients, they can be profoundly important for some, especially those with special sensitivities like the elderly.

Age alters sleep patterns in predictable ways. The older people get, the lower their ratio of SWS to total sleep, with many persons over age 70 having virtually no stage IV sleep at all. With increasing age, people also awaken more easily, commonly just after REM sleep phases. These changes are magnified by the use of alcohol and a variety of psychoactive drugs.

Many diseases cause patients to have difficult sleep due to nocturnal dyspnea, pain, muscle spasm, or side effects of prescribed medications (nocturia, hypervigilance, irritability, disturbing dreams). A few common disorders are particularly worthy of attention because of their marked worsening when coexisting with alcohol abuse or dependence.

Chronic obstructive pulmonary disease and angina are two medical problems often disrupting sleep; the precise mechanisms have not been clearly and quantitatively defined. It is recognized that arterial oxygen saturation decreases during sleep and that the highest incidence of cardiac arrhythmia occurs during the early morning hours (about 4:00 to 5:00 a.m.), when blood oxygen saturation is lowest and when hormonal and brain arousal mechanisms are being activated. It seems likely that these are the principle factors that adversely affect sleep. Chronic lung diseases (emphysema, chronic bronchitis, asthma) are very common among alcoholics and chemically dependent patients because of the high association of tobacco use with alcoholism. Eighty percent of alcoholics are or have been nicotine-dependent and the most common causes of death in *recovering* alcoholics are tobacco-related (myocardial infarction, stroke, chronic lung disease, lung cancer). Therefore, it comes as no surprise that much insomnia in alcoholic patients is directly related to their smoking dependency or to prior damage caused by years of smoking. Poor sleep may be an opportunity to help smokers contemplate a move toward quitting cigarettes. For smokers not afflicted with chronic heart or lung diseases, there is little clinical evidence that stopping smoking will help sleep very much. The literature linking poor sleep and smoking is not conclusive. Most studies are confounded by a lack of adequate segregation of cigarette use from alcohol use in the study design. Though nicotine is a stimulant drug for many areas of the brain, that property may not be a significant contributor to sleep disruption (see the discussion of smoking effects, following).

Arthritis, arthralgias, and other musculoskeletal pain disorders are well-recognized contributors to poor sleep. Many chemically dependent patients have "self-medicated" for joint pain with alcohol, other sedative drugs, or opiates for years. In early abstinence they may find an associated heightened awareness of their pain symptoms. Rebound, increased sensitivity to pain may well play a role in sleep disorders during early abstinence. Recognizing the symptom of sleep disorder as a clue to joint and skeletal pain may permit the aggressive use of antiinflammatory medications with a coincident reduction in insomnia, even though normal subjects have some sleep disruption from aspirin and NSAIDS.

Periodic limb movements (e.g., nocturnal leg cramps, hypnic jerks, myoclonus, restless legs syndrome) have frequently been associated with interruptions in sleep. Alcohol use of two or more drinks per day has been associated with a two- to threefold increase in periodic leg movements during sleep evaluation (Aldrich & Shipley, 1993); many of these patients report symptoms consistent with the restless legs syndrome. Interestingly, with heavier drinking there is a decrease in periodic leg movements (in women drinking more than four drinks/day and in men drinking more than six). A narrow window of beneficial effect appears to exist. Although alcohol is a likely candidate for inducing these findings, the study demonstrated only an association, not necessarily a causal relationship.

Sleep apnea is one of the most common problems leading to a request for a sleep lab examination. Patients with sleep apnea are known to have marked worsening of their symptoms when intoxicated by alcohol, the frequency and duration of apneic episodes being increased by alcohol. Many of these patients have loud snoring punctuated by periods of gagging-like upper airway obstruction, often loud enough to have caused a spouse to sleep in another room. During these episodes sleep architecture is disrupted, particularly showing a marked decrease in REM sleep.

Head injury patients are commonly afflicted with insomnia (Askenasy & Rahmani, 1987). Often these persons are victims of motor vehicle crashes or trauma inflicted during a time of intoxication with alcohol or other drugs; commonly their histories reveal chemical dependence antecedent to the trauma. Because a multiplicity of sleep abnormalities are found when studying these patients, it is recommended that insomniacs with a history of head injury be routinely studied in a sleep laboratory (Guilleminault, Faull et al., 1983). A large number of prisoners incarcerated for alcohol- and drug-related crimes give histories suggesting that head trauma may be a factor contributing to their sleep disorders (Friedrichs, 1996); however, the medical literature contains very few published scientific studies concerning this important observation (Bach-y-Rita & Veno, 1974; Peters, van Kammen et al., 1990; Templer, Kasiraj et al., 1992). Structural injury in young persons (15 to 25 years old) appears to produce sleep abnormalities that are similar to findings in normal elderly persons (i.e., 70 years of age or more). The injury appears to simulate a premature aging of sleep-wakefulness structures of the brainstem (George, Landau-Ferey et al., 1981).

Dementias of various types are associated with sleep problems. "Sun-downing," confusion and restlessness are often the first introduction of the physician in training to sleep disorders. Alcohol-induced Korsakoff's syndrome and Alzheimer's dementia both show insomnia associated with thalamic degeneration (Lugaresi, 1992). Parkinson's disorder and its dementia are associated with dopamine dysregulation; the cause of the associated insomnia likely also will be found to be dopamine-related.

Menopausal changes have been associated with insomnia, an effect which does not appear to be related to the change in estrogen levels (Pansini, Albertazzi et al., 1994). The complex number of hormonal changes during menopause will make it difficult to define clearly what mechanisms are involved in these changes. Nocturnal micturition, for example, appears to be one of the important factors (Asplund & Aberg, 1996). Meanwhile, trazodone (75 mg nightly) has been found to be useful not only for the insomnia, but also for anxiety and irritability, but not hot flashes (Pansini, Albertazzi et al., 1995).

FIGURE 1. A Simple Sleep Log for Patient Self-Evaluation

						Midnite							AM						Noon				
6	7	8	9	10	11	12	1	2	3	4	5	6	7	8	9	10	11	12	1	2	3	4	5
M																							
T																							
W																							
T																							
F																							
S																							
S																							

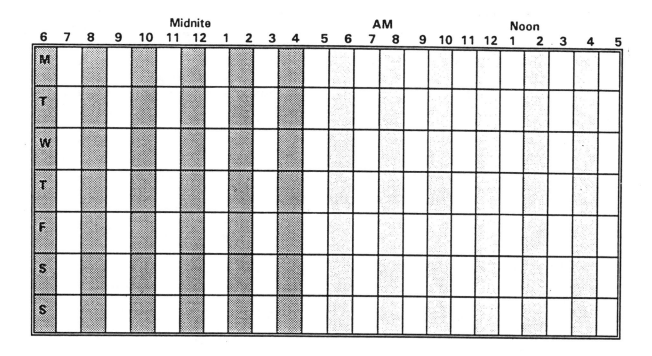

Insert appropriate symbols on chart:

● Lights out

○ Lights on or out of bed for the night

Quality

|---------------------------|

Asleep time, write in quality above line (poor, fair, good, excellent)

X------------------------X Lying down, not sleeping

Write in: **C** for each cigarette, **A** for each standard alcohol drink, **Caf** for each caffeinated drink,

Write the Initials of each medication at the time taken.

A stressful home environment is a common source for problems leading to insomnia. The physical sleep setting may not be conducive to prolonged sleep, particularly if interruptions exist by roommates coming or going or by apprehension about the failure of family members arriving home safely after drinking. Further, the learned experience of not being able to go to sleep can produce a form of conditioned anxiety. Changing the sleep environment may be helpful in dealing with these problems. The fear of being victimized by domestic violence (verbal, physical, or sexual) is a factor adversely affecting sleep for some recovering persons. Appropriate social history to identify the problem and then referral for assistance are essential to deal effectively with violence issues.

The work environment can also contribute to poor sleep, most commonly through frequent changes in shift scheduling or permanently working the night shift (Wagner, 1996). A syndrome of shift maladaptation has been described, characterized by chronic sleep disturbances and waking fatigue; gastrointestinal symptoms; alcohol/drug misuse or abuse; increased accident or near-miss rates;

depression, malaise, or personality changes; and difficult interpersonal relationships. Generally, a full week is required for workers to adapt to a shift change of 8 or 16 hours; these findings correlate with laboratory studies in circadian adjustments to shift simulation (Deacon & Arendt, 1996). Job dissatisfaction is another underlying cause of insomnia that has been documented in the occupational medicine literature. For example, sleeping tablet consumption is higher among: (1) subjects who report a bad atmosphere at work, (2) men who report little interest in their jobs, and (3) women who work under time pressure (Jacquinet-Salord, Lang et al., 1993). Dissatisfied workers have higher rates of absenteeism (a finding that may be associated with increased levels of alcohol abuse). Work disabilities also have been found to be positively associated with substance use (alcohol, sleeping pills, and tranquilizers) (Adlaf, Smart & Walsh, 1992). Finally, because substance abuse affects work performance, the chemically dependent worker also may experience more frequent job performance assessments, surveillance, and threats of job jeopardy—all problems that may be linked to disturbed sleep.

Effects of Low-Dose Benzodiazepines. Many chemically dependent patients use or request prescriptions for sleep medications, most commonly benzodiazepines. Physicians are typically reluctant to grant such requests, because this practice: (1) represents replacing one addicting substance with another, (2) commonly leads to prolonged dependence on the sleep medication, and (3) typically requires a lengthy, negotiated withdrawal to terminate the medication. A study by Schneider-Helmert provides a number of interesting observations and hypotheses concerning this situation (Schneider-Helmert, 1988). Seventy-six middle-aged and elderly chronic insomniacs were studied in the sleep lab; 40 of them met criteria for low-dose benzodiazepine dependence and were using one to two times the prescribed dose for more than six months. Withdrawal of the medications produced a perception of worsened sleep among the patients, in spite of objective evidence to the contrary. Patients demonstrated prompt improvement in REM and SWS suppression; yet, they believed they slept more while taking the medications even though the opposite finding was demonstrated on sleep EEGs. During the night after withdrawal, average sleep time increased from 211 minutes to 227 minutes, but patients estimated that sleep had decreased from 283 minutes to 241 minutes. Similar discrepancies were noted concerning sleep onset latency. The average latency estimated by patients was 53 minutes with drug and 98 without; the actual latency was 37 minutes with or without the drug. One patient, withdrawing from 0.125 mg triazolam, even estimated sleeping six hours with the drug and none without it, while the sleep EEGs showed no electrophysiologic evidence for sleep under either condition. The author hypothesizes that anterograde amnesia may be responsible for the consistent overestimation of sleep.

A study of triazolam's propensity to induce rebound insomnia in volunteers demonstrated that a gradual tapering of the drug over four nights was associated with diminished or absent rebound symptoms (Greenblatt, Harmatz et al., 1987). However, this trial was conducted in volunteers with insomnia who received only seven days of triazolam (0.5 mg per night) prior to tapering or abrupt cessation of medication. The subjects had not been chronically maintained for over six months, as in the preceding study.

Alcohol Effects in the Elderly. Physicians generally are well aware of their elderly patients' increased propensity for experiencing side effects from a wide range of drugs. Alcohol is among those implicated in many studies showing significant increases in morbidity for this age group (Dufour, Archer & Gordis, 1992); yet, physicians are disinclined to query their elderly patients concerning alcohol use. Equal doses of alcohol in elderly persons compared to younger subjects of identical mass will produce higher blood alcohol levels due to a smaller volume of distribution; older subjects have a relative increase in adipose tissue and decrease in lean body mass. Common problems recognized by gerontologists related to alcohol use include insomnia and breathing disturbances during sleep, variable responses to analgesics (sometimes increasing and other times decreasing analgesia), decrement in task performance skills, and exacerbation of cognitive dysfunctions, particularly notable in patients already with dementias.

Smoking Effects. Although cigarette smoking generally is thought to be associated with delayed sleep onset and decreased sleep duration, its causal relationship to insomnia has not been well documented in the clinical literature due to the presence of two confounding variables: concurrent alcohol and caffeine use. However, with the introduction of nicotine patches, new insights to nicotine effects on sleep have been clarified. In a study of 20 nonsmoking men and women recruited on the basis of a history of habitual snoring, nicotine patches (achieving blood nicotine levels of 7.8 ng/ml) decreased total sleep time by 33 minutes, sleep efficiency from 89% to 83%, percent rapid eye movement (REM) sleep from 19% to 15%, and prolonged sleep onset latency from seven to 18 minutes (Davila, Hurt et al., 1994). Withdrawal of nicotine from a smoker decreases sleep onset latency, increases daytime somnolence, and increases irritability, anxiety, and craving for cigarettes (Prosise, Bonnet et al., 1994).

Caffeine Effects. The relative risk of insomnia from 240 mg of caffeine per day (about four to five cups of coffee) is 1.4 times greater than for abstainers according to a logistic regression model used to analyze a sample of 4,558 Australians (Shirlow & Mathers, 1985). This association accounted for about 25% of the prevalence of insomnia in the study population. Increased risks of similar magnitude were found for tremor, headache, and palpitations. The model controlled for sex, age, adiposity, smoking, alcohol intake, and occupation.

MANAGEMENT OF INSOMNIA

The newly abstinent alcoholic commonly presents one of the truly challenging problems of patient-physician negotiation when he or she launches into complaints about poor sleep. Even the most empathic physician can be pushed to his or her limits by the encounter. The principles of motivational interviewing can be valuable at these times (Miller & Rollnick, 1991): listen carefully and reflectively to the patient's concerns; express empathy; avoid argumentation; avoid the trap of giving advice; develop discrepancies in the sleep history; and support the use of non-pharmacologic techniques the patient has tried successfully on other occasions. Patients may find useful a decisional balance approach to evaluating "the goods" and "not so goods" of pharmacologic and non-pharmacologic strategies. Both the physician and patient do well to recognize insomnia as a predictable and often annoying aspect of protracted abstinence. The quantity of time required for sleep improvement can be usefully compared to the time needed for other physical improvements, such as liver function tests. A sleep log can be another helpful aide, demonstrating week to week improvements and engendering some sense of control of the sleep process by the very act of measuring it. Both pharmacologic (Medical Letter, 1993; Medical Letter, 1996; Gillin & Byerley, 1990) and non-pharmacologic (NIH, 1996) strategies should be considered; and efforts to engage the patient in decision-making about management should be incorporated because of their likelihood of improving patient satisfaction and outcome.

PHARMACOLOGIC MANAGEMENT

Benzodiazepines and Zolpidem. Pharmacologic management has the negative appearance to doctors of substituting one addictive substance (commonly benzodiazepines) for another (commonly alcohol) and then later needing to do a second withdrawal. The clinical risk of producing a benzodiazepine dependence is probably small; but using a sleep medication may make it harder for the patient to learn that his brain can rebalance itself very well without the aid of another ingested drug. In a decisional balance assessment of benzodiazepines for sleep, the clinician can weigh as "the goods"—safety and some pharmacologic effectiveness lasting for weeks and perhaps months. The "not so goods" include decreases in SWS and REM, rebound insomnia when the drug is stopped, drug dependence, increased confusion and falls (particularly in the elderly), daytime sedation with long-acting drugs (diazepam, flurazepam), anterograde amnesia (especially with short-acting drugs like triazolam), and sleep walking and night terrors (in the case of clonazepam) (Gillin & Byerley, 1990; Medical Letter, 1996). Particularly annoying during benzodiazepine tapering is the discrepancy between the patient's impression that the medication is doing an effective job and the objective sleep measurements showing just the opposite (Schneider-Helmert, 1988).

Zolpidem, an imidazopyridine hypnotic which binds to the benzodiazepine receptor BZ_1, has a demonstrably better therapeutic profile than the benzodiazepines, which bind to receptors BZ_1, BZ_2, and BZ_3 (Medical Letter, 1993; Medical Letter, 1996). Zolpidem does not suppress SWS or REM sleep, it has fewer problems associated with the development of tolerance, and it has a relative short half-life of 2.5 hours. On the "not so good side," some rebound insomnia occurs with drug cessation; cognitive impairments, amnesia, hallucinations, and sleep walking have been reported. Tolerance and withdrawal have been demonstrated in baboons (Griffiths, Sannerud et al., 1992) and humans (Cavallaro, Regazzetti et al., 1993). It is metabolized in the liver and may accumulate more in patients with liver dysfunction or in the elderly. Public use has been too short to assess adequately the abuse potential.

Monoamine System Modulators. *Antidepressants:* Low doses of amitriptyline (15 to 25 mg), doxepine (15-25 mg), or trazodone (50 to 100 mg) are widely prescribed to aid sleep even though there are little data to support efficacy for these treatments. The antihistaminic properties of these drugs do produce a sense of drowsiness but offer little objective impact on sleep architecture. They are not associated with dependence and have no significant withdrawal problems; a potential problem with intentional overdoses and their medical complications does exist. Effective pharmacologic treatment of depression does improve depression-related insomnia, as demonstrated in numerous studies using higher doses of antidepressants than those listed above. The addition of trazodone, specifically, has been shown to be beneficial in patients with insomnia and depression who already take another antidepressant (Nierenberg, Adler et al., 1994). Trazodone alone in depressed patients does improve a number of the parameters that are also distorted in alcohol-related insomnia; notably, it decreases sleep latency, decreases intrasleep awakenings, increases total sleep duration and, at four weeks, increased SWS (Mouret, Lemoine et al., 1988). The use of antidepressants (including trazodone) for insomnia from alcoholism and withdrawal, unrelated to depression, has not been demonstrated or adequately evaluated.

Serotonin Reuptake Inhibitors (SSRIs) and Monoamine Oxidase Inhibitors. SSRIs may induce sleep disorders and are commonly administered in the morning to avoid medication-induced insomnia. Similarly, monoamine oxidase inhibitors have been associated with insomnia; trazodone is helpful in treating this complication of therapy (Nierenberg & Keck, 1989). At the present time, no data support treating insomnia in alcoholics with SSRIs.

Clonidine. Clonidine has not been studied for alcohol withdrawal insomnia but a number of studies suggest the drug may be useful, particularly during the first few weeks of abstinence.

Clonidine, an alpha 2-agonist, suppresses hyperactivity in the locus coeruleus (LC) during the withdrawal syndromes associated with alcohol or opiates. Clonidine, injected into the mouse LC, produces dose-dependent increases in SWS (Nistico, De Sarro et al., 1992) and sedation through alpha 2-adrenoreceptor-linked suppression of noradrenaline release from LC neurons projecting to the thalamus, amygdala, dorsal hippocampus, frontal cortex, and sensory-motor cortex (De Sarro, Ascioti et al., 1987). Conversely, blocking the alpha 2-adrenoreceptor in rats produces arousal, increased locomotion and exploration, and tachypnea. Stimulation of the LC (by a chronically implanted electrode in a 25-year-old man) produced profound disruptions in sleep with reductions in total sleep, REM, and non-REM (NREM) sleep (Kaitin, Bliwise et al., 1986).

TABLE 3. Important Brain Regions Regulating Sleep

Chemical Pathways

Monoamine pathways of the midbrain
- Locus coeruleus (NA)
- Raphe nuclei (5-HT)

Cholinergic neurons
- Dorsal mediolateral pontine tegmentum

Melatonin and benzodiazepine/GABA receptor circuits

Glutamate neurons
- Subcortical and cerebral cortical structures

Anatomic Locations

Ascending Reticular Activating System (NA, DA, ACh)
- Pontine tegmentum
- Periaquaductal grey matter
- Pedunculo-pontine nuclei
- Ventrolateral medulla
- Locus coeruleus
- Projections to the suprachiasmatic nucleus
- Projections to the preoptic area

Thalamus
- Dorsomedial nucleus (alcoholic Wernicke-Korsakoff's)
- Anterior nucleus (Alzheimer's)
- Both (Fatal familial insomnia)

Suprachiasmatic Nucleus and Preoptic Area

Basal Forebrain
- Nucleus basalis of Meynert

Circadian pacemaker circuits
- Suprachiasmatic nucleus
- Pineal gland (light/dark coupled)
- Hypothalamic-pituitary-adrenal axis
- Sleep-coupled (growth hormone, prolactin)
- Sleep-uncoupled (cortisol, adrenocorticotropin)

Hippocampus

Cerebral cortex

Melatonin and Circadian Rhythm Modulation. As an over-the-counter food supplement, unregulated by the Food and Drug Administration, melatonin has gathered a following of adherents in spite of a lack of evidence for its efficacy in many of the clinical circumstances for which it has been used.

In normal subjects, aged 18 to 24, given melatonin at 11:45 a.m., a direct hypnotic effect appears to be demonstrated when subjects were allowed to nap after lunch (Dollins, Zhdanova et al., 1994). These persons showed a shortened sleep onset latency and an increase in total sleep duration. Physiologic blood levels replicating nocturnal peaks were achieved with 0.1 and 0.3 mg doses.

Chronic alcohol use appears to blunt the nocturnal rise in melatonin; acute alcohol use appears to delay the melatonin peak. Total melatonin output does not appear to differ significantly among alcoholics (under age 60), controls, or depressed patients (when adjusted for sex and age) (Wetterberg, Aperia et al., 1992). Actively drinking alcoholics (men, aged 34 to 58) have higher 24-hour urinary melatonin levels than normal controls and show a disruption in the phased day-night release of melatonin (Murialdo, Filippi et al., 1991). During alcohol withdrawal, melatonin levels show a trend toward increasing but return to normal levels after two weeks of abstinence (Fonzi, Solinas et al., 1994). A temporary loss of the 24-hour periodicity of melatonin is noted at the beginning of withdrawal but resolves within two weeks.

Given the generally increased levels of melatonin present when drinking and the relatively rapid resolution of melatonin abnormalities during alcohol abstinence, little therapeutic benefit would be expected from melatonin use for alcohol withdrawal insomnia. No controlled trials of the use of melatonin in alcohol withdrawal insomnia have been published. However, melatonin may be recommended in elderly heavy drinkers, as individuals in this population have a high incidence of deficient melatonin secretion and a demonstrated likelihood of therapeutic response (Garfinkel, Laudon et al., 1995).

Other Medications (Chloral hydrate, Thioridazine, Lithium, L-tryptophan). Chloral hydrate can provide a few nights of effective sleep but potentiation of sedative effects by concurrent use of alcohol makes it potentially dangerous. Reports of overdose fatalities, withdrawal insomnia, nightmares, and drug dependency make its therapeutic profile undesirable.

Thioridazine has been used in low doses with reported utility but not in any well-controlled trials. Long-term extrapyramidal side effects could be a deleterious complication but probably not relevant for the relatively short-term use in early abstinence for chemically dependent persons.

Lithium normalizes circadian rhythms in alcoholic rats but human data in recently abstinent alcoholics are lacking. Lithium augments the effects of antidepressants in depressed subjects but has a mixed set of effects on their sleep (SWS increases, REM sleep decreases, REM latency increases and REM activity/time spent asleep decreases). Short-term therapy with lithium has been associated with small but significant delays in the sleep–wake circadian rhythm. These effects are of interest in view of polygraphic sleep abnormalities found in affective disorders and possible circadian disturbances accounting for these abnormalities. Indeed lithium might act in correcting special sleep abnormalities and/or circadian disturbances (Billiard, 1987).

L-tryptophan had been a popular over-the-counter treatment for insomnia prior to Food and Drug Administration removal of commercial preparations due to an association with eosinophilia-myalgia syndrome. A review of L-tryptophan use in insomnia (Schneider-Helmert & Spinweber, 1986) found that only subjects considered chronic insomniacs showed beneficial effects. A well-designed trial of 75 male alcoholics with depression showed (Asheychik, Jackson et al., 1989) improvement in depression was enhanced by the administration of L-tryptophan (3 gms nightly); but sleep disturbances were not significant enough to permit any clear estimation of L-tryptophan effect.

Over-the-Counter Medications (Antihistamines and Herbal Preparations). Antihistamines (diphenhydramine [Nytol®]) and doxylamine [Unisom®]) have subjective benefits lasting about a week but can be associated with daytime sedation and impaired motor performance. Their anticholinergic effects (dry mouth, urinary retention, hallucinosis) can be annoying to patients and possibly dangerous to the elderly.

Herbal preparations and other "natural remedies" generally have not been scientifically studied for efficacy. Although a popular and tasty herb and a component of the Celestial Seasonings "Sleepy Time" Tea, there is little objective data to support camomile's use. An exception is valerian root, which has been evaluated in a controlled, prospective, double-blind trial with 128 subjects (Leathwood, Chauffard et al., 1982). Valerian was associated with a subjective decrease in sleep latency and an increase in sleep quality; however, sleep EEGs in 10 relatively young, good sleepers failed to show any differences between valerian and placebo (a statistically underpowered evaluation).

Nonpharmacologic Management. An excellent review of the current literature and a set of recommendations for treating chronic pain and insomnia has been published under the sponsorship of several National Health Institutes (NIH, 1996). Benefits were found for decreased sleep onset latency and increased total sleep time, although the clinical significance of the size of the benefits was questioned. Insomnia was categorized as disturbed sleep because of: (1) an inability to fall asleep, (2) an inability to maintain sleep, or (3) early awakening. Outcomes from controlled trials generally measured sleep onset latency, number of awakenings, and total sleep time. Assessments of daytime functioning generally were not available nor were electrophysiologic confirmations of improvement nor were self-assessments of quality of life. Literature demonstrating efficacy in insomnia exists for relaxation techniques, which aim to reduce cognitive and physiological arousal through (1) a repetitive focus on a word, sound, prayer, or sensation and (2) a passive attitude toward intruding thoughts. Techniques include meditation, progressive muscle relaxation, imaging of a peaceful environment, paced respirations, and deep breathing.

The most effective behavioral techniques for insomnia were found to be: (1) sleep hygiene education (concerning how to get ready for sleep), (2) staying in bed only when sleeping, (3) using a sleep log, and (4) restricting the bedroom to activities for sleep and sex only.

NEUROBIOLOGY AND PHYSIOLOGY

Locus Coeruleus and the Pontomesencephalic Tegmentum. Sleep stages are regulated by an interplay of multiple neurotransmitters and neurocircuits acting in concert to produce the phenomenon. Analysis of the mechanisms creating the stage changes is important for understanding the role of alcohol and drug withdrawal in insomnia. For example, the change from SWS to REM is associated with a decrease in the firing rate of cells in the locus coeruleus (LC) (noradrenaline containing) and cells in the dorsal raphe nuclei (serotonin-containing). Coincident with this decreased firing is an increase in cholinergic (ACh) activity secondary to firing of cells in the neighboring pontomesencephalic tegmentum (Siegel, 1994). The pontomesencephalic tegmental cells project to the thalamocortical area and are known to facilitate activity and transmission there during wakefulness and during REM sleep. These cholinergic neurons are essential to the generation of REM. Gamma-aminobutyric acid (GABA) neurons appear to play an intermediary, coordinating role simultaneously activating tegmental cholinergic neurons and suppressing LC neurons in order to generate REM sleep (Jones, 1991).

The LC appears to have a nonessential, modulatory role during REM sleep. LC neurons have virtually no discharges during REM, a slow rate of discharge during SWS, and a tonic spontaneous firing rate during wakefulness (Aston-Jones & Bloom, 1981). It has been hypothesized that REM sleep serves to upregulate and/or prevent the downregulation of NA receptors so as to improve signal processing while the animal is awake (Siegel & Rogawski, 1988). While awake, the LC regulates attention and vigilance (Aston-Jones, Chiang & Alexinsky, 1991), complementing sympathetic nervous function through its projections to cognitive centers: the thalamus, amygdala, dorsal hippocampus, frontal cortex, and sensory-motor cortex. Interestingly, LC cells discharge more slowly during grooming and during sweet water consumption. Stimulation of mu opiate receptors on LC cells acts to prolong SWS (a subsidiary role is also played by the kappa opiate receptors); naloxone blocks this effect (Garzon, Tejero et al., 1995). In the wakeful state, whether spontaneous or induced by sleep deprivation, LC neurons show increased functional activation as measured by immediate-early gene expression (Tononi, Pompeiano & Cirelli, 1994).

In an extreme form of experimental "insomnia," spontaneous, temporal lobe, sleep epilepsy was observed during transitions from SWS to REM, effects thought to be related to a decrease in NA input from the LC to a kindled, epileptogentic focus in the temporal lobe (Shouse, Langer & Dittes, 1990). Such experimental models may help to illustrate a structural, neurobiologic connection between alcohol withdrawal (insomnia, irritability, and seizures) and epileptogenic foci related to repeated alcohol-withdrawal injury and prior closed head injuries.

Thalamus. The thalamus, which as noted above receives NA input from the LC and ACh from the pontomesencephalic tegmentum, also is essential in the generation of sleep. Ablation of the anterior or dorsomedial nuclei of the thalamus abolishes EEG sleep patterns in cats, causing decreases in REM and NREM sleep from control levels of 14% and 38% of the prior 24 hours to 1% and 2%, respectively, after ablation (Lugaresi, 1992). The dorsomedial nucleus has previously been recognized to be severely damaged in alcoholics with Wernicke-Korsakoff syndrome, many of whom suffer from insomnia. Similar findings have been observed in human beings afflicted with a familial degenerative disease of the anterior ventral and dorsomedial thalamus associated with fatal, progressive insomnia and dysautonomia (Medori, Tritschler et al., 1992). These patients showed no damage to the LC, reticular activating formation, periaquaductal grey matter, or hypothalamus. Affected subjects showed loss of SWS and REM; advanced stages showed complex hallucinations followed by stupor and coma. Further, these subjects showed loss of endocrine and autonomic homeostasis, presumed secondary to loss of inhibitory control over the hypothalamus after thalamic destruction. The clinical findings were strikingly similar to those of the alcohol withdrawal syndrome; subjects had persistently increased plasma cortisol and catecholamine levels, reduced circadian rhythms in the sleep-related hormones (growth hormone and prolactin) and in the sleep-unrelated hormones (adrenocortiotrophin and cortisol), loss of light-dark oscillations in melatonin, tachycardia, hyperthermia, and tachypnea.

Ascending Reticular Activating System and Preoptic Area. The ascending reticular activating system (ARAS) is associated with increased firing of cells during awakening. A number of grey matter brain structures and nuclei are involved which utilize a variety of neurotransmitters including dopamine, noradrenaline, and acetylcholine (Jones, 1994). The preoptic area (POA) is one nucleus affected by adrenergic inputs from two components of the ARAS, the LC and the ventrolateral medulla (VLM). Sleep-related neurons in the POA appear to be inhibited by adrenergic input to their alpha 2-adrenoreceptors; and waking-related neurons are excited by NA input to either their alpha 1- or beta-adrenoreceptors (Osaka & Matsumura, 1994). Alcohol abuse and withdrawal are likely to disrupt these inputs significantly.

Suprachiasmatic Nucleus, Pineal Gland, and Melatonin Action. The effects of alcohol and other drugs are poorly defined relative to the circadian circuits of the suprachiasmatic nucleus, the pineal gland, and melatonin release. Notably, benzodiazepine receptors, GABA-gated channels, and opiate receptors are central to the circuitry. The suprachiasmatic nucleus of the hypothalamus is the best characterized central neural pacemaker associated with circadian rhythms; however, the neurophysiological mechanisms involved in pacemaker function are not well understood. As noted previously, the ARAS projects to the suprachiasmatic nucleus. The NA input to this nucleus, part of which comes from the LC, shows a significant rhythmicity, peaking in rats at the beginning of the light period, consistent with NA playing a role in light-sensitive, oscillating patterns (Semba, Toru & Mataga, 1984). By neural connections from the retina to the suprachiasmatic, rhythmic synthesis and release of melatonin from the pineal gland become phase-linked to the light/dark cycle. Projections from the suprachiasmatic nucleus extend to the superior cervical ganglion and then to the pineal gland. NA release at the pineal induces melatonin biosynthesis (Wetterberg, Aperia et al., 1992). GABA, through its regulation of suprachiasmatic interneuron activity, is believed to play an important role in setting circadian rhythms (Borsook, Richardson et al., 1986). Melatonin binds to sites in the suprachiasmatic nucleus where it appears to act via a benzodiazepine/GABAergic mechanism. Melatonin-induced analgesia, reduction in anxiety, and changes in locomotion can be blocked by a benzodiazepine antagonist (flumazenil) (Golombek, Escolar et al., 1991; Golombek, Escolar & Cardinali, 1991). The effects on locomotion and on reduction in anxiety are mediated through a benzodiazepine/GABAergic mechanism which can be blocked by flumazenil (Tenn & Niles, 1995) (Pierrefiche, Zerbib & Laborit, 1993).

The pineal gland participates in regulating the number of benzodiazepine (BZ) receptors in the cerebral cortex. Removal of the gland creates a fall in the number of BZ binding sites without a change in binding affinity (Acuna-Castroviejo, Lowenstein et al., 1986). Supplemental intracerebroventricular melatonin will then increase BZ receptors, an effect which can be further augmented by injection of an ACTH peptide (Gomar, Fernandez et al., 1995).

Hypothalamic-Pituitary-Adrenal Axis. The hypothalamic-pituitary-adrenal (HPA) axis has circadian rhythms that are altered by alcohol withdrawal. A hyperadrenergic state is associated with acute alcohol withdrawal and results in a generalized elevation in cortisol levels and a four-hour delay in the circadian cortisol peak (Fonzi, Solinas et al., 1994). Administration of corticotropin releasing factor during withdrawal causes an accentuated response in alcoholics. Further, dexamethasone administration fails to suppress cortisol levels in actively drinking alcoholics (Murialdo, Filippi et al., 1991). Shifts in the circadian rhythm and responsiveness of the HPA axis are likely to further dysregulate sleep circuits.

CONCLUSIONS

The chemically dependent or recently abstinent patient is particularly vulnerable to insomnia and other sleep-related syndromes. Evaluating and managing these problems is a difficult challenge for clinicians.

The brain is a rich and wondrous collection of neurons, neuronal circuits, and neurochemistry. Fortunately, it has the wisdom of knowing how to repair many of the disorders we are so skillful at provoking.

To quote from Kevin Kelly's *Out of Control* (1994):

"The spirit of a beehive, the behavior of an economy, the thinking of a supercomputer, and the life in me are distributed over a multitude of smaller units. When the sum of the parts can add up to more than the parts, then that extra being (that something from nothing) is distributed among the parts. Whenever we find something from nothing, we find it arising from a field of many interacting smaller pieces. All the mysteries we find most interesting—life, intelligence, evolution—are found in the soil of large distributed systems."

. . . and so it appears to be with sleep.

ACKNOWLEDGMENT: To the memory of Dr. John P. Manges—dear friend and compassionate physician. Together we learned much about chemical dependency, medicine, and life.

REFERENCES

Acuna-Castroviejo D, Lowenstein PR, Rosenstein R & Cardinali DP (1986). Diurnal variations of benzodiazepine binding in rat cerebral cortex: Disruption by pinealectomy. *Journal of Pineal Research* 3(2):101–109.

Adlaf EM, Smart RG & Walsh GW (1992). Substance use and work disabilities among a general population. *American Journal of Drug and Alcohol Abuse* 18(4):371–387.

Aldrich MS & Shipley JE (1993). Alcohol use and periodic limb movements of sleep. *Alcoholism: Clinical & Experimental Research* 17(1):192–196.

Allen R, Wagman A & Funderburk F (1977). Slow wave sleep changes: alcohol tolerance and treatment implications. *Advances in Experimental Medicine and Biology* 85A:629–640.

Asheychik R, Jackson T, Baker H, Ferraro H, Ashton T & Kilgore J (1989). The efficacy of L-tryptophan in the reduction of sleep disturbance and depressive state in alcoholic patients. *Journal of Studies on Alcohol* 50(6):525–532.

Askenasy JJ & Rahmani L (1987). Neuropsycho-social rehabilitation of head injury. *American Journal of Physical Medicine* 66(6):315–327.

Asplund R & Aberg H (1996). Nocturnal micturition, sleep and well- being in women of ages 40–64 years. *Maturitas* 24(1–2):73–81.

Aston-Jones G & Bloom FE (1981). Activity of norepinephrine- containing locus coeruleus neurons in behaving rats anticipates fluctuations in the sleep-waking cycle. *Journal of Neuroscience* 1(8):876–886.

Aston-Jones G, Chiang C & Alexinsky T (1991). Discharge of noradrenergic locus coeruleus neurons in behaving rats and monkeys suggests a role in vigilance. *Progress in Brain Research* 88:501–520.

Bach-y-Rita G & Veno A (1974). Habitual violence: A profile of 62 men. *American Journal of Psychiatry* 131(9):1015–1017.

Billiard M (1987). Lithium carbonate: Effects on sleep patterns of normal and depressed subjects and its use in sleep-wake pathology. *Pharmacopsychiatry* 20(5):195–196.

Borsook D, Richardson GS, Moore-Ede MC & Brennan MJ (1986). GABA and circadian timekeeping: Implications for manic-depression and sleep disorders. *Medical Hypotheses* 19(2):185–198.

Cavallaro R, Regazzetti MG, Covelli G & Smeraldi E (1993). Tolerance and withdrawal with zolpidem. *Lancet* 342:374–375.

Davila DG, Hurt RD, Offord KP, Harris CD & Shepard JW Jr. (1994). Acute effects of transdermal nicotine on sleep architecture, snoring, and sleep-disordered breathing in nonsmokers. *American Journal of Respiratory Critical Care Medicine* 150(2):469–474.

De Sarro GB, Ascioti C, Froio F, Libri V & Nistico G (1987). Evidence that locus coeruleus is the site where clonidine and drugs acting at alpha 1- and alpha 2-adrenoceptors affect sleep and arousal mechanisms. *British Journal of Pharmacology* 90(4):675–685.

Deacon S & Arendt J (1996). Adapting to phase shifts, I. An experimental model for jet lag and shift work. *Physiology and Behavior* 59(4–5):665–673.

Dollins AB, Zhdanova IV, Wurtman RJ, Lynch HJ & Deng MH (1994). Effect of inducing nocturnal serum melatonin concentrations in daytime on sleep, mood, body temperature, and performance. *Proceedings of the National Academy of Science* 91(5):1824–1828.

Dufour M, Archer L & Gordis E (1992). Alcohol and the elderly. *Clinical Geriatric Medicine* 8(1):127–141.

Fonzi S, Solinas GP, Costelli P et al. (1994). Melatonin and cortisol circadian secretion during ethanol withdrawal in chronic alcoholics. *Chronobiologia* 21(1–2):109–112.

Friedrichs ES (1996). Personal communication. American Society of Addiction Medicine Conference on State of the Art in Addiction Medicine, Workshop on Sleep Disorders, October 24, 1996, Chicago, Illinois.

Garfinkel D, Laudon M, Nof D & Zisapel N (1995). Improvement of sleep quality in elderly people by controlled-release melatonin. *Lancet* 346(8974):541–544.

Garzon M, Tejero S, Beneitez AM & de Andres I (1995). Opiate microinjections in the locus coeruleus area of the cat enhance slow wave sleep. *Neuropeptides* 29(4):229–239.

George B, Landau-Ferey J, Benoit O, Dondey M & Cophignon J (1981). [Night sleep disorders during recovery of severe head injuries (author's transl)]. *Neurochirurgie* 27(1):35–38.

Gillin J & Byerley W (1990). The diagnosis and management of insomnia. *The New England Journal of Medicine* 322(4):239–248.

Gillin JC, Smith TL, Irwin M, Kripke DF, Brown S & Schuckit M (1990). Short REM latency in primary alcoholic patients with secondary depression. *American Journal of Psychiatry* 147(1):106–109.

Golombek DA, Escolar E, Burin LJ, De Brito Sanchez MG & Cardinali DP (1991). Time-dependent melatonin analgesia in mice: Inhibition by opiate or benzodiazepine antagonism. *European Journal of Pharmacology* 194(1):25–30.

Golombek DA, Escolar E & Cardinali DP (1991). Melatonin-induced depression of locomotor activity in hamsters: Time-dependency and inhibition by the central-type benzodiazepine antagonist Ro 15-1788. *Physiology and Behavior* 49(6):1091–1097.

Gomar MD, Fernandez B, Del Aguila CM, Castillo JL, Escames G & Acuna-Castroviejo D (1995). Participation of ACTH1–10 and ACTH4–10 on the melatonin modulation of benzodiazepine receptors in rat cerebral cortex. *Experientia* 51(3):209–212.

Greenblatt D, Harmatz J, Zinny M & Shader R (1987). Effect of gradual withdrawal on the rebound sleep disorder after discontinuation of triazolam. *The New England Journal of Medicine* 317(12):722–728.

Griffiths RR, Sannerud CA, Ator NA & Brady JV (1992). Zolpidem behavioral pharmacology in baboons: Self-injection, discrimination, tolerance and withdrawal. *Journal of Pharmacology and Experimental Therapy* 263:298–303.

Guilleminault C, Faull KF, Miles L & van den Hoed J (1983). Posttraumatic excessive daytime sleepiness: A review of 20 patients. *Neurology* 33(12):1584–1589.

Jacquinet-Salord M, Lang T, Fouriaud C, Nicoulet I & Bingham A (1993). Sleeping tablet consumption, self reported quality of sleep, and working conditions. *Journal of Epidemiology in Community Health* 47(1):64–68.

Johnson L, Burdick J & Smith J (1970). Sleep during alcohol intake and withdrawal in the chronic alcoholic. *Archives of General Psychiatry* 22:406–418.

Jones BE (1991). The role of noradrenergic locus coeruleus neurons and neighboring cholinergic neurons of the pontomesencephalic tegmentum in sleep-wake states. *Progress in Brain Research* 88:533–543.

Jones BE (1994). Basic mechanism of sleep-wake states. In MH Kryger, T Roth & WC Dement (eds.) *Principles and Practice of Sleep Medicine*. Philadelphia, PA: W.B. Saunders, 145–162.

Kaitin KI, Bliwise DL, Gleason C, Nino-Murcia G, Dement WC & Libet B (1986). Sleep disturbance produced by electrical stimulation of the locus coeruleus in a human subject. *Biological Psychiatry* 21(8–9):710–716.

Kelly K (1994). *Out of Control*. Reading, MA: Addison-Wesley Publishing Company.

Leathwood PD, Chauffard F, Heck E & Munoz-Box R (1982). Aqueous extract of valerian root (*Valeriana officinalis L.*) improves sleep quality in man. *Pharmacology, Biochemistry and Behavior* 17(1):65–71.

Lugaresi E (1992). The thalamus and insomnia. *Neurology* 42(Suppl 6):28–34.

Medical Letter (1993). Zolpidem for insomnia. *The Medical Letter* 35(895):35–36.

Medical Letter (1996). Hypnotic drugs. *The Medical Letter* 38(978):59–61.

Medori R, Tritschler H-J, LeBlanc A et al. (1992). Fatal familial insomnia, a prion disease with a mutation at codon 178 of the prion protein gene. *The New England Journal of Medicine* 326(7):444–449.

Miller W & Rollnick S (1991). *Motivational Interviewing: Preparing People to Change Addictive Behavior.* New York, NY: The Guilford Press.

Mouret J, Lemoine P, Minuit MP, Benkelfat C & Renardet M (1988). Effects of trazodone on the sleep of depressed subjects—A polygraphic study. *Psychopharmacology* (Berlin) 95(Suppl):S37–S43.

Murialdo G, Filippi U, Costelli P et al. (1991). Urine melatonin in alcoholic patients: A marker of alcohol abuse? *Journal of Endocrinology Investigation* 14(6):503–507.

Murphy PJ, Myers BL & Badia P (1996). Nonsteroidal anti- inflammatory drugs alter body temperature and suppress melatonin in humans. *Physiology and Behavior* 59(1):133–139.

National Institutes of Health, Treatment Assessment Panel (NIH) (1996). Integration of behavioral and relaxation approaches into the treatment of chronic pain and insomnia. *Journal of the American Medical Association* 276(4):313–318.

Nierenberg AA, Adler LA, Peselow MD, Zornberg G & Rosenthal BA (1994). Trazodone for antidepressant-associated insomnia. *American Journal of Psychiatry* 151(7):1069–1072.

Nierenberg AA & Keck PE Jr (1989). Management of monoamine oxidase inhibitor-associated insomnia with trazodone. *Journal of Clinical Psychopharmacology* 9(1):42–45.

Nistico G, De Sarro GB, Bagetta G & Mollace V (1992). Altered sensitivity of alpha 2-adrenoceptors in the brain during aging in rats. *Annals of the New York Academy of Science* 673:206–213.

Obermeyer WH & Benca RM (1996). Effects of drugs on sleep. *Neurologic Clinics* 14(4):827–840.

Osaka T & Matsumura H (1994). Noradrenergic inputs to sleep-related neurons in the preoptic area from the locus coeruleus and the ventrolateral medulla in the rat. *Neuroscience Research* 19(1):39–50.

Pansini F, Albertazzi P, Bonaccorsi G et al. (1994). The menopausal transition: A dynamic approach to the pathogenesis of neurovegetative complaints. *European Journal of Obstetrics, Gynecology and Reproductive Biology* 57(2):103–109.

Pansini F, Albertazzi P, Bonaccorsi G et al. (1995). Trazodone: A non-hormonal alternative for neurovegetative climacteric symptoms. *Clinical and Experimental Obstetrics and Gynecology* 22(4):341–344.

Peters J, van Kammen DP, van Kammen WB & Neylan T (1990). Sleep disturbance and computerized axial tomographic scan findings in former prisoners of war. *Comprehensive Psychiatry* 31(6):535–539.

Pierrefiche G, Zerbib R & Laborit H (1993). Anxiolytic activity of melatonin in mice: Involvement of benzodiazepine receptors. *Research Communication on Chemistry, Pathology and Pharmacology* 82(2):131–142.

Prosise GL, Bonnet MH, Berry RB & Dickel MJ (1994). Effects of abstinence from smoking on sleep and daytime sleepiness. *Chest* 105(4):1136–1141.

Schneider-Helmert D (1988). Why low-dose benzodiazepine-dependent insomniacs can't escape their sleeping pills. *Acta Psychiatria Scandinavica* 78(6):706–711.

Schneider-Helmert D & Spinweber CL (1986). Evaluation of L-tryptophan for treatment of insomnia: A review. *Psychopharmacology* (Berlin) 89:1–7.

Semba J, Toru M & Mataga N (1984). Twenty-four hour rhythms of norepinephrine and serotonin in nucleus suprachiasmaticus, raphe nuclei, and locus coeruleus in the rat. *Sleep* 7(3):211–218.

Shinba T, Murashima YL & Yamamoto K (1994). Alcohol consumption and insomnia in a sample of Japanese alcoholics. *Addiction* 89(5):587–591.

Shirlow MJ & Mathers CD (1985). A study of caffeine consumption and symptoms; Indigestion, palpitations, tremor, headache and insomnia. *International Journal of Epidemiology* 14(2):239–248.

Shouse MN, Langer JV & Dittes PR (1990). Spontaneous sleep epilepsy in amygdala-kindled kittens: A preliminary report. *Brain Research* 535(1):163–168.

Siegel JM (1994). Brainstem mechanisms generating REM sleep. In MH Kryger, T Roth & WC Dement (eds.) *Principles and Practice of Sleep Medicine*. Philadelphia, PA: W.B. Saunders, 125–144.

Siegel JM & Rogawski MA (1988). A function for REM sleep: Regulation of noradrenergic receptor sensitivity. *Brain Research* 472(3):213–233.

Spielman AJ, Nuners J & Glovinsky PB (1996). Insomnia. *Neurologic Clinics* 14(3):513–543.

Templer DI, Kasiraj J, Trent NH et al. (1992). Exploration of head injury without medical attention. *Perception and Motor Skills* 75(1):195–202.

Tenn CC & Niles LP (1995). Central-type benzodiazepine receptors mediate the antidopaminergic effect of clonazepam and melatonin in 6-hydroxydopamine lesioned rats: Involvement of a GABAergic mechanism. *Journal of Pharmacology and Experimental Therapy* 274(1):84–89.

Tononi G, Pompeiano M & Cirelli C (1994). The locus coeruleus and immediate-early genes in spontaneous and forced wakefulness. *Brain Research Bulletin* 35(5–6):589–596.

Wagner DR (1996). Disorders of the circadian sleep-wake cycle. *Neurologic Clinics* 14(3):651–670.

Wetterberg L, Aperia B, Gorelick DA et al. (1992). Age, alcoholism and depression are associated with low levels of urinary melatonin. *Journal of Psychiatry and Neuroscience* 17(5):215–224.

Williams H & Rundell O (1981). Altered sleep physiology in chronic alcoholics: Reversal with abstinence. *Alcoholism: Clinical & Experimental Research* 5(2):318–325.

CHAPTER 6

Medical Syndromes Associated with Specific Drugs

Alan A. Wartenberg, M.D., FASAM

Alcohol
Other Sedative-Hypnotics
Opioids
Cocaine and Other Stimulants
Marijuana
Hallucinogens
Inhalants
Miscellaneous Drugs
Polydrug Abuse

Management of medical complications in the addicted patient generally is no different from management of similar problems in any patient. However, because addicted patients may have been medically underserved, or because their addiction issues have been the patient's primary focus, or because the use of alcohol or other drugs actually has masked physical symptoms, these patients may present with more advanced illnesses, which in turn may present in unusual or atypical ways.

ALCOHOL

The patient presenting with inebriation may be disinhibited, agitated and combative, posing some risk of injury to self or others. The patient may require bed rest, with bed rails and soft restraints. Restriction should be minimized, with chemical restraints (sedating neuroleptics may be preferable to benzodiazepines in the already-intoxicated patient) used if physical restraints are required (Hackett, 1987). Provision of a calm and reassuring atmosphere is essential, with minimization of noxious stimuli, excessive or repetitive history-taking, examination and laboratory evaluation.

Nutritional status may be deficient, so provision of a diet with appropriate levels of protein, carbohydrates and fats—as well as vitamins and minerals—is critical. Formal nutritional assessment may be required in some cases, but height/weight ratio and serum albumen generally are sufficient. Supplementation with thiamine and other multivitamins is essential, and may need to include additional niacin, pyridoxine and folic acid. Vitamin A may be deficient in the alcoholic, but care should be taken in prescribing additional amounts, since high doses may be toxic. Magnesium supplements may be helpful in every debilitated patients, but caution should be exercised in prescribing calcium and Vitamin D, given the possibility of hypercalcemia and calcium nephrolithiasis. Specific supplements that purport to treat the underlying neurotransmitter substrate deficiencies are expensive and not supported by adequate data. The optimal length of treatment with vitamin and mineral supplementation is not certain: a period of several weeks to months generally is adequate, until the patient is eating a regular and balanced diet and has been away from alcohol and other drugs (Lieber, 1988). A dietician/nutritionist should be part of the treatment team.

Neurological Comorbidities. The central nervous system is the target organ for the desired effects of alcohol, but bears the brunt of its unwanted effects as well. Patients may have had "blackouts," or periods of memory loss while drinking, which typically occur with rapid elevation of blood alcohol content. These may occur without other evidence of neuropsychological impairment (Parker, 1985). Effects on memory may occur in "social" drinkers, and patients in the spectrum of alcohol amnestic syndrome through Wernicke-Korsakoff syndrome and dementia are commonly encountered (Victor,

Adams & Collins, 1989; Butters, 1982). Evaluation requires distinctions between alcohol-induced disease and other causes of dementia, including hypothyroidism, syphilis, vitamin B12 deficiency, CNS mass lesions, infectious or degenerative conditions. There is no specific treatment; provision of regular doses of thiamine and multivitamin supplementation is appropriate, with maintenance of an environment that maximizes existing function and reduces the likelihood of further alcohol or other drug use. Restorative therapies in addition to usual physical and/or occupational therapies, such as music and art, may be helpful.

Alcoholic cerebellar degeneration should be differentiated from other causes of cerebellar disease, and may respond to vitamin B complex supplementation. Marchiafava-Bignami disease, which involves a degeneration of the corpus callosum, has been reported in red wine drinkers of Italian descent and others. It produces confusion, language disturbance, seizures and dementia; there is no specific treatment (Dreyfus, 1982; Victor, Adams & Collins, 1989). Degeneration of the corpus callosum appears to be more common than previously thought (Pfefferbaum, Lim et al., 1996) and Marchiafava-Bignami disease may represent the extreme end of the degenerative spectrum. Central pontine myelinolysis, which may result in pseudobulbar manifestations of pathological crying, emotional lability and confusion, but may progress to facial paralysis, difficulty in speech and deglutition, and eventuate in quadriplegia, coma and death, is seen in nutritionally debilitated alcoholics, often in the setting of rapid correction of hyponatremia (Ayus, Krothapall & Arieff, 1987). Caution is appropriate in the provision of hypertonic saline to correct hyponatremia, with increases of 1–2 mEq/hour up to serum sodium concentrations of 125 mEq, and then more gradual correction being appropriate (Stearns, Riggs & Schochet, 1986).

A variety of neuropathies may occur. Tobacco-alcohol amblyopia, a retrobulbar neuropathy, may produce double vision and decreased acuity; it requires B vitamin supplementation and generally resolves with abstinence from the offending agent. Sensory neuropathy generally presents as burning dysesthesias of the feet and hands, with eventual hypesthesia in a stocking-glove distribution. Motor neuropathy with proximal weakness of the shoulder and hip girdle may follow; lastly, autonomic neuropathy with orthostatic hypotension and even gastric emptying abnormalities may occur. Evaluation must exclude other forms of neuropathy and may require neurological consultation with nerve conduction studies and/or electromyography. Treatment is with B vitamin supplementation, especially thiamine; physical therapy may offer some improvement (Dreyfus, 1982).

Seizures probably are the most common serious neurological problem seen in the alcoholic patient. They usually are single, although they may occur in salvos of two or three; they occur in the first two days after reduction in alcohol intake, although rarely they may occur later. They are non-focal, but may be associated with usual post-ictal changes. EEG and CT scanning usually reveal no abnormalities, and they do not recur if sobriety is continued. Patients with a first seizure that fits this description should be evaluated to exclude an underlying seizure focus, including mass lesions. There is little or no evidence that either acute or long-term use of phenytoin is helpful in the patient who does not have an underlying seizure disorder (Kasser, Kane et al., 1994); further, problems in maintaining stable drug levels in the face of continued drinking may lead to dangerous fluctuations (toxic effects of phenytoin include a variety of drug interactions, osteomalacia, gum hypertrophy, drug-induced lupus and blood dyscrasias). Consideration should be given to monitoring for and correcting any magnesium deficiency that exists, since this may decrease seizure threshold. Traditionally, 50% magnesium sulfate is given intramuscularly or intravenously (50 mg/cc of Mg^{++}, 2 to 4 cc BID-QID, for one to three days), but available oral forms, such as magnesium gluconate, may be given in equivalent doses and usually do not induce diarrhea. Prescription of drugs that reduce seizure threshold, such as phenothiazines (including prochlorperazine [Compazine®]) and antidepressants, should be undertaken with great caution in the seizure-prone patient.

There is an increased incidence of subdural hematoma in alcoholics who suffer head trauma, and the clinician should be alert to the development of mental status changes or focal neurological signs. Both hemorrhagic and thrombotic stroke may be more frequent in alcoholic patients (Gill, Shipley et al., 1991), perhaps because of underlying hypertension and/or coagulopathies. There is some evidence that elevated levels of homocysteine, which may result in hypercoagulability, may be involved (Hultberg, Berglund et al., 1993). Evaluation and treatment are no different than in the non-alcoholic patient, but long-term use of anticoagulants in alcoholics may present significant difficulties.

Gastrointestinal Comorbidities. Alcohol is an irritant, producing stomatitis, esophagitis, gastritis and duodenitis (Geokas, Lieber et al., 1981). Alcohol does not cause peptic ulcer disease, but continued use of both tobacco and alcohol may retard healing or produce exacerbations. Alcohol does act synergistically with *Helicobacter pylori* to delay ulcer healing in infected patients (Lieber, 1997). Alcohol favors colonization by *H. pylori*, which, in turn, produces ammonia, which contributes to chronic gastritis. Treatment with antibiotics to eradicate *H. pylori*, if present, is a rational therapy.

While alcohol may be an associated factor in ulcer disease, it certainly is an etiologic agent in hemorrhagic gastritis. Patients who present with dysphagia, early satiety, early morning abdominal pain, or signs and symptoms of anemia should be evaluated (particularly if they are over 40 years of age), since esophageal stricture and both esophageal and gastric malignancies may be present. The choice of endoscopic or radiographic studies depends on the expertise and facilities available, but endoscopy generally is preferred, particularly since tissue diagnosis may be needed. In younger patients whose histories are compatible with acid peptic disease, a therapeutic trial may be initiated without specific diagnosis. The presence of anemia, occult blood in the stool or significant weight loss argues for more aggressive diagnostic study.

Treatment should concentrate on avoiding inciting factors, such as alcohol and tobacco. Intensive antacid therapy works well but is poorly tolerated by patients, and may lead to diarrhea and milk-alkali syndrome. H2-blocking drugs are very effective, but should be used for a limited time until healing occurs, generally six to eight weeks. *Helicobacter pylori* may play a role in some cases of alcoholic gastritis and peptic ulcer disease (Lieber, 1997; Uppal, Lateef et al., 1991). Treatment is with bismuth salts and multiple antibiotic therapy in patients with resistant disease in whom *H. pylori* is found to be present.

Cimetidine may decrease P450 cytochrome enzyme activity, which can cause a decrease in metabolism of several drugs, including alcohol and benzodiazepines, thus leading to increased toxicity (Guram, Harden & Holt, 1991). It appears that famotidine and ranitidine do not decrease P450 activity *in vitro* at recommended doses. Use of antacids, sucralfate or famotidine may be preferred. In patients with intractable disease, particularly erosive esophagitis secondary to reflux, omeprazole may be very effective. Impaired gastric emptying secondary to autonomic neuropathy may respond to agents such as metoclopramide or cisapride. Malabsorption and diarrhea may occur, with or without pancreatic insufficiency. It is generally self-limited and resolves with abstinence; if persistent, consultation for evaluation of causes of small bowel dysfunction is appropriate, as is exclusion of *Clostridium difficile* toxin and infectious causes of diarrhea. Acute gastrointestinal bleeding is managed as it is in other patients. It is important to make a diagnosis, since the treatment of hemorrhagic gastritis, gastric ulcer, duodenal ulcer and variceal hemorrhage may differ. Rarely, significant bleeding may result from a gastric malignancy, where biopsy is required to make the diagnosis. These patients need an intensively monitored setting. Coagulation studies and type and cross-match studies should be done promptly; transfusion is required to achieve hemodynamic stability; use of vasopressin and/or somatostatin may decrease bleeding acutely (Terblanche, Burroughs & Hobbs, 1989). Treatment of esophageal variceal hemorrhage generally is with sclerotherapy or banding; emergent portacaval shunting may be required in some cases, but mortality is high, often secondary to hepatic encephalopathy. The availability of interventional radiographic techniques to effect portacaval shunting may be effective in selected cases (Conn, 1993). Prevention of bleeding in patients with known esophageal varices may be accomplished with beta-blockers (Pasta, 1988). Portal hypertensive gastropathy may cause bleeding in the absence of varices, and beta-blockers also may provide prophylactic benefit (Panes, Bordas et al., 1993). Patients with chronic acid-peptic disease generally are treated with long-term antacid and H-2 blocker therapy, but abstinence from alcohol and tobacco is critical.

Acute and chronic pancreatitis are common among abusers of alcohol (Geokas, Lieber et al., 1981; Van Thiel, Lipsitz et al., 1981). Episodes of acute abdominal pain, nausea and vomiting, often with pain radiating to the back or interscapular area, is commonly seen in association with elevated serum amylase and lipase. The urinary amylase may be helpful in some cases. Treatment is with intravenous fluids, bowel rest (nothing by mouth, with or without gastric suction), and opioids for pain. Recurrent episodes may eventuate in chronic pancreatitis, with both endocrine and exocrine insufficiency. Diabetes, malabsorption and deficiencies in some fat-soluble vitamins may be seen. Evaluation with glucose tolerance tests, tests of pancreatic function (including measurement of fecal fat and d-Xylose absorption), may be required. Treatment includes appropriate attention to diet and exercise; in mild cases, oral hypoglycemic drugs may be effective, but insulin often is required. These patients' diabetes may be very "brittle," perhaps secondary to lack of glucagon or poor compliance.

Pancreatic enzyme replacement may result in weight gain and resolution of vitamin deficiencies, and may reduce the chronic pain syndrome commonly seen in these patients. Severe chronic pain syndromes in patients with underlying alcohol abuse may be difficult to manage, since opioids also may be abused. Use of antidepressants, carbamazepine and physical measures such as nerve blocks or celiac plexus block, sometimes produce relief of pain.

Hepatic Comorbidities. The liver is the target organ of much of alcohol consumed, since it must pass through the liver via the portal circulation directly after absorption. Acute fatty metamorphosis, alcoholic hepatitis, perivenular fibrosis, and cirrhosis all may be seen (Geokas, Lieber et al., 1981). In most cases, fatty metamorphosis and acute alcoholic hepatitis are self-limited. It is recommended that enzyme studies be repeated periodically (every two to four weeks) if they are abnormal; most patients will resolve within three months. In patients who present with signs of hepatocellular insufficiency or portal hypertension, evaluation by a gastroenterologist who is experienced with alcoholic liver disease is recommended. The diagnosis of alcoholic liver disease may be problematic. In many cases, the AST will be elevated in the 100–300 IU range, and will be higher than the ALT (a ratio of 1:2 to 1:4); this is typical of alcoholic liver disease. If the ALT is greater than the AST, obtaining a test for hepatitis C antibody is worthwhile. The GGT also may be elevated: generally, two to five times higher than the AST. However, other causes of liver disease, including hemochromatosis, Wilson's disease, hepatitis B and C, alpha-1-antitrypsin deficiency, primary biliary cirrhosis and autoimmune hepatitis may need to be considered in specific cases. The definitive diagnosis may need to be made by liver biopsy; coagulation studies are needed, and care should be taken to avoid bleeding complications. Vitamin K may be given, and in some cases fresh frozen plasma may be required, if reversal of coagulopathy is urgently needed to treat bleeding diathesis or accomplish biopsies.

The treatment of alcoholic liver disease generally involves time and abstinence from alcohol. However, in cases where the disease is particularly severe or does not resolve with time and abstinence, several therapeutic options may be available. Steroids may be effective in selected cases (Carrithers, Herlong et al., 1989), and both propylthiouracil (Orrego, Blake & Blendis, 1987) and colchicine (Kershenovich, Vargas et al., 1988) have been studied. There continues to be controversy over the appropriateness of pharmacotherapy of alcoholic liver disease, so the clinician should watch current literature and engage expert consultation. Patients generally improve with abstinence from alcohol, time and appropriate nutritional intervention when required.

Treatment of ascites and edema should be with salt restriction; fluid restriction should be used only if serum sodium is less than 120 mEq/L. Aldactone usually is required to reverse secondary hyperaldosteronism; doses of up to 400 mg/day may be needed. Loop diuretics are added when aldactone does not produce adequate diuresis; weight loss of up to 1 kg/day is well-tolerated in the presence of edema, but should be limited to 0.5 kg/day if only ascites is present. High volume paracentesis with replacement of albumen may be needed in cases where respiratory embarrassment or tense ascites are present (Pinto, Amerian & Reynolds, 1988). Patients may develop spontaneous bacterial peritonitis with few or no abdominal signs; paracentesis with culture and cell count are required for diagnosis. Treatment is with appropriate antibiotics, generally aimed at anaerobic gram positive cocci and enterobacteriaceae (Crossley & Williams, 1985).

Hematologic Comorbidities. Alcohol can produce a variety of anemias, including microcytic, from ongoing upper gastrointestinal blood loss and iron deficiency; macrocytic secondary to membrane defects, premature release of red cells from bone marrow, liver disease or folate deficiency; or normocytic, normochromic secondary to marrow suppression and/or chronic disease (Herbert, 1980). In cases of severe liver disease, a variety of morphological changes in red blood cells (including burr cells and schistocytes) may occur, and frank hemolysis may be present. Immune function may be reduced and the risk of infection increased. No specific treatment can be recommended; in most cases, abstinence from alcohol results in resolution of the abnormalities. Portal hypertension may result in splenic sequestration of all cell lines, but platelets are particularly affected.

The patient with mild to moderate hematologic abnormalities generally can be managed expectantly. If the hemogram shows microcytosis, evaluation for iron deficiency or thalassemia may be appropriate, and macrocytic indices should prompt evaluation for

B12 and folate deficiency. If ring sideroblasts are seen, evaluation for sideroblastic anemia (which may be responsive to pyridoxine [Vitamin B6]) should be considered. Leukopenia generally is mild: if granulocyte levels are over 1,000, the risk of infection is low. Lymphopenia may be present in malnourished patients, as well as in HIV disease.

Mild thrombocytopenia is commonly seen and generally reverts to normal with less than a week of abstinence from alcohol. Thrombocytopenia rarely is problematic, but if values are below 50,000, there may be some risk of bleeding; values below 25,000 should be urgently evaluated; and patients with platelets below 10,000 are at high risk and may need treatment. Qualitative platelet defects also may be present and increase the risk of bleeding.

Cardiovascular Complications. Alcohol ingestion may result in a variety of supraventricular arrhythmias, including paroxysmal atrial fibrillation, often known as "holiday heart" (Greenspon & Schaal, 1983). Alcohol withdrawal is associated with high levels of circulating catecholamines, which may precipitate supraventricular and ventricular arrhythmias. Treatment with beta-blockers may be helpful, and additionally may decrease other signs and symptoms of alcohol withdrawal (Kraus, Gottlieb et al., 1985). Such patients also should be treated with appropriate benzodiazepine sedation, since patients treated only with beta-blockers may progress to delirium without warning. In general, abstinence from alcohol and observation is all that is necessary, unless there is evidence of underlying ischemic heart disease, or the arrhythmia is hemodynamically significant.

Chronic heavy use of alcohol may result in a congestive cardiomyopathy. There is insidious but progressive dyspnea, intolerance to exercise and edema, as well as other signs of congestion. Diagnosis includes echo-cardiography with findings of global hypokinesis, and exclusion of other heart disease in a patient with a significant alcohol history. Treatment is problematic, with poor results from digitalis glycosides; use of diuretics, ACE inhibitors and vasodilators is more likely to be successful. The presence of mural thrombi warrants anticoagulation, but this can be risky in the patient who continues to drink.

Regular use of alcohol is associated with arterial hypertension, which can cause all the deleterious effects of any form of hypertension (Potter & Beavers, 1984; Gitlow, Dziedzic & Dziedzic, 1986). Alcohol withdrawal can elevate blood pressure to a significant degree in patients with and without preexisting hypertension; in patients with previously elevated pressures, urgent treatment with clonidine, nifedipine or other agents may be needed. It may be appropriate to observe patients with modestly elevated blood pressure, particularly if there are no clinical signs of sequelae (left ventricular hypertrophy, proteinuria, fundoscopic changes), since blood pressure may return to normal levels with abstinence from alcohol. While use of modest amounts of alcohol (one to two drinks per day) may increase HDL cholesterol and have protective effects against coronary arteriosclerosis (Gaziano, Buring et al., 1993), heavy consumption of alcohol has adverse effects on lipids (Criqui, 1986), which—together with increased blood pressure—may increase overall cardiovascular mortality. The cardioprotective effects occur primarily in patients with LDL cholesterol above 140 mg/dl (Hein, Suadicani & Gyntelberg, 1996).

Endocrine and Metabolic Comorbidities. The effects of alcohol on the pancreas are discussed above. Acute alcohol ingestion may produce hypertriglyceridemia and lipemic serum, and (in predisposed individuals) painful abdominal crises may occur. Alcohol produces hyperuricemia by interfering with urate excretion and increasing turnover; this may result in gout and its sequelae. Since alcohol interferes with gluconeogenesis, hypoglycemia may occur, particularly in debilitated alcoholics who have used up glycogen stores; patients on insulin or oral agents are at greater risk. Vasopressin levels are inhibited with rising blood alcohol, resulting in increased urinary flow; vasopressin increases when the alcohol level is falling, which may lead to overhydration. There may be oversecretion of cortisol with impaired suppression: a "pseudo-Cushing's syndrome" (Cicero, 1981). Corticotrophin releasing factor is elevated during withdrawal and contributes also to the neurophysiologic perception of craving (Koob, 1996). Increased urinary losses of magnesium may lead to reduced parathyroid hormone secretion and hypocalcemia; both decreased magnesium and calcium may predispose to muscle weakness, tetany, seizures and cardiac arrhythmias. Alcohol use decreases the production of both male and female sex hormones, resulting in impaired fertility, menstrual irregularities or amenorrhea in women, and decreased spermatogenesis, infertility and impotence in men (Lester & Van Thiel, 1977; Van Thiel, 1983).

Miscellaneous Comorbidities. Alcohol may increase the likelihood of aspiration pneumonia by reduction in level of consciousness and reduction of cough and gag responses; the usual concomitant use of tobacco further impairs host responses, including mucociliary function. Use of alcohol increases snoring by increasing upper airway resistance through inhibition of airway motor control (Dawson, Bigby et al., 1997). There also is evidence of increased nocturnal sleep apnea in patients using alcohol (Taasan, Block et al., 1981); this may occur in normal volunteers given bedtime doses of alcohol (Dawson, Lehr et al., 1993). Such patients may have daytime drowsiness and impaired motor performance, and—eventually—increased arterial and pulmonary hypertension. Patients at risk for aspiration also are more likely to develop lung abscess. Pulmonary tuberculosis also is more common in alcoholics (Reichman, Felton & Edsall, 1979). Acute and chronic myopathy may occur, with tender muscles, pain and weakness (Perkoff, 1971). In more severe cases, rhadomyolysis and myoglobinuria may occur, particularly when the patient has been unconscious and may have pressure necrosis. Hypophosphatemia, commonly found in alcoholics, also may contribute to muscle weakness and damage. This may be secondary to a defect in renal tubular function in such patients, which appears to clear with abstinence (De Marchi, Cecchin et al., 1993).

Osteoporosis is common, leading to an increase in fractures (Bikle, Genant et al., 1985), but this may be reversible (Bikle, Stesin et al., 1993). Falls may lead to multiple rib fractures, which can be a diagnostic clue to underlying alcohol abuse (Israel, Orrego et al., 1980). There also is an increase in avascular necrosis, particularly involving the hip. A number of cancers may be associated with alcohol use (in some cases compounded by tobacco use), including oropharyngeal, esophageal, gastric, pancreatic, hepatic, colon and breast (Tuyns, 1977; Seitz, 1985). The diagnosis and treatment of all these alcohol-induced conditions is the same as in the non-alcoholic patient.

OTHER SEDATIVE-HYPNOTICS

Parenteral abuse of sedative-hypnotic drugs, particularly barbiturates, does occur; complications are discussed below. Barbiturates and barbiturate-like drugs produce respiratory depression, coma and death in overdose or when used with other CNS depressants (Gary & Tresnewski, 1983). Benzodiazepines may produce low levels of coma, but rarely cause other serious sequelae, unless taken with other central nervous system (CNS) depressants, or taken by individuals with serious chronic obstructive pulmonary disease or generalized debility (Greenblatt, Shader & Abernethy, 1983). When given by rapid parenteral injection, benzodiazepines can cause respiratory depression; their use in critical care settings may make weaning from mechanical ventilation more difficult. Use of neuroleptics for sedation may be more appropriate in such settings. Sedative-hypnotic drugs produce cognitive changes, including retrograde and anterograde amnesia; they also impair visual tracking and reflex responses, making driving or operating machinery more dangerous. There is some evidence that cognitive impairment induced by benzodiazepines—particularly in alcoholic patients—may be longer-lasting than previously had been thought (Rummans, David et al., 1993). Glutethimide may produce marrow suppression and pancytopenia. Overdose with meprobamate may cause a gelatinous bezoar in the stomach, which may require endoscopic removal. Overdose can be successfully managed in most cases with mechanical ventilation and conservative medical care; use of hemoperfusion or other extracorporeal removal should be reserved for cases in which patients fail to respond, or deteriorate, while receiving conservative management (Litovitz, 1987; Wartenberg, 1990).

OPIOIDS

Opioids generally are relatively non-toxic when used as prescribed, with constipation and sedation the major side effects (Wartenberg, 1987). Pure agonists (morphine, heroin, fentanyl, oxymorphone, hydromorphone, codeine, oxycodone, and hydrocodone) are similar in toxicity, although some may produce more pruritus secondary to release of histamine. Non-cardiac pulmonary edema can occur with use of heroin, and has been reported with other opiates as well (Frand, Shim & Williams, 1972). Heroin-induced nephropathy with glomerulonephritis, which may cause renal insufficiency, also may be seen (Cunningham, Brentjens et al., 1980). A variety of neurological syndromes may occur, including multifocal leukoencephalopathy and myelopathies, which may be secondary to both the opioid and the parenteral route of administration (Rubin, 1987).

The most serious acute effect of opioids is overdose with respiratory depression. This can be treated with naloxone; initial doses may need to be as high as 2 mg, with multiple and/or repeated doses given in cases of use of mixed agonist-antagonists, propoxyphene and methadone (Levine, Schwartz & Ungar, 1986; Wartenberg, 1990). A naloxone infusion may be needed in some cases; 0.4 mg/hour has been recommended (Linovitz, 1987). Care should be taken to titrate the dose of naloxone so as not to produce a severe withdrawal syndrome in the dependent patient. Since naloxone has a shorter half-life than most opioids (except fentanyl), the patient must be monitored in an intensive setting, and mechanical ventilation may be required.

Meperidine, propoxyphene and pentazocine may result in seizures with use of higher therapeutic doses, as well as in the overdose setting. This appears to be due to *nor* metabolites of these drugs and occasionally occurs at therapeutic doses. In other patients, agitation and confusion may occur and progress to frank delirium. Rarely, seizures may occur with other opiates, which may be secondary to cerebral hypoxia. Seizures and/or delirium should be evaluated to exclude other causes when the diagnosis is not clear; treatment generally is symptomatic but must include discontinuance of the offending drug. The use of a contaminated preparation of meperidine synthesized illicitly resulted in a number of cases of severe Parkinson's disease (Langston, Ballard et al., 1983; Bianchini & McGhee, 1985).

The use of licit opioids for sub-acute and chronic pain may lead to the development of tolerance and escalation of drug dosage. This rarely occurs in the absence of pre-existing chemical dependency or other psychiatric problems, notably post-traumatic stress disorder and victimization. The use of combination products may lead to serious salicylate or acetaminophen toxicity, and the physician should be alert to signs and symptoms of these conditions (Wartenberg, 1990). Serum levels and referral to appropriate nomograms are required for appropriate treatment. Abrupt discontinuance or reduction of dosage may lead to withdrawal symptoms, including widespread myalgias, arthralgias and abdominal cramping, which may reinforce use of the drug.

COCAINE AND OTHER STIMULANTS

The pharmacology of cocaine and other stimulants is reviewed in Section 2. These drugs have the potential to cause serious and widespread organ toxicity (Gawin & Ellinwood, 1988). Patients on cocaine binges have sleep deprivation and may exhibit paranoid behavior and become frankly psychotic. Severe hypertension, cardiac arrhythmias, angina, myocardial infarction and sudden death may be seen, as well as cerebrovascular accident with stroke (Mody, Miller et al., 1988; Kaku & Lowenstein, 1990). Seizures are not uncommon, particularly when cocaine is injected or smoked (Pascual-Leone, Dhuna et al., 1990).

While some patients with cocaine-associated ischemic events evidence underlying arteriosclerotic heart disease, studies have shown normal coronary angiography in many such patients (Minor, Scott et al., 1991). While spasm has been suspected, there is no general evidence that these patients are otherwise predisposed to coronary artery spasm; however, increased local thrombosis secondary to increased platelet aggregation may play a role (Cooke & Dowling, 1988). There may be an increase in such events in patients who use alcohol and cocaine in combination. The role of cocaethylene, a longer-acting metabolite produced when cocaine and alcohol are combined, has been investigated (Henning & Wilson, 1996; Hearn, Rose et al., 1991). Chronic cardiomyopathy with severe congestive heart failure also has occurred (Weiner, Lockhardt & Schwartz, 1986).

When cocaine is ingested through nasal insufflation (snorting), ischemic necrosis with perforation of the nasal septum may occur. When smoked as "crack" or freebase cocaine, there may be reduction of pulmonary diffusing capacity, with hypoxia and dyspnea, and possibly pulmonary edema (Hoffman & Goodman, 1989). Vigorous inhalation, particularly with the Mueller maneuver (exhaling against a closed glottis), may lead to pneumothorax and pneumomediastinum (Freudenberger, Cappel & Hiott, 1990). Pulmonary infarction, alveolar hemorrhage and vascular thrombosis also may occur (Rezkalla & Kloner, 1992). Cocaine also may cause ischemia of the gastrointestinal tract and hepatic damage (Perrino, Warren & Levine, 1987; Radin, 1992; Pellinen, Honkakoski et al., 1994); cases of massive hepatic necrosis have occurred. Acute hyperthermia, which may be associated with seizure, may develop, and may occur with muscle rigidity, severe rhabdomyolysis, myoglobinuria and renal failure (Roth, Alarcon et al., 1988).

Toxicity of amphetamines and cocaine is similar, although amphetamines sometimes produce longer periods of complications. Neuropsychiatric problems with smoked methamphetamine ("ice" or "crank") may occur more frequently than with cocaine. Occasionally, other stimulants, including caffeine, phenylpropanolamine (PPA), and ephedrine (which often are sold as legal "speed") may produce similar toxicity, including cardiovascular and cerebrovascular events (Martin, Sloan et al., 1971; Greden, 1981; Abramowicz, 1984). Other stimulants, including methylphenidate and appetite suppressants, may have significant toxicity when taken in high doses for recreational use (Gawin & Ellinwood, 1988; Parran & Jasinski, 1991).

Diagnosis of stimulant-induced complications is made by obtaining a history of use in a clinically appropriate setting, chest pain or TIA symptoms in a young patient, and by urinary toxicology. Serum levels usually are not helpful with cocaine because of the very short serum half-life of one hour. Treatment generally is symptomatic and supportive. There is controversy over the use of beta-blockers in cocaine toxicity because of the possibility of unopposed alpha adrenergic stimulation, with resultant severe hypertension (Lange, Cigarroa et al., 1990). Some authorities recommend use of calcium channel blockers and nitrates for chest pain and evidence of ischemia (Mueller, Benowitz & Olson, 1990). Severe hypertension may be treated with calcium channel blockers. Hemodynamically significant tachycardia may respond to cautious intravenous doses of propranolol; labetalol may be a better choice because it has both beta- and alpha-blocking activity, but there are little data supporting its use. Bromocriptine has been used for hyperthermia, muscle rigidity and rhabdomyolysis.

MARIJUANA

Marijuana and other cannabinoids may produce some medical comorbidity (Weil, 1970). The effects of smoking may produce pulmonary toxicity, including a decrease in vital capacity and diffusing capacity. Marijuana may be contaminated with aspergillus species, producing asthmatic symptoms, and the use of paraquat as a herbicide in the past has produced pulmonary toxicity in smokers (Landrigan, Powell & James, 1983). Older users may experience tachycardia and angina with use. There may be an increase in head and neck cancers in heavy users of cannabis (Donald, 1991). Many of the previously reported problems with gonadal dysfunction, immune suppression and long-term psychiatric problems were not supported by later studies.

Recently, marijuana has been shown to stimulate the mesolimbic dopaminergic reward circuit via opioid receptors (Tanda, Pontieri & Di Chiara, 1997). In addition, during acute pharmacologically induced marijuana withdrawal, corticotrophin releasing factor is increased greatly, a finding shown to be associated with craving in other drug withdrawal paradigms (Rodriguez de Fonseca, Carrera et al., 1997). Such neurophysiologic actions imply a greater addictive potential for marijuana than previously thought.

HALLUCINOGENS

Medical problems related to these drugs are unusual but do occur (Siegel, 1984). Lysergic acid diethylamide (LSD), mescaline, psilocin and psilocybin may produce significant tachycardia, which may be problematic in older users who have underlying cardiovascular disease. These drugs also raise the possibility of cerebrovascular constriction, with the possibility of TIA or CVA. Designer drugs, such as MDMA ("Ecstasy"), DMT and others, usually have self-limited toxicity, but there may be evidence of long-term neurological damage (Peroutka, 1987). The most significant problematic drug in this group is phencyclidine ("PCP" or "angel dust"), which is commonly associated with severe psychotic reactions, and also can cause hyperthermia, rhabdomyolysis, renal failure and intractable seizures. Severe hypertension and CVA have been reported (Peterson & Stillman, 1978). Toxicology studies are difficult to obtain for all of these drugs, except phencyclidine. Treatment is symptomatic. Use of acidification to hasten excretion of phencyclidine has been advocated (Aronow & Done, 1978), but there is little controlled evidence to support this approach and it probably is ineffective (Baldridge & Bessen, 1990); it may increase acute toxicity by increasing unbound phencyclidine in serum.

INHALANTS

Inhalants include organic solvents, anesthetic gases and nitrites. Toluene, contained in a number of products including glues, may produce serious neurotoxicity, including permanent cognitive dysfunction and neuropathy (Ron, 1986). Sniffing of volatile fluorocarbons used as propellants in aerosol cans may result in cardiac arrhythmias and sudden death. Other hydrocarbons (including those in paint thinner, degreasers, gasoline and butane) may produce pulmonary, hepatic, renal and hematologic toxicity (Barnes, 1979). Treatment is supportive. Anesthetic gases may result in asphyxiation and arrhythmias, and nitrous oxide has been reported to produce myelopathy and neuropathy with chronic use (Layzer, 1978). Amyl nitrate, isobutyl nitrate and others ("poppers"), which are used to enhance orgasm, may result in methemoglobinemia, producing oxygen desaturation in the presence of normal oxygen tension; cyanosis and dyspnea may be profound. The diagnosis should be suspected under circumstances of desaturation with a normal p02, which can be confirmed by measurement of methemoglobin; blood on filter paper may have a typical "chocolate" appearance. Treatment is with methylene blue (Wartenberg, 1990).

MISCELLANEOUS DRUGS

A wide variety of drugs may be taken for psychoactive effects, including antihistamines, anticholinergics, muscle relaxants, antidepressants and neuroleptics (Abramowicz, 1993). The major toxicity of anticholinergic drugs includes hyperthermia, delirium, and supraventricular tachycardias. Findings of confusion, mydriasis, flushed but dry skin, and fever should suggest the diagnosis. Treatment generally is supportive, but physostigmine may be helpful in cases where arrhythmias are problematic, or if seizures occur (Wartenberg, 1990). An older review of more exotic drugs of abuse by Efron, Holmstedt and Kline (1967) remains useful.

Anabolic steroid use has become widespread, particularly among high school, college and professional athletes (Ghaphery, 1995; Yesalis & Bahrke, 1995).

Cases of agitation, mania, violent behavior, suicidal ideation and personality changes are widely reported (Su, Pagliaro et al., 1993). Stunting of growth with premature virilization can occur, as can gynecomastia and early male-pattern balding. There have been case reports of myocardial infarction (McNutt, Ferenchik et al., 1988; Bowman, 1990) and cardiomyopathy and cerebrovascular accident (Mochivuki & Richter, 1988). Hepatic problems, including peliosis hepatitis and liver cancer, also may occur (Allen, 1985).

In cases where uncommon drugs of abuse are suspected, urine toxicology can be helpful, particularly if the pathologist is alerted to the drugs in question. Unusual presentations that do not fit known patterns of disease, or where the clinical course differs from that which is expected, should alert the physician to the possibility of intoxication with psychoactive drugs. In most cases, treatment requires only the removal of the offending agent and supportive care.

POLYDRUG ABUSE

In recent years it has become less common for individuals to use or abuse only one mood-altering drug (Kreek, 1987). Combinations of alcohol, cocaine and benzodiazepines are common, and users of opioids also may use cocaine, sedative-hypnotics and alcohol. Hallucinogens and inhalants are used in a variety of combinations; not uncommonly, the nature of the chemical involved is not known to the user or the physician. The possibility of sedation and respiratory depression is greater when combinations of CNS depressants are used. Alcohol and cocaine in combination may produce increased toxicity, with the formation of cocaethylene (Hearn, Rose et al., 1991). Combinations of stimulants and depressants (usually cocaine and heroin, or "speedballs") may increase the risk of seizures. Patients on methadone maintenance programs may develop significant problems with alcohol, benzodiazepines and cocaine. Marijuana sprinkled with powdered phencyclidine has been used for many years. The physician thus needs to be alert to new drugs and new combinations.

Drug-Drug Interactions. In addition to the additive, antagonistic or synergistic effects of psychoactive drugs, significant drug-drug interactions can occur (Wartenberg, 1994b). Alcohol, barbiturates, phenytoin and carbamazepine induce P450 enzyme subclasses that increase not only their own metabolism, but also that of a number of other drugs. Cimetidine and fluoxetine may decrease P450 activity, resulting in decreased metabolism of those drugs. Rifampin, used in the treatment of tuberculosis and gram-positive infections, can markedly increase the metabolism of methadone and sedative-hypnotic drugs, resulting in the abrupt appearance of a withdrawal syndrome in patients on stable doses of methadone, as well as barbiturates and benzodiazepines; it also may decrease serum concentration and efficacy of other drugs. Rifabutin, recently approved for treatment of other mycobacterial infections in HIV-infected patients, may produce the same enzyme induction, although not as dramatically. Non-prescription mood-altering drugs also can interact with prescribed psychotropic medications (Miller, 1991). Several excellent handbooks exist, and should be readily available to the clinician (Weibert & Norcross, 1988; Rizack & Hillman, 1993). Interactions also may involve certain foods with tobacco smoke; in fact, an increase in or cessation of smoking may have effects on other drug levels.

REFERENCES

Abramowicz M (1984). Phenylpropanolamine for weight reduction. *The Medical Letter on Drugs and Therapeutics* 26:55–56.

Abramowicz M (1933). Drugs that cause psychiatric symptoms. *The Medical Letter on Drugs and Therapeutics* 35:65–70.

AIDS and Chemical Dependency Committee, American Medical Society on Alcoholism and Other Drug Dependencies (1988). *Guidelines for Facilities Treating Chemical Dependency Patients at Risk for AIDS and HIV Infection, 2nd Ed.* New York, NY: American Medical Society on Alcoholism and Other Drug Dependencies.

Allen M (1985). Androgenic steroid effects on liver and red cells. *British Journal of Sports Medicine* 19:15–20.

Anastos K & Palleja S (1991). Caring for women at risk of HIV infection. *Journal of General Internal Medicine* 6(Suppl):S40–46.

Aronow R & Done AK (1978). Phencyclidine overdose: An emerging concept of management. *Journal of the American College of Emergency Physicians* 7:56–59.

Ayus JC, Krothapall RK & Arieff AI (1987). Treatment of symptomatic hyponatremia and its relation to brain damage: A prospective study. *The New England Journal of Medicine* 317:1190–1195.

Baldridge EB & Beeson HA (1990). Phencyclidine. *Emergency Medicine Clinics of North America* 8:541–550.

Barnes GE (1979). Solvent abuse: A review. *International Journal of the Addictions* 14:1–26.

Barnes PF, Le HQ & Davidson PT (1993). Tuberculosis in patients with HIV infection. *Medical Clinics of North America* 77:1369–1390.

Bartter T, Dascal A, Carrol K & Curley FJ (1988). "Toxic strep syndrome": A manifestation of group A streptococcal infection. *Archives of Internal Medicine* 140:1421–1424.

Bates JH & Stead WW (n.d.). The history of tuberculosis as a global epidemic. *Medical Clinics of North America* 77:1205–1217.

Battinelli DL & Peters ES (1992). Oral manifestations. In H Libman & R Witzburg (eds.) *HIV Infection: A Clinical Manual, 2nd Ed.* Boston, MA: Little, Brown and Co., 74–83.

Beck K (1991). Mycobacterial disease associated with HIV infection. *Journal of General Internal Medicine* 6(Suppl):S19–23.

Bianchini JR & McGhee B (1985). MPTP and parkinsonism. *Rational Drug Therapy* 19:5–7.

Biderman P & Hiatt JR (1983). Management of soft-tissue infections of the upper extremity in parenteral drug abusers. *American Journal of Surgery* 154:526–528.

Bikle DD, Genant HK, Cann CE, Recker KR, Halloran BP & Strewler GJ (1985). Bone disease and alcohol abuse. *Annals of Internal Medicine* 103:42–48.

Bikle D, Stesin A, Halloran B & Recker K (1993). Alcohol-induced bone disease: Relationship to age and parathyroid hormone levels. *Alcoholism: Clinical & Experimental Research* 17:690–695.

Blackley J & Knochel JP (1990). Fluid and electrolyte disorders associated with alcoholism and liver disease. In JP Kokko & RL Tannen (eds.) *Fluid and Electrolytes, 2nd Ed.* Philadelphia, PA: W.B. Saunders Co., 649–687.

Bowman S (1990). Anabolic steroids and infarction. *British Medical Journal* 300:750.

Butters N (1982). The Wernicke-Korsakoff syndrome. In *Alcohol and Health Monograph 2: Biomedical Processes and Consequences of Alcohol Use.* Washington, DC: U.S. Government Printing Office (ADM 82:1191), 257–287.

Carrithers RL, Herlong HF, Diehl AM, Shaw EW, Combes B, Fallon HJ & Maddray WC (1989). Methylprednisolone therapy in patients with severe alcoholic hepatitis: A randomized multicenter trial. *Annals of Internal Medicine* 110:685–690.

Centers for Disease Control (1991). Crack cocaine use among persons with tuberculosis: Contra Costa county. *Morbidity and Mortality Weekly Reports* 40:485–489.

Centers for Disease Control (1992). 1993 Revised classification system for infection and expanded surveillance case definition for AIDS among adolescents and adults. *Morbidity and Mortality Weekly Reports* 41(RR-17):1–19.

Centers for Disease Control (1993a). Recommendations for HIV testing services for inpatients and outpatients in acute care hospital settings, and technical guidance on HIV counseling. *Morbidity and Mortality Weekly Reports* 42(RR–2):1–17.

Centers for Disease Control (1993b). Sexually transmitted diseases treatment guidelines. *Morbidity and Mortality Weekly Reports* 42(RR-14):1–102.

Chambers HF, Morris L & Tauber MG (1987). Cocaine use and the risk of endocarditis in intravenous drug abusers. *Annals of Internal Medicine* 106:833–836.

Chandrasakar PH & Narula AP (1986). Bone and joint infections in intravenous drug abusers. *Review of Infectious Diseases* 8:904–911.

Cherubin CE (1971). Infectious disease problems of narcotics addicts. *Archives of Internal Medicine* 128:309–313.

Cherubin CE & Sapira JD (1993). The medical complications of drug addiction and the medical assessment of the intravenous drug user: 25 years later. *Annals of Internal Medicine* 119:1017–1028.

Cicero TJ (1981). Neuroendocrinological effects of alcohol. *Annual Review of Medicine* 32:123–142.

Conn HO (1993). Transjugular intrahepatic portal-systemic shunts: The state of the art. *Hepatology* 17:148–158.

Cooke CT & Dowling GP (1988). Test and teach number 57: Cocaine-associated coronary thrombosis and myocardia ischemia. *Pathology* 20:242, 305–306.

Criqui MH (1986). Alcohol consumption, blood pressure, lipids and cardiovascular mortality. *Alcoholism: Clinical & Experimental Research* 10:564–569.

Crossley TR & William R (1985). Spontaneous bacterial peritonitis. *Gut* 26:325–331.

Cunningham EE, Brentjens JR, Sielezny MA, Andres GA & Venuto RC (1980). Heroin nephropathy: A clinicopathologic and epidemiologic study. *American Journal of Medicine* 68:47–53.

Dans PE, Matricciani RM, Otter SE & Reuland DS (1990). Intravenous drug abuse and one academic medical center. *Journal of the American Medical Association* 263:3173–3176.

Davis BL (1982). The PCP epidemic: A critical review. *International Journal of the Addictions* 17:1137–1155.

Dawson A, Bigby BG, Poceta JS & Mitler MM (1997). Effect of bedtime alcohol on inspiratory resistance and respiratory drive in snoring and nonsnoring men. *Alcoholism: Clinical & Experimental Research* 21(2):183–90.

Dawson A, Lehr P, Bigby BA & Mitler M (1993). Effect of bedtime ethanol on total inspiratory resistance and respiratory drive in normal non-snoring men. *Alcoholism: Clinical & Experimental Research* 17:256–262.

DeGowin EL & DeGowin RL (1981). *Bedside Diagnostic Evaluation, 4th Ed.* New York, NY: Macmillan Publishing Co., 834–836.

De Marchi S, Cecchin E, Basile A, Bertotti A, Nardini R & Bartoli E (1993). Renal tubular dysfunction in chronic alcoholic abuse: Effects of abstinence. *The New England Journal of Medicine* 329:1927–1934.

DiBisceglie AM, Martin P, Kassianides C, Lisker-Melman M, Murray L, Waggoner J, Goodman Z, Banks S & Hoofnagle JH (1989). Recombinant interferon alfa therapy for chronic hepatitis C: A randomized, double-blind, placebo-controlled trial. *The New England Journal of Medicine* 321:1506–1510.

Donald P (1991). Advance malignancies in the young marijuana smoker. In H Friedman, S Specter & TW Klein (eds.) *Advances in Experimental Medicine and Biology: Drugs of Abuse, Immunity and Immunodeficiency, Vol. 288*. New York, NY: Plenum Press, 33–46.

Dowell ME, Ross PG, Musker DM, Cate TR & Baughn RE (1992). Response of latent syphilis or neurosyphilis to ceftriaxone therapy in persons infected with human immunodeficiency virus (HIV). *American Journal of Medicine* 93:481–488.

Dreyfus PM (1982). Nutritional disorders of the nervous system. In JB Wyngaarden & LH Smith (eds.) *Cecil's Textbook of Medicine, 16th Ed*. Philadelphia, PA: W.B. Saunders Co., 2045–2050.

Eckardt MJ, Harford TC, Kaelber CT, Parker ES, Rosenthal LS, Ryback RS, Salmoiraghi GC, Vendeveen E & Warren KR (1981). Health hazards associated with alcohol consumption. *Journal of the American Medical Association* 246:648–666.

Efron DH, Holmstedt B & Kline NS (1967). *Ethnopharmacologic Search for Psychoactive Drugs* (Public Health Service Pub. No. 1645). Washington, DC: U.S. Government Printing Office.

Farber HW, Fairman RP & Glauser FL (1982). Talc granulomatosis: Laboratory finding similar to Sarcoidosis. *American Review of Respiratory Diseases* 125:259–261.

Fingerhood MI, Jasinski DR & Sullivan JT (1993). Prevalence of hepatitis C in a chemically dependent population. *Archives of Internal Medicine* 153:2025–2030.

Ford M, Hoffman RS & Goldfrank LR (1990). Opioids and designer drugs. *Emergency Medical Clinics of North America* 8:495–511.

Frand MI, Shim CS & Williams MH (1972). Heroin induced pulmonary edema: Sequential studies of pulmonary function. *Annals of Internal Medicine* 77:29–35.

Freudenberger RS, Cappell MS & Hiott DA (1990). Intestinal infarction after intravenous cocaine administration. *Annals of Internal Medicine* 113:715–716.

Gary NE & Tresnewski O (1983). Clinical aspects of drug intoxication: barbiturates and a potpourri of other sedatives, hypnotics and tranquilizers. *Heart and Lung* 12:122–127.

Gawin FH & Ellinwood EH (1988). Cocaine and other stimulants: Actions, abuse and treatment. *The New England Journal of Medicine* 318:1173–1182.

Gaziano JM, Buring JE, Breslow JL, Goldhaber SZ, Rosner B, VanDenburgh M, Willet W & Hennekens CH (1993). Moderate alcohol intake, increased levels of high density lipoprotein and its subfractions, and decreased risk of myocardial infarction. *The New England Journal of Medicine* 329:1829–1834.

Geokas MC, Lieber CS, French S & Halstead CH (1981). Ethanol, the liver and gastrointestinal tract. *Annals of Internal Medicine* 95:198–211.

Ghaphery NA (1995). Performance-enhancing drugs. *Orthopedic Clinics of North America* 26(3):433–42.

Gill JS, Shipley MJ, Tsementzis SA, Hornby RS, Gill SK, Hitchcock ER & Beevers DG (1991). Alcohol consumption: Risk factor for hemorrhagic and non-hemorrhagic stroke. *American Journal of Medicine* 90:489–497.

Gitlow S, Dziedsic L & Dziedsic S (1986). Alcohol and hypertension: Implications from research for clinical practice. *Journal of Substance Abuse Treatment* 3:121–129.

Greden JF (1981). Caffeinism and caffeine withdrawal. In JH Lowinson & P Ruiz (eds.) *Substance Abuse: Clinical Problems and Perspectives*. Baltimore, MD: Williams & Wilkins, 274–286.

Greenblatt DJ, Shader RI & Abernethy DR (1983). Current status of benzodiazepines. *The New England Journal of Medicine* 399:354–358, 410–416.

Greenspon AJ & Schaal SF (1983). The "holiday heart": Electrophysiologic studies of alcohol effects in alcoholics. *Annals of Internal Medicine* 98:135–139.

Guram M, Harden CW & Holt S (1991). Further evidence for an interaction between alcohol and certain H-2 receptor antagonists. *Alcoholism: Clinical & Experimental Research* 15:1084–1085.

Hackett TP (1987). Alcoholism: acute and chronic states. In TP Hackett & NH Cassem (eds.) *Massachusetts*

General Hospital Handbook of General Hospital Psychiatry, 2nd Ed. Littleton, MA: PSG Publishing, 419–437.

Hearn WL, Rose S, Wagner J, Ciarleglio A & Mash DC (1991). Cocaethylene is more potent than cocaine in moderating lethality. *Pharmacology, Biochemistry and Behavior* 39:531–533.

Hein HO, Suadicani P & Gyntelberg F (1996). Alcohol consumption, serum low density lipoprotein cholesterol concentration, and risk of ischaemic heart disease: Six year follow up in the Copenhagen male study [published erratum appears in BMJ 1996 April 20;312(7037):1007]. *British Medical Journal* 312(7033):736–41.

Henning RJ & Wilson LD (1996). Cocaethylene is as cardiotoxic as cocaine but is less toxic than cocaine plus ethanol. *Life Sciences* 59(8):615–27.

Herbert V (1980). Hematologic complications of alcoholism. *Seminars on Hematology* 17:83–164.

Hoffman CK & Goodman PC (1989). Pulmonary edema in cocaine smokers. *Radiology* 172:463–465.

Holton PD, Larrsen RA, Leal ME & Leedon JM (1992). Prevalence of neurosyphilis in HIV-infected patients with latent syphilis. *American Journal of Medicine* 93:9–12.

Hook EW (1993). Management of syphilis in human immunodeficiency. *American Journal of Medicine* 93:477–479.

Houston MC & Hodge R (1988). Beta-adrenergic blocker withdrawal syndromes in hypertension and other cardiovascular disease. *American Heart Journal* 116:515–523.

Huemer HP, Prodinger WM, Larcher C, Most J & Dierich MP (1990). Correlation of hepatitis C virus antibodies with HIV seropositivity in intravenous drug addicts. *Infection* 18:122–123.

Hultberg B, Berglund M, Andersson A & Frank A (1993). Elevated plasma homocysteine in alcoholics. *Alcoholism: Clinical & Experimental Research* 17:687–689.

Hultberg B, Isaksson A, Berglund M & Moberg A (1993). Serum B-hexosaminidase isoenzyme: a sensitive marker for alcohol abuse. *Alcoholism: Clinical & Experimental Research* 15:549–552.

Hunyor SN, Hansson L, Harrison TS & Hoobler SW (1973). Effects of clonidine withdrawal: Possible mechanisms and suggestions for management. *British Medical Journal* 2:209–211.

Israel Y, Orrego H, Holt S, Macdonald DW & Meema HE (1980). Identification of alcohol abuse: Thoracic fractures on routine chest x-rays as indicators of alcoholism. *Alcoholism (NY)* 4:420–422.

Kaku DA & Lowenstein DH (1990). Emergence of recreational drug use as a major risk factor for stroke in young adults. *Annals of Internal Medicine* 113:821–827.

Kaplan MH, Hall WW, Susin M, Pahwa S, Salahuddin SZ & Hellman C (1991). Syndrome of severe skin disease, eosinophilia and dermatopathic lymphadenopathy in patients with HTLV-II complicating HIV infection. *American Journal of Medicine* 91:300–309.

Karan LD (1990). Primary care for AIDS and chemical dependency. *Western Journal of Medicine* 152:538–542.

Kasser C, Kane G, Gillie E & Mayo-Smith M (1994). The role of phenytoin in the management of alcohol withdrawal syndrome. American Society of Addiction Medicine, Practice Parameters Sub-Committee. *Journal of Addictive Diseases.*

Kent JH (1993). The epidemiology of multidrug-resistant tuberculosis in the United States. *Medical Clinics of North America* 77:1391–1409.

Kershenovich D, Vargas F, Garcia-Tsao G, Tamayo RP, Gent M & Riskind M (1988). Colchicine in the treatment of cirrhosis of the liver. *The New England Journal of Medicine* 318:1709–1713.

Koob GF (1996). Drug addiction: The yin and yang of hedonic homeostasis. *Neuron* 16(5):893–6.

Korenman J, Baker B, Waggoner J, Everhart JE, Di Bisceglie AM & Hoofnagle JH (1991). Long-term remission of chronic hepatitis B after alpha interferon therapy. *Annals of Internal Medicine* 114:629–634.

Kraus MG, Gottlieb LD, Morwitz RI & Ansler M (1985). Randomized clinical trial of atenolol in patients with alcohol withdrawal. *The New England Journal of Medicine* 313:905–909.

Kreek MJ (1987). Multiple drug abuse patterns and medical consequences. In HY Meltzer (ed.) *Psychopharmacology: The Third Generation of Progress.* New York, NY: The Raven Press, 1543–1553.

Landrigan PJ, Powell RE & James LM (1983). Paraquat and marijuana: Epidemiologic risk assessment. *American Journal of Public Health* 73:784–788.

Lange RA, Cigarroa RG, Flores ED, McBride W, Kim AS, Wells BJ, Bedotto JB, Danziger RS & Hillis LD (1990). Potentiation of cocaine-induced vasoconstriction by beta-adrenergic blockade. *Annals of Internal Medicine* 112:897–903.

Langston JW, Ballard P, Tetrud JW & Irwin I (1983). Chronic parkinsonism in humans due to a product of meperidine analog synthesis. *Science* 211:979–980.

Layzer RB (1978). Myeloneuropathy after prolonged exposure to nitrous oxide. *Lancet* 2:1277–1230.

Lee H, Swanson P, Shorty VS, Zack JA, Rosenblatt JD & Chen IS (1989). High rate of HTLV-II infection in seropositive i.v. drug abusers in New Orleans. *Science* 244:471–475.

Lee HH, Weiss SH, Brown LS, Mildvan D, Shorty V & Saravolatz L (1990). Patterns of HIV-1 and HTLV-I/II in intravenous drug abusers from the Middle Atlantic and central regions of the USA. *Journal of Infectious Diseases* 162:347–352.

Leen CL & Brettle RP (1991). Fungal infections in drug users. *Journal of Antimicrobial Chemotherapy* 28:83–96.

Lenehan GP, Gastfriend DR & Stetler C (1985). Use of haloperidol in the management of agitated or violent, alcohol-intoxicated patients in the emergency department: A pilot study. *Journal of Emergency Nursing* 11:72–79.

Lentner AL, Giger O & O'Rourke E (1990). Group A beta hemolytic streptococcal bacteremia and intravenous substance abuse: a growing clinical problem? *Archives of Internal Medicine* 150:89–93.

Lester R & Van Thiel DH (1977). Gonadal function in chronic alcoholism. *Advances in Experimental Medicine and Biology* 85:399–417.

Levine DG, Schwartz GR & Ungar JR (1986). Drug abuse. In GR Schwartz, P Safar, JG Stone PB Storey & DK Wagner (eds.) *Principles of Emergency Medicine.* Philadelphia, PA: W.B. Saunders Co., 1744–1757.

Levine DP (1991). Infectious endocarditis in intravenous drug users. In DP Levine & JD Sobel (eds.) *Infections in Intravenous Drug Abusers.* New York, NY: Oxford University Press, 231–185.

Levine DP & Sobel JD (1991). *Infections in Intravenous Drug Abusers.* New York, NY: Oxford University Press.

Lieber CS (1997). Gastric ethanol metabolism and gastritis: Interactions with other drugs, *Helicobacter pylori,* and antibiotic therapy (1957–1997)—A review. *Alcoholism: Clinical & Experimental Research* 21(8):1360–1366.

Lieber CS (1988). The influence of alcohol on nutritional status. *Nutrition Reviews* 46:241–254.

Litovitz T (1987). Sedatives and opiates. In ML Callahan (ed.) *Current Therapy in Emergency Medicine.* Philadelphia, PA: B.C. Decker, 962–965.

Louria D, Hensle T & Rose J (1967). The major medical complications of heroin addiction. *Annals of Internal Medicine* 67:1–22.

Magura S, Shapiro JL, Grossman J, Siddiqui Q, Lipton DS, Amann KR, Koger J & Gehan K (1990). Reactions of methadone patients to HIV antibody testing. *Advances in Alcohol and Substance Abuse* 8:97–111.

Marantz PR, Linzer M, Feiner C, Feinstein SA, Kozin AM & Friedland GH (1987). Inability to predict diagnosis in febrile intravenous drug abusers. *Annals of Internal Medicine* 106:823–828.

Martin WR, Sloan JW, Sapira JD & Jasinski DR (1971). Physiologic, subjective and behavioral effects of amphetamine, methamphetamine, ephedrine, phenmetrazine and methylphenidate in man. *Clinical Pharmacology and Therapeutics* 12:245–258.

Marzuk PM, Tierney H & Tardiff K (1988). Increased risk of suicide in persons with AIDS. *Journal of the American Medical Association* 259:1333–1337.

McNutt RA, Ferenchik GF, Kirlin PC & Hamlon NJ (1988). Acute myocardial infarction in a 22 year-old, world-class weightlifter using anabolic steroids. *American Journal of Cardiology* 62:164.

Menchel S, Cohen D, Gross E, Fragione B & Gallo G (1983). AA protein-related amyloidosis in drug addicts. *American Journal of Pathology* 112:195–199.

Miller A, Taub H, Spinak A, Pilipski M & Brown LK (1991). Lung function in former intravenous drug abusers: the effect of ubiquitous cigarette smoking. *American Journal of Medicine* 90:678–684.

Miller NS (1991). The pharmacology of interactions between medical and psychiatric drugs. In NS Miller (ed.) *The Pharmacology of Alcohol and Drugs of Abuse and Addiction.* New York, NY: Springer Verlag, 279–289.

Minor RL, Scott BD, Brown DD & Winniford MD (1991). Cocaine induced myocardial infarction in patients with normal coronary arteries. *Annals of Internal Medicine* 115:7970806.

Mochivuki RM & Richter KJ (1988). Cardiomyopathy and cerebrovascular accident associated with anabolic-androgenic steroid use. *Physicians and Sports Medicine* 16:109–114.

Mody CK, Miller BI, McIntyre HB, Cobb SK & Goldberg MA (1988). Neurological complications of cocaine abuse. *Neurology* 38:1189–1193.

Moss GB & Kreis JK (1990). The interrelationship between HIV infection and other sexually transmitted diseases. *Medical Clinics of North America* 74:1674–1660.

Mueller PD, Benowitz NL & Olson KR (1990). Cocaine. *Emergency Medical Clinics of North America* 8:665–681.

Novack DH (1987). Therapeutic aspects of the clinical encounter. *Journal of General Internal Medicine* 2:346–355.

O'Connor PG, Molde S, Henry S, Shockcor WT & Schottenfeld RJ (1993). Human immunodeficiency virus infection in intravenous drug users: A model for primary care. *American Journal of Medicine* 93:382–385.

Orrego H, Blake JE, Blendis LM, Comptom KJ & Israel Y (1987). Long-term treatment of alcoholic liver disease with propylthiouracil. *The New England Journal of Medicine* 317:1421–1427.

Ostrow DG (1986). Psychiatric consequences of AIDS: An overview. *International Journal of the Neurosciences* 29:1–3.

Panes J, Bordas JM, Pique JM, Garcua-Pagan JC, Fen F, Teres J, Bosch J & Rodes J (1993). Effects of propranolol on gastric mucosal perfusion in cirrhotic patients with portal hypertensive gastropathy. *Hepatology* 17:213–218.

Parker ES (1985). Cerebral functioning in social drinkers. In M Galanter (ed.) *Recent Developments in Alcoholism, Vol. 3.* New York, NY: Plenum Press, 203–206.

Parran TV & Jasinski DF (1991). Alcohol, cognitive dysfunction and brain damage. In *Alcohol and Health Monograph 2: Biomedical Processes and Consequences of Alcohol Use.* Washington, DC: U.S. Government Printing Office, 213–253.

Pascual-Leone A, Dhuna A, Altafullah I & Anderson DC (1990). Cocaine induced seizures. *Neurology* 40:404–407.

Pasta L (1988). Propranolol for prophylaxis of bleeding in cirrhotic patients with large varices: A multicenter, randomized clinical trial. *Hepatology* 8:1–5.

Pellinen P, Honkakoski P, Stenback F et al. (1994). Cocaine N- demethylation and the metabolism-related hepatotoxicity can be prevented by cytochrome P450 3A inhibitors. *European Journal of Pharmacology* 270(1):35–43.

Perkoff GT (1971). Alcoholic myopathy. *Annual Review of Medicine* 22:125–132.

Peroutka SJ (1987). Incidence of the recreational use of 3,4- methylenedioxymethamphetamine (Ecstacy) on an undergraduate campus. *The New England Journal of Medicine* 317:1542–1543.

Perrino LE, Warren GH & Levine JS (1987). Cocaine-induced hepatotoxicity in humans. *Gastroenterology* 93:176–180.

Perry S, Jacobsberg L & Fishman B (1990). Suicidal ideation and HIV testing. *Journal of the American Medical Association* 263:679–682.

Perry SW, Jacobsberg LB, Fishman B, Weiler PH, Gold JW & Francis AJ (1990). Psychological responses to serological testing for human immunodeficiency virus. *Acquired Immune Deficiency Syndrome* 4:145–152.

Peterson RC & Stillman RC (1978). *Phencyclidine: An Overview* (Research Monograph 21). Rockville, MD: National Institute on Drug Abuse, 1–17.

Pfefferbaum A, Lim KO, Desmond JE & Sullivan EV (1996). Thinning of the corpus callosum in older alcoholic men: A magnetic resonance imaging study. *Alcoholism: Clinical & Experimental Research* 20(4):752–7.

Pinto PC, Amerian J & Reynolds TB (1988). Large volume paracentesis in nonedematous patients with tense ascites: Its effect on intravascular volume. *Hepatology* 8:207–210.

Potter JF & Beavers DG (1984). Pressor effect of alcohol in hypertension. *Lancet* 1:119–122.

Quinn TC, Groseclose SL, Spence M, Provost O & Hook EW 3rd (1992). Evaluation of the human immunodeficiency virus epidemic among patients attending sexually transmitted disease clinics: A decade of experience. *Journal of Infectious Diseases* 165:541–544.

Radin DR (1992). Cocaine-induced hepatic necrosis: CT demonstration. *Journal of Computer Assisted Tomography* 16(1):155–6.

Regan TJ (1990). Alcohol and the cardiovascular system. *Journal of the American Medical Association* 264:377–381.

Reich P (1993). The anticoagulant quandary. *Medical Malpractice Prevention* 7:13–15.

Reichman LB, Felton CP & Edsall JR (1979). Drug dependence: A possible new risk factor for tuberculosis disease. *Archives of Internal Medicine* 139:37–339.

Rezkalla S & Kloner RA (1992). Cocaine and vascular thrombosis. *Cardiovascular Reviews and Reports* (December):54–57.

Risak MA & Hillman CDM (1993). *The Medical Letter Handbook of Adverse Drug Interactions*. New Rochelle, NY: Medical Letter.

Rodriguez de Fonseca F, Carrera MRA, Navarro M, Koob GF & Weiss F (1997). Activation of corticotropin-releasing factor in the limbic system during cannabinoid withdrawal. *Science* 276(5321):2050–4.

Ron A (1986). Volatile substance abuse: A review of possible, long-term neurological, intellectual and psychiatric sequelae. *British Journal of Psychiatry* 24:235–246.

Roth D, Alarcon FJ, Fernandez JA, Preston RA & Bourgoignee JJ (1988). Acute rhabdomyolysis associated with cocaine intoxication. *The New England Journal of Medicine* 319:673–677.

Rubin AM (1987). Neurological complications of intravenous drug abuse. *Hospital Practice* (15 April):279–288.

Rummans TA, David LJ Jr, Morse RM & Ivnik RJ (1993). Learning and memory impairment in older, detoxified, benzodiazepine-dependent patients. *Mayo Clinic Proceedings* 68:731–737.

Salanova V & Taubner R (1984). Intracerebral hemorrhage and vasculitis secondary to amphetamine use. *Postgraduate Medical Journal* 60:429–430.

Samet JH, Libman H, Stegler KA, Dhawan RK, Chen J, Shevitz AH, Dewees-Dunk R, Levinson S, Kufe D & Craven D (1992). Compliance with zidovudine therapy in patients infected with HIV type 1: A cross-sectional study in a municipal hospital clinic. *American Journal of Medicine* 92:495–502.

Samet JH, Shevitz A, Fowle J & Singer DE (1990). Hospitalization decision in febrile intravenous drug users. *American Journal of Medicine* 89:53–57.

Satel SL & Gawin FH (1989). Migraine-like headache and cocaine use. *Journal of the American Medical Association* 261:2995–2996.

Seeff LB, Cucherini JJ & Zimmerman JJ (1986). Acetaminophen hepatotoxicity in alcoholics: a therapeutic misadventure. *Annals of Internal Medicine* 104:399–404.

Seitz HK (1985). Ethanol and carcinogenesis. In HK Seitz & B Kommerell (eds.) *Alcohol-Related Diseases in Gastroenterology*. New York, NY: Springer verlag, 196–212.

Selwyn PA, Feingold AR, Iessa A, Satyadeo M, Colley J, Torres R & Shaw JFM (1989). *Annals of Internal Medicine* 111:761–763.

Selwyn PA & O'Connor PG (1992). Diagnosis and treatment of substance abusers with HIV infection. *Primary Care* 19:119–156.

Selwyn PA, Schell BM & Alcabes B (1992). High risk of active tuberculosis in HIV-infected drug users with cutaneous anergy. *Journal of the American Medical Association* 268:504–509.

Siegel RK (1984). The natural history of hallucinogens. In BL Jacobs (ed.) *Hallucinogens: Neurochemical, Behavioral and Clinical Perspectives*. New York, NY: The Raven Press, 1–18.

Small PM, Scheckter GF, Goodman PC, Sande MA, Chaisson RE & Hopewell PC (1991). Treatment of tuberculosis in patients with advanced human immunodeficiency virus infection. *The New England Journal of Medicine* 324:289–294.

Snider PE & Caras GJ (1992). Isoniazid-associated hepatitis deaths: A review of available information. *American Review of Respiratory Diseases* 145:494–497.

Stearns RH, Riggs JE & Schochet SS Jr (1986). Osmotic demyelination syndrome following correction of hyponatremia. *The New England Journal of Medicine* 314:1535–1542.

Stein MD (1990). Clinical review: Medical complications of intravenous drug use. *Journal of General Internal Medicine* 5:249–257.

Stibler H & Hultcrantz R (1987). Carbohydrate-deficient transferrin in serum of patients with liver diseases. *Alcoholism: Clinical & Experimental Research* 11:468–473.

Stockham TL & Blanke RV (1988). Investigation of an acetaldehyde-hemoglobin adduct in alcoholics. *Alcoholism: Clinical & Experimental Research* 12:748–754.

Su TP, Pagliaro M, Schmidt PJ, Pichar D, Wolkowitz O & Rubinow DR (1993). Neuropsychiatric effects of anabolic steroids in male normal volunteers. *Journal of the American Medical Association* 269:2760–2764.

Sullivan JT & Sellers EM (1986). Treating alcohol, barbiturate and benzodiazepine withdrawal. *Rational Drug Therapy* 20:1–9.

Taasan VC, Block AJ, Boyden PG & Wynne JW (1981). Alcohol increases sleep apnea and oxygen desaturation in asymptomatic men. *American Journal of Medicine* 71:240–245.

Takase S, Tsutsumi M, Kawahara H, Takada N & Takada A (1993). The alcohol-altered liver membrane antibody and hepatitis C virus infection in the progression of alcoholic liver disease. *Hepatology* 17:9–13.

Tanda G, Pontieri FE & Di Chiara G (1997). Cannabinoid and heroin activation of mesolimbic dopamine transmission by a common mu1 opioid receptor mechanism. *Science* 276(5321):2048–50.

Temey R & McLain G (1990). The use of anabolic steroids in high school students. *American Journal of Diseases of Children* 144:99–103.

Terblanche J, Burroughs AK & Hobbs KEF (1989). Controversies in the management of bleeding esophageal varices. *The New England Journal of Medicine* 320:1393–1398.

Tuyns AJ (1977). *Alcohol and Cancer* (Monograph No. HSM-42-73-116). Rockville, MD: National Institute on Drug Abuse.

Uppal R, Lateef SK, Korsten MA, Paronetto F & Lieber CS (1991). Chronic alcoholic gastritis: Roles of alcohol and Helicobacter pylori. *Archives of Internal Medicine* 151:760–764.

Van Thiel DH (1983). Ethanol: Its adverse effects upon the hypothalamic-pituitary-gonadal axis. *Journal of Laboratory and Clinical Medicine* 101:21–33.

Van Thiel DH, Lipsitz HD, Porter KE, Schade RR, Gottlieb GP & Graham TO (1981). Gastrointestinal and hepatic manifestations of chronic alcoholism. *Gastroenterology* 81:594–615.

Victor M, Adams RD & Collins GH (1989). *The Wernicke-Korsakoff Syndrome and Other Disorders Due to Alcoholism and Malnutrition, 2nd Ed.* Philadelphia, PA: Davis Press.

Wartenberg A (1987). The opiates and opiate abuse. In RE Harrington, GR Jacobson & DG Benzer (eds.) *Alcohol and Drug Abuse Handbook*. St. Louis, MO: Warren Green Inc., 19–53.

Wartenberg AA (1989). Detoxification of the chemically dependent patient. *Rhode Island Medical Journal* 42:451–456.

Wartenberg AA (1990). Clinical toxicology and substance abuse. In MS Kochar & K Kutty (eds.) *Concise Textbook of Medicine, 2nd Ed.* New York, NY: Elsevier Publishing Co., 135–160.

Wartenberg AA & Liepman MR (1990). Medical complications of substance abuse. In WD Lerner & MA Barr (eds.) *Handbook of Hospital-Based Substance Abuse Treatment*. New York, NY: Pergamon Press, 46–65.

Wartenberg AA (1994a). Into whatever houses I enter: HIV and injecting drug use (editorial). *Journal of the American Medical Association* 271.

Wartenberg AA (1994b). Drug-drug interactions. In NS Miller (ed.) *Pharmacological Therapies in Drug and Alcohol Disorders*. New York, NY: Marcel Dekker.

Wartenberg AA & Nirenberg TD (1994). Alcohol and other drug abuse in the elderly. In W Reichel (ed.) *Clinical Aspects of Aging, 4th Ed.* Baltimore, MD: Williams & Wilkins Co.

Wartenberg AA, Nirenberg TD & Clifford P (1994). Patient perceptions of adverse consequences to HIV antibody testing in the chemical dependency treatment setting: Risks of elopement, relapse, depression and suicidal ideation. *Journal of Substance Abuse*.

Watters JK, Estilo MJ, Clark GL & Lorvick J (1994). Syringe and needle exchange as HIV/AIDS prevention for injection drug users. *Journal of the American Medical Association* 271.

Weibert RT & Norcross WA (1988). *Drug Interactions Index, 2nd Ed.* Oradell, NJ: Medical Economics Books.

Weil A (1970). Adverse reactions to marijuana: Classification and suggested treatment. *The New England Journal of Medicine* 282:997–1000.

Weiner RS, Lockhart JR & Schwartz RG (1986). Dilated cardiomyopathy and cocaine abuse: Report of two cases. *American Journal of Medicine* 81:699–701.

Westermeyer J (1987). The psychiatrist and solvent-inhalant abuse: Recognition, assessment and treatment. *American Journal of Psychiatry* 144:903–907.

Williamson DJ & Young AH (1992). Psychiatric effects of androgenic and anabolic-androgenic steroid abuse in men: A brief review of the literature. *Journal of Psychopharmacology* 6:20–26.

Wright C, Moore RD, Grodin DM, Spyker DA & Gill EV (1993). Screening for disulfiram-induced liver test dysfunction in an inpatient alcoholism program. *Alcoholism: Clinical & Experimental Research* 17:184–186.

Wright C, Vatter J & Lake CR (1988). Disulfiram-induced fulminating hepatitis: guidelines for liver panel monitoring. *Journal of Clinical Psychiatry* 49:430–434.

Yesalis CE & Bahrke MS (1995). Anabolic-androgenic steroids. Current issues. *Sports Medicine* 19(5):326–40.

Young LS (1988). Mycobacterium avium complex infection. *Journal of Infectious Diseases* 157:863–867.

CHAPTER 7

HIV/AIDS, Tuberculosis, and Other Infectious Diseases

Harry W. Haverkos, M.D.

HIV/AIDS
Tuberculosis
Hepatitis Viruses

This chapter will review HIV/AIDS, tuberculosis, and hepatitis viruses in addicted persons. Infectious diseases are common among drug abusers (Cherubin & Sapira, 1993; Haverkos & Lange, 1990; Haverkos, 1991; O'Connor, Selwyn & Schottenfeld, 1993). Some—such as bone and joint infections, endocarditis, sepsis, soft tissue infections, and tetanus—occur when "dirty" or non-sterile paraphernalia or drugs are used for injection and/or the skin is not cleaned adequately before injection. Hepatitis B, C, and D virus infections, human immunodeficiency virus (HIV), HTLV-I and -II infections, and malaria occur when equipment is shared and infected blood of others is directly inoculated. Tuberculosis can be transmitted from person to person via aerial droplets. Chancroid, gonorrhea, HBV, HIV, and syphilis can result from unprotected sexual contact. Pneumonias of various etiologies also are common among drug users.

HIV/AIDS

As new treatments for HIV infection and better measures of viral load are developed, clinicians have more options than ever before to prevent and treat AIDS opportunistic illnesses and modify plasma HIV loads. Within the past few years: (1) combination antiretroviral therapies, including new classes of drugs, such as the protease inhibitors, have been developed and tested; (2) improved methods of viral load determination have been shown to have prognostic value; (3) improvements in opportunistic infection prophylaxis strategies and treatments now prolong disease-free states; (4) zidovudine for HIV-infected pregnant women has been shown to decrease vertical transmission; and (5) prophylaxis for needlestick injuries now decreases transmission in health care settings.

The nine antiretroviral agents approved by the Food and Drug Administration by January 1997 are listed in Table 1. Recent studies comparing combination antiretroviral therapy versus monotherapy have persuaded many clinicians to begin with combination therapy and change to other combinations of these agents when drug failure is documented and/or major adverse reactions develop. Combination therapy decreases HIV viral load in most patients and may delay viral drug resistance.

Many unanswered questions remain concerning currently available antiretroviral regimens. These include the optimal time to initiate therapy, the impact of combination therapy, the measurement of clinical improvement, the duration of therapeutic response, assurance of drug compliance, and the length of survival. Management of viral resistance remains a concern, as does cost. Who has legitimate access to these medications and who should pay for them are other perplexing issues.

Clinical Issues. Several new methods have been developed to directly measure HIV-1 nucleic acids in plasma (Mellors et al. 1995; Saag, Holodny et al., 1996). Plasma HIV-RNA is a reliable predictor of rapid progression to AIDS after HIV infection, independent of CD4 T-lymphocyte counts. Measurement of HIV-RNA should substantially improve prognostic accuracy in HIV disease, and antiretroviral agents that lower plasma viral load measurements may produce longer disease-free intervals and prolong survival (Mellors et al., 1995).

Important clinical advances have been made in the ability to predict, prevent, and treat many of the opportunistic infections seen among HIV-infected patients. In 1995, the U.S. Public Health Service and the Infectious Diseases Society of America published guidelines for the management of 17 opportunistic infections or groups of infections commonly

TABLE 1. Antiretroviral Therapies

Medication	Usual Adult Dose	Major Adverse Effects	Approximate Annual Cost
Zidovudine[b] [Retrovir®] (nickname: AZT)	200 mg t.i.d.	Anemia Headaches Nausea Myositis	$3,348.
Didanosine[b] [Videx®] (nickname: ddl)	200 mg b.i.d.	Pancreatitis Diarrhea Peripheral neuropathy	$2,136.
Zalcitabine[b] [Hivid®] (nickname: ddC)	0.75 mg t.i.d.	Peripheral neuropathy Pancreatitis Oral ulcers	$2,484.
Stavudine[b] [Zerit®] (nickname: d4T)	40 mg b.i.d.	Peripheral neuropathy	$4,992.
Lamivudine[b] [Epivir®] (nickname: 3TC)	150 mg b.i.d.	Nausea Headache	$2,688.
Nevirapine[c] [Viramune®]	200 mg b.i.d.	Rash Diarrhea Drug fever	$5,944.
Saquinavir[d] [Invirase®]	600 mg t.i.d.	Gastrointestinal disturbances	$6,864.
Indinavir[d] [Crixian®]	800 mg t.i.d.	Hyperbilirubinemia Nephrolithiasis	$5,940.
Ritonavir[d] [Norvir®]	600 mg b.i.d.	Gastrointestinal disturbance Perioral parasthesias	$8,016.

a. Estimated cost to the pharamacist for a 360-day supply, based on the average wholesale price in the Red Book, Montvale, NJ: Medical Economics Data, 1996.
b. Mechanism of action: Reverse transcriptase inhibitor, nucleoside analog.
c. Mecahnism of action: Reverse transcriptase inhibitor, non-nucleoside analog.
d. Mechanism of action: Protease inhibitor.

seen in AIDS. The recommendations cover prevention of exposure, prevention of first episode of the disease, and treatment of infections and relapses (Kaplan, Masur et al., 1995). These guidelines are intended for primary care providers and specialists who care for HIV-infected adults, adolescents, and children.

In November 1994, Connor and colleagues reported that the administration of zidovudine to previously untreated HIV-infected pregnant women and their newborns reduced the rate of perinatal HIV transmission by two-thirds, from one in four infected children in the placebo arm to one in 12 in the treatment group (Connor, Sperling et al., 1994). Subsequently, the U.S. Public Health Service recommended that all pregnant women be offered HIV testing and counseling. The regimen to reduce perinatal HIV transmission includes antepartum zidovudine (100 mg orally five times a day, begun after 14 weeks' gestation), intrapartum zidovudine (two mg per kilogram of body weight given intravenously over a one-hour period, then one mg per kilogram per hour until delivery) and zidovudine for the newborn (two mg per kilogram orally every six hours for six weeks, begun within 48 hours of delivery). The use of combination antiretroviral agents, including protease inhibitors, for HIV-pregnant women is under study (Connor, Sperling et al., 1994; Carmichael, 1996).

A retrospective analysis of occupational HIV exposures suggests that prophylactic zidovudine post-exposure may reduce the risk of HIV transmission to health care workers. This information prompted the U.S. Public Health Service to modify its recommendation for chemoprophylaxis after occupational exposure to HIV. For example, combination therapy with zidovudine, lamivudine, and indinavir is recommended for all percutaneous exposures with both large volumes of blood (e.g., deep injury with a hollow needle previously in the source patient's vein or artery) and blood containing high levels of HIV (e.g., a source with acute retroviral illness or late-stage AIDS). Chemoprophylaxis should be started as soon as possible after exposure and administered for four weeks, if tolerated. Chemoprophylaxis is not usually advised if more than 72 hours have elapsed since exposure (CDC, 1996; Gerberding, 1995).

Epidemiology. The changed definition of AIDS from the Centers for Disease Control and Prevention (CDC) has created difficulties in monitoring recent trends in the epidemic (CDC, 1992). The number of AIDS cases reported in 1994 (80,691) and in 1995 (74,180) declined from the number reported in 1993 (106,618), which was significantly higher than the number reported in 1992 (45,572). Because the trends for recent years may be distorted, additional methods are needed to adjust for the case definition change.

One method to assess trends is to compare rates of AIDS across populations. The epidemic is dynamic and is shifting into the heterosexual community. Although gay men still account for the largest group of new patients, less than half of new cases in 1994 and 1995 occurred among men having sex with men. The proportion of new cases attributed to injection drug use increased from 23% in 1988 to 26% in 1995. The fastest growing subset of patients continues to be heterosexuals; this group increased from 5% of new AIDS patients in 1988 to 11% of new patients in 1995.

Another method to monitor trends is to estimate the epidemic curve that would have been seen had the definition not been expanded in 1993 to include persons with severe immunosuppression; e.g., a low CD4 count. This is accomplished by using the natural history to estimate when persons with severe immunosuppression will go on to develop what used to be known as "full-blown AIDS." When this technique is employed, the incidence of AIDS-opportunistic infections is 58,200 in 1992, 59,300 in 1993, 61,200 in 1994, and 62,200 in 1995 (CDC, 1997b).

The estimated number of deaths among persons with AIDS has increased steadily to approximately 49,600 deaths in 1994. In 1995, approximately 24,900 deaths were reported in the first six months of the year, and 25,100 were reported in the last half of the year. In the first six months of 1996, approximately 22,000 deaths were reported (this represents a 13% decrease from the estimated number of deaths during the first six months of 1995). By risk/exposure category, deaths declined 18% among homosexual men and 6% for injection drug users, but increased 3% among AIDS patients who attributed their exposure to heterosexual contact. The CDC attributes the decline in AIDS deaths to both the leveling of the incidence of AIDS-opportunistic illness and improved survival among persons with AIDS as the result of improved medical care, including increased use of antiretroviral agents (CDC, 1997a).

Other CDC studies estimate the size and direction of the AIDS epidemic by monitoring HIV infection reports. Dr. Scott Holmberg (1996), CDC, reviewed more than 350 documents, several large data sets, and information from 220 public health personnel to estimate the prevalence and incidence of HIV in 96 large U.S. metropolitan areas. He estimated about 565,000 prevalent and 38,000 new HIV infections annually in these areas. Roughly half of all estimated incident infections are occurring among injection drug users, most of them in northeastern cities, Miami, and San Juan. He also estimated about 9,800 new infections annually among men who have sex with men, and 9,300 new infections among heterosexuals who do not inject drugs.

Karon and colleagues (1996) estimated the trends in HIV infection by back-calculation from AIDS surveillance data, seroprevalence studies of childbearing women, and the National Household Survey. They estimated that between 650,000 and 900,000 Americans were infected with HIV in 1992, and that the incidence of infection is increasing, although not rapidly. Approximately half of all infected persons were men who have sex with men, and another quarter were injecting drug users. The greatest relative increase was among African-Americans and Hispanics, women, and heterosexuals who did not inject drugs.

Among drug users, there are more and more reports of significant HIV infection rates among men and women who use "recreational drugs" by routes other than injection. Presumably these infections occur through sexual contact with an infected person and are potentiated by the disinhibiting effects of drugs on sexual behaviors. Studies by CDC and the National Institute on Drug Abuse (NIDA) have documented alarming HIV seroprevalence among "crack" users who have never injected an illegal drug (Ratner, 1993; Edlin, Irwin et al., 1994). Several studies also have identified a strong association of non-injectable drug use and HIV seroincidence among men who have sex with men in San Francisco, Seattle, and Chicago. Interestingly, no single drug of abuse was implicated across the studies, which included abusers of alcohol, amphetamines, cocaine, and nitrite inhalants (Harris, Thiede et al.,

1993; DiFrancisco, Ostrow & Chmiel, 1996; Stall, McKusick et al., 1996).

In summary, HIV infection and disease in the U.S. remains a serious public health problem, although it is increasing at a slower rate than during the 1980s. The HIV disease burden remains greatest among men who have sex with men and injecting drug abusers, and is growing most rapidly among minorities, women and heterosexuals, especially those who use "recreational drugs."

TUBERCULOSIS

Tuberculosis, which had decreased in the U.S. in every year since 1953 (approximately 84,000 cases), when reporting began, through 1985 (22,201 cases), began to increase in 1986 (22,575). The incidence continued to grow each year from 1986 to 1992 (26,673). From 1993 through 1996, the incidence has decreased; 24,361 tuberculosis patients were reported in 1994, 22,860 in 1995, and 21,327 in 1996 (CDC, 1997a).

There is much less optimism about controlling tuberculosis in the developing world, due to increases in active tuberculosis fostered by immunosuppression associated with the HIV pandemic and the already fragile public health infrastructure in many countries. In fact, the World Health Organization (1996) reported more deaths from tuberculosis in 1995 than in any year in history (nearly 3 million deaths).

Tuberculosis is a chronic bacterial infection caused by *Mycobacterium tuberculosis* spread from person to person via airborne particles. After a susceptible individual inhales the bacilli, the organism reaches the pulmonary alveoli and multiplies. Bacilli are ingested by macrophages and transported to regional lymph nodes. Most primary infections heal, although later reactivation may occur. Approximately 10% of individuals with TB infection develop active disease during their lifetime (about half of active cases develop disease within two years of infection). Progression to clinical disease is more common among debilitated and immunocompromised persons, including alcoholics and drug users. It is especially common among HIV-infected persons, in whom the risk of developing active tuberculosis may be as high as 10% per year without chemoprophylaxis (Selwyn, Hartel et al., 1989).

All drug users should be screened yearly for *M. tuberculosis* infection with a tuberculin skin test with purified protein derivative (PPD). All drug users infected with HIV or whose HIV status is unknown and whose PPD test reacts five or more millimeters of induration should receive isoniazid preventive therapy for 12 months, regardless of age. HIV-negative clients with skin tests 10 or more millimeters of induration should receive prophylaxis for six months, regardless of age (CDC, 1989). As of 1997, anergy testing with other antigens, i.e., mumps and Candida, is not recommended as a routine component of TB screening among HIV-infected persons (CDC, 1997b). Results from at least one U.S.-controlled trial of isoniazid in persons with anergy and HIV infection who were at high risk for tuberculosis did not support the use of isoniazid prophylaxis, unless patients had been exposed recently to active tuberculosis (Gordin, Matts et al. 1997).

Drug abuse treatment programs are ideal sites to observe prophylactic isoniazid therapy, which is given orally 300 mg daily. All patients with clinically active TB require hospitalization (including respiratory isolation for pulmonary disease) and therapy with multiple antibacterial agents. Active TB can be assessed with chest x-ray and cultures of various body fluids (such as sputum, blood, urine, and gastric aspirates) for the organism.

All isolates of *M. tuberculosis* should be evaluated by antibiotic sensitivity testing. An initial four-drug regimen (isoniazid, rifampin, pyrazinamide, and ethambutol or streptomycin) is recommended before sensitivity results are available. Compliance with self-administered therapy is poor in many populations and represents the major reason for emergence of antibiotic-resistant TB. Ideally, all patients should receive directly observed therapy that includes patient incentives and the potential for enforcement of therapy (Barnes & Barrows, 1993).

A methadone-rifampin interaction exists. Rifampin lowers plasma methadone levels as a result of hepatic microsomal metabolic activity. Methadone doses may need to be increased during rifampin therapy to avoid narcotic withdrawal symptoms (Kreek, Gutjahr et al., 1976).

HEPATITIS VIRUSES

Hepatitis viruses cause hepatic necrosis and hepatic inflammation. They are designated as hepatitis viruses because there is little evidence to suggest that they infect other organ systems to a major extent. Other viruses (such as adenoviruses, coxsackie B viruses, cytomegalovirus, Epstein-Barr virus, herpes simplex virus, measles, rubella, rubeola, and varicella-zoster virus) can secondarily affect the liver and induce a hepatitis-like syndrome. Several non-viral and non-infectious causes of hepatitis-like syndromes exist; these include alcohol abuse, amebiasis, syphilis, and vinyl chloride toxicity.

Five human hepatitis viruses (designated A, B, C, D, and E) have been identified and characterized (see Table 1). Two other viruses have been identified (designated F and G), but there is no consensus among investigators that these viruses are pathogenic in humans.

The CDC conducts extensive studies of hepatitis viruses in four counties in the United States (Jefferson County, Alabama; Denver County, Colorado; Pinellas County, Florida; and Pierce County, Washington). Of the cases of acute hepatitis reported in the U.S., HAV accounts for 32%, HBV 43%, HCV 21%, and HDV (and HBV) 2%; HEV is very rare. An additional 4% of acute hepatitis cases may be due to other viral agents or agents not yet identified. Chronic cases of viral hepatitis are caused by HBV, HCV, and HDV/HBV (Alter & Mast, 1994).

Injection drug users are at high risk for infection with several of the hepatitis viruses. In one study of 389 intravenous heroin addicts in California, 41% were positive with antibodies to HAV, 73% to HBV, 94% to HCV, and 10% to HDV (Tenant & Moll, 1995). In another study of 716 injecting drug users in Baltimore, 66% had antibodies to HBV and 77% to HCV. Among 216 participants who had injected for one year or less, 50% had antibodies to HBV and 65% to HCV (Garfein, Vlahov et al., 1996).

The management of viral hepatitis generally consists of supportive care, including rest, vitamins, especially vitamin K, avoidance of hepatotoxic drugs, and monitoring for complications. Prophylactic and therapeutic regimens for specific hepatitis virus infections are described below. Corticosteroids are *not* indicated for viral hepatitis. In addition to alcohol, medications associated with chronic hepatitis and cirrhosis include acetaminophen, aspirin, chlorpromazine, halothane, isoniazid, methyldopa, nitrofurantoin, propylthiouracil, pyrazinamide, rifampin, and sulfonamides. Complications of viral hepatitis include cerebral edema, coagulopathy, electrolyte abnormalities, hepatic insufficiency, hepatocellular carcinoma (HBV, HCV), GI bleeding, hypoglycemia, pancreatitis, peritonitis, pulmonary edema, renal failure and sepsis.

Chronic hepatitis is defined as the presence of liver inflammation that persists for at least six months. Cirrhosis and hepatocellular carcinoma may complicate chronic hepatitis with HBV and HCV infections. Hepatitis type-specific interventions are listed below.

Hepatitis A Virus (HAV). HAV is an RNA virus of the picornavirus family and sometimes is referred to as enterovirus 72. The virus is present in feces (in high titers) and in saliva and serum (in lower titers) of infected patients and generally is transmitted by fecal-oral contact. Activities associated with transmission include child care, ingesting contaminated food or water, sexual activity (especially men having sex with men), and travel to certain high-risk areas. The incubation period is two to seven weeks, and patients are most infectious during the two weeks prior to and one week after onset of clinical disease. The diagnosis is made by serology.

Measures to prevent spread of HAV include careful attention to handwashing by patients and close contacts, serum immune globulin (IG) prophylaxis, and vaccination. A single dose of IG (0.02 milliliters per kilogram body weight) is recommended as soon as possible for close contacts (i.e., household members, sexual partners) of acutely infected patients. Hepatitis A vaccine is an inactivated vaccine, given in two doses, intramuscularly. Vaccination is recommended for drug abusers, children in communities with high rates of HAV infection, international travelers, men who have sex with men, patients with chronic liver disease, and persons with clotting factor disorders (Moyer, Warwick & Mahoney, 1996).

Hepatitis B Virus (HBV). HBV, a DNA virus of the hepadnavirus family, is present in high titers in blood and exudates (e.g., skin lesions) of acutely and chronically infected patients. Moderate levels of HBV are found in saliva, semen, and vaginal secretions. The three principal modes of transmission are through blood, sexual activity, and mother-to-infant. The incubation period is six weeks to six months. The diagnosis is made by serology. The complete viral agent consists of an outer protein envelope (which contains hepatitis B surface antigen [HBsAg]) surrounding the viral nucleocapsid, which contains several components, including hepatitis B core antigen (HbcAg).

Hepatitis B vaccination is universally recommended and is given in three doses at one and six months after the initial injection. Postexposure prophylaxis for HBV is recommended for perinatal, percutaneous, ocular, mucous membrane, and sexual contacts. Although dosages and timing vary somewhat by type of exposure, hepatitis B immune globulin (HBIG) and vaccination are recommended for susceptible persons. Therapy for chronic hepatitis B infections is available, but is expensive and not generally employed. Interferon alpha (10 million units subcutaneously three time a week for 16 weeks) decreases HBV replication (Wong, Yim et al., 1995; Perrillo, Schiffer et al., 1990). The antiretroviral medication Lamivudine® (3TC) is active against HBV replication in men infected with both HBV and HIV (Benhamou, Katlana et al., 1996). Fialuridine (FIAU) decreases HBV replication, but induces life-threatening side effects (McKenzie, Fried et al., 1995).

Hepatitis C Virus (HCV). HCV, an RNA virus of the flavivirus family, circulates in low titers in the blood of infected persons and is detected inconsistently in other body fluids. The most common mode of HCV transmission is through blood; mother-to-infant and sexual transmission are less frequent (Conry-Cantilena, Van Raden et al., 1996). The incubation period generally is six to seven weeks, but ranges from two weeks to six months. HCV is a major cause of acute and chronic hepatitis and cirrhosis worldwide. Virtually all persons with acute HCV infection become chronically infected, and at least 60% develop chronic liver disease.

Serologic tests for HCV infection are improving. HCV RNA can be detected by polymerase chain reaction (PCR) as early as two weeks after infection, but is labor-intensive, expensive, and not yet licensed in the U.S. Antibodies to HCV are detectable at five to six weeks after infection in 80% of patients, and by 12 weeks in 90%. However, no tests distinguish acute from chronic infections.

Because no protective antibody response develops following HCV infection, immune globulin products do not prevent infection and vaccine development may be difficult. Interferon alfa-2b is approved by the FDA for the treatment of HCV, but it does not eradicate the virus (Hoofnagle & Di-Bisceglie, 1997; Sharara, Hunt & Hamilton, 1996). Interferon alpha (3 million units subcutaneously three times a week for 12 to 18 months) is recommended. The challenge to the clinician for chronic HBV and HCV hepatitis is to decide when to intervene with interferon. Most clinicians would agree that those patients with progressive liver disease should be treated; there is no consensus on when to intervene for those with minimal disease.

Hepatitis D Virus (HDV). HDV is an incomplete (sometimes referred to as defective) RNA virus that requires the envelope coat of HBV, HBsAg, to enter cells and replicate. Therefore, HDV infection can only occur as a coinfection with HBV or as a superinfection of chronic HBV carriers. Persons with HBV-HDV coinfection generally have more severe acute disease and a higher rate of chronic hepatitis than those with HBV infection alone. The modes of HDV transmission are similar to those of HBV, with percutaneous exposures the most efficient. Prevention of HDV can be accomplished by preventing primary HBV infection with HBV vaccination, and by educating HBV carriers about risk behaviors for HDV infection (Alter & Mast, 1994).

Hepatitis E Virus (HEV). HEV is a non-enveloped RNA virus in the Calicivirus family. It occurs in large outbreaks in areas with extremely poor sanitary conditions, such as refugee camps in developing countries. Transmission is by the fecal-oral route, with fecally contaminated drinking water the most widely documented vehicle of transmission. All cases diagnosed in the U.S. have occurred among travelers returning from endemic developing countries. The incubation period ranges from 15 to 60 days (mean, 40 days). No evidence of chronic infection has been documented in long-term follow-up. No vaccine is available, nor is immune globulin protective (Alter & Mast, 1994).

Hepatitis F Virus (HFV) and Hepatitis G Virus (HGV). Additional viruses have been identified among patients with hepatitis-like syndromes, although not all investigators agree that they represent clinically significant entities. A new enterically transmitted virus, designated HFV, had been preliminarily identified by one group of investigators, but the isolation was not reproducible. Subsequently, two other teams described presumed hepatitis agents as HGV, which are RNA viruses of the flavivirus family, distantly related to HCV. The agent appears to be blood-borne, but it is not yet clear if it induces liver disease (Alter, 1996).

ACKNOWLEDGMENT: The author expresses appreciation to Dr. Annie Umbricht for reviewing the manuscript and providing constructive comments.

REFERENCES

Alter HJ (1996). The cloning and clinical implications of HGV and HGBV-C. *The New England Journal of Medicine* 334:1536–1537.

Alter MJ & Mast EE (1994). The epidemiology of viral hepatitis in the United States. *Gastroenterology Clinics of North America* 23:437–455.

Barnes PF & Barrows SA (1993). Tuberculosis in the 1990s. *Annals of Internal Medicine* 119:400–410.

Benhamou Y, Katlama C, Lunel F et al. (1996). Effects of lamivudine on replication of HBV in HIV-infected men. *Annals of Internal Medicine* 125:705–712.

Carpenter CCJ, Fischl MA, Hammer SM et al. (1996). Antiretroviral therapy for HIV infection in 1996: Recommendation of an international panel. *Journal of the American Medical Association* 276:146–154.

Carmichael C (1996). Preventing perinatal HIV transmission: Zidovudine use during pregnancy. *American Family Physician* 55:171–178.

Centers for Disease Control (1988). Hepatitis A among drug abusers. *Morbidity and Mortality Weekly Reports* 37:297–300, 305.

Centers for Disease Control (1989). Tuberculosis and HIV infection: A statement by the Advisory Committee for Elimination of Tuberculosis. *Morbidity and Mortality Weekly Reports* 38:236–250.

Centers for Disease Control and Prevention (1992). 1993 revised classification system for HIV infection and expanded surveillance case definition for AIDS among adolescents and adults. *Morbidity and Mortality Weekly Reports* 41(RR-17):1–19.

Centers for Disease Control and Prevention (1996). Update: Provisional Public Health Service recommendations for chemoprophylaxis after occupational exposure to HIV. *Morbidity and Mortality Weekly Report* 45:468–473.

Centers for Disease Control and Prevention (1997a). Update: Trends in AIDS incidence, deaths, and prevalence—United States, 1996. *Morbidity and Mortality Weekly Reports* 46:165–173.

Centers for Disease Control and Prevention (1997b). Anergy skin testing and preventive therapy for HIV-infected persons: Revised recommendations. *Morbidity and Mortality Weekly Reports* 46(RR15):1–8.

Cherubin CE & Sapira JD (1993). The medical complications of drug addiction and the medical assessment of the intravenous drug user: 25 years later. *Annals of Internal Medicine* 119:1017–1028.

Connor EM, Sperling RS, Gelber R et al. (1994). Reduction of maternal-infant transmission of HIV type 1 with zidovudine treatment. *The New England Journal of Medicine* 331:1173–1180.

Conry-Cantilena C, Van Raden M, Gibble J et al. (1996). Routes of infection, viremia, and liver disease in blood donors found to have HCV infection. *The New England Journal of Medicine* 334:1691–1696.

DiFrancisco M, Ostrow DG & Chmiel S (1996). Sexual adventurism, high-risk behavior, and human immunodeficiency virus-I seroconversion among the Chicago MACS-CCS cohort, 1984–1992. *Sexually Transmitted Disease* 23:453–460.

Edlin B, Irwin K, Faruque S et al. (1994). Intersecting epidemics: Crack cocaine use and HIV infection among inner-city young adults. *The New England Journal of Medicine* 331:1422–1427.

Garfein RS, Vlahov D, Galai N, Doherty MC & Nelson KE (1996). Viral infections in short-term injection drug users: The prevalence of the hepatitis C, hepatitis B, human immunodeficiency, and human T-lymphotropic viruses. *American Journal of Public Health* 86:655–61.

Gerberding JL (1995). Management of occupational exposures to blood-borne viruses. *The New England Journal of Medicine* 332:444–451.

Goldschmidt RH & Moy A (1996). Antiretroviral drug treatment for HIV/AIDS. *American Family Physician* 54:574–580.

Gordin FM, Matts JP, Miller C et al. (1997). A controlled trial of isoniazid in persons with anergy and human immunodeficiency virus infection who are at high risk for tuberculosis. *The New England Journal of Medicine* 337:315–320.

Harris NV, Thiede H, McGough JP & Gordon D (1993). Risk factors for HIV infection among injection drug users: Results of blinded surveys in drug treatment centers, King County, Washington 1988–1991. *Journal of AIDS* 6:1275–1282.

Haverkos HW (1991). Infectious diseases and drug abuse: Prevention and treatment in the drug abuse treatment system. *Journal of Substance Abuse Treatment* 8:269–275.

Haverkos HW & Lange WR (1990). Serious infections other than human immunodeficiency virus among intravenous drug abusers. *Journal of Infectious Diseases* 161:894–902.

Holmberg S (1996). The estimated prevalence and incidence of HIV in 96 large U.S. metropolitan areas. *American Journal of Public Health* 86:642–654.

Hoofnagle JH & DiBisceglie AM (1997). The treatment of chronic viral hepatitis. *The New England Journal of Medicine* 336:347–56.

Kaplan JE, Masur H, Holmes KK et al. (1995). USPHS/IDSA guidelines for the preventin of opportunistic infections in persons infected with human immunodeficiency virus. *Clinical Infectious Diseases* 21(Supplement 1).

Karon JM, Rosenberg PS, McQuillan G, Khare M, Gwinn M & Petersen LR (1996). Prevalence of HIV infection in the United States, 1984 to 1992. *Journal of the American Medical Association* 276:126–131.

Kreek MJ, Gutjahr CL, Garfield JW, Bowen DV & Field FH (1976). Drug interactions with methadone. *Annals of the New York Academy of Science* 281:350–371.

McKenzie R, Fried MW, Sallie R et al. (1995). Hepatic failure and lactic acidosis due to fialuridine, an investigational nucleoside analogue for chronic hepatitis B. *The New England Journal of Medicine* 333:1099–105.

Mellors JW et al. (1995). Quantitation of HIV-1 RNA in plasma predicts outcome after seroconversion. *Annals of Internal Medicine* 122:573–579.

Moyer L, Warwick M & Mahoney FJ (1996). Prevention of hepatitis A virus infection. *American Family Physician* 54:107–13.

O'Connor P, Selwyn PA & Schottenfeld RS (1993). Medical care for injection-drug users with human immunodeficiency virus infection. *The New England Journal of Medicine* 331:450–458.

Perrillo RP, Schiffer, Davis GL et al. (1990). A randomized trial of interferon alfa-2b alone and after prednisone withdrawal for the treatment of chronic hepatitis B. *The New England Journal of Medicine* 323:295–301.

Ratner MS, ed. (1993). *Crack Pipe as Pimp: An Ethnographic Investigation of Sex-for-Crack Exchanges*. New York, NY: Lexington Books.

Saag MS, Holodny M, Kuritzkes DR et al. (1996). HIV viral load markers in clinical practice. *Nature and Medicine* 2:625–629.

Selwyn PA, Hartel D, Lewis VA et al. (1989). A prospective study of the risk of tuberculosis among intravenous drug users with human immunodeficiency virus infection. *The New England Journal of Medicine* 320:545–550.

Sharara AI, Hunt CM & Hamilton JD (1996). Hepatitis C. *Annals of Internal Medicine* 125:658–668.

Stall R, McKusick, Wiley J, Coates TJ & Ostrow DG (1986). Alcohol and drug use during sexual activity and compliance with safe sex guidelines for AIDS: The AIDS behavioral research project. *Health Education Quarterly* 13:359–371.

Tenant F & Moll D (1995). Seroprevalence of hepatitis A, B, C, and D markers and liver function abnormalities in intravenous heroin addicts. *Journal of Addictive Diseases* 14:35–49.

Wong DK, Yim C, Naylor CD et al. (1995). Interferon alfa treatment of chronic hepatitis B: Randomized trial in a predominantly homosexual male population. *Gastroenterology* 108:165–171.

World Health Organization (1996). Groups at risk: WHO report on the tuberculosis epidemic. Geneva, Switzerland: Global Tuberculosis Programme, World Health Organization.

CHAPTER 8

Special Problems of the Elderly

James W. Smith, M.D., FASAM

Age-Related Differences in Alcohol Consumption
Age-Related Factors in Alcohol Metabolism
Alcohol-Related Physical Damage
Alcohol and Nutrition
Psychiatric Manifestations
Alcohol and Sleep
General Health Status

The effects of alcohol are, in general, very similar at any age. However, the physiologic concomitants of aging together with the physiologic concomitants of "heavy" alcohol intake lead to a number of age-related differences. These differences generally are in *degree* of organ injury (or other adverse consequence) rather than in type of injury, although there does appear to be more trauma in younger people, more medical illness in older people. In studying these differences, it is perhaps wise to start at the beginning, that is, with alcohol consumption itself. See Table 1 for a summary of selected literature.

AGE-RELATED DIFFERENCES IN ALCOHOL CONSUMPTION

A good deal of research has consistently found that alcohol consumption levels are lower and alcohol misuse less prevalent in persons in their sixties and older. There are, however, studies that cast doubt on these conclusions and point out that those studies were cross-sectional in nature and compared different age groups at one point in time. When longitudinal studies are done that follow individuals over a number of years, consumption patterns do not change much at all. They tend to remain remarkably stable as the person ages (Stall, 1968). These latter findings suggest that the cross-sectional differences in consumption in older persons may represent a cohort effect influenced by different cultural and historical experiences of each generation. (Stinson, Dufour & Bertolucci, 1987; NIAAA, 1988). Nevertheless, despite the relative stability of alcohol consumption over the years, whenever changes in consumption occurred, the direction was toward a decreased intake much more often than toward an increase (Glynn, Bouchard et al., 1984). Stall reported that approximately two-thirds of older male drinkers remained stable in quantity and frequency of alcohol intake over a period of 19 years. The one-third who changed consumption levels were more than twice as likely to decrease their consumption (Stall, 1968, 1986).

There may be socioeconomic explanations for these decreases (decreased income), or unrelated chronic health problems may preclude alcohol use. Nevertheless, there are age-related changes in physiology that may also play a significant role in decreasing alcohol intake. One well-known factor is the decrease in lean body mass with aging. Between age 20 and age 70, lean body mass decreases about 10% (Bienenfeld, 1987). Because of this the total body water content accounts for a smaller percent of body weight (DuFour, Archer & Gordis, 1992). Since alcohol is distributed only in the body water (not the fat), this means that each drink of alcohol results in a higher blood alcohol level in the same person when he/she is elderly than when a young adult. Therefore, without any other age-related effect accounted for, the elderly individual gets more intoxication per drink consumed.

AGE-RELATED FACTORS IN ALCOHOL METABOLISM

Another factor is an age-related decrease in the gastric alcohol dehydrogenase enzyme (ADH). This enzyme is responsible for the first step in the metabolism of alcohol. The majority of alcohol metabolism takes place in the liver. However, a significant amount of alcohol metabolism is also known to take place in the gastric mucosa with gastric ADH. With aging, gastric ADH levels decrease. It is also noted to be lower in females of all ages. In addition, certain medications such as H_2 blockers (e.g., Tagamet®, Zantac®, Axid®, and others) further decrease gastric ADH levels and are frequently taken by elderly patients. As a consequence, less alcohol is metabolized in the stomach, which contributes further to an increased blood alcohol level per unit of alcohol consumed (Lieber, 1988; Schuckit, 1982). This also increases the alcohol burden on the liver. The metabolism of alcohol in the liver is not significantly altered with aging (Scott, 1989; Schuckit & Miller, 1976). The liver enzymes responsible for this metabolism seem to be as efficient in the aged as in the young person (Scott, 1989). Despite this, as noted above, a given dose of alcohol imposes a greater metabolic burden on the liver of an older person than on that same person when young.

Once the alcohol is in the blood stream, it affects all tissues in the body. It has been shown that measurable physical damage is detectable in *every* system of the body. Fortunately, in most systems the damage is not fatal or even permanently disabling. In others, the damage is life threatening. Some reports indicate that over 90% of actively drinking older alcoholics presented with a major health problem (Schuckit & Miller, 1976; Schuckit & Pastor, 1979).

FIGURE 1. Some Consequences of Alcoholism

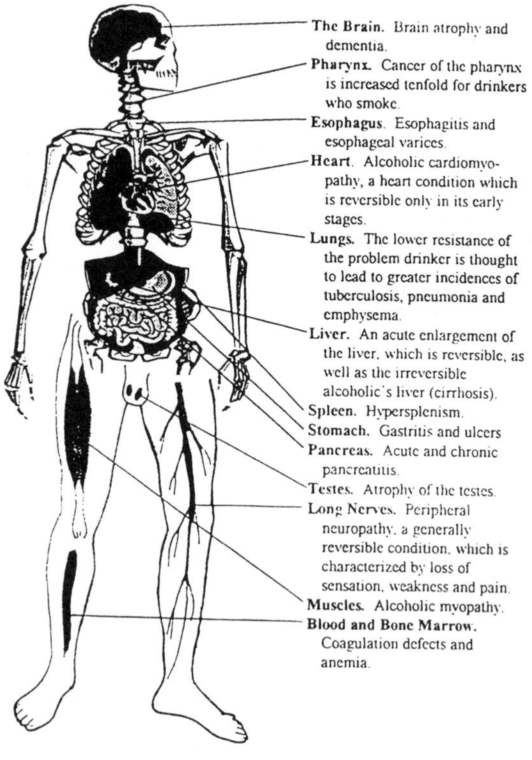

The Brain. Brain atrophy and dementia.
Pharynx. Cancer of the pharynx is increased tenfold for drinkers who smoke.
Esophagus. Esophagitis and esophageal varices.
Heart. Alcoholic cardiomyopathy, a heart condition which is reversible only in its early stages.
Lungs. The lower resistance of the problem drinker is thought to lead to greater incidences of tuberculosis, pneumonia and emphysema.
Liver. An acute enlargement of the liver, which is reversible, as well as the irreversible alcoholic's liver (cirrhosis).
Spleen. Hypersplenism.
Stomach. Gastritis and ulcers
Pancreas. Acute and chronic pancreatitis.
Testes. Atrophy of the testes.
Long Nerves. Peripheral neuropathy, a generally reversible condition, which is characterized by loss of sensation, weakness and pain.
Muscles. Alcoholic myopathy.
Blood and Bone Marrow. Coagulation defects and anemia.

ALCOHOL-RELATED PHYSICAL DAMAGE

(see Figure 1)

Skeletal System. Aging tends to be associated with a decrease in bone density (osteopenia) in both males and females. When extreme, it leads to an abnormal degree of rarefaction of bone (osteoporosis). Alcoholic drinking ("characterized by impaired control over drinking, preoccupation with the drug alcohol, use of alcohol despite adverse consequences" [Morse & Flavin, 1992]) accelerates this bone loss and may lead to compression fractures of vertebrae (Hodges, Kumar & Redford, 1986). The drinking also leads to poor mobility and a marked increase in falls (Ziring & Adler, 1991). The result is an increase in fractures. In the elderly population the fractures tend to heal more slowly than in the younger individual and tend to be associated with more complications (e.g., thromboembolism).

The head of the femur also has a rather tenuous blood supply, and even without injury, "heavy" alcohol intake can cause an interruption of circulation to the bone, resulting in aseptic necrosis of the head of the femur. This leads to deformity of the bone, fragmentation, osteoarthritis of the joint, and usually requires hip replacement surgery (Rosenkranz, 1983).

Bone Marrow and Blood. *Red Blood Cells:* Virtually no aspect of blood cell development, survival, or function escapes the toxicity of alcohol (Hillman, 1982). Interference with cell development may occur at the point of stem cell proliferation or during cell maturation. Cell survival in the circulation may be shortened because of intracellular abnormality or a change in the vascular environment.

In cases where inflammation of the liver (alcoholic hepatitis) or inflammation of the pancreas (pancreatitis) occur, the production of an essential hormone (erythropoietin) may be suppressed. This inflammatory suppression of erythropoietin leads to a lower than normal production of red blood cells leading to anemia ("hypoproliferative anemia"). A more common abnormality is a defect in red cell maturation. This leads to a progressive anemia with red blood cells that are larger than normal ("macrocytic anemia") (Beard & Knott, 1966; Eichner & Hillman, 1970). The vitamin, folic acid, appears to be a critical factor in the development of this macrocytic anemia. Folic acid is an essential vitamin for humans and is required whenever cells are actively dividing (as in the bone marrow). If the diet is severely restricted, deficiencies may occur. Elderly persons are often subject to poor nutrition. When alcoholism is added, food intake may be further reduced. Even when the diet is adequate, large amounts of alcohol interfere with absorption of the vitamin from the small intestine (Halsted, Griggs & Harris, 1967). An even more important toxic effect of alcohol involves disruption of the internal pathways of folic acid supply to marrow precursor cells and causes a dramatic drop in serum folic acid levels despite adequate supplies in the liver or diet (Hillman, McGuffin & Campbell, 1977; Eichner, Pierce & Hillman, 1973).

Even in the absence of bleeding, red cell survival is commonly reduced by alcohol ingestion. One factor is that abnormal red cells (e.g., macrocytes) have a shortened survival time in the circulation. Cell survival may also be influenced by changes in the vascular environment. Three hemolytic syndromes have been identified in alcoholics (acanthocytosis, acquired stomatocytosis [both characterized by distorted red cells] and Zieve's syndrome [a complication of alcoholic fatty liver]) (Hillman, 1973). Still another hazard to red cells is hypersplenism. With severe alcoholic cirrhosis, one concomitant may be an enlarged spleen which then traps and destroys more than the normal amount of red cells.

All of these factors lead toward anemia. When these are added to other factors that lead to anemia in the aging person, it is not surprising that significant anemia is a common finding in the elderly alcoholic (Heinz, Lorant & Stacher, 1983; An'ia, Suman et al., 1994).

White Blood Cells: Decreased levels of white blood cells (leukopenia) are frequently found in alcoholics (Eichner & Hillman, 1970). It has also been demonstrated that the granulocyte reserve available in the marrow to respond to infections is reduced in alcoholics. Not only are there fewer white cells to respond to infection, those that are present are not as effective. Alcohol reduces the ability of a granulocyte to move toward invading bacteria and engulf them (chemotoxis) (Crowley & Abramson, 1971; Brogton et al., 1970).

It is well known that pneumonia and other infectious diseases are increasing mortality risks for elderly persons. The alcohol-induced decrease in leukocyte numbers and effectiveness further increase this mortality risk.

Platelets: Decreased levels of blood platelets (thrombocytopenia) are a common laboratory finding in alcoholics (Cowan, 1969a, 1971). Older persons often take medications to inhibit the agglutination of platelets in order to prevent stroke, myocardial infarction, or other complications of inappropriate thrombus formation. It is unusual for the alcohol-induced thrombocytopenia to be severe enough (by itself) to induce bleeding. However, when these "antiplatelet" medications are added, bleeding complications become a much more real concern. Fortunately, the platelet count usually rapidly returns to normal (four to 10 days) once alcohol intake has stopped (Eichner & Hillman, 1970; Cowan, 1969a).

Immune System. The direct effect of alcohol on the immune system is difficult to determine with precision in alcoholics because of the presence of concurrent disorders in so many cases (e.g., liver disease, malnutrition). Nevertheless, numerous clinical studies have reported that alcoholics have an increased susceptibility to infection (Adams & Jordan, 1984; Andersen, 1975). Animal studies show an alcohol-related decrease in the response to infection (Colle, Foriestar et al., 1982; Bluckman, Dvorak et al., 1975). Likely factors involved in this deficient response to infection include:

- Decreased production of certain white blood cells (polymorphonuclear leukocytes [PMN]) in the bone marrow (fewer cells to fight invading organisms) (NIAAA, 1990).
- Defects in the movement toward infection (chemotoxis) (Rajkovic, Yousif-Kadara et al., 1984).
- Impaired ability of PMNs to adhere to cell surfaces (MacGregor, Spagnuolo & Lentnck, 1974; Brayton, Stolses et al., 1970) (an essential step in migration to the site of infection and ingestion of invading organisms).
- Lowered production of other white blood cells (lymphocytes) leading to deficiencies of "cell-mediated immunity" (believed to be responsible for the increased incidence of tuberculosis in alcoholics as well as an increase in virus-associated head and neck cancers) (Mutchnick & Lee, 1988; Smith & Palmer, 1976; Martinez, 1970).
- Impairment of the response of lymphocytes to infection or other activating substances. Certain lymphocytes (T-lymphocytes), which are important in fighting infection, are reduced in number in alcoholics with liver disease. The cells are also deficient in their ability to undergo transformation into an activated form, leading to a poor response to test antigens and failure to develop immune response to new antigens (Lundy, Raaf et al., 1975; Roselle & Mendenhall, 1984). This ap-

pears to be a direct effect of alcohol since incubating lymphocytes from nonalcoholics in an alcohol solution leads to the same failure of transformation (Roselle & Mendenhall, 1982)

- Alcohol by itself is shown to inhibit the function of B-lymphocytes (which produce antibodies) in humans as well as animals (Gilhus & Matre, 1982; Aldo-Benson, 1988). This inhibition may contribute to the increased incidence of pneumonia and peritonitis in alcoholics (Smith & Palmer, 1986). Alcohol also has an adverse effect on still another type of lymphocyte, the "natural killer cell." This cell is an important part of the body's defense against spontaneously arising tumors and metastases. One study showed a reduction of over 50% in mice who were fed alcohol chronically (Abdallah, Starkey, et al., 1988).

Elderly persons show a decline in immunologic competence. The additional impairment of their immune system caused by "heavy" alcohol consumption dramatically increases their risk of succumbing to pneumonia or other infections and enhances their vulnerability to cancer.

Cancer. Cancer is a worry for individuals of any age, but as one ages the risk and the worry tend to increase. Alcohol misuse adds considerably to that risk. There is substantial epidemiologic evidence linking "heavy" alcohol intake with an increased incidence of certain cancers, notably those of the liver, esophagus, larynx, nasopharynx, colon, and prostate (Decker & Goldstein, 1982; Driver & Swann, 1987; Tuyns, 1979). Alcoholics with a variety of cancers have poorer chances of survival and greater chances of developing another primary tumor than do nonalcoholics with the same cancer (Driver & Swann, 1987).

The effect of alcohol on the immune system appears to play a significant role (as noted above). In addition, alcohol may affect enzymes controlling carcinogens as demonstrated by the synergistic effect of alcohol consumption plus smoking in the development of cancer of the head, neck, and esophagus (Driver & Swann, 1987). Animal studies show an alcohol-related deficient ability to repair DNA damage produced by carcinogens, leading to the development of precancerous lesions (Garr, Espina & Lieber, 1986).

Muscles. With advancing age, the muscle mass of the body decreases (Bienenfeld, 1987). Alcohol can add to that effect. Chronic alcoholic myopathy may cause muscle wasting and weakness, most commonly involving the proximal muscles of the extremities, the pelvic and shoulder girdle, and the muscles of the thoracic cage (Smith, 1982b). Even without evidence of muscle wasting, muscle strength is diminished. One study concluded that skeletal muscle strength declined as the estimated lifetime dose of alcohol increased (Urbano-Marquez, Estrugh et al., 1989).

Acute alcoholic myopathy is a syndrome of muscle pain, tenderness, and edema occurring after an excess of alcohol ingestion (Smith, 1982b). Again, the proximal muscles of the extremities and the pelvic and shoulder girdles are the most common sites of involvement. Laboratory findings include elevated levels of the enzymes CPK, LDH, aldolase, and AST. In some cases muscle necrosis may occur and be severe enough to produce myoglobinemia which in turn may produce acute renal tubular necrosis. This is a serious complication and may lead to death unless renal dialysis is carried out (Smith, 1982b). Treatment for any type of myopathy is abstinence and nutritional repair.

Increased weakness from myopathy or any other cause can increase the possibility of falling which is a danger, even in healthy elders.

Cardiovascular System. The cardiovascular system is one of the systems of the body where "heavy" alcohol intake may result in death or permanent disability. Cardiovascular disease is the leading cause of death in the United States (Levy, 1985). Alcoholics have a marked increase in mortality from these complications. The average alcoholic man has a death rate from atherosclerotic and degenerative heart disease that is 1.74 times that of nonalcoholic men. In women, the death rate is 4.1 times that of the nonalcoholic (Schmidt & deLint, 1972). A 15-year prospective study showed a similar increased mortality with "problem drinking" (Dyer et al., 1977). These adverse effects occur as a result of both direct and indirect injury to the system.

Direct Effects on the Heart: In normal test animals, alcohol produces a decrease in contractile velocity and a decrease in peak tension of heart muscle (Mitchell & Cohen, 1970). That is, both the speed of contraction and the maximum tension produced by that contraction is reduced in the presence of alcohol. This results in the heart becoming a less efficient pump. Individuals who are alcoholic have been reported to show a similar decrease in heart function (Klatsky et al., 1977). Not only alcoholics are effected. In individuals who are not alcoholic but have cardiac disease, as little as 2 oz of whisky caused a decrease in cardiac output and a decrease in coronary artery circulation (Gould Azhir et al.,

1971). Exercise testing of nonalcoholics with known angina pectoris and proven coronary artery disease revealed that a decreased duration of exercise was required to produce angina and abnormal electrocardiographic changes (increased ischemic ST segment depression) after 2 to 5 oz of alcohol (Orlando et al., 1976).

These findings are of grave concern for the elderly population because coronary artery disease is so prevalent in that population and because alcohol has often been prescribed to treat the symptoms. Heberden, in 1786 (Heberden, 1929), first suggested the use of alcohol for the treatment of angina pectoris. As physiologists learned of the ability of alcohol to cause the blood vessels of the skin to dilate, this effect seemed to confirm the validity of alcohol as a legitimate cardiac drug, since arteriosclerotic vascular disease produces its deleterious effect on the heart by narrowing the coronary arteries, thus depriving the heart muscle of adequate blood flow. Alcohol, therefore, should dilate these vessels and improve blood flow. Unfortunately, alcohol does *not* dilate coronary arteries as it does the vessels of the skin and, as noted above, it often causes further deterioration in cardiac function. The practice of prescribing alcohol to treat angina pectoris can no longer be supported on the basis of scientific evidence despite the fact that alcohol frequently relieves the chest pain (probably because it is a rather effective analgesic).

Alcohol, at least in larger amounts, has a direct toxic effect on the heart. Injury to the walls of myocardial cells allows the leakage of intracellular contents into the blood stream, including potassium, phosphate, and cardiac enzymes. In individuals who are alcoholic, this leakage does not occur at blood alcohol levels of 0.10% (the blood level many states use as legal proof of intoxication), but leakage occurs readily at 0.20% (a level often obtained by these individuals) (Mitchell & Cohen, 1970).

The heart directly metabolizes alcohol to form a class of compounds called fatty acid ethyl esters. These compounds may cause damage to the mitochondria of the cardiac muscle and thus be a direct link to alcohol induced cardiomyopathy (Lang & Kinnanen, 1987; Klatsky, 1987). Alcoholic cardiomyopathy is defined as a syndrome of cardiac dysfunction in which the heart muscle is the site of the disease and in which the remainder of the cardiovascular system is relatively unaffected (Smith, 1982b). In the United States, up to half of all people with idiopathic cardiomyopathy are alcohol-dependent (Wang, Mallon et al., 1987). It is further estimated that 20% to 30% of all cardiomyopathy cases can be attributed to alcohol "abuse" (Regan, 1990). Regular consumption of large amounts of alcohol for 10 or more years appears to be required to produce the condition (Urbano-Marquez et at., 1989; Knott & Beard, 1982). One estimate was "at least 80 grams of ethanol daily for at least a decade" (Cohen, 1985). Electron microscopy of the heart muscle reveals swollen, fragmented mitochondria and various degrees of disruption of the contractile proteins (myofibrils) (Ferrans, 1966; Benzer, 1987). The clinical findings in alcoholic cardiomyopathy are those of congestive failure and/or arrhythmia. They include decreased exercise tolerance, tachycardia, dyspnea, and/or orthopnea, edema, palpitations, and nonproductive cough. The clinical manifestations of idiopathic and alcoholic cardiomyopathy are the same; however, the prognosis is quite different. The prognosis for idiopathic cardiomyopathy is poor regardless of treatment, but alcoholic cardiomyopathy has a better prognosis since the condition is reversible in about 30% of patients if they become abstinent (Lang & Kinnanen, 1987; Wang, Mallon et al., 1987). Even in young (age 20–24) healthy men, a single intoxicating dose of alcohol (mean blood alcohol concentration 0.123%) impeded recovery from exercise by decreased myocardial performance (Markiewicz & Cholewa, 1982) (which might be viewed as the first small step toward cardiomyopathy).

Blood Pressure: Alcohol also has an adverse effect on blood pressure even in relatively modest amounts. A significant elevation in blood pressure (with its well-known increased risk of myocardial infarction and stroke) is caused by three or more drinks a day. This effect is seen most strongly in men, Caucasians, and people over age 55 (Klatsky, 1987). Blood pressure readings in the range of definitive hypertension were more prevalent in persons over age 50 who consumed six or more drinks daily (Criqui, Wallace et al., 1981). Some individuals showed substantial or complete regression of their hypertension when they become abstinent (Klatsky, 1987; Benzer, 1987; Miller & Gold, 1987).

Coronary Artery Disease: "Heart attacks" and other complications of coronary artery disease are the leading cause of death in the United States (Levy, 1985). The risk increases with age (Levy, 1985; Wolinsky, 1985). Numerous studies show that the risk of coronary artery disease and related mortality in both men and women is increased by "heavy" drinking (Schmidt & deLint, 1972; Altura, 1986; Moore & Pearson, 1986; Knight & Smith, 1973;

Crombie, Smith et al., 1990). The issue relates to total alcohol intake (rather than type of beverage) and is incrementally increased with each average daily drinking level (Bianchi et al., 1993; Urbano-Marquez et al., 1989). Relative risk increases from 1.2 for more than one to two drinks per day, 1.4 for more than two to three drinks per day, and 2.6 for more than three drinks per day (Bianchi, Bianchi et al., 1993). Since there is no longer any question about "heavy" alcohol use causing an increase in cardiac mortality, the only remaining question is whether or not small amounts may actually be beneficial. Elderly persons are generally well aware of the fact that coronary heart disease is a leading cause of death. Many take pains to do those things that are generally believed to reduce this risk, including regular exercise, low cholesterol diets, and the like. Over a number of years, several epidemiologic studies have reported that up to one or two drinks a day may *reduce* the risk of coronary heart disease. In fact, some report that these moderate drinkers have a lower mortality rate than total abstainers (Lang & Kinnanen, 1987; Klatsky, 1987; Moore & Pearson, 1986; Hennekens et al., 1979; Coate, 1993; Yano, Rhoads & Kagan, 1977; Callen, Knuiman & Ward, 1993; Suh et al., 1992; deLabry et al., 1992; Jackson, Scragg & Beaglehole, 1992; Boffetta & Garfinkel, 1991). An argument to support the beneficial effect of moderate alcohol intake is that it leads to an increase in high-density lipoprotein (HDL) which is known to be associated with a decreased risk of coronary artery disease (Smith, 1982b; Okanoto, Fjuimori et al., 1988; Linn, Carroll et al., 1993; Razay, Heaton et al., 1992). This argument does not appear to be valid since the subfraction of HDL that is protective (HDL_2) is not appreciably affected. HDL_3, a nonprotective subfraction, is the one that is responsive to alcohol intake (Lang & Kinnanen, 1987; Moore & Pearson, 1986), and some fail to find any change in the HDL/cholesterol ratio (Seppa, Sillanouke et al., 1992). Other concepts suggest that moderate alcohol use increases fibrinolytic factors (Hendriks, Veenstra et al., 1994) and decreases platelet aggregation (Renaud & de Lorgeril, 1992), all of which decrease clot formation which, in turn, decreases risk of myocardial infarction.

Other studies question the validity of the concept of a "U-shaped curve" where moderate drinkers have a lower *total* and *cardiovascular* mortality than total abstainers or "heavy" drinkers. On the basis of a large prospective study of British men, the "light" daily drinking group (who had the lowest cardiovascular mortality rate) also had the lowest proportion of smokers, had the lowest mean blood pressure, and contained the lowest proportion of manual workers (Shaper, Wannametiiee & Walker, 1987). On the other hand, a high proportion of the abstainers had previously been "heavy" drinkers (Wannametiiee & Shaper, 1988). The ex-drinkers were also older, a high proportion were cigarette smokers and the incidence of hypertension and obesity were similar to the "heavier" drinkers (and higher than in the lifelong teetotalers, who were similar to the "light" drinkers). The former "heavy" drinkers also had the highest rates of history of angina, myocardial infarction, diabetes, and other significant illnesses assessed. The lifelong teetotalers were similar to the "light" drinkers in prevalence of hypertension and evidence of ischemic heart disease.

In a very large (11,000 subjects) prospective study comparing vegetarians with meat eaters, the issue of the "U-shaped curve" was also assessed. There was no U-shaped curve found at all. Instead, significant differences in risk were related to dietary practices, particularly in women (Gavaler, Love et al., 1991).

The official position of the Surgeon General has not changed from that of the 1988 report. That position is: "the use of alcohol, even in moderate quantities, for its possible effects on (coronary heart disease) is not recommended" (NIAAA, 1988). A similar conclusion was reached as a result of a large British study (Schaper, Wannamettiiee & Walker, 1994; Schaper, 1991).

Alcohol and Cardiac Arrhythmia: Cardiac rhythm disturbances associated with alcohol intake have been well known for years. The "holiday heart syndrome" is perhaps the best known example and consists of episodes of abnormal cardiac rhythms following a "heavy" bout of drinking. The dysrhythmia may be either atrial or ventricular (Greenspan & Schaal, 1983; Ettinger, Wu et al., 1978). In one study, 35% of all new onset atrial fibrillation was attributed to alcohol intoxication. In those under age 65, alcohol accounted for 63% of cases (Lowenstein, Gabow et al., 1983). Another study reported 62% of cases of atrial fibrillation were "heavy" alcohol users (Rich, Siebold & Campian, 1985). Ventricular arrhythmias may also be involved, with ventricular premature beats or sustained ventricular tachycardia (Greenspan & Schaal, 1993, Ettinger, Wu et al., 1978). Because these symptoms tend to occur after a binge rather than during a period of intoxication, it has been suggested that a mild degree of alcohol withdrawal syndrome may be the cause (Lang & Kinnanen, 1987).

In older age groups coronary heart disease and pulmonary disease are prominent causes of atrial fibrillation. Lowenstein et al. reported that in those over age 65 with new onset atrial fibrillation, coronary artery disease was the causative agent in 29% and pulmonary disease was the cause in 33%, while alcohol accounted for only 10% (Lowenstein, Gabow et al., 1983). Persons with established ischemic heart disease, a condition frequently encountered in older persons, are especially susceptible to arrhythmias precipitated by a "heavy" bout of drinking (Rich, Siebold & Campian, 1985; Howritz, 1975; Kentala, Luurila & Salospuro, 1976). These may result in sudden death from ventricular fibrillation (Ashley & Rankin, 1980; Frazer & Upsdell, 1981; Deutscher, Rackette & Krishnaswami, 1984).

Cerebrovascular System: Death or disability from stroke is an increasing risk as one ages. Alcohol increases the risk. Hemorrhagic strokes as well as cerebral infarctions are markedly increased in "heavy" drinkers. After adjustment for hypertension, cigarette smoking, and medication, the relative risk for stroke in the "heavy" drinkers was four times that of nondrinkers (Gill, Zezulka et al., 1986). "Heavy" alcohol intake is associated with a significant increased incidence of intracranial bleeding including subarachnoid hemorrhage as well as intracerebral hemorrhage (Altura, 1986; Monforte, Estruch et al., 1990; Colditz, 1990). Both hypertension and "heavy" alcohol use are risk factors for intracerebral hemorrhage but the lesions are in different areas. When compared to nondrinkers, even light drinkers (1–14 oz of alcohol per month) more than doubled their risk for hemorrhagic stroke (Donahue, Abbott et al., 1986). This increased risk for hemorrhagic stroke even in "moderate" drinkers has been confirmed by other studies (Stampfer, Colditz et al., 1988; Shinton, Sagar & Beevers, 1993).

Conclusions: All things considered, there seems to be nothing to recommend even moderate amounts of alcohol and much in the cardiovascular system to recommend against the use of large amounts of alcohol for older people.

Effects of Alcohol on the Reproductive and Endocrine Systems. *Men:* It is well known that alcoholic men frequently have disorders of the reproductive system including impotence, low sperm counts, low testosterone levels, and testicular atrophy (Smith, 1982a; Van Thiel, 1983; North & Walter, 1984; Cicero, 1982; Van Thiel, Gaualer & Lester, 1974). They may also show gynecomastia which may be associated with elevated estrogen levels. Alcohol appears capable of directly suppressing testosterone production in the testes (Ellingboe & Varanelli, 1979; Gordon, Vittek et al., 1980; Johnstone, Chiao et al., 1981). It has not yet been clearly determined what role alcohol effects in the hypothalamus and pituitary may play in this process. The precise role played by alcohol in alcohol-induced sexual dysfunction has not been defined but it is probably a combination of primary and secondary hypogonadism and neurotoxicity interrupting the neurogenic arc that controls sexual function (Hugues, Cofte et al., 1980).

Women: Studies involving alcoholic women suggest that they have a higher prevalence of anovulation, amenorrhea, pathologic ovarian changes, and accelerated onset of menopause (Solomon, Manepalli et al., 1993; Moskovic, 1975; Gavaler, 1985; Valimaki, Pelkonen et al., 1984). Repeated or sustained episodes of alcohol intoxication may also suppress hormonal activity in women (Mendelson, Mello et al., 1987). However, recent studies show that moderate amounts of alcohol (e.g., comparable to two drinks a day) are associated with an increase in estrogen levels and might account for the 40% to 100% greater risk of breast cancer in these women compared to alcohol abstaining women. (Reichman, Jude et al., 1993; Gavaler, Love et al., 1991).

Other Endocrine Effects: Alcohol also affects most other endocrine organs. The findings vary depending on the dose, duration, and the timing of the measurement with respect to alcohol intake. Alcoholics may have elevated plasma cortisol levels and even show pseudo-Cushing's syndrome (elevated corticosteroids with normal ACTH levels), a condition that resolves after a few weeks of abstinence (Likohri, Huttunen et al., 1978; Reese, Besse et al., 1977; Carpenter, 1990). In addition to adrenocortical effects, alcohol causes an increased output of adrenal catecholamines (epinephrine and norepinephrine) (Koob, 1983). Elevated serum catecholamines have an obvious implication in the alcohol-induced elevation of blood pressure.

Other endocrine effects include decreased thyroid hormone levels, decreased growth hormone levels, and decreased vasopressin (Hegedus, 1984). Liver disease appears to be a factor in this process (Van Thiel, Gavaler & Lester, 1974) but alcohol may also have a direct toxic effect on the thyroid since a decreased thyroid size was observed in patients with alcoholic cirrhosis but not in those with nonalcoholic cirrhosis (Hegedus, Rasmussen et al., 1988).

Conclusions: Again, alcohol, particularly in large amounts, is found to have deleterious effects on an important system (reproductive and endocrine). These effects may be most distressing to older males who may be having concerns about sexual functioning even without the added functional impairment produced by the alcohol.

Nervous System. *Central Nervous System:* Hippocrates was one of the first to associate excessive alcohol use with serious, even fatal brain dysfunction. Later Greek and Roman physicians made similar observations (Hankoff, 1972). Subsequent observations through the present time have consistently confirmed these findings. Both the physical findings and behavioral findings of this alcoholic brain syndrome closely resemble the changes induced by aging. The behavioral changes include impaired learning, difficulty concentrating, impaired abstract thinking, impaired judgment, impaired short-term memory, and impaired problem solving and perception. On tests of adaptive ability, alcoholics scored closer to brain-damaged subjects than to nonbrain-damaged controls (Fitzhugh, Fitzhugh & Reitan, 1965; Smith, Burt & Chapman, 1973). Mental aging index scores show a significant acceleration of mental aging in alcoholics. They showed more test-measured signs of mental aging at every chronological age, a finding that was more prominent in the older cohorts (Williams, Ray & Overall, 1973) This same study suggested that the alcoholics showed two distinct patterns of deterioration, one of which is consistent with general organic brain syndrome and one more closely associated with aging (Williams, Ray & Overall, 1973).

Alcohol-induced dysfunction is rather common. Alcoholic dementia accounts for 10% to 20% of all admissions to state mental hospitals in the United States (Bergman, Axelson et al., 1983; Emmerson, Dustman & Shearer, 1988; Still, Jackson et al., 1990). This condition is also found in about the same frequency in other countries and cultures where alcohol use is practiced (Park, Ko et al., 1994; Ikeda, 1991; Ishii, 1983). Neuropsychological testing reveals some degree of dysfunction in 45% to 70% of detoxified alcoholics without clinical evidence of organic brain syndrome (Eckhardt & Martin, 1986; Parsons & Leber, 1981). Some studies even suggest measurable alcohol-related cognitive impairment in nonalcoholic social drinkers in which a dose-response relationship between alcohol consumption and lower scores on certain neuropsychological tests are seen (Parker & Noble, 1977; Parker, Parker et al., 1983). Other studies, however, throw doubt on these conclusions, and the issue is still unresolved (Bergman, Axelson et al., 1983; Emmerson, Dustman & Shearer, 1988; Parsons, 1986). Studies of alcohol-induced dementia identify age as the most important risk factor in the severity of the dementia. This clinical finding is supported by CT scan reports showing significant cerebral atrophy, particularly in older alcoholics (Miller, Belkin & Gold, 1991).

Autopsy findings include brain atrophy, with histologic loss of the dendritic tree of neurons in various brain regions (including the hippocampus and cerebellum) and a variety of chemical changes of brain synaptic functions (Freund, 1984). Numerous other studies have reported cortical atrophy and/or cerebellar atrophy at autopsy in deteriorated alcoholics (Courville, 1966; Butters & Cermak, 1983). Similar antemortem findings have been demonstrated with computerized tomography (CT) scans and other imaging techniques (Tumarkin, Wilson & Snyder, 1955; Lee et al., 1979; Harper & Kril, 1985). Widening of the lateral ventricles and the third ventricle is also noted (Pfefferbaum, Rosenbloom et al., 1988; Bergman, 1987; Wilkinson & Carlen, 1980; Carlen, Williams et al., 1981). Enlargement of the third ventricle is associated with impairment of paired-associate tasks (Gebhardt, Naeser & Butters, 1984). Those with widened lateral ventricles show a consistent trend toward more neuropsychological deficits in general intelligence, verbal learning and retention, and short-term memory (Bergman, 1987). This trend is more pronounced in middle aged or older alcoholics and becomes exaggerated with age (Pfefferbaum, Rosenbloom et al., 1988; Bergman, 1987). Studies in women show changes similar to those in men but, of importance, is the finding that the evidence of brain atrophy occurs after significantly shorter and less intense periods of drinking (Jacobsen, 1986).

The issue of whether or not moderate amounts of alcohol intake are associated with structural damage is still not clear. Some CT scans show evidence of atrophy (Cala, Jones et al., 1978; Cala, 1985; Bergman, Axelson et al., 1983). So, as with the issue of cognitive deficits associated with moderate alcohol use, the findings are inconsistent and a final judgment has not been made.

Alcohol and Alzheimer's Disease: In Alzheimer's disease (AD), a special case of what has been called "pathological aging" (Freund, 1982), cognitive performance declines severely. Postmortem examination of the brain of alcoholic and nonalcoholic AD patients showed that alcoholic drinking and AD had different effects on different regions of the brain and suggested that the alcohol effects may have contributed further to the dementia of the AD patients (Freund & Ballinger, 1992).

Recovery of Function with Abstinence: A number of studies show that abstinence for months to years may lead to recovery of some or all cognitive function and even reversal of at least some brain atrophy (Bennett, 1960; Smith, Johnson & Burdick, 1971; Carlen, 1978; Carlen, Penn et al., 1996; Goldstein, Chotlos et al., 1968; Goldman, 1982; Ron, 1983). Abstinent alcoholics under age 40 have been found to recover visuospatial capacity more frequently than older abstinent alcoholics (Goldman, Williams & Glisz, 1983). On the other hand, even after five years of abstinence young alcoholics did not reverse memory and learning deficits (Brandt, Butters et al., 1983). Other studies do confirm some long-term cognitive deficits in abstinent alcoholics despite various functional improvements (Yohman et al., 1985; Fabian & Parsons, 1983).

Peripheral Neuropathy: Peripheral neuropathy is frequently seen in clinical practice. Statistics from large municipal hospitals show that alcoholic peripheral neuropathy is more common than all other forms combined (Merritt, 1979). The condition is generally believed to result from nutritional deficiency, principally of the B vitamins. The nerve lesions begin in the longest peripheral nerves (those leading to the feet and hands). Initially, demyelination of the nerves takes place, resulting in decreased conduction velocities in the affected nerves. As the process becomes more severe, degeneration of the axon occurs with a process of "dying back" from the distal end proximally.

The onset of symptoms is usually slow, extending over weeks or months, but occasionally may present rapidly over the course of only a few days (Merritt, 1979). Involvement is usually bilateral and symmetrical. The first symptoms may be pain in the calf muscles or feet. At other times the first symptoms are a burning, tingling, or prickling sensation of the lower extremities, often progressing to numbness of the feet and legs. Later, similar symptoms may occur in the hands and arms.

The sensory symptoms start peripherally and progress centrally so that the discomfort and numbness usually begins in the feet and works its way up the leg. As the process continues, muscle weakness and wasting may occur. The first noticeable effect may be a "foot-drop-gait." Later the legs may become completely paralyzed. Proprioception is often impaired and this, in concert with weakened muscles, leads to an ataxic wide-based gait.

Treatment for alcoholic peripheral neuropathy is simple and straightforward. Abstinence from alcohol, a nutritious diet, and supplementary vitamins are the main factors. Thiamine is the vitamin most heavily emphasized in the past, but it may not be the only vitamin of importance in the pathogenesis of the condition. In clinical practice doses of B vitamins (in addition to thiamine) are administered in amounts much larger than the minimum daily requirements. Recovery occurs rapidly in those early cases in which only demyelinization has occurred. When degeneration of the axon fiber has occurred, recovery is much slower, in some cases requiring months to a year or more (Merritt, 1979; Smith & Palmer, 1986).

Age-Specific Considerations: In older patients, diabetic peripheral neuropathy is often the first diagnosis considered. When this diagnosis proves false, there is too often a great deal of time and expense wasted on searching for uncommon causes of neuropathy (e.g., pharmacologic agents, toxic agents, or other metabolic diseases) while the most common cause (alcoholism) is not considered at all. This generally occurs because the patient does not fit the physician's mental image of an alcoholic.

Conclusions: Once more, it appears that alcohol, particularly in large quantities, is a further substantial burden to deficits inherent in both normal aging and "pathological aging."

Gastrointestinal System. *Esophagus:* Frequent use of alcohol may cause esophagitis, gastritis, and exacerbate existing peptic ulcers (Miller & Gold, 1987; Kurata & Halle, 1984). The relative risk of carcinoma of the esophagus is higher in alcoholics (Kamionkowski & Fleshler, 1965; Driver & Swann, 1987; Tuyns, 1979; Katlic, Wilkins & Grillo, 1990). Most studies do not calculate the increased risks. One study from China (Gao, McLaughlin et al., 1994) reported the odds ratio to be 1.4 for men who drank alcohol ("primarily heavy drinkers"). When "heavy" smoking and "heavy" drinking were combined, the effect was dramatically increased (odds ratio 12.0). In a South American study (De Stefani, Munoz et al., 1990) the relative risk was 12.2 for those drinking over 2.5 liters of a local alcoholic beverage (mate). Smoking in addition to this "heavy" alcohol intake increased the relative risk to 22.6.

Esophagitis is more prevalent in alcoholics than others because of the increased acid production in the stomach and frequent vomiting. In addition, intoxication predisposes to reflux of stomach contents into the esophagus (Fenster, 1982). Vomiting, with severe retching, may tear the mucosa at or just below the gastroesophageal junction leading to profuse bleeding and hematemesis (the Mallory-Weiss syndrome) (Fenster, 1982; Knauer, 1976).

One of the most common consequences of "heavy" alcohol intake is erosive gastritis. Alcohol increases gastric acid secretion, but of even more importance is that alcohol reduces the mucosal cell barrier, allowing back diffusion of the acid into the mucosa (Fenster, 1982; Szabo, Trier et al., 1985). The mucosal damage caused in this process leads to swelling, inflammation, and a friable surface which is prone to bleeding. If aspirin is added to this combination (as is commonly prescribed for older people), the process is accelerated (Overholt, 1969). The symptoms may include epigastric distress, nausea, and vomiting. A major complication is gastric bleeding, which may be life threatening (Fenster, 1982). Alcohol may also exacerbate existing peptic ulcer disease. If bleeding occurs, it may be more difficult to control in an older person with more rigid vessels.

Small Intestine: Chronic alcoholism leads to malabsorption of a variety of nutrients including fat, xylose, folic acid, and vitamin B_{12} (Mezey, 1975). The malabsorption syndrome thus induced may further impair the nutritional status of the individual. Alcohol also impairs normal peristalsis (Mayer, Grabowski & Fisher, 1978; Winship, Caflisch et al., 1968) and may cause a variety of structural changes including flattening of the villi, loss of certain enzymes, and inhibition of amino acid and glucose transport mechanisms (Dinda & Beck, 1977).

Pancreas: "Heavy" alcohol consumption and gallstones are the two leading causes of pancreatitis. Acute pancreatitis (inflammation of the pancreas) is manifested by severe upper abdominal pain, nausea, vomiting, ileus, fever, and sometimes hypovolemia with hypotension and electrolyte disturbances (Fenster, 1982), none of which is well tolerated by elderly people. About 20% of these patients have a much more severe form which may even lead to death (under 5%) or other severe complication such as pancreatic abscess, pseudocyst formation, or peripheral fat necrosis involving pleura, pericardium, bones, and joints (Fenster, 1982).

Chronic pancreatitis may occur insidiously, and many such patients have no previous history of acute attacks (Fenster, 1982). Over 75% of patients with chronic pancreatitis have a history of "heavy" alcohol consumption (Van Thiel, Lipsitz et al., 1981). It may be associated with chronic pain which may in turn lead to narcotic dependence (Fenster, 1982). Within three or four years of the initial attack, many of these patients develop insulin-dependent diabetes mellitus. This occurs as a result of progressive destruction of the insulin-producing cells of the pancreas. In addition, the reduced production of pancreatic digestive enzymes may lead to malabsorption, particularly of fat, leading to weight loss, malnutrition, and foul smelling bulky stools, often with diarrhea (Fenster, 1982). Both the acute effects (e.g., pain, nausea, vomiting, etc.), the stress associated with them, and the chronic effects (malabsorption and/or diabetes) are poorly tolerated by elderly patients.

Alcohol and the Liver: The liver is the principal site of alcohol metabolism. Liver damage from excessive use of alcohol has been recognized since ancient times. Descriptions of cirrhosis of the liver were given by Hippocrates (Leibowitz, 1967) and others in ancient times. There are three types of alcohol-induced liver disease. In order of increasing severity they are: (1) fatty liver, (2) alcoholic hepatitis, and (3) cirrhosis.

Among "heavy" drinkers, 90% to 100% show some evidence of fatty liver, 10% to 35% show alcoholic hepatitis, and 10% to 20% develop cirrhosis (Grant, DuFour et al., 1988). Other studies suggest that cirrhosis may be underdiagnosed since autopsy findings reveal that 40% of cirrhosis was not detected before death (Lieber, 1982).

It was assumed for many years that the principal cause of liver damage in alcoholics was their tendency to drink and neglect to eat a nutritionally adequate diet (Hartroft & Porta, 1966). This nutritional insult to the liver certainly can (and undoubtedly does) produce damage in many cases. In more recent years, however, it has been found that alcohol by itself has the capacity to cause liver cell damage in spite of a nutritionally adequate diet. This has been demonstrated in animal studies (Rubin & Leiber, 1974) and human studies both in alcoholics (Lieber, 1966) and nonalcoholics (Beckett, Livingstone & Hill, 1961; Rothschild, Oratz & Schreiber, 1989).

Fatty Liver: The precise amount of alcohol that is required to induce liver damage is still rather uncertain. One study showed that in nonalcoholic young research volunteers, the substitution of alcohol for carbohydrates in the diet for one week caused fat accumulation and ultrastructure change in liver cells (Rubin & Lieber, 1968). The alcohol intake was well below intoxication levels. The primary cause for fat accumulation in the liver appears to be simply the manner in which alcohol is metabolized in liver cells. The major route of metabolism involves the action of the enzyme alcohol dehydrogenase (ADH) which removes a hydrogen atom from the alcohol and transfers it to the coenzyme nicotinamide adenine-dinucleotide (NAD) which then converts NAD into its reduced form NADH. The NAD/NADH system is required in a multitude of metabolic processes in the liver. Metabolism of relatively large amounts of alcohol results in an excess of NADH which, in turn, leads to a variety of metabolic effects including reduced glycogen formation and both *increased* production and *decreased* oxidation of lipid (Lieber, 1966). The net effect is an accumulation of lipids within liver cells. Virtually all actively drinking chronic alcoholics show increased fat accumulation in liver cells on a liver biopsy (Fenster, 1982). This "alcoholic fatty liver" is generally not associated with distressing clinical symptoms. The liver may be enlarged and biochemical tests of liver function may be mildly deranged. Occasionally, in a binge drinking alcoholic, "acute fatty liver" may develop and be associated with abdominal pain, anorexia, and jaundice (Fenster, 1982). This may pose a diagnostic challenge since it might be confused with alcoholic or viral hepatitis or cholecystitis. The course of fatty liver of any variety is generally benign. Abstinence from alcohol and normal nutrition results in a rapid return to normal structure and function (including normal liver function tests) in a few weeks to two months or so (Fenster, 1982; Feinman & Leiber, 1974).

Alcoholic Hepatitis: In some alcoholics, for reasons not yet completely understood, continued "heavy" drinking leads to alcoholic hepatitis. Microscopic examination of liver tissue shows an active inflammatory process, areas of necrosis, fibrosis, and Mallory bodies (glassy appearing membrane structures). The process may develop insidiously and progress gradually over a period of months or years. In other cases it may present in a fulminant form, advancing to death over a course of only a few weeks (Fenster, 1982; Crabb & Lumeng, 1989; Moddrey, 1988). Clinically, the alcoholic will generally show evidence of significant liver disease with hepatomegaly, jaundice, hepatic pain, fever, and leukocytosis. These acute symptoms may lead to the erroneous diagnosis of cholecystitis (a condition not uncommon in older persons). This can be a deadly miscalculation since these patients have a high death rate following surgery and for this reason alcoholic hepatitis has been termed a "surgical trap" (Fenster, 1982; Mikkelsen et al., 1968).

Alcoholic hepatitis is a serious condition and may progress to death. Its reversibility is variable and depends on its severity and chronicity. Abstinence from alcohol is a prerequisite for healing. However, even with permanent abstinence, some degree of scarring may remain (Fenster, 1982; Moddrey, 1988).

Cirrhosis: The most advanced form of alcoholic liver disease is alcoholic cirrhosis (also known as Laennec's cirrhosis). It is characterized by fibrosis (scarring) leading to disruption of the normal liver lobular architecture in which nodules of liver parenchyma are surrounded by fibrous tissue (Rothschild, Oratz & Schreiber, 1989; Fenster, 1982). As cirrhosis progresses the patient is likely to develop portal vein hypertension, leading to esophageal varices which may rupture and bleed massively (a complication poorly tolerated by older people). In addition, edema and/or ascites may develop. In older persons with emphysema, the increased intra-abdominal pressure from ascites may seriously compromise the movement of the diaphragm and further impair respiration.

The symptoms may present insidiously with anorexia, fatigue and weakness, and a gradual onset of jaundice. The condition may progress to liver failure in which products of manufacture by the liver are no longer produced in adequate quantities (e.g., decreased serum protein levels and decreased prothrombin levels [which may lead to bleeding]). Equally dangerous is the accumulation of excessive levels of certain chemicals normally removed by the liver (e.g., bilirubin [leading to progressive jaundice] or ammonia [leading to hepatic encephalopathy and coma]). Mortality from cirrhosis is ranked as the ninth leading cause of death in the United States (NIAAA, 1988).

Individual Differences: As noted earlier, the amount and duration of excessive alcohol use that leads to liver injury has not been definitely established. It is well established, however, that there are marked individual differences in susceptibility to the alcohol damage (Moddrey, 1988). An increased risk of developing fatty liver is found with alcohol consumption of 80 grams a day for men and 20 grams a day for women (Grant, DuFour & Hartford, 1988). The severity of liver damage tends to increase with increasing daily intake to over 180 grams per day (about 14 standard bar drinks) (Grant, DuFour & Hartford, 1988). When daily alcohol consumption increases to 210 grams for 22 years, the probability of developing cirrhosis is 50% and after 33 years is 80% (Lelbach, 1974).

Genetic factors also play a role. Identical twins show an increased concordance for cirrhosis (Hrubec & Omenn, 1981). A specific gene, coding for type I collagen (the type most prominent in dense fibrosis) was found more frequently in alcoholics with cirrhosis than in those without cirrhosis (or in controls) (Weiner, Eskreis et al., 1988). Women are found to be more likely to develop alcohol-induced liver damage, and they do this with less alcohol and for a shorter duration of use than is the case with men (Maddrey, 1988).

It should be emphasized that not all cases of cirrhosis are caused by alcohol. Viral hepatitis also makes a significant contribution, particularly hepatitis B and hepatitis C. Chronic hepatitis C is also significantly correlated with the severity of alcoholic cirrhosis (Mendenhall et al., 1991) and may influence the progression of alcoholic liver disease (Schiff, 1992; Nishiguchi et al., 1991). Markers for hepatitis B have been found in some patients with alcoholic liver disease, especially those with portal hypertension, and may be a risk factor for the development or progression of alcohol-induced liver disease (Lieber, 1984). Evidence also suggests that the reverse is true and that alcohol consumption intensifies hepatitis B-induced liver disease (Nomura, Kashiwagi et al., 1988).

Age-Specific Considerations: About 25% of alcoholic liver disease is seen in persons older than 60 years (Potter & James, 1987). Of the younger persons with alcoholic liver disease, only a minority have cirrhosis. In contrast, the majority of the elderly with alcoholic liver disease have cirrhosis (Scott, 1989). Whereas the clinical finding of cirrhosis in the older alcoholic is no different than that of the younger one, the prognosis is quite different. In the first year after diagnosis of cirrhosis, 50% of those over age 60 years die, in contrast to 7% of those under age 60 (Potter & James, 1987; Scott, 1989). Treatment of cirrhosis in the elderly is similar to that of younger people; however, again there are special considerations. Diuretics are frequently required to treat edema or ascites. Great care must be used when giving diuretics to elderly cirrhosis patients since their total body water may already be decreased, making them more susceptible to fluid and electrolyte depletion (Scott, 1989). If potassium-sparing diuretics are not used, hypokalemia may occur, which may in turn lead to cardiac arrhythmia, particularly in those patients who may also be taking digitalis preparations.

If bleeding esophageal varices become one of the complications, vasopressin is sometimes used in the treatment. However, vasopressin may also compromise the blood flow in coronary arteries, a situation that is especially dangerous in the elderly (Scott, 1989). In any event, bleeding is less tolerated by the elderly. It may be necessary to treat the varices by reducing the pressure in the portal vein system by a major surgical procedure in which the portal vein is connected to the inferior vena cava (portacaval shunt). This, too, is a procedure poorly tolerated by the elderly.

If hepatic encephalopathy becomes a complication, it may pose a diagnostic dilemma. Hepatic encephalopathy progresses through four recognized stages (Scharschmidt, 1985).

1. Stage One is associated with a variety of symptoms including apathy, lack of awareness, euphoria, anxiety, restlessness, or shortened attention span.
2. Stage Two is associated with lethargy, drowsiness, and/or disorientation.
3. Stage Three is associated with deep somnolence (but at least transient arousal is possible).
4. In Stage Four, coma (absent verbal response) is present.

In Stages One and Two it may be difficult to distinguish effects of liver disease from organic brain syndrome, in which case appropriate treatment for the liver disease may be delayed with unfortunate results.

The issue of cancer is a prominent one in the older population. Primary liver cancer is relatively rare in North America and Europe; however, the disease is associated with cirrhosis. A series of studies showed that 64% to 90% percent of persons with *either* condition had *both* conditions. The reported population of alcoholics with cirrhosis who develop cancer ranges from 5% to 30% (Driver & Swann, 1987).

Skin. When the average person thinks about dermatologic manifestations of alcoholism, rosacea (also known as acne rosacea) generally is the first to come to mind, The condition is more common in later decades of life (fourth, fifth, and sixth). The central region of the face (central forehead, nose, checks, and chin) develops erythema and telangiectasias and occasionally acne-like papules. A more extreme form of rosacea, rhinophyma, involves a lobulated thickening of the lower portion of the nose and is recognized by many as the stereotypic red bulbous nose of alcoholics. Rosacea and rhinophyma are stimulated by alcohol, but the condition is not caused by alcoholism and may occur in those who never were alcoholic (Pochi, 1988). Even without rosacea, persistent redness of the face is a common finding in alcoholics ("plethoric facies") and is believed to result from chronic vasodilatation and loss of vasoregulatory control. Fine telangiectasia are also characteristic (Higgins & du Vivier, 1992).

Skin changes associated with alcoholic liver disease include jaundice, palmar erythema ("liver palms"), spider nevi, Dupuytren's contracture, white nails, and "paper money skin" (fine thread-like capillaries scattered in a random manner like the fine silk threads in paper money) (Higgins & du Vivier, 1992).

Psoriasis, while not caused by alcohol ingestion, is often made worse by "heavy" alcohol intake (Higgins, duVivier & Peters, 1992; Poikolainen, Rennal et al., 1990). Abstinence from alcohol is often associated with clinical remission of the dermatosis (Vincenti & Blunden, 1987).

Discoid eczema, characterized by well-circumscribed, nummular plaques of dermatitis, is generally found on the lower legs. The condition tends to be particularly recalcitrant to treatment and has a strong association with "heavy" alcohol intake (Higgins & du Vivier, 1992).

Skin infections, such as cellulitis, are also more frequent in alcoholics. Fungal infections are also more frequent, including tinea pedis, onychomycosis, and chronic tinea vesicolor (Higgins, Rennal et al,, 1992).

Age-Specific Considerations: Rosacea has a definite age relationship, and psoriasis was found much more frequently in alcoholics aged 65 and older than in the general population of the same age (Hurt, Finlayson et al., 1988). All of the inflammatory skin conditions (psoriasis, discoid eczema, and superficial infections) may interfere with sleep, may promote agitation and, in general, tend to be less well tolerated by older persons.

ALCOHOL AND NUTRITION

Factors Leading to Decreased Intake and Absorption. There are many ways in which excessive alcohol consumption can interfere with adequate nutrition. The first and obvious way is for the alcohol budget to compete with the food budget. In low income alcoholics the alcohol budget may win to the point where food stamps are sold to purchase alcohol (Roe, 1979), with the result that less food is purchased. If alcoholic gastritis is present, appetite may be diminished and ingested food may be vomited. Alcohol damage to the intestine and/or pancreas may impair absorption of vitamins, amino acids, and fats (Roe, 1979; Israel et al., 1969; Kuo & Shambour, 1979; Thompson et al., 1970). For example thiamine (vitamin B_1) absorption is reduced 40% to 60% after alcohol ingestion (Israel et al., 1969), and chronic alcohol intake significantly reduces protein synthesis (Sinclair, 1972). Prolonged intake of alcohol injures the mucosa of the small intestine which, among other things, intensifies folate deficiency, which separately impairs active absorption of trace nutrients (Iber, 1986; Schuckit, 1982).

Nutritional Consequences of Alcohol Metabolism. The metabolism of alcohol also places an increased demand on the utilization of thiamine (Dreyfus, 1974) as well as other water-soluble vitamins which are lost through the kidneys at an accelerated rate with "heavy" drinking. All of these factors promote malnutrition in alcoholics of all ages. Nutrient intake declines with age (Klein & Iber, 1991). Many body functions and metabolic pathways decline throughout the life cycle, with all measurably decreasing after age 65 (and many before that age) (Munro, Suter & Russell, 1987). Chronic disease is also common in the elderly and may further contribute to nutritional impairment. Social factors such as decreased income, decreased mobility, or living alone may also contribute to failure to purchase and prepare an adequate diet. The additional burden of alcoholism is cause for further concern for the nutritional status of elderly alcoholics.

Alcohol metabolism provides energy intermediate to that of fats and carbohydrates at 7 kcal per gram. However, it contains virtually no nutrients. The energy requirement for an average retired elderly person living in an apartment with no organized outings is about 1,600 to 1,800 kcal per day (Klein & Iber, 1991) The usual serving of beer or wine contains about 100 kcal, so that four or five portions (less than a six-pack of beer) may provide over 20% of the daily energy requirement in a form almost devoid of nutrients (Klein & Iber, 1991). Severe malnutrition may be expected in persons with disease or physical incapacity and/or in those consuming a high percentage of their daily caloric intake as alcohol (e.g., 25% or more) (Iber, 1990). Deficiencies in some nutrients occur after only a rather brief time (less than 21 days) of "heavy" alcohol use (e.g., folic acid, pyridoxine, potassium, phosphorous, magnesium). Others require an intermediate (one- to four-month) duration of use (e.g., thiamine, nicotinamide, ascorbic acid, zinc, selenium). Still others require a rather long (four months to several years) period of excessive intake (e.g., protein, essential fatty acids, iron, vitamins B_{12}, A, D, and E) (Iber, 1990).

Conclusions. All alcoholics are at risk for malnutrition. Elderly alcoholics are at considerably increased risk and require even greater attention to nutritional repair in the course of treatment.

PSYCHIATRIC MANIFESTATIONS

During Acute Withdrawal. Psychiatric complications of alcohol (or other drug) dependence are similar in all age groups with some shift in emphasis in the older population. Anxiety and depression are well known to be associated with alcoholism. The direct effects of alcohol (or any other depressant drug) is mood sedation. After physical dependence is established, withdrawal of alcohol leads to increased catecholamine blood levels with tremor, agitation, and sleeplessness. With more severe withdrawal symptoms, frank psychotic symptoms may develop with delusions and hallucinations. It is not possible to accurately predict what percentage of those showing symptoms of alcohol withdrawal will progress to hallucinosis since much depends on what, if any, treatment for the mitigation of those symptoms has been received. One recent study of 532 male patients in a Veteran's Administration Hospital inpatient treatment program found 10%. Those who developed hallucinosis tended to be younger at the onset of their alcohol problems, consumed more alcohol per drinking occasion, developed more alcohol-related life problems, and had higher rates of other drug experimentation than those who did not hallucinate (Tsuang, Irwin et al., 1994). It is generally agreed that alcoholic hallucinosis and delirium tremens are the result of long-term "heavy" alcohol intake (Tsuang, Irwin et al., 1994; Hemmingsen & Kramp, 1988; Benzer, 1994).

When hallucinations and/or delusions occur, they are particularly troublesome in the elderly who may already have diminished vision and hearing and are thus predisposed to misperception. Alcoholic hallucinosis generally follows a relatively benign course in which the individual remains oriented and communicative and is not generally associated with panic or paranoia (Butz, 1982). Delirium tremens is the most severe form of alcohol withdrawal and is characterized by marked tremor, anxiety, insomnia, anorexia, paranoia, disorientation, and hallucination. It may also be associated with fever, vomiting, and diarrhea. Tachycardia and tremor are the rule (Butz, 1982). In about one-third to as many as 97% of cases delirium tremens is preceded by an alcohol withdrawal seizure (Sellers & Kalant, 1982). All of these severe withdrawal reactions are physically (as well as emotionally) stressful and pose an increased mortality risk for older persons who may already have marginal cardiovascular function.

Depression. Depressed mood is present in most alcoholics, particularly in the immediate postintoxication period. Part of this is undoubtedly the result of some of the life consequences of alcoholic drinking including isolation from family and friends who will no longer put up with the drinking behavior. This leads to a spiral of loneliness and dysphoria (Bienenfeld, 1987). In addition, the neurochemical disturbances induced by a "heavy" bout of drinking lead to a depressed mood ("alcoholic sadness") which is temporary and will clear after two or three weeks of abstinence (Schuckit, 1982). However, some alcoholics have a primary depression which is present even in periods of prolonged abstinence. These individuals require treatment for their depression *in addition* to treatment for their alcoholism (Schuckit, 1982).

Suicide is a particularly common problem associated with alcohol dependence and has been estimated to be as high as 32 times the risk for the general population (Sexias, 1982). Next to advancing age, alcohol (and other drug dependence) is among the greatest risk factors for suicide. Men are more likely to commit suicide than women. In 57 countries studied, the ratio of men to women varied but suicide among the women was always "considerably lower" (La Vecchia, Lucchimi & Levi, 1994). Suicide rates for the elderly have trended upward (from 1955 to 1989), particularly in Canada and the United States, Australia, and New Zealand (La Vecchia, Lucchimi & Levi, 1994). The elderly are clearly weighted toward suicide as a complication of alcoholism (Atkinson & Schuckit, 1983).

ALCOHOL AND SLEEP

Characteristics of Normal Sleep. Sleep disturbances including frequent awakening, restless sleep, insomnia and night terrors are among the most common complaints of alcoholics (Smith, 1982c). A normal night of sleep is not a static process. Electroencephalographic studies of an entire night of sleep of healthy young adults show a predictable pattern.

It begins while awake with the eyes closed with 8–12 Hz "alpha rhythm." In the drowsy period just prior to sleep the alpha rhythm is intermittent and is finally replaced with lower frequency (4–6 Hz) "theta waves." This is Stage I sleep. After several minutes the EEG waves slow in frequency and increase in amplitude and have occasional bursts of other frequencies and patterns ("sleep spindles" and "K complexes"). This is Stage II sleep. After several minutes at this stage, higher voltage, slower waves (1–4 Hz) appear (Stage III sleep), and finally "slow wave sleep" dominates the picture (Stage IV sleep). After 20 to 30 minutes at Stage IV, the sleeper proceeds in reverse order back to a Stage I EEG pattern but now has rapid eye movements ("rapid eye movement [REM] sleep") which are associated with dreaming. During a normal night of sleep, this cycle is repeated three or more times, taking about 90 to 100 minutes to complete each REM-to-REM cycle (Smith, 1982c).

Effects of Alcohol on Sleep. Alcoholics are reported to show a characteristic deviation from this normal sleep pattern (Smith, 1982c; Johnson, Burdick & Smith, 1970). While drinking, REM sleep is suppressed and is followed by "REM rebound" (higher than normal amounts of REM sleep which may be associated with nightmares). Essentially no Stage IV sleep is present during drinking or after withdrawal. In addition, Stage III sleep is markedly diminished during drinking but tends to increase toward normal during withdrawal.

During alcohol consumption there are frequent short periods of awakening (though not usually remembered by the individual) (Smith, 1982; Johnson, Burdick & Smith, 1970). In general, sleep patterns of middle-aged alcoholics resemble those of elderly nonalcoholics. Nearly 50% of people over age 50 complain of insomnia (1987). The added sleep pattern disturbances caused by alcohol simply compound the problem despite the fact that alcohol decreases the sleep latency (they fall asleep faster) (Bienenfeld, 1987). The fragmented sleep and other disturbances of sleep physiology contribute to less "restful" sleep, leading to further problems of chronic fatigue and irritability.

Sleep Apnea: Another factor associated with sleep that is adversely affected by alcohol is sleep apnea. It is an aphorism in sleep disorder clinics that "alcohol induces snoring in normals and induces sleep apnea in snorers." Sleep apnea is an increasing problem as one ages, with nearly 40% of retirement age persons having breathing abnormalities during sleep (Charskadon, 1984). Sleep apnea may be associated with significant complications such as nocturnal enuresis, impotence, excessive sleepiness, morning headaches, personality changes, and impaired intellect (Dement, 1984). Many of these complications may be erroneously blamed on excessive alcohol use alone or on age.

GENERAL HEALTH STATUS

General health is an area of substantial concern in actively drinking elderly persons. One study showed over 90% of the actively drinking older alcoholics presented with a major health problem (Schuckit & Miller, 1976; Schuckit & Pastor, 1979). In surveys of self-perceived health status of a large stratified sample of men and women over age 60, those who were classified as heavy drinkers were most likely to see themselves as in poor health (Monk, Cryns & Cabral, 1977). The major health problems tend to be the consequence of chronic "heavy" drinking and its associated lifestyle (rather than alcohol withdrawal symptoms) (Schuckit & Miller, 1976; Schuckit, Morrissey & O'Leary, 1978).

CONCLUSIONS

Alcoholism may lead to a great many physical and mental problems in individuals of any age. Elderly alcoholics often have additional problems resulting from the interaction of age-related changes in physiology and the "heavy" alcohol intake. There seems to be no area in which even moderate alcohol intake is of positive benefit and some areas in which even small amounts are detrimental.

ACKNOWLEDGMENT: This chapter originally was published as Smith JW (1995). Medical manifestations of alcoholism in the elderly. International Journal of the Addictions *30(13&14):1749–1798. Reprinted by permission of the publisher.*

REFERENCES

Abdallah RM, Starkey JR & Meadows GG (1988). Toxicity of chronic high alcohol intake on mouse natural killer cell activity. *Research Communications in Chemical Pathology and Pharmacology* 59(2):245–258.

Adams HG & Jordan C (1984). Infections in the alcoholic. *Medical Clinics of North America* 68:179–199.

Aldo-Benson MA (1988). Alcohol directly suppresses B cell response to antigen. *Federal Proceedings* 2:6.

Altura BM (1986). Introduction to the symposium and overview. *Alcoholism* 10(6):557–559.

Andersen BR (1975). Host factors causing increased susceptibility to infection in patients with Laennec's cirrhosis. *Annals of the New York Academy of Science* 252:348–352.

An'ia BJ, Suman VJ, Fairbanks VF & Melton LJ III (1994). Prevalence of anemia in medical practice: Community versus referral patients. *Mayo Clinic Proceedings* 69(8):808–809.

Ashley MI & Rankin JG (1980). Hazardous alcohol consumption and diseases of the circulatory system. *Journal of Studies on Alcohol* 41:1040–1070.

Atkinson JH & Schuckit MA (1983). Geriatric alcohol and drug misuse and abuse. *Advances in Substance Abuse* 3:195–237.

Beard JD & Knott DH (1966). Hematopoietic response to experimental chronic alcoholism. *American Journal of Medical Science* 252:518.

Beckett AG, Livingstone AV & Hill KR (1961). Acute alcoholic hepatitis. *British Medical Journal* 2:1113–1119.

Bennett AE (1960). Diagnosis of intermediate state of alcoholic brain disease. *Journal of the American Medical Association* 172:1143–1146.

Benzer D (1987). Medical complication of alcoholism. In RE Herrington, G Jacobson & D Benzer (eds.) *Alcohol and Drug Abuse Handbook*. St. Louis, MO: Warren J. Green, Inc, 219–255.

Benzer DG (1994). Management of alcohol intoxication and withdrawal. In NS Miller (ed.) *Principles of Addiction Medicine*. Chevy Chase, MD: American Society of Addiction Medicine.

Bergman H (1987). Brain dysfunction related to alcoholism: Some results from the KARTAD project. In OA Parsons, N Butters & PE Nathan (eds.) *Neuropsychology of Alcoholism: Implications for Diagnosis and Treatment*. New York, NY: Guilford Press, 21–24.

Bergman H, Axelson G, Idestrom CM et al. (1983). Alcohol consumption and computer-tomographic findings in a random sample of men and women from the general population. *Pharmacology and Biochemical Behavior* 18(Suppl. 1):501–505.

Bianchi C, Negri E, Lavecchia C & Franceschi S (1993). Alcohol consumption and the risk of acute myocardial infarction in women. *Journal of Epidemiology and Community Health* 47(4):308–311.

Bienenfeld D (1987). Alcoholism in the elderly. *American Family Physician* 36(2):163–169.

Bluckman SJ, Dvorak VC & MacGregor RR (1975). Host defenses during prolonged alcohol consumption in a controlled environment. *Archives of Internal Medicine* 137:1539–1543.

Boffetta P & Garfinkel L (1991). Alcohol drinking and mortality among men enrolled in an American Cancer Society perspective study. *Epidemiology* 1(5):342–348.

Brandt J, Butters N, Ryan C & Bayog R (1983). Cognitive loss and recovery in long-term alcohol abusers. *Archives of General Psychiatry* 40:435–442.

Brayton RG, Stokes PE, Schwartz MS & Louria DB (1970). Effect of alcohol and various diseases on leukocyte mobilization, phagocytosis and intracellular bacterial killing. *The New England Journal of Medicine* 282:123–128.

Brogton RG et al. (1970). Effect of alcohol and various diseases on leukocyte function. *The New England Journal of Medicine* 282:123.

Butters N & Cermak LS (1983). Acute loss of autobiographical memories in an amnesic patient with Korsokoff's syndrome. *Social and Neuroscience Abstracts* 9(Part 1):29.

Butz RH (1982). Intoxication and withdrawal. In NJ Estes & ME Heinemann (eds.) *Alcoholism: Development, Consequences and Interventions*. St. Louis, MO: CV Mosby, 102–108.

Cala LA (1985). CT demonstration of the early effects of alcohol on the brain. In M Galanter (ed.) *Recent Developments in Alcoholism (Vol. III)*. New York, NY: Plenum Press, 253–264.

Cala LA, Jones B, Mastaglia FL & Wiley B (1978). Brain atrophy and intellectual impairment in heavy drinkers: A clinical psychometric and computerized tomography study. *Australian and New Zealand Journal of Medicine* 8:147–153.

Callen KJ, Knuiman MW & Ward NJ (1993). Alcohol and mortality in Brusselton, Western Australia. *American Journal of Epidemiology* 137(2):242–248.

Carlen PL et al. (1978). Reversible cerebral atrophy in recently abstinent chronic alcoholics measures by computed tomography scans. *Science* 200(4345):1076–1078.

Carlen PL, Penn RD, Fornazzari L, Bennett J, Wilkinson DA & Wortzman G (1996). Computerized tomographic scan assessment of alcoholic brain damage and its potential reversibility. *Alcoholism* 10:1–7.

Carlen PL, Wilkinson DA, Wortzman G et al. (1981). Cerebral atrophy and functional deficits in chronic alcoholics without clinically evident liver disease. *Neurology* 31:377–385.

Carpenter PC (1990). Cushing's syndrome. In RE Raket (ed.) *Conn's Current Therapy*. Philadelphia, PA: WB Saunders, 563–566.

Charskadon, MA (1984). Daytime sleepiness in the older patient. In DJ Kupfer & T Crook (eds.) *Physician's Guide to the Recognition and Treatment of Sleep Disorders in the Elderly*. New Canaan, CT: Mark Powley Associates, 18–22.

Cicero TJ (1982). Alcohol-induced deficits in the hypothalamic-pituitary luteinizing hormone axis in the male. *Alcoholism* 6:207–215.

Coate D (1993). Moderate drinking and coronary heart disease mortality: Evidence from NHANES I and NHANES I follow-up. *American Journal of Public Health* 83(6):799–801.

Cohen S (1985, November). Alcoholism: Cardiovascular consequences. *Drug & Alcoholism Newsletter* 14(8): San Diego: Vista Hall Foundation, 1.

Colditz GA (1990). A prospective assessment of moderate alcohol intake and major chronic diseases. *Annals of Epidemiology* 1(2):167–177.

Colle J, Forestier F, Quero AM, Bourrinet P & GERMAN A (1982). The effect of alcohol ingestion on the susceptibility of mice to viral infections. *Alcoholism* 6:239–246.

Courville BC (1966). *Effects of Alcohol on the Nervous System of Man (2nd edition)*. Los Angeles, CA: San Lucos Press.

Cowan DH (1969a). Effect of alcohol on circulating platelets. *Blood* 34:850.

Cowan DH (1969b). Thrombokinetics in alcoholism. *Journal of Laboratory and Clinical Medicine* 74:865.

Cowan DH (1971). Thrombocytopenia of severe alcoholism. *Annals of Internal Medicine* 74:37.

Crabb DW & Lumeng L (1989). Alcoholic liver disease. In WN Kelley (ed.) *Textbook of Internal Medicine*. Philadelphia, PA: Lippincott, 592–602.

Criqui MN, Wallace RB, Mishkel M, Barrett-Connor E & Hess G (1981). Alcohol consumption and blood pressure: The Lipid Research Clinics prevalence study. *Hypertension* 3:552–565.

Crombie IK, Smith WC, Tavendale R & Tunstall-Pedoe H (1990). Geographical clustering of risk factors and lifestyle for coronary heart disease in the Scottish Heart Health Study. *British Heart Journal* 64(3):199–203.

Crowley JP & Abramson PM (1971). Effect of ethanol on complement mediated chemotoxis. *Clinical Research* 19:415.

Decker J & Goldstein J. (1982). Risk factors in head and neck cancer. *The New England Journal of Medicine* 306:1151–1155.

deLabry LO, Blynn RJ, Levenson MR, Hermos JA, Locastro JS & Vokonas PS (1992). Alcohol consumption and mortality in an American male population: Recovering the U-shaped curve—Findings from the normative aging study. *Journal of Studies on Alcohol* 53(1):25–32.

Dement WC (1984). Disordered sleep—Why? *Diagnosis* 6(6):106–114.

De Stefani E, Munoz N, Esteve J, Vasallo A & Victor AC (1990). Mate drinking, alcohol, tobacco, diet and esophageal cancer in Uruguay. *Cancer Research* 50(2):426–431.

Deutscher S, Rackette HE & Krishnaswami V (1984). Evolution of excessive alcohol consumption on myocardial infarction risk in coronary disease patients. *American Heart Journal* 108(4):988–995.

Dinda PK & Beck IT (1977) On the mechanism of the inhibitory effect of ethanol on intestinal glucose and water absorption. *American Journal of Digestive Disorders* 22:529–533.

Donahue RP, Abbott RC, Reed DM & Yano K (1986). Alcohol and hemorrhagic stroke. *Journal of the American Medical Association* 255(7):2311–2314.

Dreyfus PM (1974). Diseases of the nervous system in chronic alcoholics. In B Kissin & H Begleiter (eds.) *The Biology of Alcoholism (31), Clinical Pathology*. New York, NY: Plenum Press, 266.

Driver HE & Swann PF (1987). Alcohol and human cancer (Review). *Anticancer Research* 7:309–320.

DuFour MC, Archer L & Gordis E (1992). Alcohol and the elderly. *Clinical and Geriatric Medicine* 8(1):127–141.

Dyer AR et al. (1977). Alcohol consumption, cardiovascular risk factors, and mortality in two Chicago epidemiologic studies. *Circulation* 56:1067–1074.

Eckardt MJ & Martin PR (1986). Clinical assessment of cognition in alcoholism. *Alcoholism* 10(2):123–127.

Eichner ER & Hillman RS (1970). The evolution of anemia in alcoholic patients. *American Journal of Medicine* 50:218.

Eichner ER, Pierce I & Hillman RS (1973). Effect of alcohol on the serum folate level. *Journal of Clinical Investigation* 52:584.

Ellingboe J & Varanelli CE (1979). Ethanol inhibits testosterone biosynthesis by direct action on Leydig cells. *Research Communications in Chemical Pathology and Pharmacology* 24:84–102.

Emmerson RY, Dustman DA, & Shearer DE (1988). Neuropsychological performance of young nondrinkers, social drinkers, and long-and-short-term sober alcoholics. *Alcoholism: Clinical & Experimental Research* 12(5):625–629.

Ettinger PO, Wu CF, Dela Cruz C, Weisse AB, Ahmed SS & Regan TJ (1978). Arrhythmias and the holiday heart: Alcohol associated cardiac rhythm disorders. *American Heart Journal* 95:555–561.

Fabian MS & Parsons OA (1983). Differential improvement of functions in recovering alcoholic women. *Journal of Abnormal Psychology* 921:87–951.

Feinman L & Lieber CS (1974). Liver disease in alcoholism. In B Kissin and H Begleiter (eds.) *The Biology of Alcoholism, Vol. 3. Clinical Pathology*. New York, NY: Plenum Press, 303–338.

Fenster LF (1982). Alcohol and disorders of the gastrointestinal system. In NJ Estes & ME Heinemann (eds.) *Alcoholism Development, Consequences and Interventions*. St. Louis, MO: CV Mosby, 136–143.

Ferrans FJ (1966). Alcoholic cardiomyopathy. *American Journal of the Medical Sciences* 252:89–104.

Fitzhugh LC, Fitzhugh KB & Reitan RM (1965). Adaptive abilities and intellectual functioning of hospitalized alcoholics: Further considerations. *Quarterly Journal of Studies on Alcohol* 26:402 411.

Frazer GE & Upsdell M (1981). Alcohol and other discriminants between cases of sudden death and myocardial infarction. *American Journal of Epidemiology* 114:462–476.

Freund G (1982). The interaction of chronic alcohol consumption and aging on brain structure and function. *Alcoholism: Clinical & Experimental Research* 6(1):13–21.

Freund G (1984). Neurotransmitter function in relation to aging and alcoholism. In JT Hartford & T Samorojski (eds.) *Alcoholism in the Elderly*. New York, NY: Raven Press.

Freund G & Ballinger WE (1992). Alzheimer's disease and alcoholism: Possible interactions. *Alcohol* 9:223–240.

Gao YT, McLaughlin JK, Blot WJ et al. (1994). Risk factors for esophageal cancer in Shanghai, China: 1. Role of cigarette smoking and alcohol drinking. *International Journal of Cancer* 58(2):192–196.

Garr A, Espina N & Lieber C (1986). Ethanol and the repair of DNA. *Alcohol Health & Research World* 10(3):26–27.

Gavaler JS (1985). Effect of alcohol on endocrine function in post-menopausal women: A review. *Journal of Studies on Alcohol* 46:495–516.

Gavaler JS, Love K, Van Thiel D et al. (1991). An international study of the relationship between alcohol consumption and postmenopausal estradiol levels. *Alcohol* (Suppl. 1):327–330.

Gaziano JM, Burning JE, Breslow JL et al. (1993). Moderate alcohol intake, increased levels of high-density lipoprotein and its subtractions and decreased risk of myocardial infarction. *The New England Journal of Medicine* 329(25):1829–1834.

Gebhardt CA, Naeser MA & Butters N (1984). Computerized measures of CT scans of alcoholics: Thalamic region related to memory. *Alcohol* 1:133–140.

Gilhus, ND & Matre R (1982). In vitro effect of ethanol on subpopulations of human blood mononuclear cells. *International Archives of Allergy and Applied Immunology* 68(4):382–386.

Gill JS, Zezulka AV, Shipley MJ, Gill SK & Beevers DG (1986). Stroke and alcohol consumption. *The New England Journal of Medicine* 315(17):1042–1046.

Glynn RM, Bouchard GR, Locastro JS & Hermos JA (1994). Changes in alcohol consumption behaviors among men in the normative aging study. In G Maddox, LN Robins & N Roseberg (eds.) *Nature and Extent of Alcohol Problems among the Elderly* (Research Monograph No. 14). Washington, D.C.: Department of Health and Human Services, 101–116.

Goldman M, Williams D & Klisz D (1983). Recoverability of psychological functioning following alcohol abuse: Prolonged visual-spatial dysfunction in older alcoholics. *Journal of Consulting and Clinical Psychology* 51:370–378.

Goldman MS (1982). Reversibility of psychological deficits in alcoholics: The interaction of aging with alcohol. In DA Wilkinson (ed.) *Cerebral Deficits in Alcoholism*. Toronto, Ontario: Addiction Research Foundation, 79–105.

Goldstein G, Chotlos JW, McCarthy RJ & Neuringer C (1968). Recovery from gain instability in alcoholics. *Journal of Studies on Alcohol* 29:38–43.

Gordon GG, Vittek J, Southern AL, Munnangi P & Lieber CS (1980). Effect of chronic alcohol ingestion on the biosynthesis of steroids in rat testicular homogenate in vitro. *Endocrinology* 106:1880–1885.

Gould L, Azhir M, Demartino A & Comprecht RF (1971). Cardiac effects of a cocktail. *Journal of the American Medical Association* 218:1799–1802.

Grant BF, DuFour MC & Hartford TC (1988). Epidemiology of alcoholic liver disease. *Seminars in Liver Disease* 8(1):12–25.

Grant BF & Zobeck TC (1989). *Liver Cirrhosis: Mortality in the United States, 1972–1986* (NIAAA Surveillance Report 11). Rockville, MD: National Institute on Alcohol Abuse and Alcoholism.

Greenspan AJ & Schaal SF (1983). The "holiday heart": Electrophysiologic studies of alcohol effects in alcoholics. *Annals of Internal Medicine* 98:135–139.

Halsted CH, Griggs RC & Harris JW (1967). The effect of alcoholism on the absorption of folic acid (H3 PGA) evaluated by plasma levels and urine excretion. *Journal of Laboratory and Clinical Medicine* 69:116.

Hankoff LP (1972). Ancient descriptions of organic brain syndrome: The "Kordiakos" of the Talmud. *American Journal of Psychiatry* 129:233–236.

Harper C & Kril J (1985). Brain atrophy in chronic alcoholic patients: A quantitative pathological study. *Journal of Neurology, Neurosurgery, and Psychiatry* 48:211–217.

Hartroft WS & Porta SA (1966). Experimental alcoholic hepatic injury. Nutrition Reviews 97–101.

Heberden W (1929). *Heberden, William 1710–1801: An Introduction to the Study of Physic*. New York: PB Hoeber.

Hegedus L (1984). Decreased thyroid gland volume in alcoholic cirrhosis of the liver. *Journal of Clinical Endocrinology and Metabolism* 58:930–933.

Hegedus L, Rasmussen N, Ravn V, Kastrup J, Krogsgaard K & Aldershvile J (1988). Independent effects of liver disease and chronic alcoholism on thyroid function and size: The possibility of a toxic effect of alcohol on the thyroid gland. *Clinical and Experimental Metabolism* 37(3):229–233.

Heinz R, Lorant P & Stacher A (1983, September). Alcohol changes in hematopoietic system: An epidemiological contribution to the problem of alcoholic anemia. *Wiener Klinische Wochenschrift* 95(17):624–628.

Hemmingsen R & Kramp P (1988). Delirium tremens and related clinical states: Psychopathology, cerebral pathophysiology and psychochemistry: A two-component hypothesis concerning etiology and pathogenesis. *Acta Psychiatrica Scandinavica Supplementum* 345:94–107.

Hendriks HF, Veenstra J, Velthuis-Te-Wierik EJ, Schaafsma G & Kluft C (1994). Effect of moderate dose of alcohol with evening meal on fibrinolytic factors. *British Medical Journal* 308(6935):1003–1006.

Hennekens CH et al. (1979). Effects of beer, wine and liquor in coronary deaths. *Journal of the American Medical Association* 242(18):1973–1974.

Higgins EM & du Vivier AWP (1992). Alcohol and the skin. *Alcohol and Alcoholism* 27(6):595–602.

Higgins EM, du Vivier AWP & Peters JJ (1992). Skin disease and alcohol abuse. *Alcohol and Alcoholism* 27(Suppl):95.

Hillman RS (1973). Hematologic disorders in alcoholism. *Journal of Clinical Investigation* 52:584.

Hillman RS (1982). Hematological disorders of alcoholism. In NJ Estes & MB Heinemann (eds.) *Alcoholism Development, Consequences and Interventions*. St. Louis, MO: CV Mosby.

Hillman RS, McGuffin R & Campbell C (1977). Alcohol interference with the folate enterohepatic cycle. *Transactions of the Association of American Physicians* 90:145.

Hodges DL, Kumar VN & Redford JB (1986). Effects of alcohol on bone, muscle and nerve. *American Family Physician* 34(5):149–156.

Horwitz LD (1975). Alcohol and heart disease. *Journal of the American Medical Association* 232:959–960.

Hrubec Z & Omenn GS (1981). Evidence of genetic predisposition to alcoholic cirrhosis and psychosis: Twin concordances for alcoholics and its biological end points by zygosity among male veterans. *Alcoholism* 5:207–215.

Hugues JN, Cofte T, Perret G, Jaryle MS, Sebaoun J & Modybani E (1980). Hypothalamo-pituitary ovarian function in 31 women with chronic alcoholism. *Clinical Endocrinology* 12:543–551.

Hurt RD, Finlayson RE, Morse RM et al. (1988). Alcoholism in elderly persons: Medical aspects and prognosis of 216 patients. *Mayo Clinic Proceedings* 63:753–760,

Iber FL (1986). Alcoholism and associated malnutrition in the elderly. In DM Prinsley & HH Sanstead (eds.) *Nutrition and Aging*. New York, NY: Academic Press, 157.

Iber FL (1990). Alcoholism and associated malnutrition in the elderly. *Nutrition and Aging*. New York, NY: Alan R. Liss, 157–173.

Ikeda H (1991, October). Clinical and epidemiological studies of alcoholic demential. *Arukoru Kenkyu to Yakubutsu Ison (Japanese Journal of Alcohol Studies and Drug Dependence)* 2695:341–348.

Ishii T (1983). A comparison of cerebral atrophy in CT scan findings among alcoholic groups. *Acta Psychiatrica Scandinavica Supplementum* 309:1–30.

Israel Y et al. (1969). Alcohol and amino acid transport in the human small intestine. *Journal of Nutrition* 98:222.

Jackson R, Scragg R & Beaglehole R (1992). Does recent alcohol consumption reduce the risk of acute myocardial infarction and coronary death in regular drinkers? *American Journal of Epidemiology* 136(7):819–824.

Jacobsen R (1986). Female alcoholics: A controlled CT brain scan and clinical study. *British Journal of Addiction* 81:661–669.

Johnson LD, Burdick JA & Smith JW (1970). Sleep during alcohol intake and withdrawal in chronic alcoholics. *Archives of General Psychiatry* 22:406–418.

Johnstone DE, Chiao YB, Gavaler JS & Van Thiel DH (1981). Inhibition of testosterone synthesis by ethanol and acetaldehyde. *Biochemistry and Pharmacology* 30:1827–1831.

Kamionkowski MD & Fleshler B (1965). The role of alcoholic intake in esophageal carcinoma. *American Journal of the Medical Sciences* 249:696.

Katlic MR, Wilkins EW & Grillo HC (1990). Three decades of esophageal squamous carcinoma at the Massachusetts General Hospital. *Journal of Thoracic and Cardiovascular Surgery* 99(5):929–938.

Kentala E, Luurila O & Salospuro MF (1976). Effects of alcohol ingestion on cardiac rhythm in patients with ischaemic heart disease. *American Journal of Epidemiology* 121:549–554.

Klatsky AL (1987). The cardiovascular effects of alcohol. *Alcohol* 22(Suppl 1):117–124.

Klatsky AL et al. (1977). Alcohol consumption and blood pressure. *The New England Journal of Medicine* 296(21):1194–1200.

Klein S & Iber FL (1991). Alcoholism and associated malnutrition in the elderly. *Nutrition* 7(2):75–79.

Knauer CM (1976). Mallory-Weiss syndrome—Characteristics of 75 Mallory-Weiss lacerations in 528 patients with upper gastrointestinal hemorrhage. *Gastroenterology* 71:5.

Knight T, Smith Z, Lockton JA et al. (1993). Ethnic differences in risk markers for heart disease in Bradford and implications for preventive strategies. *Journal of Epidemiology and Community Health* 47(2):89–95.

Knott DH & Beard JD (1982). Effects of alcohol ingestion on the cardiovascular system. In EM Pattison & E Kaufman (eds.) *Encyclopedia Handbook of Alcoholism*. New York, NY: Gardner Press, 237.

Koob G (1983). Interaction of vasopressin and corticotropin releasing factors with stress. In T Cicero (ed.) *Ethanol Tolerance and Dependence: Endocrinological Aspects*. Washington, DC: U.S. Government Printing Office, 217–230.

Kuo YJ & Shambour LL (1979). Effects of alcohol on sodium, 3-*O*-methyl glucose and L-alanine transport in the jejunum. *American Journal of Digestive Disorders* 23:51.

Kurata JH & Halle BE (1984). Epidemiology of peptic ulcer disease. *Clinical Gastroenterology* 13:289–307.

Lang LG & Kinnanen PM (1987). Cardiovascular effects of alcohol. *Advances in Alcohol and Substance Abuse* 6(3):47–52.

La Vecchia C, Lucchini F & Levi F (1994, July). Worldwide trends in suicide mortality, 1955–1989. *Acta Psychiatrica Scandinavica* 90(1):53–64.

Lee K et al. (1979). Alcohol-induced brain damage and liver damage in young males. *Lancet* 2(8146):759–761.

Leibowitz JO (1967). Studies in the history of alcoholism II: Acute alcoholism in ancient Green and Roman medicine. *British Journal of Addictions* 62:83–86.

Lelbach WK (1974). Organic pathology related to volume and pattern of alcohol use. In R J Gibbins, Y Israel, H Kolant, RE Popham, W Schmidt & RG Smart (eds.) *Research Advances in Alcohol and Drug Problems*. New York, NY: Wiley, 93–198.

Levy RI (1985). Prevalence and epidemiology of cardiovascular disease. In JB Symgaarden and LH Smith (eds.) *Cecil Textbook of Medicine*. Philadelphia, PA: WB Saunders, 155–158.

Lieber CS (1966). Hepatic and metabolic effects of alcohol. *Gastroenterology* 50:119–133. Lieber CS (1976). The metabolism of alcohol. *Scientific American* 234:25.

Lieber CS (1982). *Medical Disorders of Alcoholism: Pathogenesis and Treatment*. Philadelphia, PA: WB Saunders.

Lieber CS (1984). Alcohol and the liver: 1984 update. *Hepatology* 4(6):1243–1260.

Lieber CS (1988). Metabolic effects of ethanol and its interaction with other drugs, hepatotoxic agents, vitamins and carcinogens: A 1988 update. *Seminars in Liver Disease* 8(1):47–68.

Likohri RH, Huttunen MO, Harkonen M et al. (1978). Acute effects of alcohol on anterior pituitary secretion of the trophic hormones. *Journal of Clinical Endocrinology and Metabolism* 46:715–720.

Linn S, Carroll M, Johnson C, Fulwood R, Kalsbeek W & Biefel R (1993). High density lipoprotein, cholesterol and alcohol consumption in U.S. white and black adults: Data from NHANES II. *American Journal of Public Health* 83(6):799–801.

Lowenstein SR, Gabow PA, Cramer J, Oliva PB & Ratner K (1983). The role of alcohol in new-onset atrial fibrillation. *Archives of Internal Medicine* 143:1882–1885.

Lundy J, Raaf JH, Deakins S et al. (1975). The acute and chronic effects of alcohol on the human immune system. *Surgical Gynecology and Obstetrics* 141:212–218.

MacGregor RR, Spagnuolo PJ & Lentnek AL (1974). Inhibition of granulocyte adherence by ethanol, prednisone and aspirin, measured with an assay system. *The New England Journal of Medicine* 291:642–646.

Maddrey WC (1988). Alcoholic hepatitis: Clinicopathologic features and therapy. *Seminars in Liver Disease* 8(1):91–102.

Markiewicz K & Cholewa M (1982). The effect of alcohol on the circulatory system adaptation to physical effort. *Journal of Studies on Alcohol* 43(7):812–822.

Martinez I (1970). Retrospective and prospective study of carcinoma of the esophagus, mouth and pharynx in Puerto Rico. *Boletin—Asociacion Medica de Puerto Rico* 62:170–178.

Mayer EM, Grabowski CJ & Fisher RS (1978). Effects of graded doses of alcohol upon esophageal motor function. *Gastroenterology* 75:1133–1136.

Mendelson JH, Mello N, Cristofano P et al. (1987). Alcohol effects on naloxone-stimulated luteinizing hormone prolactin and estradiol in women. *Journal of Studies on Alcohol* 48:187–194.

Mendenhall CL et al. (1991). Antibodies to hepatitis B and hepatitis C virus in alcoholic hepatitis and cirrhosis: Their prevalence and clinical relevance. *Hepatology* 14(4):581–589.

Merritt HH, ed. (1979). *A Textbook of Neurology*. Philadelphia, PA: Lea & Febiger.

Mezey E. (1975). Intestinal function in chronic alcoholism. *Annals of the New York Academy of Sciences* 252:215.

Mikkelsen WP et al. (1968). Acute hyaline necrosis of the liver—A surgical trap. *American Journal of Surgery* 116:266.

Miller NS, Belkin BM & Gold MS (1991). Alcohol and drug dependency among the elderly: Epidemiology, diagnosis and treatment. *Comprehensive Psychiatry* 32(2):153–165.

Miller NS & Gold MS (1987). The diagnosis and treatment of alcohol dependence. *New Jersey Medicine* 84(12):873–879.

Mitchell JH & Cohen LS (1970). Alcohol and the heart. *Modern Concepts of Cardiovascular Disease* 36(Suppl. 109):13.

Moddrey WC (1988). Alcoholic hepatitis: Clinicopathologic features and therapy. *Seminars in Liver Disease* 8(1):91–102.

Monforte R, Estruch R, Graus F, Nicolas JM & Urbano-Marquez A (1990). High ethanol consumption as risk factor for intracerebral hemorrhage in young and middle-aged people. *Stroke* 21(11):1529–1532.

Monk A, Cryns AG & Cabral R (1977, November). *Alcohol Consumption and Alcoholism as a Function of Adult Age*. Presented at 30th Annual Scientific Meetings of the Gerontological Society, San Francisco, CA.

Moore RD & Pearson TA (1986). Moderate alcohol consumption and coronary artery disease: A review. *Medicine* 65(4):242–267.

Morse RM & Flavin DK (1992). The definition of alcoholism. The Joint Committee of the National Council on Alcoholism and Drug Dependence and the American Society of Addiction Medicine to Study the Definition and Criteria for the Diagnosis of Alcoholism. *Journal of the American Medical Association* 268(8):1012–1014.

Moskovic S (1975). Effect of chronic alcohol intoxication on ovarian dysfunction. *Srpski Arhiv za Celokupno Lekaarstvo* 103:752–758.

Munro HN, Suter PM & Russell RM (1987). Nutritional requirements for the elderly. *Annual Review of Nutrition* 7:23.

Mutchnick MG & Lee HH (1988). Impaired lymphocyte proliferative response to mitogen in alcoholic patients: Absence of a relation to liver disease activity. *Alcoholism* 12(1):155–158.

National Institute on Alcohol Abuse and Alcoholism (NIAAA) (1988). Alcohol and aging. 2:1–4.

NIAAA (1990, January). *Seventh Special Report to the U.S. Congress on Alcohol and Health from the Secretary of Health and Human Services*. Rockville, MD: U.S. Department of Health and Human Services, 120.

Nishiguchi S et al. (1991). Detection of hepatitis C virus antibodies and hepatitis C virus RNA in patients with liver disease. *Hepatology* 14(6):985–989.

Nomura H, Kashiwagi S, Hayashi J et al. (1988). An epidemiological study of effects of alcohol in the liver in hepatitis B surface antigen carriers. *American Journal of Epidemiology* 128(2):277–284.

North RN & Walter RM (1984). The effects of alcohol on the endocrine system. *Medical Clinics of North America* 68:133–146.

Okanoto Y, Fjuimori Y, Nakamoto H & Tsujii T (1988). Role of the liver in alcohol-induced alteration of high-density lipoprotein metabolism. *Journal of Laboratory and Clinical Medicine* 111(4):482–485.

Orlando J et al. (1976). Effect of ethanol on angina pectoris. *Annals of Internal Medicine* 84:652–655.

Overholt BF (1969). Comment on acid, aspirin, alcohol and bleeding, *Gastroenterology* 56:637.

Park J, Ko HJ, Park YN & Jung CH (1994). Dementia among the elderly in a rural Korean community. *British Journal of Psychiatry* 164(6):796–801.

Parker DA, Parker ES, Brody JA & Schoenberg R (1983). Alcohol use and cognitive loss among employed men and women. *American Journal of Public Health* 73:521–526.

Parker ES & Noble EP (1977). Alcohol consumption and cognitive functioning in social drinkers. *Journal of Studies on Alcohol* 38(7):1224–1232.

Parsons OA (1986). Cognitive functioning in sober social drinkers: A review and critique. *Journal of Studies on Alcohol* 47(2):101–114.

Parsons OA & Leber WR (1981). The relationship between cognitive dysfunction and brain damage in alcoholics: Causal, interactive or epiphenomenal? *Alcoholism: Clinical & Experimental Research* 5(2):326–343.

Pfefferbaum A, Rosenbloom M, Crusan K, Jernigan TL & Brain CT (1988). Changes in alcoholics: Effects of age and alcohol consumption. *Alcoholism* 12(1):81–87.

Pochi PE (1988). Acne vulgaris and rosacea. In RE Rakel (ed.) *Conn's Current Therapy*. Philadelphia, PA: WB Saunders, 655–659.

Poikolainen K, Rennal AT, Karvonen J, Lanharanta J & Karkkainen P (1990). Alcohol intake: A risk factor for psoriasis in young and middle aged men. *British Medical Journal* 300:780–783.

Potter JF & James OF (1987). Clinical features and prognosis of alcoholic liver disease in respect to advancing age. *Gerontology* 33:380–387.

Rajkovic IA, Yousif-Kadaru AGM, Wyke RJ & Williams R (1984). Polymophonuclear leukocyte locomotion and aggregation in patients with alcoholic liver disease. *Clinical and Experimental Immunology* 58:654–662.

Razay G, Heaton KW, Bolton CH & Hughes AO (1992). Alcohol consumption and its relation to cardiovascular risk factors in British women. *British Medical Journal* 304(6819):80–83.

Reese LH, Besse GM, Jeffcoate WJ, Goldie DJ & Marks V (1977). Alcohol induced pseudo Cushing's syndrome. *Lancet* i:726–728.

Regan TJ (1990). Alcohol and the cardiovascular system. *Journal of the American Medical Association* 264(3):377–381.

Reichman ME, Jude JT, Schatzkin A et al. (1993). Effects of alcohol consumption of plasma urinary hormone concentrations in premenopausal women. *Journal of the National Cancer Institute* 85(9):722–727.

Renaud S & de Lorgeril M (1992). Wine, alcohol, platelets and the French paradox for coronary heart disease. *Lancet* 339(8808):1523–1526.

Rich EC, Siebold C & Campian B (1985). Alcohol-related acute atrial fibrillation. *Archives of Internal Medicine* 145:830–833.

Roe DA (1979). *Alcohol and the Diet*. Westport, CN: AVI Publishing Co.

Ron MA (1983). The alcoholic brain: CT scan and psychological findings. *Psychology and Medical Monograph, Supplement* 3. Cambridge, MA: Cambridge University Press.

Roselle GA & Mendenhall CL (1982). Alteration of in vitro human lymphocyte function by ethanol, acetaldehyde and acetate. *Journal of Clinical and Laboratory Immunology* 9:33–37.

Roselle GA & Mendenhall CL (1984). Ethanol-induced alterations in lymphocyte function in the guinea pig. *Alcoholism* 8:62–67.

Rosenkranz L (1983). Aseptic necrosis of bone and chronic alcoholism. *Journal of Family Practice* 17(2):323–326.

Rothschild MA, Oratz M & Schreiber SS (1989). Alcohol-induced liver disease. In WN Kelley (ed.) *Textbook of Internal Medicine*. Philadelphia, PA: Lippincott, 592–602.

Rubin E & Lieber CS (1968). Alcohol-induced hepatic injury in nonalcoholic volunteers. *The New England Journal of Medicine* 278:869.

Rubin E & Lieber CS (1974). Fatty liver alcoholic hepatitis and cirrhosis produced by alcohol in primates. *The New England Journal of Medicine* 290:128.

Schaper, AG (1991). Alcohol and mortality: A review of prospective studies. *British Journal of Addictions* 86(4):379–382.

Schaper AG, Phillips AN, Pocock J & Walker M (1987). Alcohol and ischemic heart disease in middle aged British men. *British Journal of Medicine* 294:733–737.

Schaper AG, Wannametiiee G & Walker M (1994). Alcohol and coronary heart disease: A perspective from the British Regional Heart Study. *International Journal of Epidemiology* 23(3):482–494.

Scharschmidt BF (1985). Acute and chronic hepatic failure with encephalopathy. In JB Wyngaarden & LH Smith (eds.) *Cecil's Textbook of Medicine.* Philadelphia, PA: WB Saunders.

Schiff ER (1992). Non-alcoholic liver disease in the alcoholic. *Newer Aspects on Alcohol Nutrition and Hepatic Encephalopathy* (American Association for the Study of Liver Diseases, Postgraduate course). Thorofare, NJ: American Association for the Study of Liver Diseases, 349–360.

Schmidt W & DeLint J (1972). Causes of death in alcoholics. *Quarterly Journal of Studies on Alcohol* 33:171–185.

Schukit MA (1982). A clinical review of alcohol, alcoholism and the elderly patient. *Journal of Clinical Psychiatry* 43(10):396–399.

Schuckit MA & Miller P (1976). Alcoholism in elderly men: Survey of a general medical ward. *Annals of the New York Academy of Science* 273:558–571.

Schuckit MA, Morrissey ER & O'Leary MR (1978). Alcohol problems in elderly men and women. *Addictive Disease* 3:405–416.

Schuckit MA & Pastor PA (1979). Alcohol-related psychopathology in the aged. In OJ Kaplan (ed.) *Psychopathology in the Aging.* New York: Academic Press.

Scott RB (1989). Alcohol effects on the elderly. *Comprehensive Therapy* 15(6):8–12.

Sellers EM & Kalant H (1982). Alcohol withdrawal and delirium tremens. In EM Pattison & E Kaufmann (eds.) *Encyclopedia Handbook of Alcoholism.* New York, NY: Gardner Press, 152.

Seppa K, Sillanoukee P, Pitkajorvi T, Nikkela M & Kowula T (1992). Moderate and heavy alcohol consumption have no favorable effect on lipid values. *Archives of Internal Medicine* 152(2):297–300.

Sexias FA (1982). Criteria for the diagnosis of alcoholism. In NJ Estes & ME Heinemann (eds.) *Alcoholism: Development, Consequences and Interventions.* St. Louis, MO: CV Mosby, 49–66.

Shinton R, Sagar G & Beevers G (1993). The relation of alcohol consumption to cardiovascular risk factors and stroke. The West Birmingham stroke project. *Journal of Neurology, Neurosurgery, and Psychiatry* 56(5):458–462.

Sinclair HM (1972). Nutritional aspects of alcoholism. *Proceedings of the Nutrition Society* 31:117.

Smith FE & Palmer DL (1986). Alcoholism, infection and altered host defenses. *Journal of Chronic Disease* 28:35–49.

Smith JW (1982a). Alcohol—Its effects on sexual performance. *Consultant* 22(5):261–264.

Smith JW (1982b). Alcohol and disorders of the heart and skeletal muscles. In NJ Estes & ME Heinemann (eds.) *Alcoholism Development, Consequences and Interventions.* St. Louis, MO: CV Mosby, 176–183.

Smith JW (1982c). Neurological disorders in alcoholism. In NJ Estes & ME Heinemann (eds.) *Alcoholism: Development, Consequences and Interventions.* St. Louis. MO: CV Mosby, 144–167.

Smith JW, Burt DW & Chapman RF (1973). Intelligence and brain damage in alcoholics. *Quarterly Journal of Studies on Alcohol* 34:414–433.

Smith JW, Johnson LD & Burdick JA (1971). Sleep, psychological and clinical changes during alcohol withdrawal in NAD-treated alcoholics. *Quarterly Journal of Studies on Alcohol* 32:982994.

Solomon K, Manepalli J, Ireland GA & Mahon GM (1993). Alcoholism and prescription drug abuse in the elderly. *Journal of the American Geriatric Society, St. Louis University Grand Rounds* 41:57–69.

Stall R (1968). Respondent-identified reasons for change and stability in alcohol consumption as a concomitant of the aging process. In CR Janes, R Stall & SM Gifford (eds.) *Anthropology and Epidemiology: Interdisciplinary Approaches to the Study of Health and Disease.* Boston. MA: Reidel Publishing, 275–302.

Stall R (1986). Change and stability in quantity and frequency of alcohol use among aging males: A nineteen-year follow-up study. *British Journal of Addictions* 81:537–544.

Stampfer MJ, Colditz GA, Willett WC, Speizer FE & Hennekens CH (1988). A prospective study of moderate alcohol consumption and the risk of coronary disease and stroke in women. *The New England Journal of Medicine* 319(5):267–273.

Still CN, Jackson, KL, Brandes DA, Abramson RK & Macera CA (1990). Distribution of major dementias by race and sex in South Carolina. *Journal of the South Carolina Medical Association* 86(8):453–456.

Stinson FS, DuFour MC & Bertolucci D (1987) Alcohol related morbidity in the aging population. *Alcohol Health and Research World* 13(1):80–87.

Suh I, Shaten BJ, Culler JA & Kuller LH (1992). Alcohol use and mortality from coronary heart disease: The role of high-density lipoprotein cholesterol. *Annals of Internal Medicine* 116(11):881–887.

Szabo S, Trier JS, Brown A & Schnoor J (1985). Early vascular injury and increased vascular permeability in gastric mucosal injury caused by ethanol in the rat. *Gastroenterology* 88:228–236.

Thompson AL et al. (1970). Patterns of S-thiamine hydrochloride absorption in the malnourished alcoholic patient. *Journal of Laboratory and Clinical Medicine* 76:34.

Tsuang JW, Irwin MR, Smith TL & Schuckit MA (1994). Characteristics of men with alcoholic hallucinosis. *Addiction* 89(1):73–78.

Tumarkin B, Wilson JD & Snyder G (1955). Cerebral atrophy due to alcoholism in young adults. *U.S. Armed Forces Medical Journal* 6:67–74.

Tuyns A (1979). Epidemiology of alcohol and cancer. *Cancer Research* 39:2840–2843.

Urbano-Marquez A, Estrugh R, Navarro-Lopez F, Graw JM, Mont L & Rubin E (1989). The effects of alcoholism on skeletal and cardiac muscle. *The New England Journal of Medicine* 320(7):409–415.

U.S. Department of Health and Human Services (1988). *The Surgeon General's Report on Nutrition and Health* (PHS Pub. 988-50210). Washington, D.C.: Superintendent of Documents, US Government Printing Office.

Valimaki M, Pelkonen R, Salasporo M, Harkonen M, Hirvonene E & Ylikahri R (1984). Sex hormones in amenorrheic women with alcoholic liver disease. *Journal of Clinical Endocrinology and Metabolism* 59:133–138.

Van Thiel DH (1983). Ethanol: Its adverse effects on the hypothalamic-pituitary gonadal axis. *Journal of Laboratory and Clinical Metabolism* 101(1):21–33.

Van Thiel DH, Gavaler JS & Lester R (1974). Ethanol inhibition of vitamin A metabolism in the testes: Possible mechanism for sterility in alcoholics. *Science* 186:941–942.

Van Thiel DH, Lipsitz HD, Porter LE, Schade RR, Gottlieb GP & Graham TO (1981). Gastrointestinal and hepatic manifestations of chronic alcoholism. *Gastroenterology* 81:594–615.

Vincenti GE & Blunden SM (1987). Psoriasis and alcohol abuse. *Journal of the Royal Army Medical Corps* 133:77–78.

Wang R, Mallon J, Alterman, AI & McLellan AT (1987). Alcohol and diluted cardiomyopathy: Incidence and correlation with clinical outcome. *Journal of Substance Abuse Treatment* 4(3–4):209–213.

Wannametiiee G & Schaper AG (1988). Men who do not drink: A report from the British Regional Heart Study. *International Journal of Epidemiology* 17:307–326.

Weiner FR, Eskreis DS, Compton KV, Orrego H & Zern MA (1988). Haplotype analysis of a type I collagen gene and its association with alcoholic cirrhosis in man. *Molecular Aspects of Medicine*. Elmsford, NY: Pergamon Press, 159–168.

Wilkinson, DA & Carlen PL (1980). Relationship of neuropsychological test performance to brain morphology in amnesic and non-amnesic chronic alcoholics. *Acta Psychiatrica Scandinavica Supplementum* 286:89–103.

Williams JD, Ray GG & Overall JE (1973). Mental aging and organicity in an alcoholic population. *Journal of Consulting and Clinical Psychology* 41:392–396.

Winship DH, Caflisch CR, Zboralske FF & Hogan WJ (1968). Deterioration of esophageal peristalsis in patients with alcoholic neuropathy. *Gastroenterology* 55:173–178.

Wolinsky H (1985). Atherosclerosis. In JB Wyungaarden & LH Smith (eds.) *Cecil's Textbook of Medicine*. Philadelphia, PA: WB Saunders, 281.

Yano K, Rhoads GG & Kagan A (1977). Coffee, tea and alcohol and risk of coronary heart disease among Japanese men living in Hawaii. *The New England Journal of Medicine* 297:405–509.

Yohman JR, Parsons OA & Leber WR (1985). Lack of recovery in male alcoholics' neuropsychological performance one year after treatment. *Alcoholism* 9:114–117.

Ziring DJ & Adler AG (1991). Alcoholism: Are you missing the diagnosis? *Postgraduate Medicine* 89(5):139–144.

SECTION 11
Surgery in the Addicted Patient

CHAPTER 1

Surgical Management of the Addicted Patient **859**
George W. Nash, M.D., FASAM, and Gordon L. Hyde, M.D., FASAM

CHAPTER 2

Trauma **863**
Carl A. Soderstrom, M.D.

CHAPTER 3

Anesthesia and Analgesia **877**
Charles Beattie, M.D., Ph.D., Annie Umbricht-Schneiter, M.D. and Lynette Mark, M.D.

CHAPTER 4

Liver Transplantation **891**
Thomas P. Beresford, M.D.

SECTION COORDINATOR

GORDON L. HYDE, M.D., FACS, FASAM
Professor of Surgery and
Chief of Vascular Surgery
University of Kentucky Medical Center
Lexington, Kentucky

CONTRIBUTORS

Charles Beattie, M.D., Ph.D.
Professor and Chairman
Department of Anesthesiology
Vanderbilt University
Nashville, Tennessee

Thomas P. Beresford, M.D.
Professor of Psychiatry
University of Colorado School of Medicine
and Department of Veterans Affairs
Medical Center
Denver, Colorado

Lynette Mark, M.D.
Assistant Professor
Divisions of Critical Care Anesthesia
and Cardiac Anesthesia
Department of Anesthesiology
and Critical Care Medicine
The Johns Hopkins University
Baltimore, Maryland

George W. Nash, M.D., FASAM
Alcoholism Coordinator,
Indian Health Service;
Senior Clinical Lecturer and
Former Chief of Neurosurgery,
University of Arizona Medical School
Tucson, Arizona

Carl A. Soderstrom, M.D., FACS
Assistant Professor of Surgery
University of Maryland School of Medicine, and
Director of Physician Education
Department of Surgery/Traumatology
R. Adams Cowley Shock Trauma Center
Maryland Institute for EMS Systems
Baltimore, Maryland

Annie Umbricht-Schneiter, M.D.
Medical Director, Archway Clinic
National Institute on Drug Abuse
Intramural Research Program
Treatment Research Branch
Clinical Trials Section
Baltimore, Maryland

CHAPTER 1

Surgical Management of the Addicted Patient

George W. Nash, M.D., FASAM
Gordon L. Hyde, M.D., FASAM

Preoperative Management
Management of Acute Conditions
Postoperative Care
The Impaired Surgeon

Many special problems and needs attend the surgical management of the patient who is dependent on alcohol or other drugs, or in recovery from such dependence. The underlying addiction may be apparent or unrecognized; symptoms may be acute or delayed; clinical presentations may include acute intoxication, overdose and drug-specific withdrawal syndromes. Problems may emerge during the preoperative, operative or postoperative period. Management of the addicted trauma patient is particularly challenging.

PREOPERATIVE MANAGEMENT

Screening, Assessment and Diagnosis. Given the incidence and prevalence of addictive disease, a high index of suspicion is justified in every encounter with a surgical patient. The alcoholic or drug addict may present in either the early or late stages. The problem may be acute or chronic, minor or life-threatening, easy to diagnose or elusive. The key to diagnosis, as in any disease, is to *think about it, ask about it* and *look for it.*

Early in the disease process, there are no pathognomonic signs, symptoms or clear-cut laboratory findings. Problems of diagnosis are compounded by denial and clinical indicators may be absent. The earliest symptoms are behavioral rather than physical. They may include mood swings, marital problems, frequent loss of temper, sleep disturbance, depression, personality change, tardiness, legal difficulties and decrease in job performance.

The assessment tools utilized by the addiction medicine specialist also can become a part of the surgeon's diagnostic armamentarium. These include the patient's history, specifically including drug and alcohol use. Because the patient often is in denial, family and friends must be questioned as well.

There are a number of easy-to-administer and effective screening instruments that aid the addiction medicine specialist and surgeon in making a correct diagnosis (as reviewed in Section IV of this text).

Physical and neurologic examination may be useful in reaching a diagnosis, as are abnormalities found on routine laboratory tests. Indeed, complete neuropsychologic testing is indicated in some patients. Imaging may reveal essential information, and x-rays or EEG may be helpful.

Intervention. Once an addictive disorder has been diagnosed, the patient needs to be told of the problem. A judgmental attitude should be avoided and the information shared in a context of concern and support. A simple doctor-to-patient intervention may be all that is needed to motivate the patient to seek help. If the disease is in an early stage and the risk of withdrawal minimal, the surgeon may suggest outpatient evaluation and participation in Alcoholics Anonymous. Addiction medicine consultation should be requested in cases where the patient is reluctant to accept the diagnosis, at risk of withdrawal or evidencing other complications.

If the patient refuses consultation, this fact should be noted in the chart. In some cases, enlisting the aid of family, friends or the primary care physician may help to motivate a reluctant patient. A formal intervention may be necessary if other efforts fail. An addiction medicine specialist can facilitate this process and will be a knowledgeable consultant about attendant legal and confidentiality considerations.

MANAGEMENT OF ACUTE CONDITIONS

Intoxication with alcohol usually is obvious, but the effects of certain drugs other than alcohol may mimic psychiatric, neurologic and medical conditions. Certain drug-specific symptoms and signs may be helpful in identifying alcohol or drug use as a cause of the problem, but blood levels and urine testing are necessary to make a precise diagnosis.

Regardless of cause, intoxication is best managed by observing and protecting the patient until the alcohol or other drug is metabolized or excreted. If immediate surgery is necessary, pre-medication should provide for adequate sedation, taking into consideration the probability of increased tolerance. Opioid addicts can be stabilized prior to surgery by giving 20 mg of methadone intramuscularly. An important principle is to avoid perioperative withdrawal.

Pharmacokinetics may be altered sufficiently to influence the selection of anesthetic agent. No single anesthetic technique addresses all of the problems found in the addicted patient. (The literature concerning anesthetic requirements is summarized in Chapter 3.) In this regard, consultation with an addiction medicine specialist may be helpful.

Patients who do not require emergency surgery may need several days of voluntary or involuntary hospitalization before surgery. During this period, chemical and/or physical restraints may be necessary. High potency antipsychotics such as haloperidol—alone or in combination with a short-acting benzodiazepine—are the drugs of choice.

Overdose is not often seen in surgical patients, except in trauma cases. Those who have overdosed require intensive management, which may include resuscitation, stabilization, careful evaluation and surgical treatment as indicated. Early involvement of an addiction medical specialist is advised.

Withdrawal symptoms may become evident preoperatively, operatively or postoperatively and may be unexpected and alarming. The surgeon should consider drug withdrawal in the differential diagnosis of any physical, neurologic or psychiatric symptoms/signs that emerge during the perioperative period.

POSTOPERATIVE CARE

Abstinence syndromes typically occur after surgery and must be treated as indicated. Intervention in the addictive disease process, if not done previously, should be accomplished when the patient is stable. The services of an addiction specialist are particularly helpful at this point.

Pain management often becomes an issue in the postoperative period. Addicts/alcoholics have special needs in this regard. Proper management of these patients requires either a working knowledge of the pharmacology of addiction or consultation with a specialist in addiction medicine.

Many alcoholics/addicts have tolerance to opiates and sedative-hypnotics and require higher than usual doses; however, dosage must be individualized as tolerance is not universal. Medications must be given in adequate amounts to insure pain relief and prevent withdrawal. Methadone maintenance patients should be continued on their medication. Additional medication is added to the baseline dose as required (Beattie, 1992).

Recovering persons, though at risk for relapse, generally can be given necessary medication for relief of pain and anxiety. The danger of exacerbating an addictive disorder in recovery-stable individuals can be minimized if certain precautions are taken:

- Try nonsteroidal anti-inflammatory drugs or nerve blocks and consider continuous spinals/epidurals;
- Use drugs with the least dependence liability consistent with adequate pain relief;
- Use drugs with dependence liability for no longer than the minimum time needed;
- Involve the patient's AA sponsor (if present) and friends in his or her care;
- Encourage the patient to increase attendance at support group meetings during the pre- and postoperative period.
- If discharge medications are needed, they should be carefully selected, administered by a significant other and monitored frequently by the attending physician.

THE IMPAIRED SURGEON

In addition to caring for patients with addictive disorders, surgeons develop the disease themselves. While the precise incidence of alcohol and drug problems among surgeons is not known, preliminary data suggest that a significant number are or will become impaired through use of alcohol or drugs. Early identification, intervention and treatment rescues such physicians from a disease that can destroy careers, devastate families, ruin health and endanger patients.

Most states now have physician health or impairment programs in place. There is help for the "Wounded Healer" and it is highly effective. The medical profession can be justly proud of this accomplishment.

Every surgeon has a humanitarian and a professional obligation (and, in most states, a legal mandate as well) to intercede with a colleague who has an addictive disorder. The American College of Surgeons offers an excellent pamphlet addressing physician impairment, diagnosis, treatment and reentry.

CONCLUSIONS

The surgeon typically encounters addicted patients under less than ideal circumstances. It thus is understandable that many surgeons regard such individuals as "difficult" patients. Appropriate and timely consultation with an addiction medicine specialist can be instrumental in changing this concept.

Working with addicted patients is demanding but also can be very rewarding. Attitudes change as the surgeon becomes knowledgeable about the disease of addiction, comfortable in dealing with its various manifestations, and has the opportunity to see patients in recovery. Few things in life are more gratifying that helping someone recover from a seemingly hopeless state of mind and body.

The opinions expressed in this paper are those of the authors and do not necessarily reflect the views of the Indian Health Service.

REFERENCES

American Medical Association (1991). *Report J of the Board of Trustees: Screening for Alcohol and Other Drug Use in Trauma Patients* (Resolution 190, A-91). Chicago, IL: The Association.

American Society of Addiction Medicine (1990). *Trauma and Chemical Abuse Dependency Policy and Background Statement*. Washington, DC: The Association.

Beattie C (1992). Anesthetic considerations in both the active and recovering alcoholic/addict. In *Syllabus for the Ruth Fox Course for Physicians*. Washington, DC: American Society of Addiction Medicine.

Bourne P (1976). Acute drug abuse emergencies. In *A Treatment Manual*. New York, NY: Academic Press.

Rostenburg P (1992). Alcoholism and the surgical patient. In *Syllabus for the Ruth Fox Course for Physicians*. Washington, DC: American Society of Addiction Medicine.

Soderstrom CA, Trifillio AL & Shankar BS (1988). Marijuana and alcohol use among 1023 trauma patients: A prospective study. *Archives of Surgery* 123:733–737.

Thal ER, Bost RO & Anderson RJ (1985). Effects of alcohol and other drugs on traumatized patients. *Archives of Surgery* 120:708–712.

Westermeyer J (1986). Drug abuse. In G Winokur & P Claybon (eds.) *The Medical Basis of Psychiatry*. Philadelphia, PA: W.B. Saunders, 212–231.

Wilson B (1976). Preface to the 3rd Edition. *Alcoholics Anonymous*. New York, NY: Alcoholics Anonymous World Services Inc.

CHAPTER 2
Trauma

Carl A. Soderstrom, M.D., FACS

Trauma Centers and Emergency Departments
Alcohol and Drug Use and Injury
Screening Trauma Patients
Patient Management
The "Window of Opportunity"

An Egyptian papyrus from 1500 B.C.E. (el-Guebaly & el-Guebaly, 1981) cautions, "Make not thyself helpless in drinking in the beer shop. . . . Falling down, thy limbs will be broken, and no one will give thee a hand to help thee up." Indeed, the ancient plague of alcohol-related injury is a major health problem in the United States and abroad. McGinnis and Lee (1995) indicated that the combined deaths from alcohol-related medical diseases and injury made alcohol the third leading nongenetic cause of death in the United States. They noted that 3% to 10% of all deaths were related to alcohol use, including 40% to 50% of deaths associated with motor vehicle crashes, 16% to 67% of deaths due to occupational and domestic mishaps, fires, and drownings, and about 20,000 deaths each year from intentional injuries. Reflecting on these statistics, Angell and Kassirer (1994) observed that, "All told, this drug (alcohol) causes about 100,000 deaths yearly in the United States, about half from trauma, and when all expenses are included, it costs society $100 to $130 billion a year."

Despite the impact of alcohol use on injury, only recently have published reports begun to document the prevalence of substance use disorders among hospitalized trauma patients. This chapter focuses primarily on alcohol, but it also addresses (1) alcohol and other drug use among patients treated in emergency departments and hospital trauma centers, (2) the use of available demographic and clinical data to identify patients with substance use disorders, and (3) treatment options for problem-drinking and alcohol-dependent patients. Finally, barriers to identification of patients with substance use disorders and initiation of treatment for those patients will be examined.

TRAUMA CENTERS AND EMERGENCY DEPARTMENTS

A white paper, *Accidental Death and Disability: The Neglected Disease of Modern Society* (National Research Council, 1966) documenting that trauma was a major health care problem, provided the impetus for the development of more than 450 trauma centers (Bazzoli & MacKenzie, 1995) and systems of trauma care around the country. Approximately half of trauma center patients are vehicular crash victims (Champion, Copes et al., 1990; Treno, Cooper & Roeper, 1994; Soderstrom, Dailey & Kerns, 1994). The Committee on Trauma of the American College of Surgeons (1993) has promulgated guidelines for optimal care of injured persons treated in trauma centers and systems of care. Depending on available resources (personnel, facilities, equipment), trauma centers are classified as Level I, II, III, or IV. Level I (the highest level) and Level II centers are expected to have resources to provide "initial definitive trauma care" for severe injuries. Level I centers differ from Level II centers in that they have the most resources to treat seriously injured patients with complex injuries, and they have made a commitment to teaching and research in trauma care. Level I centers generally are university-based teaching hospitals that serve as the "regional resource trauma center" for a system of trauma care. Level III and IV centers provide care in communities that do not have immediate access to higher levels of care. After assessment, resuscitation and emergency surgical procedures, severely injured patients admitted to these facilities are transferred to Level I or II trauma centers.

The vast majority of injured patients do not require admission to a trauma center (COT, ACS,

1993; DHHS, 1992). For each person killed in a vehicular crash in 1993, another 80 were injured, for a total of more than three million individuals. Of each 80 injured persons, 41 required emergency medical attention. Of these, 33 were treated in emergency departments, and eight required hospitalization—frequently in a trauma center (NHTSA, 1988).

Before the existence of trauma centers, all injured victims were taken to the closest emergency department for treatment. Now, in areas where trauma center care is available, most seriously injured patients are triaged to trauma centers.

ALCOHOL AND DRUG USE AND INJURY

Alcohol use has been linked to all types of injury (Lowenfels & Miller, 1984; McGinnis & Lee, 1995; Secretary of Health and Human Services, 1994; Soderstrom, Triffilis et al., 1988; Soderstrom, Dischinger et al., 1995a; Zuska, 1981), particularly injury sustained in vehicular crashes (Council on Scientific Affairs, 1986; NHTSA, 1996). Approximately 15% to 25% of injured patients treated in emergency departments test positive for alcohol (NIAAA, 1991; Cherpitel, 1995; Teplin, Abram & Michaels, 1989). Alcohol-positive rates are higher among patients admitted to trauma centers. Data from trauma centers throughout California (Treno, Cooper & Roeper, 1996) document that, among more than 13,500 patients who had a blood alcohol concentration (BAC) test (test rate 60%), 53% were BAC positive (mean BAC of 180 mg/dl). Men were more frequently BAC-positive than women (men, 57% [mean BAC, 172 mg/dl]; women, 39% [mean BAC, 166 mg/dl]). Among 2,657 patients admitted to a Seattle trauma center, 36% were intoxicated (BAC ≥ 100 mg/dl) on admission (men, 40%; women, 22%) (Rivara, Jurkovich et al., 1993). Of 11,062 BAC-tested patients admitted to the University of Maryland's R Adams Cowley Shock Trauma Center in Baltimore, 29% were BAC-positive (mean BAC, 161 mg/dl) (Soderstrom, Kufera et al., 1997a). More male patients had BACs ≥ 50 mg/dl than did women (30% versus 18%), as did violence victims compared with unintentional injury victims (35% versus 24%).

Much less is known about the preinjury use of illicit drugs. A California emergency department study (Buchfuhrer & Radecki, 1996) of trauma victims revealed that, of 246 tested for drugs, the following positive results were obtained: cocaine, 16%; marijuana, 16%; amphetamines, 12%; opiates, 6%; phencyclidine (PCP), 1%. Among 452 adults admitted to a Seattle trauma center (Rivara, Mueller et al., 1989), one-half of whom were vehicular crash victims and one-fifth of whom were assault victims, urine drug screens showed that 26% were positive for cannabis, 10% were positive for cocaine, and 38% were positive for alcohol. In another study of more than 600 patients at a Chicago trauma center (Sloan, Zalenski et al., 1989), involving patients who were victims of (mostly unintentional) blunt trauma and penetrating trauma, toxicology screens showed that 17% of patients 17 to 40 years of age were positive for PCP, 5% were positive for cannabis and/or cocaine, and 41% were positive for alcohol. In yet another study from a Philadelphia trauma center (Lindenbaum, Carroll et al., 1989), in which approximately half of those tested were victims of unintentional injury and the other half were victims of assault, the following results were obtained: 37% were positive for cannabinoids, 34% for cocaine, 10% for PCP, and 41% for alcohol.

The aforementioned trauma center reports and another from Hartford, Connecticut (Cesare, Morgan et al., 1990), indicate that alcohol/drug use is higher among victims of violence compared with other trauma victims. Data from the R Adams Cowley Shock Trauma Center Clinical Toxicology Database (Soderstrom, Kufera et al., 1997a) illustrate that point. Toxicology results are presented in Table 1 for 11,028 patients admitted directly from the scene of injury and for whom results were available for alcohol, cocaine, PCP, and opiates. Alcohol is by far the most commonly detected substance among male and female victims of unintentional trauma. Cocaine and alcohol are the most commonly detected substances among men and women injured as the result of violence. Further, for all groups and substances, the rates of test positive results are higher for men than for women.

Among individuals who use health care facilities, the rates of alcohol use problems are much higher than in the general population. The combined results of six studies involving 3,406 non-trauma patients requiring care in outpatient settings or in hospitals, who were assessed using screening questionnaire/interview tests, revealed that 19% screened positive for possible alcoholism (Cyr & Wartman, 1988; Moore, Bone et al., 1989; Redmond, Richards & Plunkett, 1987; Sherin, Piotrowski et al., 1982; Solomon, Vanga et al., 1980; Yersin, Trisconi et al., 1989). The combined results of three studies involving another 1,223 non-trauma

TABLE 1. Alcohol and Other Drug Use Among Shock Trauma Center Patients, 1993–1995 (N = 11,028)

			Injury Type			
	Overall		Unintentional—72.3%		International—27.7%	
Substance	Men (73.4%)	Women (26.6%)	Men (67.3%)	Women (32.7%)	Men (88.9%)	Women (11.1%)
Alcohol[a]	30.0%	17.1%	28.5%	16.1%	32.6%	27.3%
Cocaine[b]	20.8%	9.4%	11.7%	6.2%	41.1%	35.5%
Opiates[b]	17.6%	11.2%	12.6%	9.8%	28.1%	21.8%
Phencyclidine[b]	2.4%	1.1%	2.5%	1.0%	2.3%	1.7%

a. Blood alcohol testing rate, 98%
b. Testing for drugs, 71%

SOURCE: Unpublished data from Soderstrom CA, Dischinger PC & Kerns TJ (1997). National Study Center for Trauma and Emergency Medical Systems, R Adams Cowley Shock Trauma Center, University of Maryland, Baltimore, Maryland.

patients revealed that 30% met *DSM-IIIR* criteria for alcohol dependence (Buchsbaum, Buchanan et al., 1991; Coulehan, Zettler-Segal et al., 1987; Hoffman, Harrison et al., 1989).

Despite the plethora of data linking alcohol and other drug use to injury—particularly injury resulting from vehicular crashes—documentation of the prevalence of PSUDs among trauma patients has been uncommon. In a study of preexisting disease in trauma victims, MacKenzie and colleagues (1989) found diagnoses of alcohol or other drug problems reflected in the discharge records of only 3.0% of more than 27,000 patients (both survivors and nonsurvivors). Considering that between 30% and 50% of trauma patients are intoxicated at the time of injury, that finding provides compelling evidence that trauma patients' substance use disorders are largely unrecognized and untreated. This section addresses recent reports that assess the incidence of PSUDs in injured patients.

R Adams Cowley Shock Trauma Center/University of Maryland (Baltimore). The Shock Trauma Center of the University of Maryland Medical Center (UMMC) is a free-standing Level I regional trauma care center. Although located in an urban setting, the center serves as a regional adult center for patients sustaining severe injuries in the most populated counties of central Maryland. Patients injured in rural and suburban settings outside Baltimore are transported to the center by Medevac helicopters. Most of these patients are injured as the result of unintentional trauma (motor vehicle crashes predominate, followed by falls). Shock Trauma also is an areawide trauma center for the urban communities surrounding the UMMC. Patients injured in these communities are transported to the center by ambulance. The profile of the patient population treated at Shock Trauma is similar to the aggregate of patients treated in trauma centers throughout the United States (Champion, Copes et al., 1990): approximately 75% men; age 25 to 40; three-quarters injured as the result of unintentional trauma and one-quarter injured as the result of violence (shootings, stabbings, beatings).

The prevalence of substance abuse disorders among seriously injured patients admitted to the Shock Trauma Center was studied during the period September 1994 through November 1996 (Soderstrom, Smith et al., 1997b). Study entry criteria were the following: age ≥ 18 years, admission from the scene of injury, length of stay of ≥ 2 days, and intact cognition. Diagnoses were made using the substance use disorder section of the Structured Clinical Interview for *DSM-IIIR* (SCID) (Spitzer, Williams & Gibbon, 1987). Dependence diagnoses were classified as lifetime or current. Individuals who were not in full or partial remission for at least six months were considered current alcoholics. In addition to the SCID, three alcoholism screening instruments were administered: the CAGE (Ewing, 1984), the Brief-Michigan Alcoholism Screening Test (B-MAST) (Pokorny, Miller & Lange, 1972), and the Alcohol Use Disorders Identification Test (AUDIT) (Saunders, Aasland et al., 1993; Babor, de la Fuente et al., 1992). This study, which expanded on a previous one (Soderstrom, Dischinger et al., 1992), documented for the first time the prevalence of both alcohol and drug use disorders among a large unselected group of seriously injured patients. The results are summarized below.

More than half (54%) of the 1,118 interviewed subjects had one or more lifetime PSUDs, of which 87% were for dependence (82% of alcohol diagnoses, 90% of drug diagnoses). Lifetime and current dependence diagnoses were as follows (lifetime includes current dependence): *alcohol alone*—lifetime, 36%, current, 24%; *drugs alone*—lifetime, 28%, current, 18%; *alcohol and drugs*—lifetime, 16%, current 8%.

Lifetime and current rates of alcohol dependence were significantly higher among men than women: *men*—lifetime 41%, current 28%; *women*—lifetime, 22%; current, 15%. The rate of current alcohol dependence was 27% for those 21 to 59 years of age, as compared with 13% for younger and older individuals. Lifetime and current alcohol dependence rates were higher among violence victims than among other trauma victims: *intentional injury*—lifetime, 40%, current, 30%; *unintentional injury*—lifetime, 34%, current 21%. The Shock Trauma rates of current alcohol dependence for men and women were 2.5 to 4.4 and 3.9 to 5.7 times higher, respectively, than for adult men and women in the general United States population (Grant, Harford et al., 1994; Kessler, McGonagle et al., 1994).

Lifetime drug dependence was documented in 28% of patients (current, 18%), of whom 58% were dependent on more than one drug. The lifetime (current) rates of various drug dependence were as follows: cocaine, 16% (11%); marijuana, 15% (7%); opiates, 14% (10%); hallucinogens, 2% (<1%); and stimulants, 2% (<1%). Similar to alcohol, the prevalence of both lifetime and current drug dependence diagnoses were higher among men (lifetime, 33%; current, 20%) than among women (lifetime, 17%; current, 11%) and higher among victims of violence (lifetime, 49%; current, 36%) than among other victims (lifetime, 19%; current, 10%). The lifetime and current drug addiction rates among the Shock Trauma patients were 3.8 and 6.3 times higher, respectively, than among the general population (Kessler, McGonagle et al., 1994).

The Shock Trauma study limited its scope to patients who could be interviewed and those who had lengths of stay of at least two days. Hence, the prevalence of substance use disorders among all trauma patients, particularly those who are found to have minimal injury and those with serious brain injury, was not ascertained.

Harborview Trauma Center/University of Washington (Seattle). Rivara and colleagues (1993) administered the Short Michigan Alcoholism Screening Test (SMAST) (Selzer, Vinokur & van Rooijen, 1975) to 2,422 patients admitted to the Level I Harborview Trauma Center, of whom just over three-quarters were men and victims of unintentional injury. Overall, 44% were SMAST+ for possible alcoholism, the same rate as the combined alcohol dependence and abuse diagnoses for the Shock Trauma study. Higher SMAST+ rates were found among the Harborview men (48%) and women (29%) compared with the lifetime dependence rates among the Shock Trauma patients (men, 41%; women, 22%). Further, a much greater disparity was found between the SMAST+ rates for violence victims (60%) and other patients (38%) compared with those diagnosed with a lifetime alcohol dependence in the Shock Trauma study injured as the result of intentional (40%) and unintentional (34%) trauma. The Harborview results were not corroborated against standard diagnostic criteria for alcohol abuse/dependence and the study did not include an assessment of drug diagnoses.

Michigan Emergency Departments (Ann Arbor). Maio and colleagues (1997) documented the prevalence of alcohol abuse (AA) and dependence (AD) among 1,161 patients treated in two Michigan emergency departments (one in a university hospital with a Level I trauma center). Although diagnoses were made using standardized criteria, the study population was limited to vehicular crash victims. The AA/AD rate (AA and AD were not subdivided) among patients who were treated and released was 15% compared with 30% among those admitted to the hospital. This study was limited to crash victims and did not assess drug diagnoses.

Emergency Department/University of Mississippi (Jackson). The one-year alcohol dependence rate among patients treated in a Mississippi emergency department was assessed using standardized criteria. Cherpitel (1995) found that, among drinkers (individuals who drank alcohol within 12 months), the alcohol dependence rate was the same for both injury and non-injury patients, that is, 19%. Alcohol dependence was higher among men than women, at 28% and 12%, respectively. This study consisted of a modest size sample of trauma patients (N = 247) and did not assess drug problems.

These four studies indicate that alcohol use problems are much more prevalent among injured patients treated in both emergency departments and trauma centers compared with the general population. Alcohol diagnoses are more common among men than women and appear to be more frequent among victims of violence. Additional studies are needed to more clearly define the prevalence of substance abuse disorders among all trauma victims, not just those injured as a result of interpersonal violence.

SCREENING TRAUMA PATIENTS

The best method of identifying substance use disorders in trauma patients would be to conduct an in-depth structured interview employing standardized diagnostic criteria. However, this is not practical in all trauma patients. Trauma clinicians, who have little or no expertise (and often no interest) in addiction medicine, focus their efforts on the diagnosis and management of injuries. They need to use readily available screening tools to identify patients at risk for substance use disorders, who then can be referred to addiction specialists for evaluation and treatment. This section addresses data that can be used to screen patients for substance use disorders, as well as the limitations of those data.

Alcohol Testing. BAC and other toxicology testing is a first step in identifying alcohol problems in trauma patients. For almost 20 years, such testing has been described as an "essential" diagnostic resource for Level I and II trauma centers by the American College of Surgeons' Committee on Trauma (1993). Being intoxicated under circumstances that could lead to injury, as when driving an automobile or on the job, is evidence of alcohol abuse and may identify alcohol-dependent patients.

Shock Trauma Center studies (Soderstrom, Kufera et al., 1997a; Soderstrom, Smith et al., 1997b) indicate that, for different groups of injured patients, the sensitivity of BAC+ status to detect alcohol dependence ranges from 40% to 65%, while the specificity is approximately 85% for all groups. In the Seattle trauma center study (Rivara, Jurkovich et al., 1993), 75% of BAC+ patients were SMAST+, as well as 26%+ of BAC− patients. In the emergency department studies, Maio and colleagues (1997) noted that 45% of AA/AD patients were BAC−, and Cherpitel (1995) documented that the sensitivity and specificity of an alcohol-positive status (determined by breath test) for detecting dependence were 34% and 86%, respectively. Although the presence of alcohol in the blood at the time of admission cannot be used to diagnose alcoholism, a BAC determination is an inexpensive first screening test. Indeed, these data support routine alcohol testing of trauma patients to screen for alcohol problems, provided that clinicians are aware of the limitations of BAC− results.

Floerchinger (1992) reported on 170 injury victims with BAC ≥ 80 mg/dl treated in a Portland trauma center, who were assessed for alcoholism using standardized criteria. Overall, 97% were assessed to have a problem with alcohol: 17.6% of them were considered alcohol abusers and 79.4% were classified as alcoholics. Thirty percent of the alcoholic patients did not know they had a "drinking problem." This report did not evaluate nonintoxicated patients for alcoholism or indicate whether other substance use disorders were sought.

Two observations are in order: First, in the past, the presence of alcohol in combination with injury was a reason to evaluate a patient for possible alcoholism or another substance use disorder. The data suggest that trauma alone is an adequate reason to screen a patient for such problems (Clark, McCarthy & Robinson, 1985). Second, according to current standards of practice in trauma centers, only patients who test positive for alcohol or other drugs of abuse are referred for evaluation for substance use disorders.

Surrogate Alcohol Testing. Despite promulgated guidelines, BAC testing is not conducted routinely in many trauma centers. A trauma center survey indicated that BAC was measured routinely at only 64% of 278 Level I and II centers and that only 40% tested for other drugs of abuse (Soderstrom, Dailey & Kerns, 1994).

Financial disincentives have caused BAC testing to cease in some trauma centers. At those centers, a number of third-party payers have invoked clauses that disallow payment of hospital bills for injured intoxicated patients—hence, testing stopped.

Treno and colleagues (1994) explored the possibility of developing a surrogate method to predict alcohol involvement in injury episodes as means to evaluate/monitor injury prevention efforts. Based on their findings, they concluded "that a weighting schema may be profitably used to determine changes in levels of alcohol-involved trauma in populations over time." Using linear regression techniques applied to data from a comprehensive clinical toxicology database, the author and colleagues developed a profile of indicators to predict which patients would have BACs ≥ 50 mg/dl on admission (Soderstrom, Kufera et al., 1997a). The four data points used to assign risk points for alcohol use prior to injury (BAC ≥ 50 mg/dl) among men and women injured as the result of either intentional or unintentional trauma are age ≥ 40 or < 40 years, being a Caucasian, being injured at night, and being injured on the weekend. The model may prove useful for trauma clinicians in settings where financial and/or legal concerns prevent alcohol testing.

Screening Questionnaires. Shock Trauma patients assessed for substance use disorders also were administered the CAGE, B-MAST, and AUDIT questionnaires. Results of these screening tests were correlated with PSUD diagnoses obtained using *DSM* criteria. The CAGE had the highest sensitivity (84%; B-MAST, 76%; AUDIT, 75%), the highest specificity (90%; B-MAST, 88%; AUDIT, 87%), and largest area under the curve (AUC) derived from receiver operating characteristic (ROC) curve analysis (91%; B-MAST, 89%; AUDIT, 86%) (Soderstom et al., 1997c). In her evaluation of those screening tests in "drinking" emergency patients, Cherpitel (1995) demonstrated that AUDIT and CAGE had higher sensitivities and larger AUCs than the B-MAST in detecting alcoholism: *sensitivity*—AUDIT, 90%; CAGE, 84%; B-MAST, 25%; *AUC*—AUDIT, 89%; CAGE, 86%; B-MAST, 63%. Additional research is needed on screening test results, including choice of cut points for various screening instruments among subsets of trauma populations.

In addition to alcohol screening tests, brief questionnaires are needed to assess possible drug addiction among trauma patients. In the study of Shock Trauma patients, the authors evaluated a "Drug CAGE." That instrument substutited drug(s) for alcohol in inquiring about "criticism," "annoyance," "guilt," and "eye openers." Prelimary results indicate that a Drug CAGE score ≥ 2 was 89% sensitive and 85% specific in detecting current (non-marijuana) drug dependence (McDuff, Gorelick et al., unpublished data).

Cirrhosis. Gitlow and Seixas (1988) observed "that the majority of heavy drinkers fail to develop cirrhosis despite untold numbers of debauches." As noted earlier, trauma is a disease that primarily affects patients under the age of 40; hence, one would not expect to encounter cirrhosis frequently among trauma patients. That observation is corroborated by a study (Morris, MacKenzie & Edelstein, 1990) of preexisting morbidity among almost 13,000 trauma patients treated in California hospitals: the prevalence of cirrhosis, as documented in discharge diagnoses, was 0.4%. The rate was the same for those 35 to 44 years of age and only 0.1% for those 25 to 34 years of age. Similarly, cirrhosis rarely is encountered during emergency abdominal surgery on Shock Trauma patients.

Biological Markers. *Routine Laboratory Tests:* Recent trauma center and emergency department studies indicate that the use of liver function tests and other biochemical markers are of little value in diagnosing alcoholism among trauma patients. Rivara and colleagues (1993) noted that of patients who were SMAST positive for possible acoholism, the following abnormal (elevated) results were obtained: gamma-glutamyltransferase (GGT), 25%; glutamate dehydrogenase (GDH), 32%; mean corpuscular volume (MCV), 10%. Similar results were obtained by Maio and colleagues (1997) in their study of injured crash victims treated in Michigan emergency departments. They noted that, among patients with a diagnosis of either alcohol abuse or alcohol dependence, only 8% had elevated MCVs and 10% had elevated GGT levels. In a group of 97 severely injured German men who required intensive care, Spies and colleagues (1995) found the following results of elevated biologic markers in detecting alcoholism: *AST*—sensitivity, 85%, specificity, 36%; *GGT*—sensitivity, 36%, specificity 95%; *MCV*—sensitivity, 15%, specificity 98%. In that study, in which patients who met DSM-III-R criteria for abuse or dependence were diagnosed as having "alcoholism," the prevalence of alcoholism was 55%.

The rates of elevated biochemical markers among 441 Shock Trauma Center patients, in whom alcohol diagnoses were made using *DSM-IIIR* criteria, are presented in Table 2 (Soderstrom, Dischinger et al., 1996a). The only measurement associated with an alcohol misuse diagnosis is MCV; however, only 19% of patients with a diagnosis of current dependence are MCV positive.

Carbohydrate-Deficient Transferrin (CDT): For more than two decades, CDT levels have been assessed as a biologic marker for a variety of reasons involving alcohol misuse, including diagnosing alcoholism, detecting harmful drinking, and monitoring abstinence among alcoholics in treatment (Stibler, 1991; Salaspuro, 1994). CDT levels are elevated after heavy consumption of alcohol (50 to 80 grams of alcohol per day for 1 week). In a research protocol at the Shock Trauma Center, the use of CDT levels (≥ 20 U/L) to screen patients (N = 618) for current alcohol dependence (N = 142) was found to be of little value. Although the specificity of the test was 89%, the sensitivity was only 34%. In contrast, Spies and colleagues (1995) found that the sensitivity and specificity of CDT for detecting "alcoholism" were 70% and 100%, respectively, among severely injured men who required ICU care.

Drivers' Records. According to 1995 estimates, 4.8% of drivers involved in motor vehicle crashes resulting in injuries were BAC+, while 25.5% of drivers involved in fatal crashes were BAC+ (NHTSA, 1996). In a case-controlled study, Brewer and colleagues documented that BAC+ (≥ 20 mg/dl) fatally injured drivers who were 21 to 24 years of age were 4.3 times more likely to have had at least

TABLE 2. Elevated Biochemical Markers and Alcohol Diagnoses Among Shock Trauma Patients

	AST (>84 U/L) p=NS	BILI (>1 mg/dl) p=NS	MCV + (>94m³) p<.01
No alcohol diagnosis	22%	8%	4%
Abuse	26%	11%	17%
Lifetime dependence	25%	7%	16%
Current dependence	27%	4%	19%

AST, aspartate aminotransferase; BILI, bilirubin; MCV, mean corpuscular volume

one conviction for driving while impaired in the five-year period prior to death than control drivers (25.6% versus 5.1%). The odds ratio increased to 11.7 for older fatally injured BAC+ drivers.

Maull and colleagues (1984) reported on 56 intoxicated (BACs ≥ 150 mg/dl) injured drivers who were admitted to a Richmond, Virginia, trauma center. Most were men (84%), the average age was 30, and the mean BAC was 240 mg/dl. Prior to the crashes involving injury, 16% had received one or more convictions for driving under the influence (DUI), and an additional 22% had been required to complete an alcohol education program.

Two subsequent studies of injured drivers from the Shock Trauma Center indicated that pre-injury alcohol-related or other drug-impaired driving convictions were higher among alcohol-impaired automobile (Soderstrom, Birschbach & Dischinger, 1990) and motorcycle drivers (Soderstrom, Dischinger et al., 1993) than among nonimpaired drivers. The difference was most pronounced among the motorcyclists, where a fourfold higher rate of pre-crash convictions was noted among those who were alcohol positive (BAC+) at admission compared with those who had no detectable alcohol (BAC−), at 28.9% versus 7.2%, respectively ($p < 0.0001$). The mean number of prior convictions was 2.8 for the BAC+ and 1.2 for the BAC− motorcyclists.

In the Shock Trauma studies just cited, BAC+ drivers were found to have significantly more pre-injury reckless driving and speeding convictions than BAC− injured drivers. These studies confirm the findings that Vingilis (1983) articulated in her comprehensive review of the subject, "Drinking Drivers and Alcoholics: Are They the Same Population?" She concluded that "not only are alcoholics involved in more alcohol-related violations and collisions, but with few exceptions . . . [they] have more non-alcohol related violations and collisions than the general population."

Considering that frequent drinking and driving is a characteristic of pathologic misuse of alcohol, it is not surprising that a significant number of convicted drunk drivers are problem drinkers. In an assessment of 461 convicted drinking drivers using modified *DSM-III* criteria, Miller and colleagues (1986) found that 54% had a diagnosis of alcohol abuse and 19% had a diagnosis of alcohol dependence. In a study of 490 military personnel convicted of driving while intoxicated, Kruzich and associates (1986) reported that 47% met *DSM-III* criteria for alcohol abuse and another 41% for alcoholism.

One can surmise that knowledge of a pre-injury alcohol-related driving conviction should serve as a marker of possible alcoholism in a trauma patient. Considering that fewer than 50% of drunk driving arrests result in convictions (Maull, Kinning & Hickman, 1984; Soderstrom, Birschbach & Dischinger, 1990), clinical suspicion should be heightened for an underlying alcohol diagnosis in patients with such driving records.

PATIENT MANAGEMENT

Detailed discussions of the effects of alcohol and other drug misuse on the clinical management of trauma patients can be found elsewhere (Freeland, McMicken & D'Onofrio, 1993). The salient aspects of that subject are summarized here.

The clinical impact of substance use on a patient's clinical management and course depends on a number of factors: the drug used, the number of drugs, the pattern of use (amount, duration, alone or in combination), and the patient (age, gender, pre-injury morbidity, severity of injuries) (Chou, Grant & Dawson, 1996). Hence, the expression of pathophysiology that may influence the clinical course will vary among patients.

In the treatment of the seriously injured, survival and subsequent quality of life are often determined by the clinician's ability to diagnose and treat life-threatening conditions rapidly. Intoxication obviates a patient's participation in history giving and physical examination in the resuscitation suite. Decreased sensoriums resulting from alcohol intoxication artificially lower admitting Glasgow Coma Scale scores (Jagger, Fife et al., 1984; Milzman, Jolin et al., 1992). The indication to perform many diagnostic maneuvers (diagnostic peritoneal lavage, CT scans, conventional roentgenograms, etc.) during the evaluation of trauma patients is an altered sensorium, which in addition to that resulting from head injury, includes such a state resulting from intoxication (Dunham & Cowley, 1991). Hence, it is not surprising that there is a tendency to employ more diagnostic modalities in the initial management of intoxicated patients compared with nonintoxicated patients (Jurkovich, Rivara et al., 1992).

After the initial (often frenetic) emergency phase of trauma care, significant pre-injury substance use will continue to affect patient management. Patients at risk of developing withdrawal syndromes must be identified and provided with pharmacologic prophylaxis. Choice and amount of pharmacologic agents to provide anesthesia, pain relief, sedation, and antimicrobial coverage are affected by pre-injury alcohol and other drug use.

Both acute and chronic alcohol abuse produce a constellation of pathophysiologic disorders that should impact negatively on the survival and clinical course of trauma patients. However, only recently have studies with large numbers of subjects explored that hypothesis (Waller, Stewart et al., 1986; Jurkovich, Rivara et al., 1993; McGill, Kowal-Kern et al., 1996; Maio, Waller et al., 1997). Some results are contradictory (Li, Keyl et al., 1997)—indicating the need for much more research in this area—but preliminary results suggest that alcohol abuse potentiates injury and is associated with increased morbidity and mortality. (The reader is referred to Li and colleagues' [1997] review article on this subject.) To more completely understand alcohol's effect on the clinical course of injured patients, additional studies are needed to delineate the impact of (1) pathophysiologic changes caused by acute and chronic alcohol abuse on outcomes of injury, and (2) comorbid conditions.

Intervention and Treatment. In an extensive review of current trauma center practices, Gentilello and colleagues (1995) noted that the crisis brought about by an alcohol-related injury "provides a unique opportunity to intervene and to motivate patients to examine their drinking behavior." However, there may be no "hand to help thee up" because of biases brought to the problem. In an 1894 editorial in the *Journal of the American Medical Association*, a Dr. Howle contended that lawmakers were correct in perceiving "inebriety" (drunkenness) as a vice—a problem that could be corrected by "moral suasion." This thought was affirmed in a 1910 encyclopedia discussion of "drunkenness," in which it was stated: "As a habit (as in the form of chronic alcoholism) it is one of the most degrading forms of vice which can result from the enfeeblement of the moral priniciple by persistent self-indulgence" (*Encyclopaedia Britannica*).

Some centuries-old thoughts are resistant to change. A 1989 study of medical students and residents by Geller and colleagues suggested that, as physicians proceed through their training, they develop more negative attitudes about alcoholics and the "treatability" of alcoholism as a disease. Further, a survey (Chang, Astrachan et al., 1992) of attending emergency medicine physicians who treated drunk drivers indicated that, on a scale of 1 (strongly disagree) to 7 (strongly agree), residents responded that alcoholics are difficult to treat (mean score, 6.2). However, the physicians generally agreed that alcoholism was a treatable illness (mean score, 5.3).

Gentilello and colleagues (1995) noted that, while "trauma centers are uniquely positioned to implement programs of alcohol screening, intervention, and referral" and "despite emphasis on injury control and prevention, little has been done to incorporate alcohol intervention programs into care of the injured patient." This author's trauma center surveys (Soderstrom & Cowley, 1987; Soderstrom, Dailey & Kerns, 1994) indicate that the percentage of trauma centers employing substance abuse clinicians almost doubled (32% versus 59%) in a five-year period. In addition, there is an ever-increasing number of papers concerning substance abuse treatment for trauma patients (examples: Freeland, McMicken & D'Onofria, 1993; Lowenstein, Weissberg & Terry, 1990; Parran, Weber et al., 1995; Dunn, Donovan & Gentilello, 1997). These trends suggest cautious optimism is in order relative to the trauma/emergency care environment being more receptive to identifying and treating substance-using patients.

A number of techniques are recommended to bring about a change of practice in trauma centers and emergency departments, where psychoactive substance use disorders are generally ignored. One must begin with education. This includes providing data about the magnitude of the problem relative to patients at risk and costs incurrred as the result of alcohol- or drug-related trauma. Further, it is important to educate trauma clinicians about the disease nature of substance abuse. Clinicians (including nurses) interested in substance use issues should be identified and encouraged (and given the time) to screen and refer patients for treatment. Patients should be provided with opportunities and choices to enter into treatment, obtain counseling, or join self-help groups to address their substance use problems. When presented as a means of improving overall health—including injury risk reduction—such opportunities will be viewed in a positive light by both patients and family members.

New Definitions and Treatment Options. As well articulated by Miller (1993), the time-worn "dispositional model" of alcoholism, which assigns persons to an alcoholic or non-alcoholic condition, without intermediate choices, needs to be replaced. That old model obviates using brief intervention techniques for trauma patients who are problem drinkers who may or may not eventually progress to a severe alcohol-dependent state. In fact, classifying many individuals as "abusers or dependent, healthy or diseased" is not possible (Harvard Medical School, 1996). Recently, the Institute of Medicine (1990) recommended that "alcohol problems" be the object of treatment, rather than "alcoholism" or "alcohol dependence syndrome." This allows a choice of treatment options for different groups of patients who have suffered consequences from their alcohol use, such as trauma.

Dunn and colleagues (1997) state that most "alcohol related accidents are caused by patients with mild to moderate alcohol problems." As noted above, approximately one in four trauma center patients is a current alcoholic at the time of injury. The author's research indicates that half of these patients would be classified as mild to moderately dependent and the other half would be considered severely dependent (1997, unpublished data). The latter group most likely requires traditional substance abuse consultation referral and post-discharge treatment services for severe alcohol dependence. On the other hand, studies of nontrauma patients with problematic drinking and/or diagnoses of mild to moderate alcohol dependence have shown brief interventional techniques to be of value in producing abstinence or substantially reducing harmful drinking patterns (Bien, Miller & Tanigan, 1993; Fleming, Barry et al., 1997). Dunn and colleagues (1997) recently published "practical guidelines" for brief interventions in trauma centers. One would expect that brief intervention techniques that have been used successfully in nontrauma patients should yield salutary results in the trauma center setting. As noted by Longabaugh and colleagues (1995), for intervention techniques to be effective, it is necessary to assist the patient in establishing the link between injury and substance abuse.

THE "WINDOW OF OPPORTUNITY"

A number of reports emphasize the "window of opportunity" that a substance-related trauma affords for intervention. For example, Cherpitel (1996) indicated that more than one-third of crash victims clearly associated their drinking to being injured and hence were good candidates for "brief intervention." However, in addition to clinicians' possible biases against treating trauma patients with alcohol and other drug problems, as mentioned above, operational matters hamper our ability to exploit the "window of opportunity." These obstacles will be addressed briefly.

Emergency Department versus Trauma Center. Most injured patients treated in emergency departments are discharged to home. Injured patients with PSUDs are often encountered in the emergency department in an intoxicated or post-intoxicated state and hence are not candidates for intervention when initally seen. Further, many emergency departments do not require follow-up visits. In contrast, trauma center patients represent a "captive audience" whose length of stay averages one week (often much longer). After acute care (including emergency surgery) has been rendered, enough time has passed so that the trauma patient can be seen in a sober state.

Treatment of Injuries versus Substance Abuse Disorders. Inpatient status after receiving emergency care in a trauma center would appear to provide unlimited opportunity to identify and treat an underlying alcohol/drug problem. However, our experience does not support this idea. A number of obstacles impede sustained patient interactions, including: (1) pain and pain medications; (2) physical barriers that interfere with establishing rapport (casts, external fixation devices, immobilization in bed, etc.); (3) diagnostic and therapeutic procedures (CT scans, physical rehabilitation, dressing changes, etc.); (4) visitors (family, social workers, etc.), in addition to physician/nurse rounds; and (5) psychological factors (guilt, fear, and grief) associated with being injured. These factors make it difficult to find sufficient time to interact with patients for sustained periods and thus favor the use of brief intervention techniques for trauma patients with mild to moderate alcohol problems.

CONCLUSIONS

Progress is being made toward interrupting the cause/effect relationship between substance abuse and trauma. At the national level, the percentage of fatal crashes involving alcohol has dropped from just under 60% in the early 1980s to just above 40% in the mid 1990s. The growing number of reports about substance abuse and trauma in peer-reviewed journals is the result of clinicians' increasing interest in identifying trauma patients at risk of substance use disorders and offering interventions that can break destructive patterns.

An exciting area of investigation is determining what types of treatment are applicable to which trauma patients. Further defining the role of brief intervention techniques is particularly important, as is ascertainment of their appropriate timing. In this era of cost containment, it is necessary to demonstrate the cost-effectiveness of any treatment modality, not only in relation to a trauma patient's immediate clinical needs but also in an effort to curb traumatic injury recidivism.

Finally, it is crucial to emphasize the important role that community hospitals have in injury prevention relative to substance use disorders. While most research findings come from projects in academic trauma centers and emergency medicine programs, the vast majority of patients requiring treatment for injury are not cared for in those settings. Community hospitals have a vital role in identifying and instituting treatment for injured patients with alcohol and other drug use problems. It is important to encourage and expand research initiatives in these institutions.

ACKNOWLEDGMENTS: Preparation of this chapter was supported in part by a grant from the National Institute on Alcohol Abuse and Alcoholism (RO1 AA09050). The author thanks Linda Kesselring, M.S., E.L.S., for her editorial assistance.

REFERENCES

American Psychiatric Association (1987). *Diagnostic and Statistical Manual of Mental Disorders, 3rd Ed.* Washington, DC: The Association.

Angell M & Kassirer JP (1994). Alcohol and other drugs: Toward a more rational and consistent policy. *The New England Journal of Medicine* 331:537–539.

Babor TF, de la Fuente JR, Saunders J & Grant M (1992). *AUDIT: The Alcohol Use Disorders Identification Test: Guidelines for Use in Primary Health Care.* Geneva, Switzerland: World Health Organization.

Bazzoli GJ & MacKenzie EJ (1995). Trauma centers in the United States: Identification and examination of key characteristics. *Journal of Trauma* 38:103–110.

Bien TH, Miller WR & Tonigan JS (1993). Brief interventions for alcohol problems: A review. *Addiction* 88:315–336.

Brewer RD, Morris PD, Cole TB, Watkins S, Patetta MJ & Popkin C (1994). The risk of dying in alcohol-related automobile crashes among habitual drunk drivers. *The New England Journal of Medicine* 331:513–517.

Buchfuhrer LA & Radecki SE (1996). Alcohol and drug abuse in an urban trauma center: Predictors of screening and detection. *Journal of Addictive Diseases* 15:65–74.

Buchsbaum DG, Buchanan RG, Center RM, Schnoll SH & Lawton MJ (1991). Screening for alcohol abuse using CAGE scores and likelihood ratios. *Annals of Internal Medicine* 115:774–777.

Cesare J, Morgan AS, Felice PR & Edge V (1990). Characteristics of blunt and personal violent injuries. *Journal of Trauma* 30:176–182.

Champion HR, Copes WS, Sacco WJ, Lawnick MM, Keast SL, Bain LW, Flanagan ME & Frey CF (1990). The Major Trauma Outcome Study: Establishing national norms for trauma care. *Journal of Trauma* 30:1356–1365.

Chang G, Astrachan B, Weil U & Bryant K (1992). Reporting alcohol-impaired drivers: Results from a national survey of emergency physicians. *Annals of Emergency Medicine* 21:284–290.

Cherpitel CJ (1996). Drinking patterns and problems and drinking in the event: An analysis of injury by cause among casualty patients. *Alcoholism: Clinical & Experimental Research* 2:1130–1137.

Cherpitel CJ (1995). Screening for alcohol problems in the emergency department. *Annals of Emergency Medicine* 26:158–166.

Chou SP, Grant BF & Dawson DA (1996). Medical consequences of alcohol consumption—United States, 1992. *Alcoholism: Clinical & Experimental Research* 20:1423–1429.

Clark DE, McCarthy E & Robinson E (1985). Trauma as a symptom of alcoholism (editorial). *Annals of Emergency Medicine* 14:274.

Committee on Trauma, American College of Surgeons (1993). *Resources for Optimal Care of the Injured Patient: 1993.* Chicago, IL: American College of Surgeons.

Coulehan JL, Zettler-Segal M, Block M, McClelland M & Schulberg HC (1987). Recognition of alcoholism and substance abuse in primary care patients. *Archives of Internal Medicine* 147:349–352.

Council on Scientific Affairs, American Medical Association (1986). Alcohol and the driver. *Journal of the American Medical Association* 255:522–527.

Cyr MG & Wartman SA (1988). The effectiveness of routine screening questions in the detection of alcoholism. *Journal of the American Medical Association* 259:51–54.

Department of Health and Human Services (1992). *Model Trauma Care Plan*. Rockville, MD: National Institutes of Health.

Dunham CM & Cowley RA (1991). *Shock Trauma/Critical Care Manual*. Gaithersburg, MD: Aspen Publishers, Inc.

Dunn CW, Donovan DM & Gentilello LM (1997). Practical guidelines for performing alcohol interventions in trauma centers. *Journal of Trauma* 42:299–304.

Encyclopaedia Britannica, 11th Edition, Volume VIII (1910). New York, NY: The Encyclopaedia Britannica Co.

Ewing JA (1984). Detecting alcoholism: The CAGE questionnaire. *Journal of the American Medical Association* 252:1905–1907.

Fleming MF, Barry KL, Manwell LB, Johnson K & London R (1997). Brief physician advice for problem alcohol drinkers: A randomized controlled trial in community-based primary care physicians. *Journal of the American Medical Association* 277:1039–1045.

Floerchinger SL (1992). The successful introduction of a chemical dependency evaluation and referral program in a level one trauma system (abstract). Presented at the American College of Surgeons Committee on Trauma 1992 Resident's Trauma Papers Competition, 70th Annual Meeting, Dallas.

Freeland ES, McMicken DB & D'Onofrio G (1993). Alcohol and trauma. *Emergency Medical Clinics of North America* 11:225–239.

el-Guebaly N & el-Guebaly A (1981). Alcohol abuse in ancient Egypt: The recorded evidence. *The International Journal of the Addictions* 16:1207–1981.

Geller G, Levine DM, Mamon JA, Moore RD, Bone LR & Stokes EJ (1989). Knowledge, attitudes, and reported practices of medical students and house staff regarding the diagnosis and treatment of alcoholism. *Journal of the American Medical Association* 261:3115–3120.

Gentilello LM, Donovan DM, Dunn CW & Rivara FP (1995). Alcohol interventions in trauma centers: Current practice and future directions. *Journal of the American Medical Association* 274:1043–1048.

Gitlow SE & Sexias FA (1988). The medical consequences of alcoholism. In Gitlow SE & Peyser HS (eds). *Alcoholism: A Practical Treatment Guide, 2nd Ed.* Philadelphia, PA: W.B. Saunders, 124–141.

Grant BF, Harford TC, Dawson DA, Chou P, DuFour M & Pickering R (1994). Prevalence of DSM-IV alcohol abuse and dependence: United States, 1992. *Alcohol Health and Research World* 18:243–248.

Harvard Medical School (1996). Treatment of alcoholism—part 1. *The Harvard Mental Health Newsletter* 13:1–4.

Hoffman NG, Harrison PA, Hall Jr SW, Gust SW, Mable RJ & Cable EP (1989). Pragmatic procedures for detecting and documenting alcoholism in medical patients. *Advances in Alcohol and Substance Abuse* 8:119–131.

Howle WP (1996). JAMA 100 years ago: Inebriety. *Journal of the American Medical Association* 271:482b.

Institute of Medicine (1990). *Broadening the Base of Treatment for Alcohol Problems*. Washington, DC: National Academy Press.

Jagger J, Fife D, Vernberg K & Jane JA (1984). Effect of alcohol intoxication on the diagnosis and apparent severity of brain injury. *Neurosurgery* 15:303–306.

Jurkovich GJ, Rivara FP, Gurney JG, Fligner C, Ries R, Mueller BA & Copass M (1993). The effect of acute alcohol intoxication and chronic alcohol abuse on outcome from trauma. *Journal of the American Medical Association* 270:51–56.

Jurkovich GJ, Rivara FP, Gurney JG, Seguin D, Fligner CL & Copass M (1992). Effects of alcohol intoxication on the initial assessment of trauma patients. *Annals of Emergency Medicine* 21:704–708.

Kessler RC, McGonagle KA, Zhao S, Nelson CB, Hughes M, Eshleman S, Wittchen H-U & Kendler KS (1994). Lifetime and 12-month prevalence of DSM-III-R psychiatric disorders in the United States. *Archives of General Psychiatry* 51:8–19.

Kruzich DJ, Silsby HD & Gold JD (1986). An evaluation and education program for driving while intoxicated offenders. *Journal of Substance Abuse Treatment* 3:263–270.

Li G, Keyl PM, Smith GS & Baker SP (1997). Alcohol and injury severity: Reappraisal of the continuing controversy. *Journal of Trauma* 42:562–569.

Lindenbaum GA, Carroll SF, Daskal I & Kapusnick BS (1989). Patterns of alcohol and drug abuse in an urban trauma center: The increasing role of cocaine abuse. *Journal of Trauma* 29:1654–1657.

Longabaugh R, Minugh A, Nirenberg TD, Clifford PR, Becker B & Woolard R (1995). Injury as a motivator to reduce drinking. *Academic Emergency Medicine* 2:817–825.

Lowenfels AB & Miller TT (1984). Alcohol and trauma. *Annals of Emergency Medicine* 13:1056–1060.

Lowenstein SR, Weissberg MP & Terry D (1990). Alcohol intoxication, injuries, and dangerous behaviors—and the revolving emergency department door. *Journal of Trauma* 30:1252–1258.

Lundberg GD (1984). Ethyl alcohol—Ancient plague and modern poison. *Journal of the American Medical Association* 252:1991–1912.

MacKenzie EJ, Morris JA Jr & Edelstein SL (1989). Effect of pre- existing disease on length of hospital stay in trauma patients. *Journal of Trauma* 29:757–764.

Maio RF, Waller PF, Blow FC, Hill EM & Singer KM (1997). Alcohol abuse/dependence in motor vehicular crash victims presenting to the emergency department. *Academic Emergency Medicine* 4:256–262.

Maull KI, Kinning LS & Hickman JK (1984). Culpability and accountability of hospitalized injured alcohol-impaired drivers. *Journal of the American Medical Association* 252:1880–1883.

McGill V, Kowal-Kern A, Fisher SG, Kahn S & Gamelli RL (1996). The impact of substance use on mortality and morbidity from thermal injury. *Journal of Trauma* 38:931–934.

McGinnis JM & Lee PR (1995). Healthy People 2000 at mid decade. *Journal of the American Medical Association* 273:1123–1129.

Miller BA, Whitney R & Washousky R (1986). Alcoholism diagnoses for convicted drinking drivers referred for alcoholism evaluation. *Alcoholism: Clinical & Experimental Research* 10:651–656.

Miller WR (1993). Alcoholism: Toward a better disease model. *Psychology of Addiction Behaviors* 7:129–135.

Milzman DP, Jolin SW, Boulanger BR, Domsky M, Rodriguez A & Mitchell K (1992). Positive toxicology screening predicts improved survival in severely injured neurotrauma patients (abstract). *Annals of Emergency Medicine* 21:662.

Moore RD, Bone LR, Geller G, Mamon JA, Stokes EJ & Levine DM (1989). Prevalence, detection, and treatment of alcoholism in hospitalized patients. *Journal of the American Medical Association* 261:403–407.

Morris JA Jr, MacKenzie EJ & Edelstein SL (1990). The effect of preexisting conditions on mortality in trauma patients. *Journal of the American Medical Association* 263:1942–1946.

National Highway Traffic Safety Administration (1996). *Traffic Safety Facts 1995: A Compilation of Motor Vehicle Crash Data from the Fatal Accident Reporting System and the General Estimates System*. Washington, DC: Department of Transportation (DOT HS 808 471).

National Highway Traffic Safety Administration (1988). *National Accident Sampling System–1986: A Report of Traffic Crashes and Injuries in the United States*. Washington, DC: Department of Transportation (DOT HS 807 296).

National Institute on Alcohol Abuse and Alcoholism (1991). Estimating the economic cost of alcohol abuse. *Alcohol Alert* 11(PH 293):1–4.

National Research Council, National Academy of Sciences Committee on Trauma and Committee on Shock (1966). *Accidental Death and Disability: The Neglected Disease of Modern Society*. Washington, DC: Public Health Service publication 1071-A-13.

National Research Council (1985). *Injury in America: A Continuing Public Health Problem*. Washington, DC: National Academy Press.

Parran TV, Weber E, Tasse J, Anderson B & Adelman C (1995). Mandatory toxicologic testing and chemical dependence consultation follow-up in a level-one trauma center. *Journal of Trauma* 38:278–280.

Pokorny AD, Miller BA & Kaplan HB (1972). The brief MAST: A shortened version of the Michigan Alcoholism Screening Test. *American Journal of Psychiatry* 3:118–121.

Redmond AD, Richards S & Plunkett PK (1987). The significance of random breath alcohol sampling in the accident and emergency department. *Alcohol and Alcoholism* 4:341–343.

Rivara FP, Mueller BA, Fligner CL, Luna G, Raisys VA, Copass M & Reay DT (1989). Drug use in trauma victims. *Journal of Trauma* 29:462–470.

Rivara FP, Jurkovich GJ, Gurney JG, Seguin D, Fligner CL, Ries R, Raisys VA & Copass M (1993). The magnitude of acute and chronic alcohol abuse in trauma patients. *Archives of Surgery* 128:907–913.

Salaspura M (1994). Biological state markers of alcohol abuse. *Alcohol Health and Research World* 18:131–135.

Saunders JB, Aasland OG, Babor TF, De La Fuenta JR & Grant M (1993). Development of the Alcohol Use Disorders Identification Test (AUDIT). WHO collaborative project on early detection of persons with harmful alcohol consumption, II. *Addiction* 88:791–804.

Secretary of Health and Human Services (1994). *Eighth Special Report to the US Congress on Alcohol and Health*. Rockville, MD: National Institutes of Health, NIH No. 94-3699.

Selzer ML, Vinokur A & van Rooijen L (1975). A self-administered Short Michigan Alcoholism Screening Test (SMAST). *Journal of Studies on Alcohol* 36:117–136.

Sherin KM, Piotrowski ZH, Panek SM & Doot MC (1982). Screening for alcoholism in a community hospital. *Journal of Family Practice* 15:1091–1095.

Sloan EP, Zalenski RJ, Smith RF, Sheaff CM, Chen EH, Keys NI, Crescenzo M, Barrett JA & Berman E (1989). Toxicology screening in urban trauma patients: Drug prevalence and its relationship to trauma severity and management. *Journal of Trauma* 29:1647–1653.

Soderstrom CA, Birschbach J & Dischinger PC (1990). Injured drivers and alcohol use: Culpability, convictions, pre- and post-crash driving history. *Journal of Trauma* 30:1208–1214.

Soderstrom CA & Cowley RA (1987). A national alcohol and trauma center survey: Missed opportunities, failures of responsibility. *Archives of Surgery* 122:1067–1071.

Soderstrom CA, Dailey JT & Kerns TJ (1994). Alcohol and other drugs: An assessment of testing and clinical practices in U.S. trauma centers. *Journal of Trauma* 36:68–73.

Soderstrom CA, Dischinger PC, Ho SM & Soderstrom MT (1993). Alcohol use, driving records, and crash culpability among injured motorcycle drivers. *Accident Analysis and Prevention* 25:711–716.

Soderstrom CA, Dischinger PC, Kerns TJ & Trifillis AL (1995a). Marijuana and other drug use among automobile and motorcycle drivers treated at a trauma center. *Accident Analysis and Prevention* 27:131–135.

Soderstrom CA, Dischinger PC, Smith G, Gorelick D, Hebel JR & McDuff D (1996a). Biological markers and BACs: Alcoholism in trauma patients (abstract). *Al-*

coholism: Clinical & Experimental Research 20(Suppl):139A

Soderstrom CA, Dischinger PC, Smith G, McDuff DR, Hebel JR & Gorelick DA (1992). Psychoactive substance dependence among trauma center patients. *Journal of the American Medical Association* 267:2756–2759.

Soderstrom CA, Kufera JA, Dischinger PC, Kerns TJ, Murphy JG & Lowenfels A (1997a). A predictive model to detect trauma patients with BACs ≥ 50 mg/dl. *Journal of Trauma* 42:67–73.

Soderstrom CA, Smith GS, Dischinger PC, McDuff DR, Hebel JR, Gorelick DA, Kerns TJ, Ho S & Read KM (1997b). Psychoactive substance use disorders among seriously injured trauma center patients diagnosed using a standardized interview. *Journal of the American Medical Association* 277:1769–1774.

Soderstrom CA, Smith GS, Dischinger PC, Kufera JA, Hebel JR, McDuff DR, Gorelick DA, Kerns TJ & Read KM (1997c). The accuracy of the CAGE, the Brief Michigan Alcoholism Screening Test, and the Alcohol Use Disorders Identification Test in screening trauma center patients for alcoholism. *Journal of Trauma* 43:962–969.

Soderstrom CA & Smith TC (1996b). Alcohol. In Ivatury RR & Cayten CG (eds.) *Textbook of Penetrating Trauma*. Malvern, PA: Lea & Febiger, 1033–1045.

Soderstrom CA, Trifillis AL, Shankar BS, Clark WE & Cowley RA (1988). Marijuana and alcohol use among 1023 trauma patients: A prospective study. *Archives of Surgery* 123:733–737.

Solomon J, Vanga N, Morgan JP & Joseph P (1980). Emergency-room physicians' recognition of alcohol misuse. *Journal of Studies on Alcohol* 41:583–586.

Spies CD, Emadi A, Neumann T, Hannemana L, Rieger A, Schaffartzik W, Rahmanzadek R, Berger G, Funk T, Blum S, Müller M & Rommelspacher H (1995). Relevance of carbohydrate-deficient transferrin as a predictor of alcoholism in intensive care patients following trauma. *Journal of Trauma* 39:742–748.

Spitzer RL, Williams JBW & Gibbon M (1987). *Structured Clinical Interview for DSM-III-R: Patient Version (SCID-P, 4/1/87)*. New York, NY: Biometrics Research Department, New York State Psychiatric Institute.

Stibler H (1991). Carbohydrate-deficient transferrin in serum: A new marker of potentially harmful alcohol consumption reviewed. *Clinical Chemistry* 37:2029–2037.

Teplin LA, Abram KM & Michaels SL (1989). Blood alcohol level among emergency room patients: A multivariant analysis. *Journal of Studies on Alcohol* 50:441–447.

Treno AJ, Gruenwald PJ & Poniclsi WR (1996). Use of ICD-9-CM codes in the estimation of alcohol-involved injury: Search for a surrogate, II. Estimating alcohol involvement in trauma patients: Search for a surrogate. *Alcoholism: Clinical & Experimental Research* 20:320–326.

Vingilis E (1983). Drinking drivers and alcoholics: are they the same population? In Smart RG et al. (eds.) *Research Advances in Alcohol and Drug Problems, Vol 7*. New York, NY: Plenum Press, 299–342.

Waller PF, Stewart JR, Hansen AR, Stutts JC, Popkin CL et al. (1986). The potentiating effects of alcohol on driver injury. *Journal of the American Medical Association* 256:1461–1466.

Yersin B, Trisconi T, Paccaud F, Gutzwiller F & Magnenat P (1989). Accuracy of the Michigan Alcoholism Screening Test for screening alcoholism in patients of a medical department. *Archives of Internal Medicine* 149:2071–2074.

Zuska JJ (1981). Wounds without cause. *Bulletin of the American College of Surgeons* 66:5–10.

CHAPTER 3

Anesthesia and Analgesia

Charles Beattie, M.D., Ph.D.
Annie Umbricht-Schneiter, M.D.
Lynette Mark, M.D.

Preoperative Evaluation of All Patients
Management of the Addicted Patient
Management of the Recovering Patient

Perioperative management of patients in active alcoholism or other drug addiction and of those in recovery requires careful preoperative assessment to identify comorbidities, signs of acute toxicity or withdrawal, stigmata of chronic use and, in the recovering patient, concerns regarding relapse. The standard practices of intraoperative anesthesia and postoperative pain relief must be modified to provide for the special physiologic and psychologic needs of these individuals.

PREOPERATIVE EVALUATION OF ALL PATIENTS

All surgical patients should be screened for alcohol and other drug addiction preoperatively. The CAGE and MAST tests are two screening instruments that are short, reliable and widely used (Bush, Shaw et al., 1987; Ewing, 1984; Garzotto, Baratta et al., 1988). When indicated (traumatic injuries, uncooperative patient, etc.), blood alcohol level should be determined and a toxicity screen (blood and urine) obtained to help assess the degree of tolerance, the risk for subsequent withdrawal and the specific symptoms and signs that can be expected. Such objective information can be useful later in confronting a patient's denial of an alcohol or drug problem. A nonjudgmental and compassionate but assertive approach to the patient's drug addiction lays the groundwork for a fruitful therapeutic relationship and decreases the patient's anxiety (and thus the intensity of a potential withdrawal syndrome). If the patient is lucid, the clinician should ask about previous episodes of withdrawal and clearly state that if such a complication threatens to occur, it will be acknowledged and promptly treated. This approach may encourage the patient to share past experiences, thus guiding the clinician in the choice of a therapeutic intervention. Patients usually have positive memories of clinicians who show respect for them and this also is beneficial in later clinical management.

Once good rapport has been established and the patient is confident that his or her alcohol or drug addiction will be part of comprehensive clinical management, the clinician should assess more thoroughly the extent of the problem. Because polysubstance abuse is the rule, inquiries about each class of drugs should be made. For example, many alcoholics are heavy smokers and a significant proportion have used benzodiazepines to treat their alcohol-related anxiety or insomnia. The CAGE questions can be used to detect loss of control in the use of any type of drug.

Although it may seem cumbersome to conduct such an assessment routinely for every preoperative evaluation, it is instructive to recall the high prevalence of undetected alcohol and drug abuse in hospitalized patients (Moore, Bone et al., 1989). Even if findings are negative, this assessment takes only a few minutes; if positive, the findings have the potential of saving invaluable time and resources during the perioperative period in addition to providing the opportunity for intervention and recovery.

Even as drug and alcohol abuse continue to escalate, so also does the size of the population of individuals in recovery from addiction. These persons are presenting for surgery in increasing numbers (Beattie, Moore et al., 1992) and should be identified preoperatively. Persons in recovery usually readily supply relevant historical information, with the expectation that it will be used knowledgeably to ensure their safety and comfort. A later subsection of this chapter outlines important procedures to guide the appropriate evaluation and preparation of surgical patients who have been addicted to alcohol or other drugs but who currently are abstinent.

MANAGEMENT OF THE ADDICTED PATIENT

Infection. Infections are the major complications associated with intravenous drug use (Haverkos, 1990; Haverkos & Lange, 1990). Systemic infections include viral hepatitis (A, B, Delta, and C), HIV, syphilis, bacterial sepsis and tuberculosis. A history of hepatitis has been found in 50% of addicts screened, with one-third having repeat episodes. Hepatitis B surface antigen is positive in 2.2% of addicts—four times the incidence in the general population (Gevirtz, 1988).

HIV infection and AIDS first were reported in drug abusers in the United States in 1981. By 1989, between 5% and 20% of intravenous drug users in the United States were infected with HIV and accounted for 75% of all heterosexually transmitted cases of AIDS. HIV testing therefore should be routine in this group of patients. Nonetheless, the issue of routine testing is controversial; moreover, many states require informed patient consent, which may not be possible at the time of the pàtient's initial presentation. Even before the onset of AIDS, it was recognized that the *immune responses* of alcohol- or drug-dependent persons were multifactorially impaired (Moss, 1987). For example, chronic alcoholics are predisposed to pneumococcal pneumonia, dental decay and aspiration pneumonia, often complicated by lung abscesses. Because of the AIDS epidemic, intravenous drug users are even more likely than other AIDS patients to be exposed to opportunistic infections, which tend to run a more rapidly fatal course.

Tuberculosis is again reaching epidemic proportions in this population, both as the result of worsened living conditions and the AIDS epidemic. This problem has special importance for anesthesiologists, because tuberculosis can be contracted by other patients through insufficiently decontaminated ventilators, or by the anesthesiologist by inhaling infected air droplets (for example, when suctioning a patient's airway without wearing a protective mask).

Commonly seen *localized infections* include abscesses at drug injection sites; involvement of internal organs, such as endocarditis (usually of the tricuspid valve) and lung abscesses, possibly followed by metastatic abscesses to the left heart or the brain (with a progressive or sudden change in mental status); kidney abscesses with recurrent, unexplained urinary tract infections and urosepsis; and so on.

The injection of "fillers" and other unknown contaminants into the bloodstream is responsible for other complications associated with intravenous drug use. Talc or other inert substances lodge in the pulmonary capillaries and cause an inflammatory reaction that, over time, can result in pulmonary fibrosis and restrictive lung disease. Quinidine/quinine, administered to a patient deficient in glucose-6-phosphate dehydrogenase, may cause hemolysis. Repeated injections of contaminated solutions, which are highly antigenic, stimulate the immune system chronically, resulting in an increase in circulating globulins and hyperproteinemia. False positive serologic tests are common in intravenous drug users.

Liver function tests (LFTs) are frequently abnormal secondary to hepatitis, HIV, and/or toxicity from fillers used to cut pure drugs (Gelb, Mildvan & Stenger, 1977; Klatskin, 1961). Hepatic dysfunction associated with alcohol addiction usually takes 10 to 15 years to develop. However, cirrhosis with permanent and/or reversible changes can occur in the liver following one or more acute episodes (Orkin & Chen, 1977).

Narcotic addicts have been reported in one series to have an 83% incidence of abnormal, clinically asymptomatic LFTs, with increases in alanine aminotransferase, asparate aminotransferase and alkaline phosphatase (Gervitz, 1988). Possible explanations include malnutrition and a chronic reaction to talc or other contaminants of abused drugs, concurrent infection with hepatitis C or B virus, and chronic alcohol use. This chronic toxic reaction may explain the prevalence of cirrhosis in young addicts, who have a significantly earlier onset than abusers of alcohol only (Drug Abuse Warning Network, 1982).

Special attention should be directed to *electrocardiographic abnormalities*, including atrial and ventricular rhythm disturbances, prolonged QTc interval, evidence of previous myocardial infarction (cocaine), left ventricular hypertrophy, or (as indicators of pulmonary hypertension) right ventricular hypertrophy, right atrial enlargement, and biphasic T waves. Transthoracic or transesophageal echocardiograms are invaluable techniques for viewing valve pathology, investigating sources of embolic events, and assessing cardiac function. Right-sided endocarditis and complications of septic emboli are reemerging as major problems with drug users. Issues of prophylactic antibiotic coverage or cardiac surgery may have to be addressed (Orkin & Chen, 1977).

Chest radiographs may show evidence of pneumothorax (after intrajugular or supraclavicular drug injection), interstitial infiltrate, scarring, abscesses, cardiac enlargement or hylar lymphadenopathy. Pulmonary function tests are particularly useful for assessing obstructive and restrictive lung disease, which is prevalent in this population.

Complete blood counts may reveal suppression of erythropoiesis, leukopoiesis and thrombopoiesis, which reflect the direct effect of a substance such an ethanol or secondary to poor nutrition or an infectious process. A 25% incidence of chronic anemia was reported in one series of methadone maintenance patients (Fabiani, 1991).

Serum electrolyte test results may reflect primary renal pathologic conditions or secondary effects related to poor health and nutrition, intravascular dehydration or trauma with resultant myoglobinemia from tissue necrosis and subsequent obstruction of renal tubules leading to failure. Additionally, $Na+/K+$ disturbances may reflect initial diuresis (decreased levels of antidiuretic hormone) followed by antidiuretic effects of alcohol. Rhabdomyolysis has been reported in heroin addicts, probably secondary to unknown components in adulterated heroin and diagnosed by the presence of dark urine with myoglobin and free hemoglobin (Gevirtz, 1988). Rhabdomyolysis also has been described as a reperfusion injury in cocaine users.

Withdrawal. When a patient is physically dependent on a psychoactive drug (mainly alcohol, sedative-hypnotics or opiates), a reduction or abrupt discontinuation of that drug may precipitate a *withdrawal syndrome*, the nature of which varies depending on the drug. Hospitalization for trauma or an acute illness, by causing an interruption in the patient's lifestyle, may initiate the withdrawal. The emergence of withdrawal syndrome in the perioperative period can be both confusing and dangerous. The following scenarios suggest the range of complications that can interfere with optimal treatment:

Intermittent or Recurrent Withdrawal: Although the syndrome is recognized and intervention is initiated, the process is interrupted by repeated surgical procedures and the use of various anesthetic drugs.

Complicated Withdrawal: The syndrome is recognized, but intervention is limited by the patient's cardiovascular or neurologic instability and concurrent surgical or medical stress. In the case of alcohol withdrawal, the patient's unstable condition may preclude administering the necessary sedation that optimal withdrawal management would require.

Perioperative Transition: The transition from intoxication to withdrawal, such as during a lengthy surgical procedure on a multiple-trauma victim, may express itself through diametrically opposed cardiovascular responses. Pharmacologic treatment of the first state may exaggerate the second; a narcotic overdose complicated by trauma, unknown blood loss and hypotension may require the use of vasopressors. This situation can change abruptly with the onset of withdrawal, thus confusing, for example, the estimation of volume of electrolyte solution needed to stabilize the patient.

Further complicating the situation, the same patient may evolve through more than one of these scenarios at different points during his or her hospitalization.

Both underdiagnosing and overdiagnosing withdrawal can lead to patient mismanagement. Anticipation of withdrawal syndrome by means of a thorough preoperative assessment of the patient's pattern of psychoactive drug or alcohol use therefore is essential for good patient management.

To minimize undesirable consequences of withdrawal during the perioperative period, the following principles should be applied:

Withdrawal Syndrome: Withdrawal should be considered as part of the differential diagnosis of any complication occurring during the perioperative period.

Narcotic Analgesics: These analgesics should not be withdrawn during the immediate postoperative period. On the contrary, they should be administered as required (often in larger doses and for shorter intervals than for a person who is not drug-tolerant). If an open and respectful physician-patient relationship has been developed during the preoperative evaluation, it is less likely that the patient will engage in drug-seeking behavior. Two mechanisms explain the patient's requirement for increased analgesic doses: tolerance and the hyperalgesia associated with opiate withdrawal (due to dysfunction of the endogenous opioid system). Although hyperalgesia has not been clearly demonstrated during alcohol withdrawal, the associated anxiety decreases the tolerance threshold to nociceptive stimuli. Pharmacologic and psychological tolerance can be clearly observed across different classes of psychoactive drugs.

Pharmacologic Management of Withdrawal: Management should focus on preventing serious complications (seizure, hyperthermia, hypertension with wound hemorrhage, injury to self and others); relieving subjective symptoms including anxiety; and attenuating detrimental stresses, both endogenous (fever or sepsis) and exogenous (noisy environment, bright lights). Therapy includes the use of specific pharmacologic agents, rehydration, electrolyte replacement and nutritional supplementation (thiamine and other vitamins).

After Successful Withdrawal Management and Clinical Stabilization: The clinician has a duty to confront the patient with the consequences of his or her alcohol or other drug use pattern, emphasizing the patient's loss of control over the compulsion to use drugs or alcohol in spite of otherwise sound judgment. The clinician's approach should attenuate detrimental guilt (which may externalize itself in the form of aggressive, defiant behavior) and should focus on the fact that the patient's responsibility is not for having a disease, but rather for developing a support system that is compatible with achieving abstinence. For example, rehabilitation in the setting of a methadone treatment program could be appropriate for patients dependent on opiates.

Early Consultation with an Addiction Medicine Specialist: Consultation can be used to circumvent impending disasters, accelerate recovery and facilitate discharge planning by organizing the patient's ongoing treatment.

Premedication. When premedicating alcohol- or drug-dependent patients for surgery, the most important principle is to avoid perioperative withdrawal. While accounting for the addicted patient's increased tolerance to most sedatives and narcotics, premedication should provide sufficient sedation and anxiolysis. The clinician must be cautious in recording the patient's estimation of the daily dose of "street drug" used, since addicts are themselves often misinformed: drugs are "cut" several times by dealers to increase profit, and the consumer usually receives a variable portion of the drug purchased.

The patient who is dependent on alcohol or other drugs should be premedicated as follows:

- *Alcohol-dependent patients* should be premedicated with a long-acting cross-tolerant drug such as a benzodiazepine (diazepam, chlordiazepoxide) or barbiturate (phenobarbital), given that adequate premedication will attenuate the patient's anxiety and thus limit the intensity of a potential withdrawal.
- *Opiate-dependent patients who are actively using drugs* should receive enough narcotic to manage both pain and withdrawal. The patient's daily dose should be considered a physiologic baseline to which normal premedication is added. If good communication has been established, the patient can be a reliable indicator in relating the subjective effect. A dose of 20 mg of methadone (IM) can effectively stabilize a patient before the induction of anesthesia and may attenuate symptoms of withdrawal postoperatively.
- *Opiate-dependent patients who are enrolled in a methadone program* should receive their usual oral daily dose before surgery. Physicians should not rely on patient information regarding the daily dose, but should call the program for this information. This procedure also informs the program of the patient's hospitalization.

Little information exists regarding special premedication requirements for patients with other drug dependencies. Neuroleptics and benzodiazepines may be indicated to treat psychotic states and agitation, cocaine-induced paranoia and other thought disorders. Anxiolytics with little or no reinforcing properties, such as hydroxyzine or halazepam (a benzodiazepine with slow onset of action) (Griffiths & Wolb, 1990) can provide the necessary sedation without attracting the patient to a new substance.

Premedication of the recovering patient merits special attention and is addressed below.

Anesthetic Techniques. General pharmacologic principles should be followed when planning anesthesia for addicted patients. However, altered and variable pharmacokinetics influence the type of anesthetic agents used, as well as drug doses. Drug interactions can lead to increased or decreased elimination as well as to decreased or increased toxicity (Elliott, 1975). For example, alcohol can acutely protect the liver against enflurane toxicity, but chronic alcohol ingestion may, through enzyme induction, cause significant elevation of transaminase. Similarly, a chronically damaged liver with borderline function may be precipitated into failure through the added stress of a surgical illness or the toxicity of some anesthetic agents.

Substances with high lipid solubility (such as PCP) accumulate in the fat tissues and are released unpredictably into the circulation, with consequent fluctuations in mental status over a period of time ranging from several days to weeks. Chronic use of nicotine accelerates the elimination of certain drugs (such as aminophylline) and slows the metabolism of others. Acute cessation of smoking because of hospitalization may unpredictably reverse these trends.

No single anesthetic technique addresses all the issues that relate to alcohol- and drug-dependent patients. Factors that influence the choice of technique include severity of presentation and associated illnesses, surgical requirements and ability of the anesthesiologist (Farley & Talbott, 1983). Also, the choice of agents or technique often is dictated by contraindications or limitations.

Regional anesthetic techniques are limited by the amount of patient cooperation expected, the presence of coagulopathy, infection at site of placement, intravascular dehydration, true allergy to anesthetic/narcotic or inability to metabolize the drug, neuropathy, potentially unprotected airway, technical difficulty and site of the surgical procedure. In addition, the anesthesiologist faces an increased risk of infection with every invasive procedure performed on such patients.

Limitations of general anesthesia include the use of polypharmacy, which may result in untoward drug interactions; decreased patient ability to metabolize and excrete certain classes of anesthetics, with a corresponding increase in the potential for toxicity; masking of potential withdrawal signs with anesthetics and nonanesthetic agents, which ultimately may increase the severity of the withdrawal syndrome; and the potential for profound dysrhythmogenic and depressant effects of general anesthetics on the cardiovascular system.

The selection of general anesthetic agents must be individualized based on the degree of organ dysfunction of the patient. The metabolism of inhalation agents may increase in patients with enzyme induction, resulting in toxicity. Isoflurane (with less than 1% liver metabolism) is theoretically the agent of choice, but its use may be limited by dose-dependent cardiovascular effects. Actions of nondepolarizing neuromuscular blocking agents may be increased secondary to decreased $K+$ or $Mg++$ or may be decreased secondary to altered protein binding or decreased cholinesterase activity at the motor endplate. The action of succinylcholine may be increased secondary to diminished plasma cholinesterase production. Atracurium, with partial Hoffman elimination, may be the agent of choice.

Clinical studies concerning anesthetic requirements for chronic alcoholics are confusing: does enzyme induction result in increased metabolism of anesthetic agents with subsequent increased toxicity, or does increased tolerance lead to an increase in requirements? The anesthetic requirements of chronic alcoholics for induction of anesthesia with thiopental were investigated using electroencephalographic (EEG) techniques to measure thiopental's effect on the central nervous system and pharmacodynamic modeling to relate thiopental serum concentrations to drug effect. The investigators reported no differences between alcoholics and nonalcoholics in thiopental pharmacokinetic and pharmacodynamic parameters or dose requirements. Accordingly, they suggested reconsideration of *a priori* increases in barbiturate induction doses in such patients. Although the definitive study of minimum alveolar concentration (MAC) and alcoholism has yet to be done, clinical experience affirms the broad spectrum of individual responses (Bruce, 1983).

The use of combined regional-general techniques intraoperatively with uninterrupted transition to postoperative pain management may be ideal for addicted patients. However, the literature on this subject is sparse.

General considerations for the operative management of addicted patients include difficulties assessing preoperative intravascular states and difficulties assessing ongoing fluid losses in the face of ascites and sympathomimetic effects of abused drugs. Electrolyte imbalances and problems in maintaining body temperature may predispose the patient to life-threatening arrhythmias.

Postoperative Pain. Many articles in the medical literature have impugned alcohol- and drug-dependent patients for "neurotic, even psychotic, nervous behavior," "lowered tolerance to pain" (Jage, 1988) and nagging "drug-seeking behavior." However, the scientific information on the physiological basis of addiction suggests that opiate-dependent patients should be treated on the model of corticoid-dependent patients, who have exogenously induced adrenal insufficiency and need extra corticosteroid to combat the stress of surgery. Indeed, withdrawing adequate postoperative opioid analgesia from an addicted patient induces the behavioral components of endogenous opiate deficiency.

This section provides clinicians with strategies for providing adequate analgesia to alcohol- and drug-dependent patients, with the understanding that "Attempting to change drug habits in the face of acute illness is dangerous. Proper treatment is rational therapy for the illness with full realization of the disease associated with addiction. An organized plan of approach is more important than choices in therapeutic agents" (Orkin & Chen, 1977).

For patients who actively use mu agonists, opiates such as methadone, morphine sulfate or a combination of the two are indicated for the first three to four days after surgery. Because methadone's duration of action as an analgesic is only about five hours, accumulation is likely to occur during periods of adequate pain control. If morphine is used alone, it should be administered at frequent and fixed intervals (e.g., every two to three hours) and at higher doses than for a nontolerant patient. Patient-controlled analgesia (PCA) may be indicated.

Using methadone to stabilize the patient's opioid system (10–20 mg IM, or 20–40 mg orally, once a day) and then adding morphine at the usual analgesic dose may be the most appealing option, as it clearly addresses the two problems separately. If this option is chosen, the short-acting opiate can be discontinued after the acute postoperative period and the opioid dependence then addressed (if possible with the assistance of a specialist in addiction medicine).

Patients who are enrolled in a methadone treatment program should receive their usual daily dose of methadone (they also should receive this dose on the day of surgery). Such patients also should be given short-acting opiates for analgesia in the same dose as a nonaddicted patient for three to four days. Patient care should be coordinated with the patient's methadone program: the program needs to know when to prepare the patient's dose on the first day after discharge. Some programs also can assist with basic primary care, including administration of daily medications (including antibiotics, AZT or Antabuse®) or even dressing changes.

Postoperative pain management for patients dependent on alcohol and other nonopioid substances follows similar considerations. Again, adequate analgesia is essential in preventing agitation and anxiety, both of which can precipitate or worsen an impending withdrawal syndrome. The best analgesia, which requires less medication, is obtained when withdrawal states and anxiety are prevented (Scott, Clum et al., 1983). A combination of pharmacologic, behavioral and physical approaches results in optimal patient care and minimizes the incidence of metabolic complications. Also, it prepares the patient for further drug treatment and rehabilitation.

Analgesia is provided by administering adequate narcotics in the early postoperative period. The narcotic dose should be individualized from patient to patient and from day to day. Pharmacologic cross-tolerance with other CNS depressants such as alcohol explains the possible requirement for higher doses of narcotics; alternatively, liver failure (that may be unsuspected in the face of normal transaminases) necessitates a decrease in narcotic requirements. The stress of surgery and various pharmacologic interactions may alter the narcotic requirement over time. PCA circumvents these problems and is an excellent alternative for cooperative patients. Another advantage of PCA is that it gives the patient a sense of control over his or her fate, which often has become lost in the addiction process.

Spinal and epidural narcotics are problematic in opiate tolerant patients. Doses may escalate with an increase in adverse effects.

Ketorolac®, a new nonsteroidal agent, achieves very good analgesia postoperatively in nonaddicted patients. Although theoretically attractive, its utility in patients actively using alcohol and other drugs has not been fully evaluated. Known side effects could add to the gastrointestinal toxicity of chronic alcohol abuse, although concurrent use of sucralfate may protect the gastric mucosa and circumvent this effect (Caldwell, Roth et al., 1987). A unique feature of Ketorolac is its parenteral route of administration. Other nonsteroidal drugs may be equally efficacious and synergistic with opiates.

Antidepressants generally are not necessary in treating the depression that accompanies alcohol or drug addiction, as most of its symptomatology improves dramatically with continued abstinence. However, in some circumstances (such as a prolonged hospitalization or the presence of an affective illness antedating the addiction), the use of antidepressants hastens recovery and decreases the need for long-term analgesia. Anticonvulsants such as phenytoin and carbamazepine also have a place in pain treatment by decreasing the frequency of neuronal discharge (McQuay, 1988).

Nonpharmacologic interventions also may be used to decrease analgesia requirements postoperatively (Lau, 1976). For example, patients can be taught to use transcutaneous electrical nerve stimulator (TENS) units to relieve surgical pain. When necessary, the TENS electrodes can be placed close to the surgical site before the dressing is applied during surgery, thus providing the maximum effect postoperatively. Also, biofeedback and relaxation techniques, which can be useful for a cooperating patient, are helpful. They can be started at any time and may be a welcome distraction to a patient obsessed by pain.

When treating patients who are dependent on alcohol or other drugs, it is essential that the health care team function cohesively. Clearly spelling out contracts that include behavioral incentives (for example, including punitive sanctions such as restriction to one's room for in-hospital drug abuse or abusive behavior), reinforced by consistent, randomized toxicity testing for alcohol or drugs, may prevent patients from being discharged against medical advice, spare the energy of the health care team and facilitate patient management. Discharge planning should include alcohol and drug treatment rehabilitation.

MANAGEMENT OF THE RECOVERING PATIENT

Patients recovering from drug and alcohol addiction are in remission from a debilitating chronic illness. To avoid exacerbation of their addiction by injudicious use of psychoactive agents, these patients require special care. At the same time, they need appropriate analgesia to minimize the stress of surgery, which can itself contribute to relapse.

No widely disseminated publication has addressed in detail the perioperative treatment of persons who are currently in recovery, although the issue is being considered by a committee of the American Society of Addiction Medicine. Despite the paucity of published material, clearly an extensive body of clinical experience exists among practitioners across the nation. It seems likely that the risk of relapse in the perioperative period reflects the overall risk of relapse, both being inversely proportional to the quality of the individual's recovery program. Assessments of the quality and hence the stability of a patient's recovery clearly are subjective determinations, but there has been some interest in quantifying these characteristics with psychological questionnaires such as the "Purpose in Life" Index (Jacobson, Rigger & Mueller, 1977; Lawton, 1991). If studies prove this instrument to be reliable, then the preoperative assessment of the risk of relapse will rest on a firmer foundation.

Regardless of the quality or the duration of a patient's recovery at the time of surgery, it is possible for the individual to intensify the practices of his or her program in preparation for the stressful period that lies ahead (Chambers, 1991). Recovering persons commonly draw on the resources of their fellowship (phone calls, visits from other members) during difficult times. Along with strong family relationships, this feature of the recovered person's support system constitutes a powerful defense against relapse and is exploited in the management strategies discussed below.

Fear of Pain. The almost universal fear of pain after major surgery is considered normal. This fear is exaggerated in recovering addicts, partially because they are concerned about rekindling the addictive process and partially because they believe their pain may be undertreated (Angell, 1982; Marks & Sachar, 1973; Sriwatanakul, Weiss & Alloza, 1983). Two additional considerations create a serious dilemma for recovering addicts. First, they may exhibit an elevated analgesic requirement; second, well-meaning but misinformed caregivers may withhold narcotics either from a humanitarian perspective (not wanting to trigger relapse) or because a moralistic attitude interprets requests for pain medication as drug-seeking behavior. Thus, the patient's dilemma clearly becomes the treating professional's dilemma.

There are variabilities in pain threshold, intensity of noxious stimuli and efficacy of inhibition at the receptor level that are extremely broad for humans, even for the same surgical procedure or chronic condition (Kaiko, Wallenstein & Rogers, 1983; Perry, 1985). Although clinicians repeatedly encounter instances of this fact, few alter their prescribing practice and adjust doses appropriately to ensure adequate pain relief for all patients (Mangieri, 1991; Melzak, 1990). At the same time, respiratory depression and suppression of protective airway reflexes are constant concerns in the immediate postoperative period and aggressive pain management, if accomplished with narcotics, must be balanced with heightened vigilance for complications.

Although it is commonly thought that actively addicted persons require larger doses of analgesics and sedatives (which is probably, but not universally, true), the needs of recovering addicts are unappreciated. Anecdotal information suggests that persons in recovery fall predominantly into the category of individuals who require *higher* than usual doses of analgesic drugs (Farley, 1991; Goodwin, 1991). This finding has not been formally investigated in clinical trials and must be treated with caution. Nevertheless, the possibility should be considered when determining drug requirements intraoperatively and responding to requests for analgesics postoperatively.

The reluctance by health professionals to adequately treat acute pain in the general population has been noted, analyzed and decried (Angell, 1982; Kaiko, Wallenstein & Rogers, 1983; Mangieri, 1991; Marks & Sachar, 1973; Perry, 1985; Sriwatanakul, Weiss & Alloza, 1983). Also, several publications have addressed the inadequacy of common analgesic regimens after surgery in the general population. Indeed, some consider the apparent inhumanity of treating pain inadequately to be a crisis of major proportions (Mangieri, 1991; Melzak,

1990). The recovering addict may be exposed to additional hazards in this regard. Several instances of relapse to drug use have been noted in abstinent individuals after major surgery when analgesic administration was deliberately restricted (Farley, 1991). The purported cause of return to addictive behavior in these persons was their psychological reaction to prolonged suffering, although this was, of course, superimposed on other issues of health and well-being.

The clinician confronts a medical treatment conundrum regarding anesthesia and analgesia in recovering patients: the desirability of adequate pain relief, the possibility of increased analgesic requirements, the appropriate fear of relapse and the widespread ignorance of health care professionals about these issues. By far the majority of persons closest to the issue—including persons in recovery who recently have undergone major surgery, and knowledgeable surgeons, nurses and addiction medicine specialists—report that conventional attitudes are more likely to result in inadequate perioperative pain relief rather than excessive opiate administration (Farley, 1991; Goodwin, 1991; Hyde, 1991; Radcliffe, 1991). Their collective experience may be summarized as follows:

- Recovering addicts and alcoholics should receive adequate analgesia that is appropriate to their perception of the severity of the noxious stimulus.
- When feasible, special nerve blocks, nonopiate analgesics and other alternate modalities should be considered first.
- Provided certain precautions are observed, treatment may involve opiates and yet be carried out with minimal risk of relapse.

The remainder of this chapter is devoted to elaborating and expanding on these statements with the objective of providing guidelines for the comprehensive perioperative management of recovering persons. Specific aspects of anesthetic management that will be addressed include preoperative evaluation, preoperative medication, intraoperative regional techniques, general anesthesia, postoperative narcotics, patient-controlled analgesia, other special regional techniques, and newer nonnarcotic pharmacologic therapies.

Preoperative Evaluation. The preoperative medical evaluation of recovering persons should include a search for the signs of chronic drug ingestion, which may linger for months or years. Nicotine abuse remains especially common in these patients even when they have favorably modified most other destructive personal habits—a testimony to nicotine's addictive potency.

Two pharmacologic agents employed in addiction treatment—disulfiram (Antabuse) and naltrexone—have implications for the perioperative period. Some patients taking disulfiram exhibit elevated levels of hepatic aminotransferases. Naltrexone demonstrates pure mu opiate antagonist action. Although ingestion of opiates does not cause unpleasant symptoms, the threshold to induce euphoria is greatly elevated. Patients taking naltrexone at the time of surgery have markedly elevated opiate requirements if opiates are used for pain relief. Although both naltrexone and disulfiram may be continued up to the day of surgery if this is deemed desirable, in-hospital continuance is probably not rational since access to alcoholic beverages is restricted and opiate antagonism is counterproductive.

Antagonist therapy causes selective up-regulation of mu receptors, corresponding to receptor sensitivity and to a reversal of tolerance (Gonzales & Brogden, 1988). The clinical correlation may be that after elimination of the exogenous antagonist and its active metabolites (48 to 72 hours for naltrexone), the formerly opioid-dependent patient may show no tolerance to opioids. Reexposure to opioid agonists, however, may rapidly re-induce tolerance.

Patients receiving chronic methadone therapy should have their regular daily dose ascertained and then administered as a baseline, with further opiates given to ameliorate pain as required (Hayes, 1991; Lane, 1991).

A desirable objective in the modulation of preoperative anxiety is to treat the anxiety effectively without producing a conscious euphoria that could stimulate dormant mood/thinking/behavior cycles (Mangieri, 1991). Relaxation techniques and soothing music played through personal earphones have been used in lieu of preoperative medication (Lawton, 1991). Sedatives and anxiolytics either should be avoided or else given in sufficient doses to induce hypnosis, thereby preventing a euphoric state (Mangieri, 1991).

Intraoperative Management. Intraoperative anesthesia can be administered using a broad range of agents and techniques. The advantages of using regional anesthesia in the recovering patient population are manifest: thus, this method is indicated whenever feasible and commensurate with the expertise of the practitioner. Virtually all forms of surgery may be performed using a regional technique either as a supplement to general anesthesia or as the sole modality. However, because skills and experience in administering regional anesthesia vary widely, the complete spectrum of neural blocks may not be available everywhere. Also, various relative and absolute contraindications to regional techniques exist and the failure rate is not insignificant. Fortunately, other options are acceptable.

General anesthesia in all its variations can be employed safely, provided postoperative planning has been complete. Even the use of opiates as part of a rational, balanced anesthetic need not be feared. The most difficult issues related to perioperative management begin at the termination of surgery.

Postoperative Care. Problems of the postoperative period may be divided into the time immediately after surgery, the in-hospital convalescence and the discharge medications.

If continuous regional anesthesia has been used intraoperatively, it may be continued into the postoperative period. Some authorities believe that the benefits of regional techniques are so significant (and the dangers of narcotics so serious) that postoperative pain management should virtually always involve neural blockade (Mangieri, 1991). Continuous spinals, lumbar and thoracic epidurals and even continuous plexus and axillary infusions also may be used. With this strategy, the clinician's effort to avoid narcotics includes prolonging hospital care until the patient's pain has abated sufficiently to allow discharge without medication (Mangieri, 1991). This tactic, while helpful, may not be supported by third-party payers. It also is not considered necessary by the majority of practitioners (Chambers, 1991; Farley, 1991; Hyde, 1991; Ohliger, 1991).

The large number of addicts and alcoholics recovering within the Twelve Step fellowships have resources that can be used to broaden the range of safe and acceptable analgesic methods. Thus, dependence on continuous regional anesthesia seems unnecessarily limiting. In selecting another approach, the clinician's first step should be to assess the extent and adequacy of the patient's recovery program. Sharing the details of their thinking and feeling state with others in their fellowship is standard behavior for participants in programs such as AA and NA.

An important individual in this process is the sponsor, and the patient should be encouraged to increase his or her contact with the sponsor as the time for surgery approaches (Chambers, 1991; Farley, 1991; Hyde, 1991; Ohliger, 1991). In many cases, it is helpful for the sponsor or surrogate to be introduced to the surgeon and anesthesiologist. The development of a relationship between these caregivers can help resolve questions that arise regarding analgesic requirements during the postoperative period.

Key elements of success include a knowledgeable physician who orders pain medication in response to the patient's level of discomfort and active participation by individuals important in the patient's recovery program. The second provision means that daily discussions regarding the patient's level of comfort and use of narcotics (including cumulative dosages) should involve the patient, the treating health professional and the recovery contact person. These procedures have been successfully employed for some time by several practitioners (Chambers, 1991; Farley, 1991; Hyde, 1991; Kent, 1991; Ohliger, 1991).

Intravenous PCA with opiates has been used routinely with recovering persons after major surgery (Hyde, 1991). The matter, however, is controversial. Some have objected to PCA on theoretical grounds, in particular to the harmful psychodynamics of self-administration (Mangieri, 1991; Mangieri, 1991 [letter]). Nevertheless, clinical experience has shown the method to be safe and effective for recovering alcoholics when used in the context of program intensification and daily discussions, as described above. The ethics of conducting well-designed clinical studies evaluating the use of PCA may preclude this route of investigation and the clinical community may have to rely on anecdotal reports of successful and unsuccessful cases. Neural axis narcotics have advantages over as-needed parenteral or intravenous PCA modalities, since there probably is less euphoria with spinal or epidural dosing.

Nothing in these recommendations should be interpreted to imply that narcotics are incapable of initiating relapse. These recommendations indicate only that clinical practice shows that opiate analgesia can be used effectively when combined with sensitivity to the dangers inherent in this patient population. Whether patients formerly addicted to different classes of mood-altering substances are subject to different relapse risks or would benefit from specific treatment regimens are topics of ongoing discussion (Kent, 1991; Lawton, 1991; Radcliffe, 1991).

Although it seems reasonable to believe that primary opiate abusers are at greatest risk with perioperative narcotic administration, the nature of the abused substance may or may not prove to be the overriding concern when compared with the quality of the individual's sobriety. In any case, the proportion of addicts abusing multiple substances is growing and clear distinctions frequently are not possible.

Alternate therapies that show promise for use with recovering patients have emerged. Ketorolac®, a parenteral nonsteroidal, anti-inflammatory drug (NSAID), has analgesic potencies comparable to morphine with the following intramuscular equivalence: 30 to 90 mg Ketorolac = 6 to 12 mg morphine (Buckley & Brogden, 1990). The growing literature on this drug suggests that Ketorolac is effective in treating moderate to severe pain with a rate of adverse effects similar to that for morphine, but without the risk of addiction. Side effects in some patients include somnolence and gastric upset. Ketorolac has been used successfully in recovering patients after surgery (Buckley & Brogden, 1990).

Kappa agonist/partial antagonists opiates (nalbuphine, dezocine, butorphenol, pentazocine) present lower (but finite) abuse potential while providing good analgesia (O'Brian & Benfield, 1989). These agents may be preferred, perhaps as adjuncts to Ketorolac. Buprenorphine is a partial mu agonist/kappa antagonist being investigated for the treatment of opioid dependence. Its use in hospitalized opioid-dependent patients (or patients in recovery) is attractive because of its analgesic potency, duration of action, and mild withdrawal symptoms (Walsh et al., 1992).

The $alpha_2$-receptor agonist, clonidine, or subsequently developed congeners may prove useful for both recovering addicts and active addicts during the perioperative period. In addition to its salubrious effects on the withdrawal syndrome, clonidine has been identified as: (1) an anxiolytic, (2) a sedative, (3) synergistic with anesthetic agents and (4) analgesic, especially in the epidural space (Maze & Tranquilli, 1991; Filos, Patroni et al., 1993). Further developments with this class of drugs and studies providing clear indications for their use in the amelioration of perioperative stress are needed.

If a patient continues to require analgesic medications after discharge from the hospital (a more frequent occurrence with the advent of managed care and shortened hospitalizations), a new and potentially hazardous period ensues. It is extremely unwise to allow patients to have unsupervised and unrestricted access to drugs containing opiates, regardless of the primarily abused substance, even if they are involved in a strong recovery program and have been abstinent for years. The medications should be dispensed, if possible, by the patient's spouse or friend, sponsor, or other knowledgeable person (Kent, 1991; Ohliger, 1991). The individual who accepts this responsibility must be chosen with due regard for any emotional conflicts that may exist between him/her and the patient. The doses, refills and continued need for opioid analgesics should be openly discussed by the relevant persons on a daily basis. These precautions and strict procedures will ensure that adequate pain relief is provided with effective safeguards against relapse (Hyde, 1991; Ohliger, 1991). Alternative treatments include oral NSAIDs, which should be used when possible, and transcutaneous electrical nerve stimulation (TENS), which has been employed for incision pain with intermittent success in recovering patients (Lawton, 1991).

Clinical Errors. The following anecdotes exemplify errors of omission and commission by treating physicians and their patients in recovery—errors that have led to episodes of relapse or "near miss" (Davis, 1991; Kent, 1991; Quinn, 1991):

- Narcotics were administered postoperatively in the hospital to a primary intravenous opiate user only six months into recovery. No special program intensification was provided. The patient developed drug ideation while in the hospital and returned to drug use immediately on discharge.
- Sedatives and anxiolytics were prescribed after major abdominal surgery for neoplasm in a recovering person. No program intensification was provided. The patient soon relapsed to alcohol use (his primary drug of choice).
- Tablets of acetaminophen with codeine were given to a 50-year-old physician to take home after oral surgery. He had been in stable recovery from alcoholism for 10 years. The patient experienced euphoria and drug ideation after taking the fourth tablet and immediately destroyed the remaining drug.
- After more than 10 years' sobriety, an alcoholic patient developed chronic back pain and was given unsupervised narcotics and diazepam. Though abstinent for many years, she did not actively participate in a Twelve Step fellowship or have an alternate support system. The patient relapsed and died of alcohol-related illness within the year.

These vignettes are representative of other known cases of relapse. In each instance, serious mistakes were made in patient management. Ongoing, informal surveys have failed to reveal a single incident of relapse related to perioperative medications when the treatment strategies suggested in this chapter were used.

CONCLUSIONS

Our conclusions regarding the perioperative management of patients formerly addicted to alcohol or drugs, tentatively drawn on the basis of current understanding and experience, may be summarized as follows:

- Patients in recovery from alcohol and other drug addictions should have adequate analgesia in the perioperative period. Physicians and nurses should neither unnecessarily promote nor unreasonably restrict analgesics.
- Patients who are involved in Twelve Step fellowships should intensify their program involvement preoperatively and arrange for visits and discussion of feeling state and cumulative drug dosing in the postoperative period with their sponsor or another fellowship contact.
- Optimum care is achieved by developing a trusting, cooperative relationship between a knowledgeable physician, the patient, and his or her support person.
- The risk of relapse into alcohol or drug use is real but manageable. This risk may be less for patients in an active, stable recovery program.
- Regional or regional-supplemented general anesthesia may be preferred if the technique can be performed with alacrity and maintained with vigilance. If possible, continuous infusions should extend into the postoperative period.
- Non-opiate analgesics, especially Ketorolac, should be considered first-line therapy.
- Abstinent patients may have elevated requirements for analgesia even many years following the discontinuation of mood-altering substances.
- Narcotics (opiates) may be safely and effectively used, provided they are administered by a recovery-knowledgeable practitioner and the patient intensifies his/her contact with a Twelve Step fellowship.
- Patient-controlled analgesia (PCA) has been used successfully when the patient is monitored closely (as described above). Primary opiate addicts, as compared with primary alcoholics, may or may not be at higher risk with this modality.
- Epidural and spinal narcotics, managed by a hospital's acute pain service, may have the highest margin of safety of the opiate therapies.
- Discharge medications must be supervised by Twelve Step program contacts and the treating physician. Unsupervised access to narcotic analgesics may place the patient at high risk for relapse.
- The services of an addiction medicine specialist are helpful in difficult cases, especially those involving chronic pain and the terminally ill.

Patients recovering from drug and alcohol addiction require and deserve an appropriate response to their special needs by treating physicians and other health care professionals.

ACKNOWLEDGMENTS: The authors gratefully acknowledge the contribution of Stephen A. Derrer, M.D., who participated in the original planning of this project, and Marigail Wynne, M.D., who provided encouragement and suggestions. We also would like to thank the several members of the fellowships of Alcoholics Anonymous and Narcotics Anonymous who shared their experiences with us.

The information and opinions presented with regard to recovering patients were obtained largely from interviews with surgeons, anesthesiologists, addiction medicine specialists and others with personal or professional experience. These sources are gratefully acknowledged.

REFERENCES

Alcoholics Anonymous (1976). *The Big Book, 3rd Ed.* New York, NY: Alcoholics Anonymous World Services.

American College of Physicians Health and Public Policy Committee (1985). Chemical dependence. *Annals of Internal Medicine* 102:405–408.

American Medical Association, Council on Mental Health (1972). Medical school education on the abuse of alcohol and other psychotropic drugs. *Journal of the American Medical Association* 219:1746–1749.

Angell M (1982). The quality of mercy. *The New England Journal of Medicine* 306:98–99.

Beattie C, Moore R, Mark L & Bigelow G (1992). Prevalence of abstinent and recovering alcoholics in a hospital population. *Abstract Presented at the American Society of Addiction Medicine Annual Medical-Scientific Conference*. Washington, DC.

Bruce DL (1983). Alcoholism and anesthesia. *Anesthesia and Analgesia* 62:84–96.

Buckley MMT & Brogden RN (1990). Ketorolac—A review. *Drugs* 39:86–109.

Bush B, Shaw S, Clearly P, Delbanco TL & Aronson MD (1987). Screening for alcohol abuse using the CAGE questionnaire. *American Journal of Medicine* 82:231–235.

Caldwell JK, Roth SH, Wu WC, Semble EL, Castell DO, Heller MD & Marsh WH (1987). Sucralfate treatment of nonsteroidal anti-inflammatory drug-induced gastrointestinal symptoms and mucosal damage. *American Journal of Medicine* 83 (Suppl B):74–82.

Chambers J (1991). Addictionist, Kensington, MD. Personal communication.

Davis J (1991). Director, Resource Group Counseling and Education Center, Baltimore, MD. Personal communication.

DeMarchi S, Cecchin E, Basile A, Bertotti A, Nardini R & Bartoli E (1993). Renal tubular dysfunction in chronic alcohol abuse: Effects of abstinence. *The New England Journal of Medicine* 329:1927–1934.

Drug Abuse Warning Network (1982). *1982 Annual Data*. Rockville, MD: National Institute on Drug Abuse.

Elliott HW (1975). Effects of street drugs on anesthesia. *International Journal of Clinical Pharmacology* 12:134–140.

Ewing J (1984). Detecting alcoholism. The CAGE questionnaire. *Journal of the American Medical Association* 252(14):1905–1907.

Fabiani CA (1991). From coca chewing to cocaine smoking. *Resident and Staff Physician* 37:101–110.

Farley W (1991). Medical Director, Perspectives Health Program, Hampton, VA. Personal communication.

Farley WJ & Talbott GD (1983). Anesthesiology and addiction. *Anesthesia and Analgesia* 62:465–466.

Filos K, Patroni O, Goudas LC, Bosas O, Kassaras A & Gartaganis S (1993). A dose-response study of orally administered clonidine as premedication in the elderly: Evaluating hemodynamic safety. *Anesthesia & Analgesia* 77:1185–1192.

Filshie J (1988). The non-drug treatment of neuralgic and neuropathic pain of malignancy. *Cancer Surveys* 7(1):161–193.

Garzotto N, Baratta S, Pistoso S & Faccincani C (1988). Validation of a screening questionnaire for alcoholism (MAST) in an Italian sample. *Comprehensive Psychiatry* 29(3):323–329.

Gelb AM, Mildvan D & Stenger RJ (1977). The spectrum and causes of liver disease in narcotic addicts. *American Journal of Gastroenterology* 67:314–318.

Gevirtz C (1988). The intravenous drug abuse patient. In EA Frost (ed.) *Pre-anesthetic Assessment*. Boston, MA: Birkhauser.

Goodwin G (1991). Division Medical Officer, U.S. Postal Service, Baltimore, MD. Personal communication.

Gonzales J & Brogden R (1988). Naltrexone. A review of its pharmacodynamic and pharmacokinetic properties and therapeutic efficacy in the management of opioid dependence. *Drugs* 35:192–213.

Griffiths R & Wolb B (1990). Relative abuse liability of different benzodiazepines in drug abusers. *Journal of Clinical Psychopharmacology* 10(4):237.

Griffiths RR, Evans SM, Heishman SJ, Preston KL, Sannerud CA, Wolf B & Woodson PP (1990). Low-dose caffeine physical dependence in humans. *Journal of Pharmacology and Experimental Therapy* 255(3).

Haverkos H (1990). Infectious diseases and drug abuse: Prevention and treatment in the drug abuse treatment system. In *European Symposium on AIDS and Drug Abuse: Providing Care for HIV-Infected Drug Users.* August 28–30, Vienna, Austria: World Health Organization (draft).

Haverkos H & Lange W (1990). Serious infections other than human immunodeficiency virus among intravenous drug abusers. *Journal of Infectious Diseases* 161:894–902.

Hayes MG (1991). Medical Director, Man Alive Research, Inc., Baltimore, MD. Personal communication.

Holloway M (1991). Rx for addiction. *Scientific American* 264(3):94–103.

Hyde G (1991). Professor of Surgery, University of Kentucky Medical Center, Lexington, KY. Personal communication.

Jacobson GR, Rigger DP & Mueller L (1977). Purpose in life and personal values among adult alcoholics. *Journal of Clinical Psychology* 33:314–316.

Jage J (1988). Anaesthesie und analgesie bei opiatabhngigen [Anesthesia and analgesia in opiate dependence]. *Anaesthesist* 37:470–482.

Kaiko RF, Wallenstein SL & Rogers AG (1983). Sources of variation of analgesic responses in cancer patients with chronic pain receiving morphine. *Pain* 15:191–200.

Kent M (1991). Medical Director, Oakview Treatment Center, Baltimore, MD. Personal communication.

Klatskin G (1961). Alcohol and its relation to liver damage. *Gastroenterology* 41:443–450.

Lane R (1991). Executive Director, Man Alive Research, Inc., Baltimore, MD. Personal communication.

Lau MP (1976). Acupuncture and addiction: An overview, addictive disease. *International Journal* 2(3):449–463.

Lawton MJ (1991). Associate Professor and Director, Alcohol and Drug Education/Rehabilitation Program, Department of Rehabilitation Counciling, Virginia Commonwealth University, Richmond, VA. Personal communication.

Lewis DC (1991). Comparison of alcoholism and other radical diseases. *Annals of Psychiatry* 21:256–265.

Mangieri EA (1991). *Anesthesiology News* [letter]. March 1991.

Mangieri EA (1991). Addictionist, Anesthesia and Pain Management, Inc., and Northport Hospital, Northport, Alabama. Personal communication.

Marks RM & Sachar EJ (1973). Undertreatment of medical inpatients with narcotic analgesics. *Annals of Internal Medicine* 78:173–181.

Maze M & Tranquilli W (1991). $Alpha_2$-adrenoreceptor agonists: Defining the role in clinical anesthesia. *Anesthesiology* 74:581–605.

McQuay H (1988). Pharmacologic treatment of neuralgic and neuropathic pain. *Cancer Surveys* 7(1):141–159.

Melzak R (1990). The tragedy of needless pain. *Scientific American* 262:2–8

Moore RD, Bone LR, Geller G, Mamon JA, Stokes EJ & Levine DM (1989). Prevalence, detection, and treatment of alcoholism in hospitalized patients. *Journal of the American Medical Association* 261:403–407.

Moss AR (1987). AIDS and intravenous drug use: The real heterosexual epidemic. *British Medical Journal* 294:389–390.

Narcotics Anonymous World Services (1990). Van Nuys, CA. Personal communication.

National Clearing House for Alcohol and Drug Information (NCADI) (1991). Rockville, MD. Personal communication.

National Council on Alcoholism and Drug Dependence (1991). Personal communication.

O'Brien J & Benfield P (1989). Dezocine—A preliminary review of its pharmacodynamic and pharmacokinetic properties and therapeutic efficacy. *Drugs* 38(2):226.

Ohliger P (1991). Laguna Miguel, CA. Personal communication.

Orkin LR & Chen CH (1977). Addiction, alcoholism, and anesthesia. *Southern Medical Journal* 70:1172–1174.

Perry SW (1985). Irrational attitudes toward addicts and narcotics. *Bulletin of the New York Academy of Medicine* 61:706–727.

Portenoy RK (1990). Chronic opioid therapy in non-malignant pain. *Journal of Pain and Symptom Management* 5:546–562.

Quinn J (1991). Director, Quinn Center, Inc., Baltimore, MD. Personal communication.

Radcliffe TB (1991). Physician in Charge, Chemical Dependency Recovery Program, Kaiser Hospital, Fontana, CA. Personal communication.

Scott LE, Clum GA & Peoples JB (1983). Preoperative predictors of postoperative pain. *Pain* 15:283–293.

Sriwatanakul K, Weiss FFA & Alloza JL (1983). Analysis of narcotic analgesic usage in the treatment of postoperative pain. *Journal of the American Medical Association* 250:926–929.

Walsh S, Preston K, Stitzer ML, Bigelow GE & Liebson I (1992). The acute effects of high dose buprenorphine in non-dependent humans. In LS Harris (ed.) *Problems of Drug Dependence 1991* (Research Monograph 119). Rockville, MD: National Institute on Drug Abuse, 245.

CHAPTER 4

Liver Transplantation

Thomas P. Beresford, M.D.

Early Studies of Transplantation
Evaluating Prognosis
Later Studies of Transplantation

The medical dilemma of whether and when to provide an alcoholic with a "new" liver brings many of the issues surrounding the care of alcohol-dependent persons into sharp focus (Beresford, 1997). A decade ago, the possibility of an alcoholic receiving a liver transplant seemed remote: a consensus conference at the National Institutes of Health (NIH) had concluded that although liver transplantation was becoming a viable clinical procedure, it should be offered to alcoholics only in rare circumstances (Anonymous, 1983). While this statement was intended to restrict the use of liver transplantation in alcoholic liver disease, it was the first official consideration of the possibility of alcoholics receiving "new" livers. The Consensus Panel went on to warn that only alcoholics *who were likely to remain abstinent* should be given a liver graft. Nearly 15 years later, the distribution of liver grafts to alcohol-dependent persons with liver failure has grown well beyond the NIH Consensus vision, but the concern with post-transplant abstinence persists.

A few years after the NIH pronouncement, the transplantation group at the University of Pittsburgh published data from a series of "alcoholics" who had received a liver graft: one-year survival characteristics did not differ from those of "non-alcoholic" recipients and they appeared to be maintaining an abstinent state (Starzl, Van et al., 1988). This prompted Starzl's comment in the non-medical press to the effect that liver transplantation was a "cure" for alcoholism. Few in the addictions treatment community agreed with his exuberant conclusion: clinical cases abound in which patients have undergone extensive, often painful medical procedures only to return to uncontrolled drinking. Starzl's comment also implied that the propensity to drink in an uncontrolled fashion had something to do with liver physiology or with an interaction between the liver and the brain. Most current biological research in the field of alcoholism suggests that the mechanisms that may account for tolerance, withdrawal, and loss of control of alcohol probably are confined to the brain.

At about the same time, a Michigan court established the legal precedent that alcoholism alone did not contraindicate liver transplantation (Beresford, Turcotte et al., 1990). The judge cautioned the medical profession against requiring, as a condition of an alcohol dependent patient's receiving a liver transplant, a pre-operative abstinence period that was longer than the likely natural course of the end-stage liver disease itself. Recognizing the dilemma caused by the scarcity of livers suitable for transplantation, the court challenged both the transplant and the alcohol research communities to provide a reasonable set of criteria for use in selecting alcoholic patients for liver transplantation.

EARLY STUDIES OF TRANSPLANTATION

In response to this circumstance and fueled by two medical advances—the introduction of effective immunosuppressants and improved surgical techniques that, taken together, rendered liver transplant a highly survivable procedure—the authors began to study the selection of alcoholic patients for liver transplant (Beresford, Turcotte et al., 1990). They quickly made a series of observations that required further inquiry. First, for example, it was evident that most of the persons being referred for liver transplant, who qualified for alcohol dependence by standard diagnostic criteria, were relatively young: the average age was approximately 44 years. By contrast, in the United States, cirrhosis deaths due to alcohol use reach a peak prevalence in the seventh decade of life (Grant, DeBakey & Zobeck, 1991).

At the same time, early data suggested that alcoholic women were over-represented among referrals: the ratio was approximately two men to every woman in the referral population, as compared to the four to one ratio of men to women seen for alcoholism in the general population (Schuckit, 1991). Put another way, approximately 60% more women were being referred than might have been expected from general population statistics alone. While not surprising in the context of a well-known, if unexplained, predilection toward liver injury among females, these data contradict the popular stereotype of the chronic alcoholic, who usually is pictured as a middle-aged or elderly male.

The studies also pointed out that the length of pre-evaluation abstinence for alcohol-dependent candidates, which is characterized in most studies as greater or less than six months, appeared to have little association with those factors that research on alcoholism put forth as the best prognostic indicators of long-term abstinence. In the author's experience, these indicators appeared to be: (1) a diagnosis of alcohol dependence established by standard criteria rather than by an assumption based on a probable cause for liver failure or by clinical intuition, (2) an active and unambivalent acceptance of this diagnosis of alcohol dependence by the liver transplant candidate (and, as often as possible, by the family), (3) an indication of a socially stable environment, and (4) the presence of two or more of the four prognostic factors for long-term abstinence described by Vaillant (Lucey, Merion & Beresford, 1994).

The last group of indicators includes a rehabilitative relationship with another person, one or more activities that structure time otherwise spent in drinking, a source of improved hope or self-esteem, and a certain and noxious consequence of drinking (Vaillant, 1983, 1995). The author and colleagues reported their experience with this approach in an early description of a sample of 32 alcohol-dependent candidates for liver transplantation (Beresford, Turcotte et al., 1990). These early explorations led to consideration of the following factors as useful in selecting candidates for liver transplantation. Their use has been borne out, at least partially, in later studies mentioned below.

EVALUATING PROGNOSIS

Diagnosis. The first guide to prognosis is careful diagnosis. The nosology of alcohol dependence has been described extensively elsewhere in this volume and in our published work (Lucey, Merion and Beresford, 1994). Recent codification schemes have provided more generally useful means of diagnosing alcohol dependence. The standard instrument at this time in the United States is the definition of substance dependence in the fourth edition of the *Diagnostic and Statistical Manual of Mental Disorders, 4th Edition* (*DSM-IV*; American Psychiatric Association, 1994). It requires the clinician to assess (1) physical dependence, (2) impaired control of alcohol use and (3) social and physical decline. This is not an easy task, nor is it one that can be done reliably in the absence of specific interviewing skills designed to elicit a careful drinking history (Beresford, 1994a, 1994b). Once clinical data are gathered carefully, they are matched to the *DSM-IV* criteria as establishing both physical dependence and either impaired control or social/physical decline. Some clinicians may wish to see evidence of all three before rendering a diagnosis of alcohol dependence. Practically, however, two diagnostic rules should obtain: the diagnostic scheme a transplant program chooses must be used consistently and the clinical data from the patient's history should be corroborated with a family member or significant other person who knows the patient well and sees the patient frequently.

Alcohol Dependence with Other Drug Addiction: Estimates put the lifetime prevalence of alcohol dependence at about 7% to 10% for the U.S. population (Vaillant, 1983, 1995; Schuckit, 1991). While use of other psychoactive substances may occur for many, for the great majority of alcohol-dependent persons, the addictive use of ethanol serves as the primary drug of dependence. The single exception to this may be heavy nicotine use, which often goes hand in hand with heavy drinking. There is, however, a subgroup of persons with alcohol dependence who also present a history of addiction to other substances, usually more than two substances at different times in their lives. These make up approximately 0.5% to 1% of the general population and have been described as polysubstance abusers as a primary diagnostic category (Vaillant, 1988a). Associated characteristics of this pattern of use generally include severe social or character problems before age 15 as well as beginning use of alcohol along with other drugs during adolescence followed by heavy use through their 20s and 30s. Intravenous drug use resulting in hepatitis B or C infection frequently occurs in this group.

Establishing a diagnosis of polysubstance abuse, which may include alcoholism, is vitally important in the prognosis for continued abstinence after a liver transplant. Studies of the natural history of alcoholism in the absence of polysubstance abuse and early character pathology symptoms show that pre-existing character traits do not distinguish persons who are likely to become alcoholic from those who are not (Vaillant, 1995). By contrast, similar studies of persons showing character pathology in the grade school years and early adolescence are significant predictors of subsequent polysubstance abuse including alcoholism (Glueck & Glueck, 1950). By comparison, the natural remission rates for most non-drug abusing AD persons are very hopeful, generally in the range of 30 to 60% depending on personal and treatment resources (Vaillant, 1983, 1995; Moos, Finney & Cronlsite, 1990). By contrast, the natural history of polysubstance addiction is often one of indurated behavior with little response to treatment until such time as the severity of both character problems and the polysubstance abuse wanes (Vaillant, 1966). For most affected persons, this generally occurs in the late 30s to early 40s. Prior to that time, some studies have suggested that the maximum rate of sustained abstinence will be no higher than 10% for this group (Vaillant, 1988a).

In clinical practice, liver transplant has been provided to persons with histories of polysubstance addiction and character pathology, but have not been offered to such persons when the polyaddictive style of substance use had not waned. While each case must be judged on its own merits, the author and colleagues generally have looked to a period of one to two years of abstinence from polysubstances along with evidence of a reasonable concurrent social adjustment as indicators of likely post-operative abstinence and medication compliance (Beresford, 1994a). This seems to be the only case in which pretransplant abstinence serves as a guide to posttransplant compliance and abstinence. When faced with very young patients or with acute signs and symptoms of polysubstance abuse with or without characterological problems, the author's approach has been to follow such patients over time in an effort to gauge whether or not they can refrain from injurious use of substances and maintain their compliance with prescribed regimens of medicine or diet.

Ambivalence. When considering alcohol dependence clinically, it is important to think of both the positive and of the negative aspects of habitual use (DiCicco, Biron et al., 1984). Most clinicians who are trained in recognizing and intervening in pathological states will have no trouble recognizing the injurious aspects of alcohol dependence. After all, these are well described in diagnostic schemes and in textbooks of pathology. It often is more difficult, however, to recognize those aspects of alcohol use that the alcoholic may regard as positive (Beresford, 1994a, 1994b). These can include several kinds of factors from simple avoidance of the pain and discomfort of alcohol withdrawal to complex issues like survival in a suffocating family.

The clinician must keep both the positive and the negative aspects of chronic alcohol abuse in mind in order to understand the dependent patient's own ambivalent behavior. In the clinical encounter, the physician may mention some negative effect of AD only to have the patient indicate an unwillingness to consider stopping alcohol use or attending treatment. This often is referred to as "denial," but it probably is more precise to say that the alcoholic's reaction is one of ambivalence. If one's view of alcohol is mixed with both pluses and minuses, an external force using the minuses to threaten the use of alcohol leaves the AD sufferer only the recourse of holding on to the pluses at all costs. This results in a familiar tug of war between patient and clinician and often leaves the latter with a sense of frustration, if not therapeutic nihilism. Frustration and nihilism need not be the case.

From the point of view of liver transplant allocation, a resolution of the alcoholic's ambivalence and a sustained effort at remaining abstinent is a necessity. For many patients requesting liver transplant, this ambivalence has already been resolved and is evidenced by a sustained period of alcohol-free living. For others, however, the ambivalence towards drinking may persist, often in subtle ways. Perhaps the best indicator of its presence is the clinician's own sense that a particular patient has not yet come to grips with the fact that any subsequent alcohol use is a very high-risk behavior. Another indication may be a similar sense of discomfort among family members when considering the alcoholic person. Whatever the source, in the absence of a more quantifiable measure of attitude or viewpoint towards ambivalence, the clinical sense of discomfort is often the best indicator of a referral for alcohol treatment or to a self-help support group as the patient's physical condition will allow. In the best possible circumstance, the transplant team will be afforded sufficient time to observe the patient's course as long as possible before deciding to transplant or not and will allow for a resolution of ambivalence to alcohol use.

Social Stability. The alcoholic stereotypically is a resident of Skid Row: on the streets, alone, and with no means of support. In reality, only a very small minority of alcohol dependent persons in the

United States fit this description (Vaillant, 1995; Shuckit, 1991). The vast majority have a stable residence, maintain contact with their families and have a means of earning a living. Social stability must be assessed, however, because it bears on long-term remission from AD and on compliance with an often complicated post-transplant medicine regimen. Strauss and Bacon (1951) noticed long ago that a socially stable adjustment was associated with continued participation in alcoholism treatment. In their study, persons presenting with three or more of four easily measured characteristics—employment for the previous three years, a stable residence for the previous two years, married and living with spouse, and not living alone—identified those AD sufferers who continued alcohol treatment versus those who dropped away.

One limitation of this scale is its weighting toward employment outside the home, a factor that may apply more to the preponderantly male population of alcoholics than to females. In using the Strauss-Bacon scale, we include the homemaking or child rearing, corroborated by a spouse or significant other, as evidence of gainful employment in an attempt to apply this scale equally to both genders. Another limitation will be obvious to seasoned clinicians: there is a wide range of individual variability in the areas of functioning assessed in the Strauss-Bacon scale. These data, therefore, must always be taken in context of the specific case history as well as the corroborating family discussion.

Vaillant's Prognostic Factors. In deciding to offer liver transplantation to alcohol-dependent individuals, the clinician must assess those factors that are conducive to long-term abstinence and therefore to long-term health. From longitudinal, prospective research, Vaillant identified four factors that are associated with continued long term-abstinence from alcohol (Vaillant, 1983, 1995). In his study, the presence of any two of the four factors indicated a high likelihood of abstinence for three years or more. When only one or none of the factors was present, the likelihood of abstinence was significantly less, with a maximum of two years.

The first factor is the presence of a non-drinking activity, or "substitute dependency" in Vaillant's unfortunate term. This does not refer to substituting one addictive substance with another; rather, it refers to the ability of the alcohol-dependent person to fill unstructured time with structured activities that do not involve drinking (Vaillant, 1988b). This can mean any of a series of activities, ranging from a renewed interest in work or family, through participation in self-help groups, to volunteer or recreational activities. In essence, this factor requires frequent participation in the activity for long periods of time. The rationale derives from the alcohol-dependent person's perspective: for many alcohol-dependent persons, drinking has been a pleasurable, self-reinforcing pastime. When trying suddenly to give up an important behavior, it will be easy to resume drinking unless some replacement for it is found. In practice, many persons presenting with end-stage liver failure are physically too ill to participate in time-structuring activities prior to transplant. It is important, however, for those persons who describe abstinence periods, that the clinician document the use made of the time as well as the continuing resources available that limit the amount of "dead" time that might otherwise provide occasion for drinking.

The next of Vaillant's factors is the presence of a rehabilitation relationship: i.e., one or more persons in the drinker's life who unambivalently signal their belief in the human worth of the alcohol-dependent person, while at the same time unambiguously drawing consistent limits on the drinking behavior. Many persons can fulfill this function: a spouse who has worked through the difficulties of living with an alcohol-dependent person, a knowledgeable friend, a professional therapist or counselor, a sponsor from Alcoholics Anonymous, a minister, or a number of other people who are important in the alcohol-dependent person's life. Over the short term, the staff of the transplant team may serve this purpose: they clearly signal their belief in the worth of the alcoholic patient when they give him or her a liver graft. At the same time, most programs make it clear that drinking after the operation must be avoided in order to preserve the functioning of the graft. This provides an essential focus: the responsibility for abstinence behavior rests with, and only with, the dependent person.

Operationally, each alcohol-dependent transplant candidate must demonstrate at least the presence of a person who can alert the transplant team if drinking behavior resumes. In that instance, the team can present treatment alternatives and take an active role in offering alcohol rehabilitation. A "safety" person is necessary because the effect of alcohol, especially in large amounts, on a transplanted liver is not well understood and may represent a significant medical danger. Much more to the point, it is clear that the re-establishment of continued drinking often brings with it an inattention to compliance with immunosuppressive medications, the latter of which may be followed by organ rejection, failure of the transplanted liver and death.

Vaillant's third factor involves finding a source of improved hope and self-esteem in the drinking person's life that can be used to maintain abstinence. It is important to recall that for most AD persons drinking often leads to a profound sense of guilt. Recurring thoughts of guilt over one's past behavior or lack of it can create a despondency that devalues abstinence and becomes a convenient excuse for resuming drinking. A powerful antidote is a counterbalancing sense of hope or self-esteem. At the same time it may provide a useful perspective in the way of healing past injuries through one's present behavior. As Vaillant points out, the process of doing good for others is a powerful source of self-esteem.

In daily life, improved hope and self-esteem can be found in activities that promote abstinence, such as participation in a self-help group. Other possibilities might include participating in one's religion with a renewed sense of belonging, renewing hope for the future through contact with one's children or grandchildren, or helping others who are about to undergo transplant as through participation in a support group. At interview, the clinician might ask questions such as, "If you find yourself feeling bad about things from your drinking days, what do you do to feel better?" Of the factors that Vaillant outlines, this one is probably the most difficult to assess in a quantifiable manner. Nonetheless, as other scholars have noted (Frank, 1991), the sense of hope and looking positively toward the future is of crucial importance in not only maintaining abstinence but in approaching a significant event in one's life such as surgery of this magnitude.

Vaillant's final factor involves a direct, negative behavioral consequence of the drinking. Specifically this refers to a noxious event that will happen with certainty each and every time the person imbibes alcohol. Very few drinking consequences qualify: acute pancreatic pain, returning to jail for violation of parole, or the ethanol-disulfiram reaction are the most common. Noxious results from drinking will usually occur in most of these instances. Liver failure itself rarely provides a potent negative consequence because of the subtlety and chronicity of its symptoms. The same is true for other physical derangement's such as alcohol cardiomyopathy or nerve damage. The loss of spouse or family may sometimes fit in this category depending on the firmness of their ability to set limits in the face of renewed drinking.

LATER STUDIES OF TRANSPLANTATION

Subsequent data from a series of transplant centers have accrued since these early studies (Lucey, Merion & Beresford, 1994; Beresford, 1997). The bias toward relatively younger persons and for women has remained. It also has become clear that as many as one of every four candidates referred to transplant centers as alcoholic in fact *do not* meet standard criteria for alcohol dependence (Beresford, 1994a). These individuals appear to be divided almost equally between those who have the lesser diagnosis of alcohol abuse (defined as evidence of a tolerance to alcoholism with no evidence of withdrawal symptoms, loss of control or social difficulties due to drinking) and no substance use problem at all. Conversely, previously unrecognized alcohol dependence has been found in putatively non-alcoholic patients. Finally, it is clear that the diagnoses of alcohol dependence and alcoholic liver disease, made independently, overlap only in about four of five cases (Beresford, 1994a). Data such as these underscore the need for very careful use of standard alcohol dependence diagnostic criteria, along with verification through family contact, when assessing candidates for this life-saving procedure.

After the publication of our early experience, other programs began evaluating alcoholic patients with respect to drinking risk and likely long-term prognosis. While many of these patient series are continuing, sufficient experience across centers has now been accumulated to suggest that a first year abstinence rate in the range of 90% is not unusual and is probably the norm for highly selected alcohol-dependent patient groups (Beresford and Lucey, 1994).

A careful clinical assessment of all of the prognostic factors for future abstinence may, however, result in disqualification of as many as one of every six alcohol-dependent transplant candidates because of a clinical impression of a high likelihood for resumption of sustained and uncontrolled drinking (Beresford, 1994a). A follow-up analysis of 99 alcoholic candidates for liver transplantation found that about 80% of alcohol-dependent recipients were likely to remain alive for two years. In contrast, the estimated actuarial survival of alcoholic candidates denied transplantation because of their psychiatric evaluation was significantly less and reached zero at two years (Lucey, Merion et al., 1992). No studies have examined the role of drinking versus the course of liver failure alone in the early demise of candidates not accepted for liver transplant.

Some answers have begun to appear on the clinical meaning of pre-operative abstinence for greater or less than six months: a resource utilization study done by our group found no differences, based on length of preoperative sobriety, in such measures as the number of complications post-operatively, the number of days spent in the intensive care unit, or in hospital stay after the operation (McCurry, Baliga et al., 1992). But the most salient question is whether or not a period of six months or more of abstinence prior to evaluation predicts continued abstinence after having received a new liver graft. The author and colleagues addressed this in two follow-up studies of three years or more and found that the six-month abstinence period bore no statistical relationship to the length of post-transplant abstinence among the alcohol-dependent recipients (Lucey, Merion et al., 1992; Lucey, Carr et al., 1997; Everson, Bharadhwaj et al., 1997). Contrary to expectation, we also found a relatively high rate of alcohol exposure among non-dependent recipients post-operatively: one-third to one-half had used alcohol within the follow-up period despite the fact that both alcohol-dependent and non-dependent patients had been warned specifically against alcohol use because of its unknown and potentially toxic effects on the newly transplanted liver. Other measures of post-operative functioning did not differentiate alcoholic and non-alcoholic recipients, including measures of compliance, such as missed doses of immunosuppressive medicines. Similarly, psychiatric symptoms, such as depressive episodes, did not differentiate the two groups.

Data from these follow-up studies, however, noted a relatively consistent frequency of a return to addictive drinking in about 10% of alcohol-dependent cases after three to five years and a return to any alcohol exposure in the range of about 40%. These reflect 90% and 60% remission rates. While most alcohol treatment centers would be delighted with such outcome rates at five years, these frequencies taken with the occurrence of so-called "late" deaths in association with a return to drinking well beyond the first year of transplant survival (Everson, Bharadhwaj et al., 1997) raise again the question of whether alcohol-dependent patients should receive a liver graft when donors are few and non-dependent patients have the same need. This has called upon clinicians to reexamine present selection practices and has focused necessary attention on long-term treatment and follow-up of alcohol-dependent liver graft recipients (Everhart & Beresford, 1997).

With respect to candidate selection, different centers have added different methods of assessing high risk for relapse to alcohol use. One series, for example, described an assessment based on the quantity and frequency of alcohol use and asserted that a contract, signed by the alcoholic candidate, can be a valuable adjunct in discriminating between high and low risk candidates (Gish, Lee et al., 1993). Another group has provided a mathematical calculation, based on a survey of alcoholic patients in the Department of Veterans Affairs system, that provides a coefficient claiming to predict high-risk relapse (Yates, Booth et al., 1993). These methods require further evaluation before they can be applied generally. But most transplant programs now attempt to recognize high relapse risk drinkers based on an assessment of empirical clinical data outlined above rather than simply on a clinical impression. In most programs, candidates at high risk of relapse to alcohol use make up a minority of alcoholics referred for liver transplantation.

With respect to follow-up care, the alcohol-dependent liver recipients appear to be a unique group within the overall alcohol-dependent population. Very large numbers of individuals remain abstinent for long periods, to the best of our present knowledge. Should such patients all receive a round of one or another form of standard alcohol treatment in order to prevent relapse? It is hard to argue for this if, after five years, 90% do not relapse in any case. Standard therapies are considered successful if relapse rates are above 30% and remarkably so if they approach 50%, both at one year. Liver transplant by itself seems to be much more effective. Could it be that the liver transplant itself really does cure alcoholism as Starzl suggested? Or is there another explanation that perhaps leads to a better, more creative therapeutic approach in this patient group?

As mentioned earlier, in analyzing one-year follow-up data from our first series, we noted that, during the first year, the processes of the transplant procedure and follow-up care themselves naturally incorporated all four of Vaillant's prognostic factors for stable abstinence (Beresford, Turcotte et al., 1992). In a three-year follow-up study from the second series, however, it also was clear that most of this therapeutic effort appears to wane naturally by the end of the first year and certainly in the second year and beyond (Everson, Bharadhwaj et al., 1997). Follow-up visits are much less frequent in most programs, alcohol use ceases to be a point of inquiry at those visits and alcohol dependent patients describe fewer resources available to them should they need help in avoiding drinking. Vaillant's factors likewise appear to wane. The lesson from this is obvious: if long-term abstinence and remission from alcohol use are desired in this unique group, the first method to consider is an extension of the curative aspects of the original relationship with the transplant team well beyond the first year and perhaps for as long as five years or more. Continuance of the rehabilitation relationship with the team, an extension of a renewed source of hope and self-esteem, and continued structure of time in day-to-day living all seem appropriate here through extended, if not particularly intense, contact with the transplant team. Six-or 12-week bouts of standard treatment, largely the invocation of another placebo process, should be reserved for those for whom the extended follow-up is not enough. How to effect active, long-term follow-up care for alcohol-dependent liver transplant recipients, and to prove that it works over the long term, are the challenges of the moment.

CONCLUSIONS

The conclusions to be drawn from clinical research in this area to the present time are the following:

- Carefully selected alcohol-dependent patients survive equally as well as non-alcohol-dependent patients when given a liver graft;
- Rates of relapse to alcohol dependence over the long term appear to be relatively low; and
- Despite these data, there may be a risk as high as 10% for deaths directly or indirectly due to alcohol use well beyond the first year after transplant.

Taken as a general clinical approach, the clinical data to the present time suggest that alcohol dependence is best regarded as an illness for which liver transplant, while not necessarily offering a cure, provides a reasonable and justifiable extension of life. But we must also look to improve this extension to assure the life of the liver graft and the lives of the alcohol-dependent recipients of this technological miracle of our time.

REFERENCES

American Psychiatric Association (1994). *Diagnostic and Statistical Manual of Mental and Nervous Diseases, 4th Edition*. Washington, DC: The Association.

Anonymous (1983). National Institutes of Health Consensus Development Conference Statement: Liver Transplantation. *Hepatology* 4:107S–110S.

Beresford TP, Turcotte, Merion M, Burtch G, Blow FC, Campbell D, Brower KC, Coffman K & Lucey M (1990). A rational approach to liver transplantation for the alcoholic patient. *Psychosomatics* 31:241–254.

Beresford TP, Schwartz J, Wilson D, Merion M & Lucey MR (1992). The short-term psychological health of alcoholic and non-alcoholic liver transplant recipients. *Alcoholism: Clinical & Experimental Research* 16:996–1000.

Beresford TP (1994a). Psychiatric assessment of alcoholic candidates for liver transplantation. In MR Lucey, RM Merion & TP Beresford (eds.) *Liver Transplantation and the Alcoholic Patient*. Cambridge, England: Cambridge University Press.

Beresford TP (1994b). Overt and covert alcoholism. In MR Lucey, RM Merion & TP Beresford (eds.) *Liver Transplantation and the Alcoholic Patient*. Cambridge, England: Cambridge University Press.

Beresford TP (1994c). Follow-up care of alcohol dependent liver graft recipients. In MR Lucey, RM Merion & TP Beresford (eds.) *Liver Transplantation and the Alcoholic Patient*. Cambridge, England: Cambridge University Press.

Beresford TP & Lucey MR (1994). Alcoholics and liver transplant: Facts, biases and the future. *Addiction* 89:1043–1048.

Beresford TP (1997). Predictive factors for alcoholic relapse in the selection of alcohol dependent persons for hepatic transplant. *Liver Transplantation and Surgery*. 3:280–291.

DiCicco L, Biron R, Carifio J, Deutsch C, Mills DJ, Orenstein A, Re A, Unterberger H & White RE (1984). Evaluation of the CASPAR alcohol education curriculum. *Journal of Studies on Alcohol* 45(2):160–9.

Everhart JE & Beresford TP (1997). Alcoholic liver disease and transplantation: A survey of United States liver transplantation programs. *Liver Transplantation and Surgery* 3:220–226.

Everson G, Bharadhwaj G, House R, Talamantes M, Bilir B, Shrestha R, Kam I, Wachs M, Karrer F, Fey B, Ray C, Steinberg T, Morgan C & Beresford TP (1997). Long-term follow-up of patients with alcoholic liver disease who underwent hepatic transplantation. *Liver Transplantation and Surgery* 3:263–274.

Frank J (1973). *Persuasion and Healing*. Baltimore, MD: Johns Hopkins University Press.

Gish RG, Lee AH, Keefe EB, Rome H, Concepcion W & Esquivel CO (1993). Liver transplantation for patients with alcoholism and end-stage liver disease. *American Journal of Gastroenterology* 88:1337–1342.

Glueck S & Glueck E (1950). *Unravelling Juvenile Delinquency*. New York, NY: The Commonwealth Fund.

Grant B, DeBakey S & Zobeck TS (1991). *Liver Cirrhosis Mortality in the United States (Surveillance Report #18)*. Washington, DC: Department of Health and Human Services.

Lucey ML, Merion RM & Beresford TP (1994). *Liver Transplant and the Alcoholic Patient*. Cambridge, England: Cambridge University Press.

Lucey MR, Merion RM, Henley KS, Campbell DJ, Turcotte JG, Nostrant TT, Blow FC & Beresford TP (1992). Selection for and outcome of liver transplantation in alcoholic liver disease. *Gastroenterology* 102:1736–41.

Lucey MR, Carr K, Beresford TP et al. (1997). Alcohol use after liver transplantation in alcoholics: A clinical cohort follow-up study. *Hepatology* 25:1223–1227.

McCurry KR, Baliga P, Merion RM, Ham JM, Lucey MR, Beresford TP, Turcotte JG & Campbell DA (1992). Liver transplantation for alcoholic cirrhosis: Resource utilization and outcome. *Archives of Surgery* 127:772–777.

Moos RM, Finney JW & Cronkite RC (1990). *Alcoholism Treatment*. New York, NY: Oxford University Press.

Schuckit MA (1991). *Drug and Alcohol Abuse: A Clinical Guide To Diagnosis and Treatment, Third Edition*. New York, NY: Plenum Publishing Co.

Starzl TE, Van TD, Tzakis AG, Iwatsuki S, Todo S, Marsh JW, Koneru B, Staschak S, Stieber A & Gordon RD (1988). Orthotopic liver transplantation for alcoholic cirrhosis. *Journal of the American Medical Association* 260(17):2542–2544.

Strauss R & Bacon SD (1951). Alcoholism and social stability: A study of occupational integration of 2023 male clinic patients. *Quarterly Journal of Studies on Alcohol* 12:231–260.

Vaillant GE (1966). A twelve-year follow-up of New York narcotic addicts, IV. *American Journal of Psychiatry* 123:573–584.

Vaillant GE (1983). *The Natural History of Alcoholism*. Cambridge, MA: Harvard University Press.

Vaillant GE (1988a). The alcohol-dependent and drug-dependent person. In AM Nicholi (ed.) *The New Harvard Guide to Psychiatry*. Cambridge, MA: Harvard University Press.

Vaillant GE (1988b). What can long-term follow-up teach us about relapse and prevention of relapse in addiction? *British Journal of Addiction* 83(10):1147–1157.

Vaillant GE (1995). *The Natural History of Alcoholism, Revisited*. Cambridge, MA: Harvard University Press.

Yates WR, Booth BM, Reed DA, Brown K & Masterson BJ (1993). Descriptive and predictive validity of a high-risk alcoholism relapse model. *Journal of Studies on Alcohol* 54:645–651.

SECTION 12
Pain Management and Addiction

CHAPTER 1

The Neurophysiology of Pain in Addiction **901**
Peggy Compton, R.N., Ph.D. and G. F. Gebhart, Ph.D.

CHAPTER 2

Principles of Pain Treatment in the Addicted Patient **919**
Seddon R. Savage, M.D., FASAM

CHAPTER 3

Psychological Approaches to the Management of Pain **945**
Edward C. Covington, M.D. and Margaret M. Kotz, D.O.

CHAPTER 4

Prescribing Issues and the Relief of Pain **961**
Barry Stimmel, M.D., FASAM

SECTION COORDINATORS

SEDDON R. SAVAGE, M.D., FASAM
Assistant Professor of Anesthesiology
Dartmouth Medical School
and Director, Outpatient Pain Clinic
Dartmouth Hitchcock Medical Center
Lebanon, New Hampshire

HOWARD A. HEIT, M.D., FASAM, FACP
Private Practice of Gastroenterology,
Pain and Addiction Medicine
Fairfax, Virginia

CONTRIBUTORS

Peggy Compton, R.N., Ph.D.
Assistant Professor, Acute Care Section
School of Nursing
University of California at Los Angeles
Los Angeles, California

Edward C. Covington, M.D.
Head, Section on Pain Management
Department of Psychiatry
Cleveland Clinic Foundation
Cleveland, Ohio

G. F. Gebhart, Ph.D.
Department of Pharmacology
University of Iowa
Iowa City, Iowa

Margaret M. Kotz, D.O.
Alcohol and Drug Recovery Center
Department of Psychiatry
Cleveland Clinic Foundation
Cleveland, Ohio

Barry Stimmel, M.D., FASAM
Dean for Graduate Medical Education
and Professor of Medicine
Mt. Sinai School of Medicine
of the City University of New York
New York, New York

CHAPTER 1

The Neurophysiology of Pain in Addiction

Peggy Compton, R.N., Ph.D.
G. F. Gebhart, Ph.D.

Physiological Mechanisms of Pain
Pain Modulation
Neuropathic Pain
Physiological Mechanisms of Addiction
Points of Interface between Pain and Addiction
Psychosocial Correlates of Addiction
Genetic Factors Predicting Pain and Addiction
Effects of Pain on Addiction Responses

There is a physiology underlying pain, just as there is a physiology underlying addiction. Physiology alone cannot account for the variable expression and psychosocial complexity of these two very human conditions, but its role in the experience and continuation of each cannot be minimized. It is at the physiologic level that many effective interventions for the treatment of pain and addiction act. Both conditions predominantly involve the nervous system, and both have significant involvement of central opioid systems, so it is reasonable to expect that the coexistence of pain and addiction would lead to complex responses: i.e., addictive responses altered by the physiological presence of pain, and pain responses altered by the physiological presence of addiction.

This chapter provides a comprehensive review of what is currently known about the neurophysiology of pain and addiction and presents the available evidence describing how the neurophysiology underlying addiction might overlap with or modify the expression of pain. It reviews the mechanisms of pain, giving special attention to those aspects most likely to be influenced by the physiological states associated with addictive disease. In this regard, the role of hyperalgesia, endogenous opioid systems and descending modulatory controls on the experience of pain are discussed. The neurophysiological responses to drugs of abuse also are outlined, as are the differential expression of these under acute versus chronic dosing patterns. Finally, ideas about potential sources of interaction between pain and addiction are suggested, focusing upon how the general state of addiction, changes specific to opioid abuse, and inherited characteristics of the individual might affect the co-expression of these phenomena.

PHYSIOLOGICAL MECHANISMS OF PAIN

Pain is an unpleasant sensory and emotional experience that is associated with potential or actual tissue injury or described in terms of such injury (International Association for the Study of Pain, 1979). Like addiction, pain is a unique and complex experience that is influenced by culture, by context, by anticipation and previous experience, and by a variety of emotional and cognitive factors. Accordingly, reactions to stimuli that produce pain vary from one individual to the next, and even within the same individual at different points in time. The neurophysiologic mechanisms that underlie the experience of pain may be considered in two classifications: *nociceptive pain* (pain produced by noxious stimuli) and *neuropathic pain* (pain produced by alterations in nociceptive pathways).

Nociception. The stimuli that produce pain are termed "noxious." Noxious stimuli are those that damage or threaten to damage tissue (such as pinches, cuts and burns). Pain serves to warn of potential injury and thus is an important protective mechanism. Noxious stimuli set into motion a series of events that contribute to the sensory and emotional experience of pain. They activate specific sensory receptors called *nociceptors*. Nociceptors, and the axons of neurons with which they are associated, convey nociceptive information (i.e., information about potential or actual tissue injury) to the spinal cord, where (1) autonomic and nociceptive reflexes are activated, and (2) simultaneously, the information is transmitted to the brain (supraspinally).

Autonomic reflex responses produced by noxious stimuli include increases in heart rate, blood pressure and respiration. These nociceptive reflexes are protective, withdrawal (motor) reflexes that are organized at the level of the spinal cord. For example, unexpectedly pricking one's finger with a needle produces a reflexive withdrawal, followed by conscious appreciation a pain. Such conscious appreciation that a given stimulus is painful requires integration and interpretation of information in several areas of the brain. This supraspinal integration and interpretation of peripheral events are what make pain such a unique experience.

It is important to understand the distinction between nociception and the experience of pain. Nociception describes the neural events and reflex responses produced by a noxious stimulus. It can occur in the absence of the perception of pain, just as pain can arise in the absence of nociception. For example, in paraplegics or quadriplegics, noxious stimuli applied below the level of spinal cord injury can evoke nociceptive withdrawal reflexes because the connection between the peripheral nociceptors and the spinal circuitry remain intact. However, because such nociceptive information cannot be transmitted above the spinal injury to the brain, the individual does not perceive the noxious stimuli as painful.

Sensory Channels. It is helpful to think about sensations arising from skin, joints, muscles and viscera (nociceptive or otherwise) in terms of *sensory channels*. Such channels are composed of: (1) the peripheral receptors and nerves, (2) the neurons in the spinal cord on which the peripheral nerves terminate (and transfer their message), (3) the ascending tracts in the spinal cord that carry the information supraspinally, and (4) the sites in the brain where integration and interpretation of input occurs. Activation of a sensory channel provides information about the location, onset, intensity and duration of a stimulus.

The sensory channel for pain generally is described as having two components: a sensory-discriminative component and a motivational-affective component. The sensory-discriminative component of pain is directly linked to the noxious stimulus and usually is what is meant when pain is referred to as a "sensation." Here, a noxious stimulus activates nociceptors and initiates a series of neural events that ultimately reach the cortex of the brain, allowing the individual experiencing the pain to determine the location of the stimulus, its intensity, and its duration. This exquisite ability to characterize and localize the site of pain is best developed for the skin and very poorly developed for the viscera.

The motivational-affective component of pain includes the nature and intensity of the emotional responses that make pain personal and unique to each individual. The sites in the brain that contribute to the motivational-affective component and the spinal pathways that convey nociceptive information to these brain sites are different than those associated with the sensory-discriminative component of pain. The motivational-affective component of pain is served by older, relatively indirect neural pathways that are conserved phylogenetically (i.e., are common to all vertebrates). The sensory-discriminative component of pain is organized to give information about the location, the intensity, and the duration of the nociceptive event. The motivational-affective component of pain affects the individual's response to the nociceptive input.

Overlaying the sensory-discriminative and motivational-affective components of pain are learned cultural and cognitive contributions that color the individual's interpretation of and concerns about pain. Cognitive contributions include attention, anxiety, anticipation, and past experiences and, in the case of the addict, may include concerns about drug supply, impending withdrawal, or intoxication. For example, if an addict sustains an injury in the course of obtaining or injecting a drug of abuse, his or her perception of and response to the ensuing pain is likely to be minimized by the overwhelming sense of relief anticipated on drug ingestion. On the other hand, if an addict is without a supply of drugs and fears impending withdrawal, a similar injury is likely to be experienced as relatively more painful. Thus, cognitive contributions can significantly modulate the response and reaction to a painful stimulus.

Nociceptors and the Sensory Channel for Pain. The first event in nociception is activation of a specialized sensory receptor, the nociceptor, which transduces stimulus energy into changes in nerve membrane electrical potential. Thus, receptors in skin, deep tissue, and viscera convert mechanical, thermal, and chemical stimulus energy into action potentials that are conveyed along nerve axons in the spinal cord or cranial nuclei. These sensory neurons or "primary afferent neurons," as they are called, have their cell body located in a dorsal root ganglion or ganglion of a cranial nerve.

The sensory endings of primary afferent neurons are tree-like and are distributed over a localized region of tissue. Nociceptors can be excited only by stimuli applied in the innervated region, called the "receptive field." Receptive fields of different primary afferent neurons vary in size and overlap extensively with the receptive fields of other primary afferent neurons. It is important to note that a threshold noxious stimulus that evokes one action potential in a single nociceptor is not sufficient to be perceived as painful; for pain to occur, either spatial summation (one action potential occurring simultaneously in many nociceptors) or temporal summation (many action potentials occurring closely in time in a single nociceptor) are required. Consequently, suprathreshold stimuli are required for an individual to consciously perceive a noxious stimulus as painful.

Nociceptors differ from non-nociceptors in several ways:

- The nociceptor is not macroscopically specialized and so is referred to as a free (or unencapsulated) nerve ending. In contrast, most non-nociceptors are encapsulated and have complex morphologies (e.g. Pacinian corpuscles).
- Most nociceptors are polymodal, meaning that they respond to multiple modalities of stimulation (e.g., thermal, mechanical and chemical), whereas all non-nociceptors are unimodal.
- The conduction velocity of nociceptor axons (0.5–30 m/s) is less than that of non-nociceptor axons (30–120 m/s). Conduction velocity depends on axon myelination. The axons of nociceptors are unmyelinated C-fibers or thinly myelinated Aδ-fibers. The axons of non-nociceptors are more heavily myelinated Aβ-fibers.
- Both nociceptors and non-nociceptors are heterogeneously distributed throughout the body, but their distribution varies. For example, the fingertips contain many non-nociceptors but relatively fewer nociceptors, whereas the cornea and teeth are densely innervated by nociceptors.
- The distinguishing feature of nociceptors is their ability to become sensitized when tissue is injured (i.e., the threshold intensity for activation is decreased); non-nociceptors do not sensitize when tissue is injured.

Nociceptors are present in the skin, muscles, joints, and viscera.

Cutaneous Nociceptors: The most common nociceptors in skin are the Aδ-mechanonociceptors and C-polymodal nociceptors. The receptive field of Aδ-mechanonociceptors ranges from 1 to 8 cm^2. Activation of Aδ-mechanonociceptors evokes sharp, well-localized pain. C-polymodal nociceptors are more plentiful than Aδ-mechanonociceptors, constituting over 75% of all nociceptors. The aggregated receptive field of C-polymodal nociceptors consists of three to 20 small (<1 mm^2), non-contiguous, punctuate receptive fields. C-polymodal receptors are particularly responsive to chemicals released during tissue injury and inflammation, exercise, or disease, as well as to capsaicin, the hot ingredient in chili peppers. Their absolute firing rates are typically slower than Aδ mechanonociceptors, and they rarely have spontaneous activity in the absence of a stimulus. Activation of C-polymodal nociceptors typically evokes long-lasting, burning pain.

Other Somatic Receptors: Deep somatic nociceptors occur in muscle, fascia, connective tissue and joints. Although similar to cutaneous nociceptors, deep nociceptors differ in both nomenclature and response properties. For historical reasons, afferent fibers in muscle nerves were classified as Group I, II, III, and IV, rather than using the Aβ, Aδ- and C- nomenclature employed for skin nerves. Groups III and IV are similar in myelination, conduction velocity, and response properties to Aδ- and C-fibers in skin. Deep nociceptors are well-matched to the stimuli that evoke deep pain. For example, excessive force (which can occur in traumatic injury) and chemicals that cause muscle pain (such as lactate and potassium) all effectively excite deep somatic nociceptors.

Visceral Nociceptors: It once was thought that viscera lacked nociceptors because direct manipulation (e.g., pinching) and incisions failed to produce pain when surgical anesthesia was allowed to become light. Common experience, however, instructs that the predominant (if not only) conscious sensation that arises from the viscera is pain. We now know that slowly-conducting Aδ- and C-fiber endings occur throughout visceral as well as somatic structures. The stimuli that produce pain when applied to the viscera, however, are different than those that produce pain when applied to skin. Moreover, the appropriate noxious visceral stimulus differs for different organs. For example, in hollow organs (such as the esophagus, stomach, colon, and urinary bladder), nociceptors are excited by distention, whereas in solid organs (such as the testes), compression is an effective noxious stimulus.

Central Processing of Nociception: The cell bodies of nociceptors are located principally in dorsal root ganglia that terminate in the spinal cord and synapse onto second order neurons, many of which have long ascending axons that convey the information supraspinally. It is at the first central synapse where the distinction between the sensory-discriminative and motivational-affective components of the sensory channel for pain begins.

The spinal cord can be divided anatomically and functionally into three regions: the dorsal horn, the intermediate region, and the ventral horn. Functionally, the dorsal horn processes sensory information, the ventral horn generates motor commands for spinal reflexes, and the intermediate region integrates sensorimotor information. The somatic motoneurons and preganglionic autonomic neurons in the ventral horn and spinal autonomic nuclei mediate spinal motor and autonomic reflexes, such as the protective flexion withdrawal reflex.

In the dorsal horn, several ascending pathways convey nociceptive information to supraspinal sites. The neospinothalamic tract is an evolutionarily newer pathway that mediates the sensory-discriminative component of pain. It projects to the ventrolateral and ventromedial portions of the thalamus, adjacent but non-overlapping to the projections from other sensory systems that are involved in sensory discrimination. Subsequently, the thalamus projects to the portions of the parietal lobe cerebral cortex that mediate perception and processing of both non-nociceptive and nociceptive somatosensory information.

The paleospinothalamic tract is an evolutionarily older pathway that is associated with the motivational-affective component of pain. In contrast to the neospinothalamic tract, the paleospinothalamic tract projects to intralaminar portions of the thalamus that are involved in the subjective aspects of sensory input rather than with discrimination. The intralaminar nuclei project primarily to the limbic system and cortex, which mediate motivational, subjective and affective sensations and behavior.

Lastly, spinoreticular tracts ascend to the brainstem and midbrain, where they can engage autonomic systems and descending modulation of nociception. Subsequent projections from the brainstem or midbrain to the thalamus also may contribute to the motivational-affective component of pain.

Nociceptors and non-nociceptors from adjacent regions of the body ultimately project to adjacent regions of the central nervous system, resulting in a somatotopic arrangement. In contrast, the viscera do not appear to be somatotypically represented in the thalamus or cortex, which is consistent with our difficulty in localizing visceral stimuli.

PAIN MODULATION

Pain is modulated by inputs within the nociceptive sensory channel that alter or modulate the nature and/or intensity of afferent nociceptive input, thereby changing the pain experience. Typically, pain modulation implies inhibition or relief of pain (as with drugs), but modulation also can involve enhancement or facilitation of pain. That is, pain can be made worse or non-nociceptive inputs can be altered to be perceived as painful.

Peripheral Counterstimulation. Probably the best known example of pain modulation is that based on a theory of spinal modulation introduced by Melzack and Wall (1965) in the mid-1960s, known as the gate control theory. In this model, neurons in the spinal cord that transmit nociceptive information to supraspinal sites are described as functioning as a spinal "gate." The gate is opened by, and nociception arises from, activity in small diameter afferent fibers (Aδ- and C-fibers). The gate is closed by activity in large diameter, myelinated non-nociceptive afferent fibers (Aβ-fibers). It is hypothesized that the balance in activities between nociceptive and non-nociceptive afferent fiber inputs to the spinal cord determine the position of the gate (i.e., relatively open = more pain, relatively closed = less pain) and thus modulate the intensity of pain.

The analgesia provided by dorsal column stimulation and transcutaneous electrical nerve stimulation (TENS) are generally explained by the gate control theory of pain control. For example, electrical stimulation of large diameter, myelinated fibers in the dorsal columns of the spinal cord or in peripheral nerves (through the application of TENS) is thought to close the spinal gate and thus reduce pain. Similarly, some forms of acupuncture that activate large-diameter peripheral myelinated axons may close the spinal gate.

Descending Inhibition. Subsequent modifications to the gate control theory included the addition of influences descending from the brainstem that modulate the gate. That there exist powerful descending modulatory influences on nociceptive transmission that can either attenuate or enhance pain, has become a tenet central to the concepts of pain modulation. Empirical study has revealed the complex anatomy, neurochemistry, and function of the systems descending from the brainstem (i.e., midbrain, pons, and medulla). Phylogenetic continuity of these descending systems is noted in all vertebrates.

A critical synapse exists between the midbrain and spinal cord in the rostral part of the ventral medulla. Thus, descending influences on spinal nociceptive transmission activated in the midbrain are indirect, in that there exists a relay between the midbrain and the spinal cord. From the medulla, descending influences are direct. Axons of neurons in the medulla descend in the spinal cord to terminate on the spinal neurons, from which nociceptive input from the periphery is received.

Early on, it was appreciated that descending inhibitory modulation is tonically active: that is, a moderate brake is applied to spinal neurons by the descending inhibitory system even under normal circumstances. Increases and decreases in spinal nociceptive transmission can be produced by alterations in the activity of this tonic descending system.

Endogenous Opioid Systems: A key component of the descending pain modulatory system was established in the early 1970s as a result of a number of seminal research demonstrating that the body itself could modulate nociceptive inputs and thus pain. First, stimulation through electrodes placed in the midbrain of experimental animals produced analgesia sufficient to permit surgery. This procedure, termed stimulation-produced analgesia, subsequently was tested and established as effective in relieving human pain. Additional discoveries revealed that endogenous opioid peptides (enkephalins, dynorphins and endorphins) are present in the central nervous system and that the opioid receptor antagonist naloxone attenuated the analgesic effects of stimulation-produced analgesia in humans. These discoveries established that the human body contains an anatomically restricted, opioid peptide-associated means of pain control.

The midbrain periaqueductal and periventricular gray matter is the nodal point of the opioid-mediated endogenous pain modulatory system. It is at this anatomical site that both exogenously administered opioids like morphine and endogenously released opioid peptides activate inhibitory influences that descend to the dorsal horn of the spinal cord.

Other Neurotransmitter Systems: The principal neurotransmitter chemicals that mediate descending inhibition are serotonin and norepinephrine. Serotonin is contained in the terminals of neurons that descend from the ventral medulla, while norepinephrine is contained in the terminals of neurons that descend from the dorsolateral pons (e.g., the locus coeruleus). Drugs that mimic the actions of serotonin or norepinephrine (e.g., clonidine) are analgesic when given directly into the spinal epidural or intrathecal space. While opioids, given either exogenously or released endogenously, are analgesic by an action at opioid receptors, at least part of their analgesic effect arises from activation of bulbospinal monoaminergic systems that modulate spinal nociceptive transmission. Thus, pain control by opioids ought to be enhanced by drugs that mimic or facilitate the actions of serotonin and/or norepinephrine (e.g., tricyclic antidepressants), which indeed has been documented in clinical trials.

The principal focus of investigation has been inhibitory modulation of nociceptive transmission, but research also has demonstrated that descending systems also facilitate nociceptive transmission in the spinal cord. Facilitatory modulation of spinal nociceptive transmission is a relatively recent development and thus is less well understood than inhibitory modulation. The anatomical components of facilitatory modulation in the brainstem are similar, if not overlapping, with those of inhibitory modulation. Thus, either inhibition or facilitation of spinal transmission can be produced from the same sites in the brainstem, depending upon input, although it is not yet clear how the brainstem inputs may differ. It is clear, however, that axons that mediate facilitatory influences from the brainstem descend in different spinal tracts and contain different neurotransmitters than those for inhibitory modulation. These neurotransmitters act at the cholinergic, cholecystokinin and kappa opioid receptors and can contribute to the facilitation of nociceptive transmission.

A wide variety of influences can activate inhibitory and/or facilitatory endogenous pain modulatory systems. Stress, fear, and pain itself all can activate descending systems that inhibit pain. The activation of endogenous modulation by pain itself has been interpreted as important to self-preservation by the observation that an injured animal often is able to escape a predator even in the presence of pain. In less life-threatening circumstances, pain can inhibit pain by activation of the same endogenous mechanisms, a phenomenon referred to as counter-irritation. Pathophysiology such as hypertension also can contribute to activation of descending systems and attenuation of pain. It has been documented, for example, that both experimental increases in blood pressure and pre-existing hypertension render individuals less sensitive to noxious stimuli than normotensive persons.

Descending Facilitation. Descending facilitation of pain appears to play an important role in unusual chronic pain states. It is possible, but not yet proven, that the pain-facilitating system could be activated and not turned off by normal mechanisms, thus contributing to a tonic facilitation (rather than tonic inhibition) of spinal neuron activity. Clearly, there are circumstances in which facilitation of nociceptive information has important protective value, such as during tissue repair; yet if such a system remains inappropriately activated after tissue repair is complete, normal, non-nociceptive inputs conceivably could acquire nociceptive character. Because mechanisms of chronic pain are poorly understood, there is considerable interest in better understanding the endogenous systems by which pain can be enhanced.

NEUROPATHIC PAIN

Just as continued exposure to a drug of abuse can result in neurophysiological changes in the response to that drug, perceptions of sensory stimuli are not constant, but change in response to development, environmental experience, disease and injury. These changes are collectively referred to as "plasticity." Plasticity can be brief (minutes to hours), sustained (hours to weeks), or relatively permanent.

Sustained pain always is associated with tissue injury and inflammation, such as that associated with sunburn, sprains and following surgery. One consequence of tissue injury and inflammation is the development of hyperalgesia, which is defined as an exaggerated response to a normally painful stimulus. Hyperalgesia arises because chemicals released, synthesized or attracted to the site of injury increase the sensitivity and activity of nociceptors. Consequently, increased activity of nociceptors leads to an increased release of neurotransmitters in the central nervous system, thus increasing the excitability of the central neurons on which nociceptors terminate. Accordingly, sustained pain is characterized by a change in the function and behavior of the elements that comprise the sensory-discriminative component of pain. Common experience instructs that these plastic changes are both normal and reversible. Like acute pain, sustained pain serves an important protective function. The tenderness and increased sensitivity of tissue surrounding the site of injury help to protect the tissue and prevent further damage.

A component of hyperalgesia called "allodynia" is the perception of pain in response to a normally non-painful stimulus. Like hyperalgesia, allodynia can arise from: (1) inflammatory tissue damage, (2) injury to peripheral nerves, or (3) damage to portions of the central nervous system that mediate pain sensations.

Hyperalgesia is classified as either primary or secondary. Primary hyperalgesia refers to the enhanced pain that arises from the site of injury. Secondary hyperalgesia refers to the enhanced pain that arises from uninjured tissue adjacent to the site of injury. Primary hyperalgesia typically occurs following injury, while secondary hyperalgesia sometimes is present, but usually is weaker than the primary hyperalgesia.

Inflammatory Hyperalgesia. Pain commonly arises from tissue injury. In addition to directly and briefly exciting nociceptors, the injured tissues become inflamed as a component of the repair process. During inflammation, chemical mediators such as bradykinin, serotonin, histamine, cytokines, peptides and prostaglandins are released from local and circulating cells. These chemical mediators result in local vasodilation, swelling, and the eventual removal and replacement of injured tissue. Not only do these chemical mediators directly activate nociceptors (thereby resulting in nociception), but they also sensitize nociceptors to subsequent stimuli. Nociceptor sensitization caused by inflammation contributes significantly to primary hyperalgesia.

Although both Aδ- and C-fiber nociceptors can be activated and sensitized by these chemical mediators, C-polymodal nociceptors appear particularly responsive to their effects. Recently, contributions to hyperalgesia by a previously unknown group of nociceptors have been documented. A subset of primarily C-fiber nociceptors are called "silent nociceptors" because, while normally unresponsive to noxious mechanical or thermal stimuli, following chemical sensitization these so-called silent nociceptors become spontaneously active and responsive to normal mechanical and thermal stimuli.

C-fiber nociceptors also contribute to inflammation and hyperalgesia via neurogenic inflammation. Unlike most sensory neurons, C-fiber nociceptors release neurotransmitters both centrally in the spinal cord and peripherally at receptor endings in tissue. Further, the peptide neurotransmitters released (such as substance P) enhance the inflammatory process like other inflammatory mediators, thus resulting in further activation of the C-fiber nociceptor and further release of substance P. The resulting positive feedback significantly enhances the inflammation and resulting hyperalgesia.

Neurogenic inflammation also is responsible for the spread of reddening and soreness following a localized injury. As described earlier, the receptive fields of C-polymodal nociceptors in the skin are punctate, indicating that a single C-fiber branches several times to innervate separate small patches of skin. Consequently, if a localized injury activates only one branch of the C-fiber, the evoked orthodromic action potential (traveling in the normal direction) will induce antidromic action potentials (traveling in the opposite direction) in other branches. The antidromic action potentials travel to nociceptor endings, causing substance P release, inflammation, and nociceptor sensitization.

Sensitization of nociceptors readily accounts for primary hyperalgesia (i.e., enhanced pain at the site of tissue injury), but cannot as easily explain secondary hyperalgesia (i.e., enhanced pain from uninjured tissue adjacent to the injury). The increased afferent barrage arriving in the spinal dorsal horn via Aδ- and C-fiber nociceptors, including activated silent nociceptors, releases greater than normal amounts of neurotransmitters, principally the excitatory amino acid glutamate. As a consequence, the excitability to spinal noci-receptive neurons changes and they become more easily excited (i.e., are sensitized). Recent research has shown that this central sensitization also occurs when tissue is injured. As with peripheral sensitization, central sensitization is more effectively induced by activation of C-fiber nociceptors than Aδ-mechanonociceptors.

Structural changes in the spinal cord or perhaps even in supraspinal sites may underlie chronic forms of secondary hyperalgesia such as that occurring after nerve damage. Some of the structural changes identified are:

- Death of inhibitory spinal interneurons due to toxicity arising from a powerful excitatory input.
- Rearrangement of afferent fiber terminals (e.g., non-nociceptive afferent fibers synapsing into spinal cord regions previously receiving only nociceptor input, a possible cause of allodynia).
- Proliferation of sympathetic efferent fibers into sensory ganglia.

If nociceptor activation and excessive nociceptive input to the central nervous system is responsible for central sensitization, then a logical strategy to reduce or prevent post-surgical hyperalgesia would be either to block the nociceptive pathways or decrease the response of the central nervous system. This treatment strategy, termed pre-emptive analgesia, has as its principal objective prevention of development of central sensitization. In addition to general anesthesia, the pre-emptive strategy includes the infiltration of local anesthetics or administration of opioids before surgery begins. Successful pre-emptive analgesia has been reported using morphine and, in some instances, peripheral nerve blocks. Not all reports, however, support pre-emptive analgesia treatment as a means of reducing or eliminating post-surgical hyperalgesia or post-surgical analgesic drug requirements.

Neurogenic Hyperalgesias. *Complex Regional Pain Syndrome:* Traumatic or infectious damage to peripheral nerves is a special case of tissue injury, which may result in hyperalgesia differing in symptoms and mechanisms from inflammatory hyperalgesia. The clinical syndrome associated with such injury, previously termed sympathetically-maintained pain, now is referred to as complex regional pain syndrome, or CRPS. Initially, damaged or transected peripheral nerves die back a few millimeters, then grow back toward the periphery following the pathway of the old nerve. Although growth and reinnervation of skin or other target often is successful, sometimes regrowth is blocked by an obstacle. The sprouting nerve then forms a neuroma, which acquires both mechanical and chemical sensitivity. The mechanical and chemical sensitivity, believed due to insertion of an excessive number of sodium channels in the neuroma, results in the generation of ectopic (i.e., from an abnormal point) action potentials at the neuroma. Consequently, pain can be produced by even gentle pressure or by continual release of norepinephrine from nearby sympathetic nerve endings. In other instances, even with largely successful regrowth and no apparent pathology, chronic pain occurs for reasons as yet unknown.

Phantom Pain: Amputation, an extreme form of nerve trauma, can lead to the unusual circumstance known as phantom pain. Although the pain is very real to the patient, it is labeled phantom because the patient describes it as arising from the missing tissue. Phantom limb pain is most common, but phantom breast and phantom anus pain syndromes also have been described following mastectomy and surgery for colorectal cancer. Phantom pain typically is present within the first week after amputation, but usually gradually diminishes until it disappears completely. Phantom pain has been reported to persist in 3% to 50% of amputees.

Although not well studied, it is believed that phantom pain partly arises from ectopic activity from neuromas formed by the surgically transected nerves. There also is an apparent central nervous system component to phantom pain because preemptive treatments to block nociceptor discharges during surgery have been reported to prevent or significantly reduce the incidence of phantom pain. In either case, the pain is localized to the absent body part because afferent pathways are labeled according to the region innervated early in development. Consequently, activity in that pathway is localized according to the original mapping, regardless of the origin of the activity. Vasomotor instability, temperature dysregulation, edema and autonomic dysfunction in the affected limb are characteristic of this syndrome.

Central Pain: Trauma, ischemia, or degeneration in the brain also can lead to hyperalgesia (or hypoalgesia) when the nervous tissue involved is part of the central nervous system's pain processing system. Damage to the spinothalamic tract, at any level, can lead to diminished pain perception. On the other hand, damage to some parts of the thalamus can lead to thalamic pain syndrome, a disorder characterized by hyperalgesia and allodynia. Presumably, the damaged neurons are part of a local nociceptive inhibitory system, similar to those that descend to the spinal cord from the brainstem. Central post-stroke pain syndrome is another example of pain arising in the absence of activation of peripheral nociceptors. This pain typically is deep, aching or burning and develops in the area of sensory loss or neurologic disability contralateral to the side of the cerebral infarction. Pain originating from damage to higher structures can be difficult to treat because many therapies interrupt nociceptive transmission peripheral to the central lesion (e.g., TENS).

PHYSIOLOGICAL MECHANISMS OF ADDICTION

Like pain, addiction is a multidimensional human phenomenon, the manifestations of which cannot be entirely explained by understanding its neurophysiological bases. In fact, the criteria for addictive disease of the *Diagnostic and Statistical Manual of Mental Disorders, 4th Edition* (*DSM-IV*; American Psychiatric Association, 1994) rely only minimally on the presence of recognized drug-induced physiological responses (tolerance, withdrawal), focusing instead on an inability to control use and the presence of significant disruption in social role functioning.

Also like pain, in addictive disease, chronic or sustained exposure to the stimulus (be it noxious as with pain, or rewarding as with drugs) induces changes in the central nervous system. This plasticity becomes critical to the ultimate expression, maintenance and treatment responsiveness of both pain and addiction, and have implications for the nature of each in the presence of the other.

In that a necessary stimulus for drug addiction is exposure to a drug, the physiology underlying addiction begins with an understanding of the pharmacology of addictive drugs. Effects of abused drugs can be distinguished along two domains: The drugs' discrete versus shared effects, and their effects during acute versus chronic administration (Table 1).

Discrete versus Shared Effects. The acute pharmacological effects of drugs of abuse in the CNS have been well described (Table 2). Critical to understanding how addiction might affect pain responses is discriminating between drug-specific (or discrete) mechanisms of action and the shared actions of all classes of abused drugs that contribute to their addiction liability. Thus, the effects of drugs of abuse can be understood at two levels: (1) drugs have discrete effects in certain brain regions and neurotransmitter systems, which account for their specific CNS effects (i.e., depression or stimulation), the quality of which varies widely among abused substances (i.e., barbiturates, cocaine, LSD), and (2) drugs of abuse share the ability to activate a specific locus in the brain known as the "reward center," which accounts in large part for their inherently reinforcing or rewarding nature. Acute and chronic effects at both levels have implications for nociceptive processing and the experience of pain.

The central stimulant and sympathomimetic effects of cocaine, for example, are related to its ability to block the re-uptake of norepinephrine (NE), dopamine (DA) and serotonin (5HT) in multiple brain regions (Wise, 1980; Gawin, 1991; Gold & Dackis,

TABLE 1. Domains of Addiction Physiology

	Acute	Chronic
Discrete	Various	Various, in direction to counteract acute drug effects
Shared	↑ DA transmission in reward pathways; release of endogenous opioids	↓ DA transmission in reward pathways; ? effect on endogenous opioid activity

TABLE 2. Acute Actions of Drugs of Abuse

Drug Class	Acute Clinical Effects
Opiates (heroin, methadone, morphine)	Analgesia, drowsiness, euphoria, mental clouding, depressed cough reflex, miosis, nausea and vomiting, respiratory depression
Alcohol and the CNS depressants	Dysarthria, ataxia, hyperreflexia, nystagmus and/or diploplia, impaired cognition, anterograde amnesia, intoxication, stupor to coma, decreased respirations.
Cocaine and the CNS stimulants	Euphoria, hypervigilance, anxiety, psychomotor agitation, tremor, tachycardia, pupillary dilation, increased blood pressure, anorexia, cardiac arrhythmia, generalized seizure, psychosis, delirium, transient movement disorders.
Hallucinogens (LSD, mescaline, psilocybin)	Pupillary dilation, tachycardia, perceptual alterations, tremor, acute anxiety, depersonalization.
Sedative hypnotics (benzodiazepine)	Anxiolysis, sedation, ataxia, dysarthria, impaired cognition, nystagmus, respiratopry depression.
Marijuana	Perceptual alteration, impaired time orientation, mild euphoria, decreased reaction time, decreased attention span, incoordination.

1984); likewise, amphetamine not only blocks the re-uptake of NE and DA, but increases their presynaptic release (Beil & Bopp, 1978; King & Ellinwood, 1992). Opioid drugs, acting like endogenous opioid peptides, inhibit neuronal firing when bound to opioid receptors, decreasing the release of certain other neurotransmitters, most notably glutamate and substance P in the spinal cord and monoamines in the brain. These actions account not only for centrally-mediated analgesia, but the related respiratory depression and decreased sympathetic tone produced by opioid medications. In addition to having a generalized inhibitory effect on neuronal membranes (Delin & Lee, 1992; Victor, 1992), alcohol appears to have specific and complex effects at the GABA, 5HT, NMDA, and opioid receptors (Tabakoff & Hoffman, 1992), which contribute to a generalized state of cognitive and psychomotor depression. The discrete effects of various addictive drugs differ considerably, according to their differential actions in distinct neurochemical systems. Yet all drugs of abuse have in common an ability to activate a specific dopaminergic pathway in the brain, the so-called "reward center," which is believed to underlie their overall reinforcing effects (Grunberg, 1994; Koob & Bloom, 1988; Miller & Gold, 1993; Wise, 1980). This shared action appears to be responsible for providing the subjective profound euphoria or "high" associated with drug intoxication, an effect so inherently rewarding that both animals and humans will reliably and actively seek to repeat behaviors that result in activation of these centers. Under normal circumstances, these brain systems function to reinforce behaviors necessary for the survival of the species (i.e., eating, sexual behavior) (Wise & Rompre, 1989). Surgical or pharmacological disruption of this pathway in animals significantly diminishes the reinforcing nature of all classes of abused drugs, as demonstrated in self-administration and place preference paradigms, thus illustrating its central role in drug reward (see Gardner, 1997).

This critical pathway consists of a specific set of DA neurons located within the mesolimbic area of the brain, originating in the ventral tegmental area and terminating in the nucleus accumbens (NA) of the limbic system (DiChiara & Imperato, 1988; Wise & Rompre, 1989). These neurons receive input from multiple nuclei afferent to the pathway, principally located within the lateral hypothalamus and including the noradrenergic locus coeruleus and serotonergic raphe nucleus. It is at these structures that many drugs of abuse have discrete pharmacological effects, so that the sites have been conceptualized as the "first stage" of drug reward. Within this framework, the actual release of DA in the NA has been termed the "second stage" of drug reward, and effects efferent to this DA release, most notably in endogenous opioid and GABAergic systems, as an increasingly appreciated "third stage" of drug reward. Interruption at any one of these stages of drug action has been demonstrated to notably attenuate the reinforcing properties of abused drugs (Gardner, 1997).

For certain drugs of abuse (cocaine, amphetamine and marijuana, for example), second stage reward system activation is the direct discrete effect of the drug, while for others (such as opioids, ethanol and benzodiazepines) it is a consequence of the discrete first stage of drug action. For example, the discrete effect of cocaine is to directly increase dopaminergic activity in the reward pathways by blocking the presynaptic DA uptake transporter. Opioids, CNS depressants and benzodiazepines, on the other hand, indirectly activate dopaminergic release in the reward center via their inhibitory first stage effect on noradrenergic neurons in the locus coeruleus—neurons that typically serve to inhibit DA release from VTA neurons. Whether due to a direct or an indirect discrete drug effect, dopamine release in this system underlies the reinforcement provided by all drugs of abuse, providing, at least in some part, the motivation for the individual to continue use (DiChiara & Imperato, 1988).

A principal component of the third stage of drug reward involves endogenous opioid release. When opioid receptors are pharmacologically blocked by an antagonist (naloxone or naltrexone), the reward provided by all drugs of abuse is diminished (see Gardner, 1997; Wise, 1980; Wise & Bozarth, 1984). In other words, to derive full reward from reward-relevant stimuli, opioid receptors must be activated. This opioid receptor involvement, common to all abused substances, portends a potential yet unpredictable source of interaction between addictive disease and pain across all types of drug addiction.

Acute versus Chronic Effects. By definition, drug addiction involves the repeated use of drugs over time. As noted previously, the physiology underlying addiction is characterized by changes occurring in the CNS in response to continued drug exposure and drug effects. Distinct from the evident psychosocial ramifications of repeated use, there are clear neuronal and molecular adaptations that generally serve to counteract acute drug effects so as to maintain homeostasis at the level of the organism (Hyman, 1993; Nestler, 1993). These adaptations become functional in the presence of continued drug use and may not be apparent until drug use is discontinued. Two well-described neurophysiologic adaptations to chronic drug use are *tolerance* and *physical dependence*. (It is important to emphasize that the simple presence of these neuroadaptations do not constitute addiction. A pain patient can be physically dependent on or tolerant to the effects of an opioid without being addicted. Addiction is identified by a cluster of aberrant patterns of behavior which, although they may in part be motivated by these physiological changes, are evident in much broader and more holistic domains.)

Tolerance. An important physiologic feature of addiction is the development of drug tolerance, which is defined as the reduction in response to a given dose of a drug after repeated administration (O'Brien, 1996). Three types of drug tolerance have been described: associative, dispositional and pharmacodynamic (Portenoy, 1994). Associative tolerance refers to the cognitive adaptations or learning that occur with repeated drug exposures, providing individuals with compensatory behavioral strategies to counteract drug effects. Dispositional tolerance is a decrease in drug effect due to increased rates of drug metabolism and/or excretion induced by the presence of the drug itself. Finally, and most relevant to the present discussion, is pharmacodynamic tolerance, which refers to diminished drug effect related to changes in the nervous system that serve to modulate the drug's effect. Across types of tolerance, adaptations always are evident in the direction of counteracting acute drug effects to maintain system-level homeostasis.

Pharmacodynamic tolerance involves adaptations that occur at both the site of drug action (i.e., receptor, ion channel), as well as in related systems more distal to the site of drug action. For example, pharmacodynamic tolerance to opioids is evident at both the level of the opioid receptor in the locus coeruleus (primary) and in the dopaminergic reward pathways afferent to the site of this discrete drug action (secondary). Because drugs typically act at selective receptors, tolerance has been conceptualized as a functional "uncoupling" of the receptor from its effector response (i.e., opening or closing an ion channel, initiating second messenger sys-

TABLE 3. Autonomic and Affective Withdrawal Associated with Drugs of Abuse (from Gold, 1995)

Abused Drug	Affective Withdrawal (nucleus accumbens-mediated)	Autonomic Withdrawal (locus coeruleus-mediated)
Amphetamine	+ + +	+
Cocaine	+ + + +	+
Opiates	+ +	+ + + +
Marijuana	+ +	+
Alcohol	+ +	+ + +

tems); in other words, a certain proportion of receptors are rendered nonfunctional, thus making the drug less effective (i.e., requiring a higher dose to get the same effect that was initially obtained at a lower dose). This process is referred to as "down-regulation." Clinically, the resulting tolerance provides a certain amount of protection for the user, as to the respiratory depressant effects of opioids, or the anesthetic effects of ethanol.

Although pharmacodynamic tolerance can be reliably demonstrated within a single episode of cocaine or amphetamine use (i.e., a "binge" or "run"), reverse tolerance or sensitization appears to be the physiological response to repeated CNS stimulant use over time. In reverse tolerance, drug response increases with repeated administration of the same dose, which is theorized to be due to "up-regulation" processes at receptor and molecular levels. In the case of cocaine addiction, it is believed that chronic DA depletion as a result of repeated cocaine use appears to increase the sensitivity of central DA receptors.

Physical Dependence. A related consequence of chronic drug abuse is physical dependence, which is an altered neurophysiological state that develops as a result of PT. These changes become unmasked when drug blood level falls below a critical level. Here, the adaptive changes associated with tolerance predominate and become profoundly nonadaptive (Koob, Stinus et al., 1989; Redmond & Krystal, 1984). Suddenly unopposed by drug effects, the sources of tolerance become evident at the level of the organism as the characteristic drug-specific withdrawal syndrome.

As would be anticipated, symptoms of drug withdrawal reflect changes in both the discrete and shared substrates of drug action. Gold and Miller (1995) have conceptualized these as *autonomic* and *affective* withdrawal symptoms, respectively, with the former related to withdrawal phenomena arising at the locus coeruleus and the latter arising from the dopaminergic reward pathway (Table 3). CNS depressants, opioids and benzodiazepines all acutely depress NE activity in the locus coeruleus, either via opioid receptor binding or GABAergic input. Pharmacodynamic tolerance thus results in effective up-regulation of central noradrenergic activity, which is expressed in the withdrawal state from these drugs as increased blood pressure, heart rate, peristalsis, diaphoresis and general CNS irritability.

Due to shared effects on the second stage dopaminergic reward pathway, so-called affective withdrawal is evident with all drugs of abuse. Effectively suppressed reward mechanisms predominate in the absence of drugs of abuse and include such behavioral manifestations as depression, anhedonia and intense drug craving. Although less dramatic than the autonomic withdrawal associated with alcohol and opioid withdrawal, these symptoms dominate the withdrawal syndrome of CNS stimulant abuse. The power of reward center-mediated withdrawal can be appreciated by the high relapse rates found among abusers of substances (cocaine, amphetamine) who suffer few clinically-significant somatic withdrawal symptoms.

Thus, the physiology of addiction is characterized by the related neuroadaptations of tolerance and physical dependence. These may be manifest both in the systems where drugs of abuse exert discrete actions, and at the shared reward substrate. The plasticity evidenced by psychoactive drug tolerance and physical dependence have implications for nociceptive input and processing.

POINTS OF INTERFACE BETWEEN PAIN AND ADDICTION

Drugs of abuse have multiple and distinct effects in the central nervous system and share an ability to activate the neural structures from which their "rewarding" nature arise. Primary sites of action are the brainstem (locus coeruleus) and subcortical limbic structures (mesolimbic DA pathway), which are near to, but somewhat distinct from, those central areas involved in the perception (thalamus) and/or modulation (brainstem; periaqueductal gray) of pain.

As potential points of interface between the physiology of pain and of addiction are considered, it must first be recognized that many classes of abused drugs (particularly the CNS depressants) have demonstrated analgesic properties. CNS stimulants, such as cocaine and caffeine, also produce analgesia and potentiate opioid analgesia (Hoffman & Lefkowitz, 1996), presumably by increasing neurotransmitter activity in descending pain inhibitory pathways. The NMDA antagonists, which include phencyclidine, are highly analgesic and, at high doses, alcohol has anesthetic properties. The analgesia associated with acute opioid and CNS depressant administration theoretically would be expected to diminish in the context of addiction to these substances, in the presence of tolerance. Consequently, it might by hypothesized that the acute analgesic properties of drugs of abuse are not relevant to the pain experience of the addict. Yet, careful examination of the extant literature provides evidence that physiologic states consistent with drug addiction can affect or predict nociceptive input, processing and/or modulation in several different ways.

First, there are the relatively nonspecific consequences of addictive disease, which may serve to facilitate the experience of pain via associated sympathetic arousal, negative emotional or affective mood, as well as via hypothesized but unproved changes in endogenous opioid system activity. These changes are related to both the discrete effects of certain classes of drugs, as well as the effects on reward-relevant systems of all drugs of abuse. Second, recent evidence indicates that molecular changes that accompany the development of opioid tolerance specifically appear to facilitate or increase nociceptive transmission. Finally, there appear to be patterned ways in which certain individuals process both pain (or analgesia) and the reward associated with substances of abuse, which would mediate both pain and addictive responses.

The majority of the data providing evidence for overlap between pain and addiction phenomena have been obtained in animal studies, so caution must be exercised in generalizing these to clinical populations. By definition, both pain and addiction are uniquely human conditions; the complexity of each is evident in psychosocial, cognitive and cultural domains, which cannot be replicated in animal models. Hypotheses about how the neurophysiological overlap between pain and addiction might clinically manifest must take into account how holistic human responses to their combined presence may alter or mask predicted physiological responses.

Nonspecific Effects of Addiction on Pain. *Sympathetic Arousal:* Addictive drug use is characterized by frequent and rapid fluctuations in blood levels of the drug. Abused substances tend to be ingested in short-acting formulations and via routes of rapid onset (i.e., inhalation, intravenous administration) to boost psychoactive effect. These use patterns result in relatively rapidly alternating states of intoxication and subtle (or sometimes full-blown) withdrawal. Drug intoxication and withdrawal activate the sympathetic nervous system, which is known to contribute to the pain experience. For example, intoxication with cocaine and CNS stimulants significantly increases central noradrenergic activity. Withdrawal from opioids, CNS depressants and/or sedative-hypnotics also result in an increase in central noradrenergic activity related to upregulated locus coeruleus NE discharge (Miller & Gold, 1993). Although stress-induced analgesia might be expected to be the outcome of this uncontrolled noradrenergic activity, the increased muscle tension, anxiety and irritability noted during intoxication or withdrawal from these drugs of abuse appear to augment, rather than reduce, discomfort in the addict.

Affective Withdrawal: As noted, a strong and persistent negative affective component accompanies withdrawal from all drugs of abuse. This is thought to be the result of an overall state of DA depletion in the reward pathways. When drug-free, the addicted individual suffers from such affective symptoms as anhedonia, prolonged dysphoria, and irritability (Koob & Bloom, 1988), and reports being unable to feel gratification or reward from any environmental stimuli. The degree to which these reward center-mediated affective withdrawal responses contribute to the overall drug-specific withdrawal syndrome varies, with those drugs acting more directly on DA-relevant reward pathways (i.e., cocaine, methamphetamine) (see Table 3) having a more affective withdrawal. Clearly, the negative affective/emotional states associated with drug withdrawal can augment the subjective discomfort associated with pain. Further, the DA depletion associated with cocaine addiction is marked enough to induce a clinical depression with high suicide risk. Depression has been demonstrated to increase the discomfort associated with pain in studies of chronic pain patients, with pain improving in this population with effective treatment of depression.

Drug reward relies not only on mesolimbic DA activation, but also on subsequent or consequent endogenous opioid system activation. Although not definitively demonstrated, it is reasonable to assume that changes in endogenous opioid tone in response to addictive drug use might alter pain perception. A study by Zubieta and colleagues (1996) found increased mu opioid receptor binding in the brains of recently abstinent cocaine abusers as compared to control subjects (1996), which holds interesting but unknown implications for pain perception or management. Diminished pain tolerance is reliably produced during abrupt opioid withdrawal; in fact, hyperalgesia long has been considered a cardinal symptom of the opioid withdrawal syndrome. Decreased endogenous opioid activity in reward pathways may contribute to a degree of hyperalgesia across drugs of abuse. Some evidence exists to support such an effect; in a small sample of active cocaine addicts ($N=21$), the subjects tolerated cold-pressor pain for approximately one-third less time than did abstinent (x = 39 weeks of abstinence) cocaine addicts (N = 32), whose performance was comparable to published norms (Compton, 1994).

That an effect on pain tolerance might accompany activation of reward-relevant opioid receptors was demonstrated in a series of preclinical studies over 20 years ago. Mayer and Liebeskind (1974) found considerable overlap between sites in the brain which were rewarding when stimulated electrically and provided naloxone-reversible analgesia to several different types of pain stimuli. In fact, the correlation between areas that provided analgesia and those that provided reward when stimulated was demonstrated to be 0.83, with the greatest overlap in the ventral and dorsal tegmentum (the origin of the mesolimbic reward pathways). Thus, in vivo, the experiences of pain (or pain relief) and drug reward are not entirely separate, and are, in part, due to shared involvement of opioid receptor systems within the central nervous system.

Some of the more convincing and robust findings on how addiction might affect or predict pain responses are provided for opioid addiction. Clearly, this is the drug class for which the effect of addictive disease on pain responses should be most evident, as both pain and reward are reflections of activity at the mu opioid receptor. Yet as noted above, all abused substances activate brain reward systems, which in turn are modulated by opioid activity. Thus, abuse of addictive substances that do not directly bind to opioid receptors does not rule out an effect on pain.

PSYCHOSOCIAL CORRELATES OF ADDICTION

Although not the focus of this chapter, several behavioral components of addiction may serve to augment the pain experience, and which deserve mention. Important substance-induced disorders or psychological sequelae, including sleep disorders and psychiatric illness, have in themselves been demonstrated to augment the experience of pain and decrease the efficacy of interventions for pain relief. Addiction commonly co-occurs with anxiety and affective disorders, which—if unrecognized or untreated—can increase the perception of pain (and for which neurophysiologic overlap cannot be ruled out). The interpersonal conflicts, role losses and social support losses that characterize the social context of addiction can affect the experience of chronic or acute pain, making the individual less able to manage discomfort. Further, the chaotic and drug-oriented lifestyle of the addict makes it difficult to comply with prescribed pain management regimes.

Thus, pharmacologically, abused substances can themselves provide analgesic and antianalgesic properties. Responses to the presence of certain abused drugs, or the absence of others following chronic administration, can affect neurotransmitter systems in ways that release from tonic inhibition descending pathways or increasing ascending nociceptive input, thereby increasing the pain experience. Congruence between the treatment approaches that manage pain and addiction provides further evidence that these phenomena may have similar bases and are not entirely distinct.

Opioid-Specific Changes. A relatively recent line of research provides interesting evidence for how the chronic use of opioids may decrease tolerance for painful stimuli (see Basbaum, 1995). Again, although tolerance is not addiction, it is present in opioid addiction and thus can affect pain responses. In a series of preclinical studies, Mayer and colleagues demonstrated that molecular changes associated with the development of opioid tolerance in spinal cord dorsal horn neurons are the same as those associated with the development of central hyperalgesia following tissue injury and inflammation; therefore, the presence of either state (hyperalgesia or opioid tolerance) co-induces the other (Mao, Price & Mayer, 1995b). In this work, pain-free animals given 10 micrograms of morphine over the course of eight days demonstrated analgesic tolerance on a tail flick assay, as well as less tolerance for hot plate pain when compared to control animals that received placebo (Mao, Price & Mayer, 1994). Conversely, opioid-naive animals injured so as to induce neuropathic pain and thermal hyperalgesia required nearly six times as much morphine as animals who received a sham injury to obtain analgesia to the hot plate, indicating that tolerance to morphine analgesia was induced by the processes underlying the development of hyperalgesia (Mao, Price & Mayer, 1995a). These investigators theorize that the co-occurrence of hyperalgesia and tolerance is due to both being dependent on activation of NMDA receptors, in that pretreatment with the NMDA receptor antagonist MK801 prevents the development of both phenomena (Mao, Price & Mayer, 1995b).

Mao, Price and Mayer's findings of decreased pain tolerance in the presence of morphine tolerance mirror those found in a small study of pain tolerance in opioid addicts receiving methadone maintenance. The data from that study showed that methadone-maintained (mean dose = 66 mg methadone/day) individuals (N=43) tolerated cold-pressor pain an average of 30 seconds less than matched ex-addict drug-free controls (N=26), with dose being inversely related to cold-pressor pain tolerance ($r = -0.25$, $p = 0.05$) (Compton, 1994). Given that the hyperalgesia accompanying morphine tolerance was demonstrated to occur in the spinal dorsal horn, it may be hypothesized that supraspinal pain processing and modulation is not involved in this form of opioid-induced hyperalgesia.

GENETIC FACTORS PREDICTING PAIN AND ADDICTION

Finally, it is important to consider whether individuals with a genetic propensity for addictive disease may not also possess characteristic pain responses (i.e., high versus low pain tolerance). For example, heritable differences in hepatic P450 isoenzyme activity affect both the amount of reward and analgesia individuals receive from an opioid (Gonzalez, 1991; Ingelman-Sundberg, Johansson et al., 1994; Maurer & Bartkowski, 1993; Otton, Schadel et al., 1993). Individuals who are extensive "metabolizers" of opioids (i.e., those who have high P450 activity) receive both less analgesia and reward from a given opioid dose, theoretically putting them at decreased risk for addiction, but at increased risk for undermanagement of pain. Preliminary data suggest that these extensive metabolizers of opioids are less tolerant of cold-pressor pain, possibly due to defects in the endogenous synthesis of opioids (Sindrup, Poulsen et al., 1993).

More intriguing may be the presence of heritable differences in central reward and pain processing systems. An obvious node of interface for exploring inborn differences in both pain and addiction processes is the endogenous opioid system. Because opioid systems are involved in both pain processing and psychoactive drug reward, it is likely that characteristic, inherited presentations of opioid system activity would be manifest in both pain and addiction domains. Although as yet unexplored in clinical samples, there is good evidence that certain strains of rodents, demonstrated to differ in mu opioid receptor density or endogenous opioid concentration, differ in the amount of opioid reward and analgesia they receive from a given dose of opioid, as well as on baseline tolerance for noxious stimuli (see Berrettini, Alexander et al., 1994; Crabbe, Belknap & Buck, 1994; Frischknecht, Siegfried & Waser, 1988; Marley, Elmer & Goldberg, 1992; Mogil, Marek et al., 1994; Mogil, Przemyslaw et al., 1995; Mogil, Sternberg et al., 1996; Shoaib, Spanagel et al., 1995; Shuster, 1990–91).

For example, the recombinant inbred strain of CXBK mice, which have been demonstrated to have a relatively low whole-brain density of mu opioid receptors, evidence decreased baseline pain tolerance, diminished opioid analgesia, and increased rates of opioid self-administration in the absence of pain when compared to wild type mice (Elmer, Pieper et al., 1995; Mogil, Sternberg et al., 1996; Shuster, 1990–91). DBA/2 mice, on the other hand, have relatively high whole brain concentrations of endogenous opioids and evidence greater opioid analgesia, higher baseline pain tolerance, and tend to avoid both morphine and alcohol intake (Berrettini, Alexander et al., 1994; Shuster, 1990–91). The well-known individual variations in pain tolerance, opioid analgesia (Buschbaum, Davis et al., 1981; Galer, Coyle et al., 1992; Portenoy, 1994) and drug reward in humans indicate that heritable differences in endogenous opioid activity, at endogenous peptide or receptor levels, might account for differences in clinical samples. Whether these differences in endogenous opioid activity affect drug reward from abused drugs other than opioids has yet to be explored, although based on the knowledge that endogenous opioid activity mediates reward from all drugs of abuse, such differences in reward across drugs of abuse would be suspected.

EFFECTS OF PAIN ON ADDICTION RESPONSES

What remains to be demonstrated is how the presence of pain might alter or attenuate the amount of reward provided by a given drug of abuse. Clinical lore holds that patients in pain who take opioid analgesics receive little "brain reward," at least not to the degree that they begin to seek drugs once the painful condition has resolved, with iatrogenic opioid addiction rates for persons with no history of addiction at less than 1% if present at all. Zacny and colleagues (1996) found that under experimental conditions, human subjects reported less opioid reward from a dose of opioid paired with a painful stimulus as that reported during the same opioid challenge without pain.

Similarly, it is not clear that opioid tolerance and physical dependence develop to the same degree while an individual is in pain as when the individual is pain-free. Vaccarino and colleagues (1993) provide interesting preclinical evidence that rats chronically receiving morphine paired with acute formalin-induced pain demonstrated less analgesic tolerance and naloxone-precipitated withdrawal than rats with the same chronic exposure to opioids without pain. These data parallel the anecdotal experience of many pain clinicians who report that they do not encounter opioid tolerance when providing chronic opioid analgesia to persons with malignant or nonmalignant pain syndromes, and find that doses only need be increased when pathology progresses (Portenoy & Foley, 1986). It has been observed that patients with pain who use opioids chronically at high doses for pain do not uniformly experience drug craving or relapse to use in the absence of pain following gradual cessation of use. Thus, pharmacologic tolerance and physical dependence in the absence of host factors cannot explain addiction. Conversely, the presence of nociception may interfere with the development of addiction. How the presence of pain might alter the subjective and neuroadaptive effects of drugs of abuse remains to be explored.

CONCLUSIONS

Even without considering a shared neurophysiological basis, the clinician should expect that pain responses will be complicated in the presence of addictive disease. Addiction and pain are, in every respect, *human* conditions; individual responses to these conditions are expressed holistically in biological, psychological, social and spiritual realms. The presence of addictive disease colors responses to all afferent and environmental stimuli, including pain. Beyond hypothesized and demonstrated interactions at the physiological level, the behavioral and psychosocial correlates of addictive disease cannot help but complicate pain responses.

Pain is the most modulated of the sensory modalities. How a given, quantifiable stimulus is processed by the nervous system, can be modified at the level of the nociceptor, the peripheral nerve, the spinal cord neurons and tracts, the thalamus, or the cortex; modulation typically occurs at one or more of these sites. The unique susceptibility of pain to neuro-regulation portends a significant role for addiction in modulating the pain experience. Addiction physiology underlies the processing of stimuli, which vary in the degree of reward they confer; stimuli that are extremely unrewarding, such as pain, are likely to be preferentially affected by the presence of addictive disease.

Several points of overlap exist between the physiological bases of pain and addiction. Specific avenues by which the chronic use of addictive drugs might alter the processing of noxious stimuli include the presence of sympathetic stimulation, affective withdrawal, and opioid tolerance. Less well-studied but intriguing is evidence that individuals vary in their propensity to both addiction and pain responses; the link between the two may arise from inborn differences in endogenous opioid system tone. Across this literature, a trend toward decreased pain tolerance (or decreased activity of endogenous inhibitory pain systems) can be discerned. The presence of addictive disease appears to augment the experience of pain, although further clinical study is needed to validate this observation.

Providing adequate pain relief to the addicted patient is a challenging and sometimes arduous clinical task. Consideration of the physiologic bases of pain and addiction, and how they overlap, provides direction for the management of pain in this population. The human phenomena of pain and addiction are not separate, but interrelated; knowledgeable management of the former must reflect the extent to which, even at the physiological level, its expression and response are affected by the latter.

REFERENCES

American Psychiatric Association (1994). *Diagnostic and Statistical Manual of Mental Disorders, 4th Edition*. Washington, DC: American Psychiatric Press.

Basbaum AI (1995). Insights into the development of opioid tolerance. *Pain* 61:349–352.

Beil JH & Bopp BA (1978). Amphetamine: Structure-activity relationships. In LL Iversen, SD Iversen & SD Snyderman (eds.) *Handbook of Psychopharmacology, Vol 11*. New York, NY: Plenum Press, 1–39.

Berrettini WH, Alexander R, Ferraro TN & Vogel WH (1994). A study of oral morphine preference in inbred mouse strains. *Psychiatric Genetics* 4:81–86.

Buschbaum MS, Davis GC, Coppola R & Naber D (1981). Opioid pharmacology and individual differences. I. Psychophysical pain measurements. *Pain* 10:357–366.

Compton MA (1994). Cold-pressor pain tolerance in opiate and cocaine abusers: Correlates of drug type and use status. *Journal of Pain and Symptom Management* 9:462–473.

Crabbe JC, Belknap JK & Buck KJ (1994). Genetic and animal models of drug and alcohol abuse. *Science* 264:1715–1723.

Delin CR & Lee TH (1992). Drinking and the brain: Current evidence. *Alcohol* 27:117–126.

DiChiara G & Imperato A (1988). Drugs abused by humans preferentially increase synaptic dopamine concentrations in the mesolimbic system of freely moving rats. *Proceedings of the National Academy of Science* 85:5274–5278.

Elmer GI, Pieper JO, Goldberg SR & George FR (1995). Opioid operant self-administration, analgesia, stimulation and respiratory depression in mu-deficient mice. *Psychopharmacology* 117:23–31.

Frischknecht HR, Siegfried B & Waser PG (1988). Opioids and behavior: Genetic aspects. *Experientia* 44:473–481.

Galer BS, Coyle N, Pasternak GW & Portenoy RK (1992). Individual variability in the response to different opioids: Report of five cases. *Pain* 49:87–91.

Gardner EL (1997). Brain reward mechanisms. In JH Lowinson, RM Millman & JG Langrod (eds.) *Substance Abuse: A Comprehensive Textbook, 3rd Ed.* Baltimore, MD: Williams & Wilkins, 51–85.

Gawin FH (1991). Cocaine addiction: Psychology and neurophysiology. *Science* 251:1580–1586.

Gebhart GF (1995). *Visceral Pain.* Seattle, WA: IASP Press.

Gebhart GF (1995). Somatovisceral sensation. In PM Conn (ed.) *Neuroscience in Medicine.* Philadelphia, PA: Lippincott.

Gold MS & Dackis CA (1984). New insights and treatments: Opiate withdrawal and cocaine addiction. *Clinical Therapy* 7:6–21.

Gold MS & Miller NS (1995). The neurobiology of drug and alcohol addictions. In NS Miller & MS Gold (eds.) *Pharmacological Therapies for Drug and Alcohol Addictions.* New York, NY: Marcel Dekker, 31–44.

Gonzalez FJ (1991). Human cytochrome P450: Possible roles of drug-metabolizing enzymes and polymorphic drug oxidation in addiction. *NIDA Research Monograph 111.* Rockville, MD: National Institute on Drug Abuse, 202–213.

Grunberg NE (1994). Overview: Biological processes relevant to drugs of dependence. *Addiction* 89:1443–1446.

Hoffman BB & Lefkowitz RJ (1996). Catecholamines, sympathomimetic drugs, and adrenergic receptor antagonists. In JG Hardman, LE Limbird, PB Molinoff, RW Ruddon & AG Gilman (eds.) *Goodman & Gilman's The Pharmacological Basis of Therapeutics, 9th Ed.* New York, NY: McGraw-Hill, 99–248.

Hyman SE (1993). Molecular and cell biology of addiction. *Current Opinion in Neurology and Neurosurgery* 6:609–613.

Ingelman-Sundberg M., Johansson I, Persson I et al. (1994). Genetic polymorphism of cytochrome P450. Functional consequences and possible relationship to disease and alcohol toxicity. In B Jansson, H Jornval, U Rydberg, L Terenius & BL Vallee (eds.) *Toward a Molecular Basis of Alcohol Use and Abuse.* Basel, Switzerland: Birkhauser Verlag, 197–207.

International Association for the Study of Pain (1979). Pain terms: A current list with definitions and notes on usage. *Pain* 6:249–252.

King GR & Ellinwood EH (1992). Amphetamines and other stimulants. In JH Lowinson, RM Millman & JG Langrod (eds.) *Substance Abuse: A Comprehensive Textbook, 3rd ed.* Baltimore, MD: Williams and Wilkins, 247–270.

Koob GF & Bloom FE (1988). Cellular and molecular mechanisms of drug dependence. *Science* 242:715–723.

Koob GF, Stinus L, Le Moal M & Bloom FE (1989). Opponent process theory of motivation: Neurobiological evidence from studies of opiate dependence. *Neuroscience & Biobehavioral Reviews* 13:135–140.

Mao J, Price DD & Mayer DJ (1994). Thermal hyperalgesia in association with the development of morphine tolerance in rats: Roles of excitatory amino acids receptors and protein kinase C. *Journal of Neuroscience* 14:2301–2312.

Mao J, Price DD & Mayer DJ (1995a). Experimental mononeuropathy reduces the antinociceptive effects of morphine: Implications for the common intracellular mechanisms involved in morphine tolerance and neuropathic pain. *Pain* 61:353–364.

Mao J, Price DD & Mayer DJ (1995b). Mechanisms of hyperalgesia and morphine tolerance: A current view of their possible interactions. *Pain* 62:259–274.

Marley RJ, Elmer GI & Goldberg SR (1992). The use of pharmacogenetic techniques in drug abuse research. *Pharmacology and Therapeutics* 53:217–237.

Mayer DJ & Liebeskind JC (1974). Pain reduction by focal electrical stimulation of the brain: An anatomical and behavioral analysis. *Brain Research* 68:73–93.

Maurer PM & Bartkowski RR (1993). Drug interactions of clinical significance with opioid analgesics. *Drug Safety* 8:30–48.

Melzack R & Wall PD (1965). Pain mechanisms: A new theory. *Science* 50:971–979.

Miller NS & Gold, MS (1993). A hypothesis for a common neurochemical basis for alcohol and drug disorders. *Psychiatric Clinics of North America* 16:105–117.

Mogil JS, Marek P, O'Toole LA et al. (1994). Mu-opiate receptor binding is up-regulated in mice selectively bred for high stress-induced analgesia. *Brain Research* 653:16–22.

Mogil JS, Przemyslaw M, Flodman P et al. (1995). One or two genetic loci mediate high opiate analgesia in selectively bred mice. *Pain* 60:125–135.

Mogil JS, Sternberg WF, Marek P, Sadowski B, Belknap JK & Liebeskind JC (1996). The genetics of pain and pain inhibition. *Proceedings of the National Academy of Science* 93:3048–3055.

Ness TJ & Gebhart GF (1990). Visceral pain: A review of experimental studies. *Pain* 41:167–234.

Nestler EJ (1993). Cellular responses to chronic treatment with drugs of abuse. *Critical Reviews in Neurobiology* 7:23–39

O'Brien CP (1996). Drug addiction and drug abuse. In JG Hardman, LE Limbird, PB Molinoff, RW Ruddon & AG Gilman (eds.) *Goodman and Gilman's the Pharmacological Basis of Therapeutics, 9th ed.* New York, NY: McGraw-Hill, 557–577.

Otton SV, Schadel M, Cheung SW, Kaplan HL, Busto UE & Sellers EM (1993). CYP2D6 phenotype determines the metabolic conversion of hydrocodone to hydromorphone. *Clinical Pharmacology & Therapeutics* 54:463–472.

Portenoy RK (1994). Opioid tolerance and responsiveness: Research findings and clinical observations. In GF Gebhart, DL Hammond & TS Jensen (eds.). *Proceedings of the 7th World Congress on Pain. Progress in Pain Research and Management, Vol. 2.* Seattle, WA: IASP Press, 595–619.

Portenoy RK & Foley KM (1986). Chronic use of opiate analgesics in nonmalignant pain: Report of 38 cases. *Pain* 25:171–186.

Redmond DE & Krystal JH (1984). Multiple mechanisms of withdrawal from opioid drugs. *Annual Review of Neuroscience* 7:443–478.

Shoaib M, Spanagel R, Stohr A & Shippenberg TS (1995). Strain differences in the rewarding and dopamine-releasing effects of morphine in rats. *Psychopharmacology* 117:240–247.

Shuster L (1990–91). Genetics of responses to drugs of abuse. *International Journal of the Addictions* 25:57–79.

Sindrup SH, Poulsen L, Brosen K, Arendt-Nielsen L & Gram LF. (1993). Are poor metabolizers of sparteine/debrisuquine less pain tolerant than extensive metabolizers? *Pain* 53:335–339.

Tabakoff B & Hoffman PL (1992). Alcohol: Neurobiology. In JH Lowinson, RM Millman & JG Langrod (eds.) *Substance Abuse: A Comprehensive Textbook, 3rd ed.* Baltimore, MD: Williams and Wilkins, 152–185.

Vaccarino AL, Marek P, Kest B et al. (1993). Morphine fails to produce tolerance when administered in the presence of formalin pain in rats. *Brain Research* 627:287–290.

Victor M (1992). The effects of alcohol on the nervous system. In CS Liever (ed.) *Medical and Nutritional Complications of Alcoholism.* New York, NY: Plenum Press, 413–457.

Wise RA (1980). Action of drugs of abuse on brain reward systems. *Pharmacology, Biochemistry and Behavior* 13 (Suppl. 1):213–223.

Wise RA & Bozarth MA (1984). Brain reward circuitry: Four circuit elements "wired" in apparent series. *Brain Research Bulletin* 12:203–208.

Wise RA & Rompre PP (1989). Brain dopamine and reward. *Annual Review of Psychology* 40:191–225.

Zacny JP, McKay MA, Toledano AY et al. (1996). The effects of cold-water immersion stressor on the reinforcing and subjective effects of fentanyl in healthy volunteers. *Drug and Alcohol Dependence* 42:133–142.

Zubieta JK, Gorelick DA, Stauffer R, Ravent HT, Dannals RF & Frost JJ (1996). Increased opioid receptor binding detected by PET in cocaine-dependent men is associated with cocaine craving. *Nature Medicine* 2:1225–1229.

CHAPTER 2

Principles of Pain Treatment in the Addicted Patient

Seddon R. Savage, M.D., FASAM

Clinical Pain Concepts
Management of Acute Pain in Addiction
Management of Cancer Pain in Addiction
Management of Non-Cancer Pain in Addiction
Pain Management Tools

It is widely recognized that pain of all kinds, including acute pain, cancer related pain and chronic pain of non-cancer origin, historically has been undertreated in the general population (Marks & Sacher, 1973; Morgan, 1985). And it is clear that individuals with addictive disorders are at special risk for suffering due to inadequate management of their pain (Cohen, 1980; Shine & Demas, 1984). Many factors contribute to this, including inadequate training in pain management, fear of contributing to addiction through the use of dependence-producing medications, lack of knowledge about the disease of addiction, societal prejudices against addicts, fear of regulatory sanctions related to opioid use, and others. Widespread initiatives directed at the improvement of pain treatment throughout the world have begun to improve management of pain in the general population. However, in the context of the current war on drugs and addiction, with widespread stigmatization of addicts and misunderstanding about the nature of addictive disease, individuals with addictive disorders remain at significant risk for undertreatment of pain.

In fact, the treatment of pain in individuals with addictive disorders often is challenging. Some addicted individuals identify pain as a major contributor to their addiction. The presence of pain can be an obstacle to withdrawal of alcohol or other drugs in the addicted patient because of increases in pain that accompany the physiologic stress of withdrawal. Dependence-producing medications such as opioids are potentially helpful components of pain treatment, but the addict may have difficulty controlling the use of such medications. Untreated pain represents a risk factor for relapse among persons in recovery; but exposure to some analgesics and adjunctive pain treatment medications also may place such individuals at risk for relapse. Some physiological and psychological aspects of addictive disease may make pain more difficult to treat in addicted persons than in non-addicted patients. Finally, in individuals with addictive disease who require opioids for the treatment of pain, it is sometimes difficult for both patients and their physicians to distinguish which aspect of the patient's distress represent pain and which represent opioid craving independent of pain.

CLINICAL PAIN CONCEPTS

The International Association for the Study of Pain defines pain as "an unpleasant sensory and emotional experience associated with actual or threatened tissue damage, or described in terms of such" (Mersky, 1979). Several aspects of this definition are helpful in understanding pain in the context of addiction. First, pain is an *experience*; it is subjective and essentially must be understood and accepted as what a given patient describes it to be. In an addicted person, the pain is experienced through the filter of the addictive disease process and the synergy between the two conditions may amplify the experience of pain and its associated distresses. Second, pain is not purely a sensory experience, but has emotional components as well. Emotional changes associated with addiction therefore color the experience of pain.

Finally, although pain often indicates the presence of real or potential physical injury, it can be experienced in the absence of injurious stimuli. Current neurophysiologic understanding of pain mechanisms accepts that physiologic and anatomic changes in the pathways that conduct nociceptive information may generate and sustain pain in the absence of ongoing threats to tissue integrity. In the addicted patient, concurrent neurophysiologic changes related to active chemical dependency, or pre-existing biogenetically mediated neurophysiologic idiosyncrasies associated with the disease of addiction, also may shape the experience of pain.

Pain treatment in the individual with addictive disease is most likely to be effective when the physician evaluates and addresses all components of the pain experience. This includes the physiologic (nociceptive or neuropathic) pathways of pain, the affective or emotional components of the pain experience, and the functional sequelae of pain. It is important that concurrent addictive disease, which may affect the experience of pain in all these dimensions, be appropriately addressed.

In developing clinical treatment strategies for pain, it often is helpful to view pain in three broad clinical categories: acute pain, chronic pain of noncancer origin, and cancer-related pain (or pain related to other chronic or recurrent and severely painful medical conditions). Although every pain scenario must be considered in its own unique context, pain falling within these categories tends to share certain characteristics and treatment needs that may be considered together.

Acute pain occurs in response to a specific, self-limited medical problem. Examples are pain following physical trauma; pain associated with acute painful medical conditions such as renal lithiasis, cholecystitis or dental abscess; and post-operative pain due to surgical procedures. Usually the pain gradually resolves as the underlying medical or surgical condition resolves. Acute pain is associated with autonomic arousal and, when severe, identifiable autonomic responses such as increases in blood pressure and heart rate, sweating or skin pallor often accompany acute pain. Typically, acute pain is associated with a mood state of anxiety. In the presence of acute pain, the individual's ability to function in usual roles may be retained or may diminish depending on the intensity of the pain and on a variety of other host factors.

Chronic pain of non-cancer origin (hereafter termed chronic pain) refers to pain that is not related to cancer (or to other severely painful chronic medical illnesses) and that persists for a prolonged period of time, often beyond the apparent healing of the inciting problem. Chronic low back pain, myofascial neck and shoulder pain, and persistent pelvic or abdominal pain are common examples. Neuropathic pain syndromes such as entrapment syndromes, complex regional pain syndrome, phantom pain and post stroke syndrome are other somewhat less common, but often troublesome, examples. The persistence of pain for greater than one to six months has variously been used to define chronic pain, but the choice of a duration is somewhat arbitrary. Chronic pain usually does not provoke sympathetic responses, although periodic exacerbations of the pain may do so.

Chronic pain may become a primary problem that engenders secondary clinical problems such as sleep disturbance, sexual dysfunction, physical deconditioning, and affective disturbances (including depression or anxiety). It frequently results in an individual becoming functionally disabled from customary roles, including work and domestic roles, although many individuals with chronic pain persevere in their life roles despite significant pain. Like addictive disease, chronic pain is a complex disorder with biologic, psychological and spiritual components. Independent of each other, chronic pain and addictive disease may present quite similar pictures. When they occur concurrently, chronic pain and addictive disease may synergistically act to exacerbate or reinforce each other.

A number of factors may contribute to the development of chronic pain. An undetected, untreated or untreatable somatic or visceral pathology may be present, for example a subtle inflammatory process, fascial tightness or deep muscle spasm. Physical examination and objective studies may yield only subtle, or no, confirmatory findings. The pain may represent activation of neuropathologic mechanisms of pain again yielding few objective findings. The pain may be perpetuated or reinforced by a variety of influences such as mood changes, secondary physical problems, work considerations, relationship stresses and financial issues. Addictive disease may be a strong reinforcing condition. The physical pain may be a manifestation of intrapsychic processes (somatoform or psychogenic pain). Sometimes, elements of all these factors are present.

The search for an underlying, treatable physical problem should not be abandoned when pain persists and other factors do not appear sufficient to explain an individual's pain, even while implementing management and coping strategies for other aspects of pain. Wide clinical experience suggests that the physiologic basis of pain often becomes apparent over time, either with the emergence of new or changing clinical signs or symptoms, or with the emergence of new knowledge and understanding within the clinical field of pain. This is not to recommend repetitive testing when no indications are present, but to encourage thoughtful, ongoing clinical assessment and management of an individual who continues in pain. The assumption by care providers that the etiology of pain is largely "psychogenic" when no identifiable physical cause can be found usually is erroneous and is demoralizing to patients who know from experience that their pain has a physiologic base. On the other hand, the psychological impact of persistent pain and the effects on pain of psychologic issues must be addressed.

Cancer-related pain (and other severe intractable pain due to a chronic medical illness, such as relapsing pancreatitis, sickle cell disease or some HIV-related pain syndromes) may have a variety of contributing factors. Often the most prominent is the physical disease process, which may be invasive and destructive of pain-sensitive tissues. Cancer treatments such as radiation and neurotoxic chemotherapeutic agents also can induce chronic severe pain. Secondary physical pain may result from disuse phenomena, such as muscle spasm, contractures and bedsores. Depression, anxiety, spiritual distress and grief may augment the experience of cancer-related pain. Functional limitations often are imposed by uncontrolled pain and by associated distresses. An individual with cancer and co-existing addictive disease who is actively drinking or using street drugs, or who develops an abusive pattern of use of prescribed medications, may experience increased distress associated with cancer pain. Often cancer-related pain presents with a baseline chronic component and with intermittent exacerbations related to activity or new disease expression, which must be addressed individually.

MANAGEMENT OF ACUTE PAIN IN ADDICTION

Undertreatment of pain has been shown to increase morbidity following trauma and surgery in the general population (Wattwil, 1989) and optimal pain treatment appears to shorten hospitalizations in similar contexts (Jackson, 1989). The presence of pain increases distress and anxiety and, in recovering addicts, may become a significant risk factor for relapse. Individuals with addictive disease often experience high levels of anxiety in association with the stress of trauma, illness or surgery. This may in turn affect how they experience pain. Attention to their concerns often makes pain management easier.

Physicians should inform patients with addictive disease who have acute pain that the physician is aware of the patients' addictive disease and should reassure them that this will not be an obstacle to the relief of their pain.

The individual in pain should be included in the decision-making process regarding medication choices, dosing and scheduling. This provides the patient with a sense of control and allays anxiety over whether the pain will be adequately treated. It also may give the physician valuable insights in designing an effective treatment regimen. Addicted patients and patients with therapeutic drug dependence often are experts on the drug doses they require to meet their basic dependence needs and the additional levels required to treat their acute pain. Occasionally such consultation will result in prescription of doses beyond that needed for analgesia; if patients become obviously intoxicated or sedated with prescribed doses, medications should be titrated to avoid the observed side effects while continuing to provide analgesia.

Addiction counseling should be offered when addiction is detected in the course of pain treatment and may be initiated at any time as long as acute pain is adequately controlled. Pain relief should be provided in an effective and timely manner. Without adequate control of acute pain, it is unlikely the patient will be able to engage in addiction treatment. Undertreatment of pain also may create craving for pain-relieving medications, as well as anxiety, frustration, anger and other feelings that tend to feed addiction (McCaffery & Vourakis, 1992).

If a patient is dependent on opioids, the clinician should not consider opioid discontinuation until the acute pain situation is resolved. If a patient is an actively drinking alcoholic or is dependent on non-opioid drugs, withdrawal symptoms should be treated when they occur in the course of pain treatment. Unrecognized alcohol withdrawal will make pain control difficult to achieve.

Effective Pain Treatment: When they are effective, easily available and safe, non-medication pain treatment approaches such as ice, TENS or regional anesthesia are preferred by some clinicians and patients over systemic medications to provide relief of acute pain in individuals with addictive disease. When medications are indicated to relieve pain, those that are the least likely to produce physical dependence and have the least tendency to alter mood may be used, but only if they are effective. While exposure to dependence-producing or mood-altering drugs is one component of the development of addiction or relapse to drug use, such exposure alone does not create addiction. When such drugs are needed to manage pain, they should be used effectively. In the setting of moderate to severe acute pain, opioids usually are the mainstay of treatment in all patients, including those with addictive disorders.

Scheduled or PCA administration of opioids is preferred over PRN medications for acute pain in individuals with addictive disorders. These approaches have several advantages: the patient does not have to ask for medications, which in an addict may be interpreted as drug-seeking behavior rather than a search for pain relief and thus may create friction between the patient and care providers. Delays in receiving medication are avoided, so that timely and effective pain relief is obtained and drug craving is avoided.

Because the drug administration is time-contingent rather than symptom-contingent, reinforcement of the pain symptoms is minimized.

If scheduled medications are used, PRN doses of medication should be provided initially, in addition to scheduled doses, for titration of medications to the required dosing level. Intermittent, non-scheduled medications are appropriate in the acute pain setting when an individual has little or no baseline pain, but has pain related to specific activities.

Pain treatment that does not confuse, stress or frustrate staff and/or the patient is important. For example, although an epidural infusion of local anesthesia may seem ideal for management of post-thoracotomy pain in a recovering opioid addict, if the floor nurses are unfamiliar with management of the required catheters, the patient's overall needs probably will be better met with scheduled or PCA doses of opioids, since potential failure of the epidural may leave the patient in a position of seeking opioids for pain relief.

Individuals who are on methadone maintenance or who are physically dependent on therapeutically prescribed or street opioids must have their baseline opioid requirements met in addition to the medications provided for pain (Wesson, Ling & Smith, 1993). The average baseline daily dose of opioid should be determined and either the same drug provided at the determined dose or an equianalgesic dose of an alternative opioid calculated and provided in appropriately scheduled doses (see Table 1 for an analgesic equivalence chart) (Panel, 1992).

When possible, a patient who is receiving methadone maintenance therapy for addiction should be continued on his or her baseline methadone as an inpatient and provided a different opioid for acute pain, rather than being entirely switched to an alternative opioid or having the methadone increased for pain. If necessary, methadone can be given parenterally rather than orally, in an appropriate equivalent dose. This is recommended for two reasons. First, incomplete cross-tolerance of methadone with other mu agonists has been noted and opioid withdrawal from methadone observed in some patients, even in the presence of calculated equianalgesic doses of alternative mu agonists. Second, while an increase in methadone usually is effective for pain management, the use of the same drug for addiction maintenance and for acute pain management may confuse the issues of pain treatment and addiction treatment when acute pain resolves and taper of pain medication to maintenance doses becomes appropriate.

Recovering persons often benefit from increasing their recovery activities during times of stress, such as hospitalization, trauma and pain. Many clinicians and individuals in recovery believe that exposure to opioids, sedative-hypnotics or anesthetics—even if these were not the patient's drugs of choice—may lead to relapse. However, the distress of inadequately treated physical pain may pose an even greater risk of relapse. Effective pain treatment by whatever means, coupled with an active recovery program, probably are the best supports for continued recovery during periods of acute stress, including periods of pain.

When Pain Persists Beyond Apparent Healing. When a patient continues to complain of pain and to need pain medications despite expected and apparent healing from surgery, trauma, illness or other pain-provoking pathology, several explanations should be considered.

First, the patient may have an undetected physical problem, either related to the original painful problem or to a separate process. A thorough search for such a cause should be undertaken. The search should include a review of somatic causes of pain, such as abscess or undetected fracture, as well as less common and often overlooked neurogenic causes of pain.

Second, the patient may be physically dependent on analgesic medications and may be experiencing pain related to withdrawal as the medication is discontinued. Withdrawal may mediate pain through a variety of mechanisms, including alterations in sympathetic arousal, changes in muscle tone and alterations in opiate and other receptor function. A gradual taper of medications over several days usually

TABLE 1. Equianalgesic Doses of Opioid Drugs

Drug	Approximate Equianalgesic Oral Dose	Approximate Equianalgesic Parenteral Dose
Opioid Agonists		
Morphine	30 mg q 3–4 hours (around the clock dosing) 60 mg q 3–4 hours (single dose or intermittent dosing)	10 mg q 3–4 hours
Codeine	130 mg q 3–4 hours	75 mg q 3–4 hours
Hydromorphone (Dilaudid®)	7.5 mg q 3–4 hours	1.5 mg q 3–4 hours
Hydrocodone (Lorcet®, Lortab®, Vicodin®)	30 mg q 3–4 hours	Not available
Levorphanol (Levo-Dromoran®)	4 mg q 6–8 hours	2 mg q 6–8 hours
Meperidine (Demerol®)	300 mg q 6–8 hours	100 mg q 3 hours
Methadone (Dolophine®, others)	20 mg q 6–8 hours	10 mg q 6–8 hours
Oxycodone (Percodan®, Percocet®, Roxicodone®, Tylox®)	30 mg q 3–4 hours	Not available
Opioid Agonist/Antagonist Drugs and Partial Agonists		
Buprenorphine (Buprenex®)	Not available	0.3–0.4 mg q 6–8 hours
Butorphanol (Stadol®)	Not available	2 mg q 3–4 hours
Nalbuphine (Nubain®)	Not available	10 mg q 3–4 hours
Pentazocine (Talwin®, others)	150 mg q 3–4 hours	60 mg q 3–4 hours

NOTE: Published tables vary in the suggested doses that are equianalgesic to morphine. Clinical response is the criterion that must be applied for each patient; titration to clinical response is necessary. Because there is not complete cross-tolerance among these drugs, it usually is necessary to use a lower than equianalgesic dose when changing drugs, and to re-titrate to the response.

CAUTION: Recommended doses do not apply to patients with renal or hepatic insufficiency or other conditions affecting drug metabolism and kinetics.

CAUTION: Doses listed for patients with body weight of less than 50 kg cannot be used as initial starting doses in infants younger than six months of age. Consult the AHCPR Clinical Practice Guideline for Acute Pain Management *for recommendations.*

Source: Panel on Acute Pain Guidelines (1992). *Acute Pain Management: Operative or Medical Procedures and Trauma*. Rockville, MD: Agency for Health Care Policy Research.

avoids this rebound pain phenomenon. The goal when tapering an individual who is physically dependent on medications should be to provide stable but decreasing blood levels of opioid so as to prevent intermittent withdrawal. In practice, this usually can be only approximated.

If increased discomfort occurs during the course of medication taper, the patient should be reexamined for an undetected physical origin of the pain. If none is found, the taper should be continued. Nonopioid alternatives (such as TENS, NSAIDs or block therapy) should be provided to attenuate discomfort during withdrawal of medications. In most cases, increases in discomfort will be transient during and immediately following discontinuation of medications. If pain persists and no physical cause can be identified, treatment should be as for chronic pain.

Third, the individual may be using the medication to obtain relief of symptoms other than pain, such as anxiety or depression. Opioids may in fact provide some short-term relief of such distress, but more specific treatments will be more effective and will allow tapering of pain medications.

Finally, the individual may have developed an addiction to the medication (Table 2). This is less common than the first three possibilities when treating

TABLE 2. Problems Suggesting Addiction Associated with Chronic Opioid Therapy

Adverse consequences of opioid use:
- Decreasing functionality
- Observed intoxication
- Increasing complaints of pain despite titration of medications
- Negative affective states.

Loss of control over medication use:
- Failure to bring unused medications to appointments
- Requests for early renewals
- Reports of "lost" or "stolen" prescriptions
- Appearance at clinic without appointment and in distress
- Frequent visits to emergency departments, requesting drugs
- Family reports of overuse or intoxication.

Preoccupation with opioids:
- Failure to comply wit non-drug pain therapies
- Failure to keep appointments
- Shows interest only in relief of symptoms, not rehabilitation
- Reports no effect of non-opioid interventions
- Seeks prescriptions from multiple providers.

Does not actively participate in an addiction treatment program.

a general hospital population, although it is a relatively more frequent occurrence in the population treated by addiction medicine specialists.

If addiction is suspected, the patient's drug and alcohol history should be thoroughly reviewed. If the patient is in recovery, he or she should be reengaged in the recovery system or recovery-oriented activities initiated. If the individual had an active chemical dependency problem at the time of onset of the acutely painful injury or illness, addiction treatment should be initiated. If the person has no history of addictive disorder, consideration of possibilities one, two, and three should be reexamined and further evaluation by an addiction specialist obtained. It is rare, but not unheard of, for addiction to present initially in association with the therapeutic use of opioid medications. Medication should be tapered as described above and the use of alternative methods for addressing pain implemented, if they are reasonable in terms of the individual's pain problem. Simultaneously, addiction treatment also should be undertaken.

Unless an underlying physical cause is identified, pain often resolves or improves following discontinuation of medications and treatment of addiction. If it does not, the patient should be treated for chronic pain as described below.

MANAGEMENT OF CANCER PAIN IN ADDICTION

Treatment of cancer-related pain in the patient with addictive disease is similar to that in the person without addictive disease. The comfort of the patient should be the primary goal. Opioids never should be withheld when they are needed for effective pain relief because of concerns regarding the development or perpetuation of addiction. If concerns arise regarding decreased quality of life due to active addiction, pain control should be continued and addiction issues addressed through appropriate psychospiritual interventions. Adjustment of medications may be appropriate to avoid unnecessary side effects or intoxication, but not at the expense of pain control.

The "therapeutic ladder" developed by the World Health Organization (WHO) is an accepted model for treatment of cancer pain (Panel, 1994). Stage 1 of the ladder includes use of non-opioid analgesics (usually a non-steroidal anti-inflammatory) and adjuvant medications (for sleep, mood problems, side effect management etc). Stage 2 includes use of a weak opioid preparation for mild to moderate pain, plus non-opioid analgesics and adjuvant medications as indicated. Stage 3 includes use of a titratable, potent opioid plus non-opioid analgesics and adjuvants. Treatment should start as far along the ladder as necessary to achieve pain control.

Aggressive titration of opioids is appropriate to control pain. Cancer pain usually can be managed with oral medications or with use of transdermal opioid administration. If oral or transdermal medications are not feasible because of absorption problems, vomiting, or technical problems with adherence of transdermal patches, the clinician should consider parenteral treatment, continuous or PCA intravenous or subcutaneous administration.

When WHO interventions are not sufficient to control pain, or have unacceptable side effects, more invasive approaches may be considered (Table 3). Regional anesthetic techniques such as continuous intraspinal infusions or plexus blocks may provide effective ongoing relief for many types of cancer pain (Cousins & Bridenbaugh, 1990). Neuroablative procedures such as celiac plexus block for pancreatic cancer pain, nerve root blocks for pain localized to a specific dermatome, and others may provide definitive relief in difficult cancer pain situations. Radia-

TABLE 3. Common Interventionalist Procedures for Pain

Procedure	Commonly Accepted Indications
Trigger point injections	Focal, intractable muscle spasm
Tendon, bursal or intra-articular steroid injections	Non-infectious inflammation
Peripheral nerve blocks	Neuroma Peripheral neuritis
Sympathetic blocks	Complex regional pain syndrome Ischemic pain Vasospasm
Spinal infusions	Post-operative pain control Cancer-related pain with untenable side effects on oral opioids Intractable, severe, unresponsive non-cancer related pain
Implanted peripheral nerve stimulation	Intractable peripheral nerve pain
Spinal cord stimulaion	Intractable neuropathic pain Ischemic pain unresponsive to primary treatments.

tion therapy and radiopharmaceuticals may be helpful in selected situations.

Cancer often is accompanied by significant distress such as fear, grief over impending losses, depression, anger and spiritual conflict. Because persons with addictive disorders have a tendency to use drugs to relieve such distress, cancer patients with addictive disease may be more likely than others to use therapeutically prescribed opioids in an attempt to relieve such distress. Most compassionate physicians would have no issue with such use of opioids to relieve symptoms in the setting of cancer-related pain, if they were effective. However, such use sometimes results in increased distress and greater experience of pain despite massive doses of opioids. Effective non-pharmacologic and pharmacologic means of addressing such stressors are available and should be employed to provide relief. For individuals in recovery from chemical dependence, the recovery system may provide meaningful support (McCaffery & Vourakis, 1992).

MANAGEMENT OF CHRONIC NON-CANCER PAIN IN ADDICTION

The treatment of chronic pain in individuals with addictive disease differs little from the treatment of such pain in individuals without addictive disease. The goals of chronic pain treatment are reduction of pain; improvement in associated symptoms such as sleep disturbance, depression and anxiety; restoration of function; and elimination of unnecessary dependence on medications. These goals typically are approached through non-pharmacologic means.

Addictive disease should be identified and addressed early in the treatment of chronic pain. The sequelae of addiction often include perpetuating factors for pain, such as sleep disturbance, anxiety or depressive symptoms, changes in muscle and sympathetic tone, and dysfunction in usual life roles (Savage, 1993). When treatment of addiction produces improvement in these factors, pain often resolves or improves (Finlayson, Maruta & Morse, 1986; Finlayson, Maruta et al, 1986; Brodner & Taub, 1978). When it does not, the chronic pain should be addressed in the same manner as for persons without addictive disease.

Addiction treatment generally includes detoxification from dependence-producing medications and introduction of a recovery program. This eliminates potential pain-generating or reinforcing factors inherent in physical dependence. Occasionally, however, a patient's pain symptoms may make withdrawal of medications early in treatment impossible. In such cases, stabilization of the medications may be the best option, because it avoids abrupt changes in blood levels, which in turn may avoid intermittent emergence of withdrawal phenomena (Savage, 1993; Brodner & Taub, 1978). For example, an alcoholic patient who is taking large doses of hydrocodone for back pain and who is disabled by the back pain when the hydrocodone is tapered may do better if switched to a long-acting opioid such as sustained-release morphine or methadone. Such a change ideally should take place early in treatment, so that the drug can be tapered slowly as the pain treatment progresses. Occasionally, it may be appropriate to continue long-acting opioids indefinitely.

Multidimensional Pain Management. Assessment of the patient with chronic pain must include a history of the onset of pain, treatments to date and responses to treatment, a clear description of the quality and temporal nature of the pain, and identification of factors that ameliorate or exacerbate the pain. The assessment also should include how the pain has affected the individual's life, as well as its effect on relationships, work and domestic roles, and pleasurable recreational activities. Factors known to increase or sustain pain—such as depression, anxiety, sleep disturbance, social isolation and inactivity—must be identified. A list of all factors potentially contributing to the pain and to the patient's resulting distress should be generated and a plan for addressing each component of the problem developed. Interventions that address only the physical components are unlikely to resolve the pain and its associated distress.

Physical approaches such as stretching, exercise, applications of cold or heat, peripheral electrical stimulation, manual treatments and anesthesia procedures such as nerve blocks and trigger points often are helpful in reducing pain and secondary physical symptoms. Behavioral interventions such as relaxation training, introduction of pacing of activities to minimize pain, and changes in behavioral responses to pain are used to reduce the experience of pain and associated symptoms such as anxiety. Often a multidisciplinary team of pain specialists may be involved, although many of these approaches to pain management are interventions that can be provided directly on referral by a primary care physician. More aggressive therapies, such as implanted spinal or peripheral nerve stimulators and implanted spinal infusions, are appropriate for some patients with severe intractable pain of non-cancer origin.

Opioids for the Treatment of Chronic Non-Cancer Pain. The use of long-term opioids for the treatment of chronic pain of non-cancer origin is becoming increasingly accepted as a component of chronic pain treatment when other treatments alone fail to provide adequate relief (Portenoy, 1990a; Schug, Merry & Acland, 1991; Zenz, Strumph & Tryba, 1992). However, the majority of patients with chronic non-cancer pain achieve good relief of pain and improvement of function with multidisciplinary pain treatment, including elimination of opioids. Often patients are surprised to find that they actually feel better with elimination of opioids. For most patients with chronic pain, a trial period without opioids and with a well-coordinated trial of alternative treatments should be considered before long-term opioid therapy is initiated. However, if other treatments are ineffective and long-term opioid therapy provides subjective pain relief, an improved level of function, and better quality of life, and does not result in adverse consequences, long-term opioid therapy may be the best treatment option (Table 4).

Some proponents of long-term opioid therapy for chronic non-cancer pain view a history of addiction as a relative contraindication to the implementation of such therapy because of the problems persons with addictive disorders often experience in controlling their use of potentially intoxicating medications. However, for selected patients with severe, chronic non-cancer pain and a concurrent history of addictive disease, as with other patients, opioids may in fact be the most effective and realistic pain treatment option (Dunbar & Katz, 1996; Kennedy & Crowley, 1990).

In the absence of longitudinal clinical data to guide the use of opioids for the treatment of chronic non-cancer pain, it is prudent to weigh the expected benefits of treatment against the clinical concerns associated with the use of opioids and to decide on an individual basis what is best for each patient. Among the issues that should be weighed in clinical decision making are the potential for pain relief, improvement in function, and quality of life, as opposed to issues related to physical dependence, tolerance, addiction, potential pain reinforcement, changes in pain modulation, and the potential for individuals to use opioid medications for non-pain purposes.

Drug choice and scheduling considerations in implementing opioid therapy for chronic pain are not significantly different from those involved in treating acute and cancer related pain. Selection and titration of medications should be made with the goals of reducing pain, increasing function, and minimizing unwanted side effects.

Many clinicians favor the use of a written contact when undertaking long-term opioid therapy of chronic non-cancer related pain. In individuals with a history of addiction, this is especially important, and a highly structured program using a team approach is recommended. The ideal team would include the patient's primary care physician, an addiction medicine specialist, a pharmacist and a pain specialist as well as counselors and/or therapists; in reality, however, communication most often is between one physician and a pharmacist. The written contract should specify one prescribing physician, one specific pharmacy to be used, the dose and schedule of medications, frequency of follow-up vis-

TABLE 4. Proposed Guidelines for the Management of Opioid Therapy for Nonmalignant Pain (from Portenoy)

1. Opioid therapy should be considered only after all other reasonable attempts at analgesia have failed.
2. The use of opioid therapy in an individual with a history of substance abuse is clinically complex and should be approached with great care. The inclusion of an individual experienced in addictions evaluation and treatment is recommended in such instances.
3. A single practitioner should take primary responsibility for treatment.
4. Patients should give informed consent before starting therapy; points to be covered should include recognition of the low risk of true addiction as an outcome, potential for cognitive impairment with the drug alone and in combination with sedative-hypnotics, likelihood that physical dependence will occur (abstinence syndrome possible with acute discontinuation), and understanding by female patients that children born when the mother is on opioid therapy will likely be physically dependent at birth.
5. After drug selection, doses should be given around the clock; several weeks should be agreed on as the period of initial dose titration, and although improvement in function should be continually stressed, all should agree to at least partial analgesia as the appropriate goal of therapy.
6. Failure to achieve at least partial analgesia at relatively low initial doses in the nontolerant patient raises questions about the potential treatability of the pain syndrome with opioids.
7. Emphasis should be given to capitalizing on improved analgesia by gains in physical and social function; opioid therapy should be considered complementary to other analgesic and rehabilitative approaches.
8. In addition to the daily dose determined initially, patients should be permitted to escalate dose transiently on days of increased pain; two methods are acceptable: (a) prescription of an additional four to six "rescue doses" to be taken as needed during the month; or (b) instruction that one or two extra doses may be taken on any day, but must be followed by an equal reduction of dose on subsequent days.
9. Initially, patients must be seen and drugs prescribed at least monthly. When stable, less frequent visits may be acceptable.
10. Exacerbations of pain not effectively treated by transient, small increases in dose are best managed in the hospital, where dose escalation, if appropriate, can be observed closely and return-to-baseline doses can be accomplished in a controlled environment.
11. Evidence of drug hoarding, acquisition of drugs from other physicians, uncontrolled dose escalation, or other aberrant behaviors must be carefully assessed. In some cases, tapering and discontinuation of opioid therapy will be necessary. Other patients may appropriately continue therapy with rigid guidelines. Consideration should be given to consultation with an addiction medicine specialist.
12. At each visit, assessment should specifically address: (a) comfort (degree of analgesia); (b) opioid-related side-effects; (c) functional status (physical and psychosocial); and (d) existence of aberrant drug-related behaviors.
13. Use of self-report instruments may be helpful but should not be required.
14. Documentation is essential and the medical record should specifically address comfort, function, side-effects, and the occurrence of aberrant behaviors repeatedly during the course of therapy.

Source: Reprinted with permission from RK Portenoy, "Opioid Therapy for Chronic Nonmalignant Pain: Current Status," in HL Fields and JC Liebeskind, eds., *Progress in Pain Research and Management*. Seattle, WA: IASP Press, Vol. 1, 1994: at 274.

its, expected recovery activities, and the circumstances under which treatment will be continued or discontinued. It usually is most appropriate that the contract be signed by both the patient and provider and that each have a copy. A clinical member of the treatment team should meet regularly with the patient to assess the therapeutic efficacy of the medication in terms of pain control and to monitor for addictive use of the medication or relapse to use of other drugs or alcohol. It often is helpful for the patient to bring unused medications to these appointments to document use as indicated.

In a patient with a history of addiction, periodic drug screens may be appropriate to monitor for relapse and to document that the medications prescribed actually are being used by the patient. However, short-acting opioid medications may not always be detected in urine. Discontinuation of opioid therapy may be indicated if addictive use of medications develops and persists despite expert attempts at structuring use and treating addiction.

PAIN MANAGEMENT TOOLS

As clinical knowledge of the neurophysiology of pain has increased over the past 20 years, new treatments for pain and new ways of effectively integrating pain treatment approaches have evolved. It is helpful for physicians who treat individuals with addictive disorders to have a general awareness of these options in order to help their patients, who inevitably will need help with pain management from time to time.

Extensive, in-depth information on pain treatment is available from a variety of sources. What follows is a brief overview of pain treatment approaches, with particular attention to issues relevant to their use in individuals with addictive disorders.

Pain treatment modalities may be considered in four categories: physical approaches, psychological interventions, invasive (or interventionist) therapies, and pharmacologic interventions. There is considerable overlap between these groupings, but it is helpful to consider them separately. When seeking assistance from a pain management specialist, it is important to be aware that many pain specialists and pain clinics approach the management of pain from predominately one perspective. For example, some anesthesiology pain specialists may assess patients with respect to whether their pain is likely to respond to invasive therapies and may offer primarily invasive approaches to pain treatment, while many psychiatric pain specialists offer only psychiatric and cognitive behavioral management approaches, which may help patients cope with pain but which do not directly address the physiologic aspects of pain. Increasing numbers of pain clinics are becoming multidisciplinary in their approach to both assessment and treatment. Such multidimensional assessment and treatment generally is recognized as the most effective approach, especially in establishing a program of treatment. Referral to specialty pain clinics may be helpful when specific treatments are indicated.

Physical Treatment Approaches. Physical treatment approaches include the use of therapeutic heat and/or cold treatments, stimulation analgesia (most commonly transcutaneous electrical nerve stimulation or TENS), manual treatments such as massage, manipulation and stretch, and the use of orthotic devices such as splints and braces to protect, immobilize or position body parts to reduce pain (Table 5). Physical approaches often are effective in both acute and chronic pain settings and usually can be initiated in a primary care setting. Because many such approaches can be implemented by the individual who is in pain, they provide a sense of control to the patient and encourage self-care, both of which are helpful to the individual with addictive disease. It often is helpful to give the individual specific written instructions for use of physical modalities just as one would for prescription medications. This procedure lends authority to the recommendation and affirms confidence in the procedures prescribed. This may provide a concrete behavioral substitute for habitual drug-using behavior. For example, one might write: "Apply ice pack to painful area every six hours for 20 minutes. Practice abdominal breathing/relaxation for first 10 minutes of each ice application."

TABLE 5. Physical Interventions Helpful in the Treatment of Pain

Thermal modalities:
- Cold: ice, cold packs
- Heat: hot packs, ultrasound, diathermy

Peripheral counterstimulation:
- Transcutaneous electrical nerve stimulation (TENS)
- Vibration
- Topical aromatic applications

Manual therapies:
- Massage
- Manipulation (chiropractic, osteopathic)
- Myofascial release

Active movement:
- Stretching
- Conditioning
- Strengthening

Orthotics:
- Splints, braces
- Positioning aides (pillows, supports, lifts).

NOTE: This is a partial list of available pain procedures. Decisions regarding indications for these procedures often are complex. Consultation with a pain medicine specialist usually is appropriate (except for local anesthetic trigger point injections). Other indications may be appropriate but are less widely accepted.

Cold and Heat: Thermal modalities are among the most easily available and effective, yet most underutilized tools for managing pain (Palastanga, 1994). The application of cold will temporarily relieve most musculoskeletal pain, such as pain associated with muscle, ligament or tendon strains, and is helpful in some (but not all) types of neuropathic pain. Individuals with post-herpetic neuralgia, for example, often spontaneously apply cold wet compresses to relieve pain and may find flourimethane spray helpful. Cold acts through a variety of mechanisms: it slows transmission along nociceptive neurons, reduces inflammation, reduces local circulation and may cause muscular relaxation through a reflex mechanism (Smith, 1990). It is relatively contraindicated in the presence of local ischemia and may increase sympathetically mediated pain and some forms of neuropathic pain. Cold may be employed in a variety of forms. Commercial cold packs, either containing substances that become cold with chemical activation or reusable packs requiring refrigeration, are available in a variety of designs for wrapping or applying to various body parts.

Crushed ice in a plastic bag or a plastic package of frozen peas or corn wrapped in thin material readily conforms to many body areas. Cold sprays frequently are used with gentle stretch to resolve acute muscle spasm. Direct ice massage to painful muscles, tendons and joints often is helpful. Frequently, patients experience increased discomfort for a few minutes following application of cold or ice, but generally with tissue cooling this resolves and local pain is improved.

Heat provides analgesia through several mechanisms, including increase of peripheral pain receptor firing thresholds, improvement of local circulation, and provision of general comfort, encouraging muscular relaxation and softening collagen tissues, thus permitting improved stretching of soft tissues (Palastanga, 1994; Smith, 1990). Heat can be provided in a variety of ways. Warm soaks, application of dry or moist hot packs, heat lamps, hot air and ultrasound (which provides heat to deep tissues) all may be helpful in different settings. Heat may be particularly helpful for pain in which there is a component of sympathetic maintenance and for generally sore or tight soft tissues. The question from patients as to whether to employ cold or heat sometimes leaves physicians feeling a little embarrassed, because the best answer in many settings is simply "whichever feels better." Reasonable guidelines may be that in acute injury or acutely exacerbated chronic pain, in the presence of inflammation, or with quite focal pain, cold should be used first. In the presence of more diffuse pain, reduced circulation, generalized muscle tension and chronic musculoskeletal pain not associated with inflammation, heat should be used first. There are many exceptions to these guidelines, however, and the physician must use judgment and consider the patient's preferences.

Counterstimulation: Counterstimulation has been used spontaneously to provide pain relief since the origin of pain in the species. When an individual spontaneously shakes a hand after slamming a thumb with a hammer, or rubs an ankle after a wrong landing from a jump, he or she is providing some level of analgesia through counterstimulation. Our physiologic understanding of the analgesia provided by counterstimulation is that competition of activated non-nociceptive fibers, such as touch or temperature fibers, has an inhibitory influence on transmission of nociception at the level of the spinal cord (Melzack, 1996).

Counterstimulation most often is provided in the clinical setting in the form of electrical stimulation, although vibration sometimes is used as well. Transcutaneous electrical nerve stimulation is the most widely available form of counterstimulation. Electrical stimulation typically is provided by placing a pair of electrodes adjacent to the painful area or along the afferent nerve supply from the area, or by placing a second pair of electrodes on either side of the spine just above the level of entry of the nerve supply from the painful area. However, optimum positioning of leads is highly variable. The electrical stimulation itself may be pulsed or continuous at a variety of frequencies and intensities and in a variety of wave forms. TENS appears to be effective in reducing perceived pain in some individuals for several types of pain, including peripheral musculoskeletal pain, peripheral neuropathic pain, sympathetically maintained pain and some injury-related pain, including post-operative incisional pain (Frampton, 1994; Johnson, Ashton & Thompson, 1991). However, its effects are highly variable and difficult to predict. Significant negative side-effects are not recognized, although pain sometimes can be transiently increased. Use is contraindicated in the presence of some cardiac pacemakers. TENS generally is not thought to be effective for visceral pain.

Because the individual using TENS can elect when and how to use it and can manipulate a number of variables involved in its use, TENS may provide a sense of control over pain in those individuals for whom it is effective.

Direct Musculoskeletal Interventions: Musculoskeletal interventions generally fall into two broad categories: therapeutic exercise, which tends to involve an active role on the part of the patient, and techniques involving laying on of hands, which tends toward more passive involvement. In treating acute pain in which the sole object of treatment is relief of pain based on tissue pathology, any of these approaches that are effective are appropriate for use. In treating chronic musculoskeletal pain, especially in individuals with addictive disorders in whom functional rehabilitation and responsibility for self-management of symptoms are likely to be goals, the more active approaches are preferred. Short-term use of passive modalities may be appropriate as well.

Therapeutic movement includes stretch, conditioning and strengthening approaches. Stretch is helpful for reducing painful muscle spasms, generalized muscle tension and, sometimes, in assisting in the normalization of altered biomechanics that may be present as the result of asymmetric muscle spasm. Stretch may be done actively by the patient or may be assisted by a therapist. Often, conscious breathing techniques or other forms of relaxation may be coordinated with stretch for maximum effect.

Conditioning exercises may increase general and local circulation, improving healing of injuries and assisting in the resolution of a sympathetically maintained component of pain. Such exercises also tone and strengthen muscles, which may improve posture and biomechanics. Conditioning exercise often provides a generally improved sense of well-being. Strengthening of muscles is thought to reduce their propensity for spasm and general strengthening and conditioning may improve physical capacity, leading to higher levels of function (Feine & Lund, 1997).

Pain treatment approaches that involve the laying on of hands are numerous. Massage and other soft tissue mobilization techniques encourage relaxation of muscles and release of restricted soft tissues (Basmajian, 1985). They also may provide analgesia through counterstimulation mechanisms, as well as enhancing the patient's sense of well-being through pleasant sensory stimulation (even though some techniques are transiently painful) and by providing human contact.

Joint manipulation, such as that provided through chiropractic and classic osteopathic techniques, may relieve pain by mobilizing restricted joints and stimulating reflexive muscle relaxation through triggering of joint receptors (Maitland & Brewerton, 1986; Wells, 1994).

Orthotics: Orthotic devices may offer pain relief in a variety of situations and may help to improve function (Kottke, Stillwell & Lehmann, 1982). They may reduce movement or provide support for painful body parts; for example, wrists splints may be helpful in reducing movement of the painful joint or in decreasing irritation of an inflamed median nerve; or a back brace may be used to reduce pain associated with acute compression fractures. Orthotic devices may correct biomechanics or alter weight-bearing in a way that relieves pain. For example, an appropriately selected shoelift may alter the patient's gait sufficiently to improve hip or back pain or the use of a cane may redistribute weight-bearing to relieve knee pain. Finally, pillows or other devices may be positioned to permit body parts to rest in a pain-free position; common examples are the use of a cervical pillow to support the neck in extension during sleep and an adductor pillow to reduce hip stress in a side-lying position.

Pleasure: Pleasure may serve as an effective antidote to pain by providing a sensory alternative that acts as a distraction to pain. It also may improve the quality of a life that is limited by pain. Many individuals with chronic pain have abandoned activities that they previously found pleasurable, while individuals with addictive disorders may have perceived their drug use to be their only source of pleasure. Thus, pleasurable sensory experiences may need to be prescribed in much the same manner as other treatments. Massage, a whirlpool, music, a fine meal, and other activities all may be helpful, depending on individual preferences.

TABLE 6. Psychological Interventions for Pain

- Deep relaxation
- Biofeedback (EMG, GSR, plethysmography and others)
- Cognitive-behavioral therapy
- Guided imagery
- Treatment of associated mood disorder
- Family/relationship therapy
- Functional rehabilitation.

Sexual activity often is limited in individuals with chronic pain for a number of reasons: usual body positions may exacerbate pain; loss of libido may result from pain-associated depression; and sexual function may be impaired by the distraction of pain. Problem-solving with such patients to facilitate successful reintroduction of a satisfying and pleasurable sex life may improve the overall quality of their lives.

Psychological Treatment Approaches. Psychological interventions can affect pain and the experience of pain in a variety of ways. They may directly reduce pain, they may improve the distress associated with pain (such as anxiety, depression or sleep disturbance), and they may help the individual experience a high quality of life despite the presence of some level of continued pain (Table 6). In the individual who has pain and a concurrent addictive disorder, psychological interventions directed at treatment of the addiction can improve many variables, which may increase or reinforce pain as discussed above.

Neurophysiological interventions such as relaxation training and biofeedback may directly reduce nociception (Chapman, 1983; DeGood, 1993). Elicitation of the relaxation response through techniques such as conscious breathing, meditation or repetitive vocalizing can provide both muscle relaxation and reduction of autonomic arousal, which in turn may reduce pain. Specific muscle relaxation techniques, such as progressive muscle relaxation and EMG biofeedback, may reduce muscle tone and spasm. Measures directed at reduction of sympathetic tone have been successfully used to abort migraine headaches and to improve circulation, reducing pain in complex regional pain syndrome or vasospastic disorders. Such psychophysiologic interventions thus function as direct pain treatment approaches, rather than as adjunctive techniques to improve coping or function.

Behavior modification also can directly reduce pain and improve level of function (Fordyce, 1978; Pilowski, 1975; Turk & Meichenbaum, 1984). Techniques include the identification of physical and psychological stressors that increase pain. Pacing and selection of activities can be introduced in a manner that reduces stimulation of pain, reduces rewards that reinforce the experience of pain, and implements behavioral responses to increased pain that reduce pain and pain-provoked distresses.

Depression and anxiety have been shown to increase both pain and functional disability related to pain (Haythornthwaite, Seiber & Kerns, 1991; Linton & Gotesam, 1985). Therefore, identification of these mood disturbances, and treatment when they are present, are important components of pain treatment and rehabilitation. In the context of pain treatment, depression often is treated pharmacologically in association with cognitive behavioral therapy or, if indicated, psychotherapy. Anxiety usually is addressed through cognitive behavioral therapy. Anxiolytic medications are only occasionally appropriate. In the patient with concurrent addictive disorder, benzodiazepines generally should be avoided because of their potential for abuse and dependence, unless there are specific indications. If they are used, long-acting benzodiazepines such as clonazepam are the drugs of choice.

An individual's ability to cope effectively with pain may be impaired by certain negative thought patterns (Gil, Williams et al., 1992). Cognitive restructuring, in which more adaptive thinking is introduced, may modulate the impact which pain has on the individual's life (Turk & Meichenbaum, 1984).

Psychological evaluation may help to identify painful psychological experiences or active issues that may be contributing to the experience of pain. Clinicians have come to appreciate the relatively high frequency of previous physical, sexual and/or emotional trauma and of post-traumatic stress disorder (PTSD) among individuals with chronic pain (Zayfert, Seville et al., 1997), as well as among individuals with addictive disorders (Breslau, Davis et al., 1997; Kosten & Krystal, 1988). Attention to these problems might be expected to improve pain treatment outcomes, although this has not been proven. Careful evaluation of the effect of pain on valued relationships, with the institution of therapeutic interventions to improve dysfunctional relationships, may improve pain and associated disability.

Invasive Pain Treatments. Invasive procedures often have a role in pain treatment. What have recently been termed "interventionalist" treatments fall generally into four groups: tissue injections, nerve blocks, intraspinal infusions/injections, and implanted stimulators (Table 3). Tissue injections may be performed by physicians of many disciplines, while nerve blocks and intraspinal infusions or injections generally are performed by anesthesiologists. Nerve stimulators usually are implanted by anesthesiology pain specialists and surgeons or neurosurgeons, depending on the site of implantation.

Tissue injections include intramuscular trigger-point injections and injection of inflamed bursae or tendons, as well as intra-articular injections. Trigger-point injections with local anesthetics may be helpful in resolving or improving focal muscle spasms or trigger-point pain that has not responded to first-line interventions such as physical therapy or relaxation training (Travell & Simons, 1983). Injections of botulinum toxin recently have been used, with mixed success, to provide more prolonged relief when focal spasm or pain recurs following serial local anesthetic injections. The injection of steroid into trigger points has not generally been found helpful, except when inflammation is present. The chief indication for injection of bursae, tendons or joints is the diagnosis of inflammatory bursitis, tendonitis or arthritis, in which case the use of steroids and local anesthetics in combination may be appropriate. Occasionally, even in the absence of inflammation, infiltration of chronically painful tissues with local anesthetic alone may reduce pain on a protracted basis, presumably by reducing afferent input to wound-up nociceptive pathways and reducing spontaneous neuropathic activity in these pathways.

What are commonly referred to as "nerve blocks" include peripheral nerve blocks, blocks of sympathetic ganglia (such as the stellate, lumbar or celiac ganglia), and plexus infusions. These may be helpful in a variety of contexts, both diagnostic and therapeutic (Cousins & Bridenbaugh, 1990; Moore, 1981; Raj, 1992). Peripheral nerve block or neuroma infiltration may reduce or resolve pain in the presence of a peripheral neuritis or neuroma by temporarily blocking nociceptive input and thus damping down mechanisms of hyperalgesia in nerve conduction pathways. Peripheral nerve blocks also provide effective analgesia for rib fractures and other acute pain, falling in the defined distribution of specific peripheral nerves. Infusions into the brachial plexus or lumbar plexus, which provide analgesia through the peripheral distribution of the plexi, occasionally are used for difficult-to-control upper or lower extremity pain of any origin.

Block of sympathetic ganglia, such as the lumbar or stellate ganglion, often is helpful when upper or lower extremity pain is in part mediated by reflex sympathetic mechanisms, as in complex regional pain syndrome (formerly called reflex sympathetic dystrophy) or when pain is mediated through ischemia or vasospasm. Block of the sympathetic ganglia that transmit visceral sensation, such as the celiac plexus or hypogastric plexus, may be helpful in visceral pain syndromes, such as those that involve the pancreas or lower pelvic viscera.

Carefully selected neurolytic block of peripheral nerves, which provide relief for weeks to months, may be helpful in some cancer pain presentations in which the pain is limited to the distribution of a single nerve. Neurolytic celiac plexus block often is successful in controlling pain related to pancreatic cancer. Hypogastric plexus block has been used to control pain related to invasive pelvic cancer. The use of neurolytic blocks in chronic non-cancer related pain is limited because of the potential for the development of painful regeneration neuritis or neuromas.

Spinal Infusions: Spinal infusions of local anesthetics or opioids may be helpful in a variety of pain treatment contexts. They may be used to provide continuous analgesia for post-operative, post-traumatic or acute medical pain involving the trunk, abdomen or lower extremities. Long-term percutaneous epidural infusions sometimes are used to assist in cancer-related pain when high-dose oral opioids are not well tolerated because of side effects. Implanted pumps, which infuse very low-dose opioids into the cerebral spinal fluid, have proved both clinically effective (Paice, Winkelmuller et al., 1997) and cost effective (Hassenbusch, Paice et al., 1997) in the long-term treatment of some types of cancer and severe non-cancer related pain. Serial epidural injections of local anesthetics and steroids may relieve back and radicular pain associated with disc inflammation or other etiology (Koes, Scholten et al., 1995).

Interventionalist procedures generally can be used safely in individuals with addictive disease. Intraspinal opioids act locally in the spinal cord to provide analgesia. Depending on the drug used, the dose and whether the drug is given epidurally or intrathecally (into the CSF at much lower doses), some drug may find its way into the CSF or systemic circulation. High circulating levels of opioid are much less likely with intrathecal administration because of the very low dose. For post-operative or post-traumatic pain control in a recovering opioid addict, the use of epidural local anesthetic alone, if effective, may be preferred to avoid concerns regarding opioid exposure. In managing chronic pain in recovering opioid addicts, the long-term use of intraspinal opioids by continuous infusion is controversial and should be attempted only with careful consideration and in close cooperation with pain and addiction treatment providers. It generally is agreed that long-term epidural infusion of opioids in an active opioid addict carries unacceptable risks because of the potential for systemic self-injection and/or diversion of the drug (Portenoy & Savage, 1997).

Implanted Stimulators: Spinal cord stimulation is a recently developed and effective means of providing pain control for some types of severe and intractable pain (Marchand, 1993; North, 1993). In this therapy, one or more electrodes are implanted in the epidural space at a spinal level above the level of generation of pain, and a programmable stimulating unit is implanted subcutaneously, usually over the abdominal wall. The efficacy of such stimulators has been most clearly documented for peripheral unilateral neuropathic pain and for vascular ischemic pain, but they also have proved helpful in a variety of other neuropathic pain syndromes. The mechanism of action is not certain. Despite the invasive nature of this procedure, complication rates are low. Implantation is relatively expensive, but must be weighed against the long-term costs of ineffectively treated pain and of other ongoing interventions. Implanted peripheral nerve stimulation, in which an electrode is placed in proximity to a peripheral nerve, sometimes provide analgesia in local neuropathic pain when the pain is primarily in the distribution of a specific nerve.

Invasive procedures are, for the most part, passive pain treatments. In individuals with chronic pain, they are used in conjunction with more active self-management approaches. This is particularly important in individuals with addictive disorders, who may be at risk for becoming dependent on this type of passive relief ("block junkies"), in much the same way they are at risk for becoming dependent on drugs.

Non-Opioid Medications. In treating pain, medications may be used to directly reduce pain or may

TABLE 7. Medications Commonly Used in the Treatment of Pain

- Non-steroidal anti-inflammatory drugs (NSAIDs)
- Tricyclics (antidepressants and sedatives)
- Anticonvulsants
- Muscle relaxants (short-term)
- Topical preparations:
  - Capsaicin
  - Anesthetics
  - Aromatics
- Opioids
- Other: systemic lidocaine, mexilitene, clonidine.

be used to manage distressing sequelae and perpetuating factors, such as sleep disturbance, anxiety or depression (Table 7).

When non-medication treatment approaches are easily available and likely to be effective in treating pain in an individual with addictive disease, these generally are preferred to medication. Addicts tend to view drugs as solutions to a variety of subjective distresses; the use of medications to treat pain and other symptoms tends to reinforce this view.

Although addicts are most likely to misuse medications that have the capacity to produce physical dependence or those that produce mood-altering effects, clinicians should be aware that many addicts have a propensity to misuse any medication. They often believe that "If a little is good, more must be better." Therefore, it is important to be explicit in providing instructions regarding medication use. Written instructions to the patient, with a copy included in the medical record, are recommended. Potential short-term and long-term toxic side effects should be carefully explained to the patient. The clinician also should determine in advance how lost or destroyed medications or prescriptions will be dealt with, and such actions should be documented.

Non-Steroidal Anti-Inflammatory Drugs: Analgesics that act through prostaglandin inhibition, such as the non-steroidal anti-inflammatory drugs, have mild analgesic effects with low-dose intermittent use and have additional anti-inflammatory effects with higher dose, continuous use. NSAIDs have a ceiling effect in terms of analgesic efficacy. They generally have no mood-altering effects and are appropriate in the management of pain in individuals with addictive disease. Patterns of use should be reviewed periodically. Not infrequently, addicts report taking excessive amounts of NSAIDs. The existence of a ceiling of analgesic efficacy, as well as the potential for toxicity (renal, hepatic and gastrointestinal), should be clearly explained. If an inflammatory process such as degenerative arthritis is present, continuous use is appropriate for management of inflammation. Medications should be discontinued periodically so that pain levels can be reassessed. In treating pain of non-inflammatory origin, the most appropriate use of these medications is on an intermittent basis for periodic exacerbations.

The non-steroidal anti-inflammatory, ketorolac, when given in parenteral form, has more potent analgesic efficacy than most other NSAIDs and may be a good choice for patients who wish to avoid opioids in the acute pain setting. Thirty milligrams of parenteral ketorolac is roughly equivalent to 6 to 10 mg of parenteral morphine. More selective inhibitors of prostaglandin synthesis—the cyclo-oxygenase 2 (OX2) inhibitors—which are undergoing clinical trials, may provide greater analgesic efficacy with less toxicity than traditional NSAIDs.

Tricyclics: Centrally-acting medications commonly used in the treatment of pain include tricyclics and anticonvulsants. Tricyclic antidepressant medications have been documented to have analgesic effects independent of their effect on pain-associated depression (Tollison, 1990). This may be due to facilitation of descending pain inhibitory systems, which are mediated by alterations in central serotonin and/or norepinephrine availability. Similar analgesic efficacy has not been demonstrated with selective serotonergic reuptake inhibitors or with other antidepressants. Tricyclic antidepressants may have a special effectiveness in neurogenic pain (Max, 1995).

Sedative tricyclics such as doxepine, nortriptylene and amitriptyline often are effective, not only in reducing pain, but in resolving pain related sleep disturbances. Effective doses for treatment of pain and associated sleep problems are usually in the 25 to 75 mg range for doxepine and amitriptyline though titration to antidepressant blood levels may be appropriate if analgesia is not obtained at lower doses. Tricyclics have low abuse potential. Although in high, sustained doses they are used to treat depression, in the lower doses usually used to treat pain they do not generally have direct mood altering effects. Some individuals report an unpleasant "hangover" effect in the morning. This may be disturbing to some recovering alcoholics and may limit the usefulness of these drugs in such individuals. Tricyclics do produce some physiological adaptation and should be tapered if used for a long period of time.

Anticonvulsants such as gabapentin, carbamazepine, dilantin and valproic acid may be helpful in treating neuropathic pain, including pain related to neuralgias, neuromas, neuropathies, and phantom or other deafferentation pain syndromes. Their efficacy has been documented in the treatment of post-herpetic neuralgia and trigeminal neuralgia, and they may be useful in other types of neuropathic pain as well (Swerdlow, 1981; Tobias, 1992). They have low abuse potential and may be used as needed in individuals with addictive disease.

Since its introduction four years ago, gabapentin has become a popular first-line choice for anticonvulsant pain treatment because of its relatively low toxicity and side effect profile and the ability to titrate it rapidly to high doses. Some experience suggests that carbamazepine remains the drug of choice for lancinating neuropathic pain. Systemic lidocaine administration and the use of oral mexilitene (both of which are sodium channel blocking agents) also are clinically useful in some neuropathic pain syndromes (Tanelian & Victory, 1995).

Topical Medications: Capsaicin, a derivative of the oil of red pepper, is available as a topical agent for the treatment of post-herpetic neuralgia and arthritis. Its putative mechanism of action is through depletion of the nociceptive neurotransmitter, substance P, at neuronal synapses. Application must be made three to four times a day for up to four weeks before pain relief is noted. Some patients are disturbed by the mild to moderate local burning sensation on application and may discontinue its use.

Topical local anesthetic mixtures are helpful in reducing discomfort associated with procedures such as IV insertion, but must be applied somewhat in advance of the anticipated procedure, with application of an occlusive dressing.

Some patients find topical aromatic preparations, including those containing eucalyptus, menthol or methyl salicylate, helpful in reducing local areas of somatic pain.

Opioid Medications. Opioids as a class are the most potent clinically available analgesic agents. They have wide efficacy and utility in the treatment of acute pain and cancer-related pain and are helpful as a component in the management of chronic pain of non-cancer origin. They may be used effectively and safely in individuals with addictive disorders. However, because opioids have inherent reinforcing properties, cause physical dependence and may produce pleasurable intoxication or euphoria in some individuals, they are potential objects of addiction. To facilitate appropriate decision-making regarding the use of opioids for the treatment of pain, it is helpful first to address a number of clinical and pharmacologic issues.

Concerns raised by clinicians regarding use of opioids for the treatment of pain often include the potential for development of physical dependence, tolerance, and other side effects that may complicate use of these drugs. In using opioids for the treatment of acute and cancer pain, these issues rarely are of concern, but a thorough understanding of the issues may enhance their use in these contexts. In considering the use of opioids for the long-term management of chronic, non-cancer related pain, however, consideration of these issues, as well as the potential effects of opioids on pain modulation and perception, is of some importance in determining relative risks and benefits. Each of these issues will be considered separately here.

Physical Dependence: Physical dependence on an opioid reflects a physiological state in which abrupt cessation of the drug, administration of an opioid antagonist, or precipitous lowering of drug dose will result in a withdrawal syndrome. Such dependence is an expected occurrence in all patients (both those with and without addictive disease) after two to 10 days of continuous administration of an opioid (Portenoy, 1990a). In the acute pain setting, such dependence generally is not clinically significant, because individuals tend to taper opioids naturally due to gradual reduction in pain as the acute problem (such as post-surgical pain, post-traumatic pain or medical illness) resolves. However, if pain medications are abruptly stopped or precipitously reduced, a withdrawal syndrome may follow. The character and intensity of the withdrawal varies, depending on the dose and duration of opioid administration and a variety of host factors, including previous experience with withdrawal, prior long-term administration of opioids, and the patient's expectations regarding withdrawal.

Common symptoms of opioid withdrawal include autonomic signs and symptoms, such as diarrhea, piloerection, sweating, mydriasis and mild increases in blood pressure and pulse, as well as signs of central nervous system arousal such as irritability, anxiety and sleeplessness. Craving for the medication is expected in the course of withdrawal, and pain—most often experienced as abdominal cramping, deep bone pain or diffuse muscle aching—is common (Jaffe, 1992). Patients with chronic pain may experience an intensified level of their usual pain syndrome during withdrawal. In patients who are physically dependent on opioids, the use of short-acting opioid medications may result in intermittent withdrawal between doses of medication, which may in turn cause an increase in perceived pain (Brodner

& Taub, 1978; Jaffe & Martin, 1980). This may be avoided by using long-acting or continuous medications.

Simple physical dependence occurs in any patient when opioids are administered for an extended period of time. The term "addiction" should not be used to describe such physical dependence, as it is an inaccurate description of the condition of physical dependence and it does a disservice both to persons with addictive disorders who become physically dependent on medications despite continuing in a state of recovery, as well as to individuals without addictive disorders who become physically dependent on medications without developing the true characteristics of addiction.

Tolerance: Tolerance is indicated by the need for increasing doses of a medication to achieve the initial effects of the drug (Foley, 1991). Tolerance may occur both to a drug's analgesic effects and to its unwanted side effects, such as respiratory depression, sedation or nausea.

Many characteristics of opioid tolerance remain poorly understood. Animal studies suggest that tolerance to the analgesic effects of medications occurs in some contexts but not in others (Collins & Cesselin, 1991). Human studies of the management of acute pain also document the development of progressive tolerance to the analgesic effects of opioids when they are administered on a continuous basis over a period of several days (Hill, Chapman et al., 1990; Hill, Coda et al., 1992). Over a period of weeks to months, however, some studies suggest that the continuing development of progressive tolerance to the analgesic effects of opioids may not occur. Specifically, several studies looking at the opioid management of cancer pain suggest that opioid dose requirements increase only during progression of the underlying disease process and that, with stable disease or treatment of painful tissue pathology, the need for medication remains the same or actually decreases (Foley, 1991; Twycross, 1974).

A number of studies have investigated the development of tolerance to specific opioids, with the goal of determining whether opioids of varying efficacy have different profiles with regard to the development of tolerance, but findings differ radically and no consistent relationship between intrinsic efficacy and tolerance has been demonstrated (Hill, Coda et al., 1992; Kissin, Brown & Bailey, 1991; Yaksh, 1992).

Most investigators agree that absolute tolerance to the analgesic effects of opioids does not occur (Portenoy, 1990b). That is, opioids may be used over a prolonged period of time in the face of increasing dose requirements, yet continue to provide adequate relief of pain. In general, tolerance to the side effects of morphine develops more rapidly than does tolerance to the drug's analgesic effects. Therefore, opioids may be used safely and effectively at even massive doses (such as several thousand mg of IV morphine per hour) in individuals who have gradually increased their exposure to analgesics over a prolonged period of time, with no limiting side effects. Nonetheless, all significant increases in dose should be accompanied by careful monitoring for over-sedation and respiratory depression.

Addiction: In the context of pain treatment with opioids, addiction must be defined through the observation of a constellation of maladaptive behaviors, rather than by observation of pharmacologic phenomena such as dependence, tolerance, dose escalation, etc., since these are often expected in the course of pain treatment. Addiction in the context of opioid therapy of pain is characterized by the presence of a combination of observations suggesting adverse consequences due to use of the drugs, loss of control over drug use, and preoccupation with obtaining opioids despite the presence of adequate analgesia (Sees & Clark, 1993) (Table 2). Physical dependence on opioids and the development of tolerance to their effects do not, of themselves, constitute addiction (Portenoy, 1990b; Savage, 1993; Sees & Clark, 1993). When the criteria for substance use disorder of the *Diagnostic and Statistical Manual of Mental Disorders, 4th Edition* (*DSM-IV*; American Psychiatric Association, 1994) are used to assess for addiction in the presence of pain, only the criteria that refer to function may be used as indicative of addiction (Sees & Clark, 1993), because other criteria refer only to the expected, non-pathological sequelae of chronic opioid use.

Adverse consequences suggestive of addiction may include persistent oversedation or euphoria, deteriorating level of function despite relief of pain, or increase in pain-associated distresses such as anxiety, sleep disturbance or depressive symptoms. Loss of control over use might be reflected in prescriptions used before the expected renewal date, patients who obtain multiple prescriptions or who obtain opioids from illicit sources. Preoccupation with opioid use may be reflected in noncompliance with non-opioid components of pain treatment, inability to recognize non-nociceptive components of pain, and the perception that no interventions other than opioids have any effect on pain (Savage, 1993; Sees & Clark, 1993; Wesson, Ling & Smith, 1993). It is important to recognize that such behaviors may occur on an occasional basis for a variety of reasons in the context of successful opioid therapy for pain; rather, it is a pattern of persistent occurrences that should prompt concern and further assessment.

The risk of the development of addiction to opioids in the course of opioid therapy of pain is thought to be very low, especially for individuals with no past history of addiction. Early studies of street addicts led to a misperception that the iatrogenic creation of addiction through medical use of opioids was a frequent occurrence (Kolb, 1925; Rayport, 1954). In contrast, subsequent studies of never-addicted medical patients suggested that the development of addiction in the course of long-term opioid therapy of pain is an essentially negligible risk (Perry & Heindrich, 1982; Porter & Jick, 1980). The reality likely is somewhere in between. Addiction has a multifactorial etiology, including variables that are biogenetic, psychological, sociocultural, and related to drug exposure. The lifetime prevalence of addictive disease is estimated at 3% to 16% of the general population (Regier, Meyers & Kramer, 1984). It is reasonable to expect that this portion of the population may be at some level of risk for the development of addiction when opioids are used for pain, although it has been theorized that the presence of pain may reduce this risk by attenuating the euphorigenic effect of opioids. Nevertheless, it is appropriate to use special care in implementing opioid therapy in patients who have personal or family histories of alcoholism or other addictions, but opioids never should be withheld out of fear of addiction when they are indicated for the relief of pain.

When addiction is identified in the course of opioid therapy of pain, it is important to address this aggressively, so that the pain is effectively controlled and to prevent the debilitating sequelae of addiction. Institution of appropriate psychological and spiritual recovery activities, tightening the structure of opioid prescribing in order to help the individual gain control over the medications, and involving the patient's social support system in treatment are important first steps.

Pseudoaddiction: The term "pseudoaddiction" recently has emerged in the pain literature to describe the inaccurate interpretation of certain behaviors in patients who have severe pain that is undermedicated or whose pain otherwise has not been effectively treated. Such patients may appear to be preoccupied with obtaining opioids, but their preoccupation reflects a need for pain control rather than an addictive drive. Pseudoaddictive behavior can be distinguished from addiction by the fact that, when adequate analgesia is achieved, the patient who is seeking pain relief demonstrates improved function in daily living, uses the medications as prescribed, and does not use drugs in a manner that persistently causes sedation or euphoria. It is important to recognize that such behaviors may occur on occasion even in the successful opioid therapy of pain; instead, it is a pattern of persistent occurrences that should prompt concern and further assessment.

Opioid Side Effects: Opioid side effects can be classified in three groups: respiratory depression, other physical side effects, and central nervous system side effects that may affect function.

Opioid-induced respiratory depression results from depression of brain stem respiratory responses to carbon dioxide. Although CO_2 response decreases in a dose-dependent manner with the administration of mu opioids, clinically significant respiratory depression does not usually occur in the course of treatment of healthy patients with standard analgesic doses of opioids. Respiratory depression may be significant, however, when high-dose opioids are used for acute pain in opioid-naive patients, particularly those who are elderly or debilitated. In such patients, respiratory monitoring is required. Respiratory depression rarely is a clinical problem in chronic opioid administration because tolerance to the respiratory depressant effects of opioids tends to occur more rapidly than tolerance to their analgesic effects. Patients should be closely observed, however, when abrupt doses are abruptly increased.

Common physical side effects of opioid use include constipation, nausea, urinary retention and pruritus. Such side effects sometimes can be attenuated or avoided by a trial of an alternative opioid. Side effects are minimized when opioids are prescribed in a manner that reduces the peak blood levels required to sustain analgesia, because the higher blood levels may be associated with increased side effects. To achieve stable analgesic blood levels, scheduled doses of long-acting or sustained-release opioids may be used when oral preparations are used. Continuous infusions or patient controlled analgesia (PCA) achieve the same goal when parenteral administration is required. Persistent physical side effects may be managed through pharmacological treatments, such as anti-emetics for nausea or antihistamines for pruritus. It should be remembered that these physical discomforts (with the frequent exception of constipation) usually are transient and may improve or resolve with continued use of opioids in a stable dose.

Constipation is a persistent side effect of opioid use that may not resolve without treatment. The constipating effects of opioids are thought to occur through direct action on opioid receptors in the gut wall. This causes a decrease in intestinal motility and results in dehydration of stool. It generally is advisable, therefore, to give both a stool softener and a bowel stimulant to effectively manage constipation. When long-term and/or high dose use of opioids is anticipated, introduction of such treatment on a preemptive basis is recommended.

Central nervous system side effects of opioids include sedation, cognitive dysfunction and affective changes. Sedation and mild cognitive changes are common when opioids are initially introduced or when dose is increased, but they usually resolve once a stable therapeutic dose of opioid is achieved and sustained for a period of time (Zachny, 1995). They may occasionally persist, however, when high doses of opioids are required, particularly with long-acting medications such as methadone or in elderly or frail patients. Like many other side effects, sedation and cognitive dysfunction may be managed or avoided by changing medications, by continuous administration of the minimum dose necessary to achieve analgesia, or by administration of a treatment medication. When intractable opioid-induced sedation occurs in cancer pain patients or patients with severe intractable non-cancer related pain, stimulants such as methylphenidate and dextroamphetamine may be helpful. The use of stimulant medications, which are known to be abused by some individuals, requires the same caution in patients with addictive disorder as that required by the use of opioids.

Pentazocine and other agonist/antagonists may cause dysphoria when administered on a chronic basis, probably through stimulation of sigma opioid receptors. If depression, anxiety, dysphoria or other distressing affective symptoms occur in the course of analgesic therapy, the opioids must be considered as a possible contributing factor.

Effects of Opioids on Pain Modulation and Perception: Concerns have been raised that long-term opioid exposure may actually increase pain perception in some individuals. Clinical studies and observations suggest that some individuals with pain who use opioids on a long-term basis experience improvement in pain following simple withdrawal of opioids without the institution of other major pain interventions (Brodner & Taub, 1978; Rapaport, 1988; Schofferman, 1993). These studies include observations of patients with pain and opioid dependence in both pain treatment and addiction treatment settings.

Although specific questions regarding pain sensitivity in the presence of chronic opioid administration have not been widely addressed in clinical or experimental studies, numerous studies on opioid receptor physiology in the presence of opioids suggest that changes in structure and function of receptors do occur as a result of chronic opioid exposure. Because opioid receptors are important components of endogenous pain modulatory systems, it is reasonable to raise the possibility that changes in nociceptive processing may occur as a result of chronic opioid administration, which in turn may alter pain sensitivity in individuals who are given opioids on a chronic basis. A recent study demonstrated a significantly decreased threshold for cold pressor-induced pain in methadone maintenance patients (on their usual dose of methadone), as compared to several control groups of formerly methadone-dependent individuals and persons who had no history of dependence on any drug (Compton, 1996).

The development of hyperalgesia in some patients in the presence of high-dose systemic morphine administration has been well documented (Sjogren, Jensen & Jensen, 1994). It is unclear whether these findings have any general clinical relevance for patients who use high-dose opioids on a long-term basis.

As more patients with chronic pain of non-cancer origin and normal life expectancy are prescribed opioids for long-term management of pain, controlled studies of the effects of chronic opioids on pain modulation are important to assure that such treatment does not in fact unfavorably alter pain sensitivity, ultimately increasing the experience of pain.

Pain Reinforcement: The experience of chronic pain, regardless of its nociceptive basis, may be reinforced by a variety of cognitive, behavioral, psychological and other factors (Ahles, Blanchard & Ruckdeschel, 1983; Fordyce, 1978; Gamsa, 1994; Turk & Meichenbaum, 1984). Opioids are reinforcing substances that are freely self-administered by most species of animals under experimental conditions (Johanson & Schuster, 1981). When opioid use is made contingent on the experience of pain, opioids may act as a reinforcer to the presence of pain or to the perception of pain at a sufficiently high level to justify the use of the opioid. Primary opioid reinforcement is thought to occur through the production of euphoria, tranquillity and a sense of well-being, mediated through stimulation of a dopaminergic mechanism in the nucleus accumbens (Gardner, 1992; Jaffe, 1980; Koob & Bloom, 1988).

Secondary reinforcement may occur once a subject is physically dependent through avoidance of the aversive stimulus of withdrawal. Such reinforcement of pain cannot be entirely avoided, but may be reduced by avoiding the use of opioids paired directly with the experience of increased pain. Instead of taking opioids in response to pain graded at a certain level of severity, the patient uses opioids in a time- or activity-contingent manner, taking the medication at a scheduled time or in association with a valued activity. The scheduled time is selected to coordinate with expected increases in pain or on a regular basis if continuous relief is the goal. Pairing the use of medication with a valued activity reinforces increase in activity.

Non-Pain Symptom Management: Some patients seek opioid therapy for relief of symptoms other than pain, including depression, anxiety, and sleep disturbances. These symptoms may be mislabeled as pain by the patient. A detailed evaluation of the patient's pain and related distresses often will identify such misuse of medications. More specific treatments usually are indicated.

Abuse and Diversion: Opioids have euphorigenic effects in many individuals, although other patients report dysphoria, rather than euphoria, with opioid use. Some research suggests that the presence of pain may inhibit the experience of euphoria. Nevertheless, physicians who prescribe opioids must be aware that there is a potential for abuse of these medications.

Long-acting oral medications such as methadone, Levo-Dromoran™ and sustained-release morphine tend to have a slower onset of action than short-acting medications such as hydromorphone and oxycodone. The "rush" or "high" often experienced with the more rapid onset medications is not prominent, so the longer acting opioids are less likely to be abused.

Although there often are legitimate pain-related reasons that patients may request short-acting medications, including rapid onset of relief, an adamant preference for short-acting drugs (particularly in the long-term treatment setting), may suggest opioid abuse use or diversion.

Most physicians who prescribe opioids for chronic pain occasionally are duped by individuals who seek to abuse, sell or trade the drugs. Physicians have a responsibility to do a thorough assessment of the patient to identify risk factors for such behavior, to apply reasonable structure to prescribing in order to avoid such behavior where possible, and to assess patients intermittently to develop a reasonable certainty that patients are using their medications as prescribed. Physicians should not withhold medications from patients who appear to require opioid therapy for pain control because of overconcern with diversion. Physicians cannot be held responsible for the behavior of skilled and manipulative patients who willfully deceive them. It is the legitimate role of the U.S. Drug Enforcement Administration and other regulatory bodies to identify such patients. Negative sanction of physicians who practice pain treatment in good faith and with reasonable skill is potentially harmful to the optimal medical treatment of all patients with pain (ASAM, 1997).

Opioid Maintenance Therapy of Addiction: Opioid therapy of addiction is a well-recognized and widely accepted therapy. There are major limitations, however, in the availability and structure of services provided by methadone clinics. Addicts who are seeking opioid therapy of addiction occasionally may present to physicians who prescribe opioid therapy on a long-term basis for the treatment of pain. A weekly or monthly prescription for long-acting opioids, which physicians may legally prescribe for pain, may meet the addict's therapeutic need for maintenance therapy and may in fact be medically appropriate. However, such treatment cannot be legally provided by prescription in the U.S. at this time. On the other hand, if an opioid-dependent individual has a concurrent pain problem for which opioid prescription is appropriate, opioids may be prescribed on a long-term basis for pain management (Clark, 1993).

Clinical Issues: The goal of opioid therapy of pain is to achieve effective pain control while minimizing unwanted side effects. Once it is established that an individual's pain responds to opioids and that opioids are appropriate for use, a number of variables must be considered in planning optimal treatment. These include selection of specific drug(s), identification of appropriate routes of administration and effective dose titration. In addition, it is helpful to understand how to smoothly change drugs or withdraw medications when indicated. These issues will be considered individually.

Choice of Opioid Drug: Opioids produce their pharmacologic effects (both analgesic and side effects) through stimulation of opioid receptors. Stimulation of the mu, kappa and delta receptors is associated with analgesia and with some side effects, while stimulation of the sigma receptors may be responsible for the dysphoric effects of some opioids. Most of the commonly used opioid analgesics—such as morphine, oxycodone, hydromorphone, meperidine, fentanyl and methadone—have predominantly mu receptor activity. Pure mu agonists have no ceiling analgesic effect and may be titrated as needed to achieve analgesia. Tolerance to side effects generally occurs more rapidly than tolerance to analgesia, although monitoring for respiratory depression is important in opioid-naive individuals as doses are increased.

Most mu agonists are interchangeable if attention is paid to relative dosing potencies and onset and duration of action (Table 1). However, some clinically relevant differences between mu agonists are apparent. Meperidine's usefulness is limited in pain treatment, because with high dose use, a neurotoxic metabolite, normeperidine, may accumulate, causing irritability, tremors, and seizures. This is especially relevant in opioid-dependent individuals, who may have significant tolerance and correspondingly high dose requirements. Buprenorphine is a mu agonist opioid with relatively low intrinsic analgesic efficacy and often is referred to as a partial agonist. Tramadol, also classified as a partial mu agonist, appears to provide analgesia through a second mechanism: inhibition of synaptic serotonin and norepinephrine reuptake. Both drugs have ceiling effects in terms of their ability to provide analgesia and may have lesser abuse potential than classic mu agonists, although both drugs have been abused by some individuals. Propoxyphene, a weak mu agonist, has low analgesic efficacy, some abuse potential, and little if any advantage over non-opioid analgesics. Therefore, there are few indications for its use.

Abrupt substitution of equianalgesic doses of other mu agonists to replace methadone has been observed to result in withdrawal phenomena in some patients despite pain control, suggesting incomplete receptor cross-reactivity. Therefore, it may be wise to taper methadone when substituting other opioids.

A second group of opioids, the agonist/antagonist opioids—including drugs such as pentazocine, nalbuphine and butorphanol—have predominantly kappa agonist effects, while antagonizing the mu receptor. Agonist/antagonist drugs are widely regarded as having less potential for abuse and addiction than the pure opioid agonists, although addiction to these medications has been observed. Their clinical usefulness as analgesics is limited by a number of factors: the agonist/antagonist drugs have reduced analgesic efficacy compared to pure mu agonists and exhibit a ceiling effect in terms of analgesia. Their use sometimes is associated with dysphoric reactions. Because of their antagonist activity, they may reverse analgesia and precipitate withdrawal in individuals who are physically dependent on mu opioids. Consequently, no clear advantages of agonist/antagonist drugs have been demonstrated in the treatment of pain in persons with addictive disorders.

Changing from One Opioid to Another: In order to maintain the analgesic effect when switching patients from one opioid to another, it is clinically useful to calculate the equianalgesic dose of the new medication. Parenteral morphine generally is used as the standard reference. Thus, opioid equivalence is obtained by adding the total dose of each type of opioid used in the previous 24-hour period, then (using an opioid equivalence table), converting each drug to the equivalent 24-hour dose of parenteral morphine. The next step is to calculate the equivalent 24-hour dose of the new drug to be used and providing one-half to two-thirds of this amount in appropriately divided doses. The initial dose of the new drug is given at one-half to two-thirds of the calculated dose because opioidspecific tolerance may occur and the new drug may have more relative effectiveness. This method avoids the confusion that arises in trying to compare drugs of differing half-lives and potencies.

For example, in the case of a patient who is using 30 mg of continuous-release oral morphine BID and 100 mg IV meperidine every four hours, the plan is to convert the patient to oral methadone for pain management. To determine the appropriate methadone dose, the physician first determines the 24-hour parenteral morphine equivalent of the morphine and meperidine: 60 mg oral continuousrelease MSO4 equals 20 mg parenteral morphine, while 600 mg IV meperidine equals 60 mg parenteral MSO4, for a 24-hour total equivalent dose of 80 mg morphine. According to the analgesic equivalence chart, 10 mg of parenteral morphine is equivalent to 20 mg of PO methadone. So the calculated equivalent dose is 160 mg methadone. The initial dose should be one-half to two-thirds, or 80 to 100 mg. For pain treatment, methadone generally is given every six to eight hours. Methadone therefore might be initiated at 20 mg q 6 h, titrated to obtain analgesic response.

Sometimes the transition is better tolerated if the patient is gradually "rolled over" from one medication to another: that is, the new medication is incrementally increased over a few days while the old medication is incrementally decreased.

Routes of Administration: Opioids may be administered orally, rectally, transmucosally, intravenously, subcutaneously, transdermally and intraspinally. The oral, enteral or transdermal routes generally are preferred when feasible because they are less invasive than many other routes and usually provide satisfactory analgesia, even when high doses are required. However, when these routes are not reasonable (as when patients are unable to take medications orally, or when rapid titration is necessary), parenteral routes may be preferred. IV access may be difficult in individuals with a history of injecting drug use; for such patients, surgical identification of venous access may be necessary or continuous subcutaneous infusions may be the best option. Intramuscular injections also are effective, but this route is increasingly discouraged because of the unnecessary pain of injection. If side effects of systemic use are not acceptable, intraspinal opioids may be indicated. Rectal preparations may be useful for patients with vomiting or who are unable to take oral medications. Sublingual administration of some preparations is clinically effective as well.

Dose Titration: For moderate pain requiring opioid therapy, an agonist-antagonist opioid, a relatively weak opioid such as tramadol or a weak opioid-acetaminophen preparation such as Tylenol® with codeine or oxycodone, often is appropriate. If the pain is constant, the drug should be given at scheduled and pharmacologically appropriate intervals to maintain analgesic blood levels. If the pain is intermittent, the drugs can be given on an as-needed basis. Care must be taken, however, in providing opioids on a PRN basis, particularly to an individual with an addictive or chronic pain disorder. Pairing the perception of pain with the administration of a reinforcing drug may both increase perceived pain and be viewed as legitimizing increased use of the drug (Fordyce, 1992). For constant pain at a moderate level of intensity, a relatively low dose of a long-acting pure mu agonist, such as methadone or a continuous release preparation of morphine or oxycodone, may be appropriate as an alternative to weaker or shorter acting drugs, especially if significant breakthrough pain occurs, or if the former drugs do not adequately control pain.

For severe pain, a pure mu agonist that can be titrated (i.e., not mixed with limiting doses of acetaminophen or other drugs and not having a ceiling of effectiveness) usually is indicated. If the pain is continuous, patient controlled analgesia, a continuous parenteral infusion, or long-acting or continuous release oral medications are appropriate. Rescue doses of PRN medications should be made available for breakthrough pain or exacerbations of baseline pain.

In determining the dose and interval of administration that will provide effective analgesia in a given patient for a given problem, several factors must be considered. First, the pharmacologic characteristics of each drug in terms of onset, relative potency and duration of analgesic action must be considered. Second, the marked variability among patients in intrinsic responsiveness to opioids must be assessed (Foley, 1991). The dose of a drug that will be effective for a given patient cannot be predicted without taking these factors into account.

Pain medications must be titrated based according to each patient's subjective responses. To accomplish this, the serial use of a pain scale before and after dosing and at regular intervals is helpful. Two commonly used pain scales are the verbal numerical pain report scale and the visual analogue scale. In the numerical pain scale, the patient is asked to choose a number from zero to 10 that best approximates the pain (with zero signifying no pain and 10 the worst pain imaginable). Using the visual analogue scale, the patient is presented a 10 cm line that can be demarcated into centimeters or left blank, with "no pain" written at one end and "worst possible pain" at the other. The patient then is asked to make a mark on the line to indicate the level of pain at a particular point in time.

Finally, it must be recognized that individuals who have been exposed to opioids on a prolonged basis, or who are actively using opioids for therapeutic or addictive purposes, are likely to be relatively tolerant to the analgesic effects of opioids and therefore may require relatively high doses at relatively short intervals to achieve analgesia. If opioids were used on a daily basis prior to the onset of acute pain, the individual's usual dose of opioid cannot be expected to provide any analgesia for acute pain; additional medications must be provided.

Patient-controlled analgesia (PCA) can be successfully used in individuals with addictive disease and often is the preferred method of providing post-operative and post-traumatic pain control. It is often used in the setting of advanced cancer pain as well. PCA allows the patient to self-administer small, incremental doses of opioid intravenously or subcutaneously, and thus provides stable analgesic blood levels of opioids, usually producing more uniform pain relief at a lower total dose of medications than bolus dosing or continuous infusions (Hill, Chapman et al., 1990). It avoids peaks (which may cause sedation or intoxication) and valleys (which may result in pain, anxiety and drug craving). As with scheduled dosing, the use of PCA eliminates the need for the patient to request opioids for pain relief and thus avoids potential staff/patient conflicts, which can arise when addicts request opioids. Thus, from certain perspectives, PCA is ideal for use with opioid-dependent patients.

On the other hand, because PCA requires self-administration, it may create ambivalence in recovering persons and in patients with active addiction problems, who have difficulty limiting their administration of opioids to levels that provide analgesia without intoxication. The latter problem may be managed to some degree through the physician's control of the incremental dose size and frequency and the total dose available over a period of time. In theory, PCA may reinforce pain through the pairing of pain with self-administration of opioids and thus may make cessation of analgesic doses of opioids difficult. In practice, however, these issues rarely arise, likely because the small incremental doses provided by PCA are relatively non-reinforcing.

When scheduled medications are required on an outpatient basis in individuals with addictive disease, it is helpful to give specific times for drug administration (as at 7:00 a.m., 3:00 p.m. and 11:00 p.m.) rather than indicating that a drug should be taken three times a day or every eight hours. This reduces the potential for confusion over dosing and possible resulting misuse. If an individual has difficulty controlling medication use but needs opioids for pain relief, it may be helpful to have a trusted other, such as spouse or friend, dispense the medications, either by the dose or at time-limited intervals such as every one or two days. Daily dispensing also may be arranged through a visiting nursing or pharmacy.

Management of Opioid Withdrawal: Discontinuation of opioid medications can be managed in a number of ways in order to avoid withdrawal phenomena. If the patient has been using an intermittently administered medication such as bolus parenteral morphine or oral oxycodone, the interval of administration can be decreased somewhat as the dose is decreased in order to avoid precipitously low blood levels of the drug between doses. Alternatively, the patient can be transferred to a continuous parenteral infusion or an equianalgesic dose of a long-acting oral medication such as methadone or MS Contin™ and then gradually tapered off. (Again, the substitute dose of new medication should be introduced at one-half to two-thirds the calculated equianalgesic dose.) If long-acting or continuous release opioids are not provided, the patient may experience intermittent symptoms of withdrawal as the opioid receptors are incrementally unsaturated between doses. Withdrawal phenomena may increase pain or craving (Brodner & Taub, 1978) and may make discontinuation of medications more problematic.

If abrupt cessation of opioids is necessary, an acute withdrawal syndrome may be attenuated to some degree through the prescription of alternative medications. Clonidine may be used to attenuate the autonomic signs and symptoms of withdrawal (Jasinski, Johnson & Kocher, 1985), a benzodiazepine or other sedative-hypnotic may be given to reduce irritability, anxiety and sleeplessness, and a peripherally-acting analgesic such as an NSAID may be used to attenuate pain. Since clonidine may have intrinsic analgesic effects for some types of pain, it may be continued if patients experience pain relief with its use. Benzodiazepines should be given at the usual anxiolytic dose and titrated to effect, then tapered following withdrawal. Nonsteroidal anti-inflammatory drugs are given at the usual analgesic doses.

Social Issues Related to Opioid Use: Medical, legal, public and regulatory opinion in the past has tended to discourage physicians from using opioids aggressively for the treatment of pain. This is gradually changing. Numerous initiatives to foster the aggressive treatment of pain have been active in the past decade. The Agency for Health Care Policy Research of the U.S. Department of Health and Human Services has released two guidelines for the management of acute pain and cancer pain, which encourage effective use of opioids where indicated (Panel, 1992, 1994). The Federation of State Medical Boards of the United States also has developed suggested guidelines for the use of controlled substances to manage pain; these guidelines affirm the rights of physicians to use opioids when appropriate to manage all types of pain, including chronic noncancer related pain. Unfortunately, exaggerated fears, misundertandings regarding the nature of addiction, and concerns about regulatory sanctions still prevail in many medical communities. However, it is to be hoped that over time, thoughtful and appropriate pain management efforts that integrate a variety of effective approaches, including the rational use of opioids where indicated, will help to define a clear, appropriate and accepted role for opioids in the treatment of pain.

CONCLUSIONS

Pain is a complex, highly individual experience that often has multiple components. The presence of addictive disease in a patient with pain must be considered in both the evaluation and treatment plan. The evaluation of pain must include careful identification of the nociceptive components of pain and of associated distresses such as sleep disturbance, anxiety, depression, alterations in usual roles and drug dependence. Successful treatment of pain in the addicted person must address each of the nociceptive components of pain, as well as distressing associated symptoms that may serve to perpetuate the pain.

Effective management of acute pain, chronic nonmalignant pain and cancer pain can be achieved in persons with addictive disease if both physician and patient recognize the presence of the addictive disease process and address the issues it raises. Clear and honest communication with the patient is important. Treatment of pain must address both its physical origins and associated distressing symptoms. The treatment plan must be specifically tailored to the type of pain and the nature and stage of the patient's addictive disease. A team approach that involves an addiction medicine specialist, a primary care physician and a pain medicine specialist often is valuable in successful treatment of pain in the patient with concurrent addictive disease.

REFERENCES

Ahles T, Blanchard E & Ruckdeschel J (1983). The multidimensional nature of cancer related pain. *Pain* 17:277–288.

American Pain Society (1989). *Principles of Analgesic Use in the Treatment of Acute Pain and Chronic Cancer Pain* (2nd ed.). Skokie, IL: American Pain Society.

American Psychiatric Association (1994). *Diagnostic and Statistical Manual of Mental Disorders, 4th Edition.* Washington, DC: American Psychiatric Press.

American Society of Addiction Medicine (1997). Public policy statements. *Definition Related to the Use of Opioids for the Treatment of Pain* and *On the Rights and Responsibilities of Physicians in the Use of Opioids for the Treatment of Pain.* Chevy Chase, MD: American Society of Addiction Medicine.

Basmajian J (1985). *Manipulation, Traction and Massage* (3rd ed.). Baltimore, MD: Williams & Wilkins.

Breslau N, Davis G, Peterson E & Schultz L (1997). Psychiatric sequelae of posttraumatic stress disorder in women. *Archives of General Psychiatry* 54:81–87.

Brodner RA & Taub A (1978). Chronic pain exacerbated by long-term narcotic use in patients with non-malignant disease: clinical syndrome and treatment. *Mt. Sinai Journal of Medicine* 45:233–237.

Brookoff D (1993). Abstract: Opioid abusers' evaluation of the abuse potential of various opioid formulations. Annual Meeting of the International Association for the Study of Pain.

Chapman S (1983). Relaxation, biofeedback and self-hypnosis. In S Brena & CS (eds.) *Management of Patients with Chronic Pain.* New York, NY: Spectrum, 161–172.

Clark H (1993). Opioids, chronic pain, and the law. *Journal of Pain & Symptom Management* 8(5):297–306.

Cohen F (1980). Postsurgical pain relief: Patients status and nurses' medication choices. *Pain* 9:265–274.

Collins E & Cesselin F (1991). Neurobiological mechanisms of opioid tolerance and dependence. *Clinical Neuropharmacology* 14:465–488.

Compton M (1994). Cold pressor pain tolerance in opiate and cocaine abusers: Correlates of drug type and use status. *Journal of Pain and Symptom Management* 9(7):462–473.

Cousins MJ & Bridenbaugh PO (eds.) (1990). *Neural Blockade in Clinical Anesthesia and Pain Management* (2nd ed.). Philadelphia, PA: JB Lippincott.

DeGood D (1993). What is the role of biofeedback in the treatment of chronic pain patients. *American Pain Society Bulletin* 3(3):1–5.

Dunbar S & Katz N (1996). Chronic opioid therapy for nonmalignant pain in patients with a history of substance abuse: Report of 20 Cases. *Journal of Pain and Symptom Management* 11(3):163–171.

Feine J & Lund J (1997). An assessment of the efficacy of physical therapy and physical modalities for the control of chronic musculoskeletal pain. *Pain* 71(1):5–24.

Finlayson RE, Maruta T & Morse BR (1986). Substance dependence and chronic pain: Profile of 50 patients treated in an alcohol and drug dependence unit. *Pain* 26:167–174.

Finlayson RE, Maruta T, Morse BR & Martin MA (1986). Substance dependence and chronic pain: Experience with treatment and follow-up results. *Pain* 26:175–180.

Foley K (1991). Clinical tolerance to opioids. In A Basbaum & J Besson (eds.) *Towards a New Pharmacotherapy of Pain.* New York, NY: John Wiley & Sons, 181–203.

Fordyce W (1978). Learning processes in pain. In R Sternbach (ed.) *The Psychology of Pain.* New York, NY: Raven Press.

Fordyce W (1992). Opioids, pain and behavioral outcomes. *American Pain Society Journal* 1(4):282–284.

Frampton V (1994). Transcutaneous electrical nerve stimulation and chronic pain. In P Wells, V Frampton & D Browsher (eds.) *Pain Management by Physical Therapy.* Oxford: Butterworth-Heinemann, 115–140.

Fromm G (1993). Physiologic rationale for the treatment of neuropathic pain. *American Pain Society Journal* 2:1–7.

Gamsa A (1994). The role of psychological factors in chronic pain. I. A half century of study. *Pain* 57(1):5–16.

Gardner E (1992). Brain reward mechanisms. In J Lowinson, P Ruiz, & R Millman (eds.), *Substance Abuse: A Comprehensive Text.* Baltimore: Williams & Wilkins, 70–99.

Gil K, Williams D, Keefe F & Beckham J (1992). The relationship of negative thoughts to pain and psychological distress. *Behavioral Therapy* 21:341–352.

Hassenbusch S, Paice J, Patt R, Bedder M & Bell G (1997). Economics of intrathecal therapy. *Journal of Pain and Symptom Management* 14(3S):S36–S48.

Haythornthwaite J, Seiber W & Kerns R (1991). Depression and the chronic pain experience. *Pain* 46:177–184.

Hill H, Chapman C, Kornell J, Sullivan K, Saeger L & Benedetti C (1990). Self-administration of morphine in bone marrow transplant patients reduces drug treatment. *Pain* 40:121–129.

Hill H, Coda B, Mackie A & Iverson K (1992). Patient-controlled analgesic infusions: Alfentanyl versus morphine. *Pain* 49:301–310.

Jackson D (1989). A study of pain management: Patient controlled analgesia versus intramuscular analgesia. *Journal of Intravenous Nursing* 12:42–51.

Jaffe J (1980). Drug addiction and drug abuse. In A Gilman, L Goodman, T Rall & F Murad (eds.) *The Pharmacologic Basis of Therapeutics.* New York, NY: Macmillan, 532–581.

Jaffe J (1992). Opiates: Clinical aspects. In J Lowinson, P Ruiz & R Millman (eds.) *Substance Abuse: A Comprehensive Text.* Baltimore, MD: Williams & Wilkins, 186–194

Jaffe J & Martin W (1980). Opioid agonists. In A Gilman, L Goodman, T Rall & F Mural (eds.) *The Pharmacologic Basis of Therapeutics.* New York, NY: MacMillan, 491–531.

Jasinski D, Johnson R & Kocher T (1985). Clonidine in morphine withdrawal: Differential effects on sign and symptoms. *Archives of General Psychiatry* 42:1063–1065.

Johanson C & Schuster C (1981). Animal models of drug self- administration. In N Mello (ed.) *Advances in Substance Abuse Research.* Greenwich, CT: JAAI Press, 219–297.

Johnson M, Ashton C & Thompson J (1991). An in-depth study of long-term users of transcutaneous electrical nerve stimulation (TENS): Implications for clinical use of TENS. *Pain* 44:221–229.

Joranson D, Cleeland C & Weisman D (1991). *Opioids for Chronic Cancer and Non-Cancer Pain: Survey of Medical Licensing Boards.* New Orleans, LA.

Joranson DE (1995). Intractable pain treatment laws and regulations. *American Pain Society Bulletin* 5(2):1–3, 15–17.

Kennedy J & Crowley T (1990). Chronic pain and substance abuse: A pilot study of opioid maintenance. *Journal of Substance Abuse Treatment* 7:233–238.

Kissin I, Brown P & Bailey E (1991). Magnitude of acute tolerance to opioids is not related to their potency. *Anesthesiology* 75:813–816.

Koes B, Scholten R, Mens J & Bouter L (1995). Efficacy of epidural steroid injections for low back pain and sciatica: A systematic review of randomized clinical trials. *Pain* 63(1):279–288.

Kolb L (1925). Types and characteristics of drug addicts. *Mental Hygiene* 9:300.

Koob G & Bloom F (1988). Cellular and molecular mechanisms of drug dependence. *Science* 242:715–723.

Kosten T & Krystal J (1988). Biologic mechanisms in post-traumatic stress disorder: Relevance for substance abuse. *Recent Developments in Alcoholism* 6:49–68.

Kottke F, Stillwell G & Lehmann J (1982). *Krusen's Handbook of Physical Medicine and Rehabilitation.* Philadelphia, PA: W.B. Saunders.

Linton SJ & Gotesam KG (1985). Relations between pain, anxiety, mood and muscle tension in chronic pain patients. *Psychotherapy and Psychosomatics* 43:95–98.

Maitland G & Brewerton D (1986). *Vertebral Manipulation.* London, England: Butterworth's.

Marchand S (1993). Nervous system stimulation for pain relief. *American Pain Society Journal* 2(2):103–106.

Marks J & Sacher E (1973). Undertreatment of medical inpatients with narcotic analgesics. *Annals of Internal Medicine* 78–173–181.

Max M (1995). Thirteen consecutive well-designed randomized clinical trials show that antidepressants reduce pain in diabetic neuropathy and post-herpetic neuralgia. *Pain Forum* 4(4):248–253.

McCaffery M & Vourakis C (1992). Assessment and relief of pain in chemically dependent patients. *Orthopaedic Nursing* 11(2):13–27.

Melzack R (1996). Gate control theory: On the evolution of pain concepts. *Pain Forum* 5(1):128–138.

Mersky H (1979). Pain terms: A list with definitions and notes on usage. Recommendation of the IASP Subcommittee on Taxonomy. *Pain* 6:249–252.

Moore D (1981). *Regional Block (4th Ed.).* Springfield, IL: Charles C. Thomas.

Morgan J (1985). American opiophobia: Customary underutilization of opioid analgesics. *Advances in Alcohol and Substance Abuse* 5:163.

North R (1993). The role of spinal cord stimulation in contemporary pain management. *American Pain Society Journal* 2(2):91–99.

Paice J, Winkelmuller W, Burchiel K, Racz G & Prager J (1997). Efficacy of intrathecal pain therapy. *Journal of Pain and Symptom Management* 14(3s):14–26.

Palastanga N (1994). Heat and cold. In P Wells, V Frampton & D Bowsher (eds.) *Pain Management by Physical Therapy (2nd Ed.).* Oxford, England: Butterworth-Heinemann, 177–187.

Panel on Acute Pain Management (1992). *Acute Pain Management: Operative or Medical Procedures and Trauma.* Rockville, MD: Agency for Health Care Policy Research.

Panel on Cancer Pain Guidelines (1994). *Cancer Pain Management: Clinical Practice Guidelines.* Rockville, MD: Agency for Health Care Policy Research.

Parrino M (1991a). Overview: Current treatment realities and future trends. In C Panel (ed.) *State Methadone Treatment Guidelines.* Rockville, MD: U.S. Dept of Health and Human Services, 1–9.

Parrino M (ed.) (1991b). *State Methadone Treatment Guidelines.* Rockville MD: Center for Substance Abuse Treatment.

Perry S & Heindrich G (1982). Management of pain during debridement: A survey of U.S. burn units. *Pain* 13:12–14.

Pilowski I (1975). Patterns of illness behavior in patients with intractable pain. *Journal of Psychosomatic Research* 19:279–287.

Portenoy R (1990a). Chronic opioid therapy in nonmalignant pain. *Journal of Pain and Symptom Management* 5.

Portenoy R (1990b). Pharmacotherapy of cancer pain. In *Refresher Courses on Pain Management.* Adelaide, Australia: IASP Refresher Courses, 101–112.

Portenoy R & Savage S (1997). Special therapeutic issues in intrathecal therapy of pain: Tolerance and addiction. *Journal of Pain and Symptom Management* 14(3S):S27–S35.

Porter J & Jick H (1980). Addiction rare in patients treated with narcotics. *New England Journal of Medicine* 302:123.

Raj P (1992). *The Practical Management of Pain (2nd Ed.).* St. Louis, MO: C.V. Mosby.

Rapaport A (1988). Analgesic rebound headache. *Headache* 28(10):662–665.

Rayport M (1954). Experience in the management of patients medically addicted to narcotics. *Journal of the American Medical Association* 165:684–691.

Regier D, Meyers JK & Kramer M (1984). The NIMH Epidemiological Catchment Area Study. *Archives of General Psychiatry* 41:934–958.

Savage SR (1993). Addiction in the treatment of pain: Significance, recognition and treatment. *Journal of Pain & Symptom Management* 8(5):265–278.

Savage SR (1996). Long-term opioid therapy: Assessment of consequences of risks. *Journal of Pain and Symptom Management* 11:274–286.

Schofferman J (1993). Long-term use of opioid analgesics for the treatment of chronic pain of nonmalignant origin. *Journal of Pain and Symptom Management* 8(5):279–288.

Schug S Merry A & Acland R (1991). Treatment principles for the use of opioids in pain of nonmalignant origin. *Drugs* 42(2):228–232.

Sees KL & Clark W (1993). Opioid use in the treatment of chronic pain: Assessment of addiction. *Journal of Pain & Symptom Management* 8(5):257–264.

Shine D & Demas P (1984). Knowledge of medical students, residents and attending physicians about opiate abuse. *Journal of Medical Education* 59:501–507.

Sjogren P, Jensen N & Jensen T (1994). Disappearance of morphine-induced hyperalgesia after discontinuing or substituting morphine with other opioid agonists. *Pain* 59:313–316.

Smith W (1990). The application of cold and heat. In S Michlovitz (ed.) *Thermal Agents in Rehabilitation.* Philadelphia, PA: FA Davis, 245–257.

Swerdlow M (1981). Anticonvulsant drugs and chronic pain. *Neuropharmacology* 7:51–82.

Tanelian D & Victory R (1995). Sodium channel blocking agents: Their use in neuropathic pain syndromes. *Pain Forum* 4(2):75–80.

Tobias JD (1992). Non-narcotic analgesia: Agents and mechanisms. *Anesthesiology Review* 19(2):26–32.

Tollison CD (1990). Antidepressant use in patients with chronic pain. *Drug Therapy* 20(22):50–57.

Travell J & Simons D (1983). *Myofascial Pain and Dysfunction: The Trigger Point Manual (Vol. 1).* Baltimore, MD: Williams & Wilkins.

Turk D & Meichenbaum D (1984). A cognitive and behavioral approach to pain. In P Wall & R Melzach (eds.) *Textbook of Pain.* Edinburgh, Scotland: Churchill Livingston, 787–794.

Turk DC, Meichenbaum DH & Genost M (1983). Pain and behavioral medicine: A cognitive behavioral perspective. New York, NY: Guilford Press.

Twycross R (1974). Clinical experience with diamorphine in advanced malignant disease. *International Journal of Clinical Pharmacology, Therapy and Toxicology* 9:184–198.

Wattwil M (1989). Post-operative pain relief and intestinal motility. *Acta Chirugica Scandinavica* 550:140–145.

Weissman DE & Haddox JD (1989). Opioid pseudoaddiction: An iatrogenic syndrome. *Pain* 36:363–366.

Wells P (1994). Manipulative procedures. In P Wells, V Frampton & D Bowsher (eds.) *Pain Management by Physical Therapy (2nd ed.).* Oxford, England: Butterworth-Heinemann, 187–213.

Wesson D, Ling W & Smith D (1993). Prescription of opioids for treatment of pain in patients with addictive disease. *Journal of Pain & Symptom Management* 8(5):289–296.

Yaksh T (1992). The spinal pharmacology of acutely and chronically administered opioids. *Journal of Pain and Symptom Management* 7:356–361.

Zachny J (1995). A review of the effects of opioids on psychomotor and cognitive functioning in humans. *Experimental Clinical Psychopharmacology* 3:432–466.

Zayfert C, Seville J, Schnurr P & Savage S (1997). *Trauma and PTSD among Chronic Pain Patients.* Paper presented at the International Society for Post Traumatic Stress Studies, Montreal.

Zenz M, Strumph M & Tryba M (1992). Long-term oral opioid therapy in patients with chronic non-malignant pain. *Journal of Pain & Symptom Management* 7(2):69–77.

CHAPTER 3

Psychological Approaches to the Management of Pain

Edward C. Covington, M.D.
Margaret M. Kotz, D.O.

Chronic Pain and Addiction Comorbidity
Diagnosis of Addiction in Chronic Pain Patients
Psychological Determinants of Chronic Pain
Evidence for Psychogenic Components of Pain
Persons at Risk
Treatment Approaches
Pain Management versus Addiction Recovery
Chronic Malignant Pain
Acute Recurrent Pain
Multimodality Treatment Programs

The current controversy concerning the role of opioids in the management of chronic pain makes it especially appropriate to focus on the psychological components of pain and pain management. We are embarked on a national experiment in which many state legislatures and medical boards are (appropriately) working to improve access to opioid analgesics for those in chronic pain. Recent California legislation, the so-called "Pain Patients' Bill of Rights," not only authorizes physicians to prescribe any dosage deemed medically necessary, but specifically requires those to physicians who do not wish to provide maintenance opioids to notify patients of other physicians who do. The legislation also guarantees patients the "option" to seek opioid maintenance for intractable pain. Even the most zealous proponents of this therapy will agree that it will have less than 100% efficacy, and therefore physicians will be seeing numbers of patients who have failed aggressive opioid treatment. It is likely that those whose pain was in large part functional will contribute heavily to this number, as will those who also suffer from addictive disorders.

The compassion of those who advocate opioid maintenance cannot be questioned; however, their writings may imply that the only alternative to opiates in this population is needless suffering. Were this true, the dilemma for those working with addicted chronic pain patients would be severe. Fortunately, nothing could be further from the truth. In fact, studies demonstrate remarkable reductions in pain and suffering along with increases in function following treatment approaches which utilize predominantly cognitive/behavioral components in combination with physical reconditioning.

The management of intractable pain can be quite challenging, especially when an addictive disorder complicates the situation. The presence of addiction tends to magnify and distort complaints, impeding the diagnosis of pain, while confounding results of interventions. There are risks of excessive work-ups for non-existent disease and of discounting actual pathology as another "false alarm." The presence of pain can also mask an addictive disorder, since it enables people to transition from recreational or illicit drugs to sanctioned ones. Not only is diagnosis complicated, but treatment is difficult in coexisting pain and addictive disorder. The presence of chronic pain may impede detoxification, since the hyperalgesia of withdrawal may be less tolerable (Kaplan & Fields, 1991; Noyes, Garvey et al., 1988). Pain patients usually are unwilling to identify themselves as drug-addicted, and there often is little "leverage" in the form of pressure from physicians, spouses, employers or the courts to encourage them to comply with treatment recommendations. Despite these difficulties, such patients *can* be treated successfully and they commonly demonstrate the same gratitude for their recovery as do addicted persons in whom pain is not a factor.

This chapter is concerned primarily with chronic, nonmalignant pain, as its management differs from that of acute, malignant and recurrent acute pain. Although the focus is on non-pharmacologic interventions, it should be recognized that these interventions are most commonly (and most effectively) employed in combination with (non-opiate) analgesic and non-analgesic pharmacotherapy.

CHRONIC PAIN AND ADDICTION COMORBIDITY

Many common causes of chronic nonmalignant pain are associated with substance use. The most frequent cause of disability is low back pain, which is known to be associated with nicotine and alcohol dependence (Deyo & Bass, 1989; Kelsey, Golden & Mundt, 1990; Atkinson, Slater et al., 1991). An extensive literature relates intractable headaches to the daily use of mind-altering (barbiturates, opiates, caffeine) and non-mind altering (ergots) substances (Rapoport, 1988; Mathew, Kurman & Perez, 1990; Saper, 1987). Nicotine may even worsen fibromyalgia, and the authors' personal experience (with a biased population) suggests that adult sympathetic-related pain may be more common in those with previous heavy use of alcohol or drugs. Of course, chronic pain often follows industrial or vehicular traumas, which are more common in those who are chemically dependent. Patients with so-called chronic pain syndrome also may be genetically at risk for addictive disorders (Chaturvedi, 1987; Katon, Egan & Miller, 1985). In any case, it is clear that a large number of those seen with chronic pain either abuse substances or have a true addictive disorder. Thus, *every* chronic pain evaluation should include an assessment of substance use.

King and Strain (1990) reported that among their patients, 38% were using benzodiazepines; 58% used opiates and 16% barbiturates. In studies they reviewed, 37% to 60% of chronic pain patients were using benzodiazepines, often for extended periods of time. Approximately half of our patients admitted for pain management rehabilitation require detoxification, while about 35% require formal addiction treatment as part of their pain rehabilitation program.

A distinction should be made between chronic non-malignant pain and chronic pain syndrome. Chronic nonmalignant pain as used here refers to pain that is (1) persistent, and (2) not associated with progressive tissue destruction. The common use of the term "chronic benign pain" has been challenged on the grounds that protracted suffering should not be referred to as "benign." Here, the term is used to indicate non-malignant and emphatically does not connote innocuous.

TABLE 1. Features of Chronic Pain Syndrome

- Intractable pain ≥ 6 months
- Marked alteration of behavior, depression or anxiety
- Marked restriction in daily activities
- Excessive use of medications and medical services
- No clear relationship to organic disorder
- Multiple, non-productive tests, treatment and surgeries.

Source: U.S. Commission on the Evaluation of Pain, 1987.

Some patients with chronic pain develop a pattern of difficulties, behaviors, and health care utilization that is described as *chronic pain syndrome.* This has been defined by the Social Security Administration's Office of Disabilities by the features described in Table 1 (U.S. Commission on the Evaluation of Pain, 1987).

Thus, chronic pain *syndrome* is as much a behavioral problem as one of nociception. Its major component is the excessive adoption of the sick role. Pilowsky's (1960) concept of abnormal illness behavior also is relevant to this condition. These are the patients who are infamous for difficult relationships with clinicians, leading Fordyce to characterize the syndrome as "any referral preceded by an apology." Others have been more pejorative, using such terms as "low back losers." However, virtually all of these patients are genuinely suffering and deserve our best efforts at relief. Nevertheless, since the syndrome is one in which behavioral and affective changes may be as important as nociception, treatments directed exclusively at nociception may miss the point.

It may be that much of the apparent controversy regarding opiate maintenance in chronic pain is between those who advocate its use in chronic pain and those who oppose its use in chronic pain *syndrome.* Just as it has become clear that tolerance and withdrawal are not synonymous with addiction, so too is chronic pain not synonymous with chronic pain syndrome (CPS).

Patients with both chronic pain and an active addictive disorder are likely to have chronic pain syndrome as well, since they are prone to inordinate health care utilization, increased functional impairments, and other characteristics of this condition.

DIAGNOSIS OF ADDICTION IN CHRONIC PAIN PATIENTS

When patients with chronic pain are addicted to recreational substances, the diagnosis of a substance use disorder poses no special difficulties. This contrasts with those in whom the drug of choice is an analgesic, is contained in analgesic preparations (barbiturates in headache preparations), is taken as a muscle relaxant (e.g., diazepam), or is one that, while not addictive *per se,* has addictive properties in some (e.g., meprobamate). The cornerstones of diagnosis—preoccupation, loss of control, and use despite adverse consequences—remain the same; however, their presence becomes harder to detect.

Diagnosis is hindered by the lack of consensus as to what constitutes appropriate use of opiates and sedatives in the chronic pain population. Respected authorities advocate continuous high doses of methadone to treat such conditions as chronic back pain. There are honest differences among clinicians in assessing the relative importance of outcome parameters. If a patient on maintenance opioids reports considerable benefit, yet does essentially nothing but watch television, does this constitute a good outcome? What of the patient who reports persistent pain, but resumes work, socialization, and sexual function? Who should decide which outcome is desirable? Is it possible for the untreated addict to wisely establish treatment priorities? These are difficult questions whose answers color judgements on the diagnostic criterion of "use despite adverse consequences." A definitive answer may elude us, as personal values unavoidably intrude into scientific positions on the subject.

The pain patient who uses analgesics in a nonaddictive fashion is likely to function better, while addictive use is apt to impair function. Perhaps this is because the dosage required for psychoactive effects is sufficient to produce intoxication, while the analgesic dose may not be.

A key indicator of addictive disorder is continued use of a substance after it has proved harmful. The addicted pain patient, however, has the illusion that his or her drug of choice improves his physical wellbeing, since she or he feels better after ingesting it: "It takes the edge off." This illusion of benefit is more than denial and euphoric recall. It seems to represent the inability of the patient to detect the cumulative deleterious effect of the medication when each individual dose reduces pain. It also represents the fact that peak serum levels are more comfortable than trough levels in the presence of physical dependence, and that trough levels are associated with muscle tension that can increase myalgias and autonomic arousal that can worsen neuropathic pains of several sorts.

Those addicted to recreational agents usually consume them despite the opposition of physician and family. In contrast, the physician who prescribes for a pain patient may be unaware of the deleterious effects of the drug. While some families worry about the effects of drug use and provide useful diagnostic information, others defend it as a reasonable alternative to unrelieved suffering. Our experience is that patients, their families, and their physicians are astonished at the reduction in pain and suffering that occurs after detoxification. This may suggest that in many pain patients, continued use of harmful substances is due more to ignorance than to denial.

Denial, always an impediment to the diagnosis of addiction, is especially strong in chronic pain syndrome, as exemplified by the protests, "I'm not like those people; I didn't use to get high; I only took what the doctors gave me." Many patients with chronic pain syndrome have a "need" for the sick role to legitimize their behavior and to "entitle" them to such perquisites as caretaking and disability income. A diagnosis of addictive disorder thus carries not only the usual stigma, but an additional loss of status and role.

Addiction in pain patients should be suspected when there is frequent intoxication, irritability or other mood changes. Inattention to hygiene and indifference to inappropriate behaviors are also used when, despite apparently generous analgesia, the suffering or sick role behavior seems grossly disproportionate to the organic pathology. This is a difficult clinical judgment and does not distinguish inappropriate behavior due to addictive disorder from that caused by other psychological/behavioral factors.

Loss of control may be evidenced by taking "handfuls of pills" or forgetting how much was taken. Patients who know that they have a one-month supply may be incapable of rationing themselves, use the entire amount in a few days, and suffer increased pain and withdrawal when they run out. Patients should be asked about multiple sources of drugs, forged prescriptions, whether their physicians have been concerned about their medication consumption, and whether they found it necessary to change physicians because of this.

Generally, a patient who has no history of recreational substance abuse, who becomes physically dependent on benzodiazepines or analgesics as part of a pain syndrome, who obtains the drugs legitimately, and who has not seemed drug impaired, is likely to have only an iatrogenic physical dependence. If confirmed, education and detoxification may suffice to resolve the problem. In contrast, a patient who resumes opioid use despite having experienced marked improvement in comfort and function with detoxification may have an addictive disorder.

The family's role in the patient's use may pose special difficulties. Frequently the significant other is the person who phones for prescriptions and picks them up. (One diagnostic clue to non-organic dysfunction and enabling is a call seeking drugs from the spouse or mother of a healthy patient with back pain.) Counseling may fail to convince families of the imprudence of the drug use; however, having them witness the patient's improvement with abstinence often recruits them as allies in the treatment. "Before and after" videotapes often document a dramatic change in appearance, affect, and comfort following detoxification and can aid in securing the family's "buy in" to the program.

PSYCHOLOGICAL DETERMINANTS OF CHRONIC PAIN

It is common, when considering psychology in chronic pain, to equate it with psychopathology. This overlooks the fact that, in many patients, the effects of chronic pain are mitigated by good coping and psychological strengths. Individuals such as President John F. Kennedy, who had rather severe spine pathology, have been able to lead productive and enjoyable lives despite intractable pain. Thus, psychological approaches to chronic pain may be indicated not only to identify and treat psychological factors that exacerbate or perpetuate it, but also to optimize growth and coping even when psychopathology is not apparent.

Pain as Behavior. The concepts of behaviorism were brought to pain medicine by Fordyce and others, who suggested that the behaviors associated with pain could be a response to environmental reinforcers, as opposed to being intrinsic to the stimulus of pain. Operant conditioning refers to the process in which behaviors that are reinforced increase in frequency. Elimination of reinforcement is followed by "extinction" of the behavior. The idea that such behaviors as somatically focused conversation, limping, rubbing body parts, and remaining bed bound could be maintained by environmental reinforcers led to efforts to reduce these behaviors by eliminating reinforcers and by reinforcing incompatible behaviors, such as speed-walking. Results were startling, as persons who had been disabled for years began to exercise, relinquish assistive devices, and engage in conversations about non-pain related topics. Within just a few years there were hundreds of pain management programs in the U.S. modeled to some extent on Fordyce's original program. The rapid response of severely dysfunctional people to the environmental contingencies in the programs provided indirect support to the belief that much of the pain behavior and dysfunction had been maintained by the environment more than by internal stimuli (Fordyce, Fowler et al., 1973; Fordyce, 1976).

Key points regarding operant conditioning include the facts that: (1) it often occurs without the knowledge of the trainer or trainee; (2) in most cases, repetition over time is required for the effect to occur, which probably explains why these concepts have been invoked primarily in chronic conditions as opposed to acute ones; and (3) the timing of reinforcement is critical. An immediate small reinforcer may be considerably more powerful than a larger delayed one; thus, the prospect of immediate euphoria may have more impact than the prospect of a delayed hangover.

Secondary Gain. At first glance, the life of a typical pain patient seems to provide remarkably few reinforcers. Poverty, depression, and loss of friendships and recreational activities are common. Nevertheless, much of the behavior of the pain patient, like that of the alcoholic, is maintained by initial consequences that are perceived as rewarding. Rest and inactivity initially provide relief; only later does debilitation increase pain.

Rewards for "illness behavior" include solicitous responses from others, escape from responsibility and stressful/dangerous work environments, and entitlements to narcotics, nurture, and financial compensation. These are commonly referred to as the secondary gains of the illness. Physical care may be perceived as a form of love, even if counterfeit. Avoidance of the workplace may provide stress reduction. (The authors have seen laborers whose back pain became disabling when lifting requirements diminished, but exposure of their illiteracy was threatened.) While the income from disability often is meager, it is secure. It is not contingent upon skill, ability to keep up with co-workers, or the viability of one's industry in precarious economic times. Into this equation must be placed the powerful reinforcing capacity of drugs.

Behavior also is rewarded if it (seems to) prevent the occurrence of an undesirable event or exposure to perceived danger, *whether or not the situation actually is dangerous.* This reinforcement can be insidious and debilitating; for example, each time a patient avoids some activity that he or she believes will increase pain, the patient is rewarded when the pain does not increase. This strengthens the belief that the feared behavior is to be avoided and can contribute to unwarranted invalidism (Waddell, Newton et al., 1993).

While reinforcers for "sick role behavior" can lock individuals into unnecessary invalidism, when the incentives for wellness are sufficiently powerful, even serious illness may not produce disability. Numerous studies suggest that disability with pain is more a function of job satisfaction and status than of severity of illness (Bigos, Battie et al., 1991; Osterweis, Kleinman & Mechanic, 1987).

The behavioral concept of "reinforcement" is analogous to the psychoanalytic concept of "secondary gain." Fishbain and colleagues (1995) reviewed 38 studies concerning gain and illness. Despite some conflict, results were consistent in supporting the importance of "secondary gain" in behavior. Disability benefits were addressed by five studies, four of which found them to alter behavior, although severity of illness was not controlled and secondary gain was not well determined. There was evidence that perception of pain could be manipulated by reinforcement in both chronic low back patients and healthy subjects. Studies consistently demonstrated a relationship between spouse solicitousness and pain behavior. The literature concerning compensation/litigation in pain was contradictory and weak, but it did appear that Workers' Compensation patients have poorer treatment outcome.

Rohling, Binder and Langhinrichsen-Rohling (1995) provided strong supp-analytic study of disability compensation and pain. They assessed 136 comparisons (3,802 pain patients and 3,849 controls). The clearest finding was that financial compensation was associated with greater pain and reduced treatment efficacy, whether medical or surgical.

When families foster invalidism, it usually is due to lack of knowledge about the nature of the person's pain and which activities are harmful and which are safe. Families usually have a reasonable understanding of appropriate handling of acute illness, and provide nurture, caretaking, and encouragement to rest. They may not understand when these behaviors begin to promote illness rather than recuperation. In some situations, the family may benefit from the patient's dysfunction, a phenomenon referred to as tertiary gain (Dansak, 1973). This creates an incentive to provide inappropriate support that may prolong disability. For example, a widow who enjoys security and companionship when her disabled child returns home may therefore provide excessive support that delays recovery. Similarly, a wife whose husband is an unskilled worker in a floundering industry may sense that her family is secure only so long as her husband remains disabled. She may therefore defend his disability and support his helplessness.

The political and economic climate may create a situation in which health insurance for one's family is contingent on remaining disabled. Lack of skills, education, strength or intelligence may create a situation in which a lifestyle of invalidism may seem as much a solution as a problem.

One may wonder whether helping a patient to rehabilitate meets the ethical principle of beneficence, given the alleged "profits" of the sick role. This concern is usually unwarranted, given the obvious losses associated with pain and illness. These include pride in being the breadwinner, socialization that occurs at work, money (while disability income is often secure, it rarely equals premorbid income), recreation, sex, etc. Thus, restoration of function to the greatest extent possible and safe (in view of the medical pathology) remains the *sine qua non* of good treatment for chronic pain syndrome.

Cognition. The role of cognition in psychiatric conditions has been increasingly recognized over the last 15 years. The underlying premise of most cognitive theories, whether related to depression, anxiety, or pain, is that thoughts and beliefs are major determinants of affects; i.e., we react not to events but to our interpretations of them. The person who interprets an unsuccessful job interview as an indication that the company had no open positions suffers less and is more apt to try again than the person who perceives confirmation that he is inept, undesirable, and will in all probability never find work. The terminal cancer patient who is convinced "the surgeon got it all" will be more content than the healthy hypochondriac who is certain of some occult pathology. Maladaptive cognitions have the quality of being automatic and habitual, so that they rarely are examined for validity. They are simply accepted, even when obviously (to others) illogical.

Cognitive factors impact on pain in several ways (Jensen, Turner et al., 1991; Affleck, Urrows et al., 1992). First, the aversive quality of pain is modified by its interpretation (Melzack 1986; Ahles, Blanchard & Ruckdeschel, 1983). The pain that is thought to represent a malignancy is more distressing than one thought to signal healing. Unrealistic thoughts in response to pain may include ideas such as, "My back is breaking," "The nerves are being crushed," or "I may become paralyzed." These "catastrophic" interpretations worsen the pain and hinder coping (Keefe, Brown et al., 1989).

Turk and Rudy (1986) reviewed cognitive issues in chronic pain and cited evidence that negative, maladaptive thoughts may reduce pain tolerance. Such thoughts include those emphasizing the aversiveness of the situation, the inadequacy of the person to bear it, or the physicael of learned helplessness as a cause of depression suggests that those who feel unable to control events in their lives will show passivity and lowered aggression. Beliefs in personal helplessness have been shown to be important in those disabled with pain as well (Ciccone & Grzesiak, 1984). Conversely, belief in self-efficacy is a major determinant of efforts to cope with pain (Jensen, Turner & Romano, 1991).

In fibromyalgia, self-efficacy predicted post-treatment physical activity, and improved self-efficacy was associated with reduction in pain and disease severity (Buckelew, Huyser et al., 1996). Self-efficacy was a better predictor of pain behavior than was depression (Buckelew, Parker et al. 1994). In rheumatoid arthritis, improved SE was associated with improvements in depression, pain, and disease activity (Smarr, Parker et al., 1997).

Locus of control refers to the perception that events are either a consequence of the individual's own behavior (internal control) or are contingent upon such outside forces as family members and physicians ("powerful others") or chance happenings. Those whose locus of control is internal believe that they themselves play a major role in determining their future. Such people feel and function better than those who see events as controlled by fate or other people (Harkapaa, Jarvikoski et al., 1991). Crisson and Keefe (1988) found that chronic pain patients with a "chance external" locus of control felt depressed, anxious, helpless to deal with their pain, and relied on maladaptive coping strategies. Decreased perceptions of self-control may explain much of the relationship between pain and depression (Rudy, Kerns & Turk, 1988).

Beliefs such as "I will resume living after I am well," "I can't go out if I am in pain," "I shouldn't exercise if it hurts," and a myriad of others have obvious effects on adaptation.

Depression. Although pain patients can develop classical affective disorder and recurrent unipolar depression occasionally presents as obscure pain, the preponderance of depression in chronic pain syndrome is of a different sort (Lefebvre, 1981). While pain patients attribute their depression to the fact that they hurt, studies suggest that it is the pain's interference with life activities and its ability to engender a sense of helplessness that actually lead to depression (Rudy, Kerns & Turk, 1988).

Clinically, those who acquire a sense of personal empowerment and who resume life involvements often experience a remission in depression. Maruta and colleagues (1989) reported that 98% of depressions in patients admitted to a pain management unit had resolved by the time of discharge, without antidepressants.

Anxiety/Tension. Although anxiety is painless, panic attacks may present with chest or abdominal pain. Anxiety and fear concerning injury are, however, major factors in promoting the sick role. Kori and colleagues (1990) referred to chronic pain syndrome as "kinesophobia"—fear of movement—reflecting the important role of fear in causing inactivity, which produces invalidism. They suggested that often ". . . pain behavior has more to do with phobic processes than neurological ones."

Fear also can be important in perpetuating pain, when avoidance of a feared situation is the reinforcer that helps to maintain disability (Waddell, Newton et al., 1993). For example, a person injured in a factory may fear returning to the work situation. Such fear can increase pain behavior and invalidism.

The cycle of pain/tension/pain is well known and reflects the tendency to "brace" to protect an injured part. In musculoskeletal pain, this is commonly a source of increased pain.

Anger/Blame. DeGood and Kiernan (1996) have shown what clinicians long suspected, that blaming others for one's pain, especially one's employer, is associated with greater behavioral disturbance, more emotional distress, and reduced treatment responsiveness.

It should be noted that anger, a major cause of suffering in pain patients (and those who relate with them), has been somewhat neglected in comparison with the extensive focus on depression and anxiety in these patients. It seems to significantly increase pain-related suffering, interference with life activities, and reduces response to treatment (Fernandez & Turk, 1995; Kerns, Rosenberg & Jacob, 1994). It may be that the combination of high levels of anger and low levels of anger expression are especially problematic (Burns, Johnson et al., 1996).

TABLE 2. Developmental Correlates of Chronic Pain Syndrome

In the Patient's Parents
- Chronic pain
- Depression
- Alcoholism/addiction

In the Patient's Childhood
- Abuse
- Neglect
- Abandonment
- Early responsibility

Deconditioning. Although not strictly speaking a psychological phenomenon, it is closely intertwined with psychological status. Deconditioning commonly *results* from psychological/behavioral phenomena such as unwarranted fears of self-injury and consequent excessive regression. It also *causes* psychological changes, including increased perceptions of helplessness and invalidism. A major consequence of deconditioning is that whatever one does becomes painful and reinforces the belief that one is handicapped.

Distraction. All perceptions, including pain, are more noticeable when attended to and less so when one is distracted. The life changes that pain patients make in order to feel better commonly reduce competing stimulation so that the pain becomes all-consuming.

Developmental Trauma. It follows from this discussion that psychological interventions should focus on correcting cognitions and beliefs, reinforcing healthy behaviors, and reducing such psychophysiologic components as tension and anxiety.

Unfortunately, there are other factors in chronic pain syndrome that are less amenable to therapeutic intervention. Childhood traumas may lead to low self-esteem and feelings of insecurity in competitive employment, which increase vulnerability to persistent disability (Table 2).

Among randomly selected students, childhood sexual abuse is associated with a variety of pains, and the severity of the abuse correlates with absenteeism (Bendixen, Muus & Schei, 1994). Such childhood trauma is also associated with somatization and dissociation in patients (Zlotnik, Zakriski et al., 1996). Chronic pain may be one of a myriad of symptoms in somatization disorder.

The childhood years of patients with chronic pain syndrome often are characterized by abuse, molestation, neglect, or abandonment (Payne & Norfleet, 1986; Roy, 1982a, 1982b). Many are adult children of alcoholics (Chaturvedi, 1987; Katon, Egan & Miller, 1985). More than half of female inpatients on chronic pain units may have been sexually abused (Haber & Rood, 1985).

These individuals are left with profound anger and dependence, which they may defend against with pseudo-independence. Their impaired self-esteem may lead them to struggle for a "solid citizen" image—until some illness or injury forces a temporary regression. They often have major difficulties with fears of rejection and feelings of helplessness.

EVIDENCE FOR PSYCHOGENIC COMPONENTS OF PAIN

A number of findings may support a conclusion that pain and disability are not fully explained by medical pathology. Inconsistencies should be carefully noted. Limping that is worse with the spouse present, or that changes sides with distraction is an example. A nonphysiologic examination is perhaps the strongest indicator of psychogenic complaints. Waddell's signs in back pain are the best known and supported indicators, but different findings in other conditions may demonstrate non-anatomic deficits. The finding of impairment/regression in excess of identified pathology can be a difficult judgment call—how much impairment *should* a patient with fibromyalgia have?—but some behaviors are notable. If the complaint is in a lower extremity, questionnaires should not be in the spouse's handwriting. If the patient is asked to describe the quality of the pain, he shouldn't look to the spouse for the answer. He should make his own phone calls for medications. Otherwise, there is excessive regression (not to mention enabling). Somatic preoccupation is obvious when it occurs, as it creates a strong desire on the part of almost everyone to flee from the patient. It provides a striking contrast to leave a patient with pain from terminal cancer, who may be discussing baseball, the welfare of his children, or politics, and enter the room of a patient with chronic pain syndrome who seems incapable of uttering a sentence that is not about symptoms, drugs, or doctors. The presence of active, untreated addictive disorder is an obvious clue that pain may have psychogenic components. Psychogenic pain patients may tend to focus on blame, retribution, and compensation more than on recovery, and in treatment, their wellness may seem less important to them than to the treatment team. A history of noncompliance with reasonable medical expectations and lack of effort in treatment support this conclusion. Negative reactions to compliments may be noted. A history of major trauma (molestation, abuse, neglect, abandonment) suggests vulnerability to somatization.

The presence of disincentives to function or incentives for disability often is used to challenge the organic basis of symptoms; however, Raskin, Talbott and Meyerson (1966) showed that conversion and organic patients demonstrated secondary gain, usually increased attention from family, in equal proportions. Almost all medical patients have secondary gains in the form of reduced demands, increased nurture, and, frequently, reinforcing drugs. The presence of gain, therefore, cannot be used to support a diagnosis of behaviorally maintained symptoms.

PERSONS AT RISK

Some individuals are more vulnerable than others to becoming trapped in the regression of the sick role that typifies chronic pain syndrome.

Can't Say No: The person who has an inordinate need to please others or a fear of rejection and anger may find it difficult to decline requests. Any desire to avoid a task generates an intense need for an excuse, and illness is perhaps the best. With chronic pain, the person never has to say no. He can say, "I'd love to, but unfortunately I can't." Thus, illness is reinforced by providing an "out."

Few Resources: The competitive environment of employment/business is stressful to many people, although some find it exhilarating. The less able one is to compete, the more stressful it is likely to be. Thus the person who is unable to read, to relate comfortably in the workplace, or to perform the physical or intellectual tasks of a job will find the security of a disability pension more rewarding than will the person who is doing well and expecting raises.

Trapped: Work situations that are perceived as abusive, as well as abuse in the home, may be escaped through illness. A common scenario in inordinate dysfunction due to pain is the woman whose spousal abuse stops when she is ill.

Addiction: Reinforcement of choice. Second, there is often impaired ability to cope and function at work, which causes the sick role to be more inviting.

Downsizing: While a life on disability often brings poverty, it may be perceived as secure, an important consideration when there are children who need health care, nutrition, etc. When industries are laying off or going out of business, disability is more stable than unemployment compensation.

TREATMENT APPROACHES

An important key to the non-pharmacologic treatment of pain lies in the clinician's confidence that these interventions are not merely weak substitutes for strong drugs. It may require experience for the clinician to learn that eliminating analgesics is more likely to increase comfort than to decrease it (Turner, Caslyn et al., 1982). The techniques to be described here should be seen as synergistic with detoxification rather than substitutive for narcotics.

Patients can be expected to ask, "When you take away the narcotics and sedatives, what will you give me instead?" This reflects their conviction that they are being deprived of something useful. Their skepticism may be impervious to reassurance until they have experienced diminution of their pain without opiates, tranquilizers, or sedatives.

Excessive sick role behavior is like addictive behavior, in that patients compulsively behave in a fashion that produces momentary relief, but ultimately increases suffering. They expect to suffer more when their customary adaptive strategies are taken from them, yet in fact they suffer less.

Behavior Modification. It is essential to remember that management of chronic non-malignant pain often has as much to do with behavioral changes as with perceptual ones. Pain behaviors may be separated into those that primarily affect nociception (using a heating pad) and those which primarily affect others ("pain talk"). Some behaviors do both; e.g., wearing a TENS or corset outside clothing. Unwarranted pain behaviors tend to be emitted preferentially in the presence of an audience. These include moaning, complaining, and holding body parts.

Behavioral change is initiated by changing environmental consequences of pain (contingencies, incentives). With inpatients, social reinforcers can be made contingent on healthy behaviors while pain behaviors are ignored (Turner & Chapman, 1982b). (This does not imply that the *patient* is ignored—only the pain behavior.) In physical therapy, tasks can be assigned in such a way that praise, rest and other "rewards" always follow goal completion and do not follow "trying," groaning or hurting. At home, families can be educated to see that unnecessarily coddling a family member into invalidism is a form of "enabling." They must learn to distinguish ignoring their loved one's pain from ignoring the person, and must be encouraged to provide social reinforcers for healthy behavior and not respond to pain behavior.

Education. Families and patients are unlikely to accept a behavioral approach until they have been educated about the nature of the pain and the illness underlying it. Those who see pain as mysterious cope poorly in numerous ways (Williams & Thorn, 1989). It is important that they understand the pain as genuine but benign, in the sense that it does not signal tissue destruction. It may be useful to present the analogy of pain as an alarm system and "benign" pain as a defective alarm that continues to sound after the fire is out. The patient and family should be helped to see that a protracted quest for a medical solution risks iatrogenic complications.

Cognitive Therapy. Cognitive therapies are of various types (Fernandez & Turk, 1989). One strategy involves teaching the patient to identify maladaptive cognitions as they occur and to practice alternative self-statements or interpretations that are less maladaptive. Certain patterns of self-destructive cognitions are commonly seen and addressed:

Catastrophizing describes the immediate and automatic interpretation of events in catastrophic (or at least negative) terms: if a spouse is late returning home, she or he "must have" had an accident.

Overgeneralization refers to arriving at broad (incorrect) conclusions based on a single piece of data. In this context, the conclusion is automatically negative: a single set-back shows that "I am a failure."

Selective negative abstraction or *filtering* refers to the tendency to attend only to the negative aspects of a situation—to see the thorns and not the roses. A person who made all A's except for a C in math, when asked how he did, may respond, "I blew the math final."

Personalization is a tendency to misinterpret the behavior of others as a (negative) reaction to you. Thus the surgeon's opinion that the lesion is not operable becomes, "He didn't want to give me an operation." Even the actions of bureaucracies (e.g., the Bureau of Workers' Compensation) can be personalized.

Correcting these cognitive errors requires that patients practice. One method is to have them maintain a "thought record"—a diary of automatic thoughts and their effects. *Alternative* thoughts are tried out. For each situation, the person can record the situation, thoughts occurring when the dysphoria began, the type of unpleasant feelings, how the negative thoughts can be answered realistically and constructively, what can be done to test the thoughts or handle the situation differently, and the outcome—what were the feelings after answering the thoughts? Through practice, the person can come to recognize and challenge automatic negative thoughts quickly in daily life.

Stimulus Reinterpretation. The response to pain can be reduced through reinterpretation of the stimulus. For example, "My back is breaking" can be replaced with, "It feels as though my back is breaking, but I know it isn't. I'm probably having some muscle spasm again, and it won't last forever." Catastrophic statements can be identified and reframed. "My back is killing me, I can't stand it anymore," can be changed to "Although the exercise is painful, it will ultimately help. I've coped with this much pain before and I can again. It always gets better eventually."

"Learned helplessness" and "external locus of control" must be replaced with the patient's conviction that he is and must be the playwright of his life and not just an actor or spectator. Thoughts that powerful others *will not* help and that the person is helpless can be corrected by substituting thoughts that physicians *cannot* cure everything, and that the patient has a great deal of power to manage his own pain.

Biofeedback/Relaxation Training. Clinical biofeedback therapy has evolved from evidence that animals learn to control physiological processes when an experimental apparatus provides them with information about those processes. Remarkable feats of self-control have developed, such as modifying EEG patterns or altering renal blood flow. Other, more prosaic accomplishments, such as reducing skeletal muscle tension, decreasing gastrointestinal motility, and increasing digital blood flow, have found clinical application.

It is useful to refer to biofeedback "training" (BFT) rather than "therapy." Physiologic self-control is a skill taught the patient, after which electronic monitoring no longer is required. The clinical set-up generally consists of a quiet room with comfortable seating. Skin electrodes (commonly over the frontalis, masseter, or paraspinals) transmit surface EMG activity. Thermistors on the fingers (or toes) transduce temperature and thus reflect blood flow. Palmar electrodes provide for measurement of electrical resistance and consequently sweating. Sensitive electronic equipment displays the physiologic information on gauges or digital displays for the therapist, and provides patterns of lights or sound that feed back to the patient information about the parameter being monitored. For example, lights might move to the right if a finger was warming or to the left if cooling. Sounds may soften as muscle activity diminishes. In more sophisticated set-ups, patients can control the position of objects on video games, the speed of electric trains, etc., by altering body function.

Training in warming the extremities is useful in such conditions as Raynaud's syndrome and may provide a non-pharmacologic treatment for essential hypertension (Freedman, 1991; Fahrion, 1991). EMG biofeedback often is used to teach frontalis muscle relaxation and has been used for tension headache, fibromyalgia, and back pain (Blanchard & Ahles, 1990). Both EMG and thermal biofeedback have been used extensively in headache patients, and masseter feedback may be useful for temporomandibular joint syndrome.

The indications for BFT are not fully defined and continue to expand into conditions as diverse as intractable rectal pain (Gilliland, Wexner et al., 1997; Heath, Leong et al., 1997), posttraumatic headache (Ham & Packard, 1996), cumulative trauma disorder (Spence, Champion et al., 1995), and dyspareunia attributed to vulvar vestibulitis (Glazer, Young et al., 1995).

Although widely practiced, clinical BFT has been challenged by studies showing that benefit does not necessarily correlate with the successful production of physiological changes. Some studies suggest that in patients with muscle pain and/or headache, BFT may be no more efficacious than approaches which do not require electronic equipment, such as autogenic training, progressive muscular relaxation, meditation, or self-hypnosis—all of which can facilitate a state of reduced emotional arousal and psychophysiologic quiescence (Turner & Chapman, 1982a; Linton, 1986; Roberts, 1987). Some benefits may arise as much from the *belief* in having acquired self control as from the physiologic self-regulation *per se* (Litt, 1986).

There may be a synergistic effect from combining BFT with cognitive therapies. Turk and colleagues (1996), in patients with temperomandibular disorders, found that cognitive therapy plus BFT was superior to BFT plus support in improving depression, pain, and medication use, and in showing continued improvement over time. In migraine patients, Kropp, Niederberger et al. (1997) found that BFT prior to cognitive therapy was superior to the reverse order, and felt that BFT helped patients recognize somatic effects of thoughts and feelings and thereby facilitated cognitive therapies.

Patients treated in the Chronic Pain Rehabilitation Program at Cleveland Clinic Foundation consistently rate BFT as the first or second (to physical therapy) most helpful intervention. Perhaps this is because, in addition to providing an increased sense of personal control, biofeedback helps skeptical patients understand the relationship between external and internal events. A person who witnesses a drop in hand temperature when discussing an employer may be convinced of the importance of stress management in modifying his body's responses. Thus BFT may facilitate work in other program components.

Many studies of biofeedback have confounded conclusions by combining it with other forms of relaxation training (e.g., Blanchard, Appelbaum et al., 1987). Such studies generally show quite positive effects from the combined approach.

Physical Therapy. Physical therapy is included as a reminder of its psychotherapeutic and educational effects. Lying passively while someone applies heat to one's back (1) briefly increases comfort, (2) may teach that the way to maximize comfort is to lie passively while other people work. By contrast, an active reconditioning program teaches that becoming physically reconditioned, strong, and flexible results in reduced pain and improved activity tolerance. Getting in shape is a profound antidote to feelings of helplessness. It is may be more willing to relinquish enabling when they no longer see their loved one as an invalid. Watching him/her play volleyball accomplishes this nicely.

Assertiveness Training. Assertiveness training is a form of therapy in which patients are taught direct ways of communicating their wishes and feelings. This is an important issue in chronic pain syndrome, since many patients will have come to rely on pain as a way of obtaining closeness and as an excuse to avoid unpleasant responsibilities or situations. There are strong disincentives to recover when relinquishing "pain behavior" produces re-exposure to odious tasks and a loss of attention. Therefore patients need to learn to say "no" in a kind but firm way. They must learn to set limits on how others treat them and to openly communicate needs for affection. In these ways, they can render the sick role unnecessary.

PAIN MANAGEMENT VERSUS ADDICTION RECOVERY

Treating chronic pain syndrome in a patient who also has a substance dependence is likely to be futile unless addiction recovery is achieved. Pain patients' defenses pose special obstacles.

There may be a perception of conflict between pain rehabilitation and the principles of Twelve Step programs, yet because of the frequent co-occurrence of addictive disorders and chronic pain syndrome, many patients need both (not to mention those who need adult child of alcoholics, codependence, or Al-Anon groups). Patients may use the apparent conflict to justify their resistance. In fact, the conditions are similar, in that they represent maladaptive cognitive and behavioral syndromes superimposed on an organic substrate.

The material presented on cognitive issues in chronic pain clearly supports the need to empower the patient—helping to foster an "internal locus of control," eliminating feelings of helplessness, and asking the patient to "take control" of their lives and avoid dependence on such authorities as health care professionals. This may seem contrary to needs to acknowledge powerlessness and relinquish control, which are important in addiction recovery.

The crux of the problem may be captured in the Alcoholics Anonymous counsel to "let go and let God" and to "surrender," which seem to conflict with the pain rehabilitation focus on taking charge. This contradiction is more apparent than real, and there are many overlaps between the pathology and treatment goals in pain and addiction. In the same way that addicts may be said to have a primary relationship with a substance, pain patients seem to have a primary relationship with their pain: it becomes the organizing principle of their lives, the subject of all their conversations, and results in a loss of empathy and ability to relate. Both chronic pain syndrome and addiction are maladaptive cognitive and behavioral syndromes superimposed on an organic substrate.

It may be useful to encourage patients to focus on the similarities between chemical dependence and chronic pain, rather than the differences. While these illnesses are not the patients' fault, recovery is the patients' responsibility and requires acceptance of self-responsibility. Although patients do not voluntarily contract either alcoholism or chronic pain syndrome, those with both illnesses often are blamed and criticized for their conditions and thus must overcome stigma.

An essential characteristic of both conditions is that the person's efforts to feel better lead ultimately to feeling worse. In both conditions, the patients' lifestyles cause considerable misery, yet they cling tenaciously to them. Both patients suffer loss of self-esteem. Enabling is a critical component of both syndromes—the misguided efforts of others to be helpful ultimately worsen the pathology and make it more refractory to intervention. There are struggles over the issue of control, and the more helpless the patient feels the more he or she struggles to control, dominate, or manipulate others. Prior to treatment, both groups of patients tend to be defensive, denying, projective of blame and responsibility, closed-minded, angry, and "hard to love." Both groups of patients have a high incidence of depression and suicide. Both conditions are characterized by unmanageability and powerlessness.

Dealing with chronic pain syndrome requires the patient to surrender the continual quest for a cure and accept the fact that at the current state of the art, no one can make them like they used to be. Both chronic pain and addictive disorders are lifelong illnesses that cannot be cured, but can be managed in a way that substantially reduces suffering. Resolving and letting go of resentments is an important part of recovery. In both conditions, patients are able to feel more "in control" by letting go, which is a major focus of biofeedback and relaxation training.

Projection of blame is a major issue. Just as the alcoholic spends inordinate time blaming others for his/her behavior, the patient with chronic pain syndrome may focus on attributing blame ("It is the company's fault, the foreman's, the surgeon's . . .") to the neglect of a focus on improving the situation. Pain patients and those with addictive disorders can be paralyzed by self-pity, the antidote to which is gratitude.

The families of pain patients are affected in ways similar to the families of addicts—their lives are controlled by someone else's illness. They feel bound to give, yet they receive little. Inappropriate self-blame and guilt coexist with intense resentment. They feel helpless, angry, depressed, and their own lives are unmanageable. With both groups of patients, the intervention of a recovering person has a special power that good advice from professionals "who have never been there" cannot equal. Both must learn to trust the process of recovery. With both it "is easier to act ourselves into right thinking than to think ourselves into right acting." Coping with pain "one day at a time" is an easier task to confront than the idea of accepting an eternity of incurable pain.

Pain Self-Help Groups. The American Chronic Pain Association (ACPA) is a self-help recovery program for those with chronic nonmalignant pain. Its focus is on self-management. Members are encouraged to do daily relaxation, stretching exercises, and such psychological tasks as working on goal setting, assertiveness, and avoiding pain behavior. The concept of changing "from a patient to a person" is emphasized. Workbook materials, monthly newsletters, and direction to information sources are provided. There is no cost beyond helping to pay for the coffee. This organization is 14 years old and there are less than 700 chapters worldwide. Approximately 600 are in the U.S. Thus, it may be unavailable to those who need it. Materials are available for those who wish to start new groups. AA or NA attendance are, of course, critical for pain patients with addictive disorders. ACPA attendance will not substitute for these, as its focus is not on substance use.

CHRONIC MALIGNANT PAIN

Cancer pain treatment often is thought of only in terms of pharmacological approaches; however, relaxation therapies, psychotherapy, and guided imagery can be important in malignant as well as nonmalignant pain. Physical therapy directed toward maximization of strength and flexibility can reduce discomfort and improve quality of life, as well as providing opportunities for distraction. Malignant pain, of course, is often cured and may transition into such chronic non-malignant pains as radiation plexopathy or cystitis, which require use of the approaches discussed earlier in this chapter.

ACUTE RECURRENT PAIN

Special difficulties arise in the treatment of patients with such conditions as inflammatory bowel disease, chronic pancreatitis, sickle cell disease, and other illnesses in which there is recurrent, severe, organic pain and a high incidence of addictive disorders. The literature concerning the long-term treatment of pain in these conditions (with the exception of sickle cell disease) is quite sparse. Clinical experience with patients who have Crohn's disease and opiate addiction suggest that the approach described above for chronic benign pain, combined with addiction treatment, is necessary and helpful, but the patients require extensive longitudinal care that may be intense during crises.

MULTIMODALITY TREATMENT PROGRAMS

Multiple approaches seem more effective than unitary treatments. Accordingly, combinations of interventions should be tailored to maximize comfort and function. This requires educating the patient and family about the nature of the pain and about enabling and reinforcements for healthy behavior. Environmental disincentives to recovery should be identified and, if possible, altered. To this should be added formal relaxation training, perhaps with the aid of biofeedback equipment. Cognitive errors should be addressed aggressively, with the most important issues probably being convictions of personal helplessness and "catastrophizing." Physical rehabilitation is essential.

TABLE 3. Multidisciplinary Pain Treatment: Results of Research Studies

- 14% to 60% pain reduction
- Up to 73% decrease in opioid use
- Dramatic increase in activity levels
- 43% more working after treatment than before
- 90% reduction in physician visits (one study)
- 50% to 65% fewer surgeries than untreated patients
- 65% fewer hospitalizations than untreated patients
- 35% fewer patients on disability

Pain rehabilitation programs should combine these elements and, unless they specifically exclude patients with addictive disorders, should have available primary addiction recovery treatment as a major program component. Such programs can dramatically impact on the quality of life and functional abilities of disabled pain patients.

Turk (1996) has reviewed outcome studies of multidisciplinary pain programs (Table 3) and estimated that multidisciplinary pain management led to 27 fewer surgeries per 100 patients, for an average saving of $4,050 per patient (at $15,000 per surgery). He estimated overall medical costs at over $13,000 per year pretreatment and $5,600 in the year after treatment. This suggests average savings of $7,700 per year per patient following treatment. Disability savings are striking, at an estimated $400,000 saved per person removed from permanent disability.

Physicians confronted by patients who are suffering from irreversible pathology may experience therapeutic nihilism and hopelessness. This must not be communicated to patients, for two reasons: First, the message, "There is nothing more I can do for you" confirms hopelessness and can encourage suicide. Second, it is clear that the most grateful patients are not necessarily those whose pain responded to pharmacological intervention. Many treated patients report that their pain is little changed from admission, but they laugh, walk briskly, take no habituating drugs, and report that their suffering has been largely alleviated. They are optimistic and report that "the pain is on the back burner where I don't much think about it." Thus, it is critical to communicate to patients that they can "recover" even when medical interventions have been exhausted.

The methods described in this chapter are not sufficient for all patients, even when combined with non-analgesic medications for pain reduction. Much of the challenge we face as physicians is to identify those in whom psychological and rehabilitation methods produce satisfactory results, those in whom analgesics are helpful, and those whom they harm.

When a patient demonstrates inordinate suffering, medical involvement, disability, or drug use, it is unlikely that solutions will be found external to the patient, whether through pharmacology or technology. Rather, the solution likely will come from the patient's inner resources. It is our task to help that patient find, strengthen, and trust in those resources.

REFERENCES

Affleck G, Urrows S, Tennen H & Higgins P (1992). Daily coping with pain from rheumatoid arthritis: Patterns and correlates. *Pain* 51:221–229.

Ahles TA, Blanchard EB & Ruckdeschel JC (1983). The multidimensional nature of cancer-related pain. *Pain* 17:277–288.

Atkinson JH, Slater MA, Patterson TL, Grant I & Garfin SR (1991). Prevalence, onset, and risk of psychiatric disorders in men with chronic low back pain: A controlled study. *Pain* 45:111–121.

Bendixen M, Muus KM & Schei B (1994). The impact of child sexual abuse—A study of a random sample of Norwegian students. *Child Abuse & Neglect* 18(10):837–847.

Bigos SJ, Battie MC, Spengler DM et al. (1991). A prospective study of work perceptions and psycho-social factors affecting the report of back injury. *Spine* 16(1):1–6.

Blanchard EB & Ahles TA (1990). Biofeedback therapy. In JJ Bonica (ed.) *The Management of Pain, 2nd Ed.* Philadelphia, PA: Lea & Febiger.

Blanchard EB, Appelbaum KA, Guarnieri P, Morrill B & Dentinger MP (1987). Five year prospective follow-up on the treatment of chronic headache with biofeedback and/or relaxation. *Headache* 27(10):580–583.

Buckelew SP, Huyser B, Hewett J et al. (1996). Self-efficacy predicting outcome among fibromyalgia subjects. *Arthritis Care & Research* 9(2):97–104.

Buckelew SP, Parker JC, Keefe FJ et al. (1994). Self-efficacy and pain behavior among subjects with fibromyalgia. *Pain* 59(3):377–384.

Burns JW, Johnson BJ, Mahoney N, Devine J & Pawl R (1996). Anger management style, hostility and spouse responses: Gender differences in predictors of adjustment among chronic pain patients. *Pain* 64(3):445–453.

Chaturvedi SK (1987). Family morbidity in chronic pain patients. *Pain* 30(2):159–168.

Ciccone DS & Grzesiak RC (1984). Cognitive dimensions of chronic pain. *Social Science and Medicine* 19(12):1339–1345.

Crisson JE & Keefe FJ (1988). The relationship of locus of control to pain coping strategies and psychological distress in chronic pain patients. *Pain* 35:147–154.

Dansak, D (1973). On the tertiary gain of illness. *Comprehensive Psychiatry* 14:523.

DeGood DE & Kiernan B (1996). Perception of fault in patients with chronic pain. *Pain* 64(1):153–159.

Deyo RA & Bass JE (1989). Lifestyle and low-back pain: The influence of smoking and obesity. *Spine* 14(5):501–506.

Fahrion SL (1991). Hypertension and biofeedback. *Primary Care* 18(3):663–682.

Fernandez E & Turk DC (1995). The scope and significance of anger in the experience of chronic pain. *Pain* 61(2):165–175.

Fernandez E & Turk DC (1989). The utility of cognitive coping strategies for altering pain perception: A meta-analysis. *Pain* 38:123–135.

Fishbain DA, Rosomoff HL, Cutler RB & Rosomoff RS (1995). Secondary gain concept: A review of the scientific evidence. *Clinical Journal of Pain* 11:6–21.

Fordyce WE (1976). *Behavioral Methods for Chronic Pain and Illness*. St. Louis, MO: CV Mosby.

Fordyce WE, Fowler RS, Lehman JF, Delateur BJ, Sand PL & Trieschmann RB (1973). Operant conditioning in the treatment of chronic pain. *Archives of Physical Medicine & Rehabilitation* 54(9):399–408.

Freedman RR (1991). Physiological mechanisms of temperature biofeedback. *Biofeedback and Self Regulation* 16(2):95–115.

Gilliland R, Wexner SD, Vickers D, Altomare DF & Heymen JS (1997). Biofeedback for intractable rectal pain: Outcome and predictors of success. *Diseases of the Colon and Rectum* 40(2):190–196.

Glazer HI, Young AW, Hertz R, Swencionis C & Rodke G (1995). Treatment of vulvar vestibulitis syndrome with EMG biofeedback of pelvic floor musculature. *Journal of Reproductive Medicine* 40(4):283–290.

Haber JD & Rood C (1985). Effects of spouse abuse and/or sexual abuse in the development and maintenance of chronic pain in women. *Advances in Pain Research and Therapy* 9:889–895.

Ham LP & Packard RC (1996). A retrospective, follow-up study of biofeedback-assisted relaxation therapy in patients with posttraumatic headache. *Biofeedback and Self Regulation* 21(2):93–104.

Harkapaa K, Jarvikoski A, Mellin G, Hurri H & Luoma J (1991). Health locus of control beliefs and psychological distress as predictors for treatment outcome in low-back pain patients: Results of a 3-month followup of a controlled intervention study. *Pain* 46:35–41.

Heath SM, Leong AF, Tan M & Ho YH (1997). Biofeedback is effective treatment for levator ani syndrome. *Diseases of the Colon and Rectum* 40(2):187–189.

Jensen MP, Turner JA & Romano JM (1991). Self-efficacy and outcome expectancies: Relationship to chronic pain coping strategies and adjustment. *Pain* 44:263–269.

Jensen MP, Turner JA, Romano JM & Karoly P (1991). Coping with chronic pain: A critical review of the literature. *Pain* 47:249–283.

Kaplan H & Fields HL (1991). Hyperalgesia during acute opioid abstinence: Evidence for a nociceptive facilitating function of the rostral ventromedial medulla. *Journal of Neuroscience* 11(5):1433–1439.

Katon W, Egan K & Miller D (1985). Chronic pain: Lifetime psychiatric diagnoses and family history. *American Journal of Psychiatry* 142(10):1156–1160.

Keefe FJ, Brown GK, Wallston KA & Caldwell DS (1989). Coping with rheumatoid arthritis pain: Catastrophizing as a maladaptive strategy. *Pain* 37:51–56.

Kelsey JL, Golden AL & Mundt DJ (1990). Low back pain/prolapsed lumbar intervertebral disc. *Rheumatic Disease Clinics of North America* 16(3):699–716.

Kerns RD, Rosenberg R & Jacob MC (1994). Anger expression and chronic pain. *Journal of Behavior Medicine* 17(1):57–67.

King SA & Strain JJ (1990). Benzodiazepine use by chronic pain patients. *Clinical Journal of Pain* 6(2):143–147.

Kori SH, Miller RP & Todd DD (1990). Kinisophobia: A new view of chronic pain behavior. *Pain Management* 3(1):35–43.

Kropp P, Niederberger U, Kopal T, Keinath-Specht A & Gerber WD (1997). Behavioral treatment in migraine. Cognitive-behavioral therapy and blood-volume-pulse biofeedback: A cross-over study with a two-year follow-up. *Functional Neurology* 12(1):17–24.

Lefebvre M (1981). Cognitive distortion and cognitive errors in depressed psychiatric and low back pain patients. *Journal of Consulting and Clinical Psychology* 49:517–525.

Linton SJ (1986). Behavioral remediation of chronic pain: A status report. *Pain* 24:125–141.

Litt MD (1986). Mediating factors in nonmedical treatment for migraine headache: Toward an interactional model. *Journal of Psychosomatic Research* 30(4)505–519.

Maruta T, Vatterott MK & McHardy MJ (1989). Pain management as an antidepressant: Long-term resolution of pain-associated depression. *Pain* 36(3):335–337.

Mathew NT, Kurman R & Perez F (1990). Drug induced refractory headache: Clinical features and management. *Headache* 30:634–638.

Melzack R (1986). Neurophysiology of pain. In RA Sternbach (ed.) *The Psychology of Pain, 2nd Ed.* New York, NY: Raven Press.

Noyes R Jr, Garvey MJ, Cook BL & Perry PJ (1988). Benzodiazepine withdrawal: A review of the evidence. *Journal of Clinical Psychiatry* 49(10):382–389.

Osterweis M, Kleinman A & Mechanic E (1987). *Pain and Disability: Clinical, Behavioral, and Public Policy Perspectives*. Washington, DC: National Academy Press.

Payne B & Norfleet MA (1986). Chronic pain and the family: A review. *Pain* 26:1–22.

Pilowsky I (1960). Abnormal illness behavior. *British Journal of Medical Psychology* 42:347–351.

Rapoport AM (1988). Analgesic rebound headache. *Headache* 28:662–665.

Raskin M, Talbott JA & Meyerson AT (1966). Diagnosis of conversion reactions. *Journal of the American Medical Association* 197:102–106.

Roberts AH (1987). Literature update: Biofeedback and chronic pain. *Journal of Pain and Symptom Management* 2(3):169–171.

Rohling ML, Binder LM & Langhinrichsen-Rohling J (1995). Money matters: A meta-analytic review of the association between financial compensation and the experience and treatment of chronic pain. *Health Psychology* 14(6):537–547.

Roy R (1982a). Marital and family issues in patients with chronic pain: A review. *Psychotherapy and Psychosomatics* 37:112.

Roy R (1982b). Pain-prone patient: A revisit. *Psychotherapy and Psychosomatics* 37:202–213.

Rudy T, Kerns RD & Turk DC (1988). Chronic pain and depression: Toward a cognitive-behavioral mediation model. *Pain* 35:129–140.

Saper JR (1987). Ergotamine dependency—A review. *Headache* 27:435–438.

Smarr KL, Parker JC, Wright GE et al. (1997). The importance of enhancing self-efficacy in rheumatoid arthritis. *Arthritis Care and Research* 10(1):18–26.

Spence SH, Champion D, Newton-John T & Sharpe L (1995). Effect of EMG biofeedback compared to applied relaxation training with chronic, upper extremity cumulative trauma disorders. *Pain* 63(2):199–206.

Turk DC (1996). Efficacy of multidisciplinary pain centers in the treatment of chronic pain. In MJM Cohen & NJ Campbell JN (eds.) *Pain Treatment Centers at a Crossroads: A Practical and Conceptual Reappraisal, Progress in Pain Research and Management (Vol. 7)*. Seattle, WA: IASP Press, 257–273.

Turk DC, Greco CM, Zaki HS, Kubinski JA & Rudy TE (1996). Dysfunctional patients with temporomandibular disorders: Evaluating the efficacy of a tailored treatment protocol. *Journal of Consulting and Clinical Psychology* 64(1):139–146.

Turk DC & Rudy TE (1992). Cognitive factors and persistent pain: A glimpse into Pandora's box. *Cognitive Therapy and Research* 16(2):99–122.

Turk DC & Rudy TE (1986). Assessment of cognitive factors in chronic pain: A worthwhile enterprise? *Jour-*

nal of Consulting and Clinical Psychology 54(6):760–768.

Turk DC, Meichenbaum D & Genest M (1983). *Pain and Behavioral Medicine: A Cognitive-Behavioral Perspective*. New York, NY: Guilford Press.

Turner JA & Chapman CR (1982a). Psychological interventions for chronic pain: A critical review. I. Relaxation training and biofeedback. *Pain* 12:1–21.

Turner JA & Chapman CR (1982b). Psychological interventions for chronic pain: A critical review. II. Operant conditioning, hypnosis and cognitive-behavioral therapy. *Pain* 12:23–46.

Turner JA, Calsyn DA, Fordyce WE & Ready LB (1982). Drug utilization patterns in chronic pain patients. *Pain* 12:357–363.

U.S. Commission on the Evaluation of Pain (1987). *Report of the Commission on the Evaluation of Pain, Appendix C: "Summary of the National Study of Chronic Pain Syndrome."* Washington, DC: Social Security Administration, Office of Disability.

Waddell G, Newton M, Henderson I, Somerville D & Main C (1993). A fear avoidance beliefs questionnaire (FABQ) and the role of fear avoidance beliefs in chronic low back pain and disability. *Pain* 52:157–168.

Williams DA & Thorn BE (1989). An empirical assessment of pain beliefs. *Pain* 36:351–358.

Zlotnick C, Zakriski AL, Shea MT et al. (1996). The long-term sequelae of sexual abuse: Support for a complex posttraumatic stress disorder. *Journal of Trauma and Stress* 9(2):195–205.

CHAPTER 4

Prescribing Issues and the Relief of Pain

Barry Stimmel, M.D., FASAM

Federal and State Regulations
Inadequate Physician Knowledge Base
Overprescription of Analgesics

Studies concerning the ability of persons in pain to receive adequate relief consistently demonstrate inappropriate physician prescribing patterns resulting in needless pain and discomfort. For many people, daily functioning is severely impaired, as well as their interpersonal relationships with family and friends. There are a variety of reasons why physicians may not prescribe sufficient analgesic medications (Table 1). Each must be addressed if the physician's ability to relieve pain is to be maximized.

FEDERAL AND STATE REGULATIONS

The role of the physician in initiating drug dependence (iatrogenic dependence) is of concern not only to physicians and patients but also to legislative bodies.[1,2,3] Since the beginning of the twentieth century, federal legislation has been directed toward monitoring physician prescription of dependency-producing drugs without seriously restricting access to appropriate therapies. Currently, the control of dependency-producing drugs falls under the Controlled Substances Act, with responsibility for enforcement residing with the Drug Enforcement Administration (DEA). Many states, however, have also introduced their own regulations.

The Controlled Substances Act. Under the Controlled Substances Act of 1972, drugs with the ability to produce physical or psychological dependence, associated with the potential for misuse or abuse, are classified into one of five categories. Each category represents gradations of the relative hazards and effectiveness of these agents, ranging from Schedule I substances, which have high abuse potential and no acceptable medical use, to Schedule V substances, which have little abuse potential and can be purchased without a prescription [see Appendix B of this text for a table of controlled substances]. It is important to emphasize, however, that any of the drugs that alter moods has the potential for abuse. Even some of those substances of Schedule V such as codeine, when taken inappropriately in high doses, can cause euphoria and dependence.

The Psychotropic Substances Act. This legislation, enacted in 1978, resulted in an amendment to the Controlled Substances Act and stated that the legitimate and useful prescription of these drugs for medical purposes should not be restricted. It also provided for the Secretary of Health and Human Services, in consultation with the medical and scientific communities, to determine what constituted the ethical practice of medicine with respect to prescription of these substances.

The Uniform Controlled Substances Act (UCSA). This act, initially written in 1970 and revised in 1990, forms the basis for the different states' controlled substances legislation. The revised UCSA recognizes the importance of the medical use of controlled substances, distinguishes patients from addicts, emphasizes the importance of patient confidentiality, permits the use of chronic narcotic analgesic therapy for intolerable pain, and establishes a program to detect drug diversions.

In fact, both federal and state regulations pertaining to the prescription of these drugs are so detailed and yet so vague that they often discourage physicians from prescribing these substances.[1,2,3] Physicians remain concerned that prescription of Schedule II substances for prolonged periods, even when clearly indicated, will subject them to disciplinary action. This is enhanced by the confusion that often exists between addiction and physical dependence. Many state boards require physicians to have tried all alternative means of treatment prior to placing a person on chronic narcotic therapy, with some states requiring psychiatric consultations for chronic nar-

TABLE 1. Reasons for Inadequate Prescription of Analgesics

- Inhibitory influences of federal and state regulations and disciplinary boards
- Lack of suitable knowledge base
- Fear of producing dependency and addiction
- Cultural and societal barriers to use of narcotics
- Adherence to customary prescribing behaviors
- Unconscious bias toward different groups.

cotic therapy under the premise that a need for long-term narcotic analgesics suggests a coexisting disorder. This is especially true for chronic nonmalignant pain. Since these boards often consist of physicians with inadequate knowledge bases, a physician may be called to task for prescribing what in reality is appropriate. One survey of state disciplinary boards revealed that only 75% of its members felt that prescribing opiates for an extended time to treat cancer pain was appropriate. When opiates were prescribed for more than several months for chronic nonmalignant pain, only 12% thought the practice was legal and acceptable. Since most disciplinary boards act on the basis of "customary practice" of the community's physicians and most physicians characteristically underutilize narcotics, a physician who provides appropriate analgesia may well be exposed to sanctions. This is especially true in treating severe pain, which often requires a much greater than "usual" amount of opiate for relief. Several surveys have demonstrated a reluctance of many physicians, even oncologists, to prescribe opiates in appropriate doses due to their concerns with existing regulations.[2,3]

Protection from misuse or abuse of analgesic agents really cannot be legislated but must be accompanied by an understanding of the indications and risks associated with these drugs by physicians, the public, and the regulatory agencies. Competing public interests, mainly the prevention of diversion of legal drugs to illicit use and eliminating prescribing for profit, must be balanced with relief from pain and suffering, which should be the primary concern. All too often the regulatory agencies are more concerned with their policies rather than their effect on the medical community.

INADEQUATE PHYSICIAN KNOWLEDGE BASE

The appropriate use of analgesics and other mood-altering drugs is a subject that unfortunately receives too little attention in medical school and residency training. As a physician moves further away from basic pharmacology—where most of the information concerning drug action is taught—an increasing unfamiliarity with the specific actions of analgesics and other mood-altering agents develops. Drugs may be used more frequently than necessary due to the reliance placed on the publicity given to newer agents, often accompanied by patients' requests for "nonaddictive" substances.

At times, this may result in overprescription of mild narcotic analgesics or excessive use of tranquilizers rather than a narcotic analgesic. Even today, most physicians consider propoxyphene (Darvon®) to be a nonnarcotic, effective, mild analgesic. This is despite the fact that propoxyphene is an ester of methadone and, in sufficient doses, can cause dependence, tolerance, overdose, and addictive behavior indistinguishable from more potent narcotics.[4,7] Codeine and oxycodone (Percocet®), commonly prescribed analgesics, are also capable of producing dependence or addiction. One survey found codeine to be the most frequent drug of abuse in patients without a demonstrable cause of pain.[8] In many instances, those who take codeine are not even aware it is a narcotic.

The narcotic agonist-antagonists are prescribed freely by many physicians without concern of addiction. Yet pentazocine (Talwin®), available as an analgesic since 1967, at one time was an attractive alternative to heroin.[9,10] Buprenorphine (Buprenex®), now being marketed in a noninjectable form, remains uncontrolled despite addicts reporting its effects as similar to heroin in clinical trials and its recognition as one of the leading drugs of abuse in New Zealand.

On the other hand, the use of the benzodiazepines or antidepressants is considerable despite the ability of the former to produce dependence and the latter to cause euphoria when taken inappropriately.[12–14] Surveys have documented the prescription of: (1) antidepressants to 27% of an alcoholic population, although only 7% were felt to be depressed;[12] (2) psychotropic drugs to 58% of women admitted to a metropolitan correction center, although only 23% were felt to need these medications,[13] and (3) a disproportional number of these drugs prescribed by family practitioners and internists compared to frequency of office visits.

Fear of Addiction. Fear of producing addiction to narcotics is foremost in the minds of most physicians when asked to provide medication for pain relief. This fear often interferes with their ability to provide adequate analgesia. One study demonstrated that those physicians who thought the probability of addiction was high after prescribing meperidine for ten days to a patient in pain were more likely to give lower initial doses, as well as to be less likely to respond to the need for increased medication with recurrent pain even if pain was due to terminal malignancy.[15]

A second study of 100 patients with malignant pain found 60% to be prescribed doses of meperidine of 50 mg or less, with 11% having to wait for five or more hours before another dose, with all prescriptions written for PRN administration.[16]

In fact, the risk of initiating an addiction when narcotics are prescribed appropriately for relief of pain is quite small. Although historical references attribute physicians as initiating dependence on opiates, a survey reviewing addiction among a population of Black heroin addicts found that less than 2% attributed their addiction to prescription of a narcotic for medical reasons.[17] Perhaps the largest survey of iatrogenic narcotic dependence was done as part of the Boston Collaborative Drug Surveillance Program.[18] This program monitors all drug exposures in several hospitals, with information extracted from clinical records and by interviews with patients and physicians. Of over 11,000 hospitalized medical patients who had narcotics administered during their hospital stays, only four were reported to have become addicted. A more recent analysis of publications pertaining to drug or alcohol dependence in chronic pain patients found that less than one-tenth of these publications used acceptable criteria for drug misuse or even gave percentages of dependence problems.[19]

Available data, therefore, suggest that when narcotics are utilized appropriately for acute pain in a hospital setting, the actual incidence of medically induced narcotic dependency is negligible. Even in chronic pain populations, there is little evidence that drug abuse or addiction is common. Nonetheless, this apprehension remains among many physicians and, unfortunately, narcotic analgesics continue to be underprescribed. It has been suggested that the reason for this is the metaphysical attitude toward narcotics, which endows them with mystical fearful powers that cause physician opiophobia.[3,16] This is clearly a fear that must be overcome.

Adherence to Customary Prescribing Practices. Physicians' prescribing behavior has been described as consisting of an intermix of three components or modalities: instrumental, command, and customary.[20] *Instrumental* allows for a critical assessment of the specific condition, the properties of the drugs to be used, and their effectiveness. *Command* is the modality pursued when one acts to avoid any penalties associated with noncompliance. *Customary*, or traditional, behavior reflects actions approved by the community peer group. The prescription of narcotic analgesics most commonly follows the command and customary modalities. Physicians who prescribe inappropriate doses of meperidine or mixed narcotics and benzodiazepines do so not from ignorance, but from following what has been the customary practice of using opioids as conservatively as possible, and then only as a last resort. A recent study of physicians treating patients with metastatic cancer pain highlighted such customary practices.[21] When asked which medications they would prescribe for moderate to severe cancer pain, 38% did not choose an opioid first, with 14% stating they would not choose such a drug even after palliative radiotherapy had failed.

TABLE 2. Guidelines for Prescribing Drugs with Abuse Liability

1. Set clear rules for the patient and have him/her sign a contract.
2. Set the dose of medication at the appropriate level to treat the condition and titrate as necessary. Get feedback from the patient.
3. Give enough medication, plus rescue doses.
4. Ask the patient to bring any remaining drugs to the next meeting in the original bottles. This provides information on pharmacies used and other prescribing physicians.
5. Monitor for lost or stolen prescriptions.
6. Obtain random urine screens. Know what drugs laboratory screens actually can identify.
7. Use adjunctive medications as necessary.
8. Document all your thoughts [in selecting and monitoring the pharmacotherapy] in the chart.
9. See the patient as frequently as needed.
10. Work with the patient's significant others.
11. Know how to withdraw the patient from the medications.
12. Know the pharmacology of the drugs used.
13. Limit PRN medications, since this promotes drug-seeking behavior.
14. Adequately treat acute pain to prevent the development of chronic pain.

Source: Schnoll SH & Finch J (1994). Medical education for pain and addiction: Making progress toward answering a need. *Journal of Law, Medicine & Ethics* 22(3):254. Reprinted by permission of the publisher.

Unconscious Bias. It is unfortunate but true that some of us react to a person's complaint based not on the specific complaint as much as on the characteristics of the person complaining. It has been shown that physicians' attitudes toward alcoholic or drug-dependent persons may interfere with their diagnosis and treatment.[22] Another study assessing the use of analgesics in an emergency room found Hispanic patients with bone fractures to be twice as likely as non-Hispanic patients to receive no pain medication.[23]

Similarly, persons in chronic pain who have seen many physicians without relief are, at times, thought by physicians to be less than honest concerning their symptoms. They are perceived as coming in for a visit only to request medication to allow them to get high. African-American patients have also been reported more likely to receive less than adequate analgesics. One study found patients attending cancer pain treatment clinics less likely to receive adequate analgesics when those clinics were treating primarily minority groups.[24] Patients with acute painful states, such as sickle cell disease, who may have developed a tolerance for narcotics and are in need of an increased dose, are often considered to be exaggerating their pain. Women and the elderly with metastatic cancer also were more likely to obtain less adequate analgesia than others. At times inadequate analgesics are prescribed because the patient appears less ill than the physician would expect if severe pain was present. One survey reported that 76% of physicians admit an inability to accurately assess pain, which suggests that many physicians only recognize pain when a person truly appears to be suffering or when function is severely impaired.[21]

Cultural and Social Barriers. Finally, since people's beliefs are formed by the society in which they live, often when a physician wishes to prescribe appropriately to relieve pain, the patient refuses to take this drug, also displaying opiophobia. This is frequently seen when one tries to prescribe methadone to a person in chronic pain who is not receiving relief from his or her current medication regimen. Often the person is on impressive amounts of short-acting narcotic analgesics, as well as dependency-producing amounts of benzodiazepines and other sleeping pills. Although the person remains somewhat groggy, the pain persists and prevents functioning. Yet, methadone is refused because that person feels this will incur the label of "junkie" due to the use of methadone in maintenance therapy for heroin dependency. The same person, however, will have little concern about taking large doses of Demerol® or Dilaudid®. It is difficult to overcome these biases, yet it is essential to do so in order to maximize the chances of providing effective pain relief.

OVERPRESCRIPTION OF ANALGESICS

At times, inappropriate excessive prescriptions of analgesics occur. A physician may be aware of an individual's physical dependency but, because of compassion for the patient's efforts to obtain this drug, may rationalize its prescription in order to decrease the person's anxiety or concern. Persons dependent upon various prescription drugs often are able to manipulate a physician into prescribing medication for imagined ailments without the physician realizing that these medications will only further a physical dependency. In such cases, a person may visit many physicians, requesting only a small number of pills, returning in a sequential yet "spaced" pattern to prevent arousing suspicion of drug abuse.

Physicians who themselves have become physically dependent on prescription drugs may, in an attempt to rationalize their own dependence, prescribe these drugs in increasing dosage. Finally, a small but finite number of physicians uncaring of the hazards associated with misuse and abuse of such drugs may prescribe them solely for profit. Although these physicians represent an extremely small proportion of practitioners, nonetheless, in certain instances, they may be responsible for the appearance of large numbers of drugs on the street.

SUMMARY

Existing evidence suggests that iatrogenic drug dependence is a real phenomenon but one that occurs infrequently when dependency-producing drugs are prescribed in an appropriate manner. Consistent narcotic use in chronic pain of known etiology that is unable to be relieved by other means, while associated with physical dependence, may nonetheless allow an individual to function in a productive manner. The potential for the development of iatrogenic dependence to barbiturates or other drugs used inappropriately to promote or enhance analgesics is much greater. Since physicians are often less inhibited in prescribing these medications, the indication for their use are frequently interpreted rather liberally. The many factors involved in inappropriate prescription of analgesics are all able to be identified, and when this is done, effective pain relief can occur.

ACKNOWLEDGMENT: Originally puublished as Stimmel B (1997). Unrelieved pain: The role of the physician. In B Stimmel, Pain and Its Relief Without Addiction: Clinical Issues in the Use of Opioids and Other Analgesics. *New York, NY: The*

Haworth Medical Press. Reprinted by permission of the publisher.

REFERENCES

1. Hill CS Jr (1993). The negative influence of licensing and disciplinary boards and more drug enforcement agencies on pain treatment with opioid analgesics. *Journal of Pharmaceutical Care in Pain and Symptom Control* 1:43–61.
2. Joranson DE (1993). Regulation influence on pain management: Real or imagined? *Journal of Pharmaceutical Care in Pain and Symptom Control* 1:113–118.
3. Stimmel B (1985). Underprescription/overprescription: Narcotic as metaphor. *Bulletin of the New York Academy of Medicine* 61:742–752.
4. Miller RR (1977). Propoxyphene: A review. *American Journal of Hospital Pharmacy* 34:413–423.
5. National Institute on Drug Abuse (1977, July–September). *Phase Report.* Washington, DC: Drug Abuse Warning Network, Project DAWN: U.S. Department of Justice, U.S. Department of Health, Education, and Welfare.
6. New warning on propoxyphene. *FDA Drug Bulletin* 9:22–23.
7. Smith RJ (1979). Federal government faces painful decision on Darvon. *Science* 203:857–858.
8. Maruta T, Swanson DW & Finlayson RE (1979). Drug abuse and dependency in patients with chronic pain. *Mayo Clinic Proceedings* 54:241–244.
9. Bailey WJ (1979). Nonmedical use of pentazocine (Letter). *Journal of the American Medical Association* 242:2392.
10. Inciardi JA & Chambers CD (1971). Patterns of pentazocine abuse and addiction. *New York State Journal of Medicine* 71:1727–1733.
11. Lavelle TL, Hammersley R, Forsyth A & Bain D (1991). The use of buprenorphine and temazepam by drug injectors. *Journal of Addictive Diseases* 10(3):5–14.
12. Glatt MM (1983). Alcoholism (Letter). *Lancet* 2:735.
13. Shaw A (1983, October 10). Women inmates are being overtranquilized. *The Journal,* Toronto.
14. Chambers CD, White OZ & Linquest JH (1981). *Physicians' Attitudes and Prescribing Behavior. A Focus on Minor Tranquilizers.* National Meeting on Prescribing. New York: City College of the City University of New York.
15. Marks RM & Sachar EJ (1973). Undertreatment of medical inpatients with narcotic analgesics. *Annals of Internal Medicine* 78:173–181.
16. Morgan JP & Plect DL(1983). Opiophobia in the United States. *The Undertreatment of Severe Pain in Society and Medication: Conflicting Signals for Prescribing of Patients.* Lexington, MA: Lexington Books, 313–326.
17. Chambers CD & Moffett AD (1970). Negro opiate addiction. In JC Ball, CD Chambers (eds.) *The Epidemiology of Opiate Addiction in the United States.* Springfield, IL: Charles C Thomas, 288–300.
18. Porter J & Jick H (1980). Addiction rare in inpatients treated with narcotics (Letter). *The New England Journal of Medicine* 302:123.
19. Fishbain DA, Rosomoff HL & Rosomoff RS (1992). Drug abuse, dependence, and addiction in chronic pain patients. *Clinical Journal of Pain* 8:77–85.
20. Termin P (1980). *Taking Your Medicine: Drug Regulations in the United States.* Cambridge, MA: Harvard University Press, 12–17.
21. Cleeland CS, Gonin R, Hatfield AK et al. (1994). Pain and its treatment in outpatients with metastatic cancer. *New England Journal of Medicine* 330:592–596.
22. Chappel JN & Schnoll SH (1977). Physician attitudes: Effect on the treatment of chemically dependent patients. *Journal of the American Medical Association* 237:2318–2319.
23. Todd KH, Samaroo N & Hoffman JR (1993). Ethnicity as a risk factor for inadequate emergency department analgesia. *Journal of the American Medical Association* 269:1537–1539.
24. Blendon RJ, Aiken LH, Freeman HE & Corey CR (1989). Access to medical care for black and white Americans: A matter of continuing concern. *Journal of the American Medical Association* 261:278–281.
25. Smith SN & Blachly PH (1966). Amphetamine usage by medical students. *Journal of Medical Education* 41:167–270.
26. Vaillant GE, Brighton JR & McArthur C (1970). Physicians' use of mood-altering drugs: A 20-year follow-up report. *The New England Journal of Medicine* 282:365–370.
27. Vaillant GE, Sobowale NC & McArthur C (1972). Some psychological vulnerabilities of physicians. *The New England Journal of Medicine* 287:372–375.
28. Johnson RP & Connelly JC (1981). Addicted physicians: A closer look. *Journal of the American Medical Association* 245:253–258.
29. Winick C (1961). Physician narcotic addicts. *Social Problems* 9:174–186.
30. McAuliffe WE, Rohman M & Wechsler H (1984). Alcohol, substance use, and other risk-factors of impairment in a sample of physicians-in-training. *Advances in Alcohol and Substance Abuse* 4(2):67–87.
31. Bissell L & Jones RW (1976). The alcoholic physician: A survey. *American Journal of Psychiatry* 133:1142–1146.
32. Vincent MO, Robinson EA & Latt I (1969). Physicians as patients. *Canadian Medical Association Journal* 100:403–412.
33. Green RC Jr, Carroll GJ & Buxton WD (1976). Drug addiction among physicians: The Virginia experience. *Journal of the American Medical Association* 236:1372–1375.

SECTION 13
Psychiatric Disorders in the Addicted Patient

CHAPTER 1

Substance-Induced Mental Disorders **969**
R. Jeffrey Goldsmith, M.D. and Richard K. Ries, M.D.

CHAPTER 2

Comorbid Addiction and Affective Disorders **983**
Kathleen T. Brady, M.D., Ph.D., Hugh Myrick, M.D. and Susan Sonne, Pharm.D.

CHAPTER 3

Anxiety Disorders **993**
David R. Gastfriend, M.D. and Patrick Lillard, M.D.

CHAPTER 4

Psychotic Disorders **1007**
Douglas Ziedonis, M.D., M.P.H., and Steve Wyatt, D.O.

CHAPTER 5

Attention-Deficit/Hyperactivity Disorder,
Intermittent Explosive Disorder, and Eating Disorders **1029**
Frances Rudnick Levin, M.D. and Stephen J. Donovan, M.D.

CHAPTER 6

Other Impulse Control Disorders **1047**
Susan L. McElroy, M.D., Cesar A. Soutullo, M.D. and R. Jeffrey Goldsmith, M.D.

CHAPTER 7

Borderline Personality Disorder **1063**
Linda A. Dimeff, Ph.D., Katherine Anne Comtois, Ph.D.
and Marsha M. Linehan, Ph.D.

CHAPTER 8

Integrating Psychotherapy and Pharmacotherapies
in Addiction Treatment **1081**
Joan E. Zweben, Ph.D.

SECTION COORDINATORS

Richard K. Ries, M.D.
Professor of Psychiatry
Harborview Medical Center
Department of Psychiatry and Behavioral Sciences
University of Washington
Seattle, Washington

Kathleen T. Brady, M.D., Ph.D.
Professor of Psychiatry
Center for Drug and Alcohol Programs
Medical University of South Carolina
Charleston, South Carolina

CONTRIBUTORS

Katherine Anne Comtois, Ph.D.
Behavioral Research and Therapy Clinics
Department of Psychology
University of Washington
Seattle, Washington

Linda A. Dimeff, Ph.D.
Behavioral Research and Therapy Clinics
Department of Psychology
University of Washington
Seattle, Washington

Stephen J. Donovan, M.D.
New York State Psychiatric Institute and
Columbia University
New York, New York

David R. Gastfriend, M.D.
Director of Addiction Services
Massachusetts General Hospital, and
Associate Professor of Psychiatry
Harvard Medical School
Boston, Massachusetts

R. Jeffrey Goldsmith, M.D.
Department of Veterans Affairs Hospital
Dual Diagnosis Clinic
Cincinnati, Ohio

Frances Rudnick Levin, M.D.
New York State Psychiatric Institute and
Department of Psychiatry
Columbia University
New York, New York

Patrick Lillard, D.O.
Clinical Director of Addiction Services
Massachusetts General Hospital
Instructor, Harvard Medical School
Boston, Massachusetts

Marsha M. Linehan, Ph.D.
Behavioral Research and Therapy Clinics
Department of Psychology
University of Washington
Seattle, Washington

Susan L. McElroy, M.D.
Director, Biological Psychiatry Program
Professor of Psychiatry
University of Cincinnati
College of Medicine
Cincinnati, Ohio

Hugh Myrick, M.D.
Assistant Professor of Psychiatry
Center for Drug and Alcohol Programs
Medical University of South Carolina
Charleston, South Carolina

Susan Sonne, Pharm.D.
Assistant Professor of Psychiatry
Center for Drug and Alcohol Programs
Medical University of South Carolina
Charleston, South Carolina

Cesar A. Soutullo, M.D.
Biological Psychiatry Program
Department of Psychiatry
University of Cincinnati
College of Medicine
Cincinnati, Ohio

Steve Wyatt, D.O.
Medical Director
Dual Diagnosis Program
Yale University
Connecticut Mental Health Center
New Haven, Connecticut

Douglas Ziedonis, M.D., M.P.H.
Associate Professor and
Director of the Addiction Division
Robert Wood Johnson Medical School
and Senior Researcher
Rutgers University Center for Alcohol Studies
Piscataway, New Jersey

Joan E. Zweben, Ph.D.
Clinical Professor of Psychiatry
University of California, San Francisco
and Executive Director
14th Street Clinic and
East Bay Community Recovery Project
Oakland, California

CHAPTER 1

Substance-Induced Mental Disorders

R. Jeffrey Goldsmith, M.D.
Richard K. Ries, M.D.

Substance-Induced Symptoms
Epidemiological Issues
Differential Diagnostic Process

The substance-induced mental disorders are a common problem in clinical practice. They are critical for the physician to understand because they can mimic almost every syndrome seen in psychiatry. Because they are common and because they mimic the other syndromes, they should appear in most differential diagnoses. The fourth edition of the *Diagnostic and Statistical Manual of Mental Disorders* (*DSM-IV*) of the American Psychiatric Association (1994) contains a new set of definitions of the substance-induced mental disorders, which differ slightly from the guidelines offered in the revised third edition (*DSM-III*; American Psychiatric Association, 1987). This chapter will describe the diagnostic criteria in the *DSM-IV*, review the epidemiological data, and discuss the clinical strategies needed to manage these disorders.

There are nine substance-induced disorders in the *DSM-IV.* Three are referred to generically as "organic brain syndrome": substance-induced delirium, substance-induced persisting dementia, and substance-induced persisting amnestic disorder. They will be included in other chapters and are not covered here. Three mimic many of the common Axis I disorders: substance-induced psychotic, mood, and anxiety disorders. They are covered here, as is hallucinogen persisting perceptual disorder. The last two, substance-induced sexual dysfunction and substance-induced sleep disorder, also are covered in other chapters and will not be addressed here.

SUBSTANCE-INDUCED SYMPTOMS

The occurrence of psychiatric symptoms as a result of legal and illegal drug use has been well documented. It is common medical knowledge that hallucinogens cause hallucinations, stimulants cause euphoria, and chronic sedative use can bring on depression. It is common medical knowledge that, in acute withdrawal, alcohol and sedatives cause anxiety. It is less obvious that a distinct set of symptoms appear when psychoactive substances are used over a long period of time. Symptoms reported for the major substances are reviewed below to establish a basis on which to understand the syndromes that may arise.

Caffeine is the most commonly used addictive substance. It is considered a benign drug by many consumers and professionals, and has enjoyed an increase in popularity in the 1990s. The effects of caffeine include the induction of anxiety with consumption of "large amounts"; however, the range of caffeine doses that can induce anxiety is considerable. Caffeine can increase the frequency of panic attacks in those individuals who are physiologically predisposed to them.

Nicotine is the deadliest psychoactive drug and third most popular psychoactive drug in the U.S., with about 27% of the adult population smoking cigarettes, about 5% using smokeless tobacco, and about 5% smoking pipes and cigars. While there is no indication that nicotine acutely changes mood, there is evidence that nicotine-dependent patients experience much more depression than non-users, and that some use nicotine to regulate mood. Whether there is a causal relationship between nicotine use and the symptoms of depression remains to be seen. At present, it can only be said that some persons who quit smoking do experience severe depression, which is relieved by resumption of nicotine use.

Alcohol use is common among American adolescents and young adults. While light consumption of alcohol is associated with a slight euphoria or "buzz," moderate to heavy consumption may be associated with depression, suicidal feelings, and/or violent behavior in some individuals. With prolonged drinking, the incidence of dysphoria and anxiety rises, much to the distress of the drinker. In those who are physiologically dependent, there usually is a hyperadrenergic state that is characterized by agitation, anxiety, tremor, malaise, hyperreflexia, mild tachycardia, increasing blood pressure, sweating, insomnia, nausea or vomiting, and perceptual distortions for some. After the acute withdrawal from alcohol, some persons suffer from continued mood instability, with moderate lows, fatiguability, insomnia, reduced sexual interest, and hostility. A few chronic heavy drinkers experience hallucinations, delusions, and anxiety during acute withdrawal, and some have grand mal seizures. Brain damage of several types is associated with alcohol-induced dementias and deliriums.

With *sedatives*, particularly the benzodiazepines, acute use can produce a "high" similar to that with alcohol. They are perceived as relaxing, producing a social ease, but can induce depression, anxiety, and even a psychotic-like state with prolonged use and dependence (Ashton, 1991). Withdrawal symptoms include mood instability, with anxiety and/or depression, sleep disturbance, autonomic hyperactivity, tremor, nausea or vomiting, transient hallucinations or illusions, and grand mal seizures. A protracted withdrawal syndrome has been reported to include anxiety, depression, paresthesias, perceptual distortions, muscles pain and twitching, tinnitus, dizziness, headache, derealization and depersonalization, and impaired concentration. These symptoms may last for weeks and some (anxiety, depression, tinnitus, paresthesias) have been reported for a year or more post-withdrawal.

Cocaine and *amphetamine* use often are associated with an intense euphoria or "rush," with hyperactive behavior and speech, anorexia, insomnia, inattention, and labile moods (Gold, 1993). The route of administration and the dose alter the intensity of the experience. After a binge of several days, addicts may feel "wired" or "geeked" and stop their use, or use other drugs to moderate the agitation. Individuals occasionally become paranoid and even delusional after prolonged heavy use. Unlike other psychotic states, the cocaine paranoiac has intact abstract reasoning and linear thinking, while the delusions, if analyzed, are poorly developed delusions of a non-bizarre nature (Mendoza & Miller, 1992). If abstinence is maintained for several weeks, many stimulant addicts report a dysphoric state that is prominently marked by anhedonia and/or anxiety, but which does not meet the symptom severity criteria to qualify as a *DSM-IV* disorder (Rounsaville, Anton et al., 1991). This anhedonic state may persist for weeks. Some stimulant addicts report hallucinatory symptoms that are visual ("coke snow") and tactile ("coke bugs"). Sleep disturbances are prominent in the intoxicated and withdrawn states, as is sexual dysfunction.

Opiate use is characterized by a "high" or "rush" when the drug is used intraveneously or smoked. Unlike the stimulants, the opiate euphoria usually is associated with some sedation and manifests as a mellow, sleepy state. If opiates are used for a long period of time, moderate to severe depression is common. The addict frequently experiences irritability, with craving, muscle aches, a flu-like syndrome, gastrointestinal symptoms, etc., early in withdrawal from drugs like heroin and morphine. More drug subdues the craving. In withdrawal, the opiate addict may be acutely anxious and agitated, but also may report depression and anhedonia. Anxiety, depression, and sleep disturbance, in a milder form, may persist for weeks as a protracted withdrawal syndrome. There are reports of an atypical opiate withdrawal syndrome, consisting of delirium following the abrupt cessation of methadone (Levinson, Galynker & Rosenthal, 1995). Such patients do not appear to have the typical autonomic symptoms typically seen in opiate withdrawal.

Hallucinogens such as marijuana, THC, LSD, mescaline, and DMT produce visual distortions and frank hallucinations. There can be a marked sense of time distortion and feelings of depersonalization. *Marijuana* and the cannabinoids can augment appetite and cause sedation with euphoria. All hallucinogens are associated with drug-induced panic reactions that feature panic, paranoia and even delusional states, on top of the hallucinations. There are descriptions of physiological dependence to marijuana with a mild withdrawal; however, the vast majority of users do not exhibit such problems. There is a debate in the literature concerning the existence of a marijuana-induced psychotic state (Gruber & Pope, 1994). A careful interpretation of the research still suggests that there is not such an entity. A few hallucinogen users experience chronic reactions, involving: (1) prolonged psychotic reactions; (2) depression, which can be life-threatening; (3) flashbacks; and (4) exacerbations of preexisting psychiatric illness. The flashbacks are symptoms that occur after one or more psychedelic trips, and consist of flashes of light and afterimage prolongation in the periphery. The *DSM-IV* refers to flashbacks as an "hallucinogen persisting perception disorder" and requires that they be distressing or impairing to the patient (American Psychiatric Association, 1994, p. 234).

Phencyclidine (PCP), an arylcyclohexylamine and dissociative drug, is a hallucinogen used in certain parts of the U.S. Popular in the 1970s (Giannini, 1991), PCP is known for its dissociative and delusional properties. It also is associated with violent behavior and amnesia of the intoxication (Giannini, 1991). Users who once exhibit an acute psychotic state with PCP are more likely to develop another with repeated use (Zukin & Zukin, 1992).

EPIDEMIOLOGICAL ISSUES

The epidemiology of substance-induced mental disorders is difficult to report because there is no research specifically directed at these disorders. The research literature reports on the prevalence of a particular diagnosis at a given point in time (Lydiard, Brady et al., 1992) or symptom over a period of time (Brown & Schuckit, 1988; Brown, Inaba et al., 1995), and a few mention symptoms and diagnoses over time (Dorus, Kennedy et al., 1987; Brown, Inaba et al., 1995; Rounsaville, Anton et al., 1991). Numerous case studies report the phenomena of substance-induced disorders, but not the epidemiology. Rather, they alert the general psychiatrist to the common occurrence of the disorders and the need to be cognizant. But very few studies report the prevalence of substance-induced mood, anxiety, or psychotic disorders.

However, the research suggests some estimates of the prevalence of alcohol-induced anxiety and depressive disorders. Brown and Schuckit (1988) report that 42% of their male alcoholic population displayed depressive symptoms in a range comparable to individuals hospitalized for affective disorder (more than 19 points, in the moderate-severe range of the Hamilton Depression Rating Scale). There was rapid abatement of these symptoms over the first two weeks of abstinence, with only 12% still depressed at the end of the second week—a change of 30%. In light of this rapid abatement of depressive symptoms, it is significant that the subjects averaged more than nine days of abstinence before the study began. This is a very conservative estimate of substance-induced depression, considering that some of the subjects in the mildly depressed range (11 to 19 points on the Hamilton Depression Rating Scale) could have been in the moderate-severe range at the initiation of sobriety.

Using a similar alcoholic population, who had been sober for an average of eight days, Brown and colleagues (1995) reported that 33% of the primary alcoholics (with or without secondary affective disorder) scored in the moderate-to-severe range (more than 19 points on the Hamilton Depression Rating Scale), while 81% of the subjects with primary affective disorder did so at the end of week 1. By week 4 of the study, none of the primary alcoholics were in the moderate-severe range, while 67% of the primary affective disordered group were. This suggests that all 33% of the primary alcoholism group had alcohol-induced depressive disorder, a number quite comparable to the 30% reported in the earlier study by the same group of researchers.

Dorus and colleagues (1987) used the Beck Depression Inventory rather than the Hamilton Depression Scale, making 17 the cut-off point for moderate-to-severe depression. They found that at day 1 (four or more days abstinent), 67% of their study group were depressed, while only 16% were depressed at day 24. This change suggests that over half had an alcohol-induced depressive disorder. Even more interesting, many of the subjects with a current or lifetime *DSM-III* diagnosis of major depression had scored below the 17 point cut-off level, suggesting that differentiating between the alcohol-induced and primary affective disorders may be difficult for any specific patient.

Keeler and colleagues (1979) used the Hamilton Depression Rating Scale and found that, after a week on a detoxification unit, 28% had a score of 20 or greater. Using the *DSM-II* criteria during clinical interviews with patients, fewer than 9% met the criteria for depression, suggesting that 20% had alcohol-induced depression. However, one must approach these data carefully, because the investigators used *DSM-II* criteria and arrived at diagnoses within seven days of admission.

In a study designed to examine substance-induced psychotic disorders, Rosenthal and Miner (1997) prospectively examined admissions to an acute psychiatric inpatient unit. Over the first year, they found that 30% of those admitted met the *DSM-IIIR* criteria for organic mood disorder, 8% for organic hallucinosis, and 6% for organic delusional disorder. Further, they found that 15% of schizophrenics with psychoactive substance use disorder had acute suicidal ideation, while 42% of the group with psychoactive substance use disorder and organic delusional disorder or organic hallucinosis were suicidal.

Substance-induced depression may dissipate rapidly; however, it is as dangerous or more so than major depressive disorder in terms of risk of suicide and self-injurious behavior. The rate of comorbidity is high when completed suicides are investigated. Henriksson and colleagues (1993) reported that nearly half (43%) of a group of suicide victims in Finland had alcohol dependence and that 48% of the alcoholics had comorbid depression, 42% a personality disorder, and 36% had a significant Axis III medical disorder. Young and colleagues (1994) found that persons who had major depressive disorder with both alcohol and drug dependence were at the highest risk for suicide, even in the absence of pervasive hopelessness. Pages and colleagues (in press) found that alcohol and drug dependence, as well as current use, were associated with greater severity of suicidal ideation among patients with unipolar major depressive disorder. Salloum and colleagues (1996) studied patients who had been hospitalized psychiatrically and found that over half of the subjects in all three groups (alcohol dependence, cocaine dependence, and alcohol and cocaine dependence) studied had a history of prior suicide attempts.

Elliott and colleagues (1996) found that patients with medically severe suicide attempts had a statistically higher prevalence of substance-induced mood disorder than the patients who had a less severe suicide attempt. In addition, there was no difference between the groups in their prevalence of alcohol abuse/dependence nor the prevalence of polysubstance abuse/dependence. Moreover, they found that the majority of the patients with substance-induced mood disorder did not meet the criteria for substance dependence. This is consistent with the findings of Asnis and colleagues (1993) and Murphy and Wetzel (1990), who argue that alcohol dysregulates mood independent of use, suggesting that some individuals are at risk for severe depression regardless of chronicity of use. However, among schizophrenics, Bartels and colleagues (1992) found that depression severity, not substance abuse, explained suicidal behavior. Seibyl and colleagues (1993), in contrast, reported that schizophrenics who had used cocaine prior to admission exhibited increased suicidal ideation.

Anxiety symptoms showed similar changes over the early sobriety phase. Several studies have reported high rates of anxiety symptoms for alcoholics in withdrawal. Several studies reported that 80% of alcohol-dependent male subjects had repetitive panic attacks during alcohol withdrawal (Schuckit & Hesselbrock, 1994). Further, 50% to 67% of the alcohol-dependent men had high scores on the state anxiety measures, which resembled generalized anxiety and social phobia (Schuckit & Hesselbrock, 1994). Brown and colleagues (1991) reported that 40% of recently detoxified alcohol-dependent males scored above the 75% percentile on the state-anxiety subscale of the State Trait Anxiety Inventory. At discharge after four weeks, 12% scored that high, while at three month follow-up only 5% remained above the 75% percentile. This suggests that 35% had an alcohol-induced anxiety disorder. Moreover, if 80% of alcoholic males report withdrawal panic attacks, is this alcohol withdrawal anxiety disorder or is it an independent panic disorder evoked by alcohol withdrawal? Or is it merely anxiety symptoms caused by alcohol withdrawal?

Rounsaville and colleagues (1991), using a group of cocaine addicts, studied the current and lifetime prevalence of Research Diagnostic Criteria (RDC) disorders. They used a strict criteria and a less strict criteria when evaluating the depression diagnostic data from the SADS-L. The less strict criteria made the diagnosis if the symptoms had ever been present, while the strict criteria included only those whose symptoms persisted beyond 10 days from the cessation of cocaine use. The former measure resulted in a 59% rate of major depression, while the latter yielded a 30% rate. This conservatively suggests a rate of about 30% for cocaine-induced depressive disorder during a lifetime. Further, the current rate of major depression was 4.7%, hypomania was 2% and minor mood disorders was 38% (mania was 0) (Rounsaville, Anton et al., 1991). (The current diagnoses of minor mood disorders appeared to use the strict criteria, but this is not clarified in the article.) Examining the anxiety disorders, Rounsaville and colleagues (1991) reported a 16% current rate and a 21% lifetime rate, but they did not comment about what criteria were used to include the symptoms in the diagnosis of anxiety unrelated to cocaine use.

Efforts to differentiate between substance-induced and independent depressive and anxiety disorders among a group of substance abusers (with a variety of drug dependencies) showed limited validity (Kadden, Kranzler & Rounsaville, 1995). The investigators used *DSM-IIIR* criteria, but allowed the clinicians to ask their own questions. They had two expert clinicians make a diagnosis of "independent" of "substance-induced" for each subject, based on two criteria. One criterion allowed an "independent" diagnosis as long as the symptoms satisfied the diagnostic criteria, while the other required that the symptoms precede the onset of the substance use disorder or that they occurred during a six-month period of abstinence from that substance. Use of the latter criteria produced fewer diagnoses of "independent" disorders and lower kappa values: $p<0.1$ (less agreement among raters when a comorbid diagnosis was made, only four of 18 in agreement). With the less strict criteria, there was "fair" agreement among raters, who agreed 18 out of 28 times when a comorbid diagnosis was made, for a kappa of 0.50.

DIFFERENTIAL DIAGNOSIS

Making the diagnosis is very much affected by the attitude and training of the clinician. Is the physician attuned to the prevalence of alcohol and drug use? Without this awareness, there is less inclination to search for the problem. Does the physician think that it is relevant to the current problem to take the time to elicit an alcohol and drug use history? Has the physician received adequate training to counteract the therapeutic nihilism acquired during medical school and residency training? Is the physician adversely affected by the distortions and denial which are exhibited by many alcoholics and drug addicts? Does the physician routinely seek corroboration of an alcohol and drug use history from family or friends of the patient? Will the physician order a toxic drug screen? All of these questions hint at behaviors that can make the diagnosis more apparent or leave it disguised.

Making the diagnosis of a substance use disorder is the first step in the differential diagnosis of substance-related problems. In the second step, the substance-induced symptoms must be differentiated from the symptoms of major psychoactive disorders. Finally, the substance-induced disorders must be differentiated from the dual disorders: substance abuse/dependence combined with a comorbid, nonsubstance Axis I disorder.

The *DSM-IV* contains five criteria for the substance-induced mood disorders (American Psychiatric Association, 1994):

1. A prominent and persistent disturbance in mood predominates, characterized by (a) a depressed mood or markedly diminished interest or pleasure in activities or (b) an elevated, expansive, or irritable mood;
2. There is evidence from the history, physical examination, or laboratory findings that the symptoms developed during or within a month of substance intoxication or withdrawal or medication use are etiologically related to the mood disturbance;
3. The disturbance is not better accounted for by a mood disorder;
4. The disturbance did not occur exclusively during a delirium; and
5. The symptoms cause clinically significant distress or impairment.

Mood disorders may be the most common substance-induced disorders that clinicians need to consider in their differential diagnostic process. It is important to consider, and make, the substance use diagnosis whenever it is pertinent. There are some guidelines which can help with these diagnoses. Because of denial, the patient may not understand what is happening in his or her life. If the clinician is aware of the prevalence of addictive disorders and the typical ways in which they present, he or she is more likely to take a careful history and to seek confirmation of the history from collateral informants, especially family and friends, but including health care professionals when relevant. Establishing whether there is a relationship between the use of psychoactive substances and the symptoms prominent at the moment is a crucial step. Chronic use of alcohol, sedatives, and opiates can cause depressed mood, as can withdrawal from stimulants and sedatives. Exploring the mood during periods of sustained abstinence from all depressive drugs is critical.

For the substance-induced *anxiety disorders*, the criteria are almost identical. However, the first is different: prominent anxiety, panic attacks, obsessions or compulsions predominate. The remaining four criteria are the same as for mood disorder (American Psychiatric Association, 1994). In making the diagnosis of a substance use disorder, it is helpful to order a toxic screen. Even if the results come back hours after the clinical decision is made, they can be used to confirm the presence of a substance in the face of patient denial. Such a screen also may clarify the history for use in a future episode. Sometimes addicts will report part of the story, but not all. For example, it may be useful to know that both alcohol and cocaine were used by a depressed patient. While either substance can induce anxiety (or depressed) symptoms, a slightly different treatment plan may be necessary for a patient dependent on both.

The toxic screen may be equally critical to the diagnosis of a substance-induced psychotic disorder. Again, the criteria in the *DSM-IV* are similar. Hallucinations or delusions must be prominent and are not counted if the individual has insight into the substance-induced nature of his or her cognitive problems. For this reason, the lack of insight, the toxic screen and collateral history may be important in establishing the use or absence of a psychotogenic drug.

The differentiation of psychiatric symptoms from psychiatric disorders remains elusive. The *DSM-IV* requires that the diagnosis of anxiety, affective, and psychotic disorders be made only when several criteria are satisfied. First, the symptoms—anxiety, mood, or cognitive symptoms—must be prominent. Second, there must be evidence that the substance was used within the preceding month and that the substance is known to cause the symptoms in question. Third, there should not be another cause that better explains the disorder. Fourth, the disorder cannot occur exclusively during the course of a delirium. And fifth, the disorder must cause clinically significant distress or impairment in normal functioning. While not a criteria for diagnosis, the *DSM-IV* explains that the assessment should not be made unless the symptoms are judged to be in excess of those usually associated with intoxication or withdrawal. The latter can be problematic if taken literally, since withdrawal can involve extreme symptoms such as suicidal feelings and panic attacks. In addition, intoxication can include paranoia and visual hallucinations, feelings of depersonalization and time distortion. What would it mean to be in excess of these psychotic symptoms?

Case 1. Mr. B is a 46-year-old divorced man who works as a house painter. He came to the emergency department because of suicidal ideas, which frightened him. He had become increasingly depressed over the preceding month and was afraid that he was "going crazy." He had experienced episodes of depression over the past seven years (since his divorce), but the episodes had not lasted more than a day or two. He also had experienced fleeting suicidal ideas, but had not hurt himself. He had sat with his gun on occasion during the past year and considered ending it all. At those times he felt hopeless for the moment. The suicidal and hopeless thoughts lasted for an evening, but were not continuously present for more than a day. He had never been treated psychiatrically for depression.

The clinician has gathered information suggestive of a depressive syndrome of some kind, and must clarify if there are any organic causes, the most common of which would be a substance-induced disorder.

Mr. B had been hospitalized once, four years ago, to be detoxified from alcohol, but received no treatment for alcoholism following the detoxification. Recently, his drinking had increased to about a case of beer a day. He reported that the alcohol use was the only way he could cope with his depression. He denied any loss of control, but admitted to two DUI arrests over the past 10 years. He was experiencing difficulty in getting to work on time since he became depressed and was in trouble with his supervisor. He denied morning shakes and said that he never had experienced delirium tremens.

Mr. B admitted that his ex-wife had complained about his drinking. He had only one long period of abstinence for over a year when on probation for his second DUI. He felt well during that time. He developed the depressive symptoms in his late 30s, while his heavy drinking began in his early 20s.

He denied any ongoing medical problems or thyroid problems. He had some weight loss during the past month because he was not eating regularly with his heavy drinking, and had experienced some nausea in the mornings, which made eating breakfast difficult. He denied any sedative, barbiturate, cocaine, or opiate use.

On mental status examination, Mr. B was found to be a middle-aged white man, who looked more like 55 than 46 years old. He was thin, looked depressed, and smelled of alcohol. He was vague about some details and specific about others. He was oriented to person, place, date, and purpose. He was tearful at some times, anxious at others. He seemed bewildered about his predicament. He denied having problems with alcohol. He had suicidal ideas about shooting himself, but did not seem motivated to do so. He denied hallucinations and obsessions. He denied any manic episodes. His blood alcohol concentration (BAC) was 200 mg%. A toxicology screen was negative for benzodiazepines, opiates, barbiturates, and cocaine.

Diagnostic Issues: Is there a reason to consider a diagnosis of alcohol dependence or abuse? Is depression a prominent symptom? Is there reason to connect the depressive symptoms to alcohol or drug use/withdrawal? Is the intensity of depression more severe than is usually found with alcohol intoxication? Is the depressive mood better explained by a mood disorder? Did the depressed mood occur during a delirium?

Diagnostic Considerations: At this point, the clinician has enough information to diagnose alcohol dependence. Mr. B exhibits tolerance, alcohol withdrawal, use despite adverse consequences, impairment of personal relationships, and possibly impairment of occupational functioning due to alcohol.

The mood disturbance is prominent and is more severe than that experienced by social drinkers and most alcoholics. The depressive symptoms seem severe enough to think of major depression; however, there is no evidence of depression at those times when Mr. B is not drinking heavily, suggesting alcohol-induced depressive disorder. The alcohol dependence seems to be primary; that is, it began before the depressive symptoms, also suggesting alcohol-induced depressive disorder. It still is possible that he has two independent disorders, alcohol dependence and major depression; however, there is no evidence of that at present. Finally, there is no evidence of a delirium.

Treatment Issues: Safety issues involve ongoing diagnoses, use of medications, and psychosocial therapy.

Treatment Considerations: A trial of abstinence is called for in a safe environment with a lot of support. The clinical challenge is to find a safe environment. The risk for alcohol withdrawal delirium and seizures is minimal, suggesting that this patient could be managed as an outpatient. However, there are other considerations in this decision. The ASAM *Patient Placement Criteria, Second Edition* (ASAM *PPC-2*; Mee-Lee, Shulman & Gartner, 1996) encourage evaluating the patient in six different dimensions. The first is the potential for withdrawal. The second and third are the presence of medical and psychiatric comorbidity. The seriousness of the suicidality and the degree of anergy, the inability to mobilize due to depression, are relevant in this case. The medical comorbidity is minor (possibly gastritis) and should improve with abstinence. The fourth dimension is the acceptance or rejection of treatment. This man appears to seek treatment; however, he may balk at inpatient or outpatient treatment, making his cooperation a major issue. The final two dimensions—potential for relapse and supportive environment—are very pertinent to this patient. If he has no supportive friends or family who could watch over him and ensure that he gets to therapy, or to the emergency room if his condition worsened, then outpatient therapy becomes risky, particularly given his present suicidal ideas. The potential for relapse, including motivation for abstinence, craving for alcohol while abstinent, and history of prior attempts to quit, is crucial in determining the viability of outpatient treatment.

Alcohol-induced depression should remit over the first two to three weeks of abstinence. Careful follow-up during this period is very important with outpatient treatment because of the severity of Mr. B's symptoms and the possibility that the correct diagnosis is not alcohol-induced depression. However, if he cannot or will not stay sober as an outpatient, it is likely that he will remain depressed or become even more depressed. At this point, residential treatment is essential to break the cycle of addiction and allow the mood to improve. If his mood does not improve with abstinence, a major depression should be considered, and the patient given appropriate antidepressant treatment. Anticraving medications such as naltrexone can be very helpful when the patient is cooperative, somewhat open to the idea of abstinence from alcohol, and willing to engage in some kind of psychosocial follow-up. The same is true of disulfiram. Patients with a firm commitment to sobriety may not need the assistance of such medications. Patients with a strong connection to Alcoholics Anonymous may not be motivated to take such medications because of the view that medications are not appropriate for sobriety; however, AA produces a pamphlet that is quite supportive of both psychiatrists and the use of psychiatric medications.

Case 2. Mr. M is a 45-year-old African American veteran who is divorced and unemployed. He came to the evaluation area at 9:00 a.m. because of a longstanding problem sleeping that had worsened over the past two months. He had been drinking more alcohol to fall asleep, but had been waking after only a few hours of sleep. He had hand tremors in the morning, which resolved with a few shots of whiskey. He was jumpy and irritable, tending to isolate himself from his friends.

OPTION A: Mr. M had no history of withdrawal seizures or withdrawal hallucinations. He had no history of panic attacks, chronic anxiety, or traumatic life events. His vital signs were BP 148/90, pulse 96, temperature 98.6, respirations 16.

Mr. M had been detoxified the preceding year but had refused to enter outpatient treatment. He complained that he was not going to let the doctors treat him like a "guinea pig" on detoxification, that they "just tried to lock up a Black man these days."

Diagnostic Issues: Is there a prominent symptom? If so, is this symptom related to drinking? Is there any evidence of other drug use? Is this explained better by another *DSM* disorder? Did the symptoms occur during a delirium? Has this disorder caused symptoms beyond what is normally experienced during alcohol intoxication or withdrawal?

Clinical Considerations: At this point, the clinician has information suggesting alcohol withdrawal. There also is information suggesting a sleep disturbance, which may be alcohol-induced or related to alcohol withdrawal. Because of the cross-cultural tension already reported, an effort should be made to rule out an anxiety disorder, since Mr. M may be reluctant to report anxiety symptoms. Efforts should be made to rule out other organic causes of anxiety/agitation, such as hyperthyroidism, stimulant intoxication, caffeinism, or medication-induced anxiety. A toxicology screen would be helpful to rule out stimulant intoxication, caffeinism, and opiate withdrawal. A phone call to a family member or friend may add confidence to the diagnosis and rule out chronic anxiety and paranoid disorders. The symptoms do not seem excessive for alcohol withdrawal, which is the likely diagnosis, given the available information.

OPTION B: Mr. M has no history of withdrawal seizures or withdrawal hallucinations. He has a history of panic attacks, which began after he returned from service in Vietnam in 1971. He had been in combat for six months and had seen a lot of action, which he did not wish to discuss. He became more agitated as he talked about combat, eventually cutting off the conversation. He was angry about the way he was treated when he returned to the U.S. and reported a difficult transition in the early 1970s. He demonstrated recent heavy drinking, nightmares about combat, flashbacks, relationship problems, and a significant startle reaction to loud noises. He complained of racist treatment by white soldiers and officers in Vietnam, claiming that he was sent on suicide missions by his white superiors.

Diagnostic Issues: Is there a prominent symptom? Is there a causal relationship with the symptom and drinking? Is there any drug use that could account for the disorder? Is this better explained by another *DSM* disorder? Did the symptoms occur during a delirium? Are the symptoms excessive for alcohol intoxication or withdrawal?

Diagnostic Considerations: There certainly is a prominent symptom of anxiety. However, it still is important to look for a substance dependence disorder and a substance-induced anxiety disorder. It is necessary to clarify the diagnosis of alcohol withdrawal. This patient seems to have posttraumatic stress disorder (PTSD), alcohol dependence, alcohol withdrawal and, possibly, substance-induced anxiety disorder. Since the engagement of this patient may depend on which combination of problems he has, it is important for the clinician to obtain collateral information and a toxicology screen. Because the patient's denial may be convincing, it is not sufficient to dismiss substance dependence or a substance-induced disorder based on the patient's history. If the patient's report is the only information available, the clinician must make a treatment decision, while remaining aware that new information could change the diagnosis and treatment plan. Vital signs should be monitored to pick up signs of severe alcohol withdrawal. A toxicology screen should be obtained to check for drugs that may cause agitation or anxiety. A chronic history of anxiety, tension, nightmares, etc., is excessive for alcohol-induced anxiety or alcohol withdrawal alone. With this information, the clinician can consider both posttraumatic stress disorder and alcohol withdrawal. It will be hard to diagnose alcohol-induced anxiety along with PTSD unless there is a clear history of the anxiety recently growing progressively worse, without a psychosocial trigger for the PTSD. More commonly, the clinician will see an acute improvement with sobriety as a sign that there was an alcohol-induced anxiety component.

Treatment Issues: The patient needs to be engaged in a detoxification setting (followed by an alcohol rehabilitation setting) and his denial managed to expand his awareness beyond the PTSD symptoms. His claims of racism need to be addressed as part of the engagement and assessment. Mr. M's anxiety should be managed without using benzodiazepines. His sleep disorder should be managed, and the process of relapse prevention begun.

Treatment Considerations: Treatment must be conceptualized in stages. The first stage is detoxification from alcohol (and any other drugs that may be present). With this patient, detoxification can be managed with a careful outpatient regimen if he is able to remain abstinent while outpatient. If abstinence seems unlikely, if the patient fails at outpatient detoxification, or if a comorbid problem arises that cannot be safely monitored on an outpatient basis, then residential detoxification must be considered. The next stage is the maintenance of sobriety, a stabilization phase. During this stage, the clinician should monitor Mr. M's abstinence and observe the course of the anxiety symptoms. A relapse may increase his anxiety symptoms, which would interfere with all of the treatment goals. Such a relapse would require a treatment strategy that focuses on management of denial, motivation, and relapse prevention.

If, during abstinence, the anxiety symptoms increase or stay the same, the PTSD probably is severe and medication will be needed. If the anxiety symptoms diminish or are manageable without medication, then counseling may be sufficient. Benzodiazepines are controversial with alcoholics after detoxification is achieved, even in the face of severe anxiety. The anxiolytic property of benzodiazepines is reputed to be sustained over time; however, many alcoholics request more of this medication. Moreover, craving for drugs is greatest when the drug, or a similar drug, is being used. Thus, there always is a concern that benzodiazepines will stimulate the desire for alcohol. Drinking in addition to benzodiazepine use can lead to an "out of control" binge, as well as intoxicated behaviors, which could exaggerate the PTSD symptoms of anxiety, agitation, etc.

Disulfiram is a possible safeguard to prevent drinking alcohol during outpatient treatment, but the patient must be willing to collaborate (i.e., take it regularly) if it is to be effective. The use of anti-panic medications like the selective serotonin reuptake inhibitors (SSRIs) and other antidepressants would be a safer strategy. The same problem is encountered with the complaints about insomnia. Avoiding sedatives is important; moreover, the use of sedating anti-depressants like trazadone and doxepin can be very effective without the abuse potential of other sedative drugs.

OPTION C: Mr. M has no history of withdrawal seizures or withdrawal hallucinations. He has had an episode (the day before coming to the emergency department) in which he became frightened, felt short of breath, felt his heart pounding, and worried that he was having a heart attack. This was not the first time he had experienced such an attack; he had one six months earlier when he quit drinking. He had gone to the emergency room the first time this had happened five years ago. The doctor then had checked his heart and told him that he was having a nervous attack, not a heart attack. While Mr. M felt stressed at times, he did not have these attacks regularly. When he stopped his drinking for a year, he felt well and does not recall having a spell during that time. He denies any major, traumatic life events. He was embarrassed to be worried about these anxiety spells, but he was fearful that he might have a heart attack.

Diagnostic Issues: Is there a prominent symptom? Is this symptom related to drinking? Is this symptom better explained by another *DSM* diagnosis? Is this symptom in excess of the symptoms normally encountered during intoxication or withdrawal?

Diagnostic Considerations: There is a prominent symptom of anxiety is this case, and it appears to occur only with drinking. The clinician must think about alcohol dependence, alcohol withdrawal, and alcohol withdrawal-induced panic disorder. The major anxiety disorders should be ruled out, as should PTSD (although certain events, like sexual abuse, may be denied initially). Some attempt to rule out cardiac disease as a cause of the chest pain would be important. Organic causes of anxiety also should be ruled out. It is possible that the patient has a panic disorder that is in a prodromal phase, but this is not the most likely diagnosis. While patients frequently experience anxiety during alcohol withdrawal, they usually do not experience panic attacks nor do they usually go to the emergency room in a panic.

Treatment Issues: The patient should be engaged in a detoxification program and his level of denial and motivation for treatment evaluated. The denial needs to be evaluated and the problem redefined as alcoholism, not panic or heart disease. The possibility of a comorbid anxiety disorder should be explored. The patient then needs to be engaged in an alcohol rehabilitation program. Medications that will enhance the likelihood of sobriety should be considered. The patient should be evaluated for relapse triggers and referred for relapse prevention as appropriate.

Treatment Considerations: Treatment should be designed to detoxify Mr. M safely from alcohol, to explore dependence on other drugs, and to keep him sober long enough to determine whether the anxiety disorder abates with sobriety, as an alcohol withdrawal-induced anxiety disorder would. The patient's denial and motivation are important because he must understand the connection between his drinking and his panic. If his awareness of this connection is minimal, then the treatment may have to occur in a setting where chest pain or panic is the primary focus. He may not accept the focus on his drinking. If this is the case, then referral to a rehabilitation program, either inpatient or outpatient, may not be possible at this time. Ongoing monitoring and working with his denial would be necessary before such a referral could be made. Benzodiazepine would be appropriate during detoxification only; medications that promote sobriety, such as disulfiram or naltrexone, would be appropriate if Mr. M is motivated and able to cooperate. Anti-panic medications like the SSRIs likely would be used if panic attacks persisted with sobriety.

Case 3. A 20-year-old undergraduate presented with a chief complaint of "seeing the air." The visual disturbance consists of a perception of white pinpoint specks, too numerous to count, in both the central and peripheral visual fields. These are constantly present and accompanied by the perception of trails of moving objects left behind as they pass through the patient's visual field. Attending a hockey game became difficult, as the brightly dressed players left streaks of their own images against the white of the ice for seconds at a time. The patient also described the false perception of movement in stable objects, usually in his peripheral visual fields, halos around objects, and positive and negative afterimages. Other symptoms include mild depression, daily bitemporal headache, and a loss of concentration in the last year.

The visual syndrome had gradually emerged over the past three months, following experimentation with the hallucinogenic drug LSD-25 on three separate occasions during the same period. The patient feared that he had sustained some kind of "brain damage" from the drug experience. He denied use of any other agents, including amphetamines, phencyclidine, narcotics, or alcohol, to excess. He had smoked marijuana twice a week for a period of seven months at age 17 (Spitzer, Gibbon et al., 1994).

Diagnostic Issues: Is there a reexperiencing of a perceptual symptom following the use of an hallucinogen? Does this symptom cause significant distress or impair functioning? Is this condition better explained by a delirium or another *DSM* disorder?

Diagnostic Considerations: This case appears to be hallucinogen persisting perception disorder, or flashbacks. It consists of a perceptual disturbance resembling the experience (of LSD) at some time after hallucinogen use; it requires that the patient be distressed by the experience. A toxicology screen should be obtained to rule out other drugs, despite the patient's denial. The patient appears to have insight and does not seem delusional, nor does he have negative symptoms of schizophrenia. There is no sign of delirium, but this should be considered. An evaluation of his neurological status would be an important part of this assessment. If consent is given, confirming his story with his family or a friend would be a good idea, since persons with a chronic psychotic condition can, and do, use LSD.

Treatment Issues: The patient should undergo a comprehensive assessment of his drug use. Staff need to respond to his anxiety about having caused "brain damage." He should be referred to drug rehabilitation and psychotherapy as appropriate.

Treatment Considerations: This patient is frightened by what is happening and is afraid that he has damaged his brain by using drugs. This presents a unique opportunity to engage him in some kind of treatment. The question is, what kind of treatment is most appropriate? Since his use of hallucinogens may have been months earlier, it is important to ascertain whether the current problem is anxiety about the flashbacks or is current substance abuse/dependence. According to the history supplied, he denies being dependent on LSD and does not meet the criteria for abuse or dependence; however, he may have been dependent on marijuana when he was 17 years old. A careful neurological evaluation is advised, because there are visual disturbances, difficulties in concentrating, depression and headaches, all of which can be associated with neurological illness. Outpatient therapy, either drug rehabilitation or psychotherapy for the fear, is probably sufficient; however, residential treatment may be required if the patient's panic or flashbacks are severe (that is, if they interfere markedly with his daily routine). Given the patient's anxiety, he may readily commit to abstinence from drugs. If his fears are sufficiently intense, he may develop a panic attack/PTSD-type of syndrome, which could become chronic. Classic approaches to the treatment of anxiety should be used, including those discussed in the chapter about anxiety disorders in this Section. Although research is lacking, some clinicians use anticonvulsants for such patients on the theory that "flashback" phenomena are kindled and involve some sort of focal CNS hyperactivity.

Case 4. Ms. A is a 35-year-old Caucasian divorced female who came to the emergency room because of suicidal feelings. She reported feeling very despondent that day, with suicidal ideation, and thought that she needed to be admitted to the hospital to keep her safe. On questioning, Ms. A admitted she smoked crack cocaine, about $100 worth at a time. She had recently come off of a four-day binge of crack use. She drank four to six drinks of vodka per day when she used crack, and also used marijuana.

Diagnostic Issues: Is there a prominent symptom? Is this symptom related to drug use? Is this better explained by another *DSM* diagnosis? Did this occur exclusively during a delirium? Is the symptom more severe than usually is encountered with intoxication or withdrawal?

Diagnostic Considerations: Ms. A has a prominent mood disturbance, which brought her to the emergency room. It is consistent with chronic cocaine use and temporally related to her recent binge. While her history is not consistent with a *DSM* mood disorder, it is important to evaluate the possibility. A careful history of mood swings also would be important. If she has been using crack for years, the clinician can expect that she has had transient episodes (never more than a few days) of intense depression, even suicidality, with the cessation of cocaine use in the past. At the same time, the clinician can expect that there have been no episodes of prolonged depression before the advent of crack nor during a prolonged abstinence. Because of the recent onset of this depression, it is not likely the result of metabolic problems; however, addicted individuals are not always aware of subtle changes in their bodies, which may be obscured by intoxication. A screening battery is recommended, because there often are nutritional deficiencies and, not infrequently, viral hepatitis (B or C). Unsafe sexual practices and needle sharing make AIDS a concern with the addicted population. More relevantly, the mood disturbance could be alcohol-induced. This is an important consideration during the initial work-up. It is possible that Ms. A has alcohol dependence and a depression that is alcohol-induced; however, this should not coincide with cocaine cessation. The cocaine-induced depression should last only a day or two; while the alcohol-induced depression likely would last a few days longer with sobriety. Some alcoholics experience marked depression with suicidality during intoxication, which clears with sobriety. While it is tempting to dismiss substance-induced depressions as less significant than a major depressive disorder because they go away so quickly, it is important to remember that these episodes are frightening to the individual, that some people make serious attempts, and that some people kill themselves. At this point, it appears that the patient has a cocaine withdrawal-induced mood disorder. It would be wise to obtain a toxicology screen to rule out benzodiazepine or opiate-induced depression. With the history of depression, the clinician should look for manic episodes. Without a careful history of cocaine use and its relationship to the experience of intense moods, up or down, it would be easy to think of manic depressive illness.

Another diagnostic consideration is the possibility that Ms. A has had a social crisis and is homeless. The report of suicidality could be exaggerated to gain admission to housing or hospital. In such a case, there may have been a pattern of this behavior.

Treatment Issues: Patient safety and suicidality are the primary issues here. Ms. A needs to be engaged in drug rehabilitation, her denial managed and her motivation for abstinence enhanced. She needs to be engaged in a comprehensive assessment, with her relapse triggers assessed and relapse prevention initiated, if appropriate.

Treatment Considerations: Safety is the first treatment issue in this case, because of the patient's depression (suicidality) and the possibility of alcohol withdrawal (delirium tremens). The clinician must assess the severity of the suicidal impulse and the social supports available before deciding whether a residential setting is appropriate. Clinicians should assess what type of suicidal thoughts the person is having, whether they have formulated a plan to carry out the idea, whether they have the means to complete the plan, whether they have made prior attempts and, if so, if they were serious, whether there are other alternatives, and whether the patient is very agitated.

A cocaine-induced depression usually is transient when abstinence ensues. Continued cocaine use continues the cycle of addiction and depression. Outpatient treatment is viable if the patient can refrain from using drugs and alcohol, and this often depends on the degree of support in the environment. Safety from alcohol withdrawal is a potential issue that should be considered; however, it is unlikely that a dangerous withdrawal will occur unless the patient has had delirium tremens or seizures in the past (Whitfield et al., 1978). Ongoing monitoring is the best precaution, and this can be handled on an inpatient as well as an outpatient basis if the patient is cooperative. Assessing the patient's reliability (ability to follow through) may be difficult if the patient is previously unknown to the clinician. A variety of factors enter into this assessment, including motivation, denial, awareness, craving, relapse triggers, and availability of a supportive environment. This is all part of the safety management for this patient.

Engagement in a drug and alcohol treatment program will depend on this patient's denial, motivation, awareness of the centrality of drugs and alcohol, as well as the pull of other social relationships like children, significant others, and family members who may be dependent on Ms. A. Attention to these psychosocial issues may be the key to engagement. Focusing on a comprehensive assessment, including relapse triggers, may be the way to engage a different ambivalent patient. Inclusion of the family may be the way to engage the patient. Admission to a treatment program may be a key engagement strategy with a patient who is anxious about further drug use and the sequelae. If an individual has been through rehabilitation programs in the past, has relapsed, and has a commitment to abstinence as well as a capacity to remain abstinent, then a focus on relapse prevention may be the appropriate intervention. This remains the art of medicine and hinges on the physician's style of practice, local resources, and managed care practices. It is a complex challenge each time and must be individualized with each situation.

CONCLUSIONS

The substance-induced mental disorders are common illnesses that often, but not exclusively, are associated with substance dependence. While they often are short-lived, these disorders are by no means clinically insignificant. Serious self-injury is reported with the substance-induced mood disorders, and safety is an important clinical issue. This can present a clinical dilemma in determining the proper level of care. Most patients with substance-induced mental disorders can be diverted away from traditional psychiatric inpatient treatment, either to dual diagnosis units or to inpatient or outpatient addiction treatment, where adequate substance abuse and dependence assessment and appropriate treatment is available.

Clinics and residential units that specialize in substance-dependent patients who have a comorbid psychiatric illness play an important role when there is diagnostic confusion or when the patient does not respond (or has not responded in the past) to routine psychiatric treatment. Confusion about the diagnosis can delay interventions; therefore, clarification through a comprehensive evaluation frequently is the first order of business, once safety is addressed.

While abstinence is a critical factor in recovery from a substance-induced disorder, it is not always the only factor. The regular psychosocial treatments for substance dependence are relevant as long as the person is behaviorally manageable and not psychotic or delirious. When behavior is unsafe or wild, a psychiatric unit may be necessary until the patient's behavior is less risky. If a specialized inpatient unit for dual diagnosis is available and can manage such behavior with seclusion, restraints, psychotropic medication, or a locked unit, this may be the best choice. Such patient matching is still done on an individual basis, depending on the patient's needs, the resources available, and the skills and preferences of the clinicians involved.

REFERENCES

American Psychiatric Association (1994). *Diagnostic and Statistical Manual of Mental Disorders, 4th Edition.* Washington, DC: American Psychiatric Press.

American Psychiatric Association (1987). *Diagnostic and Statistical Manual of Mental Disorders, 3rd Edition, Revised.* Washington, DC: American Psychiatric Press.

American Psychiatric Association (1980). *Diagnostic and Statistical Manual of Mental Disorders, 3rd Edition.* Washington, DC: American Psychiatric Press.

Ashton H (1991). Protracted withdrawal syndromes from benzodiazepines. In NS Miller (ed.) *Comprehensive Handbook of Drug and Alcohol Addiction.* New York, NY: Marcel Dekker, 915–930.

Asnis GM, Friedman TA, Sanderson WC et al. (1993). Suicidal Behaviors in Adult Psychiatry Outpatients, I: Description and Prevalence. *American Journal of Psychiatry* 150:108–112.

Bartels SJ, Drake RE & McHugo GJ (1992). Alcohol abuse, depression, and suicidal behavior in schizophrenia. *American Journal of Psychiatry* 149:394–395.

Brown SA, Inaba RK, Gillin JC et al. (1995). Alcoholism and affective disorder: Clinical course of depressive symptoms. *American Journal of Psychiatry* 152:45–52.

Brown SA, Irwin M & Schuckit MA (1991). Changes in anxiety among abstinent male alcoholics. *Journal of Studies on Alcohol* 52:55–61.

Brown SA & Schuckit MA (1988). Changes in depression among abstinent alcoholics. *Journal of Studies on Alcohol* 49:412–417.

Dorus W, Kennedy J, Gibbons RD et al. (1987). Symptoms and diagnosis of depression in alcoholics. *Alcoholism: Clinical & Experimental Research* 11:150–154.

Elliott AJ, Pages KP, Russo J et al. (1996). A profile of medically serious suicide attempts. *Journal of Clinical Psychiatry* 57:567–571.

Geller A (1991). Protracted abstinence. In NS Miller (ed.) *Comprehensive Handbook of Drug and Alcohol Addiction.* New York, NY: Marcel Dekker, 905–914.

Giannini AJ (1991). Phencyclidine. In NS Miller (ed.) *The Comprehensive Handbook of Drug and Alcohol Addiction.* New York, NY: Marcel Dekker, 383–394.

Gold MS (1993). *Cocaine.* New York, NY: Plenum Publishing.

Gruber AJ & Pope HG (1994). Cannabis psychotic disorder: Does it exist? *American Journal of Addictions* 3:72–83.

Henriksson MM, Aro HM, Marttunen MJ et al. (1993). Mental disorders and comorbidity in suicide. *American Journal of Psychiatry* 150:935–940.

Kadden RM, Kranzler HR, Rounsaville BJ (1995). Validity of the distinction between "substance-induced" and "independent" depression and anxiety disorders. *American Journal of Addictions* 4:107–117.

Keeler MH, Taylor CI & Miller WC (1979). Are all recently detoxified alcoholics depressed? *American Journal of Psychiatry* 136:586–588.

Levinson I, Galynker II & Rosenthal RN (1995). Methadone withdrawal psychosis. *Journal of Clinical Psychiatry* 56:73–76.

Lydiard RB, Brady K, Ballenger JC et al. (1992). Anxiety and mood disorders in hospitalized alcoholic individuals. *American Journal of Addictions* 1:325–331.

Mee-Lee D, Shulman G & Gartner L (1996). *Patient Placement Criteria, Second Edition.* Chevy Chase, MD: American Society of Addiction Medicine.

Mendoza R & Miller BL (1992). Neuropsychiatric disorders associated with cocaine use. *Hospital and Community Psychiatry* 43:677–679.

Murphy GE & Wetzel RD (1990). The lifetime risk of suicide in alcoholism. *Archives of General Psychiatry* 47:383–392.

Pages KP, Russo JE, Roy-Byrne PP et al. (in press). Determinants of suicidal ideation: The role of substance use disorders. *Journal of Clinical Psychiatry.*

Rosenthal RN & Miner CR (1997). Differential diagnosis of substance-induced psychosis and schizophrenia in patients with substance use disorders. *Schizophrenia Bulletin* 23:187–193.

Rounsaville BJ, Anton SF, Carroll K et al. (1991). Psychiatric diagnoses of treatment-seeking cocaine abusers. *Archives of General Psychiatry* 48:43–51.

Salloum IM, Daley DC, Cornelius JR et al. (1996). Disproportionate lethality in psychiatric patients with concurrent alcohol and cocaine abuse. *American Journal of Psychiatry* 153:953–955.

Schuckit MA & Hesselbrock V (1994). Alcohol dependence and anxiety disorders: What is the relationship? *American Journal of Psychiatry* 151:1723–1734.

Schultz T (1991). Alcohol withdrawal syndrome: Clinical features, pathophysiology, and treatment. In NS Miller (ed.) *Comprehensive Handbook of Drug and Alcohol Addiction.* New York, NY: Marcel Dekker, 1091–1112.

Seibyl JP, Satel SL, Anthony D et al. (1993). Effects of cocaine on hospital course in schizophrenia. *Journal of Nervous and Mental Disease* 181:31–37.

Spitzer RL, Gibbon M, Skodol AE, Williams JBW & First MB, eds. (1994). *DSM-IV Casebook: A Learning Companion to the Diagnostic and Statistical Manual of Mental Disorders, 4th Edition.* Washington, DC: American Psychiatric Press, 216.

Whitfield CL et al. (1978). Detoxification of 1,024 alcoholic patients without psychoactive drugs. *Journal of the American Medical Association* 239:1409–1410.

Young MA, Fogg LF, Scheftner WA & Fawcett JA (1994). Interactions of risk factors in predicting suicide. *American Journal of Psychiatry* 151:434–435.

Zukin SR & Zukin RS (1992). Phencyclidine. In JH Lowinson, P Ruiz, RB Millman & JG Langrod (eds.) *Substance Abuse: A Comprehensive Textbook.* Baltimore, MD: Williams & Wilkins, 290–302.

CHAPTER 2

Comorbid Addiction and Affective Disorders

Kathleen Brady, M.D.
Hugh Myrick, M.D.
Susan Sonne, Pharm.D.

Diagnostic Issues
Prevalence
Treatment

Symptoms of depression and mood instability are among the most common psychiatric symptoms seen in individuals with substance use disorders. Data also indicate that full syndromal major depression, dysthymia and bipolar disorders co-occur with substance use disorders more commonly than would be expected by chance alone. As more and more effective treatments for affective disorders are established, it is of critical importance to recognize and treat these disorders in individuals who have substance use disorders. On the other hand, because mood disturbance commonly accompanies substance use and withdrawal, and in many cases remits after a few days of abstinence, it is important to distinguish substance-induced, time-limited affective symptoms from full syndromal affective disorder. Thus, the interface of mood disorders and substance use disorders is one of critical importance to improving treatment in the substance abuse field and has received a great deal of recent attention with regard to prevalence, diagnostic issues and appropriate treatment.

Throughout this chapter, wherever diagnostic criteria are cited, it is the criteria of the *Diagnostic and Statistical Manuals of Mental Disorders (DSM-IIIR, DSM-IV)* of the American Psychiatric Association (1987, 1994) to which the reference is intended. Table 1, below, gives an overview of the *DSM-IV* schema and general guidelines for diagnosis of affective disorders.

DIAGNOSTIC ISSUES

Diagnosing an affective disorder in the face of substance abuse can be difficult because drugs of abuse, particularly with chronic use, can mimic nearly any psychiatric disorder. It also is important to note that individuals with substance use disorders often present in a primary care setting with complaints of anxiety, sleep disturbance and depression (women are particularly likely to seek help outside of the substance abuse treatment system) (Weisner & Schmidt, 1992). Both stimulant use and alcohol intoxication can cause symptoms indistinguishable from mania or hypomania, and withdrawal states often cause symptoms of anxiety and depression. More specifically, chronic use of central nervous system (CNS) stimulants (such as cocaine and amphetamines) can cause euphoria, increased energy, decreased appetite, grandiosity and sometimes paranoia, which may look very similar to mania or hypomania. Withdrawal from CNS stimulants (especially cocaine) can cause anhedonia, apathy and depressed mood with possible suicidal ideation. Chronic use of CNS depressants (e.g., alcohol, benzodiazepines, barbiturates and opiates) often is associated with depressed mood, poor concentration, anhedonia and problems sleeping, which also are symptoms of depression. Withdrawal from CNS depressants often causes symptoms of anxiety and agitation.

Addictive use of drugs is associated with lifestyles and behaviors which lead to multiple losses and stressors in one's life. These losses may precipitate a depressed affect, which is appropriate and transient. Studies have indicated that up to 98% of individuals presenting for substance abuse treatment have some symptoms of depression (Jaffe, Rounsaville et al., 1996). For the most part, these symptoms remit with time in abstinence. In a study by Dorus and colleagues (1987), depressive symptoms were monitored over a one-month period in 171 individ-

TABLE 1. Guidelines for Diagnosis of Affective Disorder

Diagnosis	Criteria
Major Depressive Episode	Symptoms severe (>5 symptoms) and persist for at least 2 weeks
Dysthymia	Symptoms less severe, more persistent (2 yrs.)
Bipoloar I Disorder	Mania usually accompanied by major depressive episodes
Bipolar II Disorder	Hypomania usually accompanied by major depressive episodes
Cyclothymia	Symptoms less severe than full diagnostic mania or depression, but persistent (2 yrs.)
Substance-Induced Mood Disorder	Direct physiological consequence of drug use/withdrawal

uals who presented for inpatient treatment for alcohol dependence. On day 1, 67% had high depression ratings, but by day 28, only 16% had high depression ratings. The national prevalence estimates for current major depressive episode is 5%. So, while it is important not to make a diagnosis too early or to overtreat depression, it also is important to recognize that the population in substance abuse treatment is at enhanced risk for depression and must be carefully assessed.

It often is easier to diagnose mania than depression in the substance abuser. During active drug use, urine drug screens can be useful in evaluating substance-induced mania, and withdrawal states generally do not mimic mania. Substance-induced mania generally lasts only for the duration of the drug's pharmacologic effect, so manic symptoms that persist for a number of days after last substance use are not likely to be substance-induced. Long-acting stimulants (methamphetamine) and hallucinogens may be an exception to this rule, as manic symptoms resulting from intoxication with these substances may last for several days. Another difficulty in the diagnosis of the bipolar disorders is the fact that bipolar spectrum disorders, such as cyclothymia, are more difficult to reliably diagnose because of the shorter duration and more subtle nature of their associated symptoms.

The best way to differentiate substance-induced, transient psychiatric symptoms from psychiatric disorders that warrant independent treatment is through observation of symptoms during a period of abstinence from drugs and alcohol. Transient substance-related states will improve with time. A key issue in this discussion is the amount of time in abstinence necessary for accurate diagnosis. It is likely that the minimum amount of time necessary for diagnosis will vary according to the comorbid condition being diagnosed. For depression, there appears to be symptom resolution about two to four weeks after last use. This means that there is a risk of overdiagnosis of psychiatric disorder if the diagnosis is made earlier. Bipolar disorder is less well studied in this regard. As mentioned earlier, it is likely, however, that one could make a diagnosis of mania with less than two to four weeks of abstinence because symptoms of mania have less overlap with withdrawal states.

Recently, diagnostic schema are evolving to address this issue. The *DSM-IV* has included a category called substance-induced mood disorder, which is designed to capture clear changes in affective state that occur only during periods of active substance use and withdrawal. While the Structured Clinical Interview for *DSM-IV* (SCID) is widely considered one of the best diagnostic instruments for psychiatric disorders, the validity of this instrument for making diagnoses in substance users is questionable. Modified versions of the SCID have been developed that are designed to overcome some of the drawbacks by developing the chronological relationships between psychiatric symptoms and substance use in order to achieve diagnostic clarity (Hasin, Endicott & Lewis, 1985).

There are many unanswered questions concerning accurate diagnoses of comorbid substance use and psychiatric disorder. A period of abstinence is optimal for diagnosis, but the necessary minimum timeframe is likely to differ for each diagnosis. A family history of affective illness, clear onset of psychiatric symptoms before onset of the substance use disorder, and the presence of sustained affective symptoms during lengthy periods of abstinence in the past all weigh in favor of making a diagnosis in cases where the diagnosis remains unclear.

PREVALENCE

Community Samples. Two major epidemiological surveys have studied the prevalence of psychiatric disorders in community samples. The first was the National Institute of Mental Health Epidemiological

Catchment Area (ECA) Study (Regier, Farmer et al., 1990), conducted in the early 1980s; the second was the National Comorbidity Study (NCS), conducted in 1991 (Kessler, McGonagle et al., 1994). Data from the ECA study estimated the lifetime prevalence rate for any nonsubstance abuse mental disorder to be 22.5%, for alcohol abuse or dependence to be 13.5%, and for other drug abuse or dependence to be 6.1%. Among those with any affective disorder, 32% had a comorbid addictive disorder. Of the individuals with major depression, 16.5% had a comorbid alcohol use diagnosis and 18% had a comorbid other drug use diagnosis. An even higher rate of comorbidity was found in individuals with bipolar disorder. Of those individuals with any bipolar diagnosis, 56.1% had an addictive disorder. The highest rate was among those individuals with bipolar disorder, 60.7% of whom had a comorbid addictive disorder, 46% of whom had a comorbid alcohol diagnosis, and 40.7% of whom had a comorbid drug use diagnosis. Bipolar I disorder was the Axis I diagnosis most likely to co-occur with a substance use disorder.

Data from the NCS estimated a lifetime prevalence of 48% for any psychiatric disorder, 14.1% for alcohol dependence, and 7.5% for drug dependence. The lifetime prevalence rate for any affective disorder was 19.3% and for any substance abuse/dependence 26.6%. An odds ratio was calculated, using the NCS data to determine the relative risk of co-occurrence by mental disorders and addictive disorders (Kessler, Crum et al., 1997). The odds ratio of finding any lifetime substance use disorder in a person with a mood disorder was 2.3 and the 12-months odds ratio was 3.0. Among those with a diagnosis of major depression, the odds ratio of comorbid substance use disorder was approximately 2.7 for lifetime co-occurrence and 3.6 for 12-month co-occurrence. The rates of addictive disorders were even higher among patients with bipolar disorder. The odds ratio of a lifetime comorbid alcohol dependence in a person with bipolar disorder was 9.7 and the comorbid drug dependence odds ratio was 8.4, while 12-month odds ratios were 6.3 and 8.2, respectively.

Affective Comorbidity in Treatment: Seeking Substance Users. *Alcohol:* The diagnostic difficulties at the interface of mood disorder and substance use disorder is reflected in the variability in prevalence estimates, but many studies have found elevated rates of affective disorders in treatment-seeking alcoholics. Powell and colleagues (1982), in a study of 565 male, alcoholic inpatients, found the frequency of current major depression to be 13.8% and that of current mania to be 2.8%. As expected, estimates of lifetime prevalence is higher, with major depression estimated at 20% to 67% and bipolar disorder estimated at 6% to 8% (Bowen, Cipywnyk et al., 1984; Hasin, Grant & Endicott, 1988; Lydiard, Brady et al., 1992).

Cocaine: A number of small studies have reported estimates of lifetime depressive disorders between 30% and 40% and lifetime bipolar spectrum disorders between 10% and 30% in samples of cocaine-dependent individuals (Gawin & Kleber, 1986; Weiss, Mirin et al., 1988; Nunes, Quitkin & Klein, 1991). Rounsaville and coworkers (1991) reported current affective disorders in 44.3% of 298 subjects. A lifetime history of affective disorder was diagnosed in 61% of the sample, with 30.5% having at least one episode of major depression and 11.1% having at least one episode of hypomania or mania. Of interest, the onset of affective disorders took place predominantly after the onset of cocaine abuse or in the same year. In a more recent study, Halikas and colleagues (1994) used the DIS and found the current and lifetime rate of affective illness to be 17% and 28% respectively in 207 cocaine abusers seeking outpatient treatment. Almost 65% of the subjects reported their first regular drug use prior to the onset of affective illness.

Opiates: There is considerable literature on affective disorder in opiate-dependent individuals. Rounsaville and colleagues (1982), in an evaluation of 533 opiate-dependent individuals, found the lifetime prevalence of any affective disorder was 74.3%. The lifetime rates for major depression and mania were 53.9% and 0.6%, while the lifetime rates for minor depression and hypomania were 8.4% and 6.6% respectively. In the largest study to date, Brooner and colleagues (1997) found that 19% of 716 opioid abusers seeking methadone maintenance met *DSM-IIIR* criteria for a lifetime mood disorder. Major depression was present in 15.8% and bipolar disorder in 0.4% of the sample.

Substance Use Comorbidity in Affective Disorder Treatment: Seeking Samples. Other investigators have explored the prevalence of substance use disorders in treatment-seeking individuals with affective disorder. Miller and Fine (1993), in a review of the epidemiological literature, found the ratio of comorbidity of patients with addictive disorders in a psychiatric setting to be 30% in depressive disorder and 50% in bipolar disorders. Hasin and colleagues (1988) assessed drug and alcohol abuse in 835 patients with affective syndromes and found that almost one-fourth of the patients had abused alcohol or drugs at a clinically significant level during their current episode. Brady and colleagues (1991) assessed substance use disorders in 100 consecutively admitted patients to a VAMC inpatient psychiatric unit, 64% endorsed current or past problems with substance use and 29% met *DSM-IIIR* criteria for a substance use disorder in the 30 days prior to admission. Of patients with major depression, 58% met criteria for a lifetime substance use disorder and 22% met criteria for a current substance use disorder. Of patients with bipolar disorder, 70% met criteria for lifetime substance use disorder and 30% met criteria for a current substance use disorder. Interestingly, only 40% of patients with current or past substance abuse had received treatment for their chemical dependency.

Prevalence and Comorbidity in the Adolescent Population. Studies of adolescents have also found high rates of comorbidity between affective and substance use disorders. Deykin and coworkers (1987) evaluated 424 adolescents and found that subjects who reported a history of alcohol abuse were almost four times as likely to have a history of major depression as the subjects who had not abused alcohol. Subjects who abused drugs were 3.3 times as likely as non-abusers to have a history of major depression. Bukstein and colleagues (1992) evaluated affective comorbidity in 156 adolescents with substance use disorders. Affective disorders were diagnosed in 51.3% of the sample. Major depression was found in 30.7% of the subjects and bipolar disorder in 7.7%. Hovens and colleagues (1994) evaluated the psychiatric comorbidity in 53 inpatient substance abusers and found major depression evident in 25% and dysthymia in 33%. More recently, Grilo and colleagues (1995) assessed 69 inpatient adolescents with substance use disorders and found that 65.2% met criteria for a mood disorder. Taken together, these data indicate that comorbidity in the adolescent population is high and patients need to be carefully assessed such that appropriate treatment can be provided.

Conclusions. The comorbidity of affective disorder and substance use disorders is impressively high when assessed from a number of differing perspectives in a variety of populations. The wide variation in estimates is likely due to differing diagnostic techniques and the different samples interviewed. A few generalizations, however, can be made. While all affective disorders are relatively common in substance users, bipolar disorder is the affective disorder most commonly associated with a substance use disorder. Depression/dysthymia are the affective disorders most commonly seen in alcoholic and opiate dependent populations. Bipolar spectrum disorders are relatively more common in the cocaine dependent population, but the substantial overlap between symptoms of mania and stimulant intoxication must be kept in mind.

TREATMENT

Pharmacotherapeutic Treatment of Depression and Substance Use Disorders. Several studies of tricyclic antidepressants (TCAs) in alcoholic populations have indicated that antidepressant treatment may be helpful in the treatment of individuals with comorbid substance use and depression. McGrath and colleagues (1996) conducted a 12-week, placebo-controlled trial of imipramine treatment in actively drinking alcoholic outpatients with depression. They found that imipramine treatment was associated with improvement in depression; and while there was no overall effect on drinking outcome, patients whose mood improved showed a more marked decrease in alcohol consumption. Mason and colleagues (1996) found that treatment of alcoholics with secondary depression (onset of depression after alcohol dependence) with desipramine led to decrease in depression and an increase in length of abstinent period. Dosage and effective blood levels of TCAs remain unclear. Lower imipramine blood levels have been reported in alcoholics on a fixed dose compared to a nonalcoholic population, which appeared to be related to differential clearance. Increased plasma imipramine levels have also been reported in patients treated with disulfiram. TCA plasma level monitoring is therefore likely to be particularly important in alcoholic populations (Weiss & Mirin, 1989).

Research investigating the use of selective serotonin reuptake inhibitors (SSRIs) in the treatment of alcoholism has shown recent promise. The serotonin system has been implicated in control of alcohol intake (Amit, Smith & Gill, 1991). A number of selective serotonin agents have been shown to have a modest effect in decreasing alcohol consumption in problem drinkers and alcoholics (Gorelick, 1989). Additionally, a recently published 12-week placebo-controlled trial of fluoxetine in depressed, alcoholic patients demonstrated significant improvement in some monitors of depression as well as alcohol-related outcomes in the fluoxetine-treated group (Cornelius, Salloum et al., 1997).

Several trials of tricyclic antidepressants have been performed with opioid-dependent patients. Doxepin has been shown in several studies in methadone-maintained patients to relieve symptoms of depression, anxiety, and drug craving. It must be noted, however, that methadone maintenance clinics have reported abuse of amitriptyline and other sedating tricyclic anti-depressants. TCA plasma level monitoring is important in methadone-maintained patients because patients receiving methadone and desipramine have been found to have plasma desipramine levels twice as high as they had been prior to methadone administration (Weiss & Mirin, 1989).

The use of tricyclic antidepressants in cocaine-dependent patients has focused primarily on the treatment of cocaine dependence rather than the treatment of depression. Several studies using desipramine have shown improvement in anhedonia and cocaine craving and increased initial abstinence in non-depressed patients, and one small study showed improvement in depression as well as cocaine use in depressed cocaine-dependent patients (Rao, Ziedonis & Kosten, 1995). Clinicians should be aware, however, that desipramine may have an activating effect in cocaine-dependent individuals, which can precipitate relapse. Also, TCAs may have additive cardiotoxicity in combination with cocaine, should relapse occur (Weiss & Mirin, 1989). Other antidepressants have shown preliminary efficacy in the treatment of cocaine dependence, but none have been explored specifically in depressed cocaine-dependent individuals.

Several treatment recommendations can be made. First, a period of abstinence is optimal before the initiation of antidepressant treatment. Even with evidence for a primary depression, it would be prudent to wait until after detoxification is complete so as not to confuse activation from antidepressants with withdrawal symptoms. The patient's aftercare plan may dictate how aggressive the clinician should be in deciding the use of antidepressant medications. If the depression is mild (dysthmia) and less clear diagnostically, the decision to postpone pharmacologic treatment for diagnostic purposes may make sense. If the depression is severe without much evidence of remission during the first few days of abstinence, early pharmacologic treatment may be justified. It is important to note that symptoms of depression that clearly predate the substance use disorder or a family history of depression may also be factors in helping the clinician to make a diagnosis of depression with shorter periods of abstinence.

After reaching the decision to use a medication, the SSRIs may be a logical first choice in alcoholic populations for several reasons. First, the SSRIs may decrease the desire to drink and help to initiate abstinence as well as treat depression. Second, SSRIs have fewer anticholinergic and cardiotoxic side effects and are therefore better tolerated and safer in a population at greater risk for noncompliance and impulsive overdosing. When using SSRIs or TCAs, one must keep in mind that higher doses may be required because of the possibility of induced hepatic microsomal activity by alcohol. When treating depression in individuals with cocaine use disorders, one may first consider using desipramine to help facilitate abstinence as well as alleviate depression. We would recommend initiating treatment with low doses to avoid activation, which may trigger relapse. The selective serotonin drugs need further investigation in the cocaine using population.

Pharmacotherapeutic Treatment and Clinical Course of Bipolar Disorder and Substance Abuse. Before treatment of the individuals with comorbid bipolar disorder and a substance use disorder can be discussed, it is important to understand the clinical course of bipolar disorder complicated by substance abuse. Sonne and colleagues (1994) compared a group of individuals with bipolar disorder and a coexisting substance use disorder to a group with bipolar disorder and no substance use disorder. They found that substance users had an earlier onset of mood disorder, were more likely to be male, have more comorbid Axis I disorders (primarily posttraumatic stress disorder and panic disorder) and were significantly more likely to have dysphoric mania at the time of interview. Blanco-Perez and colleagues (1996) found substance abuse in bipolar patients to be associated with male gender, child trauma, earlier onset of bipolar disorder, a higher number of hospitalizations, lower social support and higher frequency of attempted suicide. Still others have found that a higher percentage of patients with mixed or rapid cycling bipolar disorder had concurrent alcoholism (Keller, Lavori & Rice, 1986). Such patients also were more likely to have a slower time of recovery than patients presenting with pure depression or pure mania. These data suggest that bipolar patients with comorbid substance use disorders may have a more severe course of affective illness than bipolar patients who do not have a substance use disorder. It has been postulated that the presence of the affective syndrome, particularly mania, may precipitate or exacerbate substance abuse (Hasin, Endicott & Lewis, 1985). Alternatively, substance abuse and withdrawal are likely to worsen affective symptoms thereby forming a vicious cycle of substance abuse and affective instability.

Theoretical Implications: An interesting theoretical perspective in this area comes from the literature on neuronal sensitization, or "kindling." It has been postulated that bipolar disorder is a phenomenon of neuronal sensitization because the course of the illness is often characterized by acceleration with successively shortened periods of remission between episodes of illness (Post, Rubinow & Ballenger, 1984). Cocaine and alcohol are the most common agents of abuse in patients with bipolar disorder (Brady & Lydiard, 1992). Acute cocaine intoxication and alcohol withdrawal both appear to produce neuronal sensitization (Brown, Anton et al., 1986; Post & Weiss, 1988). Because use of both substances is associated with neuronal sensitization and it has been postulated that the course of bipolar disorder also is affected by neuronal sensitization, it is possible that this common mechanism is responsible for the morbidity and poor prognosis associated with substance abuse in bipolar patients. Carbamazepine and valproate are two anti-kindling, anticonvulsant agents which have efficacy in the treatment of acute manic states. If neuronal sensitization, or "kindling", is one consequence of substance abuse and is important in the pathophysiology of bipolar disorder, an anti-kindling agent may be particularly efficacious in patients with comorbid bipolar disorder and a substance use disorder. There is also evidence to support the use of the anti-kindling agent, carbamazepine, in the treatment of alcohol withdrawal (Malcolm, Ballenger et al., 1989), which may make the anti-kindling agents even more useful for treating substance abusing bipolar patients.

Pharmacotherapy. Unfortunately, there is currently very little published data on the treatment of bipolar disorder complicated by substance abuse. Currently, the agents that are generally used for the treatment of bipolar disorder include lithium and the anticonvulsant medications, carbamazepine and valproate. Lithium has been used as the standard treatment of bipolar disorder for several decades. However, it is effective in only 60% to 80% of classic bipolar patients (Calabrese, Rapport et al., 1993). The response rate for lithium has been estimated to be as low as 50% when all bipolar subtypes have been considered. As many as 72% to 82% of patients with the rapid cycling variant of bipolar disorder exhibit a poor response to lithium (Calabrese & Delucchi, 1989).

Substance abuse has been listed as a predictor of poor response to lithium in several studies (Tohen, Waternaux et al., 1990; O'Connell, Mayo et al., 1991; Bowden, 1995). In a four-year follow-up study of 24 bipolar patients after their first manic episode, alcoholism was found to be a statistically significant predictor of a shorter time in remission from affective symptomatology (Tohen, Waternaux et al., 1990). Another long-term lithium study (O'Connell, Mayo et al., 1991) found the incidence of substance abuse to be substantially higher in the patients with a poor outcome (36%), compared to patients with a good outcome (7%).

Both carbamazepine and valproate have shown efficacy in treating mania associated with bipolar disorder (Ballenger & Post, 1979; Post, 1990; Bowden, Brugger et al., 1994). Although other anticonvulsants are currently being studied for the treatment of mania (e.g., lamotrigine, gabapentin), only valproate (divalproex sodium) is approved by the Food and Drug Administration (FDA) for this indication (Abbott Laboratories, 1995). In addition to typical euphoric mania, many bipolar individuals have mixed manic episodes (concurrent symptoms of mania and depression) an rapid cycling episodes (>4 episodes per year).

Several studies have concluded that patients with mixed and/or rapid cycling bipolar disorder are more likely to respond to anticonvulsant medications than to lithium (Freeman, Clothier et al., 1992; Calabrese, Markovitz et al., 1992). As stated previously, bipolar patients with concomitant substance use disorders appear to have more mixed and/or rapid cycling bipolar disorder than patients with bipolar disorder who do not abuse substances. Therefore, substance abusing bipolar patients may respond better to anticonvulsant medications (e.g., valproate) than to lithium therapy. In fact, in an open-label pilot study, Brady and colleagues (Brady, Sonne et al., 1995) found valproate to be safe and effective in nine mixed manic bipolar patients with concurrent substance dependence, who previously either had not tolerated or not responded to lithium.

Both valproate and alcohol consumption are known to cause transient elevations in liver transaminases and in rare cases fatal liver failure. Therefore, it is important to frequently monitor liver function in the alcoholic receiving valproate therapy. It is recommended that valproate therapy be started only if liver transaminases are less than twice the upper limit of normal. With this practice, there is recent preliminary evidence from our site that liver transaminases do not dramatically increase in alcoholic patients who are receiving valproate, even if they are actively drinking (Sonne, Brady & Morton, 1996). Additionally, chronic alcohol use may cause decreased white blood cell and decreased platelet counts, which also may complicate the use of valproate in the alcoholic population. However, our preliminary data have not shown any clinically significant decreases in platelet counts of alcoholic individuals who were receiving valproate for as long as two years (Sonne, Brady & Morton, 1996).

Currently valproate is the only anticonvulsant medication that is FDA-approved for the treatment of bipolar disorder. However, there are a number of studies that support the use of carbamazepine in the treatment of bipolar disorder, specifically in the treatment of mixed mania and rapid cycling. A number of studies also have found carbamazepine effective in the treatment of bipolar disorder when lithium therapy has failed (Okuma, Yamashita et al., 1989).

When treating acute mania, the other traditional agents (e.g., neuroleptics, benzodiazepines) are also useful in the substance abusing population. However, when managing substance-abusing bipolar individuals with benzodiazepines on an outpatient basis, it may be prudent to use agents that have a longer onset of action (e.g., clonazepam, oxazepam) since those agents appear to have less abuse potential. It also is advisable to use benzodiazepines only in a time-limited, symptom-oriented manner and to prescribe small amounts at any one time.

Psychotherapeutic Treatments. Psychotherapeutic interventions are useful in the treatment of both affective disorder and substance use disorders and are a critical element in the treatment of a patient with comorbidity. It is fairly well accepted that the use of medications for mood stability is an essential component of patient care. While most experts agree that psychotherapy is an important adjunct to pharmacotherapeutic interventions in patients with affective disorder, there is less consensus concerning the most appropriate psychotherapeutic treatment. However, mood stabilization alone will not be an effective treatment for a substance use disorder. Adjunctive therapy and psychosocial rehabilitation is necessary.

A wide range of psychotherapeutic interventions have been used in the treatment of affective disorders. These include psychodynamic, interpersonal, cognitive, behavioral and family therapy (American Psychiatric Association, 1994). Judgments concerning the effectiveness of these treatments are based primarily on clinical consensus rather than controlled clinical trial; however, formal studies of several of these treatments are currently being conducted.

Psychotherapeutic, psychosocial and peer-oriented interventions are a mainstay in the treatment of substance use disorders. Several recent studies have demonstrated success with cognitive behavioral therapy interventions (Carroll, Rounsaville & Gordon, 1994) as well as with behaviorally oriented contingency management programs (Higgins, Budney et al., 1994). A recent treatment-matching study showed remarkably good results with all of the three most commonly used therapies including Twelve Step facilitation, brief motivational therapy and cognitive behavioral therapy (MATCH, 1996).

The psychotherapeutic/psychosocial treatment approach used should be individualized and contain elements from the substance abuse and affective disorders arena. Many of the principles of cognitive behavioral therapy are common to the treatment of affective disorder as well as substance use disorders. Alcoholics Anonymous (AA) and Narcotics Anonymous (NA) are available in all communities and active participation can be a major factor in an individual's recovery. Emphasis on developing therapies to specifically treat individuals with comorbid psychiatric and substance use disorders by combining techniques used to treat both disorders will be a fruitful area for further work. In the interim, substance use disorders should be treated aggressively in patients with affective disorders as soon as the patients are psychiatrically stable enough to participate in and benefit from treatment. It also is important to recognize that all individuals with affective disorder are at risk for developing a substance use disorder and should therefore be informed about the risks of substance abuse and counseled in the early warning signs of substance abuse. In particular, patients should be warned about the dangers of self-medication with substances of abuse.

CONCLUSIONS

Because symptoms of mood disorders are common in individuals with substance use disorders and full syndromal affective disorders are commonly comorbid with substance use disorders, this area is of much importance. Differentiating between substance-induced, time-limited mood symptoms and true affective disorder which warrants specifically tailored treatment remains an issue which justifies further investigation. Treatment options for individuals with comorbid disorders, both pharmacotherapeutic and psychotherapeutic, are promising. Improving our diagnostic and treatment approach to individuals with comorbid affective disorders is of critical importance to improvement in the treatment of substance use disorders in general.

REFERENCES

Abbott Laboratories (1995). *Divalproex Sodium (Depakote) Product Information*. North Chicago, IL: Abbott Laboratories.

American Psychiatric Association (1994). *Diagnostic and Statistical Manual of Mental Disorders, 4th Edition*. Washington, DC: American Psychiatric Press.

American Psychiatric Association (1987). *Diagnostic and Statistical Manual of Mental Disorders, 3rd Edition, Revised*. Washington, DC: American Psychiatric Press.

Amit Z, Smith BR & Gill K (1991). Serotonin uptake inhibitors: Effects on motivated consummatory behaviors. *Journal of Clinical Psychiatry* 55:55–60.

Ballenger J & Post R (1979). Therapeutic effects of carbamazepine in affective illness: A preliminary report. *Community Psychopharmacology* 159–179.

Blanco-Perez CR, Blanco C, Grimaldi JA, Rueda C, Mayo JA & O'Connell RA (1996). Substance abuse and bipolar disorder. Meeting of the American Psychiatric Association, New York, NY.

Bowden CL (1995). Predictors of response to divalproex and lithium. *Journal of Clinical Psychiatry* 56(Suppl 3):25–30.

Bowden CL, Brugger AM, Swann AC, Calabrese JR, Janicak PG, Petty F, Dilsaver SC, Davis JM, Rush AJ, Small JG, Garza-Trevino ES, Risch SC, Goodnick PJ & Morris DD (1994). Efficacy of Divalproex vs. lithium and placebo in the treatment of mania. *Journal of the American Medical Association* 271:918–924.

Bowen RC, Cipywnyk D, D'Arcy C & Keegan D (1984). Alcoholism, anxiety disorders, and agoraphobia. *Alcoholism: Clinical & Experimental Research* 8(1):48–50.

Brady K, Casto S, Lydiard RB, Malcolm R & Arana G (1991). Substance abuse in an inpatient psychiatric sample. *American Journal on Drug and Alcohol Abuse* 17(4):389–397.

Brady KT & Lydiard RB (1992). Bipolar affective disorder and substance abuse. *Journal of Clinical Psychopharmacology* 12(Suppl):17s–22s.

Brady KT, Sonne SC, Anton R & Ballenger JC (1995). Valproate in the treatment of acute bipolar affective episodes complicated by substance abuse: A pilot study. *Journal of Clinical Psychiatry* 56(3):118–121.

Brooner RK, King VL, Kidorf M, Schmidt CW & Bigelow GE (1997). Psychiatric and substance comorbidity among treatment-seeking opioid abusers. *Archives of General Psychiatry* 54:71–80.

Brown ME, Anton RF, Malcolm R & Ballenger JC (1986). Alcoholic detoxification and withdrawal seizures: Clinical support for a kindling hypothesis. *Biological Psychiatry* 43:107–113.

Bukstein OG, Glancy LJ & Kaminer Y (1992). Patterns of affective comorbidity in a clinical population of dually diagnosed adolescent substance abusers. *Journal of the American Academy of Child and Adolescent Psychiatry* 31(6):1041–1045.

Calabrese JR & Delucchi GA (1989). Phenomenology of rapid cycling manic depression and its treatment with valproate. *Journal of Clinical Psychiatry* 50(Suppl):30–34.

Calabrese JR, Markovitz PJ, Kimmel SE & Wagner SC (1992). Spectrum of efficacy of valproate in 78 rapid-cycling bipolar patients. *Journal of Clinical Psychopharmacology* 12:53–56.

Calabrese JR, Rapport DJ, Kimmel SE, Reece B & Woyshville MJ (1993). Rapid cycling bipolar disorder and its treatment with valproate. *Canadian Journal of Psychiatry* 38: 57–61.

Carroll KM, Rounsaville BJ & Gordon LT (1994). Psychotherapy and pharmacotherapy for ambulatory cocaine abusers. *Archives of General Psychiatry* 51:177–187.

Cornelius JR, Salloum IM, Ehler JG, Jarrett PJ, Cornelius MD, Perel JM, Thase ME & Black A (1997). Fluoxetine in depressed alcoholics. A double-blind, placebo-controlled trial. *Archives of General Psychiatry* 54(8):700–705.

Deykin EY, Levy JC & Wells V (1987). Adolescent depression, alcohol and drug abuse. *American Journal of Public Health* 77(2):178–182.

Dorus W, Kennedy J, Gibbons RD & Ravi SD (1987). Symptoms and diagnosis of depression in alcoholics. *Alcoholism: Clinical & Experimental Research* 11(2):150–154.

Freeman TW, Clothier JL, Pazzaglia P, Lesem MD & Swann AC (1992). A double-blind comparison of valproate and lithium in the treatment of acute mania. *American Journal of Psychiatry* 149(1):108–111.

Gawin FH & Kleber HD (1986). Abstinence symptomatology and psychiatric diagnosis in cocaine abusers. Clinical observations. *Archives of General Psychiatry* 43(2):107–113.

Gorelick DA (1989). Serotonin uptake blockers and the treatment of alcoholism. *Recent Developments in Alcohol* 7:267–281.

Grilo CM, Becker DF, Walker ML, Levy KN, Edell WS & McGlashan TH (1995). Psychiatric comorbidity in adolescent inpatients with substance use disorders. *Journal of the American Academy of Child and Adolescent Psychiatry* 34(8):1085–1091.

Halikas JA, Crosby RD, Pearson VL, Nugent SM & Carlson GA (1994). Psychiatric comorbidity in treatment-seeking cocaine abusers. *American Journal on Addictions* 3(1):1–11.

Hasin D, Endicott J & Lewis C (1985). Alcohol and drug abuse in patients with affective syndromes. *Comprehensive Psychiatry* 26:283–295.

Hasin DS, Trautman KD, Miele GM, Samet S, Smith M & Endicott J (1996). Psychiatric Research Interview for Substance and Mental Disorders (PRISM): reliability for substance abusers. *American Journal of Psychiatry* 153(9):1195–1201.

Hasin DS, Grant BF & Endicott J (1988). Lifetime psychiatric comorbidity in hospitalized alcoholics: subject and familial correlates. *International Journal of the Addictions* 23(8):827–850.

Higgins ST, Budney AJ, Bickel WK, Foerg FE, Donham R & Badger GJ (1994). Incentives improve outcome in outpatient behavioral treatment of cocaine dependence. *Archives of General Psychiatry* 51(7):568–576.

Hovens JG, Cantwell DP & Kiriakos R (1994). Psychiatric comorbidity in hospitalized adolescent substance abusers. *Journal of the American Academy of Child and Adolescent Psychiatry* 33(4):476–483.

Jaffe AJ, Rounsaville B, Chang G, Schottenfeld RS, Meyer RE & O'Malley SS (1996). Naltrexone, relapse prevention, and supportive therapy with alcoholics: An analysis of patient treatment matching. *Journal of Consulting and Clinical Psychology* 64(5):1044–1053.

Keller MB, Lavori PW & Rice J (1986). The persistent risk of chronicity in recurrent episodes of nonbipolar major depressive disorder; A prospective follow-up. *American Journal of Psychiatry*.

Kessler RC, Crum RM, Warner LA, Nelson CB, Schulenberg J & Anthony JC (1997). Lifetime co-occurrence of DSM-III-R alcohol abuse and dependence with other psychiatric disorders in the national comorbidity survey. *Archives of General Psychiatry* 54:313–321.

Kessler RC, McGonagle KA, Zhao S, Nelson CB, Hughes M, Eshleman S, Wittchen HU & Kendler KS (1994). Lifetime and 12-month prevalence of DSM-III-R psychiatric disorders in the United States. Results from the National Comorbidity Survey. *Archives of General Psychiatry* 51(1):8–19.

Lydiard RB, Brady KT, Ballenger JD, Howell EF & Malcolm R (1992). Anxiety and mood disorders in hospitalized alcoholic individuals. *American Journal on Addictions* 1(4):325–331.

Malcolm R, Ballenger RC, Sturgis ET & Anton R (1989). Double-blind controlled trial comparing carbamazepine to oxazepam treatment of alcohol withdrawal. *American Journal of Psychiatry* 146:617–621.

Mason BJ, Kocsis JH, Ritvo EC & Cutler RB (1996). A double-blind, placebo-controlled trial of desipramine for primary alcohol dependence stratified on the presence or absence of major depression. *Journal of the American Medical Association* 275(10):761–767.

MATCH (1996). Matching alcohol treatments to client heterogeneity: Project MATCH post-treatment drinking outcomes. *Journal of Studies on Alcohol.*

McGrath PJ, Nunes EV, Stewart JW, Goldman D, Agosti V, Ocepek-Welikson K & Quitkin FM (1996). Imipramine treatment of alcoholics with primary depression: A placebo-controlled clinical trial. *Archives of General Psychiatry* 53(3):232–240.

Miller NS & Fine J (1993). Current epidemiology of comorbidity of psychiatric and addictive disorders. *Psychiatric Clinics of North America* 16(1):1–10.

Nunes EV, Quitkin FM & Klein DF (1989). Psychiatric diagnosis in cocaine abuse. *Psychiatry Research* 28(1):105–114.

O'Connell RA, Mayo JA, Flatow L, Cuthbertson B & O'Brien BE (1991). Outcome of bipolar disorder on long-term treatment with lithium. *British Journal of Psychiatry* 159:123–129.

Okuma T, Yamashita I, Takahashi R, Itoh H, Kurihara M, Otsuki S, Watanabe S, Sarai K, Hazama H & Inanaga K (1989). Clinical efficacy of carbamazepine in affective, schizoaffective, and schizophrenic disorders. *Pharmacopsychiatry* 22(2):47–53.

Post R, Rubinow D & Ballenger J (1984). Conditioning, sensitization and kindling: implications for the course of affective illness. In RM Post & JC Ballenger (eds.) *Neurobiology of Mood Disorders*. Baltimore, MD: Williams & Wilkins, 432–466.

Post RM (1990). Non-lithium treatment for bipolar disorder. *Journal of Clinical Psychiatry* 51(Suppl):9–19.

Post RM & Weiss SR (1988). Psychomotor stimulant vs. local anesthetic effects of cocaine: Role of behavioral sensitization and kindling. *NIDA Research Monograph Series* 88:217–238.

Powell BJ, Penick EC, Othmer E, Bingham SF & Rice AS (1982). Prevalence of additional psychiatric syndromes among male alcoholics. *Journal of Clinical Psychiatry* 43(10):404–407.

Rao S, Ziedonis D & Kosten T (1995). The pharmacotherapy of cocaine dependence. *Psychiatric Annals* 25:363–368.

Regier DA, Farmer ME, Rae DS, Locke BZ, Keith SJ, Judd LL & Goodwin FK (1990). Comorbidity of mental disorders with alcohol and other drug abuse. Results from the Epidemiologic Catchment Area (ECA). *Journal of the American Medical Association* 264(19):2511–2518.

Rounsaville BJ, Anton SF, Carroll K, Budde D, Prusoff BA & Gawin F (1991). Psychiatric diagnoses of treatment-seeking cocaine abusers. *Archives of General Psychiatry* 48(1):43–51.

Rounsaville BJ, Weissman MM, Kleber H & Wilber C (1982). Heterogeneity of psychiatric diagnosis in treated opiate addicts. *Archives of General Psychiatry* 39(2):161–168.

Sonne SC, Brady KT & Morton WA (1994). Substance abuse and bipolar affective disorder. *Journal of Nervous and Mental Disease* 182(6):349–352.

Sonne SC, Brady KT & Morton WA (1996). Safety of Depakote in bipolar patients with comorbid alcoholism. American Psychiatric Association Annual Meeting, New York, NY.

Tohen M, Waternaux CM, Tsuang MT & Hunt AT (1990). Four-year follow-up of twenty-four first-episode manic patients. *Journal of Affective Disorder* 19(2):79–86.

Weisner C & Schmidt L (1992). Gender disparities in treatment for alcohol problems. *Journal of the American Medical Association* 268(14):1872–1876.

Weiss RD & Mirin SM (1989). Tricyclic antidepressants in the treatment of alcoholism and drug abuse. *Journal of Clinical Psychiatry* 50(7):(Suppl)4–11.

Weiss RD, Mirin SM, Griffin ML & Michael JL (1988). Psychopathology in cocaine abusers. Changing trends. *Journal of Nervous and Mental Disease* 176(12):719–725.

CHAPTER 3

Anxiety Disorders

David R. Gastfriend, M.D.
Patrick Lillard, M.D.

Prevalence of Anxiety Disorders in the Addicted Population
Major Neurotransmitter Systems Involved in Addiction and Anxiety
Diagnosing the Anxious Addicted Patient
Psychosocial Treatment
Pharmacotherapy
Integrating Treatments toward Homeostatic Balance

Anxiety is a common and confusing feature when it co-occurs with addictive behaviors. Both problems have high base rates in the general population and both problems share some underlying genetic connections. Clinically, an anxiety disorder manifests as a distorted perception running amok among impotent defenses. Similarly, addiction often is the manifestation of an attempt to shore up impotent defenses with a chemical that, ironically, causes its own distorted perceptions. Alcohol and other drugs of abuse exacerbate an anxiety syndrome. For example, alcohol may be effective in the short-term alleviation of anxiety, but in the dependent drinker it exacerbates forms of anxiety such as agoraphobia and social phobia, to say nothing of the panic precipitated in the withdrawal phase. Indeed, the relationship between addiction and anxiety is intimate and devious. Treatment of anxiety may induce iatrogenic dependence, while withdrawal frequently induces anxiety. Finally, for many patients, early recovery from addiction is a period of unmitigated stress that frequently manifests as anxiety (although this is not, of itself, a disorder).

Temporal and pharmacologic relationships between anxiety and addiction frequently cannot be simply viewed as primary or secondary. The keys to effective clinical care are: (1) an understanding of these disorders' psychopathologic similarities and differences, (2) complete clinical data from the patient and collaterals, (3) a working diagnosis and treatment contract, and (4) longitudinal monitoring of the treatment effort and response.

It is difficult to detect substance abuse, particularly in the presence of a presenting anxiety disorder. Psychiatric patients may have high rates of substance abuse (Hall, Stickney et al., 1979), and may continue to use alcohol or drugs while under close psychiatric supervision, despite the fact that their symptoms may worsen as a result of the covert substance use (McLellan, Druley & Carson, 1978).

A parallel problem is that substance abuse may lead to misdiagnosis of anxiety symptoms (Hall, Stickney et al., 1979). Table 1 indicates that most drugs of abuse are known to be capable of precipitating panic attacks, generalized anxiety, and sleep disruptions as the result of organic mental syndromes (American Psychiatric Association, 1994). Proper diagnosis is essential in treatment planning, as psychiatric inpatients with substance abuse have 10% longer lengths of stay and are three times more likely to leave against medical advice (American Psychiatric Association, 1994). In one VA psychiatric hospital study, only 7% of patients with alcohol abuse and none of the patients with drug abuse received any specific therapy for their substance abuse problems (O'Farrell, Connors & Upper, 1983).

PREVALENCE OF ANXIETY DISORDERS IN THE ADDICTED POPULATION

Among the general population, the lifetime prevalence of substance use disorders is 16.7%, higher than that of any other psychiatric disorder, with anxiety disorders a close second at 14.6% (Regier, Farmer et al., 1990). The co-occurrence of substance use disorders in individuals with anxiety disorders is about 50% higher than in the general population risk, or 23.7%. The risk calculated from community samples is a more reasonable estimate than that from individuals in treatment, for the following reasons.

In a classic example of an erroneously designed study of inpatients with addictive disorders, 84%

TABLE 1. Organic Symptoms of Anxiety and Sleep Disruption Caused by Substance Abuse and Dependence

Symptom	Substance	Temporal State
Anxiety Disorder	alcohol & sedatives	intoxication & withdrawal
	amphetamines & cocaine	intoxication
	caffeine	intoxication
	cannabis	intoxication
	hallucinogens	intoxication
	inhalants	intoxication
Sleep Disorder	alcohol & sedatives	intoxication & withdrawal
	amphetamines & cocaine	intoxication & withdrawal
	caffeine	intoxication
	opioids	intoxication & withdrawal

Source: Adapted from the American Psychiatric Association (1994). *Diagnostic and Statistical Manual of Mental Disorders, 4th Edition.* Washington, DC: American Psychiatric Press.

received another psychiatric diagnosis and 64% were diagnosed with an anxiety disorder (Ross, Glaser & Germanson, 1988). Although these diagnoses were carefully determined with structured interviews (the Diagnostic Interview Schedule), this unusually high comorbidity actually was an artifact of performing the interview within the first five days of admission. Contrast this with the 19% to 29% of the general population who received another psychiatric diagnosis in the Epidemiologic Catchment Area Study and the discrepancy becomes apparent (Robins & Regier, 1991).

The flaw in these results lies in the fact that the DIS was conducted within five days of admission for detoxification. The failure of overlapping the time period of detoxification with the assessment of anxiety is that it produces inaccurate diagnoses of anxiety in alcohol-dependent patients. This error results in wildly varying literature reports of prevalence that range from 22.6% to 68.7%. Contrast these rates with a study of 171 alcoholic male veterans in which 98% reported at least one symptom of anxiety during drinking or withdrawal, but in which only seven men (4%) fulfilled criteria for generalized anxiety disorder or panic disorder after three months of abstinence (Schuckit, Irwin & Brown, 1990).

Individuals with substance dependence may or may not have high rates of anxiety or anxiolytic abuse and need to be considered according to subgroups rather than as a unitary population. Ciraulo and colleagues reviewed various reports that from 3% to 41% of alcoholics take benzodiazepines (Ciraulo, Sands & Shader, 1988)—not a uniform pattern at all. In one study of panic patients, 28% were reported to suffer from alcoholism (Reich, Winokur & Mullaney, 1975). Kushner and colleagues, reviewing the literature, did not find elevated rates of alcoholism in patients with panic and generalized anxiety disorder, but studies reported twice the general population prevalence in agoraphobia and obsessive-compulsive disorder and nine times greater rates in social phobia (Kushner, Sher & Beitman, 1990). Anxiety disorders in heroin-dependent patients reportedly were elevated among women, at 25.4%, but were present in only 13.2% of men (Rounsaville, Weissman et al., 1982). Cocaine users have not been shown to have increased prevalence of anxiety disorders (Weiss, Mirin et al., 1986; Gawin & Kleber, 1986).

Another way to assess the comorbidity of these discrete disorders is to examine their association in family studies. Alcohol disorders may be genetically related to anxiety disorders, given that relatives of some anxiety disorder probands show increased rates of alcohol disorders (Noyes, Crowe et al., 1986). Family members of individuals with panic disorder show only slightly higher risk of alcohol problems than unaffected families (8.4% versus 5.5%), but family members of agoraphobic probands are at much greater risk for alcohol problems (17.0% versus 5.5%) (Noyes, Crowe et al., 1986).

Also, the order of onset of the anxiety disorder and addiction suggests a causal relationship. In eight studies reviewed by Kushner and colleagues, anxiety disorders tended to precede an alcohol disorder (Kushner, Sher & Beitman, 1990). No temporal relationship was consistently found between panic or simple phobia and alcohol disorders. Agoraphobia and social phobia, however, tended to be followed by alcohol problems, perhaps due to self-medication efforts.

MAJOR NEUROTRANSMITTER SYSTEMS INVOLVED IN ADDICTION AND ANXIETY

Given the close relationship between at least some anxiety disorders and addictions, it is helpful that neurobiological research has offered putative mechanisms for these connections. A useful hypothesis for understanding these interactions is the model of alarm system dysregulation that is believed to be responsible for panic disorder with agoraphobia. Fundamentally, this dysregulation occurs at the level of the locus ceruleus, a small pair of cell body groups bilaterally situated in the midbrain. These nuclei are responsible for alarm generation, which then is subject to the brain's cognitive integration into panic and the fight or flight response. A dysfunctional stress response may occur either as a complication of locus ceruleus alarm dysregulation or through an independent cortical process, e.g., in the case of social phobia. At least four distinct neurotransmitter systems take part in regulating the arousal/anxiety levels in mammalian brain: (1) the N-methyl-D-aspartate (NMDA) subtype of the excitatory glutamate receptor system, (2) the excitatory noradrenergic system, (3) the $GABA_A$ inhibitory system, and (4) the serotonin receptor systems.

Although few clinical approaches exist as yet to influence the glutamatergic system, this excitatory system is ubiquitous in the brain and directly affects the noradrenergic system (Van den Pol, Waurin & Dudek, 1990). It is highly susceptible to ethanol and intimately involved in addictive and anxiogenic processes (Tsai, Gastfriend & Coyle, 1995). Acutely, ethanol inhibits the response of one subtype of glutamate receptor, the N-methyl-D-aspartate (NMDA) glutamate receptor. Chronic heavy drinking prolongs the inhibition of the NMDA-glutamate receptor and leads to supersensitivity. Acute abstinence then causes markedly elevated post-synaptic neuronal activity in the noradrenergic system. In extreme cases, withdrawal produces glutamate-induced excitotoxicity. In sudden withdrawal from alcohol dependence, unmitigated NMDA-glutamate arousal is the mechanism responsible for withdrawal seizures and *delirium tremens* (Tsai, Gastfriend & Coyle, 1995). Cocaine is similarly associated with glutamate upregulation and seizure generation (Itzhak & Stein, 1992). Anxiety symptoms are a logical subjective consequence of this glutamatergic excitotoxicity, mediated through the glutamate's influence on the noradrenergic system.

The noradrenergic system includes the locus ceruleus alarm center. Alcohol withdrawal during chronic alcohol consumption is an acute noradrenergic hypersensitivity state (French, Palmer et al., 1975). Similarly, opiate withdrawal long has been understood to be a loss of opiate inhibition on the hypersensitized noradrenergic system (Gold, Byck et al., 1979). Alpha-2 adrenergic agonists such as clonidine (Cedarbaum & Aghajanian, 1977) and also opiates selectively inhibit neuronal activity in the locus ceruleus (Korf, Bunney & Aghajanian, 1974). Alpha-2 adrenergic antagonists (such as yohimbine) are anxiogenic (Krystal, Webb et al., 1994). Sympathomimetic agents, whether direct-acting (like the amphetamines) or indirect (like cocaine), all have some potential to provoke anxiety. Therefore, multiple agents of abuse, either during acute intoxication (stimulants) or during acute withdrawal (ethanol, opiates) have the potential to provoke anxiety. These pharmacologic stimuli may trigger anxiety in the short-term (as during stimulant intoxication), mid-term (e.g., during ethanol or opiate withdrawal), or in individuals with an underlying vulnerability for an anxiety syndrome such as panic (e.g., precipitated by an episode of marijuana use), for an extended course of illness.

GABA, the most widely distributed inhibitory neurotransmitter in the central nervous system, is a macromolecular complex that is potentiated by several drugs of abuse, including the barbiturates, benzodiazepines and ethanol. All of these increase post-synaptic Cl-influx (Suzdak, Glowa et al., 1986), producing classic hypnosedative actions of euphoria, anxiety reduction, disinhibition, and sedation (Zorumski & Isenberg, 1991). Ethanol downregulates $GABA_A$ subunits over time, reducing this inhibitory system, which may increase anxiety (Mhatre, Pena et al., 1993). The $GABA_A$ receptor also may regulate endogenous stress and this may be another source of its risk for addictive reinforcement (Koob, 1992). These agents all demonstrate cross-tolerance via the GABA receptor so that laboratory animals that have been trained to be dependent on one agent quickly adapt to self-administering another agent when the first is removed. Interestingly, GABA also may be involved in reinforcement of opiates as well as ethanol (Hubner & Koob, 1990; Koob et al, 1991; Morgenson, Jones & Yim, 1980).

Serotonin (5-HT) is a neurotransmitter involved in the regulation of mood, arousal, aggression, sleep and appetite (Dubovsky, 1994). Acutely, alcohol produces a transient rise in serotonin and accumulation of aldehydes, such as beta-carbolines, that themselves possess high lipophilicity and psychotropic activity. Serotonin also may be important in mediating some of the actions of the GABAergic inhibitory system (Traber & Glaser, 1987). Serotonin appears to play a role in the craving for ethanol (Tollefson, 1989) and possibly for cocaine, too (Branchey, Branchey et al., 1997). Direct activation of serotonin receptors attenuates alcohol consumption, whereas depletion enhances drinking. Chronic alcohol consumption reduces brain levels of serotonin, which may explain the frequent appearance of anxiety. The serotonin partial agonist MCPP produces ethanol-like effects in humans, stimulates alcohol craving in recently detoxified alcoholics, has some subjective effects similar to those of ethanol, cocaine, and marijuana, and increases nervousness (Krystal, Webb et al., 1994). Research consistently has demonstrated that serotonin-enhancing agents (such as citalopram, zimelidine, fluvoxamine) decrease alcohol consumption (Naranjo & Sellers, 1989). Thus, serotonin is another common denominator for both anxiety and alcoholism.

DIAGNOSING THE ANXIOUS ADDICTED PATIENT

Dependence syndromes mimic the symptoms of all major psychiatric illnesses (American Psychiatric Association, 1994; Galanter, Egelko et al., 1992; Hall, Stickney et al., 1979; Hasin & Grant, 1987; Lehman, Meyers & Corty, 1989; O'Farrell, Connors & Upper, 1983). When it is clear that a patient has a substance abuse problem, it is critical to conduct a basic historical review of the patient's substance abuse profile. This review must objectively characterize the setting in which abuse usually occurs (when, where and how), social network, quantity, frequency, recency and rate of consumption, perceived pressures, precipitants, and subjective responses. The assessment process itself promotes the patient's contemplation and conveys that the physician is interested, skilled, and objective. It helps to negotiate around the patient's denial, to cultivate confidence in the provider, and to educate the patient about his or her risks and complications. When the examiner is curious, straightforward, and non-judgmental about the individual (not the behavior), the patient's defenses are unprovoked and dialogue is possible. The steps to comprehensive evaluation are as follows:

Assess the symptom pattern of anxiety: Are anxiety symptoms isolated problems or do they meet criteria for a full syndrome (although meeting criteria for a syndrome may not be a definitive diagnosis without establishing the time course and excluding organic—i.e., substance-related—etiologies)? Inquire about basal tension, fears, phobias, avoidances, emotional numbing, startle reflex, tremor, hyperarousal, and associated depressive symptoms.

Assess the context: Is intoxication current, is withdrawal recent, or is early recovery (which is highly stressful in itself) in progress? Be certain to consider medical conditions and the effects of nicotine and caffeine. Theophylline must be considered when encountering panic, as should the over-the-counter nasal decongestants ephedrine and propranolamine.

Assess the temporal sequence: Did the anxiety symptoms precede, co-occur with, or only follow cessation of substance use? Were early life problems such as separation anxiety or school phobia prominent? Is a "herald attack" of panic described (i.e. the first, vivid, abrupt onset of a sense of doom with physiologic arousal that faded to fatigue over 15 minutes to an hour)? Did stressors or traumas precede or follow substance use, as frequently happens as a consequence of addiction?

Review the family history: Is the family history contributory for an anxiety disorder (e.g., reclusiveness in a first-degree relative)?

Assess the credibility of the data: Is the history corroborated by a significant other? Is the patient's self report cooperative, detailed, clear and consistent, or vague, insistent on a particular (reinforcing) pharmacotherapy and withholding of corroboration? Prior improvement of anxiety on benzodiazepines is not in itself confirmation of an anxiety disorder.

A common clinical approach to make sense of the perplexing consanguinity of anxiety and addiction is to look at the temporal sequence of signs and symptoms, in the fashion of Schuckit, and to assign "primary and secondary diagnoses based on the chronology of development of symptoms" (Schuckit, Irwin et al., 1988). Clearly a temporal approach does have clinical relevance. However, there are multilayered individual patterns of response to treatment. For example, anxiety symptoms may result from abstinence syndromes. It may be of help, then, to use a broader interpretive approach to this dilemma because the relationship is complex and marked by a vacillating interaction of many variables over time. That being the case, Engel's biopsychosocial model provides a more comprehensive and integrated approach to this relationship. As Engel postulates that each system affects, and is affected by, every other system, reducing this relationship to a simple temporal sequence yields the confusion of a biopsychosocial "who's on first?" It is helpful, therefore, to look at the common clinical syndromes from the perspective of the neurobiological substrate: the effects of psychodynamic and behavioral influences and the impact of social, cultural and environmental experience.

When anxiety symptoms precede addiction problems, the anxiety may precipitate substance abuse as the individual struggles to relieve his or her anxiety with alcohol or drugs. Important examples of such trigger symptoms include insomnia, stage fright or social phobia, post-traumatic intrusive thoughts, difficulty tolerating aloneness and obsessions. In individuals who initially became dependent on alcohol or drug use in an effort to self-medicate anxiety, recovery may be thwarted, despite motivated effort, as symptoms re-emerge and act as triggers for relapse. Different drugs of abuse may serve common goals in different ways: alcohol may be used to numb memories of sexual trauma and permit sex; cocaine may be used to disinhibit fears of humiliation to achieve sexual performance. The clinician's inquiries must be sensitive to the interactions between drug use and anxiety that are unique to each patient.

The biopsychosocial model and homeostatic paradigm help explain why panic attacks occur with certain substances. For example, research shows that cocaine affects the neurochemical system so that there is a surplus of norepinephrine and dopamine at postsynaptic receptor sites. This is received by the sympathetic nervous system as a massive threat, with the associated symptoms of a generalized sympathetic discharge. Depending on multiple factors, including the purity of the drug, the route of administration, the chronicity of use, the personality and mental health of the user, the past and present use of drugs and alcohol, the environment in which the drug is being used, and the concurrent use of other drugs (Gold & Dackis, 1984), the precipitation of a panic attack is a common side effect of cocaine intoxication. In fact, cocaine abuse can present with the clinical picture of any number of anxiety syndromes: generalized anxiety, panic and even obsessive-compulsive disorder. To maintain homeostasis, the patient will balance this chemically-induced excitatory state with upregulation of inhibitory systems, which allow the observer to predict what would happen in the period of withdrawal. The individual's response to cocaine may depend on his or her pre-morbid threshold for excitation: "whether a user enjoys or dislikes cocaine may depend on the individual's level of excitation, which is controlled by the adrenergic system, the thyroid hormone thyroxin, and other regulators" (Gold & Dackis, 1984). It is important to add that the user's psychosocial background contributes significantly to the threshold for excitation. If this information is deployed in the model in the homeostatic paradigm it yields a broader perspective on the relationship between anxiety and addiction.

Diagnostic Completeness, Precision and Revision. It does the patient a great service when the clinician enters all likely relevant diagnoses on the problem list, including organic anxiety disorder, acute intoxication, multiple or poly-psychoactive substance dependence and withdrawal. This listing serves several purposes: It educates the patient of the complexity of the risks, informs other participating caregivers (often, many are involved) of the range of issues to be addressed, and it justifies treatment utilization to managed care reviewers. Precision is important in diagnostic descriptors; for example, the patient in partial early remission from alcohol dependence may be understood to still be at risk for anxiety from intermittent relapse and withdrawal. Provisional diagnoses such as generalized anxiety disorder or agoraphobia should be listed as "rule out" and accompanied by the plan of continued evaluation and revision as the outcome indicates. This is fair to the patient, who may indeed prove to have a discrete anxiety disorder, but it also is respectful of the complexity of substance use disorders and their tendency to diminish in anxiogenesis with abstinence.

The Time Course of Anxiety Symptoms and Their Expected Resolutions. The most acute context for anxiety is stimulant intoxication, which should resolve in hours, if uncomplicated. The next earliest neurobehavioral stimulus for serious anxiety symptoms is withdrawal, the symptoms of which usually remit within days. Further along the temporal course, cessation of most drugs of abuse after chronic dependence is associated with poor frustration tolerance, dependence on quick gratification and existential malaise. These symptoms may be understood either developmentally as the consequence of years of drug-inhibited emotional stagnation, or they may represent disruption of the brain's reward system (Gold, 1994). Resolution may require weeks to months before any sense of contentment emerges for the patient.

The "Self-Medication Hypothesis" proposes that individuals choose a particular class of drug (including ethanol) because it relieves a specific intolerable affect. For example, stimulants modulate energy state and so may particularly appeal to patients who suffer from intolerable boredom, depression, hypomania, hyperactivity, frustration intolerance, or low self-esteem. Opiates produce a sense of well-being and so may be most compelling for those who suffer from disorganization, rage, and intolerable feelings of aggression. Alcohol and anxiolytics, since they acutely relieve inhibition, may be particularly dangerous for individuals who are unable to tolerate closeness, dependency, or self-assertion, or whose interpersonal communication may be characterized by "alexithymia" (Khantzian, 1990). Unfortunately, empirical research to support the self-medication hypothesis is scant, so the model remains conceptual only. Clinically, however, patients do frequently implicate self-medication as a rationalization, so this may be a fruitful area of discussion in treatment.

Chronic alcohol and benzodiazepine dependencies produce sleep cycle disruptions, particularly inhibition of rapid eye movement (REM) sleep. With abstinence, this sleep effect results in earlier and increased percentage of sleep time in the REM stage ("REM rebound"), which can last for weeks or months (Gillin, Smith et al., 1994). The patient awakens from sleep poorly rested, with progressive fatigue, irritability and tenseness, with the result that REM rebound significantly predicts alcohol relapse (Gillin, Smith et al., 1994). In the patient with recent benzodiazepine dependence, withdrawal of the depressant drug may produce symptoms of generalized anxiety and agoraphobia over three to six months; these symptoms remit over time. Therefore, pharmacotherapy may be unnecessary in this context (Schuckit, Irwin & Brown, 1990). Other causes of anxiety symptoms should be considered, such as the use of caffeine, over-the-counter diet pills and androgenic steroids. Alcohol, stimulants, marijuana and hallucinogens may provoke the onset of an anxiety disorder. Patients often discontinue marijuana and hallucinogen use when these are associated with increased anxiety, whereas alcohol dependence may persist or become substituted with anxiolytic dependence.

Understanding Anxiety as a Homeostatic Model of Arousal Dysregulation. On the theoretical level, anxiety may be thought of as the result of a threat to arousal regulation. A system may be vulnerable to such threats through genetics, congenital or environmental experience. The source of a threat may be internal or external. External threats include all substances of abuse and psychosocial stressors, such as a distorted perception that produces anxiety or panic, the recapitulation of war-time terror, or the stress of childhood separation and loss. Regardless of origin, all threats represent the same dynamic to the organism, necessarily requiring homeostatic adjustments. In the paradigm of alcohol as a depressant of the central nervous system's homeostatic mechanism, Schultz (1991) postulates that "neuroadaptation to chronic exposure would result in a compensatory downregulation of inhibitory and upregulation of excitatory systems."

On the vertical axes, this relationship includes acute, direct and primarily limbic-accessed threats and responses. On the horizontal axes, the model integrates longitudinal, indirect and more cortically-accessed mediators. These mediators may include either maladaptive social responses, such as affect isolation and social phobia, and adaptive responses, such as increased pursuit of structured daily routines and supportive social relationships. With regard to the relationship between anxiety and addiction, therefore, it is important to look beyond what is primary and secondary to see the balance between multiple factors at a particular time in the specific clinical situation.

PSYCHOSOCIAL TREATMENT OF THE ANXIOUS ADDICTED PATIENT

Whether the diagnosis is substance dependence, anxiety or both, the most empathic stance is to align with the patient's desire for health. This desire is present at some level even in the most ambivalent patient. It is helpful to maintain a persistent focus on the destructiveness of substance dependence. The effective clinician rejects non-specific treatments and integrates psychosocial and pharmacologic treatments that consider the entire range of problems. Non-specific treatments are neither effective or safe.

The elimination of psychoactive substance use is critical to the success of all therapeutic interventions. In other words, the patient must stop using uncontrolled doses of the highest potency exogenous neurotransmitters before more subtle ones at therapeutic doses can be expected to take effect. All psychotherapies, whether addiction counseling, cognitive behavioral psychotherapy or dynamic psychotherapy, require a stable capacity for learning. Dynamic psychotherapies, in particular, require the capacity to access internal dysphoria in order to succeed. All forms of substance abuse appear to sharply disrupt neurophysiologic states, learning states and the ability to access and tolerate psychological discomfort. Abstinence is therefore the starting point for all treatments.

Treatment of anxiety and/or hypnosedative dependence is longitudinal. It requires vigorous education. Often it is necessary to intensify treatment for a period of time, e.g., adding drug counseling or group to individual, or transferring the patient to an inpatient unit to stabilize and taper a benzodiazepine. The basic behavioral and cognitive techniques that can be useful for any patient with anxiety (even in the absence of a dual disorder) include:

- Diaphragmatic respiration
- Progressive muscle relaxation
- Symptom ratings
- Imagery
- Meditation
- Self-hypnosis.

For addictive diseases, most treatment modalities that stress abstinence, personal responsibility for recovery and relapse prevention show marked reductions in addiction severity and general health care costs (Gerstein & Harwood, 1990; Gerstein, Johnson et al., 1994; Gerstein, Johnson & Larison, 1997). On the other hand, no single psychosocial therapeutic approach has been demonstrated to be best, despite differential treatment outcome studies and Project MATCH's efforts to test multiple matching hypotheses (Group, 1993, 1997). Some studies, however, have indicated an advantage of professional psychotherapies for addicted patients with serious psychiatric symptomatology (McLellan, 1988; McLellan, Luborsky et al., 1983a; McLellan, Woody et al., 1983b; Woody, McLellan et al., 1985).

For anxiety disorders, the leading psychosocial modalities include the following:

- Relaxation training
- Cognitive restructuring
- Interoceptive exposure
- Situational (in vivo) exposure
- Flooding.

In panic disorder and agoraphobia, which have undergone extensive study, psychosocial treatments are at least as effective as pharmacotherapies. A meta-analysis of 43 controlled trials by the anxiety research group at the Massachusetts General Hospital found that cognitive behavioral therapy produced large effect sizes (74% of patients panic free) that were superior to results from pharmacotherapy (Gould, Otto & Pollack, 1995). Pharmacotherapy in combination with cognitive behavior therapy was not superior to cognitive behavior therapy alone. This raises the possibility that pharmacotherapy may inhibit learning from cognitive behavioral therapy or result in an attribution of the success to the medication rather than to practicing behavioral exercises. Also, effect sizes were not equal across all treatments: cognitive restructuring alone did most poorly while cognitive restructuring plus interoceptive exposure did best. Attrition was three times greater in pharmacotherapy than in cognitive behavior therapy. There is no reason to believe that dual disorder patients should not benefit from established behavioral treatments, if addictive behaviors are stabilized first. The authors know of no evidence that exposure therapies themselves pose a risk of relapse, for example, when conducted by experienced therapists.

Some unique issues arise in the patient with both addictive disease and an anxiety disorder. Agoraphobic patients will often reject inpatient treatment as anxiogenic. The clinician should recommend the optimal treatment, but it may be helpful to compromise on a less restrictive initial treatment. If the initial response is incomplete but the anxiety is partially stabilized, he or she may agree to the optimal recommendation after a time. Social phobic patients may fail to engage or even make a trial visit to self-help group meetings, for reasons of anxiety rather than resistance. Rather than a complete disruption of care, however, a "readiness" model is preferable, in which the physician closely examines the patient's obstacles over weeks. Often, this supportive but clear plan retains the clinical rapport and permits the patient to come to a realization that he must choose to enter addictions treatment or initiate exposure treatment, or no progress is possible (Rollnick, Heather et al., 1992).

An overlooked interaction is the alcoholic patient with obsessive compulsive disorder whose recovery problems appear more acute and therefore receive more attention than the anxiety symptoms and behaviors, which are more covert. The problem in such a case is that the obsessive compulsive symptoms may provoke relapse because they get overlooked. Another problematic interaction, and perhaps a common one, is the addict with post-traumatic stress disorder (Brady, Killeen, Saladin et al., 1994). In this combination, studies are examining the benefits of initiating addictions treatment first, addressing intrusive thoughts, nightmares and recollections with coping skills training, and delaying trauma exploration and resolution for an extended period of stable abstinence or perhaps indefinitely (Najavits, Weiss & Liese, 1995).

In general, with comorbid addiction and anxiety, initial treatment should engender an alliance with a therapist and a group in a highly interactive approach involving frequent contacts. The initial goal is to prepare the patient against the likely risk of relapse. Care must focus on abstinence a priori and help the patient establish new coping behaviors. These should include a schedule of daily routines, a healthy diet, elimination of caffeine and nicotine, exercise, relaxation and obtaining sober supports. Related issues for patients with addiction and anxiety are habitual negative affects, passivity, and social withdrawal (Marlatt & Gordon, 1985). Therapy should also acknowledge any ongoing threats of trauma or victimization; substance abusing individuals may be at high risk for ongoing traumatic events (Brady, Dustan et al., 1995).

Interpersonal and supportive expressive techniques that mobilize awareness of interpersonal or intrapsychic stressors may be helpful. Psychodynamic techniques such as interpretation of transference are likely to be useful during early recovery only when the relationship with the therapist is threatened. Strategically, however, this stage is fertile ground for the development of positive transference which can usefully be fostered (Blane, 1977). The patient needs help cognitively labeling anxious and depressed feelings as well as verbally expressing anger. Previously, these emotions may have been the cues for drug or alcohol craving (Galanter, 1983). Insight oriented dynamic psychotherapy may be helpful later, but the therapist must be familiar with the unique risks of previously addicted patients, in whom this treatment may induce strong dysphoric affects that may cue cravings for alcohol or drugs and provoke relapse (Childress, McLellan et al., 1987).

PHARMACOTHERAPY OF THE ANXIOUS ADDICTED PATIENT

The key criterion for instituting pharmacotherapy for anxiety symptoms in an addicted patient is: Do symptoms seriously threaten the patient's function or recovery? It helps to operationalize this question with explicit treatment goals (such as stable job performance) and objective behavioral outcomes (such as driving alone without avoidances). It avoids the moral and theoretical extremes of both pharmacologic Calvinism ("the only good drug is a dead drug") or pharmacologic Hedonism ("better living through chemistry"). In practice, these polar ideologies place patients at unnecessary risk, either influencing patients to reject psychotropics altogether or promoting iatrogenic substitute dependencies. Another ill-considered strategy is the use of the "pill transference," in which reinforcing agents are prescribed in an attempt to attach a handle to a hard-to-hold patient. A functional goal for pharmacotherapy fosters careful assessment of prior function, severity of target symptoms, recovery effort of the patient and the risk-benefit of pharmacologic agents.

Ongoing substance use makes it difficult, if not impossible, to treat anxiety with pharmacotherapy. The patient who actively continues to use alcohol or drugs lives on an unstable platform on which to build a pharmacotherapeutic homeostasis. Most pharmacotherapies require predictable pharmacokinetic (e.g., steady-state levels of medication) and pharmacodynamic (e.g., unperturbed neurotransmitter and receptor interaction) states in order to be effective.

Recovery versus Abstinence. The goal of addiction treatment is to achieve not just abstinence, but recovery. Recovery from chemical dependence is expressed as the process of restoring intrapsychic well-being and psychosocial function. In the patient with an anxiety disorder, recovery includes compliance with all treatments. As a general principle, pharmacotherapy alone is ineffective in the treatment of addicted patients and certainly in those patients with comorbid anxiety disorders.

Benzodiazepines are among the most commonly prescribed drugs in the U.S. (Rickels, Schweizer et al., 1990). Because they are themselves reinforcing, benzodiazepines pose a serious iatrogenic risk in this population, despite their efficacy and safety as anxiolytics for the general population (Busto, Sellers et al., 1986; Greenblatt & Shader, 1978).

Rapid onset benzodiazepines such as alprazolam, diazepam and lorazepam offer a degree of immediate gratification that appears to impede initiation of recovery efforts and retention of gains. In severe conditions that prove refractory to behavioral and antidepressant approaches, a slow-onset and long-acting agent such as clonazepam may be the safest of this class (Herman, Rosenbaum & Brotman, 1987). Yet, even clonazepam has addictive potential in severe drug dependence. Thus, the use of benzodiazepines should be reserved for patients with well-documented failure on antidepressants or other agents, who have demonstrated continued distress and a commitment to treatment.

Serious abuse liability is present as the result of several mechanisms when benzodiazepines are used to treat substance-abusing or substance-dependent individuals. Dependence disorders occur at low incidence when this class of agents is used to treat the general population; however, psychiatric patients are at greater risk and alcohol-, sedative-, cocaine-, and opiate-dependent or abusing individuals, including methadone maintenance patients, are at greatest risk. When their primary substance is unavailable, dependent individuals use benzodiazepines to substitute for alcohol, sedatives or opiates, or to self-medicate withdrawal. Stimulant- or cocaine-dependent individuals self-medicate cocaine paranoia. Laboratory evidence of tolerance to benzodiazepines has been shown even after single large doses (Greenblatt & Shader, 1978). This occurs through the pharmacodynamic mechanism of decreased receptor binding (Miller, Greenblatt et al., 1988a, 1988b). Physiologic dependence can occur at low doses (5 to 10 mg of diazepam or equivalent) with chronic use.

Buspirone: In contrast, buspirone has a high safety profile and has been proven in double blind trials to be as effective as benzodiazepines for primary anxiety or anxiety associated with depression (Cohn, Wilcox et al., 1992; Gammans, Stringfellow et al., 1992; Gelenberg, 1994). Buspirone, unlike the benzodiazepines, lacks anticonvulsant properties and cross-tolerance with the benzodiazepines and therefore is not appropriate as a withdrawal agent. In contrast, buspirone does not produce additive sedative or motor incoordination with other anxiolytics or alcohol, nor does it pose any dependency risk. Buspirone may be combined with antidepressants at doses of up to 60 to 80 mg per day and some data indicate that it may potentiate antidepressants adjunctively (Gammans, Stringfellow et al., 1992). The drug's lack of dependence or abuse liability makes it an advance for the at-risk anxiety population.

Despite early caveats reserving its use for "benzodiazepine virgins," buspirone indeed is effective for generalized anxiety if the patient and family are vigorously educated and reminded about the slow onset and subtle perceptibility of its unique response (Gastfriend & Rosenbaum, 1989; Kranzler, 1989). Most reports indicate benefit in substance dependence with anxiety symptoms (Bruno, 1989; Giannini, Loiselle et al., 1993; Kranzler, Burleson et al., 1994; Tollefson, Montague-Clouse & Tollefson, 1992; Udelman & Udelman, 1990), and even in non-anxious alcoholics (Bruno, 1989). Compliance requires ongoing assessment and reinforcement: buspirone and antidepressants require stable and predictable pharmacokinetic states (i.e., steady state levels of medication) in order to be effective.

Antidepressants: Tricyclic antidepressants are well established treatments for panic disorder and agoraphobia. Clomipramine has been shown to be effective for the treatment of obsessive-compulsive disorder, as have some serotonin uptake inhibitors, including fluoxetine. The antidepressants lack abuse liability, but some safety considerations are required in addiction patients. Tricyclic antidepressants have been the leading cause of medication overdose in the U.S. These agents therefore require assessment of suicide risk, adverse interactions with drugs of abuse (such as MAO inhibitors and beer or wine or cocaine) and cardiac toxicity. Tricyclic antidepressant levels must be monitored to confirm compliance and because chronic alcohol or nicotine consumption induces hepatic microsomal oxidation. Some newly abstinent anxious patients may be non-compliant with antidepressants in an attempt to procure benzodiazepines. Sedating tricyclic antidepressants, such as imipramine, may be used incorrectly on an intermittent basis by patients who seek only the sedative effect, thereby failing to achieve stable, effective levels.

Both imipramine and trazodone have been reported in one controlled trial to relieve generalized anxiety symptoms as well as diazepam, without the risk of dependence (Rickels, Downing & Hassman, 1993). Trazodone, while overly sedating for use as an antidepressant, may be adjunctively useful for anxiety symptoms in benzodiazepine withdrawal and has been reported to reduce relapse risk, in comparison with placebo (Ansseau & De Roeck, 1993). An open trial in patients with substance dependence and anxiety (many with posttraumatic stress symptoms) found that trazodone 50 to 150 mg/d relieved anxiety and was associated with decreased use of benzodiazepines (Liebowitz & el Mallakh, 1989).

A parsimonious benefit occurs if a patient is treated with serotonin uptake inhibitors, which have been shown to reduce excessive alcohol consumption. These include fluoxetine (Cornelius, Salloum et al., 1993; Naranjo & Sellers, 1989), citalopram (Naranjo, Poulos et al., 1992; Naranjo, Sellers et al., 1987), sertraline (Brands, Sellers & Kaplan, 1990), and others (Naranjo & Sellers, 1989; Naranjo, Sellers et al., 1987). Long-term studies are not yet available, however, and it is unclear to what extent "anti-craving" pharmacotherapies will be effective in patients with severe substance dependence. In all cases, these agents should be prescribed in full antidepressant doses with the expectation of a two- to four-week onset of effect. A concern among the newer antidepressants is that many serotonin reuptake inhibitors exacerbate insomnia, whereas nefazodone may promote normalization of sleep cycle problems (Sharpley, Walsh & Cowen, 1992).

TABLE 2. Key Components of a Pharmacotherapy Contract for the Dual Diagnosis Patient

1. Medication is part of a rational psychosocial treatment "package," and will be discontinued if key psychosocial components are neglected.
2. Urine or blood testing may be required at any time to provide an independent source of data about the course of the chemical dependence, or to determine if prescribed medication is reaching adequate levels in blood.
3. Medication will be used only as prescribed. Any need for changes will first be discussed with the physician. A unilateral change in medication by the patient often is an early sign of relapse.
4. Changes in medication will be prescribed one at a time, e.g. two agents will not be initiated simultaneously.
5. When used, the purpose of medication is to treat predetermined target symptoms. If medication proves ineffective for these, it will be discontinued.
6. Once target symptoms remit, a process of dose tapering may be initiated to determine the minimum dose necessary to maintain healthy function. Periodically, the medication strategy will include a period of discontinuation, or "drug holiday." Medication may not be necessary on a long term basis.

Source: Gastfriend DR (1993). Pharmacotherapy of psychiatric syndromes with comorbid chemical dependency. *Journal of Addictive Diseases* 12(3):155–170. Reprinted by permission.

Another anxiety pharmacotherapy is the beta blocker, propranolol, which is effective in low doses (10 to 30 mg prn) for performance anxiety. There is no known abuse liability associated with this use and the risk of hypotension is minimal at these doses.

Perhaps the most critical factor in effective pharmacotherapy of addiction and anxiety is painstaking psychoeducation and a treatment contract (Gastfriend, 1993). An example of such a contract is presented in Table 2. The essential principles are that pharmacotherapy targets specific symptoms, is time-limited, is modified only one change at a time, is monitored for compliance, and is provided only in the context of a comprehensive psychosocial treatment plan.

Noncompliance: In the event of noncompliance, the patient should not be administratively discharged (i.e., rejected from treatment) but should instead be told that until abstinence has been safely established, pharmacotherapies must be withheld and the focus must rest on recovery attitudes and psychotherapeutic issues. This frustrating but supportive stance can be catalytic. If a course of treatment is ineffective after sufficient duration and dosage, or if covert substance use subsequently is discovered, the treatment plan should be revised, usually with revision of pharmacotherapies and modification of psychotherapies that have either erroneously neglected the primary anxiety or overlooked impending signs of relapse to addiction.

One of the roles proposed for the pharmacotherapy of addictions has been that of trigger reducers; that is, agents to reduce anxiety symptoms that might provoke relapse (Liskow & Goodwin, 1987; Litten & Allen, 1991). This role is controversial because of a theoretical conflict with the abstinence goal: "the only good drug is a dead drug." Medications are widely used as trigger reducers despite little empirical research as to the efficacy of this approach, in the absence of a discrete dual psychiatric diagnosis. Among the anti-anxiety agents, only buspirone has the acceptable combination of non-reinforcing, efficacy and safety features. Among the sleep agents, trazodone is unique in that it may correct sleep architecture disruptions, such as REM rebound, that are common during the early ethanol and benzodiazepine post-withdrawal phase (Gillin, Smith et al., 1994; Scharf & Sachais, 1990).

INTEGRATING TREATMENTS TOWARD HOMEOSTATIC BALANCE

Although most treatment research is "deconstructionist" in that it reduces treatment to a manual-driven, single hypothesis modality, most effective clinical care is eclectic or, better still, synthetic. According to the homeostatic model of arousal regulation, the synthetic approach is most likely to succeed with uncomplicated anxiety and even more so with a complex set of disorders such as anxiety and addiction. As an example, to stabilize panic disorder with agoraphobia may require that the clinician(s) offer several or all of the following:

1. Brief benzodiazepine treatment to reduce vigilance and permit initiation of *in vivo* exposure therapy, plus
2. Antidepressant therapy to stabilize locus ceruleus firing and reduce limbic system alarm, plus
3. A cognitive behavior therapeutic approach to correct misperceptions of otherwise unprovocative stimuli such as streets and crowds, plus
4. A dynamically oriented psychotherapeutic approach to reduce the patient's stress from interpersonal friction.

In the patient with associated substance dependence or abuse, the synthetic approach is needed to a greater extent to take into account the following additional needs:

5. Pharmacologic and psychosocial treatment of substance withdrawal, plus
6. Psychoeducation, motivational enhancement and relapse prevention stabilization of abstinence, plus
7. Recovery lifestyle changes to promote predictable daily structure, sober supports and lifelong awareness of vulnerabilities, plus
8. Non-reinforcing pharmacotherapy of anxiety (e.g., buspirone) and trigger symptoms (e.g. trazodone for insomnia);
9. Anti-appetitive pharmacotherapy, as for alcoholism (e.g., naltrexone or SUI antidepressants) or opiate agonists (e.g., methadone or LAAM) or antagonists (e.g. naltrexone);
10. Pharmacotherapeutic contracting to enhance compliance and avoidance of reinforcing agents such as benzodiazepines.

These efforts usually are best achieved by a team that may include, in addition to the patient, all of the following: an addiction medicine specialist, a primary care physician, counselors and/or therapists, a case manager, self-help groups, a sponsor and the family. A well-coordinated multi-modal team approach can successfully help the patient restore an adaptive balance, allowing him or her to tolerate anxiety as an expected feature of adult life, with stable recovery, constructive coping and lifelong growth.

ACKNOWLEDGMENT: Supported by NIDA Grant DA 07693. The authors gratefully acknowledge the contributions of Jeannette Frey in editing and preparation of this manuscript.

REFERENCES

American Psychiatric Association (1994). *Diagnostic and Statistical Manual of Mental Disorders, 4th Edition.* Washington, DC: American Psychiatric Press.

Ansseau M & De Roeck J (1993). Trazodone in benzodiazepine dependence. *Journal Of Clinical Psychiatry* 54(5):189–191.

Blane H (1977). Psychotherapeutic approach. In B Kissen & H Begleiter (eds.) *The Biology of Alcoholism, Vol. 5.* New York, NY: Plenum Press, 105–160.

Brady KT, Dustan LR, Grice DE, Danksy BS & Kilpatrick D (1995). Personality disorder and assault history in substance-dependent individuals. *American Journal on Addictions* 4:306–312.

Brady KT, Killeen T, Saladin ME, Dansky B & Becker S (1994). Comorbid substance abuse and posttraumatic stress disorder. *The American Journal on Addictions* 3(2):160–164.

Branchey LB, Branchey M, Ferguson P, Hudson J & McKernin C (1997). Craving for cocaine in addicted users. *American Journal on Addiction* 6(1):65–73.

Brands B, Sellers EM & Kaplan HL (1990). The effects of the 5-HT uptake inhibitor, sertraline, on ethanol, water and food consumption. *Alcoholism: Clinical & Experimental Research* 14(2):273.

Bruno F (1989). Buspirone in the treatment of alcoholic patients. *Psychopathology* 1:49–59.

Busto U, Sellers EM, Naranjo CA, Cappell H, Sanchez CM & Sykora K (1986). Withdrawal reaction after long-term therapeutic use of benzodiazepines. *The New England Journal of Medicine* 315:854–859.

Cedarbaum JM & Aghajanian GK (1977). Catecholamine receptors on locus coeruleus neurons: Pharmacological characterization. *European Journal of Pharmacology* 44(4):375–385.

Childress AR, McLellan AT, Natale M & O'Brien CP (1987). Mood states can elicit conditioned withdrawal and craving in opiate abuse patients. In LS Harris (ed.) *Problems of Drug Dependence (NIDA Research Monograph 76).* Rockville, MD: National Institute on Drug Abuse, 137–144.

Ciraulo D, Sands B & Shader R (1988). Critical review of liability for benzodiazepine abuse among alcoholics. *American Journal of Psychiatry* 145(12):1501–1506.

Cohn J, Wilcox C, Bowden C, Fisher J & Rodos J (1992). Double-blind comparison of buspirone and clorazepate in anxious outpatients with and without depressive symptoms. *Psychopathology* 25(S1):10–21.

Cornelius JR, Salloum IM, Cornelius MD et al. (1993). Fluoxetine trial in suicidal depressed alcoholics. *Psychopharmacological Bulletin* 29(2):195–199.

Dubovsky SL (1994). Beyond the serotonin reuptake inhibitors: rationales for the development of new serotonergic agents. [Review]. *Journal of Clinical Psychiatry* 55(Suppl):34–44.

French S, Palmer D, Narod M, Reid P & Ramey C (1975). Noradrenergic sensitivity of the cerebral cortex after chronic ethanol ingestion and withdrawal. *Journal of Pharmacological and Experimental Therapeutics* 194:319–326.

Galanter M (1983). Psychotherapy for alcohol and drug abuse: an approach based on learning theory. *Journal of Psychiatric Treatment and Evaluation* 5:551–556.

Galanter M, Egelko S, De Leon G, Rohrs C & Franco H (1992). Crack/cocaine abusers in the general hospital: Assessment and initiation of care. *American Journal Of Psychiatry* 149(6):810–815.

Gammans RE, Stringfellow JC et al. (1992). Use of buspirone in patients with generalized anxiety disorder and coexisting depressive symptoms—A meta-analysis of eight randomized, controlled studies. *Pharmacopsychiatry* 25:1–9.

Gastfriend DR (1993). Pharmacotherapy of psychiatric syndromes with comorbid chemical dependency. *Journal of Addictive Diseases* 12(3):155–170.

Gastfriend DR & Rosenbaum JF (1989). Adjunctive buspirone in benzodiazepine treatment of four patients with panic disorder. *American Journal of Psychiatry* 146:914–916.

Gawin F & Kleber H (1986). Abstinence symptomatology and psychiatric diagnosis in cocaine abusers. *Archives of General Psychiatry* 43:107–113.

Gelenberg AJ (1994). Buspirone: Seven-year update. *Journal of Clinical Psychiatry* 55(5):222–229.

Gerstein DR & Harwood HJ (1990). *Treating Drug Problems*. Washington, DC: National Academy Press.

Gerstein DR, Johnson RA, Harwood H, Fountain D, Suter N & Malloy K (1994). Evaluating Recovery Services: The California Drug and Alcohol Treatment Assessment (CALDATA): Executive Summary. California Department of Alcohol and Drug Programs.

Gerstein DR, Johnson RA & Larison CL (1997). *Alcohol and Other Drug Treatment for Parents and Welfare Recipients: Outcomes, Costs, and Benefits*. Washington, DC: U.S. Department of Health and Human Services.

Giannini AJ, Loiselle RH, Graham BH & Folts DJ (1993). Behavioral response to buspirone in cocaine and phencyclidine withdrawal. *Journal of Substance Abuse Treatment* 10:523–527.

Gillin JC, Smith TL, Irwin M, Butters N, Demodena A & Schuckit M (1994). Increased pressure for rapid eye movement sleep at time of hospital admission predicts relapse in nondepressed patients with primary alcoholism at 3-month follow-up. *Archives of General Psychiatry* 51(3):189–197.

Gold M & Dackis C (1984). Clinical therapeutics: New insights and treatments: Opiate withdrawal and cocaine addiction. *Clinical Therapeutics* 7:6–21.

Gold MS (1994). Neurobiology of addiction and recovery: The brain, the drive for the drug, and the 12-step fellowship. *Journal of Subtance Abuse Treatment* 11(2):93–97.

Gold MS, Byck R, Sweeney DR & Kleber HD (1979). Endorphin-locus coeruleus connection mediates opiate action and withdrawal. *Biomedicine* 30:1–4.

Gould RA, Otto MW & Pollack MH (1995). A meta-analysis of treatment outcome for panic disorder. *Clinical Psychology Review* 15(8):819–844.

Greenblatt DJ & Shader RI (1978). Dependence, tolerance, and addiction to benzodiazepines: Clinical and pharmacokinetic considerations. *Drug Metabolism Reviews* 8:13–28.

Group PMR (1993). Project MATCH (Matching Alcoholism Treatment to Client Heterogeneity): Rationale and methods for a multisite clinical trial matching patients to alcoholism treatment. *Alcoholism: Clinical & Experimental Research* 17(6):1130–1145.

Group PMR (1997). Matching alcoholism treatments to client heterogeneity: Project MATCH posttreatment drinking outcomes. *Journal of Studies on Alcohol* 58:7–29.

Hall RC, Stickney SK, Gardner ER, Perl M & LeCann AF (1979). Relationship of psychiatric illness to drug abuse. *Journal of Psychedelic Drugs* 11:337–342.

Hasin DS & Grant BF (1987). Psychiatric diagnosis of patients with substance abuse problems: A comparison of two procedures, DIS and the SADS-L. *Journal of Psychiatric Research* 21(1):7–22.

Herman JB, Rosenbaum JF & Brotman AW (1987). The alprazolam to clonazepam switch for the treatment of panic disorder. *Journal of Clinical Psychopharmacology* 7:175–178.

Hubner CB & Koob GF (1990). The ventral pallidum plays a role in mediating cocaine and heroin self-administration in the rat. *Brain Research* 508(1):20–29.

Itzhak Y & Stein I (1992). Repeated cocaine administration in mice: sensitization to the convulsive effects involves up-regulation of the NMDA receptor, 33. Conference Proceedings, College on Problems of Drug Dependence, Keystone, CO.

Khantzian EJ (1990). Self-regulation and self-medication factors in alcoholism and the addictions. Similarities and differences. *Recent Developments in Alcoholism* 8:255–271.

Koob GF (1992). Drugs of abuse: Anatomy, pharmacology and function of reward pathways. *Trends In Pharmacological Sciences* 13(5):177–184.

Koob GF et al. (1991). In TC Napier, P Kalivas & I Hanin (eds.) *The Basal Forebrain: Anatomy to Function*. New York, NY: Plenum Press, 291–305.

Korf J, Bunney BS & Aghajanian GK (1974). Noradrenergic neurons: morphine inhibition of spontaneous activity. *European Journal of Pharmacology* 25(2):165–169.

Kranzler HR (1989). Buspirone treatment of anxiety in a patient dependent on alprazolam. *Journal of Clinical Psychopharmacology* 9(2):153.

Kranzler HR, Burleson JA, Del Boca FK et al. (1994). Buspirone treatment of anxious alcoholics. A placebo-controlled trial. *Archives of General Psychiatry* 51(9):720–731.

Krystal JH, Webb E, Cooney N, Kranzler HR & Charney DS (1994). Specificity of ethanol-like effects elicited by serotonergic and noradrenergic mechanisms. *Archives of General Psychiatry* 51(11):898–911.

Kushner M, Sher K & Beitman B (1990). The relation between alcohol problems and the anxiety disorders. *American Journal of Psychiatry* 147(6):685–695.

Lehman AF, Meyers CP & Corty E (1989). Assessment and classification of patients with psychiatric and substance abuse syndromes. *Hospital & Community Psychiatry* 40(10):1019–1025.

Liebowitz NR & el Mallakh RS (1989). Trazodone for the treatment of anxiety symptoms in substance abusers [letter]. *Journal Of Clinical Psychopharmacology* 9(6):449–451.

Liskow BI & Goodwin TE (1987). Pharmacological treatment of alcohol intoxication, withdrawal, and dependence: A critical review. *Journal of Studies in Alcohol* 48:356–370.

Litten RZ & Allen JP (1991). Pharmacotherapies for alcoholism: Promising agents and clinical issues. *Alcoholism: Clinical & Experimental Research* 15(4):620–633.

Marlatt AG & Gordon JR (1985). Relapse prevention: Maintenance strategies in the treatment of addictive behaviors. In *Relapse Prevention: Maintenance Strategies in the Treatment of Addictive Behaviors*. New York, NY: Guilford Press.

McLellan A (1988). *Patient-Treatment Matching and Outcome Improvement in Alcohol Rehabilitation.* Washington, DC: National Academy of Sciences.

McLellan A, Druley K & Carson J (1978). Evaluation of substance abuse problems in a psychiatric hospital. *Journal of Clinical Psychiatry* 39:425–430.

McLellan AT, Luborsky L, Woody GE, O'Brien CP & Druley KA (1983a). Predicting response to alcohol and drug abuse treatments. *Archives of General Psychiatry* 40:620–625.

McLellan AT, Woody GE, Luborsky L, O'Brien CP & Druley KA (1983b). Increased effectiveness of substance abuse treatment. A prospective study of patient-treatment "matching." *Journal of Nervous And Mental Disease* 171(10):597–605.

Mhatre MC, Pena G, Sieghart W & Ticku MJ (1993). Antibodies specific for $GABA_A$ receptor (alpha) subunits reveal that chronic alcohol treatment down-regulates (alpha)-subunit expression in rat brain regions. *Journal of Neurochemistry* 61:1620–1625.

Miller LG, Greenblatt DA, Roy RB et al. (1988b). Chronic benzodiazepine administration, II: Discontinuation syndrome is associated with upregulation of gamma-aminobutyric acid receptor complex binding and function. *Journal of Pharmacology and Experimental Therapy* 246:177–182.

Miller LG, Greenblatt DJ, Barnhill JG et al. (1988a). Chronic benzodiazepine administration, I: Tolerance is associated with benzodiazepine receptor downregulation and decreased gamma-aminobutyric acid A receptor function. *Journal of Pharmacology and Experimental Therapy* 246:170–176.

Morgenson GJ, Jones DL & Yim CY (1980). From motivation to action: functional interface between the limbic system and the motor system. *Progress in Neurobiology* 14(2–3):69–97.

Najavits LM, Weiss RD & Liese BS (1995). Group cognitive-behavioral therapy for women with PTSD and substance use disorder. *Journal of Substance Abuse Treatment* 13:13–22.

Naranjo CA, Poulos CX, Bremner KE & Lanctot KL (1992). Citalopram decreases desirability, liking, and consumption of alcohol in alcohol-dependent drinkers. *Clinical Pharmacology And Therapeutics* 51(6):729–739.

Naranjo CA & Sellers EM (1989). Serotonin uptake inhibitors attenuate ethanol intake in problem drinkers. *Recent Developments In Alcoholism* 7:255–266.

Naranjo CA, Sellers EM, Sullivan JT, Woodley DV, Kadlec K & Sykora K (1987). The serotonin uptake inhibitor citalopram attenuates ethanol intake. *Clinical Pharmacology And Therapeutics* 41(3):266–274.

Noyes RJ, Crowe RR, Harris EL et al. (1986). Relationship between panic disorder and agoraphobia: A family study. *Archives of General Psychiatry* 43:227–232.

O'Farrell TJ, Connors GJ & Upper D (1983). Addictive behaviors among hospitalized psychiatric patients. *Addictive Behaviors* 8:329–333.

Regier DA, Farmer ME, Rae DS et al. (1990). Comorbidity of mental disorders with alcohol and other drug abuse. Results from the Epidemiologic Catchment Area (ECA) Study. *Journal of the American Medical Association* 264(19):2511–2518.

Reich T, Winokur G & Mullaney J (1975). The transmission of alcoholism. Conference Proceedings, Annual Meeting of the American Psychopathology Association, 63:259–271.

Rickels K, Downing R & Hassman H (1993). Antidepressants for the treatment of generalized anxiety disorder: A placebo-controlled comparison of imipramine, trazodone, and diazepam. *Archives of General Psychiatry* 50:884–895.

Rickels K, Schweizer E, Case WG & Greenblatt DJ (1990). Long-term therapeutic use of benzodiazepines. I. Effects of abrupt discontinuation. *Archives of General Psychiatry* 47:99–107.

Robins LN & Regier DA (1991). Psychiatric disorders in America: The Epidemiologic Catchment Area Study. In *Psychiatric Disorders in America: The Epidemiologic Catchment Area Study*. New York, NY: The Free Press.

Rollnick S, Heather N, Gold R & Hall W (1992). Development of a short 'readiness to change' questionnaire for use in brief, opportunistic interventions among excessive drinkers. *British Journal of Addiction* 87(5):743–754.

Ross H, Glaser F & Germanson T (1988). The prevalence of psychiatric disorders in patients with alcohol and other drug problems. *Archives of General Psychiatry* 45:1023–1031.

Rounsaville B, Weissman M, Kleber H et al. (1982). Heterogeneity of psychiatric diagnosis in treated opiate addicts. *Archives of General Psychiatry* 39:161–166.

Scharf MB & Sachais BA (1990). Sleep laboratory evaluation of the effects and efficacy of trazodone in depressed insomniac patients. *Journal of Clinical Psychiatry* 51(9 Suppl):13–17.

Schuckit M, Irwin M, Howard T & Smith T (1988). A structured diagnostic interview for identification of primary alcoholism: A preliminary evaluation. *Journal of Studies on Alcohol* 49(1):93–99.

Schuckit MA, Irwin M & Brown SA (1990). The history of anxiety symptoms among 171 primary alcoholics. *Journal of Studies on Alcohol* 51(1):34–41.

Sharpley AL, Walsh AE & Cowen PJ (1992). Nefazodone—a novel antidepressant—may increase REM sleep. *Biological Psychiatry* 31(10):1070–1073.

Suzdak PD, Glowa JR, Crawley JN, Schwartz RD, Skolnick P & Paul SM (1986). A selective imidazobenzodiazepine antagonist of ethanol in the rat. *Science* 234(4781):1243–1247.

Tollefson G (1989). Serotonin and alcohol: Interrelationships. *Psychopathology* 22(Suppl 1):37–48.

Tollefson GD, Montague-Clouse J & Tollefson SL (1992). Treatment of comorbid generalized anxiety in a recently detoxified alcoholic population with a selective serotonergic drug (buspirone). *Journal of Clinical Psychopharmacology* 12(1):19–26.

Traber J, & Glaser T (1987). 5-HT 1A receptor related anxiolytics. *Trends in Pharmacological Sciences* 8:432–437.

Tsai G, Gastfriend DR & Coyle JT (1995). The glutamatergic basis of human alcoholism. *American Journal of Psychiatry* 152(3):332–340.

Udelman HD & Udelman DL (1990). Concurrent use of buspirone in anxious patients during withdrawal from alprazolam therapy. *Journal of Clinical Psychiatry* 51(9 Suppl):46–50.

Van Den Pol A, Waurin J & Dudek F (1990). Glutamate, the dominant excitatory transmitter in neuroendocrine regulation. *Science* 250:1276–1278.

Weiss RD, Mirin SM, Michael JL & Sollogub AC (1986). Psychopathology in chronic cocaine abusers. *American Journal of Drug and Alcohol Abuse* 12:17–29.

Woody GE, McLellan AT, Luborsky L & O'Brien CP (1985). Sociopathy and psychotherapy outcome. *Archives of General Psychiatry* 42:1081–1086.

Zorumski CF & Isenberg KE (1991). Insights into the structure and function of GABA-Benzodiazepine receptors: Ion channels and psychiatry. *American Journal of Psychiatry* 148(2):162–173.

CHAPTER 4

Psychotic Disorders

Douglas Ziedonis, M.D., M.P.H.
Stephen Wyatt, D.O.

Diagnosis
Acute Presentation
Drug-Specific Psychotic Symptoms
Interactions between Drugs of Abuse, Medications, and Neurobiology
Sub-Acute and Longer-Term Treatment

The presence of substance use and psychotic symptoms presents special diagnostic and treatment challenges. This chapter focuses on the tasks of assessment, diagnosis, acute management, the relation between various drugs of abuse and psychosis, and long-term and subacute treatment considerations. An improved understanding of the neurobiology of psychosis has developed through study of the neurobiology of substances of abuse, including LSD, amphetamines, cocaine, alcohol, marijuana, PCP, ketamine, and alcohol.

DIAGNOSIS

Substance abuse and psychosis commonly occur together. Transient substance-induced psychotic symptoms are not uncommon among intoxicated substance abusers, and substance use is common among psychiatric patients with schizophrenia. Whether substance abuse can actually cause a permanent psychotic disorder or even precipitate the onset of a permanent psychotic disorder in a vulnerable individual is uncertain. There does appear to be an association between frequency of drug use and the development of schizophrenia. Yet fundamental questions about this association are not fully understood: What is the association between the use of psychoactive drugs and the development of schizophrenia? Is the drug use a response to the psychopathology of schizophrenia? Is there somehow a neurobiological link between the propensity toward drug dependence and that toward schizophrenia?

The addition of drugs of abuse often increases and exacerbates psychotic symptoms in psychiatric patients. In this population, ingestion of even relatively small amounts over a short period of time may result in an exacerbation of psychiatric problems, loss of housing, frequent use of emergency room services, or increased vulnerability to exploitation (as by sexual, physical, or other abuse) within the social environment. Perhaps because of this sensitivity to psychoactive substances, individuals with schizophrenia appear to progress quickly from substance use to dependence. Substance use among psychiatric patients is associated with a worsening of prognosis, increased institutionalization, and a lowering of socioeconomic status.

Although schizophrenia is the most prevalent psychotic mental disorder, only about 1% to 2 % of the population have been so diagnosed. However, even at this rate of prevalence, the disorder poses high costs for society, for the family, and for the patient. The Epidemiological Catchment Area (ECA) study found that 47% of persons with schizophrenia have a substance use disorder in their lifetime, including 34% who have an alcohol use disorder and 28% who have a drug use disorder. Mental health treatment settings report rates of current substance use disorders in the schizophrenic population to range from 25% to 75%. It is interesting to note that somewhere between 70% and 90% of patients with schizophrenia are nicotine dependent (Ziedonis & George, 1997; Hughes, Hatsukami et al., 1986). Tobacco smoking often alters blood levels of psychiatric medications and psychiatric symptoms, and may improve cognition and stress management. However, these epidemiologic data represent a "best guess" as to the true rate of comorbidity, given the challenges of diagnosing substance abuse in the presence of schizophrenia and the problems of diagnosing schizophrenia in the context of a substance use disorder.

According to the fourth edition of the *Diagnostic and Statistical Manual of Mental Disorders* (*DSM-*

TABLE 1. Psychotic Symptoms

Delusion is a firmly held false belief based on incorrect inference about reality. **Hallucination** is a sensory perception that has the compelling sense of reality but occurs without stimulation of the relevant sensory organ.

Disorganized speech often presents as looseness of association (get off track) or, in the extreme, can be completely incoherent.

Grossly disorganized behaviors range from childlike silliness to unpredictable agitation. Disorganized behaviors include difficulty in performing activities of daily living, poor hygiene, appearing markedly disheveled, unusual dress, inappropriate sexual behavior, and unpredictable and untriggered agitation.

Negative symptoms are characterized by severe deficits in functioning and include flat affect (clearly diminished range of emotional expressiveness), alogia (poverty of speech), avolition (reduced ability to initiate and complete goals), and anhedonia (loss of interest or pleasure).

Catatonia is a marked and bizarre motor abnormality that is characterized by immobility. It may involve certain types of excessive activity, mutism, resistance to being moved, assumption of unusual body positions, and echoing the sound last heard or action last seen.

IV; American Psychiatric Association, 1994), psychotic symptoms include delusions, hallucinations, disorganized speech or behavior, "negative symptoms," and catatonia (see Table 1). Hallucinations and delusions are labeled "positive symptoms." "Negative symptoms" include flat affect, amotivation, poor attention, anhedonia, and asociality. Physicians must consider the role of general medical condition (Table 2) or substance use in association with both intoxication and withdrawal (Table 3). Psychotic symptoms may occur as the presenting symptom or may be part of a more complex syndrome of cognitive impairment (involving delirium or dementia).

Schizophrenia is the psychotic disorder that is most frequently diagnosed in psychiatric patients, but other subtypes of psychotic disorders must be considered in the differential diagnosis (Table 4). Psychotic symptoms also may occur in the context of other categories of mental disorders, particularly especially affective disorders. For example, delusions or hallucinations may be a symptom of major depression or the mania phase of bipolar disorder.

The type and duration of psychotic symptoms are important in the differential diagnosis. Psychotic symptoms that had a sudden onset and that last no more than one month are labeled "brief psychotic disorder." If the symptoms have been present for less than six months, the diagnosis is schizophreniform disorder. If the symptoms last longer than six months and include delusions, hallucinations, and other psychotic symptoms, the clinician should consider a diagnosis of schizophrenia or schizoaffective disorder. Schizoaffective disorder is diagnosed when an uninterrupted time period includes symptoms of a psychotic disorder and a mood disorder (depression, mania, or mixed states) during separate time periods. In contrast to major depression with psychotic features, schizoaffective disorder features a period of psychotic symptoms in the absence of mood disorder symptoms. A delusional disorder is diagnosed only when delusional symptoms are present.

Two common scenarios can be problematic for clinicians in establishing a diagnosis of schizophrenia and/or a substance use disorder. In the first scenario, the clinician is evaluating a new patient who presents with both psychotic symptoms and/or substance abuse. (In many cases, a definitive psychotic disorder diagnosis cannot be established and treatment of the coexisting psychosis and substance abuse must occur simultaneously.) In the second scenario, the clinician is reevaluating a known psychiatric patient with schizophrenia who presents with symptoms of an undiagnosed substance use disorder. This chapter reviews both scenarios as they relate to the acute treatment of substance-induced psychotic disorder among individuals who otherwise would not have psychotic symptoms and the chronic treatment of the dually diagnosed psychiatric patient. In many cases, a definitive diagnosis cannot be established and treatment of the coexisting psychosis and substance abuse must occur simultaneously.

ACUTE PRESENTATION

In the acute presentation of psychosis and substance abuse, there can be differences in signs and symptoms due to variations in etiology. This variation may stem from an underlying psychiatric disorder, a medical disorder, or substance abuse.

Initial Assessment. At the time of the patient's initial presentation, the clinician should have three primary goals: patient safety, staff safety, and eliciting the patient's history. Often, the most appropriate setting for the evaluation of the acutely psychotic patient is a hospital emergency department, although some psychiatric triage settings also are appropriate. Staff in such settings are trained to treat these patients in an effective and safe manner. If the patient is initially encountered outside a hospital setting, arranging an appropriate transport to the emergency department may be the most appropriate first step. An addiction medicine specialist may be asked to participate in the patient evaluation.

Patient safety should be addressed by providing a setting that will lessen the external stimuli, ensure the physical safety of patient and staff, and provide a modicum of dignity while the work-up is underway. Initial assessment of vital signs then should be obtained. Variation in pulse rate, blood pressure, and respiratory function are not uncommon in the presentation of many toxic states. The patient's mental status should be assessed. Consideration should be given to the need for protection of the airway and possible establishment of intravenous access. Physical restraints may help to ensure the initial safety of both the patient and staff; however, use of a quiet room with a sense of safety often achieves a significant reduction in the patient's level of anxiety and agitated psychotic symptoms. "Chemical restraints" may be warranted, but only after the primary assessment has taken place.

Included in the primary assessment is the gathering of history from anyone with information on the patient prior to his or her patient's arrival at the hospital. Family or friends may be very helpful in reporting the patient's psychiatric, medical, and social history. Emergency personnel should be questioned for details of the scene in which they first encountered the patient and their observations of the patient during transport. This may provide significant insight into the possible involvement of psychoactive substances (as indicated, for example, by a pattern of delirium or a waxing and waning of signs and symptoms).

Initial laboratory information should include CBC, electrolytes, liver enzymes, glucose, BUN, calcium, blood alcohol, and urine analysis with toxicology screen. If the patient lapses into coma, the administration of glucose, thiamine, and Narcan® may be appropriate even before the laboratory results are available. Computerized tomography (CT) scanning of the acutely psychotic patient's head always should be considered. Head injury, the severity of which is best confirmed by CT, often results in a confused, bizarre thought pattern that could present as psychosis and that may be associated with substance abuse. However, CT scanning is of little help in differentiating between schizophrenia and drug-induced psychosis (Wiesbeck & Taeschner, 1991). If the blood and urine evaluation is not diagnostic and the CT scan is negative, lumbar puncture may be warranted.

TABLE 2. Psychosis Secondary to Medical Conditions

Neurological conditions: neoplasms, stroke, epilepsy, auditory nerve injury, deafness, migraine, CNS infection.

Endocrine conditions: hyper- or hypothyroid, parathyroid or hypoadrenocorticism.

Metabolic conditions: hypoxia, hypercarbia, hypoglycemia.

Fluid or electrolyte imbalances

Hepatic or renal failure

Autoimmune disorders with CNS involvement (systemic lupus erythematosus).

Delirium

Dementia (Alzheimer's, vascular, HIV-related, Parkinson's, Huntington's, head trauma, etc.).

Neoplasm, lung.

Interplay between Substance Use and Psychosis. Psychotic symptoms associated with various forms and levels of drug use are well-documented. The differential diagnosis most often is determined after a period of abstinence, which may vary from hours to months, depending on the drug involved and/or the duration of use. For example, there is evidence that chronic amphetamine dependence may result in long-term neurobiologic changes, which may persist even after a prolonged abstinence and which present as a protracted psychosis that is phenomenologically similar to that of schizophrenia (Sato, 1990). By contrast, a study of cocaine-induced psychosis by Satel and Lieberman (1991) suggests that a psychosis persisting for more than several days is most likely to be an underlying psychotic disorder. However, patients who inhale or inject amphetamines at high doses, or who smoke large amounts of marijuana, PCP or formaldehyde ("illy") in combination may produce psychotic symptoms that last for months.

For many reasons, differentiating schizophrenia from a substance-induced psychotic disorder is not an easy task, especially if the physician does not know whether the patient has a chronic psychiatric history. Medication side effects can be mistaken for negative symptoms, and negative symptoms can be mistaken for depression. Substance abusers also can be poorly compliant in taking their medication, and the presenting psychotic relapse may be due to noncompliance. In one longitudinal diagnostic study of 165 patients with chronic psychosis and cocaine abuse or dependence, a definitive diagnosis could not be established in 93% of the cases (Shaner et al., 1996). To establish a definitive diagnosis of schizophrenia, the researchers required that a patient meet diagnostic criteria for schizophrenia at some point after six weeks of abstinence from psychoactive substances. The patients were interviewed at multiple points over time (using the Structured Clinical Interview and criteria of the *DSM-IIIR*) (First, Spitzer et al., 1995). Using these strict guidelines, the primary reasons for not reaching a diagnosis were insufficient abstinence (78%), poor memory (24%), and/or inconsistent reporting (20%) on the part of the patient. A review of hospital records and collateral information addressed the problems of poor memory and inconsistent reporting, leaving insufficient abstinence as the primary barrier to establishing a diagnosis. The researchers' finding that most patients continued to use substances reflects the difficulty of treating persons in this population, and underscores the need to make clinical decisions within the context of diagnostic uncertainty. Nonetheless, insufficient abstinence is the primary barrier to establishing a diagnosis. The study's finding that most patients continued to use substances reflects the difficulty in treating this subtype and the need to make clinical decisions in the context of diagnostic uncertainty.

One of the most important clues to the etiology of the psychosis, of course, is the patient history. However, the astute physician also may recognize subtle variations in presentation that will help to guide the treatment of these patients. This chapter will now focus on the unique relationship of each substance of abuse to the development of psychotic symptoms and the acute management of the psychotic symptoms.

DRUG-SPECIFIC PSYCHOTIC SYMPTOMS

The following discussion focuses on the unique relationship of certain psychoactive substances to the development and acute management of psychotic symptoms.

Alcohol and Psychosis. The most obvious psychotic symptoms associated with alcohol are most frequently associated with the withdrawal stage (Isbell, Fraser & Wikler, 1955; Mendelson, 1964; Gross, 1975). These symptoms are based in the still-undefined interplay over time of chronic alcohol dependence and the gamma-aminobutyric acid type A ($GABA_A$), N-methyl-d-aspartic acid (NMDA), and dopamine (DA) receptors (Tabakoff, 1996). Such symptoms typically are referred to as alcoholic hallucinosis; that is, auditory and visual hallucinations which occur in a clear sensorium. The auditory hallucinations are most frequently of the threatening or command type. In this condition, individuals can be in an extremely agitated and paranoid state, which is associated with the hallucinations and physical discomfort they are experiencing. The onset of this hallucinogenic state has been reported to occur from 12 hours to seven days after the onset of abstinence from long-term alcohol use. (However, there have been reports of the onset symptoms having been delayed by as much as three weeks.) The most typical time for emergence of symptoms is within two days (Victor, 1958; Scott, 1969; Schuckit, 1982). The psychotic symptoms, particularly the paranoia, may last from hours to weeks. There is some evidence to suggest that individuals with symptoms that are prolonged for weeks or months may have a predisposition to a psychotic illness (Victor, 1958). There can be tremendous similarity between this psychotic appearance and schizophrenia. Evidence of clearer sensorium noted in the withdrawing patient often is the distinguishing feature. However, this distinction may be clouded by a mild to more severe dementia associated with prolonged heavy alcohol ingestion.

The paranoia and agitation often can be treated with benzodiazepines in the same way one would treat uncomplicated withdrawal. However, in the severely agitated patient with concurrent hallucination, neuroleptics may be warranted. Withdrawal has been associated with the development of extrapyramidal symptoms, including dystonia, akathisia, choreoathetosis, and Parkinsonism (Carlen, 1981; Lang, 1982; Shen, 1984). Particular attention should be paid to the possible development of extrapyramidal symptoms in the patient treated with a neuroleptic drug during acute alcohol withdrawal or in the patient with a chronic primary psychotic illness.

Cannabis and Psychosis. The rate of cannabis dependence or abuse in the general population were estimated at a lifetime prevalence of 4.3% in the ECA study, reported in 1990. The comorbid use of cannabis in individuals with schizophrenia has been estimated at 6.0% (Regier, 1990). The most frequently reported effects of marijuana at levels of moderate intoxication are euphoria (Ames, 1958; Hollister, 1971; Chopra & Smith, 1974), an awareness of alteration in thought processes (Ames, 1958), suspiciousness and paranoid ideation (Keeler, 1968; Tart, 1970), alteration in the perception of time (Renault, 1974); a sensation of heightened visual perception (Keeler, 1971); and, at higher doses, some auditory and visual hallucinations (Beaubrun & Knight, 1973; Isbell, 1967; Keeler, 1968; Waskow, 1970). These effects have been reproducible in the laboratory and appear to be partially dose-dependent. There is some evidence that certain users seek the more psychotomimetic effects achieved through chronic administration high-dose use (Ghodse, 1986). At doses greater than 0.2 mg/kg, the potential for the development of psychotic-like symptoms increases dramatically (Isbell, 1967). Symptoms at that level of use may include suspiciousness, memory impairment, confusion, depersonalization, apprehension, hallucinations, and derealization (Ames, 1958; Talbott & Teague, 1969; Chopra & Smith, 1974; Rottanburg, 1982). These symptoms are reported to be transient, although they may recur on repeated administration of the drug (Chopra & Smith, 1974; Brook 1984; Carney, 1984). There is little evidence that chronic use of cannabis leads to a primary psychotic disorder (Chopra & Smith, 1974). First time use, large amounts, and route of ingestion (oral versus smoked) may be factors in the higher incidence of cannabis psychosis (Tennant & Groesbeck, 1972; Chaudry, 1991). A study comparing psychotic features in a group of men with psychotic symptoms and high urinary levels of cannabis, to psychotic individuals without positive cannabis urines, showed more hypomania, more agitation, less coherent speech, less flattening of affect, and fewer auditory hallucinations in the cannabis group (Rottanburg, 1982; Thacore & Shukla, 1976). Cannabis use often is associated with a more affective type of psychosis (Carny, 1984).

Typically, the psychosis associated with cannabis is acute and of short duration. However, there are case reports of chronic psychosis attributed to cannabis (Gersten, 1980). This is a difficult question to answer for a variety of reasons: Is the patient remaining abstinent? What other drugs may the patient have been exposed to? Is there predisposing psychopathology? Frequently, the evaluating physician must decide whether chronic schizophrenia is secondary to the past use of cannabis. Often this is an issue for both the patient and family. One retrospective study presented evidence showing better premorbid personalities and reduced age of onset in the cannabis-exposed individuals over the non-using schizophrenic population (Breakey, 1974). This difference, however, may be secondary to cannabis opening the "environmental window" in an already predisposed patient.

TABLE 3. Substances that Cause Psychotic Symptoms

During Intoxication:

- Sedatives (alcohol, benzodiazepines, and barbituates)
- Stimulants (amphetamine, ice, cocaine)
- Designer drugs (ecstacy, etc)
- Marijuana/THC
- Hallucinogens (LSD, Ketamine, psilosibine, etc.)
- Opioids
- Phencyclidines.

During Withdrawal:

- Sedatives (alcohol, benzodiazepines, and barbituates)
- Anesthetics and analgesics
- Anticholinergic agents
- Anticonvulsants
- Antihistamines
- Antihypertensives
- Antimicrobial medications
- AntiParkinsonian medications
- Cardiovascular medications
- Chemotherapeutic agents
- Corticosteroids
- Gastrointestinal medications
- Muscle relaxants
- Non-steroidal anti-inflammatory drugs (NSAIDs)
- Over-the-counter drugs
- Toxins (Anticholinesterase, organophosphate insecticides, nerve gases, carbon monoxide, and volatile substances such as fuel or paint).

Cocaine and Psychosis. Transient paranoia is a common feature of chronic cocaine intoxication (Manschreck, 1988; Satel, 1990), and appears in 33% to 50 % of patients. Psychotic symptoms associated with cocaine use are almost exclusively seen in the intoxication phase and rarely extend beyond the "crash" phase in the patient who does not have a primary psychotic illness. There is epidemiological evidence that men have a greater propensity toward psychosis than women and that Caucasians are affected more frequently than non-Caucasians (Brady, 1991). There are multiple indicators that high-dose use of cocaine over time has a strong association with the onset of psychotic symptoms (Brady, 1991; Satel, 1990). There also is strong evidence that sensitization occurs with chronic administration of cocaine and amphetamines (Bell, 1973; Ellinwood, 1972; Satel, 1990). This sensitization is associated with the type of psychotic symptoms that can occur with repeated use of the stimulants. The psychotic features appear to occur with repeated exposure at lower doses. Onset of psychotic symptoms has been associated with reduction in individual doses and the desire for treatment (Brady, 1991).

The most frequently reported psychotic symptoms are paranoid delusions and hallucinations. Auditory hallucinations are the most common and often are associated with the paranoid delusion. Visual hallucinations are the next most common, followed by tactile hallucinations (Brady, 1991). Visual hallucinations have been associated with chronic mydriatic pupils (Woods, 1973) and the appearance of geometric shapes. Nearly all of the hallucinations are associated with the drug use. There is evidence to suggest that the character of the psychotic symptoms experienced are associated with the setting in which the drug is ingested (Sherer, 1988). Stereotypic behavior also can be associated with psychosis. Such behavior occasionally continues after the intoxication subsides. A study of the phenomenology of the hallucinations points to an orderly progression in the development of hallucinations, from the early visual hallucinations to the tactile forms (Seigel, 1978). This comports with the observation that there is an orderly progression of the effects of cocaine intoxication from euphoria to dysphoria and finally to psychosis, and that this is related to dose, chronicity, and genetic and experiential predisposition (Post, 1975).

It is very difficult to assess the premorbid evidence of psychotic thinking in individuals who go on to use large repeat doses of cocaine, and to forecast the likelihood that they will develop psychotic symptoms. Satel and Edell (1991) did measure the level of non-drug-psychotic proneness in individuals who had a history of cocaine-induced psychosis, as compared to individuals without such a history. They found strong evidence that there is a greater incidence of low-level psychotic thinking in the abstinent patient who is prone to cocaine-induced psychosis. Whether this is evidence of proneness to the development of psychosis in some individuals as a function of their use of cocaine, or an indication of the development of persistent neurobiologic changes concurrent with the onset of cocaine-induced psychosis remains unclear. McLellan (1979) examined this question by performing a six-year follow-up study on drug-dependent individuals who had no initial psychotic symptoms, and found a strong association with psychosis in the amphetamine-dependent population. The nature of the association was unclear, but the investigators speculated that there may be some self-selection of stimulant drugs in this population or there may have been some low-level psychotic thinking that was not identified in the original evaluation.

Amphetamines and Psychosis. The first report of psychosis associated with amphetamines was made by Young and Scoville in 1938. They reported psychotic behavior in a patient who was under treatment for narcolepsy. Since that time, there have been many observations and studies of this association. Rockwell and Ostwald reviewed psychiatric hospital records in 1968 and found that the most common diagnosis of patients admitted with covert amphetamine use was schizophrenia.

Amphetamine psychosis has been described as a three-stage illness. Initially it is marked by increased curiosity and repetitive examining, searching and sorting behaviors. In the second stage, these behaviors are followed by increased paranoia. In the final stage, the paranoia leads to ideas of reference, persecutory delusions and hallucinations, which are marked by a fearful, panic-stricken, agitated, overactive state (Ellinwood, 1973). That the appearance of psychotic-like symptoms in amphetamine users would become more prevalent in the late 1960s and 1970s would fit what we now know about the pattern of use associated with these symptoms. Amphetamine-induced psychosis develops over time in association with large amounts of the drug, delivered by any route of administration. The strongest correlation has been seen in those individuals who use large amounts by intravenous injection.

A common presentation of the psychotic, amphetamine-intoxicated patient involves paranoia, delusional thinking and (frequently) hypersexuality. The hallucinatory symptoms may include visual, auditory, olfactory, and/or tactile sensations. However, the patient's orientation and memory usually remain intact. Typically, this altered mental state lasts only during the period of intoxication, although there are reports of it persisting for days to weeks.

Treatment efforts should pay particular attention to providing a safe, secure place for the patient, and reducing external environmental stimuli. Physical restraints should be avoided or used in a time-limited fashion so as not to complicate the presentation with worsening hyperthermia and/or rhabdomyolysis and possible renal failure. One should keep in mind the potential of amphetamines for lowering seizure threshold, inducing hyperpyrexia, and stimulating cardiovascular compromise, particularly in the patient who is using large amounts in a chronic pattern. Chlorpromazine should be avoided because of its potential to lower seizure threshold and worsen hyperthermia. Benzodiazepines can be

Table 4. DSM-IV Psychotic Disorders

- Brief psychotic disorder
- Schizophrenia
- Schizophreniform disorder
- Schizoaffective disorder
- Delusional disorder
- Psychotic disorder, Not Otherwise Specified

helpful in the treatment of these symptoms. A common initial dose is diazepam 10 mg, either IM or IV, then titrated to a level that sufficiently sedates the patient. Patients should be closely monitored for respiratory depression. When using benzodiazepines intramuscularly, one should wait at least one hour between doses so as to not to inadvertently overdose the patient. It is quite common to see dramatic tolerance to the benzodiazepine medications in the drug-abusing population, so that a very high dose may be needed to achieve sedation.

The question of how long the psychosis may last and how likely the patient is to develop a long-term psychotic illness as a result of the use of amphetamines is not clear. Clinical experience suggests that amphetamine psychosis may last up to three to six months in extreme cases of high-dose use. There is little evidence to suggest that these drugs cause schizophrenia. However, there is the potential for long-term affective instability, a moderate to severe anxiety state, and underlying suspiciousness.

Hallucinogens and Psychosis. Hallucinogens have a well-documented role, both ceremonial and recreational, in many societies. However, not until the synthesis of lysergic acid diethylamine (LSD) by Hofman in 1943 was a hallucinogen available in large quantities and widely used as a recreational drug. A national survey in the U.S. in 1990 yielded an estimate that 7.6% of the population over 12 years old had ever used a hallucinogen. This number rose to 8.6% in 1993. Boutros and Bowers (1996) point out in their review that the percentage of patients admitted to psychiatric hospitals with a diagnosis of "schizophrenia and paranoid disorders" at first admission was 10.9% in 1970. This number rose to 24% by 1979 and has remained around 20% since then. The increase is specific to the population between 15 and 34 years old, and correlates with the increased use of hallucinogenics during this time. This provides evidence pointing to hallucinogens as a factor in the development of schizophreniform psychosis.

The primary model for hallucinogens is LSD, an indole-type drug with structural similarities to serotonin. Included in this class of drugs are dimethyltryptamine (DMT), psilocybin, and psilocin, among others. LSD crosses the blood-brain barrier readily and has a potent affinity to the 5HT2a receptor. Its half-life is approximately 100 minutes and the effects wear off in approximately six to 12 hours. Initially, there are autonomic changes, which are associated with the early affective instability seen after administration, as in laughter and/or fearfulness. The associated alterations in perception occur subsequently, and feature hallucinations of all kinds. The most common hallucinations are visual; the least common, auditory. The occurrence of synesthesia—the blending of the senses—is uncommon but not unknown. There often is a loss of the concept of time. Paranoia and aggression can be profound, but the more frequent experience is that of euphoria and security. The "setting" may have an effect on the experience and much has been written on proper preparation for the "trip."

LSD has a large therapeutic index. Thus, the typical emergency visit secondary to the use of this class of drugs occurs as a result of the anxiety, a concurrent accident, or suicidal behavior. "Talking down" the patient is the most common way to ease his or her anxiety around the psychotic features of these drugs. The persistently agitated patient may be treated pharmacologically with a benzodiazepine. Neuroleptics have been widely and effectively used to lessen the psychotic-like experience; however, there is a report in the literature of an intensification of the experience after the administration of these drugs. If they are to be used, a suggested dose of Haloperidol 1 to 5 mg or equivalent high-potency antipsychotic medication may be appropriate.

There is no clear evidence that LSD causes a prolonged psychotic-like illness. Attempts at longitudinal studies have yielded insufficient evidence to support this occurrence. The difficulty surrounding this question is the high rate of adulterants in the formulation of these drugs, and the inability to clearly rule out any preexisting psychopathology. The incidence of the development of schizophrenia post-intoxication is not outside parameters one would expect to see in this youthful population. There is evidence that the occurrence of problems following intoxication is greater in those with a preexisting psychiatric illness. A meta-analysis of the data by Abraham (1996) helps to substantiate this conclusion. The psychiatric diagnosis most commonly associated with post-LSD psychosis is a form of schizoaffective disorder. The appearance of some affective instability—involving a feeling of an altered state of consciousness—and a recurrent perceptual disorder, primarily visual, are the most common symptoms seen in patients with associated chronic psychosis (Fink, 1966; Abraham, 1980). The schizophrenic drug user is known to have an earlier age of onset and a better premorbid social functioning than the non-drug-using schizophrenic (Bowers, 1972; Breakey, 1974).

Phencyclidine/Ketamine and Psychosis. The cyclohexylamine anesthetics, phencyclidine hydrochloride (PCP) and ketamine hydrochloride, have similar properties. Both result in psychotic-like experiences during intoxication. There is evidence that in the case of PCP, the psychotic-like state may last for prolonged periods beyond the period of intoxication. Soon after PCP was developed in 1957, it was found to produce a serene-like anesthesia in animals (Domino, 1978). This led to human experimentation and the recognition that administration of these drugs produces a dissociative state. Patients' eyes remain open and scanning during surgery, yet they appear to be "disconnected" from their environments and unable to feel pain (Johnstone, 1959; Greifenstein, 1958). More alarmingly, there were reports of bizarre hallucinations and behaviors during the postoperative period (Greifenstein, 1958). Consequently, PCP has never been released for human use.

Ketamine, at a potency 10 to 50 time lower than PCP, was shown to produce far fewer of these psychotic-like episodes and was released for use as an anesthetic. Interestingly, children do not appear to develop the associated psychotic-like symptoms.

The history of abuse of these drugs began in the mid-1960s. Street use of PCP increased when this population learned that smoking the drug, rather than ingesting it, resulted in fewer unpleasant side effects. It was then that PCP started to be smoked with cannabis (Liden, 1975). The incidence of the use of this drug increased significantly by 1976, when a survey by the National Institute on Drug Abuse found that 13.9% of 18- to 25-year-olds had experience with this drug (Lerner, 1978). At the same time, there was a concurrent increase in the number of emergency department visits associated with PCP use. Reports included numerous deaths from toxicity, homicide, suicide, and accident/bizarre behavior. A retrospective review of 80 PCP-related deaths by Helig, Diller and Nelson (1982) showed a strong association with prior affective disorders, aggressive behavior, prior arrests, and a personal crisis in the three months preceding death.

The high incidence of use of PCP has been partly due to the fact that it can be inexpensively produced and therefore often is added to the formulation of a variety of drugs sold on the street. A survey done in 1975 showed that PCP was sold 91% of the time as some other substance, most frequently as mescaline, LSD, or THC (Lundberg, Gupta & Montgomery, 1976). Since that time, the drug seems to have increased in popularity, as suggested by the fact that it is more frequently sold as PCP, although it still is found as an adulterant in other street drug formulations.

PCP and ketamine can be smoked, ingested, snorted, or intravenously injected. They are rapidly absorbed and excreted in the urine. The intoxicating effects last for approximately four to six hours. The recovery period may be highly variable.

The behavioral effects of these drugs appear to be mediated by the effects on excitatory amino acids N-methyl-d-aspartate (NMDA) subtype of glutamate receptor. The high affinity binding of PCP and ketamine to the NMDA receptor blocks ion exchange, resulting in a noncompetitive antagonism of the NMDA receptor (Cotman, 1987). Early observations of patients treated with this drug noted the similarities to dissociative and schizophrenic disorders (Davies, 1960; Luby, 1961; Cohen, 1962). The clinical appearance is that of altered sensory perception, bizarre and impoverished thought and speech, impaired attention, disrupted memory and disrupted thought processes in healthy individuals. There also may be protracted psychosis (Fauman, 1976).

There is considerable symptom variation, depending on dose. At lower doses (20 to 30 ng/ml) one is likely to observe sedation, mood elevation, irritability, impaired attention and memory mutism, hyperactivity, and stereotypy. As serum levels rise to 30 to 100 ng/ml, mood changes, psychosis, analgesia, paresthesia, and ataxia may occur. These levels are associated with profound paranoia, aggression and violent behavior. Higher levels (above 100 ng/ml) can cause stupor, hyperreflexia, hypertension, seizure, coma, and/or death.

Treatment of the acutely disturbing effects of these drugs is with benzodiazepines in doses equivalent to diazepam 10 mg and greater, titrated until the patient is satisfactorily sedated. The patient's respiratory status should be continually monitored. There may be a dramatic improvement in the aggression. There also may be significant improvement in the psychotic symptoms. Neuroleptics also can be considered for treatment of the psychotic symptoms. Most typically, a high-potency neuroleptic like haloperidol (1 to 5 mg) is used because of the decreased anticholinergic properties of these drugs. In cases of overdose, the urine may be acidified with ammonium chloride to facilitate urinary excretion. However, metabolic acidosis can result in other problems, including worsening of rhabdomyolisis, and should be considered only in the most extreme cases.

INTERACTIONS BETWEEN DRUGS OF ABUSE, MEDICATIONS, AND NEUROBIOLOGY

There are four primary findings from the literature on the interaction between disorders, substances, and medications. First, both schizophrenia and addiction appear to have a primary neurobiological defect in the mesolimbic system (ventral tegmentum, nucleus accumbens, and pre-frontal cortex). Second, substance abuse is generally associated with a more severe clinical profile, including indices of impairment, symptoms observed, and cognitive impairment. Third, some substances can impact the metabolism of medications and reduce the therapeutic effect. Fourth, there are some reported positive effects by some patients, and substances may be more frequently used by the higher prognosis patients with social skills to obtain substances.

From a biological perspective, the mesolimbic dopamine pathway appears to play an important role in reinforcement, pleasure, and reward. In the simplest sense, increased dopamine release results in increased pleasure and reward. But one must bear in mind that multiple pathways influence dopamine release, including the opioid system. The reward pathway has been identified as the dopamine pathway that includes the ventral tegmentum area, the nucleus accumbens, and the prefrontal cortex. The ventral tegmental area is linked to the prefrontal cortex, which some research has hypothesized may be hypoactive in schizophrenia (Glassman, 1993). Therefore, chemical substances may be especially reinforcing in schizophrenics due to the combined stimulation of subcortical brain reward mechanisms and the prefrontal cortex.

In addition, substances can interact with psychiatric medications used to treat the negative and positive symptoms of schizophrenia. The interactions are both pharmacokinetic and pharmacodynamic. Most of the substances of abuse interact with psychiatric medications and reduce their effectiveness; some can alter medication blood levels and increase side effects.

Coffee and tea are known to interfere with the absorption and metabolism of psychiatric medication. The metabolism of caffeine occurs through the same liver enzyme affected by cigarette use (cytochrome P450 1A2 isoenzyme).

Cigarette smoking modifies the metabolism of psychiatric medication, including its potential side effects and effectiveness. The "tar" (polynuclear aromatic hydrocarbons) in cigarettes causes this effect, not the nicotine (Jarvik & Schneider, 1992). Smoking is known to decrease the blood levels of haloperidol, fluphenazine and thiothixene, olanzapine, and clozapine (Ereshefsky et al., 1991; Ereshefsky, 1996; Hughes, 1993; McEvoy, Freudenreich et al., 1995; George et al., 1995). Abstinence from smoking increases neuroleptic medication blood levels, and smokers are usually prescribed about double the dosage of traditional neuroleptic medication as compared to non-smokers (Ziedonis, Kosten & Glazer, 1994). The impact on metabolism is important in making treatment decisions with the hospitalized patient whose smoking habits were curbed and the patient who is attempting to quit smoking. Substance abuse may be associated with earlier and more severe cases of tardive dyskinesia (Dixon et al., 1991; Olivera et al., 1990; Zaretsky et al., 1993; Binder et al., 1987). However, other studies have found that substance abuse had no effect on movement disorders when important covariables are considered (Ziedonis, Kosten & Glazer, 1994; Hughes, 1993; Goff, Henderson & Amico, 1992).

Despite all the negative consequences associated with substance abuse, some individuals with schizophrenia report that using substances helps them cope with symptoms of their schizophrenia (Mueser et al., 1995). They report using substances for pleasure, to alleviate boredom, to relieve feelings of anxiety, sadness, or distress, and to share the excitement of "getting high" with friends who are also using. In one study, the most common reason reported by the clients for using substances was "something to do with friends" (Test, Wallisch & Allness, 1989). Some individuals report that substance use reduces their social inhibitions. The self-medication theory suggests that individuals may use chemicals to self-medicate the symptoms of schizophrenia; however, the research data supporting this clinical perception is mixed (Brunette, Mueser et al., 1997). Recent studies suggest that individuals with schizophrenia may smoke to help improve their attention and concentration (Lavin, Siris & Mason, 1996). One research group has found that smoking may transiently normalize deficits in auditory physiology (P_{50}

gating), and that this gating abnormality found in individuals with schizophrenia may be caused by a genetic defect in the nicotinic cholinergic receptors in some individuals (Lavin, Siris & Mason, 1996; Adler, Hoffer & Wiser, 1993).

MEDICATION MANAGEMENT

Antipsychotic medications are an important component in the treatment of schizophrenia. They are instrumental in reducing the long-term positive symptoms of the illness. The new atypical antipsychotics appear to reduce the negative symptoms of schizophrenia, and may also assist patients in the initial stage of abstinence from substances by reducing the severity of detoxification and early protracted abstinence symptoms. Nonetheless, clinicians should have realistic expectations. Medications are not miraculous cure-alls, and this is especially true for a psychiatric illnesses such as schizophrenia, which is marked by complex symptoms and—more often than not—extreme social consequences. Thus, medications should be complemented by psychosocial therapy that engages clients, offers them practical training in interpersonal communication and crisis management, and develops their rehabilitation and recovery skills.

Medication management must first consider the best means for treating the schizophrenia or the chronic psychosis, followed by a consideration of the potential interactions between the substances abused and the possible medication choices. In general, clinicians should avoid prescribing medications that cause sedation when treating patients who abuse sedating substances. In addition, clinicians should generally avoid prescribing medications with abuse liability such as benzodiazepines.

Initially, patients presenting to an emergency room or inpatient unit may require both a detoxification from substances and the reinitiation/initiation of an antipsychotic medication. The treatment goals of detoxification are to reduce the symptoms of withdrawal and prevent serious withdrawal complications such as the development of seizures, delirium tremens, or increased psychosis. New patients who remain a diagnostic dilemma might first be detoxified and further assessed prior to the initiation of antipsychotic medications. Individuals known to have schizophrenia usually require the simultaneous administration of both antipsychotic medication and detoxification medications.

Patients presenting with active substance abuse, psychotic symptoms, and non-compliance can be difficult to manage as outpatients. Improving medication compliance in an outpatient setting can be enhanced through reducing positive and negative symptoms, providing psychoeducation and social skills training on medication management, using motivational enhancement techniques to improve compliance, and switching the route of administration of the medication from oral medication to long-acting injected medication, if patients are unable or refuse to take oral medications.

A fundamental treatment goal for these clients is to decrease and control their positive and negative symptoms through pharmacotherapy, thus allowing them to engage in psychosocial therapy and to integrate themselves into the community. One of the more promising oral medications for this dual diagnosis subtype is the newer atypical antipsychotic medication, i.e., risperidone, clozapine, olanzapine, and sertindole. In contrast to the more traditional antipsychotic medications such as haloperidol and fluphenazine, the atypicals offer three distinct advantages: (1) they treat both the positive and negative symptoms characteristic of schizophrenia and may help improve neurocognitive functioning; (2) they produce fewer acute (EPS) and long-term (TD) movement disorder side effects at therapeutic dosages; and (3) they present a different—and potentially more favorable—receptor-binding profile (Weiden, Aquila & Standard, 1996).

The presence of negative symptoms, in particular, has long been considered a problem in treating the dually diagnosed. Researchers have theorized that negative symptoms may be either a contributing factor in the development of substance abuse and in worsening the withdrawal symptoms. The "self-medication" hypothesis proposes that some patients may use substances to cope with the negative symptoms of their schizophrenia. Clinical experience lends some support to this view, as patients often show an increase in negative symptoms during the initial phase of acute withdrawal as well as the succeeding phase of prolonged abstinence. It is not surprising, then, that atypical antipsychotic medication may offer hope for improved treatment outcomes in dually diagnosed clients, especially low motivation clients, insofar as the medication jointly targets the schizophrenia and its negative symptoms. Nonetheless, the potential improved benefits of atypicals on the dually diagnosed has yet to be reported using a randomized clinical trial, despite initial research that supports their effectiveness (Kosten & Nestler, 1994; Buckley, Thompson et al., 1994). The authors' own clinical experience suggests that risperidone is the preferred choice for this dual diagnosis subtype; it is well tolerated and treats both positive and negative symptoms, but avoids the sedative qualities that may result from higher dosages of clozapine and olazapine.

A second medication option is the use of long-acting injectable medications, e.g., Haldol decanoate® or Prolixin®. Although this option is frequently ignored, it effectively solves the problem of medication compliance, and thus may be an appropriate treatment for those patients whose motivation to quit using substances is low. Further research may yield a treatment that combines the comprehensive effectiveness of atypical medications with the compliance guarantees of injectable medications. At the present time, however, the newer atypical antipsychotics are not offered in the injectable depot format.

Once clinicians have chosen a treatment option that stabilizes the schizophrenia, they may consider the use of additional medication, as necessary, to manage comorbid depression, comorbid substance abuse, or another psychiatric problem. For substance use, medications are targeted for specific purposes, including detoxification, craving reduction, relief of protracted abstinence withdrawal, and agonist maintenance. Some adjunctive medications (such as antidrepressants and mazindol) also may address the schizophrenia, helping to reduce and stabilize its negative symptoms. Despite the lack of pharmacotherapy trials among populations with a substance abuse problem and schizophrenia, a growing number of clinicians have reported the benefits of these medications.

For the treatment of alcohol use disorders, the Food and Drug Administration (FDA) has approved the use of two adjunctive medications: disulfiram (Antabuse®) and naltrexone (Revia®). The clinical record of antabuse is mixed, and it has yet to be tested in randomized control trials. The possibility of an alcohol-antabuse reaction requires patients who comprehend the risks of antabuse and are capable of not drinking in light of these risks. Furthermore, according to some clinicians, the administration of antabuse at higher dosages (1,000 mgs) has resulted in psychotic symptoms among non-dually-diagnosed patients. Clinical studies of naltrexone in this population have not been reported, however clinical experience suggests it may help reduce alcohol cravings. Naltrexone is a relatively safe medication that can be used with patients who are at higher risk to relapse to alcohol; there is no alcohol-naltrexone reaction. Naltrexone's most common side effects include headache and nausea. Naltrexone can precipitate opiate withdrawal, so clinicians should carefully assess patients' use of prescription or illicit opiates and be prepared to manage opiate withdrawal symptoms. Liver function tests should be monitored when using either disulfiram or naltrexone.

For cocaine addiction among dually diagnosed patients, clinicians have tried a variety of augmentation medications, including desipramine, selegeline, mazindol, and amantadine, all of which aim to produce an increased dopaminergic effect that will reverse or compensate for the neurophysiological changes stemming from the chronic use of cocaine. Unfortunately, no medication has been found to help reduce cocaine usage or craving among cocaine addicts without psychiatric comorbidity, and there are only a few studies that targeted individuals with schizophrenia and cocaine addiction. Two double-blind placebo-controlled trials comparing adjunctive desipramine versus placebo found some further reduced cocaine usage among individuals with schizophrenia during the third month of early abstinence using desipramine compared to placebo (Wilkins, 1997; Ziedonis & Trudeau, 1997).

In contrast to both alcohol and cocaine addiction, nicotine dependence traditionally has received less clinical attention and often has gone untreated. The recent development of treatment guidelines may correct this oversight and lead to the inclusion of tobacco dependence as a component in clinical treatment plans (APA Practice Guidelines, 1996). In addition to multicomponent behavioral therapy, treatment for nicotine cessation may include adjunctive medications such as nicotine replacements (transdermal patch, gum, spray, or inhaler) or buproprion. The new atypical antipsychotics may better treat negative symptoms and help in smoking cessation. In patients who are not receiving specific smoking cessation treatment, two studies found significant decreases in nicotine use among patients who were switched from traditional neuroleptics to clozapine (George, Sernyak et al., 1995; McEvoy, Freudenreich et al., 1995). In a study specifically aiming to treat tobacco dependence, about 20% of patients with schizophrenia were able to remain abstinent for six months with the use of nicotine replacement. This study also showed that intensive psychosocial treatment (weekly individual motivational enhancement therapy combined with weekly relapse prevention group therapy) yielded better outcomes than either individual or group therapy alone (Ziedonis & George, 1997).

SUB-ACUTE AND LONGER-TERM TREATMENT

Clinical experience has shown that some psychiatric patients will continue to simultaneously display psychotic symptoms and to actively abuse stimulants. In such cases, the abuse may be responsible for, or exacerbate, the patient's symptoms, making the task of diagnosis a difficult one. The clinician should formulate a treatment plan that initially addresses both the psychosis and the substance abuse, beginning with the use of a low-dose antipsychotic. If the patient is able to achieve prolonged abstinence, the clinician then may consider withdrawing the medication and initiating a medication-free period. Patients who continue to display an affective disorder despite a significant period of abstinence may require treatment for that disorder.

Conversely, recognizing a substance use problem in a patient previously diagnosed as schizophrenic can be problematic for several reasons. First, staff in mental health facilities may have inadequate training in screening for substance use and abuse, generally, and in diagnosing and treating dual diagnosis clients, specifically. Several studies have shown that a significant number of mental health clinicians routinely overlook substance abuse problems in their schizophrenic patients. Second, the patient may contribute to a misdiagnosis by downplaying or denying substance-related problems or pointing to other causes for such problems. One study of schizophrenic individuals who presented in emergency rooms discovered that 33% were recent cocaine users, but 50% of those reported no recent use (Shaner, Khalsa et al., 1993). Thus, urine toxicology and alcohol Breathalyzer tests are strongly advised. Finally, the physician should be careful not to dwell exclusively on the amount of substance use, as psychiatric patients may suffer more acutely from lesser amounts of a substance than non-psychiatric patients. Although further research is necessary, standard substance abuse screening instruments may be useful for this population (Hedlund & Vieweg, 1984; Drake, Osher et al., 1990; Kofoed, 1991; Westermeyer, 1992).

Clinicians also may consider a variety of behaviors that frequently underlie a substance use disorder. Cigarette smoking, for example, is linked to other substance use among schizophrenic individuals. Heavy smokers (more than 25 cigarettes per day) abuse substances at three to four times the rate for non-smokers (Ziedonis, Kosten & Glazer, 1994; Glassman, 1993). In addition, a substance use disorder may be indicated in patients who are verbally threatening, violent, noncompliant, or suicidal; patients suffering from several medical problems, with recurring hospitalizations or emergency room visits; or patients who are homeless or in legal trouble (Mueser, Yarnold et al., 1992; Bartels, Teague et al., 1993; Ziedonis & Fisher, 1996).

Independently, schizophrenia and substance use disorders each have an associated set of impairments in cognitive, interpersonal, affective, and biological functions (Ziedonis & D'Avanzo, 1998). When these disorders are seen together, the interactions of their associated impairments lead each disorder to be more intractable. The interactions occur between the underlying neurobiology, psychopathology, social correlates, treatment strategies, and health care systems associated with the two individual disorders. Hence, addicted patients with prolonged psychosis or a mental illness such as schizophrenia will generally not respond well to unmodified treatment approaches designed for patients with schizophrenia only or for patients with substance abuse only. As with all dually diagnosed patients, the most successful treatment combines medications with a psychosocial therapy that utilizes both mental health and addiction approaches. The number and variety of psychosocial interventions for the dually diagnosed is impressive, ranging from traditional self-help and Twelve Step groups to recent innovations such as community reinforcement approach (CRA). An exhaustive review of psychosocial interventions can be found in Dixon and Rebori (1995).

Dual diagnosis programs have employed psychosocial interventions in strikingly different ways, but there are core similarities. Some have favored an active outreach case management approach, while others have relied more heavily on motivational enhancement therapy in the clinical setting (Ziedonis & Fisher, 1996; Carey, 1996; Drake, Bartels et al., 1993; Drake & Noordsy, 1994; Minkoff, 1989; Noordsy, 1991; Rosenthal, Hellerstein & Miner, 1992; Schollar, 1993). Three specific substance abuse psychosocial treatments that appear fundamental to dual diagnosis treatment include Motivation Enhancement Therapy (Miller & Rollnick, 1991), Relapse Prevention (Marlatt & Gordan, 1985) and Twelve Step Facilitation. However, clinical experience suggests that these three treatment approaches need modification due to the biological, cognitive, affective, and interpersonal vulnerabilities inherent to schizophrenia. Modifications to conventional substance abuse treatments must take into account the common features of schizophrenia—

low motivation and self-efficacy, cognitive deficits, and maladaptive interpersonal skills. These limitations heighten the importance of the treatment alliance (Ziedonis & D'Avanzo, 1998).

MET, Relapse Prevention, and Twelve Step Facilitation interventions are described in therapy manuals developed by Project MATCH, and these manuals are available free of charge from the National Clearinghouse on Alcohol and Drug Information (NCADI: 1-800/729-6686). Another useful training manual that is available through NCADI is a Treatment Improvement Protocol (TIP Number 9) on *Co-Existing Mental Illness and Substance Abuse*.

Both clinical experience and research findings have demonstrated the importance of developing a positive therapeutic alliance. Patients are more responsive when the therapist consistently acts as a nurturing and nonjudgmental ally (Siris & Docherty, 1990; Docherty, 1980; Frank & Gunderson, 1990; Grinspoon, Ewalt & Schader, 1972; Rogers, Gendlin et al., 1967; Sullivan, 1962; Ziedonis & D'Avanzo, 1998). Siris maintains that dually diagnosed schizophrenics also require a positive alliance, and that premature termination and psychiatric decline will follow from a "negative" alliance; that is, one based on fear, anger, or rejection. Working with the dually diagnosed patient also requires that the therapist be realistic and direct in addressing inconsistencies, but the manner in which they approached is crucial. For example, if a patient has a recent positive cocaine urine and yet denies any use during the past month, the clinician must be understanding of the initial stage of recovery, but point out the discrepancy. If there have been overall harm reduction gains, these should be recognized and other outcomes should be assessed.

A harm reduction philosophy can be helpful and realistic with the poorly motivated client while he or she remains uncommitted and ambivalent about the goal of total abstinence (Marlatt & Tapert, 1993; Carey, 1996; Ziedonis & Fisher, 1996). The patient who is in the precontemplation or contemplation stage of change often is unwilling to commit to total abstinence as a short-term goal. Keeping such a patient engaged in treatment often requires finding extrinsic motivators to further the development of the therapeutic alliance (these might include help with obtaining food, clothing, shelter, money management, vocational/training activities, social relationships, and the like) and the use of motivational interviewing to develop intrinsic motivation to stop using substances and to maintain compliance with psychiatric treatment.

Keeping patients engaged requires attempting to treat their schizophrenia and providing encouragement and other "rewards" for small steps toward reducing drug use. Evaluating outcomes other than total abstinence is required; for example, the clinician might assess the patient for reduced quantity and/or frequency of drug use, participation in treatment or other activities, compliance with medications, following up on short-term goals, and allowing family or significant others to be involved in treatment.

Carey has suggested a five-step "collaborative, motivational, harm reduction" approach for working with the dually diagnosed patient. This approach includes: (1) establishing and developing a working alliance, (2) helping the patient evaluate the cost-benefit ratio of continued substance use (decisional balance in MET), (3) helping the patient develop individual goals, (4) helping the patient build a supportive environment and lifestyle conducive to abstinence, and (5) helping the patient learn to anticipate and cope with crises (Carey, 1996).

Several similar dual diagnosis treatment approaches have been suggested. The Motivation-Based Dual Diagnosis Treatment (MBDDT) outlines a stage matching approach that combines mental health and addiction treatments based on the patient's motivational level, severity of illness, and dual diagnosis subtype. The MBDDT approach acknowledges the distinctive factors associated with the schizophrenia-addiction subtype (Ziedonis & Fisher, 1996). The model employs Prochaska and DiClemente's stages of change in the assessment of all patients, and matching treatment strategies and goals (e.g., abstinence or harm reduction, medication compliance, session attendance, etc.) to the individual's stage of motivation.

MET is a primary psychosocial approach for the patient with low motivation. When the traditional MET approach is used with dually diagnosed patients, clinicians should recognize the need for adjustments that include the following: (1) the clinician should play a more active role in offering practical, useful solutions to the patient's concerns about everyday survival—the clinician should not assume that dual diagnosis patients have the personal tools or social resources to solve problems effectively while actively engaged in their addiction; (2) MET should be formulated as a continuing component of treatment rather than being limited to the four sessions that were envisioned for non-schizophrenic substance users; (3) the decision balance intervention, a cornerstone of MET, should be employed so that it fully accounts for the experience of substance use in relation to another and more systematic problem—schizophrenia and medication compliance; and (4) the clinician should acknowledge that dually diagnosed individuals may not consistently accept the diagnosis of schizophrenia, may vary in their willingness to maintain medication for schizophrenia, and may have greater or lesser motivation to stop their substance use.

Attending to the role of motivation is important to the success of the treatment plan. Clinicians must work to strengthen patients' motivation while confronting the effects of schizophrenia and stressing the importance of medications in managing the schizophrenia.

Prochaska and DiClemente (1992) have defined motivation in relation to a five-stage scale (precontemplation, contemplation, preparation, action, and maintenance). A recent study drawing on this scale evaluated a group of 295 patients who were diagnosed with both schizophrenia and a substance use disorder, and concluded that over half could be described as "low motivated" (in the precontemplation or contemplation stage), with the degree of motivation relative to the substance and/or number of substances abused (Ziedonis & Trudeau, 1997). Of those patients who abused alcohol, 53% were assessed as "low motivation"; the figures for cocaine and marijuana were 65% and 73%, respectively. In another study, a simple five-point Likert scale of current motivation for treatment successfully predicted the dually diagnosed patient's likelihood of achieving abstinence (Ries & Ellingson, 1990).

Certain conditions may work to accelerate a patient's motivation to change through use of external motivators, a realization that led to the development of the Community Reinforcement Approach (CRA) (Higgins, Budney et al., 1994). CRA draws on behavioral therapy principles of contingencies, rewards, and consequences. Because external motivation is frequently lacking among the dually diagnosed, CRA searches out a range of possible motivators—disability income, probation, family, etc.—and employs those motivators to engage, support, and monitor patients in treatment.

Treatment must address not only the impact of low motivation, but also potential deficiencies in the cognitive skills known as Receiving-Processing-Sending (RPS) skills, which allow individuals to act on information in a coherent and productive manner (Ziedonis & D'Avanzo, 1998). These skills assume basic levels of attention, memory, and reality awareness. For individuals with schizophrenia, these levels are often lower than normal, so that the benefits traditional relapse prevention treatment, which is built on a cognitive learning model, are sharply reduced (Marlatt & Gordon, 1985). Thus, the treatment model must be modified and tailored to the dual diagnosis patient, switching the treatment emphasis from cognitive to behavioral approaches.

Traditionally, relapse prevention and Twelve Step facilitation have been employed in addiction settings with non-schizophrenic patients, most of whom have a range of social, interpersonal, and problem-solving skills that lead to self-esteem and self-efficacy (Bandura, 1977). Self-efficacy, in particular, is directly related to the change processes that influence maintenance and relapse (Marlatt & Gordon, 1985; DiClemente, Fairhurst & Piotrowski, 1995; Velicer, DiClemente et al., 1990). Relapse prevention and Twelve Step recovery can help individuals improve self-efficacy and self-esteem. Relapse prevention therapy tends to be administered in a cognitive therapy manner, and clinical experience suggests using a more action oriented behavioral approach. This approach benefits from using the behavioral learning principles of role plays, modeling, coaching, positive/negative feedback, and homework. Traditional psychiatric approaches of social skills training use this methodology in rehabilitation programs (Liberman, Mueser et al., 1986; Foy, Wallace & Liberman, 1983). The Liberman modules include psychosis symptom management, medication management, leisure skills, dating skills, etc. Traditional substance relapse prevention can be easily adapted to work with individuals with schizophrenia with a focus on addressing difficulties in communication and problem-solving.

Dual Diagnosis Relapse Prevention (DDRP) unites substance abuse relapse prevention and psychiatric social skills training (Ziedonis & Fisher, 1996; Ziedonis, Jaffe et al., 1991; Ziedonis, 1992). The resulting treatment bolsters the patients' sense of self-efficacy, improves their social skills, and gives them tools for seeing and coping with high-risk situations. All of the training is grounded in cognitive-behavioral theory and targets the schizophrenic's cognitive difficulties (attention span, reading skills, and ability to abstract). Their ability to communicate and solve problems is developed through role plays that can be introduced in both group and individual therapy, while their understanding and management of their substance use problems is improved through an emphasis on coping strategies; e.g., how to organize one's time. The therapist gives ongoing consideration to both substance abuse and psychiatric problems, monitors their interaction, and adjusts the treatment emphasis accordingly.

The Twelve Step approach is a spiritually based program that provides participants a guide for long-term addiction recovery. This approach has been modified for dually diagnosed individuals who often reported initial difficulty in engaging in twelve-step groups given perceived stigma towards individuals with serious mental illness and the group culture against any psychiatric medications. Dual Recovery Anonymous meetings (double trudgers, MICA, MISA, etc) can provide a bridge from traditional medical model treatments to the recovery model of Twelve Step philosophy. These meetings often occur within mental health settings or social houses. They encourage recovery for both problems and the importance of taking appropriately prescribed medications. Spiritual health also is a focus of the meetings, including connecting with a Higher Power, developing a sense of community, and finding meaning and purpose in life. Clinical experience has shown that individuals with a serious mental illness want to talk about spirituality and to develop a stronger sense of hope through being in recovery.

CONCLUSIONS

In conclusion, the major psychosocial interventions for substance use disorders—MET, relapse prevention, and Twelve Step approaches—require some retooling if they are to address the problems posed by schizophrenic patients. For such patients, the prognosis for long-term improvement and recovery depends on a treatment design that addresses both their addiction and their schizophrenia, that responds to the unique vulnerabilities (cognitive, affective, social, and biological) of the schizophrenic patient, and that maintains an empathic and collaborative approach. In most cases, treatment of this dual diagnosis subtype is best suited to the mental health setting, provided that mental health staff receive adequate training in substance abuse and dual diagnosis treatment strategies.

Staff training programs should develop basic dual diagnosis assessment and treatment competencies for all staff. Clinicians should have skills and knowledge in integrating mental health and addiction therapy approaches. The specific addiction therapies include motivational enhancement therapy, relapse prevention, and Twelve Step facilitation. The specific psychiatric approaches include social skills training and behavioral therapy. Clinicians should be aware of the relevant pharmacotherapies for both psychiatric and substance use disorders, including detoxification and maintenance. Medications that best treat schizophrenia include the newer atypical antipsychotics and depot neuroleptics. Other helpful strategies include behavioral contracting, community reinforcement approaches, social skills training, money management, peer support/counseling, vocational/educational counseling, and family/network therapies.

The chief challenge in treating this population is to fashion a two-pronged treatment that gives equal care to the schizophrenia and the substance abuse—a challenge that requires a systematic approach to issues that may be of lesser concern in other settings, such as housing, entitlements, rehabilitation, and community service. Clinicians who are optimistic, empathic, and hopeful are most helpful to patients in the recovery and treatment process. Dual diagnosis treatment addresses both problems simultaneously, conducts active outreach and case management efforts, attempts to increase client motivation for abstinence or harm reduction in a realistic manner, integrates mental health and substance abuse approaches, provides broad-based and comprehensive services, and remains flexible in responding to individual needs.

ACKNOWLEDGMENT: Supported by Grants RO1-DA09127 and K20-DA00193 from the National Institute on Drug Abuse.

REFERENCES

Adler LE, Hoffer LD & Wiser A (1993). Normalization of auditory physiology by cigarette smoking in schizophrenic patients. *American Journal of Psychiatry* 150:1856–1861.

Alterman AI, Ayre FR & Williford WO (1984). Diagnostic validation of conjoint schizophrenia and alcoholism. *Journal of Clinical Psychiatry* 45:300–303.

American Psychiatric Association (1996). APA Practice Guideline for the Treatment of Patients with Nicotine Dependence. *American Journal of Psychiatry* October.

American Psychiatric Association (1994). *Diagnostic and Statistical Manual of Mental Disorders, 4th Edition*. Washington, DC: American Psychiatric Press.

American Psychiatric Association (1987). *Diagnostic and Statistical Manual of Mental Disorders, 3rd Edition, Revised*. Washington, DC: American Psychiatric Press.

Ames F (1958). A clinical and metabolic study of acute intoxication with Cannabis sativa and its role in the model psychoses. *Journal of Mental Science* 104:972–999.

Anonymous (1993). *The Dual Recovery Book.* Center City, MN: Hazelden

Bandura A (1977). Self-efficacy: Toward a unifying theory of behavioral change. *Psychological Review* 84(2):191–215.

Bandura A (1996). Self-efficacy and future research directions. Presentation at Yale University, New Haven, CT, October.

Bartels SJ, Teague GB, Drake RE, Clark RE, Bush PW & Noordsy DL (1993). Substance abuse in schizophrenia: Service utilization and costs. *Journal of Nervous and Mental Disorders* 181:227–332.

Bauer LO (n.d.). Cocaine withdrawal: Neuropsychological aspects. Grant R01 DAOJ826-01. Rockville, MD: National Institute on Drug Abuse (unpublished data).

Beaubrun MH & Knight F (1973). Psychiatric assessment of 30 chronic users of cannabis and 30 matched controls. *American Journal of Psychiatry* 130:309–311.

Beitner-Johnson D & Nestler EJ (1992). Basic neurobiology of cocaine: Actions within the mesolimbic dopamine system. In TR Kosten & HD Leber (eds.) *Clinician's Guide to Cocaine Addiction: Theory, Research, and Treatment.* New York, NY: Guilford Press, 55–83.

Bell M, Lysaker P & Milstein R (1992). Object relations deficits in subtypes of schizophrenia. *Journal of Clinical Psychology* 48(4):433–444.

Bergin AE & Garfield SL (1995). *Handbook of Psychotherapy and Behavior Change, 4th Edition.* New York, NY: John Wiley & Sons, Inc.

Binder RL, Kazamatsuri H, Nishimura T & NcNiel DE (1987). Smoking and tardive dyskinesia. *Biological Psychiatry* 22:1280–1282.

Brady K, Anton R, Ballenger JC, Lydiard B, Adinoff B & Selander J (1990). Cocaine abuse among schizophrenic patients. *American Journal of Psychiatry* 147:1164–1167.

Brook MG (1984). Psychosis after cannabis abuse. *British Medical Journal* 288:1381.

Brunette MF, Mueser KT, Xie H & Drake RE (1997). Relationships between symptoms of schizophrenia and substance abuse. *Journal of Nervous and Mental Disease* 185:13–20.

Buckley PB, Thompson P, Way L & Meltzer HY (1994). Substance abuse among patients with treatment-resistant schizophrenia: Characteristics and implications for clozapine therapy. *American Journal of Psychiatry* 151:385–389.

Calen PL (1981). Parkinsonism provoked by alcoholism. *Annals of Neurology* 9:84–86.

Carey KB (1996). Substance use reduction in the context of outpatient psychiatric treatment: A collaborative, motivational, harm reduction approach. *Community Mental Health Journal* 32(3):291–306.

Carney P & Lipsedge M (1984). Psychosis after cannabis abuse. *British Medical Journal* 288:1381.

Chappel JN(1992). Effective use of alcoholics anonymous in treating patients. *Psychiatric Annals* 22(8):409–418.

Chaudry HR (1991). Cannabis psychosis following bhang ingestion. *British Journal of Addiction* 288:1075–1081.

Chopra G & Smith J (1974). Psychotic reactions following cannabis use in East Indians. *Archives of General Psychiatry* 30:24–27.

Cohen BD, Rosenbaum G, Luby ED & Gottlieb JS (1962). Comparison of phencyclidine hydrochloride (Sernyl®) with other drugs: Simulation of schizophrenic performance with phencyclidine hydrochloride (sernyl), lysergic acid diethylamide (LSD-25), and amobarbitol (Amytal) sodium, II: Symbolic and sequential thinking. *Archives of General Psychiatry* 1:651–656.

Cotman CW & Monaghan DT (1987). Chemistry and anatomy of excitatory amino acid systems. In HY Meltzer (ed.) *Psychopharmacology: The Third Generation of Progress.* New York, NY: Raven Press, 197–210.

Croop RS (1995). A multicenter safety study of naltrexone (Abstract 585). American Psychiatric Association Annual Meeting.

Davies BM & Beech HR (1960). The effect of 1-arylcyclodexylamine (sernyl) on twelve normal volunteers. *Journal of Mental Sciences* 106:912–924.

Davis JM, Metalon L, Watanabe MD & Blake (1994). Depot antipsychotic drugs: Place in therapy. *Drugs* 47(5):741–773.

DiClemente CC, Fairhurst SK & Piotrowski N (1995). Self-efficacy and addictive behaviors. In JE Maddux (ed.) *Self-Efficacy, Adaptation, and Adjustments: Theory, Research, and Application.* New York, NY: Plenum Press.

Dilsaver SC (1987). The pathopsychophysiologies of substance abuse and affective disorders: An integrative model. *Journal of Clinical Psychopharmacology* 7:1–10.

Dixon L, Haas G, Weiden PJ, Sweeney J & Frances AJ (1990). Acute effects of drug abuse in schizophrenic patient: Clinical observations and patients' self reports. *Schizophrenia Bulletin* 16:69–79.

Dixon L, Haas G, Weiden PJ, Sweeney J & Frances AJ (1990). Acute effects of drug abuse in schizophrenic patients. *Schizophrenia Bulletin* 16:69–79.

Dixon L, Haas G, Weiden PJ, Sweeney J & Frances AJ (1991). Drug abuse in schizophrenic patients: Clinical correlates and reasons for use. American Journal of Psychiatry 148:224–230.

Dixon L, Haas G, Weiden PJ, Sweeney J & Frances AJ (1991). Drug abuse in schizophrenic patients: Clinical correlates and reasons for use. *American Journal of Psychiatry* 148:224–230.

Dixon L & Rebori TA (1995). Psychosocial treatment of substance abuse in schizophrenic patients. In CL Shiriqui & HA Nasrallah (eds.) *Contemporary Issues in the Treatment of Schizophrenia.* Washington, DC: American Psychiatric Press.

Docherty JP (1980). The individual psychotherapies: Efficacy, syndrome-based treatments, and the therapeutic alliance. In A Lazare (ed.) *Outpatient Psychiatry: Di-*

agnosis and Treatment. Baltimore, MD: Williams & Wilkins.

Donahue C, Carter MJ, Bloem WD, Hirsch GL, Laasi N & Wallace C (1990). Assessment of interpersonal problem solving skills. *Psychiatry* 53:329–339.

Dougherty RJ (1997). Naltrexone in the treatment of alcohol dependent dual-diagnosed patients. Abstract in *Journal of Addictive Diseases* 16(2):107.

Drake RE, Antosca LM & Noordsy DL (1991). New Hampshire's specialized services for the dually diagnosed. In K Minkoff & RE Drake (eds.) *An Overview in Dual Diagnosis of Major Mental Illness and Substance Disorder*. San Francisco, CA: Jossey-Bass.

Drake RE & Noordsy DL (1994). Case management for people with coexisting severe mental disorder and substance use disorder. *Psychiatric Annals* 24(8):427–431.

Drake RE, Osher FC, Noordsy DL, Hurlbut SC, Teague GB & Beudett MS (1990). Diagnosis of alcohol use disorders in schizophrenia. *Schizophrenia Bulletin* 16:57–67.

Drake RE, Osher FC & Wallach MA (1989). Alcohol use and abuse in schizophrenia: a perspective community study. *Journal of Nervous and Mental Disease* 408–414.

Drake RE, Bartels SJ, Teague GB, Noordsy DL & Clark RE (1993). Treatment of substance abuse in severely mentally ill patients. *Journal of Nervous and Mental Disease* 181:606–611.

Ereshefsky L, Saklad SR & Watanabe T (1991). Thiothixene pharmacokinetic interactions: A study of hepatic enzyme inducers, clearance inhibitors, and demographic variables. *Journal of Clinical Psychopharmacology* 11:296–300.

Ereshefsky L (1996). Pharmacokinetics and drug interactions: Update for new antipsychotics. *Journal of Clinical Psychiatry* 57(Suppl 11):12–25.

Evans K & Sullivan JM (1990). Dual diagnosis: Counseling the mentally ill substance abuser. New York, NY: Guilford Press.

Fauman B, Aldinger G, Fauman M & Rosen P (1976). Psychiatric sequelae of phencyclidine abuse. *Clinical Toxicology* 9:529–538.

First MB, Spitzer RL, Gibbon M & Williams JBW (1995). Structured Clinical Interview for Axis I DSM-IV Disorders—Version 2.0. New York, NY: New York State Psychiatric Institute, Biometrics Research Department.

Fischer DE, Halikas JA, Baker JW & Smith JB (1975). Frequency and patterns of drug abuse in psychiatric patients. *Diseases of the Nervous System* 36(10):550–553.

Fischman MW & Schuster CR (1980). Cocaine effects in sleep-deprived humans. *Psychopharmacology* 72:1–8.

Foy DW, Wallace CJ & Liberman RP (1983). Advances in social skills training for chronic mental patients. In KD Craig & MJ McMahon (eds.) *Advances in Clinical Behavior Therapy*. New York, NY: Brunner/Mazel.

Frank AF & Gunderson JG (1990). The role of the therapeutic alliance in the treatment of schizophrenia: Relationship to course and outcome. *Archives of General Psychiatry*.

Freedman R, Adler LE & Bickford P (1994). Schizophrenia and nicotine receptors. *Harvard Review of Psychiatry* 2:179–192.

George TP, Sernyak MJ, Ziedonis DM & Woods SW (1995). Effects of clozapine on smoking in chronic schizophrenic outpatients. *Journal of Clinical Psychiatry* 56(8):344–346.

Ghodse H (1986). Cannabis psychosis. *British Journal of Addiction* 81:473–478.

Glassman AH (1993). Cigarette smoking: Implications for psychiatric illness. *American Journal of Psychiatry* 150:546–553.

Glazer WM & Morgenstern H (1988). Predictors of occurrence, severity, and course of TD in an outpatient population. *Journal of Clinical Psychopharmacology* 8:10S–16S.

Glazer WM & Kane JM (1992). Depot neuroleptic therapy: An underutilized treatment option. *Journal of Clinical Psychiatry* 53:426–433.

Goff DC, Henderson DC & Amico BS (1992). Cigarette smoking in schizophrenia: Relationship to psychopathology and medication side effects. *American Journal of Psychiatry* 149:1189–1194.

Grinspoon L, Ewalt JR & Schader RI (1972). *Schizophrenia: Pharmacotherapy and Psychotherapy*. Baltimore, MD: Williams & Wilkins.

Gross MM, Lewis E & Best S (1975). Quantitative changes of signs and symptoms associated with alcohol withdrawal: Incidence, severity, and circadian effects in experimental studies of alcoholics. *Advances in Experimental Biological Medicine* 59:615–631.

Hamera E, Schneider JK, Kraenzle J & Deviney S (1995). Alcohol, cannabis, nicotine, and caffeine use and symptom distress in schizophrenia. *Journal of Nervous and Mental Disease* 183(9):559–565.

Hedlund JL & Vieweg BW (1984). The Michigan Alcoholism Screening Test (MAST): A comprehensive review. *Journal of Operational Psychiatry* 15:55–65.

Hellerstein DJ & Meehan B (1987). Outpatient group therapy for schizophrenic substance abuses. *American Journal of Psychiatry* 144(10):1337–1339.

Helzer JE & Pryzbeck TR (1988). The co-occurence of alcoholism with other psychiatric disorders in the general population and its impact on treatment. *Journal of Studies on Alcohol* 49:219–224.

Higgins ST, Budney AJ, Bickel WK, Foerg FE, Donham R & Badger GJ (1994). Incentives improve outcome in outpatient behavioral treatment of cocaine dependence. *Archives of General Psychiatry* 51:568–76.

Hilgard ER & Bower GH (1975). *Theories of Learning*. Princeton, NJ: Prentice-Hall, Inc.

Hodel B & Brenner HD (1994). Cognitive therapy with schizophrenic patients: Conceptual basis, present state future directions. *Acta Psychiatry Scandinavia* 90(Suppl 384):108–115.

Hollister LE (1971). Actions of various marijuana derivatives in man. *Pharmacology Review* 23:349–357.

Horvath AO & Greenberg LS (19940. *The Working Alliance: Theory, Research, and Practice*. New York, NY: John Wiley & Sons.

Hughes JR, Hatsukami DK, Mitchell JE & Dahlgren LA (1986). Prevalence of smoking among psychiatric outpatients. *American Journal of Psychiatry* 143:993–997.

Hughes JR (1993). Possible effects of smoke-free inpatient units on psychiatric diagnosis and treatment. *Journal of Clinical Psychiatry* 54:109–114.

Isbell H (1967). Effects of delta-9-trans-tetrahydrocannabinol in man. *Psychopharmacology* 11:184–188.

Isbell H, Fraser HF & Wikler A (1955). An experimental study of the etiology of "rum fits" and delirium tremens. *Quarterly Journal of Studies on Alcohol* 16(Suppl):1–33.

Janowsky DS & Davis DM (1976). Methylphenidate, dextroamphetamine, and levamfetamine: Effects on schizophrenic symptoms. *Archives of General Psychiatry* 33:304–308.

Jarvik ME & Schneider NG (1992). Nicotine. In JH Lowinson, P Ruiz & RB Millman (eds.) *Substance Abuse: A Comprehensive Textbook, 2nd Ed.* Baltimore, MD: Williams & Wilkins.

Johnson R (1992). Mazindol augmentation of neuroleptics in cocaine abusers. APA 1993 New Research Program and Abstracts, 92.

Karon B & Vandenbos G (1981). *Psychotherapy of Schizophrenia: The Treatment of Choice*. Princeton, NJ: Jason Aronson, Inc.

Kaufman E (1989). The psychotherapy of dually diagnosed patients. *Journal of Substance Abuse Treatment* 6:9–18.

Keeler M, Ewing J & Rouse B (1971). Hallucinogenic effects of marijuana as currently used. *American Journal of Psychiatry* 128:213–216.

Keeler M, Reifler C & Liptzin M (1968). Spontaneious recurrence of marijuana effect. *American Journal of Psychiatry* 125:384–386.

Klerman R, Bauer LO, Coons HW, Lewis JL, Peloquin LJ, Perlmutter RA, Salzman LF & Strauss J (1984). Enhancing effect of methylphenidate on normal young adults cognitive process. *Psychopharmacology Bulletin* 20:3–9.

Knoedler W (1979). How training in community living programs helps its patients work. *New Directions in Mental Health Services* 2:57–66.

Kofoed L (1991). Assessment of comorbid psychiatric illness and substance disorders. *New Directions Mental Health Services* 50:43–55.

Kosten TR & Nestler EJ (1994). Clozapine attenuates cocaine conditioned place preference. *Life Sciences* 55(1):PL9–PL14.

Kosten TR (1989). Pharmacotherapeutic interventions for cocaine abuse: Matching patients to treatments. *Journal of Nervous Mental Disease* 177:379–389.

Lang AE (1982). Alcohol and Parkinson's disease. *Annals of Neurology* 12:254–256.

Larsen E (1985). *Stage II Recovery: Life Beyond Addiction*. San Francisco, CA: Harper Collins Publishers.

Lavin MR, Siris SG & Mason SE (1996). What is the clinical importance of cigarette smoking in schizophrenia? *American Journal on Addictions* 5:189–208.

Lehman H, Nair V & Kline N (1979). Beta-endorphin and naloxone in psychiatric patients. *American Journal of Psychiatry* 136:762–766.

Liberman RP, Mueser KT, Wallace CJ, Jacobs HE, Eckman T & Massel HK (1986). Training skills in the psychiatrically disabled: Learning coping and competence. *Schizophrenia Bulletin* 12:631–647.

Liberman RP, Wallace C, Blackwell G, Eckman TA, Vaccaro JV & Kuehnel TG (1993). Innovations in skills training for the seriously mentally ill: The UCLA social and independent living skills modules. *Innovative Research* 2:43–60.

Luborsky L (1994). Therapeutic alliances as predictors of psychotherapy outcomes. In AO Horvath & LS Greenberg (eds.) The Working Alliance: Theory, Research, and Practice. New York, NY: John Wiley & Sons.

Luby ED (1959). Study of a new schizophrenomimetic drug—Sernyl®. *Archives of Neurologic Psychiatry* 81:363–369.

Lundberg GD, Gupta RC & Montgomery SH (1976). Phencyclidine: Patterns seen in street drug analysis. *Clinical Toxicology* 9:503–511.

Lysaker P, Bell M, Beam-Goulet J & Milstein R (1994). Relationship of positive and negative symptoms to cocaine abuse in schizophrenia. *Journal of Nervous and Mental Disease* 182(2):109–122.

Maany I, O'Brien CP & Woody G (1987). Interaction between thiodiazine and naltrexone. *American Journal of Psychiatry* 144:966.

Marlatt GA & Gordan JR (1985). *Relapse Prevention: Maintenance Strategies in the Treatment of Addictive Behaviors*. New York, NY: Guilford Press.

Maxwell S & Shinderman MS (1997). Naltrexone in the treatment of dually-diagnosed patients. Abstract in *Journal of Addictive Diseases* 16(2):125.

McClellan TA, Woody GE & O'Brien CP (1979). Development of psychiatric illness in drug abusers. *The New England Journal of Medicine* 301(24):1310–1314.

McDermott B (1995). Development of an instrument for assessing self-efficacy in schizophrenic spectrum disorders. *Journal of Clinical Psychology* 51.

McEvoy J, Freudenreich O, Levin ED & Rose JE (1995). Haloperidol increases smoking in patients with schizophrenia. *Psychopharmacology* 119(1):124–126.

McEvoy J, Freudenreich O, McGee M & VanderZwaag C (1995). Clozapine decreases smoking in patients with chronic schizophrenia. *Biological Psychiatry* 37(8):550–552.

McGovern MP, Kilgore KM, Melon WH & Golden DL (1993). Object relations and social functioning of schizophrenic and borderline patients: A cross-sectional developmental perspective. *Journal of Clinical Psychology* 49(3):319–326.

Mendelson JH & LaDou L (1964). Experimentally induced chronic intoxication and withdrawal in alcoholics. *Quarterly Journal of Studies on Alcohol* 2(Suppl):1–39.

Miller WR & Rollnick S (1991). *Motivational Interviewing: Preparing People to Change Addictive Behavior.* New York, NY: Guilford Press.

Miller WR, Zweben A, DiClemente CC & Rychtarik RG (1992). *Motivational Enhancement Therapy Manual.* Rockville, MD: National Institute on Drug Abuse.

Minkoff K (1989). An integrated treatment model for dual diagnosis of psychosis and addiction. *Hospital and Community Psychiatry* 40(10):1031–1036.

Minkoff K (1994). Models for addiction treatment in psychiatric populations. *Psychiatric Annals* 24(8):412–417.

Mueser KT, Bellack AS & Blanchard JJ (1992). Comorbidity of schizophrenia and substance abuse: Implications for treatment. *Journal of Consulting and Clinical Psychology* 47:1102–1114.

Mueser KT & Gingerich S (1994). *Coping with Schizophrenia.* Oakland, CA: Harbinger Publications.

Mueser KT, Nishith P, Tracy JI, DeGirolamo J & Molinaro M (1995). Expectations and motives for substance use in schizophrenia. *Psychiatric Clinics of North America* 21(3):367–378.

Mueser KT, Yarnold PR, Levinson DF, Singh H, Bellack AS, Kee K, Morrison RL & Yalalam KG (1990). Prevalence of substance abuse in schizophrenia: Demographic and clinical correlates. *Schizophrenia Bulletin* 16:31–56.

Naber D, Nedopil N & Eben E (1984). No correlation between neuroleptic-induced increase of β-endorphin serum level and therapeutic efficacy in schizophrenia. *British Journal of Psychiatry* 144:651–653.

Negrete JC, Knapp WP & Douglas DE (1986). Cannabis affects the severity of schizophrenic symptoms: Results of a clinical survey. *Psychological Medicine* 16:515–520.

Nikkel RE (1994). Areas of skill training for persons with mental illness and substance use disorders: Building skills for successful community living. *Community Mental Health Journal* 30(1).

Noordsy DL (1991). Group intervention techniques for people with dual disorders. *Psychosocial Rehabilitation Journal* 15(2):67–78.

O'Malley S (1992). Naltrexone and coping skills therapy for alcohol dependence. *Archives of General Psychiatry* 49:881–887.

Olivera AA, Kiefer MW & Manley NK (1990). Tardive dyskinesia in psychiatric patients with substance use disorders. *American Journal of Drug and Alcohol Abuse* 16(1&2):57–66.

O'Malley S, Adams M, Heaton RK & Gawin FH (1992). Neuropsychological impairment in chronic cocaine abusers. *American Journal of Drug Alcohol Abuse* 18(2):131–144.

Osher FC & Kofoed L (1989). Treatment of patients with psychiatric and psychoactive substance abuse disorders. *Hospital and Community Psychiatry* 40:1025–1030.

Penn DL & Mueser KT (1996). Research update on the psychosocial treatment of schizophrenia. *American Journal of Psychiatry* 153(5):607–617.

Pepper B, Kirshner MC & Ryglewicz H (1981). The young adult chronic patient: Overview of a population. *Hospital and Community Psychiatry* 32:463–467.

Pickworth WB (1991). Assessment of mazindol of abuse liability. *Problems of Drug Dependence 1990 (NIDA Research Monograph 119).* Rockville, MD: National Institute on Drug Abuse, 443.

Prochaska JO, DiClemente CC & Norcross JC (1992). In search of how people change: Applications to addictive disorders. *American Psychologist* 47:1102–1114.

Prochaska JO & DiClemente CC (1983). Stages and processes of self- change of smoking: Toward an integrative model of change. *Journal of Consulting and Clinical Psychology* 51(3):390–395.

Rao S, Ziedonis DM & Kosten TR (1995). The pharmacotherapy for cocaine dependence. *Psychiatric Annals* 25:363–368.

Regier DA, Farmer ME, Rae DS, Locke BZ, Keith SJ, Judd LL & Goodwin FK (1990). Comorbidity of mental disorders with alcohol and other drug abuse. *Journal of the American Medical Association* 264:2511–2518.

Renault P (1974). Repeat administration of marijuana smoke to humans. *Archives of General Psychiatry* 31:95–102.

Ries RK & Ellingson T (1990). A pilot assessment at 1 month of 17 dual diagnosis patients. *Hospital and Community Psychiatry* 41:1230–1233.

Ritz MC et al. (1987). Cocaine receptors on dopamine transporters are related to self-administration of cocaine. *Science* 44:660–669.

Roberts LJ, Shaner A, Eckman TA, Tucker DE & Vaccaro JV (1992). Effectively treating stimulant-abusing schizophrenics: Mission impossible. *New Directions in Mental Health Services* 53:55–65.

Rogers CR, Gendlin EG, Kiesler DJ & Truza CB (1967). *The Therapeutic Relationship and Its Impact: A Study of Psychotherapy with Schizophrenics.* Madison, WI: University of Wisconsin Press.

Rosenthal RN, Hellerstein DJ & Miner CR (1992). A model of integrated services for outpatient treatment of patients with comorbid schizophrenia and addictive disorders. *The American Journal on Addictions* 1(4):339–348.

Rothman RB (1990). High affinity dopamine reuptake inhibitors as potential cocaine antagonists: A strategy for drug development. *Life Sciences* 46:PL17–PL21.

Rottanburg D (1982). Cannabis associated psychosis with hypomanic features. *Lancet* ii:1364–1366.

Ryan C & Butters N (1982). Cognitive effects in alcohol abuse. In B Kissin & H Begleiter (eds.) *The Biology of Alcoholism*. New York, NY: Plenum Press, 223–250.

Satel JA & Lieberman JA (1991). Schizophrenia and substance abuse. *Psychiatric Clinics of North America* 16(2):401–412.

Sato M (1990). A lasting vulnerability to psychosis in patients with previous methamphetamine psychosis. *Annals of the New York Academy of Science* 654:160–170.

Schneier FR & Siris SG (1987). A review of psychoactive substance use and abuse in schizophrenia: Patterns of drug choice. *Journal of Nervous and Mental Disease* 175(11):641–652.

Schollar E (1993). The long term treatment of the dually diagnosed. In J Solomon, S Zimberg & E Schollar (eds.) *Dual Diagnosis: Evaluation, Treatment, Training, and Program Development*. New York, NY: Plenum Medical Book Co.

Schuckit MA (1982). The history of psychotic symptoms in alcoholics. *Journal of Clinical Psychiatry* 43:53–57.

Scott DF (1969). Alcoholic hallucinosis. *International Journal of the Addictions* 4:319–330.

Seibyl J (1993). Person communication on mazindol study.

Serper MR, Alpert M, Richardson NA, Dickson S, Dickson S, Allen MH & Werner A (1995). Clinical effects of recent cocaine use on patients with acute schizophrenia. *American Journal of Psychiatry* 152(10):1464–1469.

Sevy S, Kay SR, Opler LA & van Pragg HM (1990). Significance of cocaine history in schizophrenia. *Journal of Nervous and Mental Disease* 178:642–648.

Shaner A, Khalsa E, Roberts L, Wilkins J, Anglin D & Shih-Chao H (1993). Unrecognized cocaine use among schizophrenic patients. *American Journal of Psychiatry* 150:758–762.

Shaner A, Roberts LJ, Racenstein JM, Eckman TA, Tsuang JW & Tucker DE (1996). Sources of diagnostic uncertainty among chronically psychotic cocaine abusers. 149th Annual Meeting of the American Psychiatric Association, New York, NY, May 4–9.

Shein HM (1990). Loneliness and interpersonal isolation: Focus for therapy with schizophrenic patients. *American Journal of Psychotherapy*.

Shen WW (1984). Extrapyramidal symptoms associated with alcohol withdrawal. *Biological Psychiatry* 19:1037–1043.

Siris S (1990). Pharmacological treatment of substance abusing schizophrenic patients. *Schizophrenia Bulletin* 16:111–122.

Siris SG & Docherty JP (1990). Psychosocial management of substance abuse in schizophrenia. In MI Herz, JP Docherty, SK Klein (eds.) *Handbook of Schizophrenia, Volume 5. Psychosocial Therapies*.

Solomon J, Zimberg S & Schollar E (1993). *Dual Diagnosis: Evaluation, Treatment, Training, and Program Development*. New York, NY: Plenum Medical Book Co.

Strakowski SM, Tohen M, Flaum M & Amador X (1994). Substance abuse in psychotic disorders: Associations with affective syndromes. *Schizophrenia Research* 14(1):73–81.

Sullivan HS (1962). *Schizophrenia as a Human Process*. New York, NY: W.W. Norton & Co.

Tabakoff B & Hoffman PL (1996). Alcohol addiction: An enigma among us. *Neuron* 16:909–912.

Talbott JA & Teague JW (1969). Marijuana psychosis. *Journal of the American Medical Association* 210:299–305.

Tart CT (1970). Marijuana intoxication: Common experiences. *Nature* 226:701–704.

Taylor D & Warner R (1962). Does substance use precipitate the onset of functional psychosis? *Social Work and Social Science Review* 5(1):64–75.

Tennant FS & Groesbeck CJ (1972). Psychiatric effect of hashish. *Archives of General Psychiatry* 27:133–136.

Test MA & Wallisch LS & Allness DJ (1989). Substance use in young adults with schizophrenic disorders. *Schizophrenia Bulletin* 15:465–476.

Tracy JI, Josiassen C & Bellack AS (1995). Neuropsychology of dual diagnosis: Understanding the combined effects of schizophrenia and substance use disorders. *Clinical Psychology Review* 15(2):67–97.

Van Kammen DP, Mann LS, Sternbert DE, Scheinin M, Ninan PT & Marder SR (1982). Dopamine-beta-hydroxylase activity and homovanillic acid in spinal fluid of schizophrenics with brain atrophy. *Science* 220:974–976.

Vanover KE, Piercey MF & Woolverton WL (1993). Evaluation of the reinforcing and discriminative stimulus effects of cocaine in combination with (+)-AJ76 or clozapine. *Journal of Pharmacology and Experimental Therapy* 266:780–789.

Velicer WF, DiClemente CC, Rossi JS & Prochaska JO (1990). Relapse situations and self-efficacy: An integrative model. *Addictive Behaviors* 15:271–283.

Victor M & Hope JM (1958). The phenomenon of auditory hallucinations in chronic alcoholism. *Journal of Nervous and Mental Disease* 126:451–48.

Volpicelli JR, Alterman AL, Hayashida M & O'Brien CP (1992). Naltrexone in treatment of alcohol dependence. *Archives of General Psychiatry* 49:876–880.

Wallace CJ, Nelson CJ & Liberman RP (1980). A review and critique of social skills training with schizophrenic patients. *Schizophrenia Bulletin* 6:42–63.

Waskow IE (1970). Psychological effects of tetrahydrocannibinol. *Archives of General Psychiatry* 22:97–107.

Weiden P, Aquila R & Standard J (1996). Atypical antipsychotic drugs and long-term outcome in schizophrenia. *Journal of Clinical Psychiatry* 57(Supp 11):53–60.

Westermeyer JW (1992). Schizophrenia and drug abuse. In A Tasman & M Riba (eds.) *Review of Psychiatry, Vol 11*. Washington DC: American Psychiatric Press, 379–401.

Wiesbeck GA & Taeschner KL (1991). A cerebral computed tomography study of patients with drug-induced psychoses. *European Archives of Psychiatry and Clinical Neuroscience* 241:88–90.

Wilkins JN (1998). Pharmacotherapy of schizophrenic patients with comorbid substance abuse. *Schizophrenia Bulletin*. In press.

Zaretsky A, Rector NA, Seeman MV & Fornazzari X (1993). Current cannabis use and tardive dyskinesia. *Schizophrenia Research* 11(1):3–8.

Ziedonis D, Richardson T, Lee E, Petrakis I & Kosten T (1992). Adjunctive desipramine in the treatment of cocaine abusing schizophrenics. *Psychopharmacology Bulletin* 28(3):309–314.

Ziedonis DM & Fisher W (1996). Motivation-based assessment and treatment of substance abuse in patients with schizophrenia. *Directions in Psychiatry* 16(11):1–8.

Ziedonis DM & George TP (1997). Schizophrenia and nicotine dependence: A report of a pilot smoking cessation program and review of the literature. *Schizophrenia Bulletin* 23(2):247–254.

Ziedonis DM, Jaffe A, Davis E, Petrakis I & Hogan I (1991). Relapse prevention group therapy is effective in the treatment of mentally ill substance abusers. In 1991 New Research Program and Abstracts. Washington DC: American Psychiatric Association.

Ziedonis DM, Kosten TR & Glazer W (1994). The impact of drug abuse on psychopathology and movement disorders in chronic psychotic outpatients. In L Harris (ed.) *Problems of Drug Dependence 1992 (NIDA Research Monograph 153)*.

Ziedonis DM, Kosten TR & Glazer WM (1992). The impact of drug abuse on psychotic outpatients. New Research Program and Abstracts, 103. Washington DC: American Psychiatric Association.

Ziedonis DM & Kosten TR (1991). Pharmacotherapy improves treatment outcome in depressed cocaine addicts. *Journal of Psychoactive Drugs* 23(4):417–425.

Ziedonis DM & Trudeau K (1997). Motivation to quit using substances among individuals with schizophrenia: Implications for a motivation based treatment model. *Schizophrenia Bulletin* 23(2):229–238.

Ziedonis DM (1995). Substance abuse prevention strategies for psychiatric patients. In RH Coombs & DM Ziedonis DM (eds.) *Handbook on Drug Abuse Prevention: A Comprehensive Strategy to Prevent the Abuse of Alcohol and Other Drugs*. Boston, MA: Allyn & Bacon.

Ziedonis DM (1992). Comorbid psychopathology and cocaine addiction. In TR Kosten TR & HD Kleber (eds.) *Clinician's Guide to Cocaine Addiction: Theory, Research and Treatment*. New York, NY: Guilford Press, 337–360.

Ziedonis DM, Kosten TR, Glazer WM & Frances RJ (1994). Nicotine dependence and schizophrenia. *Hospital and Community Psychiatry* 45:204–206.

Ziedonis DM & D'Avanzo K (1998). Schizophrenia and substance abuse. In B Rounsaville & H Kranzler (eds). *Dual Diagnosis*. New York, NY: Marcel Dekker.

Zisook S, Heaton R, Moranville J, Kuck J, Jernigan T & Braff D (1992). Past substance abuse and clinical course of schizophrenia. *American Journal of Psychiatry* 149:552–553.

CHAPTER 5

Attention-Deficit/Hyperactivity Disorder, Intermittent Explosive Disorder, and Eating Disorders

Frances Rudnick Levin, M.D.
Stephen J. Donovan, M.D.

Attention-Deficit/Hyperactivity Disorder
Intermittent Explosive Disorder
Eating Disorders

This chapter examines three common psychiatric problems that have their antecedents in childhood and/or adolescence and have a connection with substance use: (1) attention-deficit/hyperactivity disorder (ADHD), (2) intermittent explosive disorder or explosive aggression and (3) eating disorders.

Attention-deficit/hyperactivity disorder (ADHD) is developmental, in that it is commonly diagnosed and treated in children and can persist into adulthood. Much of the recent research has shown that the same or similar criteria can be used to identify adults with persistent ADHD and that these adults may benefit from psychostimulant medication. Given that ADHD pathology may derive either from a delay in maturation of function or from an absence of function, it is not surprising that most children "grow out" of the problem (Mannuzza, Klein et al., 1991, 1993), whereas other do not.

Aggression, although poorly categorized in the current nosology, also has a profound impact on development. Children who are still throwing tantrums in the first grade are tracked into classrooms where they are exposed to other aggressive children. This inbreeding of aggression has fateful consequences (Kellam, 1997). Some forms of temper dyscontrol probably represent developmental delay and some, deviant development.

Other developmental disorders linked with substance abuse include the eating disorders. These disorders seem to have an intimate but obscure connection to female puberty, and clearly can change adolescent development in a deviant direction.

Development does not simply occur in childhood or adolescence but continues throughout life (Erikson, 1950). Erikson's model makes "intimacy versus isolation" the crisis of young adulthood. It is easy to imagine how the disorders discussed here would make matter worse, even in the absence of substance abuse. As comorbidities accumulate, the life trajectory may become even more warped. Identifying comorbidity thus is critical to any effort to improve traditional outcomes (as measured by treatment retention and reduction in drug use or symptom severity); it also may help individuals master age-appropriate developmental tasks.

ATTENTION-DEFICIT/ HYPERACTIVITY DISORDER

Diagnostic Criteria. *Childhood ADHD:* Attention-deficit/hyperactivity disorder (ADHD) is characterized by inattention, impulsivity, and hyperactivity. The American Psychiatric Association has changed the diagnostic criteria (and even the name) of this disorder with each revision of its *Diagnostic and Statistical Manual of Mental Disorders* (1980, 1987, 1994). This has led to ambiguities, misunderstandings and problems with generalizability of findings. Table 1 provides the criteria for childhood ADHD in the fourth edition of the *Diagnostic and Statistic Manual* (*DSM-IV*; American Psychiatric Association, 1994). Importantly, the current criteria require that some symptoms have caused impairment prior to the age of seven and that impairment must occur in more than one setting. This emphasizes both the developmental aspect of the disorder and the fact that childhood behavior problems often are situation-bound. The more settings in which de-

TABLE 1. DSM-IV Criteria for Attention-Deficit/Hyperactivity Disorder

A. Either (1) or (2):

(1) six (or more) of the following symptoms of inattention have persisted for at least 6 months to a degree that is maladaptive and inconsistent with developmental level:

Inattention

(a) often fails to give close attention to details or makes careless mistakes in schoolwork, work on other activities
(b) often has difficulty sustaining attention in task or play activities
(c) often does not seem to listen when spoken to directly
(d) often does not follow through on instructions and fails to finish schoolwork, chores, or duties in the workplace (not due to oppositional behavior or failure to understand instructions)
(e) often has difficulty organizing tasks and activities
(f) often avoids, dislikes, or is reluctant to engage in tasks that require sustained mental effort (such as schoolwork or homework)
(g) often loses things necessary for tasks or activities (e.g., toys, school assignments, pencils, books, or tools)
(h) is often easily distracted by extraneous stimuli
(i) is often forgetful in daily activities

(2) six (or more) of the following symptoms of hyperactivity-impulsivity have persisted for at least 6 months to a degree that is maladaptive and inconsistent with developmental level:

Hyperactivity

(a) often fidgets with hands or feet or squirms in seat
(b) often leaves seat in classroom or in other situations in which remaining seated is expected
(c) often runs about or climbs excessively in situations in which it is inappropriate (in adolecents or adults, may be limited to a subjective feeling of restlessness)
(d) often has difficulty playing or engaging in leisure activities quietly
(e) is often "on the go" or often act as if "driven by a motor"
(f) often talks excessively

Impulsivity

(g) often blurts out answers before questions have been completed
(h) often has difficulty awaiting turn
(i) often interrupts or intrudes on others (e.g., butts into conversations or games)

B. Some hyperactive-impulsive or inattentive symptoms that caused impairment were present before age 7 years.

C. Some impairment from the symptoms is present in two or more settings (e.g., at school [or work] and at home).

D. There must be clear evidence of clinically significant impairment in social, academic, or occupational functioning.

E. The symptoms do not occur exclusively during the course of a Pervasive Developmental Disorder, Schizophrenia, or other Psychotic Disorder and are not better accounted for by another mental disorder (e.g., Mood Disorder, Anxiety Disorder, Dissociative Disorder, or a Personality Disorder).

Code based on type:

Atention-Deficit/Hyperactivity Disorder, Combined Type: if both Criteria A1 and A2 are met for past 6 months

Attention-Deficit/Hyperactivity Disorder, Predominantly Inattentive Type: if Criteria A1 is met but Criterion A2 is not met for the past 6 months

Attention-Deficit/Hyperactivity Disorder, Predominantly Hyperactive-Impulsive Type: if criterion A2 is met but not Criterion A1 is not met for the past 6 months

Coding note: For individuals (especially adolescents and adults) who currently have symptoms that no longer meet full criteria, "In Partial Remission" should be specified.

viant behavior occurs, the more justified one is in saying that the behavior interferes with the child's functioning and therefore deserves a diagnosis.

Adult ADHD: In order to meet *DSM-IV* criteria for adult ADHD, an individual needs to have met the criteria for childhood ADHD. Adults who have ADHD symptoms but who no longer have at least six symptoms of hyperactivity-impulsivity or inattention are considered to be "in partial remission." Some clinical researchers have developed other criteria to define adult ADHD, most notably, the "Utah Criteria" (Wender & Garfinkel, 1989). The revised Utah Criteria consist of seven symptoms and require at least one of the first two symptoms and at least four of the seven total symptoms for a diagnosis of adult ADHD. Symptoms include: (1) inattention persisting from childhood, (2) hyperactivity persisting from childhood, (3) inability to complete tasks, (4) impaired interpersonal relationships or inability to sustain relationships over time, (5) affective lability, (6) explosive temper, and (7) stress intolerance. Spencer and colleagues (1994) note that because the Utah Criteria include symptoms that are not part of the *DSM-IV* criteria (such as mood lability and anxiety), they may have led to the incorrect assumption that the core childhood symptoms do not need to be present in adulthood. One way to reconcile the two diagnostic systems is to recognize that the core symptoms of ADHD remain a crucial element of the adult disorder; however, additional psychiatric symptoms (and disorders) often are found among adults with ADHD.

Validity of the Adult ADHD Diagnosis: Before discussing the association of ADHD and substance abuse, it is crucial to emphasize that, until recently, clinicians argued as to whether or not the adult syndrome was a valid disorder. The validity of a clinical diagnosis requires: (1) descriptive validity: that is, characteristic signs and symptoms; (2) predictive validity: that is, a specific course of illness and treatment response; and (3) construct validity: that is, data suggesting that an underlying etiology or pathophysiology exists (Spitzer & Williams, 1985). Prevalence and prospective studies (Weiss, Hechtman et al. 1985; Morrison, 1980; Biederman, Wilens et al., 1995; Mannuzza, Klein et al., 1993), family-genetic studies (Morrison, 1980; Biederman, Wilens et al., 1995), neuroimaging studies (Zametkin, Nordahl et al., 1990), and treatment studies (Spencer, Wilens et al., 1995; Wilens, Biederman et al., 1996) all provide data to support the three types of validity described above. Spencer and colleagues (1994) review this evidence and argue (convincingly, in the authors' opinion) that adult ADHD is a distinct clinical entity. For clinicians, it is important to accept the validity of the adult ADHD diagnosis, or they will not think to look for it. ADHD clearly is not a benign condition, and it has a plausible connection to substance use.

Possible Associations of Substance Abuse and ADHD. Meyer (1986) describes several possible relationships that may exist between addictive behavior and coexisting psychopathology. These relationships have been modified for ADHD (Levin & Kleber, 1995); they include:

- ADHD may be a risk factor for substance use disorders.
- ADHD and substance use disorders may be associated because they share some of the same risk factors.
- ADHD and substance use disorders may be associated because they specifically interact to increase each other's severity.
- ADHD symptoms may emerge as a consequence of substance use and persist into remission.
- ADHD and substance use disorders may not be specifically related and evidence to the contrary may simply be due to ascertainment bias; i.e., an individual is more likely to come to attention if he or she has two rather than one disorder, but the disorders need not be related in any other way.

Combined data from epidemiologic, prospective, and descriptive studies have helped to elucidate the relationships that exist between substance use disorders and adult ADHD.

Prevalence Studies: Within the general population, several large epidemiologic studies have found that 3% to 9% of children have ADHD (Szatmari, 1992). Unfortunately, prevalence rates of adult ADHD have not been captured in large epidemiologic surveys such as the Epidemiologic Catchment Area (ECA) study or the National Comorbidity Study (NCS). Given that 10% to 50% of affected children continue to have ADHD symptoms into adulthood (Weiss & Hechtman, 1986; Mannuzza, Klein et al., 1991), one would predict that the estimated rates for adult ADHD in the general population would be <1% to 5%. Alternatively, both the ECA Study and the NCS obtained prevalence rates for substance use disorders within the general population and found that lifetime rates for substance abuse or dependence ranged from 17% to 27% (Regier, Farmer et al., 1990; Kessler, McGonagle et al., 1994). Based on these prevalence rates, it can be determined whether substance use disorders are overrepresented among individuals seeking treatment (or not seeking treatment) for their ADHD symptoms, as well as whether adult ADHD is overrepresented among populations seeking substance abuse treatment. Biederman and colleagues (1995) have found that lifetime prevalence rates for substance use disorders among adults with ADHD was 52%, compared with 27% in comparison subjects. This elevated rate among individuals with adult ADHD is higher than the rates expected on the basis of the NCS and ECA data and suggests that an association between the two disorders may exist.

Although it is somewhat less clear, this association also appears to exist among substance abusers seeking treatment. Table 2 provides a list of studies in which psychiatric diagnoses in this population were based on *DSM* criteria. Interestingly, the pharmacologic treatment trials found that few of the patients entering treatment had childhood ADHD (Gawin, Kleber et al., 1989; Weddington, Brown et al., 1991) or residual ADHD (Gawin & Kleber, 1986; *DSM-III* nomenclature). These studies were not specifically designed to assess prevalence rates for various psychiatric disorders; therefore, certain diagnoses such as ADHD may have been overlooked. Moreover, individuals with ADHD may have been excluded from entering pharmacologic treatment protocols, not because of their ADHD symptoms, but because they had other comorbidity, such as depression. It is less obvious why Weiss and colleagues (1988) obtained low rates of adult ADHD among cocaine abusers and other drug abusers. One possible explanation is that prevalence rates were based on a clinical rather than a structured interview and this approach may have led to underdiagnosis. Further, the "diagnostic climate" at the time was not receptive toward diagnosing ADHD adult symptoms as a separate diagnostic entity.

Interestingly, Wood and colleagues (1983) found that among alcoholics seeking treatment, 33% had residual ADD (*DSM-III* criteria). Other prevalence studies have found elevated rates of childhood ADHD among different groups of substance abusers (Eyre, Rounsaville & Kleber, 1982; Rounsaville, Anton et al., 1991). However, there are no recently published data on adult ADHD prevalence rates using structured interviews in substance abusers. Levin and colleagues (Levin, Evans & Kleber, 1998a) recently completed a prevalence study in which cocaine abusers seeking treatment were evaluated for childhood and adult ADHD. Although they obtained a prevalence rate for childhood ADHD that was substantially lower than the rate found by Rounsaville and colleagues (1991)—i.e., 13% versus 35%—both rates are higher than the rate estimated in the general population. The prevalence of adult ADHD symptoms in a sample of treatment-seeking cocaine abusers ranged from 10% to 15% (Levin, Evans & Kleber, 1998a). The lower figure represents strict *DSM-IV* criteria for adult ADHD; the upper includes all individuals with clinically significant ADHD symptoms persisting from childhood.

TABLE 2. Prevalence Rate of ADHD Among Substance Abusers

Eyre et al., 1992	157 opiate abusers seeking treatment	Childhood ADHD 22%
Wood et al., 1983	33 Alcoholics seeking treatment	ADD, residual type 33%
Weiss et al., 1988	149 Cocaine abusers and 293 other drug abusers seeking treatment	ADD, residual type 5% for cocaine abusers, 1% other drug abusers
Gawin and Kleber, 1986	30 Cocaine abusers seeking pharmacologic treatment	ADD, residual type 3%
Gawin et al., 1989	72 Cocaine abusers seeking pharmacologic treatment	Childhood ADHD 0–4%
Weddington et al., 1989	54 Cocaine abusers seeking pharmacologic treatment	Childhood ADHD 0–5%
Rounsaville et al., 1991	298 Cocaine abusers seeking treatment	Childhood ADHD 35%
Carroll and Rounsaville, 1993	101 Cocaine abusers not seeking treatment	Childhood ADHD 24%
Levin et al., 1998a (in press)	281 Cocaine abusers seeking treatment	Childhood ADHD 13%, Adult and subthreshold ADHD 10–15%

One may ask if the association between ADHD and substance abuse exists only within treatment samples or whether it also is found in the general population. Carroll and Rounsaville (1993) found that the prevalence of childhood ADHD was lower among cocaine abusers not seeking treatment compared with those who were seeking treatment (22% versus 35%). However, the percentage remained higher than expected rates in the general population. Similarly, non-treatment-seeking adults with ADHD were significantly more likely to have alcohol or drug dependence than were non-treatment seeking adults who did not have histories of ADHD (Biederman, Faraone et al., 1993). Taken together, these studies suggest that ADHD and substance abuse are not independent disorders and that their association is not due to ascertainment bias. Of course, the relationship of these disorders may vary depending on the individual.

Prospective Studies: Earlier prospective studies suggested that a medicating factor, specifically conduct disorder, needed to be present for substance abuse to occur. In fact, there is substantial evidence to suggest that individuals diagnosed with childhood ADHD who also have conduct disorder as children are more likely to develop problematic substance use (Gittelman, Mannuzza et al., 1985; Mannuzza, Klein et al., 1991; Thompson, Riggs et al., 1996). However, it also is true that adolescents with ADHD may begin to use drugs even in the absence of conduct disorder. Similarly, adults diagnosed with adult ADHD are more likely to have a substance use disorder if they have antisocial personality disorder (ASP). However, a substantial proportion of individuals with adult ADHD will have an ongoing substance use disorder in the absence of ASP (Biederman, Wilens et al., 1995; Mannuzza, Klein et al., 1993). These studies suggest that, although conduct disorder and ASP may confer a substantial risk of developing a substance use disorder, a critical factor for having an ongoing substance use problem in adulthood is the persistence of ADHD symptoms. Once regular use is established, ADHD symptoms may, in and of themselves, increase the likelihood of heavy and problematic use.

Descriptive Studies: There are limited data regarding how ADHD and substance use disorders impact on each other. Carroll and Rounsaville (1993) have compared the clinical course of cocaine abuse among individuals with and without childhood histories of ADHD. Those with childhood ADHD have an earlier onset of regular cocaine use, more frequent and intense cocaine use, and have greater lifetime treatment exposure. Similarly, chronic drug use may exacerbate ADHD symptoms or may produce an ADHD-like syndrome.

Chronic use of certain substances, such as cocaine, may produce ADHD symptoms by disrupting neurotransmission (as by decreasing available dopamine and/or other neurotransmitters or by decreasing the sensitivity of certain receptors). Cocores and colleagues (1987a, 1987b) observed that several of their patients developed ADHD symptoms after continued heavy cocaine use. Similarly, in a recently completed study, Levin and colleagues (1998a) found that among cocaine abusers seeking treatment, 11% had secondary ADHD (that is, ADHD symptoms that developed after regular drug use).

Whereas chronic exposure to drugs may produce an ADHD-like syndrome, clinicians also have reported that cocaine and marijuana can reduce ADHD symptoms (Weiss, Mirin et al., 1988; Levin, Evans & Kleber, 1998a). However, any temporary improvement in symptoms may be overwhelmed by the detrimental impact of heavy continued drug use. These findings suggest that ADHD may be associated with poorer substance abuse treatment outcomes, and thus serve to highlight the need to identify this population and to develop effective treatments for them.

Difficulties in Diagnosing Adult ADHD in Substance-Abusing Populations. Although the *DSM-IV* provides clear-cut criteria for making the diagnosis of adult ADHD, diagnostic ambiguity often arises when one attempts to apply these criteria to individuals who abuse alcohol and other drugs. Perhaps the most obvious problem lies in establishing whether or not an individual had some ADHD symptoms prior to the age of seven.

Potential Reasons for Underdiagnosis: Although retrospective data typically are used when diagnosing a past psychiatric disorder, this becomes more problematic when individuals are asked to recall symptoms that began at a young age. Mannuzza and colleagues (1991) found that even among adults diagnosed with ADHD in childhood and followed repeatedly into adulthood, a substantial minority of the adults could not recall their childhood ADHD symptoms. Frequently, child psychiatrists or pediatricians seek out information from a teacher or parent to assess a child for ADHD symptoms, but these sources of information often are not available during assessment of the adult patient. Even when an older family member, preferably a parent, is available, the reliability of the information may be questionable. The older family member may have (or have had) an alcohol or drug problem or other dysfunction to a degree that his or her ability to recall the patient's childhood behavior may be limited. Another good way to obtain historical data is to ask the patient to provide elementary school report cards. These can provide valuable information and afford an accurate "snapshot" of the patient as the child. Although many parents may not have kept such school records, it is worthwhile to inquire.

In addition to the lack of good historical information, ADHD may go undiagnosed because of lack of awareness of the diagnosis on the part of patients and clinicians. Many substance abusers with adult ADHD were not diagnosed as children; thus, they do not view their problematic adult behaviors as related to having ADHD. These patients may attribute their impatience, restlessness, or procrastination to being "hot-headed," "easily-bored" or "lazy." Also confusing the picture is the fact that many of the consequences of ADHD (such as work failure and poor educational attainment) also are associated with substance use disorders. Substance abusers with undiagnosed ADHD may assume that their drug use alone prevents them from attaining their full potential. Third, patients often develop ways to partially compensate for their ADHD symptoms, so that the symptoms of the disorder may not be obvious to the evaluating clinician. Fourth, because questions regarding childhood behaviors—particularly behaviors associated with ADHD—may not be part of the "standard" assessment, it is an easy diagnosis to overlook. Unlike depression or psychosis, which may be incapacitating or require hospitalization, the negative effects of ADHD usually do not have such dramatic consequences. Finally, since depression is often episodic rather than chronic, the change in functioning is more likely to be noticed and attributed to a psychiatric problem.

Potential Reasons for Overdiagnosis: The Wender Utah Rating Scale (Ward, Wender & Reimherr, 1993) is a self-report instrument that is used to assess individuals for ADHD. Although it has been shown to have some validity among general adult patient populations, its validity among substance abusers has not been established. Some of the items used to score patients include affective symptoms, which are not part of the *DSM-IV* criteria. Therefjfore, this clinical instrument may have utility as a way to initially screen substance-abusing patients for childhood ADHD but should not replace the clinical interview.

A variety of cognitive tests have been used to distinguish children with ADHD from those without the disorder, but the usefulness of these tests in identifying adults with ADHD remains unclear. Although adults with ADHD may perform less well on a variety of cognitive tasks, at present there is no test that produces a pathognomonic response by individuals with adult ADHD. For example, substance-abusing individuals with ADHD may perform less well because of substance-induced impairment and/or attention deficits. No currently available tests have been validated in this subpopulation; therefore, any results obtained from a battery of cognitive tests need to be interpreted cautiously and in conjunction with other clinical findings.

Overdiagnosis of adult ADHD is most likely to occur if one ignores the functional impairment criterion or the requirement that impairment occur in more than one setting. Further, there must be a continuity of ADHD symptoms from childhood to adulthood. Levin and colleagues (1998a) have observed that some individuals with cocaine dependence have impairing ADHD-like symptoms that occur only after a period of regular drug use, but do not report having childhood symptoms of ADHD. These individuals would not be described as having "true" ADHD and it remains unclear whether they would respond to a pharmacologic treatment intervention. Clearly, in order to make these diagnostic distinctions, a comprehensive assessment is required.

Recommendations for Increasing Diagnostic Accuracy: As a rule, if full criteria for the diagnosis are met during elementary school years but the patient or family cannot clearly recall whether the symptoms began before the age of seven, one might incline toward diagnosing the patient with childhood ADHD. However, it is important to specifically inquire about inattention and hyperactivity, because not all disruptive behavior during the school years should be attributed to ADHD.

There also is a lack of diagnostic clarity regarding situations in which an individual may endorse four or five childhood symptoms, but not the required six symptoms from either the hyperactive-impulsive or inattentive category. For these individuals, the question arises as to whether or not they have "true" childhood ADHD. Again, one might be somewhat more lenient when making the diagnosis in substance abusers, since childhood impairment may have gone unrecognized. Using the *DSM-IV* criteria, these individuals might be diagnosed with ADHD.NOS (not otherwise specified). The potential problem with this diagnostic classification is that it may lead clinicians to incorrectly assume that individuals with ADHD.NOS do not have clinically impairing symptoms or might not benefit from a pharmacologic intervention.

As described previously, overdiagnosis of adult ADHD may occur if the clinician does not verify that functional impairment occurs in more than one setting, that ADHD symptoms produce significant impairment, and that ADHD symptoms persist from childhood into adulthood. For example, it is common for individuals to procrastinate when facing difficult projects. The difference between the person with ADHD and those without this disorder is that adults with ADHD have had significant occupational, interpersonal, or psychological impairment due to their poor ability to start tasks and complete them. Because some individuals may "explain away" their difficulties at school or work by describing themselves as having ADHD, it is incumbent upon the clinician to verify that current ADHD symptoms are not limited to one setting. An individual who is completing difficult projects at home but is unable to finish assigned projects at work may be experiencing job dissatisfaction rather than ADHD. Further, the symptoms need to be impairing, not mildly bothersome.

Finally, it is crucial that there be a continuity of symptoms from childhood into adulthood. Some clinicians interpret "continuity " of symptoms in a stricter way than simply having ADHD symptoms from childhood into adulthood. Specifically, one needs to demonstrate that an individual has the same symptoms in adulthood as those in childhood. However, it is not uncommon to find patients who learn to compensate for certain symptoms to a degree that the symptoms become less impairing. For example, adults who feel restless may learn to get up from the table and serve others as a socially appropriate way to handle their need for increased activity. Thus, the individual's restlessness may not disappear but rather it may become less impairing. Alternatively, individuals may be better able to compensate for certain symptoms in childhood than in adulthood. Patients may report that despite their difficulties with concentration, they were able to compensate by being "smart" or "well-liked" in elementary school. However, with the added cognitive demands in high school, college, or in the workplace, these same patients may report that their attentional difficulties led to poor academic and/or occupational performance. Thus, although the same ADHD symptoms may be present in childhood and adulthood, the impairment due to these symptoms may change over the lifespan of the individual.

Another area that often leads to diagnostic confusion and subsequent underdiagnosis or overdiagnosis is the issue of additional psychiatric comorbidity. The added presence of a substance use disorder can further complicate the assessment. Generally, because ADHD symptoms are present in elementary school and precede the substance use disorder, ADHD can be more readily determined as being an independent disorder, compared to those disorders that are usually episodic in nature and may occur only after heavy substance use has developed.

The last criterion for ADHD emphasizes that ADHD should not be diagnosed if the observed symptoms are better accounted for by another mental disorder. Unfortunately, some clinicians may interpret this to mean that if depression or bipolar illness is present, ADHD should not be diagnosed. In reality, these disorders may coexist. Alternatively, it is possible to diagnose ADHD when the patient simply has an affective disorder. For example, ADHD, hypomania, and mania may all share similar symptoms (e.g., distractibility, irritability) and the diagnosis of one of these disorders may be overlooked. Often, the longitudinal history can provide information to distinguish between the two disorders. Individuals with bipolar illness are more likely to describe discrete periods of increased restlessness, talkativeness, and hyperactivity, etc., whereas those with adult ADHD will be more likely to describe having a life-long constellation of these symptoms to a lesser degree. Individuals with major depression may experience symptoms of inattention but are less likely to experience other symptoms associated with ADHD, such as hyperactivity, school or work failure, or restlessness. Often adults with ADHD have first-degree relatives with ADHD, so that the presence of a first-degree relative with "ADHD" may suggest that the individual has ADHD. However, depression and bipolar illness also are overrepresented in families of individuals diagnosed with ADHD (Biederman, Faraone et al., 1990, 1992). Thus, this is not a foolproof method of confirming the diagnosis of adult ADHD. Screening tools, such as the Wender Utah Rating Scale or the Adult Behavior Checklist, are not adequate because they may not distinguish ADHD from other psychiatric disorders. Instead, as noted earlier, a comprehensive diagnostic assessment is needed before initiating any pharmacotherapy.

Treatment. Compared to other substance abusers, individuals with ADHD may have greater difficulties in processing information and may have greater problems in sitting through group meetings—a common format for substance abuse treatment. Because individuals with ADHD often act impulsively, they also may be more likely than those without ADHD to drop out of treatment. Counselors or other patients may find individuals with unrecognized ADHD to be "annoying" or "treatment-resistant" and may have less empathy for them than for those without this disorder. This also can increase the likelihood of patients with ADHD dropping out of treatment. By recognizing and treating ADHD, these problems may be alleviated and treatment outcome thus improved.

Although treatment for substance abusers with adult ADHD can be categorized as pharmacologic or nonpharmacologic, this is a somewhat artificial distinction. Both types of treatment approaches often are used concomitantly. Initially, clinicians may attempt to use nonpharmacologic interventions. However, if these interventions fail to improve symptoms, a pharmacologic intervention may be added. By using pharmacologic interventions to reduce ADHD symptoms such as distractibility or restlessness, other treatment approaches may be better utilized.

Pharmacologic Interventions. *Pharmacotherapy of ADHD:* Psychostimulants, particularly methylphenidate, are the most commonly prescribed and most efficacious medications for childhood ADHD (Barkley, 1977; Greenhill, 1992). Six studies have also evaluated the efficacy of methylphenidate in adults with ADHD (Wilens, Biederman et al., 1995). The majority of these studies report improvement in ADHD symptoms in patients treated with methylphenidate. The studies that have shown the best response to MPH have used larger doses. Spencer and colleagues (1995) found that methylphenidate (up to 1.0 mg/kg per day) produced substantial improvement in ADHD symptoms in 78% compared to 4% of those receiving placebo. Two double-blind studies comparing methylphenidate to placebo for the treatment of adult ADHD included a small number of substance abusers (Mattes, Boswell & Oliver, 1984; Spencer, Wilens, 1995). The researchers found that substance abusers with ADHD responded better to MPH than did those patients without additional substance abuse problems. However, the impact of methylphenidate on substance use was not described.

The only other medication that has been studied under double-blind, placebo-controlled conditions for the treatment of adult ADHD is desipramine. Wilens and colleagues (1996) found that desipramine produced a significant reduction in ADHD symptoms compared to placebo. Two other medications, which are currently approved for the treatment of depression, show promise for the treatment of adult ADHD: bupropion and venlafaxine. However, both medications have been evaluated only in open trials (Wender & Reimherr, 1990; Findlay, Schwartz et al., 1996). Further study of these medications under controlled conditions is needed.

Pharmacotherapy of Cocaine Dependence: At present, desipramine is the only medication in which there are both safety and efficacy data in substance-abusing populations. Desipramine has a record as a relatively safe medication among individuals who are currently using cocaine. Several double-blind placebo-controlled treatment trials have been carried out in cocaine abusers seeking treatment, without any untoward side effects or evidence of any medication abuse (Gawin, Kleber et al., 1989; Arndt, Dorozynsky et al., 1992; Kosten, Morgan et al., 1992). Findings from laboratory studies also suggest that there are few clinically significant cardiovascular effects when cocaine is administered to individuals maintained on desipramine (Fischman, Foltin et al., 1990). Unfortunately, none of the clinical treatment trials have targeted patients with adult ADHD.

Methylphenidate and bupropion have also been evaluated as potential treatments for cocaine dependence. One double-blind study using bupropion did not find the medication more effective than placebo (Margolin, Kosten et al., 1992). Similarly, Grabowski and colleagues (1997) found that sustained-release MPH and immediate-release MPH (combined dose 45 mg/day) was not more effective than placebo for the treatment of cocaine abuse among individuals without ADHD. The most common side effects were jitteriness and decreased appetite, but there were no untoward medical complications requiring discontinuation. In a recently completed laboratory study, our group found that minimal untoward cardiovascular effects occurred when repeated doses of cocaine were given to nontreatment-seeking cocaine abusers with adult ADHD who were maintained on sustained-release MPH (Evans et al., unpublished data).

Pharmacotherapy of Adult ADHD and Substance Dependence: At present, the only medications that have been reported in the treatment literature as potentially effective for the treatment of both adult ADHD and substance abuse are methylphenidate and pemoline. Bromocriptine has been given to substance abusers with ADHD, with mixed reports of benefit (Cocores, Davies et al., 1987; Cocores, Patel et al., 1987; Cavanaugh, Clifford & Gregory, 1989). Table 3 shows that most of the information is derived from a small number of case reports, mostly with cocaine-abusing patients. To date, Levin and colleagues (1998a), have provided the most promising data suggesting that methylphenidate (in the sustained-release formulation) is an effective treatment for adult ADHD in cocaine abusers seeking treatment. In patients given divided daily doses ranging from 40 to 80 mg/day of sustained-release methylphenidate, ADHD symptoms and cocaine use significantly decreased. Weekly individual relapse prevention therapy also was provided. Given the limitations of an open design, double-blind controlled trials clearly are warranted.

Special Issues in Pharmacotherapy of Substance Abusers with ADHD: Ideally, patients could be medicated with medications that are proved effective for the treatment of ADHD, have low abuse potential, and are safe when combined with other psychoactive substances. At present, there is no single medication that meets these criteria. A valid concern is the risk of methylphenidate abuse, by the patient or other family members. Some clinicians have suggested the use of pemoline rather than other stimulants because of its lower abuse potential. However, recent concerns regarding its possible hepatotoxicity may limit its use in substance-abusing patients. At present, there are no clear-cut guidelines regarding the appropriate use of methylphenidate or other psychostimulants for substance abusers with adult ADHD. Nonstimulant medications such as bupropion, venlafaxine, or desipramine are second-line treatments for childhood ADHD, primarily due to their side effect profile and less proven efficacy. However, for individuals with a current or lifetime history of substance abuse, one might initially prescribe a nonstimulant medication to avoid the possibility of abuse or diversion of the treatment medication. On the other hand, if the nonstimulant medication(s) is/are not useful, and the patient does not have a history of amphetamine or methylphenidate abuse, then stimulant medications might be considered. Generally, the threshold for use of a stimulant medication is lower for those individuals with a prolonged period of sobriety compared to those who are newly abstinent or currently abusing drugs.

For those substance-abusing adults with ADHD who are unable to become abstinent, stimulant medication may directly reduce drug craving and lead to a decrease in or cessation of drug use. Although Gawin and colleagues (1985) reported that methylphenidate increased cocaine craving and use among cocaine abusers without ADHD, this has not been confirmed by Grabowski, Roache et al. (1997). Further, the authors did not find an increase in cocaine use among cocaine abusers with ADHD who received methylphenidate (Levin, Evans et al., 1998b). Instead, preliminary results suggest that methylphenidate may reduce cocaine craving and use in this dually-disordered population.

Clearly, certain precautions are warranted when using stimulants in substance-abusing patients. First, keeping track of the prescriptions written and number of pills given is crucial. By seeing the patient on a frequent basis, the number of pills per prescription can be reduced, the patient's treatment response can be closely monitored, and any potential interactions between the stimulant and other abused substances can be identified. Further, it should be made clear to patients that urine toxicology screens will be routinely done and if the patient does not show a clinically significant reduction in alcohol or drug use, other treatment strategies will be implemented. Patients should be encouraged to ingest their medication in a regular fashion rather than on an as-needed basis to avoid inadequate and intermittent palliation of symptoms. Although some clinicians report that the sustained-release formulation of methylphenidate is less effective than the immediate-release form, it might be preferable since there

TABLE 3. Psychopharmacologic Treatment of ADHD and Substance Abuse

	Sample Size	Drug of Abuse	Method	Treatment Used	Findings
Khantzian et al., 1983	1	Cocaine	CR*	MPH	Positive
Khantzian et al., 1984	3	Cocaine	CR	MPH	Positive
Weiss et al., 1985	2	Cocaine	CR	Pemoline	Positive
Cocores et al., 1987a	4	Cocaine	CR	Bromocriptine	Positive
Cocores et al., 1987b	2	Cocaine	CR	Bromocriptine	Positive
Cavanagh et al., 1989	2	Cocaine/THC	DB**	Bromocriptine	Negative
Schubiner et al., 1995	3	Alcohol	CR	MPH	Positive
Levin et al., 1998b (in press)	10	Cocaine	OPEN	MPH – SR+	Positive

CR = case report, DB = double-blind, SR+ = susained-release

is less likelihood of abuse. Similar to other clinical areas of uncertainty, good clinical judgment becomes crucial when deciding who will benefit from a pharmacologic treatment intervention and which medication(s) should be used.

Non-Pharmacologic Interventions. Compared to the pharmacologic treatment literature, there is even less clinical data regarding what non-pharmacologic approaches work best for substance abusers with adult ADHD. Similar to substance abusers with other psychiatric disorders, it is likely that concurrently treating both the substance use disorder and ADHD symptoms is more likely to produce a positive treatment outcome than treating only one disorder. Both the treatment literature for childhood ADHD and the substance abuse treatment literature report positive outcomes with the use of behavioral approaches for these patients. These approaches include: (1) contingency management, (2) cognitive-behavioral interventions, and (3) combined pharmacologic and behavioral interventions.

Interestingly, the literature suggests that negative contingencies may be a necessary component of treatment of childhood ADHD (Pelham & Sams, 1992), whereas positive contingencies have been stressed as the appropriate treatment approach for adult substance abusers (Higgins, Delaney et al., 1994). To date, there have been no contingency management strategies targeted to substance abusers with adult ADHD. Whereas children with ADHD may lose a token for violation of a classroom rule, establishing a token economy system for ADHD behaviors manifested in adulthood might be more difficult.

Cognitive-behavioral treatment has become an integral part of many substance abuse treatment programs and the question remains whether this approach works equally well for substance abusers with ADHD. The use of cognitive interventions for children with ADHD has included "verbal self-instructions, problem-solving strategies, cognitive modeling, self-evaluation, and self-reinforcement." None of these approaches has shown any clear-cut efficacy for children with ADHD.

This contrasts the proven clinical utility of cognitive-behavioral techniques for adult substance abusers. Weinstein (1994) suggests that adults, unlike children, have a greater potential to understand the meaning of dysfunctional behavior and the effect of ADHD symptoms on his or her life and may be better able to utilize cognitive-behavioral approaches. However, these approaches may need to be modified for substance abusers with ADHD.

TABLE 4. Attention and Memory Strategies for Individuals with ADHD

Attention Strategies

- Talk to yourself to focus attention
- Write down essential information
- Ask for repetition of instructions
- Ask speakers to present information more slowly
- Break down tasks into small, simple steps
- Learn to identify and avoid overload
- Take rest periods
- Work on detailed tasks when maximally alert
- Avoid lengthy monotonous tasks
- Work in quiet space
- Try to do one thing at a time
- Practice learning to divide attention
- Develop compensatory strategies.

Memory Strategies

- Establish clear expectations in advance about what is to be learned
- Outline the sequence of a task
- Organize/categorize/chunk information
- Increase attention to material that is to be learned
- Repeat instructions to make certain message is understood
- Rehearse material to be learned
- Establish a routine doing the same task in the same order and on the same schedule
- Develop cues to aid recall
- Use a memory notebook

Source: Weinstein CS (1994). Cognitive remediation strategies: An adjunct to the psychotherapy of adults with attention-deficit hyperactivity disorder. *Journal of Psychotherapy Practice and Research* 3:44–57. Used by permission of the publisher.

There may need to be less emphasis on completion of homework tasks and more emphasis on session work. Frequently, these patients are poor self-observers and have difficulty understanding why they behave a certain way. Adapting the work of other investigators, Weinstein (1994) suggests several attention and memory strategies to help individuals cope with ADHD symptoms (Table 4). These techniques also may have clinical utility for individuals with ADHD in substance abuse treatment settings.

Two experimental approaches that might be useful for substance abusers with ADHD are nodal-link mapping and sensory integration. Often used in group settings, nodal-link mapping consists of drawing spatial-verbal displays to visually represent interrelationships between ideas, feelings, facts, and experiences (Dees, Dansereau & Simpson, 1994). Although Dansereau and colleagues (1995) did not specifically assess individuals for adult ADHD, they compared the efficacy of nodal-mapping to standard counseling among methadone-maintained patients with good or poor attention. They found that individuals who received standard therapy and/or had poor attention did less well in methadone treatment. However, mapping-enhanced counseling reduced the negative effects of poor attention. Sensory integration seeks to integrate stimuli in an organized manner. Within an inpatient substance abuse treatment setting, Stratton and Gailfus (in press) found that these techniques reduced impulsivity, increased anger control, increased attention span, and improved treatment retention. Similar to other substance abuse treatment approaches targeted to individuals with ADHD, further study is needed.

Clearly, many questions are yet unanswered regarding the diagnosis and treatment of substance abusers with adult ADHD. The reliability and validity of screening instruments for both childhood and adult ADHD still need to be established. Further, the utility of various neuropsychological tests have yet to be established. Although methylphenidate has shown to be useful for individuals with adult ADHD, its impact on ADHD symptoms and substance use among dually-diagnosed individuals has not been studied in a controlled fashion. There are even fewer data regarding the use of other pharmacologic agents as well as nonpharmacologic treatment strategies for adult substance abusers with ADHD. Given the substantial subpopulation of substance abusers with adult ADHD, further research is warranted.

INTERMITTENT EXPLOSIVE DISORDER

Clinicians often encounter aggressive patients who are not intoxicated, schizophrenic, or manic. Such patients often are diagnosed with Intermittent Explosive Disorder (IED). This diagnosis frequently is used to explain why an individual with a personality disorder or behavior problem is placed on medications such as lithium, clonidine, a beta blocker, an anticonvulsant or other medications. However, it is difficult to reconcile this practice with the actual definition. As defined, adults with IED give into irresistible urges to commit violent acts. These actions lead to reduction of tension, similar to the kleptomaniac must give into the impulse to steal. When the *DSM-IV* task force reviewed the literature, it found little support for IED as a diagnosis but noted the common use of the term to communicate information about episodic violent behavior (Bradford, Geller et al., 1996).

Episodic violent behavior is not a diagnosis; it is a commonly encountered problem in clinical practice. The common use of IED suggests that clinicians are not satisfied with the current nosology. The nosology does not formalize their intuitions about which medications to first use with different types of aggressive patients. In contrast to anxiety and mood problems, there is no *DSM-IV* classification for "types of aggressive disorders." We have argued elsewhere that perhaps there should be (Donovan, 1998). The plurality of ad hoc medications used with clinical success in explosive children, adolescents, and adults suggests a plurality of underlying biological problems (for a review, see Stowe, 1995).

Diagnostic Considerations and Pharmacologic Response. As already suggested, "episodic violent behavior" seems virtually synonymous with "explosive" aggression. In animal models, it has been compared to defensive aggression, as opposed to "predatory" aggression (Volavka, 1995). For example, a cat cornered by a dog behaves very differently from a cat stalking a bird. In animal models, explosive aggression is associated with sympathetic discharge, flailing, and global response. In contrast, predatory aggression is associated with focused concentration, low heart rate and low motor activity until the moment of the attack. Explosive aggression is "defensive" in the sense that the person acts like someone provoked and under attack. This type of aggression is not intended primarily to humiliate a rival or to prey upon a victim. It is intended to provide an escape (Volavka, 1995).

In contrast to the *DSM-IV* definition, clinicians seem to mean this type of aggression when using the term "intermittent explosive disorder." One can imagine this type of aggression emerging under a variety of biologically dissimilar situations. For example, some patients may become explosive because they are prone to paranoid misinterpretations of reality. The common clinical intuition is that such patients should receive low dose antipsychotic medications. Other patients may have a fair amount of self-hatred in addition to being quick to anger. These patients may benefit from serotonergic agents (Cocarro, 1997). Still other patients, such as those discussed in the ADHD section, probably have a problem with impulsivity. They often benefit from psychostimulants. Finally, some patients have a problem with mood regulation and are prone to temper tantrums. Our preliminary data suggests that these patients do well on valproic acid, whether they are children, adolescents, or adults. Much of our effort has been to define this latter type of explosive aggression (Donovan, 1997) and its connection to marijuana use (Donovan, 1996).

Relation to Substance Abuse. As noted earlier, Meyer (1986) describes several models of how substance use might connect to psychopathology. Before considering the problem of comorbidity, it is important to note that substance-induced violence is a common occurrence. Alcohol and cocaine are the most common offenders, although opiate withdrawal can also contribute to irritable aggressive outbursts. Alcohol in particular is a major factor in explosive violence, not only in community based studies but also in laboratory models (Volavka, 1995).

In considering comorbidity itself, however, there is circumstantial evidence that some individuals with irritable aggression who consume substances are trying to control their anger. For example, teenagers with explosive tempers report that marijuana has a specific calming effect (Tinklenberg, Roth et al., 1976). That is to say, they report they smoke marijuana in order to "chill out" (calm down). Since anger may have a direct link to substance use (Swaim, Oetting & Edwards, 1989), use of marijuana in this explosive, irritable population may represent true self-medication (Donovan, Susser & Nunes, 1996). Since marijuana plays such an important role in the start of career addiction (Kandel & Faust, 1975), it is important to address factors that initiate marijuana use.

The author's own work suggests that marijuana use in adolescents with temper outbursts and mood swings declines when the youngsters receive the mood stabilizer/anticonvulsant valproic acid. In seven adolescents self-reported marijuana use declined from an average of 24 joints at study entry per week to two joints per week at week 5 of treatment. Most reported a substantial reduction or cessation of marijuana (Donovan 1996). It is difficult to generalize these findings until they can be replicated under double blind conditions, with a more objective measure (i.e., quantitative urine testing). However, the noted improvement may be explained at the biological level. Marijuana contains over four hundred compounds, some of them are potent anticonvulsants, others have both pro and anticonvulsant properties. Because smoked marijuana is a mixture of cannabinoids, its overall effect on neuronal excitation is complex. It seems logical to expect that the mix of cannabinoids will vary by types of marijuana and the state of its metabolism (Karler & Turkanis, 1976; Weisz, Gunnell & Vardaris, 1977). Epidemiologic evidence suggests, however, that on average marijuana is a weak anticonvulsant. In a carefully designed study of first onset seizures in a major metropolitan hospital, regular marijuana use was shown to be a protective factor (Ng, Hauser et al., 1992), while regular alcohol use was a risk factor.

Marijuana may allow an irritable, violence-prone adolescent or adult to "chill out." Marijuana's weak anticonvulsant effects may mediate this effect. However, valproic acid may work better as a mood stabilizer because it does not have the same positively reinforcing effects associated with marijuana use. That these youngsters develop a problematic pattern of marijuana use is not surprising given that marijuana is also reinforced through the pleasure reward circuitry (Gardner, 1991). Further, marijuana cessation, in and of itself, may produce a withdrawal syndrome characterized by irritability, anxiety, and restlessness (Tennant, 1986) such that reduction or cessation of use is negatively reinforcing. Thus, individuals who are irritable and have an explosive temper may find quitting more difficult because they are receiving multiple reinforcements from continued marijuana use.

Potential Treatment Options. Beta blockers, serotonin uptake inhibitors, lithium, and anticonvulsants all have their place in the treatment of aggression. However, studies involving these medications have problems with methodology and generalizability. The clearest problems are referral bias and lack of double-blind, placebo controlled trials. Despite these problems, some assertions can be made. Alcohol tends to make explosive aggression worse. It increases the risk for violence during intoxication, and in theory, during sobriety as well. Therefore, clinicians should counsel patients with a history of explosive episodes (of whatever etiology) to avoid alcohol. Marijuana may be different, particularly when heavy use occurs in individuals with temper outbursts and mood swings. For these individuals there is reason to suspect that some form of self-medication may be taking place. Valproic acid, especially in its enteric form, may be particularly useful in this subgroup. In any case, clinicians should counsel heavy marijuana users to avoid the drug because of its intoxicating effects and suggest that there may be better ways to control their irritability and mood swings.

In violent non-asthmatic patients, beta blockers, in large doses, have been reported to be useful in reducing aggression (Yudofsky, Silver & Schneider, 1987). Low dose antipsychotics long have been used in violent youngsters (and adults) who are thought to have problems with reality testing. SSRIs in antidepressant doses are helpful in some irritable patients (Cocarro & Cavoussi, 1997). Data on nonpharmacologic treatments, such as anger management, suffer from the same methodologic problems found with pharmacologic studies.

In short, while many clinicians agree that episodic violent behavior is a common and serious problem, especially in deviant young people, what to do is obscured by the lack of a clinically useful taxonomy. Likewise, although it is clear that "bad kids" are prone to career addiction, it is not clear what aspect of their badness leads them down this path. Clearly more research is needed.

EATING DISORDER

Definitions. This section examines two disorders that share an adolescent onset, a marked preponderance of women patients, a distortion of body image and a set of bizarre attitudes/behaviors towards food. These disorders are anorexia nervosa (AN) and bulimia nervosa (BN). Unlike substance abuse, feeding disorders, aggression, and even attention deficit, there are no animal models for AN or BN. But remarkably, there may be historical analogues in that at various times and in various cultures, females on the edge of puberty have practiced self-starvation (Brumberg, 1988). This simultaneous lack of animal models and presence of historical models suggest that something uniquely human is involved in the pathogenesis of these disorders. It appears to be something involving the meaning of food to pubescent girls. In the previous disorders, meaning entered the equation as the person tried to cope, but with AN and BN, the pathology itself seems to be a communication or enactment.

Diagnostic Criteria. AN and BN are included in this chapter because they are linked to the idea of loss of normal impulse control (see the *DSM-IV* for definitions). Although the nature of the relationship remains unclear, eating disorders are connected to female puberty. Impulse dyscontrol in anorexia refers to excess control, for anorexia is essentially self-starvation. Bulimia (from Greek for "ox hunger") refers to too little control, for bulimia involves bingeing (and often stealing, substance use and sex). It may seem odd that individuals who will not eat and individuals who binge should be grouped together, but food can mean the same thing to people yet elicit different reactions. Both anorectics and bulimics share a distorted body image and an intense fear of what food can do. This need for therapists to understand what food means has led the various approaches from psychoanalysis to family therapy.

Epidemiology. As noted above, the one epidemiological fact no one questions is that of female predominance. The ratio is estimated at about 10 to 1 (female to male) for eating disorders. Beyond this, ascertainment and classification problems have produced varied estimates of prevalence. The most widely accepted figure is that AN is very rare, affecting about 0.4% of the adolescent female population. BN is estimated to affect 3% of the adolescent and young adult population, but this figure is open to serious question not only for the reasons mentioned, but also because bulimics fear exposure and are less likely to participate in surveys than other individuals (Fairburn & Beglin, 1990). Nevertheless, it is clear that bulimic spectrum problems are not uncommon. Dieting is very common among adolescent females, and the typical course of the BN (in 80% of the cases) is from dieting to bingeing to purging (Fairburn & Beglin, 1990).

Comorbidity Studies. The comorbidity studies show widely varying rates depending on how the sample was chosen, what criteria were employed and what eating disorder was studied (for a review, see Holderness, 1994). The rate of substance abuse among bulimics in the review ranged from 10% to 88%, with a median of 22%. Conversely, the rate of bulimia among alcohol and other substance abusers ranged from 3% to 48%, with a median of 23%. The *DSM-IV* splits AN into two subcategories, restrictors and bingers, while BN divides into purging and non-purging types. Several studies of inpatient and outpatient populations suggest that the risk for substance abuse is a function of how "bulimic" the person is (Herzog, Nussbaum & Marmor, 1996). Anorectics who binge are more at risk than are restrictive anorectics. Bulimics who purge are more at risk than bulimics who do not purge. A carefully executed family study suggested separate vulnerabilities were involved for BN and substance use disorder (Kaye, Lilenfeld et al., 1996), so the question of why there should be a co-occurrence brings the discussion back to Meyer's categories (see above).

Some argue that the eating disorders are themselves addictions (to starvation or bingeing), so the co-occurrence is a function of addiction proneness in general (Brisman & Siegal, 1984). Others argue for a common psycho-biological diathesis, perhaps involving serotonin (Goldbloom, 1993) and/or an obsessive-compulsive (OCD) spectrum problem (Rothenberg, 1990). Still others believe that the link to substance abuse is simply the consequence of shared risk factors.

The addiction to starvation model does not explain why restricting anorectics are not at increased risk for "other" addictions (Herzog, Nussbaum & Marmor, 1996). Some who support the notion of a link among risk factors point out that substance abusers and bulimics show impulsive personality profiles on the MMPI or SCID II (Herzog, Nussbaum & Marmor, 1996). Others focus on the dysfunctional family dynamics in the childhood of substance abusers and bulimics as the point of contact. Still others look to sexual trauma or depression as mediating both the substance use and the BN (Lucas, 1996). As noted above, family data suggest that the latter two disorders share the same risk factors rather than being different manifestations of the same problem (Kaye, Lilenfeld et al., 1996).

Treatment and Prognosis. Behavioral, pharmacological, psychodynamic and family treatments have been used to treat eating disordered patients. All have been reported to be helpful. One might expect that the history of substance use would worsen the prognosis, but this does not appear to necessarily be the case (Strasser, Pike & Walsh, 1992). AN is a potentially fatal disorder that follows a chronic, relapsing course in those patients who do not recover quickly. BN tends to have a better prognosis, with more spontaneous remissions, but there is a marked tendency for relapse.

In the only prospective study of the long term outcome of BN, Fairburn and colleagues (1995) found that outcome was significantly affected by the type of treatment given. Patients who received behavioral therapy did well while the therapy continued, but quickly relapsed when it ended. Fairburn describes the behavioral therapy (BT) as "a 'dismantled' form of Cognitive Behavior Therapy (CBT), which consisted solely of its behavior procedures, with the exception of those directed at one's concerns about shape and weight." Those who received cognitive therapy or interpersonal therapy did well acutely but also maintained their response over time (Fairburn, Norman et al., 1995). This superiority of psychodynamic and cognitive therapies over behavioral treatment may be the clearest evidence that meaning is central to the eating disorders.

Depression in substance users, even if it is substance-induced, probably should be treated, since it responds to medication (Nunes, Quitkin et al., 1998). Analogously, antidepressant medications have been reported to be helpful acutely in clinical trials of anorexic and bulimic symptoms (Strasser, Pike & Walsh, 1992). Therefore, it makes sense to use these medications, even if the neurotransmitter changes mentioned above are induced by the eating disorder. However, it also is true that the real problem with these disorders is the tendency to relapse, and that seems to be helped when the patient gains some insight into what food means to her personally.

CONCLUSIONS

In this chapter, the relationship of substance abuse to ADHD and other developmental disorders was presented. Diagnostic considerations and issues related to assessing substance abusers with these comorbid psychiatric disorders were discussed. Although various treatment approaches have been presented; there are no definitive treatment approaches for substance abusers with adult ADHD or other developmental disorders. As emphasized earlier, the integration of multiple treatment modalities is more likely to produce therapeutic benefits than any single treatment alone. The search for creative and clinically sound pharmacological and nonpharmacologic approaches for these dually-disordered patient populations is long overdue.

ACKNOWLEDGMENT: Both authors are supported in their scientific endeavors by Scientist Development Awards from the National Institute on Drug Abuse: Grants K-20 DA00214-01 (Dr. Levin) and K-20 DA00246-01 (Dr. Donovan).

REFERENCES

American Psychiatric Association (1980). *Diagnostic and Statistical Manual of Mental Disorders, 3rd Edition.* Washington, DC: American Psychiatric Press.

American Psychiatric Association (1987). *Diagnostic and Statistical Manual of Mental Disorders, 3rd Edition, Revised.* Washington, DC: American Psychiatric Press.

American Psychiatric Association (1994). *Diagnostic and Statistical Manual of Mental Disorders, 4th Edition.* Washington, DC: American Psychiatric Press.

Arndt IO, Dorozynsky L, Woody GE, McLellan AT & O'Brien CP (1992). Desipramine treatment of cocaine dependence in methadone-maintained patients. *Archives of General Psychiatry* 49:888–893.

Barkley RA (1977). A review of stimulant drug research on hyperactive children. *Journal of Child and Psychological Psychiatry* 18:137–165.

Biederman J, Faraone SV, Keenan K, Knee D & Tsuang MT (1990). Family-genetic and psychosocial risk factors in DSM-III attention deficit disorder. *Journal of*

American Academy of Child and Adolescent Psychiatry 29:526–533.

Biederman J, Faraone SV, Keenan SV et al. (1992). Further evidence for family-genetic risk factors in attention deficit hyperactivity disorder. *Archives of General Psychiatry* 49:728–738.

Biederman J, Faraone SV, Spencer T, Wilens T, Norman D, Lapey K, Mick E, Krifcher-Lehman B & Doyle A (1993). Patterns of psychiatric co-morbidity, cognition, and psychosocial functioning in adults with attention deficit hyperactivity disorder. *American Journal of Psychiatry* 150:1792–1798.

Biederman J, Wilens T, Mick E, Milberger S, Spencer T & Faraone S (1995). Psychoactive substance use disorders in adults with attention deficit hyperactivity disorder (ADHD): Effects of ADHD and psychiatric comorbidity. *American Journal of Psychiatry* 152:1652–1658.

Borland B & Heckman H (1976). Hyperactive boys and their brothers. *Archives of General Psychiatry* 33:669–675.

Bradford J, Geller J, Lesieur H, Rosenthal R & Wise M (1996). Impulse Control Disorders. In TA Widiger, AJ Frances, HA Pincus, R Ross, MB First & WW Davis (eds.) *DSM-IV Sourcebook, 1st Edition, Vol II*. Washington, DC: American Psychiatric Press, 1195.

Brisman J & Siegal M (1984). Bulimia and alcoholism: Two sides of the same coin? *Journal of Substance Abuse Treatment* 1:113–118.

Brumberg JJ (1988). *Fasting Girls: The Emergence of Anorexia Nervosa as a Modern Disease*. Cambridge, MA: Harvard University Press.

Carroll KM & Rounsaville BJ (1993). History and significance of childhood attention deficit disorder in treatment-seeking cocaine abusers. *Comprehensive Psychiatry* 34:75–86.

Castellanos FX, Giedd JN, Marsh WL et al. (1996). Quantitative brain magnetic resonance imaging in attention-deficit hyperactivity disorder. *Archives of General Psychiatry* 53:607–616.

Cavanaugh R, Clifford JST & Gregory WL (1989). The use of bromocriptine for the treatment of attention deficit disorder in two chemically dependent patients. *Journal of Psychoactive Drugs* 21:217–220.

Cichetti D & Cohen DJ (1995). Perspectives on developmental psychopathology. In *Developmental Psychopathology, Vol. 1: Theory and Methods*. New York, NY: John Wiley & Sons.

Coccaro EF & Cavoussi RJ (1997). Fluoxetine and impulsive aggressive behavior in personality-disordered subjects. *Archives of General Psychiatry* 54:1081–1088.

Cocores JA, Davies RK, Mueller PS & Gold MS (1987a). Cocaine abuse and adult attention disorder. *Journal of Clinical Psychiatry* 48:376–377.

Cocores JA, Patel MD, Gold MS & Pottash AC (1987). Cocaine abuse, attention deficit disorder, and bipolar disorder. *Journal of Nervous and Mental Diseases* 175:431–432.

Dansereau DF, Joe GW & Simpson DD (1995). Attentional difficulties and the effectiveness of a visual representation strategy for counseling drug-addicted clients. *International Journal on Addictions* 30:371–386.

Dees SM, Dansereau DF & Simpson DD (1994). A visual representation system for drug abuse counselors. *Journal of Substance Abuse Treatment* 11:517–523.

Donovan SJ, Susser ES & Nunes EV (1996). Divalproex sodium for use with conduct disordered adolescent marijuana users (letter). *American Journal on Addictions* 5:181.

Donovan SJ, Susser ES, Nunes EV, Stewart JW, Quitkin FM & Klein DF (1997). Divalproex sodium treatment of disruptive adolescents: A report of 10 cases. *Journal of Clinical Psychiatry* 58:12–15.

Donovan SJ (1998). New approaches to the disruptive behavior disorders and the antisocial spectrum: A review. *Medscape Mental Health*, in press.

Erikson E (1950). *Childhood and Society*. New York, NY: W.W. Norton.

Eyre SL, Rounsaville BJ & Kleber HD (1982). History of childhood hyperactivity in a clinic population of opiate addicts. *Journal of Nervous and Mental Diseases* 170:522–529.

Fairburn CG & Beglin S (1990). Studies of the epidemiology of bulimia nervosa. *American Journal of Psychiatry* 147:401–408.

Fairburn CG, Norman PA, Welch SL, O'Connor ME, Doll HA & Peveler RC (1995). A prospective study of outcome in bulimia nervosa and the long term effects of three psychological treatments. *Archives of General Psychiatry* 52:304–312.

Findlay RL, Schwartz MA, Flannery DJ & Manos MJ (1996). Venlafaxine in adults with attention-deficit/hyperactivity disorder: An open clinical trial. *Journal of Clinical Psychiatry* 57:184–189.

Fischman MW, Foltin RW, Nestadt G & Pearlson GD (1990). Effects of desipramine maintenance on cocaine self-administration in humans. *Journal of Pharmacological and Experimental Therapeutics* 253:760–770.

Gardner EL (1991). Cannabinoid interaction with brain reward systems—The neurobiological basis for cannabinoid abuse. In LL Murphy & A Bartke (eds.) *Marijuana/Cannabinoids: Neurobiology and Neurophysiology*. New York, NY: CRC Press.

Gawin F, Riordan C & Kleber H (1985). Methylphenidate treatment of cocaine abusers without attention deficit disorder: A negative report. *American Journal of Drug and Alcohol Abuse* 11:193–197.Gawin FH & Kleber HD (1986). Abstinence symptomatology and psychiatric diagnosis in cocaine abusers: Clinical observations. *Archives of General Psychiatry* 43:107–113.

Gawin FH, Kleber HD, Byck R et al. (1989). Desipramine facilitation of initial cocaine abstinence. *Archives of General Psychiatry* 46:117–121.

Gittleman R, Mannuzza S, Shenker R & Bonagura N (1985). Hyperactive boys almost grown up: I. Psychiatric status. *Archives of General Psychiatry* 42:937–947.

Goldbloom DS (1993). Eating disorders among women receiving treatment for an alcohol problem. *International Journal of Eating Disorders* 14:147–151.

Grabowski J, Roache JD, Schmitz JM, Rhoades H, Creson D & Korszun A (1997). Replacement medication for cocaine dependence: Methylphenidate. *Journal of Clinical Psychopharmacology* 17:485–488.

Greenhill LL (1992). Psychopharmacology: Stimulants. In G Weiss (ed.) *Child and Adolescent Psychiatric Clinics of North America*. Philadelphia, PA: W.B. Saunders, 411–447.

Herzog DB, Nussbaum KM & Marmor AK (1996). Comorbidity and outcome in eating disorders. *The Psychiatric Clinics of North America* 19:843–859.

Holderness CC, Brooks-Gunn J & Warren MP (1994). Comorbidity of eating disorders and substance abuse review of the literature. *International Journal of Eating Disorders* 16:1–34.

Higgins ST, Delaney DD, Budney et al. (1994). A behavioral approach to achieving initial cocaine abstinence. *American Journal of Psychiatry* 148:1218–1224.

Kandel D & Faust R (1975). Sequence and stages in patterns of adolescent drug use. *Archives of General Psychiatry* 32:923–32.

Karler R & Turkanis SA (1976). Cannabis and epilepsy. Marijuana's biological effects: Advances in the biosciences. *Proceeding of the Satellite Symposium of the 7th International Congress of Pharmacology, Paris*. Oxford, England: Pergamon Press, 619–641.

Kaye WH, Lilenfeld LR, Plotnicov K, Merikangas KR, Nagy L, Strober M, Bulik CM, Moss H & Greeno CG (1996). Bulimia nervosa and substance dependence: Association and family transmission. *Alcoholism: Clinical & Experimental Research* 20:878–881.

Kellam SG (1997). Targeting early antecedents to prevent smoking: Findings from an epidemiologically-based randomized field trial aimed at early antecedents. Paper presented at the American Academy of Addiction Psychiatry, San Antonio, Texas.

Kessler RC, McGonagle KA, Zhao S et al. (1994). Lifetime and 12-month prevalence of DSM-III-R psychiatric disorders in the United States. *Archives of General Psychiatry* 51:8–19.

Khantzian EJ (1983). An extreme case of cocaine dependence and marked improvement with methylphenidate treatment. *American Journal of Psychiatry* 140:484–485.

Khantzian EJ, Gawin FH, Riordan C & Kleber HD (1984). Methylphenidate treatment for cocaine dependence: A preliminary report. *Journal of Substance Abuse Issues* 1:107–112.

Klein DF (1989). Pharmacologic validation of psychiatric diagnosis. In DF Klein, L Robbins & Barrett (eds). *Validity of Psychiatric Diagnosis*. New York, NY: Raven Press.

Kosten TR (1992). Can cocaine craving be a medication development outcome? Drug craving and relapse in opioid and cocaine dependence. *American Journal on Addictions* 1:230–237.

Kosten TR, Morgan CM, Falcione J & Schottenfeld RS (1992). Pharmacotherapy for cocaine-abusing methadone-maintained patients using amantadine or desipramine. *Archives of General Psychiatry* 49:894–898.

Levin FR & Kleber HD (1995). Attention-deficit hyperactivity disorder and substance abuse: Relationships and implications for treatment. *Harvard Review of Psychiatry* 2:246–258.

Levin FR, Evans SM & Kleber HD (1998a). Prevalence of adult attention-deficit hyperactivity disorder among cocaine abusers seeking treatment. *Drug and Alcohol Dependence*, in press.

Levin FR, Evans SM, McDowell D & Kleber HD (1998b). Methylphenidate for cocaine abusers with adult attention-deficit hyperactivity disorder: A pilot study. *Journal of Clinical Psychiatry*, in press.

Lucas AR (1996). Anorexia nervosa and bulimia nervosa. In M Lewis (ed.) *Child and Adolescent Psychiatry: A Comprehensive Textbook*. Baltimore, MD: Williams & Wilkins, 586–593.

Mannuzza S, Klein RG, Bonagura N, Malloy P, Giampino TL & Addalli KA (1991). Hyperactive boys almost grown up: V— Replication of psychiatric status. *Archives of General Psychiatry* 48:77–83.

Mannuzza S, Klein RG, Bessler A, Malloy P & LaPadula M (1993). Adult outcome of hyperactive boys: Educational achievement, occupational rank, and psychiatric status. *Archives of General Psychiatry* 50:565–576.

Margolin A, Kosten TR, Avants SK et al. (1995). A multicenter trial of bupropion for cocaine dependence in methadone-maintained patients. *Drug and Alcohol Dependence* 40:125–131.

Mattes JA, Boswell L & Oliver H (1984). Methylphenidate effects on symptoms of attention deficit disorder in adults. *Archives of General Psychiatry* 41:1059–1063.

Mechoulam RJ & Gaoni Y (1965). A total synthesis on d-9-tetra-tetrahydrocannabinol, the active constituent of hashish. *Journal of the American Chemical Society* 87:3273–3275.

Meyer RE (1986). How to understand the relationship between psychopathology and addictive disorders: Another example of the chicken and the egg. In RE Meyer (ed.) *Psychopathology and Addictive Disorders*. New York, NY: Guilford Press, 3–16.

Morrison JR & Stewart MA (1971). A family study of the hyperactive child syndrome. *Biological Psychiatry* 3:189–195.

Morse P & Montgomery C (1994). Cognitive remediation in the neuropsychiatric setting. In JM Ellison, EJ Weinstein & T Hodel-Malinofsky (eds.) *The Psychotherapist's Guide to Neuropsychiatry: Diagnostic and Treatment Issues*. Washington, DC: American Psychiatric Press, 107–143.

Murphy K & Barkley RA (1996). Prevalence of DSM-IV symptoms of ADHD in adult licensed drivers: Implications for clinical diagnosis. *Journal of Attention Disorders* 1:147–161.

Ng SK, Hauser WA, Brust JC & Susser M (1988). Alcohol consumption and new onset seizures. *The New England Journal of Medicine* 319:66–673.

Nunes WV, Quitkin FM, Donovan SJ et al. (1998). Imipramine treatment of opiate-dependent patients with depressive disorders: A placebo-controlled trial. *Archives of General Psychiatry* 55:153–160.

Oetter P (1986). A sensory integration approach to the treatment of attention deficit disorders. *Sensory Integration SIS Newsletter* 1:1–2.

Pelham WE & Sams SE (1992). Behavior modification. In G Weiss (ed.) *Child and Adolescent Psychiatric Clinics of North America*. Philadelphia, PA: W.B. Saunders, 505–518.

Regier DA, Farmer ME, Rae DS, Locke BZ et al. (1990). Comorbidity of mental disorders with alcohol and other drug abuse: Results from the epidemiologic catchment area (ECA) study. *Journal of the American Medical Association* 264:2511–2518.

Rothenberg A (1990). Adolescence and eating disorder: The obsessive- compulsive syndrome. *Psychiatric Clinics of North America* 13:469–488.

Rounsaville B, Anton SF, Carroll K, Budde D, Prusooff BA & Gawin F (1991). Psychiatric diagnoses of treatment-seeking cocaine abusers. *Archives of General Psychiatry* 48:43–51.

Schubiner H, Tzelepis A, Isaacson JH, Warbasse III LH, Zacharek M & Musial J (1995). The dual diagnosis of attention-deficit/hyperactivity disorder and substance abuse: Case reports and literature review. *Journal of Clinical Psychiatry* 56:146–150.

Spencer T, Biederman J, Wilens T & Faraone SV (1994). Is attention-deficit hyperactivity disorder in adults a valid disorder? *Harvard Review of Psychiatry* 1:326–335.

Spencer T, Wilens T, Biederman J, Faraone SV, Ablon S & Lapey K (1995). A double-blind, crossover comparison of methylphenidate and placebo in adults with childhood-onset attention-deficit hyperactivity disorder. *Archives of General Psychiatry* 52:434–443.

Spitzer RL & Williams JBW (1985). Classification in psychiatry. In HI Kaplan & BJ Sadock (eds.) *Comprehensive Textbook of Psychiatry, 4th Edition*. Baltimore, MD: Williams & Wilkins, 591–612.

Stoewe JK, Kruesi MJP & Lelio DS (1995). Psychopharmacology of aggressive states and features of conduct disorder. *Child and Adolescent Clinics of North America* 1:359–379.

Strasser TJ, Pike KM & Walsh BT (1992). The impact of prior substance abuse on treatment outcome for bulimia nervosa. *Addictive Behaviors* 17:387–395.

Stratton J & Gailfus DA (submitted). A new approach to substance abuse treatment: adolescents and adults with ADHD.

Swaim RC, Oetting ER & Edwards RW (1989). Links from emotional distress to adolescent drug use: A path model. *Journal of Consulting and Clinical Psychology* 57:227–231.

Szatmari P (1992). The epidemiology of attention-deficit hyperactivity disorder. In G Weiss (ed.) *Child and Adolescent Psychiatric Clinics of North America*. Philadelphia, PA: W.B. Saunders, 361–384.

Tennant FS (1986). The clinical syndrome of marijuana dependence. *Psychiatric Annals* 16:225–234.

Thompson LL, Riggs PD, Mikulich SK & Crowley TJ (1996). Contribution of ADHD symptoms to substance problems and delinquency in conduct-disordered adolescents. *Journal of Abnormal Child Psychology* 24:325–347.

Tinklenberg JR, Roth WT, Kopell BS & Murphy P (1976). Cannabis and alcohol effects on assaultiveness in adolescent delinquents. *Annals of the New York Academy of Sciences* 282:85–94.

Volavka J (1995). *Neurobiology of Violence*. Washington, DC: American Psychiatric Press.

Ward MF, Wender PH & Reimherr FW (1993). The Wender Utah Rating Scale (WURS): An aid in the retrospective diagnosis of childhood attention deficit hyperactivity disorder. *American Journal of Psychiatry* 150:885–890.

Weddington WW, Brown BS, Haertzen CA et al. (1991). Comparison of amantidine and desipramine combined with psychotherapy for treatment of cocaine dependence. *American Journal of Drug and Alcohol Abuse* 17:137–152.

Weinstein CS (1994). Cognitive remediation strategies: An adjunct to the psychotherapy of adults with Attention-deficit hyperactivity disorder. *Journal of Psychotherapy Practice and Research* 3:44–57.

Weiss G, Hechtman L, Milroy T & Perlman T (1985). Psychiatric status of hyperactives as adults: A controlled prospective 15-year follow-up of 63 hyperactive children. *Journal of the American Academy of Child Psychiatry* 24:211–220.

Weiss RD, Pope HG & Mirin SM (1985). Treatment of chronic cocaine abuse and attention deficit disorder, residual type with magnesium pemoline. *Drug and Alcohol Dependence* 15:69–72.

Weiss G & Hechtman LT (1986). Adult hyperactive subjects' view of their treatment in childhood and adolescence. In *Hyperactive Children Grown Up: Empirical Finding and Theoretical Considerations*. New York, NY: Guilford, 293–300.

Weiss RD, Mirin SM, Griffin ML & Michael JL (1988). Psychopathology in cocaine abusers: Changing trends. *Journal of Nervous and Mental Diseases* 176:719–725.

Weisz DJ, Gunnell DL & Vardaris RM (1977). Effects of delta–9-THC on frequency potentiation and recurrent inhibition in rat hippocampus. *Neuroscience Abstracts* 3:433.

Wender PH & Garfinkel BD (1989). Attention-deficit hyperactivity disorder: Adult manifestations. In HI Sadock & BJ Kaplan BJ (eds.) *Comprehensive Textbook of Psychiatry*. Baltimore, MD: Williams & Wilkins, 1837–1841.

Wender PH & Reimherr FW (1990). Bupropion of attention-deficit hyperactivity disorder in adults. *American Journal of Psychiatry* 147: 1018–1020.

Wilens TE, Biederman J, Spencer TJ & Prince J (1995). Pharmacotherapy of adult attention deficit disorder: A review. *Journal of Clinical Psychopharmacology* 15:270–279.

Wilens TE, Biederman J, Prince J, Spencer TJ, Faraone S, Warburton R (1996). Six-week, double-blind, placebo-controlled study of desipramine for adult attention deficit hyperactivity disorder. *American Journal of Psychiatry* 153:1147–1153.

Wise RA (1996). Neurobiology of addiction. *Current Opinions in Neurobiology* 6:243–251.

Wood D, Wender PH & Reimherr FW (1983). The prevalence of attention deficit disorder, residual type, or minimal brain dysfunction, in a population of male alcoholic patients. *American Journal of Psychiatry* 140:95–98.

Yudofsky S, Silver J, Schneider S (1987). Pharmacologic treatment of aggression. *Psychiatric Annals* 17:397–404.

Zametkin AJ, Nordahl TE, Gross M et al. (1990). *The New England Journal of Medicine* 323:1361–1366.

CHAPTER 6

Other Impulse Control Disorders

Susan L. McElroy, M.D.
Cesar A. Soutullo, M.D.
R. Jeffrey Goldsmith, M.D.

Historical Overview
Epidemiology
Phenomenologic Similarities
Course of the Disorder
Comorbidity
Family History
Neurobiological Studies
Treatment Response

It has long been hypothesized that substance use disorders are forms of impulse control disorders (ICDs) (Esquirol, 1838; Frosch & Wortis, 1954; American Psychiatric Association, 1980, 1987, 1994). More recently, it has been suggested that ICDs are best conceptualized as addictive disorders or behavioral addictions (Bradford, Geller et al., 1996; Carnes, 1990; Fishbain, 1987; Glatt & Cook, 1987; Goodman, 1997). However, the relationship between ICDs and substance use disorders has never been fully examined. Indeed, to the authors' knowledge, no study has directly compared an ICD and a substance use disorder.

This chapter first provides an historical overview of ICDs as a family of mental disorders. It then summarizes available research suggesting that ICDs and substance use disorders may be related, and discusses the clinical and theoretical implications of such a relationship.

HISTORICAL OVERVIEW

In 1838, Esquirol introduced the term "monomania" to describe conditions in which individuals performed acts which they deplored and did not want to do in response to irresistible impulses. He cited arson, alcoholism, impulsive homicide and (later) kleptomania as examples (McElroy, Keck et al., 1995a). In the introduction to his chapter on monomanias in *Des Maladies Mentales*, Esquirol (1838) stresses the irresistible, uncontrollable, and involuntary features of the disorder:

> ". . . voluntary control is profoundly compromised: the patient is constrained to perform acts which are dictated neither by his reason nor by his emotion—acts which his conscience disapproves of, but over which he no longer has willful control; the actions are involuntary, instinctive, irresistible, it is monomania without delirium or instinctive monomania."

Later in the chapter (1838, p. 337), he writes:

> ". . . the irresistible impulses show all of the features of passion elevated to the point of delirium; the patients, furious or otherwise, are drawn irresistibly to acts which they repudiate. They can reason and judge about these acts perfectly sanely, just as well as anybody else; they deplore these acts and make efforts to conquer their impulses: are they not therefore a lucid period? Soon afterward the "paroxysm" follows the period of remission. Again prey to their delirium, these monomaniacs are carried away; they yield to their impulse, and reason no longer can control them. Obeying the impulse which presses upon them, they forget the motives that controlled them an instant earlier; they see nothing but the object of their fixation, much like a man who is prey to a powerful moral affectation and sees nothing but the object of his passion."

At the turn of the century, Kraepelin (1915) and Bleuler (1988) used the terms "pathological impulses" and "reactive impulses," respectively, to describe these conditions. They included pyromania, kleptomania, buying mania (oniomania), morbid collecting, impulses "to give everyone a present," anonymous letter writing, and impulsive poison mixing as examples (McElroy, Keck et al., 1995a). Like Esquirol, both authors stressed the impulsive features of these conditions, emphasizing how they may be enacted in an altered state of awareness. In describing buying mania, for example, Bleuler (1988, p. 540) writes:

> "The particular element is impulsiveness; they "cannot help it," which sometimes even expresses itself in the fact that not withstanding a good school intelligence, the patients are absolutely incapable to think differently, and to conceive the senseless consequences of their act, and the possibilities of not doing it. They do not even feel the impulse, but they act out of their nature like the caterpillar which devours the leaves."

Kraepelin and Bleuler also noted that these disorders had compulsive features. Specifically, they described the uncontrollable, compelling, and senseless nature of the impulses; the association of the impulses with anxiety, tension, and other negative or unpleasant affective states; and how the impulses could be resisted as well as enacted impulsively. In describing pyromania, for example, Bleuler (1988, p. 539) writes:

> "The perpetrators of the act cannot find, as a rule, any adequate reason, unless the prosecutor examines it into them; the act is so little their own that even if they are otherwise of a normal nature they cannot even display the proper regret . . . The act is sometimes preceded by distinct moodiness with anxiety, "homesickness," digestive, and similar disturbances. During the accomplishment of the act some seem to be in a kind of twilight state, while others reflect and go through a conscious struggle between their impulse and their morality."

In 1954, Frosch and Wortis examined the relationship between the irresistible impulse and impulsivity in general. They defined an impulse as "the sudden unpremeditated welling-up of a drive toward some action, which usually has the quality of hastiness and a lack of deliberation," and "morbid" impulses as further characterized by "minimal distortion of the original impulse" and an "irresistible and impelling quality in a setting of extreme tension." They divided the "impulse disorders" into two major groups based on whether the abnormal impulsivity was a discrete symptom or a pervasive characterological feature. The first group, characterized by "one or many, more or less isolated impulsive acts usually of a recurring quality," included three subgroups: (1) the impulse neuroses (kleptomania, pyromania, and addictions), (2) the perversions or impulsive sexual deviations (e.g., the paraphilias), and (3) catathymic crisis (an isolated, nonrepetitive act of violence). The second group, called the character impulse disorders and characterized by "a diffuseness of the impulse disturbance which permeates the personality without specifically attaching itself to any one kind of impulse," also included three subgroups: organic syndrome, psychopathic personality, and neurotic character disorder. Frosch and Wortis distinguished impulse disorders from obsessive-compulsive disorder by stating that the former, but not the latter, also were characterized by ego-syntonicity ("the impulse is wholly or partly in harmony with the momentary aims of the psyche") and a pleasurable component at the moment of expression.

Despite this extensive historical literature, the ICDs were not included in the *Diagnostic and Statistical Manuals of Mental Disorders* of the American Psychiatric Association until publication of the third edition (*DSM-III*; American Psychiatric Association, 1980). In the *DSM-IV*, the core feature of an ICD is defined as the failure to resist an impulse, drive, or temptation to commit an act that is harmful to the individual or to others. The *DSM-IV* also stipulates that, for most ICDs, the individual feels an increasing sense of tension or arousal before committing the act and then experiences pleasure, gratification, or relief at the time of committing the act. After the act is performed, there may or may not be genuine regret, self-reproach, or guilt. Thus, ICD symptoms may be ego-syntonic, particularly when relief or even pleasure is experienced at the moment they are enacted. But they may also be ego-dystonic, with the impulses associated with tension or anxiety and the behaviors generating self-reproach, shame, or guilt.

The *DSM-IV* (like the *DSM-III* and *DSM-IIIR*) does not have a formal category for ICDs. Rather, ICDs are listed in a residual category—the ICDs Not Elsewhere Classified, which includes intermittent explosive disorder, kleptomania, pathological gambling, pyromania, trichotillomania, and ICDs Not Otherwise Specified (NOS). Examples of ICDs NOS are compulsive buying or shopping (also called buying mania or oniomania), repetitive self-mutilation, nonparaphilic sexual addictions (also called sexual compulsions), onychophagia (severe nail biting), compulsive skin picking (also called psychogenic excoriation), and eating disorders characterized by binge eating (e.g., bulimia nervosa and binge eating disorder (McElroy, Keck et al., 1995a, 1995b). In the *DSM-IV* section on ICDs Not Elsewhere Specified, several disorders that are classified elsewhere in the *DSM-IV* are cited as examples of ICDs, although they are not defined as such in their respective categories. These disorders include the substance use disorders, as well as paraphilias, personality disorders with impulsive features, and attention deficit/hyperactivity disorder. Thus, although the *DSM-IV* does not define substance use disorders as ICDs in the section in which they are classified and defined, it cites substance use disorders as examples of ICDs in the section "ICDs Not Elsewhere Classified." In short, the *DSM-IV* considers substance use disorders to be forms of ICDs.

EPIDEMIOLOGY

ICDs generally are presumed to be rare. For example, three recent self-report surveys of hair pulling among college students found that only 0.6%, 1.0%, and 0.005%, respectively, of the populations assessed met the *DSM-IIIR* criteria for trichotillomania (Christenson, Pyle & Mitchell, 1991; Rothbaum, Shaw et al., 1993).

However, for most of the established and potential ICDs, systematic studies using operational diagnostic criteria to determine prevalence rates in the general population have not been done. Thus, there are no systematic data regarding the general population prevalence rates of intermittent explosive disorder, kleptomania, pyromania, paraphilias, nonparaphilic sexual addictions, compulsive buying, compulsive skin picking, or repetitive self mutilation; and thus, of ICDs in general. Also, studies indicate that pathological gambling—the only ICD for which systematic prevalence data are available—is common and that its prevalence is increasing (Lesieur & Rosenthal, 1991; Lopez-Ibor & Carrasco, 1995; Volberg & Steadman, 1988). A recent large-scale epidemiological survey of psychiatric morbidity in a Chinese community sample using the Diagnostic Interview Schedule, for example, found a lifetime prevalence of *DSM-III* pathological gambling of 3.0% among men and 0.16% among women (Chen, Wong et al., 1993). Indeed, among men, pathological gambling was the third most common psychiatric disorder. It is therefore noteworthy that many ICDs, including intermittent explosive disorder, kleptomania, trichotillomania, and paraphilias, have been hypothesized to be more common than realized.

Although few systematic data are available, ICDs appear to be marked by gender differences. Thus, intermittent explosive disorder, pathological gambling, pyromania, paraphilias, and nonparaphilic sexual addictions appear to be more common in men, whereas kleptomania, trichotillomania, compulsive shopping, and repetitive self-mutilation appear to be more common in women (McElroy, Keck et al., 1995a).

PHENOMENOLOGIC SIMILARITIES

It has long been recognized that ICDs and substance use disorders share phenomenologic similarities, as evidenced by the frequent inclusion of substance use disorders as forms of ICDs since the mid-1800s up to the present. Indeed, many patients with ICDs claim to be addicted to their harmful behaviors. Specifically, the irresistible impulses of ICDs resemble the cravings to drink alcohol or use drugs of substance use disorders. Drug craving has been defined as an "irresistible urge that compels drug-seeking behavior," as well as an "urgent and overpowering desire" or an "irresistible impulse" to use a substance (Halikas, Kuhn et al., 1991; Halikas, 1997). Also, alcohol and drug cravings often are associated with tension, anxiety, or other dysphoric, depressive, or negative affective states (Mathew, Claghorn & Largen, 1979; Switt & Stout, 1992; Weddington, Brown et al., 1990) and/or with arousal or excitement (Childress, McLellan et al., 1987), similar to the negative affective states and arousal that occur with ICD impulses (Griffiths, 1995). Conversely, ICD actions often are associated with pleasurable feelings, variously described by patients as feeling "high," "euphoric," a "thrill," or a "rush," which resemble the elevated mood or euphoria of alcohol and drug intoxication (Blume, 1997). For example, pathological gambling has been described as inducing "a stimulating, tranquilizing, or pain-relieving response" (Custer, 1984), as well as being an "anesthetic" with hypnotizing properties (Lesieur & Rosenthal, 1991); moreover, individuals with repetitive self-mutilation frequently report that they do not feel pain upon self-mutilation (Favazza, & Simeon 1995).

Indeed, just as substance-dependent persons use alcohol or drugs to relieve or "self-medicate" negative affective states, so do persons with ICDs achieve relief by engaging in their harmful behaviors

(Blume, 1997). Additionally, the changes in awareness that may accompany ICD acts are similar to the cognitive changes associated with intoxication (Jacobs, 1988). As Esquirol noted, "the irresistible impulses [of monomanias] show all of the features of passion elevated to the point of delirium." Thus, some persons with intermittent explosive disorder state that they develop an altered state of consciousness or "amnesia" during their explosive episodes (Maletzky, 1973), while some pathological gamblers report dissociative-like states while gambling (Blume 1997).

ICDs and substance use disorders also display similar disturbances in affective regulation (Goodman, 1997; Griffiths, 1995). As noted above, ICD impulses and behaviors often are associated with depressive and/or euphoric affective states that are similar to those of depression and intoxication. Moreover, after performance of an ICD action and resolution of the associated "high," patients with ICDs often describe the acute onset of anergic depressive symptoms similar to those that may occur in withdrawal from many substances, including depressed mood, feelings of guilt and self-reproach, and fatigue. For example, one woman with compulsive buying (which met *DSM-IIIR* criteria for an ICD NOS) reported that she experienced severe anxiety with her impulses to buy (which typically occurred when she was depressed), a "high like taking cocaine" with the act of buying, and then a prompt "crash" that was characterized by depression, guilt, anxiety, and fatigue (McElroy, Satlin et al., 1991b). Indeed, the author's research group has likened the affective dysregulation of ICDs to that of bipolar disorder (McElroy, Keck et al., 1995a; McElroy, Pope et al., 1996), just as others have noted similarities between the affective symptoms of bipolar disorder and those induced by substance abuse (Brady & Lydiard, 1992; Dilsaver, 1987). (Researchers also have noted that patients with bipolar disorder appear to be addicted to their euphoric manic symptoms, and have speculated that mania [especially euphoric mania], along with ICDs, might represent auto-addictions.)

Another phenomenologic similarity between ICDs and substance use disorders is that ICD behaviors may be associated with tolerance and withdrawal. For example, it has been reported that pathological gamblers need to gamble progressively larger sums of money to achieve the desired "high" (Anderson, 1984), and that they may develop physiological withdrawal symptoms (including insomnia, anorexia, tremulousness, headaches, abdominal pain, upset stomach, diarrhea, palpitations, nightmares, sweating, and breathing problems) (Wray & Dickerson, 1981), as well as depressive symptoms (Linden, Pope & Jonas, 1986), upon abrupt discontinuation of gambling. Indeed, "needs to gamble with increasing amounts of money in order to achieve the desired excitement" and "is restless or irritable when attempting to cut down or stop gambling," which are analogous to tolerance and withdrawal, are listed as *DSM-IV* defining criteria for pathological gambling (American Psychiatric Association, 1994; Blume, 1997). Some of the authors' patients with kleptomania have similarly described a need to steal in increasingly risky situations in order to maintain their stealing-induced "rush." Moreover, both the "self-medication" of benzodiazepine withdrawal through the thrill of kleptomanic stealing and the "switching of addictions" from alcohol and drugs to gambling have been described, suggesting that ICD acts and substances of abuse may sometimes be cross-tolerant with one another (Fishbain, 1987) or that an ICD "high" may substitute for a substance-induced "high" (Blume, 1997).

Conversely, the disinhibiting effects of ICDs and substances of abuse may be additive. Many persons with ICDs, especially those with intermittent explosive disorder, report that alcohol or drug intoxication worsens their symptoms and/or makes them more likely to act on their impulses (Maletzky, 1973; McElroy, Soutullo et al., 1998).

Yet another phenomenologic similarity between ICDs and substance use disorders is that they share similar phenomenologic features with obsessive-compulsive disorder (OCD) (McElroy, Hudson et al., 1993; Modell, Glaser et al., 1992). Obsessions are defined as persistent ideas, thoughts, impulses, or images that are experienced as intrusive and inappropriate (i.e., are ego-dystonic), and that cause anxiety or distress. Compulsions are defined as repetitive behaviors or mental acts, the goal of which is to prevent or reduce anxiety or distress.

As noted earlier, ICDs and OCD generally have been considered separate diagnostic entities, with ICD impulses and actions distinguished from OCD obsessions and compulsions by the former being considered more harmful, less senseless, more spontaneous, more likely to be associated with pleasure, and more ego-syntonic—features that ICDs share with substance use disorders. Specifically, OCD symptoms have been associated with over-estimation of risk, and thus with behaviors that aim to avoid harm or reduce risk; good insight into the absurdity or senselessness of symptoms; attempts to resist symptoms; and lack of pleasure with symptoms. Indeed, the *DSM-IV* specifies that OCD obsessions are recognized by the afflicted person as "alien, not within his or her control, and not the kind of thought he or she would expect to have," and that the goal of compulsions is "not to provide pleasure or gratification" (APA, 1994).

In actuality, however, the symptoms of all three disorders vary considerably with respect to these variables. OCD symptoms may, at times, be impulsive, associated with poor insight, and ego-syntonic (Hollander, 1993; McElroy, Hudson et al., 1993; McElroy, Keck et al., 1994). Conversely, ICD impulses (McElroy, Hudson et al., 1993) and substance cravings (Anton, Moak & Latham, 1996; Modell, Glaser et al., 1992), like OCD obsessions, are experienced as intrusive, repetitive, unwanted, associated with anxiety and as having an irresistible or compelling quality, and being difficult or impossible to resist. Indeed, the *DSM-IV* uses the term "impulse" to define an obsession, implying that obsessions and impulses are similar and may even be the same phenomenon. Moreover, ICD acts and substance abuse, like OCD compulsions, often are experienced as uncontrollable and anxiety- or tension-relieving, may be resisted, and often are followed by self-reproach or guilt.

Studies using modified versions of the Yale-Brown Obsessive-Compulsive Scale (YBOCS) (Goodman, Price et al., 1989) to assess obsessionality and compulsivity in heavy drinkers have found significant correlations between subjectively-rated craving for alcoholic beverages and several YBOCS questions regarding alcohol-related thoughts and drinking behavior (Modell, Glaser et al., 1992; Anton, Moak & Latham, 1996). Indeed, one such scale, the Obsessive Compulsive Drinking Scale (OCDS) (Anton, Moak & Latham, 1996), has proved to be a reliable instrument in quantify craving among alcohol-dependent persons. Research with the OCDS further suggests that, as severity of alcoholism increases, so does the intensity of the obsessive thoughts about alcohol and the compulsive urge to use alcohol (Anton, Moak & Latham, 1996).

In short, rather than viewing OCD symptoms as compulsive and ego-syntonic, and ICD and substance use symptoms as impulsive and ego-dystonic, all three sets of symptoms may have compulsive and ego-dystonic as well as impulsive and ego-syntonic features (McElroy, Hudson et al., 1993). As discussed later in this chapter, this conceptualization may help to explain some of the heterogeneity found in both ICDs and substance use disorders.

COURSE OF THE DISORDER

Although less systematic data are available for ICDs than for substance use disorders, both conditions often begin in adolescence or early adulthood and subsequently follow episodic and/or chronic courses (Burt, 1995; Wise & Tierney, 1994). Thus, like substance use disorders, ICD symptoms may occur in "bouts" punctuated by symptom-free intervals, or continuously over extended periods, often waxing and waning in severity. Also similar to substance use disorders, many ICDs (including intermittent explosive disorder, kleptomania, pyromania, trichotillomania, and paraphilias) may have an onset of symptoms in childhood or mid-adulthood (McElroy, Hudson et al., 1992; McElroy, Keck et al., 1995a). However, it should be acknowledged that these similarities are fairly nonspecific.

COMORBIDITY

Although preliminary, three lines of comorbidity data provide further support for a possible relationship between ICDs and substance abuse. These are: (1) findings of elevated rates of substance use disorders in patients with ICDs; (2) findings of elevated rates of ICDs in patients with substance use disorders; and (3) studies indicating that ICDs and substance use disorders display similar comorbidity patterns with other Axis I and Axis II psychiatric disorders.

The authors have found no epidemiologic or controlled clinical studies that have assessed associated psychopathology in persons with ICDs. However, more than 15 studies have used diagnostic criteria to assess Axis I psychiatric disorders in persons (mostly patients) with various ICDs, and many of these studies used structured clinical interviews. All found apparently elevated rates of associated substance use disorders. Specifically, of 24 impulsive violent offenders evaluated by one group (Linnoila, Virkkunen et al., 1983; Virkkunen, DeJong et al., 1989), 18 (75%) of whom met *DSM-III* criteria for intermittent explosive disorder, all met *DSM-IIIR* criteria for lifetime alcohol abuse. Of 22 impulsive arsonists evaluated in the same study, 20 (19%) met *DSM-IIIR* criteria for lifetime alcohol abuse. Of 14 subjects with *DSM-IV* intermittent explosive disorder evaluated by Salomen, Mazure et al. (1994), eight (57%) had abused substances in the past. Of

27 subjects with *DSM-IV* intermittent explosive disorder evaluated by the authors, 12 (48%) met *DSM-IV* criteria for a lifetime substance use disorder (McElroy, Soutullo et al., 1998). Of 20 patients with kleptomania evaluated by the authors, 10 (50%) met *DSM-IIIR* criteria for a lifetime substance use disorder (McElroy, Pope et al., 1991a). Of 140 pathological gamblers in four studies, 66 (47%) had lifetime histories of substance abuse or dependence (Linden, Pope et al., 1986; Ramirez, 1983; Specker, Carlson et al., 1996). Of 74 patients with trichotillomania in two studies, 17 (23%) had lifetime histories of substance abuse or dependence (Christenson, Mackenzie et al., 1991a; Swedo, Leonard et al., 1989). In three studies of 90 compulsive buyers, 33 (37%) displayed lifetime substance use disorders (Christenson, Faber et al., 1994; McElroy, Keck et al., 1994; Schlosser, Black et al., 1994). Of 15 men with *DSM-III* paraphilias evaluated by Kruesi (1992), eight (53%) met lifetime criteria for a substance use disorder. Of 60 consecutive male outpatients seeking treatment for a paraphilia (N = 34) or a "paraphilia-related disorder" (N = 26) evaluated by Kafka and Prentky (1994), 47% displayed a lifetime history of a substance use disorder, especially alcohol abuse (40%). Of 22 adolescent sex offenders evaluated by the authors, each of whom had at least one *DSM-IIIR* paraphilia, 23 (62%) met *DSM-IIIR* criteria for a lifetime substance use disorder (Galli, Raute et al., 1995). Further, of 36 men with compulsive sexual behaviors recruited by newspaper advertisement (seven [19%] of whose "main compulsive sexual behavior" was paraphilic) evaluated by Black and colleagues (1997), 23 (64%) reported a lifetime history of a substance use disorder.

Conversely, high rates of ICDs have been reported in persons seeking treatment for substance use disorders. In a study of 458 substance-dependent inpatients, Lesieur and colleagues (1986) found that 9% met lifetime diagnostic criteria for pathological gambling and an additional 10% reported subthreshold gambling problems. Of 100 adolescent substance-dependent inpatients evaluated by Lesieur and Heineman (1988), 14% met criteria for a lifetime diagnosis of pathological gambling and an additional 14% described subthreshold gambling problems. Similarly, of 298 cocaine abusers in treatment who were evaluated by Steinberg and colleagues (1992), 15% displayed a concurrent diagnosis of pathological gambling. In the latter study, cocaine abusers who were pathological gamblers were more likely to be dependent on alcohol and other drugs than those who were not pathological gamblers. Finally, Washton (1989) reported that 70% of outpatients entering a program for cocaine addiction also were engaging in compulsive sexual behavior.

Substantial epidemiologic and clinical data indicate that substance use disorders are highly comorbid with other Axis I disorders, especially mood, anxiety and, in women, eating disorders (Brooner, King et al., 1997; Gold, Johnson et al., 1997; Goodwin & Jamison, 1990; Regier, Farmer et al., 1990). The ICD studies noted above suggest that these disorders, like substance use disorders, also show elevated comorbidity with mood, anxiety, and eating disorders (McElroy, Hudson et al., 1992; McElroy, Keck et al., 1995a; McElroy, Pope et al., 1996; Kafka, 1995; Kafka & Prentky, 1994). Moreover, clinical studies indicating that ICDs may be associated with disproportionately high rates of bipolar relative to depressive mood disorders (McElroy et al., 1996) are consistent with the Epidemiologic Catchment Area (ECA) study finding that substance use disorders are associated with disproportionately higher rates of bipolar relative to unipolar major depressive disorders (Regier, Farmer et al., 1990).

Yet another possible comorbidity similarity between ICDs and substance use disorders is that each may be associated with elevated rates of personality disorders with impulsive features, especially antisocial and borderline personality disorders. Substantial epidemiologic and clinical data indicate that substance use disorders and antisocial personality disorder co-occur much more often than expected by chance alone (Regier, Farmer et al., 1990). Although personality disorders with impulsive features (especially antisocial and borderline) have been hypothesized to be ICDs, few studies have evaluated whether personality disorder patients perform their harmful behaviors in response to irresistible impulses (Coid, 1993; McElroy, Keck et al., 1995a). Therefore, it is not known whether ICDs and impulsive personality disorders represent separate but related conditions that are highly comorbid, identical entities (with impulsive personality disorder possibly representing the most severe cases or persons with multiple ICDs), or independent entities that may co-occur by chance, but that are easily misdiagnosed as one or the other.

Nevertheless, preliminary studies suggest that, similar to substance use disorders, some ICDs (including intermittent explosive disorder, pyromania, pathological gambling, paraphilias, nonparaphilic sexual addictions, and repetitive self mutilation) may be associated with high rates of impulsive (or cluster

B) personality disorders and/or antisocial behaviors (McElroy, Keck et al, 1995a). For example, of 54 impulsive violent offenders and fire setters evaluated by Linnoila and colleagues (1989), 29 (54%) of whom had *DSM-III* intermittent explosive disorder, 37 (69%) had borderline and nine (17%) had antisocial personality disorders, whereas six (11%) had paranoid and five (9%) had passive-aggressive personality disorders (by *DSM-III* criteria). Pathological gamblers have been shown to have elevated scores on the psychopathic deviation (pd) scale of the Minnesota Multiphasic Personality Inventory (MMPI), to engage in a wide variety of illegal behaviors, and to have possibly increased rates of antisocial and narcissistic personality disorders (Moran, 1970; Blaszczynski, McConaghy & Frankova, 1989; Lesieur & Rosenthal, 1991). Of 15 men with paraphilias evaluated by Kruesi and colleagues (1992), four (27%) met criteria for antisocial personality disorder. And of 36 men with compulsive sexual behaviors evaluated by Black and colleagues (1997) for *DSM-IIIR* personality disorders by consensus diagnosis, five (15%) subjects were determined to have a cluster A disorder, 10 (29%) a cluster B disorder, and eight (24%) a cluster C disorder.

FAMILY HISTORY

Available family history data provide tentative support for an ICD-substance abuse relationship. Family studies of probands with substance use disorders have consistently found elevated rates of substance abuse in their first-degree relatives (Anthenelli & Schuckit, 1997). Although there are no controlled family history studies of ICDs, open studies (most of which use the family history method [Andreasen, Endicott et al., 1977]) have found relatively high rates of substance use disorders in first-degree relatives of individuals with various ICDs. These disorders include intermittent explosive disorder or episodic dyscontrol (Maletzky, 1973; Linnoila, Virkkunen et al., 1983; Linnoila, DeJong & Virkkunen, 1989; Virkkunen, DeJong et al., 1989), kleptomania (McElroy, Pope et al., 1991a), pathological gambling (McCormick, Russo et al., 1984; Roy, Adinoff et al., 1988), and compulsive buying (McElroy, Phillips & Keck, 1994). For example, of 54 impulsive violent offenders and fire setters (29 of whom had *DSM-III* intermittent explosive disorder and 52 of whom had *DSM-III* alcohol abuse) evaluated by Linnoila, DeJong and Virkkunen (1989), 41 (81%) had first- or second-degree relatives with alcoholism and 35 (65%) had alcoholic fathers.

Moreover, subjects with alcoholic fathers were more often impulsive and had a lower mean cerebrospinal fluid (CSF) 5-hydroxyindoleacetic acid (5-HIAA) concentration than subjects without alcoholic fathers. Of 103 first-degree relatives (aged 16 years or older) of 20 individuals with kleptomania who were evaluated blindly by the authors with the family history method, 21 (20%) had an alcohol or substance use disorder (McElroy, Pope et al., 1991a). Ramirez and colleagues (1983) reported that 50% of 51 pathological gamblers each had a alcoholic parent. Similarly, Roy and colleagues (1988) reported that 25% of 24 pathological gamblers had a first-degree relative with alcohol abuse.

Another possible similarity is that ICDs and substance use disorders may share elevated familial rates of mood disorder. For example, of the 103 first-degree relatives of the 20 patients with kleptomania evaluated by the authors, 22 (21%) had a major mood disorder, 17% with major depression and 5% with bipolar disorder. Roy and colleagues (1988) reported that 33% of 24 pathological gamblers had a first-degree relative with mood disorder. And in a study of 17 compulsive buyers, the authors found that 16 (94%) had at least one first-degree relative with a mood disorder (McElroy, Phillips & Keck, 1994).

Other studies, however, have found relatively low rates of substance use and mood disorders in the first degree relatives of persons with ICDs. For example, of 132 first-degree relatives of 33 patients with temper outbursts (22 of whom had *DSM-III* intermittent explosive disorder), Mattes and Fink (1987) reported that 8% had alcohol or drug abuse and 11% had depression. Also, Linden and colleagues (1986) found that among 175 first-degree relatives of 25 pathological gamblers, 19 (11%) displayed alcohol abuse or dependence and 18 (10%) displayed a major mood disorder.

NEUROBIOLOGICAL STUDIES

The neurobiology of ICDs has been relatively unstudied, and few data are available that compare the neurobiology of ICDs with that of substance use disorders. Nevertheless, preliminary data suggest that some of the neurobehavioral processes and neurotransmitter systems hypothesized to be involved in addiction also may be involved in ICDs. In short, it has been suggested that the addictive process involves impaired behavioral inhibition (i.e., pathological impulsivity), aberrant function of the motivational-reward system, and impaired affect regulation, and that these three processes are associated with dysfunction in the serotonin (5HT), norepinephrine (NE), dopamine (DA), and/or endogenous opioid systems (Goodman, 1995, 1997; Miller & Gold, 1993; Nutt, 1996). It has been similarly hypothesized that interactions among serotonergic, noradrenergic, dopaminergic, and endogenous opioid neurotransmitter systems are important in the pathogenesis of ICDs, with serotonergic abnormalities possibly underlying some of their impulsive (and/or compulsive) features; noradrenergic, dopaminergic, and opioid abnormalities underlying their pleasurable or euphoric features; and abnormalities in all four systems underlying their affective dysregulation (McElroy, Pope et al., 1996; Stein, Hollander & Liebowitz, 1993; Winchel & Stanley, 1991).

Evidence of serotonergic involvement in ICDs, although mixed (Roy, Adinoff et al., 1988), comes from findings in individuals with impulsive aggression, impulsive fire-setting, self-injurious behavior, and pathological gambling (Stein, Hollander & Liebowitz, 1993). For example, in a study of 58 violent offenders and impulsive fire setters, 33 (57%) of whom had *DSM-III* intermittent explosive disorder, CSF concentrations of 5-HIAA in the impulsive offenders and fire setters were significantly lower than in the non-impulsive offenders and normal control subjects (Linnoila, Virkkunen et al., 1983; Virkkunen, DeJong et al., 1989). Moreover, low CSF 5-HIAA concentrations were associated with a lifetime history of suicide attempts. In a study of 21 patients with major depression, the five patients who exhibited self-aggressive behaviors had significantly lower CSF 5-HIAA concentrations than the other 16 patients (Lopez-Ibor & Carrasco, 1985). Similarly, in a controlled study of subjects with repetitive self mutilation and borderline personality disorder, Simeon and colleagues (1992) found that lower serotonergic activity (as measured by platelet imipramine binding sites and affinity) was related to greater severity of self-mutilation. Other findings of reduced serotonergic activity in ICDs include blunted prolactin release in response to intravenously administered clomipramine (Moreno, Saiz-Ruiz & Lopez-Ibor, 1991) and low levels of platelet monoamine oxidase (MAO) activity (Blanco, Orensanz-Munoz et al., 1996; Carrasco, Saiz-Ruiz et al., 1993) in pathological gamblers.

Evidence for abnormalities in noradrenergic and dopaminergic neurotransmission in ICDs comes from findings in pathological gamblers. Roy and colleagues (1988) reported that 24 individuals with *DSM-IIIR* pathological gambling displayed significantly lower plasma MHPG concentrations, greater centrally produced fractions of CSF MHPG, and greater urinary output of NE than did control subjects. In a subsequent study of 17 pathological gamblers, Roy, DeJong and Linnoila (1989) found highly significant positive correlations between measures of extraversion and indices of noradrenergic and dopaminergic function, including concentrations of plasma MHPG, CSF MHPG, urinary vanillylmandelic acid (VMA), and the sum of urinary NE and its major metabolites.

Further evidence suggesting dopaminergic involvement comes from findings that nearly 50% of a group of pathological gamblers carried the DRD2 gene receptor variant, which is present in 25% of the general population (Comings, Rosenthal et al., 1996). Moreover, in this population, the more severe the problem gambling, the more likely the individual was to be a carrier for this receptor variant.

The endogenous opioid system in ICDs has been relatively unstudied. Nonetheless, in one study, Coid, Allolio and Rees (1983) found that patients with habitual self-mutilation had higher mean plasma metenkephalin concentrations than control subjects. In another study, Blaszczynski and colleagues (1986) found lower baseline levels of beta-endorphins in pathological gamblers who gambled on horse races as compared to those who gambled on slot machines and normal controls. Also, preliminary evidence indicates that the endogenous opioid system may be deranged in eating disorders. As noted earlier, eating disorders, particularly those associated with binge eating, have been hypothesized to variants of ICDs (McElroy, Keck et al., 1995a, 1995b), as well as addictions to food (Stennie & Gold, 1997).

Further preliminary support for involvement of the endogenous opioid system in the pathophysiology of ICDs are reports of patients with repetitive self mutilation (Richardson & Zaleski, 1983) and bulimia nervosa (Stennie & Gold, 1997) responding to opiate antagonists (see below).

TREATMENT RESPONSE

Psychopharmacologic treatment response data provide further support for a possible relationship between ICDs and substance use disorders. Although findings are mixed, controlled studies suggest that various antidepressants may reduce craving for and overall consumption of substances in substance-dependent patients. These include serotonin reuptake inhibitors (SRIs) in alcohol abuse and dependence and cocaine dependence, and tricyclic antidepressants (TCAs) in cocaine dependence (Anton, 1995; Naranjo, Poulos et al., 1994; Rao, Ziedonis & Kosten, 1995). Similarly, various antidepressants have been reported to reduce the irresistible impulses and harmful behaviors of various ICDs. These include: SRIs in apparent intermittent explosive disorder, kleptomania, pathological gambling, trichotillomania, compulsive buying, onychophagia, nonparaphilic sexual additions, and paraphilias; tricyclics in apparent intermittent explosive disorder, kleptomania, trichotillomania, nonparaphilic sexual addictions, and paraphilias; monoamine oxidase inhibitors in kleptomania and trichotillomania; and atypical agents (e.g., trazodone or bupropion) in kleptomania and compulsive buying (Hollander, Frenkel et al., 1992; Kruesi, Fine et al., 1992; McElroy, Hudson et al., 1992; McElroy, Keck et al., 1995a, 1995b; McElroy, Pope et al., 1996; Swedo, Leonard et al., 1989; Zohar, Kaplan & Benjamin, 1994).

ICDs and substance use disorders, however, may differ in their response to mood stabilizers. Numerous double-blind, placebo-controlled studies of lithium in alcohol dependence have failed to confirm that lithium is superior to placebo in reducing abstinence. Moreover, three double-blind, placebo-controlled studies of carbamazepine in cocaine dependence have been negative (Cornish, Maany et al., 1995; Kranzler, Bauer et al., 1995; Montoya, Levin et al., 1995). (However, carbamazepine and valproate have been reported to be effective in alcohol and/or sedative hypnotic withdrawal in controlled trials [Keck, McElroy et al., 1994], and a recently completed double-blind, placebo-controlled pilot study of carbamazepine in alcohol dependence displayed treatment effects favoring carbamazepine [Mueller, Stout et al., 1997].) By contrast, there are case reports and open trials of successful lithium treatment of patients with intermittent explosive disorder, kleptomania, pathological gambling, trichotillomania, and paraphilias (e.g., transvestism and autoerotic asphyxiation) (Cesnik & Coleman, 1989; Christenson, Popkin et al., 1991b; Cutler & Heiser, 1978; McElroy, Pope et al., 1996; Moskowitz, 1980; Ward, 1975). Also, carbamazepine has been reported to be effective in intermittent explosive disorder and pathological gambling (Haller & Hinterhuber, 1994; Mattes, 1990), and valproate has been used successfully in individuals with intermittent explosive disorder, kleptomania, and compulsive buying (McElroy, Keck et al., 1991a, 1991b; Szymanski & Olympia, 1991).

Double-blind, placebo-controlled studies have shown that the opiate antagonist naltrexone reduces alcohol craving and consumption in alcohol-dependent persons (O'Brien, Volpicelli & Volpicelli, 1996; Volpicelli, Alterman et al., 1992). Although controlled studies of opiate antagonists in ICDs have not yet been done, open reports suggest these agents may reduce problem gambling, self-mutilation and binge eating in patients with pathological gambling (Kim, 1998), repetitive self mutilation (Richardson & Zaleski, 1983) and bulimia nervosa (Stennie & Gold, 1997), respectively.

ICDs and substance use disorders may share similar response to psychological treatments. In general, available data (which are very limited) suggest that individuals with ICDs, like those with substance use disorders, may not be particularly responsive to psychoanalytic or insight-oriented psychotherapies. Rather, ICDs, like substance use disorders, appear to be more amenable to psychological treatments that stress education, denial reduction, and relapse prevention and/or which employ cognitive-behavioral techniques (Blume, 1997; Goodman, 1997; Josephson & Brandolo, 1993). Also, self-help groups based on Alcoholic Anonymous (e.g., Gamblers Anonymous) have been reported to be helpful in the treatment of some people with pathological gambling and sexual addictions (Brown, 1991; Irons & Schneider, 1997).

IMPLICATIONS

Although preliminary, the evidence reviewed here indicates that ICDs and substance use disorders have many similarities. First, ICDs and substance use disorders are phenomenologically similar in that both are characterized by the repetitive performance of harmful, dangerous, or pleasurable behaviors, as well as irresistible impulses or desires to perform these behaviors. Both disorders also are characterized by impaired insight into the dangerousness or consequences of the behaviors (e.g., ego-syntonicity or denial), similar affective dysregulation (e.g., dysphoria or arousal with the impulses or cravings, relief that may be associated with euphoria with the behaviors, and depressed mood after the behaviors), and obsessive-compulsive features. Second, ICDs and substance use disorders display a similar course of illness in that both conditions often begin in adolescence or early adulthood and subsequently have an episodic or chronic course. Third, the two conditions show elevated comorbidity with each other, as well as similar comorbidity patterns with other psychiatric disorders, especially mood, anxiety, and probably antisocial personality disorders. Fourth, family history studies suggest that patients with certain ICDs, like persons with substance use disorders, have elevated rates of substance use and mood disorders in their first-degree relatives. Fifth, preliminary biological data suggest that ICDs may be associated with abnormalities in central serotonergic, dopaminergic, noradrenergic, and possibly endogenous opioid neurotransmission—the same neurotransmitter systems that have been hypothesized to be deranged in substance use disorders. Finally, some patients with ICDs, like some patients with substance use disorders, may respond to antidepressants (especially SRIs) and possibly opiate antagonists.

Indeed, some authorities have argued that ICDs should include a broader range of conditions characterized by abnormal or pathological impulsivity. Thus, this family of conditions might include not only the substance use disorders, but also other Axis I disorders with impulsive symptoms (such as ADHD and eating disorders), Axis II disorders with impulsive features (such as antisocial and borderline personality disorders), various mental disorders due to a general medical condition (such as organic personality disorder, especially the explosive type), and some neuropsychiatric disorders (such as Autistic disorder, tic disorders, and Prader-Willi syndrome) (Hollander, 1993). Conversely, because ICDs and substance use disorder also share obsessive-compulsive features, the authors and others have hypothesized that both disorders (or subsets of both disorders) may be related to OCD, and thus be members of a family of disorders related to OCD, often called OCD spectrum disorder (Hollander, 1993; McElroy, Hudson et al., 1993).

It also has been hypothesized that compulsivity and impulsivity are related, with each characterized by abnormal impulse control, and that disorders characterized by pathological impulsivity or compulsivity may constitute a family of related conditions more accurately termed compulsive-impulsive spectrum disorder (Hollander, 1993; McElroy, Pope et al., 1996). According to this model, all compulsive-impulsive spectrum disorders would be characterized by irresistible or compelling thoughts associated with anxiety, tension, or other negative affective states, and/or by repetitive behaviors aimed at reducing discomfort or eliciting pleasure. However, the differences among these disorders might be explained by the possibility that these conditions vary along a single dimension (or related dimensions) of compulsivity versus impulsivity. One extreme of this proposed dimension would consist of purely compulsive disorders further characterized by performance of harm-avoidant behaviors, insight into the senselessness of the behaviors, resistance to performing the behaviors, and absence of pleasure when the behaviors are performed (e.g., "classic" OCD and disorders thought to be closely related to OCD, such as body dysmorphic disorder and anorexia nervosa) (Phillips, McElroy et al., 1995).

The other end would consist of purely impulsive disorders further characterized by performance of harmful but potentially exciting behaviors, little insight into the dangerousness or consequences of the behaviors, automatic enactment of the behaviors, and pleasure when the behavior is performed (e.g., "classic" ICDs and substance use disorders). Various "atypical" or mixed compulsive-impulsive forms would be situated in between, such as OCD with impulsive features, ICDs and substance use disorders with prominent obsessive-compulsive features, and the co-occurrence of an ICD or a substance use disorder with OCD in the same individual. Indeed, such a model might explain some of the heterogeneity seen in both ICDs and substance use disorders (Carroll, Rounsaville et al., 1994; McElroy, Hudson et al., 1993). Thus, ICDs and substance use disorders might each have highly (or purely) impulsive (i.e., "classic") forms, highly compulsive (i.e., "atypical") forms, and mixed forms with both impulsive and compulsive features.

However, the above model does not explain the extensive overlap of ICDs, substance use disorders, OCD, and most other putative compulsive-impulsive spectrum disorders with mood disorders. To account for this overlap, we have hypothesized that most putative compulsive-impulsive spectrum disorders, or more broadly, all disorders characterized by a core disturbance in compulsivity and/or impulsivity, might belong to the larger family of affective spectrum disorder (McElroy, Pope et al., 1991; McElroy, Satlin et al., 1991; McElroy, Hudson et al., 1992; McElroy, Hudson et al., 1993; McElroy, Pope et al., 1996; Phillips, McElroy et al., 1995). Affective spectrum disorder is a hypothesized family of disorders related to mood disorders, characterized by high comorbidity with mood disorder, high familial rates of mood disorder, and response to thymoleptic agents, and thus, possibly a common pathophysiologic abnormality with mood disorder (Hudson & Pope, 1990). We have further hypothesized that compulsivity and impulsivity might be related to mood dysregulation, with depression (or unipolarity) similar to compulsivity, mania (or bipolarity) similar to impulsivity, and mixed affective states similar to mixtures of compulsivity and impulsivity (McElroy, Pope et al., 1996). Thus, compulsivity and depression each are characterized by inhibited or ruminative thinking and behavior, maintenance of insight or ego-dystonicity, and less marked fluctuations in mood state, with dysphoria alternating with relief rather than with euphoria or pleasurable feelings. Similarly, impulsivity and mania (or bipolarity) are each characterized by disinhibited or facilitated thinking and behavior, poor insight or ego-syntonicity, and more severe fluctuations in mood state, with dysphoria alternating with pleasurable affective states. Indeed, substance withdrawal and intoxication might also be viewed as representing more compulsive/depressive versus more impulsive/manic states, respectively.

If these speculations are correct, the compulsive-impulsive spectrum disorders might be arranged along an axis (or related axes) of compulsivity/unipolarity versus impulsivity/bipolarity, where disorders characterized by maximum compulsivity and unipolarity (e.g., OCD with a comorbid depressive disorder) are at one end, and those with maximum impulsivity and bipolarity (e.g., an ICD or a substance use disorder with a comorbid bipolar disorder) are at the other end. This hypothesis is supported by findings that ICDs and substance use disorders (and many other compulsive-impulsive spectrum disorders) are associated with apparently elevated rates of mood disorders, and by preliminary data suggesting that the more impulsive disorders (e.g., ICDs, substance use disorders) may be associated with higher rates of bipolar relative to depressive disorders as compared to the more compulsive disorders (e.g., OCD, body dysmorphic disorder) (McElroy, Phillips & Keck, 1994; McElroy, Keck et al., 1995a, 1995b; McElroy, Pope et al., 1996). Further preliminary support for such a dimension comes from the possible differences in thymoleptic responsiveness of various compulsive-impulsive spectrum disorders, with more compulsive forms (such as OCD) responding preferentially to SRIs, and more impulsive forms (such as ICDs) responding to a larger range of thymoleptics (e.g., SRIs, non-SRI antidepressants, and/or mood stabilizers).

This model of compulsive-impulsive spectrum disorders may have important clinical implications. For example, if pharmacologic responsiveness in fact varies along a compulsivity/unipolarity—impulsivity/bipolarity dimension (with more compulsive forms responding preferentially to SRIs and more impulsive forms responding to a wider range of thymoleptic agents), such responsiveness might be predicted based upon presenting phenomenology and comorbid affective symptoms or mood syndromes. Thus, patients with ICDs or substance use disorders with compulsive features might respond best to an SRI, especially if associated with comorbid depressive symptoms or a depressive disorder; whereas patients with more impulsive forms of these disorders might respond to a variety of antidepressants or, if accompanied by bipolar symptoms or a bipolar disorder, to mood stabilizers.

However, it is important that the concept of compulsive-impulsive spectrum disorders not be excessively broad, especially given the relative lack of empirical data on the disorders that have been hypothesized to belong to this family. At present it is not clear how similar a putative compulsive-impulsive spectrum disorder must be to OCD or to an ICD, and what these similarities should consist of. Indeed, even at this preliminary stage of knowledge, ICDs and substance use disorders may be more closely related to one another than to OCD. Further complicating this issue is the likelihood that ICDs, substance use disorders, and other putative compulsive-impulsive spectrum disorders are themselves each heterogeneous disorders. Thus, some of the putative compulsive-impulsive spectrum disorders may have subtypes that are more related to ICDs (e.g., the substance use disorders) and others that are more related to OCD (e.g., body dysmorphic disorder). Also, there are likely to be forms of compulsive-impulsive spectrum disorder, including subtypes of ICDs and substance use disorders, that are not related to affective spectrum disorder.

CONCLUSIONS

Available data, although preliminary, suggest that ICDs and substance use disorders may be related and, thus, may each belong to a larger family of disorders sharing a core disturbance in impulse control and affective regulation. Such a conceptual framework might be useful in several ways. First, awareness of the high comorbidity of these disorders with one another and with other psychiatric disorders, especially mood disorder, should increase recognition of the related disorders when a patient presents with an ICD or substance use disorder. Second, the degree of presenting impulsive versus compulsive features, as well as the type of comorbid affective symptoms or mood disorder, may help guide the choice of both psychopharmacologic and psychological treatments. Third, further research on the pathophysiologic and genetic substrates of these conditions, and of the relationships between impulsivity, addiction, compulsivity, and mood might be stimulated.

ACKNOWLEDGMENT: Supported in part by a grant from the Theodore and Vada Stanley Foundation.

REFERENCES

American Psychiatric Association (1980). *Diagnostic and Statistical Manual of Mental Disorders, 3rd Edition.* Washington, DC: American Psychiatric Press.

American Psychiatric Association (1987). *Diagnostic and Statistical Manual of Mental disorders, 3rd Edition, Revised.* Washington, DC: American Psychiatric Association.

American Psychiatric Association (1994). *Diagnostic and Statistical Manual of Mental Disorders, 4th Edition.* Washington, DC: American Psychiatric Association, 1994.

Anderson G & Brown RI (1984). Real and laboratory gambling, sensation-seeking and arousal. *British Journal of Psychology* 75:401–410.

Anderson G & Brown RI (1987). Some applications of reversal theory to the explanation of gambling and gambling addictions. *Journal on Gambling Behaviors* 3:179–189.

Andreasen NC, Endicott J, Spitzer RL & Winokur G (1977). The family history method using diagnostic inter-rater reliability and validity. *Archives of General Psychiatry* 34:1229–1235.

Anthenelli RM & Schuckit MA (1997). Genetics. In JH Lowinson, P Ruiz, RB Millman & JG Langrod (eds). *Substance Abuse: A Comprehensive Textbook.* Baltimore, MD: Williams & Wilkins, 41–51.

Anthony DT & Hollander E (1993). Sexual compulsions. In E Hollander (ed.) *Obsessive-Compulsive Related Disorders.* Washington, DC: American Psychiatric Press, 139–150.

Anton RF (1995). New directions in the pharmacotherapy of alcoholism. *Psychiatric Annals* 25:353–362.

Anton RF, Moak DH & Latham PK (1996). The Obsessive Compulsive Drinking Scale: A new method of assessing outcome in alcoholism treatment studies. *Archives of General Psychiatry* 53:225–231.

Black DW, Kehrberg LLD, Flumerfelt DL & Schlosser SS (1997). Characteristics of 36 subjects reporting compulsive sexual behavior. *American Journal of Psychiatry* 154:243–249.

Blanco C, Orensanz-Munoz L, Blanco-Jerez C & Suiz-Ruiz J (1996). Pathological gambling and platelet MAO activity: A psychobiological study. *Journal of Gambling Behavior* 5:137–152.

Blaszczynski A, McConaghy N & Frankova A (1991). Control versus abstinence in the treatment of pathological gambling: A two to nine year follow-up. *British Journal of Addiction* 86:299–306.

Blaszczynski A, Winter SW & McConaghy N (1986). Plasma endorphin levels in pathological gambling. *Journal of Gambling Behavior* 2:3–14.

Bleuler E (1988). *Textbook of Psychiatry. The Classics of Psychiatry and Behavioral Sciences Library.* Birmingham, AL: Gryphon Editions.

Blume SB (1997). Pathological gambling. In JH Lowinson, P Ruiz, RB Millman & JG Langrod (eds). *Substance Abuse: A Comprehensive Textbook.* Baltimore, MD: Williams & Wilkins, 330–337.

Boyd JH, Burke JD, Gruenberg E et al. (1984). Exclusion criteria of DSM-III: a study of co-occurrence of hierarchy-free syndromes. *Archives of General Psychiatry* 41:983–989.

Bradford J, Geller J, Lesieur HR, Rosenthal R & Wise M (1996). Impulse control disorders. In TA Widger, AJ Frances, HA Pincus, R Ross, MB First & DW Wakefield (eds.) *DSM- IV Sourcebook, Vol 2.* Washington DC: American Psychiatric Press, 1007–1031.

Brady KT & Lydiard RB (1992). Bipolar affective disorder and substance abuse. *Journal of Clinical Psychopharmacology* 12(Suppl):17–22.

Brooner AK, King VL, Kidorf M, Schmidt CW & Bigelow GE (1997). Psychiatric and substance use comorbidity among treatment-seeking opioid abusers. *Archives of General Psychiatry* 54:71–80.

Brown BR (1991). The selective adaptation of the Alcoholics Anonymous program by Gamblers Anonymous. *Journal of Gambling Behavior* 7:187–206.

Burt VK (1995). Impulse-control disorders not elsewhere classified. In HI Kaplan & BJ Saddock (eds.) *Comprehensive Textbook of Psychiatry, 6th Ed.* Baltimore, MD: Williams & Wilkins, 1409–1418.

Carnes PJ (1990). Sexual addiction: Progress, criticism, challenges. *American Journal of Preventive Psychiatry & Neurology* 2:1–8.

Carrasco JL, Saiz-Ruiz J, Moreno I & Lopez-Ibor JJ (1994). Low platelet MAO activity in pathological gambling. *Acta Psychiatrica Scandinavica* 90:427–431.

Carroll KM, Rounsaville BJ, Gordon LT et al. (1994). Psychotherapy and pharmacotherapy for ambulatory cocaine abusers. *Archives of General Psychiatry* 51:177–187.

Cesnik JA & Coleman E (1989). Use of lithium carbonate in the treatment of autoerotic asphyxia. *American Journal of Psychotherapy* 63:277–286.

Chen C-N, Wong J, Lee N, Chan-Ho MW, Tak-Fai J & Fung M (1993). The Shatin Community Mental Health

Survey in Hong Kong. II. Major findings. *Archives of General Psychiatry* 50:125–133.

Childress AR, McLellan AT, Natale M & O'Brien CP (1987). Mood states can illicit conditioned withdrawal and craving in opiate abuse patients. *NIDA Research Monograph Series* 76:137–144.

Christenson GA, Faber RJ, de Zwaan M et al. (1994). Compulsive buying: Descriptive characteristics and psychiatric comorbidity. *Journal of Clinical Psychiatry* 55:5–11.

Christenson GA, Mackenzie TB & Mitchell JE (1991a). Characteristics of 60 adult chronic hair pullers. *American Journal of Psychiatry* 148:365–370.

Christenson GA, Popkin MK, Mackennzie TB & Realmuto GM (1991b). Lithium treatment of chronic hair pulling. *Journal of Clinical Psychiatry* 52:116–120.

Christenson GA, Pyle RL & Mitchell JE (1991). Estimated lifetime prevalence of trichotillomania in college students. *Journal of Clinical Psychiatry* 52:415–417.

Coid JW (1991). An affective syndrome in psychopaths with borderline personality disorder? *British Journal of Psychiatry* 162:641–650.

Coid J, Allolio B & Rees LH (1983). Raised plasma metenkephalin in patients who habitually mutilate themselves. *Lancet* 10:545–546.

Comings DE, Rosenthal RJ, Lesieur HR et al. (1996). The molecular genetics of pathological gambling: The DRD2 gene. *Pharmacogenetics*.

Cornish JW, Maany I, Fudalla PJ, et al. (1995). Carbamazepine treatment for cocaine dependence. *Drug and Alcohol Dependence* 38:221–227.

Custer RL (1984). Profile of the pathological gambler. *Journal of Clinical Psychiatry* 45:35–38.

Cutler N & Heiser JF (1978). Retrospective diagnosis of hypomania following successful treatment of episodic violence with lithium: A case report. *American Journal of Psychiatry* 135:753–754.

Dilsaver SC (1987). The pathophysiologies of substance abuse and affective disorders: An integrative model? *Journal of Clinical Psychopharmacology* 7:1–10.

Esquirol E (1838). *Des Maladies Mentales*. Paris, France: Bailliere.

Favazza AR & Simeon D (1995). Self-mutilation. In E Hollander & DJ Stein (eds.) *Impulsivity and Aggression*. Chichester, England: John Wiley & Sons, 185–200.

Fishbain DA (1987). Kleptomania as risk taking behavior in response to depression. *American Journal of Psychotherapy* 41:598–603.

Frosch J & Wortis SB (1954). A contribution to the nosology of the impulse disorders. *American Journal of Psychiatry* 111:132–138.

Galli VJ, Raute NJ, Kizer DL, McConville BJ & McElroy SL (1995). A study of the phenomenology, comorbidity, and preliminary treatment response of pedophiles and adolescent sex offenders. New Clinical Drug Evaluation Unit (NCDEU) 35th Annual Meeting, Orlando, Florida, (abstract).

Glatt MM & Cook CCH (1987). Pathological spending as a form of psychological dependence. *British Journal of Addiction* 82:1257–1258.

Gold MS, Johnson CR et al. (1997). Eating disorders. In JH Lowinson, P Ruiz, RB Millman & JG Langrod (eds.) *Substance Abuse: A Comprehensive Textbook.* Baltimore, MD: Williams & Wilkins, 319–330.

Goodman A (1997). Sexual addiction. In JH Lowinson, P Ruiz, RB Millman & JG Langrod (eds.) *Substance Abuse: A Comprehensive Textbook.* Baltimore, MD: Williams & Wilkins, 340–354.

Goodman A (1995). Addictive disorders: An integrated approach. Part One: An integrated understanding. *Journal of Min Addiction & Recovery* 2:33–76.

Goodman WK, Price LH, Rasmussen SA et al. (1989). The Yale-Brown Obsessive-Compulsive Scale, I. Development, use, and reliability. *Archives of General Psychiatry* 46:1006–1011.

Goodwin FK & Jamison KR (1990). *Manic-Depressive Illness*. New York, NY: Oxford University Press.

Griffiths M (1995). The role of subjective mood states in the maintenance of fruit machine gambling behaviour. *Journal of Gambling Studies* 11:123–135.

Halikas JA (1997). Craving. In JH Lowinson, P Ruiz, RB Millman & JG Langrod (eds.) *Substance Abuse: A Comprehensive Textbook.* Baltimore, MD: Williams & Wilkins, 85–90.

Halikas JA, Kuhn KL, Crosby R, Carlson G & Crea F (1991). The measurement of craving in cocaine patients using the Minnesota Cocaine Craving Scale. *Comprehensive Psychiatry* 32:22–27.

Haller R & Hinterhuber H (1994). Treatment of pathological gambling with carbamazepine. *Pharmacopsychiatry* 27:129.

Hollander E, ed. (1993). *Obsessive-Compulsive Related Disorders*. Washington, DC: American Psychiatric Press.

Hollander E, Frenkel M, DeCaria C, Trungold S & Stein DJ (1992). Treatment of pathological gambling with clomipramine [letter]. *American Journal of Psychiatry* 149:710–711.

Hudson JI & Pope HG, Jr (1990). Affective spectrum disorder: Does antidepressant response identify a family of disorders with a common pathophysiology? *American Journal of Psychiatry* 147:552–564.

Irons RR & Schneider JP (1997). Addictive sexual disorders. In NS Miller (ed.) *The Principles and Practice of Addiction Psychiatry*. Philadelphia, PA: W.B. Saunders, 441–457.

Jacobs DF (1988). Evidence for a common dissociative-like reaction among addicts. *Journal of Gambling Behavior* 3:237–247.

Josephson SC, Brandolo E (1993). Cognitive-behavioral approaches to obsessive-compulsive-related disorders. In E Hollander (ed.) *Obsessive-Compulsive Related Disorders*. Washington, DC: American Psychiatric Press, 215–240.

Kafka MP (1991). Successful antidepressant treatment of nonparaphilic sexual addictions and paraphilias in men. *Journal of Clinical Psychiatry* 52:60–65.

Kafka MP (1994). Sertraline pharmacotherapy for paraphilias and paraphilia-related disorders: An open trial. *Annals of Clinical Psychiatry* 6:189–195.

Kafka MP (1995). Sexual impulsivity. In E Hollander & DJ Stein (eds.) *Impulsivity and Aggression*. Chichester, England: John Wiley & Sons, 201–228.

Kafka MP & Prentky RA (1994). Preliminary observations of DSM-III-R Axis I comorbidity in men with paraphilias and paraphilia-related disorders. *Journal of Clinical Psychiatry* 55:481–487.

Keck PE Jr, McElroy SL, Thienhaus OJ & Faedda GL (1994). Antiepileptics. In K Modigh, OH Robak & P Vestergaard (eds.) *Anticonvulsants in Psychiatry*. Wrightson Biomedical Publishing, 99–111.

Kim SW (1998). Opioid antagonists in the treatment of impulse control disorders. *Journal of Clinical Psychiatry* 59:159–164.

Kranzler HR, Bauer LO, Hersh D & Klinghoffer V (1995). Carbamazepine treatment of cocaine dependence: A placebo- controlled trial. *Drug and Alcohol Dependence* 38:203–211.

Kruesi MJP, Fine S, Valladares L, Phillips RA, Jr & Rapoport JI (1992). Paraphilias: A double-blind crossover comparison of clomipramine versus desipramine. *Archives of Sexual Behavior* 21:587–593.

Leonard HL, Lenane MC, Swedo SE, Rettew DC & Rapoport JI (1991). A double-blind comparison of clomipramine and desipramine treatment of severe onychophagia (nail biting). *Archives of General Psychiatry* 48:821–827.

Lesieur HR, Blume SB & Zoppa RM (1986). Alcoholism, drug abuse, and gambling. *Alcoholism* (NY) 10:33–38.

Lesieur HR & Heineman M (1988). Pathological gambling among youthful multiple substance abusers in a therapeutic community. *British Journal of Addiction* 83:765–771.

Lesieur HR & Rosenthal RJ (1991). Pathological gambling: A review of the literature. *Journal of Gambling Studies* 7:5–39.

Linden RD, Pope HG Jr & Jonas JM (1986). Pathological gambling and major affective disorder: preliminary findings. *Journal of Clinical Psychiatry* 47:201–203.

Linnoila M, Virkkunen M, Scheinin M, Nuutila A, Rimon R & Goodwin FK (1983). Low cerebrospinal fluid 5-hydroxyindoleacetic acid concentration differentiates impulsive from nonimpulsive violent behavior. *Life Science* 33:2609–2614.

Linnoila M, DeJong J & Virkkunen M (1989). Family history of alcoholism in violent offenders and impulsive firesetters. *Archives of General Psychiatry* 46:613–616.

Lion JR & Scheinberg AW (1995). Disorders of impulse control. In GO Gabbard (ed.) *Treatment of Psychiatric Disorders, 2nd Ed.* Washington DC: American Psychiatric Press, 2457–2472.

Lopez-Ibor JJ & Carrasco JL (1995). Pathological gambling. In E Hollander & DJ Stein (eds.) *Impulsivity and Aggression*. Chichester, England: John Wiley & Sons, 137–149.

Maletzky BM (1973). The episodic dyscontrol syndrome. *Diseases of the Nervous System* 36:178–185.

Mathew RJ, Claghorn JL & Largen J (1979). Craving for alcohol in sober alcoholics. *American Journal of Psychiatry* 136:603–606.

Mattes JA (1990). Comparative effectiveness of carbamazepine and propranolol for rage outbursts. *Journal of Neuropsychiatry and Clinical Neuroscience* 21:249–255.

Mattes JA & Fink M (1990). A controlled family study of adopted patients with temper outbursts. *Journal of Nervous and Mental Disorders* 178:138–139.

McConaghy N, Armstrong M, Blaszczynski A & Allcock C (1983). Controlled comparison of aversive therapy and imaginal desensitization in compulsive gambling. *British Journal of Psychiatry* 142:366–372.

McCormick RA, Russo AM, Ramirez LF & Taber JI (1984). Affective disorders among pathological gamblers seeking treatment. *American Journal of Psychiatry* 141:215–218.

McElroy SL, Keck PE Jr, Hudson JI & Pope HG Jr (1995a). Disorders of impulse control. In H Hollander & DJ Stein (eds.) *Impulsivity and Aggression*. Chichester, England: John Wiley & Sons, 109–136.

McElroy SL, Keck PE Jr & Phillips KA (1995b). Kleptomania, compulsive buying, and binge eating disorder. *Journal of Clinical Psychiatry* 56(4 Suppl):14–26.

McElroy SL, Keck PE Jr, Pope HF Jr, Smith JMR & Strakowski SM (1994). Compulsive buying: A report of 20 cases. *Journal of Clinical Psychiatry* 55:242–248.

McElroy SL, Hudson JI, Phillips KA, Keck PE Jr & Pope HG Jr (1993). Clinical and theoretical implications of a possible link between obsessive-compulsive and impulse control disorders. *Depression* 1:121–132.

McElroy SL, Hudson JI, Pope HG Jr, Keck PE Jr & Aizley HG (1992). The DSM-III-R impulse control disorders not elsewhere classified: Clinical characteristics and relationship to other psychiatric disorders. *American Journal of Psychiatry* 149:318–327.

McElroy SL, Phillips KA & Keck PE, Jr (1994). Obsessive-compulsive spectrum disorder. *Journal of Clinical Psychiatry* 55(10 Suppl):33–51.

McElroy SL, Pope HG Jr, Hudson JI, Keck PE Jr & White KL (1991a). Kleptomania: A report of 20 cases. *American Journal of Psychiatry* 148:652–657.

McElroy SL, Pope HG Jr, Keck PE Jr, Hudson JI, Phillips KA & Strakowski SM (1996). Are impulse control disorders related to bipolar disorder? *Comprehensive Psychiatry* 37:229–240.

McElroy SL, Satlin A, Pope HG Jr, Hudson JI & Keck PE Jr (1991b). Treatment of compulsive shopping and antidepressants. A report of three cases. *Annals of Clinical Psychiatry* 3:199–204.

McElroy SL, Soutullo CA, Beckman D, Taylor JR & Keck PE Jr (1998). DSM-IV intermittent explosive disorder: A report of 27 cases. *Journal of Clinical Psychiatry*. 59:203–210.

Miller NS & Gold MS (1993). A hypothesis for a common neurochemical basis for alcohol and drug disorders. *Psychiatric Clinics of North America* 16:105–117.

Modell JG, Glaser FB, Cyr L & Mountz JM (1992). Obsessive and compulsive characteristics of craving for alcohol in alcohol abuse and dependence. *Alcoholism: Clinical & Experimental Research* 16:272–274.

Modell JG, Mountz JM & Beresford TP (1990). Basal ganglia/limbic striatal and thalamocortical involvement in craving and loss of control in alcohol abuse and dependence. *Journal of Neuropsychiatry and Clinical Neuroscience* 2:123–144.

Montoya ID, Levin FR, Fudala PJ & Gorelick DA (1995). Double- blind comparison of carbamazepine and placebo for treatment of cocaine dependence. *Drug and Alcohol Dependence* 38:213–219.

Moran E (1970). Varieties of pathologic gambling. *British Journal of Psychiatry* 116:593–597.

Moreno I, Saiz-Ruiz J & Lopez-Ibor JJ (1991). Serotonin and gambling dependence. *Human Psychopharmacology* 6:S9–S12.

Moskowitz JA (1980). Lithium and lady luck: Use of lithium carbonate in pathological gambling. *New York State Journal of Medicine* 80:785–788.

Mueller TI, Stout RL, Rudden S et al. (1997). A double-blind, placebo-controlled pilot study of carbamazepine for the treatment of alcohol dependence. *Alcoholism: Clinical & Experimental Research* 21:86–92.

Naranjo CA, Poulos CX, Bremner KE & Lanctot KL (1994). Fluoxetine attenuates alcohol intake and desire to drink. *International Clinical Psychopharmacology* 9:163–172

Nutt DJ (1996). Addiction: Brain mechanisms and their treatment implications. *Lancet* 347:31–36.

O'Brien CP, Volpicelli LA & Volpicelli JR (1996). Naltrexone in the treatment of alcoholism: A clinical review. *Alcohol* 13:35–39.

Phillips KA, McElroy SL, Hudson JI & Pope HG Jr (1995). Body dysmorphic disorder: An obsessive-compulsive disorder, a form of affective spectrum disorder, or both? *Journal of Clinical Psychiatry* 56(Suppl 4):41–51.

Pickens RW & Johanson CE (1992). Craving: Consensus of status and agenda for future research. *Drug and Alcohol Dependence* 30:127–131.

Rao S, Ziedonis D & Kosten T (1995). The pharmacotherapy of cocaine dependence. *Psychiatric Annals* 25:363–368.

Ramirez LF, McCormick RA, Russo AM & Taber JI (1983). Patterns of substance abuse in pathological gamblers undergoing treatment. *Addictive Behaviors* 8:425–428.

Regier D, Farmer ME, Rae DS et al. (1990). Comorbidity of mental disorders with alcohol and other drug abuse. Results from the Epidemiologic Catchment Area (ECA) Study. *Journal of the American Medical Association* 264:2511–2518.

Richardson JS & Zaleski WA (1983). Naloxone and self-mutilation. *Biological Psychiatry* 18:99–101.

Rothbaum BO, Shaw L, Morris R & Ninan PT (1993). Prevalence of trichotillomania in a college freshmen population [letter]. *Journal of Clinical Psychiatry* 54:72.

Roy A, Adinoff B, Roehrich L et al. (1988). Pathological gambling: a psychobiological study. *Archives of General Psychiatry* 45:369–373.

Roy A, DeJong J & Linnoila M (1989). Extraversion in pathological gamblers. *Archives of General Psychiatry* 46:679–681.

Salomon RM, Mazure CM, Delgado PL, Mendia P & Charney DS (1994). Serotonin function in aggression: The effect of acute plasma tryptophan depletion in aggressive patients. *Biological Psychiatry* 35:570–572.

Schlosser S, Black DW, Repertinger S & Freet D (1994). Compulsive buying. Demography, phenomenology, and comorbidity in 46 subjects. *General Hospital Psychiatry* 16:205–212.

Simeon D, Stanley B, Frances A, Mann JJ, Winchel R & Stanley M (1992). Self-mutilation in personality disorder: Psychological and biological correlates. *American Journal of Psychiatry* 149:221–226.

Specker SM, Carlson GA, Edmonson KM, Johnson PE & Marcotte M (1996). Psychopathology in pathological gamblers seeking treatment. *Journal of Gambling Studies* 12:67–81.

Stein DJ, Hollander E & Liebowitz MR (1993). Neurobiology of impulsivity and the impulse control disorders. *Journal of Neuropsychiatry and Clinical Neuroscience* 5:9–17.

Steinberg MA, Kosten TA & Rounsaville BJ (1992). Cocaine abuse and pathological gambling. *American Journal of Addiction* 1:121–132.

Stennie KA & Gold MS (1997). Eating disorders and addictions: behavioral and neurobiological similarities. In NS Miller (ed.) *The Principles and Practice of Addiction Psychiatry*. Philadelphia, PA: W.B. Saunders, 433–439.

Swedo SE, Leonard HL, Rapoport JL, Lenane MC, Goldberger EL & Chescow DL (1989). A double-blind comparison of clomipramine and desipramine in the treatment of trichotillomania (hair-pulling). *The New England Journal of Medicine* 321:497–501.

Switt RM & Stout RL (1992). The relationship between craving, anxiety, and other symptoms in opioid withdrawal. *Journal of Substance Abuse* 4:19–26.

Szymanski HV & Olympia J (1991). Divalproex in post traumatic stress disorder [letter]. *American Journal of Psychiatry* 148:1086–1087.

Virkkunen M, DeJong J, Bartko J & Linnoila M (1989). Psychobiological concomitants of history of suicide attempts among violent offenders and impulsive fire setters. *Archives of General Psychiatry* 46:604–606.

Volberg RA & Steadman HJ (1988). Refining prevalence estimates of pathological gambling. *American Journal of Psychiatry* 145:502–505.

Volpicelli JR, Alterman AL, Hayashida M & O'Brien CP (1992). Naltrexone in the treatment of alcohol dependence. *Archives of General Psychiatry* 49:876–880.

Ward NG (1975). Successful lithium treatment of transvestism associated with manic depression. *Journal of Nervous and Mental Disorders* 161:204–206.

Washton A (1989). Cocaine may trigger sexual compulsivity. *U.S. Journal of Drug and Alcohol Dependency* 13:8.

Weddington WW, Brown BS, Haertzen CA et al. (1990). Changes in mood, craving, and sleep during short-term abstinence reported by male cocaine addicts. A controlled, residential study. *Archives of General Psychiatry* 47:861–868.

Winchel RM & Stanley M (1991). Self-injurious behavior: A review of the behavior and biology of self mutilation. *American Journal of Psychiatry* 148:306–317.

Wise MG & Tierney JG (1994). Impulse control disorders not elsewhere classified. In RE Hales, SC Yudofsky & JA Talbot JA (eds.) *Comprehensive Textbook of Psychiatry, 2nd Ed.* Washington, DC: American Psychiatric Press, 681–699.

Wray I & Dickerson MG (1981). Cessation of high frequency gambling and "withdrawal symptoms." *British Journal of Addiction* 76:401–405.

Zohar J, Kaplan Z & Benjamin J (1994). Compulsive exhibitionism successfully treated with fluvoxamine: A controlled case study. *Journal of Clinical Psychiatry* 55:86–88.

CHAPTER 7

Borderline Personality Disorder

Linda A. Dimeff, Ph.D.
Katherine Anne Comtois, Ph.D.
Marsha M. Linehan, Ph.D.

Defining Borderline Personality Disorder
Incidence and Prevalence
Medical Problems Among Patients with BPD
Treatment and Treatment Outcomes for BPD
Advice to Clinicians Who Work with Patients with BPD

Research over the past two decades indicates that among those persons served by community mental health agencies, a sub-population utilizes a disproportionate amount of inpatient psychiatric services. Specifically, between 6% and 18% of all persons admitted to inpatient psychiatric treatment account for 20% to 42% of admissions (Carpenter, Mulligan et al., 1985; Geller, 1986; Green, 1988; Hadley, McGurrin et al., 1990; Surber, Winkler et al., 1987; Woogh, 1986). Research by Hadley and colleagues (1992) indicates that 75% to 80% of inpatient treatment dollars are spent on 30% to 35% of patients who receive inpatient services. Persons with borderline personality disorder (BPD) frequently are among the high utilizers of inpatient psychiatric services. In fact, it is estimated that between 9% and 40% of high utilizers have been diagnosed with BPD (Geller, 1986; Surber, Winkler et al., 1987; Widiger & Weissman, 1991; Woogh, 1986).

DEFINING BORDERLINE PERSONALITY DISORDER

Borderline personality disorder is characterized by intense negative emotions including depression, anger, self-hatred, and hopelessness. In coping with these emotions, BPD individuals often engage in impulsive maladaptive behaviors, including suicidal behaviors and substance abuse (see Table 1). Linehan (1993a) has identified five domains of dysregulation that characterize BPD, corresponding to the diagnostic criteria of the *Diagnostic and Statistical Manual of Mental Disorders, Fourth Edition* (*DSM-IV*) (American Psychiatric Association, 1994; see Table 2).

- *Affective dysregulation* is characterized by high emotion reactivity and lability, where emotions fluctuate frequently and often appear to come out of nowhere. Overcontrol and undercontrol of anger is common among these individuals.
- *Interpersonal dysregulation* is characterized by a revolving door of chaotic, unstable interpersonal relationships and difficulty letting go of relationships.
- *Self-dysregulation* describes a profound sense of emptiness and identity confusion.
- *Behavioral dysregulation* includes parasuicidal acts, substance abuse, and other extreme, risky, and problematic impulsive behaviors.
- *Cognitive dysregulation* includes all non-psychotic forms of thought dysregulation, including dissociation, depersonalization, catastrophic thinking, and paranoid ideation.

BPD is the only *DSM-IV* diagnosis for which parasuicide is a criterion; parasuicide thus is considered a "hallmark" of BPD. Rates of parasuicide among patients diagnosed with BPD range from 69% to 80% (Clarkin, Widiger et al., 1983; Cowdry, Pickar et al., 1985; Gunderson, 1984). Rates of suicide among all individuals who meet the criteria for BPD—including those with no parasuicide—are 5% to 10% (Frances, Fyar et al., 1986) and are double those seen when only persons with a history of parasuicide are included (Stone, Hurt et al., 1987). More generally, parasuicide is a major health problem (Dublin, 1963; Shneidman, 1971), the rates of which have been estimated at 300 per 100,000 population per year. In Europe, the estimated rate for medically treated parasuicides is 139 per 100,000 for males and 189 per 100,000 for females (Platt, Bille-Brahe et al., 1992). From 10% to 29% of individuals who parasuicide eventually die

TABLE 1. *DSM-IV* Criteria for Borderline Personality Disorder

A pervasive pattern of instability of interpersonal relationships, self-image, and affects, and markedly impulsivity beginning by early adulthood and present in a variety of contexts, as indicated by five (or more) of the following:

- Frantic efforts to avoid real or imagined abandonment. **Note:** Do not include suicidal or self-mutilating behavior.
- A pattern of unstable and intense interpersonal relationships characterized by alternating between extremes of idealization and devaluation identity disturbance: markedly and persistently unstable self-image or sense of self.
- Impulsivity in at least two areas that are potentially self-damaging (e.g., spending, sex, substance abuse, reckless driving, binge eating). **Note:** Do not include suicidal or self-mutilating behavior.
- Recurrent suicidal behavior, gestures, or threats, or self-mutilating behavior.
- Affective instability due to a marked reactivity of mood (e.g., intense episodic dysphoria, irritability, or anxiety usually lasting a few hours and only rarely more than a few days).
- Chronic feelings of emptiness.
- Inappropriate, intense anger or difficulty controlling anger (e.g., frequent displays of tempter, constant anger, recurrent physical fights).
- Transient, stress-related paranoid ideation or severe dissociative symptoms.

Source: American Psychiatric Association (1994). *Diagnostic and Statistical Manual of Mental Disorders, 4th Edition.* Washington, DC: American Psychiatric Press, 654.

by suicide, a rate that far exceeds that of the general population (Dorpat & Ripley, 1960; Dahlgren, 1977).

The likelihood that a clinician will encounter suicidal behavior during the course of mental health treatment is especially high when he or she treats severely dysfunctional patients. Diagnosis of an Axis I or II disorder is associated with increased risk of suicide and parasuicide (Tanney, 1992).

INCIDENCE AND PREVALENCE

Between 0.2% and 1.8% of the general population (8% to 11% of outpatients seeking mental health services, and 14% to 20% of inpatients) are estimated to meet the criteria for BPD (Widiger & Frances, 1989; Widiger & Weissman, 1991; Modestin, Albrecht et al., 1997). Follow-up studies consistently indicate that BPD is a chronic condition, although the number of individuals who continue to meet diagnostic criteria slowly decreases over the life span. Two to three years after index assessment, 60% to 70% of patients continued to meet criteria (Barasch, Frances & Hurt, 1985). Other short-term follow-up studies report little change in level of functioning and consistently high rates of psychiatric hospitalization over two to five years (Barasch, Frances & Hurt, 1985; Dahl, 1986; Richman & Charles, 1976). Four to seven years after index assessment, 57% to 67% of patients continued to meet criteria (Kullgren, 1992; Pope, Jonas et al., 1983). An average of 15 years after index assessment, 25% to 44% continued to meet criteria (McGlashan, 1986; Paris, Brown & Nowlis, 1987).

Comorbidity of BPD and Substance Abuse. Substance abuse is a common problem for individuals meeting criteria for BPD. Individuals with BPD are more likely to also meet criteria for current substance abuse than individuals with other psychiatric disorders, except Anti-Social Personality Disorder (ASPD; Koenigsberg, Kaplan et al., 1985; Loranger & Tulis, 1985; McCann, Flynn & Gersh, 1992; Pitts, Gustin et al., 1985; Zanarini, Gunderson et al., 1989). In one study, 23% of inpatients with BPD met criteria for lifetime drug abuse (Links, Steiner et al., 1988). This comorbidity is not entirely due to the overlap in diagnostic criteria. For example, Dulit and her colleagues found that 67% of BPD patients currently met criteria for substance abuse disorder (Dulit, Fyer et al., 1990). When substance abuse was not used as a criterion of BPD, the incidence dropped to 57%, still a significant portion of the population. Within substance abusing populations, comorbidity with BPD has been reported to range from 5.2% (Brooner, King et al., 1997) to 32% (Weiss, Mirin et al., 1993). Within opiate-dependent populations seeking methadone treatment, BPD has been diagnosed in 12% of 150 subjects in one study (Kosten, Kosten & Rounsaville, 1989) and 5.2% of consecutive admissions (9.5% of all female admits) in another well-designed study (Brooner, King et al., 1997). Among a cocaine-dependent inpatient sample, 32% met criteria for BPD during periods of drug use *and* abstinence (Weiss, Mirin et al., 1993). In a study of 94 consecutive admissions to alcohol treatment, 13% of patients met criteria for BPD (Nace, Saxon & Shore, 1983). Within a mixed inpatient sample receiving substance abuse treatment, 17% were diagnosed with BPD (Nace, Davis & Gaspari, 1991).

Substance abusers with BPD are uniformly more disturbed than substance abusers without a personality disorder (PD). Studies comparing substance abusing patients with and without personality dis-

TABLE 2. Domains of Dysregulation in Borderline Personality Disorder

Affective Dysregulation	
	Affective lability
	Problems with anger
Interpersonal Dysregulation	
	Chaotic relationships
	Fears of abandonment
Self Dysregulation	
	Identity disturbance/difficulties with sense of self
	Sense of emptiness
Behavioral Dysregulation	
	Parasuicidal behavior/threats
	Impulsive behavior
Cognitive Dysregulation	
	Dissociative responses/paranoid ideation
	Cognitive rigidity/dichotomous thinking

Source: Linehan MM (1993B). *Skills Training Manual for Treating Borderline Personality Disorder*. New York, NY: Guilford Press. Reprinted by permission.

orders have reported that those with PD have significantly more disorders, including alcoholism, depression, behavioral dyscontrol, and legal difficulties, were at greater risk for HIV infection, and were more extensively involved in substance abuse than were patients without PD (Rutherford, Cacciola & Alterman, 1994; Nace, Davis & Gaspari, 1991). One study that discriminated BPD from other PDs found evidence that patients with BPD have more severe psychiatric problems than patients with other PDs (Kosten, Kosten & Rounsaville, 1989). Another study compared patients with BPD only, substance abuse only, or BPD with substance abuse (Links, Heslegrave et al., 1995). Individuals who were comorbid for both disorders showed significantly more psychopathology, self-destructive behaviors, and suicidal thoughts over a seven-year period than individuals who had only substance abuse or borderline personality disorder.

MEDICAL PROBLEMS AND SOMATIZATION AMONG PATIENTS WITH BPD

Individuals with BPD also report and seek services for medical problems at a higher rate compared to persons without BPD. Medical complaints frequently include asthma, diabetes, hepatitis, and ulcers, as well as chronic fatigue syndrome, irritable bowel syndrome, and fiber myalgia. While some medical conditions are the result of impulsive sexual or substance abuse behaviors or stress, others are not. A review of Medline indicated that no published research has examined medical conditions in patients with BPD, with the exception of the differential diagnosis of BPD and somatic disorders. The amount of overlap between BPD and somatization probably is at least partially related to the diagnostic approach to somatic disorders. For instance, Hudziak et al. (1996) studied a group of women with BPD and found that 45% also met criteria for somatization disorder using the *DSM-IIIR* Checklist. Importantly, 57% of their sample also met the criteria for substance abuse, but the overlap of the substance abusing subsample with somatization was not presented. In stark contrast, among substance abusers with BPD seeking treatment at the authors' clinic, only 4% were diagnosed with somatization disorder (Comtois, Pohl et al., 1996). Diagnosis of somatization was made on the basis of SCID interviews (First, Spitzer et al., 1996).

The high rate of medical problems in individuals with BPD appears to be related to being reared in a dysfunctional family environment. Prevalence estimates of a history of sexual abuse in persons with BPD range from 67% to 86% (as opposed to 22% to 34% in non-BPD individuals), while estimates of physical abuse in persons with BPD are 71%, compared to 38% in persons without BPD (Bryer, Nelson et al., 1987; Herman, Perry et al., 1989; Ogata, Silk et al., 1989; Stone, 1981; Wagner, Linehan et al., 1989). In recent years, studies conducted in primary care settings document the higher numbers of medical problems and medical costs in adults who have been abused as children (Felitti, 1991; Gould, Stevens et al., 1994; Koss, Koss et al., 1991; Lechner, Vogel et al., 1993; McCauley, Kern et al., 1997). In a current study of a randomly selected group of 1,225 adult women who sought services in a large HMO, Walker and colleagues (unpublished manuscript) conducted a self-report assessment of childhood abuse and neglect. Women who experienced childhood abuse and neglect were diagnosed by HMO physicians with significantly more minor infectious diseases (e.g., urinary tract infections, vaginitus, upper respiratory infections, sinusitis, etc.) and physical disorders (e.g., hypertension, diabetes, dermatitis, asthma, etc.). Their analysis of medical costs (Walker, Gelfand et al., 1997) parallels these results, finding significantly higher HMO costs for abused women; these findings were not due to variations in disease status or demographic variables.

While the authors are aware of no studies to date that focus exclusively on the medical problems of substance abusers with BPD, there is ample documentation in the research literature of the vast medical problems substance abusing individuals commonly experience and the cost to society when these medical conditions are not adequately treated. For example, in major metropolitan cities, emergency room visits resulting from illicit use of opiates doubled between 1991 and 1995, from 36,000 visits to 76,000, and opiate-related deaths also significantly increased during this period, from 2,300 to 4,000 (NIDA, 1997). Opiate addiction is associated with high rates of illegal behavior and a higher incidence of serious medical conditions such as HIV/AIDS, tuberculosis, endocarditis, thrombophlebitis, hepatitis B and C, and sexually transmitted diseases (see NIDA, 1997, for a review).

TREATMENT AND TREATMENT OUTCOMES FOR BPD

Achieving treatment success with BPD has been notoriously difficult. It is estimated that almost all (97%) BPD patients presenting for treatment receive outpatient treatment at some point, and that they average 6.1 therapists in their lifetime (Skodol, Buckley & Charles, 1983; Perry, Herman et al., 1990). The emotional and behavioral dysregulation experienced by these patients results in chaotic and unstable interpersonal relationships, including psychotherapy relationships. In fact, problems in treatment have been included in the *Diagnostic Interview for Borderlines* (Gunderson, Kolb & Austin, 1981).

BPD has been associated with worse outcome in treatments of Axis I disorders such as major depression (Phillips & Nierenberg, 1994), OCD (Baer, Jenike et al., 1992), bulimia (Ames-Frankel, Devlin et al., 1992; Coker, Vize et al., 1993) and substance abuse (Kosten, Kosten & Rounsaville, 1989). Randomized, controlled studies of treatments designed specifically for BPD are sparse. Other than studies examining DBT, the authors could locate only two randomized controlled trials of psychosocial interventions for BPD, neither of which specifically targeted substance abusing or suicidal patients with BPD. Marziali and Munroe-Blum (1994) found that structured, time-limited group therapy was more effective than individual psychotherapy in retaining patients in therapy, although it was not more effective on outcome variables. Turner has promising pilot data for an integrated psychodynamic/cognitive-behavioral treatment (personal communication). As noted earlier, follow-up studies of BPD individuals who have received inpatient and outpatient psychiatric care suggest that traditional treatments in the community are marginally effective at best when outcomes are measured at two to three years following treatment (Perry & Cooper, 1985; Tucker, Bauer et al., 1987).

In studies investigating pharmacotherapy for BPD, drop-out rates have been very high (Cowdry & Gardner, 1988) and medication compliance has been problematic, with more than half of patients reporting misuse of their medications and 87% of therapists reporting patient medication misuse, including patients taking other than prescribed doses or taking an overdose (Waldinger & Frank, 1989). Despite recent advances in the treatment of BPD with medications (see Soloff, 1998 and 1994 for reviews), it is widely assumed that some form of ancillary behavioral treatment is necessary for BPD patients (Skodol, Buckley & Charles, 1983; Perry, Herman et al., 1990).

DIALECTICAL BEHAVIOR THERAPY

The following discussion of Dialectical Behavior Therapy has two primary objectives: to provide a basic overview of standard DBT and DBT for Substance Abusers (DBT-S), and to offer specific recommendation for effective care and management of patients with BPD. While treatment of BPD is a complex, costly and time-intensive undertaking, the authors' hope is that the recommendations for primary care clinicians and addiction medicine specialists described in this chapter will be of assistance in promoting empathetic understanding and care of these patients.

Dialectical Behavior Therapy (DBT) is a promising treatment for individuals with BPD. In Linehan's first treatment evaluation study of suicidal women with BPD, DBT was more effective than treatment-as-usual (TAU) in the community for reducing suicidal actions, therapy drop-out, use of psychiatric inpatient beds, and anger, as well as for improving interpersonal functioning and global adjustment (Linehan, Armstrong et al., 1991). Results were maintained when numbers of outpatient psychotherapy hours, total outpatient treatment hours, and total mental health treatment hours were controlled (Linehan & Heard, 1993).

In a second study, Linehan recruited an almost identical sample, except that subjects were currently in individual psychotherapy with therapists who were committed to them and with whom they wanted to continue treatment. A DBT group skills training (only) was added to the on-going psychotherapy for a randomly selected group that equalled half of the subjects. No differences were observed between these groups at post-treatment. Inspection of means indicated that low power was not the problem. This finding suggests that DBT skills training, when isolated from the other standard DBT treatment modes, did not produce an additive treatment effect.

In a third study, Linehan and colleagues examined treatment process for four new BPD patients. Dialectical balancing of acceptance and change (as experienced by the patients) were more highly associated with subsequent reductions in suicidal behaviors than were pure change or pure acceptance techniques (Shearin & Linehan, 1992). A number of trials are in progress at various sites throughout the United States and in Europe in an effort to replicate and extend Linehan's previous findings (Barley, Buie et al., 1997; Linehan & Dimeff, 1998).

Origins of DBT. Developed by Marsha M. Linehan and colleagues at the University of Washington, DBT is a comprehensive, multi-stage cognitive-behavioral treatment for severely dysfunctional individuals with BPD. The philosophy, biosocial theory, treatment targets, structure, strategies, and protocols of standard DBT are described in two DBT treatment manuals (Linehan, 1993a, 1993b). DBT is based on a combined capability deficit and motivational model of BPD which posits that: (1) persons with BPD lack important interpersonal, self-regulation (including emotional regulation) and distress tolerance skills, and (2) personal and environmental factors often block and/or inhibit use of the behavioral skills these individuals do have, and at times reinforce their dysfunctional behaviors.

DBT treatment itself blends cognitive-behavioral interventions with Eastern mindfulness practices and teaching techniques, and has elements in common with psychodynamic, patient-centered, Gestalt, paradoxical and strategic approaches (cf. Heard & Linehan, 1994). DBT requires that the therapist balance the use of strategies within each treatment interaction, from the rapid juxtaposition of change and acceptance techniques to the therapist's use of both irreverent and warmly responsive communication styles. The emphasis on simultaneous acceptance and change leads to what could be considered a "dialectical abstinence" approach in which absolute abstinence from the dysfunctional targeted behavior is emphasized before dysfunctional episodes (such as drug use) and a harm reduction approach is emphasized after an episode, followed by rapid recommitment to abstinence.

Treatment strategies are divided into six sets: *dialectical strategies*, *core strategies* (validation, problem-solving, and behavior change procedures including contingency management, skills training, exposure and cognitive modification strategies), *communication strategies* (irreverent and reciprocal communication), *case management strategies* (consultation to the patient, environmental intervention, consultation to the therapists), *structural strategies* (targeting within sessions, starting and ending therapy), and *attachment-to-the-client strategies.* There are, as well, a number of specific behavioral treatment protocols covering crisis management, therapy-interfering behavior and compliance issues, relationship problem-solving, and clinical management of drug-replacement and psychotropic medications.

As a comprehensive treatment, DBT serves five functions. It (1) enhances behavioral capabilities, (2) improves motivation to change, (3) assures that new capabilities generalize to the natural environment, (4) structures the environment in the ways essential to support client and therapist capabilities, and (5) enhances therapist capabilities and motivation to treat patients effectively (Linehan, in press). In standard DBT, these functions are divided among modes of service delivery. For example, patients enhance capabilities by learning skills to regulate emotions, to tolerate emotional distress when change is slow or unlikely, to be more effective in interpersonal conflicts, and to control attention in order to skillfully participate in the moment.

DBT presumes that both enhancing capabilities and improving motivation are essential. In developing the treatment, however, it quickly became apparent that it was extraordinarily difficult if not impossible to simultaneously teach skills and work on behavioral motivation to die, keep taking drugs, and/or act in a borderline fashion. Consequently, these two functions are assigned to different modes, one that focuses primarily on skills training and one that focuses primarily on motivational issues, including the motivation to stop using drugs. Although new behavioral skills are learned in all forms of psychotherapy, the primary emphasis is on helping patients inhibit maladaptive behaviors and instead apply skills to problematic situations. Likewise, some attention to motivational issues occurs in DBT skills training, particularly with behavioral homework, but the fundamental emphasis is on skills acquisition and strengthening.

Dialectical Theory in DBT. DBT (and DBT-S) is defined by its philosophical base (dialectics), treatment strategies, and treatment targets. Commonly associated with the teachings of Marx and Hegel, *dialectics* refers to a process of change, a method of logic or argumentation, and a particular understanding of the nature of reality (Linehan & Schmidt, 1995). As a process of change, dialectics posits that every idea or event (thesis) contains its opposite (antithesis), which generates and transforms the thesis and ultimately leads to a reconciliation of opposites (synthesis). Importantly, achieving synthesis seldom occurs through quiet mediation or accommodation of difference (e.g., adding of black to the white pigment to achieve a medium gray), but instead occurs through a dynamic process of movement and, often, collision of opposing forces. The term *dialectical* is meant to convey both the multiple tensions that coexist and are dealt with in therapy with patients with BPD, as well as the emphasis in DBT on enhancing balanced (dialectical) patterns of behavior and thinking to replace extreme response patterns and rigid, dichotomous thinking.

As a method of logic or argumentation, dialectics can be used clinically to expose the contradictions in a patient's position or thinking in an effort to achieve synthesis or change. Consider a scenario in which the patient expresses that he or she is considering taking a lethal overdose to kill him/herself because the emotional pain and suffering has become too excruciating to bear living another moment. Earlier in the week, the patient relapsed to heroin use and then abused the benzodiazepines prescribed by a former psychiatrist in an effort to reduce the physical discomfort of opiate withdrawal. After a careful assessment, the therapist learns that the patient's behavior of overdosing is under the control of the consequence (e.g., relief from psychological suffering) and not the antecedent (e.g., the earlier relapse).

In response to the patient's comment, "I want out of this pain," the therapist might say irreverently, "How do you know that killing yourself will take away the pain and suffering? It is possible that your pain will become more intolerable if you kill yourself." Here the therapist exposes the patient's logic (e.g., death ends suffering) while simultaneously contradicting it (e.g., death by suicide might exacerbate suffering).

The overriding dialectic in DBT is the need to radically accept reality as it is (including pain and suffering) while at the same time working to change what is. It is within this dialectic that the Zen practice of observing, mindfulness, non-judgmental stance, and acceptance of the moment is integrated within a technology of change, using cognitive and behavioral techniques. This dance between the two core tensions in DBT is consistent in many respects with the notion of acceptance and change as practiced within Twelve Step programs, best exemplified in the Serenity Prayer commonly recited at Twelve Step meetings: "God, grant me the serenity to accept the things I cannot change, the courage to change the things I can, and the wisdom to know the difference." Acceptance in DBT, as exemplified in the distress tolerance skills (described later in this chapter), including radical acceptance, also is comparable to the practice of acceptance in Twelve Step programs.

> "Acceptance is the answer to *all* my problems today. When I am disturbed, it is because I find some person, place, thing, or situation—some fact of life—unacceptable to me, and I can find no serenity until I accept that person, place, thing or situation as being exactly the way it is supposed to be at this moment. Nothing, absolutely nothing happens in God's world by mistake. Until I could accept my alcoholism, I could not stay sober; unless I accept life completely on life's terms, I cannot be happy. I need to concentrate not so much on what needs to be changed in the world as on what needs to be changed in me and in my attitudes" (Alcoholics Anonymous, 1976, p. 449).

Core assumptions about the nature of reality in dialectics also form the nucleus of DBT. First, reality in dialectics is characterized by wholeness and connection. Parts are important only in relation to one another and in relation to the whole that they help create, define and give meaning to. Given the interconnectedness of all things, changes anywhere in the system result in changes throughout the system. Second, change is considered continuous in dialectics. In this sense, one can never step in the same river twice in dialectics because each moment is changed by the moments before it and the imminence of the moment after. Third, change occurs through the dynamic interactions between polarity, as captured in the creation of synthesis that is derived through the tensions between thesis and antithesis.

The spirit of a dialectical perspective is never to accept a final truth or an undisputed fact, and always to consider the question, "What is being left out of our understanding?" Truth is neither absolute nor relative, but is always evolving, developing, and constructed over time. When applied to persuasion, therapist and patient seek to arrive at new meanings within old meanings by moving closer to the essence (synthesis) of the subject/topic under consideration. The ability to see both sides of an argument as well as to reach a synthesis of both sides (which is different from a compromise) demands skills that most patients with BPD lack when entering treatment. Teaching patients how to think dialectically provides a way out of dichotomous, black-or-white thinking pattern that limits their options, and moves them from an "either-or" perspective to a "both-and" position.

Biosocial Theory in BPD. Dialectical Behavior Therapy (DBT) is based on a biosocial model where the core problem in BPD is hypothesized by Linehan as emotion dysregulation and not merely a "symptom" of the disorder. In Linehan's model, emotion dysregulation provides a framework from which other behaviors associated with BPD can be understood. Extending the work of Gottman and Katz (1989), Linehan (1993a; Fruzzetti & Linehan, in press) has hypothesized that emotion dysregulation is characterized by the following experiences: (1) extreme difficulty in changing or modulating physiological arousal associated with emotion (emotional lability); (2) extreme difficulties in orienting and reorienting attention and other cognitive processes (cognitive dysregulation); (3) extreme difficulties in inhibiting inappropriate behavior related to strong (either negative or positive) emotion (behavioral dysregulation or impulsivity); (4) abnormally high likelihood of escalating or blunting emotions (escape or avoidance); and (5) abnormally high probability of organizing behavior in the service of internal, mood-dependent goals (escape behaviors, interpersonal insensitivity) rather than external goals.

Emotion dysregulation represents a systemic dysfunction that results from the confluence of developmental factors, including genetic/biological and environmental/social learning, which in turn set the stage for later adult pathology. In Linehan's model, it is the *transaction* between a person with certain biologically-predisposed *emotional vulnerabilities* and others in his or her life that function as an *invalidating environment* that eventually produce the cluster of dysfunctional behaviors classified as BPD. Here, "transaction" refers to a reciprocal process between the individual and his or her social environment, in which the person shapes and is shaped by the response of the social environment (Linehan, 1993a): The individual engages in a particular behavior that has some impact on his or her environment; the environment then responds, shaping the behavior of the person, who again responds, thus shaping and affecting the environment (Fruzzetti & Linehan, in press).

Emotional Vulnerability: Persons with high vulnerability to emotions display the following behavioral responses to stimuli across a number of contexts:

- High sensitivity to stimuli: emotionally vulnerable individuals have a low threshold for emotional arousal and thus are more likely than non-vulnerable individuals to react emotionally to stimuli;
- More intense, extreme emotional response to stimuli: emotionally vulnerable persons respond more quickly and/or with greater intensity; and
- Slower return to baseline: compared with normative responses, emotionally vulnerable individuals take longer to "ride out" the emotion following the initial arousal before they return to baseline. Until this return to baseline has occurred, the individual remains more vulnerable still to emotional stimuli.

In many respects, the emotional vulnerability of these persons is analogous to the physical pain experienced by burn patients when their wounds are debrided. This is particularly relevant for substance abusers given the relationship between negative emotions and relapse (Marlatt & Gordon, 1985; Dimeff & Marlatt, 1998).

How emotional vulnerability develops and when it becomes pathologic in individuals with BPD also is of interest. It is possible that these individuals had fairly normative emotional functioning as infants, but their normative affective communication was persistently punished or ignored by the individuals in their environments. In a transactional manner, the emotional arousal in the child may have heightened or and continued to "escalate" until the social environment functionally attended to the child. In this fashion, emotional vulnerability develops through a transactional learning process. Alternatively, some individuals with BPD may have been born with a biological predisposition to emotional vulnerability and extreme sensitivity to their environments, such that normative parenting environments would have heightened and/or maintained their emotional sensitivity (Fruzzetti & Linehan, in press). In the latter scenario, problems emerge from the "poorness of fit" between the individual's temperament and the familial environment. This is similar to problems that arise when a child with a reading disorder participates in regular school programs for reading. While these programs are quite suitable for many children, the student with special needs may learn best in an environment tailored to that student's reading challenges.

Invalidating Environments: In Linehan's model, invalidating environments can significantly heighten emotional vulnerability and create the learning context from which BPD emerges (Linehan, 1993a). In an invalidating social or familial environment, individual communication of private experiences (such as thoughts, feelings, and physiological experiences that are not observable to others) are pervasively met by erratic, inappropriate, or extreme responses. Two primary characteristics of such an environment include: (1) the individual is told that his or her descriptions and analyses of private experiences are wrong, as are the person's understanding of what is causing these private experiences; and (2) the individual's public behavior and/or expressions of private behavior are attributed to socially unacceptable characteristics (e.g., a "disorder" such as BPD, a manipulation attempt, or paranoia).

Examples of invalidating environments include families that favor controlling or inhibiting emotional expressiveness and disapprove of expressed negative affect. Painful experiences are trivialized ("Why are you crying? There's nothing to cry about!") and are attributed to negative traits such as lack of motivation ("If you would just put your mind to it, you could do this"), without recognition that intense emotions are interfering with skillful actions. Similarly, failure to adopt a positive attitude is derided ("You want something to cry about? I'll give you something to really cry about!"). Other characteristics of the invalidating environment include restricting the demands the child may make on the environment ("If you want something, you must ask politely").

Citing experimental research investigating suppression of thoughts and emotions (cf., Cioffi & Holloway, 1993; Wegner & Gold, 1995), Fruzzetti and Linehan (in press) have described the "rebound" effect when an individual attempts *not* to think a particular thought or tries *not* to have a particular emotion in the presence of environmental invalidation. Paradoxically, such an effort *not* to experience whatever private behavior one is experiencing frequently results in a heightening of attention focused on the unwanted feeling or thought. In the presence of an invalidating environment, telling an individual not to be sad or angry, for example, actually may enhance the person's attention on his or her experience of sadness or anger, which may serve to further increase the emotion. Here, the environment has specifically instructed the individual to have less of a particular emotion, but instead the person has more of it. It is not difficult to understand how such an environment would continue to respond aversively to the individual, thus contributing to further emotional vulnerability and dysregulation.

Learned consequences of growing up in an invalidating environment are considerable and contribute to emotional dysregulation by failing to teach the child to label and modulate arousal, tolerate distress, and trust his or her own emotional responses as valid interpretations of events. When the child's own experiences are invalidated, the child learns instead to scan the environment for cues about how to act and feel. By oversimplifying the ease of solving life's problems, the child fails to learn how to form realistic goals. By punishing the expression of negative emotion and responding erratically to emotional communication only after escalation by the child, the family shapes an emotional expression style that vacillates between extreme inhibition and suppression of emotional experience on the one hand and expression of extreme emotions on the other.

Assumptions and Agreements in DBT. DBT contains a set of assumptions about patients and a set of therapist agreements that, in combination, comprise the spirit of this treatment and are applicable to clinicians treating people with BPD in a medical setting. DBT patient assumptions provide a compassionate framework in which to construct and maintain a therapeutic relationship (Linehan, 1993a). They include the following:

Patients are doing the best that they can. Even when their behavior is exasperating and inexplicable, persons with BPD usually are trying desperately to change themselves, despite any appearances to the contrary.

Patients want to improve. Emotions such as fear and shame, as well as skills deficits and other factors, frequently interfere with moving steadily forward, thereby compromising motivation to engage in behaviors that will, over time, improve the quality of patients' lives.

Patients need to do better, try harder, and be more motivated to change. The fact that persons with BPD want better lives does not mean that their efforts and motivation are sufficient to the task. One goal of therapy is to help patients determine what factors are holding them back. Clinicians may help their patients considerably by conducting an assessment of factors that compromise the patient's effectiveness, as follows: First, identify all the skills an individual would need to accomplish a task. Assess whether the patient has those skills. If the patient does not, instruct him or her in what to do. If the patient does have the skills, assess whether negative emotions are interfering with the patient's engaging in a particular behavior. For most negative emotions, the best solution is to act in a manner opposite to the emotional impulse or urge (e.g., if the urge is to avoid or move away, then the positive approach is to move toward the stimulus).

Patients may not have caused all of their own problems, but they have to solve them anyway. Persons with BPD are *not* responsible for their genes, biology, or whether they had sufficient models as children to teach them how to skillfully regulate intense emotions. Unfortunately, clinical improvements seldom occur simply by attending appointments, treating medical problems, finding a loving relationship, receiving sufficient social services support, or being saved by a doctor, psychologist, or other professional.

The lives of suicidal, drug-addicted persons with BPD are unbearable as they are being lived. Their lives are indeed a living hell, and the climb out of hell is anything but a pleasant experience.

Patients must learn new behaviors in all relevant contexts. The goal of therapy in DBT ultimately is to have a life worth living, which requires learning how to live life on life's terms rather than retreating from life through hospitalization or institutionalization. This assumption incorporates the necessity of learning how to respond effectively to usual challenges by learning and practicing (over and over again) new behavioral responses in the context in which these behavioral responses are needed. Rather than changing the environment to fit the patient, DBT always prefers to teach the individual the skillful behaviors needed to fit into the environment. This is balanced in DBT by not expecting more from a patient than he or she can reasonably be expected to learn and change.

Patients cannot fail in DBT. The therapy can fail by being insufficient to address the myriad of problems patients experience, or the therapist can fail by not applying the treatment protocol; even in the worst circumstances with the most challenging patient, the task of therapy is to enhance factors that interfere with therapy in order to become more masterful behaviorally.

Providers who treat persons with BPD need support. Treating patients with BPD can be very difficult because of the plethora of problems they present, because their behaviors interfere with the clinician's ability to provide effective treatment, and because of the very slow rate of change that frequently occurs. Therapist competence can be compromised by his or her own emotions or hopeless thoughts, which interfere with providing the most effective treatment.

Therapists in DBT also make certain agreements with the patient and to other members of the treatment team (Linehan, 1993a). Such agreements include the phenomenological empathy agreement (the therapist agrees to search for non-pejorative, phenomenologically empathic interpretations of patient's behavior when generating hypotheses about a particular behavior); the "every reasonable effort" agreement (the therapist agrees to make every reasonable effort to conduct treatment as competently as possible); the ethics agreement (the therapist agrees to conduct ethical treatment); the respect-for-the-patient agreement (the therapist agrees to respect the integrity and rights of the patient); the fallibility agreement (explicit recognition that therapists are fallible and make mistakes); the "observing limits" agreement (members of the consultation team agree that all members of the team observe their own personal and professional limits without judgment of each others limits as being "too wide" or "too narrow") (see Linehan, 1993a for a complete review of DBT agreements).

Stages and Modes of Treatment in DBT. DBT is a multi-stage treatment that begins with a set of specific pretreatment strategies aimed at engagement and commitment to treatment, then proceeds with a hierarchy of treatment stages that move from treating severe behavioral dyscontrol with a goal of increasing self-control (Stage 1) to building the capacity to sustain joy despite the suffering that is ubiquitous in living (Stage 4; Linehan, in press). While a thorough review of these stages is beyond the scope of this chapter, it is important to note that the goal of treatment during Stage 1 is stabilization and connection to caregivers. Emotional processing of traumatic past events, including sexual and/or physical abuse, is not treated until the second stage of treatment, once stabilization and behavioral self-control have been achieved.

The goals for Stage 2 of treatment in DBT focus on full emotional experiencing, which frequently involves treating PTSD using exposure and other behavioral techniques to process these past events. Treatment modes in standard DBT include individual psychotherapy, group skills training, telephone consultation, and consultation-to-the-therapist. Two modes, pharmacotherapy and case management, were added in DBT-S. We overview three of these modes below.

Individual Psychotherapy: Like other behavioral therapies, treatment targets in DBT are hierarchical, targeting the most severe behaviors first. The first of these targets is to decrease suicidal and life-threatening behaviors, including parasuicide. DBT next aims to decrease any therapist and/or patient behaviors that compromise the effectiveness of treatment. Such behaviors include missing or coming late to session, lying, coming to session sedated on prescription medications or illicit drugs, responding to a message page received during a therapy session, calling the therapist while intoxicated.

Therapy-interfering behaviors are targeted next to ensure that factors which decrease therapist and patient motivation to work diligently in treatment are adequately addressed. Unless these factors are addressed, the patient is more likely to miss treatment sessions or to drop out of therapy, and the therapist is more likely to become "burned out" and then to "give up" on a patient.

The third target involves decreasing behaviors that interfere with quality of life, with substance abuse as the top priority among individuals who abuse drugs, followed by homelessness, excessive hospitalization, unemployment, economic and health problems.

Finally, DBT seeks to increase skillful behaviors across the four skills training modules (e.g., mindfulness, interpersonal effectiveness, emotion regulation, and distress tolerance). In this manner, skillful behaviors replace disordered behaviors across the major areas of dysfunction.

Individual psychotherapy sessions of DBT begin with a review of the patient's diary card from the preceding week, a daily record of common problem behaviors (e.g., suicidal behaviors, use of illicit drugs, prescription medications, alcohol, urges to use drugs, urges to self-harm, physical discomfort, misery, lying etc.) completed by the patient throughout the week. The session agenda is largely determined by these recorded behaviors. Dysfunctional behaviors are addressed in order of their position on the DBT targets hierarchy. If no dysfunctional behaviors have occurred, the focus of the session is determined by issues the patient wishes to work on.

Regardless of the topic being discussed, the skillful DBT therapist always links all problem behaviors and therapy strategies to the patient's goals, or the "ends in view." More specifically, abstaining from drug use or self-harm behaviors is never discussed in isolation, but always is linked to the patient's reasons for quitting (e.g., improved relationships with children, to get and keep a good job, to complete a college degree, to pursue meaningful work). The question always posed is: Does this behavior bring you closer to or further from your goals for a life worth living, and in what ways? Secondly, the DBT therapist maintains a keen eye on identifying in-session dysfunctional behaviors as well as emerging dysfunctional links, while conducting a behavioral analysis of the problem behavior. Dysfunctional behaviors are highlighted and solutions to specific behaviors are generated. Finally, the DBT therapist seeks to maintain a dialectical stance throughout the session ("I know what I'm suggesting that you do is impossible, but you have to do it anyway").

DBT-S Group Skills Training: Consistent with other cognitive-behavioral approaches to addictive behaviors (Marlatt & Gordon, 1985; Monti, Abrams et al., 1989; Miller & Munoz, 1982), the assumption underlying DBT-S skills training is that many of the difficulties substance abusers with BPD have are due to behavioral skills deficits. The function of DBT skills training is acquisition and strengthening of skills necessary to decrease substance abuse and other dysfunctional behaviors.

The treatment manual for DBT skills training (Linehan, 1993b) is highly structured and provides session-by-session guidelines on content and format. DBT skills training comprises four skills modules, two of which emphasize change (emotion regulation and interpersonal effectiveness) and two of which emphasize acceptance of reality (distress tolerance and mindfulness). The core mindfulness skills include focusing attention on the immediate moment, describing these observations with words (which requires one to discriminate facts from interpretations), participating fully in the moment, assuming a non-judgmental stance, focusing awareness on the present moment, and effectiveness (focusing on what works). The interpersonal effectiveness module involves a number of skills for making requests or saying "no," and for resolving interpersonal conflicts in ways that achieve the intended goal while preserving or improving the relationship and maintaining self-respect. Emotional regulation skills teach a variety of cognitive and behavioral skills to reduce emotional vulnerability. This module emphasizes how to identify and describe emotions, how to stop avoiding negative emotions, and how to increase positive emotions. Distress tolerance training teaches a number of strategies aimed at surviving a crisis, including intense drug craving or urges, without making matters worse by engaging in dysfunctional behaviors. This set of skills teaches a number of "delaying gratification" and self-soothing techniques, "willingness" (as opposed to "willfulness") to do what is needed in the moment, and radical acceptance of that which cannot be changed or modified. Because of the central importance of behavioral principles throughout DBT, self-management techniques are woven in throughout all four skills modules.

In contrast to standard DBT skills training groups that use a 150-minute format and emphasize skills strengthening (e.g., role plays and homework review) along with skills acquisition, DBT-S skills training groups are 90 minutes in length and focus exclusively on skills acquisition. This modification to standard DBT was made because of high rates of social phobia among substance abusing patients, which compromised attendance at group and skills building. Skills strengthening activities now occur in the new Individual Skills Consultation mode described below.

DBT-S Individual Skills Consultation: This new treatment mode emphasizes skills strengthening exercises, including review of homework from prior week, behavioral rehearsal, feedback and coaching. To increase attendance at skills group, individual skills consultation ideally is conducted by one of the two group leaders, thus giving participants an opportunity to develop a strong bond with at least one of the group therapists; this eases their anxiety about attending group. The authors' experience to date is that inclusion of this mode has resulted in an increase in group attendance.

ADVICE TO CLINICIANS WHO TREAT PATIENTS WITH BPD

The following general guidelines are offered to clinicians who work with patients suffering borderline personality disorder:

Do Not Give Lethal Drugs to Lethal People. Given the incidence of suicidal behaviors and rates of successful suicides among persons with BPD, we recommend not giving lethal drugs to lethal people. This requires a thorough assessment of past suicidal behaviors and intentional and unintentional overdoses to determine whether a particular patient is at risk for using prescription medications alone or with another means to intentionally or inadvertently kill himself or herself. At the start of therapy, we advise assessing current medications used, medications being hoarded, and active (e.g., refillable) prescriptions. Just as patients are asked to get rid of other lethal means, they should be asked to dispose of lethal medications.

Evaluate the Patient for Coexisting Medical Disorders. Persons with BPD, including those who abuse substances, often have coexisting medical problems and commonly present for medical treatment. Medical complaints by individuals with BPD are not always easy to evaluate, as symptoms may be caused or exacerbated by psychotropic medication side effects (for example, blurred vision is a side effect of some mood stabilizers such as lithium, but also is a sign of diabetes) and/or emotional dysregulation. Additionally, persons with BPD are more likely to present with somatization disorder than are persons in the general population (estimates vary widely, from 4% to 45% of the population). For these reasons, it is important that a careful diagnostic assessment be performed.

While many individuals with BPD avoid seeking medical evaluation of their health problems because of excessive fear regarding their health status or because of their difficulty in interacting with professionals because of the power/status differential, some persons with BPD seek out medical services to excess. One can easily imagine a scenario in which contact with a patient's primary care provider is associated with attention and warmth, being taken seriously, and having one's concerns and perceptions validated by a credible person in a position of authority. Contact with a primary care provider thus may be highly reinforcing. In the absence of other such experiences in the patient's social environment, some patients with BPD may begin to seek contact with the primary care provider at an increased rate of frequency and frequently seek out the clinician and/or the clinic staff when in crisis or when emotionally dysregulated.

In the latter situation, the question becomes one of how best to ensure that the patient receives the necessary medical attention, while protecting the clinician from "burn out" or inadvertently reinforcing dysfunctional client behavior. One approach evaluated by Smith and colleagues (1986) involved distributing patients with somatization disorder to randomized groups, randomized to either a consultation or treatment-as-usual control condition. Consultation condition physicians were instructed by a consulting psychiatrist to see the patients on a time- versus problem-based schedule, to conduct a physical examination at each visit, and not to tell the patients their symptoms were "all in their heads." At the same time, the physicians were advised to minimize hospitalizations and the use of diagnostic and laboratory procedures unless they were clearly indicated.

As a result, medical costs were reduced by 53% as compared to the treatment-as-usual control condition. When the intervention was applied to the control condition, a 49% drop in costs was found. These cost savings were related largely to decreased hospitalizations. What is especially dialectical about this approach is that it does not represent a compromise by either the patient or the care provider (where both sides have given in half way but neither are satisfied) but rather a formulation of the problem in which everyone wins.

Some clinicians may flinch at the thought of seeing such patients more frequently, given how interpersonally unskillful these patients may be and the amount of distress they express which the physician cannot cure. As a natural consequence, many physicians put off seeing these patients. Unfortunately, a dysfunctional transaction between the patient and physician may then develop in which the patient calls in crisis and is unable to regulate his/her emotions sufficiently; this behavior affirms the physician's dislike and/or disinterest in treating the patient, which leads to further dysregulation on the part of the patient, who fears being misunderstood or rejected by the physician.

Finally, patients who seek services while in crisis may become further emotionally dysregulated if the primary caregiver is personally unavailable to provide services. By contrast, when patients with BPD are seen on a time-based rather than a crisis-based schedule, they arrive at appointments more emotionally regulated and their concerns often are taken more seriously. In this more regulated state, the patient is less aversive to the clinician and the clinician is more likely attend to and validate their concerns. In addition, scheduling allows the patient to consistently see the same provider, which keeps his or her care coordinated and minimizes crisis trips to high cost facilities such as the emergency room.

Be Alert to Parasuicidal Behaviors. As previously described, suicidal and parasuicidal behaviors are a hallmark of BPD. Parasuicidal behaviors, such as cutting or burning oneself, are frequently performed to regulate emotions during periods of intense dysregulation. There is no doubt that parasuicide, like substance abuse, is very effective (from a behavioral perspective, highly reinforcing) in regulating emotions and is frequently the patient's only reliable means of quickly doing so because of skills deficits. This highly dysfunctional behavior can be further reinforced by the response to parasuicide by the social environment by means of increased attention, warmth, caring, and validation of suffering that is commonly received by patients in medical settings. We recommend the following approach to minimize reinforcing the dysfunctional behavior of parasuicide: (1) treat the medical problem thoroughly and expediently, but keep discussion of the parasuicide or the events leading up to the parasuicide to a bare minimum; (2) use a very matter-of-fact tone and manner (e.g., do not appear overly warm or emotional); (3) ensure the patient's medical safety (e.g., assess whether the patient has any imminent plans to kill him/herself); and (4) emphasize that, while parasuicide and substance use reduces emotional pain in the moment, both result in further anguish in the next moment and do little to solve the patient's life problems.

Consult with the Patient about How to Interact Effectively with His or Her Other Care Providers (rather than intervening on the patient's behalf). Central to DBT is the goal of teaching patients with BPD how to effectively manage their own lives and interact with their environment rather than consulting with the patient's environment on how to effectively interact with the patient. Known in DBT as "Consultation-to-the-Patient Strategies," this approach involves having the physician or pharmacotherapist function as a consultant to the patient by helping the patient to identify the objective in a particular instance, then problem-solving with the patient to develop the best means to manage the situation (Linehan, 1993). While this kind of procedure is considerably more time-consuming than managing the environment for the patient, it is only by teaching patients how to effectively manage their environment in the context of their lives that they learn the necessary skills to be effective in interacting with their network.

Exceptions to the "Consultation-to-the-Patient" strategies are appropriately used in DBT when: (1) the patient is a minor, (2) he or she is unable to act on his or her own behalf and the outcome is *very* important, (3) the environment is intransigent and has an inordinate amount of power, (4) to save the patient's life or to avoid substantial risk to others, or (5) when it is the humane thing to do and will cause no harm. In our experience, environmental interventions are rare while opportunities to consult abound.

Implicit in this approach is the assumption that patients need to and can learn the necessary skills to tolerate the environment *as it is* (as perfect or imperfect as it is) or to change how he or she interacts with the environment in order to achieve the desired outcome, regardless of whether they can.

Physicians and other primary care providers can provide "Consultation-to-the-Patient" assistance in the following ways: First, help your patient identify his or her main objective(s) in a particular instance. Putting aside preference and partiality, identify what approach will work best (e.g., most effectively) in achieving the objective. Second, assist the patient in identifying an effective route to the objective. This task is similar to developing a road map for the patient to get from where they are to where they wish to go. We have found the most useful and quickest means to developing this path is to simply ask oneself, "If it were me and I were in this situation, what would I do and how would I get out (or get what I needed)?" If the topic of discussion involves the patient asking for something (e.g., hospital privileges, asking someone to be a sponsor in Narcotics Anonymous) or saying no to something (e.g., telling the dentist not to prescribe opiate-based pain medications following a painful dental procedure), the primary care provider can first model an assertive response for the patient, then ask the patient to try the response. Providing specific feedback to the patient about what aspects of the role play were effective and what could be improved is helpful. Finally (and in collaboration with the patient), the therapist seeks to identify the weak links in the plan and problem-solve solutions for these weak spots.

While this approach typically takes considerably more time and effort than intervening on the patient's behalf and may be particularly burdensome within a primary care context, we have found that such an approach, over the long term, actually reduces the number of patient crises and appointments and improves treatment compliance. In some settings, this function has been performed by a nurse or a nurse's assistant.

Treat Medication or Treatment Non-Compliance as Treatment-Interfering Behavior. Behaviors that interfere with effective therapy, including medication non-compliance, are second on the hierarchy of behavioral targets in DBT, following suicidal behaviors. When patients are non-compliant with medication regimes, the task in DBT focuses specifically on addressing this as behavior that interferes with treatment effectiveness. This rule applies regardless of whether or not the primary therapist is the patient's pharmacotherapist. Strategies to address therapy-interfering behaviors are no different from behavioral therapy strategies used to analyze and change other dysfunctional behaviors: specify the dysfunctional behavior and factors leading up to or reinforcing the dysfunctional behavior by conducting a detailed assessment. For example, are they forgetting? Are they ashamed to take the medication? Are others telling them not to take it or to double-up?

Elicit a commitment from the patient to decrease non-compliance behaviors; identify solutions that address factors that compromise compliance: What might reduce their shame about taking medication? What could be done when others tell them to stop taking the medication? Monitor prescription medication use on an ongoing basis by having the patient complete a daily record of medications used. Medication use should be targeted in medication management or psychotherapy sessions as long as the patient misuses (or does not use) the medications. The same approach applies to other medical treatment issues, including following through on a diet or exercise program, making scheduled appointments, or being more polite and agreeable with reception staff.

Focus on Safety and Effectiveness when Prescribing Psychotropics. The overarching rule that ought to guide delivery of psychotropic medications is safety (e.g., practice a "Do no harm" approach) and effectiveness (e.g., Does it work for the intended purpose? Do the benefits outweigh the potential or actual costs?). This basic principle contributed to a decision to make use of replacement medications (e.g., methadone and ORLAAM for opiates) for a group of substance abusing patients with BPD. While not without their own risks, legally marketed medications are considerably safer than illegal drugs purchased on the streets. In addition, a large body of clinical outcome research has documented the efficacy of these medications and enumerated the advantages of replacing use of illegal drugs with legally marketed drugs (see Ling, Rawson & Compton, 1994, for a review of this literature).

Clinicians at the Moncton Group in Canada have developed the following principles for use in prescribing psychotropic medications to patients. First, use safe, non-lethal drugs (e.g., SSRIs over neuroleptics, MAO inhibitors, tricyclics and other lethal drugs) and administer drugs in a safe fashion. For patients with a history of medication abuse, this may include having the patient pick up a two-day supply of a medication at the pharmacy several times a week, rather than providing a larger supply. Second, simple psychotropic medication regimens are preferred to complex ones, to avoid drug interactions and to minimize side effects, particularly those that produce cognitive disturbances (e.g., grogginess, diminished focus and attention) that interfere with the psychosocial treatment. Third, specific symptoms are targeted, using medications with a relatively "narrow" spectrum of influence. Fourth, use medications with demonstrated efficacy and change the medication if iatrogenic effects appear or in the absence of intended effects. Finally, move the patient through the induction phase to the intended maintenance level as quickly as feasible.

Referral to Psychiatric Treatment. Clearly, the authors would suggest referring patients with BPD for DBT. However, finding such treatment may not be easy. The treatment is not widely used although that is changing rapidly. Some state mental health divisions (e.g., those in Illinois and Connecticut) are training mental health staff in and mandating the use of DBT for patients with BPD, and some managed care firms are considering funding therapy for BPD only if DBT is used, on the grounds that they will only fund treatments that have been empirically validated. In addition, where DBT is available *per se*, as in Seattle and New York City, the demand for treatment often is higher than the supply of trained therapists and often the available therapists are limited in the number of sliding fee slots they can provide. When DBT is not available, an alternative is to consider some of the key aspects of DBT that uses a cognitive-behavioral approach and refer patients to treatment which have more rather than less. Some of these aspects are:

- Treatments that focus specifically on emotional regulation.
- Treatments that focus on teaching patients new skills and enhancing motivation.
- Treatments that address behaviors that interfere with therapy.
- Treatments that balance teaching patients how to tolerate their distress with a focus on how to change the circumstances of their lives to reduce situations that generate distress.
- Treatments with specified targets that are applicable to the patient's areas of behavioral dyscontrol (e.g., substance abuse, suicidal behavior, impulsivity) and preferably those that focus on more severe, life-threatening behaviors first.
- Treatments that focus on helping the patient to function for him- or herself, rather than having the clinician organize and structure the patient's life and problems.
- Following safe pharmacotherapy protocols.

CONCLUSIONS

Clinicians often are consulted by persons with BPD who are in periods of crisis, and at other times for treatment of a variety of problems, some of which are the result of self-harm; or for treatment of disorders caused by engaging in other impulsive behaviors, such as substance abuse. Providing effective care to these patients can be extremely difficult for a variety of reasons, including the patient's degree of emotion vulnerability and emotional sensitivity and resultant emotion dysregulation, patient noncompliance with aspects of treatment (including proper use of medications, attending appointments to obtain additional diagnostic tests), treatment-interfering behaviors (e.g., arriving late for clinic appointments, yelling at clinic staff, threatening to sue), as well as a compromised quality of life (e.g., transient housing or homelessness, unemployment, substance abuse).

This chapter has provided an overview of Dialectical Behavior Therapy, a comprehensive and effective treatment for individuals with BPD. While DBT was designed and empirically-validated as a psychosocial treatment, DBT theory and treatment principles can easily be tailored for use within a primary care setting. Main points reviewed in this paper with direct application to primary care physicians include the following: (1) emotional dysregulation constitutes the core problem for individuals with BPD and causes dysregulation in other domains; (2) individuals with BPD need and want help, but frequently have enormous difficulty obtaining this help because of skills and motivational deficits; (3) while somatization disorder is more prevalent in individuals with BPD, these patients more often than not have real medical problems that require medical attention; (4) while patients with BPD may indeed be more emotionally fragile than other patients, we do these patients a disservice in the end by treating them as if they are fragile; this position is balanced in DBT by teaching new skillful behaviors and treating behaviors that interfere with patients acting effectively; (5) reinforce functional behaviors (such as arriving on time for clinic appointments and using effective skills to solve problems rather than engaging in self-harm) and do not reinforce dysfunctional behaviors; and (6) for patients who are high utilizers of medical services, arranging regular medical appointments that are not contingent on illness and/or crises.

Supported by Grant DAO8674 from the National Institute on Drug Abuse, and Grant MH34486 from the National Institute on Mental Health, awarded to Dr. Linehan.

REFERENCES

Alcoholics Anonymous (1976). *Alcoholics Anonymous*. New York: Alcoholics Anonymous World Service, Inc.

Ames-Frankel J, Devlin MJ, Walsh T, Strasser TJ, Sadik C, Oldham JM & Roose SP (1992). Personality disorder diagnoses in patients with bulimia nervosa: Clinical correlates and changes with treatment. *Journal of Clinical Psychiatry* 53:90–96.

Baer L, Jenike MA, Black DW, Treece C, Rosenfeld R & Greist J (1992). Effect of axis II diagnoses on treatment outcome with clomipramine in 55 patients with obsessive-compulsive disorder. *Archives of General Psychiatry* 49:862–866.

Barasch A, Frances AJ & Hurt SW (1985). Stability and distinctness of borderline personality disorder. *American Journal of Psychiatry* 142:1484–1486.

Barley WD, Buie SE, Peterson EW, Hollingsworth AS, Griva M, Hickerson SC, Lawson JE & Bailey BJ (1993). The development of an inpatient cognitive-behavioral treatment program for borderline personality disorder. *Journal of Personality Disorders* 7(3):232–240.

Brooner RK, King VL, Kidorf M, Schmidt CW & Bigelow GE (1997). Psychiatric and substance use comorbidity among treatment-seeking opioid abusers. *Archives of General Psychiatry* 54(1):71–80.

Bryer JB, Nelson BA, Miller JB & Krol PA (1987). Childhood sexual and physical abuse as factors in adult psychiatric illness. *American Journal of Psychiatry* 144:1426–1430.

Carpenter MD, Mulligan JC, Bader IA & Meinzer AE (1985). Multiple admissions to an urban psychiatric center: A comparative study. *Hospital and Community Psychiatry* 36:1305–1308.

Cioffi D & Holloway J (1993). Delayed costs of suppressed pain. *Journal of Personality and Social Psychology* 64:274–282.

Clarkin JF, Widiger TA, Frances AJ, Hurt FW & Gilmore M (1983). Prototypic typology and the borderline personality disorder. *Journal of Abnormal Psychiatry* 92:263–275.

Coker S, Vize C, Wade T & Cooper PJ (1993). Patients with bulimia nervosa who fail to engage in cognitive behavior therapy. *International Journal of Eating Disorders* 13:35–40.

Cowdry RW & Gardner DL (1988). Pharmacotherapy of borderline personality disorder: Alprazolam, carbamazepine, trifluoperazine, and tranylcypromine. *Archives of General Psychiatry* 45:111–119.

Cowdry RW, Pickar D & Davies R (1985). Symptoms and EEG findings in the borderline syndrome. *International Journal of Psychiatry in Medicine* 15:201–211.

Dahl AA (1986). Prognosis of the borderline disorders. *Psychopathology* 19:68–79.

Dahlgren KG (1977). Attempted suicide: 35 years afterward. *Suicide and Life-Threatening Behavior* 7:75–79.

D'Aunno T & Vaughn TE (1992). Variations in methadone treatment practices: Results from a national study. *Journal of the American Medical Association* 267:253–258.

Dimeff LA & Marlatt GA (in press). Preventing relapse and maintaining change in addictive behaviors. *Clinical Psychology: Science and Practice.*

Dorpat TL & Ripley HS (1960). A study of suicide in the Seattle area. *Comparative Psychiatry* 1:349–359.

Dublin LI (1963). *Suicide: A Sociological and Statistical Study*. New York, NY: Ronald Press.

Dulit RA, Fyer MR, Haas GL, Sullivan T & Frances AJ (1990). Substance use in borderline personality disorder. *American Journal of Psychiatry* 147:1002–1007.

Felitti VJ (1991). Long term consequences of incest, rape, and molestation. *Southern Medical Journal* 84:328–31.

First MB, Spitzer RL, Gibbons M, Williams JBW & Benjamin L (1996). *User's Guide for the Structured Clinical Interview for DSM-IV Axis II Personality Disorders (SCID-II)*. New York, NY: Biometrics Research Department, New York State Psychiatric Institute.

Fruzzetti AE & Linehan MM (in press). A behavioral approach to understanding borderline personality and related disorders. In O Kernberg (ed.) *Handbook of Borderline Personality Disorder.*

Frances AJ, Fyer MR & Clarkin JF (1986). Personality and suicide. *Annals of the New York Academy of Sciences* 487:281–293.

Geller JL (1986). In again, out again: Preliminary evaluation of a state hospital's worst recidivists. *Hospital and Community Psychiatry* 37:386–390.

Grabowski J (1996). Medications for treatment of drug dependence and abuse. Paper presented at APA Workshop.

Green JH (1988). Frequent rehospitalization and noncompliance with treatment. *Hospital and Community Psychiatry* 39:963–966.

Gottman JM & Katz LF (1989). Effects of marital discord on young children's peer interaction and health. *Developmental Psychology* 25:373–381.

Gould DA, Stevens NG, Ward NG, Carlin AS & Sowell HE (1994). Self-reported childhood abuse in an adult population in a primary care setting. *Archives of Family Medicine* 3:252–256.

Gunderson JG (1984). *Borderline Personality Disorder.* Washington DC: American Psychiatric Press.

Gunderson JG, Kolb JE & Austin V (1981). The diagnostic interview for borderline patients. *American Journal of Psychiatry* 138(7):896–903.

Hadley TR, McGurrin MC, Pulice RT & Holohan EJ (1990). Using fiscal data to identify heavy service users. *Psychiatric Quarterly* 61:41–48.

Heard HL & Linehan MM (1994). Dialectical behavior therapy: An integrative approach to the treatment of borderline personality disorder. *Journal of Psychotherapy Integration* 4:55–82.

Herman JL, Perry JC & van der Kolk BA (1989). Childhood trauma in borderline personality disorder. *American Journal of Psychiatry* 146:490–495.

Hudziak JJ, Boffeli TJ, Kreisman JJ, Battaglia MM, Stanger C & Guze SB (1996). Clinical study of the relation of borderline personality disorder to Briquet's syndrome (hysteria), somatization disorder, antisocial personality disorder, and substance abuse disorders. *American Journal of Psychiatry* 153(12):1598–1606.

Koenigsberg HW, Kaplan RM, Gilmore M & Cooper AM (1985). The relationship between syndrome and personality disorder in DSM-III: Experience with 2,462 patients. *American Journal of Psychiatry* 142(2): 207–212.

Koss MP, Koss PG & Woodruff WJ (1991). Deleterious effects of criminal victimization of women's health and medical utilization. *Archives of Internal Medicine* 151:342–347.

Kosten RA, Kosten TR & Rounsaville BJ (1989). Personality disorders in opiate addicts show prognostic specificity. *Journal of Substance Abuse and Treatment* 6:163–168.

Kullgren G (1992). Personality disorders among psychiatric inpatients. *Nordisk Psykiastrisktidsskrift* 46:27–32.

Lechner ME, Vogel ME, Garcia-Shelton LM, Leichter JL & Streibel KR (1993). Self-reported medical problems of adult female survivors of childhood sexual abuse. *Journal of Family Practice* 36:633–638.

Linehan MM (1993a). *Cognitive Behavioral Therapy of Borderline Personality Disorder.* New York, NY: Guilford Press.

Linehan MM (1993b). *Skills Training Manual for Treating Borderline Personality Disorder.* New York, NY: Guilford Press.

Linehan, MM (in press). Development, evaluation, and dissemination of effective psychosocial treatments: Stages of disorder, levels of care, and stages of treatment research. In MD Glantz & CR Hartel (eds.) *Drug Abuse: Origins and Interventions.* Washington, DC: American Psychological Association.

Linehan MM, Armstrong HE, Suarez A, Allmon D & Heard HL (1991). Cognitive-behavioral treatment of chronically parasuicidal borderline patients. *Archives of General Psychiatry* 48:1060–1064.

Linehan MM & Heard HL (1993). Impact of treatment accessibility on clinical course of parasuicidal patients: In reply to R.E. Hoffman. [Letter to the editor]. *Archives of General Psychiatry* 50:157–158.

Linehan MM & Schmidt H III (1995). The dialectics of effective treatment of borderline personality disorder. In WO O'Donohue & L Krasner (eds.) *Theories in Behavior Therapy: Exploring Behavior Change.* Washington, DC: American Psychological Association, 553–584.

Linehan MM & Dimeff LA (1998). *Dialectical Behavior Therapy Manual of Treatment Interventions for Drug Abusers with Borderline Personality Disorder* (Unpublished manuscript).

Ling W, Rawson RA & Compton MA (1994). Substitution pharmacotherapies for opioid addiction: From methadone to LAAM and buprenorphine. *Journal of Psychoactive Drugs* 26:119–128.

Links PS, Heslegrave RJ, Mitton JE, van Reekum R & Patrick J (1995). Borderline personality disorder and substance abuse: Consequences of comorbidity. *Canadian Journal of Psychiatry* 40:9–14.

Links PS, Steiner M, Offord DR & Eppel AB (1988). Characteristics of borderline personality disorder: A Canadian study. *Canadian Journal of Psychiatry* 33:336–340.

Loranger AW & Tulis EH (1985). Family history of alcoholism in borderline personality disorder. *Archives of General Psychiatry* 42:153–157.

Marlatt GA & Gordon JR (1985). *Relapse Prevention: Maintenance Strategies in the Treatment of Addictive Behaviors.* New York, NY: Guilford Press.

Marziali E & Munroe-Blum H (1994). *Interpersonal Group Psychotherapy for Borderline Personality Disorder.* New York, NY: Basic Books.

McCann JT, Flynn PM & Gersh DM (1992). MCMI-II diagnosis of borderline personality disorder: Base rates versus prototypic items. *Journal of Personality Assessment* 58:105–114.

McCauley J, Kern DE, Kolodner K, Dill L, Schroeder AF, DeChant HK, Ryden J, Derogatis LR & Bass EB (1997). *Journal of the American Medical Association* 277:1362–1368.

McGlashan TH (1986). The Chestnut Lodge follow-up study, III: Long-term outcome of borderline personality disorder. *Archives of General Psychiatry* 43:20–30.

Miller A, Rathus JH, Linehan MM, Wetzler S & Leigh E (1997). Dialectical behavior therapy adapted for suicidal adolescents. *Journal of Practical Psychiatry and Behavioral Health* 3:78–86.

Miller WR & Munoz RF (1982). *How to Control Your Drinking: A Practical Guide to Responsible Drinking.* Albuquerque, NM: University of New Mexico Press.

Modestin J, Albrecht I, Tschaggelar W & Hoffman H (1997). Diagnosing borderline: A contribution to the question of its conceptual validity. *Archives Psychiatrica Nervenkra* 233:359–370.

Monti PM, Abrams DB, Kadden RM & Cooney NL (1989). *Treating Alcohol Dependence.* New York, NY: Guilford Press.

Nace EP, Davis CW & Gaspari JP (1991). Axis II comorbidity in substance abusers. *American Journal of Psychiatry* 148:118–120.

Nace EP, Saxon JJ & Shore N (1983). A comparison of borderline and nonborderline alcoholic patients. *Archives of General Psychiatry* 40:54–56.

National Institute of Health (1997). National Institute of Health Consensus Statement: Effective Medical Treatment of Heroin Addiction. Author.

Ogata SN, Silk KR, Goodrich S, Lohr NE & Westen D (1989). Childhood Sexual and Clinical Symptoms in Borderline Patients. Unpublished manuscript.

Paris J, Brown R & Nowlis D (1987). Long-term follow-up of borderline patients in a general hospital. *Comprehensive Psychiatry* 28(6):530–535.

Perry JC & Cooper SH (1985). Psychodynamics, symptoms, and outcome in borderline and antisocial personality disorders and bipolar type II affective disorder. In TH McGlashan (ed.) *The Borderline: Current Empirical Research*. Washington, DC: American Psychiatric Press, 19–41.

Perry JC, Herman JL, van der Kolk BA & Hoke LA (1990). Psychotherapy and psychological trauma in borderline personality disorder. *Psychiatric Annals* 20:33–43.

Phillips KA & Nierenberg AA (1994). The assessment and treatment of refractory depression. *Journal of Clinical Psychiatry* 55:20–26.

Pitts WM, Gustin QL, Mitchell C & Snyder S (1985). MMPI critical item characteristics of the DSM-III borderline personality disorder. *Journal of Nervous and Mental Disease* 173(10):628–631.

Platt S, Bille-Brahe U, Kerkhof A, Schmidtke A, Bjerke T, Crepet P, De Leo D, Haring C, Lonnqvist J, Michel K, Philippe A, Pommereau X, Querejeta I, Salander-Renberg E, Temesvary B, Wasserman D & Sampaio Faria J (1992). Parasuicide in Europe: The WHO/EURO multicentre study on parasuicide. I. Introduction and preliminary analysis for 1989. *Acta Psychiatrica Scandinavica* 85:97–104.

Pope HG, Jonas JM, Hudson JI, Cohen BM & Gunderson JG (1983). The validity of DSM-III borderline personality disorder: A phenomenologic, family history, treatment response, and long term follow-up study. *Archives of General Psychiatry* 40:23–30.

Richman J & Charles E (1976). Patient dissatisfaction and attempted suicide. *Community Mental Health Journal* 12(3):301–305.

Rutherford MJ, Cacciola JS & Alterman AI (1994). Relationships of personality disorders with problem severity in methadone patients. *Drug and Alcohol Dependence* 35:69–76.

Shearin EN & Linehan MM (1992). Patient-therapist ratings and relationship to progress in dialectical behavior therapy for borderline personality disorder. *Behavioral Therapy* 23:730–741.

Shneidman ES (1971). You and death. *Psychology Today* 43–45, 74–80.

Skodol AE, Buckley P & Charles E (1983). Is there a characteristic pattern to the treatment history of clinic outpatients with borderline personality? *Journal of Nervous and Mental Disease* 171:405–410.

Smith RG, Monson RA & Ray DC (1986). Psychiatric consultation in somatization disorder: A randomized controlled study. *The New England Journal of Medicine* 314(22):1407–1413.

Soloff PH (1994). Is there any drug treatment of choice for the borderline patient? *Acta Psychiatrica Scandinavica* 379:50–55.

Soloff PH (1998). Symptom-oriented psychopharmacology for personality disorders. *Journal of Practical Psychiatry and Behavioral Health* 4:3–11.

Stone MH (1981). Psychiatrically ill relatives of borderline patients: A family study. *Psychiatric Quarterly* 58:71–83.

Stone MH, Hurt SW & Stone DK (1987). The PI 500: Long-term follow-up of borderline inpatients meeting DSM-III criteria. I: Global outcome. *Journal of Personality Disorders* 1:291–298.

Strain EC, Stitzer ML, Liebson IA & Bigelow GE (1993). Methadone dose and treatment outcome. *Drug and Alcohol Dependence* 33:105–117.

Surber RW, Winkler EL, Monteleone M, Havassy BE, Goldfinger SM & Hopkin JT (1987). Characteristics of high users of acute inpatient services. *Hospital and Community Psychiatry* 38:1112–1116.

Tanney BL (1992). Mental disorders, psychiatric patients, and suicide. In RW Maris, AL Berman & JT Maltsberger (eds.) *Assessment and Prediction of Suicide*. New York, NY: Guilford Press, 277–320.

Tucker L, Bauer SF, Wagner S, Harlam D & Shear I (1987). Long-term hospital treatment of borderline patients: A descriptive outcome study. *American Journal of Psychiatry* 144(11):1443–1448.

Wagner AW, Linehan MM & Wasson EJ (1989). Parasuicide: Characteristics and relationship to childhood sexual abuse. Poster presented at the annual meeting of the Association for Advancement of Behavior Therapy, Washington, DC.

Waldinger RJ & Frank AF (1989). Clinicians' experiences in combining medication and psychotherapy in the treatment of borderline patients. *Hospital and Community Psychiatry* 40:712–718.

Walker EA, Gelfand A, Katon W, Koss M, VonKorff M & Bernstein D (unpublished manuscript). Adult Health Status of Women with Childhood Abuse and Neglect.

Walker EA, Gelfand A, Unutzer J, Saunders K, Katon W, VonKorff M & Koss M (1997). Incremental primary care costs associated with early childhood maltreatment. Poster presented at the Department of Psychiatry and Behavioral Sciences, University of Washington.

Wegner DM & Gold DB (1995). Fanning old flames: Emotional and cognitive effects of suppressing thoughts of a past relationship. *Journal of Personality and Social Psychology* 67:782–792.

Weiss RD, Mirin SM, Griffin ML, Gunderson JG et al. (1993). Personality disorders in cocaine dependence. *Comprehensive Psychiatry* 34:145–149.

Widiger TA & Frances AJ (1989). Epidemiology, diagnosis, and comorbidity of borderline personality disorder. In A Tasman, RE Hales & AJ Frances (eds.) *American Psychiatric Press Review of Psychiatry*. Washington, DC: American Psychiatric Press, 8:8–24.

Widiger TA & Weissman MM (1991). Epidemiology of borderline personality disorder. *Hospital and Community Psychiatry* 42:1015–1021.

Woogh CM (1986). A cohort through the revolving door. *Canadian Journal of Psychiatry* 31:214–221.

Zanarini MC, Gunderson JG, Frankenburg FR & Chauncey DL (1989). The revised diagnostic interview for borderlines: Discriminating borderline personality disorder from other axis II disorders. *Journal of Personality Disorders* 3(1):10–18.

CHAPTER 8

Integrating Psychotherapy and Pharmacotherapies in Addiction Treatment

Joan E. Zweben, Ph.D.

Working with Counselors and Psychotherapists
Use of Pharmacotherapies
Recovery-Oriented Psychotherapy
Dual-Disorder Patients in Self-Help Groups

The goal of this chapter is to offer assistance to the clinician who is engaged in coordinating addiction and psychosocial treatment services on behalf of a patient with dual psychiatric and addiction disorders. One of the great strengths of the addiction field is its multidisciplinary teamwork. While the physician is an essential part of the health care team, professionals who offer psychosocial interventions also play a major role. In recent years, cost constraints have restricted the physician's role far more narrowly than many would prefer, and effective interdisciplinary teamwork often makes the difference between a first rate program and an average one. This chapter addresses key elements affecting such teamwork.

Good supervision or collaboration is time-consuming and requires strong facilitation skills at the leadership level. When treatment providers are in conflict, patients suffer. This chapter will describe a variety of common situations and dilemmas and attempt to offer practical options for handling them. It is hoped that it will provide clarification to both addiction specialists and those who work in psychosocial treatment settings.

WORKING WITH COUNSELORS AND PSYCHOTHERAPISTS

Psychosocial interventions typically are provided by practitioners from a variety of disciplines. These range from non-credentialed counselors, who usually are in recovery, to licensed psychologists, social workers, and marriage, family and child counselors. Practitioners range widely in their attitudes, preparation, and skills. They also vary in the degree to which they are accustomed to working with physicians and other medical personnel. Understanding the background and orientation of specific staff can enhance communication and teamwork.

Counselors. Non-credentialed counselors have been integrated into treatment teams on inpatient units since the 1950s, when the Minnesota Model was developed at Hazelden and Wilmar (McElrath, 1997). Prior to that time, the prevailing belief was that alcoholism was a psychological vulnerability to be treated on mental health units, a theoretical framework that failed to produce effective treatment. Collaboration by the leadership of those two institutions produced an adaptation of the principles of Alcoholics Anonymous to create a new model within hospital-based treatment. Key leadership at Wilmar eventually joined Hazelden, blending their models to produce the Minnesota model, which became the prototype of 28-day inpatient programs. Proponents of the model refined their treatment practices and restructured institutional relationships to emphasize the collaboration between professionals and non-credentialed recovering persons. By 1954, non-degreed counselors shared the responsibility and the decision-making authority. Therapeutic communities (TCs), which developed and expanded in the 1960s, also relied predominantly on non-credentialed staff who were personally in recovery (Deitch, 1973; De Leon, 1995, 1994a, 1994b). Some of these gifted clinicians and managers were subsequently hired into the private, insurance-funded treatment system, where they brought their perspective on the importance of developing a subculture that supports recovery. Their appreciation of the need to strengthen environmental or micro-community forces to foster change added an important dimension to the professional model which usually assumes professional services are the main if not the sole factor in promoting change.

Programs today range widely in the extent to which they incorporate non-licensed, recovering personnel. They are prevalent in short term, Minnesota model chemical dependency inpatient programs and in a growing number of dual diagnosis programs. They are numerous in community-based addiction treatment, especially programs based on Twelve Step principles. They are also dominant in therapeutic communities, which has its own conceptual model which integrates Twelve Step elements to varying degrees. Some of these counselors return to school and obtain graduate degrees and licenses, building the cadre of professionals in recovery.

Like licensed staff members, non-credentialed counselors vary widely in talent, experience and skill. Some have little training, except for occasional in-service training sessions at the agency where they entered the job world. Others have been through comprehensive credentialing programs which may produce counselors with an addiction credential who are far more sophisticated than some licensed staff. For example, certificate programs (often attached to universities) may require 200 to 300 hours of course work, plus supervised field placement experience. Some of these programs teach from an exclusively Twelve Step perspective and do not do justice to alternative approaches or the empirical literature; others are more broad based. Some counselors have superb skills; their street savvy and experiences in recovery produce a highly sophisticated clinician. Others may tend towards rigidity: "what worked for me will work for you," and have trouble tolerating the ambiguities of the complex clinical populations seen today. In short, the physician encountering these counselors should draw conclusions about their skill level from observation, not inferences from the presence or absence of credentials. At their best, these counselors offer the additional asset of being a powerful role model, an invaluable contribution deeply valued by addicted patients, especially those coping with overwhelming feelings in early recovery.

Licensed Professionals. Within addiction treatment settings, one can find licensed professionals, both recovering and non-recovering. Some may be highly knowledgeable, others less so. Although one can usually assume basic clinical skills, ability and comfort in adapting those to the patient population can vary greatly. The rigidities of some licensed professionals come from devotion to theoretical models in which they have extensive training, in addition to personality traits of particular individuals.

Physicians likewise should be cautious about drawing optimistic conclusions from the presence of academic credentials and professional licenses. Unfortunately, it still is rare for graduate schools to integrate thorough training on the assessment and treatment of addiction into their core curriculum, despite the fact that many of the clinical populations with whom graduates will be working are abusing alcohol and drugs. Typically, it is provided as an elective (if at all) or a course tacked on in the increasing number of states that require an introductory course for initial licensure or relicensure. Many urban areas offer extensive training (through extension courses or specialized training institutes) and some graduate programs offer addiction treatment as a subspecialty. However, the physician should never assume a professional is knowledgeable in this area. Professionals may underestimate their own lack of knowledge, preferring to believe that the models they acquired in training can be adapted to treating addiction with little modification, or that specialized knowledge about addictive disorders is unnecessary.

Clinical experience alone may tell little about qualifications. Upon inquiry, therapists may say, "I've been seeing alcohol and drug users for 20 years." Many have evolved practices with which they have grown comfortable, but which bear little relation to those supported by an empirical literature or by the experience of clinicians who are addiction specialists. The comfort level of these therapists is sustained in part by the fact that they do not count, much less study their dropouts, and because they have no objective means of monitoring patient progress in becoming alcohol and drug free. Many patients report concealing or minimizing their alcohol and drug use during psychotherapy. In selecting good therapists for referral, physicians should look for evidence of recent systematic training, either through conferences or course work. This increases the likelihood that the therapist will be familiar with what are considered sound treatment practices.

Tensions may be present between recovering and non-recovering staff, and between those with and without professional training and licenses. Passions can run high and basic concepts can be used to express disapproval or discredit one's colleagues. The concepts of enabling and codependency especially lend themselves to disparaging colleagues who take certain positions. They are often used to discourage appropriate forms of helping, and to terminate treatment prematurely. It is important to remember that time in treatment is significantly correlated with positive outcome in a large number of treatment outcome studies (Gerstein & Harwood, 1990; Hubbard, Marsden et al., 1989). Thus our task is to engage and retain patients in treatment, not terminate them for manifesting symptoms of their psychiatric or addictive disorder. Physicians may also struggle in dealing with this phenomena although other chronic diseases such as asthma, diabetes and hypertension have compliance rates comparable to those of addiction treatment (McLellan, Metzger et al., 1995). They may need to be the voice of reason preventing premature termination of the patient, while being mindful of the need to avoid colluding in negative patient behaviors.

Physicians in leadership roles are advised to establish weekly in-service training sessions that address both basic and specialized topics, so as to create a multidisciplinary team that has a shared language and is knowledgeable about integrating the treatment of addictive, psychiatric and medical disorders. There are now many sources of excellent training materials, some of which are available at no charge (e.g., Treatment Improvement Protocols from the Center for Substance Abuse Treatment.) These can be used to organize on-site training sessions. Securing continuing education credits for the disciplines represented on staff enhances participation and commitment to a quality training sequence.

Collaborating with Psychotherapists in the Community. The diversity of psychotherapists in the community can make effective collaboration even more challenging. Certain key differences between general psychotherapy and addiction treatment are worth keeping in mind (see Table 1).

Addiction treatment is typically highly structured with multiple behavioral expectations. Psychotherapy usually has minimal structure other than the scheduled sessions. Psychodynamic therapists in particular may have difficulty incorporating behavioral commitments; eclectic therapists may find this more comfortable. Most outpatient addiction treatment is abstinence-oriented; although this goal may be difficult to reach, the goal itself does not usually vary. Abstinence is usually viewed as the foundation required before meaningful progress can be made on other issues.

Psychotherapy has a wider range of goals and less consistent priorities. Some psychotherapists may not even understand or endorse the need for abstinence over some form of controlled use. For example, they may share the view that drinking is "normal" and hence controlled drinking a reasonable goal, even in patients who have repeatedly demonstrated they cannot moderate their use (Brown 1985). Addiction treatment makes alcohol and drug use the primary focus; psychodynamic psychotherapy explores underlying process as a means of bringing about change. If ill-timed, this focus on process can undermine sobriety by elevating anxiety before abstinence is firmly established. Addiction treatment often includes breath and urine testing if costs permit; psychotherapists rarely arrange such testing and many consider it invasive and abhorrent. Addiction treatment has a variety of treatment components; psychotherapy usually relies on the therapy sessions themselves as the sole component. Therapists and counselors in addiction treatment are active and directive; psychotherapists in private practice have a variety of styles, which can be more or less compatible with addiction treatment. All of this poses another adaptive challenge to the physician when arranging treatment for dual disorders.

USE OF PHARMACOTHERAPIES

Recovering patients who have conditions that require psychotropic or other medications have very special needs. Their specific drug use history makes the use of certain medications highly problematic because of the potential to abuse the prescribed drug, or for precipitating relapse to the primary drug

TABLE 1. Comparison of Outpatient Alcohol and Drug Treatment and Psychotherapy

Typical Attributes of Alcohol and Drug Treatment	Typial Attributes of Psychotherapy
Structured format	Minimal structure
Goals less flexible	Wider range of goals
Alcohol and drug focus	Focus on underlying process
Monitoring by breath and urine testing	No testing; possible negative attitude
Varied treatment components	One component
Active, directive therapists	Varied clinical styles

Source: Adapted from Rawson, 1997

of abuse. Although this volume offers appropriate prescribing guidelines, patients may present for treatment taking medications prescribed by other physicians without a background in addiction medicine. In settings where patients are only seen by physicians when specific problems emerge, counselors need a screening tool which includes warning signals, such as prescriptions for benzodiazepines, that indicate the need for physician review.

Recovering patients also have complex feelings and attitudes towards medications that need to be understood and addressed. Many define recovery as living a comfortable and responsible life style without the use of psychoactive drugs; yet some disorders require the use of psychiatric medications. Family members or Twelve Step program participants may criticize the patient or pressure for discontinuation of medication, generating conflict which undermines treatment. Since physicians often lack adequate time to follow up on these issues, it is important that this task be specifically delegated to other treatment team providers, who may need some additional training to handle medication issues.

Achieving Compliance. Compliance with treatment recommendations is a key factor in successful treatment outcome; hence physicians should monitor how well the treatment team attends to this issue. Compliance with medication regimens is far from perfect, even in well-educated middle class patients who do not have a stigmatized illness. Thus it should not be surprising that addicted patients, who often have additional psychiatric and medical disorders, have difficulty in this area. It is well worth carefully eliciting patient concerns and objections; many behavioral strategies yield poor results because no one took the time to identify the real obstacles to compliance. Sympathetic listening combined with well-timed doses of information can improve medication adherence considerably. Physicians can help counselors and psychotherapists to understand and explore these issues in their counseling sessions with patients. Non-physicians vary considerably in their attitudes and education about medication; time spent educating therapists usually yields multiple benefits.

Certain forms of resistance occur frequently (Zweben & Smith, 1989). Patients on psychotropic medications often feel ashamed and guilty, that they have failed "if I can't do it myself." Because their illness is not measurable in the same manner as diabetes, it is easier for them to sustain this position. For recovering persons, there are added layers of difficulty. Taking a medication to feel better is highly charged, as many link this motive inextricably with their alcohol and drug use. Even in the case of medications such as antidepressants in which the beneficial effects are delayed, such guilt can persist. Some patients report they feel they are "cheating," despite the fact that their depression precipitated multiple relapses during the time it was untreated.

Rejecting the recommendation of medication may reflect the all-or-none thinking characteristic of the alcoholic or addict. The same patient who has at one time consumed every available substance is now horrified at the idea of "putting something foreign in my body" or "relying on drugs." With respect to disulfiram, Banys (1988) notes that patients disdainfully describe it as a crutch; the same patient who has used alcohol as a "crutch" for years is paradoxically fastidious about this one. Medications such as disulfiram or naltrexone can provide an invaluable (and life-saving) window in which to alter behavior patterns; however, patients taking them may feel unable to take credit for their achievements. Reliance on the medication undermines the sense of mastery that will ultimately promote lasting sobriety, hence the importance of handling this issue carefully when such treatment adjuncts are used.

Indeed, it is important that medication not be used as a substitute for doing the work of recovery. For example, a patient taking disulfiram can be asked to keep a daily journal describing situations which would have been hazardous if he or she were not on the medication. The patient can then be asked what behaviors need to be strengthened (often assertive behaviors) to create safety even in the absence of medication. The decision to discontinue can be implemented once the patient has developed coping skills for the high risk situations previously identified.

Compliance with medication regimens can be monitored through refill requests; patients adhering to their regimens initiate contact with their physician for refills before existing ones expire. Prescribing enough refills for a long period deprives the physician of this potential warning signal. Communication with other treatment staff is essential when noncompliance is suspected. Discontinuation of psychotropic medication is frequently a harbinger of relapse to alcohol and drugs, as distressing psychiatric symptoms begin to re-emerge. It can also be an indicator that an AOD relapse already has occurred.

It is crucial for the physician to discuss with the patient and others involved in the treatment the indications for which medication can be discontinued and the process by which this should occur. It is common to find patients with prescriptions for disulfiram who report no discussions with their physician on this topic. Physicians should clarify that disulfiram is a tool to allow other accomplishments to take place, and it is important that the patient review progress with program staff, private therapist, or prescribing physician before discontinuing the medication. Patients on antidepressants may go into denial about their psychiatric disorder once they feel better, and discontinue medication prematurely. The physician needs to educate both patients and their non-physician therapists of the dangers of both psychiatric and addiction relapse with such as decision (i.e., this is a "slippery place.")

Control issues are common. Some patients will accept the need for prescribed drugs, but will tinker with frequency and dose, much as they did with their illicit substances. Some may operate on the assumption that if one is good, three are better, as they escalate their dose of medication. Drug mixing is another common practice. "Surrendering control of medication use to your physician" is a concept that can prove useful; deviation from prescribed regimens are the subject of inquiry. Patients engaged in serious self-examination may spontaneously report such behavior as a residual part of their addictive pattern.

RECOVERY-ORIENTED PSYCHOTHERAPY

There are many forms of psychotherapy and they vary considerably in how compatible they are with addiction treatment. Therapy funded by insurance has been limited to relatively brief interventions, limited in scope. They often permit management of the initial crisis bringing the person to treatment, but little beyond that. Patients with disposable income may be working with therapists in private practice in the community, many of whom are psychodynamic in orientation. These models assume that a relatively open-ended exploration of emotionally charged issues will increase awareness and lead to change. This type of psychotherapy may certainly enhance the quality of recovery, but it has many pitfalls for the patient needing to establish and consolidate abstinence. Private therapists may refer to addiction specialists for collaborative efforts, but there are potential difficulties in the teamwork.

In a recovery-oriented model, the therapist focuses his or her activity according to the tasks faced by the recovering person. These can be conceptualized as recognizing the negative consequences of alcohol and drug use and making a commitment to abstinence, getting clean and sober, and shaping lifestyle transitions to support a comfortable and satisfying sobriety (Zweben, 1993).

For patients who sought psychotherapy unaware that their alcohol and drug use was problematic, motivational enhancement strategies have proven beneficial (Miller & Page, 1991; Miller & Rollnick, 1991; Miller, Zweben et al., 1994). The therapist identifies where the patient is on the continuum of readiness to change: precontemplation, in which the patient is unaware or barely aware that there is a problem; contemplation, in which the patient is weighing the pros and cons of tackling the problem; preparation, in which the patient is making some small forays to change behavior (such as cutting down on cigarettes or changing brands); action, in which a great deal of time and effort is devoting to making changes; and maintenance, or the consolidation of change through relapse prevention strategies and other means (Prochaska, DiClementi & Norcross, 1992). The therapist takes the position that abstinence is the foundation of progress on other issues, and makes the alcohol and drug use the primary focus, working to help the patient understand the importance of making this a priority.

Patients have many understandable reasons to resist this focus, and the therapist works carefully to examine obstacles to making an abstinence commitment, while keeping the patient engaged in the treatment. Typically, this begins with the distress that brought the patient to psychotherapy, and works to demonstrate the relationship of that stress to alcohol and drug use. For example, many seek psychotherapy for problems of self-esteem and well being. The therapist notes that regular consumption of a central nervous system (CNS) depressant like alcohol will inevitably depress mood, even though the initial effect seems like relief. Although the patient believes alcohol is a coping mechanism, it is likely exacerbating feelings of low mood and self worth. In this way, the therapist cultivates readiness to commit to at least a brief period of abstinence. To establish abstinence, effective interventions tend to be highly structured and focused on developing the behaviors which bring it about. Cognitive-behavioral strategies have been well documented to be effective (Kadden, Carroll et al., 1994; Matrix, 1995; Rawson, Obert et al., 1990). The therapist focuses on how to become and remain abstinent. Insight-oriented exploration is confined to issues relevant to obstacles to abstinence; it is not possible to formulate effective behavioral strategies without clarity on where problems lie. However, the conventionally trained therapist often tends to widen the exploration too broadly in the beginning, which may undermine abstinence in its early, fragile stages. The recovery-oriented therapist does not mechanistically focus on behavior, but blends approaches while maintaining clear perspective on the immediate goals to be achieved. Therapists who are not comfortable with a range of intervention strategies do less well with patients at this stage, and may actually undermine progress.

In prescribing medications to address withdrawal phenomena, physicians need to communicate to non-physician therapists what to expect, and what might constitute warning signs of developing problems. For example, the therapist may not be aware that the patient given three days' supply of Librium® for alcohol withdrawal by an addiction specialist may also obtain a month's supply of Valium® from his or her family physician for "back spasm" and thus be in a high-risk situation. Since therapists spend more time with their patients, they are in a good position to detect impending problems and initiate communication with the physician or clinician responsible for coordinating care.

Therapists may not understand the importance of urine and breath testing, and can weaken cooperation by conveying it is somehow degrading to the patient to comply. They need to understand that testing often functions as a key element in the support structure of outpatient treatment, permitting lapses to be identified and addressed quickly. It is helpful to inform them that patients report urine and breath testing serves as a deterrent to impulsive use, and "makes the option of using seem further removed." In addition, it can be particularly important in restoring credibility with intimates, to whom most patients have lied for considerable periods of time during periods of active drinking and drug use. Drug testing or Breathalyzer tests relieves anxiety on the part of significant others, and protects the patient from the disheartening experience of being mistrusted even though making progress. Behaviors of the early abstinence period are very similar to those of active use (difficulty structuring time, irritability, sleep disruption, moodiness), leading to mistrust on the part of others even when the patient is doing well. Testing allows everyone to know where they stand. It is preferable for the patient to sign appropriate releases for therapists outside the addiction program to be notified of test results.

Late-stage recovery issues require an examination of life style transitions need to sustain a healthy sobriety, and this period resembles conventional psychotherapy in many ways. However, it is important that the therapist have some understanding of relapse precipitants, and be able to detect relapse warning signs. Current pressures to shorten addiction treatment dramatically will place more burden on psychotherapists to handle these issues. Structured relapse prevention activities done early in addiction treatment may not "stick" because it is difficult to deal with later stage recovery issues when the person is in early recovery. The conceptual groundwork can be laid down early, but the issues are more effectively dealt with at the time they are real. Relapse prevention early in treatment is usually focused on establishing stable abstinence, and is less able to deal with dangers which can manifest after a considerable period of sobriety. Sensitivity to these later relapse issues and a willingness to again make addiction issues a priority should warning signals emerge is a necessary characteristic of the therapist capable of good work with recovering patients.

Addiction treatment providers who find themselves collaborating with mental health therapists of questionable skill in dealing with recovering patients have a delicate task. They must inform the patient of appropriate treatment practices without generating distress by criticizing another professional with whom the patient may have a strong relationship. The physician is obligated to educate the patient, but must do so with tact and sensitivity to the many complex issues involved in collaboration.

DUAL DISORDER PATIENTS IN SELF-HELP GROUPS

Self-help group participation is a major element in achieving a positive outcome, so it is important for clinicians to facilitate their use. Self-help groups are important in two ways: (1) they provide access to a culture which supports the recovery process, from which participants can recreate social networks that are not organized around alcohol and drug use, and (2) they provide a process for personal development which has no financial barriers. Although these goals can be achieved in other ways, for most people the self-help system offers the richest resource. Although there is an increasing variety of groups, the Twelve Step system is the largest self-help system in the world (Alcoholics Anonymous 1992 Membership Survey, 1993).

Many addiction treatment programs systematically promote the use of self-help or mutual-help groups, but physicians in primary care, psychiatry, or other systems need to consider how best to achieve compliance with a recommendation to participate. Resistance mirrors the patient's conflicts about acknowledging that alcohol and drugs are a problem and abstinence is necessary; hence it is not surprising that these feelings express themselves early around the issue of meeting attendance. The presence of a coexisting disorder can add additional deterrents to involvement. Health care providers' frustration and anger at non-compliance, while understandable, often results in behavior which alienates the patient. Offering an opportunity for the patient to explore these issues is more likely to promote cooperation. Improving willingness is best done by helping the patient surmount a variety of obstacles, many of which are well known.

Dual disorder patients may meet a variety of difficulties, particularly if they are severely disturbed. They may feel different in a way that reduces their sense of belonging. For them, the spirit of fellowship at the meetings may be a source of discomfort or pain. This may occur not only in those with psychotic conditions, but also in others such as combat veterans with severe PTSD, who may feel they rarely hear "their story." Specialized meetings, such as Double Trouble groups can reduce such obstacles, but there are far fewer of them than needed to provide comprehensive coverage throughout the week. Mainstreaming such patients into meetings with a wider tolerance for deviant behavior can be a way to achieve a more extensive support system. This requires some process for gathering and sharing feedback on the most hospitable and appropriate meetings in a given community for a particular patient population.

Several common forms of resistance can be anticipated, and the patient assisted in progressing beyond them. Initially, most have some form of "stranger anxiety," an understandable reluctance to enter an unfamiliar group where many or most participants appear to know each other. Encouraging patients to call central office to find someone to go with them, pairing them with other patients who attend regularly, or encouraging case managers to go with them (at least initially, and perhaps regularly) can reduce some of the awkwardness. Those with social phobias or who describe themselves as isolates may be adamant in their rejection of group activities. Practitioners should not be discouraged by this; many Twelve Step program members readily announce themselves as "loners," but nonetheless maintain active involvement. Because the meetings are generally friendly and low demand (and low intrusiveness), many objections diminish once the patient has actually taken the step of checking out meetings.

As part of the preparation, the clinician (often a program counselor) can elicit the patient's picture of what goes on in meetings, correct misconceptions, and describe some of what can be expected (opening rituals, sharing of experiences without direct feedback or "cross-talk"). Patients who object or are ambivalent about calling themselves and addict or alcoholic can be assured that AA is for anyone concerned about drinking, and that they can introduce themselves by name only or as a guest. Those who are concerned about "that religious stuff" can be encouraged to attend meetings less dominated by denominational religious overtones, and to "take what you need and leave the rest."

The concept of powerlessness in the first of the Twelve Steps ("We admitted we were powerless over alcohol—that our lives had become unmanageable.") is a point of aversion for many, particularly disempowered groups such as MICA patients, women or minorities with a painful history of being ineffective and anonymous. Clarification that one gains control over one's life by renouncing struggles to control alcohol and drug use may be reassuring, but can take some time to be fully understood. The more spiritual aspects of surrendering control are often better appreciated later in recovery. In the early stages, stressing "take what you need and leave the rest" may be one of the more effective ways to reduce this obstacle to participation. In some communities, cultural adaptations which stress empowerment may be more attractive. For example, Reverend Cecil Williams at Glide Memorial Church in San Francisco has adapted Twelve Step elements to the needs of the African-American community in a manner that regularly draws crowds from diverse groups (Smith, Buxton et al., 1993).

Medications are another issue around which there is much misunderstanding and some genuine hazards. Special preparation is needed for those on psychotropics and some other forms of medication. Despite a well articulated AA position that medication is quite compatible with recovery (Alcoholics Anonymous, 1984), it is unfortunately quite common to encounter negative attitudes from other meeting participants. Patients who are already feeling vulnerable can be quite shaken by such encounters. It is useful to give patients some history about how negative attitudes were developed: misuse of medication by addicts and alcoholics, and inappropriate prescribing practices by uninformed physicians. However, AA clearly states that members are not to play doctor. Patients should be given a copy of the AA pamphlet (The AA Member—Medications and Other Drugs: Report from a Group of Physicians in AA) and provided with an opportunity to discuss or role play handling difficult situations should they occur. It is also possible to identify meetings which are more receptive to those on medication. Hospital-based meetings are good candidates, but the wider the range of community meetings, the better. For more disturbed patients, additional supports may be useful. For example, the patient can be accompanied to initial meetings by the case manager, and as he or she becomes ready to go alone, the case manager can be available by beeper should the patient encounter problems. Some highly disturbed patients make excellent use of meetings; others incorporate elements such as the higher power into their delusional system. Meetings may be overstimulating, leading to disorganization, depending on the state of the patient and/or the nature of the particular meeting. Clinicians should be sensitive to changing patient status and possibilities, as this support system has proven highly beneficial to a wide range of patients. The therapist's conceptual orientation can present obstacles to encouraging self-help group participation. Lack of familiarity with what actually goes on in meetings can lead therapists to accept certain forms of resistance too readily. Brown (1985) discusses many ways in which a therapist's belief system can undermine encouraging both abstinence itself and Twelve Step program participation. In the case of the latter, she notes that as involvement in AA increases, the patient may cancel or miss therapy appointments, and act in other ways that reflect a shift in dependency from the therapist to the AA group. Although addiction specialists may view this as desirable, particularly in early recovery, the therapist may treat it as resistance and fall into a power struggle around loyalties. Some therapists abhor the concept of loss of control, seeing it as a defeat if the patient does not succeed in controlled use. They may dismiss Twelve Step tenets around powerlessness as antithetical to strong self-esteem. Therapists who are more knowledgeable tend to find the Twelve Step philosophy and process quite compatible with psychotherapy, and are able to translate concepts back and forth in a manner which reduces confusion and conflict for the patient.

The best preparation for practitioners is first hand familiarity with the program through a "field trip" to meetings. Interns, residents, and new staff can be asked to attend a specified number of meetings, preferably some recommended by staff or others familiar with community offerings. Those who are not alcoholics or addicts should be advised to select an open meeting and introduce themselves as a student or a guest. Subsequently, they should be provided an opportunity to share their experiences in staff meeting or supervision. Those in recovery or who have attended some meetings are encouraged to attend meetings outside of their previous focus (e.g., Overeaters Anonymous, Gamblers Anonymous). All can be instructed to notice what they felt in anticipation of going (resistances, avoidances), what they felt on arriving, throughout the meeting and afterwards, and their observations and analyses on the group process, its advantages and limitations. Sharing of these experiences in a staff meeting or training session gives some perspective on the variety of experiences possible through participation.

CONCLUSIONS

Interdisciplinary collaboration is one of the most challenging aspects of addiction medicine, but one offering the greatest possibilities of improving outcome. Like heart disease, the greatest advances are achieved through the patient's life style changes, and these must be facilitated by all members of the treatment team. Collaboration is best viewed as a clinical skill as complex as many others, worthy of time and attention to develop and apply. Members of the treatment team bring diverse attitudes, experiences, and skills which must be understood in order to handle the inevitable conflicts and draw the best from the range of resources they represent. Strong physician leadership in fostering teamwork within the program and with other treatment providers is an essential factor in achieving treatment goals.

REFERENCES

Alcoholics Anonymous (1984). *The AA Member—Medications and Other Drugs: Report from a Group of Physicians in AA*. New York, NY: Alcoholics Anonymous World Service, Inc.

Alcoholics Anonymous (1996). *Alcoholics Anonymous: 1996 Membership Survey*. New York, NY: Alcoholics Anonymous World Service, Inc.

Banys P (1988). The clinical use of disulfiram (Antabuse): A review. *Journal of Psychoactive Drugs* 20(3):243–261.

Brown S (1985). *Treating the Alcoholic: A Developmental Model of Recovery*. New York, NY: John Wiley & Sons.

Deitch D (1973). The treatment of drug abuse in the therapeutic community: historical influences, current considerations, future outlook. In *Drug Abuse In*

America: Volume IV. Rockville, MD: National Commission on Marijuana and Drug Abuse.

De Leon G (1995). Residential therapeutic communities in the mainstream: Diversity and issues. *Journal of Psychoactive Drugs* 27(1):3–15.

De Leon G (1994a). The therapeutic community: Toward a general theory and model. In FM Tims, G De Leon & N Jainchill (eds.) *Therapeutic Community: Advances in Research and Application: NIDA Research Monograph 144*. Rockville, MD: National Institute on Drug Abuse (NIH Pub. 94-3633).

DeLeon G (1994b). Therapeutic communities. In M Galanter & HD Kleber (eds.) *Textbook of Substance Abuse Treatment*. Washington, DC: American Psychiatric Press, 391–414.

Gerstein DR & Harwood HJ (1990). *Treating Drug Problems: A Study of the Evolution, Effectiveness, and Financing of Public and Private Drug Treatment Systems*. Washington, DC: National Academy Press.

Hubbard RL, Marsden ME, Rachal JV, Harwood HJ, Cavanaugh ER & Ginzburg HM (1989). *Drug Abuse Treatment: A National Study of Effectiveness*. Chapel Hill, NC: The University of North Carolina Press.

Kadden R, Carroll K, Conovan D, Cooney N, Monti P, Abrams D, Litt M & Hester R (1994). *Cognitive-behavioral coping skills therapy manual: Project MATCH: NIDA Monograph Series No. 3*. Rockville, MD: National Institute on Drug Abuse.

Matrix Center (1995). *The Matrix Intensive Outpatient Program for the Treatment of Substance Abuse and Dependence Disorders*. Los Angeles, CA: Matrix Center, Inc.

McElrath D (1997). *Journal of Psychoactive Drugs*. In press.

McLellan AT, Metzger DS, Alterman AI, Woody GE, Durrell J & O'Brien CP (1995). Is addiction treatment "worth it"? Public health expectations, policy-based comparisons. In D Lewis (ed.) *The Macy Conference on Medical Education*. New York, NY: The Macy Press.

Miller WR & Page A (1991). Warm turkey: Other routes to abstinence. *Journal of Substance Abuse Treatment* 8:227–232.

Miller WR & Rollnick S (1991). *Motivational Interviewing: Preparing People to Change Addictive Behavior*. New York, NY: Guilford Press.

Miller WR, Zweben A, DiClemente CC & Rychtarik RG (1994). *Motivational Enhancement Therapy Manual: Project MATCH: NIDA Monograph Series No. 2*. Rockville, MD: National Institute on Drug Abuse.

Prochaska JO, DiClemente CC & Norcross JC (1992). In search of how people change: Preparing to change addictive behaviors. *American Psychologist* 47(9):1102–1114.

Rawson RA, Obert JL, McCann MJ, Smith DP & Ling W (1990). Neurobehavioral treatment cocaine dependency. *Journal of Psychoactive Drugs* 22(2):159–172.

Smith DE, Buxton ME, Bilal R & Seymour RB (1993). Cultural points of resistance to the 12-step process. *Journal of Psychoactive Drugs* 25(1):97–108.

Zweben JE (1993). Recovery oriented psychotherapy: A model for addiction treatment. *Psychotherapy* 30:259–268.

Zweben JE (1995a). Early and ongoing recovery. In S Brown (ed.) *Treating Alcoholism*. New York, NY: Jossey-Bass, 197–229.

Zweben JE (1995b). Integrating psychotherapy and 12-step approaches. In AM Washton (ed.) *Psychotherapy and Substance Abuse: A Practitioner's Handbook*. New York, NY: Guilford Press, 124–140.

Zweben JE & Clark HW (1990–91). Unrecognized substance misuse: Clinical hazards and legal vulnerabilities. *The International Journal of the Addictions* 25:1431–1451.

Zweben JE & Smith DE (1989). Considerations in using psychotropic medication with dual diagnosis patients in recovery. *Journal of Psychoactive Drugs* 21:221–229.

SECTION 14
The Family in Addiction

CHAPTER 1

The Family in Addiction **1093**
Michael R. Liepman, M.D., FASAM

CHAPTER 2

A Developmental Model of the Alcoholic Family **1099**
Stephanie Brown, Ph.D. and Virginia Lewis, M.S.W.

CHAPTER 3

Children in Alcoholic Families:
Family Dynamics and Treatment Issues **1111**
Hoover Adger, Jr., M.D., M.P.H.

CHAPTER 4

Current Family Treatment Approaches **1115**
David Berenson, M.D. and Ellen Woodside Schrier, M.S.W.

SECTION COORDINATOR

MICHAEL R. LIEPMAN, M.D., FASAM
Michigan State University
Kalamazoo Center for Medical Studies
Department of Psychiatry
Kalamazoo, Michigan

CONTRIBUTORS

Hoover Adger, Jr., M.D., M.P.H.
Associate Professor of Pediatrics
The Johns Hopkins University
School of Medicine
Baltimore, Maryland

David Berenson, M.D.
Director, Family Institute of San Francisco
Sausalito, California

Stephanie Brown, Ph.D.
Co-Director
Mental Research Institute
Palo Alto, California

Virginia Lewis, M.S.W.
Co-Director
Mental Research Institute
Palo Alto, California

Ellen Woodside Schrier, M.S.W.
Family Institute of San Francisco
Sausalito, California

CHAPTER 1

The Family in Addiction

Michael R. Liepman, M.D., FASAM

Family Consequences of Addiction
Family Adjustment to Addiction
The Physician's Role with Addicted Families

People typically live in families for at least part, if not all, of their lives. Families may conceive, birth, and raise one or more children. However, not all children experience the conventional family in which two heterosexual parents produce and rear the children. Some children are adopted; some are raised in foster homes, communal groups, or institutions; some grow up in homeless shelters or on the streets of our cities; some are raised by grandparents or other relatives, or by single or homosexual parents. Some families are small and others are large; some are nuclear (parents and children only), while others live together as extended families (living with other relatives in the same home).

Some families dwell in close proximity to one another, while others may be separated by great distances geographically or by hostility and/or disinterest. Families grow by procreation, marriage and remarriage, cohabitation, adoption and foster placement. Seeking financial, child care, or emotional support, grown children return home from college, jail, military service, failed relationships, or lost jobs—often with babies, lovers, and problems of their own. Families get smaller via separation and divorce, abandonment, disappearance, institutionalization, loss of child custody, and death, as well as by launching children into adulthood and higher education. While excess morbidity and mortality always have been understood as a risk encountered by addicted persons, now more than ever, children of addicted persons also risk losing their parents and surrogate parents—their families—to AIDS.

When referring to families from the perspective of an individual, we use the term *family of procreation* to indicate a nuclear family, including the person's spouse and children. Likewise, we use the term *family of origin* to indicate the person's parents and siblings. *Extended family* refers to all the known living relatives. A *family with addiction* or *addicted family* means a family with one or more members who suffer from addictive disorders.

FAMILY CONSEQUENCES OF ADDICTION

Families can be harmed by the consequences of addiction in ways that include shifting priorities and changing values, emergence of illness and disability, violence and exposure to other dangers, experience of early losses, and the enabling of others to become affected by alcohol or other drugs.

When a person pursues the artificial "high" that alcohol or other drugs can induce, it is as an alternative to some other activity. If the time used to get high is time otherwise allocated for leisure, chores, family, work, or school, the consequence is a shift in priorities in favor of alcohol or other drug use.

Since psychoactive drugs often remain in the body longer than the time allotted for getting high, and since some drugs produce dysphoric cravings or withdrawal symptoms after use, an episode of alcohol or other drug use may spill over into times that should be, or were intended to be, dedicated to other activities. Especially as the addiction progresses, with development of toxicity, tolerance, dependence, and obsession over acquisition and ingestion, the amount of time spent impaired increases and the amount of time spent drug-free diminishes.

Human values govern behavior, but addiction often takes a toll on human values: As the addicted person becomes progressively more enslaved by the need to obtain and self-administer alcohol or other drugs repeatedly; values are compromised, as reflected in behavior and investments of time, effort, and money. Dishonesty may surface first as "white lies" to cover up indiscretions, then as stealing, drug dealing, or involvement in other illicit behavior to obtain drugs—sometimes progressing even to more serious criminal activities. Sharing alcohol and other drugs in social situations may lead to early sexual activity, poor choices in sexual partners, sexual exploitation or traumatization, trading sex for drugs, promiscuity, and prostitution. Sporadic failures to perform religious, civic, and family responsibilities because of intoxication or withdrawal may accumulate to the extent that the individual appears to shirk responsibility altogether.

Family rituals are one way that youngsters learn the values of their ancestors. Some families are more tolerant of deviance than others. Watching parents and relatives while they vacation, celebrate, or dine together permits children to observe and copy attitudes and behaviors, including those related to drug and alcohol intake, intoxication, coping with consequences, and reacting to those behaviors (Wolin, Bennett & Noonan, 1979; Wolin, Bennett et al., 1980).

An individual who abuses alcohol or other drugs has a substantially increased risk of illness or disability. Dangers such as accidents and morbidity associated with the psychological and/or physiological harm that these drugs cause to the body increase the risk of hospitalization, permanent disability and death (Burant, Liepman & Miller, 1992; Liepman, Nirenberg et al., 1987; Wartenberg & Liepman, 1987, 1990). The burden on the family increases during times when the alcohol- or drug-abusing member is ill or disabled.

Violence often erupts within addicted families, to the extent that addiction is commonly associated with increased risk of domestic violence. Intoxicated individuals may exhibit impaired judgment, which can lead to violent conflict. When alcohol or sedative-hypnotics are involved, the anxiolytic effect may numb the perception or fear of harming loved ones. The amnestic effect of these drugs also may lead to memory blackouts that prevent recall of prior hurtful acts that were committed under the influence. Opioids have been associated with increased aggression; whether this is due to the intoxication phase and/or the withdrawal phase is uncertain. Stimulants cause irritability, enhance aggression and expression of anger, and enhance paranoia.

Sometimes both the victim and the perpetrator of violence are intoxicated; this may reduce the likelihood that either partner can de-escalate the conflict before it becomes violent. Sexual violence may be associated with substance abuse; cocaine has been used as an aphrodisiac; alcohol often accompanies sexual activity and impairs judgment. The ability of an intoxicated person to remain sensitive to the subtle cues of a sexual partner and to heed warnings may be diminished, leading to the unpleasant experience of partner rape or sexual insensitivity (Nirenberg, Liepman et al., 1990).

Violence also may occur when strangers or drug associates make contact with family through the pursuit of drug transactions or sharing recreational drugs. Such individuals have no loyalty to the sanctity of a family that is not their own and may use physical or sexual assault or battery to manipulate or vent; they may be intoxicated or desperately drug-seeking when this occurs.

Alcohol or other drug abuse also can expose the entire family to danger. For example, auto crashes can involve victims other than the impaired driver; others may be affected by the intoxicated smoker or the cook who causes a fire. Attracting intoxicated unsavory characters into the home for sex, drug-sharing, drug-dealing, or partying may expose a spouse and children to risk of violence or sexual misconduct. In fact, child abuse and neglect often occur within families afflicted by addiction. There also is a risk of accidental or purposeful ingestion of drugs by children.

Death of the addicted person is all too common. While some may consider this a welcome opportunity for the family to rid itself of continuing exposure to danger and unhappiness, it tragically deprives children of parents or siblings and causes grief and loss of a valued family member. Family roles need to shift to adjust to such a loss. Some members may blame themselves or others in the family for the untimely death of the addicted parent or spouse. Loss of a role model may affect children, and loss of a spouse and sexual partner may introduce more instability or a new (all too often addicted) spouse/partner whose presence as stepparent may be resented and resisted by the children. Loss of a parent or sibling may occur in other ways, as through institutionalization (in prison, a mental hospital, a foster or group home, or a nursing home), which may result from trauma or emotional problems. Likewise, running away from home (Casey, 1991), teen pregnancy and premature marriage, divorce or separation, enrolling in school or accepting work assignments far from home, entering military service or a religious order may lead to family structural change designed to remove oneself from a dysfunctional family (Liepman, White & Nirenberg, 1986).

Participation in a family affected by addiction can lead to induction of alcohol or other drug abuse patterns in other family members. It has been observed that heterosexual women who are married to or who live with addicted men are more likely to become addicted along with their male partners (Klassen, Wilsnack et al., 1991; Lex, 1990; Wilsnack & Wilsnack, 1990, 1993); conversely, many drinking women who separate or divorce from addicted partners show a subsequent reduction in their drinking or drug use.

Children who grow up in a home where alcohol or other drugs are abused, whether out in the open or "under wraps," generally are at increased risk of developing addiction problems themselves. This may be related to hereditary risk, given recent evidence that risk of various forms of addiction may be transmitted genetically (Heath, Cates et al., 1993; Swan, Carmelli et al., 1990; Goodwin, 1979; Reich, Cloninger et al., 1988; Cadoret, Troughton et al., 1986). The "gateway theory" of drug abuse onset suggests that smoking and drinking alcohol are two early steps in an adolescent's progression into illicit drug abuse (Kandel & Faust, 1975). Exposure to drinking and smoking in the home by parents and siblings provides both behavioral role models and tacit approval for beginning to use these gateway drugs.

FAMILY ADJUSTMENT TO ADDICTION

The chronic nature of addictive disorders, coupled with the addict's resistance to the constructive influences exerted by family members, often leads to resigned acceptance of the disordered member's addiction as an unchangeable trait of the family. This is particularly so in families where the addiction has persisted for a long time (e.g., decades or generations). Such families adjust to the chronic condition of addiction so completely that adjusting to recovery may become stressful; they do so by evolving various bizarre or at least self-defeating defensive routines. For example, spouses and other family members may become so-called *enablers*; that is, persons who act as though the most important priority is helping the *active* alcoholic or addict to flourish in the short-run at a substantial long-term cost (Kaufman, 1985; Liepman, 1993; Liepman, Wolper & Vazquez, 1982).

Enablers typically become over-involved with the addicted person and align themselves with the addiction, sometimes assisting in defensive activities against others who would apply constructive influences against the addiction (Prochaska & DiClemente, 1986). Such alignments contribute to the prolongation or chronicity of the addictive disorder. Such a position may be perceived as assigning the addiction a higher priority than the family's well-being. (Al-Anon Family Groups and family therapists offer a constructive influence in overcoming the urge to persist in this destructive alliance with the disorder.)

Enabling behavior also has been characterized as including expression of hostility toward the addicted person, presumably with the laudable intention of trying to promote recovery; however, the aggressive nature of these interactions promote defensive resentments, acting out, and counterattacks rather than genuine change. Such interactions may take the focus away from the addiction and place it on family dysfunction, violence, or infidelity. Hostile interchanges may become common triggers for the next binge, providing justification for leaving home or retreating to the "basement supply."

Cultural factors influence these interactions. In an elegant ethnographic study comparing Italian-American and Irish-American Roman Catholic cultures, Bennett and Ames (1985) examined the connection between alcohol abuse by the male alcoholic and domestic violence. The Irish-American couples reported that the male did his drinking in a pub and any violent behavior seemed limited to those surroundings. Husbands and wives agreed that episodes of domestic violence would not be tolerated in their marital relationship, despite the rules of the Church concerning divorce. In contrast, the Italian-American couples described the male's drinking as limited to the home, where his violence also erupted; both husbands and wives agreed that their marriages would continue despite the violence, "until death do they part." In the United States, where there are myriad cultures of origin, and where marriages often combine different cultures within the union, families may represent an interactive mixture of cultural rules and beliefs. In families of mixed cultural background, it also is possible for dissociation of rules about use of alcohol or other drugs, or behaviors associated with such use, to result in rules with critical protective elements deleted. This finding extends the notion advanced by Wolin and colleagues (1979, 1980) that family rituals are influenced by and promote transmission of family cultural beliefs to future generations.

In families where the addiction threatens the instrumental functions of the family, other family members may "pick up the slack" by taking on the neglected responsibilities; the "martyr-spouse" or the "parentified child" usually is the one to assume these inappropriate loads. In recovery, families must readjust to normal functioning; it is threatening, in early sobriety, for such competent and responsible individuals—who have carried many responsibilities for the addicted person—to encounter the recovering addict suddenly requesting (or demanding) to assume or resume neglected roles. On such occasions, family members may express resentment over the intrusion or express skepticism about the expected duration of sobriety; at times, they may actually provoke a relapse to prevent the change.

Some families adjust to the addiction by joining in the alcohol or other drug abuse. A recovering person who returns to such a family will be challenged to maintain abstinence in the face of such an alcohol- or drug-involved family environment. The addicted family members may offer the recovering member the opportunity to relapse so as to share their alcohol or drugs; alternatively, these persons may blame the recovering person for having introduced them to alcohol or other drugs or for having encouraged or tolerated their use. In some families, a new symptomatic alcoholic or addict may emerge within the family when the formerly scapegoated addicted person begins to recover and refuses to continue his or her former role in the family; quite often this is an adolescent child or a spouse. Attempts by the newly recovering addict to inspire recovery in family members often will be frustrating and will try his or her patience. AA friends and counselors might either recommend attending Al-Anon meetings and waiting until these persons "hit rock bottom" (a frightening thought for any newly recovering person) or staying away from such family members (very difficult for those who live together in a family). Residential treatment programs can assist in separating such individuals from their dysfunctional families for awhile, but ultimately such families are likely to reunite.

Families set the agenda and inform the newcomers (children and those who marry into the family) through family rituals. Wolin and colleagues (1979, 1980) have shown that the priority status of alcoholic beverages within family rituals seems associated with transgenerational transmission of alcoholism. When families incorporate alcohol into most rituals, there is a high prevalence of alcoholism within the family in the next generation, and when alcohol is excluded from most rituals, or is used in a non-abusive manner, alcoholism within the family in the subsequent generation is rare.

Families have been observed to develop stereotyped repetitive oscillations between specific behavioral sequences that occur in association with ingestion of alcohol or other drugs and those associated with abstinence (called *family behavioral loops*: Liepman, Silvia & Nirenberg, 1989; Silvia & Liepman, 1991). The results are likened to the story of Dr. Jekyll and Mr. Hyde, one of transformation under certain conditions—in this case, under conditions of drinking or drug use. What is remarkable about such transformations is that, while the addicted person changes the character of his or her behavior, so do the other members of the family (Steinglass, Davis & Berenson, 1977). The behavior changes of family members are triggered by conditioned cues that indicate that the addicted person is currently sober or has relapsed; at times, a family member may misconstrue a situation as a relapse and behave accordingly toward the recovering person. For instance, if a recovering alcoholic has not called home at dinner time, perhaps because of a flat tire, his wife might accuse him of having been drinking when he finally arrives home late, before she discovers that he actually is sober. She might describe this hostile reaction to an innocent situation as a relapse to her former family role as a provocative enabler.

Interestingly, when one examines the family behavioral loops associated with drinking or other drug use, one typically discovers benefits to the family system contained within the loops associated with a member's drinking or other drug use. This can be useful in designing family recovery strategies. At least one distinct continuous loop can be found that traverses both sober and intoxicated intervals. While this general principle holds true for most addicted families, the specific sequences of behavior are unique to each family. Consequently, when restructuring the family behavioral loops to remove the incentive for relapse, one identifies alternative behaviors for each member of the family to perform in the situation that typically leads up to relapse and, likewise, in the situation where relapse has occurred and is prolonged, one teaches the family ways to shorten the relapse interval.

THE PHYSICIAN'S ROLE WITH ADDICTED FAMILIES

Physicians have a unique opportunity and role that can be helpful in assisting families to deal effectively with addictions. In the role of health assessor, the physician whose inquiries are aimed at screening for addiction in the patient *or* family can uncover a hidden problem. In particular, one should watch carefully for ill-defined complaints, unexplained trauma, psychic distress, and relationship problems. In the role of confidante, one can explore more deeply the nature of the problem one has uncovered, learning about the addiction and the enabling, what has been tried and what has succeeded or failed. As treatment advisor, the physician can suggest specialized resources to be used if his or her brief interventions fail to produce adequate change in a timely fashion.

A family meeting at home or in the office may be used as a means to elevate the importance of the addiction. There, the physician can reflect on the evidence collected that suggests a need for change, and share information about available relevant resources that can be accessed by the family. In such a meeting, it is important to avoid blaming or aggressive statements that might elicit defensive responses. Formal family interventions have been quite helpful in motivating initiation of recovery when properly executed (Liepman, 1993; Liepman, Wolper, Vazquez, 1982). But because they are inconvenient to arrange and carry out, this approach should be attempted only after less complex approaches to encourage the addicted person to initiate treatment have failed.

Physicians can continue to monitor the situation in the family, adding input whenever it seems appropriate to do so. Once the addicted person has received the message that the family perceives alcohol or drug use to be a problem, there still may be a need to encourage taking appropriate action; it is common for the denial of the problem to shift to denial that formal treatment would be helpful. Another pitfall is for the addicted person, often with the support of the family, to abandon recovery or treatment prematurely because the alcohol or other drug use has temporarily stopped. Persons in recovery also are at risk of drug substitutions for the drug they have eliminated; for example, quitting alcohol and replacing it with benzodiazepines, or increasing tobacco and caffeine intake. Physicians may be challenged to treat chronic pain or anxiety in such persons without prescribing addictive drugs.

As physicians watch patients and their families move through the transition points in the family life cycle, it is important to use anticipatory guidance in dealing with the stresses of such times in order to prevent relapses of recovering persons and initiation of new addictions in relatives.

This chapter has been modified from a paper originally presented at the Second Ross Roundtable on Critical Issues in Family Medicine, October 13–14, 1993, Washington, DC.

REFERENCES

Bennett LA & Ames GM (1985). *The American Experience with Alcohol: Contrasting Cultural Perspectives.* New York, NY: Plenum Publishing Co.

Burant D, Liepman MR & Miller MM (1992). Mental health disorders and their impact on treatment of addictions. In MD Fleming & KL Barry (eds.) *Addictive Disorders.* St. Louis, MO: Mosby/Year Book, 315–337.

Cadoret RJ, Troughton E, O'Gorman TW & Heywood E (1986). An adoption study of genetic and environmental factors in drug abuse. *Archives of General Psychiatry* 43:1131–1136.

Casey K (1991). *Children of Eve: The Shocking Story of America's Homeless Kids.* Hollywood, CA: Covenant House.

Goodwin DW (1979). Alcoholism and heredity: A review and hypothesis. *Archives of General Psychiatry* 36:57–61.

Heath AC, Cates R, Martin NG et al. (1993). Genetic contribution to risk of smoking initiation: Comparisons across birth cohorts and across cultures. *Journal of Substance Abuse* 5:221–246.

Kandel D & Faust R (1975). Sequence and stages in patterns of adolescent drug use. *Archives of General Psychiatry* 32:923–932.

Kaufman E (1985). *Substance Abuse and Family Therapy.* New York, NY: Harcourt Brace Jovanovich, 221.

Klassen AD, Wilsnack SC, Harris TR & Wilsnack RW (1991). Partnership dissolution and remission of problem drinking in women: Findings from a US longitudinal survey. Presented at the Symposium on Alcohol, Family and Significant Others, Social Research Institute of Alcohol Studies and Nordic Council for Alcohol and Drug Research, Helsinki, Finland (March).

Lex BW (1990). Male heroin addicts and their female mates: Impact on disorder and recovery. *Journal of Substance Abuse* 2:147–175.

Liepman MR (1993). Using family influence to motivate alcoholics to enter treatment: The Johnson Institute Intervention Approach. In TJ O'Farrell (ed.) *Marital and Family Therapy in Alcoholism Treatment.* New York, NY: Guilford Press, 54–77.

Liepman MR, Nirenberg TD, Porges R & Wartenberg AA (1987). Depression associated with substance abuse. In OG Cameron (ed.) *Presentations of Depression: Depression in Medical and Other Psychiatric Disorders.* New York, NY: John Wiley and Sons, 131–167.

Liepman MR, Silvia LY & Nirenberg TD (1989). The use of Family Behavior Loop Mapping for substance abuse. *Family Relations* 38:282–287.

Liepman MR, White WT & Nirenberg TD (1986). Children in alcoholic families. In DC Lewis & CN Williams (eds.) *Providing Care for Children of Alcoholics: Clinical and Research Perspectives.* Pompano Beach, FL: Health Communications, Inc., 39–64.

Liepman MR, Wolper B & Vazquez J (1982). An ecological approach for motivating women to accept treatment for chemical dependency. In BG Reed, J Mondanaro & GM Beschner (eds.) *Treatment Services for Drug Dependent Women, Vol. II.* Rockville, MD: National Institute on Drug Abuse, 1–61.

Nirenberg TD, Liepman MR, Begin AM et al. (1990). The sexual relationship of male alcoholics and their female partners during periods of drinking and abstinence. *Journal of Studies on Alcohol* 51:565–568.

Prochaska JO & DiClemente CC (1986). Towards a comprehensive model of change. In WR Miller & N Heather (eds.) *Treating Addictive Behaviors: Processes of Change*. New York, NY: Plenum Publishing Co., 3–27.

Reich T, Cloninger CR, Van Eerdewegh et al. (1988). Secular trends in the familial transmission of alcoholism. *Alcoholism: Clinical & Experimental Research* 12:458–464.

Silvia LY & Liepman MR (1991). Family behavior loop mapping enhances treatment of alcoholism. *Family & Community Health* 13:72–83.

Steinglass P, Davis DI & Berenson D (1977). Observations of conjointly hospitalized "alcoholic couples" during sobriety and intoxication: Implications for theory and therapy. *Family Process* 16:1–16.

Swan GE, Carmelli D et al. (1990). Smoking and alcohol consumption in adult male twins: Genetic heritability and shared environmental influences. *Journal of Substance Abuse* 2:39–50.

Wartenberg AA & Liepman MR (1987). Medical consequences of addictive behaviors. In TD Nirenberg & SA Maisto (eds.) *Developments in the Assessment and Treatment of Addictive Behaviors*. Norwood, NJ: Ablex, 49–85.

Wartenberg AA & Liepman MR (1990). Medical complications of substance abuse. In WD Lerner & MA Barr (eds.) *Handbook of Hospital-Based Substance Abuse Treatment*. New York, NY: Pergamon, 45–65.

Wilsnack SC & Wilsnack RW (1990). Epidemiology of women's drinking. *Journal of Substance Abuse* 3:133–157.

Wilsnack SC & Wilsnack RW (1993). Epidemiological research on women's drinking: Recent progress and directions for the 1990s. In ESL Gomberg & TD Nirenberg (eds.) *Women and Substance Abuse*. Norwood, NJ: Ablex, 62–99.

Wolin SJ, Bennett LA & Noonan DL (1979). Family rituals and the recurrence of alcoholism over generations. *American Journal of Psychiatry* 136(4B):589–593.

Wolin SJ, Bennett LA, Noonan DL & Teitelbaum MA (1980). Disrupted family rituals: A factor in the intergenerational transmission of alcoholism. *Journal of Studies on Alcohol* 41:199–214.

CHAPTER 2

A Developmental Model of the Alcoholic Family

Stephanie Brown, Ph.D.
Virginia Lewis, M.S.W.

Alcoholism as a Family Disease
The Stages of Family Recovery

In this chapter, we review the origins and development of the concept of the "alcoholic family" and then provide an overview of the stages of recovery from this expanded perspective.

ALCOHOLISM AS A FAMILY DISEASE

Not long ago, the field of alcoholism focused only on the drinking alcoholic, with no recognition of recovery and no attention given to those close to the drinker. For years, it was the drinking alcoholic, and the male alcoholic in particular, who received almost exclusive attention in research and treatment.

This singular focus on the alcoholic was altered in the 1950s and 1960s with the work Joan Jackson (1954), who outlined stages in a developmental process of alcoholism for the spouse and family of the alcoholic. Her work paralleled the birth and growth of Al-Anon (Al-Anon, 1984), the autonomous arm of Alcoholics Anonymous for the spouse and relatives of the alcoholic. Although the Al-Anon focus (like that of AA and, later, Alateen) was also centered on the individual, there was an implicit recognition that the attention was on the individual within a familial or interactional context (AA, 1976).

This was important institutional acknowledgment that the alcoholism of one individual has an impact on others. In a program similar to the Twelve Steps of Alcoholics Anonymous, Al-Anon provided instruction in how to detach and disengage from maladaptive and, unhealthy reactions to the alcoholic. Jackson's work and the Al-Anon program altered the field of alcoholism dramatically by expanding the primary focus to include members of the family and an interactional perspective. In 1962, Ruth Fox made a revolutionary claim: "Every member in such a family is affected by emotionally, spiritually and in most cases economically, socially, and often physically" (Fox, 1962).

Following Jackson's work, the focus of research was no longer only on the alcoholic, but also on the interactions, adjustments, and development of the family with an alcoholic member (Grisham & Estes, 1986). The disease concept, now accepted for the alcoholic, translated into "family disease," with the implication that all members of the family are affected by alcoholism (Roe & Burks, 1945; Cork, 1969).

The term *co-alcoholic*, which was later broadened to *co-dependence*, was coined to describe the maladaptive, unhealthy reactions to the alcoholic. Again, the emphasis was interactional. In its broadest sense, the term *co-dependence* defines a reactive, submissive response to the dominance of another. Individuals in Al-Anon were learning that they did not cause the alcoholism of their mates, as they had previously believed. They also were learning that their reactive response was almost certainly unhealthy for them and ineffective in changing the drinker.

Systems research broadened our understanding of the dynamics of active alcoholism to include an interactional frame, in addition to the individual disease perspective. Working on different coasts and different settings, Peter Steinglass in the research lab (Steinglass, 1980) and Stephanie Brown in the clinical realm (Brown, 1977) described the alcoholism of a parent as a central organizing principle determining interactional patterns within the family. Both of us suggested that parental alcoholism should be viewed as a governing agent affecting the development of the family as a whole and the individuals within. . . .

THE STAGES OF FAMILY RECOVERY

The family follows a developmental progression from active drinking into transition, early recovery, and finally a stable, ongoing recovery, just like the alcoholic (Brown, 1985).

The stages of recovery are all about detachment, separation and, later, new attachments and reintegration. The alcoholic must relinquish alcohol and establish a new, comfortable self in recovery. Family members must also relinquish their pathological, addictive ties to the alcoholic and to the system that perpetuates the pathology. Treatment and recovery involve the breakup of all behaviors, beliefs, distorted perceptions, and damaged self-images that have become the glue of relationship and the core of the family's identity.

It's like the breakup of a massive, airtight ship of defense. Trouble is, this terrible system that reinforces trauma and the constant sacrifice of all of its members appears to offer more security than jumping ship. The bonds of attachment and the deep loyalties we all give to family often prevent, or at least stall, individuals from challenging the view of reality organized by the individual alcoholic and the alcoholic system. But individuals and families do recover.

In the best of worlds, the family moves in concert, as each member acknowledges the reality of alcoholism and begins to detach from the unhealthy behaviors and thinking that maintain the pathology of the system and the individuals within it. The ability to move together requires a shift from the systems focus to primary attention on the individual. Although it may seem easy, it is not. In fact, there is usually hard-core resistance by every family member to breaking up the very drinking system that is destroying them.

So, families do not usually move together. It's more common for one or several family members to seek help separately. At first, the problem may not be identified as alcoholism within the family, but rather as another difficulty that is now serious enough to warrant outside help. Eventually, with the support of an outsider's view, it becomes possible to see and name the alcoholism and begin to separate from its disastrous influence. Let's follow the family through the stages.

The Drinking Stage. The alcoholic family is captured by a double bind. Dominated and organized by the realities of drinking, all members in the family must accommodate themselves to distortion, joining the family "story" that denies the alcoholism and explains it at the same time. In essence, the family says, "There is no alcoholism, and here is why we have to drink . . . because of stress in Dad's job, because the children fight, or because Mom is such a rotten wife. . . ."

The Environment: The environment includes the context of family life: the foreground, the background, the sounds, sights, smells, and moods that characterize the atmosphere of the family home. This is the description of "what it was like" that recovering alcoholics tell when they stop drinking and join AA. Within the traditional AA "story" or "drunkalogue," individuals break their denial of the past, telling "what it was like, what happened, and what it is like now." They often describe a routine of daily life dominated by the anxiety, tension, and trauma of active drinking. . . .

The ACOA popular movement expanded our knowledge base through personal descriptions of what it was like growing up with parental drinking. The alcoholic family is now recognized as one of chaos (covert or overt), inconsistency, unpredictability, bluffing of boundaries, unclear roles, arbitrariness, changing logic, and perhaps violence and incest. The "everyday" experience is one of chronic trauma, which becomes the context of "normal" family fife and family and individual development. Episodes of "acute" trauma, such as marital affairs, acts of humiliation, physical and emotional abandonment, and violence, punctuate the normalized high level of tension. The family increases defensive operations as it accommodates to this anxious, chaotic environment characterized by an absence of physical and emotional safety.

Some families may not openly demonstrate these problems. They may establish a rigid family system bound by a facade of control that perpetuates denial of serious problems. But this environment is also riddled with tension, strain, and trauma. Physical illness, psychosomatic disorders, and all variety of psychiatric disturbances provide a response to the trauma and a cover for it at the same time.

The System: The family system refers to how the family works. It includes the rules, roles, and regulatory and communication processes that allow the family to establish constancy and to sustain structures that shape predictable, patterned, and adaptive behaviors.

The family system may be stable for many years. Life with drinking becomes predictable. Drinking is "accepted" in the family lifestyle. Drinking doesn't feel out of control. Family structure is in place, routines and roles are consistent, and power dynamics are stable.

But, as we have seen, alcohol, or someone's drinking, has become the central organizing principle of the family system, controlling and dictating family beliefs, behaviors, and development (Brown, 1977). The pathology of active drinking becomes normalized, which eventually creates and reinforces considerable dissonance. What may be most visible and most problematic—the alcoholism—is also vehemently denied or explained in a way that allows it to be maintained or even to be seen as a solution to other problems. as normalization creates a terrible double bind. Family members become reactive to the dominance of the alcoholic and the systems dynamics that hold the pathology in place while they must deny that there is any problem at all. . . .

When the consequences of the alcoholism (such as illness, job loss, physical abuse, drunk driving arrests) begin to be more difficult to resolve or hide, the need for secrecy grows. The family system becomes more rigid, chaotic, and closed, cutting itself off from outside sources of help. The family also becomes arrested in its development as it grows more inflexible. The focus and energy that should go toward family life cycle maturation are centered on defensive operations that derail or detour normal growth.

Individual Development: Our developmental perspective suggests that an individual's self-view and behavior can be understood on the basis of core beliefs and experiences formed early in childhood and in ongoing development. In the alcoholic family, these core beliefs and behaviors are formed in direct relation to parental alcoholism and the overriding need for defensive adjustment within the family. In this way, alcoholism serves as a governing agent in a child's basic development and as an organizer and a reshaper of the adult's self-view in response to the alcoholism. Attachments are directly related to denial and the core beliefs and patterns of behavior formed within the family to sustain it. These defensive beliefs and behaviors then stricture subsequent cognitive, affective, and social development of the individuals within the family.

Individuals develop the same behavioral and thinking disorders as the alcoholic: they are controlled by the reality of alcoholism, and they must deny it at the same time. To preserve this inherent contradiction, all family members must adapt their thinking and behavior to fit the family's story—that is, the explanations that have been constructed to allow the drinking behavior to be maintained and denied at the same time. The story includes core beliefs, which family members share and which provide a sense of unity and cohesion, often against an outside world perceived as hostile or unsafe. Most important, individual development is shaped by and often sacrificed to the preservation of the drinking system.

The strength of this systemic organizing principle is illustrated in such family rules as "There is no alcoholism" and "Don't talk about it" or "Sure she has a few drinks, but she's not an alcoholic!' The drinking, which is often most visible and is certainly most central as an organizer, must be denied and explained as something else. Many family members in our research reported, "I never processed what I saw. I just assumed it was normal."

Key variables that affect individual development include the age of onset of parental alcoholism for both parent and child, the severity and particular circumstances, and which parent—mother, father, or both—was alcoholic. It is essential to determine the kind and quality of relationship with key family figures and the opportunities that existed for healthy bonding and development independent of the emphasis on alcohol.

Tasks of Treatment in the Drinking Stage: The process of recovery begins for one, two, or more individuals who begin to detach from the unhealthy drinking environment and system. They may label alcoholism immediately or not until later. By seeking help and focusing on themselves, even for another identified problem, they permit separation to begin (Brown & Lewis, 1993).

The tasks of treatment are:

- To challenge the behaviors and thinking that maintain the pathology of the environment, the system, and the individuals.
- To help family members shift focus from the system to themselves.
- To encourage and provide support for detachment and separation.

Beginning "cracks" in the environment, the system, or the individual signal movement into the next stage. These cracks might include a crisis such as an accident, a drunk driving arrest, school and emotional problems with children, and a rationalization that just won't hold anymore. Slowly or suddenly, the family member begins to see the reality. . . .

The Transition Stage. Transition marks the beginning of what we call the "trauma of recovery." Why? Because there is so much turmoil, disruption, and critical change. This stage includes the end of drinking and the beginning of abstinence.

During drinking, cracks form in the alcoholic system of rigid behaviors and defenses. The problems of drinking surface and shake the bedrock foundation of denial. Adjusting to the pathology doesn't work so well, or the costs can't be denied. Still, at this point, there is often a tightening in the system. Everyone tries to keep it from breaking down when, in fact, the collapse of the system is necessary for family recovery. It may come as a radical rupture or as a slow, evolutionary shift.

At the end of the drinking phase, the alcoholic hits bottom and decides to stop drinking, seeing no other alternative. . . [T]he individual accepts the loss of control and the identity as an alcoholic.

The family may or may not hit bottom at the same time, moving with the alcoholic into recovery. Or, family members go first, accepting their own loss of control over the drinker and themselves and their identity as coalcoholics, players in a pathological system. They may enter recovery alone, which is very difficult to sustain; or, their surrender may fuel the movement of others, and the family crosses into recovery together.

Abstinence marks the beginning of recovery and what we also refer to as the "trauma of recovery." Both descriptions fit. The absence of drinking is wonderful, but it is also frightening because it is unknown. The uncertainties and anxieties of the first few months and even years of recovery are hard to weather and to see as positive. Many recovering families look back to drinking with mixed feelings: it was awful, but it was known.

Families often assume that once the alcoholic stops drinking, there will be no more fighting, no more abuse, no more irresponsibility. They expect or hope to find a happy family underneath the horrors of alcoholism. But rarely does this happen. Usually, in transition the only major difference is the absence of alcohol. When family members discover that the problems continue or even get worse in early sobriety and that changes in recovery involve them too, they may become angry and discouraged.

Involvement in Twelve Step programs is enormously helpful for everyone in the family at this critical juncture. AA and Al-Anon advocate a self-focus and the development of support networks outside the family. These outside supports encourage individual separation, individual development in recovery, and the disruption of the system. They also provide a "holding" environment and structure that allow the family to maintain the system's collapse and to tolerate a temporary systems vacuum. Without individual supports, family members will be pulled back to drinking dynamics in an effort to reinstate a sense of the whole, with its illusion of security and stability.

This is the most important and most difficult task of the entire process of recovery for the family: to tolerate and hold a focus on individual separation and development while delaying repair or rebuilding of the couple and family until later in sobriety when the foundation of individual development will permit a new healthy system to form. Many people fiercely resist this delay.

In any case, as therapists, we need to help families in the transitional stage focus on:

- Breaking denial;
- Realizing that family life is out of control;
- Beginning a challenge of core beliefs;
- Hitting bottom and surrender;
- Accepting the reality of alcoholism and loss of control;
- Allowing the alcoholic system to collapse;
- Shifting the focus from the system to the individuals who begin detachment and individual recovery;
- Enlisting outside supports, such as AA, Al-Anon, Alateen, and professional treatment; and
- Learning new abstinent behaviors and thinking. . . (Brown & Lewis, 1993).

The Environment: Everything gets worse. Tension, hostility, and despair mount as family members move toward increasing chaos and loss of control (Brown, 1991b). Incidents of acute, overt trauma increase, and danger grows. Basic physical and emotional safety are chronically threatened.

As the family system moves toward collapse, the environment may become more traumatic (Brown, 1991b). The family "rubber band" is at the breaking point. Tragedies often occur.

During this time, drinking becomes overtly unpredictable and problematic. There is tremendous stress and tension. Frequently, family members will exert strong pressure on the alcoholic to quit. They may develop serious medical and psychological problems or unconsciously create crises to draw outside attention to the alcoholism within the family. In one of our research families, a spouse overdosed on prescription drugs to get her alcoholic mate into treatment.

Partners who are no longer denying the alcoholism may demand that the alcoholic choose between the bottle or them. Frequently, they do not follow through with the consequences of this challenge, which leads to repeated cycles of hollow ultimatums.

Family life may be failing apart. Individuals may miss meals, break commitments, lose their jobs, and struggle continuously with unresolvable family conflict or legal difficulties, such as drunk driving arrests. The fabric of family life unravels at a faster pace, heading for the collapse of hitting bottom.

When the drinking stops, the trauma directly related to it also stops. Mother is no longer passed out, no longer preoccupied with her supply, and no longer raging with hatred and blame at those in her family who would interfere with her drinking. But, she is not available either. She can't be emotionally present or function as she needed to during the drinking or as she will be able to in the future. Now she is just as preoccupied with herself and abstinence as she was preoccupied with drinking.

This behavior is necessary but very disappointing and frightening to family members who thought all would be well if the drinking would just stop. . . .

The atmosphere and context of family life in transition are very uncertain, unpredictable, inconsistent, and unknown. Nerves are shaky, and there may be just as much fighting, bitter resentment, and tension as ever. The threat of violence lingers. So does the new threat of relapse. Nobody knows what to do, and nobody trusts that this new state will last or lead to anything good. Children are often just as terrified with abstinence as they were with the drinking, sometimes more, because they have no familiar reactions to rely on and no defenses to bolster their anxieties about recovery.

Family members in the transition stage are typically afraid to feel excited or optimistic, afraid to expect anything now because they have been so disappointed in the past. Parents have been inconsistent and unavailable, behavior that does not change quickly. In fact, parental abandonment may continue as both adults are encouraged to seek help outside the family and to shift from the family focus to an emphasis on individual recovery. Without their own outside supports and attention to their own needs within the family, children will suffer the consequences of continuing emotional trauma in this period of important change.

The System: As we have seen, the family system grows more brittle and stretched to its limits in dealing with the crises. The alcoholic system is like a dictatorship on the verge of collapse or revolution. It simply can't hold itself together anymore. One person challenges the denial, steps out, detaches, and begins recovery, and the whole system is threatened with collapse. It doesn't always happen. Sometimes, the system finds a new balance with one person out and the rest left behind. Or, partners stabilize in a hostile battle about just what reality is: one goes into recovery, acknowledging the alcoholism, and the other steadfastly holds on to the opposing view, trying to pull the deserter back. Or, couples and families may move back and forth repeatedly in an effort to hold the family together and stabilize one point of view about reality.

Systems often collapse during this period, from a chronic buildup of stressors over many years or from multiple crises that break the brittle family system. The severe illness of a child or partner, loss of employment, or the reporting of physical or sexual abuse (usually related to alcoholism) may trigger an acute rupture. . . .

The collapse of the system is normal and necessary for family recovery. It may come as a revolution or an evolution. It may never come at all. The alcoholic may stop drinking and others may detach, but the family may never enter recovery. In our research, we see the power of outside supports to give the family a holding structure necessary to permit the collapse of the dictatorial regime. The outside supports also hold the map for redevelopment, which will help the family come back together later, or to disband, as often occurs.

In the final phase of systems collapse, the family's balance, or homeostasis, is ruptured. Family members are likely to feel crazy; life is falling apart. For many families, the system actually ceases to exist as the focus shifts radically to individual treatment.

The system is held in a vacuum state by the family's reliance on external supports such as treatment programs, AA and Al-Anon, and therapy, all of which reinforce the importance of the individual focus at this time. The intense needs of the adults are now met by outsiders, which takes stress off the marital system and adds an additional threat. The adults are literally "held" and "contained" by these resources until they can shift back to build a new, healthy couple and family system much later in recovery.

The newly abstinent family is in crisis. Equilibrium is still off balance. Everyone is vulnerable to problems, new or old. Addictive disorders, such as overeating, smoking, and alcohol and drug use, may emerge or intensify. Partners may abuse prescription pills. Children may act out their feelings of fear and confusion as a way of taking the focus off the alcoholic. Anyone may develop acute depression or anxiety. Either partner may decide to end the marriage or to have an affair.

This is a tough time. Sobriety was supposed to solve the family's problems, but it didn't. It feels more chaotic and frightening as the defenses that maintained the drinking system collapse.

Old family rules, rituals, and roles don't work, but nobody knows what does. Telling the truth and acknowledging reality are still unknown and are thought to make things worse. It will take time and the slow building of trust to reverse this thinking.

Family rituals that used to revolve around drinking, such as mealtimes and holiday celebrations, will be replaced by unstructured time and attendance at Twelve Step meetings. As parents change their patterns of functioning, the children's customary roles, which were shaped to accommodate the drinking system, will now be mismatched to the changing family structure. Although very positive in the long run, the short run will usually feel awkward, scary, and uncomfortable.

The danger is that children will end up more abandoned in transition than during drinking as the system collapses and as parents correctly turn their attention to their individual recoveries. But parents must also attend to their children. They will need help in learning what their children need and how to provide it. They will also need support, which is often lacking in our structures of treatment and our community systems.

Individual Development: As the tension mounts and the family tightens its controls to avoid collapse, the needs of individuals are often totally neglected (Brown, 1991b). The preservation of the pathological system takes precedence. Adults struggle for control, tempers flare, and danger builds. Everyone lives in a state of hyperalert anxiety and dread. Something awful is coming.

Individuals are heading toward hitting bottom, the state of surrender facilitated by despair and the experience of complete defeat. We saw earlier that the drinker must accept loss of control and the new identity as an alcoholic. The individual then substitutes behaviors of abstinence, particularly frequent attendance at AA, and begins a cognitive reconstruction process that challenges all of the defenses that maintained denial and active drinking. The focus is on the self.

Co-alcoholics will make exactly the same changes. They must disengage from their unhealthy addictive attachment to the alcoholic and focus on themselves. Co-alcoholics may be faced with a challenge sooner than they can grasp it. Their oldest belief and source of hope is now their major problem: "If only the alcoholic would stop drinking, all my problems would be solved." They aren't.

This faulty notion is often the most embedded and resistant to challenge. Partners often reject a sense of separate, independent self, believing instead that they will be fulfilled by and through their mates, who are failing them now because they are drinking. These partners often cannot see that they have a role in keeping the unhealthy environment and system going. They may be able to ask for help for the alcoholic or the children, but they are the last to seek help for themselves.

In our research, partners recall overwhelming feelings of despair, helplessness, and powerlessness. Life is unmanageable; nothing works anymore. One spouse summed it up: "I was going crazy and didn't know what to do."

At this point, recovery often represents loss as much as hope. The task for all individuals is to disengage from the addictive process that is maintained by the system. Transition places individuals face-to-face with themselves, which is where they need to stay.

Tasks of Treatment in the Transition Stage: As therapists, we work with families:

- To challenge denial and offer support for movement into recovery for all individuals;
- To support a shift in focus off the family system and on to the individuals;
- To add supports—AA, Al-Anon—outside the family; and
- To include parenting responsibilities and help parents structure their recoveries to fulfill them.

The Early Recovery Stage. Early recovery is characterized by steady abstinence and the integration of new thinking, attitudes, and behaviors (Bowlby, 1988). Individual development continues to take precedence over the family system.

New behaviors are added and expanded to support sobriety. It is a time of action, which helps individuals cope with uncomfortable feelings and impulses to drink or return to co-alcoholic behaviors. Impulses may still be strong, so quick substitute actions remain necessary. Only when new behaviors are solid and internalized can recovering people move from action to reflection, insight, and inner exploration through working the steps and perhaps insight-oriented psychotherapy.

Early recovery is a period of emerging emotions that may feel out of control. Individuals cope with emotions through the structure of the Twelve Step program, learning to identify and name feelings and accept an emotion without having to act on it or change it. The new belief structures—"I am an alcoholic and I cannot control my drinking" or "I am a co-alcoholic and I cannot control the alcoholic"—are more firmly in place.

A fear of drinking is common to all. Initially, this fear is helpful in providing the motivation and energy to establish supports and to learn new behaviors. It also keeps the focus on alcohol; such a focus is necessary to create a safe, sober environment. Later in this stage, when abstinence is strong, fear of drinking might function as a danger signal that new awareness, conflicts, or memories of the past are emerging. . . .

Our job as therapists is to help the family focus on:

- Continuing to learn abstinent behaviors and thinking;
- Stabilizing individual identities: I am an alcoholic, I am a co-alcoholic, and I have lost control;
- Continuing close contact with Twelve Step programs and working the steps;
- Maintaining a focus on individual recovery, seeking supports outside the family;
- Continuing detachment and a limited family focus; and
- Maintaining parenting responsibilities. . . (Brown & Lewis, 1993).

The Environment: Minimal change occurs in the overall context of the environment, which may still be characterized by anxiety, tension, and massive confusion. Turmoil may increase as families question why things aren't better and may feel disillusioned. The trauma of recovery—that is, adjusting to the sudden change brought by abstinence and the collapse of the family system—continues (Brown & Lewis, 1993). Abstinence is now more firmly in place, and parents are more secure in new behaviors. These beginning positive, stable changes allow for some hope and even excitement. We have seen in our research that families often move from one crisis to another for several years into recovery. The crisis orientation maintains an anxiety-driven traumatic environment long past its response to alcohol.

For some families, crisis may rescue the family system from its vacuum. Crisis may replace alcohol as a central organizing principle, particularly when the family system is not in recovery but the alcoholic or partner is. The tension, pressures, and stressors provide a pivotal focus, drawing family members back together and minimizing the realities of separation that otherwise characterize early recovery.

Family members often have a difficult time relating to each other. They simply don't know how and haven't had time yet to learn. Families in which partners and even children all belong to Twelve Step programs have a distinct advantage. The language of AA and Al-Anon provide a calming effect for anxieties, continuing chaos, and foreign emotions that now emerge. Words and slogans such as "Easy Does It," "one day at a time," and the format for the AA story, "We learn to tell what it was like, what happened, and what it is like now," help families make sense of the past and the present and thus help lift everyone above the level of pathological action and acting out so dominant during drinking and transition. Language becomes a direct antidote to the trauma of recovery by providing containment and structure (Lewis, 1977). . . .

Individuals may still feel the threat of relapse. They fear making mistakes that could leave them feeling out of control. Everything feels unknown and unfamiliar. A spouse told us he was incredibly relieved that his wife wasn't drinking and incredibly anxious that she would start again! "I've been walking on eggshells, afraid I'd say the wrong thing." Despite all the continuing uncertainties and change, however, the environment may be better; in fact, it may be vastly improved!

The System: If both parents are in recovery during this stage, they are learning new ways to behave and to experience themselves and the world. They may show a marked decrease in impulsive behaviors and a new ability to tolerate anxiety, due largely to the language of recovery that facilitates a cognitive emphasis. The therapist hopes they will be working the Twelve Steps, constructing a "drunkalogue" or Al-Anon story that incorporates the realities of the past—the drinking and all the pathological adaptations to it.

The new vocabulary and language of recovery also provide a bridge back to interaction and closer relationship. Although the focus remains on the individuals, couples often begin their rebuilding process now, going to a meeting together, sharing "program" talk and insights, and participating in Couples Anonymous if these meetings are available.

During the early recovery stage, the system is just beginning to rebuild. New roles and rules are not well developed or are still based on the needs of the individuals, especially the adults. Unfortunately, the needs of the children may still go unnoticed. We can't ignore this need. Parents must be helped to address the physical, intellectual, and emotional requirements of their children even when they are virtually incapable of doing so. They must use Twelve Step programs and the experience of what we call "family mentors" to help them with parenting.

Recovering parents must learn to hold both the individual perspective, which is essential for maintaining recovery, and the systems view, which requires them to function as responsible parents. We as therapists, in treatment centers and all kinds of community agencies, must include parenting courses and hands-on supports to enable people to maintain their recovery without sacrificing their children any further. This will have to be a truly collaborative effort. . . .

Establishing a new system raises questions and problems that require collaboration. We see the beginnings of dramatic changes as the system shifts from a polarized, hierarchical structure in which one person made all decisions to a more equal structure with shared responsibilities. Assessing changes in decisionmaking has been a consistent measure of major systemic change in recovery.

One family reported that in the first year of recovery the children took care of themselves, just as they had before. They were "alcoholic family self-sufficient" while their parents were focused on recovery. Between three and five years later, however, these parents literally "came home." They participated in school activities, attended children's sports and performances, and learned how to co-parent.

Some families don't remain intact throughout early recovery. There is a high incidence of divorce within the first three to five years as couples formally declare an end to their partnership. Sometimes, they have outgrown each other. Sometimes, the damage of the drinking can't be repaired or integrated. Often, one partner moves into strong recovery and the other simply can't come along. The split becomes intolerable after a while. Couples also find that they don't have a strong foundation to hold them through the rebuilding process once alcohol is removed. Many built their entire relationship through alcohol, and there is a painful vacuum without it.

Some couples concretize the normal separation process, deciding to end their relationship very quickly into recovery. They cannot grasp the difference between emotional separation—the breakup of the enmeshed, symbiotic alcoholic relationship—and real, physical separation. The end of the pathological system is experienced as an end to the relationship. This is an important distinction that therapists can anticipate and interpret for the couple.

As part of our research protect, we have designed a curriculum for families in recovery (Brown & Lewis, 1993). We now can offer them a "map" of what lies ahead and, particularly, what is normal and expected over a long-term process of change and new development. Within these lessons, in an informal classroom setting, we map out the need for emotional separation, the need for a focus on the individuals, and the importance of not rushing too quickly to patch up a family system. Then, we add the difficulty of managing all of this and still attending to the children. Midway through this course, we invite a "mentor family' to share their stories of drinking and recovery from a family perspective, emphasizing what it is like now in recovery.

We have found that this family class experience is enormously helpful, particularly to families with several years or more of recovery. Sometimes, families with less than a year of recovery have had trouble grasping the information, whereas those with longer sobriety are hungry for help with family matters and the integration of healthy communication and relationships.

Most important, we see that couples can tolerate the painful process of separation if they have supports and models. The shared language and new ideas of recovery also serve to hold them and provide a new foundation on which to build a healthy couple relationship. . . .

Individual Development: Individuals continue to focus on themselves, reconstructing the past and establishing a new view of self in the present. Abstinent behaviors are in place, so individuals can settle into the cognitive tasks of new learning through exchange with others, listening at meetings, and working the steps.

This is a time of intense change. As people begin to feel secure in their behavioral abstinence, they experience a window of receptivity to learn about themselves. Many can't get enough of this wonderful opportunity and the truths they can now accept. The break in denial, surrender, and initial stability achieved through the transition stage provide a strong motivation to continue.

For others, the demands of recovery and the normal difficulties of depression and anxiety that frequently occur are sometimes overwhelming. The road is painful and rocky. Relapse looms as a threat and a lure. For many, a return to drinking or to old co-alcoholic behaviors and thinking looks like a temporary painkiller.

Co-alcoholics, in their own recovery programs or not, may feel neglected, abandoned, and competitive with AA. They may also begin to feel anger at themselves for staying with the alcoholic or for joining the pathology. Now, they're told they have to change too! They may feel distrustful, unforgiving, and fearful. They may feel responsible for controlling any potential relapse in the same ways they felt responsible for the drinking.

The partner must learn that "letting go" of responsibility for the other is not equal to emotional abandonment and that it is not tantamount to separation or divorce. It is a time to focus on the self, which is hard work.

Sometimes, traumas from the drinking days or childhood interfere with people's ability to maintain forward movement. Memories or deep emotions surface and need attention. The therapist needs to help the individual maintain a recovery focus while also addressing the deep traumas (Krystal, 1978; van der Kolk, 1987). This work demands a combination of support, the building of new defensive structures, and a working through of the past.

Tasks of Treatment in the Early Recovery Stage: As therapists, we focus on the following tasks of treatment:

- Continuing to attend to behavior and cognitive change;
- Solidifying and building identities as alcoholic and co-alcoholic;
- Supporting individual focus; using couples therapy to help couples tolerate separation;
- Supporting Twelve Step programs and helping with resistance;
- Maintaining recovery assessment and watching for signs of relapse;
- Supporting parenting responsibilities; and
- Facilitating insight-oriented psychotherapy or trauma resolution as necessary (Brown & Lewis, 1993).

The work of early recovery lasts at least three years and easily into five. By then, recovery is stable. Continuing change and development take place on the new foundations of the self built during this period. . . .

The Ongoing Recovery Stage. Individual recoveries become more solid and separate during this period (Brown & Lewis, 1993). Abstinent behaviors may have long been in place and now feel routine. Individuals can enjoy the security of this stabilization while they also remain alert to the dangers of overconfidence. External behavioral controls are internalized, so people can pause and reflect on an impulse to drink or to revert back to controlling a partner. This reflection may also take the place of a need for direct action to quiet the impulse.

The identities of alcoholic and co-alcoholic become more stable and well developed through a detailed drunkalogue. The process of working the steps is much less threatening and much more a part of the structure of the self that now guides recovery and day-to-day living.

During ongoing recovery, the language of recovery becomes more familiar and can be used in a shorthand way. Couples who speak the language have already built a bridge to lead them back to focus on their relationship. The language also confirms individual identities and separation. Indeed, this can be a problem because there is no language structure within the Twelve Step program for the system, or couples partnership. It is an extremely difficult and often threatening challenge to maintain the individual perspective while adding the "we" of the couple. . . .

Stability allows people to develop new interests or to pursue old ones in more meaningful ways, to develop new relationships, and to expand the range and depth of their lives. This process of expansion is directly opposite to the constriction of the self and family that dominated the old drinking system. But this freedom to grow is often a mixed blessing: it offers new possibility and new complexity. It also can feel terribly out of control, reminding individuals of the chaotic and frightening days of active drinking.

If both individuals are anchored in recovery, it's likely they have also focused their attention on spirituality, developing a personal concept of and relationship to a higher power. This spiritual focus alters beliefs, values, and attitudes about the self and others. Control is vested in a power greater than the individual. This belief in something greater facilitates the relinquishment of a maladaptive emphasis on control between the partners. If both believe in something greater, the groundwork for an equal relationship is laid, as neither one must vest his or her deepest dependency needs completely and unrealistically in the other. . . .

Strong individual recoveries lay the foundation for a return to a couple and family focus that will accent a new relationship with healthy, open communication, equality between adults, and the possibility of greater intimacy. Much of ongoing recovery involves finding a balance between individual and couple and family growth.

Our job is to help the family:

- Continue abstinent behavior;
- Continue to build alcoholic and co-alcoholic identities;
- Maintain individual programs of recovery; to continue to work the Twelve Steps and internalize the Twelve Step principles;
- Work through the consequences of alcoholism and co-alcoholism to the self and family;
- Deepen spirituality;
- Add a focus on couple and family issues; and
- Balance and integrate combined individual and family recoveries. . . (Brown & Lewis, 1993).

The Environment: In ongoing recovery, the environment is characterized by stability, predictability, and consistency. It is less crisis-organized and crisis-dominated, and there is less, if any, regular trauma and instability, as in the drinking, transition, and early recovery stages. The atmosphere is friendly, secure, and open, rather than hostile or anxious. The context of family life reflects and reinforces the values of abstinence and recovery. Problems and crises may puncture this calming environment, but they are addressed as temporary and don't usually alter or overwhelm the solid, secure norm.

The family still has to cope with difficulties such as illness, acting-out children, employment, and financial issues. But these problems do not threaten sobriety or the structure of the new family system. In fact, problems can be dealt with, rather than denied, and they can be worked through, rather than used to cover severe family pathology. The safety of the sober environment and the solidity of the new system provide the foundation for these new healthy responses to the everyday challenges of normal life.

The System: By ongoing recovery, secure, separate individual development is in place, which becomes the foundation for a new healthy family system. Parents are better able to focus on their children and partners, although holding the multiple perspectives of self, parent, and partner is an ongoing challenge. New rules, roles, and other family regulatory mechanisms are usually in place, or their development is under way. The adults have shifted, for the most part, from an extremely polarized relationship characterized by a dominant-submissive, aggressor-victim structure to a more equal partnership, Parental decisionmaking is more likely to reflect cooperation, shared input, and responsibility.

This structural systems shift toward equality is striking. Without it, the couple tends to repeat the interactional patterns that sustained the pathology of drinking. We see that couples who do not use any external sources of help—AA, Al-Anon, treatment centers, or therapy—have tremendous difficulty making this shift. They may give up drinking but make no alterations in the system. In these families, disappointed people often express the view that nothing changed except the drinking. Unfortunately, they are right.

The change in family structure and the stability of individual growth also permit the partners to be more available to their children. As we have noted, this should not be the first time they have poked their heads up to notice the children! But what's possible now is full attention from the new security of their own healthy selves. Now, they can provide guidance, support, and modeling, as well as attachment that includes emotional attention and accurate empathy for their children's feelings and needs.

Young children may experience a safety unknown ever before and resume childhood development in the context of this healthier bond. Older children may return home, also seeking the emotional repairs and rewards of this healthier bond and system.

The family's ability to develop a new system will be influenced by each person. Severe difficulties, past and present, may thwart smooth development. Partners who are themselves adult children of alcoholics or children of other traumas may continue to bring these unresolved, painful issues to their present relationships. The trauma of the drinking years may also linger unresolved for a long time in recovery, the wounds too raw to open up for resolution. Differences in the rate of recovery by parents or a continuing crisis-dominated environment and family system can also complicate individual and family growth.

Parents who are at different stages of individual recovery have a particularly difficult time negotiating the systems changes because they are not able to feel and operate as equals. Recovery may proceed, but the system remains unchanged. In other cases, however, it may become stable with an unequal structure, which may work quite well.

Although we have seen the enormous benefits when both partners identify themselves as individuals in their own recoveries, this particular kind of structural separation is not essential for a satisfying, workable system or a happy relationship. Ultimately, the couple's sense of their own well-being is most important. We have seen a high incidence of couple dissatisfaction all through recovery when one partner chooses not to be "in recovery" or when the couple is out of sync in the development of the partners. We have also seen couples who appear out of phase to us but who are quite satisfied and report few difficulties.

One person's recovery may exist entirely outside of the marital relationship. The person builds a solid individual recovery while the system remains enmeshed, unable to resolve the pain of the drinking years. An alcoholic woman in recovery illustrates: "Alcohol is still in the house. We never changed a thing. All our friends drink, so we serve liquor. We have no complaints. Well, sometimes I do, but we are doing fine."

This couple said they have discussed the same issues for the last six years and that nothing has changed. It was evident the wife was in great pain from the drinking, but when we asked about it, her husband said, "No, those years are over. She's upset about something else."

Ironically, we have found that many couples with excellent individual recoveries have a very hard time coming back together as a mature couple. Communication may be open in certain areas, facilitated by the Twelve Step language and the commitment to honesty and a focus on the self. The expression of anger and comfortable sexuality linger as difficulties for many. Both require openness, cornmitment to resolution, a mutuality and reciprocity in communication, and a capacity to tolerate ambiguities that cannot be resolved with a right or wrong conclusion.

This is the hard work for any mature couple. The recovering couple struggles, sometimes intensely, with a deep fear of being out of control, an experience activated by unknown territories of the self or couple and the inability to achieve absolutes. Psychotherapy often stimulates the same dilemmas: the ability to experience freedom of thought and emotion is a reward of deep change, yet it can also be felt as the painful, disastrous loss of control that brought the individual and family in for help in the first place.

In ongoing recovery, the struggles and sources of tension involve conflicts and fears about intimacy, working through past hurts, and improving problem resolution. . . . The process of ongoing recovery continues over many years, although changes may be more subtle. The process is one of finding and fine-tuning a balance—between the individual and the "we" of the system and between care and caution in the service of maintaining recovery and expansive development. It is a time for attention to healthy family growth based on solid individual recovery.

Individual Development: Individual development, including reconstruction and new construction of identity as an alcoholic or a co-alcoholic, is in full swing. The early adjustments and new language are well integrated, so the focus on self in ongoing recovery can move to deep, uncovering, psychodynamic exploration and, often, a deepening in one's relationship to a higher power.

Individuals who have been involved with AA and Al-Anon now possess a structure to guide their expanding process of growth. The Twelve Steps are familiar. Their meaning has deepened from a concrete, practical interpretation to a more abstract, global source of safety, comfort, and ultimate dependence. Individuals have learned that rigorous self-honesty is essential to maintain sobriety and healthy, ongoing development. At the core of this commitment is a paradox: the individual's freedom and healthy development rest in the ongoing acceptance of loss of control, a dependence on something greater than the power of the self, and a reliance on others.

In the earlier stages, the focus of recovery remained on the self and on alcohol to the degree that it served as an organizer of the person's sense of self and a "holder" of dependency needs. For the alcoholic, the focus of dependence was alcohol; for partners and children, the focus of dependence was the alcoholic. Vesting one's dependence outside the pathological family allows for healthy dependencies on others, particularly sponsors and recovering friends, who can serve as models for healthy development.

Now, the foundation of the self is secure, with new development grounded on the Twelve Steps and, increasingly, psychotherapy. Some individuals believe they should have all of their problems solved by now and so resist the opportunity for new growth that arises as a result of sobriety. Many also remember very negative experiences with therapists while they were drinking, and they don't trust the therapeutic process or therapists to help them now. This skepticism is unfortunate because many people have the stability and insight to benefit from traditional psychodynamic therapy at this point.

Other individuals have achieved a stable, ongoing recovery because of their Twelve Step involvement and work with therapists throughout their recovery. They have managed this collaboration well, using the peer apprentice model of AA and Al-Anon and the supportive and challenging structures of psychotherapy simultaneously with different but complementary means to the same end.

Ongoing recovery allows individuals to explore their own childhood issues and their current ties with others, particularly intimate relationships. As noted, many people struggle for many years in recovery with issues of closeness. It is often threatening to come back together after the important years of detachment and disengagement. As we know, many couples and families do not survive recovery intact. . . .

In families with uneven growth, tension and problems of the earlier stages may continue. The change in one parent may be a continuing threat to the other or a reminder of the widening gap between the parents. Members of these families may cheer the idea of growth and fear it at the same time. In ongoing recovery, teens may experience their own crises related to the alcoholism of their parents, their recoveries, and their own use of alcohol. Many children will struggle with whether to drink and whether they will have to be alcoholic like their parent(s). . . .

Ongoing recovery offers the healthiest environment and family system yet possible through the drinking and recovering years. The parents' own strong individual development, their adherence to values of honesty and integrity, and their new capacity to function as a healthy couple offer their children a second chance. Parents can also help their children work through the traumas of the past as they accept responsibility for the drinking. The family constructs a story that allows everyone to make real the past and incorporate it into their lives in the present. . . .

ACKNOWLEDGMENT: Originally published as Brown S & Lewis V (1995). The alcoholic family: A developmental model of recovery. In S Brown (ed.) Treating Alcoholism. *San Francisco, CA: Jossey-Bass, 279–315. Reprinted by permission of the publisher.*

REFERENCES

Al-Anon (1984). *Al-Anon Faces Alcoholism.* New York, NY: Al-Anon Family Group Headquarters.

Alcoholics Anonymous (1976). *Alcoholics Anonymous.* New York, NY: AA World Service, Inc.

Black C (1981). *It Will Never Happen to Me.* Denver, CO: MAC.

Bowlby J (1988). *A Secure Base.* New York, NY: Basic Books.

Brown S (1991a). Adult children of alcoholics: The history of a social movement and its impact on clinical theory and practice. In M Galanter (ed.) *Recent Developments in Alcohol.* New York, NY: Plenum Press, 267–285.

Brown S (1991b). Children of chemically dependent parents: A theoretical crossroads. In T Pivinns (ed.) *Children of Chemically Dependent Parents: Multiperspectives from the Cutting Edge.* New York, NY: Brunner/Mazel, 74–102.

Brown S (1991c). Codependence and ACA's: Theoretical expansion from an interpersonal perspective. Paper presented to the National Consensus Symposium, Washington, DC.

Brown S (1977). Defining a continuum of recovery from alcoholism. Unpublished doctoral dissertation, California School of Professional Psychology, San Francisco.

Brown S & Lewis V (1993). *Maintaining Abstinence Program: A Curriculum for Families in Recovery.* Palo Alto, CA: Mental Research Institute, Family Recovery Project.

Brown S (1992). *Safe Passage.* New York, NY: John Wiley, Inc.

Brown S (1985). *Treating the Alcoholic: A Developmental Model of Recovery.* New York, NY: John Wiley & Sons.

Brown S, Beletsis S & Cermak T (1989). *Adult Children of Alcoholics in Treatment.* Orlando, FL: Health Communications.

Cork M (1969). *The Forgotten Children.* Toronto, Canada: Addiction Research Foundation, 281.

Fox R (1962). Children in the alcoholic family. In WC Bier (ed.) *Problems in Addiction: Alcoholism and Narcotics.* New York, NY: Fordham University Press, 72.

Grisham K & Estes N (1986). Dynamics of alcoholic families. In N Estes & E Heinemann (eds.) *Alcoholism: Development, Consequences, and Interventions.* St. Louis, MO: C.V. Mosby, 303–314.

Herman J (1992). *Trauma and Recovery.* New York: Basic Books.

Kaufman E (1986). The family of the alcoholic patient. *Psychosomatics* 27(5):347–360.

Krystal H (1978). Trauma and affects. In *Psychoanalytic Study of the Child.* New Haven, CT: Yale University Press, 81–116.

Jackson J (1954). The adjustment of the family to the crisis of alcoholism. *Quarterly Journal of Studies on Alcohol* 15:562–586.

Lewis M (1977). Language, cognitive development, and personality: A synthesis. *American Academy of Child Psychiatry* 16(4):646–661.

Roe A & Burks B (1945). Adult adjustment of foster children of alcoholics and psychotic parentage and the influence of the foster home. In *Memoirs of the Section on Alcoholism Studies, No. 3.* New Haven, CT: University Press.

Santostefano S (1980). Cognition in personality and the treatment process: A psychoanalytic view. In *Psychoanalytic Study of the Child.* New Haven, CT: Yale University Press, 41–65.

Steinglass P (1980). A life history model of the alcoholic family. *Family Process* 19(3):211–226.

van der Kolk B (1987). *Psychological Trauma.* Washington, DC: American Psychiatric Press.

Wegscheider S (1981). *Another Chance: Hope and Health for the Alcoholic Family.* Palo Alto, CA: Science & Behavior Books.

CHAPTER 3

Children in Alcoholic Families: Family Dynamics and Treatment Issues

Hoover Adger, Jr., M.D., M.P.H.

Effects of Alcohol and Drug Abuse on the Family
Intervention and Treatment

Of an estimated 28 million Americans who are children of alcoholics, nearly 11 million are under the age of 18. Countless other children are affected by substance-abusing parents, siblings or other caregivers. Of the under-18 group, nearly three million will develop alcoholism, other drug problems, and other serious coping problems. Many of these children are exposed to chaotic family environments that lack consistency, stability or emotional support. Some of these children may be traumatized by accidental injury resulting from parental drinking or drug use, verbal abuse or physical abuse. Poor communication, permissiveness, under-socialization, neglect and violence, all potentially devastating, are common in children who live in families affected by alcoholism and other drug dependence (National Institute on Alcohol Abuse and Alcoholism, 1992, 1997; Bavolek & Henderson, 1990).

The cycle is frequently repeated. Approximately half of all children of alcoholics marry alcoholics; thus, there is a high likelihood of recreating the same kinds of highly stressful and unhealthy families in which these individuals grew up.

Children of substance-abusing parents are at increased risk because of both genetic and environmental factors (Begleiter & Porjesz, 1997; Anthenelli & Schuckit, 1990). Children who grow up with substance-abusing parents often develop unhealthy living patterns; for example, they may not learn to trust themselves or others, how to handle uncomfortable feelings, or how to build positive relationships. Children of substance-abusing parents who lack these skills also are at higher risk for school failure, depression, and increased anxiety, as well as trouble with alcohol and other drugs (Wegscheider, 1981; Black, 1982; Johnson & Rolf, 1988).

While genetic predispositions cannot be changed, unhealthy living patterns can be countered. Children of substance-abusing parents can learn to trust, to handle their feelings in healthy ways, and to build positive, nurturing relationships. Health care professionals can help children of substance-abusing parents understand their risks and learn better social and coping skills. All children have a right to be emotionally and physically safe. No child of an alcoholic or other substance-abusing parent should have to grow up in isolation and without support. Health professionals should play a vital role in helping to optimize the health, well-being and development of children and adolescents from these families and should address, as early as possible, any associated problems or concerns.

EFFECTS OF ALCOHOL AND DRUG ABUSE ON THE FAMILY

Families often tend to act in patterned and predictable ways when one member of the family is affected by alcohol or other drug abuse and dependence. Over time, affected families may move away from the supportive relationships that characterize healthy families and move toward increasingly dysfunctional or chaotic states. Denial, secretiveness, lack of trust and honesty, and suppression of feelings are patterns that are often observed.

Denial can be a powerful but maladaptive defense and may prevent individuals from recognizing the causes of a deteriorating family relationship. Hence, actions that are obvious indicators of problems related to alcohol or drug use may become accepted by the family as normal behavior. The family's denial may be even stronger than that of the affected individual and may be related to the amount of stigmatization felt by family members. Denial may be so pervasive that, even when an alcohol or other drug problem is suspected, affected family members may unconsciously mislead health practitioners into pursuing other causes of family stress (Estes & Heinemann, 1982). Because of the power of denial, the illness may progress while health practitioners are frustrated in their attempts to confirm a suspected diagnosis, and they may react by choosing not to pursue the issue. The importance of denial is underscored by the fact that it is not uncommon for a spouse or child in the family to feel that he or she is the cause of the deteriorating family relationship. Hence, the family history and attribution may be markedly distorted.

Once family members recognize that a parent, child or spouse has a problem with alcoholism or other drug abuse and dependence, they may attempt to adapt in a number of ways to insure the integrity of the family unit. They may not discuss the problem among themselves or with others outside the family. Even young children learn not to share painful and distressing observations; instead, family members hide the problem and their reactions from each other. The drinking or drug use is not mentioned. A spouse who is abused or battered by the affected individual may tell a child that he or she fell. And the family secret grows.

The isolation that develops around such a family is both social and emotional. Children may stop inviting friends to visit because of the unpredictability of the alcoholic's or addict's behavior. A spouse may refuse social invitations or make excuses for the impaired individual's absence from work. These behavior patterns—denial, secretiveness, lack of honesty, and suppression of feelings—are amazingly similar and parallel to those of the alcoholic or drug dependent individual. The boundaries around such families can become rigid and impermeable, restricting the flow of information into and out of the family. In such situations, normal needs may be gratified in abnormal ways. For example, several studies have documented the association between child physical, emotional, and sexual abuse, neglect, family violence, and substance abuse in the family. Often the family members suffer in silence and do not reveal such abuse for many years.

Family Roles. As the family becomes increasingly preoccupied with the addicted person's drinking or drug use, there may be attempts to reorganize, and in this process various adaptive roles may be assumed. Stereotypic roles in the alcoholic family (and dysfunctional families in general) were first described by Wegscheider (1981) and since have become popularized in the lay literature. They include the alcoholic or drug addict, the "enabler," the "scapegoat," the "lost child," and the "mascot."

The *alcoholic* or *addict* is the central character in the family's drama. The *enabler*, frequently the spouse, takes control of the family and protects the affected person from the consequences of his or her actions by assuming the alcoholic's or addict's responsibilities and by shielding him or her from outside scrutiny. While the enabler usually is perceived as extremely responsible and strong-willed, he or she can harbor a number of negative feelings. Frustration, anxiety and stress-related symptoms are an understandable corollary of enabling behaviors.

The *hero* often is a high achiever and brings pride to the family through successes at school or at work. While portraying an image of self-confidence and success, the hero may feel inadequate and experience the same stress-related symptoms as the enabler.

The *scapegoat* diverts attention away from the alcoholic by acting out his or her anger. The scapegoat is considered to be at high risk for addiction because of his or her association with risk-taking activities and peers, and may be progressively involved in self-injurious and delinquent behaviors.

The *lost child*, often characterized as quiet and shy, withdraws from the family and social activities to escape the family's problems. The *mascot* seeks attention by being cute or funny, demonstrates immature behavior, and may have difficulty learning in school. While laughing on the outside, he or she may be quite sad on the inside.

For the physician, the importance of understanding these roles lies not only in the insights they provide into the dynamics of the alcoholic's or addict's family, but also their usefulness in identifying the health problems that are related to maladaptive behaviors (Duggan, Adger et al., 1991). Although the roles are stereotypical, patients may describe themselves in these terms. Hence, the physician can be more supportive of such patients if he or she understands the terms and the concepts they represent. An understanding and appreciation of family dynamics also places the physician in a better position to help patients learn more functional coping strategies.

Often, the behavior exhibited by children of substance-abusing parents brings them to professional attention before alcohol or other drug abuse or dependence is diagnosed in the parent or other family member. The impact of an alcoholic or drug-abusing parent on the child can be devastating. The younger a child is when the drinking or drug abuse begins, the more serious is its potential impact on the child's subsequent adult life (Duggan, Adger et al., 1991). When family alcohol and other drug abuse is untreated, children often carry the family rules and role-related behaviors into adulthood.

It is important to understand that, while numerous studies emphasize the illness or damage that can occur to children of substance-abusing parents, the majority of children in such families become healthy, well-adjusted adults. It appears that there are protective mechanisms that enable many children to grow into emotionally healthy adults. Children of substance-abusing parents and other drug abusing parents who do not develop serious coping problems are distinguished from their peers by more attention from a primary caretaker early in life and the absence of prolonged separation from parents. These resilient children appear to have more affectionate temperaments in childhood, have at least average intelligence, possess adequate communication skills, maintain a positive self-image, and have a more internalized locus of control (Werner, 1986).

Familial Responses. Steinglass and colleagues have found that families differ in their responses to the effects of alcoholism. Their research has highlighted that the family's rituals, priorities and behavioral styles and their use of resources and energy are altered by alcoholism. Many families are successful at maintaining their primary tasks and are not identified as problematic. In families where the alterations are the greatest, learned behaviors may be passed on to the next generation. When the family is able to resist the full effects of the disease, the children do not necessarily recreate the same kinds of highly stressful and unhealthy families in which they grew up (Steinglass, Bennett et al., 1987; Wolin, Bennett et al., 1980).

Physicians who understand these behaviors and associated symptoms can be helpful in uncovering the problem of alcoholism and other drug dependence. They can be instrumental in explaining to the family how they might be affected by the problem and can provide valuable assistance to the family and the alcohol or drug-dependent individual.

INTERVENTION AND TREATMENT

Understanding the many ways in which alcohol and other drug abuse affects families can be helpful in formulating a plan for intervention and treatment. The family can be instrumental in initiating treatment. Even when the alcoholic or drug abusing family member is highly resistant or unwilling to participate in treatment, the clinician may have another highly motivated patient: the family.

The first step in intervention and treatment is identification (Graham, 1990; Macdonald & Blume, 1986; Duggan, Adger et al., 1991). The National Association for Children of Alcoholics (NACoA) recently developed a set of core competencies to serve as a specific guide to the core knowledge, attitudes, and skills that are essential in meeting the needs of children and youth affected by family substance abuse (The White House, 1997). These competencies set forth three levels for professional involvement with children who grow up in homes where alcohol and other drugs are a problem.

Level I. For all health professionals with clinical responsibility for the care of children and adolescents:

1. Be aware of the medical, psychiatric, and behavioral syndromes and symptoms of children and adolescents in families with substance abuse present.
2. Be aware of the potential benefit, to both the child and the family, of timely and early intervention.
3. Be familiar with community resources available for children and adolescents in families with substance abuse.
4. As part of the general health assessment of children and adolescents, health professionals need to include appropriate screening for family history/current use of alcohol and other drugs.
5. Based on screening results, determine family resource needs and services currently being provided so that an appropriate level of care and follow-up can be recommended.
6. Be able to communicate an appropriate level of concern and offer information, support and follow-up.

Level II. In addition to Level I competencies, health care providers accepting responsibility for prevention, assessment, intervention and coordination of care of children and adolescents in families with substance abuse should:

1. Apprise the child and family of the nature of alcohol and other drug abuse dependence and its impact on all family members and strategies for achieving optimal health and recovery.

2. Recognize and treat, or refer, all associated health problems.
3. Evaluate resources—physical health, economic, interpersonal, and social—to the degree necessary to formulate an initial management plan.
4. Determine the need for involving family members and significant other persons in the initial management plan.
5. Develop a long-term management plan in consideration of the above standards and with the child or adolescent's participation.

Level III. In addition to Level I and II competencies, the health care provider with additional training, who accepts responsibility for long-term treatment of children and adolescents in families with substance abuse should:

1. Acquire knowledge, by training or experience, in the medical and behavioral treatment of children in families affected by substance abuse.
2. Continually monitor the child or adolescent's health needs.
3. Be knowledgeable about the proper use of consultations.
4. Throughout the course of health care treatment, continually monitor and treat, or refer for care, any psychiatric or behavioral disturbances.
5. Be available to the child or adolescent and the family, as needed, for ongoing care and support.

The complexity and diversity of problems encountered in many children of substance-abusing parents require early and comprehensive intervention. The addiction specialist needs to be acquainted with health professionals in the community who can be enlisted to assist in the evaluation, assessment and treatment of affected families. Common intervention strategies—which include delivering developmentally and age appropriate education, connecting patients with social support networks, offering training in skills development and addressing the socio-emotional needs of affected individuals—should be familiar to health practitioners.

CONCLUSIONS

Addiction medicine specialists and other clinicians are in an ideal position to identify early alcohol- and other drug-related problems in children, adolescents and families. While it is easiest to identify alcohol and other drug-related problems in those patients who are most severely affected, the challenge is to identify individuals early in their involvement and to intervene in a very timely and meaningful manner.

REFERENCES

Anthenelli RM & Schuckit MA (1990). Genetic studies of alcoholism. *International Journal of Addiction* 25:81–94.

Bavolek SJ & Henderson HL (1990). Child maltreatment and alcohol abuse: Comparisons and perspectives for treatment. In RT Potter-Efron & PS Potter-Efron (eds.) *Aggression, Family Violence and Chemical Dependency.* Binghamton, NY: Haworth Press, 165–184.

Begleiter H & Porjesz B (1997). Event-related potentials in COA's. *Alcohol Health & Research World* 21-3:236–240.

Black C (1982). *It Will Never Happen to Me.* Denver, CO: Medical Administration Company.

Duggan AK, Adger H, McDonald EM et al. (1991). Detection of alcoholism in children and their families. *American Journal of Disease of Children* 145:613–617.

Estes N & Heinemann M, eds (1982). *Alcoholism, Development, Consequences, and Interventions, Ed. 2.* St. Louis, MO: C.V. Mosby Co.

Graham AV (1990). Family Issues in Substance Abuse. Project SAEFP, Society of Teachers of Family Medicine, DHHS No. 240-89-0038.

Johnson J & Rolf JE (1988). Cognitive functioning in children from alcoholic and non-alcoholic families. *Journal of Addictions* 83:849–857.

Macdonald DI & Blume SB (1986). Children of alcoholics. *American Journal of Diseases of Children* 140:750.

National Institute on Alcohol Abuse and Alcoholism (1992). *Alcoholism Tends to Run in Families* (DHHS publication No. (ADM) 92-1914). Bethesda, MD: National Institutes of Health.

National Institute on Alcohol Abuse and Alcoholism (1997). *Ninth Special Report to the U.S. Congress on Alcohol and Health* (NIH Pub. No. 97-4017). Bethesda, MD: National Institutes of Health.

Steinglass P, Bennett LA, Wolin SJ & Reis D (1987). *The Alcoholic Family.* New York, NY: Basic Books, Inc.

Wegscheider S (1981). *Another Chance.* Palo Alto, CA: Science and Behavior Books, Inc.

Werner EE (1986). Resilient offspring of alcoholics: A longitudinal study from birth to age 18. *Journal of Studies on Alcohol* 47:34–40.

The White House (1997). Conference Proceedings, Core Competencies: Involvement of Health Care Providers in the Care of Children and Adolescents in Families Affected by Substance Abuse, The White House, September 15.

Wolin SJ, Bennett LA, Noonan DL & Teitelbaum MA (1980). Disrupted family rituals: A factor in the intergenerational transmission of alcoholism. *Journal of Studies on Alcohol* 41:199–214.

CHAPTER 4

Current Family Treatment Approaches

David Berenson, M.D.
Ellen Woodside Schrier, M.S.W.

The Roots of Eclecticism
Disease Model Perspectives
Family Systems Perspectives
Behavioral Perspectives
Toward an Integrated Approach
The Importance of Phasing
The Need for Research

Biological scientists and family systems theorists sometimes are horrified—albeit for different reasons—when addiction is referred to as a "family disease." Some biologists would like to limit the use of the term "addiction" to describing specific behaviors that are linked to a physiological substrate. They argue that if everything, including a particular relationship pattern, is potentially an addictive disease, then nothing is an addictive disease. Some systems theorists discount the idea that any addiction is a disease and hold that the disease model itself is an outdated example of cause-and-effect thinking, rather than thinking systemically. Yet, even though the "experts" may object to the validity of the concept, many laypersons feel liberated and empowered by thinking their family has a disease. To them, it serves to minimize blame and provides a bridge from which to examine and take responsibility for their own behavior.

In a similar vein, family therapists in the late 1960s began to speak of behavior or relationship patterns as dysfunctional in an attempt to develop a neutral term with no pejorative or moralistic overtones. They concluded that "sickness" had developed the connotation of "bad" and that using the word dysfunctional instead would indicate that particular patterns were merely unworkable or dissatisfying to family members. But, as the term has come to be used by the recovery movement, it also carries a connotation of being "sick" or "bad." Consequently, when authors write that 95% of American families are dysfunctional, the implication is that these families are somehow abnormal or aberrant, rather than that they do not function optimally all the time to provide full satisfaction for all family members.

Today, the situation has come full circle. At a recent conference on addiction and the family, one expert on alcohol treatment declared that we should begin to refer to families as "sick" rather than "dysfunctional" in order to seem less judgmental.

THE ROOTS OF ECLECTICISM

On reviewing the numerous family-oriented approaches to addiction treatment, one is immediately struck with the level of pragmatic eclecticism that coexists with theoretical incongruence (Kalb & Propper, 1976). This division between practice and theory is created as practitioners and patients borrow ideas and techniques from different disciplines and combine them in an *ad hoc* way without asking whether the new formulas are coherent or empirically valid, thereby enraging purists and impeding the emergence dialogue among the various camps. Although the 1990s have witnessed some diminution in the crusading zeal with which people approach the topic of the family and addiction, attention to family issues is now well established as a standard and integral part of comprehensive addiction treatment. The time has come to identify the various approaches to family treatment, to examine their effectiveness, and to describe how they might be used in practice. Despite the theoretical incongruence and overlaps that characterize much of the family-focused treatment of addiction, three main threads or models can be identified that underlie the various therapeutic approaches: disease model perspectives, family systems perspectives, and behavioral perspectives (McCrady, 1989). Before these various threads can be meaningfully combined to make a strong and vibrant tapestry, they must be disentangled and viewed separately.

DISEASE MODEL PERSPECTIVES

Family approaches based on a disease model are the most likely of the three models mentioned to have a craft orientation. They usually are developed on purely pragmatic grounds and are based on "what works," rather than empirical outcome data or theoretical consistency. Strong adherents to this perspective are typically laypersons or paraprofessionals who have experienced addictive disorders personally or in their families. These approaches sometimes are called "recovery focused" or "self-help oriented."

Disease model perspectives adopt what we term an "inside-out" approach to family factors. The emphasis is on how an individual's addictive problem disturbs family functioning, rather than on the addictive problem as a particular manifestation of a type of family organization. Thus, recovery-oriented family treatments emphasize working with individuals on family issues, rather than conjoint family therapy. Family members are most often seen in treatment apart from the addict and attend their own Twelve Step meetings. The major disease model approaches are described below:

Twelve Step Programs. In the very early days of Alcoholics Anonymous, wives of alcoholics sometimes attended meetings with their husbands. As the fellowship aspect of AA developed, spouses and other relatives were excluded from meetings and began to meet separately to discuss their common problems. By 1948, these Family Groups were listed by the AA General Service Office, and in 1951 the name Al-Anon Family Groups was given to the 50 groups moving toward independent existence (Al-Anon, 1985). From the beginning, Al-Anon has presented its members with two focuses: to deal with "the effects of the disease of alcoholism on those who live, or have lived, with an alcoholic" and "to recover from recurring symptoms of their own" (Al-Anon, 1985). The vagueness in wording allows members to adopt their own interpretation of the program. Some have seen Al-Anon as a program that supports them in helping the alcoholic recover. Others view Al-Anon as a program that provides them with the opportunity to address personal problems that may have preceded or may be contributing to the drinking problem.

Within Al-Anon, several subgroups have emerged. The first was the Alateen program, which came into existence in 1957 and was designed for teenagers with an alcoholic parent. In the 1980s, Adult Children of Alcoholics (ACOAs) began and quickly gained widespread popularity. Also in the 1980s came meetings for parents of alcoholics, which have been less popular. And, in 1993, Al-Anon officially endorsed the development of the Pre-Alateen Program, which is geared for children aged 5-12 with alcoholic parents. In addition, a separate Adult Children of Alcoholics Twelve Step program, not affiliated with Al-Anon, has emerged in various parts of the country.

Nar-Anon, which is modeled after Al-Anon, is another large, national Twelve Step program that serves families and friends of drug addicts. Co-Dependents Anonymous is gaining attention as a generic Twelve Step program for people who are not necessarily dealing with an addictive problem but who wish to address their own relational or emotional difficulties by using the Twelve Step format.

Family Intervention. Family Intervention, as developed by Johnson in the 1960s (Johnson Institute, 1987), theoretically resembles network therapy, which was developed during the same time period (Speck & Attneave, 1974). Both approaches emphasize the importance of assembling and working with the addict's social network. In practice, however, the two approaches are strikingly different. Family Intervention is tightly structured and has the very specific goal of getting the addict to agree to enter treatment as a first step toward sobriety. Family network therapy is much less structured and is directed at improving the network's overall functioning instead of focusing directly on the identified patient.

As Family interventions became more popular in the 1980s, a large number of addiction professionals and paraprofessionals were trained in the technique, but today few of them continue to conduct them. In most cities in the United States, clinicians refer families to the few practitioners who conduct such interventions on a regular basis.

Family Component of Residential Treatment. Almost all residential addiction programs now have a family component. In most, the component is conveyed largely through the education series on addiction. Family members are invited to attend lectures similar to those attended by the addicts, and information on family issues often is included in the lectures for the hospitalized addict. Some programs feature a more intensive Family Week during which family members (usually spouses) live at the facility (Laundergan & Williams, 1993). Family members are kept separate from the alcoholic or addict for most of the week and work on their own issues of co-dependence and recovery.

The work of Wegscheider-Cruse (1989) has been the single most important influence on the content and structure of facility-based programs. She postulated that children in families with alcoholism internalize limited and rigid family roles that can stay with them throughout their lives. Her descriptions of these roles (enabler, hero, scapegoat, lost child, mascot) are taught in virtually every program in the country today. She also developed the Family Reconstruction approach, which allows alcoholics, addicts, and family members in later recovery to encounter and begin to resolve unaddressed, destructive issues and patterns from their families of origin.

The Recovery Movement. The recovery movement has emerged as a unique grassroots phenomenon. It owes its existence to the synergy that developed as the Adult Children of Alcoholics Movement, the Inner Child Movement, and the Co-Dependency Movement began to borrow ideas from each other. These concepts also were combined with treatment techniques from both the addiction field and the family therapy field, and the compilation of this material spawned a cottage industry of books, magazines, tapes and workshops. Simultaneously, and in response to the growing demand, the number of psychotherapists declaring an expertise in this area increased dramatically.

FAMILY SYSTEMS PERSPECTIVES

The first self-help and research meetings on ACOAs took place in the late 1970s. The books by Black (1982) and Woititz (1983) were surprise bestsellers and fueled an upsurge of interest among people who wanted to heal the "original pain" (Bradshaw, 1990) of childhood experiences in their families. As the decade progressed, the popular literature expanded to include co-dependence (Beattie, 1987) and the wounded inner child (Whitfield, 1987). Established addiction specialists and family therapists have responded to the emergence of the movement with a mixture of tolerance and alarm. Some have viewed the increase in the number of people who are willing to look at and resolve their personal problems as positive. Others have expressed concern regarding the misuse and overly broad application of addiction and family systems concepts by people active and vocal in the movement. The degree of inept and sometimes exploitative treatment that has emerged in the name of recovery also has been questioned. Although many people clearly have used the movement as a base from which to gain a greater level of peace, understanding, and self-acceptance, others have used it as a rationale for indulging in blame, self-pity, and manipulation.

Family systems approaches occupy an intermediate position in the craft-scientific continuum. They tend to emphasize the development of theoretically informed clinical practice and pay relatively little attention to the outcome studies that validate the approach. The main point of emphasis for family systems practitioners is the overall way the problems are viewed, rather than the specific methods that may be used to intervene. To be "systemic" is to take into account the total pattern, the whole system in determining an appropriate treatment approach. Typical adherents of family systems approaches are mental health professionals (social workers, psychologists, and some psychiatrists) who are self-identified as holding this viewpoint.

Although much Al-Anon literature emphasizes the disease model, one of the pamphlets available at its meetings provides a useful example of a family systems or "outside-in" perspective. It says: "A person must have the help of at least one other person to become an alcoholic. He cannot become one by himself . . . to understand alcoholism, we must look at the illness of the alcoholic as if we were sitting in the audience watching a play and observing carefully the roles of all the actors" (Kellerman, 1969). The drinking or drug problem is seen as integral to the functioning of the entire family. It is not that the family is merely reacting to the drinking or drug abuse of an individual family member. Rather, the abuse "has become a family condition that has inserted itself into virtually every aspect of family life . . . alcoholism has become a central organizing principle" for the family (Steinglass, Bennett et al., 1987).

Until recently, most family systems therapists largely ignored addictive disorders. Family therapists who addressed addiction can be divided into two groups: those who see addiction as a family problem that can be addressed with established family systems approaches and those who see addiction as a unique problem in which there has to be a modification of standard family therapy approaches.

Family Therapy Approaches Applied to Addiction. The direct application of family systems approaches to addiction has been more common with adolescent drug abusers than with adult alcoholics. Family therapists have tended to be more comfortable addressing family problems that manifest in a child rather than a parent. Thus, the structural family therapy approach of Minuchin (1992) has been modified and expanded upon by several clinicians (Stanton & Todd, 1992; Treadway, 1989; Liddle, Dakoff & Diamond, 1992; Kaufman, 1992) to address adolescent drug abuse. While these approaches differ in emphasis, they share the common perspective that the primary treatment is family therapy and that participation in Twelve Step programs is relatively unimportant or unnecessary.

Since established practice in the addiction field traditionally has been focused almost exclusively on the treatment of adults, family therapy for adolescents with addictive disorders is potentially a welcome addition. Clearly, the treatment needs of adolescents are different from those of adults. Although family involvement is important in both adolescent and adult addiction treatment, the level and degree of such involvement vary substantially. The standard approach (which emphasizes detachment in the spouse, "hitting bottom" in the alcoholic, and spiritual awakening in both) does not translate directly to adolescent addicts. Parents need to learn the difference between appropriate involvement and enmeshment and also may need to learn how to take more active control by setting effective and realistic limits. At the same time, adolescent addicts usually need to focus more on becoming personally powerful and getting their lives together than on surrendering to a power greater than themselves.

Approaches That Integrate Family Systems Therapy and Addiction Treatment. Many of the approaches that seek to integrate a family systems perspective with addiction treatment derive from research by Steinglass and colleagues at the National Institute on Alcohol Abuse and Alcoholism, who began their research by making naturalistic observations of couples and families with alcohol problems, during periods of sobriety and intoxication. Early on, they noticed that problem drinking has adaptive, as well as maladaptive, consequences for both the drinker and his or her family (Davis, Berenson et al., 1974). They surmised that the drinking may allow the expression, often in exaggerated form, of intimate and assertive behaviors by different family members, which may be suppressed when sober. The idea that family members exhibit different sets of behavior depending on whether the alcoholic is drinking has been supported by a number of authors (Berenson, 1976; Steinglass, Bennett et al., 1987; Fossum & Mason, 1986) and has been integrated into most approaches that combine a family systems orientation with existing addiction treatment.

Berenson went on to outline a clinical family systems approach to alcohol problems that combined family therapy with the concurrent use of AA and Al-Anon (1976, 1992). He also emphasized the effectiveness of working with the non-drinking spouse when the alcoholic is resistant. Berenson's approach was further developed by Bepko and Krestan (1985) and Treadway (1989). Steinglass and colleagues (1987) outlined a therapeutic approach derived from their research findings. Although these authors present their treatment strategies and techniques in varied ways, they all share the notion that recovery progresses through a number of specific stages and that existing alcohol treatment is most usefully combined with, rather than replaced by, family therapy. All view family therapy as (usually) ancillary to participation in Twelve Step or residential programs until the drinking or drug use has stopped. They additionally hold the perspective that, once sobriety is attained, family therapy provides a unique and promising format for addressing important, unresolved family issues.

Another approach that combines a family systems perspective with existing addiction treatment is Galanter's (1993) network therapy (described in Section 8 of this text). This treatment combines direct work with the addict and a few significant members of the family or social system with participation in Twelve Step programs and the prescription of disulfiram or naltrexone.

BEHAVIORAL PERSPECTIVES

Behavioral perspectives clearly occupy the scientific end of the craft-scientific continuum. These approaches place particular attention upon rigorously describing specific therapeutic interventions and measuring their efficacy through controlled outcome studies. Adherents of these perspectives are the least numerous of the three groups, consisting principally of clinical psychologists whose background is in social learning theory. They also are the most likely to see their treatment as an alternative, rather than a supplement, to participation in Twelve Step programs.

Rather than inside-out or outside-in, behavioral marital therapy (BMT) perspectives may best be described as interactional. From this viewpoint, the interactions of the couple are seen as critical to the continuation of addictions. Both spouses are involved, "with the behavior of each partner serving simultaneously as a cue to the behavior of the other and as a reinforcer of the partner's behavior" (McCrady, 1989). Thus, behavioral marital therapy is geared to target and change the drinking-related behaviors of both spouses. The drinker learns specific behavior change techniques to help stop the drinking. The spouse learns new ways of coping with rather than reinforcing the drinking, and the couple is taught communications skills to enhance the relationship.

The two most well-developed approaches to behavioral marital alcoholism treatment have been PACT (Program for Alcoholic Couples Treatment; McCrady, 1992; Noel & McCrady, 1993) and CALM (Counseling for AlcohoLics' Marriages; O'Farrell, 1993a). PACT features 15 conjoint couples sessions, with homework and self-monitoring exercises scheduled between sessions. The behavior of the alcoholic and spouse is changed through stimulus control procedures, contingency rearrangement, cognitive restructuring, a functional analysis of the drinking, techniques to stop triggering and reinforcing drinking, and the development of alternatives to drinking. The couple's relationship is addressed through formal communications training that emphasizes the development of problem-solving and negotiating skills. CALM consists of six to eight preparatory couples sessions, followed by 10 weekly multiple couples' group meetings. In the pregroup sessions, couples establish a contract around use of disulfiram, which is monitored in the group. Group sessions also feature discussions about preventing and dealing with relapse and training in communications and negotiation skills, in combination with a focus on increasing positive couple and family activities.

Unilateral family therapy (Thomas & Ager, 1993) is a behavioral approach that seeks to produce change by working through non-abusing spouses, who are taught to decrease enabling behaviors and then to conduct nonconfrontational or confrontational interventions. It is interesting to contrast the approaches of Thomas and Ager (1993) and Berenson (1992) approaches. Both focus initially on the non-addicted spouse, but Thomas' behavioral orientation is combined with the basic message of the Johnson Family Intervention, while Berenson's family systems orientation is combined with the basic message of Al-Anon. Thomas and Ager help patients *intervene* more effectively, while Berenson focuses on helping patients to *detach* more effectively.

TOWARD AN INTEGRATED APPROACH

Each of the three overall models has unique advantages and liabilities. Disease model perspectives are the most popular and widespread, provide terms and labels that appeal to patients and—with their self-help orientation—require less professional involvement and expense. But because of their craft orientation, they have not been amenable to outcome studies. In addition, the global statements sometimes made about the personality traits of co-dependents and adult children of alcoholics may result in feelings of stigmatization. Family systems perspectives provide theoretical rigor and a more comprehensive overview, and some therapy techniques from this model already have been incorporated into addiction treatment. However, since family systems perspectives are as much ways of thinking and organizing information as they are specific therapy techniques, they, like disease model perspectives, are not easily evaluated by controlled outcome studies. Behavioral perspectives do have empirical rigor. They clearly delineate specific interventions and systematically assess their outcomes. However, in providing a precise view of the trees, they may obscure the overall panorama of the forest. Intangible, unmeasurable emotional, relational and spiritual factors do, in fact, play a role in both the development of, and recovery from, addiction. Outcome studies alone are not enough to influence patients and treatment providers, who intuitively and emotionally resonate with the disease and family systems models.

An ideal tapestry of family treatment would combine the warmth and appeal of disease model approaches with the overview of family systems approaches and the scientific rigor of behavioral approaches. At this point, we certainly fall short of that ideal, but some steps can be taken toward it. If the overall course of treatment and recovery is divided into specific phases, then the integration of the various threads becomes more possible.

THE IMPORTANCE OF PHASING

The idea of dividing treatment into discrete phases is not new. In fact, the Twelve Steps of Alcoholics Anonymous themselves can be seen as having three phases. Steps 1 through 3 concentrate on the acceptance of powerlessness as a necessary prelude to sobriety; Steps 4 through 9 deal with the need to repair the "wreckage of the past," and Steps 10 through 12 focus on developing a sense of serenity in daily life and ending the preoccupation with alcohol. We would propose a three-phase model for family treatment of drug and alcohol addiction that correlates with these different stages of individual recovery. The level of intervention within the family shifts as the various goals are addressed.

In Phase I, in order to help the patient stop drinking, it is useful to focus on helping individuals take responsibility for their own behavior and feelings. Even though family members may be seen conjointly, the emphasis is on slowing down reactivity and fostering the ability to observe one's self and the impact of one's actions on others. Coming from a disease model perspective, this approach involves helping each spouse to address his or her own addiction or co-dependence rather than worrying about what the other is doing. An intervention also may be held, with instructions for participants to stay with their own observations and feelings, rather than preaching at the drinker.

Family systems approaches might try to help the spouse disengage and define an "I position" in order to decrease the family fusion and repetitive cycling, thus setting the stage for the addict's recovery. Behavioral perspectives target the behaviors of each spouse that reinforce drinking or drug use and attempt to substitute behaviors that reinforce sobriety. Although differing in form, these approaches all recognize and support the notion that the addiction must stop before "deeper" family issues can be explored.

In Phase II, the focus can begin to shift to the wider family field, as the dysfunctional patterns that come from the family in which the patient grew up (family of origin), as well as the current household (family of procreation), are addressed. Our notion is that broadening the lens to deal with past and current relationship problems diminishes the likelihood of relapse, promotes individual and family functioning in sobriety, and may even decrease the likelihood that addiction problems will be transmitted to the next generation. Family of origin issues are well-addressed in both the recovery movement and the family therapy field. ACOA meetings, inner child work, family reconstruction weekends, and family coaching are examples of methods currently being used. Family of procreation issues, however, remain largely ignored within addiction treatment. It seems timely and advantageous to look also to the expertise that has been developing in the fields of family systems therapy and behavioral marital therapy.

Phase III therapy is the "new frontier" of addiction treatment. It is the least explored and also potentially the most controversial. Years after the cessation of drug or alcohol use, the marital relationship often continues to be strained. If both spouses are successfully participating in Twelve Step programs, they may have become more accustomed to sharing emotional or personal issues in meetings or with sponsors, rather than with each other. As a result, a fixed emotional distance may become established between them. If only one spouse is attending a Twelve Step program, the other may be jealous of the closeness he or she sees developing there. In turn, the Twelve Step participant may begin to see the marital relationship as sorely lacking, in comparison to the warmth and unconditional acceptance he or she receives from fellow Twelve Step members. This perception may drive the participant closer to his or her program and further away from the spouse, causing the spouse to become even more reactive. Marital estrangement or divorce may result. Therefore, Phase III treatment deals directly with the lack of intimacy experienced by the couple. In order to be successful, the active participation of both spouses is required.

Table 1 provides some idea of the sequencing of the family approaches. A more detailed description of our view of each phase follows.

Phase I Treatment. Clinicians consistently have observed that, in the majority of cases, a change on the part of the spouse or other intimate predated the cessation of active drug or alcohol abuse. Thus, the initial focus in Phase I often is best placed on working with the spouse, rather than on trying to get through to the addict. Typically, the spouse is overfunctioning (Bowen, 1978) and has taken on the characteristics of the emotional pursuer (Fogarty, 1976). Since spouses often are the more overworked and acutely pained of the couple, they may be more amenable to change and thus provide more potential leverage. In addition, the addict's possible nonresponsiveness in sessions or initial refusal to participate in treatment presents less of a problem, since the goal is to first initiate change in the non-addicted spouse. As the spouse shifts attention to self and pursues less, the addicted partner predictably distances less and becomes more amenable to treatment.

Since it is imperative for the spouse to stop trying to control the alcoholic's drinking, the clinician can, in early treatment, plant the seeds of powerlessness by offering three choices:

1. Continue past patterns of behavior (rescuing, persecuting, begging, not setting limits).

TABLE 1. Main Levels of Intervention in Family Systems Treatment

Phase	Goals	Main Level of Intervention
Phase I	1. Address denial	Individual
	2. Get drinking stopped	Individual
Phase II	1. Prevent relapse	Family of Origin (role as child)
	2. Stabilize family, improve functioning	Family of Procreation (role as parent)
Phase III	1. Increase marital intimacy, emotional and sexual	Couple (role as spouse)

2. Detach or emotionally distance from the situation, while staying in the marriage.
3. Physically distance by leaving.

Fairly quickly, the spouse comes to see that all of the choices presented are, initially, impossible to carry out. She or he likely will despair in recognition of personal powerlessness over emotional reactions to the alcohol and sees, perhaps for the first time, that his or her own life has become unmanageable (Berenson, 1992). With this perspective, efforts directed at connecting the spouse with Al-Anon or Nar-Anon are more likely to be successful. Attending meetings supports the development of detachment and also provides an alternative emotional support system. Spousal participation in Al-Anon, begun prior to the addict's sobriety, also minimizes the possibility of reactivity and potential sabotage in later recovery, when the addict becomes invested in his or her own Twelve Step program.

If the alcoholic or addict presents voluntarily for treatment and there is some sense of cooperation between the couple, an initial family treatment approach might feature marital behavioral therapy (Noel & McCrady 1993; O'Farrell, 1993a) or network therapy (Galanter, 1993). Here the couple or network members are encouraged to work as a team to facilitate the shift to sobriety, sometimes with the assistance of disulfiram or naltrexone contracts. If the addict subsequently becomes uncooperative or seeks to sabotage therapy, the treatment focus can shift to potentiating the bottoming-out process of the spouse, as described above.

A family intervention also may be appropriate in Phase I if the addict and family have not responded to previous treatment or if the addictive problem is creating immediate physical or financial danger for the addict or others. When talking to the family about whether to proceed with such an approach, we use an analogy to surgery for peptic ulcers: ulcers generally are managed with conservative medical treatment, but sometimes an operation is required in an emergency or when previous treatment has been ineffective. As with surgery, informed consent is important. Family members need to be told that sometimes a dramatic breakthrough results, but that in other cases the intervention leaves a residual sense of bitterness and betrayal. Requiring key family members to attend Al-Anon as a prerequisite to planning the intervention helps to prevent their seeing the intervention and subsequent residential treatment as a "magic bullet" that can "fix" the alcoholic without touching their own lives.

Phase II Treatment. The line of demarcation between Phase I and Phase II is not clear cut. As the drug or alcohol use subsides and some level of differentiation between the spouses occurs, it is valuable to begin to broaden the focus from an individual to a family perspective. If the addict and spouse have been pursuing individual approaches, they can be advised to continue in their recovery programs and also encouraged to begin looking at the dysfunctional relationship patterns and negative self-perceptions that developed in their families of origin.

With regard to marital issues, couples at this point continue to experience considerable anxiety and estrangement and may feel they are in an "emotional desert" (Steinglass, Bennett et al., 1987). Early sobriety is extremely destabilizing to the family whose members are not quite sure how to act or what to do. Tensions are high as the spouses attempt to relate to each other without their familiar but painful pattern. We compare the early stages of sobriety for couples to the first few weeks after a cast is removed from a broken bone. Even though the fracture is mended, it must be treated with care and cannot be expected to withstand the strain of running a marathon. In much the same way, the newfound sobriety is still tentative and rather fragile at this point. Both spouses are getting their footing and are not yet ready to delve into the most difficult and heavily charged areas of their marriage. AA's mottos, "Easy Does It" and "First Things First," are especially pertinent at this point. We encourage the couple to concentrate first on their roles as parents and to learn to work effectively as a team. This refocusing of attention can help the couple regain their sense of trust in each other and lay the groundwork for therapy on marital issues in Phase III.

Family of Origin Treatment in Phase II: The bulk of treatment that addresses family of origin work in Phase II is found in the recovery movement. Adult Child of Alcoholics (ACOA) work is structured to help adults who grew up with alcoholic parents to reconstruct and make sense of their pasts, which often were chaotic and damaging. The emphasis is on healing and becoming aware of patterns of relating that may have been functional in a crisis-based family but do not translate well to the outside adult world. This work typically is done in a Twelve Step group, but also can be done in psychotherapy (Cermak, 1990) or alone with workbooks and workshops (Cermak, 1989; Marlin, 1987; Woititz, 1983; Black, 1982). Spouses sometimes start ACOA work before the onset of sobriety. However, we recommend that alcoholics or addicts themselves not embark upon ACOA work until they have been sober for at least one year. It may then be beneficial for them to start by substituting an ACOA meeting for one AA or NA meeting each week.

Inner child work is another way to address painful childhood memories that have carried over into adulthood. Typically, the patient is helped through guided meditation to reconnect with his or her "inner child" and taught to nurture and heal that child. Although this work is most often done with a therapist or workshop leader, some patients can do this work on their own with the help of various books (Whitfield, 1987, 1990; Bradshaw, 1990). In making a therapy referral for inner child work, physicians should seek a therapist who understands the importance of having the patient, in meditation, remain an adult when interacting with his child, rather than regressing to become the child. Regression actually can reinforce the sense of woundedness and undermine or prolong treatment. Optimally, the bulk of ACOA and inner child work is completed within a year.

Some patients find Family Reconstruction retreats a cathartic way of healing the wounds acquired in childhood. Such retreats allow them to begin to understand the functioning of their families of origin. Wegscheider-Cruse designed the format for participants, often from families with alcoholism, to come together and, with the help of family sculpting and other experiential exercises, to recreate and let go of painful childhood memories.

Family coaching, perhaps the most elegant family of origin treatment, is yet another way to address these issues. Coaching, developed by Bowen, is particularly appropriate for people who wish to alter multigenerational family patterns with the help of a therapist, but in an individual rather than conjoint therapy setting (Bowen, 1978; Carter & McGoldrick-Orfanidis, 1976). The family coach attempts to give the patient an overview of the family field and an understanding of how his or her own actions and reactions serve to perpetuate undesirable cycles of interactions. Much as a football coach sends the quarterback into the game with specific plays, the family coach recommends specific behaviors for the patient to shift the entrenched triangular patterns. Although Bowen's model is used to intervene in the family of origin, the extended family (including the family of procreation) often improves as a result.

The genogram, or family map, is a useful tool for charting multigenerational patterns. Basically, a genogram presents a diagram of at least three generations of a family. It transmits a substantial amount of information about that particular family at a glance. When used with families with addictive disorders, genograms can help them to see how particular problems (divorce, physical abuse, addiction) tend to "run in families." This information, when presented in such a graphic and concrete way, can help the patient to validate past experience, clarify present problems, and open up to the possibilities of change (Marlin, 1987).

At present, there are no well-established behavioral approaches to addressing family of origin issues. However, Eye Movement Desensitization and Reprocessing, developed by Shapiro (1989), is a promising cognitive-behavioral method that could be used to relieve the unresolved traumas patients are carrying from their childhood.

Family of Procreation Treatment in Phase II: Addressing the marital relationship in Phase II can present a dilemma for the clinician, who may be as prone to the "walking on eggs" state as the couple. If the therapist focuses too much on relational issues or fails to address them at all, relapse may result. Both family systems and behavioral marital therapists have addressed the challenge of working with couples during this phase (O'Farrell, 1993c; McCrady, 1993; Treadway, 1989; Bepko & Krestan, 1985). The family therapists tend to focus on the rebalancing of family roles that comes with sobriety, while the behavioral marital therapists tend to focus more on integrating relapse prevention (Marlatt &

Gordon, 1985) into a couples context. Either way, the emphasis is on staying away from the full intensity of the marital issues and directing attention to the establishment of communications skills and the sharing of executive roles and responsibilities.

We find the structural family therapy distinction (Minuchin, 1974, 1992) between the parental and spousal subsystems to be a useful guide during this phase of treatment. We tell couples directly that their relationship as husband and wife likely will be the last to improve but, in the interim, they can learn to function more effectively as parents and as a team around issues such as finances.

Another way to approach family of procreation work in Phase II is through the establishment, or reestablishment, of family rituals and celebrations. Wolin and colleagues (1980) found suggestive evidence that, when alcoholic drinking leads to the disruption or discontinuation of family rituals, such as dinnertime, birthday parties and Christmas celebrations, the likelihood of alcoholism appearing in the next generation increases. The establishment of more functional and satisfying rituals gives family members a greater sense of connectedness to each other, provides ways to heal the woundedness, lessens the possibility of relapse, and may decrease the likelihood of addiction in the next generation. If patients would like to explore how to work with family rituals, they can be referred to books by Imber-Black and Roberts (1993) and Wolin and Wolin (1993), or to conjoint family therapy.

Phase III Treatment. Not all couples reach Phase III. Some find that their relationship spontaneously improves without therapy. Some ultimately are divorced. Others resign themselves to a somewhat distant relationship, preferring it to the chaos that existed during the active drug or alcohol abuse. However, a fairly large number of couples want to achieve more intimacy but are not sure how to go about it. Frequently, such couples are dealing with residual anger and distrust left over from the years of drinking or drug taking, which make it difficult for them to interact in a loving and friendly manner. And, even though participation in Twelve Step programs may have helped the couple substantially as individuals, they most likely have not been helped much in resolving their marital difficulties. In fact, we have noticed that ongoing, excessive attendance at Twelve Step meetings years into sobriety sometimes is used as a weapon against the spouse, in much the same way that the drinking or drug abuse was. In such cases, we may speak directly to the issue by recommending that the couple cut back on meetings and begin to spend more time doing things together.

Our sense is that two years of sobriety is the minimum time before a referral for Phase III treatment is appropriate. That length of time allows the personal and relational healing of Phase II to occur and also demonstrates a couple's commitment to each other. The maximum time is indefinite. Particularly since Phase III treatment is just now developing, there may be couples with five or 10 years' sobriety who may benefit from a referral for this work.

The marital relationship can be strengthened through self-help books, workshops and couples therapy. Hendrix (1990) developed a book and workshop for couples aimed at recreating the warmth and excitement of their early days together. Tannen's (1990) book can be used by couples to understand the differences in men's and women's styles of communication. And some of the ideas from Stuart's (1980) book, in particular his section on caring days, can be used by couples, even though the material is intended for professionals.

If couples are interested in professional guidance, they may be referred to marital therapy that focuses on issues of anger and intimacy. The couple in post-sobriety often needs help in learning how to productively express anger toward each other. We have observed that the direct expression of these unacknowledged feelings can help rekindle the passion and intensity that were present in the relationship during the active drug stage, without the negative or destructive consequences. Previously, angry exchanges were allowed only during periods of intoxication. Then, "no holds were barred," and the anger that may have been present at the start of the exchange quickly deteriorated into blame or resentment that left neither party feeling adequately heard or complete with the experience. When couples can master the ability to own their anger and express it appropriately, their sense of intimacy simultaneously increases. At this point, they may be ready to address and resolve long-term sexual problems.

In a recent review of the literature, O'Farrell (1990) found that, for male alcoholics, sexual dysfunction or dissatisfaction is a significant problem for couples, both before and for at least two years following alcohol treatment. At present, there are no long-term research studies that examine sexual satisfaction for couples in later stages of recovery, but our clinical impression is consistent with O'Farrell's speculation that the sexual relationship is the last area to improve for couples with addictive problems.

Thus, once the emotional climate has improved, a referral for sex therapy may be indicated in Phase III.

THE NEED FOR RESEARCH

In a review of family-involved alcoholism treatment, McCrady (1989) commented on the paucity of well-controlled research in this area and pointed out that available studies evaluate marital rather than family therapy. She concluded that studies "consistently find a small but positive benefit from family involvement in alcoholism treatment" and that "a specific focus on the marital relationship appears to have an incremental benefit beyond education of the spouse about coping with alcoholism" (McCrady, 1989).

The few controlled studies to date largely investigate behavioral approaches. There is empirical evidence for the effectiveness of unilateral family therapy and the PACT and CALM programs (O'Farrell, 1993b). O'Farrell further underlined the craft-scientific split that exists within family treatment approaches to addiction: "The most popular, most influential, and most frequently used methods—family systems and disease model approaches—have relatively weak research support for their effectiveness. Conversely, methods that have the strongest research support for their effectiveness—various BMT methods—enjoy little popularity and are used infrequently, if at all" (O'Farrell, 1993c).

REFERENCES

Al-Anon (1985). *Al-Anon Faces Alcoholism, 2nd Ed.* New York, NY: Al-Anon Family Groups.

Beattie M (1987). *Codependent No More.* San Francisco, CA: Harper/Hazelden.

Bepko C & Krestan JA (1985). *The Responsibility Trap: A Blueprint for Treating the Alcoholic Family.* New York, NY: The Free Press.

Berenson D (1976). Alcohol and the family system. In P Guerin (ed.) *Family Therapy: Theory and Practice.* New York, NY: Gardner Press, 284–297.

Berenson D (1991). Powerlessness, liberating or enslaving?: Responding to the feminist critique of the Twelve Steps. In C Bepko (ed.) *Feminism and Addiction.* Binghamton, NY: The Haworth Press, 67–84.

Berenson D (1992). The therapist's relationship with couples with an alcoholic member. In E Kaufman & P Kaufmann (eds.) *Family Therapy of Drug and Alcohol Abuse.* Boston, MA: Allyn & Bacon, 224–235.

Black C (1982). *It Will Never Happen To Me.* Denver, CO: MAC Publishing.

Bowen M (1978). *Family Therapy in Clinical Practice.* New York, NY: Jason Aronson.

Bradshaw J (1990). *Homecoming: Reclaiming and Championing Your Inner Child.* New York, NY: Bantam Books.

Carter E & McGoldrick-Orfanidis M (1976). Family therapy with one person and the family therapist's own family. In P Guerin (ed.) *Family Therapy: Theory and Practice.* New York, NY: Gardner Press, 193–219.

Cermak TL (1989). *A Time to Heal: The Road to Recovery for Adult Children of Alcoholics.* New York, NY: Avon Books.

Cermak TL (1990). *Evaluating and Treating Adult Children of Alcoholics.* Minneapolis, MN: The Johnson Institute.

Davis DI, Berenson D, Steinglass P & Davis S (1974). The adaptive consequence of drinking. *Psychiatry* 37:209–215.

Fogarty T (1976). Marital crisis. In P Guerin (ed.) *Family Therapy: Theory and Practice.* New York, NY: Gardner Press.

Fossum MA & Mason MJ (1986). *Facing Shame.* New York, NY: W.W. Norton & Co.

Galanter M (1993). *Network Therapy for Alcohol and Drug Abuse.* New York, NY: Basic Books.

Hendrix H (1990). *Getting the Love You Want: A Guide for Couples.* New York, NY: Harper Perennial.

Imber-Black E & Roberts J (1993). *Rituals for Our Times.* New York, NY: Harper Perennial.

Johnson Institute (1987). *How to Use Intervention in Your Professional Practice.* Minneapolis, MN: The Institute Books.

Kalb M & Propper MS (1976). The future of alcohology: Craft or science? *American Journal of Psychiatry* 133:641–645.

Kaufman E (1992). The application of the basic principles of family therapy to the treatment of drug and alcohol abusers. In E Kaufman & P Kaufmann (eds.) *Family Therapy of Drug and Alcohol Abuse, 2nd Ed.* Boston, MA: Allyn & Bacon, 287–314.

Kellerman JL (1969). *A Merry-Go-Round Named Denial.* Al-Anon Pamphlet.

Laundergan JC & Williams T (1993). The Hazelden residential family program: A combined systems and disease model approach. In TJ O'Farrell (ed.) *Treating Alcohol Problems: Marital and Family Interventions.* New York, NY: Guilford Press, 145–169.

Liddle H, Dakoff G & Diamond G (1992). Adolescent substance abuse: Multidimensional family therapy in action. In E Kaufman & P Kaufmann (eds.) *Family Therapy of Drug and Alcohol Abuse, 2nd Ed.* Boston, MA: Allyn & Bacon, 120–171.

Marlatt GA & Gordon JR (1985). *Relapse Prevention: Maintenance Strategies in the Treatment of Addictive Behaviors.* New York, NY: Guilford Press.

Marlin E (1987). *Hope: New Choices and Recovery Strategies for Adult Children of Alcoholics.* New York, NY: Harper & Row.

McCrady BS (1989). Outcomes of family-involved alcoholism treatment. In M Galanter (ed.) *Recent Developments in Alcoholism.* New York, NY: Plenum Press, 165–181.

McCrady BS (1992). Behavioral treatment of the alcoholic marriage. In E Kaufman & P Kaufmann (eds.) *Family Therapy of Drug and Alcohol Abuse, 2nd Ed.* Boston, MA: Allyn & Bacon, 190–210.

McCrady BS (1993). Relapse prevention: A couples-therapy perspective. In TJ O'Farrell (ed.) *Treating Alcohol Problems: Alcohol and Family Interventions.* New York, NY: Guilford Press, 327–350.

Minuchin S (1974). *Families and Family Therapy.* Cambridge, MA: Harvard University Press.

Minuchin S (1992). Constructing a therapeutic reality. In E Kaufman & P Kaufmann (eds.) *Family Therapy of Drug and Alcohol Abuse, 2nd Ed.* Boston, MA: Allyn & Bacon, 1–14.

Noel NS & McCrady BS (1993). Alcohol-focused spouse involvement with behavioral marital therapy. In TJ O'Farrell (ed.) *Treating Alcoholic Problems: Marital and Family Interventions.* New York, NY: Guilford Press, 210–234.

O'Farrell TJ (1990). Sexual functioning of male alcoholics. In RL Collins, KE Leonard, BA Miller & JS Searles (eds.) *Research and Clinical Perspectives on Alcohol and the Family.* New York, NY: Guilford Press, 244–271.

O'Farrell TJ (1993a). A behavioral marital therapy couples group program for alcoholics and their spouses. In TJ O'Farrell (ed.) *Treating Alcohol Problems: Marital and Family Interventions.* New York, NY: Guilford Press, 170–209.

O'Farrell TJ (1993b). Conclusions and future directions in practice and research on marital and family therapy in alcoholism treatment. In TJ O'Farrell (ed.) *Treating Alcohol Problems: Marital and Family Interventions.* New York, NY: Guilford Press, 403–434.

O'Farrell TJ (1993c). Couples relapse prevention sessions after a behavioral marital therapy couples group program. In TJ O'Farrell (ed.) *Treating Alcohol Problems: Marital and Family Interventions.* New York, NY: Guilford Press, 305–326.

Shapiro F (1989). Eye movement desensitization: A new treatment for post-traumatic disorder. *Journal of Behavior Therapy and Experimental Psychiatry* 20:211–217.

Speck R & Attneave C (1974). *Family Networks.* New York, NY: Basic Books.

Stanton MD & Todd T (1992). Structural-strategic family therapy with drug addicts. In E Kaufman & P Kaufmann (eds.) *Family Therapy of Drug and Alcohol Abuse, 2nd Ed.* Boston, MA: Allyn & Bacon, 46–62.

Steinglass P, Bennett LA, Wolin SJ & Reiss D (1987). *The Alcoholic Family.* New York, NY: Basic Books, Inc.

Stuart R (1980). *Helping Couples Change: A Social Learning Approach to Marital Therapy.* New York, NY: Guilford Press.

Tannen D (1990). *You Just Don't Understand.* New York, NY: William C. Morrow.

Thomas EJ & Ager RD (1993). Unilateral family therapy with spouses of uncooperative alcohol abusers. In TJ O'Farrell (ed.) *Treating Alcohol Problems: Marital and Family Interventions.* New York, NY: Guilford Press, 3–33.

Treadway DC (1989). *Before It's Too Late: Working With Substance Abuse in the Family.* New York, NY: WW Norton & Co.

Wegscheider-Cruse S (1989). *Another Chance: Hope and Health for the Alcoholic Family, 2nd Ed.* Palo Alto, CA: Science and Behavior Books.

Whitfield C (1987). *Healing the Child Within.* Deerfield Beach, FL: Health Communications.

Whitfield C (1990). *A Gift to Myself: A Personal Workbook and Guide to Healing My Child Within.* Deerfield Beach, FL: Health Communications.

Woititz JG (1983). *Adult Children of Alcoholics.* Deerfield Beach, FL: Health Communications, Inc.

Wolin SJ, Bennett LA, Noonan DL & Teitelbaum MA (1980). Disruptive family rituals: A factor in the intergenerational transmission of alcoholism. *Journal of Studies on Alcohol* 41:199–214.

Wolin SJ & Wolin S (1993). *The Resilient Self: How Survivors of Troubled Families Rise Above Adversity.* New York, NY: Villard Books.

SECTION 15

Alcohol and Drug Use in Children and Adolescents

CHAPTER 1

Screening for Substance Abuse in Children and Adolescents **1129**
Robert M. Cavanaugh, M.D., FAAP, Michelle Pickett, M.D., FAAP, and Peter D. Rogers, M.D., M.P.H., FAAP, FASAM

CHAPTER 2

Office Assessment and Brief Intervention with the Adolescent Suspected of Substance Abuse **1145**
George D. Comerci, M.D., FAAP

CHAPTER 3

Assessment of the Identified Substance-Abusing Adolescent **1153**
Susan Speraw, Ph.D., R.N. and Peter D. Rogers, M.D., M.P.H., FAAP, FASAM

CHAPTER 4

Adolescent Substance Abuse and Psychiatric Comorbidity **1161**
Marie E. Armentano, M.D.

SECTION COORDINATOR

PETER ROGERS, M.D., M.P.H., FAAP, FASAM

Associate Professor of Pediatrics
University of Tennessee College of Medicine, and
Director, Adolescent/Young Adult Medicine
T.C. Thompson Children's Hospital
Chattanooga, Tennessee

CONTRIBUTORS

Marie E. Armentano, M.D.
Child and Adolescent Psychiatry
and Addiction Services
Massachusetts General Hospital
Boston, Massachusetts

Robert M. Cavanaugh, Jr., M.D., FAAP
Associate Professor of Pediatrics and
Director, Adolescent Medicine
Department of Pediatrics
State University of New York
Health Science Center
Syracuse, New York

George D. Comerci, M.D., FAAP
Adolescent Medicine
Tucson, Arizona

Michelle Pickett, M.D., FAAP
Assistant Professor
Department of Pediatrics
University of Tennessee
College of Medicine
Chattanooga, Tennessee

Susan Speraw, Ph.D., R.N.
Associate Professor of Pediatrics
University of Tennessee
College of Medicine and
Director, Division of Behavioral Pediatrics
T.C. Thompson Children's Hospital
Chattanooga, Tennessee

CHAPTER 1

Screening for Substance Abuse in Children and Adolescents

Robert M. Cavanaugh, M.D., FAAP
Michelle Pickett, M.D., FAAP
Peter D. Rogers, M.D., M.P.H., FAAP, FASAM

Epidemiology of Adolescent Substance Abuse
Screening for Risk Factors and Substance Abuse

Screening for substance abuse in the pediatric population should begin at the prenatal visit and extend through adolescence (Fuller & Cavanaugh, 1995). *In utero* exposure to alcohol or other drugs may be teratogenic for the fetus and may be associated with an adverse pregnancy outcome (Bell & Lau, 1995). Neonates may suffer from symptoms of withdrawal, and long-term neurobehavioral problems may be seen in infants born to substance-abusing mothers (Bell & Lau, 1995). Failure to thrive, developmental delay, or poor compliance with medical recommendations during infancy may indicate exposure to a chaotic environment associated with drug abuse (Fuller & Cavanaugh, 1995). Similarly, such exposure during the toddler and preschool years may present as behavior problems, accidents, poisonings, child abuse or neglect, etc. (Fuller & Cavanaugh, 1995). Numerous manifestations of direct use, as well as of exposure to substance abusing individuals, have been described in older children and adolescents.

Clinicians should have a high index of suspicion, as the signs and symptoms of substance abuse often are subtle and easily confused with those of other physical or mental illnesses. As part of the routine medical history of every infant, child, or adolescent, it is important to inquire about exposure to any family members or friends who may have a problem with alcohol or other drugs. It also is essential to ask about conflict or fighting in the home, disruptions in the family environment, or abusive behavior. Such questions are just as basic as taking a review of systems or performing other elements of the traditional medical history on all patients within the pediatric age group.

EPIDEMIOLOGY OF ADOLESCENT SUBSTANCE ABUSE

The battery of chemicals that can be used to create an alteration in mood is extensive and adolescents have found access to all of them. Adolescent drug use includes the use of illegal substances such as marijuana, hallucinogens, cocaine, methamphetamines, and heroin. It also includes prescription drugs such as stimulants, tranquilizers and barbiturates. Other substances used and abused frequently by teenagers are legal for adults but illegal for children: alcohol and tobacco. Finally, some adolescents inhale the chemicals available in household products to produce a "high."

Abuse of alcohol, tobacco and other drugs has been well identified among American teenagers for at least two decades. Many efforts have been made to deter drug use since then and, until the beginning of this decade, there were indications that illicit drug use was declining. However, the 1990s have seen rising rates of drug use among students as young as the 8th grade. In 1975, researchers at the University of Michigan began an annual survey of substance abuse among high school seniors in the United States, the Monitoring the Future Survey (MFS). This work affords us the opportunity to observe the trends in adolescent substance use and abuse over a 22 year span. From its inception, the survey has included approximately 50,000 students in the 8th, 10th, and 12th grades at 424 public and private schools nationwide.

The Centers for Disease Control and Prevention (CDC) has administered the Youth Risk Behavior Survey nationwide in 1990, 1991, 1993 and 1995.

This survey includes questions on substance abuse. In 1995, the CDC survey distributed questionnaires in 110 schools; 10,904 questionnaires were completed, for a response rate of 60%.

Alcohol. Rates of alcohol use actually have remained stable, according to MFS data; however, the prevalence rates are disturbingly high despite the recent plateau (Johnston, 1996). Astounding proportions of high school students reported having been drunk in the 30 days prior to the survey, as well as binge drinking (five or more drinks in a row) within the preceding two weeks. Daily use, although not as high, is still of concern, as 3.7% of 12th graders report daily use and 1.6% report daily drunkenness. Again, the CDC data are comparable: almost one-third (32.69%) of students nationwide reported that they had five or more drinks on one occasion in the 30 days preceding the survey (CDC, 1996).

Illicit Drugs. Since 1991, there has been a gradual increase in the annual prevalence (use in the past 12 months) of illicit drug use. Even though there is an increase in the proportion of 10th and 12th graders using illicit drugs, the remarkable fact is that the greatest increase has been among the youngest teenagers surveyed, the 8th grade students. From 1991 to 1996, the use of any illicit drug more than doubled in the 8th-grade population, going from 11% to 24%. The increase in 10th and 12th graders is seen beginning in 1992.

Marijuana: By all measures, marijuana use has increased in all grades studied, accounting for much of the overall increase in the use of any illicit drug. Historically, marijuana use in teenagers peaked in the 1970s. In 1978, half of all seniors admitted to use in the preceding 12 months. This rate declined in the 1980s, reaching a low point of 22% in 1992. Since that time, however, there has been a strong resurgence in marijuana use.

In 1996, 23% of American 8th grade students had used marijuana in their lifetimes, more than double the percentage of 8th-grade lifetime users in 1991. The annual prevalence also increased among 10th and 12th graders, although not as dramatically. However, the rate of use remained very high: 40% and 45% of 10th and 12th graders, respectively, admitted to lifetime use.

Nationwide, 4.9% of seniors reported daily marijuana use, as did 3.5% of 10th graders and 1.5% of 8th graders. By comparison, the rate of marijuana use among 8th graders seems small, yet it represents an almost two-fold increase in 1996. Twenty percent of 10th and 22% of 12th grade students reported using marijuana in the preceding 30 days, as did 11% of 8th grade students.

LSD: Long-term increases in LSD use among students in all three grades since 1991 continued in 1996, with annual prevalence rates of 4%, 7% and 9% for 8th, 10th, and 12th grade students, respectively. Statistically significant declines in use in the past 30 days occurred from 1995 to 1996 among the 10th and 12th grade students (3% to 2.4% and 4% to 2.5%, respectively). This may represent a trend of decreasing use of LSD, since 30-day prevalence rates tend to be more sensitive to recent change.

Cocaine: The use of cocaine in any form rose slowly but significantly from 1991 to 1996. Annual prevalence rates were 3%, 4% and 5% in 8th, 10th, and 12th grades, respectively, in 1996. Many of the increases from 1995 to 1996 were not statistically significant. The use of crack cocaine followed the same trend, with rates of use in the past 12 months at 2% for each grade level.

Amphetamines: A long-term gradual increase in the use of amphetamines by 8th and 10th grade students continued in 1996, but leveled off in 12th graders in 1995 at 19%. Annual prevalence rates are 9%, 12%, and 10% for 8th, 10th, and 12th grade students, respectively, in 1996. Increases in the use of two forms of amphetamine were noted in 1995 and 1996: (1) a form of methamphetamine known as crystal meth or "ice" is burned in rock form and inhaled. Only 12th grade students were questioned about the use of this drug: 1.3% reported use in 1995, which more than doubled to 2.8% in 1996. MDMA, known as ecstasy, is the second amphetamine thought to be rising in use: in 1996, 5% of 10th and 12th grade students reported use in the preceding year, as did 2% of 8th graders.

Heroin: Increases in heroin use via noninjection routes are thought to account for recent increases in the rates of heroin use. Annual prevalence in 1996 was 1.6%, 1.2%, and 1% in 8th, 10th, and 12th graders, respectively. This represents almost a doubling of the rate of use in 8th graders since 1991.

Inhalants: The use of inhalants, a popular substance of abuse for younger teens, appears to have leveled off from 1995 to 1996 after five years of increase. Annual prevalence was 12.2%, 9.5% and 8% for 8th, 10th, and 12 graders in 1996.

Cigarettes. A brief overview of cigarette smoking is in order because nicotine has been deemed an addictive substance, yet the rate of use in the adolescent population continues to increase. According to the Monitoring the Future Survey, cigarette smoking has increased each year from 1991 to 1996 among students in the 8th, 10th, and 12th grades (Johnston, 1996). The CDC's Youth Risk Behavior Survey indicates similar rates of use (CDC, 1996). Over one-third (34.8%) of students nationwide admitted to smoking cigarettes on one or more occasions in the 30 days preceding the survey (CDC, 1996).

Attitudes and Beliefs. The researchers at the University of Michigan have included in their survey several questions that probe teenagers' attitudes and beliefs about the perceived dangers of specific substances and their degree of approval or disapproval of certain types of drug use. The Michigan researchers assert that there is a correlation between beliefs and rates of use: that is, when drugs are considered to be more dangerous or more strongly disapproved by peers, they are less likely to be used (Johnston, 1996). For example, a decrease in the perceived harmfulness and disapproval of marijuana use among 12th graders thus coincides with an increase in use since 1991. The same trend is seen for cocaine and LSD.

SCREENING FOR RISK FACTORS AND SUBSTANCE ABUSE

Cohen has refined a method for organizing the adolescent patient's history, psychosocial and medical information, which was developed by Berman in 1972 (Goldenring & Cohen, 1988). This system has been expanded and modified at the SUNY Health Science Center Adolescent Medicine Program at Syracuse. The questions are structured in an easily remembered format that stresses the importance of connecting with adolescents "HEADS FIRST," as outlined in Table 1. This approach also emphasizes that "getting into the adolescent's head" is just as necessary as performing a physical examination.

The issues outlined in Table 1 can be addressed with the traditional verbal approach, using the cue words illustrated, or by having the patient complete a self-administered personal questionnaire (see Appendices 1 and 2). The questionnaire is designed so that any responses circled in the left hand column immediately draw the physician's attention to items requiring further emphasis during preventive health counseling. With either method, the questions should be answered privately and reviewed confidentially with the examiner, unless the patient specifically requests otherwise. Most parents respect their adolescent child's need for privacy and appreciate the opportunity for them to receive one-on-one counseling with an experienced health professional.

TABLE 1. The "HEADS FIRST" Approach to Psychosocial-Medical Issues of Adolescence

Home	Separation, support, "space to grow"
Education	Expectations, study habits, achievement
Abuse	Emotional, verbal, physical, sexual
Drugs	Tobacco, alcohol, marijuana, others
Safety	Hazardous activities, seatbelts, helmets
Friends	Confident, peer pressure, interaction
Image	Self-esteem, looks, appearance
Recreation	Exercise, relaxation, TV, video games
Sexuality	Changes, feelings, experiences, identity
Threats	Harm to self or others, running away

Recent studies have shown that the items listed in Table 1 are priorities for routine adolescent health care from the point of view of both parents and adolescents (Cavanaugh, Hastings-Tolsma et al., 1993; Malus, LaChance et al., 1987). In addition, the Guidelines for Health Supervision of the American Academy of Pediatrics (Committee on Psychosocial Aspects of Child and Family Health, 1988) and the Guidelines for Adolescent Preventive Services of the American Medical Association (1994) strongly endorse a comprehensive approach to adolescent health care. A thoughtful review of these common concerns stimulates open discussions and instills among youth a feeling of security about having a medical "home." Failure to address these topics may raise unnecessary barriers and provoke a sense of eviction from the health-care system. Teenagers who expect to find help in the practitioner's office must not feel abandoned at a time when their needs for comprehensive services are greatest (Cavanaugh, 1994).

Having an organized approach for data collection and information dissemination to adolescent and young adult patients facilitates anticipatory guidance within the practice setting. For example, hobbies, interests, and career goals might be covered first to help the patient understand that the physician is interested in him or her as a whole person, as well as to serve as a buffer for more personal questions. Exercise, sports participation, and other forms of recreation then can be discussed. Activity-specific safety precautions, such as the use of bicycle helmets and swimming with a partner, are reviewed as indicated. Only then are more sensitive issues addressed.

Home. Problems at home are a leading source of stress and anxiety among adolescents (Cavanaugh & Henneberger, 1996). It is important to determine if they are receiving adequate support as they go through the separation process in an attempt to develop their own identity, autonomy, and independence. Screening for conflict, fighting, abusive behavior, or other problems at home provides valuable insight into family functioning and stability (Cavanaugh & Henneberger, 1996). It also should be determined whether the adolescent is being given adequate privacy and freedom, as well as appropriate responsibility. Asking the patient if he or she ever has thought about running away may provide additional clues to underlying concerns that should be addressed.

Adolescents frequently worry about their parents' marital relationship, as well as the physical and mental health of family members (Cavanaugh & Henneberger, 1996). The fact that more than 20% of boys and girls in a recent study believed that a family member had a problem with alcohol or other drugs is particularly noteworthy (Cavanaugh & Henneberger, 1996). In many instances, however, it is difficult for teenagers to verbalize these concerns directly (Rogers, Speraw & Ozbek, 1995; Cuda, Rupp & Dillon, 1993). Such feelings often are internalized and may be expressed through subtle symptoms and vague somatic complaints (Cuda, Rupp & Dillon, 1993; Zarek, Hawkins & Rogers, 1987). Repressed memories with delayed manifestations in adulthood also may occur (Zarek, Hawkins & Rogers, 1987). Practitioners must be willing to initiate discussions of family health issues in an effort to help reduce the emotional burdens of these young patients.

Teens who are unable to cope with family problems may attempt to compensate by using alcohol and other drugs, or they may act out sexually and risk an unintended pregnancy or acquisition of a sexually transmitted disease. They may have low self-esteem and develop unhealthy behaviors in an attempt to improve their image. They also may exercise poor safety habits and place themselves and others at risk for serious injury or death in motor vehicle crashes, etc. Such adolescents may express feelings of sadness, suicidal ideation, or thoughts of self harm. These areas should be explored as part of routine adolescent health care.

Education. School-related difficulties are another important source of distress and discomfort for adolescent patients (Cavanaugh, 1994). Manifestations may be subtle, seemingly unrelated to the educational situation, and sometimes not apparent. Thus, it is important to screen adolescents for problems at school on a regular basis. Patients should be asked if they like school or if they are having any difficulty with their classes. It is very helpful to determine if their performance meets with others' expectations and approval. In many instances, their achievements may not reach a level that they, their parents, or their teachers expected. This can be a source of considerable anxiety and tension, particularly in high achievers and/or teens who have been subjected to unrealistic expectations.

From a medical perspective, it is important to determine if the patient may have a health condition that is interfering with learning. Disorders such as hypothyroidism, depression, neurological abnormalities, decreased visual acuity, impaired hearing, etc., may contribute to poor school performance (Neinstein, 1991). Significantly, learning disabilities, attention deficit disorder, and borderline intellectual functioning often are overlooked (Neinstein, 1991). Lack of sleep, boredom, preoccupation with other thoughts, problems with teachers and other forms of difficulty in concentrating also should be considered. Study habits are another area of concern, particularly if television, video games, or computer programs are allowed to intrude.

It also is important to determine the reasons for any absences from school, which may adversely affect academic progress. Severe, prolonged, or chronic illness may result in many days lost. School phobia, avoidance, or aversion should be considered in cases of unexplained absences (Neinstein, 1991). A pattern of cutting classes, skipping school, or excessive tardiness should alert the clinician that the teenager may have an underlying problem with substance abuse (Johnston, 1996). On the other hand, adolescents who are having problems at school may turn to alcohol or other drugs as a coping mechanism. Once again, other important preventive health issues of adolescence such as safety, sexual activity, self-esteem, and suicidal ideation are closely interconnected with school issues and should be screened simultaneously.

Abuse. The importance of incorporating discussions of emotional, physical and sexual abuse into the standard health care assessment of adolescents deserves emphasis. This topic is addressed on the personal questionnaires (Appendices 1 and 2) used in the Adolescent Medicine Program at the SUNY Health Science Center, Syracuse, as follows: "Has anyone ever abused you by their actions or their words? If yes, please check all forms of abuse that apply: physical. . . . sexual. . . . emotional. . . . verbal. . . . other. . . ." In a recent study at SUNY, more than 40% of the adolescents interviewed reported that they had been abused or mistreated in some way (Cavanaugh & Henneberger, 1996). However, none of the patients presented with this complaint or volunteered this information spontaneously. Similar results were found in a study the authors conducted on first-year university students who were undergoing physical examination as a requirement of sports participation (Cavanaugh, Miller & Henneberger, 1994). Although the athletes completed the questionnaire during a relatively impersonal multistation mass screening examination, nearly a third still disclosed that they had been abused or mistreated in some way (Cavanaugh, Miller & Henneberger, 1994). These concerns would not have been identified using the forms currently recommended for the sports physical, which often is the only medical assessment that older adolescents receive (Smith, Kovan et al., 1997).

The above results reinforce the importance of routinely screening adolescents for abuse, as recently recommended by the American Medical Association (Elster & Kuznets, 1994). Although teenagers account for nearly half of all reported cases of child abuse, it is unusual for them to present with this complaint or to volunteer this information spontaneously, particularly in a multistation environment (Rosen, Xiangdong & Blum, 1990). While there may be no ability to objectively verify reported incidents, adolescents' perceptions of such traumatic experiences must be identified and addressed as soon as possible in an effort to prevent ongoing distress or injury (Cavanaugh, Miller & Henneberger, in press). Reliance on a high level of suspicion, as traditionally practiced, may delay diagnosis and postpone appropriate intervention.

The disclosure of sexual abuse by 18% of the girls in the authors' study (Cavanaugh & Henneberger, 1996) and 12% of the first-year female university students during the sports physical exams merits further consideration (Cavanaugh, Miller & Henneberger, 1994). The short-term consequences and long-term sequelae for victims of such acts are known to be severe (Berkowitz, 1992; Pokorny, 1992). The perpetrator frequently is a close family member or other person well known to the adolescent (Berkowitz, 1992). Malus and colleagues found that sexual abuse is a priority in health care from the adolescent's point of view (Malus, LaChance et al., 1987). This topic also ranks very high on the parents' agenda for routine adolescent health care, along with physical, emotional and verbal abuse (Cavanaugh, Hastings-Tolsma et al., 1993). In many instances, however, adolescents are too shy, embarrassed, or frightened to raise such issues and hope that the examiner will introduce them (Malus, LaChance et al., 1987; Cavanaugh, 1994, 1986). Thus, it is important for physicians to include a discussion of sexual abuse as part of routine preventive health counseling for teenagers and young adults.

Adolescents who have been abused may resort to alcohol or other drugs in an effort to relieve anxiety, reduce stress, or repress reality (Hoffman, Mee-Lee & Arrowood, 1993). Such individuals also frequently have feelings of guilt, low self-esteem, or thoughts of self-harm. This may place them at risk for serious injury or even death from accidental or non-accidental causes. In addition, adolescents who have been abused may pursue intimate relationships and engage in sexual activity as a source of comfort or as a means of coping with their situations. They may seek medical attention for concerns related to pregnancy or sexually transmitted diseases. These suggest numerous portals of entry into the health care system for youth who have been abused. Under such circumstances, treatment of the acute medical problem alone is not sufficient. Follow-up arrangements always should include provisions for ongoing care with a primary care practitioner who can deliver comprehensive services and screen regularly for the issues outlined in Table 1.

Drugs. There are numerous methods for taking a substance abuse history from adolescents in the office setting. Specific suggestions for performing this evaluation are outlined in Chapter 2. The screening questions used in the Adolescent Medicine Program at the SUNY Health Science Center, Syracuse, are included on the personal questionnaires at the end of this chapter (see Appendices 1 and 2). At SUNY, the questionnaire has been expanded to routinely ask about abuse of prescription drugs. In addition, patients who desire to lose weight are questioned about the use of appetite suppressants, emetics, laxatives, or diuretics. A more detailed and structured substance-abuse history is recorded as indicated. Appropriate evaluation and treatment are carefully formulated in accordance with the pattern of use.

Safety. The close association between risk-taking behavior, substance abuse, and other psychosocial-medical issues of adolescence merits special consideration (Fuller & Cavanaugh, 1995). The three leading causes of mortality among teenagers in the United States are accidents, suicide, and homicide. Each year, there are approximately 15,000 to 18,000 deaths from automobile-related injuries and 5,000 suicides among adolescents (Kempe, Silver et al., 1987; National Center for Health Statistics, 1986). Alcohol and other psychoactive drugs are factors in many of these fatalities (National Center for Health Statistics, 1986). Many of the 6,000 adolescent homicides also are committed when one or both parties are intoxicated (Christoffel, 1990).

It has been shown that many young adults have a distorted perception of alcohol-related driving risk and often underestimate the negative influence of alcohol use on driving skills (Geuna, Ravazzani & Perassi, 1995). In a recent survey of 138 first-year student athletes in a university setting, 24% of the participants reported that they had driven a motor vehicle after drinking or using drugs (Cavanaugh, Miller & Henneberger, 1994). In the same study, 43% of the students had been a passenger when the driver was drunk or "high." These findings illustrate the importance of including discussions of drugs, drinking, and driving as part of routine adolescent health care. Current standards for sports-oriented examinations have not been structured to meet this goal and should not be used as a substitute for the student athlete's routine health assessment, as commonly occurs (Goldberg, Saraniti et al., 1980; Krowchuk, Krowchuk et al., 1995; Risser, Hoffman et al., 1985). The highway safety habits of all adolescents should be ascertained and preventive strategies reinforced, including the use of designated drivers, wearing of seatbelts and avoidance of hitchhiking (Cavanaugh, 1994).

The pattern of exercise, sports participation, and other forms of recreation also should be determined on a regular basis. Most potentially hazardous activities can be readily identified by using a screening instruments such as a personal questionnaire. Activity-specific safety precautions, such as the use of bicycle helmets and swimming with a partner, should be reviewed as indicated (Cavanaugh, 1994). Ue of protective headgear when riding on a motorcycle, all-terrain vehicle, or snowmobile also should be stressed. In addition, the use of wristguards, elbow and knee pads as well as helmets are recommended for activities such as in-line skating and skateboarding (Committee on Injury and Poison Prevention, AAP, 1995). Finally, the frequent occurrence of even minor injuries, although not life-threatening, always should arouse suspicion of substance abuse (Fuller & Cavanaugh, 1995).

Friends. Difficulties with friends are a common source of stress and anxiety among adolescents (Cavanaugh, 1994). In most instances, these problems are self-limiting and do not lead to ongoing distress. However, unresolved conflicts may have serious adverse sequelae, including harm to self or others. Teens may try to cope by sexual acting out in an effort to feel wanted, turning to drugs as a source of comfort, partaking in high-risk activities to be part of the crowd, or by engaging in unhealthy patterns of behavior to enhance or improve their appearance. Thus, it is important to routinely screen adolescents for any problems regarding interaction with friends and responses to peer pressure.

It also is important to ask young adult patients if they have a friend with whom they can talk about anything at all. In general, girls appear more willing to share their innermost concerns with others than are their male counterparts. Nearly all of the young women in a recent study reported having a "friend" with whom they could talk about anything at all, but more than one-fourth of the boys said they had no such confidante (Cavanaugh & Henneberger, 1996). These results suggest that young men may have difficulty discussing their deepest feelings with someone else. The findings provide objective data to support the common belief that girls tend to have better emotional networks than boys. Teenagers who are unwilling or unable to establish such support systems may have difficulty dealing with stress. Clinicians must be able to identify such individuals so that counseling can be offered as indicated and specific referrals initiated when needed.

Image. To many adolescents, image is everything. Substance abuse, sexual acting-out/pregnancy, and other risk-taking behaviors often correlate with low self-esteem and poor body image (Cavanaugh, 1994). It is important to routinely ask young adult patients if they are happy with their looks or appearance. In a study of 854 adolescent girls, 67% were dissatisfied with their weight and 54% were unhappy with their body shape (Moore, 1988). Corresponding values for 895 adolescent boys were 42% and 35% (Moore, 1990). In many instances, teenagers resort to desperate, even dangerous measures in an effort to improve their self-esteem or enhance their image. Attempts at weight reduction often involve self-injurious behaviors such as severe caloric deprivation, excessive exercise, self-induced vomiting, and the use of appetite suppressants, diuretics, laxatives, or emetics (Fisher, Golden et al., 1995). Such problems are prevalent among adolescents and should be screened for regularly.

Participants in sports and other activities in which thinness or "making weight" is judged important to success may be particularly susceptible to unhealthy weight control practices. Such sports include body building, cheerleading, dancing (especially ballet), distance running, diving, figure skating, gymnastics, horse racing, rowing, swimming, weight-class football, and wrestling (Committe on Sports Medicine & Fitness, 1996; Garner, Garfinkel et al., 1987; Drummer, Rosen et al., 1987). As the preoccupation with thinness supersedes a desire to be healthy, physically active young women are at risk for a group of signs and symptoms known as the female athlete triad (Yeager, Agostini et al., 1993). Lack of information and the strong desire to win contribute to this condition, which consists of abnormal eating patterns, amenorrhea, and osteoporosis (Yeager, Agostini et al., 1993). The routine physical examination is an excellent opportunity to screen for body image disorders and to educate patients and parents as to healthy patterns of eating, exercise, and weight control.

At the other extreme, increasing body weight to gain a competitive edge also is a common concern of young athletes (Committee on Sports Medicine and Fitness, 1996; Committee on Sports Medicine, 1983). Adolescents who feel insecure about their bodies are very susceptible to any solicitations that may promise a better body build or improved athletic performance (Strasburger & Brown, 1991). Use of anabolic steroids to improve appearance, as well as to increase muscle size and strength is relatively common, particularly among male athletes. Those who desire greater muscle bulk and definition, such as body builders, or who want more power, such as weight lifters, shot putters, or football players, are at increased risk for using these substances (Strasburger & Brown, 1991). Many of these young athletes are not aware of the potential dangers of anabolic steroids and other performance enhancing drugs. The health maintenance examination affords the clinician an opportunity to provide factual information on this subject, as well as to review healthy practices for gaining weight when appropriate.

Sun exposure is another important concern in the image category. Many teenagers believe that they must have a suntan to feel healthy and look attractive (Cavanaugh, 1994). However, sun damage is cumulative, and blistering sunburns during adolescence have been associated with an increased risk of malignant melanoma in adulthood (Hurwitz, 1989). Additional risk factors for this rapidly increasing and serious form of skin cancer include fair skin and certain common cutaneous disorders including dysplastic nevi and congenital pigmented nevi, as well as rare dermatologic conditions such as xeroderma pigmentosum and the like (Roth & Grant-Kels, 1991). Immunodeficient children may be at increased risk for development of melanoma (Roth & Grant-Kels, 1991). It is, therefore, relevant to inquire about the sun safety habits of adolescent patients on a regular basis, particularly in susceptible individuals. Appropriate counseling can be remembered by recalling the ABCs: **A**void the sun between 10:00 a.m. and 4:00 p.m. whenever possible, **B**lock out burning rays by using a sunscreen with an SPF of 30 or higher, and **C**over-up with clothing, a hat, sunglasses, etc. as needed.

Other common sources of embarrassment to teenagers, such as acne, short or tall stature, pubertal changes, etc., should be addressed as appropriate. Issues of self-esteem are very important to the growing number of youth with disabilities and chronic illnesses. They not only face the same developmental tasks as other teenagers, but also must cope with the stress of their underlying condition. Health care providers are in a unique position to encourage these adolescents to rely on themselves for their sense of worth, rather than on the attitudes and reactions of others.

Recreation. One of the topics most teenagers and parents wish to have addressed as part of routine adolescent health care is exercise. Accordingly, it is helpful to estimate whether the amount and type of activity undertaken are appropriate. Methods of relaxation and amusement can be assessed by simple inquiry. The hours spent watching television each day, as well as time spent with video games or computer shows, can be approximated. Extreme patterns of behavior require further review, with specific recommendations provided as needed. In addition, dramatic changes in activity may be a clue to the presence of a significant underlying medical condition, such as hypothyroidism, or a psychosocial problem such as depression, eating disorder, substance abuse, etc.

Sexuality. The reasons for including discussions on sexuality as part of routine anticipatory guidance for adolescents are urgent and compelling. Each year in the United States, one in 10 adolescent girls becomes pregnant; 84% of these pregnancies are unintended (Alan Guttmacher Institute, 1989). Up to six million cases of sexually transmitted diseases are reported among adolescents annually in this country (Shafer, 1994). In addition, heterosexual transmission of the human immunodeficiency virus (HIV) is quickly becoming the predominant mode of HIV acquisition for teenagers in the United States (McGrath & Strasburger, 1995).

General questions regarding pubertal changes are asked next. Patients are asked if they think they are growing normally and if they have any questions or concerns about their sexual development. Concerns over sexual identity may be uncovered by asking male patients if they feel different from other boys, if they are interested in girls, and if they are more attracted to boys than to girls. Corresponding questions are asked for young women. Clinicians must be able to identify adolescents who are having difficulties coping with their feelings and be willing to assist when necessary.

The teens then should be asked if they have ever had any sexual experiences and, if so, what type of experiences. It is important to know if there has been oral, anal, and/or genital contact so that samples for sexually transmitted disease can be obtained from the appropriate mucosal surfaces. Teens who have been sexually active should have serological testing for syphilis and determination of HIV status, if the patient consents to the latter. Continued abstinence always should be supported for teens who are not sexually active. Information on postponing sexual involvement, contraception, and prevention of sexually transmitted diseases (STDs) should be provided as needed. The latter should stress the consistent, correct use of condoms. In addition, all young adults should be aware of the availability of emergency contraception for cases of sexual assault, isolated sexual encounters, condom leakage/breakage, etc.

The close interrelationship between sexual activity and other psychosocial issues of adolescence such as low self-esteem, depression, problems with friends or family, substance abuse, etc. must be stressed. Adolescents whose judgment is compromised by alcohol or drugs are at considerable risk for unwanted pregnancy and sexually transmitted diseases, including HIV infection (Fuller & Cavanaugh, 1995). In addition, gay and lesbian youth frequently suffer from feelings of guilt, inadequacy, and self-depreciation. Many of these adolescents turn to alcohol or other drugs as a source of comfort or to reduce emotional turmoil (Sturdevant & Remafid, 1992). Although guidelines have been available to identify these teens and deal sensitively with their special needs, few practitioners discuss concerns of sexual identity with these patients. It is time to raise this group of adolescents from the ranks of the medically underserved.

Threats. As stated earlier in this chapter, there are approximately 5,000 adolescent suicides each year in this country (Cohen, 1984). In addition, it has been estimated that there are 50 to 200 attempts for every death (Cohen, 1984). Alcohol or other drugs may serve as a catalyst in many instances (Soderstrom & Dearing-Stuck, 1993). As documented in a recent study, more than half of the adolescents surveyed during a routine screening exam reported that they got depressed or upset easily (Cavanaugh & Henneberger, 1996). Over 40% of the individuals in this sample population reported having had thoughts of running away, and 33% of the respondents thought of inflicting harm on themselves or others. Unresolved conflicts, feelings of sadness, and low self-esteem are often related to family conflicts, strained peer relationships, school difficulties, and work-related problems (Cavanaugh, 1994). It is important to assess functional status at the adolescent visit in an effort to identify not only sources of stress but predominant modes of coping with them (Schubiner & Robin, 1990; Joffe, Radius & Gall, 1988; Smith, Mitchell et al., 1990; Centers for Disease Control, 1989). Patients who are suicidal or homicidal require immediate intervention by mental health experts, legal authorities, or both.

CONCLUSIONS

It is apparent that discussions of substance abuse should be included as part of the routine health care of all infants, children, and adolescents. Practitioners must have a high index of suspicion, as signs and symptoms may be subtle, with numerous manifestations expressed throughout the pediatric age range. The close correlation between the use of alcohol and other drugs with other psychosocial-medical issues deserves emphasis, particularly in adolescents. High-risk individuals must be identified as soon as possible in an effort to minimize morbidity and mortality. This process may be enhanced by using the "HEADS FIRST" format, which can be easily recalled during the verbal interview or readily incorporated into a self-administered personal questionnaire for adolescents. Such strategies are easily adapted to the office setting and augment delivery of services to youth. Clinicians who wish to provide comprehensive care to adolescents must be as committed to meeting the psychosocial needs of these patients as they are to performing the physical examination.

REFERENCES

Alan Guttmacher Institute (1989). *Teenage Pregnancy in the United States: The Scope of the Problem and State Responses.* New York, NY: Author.

Bell GL & Lau K (1995). Perinatal and neonatal issues of substance abuse. *Pediatric Clinics of North America* 42(2):261–281.

Berkowitz C (1992). Child sexual abuse. *Pediatric Review* 13:443–452.

Cavanaugh RM, Miller M & Henneberger PK (1994). The Preparticipation Sports Physical: Are We Dropping the Ball? Presented an the annual meeting of the Ambulatory Pediatric Association, Seattle, WA.

Cavanaugh RM (1986). Obtaining a personal and confidential history from adolescents: An opportunity for prevention. *Journal of Adolescent Health Care* 7:118–22.

Cavanaugh RM, Hastings-Tolsma M, Keenan D et al. (1993). Anticipatory guidance for the adolescent: Parents' concerns. *Clinical Pediatrics* 32:542–545.

Cavanaugh RM, Miller ML & Henneberger PK (in press). The preparticipation athletic examination of adolescents: A missed opportunity? *Current Problems in Pediatrics.*

Cavanaugh RM (1994). Anticipatory guidance for the adolescent: has it come of age? *Pediatrics in Review* 15(12):485–489.

Cavanaugh RM & Henneberger PK (1996). Talking to teens about family problems: An opportunity for prevention. *Clinical Pediatrics* 35:67–71.

Centers for Disease Control (1996). Results from the National Adolescent Student Health Survey. *Morbidity and Mortality Weekly Reports* 38(9):147–150.

Christoffel KK (1990). Violent death and injury in U.S. children and adolescents. *American Journal of Diseases of Childhood* 44:697.

Cohen MI (1984). The Society for Behavioral Pediatrics: A new portal in a rapidly moving boundary. *Pediatrics* 73:791–798.

Committee on Sports Medicine (1983). *Sports Medicine: Health Care for Young Athletes.* Evanston IL: American Academy of Pediatrics, 168.

Committee on Sports Medicine and Fitness (1996). Promotion of healthy weight-control practices in young athletes. *Pediatrics* 97:752–753.

Committee on Psychosocial Aspects of Child and Family Health. (1988). *Guidelines for Health Supervision II.* Elk Grove Village, IL: American Academy of Pediatrics.

Committee on Injury and Poison Prevention, American Academy of Pediatrics (1995). Skateboard injuries. *Pediatrics* 95:611–612.

Cuda S, Rupp R & Dillon C (1993). Adolescent children of alcoholics. *Adolescent Medicine: State of the Art Review* 4:439–452.

Drummer GM, Rosen LW, Heusner WW, Roberts PJ, Counsilman JE (1987). Pathogenic weight-control behaviors of young competitive swimmers. *Physician Sportsmedicine* 15:75–86.

Elster A & Kuznets N (1994). *AMA Guidelines for Adolescent Preventive Services: Recommendations and Rationale.* Baltimore, MD: Williams and Wilkins.

Fisher M, Golden NH, Katzman DK et al. (1995). Eating disorders in adolescents: A background paper. *Journal of Adolescent Health* 16:420–437.

Fuller PG & Cavanaugh RM (1995). Basic assessment and screening for substance abuse in the pediatrician's office. *Pediatric Clinics of North America* 42(2):295–315.

Garner DM, Garfinkel PE, Rockert W & Olmsted MP (1987). A prospective study of eating disturbances in the ballet. *Psychotherapeutics and Psychosomatics* 148:170–175.

Geuna S, Ravazzani R & Perassi M (1995). Youth's perception of alcohol-related driving risk. *Journal of Adolescent Health* 16:5.

Goldberg B, Saraniti A, Witman P, Gavin M & Nicholas JA (1980). Preparticipation sports assessment: An objective evaluation. *Pediatrics* 66:736–744.

Goldenring JM & Cohen E (1988). Getting into adolescent heads. *Contemporary Pediatrics* 5:75–90.

Henshaw SK & Van Vort J (1989). Teenage abortion, birth, and pregnancy statistics: An update. *Family Planning Perspectives* 21:85–88.

Hoffmann N, Mee-Lee D & Arrowood A (1993). Treatment issues in adolescent substance use and addictions: Options, outcome, effectiveness, reimbursement, and admission criteria. *Adolescent Medicine: State of the Art Reviews* 4:371–390.

Hurwitz S (1989). There's no such thing as a "good suntan." *Contemporary Pediatrics* 6:55–66.

Joffe A, Radius S & Gall M (1988). Health counseling for adolescents: What they want, what they get, and who gives it. *Pediatrics* 82:481–485.

Johnston, LD (1996). *The Monitoring the Future Study* (1996 press release). Ann Arbor, MI: University of Michigan.

Kempe CK, Silver HK, O'Brien D et al. (1987). *Current Pediatric Diagnosis and Treatment.* Norwalk, CT: Appleton & Lange, 228.

Krowchuk DP, Krowchuk HV, Hunter DM et al. (1995). Parents' knowledge of the purposes and content of preparticipation physical examinations. *Archives of Pediatric and Adolescent Medicine* 149:653–657.

Malus M, LaChance P, Lamy L et al. (1987). Priorities in health care: The teenagers' viewpoint. *Journal of Family Practice* 25:159–162.

McGrath JW & Strasburger VC (1995). Preventing AIDS in teenagers in the 1990s. *Clinical Pediatrics* 34:46–47.

Moore DC (1988). Body image and eating behavior in adolescent girls. *American Journal of Diseases of Children* 142:1114–1118.

Moore DC (1990). Body image and eating behavior in adolescent boys. *American Journal of Diseases of Children* 144:475–479.

MMWR (1996). Youth risk behavior surveillance—United States, 1995. *Morbidity and Mortality Weekly Reports* 45(SS–4): Sep 27.

National Center for Health Statistics (1986). *Vital Statistics of the United States, Vol II: Mortality Part A.* Hyattsville, MD: Public Health Service.

Neinstein LS (1991). *Adolescent Health Care: A Practical Guide (2nd Edition).* Baltimore, MD: Urban & Schwarzenberg, 941–955.

Pokorny S (1992). Inappropriate sexual behaviors: One gynecologist's viewpoint. *Adolescent Medicine: State of the Art Review* 3:339–357.

Regale G (1988). *Surgeon General's Workshop on Drunk Driving* (Public Health Service Proceedings). Rockville, MD: Department of Health and Human Services.

Risser WL, Hoffman HM, Bellah GG & Green LW (1985). A cost-benefit analysis of preparticipation sports examinations of adolescent athletes. *Journal of School Health* 55:270–273.

Rogers PD, Speraw SR & Ozbek I (1995). The assessment of the identified substance-abusing adolescent. *Pediatric Clinics of North America* 42:351–370.

Rosen DS, Xiangdong M & Blum RW (1990). Adolescent health: Current Trends and critical issues. *Adolescent Medicine: State of the Art Review* 1:15–31.

Roth ME & Grant-Kels JM (1991). Important melanocytic lesions in childhood and adolescence. *Pediatric Clinics of North America* 38:791–809.

Schubiner H & Robin A (1990). Screening adolescents for depression and parent-teenager conflict in an ambulatory medical setting: A preliminary investigation. *Pediatrics* 85:813–818.

Shafer MA (1994). Sexually transmitted diseases in adolescents: Prevention, diagnosis, and treatment in pediatric practice. *Adolescent Health Update, American Academy of Pediatrics* 6:1–7.

Smith DM, Kovan JR, Rich BSE & Tanner SM (1997). *Preparticipation Physical Evaluation (2nd Edition).* Elk Grove Village, IL: American Academy of Family Physicians, American Academy of Pediatrics, American Medical Society for Sports Medicine, American Orthopaedic Society for Sports Medicine, American Osteopathic Academy of Sports Medicine.

Smith MS, Mitchell J, McCauley EA & Calderon R (1990). Screening for anxiety and depression in an adolescent clinic. *Pediatrics* 85:262–266.

Soderstrom CA & Dearing-Stuck BA (1993). Substance Misuse and trauma: Clinical issues and injury prevention in adolescents. *Adolescent Medicine: State of the Art Review* 4:423–438.

Strasburger VC & Brown RT (1991). *Adolescent Medicine: A Practical Guide.* Boston, MA: Little, Brown and Company, 389–390.

Sturdevant M & Remafidi G (1992). Special needs of homosexual youth. *Adolescent Medicine: State of the Art Review* 3:359.

Yeager KK, Agostini R, Nattiv A & Drinkwater B (1993). The female athlete triad: Disordered eating, amenorrhea, osteoporosis. *Medical Science, Sports & Exercise* 25:775.

Zarek D, Hawkins J & Rogers P (1987). Risk Factors to adolescent substance abuse: Implications for pediatric practice. *Pediatric Clinics of North America* 34:481–493.

APPENDIX 1. Personal Questionnaire for Young Women

Please list your favorite hobbies and interests.

What are your future plans? ____________

What is your favorite type of music? Favorite musical group? ____________

What is your favorite TV show? Favorite game? ____________

Please list your closest friends (names or initials, age, sex) ____________

What exercise do you do regularly? ____________

Which of the following activities do you participate in (check all that apply)?
☐ Biking ☐ Skateboarding ☐ Rollerblading ☐ Hunting ☐ Swimming
☐ Boating ☐ Other Water Sports

Please circle the response that best corresponds to your feelings. Y = Yes, N = No

N Y 1. Do you have a friend you can talk to about anything at all?

Y N 2. Is there a family member or friend whose physical or mental health worries you?
If yes, please explain. ____________

Y N 3. Is there a family member or friend who has a problem with alcohol or other drugs?
If yes, please explain. ____________

N Y 4. Do you have enough responsibility?

N Y 5. Do you have enough freedom?

N Y 6. Do you have enough privacy?

Y N 7. Have you ever stayed out all night without permission?

Y N 8. Have you ever felt like running away?

Y N 9. Are you having any problems with you family or friends?
If yes, please explain. ____________

Y N 10. Is there conflict or fighting in your home?
If yes, please explain. ____________

Y N 11. Do you worry about your parents' relationship?
If yes, please explain. ____________

N Y 12. Do you like school? What grade are you in?

Y N 13. Are you having any problems at school?
If yes, please explain. ____________

N Y 14. Are your grades as good as everyone expected?

N Y 15. Are your teachers OK?

Y N 16. Have you ever had to repeat a grade?

Y N 17. Have you ever cut classes, skipped school, or had any unauthorized absences?

Y N 18. Do you get depressed or upset easily?

Y N 19. Ever felt like hurting yourself?
If yes, please explain. ____________

Y N 20. Ever felt like hurting someone else?
If yes, please explain. ____________

Y N 21. Has anyone every abused you by their actions or words?
If yes, please check all forms of abuse which apply.
☐ Physical ☐ Sexual ☐ Verbal ☐ Emotional ☐ Other

Y N 22. Do you smoke cigarettes?
If yes, how many each day? ________ Age started? ________ Want to quit? ________

Y N 23. Do you use chewing tobacco, snuff, or similar products?
If yes, please list. ____________

Y N 24. Do any of your friends use alcohol or other drugs?
If yes, which ones? ________

Y N 25. Do you drink alcohol-containing beverages?
If yes, which ones? ________
If yes, how much? ________ How often? ________ Age started? ________
Last time you got drunk? ________

Y N 26. Have you ever used marijuana, cocaine, "crack," uppers, downers, inhalants (sniffed or huffed), acid, angel dust, heroin, or similar substances?
If yes, which ones? ________
Age started? ________ Do you feel you need them? ________

Y N 27. Have you every used non-prescription drugs to stay awake, go to sleep, calm down, or get high?
If yes, which ones? ________
Do you depend on them now? ________

Y N 28. Have you ever used anabolic steroids?
Please circle the response that best corresponds to your feelings:
? = Not Sure, Y = Yes, N = No

Y N 29. Have you begun to menstruate? If yes, state age you began. ________ How often do your periods occur? ________ Are they regular? ________ How long do they last? ________ Is there associated pain? ________ Distress? ________ "Blue spells"? ________ When did your last period start? ________ When did it end? ________

N Y 30. Have you heard of the toxic shock syndrome?
If yes, do you know how to prevent it? ________

Y N 31. Do you drive a car, truck, or van?

N Y 32. Do you wear a seatbelt regularly?

Y N 33. Do you ride a motorcycle, all-terrain vehicle, minibike, or snowmobile?

N Y 34. If you answered yes to question #33, do you wear a helmet regularly?
(Leave blank if does not apply.) ________

Y N 35. Ever operate a car or other motor vehicle after using alcohol or other drugs?

Y N 36. Ever been a passenger when the driver was drunk or high?

Y N 37. Do you hitchhike?

Y N 38. Are handguns, rifles, shotguns, BB guns or other firearms kept in your home?

N Y 39. If you answered yes to question #38, are the firearms kept locked up?
(Leave blank if does not apply.) ________

Y N 40. Do you ever carry a knife, gun, razorblade, club, or other weapon?

Y N 41. Have you been in a physical fight in the past 3 months?

Y N 42. Are guns or violence a problem in your neighborhood or at your school?

Y N 43. Have you ever been in trouble with the law?
If yes, please explain. ________

Y N 44. Do you fear for your personal safety or that of a family member or friend?
If yes, please explain. ________

N Y 45. Do you think you are growing normally?

Y N 46. Do you have any questions or concerns about your looks or appearance?
If yes, please explain. ________

Y N 47. Do you have any questions or concerns about your sexual development?
If yes, please explain. ________

Y N 48. Do you feel different from other girls?

N Y 49. Are you interested in boys?

Y N 50. Are you more attracted to girls than to boys?

N Y 51. Are you familiar with the term masturbation?

Y N 52. If you answered yes to question #51, do you believe it is abnormal or harmful?

Y N 53. Have you ever felt forced or pressured into having sex with anyone?
If yes, please explain. ______

Y N 54. Have you ever had any sexual experiences?
If yes, what type of experiences have you had? ______

N Y 55. If you have been involved in a sexual relationship, did you or your partner use protection?
If yes, what type of protection was used? ______

Y N 56. Have you ever been pregnant?
If yes, have you ever had a miscarriage or abortion? ______

Y N 57. Are you thinking about being sexually active with anyone sometime soon?
If yes, do you need information on contraception?
Preventing sexually transmitted diseases? ______

Y N 58. Are you worried that you may become pregnant?

Y N 59. Are you worried that you may not be able to get pregnant?

Y N 60. Are you afraid you might get AIDS?

N Y 61. Do you know how to protect yourself against getting AIDS?

Y N 62. Have you ever had any of the following sexually transmitted diseases?
(check all that apply)
☐ Herpes ☐ Chlamydia ☐ Gonorrhea ☐ Trichomonas ☐ Genital warts ☐ Syphilis
☐ HIV ☐ Other

N Y 63. Overall, do you think you are well adjusted?

N Y 64. Are you basically a happy person?

Y N 65. Do you ever worry about your physical or mental health?
If yes, please explain. ______

Y N 66. Do you have any other questions or concerns you would like to discuss with the doctor or nurse?

Name ______ Date ______

APPENDIX 2. Personal Questionnaire for Young Men

Please list your favorite hobbies and interests.

What are your future plans? ______________________________

What is your favorite type of music? ____________ Favorite musical group? ____________

What is your favorite TV show? Favorite game? ______________________________

Please list your closest friends (names or initials, age, sex) ______________________________

What exercise do you do regularly? ______________________________

Which of the following activities do you participate in (check all that apply)?
☐ Biking ☐ Skateboarding ☐ Rollerblading ☐ Hunting ☐ Swimming
☐ Boating ☐ Other Water Sports

Please circle the response that best corresponds to your feelings. Y = Yes, N = No

N Y 1. Do you have a friend you can talk to about anything at all?

Y N 2. Is there a family member or friend whose physical or mental health worries you?
If yes, please explain. ______________________________

Y N 3. Is there a family member or friend who has a problem with alcohol or other drugs?
If yes, please explain. ______________________________

N Y 4. Do you have enough responsibility?

N Y 5. Do you have enough freedom?

N Y 6. Do you have enough privacy?

Y N 7. Have you ever stayed out all night without permission?

Y N 8. Have you ever felt like running away?

Y N 9. Are you having any problems with you family or friends?
If yes, please explain. ______________________________

Y N 10. Is there conflict or fighting in your home?
If yes, please explain. ______________________________

Y N 11. Do you worry about your parents' relationship?
If yes, please explain. ______________________________

N Y 12. Do you like school? What grade are you in? ______________________________

Y N 13. Are you having any problems at school?
If yes, please explain. ______________________________

N Y 14. Are your grades as good as everyone expected?

N Y 15. Are your teachers OK?

Y N 16. Have you ever had to repeat a grade?

Y N 17. Have you ever cut classes, skipped school, or had any unauthorized absences?

Y N 18. Do you get depressed or upset easily?

Y N 19. Ever felt like hurting yourself?
If yes, please explain. ______________________________

Y N 20. Ever felt like hurting someone else?
If yes, please explain. ______________________________

Y N 21. Has anyone every abused you by their actions or words?
If yes, please check all forms of abuse which apply.
☐ Physical ☐ Sexual ☐ Verbal ☐ Emotional ☐ Other

Y N 22. Do you smoke cigarettes?
If yes, how many each day? ________ Age started? ________ Want to quit? ________

Y N 23. Do you use chewing tobacco, snuff, or similar products?
If yes, please list. ______________________________

Y N 24. Do any of your friends use alcohol or other drugs?
If yes, which ones? ______

Y N 25. Do you drink alcohol-containing beverages?
If yes, which ones? ______
If yes, how much? ______ How often? ______ Age started? ______
Last time you got drunk? ______

Y N 26. Have you ever used marijuana, cocaine, "crack," uppers, downers, inhalants (sniffed or huffed), acid, angel dust, heroin, or similar substances?
If yes, which ones? ______ Age started? ______ Do you feel you need them? ______

Y N 27. Have you every used non-prescription drugs to stay awake, go to sleep, calm down, or get high?
If yes, which ones? ______ Do you depend on them now? ______

Y N 28. Have you ever used anabolic steroids?

Please circle the response that best corresponds to your feelings:
? = Not Sure, Y = Yes, N = No

Y N 29. Do you drive a car, truck, or van?

N Y 30. Do you wear a seatbelt regularly?

Y N 31. Do you ride a motorcycle, all-terrain vehicle, minibike, or snowmobile?

N Y 32. If you answered yes to question #31, do you wear a helmet regularly? (Leave blank if does not apply.)

Y N 33. Ever operate a car or other motor vehicle after using alcohol or other drugs?

Y N 34. Ever been a passenger when the driver was drunk or high?

Y N 35. Do you hitchhike?

Y N 36. Are handguns, rifles, shotguns, BB guns or other firearms kept in your home?

N Y 37. If you answered yes to question #36, are the firearms kept locked up?
(Leave blank if does not apply.)

Y N 38. Do you ever carry a knife, gun, razorblade, club, or other weapon?

Y N 39. Have you been in a physical fight in the past 3 months?

Y N 40. Are guns or violence a problem in your neighborhood or at your school?

Y N 41. Have you ever been in trouble with the law?
If yes, please explain. ______

Y N 42. Do you fear for your personal safety or that of a family member or friend?
If yes, please explain. ______

N Y 43. Do you think you are growing normally?

Y N 44. Do you have any questions or concerns about your looks or appearance?
If yes, please explain. ______

Y N 45. Do you have any questions or concerns about your sexual development?
If yes, please explain. ______

Y N 46. Do you feel different from other boys?

N Y 47. Are you interested in girls?

Y N 48. Are you more attracted to boys than to girls?

N Y 49. Are you familiar with the terms masturbation, ejaculation, and "wet dreams"?

Y N 50. If you answered yes to question #49, do you believe these are abnormal or harmful?

Y N 51. Have you ever felt forced or pressured into having sex with anyone?
If yes, please explain. ______

Y N 52. Have you ever had any sexual experiences?
If yes, what type of experiences have you had? ______

N Y 53. If you have been involved in a sexual relationship, did you or your partner use protection?
If yes, what type of protection was used? ______

Y N 54. Are you thinking about being sexually active with anyone sometime soon?
If yes, do you need information on contraception? __________
Preventing sexually transmitted diseases? __________

Y N 55. Have you worried about getting someone pregnant?

Y N 56. Have you ever worried about not being able to get someone pregnant?

Y N 57. Are you afraid you might get AIDS?

N Y 58. Do you know how to protect yourself against getting AIDS?

Y N 59. Have you ever had any of the following sexually transmitted diseases? (check all that apply)
☐ Herpes ☐ Chlamydia ☐ Gonorrhea ☐ Trichomonas ☐ Genital warts
☐ Syphilis ☐ Other

N Y 60. Overall, do you think you are well adjusted?

N Y 61. In general, are you happy with the way things are going for you these days?

Y N 62. Do you ever worry about your physical or mental health?
If yes, please explain. __________

Y N 63. Do you have any other questions or concerns you would like to discuss with the doctor or nurse?

Name __________ Date __________

CHAPTER 2

Office Assessment and Brief Intervention with the Adolescent Suspected of Substance Abuse

George D. Comerci, M.D., FAAP

Role of the Physician
Assessing a Patient for Substance Abuse
Early Detection and Brief Intervention
Referring a Patient for Treatment

The abuse of alcohol, tobacco, and other drugs continues to be a major cause of death and disability among adolescents and young adults. Primary complications and secondary morbidity and disability resulting from alcohol and drug abuse are major public health concerns. The likelihood that the such abuse will progress to psychological or physiological dependence, or both, is a constant threat to the health and welfare of individuals in this age group. It is unacceptable that many physicians who care for adolescents and young adults abrogate their responsibility in this regard.

The true prevalence of substance abuse among adolescents and young adults is not known, but there is strong evidence of an overall increase in use following an encouraging downward trend observed in the late 1980s. Moreover, young adolescents report: (1) less concern that drug use carries certain risks; (2) an increase in availability of drugs; and (3) a perception of decreased disapproval of drug use among their peers. Research shows that attitudes and beliefs such as these are associated with increased experimentation with and abuse of alcohol, tobacco and other drugs. Data from recent national studies give cause for concern that we are at the leading edge of another upward trend in adolescent substance abuse (Substance Abuse and Mental Health Services Administration, 1996; Johnston, O'Malley & Bachman, 1996).

Current data probably understate the true dimensions of the problem, in that they depend on the accuracy of reporting by adolescent respondents and they do not reflect drug use among the 15% to 20% of adolescents who leave school before their late high school years. Such studies can be misleading regarding the abuse of certain illicit substances—such as inhalants, cocaine and heroin—which are more likely to be used in greater frequency and amounts by school dropouts, the unemployed, and those in extreme poverty. Practitioners whose patients are of average or higher than average socioeconomic status, and in school, can use information from national student surveys in their own practice settings, but should not extrapolate these data to nonstudents or to unemployed persons of lower socioeconomic status.

The harmful effects of alcohol, tobacco and other drug abuse may begin before and go beyond the adolescent period, touching all persons, regardless of socioeconomic category. Alcohol and drug abuse is a major cause of disability among adults, including pregnant women and subsequently newborns, and it affects infants, young children, and adolescents as a result of abuse and neglect, and accidental drug exposure. Intravenous drug abuse is the cause of many cases of HIV infection with subsequent transmission to the fetus. The practitioner must be aware that genetic factors may predispose to substance abuse and dependence (Cloninger, 1983), and that unhealthy childrearing practices, parental substance abuse and family dysfunction play important roles in drug abuse and require physician intervention. Thus, the practitioner has a responsibility not only for diagnosis but also for prevention, anticipatory guidance and referral and treatment.

Considering that violent deaths during adolescence and young adulthood are frequently associated with drugs and alcohol, physicians should be aware that intervention provides a reasonable chance of survival for an individual not necessarily doomed to lifelong problems with drugs and their harmful effects. Much will have been accomplished if a physician intervenes early, allowing a patient to survive through this critical period.

ROLE OF THE PHYSICIAN

Physicians who care for adolescents and young adults recognize that they are perhaps in greater need of a "medical home" than other patients. The concept of a "medical home" is certainly not a new one. The American Academy of Pediatrics defines it as care that is "accessible, continuous, comprehensive, family centered, coordinated, and compassionate. The physician should manage or facilitate essentially all aspects of care. The physician should be known to the adolescent and family and should be able to develop a relationship of mutual responsibility and trust with them" (American Academy of Pediatrics, 1992). The young person in whom alcohol, tobacco or other drug abuse is suspected, or for whom a diagnosis of abuse or dependence has been made, deserves no less.

Health care of the adolescent and young adult requires more time than that of the child or adult. This is true of routine care, but is especially true when there exists a suspicion of substance abuse. Considering the morbidity and mortality associated with substance abuse from a public and preventive health standpoint, the time spent in dealing with such problems is thoroughly justified. Practitioners must accept the fact that additional time will be needed for such patients and adjust their practice style to accommodate the needs of these patients.

When seeing a patient who is strongly suspected of substance abuse, the physician should have coverage for sick patients. Obviously, this is no small feat for the solo practitioner or two-person office partnership. Nevertheless, busy internists set aside relatively large blocks of time for patients, so pediatricians and family physicians can as well. When an adolescent is being seen for counseling and for assessment for suspected substance abuse, telephone receptionists should be notified not to disturb the physician except for emergencies. For many it will require a major change in practice philosophy, but one that, with a great deal of effort, is possible to achieve.

TABLE 1. Guidelines for Interviewing Adolescents

Approach

1. Begin by discussing more general life-style questions, including the following topic areas: home/family relations, functioning at school, peer relationships, leisure activities, employment, and self-perception.
2. Ask about dietary patterns.
3. Proceed to questions about prescribed medications.
4. Ask about over-the-counter medications.
5. Inquire about cigarettes and smokeless tobacco use.
6. Learn about the use of alcohol.
7. Question the adolescent about the use of marijuana.
8. Finally, ask about the use of any illicit drug.

Rationale

1. This approach allows time to develop or renew the patient-physician relationship.
2. It elicits a basis of general psychosocial information that is useful in identifying the patient at risk in a harmful environment.
3. The approach begins the interview with the least threatening questions.
4. It then moves to increasingly sensitive questions about substance use.
5. The order of questions recommended here provides a natural order of progression, moving from socially accepted activities to those that are socially tolerated, to the socially disapproved to the overtly illegal.

ASSESSING A PATIENT FOR SUBSTANCE ABUSE

Goals of the Evaluation. A fundamental goal of each evaluation is that the physician be able to determine whether the adolescent is using drugs and, if so, whether that use is experimental and casual or problematic. It also is important that the physician determine the patient's current stage of drug use or abuse (Macdonald, 1988).

The Interview. The manner of approach to and the content of the assessment interview for adolescents are available to the practitioner from many sources (see Table 1; also, Alderman, Schonberg & Cohen, 1992; Schonberg, 1992).

If reliable information is to be obtained from the adolescent, an atmosphere of trust must prevail. It is essential that the interview be conducted in a private setting and one in which interruptions will be kept at a minimum. The teenager or young adult must been seen separately from parents, and confidentiality and its limits must be mentioned early in the interview process. Any information from and concerns expressed by parents should, in most cases, be shared with the adolescent. Although most state statutes on substance abuse allow the adolescent to

TABLE 2. Questions to Ask an Adolescent Patient Who is Suspected of or Known to Be Abusing Drugs and/or Alcohol

1. What do your friends do at parties? Do you go to the parties? Do you drink? Get drunk? Get high?
2. Do you drive drunk? Stoned? Have you been a passenger is a car driven by someone who was drunk or stoned? Could you call home and ask for help? What would your parents say or do?
3. Do you go to rock concerts? Do you drink there? Do you get high? Who drives after the concert?
4. After drinking, have you ever forgotten where you had been or what you had done?
5. Have you recently dropped some of your old friends and started going with a new group?
6. Do you feel that lately you are irritable, "bitchy" or moody?
7. Do you find yourself getting into more frequent arguments with your friends? Brothers and sisters? Parents?
8. Have your grades recently gone down? Did you receive any F's on your last report card? Have you ever been expelled from school?
9. Do you have a boyfriend/girlfriend? How is that going? Are you having more fights/arguments with him/her lately? Have you recently broken up?
10. Do you find yourself being physically abusive to others? Your brothers or sisters? Your mother or father?
11. Have you ever been arrested for possession of drugs, burglary, vandalism, shoplifting, or breaking and entering?
12. Have you ever had to go to an emergency room or doctor's office for a drug-related accident or illness (overdose)?
13. Have you ever overdosed or intentionally tried to kill yourself?
14. Have you ever been intoxicated or high (stoned) at school?
15. Have you ever been caught at school for drug or alcohol possession?
16. Have any of your friends been admitted to a drug treatment center?
17. What drugs, if any, have you used in the past? How much?
18. What drugs, if any, are you currently using? How much?
19. Have you ever experienced blackouts while drinking heavily? (For example, have you awakened unable to remember what happened the night before?)
20. Has your alcohol or drug use caused problems with your friends or family, or both?
21. Have you ever gotten into trouble at work or at school because of alcohol or drug use?
22. Do you often wake up with a hangover?
23. Do you think your drinking or drug use is a problem? Why?

be interviewed and allow treatment to be initiated without parental consent, they do not directly address issues of confidentiality; the decision regarding what and how much to tell parents is a difficult one that each practitioner must make individually. It is vital that the adolescent know the physician's limitations with respect to confidentiality and that the patient participate in any disclosures.

A structured interview goes a long way toward improving the efficiency of the evaluation and lessens the amount of time needed to collect data. Such an interview should have definite objectives and provide the physician with specific questions to ask, while appearing to be spontaneous and flexible, and it should be targeted toward gathering certain important information (Table 2) (Anglin, 1987).

Depression and other psychiatric diagnoses should be considered. A history of physical or sexual abuse, or both, may be relevant. Information from parents often is critical (Table 3).

Use of Questionnaires. The use of questionnaires to obtain sensitive material from teenagers and young adults continues to be controversial. There is no debate that their proper use can provide reliable information and possibly increase the efficiency of an individual encounter. If honest answers are not forthcoming, however, then the information collected is, at worst, potentially life threatening to the patient. ("Efficacy is doing the right thing; efficiency is doing the right thing right.") Most adolescents answer most questionnaires honestly. Anonymous surveys are believed to be reasonably reliable.

The limitations on the use of questionnaires underscore the need for trust to be established and maintained and for privacy and confidentiality to be ensured. The adolescent and young adult are aware that if they confide in the physician regarding substantial drug abuse, such information will be used to intervene. Most persons involved in the abuse of chemicals are not interested in changing their behavior, and lying in order to avoid disclosure is not unusual.

For the physician who chooses to use questionnaires as a tool for more efficient data collection, a number of screening and assessment instruments are available (see Table 4; and Filstead, Parrella & Ross, 1992a, 1992b). Unfortunately, in the past, most available instruments, including the *Diagnostic and Statistical Manual of Mental Disorders* of the

TABLE 3. Questions to Ask the Parent(s) of an Adolescent Who is Suspected of or Known to Be Abusing Drugs and/or Alcohol

1. Does any family member, including parents, have a past or present alcohol or other drug problem?
2. Is there a family history of depression (especially bipolar affective disorder), suicide or suicide attempt, or other psychiatric illness?
3. What changes have you noted in your child's mood, affect, behavior or dress?
4. Has there been lying to cover up for absences from home or school, for missing personal or family belongings, or for no reason at all?
5. Have the child's personal belongings or family possessions or money been missing?
6. Has the child's manner of dress or personal hygiene changed?
7. Has drug paraphernalia been found in the child's possession or in the home?
8. Has there been deterioration in the child's school performance, frequent truancy, or conflict with coaches or teachers?
9. Has there been stealing, shoplifting or encounters with the police?
10. Has the child been physically abusive to family members?
11. Has the child tried to introduce drugs or alcohol to any of your other children?
12. Has the child talked about suicide or running away?

American Psychiatric Association (1994) and the popular CAGE questionnaire, were developed for the assessment of adults. Criteria developed for adults often consider tolerance and withdrawal, which are not often seen in adolescents, as important diagnostic criteria. Any assessment method for adolescents, if it is to be useful, must give attention to the special problems and characteristics of adolescents and adolescent substance abuse.

In the final analysis, valid information is more likely to result from a skilled interview than from a perfectly structured and designed questionnaire. But whatever method is used, accurate and honest responses by the adolescent or young adult are going to depend, in large part, on the degree to which trust is established and on the extent to which the patient perceives the physician as a caring, helpful and knowledgeable adult.

Laboratory Assessment. The use of urine or other body fluid testing to identify adolescents who are abusing drugs is an attractive, but deceptively simple alternative to the time-consuming interview and physical examination. The accuracy of modern testing methods notwithstanding, there are many reasons, both ethical and practical, however, why this approach remains controversial (Schwartz, 1993). The author is of the opinion that laboratory testing for drugs of abuse should not be used as a general diagnostic tool. There are special indications for voluntary testing with consent, but few if any indications for involuntary drug testing, particularly in the older adolescent and young adult. Informed consent by the adolescent, except in exceptional circumstances, is essential (American Academy of Pediatrics, 1996). Involuntary testing is justified when: (1) emergency situations exist in which a patient is unable to give informed consent (i.e., seizing, unconscious, seriously injured, or comatose patient), (2) there is altered mental status or there are acute psychiatric or behavioral states, (3) there are acute medical symptoms that may put the patient at grave risk (chest pain, dysrhythmias, hyperthermia, hypertension), (4) the competency of an older adolescent is in doubt, (5) one does not trust the veracity of the adolescent (because of conduct disorder, oppositional-defiant, anti-social, delinquent, or criminal behaviors), (6) the patient is a preadolescent or very young adolescent (with parental consent), or (7) testing is court-ordered for monitoring purposes. Scrupulous attention to collection, chain of "evidence," limited half-lives of drugs, and reasons for false positive (cross reactions) and false negatives

TABLE 4. Structured Interviews and Questionnaires for Adolescent Screening and Assessment

Structured Interviews

- Questions Concerning Drugs for the School-aged Child: A Screening Tool *(American Medical Association, 1992).*
- The "HEADS" Organized Interview (Home/Education/Activities and Affect/Drugs Sexuality) *(Goldenring & Cohen, 1988).*
- The CAGE Questions *(Bush et al., 1987)*

Questionnaires

- A Symptom Checklist for Substance Abuse *(Blum, 1987)*
- The Adolescent Assessment/Referral System (AARS) Manual *(Rahdert ER [n.d.].* ADAMHA Publication No. ADM 91-1735)
- The Problem-Oriented Screening Instrument for Teenagers (POSIT), National Institute on Drug Abuse *(ADAMHA Publication No. ADM 91-1735)*
- Substance Abuse Subtle Screening Inventory (SASSI) *(The SASSI Institute, Bloomington, IN)*
- Drug Use Screening Inventory (DUSI) *(Ralph E. Tarter, Department of Psychiatry, University of Pittsburgh Medical School, Western Psychiatric Institute and Clinic, Pittsburgh, PA).*

(specimen adulteration) is required (Woolf & Shannon, 1995).

Trust is necessary for a therapeutic alliance to be established with the adolescent. Effective ways to prevent a trusting relationship from developing are to test without the young person's knowledge, to test in spite of the adolescent's objections, or to test on parent demand. However, an out-of-control adolescent or an adolescent who shows evidence of serious dysfunction is an exception to the general rule. There is no problem with testing a patient who provides voluntary consent, but it is most unlikely that the substance-abusing adolescent will give consent for a test that may very well show that he or she is lying. The double-bind for the adolescent is that to refuse to be tested implies there is something to hide.

EARLY DETECTION AND BRIEF INTERVENTION

Early detection and intervention for the substance-abusing adolescent are necessary if the progress of the disorder, its detrimental effect on normal development and its contribution to death and morbidity are to be prevented. The leading causes of death among adolescents and young adults are accidents, homicides and suicides, a significant number of which are associated with alcohol and other drug use. The effectiveness of our interventions and treatment programs for substance abuse is uncertain.

Many physicians are skeptical of the claims of success by addiction specialists and programs, and they therefore fail to intervene or refer. Difficulties in determining outcome have to do with differences among the adolescents being referred for treatment, proper matching of treatment to a given adolescent's needs, different markers of success (e.g., total drug abstinence, return to successful life functioning, controlled use), differences between short- and long-term outcomes, differences between the assessment instruments used for adolescents and those used for adults and differences in the problem of substance abuse between adolescents and adults. Success rates vary from 15% to 45%, depending on whether short- or long-term outcome is being assessed. For juvenile drug abusers, there is a steady improvement over a seven-year period. However, the degree to which that improvement is attributable to maturational gains (the "maturing out" process) (Anglin, 1987; Donovan, Jessor & Jessor, 1978; Kandel, 1975) as opposed to treatment is not known. Short-term follow-up studies show more favorable outcomes than long-term follow-up studies (McLellan, Luborsky et al., 1982).

TABLE 5. Guidelines for Selecting an Adolescent Treatment Program

- Does the program require that the patient become totally abstinent?
- Is the program focused on substance abuse? Are appropriate professionals and therapeutic or educational activities provided?
- Does the program emphasize the importance of family involvement and family therapy?
- Does the program emphasize follow-up outpatient care? Does it acknowledge substance abuse as a chronic problem?

REFERRING A PATIENT FOR SUBSTANCE ABUSE TREATMENT

Until further research has been conducted to document treatment success, physicians must realize that is not yet possible to know which adolescents are most amenable to help; they will have to assume that some treatment, even if imperfect, is better than none at all.

Referring a Patient for Treatment. Physicians sometimes are at a loss as to how to select a treatment program for a substance-abusing adolescent. Unfortunately, because of either geographic location, affluence of a community, the limited resources of the patient's family, no or inadequate insurance, the options often are fairly limited. No specific criteria exist for selecting a program, but the guidelines in Table 5 may be helpful (American Academy of Pediatrics, 1990; Mee-Lee, Shulman & Gartner, 1994).

Accessing Community Resources. Physicians often complain that there are few community resources for substance abusing adolescents. Even where such resources do exist, physicians may not know how to access the systems that provide the services. Moreover, public health, mental health, drug abuse and social service agencies and organizations do not coordinate their patient care activities. There is interagency competition for funding, as well as cost containment pressures, which frequently lead to denial of services or exclusionary practices. Many patients have no means of paying for such services and lack adequate insurance coverage for hospital or long-term care.

The physician should be aware of a number of organizations from which information can be obtained, including local, state and federal government agencies; local and state medical societies; volunteer organizations; and citizen-parent action groups.

CONCLUSIONS

There are numerous forces acting against the involvement of primary care physicians in the diagnosis of an intervention for substance abuse. These include practical issues of time and scheduling, problems of confidentiality, reimbursement barriers and lack of incentives, inadequate training and physician discomfort and skepticism with regard to available treatment resources and outcomes. Despite these barriers, most primary care physicians acknowledge the need for their involvement and accept their obligation to adolescent patients and families (American Academy of Pediatrics, 1983).

The following appendices offer suggestions and recommendations regarding ways to overcome existing barriers and to increase the rewards of caring for patients and families affected by substance abuse and addiction.

REFERENCES

Alderman EM, Schonberg SK & Cohen MI (1992). The pediatrician's role in the diagnosis and treatment of substance abuse. *Pediatric Review* 13:314–318.

American Academy of Pediatrics (AAP) (1990). Provisional Committee on Substance Abuse. Selection of substance abuse treatment programs. *Pediatrics* 86:139–140.

American Academy of Pediatrics (AAP) (1989). Committees on Adolescence. Bioethics, and Provisional Committee on Substance Abuse. Screening for drugs of abuse in children and adolescents. *Pediatrics* 84:396–398.

American Academy of Pediatrics (AAP) (1988). Evaluation by interview. In SK Schonberg (ed.) *Substance Abuse: A Guide for Health Professionals.* Elk Grove Village, IL: The Academy, 38–46. (Second Edition: in press, 1998)

American Academy of Pediatrics (AAP) (1992). Ad Hoc Task Force on Definition of the Medical Home. *Pediatrics* 90:774.

American Academy of Pediatrics (AAP) (1983). Committee on Adolescence. The role of the pediatrician in substance abuse counseling. *Pediatrics* 72:251–252.

American Academy of Pediatrics (AAP) (1996): Testing for drugs of abuse in children and adolescents. *Pediatrics* 98:305–307, 1996.

American Medical Association (AMA) (1992). *Physician's Current Procedural Terminology. Evaluation and Management Services, 4th Edition.* Chicago, IL: The Association.

American Psychiatric Association (1994). *Diagnostic and Statistical Manual of Mental Disorders.* Washington, DC: American Psychiatric Press.

Anglin TM (1987). Interviewing guidelines for the clinical evaluation of adolescent substance abuse. *Pediatric Clinics of North America* 34:381–398.

Blum RW (1987). Adolescent substance abuse: Diagnostic and treatment issues. *Pediatric Clinics of North America* 35:530–531.

Bush B et al. (1987). Screening for alcohol abuse using the CAGE questionnaire. *American Journal of Medicine* 82:231–235.

Cloninger CR (1983). Genetic and environmental factors in the development of alcoholism. *Journal of Psychiatric Treatment and Research* 5:487–496.

Comerci GD (1993). Office assessment of substance abuse and addiction. *Adolescent Medicine: State of the Art Reviews* 4(2):277–293.

Comerci GD (1990). The role of the primary care practitioner in the diagnosis and management of substance abuse. In RR Watson (ed.) *Drug and Alcohol Abuse Prevention.* Clifton, NJ: Humana Press, 19–44.

Comerci GD (1988). The substance abuse component of primary care residency programs. *Substance Abuse* 9:84–91.

Donovan J, Jessor R & Jessor L (1978). Problem drinking in adolescence and young adulthood: A follow-up study. *Journal of Studies on Alcohol* 39:1506–1524.

Filstead WJ, Parrella DP & Ross AA (1992a). Adolescent screening tests. Part I: The assessment basis. *Addiction & Recovery* 12:31–33.

Filstead WJ, Parrella DP & Ross AA (1992b). Adolescent screening tests. II. Assessment instruments and their findings. *Addiction & Recovery* 12:7–8.

Goldenring J & Cohen E (1988). Getting into adolescent heads. *Contemporary Pediatrics* 5:75.

Joffe & Adger H (1992). Assessment methods. Department of Pediatrics, The Johns Hopkins University, Baltimore, MD, personal communication, January.

Johnston LD, O'Malley PM & Bachman JG (1996). *National Survey Results on Drug Use from the Monitoring the Future Study, December, 1996.* Rockville, MD: National Institute on Drug Abuse.

Kandel D (1975). Stages in adolescent involvement in drug use. *Science* 190:912–914.

Long WA (1990). Solutions: The role of the private practitioner, II. Financial considerations. *Adolescent Medicine: State of the Art Reviews* 1:152–155.

Lopez RI (1991). Obstacles to adolescent care: Economic issues. *Adolescent Medicine: State of the Art Reviews* 2:415–419.

Macdonald DI (1988). Substance abuse. *Pediatric Review* 10:89–94.

MacKenzie RG (1985). High-risk youth: Changing problems into solutions. In M Green (ed.) *The Psychosocial Aspects of the Family.* Lexington, MA: Lexington Books, 202–203.

McLellan AT, Luborsky L, O'Brien C, et al. (1982). Is treatment for substance abuse effective? *Journal of the American Medical Association* 247:1423–1428.

Mee-Lee D, Shulman G & Gartner L (1994). *Patient Placement Criteria for the Treatment of Psychoactive Substance Use Disorders, Second Edition.* Chevy Chase, MD: American Society of Addiction Medicine.

Substance Abuse and Mental Health Services Administration (SAMHSA) (1996). *National Household Survey on Drug Abuse, Advance Report Number 18.* Rockville, MD: SAMHSA, Office of Applied Studies.

Sanders J & Flint SS (1992). Financing of adolescent care (Strategies for the individual practitioner). In ER McAnarney et al. (eds.) *Textbook of Adolescent Medicine.* Philadelphia, PA: W.B. Saunders, 1065–1069.

Schonberg SK (1992). Substance use and abuse. In ER McAnarney et al. (eds.) *Textbook of Adolescent Medicine.* Philadelphia, PA: W.B. Saunders, 1065–1069.

Schwartz RH (1993). Testing for drugs of abuse: Controversies and techniques. *Adolescent Medicine: State of the Art Reviews* 4:353–370.

Woolf AD & Shannon MW (1995). Clinical toxicology for the pediatrician. *Pediatric Clinics of North America* 42:317–333.

Yancy WS (1992). Office practice. In ER McAnarney et al. (eds.) *Textbook of Adolescent Medicine.* Philadelphia, PA: W.B. Saunders, 154–155.

CHAPTER 3

Assessment of the Identified Substance-Abusing Adolescent

Susan Speraw, Ph.D., R.N.
Peter D. Rogers, M.D., M.P.H., FAAP, FASAM

Assessing the Adolescent
Interviewing the Family

When an adolescent has been identified as abusing drugs, including alcohol, an assessment of the young person is the logical next step. If an adolescent's substance abuse has reached significant proportions, every sphere of his or her life may be affected: psychosocial (including family, peer and school life), emotional/ behavioral, medical and spiritual.

ASSESSING THE ADOLESCENT

The purpose of the assessment is to make an accurate diagnosis, including the level and complexity of the substance abuse problem and the presence of any existing medical or psychiatric comorbidity. The authors' experience has shown that as many as 33% to 50% of substance-abusing adolescents also may have a major psychiatric disorder, such as affective disorder, thought disorders or personality disorders. This experience compares with similar estimates derived by an addiction researcher (Director, 1996).

Adolescents with dual diagnoses present a much more complicated clinical picture and often require psychiatric evaluation beyond the initial assessment. The evaluation team also may decide that the severity of an adolescent's psychiatric symptoms ultimately dictates that the child be placed in a treatment program that is psychiatrically oriented.

Only when a diagnosis is made, can there be a decision about the most appropriate intensity of treatment and setting for care. It is clear to professionals in the substance abuse field that many young people who experience relapse do so because of incomplete or inadequate initial diagnosis and treatment.

Ground Rules for Interviewing. In the process of evaluation, the adolescent must be interviewed separately, and the family must be interviewed as a unit. "Ground rules" must be explained to the adolescent and family before any formal interviews begin. These ground rules form the basis for the interaction:

Uses of Information: All information gathered in the interview becomes part of the permanent record and is shared with physicians, social workers, therapists, and others who work directly with the adolescent. Disclosing this fact prevents the physician's being drawn into a maladaptive relationship with the patient in which there is an appearance of collusion. "Secrets" regarding substance use are to be avoided. Honesty and openness are expected and strongly encouraged.

Patient Confidentiality: There are limits to confidentiality, which the physician, therapist, or other health providers are required by law to observe. Specifically, the provider is required to inform the parent, guardian and, under certain circumstances, the police or child protective agencies when a child or adolescent is engaged in behavior that is injurious or life-threatening to self or others. Similarly, a disclosure of physical, sexual or emotional abuse must be reported to the appropriate authorities, as must a strong suspicion of abuse. In these cases, reporting is *not* at the discretion of the provider; rather, it is referred to legally as "Duty to Warn" and is required by law. If a health provider fails to make a formal report regarding intent to harm, or about suspected abuse of a minor, such failure can result in revocation of the practitioner's license. Thus, limits to confidentiality are not negotiable under any circumstances.

Parents' Confidentiality: Parents are accorded the same right to confidentiality, within the same limits, with regard to personal or intimate details of their own relationship that are shared during the course of the assessment.

Refusal to Answer: Both the adolescent and parents have the right to refuse to answer any questions, although candor and honesty are encouraged in the interest of making an accurate diagnosis and formulating the best treatment plan.

Repetition: In the course of interviewing the adolescent and parents separately, and the family as a unit, some questions are repeated or asked more than once in different ways. Such repetition should not be considered redundant. Rather, repetition or rephrasing of questions should be viewed as an opportunity to expand the available data or to gain insight into how various family members view the same subject matter. When questions are asked of different individuals or repeated over time, responses may vary in critical ways. As individuals develop rapport with the physician, they may disclose facts that initially were withheld. Different family members' recollections of similar events in the family's history also may vary. Finally, during discussions that include all family members, the response of one person may trigger a thought, idea, or recollection on the part of another family member, thus helping the provider to gain a more accurate and comprehensive view of the patient in the context of his or her family system.

Approaching the Interview. The interview of the adolescent should be approached with the following question in mind: "What has happened in this young person's life that has led him or her to become dependent on drugs?" It is important to remember that young people who are heavily involved with drugs often have a core of emotional pain that predates their drug use. Adolescents often see themselves in the same ways that they believe they are viewed by significant persons in their lives. Many teens who abuse substances have little regard for themselves and see themselves as worthless. One goal of the assessment interview is to identify factors that contribute negatively or positively to the adolescent's self-image. Before change, recovery, and healing can take place, an adolescent with a negative self-image often needs to undergo a sometimes painful process of coming to understand his or her feelings of low self-worth. Such understanding is critical because an adolescent who feels worthless has little motivation to achieve or maintain sobriety.

A major focus of the interview with the substance-abusing adolescent is the quality of his or her relationships with family members, with peers of the same and opposite sex, and with spirituality. Substance abusing adolescents, however, are well guarded. Adolescents who have had counseling in the past may be sophisticated in maintaining a facade of innocence. Others may present a veneer of anger, hostility and distrust, in an attempt to distance themselves from the interviewer. Whether presenting a veneer of innocence or an armor of anger, the adolescent's motivation is to protect himself/herself, as well as the family, from exposure.

Questions. Key questions and content areas to include in the adolescent interview are:

"If your father was in the room with us, and I asked him to describe you, what would he say?" After the answer is given, repeat the question using "mother." This question may elicit information about the way the adolescent views his or her relationship with parents.

"What do *you* think about what your parents would say?"

"Do your parents spend as much time with you as you would like?" or "How interested do you feel your parents are in your future?" What these questions are asking is whether the adolescent perceives his or her parents as caring and emotionally involved. A child who perceives his/her parents as not caring begins a premature emotional drift away from the family and often engages in risk-taking behaviors such as substance abuse.

Concerning friendships with peers, the following questions might be asked: "If you like someone of the same age and sex, and would like to have this person as a friend, why would he/she want to be your friend?" "If you like someone about your age of the opposite sex, and would like to date this person, why would this person want to go out with you?" When asked with a compassionate, non-judgmental attitude and with sensitivity, these questions can elicit much information about a child's self-esteem and the nature and quality of his or her relationships.

A "spiritual assessment" to identify what resources the young person has to call upon outside of himself or herself for help, including the teenager's belief in and relationship with God or a "Higher Power." The question, "Do you consider yourself to be a 'religious' person?" often is non-threatening. Depending on the teen's response, follow-up questions regarding church affiliation and the quality of church experience are appropriate. If the teenager does have a positive relationship with God or a "Higher Power," this may be a very important strength that can help sustain the adolescent through the difficult phases of treatment and the process of recovery.

In screening for sexual abuse, the interviewer might ask: "Has anyone ever touched you or done anything to you that you think is wrong or that made you uncomfortable?" This question should be asked of teenagers of both sexes. Most children and adolescents who have been sexually abused feel shame and guilt and often are reluctant to discuss this or to admit it during an initial interview. Instances of sexual abuse, even those that involve "only" fondling or those that occurred at some time in the past, must be reported if the perpetrator has any potential for future contact with children, even if the allegation was not proved at the time or cannot now be proved.

Attempted suicide and thoughts of suicide are common among adolescents who abuse drugs. It is best to be candid when discussing this subject: "Have you ever thought about killing or hurting yourself?" or "Have you ever thought about suicide, or wished that you were dead?" "If so, did you plan how you would do it?"

Any suspicion of suicidality must be dealt with by determining whether the adolescent has a wish to be dead, a plan for killing him or herself, and a means to execute the plan. If a risk of suicide is present, the parents, guardian or authorities must be informed.

It also is worthwhile to ask the teenager if he or she is aware of either parent having a "secret" that is being kept from the family. "Secrets" are those things a young person will not readily discuss because of shame. While some are "family secrets," others are the personal secrets of the adolescent alone. Although adults often believe that their children are unaware of their "secret" activities (such as extramarital affairs), children often are acutely aware of such secrets. Young people who know that one parent has betrayed the other, or the family, may be angry, hurt, ashamed, and feel enormous stress from trying to cope with this unwelcome knowledge. Other common secrets in adolescents include having had an abortion or homosexual experience, having been raped, or having done things under the influence of alcohol or drugs that the adolescent would not have done while sober. Children and adolescents often want to share their secrets with someone and welcome an opportunity to do so. To give the patient an opportunity to speak about secrets will not "put ideas in their heads"; rather, it affords them an opportunity to talk about their concerns, gives them permission to do so, and acknowledges that they may have worries that are difficult or awkward to discuss. Although the child may not initially confide in the physician, such an invitation to talk may lead to future disclosures of personal or family "secrets" that could be the foundation for substance abuse.

Use of alcohol or drugs by at least one parent is found in 40% to 50% of adolescents in treatment for substance abuse. However, children want to be proud of their parents and often will not divulge that one parent is, for example, an alcoholic. Therefore, rather than ask a direct question about whether anyone in the family is an alcoholic or addicted to drugs, a less confrontational phrasing is preferred. For example: "Does anyone in your family drink or use drugs?" "Have you ever wished that he/she didn't drink so much?" (or "in front of your friends?"). "How do you *feel* when you know your father has been drinking?"

Questions that probe other risk-taking behaviors, such as sexual activity, must be pursued. When an adolescent has been identified as exhibiting one risk-taking behavior, such as substance abuse, he or she often is involved in other risk-taking behaviors, such as having multiple sex partners. Therefore, rather than asking if an adolescent is sexually active, which most often elicits denial, it is better to ask: "How many different sex partners have you had in the past year?" "Have you ever had sex for money or for drugs?" "Have you had sex with your dealer?" "Have you ever had sex with someone you don't know?" "Have you had sex with someone who might be using, or has used, IV drugs?" (If the adolescent is male, "Have you ever had sex with another guy?")

Depending on the answers to the above questions, HIV testing may need to be considered. If the patient has personally injected drugs, HIV testing should be done.

If recent changes of location or immigration changes have affected the family (for example, if the child is an immigrant, or if his or her parents immigrated), ask about how the adolescent is affected by adapting to changes in the community or to the dominant culture. Is language a problem? In the case of immigrants, are conflicts between "traditional" customs and attitudes and those of the new community a problem? Even if the family has simply moved from another city or state, how has the adolescent managed to cope with being "different" or with the loneliness associated with being in a new place?

Asking questions regarding parents' awareness of the adolescent's drug or alcohol use also is appropriate, as are questions about how the adolescent may have attempted to hide his or her behavior from the family. There are situations in which denial is in full force, and no one "knows" on a conscious level what the adolescent is doing. At these times, when the adolescent's behavior is a danger to him- or herself, the parents need to be involved. The adolescent should be strongly encouraged to tell his or her parents about the substance abuse. Often this step requires the direct assistance of the physician.

INTERVIEWING THE FAMILY

The interview of the adolescent, completed with care and compassion, is the first step in a process of evaluation that can eventually lead to effective diagnosis and treatment. The second step in the process is to expand the evaluation to include the greater family system by interviewing the parents as their own subsystem and then the family as a whole. General considerations for the conduct of the family interview include the following:

- Allow time to interview family members apart as well as together as a group. Sometimes a member will say things privately that he or she is not willing to say in the larger group.
- Include siblings as part of the interview process if they are available. Often siblings are more knowledgeable about what is happening in the patient's life than are the parents.
- When interviewing families, it usually is appropriate to defer to the natural authority of the parents by asking for their input first. However, if one person (such as one of the parents) is particularly resistant to the idea of intervention or family involvement, it may be useful to begin by eliciting the opinions or feelings of the most resistant family member. Such a strategy may serve to "hook" them into the process, demonstrate that the clinician views his or her contribution as valuable, and acknowledge that person's importance to the process.

Qualities in the Interviewer that Enhance Interviewing Effectiveness. The following qualities and attitudes on the part of the interviewer can greatly enhance the value of the interview experience:

Unconditional Positive Regard: An attitude of unqualified respect for the patient as a human being who has inherent worth, regardless of whether the health provider approves of all of his or her behaviors (such as drinking or drug use).

Acceptance: An attitude that is non-judgmental.

Genuineness: A feeling of real interest in the patient, conveyed with personal warmth and openness, yet with a professional manner and appearance.

Empathy: The ability to understand the experience of the patient from the patient's perspective. This does not require that the clinician agree with the patient's feelings or opinions, but rather that the clinician attempt to understand how the patient views his or her life experiences.

Self-Awareness: The clinician must be aware of his or her own response to the situation, keeping the patient's anguish separate from his own. It is important to focus on the patient's history. The interview is *not* a time for the clinician to share details of his or her own difficult life and personal struggles. Many patients with substance abuse problems are seeking every opportunity to avoid discussing their problems. They will be happy to divert attention to the interviewer, but this is not therapeutic. A well-developed self-awareness helps the health care professional avoid being drawn unwittingly into the patient's denial.

Professionalism and Maintenance of Boundaries: Patients with substance abuse problems often have great difficulty in maintaining appropriate emotional boundaries. They may attempt to ask the clinician personal questions about his or her private life, ask for a home phone numbers to use in times of "crisis," or even invite the physician home for "dinner and drinks." Maintaining a professional detachment from the patient helps the clinician to provide better care. Such detachment allows the clinician to avoid the conflict of having to confront a "friend" and avoids drawing the clinician in as an active partner in the patient's pathology.

Key Questions to Include in the Family Interview. The following questions should be included in every family interview.

Questions About Family History:

- Parents' occupations, ages, and level of education.
- How long have the parents been together?
- When were the children born? What are their current ages, living arrangements, and activities?
- Information about each parent's family of origin: age and health status of the child's grandparents, aunts, uncles, cousins. Do they live with the family?
- The history of substance use (drugs, alcohol, including prescription drugs) among any relatives or of illnesses that may be related to chronic sub-

stance use (such as cirrhosis). Does anyone in the family use substances "more than they would like?" Has anyone ever suggested attending a support group such as AA or Al-Anon?

- History of significant changes in the family (relocation/migration, births, deaths (include the deaths of pets and friends, as well as relatives), divorce, re-marriage.
- How did family members adjust to these changes? In the case of migrations, are language or traditions and customs areas of conflict or concern?
- If the family is of a cultural background different than that of the physician, or if the adolescent is first or second generation in this country, what are relationships like between the child and the immigrant family members? Are there problems with a "cultural gap" or a "generation gap?" How has the child "fit in" with peers who are not of the same cultural background?

Questions About the Substance-Abusing Child:

- When did the parents first notice a problem or change in behavior in their son or daughter that suggested substance abuse?
- Has the school reported any behavior problems?
- What has been the pattern in the child's grades? Are grades dropping over time? Has the child been truant?
- Has the child engaged in behaviors such as running away, stealing or lying?
- What is the nature of the child's relationships with his or her peers?
- What do the parents know about the child's friends?
- Have there been any changes in personality (such as acting more belligerent, "high strung," nervous, disinterested in life or depressed)?
- Does the child smoke cigarettes? Marijuana? Drink?
- Do any of the child's friends use drugs or alcohol?

Questions About the Parents:

- What is the quality of the parent's relationship? Is there tension in the home? Family violence? Divorce, separation?
- If there are step-parents, does the child visit the biological parent? What is the nature of the child's relationship with that parent? What is the nature of the child's visits with the parent; what do they do when they are together?
- Does either parent drink too much or use drugs (including prescription medications to excess), or have they done so in the past? Has either parent ever joined a self-help group such as Alcoholics Anonymous or Narcotics Anonymous? Has either parent ever tried to cut down on the amount of drugs or liquor they consume?
- What is the family's involvement with the greater community (such as church, civic groups, Little League, Girl Scouts, etc.). How satisfying do the parents find their community-related experiences?
- What is the family's idea of what form treatment should take? Have they considered hospitalization, counseling, or other treatment approaches for their child? Do they think this is part of a "medical" problem? Do they expect a recommendation? How willing are they to be included in the treatment process?

A Case Example: Lori's Family: Lori is a 15-year-old Mexican-American girl who was brought to a therapist in the community for treatment by her mother following a drug overdose with cocaine. Because the parents had no medical insurance, Lori had been observed for 24 hours in a local general hospital and released with no planned medical or psychiatric follow-up. At the first visit, three days later, Lori was sullen and withdrawn. She could give no reason for having taken an overdose, and said her drug use was sporadic, depending on the availability of funds to purchase drugs. Her drugs of choice were cocaine, methamphetamines, and LSD.

According to her mother, Lori had run away from home with her 19-year-old boyfriend for six days one year earlier. Although the mother's initial request was for individual counseling "to fix Lori's problem," the counselor refused to treat Lori unless the entire nuclear family was involved.

The next day, Lori arrived for an appointment with her mother, father, and 10-year-old sister Marta. A family history revealed that the father was born in Mexico and immigrated to the United States 20 years earlier. The mother was born in the U.S. to Mexican parents. Although both parents reported a "perfectly happy household except for Lori," the younger sister Marta provided a contrasting view. In the family session, she said that her parents often fought and that these arguments were so frightening that she would hide in the dog's house in the back yard, curled up with the dog for comfort and security.

Marta described her father's hands as "huge" and said that he had been known to hit the table, the wall, and her sister with his hand or fist. Following Marta's disclosure of violence, the mother also reported verbal abuse, stating that her husband was "just like his father" and had "old fashioned ideas" about a woman's place in the home. Moreover, she said that her husband often called her "stupid," especially when he had been drinking.

Lori's father then justified his actions by saying that if he did not set "rules," his family would get out of control. He admitted to occasional excessive drinking, but said that living with his "dumb wife" was frustrating because she had no common sense and was "too easy" on the girls. Becoming enraged with Lori, he said, was only a response to her flirtation with boys. He called her "a slut," insisted that he did not "need fixing" and suggested that the therapist was not competent to manage Lori's problem, and did not really understand his culture very well.

As the family interview came to a close, ignoring the direct order of her husband to "let's not talk about the bad things," Lori's mother tentatively asked if her child's drug problems might be related to a rape she had experienced on a school playground when Lori was seven years old. At the time of the rape, both parents had decided it was best not to discuss it, and so they never sought medical attention or spoke with Lori about her feelings about having been raped. At this disclosure, Lori began to cry and her father became irate, stating that an event that had occurred so long ago could not have any relevance in the present; moreover, he said he did not want to discuss "the family shame."

Under ideal circumstances, Lori would have benefitted from intensive inpatient evaluation and therapy for her substance abuse problems. For this family, however, such options were not available. Nine months of outpatient ("pro bono") therapy within a private therapy practice included some individual sessions for Lori as well as numerous family sessions. At the termination of therapy, Lori was drug-free, doing well in school, and had developed age-appropriate relationships with peers of both sexes. The issues of family violence and abuse, substance use, anger management, development of self-esteem, and recovery from the remembered trauma and shame associated with the childhood rape all were addressed during the course of therapy. Lori was not the only family member to benefit from intervention; all family members were able to achieve some measure of differentiation as a result of this treatment. Two years later, Lori remains drug free. Her mother, who believed herself "too stupid to learn," has graduated from vocational school, and her father's violent outbursts have diminished in frequency and intensity. Marta's grades have improved, and she no longer takes shelter in the dog house.

Without the family interview, much valuable information about this family would have remained hidden. Within their family system, Lori was the "scapegoat," involved as the third member of a triangle with her parents, and Marta was the "lost child," isolating herself in the dog house to avoid her father's rage. Lori's drug abuse served to end her parents' attacks on each other as they directed their anger and concern toward her and "her problem." By focusing on Lori, her parents were able to avoid facing directly their own conflicts and unhappiness. The interview also uncovered several family secrets: alcohol abuse, verbal abuse, physical violence and the "family shame" of the rape against Lori. Without Marta as an informant, much of this information would have been lost. Finally, by obtaining some family history, the therapist was able to identify typical coping mechanisms and cultural values and attitudes passed down through a multigenerational transmission process. The data obtained from this family interview were of critical importance in planning and implementing Lori's treatment, which was brief, yet highly effective.

CONCLUSIONS

Adolescents with substance abuse problems present numerous challenges for the physician. Considering drug and alcohol abuse as adolescent behavior that exists in the broader contexts of development, culture and family dynamics helps to remove the negative associations often linked to members of this age group.

Recognizing that their substance abuse problems are not merely another means of "annoying" adults, but reflect genuine emotional anguish and psychological distress, may help the physician summon the patience to complete a comprehensive evaluation, which can form the basis for selecting the best mode of intervention for the adolescent. With this understanding, the assessment process can be the first step toward helping adolescents come to know that there is hope, and that they can change their lives.

REFERENCES

Blum R, Harmon B, Harris L, Bergeisent L & Resnick M (1992). American-Indian-Alaska Native youth health. *The Provider* 17:137–146.

Brown S & Yalom I (1995). *Treating Alcoholism*. San Francisco, CA: Jossey-Bass.

Director L (1996). Dual diagnosis: Outpatient treatment of substance abusers with coexisting psychiatric disorders. In AM Washton (ed.) *Psychotherapy and Substance Abuse: A Practitioner's Handbook.* New York, NY: Guilford Press, 375–393.

Farrell AD, Danish SJ & Howard CW (1992). Risk factors for drug use in urban adolescents: Identification and cross-validation. *American Journal of Community Psychology* 20:263–286.

Flack J et al. (1995). Epidemiology of minority health. *Health Psychology* 14(7):592–600.

Johnson K et al. (1995). Macrosocial and environmental influences on minority health. *Health Psychology* 14(7):601–612.

Margolis R (1996). Adolescent chemical dependence: Assessment, treatment and management. In AM Washton (ed.) *Psychotherapy and Substance Abuse: A Practitioner's Handbook.* New York, NY: Guilford Press, 394–412.

Markides KS, Krause N & Mendes de Leon CF (1988). Acculturation and alcohol consumption among Mexican-Americans: A three generational study. *American Journal of Public Health* 78:1178–1181.

Markides KS, Ray LA, Stroup C & Trevino FM (1990). Acculturation and alcohol consumption in Mexican origin population of the Southwest. *American Journal of Public Health* 80(Suppl.):42–46.

May PA (1990). Alcohol and alcoholism among American Indians: An overview. In TD Watts & SJ Roosevelt (eds.) *Alcoholism in Minority Populations.* Springfield, IL: Charles C. Thomas Co., 95–119.

National Institute on Drug Abuse (1991). *National Household Survey on Drug Abuse: Population Estimates 1991* (DHHS Publication No. ADM 92-1887) Washington, DC: U.S. Government Printing Office.

Ramirez S, Wassef A, Paniagua F & Linskey AO (1996). Mental health providers' perceptions of cultural variables in evaluating ethnically diverse clients. *Professional Psychology: Research and Practice* 27(3):284–288.

U.S. Bureau of the Census (1991). *The Hispanic Population in the U.S.: March 1991* (Current Population Reports, Series P-20, No. 225). Washington, DC: U.S. Government Printing Office.

U.S. Department of Health and Human Services (1985). *Report of the Secretary's Task Force on Black and Minority Health.* Washington, DC: U.S. Government Printing Office.

CHAPTER 4

Adolescent Substance Abuse and Psychiatric Comorbidity

Marie E. Armentano, M.D.

Conduct Disorders/Antisocial Personality Disorder
Depressive Disorder
Attention-Deficit Hyperactivity Disorder
Eating Disorders
Anxiety Disorders and PTSD
Schizophrenia
Bipolar Disorder
Organic Mental Disorders
Borderline and Narcissistic Personality Disorder

Adolescents who manifest psychiatric diagnoses in addition to substance abuse and dependence are a population that have aroused increasing recognition and concern (Bukstein, Glancy & Kaminer, 1992; Costello, Costello et al., 1988; Schuckit, 1985, 1986). In this chapter, the terms "dual diagnosis" and "dually diagnosed adolescents" will be used as general terms to refer to patients who meet the criteria for a diagnosis of substance abuse or dependence and also meet the criteria for another psychiatric diagnosis on Axis I or II, using the *Diagnostic and Statistical Manuals of Mental Disorders* of the American Psychiatric Association (*DSM-IIIR* and *DSM-IV*; American Psychiatric Association, 1987, 1994). Patients who initially present for treatment for substance abuse and dependence may be different from those who present for psychiatric treatment (Mirin, Weiss et al., 1988); this chapter focuses on those adolescents who have been diagnosed and are being treated for substance problems.

Dual diagnosis issues initially were studied in adults (Fergusson, Horwood & Lynskey, 1993; Gastfriend, 1993; Kaminer, Tarter et al., 1992; Kempton, Van Hasselt et al., 1994; Minkoff, 1989), leaving the clinician to extrapolate from this work to the adolescent population. As a result, clinicians must use an imperfect system designed for adults to make substance abuse diagnoses in adolescents (Bailey, 1989). More recently, adolescent clinical populations have been studied (Bukstein, Glancy & Kaminer, 1992; Costello, Costello et al., 1988; DeMilio, 1989; Deykin, Buka & Zeena, 1992; Friedman & Glickman, 1986; Groves, 1978; Schuckit, 1985, 1986, 1994). For both adults and adolescents, some of the methodological issues are the same. For example, the course and treatment of the same two disorders may vary depending on which one is primary, i.e., which disorder preceded the other (Regier, Farmer et al., 1990; Ries, Mullen & Cox, 1994), and also depending on their relative severity. Thus, it is unhelpful to assume that all dual diagnosis patients are the same and require the same treatment (Schuckit & Chiles, 1978).

Criteria that have been developed for adults have not been validated with adolescents, and there may be some discontinuities between the adolescent and adult populations (Bukstein, Brent & Kaminer, 1992). When diagnostic criteria are based on problem behaviors, it often is unclear whether the behaviors are the result of substance use or another coexisting or preexisting problem. Although craving and loss of control are included in the *DSM-IIIR* and *DSM-IV* criteria, no studies have established whether these criteria are present in adolescents (Bukstein, Brent et al., 1993).

Although a high prevalence of comorbidity has been reported in adolescent substance abusers in inpatient treatment (Schuckit, 1985, 1986), it is unclear how many of these adolescents are exhibiting psychiatric symptoms secondary to their substance use disorder and how many have a primary or coexisting psychiatric diagnosis. Miller and Fine

(1993) argue that methodological considerations, including the length of abstinence required before the diagnosis is made, population sampled and the perspective of the examiner all affect prevalence rates for psychiatric disorders in substance abusers and account for the variability. They see the prevalence rates for psychiatric disorders as having been artificially elevated by the tendency to diagnose the patient before some of the psychiatric symptomatology secondary to substance use abates.

Despite the controversy regarding the degree of comorbidity, the clinician must treat the patient he encounters. The addiction medicine specialist or other clinician will serve these patients well if he or she:

1. Conducts a comprehensive evaluation of the patient, including a mental status examination and an inquiry into other psychiatric symptomatology, using information obtained from multiple sources.
2. Maintains a high index of suspicion for psychiatric comorbidity in adolescents who are not responding to treatment or who are presenting problems in treatment.
3. Individualizes treatment to accommodate other psychiatric diagnoses.
4. Knows when to consult a psychiatrist or other specialist.

The clinician needs to know what kind of comorbidity is likely to be seen in practice. Large-scale population studies have not yet been conducted on adolescents, but the National Institute of Mental Health's Epidemiological Catchment Area (ECA) study (Burke, Burke et al., 1990) attempted to estimate the true prevalence of alcoholism, other drug abuse disorders, and mental disorders in an adult community and an institutional sample of over 20,000 subjects standardized to the U.S. Census. The ECA study found that about 37% of persons with alcohol disorders also had another mental disorder, with the highest prevalence for affective, anxiety and antisocial personality disorders. More than half of those with drug use disorders other than alcohol had a comorbid mental disorder, 28% had anxiety disorders, 26% had affective disorders, 18% had antisocial personality disorder, and 7% had schizophrenia. The ECA study verified the widely held clinical impression that comorbidity rates are much higher in treated and institutionalized populations than in the general population.

Studies involving adolescents are smaller than those of adults and tend to involve clinical populations. Stowell and Estroff (1993) studied 226 adolescents who were receiving inpatient treatment for a primary substance abuse disorder in private psychiatric hospitals. The patients were diagnosed four weeks into their treatment, using a semistructured diagnostic interview. Of these patients, 82% met *DSM-IIIR* criteria for an Axis I psychiatric disorder, 61% had mood disorders, 54% had conduct disorders, 43% had anxiety disorders, and 16% had substance-induced organic disorder. Fully 74% had two or more psychiatric disorders. Westermeyer and colleagues (1994) studied 100 adolescents aged 12 to 20 who presented to two university outpatient substance abuse treatment programs. Of this group, 22 had eating disorders, eight had conduct disorders, seven had major depressive disorder, six had minor depressive disorder, five had bipolar disorder, five had schizophrenia, four had anxiety disorders, three had another psychotic disorder, three had an organic mental disorder, and two had attention-deficit disorder. In reviewing the distribution of diagnoses as a function of age, the researchers found that older adolescents had more eating disorder diagnoses and depressive symptoms.

Giaconia and colleagues (1994) also examined the effects of age in their study of 386 18-year-olds in a predominantly white, working class community. They compared adolescents who had met the criteria for one of six psychiatric diagnoses, including substance abuse and dependence, before and after age 14. They found that the adolescents with early onset of any psychiatric diagnosis were six times as likely to have one, and 12 times as likely to have two, additional disorders by age 18 than those with later onset. This would imply that the clinician's index of suspicion for dual diagnosis must be particularly high for his younger substance abusing patients. Burke and colleagues (1994) examined the Epidemiological Catchment Area (ECA) data to determine hazard rates for the development of disorders and concluded that ages 15 to 19 were the peak ages for the onset of depressive disorders in females and substance use disorders and bipolar disorders in both sexes.

CONDUCT DISORDERS AND ANTISOCIAL PERSONALITY DISORDER

Conduct disorders and antisocial personality disorder are the most common diagnoses coexisting with substance abuse, particularly in males (Myers, Burket & Otto, 1993; Olfson & Klerman, 1992; Schuckit, 1973). Although evidence of antisocial personality must be present by age 15, the diagnosis cannot be applied to anyone below the age of 18. The characteristic symptom of antisocial personality disorder (American Psychiatric Association, 1994) is a pervasive pattern of disregarding and violating the rights of others. Other symptoms may include deceitfulness, impulsivity, failure to conform to rules or the law, aggressiveness and irresponsibility.

The diagnostic criteria for conduct disorder are similar, but include manifestations that are likely to be seen in younger patients, such as cruelty to animals, running away, truancy and vandalism.

Many who have studied adolescent substance abuse have observed that it usually occurs as part of a constellation of problem behaviors (Bailey, 1989; Bukstein & Kaminer, 1994; Mason & Siris, 1992; Miller, 1993). Cloninger (1987) has presented an interesting schema of hereditary factors on three axes that may account for many of the interrelationships among many psychiatric diagnoses. The three axes are reward-dependence, harm-avoidance and novelty-seeking. Based on these axes, Cloninger has distinguished Type 1 and Type 2 alcoholics, defining Type 2 alcoholics as low on reward-dependence and harm-avoidance and high on novelty-seeking.

Younger alcoholics with antisocial personality fit into the Type 2 schema. The higher prevalence of antisocial personality in younger alcoholics may explain why many clinicians find adolescent substance abusers more difficult to treat. Horowitz and colleagues (1992) and Buydens-Branchey, Branchey et al. (1989) also see many young substance abusers as presenting with a combination of characteristics, including increased hostility, depression and suicidality that suggest an underlying, perhaps neurochemically determined, difficulty with self-regulation and aggression. Adolescents with co-occurring conduct and antisocial personality disorder need a strong behavioral program with clear limits. Substance-abusing adolescents with co-occurring psychiatric disorders are more likely to do well in their substance abuse treatment if their psychiatric disorder can be successfully treated (Bukstein, Brent & Kaminer, 1992).

DEPRESSIVE DISORDER

Much has been written about the interplay between depression and substance abuse and dependence (Regier, Farmer et al., 1990; Ries, Mullen & Cox, 1994; Ries, 1993; Ross, Glaser & Germanson, 1988). What seems to be emerging is an awareness that, in adolescents as well as adults (Bukstein, Brent & Kaminer, 1992), there are two groups that exhibit significant depressive symptoms: those with a substance-induced mood disorder (American Psychiatric Association, 1994) and those with primary depressive disorders. The chief symptom of depression consists of a disturbance of mood usually characterized as sadness or feeling "down in the dumps" and a loss of interest or pleasure. Adolescents may report or exhibit irritability instead of sadness. Depression also is characterized by guilt, hopelessness, sleep disturbances, appetite disturbances, loss of the ability to concentrate, a diminution of energy and by thoughts of death or suicide. In order for a patient to meet the criteria, they need to exhibit or experience depressed mood most of the day, every day, for two weeks. Patients with a substance-induced mood disorder can exhibit the same symptoms.

Schuckit (Regier, Farmer et al., 1990; Ries, 1993; Ross, Glaser & Germanson, 1988), Hesselbrock (Gastfriend, 1993) and Miller (Kandel, Raveis & Davies, 1991) stress the importance of distinguishing the two disorders. In work done with adult substance abusers (Kandel, Raveis & Davies, 1992; Katz, 1990; Ries, 1993), the substance-induced mood disorder dissipated with abstinence, but the primary depressive disorder did not. In fact it may, if left untreated, interfere with treatment of and recovery from the co-occurring substance use disorder (Olfson & Klerman, 1992). Deykin, Buka and Zeena (1997), in interviewing 223 adolescents in residential treatment for substance abuse and dependence, found that almost 25% met the *DSM-IIIR* criteria for depression. Eight percent met the criteria for a primary depression; the other 16% had a secondary mood disorder. Bukstein, Glancy and Kaminer (1992) studied adolescent inpatients on a dual diagnosis unit and reported that almost 31% had a comorbid major depression, with secondary disorder much more common than primary disorder. Unlike what has been reported in adults, they did *not* find that the secondary depression remitted with abstinence.

Depressed adolescents may present on mental status as taciturn, with poor eye contact and a sad-looking face. They may be poorly groomed or drably dressed and may become tearful during the interview. Often they deny feelings of sadness, although their demeanor bespeaks it eloquently. Depression interferes with treatment because of the characteristic lack of concentration, motivation and hope and the sufferer's tendency toward isolation. Kempton and colleagues (1994) found cognitive distortions, including catastrophizing and personalizing, to be particularly prominent in adolescents with the multiple diagnoses of conduct disorder, depressive disorder and substance abuse and dependence. A depressed adolescent may benefit from a specific cognitive intervention for depression (Bukstein & Kaminer, 1994; Kempton, Van Hasselt et al., 1994).

Research has not answered the question of whether adolescents treated for comorbid depression fare better in substance abuse treatment. At present, lacking such knowledge, treatment decisions must be made on a case-by-case basis. If the adolescent has a depressive disorder that predates his or her substance abuse or dependence, has a family history of depression, or has a mood disorder that is interfering with treatment several weeks into abstinence despite cognitive interventions, pharmacotherapy may be indicated. Serotonergic agents such as fluoxetine have a relatively safe profile of side effects and may be most appropriate, considering reports (Christie, Burke et al., 1988; Cloninger, 1987) that young substance abusers have a preexisting serotonin deficit. It would be advisable, before starting medication, to determine that:

1. The patient is abstinent from substances and his or her abstinence is secure; she or he has supports in place or is in a secure, drug-free environment.
2. The patient will be compliant with a medication regimen and/or has a family that will help him or her take medication regularly.

In looking at the referral and prescribing practices of primary care physicians (Caton, Gralnick et al., 1989; DeMilio, 1989), there is a tendency to underdiagnose and undertreat depression. If there are doubts about the diagnosis of depression or about how to treat, a psychiatric consultation with a psychiatrist experienced in treating adolescents with addictions is indicated. When the primary clinician is concerned about possible suicidality (Bukstein, Brent et al., 1993; Burke, Burke & Rae, 1994; Gastfriend, 1993; Mason & Siris, 1992), a consultation should be sought without delay.

ATTENTION-DEFICIT HYPERACTIVITY DISORDER

A large number of adolescents suffer from co-occurring attention-deficit hyperactivity disorder and substance use disorder (Kempton, Van Hasselt et al., 1994; Ries, 1993). Bukstein, Brent and Kaminer (1992) postulate that there is no direct connection, but that problems tend to be comorbid with conduct disorder. Biederman and Steingard (1989), in their studies of outpatients, note that 30% to 50% of children with the attention-deficit disorder have symptoms that persist into adulthood, contrary to the earlier belief that youngsters "mature out of it." They also report on multiple cases of attention-deficit disorder that is comorbid with affective, anxiety and antisocial disorders.

The symptoms of attention-deficit disorder (American Psychiatric Association, 1994) include inattention (as expressed in failure to listen), difficulties with organization, the tendency to lose objects, and a high degree of distractibility. Patients also may manifest hyperactivity and impulsivity, as expressed in fidgeting, restlessness and the tendency to interrupt. The diagnosis requires that these symptoms be present in more than one setting. Use of rating scales also may be helpful in establishing the diagnosis.

Treatment optimally includes behavioral intervention. Pharmacotherapy in adolescents is controversial (Blum, 1987; Fergusson, Horwood & Lynskey, 1993). It appears that adolescents respond much like younger children to medications. In addition, they may dislike the subjective effects of stimulants (Blum, 1987) and conversely, are more likely to abuse them than the younger child. The long-acting stimulant pemoline (Flory, 1996) has been suggested, as have tricyclic antidepressants and clonidine. Since the successful treatment of substance abuse involves teaching patients to plan and to delay impulses, the effective treatment of attention-deficit hyperactivity disorder is a necessary part of an integrated plan.

EATING DISORDERS

As the incidence of both eating disorders and substance abuse have increased in the adolescent population (Hicks, Batzer et al., 1993), it is not uncommon to find them occurring together; in fact, 25% of all eating disorder patients give a history of current or prior substance abuse. Anorexia nervosa, which involves weight restriction and increased activity, a distorted body image and intense fear of losing control and getting fat (American Psychiatric Association, 1994) is not as prevalent as bulimia in both the general population and in the substance abusing population. Bulimia involves recurrent episodes of binge eating, sometimes accompanied by compensatory measures such as vomiting or laxative abuse, and a preoccupation with food and weight.

About 90% to 95% of all eating disorders occur in females (Hicks, Batzer et al., 1993). While anorectics present with a characteristic emaciated appearance, bulimics can be of any weight. Patients who secrete themselves in the bathroom after meals may be purging. Eating-disordered individuals may abuse amphetamines in order to lose weight. Katz (1990) postulates that the proneness to substance abuse in bulimic patients may be due to borderline personality features.

ANXIETY DISORDER AND PTSD

Anxiety disorders include generalized anxiety disorder, panic disorder, obsessive-compulsive disorder and post-traumatic stress disorder (American Psychiatric Association, 1987; Bailey, 1989). Anxiety disorders often are not detected or treated. Sometimes patients who are resistant to going to self-help meetings may, on closer examination, be found to have social phobia or agoraphobia.

Panic attacks are periods of intense discomfort that develop abruptly and reach a peak within 10 minutes. Symptoms include palpitations, sweating, trembling, sensations of shortness of breath or choking, chest discomfort, nausea, dizziness, and fears of losing control or dying. Since some of these symptoms also may be seen in substance intoxication or withdrawal, it is important to establish abstinence before making a diagnostic assessment.

Patients with a social phobia may isolate on an inpatient unit or in a group. A careful interview in which anxiety symptoms and family history of anxiety disorders are pursued may be quite revealing. Behavioral treatment, including relaxation training, often is helpful in anxiety disorders.

The issue of pharmacotherapy is a thorny one: many experts argue that the use of benzodiazepines is contraindicated in anyone with a history of substance abuse or dependence (Gastfriend, 1993). As alternatives, buspirone and tricyclic antidepressants have been recommended as non-addicting anti-anxiety agents; however, clinical experience and anecdotal reports suggest that there are many for whom buspirone is ineffective. It is unclear whether patients who insist that only benzodiazepines are effective represent drug-seeking behavior or a *bona fide* response to pharmacotherapy. If abstinence has been established, the patient has failed an adequate trial of behavioral therapy (Olfson & Klerman, 1992) and alternative medications, and the patient is compliant with treatment and medication as prescribed, the judicious use of a long-acting benzodiazepine such as clonazepam may be justified.

Clinical and epidemiologic reports suggest that the incidence of severe trauma and symptoms of post-traumatic stress disorder are surprisingly high. If an adolescent has been acting out and abusing substances, he or she may not have dealt with past trauma, such as physical and sexual abuse or exposure to violence, or with the trauma that may be incurred in a substance abusing career (Blum, 1987). It may only be in abstinence that the symptoms and memories of trauma manifest themselves. The symptoms of post-traumatic stress disorder can be divided into three groups (American Psychiatric Association, 1994): (1) symptoms that involve re-experiencing the trauma through intrusive thoughts, dreams or flashbacks, which feel as if the event is re-occurring; (2) a numbing of general responsiveness and avoidance of thoughts about the trauma; and (3) symptoms of increased arousal, including difficulty sleeping, irritability, hypervigilance and an exaggerated startle response.

Trauma and its associated symptoms need to be considered in the assessment in order to ensure adequate identification and treatment of the adolescent substance-abusing population. Care needs to be taken to acknowledge the trauma without arousing anxiety that will interfere with substance abuse treatment and recovery. Groups that support self-care and a "first-things-first attitude" may be the best approach, because they can help the patient learn to keep him- or herself safe, with treatment for substance abuse an important aspect of safety. The patient can be told that recovery is a process that must be taken in stages, and that some of the effects of the trauma can be dealt with after the patient's safety is better established. When trauma is suspected, the clinician should obtain a psychiatric consultation if there are questions about diagnosis or management.

SCHIZOPHRENIA

Patients who simultaneously meet the criteria for schizophrenia and a substance abuse diagnosis are less likely to present for treatment on a substance abuse unit than on a psychiatric unit (Fergusson, Horwood & Lynskey, 1993). Because the late teen years are a time when many schizophrenic disorders begin, and the use of substances may precipitate an incipient psychosis, patients with this disorder may present for substance abuse treatment in the early stages of schizophrenia (King, Ghaziuddin et al.,

1996; Ries, 1993; Schuckit, 1985). The characteristic symptoms are hallucinations (usually auditory), delusions, disorganized speech, grossly disorganized or catatonic behavior, and negative symptoms such as flattening of affect, alogia or avolition (American Psychiatric Association, 1994). Therefore, the diagnosis of schizophrenia should be considered in patients who present in a bizarre manner that seems grossly different from the rest of the treatment population.

Increasingly, younger schizophrenic patients (Buydens-Branchey, Branchey & Noumair, 1989) do abuse substances, some in an attempt to manage or deny their symptoms. Such substance abuse often interferes with treatment of the psychotic disorder. These patients are best managed in special dual diagnosis facilities for psychotic patients, where the psychosis and the substance abuse or dependence can be addressed in a parallel manner (Buydens-Branchey, Branchey & Noumair, 1989; Deykin, Buka & Zeena, 1992; Fergusson, Horwood & Lynskey, 1993; Horowitz, Overton et al., 1992; Kandel, Raveis & Davies, 1992; Miller & Fine, 1993; Minkoff, 1989; Mirin, Weiss et al., 1988).

BIPOLAR DISORDER

In bipolar disorders, which often begin in late adolescence (Bailey, 1989; Caton, Gralnick et al., 1989; DeMilio, 1989), the presenting symptoms of mania include: a persistently elevated, expansive or irritable mood lasting at least one week, accompanied by grandiosity or inflated self-esteem, decreased need for sleep, pressured speech, racing thoughts, increased purposeful activity and excessive involvement in pleasurable activities such as spending money, sexual indiscretions or substance abuse. Some patients use substances, particularly alcohol, to calm themselves when manic. Clearly some of these symptoms are also seen with substance intoxication. If a patient exhibits these symptoms after a period of abstinence, the diagnosis of bipolar disorder should be considered. Bipolar disorders are treated with mood stabilizers, the most common of which is lithium carbonate. Valproic acid and carbamazepine also are used. Before treating for bipolar disorder, a psychiatric consult should be obtained.

ORGANIC MENTAL DISORDER

In some patients, the abuse of alcohol and other drugs (including marijuana, cocaine, hallucinogens and inhalants) is associated with acute and residual cognitive damage (American Psychiatric Association, 1994; Hovens, Cantwell & Kiriakos, 1994; Morrison, Smith et al., 1993; Rounsaville, Zelig et al., 1987; Schuckit, 1986). Acute symptoms may include concentration and receptive and expressive language difficulties, and irritability. Long-term interference with memory and other executive functions may occur. The possibility of a substance-induced dementia should be considered in adolescents who are having trouble coping with the cognitive and organizational demands of a structured and supportive program. Some of these young people will be able to make use of the program if instructions are simplified until they are comprehending accurately. There may be rapid improvement in cognitive functioning, but some patients continue to improve as long as a year or more after the cessation of the chemical insult to the brain. Some may be left with residual impairment.

Adolescents and their families need to be informed about the cognitive consequences of their alcohol or drug abuse in a way that does not engender despair, but one which clearly warns against further abuse. The presence of any persistent cognitive deficits needs to be considered in any rehabilitation, educational and vocational planning for the adolescent. Such patients require neuropsychological evaluation and follow-up.

BORDERLINE AND NARCISSISTIC PERSONALITY DISORDER

In addition to psychiatric diagnoses on Axis I, the personality disorders described on Axis II of the *DSM-IV* (American Psychiatric Association, 1994) are very relevant when one is treating adolescent substance abusers. Personality disorders are enduring patterns of inner experience and behavior that affect cognition, interpersonal behavior, emotional response and impulse control.

Personality factors that make an adolescent difficult to treat. Borderline personality disorder is marked by impulsivity and instability of interpersonal relationships and affects and self-image. Symptoms also include a marked sensitivity and wish to avoid abandonment; chronic feelings of emptiness; inappropriate, intense anger; and suicidal or self-mutilating behavior. Borderline patients in a treatment setting can wreak havoc because of their severe regression and tendency to engage in splitting of staff.

In narcissistic personality disorder, there is a pervasive pattern of grandiosity, need for admiration and lack of empathy. The patient with this disorder feels that he or she is unique and entitled to special treatment. It may be difficult for such a patient to participate in group therapy or to see other people as anything other than need-gratifiers.

Both of these personality disorders can present challenges to the clinician and treatment setting. Powerful and negative countertransferences (Groves, 1978) are easily aroused by patients who are draining, manipulative, rageful and entitled. Whenever a patient takes a great amount of emotional energy, it is likely that there are personality issues involved. It is essential to be aware of the effect that such patients exert, in order to take care of the clinician, the treatment setting and the patient. Expert psychiatric consultation can be very helpful in these situations.

CONCLUSIONS

Awareness of the prevalence and presentation of psychiatric diagnoses is essential to the high-quality treatment of adolescent substance abusers. An ongoing relationship with a psychiatrist who can be available for consultation as needed is helpful. Careful observation and history taking and appropriate consultation result in better detection and treatment of comorbid disorders and ultimately in better care of the patient.

REFERENCES

American Psychiatric Association (1987). *Diagnostic and Statistical Manual of Mental Disorders, 3rd Ed., Revised (DSM-IIIR).* Washington, DC: American Psychiatric Press.

American Psychiatric Association (1994). *Diagnostic and Statistical Manual of Mental Disorders, 4th Ed. (DSM-IV).* Washington, DC: American Psychiatric Press.

Bailey GW (1989). Current perspectives on substance abuse in youth. *Journal of the American Academy of Child and Adolescent Psychiatry* 151–162.

Biederman J & Steingard R (1989). Attention-deficit hyperactivity disorder in adolescents. *Psychiatric Annals* 587–596.

Blum RW (1987). Adolescent substance abuse: Diagnostic and treatment issues. *Pediatric Clinics of North America* 34(2):523–537.

Bukstein O & Kaminer T (1994). The nosology of adolescent substance abuse. *American Journal of Addictions* Winter:1–13.

Bukstein O, Brent DA, Perper JA, Moritz G, Baugher M, Scweers J, Roth C & Balach L (1993). Risk factors for completed suicide among adolescents with a lifetime history of substance abuse: A case-control study. *Acta Psychiatrica Scandinavica* 88(6):403–408.

Bukstein O, Brent DA & Kaminer Y (1992). Patterns of affective comorbidity in a clinical population of dually diagnosed adolescent substance abusers. *Journal of the American Academy of Child and Adolescent Psychiatry* 1131–1141.

Bukstein O, Glancy LJ & Kaminer Y (1992). Patterns of affective comorbidity in a clinical population of dually diagnosed adolescent substance abusers. *Journal of the American Academy of Child and Adolescent Psychiatry* 31(6):1041–1045.

Burke JD, Burke KC & Rae DS (1994). Increased rates of drug abuse and dependence after onset of mood or anxiety disorders in adolescence. *Hospital & Community Psychiatry* 45(5):451–455.

Burke KC, Burke JD, Regier DA & Rae DS (1990). Age at onset of selected mental disorders in five community populations. *Archives of General Psychiatry* 511–518.

Buydens-Branchey L, Branchey MH & Noumair D (1989). Age of alcoholism onset: I. Relationship to psychopathology. *Archives of General Psychiatry* 46:225–230.

Buydens-Branchey L, Branchey MH, Noumair D & Lieber CS (1989). Age of alcoholism onset: II. Relationship to susceptibility to serotonin precursor availability. *Archives of General Psychiatry* 46:231–236.

Caton CLM, Gralnick A, Bender S & Simon M (1989). Young chronic patients and substance abuse. *Hospital & Community Psychiatry* 1037–1040.

Christie KA, Burke JD et al. (1988). Epidemiologic evidence for early onset of mental disorders and higher risk of drug abuse in young adults. *American Journal of Psychiatry* 145:971–975.

Cloninger CR (1987). Neurogenetic adaptive mechanisms in alcoholism. *Science* 410–416.

Costello EJ, Costello AJ et al. (1988). Psychiatric disorders in pediatric primary care. *Archives of General Psychiatry* 45:1107–1116.

DeMilio L (1989). Psychiatric syndromes in adolescent substance abusers. *American Journal of Psychiatry* 146:1212–1214.

Deykin EY, Levy JC & Wells V (1987). Adolescent depression, alcohol and drug abuse. *American Journal of Pediatric Health* 178–182.

Deykin EY, Buka SL & Zeena TH (1992). Depressive illness among chemically dependent adolescents. *American Journal of Psychiatry* 149:1341–1347.

Fergusson DM, Horwood LJ & Lynskey MT (1993). Prevalence and comorbidity of DSM-IIIR diagnoses in a birth cohort of 15 year olds. *Journal of the American Academy of Child and Adolescent Psychiatry* 32(6):1127–1134.

Flory M (1996). Psychiatric diagnosis in child and adolescent suicide. *Archives of General Psychiatry* 53(4):339–348.

Friedman AS & Glickman NW (1986). Program characteristics for successful treatment of adolescent drug abuse. *Journal of Nervous and Mental Disease* 174:669–679.

Galanter M et al. (1988). Substance abuse among general psychiatric patients: Place of presentation, presentation, diagnosis and treatment. *American Journal of Drug and Alcohol Abuse* 14:211–235.

Gastfriend DR (1993). Pharmacotherapy of psychiatric symptoms with comorbid chemical dependence. *Journal of Addictive Diseases* 155–170.

Giaconia RM, Reinherz HZ, Silverman AB, Pakiz B, Frost AK & Cohen E (1994). Ages of onset of psychiatric disorders in a community population of older adolescents. *Journal of the American Academy of Child and Adolescent Psychiatry* 33(5):706–717.

Grilo CM, Becker DF, Walker ML, Levy KN, Edell WS & McGlashan TH (1995). Psychiatric comorbidity in adolescent inpatients with substance use disorders. *Journal of the American Academy of Child and Adolescent Psychiatry* 34(8):1085–1091.

Groves JE (1978). The hateful patient. *The New England Journal of Medicine* 298:883–887.

Hesselbrock MN, Meyer RE & Keener JJ (1985). Psychopathology in hospitalized alcoholics. *Archives of General Psychiatry* 1050–1055.

Hicks RD, Batzer GB, Batzer WB & Imai WK (1993). Psychiatric, developmental and adolescent medicine issues in adolescent substance use and abuse. *Adolescent Medicine* 453–468.

Horowitz HA, Overton WF, Rosenstein D & Steidl JH (1992). Comorbid adolescent substance abuse: A maladaptive pattern of self-regulation. *Adolescent Psychiatry*.

Hovens JG, Cantwell DP & Kiriakos R (1994). Psychiatric comorbidity in hospitalized adolescent substance abusers. *Journal of the American Academy of Child and Adolescent Psychiatry* 33(4):476–483.

Kaminer Y, Tarter RE, Bukstein OG & Kabene M (1992). Comparison between treatment completers and noncompleters among dually diagnosed substance-abusing adolescents. *Journal of the American Academy of Child and Adolescent Psychiatry* 31(6):1046–1049.

Kandel DB, Raveis VH & Davies M (1992). Suicidal ideation in adolescence: Depression, substance use and other risk factors. *Journal of Youth and Adolescence* 289–309.

Katz JL (1990). Eating disorders: A primer for the substance abuse specialist; 1. Clinical features. *Journal of Substance Abuse Treatment* 143–149.

Kempton T, Van Hasselt VB, Bukstein OG & Null JA (1994). Cognitive distortions and psychiatric diagnosis in dually diagnosed adolescents. *Journal of the American Academy of Child and Adolescent Psychiatry* 33(2):217–222.

King CA, Ghaziuddin N, McGovern L, Brand E, Hill E & Naylor M (1996). Predictors of comorbid alcohol and substance abuse in depressed adolescents. *Journal of the American Academy of Child and Adolescent Psychiatry* 743–751.

Mason SE & Siris SG (1992). Dual diagnosis: The case for case management. *American Journal on the Addictions* 77–82.

Miller NS (1993). Comorbidity of psychiatric and alcohol/drug disorders: Interactions and independent status. *Journal of Addictive Diseases* 5–16.

Miller NS & Fine J (1993). Current epidemiology of comorbidity of psychiatric and addictive disorders. *Psychiatric Clinics of North America* 1–10.

Minkoff K (1989). An integrated treatment model for dual diagnosis of psychosis and addiction. *Hospital & Community Psychiatry* 40:1031–1036.

Mirin SM, Weiss RD, Michael J & Griffin ML (1988). Psychopathology in substance abusers: Diagnosis and treatment. *American Journal of Drug and Alcohol Abuse* 139–157.

Morrison MA, Smith DE, Wilford BB, Ehrlich P & Seymour RB (1993). At war in the fields of play: Current perspectives on the nature and treatment of adolescent chemical dependency. *Journal of Psychoactive Drugs* 25(41):321–330.

Morrison MA & Smith QT (1987). Psychiatric issues of adolescent chemical dependence. *Pediatric Clinics of North America* 34(2):461–479.

Myers WC, Burket RC & Otto TA (1993). Conduct disorders and personality disorders in hospitalized adolescents. *Journal of Clinical Psychiatry* 54(1):21–26.

Olfson M & Klerman G (1992). The treatment of depression: Prescribing practices of primary care physicians and psychiatrists. *Journal of Family Practice* 35(6):627–635.

Regier DA, Farmer ME, Rae DS et al. (1990). Comorbidity of mental disorders with alcohol and other drug abuse. *Journal of the American Medical Association* 264(19):2511–2518.

Ries R, Mullen M & Cox G (1994). Symptom severity and utilization of treatment resources among dually diagnosed inpatients. *Hospital and Community Psychiatry* 562–567.

Ries R (1993). The dually diagnosed patient with psychotic symptoms. *Journal of Addictive Diseases* 103–122.

Ries RK (1993). Clinical treatment matching models for dually diagnosed patients. *Psychiatric Clinics of North America* 16.

Ross HE, Glaser FB & Germanson T (1988). The prevalence of psychiatric disorders in patients with alcohol and other drug problems. *Archives of General Psychiatry* 45:1023–1031.

Rounsaville BJ, Zelig SD, Babor TF & Meyer RE (1987). Psychopathology as a predictor of treatment outcome in alcoholics. *Archives of General Psychiatry* 505–513.

Schuckit MA (1985). The clinical implications of primary diagnostic groups among alcoholics. *Archives of General Psychiatry* 1043–1049.

Schuckit MA (1973). Alcoholism and sociopathy: Diagnostic confusion. *Quarterly Journal of Studies on Alcohol* 157–164.

Schuckit MA & Chiles JA (1978). Family history as a diagnostic aid in two samples of adolescents. *Journal of Nervous and Mental Diseases* 166(3):165–176.

Schuckit MA (1986). Genetic and clinical implications of alcoholism and affective disorder. *American Journal of Psychiatry* 143(2):140–147.

Schuckit MA (1994). Alcohol and depression: A clinical perspective. *Acta Psychiatrica Scandinavica* 377(Suppl):28–32.

Stowell JA & Estroff TW (1993). Psychiatric disorders in substance abusing adolescent inpatients: A pilot study. *Journal of the American Academy of Child and Adolescent Psychiatry*.

Van Hasselt VB, Ammerman RT, Glancy LJ & Bukstein OG (1992). Maltreatment in psychiatrically hospitalized dually diagnosed adolescent substance abusers. *Journal of the American Academy of Child and Adolescent Psychiatry* 31(5):868–874.

Wallen M & Weiner HD (1989). Impediments to effective treatment of the dually diagnosed patient. *Journal of Psychoactive Drugs* 161–168.

Weiss RD, Mirin SM & Frances RJ (1992). The myth of the typical dual diagnosis patient. *Hospital & Community Psychiatry* 107–108.

Westermeyer J, Specker S, Neider J & Lingenfelter MA (1994). Substance abuse and associated psychiatric disorder among 100 adolescents. *Journal of Addictive Diseases* 67–89.

Wilcox JA & Yates WR (1993). Gender and psychiatric comorbidity in substance-abusing individuals. *American Journal on Addictions* 202–206.

Young SE, Milkulich SK, Goodwin MB, Hardy J, Martin CL, Zoccolillo MS & Crowley TJ (1995). Treated delinquent boys' substance use: Onset, pattern, relationship to conduct and mood disorders. *Drug and Alcohol Dependence* 37(2):149–162.

Zamvil L (n.d.). Post-Traumatic Stress Disorder in Hospitalized Children and Adolescents (unpublished manuscript).

SECTION 16
Women, Infants and Addiction

CHAPTER 1

Understanding Addictive Disorders in Women **1173**
Sheila B. Blume, M.D.

CHAPTER 2

Social Predictors of Women's Alcohol and Drug Use: Implications for Prevention and Treatment **1191**
Edith S. Lisansky Gomberg, Ph.D.

CHAPTER 3

Treatment of the Addicted Woman in Pregnancy **1199**
Laura J. Miller, M.D.

CHAPTER 4

Treatment Options for Drug-Exposed Neonates **1211**
Stephen B. Kandall, M.D., FAAP

CHAPTER 5

Developmental Outcomes of Prenatal Exposure to Alcohol and Other Drugs **1223**
Sydney L. Hans, Ph.D.

SECTION COORDINATOR

ANDREA G. BARTHWELL, M.D., FASAM
Encounter Medical Group
Oak Park, Illinois

CONTRIBUTORS

Sheila B. Blume, M.D., C.A.C.
Clinical Professor of Psychiatry
State University of New York
Stonybrook, New York, and
Medical Director of the Alcoholism,
Chemical Dependency and
Compulsive Gambling Program
South Oaks Hospital
Amityville, New York

Edith S. Lisansky Gomberg, Ph.D.
Professor of Psychology
Department of Psychiatry
and Alcohol Research Center
University of Michigan School of Medicine
Ann Arbor, Michigan

Sydney Hans, Ph.D.
Research Associate Professor
Department of Psychiatry
The University of Chicago
Chicago, Illinois

Stephen R. Kandall, M.D., FAAP
Chief, Division of Neonatology
Beth Israel Medical Center
New York, New York, and
Professor of Pediatrics
Albert Einstein College of Medicine
Bronx, New York

Laura J. Miller, M.D.
Department of Psychiatry
University of Illinois at Chicago
Chicago, Illinois

CHAPTER 1

Understanding Addictive Disorders in Women

Sheila B. Blume, M.D., C.A.C.

Epidemiology of Addictive Disorders in Women
Pharmacology and Pathophysiologic Factors
Heredity and Addiction in Women
Psychological Factors
Sociocultural Issues
Women and Highway Safety Issues
Clinical Characteristics of Addictive Disorders
Identification of Addictive Disorders
Treatment Issues
Prognosis for Addictive Disorders in Women
Prevention of Addictive Disorders in Women

Throughout history, societies have found it necessary to develop both formal and informal rules for the acceptable use of psychoactive substances. An examination of these rules and the assumptions on which they are based reveals that—as far back as the Code of Hammurabi in 2000 B.C.—the rules have differed for men and women. Moreover, women long have been believed to react to such drugs (particularly alcohol) differently than do men. In Western culture, as far back as the Talmud and ancient Rome, alcohol was popularly believed to affect women as a sexual stimulant—a substance capable of inspiring them to lust, debauchery and promiscuity. This belief, still widespread in 20th century America, has fueled a generally negative attitude toward alcohol use by women and an intensely destructive stigma applied to those women who develop alcoholism. The stigma in turn fortifies denial: on the part of the alcoholic woman, her family, society in general, and even health professionals, leading to the under-recognition of drinking problems in women until they have reached an advanced stage. This failure to recognize alcoholism is most pronounced in middle class, educated, insured women (Moore, Bone et al., 1989).

In addition, the stereotype of the female alcoholic as a sexually aroused "fallen woman" makes her an accepted target for both physical and sexual abuse (Blume, 1991). For example, a 1982 study by Richardson and Campbell found that a rapist who is intoxicated is considered less responsible for a rape, while a victim who is intoxicated is considered more to blame (Richardson & Campbell, 1982).

Unfortunately, society's long-standing and intense interest in psychoactive substance use by women did not prompt serious study of alcohol and drug dependence in women until the last decade. Addiction was considered a problem of men. Until that time, alcohol research was confined to exclusively or predominantly male populations. Data on women often were discarded or not analyzed separately, although the results were generalized to addicts of both sexes. Treatment and casefinding models were designed for men.

Yet clinicians and researchers who have studied addicted women have regularly found that they differ from men in many important ways. Thus, this section concentrates on issues in the diagnosis and treatment of addictive disease that are specific to women, or for which there are significant male-female differences.

EPIDEMIOLOGY OF ADDICTIVE DISORDERS IN WOMEN

Surveys of the use of drugs and alcohol have uniformly found that women use less alcohol and illegal drugs than men, but are more frequent users of prescribed psychoactive drugs. In the past, cigarettes also were used more by males of all ages, but in recent studies of adolescents, girls have smoked about as much as boys (Gritz, 1987). Additionally, during the past 30 years rates of smoking have fallen more precipitously for men (52% to 28%) than for women (34% to 22%) (CASA, 1996). Smoking thus threatens to become a female-dominated form of substance abuse.

Alcohol use by American women generally has increased since the end of World War II. This trend—coupled with the growth of the addiction treatment system over the past 20 years, which brought more women into treatment—has led to a perception in the popular press of an explosive growth or epidemic of female heavy drinking and alcoholism. Population studies have not documented such an epidemic overall, although an increase in heavy drinking has been found among women in some parts of the country (Hilton & Clark, 1987) and in younger cohorts of women. Studies on college campuses (Engs & Hanson, 1985; Mercer & Khavari, 1990) have shown the clearest changes. The Engs study demonstrated both an increase in heavy drinking and in alcohol problems in university women, comparing 1982 self-report data with results of a similar survey conducted in 1974. Mercer and Khavari found evidence for a convergence of drinking patterns among male and female students, comparing a 1985 survey with one performed in 1977. Although males drank more overall, female subjects had reached or surpassed the males in the usual volume of beer and the usual volume of wine consumed at one sitting, particularly if these quantities were corrected for differences in body weight and body water.

Risk factors for alcohol problems in women have been found to vary with age. Although women aged 21 to 34 have the highest problem rates, many of these problems remit over time, whereas women aged 35 to 49 are more likely to have chronic persisting alcohol problems, including symptoms of dependence (Wilsnack, Klassen et al., 1991). Among women aged 21 to 34, those described by Wilsnack as "role-less" (never married, not full-time employed, no children) were most at risk. Risk was highest in 35 to 49 year olds who were characterized as "lost role" (divorced or separated, not employed, with children from whom they were separated). Among women in the 50 to 64 year old group, risk was highest among "role entrapment" women (married, not employed, with children who did not live with them) (Wilsnack & Cheloha, 1987). These older women fit the general description of the "empty nest" syndrome. Women's drinking patterns also have a much greater similarity to the drinking patterns of their "significant others" than do men's (Wilsnack, Klassen et al., 1991).

Women's patterns of other drug use also have changed over the years. In the late 19th and early 20th centuries, American women of all social classes were at risk for dependence on both over-the-counter and prescription medications containing opiates, alcohol and cocaine (Gomberg, 1986). Today, women remain more frequent users of prescription drugs than are men. Women who suffer from combined dependence on alcohol and other drugs are more likely to be dependent on prescription than illicit drugs (Ross, 1989). These drugs often are initially prescribed by a physician who either failed to recognize symptoms of alcohol dependence or failed to intervene successfully.

Epidemiologic studies using different methods yield different estimates of male:female ratios of addictive disorders. General population surveys have yielded a ratio of approximately 2:1 for alcohol abuse and dependence (Williams, Stinson et al., 1987). The Epidemiological Catchment Area Study (ECA), on the other hand, utilizing the Diagnostic Interview Scale (DIS), found relatively fewer females satisfying the criteria for alcohol abuse and/or dependence of the American Psychiatric Association's *Diagnostic and Statistical Manual of Mental Disorders* (Anthony, 1991). In that study, 83% of persons with a lifetime diagnosis of alcohol abuse and/or dependence in the general population were male—a ratio of approximately 4:1. Cases of other substance abuse/dependence found in the general public by the ECA were less predominantly male. Males accounted for 63% of cannabis abuse/dependence cases, 70% of hallucinogen cases, 64% of opioid cases, 50% of amphetamine/stimulant cases, 55% of cocaine cases and 54% of sedative/hypnotic/anxiolytic abuse and/or dependence cases (Anthony, 1991).

In a later study of American adults aged 15 to 54 years, the National Comorbidity Study (Kessler, McGonagle et al., 1994; Warner, Kessler et al., 1995) found male:female ratios of lifetime prevalence of 2.0:1 for any substance abuse/dependence, 2.2:1 for alcohol abuse/dependence and 1.6:1 for other drug abuse/dependence (excluding nicotine).

PHARMACOLOGIC AND PATHOPHYSIOLOGIC FACTORS

Pharmacology. Over many years, the pharmacology of alcohol and other psychoactive substances was studied in male subjects, assuming that the findings would apply to women as well. More recently, however, evidence has accumulated that this is not the case. When men and women are given equal doses of absolute alcohol per pound of body weight, women reach higher peak blood alcohol concentrations (BACs) (Goist & Sutker, 1985; Frezza, di Padova et al., 1990). This difference is related in part to the fact that women have a higher body fat and lower body water content than do men (York & Pendergast, 1990). Since alcohol is distributed throughout total body water, it is less diluted in the female. Further, the differences in BAC are more marked when alcohol is consumed orally, rather than given intravenously, because women absorb more of the alcohol they consume, particularly at low doses. This phenomenon has been shown by Frezza, di Padova et al. (1990) to be related to higher levels of alcohol dehydrogenase (ADH) in the gastric mucosa of males, leading to more active first-pass metabolism within the stomach wall and less absorption. This effect is decreased by fasting. Also, the gastric mucosa of male alcoholic patients shows less ADH activity than in normal males, and the mucosa of alcoholic women shows little or none.

Gender differences in the pharmacology of other drugs have been less well studied. The difference in body composition, with a higher proportion of body fat in women, produces a longer half life for such lipid-soluble drugs as diazepam and oxazepam (Barry, 1987). Moreover, the proportion of body fat in women increases with age, exaggerating this trend.

Evidence for variations in alcohol and other drug pharmacology with phases of the menstrual cycle has been contradictory, with some studies showing day-to-day variability of peak BACs in women with the highest BACs premenstrually, and some showing no effect. In addition, oral contraceptives may slow the rate of alcohol clearance in women (Cyr & Moulton, 1990).

Effects on the Female Reproductive System. Single doses of alcohol seem to have little effect on sex hormone levels in women. Long-term heavy drinking, however, is associated with a wide variety of reproductive dysfunctions, including inhibition of ovulation, decrease in gonadal mass, irregular menses, luteal phase dysfunction and early menopause (Mello, 1986).

Alcoholic women sometimes consult a physician for menstrual distress or infertility. Drinking during pregnancy can cause both fetal damage and spontaneous abortion, premature labor, abruptio placentae and a variety of other complications (see Chapter 5).

The general cultural belief that alcohol enhances sexual arousal in women has not been borne out by research (Blume, 1991). Physiological studies have found that alcohol has a dose-related depressant effect on both sexual arousal and orgasm in women. Also, women (unlike men) experience a dissociation between subjective feelings of arousal and physiologic responses. For example, women who received an alcoholic beverage under experimental conditions said they felt more aroused by sexual stimuli, while physiological measurements taken at the same time documented a depressed level of arousal compared to the alcohol-free state (Wilson & Lawson, 1976).

Cocaine and amphetamines are commonly believed to enhance sexual functioning. In fact, chronic use of both drugs is associated with inhibition of orgasm and loss of sexual desire in both sexes (Washton, 1989).

Heroin dependence has been reported to decrease sexual desire and to suppress ovulation (Gaulden, Littlefield & Putoff, 1964). Menstrual periods often return to normal within a few months after the institution of methadone maintenance treatment (Wallach, Jerez & Blinick, 1969). However, methadone itself may depress sexual activity, in a dose-related fashion (Crowley & Simpson, 1978). Addiction to sedative drugs and minor tranquilizers also may depress women's sexual desire and orgasm.

Sexually Transmitted Diseases. The past decade has seen a steady increase in the proportion of women among all newly reported cases of AIDS. Eighteen percent of new AIDS cases in 1995 were among females, compared to 7% in 1985. Seventy percent of present AIDS cases in women are related to illegal drug use. About half are acquired from injection drug use and another quarter from sexual contact with an injection drug user (CASA, 1996). In addition, the 1980s saw a sharp rise in the incidence of both primary and secondary syphilis, especially among women (Rolfs & Nakishima, 1990). Women's seropositivity for syphilis has been found to be associated with the use of cocaine (Minkoff, McCalla et al., 1990), as well as other drugs.

Other Aspects of Women's Health. Prolonged heavy drinking is linked to many serious medical complications in both sexes. However, there is evidence that women develop these complications more rapidly than do men (after fewer years of heavy drinking and less alcohol intake per year, even if corrected for body weight and water). Fatty liver, hypertension, anemia, malnutrition, gastrointestinal hemorrhage, and peptic ulcer requiring surgery have been shown to develop more rapidly in alcoholic women as compared with men (Ashley, Olin et al., 1977). The same has been found for both peripheral myopathy and cardiomyopathy (Urbano-Marquez, Ramon et al., 1995). The reasons for this more rapid toxicity remain unknown, although suggested mechanisms include reduced first-pass alcohol metabolism, hormonal variations (e.g., association with early menopause), and a finding by some (but not all) researchers of more rapid hepatic alcohol metabolism in women (Mishra, Sharma et al., 1989).

Several researchers have found evidence of a relationship between alcohol consumption and breast cancer, with a dose-response relationship between alcohol intake and risk (Schatzkin, Jones et al., 1987; Willett, Stampfer et al., 1987). A large meta-analysis also found a dose-response relationship (Longnecker, Berlin et al., 1988). Another study found a weak association at best (Harris & Wynder, 1988). Because breast cancer is a major cause of premature death in women, the possibility of an etiologic relationship deserves further study.

Alcohol intake in women also is linked to hypertension. A four-year longitudinal study of more than 58,000 nurses demonstrated a dose-related increase in hypertension risk, beginning at about two to three drinks per day (Witterman, Willett et al., 1990). Cardiovascular mortality in women—especially death from such disease below the age of 55—is linked to alcohol intake. Although in general men die of heart disease at a rate twice as high as women, an analysis of over 8,000 cardiovascular deaths demonstrated that women who drink heavily (14 or more drinks per week) die young of these diseases at a rate equal to that of heavily drinking men (Hanna, Dufour et al., 1992).

Nicotine dependence in women is a growing problem. The mortality for lung cancer in women, after rising steadily since the 1960s, became the most common cancer death in American women (outstripping breast cancer) in 1986. The risk for both fatal and non-fatal coronary artery disease also is greatly increased in women who smoke, as is the risk for earlier menopause, chronic obstructive lung disease, peptic ulcer disease and cancers of the larynx, esophagus, stomach, bladder and cervix (Cyr & Moulton, 1990). While the rate of smoking in men has continued to fall since reaching its peak in the mid-1960s, the rate in women has remained essentially unchanged. Today the rate of initiation of smoking among girls equals the rate for boys (Gritz, 1987).

HEREDITY AND ADDICTION IN WOMEN

The evidence for genetic influence in women is much less convincing than that for such influence in men, and there is evidence for greater importance of environmental factors in women (Sigvardsson, Bohman & Cloninger, 1996; Cloninger, Christiansen et al., 1978). For example, of the two types of genetic transmission described by Cloninger and his associates, the more strongly hereditary type is confined to males (Cloninger, Sigvardsson & Gilligan, 1988).

An Australian study, which investigated the drinking patterns of nearly 2,000 female twin pairs, highlighted the role of environment in modifying hereditary influences on women's drinking patterns. Whereas (in unmarried twins) genetic factors were estimated to account for 60% of drinking pattern variance in women age 30 or younger and about 77% of the variance in women over 30, these proportions dropped to 31% for the younger and 46% to 59% for the older cohorts of female twins who were married or cohabiting (Heath, Jardine & Martin, 1989). Thus, married or cohabiting twins showed more environmental influence. Presumably the drinking pattern of the "significant other" with whom a woman lives is an important part of that environment.

Another twin study that reexamined the role of genetics in female alcoholism reported on 1,030 female general population twin pairs (Kendler, Heath et al., 1992). Using either a broad or narrow definition of alcoholism, the authors calculated that 50% to 60% of women's liability to alcoholism is inherited. Pickens, Svikis et al. (1991) compared 114 male and 55 female same-sex twin pairs recruited from a treatment population, on *DSM III* diagnoses of Alcohol Abuse and Alcohol Dependence. Male and female patterns differed. Significant differences in concordance between monozygotic (MZ) and dizygotic (DZ) twins (indicating genetic influence) were found for both alcohol abuse and dependence in men, but only for alcohol dependence in women. Looking at other substance abuse and dependence diagnoses, MZ/DZ concordance was significantly different in males but not in females. They also found that non-shared environmental influences played a greater role than shared environment in the female twins.

An interesting analysis by Cloninger and his colleagues (1978) explored the question of whether male:female differences in the prevalence of alcoholism were due to greater genetic loading needed to produce disease in females, or to some environmental factors that protect women. They compared family history data for alcoholism with similar data for antisocial personality (ASP) in men and women. Both syndromes run in families and are more common in males. The researchers were able to infer from these data that extra-familial environmental factors account for the lower prevalence of alcoholism (but not ASP) in women.

Studies looking for biological or behavioral markers that would identify individuals at high genetic risk for alcoholism have focused primarily on male populations (Russell, Henderson & Blume, 1985). However, Lex, Lukas, and Greenwald (1988) have compared the reactions of a small group of nonalcoholic young women who had alcoholic first-degree relatives with a control group who had a negative family histories. The two groups did not differ in peak BACs after a measured dose of ethanol, nor in the rate of its metabolism. However, the family history-positive women made fewer errors on a cognitive motor task and experienced less body sway after drinking. These observations were comparable to findings in male samples, pointing to the possibility that genetically predisposed individuals of both sexes show a less vigorous response to alcohol and are therefore less able to judge their level of intoxication.

Ciraulo, Sarid-Segal et al. (1996) also reported that daughters of alcoholic parents showed more mood elevation in response to a single dose of alprazolam than matched controls. This suggests that such women may be at higher risk for abuse of this drug.

PSYCHOLOGICAL FACTORS

A variety of approaches have been used to study the relationship between alcohol and drug addiction and associated psychological or psychopathological features. Many have found male/female differences. In general, depressive and anxiety symptoms and disorders are found more frequently in female and antisocial traits and disorders more frequently in male addicts, as they are for women and men in the general public. Whether and to what degree these factors predispose an individual to addictive disorders, and to what degree these psychological dysfunctions are concomitants or consequences of alcohol and other drug-related problems, remains an open question.

Effects of Acute Alcohol Use. Men and women have been found to react differently to alcohol consumption in several ways. For example, Caudill, Wilson, and Abrams (1987) found that male social drinkers who either believed they had consumed moderate amounts of alcohol or actually did so increased self-disclosure in a social situation. On the other hand, women who believed they had been given alcohol were less likely to talk about themselves. Actually consuming alcohol had no independent effect in women. Wilsnack (1976) found that when nonalcoholic women drank, they displayed a more feminine outlook as measured on the Thematic Apperception Test (TAT). This contrasted with nonalcoholic men, who tended to become more power-oriented after alcohol consumption.

Prospective Studies of Psychological Factors. The longitudinal study of young people, evaluated before the onset of substance use and followed into adulthood, is perhaps the best method of discovering psychological factors that precede the development of addictive disorders. Unfortunately, the largest and most enlightening of such studies was limited to males (Vaillant, 1995). Only two longitudinal prospective studies have included women. The Oakland Growth Study found that feelings of low self-esteem and impaired coping ability at the junior high and high school levels predicted later problem drinking in girls (Jones, 1971), which differed from predictors for boys (Jones, 1968). Unfortunately, the small number of female problem drinkers in the group studied limited the generalizability of these results. Both women who abstained from alcohol (many from alcoholic families) and women who were problem drinkers showed similar psychological traits in childhood.

In a second longitudinal study, Fillmore, Bacon, and Hyman (1979) studied the drinking status of college-educated men and women 27 years after they had participated in a study of campus drinking practices. They found that women who had scored highest on a "feeling adjustment" scale, which contained items such as drinking to relieve shyness, drinking to get high, and drinking to get along better on dates, were most likely to have later drinking problems. This scale predicted women's adult drinking problems even better than a scale reflecting their actual drinking problems in college. Again, the predictors were different for men.

Retrospective Studies of Traumatic Events. Clinical populations of addicted women report elevated rates of sexual abuse during childhood, experiences that may predispose to their alcohol or drug dependence (Windle, Windle et al., 1995). For example, Miller and her colleagues (1987) compared 45 female alcoholics, recruited from Alcoholics

Anonymous and a treatment program, with 40 matched controls from a community sample. Sixty-seven percent of the alcoholic women reported that they had been victims of sexual abuse by an older person during childhood, while only 28% of the control women reported such abuse. The alcoholic women also reported more frequent abuse experiences and reported them over longer periods of time (especially those who were daughters of alcoholic parents). In these cases, the father was not usually the sexual aggressor. Instead, the child was abused by others due to lack of protection by the family. Miller, Downs, and Testa (1993) further explored whether or not the childhood victimization was specific to alcoholism in women by comparing two treatment samples: 178 women in treatment for alcohol problems and 92 women in treatment who had no alcohol problem history. Although both samples reported more childhood abuse of all kinds than community controls, the alcohol problem group had a significantly higher rate than did the treatment controls (members of a battered women's group and mental health outpatients), even when family background was held constant.

Reinforcing the importance of these findings is the work of Winfield, George et al. (1990), who used the framework of the Epidemiological Catchment Area Study (ECA) to explore a history of sexual assault in adult women in the general population. This study found that the lifetime prevalence of alcohol abuse or dependence was more than three times greater, and the lifetime prevalence of other drug abuse or dependence more than four times greater, in women who reported a history of sexual assault, compared with women who did not have such a history.

Comorbidity Studies: General Population. Helzer and Pryzbeck (1988), in an analysis of data from the Epidemiologic Catchment Area Study (ECA), found that American adults with a lifetime diagnosis of alcohol abuse or dependence were more likely than subjects with other diagnoses to meet criteria for one or more additional psychiatric disorders, including other drug dependence. Women suffering from alcohol abuse and/or dependence were more likely than men to have additional diagnoses. Sixty-five percent of alcoholic women and 48% of alcoholic men had such diagnoses, with major depression nearly four times as frequent (19% of alcoholic women; 5% of men). This rate of lifetime diagnosis of major depression in alcoholic women was nearly three times the general population rate for women (7%). The only diagnosis found more frequently among men with alcohol abuse/dependence was antisocial personality (ASP). ECA data also demonstrate an increased prevalence of psychiatric diagnoses in persons satisfying a diagnosis of other drug abuse/dependence, but analysis by gender is not available (Anthony, 1991).

Comorbidity Studies: Clinical Populations. The ECA study of comorbidity with alcoholism also found that persons with an additional diagnosis were more likely to have had treatment than those with alcohol abuse/dependence alone (Helzer & Pryzbeck, 1988). Thus it is not surprising that surveys of populations of addicts in treatment have found rates of both lifetime and current psychiatric diagnoses well above those in the general population. A similar finding is reported in alcoholics volunteering for research (Roy, DeJong et al., 1991). These studies are reviewed elsewhere; here, it is sufficient to observe that most (although not all) of the clinical population studies have found that female patients show a higher rate of dual diagnosis in general, higher rates of major depression and anxiety disorders (Roy, DeJong et al., 1991; Hesselbrock, Hesselbrock et al., 1988; Rounsaville, Anton et al., 1991), and lower rates of ASP and residual attention deficit disorders. This is true of adolescents as well as adults (Deykin, Buka & Zeena, 1992).

Clinical studies of dual diagnosis often have failed to screen for eating disorders. Those that have done so have found elevated rates of bulimia in both alcohol and drug addicted women (Ross, Glasser & Stiasny, 1988; Walfish, Stenmark et al., 1992). On the other hand, female addicts are less likely to be pathological gamblers than are males (Lesieur, Blume & Zoppa, 1986).

Psychiatric Diagnoses that Precede Addiction. Psychiatric disorders may be classified as *primary* (meaning developing first in time), and *secondary* (developing after the onset of the primary diagnosis, although not necessarily caused by it). Helzer and Pryzbeck (1988) analyzed ECA data concerning men and women in the general population who had a lifetime diagnosis of both alcohol abuse/dependence and major depression. The major depression was primary in 66% of the women, but in only 22% of the men. In their clinical alcoholic population, Hesselbrock, Meyer, and Keener (1985) found a similar contrast: 52% of the alcoholic women satisfied a lifetime diagnosis of major depression, compared with 32% of the men. In 66% of these female patients, the major depression was primary, compared with 41% of the males. Likewise, adolescent girls in addiction treatment were more likely than boys to have a history of depression. Since these patients had early onset of both depression and addiction, it is of interest that in 58% of the boys (but only 28% of the girls) with both diagnoses, the alcohol/drug disorder was clearly primary (Deykin, Buka & Zeena, 1992).

Survey evidence also documents a relationship between depression and alcohol use in women. In a meta-analysis of eight general population longitudinal surveys that recorded both drinking patterns and depressive symptoms, Hartka, Johnstone et al. (1991) found male/female differences in the relationship between alcohol use and depression. For women (but not men), depressive symptoms at the time of the first survey predicted quantity of alcohol consumed several years later. Quantity of alcohol consumed also predicted later depressive symptoms in women, especially over shorter intervals. In a longitudinal survey of a general population sample of 143 female problem and 157 female non-problem drinkers, Wilsnack, Klassen et al. (1991) discovered that both sexual dysfunction and depression were predictors of chronicity (the persistence of problem drinking over a five-year period).

Taken together, these studies suggest that in women, depressive symptoms may represent a psychological condition that in some way predisposes to increased drinking, alcohol addiction, and perhaps other drug dependence. In addition, the increased risk in women associated with traumatic events such as sexual assault might be mediated through such symptoms as discouragement, low self-esteem and demoralization, often associated with depression.

A four-year longitudinal study of 457 college students found that low self-esteem in freshmen year predicted alcohol use disorder in senior year for female, but not male students (Walitzer & Sher, 1996).

Less is known about temporal relationships with other psychiatric diagnoses, but their study may unearth other information important to improving the treatment of women.

Clinical Implications of Research on Psychological Factors in Addicted Women. The discussion of psychological factors and psychopathology has implications for clinical practice. Assessment of adolescent girls and adult women with addictive disorders must include a good psychiatric history, with emphasis on traumatic life events such as physical and sexual abuse, as well as symptoms of anxiety, depression, eating disorder and other pathology. In addition, a careful history should attempt to establish whether the addiction is primary. Women suffering from psychiatric disorders that precede the addiction (primary major depression, for example) are less likely to recover from their psychiatric symptoms with treatment for their addictive disorder alone. They not only may require more vigorous treatment of the primary disorder concurrent with addiction treatment, but they also may need help learning to recognize symptoms of recurrence of the primary disorder, once alcohol and drug abstinence is achieved. Prompt and specific treatment of any recurrence will avoid relapse of the addictive disorder and allow recovery to proceed.

SOCIOCULTURAL FACTORS

As mentioned earlier, current evidence supports a significant influence of environment on both patterns of use and problems related to alcohol and other drugs in women. Societal attitudes and customs function as a double-edged sword in American society. On one hand, the expectation that women will follow different drinking norms than men protects women from alcohol problems (e.g., Kubicka, Csemy & Kozeny, 1995; Klee & Ames, 1987; Celentano & McQueen, 1984). On the other hand, social attitudes based on incorrect information (for example, that alcohol makes women lustful and promiscuous) produces negative stereotypes, a pervasive stigma, and a socially accepted rationalization for the victimization of women who drink.

Several studies have explored this victimization. For example, in Wilsnack's large general population study, female subjects completed a questionnaire about the relationship between their drinking and sexual experiences. Among women who used alcohol to some extent, only 8% said they had ever become less particular in their choice of sexual partner when they had been drinking. On the other hand, 60% of the women surveyed said that someone else who was drinking had become sexually aggressive toward them (Klassen & Wilsnack, 1986). In another study of social victimization, Fillmore (1985) found that women in the general population were more likely than men to be the victims of negative behavior associated with the drinking of another person. This was particularly true for women who drank heavily or had alcohol problems. Women who drank in bars (that is, who were exposed to others while drinking) also were more likely to be victimized, even if they were not themselves heavy or problem drinkers.

In a New York State study, 96 alcoholic women in treatment (age 18 to 45) were found to be significantly more likely than 92 nonalcoholic women in the general population to have been the victim of a violent crime by other than a spouse or partner (61% versus 20% of controls), including rape (33% versus 8%) (Miller, Downs & Testa, 1991). This high prevalence makes questions about victimization an important part of the medical history for any woman with addictive disorder.

Changes in attitudes toward women in American society over the past few decades also have affected their drug-taking patterns. Women seek the help of physicians more frequently than men in general, and are more likely to receive a prescription for a psychoactive drug. A generation ago, pharmaceutical manufacturers advertised some of these medications to physicians as ways to rid their waiting rooms of troublesome complaining female patients. This kind of advertising was withdrawn after protests by feminist and consumer groups. Quite possibly a significant portion of the troublesome patients with vague but persistent complaints were undiagnosed alcoholics or other drug addicts. Improved physician education in the identification and treatment of alcohol and other drug problems in women is a primary ingredient in overall addiction prevention.

WOMEN AND HIGHWAY SAFETY ISSUES

Driving while intoxicated (DWI) and driving while alcohol-impaired (DWAI) have been appropriately identified as problems far more common in men than in women. Reducing the mortality and morbidity attributable to drinking and driving has been a major national public health objective (USPHS, 1992). A recent progress report documents continued success in decreasing alcohol-related highway deaths. However, analysis of these rates by sex reveals a disturbing trend. On the national level, the decrease in alcohol-involved fatal crashes between 1982 and 1991 was 15% for men but only 4% for women (CDC, 1992). In New York State, a study of DWI and DWAI convictions during the period 1978 to 1988 revealed that while the proportion of male offenders aged 16 to 20 decreased, the proportion of female offenders aged 21 and over increased (Yu, Essex & Williford, 1992). In 1980, 8.8% of convicted offenders were female. The proportion grew progressively to 13.9% by 1986, and stabilized at about 13% thereafter. Moreover, while recidivism rates for males (defined as a repeat offense within 36 months) were much higher than for females in 1980 through 1982, in 1985 and 1986 the recidivism pattern for women changed drastically and actually slightly exceeded the rate for men. In order to reverse this trend, more research on female drinking and driving and better educational efforts targeted at women will be required.

CLINICAL CHARACTERISTICS OF ADDICTIVE DISORDERS IN WOMEN

Studies of clinical populations usually have compared male and female patients in addiction treatment (e.g., Beckman, 1975; Gomberg, 1986; Schmidt, Klee & Ames, 1990; Ross, 1989; Griffin, Weiss et al., 1989; Rounsaville, Anton et al., 1991; Cyr & Moulton, 1990; Wallen, 1992). Others have studied female addicts alone (Corrigan, 1980) or have compared such women with non-addicted women (Gomberg, 1991). Important findings include:

Course of the Illness. Women usually begin their use of alcohol and have their first symptoms of alcohol-related problems at a later age than men. They enter treatment, however, at about the same age and with the same severity of symptoms. This is evidence of a more rapid development of the alcoholism once it begins, a phenomenon sometimes referred to as "telescoping" of the illness (Smart, 1979; Corrigan, 1980; Ross, 1989). Telescoping seems to be particularly characteristic of women who suffer from primary depression and later develop alcoholism (Smith & Cloninger, 1981). As mentioned earlier, the chronic medical complications of alcoholism also develop more rapidly in women.

Whether or not the same telescoping occurs in other addictions is not clear. Griffin, Weiss et al. (1989) found that cocaine-addicted women both began cocaine use earlier and reached treatment earlier than males. The 34 female patients had used cocaine for an average of 3.7 years, versus 5.4 years for the 95 males, a significant difference. In contrast, the 42 female opiate addicts treated during the same period at the same clinical site were slightly older than the 163 males and had begun use later (Griffin, Weiss et al., 1989). Whether these findings from a private hospital will apply as well to addicts in poverty populations is not yet clear.

Female alcoholics are more likely than males to date the onset of their aberrant drinking patterns to a specific event or stressful situation (Corrigan, 1980). Likewise, Griffin, Weiss et al. (1989) found female cocaine addicts more likely than males to cite specific reasons for their drug use, such as depression or family, job and health problems.

Marital Status. Women addicts in treatment are more likely to be married to or living with an alcoholic or addicted sexual partner, or to be divorced or separated, whereas men entering treatment are more likely to be married to a non-addicted spouse (Jacob & Bremer, 1986; Griffin, Weiss et al., 1989). Again, the influence of a "significant other" on patterns of women's drug use is evident. Married or cohabiting alcoholic women often are the victims of battering (Silva & Howard, 1991).

Alcohol Dependent Women Drink Significantly Less than Men. This is an important finding that reminds us that alcoholism should not be diagnosed by quantity of intake alone, particularly in women. The lower alcohol intake in alcoholic women is significant, even if corrected for body weight. For example, York reported on a treatment sample of 51 female and 105 male alcoholics. The men reported a lifetime alcohol consumption of 15.4 kg per kg of body weight versus 10.1 kg/kg body weight for women, and an average daily intake of 2.3 grams/kg body weight versus 1.5 grams/kg body weight for women. These differences were both clinically and statistically significant (York, 1990). In addition to gender differences in absorption and body water, concurrent use of other sedative drugs may help explain women's lower intake. The equivalent of the male alcoholic's morning drink may be a morning diazepam for an alcoholic woman. Her "nightcap" may contain less alcohol and more of a sedative drug. As the alcoholic woman ages, her tolerance for both alcohol and other drugs decreases and she drinks even less than before, while still experiencing adverse health and social consequences from her drinking. Corrigan (1980) reported that while 25% of 150 alcoholic women in treatment reported their "usual quantity consumed when drinking" as 15 or more drinks a day, 17% reported less than five drinks a day. When asked about the most they ever drink, 60% of these women (10% of the total study group) said they did not exceed five to seven drinks.

Psychiatric Symptoms. As discussed earlier, women suffering from addictive disorders are more likely than men to satisfy criteria for additional psychiatric diagnoses, both in general and clinical populations. Women also score higher on a variety of measures of anxiety and depressive symptoms during addiction treatment, and are more likely to suffer from eating disorders than men. The higher prevalence of depression echoes the higher rates of depression among women in general, but women with addictive disorders are more likely to be depressed than women who do not suffer from diagnosable alcohol or other drug problems (Helzer & Pryzbeck, 1988; Gomberg, 1991). Turnbull and Gomberg (1990) analyzed the symptomatic structure of depression in 301 depressed alcoholic compared to 137 depressed non-alcoholic women. They found no differences in the manifestations of depression in the two groups, and further noted that 88% of the alcoholic women attributed their entry into treatment to "feeling very low and depressed." Increased rates of depression also are seen in female cocaine and opiate addicts (Griffin, Weiss et al., 1989).

Suicide attempts are frequent among women with addictive disorders, compared with women controls (Gomberg, 1989), and with men in treatment (Hesselbrock, Hesselbrock et al., 1988). Most at risk are alcoholic women aged 20 to 29, who were found to be twice as likely to attempt suicide as alcoholic women aged 40 to 49. These age differences in suicide risk were not observed in female controls (Gomberg, 1989).

Polydrug Dependence. Alcoholic women reaching treatment are more likely than men to report misuse of other drugs, particularly prescribed medicines such as minor tranquilizers, sedatives, analgesics and stimulants (Schuckit & Morrissey, 1979). This may be due in part to the tendency of alcoholic women to obtain medical care outside of the alcohol-specific treatment system (for example, in mental health and general health facilities) (Weisner & Schmidt, 1992).

Motivation for Treatment. Women addicts often are more motivated to seek treatment by problems with health (mental and physical) (Gomberg, 1991) and problems with family members, in contrast with men, whose most frequent motivations are problems on the job and with the law (Ross, 1989).

IDENTIFICATION OF ADDICTIVE DISORDERS IN WOMEN

Women frequently are referred to as "hidden" alcoholics, more often drinking alone than in company and kept from seeking alcohol-specific treatment by individual and family denial, reinforced by an inaccurate and destructive societal stigma. It is therefore not surprising that women tend to be underrepresented in alcoholism treatment. However, there are additional reasons for this inequity (see the following discussion of barriers to treatment), one of which involves casefinding. The most prevalent organized systems for motivating alcohol- and drug-dependent people to seek treatment are employee assistance programs and criminal justice diversion programs such as those for intoxicated or impaired drivers. These intervention models are far more effective at reaching male than female addicts. Since research shows that women most often enter treatment in response to physical and mental health problems (Gomberg, 1991), it is not surprising that effective casefinding for alcoholic women can be performed in medical settings. Examples include:

- Halliday, Bush et al. (1986) found that 12% of women seeking routine gynecological care and 21% seeking help for premenstrual syndrome were alcoholics.
- Moore, Bone et al. (1989) found that 12.4% of 556 obstetric and 242 gynecology inpatients screened positive for alcoholism.
- Cyr and Wartman (1988) found that 17% of women making a first visit to an ambulatory primary care clinic screened positive for alcoholism.
- Cleary, Miller et al. (1988) reported that 11% of female medical outpatients met criteria for alcoholism.
- Hoffman, Harrison et al. (1989) found that 14% of female medical and surgical inpatients met diagnostic criteria for active alcohol abuse or dependence and an additional 9% for an alcohol use disorder in remission.
- Chasnoff, Landress, and Barrett (1990) studied obstetric patients in both private and public care in Pinellas County, Florida. About 13% of those in private and 16% in public clinics tested positive for illegal drugs.

TABLE 1. "TWEAK" Test

Do you drink alcoholic beverages? If so, please take our "TWEAK Test"

T **Tolerance:** How many drinks does it take to make you feel high? (Record number of drinks) ____

W **Worry:** Have close friends worried or complained about your drinking in the past year? (If yes, enter 2 points) ____

E **Eye-Opener:** Do you sometimes take a drink in the morning when you first get up? (If yes, enter 1 point) ____

A **Amnesia (Blackouts):** Has a friend or family member ever told you about things you said or did while you were drinking that you could not remember? (If yes, enter 1 point) ____

K **(C)** Do you sometimes feel the need to **cut down** on your drinking? (If yes, enter 1 point at right) ____

Scoring: To score the test, a seven-point scale is used. The tolerance question scores two points if a woman reports it takes two or more drinks for her first to feel the effects of alcohol. (Think of the song, "tea for two.") A positive response to the worry question scores two points. Each of the last three questions scores one point for positive responses. A total score of three or more points indicates the woman is likely to be a heavy/problem drinker.

Source: Russell M, Martier SS & Sokol RJ (1991). Screening for pregnancy risk-drinking: Tweaking the tests. *Alcoholism: Clinical & Experimental Research* 15:268. Reprinted by permission.

All of the above rates of positive screening and/or diagnosis are well above the general population prevalence of addictive disorders in women.

Several screening instruments have been developed specifically for use in women, such as the SWAG (Spak & Hallstrom, 1996), the TWEAK (Table 1) (Russell, Martier & Sokol, 1991) and the T-ACE (Sokol, Martier & Ager, 1989). Both the TWEAK and the T-ACE may be given as written questionnaires, but also are usefully incorporated into routine history-taking. In using the TWEAK, T-ACE or CAGE (Ewing, 1984) test with women, the "E" question (use of alcohol as an "eye opener"—the same in all three tests) might best be worded, "Have you ever needed a drink *or medication of some kind* first thing in the morning to steady your nerves or get over a hangover?" This recognizes the frequency of polydrug use in women.

Another screening tool, the Health Questionnaire, was developed by Marcia Russell at the New York State Research Institute on Addiction for the State's Fetal Alcohol Syndrome Prevention Program (Figure 1). This questionnaire, designed to be completed by the patient, is not scored numerically, but gathers information useful in evaluating women for addictive disease.

Laboratory screening tests also can be of value in women. For example, among 100 first admissions to an outpatient alcoholism clinic for women in Sweden, 48% of the patients had an increased red cell mean corpuscular volume (MCV) and 42% had an increase in serum gammaglutamyl transferase (GGT). A screening criterion of elevated MCV or GGT, or both, correctly identified 67% of the alcoholic women, who were relatively early in their disease and in relatively good overall health (Hollstedt & Dahlgren, 1987). The same two laboratory tests in pregnancy were found to correlate with levels of drinking and to predict alcohol-related birth defects (Ylikorkala, Stenman & Halmesmaki, 1987). Urine testing for both prescription and illegal drugs of dependence should be a routine part of the diagnostic assessment of any female patient whose presenting complaints, family history or present situation indicate a risk for addictive disorder.

FIGURE 1. Health Questionnaire

Please check answers below

1. When you are depressed or nervous, do you find any of the following helpful to feel better or to relax?

	VERY HELPFUL	NOT HELPFUL	NEVER TRIED
a. Smoking cigarettes	_____	_____	_____
b. Working harder than usual at home or job	_____	_____	_____
c. Taking a tranquilizer	_____	_____	_____
d. Taking some other kind of pill or medication	_____	_____	_____
e. Having a drink	_____	_____	_____
f. Talking it over with friends and relatives	_____	_____	_____

2. Think of the times you have been most depressed; at those times did you:	YES	NO
a. Lose or gain weight	_____	_____
b. Lose interest in things that usually interest you	_____	_____
c. Have spells when you can't seem to stop crying	_____	_____
d. Suffer from insomnia	_____	_____
3. Have you ever gone to a doctor, psychologist, social worker, counselor or clergyman for help with an emotional problem?	_____	_____

4. How many cigarettes a day do you smoke? Check one.
_____ More than 2 packs _____1-2 packs _____ Less than 1 pack _____ None

5. How often do you have a drink of wine, beer, or a beverage containing alcohol?
_____3 or more times a day _____ Once or twice a week
_____ Twice a day _____ Once or twice a month
_____ Almost every day _____ Less than once a month _____ Never

6. a. If you drink wine, beer or beverages containing alcohol, how often do you have four or more drinks?
_____ Almost always _____ Frequently _____ Sometimes _____ Never

b. If you drink wine, beer or beverages containing alcohol, how often do you have one or two?
_____ Almost always _____ Frequently _____ Sometimes _____ Never

7. What other prescribed medications do you take? _______________

8. What other drugs or medications do you use? _______________

	YES	NO
9. Does your drinking or taking other drugs sometimes lead to problems between you and your family, that is, wife, husband, children, parent, or close relative?	_____	_____
10. During the past year, have close relatives or friends worried or complained about your drinking or taking other drugs?	_____	_____
11. Has a friend or family member ever told you about things you said or did while you were drinking or using other drugs that you do not remember?	_____	_____
12. Have you, within the past year, started to drink and found it difficult to stop before becoming intoxicated?	_____	_____
13. Has your father or mother ever had problems with alcohol or other drugs?	_____	_____

TREATMENT ISSUES

The overall treatment of addictive disorders is discussed elsewhere in this text. Special needs and considerations in treating female patients are outlined below:

Intervention. The need for and value of systematic screening in medical settings was discussed earlier. Once a problem has been identified, intervention and referral may be attempted either directly by the physician and/or treatment team, or through family and friends. In preparing to intervene with a female patient, sensitivity to issues of shame and stigma, and awareness of the possibility of depression and suicidality are important. It often is crucial to the success of such a treatment plan that the patient's "significant others" are included in the planning process and are counselled so that they support the female addict in her treatment. Often one or more of these family members also will need help for an addictive disorder.

Assessment. Factors that merit special consideration in the assessment of addicted women include:

Exploration of a Physical and/or Sexual Abuse History. Such abuse often is missed in routine history-taking, yet is an important factor in planning treatment and influencing the establishment of trust, self-esteem, marital and sexual functioning and relapse potential.

Diagnosis of Accompanying Physical and Psychiatric Disorders. Because of the higher rates of dual diagnosis in women, including polydrug dependence, depression, eating disorders and other psychiatric disorders, special attention must be given to the psychiatric history and mental status examination. As discussed earlier, it is important to determine whether or not other psychiatric disorders were present before the development of addiction symptoms, since such primary disorders may recur and become factors in alcohol/drug relapse if not recognized and treated appropriately.

Because of the tendency for alcoholic women to develop physical complications rapidly, these should be evaluated. For women with a history of intravenous drug use or sexual relations with an intravenous drug user, HIV and hepatitis B testing should be recommended.

Evaluation and treatment of the entire family is sometimes possible and almost always desirable. Spouses of female addicts are likely to have addiction or other psychiatric problems of their own, and their children may suffer from fetal alcohol or drug effects, congenital HIV infection and/or other problems related to growing up in a disrupted family.

Detoxification. Care must be taken to look for a history of multiple drug dependence so that withdrawal symptoms are appropriately anticipated. It is not unusual for a woman undergoing alcohol detoxification to have a delayed seizure, and only then to admit to significant benzodiazepine use.

Rehabilitation. Alcohol and drug education should include information about the teratogenic effects of these substances, about birth control, and about the prevention of AIDS and other infectious diseases transmitted through blood and body fluids.

Conjoint couples' counseling and family therapies are sometimes helpful, particularly in couples or families with more than one addicted member, families that have entrenched patterns of domestic violence or enabling, and families that attempt to pull the female patient out of treatment because she is so "loved and needed" at home.

Parenting education is sometimes a critical adjunct to treatment for women, who often are single parents. Women raised by alcoholic or addicted parents may have no adequate role models for parenting and may feel inadequate and overwhelmed as parents.

The female addict should be helped to explore the consequences of sexism in her life. Societal undervaluing of women's contributions to both workplace and family functioning may contribute to problems in self-esteem and confidence. Vocational counseling and rehabilitation may be useful components in the recovery process for women who have had limited vocational opportunity. Success in addiction rehabilitation for women should not be measured merely in how well the patient adjusts to societal expectations of the stereotypical female role. If encouraged to explore her feelings about individuality and independence, she may be able to enlarge her horizons.

Other approaches to self-esteem problems include assertiveness training and exposure to positive role models—often recovering female staff members, female self-help group members and sponsors—and through reading the autobiographies of recovering women (Allen, 1978; Ford, 1987; Robertson, 1988).

Minority women often have special needs related to cultural attitudes toward addicted women (Carter, 1987; Fernandez-Pal, Bluestone et al., 1986). An understanding of the patient's culture may be critical to recovery. For example, the extended family structure in some social groups may be helpful in maintaining abstinence. On the other hand, recommending that a woman attend a mixed-sex self-help group or go to meetings at night by herself may be an untenable approach in her cultural group.

Special care should be taken to avoid iatrogenic drug dependence. Benzodiazepines, other sedative drugs, and analgesics capable of producing dependence should be avoided wherever possible. When these medications are absolutely necessary, their use should be kept to a minimum and closely monitored.

Special Treatment Modalities for Women. Because of the intense social sigma applied to female addicts and the shame often felt by such women, a number of women-only programs and all-female therapy groups within mixed-sex programs have been developed. Unfortunately, there is little research base to guide our clinical choice of the most effective approach for an individual female patient. A Swedish study found a better two-year outcome for 100 alcoholic women randomly assigned to a specialized women's outpatient program, compared to 100 assigned to a standard mixed-sex outpatient clinic (Dahlgren & Willander, 1989). A New York study found better retention in treatment for cocaine dependent women in a specially-designed women's day program, compared to mixed-sex outpatient care or residential treatment (Roberts & Nishimoto, 1996). If the addicted woman is treated in a facility that serves both sexes, it is important that she have adequate opportunity to explore issues that she may find hard to discuss with male patients. This may be accomplished either in individual counseling sessions or in an all-female group. Coeducational residential facilities should be managed so as to avoid role assignments based on societal stereotyping. Men and women should share equally in housekeeping, shopping, cooking, fiscal management, building maintenance, and other jobs. Both sexes should have the opportunity to learn new and unfamiliar skills. Staff training and ongoing supervision often will be needed to achieve a non-sexist milieu in residential addiction units.

Barriers to Treatment for Women. The absence of adequate child care is a special barrier affecting a disproportionate number of women in need of residential addiction treatment. Since most single parents are female, and many female addicts are divorced or separated mothers, the lack of facilities that can accommodate both a woman and her children is an important societal problem. Although models for treatment with child care exist (Reckman, Babcock & O'Bryan, 1984), funds for their support are lacking. In addition, legal definitions equating alcohol/drug misuse with child abuse or neglect can put women at risk of loss of custody if they ask for assistance with child care from local government child protective services while they undergo residential care. Changes in definition and public policy can remove this barrier and encourage women to enter treatment (Blume, 1986; Blume, 1997).

Another important barrier for women is a lack of insurance coverage, since women are more likely to be unemployed or employed in part-time or low-paying jobs that do not supply benefits (Blume, 1997).

A final barrier is the threat of civil or criminal prosecution. The past decade has seen a number of widely publicized cases of pregnant or postpartum women who were arrested and prosecuted for prenatal child abuse, homicide or the delivery of a controlled substance to a minor (through the umbilical cord). More than 150 criminal cases had been initiated in 24 states as of 1992 (ACLU, 1992). Cases continued to be reported in the press throughout the 1990's. Although many cases have been thrown out of court or overturned on appeal, the publicity they have received and the fear they have generated have deterred pregnant addicts from seeking addiction treatment and obstetric care. Regulations requiring the testing and reporting of pregnant addicts to government agencies (who then act to remove child custody rather than offer treatment to mother and child) reinforce this fear. Society's failure to identify and treat alcohol/drug problems in women of childbearing age, and the lack of facilities for the treatment of pregnant addicts, will not be corrected by turning such women into criminals. Enlightened public policy can remove this barrier as well (Blume, 1997; ASAM, 1989).

PROGNOSIS FOR ADDICTIVE DISORDERS IN WOMEN

The effectiveness of addiction treatment in women has received far less attention than such treatment in male populations. Generally, studies that have compared male and female patient outcomes show that men and women treated together for alcoholism and other drug dependence do about equally well when the data are corrected for demographic and clinical variables (Vannicelli, 1986; McLellan, Luborsky & O'Brien, 1986). A meta-analysis of 20 alcoholism treatment follow-up studies, in which data were analyzed by gender, found that there were some significant sex differences (Jarvis, 1992). Women did better for the first 12 months, while men showed more improvement than women in longer-term outcome.

Factors that influence treatment effectiveness for women include the presence or absence of a supportive social network and the number of life problems encountered (MacDonald, 1987).

Mortality rates among alcohol-dependent women are high, both when compared with the general population of women and with rates of excess mortality in alcoholic men (Klatsky, Armstrong & Friedman, 1992; Hill, 1986). For example, a longitudinal study of 4,000 men and 1,000 women who had been treated for alcoholism in Sweden found that the mortality rate in women was 5.2 times the expected rate, while for men it was 3 times the expected rate (Lindberg & Agren, 1988). Smith, Cloninger, and Bradford (1983) followed 103 women who underwent inpatient treatment for alcoholism. After 11 years, the study subjects had a mortality rate 4.5 times higher than expected. However, those women who attained abstinence did not experience excess mortality.

PREVENTION OF ADDICTIVE DISORDERS IN WOMEN

Secondary prevention—that is, identifying women with alcohol or drug problems at an early stage and providing effective intervention—was discussed earlier. *Primary prevention* designed specifically for women is a subject that has received relatively little attention. As discussed earlier, societal attitudes and customs related to alcohol/drug use by women is a "double edged sword" which, on the one hand, protects women by dictating lesser levels of alcohol consumption, and on the other harms them by stigmatizing those who drink and condoning violence. Therefore, societal efforts at prevention must be delicately crafted to combat the stigma while preserving the customs of abstinence or moderation for women. A preferred strategy would be widespread education about women's special sensitivity to alcohol, the teratogenicity of alcohol, the risk involved in using alcohol to medicate feelings of inadequacy or other dysphoric states, the risks of mixing alcohol and sedatives, and similar issues. Such an approach should include education about the properties and appropriate use of prescription drugs and the dangers of tobacco and illicit substances for women and their offspring.

As discussed earlier, the average per capita alcohol consumption of American women is approximately half that of men. Because of their lower body weight, greater sensitivity to alcohol, and special risk during pregnancy, if women were ever expected to match "drink for drink" with men, they would be likely to have more alcohol problems than men instead of fewer. Unfortunately, drinking customs in contemporary American society are changing. The advertising and marketing of alcoholic beverages sends messages that can, and do, change cultural norms. Manufacturers of these beverages see women as a "growth market" (Jacobson, Hacker & Atkins, 1983). Advertisements portray drinking as part of being a modern, high achieving, unconventional and liberated woman. Alcohol beverage advertising budgets dwarf the funds available for prevention and education. In addition, new alcoholic drinks in fruit flavors have been designed to appeal specifically to women. If advertising is successful, the cultural norms that have protected women will become blurred and drinking by women will increase. The need for controls on beverage marketing and much intensified alcohol education is particularly acute as we head toward the 21st century (Blume, 1997).

In addition to generally targeted education, culturally appropriate programs are needed for high-risk special populations such as Native American women. All women can be helped to develop coping skills and self-esteem, so that they are able to negotiate stressful life events and transitions without the use of alcohol or other drugs. School-based counseling, individual and group support for women involved in separation, divorce or widowhood, supports for single parents, working mothers, caretakers of the elderly or chronically ill, and other similar sources of help for women who find themselves in stressful situations have the potential to prevent addiction.

Physicians have a unique opportunity to educate patients and their families about the characteristics, properties and dangers of the drugs they may encounter. Physicians can help with stress-reduction counseling and referral. In addition, through the identification, referral and treatment of addicts and their families, physicians can help to break the chain of alcohol and drug addiction that runs through many generations of American families.

REFERENCES

Allen C (1978). *I'm Black and I'm Sober.* Minneapolis, MN: Comp Care.

American Civil Liberties Union (1992). *Criminal Prosecutions Against Pregnant Women: National Update and Overview.* New York, NY: ACLU.

American Society of Addiction Medicine (1989). *Policy Statement on Chemically Dependent Women and Pregnancy.* Washington, DC: The Society.

Anthony JC (1991). The epidemiology of drug addiction. In NS Miller (ed.) *Comprehensive Handbook of Drug and Alcohol Addiction.* New York, NY: Marcel Dekker, 55–86.

Ashley MJ, Olin JS, LeRiche WH, Kornaczewski A, Schmidt W & Rankin JG (1977). Morbidity in alcoholics: Evidence for accelerated development of physical disease in women. *Archives of Internal Medicine* 137:883–887.

Barry PP (1987). Gender as a factor in treating the elderly. In RA Ray & MC Braude (eds.) *Women and Drugs: A New Era for Research (NIDA Research Monograph 16).* Rockville, MD: National Institute on Drug Abuse, 65–69.

Beckman LJ (1975). Women alcoholics: A review of social and psychological studies. *Journal of Studies on Alcohol* 36:797–824.

Blume SB (1986). Women and alcohol: Public policy issues. *Women and Alcohol: Health-Related Issues (NIDA Research Monograph 16).* Rockville, MD: National Institute on Drug Abuse, 294–311.

Blume SB (1991). Sexuality and stigma: The alcoholic woman. *Alcohol Health and Research World* 15(2):139–146.

Blume SB (1997). Women and alcohol: Issues in social policy. In RW Wilsnack & SC Wilsnack (eds.) *Gender and Alcohol.* Piscataway, NJ: Rutgers Center of Alcohol Studies.

Carter CS (1987). Treatment of the chemically dependent black female: A cultural perspective. *Counselor* 5:16–18.

Caudill BD, Wilson GT & Abrams DB (1987). Alcohol and self-disclosure: Analyses of interpersonal behavior in male and female social drinkers. *Journal of Studies on Alcohol* 48:401–409.

Celentano DD & McQueen DV (1984). Alcohol consumption patterns among women in Baltimore. *Journal of Studies on Alcohol* 45:355–358.

Center on Addiction and Substance Abuse (CASA). (1996). *Substance Abuse and American Women.* New York, NY: CASA.

Centers for Disease Control (1992). Trends in alcohol-related traffic fatalities by sex—United States. *Journal of the American Medical Association* 268(3):313–314.

Chasnoff IJ, Landress HJ & Barrett ME (1990). The prevalence of illicit drug or alcohol use during pregnancy and discrepancies in mandatory reporting in Pinellas County, Florida. *The New England Journal of Medicine* 322(17):1202–1206.

Ciraulo DA, Sarid-Segal O, Knapp C, Ciraulo AM, Greenblatt DJ & Shader RI (1996). Liability to alprazolam abuse in daughters of alcoholics. *American Journal of Psychiatry* 153:956–958.

Cleary PD, Miller M, Bush BT, Warburg MM, Delbanco TL & Aronson MD (1988). Prevalence and recognition of alcohol abuse in a primary care population. *American Journal of Medicine* 85:466–471.

Cloninger CR, Christiansen KO, Reich T & Gottesman II (1978). Implications of sex differences in the prevalences of antisocial personality, alcoholism, and criminality for familial transmission. *Archives of General Psychiatry* 35:941–951.

Cloninger RJ, Sigvardsson S & Gilligan SB (1988). Genetic heterogeneity and the classification of alcoholism. *Advances in Alcohol and Substance Abuse* 3/4:3–16.

Corrigan EM (1980). *Alcoholic Women in Treatment.* New York, NY: Oxford University Press.

Crowley TJ & Simpson R (1978). Methadone dose and human sexual behavior. *International Journal on Addictions* 13:285–295.

Cyr MG & Moulton AN (1990). Substance abuse in women. *Obstetric Gynecologic Clinics of North America* 17(4):905–925.

Cyr MG & Wartman SA (1988). The effectiveness of routine screening questions in the detection of alcoholism. *Journal of the American Medical Association* 259:51–54.

Dahlgren L & Willander A (1989). Are special treatment facilities for female alcoholics needed? A controlled 2-year follow-up study from a specialized female unit (EWA) versus a mixed male/female treatment facility. *Alcoholism: Clinical & Experimental Research* 13(4):499–504.

Deykin EY, Buka SL & Zeena TH (1992). Depressive illness among chemically dependent adolescents. *American Journal of Psychiatry* 149(10):1341–1347.

Engs RC & Hanson DJ (1985). Drinking patterns and problems of college students. *Journal of Alcohol and Drug Education* 31:65–83.

Ewing JA (1984). Detecting alcoholism: The CAGE questionnaire. *Journal of the American Medical Association* 252(14):1905–1907.

Fernandez-Pal B, Bluestone H, Missouri C, Morales G & Mizruchi MS (1986). Drinking patterns of inner-city black Americans and Puerto Ricans. *Journal of Studies on Alcohol* 47:156–160.

Fillmore KM (1985). The social victims of drinking. *British Journal of Addictions* 80:307–314.

Fillmore KM, Bacon SD & Hyman M (1979). The 27-year longitudinal panel study of drinking by students in college. *1979 Report to Congress from the National Institute of Alcoholism and Alcohol Abuse* (Contract No. ADM 281-76-0015). Rockville, MD: National Institute on Alcohol Abuse and Alcoholism.

Ford BB (1987). *Betty: A Glad Awakening.* New York, NY: Doubleday.

Frezza M, di Padova C, Pozzato G, Terpin M, Baraona E & Lieber CS (1990). High blood alcohol levels in women: The role of decreased gastric alcohol dehydrogenase activity and first-pass metabolism. *The New England Journal of Medicine* 322(2):95–99.

Gaulden EC, Littlefield DC & Putoff OE (1964). Menstrual abnormalities associated with heroin addiction.

American Journal of Obstetrics and Gynecology 90:155–160.

Goist KC & Sutker PB (1985). Acute alcohol intoxication and body composition in women and men. *Pharmacology, Biochemistry and Behavior* 22:811–814.

Gomberg ESL (1986). Women: Alcohol and other drugs. In B Segal (ed.) *Perspectives on Drug Use in the United States.* New York, NY: The Haworth Press.

Gomberg ESL (1989). Suicide risk among women with alcohol problems. *American Journal of Public Health* 79:1363–1365.

Gomberg ESL (1991). Alcoholic women in treatment: New research. *Substance Abuse* 12(1):6–12.

Griffin ML, Weiss RL, Mirin SM & Lange U (1989). A comparison of male and female cocaine abusers. *Archives of General Psychiatry* 46:122–126.

Gritz ER (1987). Which women smoke and why? *Not Far Enough: Women vs. Smoking* (NIH 87–2942). Washington, DC: U.S. Department of Health and Human Services, 15–19.

Halliday A, Bush B, Cleary P, Aronson M & Delbanco TL (1986). Alcohol abuse in women seeking gynecologic care. *Obstetrics and Gynecology* 68:322–326.

Hanna E, Dufour MC, Elliott S, Stinson F & Harford TC (1992). Dying to be equal: Women, alcohol, and cardiovascular disease. *British Journal of Addiction* 87:1593–1597.

Harris RE & Wynder EL (1988). Breast cancer and alcohol consumption: A study in weak associations. *Journal of the American Medical Association* 259:2867–2871.

Hartka E, Johnstone B, Leino EV, Motoyoshi M, Temple MT & Fillmore KM (1991). A meta-analysis of depressive symptomatology and alcohol consumption over time. *British Journal of Addiction* 86:1283–1298.

Heath AC, Jardine R & Martin NG (1989). Interactive effects of genotype and social environment on alcohol consumption in female twins. *Journal of Studies on Alcohol* 50:38–48.

Helzer JF & Pryzbeck TR (1988). The co-occurrence of alcoholism with other psychiatric disorders in the general population and its impact on treatment. *Journal of Studies on Alcohol* 49:219–224.

Hesselbrock M, Hesselbrock V, Syzmanski K & Weidenman M (1988). Suicide attempts and alcoholism. *Journal of Studies on Alcohol* 49(5):436–442.

Hesselbrock MN, Meyer RE & Keener JJ (1985). Psychopathology in hospitalized alcoholics. *Archives of General Psychiatry* 42:1050–1055.

Hill SY (1986). Physiological effects of alcohol in women. *Women and Alcohol: Health-Related Issues* (Research Monograph 16, ADM 86–1139). Washington, DC: U.S. Department of Health and Human Services.

Hilton ME & Clark WB (1987). Changes in American drinking patterns and problems. *Journal of Studies on Alcohol* 48:515–522.

Hoffmann NG, Harrison PA, Hall SW, Gust SW, Mable RJ & Cable EP (1989). Pragmatic procedures for detecting and documenting alcoholism in medical patients. *Advances in Alcohol & Substance Abuse* 8(2):119–131.

Hollstedt C & Dahlgren L (1987). Peripheral markers in the female "hidden alcoholic." *Acta Psychiatrica Scandinavica* 75:591–596.

Jacob T & Bremer DA (1986). Assortative mating among men and women alcoholics. *Journal of Studies on Alcohol* 47:219–222.

Jacobson M, Hacker G & Atkins R (1983). *The Booze Merchants: The Inebriating of America.* Washington, DC: Center for Science in the Public Interest.

Jarvis TJ (1992). Implications of gender for alcohol treatment research: a quantitative and qualitative review. *British Journal of Addiction* 87:1249–1261.

Jones MC (1968). Personality correlates and antecedents of drinking patterns in adult males. *Journal of Consulting Clinical Psychology* 32:2–12.

Jones MC (1971). Personality antecedents and correlates of drinking patterns in women. *Journal of Consulting Clinical Psychology* 36:61–69.

Kendler KS, Heath AC, Neale MC, Kessler RC & Eaves LJ (1992). A population-based twin study of alcoholism in women. *Journal of the American Medical Association* 268(14):1877–1882.

Kessler RC, McGonagle KA, Shanyang Z et al. (1994). Lifetime and 12-month prevalence of 14 DSM-III-R psychiatric disorders in the United States: Results from the national comorbidity survey. *Archives of General Psychiatry* 51(1):8–19.

Klassen AD & Wilsnack SC (1986). Sexual experience and drinking among women in a U.S. national survey. *Archives of Sexual Behavior* 15:363–392.

Klatsky AL, Armstrong MA & Friedman GD (1992). Alcohol and mortality. *Annals of Internal Medicine* 117:646–654.

Klee L & Ames G (1987). Reevaluating risk factors for women's drinking: A study of blue collar wives. *American Journal of Preventive Medicine* 3:31–41.

Kubicka L, Csemy L & Kozeny J (1995). Prague women's drinking before and after the 'velvet revolution' of 1989: A longitudinal study. *Addiction* 90:1471–1478.

Lesieur HR, Blume SB & Zoppa RM (1986). Alcoholism, drug abuse, and gambling. *Alcohol: Clinical & Experimental Research* 10(1):33–38.

Lex BW, Lukas SE & Greenwald NE (1988). Alcohol-induced changes in body sway in women at risk for alcoholism: A pilot study. *Journal of Studies on Alcohol* 49:346–356.

Lindberg S & Agren G (1988). Mortality among male and female hospitalized alcoholics in Stockholm 1962–1983. *British Journal of Addiction* 83:1193–1200.

Longnecker MP, Berlin JA, Orza MJ & Chalmers TC (1988). A meta-analysis of alcohol consumption in relation to risk of breast cancer. *Journal of the American Medical Association* 260(5):652–656.

MacDonald JG (1987). Predictors of treatment outcome for alcoholic women. *International Journal on Addiction* 22:235–248.

McKirnan DJ & Peterson PL (1989). Alcohol and drug use among homosexual men and women: Epidemiology and population characteristics. *Addictive Behaviors* 14:545–553.

McLellan AT, Luborsky L & O'Brien CP (1986). Alcohol and drug abuse treatment in three different populations: Is there improvement and is it predictable? *American Journal of Drug and Alcohol Abuse* 12:101–120.

Mello NK (1986). Drug use and premenstrual dysphoria. In BA Ray & MC Braude (eds.) *Women and Drugs: A New Era for Research (NIDA Research Monograph 65)*. Rockville, MD: National Institute on Drug Abuse, 31–48.

Mercer PW & Khavari KA (1990). Are women drinking more like men? An empirical examination of the convergence hypothesis. *Alcohol: Clinical & Experimental Research* 14(3):461–466.

Miller BA, Downs WR, Gondoli DM & Keil A (1987). The role of childhood sexual abuse in the development of alcoholism in women. *Violence and Victims* 2:157–172.

Miller BA, Downs WR & Testa M (1991). Violent Victimization of Alcoholic Women. Paper presented at the annual meeting of the Research Society on Alcoholism, Marco Island, FL, June 8–13, 1991.

Miller BA, Downs WR & Testa M (1993). Interrelations between victimization experiences and womens alcohol/drug use. *Journal of Studies on Alcohol* 11(suppl):109–117.

Minkoff HL, McCalla S, Delke I, Stevens R, Salwen M & Feldman J (1990). The relationship of cocaine use to syphilis and human immunodeficiency virus infections among inner city parturient women. *American Journal of Obstetrics and Gynecology* 163(2):521–526.

Mishra L, Sharma S, Potter JJ & Mezey E (1989). More rapid elimination of alcohol in women as compared to their male siblings. *Alcoholism: Clinical & Experimental Research* 13(6):752–754.

Moore RD, Bone LR, Geller G, Mamon JA, Stokes EJ & Levine DM (1989). Prevalence, detection and treatment of alcoholism in hospitalized patients. *Journal of the American Medical Association* 261:403–408.

Pickens RW, Svikis DS, McGue M, Lykken DT, Heston LL & Clayton PJ (1991). Heterogeneity in the inheritance of alcoholism: A study of male and female twins. *Archives of General Psychiatry* 48:19–28.

Reckman LW, Babcock P & O'Bryan T (1984). Meeting the child care needs of the female alcoholic. *Child Welfare League of America* 63:541–545.

Richardson D & Campbell J (1982). The effect of alcohol on attributions of blame for rape. *Personality and Social Psychology Bulletin* 8:468–476.

Roberts AC & Nishimoto RH (1996). Predicting treatment retention of women dependent on cocaine. *American Journal of Drug and Alcohol Abuse* 22(3):313–333.

Robertson N (1988). *Getting Better Inside AA*. New York, NY: William Morrow.

Rolfs RT & Nakishima AK (1990). Epidemiology of primary and secondary syphilis in the U.S. 1981 through 1989. *Journal of the American Medical Association* 246:1432–1437.

Ross HE (1989). Alcohol and drug abuse in treated alcoholics: A comparison of men and women. *Alcohol: Clinical & Experimental Research* 13:810–816.

Ross HE, Glaser FB & Stiasny S (1988). Sex differences in the prevalence of psychiatric disorder in patients with alcohol and drug problems. *British Journal of Addiction* 83:1179–1192.

Rounsaville BJ, Anton SF, Carroll K, Budde D, Prusoff BA & Gawin F (1991). Psychiatric diagnoses of treatment-seeking cocaine abusers. *Archives of General Psychiatry* 48:43–51.

Roy A, DeJong J, Lamparski D et al. (1991). Mental disorders among alcoholics. *Archives of General Psychiatry* 48:423–427.

Russell M, Henderson C & Blume SB (1985). *Children of Alcoholics: A Review of the Literature*. New York, NY: Children of Alcoholics Foundation.

Russell M, Martier SS & Sokol RJ (1991). Screening for pregnancy risk-drinking: Tweaking the tests. *Alcohol: Clinical & Experimental Research* 15:268.

Schatzkin A, Jones DY, Hoover RN et al. (1987). Alcohol consumption and breast cancer in the epidemiologic follow-up of the first national health and nutrition examination survey. *The New England Journal of Medicine* 16:1169–1173.

Schmidt G, Klee L & Ames G (1990). Review and analysis of literature on indicators of women's drinking problems. *British Journal of Addiction* 85:179–192.

Schuckit MA & Morrissey ER (1979). Drug abuse among alcoholic women. *American Journal of Psychiatry* 136:607–611.

Sigvardsson S, Bohman M & Cloninger CR (1996). Replication of the Stockholm adoption study of alcoholism: Confirmatory cross- fostering analysis. *Archives of General Psychiatry* 53(8):681–687.

Silva NM & Howard MC (1991). Woman battering: The forgotten problem in alcohol abuse treatment. *Family Dynamics of Addiction Quarterly* 1(2):8–19.

Smart RG (1979). Female and male alcoholics in treatment: Characteristics at intake and recovery rates. *British Journal of Addiction* 74:275–281.

Smith EM & Cloninger CR (1981). Alcoholic females: Mortality at twelve-year follow-up. *Focus on Women* 2:1–13.

Smith EM, Cloninger CR & Bradford S (1983). Predictors of mortality in alcoholic women: A prospective follow-up study. *Alcohol: Clinical & Experimental Research* 7:237–243.

Sokol RJ, Martier SS & Ager JW (1989). The T-ACE questions: Practical prenatal detection of risk-drinking. *American Journal of Obstetrics and Gynecology* 160:863–870.

Spak F & Hallstrom T (1996). Screening for alcohol dependence and abuse in women: Description, validation, and psychometric properties of a new screening instrument, SWAG, in a population study. *Alcoholism: Clinical & Experimental Research* 20(4):723–731.

Turnbull JE & Gomberg ESL (1990). The structure of depression in alcoholic women. *Journal of Studies on Alcohol* 51:148–155.

Urbano-Marquez A, Ramon E, Fernandez-Sola J, Nicolas JM, Pare JC & Rubin E (1995). The greater risk of alcoholic cardiomyopathy and myopathy in women compared with men. *Journal of the American Medical Association* 274(2):149–154.

U.S. Public Health Service (1992). *A Public Health Service Progress Report on Healthy People 2000: Alcohol and Other Drugs.* Washington, DC: USPHS.

Vaillant GE (1995). *The Natural History of Alcoholism Revisited.* Cambridge, MA: Harvard University Press.

Vannicelli M (1986). Treatment considerations. *Women and Alcohol: Health-Related Issues* (Research Monograph 16, ADM 86–1139). Washington, DC: Department of Health and Human Services, 130–153.

Walfish S, Stenmark DE, Sarco D, Shealy JS & Krone AM (1992). Incidence of bulimia in substance misusing women in residential treatment. *International Journal of the Addictions* 27(4):425–433.

Walitzer KS & Sher KJ (1996). A prospective study of self-esteem and alcohol use disorders in early adulthood: Evidence for gender differences. *Alcoholism: Clinical & Experimental Research* 20(6):1118–1124.

Wallach RC, Jerez E & Blinick G (1969). Pregnancy and menstrual function in narcotics addicts treated with methadone. *American Journal of Obstetrics and Gynecology* 105:1226–1229.

Wallen J (1992). A comparison of male and female clients in substance abuse treatment. *Journal of Substance Abuse Treatment* 9:243–248.

Warner LA, Kessler RC, Hughes M, Anthony JC & Nelson CB (1995). Prevalence and correlates of drug use and dependence in the United States. *Archives of General Psychiatry* 52(3):219–228.

Washton AM (1989). *Cocaine Addiction.* New York, NY: WW Norton.

Weisner C & Schmidt L (1992). Gender disparities in treatment for alcohol problems. *Journal of the American Medical Association* 268(14):1872–1876.

Willett WC, Stampfer MJ, Colditz GA, Rosner BA, Hennekens CH & Speizer FE (1987). Moderate alcohol consumption and the risk of breast cancer. *The New England Journal of Medicine* 316:1174–1179.

Williams GD, Stinson FS, Parker DA, Harford TC & Noble J (1987). Demographic trends, alcohol abuse and alcoholism, 1985–1995. *Alcohol Health and Research World* 11:80–91.

Wilsnack RW & Cheloha R (1987). Women's roles and problem drinking across the life span. *Social Problems* 34:231–248.

Wilsnack SC (1976). The impact of sex roles on women's alcohol use and abuse. In M Greenblatt & MA Schuckit (eds.) *Alcoholism Problems in Women and Children.* New York, NY: Grune & Stratton.

Wilsnack SC, Klassen AD, Schur BE & Wilsnack RW (1991). Predicting onset and chronicity of women's problem drinking: A 5-year longitudinal analysis. *American Journal of Public Health* 81(3):305–318.

Wilson GT & Lawson DM (1976). Effects of alcohol on sexual arousal in women. *Journal of Abnormal Psychology* 85:489–497.

Windle M, Windle RC, Scheidt DM & Miller GB (1995). Physical and sexual abuse and associated mental disorders among alcoholic inpatients. *American Journal of Psychiatry* 152(9):1322–1328.

Winfield I, George LK, Swartz M & Blazer DG (1990). Sexual assault and psychiatric disorders among a community sample of women. *American Journal of Psychiatry* 147:335–341.

Witteman JCM, Willett WC, Stampfer MJ et al. (1990). Relation of moderate alcohol consumption and risk of systemic hypertension in women. *American Journal of Cardiology* 65:633–637.

Ylikorkala O, Stenman U & Halmesmaki E (1987). Gammaglutanyl transferase and mean cell volume reveal maternal alcohol abuse and fetal alcohol effects. *American Journal of Obstetrics and Gynecology* 157:344–348.

York JL (1990). High blood alcohol levels in women (Letter). *The New England Journal of Medicine* 323(1):59–60.

York JL & Pendergast DE (1990). Body composition in detoxified alcoholics. *Alcohol: Clinical & Experimental Research* 14(2):180–183.

Yu J, Essex DT & Williford WR (1992). DWI/DWAI offenders and recidivism by gender in the eighties: A changing trend? *International Journal on Addictions* 27(6):637–647.

CHAPTER 2

Social Predictors of Women's Alcohol and Drug Use: Implications for Prevention and Treatment

Edith S. Lisansky Gomberg, Ph.D.

Social Predictors
Stages in the Life Course
Implications for Prevention and Treatment

The term "addiction" traditionally has been used to refer to drug and alcohol addiction. More recently, the term has been expanded to embrace eating disorders, gambling, work addiction, relationship addiction, and the like. This chapter addresses only the social predictors of drug and alcohol abuse; these addictive patterns of behavior are complicated enough, embracing as they do a wide variety of substances.

Most research and publications on the subject deal with women's use and abuse of alcohol and this, too, embraces a heterogeneity of persons and drinking patterns. Alcohol, like nicotine and caffeine, is the "social drug" that is more or less accepted in most Western societies. Addiction to nicotine and the difficulties of smoking cessation has grown into a major societal and individual problem in recent decades (Hughes, Gust et al., 1991). Addiction to caffeine has remained a relatively minor issue, although there are problems associated with overuse (Greden & Walters, 1992). In the use and abuse of alcohol, there are consistent gender differences, with men beginning to drink earlier in life, drinking larger quantities, developing more alcohol-related problems. The picture is less clear as to the use of nicotine and caffeine, and community studies of use vary in the results of gender comparisons.

There is, too, the question of women's use of medications and controlled substances. Whereas men are more likely to use "street drugs" such as heroin and crack cocaine, women are more frequent users of prescribed psychoactive medications and are more likely to develop drug-related problems with medications such as the sedatives. The gender comparison is less clear with stimulant drugs and the antidepressants. Some community studies of current use are needed.

There are, of course, wide variations in the drug and alcohol patterns of women, varying with socioeconomic class, gender, ethnicity, age, and with regional location within the United States. From one of the earliest epidemiological survey of American drinking practices (Cahalan, Crisin & Crossley, 1969), which analyzed percentage of drinkers and abstainers by family income, virtually all community and national studies include analysis by income. Gender studies showing differences in usage of alcohol and other drugs are included in both clinical and epidemiological research (Gomberg & Nirenberg, 1993). Ethnicity studies have increased in the last decades and a NIAAA monograph summarizes some of the progress (Spiegler, Tate et al., 1989). Age differences in drug and alcohol use are well studied, ranging from systematic reports of adolescent drinking and drug use patterns (Johnston, O'Malley & Bachman, 1993) to many recently written reviews of older persons' drinking and drug use (e.g., Gomberg, 1990). Finally, regional differences are frequently analyzed in federal reports of drinking behavior; often these are state-by-state analyses. We are presenting here gender patterns of alcohol and drug use and abuse and the social predictors of abuse by women. Although the discussion includes the predictive role of positive family history and potential difficulties in childbearing, we are not including premenstrual problems, which were—for a period of time—held to be important etiologically. We are not including the many biological studies which report on differing physiological response of men and women to alcohol (e.g., Frezza, di Padova et al., 1990).

SOCIAL PREDICTORS

A significant role in prediction of alcohol/drug abuse among women is played by *positive family history.* The extent to which this factor is biological, i.e., involving a biochemical predisposition to use alcohol/drugs or involving a chaotic, stress-filled early life in the family of origin, or both, is not resolved. In a study of alcoholic women in clinical treatment (Gomberg, 1986), the alcoholic women were compared with a control group of nonalcoholic, age-matched, class-matched women, there were significant differences in report of father or sibling who manifested heavy or problem drinking in the respondent's childhood between alcoholic and control women; there were differences, not as large, between report of maternal heavy/problem drinking. Interestingly enough, when the women in treatment and the control women are combined, and compared by positive versus negative family history, significant differences appear in level of educational achievement, and in psychiatric, anxiety and depressive symptoms (Gomberg, 1991).

This brings us to the question of an early life dysfunctional family history. In the same study cited above, difference between the alcoholic women and the control women in report of early life negative events is modest (Gomberg, 1989a). Apart from alcohol/drug problems within the family, there are significant differences in two items: "adults did not get along well" and "someone in the family had a nervous breakdown." The other negative events queried about an absent parent, poverty, extreme religious discipline, etc. showed no differences. One may speculate that the women who become alcoholic are more vulnerable to early life distress but not necessarily different in childhood negative events.

Abuse and Violence as Predictors of Women's Alcohol and Drug Misuse. To what extent do abuse and violence have a role as predictors of women's alcohol and drug misuse? First, there is a question of definitions:

- Incest is almost always child abuse phenomenon; rape may occur in early life, adolescence or later.
- Violent aggression or "battering" may occur either in early life or later; there is a distinction, however, between child abuse and woman abuse (Flitcraft, 1992).
- Violence may take the form of "parental physical violence" (Downs, Miller & Gondoli, 1987).
- Violence and female drinking, intoxication, and alcohol abuse: a study of alcoholic women in treatment showed that 13.6% of the women reported a recent history of assault, compared with 1.5% of the matched, nonalcoholic control women (Gomberg, 1990). The younger women in treatment, who do more drinking in public places, are significantly more likely to be assaulted than the older women.
- Abuse is sometimes used to cover the area of neglect as well as violence.
- There are some students of female addiction who find "victimization" in the "patriarchal society" of the United States (Van Den Bergh, 1991).

The question remains: is childhood sexual abuse a causal factor in development of female alcohol abuse? There is a fair amount of evidence to answer "yes" (Wilsnack & Wilsnack, 1993). Women problem drinkers more frequently give a history of such abuse than nonproblem drinkers. However, it should be noted that early sexual abuse also is associated with depression among problem drinkers, and that suicidal thoughts, use of drugs other than alcohol and violent relationships characterize the adult lives of both problem drinkers and nonproblem drinkers alike (Wilsnack & Wilsnack, 1993). Perhaps it is the intervening effect of depression that is the key.

Social Predictors in Adolescence. What are social predictors in adolescence which appear to be antecedent in the development of alcohol problems? There is more information in the research literature about male adolescents than about female. Distinction needs to be made between the early years of adolescence and the later years; parents and peer group influence becomes more of an influence as they move into later adolescence (Kandel & Andrews, 1987). For both boys and girls, there is an increase in alcohol use and in heavy drinking as they move from 8th grade through 10th grade to 12th grade (Johnston, O'Malley & Bachman, 1993). Asked about alcohol use in the last 10 days, the gender gap is modest but when the percentage reporting heavy drinking is compared, it is considerably larger with boys doing more heavy drinking.

A gender difference which appears in adolescence and throughout the life span, is the greater susceptibility of the females to peer influence. While "individual susceptibility" is related to alcohol misuse in both men and women (McLaughlin, Baer & Burnside, 1985; Schulenberg, Dielman & Leech, 1993), it is relatively more of an influence on male adolescent drinkers.

Positive Family History and Early Life Alcohol Misuse: Marital conflict between parents, inadequate parenting, and limited attachment to parents characterize the dysfunctionality of the family of origin (Gomberg, 1986; Zucker & Fitzgerald, 1991). Trouble with school authorities, low educational achievement and early dropout from school are frequently accompanied by or followed by alcohol/drug misuse. Behavior problems e.g., heightened impulsivity, antisocial or aggressive acting out frequently predict alcohol/drug problems (Zucker & Fitzgerald, 1991; Gomberg, 1986; Ellickson & Hays, 1991; Windle, 1990). Relatively early and heavy use of alcohol and early use of marijuana also are related to substance abuse problems.

Risk factors for problem drinking among female adolescents may be summarized as follows: (1) peer use of alcohol; (2) behavior problems and problems in school; (3) alienation and symptoms of stress/distress; (4) early experience of intoxication and early use of marijuana; (5) positive family history and/or dysfunctional family; and (6) positive expectancies about alcohol

Late Adolescence, College Student Status, and Life Adjustments in the 20s: Career, marriage, childbearing, produce role shifts and, frequently accompanying these shifts are changes in alcohol-related behavior. In the late teens and during college years, there are data which suggest that males underreport the quantity of drinking more than women do. Women in college drink more often and in larger quantities than they will after they graduate and marry and/or find a job (Gomberg, 1994). Marital status also may be an important social predictor: young women who are single, divorced or separated, or in a cohabiting relationship drink more frequently and in larger quantities than married women (Wilsnack & Wilsnack, 1991). A particularly vulnerable subgroup of young women are those who are divorced, depressed, unemployed and raising young children by themselves. Finally, as is true of all age groups and both genders, smoking clearly is linked with alcohol dependence among women (Prescott & Kendler, 1995).

Workplace Issues. Are women in the workplace or women at home more likely to be drinkers? Answers are ambiguous and everyone agrees that gender, work and drinking are a complex combination. Reported data include Johnson's (1982) report that, "employed women who are married showed significantly higher rates [of alcohol-related problems] than single employed women or married women not employed outside the home" (Johnson, 1982, p. 93) to more recent work (Wilsnack, Wilsnack & Klassen, 1984) showed unemployed women seeking work to report most alcohol dependence symptoms, and women in part-time employment ranking second. A recent critique (Wilsnack & Wilsnack, 1992) summed the situation up well: it was titled: "Women, Work, and Alcohol: Failures of Simple Theories." Recent reviewers of the literature in this area have concluded that both workplace and individual variables are multifaceted and interact in complex ways (Ames & Rebhun, 1996).

Marital Status. To what degree are marriage and relations with the opposite sex social predictors of alcohol problems? The literature on this issue is filled with non-answers and writers speak of the paucity of information, theory and good methodological techniques. It is an extremely complex issue just as the relationship among work, gender and alcoholism a complex question.

For both genders, married persons tend to drink less and avoid problem drinking to a greater extent that individuals who are single, separated or divorced: for women, the most drinking occurs among those who are cohabiting. Marriage may be a stress or a support, increasing risks or providing protection from negative outcomes (Roberts & Leonard, 1997). There are some data indicating that male heavy drinkers marry earlier than other men (Power & Estaugh, 1990) and data as well indicating that female heavy drinkers enter marriage at an early age (Gomberg, 1986) and are more likely to enter cohabiting and relationships (Bachman, O'Malley & Johnston, 1984).

The basic question is: which comes first for women, the heavy/problem drinking or divorce/separation? Hanna, Faden, and Harford (1993) found differences among younger women (24 to 32); divorce or separation led to increased drinking but those who married or remarried during the same time period showed a increase in drinking. The Wilsnacks (1993) also tracked women in two time periods, 1981 and 1986. In their sample of women with no signs of problem drinking in 1981, divorce or separation were more likely to *follow* than to *precede* heavy drinking. Among women identified as problem drinkers in 1981, divorce and separation predicted a *reduction* in problem drinking. If the question is posed whether divorce is a risk or a remedy, the Wilsnacks conclude that it may be both.

The issue of influence on the spouse? Because there are many more male alcoholics than female, with supporting evidence from clinical research, it has been posited that husband-to-wife transmission is far more frequent than wife-to-husband. Roberts and Leonard (1997), in their review of the relationship between marriage and alcohol use, state that "wives are more likely to have problem-drinking partners than are husbands. Women are rarely married to men who drink less than they do. Consequently, husbands are likely to influence wives to drink more, while wives are likely to influence husbands to drink less" (Roberts & Leonard, 1997).

It has been illuminating to see this dynamic in operation among older problem drinkers (Gomberg, 1995) as well as younger and middle-aged ones. Throughout the life span, transmission of heavy/problem drinking, is more likely to be male-to-female than the other way round. This holds for the abuse of illegal substances as well.

Pregnancy, Childbirth and Child-Rearing. There is a voluminous literature on female problem drinking and its effects on children (e.g., Williams & Klerman, 1984; Little & Wendt, 1993). There is a good deal of publication about heavy drinking and reproductive dysfunction (e.g., Wilsnack, 1984). And there are volumes written about the fetal alcohol syndrome and fetal alcohol effects. All of this work deals with heavy/problem drinking and its effects, its consequences and it is likely that these negative events often facilitate continuation of heavy drinking.

Generally, when women are pregnant, there is a decline in drinking (Passaro & Little, 1997). There are, however, a number of situations which may act as precipitant to female heavy drinking. First, there is difficulty in conception and an inevitable disappointment, particularly in a subgroup of vulnerable women who value the maternal role very highly. Second, some women respond to stillbirth or a miscarriage with depression, which may in turn lead to an increase in drinking. Third, there are women, particularly those with young children, raising children with a minimum of social support. Finally, there is the "empty nest," a phenomenon much exaggerated but nonetheless occasionally present as precipitant to increased drinking, particularly if it occurs during the same years as a painful divorce or separation.

Depression. The question is whether the linkage between depression and problem drinking in women is depression-as-etiology or depression-as-consequence. In all age groups, depression and problem drinking are linked. Schuckit (1972) made a useful distinction between primary and secondary alcoholism in women; in primary female alcoholism, the alcoholism precedes the depression and in secondary female alcoholism, depression is antecedent to the heavy drinking which produces depression. In the latter instance, depression is both pharmacological and psychological.

Depression as Antecedent: While the depressing pharmacological effects of heavy intake of alcohol should work for both genders, male alcoholics were only slightly more likely to receive a diagnosis of depression than men in the general population (2%); women alcoholics, on the other hand, were more likely to be diagnosed with depression as comorbidity than women in the general population, (12%) (Helzer & Pryzbeck, 1988). Where depression and alcoholism occur together in women, in 66% of the women in the study sample, depression preceded the alcoholism (Helzer, Burnam & McEvoy, 1991). Women who qualify as secondary alcoholics differ from primary alcoholics in several ways: less frequency of positive family history (positive for alcoholism/substance abuse), a shorter duration of the problematic drinking, and a more favorable prognosis (Turnbull, 1988).

A study of age differences among alcoholic women in treatment, aged 20 to 50, showed the alcoholic women to report significantly more current depression than an age-matched control group; there were no significant age differences, however, among the treatment women in their twenties, thirties and forties (Gomberg, 1986). In the same study, the women in treatment were asked about recent events which led them to seek treatment; the largest percentage reported "increasing depression," 87.8%, with "blackouts, DTs, medical problems" reported by 67.4% and "love relationship problems" reported by 65.4%.

Support for the linkage between female alcoholism and depression comes from both epidemiological studies of the general population and clinical studies of women in treatment. These include Schuckit and Morrissey (1986); Beckman (1980); Corrigan (1980); Gomberg and Lisansky (1984); Hesselbrock, Meyer, and Jeener (1985); etc.

Unconventional, Nontraditional Lifestyle. Data from epidemiological surveys indicate that women who drink heavily are more likely to have earlier sexual experience, live in a cohabiting relationship, and use drugs other than alcohol more than abstainers or light drinkers. Wilsnack and Wilsnack (1993) comment on these data as follows: "Cohabiting and nontraditional sexual behavior may be indicators of a relatively nontraditional or nonconventional life style. The increased drinking opportunities and greater freedom from traditional moral constraints associated with such a lifestyle may increase women's risk of hazardous drinking behavior. Low self-esteem or a lifetime pattern of using drugs to feel good or deal with problems may increase these risks further (Wilsnack & Wilsnack, 1993).

For both men and women, the more frequent and heavier use of nicotine is associated with heavier patterns of drinking (Schiffman & Balabanis, 1995). A comparison of alcoholic women in treatment with a control group of matched nonalcoholic women showed the alcoholic women reporting significantly more smoking, past and current than the controls (Gomberg, 1989a, 1989b). A current study of an elderly community sample of former drinkers now abstinent show those with a past history of heavy drinking reporting significantly heavier current smoking than those with a history of light drinking (Gomberg, Walton et al., 1997b).

The comparison of alcoholic women in treatment with matched control women (Gomberg, 1989b) showed the alcoholic women reporting significantly more use of benzodiazepines, prescription analgesics and stimulants, over-the-counter products such as NyQuil, psychodelics, cocaine and heroin. The two groups were similar only in the reported past use of marijuana. While the patterns may vary with age, there is no question but that women who are heavy/problematic drinkers are more likely to be using drugs other than alcohol.

Stresses in Special Life Situations. There are a number of special life situations which have a high degree of association with alcohol and/or drug abuse.

First, there is general agreement (although empirical evidence is scarce) that homosexual individuals have relatively high rates of heavy/problematic drinking. This has been attributed to stigma and societal rejection, to bars as important meeting places for homosexuals, etc. Whatever the antecedents may be, there does appear to be a significant number of lesbians who are heavy/problem drinkers. However, this finding awaits more verification.

Second, there appears to be relatively heavy drinking among male military personnel. There is a difference in the alcohol/drug use of younger, enlisted men and older noncommissioned officers, women in the military show similar differences between younger and older personnel. This is in need of study.

Third, there are relatively high rates of alcohol and drug abuse among women in the correctional system. As is true among male prisoners, too, the high degree of linkage between alcohol and drug problems and the reasons for incarceration, seems to hold for women in prison as well as men. Once again, this is a research area that needs work.

Finally, there is the chaos and precariousness of life among the poor, the near-poor and the underclass (Howell, 1973). Howell's ethnographic description of "hard living on Clay Street" contains portraits of blue collar families who are on the fringe of poverty; for the most part, the families are Caucasians. While epidemiological data are gathered with analyses sometimes in terms of income, ethnographic description of how life is lived in the poverty population, minority or Caucasian is scarce. The blue collar and poverty worlds and their consequences in lowered expectations and despair as facilitating the use of drugs and alcohol as escape are neglected in research and policy.

STAGES IN THE LIFE COURSE

To sum up the risk factors that play prominent roles in the alcohol and/or drug misuse by women, three life stages of women are differentiated.

Risk Factors for Adolescents and Young Women. First, the risk factors for adolescents and young women need not *all* be present to be concerned, but the more of these risk factors that are present, the greater the likelihood of development of substance abuse problems. These risk factors are:

- A family history positive for substance abuse.
- Dysfunctional, disruptive, often chaotic early family life in the family of origin. Vulnerable young women often report early life unhappiness, depression, and feelings of deprivation.
- School-related problems, including low achievement drive and expectations and trouble with school authorities. Young women with substance abuse problems also manifest lesser school achievement than their age peers, and so come into the job market with fewer skills and are employed at relatively lower status jobs than their age peers.
- Positive expectancies about alcohol and drugs. There is evidence that positive expectancies about alcohol/drugs are strong predictors of adolescent drinking (Gomberg, 1994).
- Peer pressure and participation in social groups in which use of alcohol and/or drugs is facilitated both by encouragement and availability.
- Early experience with alcohol intoxication, marijuana use; early sexual experience.
- Behavior problems: e.g., difficulties in impulse control, shoplifting, vandalism, temper tantrums, etc. These include antisocial aggressive behavior and rejection of authority.

Risk Factors for Adult and Middle-Aged Women. Risk factors specific to adult and middle-aged women include:

- A family history positive for substance abuse.
- Marital status: there is a greater likelihood of heavy drinking among single women, divorced/separated women and those who are in cohabiting relationships. Married women are less likely to develop heavy drinking problems although a spouse's heavy drinking may be a factor for young and middle-aged women.
- Participation in a social group where there is heavy drinking. Although this is more likely to be a mixed gender group, there are social groups of women who facilitate each others' drinking.
- Gynecological/obstetrical problems are sometimes antecedent to high risk drinking. In a study of alcoholic women in treatment, compared with a matched nonalcoholic control group, the problem drinking women reported significantly more miscarriage and hysterectomy; whether those preceded or followed upon heavy drinking is not clear.
- Depression is reported as antecedent to problem drinking among a large proportion of women problem drinkers. Other antecedent symptomatic behaviors include eating disorders, phobias, panic states and anxiety attacks.
- Use and abuse of prescribed psychoactive drugs may precede, accompany or follow upon problematic drinking.
- Among middle-aged women (45 to 60), difficulty in redefining one's role—marital, occupational, maternal—may create conditions for the development of problem drinking. While the loss of youth produces, in most women, adaptations of one sort or another, this adjustment in role is difficult for some middle-aged women.

Risk Factors for Elderly Women. Risk factors for elderly women include:

- While there are elderly women problem drinkers of long duration, relatively later, more recent onset is more frequent among female older drinkers than among male elderly problem drinkers. When they present for treatment, they come with a shorter duration of alcohol-related problems than do men.
- Marital disruption is present among elderly women problem drinkers more than it is among males. The disruption often takes the form of widowhood rather than divorce of separation. Widowhood and its accompanying sense of loss and depression appears to be an antecedent.
- Work situation: for those women who have been employed outside the home most of their adult lives, retirement from the work force may act as antecedent to problematic use of alcohol. This is probably so because for those women, most of their social networks have been within the workplace.
- Throughout their lives, women have been bigger users of prescribed psychoactive drugs than men. There may, in fact, be more elderly women with psychoactive drug misuse than those manifesting misuse of alcohol. Elderly women problem drinkers report more dependence on such drugs than elderly male problem drinkers.
- Depression, associated with aging or losses, may clearly act as antecedent.
- Among elderly women alcohol abusers, there are frequent reports of drinking with the spouse or a significant other. This may well be, again, the transmission of problem drinking from male to female.

IMPLICATIONS FOR TREATMENT

It is consistently reported that a smaller proportion of women alcoholics present for treatment than do males. Women are less likely to come to a substance abuse facility but they will apparently consult with their physicians; the presenting complaint is not substance abuse but more likely gastric difficulties, depression, or insomnia.

When alcoholic women in treatment are asked about recent events in their lives which brought them to treatment, the largest proportion cite "increasing depression," with problems with a spouse or lover as next in percentage. Death of a loved one often is cited. Among women in their forties, a child moving away from home is cited frequently and, among the youngest women—in their twenties—blackouts and delirium tremens, trouble with the police or at work often are cited as pre-treatment events (Gomberg, 1997a).

Most women alcoholics enter treatment presenting a clinical picture of depression, low self-esteem, guilt and shame. Often, they are angry, resentful and distrustful and it is important for the therapist to be aware of these mixed feelings.

Adjunctive services need to be enlisted: the woman may need help with medical problems, vocational problems, child-rearing problems. She may need legal advice and economic help. Referral to facilities for evaluating and treating children may be important. This can be helpful for the woman client and a line of primary prevention with children of alcoholic mothers.

Generally, those treatment modalities which are most effective with male alcoholics are likely to be most effective with women clients as well. Whatever treatment modalities offered by any resource, the most critical aspect of treatment for alcoholic women is the therapists' attitude toward women and toward women substance abusers. Sympathetic acceptance and support (while setting limits) is critical.

Do women respond better to female therapists? This may be so but there is little empirical evidence for it. Should women be treated in all-female facilities? Besides the obvious limitation of funding for gender-specific clinics, the evidence is mixed. What is recommended is woman's group therapy—such groups often are maintained within a mixed-gender treatment facility or self-help group.

REFERENCES

Ames GM & Rebhun LA (1996). Occupational culture, drinking, and women: An incomplete research picture. In JM Howard, SF Martin, PD Mail, ME Hilton & ED Taylor (eds.) *Women and Alcohol: Issues for Prevention (Research Monograph No. 32)*. Rockville, MD: National Institute of Health, 361–380.

Bachman JC, O'Malley PM & Johnston LD (1984). Drug use among young adults: The impacts of role status and social environment. *Journal of Personality and Social Psychology* 47:629–645.

Beckman LJ (1980). Perceived antecedents and effects of alcohol consumption in women. *Journal of Studies on Alcohol* 41:518–530.

Cahalan D, Cisin IH & Crossley HM (1969). *American Drinking Practices* (Monograph 6). New Brunswick, NJ: Rutgers Center of Alcohol Studies Publications Division.

Corrigan EM (1980). *Alcoholic Women in Treatment.* New York, NY: Oxford University Press.

Downs WR, Miller BA & Gondoli DM (1987). Childhood experiences of parental physical violence for alcoholic women as compared with a randomly selected household sample of women. *Violence and Victims* 2:225–240.

Ellickson PL & Hays RD (1991). Antecedents of drinking among young adolescents with different alcohol use histories. *Journal of Studies on Alcohol* 52(5):398–408.

Flitcraft AH (1992). Violence, values and gender (Editorial). *Journal of the American Medical Association* 267(23):3194–3195.

Frezza M, di Padova C, Pozatto G et al. (1990). High blood alcohol levels in women: The role of decreased gastric alcohol dehydrogenase activity and first-pass metabolism. *The New England Journal of Medicine* 322:95–99.

Gomberg ESL (1986). Women and alcoholism: Psychosocial issues. *Women and Alcohol: Health-Related Issues (Research Monograph No. 16)*. Rockville, MD, National Institute on Alcohol Abuse and Alcoholism, 78–120.

Gomberg ESL (1989a). Alcoholic women in treatment: Early histories and early problem behaviors. *Advances in Alcohol & Substance Abuse* 8(2):133–147.

Gomberg ESL (1989b). Alcoholism in women: Use of other drugs. *Alcoholism: Clinical & Experimental Research* 13:338 (Abstract 215).

Gomberg ESL (1990). Alcoholic women in treatment: Report of violent events. *Alcoholism: Clinical & Experimental Research* 14:312 (Abstract 289).

Gomberg ESL (1991). Comparing alcoholic women with positive vs. negative family history. *Alcoholism: Clinical & Experimental Research* 15(2):363 (Abstract 307).

Gomberg ESL (1994). Risk factors for drinking over a woman's life span. *Alcohol Health and Research World* 18(5):220–227.

Gomberg ESL (1995). Older women and alcohol: Use and abuse. In M Galanter (ed.) *Recent Developments in Alcoholism* (Vol. 12). New York, NY: Plenum, 61–79.

Gomberg, ESL (1997a). Alcohol abuse: Age and gender differences. In RW Wilsnack & SC Wilsnack (eds.) *Gender and Alcohol, Individual and Social Perspectives.* New Brunswick, NJ: Rutgers Center of Alcohol Studies, 225–244.

Gomberg ESL & Lisansky JM (1984). Antecedents of alcohol problems in women. In SC Wilsnack & LJ Beckman (eds.) *Alcohol Problems in Women.* New York, NY: Guilford Press, 233–259.

Gomberg ESL & Nirenberg TD (eds.) (1993). *Women and Substance Abuse.* Norwood, NJ: Ablex Publishing.

Gomberg ESL, Walton MA, Bandekar R, Coyne JM & Blow FC (1997b). Alcohol and elderly health: Gender differences for lifetime abstainers versus former drinkers. *Alcoholism: Clinical & Experimental Research* 21: 24A (Abstract 122).

Greden JF & Walters A (1992). Caffeine. In JH Levinson, P Ruiz, RB Millman et al. (eds.) *Substance Abuse: A Comprehensive Textbook (2nd Edition).* Baltimore, MD: Williams & Wilkins.

Hanna E, Faden V & Harford T (1993). Marriage: Does it protect young women from alcoholism. *Journal of Substance Abuse* 5:1–14.

Helzer JE, Burnam A & McEvoy LT (1991). Alcohol abuse and dependence. In L Robins & DA Regier (eds.) *Psychiatric Disorders in America: The Epidemiologic Catchment Area Study.* New York, NY: The Free Press, 81–115.

Helzer JE & Pryzbeck TR (1988). The co-occurrence of alcoholism with other psychiatric disorders in the general population and its impact on treatment. *Journal of Studies on Alcohol* 49(3):219–224.

Hesselbrock MN, Meyer RE & Jeener J (1985). Psychopathology in hospitalized alcoholics. *Archives of General Psychiatry* 42(11):1050–1055.

Howell JT (1973). *Hard Living on Clay Street: Portraits of Blue Collar Families.* Garden City, NY: Anchor Books.

Hughes JR, Gust SW, Skoog K et al. (1991). Symptoms of tobacco withdrawal. *Archives of General Psychiatry* 48:52–59.

Johnson PB (1982). Sex differences: Women's roles and alcohol use: Preliminary national data. *Journal of Social Issues* 38(2):93–116.

Johnston LD, O'Malley PM & Bachman JG (1993). *National Survey Results on Drug Use from Monitoring the Future Study, 1975–1992, Volumes I and II* (NIH Publication No. 93-3597 and 93-3598). Rockville, MD: National Institute on Drug Abuse.

Kandel DR & Andrews K (1987). Processes of adolescent socialization by parents and peers. *International Journal of the Addictions* 22(4):319–342.

Little RE & Wendt JR (1993). The effects of maternal drinking in the reproductive period: An epidemiological review. In ESL Gomberg & TD Nirenberg (eds.) *Women and Substance Abuse.* Norwood, NJ: Ablex Publishing, 191–213.

McLaughlin RJ, Baer PE & Burnside MA (1985). Psychosocial correlates of alcohol use at two age levels during adolescence. *Journal of Studies on Alcohol* 46(3):212–218.

Passaro KT & Little RE (1997). Childbearing and alcohol use. In RA Wilsnack & SC Wilsnack (eds.) *Gender and Alcohol: Individual and Social Perspective.* New Brunswick, NJ: Rutgers Center of Alcohol Studies Publications, 90–113.

Power C & Estaugh V (1990). The role of family formation and dissolution in shaping drinking behavior in early adulthood. *British Journal of Addictions* 85:521–530.

Prescott CA & Kendler KS (1995). Genetic and environmental influences on alcohol and tobacco dependence among women. In JB Fertig & JP Allen (eds.) *Alcohol and Tobacco: From Basic Science to Clinical Practice (Research Monograph 30).* Rockville, MD: National Institute on Alcohol Abuse and Alcoholism, 59–88.

Roberts LJ & Leonard KE (1997). Gender differences and similarities in the alcohol and marriage relationship. In RA Wilsnack & SC Wilsnack (eds.) *Gender and Alcohol: Individual and Social Perspectives.* New Brunswick, NJ: Rutgers Center of Alcohol Studies Publications, 289–311.

Schiffman S & Balabanis M (1995). Associations between alcohol and tobacco. In JB Fertis & JP Allen (eds.) *Alcohol and Tobacco: From Basic Science to Clinical Practice (Research Monograph 30).* Rockville, MD: National Institute on Alcohol Abuse and Alcoholism, 17–36.

Schuckit MA (1972). The alcoholic woman: A literature review. *Psychological Medicine* 3:37–43.

Schuckit MA & Morrissey ER (1986). *Women and Alcohol: Health Related Issues (Research Monograph 16).* Rockville, MD: National Institute on Alcohol Abuse and Alcoholism, 226–259.

Schulenberg J, Dielman TE & Leech SL (1993). Individual vs. Social Causes of Alcohol Abuse During Early Adolescence: A Three Way Prospective Study. Paper presented at the Research Society on Alcoholism, San Antonio, TX, June 1993.

Spiegler D, Tate D, Aitken S et al. (eds.) (1989). *Alcohol Use Among U.S. Ethnic Minorities (Research Monograph 18).* Rockville, MD: National Institute on Alcohol Abuse and Alcoholism.

Turnbull JE (1988). Primary and secondary alcoholic women: Social casework. *Journal of Contemporary Social Work* 69(3):290–297.

Van Den Bergh B (ed.) (1991). *Feminist Perspectives on Addictions.* New York, NY: Springer.

Williams CN & Klerman LV (1984). Female alcohol abuse: Its effects on the family. In SC Wilsnack & LJ Beckman (eds.) *Alcohol Problems in Women: Antecedents, Consequences and Interventions.* New York, NY: Guilford Press, 280–312.

Wilsnack RA & Wilsnack SC (1992). Women, work and alcohol: Failures of simple theories. *Alcoholism: Clinical & Experimental Research* 16:172–179.

Wilsnack RA, Wilsnack SC & Klassen AD (1984). Women's drinking and drinking problem patterns from a 1981 national survey. *American Journal of Public Health* 74:1211–1238.

Wilsnack SC (1984). Drinking, sexuality, and sexual dysfunction in women. In SC Wilsnack & JL Beckman (eds.) *Alcohol Problems in Women: Antecedents, Consequences and Interventions.* New York, NY: Guilford Press, 189–227.

Wilsnack SC & Wilsnack RA (1991). Epidemiology of women's drinking. *Journal of Substance Abuse* 3(2):133–158.

Wilsnack SC & Wilsnack RA (1993). Epidemiological research on women's drinking: Recent progress and directions for the 1990s. In ESL Gomberg & TD Nirenberg (eds.) *Women and Substance Abuse.* Norwood, NJ: Ablex Publishing, 62–99.

Windle M (1990). A longitudinal study of antisocial behaviors in early adolescence as predictors of late adolescence substance use: Gender and ethnic group differences. *Journal of Abnormal Psychology* 99(1):86–91.

Zucker RA & Fitzgerald HE (1991). Early developmental factors and risk for alcohol problems. *Alcohol Health and Research World* 15(1):18–24.

CHAPTER 3

Treatment of the Addicted Woman in Pregnancy

Laura J. Miller, M.D.

Medical Stabilization
Detoxification from Alcohol
Detoxification from Sedative-Hypnotics
Detoxification from Opioids
Detoxification from Cocaine
Methadone Maintenance

The use of alcohol and other illicit drugs during pregnancy has been associated with increased morbidity and mortality for the mother, the fetus and the subsequent infant. Viewed critically, however, it becomes apparent that this increase in morbidity and mortality most often is due to a complex interaction of multiple factors and not always due *directly* to the effect of the substance. In addition, lifestyle factors contribute greatly to the adverse outcomes seen in alcohol and drug-using women and need to be reviewed. Many women perceive pregnancy as a stressful life event; indeed, some women feel extreme emotional conflicts on discovering they are pregnant. Concurrently, they may view the pregnancy as motivation to pursue recovery and thus gain control over their lives. This may lead them to seek treatment of their addiction and medical care for their pregnancy. However, their ability to follow through may be compromised by their guilt, the lack of supportive significant others (including family) and their ambivalence about the success of drug treatment (Mitchell, 1994). This chapter is intended as a guide to decisions about detoxification and treatment during pregnancy.

Prenatal Care. Prenatal care of addicted women is best provided under the supervision of physicians who are knowledgeable about both high risk obstetrics and addiction medicine. However, the number of physicians with both qualifications is small. Alternatively, optimal prenatal care can be a collaborative process between an obstetrical service and addiction treatment program(s), so as to provide the best treatment for the medical disease of addiction and close monitoring of the progress of the pregnancy. Whether an inpatient or outpatient program, collaboration is essential to assure continuation of the addiction treatment after childbirth (Mitchell, 1994).

Certain general concepts should be kept in mind when providing obstetrical care for addicted women. Most will enter care late in their pregnancies. Their ambivalence about continuing an unintended pregnancy, their fear and guilt associated with exposing the fetus to alcohol or drugs, unpleasant past experiences with institutions and agencies, and uncertainty about the father may provide the impetus to delay seeking care. Further, because of the menstrual dysfunction often associated with addiction, addicted women may not realize that they are pregnant for many months (Mitchell & Brown, 1990). Others, who have unsuccessfully sought abortions, find that their pregnancies are beyond the legal time allowed or no that no pregnancy termination services are available to them. These issues often prevent women from following through with appointments and prescribed treatments, especially if their motivation to seek treatment is based largely on concern for the pregnancy and not on recognition that the addictive disorder requires treatment. Similar issues also contribute to an inability to bond to the fetus during pregnancy and after birth (Mitchell, 1994).

Weekly visits should include (but not be limited to) taking weight; urine dipstick for sugar, acetone and protein; and toxicology, blood pressure, fundal height, and fetal heart rate. Random blood toxicologies for alcohol are helpful as appropriate. Women who are HIV-positive should be referred to the infectious disease clinic for evaluation and treatment (Mitchell, 1994).

TABLE 1. Guidelines for Medical Withdrawal from Alcohol

At Admission:
Obtain a detailed health history, including alcohol and other drug use; make arrangements for prenatal care.

Conduct a comprehensive physical examination, including weight, vital signs, and an obstetrical examination.

Obtain laboratory tests, including an initial blood workup that includes, but is not limited to:
- Blood group, Rh factor determination, and antibody screen;
- Serological test for syphilis;
- Hepatitis B and C screens; and
- Complete blood count with indices.

Also obtain other laboratory tests that include, but are not limited to:
- Cervical cytology smear (Pap smear), unless the provider has results of a test performed within the past three months;
- Cervical culture for gonorrhea;
- Urine screen for urinary tract infection, kidney disease, protein, and glucose; and
- Chlamydia screen.

Obtain purified protein derivative of tuberculin (IPPD) test with antigen panel, as well as urine and/or blood toxicologies.

Provide for HIV antibody counseling and testing.

Obtain baseline sonogram, if appropriate.

Dosing Strategy:
Evaluate the pattern, frequency and amount of alcohol or other drug use.

Obtain a detailed history of alcohol and other drug use within the preceding 24 hours and of any previous alcohol withdrawal reaction.

Begin initial treatment with thiamine, folic acid, and prenatal iron and vitamins. Obtain laboratory tests listed earlier, including CBC, electrolytes, and magnesium level; when indicated, obtain an EKG.

Obtain an initial blood alcohol level to determine:
- Extent of intoxication at admission;
- Safe time to begin medication; and
- Expected time for full withdrawal to begin. (The usual rate of elimination of alcohol from a healthy alcohol dependent person is 30 mg/dl/hr. This rate may be increased during pregnancy.)

Provide for nonpharmacological interventions designed to:
- Reduce stimuli;
- Maintain hydration;
- Maintain reality orientation;
- Provide reassurance and positive reinforcement;
- Provide nutritional support;
- Maintain physical comfort;
- Maintain body temperature; and
- Encourage sleep and rest.

Follow the appropriate withdrawal schedule:
- *Phenobarbital*: typically, 15 to 60 mg by mouth every 4–6 hours as needed for the first two days, decreasing gradually to 15 mg by the fourth day;
- *Diazepam*: typically, 10 mg four times a day; 10 mg every two hours as needed for withdrawal symptoms with a maximum of 150 mg/24 hours; decreasing gradually at a rate of 20–25% over approximately five days. The loading dose protocol with diazepam is accomplished with doses given according to withdrawal symptoms: when symptoms are stabilized, diazepam's long half-life alleviates the need for further medication in most cases.
- *Chlordiazepoxide*: typically, 25 to 50 mg four times a day for days eight through 10.

Monitor for signs and symptoms of alcohol withdrawal syndrome, including:
- Vital signs (temperature, blood pressure, pulse);
- Delirium (orientation);
- Wernicke's encephalopathy (nystagmus);
- Psychosis (hallucinations, inappropriate thinking);
- Irritability (tremors, increased reflexes);
- Autonomic reflexes (goosebumps, sweating); and
- Fetal well-being (fetal heart tones, sonograms, or Nonstress Test) as appropriate for gestational age.

Reduce medication dose if the patient shows signs of oversedation.

Provide for positive social support for the patient to help manage stress.

Discharge the patient after medical withdrawal to the care of a case manager for continuing treatment and prenatal care.

Source: Center for Substance Abuse Treatment (1993). *Treatment Improvement Protocol for Pregnant, Substance-Using Women.* Rockville, MD: CSAT, 16–17.

Detoxification. The issue of whether, and how, to detoxify the patient from alcohol or drugs during pregnancy is a complicated one. The clinician must take into account not only the effects of withdrawal symptoms and pharmacologic agents on the woman, but on her fetus and neonate as well. Potential risks to offspring exposed to alcohol and other drugs *in utero* include morphologic teratogenicity (physical anomalies), behavioral teratogenicity (enduring behavioral changes resulting from alterations in the developing central nervous system), fetal or neonatal withdrawal, fetal or neonatal toxicity, and miscarriage or stillbirth. However, in research as in clinical practice, it is impossible to separate the direct adverse effects of these substances from associated changes in lifestyle, nutrition, medical illness and social support.

This chapter is intended as a guide to decisions about detoxification during pregnancy. It will cover detoxification from alcohol, sedative-hypnotics, opioids and cocaine.

MEDICAL STABILIZATION

The initial stabilization as well as the medical withdrawal of pregnant women from their drug(s) of abuse are recognized means of reducing the acute illness associated with the use of alcohol and other drugs. The federal Center for Substance Abuse Treatment (1993) advises that initial stabilization of the patient should be accomplished within 10 days of first contact, or earlier if medically necessary.

During the period of stabilization, caregivers need to monitor the mother and fetus for adverse signs of drug withdrawal, establish a basis for ongoing alcohol and other drug treatment and recovery, and initiate a relationship between the mother and available supportive services within the community.

Protocols for prenatal care are presented below, and apply to all of the specific medical withdrawal guidelines that follow.

DETOXIFICATION FROM ALCOHOL

In addition to the profound health risks of alcohol addiction to the pregnant woman herself, alcohol may have devastating consequences for exposed offspring (see Chapter 4 for a more detailed discussion). Given the risks to both the woman and her fetus of continuing alcohol use during pregnancy, controlled detoxification clearly is indicated. Guidelines for such detoxification are presented in Table 1.

According to the federal Center for Substance Abuse Treatment (CSAT, 1993), any pregnant woman who consumes over 8 ounces of alcohol (one pint of liquor) daily should be assumed to have developed tolerance. (However, tolerance may develop at lower levels of consumption in some women, particularly those using multiple drugs.) CSAT recommends that medical withdrawal of an alcohol-dependent pregnant woman be conducted in an inpatient setting and under medical supervision that includes collaboration with an obstetrician.

TABLE 2. Similarities and Differences between Symptoms Associated with Pregnancy and Symptoms Associated with Alcohol Withdrawal

Signs and Symptoms Common to Both Pregnancy and Alcohol Withdrawal:
Hypertension
Nausea and vomiting
Restlessness
Seizures
Sleep disturbance
Tachycardia
Tachypnea and respiratory alkalosis
Signs and Symptoms of Alcohol Withdrawal Not Commonly Associated with Pregnancy:
Agitation
Distractibility
Fever
Hallucinosis
Impaired memory
Marked diaphoresis
Tremor

The sudden cessation of drinking can precipitate withdrawal symptoms that are life-threatening to both the mother and the fetus. If this occurs or the physician feels that the potential for a life-threatening situation exists, medications should be used to control the withdrawal.

Signs of Alcohol Withdrawal in Pregnancy. The physiologic changes accompanying normal pregnancy can make it more difficult to recognize early signs of alcohol withdrawal. During normal pregnancy, tachycardia and tachypnea often are present, with the latter causing a mild respiratory alkalosis. Sleep disturbances are common, with decreased Stage 4 sleep as pregnancy progresses. Nausea and vomiting are frequent, particularly in the first trimester. Physical restlessness and difficulty in sitting still often are experienced. In the context of preeclampsia or eclampsia, hypertension and/or seizures also may occur. Since all of the above also may be symptoms or signs of alcohol withdrawal, the diagnosis of withdrawal may be obscured.

Obtaining a thorough history of alcohol consumption and cessation is the most reliable way to diagnose withdrawal during pregnancy. Certain symptoms and signs also are characteristic of withdrawal and atypical during normal pregnancy. For example, pronounced tremor and diaphoresis, fever, agitation, distractibility, impaired memory and hallucinosis should all raise the suspicion of alcohol

Protocol for Prenatal Care of the Pregnant Woman with an Alcohol or Drug Use Disorder

At the first prenatal visit:

1. Perform a complete history and physical examination;
2. Order a baseline sonogram;
3. Order baseline laboratory tests, to include but not be limited to:
   a. Complete blood count with Hgb electrophoresis
   b. Serological test for syphilis
   c. Cervical cultures for gonorrhea and chlamydia
   d. PPD with anergy panel
   e. SMA 12
   f. PAP smear
   g. Rubella titer
   h. Blood type and RH titers
   i. Screen for hepatitis B and C;
4. Initiate HIV counseling;
5. Make other appropriate referrals, as for genetic counseling for women who may be age 35 or older at delivery;
6. Order an initial psychological evaluation;
7. Make a social service referral;
8. Refer the patient to a drug treatment program;
9. Refer opioid addicts for methadone maintenance for the duration of pregnancy; and
10. Establish rules, requirements and goals with the patient and her significant other(s).

At follow-up visits:

28 weeks

1. Order a follow-up sonogram;
2. Screen for diabetes;
3. Repeat the complete blood count;
4. Repeat the serological test for syphilis;
5. Establish an ongoing relationship with the patient's drug treatment providers (for obstetric personnel) or obstretrical caregivers (for addiction specialists);
6. Establish a good working relationship with the patient's significant other(s); and
7. Begin to discuss contraceptive methods.

36 weeks

1. Repeat the complete blood count and serological test for syphilis;
2. Repeat the screens for hepatitis B and C, if the initial test results were negative;
3. Repeat the test for HIV, if the initial results were negative; and
4. Begin antepartum testing of women on methadone maintenance and those who have consistently positive urine toxicologies.

At labor and delivery:

1. Perform a complete history and physical (especially a recent drug history);
2. Repeat the hepatitis screen and serological tests for syphilis;
3. Order a urine toxicology;
4. Alert pediatric medical and nursing staff;
5. Alert social service personnel;
6. Provide pain management as appropriate; and
7. Select a method of delivery based solely on obstetric considerations.

During the post-partum period:

1. Encourage the patient to continue in a drug treatment program;
2. Encourage use of an appropriate contraceptive method; and
3. Remember that breastfeeding is *not* contraindicated in methadone-maintained women.

Source: Mitchell JL (1994). Treatment of the addicted woman in pregnancy. In NS Miller (ed.) *Principles of Addiction Medicine*. Chevy Chase, MD: American Society of Addiction Medicine.

TABLE 3. Guidelines for Withdrawal from Sedative-Hypnotic Drugs

At Admission:

Obtain a detailed health history, including alcohol and other drug use; make arrangements for prenatal care.

Conduct a comprehensive physical examination, including weight, vital signs, and an obstetrical examination.

Obtain laboratory tests, including an initial blood work-up that includes, but is not limited to:

- Blood group, Rh factor determination, and antibody screen;
- Serological test for syphilis;
- Hepatitis B and C screens; and
- Complete blood count with indices.

Also obtain other laboratory tests that include, but are not limited to:

- Cervical cytology smear (Pap smear), unless the clinician has results of a test performed within the past three months;
- Cervical culture for gonorrhea;
- Urine screen for urinary tract infection, kidney disease, protein, and glucose; and
- Chlamydia screen.

Obtain purified protein derivative of tuberculin (IPPD) test with antigen panel, as well as urine and/or blood toxicologies.

Provide for HIV antibody counseling and testing.

Obtain baseline sonogram, if appropriate.

Dosing Strategy:

Evaluate the pattern, frequency, and amount of drug use.

Obtain a detailed history of drug use within the preceding 24 hours.

Document signs and symptoms of withdrawal. The regular use of a standardized withdrawal assessment scale can be helpful.

Administer drugs for medical withdrawal. The drugs used may vary. For medical withdrawal of patients dependent on barbiturates, minor tranquilizers, or other sedatives, some programs suggest administering the drug of use. The use of a long-acting drug, such as phenobarbital, diazepam, or clonazepam, may be helpful.

Stabilize the patient to suppress withdrawal symptoms. Supportive measures should include a safe environment, with proper nutrition and rest. Frequent reassurance and encouragement are vital.

Withdraw the pregnant patient in regular decrements of 5% to 10% of dose daily.

Source: Center for Substance Abuse Treatment (1993). *Treatment Improvement Protocol for Pregnant, Substance-Using Women*. Rockville, MD: CSAT, 25.

withdrawal. Table 2 summarizes pregnancy-related and withdrawal-related symptoms.

Pharmacologic Treatment of Withdrawal Signs and Symptoms. Uncontrolled withdrawal seizures, hypertension, tachycardia and agitation pose risks to both the pregnant woman and her fetus, and often require pharmacologic intervention. However, some medications used to treat alcohol withdrawal introduce risks as well. Known effects of such agents are as follows:

Benzodiazepines: Benzodiazepines often are indicated to control agitation, seizures and delirium from alcohol withdrawal. When high doses are required (the equivalent of 30 mg of diazepam or more), fetal or neonatal toxicity may result. Fetal toxicity can be detected by external cardiac monitoring, and manifests itself as decreased beat-to-beat variability and absence of accelerations. Newborns who are toxic appear lethargic and like "floppy babies," with hypotonia, hyporeflexia, difficulty sucking, poor respiratory efforts and difficulty maintaining body temperature in cold environments. These problems can be reversed by the benzodiazepine inhibitor flumazenil.

When benzodiazepines are needed for more than a few days near the end of a pregnancy, the newborn may show signs of benzodiazepine withdrawal. These begin hours to days after birth, and include increased tone, hyperreflexia and tremor. Neonatal benzodiazepine withdrawal resolves spontaneously and does not require specific treatment.

Benzodiazepines for intravenous administration are usually stored in a sodium benzoate/benzoic acid buffer preservative. This preservative is a potent uncoupler of bilirubin and albumin. When benzodiazepines are given intravenously during pregnancy, free bilirubin levels may rise in the fetus or neonate, risking kernicterus.

Studies of benzodiazepine teratogenicity in humans have had conflicting results. Some studies have linked first trimester exposure to diazepam with oral clefts,while others have not. One group has found delays in both mental and motor development in toddlers exposed to benzodiazepines *in utero*, but the studies on which these conclusions are based have major methodologic flaws. Other studies have found that benzodiazepine use during pregnancy does not adversely affect offsprings' intelligence scores or increase their risk of mental retardation. The bulk of the evidence suggests that short-term use of benzodiazepines, as in alcohol detoxification, does not have enduring adverse effects on offspring.

In sum, the risks of uncontrolled withdrawal seizures, agitation and delirium outweigh the risks of benzodiazepine use for both the woman and her fetus in most cases. To avoid fetal or neonatal toxicity, doses should be kept as low as possible. If significant toxicity occurs despite this, flumazenil can be administered to the neonate. The newborn should be monitored carefully for recurring signs of toxicity, since flumazenil has a short half-life and repeat doses often are required. Prolonged use of intravenous benzodiazepines should be avoided during pregnancy.

Phenobarbital: Although phenobarbital sometimes has been recommended as a replacement for benzodiazepines in alcohol detoxification during pregnancy, it confers no significant advantage. Like benzodiazepines, it can cause fetal or neonatal toxicity. Fetal intoxication can reduce intrauterine movements, increasing the risk of malpresentation. In addition, most studies suggest phenobarbital is a weak teratogen, causing an increase in minor craniofacial anomalies and possibly an increase in nonspecific major anomalies.

Chloral Hydrate: As with phenobarbital, there is no evidence that chloral hydrate is safer during pregnancy than benzodiazepines. Limited data suggest that it may have nonspecific teratogenic effects, and that it may have more side effects in the newborn than benzodiazepines.

Carbamazepine: Carbamazepine sometimes is used to prevent and control symptoms of alcohol withdrawal. During pregnancy, its use poses a number of risks. During the first trimester, it is weakly teratogenic, increasing the risk of minor congenital anomalies, neural tube defects, and possibly developmental delay. Given later in pregnancy, in rare instances it can increase the risk of neonatal hemorrhage by lowering vitamin K-dependent coagulation factors, or cause transient neonatal hepatic dysfunction.

For these reasons, benzodiazepines are preferred to carbamazepine in most cases of alcohol detoxification. Nevertheless, in cases where carbamazepine is needed, its risks can be minimized by vitamin supplementation. During pregnancy, folate requirements increase, and folate supplementation can significantly decrease the risk of neural tube defects. Folate deficiency is especially common in the context of alcoholism, so folate supplementation is recommended whether or not carbamazepine is prescribed. In addiction, vitamin K supplementation for pregnant women who have received carbamazepine can prevent neonatal hemorrhage. Vitamin K (phytonadione) should be given at a dose of 20 mg po qd during the last one to two months of pregnancy, and 1 mg IM should be given to the newborn.

Neuroleptic Agents: Antipsychotic drugs sometimes are prescribed for alcohol hallucinosis. If these agents are used near the end of a pregnancy, a mild neonatal withdrawal syndrome is not uncommon. Signs include tremor, increased tone, and motor immaturity. Much more rare is withdrawal dyskinesia, which can include the above symptoms as well as irritability, hyperreflexia, abnormal posturing, tongue thrusting, and irregular breathing. These difficulties begin within hours to days after birth, last up to several weeks and resolve spontaneously, with no lasting effects on motor development. In severe cases, diphenhydramine elixir can be given to alleviate symptoms.

During pregnancy, haloperidol or trifluoperazine are preferable to other neuroleptics, because they are relatively well studied and have not been associated with teratogenicity, and because they are less likely than low potency agents to cause hypotension and decreased placental perfusion. There is some evidence to suggest that relatively low serum calcium levels can contribute to the development of extrapyramidal side effects from neuroleptics. Since pregnancy is a state of high calcium demand and many addicted women have poor nutrition, calcium supplementation is recommended (500 mg BID or TID, depending on dietary intake).

Beta-Adrenergic Blocking Agents: Hypertension often accompanies alcohol withdrawal and can adversely affect pregnancy outcome if untreated. The beta-adrenergic blocking agents propranolol and atenolol have been relatively well studied during pregnancy, and have not been associated with adverse effects. Propranolol can have a greater effect on heart rate during pregnancy than in the nonpregnant state, so heart rate should be closely monitored. Atenolol has a theoretical advantage over propranolol because it is a selective beta-1 receptor blocker, so it does not block beta-2 uterine receptors to increase myometrial tone. In sum, untreated withdrawal symptoms in pregnancy clearly pose a greater risk than treatment with atenolol or propranolol.

Note: Disulfiram has been associated with birth defects and should not be used in pregnancy.

TABLE 4. Guidelines for Withdrawal from Cocaine

At Admission:
Obtain a detailed health history, including alcohol and other drug use; make arrangements for prenatal care. Conduct a comprehensive physical examination, including weight, vital signs, and an obstetrical examination.

Obtain laboratory tests, including an initial blood work-up that includes, but is not limited to:
- Blood group, Rh factor determination, and antibody screen;
- Serological test for syphilis;
- Hepatitis B and C screens; and
- Complete blood count with indices.

Also obtain other laboratory tests that include, but are not limited to:
- Cervical cytology smear (Pap smear), unless the provider has results of a test performed within the past three months;
- Cervical culture for gonorrhea;
- Urine screen for urinary tract infection, kidney disease, protein, and glucose; and
- Chlamydia screen.

Obtain purified protein derivative of tuberculin (IPPD) test with antigen panel, as well as urine and/or blood toxicologies.

Provide for HIV antibody counseling and testing.

Obtain baseline sonogram, if appropriate.

Dosing Strategy:
Evaluate the pattern of drug use, route of administration, and frequency and amount of use.

Obtain a detailed history of drug use within the past 24 hours.

To withdraw a pregnant woman dependent on cocaine, the following are options:

No medications: Pregnant patients who are withdrawing from cocaine should not be medicated except in cases of extreme agitation and by order of the physician.

Anxiolytics: If medication is needed, low doses of diazepam (Valium) or chlordiazepoxide (Librium) (25 mg by mouth, 4 times a day x 6 doses) may be used.

Antidepressants: A typical withdrawal guideline for cocaine-dependent women uses doxepin (Sinequan) or desipramine (Norpramin). For example:
- Days 1–2: Doxepin 25 mg (one tablet) by mouth two times a day, 50 mg maximum;
- Days 3–5: Doxepin 25 mg (one tablet) by mouth two times a day, then discontinue;
- Further therapy should be determined by the treating physician after an initial period of observation;
- No drug therapy usually is indicated after the first five days.

Barbiturates: For cocaine withdrawal symptoms:
- Days 1–2: Phenobarbital 30-60 mg every 4 hours, as needed;
- Days 3–4: Phenobarbital 30-60 mg every 6 hours, as needed.

Bromocriptine: The use of bromocriptine in pregnant women is *not recommended* because of the lack of proven efficacy and unknown effects (both short- and long-term) on the fetus.

Source: Center for Substance Abuse Treatment (1993). *Treatment Improvement Protocol for Pregnant, Substance-Using Women.* Rockville, MD: CSAT, 23.

DETOXIFICATION FROM SEDATIVE-HYPNOTIC DRUGS

Medical withdrawal from sedative-hypnotics can include substitution of a long-acting agent, with subsequent controlled, slow withdrawal of that agent, or by controlled, slow withdrawal of the addicting agent. The method chosen usually depends on an assessment of the risk that the woman might experience *severe* withdrawal symptoms, which can include status epilepticus and fetal respiratory arrest. In such cases, immediate obstetrical intervention and hospitalization are warranted (CSAT, 1993). Untreated, withdrawal symptoms can progress to hyperpyrexia, electrolyte abnormalities, cardiovascular collapse, and death.

Thus, inpatient medical withdrawal from barbiturates, benzodiazepines, and other sedative-hypnotic drugs is recommended because continual monitoring of the mother and fetus is required. Drug doses must be tapered so that mother and fetus arrive at a drug-free state without experiencing an uncontrolled withdrawal (CSAT, 1993). Guidelines for detoxification from sedative-hypnotics during pregnancy are presented in Table 3.

The occurrence of seizures associated with unsupervised or rapid withdrawal of barbiturates in addicted persons can lead to respiratory arrest in both the mother and fetus. Although the use of dilantin is associated with birth defects, it is quite commonly used in pregnancy because of its superior anti-seizure effects. The birth defect issue in pregnancy is not clear, since epileptics not on dilantin also have increased risk of birth defects similar to those associated with the use of dilantin.

TABLE 5. Opioid Conversion and Methadone Stabilization

At Admission:
Obtain a detailed health history, including alcohol and other drug use; make arrangements for prenatal care.

Conduct a comprehensive physical examination, including weight, vital signs, and an obstetrical examination.

Obtain laboratory tests, including an initial blood work-up that includes, but is not limited to:
- Blood group, Rh factor determination, and antibody screen;
- Serological test for syphilis;
- Hepatitis B and C screens; and
- Complete blood count with indices.

Also obtain other laboratory tests that include, but are not limited to:
- Cervical cytology smear (Pap smear), unless the provider has results of a test performed within the past three months;
- Cervical culture for gonorrhea;
- Urine screen for urinary tract infection, kidney disease, protein, and glucose; and
- Chlamydia screen.

Obtain purified protein derivative of tuberculin (IPPD) test with antigen panel, as well as urine and/or blood toxicologies.

Provide for HIV antibody counseling and testing.

Obtain baseline sonogram, if appropriate.

Dosing Strategy:
Evaluate the pattern of drug use, route of administration, and frequency and amount of use. Know something about the purity of the street product and the other substances (such as quinine or diazepam) with which the product may be cut or diluted.

Obtain a detailed history of drug use within the preceding 24 hours.

Give an initial oral methadone dose of 10–40 mg. Because it is imperative to reverse any opioid abstinence symptoms as quickly as possible, an additional dose of methadone may be required in the range of 5–10 mg if objective signs of withdrawal persist after 3 to 4 hours (time to allow the methadone to reach a peak blood level). This 5–10 mg dose can be repeated at 3 to 4 hour intervals, until objective signs of withdrawal no longer are present.

Adjust the dose by 5 to 10 mg daily, based on physical signs and symptoms of opioid withdrawal and patient comfort. **Even minimal symptoms in the mother may indicate distress in the fetus.**

After the stabilization dose has been established, keep the patient at this level for several days.

If there is simultaneous dependence on other drugs such as alcohol, cocaine, and sedatives, methadone induction should proceed as outlined above, while concurrent medical withdrawal procedures are initiated. The other drug withdrawals can be managed as usual against the background of methadone maintenance. Ideally, this is an inpatient procedure.

Important warning: NARCAN (or any narcotic antagonist) *never* should be given to a pregnant woman except as a last resort to reverse severe narcotic overdose. Administration of a narcotic antagonist to a pregnant woman could result in spontaneous abortion, premature labor, and/or stillbirth.

Source: Center for Substance Abuse Treatment (1993). *Treatment Improvement Protocol for Pregnant, Substance-Using Women*. Rockville, MD: CSAT, 19–20.

DETOXIFICATION FROM COCAINE

The effects of *in utero* cocaine exposure are not fully understood; however, use of cocaine during pregnancy is associated with intrauterine growth retardation, perhaps due to vasoconstriction of placental and umbilical blood vessels. Crack cocaine increases the risk of premature labor and placental abruption by increasing uterine contractility. Exposed offspring may exhibit neurobehavioral abnormalities, but it is unclear whether these are directly due to cocaine.

Detoxification from cocaine during pregnancy is clearly indicated. The difficult question in this case is whether to use pharmacologic agents for detoxification of a pregnant woman. However, because the efficacy of the many drugs used in the treatment of cocaine addiction is still under debate and the safety of many of the drugs in pregnancy is unknown, there currently are no commonly embraced protocols for cocaine withdrawal in pregnancy. (Guidelines for medical withdrawal from cocaine are presented in Table 4.)

DETOXIFICATION FROM OPIOIDS

It is recommended that opioid addiction during pregnancy be treated with methadone maintenance in nearly all cases. The goal of the methadone strategy is to stabilize the patient without producing any indication of opioid abstinence syndrome. According to the federal Center for Substance Abuse Treatment (1993), such a strategy provides the following advantages:

- It reduces illegal opioid use, as well as use of other drugs;

TABLE 6. Guidelines for Medical Withdrawal from Methadone

Timing of Withdrawal:	Withdrawal Schedule:
There are no research data to suggest that withdrawal during one trimester is worse than the others. Some clinical practitioners indicate concerns regarding methadone withdrawal prior to 14 weeks or after 32 weeks. These concerns are based on the theoretical possibility of an increased incidence of spontaneous abortion and premature labor. Other clinicians believe that withdrawal can be performed in all trimesters.	Medical withdrawal from methadone usually is done in decrements of 2 to 2.5 mg every 7 to 10 days. This procedure only should be done in conjunction with an obstetrician who can monitor the effects on the fetus.
Patients should be allowed to discontinue withdrawal at any time, for any reason, without feelings of guilt. They then should be placed into a methadone maintenance program at a therapeutically sound dose. Clinicians need to be particularly aware that a decrease in methadone dose could precipitate a relapse to drug use.	Intrauterine demise (death of the fetus *in utero*) has been documented as a complication of medical withdrawal even when done under optimal conditions, such as hospitalization and close fetal monitoring.
Patients in continuous treatment who return to illegal drug use should be placed back on methadone. Methadone is preferable to the use of illegal street drugs.	**Opioid Withdrawal Using Clonidine:** The long-term effects of the use of clonidine in pregnancy are still unknown. Although clonidine hydrochloride has been used safely and effectively for rapid medical withdrawal in nonpregnant, opioid-dependent individuals, there are no data concerning its safety in pregnancy. Further research in this area needs to be performed before this technique can be recommended as a standard of care for pregnant women.

Source: Center for Substance Abuse Treatment (1993). *Treatment Improvement Protocol for Pregnant, Substance-Using Women.* Rockville, MD: CSAT, 21.

- It helps to remove the opioid-dependent woman from the drug-seeking environment and eliminates the need for illegal behavior;
- It prevents fluctuations of the maternal drug level that may occur throughout the day;
- It improves maternal nutrition, increasing the weight of the newborn;
- It improves the woman's ability to participate in prenatal care and other rehabilitation efforts;
- It enhances the woman's ability to prepare for the birth of the infant and begin homemaking; and
- It reduces obstetrical complications.

Guidelines for opioid conversion and methadone stabilization are presented in Table 6.

If a woman is highly motivated for detoxification, or a methadone maintenance program is unavailable, detoxification may be attempted. During pregnancy, detoxification should be slow and individualized. It is preferable to use methadone alone and to avoid the use of clonidine or naltrexone. Typically, the methadone dose is reduced by about 0.2 mg to 1 mg per day, and detoxification requires two to eight weeks. As pregnancy progresses and total body water increases, it is not uncommon for dosage requirements to be higher, so that detoxification must proceed more slowly. Fetal heart rate monitoring and uterine tocodynamometry are added to the usual monitoring.

Nonstress tests are commonly used to assess fetal well-being. These tests are performed by asking the pregnant woman to mark perceived fetal movements, while fetal heart rate and uterine activity are continually recorded. A normal (reactive) pattern is one in which fetal heart rate accelerates with fetal movements. After a dose of methadone, it is common to obtain false positive (nonreactive) patterns, which may give an erroneous impression of fetal distress. Nonstress tests are useful for monitoring during detoxification, but should be performed just before, rather than after, methadone is ingested.

CONCLUSIONS

Providing care to pregnant addicted women requires the skills of a multidisciplinary team to provide all needed medical services, including appropriate treatment of alcohol and other drug problems. Assessment and appropriate treatment of psychosocial and mental health issues, as well as social services for the children (if any) also is essential.

REFERENCES

Aarskog D (1975). Association between maternal intake of diazepam and oral clefts. *Lancet* 2:921.

Allen MH (1991). Detoxification considerations in the medical management of substance abuse in pregnancy. *Bulletin of the New York Academy of Medicine* 67:270–276.

Anderson PO & McGuire GG (1989). Neonatal alprazolam withdrawal—Possible effects of breast feeding. *Drug Intelligence and Clinical Pharmacology* 23:614.

Archie CL, Lee MI, Sokol RJ et al. (1989). The effects of methadone treatment on the reactivity of the nonstress test. *Obstetrics and Gynecology* 74:254–255.

Athinarayanan P, Peirog SH, Nigam SK et al. (1976). Chlordiazepoxide withdrawal in the neonate. *American Journal of Obstetrics and Gynecology* 124:212–213.

Auerbach JG, Hans SL, Marcus J et al. (1992). Maternal psychotropic medication and neonatal behavior. *Neurotoxicology and Teratology* 14:399–406.

Bergman U, Rosa FW, Baum C et al. (1992). Effects of exposure to benzodiazepine during fetal life. *Lancet* 340:694–696.

Bertollini R, Kallen B, Mastroiacovo P et al. (1987). Anticonvulsant drugs in monotherapy: Effect on the fetus. *European Journal of Epidemiology* 3:164–171.

Brockington IF & Kumar R (1982). Drug addiction and psychotropic drug treatment during pregnancy and lactation. In IF Brockington & R Kumar (eds.) *Motherhood and Mental Illness.* London, England: Academic Press, 239–255.

Center for Substance Abuse Treatment (1993). *Treatment Improvement Protocol for Pregnant, Substance-Using Women.* Rockville, MD: CSAT.

Cleary MF (1992). Fluphenazine decanoate during pregnancy. *American Journal of Psychiatry* 134:815–816.

Cree JE, Meyer J & Hailey DM (1973). Diazepam in labour: Its metabolism and effect on the clinical condition and thermogenesis of the newborn. *British Medical Journal* 4:251–255.

Crombie DL, Pinsent RJ, Fleming DM et al. (1975). Fetal effects of tranquilizers in pregnancy. *The New England Journal of Medicine* 293:198–199.

Czeizel A & Lendvay A (1987). In-utero exposure to benzodiazepines. *Lancet* 1:628.

Dansky LV, Rosenblatt DS & Andermann E (1992). Mechanisms of teratogenesis: Folic acid and antiepileptic therapy. *Neurology* 42(Suppl. 5):32–42.

Dubois D, Peticolas J, Temperville B et al. (1983). Treatment with atenolol of hypertension in pregnancy. *Drugs* 25(Suppl 2):215–218.

Finnegan LP & Kandall SR (1992). Maternal and neonatal effects of alcohol and drugs. In JH Lowinson, P Ruiz & RB Millman (eds.) *Substance Abuse: A Comprehensive Textbook (2nd Ed).* Baltimore, MD: Williams & Wilkins, 628–656.

Gillberg C (1977). "Floppy infant syndrome" and maternal diazepam. *Lancet* 2:244.

Hartz SC, Heinonen OP, Shapiro S et al. (1975). Antenatal exposure to meprobamate and chlordiazepoxide in relation to malformations, mental development, and childhood mortality. *The New England Journal of Medicine* 292:726–728.

Heinonen OP, Slone D & Shapiro S (1977). *Birth Defects and Drugs in Pregnancy.* Littleton, MA: Publishing Sciences Group.

Hill RM, Desmond MM & Kay JL (1966). Extrapyramidal dysfunction in an infant of a schizophrenic mother. *Journal of Pediatrics* 69:589–595.

Jones KL, Lacro RV, Johnson KA et al. (1989). Pattern of malformations in the children of women treated with carbamazepine during pregnancy. *The New England Journal of Medicine* 320:1661–1666.

Koch S, Losche G, Jager-Roman E et al. (1992). Major and minor birth malformations and antiepileptic drugs. *Neurology* 42(Suppl 5):83–88.

Kuny S & Binswanger U (1989). Neuroleptic-induced extrapyramidal symptoms and serum calcium levels: Results of a pilot study. *Pharmacopsychiatry* 21:67–70.

Kuzemko JA & Hartley S (1972). Treatment of cerebral irritation in the newborn: Double-blind trial with chloral hydrate and diazepam. *Developmental Medicine and Child Neurology* 14:740–746.

Laegreid L, Hagberg G & Lundberg A (1992). Neurodevelopment in late infancy after prenatal exposure to benzodiazepines—A prospective study. *Neuropediatrics* 23:60–67.

Laegreid L, Olegard R, Wahlstrom J et al. (1987). Abnormalities in children exposed to benzodiazepines in utero. *Lancet* 1:108–109.

Lowinson J, Oliveira A, Selwyn P et al. (1991). Workshop on detoxification policies and directions. *Bulletin of the New York Academy of Medicine* 67:308–310.

Maas U, Kattner E, Weingart-Jess B et al. (1990). Infrequent neonatal opiate withdrawal following maternal methadone detoxification during pregnancy. *Journal of Perinatal Medicine* 18:111–118.

Mazzi E (1977). Possible neonatal diazepam withdrawal: A case report. *American Journal of Obstetrics and Gynecology* 129:586–587.

Merlob P, Mor N & Litwin A (1992). Transient hepatic dysfunction in an infant of an epileptic mother treated with carbamazepine during pregnancy and breastfeeding. *Pediatrics* 26:1563–1565.

Mitchell J (1994). Treatment of the addicted woman in pregnancy. In NS Miller (ed.). *Principles of Addiction Medicine.* Chevy Chase, MD: American Society of Addiction Medicine.

Mitchell JL & Brown G (1990). Physiological effects of cocaine, heroin, and methadone. In RC Engs (ed.) *Women: Alcohol and Other Drugs.* Dubuque, IA: Kendall/Hunt Publishing Co., 53–60.

Moslet U & Hansen ES (1992). A review of vitamin K, epilepsy and pregnancy. *Acta Neurologica Scandinavica* 85:39–43.

O'Connor MO, Johnson GH & James DI (1981). Intrauterine effect of phenothiazines. *Medical Journal of Australia* 1:416–417.

Omtzigt JGC, Los FJ, Meijer JWA et al. (1993). The 10, 11-epoxide-10, 11-diol pathway of carbamazepine in early pregnancy in maternal serum, urine, and amniotic fluid: effect of dose, comedication, and relation to outcome of pregnancy. *Therapeutic Drug Monitor* 15:1–10.

Ray D & Singh M (1988). Anticonvulsants during pregnancy and lactation: Fetal and neonatal hazards. *Indian Pediatrics* 25:185–191.

Rosa F (1991). Spina bifida in infants of women treated with carbamazepine during pregnancy. *The New England Journal of Medicine* 324:674–677.

Reynolds B, Butters L, Evans J et al. (1984). First year of life after the use of atenolol in pregnancy associated hypertension. *Archives of Diseases of Children* 59:1061–1063.

Rosenberg L, Mitchell AA, Parsells JL et al. (1983). Lack of relation of oral clefts to diazepam use during pregnancy. *The New England Journal of Medicine* 309:1282–1285.

Rubin PC (1981). Beta-blockers in pregnancy. *The New England Journal of Medicine* 305:1323–1326.

Rubin PC, Butters L, McCabe R et al. (1987). The influence of pregnancy on drug action: concentration-effect modelling with propranolol. *Clinical Sciences* 73:47–52.

Ryan CL & Pappas BA (1990). Prenatal exposure to antiadrenergic antihypertensive drugs: Effects on neurobehavioral development and the behavioral consequences of enriched rearing. *Neurotoxicology and Teratology* 12:359–366.

Safra MJ & Oakley GP (1975). Association between cleft lip with or without cleft palate and prenatal exposure to diazepam. *Lancet* 2:478–480.

Saxen I (1975). Associations between oral clefts and drugs taken during pregnancy. *International Journal of Epidemiology* 4:37–44.

Schiff D, Chan G & Stern L (1971). Fixed drug combinations and the displacement of bilirubin from albumin. *Pediatrics* 48:139–141.

Sexson WR & Barak Y (1989). Withdrawal emergent syndrome in an infant associated with maternal haloperidol therapy. *Journal of Perinatology* 9:170–172.

Shannon RW, Fraser GP, Aitken RG et al. (1972). Diazepam in preeclamptic toxaemia with special reference to its effect on the newborn infant. *British Journal of Clinical Practice* 26:271–275.

Stahl MM, Saldee P & Vinge E (1993). Reversal of fetal benzodiazepine intoxication using flumazenil. *British Journal of Obstetrics and Gynecology* 100:185–188.

Viggedal G, Hagberg BS, Laegreid L et al. (1993). Mental development in late infancy after prenatal exposure to benzodiazepines—A prospective study. *Journal of Child Psychology and Psychiatry* 34:295–305.

Whitelaw AGL, Cummings AJ & McFadyen IR (1981). Effect of maternal lorazepam on the neonate. *British Medical Journal* 282:1106–1108.

Yeh SY, Paul RH, Cordero L et al. (1974). A study of diazepam during labor. *Obstetrics and Gynecology* 43:363–373.

Yerby MS, Leavitt A, Erickson DM et al. (1992). Antiepileptics and the development of congenital anomalies. *Neurology* 42(Suppl 5):132–140.

CHAPTER 4

Treatment Options for Drug-Exposed Neonates

Stephen R. Kandall, M.D., FAAP

Opiate Abstinence Syndrome
Neurotoxicity Related to Alcohol
Cocaine
Amphetamines
Other Drugs

Recent attention to women and drugs has derived, in part, from anecdotal reports and clinical studies that have made it obvious that drug use during pregnancy is associated with significant morbidity in the fetus, neonate, and young infant.

The common practice of using multiple drugs during pregnancy has hindered delineation of the perinatal effects of specific individual drugs. Since the clinical sequelae of intrauterine exposure to different drugs may appear similar in the neonate, the appropriate treatment of the drug-exposed newborn must rest on accurate determination of the pattern of maternal alcohol or other drug use. This determination, however, is far from easy. Maternal histories of drug use may be unreliable; obstetric care providers may not fully, skillfully and nonjudgmentally question women about their drug use habits; and women may not admit to drug use, often fearing repercussions in the legal and child welfare arenas. In the newborn period, unskilled observers may miss signs of non-opiate drug exposure, which often are less dramatic than a full-blown opiate abstinence syndrome.

In addition, a positive urine toxicologic analysis in an infant—considered the "objective" benchmark of drug exposure—actually reflects maternal drug use for only a few days prior to delivery. Moreover, policies governing drug testing of mothers and neonates may not be applied uniformly. Such policies may range from universal testing to selective testing based on combinations of maternal self-report, behavior, lifestyle indices, and obstetric conditions, as well as non-specific neonatal conditions such as prematurity, intrauterine growth retardation, and subjective assessment of neurologic dysfunction.

Confusion also arises from terminology that often equates two vague terms: "drug-exposed" infants, who may not show immediate effects of drug exposure, and "drug-addicted" infants, defined as only those infants who have been diagnosed by hospital staff in the neonatal period as having suffered the effects of intrauterine drug exposure.

This chapter discusses clinical aspects and treatment of the neonatal opiate abstinence syndrome and the neurotoxicity seen following intrauterine exposure to alcohol, cocaine, amphetamines and other drugs.

NEONATAL OPIATE ABSTINENCE SYNDROME

Infants born to mothers who are chronically dependent on opioids during pregnancy frequently are born with a passive dependency on those agents. The opioids involved include powerful opiates such as heroin, morphine, and methadone, as well as less potent opioids such as codeine, pentazocine, and propoxyphene hydrochloride. Transplacental passage of the drugs leads to fetal biochemical adaptation to these substances. When the umbilical cord is cut, the supply of drug is abruptly terminated, setting the stage for neonatal abstinence.

Fetal exposure to these drugs varies according to the amount of drug used by the mother, the purity of the drug (if used illicitly), and the length of use. Abstinence from heroin and other short-acting opioids usually begins within 48 to 72 hours of birth. Abstinence from methadone also usually begins within a few days after birth, but since methadone is stored in fetal tissue and its rate of tissue clearance and excretion postnatally varies, the occurrence, time of onset, and severity of abstinence symptomatology is less predictable. Rosen and Pippenger (1976) found that neonatal methadone abstinence began when serum levels of methadone dropped to 0.06 micrograms/millimeter. The time after birth at which this level is reached may vary from infant to infant and, in a few cases (usually those in which a mother has been treated with doses of methadone exceeding 100 mg daily), the onset of major signs of neonatal abstinence may be delayed for as long as one to two weeks (Kandall & Gartner, 1974).

Controversy still exists as to the relationship between neonatal abstinence, maternal drug dose and serum levels of drugs. A recent study found that a spectrum of relationships does exist between these variables (Doberczak, Kandall & Friedmann, 1993), strengthening the general impression that lower maternal drug doses are associated with reduced severity of neonatal abstinence. It is important to stress, however, that reduction of the maternal methadone dose may lead to an increase in use of street drugs, with an attendant increase in the risk of adverse health conditions, such as HIV acquisition. Evidence suggests that the increased maternal fluid space, large maternal tissue reservoir, and altered drug metabolism by the placenta and fetus during pregnancy would argue for increasing, rather than decreasing, the maternal methadone dose (Pond, Kreek et al., 1985). Data also suggest that higher maternal methadone dosages in the first trimester may lead to higher birthweights in offspring, reversing the growth retardation often seen with maternal heroin use (Kandall, Albin et al., 1976). The most important consideration remains that maternal methadone doses should be individualized and should be adequate to ensure maternal and fetal well-being.

Neonatal opiate abstinence occurs in about 60% to 80% of heroin-exposed infants and methadone-exposed infants (Kandall, Albin et al., 1977; Finnegan & Ehrlich, 1990). Individual symptoms occur with the same frequency in the two groups of infants, although severity of abstinence from methadone and from heroin cannot be compared on a milligram to milligram basis. One study found that, probably because of differing pharmacokinetics, methadone-exposed infants more often required treatment with higher dosages of medication for longer periods of time than did heroin-exposed infants (Kandall, Albin et al., 1977). Another study found that more full-term infants required treatment for abstinence than did premature infants, either due to differing degrees of central nervous system maturation, differences in total drug exposure during gestation, or the insensitivity of testing techniques to detect gestation-related manifestations of abstinence (Doberczak, Kandall & Wilets, 1991).

Signs of neonatal opiate abstinence usually are grouped into four categories. *Central nervous system signs* of neonatal abstinence usually are the most obvious clinically. These signs include irritability, tremulousness, hypertonia, and excessive crying. Opiate-exposed infants often show a voracious appetite and an exaggerated sucking drive, but coordination between sucking and swallowing frequently is abnormal (Kron, Litt et al., 1976). This incoordination poses a risk to the newborn infant of poor nutrient intake, excessive weight loss and suboptimal weight gain, as well as the potentially more serious complications of regurgitation and pulmonary aspiration.

The most dramatic central nervous system manifestation is the occurrence of abstinence-associated seizures, which occur in about 1% of heroin-exposed infants and about 5% to 7% of methadone-exposed infants (Herzlinger, Kandall & Vaughan, 1977). The etiology of these seizures is not well understood. Abstinence-associated seizures occur unpredictably, tend to be myoclonic in type, generally occur between one and two weeks after birth, and are more common when either phenobarbital or no drug, rather than paregoric, is used to treat early signs of opiate abstinence. Part of the reason studies cite different incidences of these seizures may be explained by the fact that the seizures may not be detected if the infants are tightly swaddled in a dimly-lit room.

If seizures occur, the infant should have a full sepsis workup, including lumbar puncture, to rule out systemic or central nervous system infection. A complete metabolic evaluation, including blood sugar, electrolytes, calcium, phosphorus, and magnesium levels, also should be performed. Central nervous system imaging, as by ultrasound and CT scanning or MRI, should be obtained. An electroencephalogram (EEG) will be abnormal in about half of the infants (Doberczak, Shanzer et al., 1988). Serial EEGs may be useful as a guide to further assessment, treatment, and follow-up.

Gastrointestinal signs include vomiting and diarrhea, which may further exacerbate a catabolic state. *Respiratory signs* include tachypnea and hyperpnea, which will increase insensible water loss, respiratory alkalosis, cyanosis, and apnea. *Autonomic nervous system signs* include sneezing, yawning, tearing, sweating, and hyperpyrexia.

The analgesic propoxyphene (Darvon®) has a marked structural similarity to methadone. Anecdotal reports of neonatal abstinence from propoxyphene have described irritability, tremors, high-pitched crying, watery stools and, in one case, a generalized clonic-tonic seizure at 36 hours of age. Similar symptomatology has been described following prolonged intrauterine exposure to codeine and pentazocine (Talwin®).

Treatment. The appropriate treatment of opioid-exposed infants rests on sound principles of diagnosis and assessment. Since the individual signs and symptoms of neonatal abstinence tend to be nonspecific, consideration of other diagnoses such as sepsis, electrolyte imbalance, hypoglycemia, and central nervous system hemorrhage and ischemia must always be part of the infant assessment. This is especially relevant because maternal drug abuse frequently occurs in a clinical and socioenvironmental setting that poses multiple medical risks to the infant.

It also is important to gather objective information as to the mother's drug use to provide optimal treatment for the infant. Data-gathering should rely on a comprehensive interview with the mother, reports from drug treatment facilities and social service agencies, and more objective measures such as toxicologic assays of drugs and their metabolites. Since, as noted earlier, urine testing imposes methodologic limitations, it should be noted that analysis of infant meconium provides a much broader picture of fetal drug exposure (Ostrea, Brady et al., 1992). This is based on the concepts that (1) drugs are metabolized by the fetal liver and excreted into bile, and (2) since the fetus does not usually pass stool *in utero*, drug metabolites accumulate in meconium throughout gestation. More recently, assay techniques applied to infant and maternal hair samples have broadened even further the ability to detect intrauterine drug exposure (Callahan, Grant et al., 1992).

Since the occurrence, time of onset, and ultimate severity of neonatal abstinence is not totally predictable, the use of a semi-objective "abstinence score" is strongly recommended. This scoring system should be used to monitor the onset, progression, and spontaneous regression of symptoms or response to treatment of neonatal abstinence.

Although a number of scales have been proposed, the most comprehensive scoring system is that proposed by Finnegan (Finnegan & Kaltenbach, 1992; reproduced in Kandall, 1993) (Figure 1). This scoring system assigns a weighted score to 21 symptoms commonly seen in neonatal abstinence, based on their postulated relationship to the outcome variables of morbidity and mortality. Infants are scored at two hours after birth and every four hours thereafter. Infants may be scored every two hours if the total severity score exceeds 8, but scoring every four hours may be resumed if the severity score decreases. All symptoms exhibited during the entire two-hour or four-hour interval should be included. In addition to the quantitative scoring, relevant clinical observations should be noted in the "Comments" column on the scoring sheet.

Using the Finnegan scale, specific pharmacologic treatment to control opiate abstinence usually is initiated when the total severity score exceeds 8 for three consecutive scoring periods, or when the average of three consecutive scores is 8 or higher.

While the infant is undergoing assessment with the aid of this scoring scale to determine whether specific treatment will be necessary, general treatment measures should be instituted. Environmental modification, such as loose swaddling in a side-lying position in a quiet, dimly-lit room usually is recommended, despite the lack of firm evidence as to its efficacy in controlling the severity of neonatal abstinence (Ostrea, Chavez & Strauss, 1976). Such management also places additional burdens on medical and nursing staff to monitor vital signs, prevent hyperthermia, note skin excoriations, and detect seizures. Placing infants in the prone position for sleep, especially on a soft bedding material, recently has been implicated in higher rates of Sudden Infant Death Syndrome (SIDS; AAP Task Force on Infant Positioning and SIDS, 1992). This is especially relevant in opiate-exposed infants, since their risk of SIDS is approximately three- to fourfold that of infants who were not drug-exposed (Kandall, Gaines et al., 1993).

Gentle handling based on individual infant cues and control of external stimulation appears to benefit the opiate-exposed infant. One study has suggested that opiate-exposed infants benefit from being placed on nonoscillating waterbeds (Oro & Dixon, 1988). Infants treated with medication and waterbeds as an adjunctive therapy had lower severity scores on day 5 and a better pattern of weight gain than infants conventionally treated with pharmacotherapy alone.

Supportive treatment measures also include provision of adequate fluids and calories based on the

FIGURE 1. Neonatal Abstinence Score

DATE: DAILY WEIGHT:

SYSTEM	SIGNS AND SYMPTOMS	SCORE	AM	PM	COMMENTS
CENTRAL NERVOUS SYSTEM DISTURBANCES	Excessive High Pitched (other) Cry Continuous High Pitched (other) Cry	2 3			
	Sleeps < 1 hour after feeding Sleeps < 2 hours after feeding Sleeps < 3 hours after feeding	3 2 1			
	Hyperactive Moro reflex Markedly Hyperactive Moro reflex	2 3			
	Mild Tremors Disturbed Moderate-Severe Tremors Undisturbed	1 2			
	Mild Tremors Undisturbed Moderate-Severe Tremors Undisturbed	3 4			
	Increased Muscle Tone	2			
	Excoriation (specific areas)	1			
	Myoclonic Jerks	3			
	Generalized Convulsions	5			
METABOLIC/VASOMOTOR/ RESPIRATORY DISTURBANCES	Sweating	1			
	Fever < 101 (99-100.8F/37.2-38.2C) Fevers > 101 (38.4C and higher)	1 2			
	Frequent Yawning (>3-4 times/interval)	1			
	Mottling	1			
	Nasal Stuffiness	1			
	Sneezing (>304 times/interval)	1			
	Nasal Flaring	2			
	Respiratory Rate > 60/min. Respiratory Rate > 60/min with retractions	1 2			
GASTRO-INTESTINAL DISTURBANCES	Excessive Sucking	1			
	Poor Feeding	2			
	Regurgitation Projectile Vomiting	2 3			
	Loose Stools Water Stools	2 2			
TOTAL SCORE					
INITIALS OF SCORER					

infant's individual needs. Abnormal postnatal weight changes should be anticipated because of the infant's hypermetabolic state, excessive fluid loss and suboptimal nutrient intake. One study (Weinberger, Kandall et al., 1986) showed that infants with mild abstinence lost an average of 4% of their birth weight, reached a nadir on day 3, and regained their birth weight by the end of the first week. Newborns who developed more severe abstinence lost more weight and required a longer period of time to regain their birth weight. These data support both the need for prompt initiation of specific pharmacologic treatment of neonatal abstinence and the importance of nutritional support of those infants.

Breast-feeding should be offered, and may even be encouraged in those infants born to mothers who are well maintained on methadone, not abusing other substances, and who are HIV-negative. Breast-feeding enhances the mother-infant bond, an important consideration when mothers and babies are separated because of prolonged hospitalization. Although methadone does pass to the infant in breast milk, no study has documented the impact of breast feeding on the course of neonatal abstinence.

Pharmacotherapy. Naloxone often is used in the delivery room to reverse the depressant effects on the newborn of maternal medications such as meperidine, which may be used to provide analgesia for the parturient. Naloxone usually is contraindicated in opiate-exposed infants because its use may precipitate an acute abstinence syndrome. Naloxone is not specifically contraindicated following intrauterine exposure to cocaine, but caretakers must remember that cocaine use may be accompanied by opioid use.

In the neonatal period, specific pharmacotherapy to control opiate abstinence should be provided when the severity score (discussed earlier) reaches a predetermined level. Therapy is aimed at clinical stabilization of narcotic-exposed infants who require specific treatment, followed by gradual reduction of the medication, accompanied by close and objective assessment. Failure to treat neonatal abstinence may result in significant morbidity or even mortality from excessive fluid loss, respiratory distress, seizures, vomiting and aspiration, or hyperpyrexia.

The pharmacotherapeutic control of neonatal opiate abstinence can be accomplished with either (1) a substitute opiate such as paregoric (camphorated tincture of opium), or (2) a non-specific central nervous system depressant such as phenobarbital. Following some initial enthusiasm over the use of diazepam, it is now recognized that diazepam may cause respiratory and central nervous depression in the neonate. In addition, diazepam has been shown to provide poor prophylaxis and treatment of abstinence-associated seizures (Herzlinger, Kandall & Vaughan, 1977). The use of chlorpromazine to treat neonatal opiate abstinence is limited by the drug's potential hepatotoxicity and its adverse effect on the extrapyramidal tracts of the central nervous system. Short-acting opiates such as morphine and laudanum and longer-acting opioids such as methadone have been used to treat neonatal abstinence, but insufficient data exist with which to assess their efficacy and limitations.

Paregoric: A consensus panel convened in 1992 by the Center for Substance Abuse Treatment has promulgated useful guidelines for the treatment of opioid-exposed infants (Kandall, 1993). The panel recommended paregoric as the treatment of choice (Figure 2). The advantages of paregoric include its oral administration, its lack of significant adverse effects, and its wide margin of safety because of the low dose needed to control abstinence and its short half-life.

Paregoric treatment usually is initiated with a dose of 0.2 ml every three hours by mouth. If the severity of abstinence does not decrease, the stabilizing dose is raised by 0.05 ml at each succeeding dose, to a maximum dose of 0.4 ml, until the severity score begins to decrease. Once the infant is stabilized, the stabilizing dose is maintained for three to five days. Following stabilization, paregoric may be slowly decreased by 0.05 ml every other day, as dictated by the severity score. While the dose is being reduced, the dosing interval (every three hours) should remain the same. Paregoric may be discontinued once the infant is stable on 0.05 cc every three hours. Following this treatment, the infant should be observed, using the severity scale, for one to two days in the hospital to observe for "rebound symptomatology."

A slightly different treatment regimen has been suggested by Finnegan (Finnegan & Kaltenbach, 1992). Paregoric is administered every four hours, with the dose based on the severity score and the infant's weight. Infants with abstinence scores of 8 to 10 are treated with a total dose of 0.8 ml/kg/day; those with scores of 11 to 13 receive 1.2 ml/kg/day; those with scores of 14 to 16 receive 1.6 ml/kg/day; and those with scores of 17 or above receive 2.0 ml/kg/day. Once the infant is stabilized, paregoric may be slowly reduced by 10% of the total daily dose every 24 hours, guided by the severity score. Paregoric therapy may be discontinued once the infant is stable on a dose of 0.5 ml/kg/day. Following discontinuance of treatment, the infant should be observed in the hospital for two days.

The anticipated length of treatment of opiate abstinence with paregoric cannot be predicted with certainty. Although dose equivalencies obviously cannot be calculated for heroin and methadone, the pharmacokinetics of the two drugs suggest that treatment time would be longer following methadone exposure. Kandall and co-workers (1977) found a mean treatment time of 10 days for heroin abstinence, compared to 20 days for abstinence from heroin and methadone in combination, and 29 days for abstinence from methadone alone. Finnegan and Ehrlich (1990) confirmed a mean treatment time for opiate abstinence to be 24 days with paregoric and 20 days with phenobarbital.

Phenobarbital: The CSAT Consensus Panel also found phenobarbital to be a useful agent in the treatment of neonatal abstinence (Kandall, 1993). Phenobarbital controls the major signs of abstinence quite adequately, and provides much broader coverage in those cases of exposure to both opiates and depressants. Phenobarbital, however, has the potential disadvantages of producing depression of neonatal respiration and neonatal sucking, especially when the medication is used at higher doses.

FIGURE 2. Pharmacologic Treatment of Opiate Withdrawal

Drug	Dose	Considerations
Paregoric (0.4 mg MS/cc)	0.2 mL every 3 hours (PO) up to max of 0.4 mL every 3 hours. Gradually decrease dose every other day by 0.05 mL/dose as tolerated. After stabilization for 5 days, taper the dose cautiously.	If abstinence syndrome remains uncontrolled, add phenobarbital. Observation of infant should be maintained for 1—2 days after discontinuing drugs.
Phenobarbital	**Loading dose**: 5 mg/kg IM, IV. **Maintenance dose**: 3—5 mg/kg/day (PO, IM or IV), divided into doses every 8 hours. Increase as needed by 1 mg/kg to maximum of 10 mg/kg for 5 days, then reduce by 1 mg/kg every other day or as clinically indicated.	After stabilization for 5 days, taper the dose cautiously. Serum phenobarbital should be monitored when clinically indicated. Excessive phenobarbital dose may cause poor feeding behavior and lethargy.

Phenobarbital treatment usually can be started at 5 mg/kg/day as a loading dose, given either intramuscularly or intravenously to assure effective absorption (Figure 2). Using the same severity scale as described above, an oral maintenance dose is reached by increasing the dose by 1 mg/kg to a maximum of 10 mg/kg/day until a decrease in the severity score indicates that the abstinence symptoms are being controlled. Because of its longer half-life compared to paregoric, phenobarbital is administered every eight hours in this regimen. Following stabilization for about five days, the phenobarbital dose may be lowered by 1 mg/kg/day every other day, with monitoring of the severity score. In this regimen, phenobarbital levels are monitored only when clinically indicated, as in the case of poor control of abstinence symptoms or excessive sleepiness of the infant.

The phenobarbital treatment regimen proposed by Finnegan and Kaltenbach (1992) is somewhat more rigorous. This regimen relies more heavily on frequent monitoring of plasma phenobarbital levels, with titration of the dose to both the drug level and severity score. A loading dosage of 20 mg/kg/day is followed by a maintenance dosing regimen of 2 to 6 mg/day daily, if the plasma phenobarbital level is therapeutic and the infant is clinically stable. If an optimal plasma level is obtained (approximately 20 mcg/ml) and the severity score is less than 8, the phenobarbital dose is maintained for 72 hours.

If the total score continues to exceed 8, Finnegan recommends increasing the phenobarbital dose by administering 10 mg/kg of phenobarbital every 12 hours until control is achieved, the blood level reaches 70 mcg/ml, or the infant becomes clinically toxic. Following a clinically stable period of 72 hours, reduction of the phenobarbital level by about 15% per day usually can be accomplished by administering phenobarbital at a dose of 2 mg/kg/day. Phenobarbital is discontinued when the serum level falls below 10 mcg/ml and the severity score is less than 8. In the next 72 hours, if the infant remains stable, he may be discharged home.

The regimen detailed by Finnegan offers the advantage of extremely careful assessment and documentation of the therapeutic response of the infant in withdrawal. It has the disadvantage, however, of requiring frequent clinical assessments by trained personnel, as well as the need to draw blood for drug levels, which is expensive, time-consuming, and painful to the infant.

Comparison of phenobarbital and paregoric suggest the superiority of the latter in the treatment of neonatal opiate abstinence. Kaltenbach and Finnegan (1986), in a study of infant outcomes following intrauterine drug exposure, found that treatment with paregoric was far more successful in controlling neonatal abstinence than was either phenobarbital or diazepam. A later study of 176 infants (Finnegan & Ehrlich, 1990) showed that, although the treatment period with paregoric was slightly longer than with phenobarbital, paregoric was more effective in controlling the signs of opiate abstinence.

Another comparative study (Kandall, Doberczak et al., 1983) found that paregoric and phenobarbital, administered randomly to 153 passively addicted infants, initially controlled signs of abstinence equally well. Of the 12 infants who developed abstinence-associated seizures, however, 7 occurred among the 62 infants treated with phenobarbital, while none occurred among the 49 infants treated with paregoric. The authors postulated that, since a low-dose phenobarbital regimen was used, a protective blood level of the drug may not have been achieved in light of phenobarbital's ability to induce microsomal enzymes and speed the disposition of methadone from tissue stores in the neonate.

Since disorders of sucking frequently are seen in neonatal opiate abstinence, and since sucking represents an important function of neurobehavioral integration in the neonate, Kron and co-workers (Kron, Litt et al., 1976) compared the effect of treatment regimens on this behavior. Opiate-exposed infants treated with paregoric tended to suck more vigorously and with more normal periodicity than those infants treated either with phenobarbital or with no specific therapy.

Abstinence-associated seizures initially should be treated with intravenous phenobarbital at a loading dose of 10 to 20 mg/kg (Kandall, 1993). If the lower dose is used, a second dose of 10 mg/kg can be administered 10 minutes later, if seizures persist. If seizures are controlled, a serum phenobarbital level should be obtained in 24 hours, just prior to starting maintenance therapy at 3 to 5 mg/kg/day, divided into two doses. Paregoric therapy also should be started if the infant has not already been so treated.

Ongoing management of infants should be based on clinical and laboratory assessments. If other neuropathology is excluded, these seizures tend to be self-limited. If the first EEG is normal or the follow-up EEG becomes normal in the course of the infant's neonatal stay, medication doses may be slowly reduced under close observation. Once paregoric has been given, phenobarbital may be slowly discontinued at the rate of 1 mg/kg every other day. Following discontinuation of the phenobarbital, paregoric may be slowly discontinued, as outlined above.

If the seizures are not easily controlled and other anti-convulsant medications such as diphenylhydantoin are required, it is likely that another cause of the persistent seizures will be found. If the EEGs do not normalize in spite of good clinical control of seizures, the infant should be discharged from the hospital on maintenance anti-convulsant treatment and further management decisions should be made jointly with a pediatric neurologist.

Serial observations of these infants, as well as follow-up studies at one year of age, suggest that the seizures carry an excellent prognosis in the short term. A follow-up study (Doberczak, Shanzer et al., 1988) found normalization of neurologic and electroencephalographic abnormalities in these infants during the first year of life. In addition, Bayley developmental test scores remained normal during the period of observation. In that study, 7 of the 14 infants were able to be discharged from the nursery without anti-convulsant medications.

Despite some methodologic variations, therapeutic regimens for the treatment of neonatal opiate abstinence should be based on the following principles: complete assessment of the patterns of prenatal drug use, objective testing for drug exposure in the neonate, use of an abstinence scoring system to guide the initiation, maintenance, and discontinuation of drug treatment, and supportive care of the drug-exposed neonate.

NEUROTOXICITY TO DRUGS AND ALCOHOL

Because intrauterine alcohol exposure is now known to pose significant risks to the developing fetus, inclusion of this short discussion seems appropriate. Although estimates of alcohol use in pregnancy vary widely, the National Pregnancy & Health Survey has estimated that 757,000 babies annually are born following intrauterine exposure to alcohol. Fetal alcohol syndrome (FAS), first described by Lemoine in 1968 and Jones and Smith in 1973, can be identified in approximately 1 in 300 to 1 in 1,000 births in the United States; less severe manifestations, often termed fetal alcohol effects (FAE), may occur in as many as 1 in 100 births. Fetal alcohol-related damage cannot be confidently predicted, and no absolutely safe level of alcohol consumption during pregnancy has been established, but it is generally believed that daily consumption of more than three ounces of absolute alcohol, especially in conjunction with "binge drinking," may be particularly dangerous to the fetus.

In the context of maternal alcohol intake, the diagnosis of FAS can be made in an infant with findings in each of three categories (Day, Jasperse et al., 1989; Golden, Sokol et al., 1982; Ouellette, Rosett et al., 1977; Smith, 1979; also see Chapter 4 of this Section).

First, fetal growth retardation, typically in all three parameters of weight, length and head circumference, often is compounded by postnatal growth failure.

Second, facial dysmorphism is characterized by short palpebral fissures, hypoplastic maxilla, short upturned nose, flat philtrum, thin upper vermillion border, and micrognathia or retrognathia. Other features, such as ptosis, strabismus, microphthalmia, posteriorly rotated ears, and cleft lip or palate, also may be seen. Other congenital abnormalities of the cardiac, renal and skeletal systems have been described in FAS.

Third, severe central nervous system dysfunction may be evident in the neonatal period, with irritability, tremulousness, inconsolable crying, hypertonia, and seizures (Coles, Smith et al., 1984; Pierog, Chandavasu & Wexler, 1977). Microscopic examinations of infant brains have revealed cerebral malformations, neurologic heterotopia and disordered neuronal migration (Clarren, Alvord et al., 1978); MRI examinations have revealed a high incidence of midline brain anomalies (Swayze, Johnson et al., 1997) ascribed to alcohol exposure. One study found that alcohol-exposed premature infants had an increased risk of brain hemorrhage and white matter damage (Holzman, Paneth et al., 1995).

Later in life, FAS children may show a wide range of neurologic deficits, including cerebellar dysfunction, hypotonia, hyperactivity and speech problems. Mental retardation occurs in about 85% of FAS children; problems in intellectual functioning and attentional and behavioral problems in structured learning situations are very common. A landmark study (Streissguth, Aase et al., 1991) found that FAS and FAE patients aged 12 to 40 had an average IQ score of 68; 58% of the group had an IQ below 70. Only 6% of the patients were in regular school classes and all showed maladaptive behavior.

COCAINE

Although the use of cocaine in the U.S. dates back to the 1870s, the recent epidemic of smokeable ("crack") cocaine in the 1980s, coupled with an increase in the birth of cocaine-exposed babies and the epidemic of perinatal HIV/AIDS, has brought a new level of concern about the effects of cocaine use during pregnancy.

As with opiates, life circumstances of the cocaine-using mother often place the fetus and newborn infant at increased risk for suboptimal perinatal outcome. Many obstetric-related complications stem from the potent vasoconstrictive properties of cocaine, due to the drug's inhibition of neurotransmitter uptake in the synaptic cleft. Vasoconstriction in the uteroplacental circulation may lead to acute and chronic fetal hypoxia (Moore, Sorg et al., 1986; Woods, Plessinger & Clark, 1987). Vasoconstriction also may be the underlying mechanism for intrauterine growth retardation (Petitti & Coleman, 1990; Frank, Bauchner et al., 1990) and congenital anomalies, often termed "fetal vascular disruption" (Hoyme, Jones et al., 1990).

Cocaine's low molecular weight and high solubility in both water and lipids allow it to cross the placenta easily and enter fetal compartments. Similar to opiates, treatment of the cocaine-exposed neonate rests on an objective assessment of the impact of intrauterine drug exposure. Unlike opiate-exposed infants, cocaine-exposed infants do not undergo a physical abstinence or "withdrawal." These infants do, however, show signs of neurotoxicity, such as transient irritability and tremulousness (Chasnoff, Burns et al., 1985; Doberczak, Shanzer et al., 1988). Following this period of central nervous system irritability, cocaine-exposed infants tend to show a period of hyporeactivity, lethargy, and poor interaction with caretakers. In addition, specific neurobehavioral testing has led to a general agreement that these infants evidence lability of state, with wide swings from hyperalertness to reduced reactivity, decreased habituation, and visual tracking difficulties (Chasnoff, Griffith et al., 1989; Eisen, Field et al., 1991; Mayes, Granger et al., 1993). One study found that cocaine-exposed infants had fewer cry utterances, more short cries, and less crying in the hyperphonation mode, suggesting a pattern of underaroused neurobehavioral function (Corwin, Lester et al., 1992).

Cocaine-exposed infants show a very wide spectrum of effects, ranging from a lack of obvious symptoms to neurobehavioral dysfunction described above to more dramatic but less common complications such as seizures (Kramer, Locke et al., 1990) and cerebrovascular accidents (Chasnoff, Bussey et al., 1986). These serious events may be due either to an ischemic insult secondary to vasoconstriction or to hemorrhage from acute hypertension. Electroencephalographic abnormalities have been reported in as many as 50% of cocaine-exposed infants in one study (Doberczak, Shanzer, Senie et al., 1988), but this observation was not confirmed in another study (Legido, Clancy et al., 1992).

In addition, echoencephalographic abnormalities have been reported in 35% of infants exposed to either

either cocaine or methamphetamines (Dixon & Bejar, 1989). These abnormalities include ischemic injury with cavitary lesions (8%), intraventricular hemorrhage (12%), subependymal hemorrhage (11%), subarachnoid hemorrhage (14%), and ventricular dilatation (10%). In another study of infants with birth weights under 1,500 grams, however, cocaine exposure did not increase the incidence of intraventricular hemorrhage or periventricular leukomalacia, compared to controls (Dusick, Covert et al., 1993). Intrauterine exposure to cocaine also has been linked, usually through case reports, to other neonatal complications, including necrotizing enterocolitis, bowel perforation, arterial thrombosis and hypertension, transiently decreased cardiac output and myocardial ischemia, and persistent hypertension.

Treatment. Since cocaine-associated neurotoxicity is quite different from opiate abstinence, use of the previously described opiate abstinence severity scale to assess cocaine exposure is inappropriate. The subtlety of cocaine-related signs and the nature of those neurologic abnormalities suggest the need for an assessment instrument such as the Brazelton Neonatal Behavioral Assessment Scale. An appropriate assessment should focus on areas such as habituation, responsivity, state, and quality of motor function, as well as a more general neurologic evaluation.

Although most cocaine-exposed infants do not require treatment with pharmacotherapeutic agents, some infants who are excessively irritable appear to benefit from a short course of treatment with phenobarbital. In such instances, phenobarbital treatment is rarely needed for more than a few days and, following control of the infant's irritability, therapy may be discontinued without tapering.

Seizures due to cocaine neurotoxicity should be treated acutely with a loading dose of 10–20 mg/kg of phenobarbital administered intravenously. If the lower dose of 10 mg/kg is used and seizures persist, that dose should be repeated in 10 to 15 minutes. While seizure control is being accomplished, diagnostic work-up should be initiated; this evaluation usually includes determination of electrolytes and serum glucose levels, full sepsis workup—including lumbar puncture, EEG, and central nervous imaging by ultrasound and either CT scan or MRI.

If seizures are controlled with phenobarbital, continued seizure management should be based on clinical assessment and results of the diagnostic work-up. Phenobarbital levels should be drawn 24 hours after completion of the loading dose; if levels are in the therapeutic range, maintenance therapy, usually at a dose of 5 mg/kg/day should be started. Refractory seizures, such as those that may occur following a cerebrovascular accident, may require the addition of other anti-convulsants, such as phenytoins, to the treatment regimen.

An important part of the therapeutic management of cocaine-exposed infants is the provision of an appropriate nursery environment. In contrast to opiate-exposed infants, whose irritability draws the attention of the nursery staff, cocaine-exposed infants tend toward hyporeactivity and decreased social responsiveness. This may result in their being left for periods of time without appropriate attention. Cocaine-exposed infants should be provided with an individualized program of structured physical contact, including gentle handling with support of the head and body, soft social talking, and eye contact without overstimulation.

As with maternal opiate use, interventional programs for cocaine-exposed infants should include mothers and fathers of the infants as much as possible. Parents benefit significantly from inclusion in the assessment and treatment of their infants. This should be accomplished with the involvement of trained personnel who are skilled in both assessing the infant and working with the parents in a supportive and non-judgmental manner.

Breast-feeding, which could foster mother-infant bonding, is contraindicated if the mother is actively using cocaine. Cocaine may readily pass to the infant through breast milk, and may produce a neonatal neurotoxic syndrome, including hypertonia, tremors, apnea and seizures (Chaney, Franke & Wadlington, 1988). In addition, breast-feeding is contraindicated when the mother is HIV positive due to transmissibility of the virus in breast milk.

AMPHETAMINES

Similar to the action of cocaine, amphetamine (racemic-B-phenylisopropyl-amine) stimulates the release and blocks the reuptake of neurotransmitters. Methamphetamine is structurally similar to amphetamine but has relatively greater central effects and less prominent peripheral actions.

The impact of cocaine and amphetamines on pregnancy appear to be similar. Two studies from Sweden by Eriksson and coauthors (1978, 1981) report a high perinatal mortality rate, an increased incidence of low birthweight babies and congenital malformations, and neurologic abnormalities that include drowsiness, poor feeding, and seizures in amphetamine-exposed infants. Neither of the reports comments on the need for specific treatment in the newborn period.

More recently, Oro and Dixon (1987) found a wide range of abnormalities, including abnormal sleep patterns, tremors, poor feeding, hyperactive reflexes, abnormal cry, state disorganization, vomiting, sneezing, and tachypnea, in a group of 46 infants following intrauterine exposure to cocaine and methamphetamines. Despite these findings, only one of 28 methamphetamine-exposed infants required specific treatment.

In a study cited previously, Dixon and Bejar (1989) found ECHO abnormalities in 35% of infants following intrauterine exposure to cocaine and methamphetamines. Despite these impressive findings, neurobehavioral assessment of the infants did not correlate well with ECHO abnormalities, perhaps because damage in the frontal lobes and basal ganglia may produce clinical abnormalities only later in infancy.

Some studies have suggested that the spectrum of neonatal cocaine-associated neurologic abnormalities should be broadened to include aberrant brainstem and auditory responses and abnormal ophthalmologic findings.

OTHER DRUGS

Barbiturates. Neonates exposed to maternal doses of phenobarbital of at least 90 mg/day for 12 weeks prior to delivery also may undergo abstinence. Barbiturate-dependent infants may show signs similar to opiate abstinence, such as hyperactivity, tremors, crying, vomiting, and diarrhea, which usually begins four to eight days after birth (Desmond, Schwanecke et al., 1972). Control of abstinence usually can be effected with phenobarbital treatment. Infants may show a prolonged abstinence, in which obvious central nervous system dysfunction may persist for two to six months.

Benzodiazepine Derivatives and Related Drugs. Case reports have described neonatal abstinence from diazepam (Valium®), chlordiazepoxide (Librium®), ethchlorvynol (Placidyl®), glutethimide (Doriden®), and hydroxyzine (Atarax®). Neonatal signs referable to the central nervous system dominate the picture of abstinence following all of these intrauterine exposures.

Hallucinogens. Little is known regarding neonatal symptomatology following exposure to hallucinogens. Prenatal exposure to marijuana has been reported to cause increased startles and tremors in the newborn that persist through the first year of life. Phencyclidine (PCP, angel dust) also has been reported to produce hypertonia, hyperreflexia, and coarse tremors.

CONCLUSIONS

Although the precise dimensions of intrauterine drug exposure are not known, the problem appears to be of major proportions. In addition to the drugs discussed above, other substances such as tobacco, marijuana, lysergic acid diethylamide (LSD), and an array of newer "designer drugs" not covered in this summary chapter merit consideration. Careful assessment of maternal drug-taking patterns and objective, scientifically-validated examination of substance-exposed infants should be strongly encouraged to delineate the effects of these substances on the fetus, neonate and young infant.

ACKNOWLEDGMENT: This chapter is based partially on material published in a chapter by the author, Treatment options for drug-exposed infants, in CN Chiang & LP Finnegan (1995). Medications Development for the Treatment of Pregnant Addicts and Their Infants (NIDA Research Monograph 149). *Rockville, MD: National Institute on Drug Abuse.*

REFERENCES

AAP Task Force on Infant Positioning and SIDS (1992). Positioning and SIDS. *Pediatrics* 89:1120–1126.

Callahan CM, Grant TM, Phipps P et al. (1992). Measurement of gestational cocaine exposure: sensitivity of infants' hair, meconium, and urine. *Journal of Pediatrics* 120:763–768.

Chaney NE, Franke J & Wadlington WB (1988). Cocaine convulsions in a breast-feeding baby. *Journal of Pediatrics* 112:134–135.

Chasnoff IJ, Burns WJ, Schnoll SH & Burns K (1985). Cocaine use in pregnancy. *The New England Journal of Medicine* 313:666–669.

Chasnoff IJ, Bussey ME, Savich R & Stack CM (1986). Perinatal cerebral infarction and maternal cocaine use. *Journal of Pediatrics* 108:456–459.

Chasnoff IJ, Griffith DR, MacGregor S, Dirkes K & Burns KA (1989). Temporal patterns of cocaine use in pregnancy. *Journal of the American Medical Association* 261:1741–1744.

Clarren SK, Alvord EC, Sumi M, Streissguth AP & Smith DW (1978). Brain malformations related to prenatal exposure to ethanol. *Journal of Pediatrics* 92:64–67.

Coles CD, Smith IE, Fernhoff PM & Falek A (1984). Neonatal ethanol withdrawal: characteristics in clinically normal, nondysmorphic neonates. *Journal of Pediatrics* 105:445–451.

Corwin MJ, Lester BM, Sepkoski C, McLaughlin S, Kayne H & Golub HL (1992). Effects of in utero cocaine exposure on newborn acoustical cry characteristics. *Pediatrics* 89:1199–1203.

Day NL, Jasperse D, Richardson G et al. (1989). Prenatal exposure to alcohol: effect on infant growth and morphologic characteristics. *Pediatrics* 84:536–541.

Desmond MM, Schwanecke RP, Wilson GS, Yasunaga S & Burgdorff I (1972). Maternal barbiturate utilization and neonatal withdrawal symptomatology. *Journal of Pediatrics* 80:190–197.

Dixon SD & Bejar R (1989). Echoencephalographic findings in neonates associated with maternal cocaine and methamphetamine use: incidence and clinical correlates. *Journal of Pediatrics* 115:770–778.

Doberczak TM, Kandall SR & Friedmann P (1993). Relationships between maternal methadone dosage, maternal-neonatal methadone levels, and neonatal withdrawal. *Obstetrics and Gynecology* 81:936–940.

Doberczak TM, Kandall SR & Wilets I (1991). Neonatal opiate abstinence syndrome in term and preterm infants. *Journal of Pediatrics* 118:933–937.

Doberczak TM, Shanzer S, Cutler R, Senie R, Loucopoulos J & Kandall SR (1988). One-year follow-up of infants with abstinence-associated seizures. *Archives of Neurology* 45:649–653.

Doberczak TM, Shanzer S, Senie RT & Kandall SR (1988). Neonatal neurologic and electroencephalographic effects of intrauterine cocaine exposure. *Journal of Pediatrics* 113:354–358.

Dusick AM, Covert RF, Schreiber MD et al. (1993). Risk of intracranial hemorrhage and other adverse outcomes after cocaine exposure in a cohort of 323 very low birth weight infants. *Journal of Pediatrics* 122:438–445.

Eisen LN, Field TM, Bandstra ES et al. (1991). Perinatal cocaine effects on neonatal stress behavior and performance on the Brazelton scale. *Pediatrics* 88:477–480.

Eriksson M, Larsson G, Winbladh B & Zetterstrom R (1978). The influence of amphetamine addiction on pregnancy and the newborn infant. *Acta Paediatrica Scandinavica* 67:95–99.

Eriksson M, Larsson G & Zetterstrom R (1981). Amphetamine addiction and pregnancy. *Acta Obstetricia et Gynecologica Scandinavica* 60:253–259, 1981.

Finnegan LP & Ehrlich SM (1990). Maternal drug abuse during pregnancy: Evaluation and pharmacotherapy for neonatal abstinence. *Modern Methods of Pharmacologic Testing in the Evaluation of Drugs of Abuse* 6:255–263.

Finnegan LP & Kaltenbach K (1992). Neonatal abstinence syndrome. In RA Hoekelman, SB Friedman, N Nelson & HM Seidel (eds.) *Primary Pediatric Care (2nd Edition)*. St. Louis, MO: CV Mosby, 1367–1378.

Frank DA, Bauchner H, Parker S et al. (1990). Neonatal body proportionality and body composition after in utero exposure to cocaine and marijuana. *Journal of Pediatrics* 117:622–626.

Golden NL, Sokol RJ, Kuhnert BR & Bottoms S (1982). Maternal alcohol use and infant development. *Pediatrics* 70:931–934.

Gomby DS & Shiono PH (1991). Estimating the number of substance-exposed children. *The Future of Children*. Center for the Future of Children, 1:17–25.

Herzlinger RA, Kandall SR & Vaughan HG (1977). Neonatal seizures associated with narcotic withdrawal. *Journal of Pediatrics* 91:638–641.

Holzman C, Paneth N, Little R et al. (1995). Perinatal brain injury in premature infants born to mothers using alcohol in pregnancy. *Pediatrics* 95:66–73.

Hoyme HE, Jones KL, Dixon SD et al. (1990). Prenatal cocaine exposure and fetal vascular disruption. *Pediatrics* 85:743–747.

Kaltenbach K & Finnegan LP (1986). Neonatal abstinence syndrome, pharmacotherapy and developmental outcome. *Neurobehavioral Toxicology and Teratology* 8:353–355.

Kandall SR (1993). *Improving Treatment for Drug-Exposed Infants* (Treatment Improvement Protocol Series). Rockville, MD: Center for Substance Abuse Treatment, 14–15.

Kandall SR & Gartner LM (1974). Late presentation of drug withdrawal symptoms in newborns. *American Journal of Diseases of Children* 127:58–61.

Kandall SR, Albin S, Lowinson J, Berle B, Eidelman AI & Gartner LM (1976). Differential effects of maternal heroin and methadone use on birthweight. *Pediatrics* 58:681–685.

Kandall SR, Albin S, Gartner LM, Lee KS, Eidelman A & Lowinson J (1977). The narcotic-dependent mother: fetal and neonatal consequences. *Early Human Development* 1/2:159–169.

Kandall SR, Doberczak TM, Mauer KR, Strashun RH & Korts DC (1983). Opiate v CNS depressant therapy in neonatal drug abstinence syndrome. *American Journal of Diseases of Children* 137:378–382.

Kandall SR, Gaines J, Habel L, Davidson G & Jessop D (1993). Relationship of maternal substance abuse to subsequent sudden infant death syndrome in offspring. *Journal of Pediatrics* 123:120–126.

Kramer LD, Locke GE, Ogunyemi A & Nelson L (1990). Neonatal cocaine-related seizures. *Journal of Child Neurology* 5:60–64.

Kron RE, Litt M, Phoenix, MD & Finnegan LP (1976). Neonatal narcotic abstinence: effects of pharmacotherapeutic agents and maternal drug usage on nutritive sucking behavior. *Journal of Pediatrics* 88:637–641.

Legido A, Clancy RR, Spitzer AR & Finnegan LP (1992). Electroencephalographic and behavioral-state studies in infants of cocaine-addicted mothers. *American Journal of Diseases of Children* 146:748–752.

Mayes LC, Granger RH, Frank MA, Schottenfeld R & Bornstein MH (1993). Neurobehavioral profiles of neonates exposed to cocaine prenatally. *Pediatrics* 91: 778–783.

Moore TR, Sorg J, Miller L, Key TC & Resnik R (1986). Hemodynamic effects of intravenous cocaine on the pregnant ewe and fetus. *American Journal of Obstetrics and Gynecology* 155:883–888.

Oro AS & Dixon SD (1987). Perinatal cocaine and methamphetamine exposure: maternal and neonatal correlates. *Journal of Pediatrics* 111:571–578.

Oro AS & Dixon SD (1988). Waterbed care of narcotic-exposed neonates. *American Journal of Diseases of Children* 142:186–188.

Ostrea EM, Chavez CJ & Strauss ME (1976). A study of factors that influence the severity of neonatal narcotic withdrawal. *Journal of Pediatrics* 88:642–645.

Ostrea EM, Brady M, Gause S, Raymundo AL & Stevens M (1992). Drug screening of newborns by meconium analysis: a large-scale, prospective, epidemiologic study. *Pediatrics* 89:107–113.

Ouellette EM, Rosett HL, Rosman NP & Weiner L (1977). Adverse effects on offspring of maternal alcohol abuse during pregnancy. *The New England Journal of Medicine* 297:528–530.

Petitti DB & Coleman C (1990). Cocaine and the risk of low birth weight. *American Journal of Public Health* 80:25–28.

Pierog S, Chandavasu O & Wexler I (1977). Withdrawal symptoms in infants with the fetal alcohol syndrome. *Journal of Pediatrics* 90:630–633.

Pond SM, Kreek MJ, Tong TG et al. (1985). Altered methadone pharmacokinetics in methadone-maintained pregnant women. *Journal of Pharmacology and Experimental Therapeutics* 233:1–6.

Rosen TS & Pippenger CE (1976). Pharmacologic observations on the neonatal withdrawal syndrome. *Journal of Pediatrics* 88:1044–1048.

Smith DW (1979). The fetal alcohol syndrome. *Hospital Practice* 14:121–128.

Streissguth AP, Aase JM, Clarren SK, Randels SP, LaDue RA & Smith DW (1991). Fetal alcohol syndrome in adolescents and adults. *Journal of the American Medical Association* 265:1961–1967.

Swayze VW II, Johnson VP, Hanson JW et al. (1997). Magnetic resonance imaging of brain anomalies in fetal alcohol syndrome. *Pediatrics* 99:232–240.

Weinberger SM, Kandall SR, Doberczak TM, Thornton JC & Bernstein J (1986). Early weight-change patterns in neonatal abstinence. *American Journal of Diseases of Children* 140:829–832.

Woods JR, Plessinger MA & Clark KE (1987). Effect of cocaine on uterine blood flow and fetal oxygenation. *Journal of the American Medical Association* 257:957–961.

CHAPTER 5

Developmental Outcomes of Prenatal Exposure to Alcohol and Other Drugs

Sydney L. Hans, Ph.D.

Extent of the Problem
Alcohol
Opioids
Cocaine
Nicotine
Marijuana
Summary of the Data
Social-Environmental Factors

The extent of scientific knowledge available on the development of children prenatally exposed to cocaine, alcohol, and other drugs remains largely focused on health, physical development, and behavior during the first days of life. This chapter will review the state of current knowledge about the consequences of women's use of alcohol and drugs during pregnancy on the development of their children's behavior during later infancy and childhood.

A teratogen is broadly defined as any factor associated with the production of physical or mental abnormalities in the developing embryo or fetus. (The word teratogen is derived from the Greek words "terato", monster, and "genesis", origin or beginning.) Most known teratogenic factors are either drugs, environmental toxins, radiation, or infections. It is estimated that some type of teratogenic effect can be found in 2% to 3% of all live births and that teratogenic effects, at least in part, account for 20% of the deaths that occur during the first five years of life. These effects, which can be acute and self-limiting or irreversible and long-term, may be displayed in a variety of ways among developing infants and children (Pagliaro & Pagliaro, 1995).

Many psychotropic drugs that are widely used in human populations are suspected of having teratogenic effects (Table 1). Although many prescribers and other health care providers are paying closer attention to the potential teratogenic effects associated with the use of selected drugs during pregnancy (see Pagliaro & Pagliaro, 1995), their general knowledge and understanding of the possible teratogenic effects associated with the abusable psychotropics may be limited.

The study of how prenatal exposure to drugs and toxic substances affects postnatal behavior is called behavioral teratology (Vorhees, 1986). Much research in the field of behavioral teratology uses experimental models in which pregnant laboratory animals are given carefully controlled doses of the substance being studied and then the offspring are cross-fostered to normal females for rearing. While animal studies are important for identifying drugs with teratogenic potential and for elucidating biological mechanisms of teratological action, studies of human populations are essential to understanding the effects of substances on human behavioral development. Studies of human populations, however, present numerous methodological challenges because research designs are limited to those in which the scientist has no control over the timing and amount of drug exposure and may even have difficulties determining the exact nature of that exposure, particularly when the drug of interest is illegal. Mothers who use drugs during pregnancy are a self-selected group who may differ from other women in terms of genetics, health practices, psychopathology, social class, life experiences, and capacity to provide parental care. In order to isolate the effects of exposure to a particular drug during pregnancy, scientists working with human populations must statistically control for mothers' use of other drugs and for other biological and social risk factors.

The data to be reviewed in this chapter come, for the most part, from studies that have attempted to

TABLE 1. Psychotropics with Suspected Teratogenic Effects

Central Nervous System Depressants
- Opioids (codeine, heroin, meperidine, morphine, pentazocine)
- Sedative-hypnotics (including alcohol [beer, wine, distilled spirits]; barbiturates; benzodiazepines; miscellaneous)
- Volatile solvents and inhalants (e.g., gasoline; glue).

Central Nervous System Stimulants
- Amphetamines (e.g., dextroamphetamine)
- Caffeine (including caffeinated soft drinks; coffee, tea)
- Cocaine (cocaine hydrochloride and crack cocaine)
- Nicotine (tobacco cigarettes and cigars).

Psychedelics (partial list)
- Lysergic acid diethylamide (LSD)
- Mescaline (peyote)
- Phencyclidine (PCP)
- Psilocybin (hallucinogenic mushrooms)
- Marijuana.

adhere to current best methodological standards for human behavioral teratology. Such standards include: recruiting a sample during pregnancy (to avoid biases of retrospective recall), determining drug use through multiple methodologies (usually self-report and biochemical assay), assessing infants and children longitudinally by examiners blind to knowledge of the children's histories of prenatal drug exposure, directly assessing unexposed comparison children rather than relying on published norms for behavior, and employing appropriate statistical controls for potentially confounding variables.

The chapter summarizes what is known about the long-term consequences of women's use during pregnancy of five classes of substances commonly abused in the United States: alcohol, opioids, cocaine, tobacco and marijuana. It concludes with a discussion of non-teratological factors, particularly environmental factors, that also may affect the development of children whose mothers use drugs and alcohol.

EXTENT OF THE PROBLEM

Although it is extremely difficult to estimate the numbers of children exposed to drugs and alcohol *in utero* (cf. NICHD, 1993), conservative estimates from the National Pregnancy and Health Survey collected in 1992 indicate a high percentage of American infants are born each year having been exposed prenatally to substances of abuse (NIDA, 1996). These estimates include 18.6% (762,000) exposed to alcohol; 20.2% (826,100) to tobacco; 2.9% (118,700) to marijuana; and 1.1% (45,100) to cocaine. *In utero* exposure to opioids lags considerably behind, with 0.1% (3,600) exposed to heroin and 0.1% (3,400) to methadone, but has been rapidly increasing in recent years as the use of cocaine decreases and as purer, inhalable forms of heroin have been introduced (Martin, Hecker et al., 1991). Recent data suggest that most reported statistics on the prevalence of drug abuse in America underestimate actual rates of use, particularly for urban populations (Bendavid, 1997).

Alcohol. Research on the consequences for human children of maternal substance abuse during pregnancy began with the identification of Fetal Alcohol Syndrome more than two decades ago (Jones & Smith, 1973). Fetal Alcohol Syndrome (FAS) is defined by a cluster of infant characteristics that include: (1) growth deficiency both prenatally and postnatally, (2) craniofacial anomalies including short palpebral fissures, flat midface, thin upper vermilion lip, and hypoplastic maxilla and/or mandible, and (3) central nervous system anomalies such as microcephaly and mental retardation (Sokol & Clarren, 1989). The full constellation of FAS symptoms are observed only in offspring of heavily drinking women. Only 7% of alcoholic women deliver children with full FAS (Abel & Sokol, 1991), although a much higher proportion of their children are born with some of the symptoms, a condition sometimes referred to as Fetal Alcohol Effects (FAE) (Sokol, Miller & Reed, 1980). The incidence of FAS is estimated to be between one and three cases per 100 live births (National Institute on Alcohol Abuse and Alcoholism, 1990), although FAS is probably considerably underdiagnosed (Little, Snell et al., 1990).

Since the identification of FAS, efforts have been made to determine the extent of the teratological effects of alcohol within epidemiological samples of pregnant women whose use of alcohol includes levels of alcohol consumption generally considered to be "social drinking" within the U.S. The first epidemiological study of drinking during pregnancy and the one that has served as the model for subsequent research in human behavioral teratology was the Seattle Longitudinal Prospective Study on Alcohol and Pregnancy (Streissguth, Martin et al., 1981). In this predominantly white middle-class sample recruited prenatally, maternal alcohol use was associated with poorer mental and motor development in eight-month-old infants (Streissguth, Barr et al., 1980). The threshold of alcohol consumption at which effects were seen at eight months was approximately four or five drinks per day. The effects of lower levels of maternal alcohol use during pregnancy were seen at later ages in reduced general intelligence. When the children were four years of age (Streissguth, Barr et al., 1989), their IQ scores were reduced by five points with each 1.5 ounces of daily absolute alcohol (approximately three drinks) consumed by their mothers during pregnancy compared to children whose mothers did not consume alcohol. Maternal consumption of two or more drinks a day was related to IQ decrements of 7 points when the children were 7½ years old, with binge drinking patterns particularly strongly related to learning problems (Streissguth, Barr & Sampson, 1990).

In the Seattle Longitudinal Prospective Study, many of the most consistent findings across age have come from assessments of attention, hyperactivity and impulsivity in their subjects. Computerized vigilance tasks, adapted from the Continuous Performance Test (Rosvold, Mirsky et al., 1956), were used to assess attention. In vigilance tasks children are exposed to long series of briefly presented visual stimuli and asked to respond to a particular target stimulus by pressing a button. The task yields indices of children's inability to sustain attention over time (errors of omission), impulsive responding (errors of commission or false alarms), and speed of response. In the Seattle study, four-year-olds whose mothers drank during pregnancy were less attentive with longer reaction times on a laboratory vigilance task (Streissguth, Martin et al., 1984) and less attentive and more active during home observations (Landesman-Dwyer, Ragozin & Little, 1981). Alcohol-exposed children remained poorer on vigilance tasks (CPT) at 7½ years (Streissguth, Barr et al., 1986), with increased errors of omission and commission and, in particular, slower reaction time. In the Seattle study, at age 14, prenatal alcohol exposure related to a composite pattern of neurobehavioral problems associated with fluctuating attentional states, problems with response inhibition and spatial learning (Streissguth, Sampson et al., 1994; Hunt, Streissguth et al. 1995).

Data from other well-controlled longitudinal studies sampling from diverse populations have fairly consistently suggested delays in global mental and motor development during infancy related to maternal alcohol use during pregnancy. Such delays were observed in a predominantly poor African-American Atlanta sample at 6 and 12 months (Coles, 1993a); an upper middle-class Los Angeles sample at one year of age (O'Connor, Brill & Sigman, 1986; O'Connor, Sigman & Kasari, 1993); a largely middle-class sample from Ottawa at 13- and 24-months (Gusella & Fried, 1984; Fried & Watkinson, 1988); and a Detroit lower-income African-American sample at 12 months (Jacobson, Jacobson et al., 1993). In addition, a recent study examining specific cognitive functions during infancy, rather than global developmental indices, reported alcohol-related functional deficits on infants' reaction time (Jacobson, Jacobson & Sokol, 1994) and efficiency of information processing (Jacobson, Jacobson et al., 1993). Two major studies (Richardson, Day, & Goldschmidt, 1995; Parry & Ogston, 1992) failed to find alcohol effects on mental or motor development during infancy.

Several studies also have replicated the Seattle Longitudinal Prospective Study finding of reduced intelligence after infancy. In the Atlanta sample, prenatal exposure was related at five years of age to poorer performance on cognitive tasks, especially overall mental processing and sequential memory processing (Coles, Brown et al., 1991). In the Ottawa sample, moderate drinking was related to lower cognitive scores at 36, but not 48 months (Fried & Watkinson 1990), 60 months or 72 months (Fried, O'Connell & Watkinson, 1992). In a French sample identified during pregnancy, Larroque, Kaminski et al. (1995) reported a deficit of 7 points in general IQ at 4½ years of age in the children whose mothers' average daily consumption was at least 1.5 ounces absolute alcohol. In contrast to these other findings, a study of a low-income Cleveland sample (Greene, Ernhart et al., 1991) found no relation between prenatal alcohol exposure and intellectual development at 4 years 10 months.

Attempts to replicate the findings of the Seattle Longitudinal Prospective Study sample in the domain of attention using vigilance tasks have yielded very inconsistent results. In the Atlanta sample prenatal exposure was related to difficulties in sustaining attention but not to impulsive responding (Brown, Coles et al., 1991), in the Cleveland sample prenatal alcohol exposure was unrelated to attention (Boyd, Ernhart et al., 1991) and, in the Ottawa study, prenatal alcohol exposure was unrelated to sustained attention and related to *decreases* in impulsive responding (Fried, Watkinson & Gray, 1992). Although some of the failure of later studies to find prenatal alcohol exposure effects on vigilance tasks may be due to the somewhat lower exposure levels of the later studies than those in the Seattle Longitudinal Prospective Study, Fried, Watkinson and Gray (1992) conclude that, taken together, these studies suggest that on vigilance tasks, children prenatally exposed to alcohol show a tendency for slow, delayed, non-impulsive responding, which is in sharp contrast to the rapid impulsive responding typical of children with attention deficit hyperactivity disorder.

OPIOIDS

Prenatal opioid exposure results in a clear and dramatic neonatal narcotic abstinence syndrome (withdrawal) that can be life-threatening (Desmond & Wilson, 1975; Finnegan, Connaughton et al., 1975), and numerous investigations have been focused on opioid-exposed children during the neonatal period. Yet, only a small number have followed the development of opioid-exposed children longitudinally.

Studies of infants whose mothers used opioid drugs—heroin or methadone—during pregnancy generally have reported either very small lags in exposed compared to unexposed children on global mental and motor development as assessed on standardized tests (Hans, 1989; Rosen & Johnson, 1982; Johnson, Diano & Rosen, 1984; Wilson, 1989) or no differences (Kaltenbach & Finnegan, 1987; Strauss, Starr et al., 1976).

Investigators who have examined aspects of infant behavior other than global developmental progress in opioid-exposed children have reported problems with fine motor coordination and short span of attention at nine months (Wilson, Desmond & Wait, 1981); problems in increased activity level, poorer motor coordination and shorter attention during the first two years of life (Hans, 1989; Marcus, Hans & Jeremy, 1982; Hans & Marcus 1983; Hans, Marcus et al., 1984); and an increased incidence of abnormal neurological findings at 18, 24, and 36 months (Rosen & Johnson, 1982; Johnson, Diano & Rosen, 1984; Johnson, Glassman et al., 1987). Grattan and Hans (1996) reported motor coordination difficulties in children exposed to opioids during pregnancy at ages eight and nine years, but not ten and eleven years.

Although some studies have reported intellectual deficits in preschool age children of opioid users (Wilson, McCreary et al., 1979), most have not found such differences (Strauss, Lessen-Firestone et al., 1979; Johnson, Glassman et al., 1987; Kaltenbach & Finnegan, 1987; Lifschitz, Wilson et al., 1985). Several studies, however, report high activity, impulsivity, poor self-control, and poor performance on cognitive tests requiring focused attention. Wilson, McCreary et al. (1979) reported that preschool children who had been heroin exposed were rated by parents as having difficulty in adjustment, particularly uncontrollable temper, impulsiveness, and aggressiveness. In the only prospective study in which laboratory measures of vigilance were administered to opioid-exposed children (Hans, 1997), prenatal opioid exposure was related to more errors of omission and commission at age ten years. In a cross-sectional study of seven- to 12-year-old boys, children exposed prenatally to opiates made fewer correct responses on a vigilance task than unexposed children, although poorer scores also were observed in children being raised by opiate-using mothers who reported that they did not use illicit drugs during their pregnancies (Hickey, Suess et al., 1995).

A number of cross-sectional investigations have reported an increased incidence of behavior problems in school-age children whose parents are users of opioid drugs, but none of these studies were able to separate out the effects of prenatal exposure from other factors. Sowder and Burt (1980) found that children of heroin abusing parents were at risk for neurological deficits and emotional problems during early childhood, and delinquency, behavior problems, grade retention, and truancy as adolescents. Ornoy, Michailevskaya and Lukashov (1996) reported a high proportion of children born to heroin dependent women (74%) have hyperactivity, inattention and a variety of behavioral problems during early childhood, but behavior problems also were high in children born to heroin-dependent fathers (42%) and relatively low in children born to heroin-using mothers but raised by adoptive parents (20%). De Cubas and Field (1993) examined six- to 13-year-olds whose mothers were in methadone treatment and reported that, while similar in intellectual ability, children of methadone-using women rated higher on anxiety, aggression, and a host of behavior problems. Wilens, Biederman et al. (1995) found higher levels of both internalizing problems (such as depression) and externalizing problems (such as hyperactivity and conduct problems) in children of opioid abusers compared to children of parents who did not use drugs.

COCAINE

In the late 1980s, as the use of cocaine, particularly in its "crack" form, became more widespread in the U.S., there was a sharp increase in public alarm over the consequences of women's use of cocaine during pregnancy on the long-term development of their children (Hopkins, 1990; Kantrowitz, 1990; Toufexis, 1991). Concern focused particularly on whether *in utero* cocaine exposure might create permanent cognitive deficits and behavior problems in children that would make them uneducable or incapable of forming normal human social relationships. Such dire predictions no longer seem warranted, as the first long-term follow-up data on children exposed prenatally to cocaine have become available (Mayes, Granger et al., 1992; Coles, 1993b; Richardson & Day, 1994; Gavzer, 1997; Hager, 1997).

A large number of prospective studies focusing on prenatal exposure to cocaine emerged as a result of the rise in crack cocaine use in the late 1980s; many of these have followed children through infancy and even into the preschool years.

Most studies have not found any global developmental deficits during infancy associated with prenatal cocaine exposure (Chasnoff, Griffith et al., 1992; Hurt, Brodsky et al., 1995; Chiriboga, Vibbert et al., 1995; Jacobson, Jacobson et al., 1996), although there have been reports of poorer general motor development in cocaine-exposed infants who were assessed on standard instruments in two independent studies (Mayes, Bornstein et al., 1995; Arendt, Minnes & Singer, 1996). Several investigators have reported specific problems in motor functioning during infancy in cocaine-exposed infants in areas such as volitional movements, tone, and reflexes (Schneider & Chasnoff, 1992; Rose-Jacobs, Frank et al., 1994; Fetters & Tronick 1996; Piazza, Lanza, & Dweck, 1989).

Cocaine exposure has been found to be related to state regulatory processes during infancy. For example, Mayes, Bornstein et al. (1995) found that in a habituation task, three-month-old infants who had been prenatally exposed to cocaine were more labile and reactive to stimuli and less likely to finish tasks. Prenatal cocaine exposure also may be related to infants' inability to recover once frustrated or upset (Alessandri, Sullivan et al., 1993; Bendersky, Alessandri & Lewis, 1996).

In the domain of early cognition, contingency learning at four and eight months (Alessandri, Sullivan et al., 1993), and visual recognition memory (Jacobson, Jacobson et al., 1996; Struthers & Hansen, 1992) both are related to *in utero* cocaine exposure. Jacobson, Jacobson et al. (1996) reported that heavy cocaine use (at least twice a week) in early pregnancy related to poor recognition memory. Heffelfinger, Craft and Shyken (1997) reported that cocaine-exposed infants were slower to orient to stimuli in their right visual field, suggesting a left hemisphere visual attention system deficit.

Prospective studies that have followed samples of cocaine-exposed infants to early childhood have not reported effects on global intellectual functioning (Griffith, Azuma & Chasnoff, 1994; Morrow, Bandstra et al., 1997; Richardson, Conroy & Day, 1996; Hurt, Malmud et al., 1997). In the sample of cocaine-exposed children who have been followed prospectively for the longest period of time, IQ scores were not decreased relative to comparison children, but there was evidence of language delay during the preschool years (Azuma & Chasnoff, 1993). Similarly, a cross-sectional study comparing adopted cocaine-exposed children to non-cocaine-exposed children found no differences in global IQ, but verbal comprehension and expressive language deficits during the toddler and preschool years were related to *in utero* cocaine exposure (Nulman, Rovet et al., 1994). In comparing four- to six-year-old children who were prenatally exposed to cocaine to a similar group of children who were not exposed, investigators found that prenatal exposure was not related to deficits in expressive language, but was related to deficits in receptive language and visual motor performance (Bender, Word et al., 1995).

In the only study to report on the performance of cocaine-exposed children on a computerized vigilance task, Richardson, Conroy and Day (1996) found that six-year-olds who had experienced light to moderate prenatal cocaine exposure showed deficits in ability to sustain attention.

NICOTINE

The earliest prospective data on the effects of prenatal tobacco exposure came primarily from the Ottawa Prenatal Prospective Study (Fried & Makin, 1987), a longitudinal investigation of a predominantly middle-class Canadian sample. In the Ottawa Prenatal Prospective Study, prenatal tobacco exposure was related to global mental development at age 12 months, but not 24 months (Fried & Watkinson, 1988). Thirty-nine percent of one-year-old infants born to heavy smokers had mental development indices under 85, compared to 6% of other infants in the sample. In the Ottawa study, there was a dose-response association between maternal smoking during pregnancy and general cognitive abilities at ages three (Fried & Watkinson, 1990), five, and six years (Fried, O'Connell & Watkinson, 1992), with offspring of heavily smoking women having IQ scores approximately six points lower than offspring of nonsmoking mothers.

The Ottawa Prenatal Prospective Study has found consistent patterns of problems in the auditory domain during infancy associated with prenatal tobacco exposure, beginning with alterations in auditory responsiveness and habituation (Fried & Makin, 1987) during the neonatal period and differences in ratings of auditory responsiveness at ages 12 and 24 months (Fried & Watkinson, 1988). During early childhood, cognitive deficits associated with prenatal tobacco exposure were strongest for tests involving language (Fried & Watkinson, 1990) and verbal memory (Fried, Watkinson & Gray, 1992).

Data from other prospective studies do not consistently replicate the Ottawa findings of cognitive deficits during infancy. The Pittsburgh Maternal Health Practices and Child Development Study (Richardson, Day & Goldchmidt, 1995) reported that prenatal tobacco exposure was associated with lower global mental scores in offspring at 19 months, but not nine months of age. Other investigators have found no effects of prenatal tobacco exposure on assessments of global infant development after controlling for covariates (Streissguth, Barr et al., 1980; Forrest, Florey et al., 1991).

On the other hand, numerous studies have found a relation between parental smoking and lowered general cognitive skills in older children (Rush, 1992), although not all have carefully controlled for other variables, including postnatal passive smoke exposure, and most have not been prospective and longitudinal in design. At least two studies that found correlations between tobacco exposure prenatally and later cognitive outcomes were able to explain these differences in terms of children's social class and home environments (Baghurst, Tong et al., 1992; Fergusson & Lloyd, 1991).

In addition, several studies of smoking cessation during pregnancy reported higher IQ scores in preschool children of heavily smoking women who stopped smoking during pregnancy than in those who continued to smoke, after controlling for other variables (Sexton, Fox & Hebel, 1990; Olds, Henderson & Tatelbaum, 1994; Isohanni, Oja et al., 1995).

Data from a variety of other prospective investigations link maternal smoking during pregnancy to motor hyperactivity and impulsive responding on vigilance tasks. In the Ottawa Prenatal Prospective Study (Kristjansson, Fried & Watkinson, 1989; Fried, Watkinson & Gray 1992), prenatal smoking was related to activity level (wiggling in chair) and errors of impulsive responding on a vigilance task in four- to seven-year-old children. In the Seattle Longitudinal Prospective Study (Streissguth, Martin et al., 1984), maternal smoking was significantly related to more errors of omission and commission and slower reaction times on a vigilance task at age four. Data from the National Collaborative Perinatal Study of the National Institute of Neurological and Communicative Disorders and Stroke, a large prospective study, found child hyperactivity, short attention span and poor verbal achievement in children whose mothers smoked during pregnancy (Naeye & Peters, 1984). Data from retrospective reports (Milberger, Biederman et al., 1996) also suggest problems in attention related to prenatal tobacco exposure.

Recently there have been reports of an increased incidence of serious conduct problems in offspring of smoking mothers (Fergusson, Horwood & Lynskey, 1993; Wakschlag, Lahey et al., 1997; Weitzman, Gortmaker & Sobol, 1992), even after controlling for confounding variables.

MARIJUANA

Even though marijuana is the illicit drug most commonly used during pregnancy, information on its effects on the child is extremely limited, coming primarily from the Ottawa Prospective Prenatal Study and the Pittsburgh Maternal Health Practices and Child Development Study.

Available data consistently have suggested that prenatal exposure to marijuana has little effect on infant development as assessed by standard tests of motor and mental milestones (Tennes, Avitable et al., 1985; Fried & Watkinson, 1988; Richardson, Day & Goldschmidt, 1995).

Data somewhat more strongly suggest effects of prenatal marijuana on child development past the infancy age period. In the Pittsburgh Maternal Health Practices and Child Development Study, maternal exposure to marijuana was related to poorer functioning on the short-term memory and verbal reasoning subscales of the Stanford-Binet at age three years (Day, Richardson et al., 1994). Similarly, in the Ottawa Prenatal Prospective Study marijuana exposed children had lower scores on verbal and memory performance tests at 48 months of age (Fried & Watkinson, 1990). At ages nine through 12 years (Fried, Watkinson & Siegel, 1997), in the Ottawa Prenatal Prospective Study sample there was a relationship between prenatal marijuana exposure and poorer language and reading scores.

In the Ottawa Prenatal Prospective Study, prenatal marijuana exposure was related to poorer performance on a computerized vigilance task, particularly increased errors of omission, and to maternal reports of impulsive/hyperactive behavior at age six (Fried, Watkinson & Gray, 1992). From ages six to nine years, prenatal marijuana exposure was related to conduct problems and distractibility (O'Connell & Fried, 1991). Fried (1996) has suggested that these findings are consistent with executive functioning deficits linked to prefrontal lobe function.

DATA ON TERATOLOGIC EFFECTS OF PRENATAL EXPOSURE

Taken together, studies of the effects of maternal drug use during pregnancy have produced a remarkable amount of scientific progress during the relatively short period of time since the first reports of Fetal Alcohol Syndrome in 1973. The strongest findings to emerge from human behavioral teratology remains the devastating effects on some children of mothers' heavy drinking during pregnancy. Fetal Alcohol Syndrome today is the number one identifiable cause of mental retardation in the U.S., leading both Down syndrome and spina bifida (Abel & Sokol, 1987), and alcohol is the only commonly used drug that also has been shown to produce physical birth defects. Yet there is much we do not know about drinking during pregnancy, including whether there is any safe level of alcohol consumption, what patterns of use are most likely to affect the child, and why some children are more seriously affected than others.

There is suggestive evidence for some negative effects of prenatal exposure to all other drugs of abuse that have been studied in humans, although no drug other than alcohol has been clearly linked to serious mental retardation or physical birth defects. There is actually relatively little evidence, except perhaps for tobacco, that prenatal exposure to these other drugs leads to deficits in global intelligence. Much remains to be learned about the more subtle effects that tobacco, marijuana, cocaine, and opioids have on the long-term development of children and on the domains in which these effects are likely to be seen. It is notable that studies of all drugs of abuse have found exposure-related problems in the areas of attention, impulsivity, and motor control, suggesting that brain processes that modulate arousal, attention, and inhibitory control may be particularly vulnerable to the teratological effects of a variety of substances.

Lester, Freier and LaGasse (1995) have noted that the areas that seem to be affected most by prenatal substance abuse are the "four As of infancy": **A**ttention, **A**rousal, **A**ffect, and **A**ction. Data suggest that the four As also may be relevant to long-term behavioral teratological effects, although performance in other domains, such as language and reading, also may be especially relevant in examining outcomes in older children. The similarity of findings across different substances suggests that the source of their actions may include some general process, such as prenatal hypoxia, rather than a mechanism more specific to a particular drug's actions, such as the effects of a drug on the development of a particular neurotransmitter system. Data from the longitudinal studies also suggest that even when behavioral teratological effects are minimal during infancy, they may emerge at later ages. Such "sleeper" effects might be reflections of the relatively crude techniques that scientists have had available for assessing behavior during infancy or to the possibility that teratogens may have their strongest impact on complex cognitive skills (such as those involving language, reading, executive functioning) that can be observed only after early childhood (Hans, 1996).

Nevertheless, there is provocative evidence in studies to date that particular drugs may lead to specific types of developmental problems: alcohol to slowed reaction times and lowered IQ; marijuana to problems in processing of auditory information and executive functioning; cocaine to motor dyscoordination, difficulties modulating affective arousal, and language delays; tobacco to impulsive behavior and conduct problems; opioids to attention and motor problems. Because opportunities for replication of findings have been limited, the extent to which these patterns of findings are drug-specific, or whether they simply are specific to particular samples, is not clear.

Finally, the human studies remain difficult to interpret because the application of stringent controls to data about children's social environment often causes the reported effects to diminish or disappear. This leads to a need to consider effects of the parenting environment on the development of children whose mothers use alcohol and other drugs.

SOCIAL-ENVIRONMENTAL ISSUES

Although most research on children who are exposed prenatally to drugs has been conducted with the goal of understanding the possible teratological effects of *in utero* exposure, there is a related question as to whether maternal substance abuse may place the children at environmental risk by affecting the mothers' parenting abilities. Indeed, this question is of paramount importance in interpreting the teratological studies and, more importantly, intervening in the lives of children who may need help (Mayes, 1995).

A small number of studies have suggested that the incidence of child abuse and neglect is high when a parent abuses alcohol or drugs. Wasserman and Leventhal (1993), in a historical cohort study of 47 prenatally drug-exposed children, concluded that by 24 months of age, children whose mothers had a documented history of cocaine dependency during pregnancy had a 23% incidence of maltreatment, compared to only 4% for case-matched comparison infants. Jaudes, Ekwo and Voorhis (1995) report that the risk of child abuse is two to three times greater in children who are prenatally exposed to drugs than in a general population of children from the same geographic area. Hawley, Halle et al. (1995) also reported a high incidence of emotional and physical neglect among a group of 25 addicted mothers, compared to 25 nonaddicted controls. In a review of case records from a large juvenile court, Famularo, Kinscherff and Fenton (1992) reported an association between parental alcohol abuse and child physical maltreatment and between cocaine abuse and child sexual maltreatment.

Several studies, most using very small samples and looking at limited aspects of parenting behavior, have detected differences between drug-using and comparison mothers in interactions with their children. Householder (1980) reported that opioid-using mothers with three-month-old infants exhibited more physical activity and less emotional involvement in communicating with their infants than did comparison mothers. The opioid-using mothers seemed to enjoy the mothering role less and gazed into their infants' eyes less often. Bauman and Dougherty (1983)—who had found no drug-related differences in parenting attitudes—did find that in actual interactions with their preschool children, drug-using mothers were more likely to use a threatening disciplinarian approach and less likely to employ positive reinforcement.

Bernstein and colleagues (Bernstein, Jeremy et al., 1984; Bernstein, Jeremy & Marcus, 1986; Jeremy & Bernstein, 1984) reported that methadone-using mothers were less responsive to their infants and less encouraging of their infants' communicative behavior. Fitzgerald, Kaltenbach and Finnegan (1990) reported that opioid-using women were less socially engaged and showed less positive affect toward their neonates. Rodning, Beckwith and Howard (1991) found that women who used PCP and cocaine during pregnancy differed from comparison women on a number of dimensions of parenting (effectiveness in soothing, quality of physical contact, acceptance/rejection, accessibility, cooperation/interference, sensitivity/insensitivity to baby's communications, amount of physical contact) assessed when the children were three and nine months of age.

A high proportion (80%) of the children born to drug-using women and who remained in their care were insecurely attached to their mothers at 15 months. At least two investigations have reported no statistically significant effects of maternal drug use on mother-infant interaction, but these investigators qualified their findings in terms of limited sample size (Black, Schuler & Nair, 1993) and appropriateness of their assessment instruments (Johnson & Rosen, 1990).

Despite this generally negative picture of the interaction between drug-using women and their children, investigators and clinicians frequently have pointed to the variability in parenting skills of drug-using women, including their potential for good childrearing (Finnegan, Oehlberg et al., 1981; Johnson & Rosen, 1990; Jeremy & Bernstein, 1984). Few data exist on the potential sources of variability among drug-using women in parenting skills and relationships with their children. Bernstein and colleagues (Jeremy & Bernstein, 1984; Bernstein, Jeremy & Marcus, 1986; Bernstein & Hans, 1994) have documented that cumulative psychosocial risks, and particularly maternal psychopathology (Hans, Bernstein & Henson, 1990), are related to problems in mother-infant communication. Finnegan, Oehlberg et al. (1981) concluded that polydrug abuse, psychological problems, and stressful life events are strong indicators of poor parenting behavior among drug-using parents. Howard and colleagues (1995) found that among cocaine-using mothers with infants, signs of disturbed personality (histrionic, narcissistic, borderline, paranoid) correlated with insensitive parenting. Among women in methadone maintenance, Regan, Ehrlich and Finnegan (1987) report that those mothers with a personal history of violence or abuse are most likely to have their own children placed in foster care.

Strong evidence suggests that the quality of parenting and the psychological functioning of the parent has a major impact on the development of children born to drug-abusing parents. Bernstein and Hans (1994) found that the quality of interaction between mother and child during infancy was related to child developmental outcomes at age two and that this effect was stronger for methadone-exposed children than for children who were not exposed to drugs prenatally. In the same sample (Wakschlag & Hans, 1997), the investigators found that the quality of early parenting was a good predictor of children's disruptive behavior problems at age 10. Singer, Arendt et al. (1997) reported that maternal psychological distress was related to poorer infant development, independent of prenatal drug exposure. Johnson and colleagues (1987) found that family social disorganization, including frequent moves, crowded housing conditions, and family violence, was related to mental functioning of children at age three. Rodning, Beckwith and Howard (1991) found that children of drug (cocaine and PCP) using women had more disorganized attachment patterns and that the security of the children's attachment to their mothers was related to the mother's postnatal abstinence from drugs. In the same sample, infant cognitive and motor development at six months of age was related to maternal sensitivity (Howard, Beckwith et al., 1995). In a sample of substance-abusing women who received intervention, Hofkosh and colleagues (Hofkosh, Pringle et al., 1995) reported that developmental outcomes in children who were prenatally exposed to cocaine and other drugs during pregnancy was related to the quality of the home environment provided by the mother, especially maternal responsiveness, maternal involvement with the child, and provision of appropriate play materials.

Taken together, these studies suggest the great importance the caregiving environment plays in the development of children of substance-abusing parents. They also suggest that findings implicating teratological factors in child development can be trusted only to the extent that careful controls have been introduced for postnatal environmental factors.

IMPLICATIONS FOR PREVENTION AND INTERVENTION

Although many questions remain unanswered about the behavioral teratological effects of alcohol, tobacco, and other drugs, the data presently available document clear harmful consequences of drinking during pregnancy. These data also suggest negative, albeit more subtle, effects of exposure to use of tobacco and other drugs. The problem of substance use and abuse during pregnancy must be addressed on several fronts. A solution will include: (1) substance abuse prevention targeted at girls; (2) increased attention to substance abuse screening, intervention, and referral by primary care physicians who treat young women, particularly pregnant women; (3) substance abuse treatment that is sensitive to the needs and concerns of pregnant and parenting women; (4) integration of mental health services into substance abuse treatment for women; and (5) implementation of parenting interventions and child development screening within substance abuse treatment settings. Each of these points of attack is appropriate, regardless of whether the effects of maternal alcohol and drug use on child development derive from exposure during pregnancy or childrearing by an alcohol- or drug-using parent.

Clearly, the ideal solution to preventing the negative consequences of maternal alcohol, tobacco, and other drug use on child development is to prevent the use of these substances by women in the childbearing years. If women wait until they recognize they are pregnant to reduce their alcohol or drug use, their children already will have been exposed to these substances during the critical early period of gestation when organ structures are formed and physical birth defects have their origin (Coles, 1994). Since the two most commonly used substances—alcohol and tobacco—have the most well-documented harmful effects on children's long-term development, and because they may serve as gateways to other substance abuse (Kandel, 1975), they also should be the focus of prevention efforts.

Primary care physicians can serve an important role in preventing initiation of tobacco and alcohol use in young people (Epps & Manley, 1992; Kaufman, 1994; Kendrick & Merritt, 1996). American adolescent females typically have several primary care contacts each year and more than 80% have at least one contact a year (Adams & Marano, 1995).

After prevention, the next line of attack needs to be the identification of tobacco, alcohol and other drug use in all women during the childbearing years, particularly those who already are pregnant. Primary care medical providers, including obstetricians, are well-situated to screen for substance use and abuse and to encourage treatment. However, women's substance abuse, even of legal substances, is a highly stigmatized subject (Finkelstein, 1993; Farkas & Parran, 1993) and women are reluctant to speak openly about the topic. Similarly, providers may be reluctant to ask questions about substance abuse, in part because of their own feelings of inadequacy at treating problems they have not been well-trained to handle. Yet clinicians who ask questions in an objective, non-judgmental way can receive remarkably reliable responses from patients (Rankin, 1990; Zuckerman, Amaro & Cabral, 1989).

Physicians and other medical providers need to be better educated about the importance of substance abuse screening during pregnancy, how to conduct screening to gather the most accurate information, and how to recognize signs of substance abuse even when patients do not admit to use. It has been suggested that monitoring of smoking habits should be just as much a part of routine collection of vital signs at every health encounter as is measurement of blood pressure (Kendrick & Merritt, 1996; Robinson, Laurent & Little, 1995).

CONCLUSIONS

Accumulating evidence from studies of human populations suggests that substances of abuse may have long-term teratological effects on the development of children. Alcohol appears to have the strongest negative impact on child development, but data suggest that marijuana, cocaine, opioids, and particularly tobacco also may have adverse effects. The effects of prenatal drug exposure may be subtle and are most likely to be seen in behavioral domains related to attention, arousal, and inhibitory controls. It also is clear that postnatal environmental experiences, many of which are related to parental substance abuse, contribute to developmental problems more strongly than do teratological influences.

Regardless of the relative contribution of teratological and environmental factors, it is evident that prevention and treatment of maternal substance abuse should have a positive effect on children's behavioral development. Efforts need to focus on prevention of substance use, particularly tobacco and alcohol, in young women, on effective screening for prenatal tobacco, alcohol and drug use in primary medical care settings, on appropriate treatment programs for drug-dependent pregnant women, on integration of mental health interventions into substance abuse treatment programs, and on parenting support for women in treatment and developmental screening and intervention for their children. One should not be lulled into complacency by the relatively subtle teratologic effects on the child of cocaine, opioids, and other illicit drugs. Environmental factors associated with the substance-abusing lifestyle place these children at serious risk for problems in development. Children born into families affected by substance abuse, whether legal or illegal, deserve attention and assistance.

ACKNOWLEDGMENTS: During the preparation of this chapter, the author's time was supported by Grants R01 DA05396 and R01 DA09595 from the National Institute on Drug Abuse. The author thanks Holly Furdyna, Linda Henson, Victor Bernstein, and Janet Chandler for their comments on the manuscript as it was being prepared.

REFERENCES

Abel E & Sokol R (1991). A revised conservative estimate of the incidence of FAS and its economic impact. *Alcoholism: Clinical & Experimental Research* 15:514–524.

Abel EL & Sokol RJ (1987). Incidence of fetal alcohol syndrome and economic impact of FAS-related anomalies. *Drug and Alcohol Dependence* 19:51–70.

Adams PF & Marano MA (1995). Current estimates from the National Health Interview Survey, 1994. *Vital Health Statistics* 10:193.

Alessandri SM, Sullivan MW, Imaizumi S & Lewis M (1993). Learning and emotional responsivity in cocaine exposed infants. *Developmental Psychology* 29:989–997.

Arendt RE, Minnes S & Singer LT (1996). Fetal cocaine exposure: Neurologic effects and sensory-motor delays. *Physical and Occupational Therapy in Pediatrics* 16:129–144.

Azuma SD & Chasnoff IJ (1993). Outcome of children prenatally exposed to cocaine and other drugs: A path analysis of three-year data. *Pediatrics* 92:396–402.

Baghurst PA, Tong SL, Woodward AJ & McMichael AJ (1992). Effects of maternal smoking upon neuropsychological development in early childhood: Importance of taking account of social and environmental factors. *Paediatric and Perinatal Epidemiology* 6:403–415.

Bauman PS & Dougherty FE (1983). Drug-addicted mothers' parenting and their children's development. *International Journal of the Addictions* 18:291–302.

Bendavid N (1997, December 12). 333,000 labeled hardcore users. *Chicago Tribune*, 1–28.

Bender SL, Word CO, DiClemente RJ, Crittenden MR, Persaud NA & Ponton LE (1995). The developmental implications of prenatal and/or postnatal crack cocaine exposure in preschool children: A preliminary report. *Developmental and Behavioral Pediatrics* 16:418–424.

Bendersky M, Alessandri SM & Lewis M (1996). Emotions in cocaine-exposed infants. In M Lewis & MW Sullivan (eds.) *Emotional Development in Atypical Children*. Hillsdale, NJ: Erlbaum, 89–108.

Bernstein VJ & Hans SL (1994). Predicting the developmental outcome of two-year-old children born exposed to methadone: The impact of social-environmental risk factors. *Journal of Clinical Child Psychology* 23:349–359.

Bernstein VJ, Jeremy RJ, Hans SL & Marcus J (1984). A longitudinal study of offspring born to methadone-maintained women. *American Journal of Alcohol and Drug Abuse* 10:161–193.

Bernstein VJ, Jeremy RJ & Marcus J (1986). Mother-infant interaction in multiproblem families: Finding those at risk. *Journal of the American Academy of Child Psychiatry* 25:631–640.

Black M, Schuler M & Nair P (1993). Prenatal exposure to cocaine: Neurodevelopmental outcome and parenting environment. *Journal of Pediatric Psychology* 18:605–620.

Boyd TA, Ernhart CB, Greene TH, Sokol RJ & Martier S (1991). Prenatal alcohol exposure and sustained attention in the preschool years. *Neurotoxicology and Teratology* 13:49–55.

Brown RT, Coles CD, Smith IE et al. (1991). Effects of prenatal alcohol exposure at school age. II. Attention and behavior. *Neurotoxicology and Teratology* 13:369–376.

Chasnoff IJ, Griffith DR, Freier C & Murray J (1992). Cocaine/polydrug use in pregnancy: Two-year follow-up. *Pediatrics* 89:284–289.

Chiriboga CA, Vibbert M, Malouf R et al. (1995). Neurological correlates of fetal cocaine exposure: Transient hypertonia of infancy and early childhood. *Pediatrics* 96:1070–1077.

Coles C (1994). Critical periods for prenatal alcohol exposure: Evidence from animal and human studies. *Alcohol Health and Research World* 18:22–29.

Coles CD (1993a). Impact of prenatal alcohol exposure on the newborn and the child. *Clinical Obstetric and Gynecology* 36:255–266.

Coles CD (1993b). Saying "goodbye" to the "crack baby." *Neurotoxicology and Teratology* 15:290–292.

Coles CD, Brown RT, Smith IE, Platzman KA, Erickson S & Falek A (1991). Effects of prenatal alcohol exposure at school age. I. Physical and cognitive development. *Neurotoxicology and Teratology* 13:357–367.

Day NL, Richardson GA, Goldschmidt L et al. (1994). Effect of prenatal marijuana exposure on the cognitive development of offspring at age three. *Neurotoxicology and Teratology* 16:169–175.

De Cubas MM & Field T (1993). Children of methadone-dependent women: Developmental outcomes. *American Journal of Orthopsychiatry* 63:266–276.

Desmond MM & Wilson GS (1975). Neonate abstinence syndrome: Recognition and diagnosis. *Addictive Diseases* 2:113–121.

Epps RP & Manley MW (1992). The clinician's role in preventing smoking initiation. *Medical Clinics of North America* 76:439–449.

Famularo R, Kinscherff R & Fenton T (1992). Parental substance abuse and the nature of child maltreatment. *Child Abuse and Neglect* 16:475–483.

Farkas KJ & Parran TV (1993). Treatment of cocaine addiction during pregnancy. *Clinics in Perinatology* 20:29–45.

Fergusson DM, Horwood LJ & Lynskey MT (1993). Maternal smoking before and after pregnancy: Effects on behavioral outcomes in middle childhood. *Pediatrics* 92:815–822.

Fergusson D & Lloyd M (1991). Smoking during pregnancy and its effect on child cognitive ability from the ages of 8 to 12 years. *Paediatric and Perinatal Epidemiology* 5:189–200.

Fetters L & Tronick EZ (1996). Neuromotor development of cocaine-exposed and control infants from birth through 15 months: Poor and poorer performance. *Pediatrics* 98:938–943.

Finkelstein N (1993). Treatment programming for alcohol and drug-dependent pregnant women. *International Journal of the Addictions* 28:1275–1309.

Finnegan LP, Connaughton JF, Kron RE & Emich JP (1975). Neonatal abstinence syndrome: Assessment and management. *Addictive Diseases* 2:141–158.

Finnegan LP, Oehlberg SM, Regan DO'M & Rudrauff ME (1981). Evaluation of parenting, depression and violence profiles in methadone maintained women. *Child Abuse and Neglect* 5:267–273.

Fitzgerald E, Kaltenbach K & Finnegan L (1990). Patterns of interaction among drug dependent women and their infants. *Pediatric Research* 10A.

Forrest F, Florey C du V, Taylor D, McPherson F & Young J (1991). Reported social alcohol consumption during pregnancy and infants' development at 18 months. *British Medical Journal* 303:22–26.

Fried PA (1996). Behavioral outcomes in preschool and school-age children exposed prenatally to marijuana: A review and speculative interpretation. *NIDA Research Monograph* 164:242–260.

Fried PA & Makin JE (1987). Neonatal behavioral correlates of prenatal exposure to marihuana, cigarettes, and alcohol in a low risk population. *Neurotoxicology and Teratology* 9:1–7.

Fried PA, O'Connell CM & Watkinson B (1992). 60- and 72-month follow-up of children prenatally exposed to marijuana, cigarettes, and alcohol: Cognitive and language assessment. *Developmental and Behavioral Pediatrics* 13:383–391.

Fried PA & Watkinson B (1988). 12- and 24-month neurobehavioural follow-up of children prenatally exposed to marihuana, cigarettes and alcohol. *Neurotoxicology and Teratology* 10:305–313.

Fried PA & Watkinson B (1990). 36- and 48-month neurobehavioral follow-up of children prenatally exposed to marijuana, cigarettes and alcohol. *Developmental and Behavioral Pediatrics* 11:49–58.

Fried PA, Watkinson B & Gray R (1992). A follow-up study of attentional behavior in 6-year-old children exposed prenatally to marihuana, cigarettes and alcohol. *Neurotoxicology and Teratology* 14:299–311.

Fried PA, Watkinson B & Siegel LS (1997). Reading and language in 9- to 12-year olds prenatally exposed to cigarettes and marijuana. *Neurotoxicology and Teratology* 19:171–183.

Gavzer B (1997, July 27). Can they beat the odds? *Parade*, 4–5.

Grattan MP & Hans SL (1996). Motor behavior in children exposed prenatally to drugs. *Journal of Occupational and Physical Therapy in Pediatrics* 16:89–109.

Greene T, Ernhart CB, Ager J, Sokol R, Martier S & Boyd T (1991). Prenatal alcohol exposure and cognitive development in the preschool years. *Neurotoxicology and Teratology* 13:57–68.

Griffith DR, Azuma SD & Chasnoff IJ (1994). Three-year outcome of children exposed prenatally to drugs. *Journal of the American Academy of Child and Adolescent Psychiatry* 33:20–27.

Gusella J & Fried P (1984). Effects of maternal social drinking and smoking on offspring at 13 months. *Neurobehavioral Toxicology and Teratology* 6:13–17.

Hager M (1997). Hope for "snow babies." *Newsweek* September 29:62–63.

Hans SL (1989). Developmental consequences of prenatal exposure to methadone. *Annals of the New York Academy of Sciences* 562:195–207.

Hans SL (1996). Prenatal drug exposure: Behavioral functioning in late childhood and adolescence. *National Institute on Drug Abuse Research Monograph* 164:261–276.

Hans SL (1997, June). *Effects of Prenatal Exposure to Opiates on Attention During Middle Childhood.* Paper presented at the meetings of the Neurobehavioral Teratology Society. Palm Beach, FL.

Hans SL, Bernstein VJ & Henson LG (1990). Interaction between drug-using mothers and their toddlers. *Infant Behavior and Development* 13(Special):190.

Hans SL & Marcus J (1983). Motor and attentional behavior in infants of methadone maintained women. *National Institute on Drug Abuse Research Monograph* 43:287–293.

Hans SL, Marcus J, Jeremy RJ & Auerbach JG (1984). Neurobehavioral development of children exposed in utero to opioid drugs. In J Yanai (ed.) *Neurobehavioral Teratology.* New York, NY: Elsevier, 249–273.

Hawley TL, Halle TG, Drasin RE & Thomas NG (1995). Children of addicted mothers: Effects of the 'crack epidemic' on the caregiving environment and the development of preschoolers. *American Journal of Orthopsychiatry* 65:364–379.

Heffelfinger A, Craft S & Shyken J (1997). Visual attention in children with prenatal cocaine exposure. *Journal of the International Neuropsychological Society* 3:237–245.

Hickey JE, Suess PE, Newlin DB, Spurgeon L & Porges SW (1995). Vagal tone regulation during sustained attention in boys exposed to opiates in utero. *Addictive Behavior* 20:43–59.

Hofkosh D, Pringle JL, Wald HP, Switala J, Hinderliter SA & Hamel SC (1995). Early interactions between drug-involved mothers and infants: Within-group differences. *Archives of Pediatric and Adolescent Medicine* 149:665–672.

Hopkins E (October 18, 1990). Childhood's end. *Rolling Stone*, 66–72, 108–110.

Householder J (1980). *An Investigation of Mother-infant Interaction in a Narcotic-addicted Population.* Unpublished doctoral dissertation, Northwestern University.

Howard J, Beckwith L, Espinosa M & Tyler R (1995). Development of infants born to cocaine-abusing women: Biologic/maternal influences. *Neurotoxicology and Teratology* 17:403–411.

Hunt, E, Streissguth AP, Kerr B & Olson HC (1995). Mothers' alcohol consumption during pregnancy: Effects on spatial-visual reasoning on 14-year-old children. *Psychological Science* 6:339–342.

Hurt H, Brodsky NL, Betancourt L, Braitman LW, Malmud E & Giannetta J (1995). Cocaine-exposed children: Follow-up through 30 months. *Journal of Developmental and Behavioral Pediatrics* 16:29–35.

Hurt H, Malmud EK, Betancourt LM, Braitman LE, Brodsky NL & Giannetta JM (1997). Children with in utero cocaine-exposure do not differ from controls on intelligence testing. *Archives of Pediatric and Adolescent Medicine* 151:1237–1241.

Isohanni M, Oja H, Moilanen I, Koiranen M, Rantakallio P (1995). Smoking or quitting during pregnancy: Associations with background and future social factors. *Scandinavian Journal of Social Medicine* 23:32–38.

Jacobson SW, Jacobson JL & Sokol RJ (1994). Effects of fetal alcohol exposure on infant reaction time. *Alcoholism: Clinical and Experimental Research* 18:1125–1132.

Jacobson JL, Jacobson SW, Sokol RJ, Martier SS, Ager JW & Kaplan-Estrin MG (1993). Teratogenic effects of alcohol on infant development. *Alcoholism: Clinical & Experimental Research* 17:174–183.

Jacobson SW, Jacobson JL, Sokol RJ, Martier SS & Chiodo LM (1996). New evidence for neurobehavioral effects of in utero cocaine exposure. *Journal of Pediatrics* 129:581–590.

Jaudes PK, Ekwo E & Voorhis JV (1995). Association of drug abuse and child abuse. *Child Abuse and Neglect* 19:1065–1075.

Jeremy RJ & Bernstein VJ (1984). Dyads at risk: Methadone-maintained women and their four-month-old infants. *Child Development* 55:1141–1154.

Johnson HL, Diano A & Rosen TS (1984). 24-month neurobehavioral follow-up of children of methadone-maintained mothers. *Infant Behavior and Development* 7:115–123.

Johnson HL, Glassman MB, Fiks KB & Rosen T (1987). Path analysis of variables affecting 36-month outcome in a population of multi-risk children. *Infant Behavior and Development* 10:451–465.

Johnson HL & Rosen TS (1990). Difficult mothers of difficult babies: Mother-infant interaction in a multi-risk population. *American Journal of Orthopsychiatry* 60:281–288.

Jones KL & Smith DW (1973). Recognition of the fetal alcohol syndrome in early infancy. *Lancet* 2:999–1001.

Kaltenbach K & Finnegan LP (1987). Perinatal and developmental outcome of infants exposed to methadone in utero. *Neurotoxicology and Teratology* 9:311–313.

Kandel D (1975). Stages in adolescent involvement in drug use. *Science* 190:912–914.

Kantrowitz B (1990). The crack children. *Newsweek* February 12:62–63.

Kaufman NF (1994). Smoking and young women: The physician's role in stopping an equal opportunity killer. *Journal of the American Medical Association* 271:629–630.

Kendrick JS & Merritt RK (1996). Women and smoking: An update for the 1990s. *American Journal of Obstetrics and Gynecology* 175:528–535.

Kristjansson EA, Fried PA & Watkinson B (1989). Maternal smoking during pregnancy affects children's vigilance performance. *Drug and Alcohol Dependence* 24:11–19.

Landesman-Dwyer S, Ragozin AS & Little RE (1981). Behavioral correlates of prenatal alcohol exposure: A four-year follow-up study. *Neurobehavioral Toxicology and Teratology* 3:187–193.

Larroque B, Kaminski M, Dehaene P, Subtil D, Delfosse M & Querleu D (1995). Moderate prenatal alcohol exposure and psychomotor development at preschool age. *American Journal of Public Health* 85:1654–1661.

Lester BM, Freier K & LaGasse L (1995). Prenatal cocaine exposure and child outcome: What do we really know? In M Lewis & M Bendersky (eds) *Mothers, Babies, and Cocaine: The Role of Toxins in Development.* Hillsdale, NJ: Erlbaum, 19–39.

Lifschitz MH, Wilson GS, Smith EO & Desmond E (1985). Factors affecting head growth and intellectual function in children of drug addicts. *Pediatrics* 75:269–274.

Little BB, Snell LM, Rosenfeld CR, Gilstrap LC & Gant NF (1990). Failure to recognize fetal alcohol syndrome in newborn infants. *American Journal of Diseases of Children* 144:1142–1146.

Marcus J, Hans SL & Jeremy RJ (1982). Patterns of 1-day and 4-month motor functioning in infants of women on methadone. *Neurobehavioral Toxicology and Teratology* 4:473–476.

Martin M, Hecker J, Clark R et al. (1991). China white epidemic: An eastern United States emergency department experience. *Annals of Emergency Medicine* 20:158–164.

Mayes LC (1995). Substance abuse and parenting. In MH Bornstein (ed.) *Handbook of Parenting. Volume 4: Applied and Practical Parenting.* Mahwah, NJ: Erlbaum, 101–126.

Mayes LC, Bornstein MH, Chawarska K & Granger RH (1995). Information processing and developmental assessments in 3-month old infants exposed prenatally to cocaine. *Pediatrics* 95:539–545.

Mayes LC, Granger RH, Bornstein MH & Zuckerman B (1992). The problem of cocaine exposure: A rush to judgment. *Journal of the American Medical Association* 267:406–408.

Milberger S, Biederman J, Faraone SV, Chen L & Jones J (1996). Is maternal smoking during pregnancy a risk factor for attention deficit hyperactivity disorder in children? *American Journal of Psychiatry* 153:1138–1142.

Morrow CE, Bandstra ES, Johnson AL, Hagues ME, Ojeda-Vaz MM & Churchill SS (1997). Cognitive functioning in 3-year-old children exposed prenatally to cocaine. *Pediatric Research* 41:205A.

Naeye RL & Peters EC (1984). Mental development of children whose mothers smoked during pregnancy. *Obstetrics and Gynecology* 64:601–607.

National Institute on Alcohol Abuse and Alcoholism (1990). *Seventh Special Report to the U.S. Congress.* Washington, DC: US Department of Health and Human Services.

National Institute on Child Health and Development (1993). Effects of in utero exposure to street drugs. *American Journal of Public Health* 83 (Suppl.):9–32.

National Institute on Drug Abuse (1996). *National Pregnancy and Health Survey: Drug Use among Women Delivering Livebirths: 1992.* Washington, DC: US Department of Health and Human Services.

Nulman I, Rovet J, Altmann D, Bradley C, Einarson T & Koren G (1994). Neurodevelopment of adopted children exposed in utero to cocaine. *Canadian Medical Association Journal* 151:1591–1597.

O'Connell CM & Fried PA (1991). Prenatal exposure to cannabis: A preliminary report of postnatal consequences in school-age children. *Neurotoxicology and Teratology* 13:631–639.

O'Connor MJ, Brill NJ & Sigman M (1986). Alcohol use in primiparous women older than 30 years of age: Relation to infant development. *Pediatrics* 78:444–450.

O'Connor MJ, Sigman M & Kasari C (1993). Interactional model for the association among maternal alcohol use, mother-infant interaction, and infant cognitive development. *Infant Behavior and Development* 16:177–192.

Olds DL, Henderson CR & Tatelbaum R (1994). Prevention of intellectual impairment in children of women who smoke cigarettes during pregnancy. *Pediatrics* 93:228–233.

Ornoy A, Michailevskaya V & Lukashov I (1996). The developmental outcome of children born to heroin-dependent mothers, raised at home or adopted. *Child Abuse and Neglect* 20:385–396.

Pagliaro LA & Pagliaro AM (1995). Drugs as human teratogens. In LA Pagliaro & AM Pagliaro (eds.) *Problems in Pediatric Drug Therapy (3rd Edition).* Hamilton, IL: Drug Intelligence.

Parry GJ & Ogston SA (1992). Results: Child development at age 18 months. *International Journal of Epidemiology* 21(Suppl 1):S72–S78.

Piazza SF, Lanza B & Dweck HS (1989). Neurological abnormalities and developmental delays in infants of substance abusing mothers. *Pediatric Research* 25:1546.

Rankin H (1990). Validity of self-reports in clinical settings. *Behavioral Assessment* 12:107–116.

Regan DO, Ehrlich SM & Finnegan LP (1987). Infants of drug addicts: At risk for child abuse, neglect, and placement in foster care. *Neurotoxicology and Teratology* 9:315–319.

Richardson GA, Conroy ML & Day NL (1996). Prenatal cocaine exposure: Effects on the development of school-age children. *Neurotoxicology and Teratology* 18:627–634.

Richardson GA & Day NL (1994). Detrimental effects of prenatal cocaine exposure: Illusion or reality? *Journal of the American Academy of Child and Adolescent Psychiatry* 33:28–34.

Richardson GA, Day NL & Goldschmidt L (1995). Prenatal alcohol, marijuana, and tobacco use: Infant mental and motor development. *Neurotoxicology and Teratology* 17:479–487.

Robinson MD, Laurent SL & Little JM (1995). Including smoking status as a new vital sign: It works! *Journal of Family Practice* 40:556–561.

Rodning C, Beckwith L & Howard J (1991). Quality of attachment and home environments in children prenatally exposed to PCP and cocaine. *Development and Psychopathology* 3:351–366.

Rose-Jacobs R, Frank DA, Brown ER, Cabral H & Zuckerman BS (1994). Use of the Movement Assessment of Infants (MAI) with in-utero cocaine-exposed infants. *Pediatric Research* 35:26A.

Rosen TS & Johnson HL (1982). Children of methadone-maintained mothers: Follow-up to 18 months of age. *Journal of Pediatrics* 101:192–196.

Rosvold HE, Mirsky AF, Sarson I, Bransome ED & Beck LN (1956). A continuous performance test of brain damage. *Journal of Consulting Psychiatry* 20:343–350.

Rush D (1992). Exposure to passive cigarette smoking and child development: An updated critical review. In D Poswillo & E Alberman (eds.) *Effects of Smoking on the Fetus, Neonate, and Child.* Oxford: Oxford University Press.

Schneider JW & Chasnoff IJ (1992). Motor assessment of cocaine/polydrug exposed infants at age 4 months. *Neurotoxicology and Teratology* 14:97–101.

Sexton M, Fox NL & Hebel JR (1990). Prenatal exposure to tobacco: II. Effects on cognitive functioning at age three. *International Journal of Epidemiology* 19:72–77.

Sexton M & Hebel JR (1984). A clinical trial of change in maternal smoking and its effect on birth weight. *Journal of the American Medical Association* 251:911–915.

Singer LT, Arendt R, Farkas K, Minnes S, Huang J & Yamashita T (1997). The relationship of prenatal cocaine exposure and maternal psychological distress to child developmental outcome. *Development and Psychopathology* 9:473–489.

Sokol RJ & Clarren SK (1989). Guidelines for use of terminology describing the impact of prenatal alcohol on the offspring. *Alcoholism: Clinical & Experimental Research* 13:597–598.

Sokol R, Miller S & Reed G (1980). Alcohol abuse during pregnancy: An epidemiological study. *Alcoholism: Clinical & Experimental Research* 4:135–145.

Sowder BF & Burt MR (1980). *Children of Heroin Addicts: an Assessment of Health, Learning, Behavioral and Adjustment Problems.* New York, NY: Praeger.

Strauss ME, Lessen-Firestone JK, Chavez CJ & Stryker JC (1979). Children of methadone-treated women at five years of age. *Pharmacology, Biochemistry, and Behavior* 11:3–6.

Strauss ME, Starr RH, Ostrea EM Jr, Chavez CJ & Stryker JC (1976). Behavioral concomitants of prenatal addiction to narcotics. *Journal of Pediatrics* 89:842–846.

Streissguth AP, Barr HM, Martin DC & Herman CS (1980). Effects of maternal alcohol, nicotine, and caffeine use during pregnancy on infant mental and motor development at eight months. *Alcoholism: Clinical & Experimental Research* 4:152–164.

Streissguth AP, Barr HM & Sampson PD (1990). Moderate prenatal alcohol exposure: Effects on child IQ and learning problems at age 7 years. *Alcoholism: Clinical & Experimental Research* 14:662–669.

Streissguth AP, Barr HM, Sampson PD, Darby BL & Martin DC (1989). IQ at age 4 in relation to maternal alcohol use and smoking during pregnancy. *Developmental Psychology* 25:3–11.

Streissguth AP, Barr HM, Sampson PD, Parrish-Johnson JC, Kirchner GL & Martin DC (1986). Attention, distraction, and reaction time at age 7 years and prenatal alcohol exposure. *Neurobehavioral Toxicology and Teratology* 8:717–725.

Streissguth AP, Martin DC, Barr HM, Sandman BM, Kirchner GL & Darby BL (1984). Intrauterine alcohol and nicotine exposure: Attention and reaction time in 4-year-old children. *Developmental Psychology* 20:533–541.

Streissguth AP, Martin DC, Martin JC & Barr HM (1981). The Seattle Longitudinal Prospective Study on Alcohol and Pregnancy. *Neurobehavioral Toxicology and Teratology* 3:223–233.

Streissguth AP, Sampson PD, Olson HC et al. (1994). Maternal drinking during pregnancy: Attention and short-term memory in 14-year-old offspring—A longitudinal prospective study. *Alcoholism: Clinical and Experimental Research* 18:202–218.

Struthers JM & Hansen RL (1992). Visual recognition memory in drug-exposed infants. *Developmental and Behavioral Pediatrics* 13:108–111.

Tennes K, Avitable N, Blackard C et al. (1985). Marijuana: prenatal and postnatal exposure in the human. *National Institute on Drug Abuse Research Monograph* 59:48–60.

Toufexis A (1991, May 13). Innocent victims. *Time* 137(19):56–60.

Vorhees CV (1986). Origins of behavioral teratology. *Handbook of Behavioral Teratology.* New York, NY: Plenum Press, 3–22.

Wakschlag LS & Hans SL (1997, April). *Early Parenting and its Relation to Disruptive Behavior Disorders in High Risk Youth.* Paper presented at the meetings of the Society for Research in Child Development. Washington, DC.

Wakschlag LS, Lahey BB, Loeber R, Green SM, Gordon RA & Leventhal BL (1997). Maternal smoking during pregnancy and the risk of conduct disorder in boys. *Archives of General Psychiatry* 54:670–676.

Wasserman DR & Leventhal JM (1993). Maltreatment of children born to cocaine-abusing mothers. *American Journal of Diseases of Children* 147:1324–1328.

Weitzman M, Gortmaker S & Sobol A (1992). Maternal smoking and behavior problems of children. *Pediatrics* 90:342–349.

Wilens TE, Biederman J, Kiely K, Bredin E & Spencer TJ (1995). Pilot study of behavioral and emotional disturbances in the high-risk children of parents with opioid dependence. *Journal of the American Academy of Child and Adolescent Psychiatry* 34:779–785.

Wilson GS (1989). Clinical studies of infants and children exposed prenatally to heroin. *Annals of the New York Academy of Sciences* 562:183–194.

Wilson GS, Desmond MM & Wait RB (1981). Follow-up of methadone-treated and untreated narcotic-dependent women and their infants: Health, developmental, and social implications. *Journal of Pediatrics* 98:716–722.

Wilson GS, McCreary R, Kean J & Baxter JC (1979). The development of preschool children of heroin-addicted mothers: A controlled study. *Pediatrics* 63:135–141.

Zuckerman B, Amaro H & Cabral H (1989). Validity of self-reporting marijuana and cocaine use among pregnant adolescents. *Journal of Pediatrics* 5:812–815.

SECTION 17
Alcohol and Drug Use in the Workplace

CHAPTER 1

Overview of Drug-Free Workplace Programs **1241**
Barbara L. Johnson, Esq. and Jonathan D. Quander, Esq.

CHAPTER 2

The Role of the Medical Review Officer **1255**
Donald Ian Macdonald, M.D., FASAM, and Robert L. DuPont, M.D., FASAM

CHAPTER 3

Impairment and Recovery in Physicians and Other Health Professionals **1263**
G. Douglas Talbott, M.D., FASAM, Karl V. Gallegos, M.D., and Daniel H. Angres, M.D.

SECTION COORDINATOR

DONALD IAN MACDONALD, M.D., FASAM
Chairman and CEO
Employee Health Programs
Bethesda, Maryland

CONTRIBUTORS

Daniel H. Angres, M.D.
Director, Rush Behavioral Health, and
Assistant Professor of Psychiatry
Rush Medical College
Chicago, Illinois

Robert L. DuPont, M.D., FASAM
President, Institute for Behavior and Health, Inc.
Rockville, Maryland, and
Clinical Professor
Georgetown University School of Medicine
Washington, D.C.

Karl V. Gallegos, M.D.
Talbott Recovery Systems
Atlanta, Georgia

Barbara L. Johnson, Esq.
Wickliff & Hall, P.C.
Houston, Texas

Jonathan D. Quander, Esq.
Wickliff & Hall, P.C.
Houston, Texas

G. Douglas Talbott, M.D., FASAM
Founder and Medical Director
Talbott Recovery Systems
Atlanta, Georgia

CHAPTER 1

Overview of Drug-Free Workplace Programs

Barbara L. Johnson, Esq.
Jonathan D. Quander, Esq.

Rationale for Workplace Alcohol and Drug Programs
Types of Drug Testing
Testing Methods, Reliability, and Selection of Laboratories
The Employer's Right to Implement Testing
The Employer's Potential Tort Liability
Federal and State Legislation
Implementation and Enforcement of Policies

Responding to current concerns about the use and abuse of drugs and alcohol in the workplace, many employers have introduced new workplace drug and alcohol testing programs, revamped outdated programs, or addressed problems arising out of the enforcement of existing drug and alcohol testing programs. This chapter reviews a number of issues related to such programs, including the statutory and case law that may affect an employer's implementation and enforcement of drug and alcohol testing programs, regulations that mandate drug and/or alcohol policies and testing in the workplace, and the types of drug or alcohol tests and testing procedures currently in use. It concludes with general guidance on how to design a drug and alcohol abuse policy.

RATIONALE FOR WORKPLACE ALCOHOL AND DRUG PROGRAMS

The "War on Drugs" in the American workplace has become a priority for many employers in the 1990s (Carr, 1989). In fact, alcohol and other drug abuse has replaced AIDS as the primary workplace concern, according to a *Wall Street Journal* survey of 257 industrial relations executives. Moreover, substance abuse reportedly costs employers approximately $100 billion annually through lost productivity, increased absenteeism and drug related injuries. The courts have found that employers have a duty to provide a safe workplace, and they also have a right to expect employees to perform their work in a safe and efficient manner.

Insofar as alcohol and drug use impairs an individual's mental and physical faculties and thus his or her ability to perform work, employers have responded by implementing drug and alcohol use policies. In addition, the federal government now enforces various laws designed to prevent, detect and eliminate illegal drug use in the workplace. More than 80% of manufacturing firms in a variety of high technology industries have corporate drug and alcohol policies, with 93% of the firms testing job applicants and about 75% of the firms testing current employees (Anonymous, 1990).

According to a report prepared for the Institute for a Drug Free Workplace by SmithKline Beecham (1990), a major drug testing company, drug testing garners positive results in many respects. Employer drug testing and drug abuse prevention programs have resulted in significantly fewer employees using illicit drugs in the workplace, as evidenced by the fact that the rate of "positive" drug tests of employees and job applicants has decreased by nearly one-fourth since 1994. The report asserts that 13.8% of a sample of approximately one million employees and job applicants' drug tests conducted in the first six months of 1990 were "positive," appreciably lower than the 18.1% positive rate in a comparable sample in 1987 (SmithKline Beecham, 1990).

TYPES OF DRUG TESTING

Pre-Employment Testing. Pre-employment testing is considered preventive because it denies employment to persons who are identified as drug users before they begin work. Almost all companies that conduct any type of drug testing use pre-employment testing, which is the most frequently used form of situational testing. For the most part, pre-employment testing exposes the prospective employer to less liability involving labor grievances and litigation, given that an employer generally has no obligation to non-employees.

Reasonable Cause Testing. "Reasonable cause" testing is used when an employee's unsafe or unacceptable job conduct clearly points to a problem, which may involve drug use. This form of testing is conducted when an employer believes, based on objective facts, that a particular employee is unable to perform his or her duties satisfactorily by virtue of impairment from drugs or alcohol. Such inability to perform may include, but is not limited to, a decrease in the quality or quantity of the employee's productivity, judgment, reasoning, concentration, and psychomotor control, as well as marked behavioral changes. Accidents, deviations from safe working practices, and erratic workplace conduct—indicative of impairment—are other examples of reasonable cause situations.

The major obstacle to reasonable cause testing is that supervisors may lack sufficient training and motivation to detect employee alcohol or drug use. Supervisors also avoid reasonable cause testing because of legitimate concerns that: (1) such testing will hamper efforts to build team spirit or employee unity, thus decreasing productivity; or (2) the supervisor's decision to test will be challenged by the employee's union or questioned by upper management.

Random Testing. Random testing is the most controversial drug testing option because it pits the employer's desires, which often mirror broad societal interests, against the employee's privacy interest. Random testing also is referred to as "unannounced testing" because the salient feature is the absence of advance notice. It also is called "no-cause testing" because the selection of tested employees is unrelated to a specific performance problem. These two factors—no notice and no cause—are responsible for the unpopularity of this testing method.

A random selection technique is one in which all persons from a defined population have an equal chance of being tested. The percentage of persons chosen from the total population sometimes is proportional to an employer's perception of drug abuse; namely, a perception of widespread abuse requires the random selection of a high proportion of employees. This technique can be applied to the selection of either one or a few sites among many work sites.

Post-Accident Testing. Post-accident testing involves employer-mandated testing of an individual who is directly involved in a motor vehicle crash or other accident or near-miss. Post-accident testing resembles reasonable cause testing because both are based on events that automatically require testing. However, in post-accident testing, indicators of employee impairment need not be present for testing to occur.

Periodic Testing. Periodic testing is a catch-all category that includes drug tests conducted at designated intervals. Such tests usually are conducted as an adjunct to routine checkups or recertification of occupational licenses. However, periodic testing has limited efficacy in deterring or detecting on-the-job alcohol or drug use because users can simply abstain from use prior to the scheduled test. Also, the health professionals who collect drug test specimens as part of a medical evaluation do not always adequately guard against specimen substitution.

Rehabilitation Testing. The frequency and manner of testing employees in rehabilitation programs before they return to work are determined by rehabilitation program professionals. The key person could be a medical review officer (MRO) or a substance abuse professional (SAP) who is employed by the company. Although the principal role of the MRO usually is to evaluate positive test results, this role could be expanded to include rehabilitation functions (such as setting an unannounced testing schedule for the employee and deciding when an employee is fit to return to work).

The use of unannounced testing after an employee returns to work from a rehabilitation program is determined by management or senior supervisors close to the job and familiar with the employee's duties. When the job involves safety-sensitive duties, unannounced testing should occur more frequently and be more unpredictable; the period of aftercare monitoring also should be longer. These steps are taken to maximize assurances that an employee will remain drug-free. The frequency of unannounced testing following rehabilitation can vary from once every three months to once every three days, with the norm about once a month. The length of post-treatment monitoring usually ranges from one to five years.

TESTING METHODS, RELIABILITY AND SELECTION OF LABORATORIES

Alcohol Tests. Alcohol intoxication can be measured by a number of testing methods, involving the use of blood, breath, urine and saliva. In the past, blood specimens were analyzed most often to measure "blood alcohol concentration" (BAC), which is expressed as a percentage. However, other methods are now being used more frequently. Breath analysis by infrared spectrometry measures the amount of alcohol in the breath, from which the blood/alcohol level is inferred. Breath specimens also can be taken through the use of portable breath testing devices (e.g., Breathalyzer®), which law enforcement agencies commonly use for forensic and evidentiary purposes. Additionally, urine testing often is conducted by rehabilitation programs to monitor an individual's continued sobriety. Many states authorize the use of urine for alcohol testing for DWI offenses and to regulate commercial drivers.

Saliva tests are completed by using test strips and other devices that measure alcohol levels in a person's saliva. While saliva tests facilitate immediate on-site testing, under Department of Transportation rules, training and extensive recordkeeping on the part of test administrators is required.

Drug Tests. Unlike blood/alcohol levels, drug tests cannot measure impairment, because drug concentrations in urine or blood do not correlate with the degree of impairment. All test manufacturers emphatically recommend that positive test results from a screening test be confirmed with an equally sensitive test that uses a different chemical process.

A standard screening test, such as the Enzyme Multiplied Immunoassay Technique (EMIT®), has become the most widely used drug test because it is easy to administer and inexpensive. Because EMIT tests only for the presence of a drug metabolite, positive test results should be confirmed by another method. Radio-immunoassay has approximately the same specificity as EMIT. Gas Chromatography/Mass Spectrometry (GC/MS) is a state-of-the-art analytic technique that can test and specifically identify a wide spectrum of drugs. It is by far the most accurate testing technique, but also the most expensive. Hair analysis is a relatively recent technology for determining drug use. The advantage of hair analysis is that there is a long window for detection, meaning that drug use months or even years prior to the test date can be detected. The disadvantage to hair testing is that the testing does not always show current drug use. Therefore, in a post-accident test, hair analysis should be combined with a urinalysis.

Saliva testing is another relatively recent method for detecting drugs and/or alcohol. An advantage of saliva testing is that the active drug is present in the saliva, and a saliva test may be more useful in determining degree of impairment. A disadvantage of saliva testing is that, for some drugs, the pH level in the saliva can affect the test result.

Selecting a Laboratory. It is important for an employer to choose a good testing laboratory in order to ensure accuracy and obtain protection against test result challenges. First-hand review of testing procedures by qualified personnel is beneficial. The employer should consider:

- Whether the laboratory is certified by the National Institute on Drug Abuse (as is required of all laboratories processing federally mandated drug and alcohol tests);
- The size and credentials of the laboratory's staff;
- The laboratory's testing volume and experience;
- The screening and confirmation methods used;
- The number and types of drugs the laboratory is capable of detecting;
- The laboratory's management software;
- The laboratory's chain of custody procedures and documentation;
- The type of litigation support provided by the laboratory;
- The turnaround time to process specimens;
- The laboratory's security procedures;
- The laboratory's method of reporting and reputation for service; and
- The laboratory's charges for performing the desired testing procedures.

THE EMPLOYER'S RIGHT TO IMPLEMENT TESTING

Non-Union Contract Employees. It is well understood that when an employee has a written contract, the discharge of that employee in violation of the terms of the contract gives rise to liability under ordinary breach of contract principles. In such a circumstance, to establish a cause of action for wrongful discharge, the employee must prove: (1) the existence of a contract that specifically provides that the employer cannot terminate at will, and (2) the existence of a written employment agreement.

An employment contract may be based on either written or oral representations made to the employee by management. The statute of frauds is inapplicable where the employment is for an indefinite period of time, since the employment relationship is not one that must be longer than one year. If the contract promises employment for a definite term, the employer has the burden of showing good cause for the discharge.

Under an employment contract, an employer always may discharge an employee for good cause. "Good cause" includes dishonesty, immoral conduct, negligence, incompetence, or disobedience of reasonable work rules. If a contract for a definite term does not specifically state that an employer can terminate an employee for failing to abide by the employer's drug and alcohol policy, the employer may be faced with a breach of contract claim. An employer also may raise traditional contract defenses to a breach of contract claim, such as disobedience of a reasonable work rule. Clearly, an employer can avoid liability for a breach of contract claim arising from the discipline or discharge of an employee who refuses to take a drug test, or who tests positive, by specifically including a term addressing drug and alcohol testing in any employment contract.

An employee may attempt to rely on a written employee handbook as the basis of an implied contract.

Employees Covered by Collective Bargaining Agreements. *Employer's Obligation to Bargain under the National Labor Relations Act:* Section 8(c) of the National Labor Relations Act (NLRA) requires that the union and employer negotiate over "wages, hours and other terms and conditions of employment" (*29 U.C.S.A. 158(d)(1982)*). Furthermore, Section 8(a)(1) makes it an unfair labor practice "to interfere with, restrain, or coerce employees" (*29 U.C.S.A. 158(a)(5)*). Therefore, an employer violates the NLRA if material changes in the conditions of employment occur without consulting the employee's bargaining representative and providing a meaningful opportunity to bargain. Thus, a private employer would violate the NLRA by unilaterally implementing a drug or alcohol testing program without engaging in collective bargaining.

Job Applicants: Bargaining May Not be Required: The National Labor Relations Board (NLRB) has ruled that employers must bargain prior to establishing drug and alcohol testing programs for current employees, but bargaining is not required before testing job applicants (*Minneapolis Star Tribune*, 1989; *Johnson-Bateman Co.*, 1989). The NLRB reasoned that job applicants are not "employees" represented by a union, and an employer's use of drug testing, as part of the hiring criteria, does not affect the working conditions of current employees so as to bring such actions within the scope of the NLRA.

Current Employees: Bargaining Is Required: Work rules and conditions of employment are mandatory subjects of bargaining under the NLRA, such that unilateral implementation of a drug and alcohol policy, without first bargaining with the union, may be an unfair labor practice (*National Football League Players Assn. v. N.L.R.B.*, 1974 [employee misconduct rules]; *N.L.R.B. v. Gulf Power Co.*, 1967 [safety rule]). On September 8, 1987, the General Counsel for the NLRB, in Memorandum GC87-5, indicated that the development of a testing program was a substantial change in working conditions and, absent either specific union consent or bargaining impasse, the NLRB would litigate an employer's unilateral implementation of a drug and alcohol policy as an unfair labor practice. Consistent with this 1987 opinion by the NLRB's General Counsel, the NLRB has ruled that testing of current employees is a mandatory subject of bargaining because it affects the "terms and conditions of employment" (*Minneapolis Star Tribune*, 1989; *Johnson-Bateman Co.*, 1989).

Impact of the Employer's Duty to Implement Drug Testing under Federal Law on the Employer's Duty to Bargain: The question of whether an employer's duty to implement drug testing under federal law affects the employer's obligation to collectively bargain with the union has not yet been addressed by the NLRB or the courts. It is reasonable to assume that certain aspects of a company's drug testing program that are specifically required by federal regulation cannot be bargained away (*Oil, Chemical and Atomic Workers*, 1988). However, aspects of a company's program that are permitted but not mandated (e.g., a company-sponsored employee assistance program as part of the company's implementation of DOT drug testing regulations) probably are subject to mandatory bargaining.

Contract Arbitration: Unions have challenged employers' drug and alcohol abuse policies on various fronts, with varying degrees of success. In general, courts have been reluctant to enjoin private employers from implementing drug testing programs prior to arbitration of the validity of the policy, as provided for by the terms of a collective bargaining agreement (*Niagra Hooker Employee's Union v. Occidental Chemical Corp.*, 1991; *International Brotherhood of Teamsters, Local 19 v. Southwest Airlines*

Co., 1989). Most collective bargaining agreements require a grievance and subsequent arbitration of disputes. Even when an arbitrator upholds a company's overall drug policy and drug testing program, unions often grieve and arbitrate the employer's right to discharge a union employee for violation of the policy.

In general, arbitrators have invalidated drug and alcohol testing programs where the contract does not define employer and employee rights related to the testing program. In one case, an employee who was discharged for refusal to submit to a post-accident drug test was reinstated because the contract failed to articulate that automatic post-accident testing was required as a condition of employment (*Tribune Co.*, 1986).

Implicitly, an arbitrator must find a testing program reasonable before accepting the program as a work rule (Elkouri & Elkouri, 1985). Arbitrators typically approve a drug and alcohol abuse program if it: (1) promotes employee safety and health protection (*Concrete Pipe Products Co.*, 1986); (2) follows on-the-job accidents (*North County Transit District*, 1987); and (3) does not discriminate (*Concrete Pipe Products Co.*, 1986).

In examining the reasonableness of a work rule, arbitrators have looked at several factors, including the intrusive nature of the drug testing in question, to determine the reasonableness of the rule (*Houston Lighting & Power Co.*, 1986; *Ashland Oil Co.*, 1987). Random alcohol and drug testing without evidence of drug use generates significant controversy. Without suspicious behavior providing sufficient cause to test, random test results may not provide just cause for termination. In *Vulcan Materials Co.* (1988), the arbitrator found that:

> ". . . when an employee is required to undergo urinalysis for drug or alcohol test without probable cause or reasonable suspicion, he is required to give evidence against himself. He must prove his innocence before any discipline has ever been imposed. The rule of random testing is contrary to the normal and customary rule of discipline that an employee is presumed to be innocent of the particular offense."

Where random testing is fair, thorough, and applied in a nondiscriminatory manner, the resulting discipline or discharge for a positive test may be upheld. For example, in *Dow Chemical Co.* (1989), the arbitrator examined the issue of whether the employer properly implemented a random drug testing program at a petrochemical plant, where the sale and use of drugs was widespread throughout the plant. Using the "balancing of interests" test, the arbitrator held that the privacy intrusion created by the random testing was outweighed by the need for a more effective testing tool. The arbitrator determined that "for cause" testing was inefficient to solve the widespread problem of drug abuse and sales. Moreover, the company did not violate any existing collective bargaining agreements or past practices by implementing random testing as part of its alcohol and drug abuse policy (*Texas City Ref., Inc.*, 1987).

Even in cases where the union and employer have agreed to drug testing, an employee's subsequent discipline or discharge may not be sustained unless "just cause" existed for administering the test. Arbitrators differ on the proper circumstances required to satisfy the reasonable cause standard. While the standard probably does not rise to the level of constitutionally required "probable cause," an objective basis must exist before the testing order can be sustained.

To support reasonable cause to test, an arbitrator generally evaluates an employer's indication that an employee is "under the influence." In *American Standard* (1981), the arbitrator determined that the employer had the right to require a drug test because several witnesses stated that the employee had difficulty parking her car, the employee appeared glassy-eyed and unsteady, she staggered and slurred her speech, the employee had a history of drug-related experiences requiring medical leaves of absence, and the collective bargaining agreement contained a provision authorizing a medical examination at any time.

Most collective bargaining agreements require that an employee may be disciplined or discharged only for "just cause." Therefore, even if a valid drug and alcohol abuse testing policy exists, and even if an employer has the right to conduct testing, the employer also must establish that the discipline or discharge of the tested employee was for "just cause." Arbitrators determine, on a case-by-case basis, whether there was "just cause" to discipline or discharge an employee who tests positive (*Poly Tech, Inc.*, 1988; *General Dynamics Corp.*, 1988).

Preemption of State Tort Claims: The National Labor Relations Act preempts state tort claims arising from drug and alcohol testing under a collective bargaining agreement, if the agreement calls for arbitration of disputes concerning working conditions. In *Strachan v. Union Oil Co.* (1985), the Fifth Circuit Court of Appeals reviewed a situation in which an employer suspected two union employees of being under the influence of drugs at work; the employer required the two employees to undergo blood and urine drug tests. However, the laboratory results indicated that drugs were not present in their systems, and the employees returned to work. Subsequently, the two employees filed state tort claims against the employer for invasion of privacy, defamation, assault, and intentional infliction of emotional distress. Ultimately, the court held that "the law is completely clear that employees may not resort to state tort or contract claims in substitution for their rights under collective bargaining agreements." The court also noted that issues concerning medical examinations and blood and urine tests are clearly within the employer's authority, under the collective bargaining agreement, to insist upon medical examinations when the physical condition of an employee is in doubt.

Public Employees. The Fourth Amendment of the United States Constitution protects employees of federal, state and local government from unreasonable searches conducted by the government, even when the government acts as an employer (*National Treasury Employees Union v. Von Raab*, 1989; *Skinner v. Railroad Labor Executives' Assn.*, 1989). The United States Supreme Court has included within the definition of searches "the collection and subsequent analysis of biological samples [blood, urine, breath]," in addition to more conventional searches of possessions and tangible objects (*National Treasury Employees Union v. Von Raab*, 1989). Therefore, government employers must consider the special protection afforded government employees by the Fourth Amendment in the implementation and enforcement of a drug and alcohol testing program.

The United States Supreme Court has determined that, subject to constitutional constraints, public employers can implement drug and alcohol testing programs (*Skinner v. Railway Labor Executives' Association*, 1989). The Court has held that such testing may occur, subject to the Fourth Amendment's reasonableness requirement, which relates to an individual's right to be secure from "unreasonable searches and seizures" (*Skinner v. Railway Labor Executives' Association*, 1989).

Random and "Reasonable Suspicion" Drug and Alcohol Testing in Safety-Sensitive Industries: In general, courts have upheld random and "reasonable suspicion" drug and alcohol testing of public employees in safety-sensitive or highly regulated industries. Further, the Supreme Court has denied review of three cases that allowed random and "reasonable suspicion" testing for police officers and mandatory, pre-employment drug testing for applicants for nuclear power plant jobs (*Alvarado v. Washington Pub. Power Supply Sys.*, 1989; *Copeland v. Philadelphia Police Dept.*, 1989).

Non-Safety Sensitive Positions: Courts are divided, however, on the legality of drug testing of public employees in non-safety sensitive positions (*Bangert v. Hodel*, 1989; *AFGE, Local 1616 v. Thornburgh*, 1989).

Reasonable Suspicion Testing: Courts have regularly upheld testing of public employees based on a reasonable suspicion that the tested employees were under the influence of alcohol or drugs (*Everett v. Napper*, 1987).

Due Process Issues: Drug and alcohol testing of public employees requires consideration of substantive and procedural due process issues. For example, a court may review the accuracy and reliability of the actual testing methods and procedures used for a public employee with a higher level of scrutiny than for a private-employee. In *Banks v. Federal Aviation Administration* (1982), the court overturned the dismissal of two public employees because they were not given an opportunity to challenge and examine the laboratory reports. The court determined that it was *not* proper for the Board to introduce the results of government-sponsored tests of the controllers' voluntarily submitted urine samples, when the samples were destroyed and unavailable for independent testing. Thus, in the absence of the properly admitted test results, the evidence was insufficient to support the employees' discharge.

Confidentiality of Test Results. The Fourth Amendment's ban on unreasonable searches, under the balancing of interests standard, is less likely to prohibit drug and alcohol testing if the privacy invasion is lessened by protecting the confidentiality of test results (*Skinner v. Railway Labor Executives' Assn.*, 1989).

THE EMPLOYER'S POTENTIAL TORT LIABILITY

Defamation. An employee establishes a *prima facie* case of libel (written defamation) or slander (oral defamation) by proving that a defamatory statement about him or her was communicated to a third person. Generally, truth is a defense to a cause of action for defamation. While an employee may bring a cause of action for defamation arising out of drug or alcohol testing, a qualified privilege exists for statements made by the employer to other persons in the employment context, where such persons have a "corresponding interest or duty to which the communication relates" (*Gulf Construction Co. v. Mott,* 1969). This privilege can be lost if the statements made were motivated by malice.

False written statements of an employee's drug use created liability for the employer in *Houston Belt & Terminal Ry. Co. v. Wherry* (1976). In *Wherry*, a former railroad switchman sued his employer for defamation after the employer falsely accused him of using drugs. The employee was discharged when a urinalysis test showed the presence of methadone. A subsequent test revealed the presence of methadone, but established that the compound was not methadone. However, despite the second, negative urinalysis report, the employee was terminated for being an "unsafe employee." Knowing the report's falsity, the employer published a report stating that methadone traces were found in the plaintiff's system; the inaccurate report then was sent to seven company officials. It is important to note that liability was found in *Houston Belt*, even though the communications, in part, were made to *internal* management personnel.

Invasion of Privacy. Although an employee may fail to establish a defamation claim against an employer because of veracity, an employee may prevail in an invasion of privacy cause of action, if the investigation conducted in connection with drug and alcohol testing is unreasonable. Contrary to defamation claims, truth is not a defense to an invasion of privacy claim. "One who gives publicity to a matter concerning the private life of another is subject to liability to the other for invasion of his privacy, if the matter publicized is of a kind that: (1) would be highly offensive to a reasonable person, and (2) is not of legitimate concern to the public" (*Restatement of the Law*).

An unreasonable search for drugs also may give rise to a common-law tort action for invasion of privacy. In *K-Mart Corporation Store No. 7441 v. Trotti* (1985), an employee brought suit against her employer for invasion of privacy, claiming that the employer had violated her reasonable expectation of privacy by forcibly entering her company locker without her knowledge. While the company allowed employees to provide their own personal locks, it was never communicated to employees that the company reserved the right to enter the lockers at any time. The court of appeals held that the employee was entitled to recover because the employer intruded into an area where the employee had a reasonable expectation of privacy. The court noted that had the lock been supplied by the employer, the court's decision would have been different (*O'Brian v. Papa Gino of America, Inc.*, 1986).

Intentional Infliction of Emotional Distress. Employees often include the tort of intentional infliction of emotional distress in lawsuits against employers. Lawsuits arising out of drug and alcohol testing are prime candidates for claims of intentional infliction of emotional distress. A plaintiff can recap enormous monetary damages by prevailing on a claim of intentional infliction of emotional distress because of possible punitive damages. Generally, to establish a cause of action for intentional infliction of emotional distress, a plaintiff must show that the employer acted intentionally or recklessly; that the defendant's conduct was extreme and outrageous; the defendant's actions caused the claimant's emotional distress; and the emotional distress was severe (*Bushell v. Dean*, 1989).

FEDERAL AND STATE LEGISLATION

Federal Drug-Free Workplace Legislation and Regulations. *Executive Order 12,564* requires the head of each federal agency to develop a five-point plan for achieving the objective of a drug-free federal workplace. The plan should include a policy statement setting forth the agency's expectations regarding drug use and the anticipated action in response to identified drug use. EAPs must emphasize high-level direction, education and counseling, referrals to rehabilitation, and coordination with available community resources. Additionally, supervisory training should be available to assist in identifying and addressing illegal drug use by agency employees. The plan also should provide for referrals (self and supervisory) to treatment facilities, with maximum respect for individual confidentiality and consistent with safety and security issues. The final point is that provisions for identifying illegal drug users, including controlled and carefully monitored testing, should occur in accordance with the order. However, despite the requirements of Executive Order 12,564, courts have limited the government's ability to conduct random drug testing, unless a strong justification is demonstrated.

Drug-Free Workplace Act of 1988. This Act, which became effective after March 18, 1989, requires contractors and grantees of federal agencies to certify that they will provide drug-free workplaces. To be in compliance with the Act, an employer must publish a statement notifying employees that the manufacture, distribution, dispensation, possession, or use of an unlawful controlled substance is prohibited in the workplace. Additionally, employers must establish a drug-free awareness program to inform employees about the following: the dangers of drug abuse in the workplace; the employer's policy of maintaining a drug-free workplace; available drug counseling, rehabilitation and employee assistance programs; and the penalties to be enforced for employee drug abuse violations. The employer is required to make a good faith effort to maintain a drug-free workplace.

The Act requires an employer to conduct employee drug tests. The employer also is required to notify the contracting or funding agency within 10 days after receiving notice of an employee's conviction for violating a criminal drug offense in the workplace. After such an occurrence, each federal contract or grant shall be subject to payment suspension, and the employer will be subject to suspension or disbarment if the head of the agency determines that the employer offered a false certification; violated the certification by failing to implement the requirements of the Act; or, that such a number of employees have been convicted of violating criminal drug offenses in the workplace to indicate that the employer did not make a good faith effort to provide a drug-free workplace. Thereafter, an employer will be ineligible for any federal agency contract or grant award and for participation in any federal agency procurement or grant for a period not to exceed five years.

Department of Defense (DOD) Interim Drug-Free Workforce Rule. The DOD Act applies only to defense contractors. There are two categories of defense contracts subject to the requirements of the rule: (1) all contracts involving access to classified information; and (2) any other contracts that the contracting officer determines that inclusion of a drug-free workforce clause is necessary for reasons of national security, or protection of the health and safety of those affected by the product or performance of the contract (except for commercial or commercial-type products).

Each contract with the DOD subject to the drug-free rule must contain a clause in which the contractor agrees to institute a drug-free workforce program. The program must provide employee assistance that emphasizes high-level direction, education, counseling, rehabilitation, and coordination with available community resources. Supervisory training should also be provided to address illegal drug use by contractor employees, along with self and supervisory referrals for substance abuse treatment. The program also should include the means to identify illegal drug users.

Drug testing programs under the DOD regulations are mandated for employees in safety-sensitive positions. Although the rule does not specifically state that random testing is required, the DOD's published "Questions and Answers" indicate that employees in safety-sensitive positions must be tested on a random basis. Further, the extent and criteria of random testing is the responsibility of the contractor. Although not required, the rule also authorizes drug testing when there is reasonable suspicion of employee drug use; where an employee has been involved in an accident or unsafe practice; as a follow-up to counseling or rehabilitation programs; and on a voluntary basis.

Department of Transportation Drug-Free Workforce Rule. The Department of Transportation (DOT) has promulgated comprehensive procedures for federal workplace testing programs affecting several of its operating administrations and their regulated industries. Specifically, the DOT has issued drug testing regulations for the Federal Aviation Administration, Federal Highway Administration, Federal Railroad Administration, United States Coast Guard, Urban Mass Transportation Administration, and Research and Special Programs Administration. In addition to drug testing procedures applicable to these six agencies, each agency has its own set of drug testing regulations for industry employees.

The DOT regulations represent the most comprehensive and detailed rules for drug testing in the private sector to date. The DOT rules have been subjected to many court challenges, even prior to their effective date (*Intl. Brotherhood of Teamsters, Chaffeurs v. Dept. of Transportation*, 1991; *Transportation Institute v. U.S. Coast Guard*, 1989).

Under the DOT rules, public and private employers in the transportation industries are required to test individuals in safety-sensitive positions for certain controlled substances. Covered employees are required to take random drug tests, pre-employment drug tests, reasonable suspicion drug tests, drug tests during routine physicals, and upon suspicion of use, following an accident.

The DOT rules require an employer to test for the presence of five drugs: marijuana, cocaine, opiates, amphetamines and PCP. The testing procedures must be performed in accordance with the guidelines set forth by U.S. Department of Health and Human Services regulations, entitled "Mandatory Guidelines for Federal Workplace Drug Testing Programs." The regulations require that all drug test analyses be performed at a laboratory certified by the National Institute on Drug Abuse (NIDA).

The Department of Transportation also has promulgated regulations requiring alcohol testing of employees and independent contractors in safety-sensitive positions. While the regulations met considerable opposition, they became effective in 1994.

Nuclear Regulatory Commission's Fitness for Duty Rule. The Nuclear Regulatory Commission (NRC) requires all private-sector employers with NRC licenses that construct or operate nuclear power reactors to implement a fitness-for-duty program that includes alcohol and drug testing. The program applies to all individuals who are granted unescorted access to the plant, including vendors and contractors that provide services within the protected area.

The NRC regulations require both alcohol and drug testing. Random tests must be conducted at a rate equal to at least 100% of the workforce; they also must be administered on a nominal weekly frequency and at various times during the day, to enhance discovery of lunchtime drinking and drug use. Thereafter, employees who test positive must be removed from access to the site for at least 14 days and placed in an EAP. Employees who are denied access for any subsequent positive test are to be denied access to unescorted areas for a minimum of three years. Additionally, anyone involved in the sale, use, or possession of illegal drugs while in a protected area must be removed from the workplace for a minimum of five years.

Rehabilitation Act of 1973. This Act may affect an employer's right to discharge or discipline an alcohol- or drug-dependent person. The Rehabilitation Act of 1973 prohibits the federal government, federal contractors, and employers receiving federal financial aid from discriminating against "otherwise qualified individuals" solely on the basis of their handicap. The Act defines a "handicapped individual" as any person who (i) has a physical or mental impairment which substantially limits one or more of such person's major life activities, (ii) has a record of such an impairment, and (iii) is regarded as having such an impairment.

Alcoholism and drug dependence are defined as handicaps in interpretive regulations and have been held to be handicaps by federal courts (*29 CFR 32.3*, 1989; *28 CFR 41.32*, 1989; *Davis v. Bucher*, 1978). However, the Act excludes workers with current drug or alcohol problems from its "handicapped" definition, if the impairment interferes with their ability to work or poses a danger to persons or property (*29 U.C.S.A. 706(8)(B)*). Because the Act prohibits "discrimination" against a "handicapped individual," an employer who implements and enforces a drug testing program in a non-discriminatory manner should not run afoul of the Act (*Burka v. New York City Transit Authority*, 1988). The court determined, from a review of the legislative history of 1978 Amendments to the Act, that the amendments to the Act were not intended to cover all alcoholics and drug abusers.

Because the Office of Federal Contract Compliance Programs is charged with enforcement of the Act, an employee who alleges discrimination has no private cause of action.

Americans with Disabilities Act of 1990 (ADA). Signed into law on July 26, 1990, the ADA became effective for employers with 25 or more employees on July 26, 1992, and for employers with 15 or more employees on July 26, 1994. The ADA provides much greater protection to individuals with handicaps than the Rehabilitation Act of 1973, because the ADA covers all employers with more than 15 employees, not just federal contractors.

Employer Prohibitions on Alcohol and Drug Abuse: The ADA specifically permits employers to ensure that the workplace is free from the illegal use of alcohol and other drugs, and to comply with other federal laws and regulations regarding drug and alcohol use under the ADA. An employer may require employees not to be under the influence of drugs or alcohol in the workplace. Similarly, an employer may require that employees conform with the requirements of the Drug-Free Workplace Act of 1988 (*41 U.S.C. 701*). The ADA also provides that employers may hold a drug user or alcoholic to the same standard for job performance and behavior that the employer holds other employees, even if unsatisfactory performance or behavior is related to the employer's drug use or alcoholism. Finally, an employer may require that employees comply with federal agency standards, such as the DOT and NRC (*42 U.S.C. 12114(c)*).

Protection of Alcoholics and Recovering Drug Addicts: The ADA does not protect an employee or applicant who currently engages in the use of illegal drugs (*42 U.S.C. 12114(c)*). Accordingly, an employer may take adverse action against an employee if the action is taken because of current drug use. The EEOC defines "currently engaging" as a term that "is not intended to be limited to the use of drugs on the day of, or within a matter of days or weeks before the employment action in question. Rather, the provision is intended to apply to the illegal use of drugs that has occurred recently enough to indicate that the individual is actively engaged in such conduct."

The ADA's definition of a "qualified individual with a disability" specifically includes an individual who: (1) has successfully completed a supervised drug rehabilitation program and is no longer engaging in the illegal use of drugs, or has otherwise been successfully rehabilitated and no longer uses drugs; (2) is participating in a supervised rehabilitation program and no longer uses drugs; or (3) is mistakenly regarded as using drugs (*42 U.S.C. 12114 (c)*).

The ADA does not specifically exclude someone who is currently using alcohol from the definition of a "qualified individual with a disability." Moreover, ADA regulations specifically state that alcoholics are protected by the Act (*29 C.F.R. 1630.2(o)*). Therefore, alcoholics and rehabilitated drug users satisfying the ADA's criteria are "qualified individuals with a disability" and are protected by the ADA.

Requirement of Reasonable Accommodation: If an individual is a qualified person with a disability, the ADA imposes a reasonable accommodation requirement on the employer. The ADA does not require an employer to provide a rehabilitation program or an opportunity for rehabilitation to any applicant who is a drug addict or alcoholic. Likewise, an employer need not provide a rehabilitation program or an opportunity for rehabilitation to an employee against whom employment action is taken for violating workplace rules regarding substance abuse. However, employers have a general duty to reasonably accommodate an alcoholic or drug-addicted employee who is not currently using illegal drug use. Such accommodations may include granting a leave of absence so that the individual may undergo rehabilitation treatment for alcoholism or addiction to prescription drugs, job restructuring or a modified work schedule (*29 C.F.R. 1630.2(o)*). However, while these types of reasonable accommodations must be implemented by an employer, the employer is not be required to lower the normal performance standard when evaluating an alcoholic or rehabilitating drug user.

Drug and Alcohol Testing by Employers: An employer may not inquire as to whether an applicant is a drug addict or alcoholic, and whether the applicant has been in drug or alcohol rehabilitation. However, the employer may inquire whether an applicant drinks alcohol or whether the individual currently engages in illegal drug use. The employer also may inquire about the applicant's ability to perform the job (*42 U.S.C. 12112(d)(2)(B)*).

The ADA provides specific parameters for medical examinations conducted by employers. Employers are permitted to conduct pre-employment medical examinations only after a job offer has been extended, but before the commencement of employment (*42 U.S.C. 12112(d)(3)*). Further, the employer may condition the offer of employment on the results of the medical examination if all entering employees are subjected to such an examination, regardless of disability; information obtained regarding the medical condition or history of the applicant is collected and maintained on separate forms and in separate medical files and is treated as a confidential medical examination; and the results of the examination are used only pursuant to the ADA (*42 U.S.C. 12112(d)(3)*).

Drug Tests Are Not Medical Examinations under the ADA: The ADA is neutral with respect to drug testing; it neither grants nor denies an employer's authority to test employees and applicants for evidence of current illegal drug use, and subsequently, base employment decisions on the results of such tests (*42 U.S.C. 12114(d)(2)*). However, despite this proclamation of neutrality, the ADA expressly provides that a test to determine illegal drug use is not considered a medical examination (*42 U.S.C. 12114(d)(1)*).

The ADA defines the illegal use of drugs to include using, selling, or distributing drugs in violation of the federal Controlled Substances Act (*42 U.S.C. 12111(6)(A)*). In contrast, the use of drugs taken under the supervision of a licensed physician is not considered illegal use. Because the ADA provides a number of restrictions regarding employer medical examinations, employers are relieved of the necessity of satisfying the statutory requirements for medical examinations when testing for illegal drug use. Pre-offer employment drug testing and random employment drug testing are arguably permissible under the ADA (*42 U.S.C. 12112(d)*).

To determine the presence of an illegal drug, an employer may need to inquire about what prescription drugs an applicant uses. Therefore, drug testing should occur after a conditional employment offer is made.

The ADA provides that an employer may adopt or administer reasonable policies, including testing, to ensure that a rehabilitating drug user is no longer engaging in the use of illegal drugs (*42 U.S.C. 12114(b)*). The Act permits employers to test employees while they are participating in a drug rehabilitation program and after having completed a program. However, any information obtained from a drug test about an individual's medical condition or history, other than information pertaining to illegal drug use, must be treated as a confidential medical record. As such, the information is subject to the same recordkeeping and nondisclosure requirements that apply to information obtained during a medical examination (*29 CFR 1630.16(c)*).

Alcohol Testing Must Meet ADA Criteria: The ADA does not state whether tests to determine alcohol use are medical examinations. However, the Technical Assistance Manual for the ADA (1992) states that a test to determine an individual's blood alcohol content is a medical examination and subject to the ADA's restrictions on such examinations. Accordingly, if an employer uses a blood test to determine alcohol use, the employer should administer the test only after a conditional offer of employment is made. Moreover, since a medical examination, under the ADA, may be administered when it is job-related and consistent with a business necessity, the most conservative course of action would be for employers to conduct only post-offer and reasonable cause blood tests for alcohol.

The ADA is ambiguous as to whether Breathalyzer tests or other less invasive methods of determining alcohol use will be considered medical examinations and restricted in the same manner as blood tests. However, the ADA does not interfere with preemployment or post-employment alcohol tests conducted pursuant to the Department of Transportation regulations. The Department of Transportation has implemented regulations requiring random alcohol testing of individuals in safety-sensitive positions.

Medical Examination of Current Employees: The ADA limits the examinations of current employees. After an individual is hired, an employer may not require a medical examination and may not inquire as to whether an employee has a disability and, if so, its nature or severity, unless the examination is job-related and consistent with business necessity (*42 U.S.C. 12112(c)(4)(B)*). However, an employer may inquire about an employee's ability to perform job-related functions (*29 C.F.R. 1630.14(c)*).

False Positive Test Results: An individual who is disciplined on the basis of a false positive test result likely can assert a cause of action under the ADA. Therefore, employers should be particularly concerned with the accuracy and reliability of their drug testing procedures to avoid false positive results. Any drug or alcohol testing should comply with applicable federal, state and local laws or regulations regarding quality control.

Title VII of the Civil Rights Act of 1964 (Title VII). This Act prohibits employers, both public and private, from discriminating against employees because of race, color, religion, sex, or national origin (*42 U.S.C.A. 2000e-2-17*, 1982). Thus, an employment practice that has a disparate impact on a protected minority group may violate the Act. Therefore, a drug or alcohol testing program that has a discriminatory impact on a protected group may give rise to a cause of action against an employer under Title VII.

In *Chaney v. Southern Railway Co.* (1988), the court ordered reconsideration of an employee's claim that the employer's sole reliance on the seemingly unreliable EMIT drug test had a discriminatory impact on African-American employees. The court stressed that if the EMIT test, in fact, has a substantial adverse impact on a protected group, the employer must show that use of a particular drug test is a business necessity. Even if drug and alcohol testing has a disparate impact on a protected group, the business necessity defense is ordinarily available.

National Labor Relations Act. The National Labor Relations Board has determined that the drug and alcohol testing of current employees is a mandatory subject of bargaining.

IMPLEMENTATION AND ENFORCEMENT OF POLICIES

The formulation and implementation of a comprehensive drug and alcohol abuse policy is a useful means of defining and correcting problems that might exist in order to maintain a productive workforce. It is essential that an employer design a drug and alcohol abuse policy that fits the company's specific needs. The company should seek input from a variety of sources about its need to conduct substance abuse testing. An employer also should consider federal drug testing requirements and potential tort liability because of drug-related accidents in the workplace. Ultimately, the employer should determine what testing method best addresses the substance abuse problem in the company's workforce, choosing from among reasonable suspicion testing, post-accident testing, and random testing.

The employer's substance abuse policy should state, in writing, what conduct is prohibited on company property and during working hours, including trafficking, possession, use, being under the influence, and presence in one's system of a detectable amount of alcohol or an illegal drug. Further, the employer should indicate what disciplinary action will be taken against employees who violate the policy, while also discussing exemptions for over-the-counter and prescription medication. The policy should provide that an employee's refusal to submit to a test or search may result in termination of employment for violations of the policy and insubordination; it also should state the potential consequences, including termination, for positive test results.

An employer should communicate the new policy and program to all current employees well in advance of implementation. Employees should sign a statement, to be maintained in their personnel files, verifying that they have received, read, understand and will abide by the policy. The policy also should be included in the company's employee handbook.

Thereafter, employee questions should be handled confidentially. It also is vital for an employer to communicate information about a specific employee's drug or alcohol test, and any related investigation and discipline, only to those individuals who "need to know" the information as part of their job function. Additionally, information about suspected drug or alcohol abuse should be placed in locked files separate from routine personnel files or medical files.

Supervisors should receive extensive training on the company's substance abuse policy, the physical appearance of various illegal drugs, and the physical and psychological symptoms of an individual under the influence of alcohol or drugs. Employers should educate supervisors about the importance of developing and articulating performance standards; assessing performance against those standards; and, if necessary, disciplining employees for poor work performance. If an employee is suspected of being under the influence of alcohol or drugs, two or more supervisors should observe the employee, if possible.

Before an applicant or employee is tested, the individual should sign a new consent form, under no coercion, authorizing the test and communication of the test results to the company. Consent obtained far in advance of testing may not be valid, especially for public employees. Upon testing, chain of custody procedures should be followed to avoid legal challenges to the identity of the tested sample. Guidelines should be established to assure that an employee suspected of being under the influence of drugs or alcohol is removed from the job, and safe transportation to the testing facility and the employee's home should be provided by the employer.

ACKNOWLEDGMENT: The authors thank John Fay, author of Drug Testing *(Butterworth-Heinemann) for his contributions to this chapter.*

REFERENCES

AFGE, Local 1616 vs. Thornburgh, 713 F.Supp. 359 (N.D. Cal. 1989) [INS employees successfully enjoined random and post-accident testing components of drug testing program].

Alvarado v. Washington Pub. Power Supply Sys., 111 Wash.2d 424, 759 P.2d 427, cert. denied, 490 U.S. 1004 (1989) [Washington Public Power Supply System did not violate Fourth Amendment by requiring applicants for repair jobs to pass pre-employment drug tests to obtain access to the plant's secured areas].

Americans with Disabilities Act, 41 U.S.C. 12114(d)(2); 29 C.F.R. 1630(c) [the Equal Employment Opportunity Commission maintains that the ADA is neutral with respect to employee and applicant drug tests].

Anonymous (1990). *The Drug Free Workplace: A MAPI Progress Report*, February.

Ashland Oil, Inc., 89 L.A. 795, 798 (1987) (Flanagan, Arb.) [management has the right to establish reasonable rules when its legitimate concern is on-the-job safety resulting from off-duty use of drugs].

Bagby v. General Motors Corp., 976 F.2d 919 (5th Cir. 1992) [employer's state law claims for defamation and intention infliction of emotional distress were preempted by Labor Management Relations Act].

Bangert v. Hodel, 705 F. Supp. 643 (D.D.C. 1989) [Interior Department enjoined from randomly testing employees holding "sensitive" jobs].

Burka v. New York City Transit Authority, 680 F. Supp. 590 (S.D.N.Y. 1988).

Bushell v. Dean, 781 S.W.2d 652 (Tex. App.—Austin, 1989), reversed on other grounds (per curiam), 803 S.W.2d 711 (1991).

Carr AR (1989). A special news report on people and their jobs. *The Wall Street Journal* April 11.

Chaney v. Southern Railway Co., 847 F.2d 718 (11th Cir. 1988).

Concrete Pipe Prods. Co., 87 L.A. 601, 605 (Caraway, Arb.).

Copeland v. Philadelphia Police Dept., 840 F.2d 1139, cert. denied, 109 S. Ct. 1636 (1989) [compulsory urinalysis examination of officer was supported by reasonable suspicion that he was an illegal drug user and had been afforded substantive and procedural due process].

Davis v. Bucher, 451 F.Supp. 791, 796 (E.D. Pa. 1978).

Elkouri F & Elkouri EA (1985). *How Arbitration Works, 4th Ed.* Washington, DC: BNA, 414–436.

Equal Employment Opportunity Commission (1992). *EEOC Technical Assistance Manual on the Employ-*

ment Provisions of the ADA, VIII–7. Washington, DC: U.S. Government Printing Office.

Everett v. Napper, 833 F.2d 1507 (11th Cir. 1987) [city had reason to suspect that a fire fighter might be using illegal drugs, and could order him to submit to urinalysis and terminate him for refusal to comply].

General Dynamics Corp., 91 L.A. 539 (1988) (Marcus, Arb.) [where employee's agitation over work requirement to maintain certain tools could have caused certain symptoms such as loud voice, anger, raised blood pressure, and where evidence of alcohol on employee's breath was disputed, and where employee's physical movements and control were not impaired, no just cause for termination existed].

Gulf Construction Co. v. Mott, 442 S.W.2d 778, 784–785 (Tex. Civ. App.—Houston [14th Dist.] 1969, no writ).

Houston Belt & Terminal Ry. Co. v. Wherry, 548 S.W.2d 743 (Tex. Civ. App.—Houston [1st Dist.] 1976, writ ref's n.r.e.), cert. denied, 434 U.S. 962 (1977).

Houston Lighting & Power Co., 87 L.A. 478, 483 (1986) (Howell, Arb.) [a work rule should reasonably relate to a legitimate objective of management].

International Brotherhood of Teamsters, Chauffeurs v. Department of Transportation, et al., 932 F.2d 1292 (D.C. Cir. 1991) [regulations calling for random, biennial, pre-employment and post-accident testing of urine samples of truck drivers did not violate Fourth Amendment freedom from search and seizure].

International Brotherhood of Teamsters, Local 19 v. Southwest Airlines Co., 875 F.2d 1129 (5th Cir. 1989) [insufficient showing of irreparable harm in regard to employers' unilateral enactment of drug testing policy to warrant an injunction].

Johnson Bateman Co., 295 N.L.R.B. 26 (1989) [union did not waive right to contest employer's drug testing program by agreeing to management rights clause in current contract or by acquiescing to employer's earlier testing of job applicants].

Minneapolis Star Tribune, 295 N.L.R.B. 63 (1989).

National Football League Players Association v. N.L.R.B., 503 F.2d 12 (8th Cir. 1974) [employee misconduct rules].

National Treasury Employees Union v. Von Raab, 489 U.S. 656 109 S. Ct., 103 L.E.2d 685 1384 (1989) [U.S. Customs Service's drug testing program was subject to Fourth Amendment's reasonableness requirement; however, a warrant was not needed after balancing the individual's privacy expectations with the government's interests to determine whether it is impractical to require a warrant or some level of individualized suspicion in the particular context].

Niagra Hooker Employee's Union v. Occidental Chemical Corp., 935 F.2d 1370 (2nd Cir. 1991).

N.L.R.B. v. Gulf Power Co., 384 F.2d 822 (5th Cir. 1967) [safety rule].

North County Transit District, 89 L.A. 768 (1987) (Caraway, Arb.).

O'Brian v. Papa Gino of America, Inc., 780 F.2d 1067 (1st Cir. 1986) [employer's investigative techniques would be highly offensive to a reasonable person and were an invasion of plaintiff's privacy].

Oil, Chemical and Atomic Workers, 88-1 Lab. Arb. Awards (CCH) Par. 8084, at p. 3401 (January 11, 1988) [management has the fundamental right to unilaterally establish reasonable work rules not inconsistent with the law or the collective bargaining agreement].

Poly Tech, Inc., 91 L.A. 512 (1988) (Gunderson, Arb.) [where employer failed to prove that can contained beer, and where employee denied drinking beer on the premises, and where employee had a good employment record for eight years, discharge was not for good cause].

Skinner v. Railway Labor Executives' Association, 489 U.S. 602, 109 S. Ct. 1402, 103 L.E.2d 639 (1989) [Fourth Amendment was applicable to drug and alcohol testing of railroad employees, although railroad was a private company, because testing was mandated by federal regulations; yet, drug and alcohol tests, mandated or authorized by the regulations, were reasonable under the Fourth Amendment. Privacy intrusion was lessened by the fact that the regulations provided for the confidentiality of information obtained as a result of drug testing.].

SmithKline Beecham (1990). *The Drug Free Workplace Report*. Philadelphia, PA: SmithKline Beecham.

Southwestern Bell Telephone Co. v. Dixon, 575 S.W.2d 596 (Tex. Civ. App.—San Antonio 1978, writ dismissed w.o.j.) [company has qualified privilege to make inquiries and conduct investigations about suspected employee wrongdoing, provided it is done without malice].

Texas City Ref. Inc., 89 L.A. 1159, 1162 (Milentz, Arb.) [one year of retesting with counseling after a positive random test upheld].

Transportation Institute v. U.S. Coast Guard, 727 F.Supp. 648 (D.D.C. 1989) [court struck down Coast Guard's random drug testing provisions as being overly broad].

Tribune Co., 93 L.A. (1986) (McKay, Arb).

Vulcan Materials Co., 90 L.A. 1161 (1988) (Caraway, Arb.).

CHAPTER 2

The Role of the Medical Review Officer

Donald Ian Macdonald, M.D., FASAM
Robert L. DuPont, M.D., FASAM

Contractual Issues
Laboratory Selection
Initiating the Medical Review Process
Interpreting Test Results
Issues in Specimen Collection
Reporting Results
The Future of Workplace Programs

Medical review of workplace drug tests brings new challenge and opportunity to the field of addiction medicine. Thousands of physicians who act as medical review officers (MROs) are convinced that the expertise they offer makes drug-free workplace programs more effective and that such programs are deterrents to casual drug use and of benefit to those workers with alcohol or other drug problems who are detected and referred to treatment earlier in the course of their disease than they otherwise would be.

A 1986 Presidential Executive Order directed the Department of Health and Human Services (HHS) to develop and publish scientific and technical guidelines for workplace drug testing of federal employees (U.S. Department of Health and Human Services, 1988). These guidelines significantly increased public acceptance of drug testing by establishing rigid certification procedures for laboratories and placing final responsibility for the review of drug tests with a physician—called, for the first time, an MRO. The field grew dramatically when, in late 1989, the federal Department of Transportation (DOT) mandated widespread testing of transportation workers in safety-sensitive positions (U.S. Department of Transportation, 1989) and included the requirement for medical review. Further growth occurred as the courts and other government agencies and private employers acknowledged the protection offered by the expertise of a physician and as more and more employers added MROs to their testing programs, even when not required to do so.

There are significant variations in the rules under which MROs function, even within DOT programs. In non-mandated programs, the variations may be even greater, reflecting federal rules as well as any relevant state or municipal rules. In general, the programs that are most closely modeled after the federal guidelines are the safest legally because of their success in withstanding court challenges.

In the original regulations promulgated by the Department of Health and Human Services (1988), the only qualifications specified for MROs specified are that the MRO must be a "licensed physician with a knowledge of substance abuse disorders." However, it quickly became apparent that additional qualifications would be needed. The American Society of Addiction Medicine and other organizations responded to this need by offering education and certification programs to prepare physicians for this new field of activity. As the laws and regulations governing workplace drug testing change and as drug-using individuals devise ever-changing ways to "beat" the testing system, the practicing MRO must find a way to keep his or her knowledge up to date. For this purpose, periodic attendance at training sessions and subscription to one or more of the MRO update services is recommended.

CONTRACTUAL ISSUES

Before beginning the process of medical review, the MRO should have a written contract with the employer, spelling out in detail the services to be provided. Medical review is only one of many components of a drug-free workplace program and the successful MRO will either provide the other components or be able to direct the client to them. Organizations called third-party administrators (TPAs) provide overall program management, policy review, educational materials, training programs, and random sampling of employees, and contract out for laboratory, MRO, and collection services. MROs may function as TPAs, but must be cautious of the regulations that prohibit them from having a financial relationship with the laboratories whose tests they review (U.S. Department of Transportation, 1989).

LABORATORY SELECTION

It is strongly recommended that MROs work only with laboratories that have been certified under the HHS rules requiring academic credentials, regular inspections, and satisfactory performance on the testing of regularly submitted blind proficiency specimens (DuPont, 1989, 1990). Before a test may be called positive, its designated analyte has to be positive both by an approved immunoassay and by confirmation with gas chromatography/mass spectrometry (GC/MS). The GC/MS is so specific that some have called it a chemical fingerprint. Screening tests are less specific than GC/MS and may be positive on the basis of compounds that are in some way chemically similar to the sought after analytes. HHS has established testing cut-off levels, below which an analyte could be present but not reportable, to discount the possibility of drug tests be read as positive in individuals who may have passively inhaled marijuana or cocaine.

The HHS certification program includes only the so-called "NIDA Five" drugs (cocaine, marijuana, PCP, amphetamines, and opiates) and does not include certification for the testing of additional drugs, such as benzodiazepines and barbiturates, which often are included in non-federally mandated testing panels.

On-site testing kits are widely advertised and sold, but are not allowed under DOT or HHS rules, principally because they are screening tests only and may not confirm. When an individual who screens positive for amphetamines because of a non-prescription cold medicine is held under suspicion, even temporarily, harm is done. Unlike breath alcohol determinations, which have some direct correlation with impairment, positive urine drug screens, even when confirmed, do not. In recognition of this, HHS and DOT programs have been set up to deter drug use and are not well suited for determining fitness for duty on any given day. On the other hand, the Nuclear Regulatory Commission, with higher safety requirements, does use on-site screening as a condition of work.

INITIATING THE MEDICAL REVIEW PROCESS

The medical review process begins when the MRO receives a drug test result from a laboratory and ends when he or she reports the result. The specific duties, however, vary according to the status of the test result.

Negative Results. For negative test results, the MRO's role is administrative only and is limited to inspection of the chain of custody forms from the laboratory and from the collection sites, with particular attention to proper signatures and comments.

Indeterminate Results. Some tests are not positive, but are in some way suspicious (such as those involving dilute specimens or specimens that the laboratory finds unsuitable for testing). Such tests require MRO review and comment.

Positive Results. The review of positive drug test results is the principal MRO function. Before reporting a result as positive, the MRO should be satisfied that: (1) the correct specimen was tested (and not somehow mixed up with someone else's, for example); (2) the laboratory correctly followed chain-of-custody procedures and accurately performed the necessary analyses; and (3) there was no legitimate medical explanation for the positive test result. To resolve these questions, the MRO must understand forensic collection and chain-of-custody procedures, know what the toxicology laboratory does, and be familiar with the relevant laws and regulations. Each employee who has a laboratory-confirmed positive test must be interviewed and the relevant paperwork from the laboratory and collection sites reviewed. During this review, the MRO may find it necessary to speak with the "communicator" (the employer's designated representative), with the individual who collected the urine, with the laboratory personnel, and/or with the employee's physician or pharmacy. Additional laboratory testing may be required, possibly including reanalysis of the specimen.

Recordkeeping: When a positive test result arrives, a chart should be prepared to track all of the relevant paperwork and notes of all MRO interactions with the employee and others. Because the information on this chart may be subpoenaed, the MRO should treat it with at least as much care as is used in a clinical chart. Under federal testing programs, the MRO is required to keep records of all positive tests for five years. In practice, this is a good rule for unregulated programs as well. Many MROs keep the records even longer.

The MRO Interview: As soon as the MRO has obtained the worker's phone number from the collection site paperwork or from the company communicator, a call to the donor is placed, preferably at home. (If, after a reasonable effort by the MRO and the company to find the employee, no contact is made within 14 days, the MRO should call the test positive. If the employee is reached but fails to return the phone call within five days, the test may be called positive.) When contact is made, the MRO should identify himself or herself and tell the individual that the call concerns a drug test result. The donor then should be asked to provide further identification by giving the ID number (usually the Social Security number) that was placed on the collection site paperwork. When this is satisfactory, the donor should be told—in what some have called a "Miranda notification"— that, under some circumstances, what is learned in the course of the interview may have to be reported to the employer or a government agency.

If the donor is willing to proceed with the interview, the MRO then should relay the test result and make note of the individual's reaction or lack of reaction to the news.

INTERPRETATION OF TEST RESULTS

For four of the "NIDA Five" drugs (the exception being PCP), there may be a legitimate medical explanation for a positive test result (Hawks & Chiang, 1986). To properly assess this possibility, the MRO should develop, use, and document a standard protocol for positive test results with each class of drugs. When a possible explanation involving medical use is suggested, the MRO should secure documentation in the form of a conversation with the prescribing physician or pharmacy, with written follow-up for the record.

Alcohol. Breathalyzer alcohol testing has been mandated by DOT (Anonymous, n.d.[d]) for most of the individuals who fall under the drug testing rules. DOT does not require medical review of these tests, reasoning that there is no legitimate medical explanation for having a level of 0.04 while on duty. DOT does not accept alcohol tolerance as a defense against actions under these rules.

Marijuana. Marinol®, a synthetic form of delta-9-THC, is legally prescribed for nausea related to chemotherapy and for appetite stimulation in AIDS. Either of these indications may be a legitimate medical explanation for a positive test. So too is marijuana use that has been court-approved for the treatment of glaucoma. The enactment of Propositions 215 in California and 200 in Arizona in November 1996, calling for legal use of marijuana for a much wider set of medical circumstances, may complicate the MRO's decision in private industry. In federal testing programs, however, DOT and HHS have advised MROs not to consider use under these propositions as legitimate medical use and therefore not to consider such use reason to reverse a positive test result for cannibinoids (Interagency Coordination Group, 1997).

Marijuana, because of its lipid solubility, may remain in the body for extended periods of time, but it will not remain at levels above the cut-off for very long. It has been shown that, at the HHS-recommended screening cut-off level of 50 ng/mL, mean detection time after a single high-dose marijuana cigarette is less than two days (Interagency Coordination Group, 1997). In the chronic user, higher levels have been reported for as long as 70 days but, in most cases, allowing any more than a month for this possibility is generous. In any case, this explanation does not change the test result.

The employee may try to convince the MRO that the reason for the positive test was marijuana smoked years ago or exposure to marijuana smoked by a friend or co-worker. In establishing its guidelines, HHS set its testing cut-off levels high enough to discount both of these possibilities. Subsequent studies showing that passive exposure accounts for only very low urine levels of cannabinoids allowed HHS to lower the cut-off levels from those written into its initial guidelines. Although positive tests may result from eating marijuana brownies, such ingestion, even if proven, is not considered legitimate medical use or a reason to reverse a positive test report. (The same is true of hemp cookies and a confection called "Seedie Sweeties.")

Cocaine. Cocaine is never prescribed but may be legally used by emergency physicians as a topical anesthetic in a compound called TAC (tetracaine, adrenalin, and cocaine) or by ophthalmologists, dentists, and ENT physicians as a 1% to 4% solution. The MRO should ask the donor who tests positive for cocaine if he or she has recently been seen by a doctor, dentist, or in an emergency room. If the answer is yes, the MRO should ask about procedures that might have required local anesthesia. If a history of possible use within two to three days of the drug test is obtained, the donor should be asked to have the treating physician call the MRO or send a copy of the pertinent medical record.

The names of many drugs with anesthetic properties incorporate the "-caine" suffix (such as lidocaine and procaine), but none of them test positive for benzoyl ecognine, the metabolite of cocaine that is monitored in the urine.

Amphetamines. A number of widely used over-the-counter medications, such as pseudoephedrine and phenylpropanolamine, have chemical structures similar to the amphetamines and may test positive on the screening test, but only amphetamine and methamphetamine and drugs that metabolize to them will be confirmed by the GC/MS test.

The MRO should be aware of the long list of medications that do result in positive GC/MS confirmation, including those that contain amphetamine (e.g., Dexedrine®) and methamphetamine (Desoxyn®) and those that the body breaks down to methamphetamine (e.g., Benzphetamine® and Selegiline®) and amphetamine (e.g., Amphetaminil®). This list is only partial and does not include amphetamine-containing prescriptions from Mexico and other countries.

Among non-prescription medications, only the Vicks nasal inhaler causes a GC/MS confirmed positive test. Further laboratory analysis can distinguish Vicks from the form of methamphetamine with high abuse potential. (Amphetamines come in two forms, with those that refract light to the right—the most psychoactive forms—called "dextro" or "d-forms." The methamphetamine in Vicks refracts to the left and is called "levo" or "l-methamphetamine." Some MROs routinely request and some laboratories routinely perform d-l (chiral) separations on all tests that are positive for methamphetamine. If less than 80% l-methamphetamine is present, the MRO cannot accept that the Vicks inhaler caused the positive result and must call the test positive (U.S. Department of Transportation, 1997a).

Opiates. Interpretation of opiate positives can be confused by the ingestion of poppy seeds and poppy seed pastes, because they are products of the same plants that yield morphine and codeine. Because of this possibility, there is an HHS requirement that before an opiate positive may be reported to the employer, the MRO must find clinical evidence of inappropriate use in addition to having a positive drug test (U.S. Department of Health and Human Services, 1988). The only exception is in cases in which the laboratory is able to identify the heroin metabolite, 6-monoacetylmorphine (also called 6-AM, 6-MAM, and MAM). Much of the problem with interpretation of poppy seed ingestion and confusion about how to handle prescription medications will be avoided when HHS implements it proposed change that will raise the opiate cut-off levels to 2,000 nanograms/ml.

Although documentation of legitimate prescriptions usually is sought and frequently obtained, the donor is not required to prove legitimate prescription use. Because federal programs test only for morphine and codeine, prescriptions for other opiates such as hydrocodone, Dilaudid®, and hydromorphone, which do not contain or metabolize to morphine or codeine, cannot explain the positive test. Physical examination of individuals who test positive for opiates has largely been abandoned by MROs because only rarely did they yield sufficient evidence of current use. For "evidence," the MRO often must rely on the history given by the donor; this may, but rarely does, include an admission of heroin use.

Most often the clinical evidence comes as an admission of taking a drug prescribed for another. DOT would like MROs to consider such an admission sufficient evidence of "inappropriate use," but some MROs disagree. Part of their concern involves the severity of the assessed penalty (i.e., job loss) relative to the gravity of the offense, their belief that they had not adequately warned the worker against self-incrimination, and that such use is not what the program was designed to deter. A compromise position (which usually requires a change in company policy) is to call the test result positive but to expedite a speedy assessment and return to work.

Other Drugs. Although the federal laboratory certification program and testing are limited to the "NIDA Five" (phencyclidine [PCP], marijuana, cocaine, amphetamines, and opiates), MROs often are asked to review drug tests that are positive for a variety of other compounds, the yield for which is low in terms of reportable abuse. Most often these panels include testing for the benzodiazepines or barbiturates. MROs who express concern about prescription drug abuse must recognize that most workplace testing programs were set up to deter the use of "street" drugs and accept the fact that such programs are not effective at dealing with the problem of prescription abuse.

If a legitimate medical explanation is found and documented, the test should be reported to the employer as a negative test.

Foreign Medications. The DOT policy on foreign medications (Huestis, Mitchell & Cone, 1995) allows reversal of a positive drug test for medications that were imported for personal use consistent with an indicated medical condition, provided there is adequate documentation of foreign travel and verification of a legal prescription or evidence of nonprescription status in the country of issue.

See Table 1 for the window of detection for some commonly abused drugs other than alcohol.

Safety Concerns. Even though there may be a legitimate medical explanation for a drug test result, the MRO may be concerned about use of the drug by an individual who works in a safety-sensitive position. To deal with this possibility, DOT regulations specify that "the MRO *may* disclose such information to the employer, a DOT agency or other Federal safety agency, or a physician responsible for determining the medical qualification of the employee under an applicable DOT agency regulation, as applicable, only if, . . . in the MRO's reasonable medical judgment, . . . the information indicates that continued performance by the employee of his or her safety-sensitive function could pose a significant safety risk" (U.S. Department of Health and Human Services, 1988). Under this provision, an MRO might reverse a positive test result when there is a legitimate prescription for amphetamine, but may contact the employer to express his or her concern about the narcolepsy for which the amphetamine was prescribed.

ISSUES IN SPECIMEN COLLECTION

Although federal guidelines minimize the MRO's responsibility in this area, the MRO is required to check each collection form for signature and collector remarks. In addition to this administrative function, the MRO should satisfy himself or herself that, in cases involving positive test results, the chain-of custody was not broken. The MRO also should be prepared to deal with problems of "shy bladder," and with issues of dilution, substitution, and adulteration.

Chain of Custody. The employee being tested should not lose sight of his or her specimen from the moment the cup is filled until the specimen is securely and forensically sealed. For each DOT collection, a DOT-approved printed form should be used to identify the sample, with an identifying number

TABLE 1. Approximate Duration of Detectability of Selected Drugs in Urine

Drug	Approximate Duration of Detectability*	Limits of Sensitivity of Analytic Techniques (μmo-iL)
Amphetamine	48 h	0.5 μg/mL
Methamphetamine	48 h	0.5μg/mL
Barbiturates		
Short Acting	24 h	
Hexobarbital		1.0μg/mL
Pentobarbital		0.5μg/mL
Secobarbital		0.5μg/mL
Thiamylal		1.0μg/mL
Intermediate Acting	48-72 h	
Amobarbital		1.0μg/mL
Aprobarbital		1.5μg/mL
Butabarbital		0.5μg/mL
Butalbital		1.5μg/mL
Long Acting	≥7 d	
Barbital		5.0μg/mL
Phenobarbital		1.0μg/mL
Benzodiazepines	3 d†	1.0μg/mL
Cocaine metabolites	2-3 d	
Benzoylecgonine		0.5μg/mL
Ecgonine methyl ester		1.0μg/mL
Methadone	≈3 d	
1,5-Dimethyl-3, 3-diphenyl -2-pyrrolidine(metabolite of methadone)		0.5μg/mL
Codeine	48 h	0.5μg/mL
Morphine		1.0μg/mL
Propoxyphene	6-48 h	0.5μg/mL
Norpropoxyphene		1.5μg/mL
Cannabinoids (11-nor-Δ9-tetra-hydrocannabinol-9-carboxylic acid)	3d,‡5d,§ 10d,‖ 21-27d¶	20μg/mL
Methaqualone	≥7 d	1.0μg/mL
Phencyclidine	≈8 d	0.5μg/mL

*Interpretation of the duration of detectability must take into account many variables, such as drug metabolism and half life, subject's physical condition, fluid balance and state of hydration and route and frequency of ingestion. These are general guidelines only.

† Using therapeutic dosages
‡ Single use
§ Moderate smoker (4 times/wk)
‖ Heavy smoker (smoking daily)
¶ Chronic heavy smoker.

Source: American Academy of Pediatrics and Center for Advanced Health Studies (1988). *Substance Abuse: A Guide for Health Professionals.* Elk Grove Village, IL: American Academy of Pediatrics, 55. Reprinted by permission of the publisher.

unique to that form and with seven or eight copies attached.

The specimen bottle should be sealed with tamper-evident tape that is dated by the collector and that contains the unique number from the individual's collection site form, which should be initialed by the sample donor. In some testing programs, mandated and otherwise, collection of a split specimen is required. A split specimen is a single-void specimen that has been divided into two bottles, each forensically identified and sealed, and sent together to the laboratory (U.S. Department of Transportation, Office of Drug Enforcement and Program Compliance, 1995). During its progress through the laboratory, strict chain-of-custody procedures continue and are carefully documented.

Privacy Issues. Because drug users continually seek ways to beat the drug testing system, observed collections are a part of testing programs for the military and in the criminal justice and treatment systems. To increase the acceptance of testing programs in the civilian workplace, collections are not routinely observed but, to provide the system with some protection, there have been "privacy trade-off" measures. Among these are turning off the water supply to the area of the collection, adding blueing to the water in the commode, and taking the temperature of the freshly voided urine specimen.

"Shy Bladder": The DOT rules (1994a) state that an employee who does not produce an adequate volume of urine may be given fluids in an amount not to exceed 40 ounces and be given up to three hours to complete the collection. For current employees (but not for pre-employment donors) who are unable to provide an adequate specimen within three hours, it is the employer's responsibility to see that a medical evaluation is performed by an evaluator of the employer's choosing. The MRO is responsible for making the final report to the employer, based on his or her own evaluation or a copy of the evaluation by another physician. The consequences of an unexplained "shy bladder" are the same as the consequences of a "refusal to test," which in most cases is the same as the consequences of a positive test result.

DOT rules limit acceptable medical explanations for failure to provide a specimen to (1) physiological causes (e.g., urinary system dysfunction) and (2) pre-existing and documented psychological conditions (i.e., one designated by the *Diagnostic and Statistical Manual of Mental Disorders, 4th Ed.* (*DSM-IV*; American Psychiatric Association, 1994). Assertions of "situational anxiety" and dehydration are considered unverifiable and not an acceptable medical explanation.

Dilution, Substitution, or Adulteration. The tabloid *High Times* and other drug-oriented publications keep users informed as to ways to escape detection in drug tests. As solutions to one strategy emerge, new strategies appear and are marketed.

Dilution of the Specimen: One of the most commonly used ways to avoid detection involves diluting the urine so that the concentration of the analyte falls below the cut-off level. Because it is very difficult to maintain the temperature of a specimen that is substituted for the user's own urine or to maintain the temperature of a specimen to which water has been added, the temperature of each specimen should be measured within four minutes of the time of void. If the temperature falls outside the 90 degree to 100 degree range, a note should be made on the chain-of-custody form and the individual's body temperature (oral or ear) taken. If the body temperature is not within 1.8 degrees Fahrenheit of the specimen, an observed collection should be obtained immediately. Both the first and second specimens should be sent to the laboratory for analysis.

While temperature measurement will detect the specimen to which water has been added at the collection site, the most commonly used way to dilute the specimen is by drinking a large quantity of fluids. Dilute specimens produced in this fashion are of normal temperature and can be reported by the laboratory as dilute if they have a specific gravity below 1.003 and a creatinine of less than 0.2 Gm/dL. Although many dilute specimens represent attempts to beat the test, it is important to exercise judgment in their interpretation because most of them contain no measurable amount of drug. The DOT rules (1989) allow for an observed collection on the next occasion at which such individuals are tested, but they do not allow the employer to send the individual back for another test on the basis of the dilute urine. In either case, the provision to observe was designed to deal with the individual who adds water to his specimen and does not deal with the individual who drinks water on the way to the collection site. Some combination of escorting an individual to the site and restricting fluids on the way to the site is recommended.

Adulteration of the Specimen: When attempts to adulterate are noted by the collector, an observed collection should be performed immediately after reviewing the circumstances with the collector's supervisor, the employer, or the MRO. Some, but not all, adulterated specimens interfere with the laboratory's ability to conduct the usual screening immunoassays. When a laboratory reports that a specimen is "unsuitable for testing," the MRO should call the laboratory director to get the director's advice as to how best to proceed.

Urinaid®, the trade name for glutaraldehyde, was a popular additive that increased the light absorbency of the most commonly used screening test, the enzyme multiplied immunoassay (EMIT®), and made the test unreadable. Urinaid became less popular when it was discovered that alternate screening immunoassay tests could be used and that glutaraldehyde could be detected by GC/MS. It was quickly replaced by "MaryJane Superclean 13," which turned out to be clear detergent and was detected by its ability to make suds. Next was "Klear," which is probably potassium nitrite and which interferes with the GC/MS. DOT rules allow for obtaining an observed collection sample from anyone who has a specimen that is unsuitable for testing.

Flaws in the Collection Process. When the MRO finds evidence of possible flaws in the collection process, he or she should report them to the employer. Flaws such as no blue dye in the commode or requiring an individual to disrobe for collection are important, but do not affect the chain of custody nor the validity of a positive test.

At the time of the first interview with the donor, the MRO should ask about the collection procedure, to ascertain whether the donor handed his or her specimen to the attendant and whether the attendant sealed the package in the presence of the donor and had the donor initial the sealed package. Frequently, the donor will not recall these details. Grounds for cancellation exist if the MRO is told that a donor's unsealed specimen was placed on a counter on which there were other unsealed specimens, and that the donor was dismissed before the specimen was sealed. Other grounds for cancellation might include sending the donor home or to the waiting room while the collector sealed the specimen package, or that the donor was unable to fill the specimen bottle on first effort and over the course of time added urine to the original bottle. In each of these cases, the MRO should call the collector and check the story. If the collector denies the story and is able to convince the MRO of his or her competence and experience, the MRO would notify the client that the collection has been questioned, but sounds defensible. If, on the other hand, the MRO has a reasonable doubt as to whether the specimen could have been switched, he or she should discuss the problem with the employer. In DOT testing, these collection site errors are not reason to cancel the test but, for non-DOT specimens, the MRO working with the employer may decide to cancel the test because of sufficient doubt about its validity and legal defensibility.

Re-analysis of Results. During the course of an interview with a donor, the MRO may notify the individual that the specimen or "split" specimen is being kept at the laboratory and may be shipped to another laboratory for re-analysis if the donor requests re-analysis within 72 hours. There is no standard as to who pays for this; however, for DOT tests, the MRO must honor the request and make payment the employer's responsibility. The specimen sent to the second laboratory is sent directly to GC/MS without screening and there is no cut-off level other than the laboratory's scientific limit of detection. If the initial result is confirmed, there is no action except notification of the donor and the employer. If it is not confirmed, both the original and the re-analysis are canceled and DOT is notified. During the time that the re-analysis is being processed, the donor may not occupy a safety-sensitive position.

REPORTING RESULTS

At the conclusion of an interview with an employee whose urine has tested positive for drugs, the MRO notifies the donor of the outcome of the drug test. The findings may be:

- *Negative* (including reversals on the basis of legitimate medical explanations);
- *Positive* (including positives confirmed on re-analysis);
- *Canceled*, on the basis of a specified administrative error in the chain of custody, with failure to re-confirm on re-analysis;
- *Unsuitable for testing* for various reasons; or
- *Adulterated*, in cases in which the laboratory is able to confirm the presence of a named adulterant.

These findings are promptly reported to the employer.

THE FUTURE OF WORKPLACE PROGRAMS

The contemporary understanding of alcohol and drug abuse in the workplace is rooted in the new understanding of addiction as a biopsychosocial disease, with a renewed emphasis on brain biology (Nahas & Burks, 1997; DuPont, 1997). As a consequence, MRO practice is challenging and constantly changing, providing physicians who specialize in addiction medicine with an additional arena in which to exercise their expertise and interest.

The major challenge for the future of addiction prevention and treatment in the workplace is to develop comprehensive programs that are compassionate as well as tough. These programs must operate in the public interest in ways that respect not only the interests of all involved, but also the dignity of workers and their families, including the dignity of persons with addictive disorders.

In a free and open society, many hurdles faced by workplace alcohol and drug programs will not be dealt with easily, but they must be addressed if the workplace programs are to achieve their full life-saving potential.

REFERENCES

American Correctional Association and Institute for Behavior and Health, Inc. (1991). *Monograph: Drug Testing of Juvenile Detainees.* Washington, DC: Office of Juvenile Justice and Delinquency Prevention, Office of Justice Programs, U.S. Department of Justice.

American Psychiatric Association (1994). *Diagnostic and Statistical Manual of Mental Disorders, 4th Ed.* Washington, DC: American Psychiatric Press.

Anonymous (1998). Scientists combat effects of popular adulterant on workplace testing programs. *Workplace Substance Abuse Advisor* 12(7).

Anonymous (n.d.[a]). An evaluation of preemployment drug testing. *Journal of Applied Psychology* 75:629–639.

Anonymous (n.d. [b]). Medical Review Officer training. *MRO Alert.*

Anonymous (n.d. [c]). *MRO Update.* Arlington Heights, IL: American College of Occupational and Environmental Medicine.

Anonymous (n.d. [d]). *The Medical Review Officer Handbook, Sixth Edition.* Research Triangle Park, NC: Quadrangle Research LLC.

DuPont RL (1989). Drugs in the American workplace: Conflict and opportunity, part II: Controversies in workplace drug use prevention. *Social Pharmacology* 3:147–164.

DuPont RL (1990). Medicines and drug testing in the workplace. *Journal of Psychoactive Drugs* 22:451–459.

DuPont RL (1997). *The Selfish Brain: Learning from Addiction.* Washington, DC: American Psychiatric Press.

Hawks RL & Chiang CN (1986). *Urine Testing for Drugs of Abuse: Research Monograph* 73. Rockville, MD: National Institute on Drug Abuse.

Huestis MA, Mitchell J & Cone EJ (1995). Detection times of marijuana metabolites in urine by immunoassay and GC/MS. *Journal of Analytical Toxicology* October:19.

Interagency Coordination Group (1997). *Action Regarding California Proposition 215 and Arizona Proposition 22.* Washington, DC: Office of National Drug Control Policy, U.S. Department of Justice, Office of Personnel Management & U.S. Department of Health and Human Services.

Nahas GG & Burks TF (1997). *Drug Abuse in the Decade of the Brain.* Amsterdam, The Netherlands: IOS Press.

National Treasury Employees Union v. Von Raab, 489 U.S. 656 (1989).

Schwartz RH (1988). Urine testing in the detection of drugs of abuse. *Archives of Internal Medicine* 148:2407–2412.

Skinner v. Railway Labor Executives' Association, 489 U.S. 602 (1989).

U.S. Department of Health and Human Services (1988). Mandatory guidelines for federal workplace drug testing programs. *Federal Register* 1988;53:11970

U.S. Department of Health and Human Services (1998). Substance Abuse and Mental Health Services Administration, Testing Split (Bottle B) Specimens for Adulterants, March 9.

U.S. Department of Transportation (n.d.). 49 CFR Part 40 Procedures for Transportation Workplace Drug Testing Programs, Section 40.33,i.

U.S. Department of Transportation (1997a). Guidance on Recent Drug Initiatives in California and Arizona, January.

U.S. Department of Transportation (1994a). Limitation on alcohol use by transportation workers. *Federal Register* 1994:59:7302

U.S. Department of Transportation (1996). Procedures for Transportation Workplace Drug and Alcohol Testing Programs; Insufficient Specimens and Other Issues. *Federal Register* 1996:61:37693

U.S. Department of Transportation (1994b). *Urine Specimen Collection Procedures Guidelines for Transportation Workplace Drug Testing Programs.* Washington, DC: Government Printing Office.

U.S. Department of Transportation (1997b). Procedures for Workplace Testing Programs, 49 CFR Part 40, Section 40.25 Procedures (E)(2)(B)(ii), January 10.

U.S. Department of Transportation (1989). Procedures for transportation workplace drug testing programs. *Federal Register* 1989;54:11979

U.S. Department of Transportation, Office of Drug Enforcement and Program Compliance (1995). 49 CFR Part 40 Interpretation, December 14.

CHAPTER 3

Impairment and Recovery in Physicians and Other Health Professionals

G. Douglas Talbott, M.D., FASAM
Karl V. Gallegos, M.D.
Daniel H. Angres, M.D.

Historical Perspective
Prevalence
Etiology
Identification
Intervention
Assessment
Treatment
Aftercare and Monitoring
Outcomes

In the first half of this century, the medical profession slowly and painstakingly acquired a special position in society as providers of health care services. Through a series of strategic efforts, the profession gained autonomy, monopoly and expertise over the practice of medicine (Starr, 1982). Physicians assumed the moral responsibility of caring for their patients, not only by direct care and precept, but also through the example of their own lives and personal conduct. The misuse of alcohol and drugs by a member of the medical profession thus is an occupational, social, and personal problem that demands action to ensure early detection, treatment, and rehabilitation.

The majority of all health consumers are concerned about the effect of alcohol and drug use by their physician on the quality of the care they receive (Harris, 1987). The Florida "sick doctor statute" (Nesbitt, 1970) was a pioneering legislative effort to define the inability to practice medicine with reasonable skill and safety, and to revise the grounds for professional discipline under that state's medical practice act. Addiction to alcohol and other drugs of abuse has been a priority issue for the profession for many years, with organized activity dating to formal initiatives by the American Medical Association (AMA) in the early 1970s (Steindler, 1974). In 1973, the AMA Council on Mental Health adopted a landmark report on "The Sick Physician" (1973), which recommended, first, that state medical societies establish programs or committees devoted to identifying and helping impaired physicians and, second, that the AMA develop model legislation to amend state practice acts so that treatment could be made available in place of punitive disciplinary measures.

Prior to the Council's report, the AMA conducted two national surveys on the subject. One asked state medical societies if they had a committee to deal with physicians who were addicted or psychiatrically impaired: the survey found that only seven states had such committees. The second survey examined disciplinary actions by three state Boards of Medical Examiners. From its results, the Council concluded that little was being done to address the problem of physician impairment.

Extensive information has accumulated over the past two decades regarding the pathologic use of alcohol and other drugs of abuse by physicians (Wright, 1990; Robertson, 1986; American Medical Association, 1996; Centrella, 1994). Organized medicine has carefully and systematically begun to evaluate the extent to which drug addiction, alcoholism, and psychiatric disorders among physicians affect their professional performance. The conceptualization of impaired performance as a medical rather than a legal, moral or ethical problem has led to the development of programs and policies that integrate medical rehabilitation with professional peer review (Watry, Morgan et al., 1996).

This chapter will focus solely on impairment caused by dependence on alcohol and other drugs. The authors will identify assumptions underlying the concept of physician impairment; outline the characteristics of an impaired physician; describe the identification, intervention, treatment, rehabilitation, outcome monitoring of such physicians, and the effectiveness of the treatment methods currently available; present the evolution, progress and policies that link organized concern for sick physicians to social, legal, and political pressures for professional accountability; and examine the practice of medical supervision of problem physicians in terms of its compatibility with professional values and interests.

This review of the impaired physicians' movement is undertaken at a time when the social and cultural components of professional self-governance are undergoing rigorous re-evaluation. The nation's health care system is undergoing rapid and dramatic change, and the coming century promises increasing regulation of all components of patient care, heightened peer review, changes imposed on the practice of medicine by managed care, and the emergence of the capability to micro-monitor financial and professional performance of individual physicians.

HISTORICAL PERSPECTIVE

Before looking forward, however, it is useful to look back to the antecedents of the contemporary impaired physician movement. More than a century ago, for example, Professor William Oster chronicled, in his "Inner History of The Johns Hopkins Hospital," his observations of and concerns for his friend, Professor William Stewart Halstad:

> "The proneness to seclusion, the slight peculiarities amounting to eccentricities at times (which to his old friends in New York seemed more strange than to us) were the only outward traces of the daily battle through which this brave fellow lived for years. When we recommended him as full surgeon to the hospital in 1890, I believed, and Welch did too, that he was no longer addicted to morphia. He had worked so well and so energetically that it did not seem possible that he could take the drug and done so much.
>
> "About six months after the full position had been given, I saw him in severe chills, and this was the first information I had that he was still taking morphia. Subsequently, I had many talks about it and gained his full confidence. He had never been able to reduce the amount to less than three grains daily; on this, he could do his work comfortably and maintain his excellent physical vigor (for he was a very muscular fellow). I do not think anyone suspected him, not even Welch." (Noland & Halstad, 1991)

This excellent description of an opiate-addicted physician, recorded in a small locked black book that was not even opened until 1969, is classic, yet rarely taught to students of medicine. Paget's early (1869) report on the fate of 1,000 medical students, articles by Mattison (1884), Harris (1914), De-Quincy (1950), and others (Pacsor, 1942; Stimson, Oppenheimer & Stimson, 1984; Ehrhardt, 1959; Modlin & Montes, 1964), could well be used by medical educators to begin the study of substance abuse and occupational risk. Instead, these writings have incited public concern and scandal about pharmacologic excess by physicians.

After the Flexner report on medical education in the United States (1910), state medical societies and legislatures began to regulate medical practice and to pass laws and regulations requiring that physicians and surgeons be free of "vice, moral turpitude and the intemperate use of alcohol and drugs." In 1906, the U.S. Congress enacted the Pure Food and Drug Act, thus initiating the federal role in drug regulations (Musto, 1973). The Harrison Narcotics Act began the process of classifying, regulating, and controlling drugs that have a potential for abuse (P.L. 233, 1914). The act also criminalized the use of certain drugs and forbade drug maintenance treatment.

In 1920, the English Parliament passed the Dangerous Drug Control Act (Stimson, Oppenheimer & Stimson, 1984) in an attempt to control addiction through the registration of addicts. Nearly 25% of the addicts who registered were doctors, dentists, nurses, or veterinary surgeons. In the United States, legislation such as Prohibition (Caston, 1981) and the Marihuana Tax Acts (P.L. 238, 1937) helped form the public view of addiction as a legal and social issue rather than a medical illness. There was a relative absence of teaching and research about alcohol and drug dependence in medical schools until the past two decades, and negative attitudes still permeate much of the health care system.

PREVALENCE

Literature on alcohol and drug problems in the U.S. from the mid-1950s to the mid-1980s consistently documented an apparent excess prevalence of these disorders among physicians (Keeve, 1984). Reports of physician substance abuse from Britain, Germany, Holland, France, and Canada from the same study period also revealed higher than expected rates of physician addiction (Ehrhardt, 1959; Wollot & Lambert, 1982; East, 1947; Clatt, 1968; A'Brook, Hailstone & McLauchlan, 1967; Watterson, 1976; Vincent, Robinson & Latt, 1969; Brewster, 1986; Hughes et al. 1992; Robins & Regier, 1991). In a 1986 study, Brewster (1986) reviewed the existing, mostly English, written literature to estimate the prevalence of drug and alcohol problems among physicians. She concluded that "extreme statements regarding the prevalence of physician problems with alcohol and other drugs have been made without firm empirical supports." Her principal finding was that the prevalence of substance abuse problems among practicing physicians is unknown. She noted that, when alcohol and other drugs are considered together, the prevalence among physicians may be no higher than that of the general population.

Hughes and colleagues (1992) mailed an anonymous, self-report survey to a sample of 9,600 physicians, who were stratified by specialty and career stage and randomly selected from the AMA Physician Masterfile. They concluded that a higher prevalence of alcohol use among physician respondents was more an artifact of socioeconomic class than of profession. On the other hand, the researchers found a high rate of reported self-treatment with controlled substances.

Several major surveys in the U.S. and internationally have assessed the prevalence of substance abuse and dependence disorders within the general population. One of the largest is the National Institute of Mental Health's Epidemiologic Catchment Area (ECA) survey (Robins & Regier, 1991). ECA data provide information on diagnoses of substance abuse and dependence according to criteria from the *Diagnostic and Statistical Manual of Mental Disorders, 3rd Edition, Revised* (*DSM-IIIR*; American Psychiatric Association, 1987). The lifetime rate of alcohol disorders was 13.5% overall (Regier et al., 1990), 23.8% for men and 4.7% for women (Halzer, Burnam & McEvoy, 1991). The ECA surveys found a lifetime prevalence of drug abuse and dependence of 6.2% overall (Anthony & Hetzer, 1991), with a 7.7% rate for the men in the study population and a 4.8% rate for women (Halzer, Burnam & McEvoy, 1991).

Currently, there are more than 684,400 physicians in the United States, 19.5% of whom are women. Based on ECA data, it can be estimated that 137,397 physicians (131,124 men and 6,273 women) will experience an alcohol disorder during their lifetime, and 48,829 physicians (42,423 men and 6,406 women) will have a drug disorder.

It is thus clear that even though physicians are believed to have essentially the same incidence and prevalence rates for alcohol and drug disorders as the general population, the number of lives affected is significant. Moreover, chemical dependence appears to be the single most frequent disabling illness among medical professionals (Talbott & Wright, 1987) and thus poses a major problem for the profession and for society alike.

ETIOLOGY

The existence of a premorbid "professional" personality type that predisposes a physician to addiction has been postulated but not demonstrated. There also is no evidence that medicine selects those with special risk for addiction. Who, then, is at risk for becoming addicted? Vaillant (1992) has reported psychological vulnerabilities including passivity and self-doubt, dependency and pessimism. Physicians whose childhood and adolescence were unstable also appear to have excess risk for addiction. A narcissistic personality type (Richman, 1912), non-Jewish ancestry and a lack of religious affiliation (Moore, 1990), cigarette use of more than a pack a day, the regular use of alcohol, a personal history of alcohol-related difficulties, and a family history of alcoholism, substance dependence and/or mental illness all have been identified as risk factors for physicians (Gallegos, Browne et al., 1988). Jex and colleagues (1992) have reported that certain specialty groups and physicians in academic medicine have excess risk for addiction. Hughes and colleagues (1992) found that physicians were five times more likely than controls to take sedatives and minor tranquilizers without medical supervision, and Vaillant (1992) has identified self-prescribing (and self-treatment with prescription drugs) as a risk factor for chemical dependence.

In a large study of physicians and medical students, McAuliffe (1987) identified risk factors as: (1) access to pharmaceuticals, (2) a family history of substance abuse, (3) emotional problems, (4) stress at work or at home, (5) thrill-seeking, (6) self-treatment of pain and emotional problems, and (7) chronic fatigue. Talbott and colleagues (1987) reviewed the medical records of 1,000 physicians with chemical dependence and concluded that age, specialty, drug access, genetic predisposition, stress and poor coping skills, the lack of education regarding substance abuse, the absence of effective prevention and control strategies, drug availability in the context of a permissive professional and social environment, and denial all were risk factors for physician substance abuse. Wright (1990) postulated that physicians who have excess risk for addiction are those with a history of illicit substance use (including self-prescribing of controlled substances), those in high-risk specialties, those who have a pattern of over-prescribing, and those with an urge to succeed in an academic setting who overwork and have the combined problems of grandiosity and excessive guilt.

These populations studies aside, researchers have not examined physician risk factors in terms of genetic predisposition, the psychobiology of craving, the relationship of classically conditioned factors, brain reward mechanisms, and psychodynamic factors, and sociocultural determinants of addiction in physicians as compared with their non-physician peers.

IDENTIFICATION

Detection of the physician with an alcohol or drug disorder often is delayed by the ability of the physician to protect his or her job performance at the expense of every other dimension of his or her life. Clinical studies (Bissell & Haberman, 1984; Vaillant, Clark et al., 1983) suggest that the first realm to be adversely affected by the physician's addiction is family, followed by community, finances, spiritual and emotional health, physical health, and only then, job performance.

As with any potentially fatal illness, early detection is critical. Physicians who are afflicted with alcohol or drug disorders demonstrate a predictable constellation of signs and symptoms, as listed in Table 1.

Early identification and diagnosis are critical. Barriers to early diagnosis are the widely-remarked "conspiracy of silence" and denial on the part of family, friends, peers, and even patients. Such barriers are products of a lack of education concerning the true nature of the primary, psychosocial, biogenetic disease of addiction.

INTERVENTION

Denial is an almost universal characteristic of the disease of addiction. Denial absolves the addict of personal accountability; at the same time, denial—both the deliberate conscious deception and the unconscious defense mechanism—fills the addicted physician with guilt, shame, and remorse so that most addicted physicians cannot reach out for help. It is the nature of the disease of addiction for the denial system to progress as the addiction impairs the individual's functioning. This distortion of the truth is an unconscious defense mechanism that protects a damaged self-esteem while allowing the underlying disease to progress. The denial system, as well as the addictive process itself, can prevent the addicted physician from wanting or even feeling the need for treatment.

Intervention is a procedure that is necessary when an individual is either unaware of his or her addiction or, because of denial, is psychologically unable to recognize the seriousness of the disease and to seek treatment (Talbott & Gallegos, 1990). Intervention generally is used as a component of a comprehensive assessment. Once addiction is suspected by colleagues, intervention needs to be carefully planned and swiftly executed. However, careful preparation is essential. Intervention is a very serious experience that can prevent the addicted individual from hitting a personal "bottom"; however, the authors have seen improperly conducted interventions result in death. Over the past two decades, intervention has been redefined into a science and an art. Successful intervention has several components:

Use of a Trained and Experienced Intervention Leader. Proper preparation for an intervention is essential. The interventionist must select individuals to do the intervention, train the intervenors to present relevant information, set goals for the intervention, and expedite the patient's prompt referral for recommended treatment.

Selection of the Intervention Team. The leader of the intervention team must involve the most significant persons in the patient's life. An intervention team for a physician might include family members, peers, supervisors, close friends, clergy, hospital administrators, medical society members, court officials, and members of the licensing board. The team

TABLE 1. Signs and Symptoms of Addictive Disorder in Physicians, by Life Area

Family
1. The physician withdraws from family activities; there are unexplained absences.
2. The spouse becomes a caretaker.
3. Fights increase in frequency; there is dysfunctional anger; the spouse tries to control the physician's substance abuse.
4. The spouse becomes isolated, angry, and physically and emotionally unable to meet the demands of the addict's illness.
5. There is child abuse.
6. The children assume responsibility for maintaining normal family functioning.
7. The children develop abnormal, antisocial behavior (depression, promiscuity, running away from home, substance abuse).
8. Sexual problems emerge, including impotence and extramarital affairs.
9. The spouse disengages, abuses drugs and/or alcohol, or enters recovery.

Community
1. The physician becomes isolated and withdraws from community activities, church, friends, leisure, hobbies, and peers.
2. He or she exhibits embarrassing behavior at clubs or parties.
3. The physician receives DUI citations, experiences legal problems, and exhibits role-discordant behaviors.
4. The physician's behavior is unreliable and unpredictable in community and social activities.
5. The physician is unpredictable in personal behavior, engaging in excessive spending, risk taking behaviors.

Physical Status
1. The physician's personal hygiene deteriorates.
2. His or her clothing and dress habits deteriorate.
3. The physician has multiple physical signs and complaints.
4. The physician writes numerous prescriptions for personal use.
5. The physician experiences frequent hospitalizations.
6. The physician has numerous visits to physicians and dentists.
7. The physician is involved in multiple episodes of accidents and trauma.
8. There is evidence of a serious emotional crisis.

Office
1. Patient appointments and schedule become disorganized and progressively later.
2. The physician's behavior toward staff and patients is hostile, withdrawn, or unreasonable.
3. The physician spends time behind "locked doors."
4. The physician orders excessive office supplies of drugs.
5. Patients complain to staff about the physician's behavior.
6. The physician is frequently absent from the office or has unexplained or frequent illnesses.

Hospital
1. The physician makes rounds late or exhibits inappropriate or abnormal behavior.
2. There is a decrease in the quality of the physician's performance in staff presentations, writing in charts, etc.
3. The physician enters inappropriate orders for or overprescribes medications.
4. Nurses, secretaries, orderlies, and other staff report that the physician's behavior has changed.
5. The physician becomes involved in malpractice suits and legal sanctions against the physician or hospital.
6. Emergency department staff report that the physician is unavailable for or responds inappropriately to telephone calls.
7. The physician does not respond to pages, or is slow to do so.
8. He or she is reluctant to undergo immediate physical examination or to submit to urine drug screens.
9. The physician engages in heavy drinking at staff functions.

Professional History
(Clues from the Curriculum Vitae)*
1. The physician has changed jobs numerous times within the preceding five years.
2. The CV documents frequent geographic relocations without clear explanations.
3. There is a history of frequent hospitalizations.
4. The physician has a complicated and elaborate medical history.
5. The CV shows unexplained time lapses between jobs.
6. The physician submits indefinite or inappropriate medical references and vague letters of reference.
7. The physician has been employed in one or more positions that are not appropriate to his or her qualifications.
8. There is a decline in the physician's professional productivity.

*If any three of the above are present on an application for employment or staff privileges, the index of suspicion should be high.

must exclude individuals who are resentful and/or hostile. The best intervenors are individuals who are knowledgeable about the disease of addiction, able to maintain objectivity, yet express an attitude of caring and concern. Intervenors must be emotionally stable, believe in the progressive nature of addictive disease, and understand that the illness is treatable. An intervention should never be done alone.

Selection of the Intervention Site. The site of the intervention needs to be non-threatening and quiet. Time and experience have taught that an early morning intervention, prior to the intake of alcohol or other drugs by the physician, is best accomplished in the patient's home with the cooperation of the spouse and children. Occasionally, guilt and shame are present to such a degree that intervention needs to be away from the home and can be conducted at some neutral site. Some spouses believe that their participation in an intervention will result in divorce. If the spouse is not convinced that addiction is a progressive, potentially fatal but treatable illness that affects the entire family, it may be better for that person not to participate in the intervention, as it is essential for all members of the intervention team to present a consistent understanding of the problem.

Establishment of Intervention Goals. Such goals must be established in advance and accepted by all the members of the intervention team. Intervenors must decide what choices they will give the physician, and what they will commit to do if the physician refuses all offers of help. Frequently, the perception of reality is grossly distorted by the effects of alcohol and drugs on the brain. Intervenors need to review the pain and consequences they have experienced as a result of the addict's behavior.

Documentation of Information. It is critical that the information to be presented be carefully documented. Use of gossip or innuendo may reduce the chances of a successful intervention. The intervention team members should write down and present to the physician their experiences with his or her addiction-influenced behaviors. The addict should be told why the intervention is necessary, as well as the legal, social, personal, health-related and professional implications of the illness. The team also should consider presenting advocacy and immunity regulations of the state medical board, to prepare the way should the physician voluntarily seek treatment as a result of the intervention.

Availability of Adequate Time. It is extremely important to allow enough time for the intervention, so that neither the physician nor the intervenors feel rushed. The impaired physicians should not be intoxicated at the time of the intervention. Timing is important: an intervention done soon after an addiction-precipitated crisis often is successful. If the impaired physician refuses the recommended help, the interventionist may negotiate a behavioral contract, so that the next relapse or crisis triggers another intervention.

Rehearsal. Careful planning, including rehearsal, is critical. Each member of the intervention team must know and practice his or her role and what he or she will say during the intervention. It is helpful to anticipate the impaired physician's reaction, including hostility and flight, and plan appropriate responses.

Outcomes. At the conclusion of a successful intervention, the physician-patient will follow the team's recommendations for assessment or treatment. Referral options, transportation, and an action plan should be in place before the intervention is initiated. The authors have seen more than one intervention that at first appeared successful, but in which allowing the physician to negotiate his or her own arrangements tragically ended in suicide.

Intervention sometimes must be repeated. Even if the physician does not initially accept the information presented, the intervention is not a failure, for a seed has been planted. The impaired physician may reject, refuse, or even leave the intervention, but he or she is at least aware that his or her support systems are aware of the problem and concerned.

Some interventions fail. A cohesive team can develop an action plan for the next time the addicted doctor is in an addiction-precipitated crisis.

No matter what the outcome of the intervention, it is important that the team regroup so that members can process their feelings and thoughts about the experience.

ASSESSMENT

Experienced interventionists, most state medical society Impaired Physician Committees, and many state medical licensing boards recommend a comprehensive assessment in a specified treatment facility to determine the extent of the impaired physician's illness and treatment needs. Physicians who voluntarily seek the recommended treatment after assessment, who successfully complete their treatment program and who enter into a state medical society-sponsored monitoring program often receive advocacy rather than punitive sanctions. Ideally, the recovering physician allows the experienced treatment team to make the best choices about his or her recovery, rather than attempting to treat him- or herself or undertreat the illness.

Many specialized treatment programs have evolved to meet the needs of the addicted and/or psychiatrically impaired physician. The Georgia Program has refined its 96-hour assessment, which is used to evaluate the scope of illness and to place the patient in an appropriate intensity of service and level of care (Mee-Lee, Shulman & Gartner, 1996). The assessment program is composed of five teams, which provide an interdisciplinary composite diagnostic score, on the basis of which treatment recommendations are formulated. This interdisciplinary approach permits the optimal use of skills, coordination, flexibility, synergy, support, and communication (Talbott & Martin, 1986). The five teams used in the Georgia Program are:

The Medical Team. Headed by a physician who is trained in addiction medicine, the members of this team are certified, knowledgeable, and experienced in addiction medicine and are trained to identify and treat the medical consequences of alcohol and drug abuse. They perform a detailed history and physical examination and order the appropriate diagnostic and confirmatory laboratory, radiologic, and other tests. Inherent in the functioning of the medical team is appropriate consultation for specific medical complications.

The Addiction Medicine Team. This team is led by a certified addiction medicine specialist who is trained to diagnose and recommend a range of addiction medicine services. Team members provide needed detoxification services after a comprehensive addictive disease assessment has been obtained. They evaluate the psychological and behavioral effects of the drugs used by the patient, assess the severity of the patient's addiction from a biopsychosocial perspective, and collect and collate information from persons in the individual's support system to validate the patient's historical information. This rapid data acquisition effort, followed by presentation of the information to the patient and family, often is critical for rapid decompression of the impaired physician's denial system.

The Psychiatric Team. Addicted patients frequently manifest multiple co-occurring addictive and psychiatric disorders (Kosten & Kleber, 1988). Consequently, a comprehensive psychiatric assessment is a critical component of the assessment process. It is necessary to determine whether a definitive psychiatric diagnosis is present, or to achieve a working differential diagnosis that is contingent on additional evaluation. Treatment research has documented that patients with untreated psychiatric comorbidities are more likely to relapse after addiction treatment than are patients with psychiatric comorbidities (Catalano, Howard et al., 1986).

The Neuropsychological Team. The addicted physician may appear cognitively unimpaired, particularly if he or she has had training in psychiatry or psychology. However, neuropsychological testing often reveals significant deficits in reasoning and memory (Robinson, Fitzgerald & Gallegos, 1985). After a focused clinical interview, psychological testing should involve the Halstead-Reitan Neuropsychological Test Battery (HRNB), which includes the Booklet Category Test, the Tactile Performance Test, the Reitan-Indiana Aphasia Screening Test, the Trailmaking Test, the Reitan-Klove Sensory Examination, and the Seashore Rhythm Test. Useful adjuncts to the HRNB include the Wechsler Adult Intelligence Scale (WAIS), the Wechsler Memory Scale Revised (WMS-R), the Graham-Kendal Memory for Design Test, the Minnesota Multiphasic Personality Inventory (MMPI) and the Rorschach Test. Often missed in standard evaluations are neuropsychological deficits, which may become apparent with more sensitive evaluation techniques.

The Family Therapy Team. The family is critical to treatment success. Interviews with the patient's spouse or significant other, children, parents, and siblings are very helpful in achieving a definitive diagnosis. Enlistment of these individuals in the treatment and recovery program is coordinated by family therapists.

If possible, assessments are done in the hospital, where close and constant observation facilitates documentation of withdrawal symptoms, medical symptoms, and complications. This method also permits detection of self-medication by the patient. Team members see the patient for testing and evaluation, which are completed independently. The team then meets for discussion of their diagnosis and treatment recommendations. Differences in tentative diagnoses are discussed and resolved. It is in this forum that collateral information from other sources, particularly from the family therapist and the addiction medicine team member, becomes critical. (Obviously, informed consent must be obtained from the patient to obtain this information.) Finally, a primary Axis I diagnosis and sub-diagnosis are arrived at by the team members and a detailed plan of treatment recommended.

At this point, the team meets with the patient. It is useful to have not only the spouse or significant other, but often other family members present for the presentation and discussion of the diagnostic and therapeutic recommendations of the assessment team. If inpatient treatment is indicated, the patient may be offered a choice of treatment at several different facilities. Adequate time should be allowed for questions and answers, as well as discussion of treatment options and the problems that can be expected if the patient refuses treatment. (It is not appropriate for the assessment team to comment on issues related to licensure or registration with the Drug Enforcement Administration [DEA], which should be left to the appropriate organizations. The appropriate role for the assessment and treatment team is as advocate for the patient, not prosecutor. Moreover, assurance of patient confidentiality is of the highest priority.)

TREATMENT

Treatment of the impaired physician has many special features that combine the highest clinical standards and serve as a benchmark for the field of addiction medicine. The goal of treatment should be abstinence from alcohol and other psychoactive substances and recovery from associated medical and psychiatric disorders.

Treatment centers that specialize in the care of impaired physicians generally offer levels of care that are consistent with the ASAM *Patient Placement Criteria* (Mee-Lee, Shulman & Gartner, 1996). While some impaired physicians have attained true sobriety through intense and focused long-term participation in Alcoholics Anonymous, the most successful programs feature residential outpatient treatment, with sufficient time to work through denial. Treating the impaired physician in a peer group setting appears to facilitate the recovery process (Angres, Talbott & Angres, in press). Outpatient programs, which lack a residential component, have not been found to be as successful in the Oklahoma and Oregon impaired physician programs.

The treatment team should be experienced in dealing with impaired physicians and other health professionals, and knowledgeable about the legal and professional issues that confront such physicians, including reporting requirements of the National Physician Data Bank, malpractice insurance, DEA certification, and issues related to state medical boards. They need to be experienced in setting firm limits and boundaries, skilled at helping physicians and other health professionals solve re-entry problems, and available for frequent consultation.

Elements of Successful Treatment Programs. Successful treatment of the impaired physician has several significant elements:

Understanding and Acceptance of the Disease Concept: For the impaired physician to both understand and accept that he or she has a primary psychosocial biological genetic disease has proved to be the most critical and elementary aspect of recovery. Acceptance of the disease concept begins to resolve the guilt, shame, and fear that attend addictive disorders in physicians. Initially, this is accomplished by education, because understanding of the disease of addiction dispels the shame.

Compulsivity is a primary symptom of chemical dependence. Thus, the recovering physician must be carefully schooled in the neurochemistry of addiction and the medical and sociocultural consequences of the disease. Only then can the impaired physician understand that while he or she is not responsible for the disease, he or she is responsible for the recovery. An intellectual understanding of this concept may come rather readily, but to accept it in depth is a process requiring time and the proper environment. Physicians, by training, wish to solve all their problems intellectually, but addiction is not a disease that responds to intellect alone.

Identification of the Trigger Mechanisms: Appreciating that abuse of alcohol or drugs, in combination with a genetic predisposition produces the disease of addiction, identification of triggers that produce abuse is critical to recovery, as demonstrated by recent research into the psychology of craving, conditioning factors and brain reward mechanisms. Each impaired physician must, over a period of time, learn to identify his or her own triggers. With this knowledge, the physician can begin to learn more about relapse thinking and behavior and develop coping skills to prevent relapse.

Development of Non-Chemical Coping Methods: Basic to recovery is the ability to develop nonchemical coping skills. For example, one of the most widespread and troublesome symptoms of drug withdrawal is insomnia. Addicted physicians have to be taught that this common withdrawal symptom must be dealt with by nonchemical coping mechanisms. These might include: (1) a quiet restful environment, (2) small, balanced, multiple meals during the day, (3) abstinence from caffeine and nicotine and a reduction in salt and protein intake, (4) a prescribed time for trying to fall asleep and then two-hour increments of planned insomnia time, during which planned activities are scheduled, (5) a hot bath, (6) massage, (7) light reading, (8) counseling every evening to anticipate the coming night and periods of activity during planned insomnia time, (9) charting the insomnia activities in an attempt to relate it to specific thought processes, and (10) reading self-help books or listening to audiotapes about insomnia.

These simple nonchemical coping methods must be learned by the impaired physician for a variety of emotions, including anxiety, grief, guilt, depression, and situational crisis such as divorce, loss of job, death in the family, personal problems or physical problems. The impaired physician, therefore, must develop a multitude of nonchemical coping skills, abilities and capabilities to deal with stresses without chemicals. For all of their professional lives, physicians have been taught that drugs and chemicals are a powerful part of their therapeutic armamentarium, so that adoption of nonchemical coping requires extended practice to "unlearn" the earlier behaviors.

Achieving Balance by Changing Priorities: Many impaired physicians place their careers and their physician's role as the first priority in their lives. Almost by definition, they are both workaholics and perfectionists. For many, this behavior becomes a major "trigger" for substance abuse. The impaired physician is taught that recovery and growth are first; family is second, and professional concerns third. Leisure time and fun are critical to recovery, yet many impaired physicians have lost the ability to have fun and have forgotten how to play. Achieving recovery involves learning to balance these elements.

Family Involvement: Family involvement is critical to the diagnostic, treatment and recovery processes. Most often, the family knows of the disease long before friends or professional peers. If the family is involved early, they can be a powerful factor in recovery. The pain and discomfort they have suffered as a result of the physician's addiction must be dealt with in a manner that shows them how to help the impaired physician, as well as how to help themselves. Basic to this process is their own understanding and acceptance of the disease, as well as specific suggestions as to how they can modify their own responses and behaviors toward the recovering physician who returns home after treatment.

Involvement in Mutual Help Groups: Successful health professional programs have been based on Alcoholics Anonymous and other Twelve Step programs. The merits of Twelve Step programs are that they are widely available, free, and available at all times of the day and night.

Peer-Oriented Therapy: The addicted physician often over-identifies with his or her professional persona as a defense against increasing distress and dwindling self-esteem. Other physicians in treatment can effectively confront these defenses as they confront their own. The physician's sense of uniqueness can be dealt with in a productive way in a peer group setting.

AFTERCARE AND MONITORING

Because substance abuse is a chronic illness, treatment is but the beginning of recovery. Most treatment centers have developed structured aftercare programs so that patients can continue to work on issues identified during their treatment. Initially, many recovering physicians regard aftercare as punitive, hostile, or intrusive. However, when the physician understands and accepts the relapsing nature of the disease of addiction, and when aftercare monitoring is presented as a legal and licensing advocacy issue, the degree of compliance, acceptance, and gratitude usually improves.

The planning of aftercare and monitoring should begin on the first day of treatment and involve the family and all other support systems of the impaired physician.

Stages of Recovery. The milestones in recovery from addiction are both similar to and different from the process of recovering from any chronic, life-threatening illness. Each individual has a unique combination of risk and protective features and resiliencies that can be engaged in the recovery process. Treatment and aftercare ideally combine to improve outcome by changing a relapse-prone individual into a recovery-prone one.

The needs of every recovering physician change over time. Without appropriate problem-solving strategies, the willingness to reach out for help and respond appropriately to feedback, and the ability to successfully cope with "stuck points" (Gorski, 1986) and stressors, relapse is likely. A thorough recognition of the stages through which the recovering physician must pass and ways to overcome "stuck points" in the journey of recovery are essential.

Recovery is a long-term process with clearly defined stages. Although the recovery time course is unique for each individual, Gorski (1989a, 1989b) has defined the major recovery stages as:

1. *Transition:* This stage starts when the individual begins to believe that he or she may have a prob-

lem with alcohol or drugs. It ends when the individual becomes willing to reach out for help.

2. *Stabilization:* In this stage, the patient completes the physical withdrawal and post-acute withdrawal processes. Both physical and emotional healing begin. Obsession with drug and/or alcohol use subsides. The physician begins to feel hope and develop motivation for recovery.
3. *Early Recovery:* This stage marks a time of internal change, when the recovering physician begins to let go of painful feelings (such as guilt, shame, fear and resentment) about the addictive disease. Compulsion to use alcohol and/or drugs subsides, while reliance on non-chemical coping skills to address life problems and situations strengthens.
4. *Middle Recovery:* In this stage, balance begins to be restored. The wreckage of the past is cleaned up. Relationships are developed that positively reinforce learned skills so as to ensure continued personal growth.
5. *Late Recovery:* At this point, resolution of painful events and issues related to growing up in a dysfunctional family must occur.
6. *Maintenance:* The recovering physician begins to practice the principles of successful recovery in all daily activities.

This evolving process requires changes that are perceptible to those around the recovering physician. Programs that are responsive to the changing needs of the recovering physician, monitor the stages of recovery thoroughly, and use every resource available to help each individual physician become recovery-prone, are likely to be the most successful.

Role of Physician Health Programs (PHPs). In many states, physicians are expected to participate in their state medical society-sponsored PHP for post-treatment monitoring, in addition to the aftercare provided by their treatment programs. PHPs operate from the premise that impaired physicians may be unable to seek help spontaneously due to the nature of their illness and, therefore, that their colleagues have a special obligation to take the initiative in encouraging voluntary treatment. These programs have a dual function: to protect the public from the impaired physician and to help the impaired individual achieve recovery. Such programs typically provide low cost or no cost services to the physician. Their services typically include:

1. Receiving requests to investigate questions surrounding impairment of specific individuals.
2. Training intervention specialists and organizing interventions.
3. Seeking assistance for physicians who need financial aid during the treatment or rehabilitation process.
4. Establishing a registry of the appropriate resources for treatment of alcoholism, other drug dependence, mental health, geriatric issues and other problems resulting in physician impairment.
5. Establishing liaison with hospital administrations, medical staffs, managed care organizations and medical societies throughout the state.
6. Liaising with the directors of approved addiction treatment programs.
7. Recommending appropriate treatment to physicians seeking help.
8. Monitoring the progress of physicians after treatment.
9. Collaborating with other state Physician Health Programs to improve standards of recovery monitoring, data collection, process refinements, and to plan and conduct research to evaluate the effectiveness of treatment and monitoring.
10. Reporting to appropriate individuals, committees, or organizations, funding sources, and credentialing agencies regarding the success of the monitoring program.
11. Conducting educational programs to educate physicians and their families, hospital staffs, county medical societies, medical auxiliaries, and other appropriate groups or agencies about physician impairment.

Several state PHPs also provide individual, group, and family counseling.

PHPs attempt to provide quantitative documentation of each physician's progress in recovery by obtaining data from face-to-face interviews with the recovering physician. Data for surveillance of recovery are obtained by the PHP at regularly scheduled two-week intervals in the first year after treatment. The evaluation schedule gradually lengthens to twice-yearly monitoring and face-to-face interviews toward the end of five years. Aftercare monitoring of recovering physicians has become an essential part of continued recovery.

In many states, including Florida (Goetz, 1996), New Jersey (Reading, 1992), Maryland (Alpern et al., 1992), Oregon (Ulwelling, 1991), Georgia (Gallegos, Keppler & Wilson, 1989), New Mexico (Miscal, 1991), Alabama (Summer, 1996), and Oklahoma (Smith & Smith, 1991), the PHP assists physicians who voluntarily seek treatment and monitoring with advocacy before the state medical board. By contrast, physicians who are reported directly to the state medical board are required to have a formal, disciplinary relationship with that agency. Most PHPs supervise physicians for a minimum of five treatment years.

Recently, an organization of full and part-time medical directors of PHPs has gathered to form the Federation of State Physician Health Programs, Inc. (FSPHP). The Federation provides a forum for the exchange of information among State Physician Health Programs (PHPs) and promotes the safety and well-being of the public and the state medical associations' PHPs. The final goal of the Federation is to promote early identification prior to the illness impacting upon the care of patients. The FSPHP is developing a closer relationship with the AMA and the FSMB. Encouragement has attended the formation of the FSPHP. A common ground can be established that links organized concern for sick doctors to social, legal, and political pressures of professional accountability. The medical profession has recognized alcoholism and drug addiction as a disease. The medical control of impaired physicians in terms of compatibilities with professional values and interests has demonstrated that when conflicting but overriding considerations are put into action, a partnership can form. This partnership is capable of meeting the demands of disparate forces, ultimately resulting in improved safety to the public while maximizing the personal rights of recovering physicians.

Factors that Influence Recovery. Close and careful monitoring by the state medical society PHP is thought to be necessary to help physicians safely through the stages of recovery and to avoid "stuck points." Galanter et al. (1990) studied 100 recovering physicians who were successfully treated in a program that combined professionally directed psychotherapeutic treatment and peer-led self-help groups. An average of 37.4 months after admission, all of the physicians reported being abstinent. They rated participation in Twelve Step groups as the most important element in their recovery, followed by physician counseling, the desire to do well at work, family therapy and regular urine drug screens. In this group, feelings of affiliation with AA and identification with the role of caregiver in addiction treatment appeared to be central to recovery.

Gallegos et al. (1992) reported that all physicians (N = 100) in a study signed a continuing care contract that included witnessed urine screens, assignment to a primary care physician, attendance at five Twelve Step meetings and one Caduceus meeting per week, participation in individual and family therapy as indicated, engagement in a spiritual program, a physical fitness program and a leisure activity program. Those who relapsed within the first year were: (1) likely not to have accepted the disease concept, (2) did not believe that they needed the recommended help, and (3) felt that they would not have difficulty staying sober. Those who relapsed in the second year most often reported family and emotional issues as triggers for relapse. For all who relapsed (N = 22), behavioral changes and denial of their condition elevated their stress, increased their isolation and impaired their judgment. All of the physicians who relapsed reported that they had stopped attending their AA group. They also felt that neither their fear of losing their license to practice medicine, nor any other legal, marital or professional sanction could have inhibited the progression of their relapse or promoted recovery once substance use was re-initiated.

Based on experience in the Georgia Program, Talbott has postulated that 16 factors appear to have predictive value in maintaining successful recovery. They include:

1. The number of Twelve Step meetings attended per week.
2. A working relationship and frequent contact with a sponsor.
3. Random urine drug screens.
4. Monitoring milestones in each stage of recovery to help the physician avoid "stuck points" or emotional traps (such as anger, guilt, depression, anxiety, insomnia, etc.).
5. Monitoring for the emergence of compulsive behaviors (involving sex, work, food, nicotine, gambling, etc.).
6. Evaluate the status of current therapies/treatments and medications.
7. Assessment of family relationships.
8. Attention to physical health status.
9. Participation in a number of leisure activities each week.
10. Compliance with all monitoring activities, and timely attendance at recommended therapies and Twelve Step meetings.
11. Time spent in physical exercise each week.
12. Evaluation of work-related stressors (professional status, job duties, and workplace attitudes)
13. Changes in financial status.

14. Enrollment in additional training and/or continuing medical education.
15. Quality of the recovery program.
16. Identification of "soft parts" of the recovery program.

Contingency contracting also has been found to be helpful in reducing the risk of relapse (Crowley, 1986). State PHPs or a therapist obtains a license-surrendering letter from the physician being monitored. The physician agrees that if a urine drug screen is positive, the letter will be sent to the state licensing agency and professional sanctions will be issued by the licensing agency.

One common element among successfully recovering physicians appears to be the extent to which the physician is able to internalize the treatment experience (Centrella, 1994). Physicians who are most successful in their recovery avoid emotions such as anger, guilt, depression, and anxiety by using Twelve Step recovery program principles (Kurtz, 1982). They avoid compulsive behaviors and learn to become skillful in participating in important relationships (family, sponsor, spouse, parents, children, friends, etc). They also develop a profound and abiding attitude of gratitude. They learn to have open and honest communication with family members. They are regular in their attendance at AA (or other Twelve Step meetings), they communicate with their sponsors, and check out their behavior with other family members and recovering friends. These behaviors must become part of the recovering physician's routine patterns of life.

OUTCOMES

The primary goal of treatment is to help the physician achieve and maintain long-term remission of the addictive disease (Gordis, 1989). Reported recovery rates vary considerably, with rates of complete abstinence from mood-altering substances ranging from 27% (Wall, 1958) to 92% (Jones, 1958). The interpretation of these outcomes, however, requires explanation.

Many methodologic problems exist when comparing different outcome studies of physicians who have been treated for addictive disorders (Gallegos, 1987). Notable differences among studies that affect outcome rates are:

1. Patient selection: some study populations are restricted to physicians, while others include nurses, dentists, and medical students;
2. Significant differences in the types, intensity, and duration of treatment given (there is no standard way to retrospectively evaluate intensity, quantity, and quality of treatment);
3. Some studies rely on self-reports from physicians about abstinence versus relapse;
4. Positive urine drug test results are based on random urine drug screens that are performed within 24 hours of notification of the recovering physician (alcohol and some drugs of abuse taken a day or two before notification might not be detected);
5. The data used to select subjects for study may be incomplete;
6. Some studies fail to adequately account for treatment dropouts in their analysis of treatment outcome data;
7. Some studies fail to follow patients for adequate lengths of time post-treatment; and
8. Some studies fail to provide for adequate, multidimensional treatment outcome measures that map a full range of patient behaviors.

These methodologic differences have made meta-analysis impossible. However, there has been a steady progression in the cohesiveness of findings in all investigations published over the past decade. Physicians appear to have better treatment outcomes than the general population, when long-term aftercare and monitoring are in place. There also are sufficient data to conclude that most physicians can be successfully rehabilitated and re-enter medical practice with reasonable skill and safety for their patients.

Reading (1992) reported that, given two years of program involvement after formal treatment, New Jersey physicians had a recovery rate of 83.8% without relapse. Gallegos et al. (1992) studied one hundred physicians who entered into a continuing care contract with the Georgia Impaired Physicians Program between July 1982 and June 1987. Of these, 77 physicians maintained documented abstinence from all mood-altering substances from 5 to 10 years after initiation of the continuing care contract. One physician was lost to follow-up, and 22 relapsed. Of those who relapsed, one died during relapse. One physician was involved in a pattern of continuous relapses and was unable to return to medical practice. All but four of the remaining physicians who relapsed had at least two years of continuous sobriety since their most recent relapse.

Angres (in press) describes a population of 101 physicians followed over a six-year period, in which

80% demonstrated continued abstinence. Of those who relapsed, a significant percentage had comorbid personality disorders, particularly Narcissistic Personality Disorder. Over half of those who relapsed went on to achieve sustained sobriety following an appropriate treatment intervention.

Shore (1987) reported on 63 impaired physicians who had been placed on probation by the Oregon Board of Medical Examiners. These physicians were followed for eight years. This investigation allowed the evaluation of the effectiveness of monitored outpatient supervision by comparing monitored and unmonitored subgroups. There was a significant difference in the abstinence rate for monitored subjects (96%) as compared with the treated but unmonitored addicted physicians (64%). Shore concluded that "there is increasing evidence that random urine monitoring during a two- to four-year period is positively correlated with treatment outcome."

Smith and Smith (1991) reported on treatment outcomes for impaired physicians in the Oklahoma program. Physicians were categorized by length of time in treatment: Type I had treatment for three to four months in a program specializing in the care of health professionals. Type II had inpatient treatment for four to six weeks. Type III had other treatment, including outpatient treatment, psychiatric or psychological therapy, and/or Twelve Step groups without prior addiction treatment. Of those with Type I treatment, 85% had a favorable outcome, as compared with favorable outcomes for 46% of those Type II treatment and 38% of those with Type III treatment.

Other studies demonstrate similar results. Gallegos and Norton (1984) reported on 250 consecutive physicians who had completed a specialized treatment program for impaired physicians, with a minimum of four months' supervised treatment. These were the first physicians to be treated in the Georgia program, between 1974 and 1982. Complete abstinence was reported by 73.9% at two years' follow up. Twenty-nine (11%) of the 250 physician were lost to follow-up and counted as treatment failures.

Morse et al. (1984) compared recovery rates of 73 physicians with 185 middle-class patients treated in a hospital-based program. Of the physician group, 83% of those who completed treatment had favorable outcomes at one or more years after treatment, compared with 68% of nonphysicians. Morse concluded that close monitoring may account, in part, for the better outcome among physicians.

Harrington et al. (1982) reported that 31 of 33 physicians who completed treatment (94%) had returned to full practice. Twenty-two (67%) had experienced no relapse, and 15% had a very brief period of relapse during the two-year follow-up period.

Johnson and Connelly (1981) evaluated and treated 50 physicians in a psychiatrically oriented, short-term addiction program. The criteria for a successful treatment outcome were abstinence and a return to effective job functioning. A "brief relapse" was not considered a treatment failure. Patients were followed for varying periods, ranging from nine to 54 months. Thirty-two (64%) of the study population were sober and practicing medicine at the time of follow-up. Of significant concern, four (8%) were dead: three of suicide and one of subdural hematoma.

Kliner, Spicer and Barnett (1980) studied treatment outcomes of alcoholic physicians with a multiple-choice questionnaire sent to each patient one year after discharge from an inpatient 30-day alcoholism treatment program. Of the 85 patients, 10 had died, four did not return the questionnaire, three refused permission to be contacted, and one could not be located. Fifty-one (76%) reported abstinence since treatment, and 53 (79%) of those who returned the questionnaire reported general improvement in their professional performance. The response to treatment was more favorable than that in the general patient population (only 61% remained abstinent at one year).

Goby et al. (1979) identified 51 physicians who had undergone treatment between 1967 and 1977, with one to 10 years of follow-up. Only 43 were interviewed, by telephone phone. Of those not included in the follow-up, one was incarcerated and seven were dead (only one of seven deceased physicians had been abstinent since treatment). Only 19 (44%) of those interviewed reported no use of alcohol since treatment.

The following conclusions can be drawn from these treatment outcome studies:

1. Treatment does work;
2. Long-term abstinence and personal well-being correlate with strict aftercare monitoring and improved recovery surveillance techniques;
3. Death is more prevalent among those who leave treatment prematurely and those who relapse; and
4. The majority of physicians who successfully complete treatment and participate in aftercare monitoring can successfully return to the practice of medicine.

CONCLUSIONS

In recent years, many stakeholders who guard the public safety and the practice of medicine (including the AMA, FSMB, medical and specialty societies, ASAM, regulatory agencies, FSPHP and others) have joined forces to find solutions to the challenge of physician substance abuse. As described earlier, the American Medical Association has provided leadership in developing programs to prevent and treat physician impairment. Through the AMA's efforts, every state medical society now has a stated policy and a committee on physician impairment. The Federation of State Medical Boards has suggested guidelines for the relationship between these impaired physician programs (Physician Health Program or PHP) and the state regulatory entities (Rasseth et al., 1994).

The standardization of terms and language required for effective communication between treatment providers and regulatory boards has been documented (Rinaldi, Steindler et al., 1988). Standardization of diagnoses (American Psychiatric Association, 1987), the measurement of illness severity (Mee-Lee, 1985), and the levels of care and intensities of treatment have been established (Mee-Lee, 1974). The science of matching addicted patients to specific kinds of treatment and treatment outcome research that links process with outcome (Filstead, Parrella et al., 1994) is evolving. A computerized masterfile of physician characteristics for comparative, randomized, stratified and/or case-control studies has been developed and refined (Robeck, Randolph et al., 1993).

Wright (1990) has stated that "impaired physicians are to the rest of the profession as the canary was to the coal miners of another generation. Until we can determine the risk of addiction to drugs for a specific individual before the individual is exposed to them, we must rely on the experience of the most vulnerable individuals in our occupational cohort to learn how to protect ourselves from the chemical tools of our trade."

A uniform mechanism for data collection and the development of a collaborative process to investigate physician impairment have been proposed (Gallegos, 1987). Such research would build on prior multiprogram, clinically-based research. Information gleaned would provide a foundation for improving addiction abuse treatment into the next century. This research also would have broad implications for the development of strategic prevention initiatives for the medical profession, for high-risk specialties, and for the general public.

REFERENCES

A'Brook M, Hailstone J & McLauchlan I (1967). Psychiatric illness in the medical profession. *British Psychiatrist* 113:1013–1023.

Ackerman T (1996). Chemically dependent physician and informal consent disclosure. *Journal of Addictive Disease* 15:25–42.

Alcoholics Anonymous World Service, Inc. (1972). *Alcoholics Anonymous* (2nd edition). New York, NY: Author.

Alpern F et al. (1992) A study of recovering Maryland physicians. *Maryland Medical Journal* 41:301–303.

American Medical Association (1996). *Uncertain Times: Preventing Illness, Promoting Wellness* (Abstracts). 1996 International Conference on Physician Health, Chandler, Arizona.

American Medical Association, Council on Mental Health (1973). The sick physician: Impairment by psychiatric disorders, including alcoholism and drug dependence. *Journal of the American Medical Association* 233:684–687.

American Psychiatric Association (1987). *Diagnostic and Statistical Manual of Mental Disorders, 3rd Edition, Revised.* Washington, DC: American Psychiatric Press.

Americans With Disabilities Act of 1990. Public Law 101–336, 104 Stat 327.

Angres DH, Talbott D & Angres K (in press). Chemical dependency for professionals: The Rush and Talbott Recovery System Programs. *Healing the Healer, Treating the Chemically Dependent Physician.* Madison, CT: Psychosocial Press.

Anthony J & Hetzer J (1991). Syndrome of drug abuse and dependence. In LN Robins & DA Regier (eds.) *Psychiatric Disorders in America.* New York, NY: The Free Press, Macmillan, 116–154.

Bissell L & Haberman P (1984). *Alcoholism in the Professions.* New York, NY: Oxford University Press.

Bissell L & Skorina J (1987). One hundred alcoholic women in medicine: An interview study. *Journal of the American Medical Association* 57:2939–2944.

Blume S (1991). Women, alcohol, and drugs. In NS Miller (ed.) *Comprehensive Handbook of Drug and Alcohol Addiction.* New York, NY: Marcel Dekker, 147–177.

Brewster J (1986). Prevalence of alcohol and other drug problems among physicians. *Journal of the American Medical Association* 255:1913–1920.

Caston S (1981). *Prohibition: The Lie of the Land.* New York: The Free Press.

Catalano R, Howard M, Hawkins J & Wells E (1986). Relapse in the addictions: Rates, determinants, and promising prevention strategies. *1988 Surgeon General's Report on Health Consequences of Smoking.* Washington, DC: Office on Smoking and Health.

Centrella M (1994). Physician addiction and impairment—Current thinking: A review. *Journal of Addictive Disease* 13:91–105.

Clatt M (1968). Alcoholism and drug dependence in doctors and nurses. *British Medical Journal* 1:380–381.

Crowley T (1986). Doctor's drug abuse reduced during contingency-contracting treatment. *Alcohol and Drug Research* 6:299–307.

DeQuincy T (1950). *Confessions of an English Opium Eater.* New York, NY: Heritage Press, 38–39.

Doll T & Hill S (1964). Mortality in relation to smoking: Ten years' observation of British doctors. *British Medical Journal* 1:1399–1410, 1460–1467.

East W (1947). The British government report to the United Nations on the traffic of opium and other dangerous drugs. *British Journal of Addiction* 46:38–39.

Ehrhardt H (1959). Drug addiction in medical and allied professionals in Germany. *Bulletin on Narcotics* 11:18–26.

Filstead W, Parrella D, Ross A & Norton E (1994). Management of addiction treatment: Key issues in outcomes research. In NS Miller (ed.) *Principles of Addiction Medicine.* Washington, DC: American Society of Addiction Medicine.

Flexner A (1910). *Medical Education in the United States.* New York, NY: American Association of Medical Colleges.

Galanter M, Talbott G, Gallegos K & Rubenstone E (1990). Combined alcoholics anonymous and professional care for addicted physicians. *American Journal of Psychiatry* 147:64–68.

Gallegos K (1987). The Pilot Impaired Physicians Epidemiologic Surveillance System (PIPESS). *New Mexico Medical Journal* 36:264–266.

Gallegos K, Browne C, Veit F & Talbott G (1988). Addiction in anesthesiologists: Drug access and patterns of substance abuse. *Quality Review Bulletin* 116–122.

Gallegos K, Keppler J & Wilson P (1989). Returning to work after rehabilitation: Aftercare, follow-up and workplace reliability. *Occupational Medicine: State of the Art Reviews* 4:357–371.

Gallegos K, Lubin B, Bowers C et al. (1992). Relapse and recovery: Five to ten year follow study of chemically dependent physicians—The Georgia experience. *Maryland Medical Journal* 41:315–319.

Gallegos K & Norton, M (1984). Characterization of Georgia's impaired physicians program treatment population: Data and statistics. *Journal of the Medical Association of Georgia* 73:755–758.

Goby M, Bradley N & Bespalec D (1979). Physicians treated for alcoholism: A follow-up study. *Alcoholism: Clinical & Experimental Research* 3:121–124.

Goetz R (1996). Personal communication, June.

Gordis E (1989). Relapse and craving. *Alcohol Alert.* Rockville, MD: National Institute on Alcohol Abuse and Alcoholism, 6:3.

Gorski T (1986). *Staying Sober: A Guide for Relapse Prevention.* Independence, MO: Independence Press.

Gorski T (1989a). *Passages Through Recovery : An Action Plan for Preventing Relapse.* Center City, MN: Hazelden.

Gorski T (1989b). *The Relapse and Recovery Grid.* Center City, MN: Hazelden, 1989.

Halzer J, Bumam A & McEvoy L (1991). Alcohol abuse and dependence. In LN Robins & DA Regier (eds.) *Psychiatric Disorders in America: The Epidemiologic Catchment Area Study.* New York, NY: The Free Press/Macmillan, 81–115.

Harrington R et al. (1982). Treating substance-use disorders among physicians. *Journal of the American Medical Association* 2253–2257.

Harris L (1987). *Consumers' Perception of Substance Abuse by Health Care Providers.* Research abstracts presented at the AMA Eighth National Conference on Impaired Health Professionals. Chicago, IL.

Harris S (1914). Alcoholism and drug addiction among physicians of Alabama. *Transactions of the Medical Association of Alabama* 685–691.

House of Representatives Rep. No 485, 101st Congress, 2nd Sec. (part 2) 56, (part 3) 46 (1990). Reprinted in U.S. Code Cong Admin. News, 1990 4:338–469.

Hughes P, Brandenburg N, Baldwin D et al. (1992). Prevalence of substance use among U.S. physicians. *Journal of the American Medical Association* 1267:2333–2339.

Ikoda R & Pelton C (1990). Diversion programs for impaired physicians. *Western Journal of Medicine* 152:617–621.

Jex S et al. (1992). Relations among stressors, strains, and substance use among resident physicians. *International Journal of the Addictions* 27:479–494.

Johnson R & Connelly, J (1981). Addicted physicians: A closer look. *Journal of the American Medical Association* 245:253–257.

Jones L (1958). How 92% beat the dope habit. *Bulletin of the Los Angeles County Medical Society* 19:37–40.

Keeve J (1984). Physicians at risk: Some epidemiologic considerations of alcoholism, drug abuse, and suicide. *Journal of Occupational Medicine* 26:503–508.

Kliner D, Spicer J & Barnett P (1980). Treatment outcome of alcoholic physicians. *Journal of Studies on Alcohol* 41:1217–1220.

Kosten T & Kleber H (1988). Differential diagnoses of psychiatric comorbidity in substance abusers. *Journal of Substance Abuse Treatment* 5:201–206.

Kurtz E (1982). Why AA works. *Journal of Studies on Alcohol* 43:38–80.

Mattison J (1984). Morphinism in medical men. *Journal of the American Medical Association* 23:186–188.

McAuliffe W (1987). Risk factors in drug impairment in random samples of physicians and medical students. *International Journal of Addiction* 22(9):825.

Mee-Lee D (1974). Clinical overview of addiction treatment: Patient placement criteria and patient-treatment matching. In NS Miller (ed.) *Principles of Addiction Medicine.* Chevy Chase, MD: American Society of Addiction Medicine.

Mee-Lee D (1985). The Recovery Attitude and Treatment Evaluator (RAATE): An Instrument for Patient Progress and Treatment Assignment. Presented at the 34th International Congress on Alcoholism and Drug Dependence.

Mee-Lee D, Shulman G & Gartner L (1996). *Patient Placement Criteria for the Treatment of Psychoactive Substance Use Disorders, Second Edition.* Chevy Chase, MD: American Society of Addiction Medicine.

Miscal B (1991). Monitoring recovering physicians: The New Mexico experience. *American College of Surgeons' Bulletin* 76:22–40.

Modlin H & Montes A (1964). Narcotic addiction in physicians. *American Journal of Psychiatry* 121:358–363.

Moore R (1990). Youthful precursors of alcohol abuse in physicians. *The American Journal of Medicine* 88:332–336.

Morse R et al. (1984). Prognosis of physicians treated for alcoholism and drug dependence. *Journal of the American Medical Association* 251:743–746.

Musto D (1973). *The American Disease: Origins of Narcotic Control.* New Haven, CT: Yale University Press.

Nesbitt J (1970). The sick doctor statute: A new approach to an old problem. *Federation Bulletin* 70:266–279.

Noland S & Halstad W (1991). Idiosyncrasies of a surgical legend. *Harvard Medical Alumni Bulletin* 65:17–23.

Paget J (1869). What becomes of medical students? *St. Bartholomew's Hospital Report* 5:238–242.

Pascor M (1942). Physician drug addicts. *Diseases of the Nervous System* 3:2–3.

Rasseth H et al. (1994). Ad hoc committee on physician impairment (Report). *Federation of State Medical Boards.*

Reading E (192). Nine years' experience with chemically dependent physicians: The New Jersey experience. *Maryland Medical Journal* 41:325–329.

Regier D et al. (1990). Co-morbidity of mental disorders with alcohol and other drug abuse: Results of the Epidemiologic Catchment Area (ECA) study. *Journal of the American Medical Association* 264:2511–2518.

Richman J (1912). Occupational stress, psychological vulnerability and alcohol-related problems over time in future physicians. *Alcoholism: Clinical & Experimental Research* 16(2):166–171.

Rinaldi R, Steindler M, Wilford BB, Goodwin D et al. (1988). Clarification and standardization of substance abuse terminology. *Journal of the American Medical Association* 254:555–657.

Robeck G, Randolph L, Mead D et al. (1993). *Physician Characteristics and Distribution in the U.S.* Chicago, IL: American Medical Association.

Robins L & Regier D (1991). *Psychiatric Disorders in America: The Epidemiologic Catchment Area Study.* New York, NY: The Free Press/Macmillan Inc.

Robinson E, Fitzgerald J & Gallegos K (1985). Brain functioning and addiction: What neuropsychologic studies reveal. *Journal of the Medical Association of Georgia* 73:74–79.

Robertson J (1986). *Annotated Bibliography on Physician Impairment and Well-Being.* Chicago, IL: American Medical Association.

Shore J (1987). The Oregon experience with impaired physicians on probation. *Journal of the American Medical Association* 257:2931–2934.

Smith P & Smith D (1991). Treatment outcomes of impaired physicians in Oklahoma. *Journal of the Oklahoma State Medical Association* 84:599–603.

Starr P (1982). *The Social Transformation of American Medicine.* New York, NY: Basic Books.

Steindler E (1974). Physician impairment: Past, present, and future. *Journal of the Medical Association of Georgia* 73:741–743.

Stimson G, Oppenheimer B & Stimson C (1984). Drug abuse in the medical profession. *British Journal of Addiction* 79:395–402.

Summer G (1996). Personal communication, June.

Summer G (1996). Federation of State Physicians Health Programs, Inc. (letter), June 19.

Talbott G (1996). Letter summarizing the American Medical Association's Physician Health Committee meeting. Atlanta, GA.

Talbott G & Gallegos K (1990). Intervention with health professionals. *Addiction & Recovery* 10(3):13–16.

Talbott G, Gallegos K, Wilson P & Porter T (1987). The Medical Association of Georgia's impaired physician program—Review of the first 1,000 physicians: Analysis of specialty. *Journal of the American Medical Association* 257:2927–2930.

Talbott G & Martin C (1986). Treating impaired physicians: Fourteen keys to success. *Virginia Medical Journal* 113:95–99.

Talbott G & Wright C (1987). Chemical dependence in healthcare professionals. *Occupational Medicine: State of the Art Reviews* 2:581–591.

Ulwelling J (1991). The evolution of the Oregon program for impaired physicians. *American College of Surgeons Bulletin* 76:18–2 1.

U.S. Congress, Public Law No. 233. Approved December 7, 1914.

U.S. Congress, Public Law No. 238. Approved, August 2, 1937.

U.S. Department of Health and Human Services (1989). *Reducing the Health Consequences of Smoking: 25 Years of Progress. A Report of the Surgeon General.* Rockville, MD: Office on Smoking and Health.

Vaillant G (1983). *The Natural History of Alcoholism.* Cambridge, MA: Harvard University Press.

Vaillant G (1992). Physician, cherish thyself. The hazards of self prescribing. *Journal of the American Medical Association* 267:2373–2374.

Vaillant G, Clark W et al. (1983). Prospective study of alcoholism treatment. *American Journal of Medicine* 75:455–463.

Vaillant G, Soborale N & McArthur C (1992). Some psychologic vulnerabilities of physicians. *The New England Journal of Medicine* 287:372–375.

Vincent M, Robinson E & Latt L (1969). Physicians as patients: Private psychiatric hospital experience. *Canadian Medical Association Journal* 100:403–412.

Wall J (1958). The results of hospital treatment of addiction in physicians. *Federation Bulletin* 45:144–152.

Watry A, Morgan D, Earley P et al. (1996). *Georgia Composite State Board of Medical Examiners Guidelines for Problem Physicians.* Atlanta, GA: Board of Medical Examiners.

Watterson D (1976). Psychiatric illness in the medical profession: Incidence in relation to sex and field of practice. *Canadian Medical Association Journal* 115:311–317.

Wollot H & Lambert J (1982). Drug addiction among Quebec physicians. *Canadian Medical Association Journal* 126:927–930.

Wright C (1990). Physician addiction to pharmaceuticals: Personal history, practice setting, access to drugs and recovery. *New Mexico Medical Journal* 39:1021–1025.

APPENDIX A

Policy Statements of the American Society of Addiction Medicine

The statements listed here have been adopted as policies of the American Society of Addiction Medicine. Copies may be obtained by contacting the ASAM office.

Abstinence (1974)

The Definition of Alcoholism (NCADD/ASAM) (1990)

Labeling (1979)

Self-Help Groups (1979)

Increasing the Availability of Appropriate High-Quality Alcoholism Services to All Americans, Delivered in a Cost-Effective Way (1980)

Fetal Alcohol Syndrome (1980)

Treatment for Alcoholism and Other Drug Dependencies (1980, 1986, 1987)

Medical Needs of the Public Inebriate (1980)

NIAAA and Alcoholism Research (1982)

State of Recovery (1982)

Advertising (1983, 1996, 1998)

Alcoholism as a Primary Disease (1983)

The Impaired Health Professional (1984)

Prevention (1984, 1989, 1990)

The Treatment of Patients with Alcoholism or Other Drug Dependencies, and Who Have or Are at Risk for Acquired Immunodeficiency Syndrome (AIDS) (1985)

How to Identify a Physician Recognized for Expertness in Diagnosis and Treatment of Alcoholism and Other Drug Dependence (1986)

Mandatory Insurance Coverage (1986)

Clean Air Policy (1986)

Children of Parents Suffering from Alcoholism and Other Drug Dependencies (1987)

Transplantation (1987)

Highway Safety in Relation to Alcoholism and Other Drug Dependencies (1987)

Marijuana (1987, 1997, 1998)

Nicotine Dependence and Tobacco (1988, 1989, 1996)

The Use of Alcohol and Other Drugs During Pregnancy (1988)

Measures to Counteract Prescription Drug Diversion (1989)

Nicotine Dependence: Documentation of Nicotine Dependence on Death Certificates and Hospital Discharge Sheets (1989)

Returning to Work People Treated for Alcoholism and Other Drug Dependencies (1989)

Medical Care in Recovery (1989)

Chemically Dependent Women and Pregnancy (1989)

Methadone Treatment (1990, 1991)

Reimbursement for the Treatment of Nicotine Dependence (1990)

Third-Party Coverage for Addiction Treatment (1990)

Managed Care and Addiction Medicine (1990)

Trauma and Chemical Misuse/Dependency (1991)

The Role of Medical Review Officers (1991, 1992)

Addiction Medicine and Health Insurance Reform (1992)

Recommendations for Design of Treatment Efficacy Research With Emphasis on Outcome Measures (1992)

Clinical Applications of the Nicotine Patch (1992)

Principles of Medical Ethics (1992)

Core Benefit for Primary Care and Specialty Treatment and Prevention of Alcohol, Nicotine and Drug Abuse and Dependence (1993)

The Practice of Addiction Medicine (1993)

Discrimination on the Basis of Sexual Orientation (1993)

National Drug Policy (1994)

Persons with Alcohol & Other Drug (AOD) Problems and the Criminal Justice System (1994)

Mutually Accepted Sanctions by State Boards of Medical Examiners (1994)

Inquiring into Physicians' Health on Applications for Licensure, Examination and Privileges (1994)

Primary Medical Care for HIV Infected Patients in Addiction Treatment (1994)

HIV Testing of Patients in Addiction Treatment Facilities (1994)

Needle Exchange (1994)

HIV/AIDS Education for Drug and Alcohol Treatment (1994)

Federal Funding for Addiction Prevention, Treatment and Rehabilitation (1995)

Fair Treatment of Persons Whose Job Performance is Impaired by Alcoholism and Other Drug Dependencies (1996)

Rights and Responsibilities of Physicians in the Use of Opioids for the Treatment of Pain (1997)

Definitions Related to the Use of Opioids in Pain Treatment (1997)

Screening for Addiction in Primary Care Settings (1997)

Effective Treatment of Addictive Disorders: A Basis for a Dialogue Between the American Society of Addiction Medicine and the American Managed Behavioral Healthcare Association (1997)

Parity in Benefit Coverage: A Joint Statement by the American Society of Addiction Medicine and the American Managed Behavioral Healthcare Association (1997)

Relationship Between Treatment and Self Help: A Joint Statement of the American Society of Addiction Medicine, Inc., the American Psychiatric Association and the American Academy of Addiction Psychiatry (1997)

Buprenorphine (1998)

Documenting the History of Substance Use in the History and Physical Examination (1998)

APPENDIX B

Section 1. Screening Instruments

Addiction Severity Index (ASI)
Alcohol Dependence Scale
Alcohol Use Disorders Identification Test (AUDIT)
CAGE
Clinical Institute Withdrawal Assessment for Alcohol, Revised (CIWA—Ar)
Drinker Inventory of Consequences (DrInC)
Michigan Alcohol Screening Test (MAST and SMAST)
Problem Oriented Screening Instrument for Teenagers (POSIT)
Self-Administered Alcoholism Screening Test (SAAST)

ADDICTION SEVERITY INDEX (ASI)

The Addiction Severity Index (ASI) is a semistructured interview designed to address seven potential problem areas in substance abusing patients: medical status, employment and support, drug use, alcohol use, legal status, family/social status, and psychiatric status. In one hour, a skilled interviewer can gather information on recent (past 30 days) and lifetime problems in all of the problem areas.

Uses. The ASI provides an overview of problems related to substance abuse, rather than focusing on any single area (McLellan, Luborsky et al., 1980, 1985; McLellan, Kushner et al., 1992). The ASI thus can be used effectively to explore problems within any adult group of individuals who report substance abuse as their major problem. It has been used with psychiatrically ill, homeless, pregnant, and prisoner populations, but its major use has been with adults seeking treatment for substance abuse problems. The ASI also has been used extensively for treatment planning and outcome evaluation. Outcome evaluation packages for individual programs or for treatment systems are available.

Design. The ASI contains approximately 200 items and seven subscales. Time required for administration is 50 minutes to one hour. Training is required to administer the instrument, and a self-training packet is available. Scoring time is about five minutes for the severity rating. Computerized scoring or interpretation are available.

The ASI provides two scores: severity ratings are subjective ratings of the client's need for treatment, derived by the interviewer, while composite scores are measures of problem severity during the preceding 30 days and are calculated by a computerized scoring program.

Validity. The ASI has been normed on multiple treatment groups (alcohol, opiate, cocaine; public and private; inpatient and outpatient) and subject groups (men, women, psychiatrically ill substance users, pregnant substance users, gamblers, homeless persons, probationers, and employee assistance clients). The following reliability studies have been conducted for the ASI: test-retest, split half, and internal consistency. Measures of utility derived include: content, criterion (predictive, concurrent, "postdictive"), and construct (Allen & Columbus, 1995).

Availability. There is no charge for the instrument, although a minimal fee for photocopying and mailing may apply. A free computerized scoring disk is provided with the training materials. Copies of the ASI and related materials may be obtained from the DeltaMetrics/TRI ASI Information Line at 1-800/238-2433.

ALCOHOL DEPENDENCE SCALE (ADS)

The Alcohol Dependence Scale (ADS) provides a quantitative measure of the severity of alcohol dependence consistent with the concept of the alcohol dependence syndrome.

Uses. Because the test can be administered in approximately five minutes, it can be used for screening and case-finding in a variety of settings. The ADS also is widely used as a research and clinical tool (Skinner & Allen, 1992).

Use of the ADS has been reported primarily for clinical adult samples; however, researchers also have used the instrument in general population and correctional settings. The ADS has been found to have excellent predictive value with respect to a *DSM* diagnosis. Moreover, the ADS yields a measure of the severity of dependence that is important for treatment planning, especially with respect to the intensity of care (Allen & Columbus, 1995).

Design. The 25 items cover alcohol withdrawal symptoms, impaired control over drinking, awareness of a compulsion to drink, increased tolerance to alcohol, and salience of alcohol-seeking behavior (Skinner & Horn, 1984).

The printed instructions for the ADS refer to the preceding 12-month period. However, instructions can be altered for use as an outcome measure at selected intervals (for example, at 6, 12, or 24 months) following treatment.

Validity. The ADS has been found to be reliable and valid. Research shows that it has excellent predictive value with respect to *DSM* diagnoses (Allen & Columbus, 1995).

Availability. The ADS is copyrighted by the Addiction Research Foundation and cannot be copied without permission. In addition to the questionnaire version, a computer-administered version is available as part of the Computerized Lifestyle Assessment (Alcohol Module). Information is available from Marketing Services, Addiction Research Foundation, 33 Russell Street, Toronto, Ontario, Canada M5S 2S1, or by telephone at 416/545-6000.

ALCOHOL USE DISORDERS IDENTIFICATION TEST (AUDIT)

The Alcohol Use Disorders Identification Test (AUDIT) was developed by the World Health Organization in 1989 to identify persons whose alcohol consumption has become hazardous or harmful to their health (Allen & Columbus, 1995).

Uses. The test is appropriate for a variety of populations and in multiple settings, including primary care, emergency departments, surgery and psychiatric units. It also has been used with criminal justice populations, military personnel, and in workplace programs.

Design. The AUDIT is a 10-item screening questionnaire that can be incorporated into a medical history. It contains questions about recent alcohol consumption, dependence symptoms, and alcohol-related problems (Allen & Columbus, 1995).

Validity. The test has been normed on heavy drinkers and alcoholics. Test-retest reliability and internal consistency have been validated. Measures of validity include content, criterion (predictive, concurrent, "postdictive"), and construct.

Availability. The AUDIT is copyrighted by the World Health Organization. The test and module are free; the training materials cost $75. Information is available from the WHO Programme on Substance Abuse, 1211 Geneva, Switzerland, or from Thomas F. Babor, Alcohol Research Center, University of Connecticut, Farmington, CT 06030.

CAGE

The CAGE is a simple, four-question screening instrument that can be used in a variety of settings. The CAGE questions are:

- Have you ever felt you ought to **C**ut down on your drinking?
- Have people **A**nnoyed you by criticizing your drinking?
- Have you ever felt **B**ad or guilty about your drinking?
- Have you ever had a drink first thing in the morning (**E**ye opener) to steady your nerves or get rid of a hangover?

Two or more affirmative answers are considered indicative of probable alcoholism, while one affirmative answer indicates that the patient's alcohol use deserves further evaluation (Ewing, 1984).

CLINICAL INSTITUTE WITHDRAWAL ASSESSMENT FOR ALCOHOL, REVISED (CIWA—Ar)

The Clinical Institute Withdrawal Assessment for Alcohol, Revised (CIWA—Ar) was developed by the Addiction Research Foundation.

Uses. The CIWA—Ar is widely used in clinical and research settings for initial assessment and ongoing monitoring of alcohol withdrawal symptoms.

Validity. The CIWA—Ar has been studied only in alcohol treatment programs; efficacy outside such program settings is not clear (Kasser, Geller et al., 1997).

Availability. The CIWA—Ar is not copyrighted. Information is available from Marketing Services, Addiction Research Foundation, 33 Russell Street, Toronto, Ontario, Canada M5S 2S1, or by telephone at 416/545-6000.

DRINKER INVENTORY OF CONSEQUENCES (DrInC)

The DrInC is a self-administered 50-item questionnaire designed to measure adverse consequences of alcohol abuse in five life areas: Interpersonal, Physical, Social, Impulsive, and Intrapersonal.

Uses. The test has been used in a variety of settings, including inpatient and outpatient alcohol treatment facilities, homeless shelters and college campuses. It can be used for treatment planning, and has been used in alcohol treatment clinical trials as an outcome measure.

Design. DrInC items span a full spectrum of adverse consequences, ranging from those encountered by heavy social drinkers to those seen in severely alcoholic populations. Each of the five life-area scales provides a lifetime and past three months measure of adverse consequences. Scales can be combined to assess total adverse consequences.

Validity. Normative data are available for interpretation of client scale scores, and a brief version of the DrInC, the Short Index of Problems (SIP), is available when assessment time is limited.

A test manual is available that provides normative data for interpretation of total and subscale scores for a number of different populations (e.g., male, female, inpatient, outpatient). Simple directions are provided for scoring the DrInC.

Availability. The DrInC is not copyrighted. Copies can be obtained from the National Clearinghouse for Alcohol and Drug Information, P.O. Box 2345, Rockville, MD 20847-2345, or by telephone at 1-800/729-6686.

MICHIGAN ALCOHOL SCREENING TEST (MAST AND SMAST)

The Michigan Alcoholism Screening Test (MAST), which is one of the most widely used measures for assessing alcohol use, is a 25-item questionnaire designed to provide a rapid and effective screen for lifetime alcohol-related problems and alcoholism.

Uses. Clinically, the MAST can be used to screen for alcoholism with a variety of populations. In research studies, it is useful in assessing the extent of lifetime alcohol-related problems.

Design. The MAST can be used in either a paper-and-pencil or interview format. Its target population is adults. The instrument consists of 25 questions and requires 10 minutes to administer.

Also available are briefer versions of the MAST, including the 10-item Brief MAST, the 13-item Short MAST (SMAST), and a nine-item modified version called the Malmo modification (Mm-MAST). A geriatric version, called the MAST-G, also has been developed.

Validity. Reliability studies on the MAST include test-retest reliability and internal consistency. Measures of validity have been derived for both content and criterion (predictive, concurrent, "postdictive").

Availability. The MAST is not copyrighted and there is no fee for its use. Copies are available at $5 each from Melvin L. Selzer, M.D., 6967 Paseo Laredo, La Jolla, CA 92037.

PROBLEM ORIENTED SCREENING INSTRUMENT FOR TEENAGERS (POSIT)

The POSIT is a simple, cost-efficient problem screen for use with troubled adolescents who may have one or more problems amenable to treatment or to a combination of preventive services.

Uses. The POSIT can be administered to populations in schools, the juvenile and family court system, and medical, psychiatric, alcohol and drug treatment programs as the first step toward identifying problem areas that require a more comprehensive diagnostic assessment. The target population is adolescents 12 through 19 years of age.

Design. Available in English and Spanish language versions, the POSIT is a brief screening tool designed to identify problems and the potential need for service in 10 functional areas, including substance use/abuse, mental and physical health, family and peer relations, vocation, and special education.

The test can be administered by any office personnel (no special qualifications are necessary). Computerized scoring and interpretation are available.

Availability. The POSIT is not copyrighted. Copies of the test and a related scoring template can be obtained from the National Clearinghouse for Alcohol and Drug Information, P.O. Box 2345, Rockville, MD 20847-2345, or by telephone at 1-800/729-6686.

SELF-ADMINISTERED ALCOHOLISM SCREENING TEST (SAAST)

The Self-Administered Alcoholism Screening Test (SAAST) is a 37-item instrument derived from the MAST.

Uses. The SAAST is used as a screening instrument for alcoholism in medical inpatient and outpatient settings.

Design. The SAAST was derived by adding items to the MAST to make it suitable for use in general medical populations. The test is available in a form suitable for administration to the patient, as well as in a form for use with the patient's spouse, friend, et al. Domains include loss of control, occupational and social disruption, physical consequences, emotional consequences, concern on the part of others, and family members with alcohol problems.

Validity. Reliability studies have examined internal consistency. Measures of validity include predictive, concurrent, and "postdictive" criteria. Factor analysis has been done.

Availability. The instrument is copyrighted by the Mayo Foundation. Information can be obtained from the Mayo Foundation, Rochester, MN.

ACKNOWLEDGMENT: Much of the information in this section is excerpted from Allen JP & Columbus M (1995). Assessing Alcohol Problems: A Guide for Clinicians and Researchers (NIAAA Treatment Handbook, Series 4). *Rockville, MD: National Institute on Alcohol Abuse and Alcoholism. Appreciation is expressed to the authors and publisher.*

REFERENCES

Allen JP & Columbus M (1995). *Assessing Alcohol Problems: A Guide for Clinicians and Researchers (NIAAA Treatment Handbook, Series 4)*. Rockville, MD: National Institute on Alcohol Abuse and Alcoholism.

Babor TF, de la Fuente JR, Saunders J & Grant M (1992). *AUDIT: The Alcohol Use Disorders Identification Test: Guidelines for Use in Primary Health Care.* Geneva, Switzerland: World Health Organization.

Ewing JA (1984). The CAGE questionnaire. *Journal of the American Medical Association* 252:1907.

Hedlund JL & Vieweg BW (1984). The Michigan Alcoholism Screening Test (MAST): A comprehensive review. *Journal of Operational Psychiatry* 15:55–64.

Kasser CL, Geller A, Howell EF & Wartenberg AA (1997). Detoxification: Principles and protocols. In *Topics in Addiction Medicine.* Chevy Chase, MD: American Society of Addiction Medicine.

McLellan AT, Kushner H, Metzger D, Peters F et al. (1992). The fifth edition of the Addiction Severity Index. *Journal of Substance Abuse Treatment* 9:199–213.

McLellan AT, Luborsky L, Cacciola J & Griffith J (1985). New data from the Addiction Severity Index: Reliability and validity in three centers. *Journal of Nervous and Mental Disease* 173:412–423.

McLellan AT, Luborsky L, O'Brien CP & Woody GE (1980). An improved diagnostic instrument for substance abuse patients: The Addiction Severity Index. *Journal of Nervous and Mental Disease* 168:26–33.

Miller WR, Tonigan JS & Longabaugh R (1995). *The Drinker Inventory of Consequences (DrInC): An Instrument for Assessing Adverse Consequences of Alcohol Abuse; Test Manual (NIAAA Project MATCH Monograph Series 4)*. Washington, DC: National Institute on Alcohol Abuse and Alcoholism.

Selzer ML (1971). The Michigan Alcoholism Screening Test: The quest for a new diagnostic instrument. *American Journal of Psychiatry* 127:1653–1658.

Skinner HA & Allen BA (1982). Alcohol dependence syndrome: Measurement and validation. *Journal of Abnormal Psychology* 91:199–209.

Skinner HA & Horn JL (1984). *Alcohol Dependence Scale: Users Guide.* Toronto, Canada: Addiction Research Foundation.

APPENDIX B

Section 2. Summary of the DSM-IV Diagnostic Criteria

DSM-IV Criteria for Substance Dependence
DSM-IV Criteria for Substance Abuse
DSM-IV Criteria for Substance Withdrawal

The following criteria for substance dependence, substance abuse and substance withdrawal are excerpted from the fourth edition (*DSM-IV*) of the American Psychiatric Association's *Diagnostic and Statistical Manual of Mental Disorders* (*DSM-IV*; 1994).

The *DSM-IV* divides substance-related disorders into two groups: Substance Use Disorders (including Substance Dependence and Substance Abuse) and the Substance-Induced Disorders (including Substance Intoxication, Substance Withdrawal, Substance-Induced Delirium, Substance-Induced Persisting Dementia, Substance-Induced Persisting Amnestic Disorder, Substance-Induced Psychotic Disorder, Substance-Induced Mood Disorder, Substance-Induced Anxiety Disorder, Substance-Induced Sexual Dysfunction, and Substance-Induced Sleep Disorder). The diagnoses associated with each specific group of substances are shown in Table 1.

DSM-IV CRITERIA FOR SUBSTANCE DEPENDENCE

The *DSM-IV* defines substance dependence as a syndrome characterized by a maladaptive pattern of substance use, leading to clinically significant impairment or distress, as manifested by three (or more) of the following, occurring at any time in the same 12-month period:

1. Tolerance, as defined by either of the following:
   (a) a need for markedly increased amounts of the substance to achieve intoxication or desired effect, or
   (b) markedly diminished effect with continued use of the same amount of the substance.
2. Withdrawal, as manifested by either of the following:
   (a) the characteristic withdrawal syndrome for the substance (refer to Criteria A and B of the criteria sets for Withdrawal from the specific substances), or
   (b) the same (or a closely related) substance is taken to relieve or avoid withdrawal symptoms.
3. The substance is often taken in larger amounts or over a longer period than was intended.
4. There is a persistent desire or unsuccessful efforts to cut down or control substance use.
5. A great deal of time is spent in activities necessary to obtain the substance (e.g., visiting multiple doctors or driving long distances), use the substance (e.g., chain-smoking), or recover from its effects.
6. Important social, occupational, or recreational activities are given up or reduced because of substance use.
7. The substance use is continued despite knowledge of having a persistent or recurrent physical or psychological problem that is likely to have been caused or exacerbated by the substance (e.g., current cocaine use despite recognition of cocaine- induced depression, or continued drinking despite recognition that an ulcer was made worse by alcohol consumption).

Specify if:

With Physiological Dependence: evidence of tolerance or withdrawal (i.e., either Item 1 or 2 is present).

TABLE 1. DSM-IV Diagnoses Associated with Specific Classes of Substances

	Dependence	Abuse	Intoxication	Withdrawal	Intoxication Delirium	Withdrawal Delirium	Dementia	Amnestic Disorder	Psychotic Disorders	Mood Disorders	Anxiety Disorders	Sexual Dysfunctions	Sleep Disorders
Alcohol	X	X	X	X	I	W	P	P	I/W	I/W	I/W	I	I/W
Amphetamines	X	X	X	X	I				I	I/X	I	I	I/W
Caffeine		X									I		I
Cannabis	X	X	X		I				I		I		
Cocaine	X	X	X	X	I				I	I/W	I/W	I	I/W
Hallucinogens	X	X	X		I				I	I	I		
Inhalants	X	X	X		I		P		I	I	I		
Nicotine	X			X									
Opioids	X	X	X	X	X	I			I	I		I	I/W
Phencyclidine	X	X	X		I				I	I	I		
Sedatives, hypnotics, or anxiolytics	X	X	X	X	I	W	P	P	I/W	I/W	W	I	I/W
Polysubstance	X												
Other	X	X	X	X	I	W	P	P	I/W	I/W	I/W	I	I/W

* Also Hallucinogen Persisting Perception Disorder (Flashbacks).

Note: X, I, W, I/W, or P indicates that the category is recognized in DSM-IV. In addition, I indicates that the specifier With Onset During Intoxication may be noted for the category (except for Intoxication Delirium); W indicates that the specifier With Onset During Withdrawal may be noted for the category (except for Withdrawal Delirium); and I/W indicates that either With Onset During Intoxication or With Onset During Withdrawal may be noted for the category. P indicates that the disorder is Persisting.

Source: American Psychiatric Association (1994). *Diagnostic and Statistical Manual of Mental Disorders, 4th Edition.* Washington, DC: American Psychiatric Press.

Without Physiological Dependence: no evidence of tolerance or withdrawal (i.e., neither Item 1 nor 2 is present).

Course specifiers:

Early Full Remission: This specifier is used if, for at least 1 month, but for less than 12 months, no criteria for Dependence or Abuse have been met.

Early Partial Remission: This specifier is used if, for at least 1 month, but less than 12 months, one or more criteria for Dependence or abuse have been met (but the full criteria for Dependence has not been met).

Sustained Full Remission: This specifier is used if none of the criteria for Dependence or Abuse have been met at any time during a period of 12 months or longer.

Sustained Partial Remission: This specifier is used if full criteria for Dependence have not been met for a period of 12 months or longer, however, one or more criteria for Dependence or Abuse have been met.

On Agonist Therapy: This specifier is used if the individual is on a prescribed agonist medication, and no criteria for Dependence or Abuse have been met for that class of medication for at least the past month (except tolerance to, or withdrawal from, the agonist). This category also applies to those being treated for Dependence using a partial agonist or an agonist/antagonist.

In A Controlled Environment: This specifier is used if the individual is in an environment where access to alcohol and controlled substances is restricted, and no criteria for Dependence or Abuse have been met for at least the past month. Examples of these environments are closely supervised and substance-free jails, therapeutic communities, or locked hospital units.

DSM-IV CRITERIA FOR SUBSTANCE ABUSE

According to the *DSM-IV* criteria, substance abuse is characterized by:

1. A maladaptive pattern of substance use leading to clinically significant impairment or distress, as manifested by one (or more) of the following, occurring within a 12-month period:
   (a) Recurrent substance use resulting in a failure to fulfill major role obligations at work, school, or home (e.g., repeated absences or poor work performance related to substance use; substance-related absences, suspensions, or expulsions from school; neglect of children or household); or
   (b) Recurrent substance use in situations in which it is physically hazardous (e.g., driving an automobile or operating a machine when impaired by substance use); or
   (c) Recurrent substance-related legal problems (e.g., arrests for substance-related disorderly conduct); or
   (d) Continued substance use despite having persistent or recurrent social or interpersonal problems caused or exacerbated by the effects of the substance (e.g., arguments with spouse about consequences of intoxication, physical fights).
2. The symptoms have never met the criteria for Substance Dependence for this class of substance.

DSM-IV CRITERIA FOR SUBSTANCE WITHDRAWAL

DSM-IV criteria for substance withdrawal are three:

1. The development of a substance-specific syndrome due to the cessation of (or reduction in) substance use that has been heavy and prolonged.
2. The substance-specific syndrome causes clinically significant distress or impairment in social, occupational or other important areas of functioning.
3. The symptoms are not due to a general medical condition and are not better accounted for by another mental disorder.

REFERENCE

American Psychiatric Association (1994). *Diagnostic and Statistical Manual of Mental Disorders, 4th Edition.* Washington, DC: American Psychiatric Press.

APPENDIX B

Section 3. ICD-10 Diagnostic Criteria for Harmful Use of Alcohol or Drugs and the Dependence Syndrome

The following diagnostic criteria are excerpted from the World Health Organization's *International Classification of Diseases, Tenth Revision* (Clinical Description and Diagnostic Guidelines Version).

This block contains a wide variety of disorders that differ in severity (from uncomplicated intoxication and harmful use to obvious psychotic disorders and dementia). All are attributable to the use of one or more psychoactive substances (which may or may not have been medically prescribed). They are classified as follows:

MENTAL AND BEHAVIORAL DISORDERS DUE TO PSYCHOACTIVE SUBSTANCE USE

F10. Mental and behavioural disorders due to use of alcohol

F11. Mental and behavioural disorders due to use of opioids

F12. Mental and behavioural disorders due to use of cannabinoids

F13. Mental and behavioural disorders due to use of sedatives or hypnotics

F14. Mental and behavioural disorders due to use of cocaine

F15. Mental and behavioural disorders due to use of other stimulants, including caffeine

F16. Mental and behavioural disorders due to use of hallucinogens

F17. Mental and behavioural disorders due to use of tobacco

F18. Mental and behavioural disorders due to use of volatile solvents

F19. Mental and behavioural disorders due to multiple drug use and use of other psychoactive substances

The substance involved is indicated by means of the second and third characters (i.e., the first two digits after the letter F), while the fourth and fifth characters specify the clinical states. To save space, all the psychoactive substances are listed first, followed by the four-character codes; these should be used, as required, for each substance specified, but it should be noted that not all four-character codes are applicable to all substances.

Diagnostic Guidelines. Many drug users take more than one type of drug, but the diagnosis of the disorder should be classified, whenever possible, according to the most important single substance (or class of substances) used. This may usually be done with regard to the particular drug, or type of drug, causing the presenting disorder. When in doubt, code the drug or type of drug most frequently misused, particularly in those cases involving continuous or daily use. Only in cases in which patterns of psychoactive substance taking are chaotic and indiscriminate, or in which the contributions of different drugs are inextricably mixed, should code F19 (disorders resulting from multiple drug use) be used.

Misuse of other than psychoactive substances, such as laxatives or aspirin, should be coded by means F55 (abuse of non-dependence-producing substances), with a fourth character to specify the type of substance involved.

Cases in which mental disorder (particularly delirium in the elderly) are due to psychoactive substances, but without the presence of one of the disorders in this block (e.g., harmful use or dependence syndrome), should be coded in F00–F09. Where a state of delirium is superimposed upon such a disorder in this block, it should be coded as F1x.3 or F1x.4.

DIAGNOSIS OF HARMFUL USE (F1x.1)

This diagnosis reflects a pattern of psychoactive substance use that is causing damage to health. The damage may be physical (as in case of hepatitis from the self-administration of injected drugs) or mental (e.g., episodes of depressive disorder secondary to heavy consumption of alcohol).

Diagnostic Guidelines. The diagnosis requires that actual damage should have been caused to the mental or physical health of the user. The fact that a pattern of use of a particular substance is disapproved of by another person or by the culture, or may have led to socially negative consequences such as arrest or marital arguments, is not in itself evidence of harmful use.

Similarly, acute intoxication (F1x.0), or "hangover," is not in itself sufficient evidence of the damage to health required for coding harmful use. Harmful use should *not* be diagnosed if dependence syndrome (F1x.2), a psychotic disorder (F1x.5), or another specific form of drug- or alcohol-related disorder is present.

DIAGNOSIS OF DEPENDENCE SYNDROME (F1x.2)

This diagnosis reflects a cluster of physiological, behavioral and cognitive phenomena in which the use of a substance or a class of substances takes on a much higher priority for a given individual than other behaviours that once had greater value. A central descriptive characteristic of the dependence syndrome is the desire (often strong, sometimes overpowering) to take psychoactive drugs (which may or may not have been medically prescribed), alcohol or tobacco. There may be evidence that return to substance use after a period of abstinence leads to a more rapid reappearance of other features of the syndrome than occurs with nondependent individuals.

Diagnostic Guidelines. A definite diagnosis of dependence should usually be made only if three or more of the following have been experienced or exhibited at some time during the previous year:

(a) a strong desire or sense of compulsion to take the substance;

(b) difficulties in controlling substance-taking behaviour in terms of its onset, termination or levels of use;

(c) a physiological withdrawal state (F1x.3 and F1x.4) when substance use has ceased or been reduced, as evidenced by: the characteristic withdrawal syndrome for the substance; or use of the same (or a closely related) substance with the intention of relieving or avoiding withdrawal symptoms;

(d) evidence of tolerance, such that increased doses of the psychoactive substance are required in order to achieve effects originally produced by lower doses (clear examples of this are found in alcohol- and opiate-dependent individuals who may take daily doses sufficient to incapacitate or kill nontolerant users);

(e) progressive neglect of alternative pleasures or interests because of psychoactive substance use, increased amount of time necessary to obtain or take the substance or to recover from its effects;

(f) persisting with substance use despite clear evidence of overtly harmful consequences, such as harm to the liver through excessive drinking, depressive mood states consequent to periods of heavy substance use or drug-related impairment of cognitive functioning; efforts should be made to determine that the user was actually, or could be expected to be, aware of the nature and extent of the harm.

Narrowing of the personal repertoire of patterns of psychoactive substance use has also been described as a characteristic feature (e.g., a tendency to drink alcoholic drinks in the same way on weekdays and weekends, regardless of social constraints that determine appropriate drinking behaviour).

It is an essential characteristic of the dependence syndrome that either psychoactive substance taking or a desire to take a particular substance should be present; the subjective awareness of compulsion to use drugs is most commonly seen during attempts to stop or control substance use. This diagnostic requirement would exclude, for instance, surgical patients given opioid drugs for the relief of pain, who may show signs of an opioid withdrawal state when drugs are not given but who have no desire to continue taking drugs.

The dependence syndrome may be present for a specific substance (e.g., tobacco or diazepam), for a class of substances (e.g., opioid drugs) or for a wider range of different substances (as for those individual who feel a sense of compulsion regularly to use whatever drugs are available and who show distress, agitation and/or physical signs of a withdrawal state upon abstinence).

REFERENCE

World Health Organization (1992). *International Classification of Diseases, Tenth Revision* (Clinical Description and Diagnostic Guidelines Version). Geneva, Switzerland: World Health Organization.

APPENDIX B

Section 4. Crosswalks of the ASAM Patient Placement Criteria for the Treatment of Psychoactive Substance-Related Disorders

This overview of the Adult Admission Criteria is an approximate summary to illustrate the principal concepts and structure of the criteria.

Source: Based on Mee-Lee D, Shulman G & Gartner L (1994). *ASAM Patient Placement Criteria for the Treatment of Psychoactive Substance-Related Disorders, Second Edition.* Chevy Chase, MD: American Society of Addiction Medicine.

Adult Admission Criteria: Crosswalk of Levels 0.5 through IV

Criteria Dimensions	Levels of Service				
	Level 0.5 Early Intervention	**OMT Opioid Maintenance Therapy**	**Level I Outpatient Services**	**Level II.1 Intensive Outpatient**	**Level II.5 Partial Hospitalization**
DIMENSION 1: Alcohol Intoxication and/or Withdrawal Potential	No withdrawal risk	Patient is physiologically dependent on opiates and requires OMT to prevent withdrawal	I-D, Ambulatory detoxification without extended on-site monitoring Minimal risk of severe withdrawal	Minimal risk of severe withdrawal	II-D, Ambulatory detoxification with extended on-site monitoring Moderate risk of severe withdrawal
DIMENSION 2: Biomedical Conditions and Complications	None or very stable	None or manageable with outpatient medical monitoring	None or very stable	None or not a distraction from treatment and manageable in Level II.1	None or not sufficient to distract from treatment and manageable in Level II.5
DIMENSION 3: Emotional/Behavioral Conditions and Complications	None or very stable	None or manageable in outpatient structured environment	None or very stable	Mild severity, with potential to distract from recovery; needs monitoring	Mild to moderate severity, with potential to distract from recovery; needs stabilization
DIMENSION 4: Treatment Acceptance/ Resistance	Willing to understand how current use may affect personal goals	Resistance high enough to require structured therapy to promote treatment progress but will not render outpatient treatment ineffective	Willing to cooperate but needs motivating and monitoring strategies	Resistance high enough to require structured program but not so high as to render outpatient treatment ineffective	Resistance high enough to require structured program but not so high as to render outpatient treatment ineffective

Adult Admission Criteria: Crosswalk of Levels 0.5 through IV (continued)

Criteria Dimensions	Levels of Service				
	Level 0.5 Early Intervention	**OMT Opioid Maintenance Therapy**	**Level I Outpatient Services**	**Level II.1 Intensive Outpatient**	**Level II.5 Partial Hospitalization**
DIMENSION 5: Relapse/ Continued Use Potential	Needs understanding of, or skills to change, current use patterns	High risk of relapse or continued use without OMT and structured therapy to promote treatment progress	Able to maintain abstinence or control use and pursue recovery goals with minimal support	Intensification of addiction symptoms, despite active participation in Level I, and high likelihood of relapse or continued use without close monitoring and support	Intensification of addiction symptoms, despite active participation in Level I or II.1; high likelihood of relapse or continued use without monitoring and support
DIMENSION 6: Recovery Environment	Social support system or significant others increase risk for personal conflict about alcohol/drug use	Supportive recovery environment and/or patient has skills to cope with outpatient treatment	Supportive recovery environment and/or patient has skills to cope	Environment unsupportive, but with structure and support, the patient can cope	Environment is not supportive but, with structure and support and relief from the home environment, the patient can cope

Adult Admission Criteria: Crosswalk of Levels 0.5 through IV (continued)

Criteria Dimensions	Levels of Service				
	Level III.1 Clinically-Managed Low Intensity Residential Services	**Level III.3 Clinically-Managed Medium Intensity Residential Services**	**Level III.5 Clinically-Managed Medium/High Intensity Residential Services**	**Level III.7 Medically-Monitored Intensive Inpatient Services**	**Level IV Medically-Managed Intensive Inpatient Services**
DIMENSION 1: Alcohol Intoxication and/or Withdrawal Potential	No withdrawal risk	Level III.3-D, Clinically-Managed Residential Detoxification Services No severe withdrawal risk, but moderate withdrawal manageable in III.2-D	Minimal risk of severe withdrawal for Level III.3 and III.5. If withdrawal is present, meets Level III.2-D criteria	III.7-D, Medically-Monitored Inpatient Detoxification Services Severe withdrawal, but manageable in Level III.7-D	IV-D, Medically-Managed Inpatient Detoxification Services Severe withdrawal risk
DIMENSION 2: Biomedical Conditions and Complications	None or stable	None or stable	None or stable; receiving concurrent medical monitoring	Patient requires medical monitoring but not intensive treatment	Patient requires 24-hour medical and nursing care
DIMENSION 3: Emotional/Behavioral Conditions and Complications	None or minimal; not distracting to recovery	Mild to moderate severity; needs structure to allow focus on recovery	Repeated inability to control impulses; personality disorder requires high structure to shape behavior	Moderate severity; patient needs a 24-hour structured setting	Severe problems require 24-hour psychiatric care with concomitant addiction treatment
DIMENSION 4: Treatment Acceptance/ Resistance	Open to recovery, but needs structured environment to maintain therapeutic gains	Little awareness; patient needs interventions available only in Level III.3 to engage and keep in treatment	Marked difficulty with or opposition to treatment, with dangerous consequences if not engaged in treatment	Resistance high and impulse control poor, despite negative consequences; patient needs motivating strategies available only in 24-hour structured setting	Problems in this dimension do not qualify the patient for Level IV services

Adult Admission Criteria: Crosswalk of Levels 0.5 through IV (continued)

Criteria Dimensions	Levels of Service				
	Level III.1 Clinically-Managed Low Intensity Residential Services	**Level III.3 Clinically-Managed Medium Intensity Residential Services**	**Level III.5 Clinically-Managed Medium/High Intensity Residential Services**	**Level III.7 Medically-Monitored Intensive Inpatient Services**	**Level IV Medically-Managed Intensive Inpatient Services**
DIMENSION 5: Relapse/ Continued Use Potential	Understands relapse but needs structure to maintain therapeutic gains	Little awareness; patient needs interventions available only in Level III.3 to prevent continued use	No recognition of skills needed to prevent continued use, with dangerous consequences	Unable to control use, with dangerous consequences, despite active participation in less intensive care	Problems in this dimension do not qualify the patient for Level IV services
DIMENSION 6: Recovery Environment	Environment is dangerous, but recovery achievable if Level III.1 structure is available	Environment is dangerous; patient needs 24-hour structure to learn to cope	Environment is dangerous; patient lacks skills to cope outside of a highly structured 24-hour setting	Environment dangerous for recovery; patient lacks skills to cope outside of highly structured 24-hour setting	Problems in this dimension do not qualify the patient for Level IV services

Note: This overview of the Adult Admission Criteria is an approximate summary to illustrate the principal concepts and structure of the criteria.

Adolescent Criteria: Crosswalk of Levels 0.5 through IV

Criteria Dimensions	Levels of Service				
	Level 0.5 Early Intervention	Level I Outpatient Treatment	Level II Intensive Outpatient Treament	Level III Medically-Monitored Intensive Inpatient Treatment	Level IV Medically-Managed Intensive Inpatient Treatment
DIMENSION 1: Acute Intoxication and/or Withdrawal Potential	No withdrawal risk	No withdrawal risk	Manifests no overt symptoms of withdrawal risk	Risk of withdrawal syndrome is present but manageable in Level III	Severe withdrawal risk
DIMENSION 2: Biomedical Conditions and Complications	None or very stable	None or very stable	None or, if present, does not distract from addiction treatment; manageable at Level II	Require medical monitoring but not intensive treatment	Requires 24-hour medical and nursing care
DIMENSION 3: Emotional/Behavioral Conditions and Complications	None or very stable	None or manageable in an outpatient structured environment	Mild severity, with the potential to distract from recovery efforts	Moderate severity; requires a 24-hour structured setting	Severe problems require 24-hour psychiatric care, with concomitent addiction treatment
DIMENSION 4: Treatment Acceptance/ Resistance	Willing to understand how current use may affect personal goals	Willing to cooperate but needs motivating and monitoring strategies	Resistance high enough to require structured program but not so high as to render outpatient treatment ineffective	Resistance high despite negative consequences; needs intensive motivating strategies in a 24-hour structured setting	Problems in this dimension do not qualify patient for Level IV treatment
DIMENSION 5: Relapse/ Continued Use Potential	Needs understanding of, or skills to change, current use patterns	Able to maintain abstinence and recovery goals with minimal support	Intensification of addiction symptoms; high likelihood of relapse without close monitoring and support	Unable to control use despite active participation in less intensive care; needs 24-hour structure	Problems in this dimension do not qualify patient for Level IV treatment
DIMENSION 6: Recovery Environment	Social support system or significant others increase risk of personal conflict about alcohol/other drug use	Supportive recovery environment and/or patient has skills to cope	Environment unsupportive but, with structure or support, patient can cope	Environment dangerous for recovery, necessitating removal from the environment; logistical impediments to outpatient treatment	Problems in this dimension do not qualify patient for Level IV treatment

This overview of the Adolescent Admission Criteria is an approximate summary to illustrate the principal concepts and structure of the criteria.

APPENDIX B

Section 5. Federal Schedules of Controlled Drugs

NOTE: The following table is based on federal law. State regulations may result in different classifications.

	Schedule I	**Schedule II**	**Schedule III**	**Schedule IV**	**Schedule V**
OPIOIDS	Benzylmorphine Dihydromorphinone Heroin Ketobemidone Levomoramide Morphine-methylsulfanote Nicocodeine Nicomorphine Racemoramide	Codeine *various compounds* Fentanyl *Sublimaze®* Hydromorphone *Dilaudid®* LAAM Meperidine *Demerol®* Methadone Morphine Oxycodone *Percocet®* *Percodan®* Oxymorphone *Numorphan®* Pantopon	Codeine *Tylenol #3®* *Tussionex®*	Propoxyphene *Darvon®* *Darvocet®*	Butalbital *Fiorecet®* Diphenoxylate *Lomotil®* Opium *Donnagel PG®*
OPIOID ANTAGONISTS				Pentazocine *Talwin®*	Buprenorphine *Buprenex®*
STIMULANTS	N-methyl-amphetamine	Amphetamines Cocaine Dextro-amphetamine *Dexedrine®* Methamphetamine *Desoxyn®* Methylphenidate *Ritalin®* Phenmetrazine *Preludin®*	Benzphetamine *Didrex®* Phendi-metrazine *Plegine®*	Diethylpropion *Tenuate®* Fenfluramine Mazindol Phentermine *Fastin®*	1-deoxy-ephedrine *Vicks Inhaler®*
HALLU-CINOGENS, OTHER	Lysergic acid diamine *LSD* Marijuana Mescaline Peyote Phencyclidine Psilocybin Tetrahydrocan-nabinols	Dronabinol *Marinol®*	Testosterone		

	Schedule I	Schedule II	Schedule III	Schedule IV	Schedule V
SEDATIVE-HYPNOTICS	Methaqualone *Quaalude®*	Amobarbital *Amytal®* Butabarbital *Butisol®* Pentobarbital *Nembutal®* Secobarbital *Seconal®*	Butalbital *Fiorinal®* Glutethimide *Doriden®* Methyprylon *Noludar®*	Alprazolam *Xanax®* Chlordiaze-poxide *Librium®* Chlorazepate *Tranxene®* Clonazepam *Klonopin®* Chloral betaine Chloral hydrate *Noctec®* Diazepam *Valium®* Estazolam *Prosom®* Ethchlorvynol *Placidyl®* Ethinamate Flurazepam *Dalmane®* Halazepam *Paxipam®* Lorazepam *Ativan®* Mazindol® *Sanorex®* Mephobarbital *Mebaral®* Meprobamate *Equanil®* Methohexital *Brevital Sodium®* Methyl-phenobarbital Midozolam *Versed®* Oxazepam *Serax®* Paraldehyde *Paral®* Pemoline *Cylert®* Phenobarbital *Luminal®* Prazepam *Centrax®* Temazepam *Restoril®* Triazolam *Halcion®* Zolpidem *Ambien®*	Chlordiaze-poxide *Librax®*

Sources: Stimmel B (1997). *Pain and Its Relief Without Addiction: Clinical Issues in the Use of Opioids and Other Analgesics.* New York, NY: The Haworth Medical Press, 335; Keltner NM & Folks DG (1997). *Psychotropic Drugs.* St. Louis, MO: C.V. Mosby, 442–531.

APPENDIX B

Section 6. ASAM Addiction Terminology

Emanuel M. Steindler

The Definition of Alcoholism
32 Definitions Approved by ASAM

In an effort to resolve disagreements and confusion in the addictions field over the use and meaning of terms, the American Society of Addiction Medicine, in 1990, formed a Committee on Nomenclature to select terms it believed were important to the practice of addiction medicine and to come to agreement on how those terms should be defined.

Earlier, the American Medical Association, in a Delphi study, had produced a list of 50 terms that were adjudged by a representative group of respondents to be most significant, as then currently used by the field (Rinaldi, Steindler et al., 1988). The most agreed-upon definition also was determined for each of the terms.

Working primarily with the AMA list, but also selecting terms from their own experience as addiction specialists, members of the ASAM Committee compiled a list of 32 high-priority terms and established a definition for each. The terms and definitions then were approved by the ASAM Board of Directors as recommended terminology for use in all ASAM scientific publications and for dissemination to the field. The Committee and Board also endorsed the definition of alcoholism that had been developed by a special joint committee of ASAM and the National Council on Alcoholism and Drug Dependence (Morse, Flavin et al., 1992). The Nomenclature Committee's work of selecting and defining additional significant terms continues.

Following are the 32 terms and definitions that have been approved through 1993 by the ASAM Board, as well as the definition of alcoholism prepared by ASAM and the National Council on Alcoholism (see note).

THE DEFINITION OF ALCOHOLISM

As defined by ASAM and the National Council on Alcoholism (Morse, Flavin et al., 1992), alcoholism is a primary, chronic disease with genetic, psychosocial, and environmental factors influencing its development and manifestations. The disease is often progressive and fatal. It is characterized by impaired control over drinking, preoccupation with the drug alcohol, use of alcohol despite adverse consequences, and distortions in thinking, most notably denial. Each of these symptoms may be continuous or periodic.

"Primary" refers to the nature of alcoholism as a disease entity in addition to and separate from other pathophysiologic states that may be associated with it. It suggests that as an addiction, alcoholism is not a symptom of an underlying disease state.

"Disease" means an involuntary disability. Use of the term *involuntary* in defining disease is descriptive of this state as a discrete entity that is not deliberately pursued. It does not suggest passivity in the recovery process. Similarly, use of this term does not imply the abrogation of responsibility in the legal sense. "Disease" represents the sum of the abnormal phenomena displayed by the group of individuals. These phenomena are associated with a specified common set of characteristics by which certain individuals differ from the norm and which places them at a disadvantage (Campbell, Scadding & Roberts, 1979).

"Often progressive and fatal" means that the disease persists over time and that physical, emotional, and social changes are often cumulative and may progress as drinking continues. Alcoholism causes premature death through overdose; through organic complications involving the brain, liver, heart, and other organs; and by contributing to suicide, homicide, motor vehicle crashes, and other traumatic events.

"Impaired control" means the inability to consistently limit, on drinking occasions, the duration of the drinking episode, the quantity of alcohol consumed, and/or the behavioral consequences.

"Preoccupation," used in association with "alcohol use," indicates excessive, focused attention given to the drug alcohol and to its effects or its use (or both). The relative value the person assigns to alcohol often leads to energy being diverted from important life concerns.

"Adverse consequences" are alcohol-related problems, "disabilities," or impairments in such areas as physical health (e.g., alcohol withdrawal syndromes, liver disease, gastritis, anemia, and neurologic disorders), psychologic functioning (e.g., cognition and changes in mood and behavior), interpersonal functioning (e.g., marital problems, child abuse, and troubled social relationships), occupational functioning (e.g., scholastic or job problems), and legal, financial, or spiritual problems. Although the alcohol dependence syndrome may theoretically occur in the absence of adverse consequences, we believe that the latter are evident in virtually all clinical cases.

"Denial" is used in the definition not only in the psychoanalytic sense of a single psychologic defense mechanism disavowing the significance of events, but more broadly to include a range of psychologic maneuvers that decrease awareness of the fact that alcohol use is the cause of a person's problems rather than a solution to those problems. Denial becomes an integral part of the disease and is nearly always a major obstacle to recovery. Denial in alcoholism is a complex phenomenon determined by multiple psychologic and physiologic mechanisms. These include the pharmacologic effects of alcohol on memory, the influence of euphoric recall on perception and insight, the role of suppression and repression as psychologic defense mechanisms, and the impact of social and cultural enabling behavior.

This proposed definition should not be interpreted as a new set of criteria for making the diagnosis of alcoholism, even though certain criteria are implied in its terminology.

32 DEFINITIONS APPROVED BY ASAM

Following are the 32 terms and definitions approved by the ASAM Board.

Abstinence. Non-use of a specific substance. In recovery, non-use of any addictive psychoactive substance. May also denote cessation of addictive behavior, such as gambling, over-eating, etc.

Abuse. Harmful use of a specific psychoactive substance. The term also applies to one category of psychoactive substance use disorder. While recognizing that "abuse" is part of present diagnostic terminology, ASAM recommends that an alternative term be found for this purpose because of the pejorative connotations of the word "abuse."

Addiction. A disease process characterized by the continued use of a specific psychoactive substance despite physical, psychological or social harm.

Addictionist. A physician who specializes in addiction medicine.

Alcoholics Anonymous. "A fellowship of men and women who share their experience, strength and hope with each other that they may solve their common problem and help others recover from alcoholism. The only requirement for membership is a desire to stop drinking" (from the *Alcoholics Anonymous Preamble*).

Blackout. Acute anterograde amnesia with no formation of long-term memory, resulting from the ingestion of alcohol or other drugs; i.e., a period of memory loss for which there is no recall of activities.

Chemical Dependency. A generic term relating to psychological or physical dependency, or both, on one or more psychoactive substances.

Cross-tolerance. Tolerance, induced by repeated administration of one psychoactive substance, that is manifested toward another substance to which the individual has not been recently exposed.

Decriminalization. Removal of criminal penalties for the possession and use of illicit psychoactive substances.

Dependence. Used in three different ways: (1) physical dependence, a physiological state of adaptation to a specific psychoactive substance characterized by the emergence of a withdrawal syndrome during abstinence, which may be relieved in total or in part by readministration of the substance; (2) psychological dependence, a subjective sense of need for a specific psychoactive substance, either for its positive effects or to avoid negative effects associated with its abstinence; and (3) one category of psychoactive substance use disorder.

Detoxification. A process of withdrawing a person from a specific psychoactive substance in a safe and effective manner.

Drug Intoxication. Dysfunctional changes in physiological functioning, psychological functioning, mood state, cognitive process, or all of these, as a consequence of consumption of a psychoactive substance; usually disruptive, and often stemming from central nervous system impairment.

Enabling. Any action by another person or an institution that intentionally or unintentionally has the effect of facilitating the continuation of an individual's addictive process.

Familial Alcoholism. A pattern of alcoholism occurring in more than one generation within a family, due to either genetic or environmental factors, or both.

Family Intervention. A specific form of intervention, involving family members of an alcoholic/addict, designed to benefit the patient as well as the family constellation.

Impairment. A dysfunctional state resulting from use of psychoactive substances.

Intervention. A planned interaction with an individual who may be dependent on one or more psychoactive substances, with the aim of making a full assessment, overcoming denial, interrupting drug-taking behavior, or inducing the individual to initiate treatment. The preferred technique is to present facts regarding psychoactive substance use in a caring, believable and understandable manner.

Legalization. Removal of legal restrictions on the cultivation, manufacture, distribution, possession and/or use of a psychoactive substance.

Loss of Control. The inability to consistently limit the self-administration of psychoactive substances.

Misuse. Any use of a prescription drug that varies from accepted medical practice.

Overdose. The inadvertent or deliberate consumption of a dose much larger than that either habitually used by the individual or ordinarily used for treatment of an illness, and likely to result in a serious toxic reaction or death.

Polydrug Dependence. Concomitant use of two or more psychoactive substances in quantities and with frequencies that cause the individual significant physiological, psychological and/or sociological distress or impairment.

Prevention. Social, economic, legal, medical and/or psychological measures aimed at minimizing the use of potentially addicting substances, lowering the dependence risk in susceptible individuals, or minimizing other adverse consequences of psychoactive substance use. Primary prevention consists of attempts to reduce the incidence of addictive diseases and related problems in a general population. Secondary prevention aims to achieve early detection, diagnosis and treatment of affected individuals. Tertiary prevention seeks to diminish the incidence of complications of addictive diseases.

Problem Drinking. An informal term describing a pattern of drinking associated with life problems prior to establishing a definitive diagnosis of alcoholism. Also, an umbrella term for any harmful use of alcohol, including alcoholism. ASAM recommends that the term not be used in the latter sense.

Recovery. A process of overcoming both physical and psychological dependence on a psychoactive substance, with a commitment to sobriety.

Rehabilitation. The restoration of an optimum state of health by medical, psychological and social means, including peer group support, for an alcoholic/addict, a family member or a significant other.

Relapse. Recurrence of psychoactive substance-dependent behavior in an individual who has previously achieved and maintained abstinence for a significant period of time beyond withdrawal.

Sobriety. A state of complete abstinence from psychoactive substances by an addicted individual, in conjunction with a satisfactory quality of life.

Tolerance. A state in which an increased dosage of a psychoactive substance is needed to produce a desired effect.

Treatment. Application of planned procedures to identify and change patterns of behavior that are maladaptive, destructive and/or injurious to health; or to restore appropriate levels of physical, psychological and/or social functioning.

Withdrawal Syndrome. The onset of a predictable constellation of signs and symptoms following the abrupt discontinuation of, or rapid decrease in, dosage of a psychoactive substance.

NOTE: The definition of alcoholism was prepared by Robert M. Morse, M.D., Daniel K. Flavin, M.D., and the Joint Committee of the National Council on Alcoholism and Drug Dependence and the American Society of Addiction Medicine to Study the Definition and Criteria for the Diagnosis of Alcoholism. Members of the committee were Daniel J. Anderson, Ph.D., Margaret Bean-Bayog, M.D., Henri Begleiter, M.D., Ph.D., Sheila B. Blume, M.D., FASAM, Jean Forest, M.D., Stanley E. Gitlow, M.D., FASAM, Enoch Gordis, M.D., James E. Kelsey, M.D., Nancy K. Mello, Ph.D., Roger E. Meyer, M.D., Robert G. Niven, M.D., Ann Noll, Barton Pakul, M.D., Katherine M. Pike, Lucy Barry Robe, Max A. Schneider, M.D., FASAM, Marc Schuckit, M.D., David E. Smith, M.D., FASAM, Emanuel M. Steindler, Boris Tabakoff, Ph.D, and George Vaillant, M.D. Ex officio members were James F. Callahan, D.P.A., Jasper

Chen-See, M.D., and Robert Sparks, M.D. Frank Seixas, M.D., was emeritus consultant.

REFERENCES

Campbell EJM, Scadding JG & Roberts RS (1979). The concept of disease. *British Medical Journal* 2:757–762.

Morse RM, Flavin DK et al. (1992). The definition of alcoholism. *Journal of the American Medical Association* 268:1012–1014.

Rinaldi RC, Steindler EM, Wilford BB & Goodwin D (1988). Clarification and standardization of substance abuse terminology. *Journal of the American Medical Association* 259:555–557.

Index

Abstinence
from alcohol
in liver transplant recipients, 892–897
and outcomes, 304–305
return of cognitive function in, 841
ambivalence toward addiction and, 893
conditioned, 654
definition of, 1302
patterns of recovery in, 302–303
from polydrug abuse, 893
predictors of, 892, 894–895
in progressive course of addiction, 299
before psychiatric assessment, 285
psychotherapy and, 647, 653–654
sleep patterns in, 798, 801
Acamprosate, xxv, xxxi, 506–507, 511
Access to care, 324
recruitment issues, 597–598
women's issues, 1185
Access to substances of abuse
in addiction process, 296
cost of substances as a factor in, xxiv, xxx, 296
Acetaldehyde
alcohol sensitizing agents, 501
alcohol use-related, xxii, xxviii, 105
gender differences in metabolism of, 760–761
production of, 756
toxicity of, 746, 759–763
Acetaminophen, 758
Acidosis, alcohol-related, 743
Acupuncture, 373–374, 375–376
Addiction counselor certification, 320
Addiction processes, 295
alarm system dysregulation theory of, 995
with alcohol
brain function in, xxvii, xxx, xxxvi, xxxvii–xxxvii
gene-environment interaction, xxvi–xxvii, xxxvii–xxxii
with amphetamines, 140
beginning of, 295–296
behavioral models, 37–48
brain stimulation reward model, 42–44, 46
conceptual development of, 37–39
conditioned place-preference paradigm, 38, 40–42, 46
drug self-administration paradigm, 39–40, 46, 84
progressive ratio paradigm, 39
recent dependence model, 45–46
reinstatement paradigm, 44–45
with benzodiazepines, 121–122, 523
biopsychosocial model, 207–208
clinical conceptualization of, 305–306, 309
with cocaine, 140
conceptual development of, 37–39
conditioned withdrawal, 654–655
current understanding and research, 195–198, 199–200
dependence syndrome and, 645–646
detoxification effects, 301–302
dopaminergic system in, 195, 196
drive models, 37
drug-centered models, 83
drug efficacy and, 52
endorphin model, 375–376
in families, 1095
gender differences, 298, 299
genetic factors, 28–29
heroin *vs.* alcohol, 295
incentive models, 37
individual-centered models, 83
monoamine oxidase system in, 23
natural history, 295–306
neuroadaptation in, 57, 910. *See also* Neuroadaptation
neurochemical, 51–54
neurocircuitry reinforcement, 75–78
with nicotine, 148–149, 571–573
as "occupation," 302
operant conditioning model, 675, 687
with opioids, 135, 558–559
pain physiology and, 911–913, 914–915
pharmacokinetic factors, 52–53
physiological mechanisms, 908–911
progressive course, 298–299
psychosocial correlates, 913–914
reinforcement processes, xxxi. *See also* Reinforcement
research prospects, xxxiv–xxxv, 199–200
risk factors for addiction, 296–298. *See also* Risk
with sedative-hypnotics, 518–519
serotonergic system in, 195–196, 995–996
stress theory, 85–92
voluntariness, 309
vs. other medical disorders, 309–310
Addiction Severity Index, 275, 1283
Addictive Voice Recognition Technique[sm], 720
Adenylate cyclase, 23, 198
Adjunctive withdrawal management, 452
Adolescent Drinking Inventory, 265, 266
Adolescents
alcohol use
assessment, 265
patterns of addiction, 299–301
perceptions and understanding, 1131, 1134
trends, xxix, 1130
antisocial personality disorder in, 1162–1163
anxiety disorders in, 1165
assessment of, 1145–1152, 1285
alcohol use, 265
depression, 1163–1164
home life, 1132, 1156–1158
of identified substance user, 1153–1158
instruments, 263–278, 1283–1286
laboratory, 1148–1149
peer relationships, 1134, 1154
school stress, 1132
sexual behavior, 1155
substance use, 236–237, 1131–1137, 1146–1150
attention disorders, 1164
attitudes toward substance use, 1131
bipolar disorder, 1166
borderline personality disorder, 1166–1167
brief intervention, 1149
cocaine addiction, pharmacotherapy for, 539
community resources for treatment, 1149–1150
confidentiality issues, 1146–1147, 1153–1154
depressive disorders, 1163–1164
detoxification, 427
developmental considerations in family therapy, 210

drug use
assessment, 1133
trends, 1130, 1145
eating disorders, 1164–1165
epidemiology of substance abuse, 265, 1129–1131, 1145
family systems therapy, 1117–1118
home life assessment, 1132
identified substance abuser
assessment, 1153–1156
family assessment, 1156–1158
inhalant abuse, 187–189
mass media exposure, 211
narcissistic personality disorder, 1166–1167
parental substance use, 1155
peer relationships, 1134, 1154
peer resistance training, 210
physical abuse of
assessment for, 1132–1133
help-seeking behaviors, 1133
predictors of substance abuse, 207
alcohol use in women, 1192–1193
research methodology, 218
prevention programs
design, 208–209
life skills enhancement, 221
mentoring, 222–223
resiliency-focused, 211–212
psychiatric comorbidity, 1161–1167
mood disorders, 986
referrals for treatment, 1149
religion/spirituality, 1154–1155
safety assessment, 1133–1134
schizophrenia, 1165–1166
school stress, 1132
self-esteem, 221
self-image, 1134–1135, 1154
sexual behavior, 1135–1136
assessment, 1155
steroid use, 174–175, 176–177
therapeutic relationship, 1131–1132, 1146–1147, 1149
tobacco use, 237–238
marketing strategies, 235–236
trends, 235, 1130–1131
weight control issues, 1135
withdrawal management, 480
Adrenergic system, in alcohol withdrawal, 432
Adult Children of Alcoholics, 700–701, 1100, 1116
physician referrals, 702
treatment goals, 1122
See also Families
Affective functioning
alcohol relapse prevention, 507–511
assessment of, 636
in borderline personality disorder, 1069–1070
conditioned withdrawal and, 655
dysphoric, 639
in early stage of alcoholism recovery, 1104–1105
in impulse control disorders, 1049–1050
motivation for change, 601
painful affect in abusers, psychotherapy for, 639
in patients with medical problems, 731–732
as recovery outcome determinant, 1274
relapse risk and, 639
in emotional distress, 596–597
See also Mood disorders
Age
AA membership, 708, 712
developmental considerations in family therapy, 210
drug use disorder epidemiology, 4
at first alcohol exposure, and risk of addiction, xvii
of onset of addiction
alcohol disorder classification, 301
diagnostic significance, 287
prevalence of alcoholism and, 299
steroid use patterns and, 174
substance use risk and, 5
Aggressive/violent behavior
alcohol-/drug-related, xxix, 406, 864
gender differences in, 5
consequences of addiction in families, 1094
intermittent explosive disorder, 1039–1041
marijuana and, 166–167
paradoxical reaction to benzodiazepines, 521–522
PCP effects, 476
predictors of substance abuse, 207
among women victims, 1192
self-medication for, 1040
serotonergic system in, 505
steroid use-related, 179–180, 584
in stimulant intoxication/overdose, 467, 468
stress effects, 87–88
trauma center admissions, 864
victimization of women with addictive disorders, 1179–1180
Agoraphobia, 999
AIDS/HIV
adolescent risk for, 1135–1136
among drug users, 827–830
among women, 1175
antiretroviral agents and, 825
assessment of, 735, 825
case definition of, 827
chemoprophylaxis of, 826–827
detoxification considerations, 426
epidemiology of, 827–830
harm reduction strategies, 399–400, 401–402
methadone maintenance and, 550
mortality, 827
needle exchange programs, 396
in harm reduction, 400
opportunistic infections, 825–826
perinatal transmission, 826
preoperative testing, 878
prevalence in intravenous drug users, 878
in primary care treatment settings, 354–355
risk for, 735
syphilis and, 734, 735
testing for, 735
treatment of, 735–736
research in, 825
tuberculosis and, 830
Al-Anon, 698–700
conceptual basis of, 1116
family systems perspective and, 1117
historical development of, 1099
physician referrals to, 702
Alanine aminotransferase, 267
Alarm signal dysregulation, 995
Alateen, 700, 1116
Alcohol dehydrogenase enzyme, 105, 833–834, 843
Alcohol Dependence Scale, 265, 1283–1284
Alcohol (alcohol use)
acetaldehyde toxicity, 759–763
alpha-/beta-carotene interactions, 759
among adolescents, 1130
adolescent perceptions of, 1134
comorbid personality disorder and, 1162–1163
among elderly, 762, 833
medical effects. *See also* Elderly, alcohol effects
among women
depression and, 1194
epidemiology of, 1173–1174, 1191
genetic factors in, 1176–1177
medical complications of, 731–856, 1175–1176
outcomes of, 1185–1186
pharmacology of, 1174–1175
predictors of, 1192–1196
preventive intervention for, 1186
psychological factors and, 1177–1179

stereotypes of, 1173, 1175
treatment considerations, 1184–1185
victimization and, 1179–1180
antagonists, 333–334, 432
appetite effects, 742
beneficial effects, 765
benefits of, xxi–xxii, xxvii–xxviii
alcohol user's perception, 893
cardiovascular, 838
benzodiazepine use and, 447–448, 519
blackouts, 778–779
brief intervention
assessment, 624, 625
effectiveness, 617–624
carcinogenicity, 758–759
cocaine use and, 141
collateral psychopathology, 266
conditioned behaviors in, 668
continuum, 616–617
delirium induced by, 434
management of, 439–440
depression and, 297–298, 846
epidemiology of, 971, 972
endocrine pathology, 765, 813
energy content of alcohol, 755
family rituals using, 1094, 1096
stress of recovery, 1098
therapeutic role, 1123
gender differences, 1180–1181
genetic predisposition, 762–763
harm reduction measures, 395–396
health effects, xxi–xxiii
incidence of disorders, 3
intoxication
as addiction risk predictor, 26–27
assessment of, 431, 1257
clinical effects of, 53–54, 431
management of, 431–432, 809
testing for, 1243
lifestyle risk assessment, 625
mental processes in, xviii
metabolic effects, 741–742
methanol treatment and, 758
moderate, 765, 767, 838
molecular sites of action in brain, 106–112
mortality, 863
motor vehicle crashes related to, 863, 868–869
negative outcomes, xvii
neurological comorbidities, 809–810
neuronal sensitization, 988
nutritional effects, 742–743, 755–756, 845–846
assessment of, 809
liver disease, 748–749
nutritional value of alcoholic beverages, 741
perception of hangover, 667
pharmacology, 105–112
by physicians, 1265
predictors of abstinence, 892
in pregnancy, 104, 1217. *See also* Fetal alcohol syndrome
treatment, 1201–1204
prevalence of disorders, 2–3
preventive intervention
educational, 210
research trends, xxix–xxx
product cost and, xxiv, xxx
psychopathology related to, 969–970
readiness to change (assessment), 625
replacement activities, 894
screening, 249–250, 615
biochemical markers and, 266–268
goals of, 269
instrument selection for, 265–266
objectives of, 263
in primary care setting, 626–627
self-reports in, 263–265
test combinations, 268
in trauma patients, 867–868
sleep apnea and, 798, 847
social costs of, xvii, 103, 863
suicide and, 846
therapeutic use of, 103
for angina pectoris, 837
in withdrawal, 438
tobacco use and, 148, 758
toxicity
mechanisms, 755–763
metabolites, 756–758
research, xviii–xxv
toxicology research, xviii–xix
trauma and, xxiii, 864–866, 870
trends
consumption, 767
treatment, 767–768
See also Alcoholism
Alcohol Use Disorders Identification Test (AUDIT), 264, 265–266, 1284
Alcoholic dementia, 781–782, 840
sleep behavior and, 798
Alcoholics Anonymous
anniversaries, 695–696, 704
change processes, 317–319, 712–713
compliance, 703
court-ordered participation in, 710
cue recognition and avoidance in, 656
dropout rate, 697
empirical research, 707, 716
measurement issues, 715
growth, 707
history, 693
international comparison, 707–716
limitations, 703
meetings, 694–695
membership demographics, 708
network therapy and, 663
organizational structure and operations, 694, 707–709, 715
outcomes, 304, 331, 697, 713–715, 716
pharmacotherapy and, 260
philosophy, 693–694, 709, 727
physician support for, 577, 696, 697, 709
referrals, 701, 703–704
promises, 696–697
serenity prayer, 696
slogans, 696
social cohesiveness in, 656
special groups, 695, 708, 711–712, 716
spiritual component of, 304
sponsorship in, 695
Twelve Steps, 693–694
Twelve Traditions, 694
utilization, 709–711, 715
See also Self-help groups; Twelve Step programs
Alcoholism
abstinence effects, 304–305
addiction process, 295, 995–996
neurocircuitry reinforcement, 73, 75–78
serotonergic system in, 195–196
alcoholic's perception of, 893
among Native Americans, 6, 385
ASAM terminology, 1301–1302
attention disorder and, 1032
aversion therapy for, 667, 668, 669–670
biomarkers of, 868
biomarkers of risk
current prospects, 22–28
rationale, 19
carbohydrate-deficient transferrin levels, 868
cellular adaptation in, xxi, xxvii
clinical conceptualizations of, xviii, xxix, xxxv

controlled drinking and, 305
cultural risk factors for, 297
definition of, 73
dependence syndrome concept, 645–646
diagnosis of, 892–893, 895
  subtypes, 21–22, 103–104, 287
endogenous opioids pathways in, 112, 504–505
in families
  disease model, 1099
  ongoing recovery, 1107–1110
  risk factors, 7
  stages of recovery from, 1100–1107, 1119–1124
  twin/adoption studies, 18–19, 29
family support groups, 698–701
genetic research, xviii, xxv–xxvii, xxxi
  adoption studies, 18–19
  in families, 17–18
  risk factors, xxvi, 297
  twin studies, 18
hospital admissions for, 864–865
incidence of, 3
liver transplantation and, 891–897
marital relations and, 296
medical complications of, xxvii–xxix, 103, 104
  blood pressure, 251
  cardiovascular, 732–733, 765–766, 813, 836–839
  cerebellar degeneration, 783
  cerebrovascular, 839
  coma, 431
  dermatologic, 765, 844–845
  diabetes, 733–734
  endocrine system, 839–840
  esophageal, 841–842
  ethanol oxidation, 756–758
  gastrointestinal, 764, 811–812, 841–842
  hematologic, 765, 812–813
  hepatic, 763–768, 812, 842–844, 878
  hypertension, 813
  individual differences, 843–844
  musculoskeletal, 765
  neurological, 784, 840–841
  nutrition-related liver disease, 748–749
  optic neuropathy, 784
  pancreatic, 765, 811–812, 842
  peripheral neuropathy, 841
  renal, 765
  reproductive system, 839–840
  respiratory, 813–814
  risks for elderly. *See also* Elderly, alcohol effects
  stroke, 784
  trauma, xxix
  vitamin-mineral status, 743–748
  in women, 1175–1176
neurochemistry
  opioid receptor reinforcement, 504
  research trends, xviii, xxi, xxvii
neurologic complications, 766–767, 775–776
polydrug dependence, 892–893
  cocaine, 537–538
  nicotine, 586
  opioids, 587
prevalence, xvii, 3, 698, 784, 892
  age-mediated, 299
protective factors, xx, xxvi
psychiatric comorbidity, 507, 511
  borderline personality disorder, 984–985
  diagnostic classification, 20–21
  obsessive-compulsive disorder, 999
  prevalence, 985, 994
psychopathology induced by, 969–970
psychotic disorder and, 1010
reinforcement models, xxi, xxvii, 112–113
relapse, neurocircuitry reinforcement in, 78–79
research
  advances, xvii–xviii, xxv, xxxi, xxxvii
  animal, xx, xxvi
  goals, xix, xvii, xxv
  prevention, xxix–xxx, xxv
  treatment, xxiv–xxvi, xxx–xxvi
risk
  age at first exposure, xvii
  age factors, 5
  employment-related factors, 7
  family factors, 7
  gender differences, xx, xxvi, 4–5, 250
  gene-environment interaction, xx–xxi, xxvi–xxvii
  genetic, xx, xxvi, 297
  marital status correlates, 7–8
  psychopathology, 297–298
  race/ethnicity and, 5–6
  sensitivity to effects, xx, xxv
seizures in, 785, 810
sleep patterns in, 104, 793–794, 795–796, 846–847
social stability, 893–894
substance-related risk factors, 296
in surgical patients
  anesthesia, 867, 880
  postoperative pain management, 881, 882–883
  premedication, 880
thiamine deficiency, 438
treatment
  acupuncture, 376
  affective functioning, 507–510
  Alcoholics Anonymous, 707–716, 727
  alternative programs, 693, 719, 721–722. *See also specific program*
  brief intervention, 340
  contingency management, 679, 681
  detoxification. *See* Alcoholism, withdrawal
  disulfiram, xxiv–xxv, xxx–xxxi, 303–304, 311, 333, 667, 1017
  family therapy approaches, 1115–1119
  herbal remedies, 381–382
  inpatient *vs.* outpatient, 329–330
  integrated approaches, 1119
  non-abstinence-based, 693, 719, 721
  nutrition-focused, 377–378
  outcomes, 722
  pharmacotherapies, 501–592
  psychiatric comorbidity, 507, 511
  research trends, xix, xxiv–xxvi, xxv, xxx–xxvi
  traditional models, 315–325
    See also Alcoholics Anonymous, Pharmacotherapy, Twelve Step programs, alcohol relapse prevention
  vitamin deficiencies, neurological manifestations of, 782–783
withdrawal, 104
  alarm system dysregulation theory, 995
  assessment, 434–435
  clinical features, 432–434
  in continuum of care, 440
  magnesium levels, 438
  nausea in, 54
  See also Detoxification
NMDA receptor complex, 54, 110, 197–198
pharmacological management of, 435–438, 1017
psychological disorders in, 972, 1010
repeated, 434
seizures in, 433–434, 439, 766, 784–785
settings for, 438–439
and sleep patterns, 793
therapeutic use of alcohol for, 438
Aldehyde dehydrogenase enzyme, 22–23
Allodynia, 906
Alpha-adrenergic blocking agents
  for alcohol withdrawal, 436–437
  for opioid withdrawal, 460–461
  for stimulant intoxication, 469

See also specific agent
Alpha-/beta-carotene, 759
Alpha-theta brainwaves, 376–377
Alprazolam, 118
alcohol relapse prevention, 509
dependence risk, 518
for panic disorder, 517–518
See also Benzodiazepines
Alternative medicine
acceptance by clinicians, 372–373
acupuncture, 373–374, 375–376
aromatherapy, 385
biofeedback, 376–377
current perceptions, 371
definition and characteristics, 372
effectiveness, 386–387
eye movement desensitization and reprocessing, 383–384
flower essence elixirs, 385
future prospects, 387
herbal remedies, 381–382
historical developments, 372
homeopathy, 384
hypnosis, 378–379
light therapy, 383
nutrition therapies, 377–378
placebo effects, 374–375
relaxation training, 384
restricted environmental stimulation, 382
standardization issues, 373
Tai-chi, 383
transcendental meditation, 380–381
transcranial neuroelectric stimulation, 382
utilization, 371–372
yoga, 383
Alzheimer's disease, xxx, xxxvi, 840–841
Amantadine HCl
in cocaine recovery, 534–535
teratogenicity, 539
Ambien® (zolpidem). *See* Benzodiazepines
Amblyopia, 810
American Society of Addiction Medicine
addiction terminology, 1301–1303
patient placement criteria. *See Patient Placement Criteria* (ASAM)
policy statements, 1281–1282
Americans With Disabilities Act, 1249–1251
Amino acids, 378, 536
Amobarbital. *See* Sedative-hypnotics
Amnesia
alcohol-related, 778–779
benzodiazepine-related, 521
Amphetamines. *See also* Stimulants
addiction liability, 140
adolescent use trends, 1130
aversion therapy for dependence, 670–671
concurrent psychotic disorder, 1009
detoxification, urine acidification for, 470
fetal exposure, 1219–1220
misuse of, 137
neuroadaptations in addiction, 65–66
pharmacology of, 141, 142–143
psychopathology related to, 970
psychosis related to, 1009, 1012–1013
reinforcing properties, 143
specimen testing for, 1258
therapeutic uses of, 137
Amyl nitrate, 816–817
See also Inhalants, volatile
Amytal® (amobarbital). *See* Sedative-hypnotics
Anabolic steroids. *See* Steroids
Anandamide, 164, 167
Anemia, alcoholic, 765, 812
in elderly, 834–835
Anesthesia
for addicted patients, 880–881
for recovering patients, 884–885
Anger, 950
Angina pectoris, 837
sleep patterns, 797
Animal research
addiction processes
behavioral models, 37–46
drug self-administration, 84
alcohol, xxvi
dopaminergic system, xxvi
genetically-mediated addiction risk, 28–29
neurocircuitry reinforcement, 75, 79
reinforcing properties of drugs, 195–196
steroid self-administration, 183
Anorexia nervosa, 1041–1042, 1164–1165
See also Eating disorders
Anosognosia, 785–786
Antabuse®. *See* Disulfiram
Anthropology, 234, 235, 242
Anticholinergic drugs
hallucinogen interactions, 475
toxicity, 817
Anticonvulsants, 933–934
Antidepressant medications
for addicted medical patients, 933–934
in alcohol relapse prevention, 507–510
for anabolic steroid abuse, 584
for anxiety disorder in addiction, 1001–1002
for cocaine addiction, 532–534, 987
for impulse control disorders, 1054–1055
for mood disorders in addiction, 986–987
for nicotine withdrawal, 576–578
opioid maintenance therapy and, 561
for postoperative pain, 882
prescribing practices, 962
side effects of, 533
sleep effects of, 797
for stimulant withdrawal, 472
Antisocial personality disorder
in adolescent substance abusers, 1163
alcoholism risk and, 298
concurrent attention disorder, 1033
diagnosis of, 1162–1163
Anxiety disorders, 993–1004
in alcohol withdrawal, 972
as arousal dysregulation, 998
treatment of, 1002–1003
benzodiazepine therapy, 118
in chronic pain, 950
neurotransmitter systems in, 994–996
substance abuse comorbidity
in adolescents, 1164–1165
assessment of, 993, 996–998
diagnosis of, 996–999
interaction/relationship of disorders, 993, 996–997
pharmacotherapy of, 1000–1003
prevalence of, 993–994
psychosocial treatment, 998–1000, 1002–1003
relapse prevention, 999–1000
Aromatherapy, 385
Arrhythmias, alcohol-related, 813, 838–839
Ascites, 747
treatment of, 812
Aspartate aminotransferase, 267
Assertive Community Team Model, 358
Assertiveness training, 954
Assessment, 273–277
AA involvement, 715
addicted family, 1096
for adolescent substance abuse, 1129, 1133
family, 1156–1158
goals, 1146
instruments, 273–276, 1147–1148, 1283–1286

interview, 1146–1147
laboratory, 1148
peer relationships, 1134, 1154
patient history, 249–261
physical/sexual abuse, 1132–1133
physician attitude, 1158
psychiatric comorbidity, 1161–1167
recreational behaviors, 1135
safe behavior, 1133–1134
screening, 263–271, 1129, 1136–1137, 1149
self-image, 1134–1135
sexual behavior, 1135–1136
stress, 1132
suicidal ideation/behavior, 1136, 1155
young men's personal life, 1243–1245
young women's personal life, 1240–1243
affective functioning, 731–732
AIDS/HIV, 825
case definition, 827
alcohol use/alcoholism, 892–893
brief intervention, 624
cardiomyopathy, 766
diagnostic classification, 20–22
goals, 269
intoxication, 431, 1243, 1257
lifestyle risk, 625
treatment matching, 273–274
withdrawal, 268–269, 434–435
withdrawal seizures, 439
alcoholic family, 1113
family denial as obstacle to, 1112
anxiety disorders in substance abuse, 996–999
attention deficit/hyperactivity disorders, 1029–1031, 1033–1035, 1164
aversion therapy for, 671
biochemical basis of, 286
for alcoholism, 266–268
bipolar disorder, 1166
borderline personality disorder, 1063–1064, 1073–1074
CAGE questionnaire, 249, 250, 1284
cancer, 734
cardiovascular function, 732
chronic pain, 926, 946, 947–948, 951
co-occurring disorders, 353
continuum of care, 324
dependence, 423
vs. substance use disorder, 520–521
depression in adolescents, 1163–1164
for detoxification placement, 428–429
diabetes mellitus, 733
diagnostic classification systems, 279–282
interview strategies, 284
reliability of, 282, 283–284
subtyping, 21–22, 286–287
validity of, 283–284
eating disorders, 1164–1165
electrocardiographic, 878
fetal exposure, 1231–1232
alcohol, 1217–1218
cocaine, 1218–1219
follow-up care, 259–260
future research, 287–288
history taking, 251
of identified adolescent abuser
confidentiality issues, 1153–1154
goals, 1153
interview, 1153–1156
psychiatric comorbidity, 1153
impaired professionals, 1266, 1268–1270
impulse control disorders, 1051
infant substance exposure, 1129
infection risk, 737
for inpatient/outpatient treatment, 330
intermittent explosive disorder, 1039–1040
of intoxication
alcohol, 1243, 1257
laboratory tests, 1243
Korsakoff's psychosis, 780
laboratory evaluation, 251, 266
intoxication, 1243
specimen analysis, 1256
for women, 951
for liver transplantation in alcoholics, 892–897
medical, 731
methadone dose, 564–565
Minnesota Model, 315–316, 321–322
neonatal opiate abstinence syndrome, 1213
neurologic dysfunction in alcoholism, 809–810
objectives, 263
pain, for management of addicted patient, 920
of patient readiness to change, 254–255, 256–257, 275, 1085
physical examination, 251
pontine myelinolysis, 782, 810
posttraumatic stress disorder, 562
practice guidelines, 241–242
preoperative, 877, 878–879
of addicted patient, 859
recovering addict, 884
preventive intervention, 211, 212
primary care, 241–242, 249
follow-up, 259–260
protective factors, 250
psychiatric comorbidity
anxiety disorders, 993, 996–998
mood disorders, 983–984
psychological functioning, 635–636
concurrent alcoholism, 266
obstacles to, 284–286
psychopathology, substance-induced, 969–971
anxiety disorders, 973
case examples, 974–980
mood disorders, 973
psychotic disorders, 973–974
psychotic disorder, 1007–1010
substance use, 1018
readiness to change, 625, 638
recovering addicts, 883
recovery monitoring, 703–704
red flags, 250
reporting diagnosis to patient, 251–254, 255
risk categorization, 218–219, 241
schizophrenia, 1165–1166
screening, 249–250
of children and adolescents, 1129, 1131–1137
of infants, 1129
screening instruments, 236–237, 241, 1283–1286
See also specific instrument
for child/adolescent substance abuse, 1131–1132
combining, 268
diagnostic classification, 284
good qualities of, 275
reliability of, 275
selection of, 265–266
self-reports, 263–265, 275–276, 284
for treatment planning, 274–277
validity of, 275
vs. clinical interview, 274
secondary hypertension, 733
severity of use/abuse, 251, 274–275
sexually transmitted diseases, 734–735
sleep patterns, 793, 794–795
social stability in alcoholics, 893–894
stimulant intoxication, 468–469, 470
therapeutic relationship, 249
trauma patients, 869–870
screening, 867–868
for treatment matching, 273–274, 335

for treatment planning, 274–275
standardized instruments, 274–277
treatment response and, 286
tuberculosis, 736–737
screening, 830
uncommon drugs of abuse, 817
withdrawal, 423, 424, 425
alcohol, 268–269, 434–435
with psychiatric comorbidity, 426
of women, 1181–1182, 1184
in workplace. *See* Workplace, drug testing
Atenolol, 436
efficacy, 505
Athletics
adolescent assessment, 1135
steroid use, 173–174, 175–176
Ativan® (lorazepam). *See* Sedative-hypnotics
Attention deficit/hyperactivity disorder, 207, 1029–1044
in adolescent substance users, 1164
in adults, 1031, 1033–1035
alcoholism risk and, 298
associated substance abuse, 1031–1033
concurrent conduct disorder, 1033
concurrent personality disorder, 1033
diagnosis of, 1029–1031, 1033–1035
prevalence of, 1031
treatment of, 1035–1036
contingency management, 1038
pharmacotherapy, 1036–1038
psychosocial, 1038–1039
Aversion therapy, 667–673
acceptability, 672
for alcohol dependence, 669–670
criticisms of, 672
faradic, 669, 670, 671
goals of, 667
for heroin dependence, 671
for marijuana dependence, 670
mechanism of change, 667–668
in multimodal treatment program, 672–673
nausea, 669–670
principles of treatment, 668
safety of, 671–672
for smoking cessation, 668–669
spontaneous aversions, 668
for stimulant dependence, 670–671
vs. punishment, 667
Ayurvedic medicine, 380
AZT. *See* Zidovudine

Barbiturates. *See also* Sedative-hypnotics
fetal exposure to, 1220
withdrawal from, 443
Behavior models, 37–48
addiction processes
brain stimulation reward model, 42–44, 46
conceptual development, 37–39
conditioned place-preference paradigm, 38, 40–42, 46
drug self-administration paradigm, 39–40, 46, 84
progressive ratio paradigm, 39
recent dependence model, 45–46
reinstatement paradigm, 44–45
stress theory, 83–92
conditioned reinforcement, 43–44, 61
of pain, 948–949
priming effects, 42
secondary gain, 949
Behavioral therapies, 595–674
for alcohol dependence, xxx
brain changes in, xxxiii
chronic pain management, 952–953
for cocaine dependence, 644
for eating disorders, 1042
family treatment, 1118, 1119
marital therapy, 1118–1119, 1122–1123
for nicotine dependence, 571
with pharmacotherapy, 578–579
for opioid dependence, 642–643
for pain management, 948
with pharmacotherapy, xxxiii
See also Dialectical behavior therapy
Benzocaine, for nicotine withdrawal, 487
Benzodiazepines. *See also* Sedative-hypnotics
abuse potential of, 53, 119, 121, 519
for acute psychosis in amphetamine use, 1012–1013
addiction liability, 121–123
adverse effects of, 119–121
for alcohol intoxication, 432
for alcohol relapse prevention, 508–509
for alcohol withdrawal, 435–436, 439–440
monitoring, 268–269
in pregnancy, 1203–1204
for anxiety disorder, 118, 121
assessment of use, 458
chemical types, 123
for chronic pain management, 946
for depression, 118, 121
dosimetry, 118
federal classification of, 1300
GABA complex interactions, 445–446, 518
for hallucinogen intoxication, 473
for insomnia, 119
intoxication, 441–454
for marijuana intoxication, 476
mechanisms of action, 123–126
memory effects, 521
for nicotine dependence, 578
for nicotine withdrawal, 487
onset of action, 53, 436
for panic disorder, 118, 517–518
paradoxical reactions to, 521–522
for PCP intoxication, 477–479, 480
pharmacokinetics of, 123
pharmacology of, 117–130
pharmacotherapy for dependence, 517–530
polydrug use, 447–448, 457–458
relapse, 122–123
risk of abuse, 509, 1000–1001
for schizophrenia, 119
sleep patterns and, 800
specimen testing for, 1258
for stimulant intoxication/overdose, 467–468
for stimulant withdrawal, 470–472
teratogenicity of, 1203–1204
therapeutic use of, 517, 521, 527
toxicity, 441
withdrawal, 122, 441–454
assessment, 448–449
clinical features, 443–445, 522
continuing care, 526–527
co-occurring substance abuse, 447–448
demographic considerations, 448
dose effects, 522–526
management of, 449–453
natural history of, 523–524
neurochemical processes, 445–446
onset and duration, 446–447
pharmacologic management, 524–526
protracted, 522–523
substitution therapies, 450–451
See also specific drug
Best estimate procedure, 286
Beta blockers
in alcohol withdrawal management, 436–437
in pregnancy, 1204
for cocaine intoxication, 816
risks, 732
sleep patterns and, 797

for stimulant intoxication management, 469
See also specific agent
Biofeedback, 376–377
pain management, 953–954
Biomarkers
alcohol challenge studies, 25–26
of alcoholism, 266–268, 868
risk predictors, 22–28
aldehyde dehydrogenase, 22–23
cognitive function, 24–25
electrophysiological, 24
genetic polymorphisms, 23–24
monoamine oxidase, 23
personality, 25
platelet adenylate cyclase, 23
research methodology, 19–22
role of, 19
Biopsychosocial model
addiction processes, 207–208
treatment planning, 425
Bipolar disorder, 987–989, 1050, 1166
See also Psychiatric comorbidity
Birth defects, 1223–1236
fetal alcohol syndrome research, xxii–xxiii
Blackouts, 778–779, 1302
Blame, 950, 955
Blood alcohol levels
effects, 431
in elderly, 833
fatal, 431
testing methods, 1243
trauma center admissions, 864–866
predictive modeling, 867
screening, 867–869
Blood disorders
alcohol-related, 765
in elderly, 834–835
assessment, 879
Blood pressure
alcohol effects, 251, 837
See also Hypertension
Body image disorders, 181
Bones/joints
alcohol-related disorders and, 765
alcohol use among elderly and, 834
Borderline personality disorder, 1063–1078
in adolescent substance abusers, 1166–1167
biosocial theory, 1069–1070
clinical features, 1063
epidemiology, 1064
inpatient service utilization, 1063
medical problems, 1065–1066, 1073–1074
prognosis, 1064, 1066
substance abuse comorbidity, 1064–1065
suicidal behavior/ideation, 1063–1064, 1074
treatment, 1066
dialectical behavior therapy, 1066–1073
medications, 1073, 1075–1076
outcomes, 1066
See also Psychiatric comorbidity
Brain. *See also* Neurochemical processes
addiction biomarkers, 24
alcohol effects
addiction processes, xxvii, xxxvi, xxxvii–xxxvii
molecular sites of action, 106–112
neuropsychological effects, xxviii
behavior therapy effects, xxxiii
biofeedback therapy, 376–377
extended amygdala, 78
locus ceruleus, 60, 64, 995
marijuana effects, 165–166
neuroadaptation
in gene expression, 64–65
in glutamatergic neurons, 62
stimulation reward model of addiction, 42–44, 46
Brain injury, 198–199
alcohol-related
cerebellar degeneration, 783, 810
individual differences, 776
pathogenesis, 775–776
pontine myelinolysis, 782, 810
reversibility, 778, 841
syndromes, 776. *See also specific syndrome*
trauma, 782
cocaine-related, 786
detoxification considerations, 426
in elderly, alcohol use and, 840
nfections, 737
inhalant-related, 189
insomnia related to, 798
stimulant-related, 466
Breast cancer, 1176
Breastfeeding
contraindications, 426
detoxification considerations, 425–426
in neonatal opiate abstinence syndrome, 1214
Breath analysis, 1243, 1257
Brief intervention, 249–262
with adolescents, 1149
assessment in, 624, 625
definition of, 253
effectiveness of, 340
follow-up on, 259–260
goals of, 626
indications for, 615, 628
mechanism of change, 340–341
motivation enhancement, 615–616
outcomes of, 617–624
in primary care setting, 626–628
procedure for, 253–254
rationale for, 615
training for clinicians, 627
Brief Symptom Inventory, 266
Bromocriptine, 505
for attention disorder, 1036
for cocaine recovery, 534
side effects, 534
teratogenicity, 539
Bulimia, 1041–1042, 1164–1165
See also Eating disorders
Buprenorphine, 333, 886, 962
for opioid detoxification, 462, 537–38, 547–548, 566–567
for opioid maintenance, 552–553
for polydrug treatment, 537–538
See also Opioids
Bupropion HCl
for cocaine recovery, 534
for nicotine withdrawal, 488, 576–577
Buspirone HCl, 118
for alcohol relapse prevention, 509
for anxiety disorder in addiction, 1001
for benzodiazepine dependence, 527
for nicotine withdrawal, 487, 578
for sedative-hypnotic withdrawal, 452
Butabarbital. *See* Sedative-hypnotics
Butisol® (butabarbital). *See* Sedative-hypnotics

Caffeine, 584–585
effects on sleep, 801
mental disturbances induced by, 969
CAGE questionnaire, 249, 250, 263, 265, 1284
Calcium channel blockers, 732
for cocaine recovery, 536, 816
Calcium metabolism, alcohol-related abnormalities, 746
California Drug and Alcohol Treatment Assessment, 414
CALM. *See* Counseling for Alcoholics' Marriages
Calories. *See* Nutrition.

cAMP pathway. *See* Cyclic adenosine monophosphate; Neuroadaptation
Cancer
adolescent assessment, 1135
alcohol-related, 758–759, 814
alcohol use among elderly and, 836
assessment of, 734
lung, marijuana-related, 164
pain management in addicted patient, 921, 924–925
risk of, 734
treatment of, 734
vitamin A metabolism in, 758–759
See also specific type or anatomical site
Capsaicin, 933, 934
Carbamazepine, 933, 934
for alcohol withdrawal, 437
in pregnancy, 1204
for benzodiazepine dependence, 527
for bipolar disorder in substance use, 988, 989
for cocaine dependence, 536
for impulse control disorder, 1055
for sedative-hypnotic withdrawal, 452
Carbimide, 503–504
mechanisms of action, 501–502
Carbohydrate-deficient transferrin, 267–268, 868
Carbohydrate metabolism, 742–743
Cardiovascular system
alcohol effects, xxii, xxviii, 765–766, 813, 836–839
alcoholic cardiomyopathy, 766, 837
arrhythmias, 813, 838–839
cocaine effects, 138, 815
detoxification considerations, 426
inhalant effects, 189
ischemic heart disease, 732–733
marijuana effects, 164
steroid effects, 178, 179
use of antidepressants in cocaine addiction management, 533
Case management
integrated mental health—substance abuse treatment, 358
preventive intervention in, 222–223
Catecholamines
interventions for alcohol relapse prevention, 505
stimulant intoxication, 466
Center for Substance Abuse Prevention, guidelines for prevention programs, 220
Center for Substance Abuse Treatment, guidelines for care of the addicted pregnant woman, 1202–1208
Centrax® (prazepam). *See* Benzodiazepines
Certification and licensure
addiction counselor, 320
as outcome factor, 332, 609–612
Change processes
action-oriented paradigm, 597–598
in brief intervention, 340–41
dialectical behavior therapy, 1067–1071
mechanisms of, 338
Minnesota Model, 317–319
motivation and, 615
outcome measures, 322
perceived costs and benefits, 601
proactive approach, 598, 606
readiness assessment, 625
stages of, 595–597, 625
implications for treatment, 598–603, 638
in Twelve Step programs, 712–713
Child abuse
assessment for, 1132–1133
chronic pain syndrome related to developmental trauma, 951
in addicted women, 1177–1178, 1192
maternal substance abuse and, 1230
physician reporting rules, 1153
Children
alcohol use trends, xxiii
developmental effects, 1223–1237
fetal alcohol syndrome, xxii–xxiii
See also Adolescents
Children of alcoholics
adult, risk of benzodiazepine use, 448
benzodiazepine effects, 519
developmental patterns, 1113
genetically-mediated biomarkers, 27–28
maladaptive roles, 1112–1113, 1117
prevalence, 1111
professional competencies for intervention, 1113–1114
risks for, 1111, 1112–1113
See also Adult children of alcoholics; Fetal alcohol syndrome
Chloral hydrate, 1204
See also Sedative-hypnotics
Chlordiazepoxide
alcohol relapse prevention, 509
for alcohol withdrawal, 435–436, 766
monitoring, 269
See also Benzodiazepines
Chlorpromazine
management of hallucinogen intoxication, 475
stimulant intoxication/overdose management, 468
Choline deficiency, 747
Chronic pain syndrome, 946
denial in, 947
depression in, 950
risk of, 952
treatment approaches, 952–954
addicted patient, 954–956
See also Pain, chronic
Circumstances, Motivation, Readiness, and Suitability Scale, 275
Cirrhosis, 878
in elderly patients, 844
genetic predisposition for, 763
hepatitis C infection and, 736
individual differences in risk of, 843–844
mortality, 755, 762, 843
pathogenesis, 763, 843
nutrition-related, 748–749
prevention of, 747
trauma admissions, 868
zinc deficiency in, 748
Citalopram, 505–506
Civil Rights Act of 1964, 1251
Classical conditioning, 668
Clinical Institute Withdrawal Assessment of Alcohol—Revised, 268–269, 277, 424, 435, 1284
Clocinnamox, 52
Clomipramine, 1001
Clonazepam, 1000
See also Benzodiazepines
Clonidine
with naltrexone, 461
for nicotine withdrawal, 488
for opioid detoxification, 546–547
for opioid withdrawal, 461
in perioperative pain management, 886
for sedative-hypnotic withdrawal, 452
See also Alpha-adrenergic blocking agents
Clorazepate, 509
See also Benzodiazepines
Clozapine, 1016–1017
See also Benzodiazepines
Co-dependence
concept, 1099
in recovery, 1104, 1106–1107
Cocaine Anonymous, 331, 698
Cocaine (cocaine use). *See also* Stimulants
addiction liability, 140
addiction processes, 45
adolescent trends, 1130
assessment red flags, 250
attention disorder and, 1033, 1036, 1037

aversion therapy for dependence, 670–671
behavioral treatments, 644
blocking agents, 333
cognitive-behavioral treatment for addiction, 336
Community Reinforcement Approach, 681–682
conditioned responses, 668
contingency management for, 682–684
convulsions related to, 786
crack form, 414–415
medical complications, 138
craving, 536
criminalization, 405–406
race as an issue in, 414–415
dopaminergic system in, xxxi
drug interactions, 141
fetal exposure, 1218–1219
developmental outcomes, 1226–1227
gender risk factors, 5
heart disease medications for users of, 732
maintenance therapy, 535
mechanisms of action, 141–142
medical comorbidity, 538
medical effects, 138–139, 469, 786, 815–816
misuse of, 137
neuronal sensitization, 988
neuropharmacological action, 532
anxiety and, 997
pharmacokinetics of, 140–141
pharmacotherapy for dependence
adolescents, 539
amino acids, 536
anticonvulsants, 536
antidepressants, 532–534, 987
calcium channel blockers, 536
current practice, 531
dopamine agonists, 534–535
future prospects, 539
gender issues, 538–539
goals, 531–532
lithium, 536
maintenance treatment, 535
medical comorbidity, 538
medication combinations, 536–537
neuroleptics, 535
pharmacokinetic approach, 539
polydrug addictions, 537–538, 587
psychiatric comorbidity, 538, 1017
psychosocial component, 532
in psychotic patient, 1017
strategies, 532
polydrug dependence and, 537–538
opioids and, 587
polydrug use, 141
in pregnancy, 138–139
detoxification from, 1206
psychiatric comorbidity, 139, 538
borderline personality disorder, 984
mood disorders, 985
psychological effects, 141
psychopathology related to, 139–140, 970, 1011–1012
epidemiology, 972
psychotherapy, 644, 646–647
reinforcing properties, 143
social costs, 140
specimen testing, 1257–1258
therapeutic use, 137
trauma center admissions, 864
treatment, 323
nutrition-focused, 378
See also Cocaine, pharmacotherapies
settings for, 329–330
withdrawal, 142
Codeine, 962. *See also* Opioids
Coerced treatment, 409–410
Cognitive-behavioral therapy
attention disorder treatment, 1038
benzodiazepine effects, 120
chronic pain management, 953
for cocaine dependence, 336
eating disorder, 1042
for opioid dependence, 641–642
in sedative-hypnotic withdrawal management, 452
Cognitive functioning
AA outcomes, 714
as addiction biomarker, 24–25
addiction processes, xxxi–xxxii
knowledge deficits in, 316–317
addictive voice recognition technique, 720
alcohol use
aging and, 762
among elderly, 846
anosognosia, 785–786
early research, 775
effects of consumption, xxii, xxviii
mechanisms of, 775–776
pathologies, 776. *See also specific pathology*
psychological processes in addiction, xviii, xxxiii
reversibility in abstinence, 778, 841
withdrawal from, 434
assessment of impaired physicians, 1269
in attention disorder, 1034
benefits of spirituality, 725–726
cocaine effects, 141
denial, xxxiii
dialectical analysis, 1068
hallucinogen effects, 472, 585–586
marijuana effects, 165–166, 475
nicotine effects, 147, 572
obstacles to substance use assessment, 283–284
pain, 949–950
management, 931, 953
patient readiness to change, 254–255, 256–257, 275, 596, 601–602, 1085
PCP effects, 476, 479
in recovery, 1106–1107
recovery process, 317–319
for resiliency, 211–212
steroid effects, 179–180
stimulant intoxication, 466–467
substance use-related damage, 1166
treatment research issues, xxxiii–xxxiv
See also Psychiatric comorbidity; Psychopathology
Collaborative Study on the Genetics of Alcoholism, xix–xx, xxv–xxvi
Coma, alcohol-induced, 431
Community coalitions, 209, 220, 227–231
advantages, 227–228
defining, 227
membership, 228
outcomes assessment, 230–231
rationale for, 227
resources for, 228
external, 228–229
role of health professionals, 211, 228
skills, 228
successful, characteristics of, 229–230
Community Reinforcement Approach, 687–688, 1020
in cocaine dependence treatment, 681–682
conceptual basis of, 675–676
disulfiram therapy in, 678
in opioid dependence treatment, 684–685
outcomes of, 676, 677
significance of, 678
social club, 677–678
technical development of, 676
Comorbid disorders
addiction processes, 297–298
among adolescents, 1153

assessment of, 353, 635–636
chronic pain, 946
assessment of, 947
detoxification considerations, 426
diagnostic subtyping and, 287
genetic biomarkers for, 20–21
medical. *See* Medical complications
neurologic, 809–810
psychiatric. *See* Psychiatric comorbidity
risk for, 8–9
self-help groups for, 1086–1088
withdrawal assessment, 426
See also Polydrug use; *specific disorder*
Complementary medicine. *See* Alternative medicine
Compliance
AA dropout rate, 697
contingency management for increasing, 679–680
determinants of, 311
in dialectical behavior therapy, 1075
disulfiram, 503, 657–658
importance of, 311, 312
methadone maintenance, 558
naltrexone, 505
obstacles to research, 216
strategies for, 1084–1085
Comprehensive Drug Abuse and Control Act, 406
Compulsive disorders, 320
compulsive buying
affective regulation, 1050
substance use comorbidity, 1052
Conditioned response
in addiction, 668
behavioral models of addiction, 37–39, 61
classical conditioning, 668
mood-related cues, 655
operant conditioning, 668
withdrawal, 654–655
Conduct disorders, 1029–1044
in adolescent substance abusers, 1162–1163
concurrent attention deficit disorders, 1033
Confabulation, 780, 785
Confidentiality and privacy
adolescent rights, 1146–1147, 1153–1154
drug testing
employer tort liability, 1247
random application, 1242, 1245
results, 1246
referral from primary care, 628
Congestive heart failure, 732
Consultations, 360
Contingency management, 675–690
application, 602–603, 687–688
attention disorder treatment, 1038
cocaine dependence treatment, 682–684
compulsory, 680
conceptual basis, 675–676
to directly reduce drinking, 679
features, 678–679
for increasing treatment compliance, 679–680
indications, 681
in methadone therapy, 685–687
in network therapy, 660–661
treatment goals, 678
Control
change processes in AA, 317–318
as diagnostic criterion, 281
in impulse disorders, 1047–1049
issues for adult children of alcoholics, 700
locus of, in pain experience, 950
pharmacotherapy compliance, 1085
Controlled Substances Act (1972), 961, 1299–1300
Controlled use, 596, 638
alcohol, 305, 765, 767, 838
forms of recovery, 302–303
Conversion experiences, 304
Corpuscular red cell volume, 267
Correctional Drug Abuse Treatment Effectiveness, 414
Corticosterone secretion, 89
Corticotrophin-releasing factor, xxxi
addiction processes, xxxi
Cost of abuse
alcohol, xvii, 103, 615, 863
vs. cost of treatment, 310–311
workplace, 1241
Cost of care
adjunctive services, 337
assessment for brief intervention, 624
complementary and alternative medicine, 371
cost-effectiveness, 310–311, 327
current health care environment, 273
detoxification decisions, 428
group psychotherapy, 634
vs. cost of abuse, 310–311
Counseling for Alcoholics' Marriages (CALM), 1119
Counselors, non-credentialed, 1081–1082
Counterconditioning, 602
Couples therapy. *See* Marital/couples therapy
Court-ordered services, 405–420
Alcoholics Anonymous, 710
contingency management, 680
treatment
efficacy, 409–410
monitoring, 410
See also Criminal justice system
Crack lung, 138
See also Cocaine
Craving
conditioned, 654–655
definition, 1049
extinction of conditioned response, 643
Crime/criminal behavior
drug-related crimes, 406–407
effects of drug abuse treatment, 407
race issues in sentencing, 414–415
temporal relationship to drug use, 406
See also Criminal justice system
Criminal justice system
arrest trends, 415
attitudes toward abuse, 405
controlled substances law, 961–962
detoxification considerations, 427
drug courts, 410
evolution of drug law, 405–406
incarceration of drug abusers, 405
parole/probation, 303, 407–408
physician role, 416
prison statistics, 408
racial issues, 414–415
responsibilities, 415–416
sentencing guidelines/mandates, 406, 407–408, 414–415
structure and operations, 407
treatment
coerced, 409–410
methadone maintenance, 412–413
modalities, 408
monitoring, 410
outcomes, 409
outpatient, 413
plea-bargain for, 407
program evaluation, 413–414
therapeutic communities, 410–412
trends, 408–409
See also Legal issues
Crisis intervention, 259
See also Emergency medicine
Cross-tolerance, 99–102, 425, 435–436
Cultural issues. *See* Sociocultural factors
Cyclic adenosine monophosphate (cAMP), 198

alcohol pharmacology, 111
neuroadaptation, 58–61
response element binding protein, 64–65
Cytochrome P–450, 99–100, 638, 756–757, 758, 762, 811, 914
Cytokines, xxviii
and liver damage, xxii

Dalmane® (flurazepam). *See* Sedative-hypnotics
D.A.R.E., 222
Deconditioning, 951
Definitions. *See* Terminology
Delirium tremens, 315, 434, 846
pharmacotherapy, 439–440, 766
Dementia, alcoholic, 781–782, 840
sleep behavior and, 798
Demerol® (meperidine). *See* Opioids
Demographics
Alcoholics Anonymous, 655, 708, 709, 711–712
membership, 708
predictors of affiliation, 710–711
subgroups, 716
benzodiazepine use, 448
model of prevention, 234–235
prevention program design, 212
Denial, xxxiii, 317
acceptance of blackouts, 779
in addicted physician, 1266
in alcoholic families, 1111–1112
in chronic pain syndrome, 947
as obstacle to assessment, 1112
organic causes, 785–786
recovery processes, 318
treatment outcomes and, 697
vs. ambivalence, 893
Department of Defense, U.S., 1248
Department of Transportation, U.S., 1248–1249, 1255, 1260
Dependence
alcohol, 103–114
benzodiazepines, 117–130
cocaine, 142
current understanding, 196–197
definition, 1302
diagnosis, 423
diagnostic classification systems, 282–284
DSM conceptualizations, 279–280, 1287–1289
ICD-10 diagnostic criteria, 1292–1293
marijuana, 163–164, 166
neuroadaptation in, 911
nicotine, 571–572
opioids, 131–135
screens for, 263–272, 1283–1286
sedative-hypnotic, 442
steroids, 180–181
stimulants, 137–145
syndrome concept, 645–646
vs. substance use disorder, 520–521
Depression
in adolescent substance abuser, 1163–1164
alcohol use and, 507, 846
epidemiology, 971, 972
in women, 1194
alcoholism risk and, 297–298
in chronic pain, 950
comorbid opioid dependence, 561
eating disorder and, 1042
impulse control disorders and, 1057
pharmacotherapy, 118, 507–508
in recovery, 260
in stimulant withdrawal, 472
in substance abuse
assessment, 984
epidemiology, 983–984
treatment, 986–987, 989
suicidal ideation, 972
therapeutic hallucinogen use, 588
tobacco use and, 577–578
See also Mood disorders
Dermatologic disorders, 765, 844–845
adolescent assessment, 1135
"Designer Drugs." *See* MDMA
Desipramine
for adult attention disorder, 1036
for alcohol relapse prevention, 507, 508
for cocaine addiction, 532–533
methadone and, 987
Desoxyn® (methamphetamine). *See* Stimulants
Detoxification, 423–496. *See also* Withdrawal
of adolescents, 427, 480
and comorbid conditions
medical, 426
psychiatric, 426
in continuum of care, 424, 425
in criminal justice settings, 427
definition of, 423, 1302
duration of, 424–425
emergency intervention, 428
goals of, 328, 423–424
harm reduction strategies, 398
individualized plan of care, 425
inpatient, 427
methadone, 546
in natural history of addiction, 301–302
of older patients, 427
opioid, 460–462
rapid, 548
outpatient, 427–428
patient expectations of, 425
of persons with AIDS/HIV, 426
of pregnant/nursing women, 425–426, 1200–1207
from alcohol, 1200–1201
from cocaine, 1206
from opioids, 1206–1207
from sedative-hypnotics, 1205
principles of, 423–428
of psychotic patients, 1016
rapid, from opiates, 548
tapering methods, 449–451
and treatment planning, 428–429
See also specific substance
Developmental disorders, 1029, 1223–1236
Dexedrine® (dextro-amphetamine). *See* Stimulants
Diabetes, 733–734
Diagnosis, 249–288
Diagnostic and Statistical Manual of Mental Disorders, 1287–1290
ADHD, 1029
alcohol dependence, 73, 892
withdrawal syndrome, 433
ASAM *Patient Placement Criteria* and, 365
assessment instruments, 274, 276
concepts of abuse and dependence, 520–521
current, 280–281
historical evolution, 279–280
diagnostic subtyping in, 286–287
distinctions among substances, 279, 281
impulse control disorders, 1030–1031
mood disorder criteria, 983, 984
substance abuse criteria, 1289
substance dependence criteria, 1287–1289
substance-induced mental disorders, 969, 973–974
substance withdrawal criteria, 1289
Diagnostic Interview Schedule, 274
Dialectical behavior therapy
access to care, 1076
assumptions, 1070–1071, 1076
borderline personality disorder, 1066–1073
effectiveness, 1066
group skills training, 1072–1073

method, 1071–1073
noncompliance in, 1075
patient consultation in, 1074–1075
theoretical/technical development, 1067–1069
Diazepam
alcohol relapse prevention, 509
for alcohol withdrawal, 435–436, 439
stimulant intoxication management, 469
See also Benzodiazepines
Diethylproprion, 535
Digitalis, 732
Dilantin®. *See* Phenytoin
Dilaudid® (hydromorphone). *See* Opioids
Diltiazem, 536
Disability law, 1249–1251
Discrimination law, 1251
Disease model, 309–310, 315–316, 322
acceptance of, by impaired physician, 1270
alcoholic family, 1099
alcoholism, xviii, xxix–xxxi
continuum of care, 233
family disease concept, 1115, 1116–1117
historical development, 315–316
treatment in, 322
Disulfiram, xxiv–xxv, xxx–xxxi, 303–304, 311, 333, 667, 1017
adverse effects, 501, 502
in Community Reinforcement Approach, 678
compliance, 503, 657–658
contingency management for increasing compliance, 679–680, 687
dosimetry, 503
efficacy, 502–503, 646
mechanisms of action, 501, 766–767
in network therapy, 657–658
pharmacokinetics, 502
polydrug dependence treatment, 538
preoperative, 884
with psychosocial intervention, 646
teratogenicity, 1204
Dopamine agonists, 111–112
for alcoholism recovery, 509–510
for cocaine recovery, 534–535
Dopaminergic system
in addiction processes, xxx, xxxvi, 51, 75–77, 1015
depletion hypothesis, 45–46
genetically-mediated biomarkers, 23–24
neurochemical action, 51
neurotransmitter-receptor adaptation, 61–62
reinforcement model, 113
stress response, 88–89, 91
in affective withdrawal, 912
alcohol effects, 111–112
implications for recovery, 505
discrete effects of drugs, 909–910
disulfiram effects, 502
in impulse control disorder, 1054
neuroadaptation, 61–62
in reinforcing properties of drugs, 195, 196
in schizophrenia, 1015
shared effects of drugs, 908–909
stimulant withdrawal, 470
uptake blockers, 51
in withdrawal, 61
Dose-response relationship
alcohol and breast cancer, 1176
in brain stimulation reward model of addiction, 43
fetal alcohol syndrome, 1224–1225
in neonatal opiate abstinence syndrome, 1212
research methodology, 216
in reverse tolerance, 911
social stress effects, 86–87
in tolerance, 910–911
Doriden® (glutethimide). *See* Sedative-hypnotics
Doxepin, 987
DRD2, 23–24
Drinker Inventory of Consequences (DrInC), 275, 1285
Dronabinol, 163
Drop-outs
motivation, 598
predictors, 598–599
Drug Abuse Reporting Program, 413
Drug Abuse Treatment Outcome Study, 414
Drug Enforcement Administration, U.S., 961–962
Drug-Free Workplace Act of 1988, 1247–1248
See also Workplace drug and alcohol programs
DSM. *See* Diagnostic and Statistical Manual
Dual diagnosis relapse prevention, 1020–1021
Duty to warn, 1153

Eating disorders, 1029
in adolescent substance abuser, 1164–1165
assessment, 1135
definition, 1041
diagnosis, 1041
epidemiology, 1041
possible associations with substance abuse, 1041–1042
treatment, 1042
Ecstasy. *See* MDMA
Educational intervention, 208
chronic pain management, 953
effectiveness, 210
historical evolution, 208
hypertension, 733
integrated approach, 210
life skills training, 221
in opioid maintenance, 567–568
role of health care professionals, 211
successful, 223
Efficacy, drug, 52
Elderly, 833–852
alcohol effects, 762
age-mediated metabolism, 833–834
cancer risk, 836
cardiovascular system, 836–839
hematology, 834–835
immune system, 835–836
muscle problems, 836
nutritional, 845–846
psychiatric, 846
skeletal system, 834
sleep patterns, 800
alcohol use, 833
among women, 1196
morbidity/mortality, 299
prevalence, 299
withdrawal, 434, 846
benzodiazepine withdrawal, 448
detoxification, 427
general health concerns, 847
sleep patterns, 797, 847
substance use disorders in, 5
withdrawal considerations, 480–481
Electro-acupuncture. *See* Acupuncture
Electrocardiography, 732, 878
Electroencephalography, 24
alcohol intoxication response, 27
Electrolyte levels, 747–748, 765
Emergency medicine
acute psychosis, 1008–1010
addiction professionals in, 870
alcohol as outcome factor, 870
assessment, 869–870
cirrhosis, prevalence, 868
clinician knowledge of addiction, 870–871
detoxification, 428
hallucinogen intoxication, 472–475
intervention for addiction in, 870–872
opioid intoxication/overdose, 458–459

patient management, 869–871
PCP intoxication, 476–477
sedative-hypnotic overdose, 441–442
substance use among admitted patients, 864–866
substance use screening, 867–868
trauma center system, 863–864, 871
Wernicke's disease, 438
See also Crisis intervention, Trauma
Emetine, 671
Enablers/enabling behavior
definition, 1095, 1302–1303
family accommodations for addicted member, 1095–1096
role of, 1112
Endocarditis, 737
Endocrine system
alcohol effects, 839–840
alcohol use effects, xxii, xxviii, 765, 813
Endorphins, acupuncture stimulation, 373, 375
Environmental factors, 296
alcohol use, xxvi–xxvii
alcoholic families, 1100
early recovery, 7, 1102–1103
ongoing recovery, 1108
biopsychosocial model of addiction. *See* Biopsychosocial model
in borderline personality disorder pathogenesis, 1070
development of resiliency, 211–212
in reinstatement model of relapse, 45
relapse risk, 302
risk assessment, 218
tobacco use, 572
addiction liability, 148
Enzyme Multiplied Immunoassay Technique, 1243
Epidemiologic Catchment Area survey, 2, 3–4
Epidemiology, 3–14
addiction comorbidity in chronic pain, 946
addictive disorders in women, 1173–1174, 1191
adolescents
pregnancy, 1135
sexually transmitted diseases, 1135–1136
substance abuse, 1129–1131
alcohol-induced mood disorders, 971, 972
alcohol-related liver damage, 842
alcoholism, xvii, 784, 892
among elderly, 299
incidence, 3
prevalence, 2–3
attention disorder, 1031–1032
borderline personality disorder, 1064–1065
drug use disorders, 3–4
eating disorders, 1041
fetal alcohol syndrome, 1224
fetal exposure, 1224
hallucinogen use, 1013
HIV infection, 827–830
impaired professionals, 1265
impulse control disorders, 1049
inhalant abuse, 187–189
opioid abuse, 131–132
parasuicide, 1063–1064
prevention research, 234, 235, 242
psychiatric comorbidity, 355
anxiety disorders, 993–994
depressive symptoms, 983–984
mood disorders, 984–986
psychopathology
in adolescent substance abusers, 1161–1162
substance-induced, 971–973
sexually transmitted disease among adolescents, 1135–1136
steroid use/abuse, 174
terminology, 1
tuberculosis infection, 830
types of studies, 1–2
Epilepsy, alcohol withdrawal seizures and, 784
Esophagus
alcohol-related problems, 841–842
variceal bleeding, 844
Estazolam. *See* Benzodiazepines
Ethanol. *See* Alcohol
Ethical issues, xxxiv
liver transplantation and alcoholism, 891
in prevention research, 217
Event-related potentials, 24
Excitotoxicity, 199
Eye Movement Desensitization and Reprocessing, 383–384, 1122

Families, 1093–1124
with addiction
conceptual approaches, 1115
definition, 1093
disease model, 1115, 1116–1117
functional/structural accommodation, 1095–1096, 1112
intergenerational transmission, 1095
physician role, 1096–1097
with recovering member, 1096
resources for, 259
risks, 1093–1095
addiction risk factors, 7, 297
among women, 1192–1193
adolescent assessment, 1132
alcoholism in
adult children of alcoholics, 700–701
denial in, 1111–1112
disease model, 1099, 1115
early recovery stage, 1104–1107
environmental features, 1100, 1102–1103, 1105
extent, 698
individual development in, 1101, 1104, 1109–1110
maladaptive roles, 1112–1113, 1117
ongoing recovery, 1107–1110
physician competencies for intervention, 1113–1114
recovery mechanism, 1100
resistance to change, 1100
systemic functioning, 1100–1101, 1105–1106, 1108–1109, 1115–1116
transition to recovery, 1101–1104
Twelve Step support programs, 698–701
See also Children of alcoholics
assessment, 1132, 1156–1158
behavioral loops, 1096
of chronic pain patients, 948, 949
extended, definition, 1093
functional/structural variation, 1093
gateway exposure in, 1095
genetic research in addiction, 17–19
of impaired physician, 1269–1270, 1271
invalidating environment, 1070
of origin
definition, 1093
therapy issues, 1122
preventive interventions
benefits, 209–210, 220
neglect of, 209
parenting skills, 222
of procreation
definition, 1093
therapy issues, 1122–1123
protective factors, 208
in recovery process, 318, 321
risk factors, substance abuse, 208
ritualized behavior, 1094, 1096
stress of recovery, 1098
secrets in, 1155
terminology, 1093
See also Family treatment; Parenting
Family Intervention, 1116
Family Reconstruction therapy, 1122

Family treatment
approaches, 1116–1117
behavioral approaches, 1118–1119
behavioral loops in, 1096
coaching, 1122
conceptualizations of addiction, 1115
eclectic approach, 1115–1116, 1119
developmental considerations in, 210
family of origin issues, 1122
genogram mapping, 1122
rationale, 658
recovery movement, 1117
research needs, 1124
residential treatment, 1116–1117
stages of recovery, 1100, 1119–1124
systems perspective, 1117–1118
in transition from alcoholism, 1096
unilateral family therapy, 1119
See also Network therapy; Families
Faradic aversion, 669, 670, 671
Federal Drug-Free Workplace Legislation and Regulations, 1247
Fenfluramine, 536
Fentanyl. *See* Opioids
Fetal alcohol syndrome
clinical features, xxii–xxiii, xxviii–xxix, 222, 1217–1218, 1224
developmental outcomes, xxix, 1113, 1224–1226
epidemiology, 1224
long-term outcomes, xxiii
Fetal exposure, 1220
alcohol, 1217
developmental outcomes, 1224–1226
See also Fetal alcohol syndrome
amantadine, 539
amphetamines, 1219–1220
assessment, 1211, 1231–1232
barbiturates, 1220
bromocriptine, 539
cocaine, 1218–1219
developmental outcomes, 1226–1227
developmental outcomes, 1224–1232
knowledge base, 1113, 1223–1224
disulfiram, 1204
epidemiology, 1224
hallucinogens, 1220
lithium, 539
management of, 1211–1221
marijuana, 1228–1229
methadone, 549
neonatal opiate abstinence syndrome
assessment, 1213
breastfeeding, 1214
clinical features, 1211–1213
treatment, 1213–1217
neuroleptics, 539
nicotine, 1227–1228
opioids, 1226
perinatal transmission of HIV, 826
prevention, 1231
preventive intervention with pregnant mothers, 221–222
screening for, 1129
sedative-hypnotics, 1220
teratogenicity, 1113, 1223
Fiorinal® (butalbital). *See* Sedative-hypnotics
First time offender, 410
Flashbacks
definition, 970–971
LSD-related, 155, 586
PCP-related, 479–480
Flower essence elixirs, 384
Flumazenil, 519
as alcohol antagonist, 432
for sedative-hypnotic intoxication, 442
See also Benzodiazepines
Flurazepam. *See* Benzodiazepines
Fluoxetine, xxv, xxxi, 986, 1164
alcohol relapse prevention, 505–506, 508
for cocaine recovery, 533
Flupenthixol, for cocaine recovery, 535
Fluvoxamine, 506
Folic acid, 744, 765
alcohol effects, 835
function, 834–835
See also Nutrition
Follow-up
after brief intervention, 259–260
after inpatient treatment, 341
benzodiazepine withdrawal, 526–527
of impaired physician, 1271–1274
liver transplantation, 896–897
opioid intoxication/overdose, 459
opioid withdrawal management, 462
as outcome factor, 341
outpatient rehabilitation, 329
rationale, 341
Free radicals, 746
alcohol use-related, xxii, xxviii

G protein, 63–64
GABA. *See* Gamma-amino-butyric acid
Gabapentin, 933–934
Gambling addiction
affective regulation, 1049
substance use comorbidity, 1052
withdrawal symptoms, 1050
See also Impulse control disorders
Gamma-amino-butyric acid (GABA)
in addiction process, 198, 995
alarm signal dysregulation, 995
alcohol effects, 53–54, 107, 108–109, 198, 519
neurocircuitry reinforcement, 75, 77–78
withdrawal, 432
antagonists, 75
benzodiazepine effects, 435, 445–446, 518, 519
pharmacology, 123–126
function, 518
Gamma-glutamyl transpeptidase, 266–267
Gas chromatography/mass spectrometry, 1243, 1256, 1258
Gastritis, alcoholic, 811
Gastrointestinal complications, 764–765, 811–812, 841–842
Gateway theory, 1095
marijuana in, 164, 166
tobacco in, 148
Gays and lesbians, 1195
AA participation, 712
Gender differences
AA membership, 708
acetaldehyde metabolism, 760–761
addiction processes, 298, 299
alcohol-related injury, 866
alcohol-related liver dysfunction, 761–762
alcohol use disorder, xxvi, 2, 250, 1180–1181, 1191
alcoholics, social stability assessment, 894
alcoholism risk, xx
benzodiazepine use, 448
clinical characteristics of addictive disorders, 1180–1181
cocaine pharmacotherapy, 538–539
drug use disorder epidemiology, 4
liver transplantation candidates, 891–892
pharmacology, 1174–1175
in preventive intervention, 237
substance use risk, 4–5
treatment outcomes, 1185–1186
withdrawal management, 480
See also Women's issues
Genetics, 17–35
addiction in women and, 1176–1177
in addiction processes, 28–29, 1095

research limitations, 28
addiction risk, 7, 297
alcohol effects, 105–106, 762–763
alcohol-related liver disease, 844
alcoholism research, xviii, xxv–xxvii, xxxvii
adoption studies, 18–19, 29
biomarkers, 19–27
family studies, 17–18
gene-environment interaction, xxvi–xxvii
receptivity to alcohol effects, 105–106
twin studies, 18, 29
biopsychosocial model of addiction, 207–208, 425
current understanding, 30
gene-environment interaction
alcohol research, xx–xxi
gene polymorphisms and addiction risk, 23–24
immediate-early genes, 197
in neuroadaptation, 66–67
opioid addiction risk, 558–559
in pain processes, 914
quantitative trait loci, xx, xxvi
in tobacco addiction, 29–30
Genogram, 1122
Glucocorticoid hormones, 88–89, 91
Glutamatergic system, 54, 995
alcohol effects, 108
neuroadaptation, 62–63
Glutamic pyruvic transaminase, 267
Glutathione metabolism, 758
Glutethimide. *See* Sedative-hypnotics
Glycine receptors, alcohol effects, 109
GOAL Project, 624
Gonorrhea, 734
Government intervention
research program, 215
resource allocation, 208
Group therapies
advantages, 634
dialectical behavior therapy, 1072–1073
gender-segregated, 1185
non-Twelve Step programs, 693, 719. *See also specific program*
vs. individual psychotherapy, 634–635
See also Network therapy; self-help groups; Twelve Step programs
Growth factors, 58

Hair analysis, 1243
Halazepam
in alcohol relapse prevention, 509
See also Benzodiazepines
Halcion® (triazolam). *See* Benzodiazepines
Haldol decanoate, 1017
Hallucinations
in alcohol withdrawal, 433, 846, 1010
in hallucinogen intoxication, 472, 970
PCP flashbacks, 479–480
in stimulant intoxication, 466, 1012
Hallucinogen use
clinical features of intoxication, 472
fetal exposure, 1220
management of effects, 473–475
medical effects, 472–473, 816
persistent symptoms, 475
pharmacokinetics, 158–159
pharmacotherapy of, 585–586
prevalence, 1013
psychological/behavioral effects, 472, 585–586, 970–971
psychosis, 1013–1014
psychopathology related to, 970–971
serotonergic effects, 379
therapeutic
for addiction, 379–380, 587–588
for depression, 588
types of, 153
withdrawal, 475
Haloperidol, 432, 437
hallucinogen intoxication management, 473
preoperative management of addicted patient, 860
stimulant intoxication/overdose management, 467–468
See also Neuroleptic agents
Hangover, alcoholic's perception, 667
Harm reduction, 395–403
definition, 395
goals, 395
historical development, 395–396
law enforcement and, 396–398
outcomes, 399–400
techniques, 396–397, 400–403
Harrison Narcotics Act, 297, 406, 1264
Hazelden. *See* Minnesota Model
Headaches, cocaine-related, 786
HEADS FIRST assessment, 1131–1136
Healing, culturally specific practices, 385
Health care professionals
in community coalitions, 211, 227–228
impaired, 860–861, 1263–1278
assessment, 1268–1270
etiology, 1265–1266
historical perspective, 1264–1265
identification of, 1266
intervention with, 1266–1268
outcomes, 1274–1275
posttreatment care, 1271–1274
prescribing practices, 964
prevalence, 1265
professional concern, 1263–1264
research needs, 1276
social concerns, 1263
treatment, 320–321, 1270–1271
interdisciplinary treatment for psychiatric comorbidity, 1081–1088
intervention with addicted families, 1096–1097
assessment, 1111–1112
professional competencies for, 1113–1114
intervention with adolescents
physician roles, 1146
rationale, 1145–1146, 1149
intervention with children of alcoholics, 1111
mandated reporting, 1153
pain management knowledge base, 962–964
patient advocacy, 273
pharmacological knowledge needs, 99, 102
physician health programs, 1272–1273
role in preventive interventions, 210–211, 241–242
fetal exposure, 1231–1232
role in Twelve Step recovery programs, 696, 697, 709
referral, 701–704
substance use beliefs, 870–871
treatment recruitment techniques, 597–598
See also Medical Review Officer (MRO)
Heart disease
assessment, 732
ischemia, 732–733
pharmacotherapy, 732–733
See also Cardiovascular system
Helicobacter pylori, 764, 811
Help-seeking behaviors
abused children/adolescents, 1132–1133
attractiveness of programs, 339–40
gender differences, 1181–1182, 1196
mental health patients, 355–356
patterns, 709–710
precontemplation stage, 595–596, 599
in pregnant women, 1199
stages, 595–596
Hepatitis
alcoholic, 843

among injection drug users, 831
chronic, 831
clinical features, 896–897
complications, 831
management, 831
prevalence in addicts, 878
virus types, 831. *See also specific type*
Hepatitis A, 831
Hepatitis B, 736, 831–832, 844
Hepatitis C, 560–561, 736, 763–764, 832, 844
Hepatitis D, 832
Hepatitis E, 832
Hepatitis F, 832
Hepatitis G, 832
Herbal remedies, 381–382
Hero role, 1112
Heroin
adolescent use trends, 1130
associated criminal activity, 406
aversion therapy for dependence, 671
criminalization, 405
familial risk factors, 297
genetic risk, 297
medical effects, 786–787
methadone treatment for, 557–568
outcomes, 131–132
psychopathology as risk factor, 298
See also Opioids, Methadone
Hierarchical linear modeling, 216
High density lipoproteins, 765–766, 838
HIPATHE, 210
"Hitting bottom," 596, 1096, 1102
Homeopathy, 384
Homosexuality. *See* Gays and lesbians
5HT$_3$ receptors, 110–111, 112. *See also* Serotonergic system
Hydromorphone. *See* Opioids
Hyperalgesia, 906
Hyperglycemia, alcohol effects, 742–743
Hyperlipidemia, 743
Hypertension
alcohol-related, 783, 813, 837, 1176
assessment, 733
PCP-induced, 476–477
stimulant-induced, 469
treatment, 733
sleep patterns and, 797
Hyperthermia
in hallucinogen intoxication, 472, 473
in stimulant intoxication, 468–469
Hypervigilence, in stimulant intoxication, 466
Hypnotherapy, 378–379
Hypoglycemia, 813
alcohol effects, 742–743

Ibogaine, 379, 380
therapeutic use for addiction, 588
Imipramine, 1001
for benzodiazepine addiction, 527
clearance in alcoholics, 507, 508
for panic disorder, 517–518
Immediate-early genes, 197
Immune system
alcohol effects, xxii, xxviii
in elderly, 835–836
marijuana effects, 165
Impaired physicians. *See* Health professionals, impaired
Impulse control disorders, 1047–1060
conceptual evolution, 1047–1048
diagnostic classification, 1048–1049, 1056
epidemiology, 1049
neurobiological studies, 1053–1054
substance use comorbidity, 1051–1053
family history factors, 1053
substance use disorders related to, 1049–1051, 1055–1058
treatment response, 1054–1055
and withdrawal symptoms, 1050
Impulsive behavior, stress-induced, 89
Individual differences
addiction risk, 297–298
alcohol-related brain injury, 776
benzodiazepine effects, 519
detoxification planning, 425
medical effects of alcohol, 843–844
nicotine sensitivity, 573
susceptibility, 219
treatment planning, 321
treatment response, 286
Infant health. *See* Fetal exposure
Infection
alcohol use among elderly and, 835–836
intravenous drug use-related, 737–738, 878
opioid use-associated, 549
opportunistic, in AIDS/HIV, 825–826
preoperative management, 878–879
retroviral, 735–736
risk among drug abusers, 825
See also Sexually transmitted diseases; *specific pathogen or anatomic site*
Inflammation, 906–907
Informed consent
adolescents
confidentiality issues, 1146–1147
urine testing, 1148–1149
aversion therapy, 672
Inhalants, volatile
addiction liability, 189–190
adolescent use trends, 1130
adverse effects, 189
assessment for abuse, 189
delivery, 187
epidemiology, 187–189
intoxication, 191
mechanisms of action, 190–191
medical effects, 816–817
neurological effects, 788
pharmacokinetics, 190
pharmacology of, 187–193
pharmacotherapy of, 586
psychiatric comorbidity, 190
reinforcing properties, 191
research needs, 191
tobacco smoke, 572
replacement therapy, 575–576
types of, 187
Inhibition deficit, 89
Inner child therapy, 1122
Institute of Medicine risk categorization, 218–219
Insurance
access to care, 324
addiction treatment coverage, 320
alcohol use screening and, 626
detoxification placement, 428
inpatient treatment, 342
intoxication-related injury, 867
Integrated definition modeling, 238–241
Interferon, 736
Intermediate brain syndrome, 776–778
Intermittent explosive disorder, 1039–1041, 1048, 1049
changes in awareness, 1050
See also Impulse control disorders
International Classification of Diseases, 281–282
diagnostic criteria, 1291–1293
International Doctors in AA, 695
Interpersonal interaction
adolescent assessment, 1134
children of alcoholics, 1111
co-dependence concept, 1099
consequences of addiction in families, 1093–1094

crisis intervention, 259
life skills in development, 221
maladaptive roles in alcoholic families, 1112–1113
prevention programs based on, 222–223
recovery process, 318
rehabilitation relationship, 894–895
social cohesiveness, 656
social stability of alcoholics, 893–894
support for clinical change, 603
support in psychotherapy, 639–640
support in recovery, 883
treatment milieu, 317
Intoxication
with alcohol, 430–440
with hallucinogens, 465–484
with opioids, 457–463
with sedative-hypnotics, 441–454
with stimulants, 465–484
Intravenous drug use
and AIDS/HIV
incidence, 827–830
risk, 735
drug impurities, 738
hepatitis risk, 831
infection and, 550, 878
local infections related to, 737
in steroid abuse, 177
systemic infections related to, 737–738
tuberculosis risk, 736
Ion channel, calcium, 106–107
Iron deficiency, 748, 765
Ischemic heart disease, 732–733
Isoniazid, 830

Johnson Institute Intervention. *See* Family Intervention
Juvenile justice system. *See* Criminal justice system
Juveniles. *See* Adolescents

Kappa agonists/antagonists, 886
Ketamine use
PCP intoxication management, 479
psychosis related to, 1013–1014
Ketorolac, 882, 886
Kidney(s)
detoxification considerations, 426
preoperative assessment, 879
Kindling phenomenon. *See* Neuronal sensitization
Kleptomania, 1050
Klonopin® (clonazepam). *See* Benzodiazepines
Korsakoff's psychosis, 438, 775, 780–781, 782
Kudzu, 381–382

L-dopa
for cocaine recovery, 536
stimulant withdrawal treatment, 470
LAAM. *See* Levo-alpha-acetylmethadol
Law enforcement
harm reduction and, 396
See also Criminal justice system
LEAD procedure, 286
Learned behavior, 675
stress-induced self-administration and, 91
Lecithin, 747
Legal issues
adolescent confidentiality rights, 1146–1147, 1153–1154
classification of controlled substances, 961
disability law, 1249–1251
duty to warn, 1153
historical development of anti-drug laws, 405–406
impaired physicians, 1264–1265
liver transplantation and alcoholism, 891
methadone detoxification of adolescents, 427
prescribing for pain relief, 961–962
workplace drug testing
emotional distress claims, 1247
employee/employer rights, 1243–1246
employer tort liability, 1246–1247
mandated, 1241, 1244, 1248–1249, 1255
relevant legislation, 1247–1251
See also Criminal justice system
Legalization of drugs, 396
Length of stay
detoxification, 439
as outcome factor, 330–331, 341
Levo-alpha-acetylmethadol (LAAM), 53, 551–552, 566
Librium® (chlordiazepoxide). *See* Sedative-hypnotics
Licensure and regulation
evaluating professional qualifications, 1082
non-credentialed counselors, 1081–1082
Life skills training, 221
Lifestyle factors, 1194–1195
Ligands, 100
Light therapy, 383
Lisuride, 472
Lithium
for alcohol relapse prevention, 510
for bipolar disorder in substance use, 988
for cocaine recovery, 536
for impulse control disorder, 1055
teratogenicity, 539
Liver
acetaminophen injury, 758
alcohol effects, xxii, xxviii, 743, 812, 878
acetaldehyde metabolism, 746
alcoholic hepatitis, 843
assessment, 812
course of dysfunction, 763–764
epidemiology, 842
fat accumulation, 743, 749, 755–756, 762, 842–843
gastrointestinal complications, 764–765
gender differences, 761–762
genetic predisposition, 762–763
individual differences, 843–844
mechanisms of toxicity, 758
prevention, 764
treatment, 764
See also Cirrhosis
cancer, 844
detoxification considerations, 426
gamma-glutamyl transpeptidase assessment, 266–267
hepatic encephalopathy, 844
hepatitis C infection, 736
hyperlipidemia, 743
nutrition-related pathogenesis, 748–749
opioid effects, 550
peroxidation, 746
steroid effects, 179
transplantation. *See* Liver transplantation
vitamin effects, 746–747
Liver transplantation, 891–896
abstinence in alcoholic recipients, 892–897
follow-up care, 896–897
gender differences, 891–892
patient selection, 891–892, 896
to polydrug abusers, 893
public policy issues, 891
survival rates, 895
Lobaline, 487
Locus ceruleus, 60, 64, 995
in opiate withdrawal, 133–134
Locus of control, 950. *See also* Control
Lofexidine, 461
Lorazepam
alcohol relapse prevention, 509
for alcohol withdrawal, 436, 439, 440
management of hallucinogen intoxication, 473
See also Benzodiazepines
Lost child role, 1112

LSD (lysergic acid diamine)
adolescent use trends, 1130
adverse effects, 155
dependence on, 158
flashbacks, 155, 586
mechanisms of action, 159
pharmacology of, 153–161
pharmacotherapy of, 585
psychological effects, 155
reinforcing properties, 160
research, xxxiv
serotonergic effects, 379
therapeutic use, 154
for addiction, 379–380, 587–588
tolerance, 156
See also Hallucinogens

M. avium-intracellular complex, 737
MacAndrew Alcoholism Scale, 264, 266
Magnesium, 748
in alcohol withdrawal, 437
Managed care, 321, 324
and alcohol use screening in primary care, 627
and patient assessment, 274
and detoxification, 428
and patient placement criteria, 365, 367
and accountability, xvii
Mania, substance-induced, 984
Marchiafava-Bignami disease, 782, 810
Marijuana
addiction liability, 166–167, 816
adolescent use trends, 1130
aggressive behavior and, 166–167
aversion therapy for, 670
carcinogenicity, 164
cognitive effects, 166
dependence and withdrawal, 163–164, 166, 476
fetal exposure to, 165, 1228–1229
federal classification of, 1299
as gateway drug, 164, 166
intoxication, 465–484
management, 476
mediators, 475
medical effects, 475–476
psychological/behavioral effects, 475
mechanisms of action, 167–168
medical complications, 164–165, 816
memory effects, 787
pharmacokinetics, 167
pharmacology of, 163–171
pharmacotherapy of, 583–584
physiological effects, 164–165, 787
psychological effects, 165–166, 970–971, 1010–1011
receptor antagonist, 476, 584
reinforcing properties, 168
self-medication to control anger, 1040
specimen testing, 1257
therapeutic use, 163
trauma center admissions, 864
use trends, 163
adolescent, 1130
withdrawal, 197
Marinol, 1257
Marital/couples therapy. *See also* Families
disulfiram compliance, 657–658
effectiveness, 337
initiating treatment, 658
network therapy, 657–658
Marriage
addiction processes in, 296
addiction risk and, 7–8
anger, 1123
behavioral therapies, 1118–1119, 1122–1123
gender difference in addictive disorders, 1180–1181
intimacy issues in recovery, 1123–1124
in phases of addiction recovery, 1120–1124
predictors of alcohol use in women, 1193–1194
risk of divorce in recovery, 1106, 1120
risks for spouse of addicted person, 1094–1095
self-help books, 1123
See also Marital/couples therapy; Families
Mascot role, 1112
Mass media
effect on children, 211
tobacco marketing, 235–236
MAST. *See* Michigan Alcohol Screening Test
MATCH, Project, 327–343, 609
Mazindol, 535
MDMA, 475
adverse effects, 155
mechanisms of action, 159
pharmacology, 158–159
reinforcing properties, 160–161
therapeutic use, 154
for addiction, 588
tolerance, 156
Mean corpuscular red cell volume, 267
Medical complications, 731–852
blood pressure, 251
cardiovascular, 732–733, 765–766, 813, 836–839
cerebellar degeneration, 783
cerebrovascular, 839
coma, 431
dermatologic, 765, 844–845
diabetes, 733–734
in the elderly, 762, 833–846
stroke, 784
trauma, xxix
vitamin-mineral status, 743–748
endocrine system, 839–840
esophageal, 841–842
ethanol oxidation, 756–758
gastrointestinal, 764, 811–812, 841–842
hematologic, 765, 812–813
hepatic, 763–768, 812, 842–844, 878
hypertension, 813
individual differences, 843–844
musculoskeletal, 765
neurological, 784, 840–841
nutrition-related liver disease, 748–749
optic neuropathy, 784
pancreatic, 765, 811–812, 842
peripheral neuropathy, 841
renal, 765
reproductive system, 839–840
respiratory, 813–814
trauma, 863–874
in women, 1175–1176
Medical Review Officer (MRO), 1255–1261
continuing education of, 1255
contractual issues, 1255–1256
drug testing role
in rehabilitation program, 1242
reporting results, 1261
specimen collection concerns, 1259–1261
function, 1255
future challenges, 1261–1262
historical development, 1255
interpretation of test results, 1257
laboratory selection, 1256
recordkeeping, 1256–1257
regulation, 1255
review process, 1256–1257
third-party administrators and, 1256
Memory
alcohol-related effects
blackouts, 778–779
syndromes, 775. *See also specific syndrome*

withdrawal, 778
benzodiazepine effects, 119–120, 521
marijuana effects, 165, 787
Menopause, sleep changes in, 798
Menstruation, 761
Mentoring programs, 222–223
Meperidine, 815
See also Opioids
Mescaline. *See* Hallucinogens
Methadone, 323
adjunctive services, 336
for adolescent detoxification, 427
AIDS/HIV and, 550
alcohol use and, 758
alternatives, 551
attitudes, 557
blood level measurement, 564–565
with contingency management, 679, 685–687
in the criminal justice system, 412–413
desipramine and, 987
detoxification, 546
dosimetry, 333, 399, 549, 562–566
drug interactions, 566
duration of treatment, 562
effectiveness, 311
effects, 311
experience of, *vs.* heroin, 562
historical development, 408
international utilization, 397–398
legal sources, 428
limitations, 684
medication interaction, 550
neonatal opiate abstinence syndrome, 1211–1212
nursing mothers, 1214
opioid withdrawal management, 460–461
outcomes, 333, 399–400
pain management and, 938
pain tolerance and, 913–914, 922
pharmacokinetics, 549–550
polydrug treatment, 537
positive contingencies, 643
postoperative addict, 881–882
preoperative dose, 880
program effectiveness, 551
with psychotherapy, 331–332, 550–551, 633, 641–642
rationale for, xxxii, 396–397, 549
side effects, 549
take-home delivery, 685–686
teratogenicity, 549
tuberculosis treatment and, 830
withdrawal, 427
See also Opioid use, maintenance treatment
Methamphetamine, 199. *See also* Stimulants
Methaqualone. *See* Sedative-hypnotics
N-methyl-D-aspartate receptor, 779, 995. *See also* NMDA
Methylphenidate, 137, 141, 143, 535
for attention disorder, 1036, 1037
See also Stimulants
Michigan Alcohol Screening Test (MAST), 1285
Microsomal ethanol oxidizing system, 756–757
Midozolam. *See* Benzodiazepines
Mineral metabolism, 747–748
Minimization, 317
Minnesota Model treatment
change process, 317–319
criticism of, 321–322
design variations, 319–321
goals, 316–317
historical development, 315–316
Moderate alcohol use, 765, 767, 838
Moderation Management, 693, 719, 721
Monoamine oxidase, alcoholism risk marker, 23
Monoamine oxidase inhibitors
for cocaine recovery, 533–534
sleep effects, 797
Monoclonal antibodies, PCP treatment, 477
Monomania, 1047
Mood disorders. *See also* Psychiatric comorbidity
comorbid substance use disorder
in adolescents, 986
clinical significance, 983, 989–990
diagnosis, 983–984
pharmacotherapy, 986–989
prevalence, 984–986
psychotherapy, 989
impulse control disorders and, 1052, 1053, 1056–1057
substance-induced, 973
See also specific disorder
Morphine. *See* Opioids
Mortality
adolescent risk, 1133–1134
AIDS, 827
alcohol-related, 299, 863
cardiovascular disease, 836
cirrhosis, 755, 762, 843
delirium tremens and, 439
fatal blood alcohol levels, 431
gender differences, 1186
heroin addicts, 131–132
moderate alcohol use and, 765
parasuicide, 1063–1064
tobacco-related, 148, 571
tuberculosis, 830
Motivation
in brief intervention, 615–616
clinical enhancement of
matched to stage of change, 599–603
recruitment, 597–598
retention in treatment, 598–599
clinical focus, 638
implications for treatment, 595
neurobiological context, in addiction, 60–61
patient readiness for treatment, 254–255, 275, 597–598
gender differences, 1181–1182
psychotic patient, 1019
perceived costs/benefits of change, 601
in pregnant women, 1199
psychotherapy assessment, 638
recruitment into treatment, 597–598
self-image, 602
treatment research, 323
Motivation-Based Dual Diagnosis Treatment Model, 358, 1019
Motivation enhancement therapy, 1019–1020, 1085
Motor vehicle crashes
alcohol-related, xxix
adolescent perception, 1134
as alcohol use disorder indicator, 868–869
outcomes, 863, 868
emergency care system, 863–864
marijuana and, 165
post-accident drug testing, in workplace, 1242
women's issues, 1180
MRO. *See* Medical Review Officer
Mu receptors, 100–101, 133, 167
opioid analgesics, 938–939
Mycobacterial disease, 737
Myelinolysis, pontine, 782, 810
Myocardial infarction, stimulant-induced, 138, 469
Myocardial ischemia, stimulant-induced, 469

Nalmefene, xxv, xxxi
Naloxone, 197
mechanisms of action, 133
for newborns, 1214–1215
for opioid intoxication/overdose, 459, 814–815
Naltrexone, xxv, xxxi, 311–312, 333, 767, 1017
for alcohol relapse prevention, 504–505, 511
compliance, 505

gastrointestinal side effects, 549
for impulse control disorder, 1055
for opioid treatment
detoxification, 547–548
with individual psychotherapy, 641, 646
maintenance, 548–549
withdrawal management, 461
for PCP flashbacks, 480
polydrug treatment, 537–538, 538
preoperative, 884
Narcissistic personality disorder, 1166–1167
Narcotic Addict Rehabilitation Act, 408
Narcotics Anonymous, 697–698
physician referrals, 701–702
National Institute on Drug Abuse, principles of prevention, 219–220
National Institutes of Health, 2, 3–4
National Labor Relations Act, 1244, 1251
Native Americans, 385
Needle exchange programs, 396, 397, 400, 735, 738
Network therapy, 653–665, 1116, 1118
conceptual basis, 655–656
conceptual development, 654
with couples, 657–658
family in, 658–660
goals, 653
with individual therapy, 661
initiating, 662
maintaining, 663
self-help groups and, 663
social cohesiveness in, 656–657
standardization, 661–662
techniques for sustaining, 660
training effects, 662
treatment principles, 662–663
in withdrawal stage, 660–661
Neuroadaptation
in addiction, 57–70, 910
cAMP pathway model, 58–61
in dependence, 911
in gene expression, 64–65
implications for treatment, 66–67
neurobiological context, 57–58
in neuronal morphology, 65–66
in neurotransmitter-receptor systems, 61
dopaminergic, 61–62
endogenous opioid pathways, 63
G protein-coupled, 63–64
glutamatergic, 62–63
nicotine dependence, 572
research needs, 57
sedative-hypnotic addiction, 518–519
in tolerance, 910–911
types of, 57
Neurochemical processes
acupuncture action, 375–376
addiction biomarkers, 24
alarm signal dysregulation, 995
in alcohol use, 775–776
anosognosia, 785–786
autonomic system dysfunction, 783–784
central nervous system dysfunction, 840
clinical conceptualization, xxix–xxxi, xxxv–xxxi
clinical effects, 53–54, 431
interventions for relapse prevention, 504–507
ligand-gated ion channels, 106–108
memory dysfunction, 779
nerve trauma, 784
neurocircuitry reinforcement, 75–79, 113
neuropsychological disorders, xxii, xxviii
neurotransmitter systems, 432
pathologies, 766–767, 776, 809–810. *See also specific pathology*
polyneuropathy, 783
reinforcement, 75–79, 113
research prospects, xxvi
research trends, xviii, xxvi, xxxi
vitamin deficiency-related pathology, 782–783
in anxiety and addiction, 994–996
benzodiazepine-GABA complex interactions, 445–446
brain changes in behavioral therapies, xxxiii
breadth of drug effects, 788
catecholaminergic agents, 505
cocaine action, 141–142, 532, 786
cocaine withdrawal, 142
common drug pathways
dopaminergic, 51
endogenous opioids, 51–52
sites of action, 51
discrete effects of drugs, 909–910
disulfiram effects, 502
drug characteristics, 52–54
endogenous opioids in alcoholism, 504–505
endorphin release, 375–376
first/second messenger systems, 58, 198
heroin use, 787
implications for treatment research, xxxii–xxxiii
in impulse control disorder, 1053–1054
in inflammatory pain, 906–907
inhalant abuse, 788
long-term effects of substance use, 197
marijuana, 163
antidote, 476
intoxication, 167, 475
neuroadaptation, 57, 425
neuropsychological functioning, xxviii, xxxiii
nicotine kinetics, 572
nociception, 901–904
opioid intoxication/overdose, 457, 459
pharmacology, 132–134
withdrawal, 459
pain modulation, 904–906
receptor pharmacology, 100
in relapse, 78–79
research needs, 788–789
sedative-hypnotic dependence, 518–519
shared effects of drugs, 908–909
signal transduction, 57–58
in sleep behavior, 793
steroid effects, 182–183
stimulant intoxication, 466
stress response, 88–91
drug use and, 84
See also Brain; Brain injury; Neuroadaptation
Neurocircuitry, 73–81
Neuroleptic agents
for alcohol intoxication, 432
for alcohol withdrawal, 437, 440
in pregnancy, 1204
for anabolic steroid abuse, 584
for cocaine recovery, 535
for PCP intoxication, 479, 480, 1014–1015
for stimulant intoxication/overdose, 467–468
for stimulant withdrawal, 472
teratogenicity, 539
Neuronal sensitization (kindling phenomenon), 536, 988
Niacin, 782
Nicotine
abstinence, 311
addiction liability, 148–149
addiction process, 571–573
adolescent use trends, 1130–1131
adverse effects, 147–148
alcohol use and, 148, 758
in women, 1195
aversion therapy for addiction, 668–669
cessation outcomes, 492–493, 603–606, 731
cessation research, 492

cessation trends, 579
cognitive effects, 147, 969
fetal exposure, 1227–1228
as gateway drug, 148
genetic risk of abuse, 29–30
harm reduction strategies, 398–399
marketing strategies, 235–236
mechanisms of action, 150–151
mortality, 571
nicotine replacement therapy, 573–574
advice to patients, 491–492
with behavioral therapy, 579
combination of delivery methods, 578
comparison of products, 574, 576
detoxification schedule, 491
dosimetry, 492
polacrilex/gum, 489, 491, 493, 574
sprays/inhalers, 489, 575–576
sublingual tablet, 577
transdermal patches, 489–492, 574–575
pharmacokinetics, 149–150, 572
pharmacotherapy for addiction
with behavioral therapy, 578–579
bupropion for, 576–577, 576–578
combination of therapies, 578–579
with concurrent alcoholism, 586
current trends, 571
non-nicotine products, 576–578
with other addiction, 586–587
in psychotic patient, 1017
preventive interventions with youth, 237
receptor mechanics, 572
recruitment into treatment, 597–598
reinforcing properties, 151
research, xxx, xxxvi
schizophrenia and, 1015–1016
pharmacotherapy for addiction, 1017
sleep behavior and, 797–798, 800–801
tolerance, 149, 573
treatment research, 323
trends among women, 1176
use assessment
findings among youth, 237–238
survey instrument, 236–237
withdrawal, 149
pharmacotherapies for, 487–488
in surgical patient, 492, 866
symptoms, 487, 573
Nifedipine, 536
Night blindness, 745, 748
Nimodipine, 536
Nitrate medications, 732
Nitroglycerine, 732
NMDA receptor system, 995
in addiction process, 197, 198, 913
in alcohol intoxication, 54, 107, 109–110
in alcohol withdrawal, 54, 110, 197–198
drug antagonists, 62–63
excitotoxicity, 199
phencyclidine/ketamine action, 1014
treatment implications, 199
Nociception, 901–904
Nodal-link mapping, 1038–1039
Noradrenergic system
alarm signal dysregulation, 995
in impulse control disorder, 1054
Norepinephrine
alcohol effects, 432
in pain modulation, 905
Nuclear Regulatory Commission, 1249
Nutrition
adolescent assessment, 1135
alcohol effects
appetitive, 742
alcohol use effects, 103, 742–743, 755–756, 845–846
intoxication management, 809
alternative medicine, 377–378
calories, 741, 742
in liver pathogenesis, 748–749
nutritional value of alcoholic beverages, 741–742
small intestine dysfunction, 842
therapy for alcoholism, 749–750
vegetarian diet, 838

Obesity, 741
Obsessive-compulsive disorders, 1047–1061
in alcoholic, 999
impulse control disorders and, 1050–1051, 1056
Olanzapine, 1016–1017
Ondansetron, 163
for nicotine withdrawal, 487–488
Operant conditioning, 668
in Community Reinforcement Approach, 675
in drug self-administration paradigm, 39–40, 84
mechanism, 39
for pain management, 948
treatment goals, 675–676
Ophthalmologic complications, in alcoholism, 784
Opioids
addiction liability, 132
addiction symptoms, 935–936
adverse effects, 132
agonists, 52, 133
antagonists, 52, 133, 333–334
pharmacology, 101
cAMP pathway regulation, 60
CNS effects, 937
Community Reinforcement Approach, 684–685
contingency management for dependence, 685–687
criminalization, 405–406
dilutants, 458
endogenous, 375–376
in addiction processes, 51–52
in affective withdrawal, 912–913
in alcoholism, 112, 504–505
in impulse control disorder, 1054
neuroadaptation in addiction, 57
pain experience and, 914
in pain physiology, 905
familial risk, 29
federal classification of, 1299
heroin experience, 562
historical, 131
intoxication/overdose, 814–815
clinical features, 457
complications, 458–459
diagnosis, 457–458
follow-up care, 459
management, 458–459
maintenance treatment, 938. *See also* Methadone therapy
buprenorphine, 462, 552–553, 566–567
clinician role, 567–568
compliance, 558
conceptual basis, 558
effectiveness, 558
goals, 559
hepatitis C, 560–561
initial dose, 559
LAAM, 551–552, 566
medical maintenance, 559–560
naltrexone, 548–549
pain management, 560
patient perspective, 557–558
physician attitudes, 557
pregnancy and, 560
psychosocial component, 567
public attitudes, 557
regulatory issues, 568

utilization, 557, 568
mechanisms of action, 132–134
medical effects, 550, 786–787, 814–815, 936–937
misuse, 131–132
neonatal opiate abstinence syndrome
clinical features, 1211–1213
treatment, 1213–1217
pain tolerance and, 913–914
pharmacokinetics, 53, 132
pharmacology of, 131–135
pharmacotherapy of, 545–555
acute withdrawal, 546–548
combined medication detoxification, 548
hallucinogens for, 588
with individual psychotherapy, 641
intoxication/overdose, 459
polydrug addiction, 587
withdrawal, 460–462
polydrug addiction
alcohol, 587
cocaine, 537, 587
withdrawal management, 480
postoperative addict, 881–882
in pregnancy, 425–426
detoxification, 1206–1207
developmental outcomes, 1226
preoperative assessment/management, 878
of addict, 880
of recovering patient, 884
protracted abstinence, 545–546
pseudoaddiction, 936
psychiatric comorbidity, 561–562
borderline personality disorder, 984
mood disorders, 985
psychopathology related to, 970
psychosocial treatment, 640–643, 646
receptors
alcohol interaction, 504
interventions for alcohol relapse prevention, 504–505
mu subclasses, 549
pharmacology, 100–101
recovery natural history, 545
reinforcing properties, 134
specimen testing, 1258
therapeutic, 131
alternatives, 945
chronic pain management, 926–927, 934
pain management in addicted patient, 921, 934–942
treatment trends, 945
trauma center admissions, 864
tuberculosis treatment in, 830
types of, 131, 457
unique features of addiction, 558–559
withdrawal
cAMP pathway upregulation in, 60
clinical features, 459, 934–935
concurrent medical conditions, 460
diagnosis, 459–460
follow-up, 462
locus ceruleus in, 133–134
management, 460–462, 941
pain physiology in, 912–913
pharmacotherapies, 546–548
syndrome, 134–135
Oral behavior, 597
Organic brain syndrome, 466, 969–982
Osteomalacia, 746
Osteoporosis, 814
Outcome studies, 310–311, 322, 338
acamprosate, 506–507
adjunctive therapies, 334–335
adolescent intervention, 1149
Alcoholics Anonymous, 304, 713–715, 716
alcoholism, 722
borderline personality disorder, 1066
brief interventions, 340, 617–624
bromocriptine, 505
carbimide, 504
coerced treatment, 409–410
community coalitions, 230–231
Community Reinforcement Approach, 676, 677
compliance factors, 312
cost-effectiveness, 327
disulfiram, 502–503
evaluation of public programs, 413–414
findings, 337–338, 342
follow-up outpatient care, 341
gender differences, 1185–1186
harm reduction, 399–400
homeopathy, 384
hypnotherapy, 379
impaired physicians, 1274–1275
individual psychotherapy, 640–645
length of treatment, 330–331, 341
literature review, 327–328
methodological issues, 216
Minnesota Model, 322
naltrexone, 505
nicotine cessation, 492–493
nutrition interventions, 377–378
pain management, 956
patient placement criteria for, 367–368
pharmacotherapy, 332–334
prevention programs, 220–222
multidisciplinary approach, 237
psychotherapy, therapist effects, 609–613
severity of addiction, 299
stage of change, therapy matched to, 603–606
therapeutic communities for criminals, 411
therapist factors, 331–332
transcendental meditation, 381
treatment in criminal justice system, 409
treatment matching, 335–337
treatment variables, 337
process factors, 329
setting, 329–330
Twelve Step programs, 713–714
Overdose
on alcohol, 431–438
definition, 1303
on opioids, 457–459, 814–815
pharmacotherapeutic strategies, 465
on sedative-hypnotics, 441–442
on stimulants, 465–470
in surgical patients, 860
Oxaloacetic transaminase, 267
Oxandrolone, 764
Oxazepam
for alcohol relapse prevention, 509
See also Benzodiazepines
Oxycodone. *See* Opioids

PACT. *See* Program for Alcoholic Couples Treatment
Pain
acute, 920
recurrent, 956
allodynia, 906
anger and blame in, 950, 955
behavior theory, 948–949
cancer-related, 921
psychosocial intervention, 956
central pain syndrome, 908
chronic, 920–921. *See also* Chronic pain syndrome
addiction comorbidity, 946
assessment, 926, 946, 947–948, 951
cognitive functioning in, 950
family functioning, 948, 949
management, 925, 926–927

mood disturbances in, 950
outcomes evaluation, 947
psychological determinants, 948–951
clinical characteristics, 919
cognitive functioning in, 949–950
treatment focus on, 953
complex regional pain syndrome, 907
deconditioning in, 951
descending facilitation, 906
descending inhibition, 904–905
distraction effects, 951
genetic factors in, 914
hyperalgesia, 906
inflammatory, 906–907
neurogenic, 907–908
locus of control, 950
management. *See* Pain management
modulators, 904, 915
opioid use and tolerance of, 913–914
peripheral counterstimulation, 904
phantom, 907–908
physiological mechanisms of, 901, 906, 919–920
addiction processes and, 911–913, 914–915
nociception, 901–902, 904
nociceptor classification, 903
sensory channels, 902–903
plasticity in perceptions of, 906
psychogenic component, 951–952
reinforcement, 948–949
sleep dysfunction and, 798
sustained, 906
Pain management
in addicted patients, 919–940
acute pain, 921–924
assessment, 920
cancer-related, 921, 924–925
challenges, 919, 945–946
chronic pain, 925–927
goals, 942
invasive procedures, 931–932
non-opioid medications, 932–933
opioid medications, 934–942
pharmacological approaches, 928–930
psychological approaches, 930–931, 945–956
treatment options, 927–928
treatment planning, 942
withdrawal pain, 922–923
addiction liability, 914–915
addiction resulting from, 923–924
after discharge, 886
assertiveness training for, 954
biofeedback/relaxation training, 953–954
chronic
detoxification considerations, 426
multimodal treatment, 956–957
chronic pain syndrome, 946, 947, 952–954
in addiction, 954–956
controlling legislation, 961–962
counterstimulation, 929
gate control theory, 904
implanted stimulators, 932
marijuana use, 163
massage, 930
multimodal treatment, 956–957
nerve blocks, 931–932
non-narcotic analgesics, 886
opioid maintenance therapy, 560
orthotic, 930
outcome studies, 956
patient-controlled analgesia, 885, 940–941
patient participation in planning, 921
pharmacological approaches, 928–930
physical therapy, 954
physician knowledge base, 962–964
physiologic principles, 904–906
postoperative addict, 860, 881–883
prescribing practices, 961–965
psychological approaches, 945, 951–952
recovering surgical patients, 883–886
reinforcement of pain through, 937–938
self-help groups, 955–956
spinal infusions, 932
therapeutic exercise, 929–930
therapeutic stance, 956–957
thermal treatments, 928–929
transcutaneous electrical nerve stimulation, 882, 886
Twelve Step program goals and, 955
Pancreatitis
alcoholic, 765, 811–812, 842
Panic disorder
in adolescent substance abuser, 1165
alcoholism risk and, 298
in cocaine intoxication, 997
pharmacotherapy of, 118, 517–518
Pantothenic acid, 782–783
Paradoxical reaction, 521–522
Paregoric, 1215
Parenteral therapy, 749–750
Parenting
confidentiality rights, 1153–1154
maternal substance abuse, 1229–1231
preventive interventions in, 222
in recovery, 1105–1106
See also Families
Parole, 303
Paroxetine, 518
PATHE, 210
Patient-controlled analgesia, 885, 940–941
Patient Placement Criteria (ASAM), 323–324, 330, 339, 428–429, 1293–1298
application, 364–365
evolution of, 363–366
in individualized treatment, 366–367
in managing care, 367
in monitoring care, 367–368
rationale for, 338, 363
validation of, 364
Paxipam® (halazepam). *See* Benzodiazepines
PCP. *See* Phencyclidine
Peer relationships
as addiction risk factor, 296
preventive interventions, 210, 223
risk factors, substance abuse, 208
See also Interpersonal interaction
Peer resistance training, 210
Pellegra, 782
Pemoline, 535
for attention disorder, 1036
Pentazocine, 815. *See also* Opioids
Pentobarbital, in sedative-hypnotic detoxification, 451
See also Sedative-hypnotics
Percodan® (oxycodone). *See* Opioids
Peripheral neuropathy, 841
Personality disorders
in adolescent substance abuser, 1162–1163, 1166–1167
comorbid opioid dependence, 561–562
impulse control disorders and, 1052–1053
Personality traits
predictors of dependence, 25, 892–893
resiliency, 211–212
steroid abusers, 177
Pharmacology, 99–202
agonist/antagonist effects, 101
alcohol, 105–112
clinical practice guidelines, 101–102
cocaine, 140–142
disulfiram, 502
gender differences, 1174–1175

hallucinogens, 158–159
inhalants, 190–191
knowledge base, 99, 102
marijuana, 163, 167–168
metabolic enzymes, 99–100
methadone, 549–550
nicotine, 149–151, 572
opioids, 53, 132–134
pharmacodynamics, 100–101
defined, 99
pharmacokinetics, 99–110
defined, 99
phencyclidine, 158
protein binding, 100
receptor function, 100
sedative-hypnotics, 117, 123–126
steroids, 181–183
Pharmacotherapy, 501–590
acute psychosis with amphetamine use, 1012–1013
for addicted patient
perioperative withdrawal, 879–880
postoperative pain, 860
preoperative management, 860
addiction resulting from, 923–924
pain management, 962–963
adolescent substance abuser
with anxiety disorder, 1165
with attention-deficit disorder, 1164
with depression, 1164
agonists, 52, 100, 333, 633
AIDS/HIV, 825
alcohol intoxication, 432
alcohol relapse prevention
affective functioning, 507–510
alcohol sensitizing agents, 501–504
compliance enhancement, 503, 505
future prospects, 510–511
neurotransmitter system interventions, 504–507
policies of self-help groups, 722
with psychotherapy, 511
research trends, xxx–xxxi
strategies, 501
alcohol use disorder
research trends, xxiv–xxv
alcohol withdrawal, 435–438
assessment, 268–269
delirium tremens, 439–440, 766
dosimetry/delivery, 436
in psychotic patient, 1017
seizures, 785
alcoholic liver disease, 812
cirrhosis, 764
anabolic steroid abuse, 584
antagonists, 52, 100, 333–334, 633, 654
attention disorder, 1036–1038
with behavioral therapy, xxxiii, 578–579
benzodiazepine withdrawal, 524–527
blocking agents, 333
borderline personality disorder, 1066, 1073, 1075–1076
caffeine dependence, 584–585
cocaine addiction. *See* Cocaine/cocaine use, pharmacotherapy for addiction
compromised liver function and, 549
cross-tolerant, 425
detoxification of elderly, 427
drug interactions, 817
hallucinogen abuse, 585–586
hallucinogen intoxication, 473–475
harm reduction, 395
heart disease, 732–733
hypertension, 733
inhalant abuse, 586
intermittent explosive disorder, 1040–1041
intoxication/overdose, 465
Korsakoff's psychosis, 781
legal issues in prescribing for pain relief, 961–962
limitations, 466
marijuana
abuse treatment, 583–584
intoxication management, 476
multidisciplinary psychopharmacology, 1081–1088
neonatal opiate abstinence syndrome, 1214–1217
nicotine addiction. *See* Nicotine, pharmacotherapy for addiction
opioid addiction. *See* Opioid use, pharmacotherapy for addiction
outcomes, 332–334
overprescription of analgesics, 964
pain management, 932–1042
risk of addiction in, 962–963
panic disorder, 517–518
PCP abuse, 477–479, 585
physician knowledge base for pain management, 962–964
polydrug withdrawal, 480
in pregnancy, 539
alcohol withdrawal, 1203–1204
preoperative recovering addict, 884
prospects, xxxii
psychiatric comorbidity
anxiety disorders, 1000–1003
mood disorders, 986–989
psychiatric medications and detoxification, 426
psychological dysfunction, 507–508
psychotherapy and, 633–634
in recovery phase, 260
research base, 589
research needs, xxxii–xxxiii
schizophrenia, 1016–1017
substance interactions, 1015, 1018
sedative-hypnotic withdrawal, 450–451
self-administration of narcotic analgesics, 885
sleep disorder related to, 796–797
specimen testing for substance abuse, 1258–1259
stimulant intoxication/overdose, 466, 467–468
withdrawal management, 470–472
strategies, 583
symptom-triggered therapy, 436
therapeutic hallucinogens, 379–380, 587–588
treatment compliance, 311–312
tuberculosis, 830
Twelve Step programs and, 636–637, 1087–1088
withdrawal, generally
goals, 425
special populations, 480–481
strategies, 465
See also specific medication; specific class of medication
Phencyclidines
adverse effects, 154–155
antibody therapy, 477
federal classification of, 1299
fetal exposure, 154–155, 156–157
flashbacks, 479–480
intoxication, 476–477, 816
acute presentation, 154
management, 477–479
mechanisms of action, 159
mental disturbances related to, 971
misuse, 153–154
pharmacokinetics, 158
pharmacology of, 153–160
pharmacotherapy of, 585
polydrug abuse, 585
psychosis related to, 1013–1014
reinforcing properties, 159–160
therapeutic, 153
tolerance, 156
trauma center admissions, 864
withdrawal, 156–158, 479

Phenelzine, 533
Phenmetrazine, 535
  See also Stimulants
Phenobarbital
  for alcohol withdrawal in pregnancy, 1204
  for benzodiazepine withdrawal, 524–525
  for neonatal opiate abstinence syndrome, 1215–1217
  See also Sedative-Hypnotics
Phenothiazines
  for alcohol relapse prevention, 509–510
  for alcohol withdrawal, 437
  for hallucinogen intoxication, 473–475
  See also Neuroleptic agents
Phenytoin
  alcohol withdrawal management and, 438, 439
  for alcoholic seizures, 785
Phosphorylation, 58, 63–64
Physical examination, 251
  adolescent, 1135–1136, 1148–1149
  pre-employment, 1250–1251
Physician health programs, 1272–1273
Placebo effects, 374–375
Placidyl® (ethchlorvynol). *See* Sedative-hypnotics
Pneumonia, 813–814
Polydrug use, 817
  alcoholism, 537–538, 892–893
    epidemiology, 8–9
    nicotine use and, 586
  assessment for, 458, 877, 892–893
  benzodiazepines, 447–448
  cocaine, 537, 585
  definition, 1303
  gender differences, 1181
  nicotine use
    alcoholism and, 586
    pharmacotherapies, 586–587
  opiate addiction, 457–458, 537
    with alcoholism, 587
  PCP, 585
  prospects for recovery, 893
  sedative-hypnotics, 480
  withdrawal, 480
Poppy seeds, 1258
Positive reinforcement, 37
Posttraumatic stress disorder
  in adolescent substance abusers, 1165
  assessment of, 562
Potassium, 747
Prazepam. *See* Benzodiazepines
Pregnancy
  addicted mother, 1199–1209
    alcoholism, 104, 1201–1204
    cocaine dependence, 138–139, 1206
    detoxification, 425–426, 1200–1201
    methadone effects, 549
    motivation to change, 1199
    opioid dependence, 1206–1207
    opioid maintenance therapy, 560
    prenatal care, 1199
    sedative-hypnotic dependence, 1205
    stabilization, 1201
    withdrawal considerations, 480
  blood pressure, 733
  HIV transmission, 826
  marijuana smoking in, 165
  pharmacotherapy considerations, 539
  predictors of alcohol use in women, 1194
  preventive intervention during, 221–222
  See also Fetal exposure
Prevention, 207–244
  adolescent abuse, early intervention rationale, 1145–1146, 1149
  alcohol use, research trends, xxv, xxix–xxx
  among individuals with psychiatric disorder, 358–359
  community-based framework, 236–238. *See also* Community coalitions
  continuum of care, 207, 233, 241, 242
  definition, 1303
  demand reduction strategies, 208
  demographic research for, 234–235
  educational intervention, 208
  fetal exposure, 1231
  gender differences, 237
  goals, 207, 242
  hepatitis A, 831
  hepatitis B, 831
  historical evolution, 208
  HIV infection, 826–827
  intervention with addicted family, 1096–1097
  interventions with women, 1186
  liver fibrosis, xxii, xxviii
  multidisciplinary approach, 234–236, 242
  outcomes, 220–222
    mediators, 223
  primary, 207, 233, 242
  program design, 208
    diversity in, 212
    focus/setting, 209–210
    integrated definition modeling, 238–241
    multicomponent approaches, 223
    principles, 219–220
    risk categorization, 218–219
    social context considerations, 238
  public health approach, 233–234
  relapse, 303
  repeat exposure, 222
  research, xxix–xxx, xxv
    anthropologic, 234
    challenges, 215–217
    epidemiologic, 234, 235
    ethical issues, 217
    historical development, 215, 223
    methodological validity, 217–218
    needs, 209, 223, 242
    objectives, 215
    prospects, 215, 222–223
  resiliency-focused, 211–212
  risk categorization, 218–219
  role of health care professionals, 210–211, 241–242
  screening of children/adolescents, 1129, 1131–1137
  secondary, 207, 233
  sequencing of interventions, 223
  steroid abuse, 177
  substance abuse precursors, 207, 212, 218–219
  supply reduction strategies, 208
  tertiary, 207, 233
  tobacco use, 237
  tuberculosis, 830
  in workplace. *See* Workplace alcohol and drug programs
  See also Harm reduction
Primary care
  assessment, 241–242, 249
  brief intervention in, 626–628
  communications with addiction specialists, 628
  follow-up care, 259–260
  prevention of fetal exposure, 1231–1232
  in substance abuse treatment, 353–355
Priming effects, 42
PRISM, 285
Prisons/prisoners
  detoxification consideration, 427
  number of, 408
  treatment needs, 408
  See also Criminal justice system
Problem Oriented Screening Instrument for Teenagers (POSIT), 1285
Prodrugs, 53
Program for Alcoholic Couples Treatment (PACT), 1119

Prolixin, 1017
Propanolol, 436
Propoxyphene, 815, 962
in neonatal abstinence syndrome, 1213
See also Opioids
Propranolol, 1002
in sedative-hypnotic withdrawal management, 452
Propylthiouracil, 764
Prosom® (estazolam). *See* Benzodiazepines
Protective factors
alcohol abstinence, 894–895
alcoholism, genetic, xx, xxvi, 297
assessment, 250
familial, 208, 1111–1113
life skills training for, 221
resiliency-focused prevention, 211–212
self-esteem as, 221
Protein/protein metabolism, 742
alcohol, mechanisms of action, 106–107
neuroadaptation in addiction, 63–64, 65
in neurotransmitter-receptor activation, 58
pharmacokinetics, 100
Protracted abstinence syndrome, 425, 545–546, 793
Pseudoaddiction, 936
Pseudowithdrawal, 445
Psilocybin, 473
See also Hallucinogens
Psychiatric comorbidity, 969–1090
in alcoholism, 20–21, 266, 507, 511
mood disorders, 985
among adolescents, 1161–1167
antisocial personality disorder, 1162–1163
anxiety disorders, 1164–1165
assessment, 1161
bipolar disorder, 1166
conduct disorders, 1162–1163
depressive disorder, 1163–1164
eating disorders, 1164–1165
mood disorders, 986
personality disorders, 1166–1167
physician role, 1162
prevalence, 1161–1162
schizophrenia, 1165–1166
assessment, 284–286
in cocaine addiction, 538
mood disorders, 985
detoxification, 426
epidemiology, 355
mood disorders, 984–986
prevalence among adolescents, 1161–1162
gender differences, 1178–1179, 1181
in impulse control disorder, 1051–1052
in inhalant abuse, 190
neurobiology, 994–996
in opioid addiction, 561–562
self-medication theory, 295
suicidal ideation in, 971–972
treatment
delivery, 355–359
matching, 335
multidisciplinary approach, 1081–1088
in women, 1178–1179
See also specific psychiatric disorder
Psychiatric Research Interview for Substance and Mental Disorders, 285
Psychoanalytic psychotherapy/theory, 322
secondary gain, 949
Psychopathology
as addiction risk factor, 297–298
chronic pain syndrome related to developmental trauma, 951
comorbid substance abuse. *See* Psychiatric comorbidity
disulfiram effects, 502
preventive intervention, 358–359
psychotherapies for addiction, 322–323
sleep disorders in, 796
steroid use-related, 179–180
substance-induced, 1166
alcohol, 969–970
amphetamines. *See* Psychopathology, substance-induced, stimulants
assessment of impaired physician, 1269
benzodiazepines, 447
caffeine, 969
clinical significance, 969, 980
cocaine, 139, 970, 972. *See also* Psychopathology, substance-induced, stimulants
diagnostic classification, 969
differential diagnosis, 972–980, 983
epidemiology, 971–973
hallucinogens, 155, 472, 475, 585–586, 970–971
ICD-10 diagnostic criteria, 1291–1292
marijuana, 165–166
nicotine, 969
opioids, 970
PCP, 479
sedative-hypnotics, 970
stimulants, 466–467, 970
symptoms, 969–971
treatment, 980
treatment matching, 335
women's alcohol/substance use and, 1177–1179
Psychotherapy, 631–651
addiction, 322–323, 331–332
anxiety disorder in addiction, 998–1000, 1002–1003
attention disorder, 1038–1039
borderline personality disorder, 1066–1073
changing reinforcement contingencies, 639
chronic pain syndrome, 946
cocaine addiction
pharmacotherapy and, 532, 644, 646–647
conditioned abstinence, 655–656
controlled use issues, 638
dynamic, 631–632
eating disorder, 1042
effectiveness, 653
family approaches, 1115–1124
impulse control disorder, 1055
indications for, 632–633
individual
advantages, 634–635
as ancillary treatment, 645–646
current status, 632
effectiveness, 640–645
following achievement of abstinence, 647
historical development, 631–632
indications, 645, 647
as introduction to treatment, 645
with network therapy, 661
opioid dependence, 640–643, 646
special needs of drug abusers, 635–637
treatment goals, 632
vs. group, 634–635
inner child therapy, 1122
intoxicated patient, 636
management of painful affect, 639
manualized approach, 612
network therapy, 661–662
with methadone treatment, 550–551, 633
monitoring medication use in, 1086
multidisciplinary psychopharmacology, 1081–1088
non-credentialed counselors, 1081–1082
opioid maintenance treatment, 567
outcome studies, 335–336
pain management, 930–931, 945, 951–952
pharmacotherapy and, 633–634
for alcoholism, 511
psychiatric comorbidity
mood disorders, 989

psychotic disorders, 1018–1021
psychoanalytic, 322, 949
recovery-oriented, 1085–1086
relations with physicians, 1083
in sedative-hypnotic withdrawal management, 452
service linkages with substance abuse treatment, 355–359
social supports and, 639–640
supportive-expressive, 641–642
teaching coping skills, 638–639
therapist effects, 609–613
treatment goals, 637–638
trends, 644–645, 653–654
Twelve Step programs and, 636–637
utilization, 653
See also Network therapy
Psychotic disorders, 1007–1027
acute presentation, 1008–1010, 1016
alcohol and, 1010
pharmacotherapy for addiction, 1017
assessment, 1007–1010
for substance use, 1018
cocaine and, 1011–1012
pharmacotherapy for addiction, 1017
hallucinogens and, 1013–1014
ketamine and, 1013–1014
marijuana and, 1010–1011
nicotine and, pharmacotherapy for addiction, 1017
pharmacotherapy, substance interactions, 1015, 1018
phencyclidine and, 1013–1015
psychosocial intervention, 1018–1021
stimulants and, 1009–1010, 1012–1013
substance-induced, 973–974
assessment, 1007–1008
Public opinion/understanding, 1130–1134
about addiction, xxxii, xxxv–xxxi, 309
sociocultural differences, 712
Alcoholics Anonymous, 697
complementary and alternative medicine, 371–372
criminality of drug use, 414
harm reduction, 398
methadone maintenance, 557
Pulmonary function
cocaine effects, 138
inhalant abuse effects, 189
marijuana effects, 164
preoperative assessment, 878–879
Pyridoxine, 744, 782–783

Quaalude® (methaqualone). *See* Sedative-hypnotics
Quality improvement/management, 627–628
Quantitative trait loci, xx, xxvi
Quitting (substance abuse)
acceptance of need for, 1068
See also Treatment; Recovery

RAATE-CE, 275
Race/ethnicity
AA participation, 711–712
addiction risk and, 5–7
alcohol use patterns, 105
alcoholism risk, 297
conceptualizations of addiction, 711–712
criminal justice system drug interventions, 414–415
discrimination in workplace drug-testing, 1251
Rational-emotive behavior therapy, 693, 719, 720
Rational Recovery[sm], 720
Rebound, benzodiazepine, 444–445, 522
Recovery
in alcoholic family
early stage, 1104–1107
mechanism of change, 1100
ongoing, 1107–1110
resistance to, 1100
risk of divorce, 1106
transition stage, 1101–1104
benzodiazepine addiction, 526–527
cognitive change, 317–319
definition, 1303
determinants of, 302, 303–305
diabetic patient, 734
drug testing in workplace, 1242–1243
family functioning in phases of, 1119–1124
in family with addiction, 1096
impaired physician, 1271–1274
outcomes, 1274–1275
integrated psychopharmacological approach, 1085–1086
late-stage, 1086
outcome determinants, 1273–1274
parents in, 1105–1106
patterns of, 302–303
perioperative management, 883–887
pharmacotherapy in, 260
problems in, 260
religion/spirituality in, 304, 725
secondary reinforcers in, 303
sleep patterns after, 796
social support, 883
alcoholism, 894–895
stages, 1271–1272
substitute dependencies, 303–304
successful, 597
supervision for, 303
in Twelve Step programs, 703–704
See also Treatment
Recovery-focused treatment, 1085–1086, 1116
Recovery movement, 1117
Recruitment into treatment, 597–598
Referrals
from primary care, 628
to Twelve Step programs, 701–702, 703–704
potential problems, 702–703
Rehabilitation Act of 1973, 1249
Reinforcement
addiction processes, xxxi, 73
alcoholism models, xxi, xxvii, 112–113
amphetamine properties, 143
behavioral models of addiction, 37–39.
See also specific model
cocaine properties, 143
current understanding, 195–196
inhalant properties, 191
LSD properties, 160
marijuana properties, 168
MDMA properties, 160–161
neural basis, 113
neurocircuitry targets in alcoholism, 75–79
nicotine properties, 151
opioid properties, 134, 135
of pain, 948–949
through medications, 937–938
phencyclidine properties, 159–160
secondary gain theory, 949
sedative-hypnotics, 126
steroid properties, 183
Reinstatement
model of, 44–45
relapse research, 84, 87
stress-induced, 87, 89–91
Relapse, 425
alcoholic
after liver transplantation, 896
See also Pharmacotherapy, alcohol relapse prevention
alternative therapies for prevention of, 387
behavioral indicators, 255
benzodiazepine, 122–123
conditioned drug-seeking, 654–655
definition, 1303
early treatment program outcomes, 408

neurochemical processes, 78–79
patterns of, 298–302, 305
perioperative risk, 883–884, 885–886
prevention, 303
in anxious addicted patient, 999–1000
coping skills for, 638–639
cue recognition and avoidance, 655
dual diagnosis, 1020–1021
individual behavior therapy, 644
preparation for, 596–597
in psychotic patient, 1020
protracted abstinence and, 545–546
reinstatement model of, 44–45
reinstatement studies, 84, 87
risks
affective functioning, 639
emotional distress, 596–597
family functioning, 1095–1096
symptoms, 703
tobacco cessation, 492–493
trigger mechanisms, 301–302, 1270
Relative risk, defined, 1
Relaxation training, 384
pain management, 953–954
Reliability
of diagnostic classification systems, 282, 283–284
test, 275
Religion/spirituality
adolescent assessment, 1154–1155
in Alcoholics Anonymous, 693, 694–695
international comparison, 708
alternative Twelve Step programs, 693, 719
attainment of spiritual health, 726–727
benefits, 725–726
clinical significance, 385–386
conversion experiences, 304
empirical research, 725
health professionals and, 725
implications for clinical practice, 727–728
significance of, in recovery, 725
treatment programs based on, 386
Replacement therapy
buprenorphine for opioid maintenance, 552–553, 566–567
cocaine, 535
LAAM for opioid maintenance, 552–553, 566
naltrexone for opioid maintenance, 548–549
nicotine. *See* Nicotine, nicotine replacement therapy
prospects, xxxii
with psychosocial component, 567
rationale, xxxii
See also Methadone, methadone replacement therapy
Reproductive function
alcohol use effects, xxii
Reproductive system
alcohol effects on, xxviii, 839–840, 1175
marijuana effects on, 164–165
opioid effects on, 1175
steroid effects on, 178–179
stimulant effects on, 1175
Research methodology
AA measurement, 715
challenges, 215–217
for complementary and alternative medicine, 372–373
integrated definition modeling, 238–241
nicotine cessation, 492
outcome measures, 322
outcomes studies, 338
social epidemiology, 234
therapeutic hallucinogens, 587–588
validity issues, 217–218
See also Prevention, research
Residential treatment, 1116–1117
Resiliency-focused prevention, 211–212
Restoril® (temazepam). *See* Benzodiazepines
Restraints
management of hallucinogen intoxication, 473
management of stimulant intoxication, 468
Restricted environmental stimulation, 382
Retroviral infection, 735–736
Revia. *See* Naltrexone
Riboflavin, 744, 782
Risk
of abuse disorders/addiction, 295–296
adolescent behavior assessment, 1133–1134
age at first alcohol exposure, xvii
age correlates, 5
alcohol, xxvi–xxvii
alcohol problems in women, 1174
benzodiazepines, 509
biomarkers, 19–20
categorization, 218–219
for children of alcoholics, 1111, 1113
concurrent attention and conduct disorder, 1033
developmental predictors of alcohol use in women, 1195–1196
employment-related factors, 7
environmental factors, 296–297
family factors, 208
family history factors, 7
gender correlates, 4–5
gender differences, xxvi, 250
genetic, xxvi
individual differences, 219
individual factors, 4–8, 297–298, 299
lifestyle assessment, 625
peer relationship factors, 208, 1154
in physicians, 1265–1266
in prescribing for pain management, 936, 962–963
psychological factors, 1177
race/ethnicity and, 5–7
risk of recovery *vs.*, 295
school factors, 208
sedative-hypnotic overdose, 441
sensitivity to alcohol effects, xxv
sensitivity to nicotine effects, 573
social predictors of alcohol use in women, 1192–1195
sociocultural factors, 208
substance characteristics, 296
addiction comorbidity in chronic pain, 946
adolescent mortality, 1133–1134
AIDS/HIV, 735
alcohol-related liver disease, 762–763
chronic pain syndrome, 952
comorbidity in addiction, 8–9
for families with addiction, 1093–1095
of infection, 825
relative, defined, 1
severe alcohol withdrawal, 434
sexually transmitted disease, 734
suicide, 846
adolescent assessment, 1155
Risperidone, 1016–1017
Ritalin® (methylphenidate). *See* Stimulants
Ritanserin, 534
RO *15-4513*, 105
Rosacea, 844–845

Scapegoat role, 1112
Schedule for Affective Disorders and Schizophrenia, 274
Schizoaffective disorder, 1008
Schizophrenia, 1165–1166. *See also* Psychiatric comorbidity
assessment, 1007, 1008–1010
concurrent substance use disorder, 1007
self-medication theory, 1015–1016
treatment, 1017–1021
neurobiology, 1015
nicotine and, 1015–1016
opioid dependence and, 561

pharmacotherapy, 119, 1015, 1016–1017
suicidal ideation, 971, 972
vs. hallucinogen intoxication, 472
vs. stimulant intoxication, 466, 538
Schizophreniform disorder, 1008
Schools
adolescent assessment, 1132
educational attainment, 8
preventive interventions, 210, 220, 222
risk factors, 8, 208
Scopolamine, 487
Seasonal affective disorder, 383
Secobarbital. *See* Sedative-hypnotics
Secondary gain, 949, 952
Secular Organizations for Sobriety, 720
Sedative-hypnotics
addiction process, 518–519
assessment for dependence, 519
dependence risk, 518, 519
as depressants, 517
federal classification of, 1300
fetal exposure, 1220
intoxication, 441–454
medical effects, 814
neurological effects, 787–788
overdose risk, 441
pharmacology of, 123–126
pharmacotherapy of, 517–530
psychopathology related to, 970
reinforcing properties, 126
therapeutic, 117, 517
treatment for dependence
initiating withdrawal, 520–522
sedative-hypnotic dependence, 519–520
types of drugs, 117
withdrawal, 441–454
addiction treatment, 452
adjunctive withdrawal management, 452
clinical features, 442–445
detoxification medications, 450–451
indications for initiating, 520–522
management, 441–442, 449–453
polydrug use, 480
in pregnancy, 1205
prolonged, 452–453
symptoms, 970
tolerance testing, 451
See also specific drug
Seizures
in alcohol withdrawal, 433–434, 439, 766, 784–785, 810
in neonatal opiate abstinence syndrome, 1212
stimulant-induced, 469, 786
Selegiline, 534
Selenium, 746, 747
Self-Administered Alcoholism Screening Test (SAAST), 263–264, 266, 1286
Self-concept, 317–318, 1101–1110
Self-efficacy
pain experience and, 950
therapy with psychotic patient, 1020
Self-esteem
in aversion therapy, 667
as predictor of abstinence, 895
as preventive factor, 221
treatment of women with addictive disorders, 1184
Self-help groups, 693–717
advantages, 1086
chronic pain management, 955–956
dual-diagnosis patients in, 1086–1088
See also Twelve Step programs
Self-medication, 997–998
in addiction process, 296
controlling anger, 1040
opioid use as, 295
substance use in schizophrenia, 296
Sensitivity to effects
alcohol, xxv, 297
as addiction risk predictor, 26–27
nicotine, 573
in reinforcement of drug-taking behavior, 196
self-administration studies, 84
Sensitizing agents
alcohol, 501–504
efficacy, 502
Sensory deprivation, 382
Sensory integration, 1038–1039
Sentencing Reform Act, 406
Serax® (oxazepam). *See* Benzodiazepines
Serindole, 1016–1017
Serotonergic system, xxxi
in addiction processes, 75–76, 995–996
in alcohol use, xxi, xxvii, 112
implications for treatment, 505–506, 986
hallucinogen action, 379
in impulse control disorder, 1054
in pain modulation, 905
in reinforcing properties of drugs, 195–196
See also 5-HT_3 receptors
Serotonin reuptake inhibitors
for alcohol relapse prevention, 508, 986–987
for anxiety disorder in addiction, 1001
for cocaine recovery, 533
for panic disorder, 518
sleep effects, 797
Sertraline, xxv, xxxi
Severity of use/abuse
assessment, 251, 274–275
as outcome indicator, 299
Sexuality/sexual behavior
adolescent assessment, 1135–1136, 1155
alcohol use and, xxiii, xxix, 839, 1175
assessment, 734
chronic alcohol effects, 784
cocaine effects, 138, 1175
HIV epidemiology, 827
marital therapy in recovery, 1123–1124
opioid effects, 1175
recovery problems, 260
risks for families with addiction, 1094
stereotypes of women and substance use, 1173, 1175
Sexually transmitted diseases, 734–735
among adolescents, 1135–1136
assessment, 734–735
risk, 734
among women, 1175
syphilis, 734–735
treatment, 735
See also AIDS/HIV
Silver acetate, 487
Sleep, 793–806
alcohol effects on, 798, 847
in elderly, 800
in alcoholics, 104, 795–796, 846–847
anxiety and substance use in, 998
assessment, 793, 794–795
benzodiazepine effects, 800
caffeine effects, 801
disorders, 784
benzodiazepine therapy, 119
environmental effects, 799
insomnia management, 801
medical conditions affecting, 796–800
medication effects, 796–797
in menopause, 798
neurobiologic systems in, 793
nicotine dependence and, 797–798, 800–801
in psychopathology, 796
shift work, 799–800

snoring, 814
stages of sleep, 795
trauma effects, 798
SMART Recovery[sm], 720–721
Societal costs
of alcohol abuse, xvii, 863
of cocaine use, 140
Sociocultural factors
and AA participation, 711–712
and addiction risk, 296–297
community-focused prevention, 209, 220, 236–238
role of health professionals, 211
culturally-specific healing practices, 385
family accommodations for addicted member, 1095
international comparison of AA operations/outcomes, 707–716
mass media exposure, 211
pain management practices, 964
in prevention
program design, 212, 238
research methodologies, 234–235
relapse prevention, 303, 304
social change, alcoholism and, 297
social stressors, drug use and, 85–87
substance abuse risk, 208
treatment of women with addictive disorders, 1184–1185
victimization of women with addictive disorders, 1179–1180
women and substance use, 1173
Socioeconomic factors
AA membership, 708
alcohol/drug addiction risk, 6–7
alcohol use/abuse
access, 296
prevention, xxiii–xxiv, xxix–xxx
risk assessment, 218
Solvent abuse, 788, 816
See also Inhalants, volatile
Somatization disorder, 1065
Spirituality, 725–727
Spleen, 835
Spontaneous recovery
from alcohol addiction, 669
from nicotine addiction, 668
Stages of Change Readiness and Treatment Eagerness Scale, 275
Steroids, 584, 817
access to, 174–175
addiction liability, 180–181
adolescent assessment, 1135
adverse effects, 177–180
assessment, 181
at-risk population, 174
federal classification of, 1299
to improve physical appearance, 176–177
mechanisms of action, 182–183
personality traits of abusers, 177
pharmacokinetics, 181–182
pharmacology of, 173–185
psychological effects, 179
reinforcing properties, 183
in sports, 173–174, 175–176
therapeutic use, 175
types of, 173, 175
urine testing, 174
work-related use, 177
Stimulants
alcohol intoxication management, 432
federal classification of, 1299
intoxication
management of, 466–468, 469–470
medical consequences, 468–469
psychological/behavioral consequences, 466–468
vs. psychopathology, 983
maintenance therapy for, 535
medical effects, 138–139, 815–816
pharmacology of, 137–145
pharmacotherapy of, 531–541
psychosis related to, 1009–1010, 1012–1013
therapeutic use of, 137
trauma center admissions, 864
types of, 137
withdrawal from
clinical features, 470
management, 470–472
medical effects, 470
See also specific stimulant
Stimulus control, 603
Stress, 83–93
behavioral research, 84
biological research, 84
drug self-administration and, 85–87, 91–92
experimental research, 83–85
impulsivity induced by, 89
in induction of drug-prone phenotype, 91
intensity, 87
mechanisms of action, 88–91
obstacles to research, 83
physical *vs.* psychological, 87–88
predictability, 87
predictors of alcohol use in women, 1195
in reinstatement model of relapse, 44–45
time contingencies, 88
Stroke, 839
alcohol and, 784
Structured Clinical Interview for *DSM-IV* (SCID), 274, 276
psychiatric assessment, 285
Sublimaze® (fentanyl). *See* Opioids
Substitution therapies for withdrawal, 303–304
benzodiazepine dependence, 524–525
sedative-hypnotic dependence, 450–451
See also Replacement therapy
Suicidal behavior/ideation
adolescent assessment, 1136, 1155
alcohol use and, 846
in borderline personality disorder, 1063–1064, 1074
psychopathology and substance abuse, 971–972
Supply reduction strategies, 208, 400–401, 402–403
Support groups
families of alcoholics, 698–701
pharmacotherapy for alcoholism and, 511
See also Twelve Step programs; *specific group*
Surgeons, impaired, 860–861
Surgery in addicted patients, 859–862
acute conditions, 860
anesthesia, 880–881
challenges, 859, 861, 877
narcotic analgesics, 879
postoperative, 881–882
nicotine withdrawal, 492
opioid maintenance therapy, 560
patient-controlled analgesia, 885
physician errors in pain management, 886
post-discharge pain management, 886
postoperative pain, 860, 881–883
recovering patient, 884–886
preoperative assessment/management, 859, 877, 878–879
premedication, 880
recovering patient, 884
recovering addicts, 883–887
relapse risk, 885–886
therapeutic relationship, 859, 877, 880
transition from intoxication during, 879
withdrawal management, 879–880
See also Pain management, in addicted patient
Symptom-triggered therapy, 436
Synanon, 408
Syphilis, 734–735

Tachycardia, PCP-induced, 476–477
Tai-chi, 383
Tapering
methadone, 546
polydrug withdrawal, 480
sedative-hypnotic detoxification, 449–451
Temazepam, 117
See also Benzodiazepines
Temposil®. *See* Carbimide
Terminology, addiction, 1301–1303
Testosterone, 173–174, 181–182. *See also* Steroids
Tetrahydrocannabinol. *See* Marijuana
Therapeutic communities, 323, 328
historical development, 1081–1082
Therapeutic relationship, 731
adolescent assessment/intervention, 1131–1132, 1146–1147, 1149
alcoholic's perception of alcohol use, 893
for assessment, 249
in dialectical behavior therapy, 1070, 1071, 1074–1075
in dynamic individual psychotherapy, 632
liver transplantation follow-up, 896–897
medical care and, 738
objectives, 260
in opioid maintenance treatment, 567–568
as outcome factor, 331–332, 611–612
in pain management, 956–957
preoperative management of addicted patient, 859, 877, 880
psychotic patient, 1019
reporting diagnosis to patient, 251–254, 255
special needs of drug abusers, 635, 637
spiritual issues, 727–728
Thiamine
in alcohol-related cognitive dysfunction, 775
alcohol withdrawal management, 438
deficiency, alcohol-related, 743–744
cause of, 845
treatment, 749–750
in Wernicke's encephalopathy, 779–780
Thiopental, 867
Third-party administrators, 1256
Tiapride, 510
Tobacco. *See* Nicotine
Tolerance
to cocaine, 142
definition, 423, 1303
DSM conceptualizations, 280, 281
in impulse control disorder symptoms, 1050
to LSD, 156
to marijuana, 167–168
to MDMA, 156
metabolic adaptation, 757
neuroadaptation in, 910–911
to nicotine, 149, 573
to opioids, 935
to phencyclidine, 156
reverse, 911
to steroids, 180
testing for, 451
types of, 910
Traffic accidents. *See* Motor vehicle crashes
Training and education of practitioners
for brief intervention, 627
for individual psychotherapy with drug abusers, 635–636
as a multidisciplinary team, 1083
for network therapy, 662
and therapist effectiveness, 612–613
Transcendental meditation, 380–381
Transcranial neuroelectric stimulation, 383
Transcutaneous electrical nerve stimulation, 882, 886, 929
Transdermal drug delivery
of nicotine, 489–492, 574–575
of nitroglycerine, 732
Transference, 632
Transferrin, 748
Transtheoretical model of change, 596
Trauma, 863–874
alcohol-related, xxiii, xxix
cerebral injury, 782
mortality, 863
Trazodone, 583–584. *See also* Benzodiazepines
for anxiety disorder in addiction, 1001
TrEAT, 624
Treatment
of abused children, 1133
by acupuncture, 373–374, 375–376
adjunctive services, 353
of adolescents
brief intervention, 1149
community resources, 1149–1150
referrals, 1149
of AIDS/HIV, 735–736
of alcohol intoxication, 431–432, 809
of alcoholism
aversion therapy, 667, 668
goals, xxiv, xxx, xxi–xxvi
implications of cognitive impairment, 778
liver disease, 764, 812
nutritional issues, 749–750
pregnant woman, 1201–1204
research trends, xix, xxiv–xxvi, xxx–xxvi
treatment matching, xxv, xxxi, 273–274
trends, 767–768
withdrawal, 435–440
women, 1196–1197
of anxiety disorder, 1002–1003
ascites, 812
of attention disorder, 1035–1036
pharmacotherapy, 1036–1038
psychosocial, 1038–1039
behavioral. *See* Behavioral therapies
biofeedback, 376–377
of borderline personality disorder, 1066, 1073–1076
of cancer, 734
of cirrhosis, 844
salt/water retention in, 747–748
clinical conceptualization, 305–306, 309, 313, 315
clinician qualifications for, 423
coerced, 409–410
compliance. *See* Compliance
continuum of care, 324
cost-effectiveness, 310–311, 327
in the criminal justice system
methadone maintenance, 412–413
modalities, 408
outcomes, 409
outpatient, 413
program evaluation, 413–414
therapeutic communities, 410–412
trends, 408–409
crisis intervention, 259
culturally-specific, 385
definition of, 1303
and diabetes mellitus, 733
diagnosis, 321–322
disease model, 309–310
duration of, 320
eating disorder, 1042
effects on criminal behavior, 407
in emergency settings. *See* Emergency medicine
of families with addiction
physician's role in, 1096–1097
professional competencies for, 1113–1114
referral resources, 259
of fetal alcohol/drug effects, 1211–1221
goals of, 328
of hallucinogen use, 379–380
harm reduction and, 398–399

of hepatitis, 736, 831
historical development, 315, 408, 1081–1082
of impaired physicians, 1270–1271
  aftercare, 1271–1274
  assessment, 1268–1270
  intervention, 1266–1268
of impulse control disorder, 1054–1055
individual differences in, 321
  outcomes, 286
of inhalant abuse, 816–817
initiation, 645
  couples, 658
inpatient settings, 319
  methods, 328
  as outcome variable, 329–330
  outpatient care after, 341
  utilization, 1063
and insomnia, 801
intensity of, 323–324, 325, 335
interactive *vs.* non-interactive, 605–606
length of, 330–331, 341
linkages across settings, 353
  mechanisms to improve, 359–360
  with mental health services, 355–359
  with primary care, 354–355
  rationale, 360
and managed care, xvii, 321
matched to stage of change, 598–600, 601–603
  effectiveness, 603–606
Minnesota Model, 315–319, 325
motivational issues, 595
multidisciplinary psychopharmacology, 1081, 1088
of neonatal opiate abstinence syndrome, 1213–1214
of nicotine withdrawal, 487–493
of opioid overdose, 814–815
outcomes
  expectations, 329
  outpatient, 329–330
  predictors, 646
  variables, 329
  See also Outcome studies
outpatient, 328–329
  after inpatient care, 341
  outcomes, 329–330
pharmacotherapies. *See* Pharmacotherapy
planning
  assessment for, 287
  goals, 259
  negotiated model, 255–256
  options, 257–259
plea-bargained, 407
in pregnancy, 1201–1204
primary care settings, 353–355
proactive approach, 598, 606
prognostic factors, 256, 310
psychopathology, substance-induced, 980
psychosocial, xxxiv
psychotherapeutic, 322–323
public policy issues, 342
public sector *vs.* private sector, 324
recruitment, 597–598
replacement therapy, xxxii
reporting diagnosis to patient, 251–254, 255
research trends/prospects, xxxii–xxxiv, 369–370
retention, 598–599
role of patient placement criteria, 366–369
of sedative-hypnotic dependence, 452
  health care environment, 519–520
  initiating withdrawal, 520–522
  intoxication/overdose, 441–442
  withdrawal, 449–453
setting of, 329–330, 345–350
sexually transmitted diseases, 735
social milieu, 317
stimulant intoxication/overdose, 466–468, 469–472
thiamine deficiency, 779
tuberculosis, 736–737
Wernicke's disease, 438, 780
of women, 1184–1185, 1196–1197
See also Detoxification; Psychotherapy; Pharmacotherapy; Recovery
Treatment Alternatives to Street Crime, 410
Treatment matching
  assessment for, 273, 274–275, 287
  limitations, 337
  matching variables, 273
  outcome studies, 335–337
  patient placement criteria in, 363–369
  practice trends, 273
  rationale, 325
  standardized criteria, 273–274
Treatment Outcome Prospective Study, 413–414
Triazolam, 117, 800
  See also Benzodiazepines
Tuberculosis, 736–737, 830, 878
Twelve Step programs, 693
  acceptance in, 1068
  for alcoholic family in recovery, 1096
  alternative programs, 719, 721–722. *See also specific program*
  change processes, 713
  group problems, 702–703
  group/sponsor selection, 703
  limitations, 703
  outcome studies, 331, 713–714
  pain management goals and, 955
  patient objections, 702
  pharmacotherapy and, 636–637, 1087–1088
  physician role, 701
    monitoring recovery, 703–704
    referrals to programs, 701–703
    support, 703, 704
  powerlessness concept, 1087
  psychotherapy compatibility, 636–637
  psychotic patient, 1020, 1021
  stages of recovery, 1119–1120
  support for surgical patients in recovery, 885

Ulcer disease, gastrointestinal, 811, 842
Uncommon drugs of abuse, 817
Uniform Controlled Substances Act (1970/1990), 961–962, 1299–1300
Unilateral family therapy, 1119
United Nations, 397
University of Mississippi, 866
University of Rhode Island Change Assessment Scale, 275
Urine acidification
  PCP intoxication management, 477
  stimulant intoxication management, 470
Urine testing
  adolescent, involuntary, 1148–1149
  alcohol use, 1243
  collection, 1259–1261
  employees, 1241
  false-positive, 1251
  medical review process, 1256–1257
  specific drugs, 1257–1259
  for steroids, 174
  trauma center admissions, 864–865
  See also Workplace drug testing

Vagal neuropathy, 783–784
Validity
  of diagnostic classification systems, 283–284
  test, 275
Valium® (diazepam). *See* Benzodiazepines
Valproate
  for bipolar disorder in substance use, 988–989

in sedative-hypnotic withdrawal management, 452
Valproic acid, 536
Vegetarian diet, 838
Versed® (midozolam). *See* Benzodiazepines
Violent behavior. *See* Aggressive/violent behavior
alcohol-related, xxiii
Viqualine, 506
Vitamin A, 745–746
carcinogenesis and, 758–759
Vitamin B_{12}, 744–745
Vitamin C, 745
Vitamin D, 746
Vitamin E, 746–747
Vitamin K, 746
Vitamins
alcohol effects, 743–748
treatment, 749–750, 841
deficiencies in alcoholism, 782–783
See also specific vitamin

Wernicke-Korsakoff syndrome. *See* Korsakoff's psychosis
Wernicke's encephalopathy, 775, 779–780
clinical features, 438
Korsakoff's psychosis and, 780
management, 438
Withdrawal. *See also* Detoxification
addiction processes and, xxxi
alarm system dysregulation theory of, 995
from alcohol, 104, 431–438
assessment and diagnosis, 268–269, 423, 424, 425
from barbiturates, 443
from benzodiazepines, 122, 443–449, 522–524
from caffeine, 584–585
from cocaine, 142, 465–484
conditioned, 654–655
definition of, 1303
dopaminergic system in, 61
DSM conceptualizations of, 280, 281, 1289
in elderly patients, 480–481
gender differences in, 480
from hallucinogens, 475
impulse control disorder symptoms in, 1050
from inhalants, 190–191
from LSD, 158, 465–484
from marijuana, 163–164, 166, 197, 476
from methadone, 427
network therapy and, 660–661
from nicotine, 149
non-chemical coping methods, 1270–1271
from opioids, 131–135, 459–462, 545, 562, 934–935, 941
pain physiology in, 912–913
perioperative, 879–880
pharmacologic management of
goals, 425
strategies, 465
from phencyclidines, 156–158, 479–480
from polydrugs, 480
in pregnancy
symptoms, 1201–1203
treatment, 1203–1204
preoperative management, 860
protracted, 425, 452–453, 507, 522–523
relapse risk factors, 301–302
risks, 424
from sedative-hypnotics, 442–453, 520–522, 1205
from steroids, 180–181, 584
from stimulants, 470–472
See also Detoxification
Women For Sobriety, 719–720
Women's issues
AA utilization, 711
alcohol use
alcoholism risk, 298
alcoholism treatment, 1196–1197
heredity and, 1176–1177
medical complications, 1175–1176
modern trends, 1174
pharmacology, 1174–1175
psychological factors, 1177–1179
risk factors, 1174
stereotypes, 1173
assessment for addictive disorders, 1181–1182, 1184
barriers to treatment, 1185
child abuse experience, 1177–1178
course of addiction, 298, 299
epidemiology of addictive disorders, 1173–1174
heredity and addiction, 1176–1177
highway safety, 1180
HIV infection, 736
pharmacologic research, 1174–1175
postmenopausal alcohol use, xxii, xxviii
predictors of alcohol/drug use
developmental, 1195–1196
social, 1192–1195
prevention of addictive disorders, 1186
reproductive health
alcohol/drug use and, 839, 1175
sexually transmitted diseases, 1175
sleep changes in menopause, 798
tobacco use, 1176
treatment for addictive disorders, 1184–1185
victimization, 1179–1180
withdrawal management, 480
See also Gender differences; Pregnancy
Workplace
addiction risk related to employment status, 7
alcohol and drug programs
federal/state laws, 1247–1251, 1255
future prospects, 1261–1262
hiring practices, 1242, 1244, 1251
policy implementation and enforcement, 1251–1252
rationale, 1241
Drug-Free Workplace Act of 1988, 1247–1248
drug testing
confidentiality of findings, 1246
effects of, 1241
employee/employer rights, 1243–1246
employer tort liability, 1246–1247
interpretation of results, 1257–1259
laboratory selection, 1243, 1256
methods, 1243
periodic, 1242
post-accident, 1242
pre-employment, 1242, 1244
public employees, 1246
random, 1242, 1245
for reasonable cause, 1242, 1245
reasons for, 1242–1243
in rehabilitation programs, 1242–1243
relevant legislation, 1247–1251
specimen collection, 1259–1261
predictors of alcohol use in women, 1193
See also Medical Review Officer (MRO)
World Health Organization, 281
See also ICD-10 diagnostic criteria

Xanax® (alprazolam). *See* Benzodiazepines

Yoga, 383

Zidovudine (AZT)
for pregnant women, 826
prophylactic, 826–827
Zieve's syndrome, 835
Zinc, 745, 748
Zolpidem, 117, 800
See also Benzodiazepines